ON
TRIAL

ON TRIAL

BLITZ EDITIONS

Published by Blitz Editions
an imprint of Bookmart Ltd
Registered Number 2372865
Trading as Bookmart Ltd
Desford Road
Enderby
Leicester LE9 5AD

ISBN 1 85605 114 5

This material has previously appeared in *Crimes and Victims*

50 934

Every effort has been made to contact the copyright holders for the pictures.
In some cases they have been untraceable, for which we offer our apologies.
Thanks to the following libraries and picture agencies which supplied pictures:

Associated Press, AP Worldwide, AGIP, Black Museum, Culver Pictures,
Mary Evans Photo Library, Jack Hickes Photography, Fairfax Ltd,
Illustrated London News, Hulton-Deutsch Collection, News Ltd of Australia,
Popperfotos, Press Association, Rex Features, Frank Spooner Pictures,
Syndication International, Suddeutscher Verlag, Topham, UPI/Bettmann

The Authors
Frank Smyth is the consultant editor of *On Trial* and also wrote the chapters *Crimes of Horror*
and *Crimes of Passion*. He began his career as a crime reporter in Yorkshire,
and has since written numerous books on all aspects of crime,
including *Detectives in Fact and Fiction*, *I'm Jack: The Police Hunt for Jack the Ripper*
and *Cause of Death: A History of Forensic Science*.

J. Anderson Black is the author of *Murder Most Foul*.
He is a fine arts graduate from Edinburgh University.
He has been a professional writer for more than twenty-five years,
and his published work covers a wide range of topics from art to crime,
as well as three novels and several screenplays for feature films.

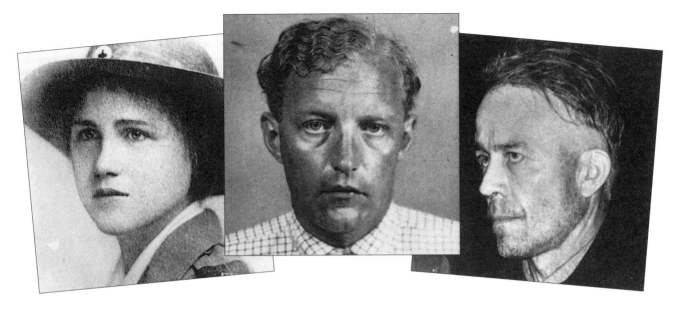

Contents

ON TRIAL

O N TRIAL concentrates on the act of murder, that most final of all acts – extinguishing life in another person. Sometimes it is the murder of a complete stranger, sometimes it is the person closest to the murderer. And perhaps the most disquieting element of all is that we all wonder if we, too, might not be capable of such an atrocity, such an act of madness.

The criminals in these stories were often men and women whom their neighbours and friends took to be perfectly ordinary and decent, but who in fact were locked into a grotesque and monstrous world. They may have committed a single murder, or they may have been serial murderers for many years.
After weeks, months or years of secrecy, the culprit is finally cornered and exposed, dragged out from obscurity into the blinding light of the world's shocked attention.
Complete nonentities are suddenly rocketed into a grim light and their names become part of the folklore of crime and depravity –
Dr Crippen, Ruth Ellis, Peter Sutcliffe, Donald Neilson and many others.

ON TRIAL tells the tales of those who were caught and brought to justice, but perhaps the most disturbing thought of all is how many of these deranged men and women are still walking freely amongst us – unchecked, unsuspected and looking for their next victim.

MURDER
MOST
FOUL

Dr CRIPPEN
Hen-pecked Killer

Dr Crippen is notorious as the first murderer to be arrested with the help of Marconi's newly invented wireless telegraphy. This quiet little patent-medicine salesman was hanged in 1910 for poisoning a wife who had treated him shamefully

Early in 1900 a slight, modest gentleman enquired about an flat in Shore Street, Bloomsbury. He had a high-domed, bald head, a large sandy moustache, and greyish eyes which bulged behind a pair of gold-rimmed spectacles. With him, and seeming to loom over him, was his wife, a florid, full-figured woman in garish silks.

The oddly assorted pair were American, they explained. They had just arrived on the boat from New York, she to make a name on the music-hall stage, he to manage a patent medicine firm. Their names were Dr Hawley Harvey and Mrs Cora Crippen, and they were to become almost synonymous with twentieth-century murder.

THE MEDICAL MAN

Hawley Crippen was born in 1862, the son of a dry goods merchant in Coldwater, Michigan, who had ambitions for his son to be a doctor. In 1879, when he was just seventeen, the young Crippen embarked on his medical training.

In subsequent years he was to be reviled as an out-and-out quack, or defended as a highly qualified medic who was simply unlicensed to practise in England. The truth lies somewhere in between.

He received a general scientific

Above: *Mrs Cora Crippen, an extravagant woman who totally dominated her husband.*

Opposite: *Dr Hawley Harvey Crippen, the mild-mannered purveyor of patent medicines who was driven to murder.*

Left: *39 Hilldrop Crescent, Kentish Town, the Crippen family home where the murder was committed.*

Above: *39 Hilldrop Crescent, London.*

background at the California University, Michigan, and then went on to study medicine at the Hospital College in Cleveland, Ohio. Probably, though not certainly, he left without a degree.

In 1883 he sailed for England and spent some time attending lectures at Guy's and St Thomas's hospitals in London, before returning to New York and enrolling at the Opthalmic Hospital there, gaining a diploma in 1885.

While in Santiago in 1887 he met and married a woman named Charlotte Bell, and the following year their son, Otto Hawley Crippen, was born. This boy was to spend his life in Los Angeles.

The Crippens moved to Salt Lake City, where, in 1890, Charlotte died. Hawley drifted back to New York. Two years later he met a striking young woman of seventeen who called herself Cora Turner and was the mistress of a rich stove manufacturer.

Crippen fell in love with her, and for her part she seemed to like the idea of being a doctor's wife. In 1893 he married her and took her with him to St Louis, where he was working as consultant physician to an optician. There he learned that his wife's real name was Kunigunde Mackamotzki. She was the daughter of a Russian Polish father and a German mother.

Despite the strong prejudice then current among 'White Anglo-Saxon Protestants' against mid-European Catholics, the revelation did little to

WASP PREJUDICE AGAINST CENTRAL EUROPEAN CATHOLIC IMMIGRANTS DID NOTHING TO DIMINISH CRIPPEN'S ARDOUR FOR HIS YOUNG WIFE.

affect Crippen's passion for Cora.

For her part, Cora was growing dissatisfied with Crippen's earnings as an orthodox doctor, pointing out that there was much more money to be made in the world of 'patent' medicines. One of the best-selling of these was 'Professor Munyon's Pills for Piles'. In 1897, Crippen joined the firm in New York and parted company with the mainstream of medicine for ever.

When Munyon's opened an office in Shaftesbury Avenue, London, Crippen was appointed first manager. The summer of 1900 saw him and Cora taking the lease on the flat in Shore Street, Bloomsbury.

AMBITIONS

Bloomsbury was at the heart of the London music hall world. Cora lost no time in introducing herself into the pubs and restaurants in which the music-hall artistes met, and even hired herself an agent, 'billing' herself under the stage name of Belle Ellmore.

She looked the part. Cora was pretty enough, with dark eyes and raven hair. Her looks, together with her American accent, described as 'twangy', and the stagey clothes she affected reeked of the American vaudeville theatre of which she claimed to have been a part.

The trouble was that Belle Ellmore could not sing – at least she could not project her voice to reach the far corners

*Left: **Cora Crippen had a passion for the music hall and a taste for garish fashion.***

WOULD-BE MUSIC-HALL ARTISTE CORA WAS BOOED FROM THE STAGE – PARTLY FOR STRIKE-BREAKING AND PARTLY FOR BEING DREADFUL

*Below: **Cora hired herself out as an artiste's agent under her stage name of Belle Ellmore.***

of a theatre. Once, during a music-hall strike, she obtained work at the Euston Palace. But she was hissed and booed from the stage, partly for being a 'blackleg', and partly for being dreadful. After that distressing experience, Cora's active theatrical days were over.

Despite this she remained friendly with such artistes as Marie Lloyd. She also became a member and later honorary treasurer of the Music Hall Ladies' Guild, a charitable organization. And she took to wearing expensive jewellery, which she bullied Hawley Crippen into buying.

In 1901, urged on by Cora to 'better' himself, he took an appointment as consultant to a dubious firm of ear specialists named the Drouet Institute. Its bookkeeper-secretary was a seventeen-year-old named Ethel Neave who shared with Cora a dissatisfaction with her surname and called herself LeNeve. Two years after Crippen joined, the Institute was bankrupted after a charge of negligence was levelled against it – the charge did not involve Crippen. By this time he had fallen in love with Ethel.

Under any name, Ethel LeNeve does not seem to have been particularly prepossessing. Despite her pretty face she was a mousey child with a slight limp who suffered from chronic catarrh.

But, like Cora, she had a strong dominant trait which seemed to appeal to Crippen. And there is no doubt that she loved the by-now infatuated doctor as much as he loved her.

She followed him, as secretary, to the Sovereign Remedy Company, which failed, then to the Aural Company, which also failed, and then back to Professor Munyon's, where he took up his old post as manager.

Later, she became secretary to a dental practice which Crippen set up as an extra source of income at Albion House, New Oxford Street, with a dental surgeon named Dr Rylance.

HEN-PECKED HUSBAND

In 1905, the Crippens left Shore Street and moved north to a leased semi-detached villa at 39 Hilldrop Crescent, off the Camden Road in Kentish Town. By this time Crippen was making money,

ONCE THE LODGERS WENT, THE CRIPPENS LIVED IN THE KITCHEN SURROUNDED BY THE UNTOUCHED FILTH OF EVERYDAY EXISTENCE

Below: *Ethel LeNeve, Dr Crippen's lover, thinly disguised as a boy for their flight to America.*

most of which was spent on entertaining Cora's friends and on buying Cora's dresses and jewellery. However, by now the couple slept in separate bedrooms and were polite to each other only in company. Cora openly had men friends, and occasionally took them to bed in the afternoons when Crippen was at work.

When her interest in the new house waned a little, Cora took in four lodgers. She had an antipathy towards 'living in' domestic servants, so she buckled down to the task of being a landlady herself, with the help of a daily cleaner.

Crippen was ordered up at six in the morning to clean the lodgers' boots, lay and light the fires, and prepare the breakfast – all before he set off for his office at 7.30.

Incredibly, the doctor continued to pay all the household bills, while the lodgers' rents went into Cora's dress and jewellery account.

In December 1906 Crippen came home to find Cora in bed with one of the lodgers, a German. The following day he told Ethel, and for the first time in their four-year relationship she consented to go to bed with him. Their affair was consummated in a cheap hotel one afternoon on Ethel's day off.

Soon after this, Cora tired of the game of being a landlady and dismissed the lodgers. Instead she entertained her friends on two or three evenings a week. For the rest of the time, she and her husband virtually lived in the kitchen. Both of them gave up housework, and cleaning was done only spasmodically.

Over the next four years Crippen continued to live at Hilldrop Crescent, though life with Cora became more and more intolerable. There was no longer any pretence at amiability. Cora mocked him in front of her friends and Hawley Crippen bore it all stoically, buoyed up by his love for Ethel LeNeve.

Cora was by now aware of the affair. At one point Ethel became pregnant and decided to have the baby, thus forcing matters to a crisis. But she miscarried.

Cora's response was to speculate, to a group of her music-hall friends and in her husband's hearing, as to which of Ethel's many lovers was responsible for the child. It may have been at that moment that Hawley Harvey Crippen's patience came abruptly to an end.

THE WORM TURNS

On 1 January 1910 he went to the firm of Lewis and Burrows, wholesale chemists, and ordered seventeen grains of the vegetable drug hydrobromide of hyoscine. It was, he said, on behalf of Munyon's – though the American company did not manufacture in Britain. On 19 January he took possession of the drug, which he had seen used to calm violent patients in mental hospitals. It was also an anaphrodisiac – it killed sexual ardour.

On 31 January the Crippens entertained a couple named Martinetti, theatrical friends of Cora's, to dinner.

During the course of the evening Cora picked a quarrel with her husband because he had not shown Mr Martinetti to the lavatory. It was an odd grudge, even for Cora. But, according to Crippen's later evidence, she took it as a 'last straw' and threatened to leave him.

It is doubtful whether Crippen would have worried overmuch if his wife had simply walked out of his life. But she had access, through their joint account, to his savings, and she would also have taken her valuable jewellery and have had a legal right to their joint property. She had threatened before to leave and take 'her' money – though in fact, apart from the abortive night treading the boards of the Euston Palace, she had never earned a penny in her life.

At 1.30 on the morning of 1 February the Martinettis bade Cora and Hawley goodbye. Cora Crippen was never seen alive again. That afternoon, Crippen called on the Martinettis, as he often did, and remarked that Cora was well.

On 2 February, Crippen pawned for £80 a gold ring and a pair of earrings belonging to his wife. The same evening Ethel LeNeve came to Hilldrop Crescent for the first time and stayed overnight.

The same day a letter arrived at the Music Hall Ladies' Guild office, apparently from their treasurer, Belle Ellmore. It said that she was leaving immediately for America to nurse a sick relative and was therefore tendering her resignation.

On 9 February Crippen pawned more jewellery, this time for £115. At his trial Crippen was to point out indignantly that he had every right to dispose of his wife's

Above: The SS Negantic is towed into port with Crippen and LeNeve on board. They were initially arrested aboard the SS Montrose.

Below: Police accompany Dr Crippen and Ethel LeNeve down the gangway of the SS Negantic after his arrest in 1910.

jewellery in any way he thought fit, since he had bought it.

On 20 February Crippen carried openness to potentially dangerous lengths when he escorted Ethel LeNeve to the Music Hall Ladies' Guild ball. She was decked out in some of Belle Ellmore's finest jewels – a fact not lost on the Martinettis, among other guests present.

Ostensibly Ethel was still simply Crippen's secretary, standing in for his absent wife at a social occasion. But on 12 March caution was thrown to the winds. Ethel moved in permanently to 39 Hilldrop Crescent.

FAKED DEATH, SUSPICIOUS FRIENDS

On 20 March, with Easter approaching, Crippen wrote to the Martinettis to say that he had heard from his wife and that she was seriously ill with pleuro-pneumonia. He was thinking, he said, of going to the United States to look after her. Contemporary writers have suggested that this may have been his original plan – to go to America and then quietly disappear. But something stopped him, and that something was probably Ethel LeNeve.

At this stage, it seems unlikely that Ethel knew that Cora was dead. But she knew that she was finally with the man

she loved and she was not going to let him leave her, even for a short while.

On 23 March, instead of going to America, Crippen and Ethel took a cross-Channel ferry to Dieppe, where they stayed during Easter week.

But from Victoria station he sent the Martinettis a telegram: 'BELLE DIED YESTERDAY AT SIX O'CLOCK. PLEASE PHONE ANNIE. SHALL BE AWAY A WEEK – PETER.' 'Peter' was a nickname for Crippen used by Belle Ellmore's theatrical friends.

When he returned, Crippen was inundated with enquiries from his wife's friends. Where exactly had she died? Where could they send a wreath? Crippen told them that he was having her cremated in America. When her ashes were shipped back 'we can have a little ceremony then'.

Lil Hawthorne, the well-known music hall comedy singer who had been one of Belle Ellmore's closest friends, was not satisfied. She checked with shipping lines but could find no record of either a Cora Crippen or a Belle Ellmore embarking for the States around the first week in February. Lil and her agent husband, John Nash, had to go to New York on business in March, and their enquiries there also drew a blank.

On his return to London, Nash confronted Crippen. Under questioning, Crippen broke down and sobbed pathetically. Nash, knowing of the doctor's kindly nature and tolerance of what even her friends had to acknowledge as his wife's often outrageous treatment of him, was almost convinced of the truth of Crippen's story.

And yet if Crippen was so distressed, why was his mistress living openly with him? Eventually Nash went to Scotland Yard and, on 30 June, poured out the whole tale.

INTERVIEWED BY THE YARD

A week later, on 8 July, Detective Chief Inspector Walter Dew, accompanied by Detective Sergeant Mitchell, went to call on Crippen at Albion House. Dew was one of the Yard's most experienced detectives. He was impressed, by Dr Crippen's demeanour.

Above: *Crippen arrives at the police station after his arrest in a taxi.*

Below: *Superintendent Frost, head of the Crippen investigation, discusses evidence with his colleagues.*

Asked about his wife's disappearance and alleged death, Crippen immediately confessed that the whole story was untrue. In fact, he said, Belle Ellmore alias Cora Crippen had run off to Chicago with an old prize-fighter lover of hers. Crippen had been so ashamed, and so worried about damaging his medical career with a scandal, that he had invented the story of her fatal illness.

Dew spent all day with Crippen, sitting in the waiting room between Crippen's periodic surgery calls to dental patients.

In the evening, Crippen took the two policemen to Hilldrop Crescent and showed them over the house, from attic to basement. All seemed perfectly normal.

'Of course,' said Dew, 'I shall have to find Mrs Crippen to clear the matter up.'

'Yes,' agreed the doctor, 'I will do everything I can. Can you suggest anything? Would an advertisement be any good?' Dew thought an advertisement in the Chicago papers an excellent idea, and helped Crippen draft one before finally saying goodnight.

In fact, Dew later admitted, the advertisement was unnecessary. He was convinced by that time that Crippen was telling the truth at last, and that the flighty Belle Ellmore had run off.

The investigation was to all intents and purposes finished. However, Crippen had no means of knowing this.

THE FATAL MISTAKE

Despite numerous theories, no one has ever given a satisfactory reason why Crippen, whose nerve had so far held, should suddenly at this point make the mistake of flight. But flee he did.

After carefully putting his affairs in order Crippen and LeNeve took the boat to Rotterdam on the night of 9 July. From there they made their way to Antwerp, where they embarked on the SS *Montrose,* bound for Quebec, under the names of Mr and Master Robinson.

Ethel had had her hair cropped short and was wearing cut-down men's clothes, probably Crippen's, and they kept under cover as much as possible before the ship sailed on 20 July.

Even now, the fleeing lovers might have got away but for a fluke. Chief Inspector Dew had forgotten some minor point during his questioning of Crippen. It was not important and there was no urgency. But on Monday 11 July, finding himself in the vicinity of Albion House, he decided to drop in and check it out. There he was told that Crippen had left.

Suddenly alarm bells were beginning to ring, and Dew dashed up to Hilldrop Crescent. All seemed to be in order, but he carried out a thorough search, checking the garden for recent signs of digging and testing the bricks in the empty basement coal cellar with his foot.

All was solid and normal. But Dew was certain that somewhere in this ordinary little house and its garden lay

> THE TENACIOUS DEW WAS CONVINCED THAT THIS ORDINARY SUBURBAN HOUSE AND GARDEN CONTAINED THE ANSWER TO CORA'S DISAPPEARANCE

the solution to Cora's disappearance.

On the following day he returned with extra men. Again they searched, digging and probing. Again nothing. On Wednesday the 13th they were there again, but towards evening it began to look as if Dew's instinct was wrong. Then, standing in the brick-floored cellar, he probed one of the cracks with a poker and found that the brick was loose. He prised it out, and found loosely packed soil underneath. This time he got a spade, removed the rest of the bricks, and dug. Eight inches down he found what he described at the trial as 'a mass of flesh' wrapped in a striped pyjama top.

On preliminary examination by Dr

Right: *August 1910 – crowds gathered outside Bow Street Court as Crippen stood before magistrates.*

Below: *The trial of Dr Crippen and Ethel LeNeve at the Old Bailey in October 1910 attracted huge public interest.*

Above: Dr Crippen in the dock at the Old Bailey during his trial for the murder of his wife.

THE 'MASS OF FLESH' IN THE CELLAR PROVED TO BE A BODY THAT HAD BEEN FILLETED, WITH SURGICAL PRECISION, JUST LIKE A FISH

IN COURT, THE DISPUTED PIECE OF HUMAN FLESH WAS EXHIBITED TO JUDGE, JURY AND COUNSEL ON A SOUP PLATE

Marshall, the police surgeon, it proved to be a human torso from which the neck and head, arms and legs had been severed. The vagina and uterus had been excised, and the trunk had been neatly filleted – all the bones had been removed – with considerable surgical skill.

On 15 July, Marshall and Dr Augustus J. Pepper, a Home Office pathologist based at St Mary's Hospital, Paddington, removed the remains for further examination. The following day a warrant was issued for the arrest of Crippen and LeNeve.

On 20 July, the westward-bound SS *Montrose* steamed out of Antwerp. Sharing a cabin were a Mr John Robinson and his son, who between them had only one small valise as luggage. The ship's master, Captain Henry Kendal, thought them an odd couple, and kept an eye on them.

Among other things he noticed that 'Mr Robinson' was reading a copy of Edgar Wallace's *Four Just Men*, a famous murder yarn of the time. But he also noticed that the 'son' wore an ill-fitting hat and trousers, which were held together with safety pins at the back, and that the couple held hands in a manner most unusual for a father and son. When he saw a picture of Crippen in a copy of the *Daily Mail* which had been brought aboard just before the *Montrose* sailed, Captain Kendal despatched a wireless message which began: 'Have strong suspicion that Crippen London cellar murderer and accomplice are among saloon passengers....'

The message went out on 22 July, and the following day Dew and Mitchell embarked on the SS *Negantic* at Liverpool just before she sailed. On 31 July, Dew boarded the *Montrose* as she lay at anchor off Father Point, Quebec, and arrested the pair.

Crippen's first words were: 'I am not sorry. The anxiety has been too much.' He was the first murderer to be arrested by wireless telegraphy, for which Marconi had received the Nobel Prize the previous year.

Back in London Dr Pepper, assisted by his colleagues Dr William Willcox and Dr Bernard Spilsbury, had conducted a thorough examination of the remains from the cellar. They contained at least five grains of hyoscine which, as Willcox the toxicologist was to point out, was derived from henbane. When used as a sedative, one-fortieth of a grain had been known to produce 'severe symptoms'.

The defence were to claim that these remains were not those of Belle Ellmore-Cora Crippen, but of some previous murder, coincidentally committed in the house before the arrival of the Crippens. Even this credulity-stretching defence was scotched when pubic hairs on the torso were matched for colouring with Cora's head hair, and Bernard Spilsbury showed that a mark on the skin was not a fold, as alleged by the defence, but the scar of an ovariotomy such as Cora was known to have undergone. At the trial, the piece of flesh and skin showing the scar was handed about, to the judge, jury, defence and defendant Crippen, on a soup plate.

Finally, Crippen was caught out in a direct lie when he claimed that the pyjamas in which the body was wrapped were not his. They were proved to have been bought by him in 1909.

Left: *Ethel LeNeve leaves Bow Street Magistrates Court.*

Below: *Ethel LeNeve, Crippen's lover, was a mousey young woman with a limp and chronic catarrh.*

CRIPPEN'S PATCH

The trial had begun at the Old Bailey on 18 October before the Lord Chief Justice, Lord Alverstone, and the jury took twenty-seven minutes to reach their verdict. Crippen was sentenced to hang, while Ethel LeNeve, tried separately, went free.

Crippen's only concern, after his arrest, had been for the welfare of his mistress. He told Dew: 'She has been my only comfort for the last three years.' In jail at Pentonville his courtesy and pleasant nature almost endeared him to his warders. When he asked the Governor that a photograph and two letters from Ethel LeNeve be buried with him, the Governor readily complied.

Crippen was hanged on 23 November 1910. To this day the graveyard within the walls of Pentonville prison in which he and other executed prisoners were buried is known to staff and inmates as 'Crippen's Patch'.

Exactly when he killed his wife, and how he disposed of the body, remains a mystery. It was most probable that he poisoned her on either the night of 31 January or the following morning. He then cut her up in the bath, and dropped the missing head and limbs overboard in a suitcase during his subsequent trip to Dieppe.

The other abiding mystery is exactly why, after tolerating his apparently intolerable wife for so long, he suddenly decided to kill her. Many theories have been produced over the years, but none have resolved the mystery satisfactorily.

After her acquittal, Ethel LeNeve emigrated to Canada until the fuss died down, and then quietly returned to England in 1916. She took a job as bookkeeper for a company in Trafalgar Square, and married a man who was said to look remarkably like Crippen. They lived in East Croydon.

In 1954, novelist Ursula Bloom published a book entitled *The Woman Who Loved Crippen*. Afterwards, she was approached by an elderly lady who revealed herself to be Ethel. She told Miss Bloom that she had never ceased to love her little doctor. Ethel LeNeve died in 1967, aged eighty-four.

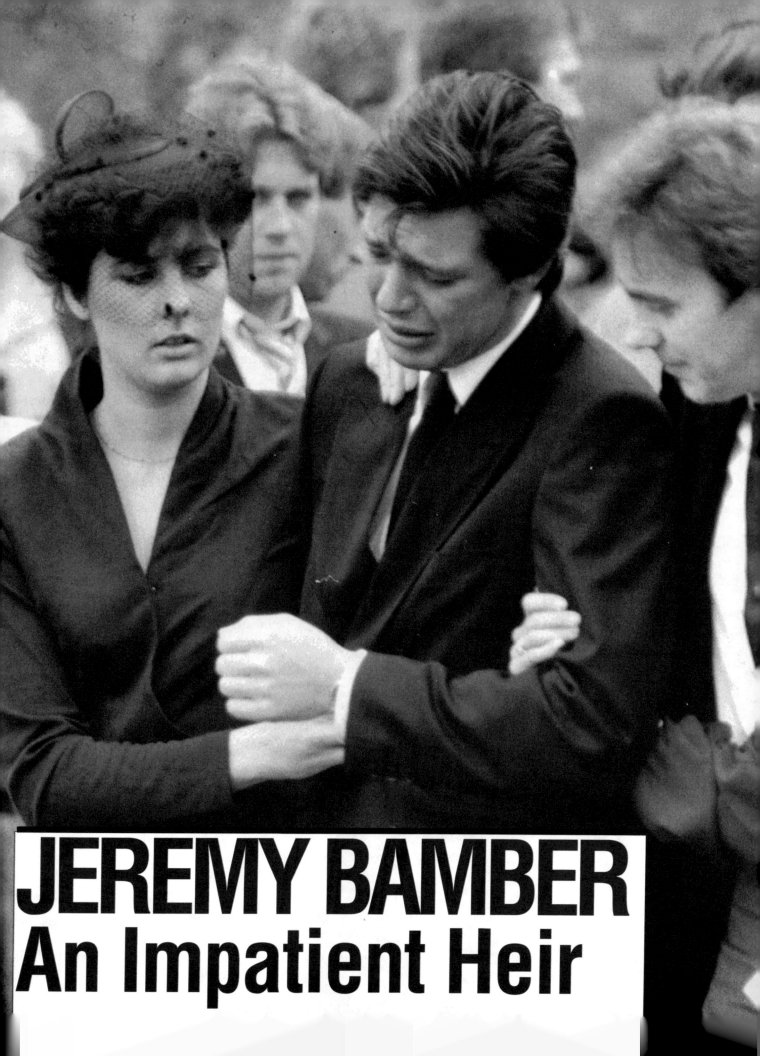

JEREMY BAMBER
An Impatient Heir

The horrific mass killing seemed to be the work of a deranged family member who had then committed suicide. Eventually the real murderer was nailed – but no thanks to the police who jumped to conclusions and destroyed vital evidence

A t 3.26 in the morning of 7 August 1985, the duty officer at Chelmsford police station in Essex received a phone call from a young man calling himself Jeremy Bamber. The caller sounded agitated.

He explained to the policeman that he was calling from his home at Goldhanger and that he had just received a frantic call from his father who lived in the nearby village of Tolleshunt D'Arcy. According to Bamber, his father had shouted: 'Come over. Your sister's gone crazy and she's got a gun....'

Bamber had then heard a shot and the line had gone dead. He had tried to call back, but the telephone was off the hook. What should he do?

The duty sergeant told Bamber to go to his father's farm and wait for the police.

*Above: **Sheila 'Bambi' Caffell** was a pretty young woman but was dogged by psychological problems.*

*Opposite: **Jeremy Bamber** is consoled by his girlfriend, Julie Mugford, after the funeral of his family.*

*Left: **White House Farm at Tolleshunt D'Arcy** where the Bamber family were slaughtered.*

Under no circumstances should he enter the building. Within minutes Detective Inspector Bill Miller had assembled an armed squad of forty men which included Special Firearms Unit marksmen.

The police reached White House Farm shortly after 4a.m. There were lights in some of the windows but everything seemed peaceful. Marksmen took up their positions and covered every door and window in the elegant Georgian farmhouse. There was still no sign of life.

Minutes later, Jeremy Bamber arrived at the farm. He was hurried over to Inspector Miller who wanted to know what they were dealing with. Was there

normally a gun in the house?

Yes, Jeremy explained. His father, Nevill Bamber, was a keen shot and kept a rifle, a high velocity semi-automatic .22 Anchutz, which he used for rabbitting.

What about his sister? From the start, Jeremy made it clear that there was no love lost between them. He stressed that they were not really brother and sister, but that they had both been adopted.

'My sister is a nutter,' Jeremy explained. 'She could go mad at any time...She's gone mad before.'

WAITING GAME

The police kept their vigil for a while longer and then made a series of appeals over a loud hailer. There was no response.

Above: *Sheila 'Bambi' Caffell with her adoptive mother, June Bamber, and her two sons, Nicholas and Daniel. All of them died at White House Farm.*

Above right: *Colin Caffell, Sheila's estranged husband, with their two children.*

> 'MY SISTER IS A NUTTER,' JEREMY BAMBER EXPLAINED. 'SHE'S GONE MAD BEFORE.'

The basic brief in circumstances like these is for police to minimize the risk of loss of life. Since there was a possibility that members of the family were being held hostage, they opted to wait it out.

Bamber, meanwhile, provided police with a detailed picture of the house and family. His adoptive parents, Nevill and June Bamber, both sixty-one, lived there and farmed the surrounding 400 acres. His adoptive sister, twenty-seven-year-old Sheila Caffell, nicknamed 'Bambi', had been staying with them since March with her six-year-old twins, Daniel and Nicholas. Bambi, Jeremy explained, had a long history of depression and had recently come out of mental hospital after a 'nervous breakdown'.

As dawn broke there was still no sign of life in the farmhouse, and the police decided to move in. A squad of ten armed officers inched their way towards the kitchen door. One of the assault team then smashed down the door and the others moved quickly into the building.

But there was no sign of violence – in fact no sign of life at all.

SCENES OF CARNAGE

As the police reached the sitting room, however, they were confronted with a glimpse of the carnage which was to come. The room was a shambles, and lying near the telephone was the body of Nevill Bamber. He had been shot six times in the head, once in the shoulder and once in the arm. He had also been brutally beaten about the head and face.

Other officers moved upstairs. In one of the bedrooms they found the bodies of the twins, Daniel and Nicholas. Both had died from multiple gunshot wounds. They had obviously been murdered while they slept; Daniel was still sucking his thumb.

The master bedroom was the scene of more horror. June Bamber was sprawled in her nightdress on the floor beside the door, a Bible lying open by her side. She had been shot seven times, once directly between the eyes.

And by the window was the body of Sheila 'Bambi' Caffell. She was lying on her back in her nightdress. She had one gunshot wound in the throat and another in her jaw. Across her lap was lying a .22 Anchutz rifle, its butt splintered and its magazine empty.

BERSERK

The forensic team, led by Detective Inspector Ronald Cook, moved into the house together with police surgeon Dr Ian Craig. Craig examined each of the five bodies in turn.

Nevill Bamber had multiple wounds to the head and had probably been beaten unconscious before he was shot. Upstairs, the children and June Bamber were quite obviously victims of a surprise attack.

That left Bambi. Dr Craig examined her two wounds. The shot to her throat had severed her jugular vein. The other had passed through her chin and entered her brain. This would have killed her instantly. Bambi had one impact bruise to her cheek but was otherwise unmarked. Her long fingernails had survived the night of violence unscathed.

Dr Craig went downstairs and joined Detective Inspectors Cook and Miller. There was no sign of a break-in and the

THE SIX-YEAR-OLD TWINS HAD BEEN SHOT WHILE THEY SLEPT — ONE OF THEM WAS STILL SUCKING HIS THUMB

Below: *Whitehouse Farm, a monument to upper-middle class respectability, and scene of one of the worst mass murders of recent times.*

three men agreed that the most obvious scenario was that Sheila Caffell had gone beserk, murdered her entire family and then turned the gun on herself.

They expressed this opinion to Detective Chief Inspector Tom 'Taff' Jones when he arrived at the farm later that morning. Jones was apparently happy to accept their conclusions.

Having 'solved' the case to their own satisfaction, Cook and his forensic team apparently decided that a detailed examination of the house and its contents was surplus to requirements – a decision which would later attract violent criticism from both the press and the judiciary.

The police did remove the rifle and some other items of evidence, but officers failed to wear gloves, and no fingerprints were ever taken of the dead family members, or of Jeremy Bamber, for elimination purposes. The only rooms that were searched were the sitting room and the two bedrooms where the bodies had been found.

Then, in an act of misplaced kindness to Jeremy Bamber, the police destroyed the very evidence they had already failed to examine properly. They washed bloodstains from the walls. Then they removed bedding and carpets from the living room and bedrooms and burned them on a bonfire.

Jeremy Bamber remained outside while his family's bodies were removed from the scene. He remained calm and subdued. The only person he wanted to see was his girlfriend, Julie Mugford. A police officer was despatched to collect her from her home in Colchester.

When Julie was told of the massacre, she looked grim but made no comment. She was driven to White House Farm and she and Jeremy Bamber held each other as they watched evidence being carried from the house and destroyed.

As police moved the focus of their enquiries to neighbours and friends, everything they heard seemed to confirm what they already suspected. The wealthy and eminently respectable Bamber family had died tragically at the hands of a deranged family member.

The suggestion that Bambi might have been involved with drugs was raised by several of the Bambers' neighbours. The

Above: *Police fingerprint Jeremy Bamber's Citroën estate car outside his home at Goldhanger, Essex.*

Below: *A police officer holds up the .22 Anchutz rifle and silencer used in the Bamber murders.*

press were quick to accept salacious village gossip as fact, and this case had everything the tabloids could ask for – a glamorous, drug-crazed heiress had apparently murdered her own children and her adoptive parents.

THE SCEPTICS TAKE ACTION

The police and press had effectively convicted Bambi of murder. Not everyone felt comfortable with that idea, however.

Nevill Bamber's nephew, David Boutflour, had been very fond of his adoptive cousin. He was horrified by the allegations being made against her.

Boutflour said the very idea that Bambi could have carried out the killings was preposterous. He knew from police reports that twenty-five shots had been fired. This would have meant reloading twice in a situation of mayhem, an operation which would have required skill and co-ordination. 'Sheila,' said Boutflour, 'couldn't put baked beans on toast without knocking them over.'

Boutflour's protests fell on deaf ears so he decided it was up to him to obtain evidence which would exonerate Bambi and, he hoped, identify the real killer.

On Sunday, 11 August, while a service for the Bambers was being held at St Nicholas's Church in Tolleshunt D'Arcy, David and his sister, Mrs Christine Eaton, went to White House Farm. They worked their way methodically through the house, looking for possible clues.

Much of the evidence had already been removed or destroyed, but the amateur sleuths found two vital clues. At the back of the gun cabinet David Boutflour discovered a .22 silencer with some specks of blood on it. Christine noticed scratches on the kitchen window-ledge which suggested that the window had been closed and locked from the outside.

Boutflour immediately informed the police of their findings. Detectives were polite but unimpressed, and it was two days before they even bothered to go out to the farm to collect the silencer.

More doubt was cast on the murder-suicide theory two days later by the Home Office pathologist. He reported to detectives involved in the case that, in his opinion, their scenario was absurd.

Firstly it required slender, 5ft 7in Sheila Caffell to bludgeon 6ft 4in Nevill Bamber unconscious. And the 'suicide' shots didn't add up either. The first shot,

Above: *Jeremy Bamber is every inch the grief-stricken son as he follows his father's coffin.*

'SHEILA,' SAID DAVID BOUTFLOUR, 'COULDN'T PUT BAKED BEANS ON TOAST WITHOUT KNOCKING THEM OVER'

Right: *Bamber was a spoiled, vain young man who wanted to live the high life, but wasn't prepared to work for it.*

THE HOME OFFICE PATHOLOGIST FOUND SEVERAL REASONS WHY SHEILA COULD NOT HAVE FIRED THE GUN, BUT THE POLICE IGNORED HIM

WITH BAMBER AWAY IN FRANCE, JULIE MUGFORD WENT TO THE POLICE AND TOLD A VERY DIFFERENT STORY

Below: *Jeremy Bamber handcuffed to a prison officer as he leaves court in a police van.*

through her jugular vein, would have rendered her incapable of firing the second into her brain. In addition, the second shot had been fired with a silencer, and there was no sign of a silencer near Bambi's body. And if the rifle had been fitted with a six-inch silencer, the weapon would have been so long that Bambi would not have been able to reach the trigger while the muzzle was pressed under her chin. She could not possibly have fired that shot.

Despite these glaring inconsistencies, detectives ignored the pathologist's findings. No mention was made of them at the coroner's inquest, which was held at Chelmsford on 14 August.

The bodies of Nevill and June Bamber were released to Jeremy Bamber. Two days later friends and relatives of the Bambers returned to St Nicholas's church for the funeral service. Then the coffins were driven to Colchester for cremation.

THE TRUTH FILTERS OUT

On 8 September, three weeks after his family's funeral, Jeremy Bamber was arrested – not for murder, but for an unrelated burglary which dated back some six months. He was charged with stealing £980 from a caravan park which he co-owned with his late parents.

The following day, Bamber appeared at Chelmsford court and was refused bail. This was extremely unusual for a first offender accused of a non-violent crime, and it suggests that the police were starting to look at the White House killings in a new light. Jeremy was held in gaol for five days before being released in his own recognizance.

Jeremy left immediately for a holiday on the French Riviera. Surprisingly, he went with a friend, Brett Collins, rather than his girlfriend. This would prove Bamber's most expensive mistake.

A few days after Jeremy left for France, Julie Mugford went to see the Essex police. She told them she was certain that Jeremy had killed his family.

According to Julie, Jeremy had been planning the murders for months. She explained that Jeremy loathed his parents and he resented the fact that he had not been given his inheritance while he was young enough to enjoy it.

Julie said that on the night of the massacre Jeremy had telephoned her and said: 'It's got to be tonight or never.' Julie said she had told him not to be stupid, but that he had hung up. At three the following morning, Jeremy had rung again and said: 'Everything is going well.'

At first, detectives were inclined to believe that they were listening to the bitter rantings of a spurned woman. After all, hadn't Jeremy just taken off to France without her? But, as her story unfolded, they were reminded of the pathologist's findings and the evidence submitted by David Boutflour and Christine Eaton. It was becoming increasingly obvious that they had made a terrible mistake.

On 30 September, police were waiting at Dover ferry terminal when Jeremy Bamber returned from his holiday. He was arrested and charged with murdering Nevill and June Bamber, together with Sheila, Daniel and Nicholas Caffell.

GREED AND EXTRAVAGANCE

On Tuesday, 2 October 1986, more than a year after the massacre at White House Farm, the trial of Jeremy Bamber opened at Chelmsford Crown Court. Bamber had secured one of the country's best criminal solicitors, Sir David Napley, and he in turn had briefed Geoffrey Rivlin QC to conduct the defence. Bamber pleaded not guilty to five charges of murder.

The prosecution, led by Anthony Arlidge QC, opened by describing the massacre in graphic detail. He said that he would prove beyond all reasonable doubt that the perpetrator of the five killings was Jeremy Bamber. His motive, Arlidge claimed, was greed. Bamber knew that if all his family died, he would inherit almost half a million pounds.

The prosecution produced a plethora of evidence and expert witnesses. It all indicated that Sheila Caffell could not have committed the murders, and suggested that Jeremy Bamber might well have done so. The evidence against Bamber was, at best, circumstantial. Mr Arlidge chastised the police for their handling of the case, saying that if they had done their job properly his own job would have been made simpler.

On the morning of 9 October, Arlidge put his star witness on the stand. Julie Mugford wept as she told the jury of the months during which Jeremy Bamber's

Left: *Jeremy Bamber is remanded in custody at Maldon Magistrates' Court.*

IF BAMBER'S WHOLE FAMILY
DIED, EXPLAINED THE
PROSECUTING COUNSEL,
HE WOULD STAND TO
INHERIT £500,000

Below: *May 1986 – Jeremy Bamber arrives at Maldon Magistrates' Court for the committal proceedings.*

fantasies of killing his family had threatened to become a horrifying reality. Her answers during cross-examination were precise and consistent, and bore an unmistakeable ring of truth.

On 16 October, Rivlin opened the defence. He set out to prove that Sheila Caffell was a more likely murderer than he was. His argument came unstuck, however, when he was unable to discredit evidence submitted by the ballistics expert and the Home Office pathologist.

The following day, Rivlin put Jeremy Bamber on the witness stand. Bamber denied the killings and claimed to have had a loving relationship with his family. Under cross-examination, however, Bamber displayed a petulant, arrogant streak which did nothing to help his case.

Arlidge went to town on Bamber's character, portraying him as a greedy, vain and idle young man. None of this was very flattering, but it didn't prove that Jeremy Bamber had killed his family. In the final analysis, it all came down to who the jury chose to believe – Jeremy Bamber or Julie Mugford.

In the afternoon of 27 October, the jury retired to consider their verdict. Two days later they returned a verdict of 'guilty' on all five counts by a majority of 10–2.

Sentencing Bamber to five concurrent life sentences, the judge recommended that he should not be released for at least twenty-five years.

REIGN OF TERROR
The Boston Strangler

In 1963 a serial killer stalked the streets of Boston. His female victims were first sexually assaulted, then strangled and left lying in obscene postures. And this demented psychopath left no clues ...

Just before seven o'clock on the evening of 14 June 1962 Juris Slesers, a twenty-five-year-old research engineer, climbed the stairs to his mother's third-floor apartment at 77 Gainsborough Street in Boston. He had arranged to drive her to a memorial service at the Latvian Lutheran church in nearby Roxbury.

Mrs Slesers, a petite fifty-five-year-old divorcee, had fled Soviet-occupied Latvia with her son some twenty years earlier and settled in Boston, where she worked as a seamstress. For the past three months, since Juris had moved out, she had lived alone in this tiny apartment.

Juris knocked on the door and waited. There was no answer. He knocked again, pressed his ear to the metal door and listened. There was no sound from within.

He presumed his mother had popped out to do some shopping and went downstairs. He sat on the front steps and waited. Three-quarters of an hour passed and Juris was becoming concerned. He went back upstairs, hammered on the door and shouted his mother's name. There was still no response.

He put his shoulder to the door, backed

Opposite: *Albert de Salvo. Was he indeed the Boston Strangler?*

Below: *Massachusetts State Troopers search for the Strangler.*

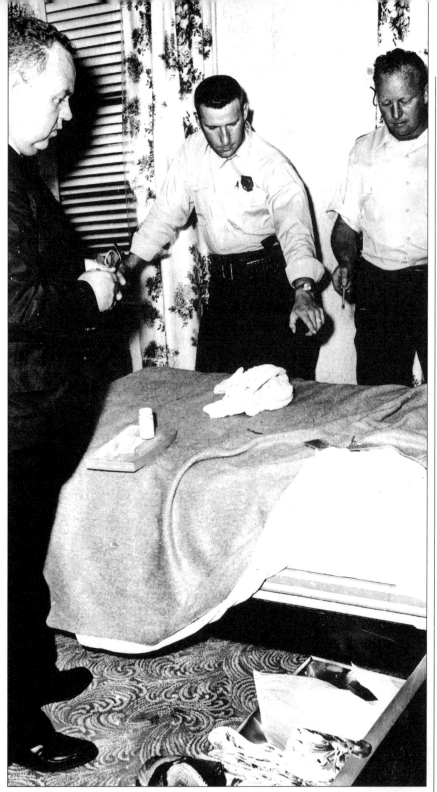

hallway and headed for the bathroom.

Anna Slesers was lying just outside the bathroom door. She was wearing her blue taffeta housecoat which was spread wide apart at the front, leaving her effectively nude. She lay with her left leg stretched straight out and her right flung at right-angles with the knee bent so that she was grossly exposed. The cord of her housecoat was knotted tightly round her neck and then fastened under her chin in the fashion of a crude bow. She was quite obviously dead.

The police, led by Special Officer James Mellon, arrived on the scene within minutes of receiving Juris Slesers's call.

Despite the fact that there was little sign of disturbance, it was immediately obvious to Officer Mellon that he was dealing with homicide. Mrs Slesers had been sexually assaulted and then strangled.

His initial suspicion was that someone had broken into the apartment with the intention of committing a robbery, had found Mrs Slesers in a state of undress – she looked younger than her years – and was seized by an uncontrollable sexual urge. He had raped Mrs Slesers and then strangled her to prevent her from identifying him.

The police conducted a thorough investigation. House-to-house enquiries were carried out. Relatives and friends were interviewed. A few possible candidates for the crime were picked up and questioned.

But the officers made no headway and, gruesome though the crime was, it soon became just another statistic. Boston averaged more than a murder a week at that time and, with a total lack of clues, the police accepted that their chances of ever finding the man responsible for Anna Slesers's death were very slim.

up and then rammed it with all his strength. The door sprang open.

JUST ANOTHER STATISTIC

Inside the apartment it was quite dark, and Juris tripped over a chair which had unaccountably been left in the middle of the narrow hallway. He looked into the living room and the bedroom, both of which were oddly untidy. There was no sign of his mother. He returned to the

Above: *The police search for clues in Helen Blake's apartment.*

THE FIFTY-FIVE-YEAR-OLD
WOMAN HAD BEEN RAPED
AND THEN STRANGLED WITH
HER HOUSECOAT CORD

SEXUAL PSYCHOPATH

At five o'clock on 30 June, two weeks after the murder at Gainsborough Street, Nina Nichols, a sixty-eight-year-old retired physiotherapist, returned home to 1940 Commonwealth Avenue in Boston. She had just spent a pleasant few days in the country staying with friends.

As soon as she got into her apartment Mrs Nichols called her sister, Marguerite Steadman, to say that she was back safely and that she would be over for dinner at six o'clock as planned. The sisters chatted for a while but then Nina Nichols cut their conversation short, saying: 'Excuse me, Marguerite, there's my buzzer. I'll call you right back.'

Mrs Nichols didn't call her sister back, nor did she arrive for dinner at six o'clock. By seven, her sister was becoming concerned and asked her husband, attorney Chester Steadman, to telephone and make sure everything was all right. There was no reply to his call.

Another half an hour passed, and the Steadmans were becoming really alarmed. Maybe she had been been taken ill? Chester Steadman called the janitor of the building, Thomas Bruce. Would he go up to Mrs Nichols's apartment and see if she was still there?

Bruce went upstairs, knocked on the door and, when there was no reply, opened it with his pass-key. He never set foot inside. What he saw from the doorway was enough.

The apartment had obviously been burgled. Drawers had been pulled out, and clothes strewn all over the floor.

But there was worse, much worse. Directly ahead of him, Bruce could see into the bedroom. And on the floor, legs spread wide apart, was the nude body of Nina Nichols. Around her neck, tied so tightly that they cut into her flesh, were a pair of stockings. They were knotted under her chin in a clumsy bow.

Police Lieutenant Edward Sherry was soon at the scene with medical examiner Dr Michael Luongo. The similarities to the Slesers murder were immediately obvious to both men.

Nina Nichols had been sexually molested and then strangled. Both women had been left in a grossly exposed state. And then there were the tell-tale bows in the ligatures. There had been no sign of forceable entry to either apartment. Both had been ransacked but apparently nothing had been stolen in either case, despite the fact that high-value, easily disposable items like jewellery and cameras had been lying around. And there was no reason to

Above: *District Attorney John Burke and homicide officers search the scene where the body of Carrol Anne Donovan, one of the Boston Strangler's victims, was discovered.*

'EXCUSE ME, MARGUERITE,' SAID NINA NICHOLS, 'THERE'S MY BUZZER. I'LL CALL YOU RIGHT BACK.' BUT SHE NEVER DID

believe that the intruder had been interrupted on either occasion.

The police came to the conclusion that the murderer had never intended to commit a robbery – he had merely wanted to give the impression of committing a robbery. So what were they dealing with? Two murders did not constitute a serial, but Sherry and his colleagues had a gut feeling that there was a sexual psychopath at large in Boston.

They did not have to wait long before their fears were confirmed. On 2 July, two days later, police received a call from the neighbours of Helen Blake, a sixty-five-year-old retired nurse.

Helen had not been seen for a couple of days. Her friends had been concerned and borrowed a pass-key from the building supervisor. They had opened the door of her apartment, seen signs of a burglary and been afraid to go in.

The police entered the apartment and found Helen Blake lying face down on her bed. She was naked except for a

'OH GOD,' SAID THE POLICE COMMISSIONER WHEN TOLD OF THE THIRD MURDER. 'WE'VE GOT A MADMAN LOOSE!'

Below: *Mary Sullivan, 19, was found strangled on 5 January 1964 in her Beacon Hill apartment.*

pyjama top, which had been pushed up to her shoulders. She had been sexually assaulted and strangled with a pair of stockings. A brassiere was also tied around her neck, and fastened under her chin in a bow. The medical examiner estimated that she had been dead for about three days.

Police Commissioner McNamara was winding up a conference on the murders of Anna Slesers and Nina Nichols when Lieutenant Donovan told him that Helen Blake's body had been found. As Donovan gave him the details, McNamara expressed the feelings of the whole police department. 'Oh God,' he said. 'We've got a madman loose!'

What McNamara could not know was that these three murders were just the beginning and that, over the next year and a half, a total of eleven women would be strangled and sexually assaulted in Boston. The city would become a town paralysed by terror.

As the public screamed for a solution to the atrocities, the police mounted the greatest man-hunt known in modern crime, using every known detection technique, both natural and supernatural. They would use computers, clairvoyants and psychometrists, psychiatrists with hypnotic drugs and truth serums, psychologists, experts on anthropology, graphology and forensic medicine, as they found themselves confronted by a man whose brutality and insanity were matched by enormous cunning. He appeared to be able to gain access to locked apartments, molest and kill women, and never leave a single clue.

EXHAUSTIVE ENQUIRIES

The day after the discovery of Helen Blake's body, Commissioner McNamara cancelled all police leave. All his detectives were reassigned to homicide. There was a round-up of all known sex offenders. And anyone between eighteen and forty who had been released from a mental institution in the previous two years was investigated.

The police held a press conference during which they appealed to women, particularly women living alone, to keep their doors and windows locked, to admit no strangers, and to report any prowlers, obscene phone calls and letters.

Over the next few weeks the police were deluged with telephone calls and letters conveying tips, suspicions and alarms, both genuine and spurious. Lieutenants Sherry and Donovan, Special Officer Mellon and Detective Phil DiNatale, together with scores of other detectives, spent long hours and weekends covering leads and tracing and picking up possible suspects. The police held identity parades and administered lie-detector tests on scores of men. None of them was the strangler.

By mid-August there had been no more killings, and McNamara was beginning to hope that the strangler had sated his hideous cravings. Then, on 21 August, they found Ida Irga.

A seventy-five-year-old widow, Mrs

Irga had been dead for two days. She had been strangled by human hands, but a pillow case had also been tied round her neck in a bow. Like the other victims, she had been sexually molested and, in her case, the murderer had added an appalling refinement to his attack. He had placed two chairs widely apart and tied one ankle to each in an obscene parody of a gynaecological examination. Again, the apartment had been ransacked yet no property had been removed.

Ten days later, the strangler struck again. His victim was Jane Sullivan, a sixty-seven-year-old nurse. She was found in the bathroom of her apartment; she had been dead for more than a week.

Her body was half kneeling in the tub, her face and arms submerged in six inches of water so that her buttocks were exposed. She had been strangled with two of her own stockings and placed in the bath after death.

UNBRIDLED HYSTERIA

Three months passed without a strangling but, far from relaxing, the people of Boston built themselves up to a state of unbridled hysteria. Every prowler, every flasher, every obscene phone caller was automatically presumed to be the strangler. A housewife in Brockton dropped dead of a heart attack when she found herself confronted with a stranger

*Above: **Police remove the body of Mary Sullivan from her apartment.***

THE FOURTH BODY WAS LEFT LYING IN A POSITION THAT OBSCENELY PARODIED THAT OF A GYNAECOLOGICAL EXAMINATION

ONE HOUSEWIFE DIED OF HEART FAILURE WHEN SHE OPENED THE DOOR TO A STRANGER. HE WAS ONLY SELLING ENCYCLOPAEDIAS

---

on her doorstep. He turned out to be selling encyclopaedias.

The police, with the help of a host of experts, had built up a complex psychological profile of the strangler. He was, they decided, between eighteen and forty years old, white, highly intelligent but psychopathic. He might well be homosexual or bi-sexual. He probably suffered from schizophrenia. He hated women, particularly older women, and had probably been brought up by a domineering mother. To his actual identity, however, they still had no clue.

When the next killing occurred, on 5 December 1962, even their psychological profile proved at least partially inaccurate. The latest victim, Sophie Clark, could not have been more different from the established strangler 'type'. She was an attractive black student of twenty who shared a flat with two other women. And Patricia Bisset, who was found strangled and sexually assaulted on New Year's Eve, was twenty-three and white.

It was now obvious that the strangler struck at random and no woman in Boston, young or old, black or white, living alone or living with others, was safe from him.

FURTHER GROTESQUE ATTACKS

On Wednesday, 8 May 1963, thirty-three-year-old Oliver Chamberlin called round to see his fiancée, Beverly Samans, a graduate student at Boston University. There was no answer when Chamberlin rang the bell of Beverly's apartment, so he let himself in with his own key.

He saw her at once. She was sprawled on a sofa bed in the living room, naked, her legs spread wide apart. Her wrists were tied behind her back with sequin-studded silk scarves. A bloodstained stocking and two handkerchiefs were knotted around her neck.

Beverly, however, had not died of stangulation. She had been stabbed twenty-two times in the throat and left breast. There was no doubt, however, that this was the work of the strangler, whose body count had now risen to eight.

Three months passed before the strangler struck again. Number nine was a vivacious fifty-eight-year-old divorcee called Evelyn Corbin. Strangled, assaulted and grossly exposed, she was found by a neighbour. Again the police found no clues, save a doughnut on the fire escape outside Mrs Corbin's apartment.

Friday 22 November 1963 is a day that no American will ever forget. President Kennedy was gunned down in Dallas, Texas. The following day, the entire nation was reeling from the blow, but for the strangler it was business as usual. This time his victim was a shy twenty-three-year-old, Joann Graff. He strangled her with her own black leotard and left her nude body on a day bed in her apartment.

Christmas came, and the people of Boston did their level best not to let the strangler ruin the holiday season. Indeed he did not strike over that period. But shortly after New Year Pamela Parker and Patricia Delmore returned from work to find their nineteen-year-old flatmate, Mary Sullivan, brutally murdered. It was the most grotesque and macabre killing so far.

Mary's body – in the words of the police report – was 'on the bed in a propped position, buttocks on pillow, back against headboard, head on right shoulder, knees up, eyes closed, viscous liquid dripping from mouth to right breast, breasts and lower extremities exposed, broomstick handle inserted in vagina...' Knotted round her neck were a stocking and a silk scarf tied together in a huge, comic bow. A bright greetings card which read 'Happy New Year!' was propped against her left foot.

The public outrage was intense, and two weeks later the Attorney General, Edward W. Brooke Jnr, announced that the Attorney General's Office of the Commonwealth of Massachusetts was taking over the investigation.

NO LONGER TOLERABLE

The strangler task force worked tirelessly throughout 1964. There were no further stranglings, but the police force's determination to identify and convict the man responsible was undiminished. But, by the autumn of 1964, the authorities were no nearer catching the strangler. It

Top: *Newsmen and photographers gather outside the apartment of Strangler victim Mary Sullivan.*

Above: *Police officers look for clues on the roof of Mary Sullivan's apartment.*

THE ONLY CLUE LEFT BY THE STRANGLER AT THE SCENE OF HIS NINTH MURDER WAS A DOUGHNUT DROPPED ON THE FIRE ESCAPE

---

was now nine months since he had struck and there was a feeling that the killer might have moved from the area, committed suicide or merely quit.

Then, on 27 October, the police in Cambridge, Massachusetts received a complaint from a young housewife. It was destined to open a whole new avenue of enquiry.

She told detectives that she was dozing in bed, after seeing her teacher husband off to work, when a man appeared at the bedroom door. He was about thirty, of medium build, wearing green slacks and large sunglasses.

The man had come slowly towards her and said: 'Don't worry, I'm a detective.' The young woman had yelled at him to get out, but the man had leaped forward, pinned her to the bed and held a knife to her throat. 'Not a sound,' he had commanded, 'or I'll kill you.'

The intruder had gagged his victim with her underwear, then tied her ankles and wrists to the bedposts so that she was spread-eagled. He had proceeded to kiss and fondle her body. Suddenly he had stopped, got to his feet and loosened her bonds slightly.

'You be quiet for ten minutes,' he said. 'I'm sorry,' he added and then fled from the apartment.

After she had finished giving her statement to detectives, the young woman spent several hours with a police artist trying to establish a likeness of her attacker. Between them they did a good job. One of the detectives recognized the face immediately. 'That,' he said, 'looks like the Measuring Man.'

THE MEASURING MAN

This was a character well known to the Boston police. He had been convicted and gaoled in 1960 for breaking and entering and indecently assaulting young women. He had gained his nickname because he had a habit of posing as an artist's agent, calling on young women and taking their measurements for supposed employment as models. The Measuring Man's real name was Albert H. De Salvo.

Thirty-three-year-old maintenance man De Salvo was picked up and brought to the police headquarters at Cambridge. He denied assaulting the young woman, but she identified him immediately. De Salvo was charged and taken into custody. As a matter of routine, the Cambridge police teletyped De Salvo's picture to neighbouring states. The response was astounding.

Messages poured in from New Hampshire, Rhode Island and Connecticut to say that De Salvo had been identified by scores of women as being the man who had sexually assaulted them. In some areas he was known as the Green Man because of his penchant for green trousers.

De Salvo denied everything and refused to answer any questions until he had spoken to his German-born wife, Irmgard. She was duly delivered to him and detectives watched them as they whispered together.

The police got the impression that Irmgard knew her husband had been 'up to something with women'. She confirmed their suspicions by saying aloud: 'Al, tell them everything. Don't hold anything back.'

De Salvo heeded his wife's advice and told detectives: 'I have committed more than four hundred breaks [breaking and entering], all in this area, and there's a couple of rapes you don't know about.'

As the investigation widened,

Below: *Police Commissioner McNamara with the special tactical squad he formed to catch the Boston Strangler.*

detectives soon realized that De Salvo was not exaggerating. They estimated that in the past two years he had committed sexual assaults on more than three hundred women.

De Salvo was shipped to Boston State Hospital for observation while he awaited trial for the Green Man offences. Doctors found him to be 'overtly schizophrenic and potentially suicidal', and on 4 February 1965 Judge Edward A. Pecce ordered him to be committed to a hospital for the criminally insane 'until further orders of the court'.

Al De Salvo should really have been caught up in the 'strangler dragnet' three years earlier. But, because of an administrative anomaly, he had been listed on the computer as a breaking-and-entering man rather than as a sex offender. So he had been overlooked when Boston police were conducting routine questioning early in the case. Now they wanted to know if he was involved.

But De Salvo was horrified at the suggestion that he might be connected with the killings. 'No, no' he wept, 'I've

done some terrible things with women – but I've never killed anyone.' Detectives were initially inclined to believe him. De Salvo didn't fit their profile of the Strangler, and he simply wasn't smart enough to have got away with it.

In hospital, De Salvo befriended a convicted killer named George Nassar. Soon he was using him as a confidant.

He did not come straight out and say he was the strangler, but his hints were sufficiently pointed for Nassar to get a distinct impression that he might be. A $110,000 reward had been offered to anyone giving information which led to the capture and conviction of the strangler, and Nassar saw this as a perfect chance to make a fast buck. He informed his attorney, F. Lee Bailey.

Bailey went to see De Salvo and recorded his confession to all eleven Boston stranglings, plus another two killings which the police had not previously connected with the strangler. Bailey turned a copy of his tape over to the police and the Attorney General's Office.

At first everyone was sceptical about

Below: *Store which DeSalvo held up, for which he was later arrested and convicted.*

De Salvo being the strangler. Not only did he not fit their profile, he had also gained a reputation as a braggart.

But when he was questioned at length, he started to disclose facts about the killings that only the strangler could have known – facts that had been deliberately kept secret to catch out the 'confessors'. De Salvo drew diagrams of the various apartments where the killings had taken place, and under hypno-analysis described the actual stranglings in gruesome detail.

Finally, the authorities were forced to accept that he might indeed be the Boston Strangler.

NO CASE

It was now the spring of 1965. The manhunt, now in its third year, was wound down, and the investigation team was reduced to two men. Assistant Attorney General John Bottomley spent the next seven months interviewing De Salvo, talking him through each crime in minute detail. De Salvo proved to have an incredible memory and his descriptions of the various murders left Bottomley in absolutely no doubt that Albert De Salvo and the Boston Strangler were one and the same person.

Bottomley had his confession, but he had no one to corroborate it. De Salvo's victims could not testify against him and there were no eye-witnesses to identify him, and in America no one can be convicted solely by their own uncorroborated testimony. After all that effort, the state still had no case.

De Salvo had committed other crimes, however, for which the police had ample evidence. On the last day of June 1966 Albert De Salvo attended a hearing at Middlesex County Courthouse in East Cambridge, which was designed to determine whether he was mentally fit to stand trial for the Green Man offences.

It was his first public appearance since he had been committed to the institution at Bridgewater on 4 February 1965. Everyone in the court knew that De Salvo was probably the Boston Strangler, yet that case was not allowed to be mentioned.

Dr Mezer and Dr Tartakoff appeared as expert witnesses for the prosecution. They said that in their opinion Albert De Salvo was suffering from a committable mental illness, but was quite capable of standing trial.

Dr Robey, however, who had originally committed De Salvo to Bridgewater, disagreed completely: 'He is suffering from schizophrenic reaction, chronic undifferentiated type with very extensive signs of sexual deviation...My opinion is that I cannot – repeat – cannot consider him competent to stand trial....' Dr Robey added that, in his opinion, De Salvo would react to cross-examination by getting 'in such a state that he would not be making sense'.

Ten days later Judge Cahill accepted the prosecution argument and found Albert De Salvo competent to stand trail. The following year De Salvo was tried and convicted of armed robbery, breaking and entering, theft, assault and sexual crimes against four women, all of whom were lucky enough to live to identify their attacker. He was sentenced to life imprisonment.

While Albert De Salvo was never to stand trial as the Boston Strangler, the system had made sure he would never be free again. As it turned out, the length of his sentence was academic. On 26 November 1973, Albert De Salvo was found dead in his cell in Walpole State Prison. He had been stabbed sixteen times. The identity of his killer has never been established.

Above: *Women of all ages crowd into the Middlesex Superior Courtroom, hoping to catch a glimpse of the Strangler.*

FREDERICK SEDDON
Murdering for Gold

Greed was a clear motive for the killing of a rich, elderly spinster, and there was an obvious suspect. But his conviction on the basis of new and unproven scientific evidence raised a public outcry

Frederick Seddon was an avaricious man. At the age of thirty-eight, he was district superintendent for a large insurance company and was already quite prosperous. He had an annual income of more than £400 a year – a substantial sum in 1910. Seddon also had successful property investments, substantial savings in cash, and shares. But like all greedy men, he wanted more.

ROOMS TO LET

Seddon lived in a large, comfortable house in Tollington Park, Islington, North London with his attractive wife Margaret and his five children. Despite his circumstances and the size of his family, Seddon employed no domestic help.

Additionally, he considered the empty rooms on the top floor of the house to be wasteful. With no regard for his already overworked wife, he decided to take in lodgers. To this end, he placed an advertisement in the local newspaper.

On 10 July 1910, Seddon opened his front door to Miss Eliza Barrow and some companions who had come about the lodgings. Miss Barrow, a forty-nine-year-old spinster, was loud, hard of hearing and considerably overweight. She was accompanied by Ernie Grant, the eight-year-old orphaned son of a woman friend, and a slightly drunk, middle-aged couple named Hook.

This unprepossessing little group had been lodging with Miss Barrow's cousins, a Mr and Mrs Frederick Vonderahe, but had left hurriedly after a row.

Many potential landlords would have turned them away without a second thought, but Frederick Seddon was not interested in social niceties. He was interested in money, and when Miss Barrow offered him cash in advance from a well-stocked strong box, he welcomed the unlikely foursome into his home.

It was obvious to Seddon from the outset that Eliza Barrow was supporting the other three. So when, after a blazing row a week later, she asked Seddon to evict the Hooks, he readily agreed.

Mr Hook responded angrily, accusing Seddon of being 'after her money'. As he left 63 Tollington Park, Hook delivered a parting shot to his erstwhile landlord: 'I defy you and a regiment like you to get it.'

WEALTHY SPINSTER

Seddon, who up to this point had merely seen his tenant as someone who could be relied upon to pay her rent, decided that her affairs deserved more serious investigation.

Eliza Barrow might have been a slob, but at least she had no illusions about her charm. In the light of this self-realization, she mistrusted anyone who showed her good will, let alone attempted to befriend her. She assumed, and usually rightly, that they were only interested in her money.

Despite Miss Barrow's suspicious nature, however, Seddon managed to find out a great deal about her finances in the ensuing weeks. This was perhaps because Miss Barrow saw in him a kindred spirit, a man who worshipped money and had clearly done well for himself. She thought it might be worth picking his brains with the aim of maximizing the potential of her capital.

Miss Barrow confided in Seddon that some years earlier she had received a small inheritance whose value she had managed to multiply several times over. At this moment, she owned £1600 worth of India stock, and leases on the Buck's Head public house in Camden Town, a barber's shop and a tenement building. These investments yielded her an annual

Above: *Margaret Seddon was a hard-working, decent woman who bore her husband five children.*

Opposite: *Frederick Seddon was a man of property and insatiable greed.*

WITH FIVE CHILDREN AND NO DOMESTIC HELP SEDDON HEAPED YET MORE WORK ON HIS WIFE BY ADVERTISING FOR LODGERS

MISS BARROW SAW IN HER NEW LANDLORD A MONEY-WORSHIPPING KINDRED SPIRIT AND DECIDED TO CONFIDE IN HIM

income of about £120.

In addition to that, she had a £216 on deposit at the Finsbury and City of London Bank, and some £400 in gold and banknotes which she kept in a strong box in her rooms. She realized that it was risky to keep so much cash in the house, but told Seddon that young Ernie shared her bed as a security measure.

The confidence that Miss Barrow shared with her landlord soon developed into a genuine trust. Not only did she

Above: *Margaret Seddon was initially under suspicion of murder, along with her husband, but it was soon obvious to the court that she too was an innocent victim.*

respect Seddon's business acumen, she got on particularly well with his wife. Margaret Seddon was a northerner, a sensible, hard-working woman with whom she could readily relate.

FINANCIAL ADVISER

By early October, Miss Barrow felt confident enough to ask for advice outright. She told Seddon that she was anxious about her investments and wondered if he had any suggestions.

He said he would consider the matter, and some days later advised her to take out an annuity. This was, he explained, a particularly appropriate form of investment for a spinster without dependants. It paid a very high annual dividend for as long as the holder lived, and then the policy died with them.

On 14 October 1910, Miss Barrow and Frederick Seddon signed an agreement whereby she surrendered her India stock for an annuity of £103 4s. Three months later, she turned over the leases of the pub and the barber's shop for a further £50 per annum.

Seddon's terms were, in fact, fair to the point of being generous. Miss Barrow's annuity amounted to at least £30 a year more than she would have received if she had invested in an insurance policy or deposited her money in the Post Office. The instalments were paid regularly and in full, usually in the form of gold coins. Seddon had a passion for gold and made a practice of paying all his debts in that form, merely for the pleasure of handling the metal.

Nine months later Miss Barrow, well pleased with her new financial arrangements, expressed concern about her remaining investments.

On 9 June 1911, Seddon took possession of her tenement building in exchange for a further annuity of £150. Ten days later, he claimed to have heard that the Finsbury and City of London Bank was in trouble, and suggested that Miss Barrow close her account.

The following morning, accompanied by Margaret Seddon, Miss Barrow duly went down to her bank and drew out all her savings of £216 in gold coins. Then she added these to the other ready cash which she kept in her strong box.

From this point on, everything Eliza Barrow owned was either controlled by Frederick Seddon or stored under his roof.

HOT WEATHER

Miss Barrow and young Ernie lived a solitary existence in their rented rooms. Ernie went to school, but otherwise they rarely left 63 Tollington Park. Even their meals were brought upstairs.

August 1911 was hot and humid, and neither Miss Barrow nor her young charge was particularly fussy about personal hygiene or domestic cleanliness. Their rooms soon became infested with flies and, to combat this, chemical fly papers were hung up. Whether Miss

---

MISS BARROW'S ROOMS WERE SOON INFESTED WITH FLIES, ATTRACTED BY THE STENCH OF VOMIT AND FAECES

Below: *Number 63 Tollington Park, home of the Seddon family, where Miss Eliza Barrow took lodgings.*

Barrow or the Seddons installed the papers is open to question, but it was a matter which would be hotly debated some months later.

On 1 September 1911, Miss Barrow was taken ill with stomach pains, nausea and diarrhoea. Mrs Seddon summoned their own family doctor, Dr Henry Sworn, to examine her. He said it was nothing serious and prescribed a variety of stomach mixtures, including a nightly dose of Valentine's Meat Juice.

Days passed, but Miss Barrow showed no sign of improvement. Dr Sworn suggested she should go into hospital for tests but, balking at the cost, Miss Barrow said that she would prefer to be treated at home by Margaret Seddon. The long-suffering Mrs Seddon agreed to take on this additional responsibility provided Dr Sworn made regular house calls. And so it was agreed.

In the next couple of weeks, the condition of Miss Barrow's rooms deteriorated from merely unpleasant to truly squalid. They were now infested with flies, attracted by the constant stench of vomit and faeces. Despite her infirmity, Miss Barrow never forgot about the security of her strong box and insisted that the unfortunate Ernie continue to share her bed.

Mrs Seddon did her best to ensure that her patient was comfortable and took her medicine. But, despite her best offices and frequent visits from Dr Sworn, Miss Barrow seemed to get progressively worse.

On 13 September, two weeks after Miss Barrow first fell ill, Frederick Seddon took a rare trip to the theatre. While he was out, Ernie came downstairs and asked Mrs Seddon for help. She followed the boy upstairs and found Miss Barrow writhing around on the floor in agony. 'I'm dying!' she moaned.

Mrs Seddon managed to get her lodger back to bed and sat with her through the night. At 6.30 the following morning, rasping thickly, Eliza Barrow died.

Later that morning, Frederick Seddon went down to the surgery where the doctor handed him a death certificate without even seeing his erstwhile patient. The certificate gave the cause of death as epidemic diarrhoea.

SUSPICIOUS RELATIVES

That same evening, Seddon packed young Ernie Grant off to relatives in Southend and started to make arrangements for Miss Barrow's funeral. She had told the Seddons that she had a place reserved in her family vault, but Seddon opted for a cheaper, quicker burial at Islington cemetery in North Finchley.

The funeral took place two days later on Saturday 16 September. None of Eliza Barrow's relatives had been informed of her death, let alone her interment. Frederick Seddon assumed, wrongly as it transpired, that no one would be particularly interested.

However, Miss Barrow's cousins, the Vonderahes, were very interested. Eliza might have been distinctly unlovable, but she was family. They were incensed at Seddon's failure to inform them of her death before the funeral took place. They were also suspicious.

When they looked into her affairs and found that she had transferred all her capital to Seddon in exchange for annuities – annuities which no longer needed to be paid – they went straight to the police.

Two days later, the police obtained an order to exhume Miss Barrow's body. Sir William Willcox, a Home Office pathologist, conducted an autopsy. His examination revealed that the body contained two and a half grains of arsenic.

On 4 December 1911 the police arrested Frederick Seddon and charged him with the murder of Eliza Barrow.

BEWILDERED OUTRAGE

Seddon's reaction to the charge was one of bewildered outrage 'Absurd,' he blustered. 'What a terrible charge, wilful murder....Are you going to arrest my wife as well?' They were.

On 15 January, Mrs Margaret Seddon was arrested and charged with conspiring to murder Miss Eliza Barrow. And on 2 February she and her husband were committed for trial.

Seddon appeared quite confident that he would be acquitted of the charge. And

Above: *Eliza Barrow, a forty-nine-year-old spinster, was loud, hard of hearing and considerably overweight.*

while he awaited trial, he gave the impression of trying to cooperate with the investigating officers.

Some of the questions he asked, however, made the police even more convinced that he had indeed committed the murder. On one occasion, for instance, he asked detectives: 'Have they found any arsenic in the body?' If he had been privy to the autopsy report, he would have known that they had. If he

hadn't seen the report, why had he assumed that arsenic was the cause of death? There were scores of other toxic substances which could have accounted for Eliza Barrow's untimely death.

Seddon also mentioned arsenic to his lawyer, saying that 'the old girl' had had some very odd habits. For instance he had seen her drinking soaked fly papers – in those days fly papers were frequently impregnated with arsenic.

His preoccupation with arsenic certainly aroused the interest of the police, but it proved absolutely nothing. There was no forensic evidence against the Seddons, and the detectives soon realized that, if they were to build a successful case, they would have to follow Miss Barrow's missing fortune.

PICTURE OF MIDDLE-CLASS RESPECTABILITY

Seddon was a wizard with figures. His accounts were always meticulously kept,

and his memory for the details and dates of transactions was truly phenomenal. And when his trial opened at the Old Bailey on 4 March 1912, he must have been confident that he could run circles round any barrister on matters of accountancy.

It was to Frederick Seddon's misfortune that the prosecutor in this case was Sir Rufus Isaacs KC, the Attorney General. Isaacs had spent his early years working in the City of London as a trader, and as a barrister he had specialized in commercial cases. He was every bit Seddon's match when it came to matters of finance.

For his defence Seddon had obtained the services of Sir Edward Marshall Hall, a fiery showman who was famous for his court room gamesmanship. Mrs Seddon was defended by a young counsel named Gervais Rentoul, though in reality Marshall Hall ended up conducting the defence for both of them.

Frederick and Margaret Seddon sat

UNFORTUNATELY FOR SEDDON, THE PROSECUTING COUNSEL HAD ONCE WORKED IN THE CITY AND KNEW ALL ABOUT FINANCIAL WHEELER-DEALING together in the dock, attended by a policeman and a female warder. Seddon was the picture of middle-class respectability in his dark business suit, while his wife wore a dark coat and hat with a veil. As the charges were read, both of them pleaded Not Guilty to murdering Eliza Barrow.

Sir Rufus Isaacs showed enormous patience as he carefully guided the jury through a myriad of financial transactions which had taken place between Seddon and Miss Barrow over a period of eighteen months. He also plotted the ongoing movement of gold coins and banknotes in and out of various bank accounts and from one part of 63 Tollington Park to another.

Much of this had happened just as Seddon had claimed, conceded Isaacs. But there were several financial questions which remained unanswered.

Where, for instance, was the £400 which Miss Barrow had brought with her in a strong box to the Seddons' house in July 1910? And where had Seddon acquired the large quantity of gold found in his possession shortly after Miss Barrow's death? A close examination of Seddon's accounts showed no withdrawal which could account for it.

Isaacs went on to suggest that the two mysteries were indeed directly connected, and that the gold in Seddon's possession had come from Miss Barrow's strong box.

The first witness called was Home Office pathologist William Willcox. He testified that, according to the 'Marsh test' he had conducted, some five grains of arsenic had been administered to Miss Barrow shortly before her death. This, he said, was twice the minimum lethal dose for a woman of Miss Barrow's age.

The 'Marsh test' was a comparative innovation and it was the first time its

Below: *March 1912 – huge crowds gathered outside the Old Bailey during the Seddon murder trial.*

results had been offered as evidence in a British court. Sir Edward Marshall Hall, for the defence, set about discrediting it.

He suggested that Miss Barrow might have died of long-term arsenic poisoning, rather than the acute form, and that traces of the toxin in her hair suggested that she had been ingesting arsenic for more than a year.

Sir William Willcox countered this claim with another test which indicated that the poison on the victim's hair could have been deposited via the fluid in her coffin.

On Friday, 8 March, six days into the trial, Frederick Seddon went into the witness box. It is a measure of the accused's arrogance that he actually boasted to his solicitor that he was looking forward to locking horns with Sir Rufus Isaacs.

He was expecting questions about finance, but the prosecution's first question was intensely personal. 'Miss Barrow lived with you from 26 July 1910 until the morning of 14 September 1911....Did you like her?' Isaacs asked.

Seddon was so astonished by the question that all he could do was to repeat it: 'Did I like her?' After a long, embarrassing pause, he replied to the effect that while Miss Barrow 'was not the sort of woman you could be in love with', he had deeply sympathized with her. Seddon gave the distinct impression that he was a man uncomfortable with basic sensitivities.

Satisfied with the impression he had made, the Attorney General moved on to matters of finance. Hour after hour, he questioned him about his business dealings.

Seddon had every fact at his fingertips. He could describe in minute detail how constantly changing sums of money came into his possession at any given time.

It was an efficient display, but showed Seddon to be a cold, calculating man, with no feeling for people. It did nothing to endear him to the jury. They finally saw the passionate side of Frederick Seddon's nature when it came time to talk about gold.

The prosecution questioned him about counting gold in the house, hours after Miss Barrow's death. Seddon, aware of the impression this would have on the court, snapped: 'I am not a degenerate....That would make it out that I was a greedy, inhuman monster...the suggestion is scandalous.'

Margaret Seddon then took the stand. She broke down several times as she tried to support her husband's testimony. Despite her efforts, she was not an asset to Seddon's defence. She was extremely nervous and had an unfortunate habit of smiling when she was in distress.

What was clear from her testimony, however, was that, assuming a murder had taken place, she had played no part in it. Even Sir Rufus Isaacs suggested that he did not expect a conviction in the case of Mrs Seddon.

On 14 March, the tenth day of the trial, the judge, Mr Justice Bucknill, summed up and the jury retired to consider their verdict. Less than an hour later, they returned to court. Frederick Seddon was found guilty. His wife was acquitted.

Seddon kissed his wife, then turned to the court and delivered a speech denying his guilt. He ended his monologue by raising his arm in a masonic salute – he knew full well that Mr Justice Bucknill was a brother of the same order – 'I declare before the Great Architect of the Universe, I am not guilty, my Lord,' he declared.

The judge, who abhorred the death penalty, was close to tears as he told Seddon to make peace with his maker. 'I am at peace,' Seddon replied. Then Bucknill summoned the black cap.

Frederick Seddon's conviction and subsequent sentence caused considerable public debate. The press were unhappy that his guilt was founded on new and unproven scientific evidence, and a petition demanding a reprieve attracted thousands of signatures. Encouraged by this wave of public support for their client, Seddon's own solicitors lodged an appeal. But it was dismissed at the Appeal Court on 2 April 1912.

Seddon's execution was set for 18 April at Pentonville prison. The previous evening Seddon summoned his solicitors. Mercenary to the last, his only concern was to find out what his furniture had fetched at auction. When told of the low prices, Seddon seemed despondent.

HIS FACT-PERFECT PERFORMANCE IN THE WITNESS BOX SHOWED SEDDON TO BE A COLD, CALCULATING PERSONALITY

IT WAS QUITE CLEAR FROM MARGARET SEDDON'S NERVOUSLY GIVEN EVIDENCE THAT SHE HAD HAD NO PART IN ANY MURDER

AT THE END OF HIS IMPASSIONED MONOLOGUE TO THE COURT THE CONDEMNED MAN RAISED HIS ARM IN A MASONIC SALUTE

GEORGE HAIGH
Acid-Bath Murders

The dapper thirty-nine-year-old charmed the ladies of a London hotel – until one of them disappeared. The suspicions of her best friend led to the conviction of one of the most shocking murderers of the century. Not content with robbing his victims, he also did sickening things to their bodies

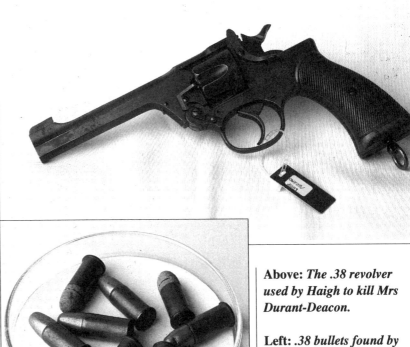

Mr John George Haigh was something of an odd-man-out at the Onslow Gardens Hotel in South Kensington. In 1949 this genteel establishment in a fashionable part of London was the haunt almost exclusively of elderly, well-heeled, upper-class ladies.

Not that Mr Haigh's presence was in any way resented by the other permanent residents of the hotel. On the contrary, for the most part they found the dapper thirty-nine-year-old engineer handsome, charming and meticulously well-mannered.

One of his particular fans was Mrs Helen Olivia Robarts Durant-Deacon, a well-preserved, buxom sixty-nine-year-old widow. She was quite smitten with 'young Haigh' and confided in him freely.

Mrs Durant-Deacon's husband, a colonel in the Gloucester Regiment, had died some years earlier and left her a legacy of £40,000. It was enough to allow her to live in some comfort for the rest of her life. But, as she explained to Haigh, she wasn't the sort of person to sit around doing nothing.

She was thinking of starting a business, designing and manufacturing artificial fingernails. She had already made some paper prototypes, but she knew absolutely nothing about the technical side of things. Perhaps Mr Haigh, as an engineer, could give her some pointers?

Above: The .38 revolver used by Haigh to kill Mrs Durant-Deacon.

Left: .38 bullets found by the police at the scene of the crime.

Opposite: George Haigh took elaborate precautions while handling the acids he used to dissolve his victims' bodies.

Below: Mrs Durant-Deacon's handbag was one of many clues found by police at Haigh's workshop.

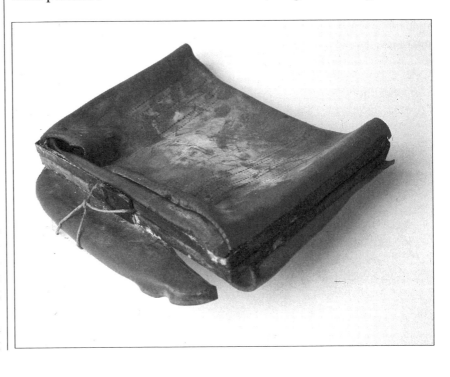

APPOINTMENT WITH DEATH

In reality, Mrs Durant-Deacon's idea was a commercial non-starter in ration-bound post-war England. But Haigh feigned enthusiasm. Of course he would be delighted to help. Perhaps she would like to come out to his factory in Essex some time, and they could look at some possible materials from which the nails could be made.

At about 3p.m. on Friday, 18 February 1949, Haigh picked up Mrs Durant-Deacon and drove her down to a factory in Crawley, Sussex. He did not, as he had claimed, own the factory, but he did know the owner, and had the use of a storeroom for his 'experimental work'.

The grimy brick shed was cluttered with bottles, vats and drums. It was not what Mrs Durant-Deacon had expected, but Haigh reassured her. Experimental laboratories were always chaotic.

Mrs Durant-Deacon took his word for it and reached for her handbag, which held her designs. As she turned away from Haigh, he pulled a .38 Enfield revolver from his jacket pocket. He calmly shot her through the nape of the neck, killing her instantly.

Haigh then kneeled by his victim's body and made an incision in her neck with a knife. He collected a glassful of her still coursing blood and drank it.

Having quenched this gross thirst, Haigh gathered Mrs Durant-Deacon's valuables – a Persian lamb coat, rings, a necklace, earrings and a gold crucifix – and stowed them in his car.

Now it was time to get rid of the body. The very clutter which had offended Mrs Durant-Deacon was, in fact, the paraphernalia of her destruction. There were vats of sulphuric acid, a specially lined metal drum, rubber gloves and a rubber apron, a gas mask and a stirrup pump. Haigh needed all these things to dissolve his victim's body. He knew precisely what to do. He'd done it before.

He laid the forty-five gallon drum on its side and pushed Mrs Durant-Deacon's head and shoulders inside. Then he righted the drum so that the whole body slumped down to the bottom. He donned his rubber apron and gloves, his wellington boots and gas mask and

LEAVING THE BODY TO DISSOLVE IN A DRUM FILLED WITH SULPHURIC ACID, HAIGH DROVE TO A RESTAURANT TO EAT SOME POACHED EGGS

Below: *Haigh's apron found in the Crawley workshop.*

proceeded to pour concentrated sulphuric acid into the drum.

Using the stirrup pump, Haigh adjusted the level of acid to cover the entire body. Once satisfied, all he had to do was wait for the flesh and bone to dissolve. He knew this would take at least two days. So, tired and hungry after his exertions, he drove to Ye Olde Ancient Priors restaurant in Crawley for a little supper, before driving back to London.

NAGGING SUSPICIONS

At breakfast the following morning several residents of the Onslow Court Hotel remarked on Mrs Durant-Deacon's

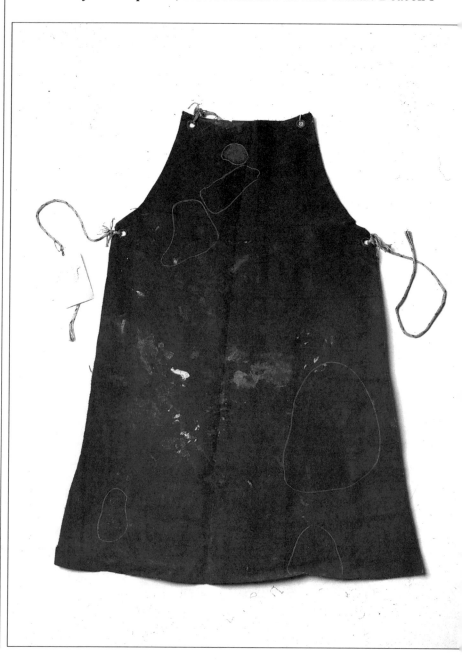

Above: *The gas mask worn by George Haigh to protect himself from acid fumes.*

Left: *Haigh wore these rubber gloves as he man-handled Mrs Durant-Deacon into her acid bath.*

absence. Her closest friend at the hotel, Mrs Constance Lane, was particularly concerned and started to make some discreet enquiries. The chambermaid told Mrs Lane that Mrs Durant-Deacon's bed had not been slept in.

Later that morning Mrs Lane was approached by John Haigh who solicitously enquired about Mrs Durant-Deacon's whereabouts. He said that he

Below: *The barrel used by Haigh to dissolve his victim's body.*

had had an appointment with her the previous day, and that Mrs Durant-Deacon had failed to show up.

Mrs Lane already knew about the trip to Crawley. She had seen her friend just as she was about to leave the hotel. She couldn't understand how Mrs Durant-Deacon could have 'failed to show up'. Mrs Lane had never liked Haigh. He was too oily for her taste, and his involvement with Mrs Durant-Deacon had always made her uneasy. Now she had a creeping feeling that something awful had happened to her friend.

Mrs Lane toyed with the idea of going to the police. But she was afraid that there might be some perfectly good reason for Mrs Durant-Deacon's absence and was anxious not to embarrass her friend – or to make a fool of herself. She decided to wait.

The following morning there was still no sign of Mrs Durant-Deacon. Mrs Lane was at breakfast, pondering her next move, when she was again approached by Haigh, expressing concern. Mrs Lane was suddenly galvanized into action. She told Haigh that she was going down to the police station, and that she would like him to go with her. Haigh had little choice but to agree, so he drove her to Chelsea Police Station.

The report Haigh made to the police was plausible enough. He had arranged to meet Mrs Durant-Deacon outside the Army and Navy Stores in Victoria Street at 2.30p.m. on 18 February. He had waited there until 3.30. Mrs Durant-Deacon had never materialized, and he had driven down to his workshop in Crawley alone.

He was, of course, extremely concerned about Mrs Durant-Deacon's welfare, and would do anything he could to help them locate her. The police thanked Haigh for his cooperation and said that they would be in touch if they thought of anything else.

Haigh drove Mrs Lane back to the Onslow Court and hoped against hope that that was the last he would hear of the matter. It wasn't. Four days later, on Thursday, 24 February, Woman Police Sergeant Alexandra Lambourne went to the hotel to gather additional background information on Mrs Durant-Deacon. She

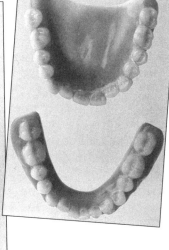

*Above: **Haigh's acid bath failed to dissolve Mrs Durant-Deacon's dentures.***

*Above left: **Home office pathologist Keith Simpson immediately identified three round 'pebbles' as Mrs Durant-Deacon's gallstones.***

interviewed Haigh at some length.

Like Mrs Lane, she was immediately repelled by his superficial charm and his unctuous concern for the well-being of the missing widow. She was an experienced police officer and was convinced that Haigh was lying.

WPS Lambourne had no evidence to support her gut feeling, but she felt strongly enough about it to mention it in her report to her divisional Detective Inspector, Shelley Symes. 'Apart from the fact I do not like the man Haigh and his mannerisms,' she wrote, 'I have a sense that he is "wrong", and there may be a case behind the whole business.'

Symes had sufficient respect for Sergeant Lambourne's judgement to ask the Criminal Record Division at Scotland Yard to run a check on Haigh. Within a matter of hours, they came back to him with a file which showed that John George Haigh had been jailed three times, twice for obtaining money by fraud and once for theft. Further enquiries in London and Sussex showed that he owed substantial sums of money – to the Onslow Court Hotel, among others.

On Saturday, 26 February, Sergeant Pat Heslin of the West Sussex Constabulary, accompanied by Police Sergeant Appleton, went to see Mr Edward Jones, owner of Hurtslea Products, a small engineering company located on Leopold Street in Crawley. Jones told the police that he had known John George Haigh

for some years. Over the past few months he had let him use a store-house at the back of the factory for a nominal rent. Haigh had been using the premises for 'experimental work', but had never said precisely what that entailed.

The police were anxious to look round the shed, but Jones told them that Haigh had the only set of keys. So Heslin picked up a steel bar and prised the padlock off the door. At first glance, the whitewashed interior looked ordinary enough. There was the usual clutter – paint pots, old bits of wood, a couple of work benches, vats of chemicals, protective clothing.

Then something caught the sergeant's eye. On one of the workbenches there was a small hatbox and an expensive leather briefcase. They simply didn't belong.

Heslin looked through the case. He found a variety of papers and documents, including ration books and clothing coupons. The contents of the hatbox were even odder. It contained several passports, driving licences, diaries, a cheque book and a marriage certificate, none of which bore the name of Haigh. At the bottom of the box was the most alarming find of all, a .38 Enfield revolver and a small white envelope containing eight bullets.

*Below: **George Haigh's diary was scrutinized by police.***

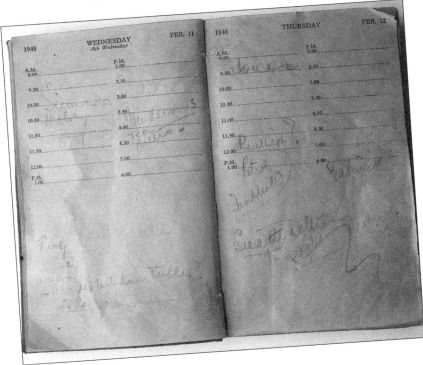

Above: *The basement flat in Kensington where Haigh is believed to have killed Dr and Mrs Archibald Henderson.*

Below: *Police search a cellar in Gloucester Road for clues in the Haigh murders.*

The following evening, 27 February, Haigh was invited back to Chelsea Police Station to answer further questions. He appeared totally unconcerned as he was led into an office and given a cup of tea. He had dozed off by the time Detective Inspector Shelley Symes, Inspector Albert Webb, and Superintendent Barratt arrived to interview him at 7.30.

They came at him well-armed with evidence. Not only did they have the obviously stolen documents from the Crawley workshop, they had also traced Mrs Durant-Deacon's jewellery to a dealer in Horsham, Sussex. His description of the seller matched John George Haigh precisely. As did that of a dry-cleaner to whom he had taken Mrs Durant-Deacon's Persian lamb coat.

THE AWFUL TRUTH EMERGES

Confronted with this, Haigh was barely ruffled. Puffing on a cigarette, he said, 'I can see you know what you're talking about. I admit the coat belonged to Mrs Durant-Deacon and that I sold her jewellery.'

'How did you come by the property?' asked Symes, 'And where is Mrs Durant-Deacon?'

Haigh thought for a while before replying. 'It's a long story,' he confided. 'It's one of blackmail and I shall have to implicate many others.'

Just then the telephone rang, and Symes and Barratt were summoned from the room. Left alone with Inspector Webb, the most junior of his interrogators, Haigh changed his tack. 'Tell me frankly,' he asked. 'What are the chances of anyone being released from Broadmoor?'

Webb's immediate reaction to Haigh's extraordinary question was to caution him and advise him of his rights. Haigh dismissed the warning with a wave of the hand. 'If I told you the truth,' he continued, 'You would not believe it. It is too fantastic for belief. I will tell you all about it....

'Mrs Durant-Deacon no longer exists. She has disappeared completely and no trace of her can ever be found. I have destroyed her with acid. You will find sludge that remains at Leopold Road. Every trace has gone. How can you prove a murder if there is no body?' Haigh added, obviously pleased with himself.

Webb's first reaction was to disbelieve Haigh's confession. It was simply too fantastic, too grotesque. Haigh was obviously setting himself up for an insanity plea. After all, he had already mentioned Broadmoor.

When Symes and Barratt returned to the interview room, Webb asked Haigh to repeat what he had said. Haigh did so. Symes cautioned him again, but there was no stopping Haigh now. He talked for two-and-a-half hours. And Inspector Symes wrote it all down.

He described the events of Friday, 18 February, in meticulous detail. He told how he had shot Mrs Durant-Deacon, how he had drunk her blood, put her in the acid bath, and then gone to the Ancient Priors for tea and poached eggs. He explained how, on Monday, he had disposed of her jewellery for £110. Then he had returned to Crawley and emptied the sludge – Mrs Durant-Deacon's decomposed body – out of the drum with a bucket, and poured it on to some wasteground at the back of the shed.

The police said nothing as Haigh told his terrible story of murder and theft, vampirism and genteel cups of tea. When he had finished the story of Mrs Durant-Deacon's death, Haigh moved back in time. By the early hours of 1 March he had confessed to five additional murders.

The first, he claimed, had been committed on 9 September 1944. The victim had been an old acquaintance, William McSwan. He had killed him at a basement flat in Gloucester Road. A year later, he had lured William's parents, Donald and Amy McSwan, to the same flat. There he had beaten them to death.

He had forged Donald's signature to gain power of attorney over the McSwans' estate. While selling one of their properties in February 1948, he had met Dr Archibald Henderson and his wife Rosalie. He had killed them in a storeroom in Giles Yard.

In each case, he had acquired money or other property belonging to his victims by skilful forgery and deception. Years after he had disposed of their remains, he had written forged personal and business letters, 'successfully staving off enquiries from relatives, friends and associates.'

Haigh added that he had destroyed all the bodies by his acid bath method – after drinking a glass of their blood.

The arrest of John George Haigh caused an immediate public sensation. His remand at Horsham magistrates court drew huge crowds – predominantly of jeering women.

BUT WHERE IS THE PROOF?

On 4 March, after being transferred from the Chelsea police cells to Lewes Prison, Haigh sprang more surprises. He asked to see Inspector Webb, with whom he clearly felt some sort of affinity. He confided in the young detective that he had committed three murders which he hadn't mentioned in his earlier statement – a woman and a young man in West London, and a girl in Eastbourne. This brought his total to nine.

The police, however, were having their time cut out establishing a case against Haigh for the murder of Mrs Durant-Deacon. Even though he had admitted to the crime, to be certain of a conviction, the prosecution needed proof that the woman was, in fact, dead, and that Haigh really had killed her.

The Home Office pathologist, Dr Keith Simpson, first carried out routine blood tests at the workshop in Crawley. He

Above: *Rosalie Henderson – she died at Haigh's hands along with her husband Archibald.*

THE PATHOLOGIST SEARCHED FOR THE HUMAN 'SLUDGE' ON WASTEGROUND NEAR HAIGH'S LABORATORY OF DEATH

established that blood stains found there were of the same group as Mrs Durant-Deacon. He then turned his attention to the wasteland where Haigh claimed to have deposited the 'sludge' from his acid bath. Soon he found a stone 'the size of a cherry'. It was a gallstone.

Simpson soon found more human remains, including fragments of a left foot. He managed to reconstruct it and cast it in plaster. The cast fitted one of Mrs Durant-Deacon's shoes perfectly.

He discovered other, non-human remains – the handle of a handbag, a lipstick container, a hairpin and a notebook. All of these could be traced back to the victim. His most sensational find, however – the clincher – was a set of dentures which were positively identified as having belonged to the missing woman.

In Lewes Prison, Haigh was well aware of the forensic evidence being amassed against him, but he still remained optimistic. He was certain that he could escape the gallows by convincing a jury that he was insane. And on being told that the eminent barrister Sir Maxwell Fyfe was to represent him, Haigh was delighted. He wrote: 'I'm very glad to see we have got old Maxy. He's no fool.'

THE MIND OF A KILLER

The trial of John George Haigh for the murder of Mrs Durant-Deacon – that was the only charge ever brought against him – opened at Lewes Assizes on 18 July 1949 and lasted less than two days.

There was no real question as to whether Haigh had killed Mrs Durant-Deacon. The case rested on whether or not he was sane. The defence called Dr Henry Yellowlees, a consultant psychiatrist at St Thomas's Hospital, as an expert witness.

Dr Yellowlees was no doubt an able man in his field, but he was a rotten witness. He was a pompous windbag. 'In the case of pure paranoia,' Yellowlees explained, 'it really amounts, as it develops and gets a greater hold, to practically self-worship, and that is commonly expressed by the conviction in the mind of the patient that he is in some

summoned the black cap and condemned him to death. Haigh was taken to Wandsworth Prison to await execution.

While there was no expression of pity for him from the press, there was a great deal of editorial speculation. How was it, they wondered, that an intelligent boy from a good home – his parents were members of the Plymouth Brethren – could grow into a monster like Haigh?

Haigh himself went some way to answering them. He wrote from prison: 'Although my parents were kind and loving, I had none of the joys, or the companionship, which small children usually have. From my earliest years, my recollection is of my father saying "Do not" or "Thou shalt not". Any form of sport or light entertainment was frowned upon and regarded as not edifying. There was only condemnation and prohibition....

'It is true to say that I was nurtured on Bible stories but mostly concerned with sacrifice. If by some mischance I did, or said, anything which my father regarded as improper, he would say: "Do not grieve the Lord by behaving so." '

On 24 July, five days after his trial ended, Haigh's mother sent him a fortieth birthday card, but he rejected any suggestion that she visit him in prison.

mystic way under the control of a guiding spirit which means infinitely more to him and is of infinitely greater authority than any human laws or rules of society.'

Dr Yellowlees rambled on in this vein for some considerable time. He was frequently interrupted by both Sir Travers Humphry, the judge, and Sir Hartley Shawcross, counsel for the prosecution, neither of whom had the faintest idea what he was talking about.

As for the jury, he had lost them after the first few sentences. It took them only fifteen minutes to return a verdict of Guilty on John George Haigh. Sir Travers Humphry was equally speedy as he

Top and above: *George Haigh leaves Horsham Court with his police escort. Haigh is besieged by photographers as he leaves court.*

Right: *Dr Keith Simpson, the Home Office pathologist, was the greatest forensic scientist of his day.*

As the day of his execution approached, Haigh's apparently limitless poise began to crumble. He started to suffer from depression and complained of recurrent nightmares about blood.

Despite his depression, Haigh maintained his sense of theatre. He bequeathed his favourite suit and tie to Madame Tussauds, ensuring himself a place in the Chamber of Horrors. He even requested his model should show at least one inch of shirt cuff.

Then Haigh became concerned about the hanging itself. He contacted the prison governor, Major A.C.N. Benke, and requested to rehearse his own execution. 'My weight is deceptive,' Haigh insisted, 'I have a light springy step and I would not like there to be a hitch.'

The governor turned down his request, assuring him that the executioner was highly experienced and that there would be no hitches.

On 9 August, the eve of his execution, Haigh wrote a letter to his parents. It began: 'My dearest Mum and Dad, Thank you for your very touching letter which I received this morning and which will, I suppose, be your last....'

He went on to say that he had found parts of his upbringing very restrictive: 'There was much that was lovely.... We cannot change the inscrutible predictions of the eternal.... I, that is my spirit, shall remain earthbound for some time: my mission is not yet fulfilled....'

Haigh did not go on to explain what he thought his mission was, nor expressed any remorse for his terrible crimes. In the end, the ultimate mystery of Haigh's life – what was going on inside his mind? – would go to the grave with him.

At 9a.m. on 10 August, John George Haigh was executed. His depression had left him and he was his old self, all swank and swagger, as he faced the gallows. He was buried the same day inside the prison walls, as is the custom in cases of execution.

Below: *10 August 1949. A crowd gathers outside Wandsworth Prison as John George Haigh is executed.*

NEVILLE HEATH
An Unlikely Killer

Who was the elegant, urbane Air Force officer who cruelly mutilated and then murdered his young female victims? Was he insane, or was he, as the prosecution alleged at his trial, just a sadist?

In the early hours of the morning of 21 June 1946, a dashing young ex-RAF pilot and an aspiring actress took a taxi from the Panama Club in South Kensington to the Pembridge Court Hotel in Notting Hill. The young man paid the 1s 9d fare and disappeared into the hotel with his arm round the young woman's waist. The cabbie noticed that they were both fairly drunk, but thought they seemed to be in high spirits.

SAVAGERY IN NOTTING HILL

The following day, at around 2p.m., there was still no sign of life from Room 4 at the Pembridge Court. The chambermaid responsible for cleaning that particular room was keen to get her duties finished and was becoming irritated. She knocked on the door and received no response. Then she bent down and peered through the keyhole, but she could see nothing in the darkened room. She knocked again, harder this time, and when there was still no answer she sought out the hotel's assistant manager, Mrs Alice Wyatt.

Mrs Wyatt let herself into Room 4 with her pass key and drew back the curtains. One of the beds in the twin-bedded room was empty. In the other, sheets and blankets pulled up around her neck, lay a

Opposite: *Handsome and charming, Neville Heath had a way with women.*

Below: *R.A.F. Officer Neville Heath with his squadron in 1936.*

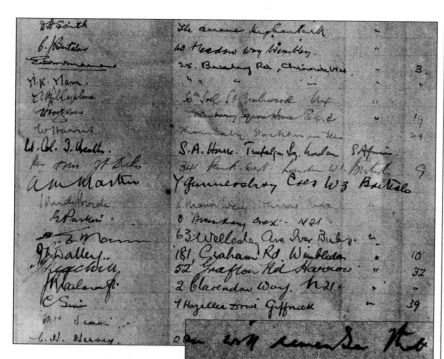

*Above: **Heath signed the visitors books at the Ocean Hotel, Worthing with his own name. Only the rank was fictional.***

*Right: **A fragment of Heath's flowing hand.***

MRS WYATT DREW BACK THE BEDCLOTHES AND SAW ON THE YOUNG WOMAN'S FACE THE UNMISTAKABLE BLUE TINGE OF DEATH

'IF YOU FIND THAT WHIP,' SAID THE HOME OFFICE PATHOLOGIST TO THE POLICE, 'YOU'VE FOUND YOUR MAN '

---

young, dark-haired woman. Mrs Wyatt pulled the bedclothes a few inches to one side and looked down at the young woman's face. It bore the unmistakable blue tinge of death.

Mrs Wyatt backed out of the room, went downstairs and called the Notting Hill Gate police station in nearby Ladbroke Grove.

Ten minutes later, Sergeant Fred Averill arrived at the scene. He pulled back the bed covers to reveal a gruesome sight – the naked, trussed and grotesquely mutilated body of a young woman.

He checked the room thoroughly but could see no sign of a struggle. The woman's clothes were neatly folded over a chair. Her rings were on her fingers and her handbag still contained her purse, cash and a wartime identity card identifying her as Margery Aimee Brownell Gardner.

The victim's body, for this was undoubtedly a murder, was removed to Hammersmith Mortuary where Dr Keith Simpson, the Home Office pathologist, conducted a post-mortem. 'Even without

the seventeen lash marks,' Simpson wrote in his report, 'the girl's injuries were appalling. Both nipples and some of the soft breast tissue had been bitten away and there was a seven-inch tear in her vagina and beyond.'

The lash marks Simpson referred to had been made with a leather riding whip with a distinctive diamond-pattern weave. 'If you find that whip,' said Simpson, 'you've found your man.' Nine of the wounds were on the back between the shoulder blades, two across the breasts and abdomen, and two on the forehead.

The injuries to the vagina had been caused by a tearing instrument. Simpson pointed to a missing poker from the fire-iron set as a possible weapon.

Death had not resulted from Miss Gardner's injuries, however, but from suffocation. Simpson thought this could have been caused either by a gag, or by the victim's face being pressed into a pillow.

HUNTING THE KILLER

While the post-mortem was under way, the police were starting on their hunt for the killer. On the face of it, it looked remarkably straightforward. On Sunday, 16 June, five days before the murder, Room 4 at the Pembridge Court had been let to a man and woman (not Margery Gardner) who had signed the register as Lieutenant-Colonel and Mrs N.G.C. Heath, giving an address in Hampshire.

Within hours of the crime being discovered, Superintendent Thomas Barratt, who was heading the case, had established that N.G.C. Heath was in fact Neville George Clevely Heath, a twenty-nine-year-old ex-Air Force officer who had been cashiered by both the RAF and the South African Air Force for fraud and other offences 'prejudicial to good order and military discipline'.

He also had a civilian criminal record stretching back almost ten years, but had never been convicted of violent crime. His file described him as being: '5 ft 11½ ins tall, fresh complexion, blue eyes, square face, broad forehead and nose, firm chin, good teeth, military gait'.

The victim, Margery Gardner, was also

known to the police. The previous year she had been questioned when she was found to be the passenger in a stolen car that was chased and stopped at Hyde Park Corner. The police had accepted her story that she had had no idea that the car was stolen, and she had been released without charge.

Margery was thirty-one at the time of her death. She had recently abandoned her husband and child in Sheffield for the lure of fame and fortune in London. Her dream of film stardom had so far resulted in a few days' work as a film extra.

She associated with the demi-monde of thieves, pimps and black marketeers. But while she certainly slept with a great number of men, she never actually resorted to prostitution to support herself.

Margery Gardner had never met Neville Heath before the evening of 20 June. The couple met in the Trevor Arms pub in Knightsbridge and spent the evening together – a pub crawl, followed by dinner at the Normandie Hotel, more drinks and dancing at the Panama, and finally her rendezvous with death at the Pembridge Court Hotel. She was, to the very last, one of life's victims.

To the police the case presented few problems. It was just a matter of picking up Neville Heath. To this end it was decided to release Heath's name and description to the press as a man who, using the time-honoured police euphemism, they would like 'to assist them with their enquiries'.

The police also had a picture of Heath, but they were in two minds whether to release it to the newspapers. It would improve their chances of achieving a speedy arrest. But identification would be a critical issue at his trial, and the widespread publication of his likeness might be seen as prejudicial. They had to weigh this risk against the risk of having a vicious killer on the loose.

In the end they withheld the photograph. As a direct result of this decision, another young woman was destined to meet a horrible death.

By the time Heath's name and description were circulated, he was registered under his own name at the Ocean Hotel in the resort town of Worthing, Sussex. He had travelled down to the South Coast on the morning of 21 June, hours before Margery Gardner's body had been discovered.

The purpose of Heath's trip was to meet up with Yvonne Symonds, another of the many women in his life. He had met Yvonne at a dance in Chelsea a week earlier. Like Margery Gardner, she had gone drinking with him afterwards at the Panama Club. Heath had tried to persuade her to spend the night with him, but she had refused.

The following evening, however, he had proposed to her, and she had accepted both his proposal and his invitation to bed. Yvonne Symonds was the 'Mrs N.G.C. Heath' who had spent the previous Saturday night in Room 4 of the Pembridge Court Hotel.

By the time Heath and Yvonne sat down to dinner in the Blue Peter Club in Worthing on the evening of 21 June, he knew the police must be looking for him. He decided to preempt the publicity by confiding in his 'fiancée'.

'Yvonne, there's been a nasty murder in London,' he said. 'It took place in the room we stayed in last weekend. I knew the girl. She was with some man called Jack. They had nowhere to stay so I gave them the key.'

Since the room was still booked in his name, Heath went on, the police had naturally wanted to talk to him. He had spoken to an Inspector Barratt of Scotland Yard – it should have been Superintendent Barratt – and told him everything he knew. He had even visited the scene of the crime to see if he could be of any more help. He couldn't, but the police were very grateful for his cooperation.

Heath was extremely plausible, and Yvonne took everything he said at face value. After all, with his impeccable manners and charm, Neville Heath was hardly a girl's idea of a sex killer.

At the end of their evening together Heath saw Yvonne home, kissed her on the cheek and returned to the Ocean Hotel. The following morning, he received a phone call. It was Yvonne in a state of high anxiety. Her parents had read in the Sunday newspapers that the police wanted to interview him on a matter of urgency.

WITH HIS IMPECCABLE MANNERS AND CHARM, NEVILLE HEATH WAS HARDLY A GIRL'S IDEA OF A DEPRAVED SEX KILLER

'Yes,' said Heath, calmly. 'I thought they would...I've got a car and I'm driving back to London to sort things out. I'll probably give you a ring this evening.'

But he didn't return to London, nor did he ring Yvonne. She never saw or heard from her 'fiancé' again.

THE SECOND VICTIM

On Monday morning, 24 June, a letter landed on Superintendent Tom Barratt's desk at Scotland Yard. It was postmarked Worthing and, despite a flood of crank communications already received, Barratt had no doubt that it came from the real Neville Heath.

The letter began: 'Sir, I feel it is my duty to inform you of certain facts in connection with the death of Mrs Gardner at Notting Hill Gate....' Heath went on to relate a slightly more elaborate version of the story he had told to Yvonne Symonds two days earlier.

He had lent his room key to Mrs Gardner and a friend called Jack, a man of approximately thirty, 5 ft 9 ins tall with a slim build, dark hair and a small moustache. Heath claimed to have returned to his room at about 3a.m. and found Margery Gardner already dead. He had panicked, run away, and was now living under an assumed name.

The police search for Heath now moved to Worthing. Yvonne Symonds and her parents told the police about his overnight stay at the Ocean Hotel, but a search of his room produced only an Air Force uniform and some medals. It was obvious that he was long gone.

Over the next few days, scores of false sightings of Neville Heath were reported to Scotland Yard. He had been seen in London, Hampshire, Wiltshire, even in Dublin.

In reality, Neville Heath was comfortably ensconced in the Tollard Royal Hotel in Bournemouth, where he was registered under the unlikely name of 'Group Captain Rupert Brooke'. He could be found in the lounge bar any evening regaling his fellow guests with stories of wartime heroism and life in South Africa.

As the days passed, and he continued

WHILE DETECTIVES SEARCHED HIGH AND LOW, HEATH, ALIAS 'GROUP CAPTAIN RUPERT BROOKE', WAS STAYING AT A BOURNEMOUTH HOTEL

Below: *Heath leaves West London Police Court, charged with murdering Margery Gardner.*

to elude detection, Heath's confidence grew and he ventured out on to the Bournemouth promenade. In the height of summer, it was an ideal place for a young, good-looking Air Force officer to find female companionship.

The first girl who caught Neville Heath's eye was a pretty, nineteen-year-old former Wren, Doreen Marshall. She was in Bournemouth for a week, recuperating from a bad dose of measles and flu. Heath, with his easy manner, had no difficulty picking her up and persuading her to join him for tea at the Tollard Royal.

Tea became dinner and Doreen, a shy, rather naive girl, was initially captivated by chivalrous Group Captain Brooke. Towards the end of the meal, however, some of the other guests noticed a sudden change in Doreen's mood. It was as though Heath had done or said something to offend her. Perhaps it was just that he had drunk rather too much.

After dinner, Doreen said she wanted to get back to her own hotel, the Norfolk. Heath persuaded her to take coffee in the writing room where they were joined by some fellow guests, Miss Parfitt and a Mr and Mrs Phillips.

When they had finished their coffee, Doreen asked Mr Phillips if he would order her a taxi. But Heath intervened, saying that he would walk his guest home. At about 12.15a.m., they left the Tollard Royal together.

'I'll be back in half an hour.' Heath told the hall porter.

'He'll be back in quarter of an hour.' Doreen Marshall snapped.

The hall porter waited up for the guest to return, but at 4a.m. there was still no sign of him. The porter went up to his room and, to his surprise, found him in his bed sound asleep. The following morning Heath chuckled as he told the hotel manager, Ivor Relf, that he had played a practical joke on the hall porter.

There had been a ladder outside the hotel and he had used it to let himself into his bedroom window. Mr Relf probably thought this a pretty infantile jape, but ascribed nothing more ominous to it than that.

On Friday, 5 July, two days after Doreen Marshall had dined with Heath, Ivor Relf received a call from the manager of the Norfolk Hotel. He was concerned about one of his guests, a young woman from Pinner, who had apparently disappeared.

The following morning, Relf mentioned the call to Heath. Could the missing girl possibly be the same girl who had dined at the Tollard Royal on Wednesday evening? Heath was certain it could not be: 'Oh, no,' he said, 'I have known that lady for a long while, and she certainly doesn't come from Pinner.'

Relf, however, was unconvinced and suggested that his guest should at least get in touch with the police. Heath had no real choice but to agree.

Introducing himself as Group Captain Rupert Brooke, he contacted Detective Constable George Souter at Bournemouth police station. Souter suggested he come down to the station to look at some

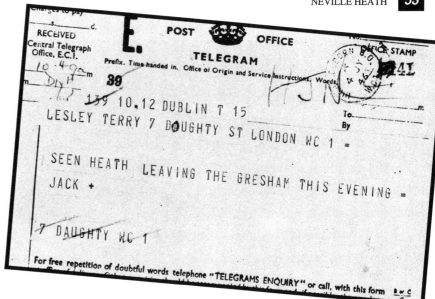

photographs, and Heath agreed to do so.

Heath appeared completely at ease as he confirmed that the missing girl and the girl with whom he had had dinner were one and the same person. On the night in question, he said he had walked her part of the way to the Norfolk Hotel and then returned to the Tollard Royal. He also claimed to have seen Doreen going into a shop the following morning.

He had no idea where she might be now, but added that he had got the impression that she had a number of other 'men friends' in Bournemouth. Perhaps she was with one of them.

Heath was just leaving the police station when Charles Marshall, Doreen's father, and Mrs Cruickshank, her elder sister, walked in. Mrs Cruickshank bore a striking resemblance to Doreen and her appearance shocked Heath. He broke into a cold sweat and started to shake.

After a few seconds he recovered his composure and offered Doreen's family a few words of comfort. But his moment of panic had not gone unnoticed by Detective Constable Souter. Suddenly he remembered where he had seen this man before. 'Isn't your name Heath?' he asked.

'No,' said Heath.

Souter, still friendly and polite, pretended to accept Heath's word for it. But he added that he looked very like the picture of the man who the police were looking for in the Margery Gardner case.

Heath agreed. Yes, people had commented on the likeness.

The trap was sprung. Since Heath's photograph had been withheld, the only people in Bournemouth who knew what

Above: *A cable from Dublin suggested that Heath might be hiding in Ireland.*

HEATH HAD RETURNED TO HIS ROOM BY A CONVENIENT LADDER, LEAVING THE HALL PORTER WAITING UP UNTIL 4A.M.

WHEN DOREEN MARSHALL'S SIMILAR-LOOKING SISTER WALKED INTO THE POLICE STATION HEATH BROKE OUT IN A COLD SWEAT

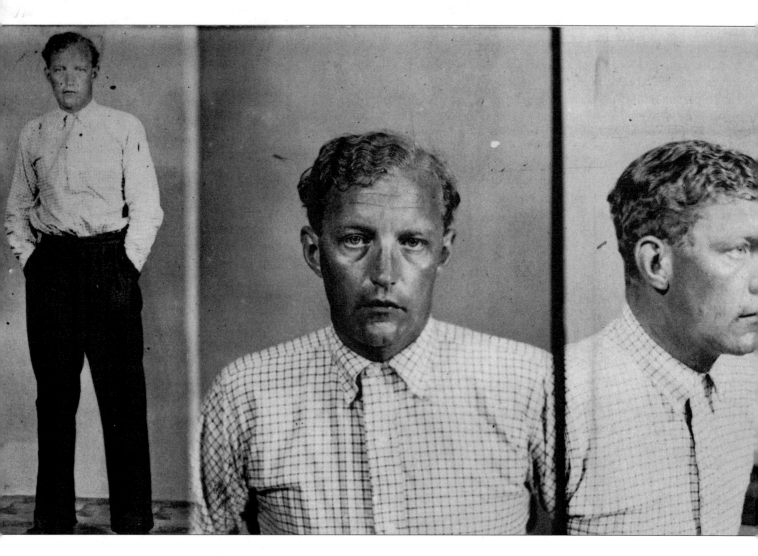

Above: *George Neville Heath, photographed by Poole police shortly after his arrest.*

HEATH'S SUITCASE
CONTAINED A LEATHER
RIDING WHIP WITH A
DISTINCTIVE DIAMOND-
PATTERN WEAVE

Neville Heath looked like were the police and Heath himself.

Heath was detained until 9.45p.m. that evening when Detective Inspector George Gates of the Hampshire Police arrived. After a few minutes with his suspect, Gates said, 'I am satisfied that you are Neville George Clevely Heath and I am going to detain you pending the arrival of officers of the Metropolitan Police.'

'Oh, all right,' Heath muttered, apparently unconcerned. He was more worried about being cold than he was about the police, and asked if he could fetch his sports jacket from his room at the Tollard Royal.

Gates went personally to collect the jacket. In one pocket he found a left-luggage ticket issued at Bournemouth West Railway Station. In the other he found the return half of a first-class ticket from Waterloo to Bournemouth – a ticket which later proved to have been issued to Doreen Marshall.

Gates went to Bournemouth West station and redeemed Heath's suitcase from the cloakroom. It contained a few items of clothing, a bloodstained scarf, and a leather riding whip with a diamond-pattern weave.

Shortly before midnight, Heath started writing his statement in which he repeated his version of the events of the night of Wednesday, 3 July. He had left Miss Marshall at the pier at 1a.m. and watched her walk towards the Norfolk Hotel. He had not seen her to speak to since, although he thought he had seen her entering Bobby's Ltd., on the Thursday morning.

A few hours after Heath finished his statement, Detective Inspector Spooner of Scotland Yard arrived and took him back to London. Here he was to be questioned concerning the death of Margery Gardner.

Later that day he appeared at West

London Magistrates' Court and was charged with her murder. Asked if he required legal aid, Heath replied: 'I think I can just about manage, sir.'

That same morning, a woman's body was discovered in a clump of rhododendron bushes at Branksome Chine, Bournemouth. Naked except for her left shoe, the woman was covered with her own clothing – a black dress, a camelhair coat and some underwear. She had been dead for some days.

Her throat had been cut, and there were bruises to the head. Her right nipple had been bitten off and there were jagged cuts the length of her torso. Her hands were also cut in such a way that suggested that she had tried to fight off her assailant. The search for Doreen Marshall was over.

GAME TO THE LAST

In 1946, English law dictated that a person could only be tried for one murder at a time. And although Heath had been charged with both killings, the Crown decided to proceed with the stronger of the two cases, the murder of Margery Gardner.

The defendant retained the services of a top criminal lawyer, Ian Near, who in turn briefed J.D. Casswell KC to appear for the defence.

Heath appeared resigned to his fate. 'Why shouldn't I plead Guilty?' he asked his barrister.

'You've a mother, father and brothers alive,' Casswell replied. 'Do you want it

> THE EVIDENCE WAS SO OVERWHELMING THAT THE DEFENCE'S ONLY HOPE WAS TO PROVE THEIR CLIENT INSANE

> WHEN THE EXECUTIONER ARRIVED, EX-AIR FORCE OFFICER HEATH JOKED: 'COME ON, BOYS, LET'S GET ON WITH IT!'

Below: *Crowds of people queued all night in the hope of witnessing the Heath trial at the Old Bailey.*

said that a man in his right mind could commit two such brutal murders?'

Heath thought about it for a moment, and then shrugged, 'Put me down as Not Guilty, old boy,' he said.

When the trial opened on 24 September 1946, the case against Neville Heath was so overwhelming that the defence pinned all their hopes of cheating the gallows on proving that their client was insane. Casswell produced an expert witness, William Henry Hubert BA, MRCP, MRCS, who had diagnosed Heath as being periodically insane.

Anthony Hawke for the prosecution, anticipating this line of defence, had experts of his own. Dr Hugh Grierson, Senior Medical Officer at Brixton Prison, took the stand and testified that, in his opinion, Heath was a sadist but sane. His view was endorsed by Dr Hubert Young, Senior Medical Officer at Wormwood Scrubs.

On balance, the argument presented by the two prison doctors proved the more convincing, and it took the jury less than an hour to reach their Guilty verdict

On 26 September, Neville Heath was sentenced to death. He was taken to Pentonville Prison to await execution, but showed complete indifference to his fate.

He refused to see his family, but on 15 October, the day before his execution, he wrote two letters to his mother. The first said: 'My only regret at leaving the world is that I have been so damned unworthy of you both.' In the second he wrote: 'I shall probably stay up reading tonight because I'd like to see the dawn again. So much in my memory is associated with the dawn – early morning patrols and coming home from night clubs. Well, it really wasn't a bad life while it lasted....Please don't mourn my going – I should hate it – and don't wear black.'

On the morning of 16 October, huge crowds gathered outside Pentonville Prison. Inside, Neville Heath sat calmly in his cell, and, when the public executioner, Albert Pierrepoint, arrived, Heath is reported to have said, 'Come on, boys, let's get on with it!' Later, when offered the traditional glass of whisky to steady his nerves, he joked: 'While you're about it, you might make that a double.'

SIR HARRY OAKES
A Mysterious Death

A rich man's brutal murder in a tropical paradise is a tabloid journalist's dream. Did the ex-King of England buy off the police and instigate a frame-up? Were voodoo rites involved? Or was it the Mafia?

Above: *The Bahamas: murder was an anathema in this rich man's playground.*

Opposite: *Sir Harry Oakes was one of the Bahamas' richest and most influential residents. He was also a close friend of the Duke of Windsor.*

A t 7a.m. on Thursday, 8 July 1943, Sir Harry Oakes, the Bahamas' richest and most influential resident, was found battered to death. His body was discovered lying on his bed at Westbourne, one of several homes that Oakes owned in Nassau, by his friend Harold Christie.

Christie, who had spent the night as a house guest at Westbourne, immediately called for help. He contacted not the police but the Governor of the island, the Duke of Windsor, formerly King Edward VIII of England. The Duke was a close friend of both Oakes and Christie.

Christie could smell a scandal, and he thought that if anyone could minimize the effects for all of them it would be the Duke of Windsor. Christie, however, overestimated his friend. After hearing the news, the Duke did nothing for two hours and then made a series of telephone calls in an attempt to muzzle the press.

He was too late. During those two hours, Christie had panicked and called several other leading figures in Nassau.

In his capacity as Governor, the Duke had three possible courses of action. He could instruct the Bahamian police to conduct an investigation. He could seek assistance from the FBI – the USA was only 90 miles away. Or, since the islands were a Crown Colony, he could call in Scotland Yard.

Inexplicably, he did none of these things. Instead, at 10.50, almost four hours after he had heard about Oakes's death, he telephoned Captain Edward Walter Melchen in Miami.

INVESTIGATING A 'SUICIDE'

Melchen, head of the Miami Homicide Bureau, was apparently selected on a personal whim of the Duke's. He had once acted as the Duke's bodyguard during a visit to Florida.

According to Melchen, the Duke initially told him that one of the leading

> WHILE THE DUKE OF WINDSOR DELAYED, CHRISTIE HAD PANICKED AND TOLD PEOPLE. NOW THE NEWS AGENCIES HAD GOT THE STORY

Left: *The Duke and Duchess of Windsor. Were they involved in an elaborate cover-up?*

citizens of the Bahamas had apparently committed suicide. He asked Melchen to fly over to Nassau to confirm the details. Melchen arrived in the Bahamas at 2p.m. accompanied by Captain Otto Barker, head of the Miami Police Department's Bureau of Criminal Investigation.

On arriving at Westbourne, it was obvious to the two American detectives that the sixty-nine-year-old baronet could not possibly have committed suicide. He

had been brutally battered and burnt. Around the left ear he bore four triangular wounds, three of which had penetrated his skull. The chest and abdomen of his pyjama-clad body were covered with burns. The mattress under the body had been scorched. The mosquito netting over the bed had been burnt away. And the body itself was covered with feathers.

It was clear that the killing had not taken place in this position. Blood and soot were everywhere. There were

started to piece together the last hours of Sir Harry Oakes's life. He had spent the previous afternoon at the office of the Colonial Secretary obtaining an exit visa to the United States – a temporary wartime measure – to enable him to travel to Bar Harbor, Maine where his wife was staying.

After his meeting Oakes had picked up Christie, and the two men had returned to Westbourne for a game of tennis. In the evening, several friends had arrived for an informal cocktail party.

By 11p.m., all the guests had left except for Christie, who had decided to stay the night. Christie had woken shortly before 7a.m. and walked out on to a balcony which connected his bedroom to that of his host. He knocked on the door of Sir Harry's room and walked in.

Even in the semi-darkness he realized something was dreadfully wrong. Sir Harry was sprawled on the charred bed, covered in blood. Christie had lifted up his friend's head and pressed a glass of water to his lips. The body was still

Below: *The walls and floor of Sir Harry Oakes' bedroom were scorched and splattered with blood.*

bloody handprints, some still wet, on the walls of the bedroom and on the door leading to the balcony. Next to the bed there was a Chinese folding screen.

After a cursory examination of the scene of the crime, Melchen and Barker interviewed Harold Christie.

They already knew from the Duke of Windsor that Christie was a man above suspicion. Aged forty-seven, Harold Christie was a vastly wealthy property developer whose family was among the leading lights of Nassau society.

With Christie's help, the two detectives

warm. He dabbed his face with a towel.

Realizing that his friend was dead, Christie said he ran downstairs, shouting for the servants.

UNBELIEVABLE INEPTITUDE

Satisfied with Christie's statement, Melchen and Barker began their investigation. Between them the two Miami detectives were to demonstrate an extraordinary degree of ineptitude.

While Melchen routinely questioned

WITHIN TWO HOURS OF THE DUKE'S CONFIDENTIAL TALK WITH THE MIAMI DETECTIVE A SUSPECT WAS ARRESTED

Left: *Harold Christie, Sir Harry's friend and business partner. He found the body.*

Below: *Westbourne, one of several properties belonging to Sir Harry Oakes. Was he killed here or elsewhere?*

everyone who had attended the cocktail party on the night of the murder, Barker set about looking for clues.

Considering he was the head of Miami's Fingerprint Division, Barker's approach was astonishing. He had forgotten his fingerprint camera and, rather than borrow one, he dusted wet prints with fingerprint powder, thus destroying them.

The following morning, Melchen began interviewing the staff and assorted friends of the deceased. Then, at 4 p.m., the Duke of Windsor arrived.

The Duke went upstairs and had a long, confidential meeting with Captain Barker. No one will ever know what the Duke told the detective, but within two hours of them parting company a suspect was arrested.

The man taken into custody was one of the guests being interviewed in the living room by Captain Melchen. He was Count Marie Alfred Fouquereaux de Marigny, a French aristocrat, Olympic yachtsman and chicken farmer. He was also the husband of Sir Harry's daughter Nancy.

Eighteen-year-old Nancy Oakes had caused a sensation the previous year by

eloping with the thirty-two-year-old Frenchman.

It would not be accurate to say that Sir Harry and Lady Oakes approved of the marriage – Lady Oakes fainted when she was told about it – but it was not as acrimonious as one might have expected. It was soon clear to Sir Harry that de Marigny was not after the Oakes fortune. He was a hard-working man, determined to make his own way in the world.

Oakes and de Marigny did have their problems, however. The Frenchman was arrogant and self-opinionated. And he despised the Duke of Windsor – a feeling which he concealed badly, if at all. This embarrassed and infuriated Sir Harry.

Once in police custody Count Alfred de Marigny was dignified and aloof. He told the detectives that he had spent the early part of the evening of 7 July at the Prince George Hotel, where he had met up with some friends. They included his lodger, the Marquis Georges de Visdelou Guimbeau, the Marquis's girlfriend Betty Roberts, and the wives of two Canadian Air Force officers, Dorothy Clark and Jean Ainslie. After a few drinks the entire party, eleven in all, had returned to de

Above: *Superintendent Edward Sears, whose evidence in the case was totally ignored.*

Marigny's house for dinner. Countess Nancy de Marigny was away visiting her mother in Maine.

About midnight, Mrs Clark and Mrs Ainslie were ready to go home. They were going to call a taxi, but de Marigny had insisted on driving them across Nassau to the women's billet at Hubbard's Cottage, a stone's throw from Westbourne.

The police searched de Marigny's house but found nothing incriminating.

OTHER INFORMATION IGNORED

Despite their lack of evidence, the two Miami detectives seemed determined to prove that the Count was the killer. They virtually ignored other information including two interesting stories.

The first came from a caretaker at Lyford Cay, a small port some 17 miles from Nassau. He reported that, on the night in question, a powerful motor launch had moored at the pier and several men, strangers to the island, had come ashore. They had driven away in a station wagon. Some time after midnight they had returned and sailed away.

The second came from Superintendent Edward Sears, a traffic controller and lifelong acquaintance of Harold Christie. He reported that, at about midnight on 7 July, he had been driving though Nassau when a station wagon passed. Sears could not identify the driver, but he was certain the passenger was Harold Christie.

Shortly after de Marigny was arrested, the autopsy on Sir Harry Oakes was being completed at Nassau mortuary. The examination was performed by two local doctors. They stated that Sir Harry Oakes had died as a result of head wounds caused by a blunt instrument, triangular in section. All the wounds had been caused by a forward and downward thrust. In other words, they could not have been inflicted while Sir Harry was lying on his bed. They put the time of death at between 1.30 and 3.30a.m.

On 15 July, Sir Harry Oakes's body was flown from Nassau to Bar Harbor, Maine for burial. After the funeral a dozen mourners, including Nancy de Marigny and Captains Melchen and Barker, went back to the Oakes house. In a display of appalling taste, Captain

Right: *Nancy de Marigny, Sir Harry's daughter and wife of the man accused of his murder.*

AMAZINGLY, STRAIGHT AFTER THE FUNERAL CAPTAIN BARKER CONDUCTED A DRAMATIZED RE-ENACTMENT OF THE MURDER

Below: *Count Alfred de Marigny is escorted to court by Bahamian police, accused of his father-in-law's murder.*

Barker suddenly took it into his head to use the gathering as an audience for his version of the murder of Sir Harry Oakes.

Acting out each part, he demonstrated to the stunned group how de Marigny had taken a railing from the Westbourne fence, climbed into Sir Harry's bedroom and struck the baronet. Barker finished his charade with a stunning statement: he had found several of de Marigny's fingerprints at the scene of the crime.

For Countess Nancy de Marigny, it was all too much. She was certain that her husband had not killed her father. She stormed out of the house and caught the first flight to New York. There she made contact with one of America's most famous private detectives, Raymond Campbell Schindler.

CONSPIRACY

Three days later, Schindler and his team flew into Nassau to be greeted by a hostile, uncooperative Bahamian police force. After considerable difficulty, Schindler gained access to Westbourne.

Many aspects of the investigation dismayed Schindler. The 'several' fingerprints of de Marigny which Barker claimed to have found turned out to be a single print of the Count's little finger. Barker claimed it had been 'lifted' from the folding Chinese screen.

On seeing this so-called evidence, Schindler immediately called on the services of Maurice B. O'Neil of the New Orleans Police Department, one of the world's experts on fingerprints. It was obvious to Schindler that the Miami detectives were at best incompetent and probably guilty of conspiracy to pervert the course of justice.

By the time Count de Maringy was brought to trial in October 1943, Schindler was ready. Much of the evidence levelled against the defendant was purely circumstantial. The only concrete fact offered by the prosecution was Barker's fingerprint evidence. As an expert witness, Maurice O'Neil tore it, and Barker's reputation, to shreds.

The defence cast doubt on whether the print had indeed been lifted from the screen at all. The lawyers suggested instead that it might well have come from the cellophane wrapper on a cigarette packet given to de Marigny by Captain Melchen during their interview the day after the murder. Asked if this was possible, O'Neil answered, 'Yes.'

Sir Oscar Daly, Chief Justice of the Bahamas, presiding, spent five and a half hours summing up, but it was obvious that O'Neil's evidence had totally undermined the prosecution case.

The jury agreed with the Chief Justice and found de Marigny Not Guilty by nine votes to three.

WHO KILLED HARRY OAKES?

And there the matter has rested for almost half a century. But the question remains, who did kill Sir Harry Oakes?

There was a school of thought which suggested that Harold Christie killed Sir Harry Oakes. He was at the scene of the crime, and his bloodstained handprints were found on the wall. But the fact is that Christie was the baronet's closest friend and had absolutely nothing to gain by his death.

A more bizarre theory is that Oakes was killed by black dissidents, and that the burning and 'feathering' of the body had been part of a voodoo ritual. But voodoo is not widely practised in the Bahamas; the killing bore no resemblance to any known voodoo ritual, and Sir Harry Oakes, a noted philanthropist, was liked and respected by black Bahamians.

The most plausible theory was advanced in 1972 by Marshall Houts, a former judge and FBI agent, in his book *Kings X*. Basing his conclusion on information from unnamed persons, Houts claims that Oakes died at the hands of a crime association headed by Charlie 'Lucky' Luciano, Benjamin 'Bugsy' Siegel and Meyer Lansky.

In 1943, the Mob had just established themselves in Las Vegas and were looking for other locations for their gaming interests. Nassau seemed ideal. According to Houts, Meyer Lansky, the Mob's money man, approached Harold Christie and, through him, the Duke of Windsor with a view to gaining a toe-hold on the island.

Christie had seen a chance to make a great deal of money and had readily agreed. The Duke, an inveterate gambler, posed no problem. Sir Harry Oakes, however, was another matter. He had more money than he knew what to do with, and he disapproved of gambling.

Christie reported Sir Harry's opposition to Lansky, and he in turn put pressure on the Duke. There were only two ways to resolve the situation: to 'persuade' the cantankerous baronet, or to get rid of him.

On the night of 7 July, Houts's story continues, a boatload of Lansky's heavies landed at Lyford Cay. After the other guests left Westbourne, Christie persuaded Sir Harry to accompany him to the boat to discuss the casino business. Sir Harry reluctantly agreed, taking along his automatic pistol as a precaution.

Once on board the boat, the mobsters threatened Oakes and he in turn pulled his gun on them. One of the crew then hit him on the head with a pronged winch handle – causing the curiously shaped wounds to his head. The heavies then bundled Sir Harry's unconscious body into the back of a waiting estate car and drove back through Nassau towards Westbourne. En route, Christie was spotted in the passenger seat by Sears.

Back at Westbourne, the mobsters told a terrified Harold Christie to go to bed and stay there until his normal time of rising. They set fire to the bed and placed Sir Harry's body on the flames. Presumably they ripped a pillow in the process and covered him with feathers.

In the morning Christie 'discovered' the body and then called the Duke of Windsor. The two men then set about framing a suitable suspect – the man they both hated, Count Alfred de Marigny.

Above: Sir Harry Oakes and his family.

Below: Count Alfred de Marigny leaves court, cleared of killing Sir Harry Oakes.

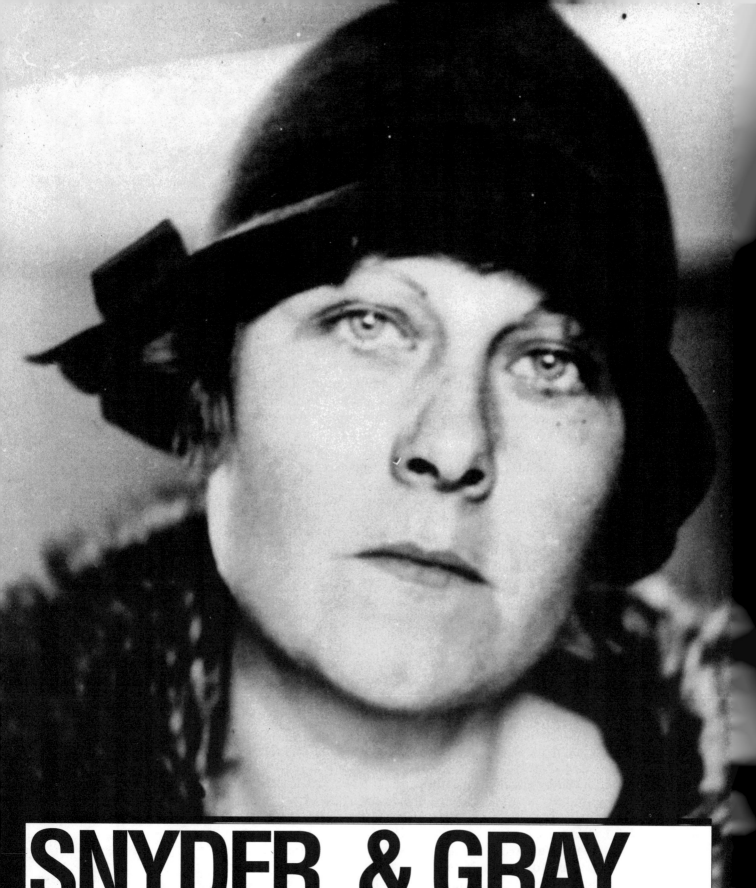

SNYDER & GRAY
Momsie and Loverboy

The mousey little underwear salesman wanted a passionate woman to dominate him. The blonde good-time girl was after a man whom she could control utterly. It seemed the perfect match – but after sex came murder

They were an odd couple. He was a submissive traveller in ladies' underwear; she was a domineering good-time girl. Dubbed 'Putty Man' and 'Granite Woman', they fulfilled a need in each other and, while their relationship was always faintly ludicrous, it was also to prove ultimately deadly.

ATTRACTION OF OPPOSITES

Judd Gray and Ruth Snyder first met in June 1925 at Henry's, a small Scandinavian restaurant in New York City. It was a blind lunch date set up by two of Ruth's friends, Karin Kaufman and Harry Folsom.

Judd and Ruth hit it off from the start. It was an attraction of opposites. She was an attractive twenty-eight-year-old blonde, an extrovert who enjoyed drinking, dancing and sex. He was thirty-one, slight, shy and myopic. He too had a thirst for excitement which he had never had either the courage or the opportunity to slake. In Ruth he saw the chance for a passionate affair, an escape from the drudgery of his bourgeois life.

Judd and Ruth spent their first three hours together in the restaurant booth swapping personal and marital histories. She explained that she was married with a seven-year-old daughter, Lorraine, and lived in the suburb of Queens with her husband, Albert, who was much older than she. Art editor with *Motor Boating* magazine, he was a great outdoors man and spent most of his time and money on boating and fishing.

In fact, he was away on one of his trips as they spoke. She didn't care for the outdoor life. She preferred dining in good restaurants and dancing – not that Albert cared. In all, she painted her marriage in fairly grim terms with herself as the grass widow to a selfish and insensitive man.

What she neglected to mention to Judd Gray was that he was merely the latest in a long string of 'men friends' whom she had cultivated to compensate herself for her marital dissatisfaction.

Judd responded by saying that he too was married with a daughter and lived in East Orange, New Jersey. He described his wife Isabel as a good mother and a

Opposite: *'Granite Woman', Ruth Snyder was a good-time girl who liked to dominate the men in her life.*

Below: *Judd Gray, 'Putty Man', was an ineffectual underwear salesman who lusted after excitement. He found it in Ruth Snyder.*

Above: *The Snyder house in East Orange, New Jersey.*

Opposite: *In her younger years, Ruth Snyder cut a glamorous figure.*

meticulous housekeeper, but made it plain that she did not provide the excitement he wanted from life.

The one bright spot in his otherwise dull existence was his job. As a travelling salesman for the Bien Jolie Corset Company, he spent much of his time on the road. The company's headquarters were in New York and so he came to the city on a regular basis. Would Ruth like to meet him again? Yes, she would.

By the time Ruth and Judd parted company on the sidewalk outside Henry's it was after 4p.m., and both of them had found what they had been searching for: Judd, a passionate affair in which he could be led and dominated; Ruth, a man she could control utterly.

CONSUMMATION ON THE OFFICE FLOOR

Despite this obvious mutual attraction, it was almost two months before the couple met again for their first real date. On 4

August, Judd called Ruth and asked if she would care to join him for dinner at 'their place' – Henry's Swedish restaurant. After the meal Judd, fortified with copious quantities of rye whiskey, invited Ruth back to the Bien Jolie offices on Fifth Avenue. 'I have to collect a case of samples,' he explained lamely.

Once inside the empty office, Judd made his move. 'You really ought to try one of the new glamour corsets,' he suggested. 'I'll fit it for you if you like.'

Ruth took off her coat. 'Okay,' she said. 'You can do that. And from now on you can call me Momsie.'

And so, on the floor of the Bien Jolie Corset Company, Ruth Snyder and Judd Gray consummated their affair, an affair which was to burn with increasing ardour for almost two years. Soon after their first tryst, Judd and Ruth started to meet regularly, spending nights – or parts of nights – together in Manhattan hotel bedrooms. While Judd needed no excuse to be away from home, Ruth would tell

Albert that she was visiting girlfriends. Despite the fact that the meetings became increasingly frequent, Albert suspected nothing – or perhaps he didn't care.

As the relationship developed, its true nature became more apparent. Ruth became increasingly dominant and Judd became correspondingly more besotted. He would sink to his knees and caress her feet and ankles. 'You are my queen, my Momsie!' he would simper, gazing up into her imperious face. 'And you are my baby, my Bud, my Lover Boy,' she would reassure him.

By the end of 1925 the couple had abandoned the last vestiges of discretion and Judd started to visit Ruth at home. Ruth took little Lorraine on her visits to New York, leaving her in the care of the hotel concierge while she went upstairs to spend a few hours with her Lover Boy.

From their first meeting, Ruth had made it clear that her marriage was not happy. As time passed she amplified this point with frequent references to Albert's cruelty, claiming that he beat and humiliated her. When she spoke of these things, she always made a point of saying how wonderful things would be if only she and Judd were both free and could be together all the time.

'ACCIDENTS'

Ruth did not come right out and say that she wished her husband was dead, but she was soon sowing the seeds of the idea in her lover's mind. Just before Christmas 1925, Ruth told Judd about a series of strange 'accidents' which had befallen her husband in recent months.

On one occasion, while he had been changing a tyre, the jack had slipped and the car had almost crushed him to death. A few days later, he had been in the garage stretched under the car with the engine running. Ruth, the ever-dutiful wife, had brought him a glass of whiskey and, not thinking, had closed the garage door after her. A few minutes later Albert had felt very dizzy, and he had just managed to escape from the garage before being asphyxiated by exhaust fumes.

Albert might have seen nothing ominous about these incidents, but Judd

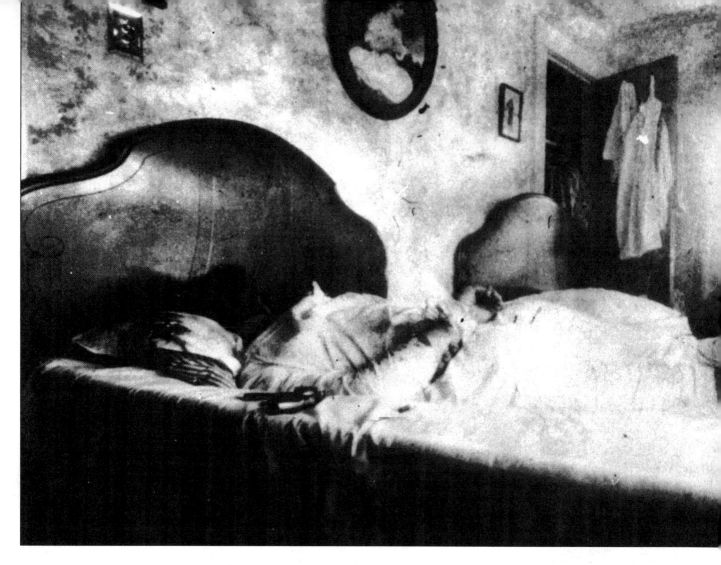

Gray certainly did. 'What are you trying to do?' he asked, horrified. 'Kill the poor guy?'

Ruth pouted: 'Momsie can't do it alone. She needs help. Lover Boy will have to help her.' They had both been drinking heavily and Judd wrote off this first suggestion of murder as alcoholic bravado.

The next time the couple met, however, Judd realized that she was deadly serious. 'We'll be okay for money,' Ruth said. 'I've just tricked Albert into taking out some hefty insurance. He thinks it's for $1000, but it's really for $96,000 with a double indemnity clause.'

Judd made light of the idea and changed the subject, but Ruth was not about to be dissuaded. Over the next few months she gradually chiseled away at Judd's resistance.

In December she told him that Albert had bought a gun and was threatening to kill her. She appealed to Judd directly to help her kill Albert. When he refused, she said she would do it by herself.

> TIRED OF HER LOVER'S NON-COMPLIANCE IN HER MURDER PLANS, RUTH ORDERED HIM TO BUY SOME CHLOROFORM AND PICTURE WIRE

THREATS AND BULLYING

Finally Ruth tired of trying to persuade and cajole her lover into action. It was time, she decided, to capitalize on her dominant position in the relationship and to give a few outright orders.

In February 1927 the couple spent the night together in the Waldolf-Astoria Hotel. Ruth instructed Judd to purchase some chloroform, a sash weight and a length of picture wire. These, she explained, were to be their murder weapons: 'That way,' she explained gleefully, 'we have three means of killing him. One of them must surely work.'

But again Judd baulked at the idea of becoming involved in murder. Ruth flew into a rage and threatened him: 'If you don't do as I say, then that's the end of us in bed. You can find yourself another Momsie to sleep with – only nobody else would have you but me!'

Cowed by the prospect of losing Ruth and returning to his old, dull life, Judd reluctantly agreed to help. Two days later, while passing through Kingston in

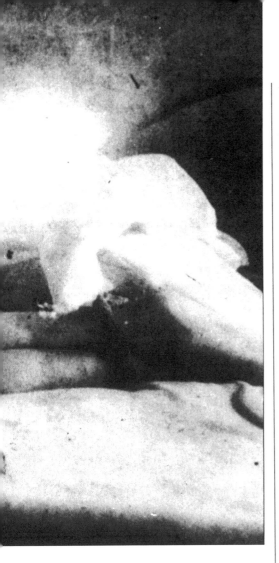

New York State, he bought a bottle of chloroform in a drug store. He then walked a few doors further along the street to a hardware store and bought a foot-long, lead sash weight and a coil of picture wire.

The next day, Judd returned to New York City and met Ruth at Henry's Restaurant. There he handed over a parcel containing his purchases. Despite the fact that Ruth had brought her daughter with her she was anxious to get on with things, and so the couple discussed the murder of Lorraine's father by exchanging notes scribbled on table napkins. By the time they got up from the table, a date for the killing had been set – Saturday, 19 March.

THE PLAN TAKES SHAPE

On Friday the 18th, Judd Gray registered at the Hotel Onondaga in Syracuse, New York State. In the lobby he bumped into an old friend, Haddon Gray (no relation). Judd saw this as a piece of good fortune and decided to use him as an alibi for the following night.

He told Haddon that he had an assignation with a lady in New York. Would he cover for him? He asked Haddon to 'muss up' his bedclothes and to hang a 'Do Not Disturb' sign on the bedroom door. Haddon readily agreed to this 'manly' conspiracy.

Having thus established his alibi – and, in the process, established the premeditation of his crime – Judd set off by train for New York City.

He arrived at Grand Central Station at 10.20p.m. on the evening of 19 March. After stopping briefly at the Pullman window to purchase a return ticket to Syracuse on the morning train, he walked out on to 42nd Street.

It was raining, but Judd chose to walk the four miles to Queens rather than risk being recognised by a cab driver. He made frequent stops along the way to drink from his hip flask, and he was already quite drunk when he reached his destination.

Judd reached the Snyders' three-storey, clapboard house shortly after midnight. He knew that Ruth and her family would be out at a party until very late, and he let himself into the house by a side door, using a key that Ruth had hidden for him. He went upstairs and into the spare bedroom. Keeping on his buckskin gloves, he removed his hat and coat and hung them in the wardrobe. Then he felt under the pillow and retrieved the sash weight, chloroform, picture wire and a bottle of whiskey which had been left there by Ruth. He laid these props on the bed along with various other items which he had brought with him – a handkerchief, some cheesecloth and an Italian newspaper he had found on the train.

Judd opened the whiskey, took a long slug and settled down to wait.

At about 2am, Judd was woken from his drunken sleep by the sound of the Snyders' car pulling up outside. He heard the front door open, and then footsteps on the stairs. He recognized the voices of Ruth and Lorraine. Ruth slipped into the room where Judd was hiding.

She kissed him and whispered: 'Have you found the sash weight?' Judd nodded. 'Good,' she said. 'Keep quiet and I'll be right back.'

JUDD'S ALIBI HAD ANOTHER, LESS DESIRABLE EFFECT: IT ESTABLISHED THAT THE MURDER OF RUTH'S HUSBAND WAS PREMEDITATED

She returned a few minutes later in her negligee. 'He's just brushing his teeth.' she said, and slipped away again. And so the farce continued for half an hour with Ruth toing and froing, updating Judd on the status in the master bedroom.

'He's getting undressed now.... He's in bed but he's still awake.... I think he's dropped off, but we'd better leave him to settle for a while....'

It was almost 3a.m. before Ruth decided the time was right and joined Judd in the bedroom. He was sitting on the floor and, having almost finished the bottle of whiskey, was very drunk.

'You are going through with it tonight, aren't you?' Ruth asked him.

'I don't know whether I can or not. I'll try.' he replied. Ruth helped him to his feet. 'Now,' she said.

Judd removed his buckskin gloves and pulled on a pair of rubber housegloves in their place. He picked up the sash weight with one hand and with the other took Ruth's arm. And so the odd couple picked their way along the darkened corridor towards the master bedroom.

Ruth led Judd over to the bed where Albert was sleeping. Judd lifted the sash weight above his head and brought it down with all the force he could muster. The blow should have smashed Albert's skull but Judd's aim was off. The weight only glanced the side of Albert's head and crashed into the wooden bedhead.

Albert sat bolt upright and started lashing out at his unseen assailant. Judd hit him again, harder this time, but Albert continued to struggle. Judd dropped the weight and climbed on to the bed, trying to smother his victim with the bedclothes. Albert managed to get his hands round Judd's throat and started to throttle him. Judd screamed at Ruth: 'Momsie, Momsie, for God's sake help me!'

Ruth picked up the sash weight and smashed it into her husband's skull, time and time again. Once Albert stopped struggling, Judd climbed off the bed and watched Ruth put the finishing touches to the job. She tied Albert's hands and feet with a towel and a tie and stuffed his mouth and nostrils with cotton rags soaked in chloroform. Then, just for good measure, she garotted him with the length of picture wire.

'HE'S CLEANING HIS TEETH... HE'S GETTING UNDRESSED... HE'S IN BED BUT HE'S STILL AWAKE...'

'MOMSIE, MOMSIE, FOR GOD'S SAKE HELP ME!' CRIED THE INCOMPETENT WOULD-BE MURDERER AS HIS VICTIM STARTED TO THROTTLE HIM

Below: *Ruth Snyder and her defence team. Their argument failed to convince the jury.*

There was blood everywhere, and Ruth and Judd spent the next half-hour cleaning themselves up. Ruth changed nightdresses and Judd borrowed one of Albert's shirts to replace his own, which was ripped and bloodstained.

Ruth then reminded Judd that they had agreed to ransack the house to make it look like a robbery. They overturned furniture in the living room and scattered the contents of various drawers around the floor. Ruth took all the money out of Albert's wallet and gave it to Judd, and then offered him her jewellery. He refused, and suggested she hide it under the mattress.

In an equally futile attempt to destroy the evidence, Ruth went down to the cellar. There she burned the bloodstained shirt and nightdress in the furnace, and hid the sash weight in a tool box.

Satisfied that everything was just so, Ruth gave Judd another bottle of whiskey for the journey, and told him to knock her out, so that it would look as if she too had been a victim of a robbery.

Judd could not bring himself to do this, but tied her hands and feet and gagged her with a piece of cheesecloth. He left her on the spare bed, with the Italian newspaper – his idea of a false clue – by her side.

As he left, he looked back at Ruth and

Above: *Huge crowds gathered outside the court hoping to gain access to the Snyder-Gray trial.*

was momentarily overcome with disgust and guilt. 'It may be two months,' he said, 'it may be a year, and it may be never before you see me again.'

CLUMSY LIES, SCATTERED CLUES

The murder of Albert Snyder must have been a noisy affair, but little Lorraine Snyder apparently slept through the whole thing. She was woken at 7.45 by a knocking at her bedroom door. She opened the door and found her mother, bound and gagged, lying on the floor in the hallway.

Lorraine undid the cheesecloth gag, and her mother told her to run and get help. Minutes later, the child returned with Louis and Harriet Mulhauser, their friends and neighbours.

'It was dreadful, just dreadful!' Ruth screeched at the Mulhausers. 'I was attacked by a prowler.... He tied me up.... He must have been after my jewels.... Is Albert all right?' Louis Mulhauser crossed the hall and went into the master bedroom. Seconds later, he returned with the awful news. Albert had been battered to death.

Ruth Snyder repeated her version of events twice more that morning, elaborating a little with each successive version. 'He was a big, rough-looking

---

'IT MAY BE TWO MONTHS, IT MAY BE A YEAR, AND IT MAY BE NEVER BEFORE YOU SEE ME AGAIN'

SHE HAD POWER OVER ME. SHE TOLD ME WHAT TO DO AND I JUST DID IT

---

guy of about thirty-five with a black moustache,' she told Dr Harry Hansen. 'He was a foreigner, I guess. Some kind of Eyetalian.'

Dr Hansen was not convinced by her story, and nor were the police when they arrived. Police Commissioner George V. McLaughlin, heading the investigation, had investigated enough robberies to know the real thing when he saw it. And this definitely was not the real thing.

It had all the hallmarks of an inside job, carried out with the help of an accomplice, probably a man.

A clue to that man's identity came when one of the detectives found a tiepin with the initials JG on the floor of the master bedroom. Then another detective found Ruth's address book which contained the names of twenty-eight of her men friends; the most recent entry was one Judd Gray. Then they found a cancelled cheque made out to Gray by Ruth Snyder in the amount of $200.

By this time, other detectives had discovered the bloodstained sash weight in the cellar and Ruth's jewellery stuffed under the mattress in the spare bedroom. They also found insurance policies taken out on Albert Snyder's life to a total of $96,000.

After twelve hours of questioning, Ruth caved in and admitted that she had been present at her husband's murder, but she denied playing any part in the actual killing. That was all Judd's doing. She was shipped off to the Jamaica Precinct police station and charged.

Acting on information from Ruth Snyder, police arrested a snivelling and terrified Judd Gray at the Onondaga Hotel later that evening. They brought him back to New York City by train.

By the time they arrived, Judd too had confessed to being a party to the murder, but he did not cover up for Ruth. 'I would never have killed Snyder, but for her,' he wept as he completed his statement. 'She had power over me. She told me what to do and I just did it.'

GOOD NEWS FOR THE TABLOIDS

From then on, the case against Snyder and Gray proceeded with all the implacability of the law. Their trial opened on 18 April at the Queens County Courthouse and lasted eighteen days.

The central issue at stake for the jury was not whether the defendants were guilty of killing Albert Snyder. They had both confessed to being present and playing a part in the murder. What had to be decided was whether the crime was premeditated, and whether or not it had been executed for financial gain. Both these factors would have a bearing on the eventual sentencing.

The two defence teams tried to push the blame on to each other's clients to a point where the case became not so much the State v Snyder & Gray as one of Ruth Snyder v Gray. This did nothing for the cases of the two defendants.

On 9 May, Snyder and Gray were duly found guilty of murder in the first degree and sentenced to die in the electric chair at Sing Sing prison in upstate New York.

CHANGED CHARACTERS

Immediately after sentencing, both teams of defence lawyers filed appeals. Ruth's appeal was heard on 27 May, Judd's on

> FROM THE CONDEMNED CELL RUTH TOLD A REPORTER: 'I ALWAYS WANTED AN ELECTRIC HEATER, BUT MY HUSBAND WAS ALWAYS TOO STINGY TO BUY ME ONE'

> 'I NEVER SAW ANYTHING MORE TERRIBLE,' SAID RUTH'S LAWYER. 'I CANNOT DESCRIBE HER AGONY, HER MISERY, HER TERROR'

Below: *Ruth Snyder being followed by jail matron, Mrs Irene Wolf.*

10 June. On 23 November both appeals were rejected and Snyder's original sentence was upheld.

With all legal means for clemency now closed to her, Ruth started writing her autobiography, My Own True Story – So Help Me God! which was syndicated by the Hearst newspaper chain.

She also promoted herself in the media by granting audiences to press men from her condemned cell. She even managed moments of black humour. Talking of her forthcoming execution, she told reporter Jack Lait: 'I always wanted an electric heater, but my husband was always too stingy to buy me one.'

While awaiting execution, Ruth had a regular flow of fan mail. It included 164 proposals of marriage, mainly from men desperate to take Judd Gray's place as her slave.

For all her bravado, however, the 'Granite Woman', as the press had dubbed her, was terrified of dying. Screams could be heard coming from her Sing Sing cell at night.

Judd Gray, in contrast, appeared totally resigned to his fate. He spent much of his time writing letters to his family and friends. When he was not busy with his correspondence, he studied the Bible and discussed religious matters with the prison chaplain.

The execution was set for 11 p.m. on 12 January 1928. At 7.30 p.m., Ruth Snyder was moved to her death cell, 30 feet from the execution chamber.

Shortly before the evening meal she was visited by her lawyer, Edgar Hazleton. Her condition was pitiful, he recalled. 'She was too far gone to know what she was doing. I never saw anything more terrible. I cannot describe her agony, her misery, her terror.'

A little later Samuel Miller, Judd Gray's attorney, visited him in his death cell, a few feet away from that of his erstwhile lover. Miller painted a very different picture of his client to that of Hazleton. 'He is absolutely resigned and courageous,' Miller said. 'He indulges no self-pity. He realizes the enormity of his act.'

A few minutes before 11 p.m. twenty-four witnesses, most of them reporters, were shown into the death chamber.

Among those who took their seats opposite the electric chair was a young photographer, Thomas Howard. Cameras were strictly forbidden in the chamber, but Howard had managed to smuggle in a tiny one strapped to his ankle.

At precisely 11 p.m. Ruth Snyder, her head shaved, was led from her cell by two female warders. As she was strapped to the chair, she wept: 'Father, forgive them, for they know not what they do.' Seconds later the state executioner, Robert Elliot, threw the switch and a massive surge of electricity shot through Ruth's body. At precisely that moment, Thomas Howard released the shutter of his hidden camera, recording the death of Ruth Snyder on film and guaranteeing for himself a place in journalistic folklore.

At 11.10, after Ruth Snyder's body had been removed to the nearby autopsy room, Judd Gray was brought into the death chamber. He stood between two warders, calm and composed. A priest stood by him as he was strapped into the chair, and they recited the Beatitudes together. Gray continued to pray as the electrodes were fitted and a mask was pulled over his face.

Ten minutes later, Judd Gray was reunited with Ruth Snyder for the first and last time since the fateful night of Albert Snyder's murder. This time they lay side-by-side on a slab in the Sing Sing prison morgue.

Above: *Ruth Snyder at the moment of her death in the electric chair: taken by a camera smuggled into the death chamber strapped to the photographer's leg.*

GRAY CONTINUED TO PRAY EVEN AS THE ELECTRODES WERE FITTED AND A MASK WAS PULLED OVER HIS FACE

DONALD NEILSON
The Black Panther

For three years police pursued a man who committed sixteen robberies and four murders and terrorized a large part of England. But the real Donald Neilson was very far from the hooded 'Black Panther' image of popular imagination

O n the evening of 13 January 1975, seventeen-year-old Lesley Whittle was at home alone and went to bed early. She lived with her widowed mother, but on this particular night Mrs Dorothy Whittle was out for the evening. When she did return to her comfortable home in the village of Highley, Shropshire at 1.30a.m., Mrs Whittle made a point of checking her daughter's bedroom. Lesley was sound asleep.

HOODED FIGURE CLAD IN BLACK

Shortly after Mrs Whittle herself retired to bed, a man forced the lock on the garage door. He was dressed from head to foot in black and was wearing a hood. Working silently and in total darkness, the intruder cut the telephone line and then moved into the house. Passing through the living room, he climbed the stairs and made his way directly to Lesley's room.

Lesley Whittle was woken by a hand shaking her roughly. She looked up to see the black-clad figure standing over her, pointing a sawn-off shotgun in her face. Lesley lay transfixed as the intruder taped her mouth, and indicated that she should get out of bed. He led Lesley downstairs and outside to a waiting car, a green Morris 1300. He laid her on the back seat, bound her wrists and ankles and placed tape over her eyes.

The intruder then removed his hood, got into the driving seat and set off on a sixty-mile trip to his hiding place. He drove down the M6 motorway, turned off at Junction 16 and drove to Bathpool Park, near Kidsgrove. He parked the car alongside the access shaft of the town's drainage system, removed the manhole cover and forced Lesley to climb 65 feet down a rusty ladder.

When they reached a tiny platform, on which he had installed a foam rubber mattress, the kidnapper removed Lesley's dressing gown, placed a wire noose around her neck and clamped it to the wall. Below, the access shaft fell away. If Lesley were to slip she would hang.

The kidnapper then made his next move in an elaborate plan to extort money from his victim's family. He

Above: Lesley Whittle's disappearance prompted a nation-wide hunt.

Opposite: The Black Panther. A model dressed in the outfit adopted by Donald Neilson.

uncovered Lesley's eyes, proffered a memo machine, and instructed her to read two messages which he had written on a pad.

Lesley did not know her kidnapper. She had never laid eyes on him before in her life. His name was Donald Neilson.

The name would have meant nothing to her. It would have meant little to the police either, even though they had been chasing him for more than three years, during which time he had been responsible for armed robberies and the murder of three sub-postmasters. Yet they only knew him by a nickname.

No one knew it yet, but Lesley Whittle had been kidnapped by the 'Black Panther'.

HOAXES AND MISTAKES

On the morning of 14 January, Mrs Dorothy Whittle woke to find her daughter missing. She was more puzzled than alarmed. Lesley had been safely tucked up in her bed at 1.30. Nothing bad could have happened to her since then. Mrs Whittle checked round the house and then tried to telephone her son, Ronald.

The phone, of course, had been cut. But, assuming it was merely out of order, Dorothy Whittle drove to her son's house at the other end of the village.

Neither Ronald nor his wife Gaynor had seen Lesley that morning. Mrs Whittle was now becoming uneasy.

Gaynor drove back home with Mrs Whittle, and the two women checked the house more carefully in the hope of finding a note. They found a note all right, but it wasn't from Lesley.

In a cardboard box, resting on a flower vase in the lounge, they discovered a long roll of Dymo tape. There were three messages carefully typed into the coloured plastic. The messages were ransom demands.

The first read: 'No police £50,000 ransom to be ready to deliver wait for phone call at Swan shopping centre telephone box 6 p.m. to 1 a.m. if no call return following evening when you answer give your name only and listen you must follow instructions without argument from the time you answer you are on a time limit if police or tricks death.'

Above: *The access shaft to the sewer system at Bathpool Park where Neilson held, and finally murdered, Lesley Whittle.*

Despite the warning in the note, Mrs Whittle did not hesitate to call the police. Within an hour the case was being led by the head of West Mercia CID, Detective Chief Superintendent Bob Booth.

He was in no doubt that this was a professional kidnapping. Lesley was a logical target. Two years earlier she had been the beneficiary of a large and highly publicized inheritance.

Booth advised the Whittle family that their best chance of getting Lesley back alive was to comply fully with the kidnapper's demands.

While Ronald Whittle, who owned a successful coach company, was raising the money, Booth had his own elaborate arrangements to make. He installed taps on the phones at Mrs Whittle's home and the phone box at Kidderminster.

After midday, Booth and his detectives were joined by a team of kidnap specialists from Scotland Yard.

Shortly after 5p.m. Ronald Whittle, armed with a white suitcase full of money, installed himself in the phone box at Kidderminster, and waited.

The police, who were watching Whittle from a discreet distance, hoped to have the whole episode dealt with that night, but it was not to be. A freelance journalist had somehow got wind of the operation and started making a nuisance of himself.

Rather than alerting the kidnapper to the fact that the police were indeed involved, Booth decided to abort the mission.

The following evening, Ronald Whittle returned to the phone box with the money. Shortly after 8 p.m., the police called him out again. They had received a call from a man claiming to be the kidnapper and had been given delivery instructions for the ransom money. The call, however, proved to be a hoax.

Meanwhile, another drama was unfolding. Donald Neilson left his hideout in the drains of Bathpool Park and did a dummy run of the route he had mapped out for the ransom carrier. He travelled to Dudley in Worcestershire, stopping at various telephone boxes to conceal more Dymo tape instructions.

In Dudley itself, he decided to check over the final drop-off point, the Freightliner depot. He was browsing around when he was challenged by the night supervisor, Gerald Smith.

Neilson shot Smith six times. He then ran from the scene, abandoning his stolen Morris car.

When local police investigated the shooting, they failed to check the car. This was a tragic oversight, because the boot of the car was a positive treasure trove of clues.

Amazingly, Gerald Smith survived the shooting – though he died fourteen months later as a result of his wounds – and was able to give the police a description of his assailant. What he told them left police in no doubt that he was the victim of the 'Black Panther'.

At 11.45 p.m. on the night of 16 January, the third day of the kidnap, Leonard Rudd, transport manager of Whittle's Coaches, received a telephone call. On the other end of the line was Lesley Whittle's recorded voice instructing the courier to take the ransom money to a phone box at Kidsgrove.

Ronald Whittle was extensively briefed by Detective Chief Superintendent Lovejoy of Scotland Yard.

Whittle reached the Kidsgrove telephone box shortly after 3 a.m., and waited there for half an hour before discovering another Dymo message. It read: 'Go up road to Acres Nook sign. Go up Boathouse Road turn right into public footpath deadend go into entry service area. Drive past wall and flash headlights looking for torchlight run to torch instructions on torch. Go home wait for telephone.'

Below: The boot of Neilson's Morris car yielded a host of clues for police.

Ronald Whittle got back into his car and followed the directions. After a few minutes he arrived at Bathpool Park. He flashed his headlights and waited for the torch signal. It never came.

Donald Neilson had been watching as Ronald Whittle arrived, and was immediately suspicious. He could smell police.

Certain that he would never now get his hands on the ransom money, he flew into a rage. As soon as Whittle had left he climbed back down the drainage access shaft, pushed Lesley Whittle off her precarious platform and left her to hang by her neck until she died.

By dawn, he was on the train north to his home in Bradford.

VITAL NEW EVIDENCE

Most of Booth's and Lovejoy's efforts now centred around the village of Highly, where the abduction had taken place. Everyone in the village and the surrounding area was interviewed. But this revealed absolutely nothing.

And then, on 23 January, a week after the last abortive attempt to deliver the ransom money, a police constable patrolling the Freightliner depot at Dudley became interested in a green Morris 1300. He noticed it had been parked in the same spot for several days.

The car was towed into the police station and searched. The boot revealed startling new evidence. There were a tape recorder containing a tape of Lesley Whittle's voice, a gun, torches and a foam mattress. A ballistic examination of the gun confirmed that it had been used in the 'Black Panther' raids.

As the days passed, Detective Chief Superintendent Booth felt sure that Bathpool Park was probably the most important location they had encountered in their investigation, and he was determined to search it thoroughly. To this end, he planned an elaborate ruse.

On the evening of 5 March, Booth appeared on a television news programme with Ronald Whittle and the two men acted out a pre-rehearsed confrontation. Whittle described how he had gone to Bathpool Park on the night of 16 January. Booth, pretending this was

Above: *A press conference given by the police during the hunt for the 'Black Panther'.*

the first he had heard of the abortive rendezvous, flew into a rage and stormed out of the studio. The effect was to make Booth look extremely foolish. In fact, the deception gave him the excuse he had been looking for to search the park.

At dawn the following day, the police moved into Bathpool Park. At first their search yielded nothing. But then, two schoolboys came forward with a torch they had found there a few weeks earlier. Wrapped around the handle was a strip of Dymo tape which read: 'Drop suitcase into hole.'

On the next day, Friday, 7 March, Police Constable Paul Allen removed the manhole cover of the drainage system and climbed slowly down. He had descended about twenty feet when he paused and shone his torch downwards.

He was confronted with the grisly spectacle of Lesley Whittle's naked body, hanging from its wire noose.

UNITED AGAINST THE PANTHER

Up to this point, different teams of police had been working on 'Black Panther' murders in Accrington, Harrogate and Langley, as well as the team investigating the kidnap of Lesley Whittle. There had been close cooperation between the forces, but now it was decided to form a single 'Black Panther' task force under Scotland Yard's murder squad.

Above: *Police sniffer dogs search for clues in the murder of Lesley Whittle.*

The murder squad took over Kidsgrove police station, and 800 officers were drafted in to interview every one of the town's 22,000 population.

In an attempt to solicit help from the public, a local actor was dressed in black and drove the green Morris along the route thought to have been taken by the Panther. The reconstruction was shown on national television and attracted more than a thousand phone calls. Scores of names were submitted but the name Donald Neilson was not among them.

Nine months passed, and the murder squad were no nearer identifying the 'Black Panther'.

On Thursday, 11 December, Donald Neilson finally obliged them. It was 11 p.m. and Constables Stuart McKenzie and Tony White were sitting in their Panda car in Mansfield Woodhouse, Nottingham, when they caught sight of a man with a hold-all loitering outside the Four Ways public house.

McKenzie did a U-turn and pulled up alongside Neilson. White got out of the car and asked him what his name was, and what he was doing. Neilson smiled, gave them a name and a local address, and said he was on his way home from work. Still suspicious, White asked him to write down his particulars.

Suddenly Neilson produced a sawn-off shotgun from under his coat. He forced White into the back seat of the Panda car and got into the front passenger seat himself. He instructed McKenzie to drive to Blidworth, a village six miles away.

As they drove, White in the back noticed the shotgun waver away from his partner's side. He lunged forward and grabbed the barrel of the gun. McKenzie slammed on the brakes; the shotgun went off, blowing a hole in the roof of the car.

The Panda screeched to a halt outside a fish and chip shop, which was still open. As the two constables wrestled with Neilson, two customers, Keith Wood and

> As White grabbed the gun barrel his partner slammed on the brakes – the shotgun blew a hole in the car roof

Above: The diminutive figure of Donald Neilson, head covered, is led away from the committal proceedings.

THE JURY WATCHED IN OPEN-MOUTHED HORROR AS THE DEFENDANT RELATED HIS GHASTLY CRIMES IN MATTER-OF-FACT DETAIL

Roy Morris, rushed over to help.

Despite his diminutive stature, Neilson fought ferociously and it took all four of them to subdue him. A few minutes later, other police cars arrived on the scene. Donald Neilson was driven the 70 miles to Kidsgrove police station.

Neilson was questioned for twelve hours before he finally admitted to the abduction of Lesley Whittle.

The burning question for the police was, just who was this man Donald Neilson? For a man who had terrorized an entire region, he did not cut a very impressive figure – forty years old, 5 ft 4 ins tall, and slightly built.

Yet, over the previous ten years, he had committed more than four hundred robberies – sixteen on sub-post offices – and had killed four people. All this, and he had never so much as been questioned by police.

The secret of his 'success', the police were to discover, was discipline and meticulous planning, qualities he had developed courtesy of Her Majesty's armed forces. In 1955–7 Neilson had

spent his National Service in the King's Own Yorkshire Light Infantry, where he rose to the rank of lance corporal and served in Kenya, Aden and Cyprus.

At the time of his arrest, Neilson lived a quiet life with his wife Irene and their fifteen-year-old daughter Kathryn at their terraced house on the outskirts of Bradford. He made a modest living as a jobbing carpenter and, according to his neighbours, had no enemies and few friends.

WHEN LIFE MEANS LIFE

The trial of Donald Neilson began on 14 August 1976 at Oxford Crown Court. In addition to the murder of Lesley Whittle, Neilson stood charged with the murder of three sub-postmasters – Donald Skepper of Harrogate, Derek Askin of Accrington and Sidney Gray-land of Langley – all of whom had been shot to death in 1974. He was defended by Gilbert Gray QC and entered a plea of Not Guilty to all four charges.

Neilson's behaviour in court was nothing short of extraordinary. He maintained his military posture throughout the trial, standing smartly to attention and answering questions with a brisk 'Yes, sir,' or 'No, sir'.

Neilson seemed to have the idea that by being calm, precise and matter-of-fact he could persuade the court that he was the victim of a ghastly misunderstanding. At no time did he show one iota of sadness or remorse.

When it came to the murder of the three sub-postmasters, Neilson again tried to portray himself as the victim of misfortune. On all three occasions, he claimed, the gun he was carrying had gone off accidentally.

All in all, it was one of the most feeble defences ever presented to a British criminal court, and the jury wasted no time in returning a verdict of Guilty on all charges.

Sentencing Donald Neilson to life imprisonment, Mr Justice Mars-Jones would not set a minimum number of years. 'In your case,' he said, 'life must mean life. If you are ever released from prison it should only be on account of great age or infirmity.'

CRIMES
OF
HORROR

CONSTANZO
Voodoo Murders

In 1989 a Texan student's end-of-term spree 'down Mexico way' ended with his nightmarish execution. He had run into members of a maniacal voodoo cult, as devoted to diabolic ritual as they were to criminal profit

The air of the American southwest is already warm in the middle of March, when the University of Texas at Austin takes its spring break. Students pile into cars and head to the border to revel in the bars of Brownsville, its beach suburb South Padre on the banks of the Rio Grande, and the cantinas of Matamoros, across the Gateway International Bridge in Mexico.

Mark Kilroy, Bill Huddleston, Brent Martin and Bradley Moore drove south on 11 March 1989. Five days later the four friends, all in their twenty-first year, all from the same hometown, Santa Fe near Houston in Texas, were still staggering around the hot spot in a collective euphoric haze.

Above: *Constanzo as a young man in Florida. He was the child of Cuban immigrants who brought their Santeria religion with them.*

Opposite: *Adolfo de Jesus Constanzo, handsome, charismatic and totally evil.*

Left: *Mark Kilroy, a student at the University of Texas. A day trip to Mexico with friends had a horrific ending for him.*

VANISHED

At about two o'clock on the morning of 15 March, the boys joined the crowds of young Americans filtering back up the main street of Matamoros towards the border bridge. Martin and Moore had wandered ahead, and Bill Huddleston paused in an alley to urinate. While doing so he glimpsed Mark Kilroy talking to some Mexicans. When he came out of the alley Mark had vanished.

Rejoining his two friends at the bridge, Bill urged them to hang around in the hope that Mark would join them. When he did not, the trio walked back into Matamoros and searched the bars until dawn. Then they returned to their hotel in South Padre, before filing a missing persons report with the local police.

In fact, Mark Kilroy was in desperate trouble. Like most of his fellow American students, Kilroy shunned the company of the hard, streetwise Mexicans of his own age who drove around Matamoros in their battered pick-

Above: *The shack on the Santa Elena ranch contained a bloodstained altar. The building was later destroyed on police orders.*

IN HIS DRUNKEN AND TIRED STATE, MARK KILROY WAS UNABLE TO RESIST THE MEXICANS WHO BUNDLED HIM INTO THEIR TRUCK

up trucks. But on the night of his disappearance, Mark was approached by a couple of young Mexicans, who asked him if he wanted a ride.

Slowed by alcohol and fatigue, Kilroy barely had time to reply before he was bundled into a pick-up truck between the two men and driven off down the still busy main street. Kilroy realized that he was in some kind of peril. When the driver got out to relieve himself, he summoned all his wits and ran.

But two other Mexicans were following in a Chevrolet Suburban station wagon. The American was dragged in and driven off once more, this time with a knife at his throat.

The leader of the kidnap team was a twenty-seven-year-old drug smuggler named Serafin Hernandez Garcia, who had turned to the profitable world of crime under the patronage of a Cuban Padrino – 'Godfather' – thirty-seven-year-old Adolfo de Jesus Constanzo.

Constanzo, his underlings believed, was a powerful black magician. He used the spells of Palo Mayombe, the darker side of Santeria, which was the old slave religion of Cuba, to confer on his illegal operations an air of invulnerability from police and rival gangs. He needed a blond-haired, blue-eyed 'Anglo' such as Mark Kilroy as a human sacrifice.

The two battered vehicles drove to a derelict smallholding named the Rancho Santa Elena, about twenty miles south of the border; it was the headquarters of the Constanzo outfit. Kilroy was tied up and bundled into a barn in which the gang stored marijuana. Meanwhile Garcia rang Constanzo, who was at a Brownsville hotel, to say that his sacrifice was ready.

What happened next was described later to the police by David Serna Valdez, one of the kidnappers. Set up inside a shack on the ranch was an altar, on which stood cheap images of Catholic saints, lighted candles, a chalice and seven strips of coloured cloth to represent the seven principal African gods.

LET THE CEREMONY BEGIN

At midday Mark Kilroy was given a meal of bread and scrambled eggs. Then, at two o'clock in the afternoon, he was dragged into the 'temple'. Constanzo was dressed in a white robe, with coloured glass beads around his neck. He was attended by Elio Hernandez Rivera, known in the underground world of drug smugglers as 'Little Elio'. Elio was also known as 'The Executioner' and bore brand marks on his arms, made with the tip of a red hot knife, to mark him for this role. The third man present was Alvaro de Leon Valdez, another of Constanzo's criminal lieutenants.

Mark Kilroy was brought in and forced to kneel over an orange-coloured tarpaulin, while Constanzo lit a cigar. The 'high priest' blew cigar smoke over the bound captive. Next he raised a rum bottle, took a swig and blew the rum out in a fine spray over Mark's head. The victim was thus 'purified'.

Then, as Mark knelt, Constanzo swung a heavy machete and cut off the back of his skull 'with a sound,' David Valdez

Left: *The weapons with which Mark Kilroy was killed and butchered.*

Below: *Titled 'La Padrona' (the Godmother) by Constanzo, Sara Maria Aldrete was once a straight-A student in Texas.*

El Coqueto's reaction was to slam his foot on the accelerator and crash his way through, roaring off in his powerful car with the lawmen in hot pursuit.

CAPTURE OF THE UNCATCHABLE

Valdez drove like a demon, but the Federales were dogged in their pursuit and they were helped by the fact that Valdez was high on more than mere drugs. Since the sacrificial ceremony he was convinced, like the rest of the Constanzo gang, that he was under demonic protection and thus invulnerable to arrest and capture. He led the police straight to the Santa Elena ranch.

later recalled, 'like a ripe coconut being split open'.

Constanzo then scooped out the brain and threw it into a cauldron which bubbled over an open fire. The cauldron, already containing a potion of blood, chickens' feet, feathers and a goat's head, was called a *n'ganga* – simply an African cooking pot. For a while, the 'priest' chanted over the sickening stew. Then he encouraged his followers to mutilate Kilroy's body, cutting off facial features, fingers and genitals.

Some three weeks after the terrible events at Santa Elena ranch, David Serna Valdez, who had taken part in the kidnapping of Kilroy and was known as 'El Coqueto' – 'the Flirt' – by his homosexual friends, was driving his Chevrolet Silverado when he came across a police roadblock, manned by members of the Mexican Army and the Federal Judicial Police – the Federales.

Above: *Texas Attorney General Jim Mattox looks down at the blood-stained* n'ganga *which contained Mark Kilroy's brain.*

Above right: *The shack at Santa Elena where Mark Kilroy spent his last horrific hours.*

THE BODIES IN THE GRAVES HAD HAD THEIR FINGERS, LIMBS AND GENITALS SEVERED AND THEIR BRAINS SCOOPED FROM THEIR SKULLS

There, Valdez was arrested, and in the ramshackle buildings of the ranch the police found a sizeable reward for their persistence. In addition to large quantities of marijuana and cocaine, they found an arsenal of firearms and ammunition and eleven brand new cars.

Also at the farm was an old caretaker; when the police routinely showed him a photograph of the missing Mark Kilroy, the old man nodded recognition. Yes, he said, the boy had been brought here some weeks ago. The old man had made him a meal of eggs and bread.

A computer search yielded the names and addresses of what appeared to be a large and powerful gang. Within days the police were making arrests. Among others hauled in were Sergio Martinez, known as 'La Mariposa' – 'the Butterfly' – along with Serafin Hernandez Jnr and Elio Hernandez Rivera – Little Elio – who was one of the most prominent names on the Federales' wanted list.

On Tuesday 11 April the Federal Judicial Police took the principal arrested gang members out to the ranch and demanded a guided tour. They found the evil-smelling shack with its breeze-block altar and orange tarpaulin, and noted the paraphernalia of Santeria.

They also found the cast iron *n'ganga* containing the now congealed and decaying lumps of vegetable and animal and human flesh in a soup of black blood.

Eventually thirteen bodies were discovered in nine graves. Mark Kilroy lay three feet under the ground and was identified only through dental records of his lower jaw. Most of the other bodies had been mutilated in a similar fashion to Mark's. Fingers, limbs and genitals were severed, faces obliterated, brains scooped from skulls.

The thirteenth grave was exhumed for the benefit of TV cameras and press photographers. The police made a gang member, Sergio Martinez, do the digging. The grave contained the corpse of a fourteen-year-old whose rib cage had been hacked open. The heart was missing.

With the grim secrets of the Santa Elena ranch laid bare, the police began an intensive search for Adolfo de Jesus Constanzo and his high priestess, Sara Maria Aldrete.

VOODOO CHILD

Constanzo had been born on 1 November 1962 in Miami, Florida, to Delia Gonzales Del Valle and her lover, both of whom had fled Castro's Cuba. Adolfo's father abandoned Delia and the baby soon after the child's birth, and his mother married a Puerto Rican, who brought the boy up as a devout Catholic.

When he was ten, his stepfather died and his mother reverted to old habits to make money. She was the daughter of a priestess of Palo Mayombe back in Cuba, from whom she had learned her craft. Now she began to practise as a magician again, casting spells and charms for the expatriate Cuban community.

As he grew up, his mother taught Adolfo the family magical secrets. But Adolfo also had natural charm and film-star good looks. By the time he was fourteen he had attracted a bevy of women to him.

In 1983, when he was twenty-one, Adolfo moved with his mother to Mexico City, where he became a male model. Soon he was a familiar figure in the city's fashionable circles. As a bisexual, he cultivated links with homosexuals in government and legal circles, and he began to work his way into the lucrative world of drug-dealing. At the same time, according to his mother, he was studying the black arts under a major 'santero' known as 'The Great One', apparently the most powerful magician in Central America. From him, Adolfo learned the use of human sacrifice.

Sara Maria Aldrete had been born in Matamoros on 6 September 1964 and

Above: *Mexican federal policeman, Martin Solozar, examines human remains in one of several shallow graves at the ranch.*

Below: *Police unearth dismembered human remains.*

grew up there. She married at eighteen, divorced at twenty and a year later, in 1985, was accepted into Texas Southernmost College in Brownsville on a two-year physical education course. The tall brunette was extremely attractive and soon caught the attention of Serafin Hernandez Jnr, a smart young man who made his money from the family trade of drug smuggling.

The Hernandez family operated in two 'divisions'. Serafin Snr handled the USA side, until his arrest in February 1987. Serafin Jnr worked out of Matamoros for his young uncle, the feared 'Little Elio' Hernandez Rivera.

Sara Aldrete and Serafin Jnr saw each other at weekends, when Sara came home across the Gateway International Bridge to Matamoros. But one weekend in the autumn of 1986, a Mercedez cut in front of her car, and the handsome Constanzo got out. Using his easy charm instead of the usual Mexican macho approach, Constanzo invited Sara to a café and read her fortune from tarot cards. He told her that someone close to her would come to her with a 'terrible problem'.

Sure enough, two weeks later Serafin Jnr told her how the Hernandez family business was in danger of collapse. Sara was impressed by this demonstration of Constanzo's 'powers', while he saw an opportunity of worming into the confidence of the drugs barons of Mexico City. Soon he was Sara's lover.

Sara was now completely under

Left: *Martin Quintana was one of Constanzo's many homosexual lovers.*

Below: *Constanzo and Quintana lie together in death after their suicide pact.*

Constanzo's spell. During the coming months he took her to his Mexico City home, where he had already begun to dabble in human sacrifice.

SLAUGHTER: A WAY OF LIFE – AND DEATH

In the early part of 1988, acting on Constanzo's instructions, Sara seduced Little Elio. Before long she was convincing him that what he needed was the help of a powerful sorcerer to help him with his family problems. The drugs boss, as superstitious as most of his countrymen, needed little persuasion to meet Constanzo. And, like his nephew and his new mistress, he was instantly impressed.

Constanzo initiated him into the dark rituals of Palo Mayombe, branding him on the shoulders, back and chest with a hot knife to denote his new rank of executioner. Now, Constanzo and Little Elio became joint ceremonial killers, using one of Elio's gang hideouts – the Santa Elena ranch.

Gradually, true to Constanzo's predictions, the Mexican side of the drug business began to improve. Now they needed to place the US side on a solid footing once more. To do this, Constanzo ordered the kidnapping of an 'Anglo' for sacrifice, his white blood being deemed to have better protective powers over Anglo policemen than the Mexican variety. And so Mark Kilroy met his savage end.

No one knows exactly how many ritual

sacrifices were made by Constanzo and his cult, but one informed estimate was that the total was nearer thirty than the thirteen discovered at the ranch. In any case, time was now running out for the black magician and his depraved coterie.

Commandante Benitez Ayala of the Federales led a posse of policemen to Sara's house in Matamoros even before the last of the Santa Elena bodies had been exhumed. Her father showed them her apartment and they burst in. Inside

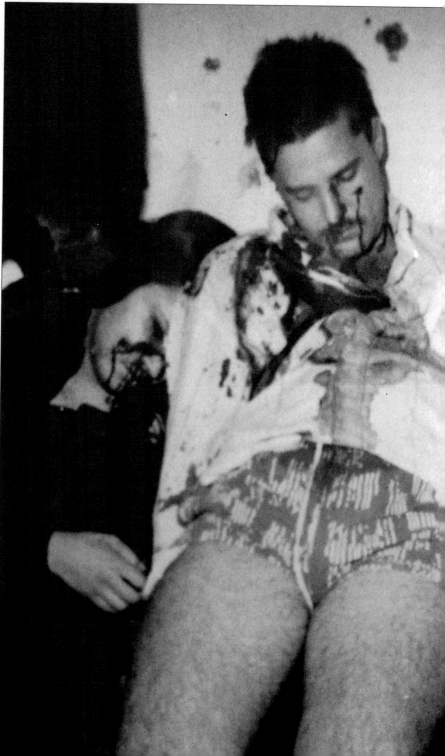

was an altar with candles, blood and bloodstained clothing – but no sign of the sorceress.

That afternoon Commandante Ayala, who himself kept 'white' Santeria charms on his desk at headquarters, summoned a 'curandero' – a Santeria priest. They went out to the ranch, and Ayala called an end to the digging. The curandero sprinkled holy water around the shack which contained the altar and chanted spells. Then he poured petrol over the red tarpaper of the walls, and set fire to the place, burning it to the ground.

As his black magic headquarters burned, Constanzo was on the run with his high priestess. Sara met him at Brownsville, where they boarded an aeroplane for Mexico City. When they arrived there, however, the Federales had already raided his flat, picked up notebooks which named important clients and laid a trap for him.

Constanzo, Sara, Alvaro de Leon Valdez and a number of others collected money at gunpoint from criminal associates, then drove in a convoy to the resort of Cuernavaca, fifty miles south of Mexico City. For three weeks they kept on the move, eluding police and police informers and finally returning to Mexico City by a circuitous route. There they holed up in a friend's apartment.

There is evidence that by this time Sara regretted any connection she had with the gang, and may have made an effort to contact the police. In any case, on 5 May 1989 the police became aware of a woman answering Sara's description, buying a large amount of groceries from various food stores. Gradually the police's net tightened.

On the morning of 6 May a lookout spotted a known police officer in plain clothes. Constanzo joined the lookout at the window and was able to pick out a number of officers moving into strategic positions. Suddenly Constanzo went berserk. 'They're here! Why run? Don't hide!' screamed the Godfather. He began to run around the flat, gathering up piles of coins and sheaves of US $20, $50 and $100 bills, flinging them through the window into the street.

Then, as passers-by ran forward to get at the money, he thrust an AK-47 out and began firing wildly, chipping chunks of masonry from the walls opposite and reducing a tamale cart to matchwood.

There followed an intense forty-five minute gunbattle, with Alvaro de Leon Valdez taking over Constanzo's gun while the Godfather himself continued to panic, burning wads of money on the gas stove and screaming, 'Let's all die!'

Finally Constanzo grabbed his homosexual lover, Martin Quintana, and hustled him into a cupboard, where the two men embraced before Constanzo ordered Valdez to kill them both.

After some persuasion, Valdez turned the AK-47 on to his chief, and sprayed the two men with bullets, killing them instantly. Valdez, Sara and the rest surrendered shortly afterwards.

In the early 1990s, the trials arising from the bizarre Constanzo affair are still proceeding. In August 1990 Alvaro de Leon Valdez was sentenced to thirty years for killing Constanzo and Quintana. Sara Maria Aldrete was acquitted on these charges but given six years for criminal association. Most of the other gang members remain in jail, awaiting final sentence.

The reaction of Helen Kilroy, Mark's mother, to the horrors of the Santa Elena ranch was almost superhumanly charitable. 'I think they must be possessed by the devil,' said the Catholic Irishwoman. 'That is the only explanation for what they did. I pray for all of them.'

COMMANDANTE AYALA TURNED WHITE MAGIC AGAINST BLACK TO DESTROY THE VOODOO TEMPLE

'LET'S ALL DIE!' SCREAMED THE HYSTERICAL CONSTANZO AS HE BURNED WADS OF MONEY ON A GAS STOVE

Below: *El Dubi is arrested in Mexico City following a shoot-out between police and Constanzo's cult members.*

PETER SUTCLIFFE
The Yorkshire Ripper

Left: *Peter Sutcliffe at seven years old.*

Opposite: *Peter Sutcliffe, the Yorkshire Ripper, on his wedding day.*

In the 1970s Yorkshire women were terrorized by a serial killer who, like the notorious Jack the Ripper, inflicted hideous mutilations on his victims. Was Peter Sutcliffe a paranoid schizophrenic, or just 'a wilfully evil bastard'?

Late on the afternoon of 22 May 1981, a dark-haired, bearded, scruffy little man rose to his feet in the dock beneath the dome of Number One Court at the Old Bailey to hear judgement passed upon him.

Found guilty of murdering thirteen women, and attempting to murder seven others, thirty-five-year-old Peter William Sutcliffe was sentenced to life imprisonment by Mr Justice Boreham with a recommendation that he should serve at least thirty years.

And yet, as the police knew to their unease, it was only by fluke that the 'Yorkshire Ripper' had been finally brought to book.

AN ORDINARY MURDER

The Ripper murders began in 1975 on a bitter morning of freezing fog in the run-down Chapeltown area of Leeds. A milkman making deliveries in Harrogate Road spotted a frosted bundle of what appeared to be rags on the white-rimed grass. He went and peered at it. It was a woman's body.

She lay on her back, her dyed blonde hair dark and spiky with dried blood. Her jacket and blouse had been torn open and her bra pulled up, revealing breasts and abdomen, and her trousers were round her knees, though her pants were still in position. Her torso had been stabbed and slashed fourteen times, after her death from two crushing hammer blows to the back of the skull.

The dead woman's name was Wilma McCann. She was twenty-eight years old, the mother of four young children, and separated from her husband.

Because Mrs McCann's purse was missing, West Yorkshire Metropolitan Police treated the case as murder in the pursuance of robbery. Despite the brutality of the attack there seemed no other motive.

DEATH OF A 'GOOD-TIME GIRL'

Just over two and a half months later, forty-two-year-old Emily Jackson set out with her husband from their home in the

THE MILKMAN THOUGHT THE PILE OF RAGS WAS AN ABANDONED GUY FAWKES FIGURE — WHEN HE LOOKED, HE SAW IT WAS A WOMAN'S BODY

Below: *Peter and Sonia Sutcliffe with friends on holiday.*

respectable village of Churwell, three miles south-west of Leeds, for a drink at the Gaiety pub on the Roundhay Road, Chapeltown.

In the 1970s Chapeltown was a red light area with a long pedigree. But not all the girls were local, nor were they all 'professionals'. Emily Jackson was one of many women who came to Chapeltown once or twice a week to sell herself on a casual basis. The police categorized these amateur prostitutes – and Wilma McCann had been an occasional member of their ranks – as 'good-time girls'.

On the early evening of 20 January 1976 Emily and her husband arrived at the Gaiety and had a drink together before Emily went off 'trolling' for custom. An hour after her arrival, her husband saw her get into a Land Rover in the pub car park. He drank in the pub until closing time, and then went home.

Early next morning a worker going onshift came across a bundle with a coat over it. He lifted the coat and found Emily Jackson, lying on her back.

Like Wilma McCann she had been killed from behind by two blows from a heavy hammer. Her breasts were exposed and her trousers pulled down, though again her pants were in place. On her right thigh was stamped the impression of a heavily ribbed wellington boot.

The similarity of her wounds with those of Wilma McCann was so close that police knew they were dealing with a

Above: *The Royal Standard pub where Peter and Sonia Sutcliffe first met.*

Below: *Peter Sutcliffe prepares to carry his new bride over the threshold.*

double murderer. The only solid clue they had so far was that the perpetrator took size seven in shoes.

SERIAL KILLER ON THE LOOSE

Over a year went by. Though the murder files remained open at Millgarth, the Leeds headquarters of the West Yorkshire police, no progress was made. Then, on 5 February 1977, the killer struck again.

His third victim was twenty-eight-year-old Irene Richardson, another 'good-time girl'. She was discovered by a jogger on Soldiers' Field, not far from Chapeltown. She was lying on her face and had died from three hammer blows to the back of her skull. Her killer had stripped her from the waist downwards. Her neck and chest had been subjected to a frenzied knife attack.

The pattern of wounds now left no doubt that the police were dealing with a serial killer.

As details of the killings spread through the street-girl population, many prostitutes, amateur and professional, began either to stay off the streets or to move to other cities.

Not so, however, with the Manningham

VICTIM 2
Joan Harrison, 26,
Preston prostitute

VICTIM 1
Wilma McCann, 28,
Leeds prostitute

VICTIM 3
Emily Jackson, 42,
Leeds prostitute

VICTIM 4
Irene Richardson, 28,
Leeds prostitute

VICTIM 5
Pat Atkinson, 33,
Bradford prostitute

VICTIM 6
Jayne MacDonald, 16,
Leeds shopgirl

VICTIM 7
Jean Royle,
prostitute, 21

VICTIM 8
Helen Rytka
prostitute, 16

VICTIM 9
Yvonne Pearson, 21,
Bradford prostitute

VICTIM 10
Vera Millward,
prostitute, 40

VICTIM 11
Jane Whitaker, 19,
Halifax clerk

VICTIM 12
Barbara Leach, 20,
Bradford student

Jacqui, the last victim

Lane–Lumb Lane–Oak Lane triangle which served as the red light district of Bradford, some ten miles away. By the 1970s the district had been largely colonized by Asian immigrants who were making valiant efforts to modernize the semi-derelict properties.

But prostitutes did a steady trade there, often catering to the Asian businessmen whose religion and customs forbade them to sleep with their own women before

Above: *Ten of Sutcliffe's thirteen victims were prostitutes from Leeds or Bradford.*

ONCE AGAIN, THE KILLER HAD LEFT HIS 'SIGNATURE' - THE IMPRINT OF A SIZE SEVEN WELLINGTON BOOT

marriage. One such girl was thirty-two-year-old Patricia Atkinson.

On Saturday, 23 April, 'Tina' Atkinson set out for her local, the Carlisle. She enjoyed the noisy, friendly boozing spree, and lurched rather drunkenly back to her flat alone when the pub closed.

The following evening friends called for her, but got no answer to their ring on the doorbell. Since the door was ajar, they went in. Tina lay on her bed, the back of her head crushed by four hammer blows. She was naked. Seven knife wounds had lacerated her stomach, and her left-hand side had been slashed open.

Any doubts about the killer's identity were dispelled by a clue found imprinted on the bottom bedsheet. It was the mark of a size seven wellington boot, identical with the imprint found on Emily Jackson's thigh.

This serial killer seemed to have a particular antipathy towards prostitutes. The police began touring Chapeltown and Lumb Lane, questioning street girls about any regulars who might have acted suspiciously. Then, on Sunday, 26 June 1977, came an even nastier shock.

THE RIPPER SPREADS HIS NET

At 9.45a.m., a sixteen-year-old girl named Jayne MacDonald was found slumped and dead in Reginald Terrace, a street on the fringes of Chapeltown. Her long blonde hair was stained and tangled with blood from at least three hammer blows. She had been stabbed once in the back and several times through the chest. But Jayne MacDonald was no prostitute or good-time girl.

It now seemed certain that the Yorkshire Ripper regarded any woman out alone at night as fair game. A fortnight later this was emphasized when a Bradford housewife, Maureen Long, was struck down near her home but miraculously survived.

In the face of increasing public outcry the police stepped up their enquiries. Three hundred and four officers were assigned to the case. And to head them, veteran detective George Oldfield, Assistant Chief Constable (Crime), came out from behind his desk at administrative headquarters in Wakefield.

THE FIRST CLUE

The next time the Ripper struck he changed his location and killing pattern, but left a clue which was to bring him face to face with his hunters. Unfortunately for them, he slipped the net.

On 1 October 1977, a Saturday night, Jean Bernadette Jordan, a frail but experienced prostitute, was picked up near her home in Moss Side, Manchester and driven by her murderer to the Southern Cemetery two miles away. She demanded £5 in advance and was paid with a crisp new note, which she hid in a 'secret' pocket of her purse.

As she climbed from the Ripper's car on to allotment land adjoining the large cemetery, Mrs Jordan was knocked to the ground with a hammer blow and beaten eleven times more. Then she was pulled into a clump of bushes. But the killer was disturbed by the arrival of another car and made off.

The £5 note had been given to the Ripper in his wage packet two days before the attack. He realized that it might be a valuable clue, and eight days later returned to the Southern Cemetery area. After searching in vain for his victim's handbag, the Ripper attacked the decaying body with a ragged shard of broken glass.

Two days after the second attack, Mrs Jordan's remains were discovered, along with the missing handbag which had fallen among the bushes. The £5 note, serial number AW51 121565, had been used in the wage packets of the road haulage firm T. and W.H. Clark. And one of Clark's drivers was Peter Sutcliffe, who had worked there since October 1976.

LIVING VICTIMS

A month after he killed Jean Jordan, detectives visited Sutcliffe at his spacious detached home at 6 Garden Lane, Heaton, in one of the greener areas of Bradford.

Sutcliffe told them that he had lived there for three years since marrying his wife Sonia in 1974. He seemed a steady, quiet man, and the officers left, satisfied.

But had they had time and reason to do so, they would have discovered from old

*Above: **Police examine the scene where Emily Jackson, the Ripper's third victim, was murdered.***

IT WAS WOUNDED MALE PRIDE THAT HAD LED SUTCLIFFE TO CARRY OUT HIS FIRST 'REVENGE' ATTACK ON A PROSTITUTE

*Below: **Assistant Chief Constable George Oldfield and Superintendent Richard Holland at a 'Ripper' press conference.***

Bradford City Police files that Peter Sutcliffe had attacked his first victim in August 1969, and had been questioned by the police as a result. This first attack was not quite motiveless. Earlier that summer he had suspected his girlfriend Sonia of seeing another man.

To 'get even', he had approached a Bradford prostitute, but had been unable to maintain an erection. The woman had laughed at him, taken his £10, and got her pimp to chase him away.

In August he had seen her in the St Paul's red light district, crept after her, and hit her violently on the back of the head with a stone in a sock. The woman had noted the number of his van, and

Sutcliffe had been traced. But because he had no record, he had been let off with a caution.

Since then he had left five women damaged but alive. The first was Anna Rogulskyj, beaten with a hammer on 5 July 1975 in Keighley. The next victim was Olive Smelt, who was beaten down and slashed with a knife near her Halifax home on 15 August of the same year. On 9 May 1976 he had struck down Marcella Claxton, a West Indian prostitute from Chapeltown, and a fortnight after killing Jayne MacDonald he had attacked a woman named Maureen Long in Bradford. Later that year, on 14 December, he struck at Marilyn Moore in Leeds.

Each of these living victims had tried to describe their attacker. Mrs Smelt had been on the right track when she described him as thirtyish, about 5 ft 10 ins tall, and bearded. Marcella Claxton had described him accurately as having a black, crinkly beard, but because she was educationally subnormal her statement was treated less seriously.

DESPERATION

On the evening of 21 January 1978, a twenty-two-year-old 'career' prostitute named Yvonne Pearson went into Bradford to the Flying Dutchman pub in Lumb Lane.

At 9.30p.m. she left the pub and was

Below: *Police search the alley where the body of Barbara Leach was discovered. A 20-year-old student, she was the Ripper's penultimate victim.*

Bottom: *Police search for clues in their hunt for the Yorkshire Ripper.*

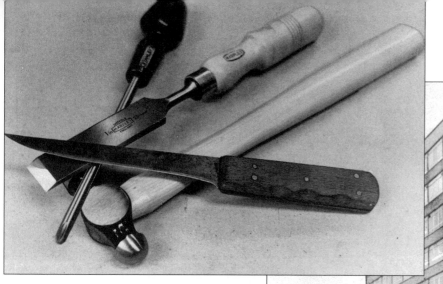

seen climbing into a car driven by a man described as having a dark beard and black, piercing eyes. It was Sutcliffe, who took her to waste ground in Arthington Street, killed her with a club hammer and jumped on her chest until her ribs cracked. He then piled an old abandoned horsehair sofa on top of her. About a month later, when the body remained undiscovered, Sutcliffe was to return and place a current copy of the *Daily Mirror* under one of her mouldering arms. But between the killing and the newspaper incident he had paid a visit to Huddersfield.

Helen and Rita Rytka were pretty eighteen-year-old twins, the product of an Italian mother and a Jamaican father. They had gained places at West Yorkshire art schools and had done well. Economic pressures, however, had forced them into a squalid Huddersfield bedsitter, and a life of prostitution.

Because of the Ripper publicity, Helen and Rita had worked out 'safety measures' including the taking of car numbers and the timing of 'tricks'. But on the snowy night of Tuesday, 31 January 1978, the safety net broke down.

While Rita was off with a client, Sutcliffe picked up Helen. They went into a timber yard under railway arches near the centre of the town and, uncharacteristically, Sutcliffe managed to have intercourse with her before killing her in his usual fashion.

Immediately after Helen Rytka's murder, the police were optimistic. Her abduction had taken place in the early evening on a busy street. But despite tracing a hundred passers by, and with all but three cars and one man eliminated, there was no real result.

Above left: *Peter Sutcliffe's murder weapons could have been bought at any local hardware store.*

Above: *The bus stop at Leeds' Arndale Shopping Centre where Jacqueline Hill was accosted and murdered by the Yorkshire Ripper.*

The police were convinced that the Ripper lived in the locality of Leeds or Bradford, but they little realized that, by the end of 1978, they had interviewed him no fewer than four times. Apart from two visits concerning the £5 note clue, they had called at Garden Lane because routine checks had turned up Sutcliffe's car registration in red light areas. They also called to check on tyre tracks to compare them with some found near the scene of Irene Richardson's murder.

But they did not check two vital clues they knew about the Ripper against Sutcliffe. The Ripper was a B secretor – a rare blood type. And he took size seven boots – very small for a man.

On the night of 16 May 1978, two months after Yvonne Pearson's body was found, Sutcliffe killed Vera Millward, a forty-one-year-old prostitute. Then, for eleven months, he lay quiet.

Then, as women were beginning to venture abroad again tragedy befell an ordinary Halifax family. Nineteen-year-old Josephine Whittaker, a clerk in the Halifax Building Society headquarters, was hurrying home across Savile Park playing fields when she was attacked and killed with sickeningly familiar ferocity. She was the second non-prostitute to die.

TAUNTS AND HOAXES

Between Josephine Whittaker's death in May 1979 and September of the same year there was another lull. This time it was filled by a brutal hoax which almost certainly cost three women their lives.

Since March 1978 George Oldfield had received two letters purporting to come from the Ripper. Shortly before the Whittaker murder a third letter came, mentioning Vera Millward's death. All three letters were postmarked from Sunderland in the north-east. On the third traces of engineering oil, similar to traces found on Josephine Whittaker's body, were discovered. To the beleaguered detectives, this seemed to confirm that the letters were written by the Ripper.

When, on 18 June 1979, a tape recording addressed in the same handwriting as the letters was received, West Yorkshire police were convinced that they had all but got their man. The tape, a taunting message to Oldfield personally, was in a broad Geordie accent, narrowed down by experts to one small town in Sunderland called Castletown. The West Yorkshire police became convinced that anyone without a Geordie accent could be eliminated from their enquiry. This, of course, put Sutcliffe temporarily in the clear.

In July he was visited by Detective Constable Laptew, who had noticed that Sutcliffe's car had been spotted in the Lumb Lane area on thirty-six separate occasions. Laptew was deeply suspicious of Sutcliffe, but because of the Sunderland connection he went unheeded by his superiors.

On the late evening of 1 September 1979 Sutcliffe ambushed a social sciences student named Barbara Leach in the residential area of Little Horton in

*Above: **Peter and Sonia Sutcliffe's house in Garden Lane, Heston, Bradford.***

> OBSESSED WITH THE 'SUNDERLAND CONNECTION', THE POLICE DISREGARDED ONE OFFICER'S DEEP SUSPICIONS OF SUTCLIFFE

*Left: **Police dig up Peter Sutcliffe's garden shortly after his arrest on suspicion of being the Yorkshire Ripper.***

Bradford as she left a friendly pub called the Mannville Arms.

On 18 August 1980 Sutcliffe killed for the twelfth time, his victim was forty-seven-year-old civil servant Margaret Walls. Because she had been bludgeoned and strangled, but not mutilated further, the Ripper Squad were reluctant to add her to their list of victims. But there was no question of the authenticity of his thirteenth and final slaying.

Twenty-year-old Jacqueline Hill, a language student at Leeds University, was walking home to Lupton Flats, a hall of residence in respectable Otley Road, Leeds, when she was spotted by Peter Sutcliffe. He dragged her on to waste land and savaged her with a hammer, a knife and a screwdriver.

The casual pointlessness of Jacqueline Hill's brutal death caused a backlash of frustration among the public and police.

As a sop to police feeling, the Home Office set up a 'super squad' of four outside detectives and a forensic scientist, Mr Stuart Kind. The idea was that this team should review the evidence, and in fact they made some progress. For instance, they deduced that the 'Geordie' letters and tape must be a hoax, and computer calculations pinpointed the 'centre of gravity' of the Ripper's operations as Bradford. A final sweep, using blood group, shoe size, tyre tracks and the £5 note 'wage packet' clue might well, inexorably, have nailed the wretched Sutcliffe.

As it was, he was caught by chance. On 2 January 1981, Sergeant Robert Ring and Police Constable Robert Hydes of South Yorkshire Police were cruising along Melbourne Avenue, Sheffield – a haunt of prostitutes – when they saw a girl getting into a Rover V8 3500.

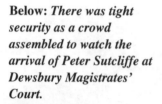

Below: *There was tight security as a crowd assembled to watch the arrival of Peter Sutcliffe at Dewsbury Magistrates' Court.*

Left: *Police help Sonia Sutcliffe as she enters Dewsbury Court for her husband's hearing.*

SUTCLIFFE CLAIMED THAT A VOICE IN A GRAVEYARD HAD ORDERED HIM TO GO OUT AND KILL PROSTITUTES

Below: *Peter Sutcliffe after being attacked in prison.*

told him to go out and kill prostitutes.

Some experts argued that he was a paranoid schizophrenic who had little control over the delusions and impulses that haunted him, while one of the Home Office pathologists who worked on the case echoed the thoughts of the general public: 'He was quite simply a wilfully evil bastard.'

While awaiting trial in Armley gaol, Leeds, Sutcliffe was overheard by a warder planning with his wife Sonia that he would fake 'madness' and 'be out in ten years'. As it was, his plot failed. He was sent to Parkhurst maximum security prison on the Isle of Wight.

Peter Sutcliffe's mental condition did begin to deteriorate, and in March 1984 he was moved to Ward One of Somerset House, Broadmoor Institution for the Criminally Insane, where, in the early 1990s, he remains.

The driver, a short, bearded man, gave his name as Peter Williams and asked if he could relieve himself before answering further questions. Bob Ring nodded, and the man disappeared into bushes by the side of the road.

After being interviewed at Sheffield, 'Williams' was driven to Dewsbury in West Yorkshire for further questioning, because it had been discovered that his number plates were false and had been stolen from that town. Later that day, when Sergeant Ring heard that the driver was still being held at Dewsbury, the implication struck him.

He dashed back to Melbourne Avenue and searched the bushes. There he found a ball-peen hammer and a knife, which eventually were to be matched to the Ripper's crimes.

'Well, it's me,' he told the Dewsbury police. 'I'm glad it's all over. I would have killed that girl if I hadn't been caught.'

What made him do it? Sutcliffe himself told how he had been cheated by the prostitute back in 1969, later claiming that, when he was a gravedigger in the early seventies at Bingley cemetery, a voice emanating from a gravestone had

JOHN CHRISTIE
10 Rillington Place

Ridiculed for sexual inadequacy, the warped John Christie developed into a necrophiliac murderer, walling up his victims in a squalid London flat. In the process, he was a part in one of Britain's worst-ever miscarriages of justice

In March 1953 a Jamaican couple, Mr Beresford Brown and his wife, received good news from their landlord. For some years the Browns had rented cramped rooms on the third floor of 10 Rillington Place, a decaying property in the Ladbroke Grove area of North Kensington in west London.

Would the Browns like to move to the ground floor? Mr and Mrs Brown were delighted. The ground-floor flat had a

front room, a bedroom and a kitchen as well as a wash house, and the single lavatory shared by all the tenants was on the ground floor too. There was even a small garden out at the back.

The only slight misgiving was felt by Mrs Brown. She had often seen John Christie sprinkling strong disinfectant around the flat and along the corridor which connected the front door with the back yard.

There was also the reputation of 10 Rillington Place. Five years previously the second-floor tenant, Timothy Evans, had been charged with killing his wife and infant daughter in the house. He had been hanged for the murders in 1949.

For some days Beresford Brown worked hard, removing piles of old clothes, decaying furniture and general rubbish from the kitchen and heaping it in the back garden. Finally, on 24 March, the room was stripped to its bare walls. Brown began tapping the plaster of the rear wall, but it sounded strangely hollow. He stripped off a piece of mouldering wallpaper and found that it covered a cupboard door. Behind the wooden door was an alcove, and Brown's torch shone on the bare back and buttocks of a woman. She was hunched forward, and wore only a bra, a white cotton coat, stockings and suspender belt. The unnatural colour of her flesh, and the stench, clearly indicated that she had occupied her impromptu tomb for some time.

Right: *The body of Mrs Ethel Christie was found under the floorboards in the living-room of 10 Rillington Place.*

THEY HAD UNCOVERED, SAID THE POLICE, 'THE MOST BRUTAL MASS KILLING KNOWN IN LONDON'

The police came around quickly to continue the search. Behind the first body they found a second corpse, wrapped in a blanket, and beyond that a third, also wrapped in a blanket which had been tied with electric flex.

The search went on into the night, and in the early hours of the following day a fourth body was found wrapped in a blanket and stuffed beneath the floorboards of the front room. She was identified as Mrs Ethel Christie, and like the rest of the corpses she had been strangled.

As forensic experts were called in, the police called a press conference. They had uncovered, they said, the 'most brutal mass killing known in London', and they were looking for a 'vital witness'. His name was John Reginald Halliday Christie, aged fifty-four. He and his wife had lived at 10 Rillington Place since 1938.

Digging in the garden revealed two more female skeletons. The skull of one was missing, and the thigh bone of another had been used to prop up a fence. Meanwhile, undetected, John Christie wandered around London.

On 31 March, Police Constable V100 Thomas Ledger made himself the most famous copper in the land. On his beat near Putney Bridge he saw a short, middle-aged man in a trilby hat leaning over the embankment railings by the Star and Garter Hotel.

'Can you tell me who you are?' asked PC Ledger.

'John Waddington, 35 Westbourne Grove,' said the man.

PC Ledger asked him to remove his hat. The bald head thus revealed confirmed the officer's suspicions, and John Christie was under arrest.

YORKSHIRE ORIGINS

Christie was born on 8 April 1898 in Halifax, West Yorkshire, where his father Ernest was a designer for one of the town's leading firms, Crossley Carpets. Ernest Christie was an upright, no-nonsense Victorian figure, a founder of the Halifax Conservative Party.

Not surprisingly John, one of seven children, lived in mortal fear of his father.

On the other hand his mother enveloped her children with affection. Four of Christie's siblings were sisters, three of them older than himself. They, too, tended to suffocate young John with perhaps misguided kindness.

John Christie went to Sunday School, sang in the choir and became a Boy Scout, rising to the rank of assistant

scoutmaster. At secondary school he was good at arithmetic and algebra and meticulously neat in his work. He was also good with his hands, making toys and repairing watches.

After he left school at fourteen, Christie's early facade of respectability seemed to crumble. One day, working in the Gem Cinema in Halifax, he was picked up by an older, sexually experienced girl and taken to an alley known locally as the Monkey Run. Christie failed to get an erection, and the girl spread the word; overnight he was known as 'Reggie-No-Dick' or 'Can't-Do-It-Reggie'.

There is no doubt that this incident had a direct bearing on the direction of his feelings towards women. 'Women who give you the come-on look,' he told a psychiatrist while in Brixton, 'wouldn't look nearly so saucy if they were helpless and dead.'

FROM PETTY CRIME TO MURDER

Sex was only the first of a line of disasters. At seventeen he got a job as civilian clerk with the West Riding Constabulary, but was sacked for fiddling the petty cash.

For the next few months he drifted from job to job, mainly as a clerk, until in 1916, during the First World War, he was called up and sent to France. In June 1918 he was gassed and invalided out of the army.

Marriage in May 1920 to a plump, amiable girl from Leeds named Edith Waddington seemed to do little to curb Christie's petty criminal ways. A job as postman ended when he was caught stealing money from packets and imprisoned for nine months. Two years later he was bound over for violence and in 1924, having drifted south, he was jailed for a further nine months for larceny at Uxbridge Petty Sessions.

For the next ten years, Christie's life continued its aimless course. Ethel left him, and for a while he lived with a prostitute until he beat her up so badly that he was sentenced to six months' hard labour. Magistrates called it a 'murderous attack'. It was not to be the last.

The placid Ethel returned to him, however, and seems to have kept him at least outwardly respectable as they settled at Rillington Place.

Despite his criminal record, Christie spent the Second World War in the Emergency Reserve as a special constable at Harrow Road police station in west London.

It was in the early summer of 1943, looking for a man wanted for theft, among the low-life cafés and pubs of Notting Hill, that John Christie met his first victim. Her name was Ruth Fuerst and she was a tall, dark-haired Austrian, a refugee from Hitler.

Curiously enough, Christie had a knack for drawing out confidences from women. He sat with Ruth in a café and listened sympathetically to her problems, even lending her ten shillings.

They continued to meet for several

Above: *Rillington Place in Notting Hill, an address made famous by Ludovic Kennedy in his book of the same name.*

IN SPITE OF HIS RECORD OF THEFT AND VIOLENCE, DURING THE SECOND WORLD WAR CHRISTIE WAS TAKEN ON AS A SPECIAL CONSTABLE

months. And then one hot afternoon in August, when Ethel was safely away visiting relatives in Sheffield, he invited Ruth back to 10 Rillington Place.

'I was rather backward and shy about the act of lovemaking on this occasion,' he was to admit, 'but she was encouraging.' The couple went to the Christies' matrimonial bed, and there, during intercourse, he strangled her with a piece of rope.

As Christie struggled to clean up the evidence of his act, the doorbell rang. It was a telegraph boy with a message announcing that Ethel was coming back.

Christie hastily prised up the floorboards of the front room and hid the body and clothes there.

Ethel returned with her brother Henry. That night Henry slept in the front room, inches above the stiffening corpse of Ruth Fuerst, while Ethel and Christie lay together in the murder bed.

The next day Christie removed the body to the wash house, and spent the afternoon digging a grave in the garden. Neighbours, he recalled, waved to him at his labours. Under cover of darkness he buried Ruth.

THE SECOND VICTIM

At the end of 1943 Christie, perhaps uneasy about what he had done, applied for a release from the police force. In January 1944 he took a civilian job at the Ultra Radio Works in Park Royal, Acton.

There he befriended a girl from the despatch department named Muriel Amelia Eady.

Muriel was thirty-one and a highly respectable spinster who lived with her aunt in Putney. She often sat next to Christie in the canteen, and soon, with his knack of inspiring confidences, he learned that her father was in the Royal Navy and she had a boyfriend.

The boyfriend gave Christie cover – an excuse to invite them both to tea at Rillington Place to meet Ethel. He had already decided that plump and homely Muriel was to go the way of Ruth Fuerst.

First, however, he had to find a method of getting her alone and subduing her without violence. In the autumn, he saw a solution to both problems. Muriel suffered from chronic catarrh, and Christie was able to convince her, with his knowledge of first aid, that he had a remedy.

In October Ethel went off to Sheffield again, and Christie seized his opportunity. He had rigged up a screw-top jar with two rubber tubes leading from it, one to a face mask and the other, secretly, to a gas tap.

Christie invited Muriel round, and, over a cup of tea, persuaded her that the apparatus would help her catarrh.

IN THEIR CRAMPED QUARTERS MARRIED BLISS COULD NOT LAST, AND SOON TIMOTHY AND BERYL WERE HAVING VIOLENT QUARRELS

Below: Chief Inspector Griffin and Inspector Kelly leaving 10 Rillington Place after the discovery of the bodies.

Obediently, Muriel inhaled – the jar was filled with Friar's Balsam, to mask the smell of gas – and when she lapsed into unconsciousness, he carried her into the bedroom and strangled her during the sexual act. Afterwards he buried her alongside Ruth Fuerst.

At Easter 1948 a young couple named Timothy and Beryl Evans rented the top flat at Rillington Place. Beryl was pregnant, and the pair were eager to settle anywhere.

In October 1948 Beryl gave birth to a baby daughter. She was named Geraldine, and both Timothy and Beryl adored her.

For a while the trio were happy at Rillington Place. Unfortunately, it was not to last. Like other married couples in cramped quarters the Evanses had their quarrels, sometimes violent.

On one occasion, Beryl invited a girlfriend to stay. The two women slept in the bed, which meant that Timothy had to rough it on the floor. The following day a flurry of blows were struck. To make matters worse, Beryl began to neglect the housework, and the tiny flat became untidy and dirty.

THE ABORTION THAT WENT WRONG

In the summer of 1949 Beryl, to her horror, became pregnant again. She wanted an abortion, but Timothy and his mother, both Catholics, were against it. In desperation Beryl told Christie. He persuaded her that, with his 'medical training', he could do the operation.

Evans was furious when Beryl told him, but was somewhat mollified when Christie showed him one of his 'medical books' – an old St John Ambulance Brigade manual. Timothy, who was almost totally illiterate, was impressed by the pictures and reluctantly agreed to Christie 'taking care of' Beryl.

On either 6 or 7 November 1949, Evans came home to find Christie waiting for him. The operation had gone wrong, and Beryl was dead.

Without giving the bewildered Timothy time for grief or remonstrance, Christie told him that if he went to the police he, Christie, would be charged with manslaughter or possibly murder, as

Above: *The house where Christie lived as a child.*

Left: *Christie in his uniform. He served as a special constable during the Second World War.*

abortion was illegal. Slyly he got Evans to help him move Beryl's body to the second floor flat whose occupant was in hospital. Now Timothy Evans was an accessory to murder.

Christie promised that he and Ethel would find someone to look after Evans' baby daughter. He also promised to help Evans by putting Beryl's body down a drainage shaft in the street outside.

During the next few days, Evans sold the furniture – which was still on hire

> CHRISTIE GOT EVANS TO HELP HIM MOVE BERYL'S BODY TO AN EMPTY FLAT - NOW EVANS WAS AN ACCESSORY TO MURDER

purchase – for £40, and destroyed the bloodstained sheets on which his wife had died. He then told Christie he was going to Bristol, but instead went to South Wales, where he stayed with his aunt and uncle.

If Evans naively expected to leave his troubles behind and find peace in his native valleys, he was mistaken. He told his family that Beryl had walked out.

Finally, on 30 November 1949, he decided to go to Merthyr Vale police station. There, his habitual lying got him into an inextricable mess.

First, he told a detective constable that he had disposed of his wife. Then he said that it had been an accident, that, to procure a miscarriage, he had bought a bottle of chemicals from a man in a transport café in East Anglia.

He had told his wife not to drink the contents of the bottle, but she had done so. When he got home he had found her dead and had thrust her body, under cover of darkness, down a drainage manhole in the road outside the house.

The Merthyr Vale police contacted the Metropolitan Police, and men from Notting Hill station went to Rillington Place. The drain was empty. Faced with this weighty contradiction, Evans made another statement, implicating Christie in the abortion.

FRAMED FOR MURDER

When interviewed, Christie skilfully used his knowledge of the police mind to slip Evans into trouble while extricating himself. He told of the couple's rows and the exchange of blows. He said that Beryl had accused her husband of trying to throttle her.

A search of the premises revealed Beryl's body in the wash house, wrapped in a green tablecloth behind a stack of wood. The body of baby Geraldine was found behind the door, with a tie tightly knotted around her neck.

The Home Office pathologist, Dr Donald Teare, reported that both victims had died of strangulation. Beryl's right eye and upper lip were badly swollen and there were signs of bruising in her vagina, though Dr Teare omitted to take a vaginal swab. Had he done so, things might have turned out differently, in view of John Christie's sexual habits.

As it was, the police now viewed the case as a simple 'domestic' which had turned into murder. Evans was brought back to Notting Hill and made two lengthy statements in the course of the afternoon of Friday, 2 December.

In his first, he claimed to have strangled Beryl and Geraldine while the Christies were in bed. In the second, he added that Beryl had been getting deeper and deeper into debt. The Crown decided to proceed only on the killing of Geraldine, a crime for which Evans could expect little sympathy.

Timothy Evans's trial for murder began at Number One Court at the Old Bailey on 11 January 1950, before Mr Justice Lewis.

In the witness box, Christie won the judge's sympathy when he told him that First World War gas had left him with difficulty in speaking. He also impressed him with an account of his wartime service as a special constable.

In the end the jury took just forty minutes to find Evans guilty of murder, and he was sentenced to death.

Thereafter – to his solicitors, counsel, family, priests and prison officers – Evans maintained the story that Christie had killed both Beryl and Geraldine. Already there was some public disquiet, and a petition with about 1800 signatures was presented to the Home Secretary.

But no reprieve was forthcoming. On 9 March, 1950, a bewildered Timothy Evans walked to the gallows. To the end he repeated his protest: 'I didn't do it. Christie done it.'

CHRISTIE ON THE LOOSE AGAIN

Almost two years after Timothy Evans's execution, the urge to kill came upon John Christie once again. This time, the victim was his wife Ethel.

On 14 December 1952, Christie was to claim that he was awakened by his prematurely elderly and arthritic wife having convulsions. To put her out of her misery 'in the kindest way', he strangled her. 'For two days I left my wife's body in bed. Then I pulled up the floorboards of the front room and buried her.'

Afterwards, said Christie, he was sorry. 'From the first day I missed her. The quiet love she and I bore each other happens only once in a lifetime.'

During the few weeks after Ethel's killing, he sold most of his furniture and lived with a few bare essentials, accompanied only by his cat and mongrel bitch Judy, to which he was devoted. At Christmas he sent Ethel's sister and her husband in Sheffield a Christmas card signed 'From Ethel and Reg'.

That winter he prowled the streets and cafés of Notting Hill as he had done in

Above: *Timothy Evans, Christie's tragic dupe, gave himself up to police in Merthyr Vale and was shipped back to London to face murder charges.*

wartime. By March 1953, he had lured three more women to their deaths in 10 Rillington Place.

The first was a twenty-six-year-old Southampton-born prostitute named Kathleen Maloney. After giving her the 'gas' treatment, as she lolled semi-conscious in a deckchair, Christie strangled her during sex. Then, after wrapping her in a blanket, he thrust her into the kitchen alcove and papered over the door.

A few days later, Christie struck again. This time his victim was a twenty-five-year-old Belfast street-walker named Rita Nelson whom he met in a café. She was gassed, strangled and ravished, then pushed in behind Kathleen Maloney.

Towards the end of February Christie came across Hectorina MacLennan, fated to be his last victim. Hectorina, a twenty-six-year-old originally from Scotland, was living with her lorry driver boyfriend Alexander Baker, but the couple had been locked out of their flat. Christie invited Hectorina back to Rillington Place, but was disconcerted when she turned up with Baker in tow.

The three of them spent an extremely uncomfortable three days together in the first week in March. Although the couple were lovers, Christie would not allow them to use his mattress. While one slept, the other sat up with him in the kitchen – for despite his necrophiliac preferences, a streak of puritanism from his long-gone Sunday school days in Halifax remained.

On 6 March Christie apparently accompanied the couple to the labour exchange. When Baker went in to sign for his dole money, Christie whisked Hectorina back to Rillington Place with him. When it was over, Christie shoved the still-warm MacLennan into the cupboard alcove, clipping her bra strap round Maloney's knees to hold her body upright. Then he sealed up the door again.

CONFESSION TIME

And then, it seemed, Christie had had enough of the dilapidated house and its mouldering ghosts. He fled, he was arrested and he began to confess – in letters to friends, to newspapers and to the police.

But even now the wily streak in his character was not subdued, for his very confessions were preparations towards the defence which he was convinced would see him clear of the gallows. He intended to prove that he was insane.

Christie's trial began on 22 June 1953 in the same Old Bailey court in which Evans had stood trial three years before.

Derek Curtis-Bennett QC, his distinguished defence counsel, was out to prove insanity on Christie's behalf. To this end Christie had admitted to all the women's murders, even that of Beryl Evans – 'The more the merrier,' he remarked. But, like Evans, he could expect scant sympathy for killing a child, so Curtis-Bennett tried to keep Geraldine's death out of the way.

The legal establishment were not, in any case, eager to awaken the spectre of a man who had perhaps been wrongly convicted and executed.

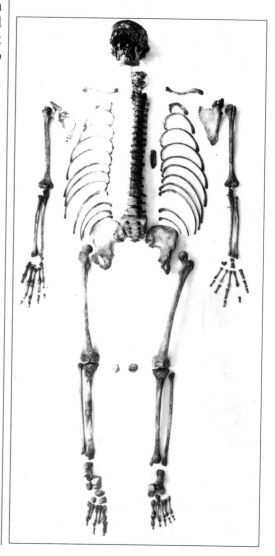

Right: *The skeleton of Ruth Fuerst found in the garden at 10 Rillington Place.*

efforts of his defence team, his trial lasted only four days, and at the end of it, on 25 June 1953, Christie was sentenced to death.

CAMPAIGN FOR TIMOTHY EVANS

Almost immediately, a clamour went up for a review of the Evans case. Under pressure from the Labour opposition the Home Secretary, Sir David Maxwell Fyfe, appointed the Recorder of Portsmouth, John Scott-Henderson, to study 'whether there is any ground for thinking there may have been a miscarriage of justice'. It was a monumental task which had to be completed in under twenty days, before sentence on Christie was carried out.

Surprisingly, when the hastily assembled report appeared it claimed that Evans had indeed carried out the murder of his daughter, as charged. But it added that he had also killed his wife. In other words, according to Scott-Henderson, Christie had told the truth at Evans's trial but lied at his own.

Although some criminologists have continued to have misgivings as to Evans's total innocence, a sustained campaign throughout the 1950s and into the 1960s by such journalists as Harold Evans and Ludovic Kennedy eventually bore fruit.

In 1966, a year after he had successfully called for the temporary abolition of capital punishment, Labour Home Secretary Roy Jenkins granted Timothy Evans a posthumous free pardon. On 18 October of that year, his remains were reburied at St Patrick's Cemetery in Leytonstone in east London. Four years later, capital punishment was abolished entirely.

Rillington Place lingered on for another half dozen years under a new name, Ruston Close. Finally it was demolished, and a new street, Bartle Road, built on its site. There is no number 10 at Bartle Road. A garden marks the spot, between number 9 and number 11, where the most infamous house in British criminal history once stood.

On 18 May, Beryl Evans's body had been exhumed from Kensington Borough Cemetery in Gunnersbury for examination by a trio of the leading Home Office consultant pathologists. The body of Geraldine, which lay alongside that of her mother, had not been exhumed.

The bones in the garden had been reassembled, and the heat-shattered skull of Ruth Fuerst was pieced together like a jigsaw puzzle. In post-mortem examinations, the bodies of Maloney, Nelson and MacLennan had been found to contain samples of Christie's sperm. But whether intercourse had taken place before, after or during the murders was impossible to prove.

In court, when he was asked if he had killed the baby Geraldine, Christie replied 'No.' He was constantly evasive about the evidence he had given in the Evans trial. In any case, despite the best

Above: *The wash house where baby Geraldine's body was found.*

THE REVIEW OF THE TIMOTHY EVANS CASE HAD TO BE COMPLETED IN A STAGGERING TWENTY DAYS, BEFORE CHRISTIE WAS DUE TO BE EXECUTED

PETER KURTEN
Düsseldorf Monster

Vampirism, cannibalism, rape and torture were all part of the depraved Peter Kurten's repertoire. After forty years of violence, bestiality and blood-lust he became the first serial killer to be examined in depth by a criminal psychiatrist

' I have no remorse. As to whether recollection of my deeds makes me feel ashamed, I will tell you. Thinking back to all the details is not at all unpleasant. I rather enjoy it.'

Thus, in the summer of 1931, spoke a polite, quiet-voiced, neat little man of forty-eight named Peter Kurten, who in a career spanning over thirty years had turned his adopted city of Düsseldorf into the murder centre of Europe. Kurten's name entered the annals of criminology through the fact that, after his conviction, he became the first serial killer ever interviewed in depth by a psychiatrist.

Professor Karl Berg concluded, after listening to Kurten's lucid and rational confession, that, though sane under German law, Kurten was a 'narcissistic psychopath' whose sole reason for being was the gratification of his own desires. It was the horrific variety of those desires that appalled the pre-Hitler German people: vampirism, cannibalism, bestiality, rape, sadism and murder in many forms.

PRECOCIOUS SEXUALITY

Peter Kurten was born in Köln-Mulheim in 1883 into a family of thirteen children. His father was a violent drunk, who often forced his wife to have sexual intercourse in front of his children. When finally he attempted sex with one of his daughters, his wife had him arrested and he was imprisoned.

But there is little doubt that a strange seed had been sown in the mind of Peter by the activities of his father. And that seed was nurtured by the town dog-catcher, who moved in as lodger when his father went to jail.

Kurten was a precociously sexual child. When his father was taken away he tried to molest the sister who had been attacked, imitating what he had seen his father do. The dog-catcher taught him to masturbate dogs and torture them.

Kurten was also a murderer very early on. At the age of nine, on a school outing in Düsseldorf, to which city the family had moved, he managed to push a friend off a raft. The friend could not swim, and when another boy dived in Kurten held his head under. Both boys drowned, but the blame was not lodged with Kurten until he confessed all to Professor Berg nearly forty years later.

At thirteen, Kurten began to practise bestiality with sheep, pigs and goats. Three years later he ran away from home to Koblenz, where he moved in with a prostitute. After stealing money from her he was jailed, the first of several prison sentences which were to take up over twenty years of his life.

EVIL FANTASIES

While in jail – much of the time in solitary confinement for insubordination – he began to fantasize. Once out, he tried an experiment by strangling a girl in a wood while having sex with her. As no body was ever found, it is presumed that this first victim, at least, escaped with her life and recovered.

By 1900 Kurten, just seventeen, was back in jail serving four years for theft. When he was released in 1904 his dark fantasies bore fruit. He committed his first recorded sex murder, getting away with it almost by fluke.

A ten-year-old girl named Christine Klein lived with her father in the family tavern at Köln-Mulheim, on the Rhine. One summer morning the girl was found dead, throttled into unconsciousness, and then slashed across the throat with a sharp knife. She had not been raped, but had suffered some sexual molestation.

Twice after the Klein killing, Peter Kurten struck down strangers in the street with an axe. Both victims survived. Kurten said he derived sexual pleasure from watching their blood flow.

In 1921 he was released from prison for burglary, and at his sister's house in Altenburg met his future wife. Posing as a prisoner of war recently released by the Russians, he wooed her with a mixture of sexual flattery and threats of violence.

Frau Kurten remains a shadowy figure. It appeared that she had been a prostitute for a time, and had been imprisoned for four years for shooting dead a man who had jilted her after promising marriage.

Kurten treated her with a kind of rough

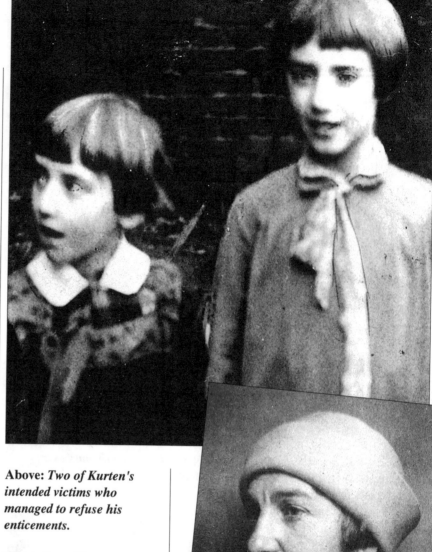

Above: *Two of Kurten's intended victims who managed to refuse his enticements.*

Right: *Frau Meurer was walking home one night when she was approached by a 'respectable' man.*

A MURDERER AT NINE, FOUR YEARS LATER KURTEN WAS INDULGING IN TORTURE AND BESTIALITY WITH FARMYARD ANIMALS

ARMED WITH AN AXE, KURTEN ATTACKED STRANGERS IN THE STREET - WATCHING THEIR BLOOD FLOW, HE SAID, GAVE HIM SEXUAL PLEASURE

affection, and although he was unfaithful always returned. For four years the couple lived in Altenburg, and Kurten made an effort to reform. He worked as a moulder, became a trade unionist, and was politically active in the troubled days of the ill-fated Weimar Republic.

From time to time, however, he still went on the prowl, seeking out women either to beat or to strangle into submission. Often, if he achieved orgasm before they passed out, he would apologize, saying; 'Ah well, that's the way love is.' Occasionally his wife intervened to save him from charges of assault.

NOCTURNAL ATROCITIES

Kurten realized, however, that his strange desires were growing again, and that Altenburg was too small a town for them to go undetected. In 1925 the Kurtens moved to Düsseldorf and settled in a top-floor flat at 71 Mettmannerstrasse. Almost at once, a series of sexual atrocities and murders made police aware that a maniac was roaming the streets.

They began on the night of 3 February 1929, when Kurten sprang from the shadows at a woman walking home and stabbed her twenty-four times with a pair of scissors. Miraculously, she survived. On 13 February, a forty-five-year-old mechanic named Rudolf Scheer was attacked on his way home from a beer cellar. He was stabbed repeatedly in the head and neck before being left to die in the road.

On the night of 9 March, Kurten had time to kill undisturbed. His victim was an eight-year-old girl named Rosa Ohliger, who was dragged behind a hedge and stabbed thirteen times.

Soon after this, Kurten had another lucky break. Two women were attacked by a man with a noose but escaped, badly bruised. They described their attacker as an 'idiot' with a hare-lip.

The police found a man named Stausberg who fitted the description. After confessing not only to the noose attacks but to the recent murders, he was confined to a mental home. For the next few months the attacks ceased and the police relaxed their vigilance.

But early in August 1929 they began again. Two women and a man were attacked as they walked home late at night. They survived.

Then, on the 24th, two children were found dead on an allotment in Düsseldorf. Like Christine Klein sixteen years before, they had been first throttled, then slashed across their throats.

That same afternoon, a serving maid named Gertrude Schulte was walking home when she was accosted by what she described as a 'pleasant-looking, ordinary man' of about forty. The man asked her outright to have sexual intercourse with her, walking by her side and almost pleading.

Above left: *Gertrude Schulte survived an attack by Kurten despite being stabbed in the neck several times.*

Above: *Frau Meurer was another who survived a vicious attack by Kurten.*

'I'd rather die!' said Gertrude. 'Well, die then!' said the man, and stabbed her several times before running off. She survived to give the police their first good description of the man they sought.

Kurten's next victim was not discovered until the late autumn. Another servant girl, twenty-year-old Maria Hahn, had been stabbed to death with twenty knife blows, and buried on the banks of the Rhine.

The following day Kurten returned to the site and dug up the body, intending, he said, to crucify it on a tree 'to shock passers-by'. But the body was too heavy, so, after stabbing it again, he dragged it to a new site for reburial.

Early in September a thirty-one-year-old servant girl named Ida Reuter was raped and battered to death with a hammer. A few days later yet another servant girl, a half-gypsy named Elisabeth Dorrier, suffered the same fate.

In October a housewife, Frau Meurer, was walking home when a 'respectable' man asked her if she was not afraid to be walking out alone so late at night. Before she could reply, he beat her to the ground with a hammer. The same day a prostitute was similarly attacked, but like Frau Meurer, she survived.

It was probably the sheer casual bravado of the attacks which kept Peter Kurten from arrest for so long, for by the end of 1929 he was the world's most

'I'D RATHER DIE!' SAID THE SHOCKED GIRL WHEN KURTEN BEGGED TO HAVE SEX WITH HER. 'WELL, DIE THEN!' HE REPLIED, STABBING HER

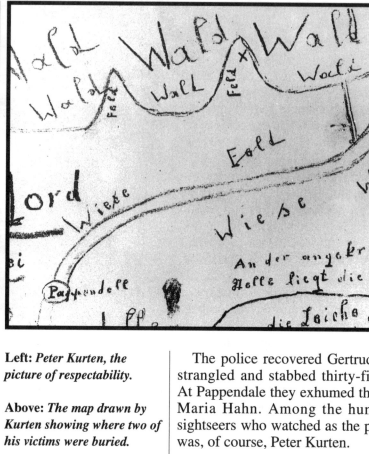

Left: *Peter Kurten, the picture of respectability.*

Above: *The map drawn by Kurten showing where two of his victims were buried.*

infamous murderer. Foreign journalists flocked to Düsseldorf, while police interviewed over nine thousand people and followed up a further two thousand clues. Still they got nowhere, and the attacks continued.

The last murder took place on 7 November, when five-year-old Gertrude Albermann disappeared. Two days later, Kurten wrote to the Communist newspaper *Freiheit* (Freedom). He enclosed a map showing the location of the body, along with a plan of the Pappendale Meadows with the position of another burial site marked.

The police recovered Gertrude's body, strangled and stabbed thirty-five times. At Pappendale they exhumed the body of Maria Hahn. Among the hundreds of sightseers who watched as the police dug was, of course, Peter Kurten.

IDENTIFIED THROUGH A FLUKE

His capture came about by an unlikely chance. On 19 May 1930 a certain Frau Brugmann opened and read a letter which arrived wrongly at her address.

It was from a twenty-year-old servant girl named Maria Budlick who had gone back with a man to his apartment at Mettmannerstrasse.

During the course of the evening he had turned nasty, demanding sex. Frightened, Maria had complied, and the couple had copulated standing up in a doorway. He then led her back to a tram stop and left her to find her way to a convent, where the nuns had given her a bed.

In view of the intense police hunt then going on for a sex maniac, Fraù Brugmann felt she ought to hand this extraordinary letter to the authorities. A Chief Inspector Gennat, who was in charge of the case and was by now clutching at straws, sought out Maria Budlick. In turn, she led the policeman to the address 71 Mettmannerstrasse where the man had taken her, and showed

Gennat the empty room into which she had been led. On the way downstairs she met the man who had raped her. He went pale. Later, the landlady told her that his name was Peter Kurten.

Looking through his files, Gennat found that Kurten had been among the thousands of people interviewed after a woman had accused him of attacking her. So flimsy was the evidence against the respectable tradesman, however, that the police had fined the woman for wasting their time. When questioned, the neighbours assured Gennat that Kurten was a pleasant, likeable man whom children seemed to take to instantly.

Kurten heard of these enquiries and knew instinctively that the game was up. Indeed his behaviour suggests that, like many subsequent serial killers, he had reached a point where his principal urge was to be caught.

On 23 May he told his long-suffering wife that he was the 'monster of Düsseldorf' and had killed even more victims than the police thought – the final estimation was about twenty-two or twenty-three.

Frau Kurten's reaction was of horror and dismay and she suggested a suicide pact. But Kurten had a better idea. There was a large reward offered for the capture of the killer. If his wife could claim that, she could live in comfort. And so on the afternoon of 24 May, outside the St Rochus church and almost by appointment, Peter Kurten was finally arrested.

TEXTBOOK SERIAL KILLER

In prison, he gave a long and highly detailed confession to the police psychiatrist, Dr – later Professor – Karl Berg. He even admitted to setting a number of fatal fires in 1911 and 1912. Peter Kurten's confession was to provide the basis for later analysis into the minds of serial killers.

Most people, of course, were horrified when details of Kurten's career came to light, but many were not. For every letter abusing him which arrived at Düsseldorf jail, there was at least one other which was a love letter or a request for an autograph. Kurten revelled in them all.

His trial opened at Düsseldorf Criminal Court on 13 April 1931 and lasted ten days. His defence was insanity, but after listening to complex psychiatric evidence the jury retired for only ninety minutes before returning a Guilty verdict on nine counts of murder.

Kurten was sentenced to death. His lawyer formally appealed, but the appeal was turned down on 30 June, and the execution was set for 2 July at 6 a.m.

It was to be only two years before Adolf Hitler swept to power, but meanwhile liberalism ran deep in the dying Weimar republic and the death penalty was rarely used. The last condemned man actually to die was a double murderer named Bottcher, executed in Berlin in 1928. The German Humanitarian League protested against the Kurten sentence, and letters of support poured into the prison.

But for a killer of Kurten's notoriety there could be no reprieve – and in any case, the last person to wish for such an outcome was Peter Kurten himself. Execution in Germany was by guillotine, and he was fascinated by the instrument. Would he, he asked Dr Berg, be able – even for an instant – to hear the gushing of his own blood when the blade fell?

Berg said that he thought that this was physiologically possible, and Kurten was delighted. After eating an outsized last 'breakfast' of Wiener schnitzel, fried potatoes and white wine, the monster of Düsseldorf went to his fate smiling and replete.

UNABLE TO FACE BEING A MURDERER'S WIDOW, FRAU KURTEN SUGGESTED A SUICIDE PACT. NO, SAID KURTEN, SHE SHOULD TURN HIM IN AND COLLECT THE REWARD

KURTEN WAS FASCINATED BY THE PROSPECT OF HEARING HIS OWN BLOOD GUSH OUT AS THE GUILLOTINE FELL

Below: *Kurten listening to proceedings during his trial.*

EDWARD GEIN
The Secret Hunter

Warped and perverted by an emotionally disturbed childhood, Edward Gein was to turn his small-town rural community into the centre of a ghoulish murder case – inspiration for *The Silence of the Lambs* and Hitchcock's thriller *Psycho*

Above: *Mary Hogan, one of Gein's victims. She was running a local bar when she disappeared.*

Above right: *Hogan's Tavern, a barn-like saloon, exalts its regulars to drink Blatz Beer.*

Opposite: *Edward Gein, the handyman from Plainfield, Wisconsin, who was charged with mass murder.*

Below: *The farmhouse where Edward Gein lived and killed. Bernice Worden's corpse was found here.*

The central plain of Wisconsin is one of the most melancholy and uninspiring tracts of land in the United States. It consists of flat, stony farmland about 120 miles square, fit only for raising scrubby cereal crops and equally lean livestock. In the 1950s it was scattered with dilapidated farmsteads clustered around a few small towns.

One of these was Plainfield, which, founded by German settlers in 1849, had grown in a hundred years to accommodate about 800 souls. In an area of clapboard houses and gloomy non-conformist chapels, about the only place of human warmth and interest was Hogan's Tavern, and even that was no stately pleasure-dome.

BLOODSTAINS AT HOGAN'S TAVERN

The tavern was presided over by its eponymous owner, Mary Hogan. She was a big, buxom woman in her early fifties with a broken nose and a colourful past.

She had come to Plainfield before the Second World War from Chicago, where, it was rumoured, she had run a speakeasy and brothel for one of the Prohibition

Above: *Plainfield, Wisconsin was a small farming community. Founded in 1849, its population never reached a thousand.*

DURING THE DEER-HUNTING SEASON CARCASSES WERE DISEMBOWELLED IN THE OPEN AND THE BLOODSTAINED REMAINS ABANDONED IN THE SNOW

mobs. Most of the local menfolk would gather at Hogan's to drink beer and yarn away the long evenings.

On the afternoon of 8 December 1954, a local farmer named Seymour Lester entered the deserted bar room, stamping his boots on the floor and calling for service. There was no reply. Seymour's eye was drawn to a large dark patch on the floor leading into a back room. It was blood, soaking into the pine floorboards.

Seymour scuttled to the telephone and soon Wautoma County Sheriff Harold S. Thompson arrived, followed by a couple of deputies. A search of the premises revealed a .32 calibre rifle cartridge case near the blood patch. Further bloodstains led out through the back door and across the snow to where tyre tracks indicated that a vehicle about the size of a pick-up truck had been parked.

The cash register had not been interfered with, and it seemed to Sheriff Thompson that Mary Hogan had been shot down and spirited away.

UNEXPLAINED DISAPPEARANCES

It was not the first time that the area had experienced sudden disappearances. In May 1947 a schoolgirl from the nearby hamlet of Jefferson had vanished after being given a lift home by a neighbour. In November 1952 Victor 'Bunk' Travis, a Plainfield farmer, set off with his friend Ray Burgess to hunt deer during the Wisconsin open season. Both men subsequently vanished.

Of more interest to the men investigating the Hogan case was the affair of fifteen-year-old Evelyn Hartley, who had apparently been abducted while baby-sitting for a neighbour in November 1953. As in the Hogan disappearance, there were signs of a scuffle and bloodstains had been found leading from the house.

The Travis–Burgess case was perhaps the most explicable. During the nine-day deer-hunting season, tourists flocked in from Milwaukee and Chicago to track their prey through the snowy woodlands of central Wisconsin.

Many of them had little experience of either woodcraft or firearms, and accidents were frequent. In 1957, for instance, thirteen hunting visitors died in the Plainfield area from stray bullets.

At the best of times, the deer-hunting season was not for the squeamish. Hunters 'gralloched' their kill in the open, stringing up the carcasses from

trees, porches or any suitable structure, slitting up their abdomens. Edible portions such as liver, kidneys and hearts would be removed, and the rest of the offal abandoned. The empty husk of the carcase would then be lashed across the radiator of the hunter's truck and driven away for skinning and quartering elsewhere.

One of the few Plainfield farmers to express his disgust at this slaughter was a slightly built bachelor named Edward Theodore Gein.

LOVELESS CHILDHOOD

Gein was descended from the first wave of German settlers, though the two sides of his family were diametrically different in outlook. Edward's father, George Gein, was an orphan who had been brought up on a farm near the township of La Crosse by his god-fearing grandparents. In 1899 he had married. His wife, Augusta, ran the family grocery store in La Crosse.

A strict Lutheran, Augusta soon grew to dread and despise her husband's drinking and violence. Nevertheless the couple had two sons, Henry, born in 1902, and Edward Theodore, born on 27 August 1906.

In 1913 George Gein inherited his grandparents' farm near La Crosse, and the family moved out to work it. A year later they bought a larger spread just outside Plainfield. George Gein died of alcoholic excess in 1940, aged sixty-six, and was buried in the Plainfield cemetery.

George had given love to no one. Augusta seemed incapable of doing so. Instead of affection, she showered scriptural texts on her sons, reminding

*Above: **Gein used Bernice Worden's own pick-up to move her body.***

*Below: **Sheriff Art Schley. The Gein investigation was his first murder case.***

them constantly that they were sinners.

Henry seemed able to detach himself from his mother's hide-bound views, but his brother Edward grew morose and solitary.

In the spring of 1944, Henry and Eddie Gein suffered a brush fire on their farm and were separated by the smoke. Eddie ran for help, and managed to lead a search party directly to where his brother lay dead. Henry had bruising to his forehead, but an autopsy gave the cause of death as smoke inhalation.

LONE SURVIVOR

Shortly after Henry's death, Augusta suffered a stroke. For twelve months Eddie nursed her tenderly back to what seemed like full health, but in December 1945 she suddenly collapsed and died. Eddie was left by himself in the big old 'L'-shaped timber farmhouse, with its annexe at the rear which he called his 'summer kitchen'.

He was known as a hard-working and honest man, but was not talkative. Unlike his father Eddie was never a heavy drinker, though he enjoyed the odd evening sitting over a beer or two down at Hogan's Tavern, and seemed to miss Mary Hogan when she was gone.

This point was made to Eddie one morning by Elmo Ueeck, who owned the Plainfield sawmill, when Eddie was over at the mill fixing fences some weeks after Mary's disappearance. If Eddie had taken a shine to Mary Hogan, Ueeck teased, why hadn't he said so when she was still around? Then maybe she would have been back at Gein's farm cooking supper for him, instead of being missing and maybe lying dead somewhere.

Gein, Ueeck was to recall later, rolled his eyes and shifted his weight from foot to foot, before giving one of his strange, tooth-baring, lopsided grins. 'She ain't missing,' he said after some deliberation. 'She's at the farm right now.'

Elmo Ueeck thought no more about Eddie's odd fancy. It was just the sort of strange remark he would make.

DEATH AT THE HARDWARE STORE

Three years went by, and the time of the annual deer cull approached again. One woman who always looked forward to the increased trade was Bernice Worden. A plump and homely widow in her late fifties, she ran Worden's Hardware and Implement Store, selling everything from agricultural tools to ammunition.

Bernice was now preparing to hand over the store to her son, Frank, who served as deputy sheriff of Plainfield, and settle down to enjoy her retirement in the company of her grandchildren.

Recently, Bernice had been vaguely troubled by the presence of Eddie Gein. For the last few weeks he had taken to sitting in his pick-up outside the store, or standing opposite, gazing across at her.

On Friday, 15 November 1957, just before she closed for the night, Gein had wandered in, looked around vaguely and asked her the price of anti-freeze. When she told him he wandered off again without a word.

Saturday, 16 November, was the first day of the deer-hunting season. When dawn broke, the town emptied of its menfolk as they made for the woods in their pick-up trucks, rifles racked behind them. Only one customer appeared at Worden's store as Bernice opened up at 8.30a.m.: Eddie Gein.

This time Eddie had an empty half-

Above: *Edward Gein adored his dominant mother. He professed to hating violence in any form.*

'SHE AIN'T MISSING,' SAID EDDIE OF THE MURDERED MARY. 'SHE'S AT THE FARM RIGHT NOW'

Below: *Police found Mary Hogan's face and scalp behind rubbish stacked in Gein's summer house.*

gallon jug, which he asked Bernice to fill with anti-freeze. He paid for it and left by the back door, while Bernice returned to the front of the store to fill out a sales slip with Eddie's name and purchase.

At this point, according to Eddie's later testimony, he walked back in, picked up a hunting rifle and, while pretending to admire it, loaded it and shot Bernice. He then dragged her out to her own pick-up truck and drove off with her body.

Bernard Muschinski, who managed the filling station just down and across the street from Worden's store, looked out of his office at 8.45a.m. and saw Bernice's pick-up truck pull out from the store's back yard and roar away. At lunchtime he walked past the store and was surprised to see that the lights were still on, though the door was locked. Bernice he guessed was growing forgetful.

In mid-morning, Elmo Ueeck had caught sight of Eddie Gein in slightly embarrassing circumstances. The sawmill owner had chased a deer off his own property and on to Eddie's, where he had managed to shoot it.

He had brought his truck round on to Eddie's land to whisk the carcass away, when he saw Eddie's old Ford sedan bouncing down the rutted track towards him. Eddie clearly saw the dead deer tied across Ueeck's front fender, but merely gave a friendly wave and roared past in a flurry of frozen slush. At lunchtime he drove back to apologize, but Eddie

cheerfully waved away Elmo Ueeck's explanation.

That afternoon Bob Hill and his sister Darlene, Eddie's cousins, walked across to see him. They wanted him to run them into town to pick up a new car battery, as theirs had gone flat.

Gein stepped out briskly on to the porch to greet them. He was in his shirtsleeves and, to their surprise, his hands and arms were dappled with blood.

Bob knew of Gein's often expressed horror of blood and butchery, but his cousin seemed calm as he told them he had been dressing a deer. After going indoors to wash his hands, he came out and drove them into Plainfield. When he drove them back home, their mother, Irene, invited him to stay for supper.

Meanwhile, Frank Worden had called at Bernard Muschinski's gas station to fill up his car. There he heard that his mother's store was still locked, though the lights were on.

Frank opened the door with a spare key and viewed the scene with a sinking heart. There was a large patch of blood on the floor, and the cash register had been torn from its screws on the counter.

He rang the new sheriff of Wautoma County, thirty-two-year-old Art Schley, and then set about searching the store. By the time Schley arrived, Frank had found his mother's last sales slip. It had Gein's name on it.

'He's done something to her,' Worden told the sheriff and his deputy.

'Who?' the sheriff asked.

Worden held out the docket. 'Ed Gein,' he said. Sheriff Schley put out a radio call for Gein to be brought in, as news of the dramatic and not unprecedented events spread around the town.

Up at the Hills' farm, Eddie Gein was just finishing his supper when a neighbour called by with the news of the disappearance.

'It must have been somebody pretty cold-blooded,' commented Eddie.

Irene Hill turned to her cousin. 'How come,' she asked jocularly, 'that every time someone gets banged on the head and hauled away, you're always around?

In reply, she was to remember, Gein shrugged his shoulders and grinned his toothy grin.

Bob Hill suggested that he and Eddie should drive into town to see what was going on. Gein cheerfully agreed, but as the two men stepped across the freezing, starlit yard a police squad car skidded to a stop. Traffic Officer Dan Chase and

Above: *A police officer sorts through trash in Gein's kitchen. It was described by one writer as 'mental disorder as decor'.*

A WOMAN'S BODY WAS HANGING BY ITS HEELS FROM THE RAFTERS — SHE HAD BEEN BEHEADED AND DISEMBOWELLED JUST LIKE A DEER

Deputy 'Poke' Spees got out, and Gein was taken in for questioning.

On the way into town, Chase asked him what he had been doing that day. Gein told him. Questioned on details, however, Gein became muddled, and then said: 'Somebody framed me.'

'Framed you for what?' Chased asked.

'Well, about Mrs Worden,' Gein replied. 'She's dead, ain't she? I heard it. They told me in there.'

SECRETS OF THE 'SUMMER KITCHEN'

With Gein in custody, Sheriff Schley called in a more experienced colleague, Captain Lloyd Schoephoerster of the nearby Green Lake County Sheriff's office. Together they drove to Gein's farmhouse. The yard was dark and deserted as the headlights of their car illuminated the dark wooden walls of Gein's 'summer kitchen'.

Flashlights in hand, the two men walked up the steps and pushed open the creaking door. As he entered the room, Art Schley felt something brush his shoulder. He whirled around. The beam of his torch fell on the bloody stump of a human neck. It belonged to the naked torso of a stout woman, hanging by the tendons of her heels from the rafters. She had been beheaded and cleanly disembowelled – 'gralloched' like a deer.

When the two officers had radioed for reinforcements, they ventured back into the house. They could find no lights, and until a mobile generator was rigged they and their helpers searched by torchlight.

It was a cesspit, a rotting rubbish dump of old metal and organic remains. Apart from the grisly corpse hanging from the ceiling there were piles of old clothes, dirty pans and dishes, broken chairs, dusty packages of half-eaten, mouldering food, and heaps of gaudy-covered magazines.

These proved to be a mixture of garish horror comics which dealt with stories of torture and flagellation, war crimes and 'true' detective magazines, and more or less 'straight' pornography. The kitchen sink was filled with sand, and there was a sinister, grinning row of dentures on the mantlepiece.

The full horror of the scene was only revealed when the generator was rigged. As the powerful light chased shadows away, it shone in the eye sockets of a number of skulls. Some lay tumbled under the table, others had been sawn in half and were apparently used as bowls. Two of them were impaled on the posts of a rag- and fur-strewn bed in which Gein presumably slept.

Then came the skin. As forensic scientists arrived and poked around in the growing dawn, they realized that a kitchen chair had a seat of human hide. Soon they had turned up lampshades, the sheath of a hunting knife, a drum, a bracelet and a wastepaper basket – all made from crudely tanned human skin.

There was a skin shirt, the pendulous dried breasts still attached, clearly made from the top half of a woman's body, and several pairs of human skin 'leggings'. And in cardboard boxes were bones and pieces of dried flesh, the debris of this ghoulish tannery.

But the biggest shocks were still to come, for Eddie Gein had a collection of 'shrunken heads'. They hung on the walls of his bedroom, some by their hair, some from hooks thrust through their ears. Gein had obviously peeled the flesh away from the skulls and stuffed the resulting faces and scalps with old rags and newspapers. All seemed, by the length of the hair, to be women's faces. One bore the still recognizable features of Mary Hogan.

By now the heat of the arc lamps had made the stench almost unbearable, despite the freezing weather outside. But the searchers had a few more vital items to discover. They finally found them in and around the cold and rusted kitchen stove.

Bernice Worden's heart was in a plastic bag and the rest of her entrails lay nearby, wrapped in an old coat. In a meal bag lay her head, bloodied around the nostrils but with a strangely peaceful expression on her face. Her ears, however, had already been pierced with hanging hooks...

Less dramatic, but still surprising, was the main part of the house. This, locked and boarded off from the chamber of horrors at the rear, proved to be a perfectly ordinary, though dust-covered,

THE HORRIFIED POLICE REALIZED THAT GEIN'S CLOTHING, FURNITURE AND HOUSEHOLD EFFECTS HAD ALL BEEN FASHIONED FROM HUMAN SKIN

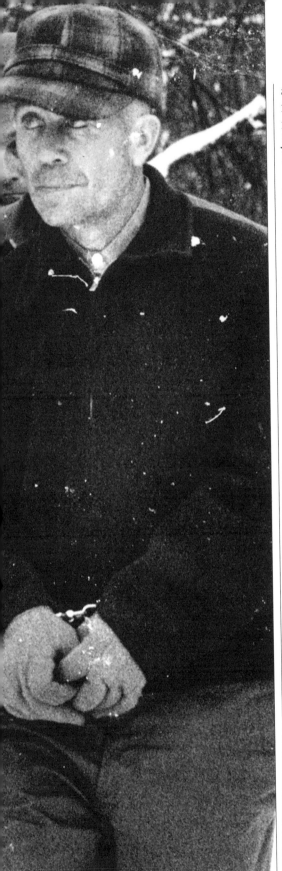

and despatched to Gault's Funeral Home for post-mortem examination. Gein, meanwhile, sat silently in the town's jailhouse, his stubbled jaw hanging and his eyes rolling damply.

For twelve hours he uttered not a word, even when Sheriff Schley, fresh from the mayhem of the ranch, lost control and struck him. During the afternoon, however, an initial autopsy showed that Bernice Worden had been shot in the head with a .22 bullet.

NEED FOR HUMAN REMAINS

On 18 November, Monday morning, Gein slowly began to reply to the questioning of the local District Attorney, Earl Kileen. He confessed to having shot Mrs Worden and loaded her body into her own pick-up truck, along with the cash register which, he said, he wanted to 'strip down to see how it worked'.

After dumping the pick-up in the woods near his home, he had transferred the body to his Ford sedan and strung it up with a sharpened branch through the ankle tendons. He had bled the corpse into a bucket, afterwards burying the fresh blood in the ground. Asked by Kileen if he thought he had been dressing a deer, he replied, 'That is the only explanation I can think of.'

Mrs Worden, he claimed, was the only person he ever remembered killing, but during the past few years he had felt the need for human remains. Sometimes he watched the newspapers for the funerals of people he knew had died, and then went to the graveyard and stole the corpses. He always, he claimed, 'then left the graves in apple-pie order'.

Which neatly introduced a topic that had preyed on Kileen's mind. Had Gein ever eaten any parts of the corpses?

The farmer looked genuinely horrified, and vigorously shook his head.

Had he then ever had sexual relations with any of them?

'No! No!' replied Gein. 'In any case, they smelt too bad.'

That afternoon Gein was held on a charge of armed robbery – stealing the cash register – and then spent the rest of the day helping the police with their enquiries.

family home. It was a shrine to Augusta Gein, untouched and unseen by outside eyes since her death over a decade previously.

During the morning of Sunday, 17 November, the human relics from Gein's hellish kitchen were bagged and tagged

Left: November 1957 – Edward Gein stands handcuffed on the farmland where human remains were discovered.

He pointed out the spot where he had poured away Bernice Worden's blood. Later he was interviewed about the four-year mystery of the disappearance of Evelyn Hartley, the fifteen-year-old baby sitter. Gein seemed never to have heard of her.

When questioned about Mary Hogan, however, whose head had been found on his premises, Gein lapsed into silence again. Then, in a faltering voice, he admitted that he had 'called into her bar for a drink, once or twice'.

The following day, Tuesday, the hoard of pressmen which had converged on Plainfield and had been filing wildly speculative stories ever since, was finally allowed up to Gein's property. Sheriff Schley promptly got into a fist fight with a number of reporters.

Gein was taken to the State Central Crime Laboratory in the state capital, Madison, for lie detector tests. Strapped to the equipment for almost nine hours, Eddie Gein readily admitted to making and wearing the 'garments' of human skin, and said that he thought that he 'may have murdered Mary Hogan, but was very hazy' about it.

On the subject of Bernice Worden, however, he claimed that this was an accident. He was to keep up the protest for the remainder of his life.

On Thursday, 21 November, Gein was formally charged with the first degree murders of Worden and Hogan. His attorney entered a plea of insanity, and the judge committed the accused to the Central State Hospital for the Criminally Insane in Waupun, pending psychological tests.

By now, DA Kileen had obtained from Gein a list of the persons whose graves he remembered robbing, and the focus of interest moved to Plainfield Town Cemetery. Pat Danna, the sexton, claimed that none of the graves had been disturbed, but the exhumation party chose to examine the tomb of Mrs Eleanor Adams – who was, coincidentally, buried a few feet from Gein's parents. (Later it was explained that, had he tried to disturb his own mother, he would have to break into a concrete vault to get at her.)

As the frozen soil was scraped away

Above: *Gein was incarcerated in Mendota Mental Health Institute, a gothic pile near Madison, Wisconsin.*

Right: *Sheriff Art Schley steers Edward Gein into the Central State Hospital at Waupun, Wisconsin.*

GEIN WAS APPALLED WHEN THE DISTRICT ATTORNEY ASKED IF HE HAD EVER EATEN CORPSES OR MADE LOVE TO THEM

from Mrs Adams's casket, the lid was seen to be split in two. The coffin itself proved to be empty except for rotting bits of burial shroud and a 12-inch steel crowbar.

Digging continued at Gein's farm. In a rubbish dump, the near complete skeleton of a woman with a gold tooth was discovered. In another burial trench a jumbled mass of bones had been interred.

After further lie detector and psychological tests, forensic scientist Joe Wilimovski became convinced that Gein had killed only Hogan and Worden, and had otherwise confined his hobby of mutilation to the bodies of already dead women. Nine corpses had by now been assembled from the unidentified portions, all of them middle-aged women.

During his questioning, Gein spoke calmly and apparently rationally about the dismemberments and flayings. He seemed to find little wrong with what he had done, and was apparently rather proud of his unsuspected anatomical knowledge.

The standard Wechsler adult intelligence test showed that Eddie Gein was 'quite bright' and in some ways above average, except for his almost total inability to communicate with other people in any but the most basic terms.

Psychologists at the hospital put this down to a 'severe emotional disturbance' in his early development. This had retarded his normal sexual-emotional development causing him to retreat into a bizarre fantasy world in which his sexual urges became confused by grief over the death of his mother, combined with fear of transgressing the strait-laced moral code she had imbued in him while she was alive.

As one expert, Dr Milton Miller, put it: 'In many ways, the patient has lived a psychotic life for years. He has substituted human parts for the companionship of human beings.'

On 6 January 1958, as Eddie Gein sat blankly chewing gum, Circuit Judge Herbert Bunde briefly heard the comments of three psychologists and committed him indefinitely to the state hospital. Almost three months later Gein's farm, which was due to be put up for auction, was mysteriously consumed by fire while many of Plainfield's leading citizens – including Deputy Sheriff Frank Worden – looked on. Gein's comment was: 'Just as well.'

As the Gein case unfolded, Robert Bloch, a writer living in Weyauwega, 30 miles east of Plainfield, followed it with interest. He was intrigued by the psychologists' report that the influence of a long-dead mother could drive a man to commit such strange and inhuman crimes.

But, like other Mid-West dwellers, he was even more astonished that 'a ghoulish killer with perverted sexual appetites could flourish almost openly in a small rural community where everybody prides himself on knowing everyone else's business'.

Bloch's resulting novel *Psycho* was filmed by Alfred Hitchcock in 1960. And nearly thirty years later another novel-based film, *The Silence of the Lambs*, which featured a man who made suits out of female skin, also echoed the bizarre doings at Plainfield.

In January 1968, District Judge Robert Gollmar heard from the hospital authorities that their patient was now deemed sufficiently sane to stand trial, and Eddie Gein was marched into the dock. It was a short-lived appearance. Eddie was found guilty but insane, and returned to hospital.

There, despite being a model inmate, he was to remain for the rest of his life. He died in the geriatrics wing of Mendota Mental Health Institute on 26 July 1984, and was buried in an unmarked grave at Plainfield, beside his mother.

ONE NIGHT THE FARM BURNT DOWN, WATCHED BY PROMINENT PLAINFIELD CITIZENS. 'JUST AS WELL,' WAS GEIN'S COMMENT FROM THE MENTAL HOSPITAL

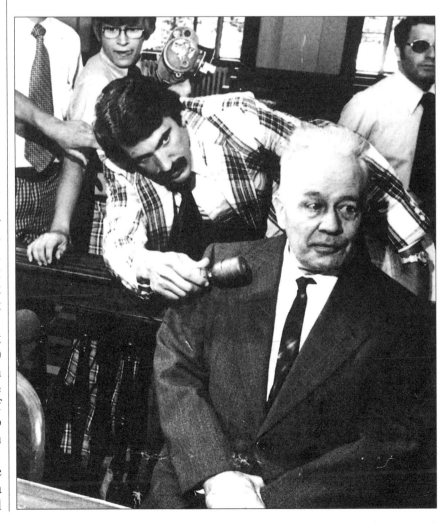

Below: *Edward Gein awaits the start of his unsuccessful petition for release from Central State Hospital in 1974.*

GARY HEIDNIK
The Baby Farmer

Gary Heidnik believed God wanted him to people the world. So he kidnapped women to start his 'baby farm', feeding them on dog food and human flesh. Was he insane, or, as the judge said at his trial, merely 'possessed of a malignancy in his heart'?

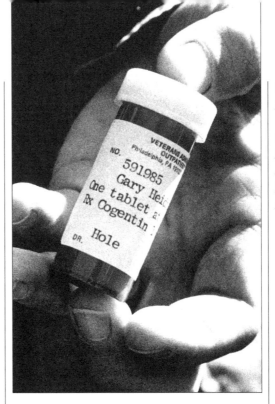

Left: *Medicine prescribed for Heidnik by Dr Hole.*

Opposite: *Gary Heidnik believed that he had a divine calling to procreate. He kidnapped women and started his 'baby farm'.*

On the freezing cold night of 24 March 1987, Philadelphia police received a telephone call from a box in the neighbourhood of Sixth and Girard Streets. The caller, who identified himself as Vincent Nelson, was excited but apologetic, as if he found the story he had to tell difficult to believe.

His ex-girlfriend, Josefina Riviera, a half-black, half-Puerto Rican prostitute, had turned up at his house after a long absence. 'She was...you know...talking real fast about this guy having three girls

Below: *Josefina Riviera (right) leaves court with another of Hednik's victims, having given evidence at his trial.*

'SHE SAID THAT HE WAS BEATING THEM UP, RAPING THEM, HAD THEM EATING DEAD PEOPLE...'

chained up in the basement of this house and she was held hostage for four months....She said that he was beating them up, raping them, had them eating dead people just like he was a cold blooded nut....I thought she was crazy.'

HORROR IN THE BASEMENT

The police switchboard operator was inclined, on the evidence, to side with the latter point of view. Nevertheless he despatched a patrol car. Officers David Savidge and John Cannon picked up Nelson and the distressed Josefina and took them to the precinct house.

There, a brief examination of Josefina's skinny body convinced the police that something untoward had happened to her. Her ankles, in particular, bore the marks where shackles had eroded the flesh.

She managed to tell them that her captor was named Gary Heidnik, and that he was due to pick her up in his new grey and white Cadillac Coupe de Ville, with his initials 'GMH' on the door, at the gas station on Sixth and Girard.

Officers Savidge and Cannon cruised around to the filling station. There, sure enough, was the Cadillac. The driver was a greasy-haired man with cold blue eyes, dressed in a fringed buckskin jacket and gaudy shirt. After admitting that he was Gary Heidnik, he was taken to the Philadelphia Police Department Sex Crimes Unit for further questioning.

At 4.30a.m. on 25 March, a squad of officers bearing a search warrant, crowbars and a sledge hammer arrived at Heidnik's address – 3520 North Marshall Street.

The foetid stench hit them as they broke the locks of the door. Following

Below: *Searching for evidence of Heidnik's crimes in the basement of his house.*

two evils. In an aluminium pot were boiled human ribs, while the fridge contained a jointed human arm. Officer Savidge, hardened as he was, had to run outside for air.

Back at the precinct house, Josefina Riviera slowly began to piece together a statement. She explained that Gary had a notion of starting a 'baby farm' in his basement. A religious freak, he claimed that God had commanded him to collect women so that, 'like a bee to flowers', he could move from one naked woman to another, impregnating them.

Josefina herself was twenty-five years old and had been brought up in an orphanage by nuns. Since her early teens she had worked the streets as a prostitute.

On 26 November 1986 Josefina met Gary Heidnik for the first time. Heidnik took her to a McDonald's where he had a coffee, ignoring Josefina. Finally he suggested they go back to his house in North Marshall Street.

As he parked in the garage she noticed a 1971 Rolls Royce, and in the house itself the hallway was papered with $1 and $5 bills. But again, these signs of opulence were spoilt by the squalor of the bedroom, which contained only two battered chairs, a table and a big waterbed.

The pair then stripped, and the sex act was over in minutes. Gary handed her a $20 bill, and Josefina reached for her jeans. Then her nightmare began.

THE 'BABY FARM'

Heidnik leaped from the bed, grabbed her wrists and handcuffed her. Before she realized what was happening he dragged her out and down several flights of stairs to a dim and filthy cellar, lit only by narrow windows set near the ceiling. Metal heating pipes ran around the room, and he shackled her ankle to one of these, using a U-shaped link and a length of chain. Then he slapped her down on to an evil-smelling mattress, placed his head in her naked lap, told her to be quiet and slept. Josefina noticed a shallow pit in the centre of the room. This, covered by boards, was to be used by Heidnik as a 'punishment pit'.

Three days later Heidnik went out again. He was looking for his former

Josefina's instructions they made their way down to the basement, where their torches picked out the terrified faces of two black women huddled under a blanket on a dirty mattress. The women were shackled, chained, filthy and naked apart from skimpy vests, and they cringed and whimpered in the light.

When they were calmer, they indicated a shallow pit in the floor. In it was another black woman, naked and with her hands handcuffed behind her back.

But when the officers examined the kitchen, they began to believe that starvation would have been the lesser of

Above: *Police sift through the debris in Heidnik's house.*

APPALLED AT THE FILTHY, EMACIATED WOMEN, THE OFFICERS HAD WORSE TO COME WHEN THEY EXAMINED THE CONTENTS OF THE KITCHEN

Above: *Heidnik believed he was carrying out God's will.*

To punish Sandra Lindsay Heidnik hung her from a beam and force-fed her bread until she choked and died

lover, a slightly retarded black girl of twenty-five named Sandra Lindsay. Some time before, Heidnik was to explain to Josefina, he had paid Sandra $1000 to have his baby but she had aborted it.

That evening he came back with the terrified Sandra, and she too was stripped and shackled. The women, forced to perform various sexual acts, were told by Heidnik that they were the nucleus of his 'baby farm'.

The following day the two girls had a moment of hope when they heard pounding on the front door. Gary told them later that the callers had been Sandra's sister, Teresa, and two cousins, searching for her in her old haunts.

Over the next few weeks, more women were lured back to join Heidnik's 'baby farm'. Lisa Thomas, aged nineteen, was picked up on 22 December. On New Year's Day 1987, twenty-three-year-old Deborah Dudley became his fourth victim, while his fifth and youngest, nineteen-year-old Jacquelyn Askins joined the unwilling harem on 18 January. Another girl, Agnes Adams, known on the streets as 'Vickie', was tricked by Gary Heidnik into going back with him through her acquaintance with Josefina. She arrived the day before the latter's escape.

Every day, Heidnik beat the girls and forced them to perform sexual acts with both him and each other. He fed them a curious diet of bread, dog food and ice cream, which he kept in a deep freeze in the corner of the cellar. Later, another ingredient was to be added.

At some time during the New Year Sandra Lindsay annoyed Heidnik. To punish her, he strapped her by one wrist to an overhead beam and then forced her to eat lumps of bread, holding her lips together until she swallowed. For a week the half-witted girl dangled feverishly from the beam, until finally she choked on a piece of bread and died.

He carried the body upstairs. Soon the girls in the cellar heard the whine of an electric saw, followed by the pungent odour of cooking flesh.

That night Deborah Dudley had a bout of rebelliousness, and physically fought Heidnik when he tried to force himself upon her. In reply, the furious man unshackled her and dragged her upstairs.

A few minutes later she came down, silent and shocked. When she could speak, she told the others: 'He showed me Sandra's head in a pot. And he had her ribs in a roasting pan, and a bunch of her other body parts in the freezer. He told me if I didn't start listening to him, that was going to happen to me too.'

But despite the horror of what she had seen, Deborah rebelled again. This time she was thrust down into the pit in the floor, and water was poured in on top of her. Then Heidnik made Josefina push a live electric wire through a hole in the boards covering the pit. Deborah gave one terrible scream. When the boards were removed, she lay dead in the water.

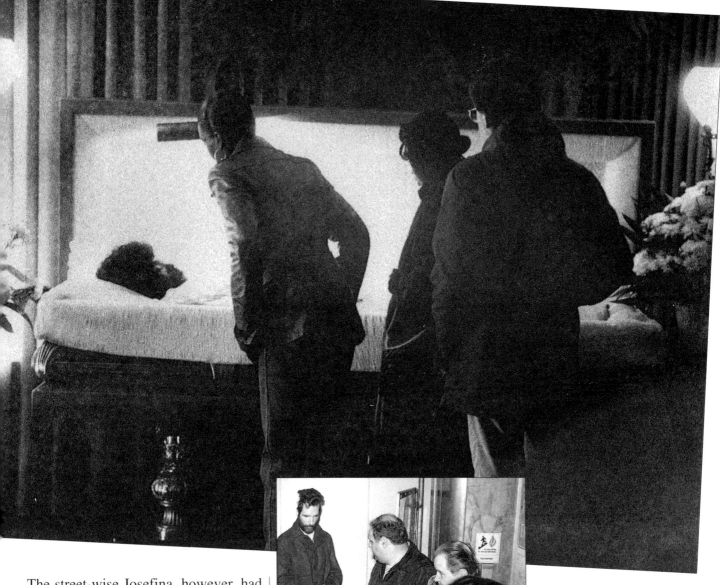

The street-wise Josefina, however, had a streak of cunning. Gradually she worked at winning Heidnik's trust, until he began taking her out on little expeditions to McDonald's and even buying her clothes and wigs. Finally, she begged him to let her see her three children who, she claimed, she had left with a babysitter. Instead she ran to her old boyfriend, Vincent Nelson.

What kind of a monster had the Philadelphia police netted?

BACKGROUND OF A MANIAC

Gary Michael Heidnik had been born on 21 November 1943 in the suburb of Eastlake in Cleveland, Ohio.

At the age of thirteen he became fascinated with things military – he had been a keen Boy Scout – and with his father's profound approval enrolled at the Staunton Military Academy in Virginia. There he scored consistently high marks until, quite suddenly, he dropped out.

In October 1961, as soon as he was old enough, Gary Heidnik joined the US Army. After basic training he was transferred to Landsthul in Germany.

Less than a year later he developed nausea, dizzy spells, headaches and blurred vision. Doctors noticed a series of nervous tics, including sudden head spasms, and he developed a habit of saluting in an exaggeratedly smart fashion at inappropriate moments.

Despite recording his IQ as up to 148 – a 'near genius' level – the army psychiatrists could do little to help Gary out of the slough into which he had fallen. In January 1963 he was given an

Above: *The viewing of Deborah Dudley's body.*

Left: *Heidnik being brought into the sheriff's office after his arrest.*

US ARMY PSYCHIATRISTS FAILED TO DEAL WITH HEIDNIK'S DEPRESSION OR TO NOTICE HIS EXCESSIVE SEX DRIVE honourable discharge and, with it, a pension of almost $2000 a month.

Neither the Army nor his civilian psychiatrists noticed Gary Heidnik's extraordinary sexual drive. Even in his forties, shortly before his arrest, he was regularly having sex four times a day, and he spent a great deal of money on prostitutes and sex videos. His only other material interest was in cars.

After his discharge from the army, what friends he had were invariably black. The prostitutes he consorted with were also black, and with rare exceptions, like Josefina Riviera, simple-minded. And it was among these women that he looked for mothers – the mothers of his children.

His obsession that God wanted him to father children led Heidnik, on 12 October 1971, to start a religion to be known as the United Church of the Ministers of God. Gary was the Church's 'Bishop', and his brother Terry a member of the board. The church was registered with the state, and under US law was exempt from taxes.

The congregation was largely comprised of black physical and/or mental cripples. All the evidence shows that Heidnik treated these people with generosity and kindness.

In 1977 he impregnated an illiterate

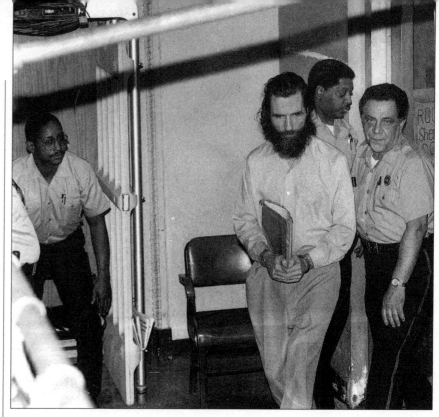

Above: *Heidnik is led into court for his trial at city hall in Philadelphia.*

Below: *The formal charges against Heidnik were all-encompassing.*

black girl named Aljeanette Davidson. She had an IQ of 49, and was completely under Heidnik's thrall. The baby girl was immediately fostered by the state.

Undeterred, Heidnik hatched a wicked plan. Aljeanette's sister, Alberta, was thirty-five and had for twenty years been an inmate of an institute for the mentally handicapped in Harrisburg, Pennsylvania. Gary took Aljeanette to see Alberta, and the elder sister was delighted when her sister's kindly boyfriend suggested they go for 'an outing'.

Alberta failed to return, and the institute officials became worried. Days later the hospital authorities, accompanied by police, broke into the house in North Marshall Street and found the wretched Alberta crammed into a garbage bin in the cellar.

Because she was not deemed fit to give evidence, Heidnik could only be tried on the comparatively trivial charges of assault and abduction. But Judge Charles Mariarchi spotted something 'evil and dangerous' about Heidnik.

Heidnik spent most of the sentence in mental hospitals. For at least six years after his release from jail, Gary Heidnik vanished from all official records except those of the stock market. When he registered his Church in 1971 its total assets were $1500, but twelve years later, despite its founder's curious habits, the funds had multiplied to $545, 000.

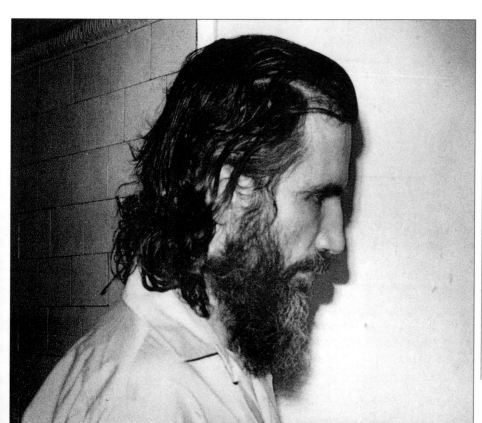

TRIAL BY JURY

His trial opened at City Hall, Philadelphia, on 20 June 1988 before Judge Lynne M. Abrahams. The charges against Heidnik were murder, kidnapping, rape, aggravated assault, involuntary deviate sexual intercourse, indecent exposure, false imprisonment, unlawful restraint, simple assault, making terroristic threats, recklessly endangering another person, indecent assault, criminal solicitation, possession, and abuse of a corpse. The judge proved very dubious of arguments presenting Heidnik's acts as 'excusable' because of his alleged mental sickness.

In a three-hour stint in the witness box, Josefina Riviera told how Heidnik had set up his basement baby farm 'because the city was always taking his babies away'. She described in graphic detail the horrors of life in the Heidnik basement.

Food consisted of crackers, oatmeal, chicken, ice-cream, bread, water, and – after the murder of Lindsay – dog food 'mixed with minced body parts'. Very occasionally, their captor would take one of the girls upstairs for a bath, have sex with her, and then bring her down again.

The tiny figure of Jacquelyn Askins presented the most forlorn figure on the witness stand. She was so small that Heidnik had used handcuffs to shackle her ankles, and his lawyers tried to suggest that a degree of compassion had been shown in the extra length of chain he had used to link them. 'Oh no,' said Jacquelyn, 'he did that so I could open my legs for sex.'

After two and a half days the jury brought in a verdict of Guilty on all counts. Heidnik was sentenced to death on two charges – the death penalty was in abeyance in Pennsylvania – and a total of 120 years' imprisonment on the rest.

He was, said Judge Abrahams, possessed 'not of an illness in his head, but a malignancy in his heart. I don't want any parole order to put Mr Heidnik back on the streets as long as he's breathing,' she concluded.

In January 1990 the State Supreme Court refused Heidnik's request to be executed, and almost simultaneously the US Bankruptcy Court divided his $600,000 among his creditors. Each of his surviving victims was awarded $34,540 for her bizarre ordeal.

Above: *Friends and relatives of the victims hurry from the courtroom after the jury finally returned their verdict of guilty on all charges.*

DID THE LONGER CHAIN ON ASKINS'S ANKLES IMPLY COMPASSION ON HEIDNIK'S PART? NO, SHE REPLIED, IT WAS TO ENABLE SEX TO TAKE PLACE

ED KEMPER
The Headhunter

He started with family pets. Then he moved on to assorted hitch-hikers, his grandmother and mother, carving up the bodies to prevent detection.
Ed Kemper was a paranoid schizophrenic with a John Wayne macho fixation, and he was loose in California

Someone, in a state so conscious of psychiatry, psychotherapy and general mental maintainance as California, should have spotted Ed Kemper sooner. He started young enough, after all.

When he was nine years old, Ed buried the family cat alive in the back yard. Later he dug up its body, cut off its head,

stuck it on a pole and, taking the strange totem to his bedroom, prayed to it.

In 1961, when he was thirteen and in summer camp, Ed was taught to shoot. He celebrated by shooting dead a

Left: *Kemper arriving at court.*

Opposite: *Edmund Emil Kemper III, the six-foot-nine giant who loved killing things.*

ALL HIS LIFE ED KEMPER BELIEVED HE BEHAVED REASONABLY SO LONG AS NO ONE CROSSED HIM — AND THE SIAMESE CAT HAD CROSSED HIM

Below: *609A Ord Drive in Aptos, California was the Kempers' comfortable lower-middle-class home.*

classmate's pet dog. But instead of it giving him a macho image – his hero John Wayne was fast with a gun, but always popular – Kemper was reviled for the deed.

Shortly afterwards he wreaked revenge on the new family pet, a Siamese cat. This time he sliced off the top of the animal's skull with a machete, and then stabbed the body. Parts of the cat were hidden in his bedroom cupboard.

BIZARRE BACKGROUND

But if Ed was odd, his family were at least partly to blame.

Ed – Edmund Emil Kemper III, known at home as 'Guy' – was the only son of an ex-Marine who had served with the Special Forces Unit in Europe during the Second World War. Ed III was born on 18 December 1948, and worshipped his 6 ft 8 ins tall father.

In 1957 the father, who despite his size tended to be dominated by Ed's mother Clarnell, left his wife and three young children for another woman. Clarnell sold the family home in California, and moved to Helena, Montana.

Clarnell Kemper herself stood over 6 ft tall, and was a hard drinker. When Ed mourned the departure of his father, his mother feared that he was 'going soft' and might develop into a homosexual. To pre-empt this, she made him sleep in the cellar, locking him in and placing the kitchen table over the trapdoor.

In the summer of 1964, Ed's father felt that the boy needed a complete change. The answer seemed to be his own parents, Edmund and Maude Kemper.

Edmund Kemper I was a quiet, rather colourless man who had worked most of his life for the California State Division of Highways. Now, at seventy-one, he lived in retirement on his smallholding in the foothills of the Sierra Nevada. His wife Maude, sixty-five, was an entirely different creature. Everything and everyone within her sphere of influence was controlled with an iron hand.

On 8 August 1964, Maude's grandson Ed III arrived at the ranch. Maude took against her grandson from the outset. She had to suffer him, in the event, for just sixteen days.

Above: *Anita Luchessa was eighteen and in her first year at Fresno State University when she made the fatal error of accepting a lift from Ed Kemper.*

> TO PRE-EMPT ANY 'SOFTNESS' OR HOMOSEXUAL TENDENCIES ED'S MOTHER MADE HIM SLEEP LOCKED UP IN THE CELLAR

SHOOTING GRANDMA

On the hot, airless morning of 27 August 1964, old Ed Kemper set out to fetch the shopping while Maude settled to her typewriter at the kitchen table. Young Ed shuffled around listlessly in the yard for a while, then came in and took his grandfather's .22 rifle from the kitchen door. Loading it, he told his grandmother he was going out to shoot rabbits.

'Just don't shoot any birds,' she snapped. Young Kemper stopped on the threshold. Something about her tone induced an instant surge of white-hot rage. Whipping around he flung the rifle up to his shoulder and fired a shot into the back of her head. As she fell forward he loosed off two more into her back. Then he put down the gun, selected a sharp kitchen knife, and stabbed her repeatedly until his fury drained away.

Then he wrapped a towel around the dead woman's head to soak up the blood, and carried her body into the bedroom.

Above: *Mary Ann Pesce was Anita Luchessa's roommate at university. The two girls were hitch-hiking when they met with Kemper.*

He realized that he was in trouble. As his grandfather drove up outside, Kemper killed him with a single shot to the head in order, he said later, to spare him the sight of his murdered wife.

After a desultory attempt to clean up the kitchen, Ed rang his mother Clarnell for help. 'There's been an accident,' he said. 'Grandma's dead. So is Grandpa.'

Clarnell, who immediately suspected that her son was responsible, told him to ring the local sheriff. When the lawman arrived, Ed admitted what he had done.

After a session with a court psychiatrist, Ed Kemper was pronounced a paranoid schizophrenic. Without much further examination, it was decided to send him to the State Hospital at Atascadero.

BAD INFLUENCE

The boy murderer was to stay at Atascadero for the next five years, and all in all he enjoyed the experience. The

LISTENING TO THE SEX OFFENDERS, KEMPER UNDERSTOOD THAT TO GET AWAY WITH RAPE IT WAS NECESSARY TO KILL THE VICTIM

Research Director, Dr Frank Vanasek, took him under his wing and Ed soon became a trusted inmate.

Gradually he acquired a basic working knowledge of psychological conditions, including his own. He knew what the doctors wanted him to say, and he said it.

But he also learned a lot about sex. Eagerly he listened to sex offenders of every kind, fantasizing at night about their experiences. He was particularly interested in the testimony of the rapists, noting that almost all of them had been caught because a victim had identified them. The moral seemed to be that to get away with rape, the victim should not be allowed to live.

These, of course, were very private thoughts. To the doctors, he tried to present the portrait of a rapidly improving, integrated human being.

Although the possibility of explosiveness was 'certainly evident', the doctors decided that he would be safe in the community. He was first released into the care of the California Youth Authority in 1969, and stayed there for three months while he attended college.

Most of his reports at Atascadero had noted that his mother was probably a causative influence of his problems, and recommended that Ed should in future be kept apart from her. But on his final release from the halfway house he was placed back in the custody of the formidable Clarnell Kemper just in time for his twenty-first birthday.

His mother had by now moved to the coastal town of Santa Cruz. She had an administrative job at the University of California and an apartment in the suburb of Aptos.

Across from the courtroom at Aptos was a bar named the Jury Room, where off-duty local policemen congregated. Kemper began drinking there, and his size, clipped hair, short, police-style moustache and conservative attitudes helped him fit in very well. The police liked him, and he became known to them as 'Big Eddie'.

Kemper, with his John Wayne fixation, fancied the idea of a career as a lawman himself, but was told that he would be too big for the California law agencies. He became depressed and took a job as

Above: *Fifteen-year-old Aiko Koo was standing at a bus stop in Berkeley, California when she was picked up by Ed Kemper.*

flagman with the Division of Highways.

His mother had other ideas. His marks had been good in college, during his treatment period, and she wanted him to enter university and 'better himself'. Inevitably they had rows.

The monotonous but steady job of flagman meant that Ed had independent money for the first time in his life. He bought a black and yellow 1969 Ford Galaxie sedan, and rented a room in a friend's flat in Alameda, a suburb of San Francisco.

PROWLING THE HIGHWAYS

For the next eighteen months or so, Ed Kemper spent his leisure time cruising the highways and byways of California, pondering in his unquiet mind lubriciously upon sex.

At the tail end of the 'flower power'

era, San Francisco and its environs were full of free-spirited young women who habitually hitch-hiked. Ed made a practice of picking them up and chatting to them, using all the psychological wiles he had learned in Atascadero.

His 'straight' looks led girls to trust him, and he made things easier for himself by getting his mother to fix him up with a University of California permit for his windscreen, giving him access to the university's campuses. He had given about 150 girls 'safe' lifts before he was ready for what he had in mind.

On Sunday, 7 May 1972, Kemper took to the access roads around the freeways outside San Francisco in his Ford Galaxie. Under his seat were a hunting knife, a plastic bag, a pair of handcuffs and a Browning 9mm automatic pistol, borrowed from a workmate. At 4 p.m. he spotted two pretty young girls thumbing by the side of the road, and Kemper drew alongside them.

Mary Ann Pesce and Anita Luchessa were eighteen years old, first-year students at Fresno State College. They were, as they told Kemper, going to see a friend at Stanford University, about an hour's drive away. The girls were unfamiliar with those parts, they admitted, and did not know the area.

As they talked, Kemper had been taking advantage of the girls' lack of local knowledge to drive out of town. Now he pulled down a side road. Mary Ann suddenly realized something was wrong and asked, from the back seat, 'What do you want?'

Kemper held up the Browning pistol in reply and said: 'You know what I want.'

Mary Ann talked calmly to Kemper in the approved fashion that she had learnt during university safety lectures, trying to get her potential attacker to see her as

Above: *Ed Kemper helps police locate the body of his victim, Aiko Koo.*

Below: *Police dig up the remains of fifteen-year-old Aiko Koo.*

a person rather than a victim. Unfortunately Kemper, with his experience at Atascadero, knew the ruse.

In fact he used a piece of psychology of his own. He told the girls that he was going to lock one of them in the boot and hide the other in the back seat, before taking them both back to his apartment. He had, of course, no such intention, but the girls went along with his wishes.

After locking the terrified Anita in the boot, he handcuffed Mary Ann's hands behind her back. Then he pulled a plastic bag over her head and began to strangle her with a dressing gown cord. Mary Ann put up a tremendous fight. She bit through the plastic bag and managed to get her mouth to the rope, keeping it from its choke-hold.

Kemper took up the hunting knife and stabbed her twice in the back. She turned over and he stabbed her once more, but she managed to shake the bag off and tried to sit upright. Finally Kemper grabbed her by the chin and slashed her throat.

With Mary Ann dead, Kemper went to deal with Anita, who must have heard the struggle and thus, he considered, would have to be slaughtered with despatch. He was right. When she saw the blood on his hands she began to scream and struggle and he stabbed frantically.

With both girls dead he drove the bodies back to his room in Alameda, knowing his flatmate was out. It was about 6 p.m. He carried them in, wrapped in blankets, and first undressed them, taking copious photographs with a Polaroid, and then dissected and decapitated them. He copied down the information from their ID cards and then destroyed their clothes and possessions, retaining only their ready cash – $8.28.

That same evening he took the segmented bodies out to the wilds of Santa Cruz, where he buried them. The heads he kept for a while. They were trophies, but they were also small guards against dental identification. Some time later he drove up into the hills and tumbled them into a ravine.

To the Californian police forces, the two girls were free spirits who had gone their own ways, regardless of parental admonitions. Mary Ann and Anita were, for a while, just a couple of runaways.

For four months Kemper gloated over his Polaroid photographs, slaking his sadistic urges by recalling in detail the things he had done to the two girls. Any intention to kill was further curbed by another motorcycle accident, which left him with a broken left arm.

And Kemper had another priority on his mind. Any prospect of a better job was hampered by his record, for even in California few people fancied employing a double murderer who had served five years in a mental institution. Until he had his juvenile record declared sealed, he was unable to buy a gun easily. Meanwhile he had managed to borrow a .357 Magnum.

THE KILLER STRIKES AGAIN ... AND AGAIN

As dusk fell on 14 September, fifteen-year-old Aiko Koo was standing at a bus-stop in University Avenue, Berkeley, trying to thumb a lift.

Ed Kemper picked her up, but instead of taking her towards San Francisco, her destination, he set off fast down the coast highway. Aiko instantly realized she was in trouble and began to scream. Kemper pulled out his pistol and thrust it into her ribs, telling her that he meant her no harm. He was, he said, contemplating suicide, and wanted someone to talk to.

He drove her up into the mountains and stopped the car. Like her predecessors, Aiko struggled against his colossal weight, but in the end was overcome. He suffocated her into unconsciousness, raped her and then strangled her.

After wrapping the small body in a blanket and stowing it in the boot of his car Kemper drove off, glowing with satisfaction and the knowledge of his secret. A few miles down the road he stopped off at a bar for a beer, in order to savour his 'conquest' at leisure.

At about eleven that night he arrived back at Alameda and carried the body indoors. Then he dissected it and scattered the pieces in the Santa Cruz mountains. He retained only the head, which he carried around in the boot of his car.

On 15 September, a panel of juvenile psychiatrists examined Kemper and declared him mentally fit. Two months later a court, acting on the panel's instructions, 'sealed' his juvenile record. He was now entitled to go out to a gun shop, sign a form, wait five days and purchase a gun.

For the moment, however, Kemper had

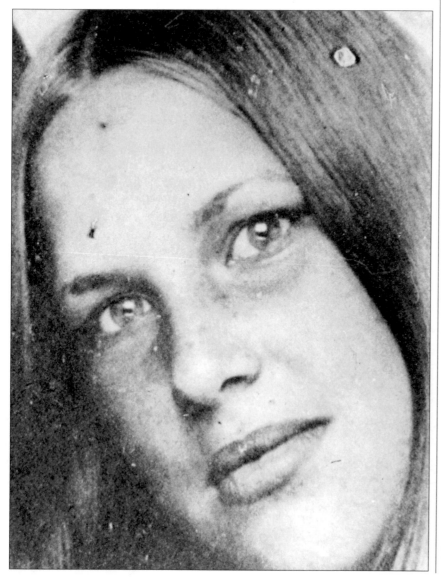

Below: *Eighteen-year-old Cindy Schall was picked up by Kemper on the outskirts of Santa Cruz.*

Mission Avenue in Santa Cruz, he saw a short, shapely blonde named Cindy Schall.

Cindy was eighteen, a native of Marin County, near San Francisco. She was in her second year at Cabrillo College, on the outskirts of Santa Cruz, where she was studying to become a teacher. When Kemper picked her up she was on her way to an evening class.

As soon as she got into the car, he showed her the gun. Then he told her a similar 'suicide' story to the one he had told Aiko Koo. For three hours he drove, heading east to Watsonville and then turning into the hills at the township of Freedom. He persuaded her to get into the boot, and then killed her with a single shot to the head.

Kemper's mother was out for the evening, but even without the danger of prying eyes, Kemper had a difficult job manoeuvring the 11 stone corpse indoors with his injured arm. As it was, his plaster cast was splashed with blood, which he covered up with his mother's white shoe polish. Overnight, Cindy Schall lay in Kemper's bedroom cupboard.

The following morning, when his mother left for work, Kemper lugged the body into the bathroom and began cutting it into disposable pieces.

Later in the day, Kemper placed the pieces of flesh in plastic bags and threw them into a ravine near Monterey. As souvenirs he kept Cindy's outsize man's work shirt, and a small handmade ring. He also kept her head in his cupboard.

A day later, newspapers carried details of a Highway Patrolman's find on the road out of Monterey – two arms, a hand, and portions of two legs. Some time after that a ribcage was washed ashore. Enough of the body was recovered for Cindy Schall to be positively identified. Caution dictated that Ed get rid of the head, so he buried it outside his mother's window.

Just a month after the slaying of Cindy Schall, the Kempers – mother and son – had another mammoth row. The effect on Ed was familiar: rage and frustration. He stormed out of the house and threw himself into the Ford, tucking the pistol under his right thigh as he drove. It was another wet night.

Rosalind Thorpe was just emerging

other problems. His broken arm had kept him off work, and he was unable to pay the rent in Alameda. Reluctantly, he moved back to his mother's flat at 609A Ord Drive in Apatos. They began to quarrel again almost instantly, and the old frustrations began to build up.

On 8 January 1973, Kemper bought a .22 Rutgers automatic with a 6 inch barrel. Itching to try it out, he took to cruising the roads that same evening. Weather conditions seemed ideal, with heavy rain forcing girls who would otherwise avoid the risk to get any ride they could. He picked up two or three, but the streets were busy and he decided to make no untoward moves.

He had almost given up when, in

Above: *Student IDs of Rosalind Thorpe and Alice Liu, the last two students to fall prey to Ed Kemper.*

KEMPER USED HIS MOTHER'S WHITE SHOE POLISH TO COVER UP THE BLOODSTAINS ON HIS PLASTER CAST from a lecture theatre as Kemper drove by. Normally the twenty-three-year-old linguistics and psychology student rode her bicycle everywhere, but tonight the rain had put paid to that, she told Kemper. Seeing his campus sticker, she assumed him to be a fellow student.

As they chatted, Kemper spotted a small Chinese girl thumbing by the side of the road. He stopped and she got into the back seat. She was, she said, Alice Liu. She was twenty-one.

As they reached the hill overlooking the town of Santa Cruz, Kemper slowed the car as if to admire the lights reflected in the ocean. Then he picked up his gun in his good right hand and shot Rosalind smartly in the temple.

As she fell he turned to Alice, who was writhing in the back, screaming. Kemper fired twice at her and missed, then managed to hit her in the head. Alice lay unconscious, though making soft moaning sounds, as he drove at speed out of town.

For the first time in his 'adventures' Kemper felt sick and frightened at what he had done. Alice's moaning did not help, and as soon as he was far from any street lights he stopped the car and shot her once more in the head. For a time she was quiet, and then the terrible moaning began again. He pulled off the road and carried both bodies to the boot of his car.

His plaster cast was again sprayed with blood by the 'blow-back' as the bullet entered Rosalind's skull, and he stopped in a filling station toilet to scrub it off as best he could. Then he went home.

His mother was up, watching TV. He told her that he was going out for cigarettes, but before going to the shop he stopped by the car, opened the boot and hastily decapitated both bodies with his hunting knife. It was between 10 and 11p.m., but no one was around.

The following morning he carried Alice's headless body into his bedroom and had sexual intercourse with it, before cutting off her hands 'as an afterthought'. Later that day he dumped the bodies near San Francisco, in the hope that police would think the perpetrator a local man. Then he drove back to the town of Pacifica and threw the heads and hands over a bluff called Devil's Slide.

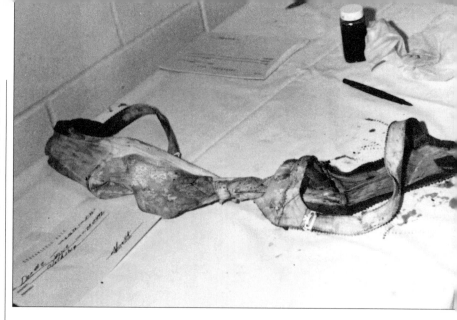

Above: *Rosalind Thorpe's bloodstained bra was introduced as evidence at Kemper's trial.*

TROUBLE NOW CAME FROM AN UNEXPECTED QUARTER - ANOTHER MASS MURDERER WAS WORKING OUT OF SANTA CRUZ

HIS MOTHER ASKED HER SON IF HE WANTED TO TALK. 'NO,' HE REPLIED, AND WENT TO FETCH A KNIFE AND HAMMER

He also felt that things were getting more difficult for him. At the end of January a woman's skeleton was found in the mountains. She was identified as Mary Guilfoyle, a twenty-three-year-old English student who, like Cindy Schall, had attended Cabrillo College.

She was a victim not of Kemper but of another mass murderer, Herbert Mullin, who had started killing at the same time as Kemper and also lived in Santa Cruz. Mullin was to kill thirteen victims and eventually ended up in the same prison as Ed Kemper. Meanwhile he was causing Kemper trouble.

FINAL BLOODBATH

In the middle of April, Kemper packed up all the documents and personal belongings he had taken from his victims, together with his prized .22 pistol, and threw them in the ocean. He had stomach trouble, which turned out to be ulcers, and his nerves were in shreds. It was time, he felt, to bring his career to a massive climax, perhaps killing everyone in his neighbourhood in one night of slaughter.

On 20 April, Good Friday, Kemper went home and drank beer in front of the television while pondering what to do next; his mother was working late. At about four in the morning of Easter Saturday he went into his mother's bedroom. She was awake, and asked him if he wanted to talk. He told her no, and went back to his own room to fetch a pocket knife and a hammer.

When he was sure his mother was sleeping he crept back in and brought the hammer down with all his force on the right side of her head. She did not move, but as the blood welled up Ed saw that she was still breathing. Turning her over on to her back, he sawed into her trachea with his pocket knife, continuing to cut until the head rolled free.

For the rest of that day he felt sick, giddy and restless. The killing this time had done nothing to calm his confused feelings. He cleaned up the bloody mess as best he could, and then went out drinking with a friend.

Towards the evening, in a muddled attempt to disguise his mother's absence over the Easter holiday, he decided to kill her best friend, Mrs Sally Hallett. He hoped that the joint disappearance would confuse the police. Kemper rang Mrs Hallett, and told her he was preparing a surprise dinner for his mother. Mrs Hallett agreed to come over that evening.

She arrived exhausted after the journey. 'Let's sit down,' she said. 'I'm dead!' They were her last words.

After strangling and decapitating her, Kemper went for a drink at the Jury Room. He had, he knew, reached the very end of the trail. There was no way he could cover up the slaughter just across the road from the policemen's bar.

On Easter Sunday morning he packed Mrs Hallett's body into his bedroom cupboard, and then loaded his weapons into her car.

He headed east to Reno and then hired a car, leaving Mrs Hallett's vehicle at a garage. He drove for the rest of the day and night. Just before midnight on Monday, 23 April, he stopped at a payphone in the town of Pueblo, Colorado, 1200 miles away from Santa Cruz.

Then he rang the Santa Cruz police and asked for Lieutenant Charles Scherer, who was in charge of the student murder investigations. It was not until three telephone calls and five more hours had passed, however, that Ed Kemper convinced his old police drinking buddies that he was the man they were looking for. They sent a Colorado patrol car out to pick him up, and he was arrested in Denver by Santa Cruz police.

Ed Kemper's confession was long, articulate and complete in every detail, for he had savoured each killing over and over in his head. When the details of his release from Atascadero were made public there was sudden public loss of confidence in psychiatric criminal evaluation. It was already shaky after revelations that Herbert Mullin, the other Santa Cruz murderer, who had also been arrested, was likewise a former mental hospital inmate. Typically Ed Kemper detested Mullin because 'he had killed people for no good reason'.

On 25 October 1973 Ed Kemper was charged with eight counts of first degree murder at Santa Cruz Court House. On 8 November he was found guilty and sentenced to life imprisonment in California Medical Facility at Vacaville. He escaped the death penalty because it was suspended in California at that time.

All parole recommendations for Kemper have been turned down since then, and it is unlikely that he will ever be released. Since entering the Facility, Kemper has worked at recording books for the blind, supervising fifteen fellow inmates. He received a public service award for this work in 1981.

'LET'S SIT DOWN,' SAID HIS MOTHER'S FRIEND AFTER HER EXHAUSTING JOURNEY. 'I'M DEAD!' A FEW MINUTES LATER, SHE WAS

Below: *Ed Kemper towers above his police escort in court.*

DENNIS NILSEN
A Quiet Civil Servant

Was it fear of desertion that caused Dennis Nilsen to become a mass murderer in the most gruesome of circumstances? And was he merely evil, or was he himself one of life's victims – a schizophrenic?

A t 6.25 on the morning of 8 February 1983, Michael Cattran parked his Dyno-Rod van outside 23 Cranley Gardens in the north London suburb of Muswell Hill. It was a routine call. Jim Allcock, one of the residents of No. 23, had phoned to say that the drains had

Above: *A police constable stands guard at the back of 23 Cranley Gardens, Muswell Hill, where Dennis Nilsen rented an attic flat.*

Opposite: *Dennis Nilsen, the quiet civil servant who became Britain's most prolific mass murderer.*

AT THE BOTTOM OF THE STINKING SHAFT WAS A GLUTINOUS, GREYISH-WHITE SUBSTANCE

Left: *The front of 23 Cranley Gardens.*

been blocked for five days. After a quick examination of the interior plumbing, Cattran decided the problem lay outside the house itself. He walked round to the side of the house and removed the manhole cover.

The smell was nauseating as Cattran climbed down the 12-foot inspection shaft. At the bottom he found a glutinous greyish-white mass.

Cattran told Jim Allcock that it was nothing serious and that he would be back shortly to straighten things out. When he called his boss, however, he voiced his real suspicions. The matter which was clogging the drains at 23 Cranley Gardens was, in his opinion, human flesh.

Cattran and his boss returned to Muswell Hill the following morning. To Cattran's surprise, the glutinous mass had vanished. He knew that, even though it had been raining the previous day, the drains could not possibly have cleared themselves. Cattran reached deep into the drainpipe and pulled out several pieces of meat and a number of bones.

Cattran explained the mystery of the missing sludge to Jim Allcock and another tenant, Fiona Bridges. They told

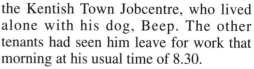

him they had heard someone moving the manhole cover in the early hours of the morning. They thought it might be Mr Nilsen who lived above them in the attic flat. Cattran and his boss decided it was time to call the police.

Detective Chief Inspector Peter Jay arrived on the scene shortly after 11a.m. and collected the meat and bones for forensic examination. At Charing Cross Hospital, it took pathologist Professor David Bowen only minutes to confirm that the meat was indeed human flesh and that the bones were from a man's hand.

THE TENANT OF THE ATTIC FLAT

Police attention immediately focused on the occupier of the attic flat, Dennis Andrew Nilsen, an executive officer at

Above left: *The stove in Nilsen's kitchen was caked with grease. Forensic examination determined that this was human fat.*

Above: *Black plastic bags in Nilsen's wardrobe contained the remains of two bodies.*

Right: *Two bodies had been dissected in Nilsen's bath, and the remains of Stephen Sinclair had been hidden under it.*

Below: *A cooking pot used by Nilsen to simmer the head of one of his victims.*

the Kentish Town Jobcentre, who lived alone with his dog, Beep. The other tenants had seen him leave for work that morning at his usual time of 8.30.

Peter Jay, together with Detective Inspector McCusker and Detective Constable Butler, waited outside 23 Cranley Gardens for Nilsen to return.

When he walked up to the front door at 5.40, Peter Jay intercepted him. Nilsen, a polite, quietly spoken man in his late thirties, seemed surprised but not alarmed when Jay introduced himself and his colleagues as police officers.

The four men went inside the house and climbed the stairs to Nilsen's tiny flat. Once inside, Jay told Nilsen about the human flesh which had been found in the drain outside. Nilsen feigned horror, but Jay was not remotely convinced. 'Stop messing about,' he said. 'Where's the rest of the body?'

Nilsen didn't even bother to protest his innocence. 'In two plastic bags in the wardrobe. I'll show you,' he said, unlocking the doors. The awful stench from the cupboard confirmed that Nilsen was telling the truth.

He arrested Nilsen, charged him with murder and shipped him off to Hornsey Police Station.

En route, Inspector McCusker asked Nilsen if there was anything he wanted to say. Nilsen replied, 'It's a long story. It goes back a long time. I'll tell you everything. I want to get it off my chest.'

'Are we talking about one body or two?' McCusker asked Nilsen.

'Fifteen or sixteen,' Nilsen replied calmly. 'Since 1978.... Three at Cranley Gardens and about thirteen at my previous address, 195 Melrose Avenue in Cricklewood.'

CONTENTS OF A WARDROBE

Detective Chief Inspector Jay returned to 23 Cranley Gardens with Detective Chief Superintendent Chambers and the pathologist, Professor Bowen. They removed the two stinking black plastic bags from Nilsen's wardrobe and took them to Hornsey mortuary.

When Bowen opened the first he found it contained four smaller shopping bags. In the first of these was the left-hand side of a man's chest with the arm attached. The second contained the right-hand side of a chest. The third held a torso, and the fourth an assortment of human offal.

In the other black bag, Bowen found two human heads and another torso with the arms attached but missing the hands. One of the heads had most of the flesh boiled away.

Nilsen told the police that one of the heads belonged to a young drug addict called Stephen Sinclair. The second he knew only as 'John the Guardsman'. He could put no name to a third victim whose remains were later found in a tea chest at his flat.

Nilsen seemed willing, even anxious, to help the police. On 11 February, three days after his arrest, he accompanied Peter Jay to the ground-floor flat at 195 Melrose Avenue which he had occupied from 1976 to 1981.

'ARE WE TALKING ABOUT ONE BODY OR TWO?' ENQUIRED THE POLICEMAN. 'FIFTEEN OR SIXTEEN,' WAS THE CALM REPLY

Below: *Nilsen's obsession with death was already evident during his days in the National Service.*

He told Jay that he had cut up the bodies and burnt them on a series of huge bonfires in the back garden. He even pointed out where the fires had been and where they should look for human remains.

Using this information, forensic teams started the laborious task of sifting through the earth for evidence. A day later they had found enough human ash and bone fragments to establish that at least eight people had been cremated in the garden.

Despite his willingness to cooperate with the police, Nilsen was unable to identify many of his early victims. None of them had ever been more than casual acquaintances. They had been, for the most part, young, homeless homosexuals – social misfits, drug addicts or alcoholics, men who could simply disappear without anyone knowing or caring. However, based on dates and

physical descriptions given by Nilsen, and comparing them with missing persons' records, the police were eventually able to identify six victims with reasonable certainty.

The question now for the police and Nilsen's lawyer was not if Nilsen was a mass murderer, but rather why he had killed more than a dozen young men. On this point, Nilsen could not help. 'I am hoping you will tell me that,' he said.

FOUR YEARS OF CARNAGE

Nilsen was questioned for the next few weeks, during which time he gave a meticulous account of his four years of carnage. It was a story so monstrous and grotesque that it made even case-hardened police interrogators physically ill to listen to it.

It had all started on New Year's Eve 1978. Nilsen had met a young Irish boy in a pub in the West End and taken him back to his flat in Melrose Avenue. After seeing in the New Year, the two men had gone to bed together. They were both stupefied with drink, and no sex took place between them.

In the morning, according to Nilsen, he woke to find the young Irishman still asleep beside him. He was suddenly overcome with terror that the boy would want to leave as soon as he too awoke. Nilsen desperately wanted him to stay, and could only think of one way to ensure that he did so.

Nilsen picked up a tie from the floor, straddled the boy's chest, placed the tie around his neck and pulled. The boy woke and a mighty struggle ensued before he finally passed out.

But he was not dead yet. So Nilsen went to the kitchen, filled a bucket with water and held the boy's head under the water until he drowned.

Nilsen then bathed the boy's body, dressed it in clean underwear and socks, took it back to bed with him and masturbated. For the next week, Nilsen went off to work as usual. He returned each evening to his dead companion who would be sitting in an armchair, waiting for him.

After eight days, Nilsen prised up some floor boards and hid the corpse. It

Above: *After a brief stint with the police, Nilsen, aged 28, spent three months working as a security guard.*

Below: *In the winter of 1975, Nilsen moved into a ground floor flat at 195 Melrose Avenue. It was here that he committed a dozen murders.*

remained there for seven months before Nilsen dissected it and burnt it on a bonfire in his back garden.

On the evening of 3 December 1979, almost a year later, Dennis Nilsen was cruising the gay bars of Soho when he met a twenty-six-year-old Canadian tourist, Kenneth Ockendon. Ockendon, who was staying at a cheap hotel in King's Cross, was due to fly home the following day.

Nilsen persuaded him to accompany him back to Melrose Avenue for a meal. He could stay the night if he wanted, and pick up his things from the hotel the following morning.

By the early hours of the morning the two men were in Nilsen's sitting room, both much the worse for drink. Nilsen was watching Ockendon as he listened to music through a set of headphones.

His feelings of imminent desertion were similar to those he had experienced a year earlier.

So Nilsen walked behind Ockendon's chair, grabbed the flex of the headphones and strangled him with it. Again he

*Above: **Police remove human remains from Nilsen's flat at Melrose Avenue.***

built an enormous bonfire which was constructed in part from human remains wrapped in carpet. He crowned the fire with an old car tyre to disguise the smell of burning flesh.

At the end of 1981, Nilsen was planning to move. By this time he had accumulated a further five bodies and, shortly before he left, he had another massive fire.

No. 23 Cranley Gardens, Nilsen's new home, presented some real problems for a mass murderer of his ilk. It was an attic flat with no floorboards and no garden – in fact nowhere decent to hide a body at all. But this didn't stop him.

Within weeks of his move to Muswell Hill, Nilsen strangled John Howlett with an upholstery strap and then drowned him. Graham Allen was the next to die. Nilsen couldn't actually recall killing him, but thought he had strangled him with a tie while he was eating an omelette.

On 26 January Nilsen met his last victim. Stephen Sinclair, a drug addict and petty criminal, was wandering the streets of Soho looking for a hand-out. Nilsen offered to buy him a hamburger and then persuaded him to go back to Cranley Gardens with him.

Two weeks later, Michael Cattran of Dyno-Rod found what was left of Stephen in the drain outside 23 Cranley Gardens.

NO EMOTION, NO REMORSE

On 24 October 1983, Dennis Andrew Nilsen stood before Mr Justice Croom-Johnson at No. 1 Court in the Old Bailey. He was charged with six murders and two attempted murders.

There was no doubt that Nilsen had committed the offences. What the court had to evaluate was Nilsen's mental state at the time when he committed them.

If Nilsen had pleaded Guilty, as he originally intended, he would have saved the jury a considerable ordeal. Instead, they were forced to spend two weeks listening to detailed evidence of Nilsen's gruesome acts.

Detective Chief Superintendent Chambers spent almost an entire day reading out a transcript of Nilsen's

washed the body, dressed it in clean underwear, placed it next to him in bed and went to sleep.

Ockendon's corpse remained his constant companion for the next two weeks. Nilsen spent the evenings watching television with the body in an armchair next to him. When he was ready for bed, he would wrap it in a curtain and place it under the floorboards for the night.

Unlike the Irish boy, Ockendon's disappearance caused a considerable stir. Several of the tabloids carried his picture and Nilsen felt sure that his days were numbered. But the police didn't come. And over the next eighteen months eleven more young men were destined to die at Melrose Avenue.

By the end of 1980, Nilsen had accumulated six bodies. Three were stowed under the floorboards, while the others were cut up, stuffed in suitcases and stored in a garden shed.

At the beginning of December, Nilsen

EVERY EVENING NILSEN WOULD WATCH TELEVISION WITH OCKENDON'S BODY IN AN ARMCHAIR NEXT TO HIM

WITH NO FLOORBOARDS AND NO GARDEN, HOW WAS NILSEN GOING TO DISPOSE OF HIS VICTIMS AT HIS NEW ADDRESS?

confession. The graphic descriptions of decapitations and dissections, of the boiling and mincing of human flesh, and of necrophilia, sickened and enraged the jury. Nilsen, for his part, sat through the evidence without betraying a single vestige of emotion.

The prosecution called three witnesses to give evidence that Nilsen had attempted to kill them. Paul Nobbs, a university student, told how he had been rescued by Nilsen from the unwanted attentions of another man.

Nilsen had taken him back to Cranley Gardens and had shown him genuine kindness. He had not tried to ply him with drink or force him to have sex. He had even suggested that he call his mother so that she would not be worried. Nobbs had gone to bed alone but had woken in the early hours of the morning with a splitting headache. He had looked in the mirror and had seen that his eyes were completely bloodshot and that there was a bruise around his neck.

Nilsen had feigned concern, saying that Nobbs looked awful and should go straight to a doctor.

At the casualty department of the hospital he went to, Nobbs was told that he had been partially strangled. He had realized that Nilsen must have been his attacker, but had been reluctant to report the incident to the police because he felt sure that he would not be believed.

The defence made much of Nobbs's testimony. It demonstrated that Nilsen could behave perfectly normally one minute and then be possessed of murderous impulses the next, without provocation or reason. It proved, they said, that Nilsen was clearly insane.

If Nobbs's story was difficult to credit, Karl Strotter's encounter with Nilsen was nothing short of fantastic. Strotter had met Nilsen in a pub in Camden Town. He was depressed after the break-up of a relationship and, like Nobbs, described Nilsen's behaviour towards him as sympathetic and undemanding.

They had gone back to Cranley Gardens together and Nilsen had put him to bed in a sleeping bag. Strotter described what happened next: 'I woke up feeling something round my neck. My head was hurting and I couldn't breathe

Above: *Having confessed his crimes, Nilsen is remanded at Highgate Magistrates' Court in north London.*

NOBBS WOKE UP WITH BLOODSHOT EYES AND A SPLITTING HEADACHE. DOCTORS TOLD HIM SOMEONE HAD TRIED TO STRANGLE HIM

properly and I wondered what it was.

'I felt his hand pulling at the zip at the back of my neck. He was saying in a sort of whispered shouting voice, "Stay still. Stay still." I thought perhaps he was trying to help me out of the sleeping bag because I thought I had got caught up in the zip, which he had warned me about. Then I passed out.

'...the pressure was increasing. My head was hurting and I couldn't breathe. I remember vaguely hearing water running. I remember vaguely being carried and then felt very cold. I knew I was in the water and he was trying to drown me. He kept pushing me into the water....I just thought I was dying. I thought: "You are drowning. This is what it feels like to die." I felt very relaxed and I passed out. I couldn't fight any more.'

Strotter said he was amazed to awake lying on a sofa with Nilsen massaging him. Nilsen had then helped him to the underground station and wished him luck.

This apparent detachment from reality was echoed in Detective Chief Inspector Jay's evidence as he described Nilsen's behaviour during his interrogation. He was, Jay said, relaxed, cooperative and matter-of-fact. He did not, however, show any remorse. It was as though he was talking about someone else.

Both the prosecution and defence trotted out their 'expert witnesses', a mandatory feature of insanity pleas. Two equally well-qualified psychiatrists proceeded to give directly conflicting evaluations of the mental condition of the accused, thus effectively cancelling one another out in the eyes of the jury.

The judge spent four hours summing up, addressing himself in particular to the question of Nilsen's personality. 'A mind can be evil without being abnormal,' he advised the jury. 'There must be no excuses for Nilsen if he has moral defects. A nasty nature is not arrested or retarded development of the mind.'

The implication of what Mr Croom-Johnson was saying was obvious. Dennis Nilsen was, in his opinion, evil rather than insane, and the jury should therefore find him guilty of murder.

The jury retired on the morning of Thursday, 3 November 1983. Despite the clear guidance given by the judge, they returned the following morning to say that they were unable to reach a

Above: *Two that got away: Douglas Stewart (left); Karl Stotter (right). Both testified at the trial that they had been victims of attacks by Dennis Nilsen. Their evidence was vital for the prosecution as it argued that Nilsen was not technically insane.*

Below: *Nilsen's face bears the scar from an attack by a fellow prisoner.*

consensus about Nilsen's state of mind at the time of the various murders.

Mr Croom-Johnson said that he would accept a majority verdict. At 4.25 that afternoon the jury returned to court with a verdict of Guilty on all six counts of murder, by a majority of ten to two.

The judge condemned Dennis Andrew Nilsen to life imprisonment, with the recommendation that he should serve no less than twenty-five years.

Nilsen spent the first nine months of his sentence in Parkhurst Prison on the Isle of Wight.

In the summer of 1984 Nilsen was transferred to Wakefield Prison. He remains there to this day, sharing his cell with a budgerigar called Hamish.

DR PERERA
The Arrogant Dentist

A smooth and well-educated murderer thought he could outwit a simple Yorkshire detective. But he had not bargained for police perseverance and expert assistance in putting together the gruesome evidence that eventually convicted him

In 1935 Bukhtyar Hakim, a Parsee doctor who had changed his name to Buck Ruxton when he settled in the northern English town of Lancaster, strangled his wife Isabella in a fit of jealous rage. The sound of the struggle brought her maid, Mary Rogerson, to the scene. Ruxton killed her too.

He took the bodies upstairs and cut them into small pieces in the bath before wrapping them in newspapers and strips of cotton sheet. Then he drove north and scattered the packages along the side of the Edinburgh–Moffat road.

Ruxton was eventually arrested and brought to the gallows at Lancaster Gaol.

At some time during the early winter of 1983 history, in the person of Dr

Above: DI Tom Hodgson, who spent a year gradually building up a case against Dr Perera.

Opposite: Dr Perera is taken away by the police.

Below: Perera's house in Sitwell Close, in the Wakefield suburb of Sandal.

Samuel Perera, repeated itself almost detail for detail when Perera killed and cut to pieces his adopted daughter.

Like Ruxton, Perera was a native of the Indian subcontinent, having been born in Sri Lanka, at that time the British colony of Ceylon. He too was a doctor, a specialist in oral biology at Leeds University School of Medicine. He lived near Wakefield, West Yorkshire, just fifty miles from Lancaster. And, like Ruxton, he was astonishingly arrogant.

As one detective who worked on the case was to put it: 'He must have known of Ruxton from his medical studies. All doctors do a course in forensic medicine, and Ruxton is a standard text. You'd have thought that he would have learned from Ruxton's mistakes.'

Perera was born in 1943. After graduating from Colombo University he travelled to England to take up a three-year research scholarship at Newcastle University dental school. There he met and married his Hindu wife Dammika, converting her to Roman Catholicism.

In the early seventies he successfully applied for a post as lecturer in oral biology in the Dental Department of the Leeds School of Medicine, and travelled to England to settle in the middle-class suburb of Sandal, near Wakefield.

Above: *Nilanthe 'Philomena Perera', the Sri Lankan girl adopted by Dr Perera.*

PERERA, WHO HAD PAID
MONEY TO HER FATHER,
MAY HAVE INTENDED TO USE
HIS ADOPTED DAUGHTER AS
A HOUSEHOLD SLAVE

JUNGLE GIRL

Mrs Perera gave birth to two daughters during the latter part of the 1970s. But in December 1981, for reasons which were never satisfactorily explained, her husband decided he wanted to adopt a further child. He and his wife went back to Sri Lanka and returned with a ten-year-old girl named Nilanthe, giving her the adoptive name of Philomena. Perera may have had long-term plans to use Philomena as a sort of household slave. He had paid money to her natural father and, as he was later to tell police

dismissively, 'in any case she was only a jungle girl'.

Over the next couple of years the little 'jungle girl' became known and liked by the other residents of Sitwell Close. Her lack of English gave her a somewhat forlorn attitude, but her waif-like figure, large doe eyes and long, glossy hair held the promise of great beauty.

In November 1983, Nilanthe 'Philomena' Perera disappeared. 'My husband is very strict,' Mrs Perera told a neighbour. 'He has banned her from going out because she would make eyes at the men.'

But Christmas came and went, winter gave way to spring and there was still no sign of little Philomena.

The neighbours' curiosity began to stir again and finally, in April 1984, Mrs Perera told them: 'She's gone home. She grew very homesick and my husband decided it was kindest to send her back to her father in Sri Lanka.'

LETTER TO THE LAW

But the neighbours were not satisfied, and so they did a rather un-English thing. They called a meeting and, after discussing the matter, decided to send a letter laying out the facts to the authorities. The letter was opened at Wood Street Police Station in Wakefield, by a fifty-one-year-old detective inspector named Tom Hodgson.

Hodgson was a burly, snub-nosed man with a stubborn, cleft chin. His receding hairline and the bags under his amiable eyes bespoke years of police service, mostly as a detective officer.

It was a warm summer morning in July 1984 when Detective Inspector Hodgson drove up to 16 Sitwell Close, at the beginning of what was to be a year-long investigation – and Hodgson's last case.

From that first meeting, the detective later claimed, he was struck by the smooth doctor's exaggerated sense of his own importance. As he ushered his visitor through the front door, Perera snapped at his wife: 'Get upstairs with the children.'

'She's only a wife, after all,' he told Hodgson. Seated in Perera's front room, the policeman told him that he was

Above: *Philomena's home in Sri Lanka.*

Left: *Philomena's mother.*

FROM THEIR FIRST MEETING DETECTIVE INSPECTOR HODGSON WAS STRUCK BY PERERA'S ARROGANT SELF-ASSURANCE

making routine enquiries about the missing girl Nilanthe Philomena. Dr Perera was easy in his reply. Philomena, he said, had failed to settle, growing more and more homesick as the months passed. 'After all she was only a jungle girl.'

In April, he said, he had decided to take her home. He had taken her with him on a weekend trip to Catania in Sicily, where his brother lived. From there, the brother was to have put her on a flight to Sri Lanka.

Tom Hodgson returned to his desk at Wood Street to set in motion a long and careful series of checks, first with the airport authorities and then with Interpol.

First, the airport authorities: had Dr Perera booked a flight to Sicily with his adopted daughter from any British airport at any time in the early months of the year? No.

Next, Interpol came back to Hodgson with the result of their enquiries in Sicily and Sri Lanka. The girl had not turned up there. It seemed likely, therefore, that she must still be in the British Isles.

Meanwhile, Hodgson had paid several surreptitious visits to the Dental Department of Leeds Medical School, winkling out details of Dr Perera and his ways. 'Arrogant' was the word repeatedly used by his colleagues of Perera.

SEARCH FOR THE BODY

By now, Hodgson had no doubt in his own mind that Perera was a murderer. But where was the body? Hodgson's best course of action seemed to lie in shaking Perera into making some kind of a move – perhaps shifting the body to a safer hiding-place. To this end the tenacious

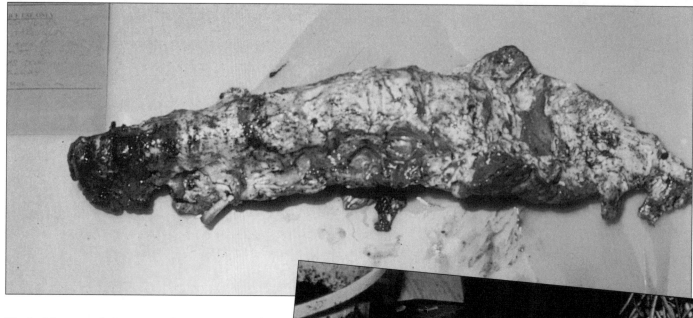

Yorkshireman began to play a cat and mouse game with the doctor, making it clear to him that he was being watched – 'showing out', in police parlance – and making several personal calls at his home to interview him on small points.

Just before Christmas 1984, Inspector Hodgson decided to give his quarry a good shake-up. 'I knew by this time that something was seriously wrong, so I started to put pressure on him. I told him I was coming to see him at the university on the first day of the new term in January 1985. Perera started blustering, saying I was making assertions I could not prove.'

And then, on 4 February 1985, came dramatic evidence to justify Hodgson's pressure tactics. A colleague of Perera's who shared a desk and cupboards with him noticed a large brown envelope in one of the desk drawers. It contained a human jawbone with several teeth present, and a number of pieces of human skull. Aware of the police interest in Dr Perera, the lecturer made a rapid search of other drawers and cupboards used by the Sri Lankan. He found a five-litre glass beaker, a coffee jar with a screw-top lid, and a shallow, stainless steel tray. Each of these contained small bones and bone fragments, immersed in a bluish liquid which later proved to be a decalcifying fluid which would ultimately have dissolved the bones completely. None of these bones appeared to have anything to do with orthodox dental research.

Top: *A piece of human spine found in a plant pot in Perera's house.*

Above: *Pieces of human flesh were found under geranium plants in two other pots.*

A UNIVERSITY COLLEAGUE NOTICED AMONG PERERA'S BELONGINGS A BROWN ENVELOPE CONTAINING HUMAN BONES

The lecturer telephoned Wood Street Police Station, and Hodgson arranged for the remains to be transferred to Wakefield. He also arranged for Dr Perera to come to the station to assist the police with their enquiries.

Early the next morning, Mrs Perera and her two children were taken into care from the house in Sitwell Close. Overall-clad policemen arrived at their home with spades, trowels and gardener's riddles.

THE SEARCH FOR EVIDENCE

The police eventually turned to the Department of Forensic Medicine at Sheffield University. Head of the department and holder of the chair of forensic pathology at the university was Professor Alan Usher, whose active career spanned over thirty years.

Several identical 'murder bags' containing equipment for on-site investigation were always kept packed and ready in Professor Usher's office. On receiving Hodgson's call he picked one up, loaded it into his car, and set off on the hour-long drive to Wakefield and the suburb of Sandal.

When he arrived, the police were already digging in the garden at Sitwell Close. Between the rear of the garage and the garden fence they had excavated an oblong hole about five feet by three feet, and were sieving the earth through large garden riddles. On a plastic sheet by the hole lay a tooth, a small bone and a long hank of dark, earth-clotted hair.

A brief examination convinced Usher that the bone and tooth were human. They were docketed and placed in samples envelopes for later scrutiny.

As the police continued their digging outside, Usher and the two senior detectives entered the hallway of the house. The first objects to confront them were three large plastic plant pots. The central one was raised, and contained a narrow leaved plant. The other two, containing geraniums, stood on the floor on either side.

'The plants seemed very small for such large pots,' recalled Professor Usher, 'and they didn't seem to be doing terribly well. They were wilting somewhat.' When the professor bent to examine them further he caught a distinct whiff of the sickly-sweet stench of decaying flesh.

Ouside the door stood a plastic dustbin. Usher placed its upturned lid on the ground and very carefully decanted the contents of the central plant pot on to this ad hoc examination table.

What met their eyes gave Chief Superintendent Walter Cowman, at least, one of the more unpleasant frissons of his long career. 'I don't think I shall ever forget,' he said later, 'the sight of a virtually complete human spine curled around the roots of the plant.'

The two geranium pots were emptied in turn. Plant, earth and roots slid out in a solid lump, revealing that the geraniums were embedded in some browning, slimy material. It was rotting human flesh.

Eventually Professor Usher's team were to identify a total of 106 bony fragments which, in their opinion, came from 77 individual bones or parts of bones. They had been gathered from eight different sites – four at home, four in the Leeds lab – accessible to Samuel Perera.

PIECING TOGETHER A HUMAN JIGSAW

But that was in the future. In that second week of February 1985, Usher was faced with the long and tedious task of 'defatting' the bones. This meant stripping them of their remaining fat and flesh, and then with infinite care attaching numbers to them so that each tiny piece of the jigsaw could be identified, and the source not be lost, as attempts were made to rearticulate them into the semblance of a skeleton.

It was a colossal project, and one of the most complex ever undertaken. Over a period of time Usher assembled a

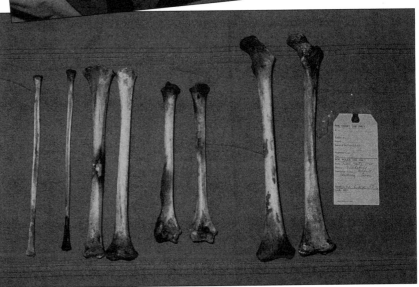

Left and below: *A holdall was found containing a collection of human bones.*

seven-man team of distinguished experts, headed by himself.

The anatomist's role was filled by Professor G.N.C. Crawford. Then there were Professor R.D. Grainger, Professor of Radiodiagnosis at Sheffield Medical School; Dr G.T. Craig, senior lecturer in oral pathology at Sheffield University and an expert in forensic dentistry; Dr Y.Z. Erzinclioglu, an entomologist from Cambridge University – brought in to study organisms in the soil; Dr P.J. Tarff, a postgraduate student, and Mr D.R. Jarvis, Usher's senior medical scientific officer.

SCIENTIFIC KNOW-HOW

The deliberations of the seven experts took several months, for they had several vital points to establish: points which should eventually satisfy a court of law.

First, were the bones human, and were they the bones of one person only? The answers to both questions were affirmative. Second, what of sex? In general the bones were gracile and slender, with little evidence of any strong muscular markings: 'Though not conclusive in themselves, the delicacy of the bones and the lack of muscular development are predominantly female characteristics,' said Professor Usher, 'and these facts, coupled with the pelvic angles and Professor Grainger's radiological studies, satisfied us that these were the bones of a female.'

Like sex, the determination of age was difficult from the incomplete remains. In the end, Usher took data from previous

Above: *A tray of bone fragments in decalcifying fluid was found in the laboratory where Perera worked.*

Below: *Police digging up Perera's garden in the search for evidence.*

enquiries in conjunction with independent assessments made by Professor Grainger, radiologically, and Dr Craig, using dental methods, and came to the firm conclusion that the remains were those of a person 'certainly not seventeen years old and most probably between twelve and fifteen years old at the time of death'.

The establishment of the exact race of the dead person proved, in the end, impossible. Again the bones were so fragmented that little significance could be made of, for instance, skull shape. However, Dr Craig found certain deposits on the front upper and lower molar to be so unusual as to suggest that the skeleton was not Caucasian.

As this complicated work was being carried out at the Sheffield Medico-Legal Centre, a team from the University's Department of Television and Graphics was preparing a series of charts showing the bones recovered in relation to the average human skeleton. These charts would later prove invaluable in court.

For it was towards the criminal courts, of course, that these enquiries were inexorably heading.

The entomological studies performed by Dr Erzinclioglu were in themselves proving quite damning to Dr Perera. Tiny insect pupae on many of the bones showed that they had first been buried at an outdoor site – and soil samples matched those of the Sitwell Close garden – before being transferred indoors, first beneath the house floor and then into the oral biology laboratories at Leeds University.

The degree of putrefaction found in the

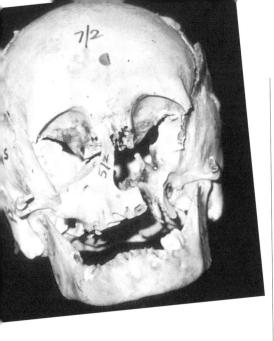

Left: *The reconstructed skull of the victim.*

THE SUSPECT CLAIMED THAT THE FLESH IN THE FLOWER POTS WAS PORK, WHICH HE WAS EXPERIMENTING WITH AS A FERTILIZER

claimed that the flesh in the flower pots had been pork, which he was trying as a new kind of fertilizer. Analysis of the flesh proved this to be palpable nonsense.

Then he claimed that the partial destruction of bones in his laboratory was necessary to his research work. While it is true that decalcification of bone does play a part in dental pathology, the samples used are invariably small – usually no bigger than a postage stamp. And the study of ribs, pelvises and long bones is hardly relevant to dental medicine.

'It simply wasn't possible, due to the fragmentary nature of the remains, to come to any firm conclusion as to the cause of the young girl's death,' admitted Professor Usher.

'But from the systematic attempts made to destroy and dispose of her body, I would strongly deduce that she died of foul play. All indications were that this was the body of Nilanthe Philomena Perera.'

In desperation, Perera tried one last ploy. His new story was that he had

mass of flesh in the central plant pot meant that death had occurred at least six months prior to discovery and possibly a great deal earlier than that. 'What it all came down to,' remarked Professor Usher dryly, 'was that I could conceive of no legitimate purpose for what was literally half a human torso being concealed in a domestic flower pot.'

By now Perera was, as one detective put it, 'losing some of his cool'. First, he

Below: *Professor Usher sifting through the contents of the plant pots.*

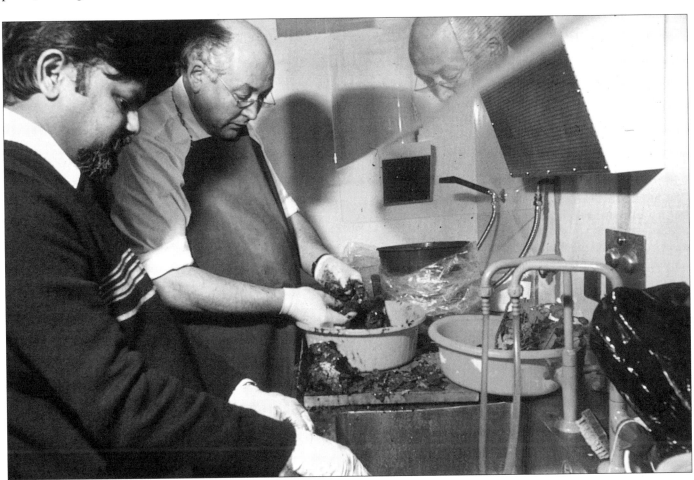

obtained the corpse of a young girl legitimately from a Sri Lankan university for medical purposes and had brought it to England in his suitcase, knowing that open importation would be prohibited.

'Again,' said Usher, 'the idea that someone would voluntarily carry such a huge mass of mouldering flesh and bone about, in hand luggage, was to my mind quite preposterous.'

Nevertheless, Cowman and Hodgson decided to check out this latest tale and travelled to Sri Lanka to interview the university authorities. They discovered that Perera had never been given a body for research, for export or otherwise.

'In many ways,' said Cowman, 'Sri Lankan society is living under Victorian standards, but their ledgers were a policeman's dream. Everything was written out in copperplate longhand.'

The two West Yorkshire policemen also met Nilanthe's grieving father, who confirmed that she had left for England with the Pereras and had never returned.

So what were Perera's motives for killing his adopted 'jungle girl'? Some sort of sex angle seemed likely, in view of Mrs Perera's earlier comments to the neighbours when Nilanthe first vanished. In any case, a jury at Leeds Crown Court found him guilty of unlawfully killing the girl, and on 11 March 1986 Dr Samuel Perera was gaoled for life.

In every way it had been a classic murder investigation, an immaculate piece of scientific and lay detection. Walter Cowman, who became head of Lincolnshire CID after the trial, commented: 'If Tom Hodgson had not been determined, had not refused to accept explanations which others may have accepted, who knows how things may have turned out?'

For Tom Hodgson, it set the seal on his police career. He retired soon afterwards. For Professor Usher the scientific side of the investigation was a personal triumph, but he is quick to point up Hodgson's part in the affair. 'To me, the abiding delight of the case was that this arrogant intellectual murderer obviously thought he was vastly superior to the hick Yorkshire copper who came to question him. But the final score was a resounding game, set and match to Tom.'

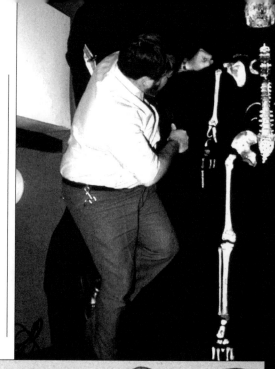

Right: *A team of experts spent several months reconstructing the victim's skeleton.*

Below: *The diagram shows which bones were found in Perera's laboratory and which in his house.*

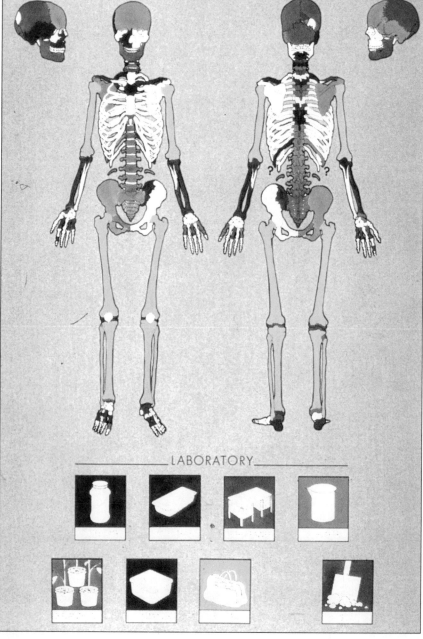

LABORATORY

CRIMES
OF
PASSION

RUTH ELLIS
Spurned in Love

On a summer's day in 1955 a woman walked out of the condemned cell in Holloway prison to await the hangman's noose. Having shot to death a lover who had treated her appallingly, Ruth Ellis became the last woman in Britain to be executed.

F or most of the year, the north London suburb of Hampstead keeps to itself on the edge of its leafy and spacious Heath. But at Easter the area's tranquillity is jovially disrupted. Outsiders flock in, as they have done for 150 years, to enjoy the fun of the fair. Lights and music flicker and boom across the green slopes, and the balmy spring air is scented with the pungent odour of fried onions from the fast food stalls.

On the evening of Easter Sunday, 10 April 1955, everything was running true to form. Downhill from the fairground, the Magdala pub in South Hill Park was packed and boisterous. Just after nine o'clock two young men parked their grey green Vauxhall Vanguard van and crossed the road to push into the saloon bar.

AS THE TWO MEN LEFT THE PUB A SMARTLY DRESSED BLONDE EMERGED FROM THE SHADOWS WITH A SMITH AND WESSON IN HER HAND

Twenty-six-year-old David Blakely and his friend Clive Gunnell had been to the fair, and were now after a quick drink before buying beer to take out to a nearby party.

As they re-emerged, neither of them noticed the slender blonde standing with her back to the wall of the pub. She was twenty-nine, her name was Ruth Ellis, and she had had a stormy relationship with Blakely which had lasted for two years. That evening, her pale, pretty face was grim behind her horn-rimmed spectacles as she called out: 'David!'

Blakely had been intent on avoiding Ruth all day. Now he ignored her. 'David!' she said again, sharply. Clive Gunnell looked up and saw that she was holding a .38 Smith and Wesson service revolver which was levelled at his friend.

David Blakely turned from the door of his van, opened his mouth, and then dropped his car keys and the bottle of beer he was holding as the first bullet slammed into his white shirt. A second bullet knocked Blakely on to his back.

'Clive!' Blakley's voice was a gurgled choke.

'Get out of the way, Clive,' said Ruth, deadly calm. She pulled the trigger again. Blakely, crawling on his stomach by now, was slammed into the tarmac. She

Above: *Ruth had a brief and not very successful stab at modelling.*

Right: *David Blakely, Ruth Ellis's lover and eventual victim.*

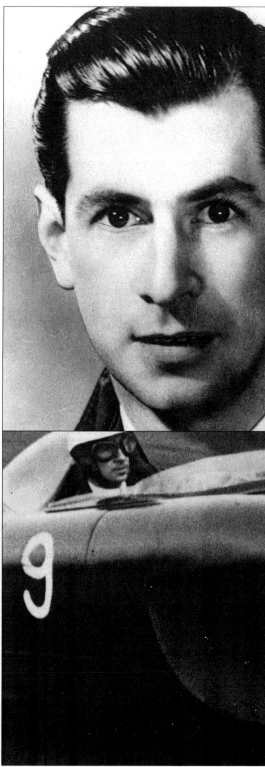

Leonard Crawford at Hampstead's Haverstock Hill police station, David Blakely was being declared dead on arrival at nearby New End Hospital.

When cautioned by DCS Crawford, Ruth Ellis was detached and composed. 'I am guilty,' she said. 'I am rather confused.' Then, little by little, she began to spill out her story...

positioned herself beside him, and then she fired twice more, sending fragments flying from the back of his jacket.

David Blakely lay prone and still. Ruth unfocussed from what she had done, looked Gunnell blankly in the eye, raised the pistol to her own temple, and pulled the trigger. Amazingly, the 'four-inch Smith', renowned for its reliability, did nothing.

She lowered the gun to her side and almost absent-mindedly tried the trigger again. The sixth and last bullet splintered the pavement, whined off up the road and clipped the hand of a passer-by, Mrs Gladys Kensington Yule.

Ellis and Gunnell stood facing each other. The whole bloody little drama had lasted less than ninety seconds, but those six shots were to reverberate for an unconscionable time in criminal history.

Someone had already called for the police and an ambulance when Ellis herself seemed to come out of a trance to tell a young man nearby: 'Fetch the police.'

'I am the police,' said Alan Thompson, an off-duty Hampstead officer who had been drinking in the pub. He took the pistol from her hand – inadvertently smudging latent prints, as it later proved – and led her off to await the squad car.

By the time it delivered Ruth into the hands of Detective Chief Superintendent

'FETCH THE POLICE,' SAID ELLIS TO A BYSTANDER. 'I AM THE POLICE,' REPLIED THE OFF-DUTY OFFICER AS HE TOOK THE GUN FROM HER

FROM FACTORY WORKER TO CLUB HOSTESS

It had begun a quarter of a century previously in Rhyl, North Wales, where Ruth was born the daughter of dance band musician Arthur Neilson and his wife Bertha on 9 October 1926. When Ruth was fifteen the family moved to Southwark in south London, and the girl found work in the local Oxo factory. She was ordered to take a year off work after contracting rheumatic fever. As part of her convalescence she took up dancing.

By 1943 she was working as a dance hall photographer's assistant when she met a Canadian soldier named Clare, and in September 1944, she bore him a son, christened Andria. Unfortunately Clare proved to have a wife back home, and Ruth, her mother Bertha and her older married sister Muriel were left to care for the boy.

In 1945, with the war in Europe ending and Ruth in her nineteenth year, she found another kind of career when she met Morris Conley.

Conley was a property racketeer, pimp and gangster who was to be dubbed 'Britain's biggest vice boss' by the press. But he did not attempt to draw Ruth into prostitution. Astutely, he spotted her greater potential as a club hostess.

At that time Britain's licensing laws were stringent. Pubs were permitted to open for only nine hours or less a day.

To beat the drinks ban, afternoon and late-night drinking clubs were set up, often in seedy basements and garret rooms. Usually there were rooms off the main bar where the prostitutes who were an integral part of such places could entertain their clients.

Conley owned a number of these dives in Soho, Bayswater and Kensington. Most were sleazy, but a few, like his Court Club in Duke Street near Marble Arch, catered for the raffish 'officer classes' with money to spend. He set Ruth up as hostess at the Court, and her rather tinsel good looks and natural wit were soon drawing in a fast set of hard-spending drinkers.

Ruth herself was soon earning up to £20 a week – about ten times the national average. For a time, she and her infant son lived well.

> A SINGLE MOTHER AT SEVENTEEN, RUTH TURNED TO NUDE MODELLING TO SUPPORT HERSELF AND HER CHILD

Below: *For a while, David Blakely had the money to race cars but lacked the talent to do it particularly well.*

SHORT-LIVED RESPECTABILITY

Despite her lifestyle, Ruth Neilson's maternal instincts, though erratic, were strong. She yearned for respectability not only for herself but for Andria. When she met George Johnston Ellis, a forty-one-year-old-dentist with a practice in Surrey, she thought she had it within her grasp.

Ellis was a bore and a drunk, but Ruth pursued him, moved in with him and finally, in November 1950, married him.

In October 1951 the couple had a daughter, Georgina, though by then the marriage was over. Ruth now had two young children to support. After recovering from Georgina's birth, she went back to London. Morris Conley was delighted to see her, and in October 1953 he made her manageress of his Little Club in Brompton Road, Knightsbridge.

A NEW JOB AND NEW ADMIRERS

She was paid £15 per week plus commission, with a £10 per week entertainment allowance, and a rent-free two-bedroom flat above the club rooms. Even if the job lacked respectability, it

was security of a sort. But among her first customers were two men destined to be fatal to her very existence.

Desmond Cussen was a rich and well-established businessman, with a large car and an elegant bachelor flat in Devonshire Place, near Baker Street. Aged thirty-two, he had had several minor affairs, but when he set eyes on Ruth Ellis it was love at first sight.

For her part she was fond of him – with his money and status he fitted her needs very nicely. But within hours of their first meeting a complication in the shape of a handsome young drone named David Blakely was to enter the picture.

The first time Blakely came to the Little Club he was drunk and abusive. Ruth had him thrown out, commenting: 'I hope never to see that little shit again.'

But Blakely came back to apologise, and Ruth let him buy her a drink. Within a month, Blakely had moved into Ruth's flat above the club.

David Blakely was twenty-four when he first entered Ruth Ellis's life. He had been born on 17 June 1929 in Sheffield, the fourth child of a Scottish doctor. In 1940 his parents divorced, and David's mother married a well-to-do racing driver named Humphrey Cook, who imbued his stepson with a love of his sport.

Blakely's real father had left him £7,000 – then a considerable sum. Between about 1951 and his death David was to spend all of that and more on his dream, a prototype racing car that he called the Emperor. The Emperor was probably his only real love, though Ruth Ellis learned this too late.

So Blakely moved into Ruth's rooms above the Little Club, and they began a turbulent affair. Blakely had a fiancée, Linda Dawson, the daughter of a rich Halifax millowner, whom he tried to string along for a while, but he lost her as his life became more and more centred on Ruth.

Ruth Ellis's first judgement of Blakely had in fact been the correct one. Most of his acquaintances thought him a 'little shit' and he proved it by living off his new mistress, cadging drinks from her club and openly flirting with her female customers.

The pair had violent rows, but Ruth

BLAKELY'S PROTOTYPE RACING CAR, AFFECTIONATELY KNOWN AS THE EMPEROR, WAS PROBABLY HIS ONLY REAL LOVE

Below: *Ruth had a passion for night life.*

---

tolerated Blakely's behaviour until it started driving customers away. She had a confrontation with Morris Conley about it and, favourite or no, she was fired.

Meanwhile, Desmond Cussen had proved a faithful friend to Ruth, constantly by her side whenever she felt the need of a shoulder to cry on. When Conley threw her out of her job and her flat, it was he who took her into his own apartment along with Andria – Georgina had by then been adopted. Cussen and Ellis slept together, but her benefactor was by no means possessive. He allowed her to go on seeing Blakely, and even connived at the pair sleeping in his flat.

A CYCLE OF BETRAYAL, VIOLENCE AND RECONCILIATION

In August 1954 Blakely finally broke off his engagement with Linda Dawson. Ruth thought, wrongly, that this was for her benefit. Blakely took her to Buckinghamshire and his family, but she was treated there as a London tart. And she discovered that he was in any case sleeping with other women.

One of these was Carole Findlater, wife of Anthony 'Ant' Findlater, a skilled amateur mechanic who worked on Blakely's Emperor. He and Clive Gunnell, another skilled mechanic, were almost as keen as Blakely on the expensive racing car.

After every betrayal there followed

gin-soaked acrimony, violence and finally reconciliation. But it was a punishing cycle which must have damaged Cussen almost as much as the two principals.

In any case, in January 1955 he paid for a one-bedroom service flat at 44 Egerton Gardens, Kensington. Ruth – and by tacit agreement Blakely – could now have privacy, of a sort, for their rows.

That spring, Ruth discovered she was pregnant. Her divorce from George Ellis was almost final, and Blakely was free, but when she brought up the subject of marriage his response was to beat her so badly that she miscarried. The usual boozy, tearful remorse followed, with Blakely sending a bunch of red carnations and a note of apology.

On Good Friday, 7 April, they spent what was to be their last night together. Over breakfast Blakely gave her a signed photograph proclaiming his love, and finally proposed to her. They parted with Ruth blissfully happy, and with Blakely promising to take her to drinks with the Findlaters that evening. But he failed to keep his promise.

Instead, he went alone to meet the Findlaters at the Magdala. He told them that Ruth had him trapped, that he wanted to leave her, but that he feared the consequences. And he had a sympathetic audience. Both Ant and Carole thought Ellis a grasping, vulgar woman, totally unsuitable for their friend. They suggested that Blakely stay with them for the Easter holiday.

The following morning was Easter

> WHEN RUTH TOLD BLAKELY SHE WAS PREGNANT HE BEAT HER UP SO BADLY THAT SHE SUFFERED A MISCARRIAGE

Saturday, and the fair on Hampstead Heath was in full swing. Blakely, the Findlaters, Clive Gunnell and other friends spent a jovial day.

Ruth Ellis spent a distracted one. On the previous evening, she had insisted that Cussen drive her to Hampstead in search of Blakely, but she was turned away from the Findlaters' house in Tanza Road, just up from the Magdala.

Now she returned, banging vainly on the Findlaters' front door and ringing them from a telephone box nearby – only to have them hang up on her. In the afternoon she began to kick Blakely's Vanguard van, screaming at the top of her voice, and the police were called to send her away.

Finally, on Sunday evening, she took a taxi to Tanza Road, spotted Blakely and Gunnell getting into the van, and followed them to the Magdala. She had a revolver in her bag....

ARREST AND TRIAL

That, in essence, was the story Ruth Ellis told DCS Crawford. She remembered little, she said, about Sunday afternoon, other than that 'I intended to find David, and shoot him.'

And therein lay the whole case, as far as the police were concerned. Ruth Ellis had cold-bloodedly gunned down her lover in front of a pub full of witnesses, and then admitted to the crime. But where had she got the gun? Unfortunately PC Thompson, in taking the weapon from her, had accidentally

Above: *Ruth and Desmond enjoy an evening out with friends.*

wiped all prints from it.

However, Ruth said that she had had the gun and ammunition for three years. It had been left with her as a pledge against a bar bill by one of her customers. The police were satisfied with her story.

So Ellis was charged with murder and removed to Holloway women's prison to await trial.

On 11 May 1955 she was arraigned at the Central Criminal Court of the Old Bailey before Mr Justice Barrie. The defence team was a distinguished and formidable one: Melford Stevenson QC, Sebag Shaw and Peter Rawlinson. Melford Stevenson asked for, and was granted, an adjournment of forty days in order to look for a precedent which would allow his client to plead guilty to manslaughter provoked by jealousy.

Unfortunately, no precedent could be found. Accordingly, when the trial proper began on 20 June, Ruth was advised to plead not guilty in the hope that her story would sway the jury to pity. But Stevenson had reckoned without Ruth's vanity.

Throughout her stay in Holloway, her main concern seems to have been that mousy roots were beginning to show through her platinum hair, and the day before her trial the Governor, Dr Charity Taylor, allowed her to bleach it. The result was that when she appeared in court she cut an impossibly glamorous figure in her smart black suit. Her lawyers were convinced that her dazzling

Right: *Mr and Mrs Neilson, Ruth Ellis's parents, leave their home in Hemel Hempstead to visit Ruth on the eve of her execution.*

appearance alienated half the jury before the evidence was heard.

As it was, the trial lasted barely two days. On 21 June the jury took just twenty-three minutes to return a verdict of guilty, and made no recommendation for mercy. Ruth Ellis was sentenced to death by hanging.

PUBLIC OUTRAGE

Back in Holloway she refused her solicitor, Victor Mishcon, permission to appeal on her behalf, though he wrote in vain to the Home Secretary begging for mercy. Instead she asked her brother, Granville, to smuggle in poison so that she could kill herself. He refused.

Granville Neilson, in fact, rightly mistrusted Ruth's story of how she had come by the fatal gun, and spent his time in a frantic search for its real owner.

Meanwhile the general public – women in particular – launched an outcry against the sentence. Letters were written to MPs and petitions were launched.

It was all to no avail. As the clock began to strike nine on the morning of 13

July 1955, Ruth drank a last glass of brandy and walked steadfastly to the Holloway gallows.

There is no retrospective doubt that Ellis's death was a turning point in the anti-hanging campaign, though another decade was to pass before the rope was abolished competely.

THE MISSING DETAILS EMERGE

It took even longer for what seems to have been the real truth to emerge. On the night before her death, Ruth summoned Victor Mishcon to the condemned cell and dictated her account of what she said really happened on that fateful Easter Sunday.

Desmond Cussen, she said, had given her the gun. The pair had been drinking Pernod in Cussen's flat while Ruth poured out her misery. Cussen drove her and the boy Andria out to Epping Forest, where he had shown her how to load the weapon and had given her tips on aiming and firing.

Later that afternoon, after having more to drink, she had taken the loaded pistol and demanded that Cussen – not a taxi, as she had stated – drive her to the Findlaters' house in Tanza Road. From there she had made her way to the Magdala.

If this was true, what were Cussen's motives? He was certainly besotted with Ruth, lavishing money, presents and offers of marriage upon her. He had never refused her slightest whim. Perhaps he was simply going along blindly, as usual, with her wishes.

Or, as has been suggested, did he simply give her the gun, knowing that in her mood of jealous, drink-fuelled rage she would kill his rival Blakely. In which case, was he also convinced that she would be acquitted?

Desmond Cussens visited Ruth Ellis every day during her remand in Holloway prison, bringing her flowers, chocolates and other presents. But as soon as the guilty verdict was pronounced he broke all contact with her. He died twenty years after his troubled lover, in Australia, without apparently ever having told his side of the story.

Below: *Huge crowds gathered outside Holloway Prison on the morning of Ruth Ellis's execution.*

MADAME FAHMY
Driven to Kill

The fashionable French society woman had no idea of the horrors that awaited her after her marriage to a rich and elegant Egyptian. But it was not the fact that she murdered him so much as the nature of the trial defence that caused a furore

Opposite: *Born Marie Marguérite Alibert, Madame Fahmy found wealth and respectability in her marriage to a wealthy Egyptian, Prince Ali Kamel Fahmy Bey.*

Right: *The .25 Browning automatic which killed Prince Ali Kamel Fahmy Bey.*

Below: *Prince Ali Kamel Fahmy Bey was charming and vastly wealthy. His annual income in the 1920s was estimated at more than £100,000.*

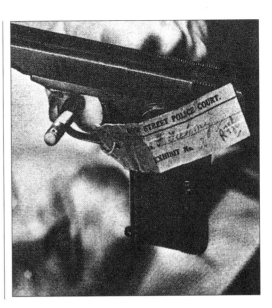

O n 10 July 1923, the *Daily Telegraph* reported the worst thunderstorm in London's memory.

'The outbreak appeared to travel from the direction of Kingston and Richmond. Soon afterwards the storm reached London itself, and broke with all its fury...the lightning was vivid to a degree ...heavy crashes of thunder grew in a mighty crescendo, intense and majestic...as the storm swept irresistibly over the city....'

As this celestial turmoil began to die away a mundane, human one was reaching its peak in the Savoy Hotel, and for years afterwards Londoners who remembered the 'night of the great storm' were also to remember it as 'the night that Madame Fahmy killed her Prince'.

THE TAXI DRIVER'S DAUGHTER

As it chanced, the most celebrated husband killer to escape the gallows in the history of twentieth-century British crime could speak not a word of English. She was born Marie Marguérite Alibert on 9 December 1890, the daughter of a Paris cab driver, and from an early age was known as Marguérite, shortened by her friends to Maggie.

She reached her early teens tall, slender and elegant, with striking chestnut hair that fell to her knees. But

Right: *A lover of high fashion, Mme Fahmy photographed in September 1923, days before her trial for murdering her husband.*

BY THE AGE OF SIXTEEN THE WELL-EDUCATED (AND WELL-DEVELOPED) CONVENT GIRL HAD A BABY

she was also sexually forward, and by her sixteenth birthday had an illegitimate daughter whom she called Raymonde.

The daughter was sent to live with an aunt in the Paris suburbs, while Maggie herself was despatched to Bordeaux to live with family friends. There she met a rich admirer, Paul Channon, who proposed to her. Unfortunately he was married, and when his wife refused him a divorce he consoled Maggie, by then twenty-three years old, with gifts of property, including a villa in Deauville and an elegant flat in Paris.

The following year, the Great War swept across Europe. Maggie put herself, her Renault car and her new flat at the service of the Red Cross, and in her spare time sang in charity concerts.

During this busy wartime service she re-encountered an old friend from Bordeaux, Charles Laurent, and the pair were married in 1919. Charles worked at the Japanese Consulate in Paris. When, a couple of years later, he was offered a post in Tokyo, he was delighted, but Marguérite flatly refused to leave France.

There was no question of where Charles's heart lay. He offered his wife a divorce, his house in Paris and a generous allowance until she remarried. Then he set off for the Orient.

If Maggie was upset, she managed to conceal it very well. She gave lavish parties, bought clothes at the top fashion houses and was escorted to the opera, fashionable restaurants and galleries by the most eligible young men in Paris.

ENTER THE EGYPTIAN PRINCE

In January 1922 Maggie and a party of women friends took a limousine and drove to the Mediterranean, where they embarked for Egypt. Putting up at the Shepheard's Hotel in Cairo, they set about exploring the sights and night life.

Towards the end of their stay they were attending a soirée, when one of the Egyptian guests sent a message to Maggie asking to be allowed to organize a 'fête Vénitienne' on his yacht in her honour. The generous would-be party giver was twenty-one-year-old Prince Ali Kamel Fahmy Bey, who had recently inherited from his father vast cotton plantations, property and shares in shipping and banking which brought him an estimated income of £100,000 per year.

Swarthily handsome, and dressed in white and gold robes set off by a red fez, Prince Ali – the title was an honorary one granted by the Egyptian government in recognition of his gifts to charity – was unused to being turned down. But in this instance he got the cold shoulder. Madame Laurent was greedy for neither money nor admirers and in any case she was missing Paris and eager to go home.

Back home, Maggie launched into the joys of Paris in the spring. But towards the beginning of May she caught sight of a familiar figure eyeing her from across a smoky salon. Despite his pin-stripe Savile Row suit and temporary lack of fez, there was no mistaking Prince Ali Fahmy Bey. She ignored him, or at least appeared to do so.

In fact, as she was to confess to the *People* newspaper, she had by this time checked him out thoroughly. Ali had been sired by a noble Turkish Muslim – hence the hereditary title 'Bey'. His father, besides inheriting wealth, had made even more money after being trained by the British as an engineer. In the hope that young Ali would make some sort of career for himself, the boy had been sent to public school in England, and to a Paris academy. As a result he was fluent in both these languages.

Still, for the next few weeks she shunned his company, though he seemed to crop up at every reception she attended. The crunch came in July when she went to spend a few days in Deauville. There she was approached by a rich Moroccan woman, who told her that an admirer wished to meet her when

they got back to Paris. According to Marguérite's unlikely testimony, 'the thought had never occurred' when they met for tea in the lounge of the Majestic Hotel on 30 July 'that the individual who so longed to meet me was this Egyptian "Prince"'.

But, she admitted, most of that first meeting was taken up with 'gentle raillery concerning me having avoided him for so long'. When, after tea, he suggested a drive to the Château de Madrid, giving her the choice of riding in either a Rolls Royce limousine or a Bugatti 'torpedo', she was captivated. She chose the Rolls.

For the next fortnight they spent almost every day together, driving and dining and meeting mutual friends. He was, as she told the *People* reporter, 'a man of exceptional powers of fascination. Never have I met a man who possessed to such a degree that kind of charm which we are accustomed to call Oriental.

'His eyes were remarkably expressive, striking one with the exceptionally caressing quality of their glance....' But, she added, she had already noticed that those eyes were capable of 'suddenly hardening on occasions into a ferocity which was positively terrifying'.

She was also rather intimidated by Ali's personal entourage. Led by Said Enani, his right-hand man and private

Below left: *Prince Ali Fahmy Bey was a gift to contemporary cartoonists.*

Below: *Madame Fahmy, later described as a 'charming and attractive woman' by her defence counsel.*

secretary, it included a second secretary, a valet, a lawyer and a chauffeur-cum-bodyguard whom Marguérite was to describe as a 'chocolate-coloured Colossus'.

THE ORIENTAL CHARMER TURNS SERIOUS

It was not until mid-August, when Ali followed her to Deauville that his hitherto light-hearted approach took a serious turn. Or, as she put it, 'he made "des avances furieuses"'. When Marguérite resisted, Ali gathered together his entourage and swept off in a huff for a holiday in Italy.

From there he sent letters and presents – 'ransacking Cartier's for the latest in jewellery' – and proposals of marriage. Still she refused to join him. By the end of September he was back in Egypt, writing that he was 'sick with despair' that he was 'dying', and that 'your name alone is on my lips'.

Finally, on 17 November she agreed to visit him. Marguérite reached Alexandria on 22 November and was immediately whisked off to the palace of Zamalik on the Nile outside Cairo. Its splendour certainly lived up to Ali's promises.

Marguérite's suite had, she discovered, been designed for the pre-1914 King of

Above: London's fashionable Savoy Hotel where Prince Ali Fahmy Bey was shot to death.

ALI'S PERSONAL ENTOURAGE INCLUDED A CHAUFFEUR-CUM-BODYGUARD WHOM MARGUÉRITE DESCRIBED AS A 'CHOCOLATE-COLOURED COLOSSUS'

ONLY WEEKS AFTER THE WEDDING MARGUÉRITE SENT HER LAWYER A LETTER STATING THAT ALI HAD VOWED TO AVENGE HIMSELF ON HER

Serbia. The bed was huge and shaped like a ceremonial boat, the bath was of solid silver with white marble surrounds, and the whole thing was swagged in white and gold silk. On the elegant Empire dressing table was a toilet set made of gold and tortoiseshell, with Marguérite's initials in diamonds.

A QUEER KIND OF MARRIAGE

Amidst this elaborate splendour Ali proposed, and Marguérite, after a few days' thought, accepted. On 26 December the wedding was celebrated with a lavish reception at Shepheard's Hotel. During the proceedings the couple were married according to Muslim rights, and Marguérite was asked to swear that she would waive the right to divorce. This meant that, although Ali could at any time end their marriage by simply renouncing her in front of witnesses, Marguérite was now bound to him till death them did part.

The marriage was in trouble almost from the time that Ali's yacht steamed out of Cairo, bound up-river for Luxor on their honeymoon voyage. Ali immediately became brutal and literally perverse.

Despite her own sexual experience, Marguérite had so far allowed no intimacy between herself and Ali, who was ten years her junior.

Now, on her wedding night, she got a violent shock. The muscular Ali threw her face down on the bed and had anal intercourse with her. As she was later to explain to her English defence team, she tried to reason rather than remonstrate with her husband, but the following night he sodomized her again, causing her intense pain. Too late, she realised that Ali's entourage had mostly consisted of handsome young men.

From Zamalik on 22 January 1923, two months to the day after her arrival at Alexandria and less than a month since her nightmare union began, she managed to send a letter to her lawyer in Paris. It was to be produced at her trial and, headed 'THE SECRET DOCUMENT', was destined to make world headlines.

'I Marie Marguérite Alibert, of full age, of sound mind and body, formally accuse, in the case of my death, violent

Mme. Said, sister of the dead man, with her husband, Dr. Said (centre), and Abdul Faath Razal Bey, an Egyptian lawyer, representing Mme. Said.

Sir Henry Curtis Bennett, K.C., one of the counsel engaged for the defence.

Mr. Cecil Whiteley, K.C., who held a watching brief, arriving at the Old Bailey.

Said Enani, the dead man's secretary, said the couple were not very happy.

A new portrait, received from Paris last night, of Mme. Fahmy, who is charged with the murder of her husband, Ali Kamel Fahmy Bey (inset), a wealthy young Egyptian.

The large crowd that waited outside the Old Bailey in the hope of gaining admittance for the opening of the trial. Many fashionably-dressed women were present

SAVOY SHOOTING: MME. FAHMY'S TRIAL OPENS

The Daily Mirror

NET SALE MUCH THE LARGEST OF ANY DAILY PICTURE NEWSPAPER

No. 6,194. TUESDAY, SEPTEMBER 11, 1923 One Penny.

or otherwise, Ali Fahmy Bey of having contributed to my disappearance.

'Yesterday, 21 January, 1923, at three o'clock in the afternoon, he took his Bible or Koran – I do not know how it is called – kissed it, put his hand on it, and swore to avenge himself upon me tomorrow, in eight days, a month, or three months, but I must disappear by his hand. This oath was taken without any reason, neither jealousy, bad conduct, nor a scene on my part. I desire and demand justice for my daughter and for my family...' And there was a telling PS: 'Today he wanted to take my jewellery from me, hence a fresh scene.'

Ali's behaviour towards his wife seems to have improved during the rest of the winter, and when, in May, he was offered a minor diplomatic post in Paris, both were light-hearted as they booked in at the Majestic. To the entourage had been added another giant bodyguard named Le Costaud, whom Marguérite dubbed the 'Black Hercules'. Le Costaud took turns in guarding both Ali and his wife, but

Above: Madame Fahmy's trial dominated the popular press.

seems to have been hired more to keep an eye on the Fahmy jewels than on Marguérite herself. In any case Ali was sufficiently concerned about their mutual safety to buy a pair of neat little Browning .25 automatic pistols – 'his and hers' – to be kept by their bedsides.

Alongside her pleasure at being in her home town, Marguérite had a further reason for being glad to be in Paris: she needed medical attention. Ali Bey's continued sexual perversity had left her with piles, which a French doctor now told her would require surgical treatment. But before she could book an appointment in a clinic, her husband's exotic caravan was on the move again.

ANGRY SCENES AT THE SAVOY

On Sunday, 1 July Ali and Madame Marguérite Fahmy Bey booked into a suite of rooms on the fourth floor of the Savoy Hotel, London.

One of Marguérite's first acts was to contact a doctor to continue her treatment. Dr Edward Gordon listened sympathetically to her problem and was able to treat her on a daily basis.

On the morning of Monday, 9 July Dr Gordon, arrived with a specialist to see Marguérite. The specialist examined her, and advised her to have surgery without delay.

That day Marguérite, Ali, and the secretary Said Enani had lunch at the Savoy Grill. According to Said, who took no part in the noisy discussion, the couple argued about Marguérite's determination to go back to Paris for her operation. Fahmy suggested she should enter a Harley Street clinic.

In the evening the same trio shared an after-theatre supper at the Savoy. There, the lunchtime dispute began again. At one point, fellow diners were startled when Marguérite suddenly picked up an empty bottle and yelled to her husband, in French: 'Shut up – or I'll smash this over your head!'

A NIGHT OF VIOLENCE

At midnight the thunderstorm broke as Ali Fahmy Bey boarded a taxi and was swept off to Soho apparently to a

Above: *Detective Inspector Grosse attends the inquest into the shooting of Prince Ali Fahmy Bey.*

homosexual club. At about two o'clock, Ali returned to the hotel.

Half an hour later a night porter, John Beattie, was wheeling a luggage trolley along the corridor on the fourth floor, when he saw a swarthy man, clad in mauve silk pyjamas and green velvet slippers, step out into the corridor. As Beattie drew near, the man said: 'Look at my face! Look what she has done!'

Obediently, Beattie looked and saw a faintly ruddy mark on the guest's left cheek. He noticed that the suite door was open, and that the room was lit only by a table lamp. Suddenly, another door to the suite was flung open, and a woman in a low-cut evening dress which seemed to consist entirely of white pearls came out and began screaming in French.

Beattie vainly tried to persuade the agitated pair to return to their suite, then decided to leave them to it. He had just turned a corner in the corridor, when he heard three loud bangs – distinct, separate, nothing to do with the storm.

Beattie ran back, then stopped, stock still. The woman was standing with a small automatic pistol clutched in her hand. The hem of her glistening white gown was freckled with crimson.

At her feet lay the pyjama-clad Ali Fahmy Bey. He was flat on his back, his arms thrown defensively over his face, which was pouring with blood. Deadly little .25 bullets had pierced both upflung arms before tearing through his forehead and cheekbones. When Beattie reached him he was dying.

Madame Fahmy went back into her suite. She made two telephone calls, the first to Said Enani and the second to Dr Gordon. Then she fell into a tremulous fit of weeping.

Dr Gordon arrived almost simultaneously with Detective Inspector Edward Grosse, who took her to Bow Street police station, where she was charged with the murder of her husband. After the initial hearing, she was taken to Holloway gaol to await trial. The attentive Dr Gordon hired a limousine to take her there.

More importantly, the doctor spoke to London's most celebrated criminal solicitor, Freke Palmer, who agreed to organize Marguérite Fahmy's defence. He could not have picked a better team. To assemble the background and basics of the case he chose Sir Henry Curtis-Bennett and, as junior counsel, Roland Oliver. They were united under the leadership of the third team member, the celebrated and wildly histrionic defence counsel Sir Edward Marshall Hall KC.

Madame Fahmy's trial opened at the Old Bailey on Monday, 10 September, before Mr Justice Rigby Swift. The leading Crown counsel was Percival Clarke, and there were two women on the jury. The trial was to last for six days, extended because of the time taken to translate the proceedings between the defendant and the court – two translators worked turn and turn about.

In a firm, clear voice, Marguérite pleaded 'Non coupable.'

Briefly, Marshall Hall's task was to convince the jury that Marguérite had been abominably treated by her husband, and that she had killed him when she thought her life to be in danger.

After bullying Said Enani, and producing the celebrated gunsmith Robert Churchill to show that an inexperienced person could have fired three shots from a Browning automatic unwittingly, Sir Edward closed Tuesday's hearing with a speech which set the tone of his defence.

'Fahmy Bey, shortly before he was shot, attacked his wife like a raving, lustful beast because she would not agree to an outrageous suggestion he made – a suggestion which would fill every decent-minded person with utter revulsion. Almost throughout their miserably tragic life of six months, this treacherous Egyptian beast pursued his wife with this unspeakable request...until she was changed by fear from a charming, attactive woman to a poor quaking creature hovering on the brink of nervous ruin.'

The following day, Marguérite took the stand. To a hushed court, and through her interpreters, she told her story. Her sister Yvonne and her maid, Amy Pain, told of the bruises and lacerations they had seen on the defendant's body. Racism continued to be Marshall Hall's weapon: 'She made one mistake,' he said quietly, 'possibly the greatest mistake any woman of the West can make. She married an Oriental.' He went on to attack Egyptian morals and those of Ali Bey in particular.

Mr Justice Swift summed up, saying that he had been 'shocked, sickened, and disgusted' by some of the evidence. But it was Marshall Hall's eloquence which

> MARGUÉRITE'S HISTRIONIC DEFENCE LAWYER SPOKE PASSIONATELY OF LUST, REVULSION AND TRAGEDY IN THE COUPLE'S SHORT LIFE TOGETHER

Below: *Madame Fahmy at Chamoix, six months after she was acquitted of the murder of her husband.*

had settled matters. The jury gave a verdict of 'Not Guilty'.

After the trial the Egyptian Bar, as well as ambassadors and High Commissioners throughout the Middle East, lodged furious formal complaints with the Foreign Office about the nature of Marshall Hall's defence. The urbane advocate was eventually prevailed upon to sign a letter of apology to the offended governments – a small price to pay.

Madame Fahmy left the Savoy and put up at a discreet hotel in Jermyn Street, where she gave interviews to selected newspapers. Then, after paying private visits to friends, including Marshall Hall, to thank them for their support, she left for Paris. Two or three years later her name finally vanished from the gossip columns, as she herself disappeared into obscurity. The final destination of this most elegant of killers remains a mystery.

HARRY THAW
A Jealous Husband

New York society was thrown into uproar in the 1900s when a fashionable architect and notorious womanizer was publicly shot by a jealous husband. But the husband had grotesque sexual tastes and the subsequent revelations were sensational

One balmy summer evening in 1906, thirty-five-year-old New York playboy Harry Thaw fired three .44 calibre bullets into the teeth, neck and left eyeball of Stanford White, America's leading architect. The public sensation that followed was enormous.

First the shooting took place in full view of a fashionable society crowd packing the open air roof restaurant–theatre of Madison Square Garden for the opening of a new musical *Mam'zelle Champagne*. The killing was literally – though paradoxically – 'live' drama.

A fact which added extra zest was that those 'in the know' – which meant most of the trendy crowd present – had heard rumours that fifty-two-year-old White had been the lover of twenty-one-year-old Evelyn Thaw long before her husband set eyes upon her.

This was no murder, they suggested. Thaw had simply acted according to the unwritten law of the Old West, defending his wife's honour with an 'American' model .44 Smith and Wesson, the revolver favoured by Jesse James.

The Thaw-White affair took a considerable time for the courts to sort out. With hindsight, the threads are easier to unravel.

The dominant figure was undoubtedly Stanford White, standing over six feet

Above and right: *An object of desire. Evelyn Thaw, Harry's 21-year-old wife, was the cause of the animosity between Harry Thaw and Stanford White.*

Opposite: *Harry Thaw, the New York playboy who shot prominent architect, Stanford White, in front of hundreds of witnesses at Madison Square Gardens.*

REPORTERS FELT THAT IN SHOOTING HIS WIFE'S LOVER HARRY THAW HAD ACTED ON THE UNWRITTEN LAW OF THE WILD WEST

tall. At the time of his death his waxed handlebar moustache, long mutton-chop sideburns and smooth, neatly cropped hair were fading from their natural sandy colour to red-pepper-and-salt.

His works were enduring too. The Romanesque house for Tiffany on Madison Avenue, the Memorial Arch in

Right: *Stanford White was one of America's leading architects. He was also a legendary womanizer.*

Below: *Evelyn Thaw, a model since her early teens, was fond of being photographed in sensual and provocative poses.*

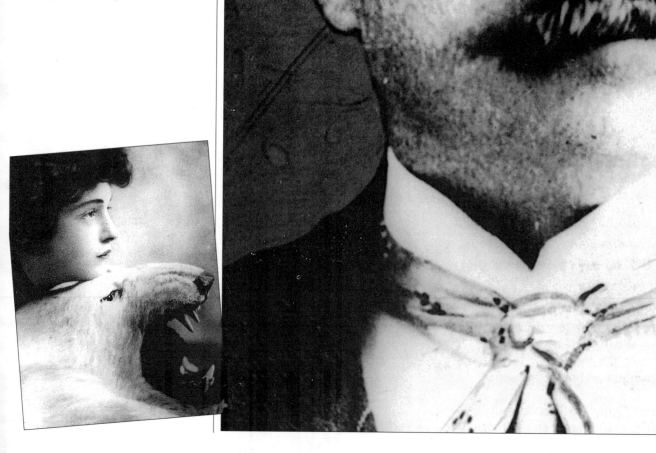

Washington Square, the domed Madison Square Presbyterian church and the Hall of Fame at New York University were all the products of Stanford White's fertile drawing board.

White was a New Yorker, born there in 1853. By the turn of the century Stanford White was living an elegant bachelor life, dividing his time between his mansion on Long Island, a luxury suite in Madison Square Garden and a studio apartment on East 22nd Street. At the last two addresses, White indulged his taste for young teenage girls – sometimes prostitutes, occasionally actresses – whom he picked up in the strictest secrecy; for by now his public profile was very high. In 1901 he met his ideal in the person of Evelyn Nesbit.

A CARRIAGE ARRIVED TO TAKE EVELYN TO A 'PARTY', BUT WHEN SHE ARRIVED AT HER 'GUARDIAN'S' STUDIO THERE WERE NO OTHER GUESTS

Below: *Harry Thaw as a young buck.*

FROM FATHER FIGURE TO SUGAR DADDY

Evelyn had been born on Christmas Day, 1884. By the age of fourteen, she was attracting the attention of photographers and painters in New York. She became precociously successful as a model, and a year later, in 1901, she joined the chorus of a popular musical *Floradora*. In August, White, an avid theatregoer, saw her and contrived an introduction.

Although sixteen, Evelyn looked younger, and appealed to both White's erotic and aesthetic tastes. White first courted her mother, Winifield Holman, and gradually convinced her that he was a suitable father-figure for Evelyn.

He began to groom the girl, buying her expensive clothes and schooling her in manners and deportment, and he also paid for her to complete her formal education at a college in New Jersey. Eventually, in the autumn of 1901, Winifield Holman was confident enough to leave her daughter in White's care while she herself went on a visit to Pittsburgh.

What Evelyn alleged happened while her mother was away was to be described by the girl in court six years later. His real intentions, according to Evelyn, were fully revealed one evening when a carriage arrived to take her to a party. On arrival, she found that she and White were the only guests. White explained that the others had failed to show up.

White asked her to go and see the back room. The back room turned out to be furnished with a large bed, two chairs and a 'tiny little table. There was a bottle of champagne, a small bottle, and one glass...'

'Mr White picked up the bottle and poured the glass full of champagne...then he came to me and told me to finish my champagne. I don't know whether it was a minute or two after, but a pounding began in my ears, then the whole room seemed to go round...'

For a while she lost consciousness. 'When I woke up, all my clothes were pulled off me, and I was in bed. I sat up in the bed and started to scream. He said, "It is all over, it is all over." He was in the bed, completely undressed.'

CRIMES OF PASSION

At the trial, Evelyn claimed that after this she had 'hated' White. But she admitted that she had continued to see him, sometimes several times a week, for a further year and had accepted money from him until the spring of 1903. By this time she was firmly enmeshed with her husband-to-be, Harry Kendal Thaw.

THE WRONGED HUSBAND

Thaw, who was to be cast, at least by his own lawyers, as the virtuous if vengeful husband, was if anything odder in his sexual tastes than his victim. Though equal in social rank to White, he had none of the architect's industry and certainly none of his talent.

Thaw had been born on 12 February 1871 near Pittsburgh in Pennsylvania.

ALTHOUGH SHE CLAIMED TO HAVE HATED WHITE AFTER HE FIRST DRUGGED AND THEN SEDUCED HER, EVELYN CONTINUED TO SEE HIM REGULARLY

Below: *Evelyn Thaw had a long list of admirers.*

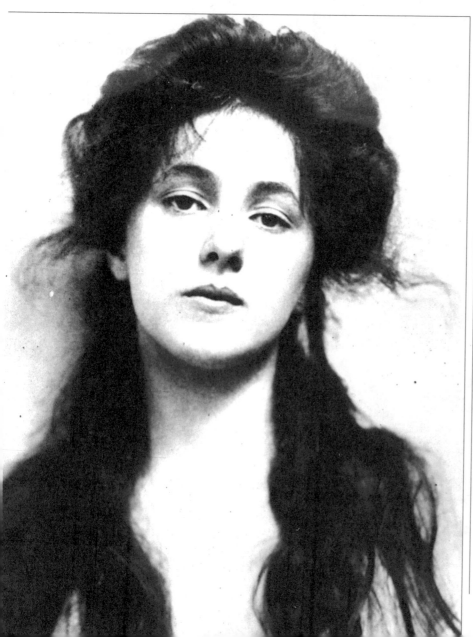

William Thaw, Harry's father, had built up coke smelting plants and then expanded into railway building. By the time of Harry's birth his family had a personal fortune of $40 million and a large mansion in Cresson, Pennsylvania.

Only the financial side of this interested the young Harry. His father, a typically bluff self-made man had little patience with the pale-faced boy, who tended to cling to his mother's skirts. At the age of seven Harry went to boarding school at Lititz, Pennsylvania, and then on to a Presbyterian college at Wooster, Ohio. He hated the place, did almost no work, and was soon sent down. Back in Pittsburgh, at Western University, he did enough to qualify for a place at Harvard. But once there he dropped all attempts at industry and took up a life of drinking, poker playing, and building up a wardrobe of elegant clothes.

Like his mother, Harry Thaw was a snob. He wormed his way into high society and mixed, where possible, with titled students from Europe. He liked causing what he called 'rumpuses' – going into bars and deliberately picking fights.

'One night I was drinking,' he was to write. 'I went into Molly's bar, and took a notion to dislike one of three men in the next room, so I wandered in and swatted this man's hat violently.' On that occasion he was chased into the street, but often he was caught in a brawl of his own making and ended up badly beaten and covered in blood.

Later, he developed a taste for whipping naked girls and, in at least one instance, a seventeen-year-old-boy. At Wooster College he had landed in trouble for paying a visiting group of pre-pubescent girls to wear garters in the college colours. He also wrote gushing 'poetry' to girls who took his fancy but to whom he had not been introduced.

After leaving Harvard, Thaw worked briefly in a Pittsburgh lawyer's office. But he found the work boring, and eventually left to lead a hedonistic existence in New York. When Harry was in his mid-twenties his father died. To the son's horror, he had added a codicil to his will refusing Harry his expected $5 million inheritance until such a time

Left: *Evelyn Thaw in costume for her role in 'The Wild Rose'.*

ON HIS EUROPEAN TRIP HARRY ENJOYED A 'BEAUTY DINNER' AT WHICH HE WAS THE ONLY MAN, SURROUNDED BY THE YOUNGEST PARIS WHORES

'Beauty Dinner' at which Harry sat, a lone male in one of the finest hotels, surrounded by the cream of the city's youngest whores.

In New York he made a nuisance of himself with his 'rumpuses', on one occasion trying to ride a horse into a club, and on another driving a motor car through a Fifth Avenue shop window. And then, one evening in the spring of 1902, he went to see *Floradora* and fell in love with Evelyn Nesbit.

A STAGE DOOR JOHNNIE IN LOVE

Harry Thaw was by this time an expert 'stage door johnnie' and sent flowers, clothes and candy to pretty Evelyn at the

as he had 'settled down'.

Harry immediately went to work on his mother and persuaded her to increase his allowance to $80,000 a year while he searched for a suitable wife. The way in which he set about this task can hardly have been reassuring, for he sailed to Paris and spent a reported $50,000 on a

Right: *Judge Fitzgerald, who presided at the Harry Thaw trial.*

Below: *Large crowds assembled outside the courthouse.*

Above: *Evelyn listens intently to the Judge during the trial.*

but Thaw did not care. For once he seemed deeply involved with someone other than himself, which made Evelyn's revelations to him all the harder to bear. For Evelyn decided to make a clean breast of the Stanford White affair.

When she told him of the drugged champagne followed by seduction at White's hands, Thaw was distraught. He paced their hotel room clutching his head, biting his nails and sobbing, 'Oh God! Oh God!' Some time afterwards, he recovered himself, ordered her to strip, and flogged her with a bullwhip.

Two months after that, according to her later testimony, he forgave her. 'White has ruined my life,' he said, 'but it it not your fault. I can love and marry no one but you.'

Unknown to Thaw, when Evelyn returned to New York, she took up with her sugar daddy Stanford White again, telling him everything that had occurred in Paris. Stannie, as she called him, immediately called a lawyer named Abraham Hummel and ordered him to take a statement from Evelyn about the whipping she had endured from Thaw.

Evelyn was already taking on the character laid upon her by a lawyer at Thaw's trial, that of 'a tigress between two men, egging them on'.

In her autobiography, Evelyn was to claim that she had loved Stannie, and when she came across a notebook 'in which he had recorded the birthday of every pretty girl he knew, I became violently jealous. Like a silly child, I wanted to make him jealous of me.'

Hitting back, she told Harry Thaw about Stannie's notebook. Thaw reported White's activities with under-age girls to Anthony Comstock, president of a curious organization named the Society for the Suppression of Vice.

While Comstock began – unsuccessfully – to try to gather incriminatory evidence against White, the architect was himself adding to his anti-Thaw dossier. He had found a woman named Ethel Thomas who testified that, in 1902, Thaw had seduced her with presents of jewellery and flowers, and then beaten her with a bullwhip in the familiar manner.

The whole situation was assuming an almost farcical tit-for-tat air when Thaw,

theatre, before coaxing her out to dine with him. Thaw was notorious from the gossip columns, and Evelyn was flattered by his attentions. Later, she claimed, she fell genuinely in love with him.

For his part, Harry thought her 'a gallant, immovable, steadfast creature'. His mother thought differently, branding her a hussy who was not good enough for Pittsburgh 'society', and considering her mother Winifield 'low bred and uncouth'.

Nevertheless, despite strong parental opposition, Harry took Evelyn to Paris with him early in 1903. Her youth caused a stirring of scandal in the newspapers,

*Top and above: **Harry Thaw in the courtroom, and giving evidence during his trial.***

in defiance of his mother, married Evelyn in Pittsburgh on 5 April 1905.

There is some evidence that White continued to see Evelyn after her marriage. Certainly he did not go out of his way to avoid her, for all three parties continued to use the same fashionable eating places, bars and theatres.

Evelyn may have tried to frighten White by telling him that Harry had acquired the Smith and Wesson .44 'American', a powerful hand gun. But White's attorney was to recall the architect saying: 'That dude won't attack me with a pistol. He hasn't nerve enough.' Nevertheless, White began to carry a short barrelled pistol in his own right hip pocket. So now the scene was set for tragedy. It would be instigated, as usual, by the teenage siren Evelyn.

CRIME OF PASSION – WITH AN AUDIENCE OF THOUSANDS

On Monday, 25 June 1906 a new musical, *Mam'zelle Champagne*, was due to open at the alfresco roof theatre of Madison Square Garden in the heart of Manhattan, and as usual the leaders of New York society were to be present. Harry and Evelyn Thaw, who had been spending some time in Pittsburgh, decided to see the show immediately before embarking for a trip to Europe.

At 9.15 the Thaw party arrived at Madison Square Garden, where the vine-covered trellises and potted palms were bedecked with Chinese lanterns. A buzz of excited conversation arose from the busy tables as young men in striped blazers and straw boaters pointed out fashionable arrivals to their demurely clad ladies.

Stanford White had already attracted attention. The tall and languid figure, clad in impeccable evening dress and familiar from the society pages, was leaning back nonchalantly in a basket chair at a table by the stage. Sipping champagne and smoking a cheroot, he was alone. He had arranged to meet one of the girls from the show after the performance.

The Thaws settled at a table some distance away, though Harry seemed preoccupied and sat slumped in his incongruously heavy overcoat despite the warm evening air. Several times during the early part of the performance he got up and wandered aimlessly between the tables before returning to join his wife.

At about ten past ten the Thaws and their guests had had enough of the show and decided to leave. Thaw dropped behind and sauntered towards the table where Stanford White sat alone, abstractedly gazing at the stage.

At the elevator Evelyn turned to look for the rest of the party, and caught sight of her husband just as he stopped by White's side.

White raised his head, and his eyes met those of Harry Thaw for the last time. As Thaw recalled a few days later: 'He smiled slowly, showing all his big white teeth in a horrible leer. His very hair was bristling.'

Harry Thaw drew the long-barrelled pistol from the inside breast pocket of his overcoat, placed it deliberately to White's left eye and pulled the trigger. As White's head jerked back, Thaw put the muzzle to

Left: *April 1924 – Harry Thaw at the opening of his hearing at Philadelphia.*

Right: *Evelyn Thaw at her husband's trial. She fought actively for his conviction.*

AT THAW'S TRIAL EVELYN WAS DESCRIBED BY ONE LAWYER AS 'A TIGRESS BETWEEN TWO MEN, EGGING THEM ON'

the grimacing white teeth and fired again. Then he got off a third and final shot which hit the architect in the left shoulder as he crashed to the floor, turning table, glass and bottle over with him.

Panic swept the roof garden. Women screamed, men dived under tables, glasses shattered. The manager of the theatre, in a futile bid to avoid panic, urged the orchestra to keep playing. Then he gave up and addressed himself to seeing out the audience in as orderly a fashion as possible.

At the elevator, Evelyn grabbed at Thaw's lapels: 'My God, Harry, what have you done?'

Thaw was unnaturally nonchalant. 'It's all right, dearie,' he told her, 'I have probably saved your life.'

A fireman on duty at the theatre took the pistol from Thaw, who handed it over almost absent-mindedly. Then police officer Anthony Debes arrived and took him down in the elevator.

On Thursday 28 June Stanford White was quietly buried at St James's churchyard, Long Island, and his killer was indicted by the Grand Jury and committed for trial on a charge of first degree murder. Conviction would mean the electric chair.

For the next six months, Thaw's lawyers examined all the possibilities for his defence. They were urged on by his mother, the imperious figure to whom he

Below: *Russell Thaw, Harry and Evelyn's fifteen-year-old son. It was in his interests that the couple eventually effected a reconciliation.*

had clung since childhood. Mrs Thaw's pledge to spend $1 million to save her son from execution led to the newspaper jeer: 'You can't convict a million dollars.'

When the trial finally opened at 10 a.m. on Wednesday, 23 January 1907 it

attracted worldwide attention. The number one court room of New York's Criminal Courts Building was packed. Accommodation had been provided for over fifty journalists, and a hundred-strong police detachment kept order outside the court for the duration – an eventual nine and a half weeks.

The jury retired on the early evening of 10 April, and re-emerged on the afternoon of the 12th. After forty-seven hours of deliberation they announced that they could not agree. A second trial had to be arranged.

This time the judge was convinced of Thaw's mental state. He ordered Thaw to be detained in an asylum for the criminally insane, and Thaw was sent to Matteawan Prison Hospital in upper New York State.

In 1913 Thaw made a sensational escape from Matteawan, and took refuge first in Canada and then in Vermont. In the latter state a jury found that he was sane, and he was formally freed.

By 1917 Thaw was back inside again. He had imprisoned a teenage boy and brutally whipped him. This time it was Mrs Thaw who had him committed as insane. He emerged in 1924 – only to be prosecuted twice more, in 1929 and 1939, for assault.

For the rest of his life Thaw used his vast wealth to indulge his sadistic pleasures. In 1947 he collapsed and died in Florida, aged seventy-six.

Evelyn wrote her memoirs in the 1930s, and emerged in 1955 to appear at the premiere of a film, based on her life with White and Thaw, entitled *Girl on a Red Velvet Swing*. She was played by the young Joan Collins.

A few years later Evelyn Nesbit, last surviving principal of one of America's most bizarre sex dramas, died in her seventies.

Above: *Harry Thaw and Evelyn Nesbit announce that they will remarry in Atlantic City, New York.*

ALMA RATTENBURY
The Price of Passion

To protect her jealous young lover Alma Rattenbury confessed to the brutal murder of her elderly husband. But though she was freed by the courts, prurient 1930s' society condemned her as an adulteress. There was only one possible outcome

On 24 September 1934, a small advertisement appeared in the 'Staff Wanted' column of the *Bournemouth Evening Echo*. 'Daily willing lad, 14–18, for housework. Scout trained preferred.'

It was answered by seventeen-year-old George Percy Stoner, a shy young lad who had been working as a garage attendant. He made his way to Manor Park Road, a genteel thoroughfare leading down to the sea, and thence to the

Opposite: *Alma Rattenbury, essentially a middle-class housewife, flew in the face of acceptable morality by taking a young lover.*

OUTDATED VICTORIAN MORAL VALUES WERE TO PLAY A LARGE PART IN THE EVENTS THAT FOLLOWED THE MURDER

Below and right: *Villa Madeira in Bournemouth was home to Alma and Francis Rattenbury.*

Villa Madeira, a small, white-stuccoed house with pine trees in its front garden.

The mistress, Mrs Alma Victoria Rattenbury, liked the look of Stoner immediately. When she learned that he could drive as well as service a motor car, and that he had experience as a carpenter and general odd-jobber, she engaged him.

Exactly nine months later Alma Rattenbury and Percy Stoner were to stand trial at the Old Bailey, charged jointly with killing Francis Mawson Rattenbury, Alma's elderly husband.

MUSICAL TALENT

The Villa Madeira was small for the middle-class district in which it stood. On the ground floor were the kitchen, dining room and drawing room, off which was Mr Rattenbury's study-cum-bedroom. Upstairs was a master bedroom in which Mrs Rattenbury slept, three spare bedrooms, and a room occupied by Miss

Irene Riggs, Mrs Rattenbury's companion-housekeeper.

Both the Rattenburys had been married before and had had children. Between them they had had a son, John, who in 1934 was just five years old.

Mrs Rattenbury was born Alma Victoria Clark in Victoria, British Columbia in 1896. Her father was a small-town printer, not rich, but able to give his musically talented daughter a first-class grounding in the piano. By the time she was twelve she had played at concerts all over western Canada.

As she reached maturity she already had the good looks which were to remain with her throughout her life. Although she was what the newspapers described as a 'man's woman' she got on with women, too, and her generous, kindly, sentimental and easy-going nature made her widely liked.

In 1915, when she was just seventeen, Alma fell in love with and married a young Englishman. She moved to England where she got a job as a government secretary in Whitehall.

After the death in action of her first husband, Alma met a man whose wife divorced him, citing Alma, and she remarried. It was a brief romance, and shortly after her son Christopher was born, in 1922, Alma divorced her second husband and returned to Canada to live with an aunt in Victoria. Soon she made the acquaintance of Francis Mawson Rattenbury.

THE THIRD HUSBAND

Rattenbury was an English architect who had spent most of his life working in Canada and the United States, and was married to a Canadian woman of about his own age. When he met Alma he was bowled over, and she took to him as well. Rattenbury divorced his wife, and in 1927, when he was sixty and Alma was thirty-one, they were married.

In western Canada the scandal was too much for Rattenbury's business to bear, however. So the same year they sailed for England, where Rattenbury bought the Villa Madeira.

The following year his son by Alma, John, was born. From then on all physical

love ceased between the Rattenburys, and Francis took to sleeping downstairs. He was naturally a lugubrious sort of man, whose only real interest was his architectural work, and his unsociability was emphasized by his growing deafness.

On the whole it was a contented, if not a blissfully happy, household. There were, of course, quarrels from time to time, usually about money. But only once did a combination of drink and arguments over money lead to violence between the Rattenburys.

One afternoon in July 1934 Mr Rattenbury had been drinking and moaning about the state of his finances. Francis Rattenbury was, in fact, a chronic pessimist, much given to talk of suicide when drunk. As the evening wore on, he once more broached the subject of killing himself. Alma, who had also been drinking, asked him why he didn't do it instead of just talking about it.

To her astonishment, Rattenbury lashed out and hit her, giving her a black eye, before storming off into the night, only to return at two in the morning.

HIGHLY SEXED

The fact was that Alma Rattenbury, still only thirty-eight, was a highly sexed woman who had had no satisfaction for six years. The need for a chauffeur-handyman at Villa Madeira was genuine enough. But Alma immediately saw other possibilities in Percy Stoner. Originally hired as a 'day' worker, he had moved into one of the spare rooms within weeks. Percy Stoner was a virgin when he moved into the Villa Madeira.

In a household as compact as the Rattenburys' secrecy was difficult to preserve, and from the beginning of her affair Alma decided to make a clean breast of things to Irene Riggs. 'Ratz' – Alma's pet name for her husband – seemed unaware of what was going on under his roof.

At the trial Mr Justice Travers Humphreys thought that he was probably, in the French phrase, *un mari complaisant* – meaning that he knew but took no notice for the sake of peace. In fact, those who knew him better claimed that by now deafness and drink, plus

Above: *Alma and Francis Rattenbury with their son on the beach at Bournemouth.*

concern for his business, had left him almost totally unaware of anything outside his personal interest.

Certainly he showed little concern when, on Monday, 18 March 1934, Alma announced that she was going to have Stoner drive her up to London 'for medical treatment'.

That evening they booked in at the Royal Palace Hotel, Kensington – not as mistress and chauffeur but as brother and sister. Their rooms faced each other across a corridor.

Over the next couple of days Alma delighted in taking Percy around town. They breakfasted and dined together at the hotel, dancing in the evenings to the band. Percy revelled in the fact that, for the first time in his life, servants called him 'Sir'.

And, of course, every night they made love with a frenzy and frequency, according to Alma, which later caused the prosecution to ask a medical witness 'whether such regular sexual intercourse with a member of the opposite sex by a boy of eighteen or onwards, would be likely to do him good or harm?'

GLOOM AND DESPONDENCY

Naturally it was with deflated spirits that Stoner, once more simply a chauffeur, drove his mistress back to Bournemouth on Friday 22 March.

When they arrived Mr Rattenbury was already drunk, and brooding about the contract for a block of flats he was expecting and which had not arrived. He did not ask about the 'operation', and barely acknowledged Alma's return.

By Sunday, Rattenbury was still filled with gloom, even after Alma had taken him for a morning drive. Because of a slight feeling of guilt, Alma was patient and indulgent with him. She suggested telephoning his friend, Mr Jenks, to ask if they might call on him in Bridport the following day. Ratz perked up slightly, and asked Alma to make the call.

The telephone was in Rattenbury's den-cum-bedroom, which opened off the drawing room. Alma dialled and got through to Jenks, who was delighted at the idea and suggested they stay overnight. As she put the telephone

'RATZ', ISOLATED BY DEAFNESS AND DRINK, SEEMED TO BE UNAWARE OF THE AFFAIR GOING ON UNDER HIS ROOF

Above: *After her acquittal, Alma Rattenbury left the Old Bailey by taxi. She was roundly booed by the waiting crowd.*

down, Alma saw that Percy Stoner had followed her in and had heard the call.

For the next few hours Alma and Percy were locked in the first – and as it chanced only – major row of their relationship.

INSANE JEALOUSY

At one point he waved an air pistol at her and threatened to kill her if she and Francis went to Bridport. He accused her of having sex with her husband that afternoon, an impertinent but – as it happened – baseless accusation, and said he would refuse to drive them the following day.

It became clear to Alma that Percy was in the throes of desperate, semi-articulate jealousy. If they went to Bridport he would go as chauffeur, would eat in the servants' hall and would sleep 'below stairs', while she and Francis slept together as his master and mistress. The spell in London with her might as well have been a dream.

Alma tried to reassure him. Gradually she seemed to soothe Stoner's temporarily savage breast, and at eight o'clock he walked to his grandparents' house. Apparently he chatted affably with them, and then casually asked to borrow a wooden carpenter's mallet which his grandfather owned.

Meanwhile, Alma Rattenbury played a hand of cards with her husband before saying goodnight at about nine o'clock.

'DON'T GO AND SEE YOUR HUSBAND. THE SIGHT MIGHT UPSET YOU!'

At about 10.15 Irene came in from her night off and, after going upstairs, came down again to the kitchen for something to eat. She heard heavy breathing coming from the drawing room, and concluded that Mr Rattenbury had fallen asleep in his chair – a not uncommon occurrence.

On her way upstairs again, she found Stoner leaning over the balcolny at the head of the stairs, head cocked, as if listening.

'What's the matter?' asked Irene. 'Nothing' said Stoner. 'I was looking to see if the lights were out.'

At about 10.30, Alma went and got ready for bed. She had been lying there for about ten minutes when Stoner crept into the room and slid into bed beside her. He was clearly upset.

'What's the matter, darling?' she asked.

'You won't be going to Bridport tomorrow. I've hurt Ratz,' he mumbled. He added that he had hit him over the head with a mallet, which he had hidden in the garden.

Even now, Alma was to testify, she thought that Stoner was sulkily trying to throw cold water on the Bridport idea. She said that she would go and see her husband, to which Stoner replied: 'No, you mustn't. The sight will upset you.'

Something about the sullen youth's manner, even in the darkened bedroom, was suddenly very alarming. She jumped out of bed and, without pausing to snatch up her dressing gown, ran down the stairs in her pyjamas and bare feet. A minute later the sound of her mistress's shriek brought Irene dashing down.

'LOOK AT THE BLOOD'

In the drawing room Mr Rattenbury was slumped, head back in his armchair, breathing stertorously. His head, face and shirt were covered in blood, and one eye was swollen and blackened. Blood was spreading in a large pool on the floor.

Alma was hysterical; as Irene Riggs later described it: 'She went raving about the house.'

Snatching up Rattenbury's whisky bottle, she poured herself a large glass and downed it, calling for Irene to telephone the doctor at once. She also told her to wipe up the blood: 'Little John must not see any blood!' Then she vomited violently, but immediately refilled her glass and drank it off.

At about 11.45, in answer to Irene's call, Dr O'Donnell arrived at the villa. Mrs Rattenbury was, in his opinion, already very drunk. 'Look at the blood!' she kept saying. 'Look at the blood! Someone has finished him!'

After a cursory examination of Rattenbury's wounds, hampered all the time by the intoxicated Alma, the doctor telephoned for a surgeon named Mr Rooke. The two medical men agreed that the nearest place in which to treat Mr Rattenbury was the Strathallen Nursing Home, in nearby Manor Road.

They called an ambulance, and the unconscious man was carried out. His ranting wife was left in the care of Irene Riggs. Stoner, who had dressed himself in his chauffeur's uniform, drove Dr O'Donnell behind the ambulance.

On arrival at the nursing home, Rattenbury was rushed to the operating theatre where his head was shaved. Three large wounds to his scalp and skull, each obviously the result of separate blows, were discovered. O'Donnell went to the telephone and dialled Bournemouth Central Police Station.

After giving his name and location, he said: 'Mr Rooke and myself have just taken Mr Rattenbury from 5 Manor Park Road to the nursing home. On examination we find three serious wounds on the back of his skull, due to external violence, which will most probably prove fatal.'

'You want an officer?'

'Yes, at once,' replied O'Donnell.

A DOUBTFUL CONFESSION

An Inspector Mills was sent to the Villa Madeira and arrived just after two. Even the experienced police officer was surprised at what he found. All the lights of the house were blazing, the gramophone was going full blast, and Mrs Rattenbury was dancing around the bloodstained drawing room in her bare feet and pyjamas with the much-depleted

Below and bottom: *On the evening of her acquittal, Mrs Rattenbury checked into a private nursing home in the West End of London.*
A few days later she checked out again and returned to Bournemouth.

whisky bottle clutched in her hand. She grabbed at the Inspector, told him that she had 'killed her husband', and tried to get him to dance with her.

Mills called for two or three constables to guard the scene, before setting off for the nursing home to fetch O'Donnell. When they arrived back, driven by Stoner in the Rattenburys' car, Alma was still drinking and trying to kiss the constables.

O'Donnell turned off the gramophone, removed the bottle from Alma's grasp – none of the police had thought to do this – and tried to explain to her what had happened. Inspector Mills told her that her husband had been seriously injured and was now in the nursing home. 'Will that be against me?' she asked.

Mills then cautioned her, and Alma said: 'I did it. He had lived too long. I will tell you in the morning where the mallet is. Have you told the coroner yet? I shall make a better job of it next time. Irene does not know. I have made a proper muddle of it. I thought I was strong enough.'

Dr O'Donnell protested that Alma did not know what she was saying and was in no condition to be questioned; Mills must wait until the morning. He then took her to her bedroom and injected her with half a grain of morphine – a large dose. Two hours later she was awakened by a police inspector named Carter, who realized that she was ill and sent for a police matron.

Alma was given coffee and then, clearly still under the influence of the whisky and morphine, made a second statement in which she said that, while playing cards with her husband, he had dared her to kill him, as he wanted to die.

Before she was taken to Bournemouth Central she whispered to Riggs: 'You must get Stoner to give me the mallet.'

At the police station she was charged with grievous bodily harm with intent to murder, and sent to Holloway Prison where, according to the prison doctor, she remained under the influence of drink and the morphine for a full three days.

MEANWHILE, BACK AT THE VILLA...

Stoner and Irene Riggs were left in charge of the Villa Madeira by Mr Rattenbury's solicitors, though Dr O'Donnell also took it upon himself to call daily. Irene wanted to speak to O'Donnell, for she knew Mrs Rattenbury was not guilty. Either, she reasoned, a burglar had broken in and done the deed, or Stoner was the killer.

Irene wanted to tell all this to the doctor, but the lumpen Stoner was ever-present. Eventually, on Tuesday, Irene asked her mother and brother to move in to keep her company. On Wednesday Irene, though not a Catholic, felt that she had to tell someone what she knew, and went to see a priest.

When she returned her mother told her that there had been more excitement. Stoner, who not only was teetotal himself but had piously disapproved of his mistress's drinking, had got blind drunk and had been marching up and down the road outside, shouting: 'Mrs Rattenbury is in jail, and I've put her there!'

The following day, Thursday 28 March, Stoner got groggily out of bed and caught the train to London to see his mistress in Holloway. This time, when Dr O'Donnell called, Irene told him that she had known Mrs Rattenbury was innocent. Now Stoner had confirmed it by confessing to Irene while drunk, telling her where the mallet was to be found.

The police were called, and while some officers searched for and found the mallet, others waited at Bournemouth station for Stoner's return. When he

To THE SURPRISE OF THE POLICE INSPECTOR, THE VICTIM'S WIFE WAS BLIND DRUNK AND DANCING BAREFOOT IN HER NIGHTWEAR

Below: *On 3 June 1935, Mrs Rattenbury stabbed herself several times and then threw herself into the river near Christchurch. Her body was found by Mr Mitchell and Mr Penny.*

stepped off the train that evening he was charged with murder, for Francis Rattenbury had died that afternoon.

CHARGED WITH MURDER

Now began a curious battle for both parties' solicitors. For Alma Rattenbury refused to withdraw her confession that it was she who had killed her husband. Stoner, for his part, stated that he had acted alone in the murderous attack, and had not been influenced by Alma in any way.

On Monday, 27 May 1935, Alma Victoria Rattenbury and George Percy Stoner were jointly charged at the Central Criminal Court with the murder of Francis Mawson Rattenbury. Throughout the week-long trial Stoner sat in the dock with his head resting on his hand, his eyes 'downcast and his face immovable'.

The two were represented individually, but it was Patrick O'Connor, Mrs Rattenbury's defence counsel, who encapsulated the case. After drawing a picture of Alma as a woman who 'has sinned...her sin has been great' and sketching Stoner as ' a lad who was melodramatic...violent sometimes, impulsive, jealous...a lad whose antecedents had been quiet...who never mixed with girls...,' he reached his conclusion.

'You may as moral men and women, as citizens, condemn her in your soul for the part she has played...she will bear to

Above: *A large crowd gathered outside the Law Courts in the Strand to hear George Stoner's appeal.*

her grave the brand of reprobation, and men and women will know how she acted. That will be her sorrow and her disgrace so long as she lives. You may think of Mrs Rattenbury as a woman, self-indulgent and wilful, who by her own acts and folly had erected this poor young man a Frankenstein of jealousy which she could not control.'

SOCIETY'S FINAL JUDGEMENT

On Friday, 31 May, the jury found Mrs Rattenbury not guilty, and she went free. Percy Stoner was sentenced to hang. He was refused leave to appeal, but his sentence was later commuted to life imprisonment, a decision almost certainly influenced by what happened three days after the verdict.

On Monday 3 June, Alma Rattenbury took a train to Christchurch in Hampshire and walked to a meadow by a stream, one of the spots to which she had come with both Percy and Ratz. After writing copious notes on pieces of paper and used envelopes, apparently trying to express her feelings about what had happened, she took out a clasp knife and stabbed herself six times in the breast. Her body was found as night was falling.

Dr Geoffrey Jones, who carried out the post mortem, noted that no fewer than three of the knife blows had pierced the heart. It was one of the most unbelievably rigorous suicides in the history of forensic pathology.

F. Tennyson Jesse, perhaps the leading criminologist of her era, described Alma Rattenbury as: 'in some ways a vulgar and silly woman, but she was a generous, kindly, lavish creature, capable of great self-sacrifice. She was innocent of the crime of which, entirely on the strength of her own drunken maunderings, she was accused, but, nevertheless, though her life was handed back to her, it was handed back to her in such a shape that it was of no use to her. For the world had progressed very little since Ezekiel wrote: "And I will judge thee as women that break wedlock and shed blood are judged, and I will give thee blood in fury and jealousy." Such was the judgement of society on Mrs Rattenbury, and she knew it.'

MRS MAYBRICK
A Cause Célèbre

The trial of an American woman accused of poisoning her husband became a *cause célèbre* in late Victorian England. But he was a known arsenic addict – so was she convicted by a bigoted court simply because of her adultery with another man?

The stricter control of dangerous drugs during the latter half of the twentieth century means that poison has all but disappeared from the murderer's armoury. But even in Victorian times, when such poisons as

Above: *James Maybrick was 41 when he met and proposed to 17-year-old Florence Chandler.*

Left: *Battlecrease House, the Maybricks' splendid home in Aigburth, an upper-class suburb of Liverpool.*

Opposite: *Mrs Florence Maybrick, convicted as much by Victorian bigotry as by hard evidence.*

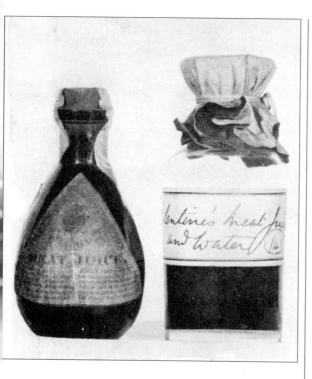

Left: *Two bottles of Valentine's Meat Juice which were exhibits at Mrs Maybrick's trial.*

Opposite: *Mr and Mrs James Maybrick, circa 1889.*

strychnine, cyanide and arsenic were comparatively easy to obtain, poisoning was always a risky affair from the killer's point of view.

Because of its very intimacy, police knew that the poisoner had to be close to his or her victim. The trial of Florence Elizabeth Maybrick, one of the most famous of all Victorian arsenic cases, was complicated by the fact that the victim, James Maybrick, had been poisoning himself with the substance for years.

A SOUTHERN BELLE AND THE LIVERPOOL COTTON BROKER

Florence Elizabeth Maybrick was born on 3 September 1862 in Mobile, Alabama. Her father William G. Chandler was a successful cotton dealer. When Florence was barely one-year-old, William Chandler died suddenly, and her mother, Caroline, took her infant daughter and young son Holbrook to live in Macon, Georgia. Here she married a Confederate naval officer, Captain Franklin Bache du Barry. Captain du Barry died too in 1864, and his widow took the children to Paris.

There in 1872 she married for the last time, her third husband being Baron Adolph von Roques, a Prussian cavalry officer. When she and her husband separated after seven years, the Baroness began to divide her own and her

FLORENCE'S MOTHER MARRIED THREE TIMES, ENDING UP A BARONESS, AND ENJOYED NUMEROUS LOVE AFFAIRS

FLORENCE'S EYES, SAID A FRIEND OF HER HUSBAND'S, LACKED EXPRESSION, 'AS IF YOU WERE GAZING INTO THE EYES OF A CORPSE'

AFTER A RECURRENCE OF MALARIA JAMES ACQUIRED HIS SECOND ARSENIC SUPPLIER, THIS TIME ON THE BRITISH SIDE OF THE ATLANTIC

children's time between Europe and the United States.

By her late teens, Florence Chandler had developed a curious power of fascination. An American friend of her husband was later to describe it rather chillingly: 'Her eyes,' he said, 'would appear to be entirely without life or expression, as if you were gazing into the eyes of a corpse...then again her eyes seemed to grow larger, more round, with a look of childish wonder, amazement, and astonishment.'

Perhaps it was this startling ocular sorcery which so swiftly captured the heart of forty-one-year-old James Maybrick when the pair met in the tea lounge of the White Star liner *Baltic* as she steamed out of New York harbour one spring afternoon in 1880, bound for Liverpool. The seventeen-year-old Florence was travelling, as usual, with her mother and brother, heading eventually for Paris. James Maybrick was on his way home after one of his regular transatlantic business trips.

Maybrick had been born in Liverpool in 1839, the third of five sons of a parish clerk. He had a moderately good education which developed his flair for figures, and he was apprenticed, with his brother Edwin, into the world of commerce.

He and Edwin, and later their younger brother Michael, took up cotton broking. After a survey of the Southern states following the Civil War, James set up a purchasing office in Norfolk, Virginia.

Perhaps the details of his business gave him his allure. For his physical appearance – whey-faced and rather portly – cannot have contributed much in the way of attraction.

For the rest of the eight-day voyage, Florence ignored the disapproving glances of English matrons in her relentless pursuit of Maybrick. When the *Baltic* docked it was his turn to pursue her, taking valuable time off from business for a trip to Paris.

The swift upshot was that they became engaged, and on 27 July 1880 they were married at the fashionable London church of St James's, Piccadilly. Their first child, James Chandler Maybrick was born eight months later on 24 March 1881.

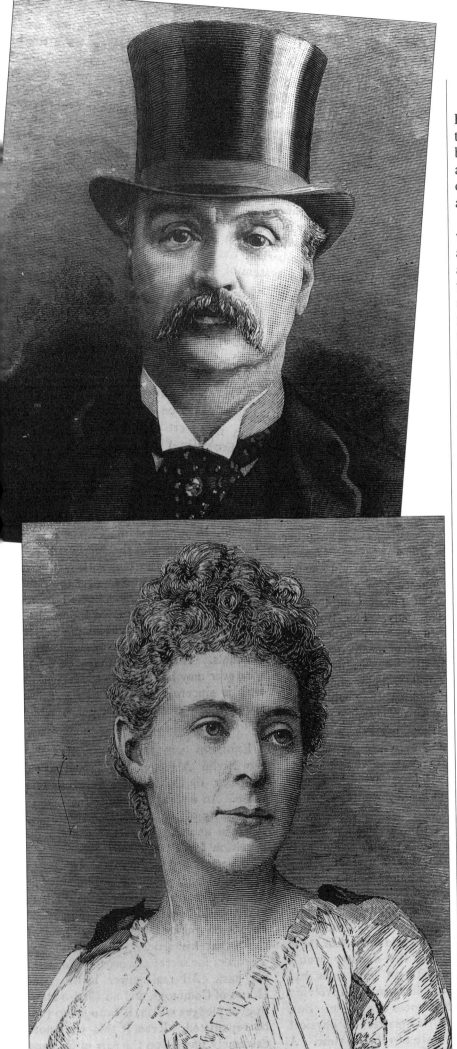

A RESPECTABLE MARRIED COUPLE

For the first three years of their marriage the Maybricks virtually commuted between Liverpool and Norfolk, Virginia, as James consolidated the American side of his business. By now he was probably addicted to arsenic.

In 1877, three years before he met his wife, Maybrick had contracted malaria, and had been treated with doses of arsenic. For years, doctors had used traces of the chemical element as a specific against fever and in stomach mixtures and general tonics. Maybrick by this time was taking a daily dose and apparently enjoying it.

By March 1884, Florence was beginning to weary of their constantly nomadic life, and James decided to settle permanently in Liverpool. He took a lease on Battlecrease House, a three-storey mansion in Riversdale Road in the prosperous suburb of Aigburth.

The house was set in a large garden, with a well-stocked vegetable garden and orchard at the rear. They employed five servants in all, the most dominant being twenty-eight-year-old Alice Yapp, a nurse hired to look after young James.

One of their circle of acquaintances was Dr Arthur Hopper, who not only became a family friend but ministered to their health. It was Dr Hopper who, on 20 June 1886, delivered the Maybricks' second child, a daughter named Gladys Evelyn. He also began prescribing an arsenic-based drug for James Maybrick when a recurrence of his 'swamp fever' laid him low.

During the autumn of 1888, James Maybrick junior contracted scarlatina during an epidemic. While his father took young Gladys to Wales, out of harm's way, Florence stayed behind to look after the boy.

DRAMATIC REVELATIONS

During her husband's absence, Florence made a discovery which effectively ended the sexual side of her marriage. Her husband had had a long-standing affair with a woman on the other side of Liverpool who had borne him five children – two since his marriage.

Though all had died early they were, to Florence, an unforgivable affront.

By New Year's Eve all pretence at civilized discussion had gone by the board. After a screaming row James tore up his will, which had named Florence as sole legatee.

There were other sources of argument at that time. Both James and Florence took exception to Alice Yapp's surly moods – James particularly so, since he was beginning to suffer headaches and pains in his stomach and joints. Dr Hopper questioned his irregular use of arsenic-based medicines, but James pooh-poohed him. He was by now picking up prescriptions from at least two other doctors, and he also had a source of 'raw' arsenic.

Florence had mentioned to his younger brother Michael 'some sort of drug' that James was taking, but when Michael brought the matter up James flew into one of his increasingly frequent tantrums.

Meanwhile, Florence had found a source of solace in the midst of all these troubles. Just before Christmas, James had brought a thirty-eight-year-old cotton broker to dinner at Battlecrease House. Alfred Brierley was a bachelor and, like James, he was very rich. Soon Florence was smitten and, while James was away on business, she agreed to spend a clandestine weekend away with him. On 21 March, the couple booked into Flatman's Hotel in Cavendish Square in London.

On 29 March, on their return, Brierley and the Maybricks were at Aintree racecourse together, in a party for the Grand National. Alfred escorted Florence in the grandstand private enclosure, while James accompanied Gertrude Janion, a gossipy friend of Brierley's. Somehow, Gertrude managed to spill the beans.

The row which broke loose when the Maybricks returned home rivalled Victorian melodrama at its most baroque. According to Alice Yapp's evidence at the trial, James yelled: 'Such a scandal will be all over town tomorrow! Florrie, I never thought you would come to this!'

After further sounds of mayhem from the bedroom, Florrie descended the main staircase, donning her fur cape and hat. Her dress was torn, and she was in tears.

Above: *Wokes the chemists where Mrs Maybrick bought the chemically treated fly papers.*

'BY HEAVEN FLORRIE! IF YOU CROSS THAT THRESHOLD YOU SHALL NEVER ENTER THIS HOUSE AGAIN!'

James rushed after his wife crying: 'By heaven, Florrie! If you cross that threshold you shall never enter this house again!'

Eventually, Mrs Maybrick went upstairs to sleep in her dressing room, appearing next morning with bruised arms and a black eye. Dr Hopper was called, and after tending her wounds acted, at first successfully, as a mediator. Unfortunately the next day, Sunday, 31 March, the quarrelling resumed until Florence collapsed under the strain.

After a week's rest in bed, Florence went into Liverpool to see Brierley at his apartment. But she found that his ardour seemed to have cooled considerably. A few days later, on 13 April, she visited a local chemist, Wokes of Aigburth, and bought a dozen fly papers containing an arsenic base. A common brand at the time, they were often soaked in water, and the resultant mixture used by women as a cosmetic.

This, in fact, was exactly what Florence Maybrick did with them, a detail noticed by Alice Yapp. At about the same time James Maybrick returned from a trip to London and made a new will which left almost everything in trust to the children, with an allowance for Florence.

But on Friday, 26 April a bottle of medicine arrived from London, and that evening James dined with Florrie and brother Edwin as if nothing had ever come between them. These rare good spirits were short-lived.

STRANGE SYMPTOMS

The following morning Maybrick felt numb, and he began to vomit. By Monday morning Maybrick was so ill

Below: Two views of the interior of Wokes the chemists.

that Florence called a local practitioner, Dr Richard Humphreys, and told him of a 'white powder' that her husband had been taking. But Humphreys diagnosed chronic indigestion and placed James on a diet.

Sure enough, the symptoms seemed to ease a little, and on Tuesday, 30 April he felt well enough to go to the office in Liverpool. While he was away, Florence visited another local chemist, Hansons of Cressington, and bought another two dozen fly papers.

On 3 May, Dr Humphreys prescribed morphine for Maybrick's worsening leg pain, but this made little difference. On 6 May, ignoring what he had heard from Florence, Dr Humphreys prescribed Fowler's Mixture, a patent medicine containing carbonate of potash and arsenic.

By Wednesday, 8 May, James was ill and confined to bed, and Florence called a nurse to tend him. After sending for his two brothers, Alice Yapp saw her tidying his bedside table and pouring medicine from one bottle to another.

That afternoon a family friend, Matilda Briggs, called at the house and Yapp cornered her. 'Thank God you have come,' she said, 'for the mistress is poisoning the master.' Nurse Yapp told her about the fly papers she had seen soaking, as well as Florence's 'interference' with the medicine bottles.

CONDEMNED AS AN ADULTERESS AND A POISONER

That evening Florence unwittingly handed Yapp all the ammunition that the spiteful nurse could need. It was in the form of a letter to Alfred Brierley. Yapp later claimed that the letter was dropped accidentally into a puddle and that she opened it to change the envelope. However she came to open it, Yapp noticed that it called Alfred 'dearest', that it said Maybrick was 'sick unto death', and that it swore that the lovers would be 'free of all fear of discovery now and in the future'.

When, instead of posting it, Yapp unctuously handed it to Michael Maybrick on his arrival that evening, James's brother declared: 'The woman is an adulteress!' Michael Maybrick told Dr Humphreys of the letter. The doctor was at first sceptical of the idea that Florence could have poisoned her husband.

Dr Humphreys then tested James's urine and faeces for traces of arsenic, but found none. 'James must have made a grave error of diet,' he told Michael. When he tried a similar test on a bottle of Valentine's meat juice, a popular convalescent aid which he found on James's bedside table, traces of arsenic were present. But by that time such considerations were irrelevant. On Saturday, 11 May Maybrick became delirious, and at 8.40 p.m. he died.

The grief-stricken brother locked Florence in her room and called the police, who searched the house from attic to basement. During the next two days they found 117 items from 29 different chemists, all prescribed for 'J. Maybrick'. Altogether there was enough arsenic in Battlecrease House to have seen off about 150 able-bodied people.

The autopsy, after the fashion of the times, was held in the dead man's bedroom. Maybrick's stomach and bowels were opened and found to be inflamed, and it was decided that death was due to some non-specified 'irritant poison'. A few days later he was buried, only to be exhumed within the week on the order of the coroner. At the second

*Right: **Michael Maybrick, James's brother, who was instrumental in bringing his sister-in-law to justice.***

WHEN THE POLICE SEARCHED BATTLECREASE HOUSE THEY FOUND ENOUGH ARSENIC TO KILL SOME 150 HEALTHY PEOPLE

*Below: **The Aigburth Hotel, Liverpool, where the inquest on James Maybrick was held.***

post-mortem, a different team of medical examiners found traces of arsenic – a total of one-tenth of a grain – in the body. The average fatal dose is two grains, and presumably Maybrick's tolerance of the drug meant that he would have required much more than that to kill him outright.

However, the coroner's jury found that in all probability Maybrick had been deliberately poisoned by his wife. On 6 June 1889, Florence Chandler Maybrick was formally charged with his murder.

ON TRIAL FOR MURDER

The trial opened at St George's Hall, Liverpool, on 31 July before Mr Justice Stephen and an all-male jury.

It was a complex case. To convict Mrs Maybrick, the prosecution had to establish that Maybrick had died from arsenic poisoning, and also that he had been killed by one final, fatal dose deliberately administered with the intention of finishing him off. And given his record of eating arsenic more or less for pleasure, was it Maybrick himself, or his wife, who had delivered this final dose?

The medical evidence, too, was highly technical. Both sides agreed that Maybrick had died of gastro-enteritis, but could not, or would not agree on whether or not the half grain of arsenic found in the body was the remains of a single, large dose or the residue of an arsenic 'habit' lasting years.

The turning point came when Alice Yapp told of the letter she had intercepted to Alfred Brierley, and of how she had subsequently seen Mrs Maybrick apparently tampering with bottles on her husband's bedside table.

In explaining the incident, Mrs Maybrick made a statement which irreparably damaged her case. Talking of events on 9 May, two days before her husband died, she began to weep as she told the court: 'He complained to me of being very sick and very depressed, and he implored me then to give him this powder. He told me that the powder would not harm him, and that I could put it in his food. I then consented.'

She explained that while giving him the powder she had spilled some of the Valentine's meat juice on his table and had made up the quantity with water. This, she said, was the incident that had aroused Yapp's suspicions. Now it seemed, Florence had confirmed those suspicions to the judge and jury by admitting that she had given James Maybrick the mysterious white powder.

Her defence barrister, Sir Charles Russell, fought back hard but to no avail. On 6 August Mr Justice Stephen, in a rambling and biased summing up, told the jury: 'You must remember the intrigue that she carried on with this man Brierley...it is easy enough to conceive how a horrible woman in so terrible a position might be assailed by some fearful and terrible temptation....'

The jury took only forty-five minutes to find Florence Maybrick guilty, and she was sentenced to hang. Sir Charles Russell was now placed in a difficult position, for those were the days before the establishment of the Court of Appeal. Nevertheless, by skilful lobbying of MPs and newspaper editors a massive public appeal was launched. Letters were sent to the Home Office and Queen Victoria.

Four days before Mrs Maybrick's scheduled execution, on 22 August 1889, the Home Office announced that, though her conviction still stood, there was some doubt about the exact cause of her husband's death. Her sentence was therefore commuted to life imprisonment.

Sir Charles Russell continued to campaign for Mrs Maybrick's release until his own death in 1900, by which time he was Lord Chief Justice. He was supported by pressure groups in the United States, and by two personal appeals from Presidents Cleveland and McKinley.

Finally, in 1904, Florence was released on parole from Aylesbury Prison after spending fifteen years in jail. She returned to the United States, where she wrote a book about her years in jail and lectured on prison reform before disappearing into obscurity. She never saw her children again, and on 23 October, 1941, she died in her little clapboard house in Connecticut.

Below: *Mrs Maybrick stands accused of murder.*

EDITH THOMPSON
Lovers on Trial

Trapped in a dull marriage, Edith Thompson conducted a steamy affair with a dashing merchant seaman. High on bodice-ripper novelettes, she hatched farcical murder plans that were doomed to failure – but the hangman's noose still awaited her

At around midnight on the misty evening of 3 October, 1922 the streets on the outskirts of the East London suburb of Ilford were all but deserted. The few people still about had just left the last train from Liverpool Street, and were making their quiet way home in twos and threes along gas-lit Belgrave Road, which led from the station to the smart middle-class villas of the town itself.

The sudden piercing sound of the woman's scream was, therefore, all the more dramatic: 'Oh, don't! Oh, don't!'

A group of people at the Ilford end of the road heard the erratic clatter of her high-heeled shoes echoing in the empty road as she ran to catch them up. 'Oh, my God!' she gasped. 'Will you help me? My husband is ill. He is bleeding!'

The startled group followed the sobbing, smartly dressed woman in the fur coat and cloche hat as she hurried back the way she had come. At the junction with Endsleigh Gardens they found a man lying on the pavement. His face was white and shining with blood in the light of the street lamp.

Asked what had happened, the distracted woman, now kneeling by the body, cried: 'Oh, don't ask me. I don't know. Somebody flew past and when I turned to speak to him blood was pouring from his mouth!'

In fact the apparently distraught woman, whose name was Edith Thompson, knew very well what had happened. Her lover Freddy Bywaters had just stabbed her husband Percy to death.

The exact nature of her knowledge, and whether the stabbing had occurred with or without her consent, was a matter which was to divide the nation.

PRECOCIOUS TALENTS

Edith Graydon, was born on Christmas Day 1893. When Edith was five, her parents moved from Dalston to Manor Park, East Ham, then a new development area with parks and good schools – a healthy environment for a talented girl. For Edith was already showing a precocious gift for dancing, acting and generally making the most of the good looks which were to bring about her downfall.

She also had a natural ability for figures, and before she was twenty had become chief buyer for the City firm of Cracknell and Prior, importers of fabrics and women's fashions. Edith picked up a smart dress sense and a street-wise

Above: *The knife with which Percy Thompson was killed.*

Opposite: *Mrs Edith Thompson.*

'SOMEBODY FLEW PAST, AND WHEN I TURNED ROUND TO SPEAK TO HIM BLOOD WAS POURING FROM HIS MOUTH!'

ANXIOUS TO ESCAPE CONSCRIPTION, PERCY SMOKED FIFTY CIGARETTES A DAY TO GIVE HIMSELF A RACING HEARTBEAT

Left: *Twenty-year-old merchant seaman, Frederick Bywaters, was Edith Thompson's lover.*

Above: *Percy Thompson in full battle dress at the beginning of the First World War.*

stockily handsome and a year older than the pretty young fashion buyer, whom he seems to have met while commuting to and from the City in 1910.

A LOVELESS MARRIAGE

It was an odd match – Edith vibrant, witty and worldly-wise, Percy dull and, at eighteen, already set in his ways. But the fact that he was a coward indubitably helped.

In 1914, with the outbreak of the First World War, Percy, like thousands of other young men, received his call-up papers. For a month he smoked fifty cigarettes a day, so that by the time he went for his medical his heart was racing unnaturally. He was excused service on the grounds of a weak heart.

Two years later, when he proposed to Edith, he had little competition. Most of his contemporaries were either dead or facing death in Flanders.

Edith accepted his proposal, and they were married in January 1918. Shortly afterwards they bought an eight-roomed villa at 41 Kensington Gardens, Ilford, and lived in considerable comfort and reasonable content for two years. After that, Edith was to claim, the marriage had become 'loveless'.

Two years later, in 1920, when Edith was twenty-seven, she met a nineteen-year-old merchant seaman petty officer named Freddy Bywaters. The two were instantly attracted. In fact, it was a renewal of acquaintanceship. Nine years previously Edith had known Freddy as a friend of her ten-year-old brother, and now he was again visiting Edith's family home, this time as a friend of her younger, unmarried sister Avis.

Freddy Bywaters was about as unlike Percy Thompson as it was possible to be. Like Edith, he had a lower middle-class background, and combined a head for figures with the body of an athlete. He had gained a reputation at school as a defender of weaker boys against school bullies, and at the age of fifteen – too young for military service – had enlisted in the Merchant Navy.

Four years later he was chief clerk on the freighter SS *Morea,* a position which gave him chief petty officer status, and

attitude and was soon making regular trips to Paris.

By the time of her husband's death she was earning over £6 of their joint £10-a-week income – a formidable sum at a time when the average senior clerk took home about £3 10s (£3.50).

Percy Thompson was a little above average, but not much. Born in Manor Park, with a father who died when Percy was thirteen, the boy left school early to keep his family. Like Edith he was good at figures, and he became a shipping clerk in Eastcheap. He was smart and the survivor of numerous Atlantic convoys and U-Boat attacks. As if to emphasize his bravery, he had, while on leave, dashed through a Zeppelin bombing raid on east London and rescued his sister from their burning home. Freddy was also extremely handsome.

Edith was not alone in being attracted to the gallant Freddy. Her husband Percy, he of the phoney weak heart and tedious City life, at first found young Bywaters fascinating. During the next year, Freddy and Avis were regular visitors to the Kensington Gardens villa whenever the SS *Morea* docked at Tilbury, and in June 1921 the couple were invited by Percy to join him and Edith on their annual holiday at Shanklin in the Isle of Wight. It was on this holiday that he and Edith confessed their feelings for each other.

BRAVE, HANDSOME FREDDY HAD HAD AN ADVENTUROUS WAR DURING WHICH HE HAD RESCUED HIS SISTER FROM A ZEPPELIN RAID

AFTER THE ROW WITH HER HUSBAND, EDITH WROTE HER LOVER THE FIRST OF A SERIES OF DANGEROUSLY DAMNING LETTERS

Below: *Frederick Bywaters, the dashing young seaman.*

MÉNAGE À TROIS

With the holiday over, Freddy had several weeks to wait until his next voyage, and Edith suggested that he move in as lodger until he sailed. Percy, with some reluctance, agreed, and on 18 June 1921, Freddy Bywaters moved into Kensington Gardens.

For the six weeks that he was there Freddy happily played slave to Edith, to the growing disgruntlement of Percy. If she wanted a book, a chocolate or a cup of tea, Freddy leaped to fetch it.

Matters came to a head on 1 August, a Bank Holiday, when Edith insisted that Percy, rather than Freddy, fetch her a pin. When Percy grumpily refused, Edith yelled at him. It was the final straw: Percy's reply was to leap to his feet, pick Edith off her chaise-longue and throw her bodily across the room.

Freddy pushed Percy away, and took the sobbing Edith in his arms. He told Thompson that he was leaving and going back to his ship – but that perhaps he should grant his wife a divorce, as they were so obviously incompatible.

Despite the violence of the row, and Bywaters's comments, he did not leave that night. As one contemporary writer was to comment, it was difficult in those days for a man whose wife earned £6 per week to push her about for long. So Bywaters returned to his room, and the no-doubt shaken Thompson went to his.

Left alone, Edith began the first of a long series of letters which were eventually to condemn her. She sent Freddy a slushily sentimental romantic novel, with certain passages marked, and accompanied it with the commentary:

'The part about "a man to lean on" is especially true. Darlint [this was a lover's usage that both adopted, and was apparently short for 'darlingest'] it was that about you that first made me think about you in the way that I do now....Note the part "always think of her first, always be patient and kind, always help her in every way he can, he will have gone a long way to helping her love him."

'Such things as wiping up, getting pins for me, etc., all counted. Do you remember the pin incident...and the

subsequent remark from him, "You like to have some one always tacked on to you to run all your little errands." That was it, darlint, that counted, obeying little requests – such as getting a pin, it was a novelty – he'd never done that. It is the man who has no right who generally comforts the woman who has wrongs....'

The message brought matters to a head, as a surviving letter from Freddy to Edith shows: 'Darlint Peidi [pet name for Edith] Mia – I do remember you coming to me in the little room and I think I understand what it cost you – a lot more

IN THE MONTH BEFORE FREDDY SAILED, HE AND EDITH MADE LOVE DAILY IN PARKS, RAILWAY CARRIAGES AND EMPTY BUILDINGS

Below: *Mrs Edith Thompson at twenty-eight.*

then, darlint, than it could ever now.'

In other words, the lovers consummated their affair in Freddy's 'little room'. On 4 August, Freddy finally left the villa. For the next month, before he sailed, he met Edith almost every day, and they made love in a variety of parks, railway carriages and empty buildings.

During the next year Bywaters made five voyages in the *SS Morea*, and spent a total of eighty-four days in England. On most of them he and Edith managed to see each other.

That Percy Thompson was pretty sure of what was going on was attested by his wife. One evening when she returned from a tryst Percy fell back on the sofa and, echoing his wartime behaviour, staged a 'heart attack'. Edith laughed at him and swept up to bed.

However, according to Edith, Percy continued to insist on his rights as a husband. Apparently his suspicions had heightened his ardour, and Edith, as she told Freddy, 'thought it best' to comply with his wishes rather than cause a complete break. In all probability she enjoyed being the focus of attention of two men.

SINISTER PLANS

It was also probable that at this point Edith Thompson conceived her 'murder plan', but it was almost certainly not as straightforward as appeared on the surface, though the courts were to think otherwise.

She was a fashionable young woman with security, and she was not about to lose Thompson without being sure of his replacement. Divorce, for the lower middle classes in those days, was still a cause of scandal and could easily mean that both she and Percy would lose their jobs. It might even mean that Freddy Bywaters, named as co-respondent, could be dismissed too.

On the other hand Freddy was a handsome young man – nine years younger than she was – and though he seemed devoted to her he was a sailor, and traditionally supposed to have a 'girl in every port'.

So Edith hit on an idea to retain his interest. She suggested to Freddy that she should kill her husband. She would set herself a five-year limit, and if she had failed by then, she and Freddy would commit suicide together.

All this was decided by letter between the two of them. Edith destroyed all but three of Freddy's letters to her. Unfortunately, Freddy kept a number of hers. They were, on the face of it, damning.

She discussed slipping something 'with a bitter taste' into Percy's tea, but he noticed. 'Now I think whatever else I try it will still taste bitter he will recognize it and be more suspicious still.' On the top of the page she had written: 'Don't keep this piece.'

From the mysterious 'bitter' substance she turned to glass: 'I used the light bulb three times [in his porridge] but the third time he found a piece so I've given it up until you come home.'

In another letter she explained: 'I was buoyed up with the hope of the light bulb and I used a lot – big pieces too – not powdered – and it has no effect...Oh darlint, I do feel so down and unhappy...'

Later she expressed doubts, fearing that Freddy might lose interest if she ever actually became a murderess. 'This thing that I am doing for both of us will it ever – at all, make any difference between us darlint, do you understand what I mean. Will you ever think any the less of me – not now, I know darlint, but later on....'

She also reverted to her practice of sending him significantly marked copies of pulp novelettes. In one, *Bella Donna*, a tale in which the eponymous heroine kills her husband Nigel with digitalin, she had copied out the head-note:'It must be remembered that digitalin is a cumulative poison and that the same dose, harmless if taken once, yet frequently repeated, becomes deadly.'

Interestingly, Edith commented on the character and motives of the anti-heroine: 'If she had loved Baroudi enough she could have gone to him – but she liked the security of being Nigel's wife – for the monetary assets it held....'

Edith Thompson's letters to Freddy Bywaters might have been more touching if she had been totally faithful to him – but she was not. Once, after spending £27 on a fur coat, she went off to the Waldorf Hotel in the Aldwych and allowed herself to be 'picked up'.

On another occasion she met a man at the Regent's Palace Hotel in Piccadilly and allowed him to buy her lunch and a box of marrons glacés. He expected, she confessed to Freddy, 'something in return'. Freddy begged her to avoid the Regent's Palace in future.

'LOWER THAN A SNAKE'

Matters were now moving towards a climax. However secretive Edith thought she had been, her affair with Freddy was apparent not only to Percy but to her own parents. On one occasion Percy saw the lovers locked in embrace at Ilford station, and when Edith returned home he told her: 'Bywaters is not a man or he would ask my permission to take you out.'

When Edith told Bywaters about the comment, Freddy stormed round to see him. He told Edith's husband that he intended to see Edith at every opportunity whether he liked it or not, and that he, Thompson, ought to do the decent thing and arrange for a divorce or a separation.

Freddy Bywaters returned from what was to be his last voyage on the *SS Morea* at the end of September 1922. He met Edith on a Friday evening, and they made love before she went home to Percy for the weekend. During the weekend she wrote her last letter to Freddy, or at least the last he was to receive.

'Darlingest lover, what happened last night? I don't know myself I only know how I felt – no not really how I felt but how I could feel – if time and circumstances were different. It seems like a great welling up of love – of feeling – of inertia, just as if I am wax in your hands – it's physical purely and I can't really describe it...Darlingest when you are rough I go dead – try not to be, please.'

She finished the letter by telling Bywaters that her husband had insisted on sex at the weekend. On the evening of 2 October the lovers met, and Freddy referred to Percy as 'several degrees lower than a snake'.

On 3 October, Percy Thompson had

Above: *One of a pair of matching watches. The smaller one belonged to Edith Thompson, the larger one she gave to Freddy Bywaters.*

HAVING FAILED TO POISON PERCY'S TEA, EDITH TRIED SLIPPING SLIVERS OF LIGHTBULB INTO HIS PORRIDGE

DESPITE HER PASSIONATE AFFAIR WITH FREDDY, EDITH ALLOWED HERSELF TO BE PICKED UP BY MEN IN WEST END HOTELS obtained two tickets for a performance that evening of the popular Ben Travers farce *The Dippers* at the Criterion Theatre in the West End. Edith, always a girl for fun, admitted to Freddy, when she met him for tea that afternoon, that she was looking forward to it.

After tea, while Edith went home to change for the theatre, Freddy went to the Graydons' home for the evening. As an old family friend he was not only still tolerated there, but Edith's parents seemed tacitly to approve of his affair with their married daughter.

According to testimony in court, Mr Graydon had got some special pipe tobacco for Freddy. When he pulled out his pouch to fill it, Mrs Graydon recognized it as one which Edith had bought some days before.

'You've got a new pouch, Freddy. From a girl, I expect?'

'Yes.'

'I expect the same girl gave you that as gave you the watch?'

'Yes, the same girl gave it me.'

'I know who it is, but I'm not going to say. Never mind, we won't argue about it. She's one of the best.'

'There is none better,' agreed Freddy.

JEALOUSY ERUPTS INTO BLOODSHED

Freddy and the Graydons said goodnight at about eleven o'clock, and Bywaters walked out into the mist. He was staying with his mother in Upper Norwood, so he headed towards East Ham station to catch a train. Then he changed his mind and walked on to Ilford.

'I went to see the Thompsons to come to an amicable understanding for a separation or divorce,' he was to explain in court. 'I had no previous intention at all of going to Ilford that night. It kind of came across me all of a sudden.'

It may or may not have been sudden impulse, but in any case he carried in his overcoat pocket a seaman's sheath knife with a six-inch double-edged blade. By a quarter to twelve he was hidden by the privet hedge of 59 Endsleigh Gardens, just off Belgrave Road.

As Percy and Edith Thompson walked arm in arm towards him down the lamp-lit road, Freddy flung himself in their

Above: *Frederick Bywaters arrives at the Old Bailey for his trial.*

> HE HAD NO INTENTION OF GOING TO ILFORD THAT NIGHT, SAID FREDDY. 'IT CAME ACROSS ME ALL OF A SUDDEN'

path. Edith grabbed at him, and he pushed her with such force that she sat down abruptly on the pavement, banging her head.

In a daze, she heard Freddy shout: 'Why don't you get a divorce from your wife, you cad?'

'I've got her,' shouted Percy in reply. 'I'll keep her, and I'll shoot you!'

Percy's knife flashed out, as Edith screamed, 'Oh, don't! Oh, don't!'

Freddy slashed his hated rival deep across the cheek and neck before thrusting the blade almost up to the hilt in his throat. As Edith began to scream over her dying husband, Freddy ran off towards the station. He dropped the bloody knife down a drain and then made his way home to his mother's, sneaking in without waking her.

LOVERS ON TRIAL

The following day Freddy calmly took his mother shopping in the West End, and after lunch left her while he dropped in on his shipping office in the City. Outside, he bought an *Evening News*, which had a headline 'Ilford tragedy' splashed across the front page.

Freddy hurried to the Graydons' house and asked Edith's father if the news was true. Mr Graydon replied that it was only too true, and that his daughter had already been arrested. As they talked, the police arrived, and Freddy Bywaters was taken into custody too. Edith had talked, and the police had recovered the murder weapon.

The charge sheet read that Edith and Freddy 'the 4th day of October, 1922, in the County of Essex, and within the jurisdiction of the Central Criminal Court murdered Percy Thompson'.

The trial began on 6 December 1922 at the Old Bailey, and by this time the case had aroused such popular clamour that seats were being touted at £5 a time. Leading for the prosecution was Mr Traverse Humphreys, and for the defence Sir Henry Curtis-Bennett, who had a grim task ahead of him.

In fact, Curtis-Bennett's only real chance of getting at least Edith off was to move for a separate trial. But the judge, Mr Justice Shearman, refused the motion.

There was little doubt about Freddy Bywaters' guilt. A feeble plea of self-defence was registered, but when it was shown that the dead man had two stab marks on the back of his neck Freddy had no chance.

Then Mr Traverse Humphreys read out the letters from Edith to Freddy, with their plans for poisoning her husband. The fact that Dr Bernard Spilsbury, the pathologist, had found no sign of any poisoning attempt on Thompson was unaccountably

Right: *Sir Henry Curtis-Bennett, counsel for the defence.*

EDITH BYWATERS WAS HANGED LESS FOR A MURDER SHE DID NOT COMMIT THAN FOR IMMORALITY AND SHEER FOOLISHNESS

Below: *Detective Inspector Hall and Superintendent Wensley, the officers heading up the Thompson/Bywaters case.*

ignored by Curtis-Bennett.

When he allowed Ethel to testify on her own behalf, the effect was disastrous. By turns hysterical and flirtatious – the jury consisted of eleven men and one woman – she tried to save her neck by throwing Freddy to the wolves.

On 11 December the jury took only two hours to find both parties guilty, and they were sentenced to hang. Freddy Bywaters took the decision stoically. But Edith screamed hysterically: 'I am not guilty! Oh God, I am not guilty!'

In retrospect, it seems unlikely that there was any real substance in Edith's 'murder plan'. Although she was a highly efficient businesswoman, on another level she lived in a world of fantasy fuelled by cheap fiction. As many commentators have observed, in the end she was probably hanged for immorality and sheer foolishness.

And it is possible that Freddy Bywaters meant only to threaten, rather than harm, his hated rival, though the carrying of such a deadly weapon militates against this.

In any case, at nine o'clock on the morning of 9 January 1923 Freddy Bywaters walked to the gallows at Pentonville gaol 'like a gentleman', according to hangman Tom Pierrepoint. At the same time in Holloway, Edith Thompson went less easily to her fate.

MADAME CAILLAUX
Accident or Murder?

On the Eve of the First World War the author of a vicious press campaign against a French politician was gunned down by his victim's wife. Was it a crime of passion committed by a devoted spouse, or a cold-blooded, calculated murder?

Opposite: *Madame Henriette Caillaux, wife of French Finance Minister, Joseph Caillaux.*

Left and below: *Gaston Calmette, the victim, was editor-in-chief of* Le Figaro *and a close friend of Marcel Proust.*

For over 180 years, apart from a short period in the early nineteenth century when publication was suspended, *Le Figaro* has loomed large in French politics. Although it is nominally a right-wing journal, its editors wielded a power all of their own. Many top figures of right, left and centre have felt the sting of its editorial lash.

On Monday, 16 March 1914, as the very first tremors of the earthquake which was to become the First World War were felt throughout Europe, the editor-in-chief of *Le Figaro* was Gaston Calmette. Calmette was the friend and son-in-law of the proprietor. He was also a leading social figure and a friend of the author Marcel Proust, who had dedicated his novel *Swann's Way* to him.

A LAST WORKING LUNCH

At midday on 16 March Calmette had gone for a pleasant working lunch, and had continued talking to his guests far into the afternoon. He was looking forward to a meeting later with the currently popular novelist Paul Bourget, to whom he was giving dinner. Gaston Calmette was a happy man. Unfortunately he was living out the last hours of his existence.

At about 5p.m. a fashionably dressed woman arrived at the front desk of *Le Figaro* and asked to speak to Calmette.

Above: *Mme Caillaux, devoted wife or cold-blooded killer?*

Right: *News of the Caillaux affair dominated the French newspapers.*

The doorman told her that the editor was out, and politely asked her name. The woman withdrew one of her hands from the large fur muff she carried and handed him a card in an envelope. She was shown into a waiting room and told that her card would be given to the editor as soon as he returned.

Almost an hour passed, during which time the woman sat impassively, her hands hidden by the muff, beneath the portrait of King George I of Greece, who had been assassinated the year before.

At about 5.45 the writer Bourget arrived, closely followed by Calmette himself. They were just about to leave again for dinner when a secretary remembered the silent woman sitting in the waiting room. Her card was taken to Calmette. When he saw the name on the card, Calmette was startled. It was from Madame Henriette Caillaux, present wife of the Finance Minister, Joseph Caillaux.

Le Figaro, under Calmette's direction, had for the past three months been lashing at Caillaux almost daily. As time went by, the campaign had become dirtier and more underhand. Only that morning Calmette had published a love letter written by Caillaux to his ex-wife a dozen years previously, and further, similar revelations had been promised.

Under the circumstances, the present Madame Caillaux was the last person he expected to see. However, Madame Caillaux was ushered into the office, her hands still hidden in the fur muff.

'THERE IS NO LONGER ANY JUSTICE'

Almost as soon as the door closed behind her, there followed a sound described by one witness as 'like that of a heavy ruler being repeatedly slapped on a desk'.

Below: *The funeral of Gaston Calmette attracted huge crowds.*

Madame Caillaux had produced a 9mm Browning automatic from her muff, thumbed off the safety catch and fired five times. One bullet missed, but four hit Gaston Calmette squarely in the chest, throwing him back in his chair. She then placed the smoking weapon on the mantelpiece and turned to face the horrified staff already clamouring about the office door.

As *Le Figaro* employees milled around the wounded man, Henriette said calmly: 'There is no longer any justice in France...all these horrors will come out at the assizes....'

When someone took her arm, she snapped imperiously: 'How dare you! Don't touch me! I am a minister's wife. My car is waiting below to take me to the police station!'

When the police arrived they seemed overawed, and it was twenty minutes before they formally arrested Henriette. Even then she took charge of the situation, pointing out the gun on the mantelpiece and insisting that she travel in her own car to the police station. 'One of you may sit beside the chauffeur.'

Top: *The prison at St Lazare.*

Above: *The grim 6' by 8' cell where Madame Caillaux was held.*

'I ONLY MEANT TO FRIGHTEN HIM,' CRIED HENRIETTE. BUT CALMETTE HAD ALREADY BLED TO DEATH

CONFUSION AND RESIGNATION

In comparison with his attacker, the mortally injured Calmette received tardy attention. The newspaper's own doctor removed the wounded man's jacket and shirt and tried to staunch the blood as Calmette slipped into unconsciousness.

A local physician, Dr Emile Reymond, arranged for Calmette to be taken to a clinic at Neuilly. But he did not arrive there until about 8p.m. When he did arrive, no facilities for blood transfusion had been made. And, despite the attentions of three doctors, one of his wounds, which had caused abdominal bleeding, went completely unnoticed.

Not surprisingly, when he was finally wheeled into the operating theatre he was found to be dead.

Meanwhile, Henriette had arrived at the police station in the Rue du Faubourg in Montmartre. The Commissaire, Monsieur Carpin, had contacted Minister Caillaux and given him brief details of what had occurred.

When the minister arrived, he confronted his wife angrily: 'What have you done?' By this time, some of Henriette's grand manner had left her. 'I only meant to frighten him. I hope I haven't killed him,' she said.

Caillaux's anger faded, and he comforted Henriette as best he could before calling for a telephone. As an important minister his first duty, he felt, was to tender his resignation to the Prime Minister, Gaston Doumergue.

Doumergue's reaction was to call a two-hour emergency cabinet meeting to discuss the implications. The ministers decided that the gravity of the general political situation in Europe outweighed everything else, and that Caillaux should be persuaded to withdraw his resignation. Caillaux, however, refused.

Meanwhile, at the Rue du Faubourg, Commissaire Carpin held a press conference. Madame Caillaux, he said, had spoken of Gaston Calmette's vendetta against her husband, and of how she had campaigned peaceably to stop it. She had told Carpin: 'This morning I bought a revolver, and this afternoon I went to the office of *Le Figaro*. I had no intention of killing Monsieur Calmette. This I affirm, and I regret my action deeply.'

Shortly after the police chief's announcement to the press, the Examining Magistrate officially ordered Madame Caillaux to be detained. She was driven through the cat-calling mob to the women's prison of St Lazare.

THE VITAL BACKGROUND DETAILS

Only a handful of colleagues and close friends of the Caillaux knew the full background to the events, both personal and political, which had led to Calmette's public attack on Joseph Caillaux and thus to his own bloody end.

Caillaux had been born in 1863, the son of a rich Paris engineer who had been Minister for Public Works. Joseph inherited his father's political interests and entered the French Parliament in 1898, at the age of thirty-five. He was appointed Minister of Finance a year later.

In 1900 Caillaux had begun an affair with Madame Berthe Dupré, née Gueydan, the wife of a minor Board of

Trade official. For several years the affair was mutually satisfactory until 1904, when Berthe decided to divorce her husband and marry Caillaux.

Almost immediately he realized that he had made an appalling mistake. Berthe had become even more domineering and moody, not to mention extravagant.

And besides, by now Joseph was involved in another liaison, this time with Madame Henriette Clairtie, the wife of a distinguished journalist.

Geneviève-Josephine-Henriette Rainouard was born on 6 December 1874. At the age of nineteen, she married Léo Clairtie. The couple had two daughters, one of whom died in infancy, but were never really happy. They divorced in 1909, shortly after Henriette had begun her affair with Joseph.

If she thought that her divorce from Léo would simplify her emotional life, Henriette was in for a shock. Shortly afterwards, Berthe discovered a batch of love letters signed 'Riri' – Joseph's pet name for Henriette – in a locked writing desk.

Joseph wanted a divorce, but important elections were pending in April 1910 and he could not afford a scandal. So, with Berthe holding the 'Riri' letters like a club over his head, he agreed to her bizarre proposals.

She would destroy the dangerous letters, she said, in front of a legal witness, if he would give their authoress up. Joseph agreed. However, as soon as the elections were safely over Joseph sued for a divorce.

Under the divorce agreement in March 1911, Joseph agreed to pay Berthe a down payment of 200,000 francs and a further 18,000 per annum if she agreed to a second letter-burning – for, of course, she had made copies of the 'Riri' correspondence.

On 31 October 1911 Joseph and Henriette were finally married, and embarked on a period of contentment rare for either of them. On their return Joseph briefly became Prime Minister in 1911-12.

But unknown to either of them, the wretched Berthe had yet more copies of the letters. Now she began hawking them around the Paris newspapers.

Above: *The two nuns who were responsible for Madame Caillaux.*

AS SOON AS THE PHILANDERING CAILLAUX MARRIED HIS MISTRESS HE REALIZED HE HAD MADE A DREADFUL MISTAKE

WITH AN ELECTION IN THE OFFING CAILLAUX COULD NOT RISK THE SCANDAL OF DIVORCE AND GAVE IN TO BERTHE'S BLACKMAIL THREATS

BITTER ENEMIES, SAVAGE ATTACKS

During the next two years, Caillaux found himself politically under attack on two fronts. As a member of the Radical-Socialist party he was hated by the right wing for his proposal of vigorous income tax reforms that would mainly affect the very rich. But on a wider front, he was bitterly opposed by the French Nationalists for his policy of appeasement towards the Kaiser's Germany.

When, in December 1913, he played a major part in bringing down the right-wing government of Louis Barthou, both factions turned their hatred against him.

So strong was the bitterness, that Henriette begged him not to accept the post of Minister of Finance in Gaston Doumergue's new administration. Caillaux, however, shrugged off his wife's protests.

The fallen Barthou was a great friend of Gaston Calmette, and it was perhaps natural that the editor should use *Le Figaro* to attack the usurper Caillaux.

By March 1914 the paper had published vindictive and savage attacks on Caillaux in no fewer than ninety-two consecutive issues. Caillaux shrugged off the attacks at first, but when Henriette returned home from her dressmaker in tears, having heard a fellow customer whisper that her husband was 'a thief', Caillaux started to get annoyed. When Henriette became ill, he grew concerned.

DISHING THE DIRT

Then, on Friday, 13 March 1914, the nature of the *Le Figaro* attacks changed when Calmette published a letter on the front page. The letter was one that Caillaux had written to Berthe in July 1901, near the beginning of their affair, and was signed 'Ton Jo' – 'Your Little Joey'. Although it was over a dozen years old, the fact that it had been written to a married woman was still embarrassing to Caillaux.

But worse was to come. On 16 March, Calmette published a paragraph announcing a 'comic interlude' which would be provided by 'Monsieur Caillaux's imprudent correspondence'.

At breakfast that morning, Henriette shook the newspaper under her husband's nose.

'Aren't you going to do anything?' she cried. 'Are you going to let these wretches defile our home?'

Caillaux agreed that something must be done, and while he went personally that morning to President Poincaré to see if there was some way of restraining Calmette through government channels, Henriette consulted Fernand Monier, Chief Justice of the Seine Assizes, about the possibility of taking out a legal injunction.

When the couple met again at lunch, they shared dismal news. Both had drawn blanks. 'If Calmette publishes any of those letters,' said Caillaux, finally losing some of his savoir-faire, 'I shall go round and smash his face.'

Naturally, Henriette's movements on that fatal afternoon were to be the subject of rigorous legal scrutiny. Was the shooting of Gaston Calmette deliberately planned, or was it the spur-of-the-moment act of a righteously indignant wife defending her beloved husband's honour?

According to Henriette, she had had several errands planned, plus an appointment for tea at the Ritz with friends. In fact she dressed carefully for

BY SPRING 1914 *LE FIGARO* HAD VEHEMENTLY ATTACKED CAILLAUX IN NO FEWER THAN 92 CONSECUTIVE ISSUES

Right: *Monsieur Labori, counsel for the defence.*

Below: *Dr Raymond gives evidence at the Caillaux trial.*

the latter appointment, but cancelled it before setting out.

Instead she went to Gastin-Renette's, a well known gunsmith's in the Rue d'Antin, and asked to see a selection of handguns. Choosing a Browning automatic, she was taken to the shooting gallery and managed to put three out of five shots into a silhouetted human figure-target at ten paces.

At about 4.30 she returned home to write a note. She handed it to her daughter's English governess, Miss Baxter, with instructions to give it to her husband should she not return by 7p.m. In it she expressed her fears that her husband would attack Calmette physically, and thus damage his career.

'France and the Republic need you,' she said. 'It is I who must do this deed. If this letter is handed to you, it will mean that I have performed or attempted to perform the act of justice. Forgive me, but my patience is at an end....'

WATCHED BY THE WORLD

The examining magistrate Monsieur Boucard pronounced himself satisfied with the evidence on 11 May, and set 20 July as the date for the trial.

Henriette's trial began on the decreed day at the Palais de Justice before presiding judge Albanel. The first part of the trial concerned Henriette's claim, firstly that her visit to the *Le Figaro* offices was a spur-of-the-moment affair, and secondly that the actual shooting was an accident and that she had merely intended to frighten Calmette.

The note to her husband, she claimed, was both proof of her indecision concerning the Ritz appointment, and also threw light on subsequent events. 'If, as certain people have said, I had coldly determined to go to *Le Figaro* to kill, I wouldn't have been so stupid as to leave something that could have been used against me.'

She also reasserted her claim that the actual shooting had been an accident. 'I aimed at his feet, meaning only to frighten him...but I could not control the gun...it went on firing, and each shot rose higher than the last.'

That this part of her evidence made sense was confirmed by both medical and firearms experts. Colonel Aubrey of the 21st Artillery Regiment pointed out that the Browning 9mm automatic was an awkward weapon to handle. The strong recoil made it virtually impossible for an amateur marksman to fire a single round, and as it bucked in the hand it caused a rising trajectory in its bullets – each shot tended to rise higher than the last.

Dr Paul, a forensic pathologist, admitted that one bullet had hit the ground, and the other four had risen in just such a manner. The final bullet had been deflected by a briefcase into Calmette's stomach, and had caused the abdominal bleeding which finally killed him. Calmette had, in fact, been particularly unlucky. Seeing the gun, his natural instinct had been to duck down, thus taking the bullets higher in his torso.

'Had he remained standing, he would probably have escaped serious injury,' said the doctor.

After hearing evidence from eye-witnesses to the shooting – mostly *Le Figaro* employees, who added gratuitous testimony of Calmette's wonderful personality – a deposition from President Poincaré was read out.

His statement provided a useful indication of Caillaux's state of mind at the time of the shooting, and helped justify his wife's fears that she had thought him about to do violence of some kind to Calmette. Poincaré told of Caillaux's visit to him on the morning of 16 March, and how he had tried to reassure the minister that Calmette was a gentleman who would never 'publish letters that compromised a lady'. Caillaux had shouted: 'If he publishes a single one of those letters, I shall kill him!'

Caillaux's personal evidence followed the President's deposition. He gave a detailed account of his marriage to Berthe and its break-up, and the stolen letters episode. As early as November 1911, he said, he had heard that the letters had been offered for sale by his ex-wife to newspapers. In a way he blamed himself, he said, for Calmette's death, for he should have noticed the depth of his wife's distress.

The last main witness was Berthe Gueydan, she of the purloined letters. Her obvious bitterness to Caillaux and Henriette belied the claim she made that it was her sister, not she, who had first copied and then sold the letters.

She had no idea, she said, how the editor of *Le Figaro* had managed to acquire them. This was palpable nonsense, even to the more reasonable members of the prosecution team.

But then her spite got the better of her. She produced two of the letters, written by Joseph to Henriette while he was still married to Berthe, and asked that they should be read out. At first it seemed that Calmette had won from the grave, for these were a sample of the letters for which, in effect, he had died.

They turned out to be long, boring and detailed accounts of Caillaux's plans for breaking with Berthe after the elections of 1910, and then marrying Henriette. As a basis for murder, they were pathetic.

In vain, the prosecution now tried to argue that Calmette had died not because of the letters, but because he was about to publish damaging political material about the Minister of Finance.

Defence counsel Labori pooh-poohed this new sideline. 'Let us,' he said, 'reserve our anger. Let us keep it for our enemies outside.'

The jury agreed, taking an hour and ten minutes to acquit Henriette Caillaux completely.

HAD CALMETTE NOT DUCKED TO THE FLOOR, SAID THE DOCTOR IN EVIDENCE, HE WOULD HAVE AVOIDED FATAL INJURY

WAS CALMETTE'S SHOOTING COLDLY PLANNED, OR WAS IT THE EMOTIONAL RESPONSE OF A RIGHTEOUSLY INDIGNANT WIFE?

Below: *Madame Caillaux's likeness at Madame Tussaud's Wax Museum.*

MME CHEVALLIER
The Wronged Wife

A high-principled woman from a straightlaced background, Yvonne Chevallier was left behind socially by her ambitious, successful husband. Ignored, reviled and passed over for a more glamorous woman, finally she delivered due punishment....

Despite popular belief, which extends even to France itself, there is no such defence as a plea of *crime passionel* under French law. Such is the romantic French temperament, however, that over the years French juries have become reluctant to convict even the most blatant of murderers – or more often murderesses – where a strong motive in the form of bruised affection or unrequited passion is involved.

Such was the case of Yvonne Chevallier, the leading figure in one of the most infamous of post-war *crimes passionel*s.

A CLEAR-CUT CASE

At about 9.30 on the morning of Sunday, 12 August 1951 Commissaire Gazano, chief of the Orleans police, was finishing his breakfast coffee when the telephone rang. On the other end he recognized the voice of Yvonne Chevallier, wife of the mayor, Dr Pierre Chevallier. 'Come immediately to the mayor's house,' said Yvonne. 'He wants you urgently.'

Above: *Orleans, home of Dr Chevallier and scene of his murder.*

Opposite: *Yvonne Chevallier, an abused wife who could take no more.*

Below: *The French Cabinet which included Dr Pierre Chevallier.*

The previous day, Dr Chevallier had been appointed France's Secretary of State for Technical Education, Youth and Sport. Presumably, reasoned Commissaire Gazano, the new post carried with it added requirements as far as security was concerned. He drove round to the Chevalliers' home.

When he rang the doorbell, Yvonne answered. Slightly drawn but composed, she said: 'Please come in. I have just killed my husband.'

Silently, Yvonne led the way upstairs and into the master bedroom. On his back on the carpet lay Pierre Chevallier, his white shirt front soaked in fresh blood. Yvonne picked up and handed to Gazano an automatic pistol from which five shots had been fired. It seemed as clear and cool a case of murder as Commissaire

Above: *Jeanne Perreau, Pierre Chevallier's lover.*

Right: *Dr Pierre Chevallier was only forty-two when he was made a member of the French Cabinet.*

'PLEASE COME IN,' SAID THE MAYOR'S WIFE TO THE POLICE CHIEF. 'I HAVE JUST KILLED MY HUSBAND'

Gazano had ever encountered.

Gazano called in detectives and forensic experts. While they worked he interrogated Madame Chevallier for several hours before despatching her, heavily veiled, to the town gaol.

Once there, she was seen by both an ordinary police surgeon and a psychiatrist, for to Gazano the woman seemed to be in a highly neurotic state. The story told to him by the servant seemed to confirm that she was not in her right mind.

THE HOUSEKEEPER'S STORY

According to the housekeeper, Dr Pierre had returned home that morning at just after nine o'clock. He had come from Paris, where he had stayed after the excitement of his appointment the previous day.

He had informed Yvonne that he was not staying. He had only called in for a change of clothes before driving on to Châtillon-sur-Loire for an agricultural conference.

Madame Chevallier had followed him up to the bedroom, and the housekeeper had heard the sound of a heated argument followed by four clear gunshots. The couple's young son Mathieu had rushed upstairs to his parents' bedroom and screamed: 'Papa! What's the matter with your chest?'

Quite calmly, his mother had led Mathieu back down the stairs, handed him over to the housekeeper and gone back up again. Seconds later, the servant had heard a final, fifth shot.

A brief check through the Orleans police files showed that Yvonne Chevallier had applied for a gun licence at the main police station the previous week. Because of her status she had been granted one immediately.

On 9 August, the Thursday before the shooting, she had gone to one of the leading Orleans sports shops and had asked to see a selection of handguns. According to the owner, she had asked him: 'Which is the most dangerous? Which is most sure to kill?'

RESISTANCE BACKGROUND

Yvonne had been born into a prosperous farming family named Rousseau in the Loiret district in 1911. Though not particularly bright at school, she went into the nursing profession and qualified in midwifery. In 1935 she obtained a post as midwife at Orleans hospital, where she met her future husband.

Pierre Chevallier was born in January 1909. His father was a rich industrialist, but Pierre fulfilled a boyhood ambition and became a doctor. Working at Orleans hospital, he fell in love with Yvonne Rousseau and proposed to her. They were

married in 1939, despite his family's rigorous opposition to the match.

Then came the war. By late 1940, after Dunkirk and the German occupation of northern France, resistance groups were coming into being, aided and supplied by agents and saboteurs who were parachuted in from England. One of the prime movers in Orleans was Pierre Chevallier, assisted by his wife and other members of the hospital medical staff.

In 1944, as the Allies landed along the Normandy coast, Chevallier led his band of resistance fighters in armed attacks on the retreating Germans. Very much a local hero, at thirty-six the dashing doctor was elected first post-war mayor of Orleans.

Yvonne Chevallier had never been one for the limelight, and her husband's new role in French politics began to drive a wedge between them. The birth of Mathieu in 1946 did little to patch things up, though Pierre apparently doted on his baby – the couple also had an older boy, born during the war.

THE MAYOR'S AFFAIR

Then, in 1947, Chevallier met a pretty young married woman named Jeanne Perreau, who worked for a Paris publishing house. Over the next three years, red-headed Jeanne and her husband Léon became fairly frequent visitors to the Chevallier household.

Above: *Jeanne and Léon Perreau.*

YVONNE CALMLY HANDED OVER HER HYSTERICAL CHILD TO THE HOUSEKEEPER BEFORE RETURNING UPSTAIRS TO FIRE A FINAL SHOT

Below: *Yvonne Chevallier.*

When, in 1950, Pierre and Jeanne ran into each other on a train to Paris, it was natural that he should invite her out to dinner. Soon, they were involved in an affair.

All this slowly emerged as the Orleans examining magistrate, Monsieur Berigault, questioned Yvonne in the aftermath of the shooting. How had she first learned of the affair?

There had, said Yvonne, been a number of poison pen letters, probably from one or more of her husband's political opponents. They suggested that during his frequent trips to Paris her husband did not sleep alone in his flat in the Rue Cambronne.

Many Frenchwomen of Yvonne's generation might well have shrugged off such insinuations. Not Yvonne. To begin with, she retained the deeply ingrained Catholic morality of the country girl.

But most of all, as her housekeeper was to tell the press: 'Madame was devoted to her husband. She talked about him all the time he was away, but she found it increasingly hard to bear his long absences from home.'

All through the summer and autumn of 1950, matters deteriorated. Yvonne found a letter addressed to 'Pierre darling' and signed 'Jeanette'. She was pretty certain that 'Jeanette' was in fact Jeanne Perreau. When she approached her husband with the letter he was brusquely dismissive.

By this time Yvonne was at breaking point. Each night she took a heavy dose of sleeping pills, while during the day she washed down stimulants with strong black coffee and chain-smoked Gauloises.

YVONNE HAD FIRST LEARNED OF HER HUSBAND'S 'OTHER WOMAN' VIA POISON PEN LETTERS

By June 1951, Yvonne's husband was spending every Tuesday and Wednesday night in Paris – sometimes longer – and there was no longer any question but that Jeanne kept him company.

For over a month Yvonne Chevallier wallowed in self-pity. Then, finally, the first spark of anger against her husband began to glow. She made enquiries about buying a gun. She bought the gun.

On Saturday, 11 August she heard on the radio the news of her husband's election to the post of minister. She stayed awake all night, thinking, remembering, until at nine o'clock the next morning she heard the purr of the ministerial Citroën at the front door....

WHO EXACTLY WAS ON TRIAL?

For almost thirteen and a half months Yvonne Chevallier remained in custody while the prosecution prepared a case

Right: *Yvonne Chevallier stands in the dock.*

Below: *The murder weapon is introduced as evidence.*

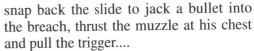

against her and her lawyers worked on a defence. Because of the obvious fear of prejudice in an Orleans jury, the venue of her trial was moved to Rheims. The hearing opened at the Palais de Justice on 5 November 1952.

Judge Jadian opened by giving an outline of the Chevalliers' marriage, their early days in Orleans, Pierre's wartime heroics, and his subsequent political career.

But as the judge's dispassionate voice recited the story it became clear that the facts themselves militated against the arrogant mayor. While he rose in public office he had made little attempt to carry the timid partner of his earlier years with him, or to help her adapt.

On the day of the shooting Pierre's contempt, and the words in which it was expressed, had been clearly audible to the housekeeper. When Yvonne followed her husband up to the bedroom and accused him of going off with Jeanne Perreau, he had told her: 'I will not allow you to insult that woman. We are going to divorce, and you are going to stay in your shit.'

She had asked him to consider the children: 'I don't give a fig for the children,' he said. 'We'll put them in a boarding school.'

She had then gone on to try and tell him of her misery, and how she wanted to kill herself.

'Go ahead!' he had yelled. 'It will be the first sensible thing you've done in your life.' According to Yvonne he had emphasized this with an obscene guesture. It was the guesture which had finally caused her to pull out the gun,

*Above: **The press gather at Madame Chevallier's trial.***

*Below: **Madame Chevallier is congratulated after her acquittal.***

snap back the slide to jack a bullet into the breach, thrust the muzzle at his chest and pull the trigger....

The psychiatrist who had examined her immediately after the killing, Dr Gourin, told of her traditional – almost Old Testament – attitude to adultery.

When Jeanne Perreau took the stand, there were hisses from the crowd. Already popular feeling was turning in sympathy with the tortured, ghastly-faced figure in the dock. By contrast, Jeanne Perreau, with her glossy, copper-coloured hair and jaunty green beret, looked almost obscenely frivolous.

Two witnesses, colleagues of the dead man, told how trying Yvonne's personality had become, and how difficult it had been for Chevallier to live with her. But in view of the evidence which had gone before, their testimony seemed almost impertinent.

The jury took less than forty-five minutes to acquit Yvonne Chevalier on all charges. She walked from the courtroom a free woman, to the tumultuous cheering of a crowd which, only fourteen months before, had considered her a brutal murderess.

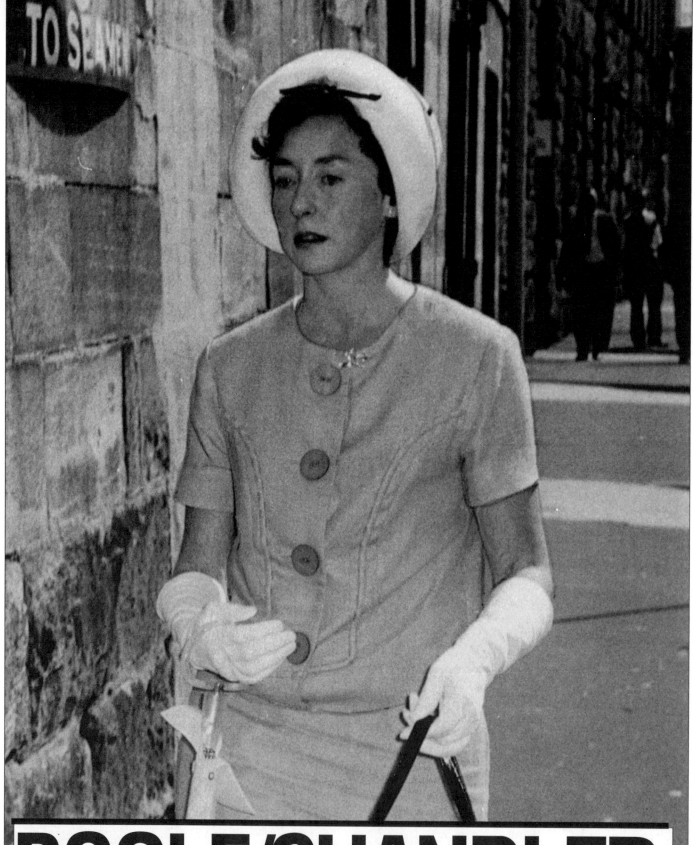

BOGLE/CHANDLER
The Riddle Remains

After a New Year's Eve party hosted by loose-living Sydney socialites, two lovers were found dead on a muddy river bank. But both police and forensic scientists were baffled and could find no physical reason for their death

To snobbish Europeans, the idea of an Australian 'society' party seems a contradiction in terms. Canned lager, prawns from the barbie and raucous vulgarity would fit the popular image.

Yet in the late fifties and early sixties, the Sydney 'push' – a trendy set of professional people – was almost self-consciously sophisticated. Among its leading members were Kenneth Nash and his wife Ruth, whose home in the suburb of Chatsworth was one of the most popular venues for elegant gatherings.

Nash was a photographer at the Commonwealth Scientific and Industrial Research Organization (CSIRO) and a keen amateur painter. Searching for a 'theme' for his 1962 New Year's Eve party, he and Ruth hit upon the idea of asking each of their twenty-two guests to bring a 'modern art' painting done by themselves. Each painting would then be criticized, and at the end of the evening, the best painting and the best critic would win prizes.

It seemed a rather silly and naive idea on the face of it, but in fact each guest knew that it was an excuse for banter about private lives and sexual proclivities. For the Sydney 'push' was a sexually complex group.

Another of its leaders was thirty-eight-year-old Dr Gilbert Bogle, a scientist with CSIRO. One of Australia's leading physicists, Bogle was also an

Above: *Dr Gilbert Bogle was talented and good looking, and highly attractive to women.*

accomplished jazz and classical clarinettist and spoke several languages. Bogle had dark, rather brooding good looks, and a smooth manner which made him highly attractive to women.

THE NEW YEAR'S EVE PARTY

Bogle arrived at the Nashes' party alone. His wife had stayed at home to look after one of the children, who was sick. One of the next arrivals was Geoffrey Chandler, another CSIRO scientist, with his pretty twenty-nine-year-old wife Margaret.

Margaret Chandler and Gilbert Bogle had met ten days previously at the CSIRO Christmas party. She had found Bogle attractive, and, on the way to the Nashes' New Year party, asked her husband if he would mind if she had an affair with his colleague.

Having been given the go-ahead by her husband, she used all her charm on Gilbert Bogle, and he responded eagerly. They spent most of the evening together.

Geoffrey Chandler left them to their own devices. At about eleven o'clock he announced that he was going out to buy cigarettes, and after doing so he called in at a rival party at the home of a friend, Ken Buckley, in the suburb of Balmain. There he met a girlfriend, Pamela Logan, his former secretary, and just after midnight Geoffrey and Pamela went back to her flat for sex.

At about 2.30 a.m., Chandler drove back to the Nashes' party and rejoined Bogle and Margaret. The trio chatted until about 4 a.m., when Chandler bade everyone a cheery goodbye and drove off. A few minutes later Bogle and Margaret Chandler also left, and were seen getting into Bogle's car.

At about 4.20 a.m. they were spotted driving into Lane Cove River Park. At 8 a.m. two youths, Michael McCormick and Denis Wheway, arrived at the park bent on finding golf balls. Instead they found a man lying face down on the river bank. They ran off to telephone for the police.

The first officer to arrive, just before 10 a.m., was Sergeant 'Andy' Andrews. As he said later, he was so struck by the bizarre arrangement of the body that he made careful notes and sketches in his notebook before attempting to identify it.

The man was wearing a shirt, tie, shoes and socks, but no underpants, trousers or jacket. From neck to buttocks he was covered with a piece of old carpet about three feet long and two feet wide. On top of this his jacket and trousers had been neatly laid, giving the casual impression that the body was fully clothed.

Sergeant Andrews noted that the face was deep purple and that rigor mortis was well advanced. Having noted this, he examined the dead man's pockets, and found identifying documents. It was Dr Gilbert Bogle.

The Sydney Criminal Investigation Bureau (CIB) had been notified, and Detective Inspector Ron Watson and two of his men arrived on the scene. Beginning a search of the area for clues, they came across a second body.

Margaret Chandler was lying in a shallow depression about fifteen yards from Bogle, sprawled on her back. Her floral dress had been pulled down from her shoulders, exposing her breasts, and its skirt was rucked up around her waist.

Her legs were bare and her knickers were missing, along with her shoes, but

ON NEW YEAR'S DAY TWO TEENAGERS WENT OUT TO LOOK FOR LOST GOLF BALLS. INSTEAD THEY FOUND A DEAD MAN

THE BODIES WERE COVERED WITH OLD CARPET AND CARDBOARD BOXES, AS IF SOMEONE HAD TRIED TO MAKE THEM LOOK DECENT

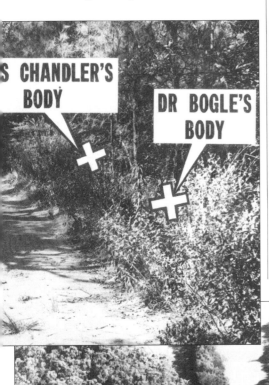

Left: *The two bodies were found about fifteen yards apart on the riverbank.*

Below: *The couple drove to Cove Lane River Park, where their bodies were discovered a few hours later.*

between her ankles was a pair of male underpants later identified as Bogle's. And, like Bogle's, her body had been covered, as if to preserve a vestige of decency – in Mrs Chandler's case with three flattened cardboard beer cartons.

NO OBVIOUS CAUSE

DI Watson was naturally puzzled by the curious way in which the bodies had been covered, but he was pretty certain that his investigation would be fairly straightforward. It was a double suicide, or murder and then suicide, or a double accidental death from an overdose.

The results of the autopsy, however, baffled police and pathologists alike. There were no external signs of serious injury – no shooting, bludgeoning, strangling or stabbing. Opened up, the two bodies showed no internal signs of violent injury, nor of any disease.

Their final verdict on both bodies was that they had died from 'acute cardiac failure associated with anoxia and pulmonary oedema'. In other words, said the experts, Bogle and Chandler had died either because their hearts failed and they stopped breathing, or because they stopped breathing and then their hearts failed. Even the order in which these events had occurred was uncertain.

The inquest opened on 21 March 1963, before coroner J.J. Loomes. The real interest centred on the evidence of three people. First Geoffrey Chandler and then Pamela Logan took the stand to tell how Margaret Chandler had set her sights on Bogle on New Year's Eve, and how subsequently Chandler and Logan had met for sex. But there was more to come when a mystery witness named Margaret Fowler took the stand.

She stepped into the box and took the oath, and then, with reporters agog, there was a flurry of legal activity. Three counsels – her own, and representatives appearing for the Bogle and Chandler families – all objected to her evidence being heard. After a private consultation with them, the coroner agreed.

The inquest ended on 29 May. In his summing up, the coroner said that the inquiry had been as exhaustive as possible. 'It gives me no satisfaction to

sit here and tell you that all we know is that the two people died of acute circulatory failure, the cause of which is still unknown.' And there, officially, the matter rested.

However, on 18 June 1977 Margaret Fowler, the mystery witness at the Bogle-Chandler inquest, died in London after a short illness.

THE MYSTERY WITNESS RE-EMERGES

Immediately, Marian Wilkinson, crime reporter for the *Australian National Times,* began digging into Fowler's role in the affair. Her findings were sensational.

In brief, Ms Wilkinson discovered that Bogle and Fowler had had an affair, after which Bogle had callously dumped her. Fowler was obsessed with her former lover and heard about his relationship with Margaret Chandler. She had told friends at the CSIRO, where she was employed in administration, that Bogle and Chandler were 'going to cop it'. Fowler had reportedly been seen outside the Nashes' house shortly after midnight on New Year's morning. At least one senior detective was convinced that Fowler was the murderer.

Fowler had, in fact, tried to make a break from Bogle during their affair, taking a new job in North Sydney. But she kept in touch with Bogle's doings through a mutual friend named Jenny

Above: *The police team arrives to start an extensive search of the area.*

Below: *Dr Bogle's car being examined for clues.*

Newbold. According to Newbold, when Fowler heard about Bogle's projected move to a new job in the United States she became hysterical, swearing that she loved him and could not live without him.

Then came the CSIRO Christmas party and Bogle's interest in Margaret Chandler. Fowler was at the party, and her jealous eye took everything in. She told Newbold: 'I pity that Bogle if he's going to get mixed up with the Chandlers.'

Detectives investigating the deaths first interviewed Fowler on 7 January 1963, and were to see her four times more. She admitted being miserable over the Bogle affair, and stated that on several occasions she had thought of killing herself with phenobarbitone.

She also made a surprising observation to the investigating officers. Bogle, she speculated, 'might have taken a "sex drug"'.

VICTIMS OF A SEX DRUG?

At the time of the police interviews a colleague, Graham Carlton, had found Fowler in a state of distress. Asked what was the matter, she mentioned the deaths and said: 'It's all going to come out, you'll see.'

Later, he was to tell the press that he

had not believed a word Fowler said, and that she was a very bright woman.

However, Margaret Fowler's mention of a 'sex drug' intrigued journalist Marian Wilkinson. Digging into Bogle's background she discovered that despite his reputation as a womanizer, Bogle had had sexual problems. The 'sex drug' mentioned by Fowler could have been LSD – a substance popularly supposed to be an aphrodisiac.

So Bogle and Chandler might well have overdosed, either accidentally or as the result of a bad joke. At this point, Margaret Fowler entered Marian Wilkinson's scenario. Either she followed the couple to the park after leaving her own party and watched them having sex. Or she came upon them when they were dead or dying, and covered their bodies in the manner in which they were found.

Forensic psychiatrists consulted by Ms Wilkinson readily concurred with this part of the theory. Whoever had covered Bogle's body, they suspected, had done it out of compassion. By the same token, whoever had disarranged Margaret Bogle's clothing to expose her breasts and genitals had done it out of hatred and contempt.

But like many another case, the real truth of Dr Gilbert Bogle's final New Year may never be known.

Left: *Police spent the morning searching the area.*

Below: *They were unable to find any evidence that helped to explain how the couple died.*

SAM SHEPPARD
A Travesty of Justice

A well-respected citizen is arrested for the brutal murder of his pregnant wife. Vital forensic evidence is ignored and the trial is a travesty of justice. In this, as in so many murder cases, there are no winners, only losers

Saturday, 3 July 1954 – the eve of Independence Day – was a busy one for Dr Sam Sheppard, though his wife, four-and-a-half-months pregnant Marilyn, took things rather more easily. Dr Sheppard was on call at his father's Bay View Hospital in Bay Village, Cleveland, Ohio and split his day between work and socializing with their close neighbours, Don and Nancy Ahern.

THE FATAL EVENING

The Aherns' two young sons and seven-year-old Chip Sheppard ate first, while their parents sat on the porch overlooking the lake and sipped drinks. Later the Ahern boys were sent home and Chip went to bed, after which the four adults spent a relaxed evening.

By midnight Marilyn and Sam were drowsing. The Aherns decided to go home to bed. Before leaving, Nancy Ahern locked the lakeside door of the house for Marilyn. Then she and her husband went out by the main door on to the road. Marilyn had gone upstairs to the bedroom, Sam was snoring on the sofa.

At 5.45a.m. John Spencer Houk, a businessman friend of Sheppard's who

Above: *The Sheppards' clapboard house in Bay Village, Cleveland, Ohio.*

Opposite: *Dr Sam Sheppard on his way to court.*

Below: *A detailed diagram of the Sheppard house shows the scene of the crime.*

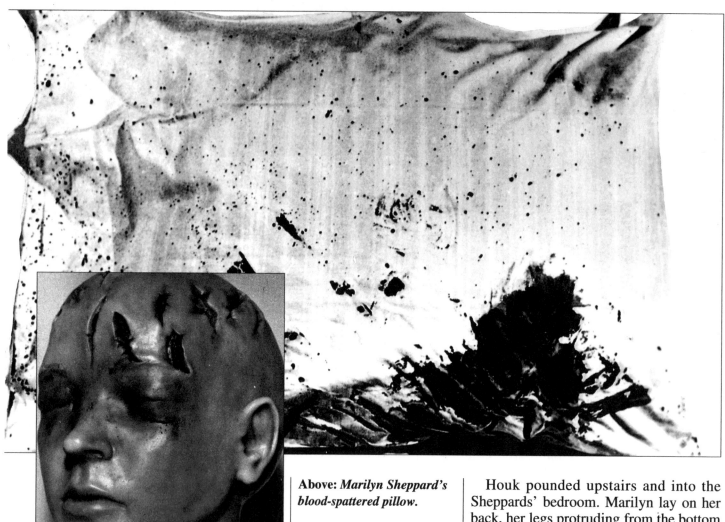

Above: *Marilyn Sheppard's blood-spattered pillow.*

Left: *A model shows the horrific wounds inflicted on Marilyn Sheppard's skull.*

was also mayor of Bay Village, was awakened by the shrilling noise of his bedside telephone. Sleepily he picked it up and heard the voice of Sam Sheppard: 'For God's sake, Spen, come quick! I think they've killed Marilyn!'

SCENES OF VIOLENCE

Houk's house was just 100 yards from that of the Sheppards. He and his wife arrived at 5.55 to a scene of chaos. The roadside door was open and Sheppard's medical bag lay inside, its contents scattered around. A desk drawer hung open, and the immediate impression was of a burglary. Sam Sheppard sat, stripped to the waist, in his den. His trousers were wet and his face was bruised. His neck was contorted with agony.

IT WAS A COSY, RELAXED, EVE-OF-INDEPENDENCE-DAY SUPPER WITH A COUPLE OF CLOSE NEIGHBOURS

Houk pounded upstairs and into the Sheppards' bedroom. Marilyn lay on her back, her legs protruding from the bottom of the bed. Her face, hair and pillow were plastered with blood from over thirty deep head wounds.

Three minutes after sunrise Patrolman Fred Drenham arrived. He was closely followed by Richard Sheppard, one of Sam's elder brothers, and his wife, and by the other brother Stephen and the local Chief of Police, John Eaton. At 6.30a.m., as police began their systematic work at the murder scene, Sam was driven by Stephen and John Eaton to Bay View Hospital for a check-up. Nurses who tended Sam were later to testify that his lips were badly cut and swollen, and his front teeth were loose.

By 9a.m. Sam had been fitted with a neck brace and was heavily sedated. He was, however, able to answer questions from the coroner of Cuyahoga County, Dr Samuel Gerber, who had already made a brief visit to the house. At 11a.m., Detectives Robert Schottke and Patrick Gareau of Cleveland Police took over the questioning.

The two detectives had already noted that there had been no signs of forced entry into the Sheppard house, and the only fingerprint was a thumb-mark which subsequently turned out to be Chip's. Sam's corduroy jacket, which the Aherns had seen him wearing the night before, was neatly folded and lying on the sofa. No bloodstained weapon had been found, and, despite the confusion, the detectives were pretty sure that the motive had not been burglary.

They were not happy that Sheppard had been taken to his family-run hospital, and they were certainly not happy with his uncorroborated story. As Schottke was to tell him: 'The evidence points very strongly at you. I don't know what my partner thinks, but I think you killed your wife.'

By that evening the murder was headline news, not merely because of its bloody drama but because it involved the Sheppards, one of Ohio's most prominent and controversial medical families.

PROMINENT MEDICAL FAMILY

Samuel Holmes Shepherd was born in Cleveland on 29 December 1923, the youngest of Dr Richard and Ethel Sheppard's three boys. Richard Sheppard was a general surgeon who was beginning to gain a reputation as an osteopath, at a time when this holistic form of medicine was little known in the United States.

Academically Sam was not particularly bright, but he had an ability for hard work which got him through his exams. In 1943, as an alternative to military service, he began to study medicine at the Western Reserve University in Cleveland, at Hanover College, Indiana, and finally at the Osteopathic School of Physicians and Surgeons in Los Angeles.

In the meantime he had met and fallen in love with Marilyn Reese, and in November 1945, when she was nineteen, the couple were married at the First Hollywood Methodist Church in Los Angeles.

In 1948 Sam graduated as a doctor of medicine, and he and his wife intended to stay in California. Sam's father, however, had that same year founded the Bay View Hospital back in Cleveland, and Sam,

'I DON'T KNOW WHAT MY PARTNER THINKS, BUT I THINK YOU KILLED YOUR WIFE'

Below: *Newsmen pack the courtroom during the trial.*

with his two brothers, was pressured into joining the family 'firm'.

Within months, business was booming. By 1954 Bay View was one of the most prestigious hospitals in the state.

Now, despite their suspicions, the police were reluctant to arrest one of the Dr Sheppards of Bay View. As his attorney, William Corrigan, told him: 'The only way to convict yourself, Sam, is by opening your mouth.'

PRESS CAMPAIGN

There was one man, however, who was unimpressed by Sheppard's status in the community. He was Louis Benson Seltzer, editor of the *Cleveland Press*, and well known for his hard-hitting campaigns against crooked politicians and 'soft' police departments.

On 21 July, seventeen days after the killing, the *Cleveland Press* ran a splash headline: 'Why No Inquest? Do It Now, Dr Gerber.'

Dr Gerber, the fifty-seven-year-old coroner for Cuyahoga County, had felt Seltzer's righteous wrath before. The next day he called an inquest. Gerber refused witnesses the right to counsel, and when William Corrigan protested he had him thrown out to tumultuous cheers.

Above: *Police search Dr Sheppard's medical bag after the murder.*

Sheppard was knocked out from behind. When he regained his senses he saw on the floor his own police surgeon's badge – he was unpaid police surgeon for the Bay Valley force – which he normally kept in his wallet. He took Marilyn's pulse 'and felt that she was gone'.

After checking that his son Chip was still asleep and safe, Sheppard had heard a noise, ran downstairs and saw 'a form rapidly progressing somewhere'. Sheppard had chased the figure down from the porch to the lake, where he had grappled with a large man with bushy hair. The man had caught his neck in an armlock, and he had passed out.

When he came to he had woken up on his face by the water's edge. His T-shirt was missing, though he could not recollect what had happened to it.

Also missing from his wrist was his gold watch, which was later found, spattered with Marilyn's blood, in a duffle bag in the Sheppards' boat-house by the lake. This watch was to be the centre of vigorous controversy later. Sheppard had then staggered back to the house.

TRIED FOR FIRST DEGREE MURDER

The trial of Sam Sheppard on the charge of first degree murder began in the Court of Common Pleas, Cleveland, on Monday 18 October 1954. But because of delay in jury selection – many admitted that they had firm ideas on the case – it did not properly get under way until 4 November. The judge was Edward Blythin, and Sheppard pleaded Not Guilty.

The main thrust of the case against Sheppard was indicated by prosecuting counsel John Mahon in his opening address: 'The state will prove that Sheppard and Miss X talked together about divorce and marriage. No one was in that house that morning on 4 July attempting to commit a burglary. No evidence has been found that any burglar or marauder was there.'

The Aherns were called early in the trial. Don said that he had never seen the placid Sam Sheppard lose his temper, though Nancy introduced a hesitant note when she said that, though she was sure

Sam Sheppard waived his right not to give evidence, and was questioned for eight hours by Gerber. Among other things, Sheppard denied having committed adultery with a mystery woman in California named only as 'Miss X'. Finally, on 30 July, he was arrested, even before Gerber recorded his verdict that Marilyn had been murdered.

Sheppard's statement at the time of his arrest was essentially the same as he had made shortly after the crime was committed. He said that he had been awakened, as he lay on the sofa, by his wife's screams from upstairs. He refused to guess what time it might have been.

'I charged into our room and saw a form with a light garment,' he said. 'It was grappling with something or someone....'

He and this person had wrestled, until

Marilyn was very much in love with her husband, she had never been sure of Sam's feelings towards Marilyn.

Dr Samuel Gerber, the coroner, caused a sensation when he spoke of a 'blood signature' on the yellow pillowcase under Marilyn's battered head. 'In this bloodstain I could make out the impression of a surgical instrument,' he said. The instrument, he suggested, 'had two blades, each about three inches long, with serrated edges'.

No weapon of any kind had been found at the house, but, said Gerber, 'the impression could only have been made by an instrument similar to the type of surgical instrument I had in mind'. Curiously, he was not asked to specify just what the mysterious instrument was.

On 1 December came another sensation, when Miss X entered the witness box. She identified herself as Susan Hayes, a twenty-four-year-old laboratory technician who had worked at the Bay View Hospital and met Sam there in 1951.

They had begun their affair in California, after she had left Bay View to work in Los Angeles in 1954. She admitted that they had slept together, as well as making love in cars. 'He said that he loved his wife very much but not as a wife, and was thinking of getting a divorce,' she testified.

This evidence meant that Sam was not only a perjurer – he had denied adultery at the inquest – but guilty of the then criminal offence, under Ohio law, of adultery.

On the stand, Sam now admitted lying at the inquest, saying that he had done so to protect Susan Hayes rather than himself. In any case, he went on, he had never truly been in love with her, and had never discussed divorce with either her or his wife. He admitted that he had committed adultery with women other than Susan Hayes, but refused to name them.

Summing up for the prosecution, Thomas Parrino, an assistant prosecutor, said: 'If the defendant would lie under oath to protect a lady, how many lies would he utter to protect his own life?'

Corrigan's defence was, on the face of it, poor. He made no mention of one or

Above and right: *Police examine evidence during the investigation of the case.*

THE CORONER CAUSED A SENSATION WHEN HE SPOKE OF A 'BLOOD SIGNATURE' ON THE PILLOWCASE UNDER MARILYN'S BATTERED HEAD

IF THE DEFENDANT WOULD LIE UNDER OATH TO PROTECT A LADY, HOW MANY LIES WOULD HE UTTER TO PROTECT HIS OWN LIFE?

two curious pieces of evidence which might have helped Sam.

Tooth chippings had been found on the bedroom floor which belonged neither to Sam nor to Marilyn. There was firm evidence that Marilyn had bitten her attacker savagely, though Sheppard bore no bite marks. There was the business of the mysterious surgical instrument. And there were wool threads, found under Marilyn's nails, which matched no clothing in the house – not hers, not Sam's, not Chip's. Above all, there was the blood-spattered watch.

Instead, Corrigan took up the prosecution's sex theme and made a negative mess of it. 'Is sex the only thing in a marriage?' he asked. 'Sheppard wandered from the path of rectitude. That didn't prove he didn't love his wife, his home, or his family.'

After a briefing from Judge Blythin on the laws governing circumstantial evidence, and the difference between first and second degree murder, the jury retired. They returned on Tuesday, 21 December after over four days' deliberation. Their decision was that Sam Sheppard was guilty of second degree murder, and Judge Blythin sentenced him to life imprisonment.

After what must have been a melancholy Christmas for the Sheppard family, William Corrigan retrieved the keys of Sam's house from the police and handed them over to Dr Paul Leland Kirk. One of the country's leading forensic scientists, he had undertaken to do independent tests.

EXHAUSTIVE FORENSIC WORK

Dr Kirk began work in the Sheppards' house in January 1955, and after studying the results in his California headquarters produced a 10,000-word report three and a half months later.

Among the detailed facts examined in the report the most important was Dr Kirk's emphatic assertion that a fourth person, other than Sam, Marilyn or Chip, had been in the house on the night of the murder. Blood on the wardrobe door demonstrably did not match that of any of the Sheppards. And teeth fragments on the carpet showed that Marilyn had bitten her attacker very deeply, though, as had been shown at the trial, Sheppard bore no such scars.

Dr Kirk was able to show that whoever delivered the death blows to Marilyn would have been covered in her flying blood, but the only stain on Sam's clothing was a spot on the knee of his trousers – gained, he claimed, when he had knelt to take his wife's pulse.

Furthermore, bloodstains on the walls showed that the killer had struck with his left hand, while Sam was right-handed. The blows had undoubtedly been made with a blunt instrument such as a piece of piping, which made nonsense of the coroner's 'surgical instrument' theory.

'No actual proof of a technical nature

was ever offered indicating the guilt of the defendant,' he concluded.

Despite what seemed to be Kirk's irrefutable report, Judge Blythin refused, on 10 May 1955, to grant a retrial. Six weeks later the Ohio Court of Appeals praised 'the originality and imagination' of Dr Kirk, but nevertheless turned down an appeal for a new trial.

The following summer, on 31 May 1956, the Ohio Supreme Court upheld Sheppard's conviction by five votes to two. Hope was raised, however, by the two dissenting judges, who expressed the view that there had been little real evidence to prove Sheppard guilty, and that Judge Blythin had accepted gossip as evidence.

But on 19 December the highest judicial body in the land, the United States Supreme Court, refused to review the case on technical grounds. Again, however, doubts were expressed about the conduct of the Ohio judiciary.

A CONVICT'S CONFESSION

Sheppard's hopes were raised once more six months later, when, in June 1957 a convict named Donald Wedler, who was serving a ten-year sentence for a Florida hold-up, confessed to the murder. He claimed that he had been in Cleveland, Ohio on the day of Marilyn's killing, and after taking heroin had stolen a car and driven around looking for a house to burgle.

He had found a suitable one, a large white house on a lake front, had broken in, crept past a man asleep on a settee and gone upstairs.

A woman in an upstairs bedroom had awakened as he was preparing to rifle her dressing table, and he had beaten her repeatedly with an iron pipe. Then, as he fled downstairs, he had encountered a man, whom he had struck down with the pipe, before flinging the impromptu weapon into the lake and driving away.

The coroner was quick to point out discrepancies in the story. Sheppard had said that he was struck down from behind in the bedroom, not on the stairs, and Wedler had made no mention of a struggle in the garden by the lake. Nor was Wedler a burly man with the 'bushy' hair mentioned by Sheppard – he was slight, though he did have unruly, curly hair.

What interested Sheppard's lawyers most was the fact that a lie-detector expert who tested Wedler was quite certain that he was telling the truth, 'or what he believed to be the truth'.

Unfortunately, there were many imponderables about the Wedler story. As a heroin user, he might have been telling the truth and have confused the details, but equally he might have invented the whole thing after reading newspaper accounts of the case, and convinced his

'

Below: *Susan Hayes. It was revealed that she was Sam Sheppard's mistress.*

drug-addled mind that he was the murderer.

In the end, it was the plethora of newspaper speculation surrounding the original event which led to a successful appeal – but only after Sheppard had served ten years in jail. In 1961 William Corrigan died, and in his place Stephen Sheppard hired a smart, fast-talking young attorney from Boston named F. Lee Bailey.

RETRIAL AT LAST

In April 1963, after a series of legal moves, Bailey lodged a petition with the US District Court, a federal rather than state body, that the case be reopened. This time he was successful. After almost a year's deliberation, Judge Carl Weinman delivered his verdict on 15 July 1964. The original trial, he said, had been a 'mockery of justice'. He ordered Sheppard to be released pending a retrial.

Lawyer F. Lee Bailey immediately swept into the attack. Quoting the exhaustive inquiry undertaken by Dr Kirk, he compared it with the muddled and pathetic attempts of the Cleveland Police, whose search for clues, he forced them to admit, had been perfunctory to a degree. Their check for fingerprints had been particularly casual. They had not even tried to get prints from the bloodstained watch found in the duffle bag, and had also ignored a key-ring and chain which accompanied it.

Bailey produced a photograph of the watch, which had blood speckles across the face such as could have been caused had Sheppard been wearing it when he battered his wife to death. But, as Bailey pointed out, there were also speckles of blood on the back of the watch and the inside of the wristband, which certainly could not have got there if he really had been wearing it under such conditions.

On 6 June, 1966, the United States Supreme Court overturned Sheppard's conviction, and he walked free.

UNANSWERED QUESTIONS

There were, of course, still questions which remained unanswered. One was the old Sherlock Holmesian puzzle of the

Above: *Sam Sheppard outside Ohio Supreme Court.*

'THE ANSWER TO THE SHEPPARD CASE RIDDLE,' WROTE A PRIVATE DETECTIVE, 'LIES IN BAY VILLAGE'

dog that did nothing in the night.

For if an unknown intruder had indeed broken in, why had the family dog Koko not barked a warning? Although neither police nor defendants thought fit to bring their suspicions into the open, privately they admitted that, if Sam did not kill his wife Marilyn, then it was someone who knew her, and the house, well.

As Harold Bretnall, a New York private detective hired by the Sheppard family, wrote in a report dated 1955: 'The answer to the Sheppard case riddle lies in Bay Village.' At the first trial, the jury had heard part of a statement made by Sam to detectives, in which he had said that Marilyn had 'spurned lovers – potential lovers...three that I know of and I am pretty sure more'.

Although not named at the trial, the men had, it was claimed, been identified to the investigating officers. Bretnall also claimed that a pair of Marilyn's bedroom slippers bore evidence that she had left the house during the night of 4 July 1954 while she was wearing them. 'Marilyn Sheppard was murdered by someone who was a frequent visitor to the Sheppard home,' wrote Bretnall.

The blood-speckled watch, too, posed unanswered questions. For if it had been splashed with Marilyn's blood, it must surely have been lying on the bedside table when she was killed – when it should have been downstairs on her husband's wrist. Did he come to bed, leaving his corduroy jacket downstairs, place his watch on the bedside table and batter his wife to death?

Or did he come to bed, take off his watch, hear an intruder, put on his trousers to investigate, get himself laid out – and then inexplicably lie to the police about his movements?

FURTHER TRAGEDY

One thing was sure: Marilyn's death and Sam Sheppard's ruined career were not the only tragedies involved in the drama. Sam's mother Edith was deeply shocked by the event, and took an overdose of sleeping pills during the first trial. She recovered at the family hospital.

But on 17 January 1955, soon after her youngest son was convicted of murder, she shot herself. Eleven days later Sam's father, Dr Richard Sheppard, died at the age of sixty-five of a bleeding gastric ulcer. Almost exactly eight years after Mrs Sheppard's suicide, Marilyn's father, Thomas Reese, also shot himself.

Soon after his release, Sam married Ariane Tebbenjohanne, who had supported his cause. In December 1967, after a vigorous fight to regain his medical licence, it was granted, and Sheppard joined the staff of the Youngstown Osteopathic Hospital, Ohio. His appointment lasted a year, until a malpractice claim was made against the hospital. The insurance company refused to pay out until Sam resigned.

On the day of his resignation, 3 December 1968, Sheppard was sued for divorce by Ariane. She claimed that she had suffered mental and physical cruelty at the hands of 'that maniac'.

Sheppard had authorized a ghost-written autobiography entitled *Endure and Conquer*, but most of the proceeds went to pay F. Lee Bailey's legal fees. While fighting once more to re-establish his medical career, he took up wrestling. In October 1969 he married his manager's daughter, a twenty-year-old named Colleen Strickland.

For a while his wrestling career and the third marriage seemed to prosper, but Sheppard was consuming heavier and heavier amounts of vodka. On 5 April 1970 he died of liver failure.

Antología
DE
TEXTOS LITERARIOS

Carlos Alberty ● Vivian Auffant ● Sofía Cardona
Susana Matos ● Aurea María Sotomayor
EDITORES

ANTOLOGÍA DE TEXTOS LITERARIOS

Departamento de Español
FACULTAD DE ESTUDIOS GENERALES
Universidad de Puerto Rico

EDUPR
EDITORIAL DE LA UNIVERSIDAD
DE PUERTO RICO
1994

Primera edición, 1994

© 1994 Universidad de Puerto Rico

Catalogación de la Biblioteca del Congreso
Library of Congress Cataloging-in-Publication Data

Antología de textos literarios / Departamento de Español, Facultad
    de Estudios Generales, Universidad de Puerto Rico, editores, Carlos
    Alberty ... [et al.].
        p.   cm.
    Includes bibliographical references and index.
    ISBN 0-8477-0181-6
    1. Spanish language--Readers. I. Alberty, Carlos R., 1957-
II. University of Puerto Rico (Río Piedras Campus). Departamento
de Español.
PC4117.A7385.   1993   93-29202
468.6--dc20   CIP

ISBN: 0-8477-0181-6
Portada: Nivea Ortiz
Tipografía y diseño: Ninón L. de Saleme/Saleme y Asociados

Impreso en los Estados Unidos de América
Printed in the United States of America
EDITORIAL DE LA UNIVERSIDAD DE PUERTO RICO

Apartado 23322
Estación de la Universidad
Río Piedras, Puerto Rico 00931-3322

Contenido

NARRATIVA

Prólogo

Encontrar el texto que ilustre, asombre, ilumine y conmueva, ha sido nuestro propósito, como el de todo antólogo, especialmente el de aquél que piensa en el lector universitario. Movidos por ese deseo, celosos de nuestro curso y de la libertad de cátedra, confiados en los beneficios del común propósito, se han compilado los textos que hoy llegan hasta ustedes.

La *Antología,* por décadas el corazón de este curso, tiene su historia y sus objetivos. Creemos oportuno aquí ofrecer unas notas aclaratorias para inscribirnos en la tradición y asegurar la continuidad —memoria y proyecto— requisitos fundamentales de todo quehacer universitario.

Su historia

La *Antología* ha estado estrechamente vinculada a la estructura curricular del curso de Español Básico. Después de tres décadas, la edición de 1988 fue la primera en promover un cambio abrupto en el concepto de la Antología. Las discusiones sobre ese libro culminaron en la creación de un Comité que se ocuparía de la producción de una antología de lecturas para la revisión curricular.

Esta vez quedó en manos de Carlos Alberty, Vivian Auffant, Susana Freire, Aurea María Sotomayor (quien había colaborado extensamente en la edición de 1988) y Sofía Irene Cardona, timonear la recolección de textos y cuidar de la edición. Las antologías de 1977 y la del 1988, sirvieron de punto de partida para garantizar la continuidad. Gran parte de las lecturas proviene de la experiencia de algunos compañeros profesores que tenían sus antologías personales o sus textos predilectos. Otras lecturas fueron sugeridas por miembros del mismo Comité quienes tuvieron la última palabra en el destino de más de mil doscientas páginas de buena literatura.

De ahí se partió a darle forma, confiando en la coherencia que daría el propósito común y todas las otras comunidades que hacen del Departamento de Español un grupo de trabajo. Más adelante surgió la idea de los índices alternos: trayectorias de posibles viajes entre los textos. Se propusieron dos tipos de índices, unos que atendieran el contenido temático y otros, los asuntos retóricos que ilustraran o problematizaran las lecturas. Los índices, que a manera de apéndice concluyen el libro, sirven de guía para que el profesor pueda planificar su curso y el estudiante explore individualmente la colección.

Esta antología corresponde a las ideas que sobre el curso tienen los profesores. A tono con el proceso de reflexión que orienta actualmente nuestras discusiones, se intentó producir una antología que correspondiera a los propósitos y perspectivas que han ido desarrollando los profesores y sirviera como instrumento al proceso creativo de la docencia. Notarán que rigen varias directrices: incluimos autores de Puerto Rico, Hispanoamérica y España, de diferentes generaciones, tratamos de balancear el escogido de escritores y escritoras en los distintos géneros, contamos con la modernidad y contemporaneidad de las selecciones y sobre todo, pensamos en las provocaciones que los textos hagan surgir en el estudiante universitario.

A la amplitud de la selección de la *Antología* le hemos visto fundamentalmente dos ventajas. En primer lugar, se coleccionaron textos con los cuales podrían diversificarse los enfoques del curso. En segundo lugar, pensamos que uno de nuestros principales objetivos, el de ganar al estudiante para la lectura, se lograría con un libro que invitara a la exploración mediante referencias a otros textos, de manera que persuada al lector a buscar en otros libros su disfrute personal

Su propósito*

El curso para el cual se produce esta *Antología* estudia la lengua y el discurso** a través de la lectura de textos lite-

---

*El texto de este apartado se fundamenta en el informe del Seminario de Autoestudio de la Facultad de Estudios Generales, redactado en gran parte por la Prof. Ileana Viqueira, coordinadora del Comité de Currículo del Departamento de Español 1990-91.

rarios y no literarios en español. Sus objetivos son fundamentalmente: "el desarrollo de la competencia lingüística y analítica del estudiante en un contexto de responsabilidad éticosocial; y la educación de la conciencia lingüística, humanística y estética". Sin embargo, esta *Antología* sirve específicamente al componente de análisis del discurso***, sobre lo cual queda establecido lo siguiente:

> El objetivo principal de este componente del curso es la comprensión y producción del discurso a través de la lectura, el análisis y la discusión de texto. En el desarrollo de esta competencia lingüística, se entiende que deben atenderse los aspectos de la observación, la percepción, la organización, la expresión y el análisis.

En armonía con estos propósitos, la *Antología de textos literarios* sirve para exponer al estudiante a distintos géneros y precisar diversos métodos de lectura y análisis. Según se expone en el documento citado: "La preferencia por el discurso literario se basa en la rica y profunda experiencia cognoscitiva de esta lectura: desarrollo de la imaginación, intensa experiencia del pensamiento y del lenguaje analógico, profundidad y alcance ético y estético".

Dedicamos gran parte del esfuerzo a ampliar la selección de obras literarias según su variedad de temas, niveles de dificultad, técnicas y posibilidades de provocación. La colección continuará modificándose a medida que, en futuras revisiones, se evalúen las lecturas y se presenten textos nuevos con los cuales puedan cumplirse los mismos objetivos.

Agradecimientos

En la mejor tradición prologal, concluimos este apartado agradeciendo a todos los miembros del Departamento de Español que colaboraron en las dos consultas de las cuales el Comité extrajo las directrices y el corpus básico de la selec-

---

**El término, ampliamente discutido tanto en la teoría literaria como en filosofía, se refiere aquí al conjunto de convenciones (expectativas que se tienen de una determinada clasificación de género) que distingue una realización comunicativa de otra. Los textos que se agrupan bajo determinada clasificación de discurso comparten un mismo sistema retórico y se inscriben en una tradición común.

***El estudio específico de la lengua se realiza desde distintas perspectivas interdisciplinarias, mayormente en su realidad discursiva, una vez se ha presentado el tema desde perspectivas lingüístico-teóricas e histórico-sociales. Es esta diversidad una de las razones por las cuales decidimos que atenderíamos el tema de la lengua en un libro aparte de la *Antología de textos literarios*.

ción de textos, muy especialmente a la compañera Norma Urrutia de Campo, quien ayudó a insertarnos en la tradición departamental, y a Isabelo Zenón Cruz, director del Departamento, quien depositó en nosotros su confianza al designarnos editores de esta antología. También agradecemos la entusiasta colaboración de los miembros de la Editorial de la Universidad de Puerto Rico, Marta Aponte, y Gloria Madrazo, que permitieron que este libro llegara a sus manos.

Los Editores
Aurea María Sotomayor, Susana Matos Freire,
Vivian Auffant, Carlos R. Alberty y Sofía Irene Cardona

Queremos reconocer
en este espacio
la labor de los principales
responsables de las
sucesivas antologías
que precedieron a ésta:

María Arrillaga
Sylvia Bigas
Miriam Curet de Anda
Juan Ramón Duchesne Winter
Mariano Feliciano
Ruth García de Padilla
Agustina G. de Gaztambide
Rafael González Torres
Juan Edgardo López Román
Jorge Luis Morales
Carmen Muñiz de Barbosa
Nilda S. Ortiz García
Jorge Luis Porras Cruz
Alicia Raffucci
Rosario Rangel
Eladio Rivera Quiñones
Mariana Robles de Cardona
Edgardo Sanabria Santaliz
Luis Rafael Sánchez
Aurea María Sotomayor
Norma Urrutia de Campo
José Luis Vivas Maldonado
Isabelo Zenón Cruz

ENSAYO

Tomás Blanco
1900—1975
Puerto Rico

Elogio de la plena
(Variaciones boricuas)

Ateneo Puertorriqueño. 1935

E NTRE los españoles y sudamericanos a quienes he hecho oír selecciones de música popular puertorriqueña —danzas seises, plenas, aguinaldos, marumbas y mariandás—, no ha habido uno que no señalara la *plena* como lo más original o lo más fuerte. Casi todos se han entusiasmado con *Santa María o Temporal.* Una de estas personas —prestigioso valor intelectual que ha pasado algún tiempo en la Isla—, se maravilla de que, durante su estancia allí, ninguno de sus amigos o amigas le diera a conocer las *plenas.*

A mí no me maravilla. Es indudable que en Puerto Rico se goza la *plena;* pero no se la valoriza como es debido. Se la posterga. Salvo contadas excepciones, a nadie se le ocurre exhibirla ante extranjeros, y los que tal hacen no son nada bien mirados por muchos espíritus de apolillada prosopopeya que llevan bombo y levita en el alma.

Ojalá me equivoque, pero, al parecer, nadie ha intentado estudiar musicalmente la *plena* y sacarle provecho. Y casi nada escrito sobre ella ha llegado hasta mis manos. La Doctora Cadilla, en su voluminoso libro, le dedica exactamente seis líneas, más un ejemplo en pauta. En *Insularismo,* obra reciente del Doctor Pedreira, apenas si se la nombra al pasar. José A. Balseiro —nuestro crítico musical y académico correspondiente de la Española de la Lengua— no sé yo que haya publicado nada sobre ella. Monserrate Deliz, que también entiende profesionalmente de música y quien, como María Cadilla, se interesa por lo popular, le ha dedicado algunos breves párrafos en un ensayo sobre música popular puertorriqueña.

"*La plena* es cosa de negros salvajes", me dijo cierta vez un buen señor, indignado de que yo la defendiera. Cosa de negros salvajes. En esa creencia estriba, a mi ver, el secreto de nuestra timidez frente a la *plena* y ante extraños. La frase parece darle la razón a un agudo visitante norteamericano que veía en el menosprecio de la *plena* indicios de antagonismos raciales. No andaba descaminado el estadounidense, aunque exageraba en su apreciación del prejuicio de raza.

Echar ahora un cuarto a espadas sobre el prejuicio racial en Puerto Rico necesitaría una digresión demasiado extensa para no recabar artículo aparte. Estimo, sin embargo, imprescindible hacer algunas consideraciones respecto al asunto antes de pasar adelante.

Creo que nuestro prejuicio racial, en la mayoría de los casos, se reduce exclusivamente a un horror irrazonable de ser tomado por mulato. Cada cual teme infundir sospechas de que en su genealogía pueda haber alguna gota de rítmica sangre de color. Se diría que vivimos subconscientemente asustados de pasar por negros bozales, y actuamos como si creyéramos que el mejor medio posible para neutralizar ese temor es el mostrar frecuentemente mezquinas puntas y ñoños ribetes de prejuicios raciales.

El auténtico veneno, el verdadero prejuicio racial, es agresivo, intransigente, cruel hasta llegar a lo cruento, y expresado en tono mayor. Nuestro llamado prejuicio es por lo común apologético, ruboroso y de tono menor. En la realidad efectiva de la vida boricua, el decantado prejuicio se manifiesta —a Dios gracias— paradójicamente tolerante y, en definitiva de casos concretos, parece un eco ofensivo de aberraciones forasteras.

No se explican estas pueriles manifestaciones del prejuicio sino como protesta irreflexiva de que se nos pueda considerar negros salvajes. Y esto parece ocurrir no sólo en cada caso individual, sino sobre todo, o por mal entendido patriotismo, cuando se trata del conjunto de nuestro pueblo.

Y, sin embargo, ni somos salvajes, ni somos negros tampoco; que es cosa muy aparte, también, de ser salvajes. A pesar de lo que matemáticamente pueda aseverar el censo oficial, creo que ningún observador cuidadoso negará que, entre nosotros, casi no existen negros puros. Para cerciorarse de esto basta comparar nuestros pardos más prietos con algunos cocolos barloventeños, con determinados jazz-bandistas de Norteamérica, o con los afrancesados senegaleses que se pasean por Europa.

Tampoco me convence por completo el censo oficial en cuanto a las cifras y porcentajes que adjudica a los blancos puros. Supongo que no convencerá a nadie que, sobre el terreno, haya contrastado la variedad de matices de piel y grados de pelo crespo; y, que, al mismo tiempo, sepa la manera dúctil, complaciente, esquemática, arbitraria y fácil como se hacen oficialmente —al buen tuntún— esas tontas clasificaciones pedantes.

En general, debe parecer evidente a todo el que tenga ojos y haya considerado el asunto con alguna objetividad, que Puerto Rico es la más blanca de todas las Antillas: que casi no tenemos negros puros; y que el número de blancos puros —computados *a grosso modo,* pero con mayor fidelidad que en el censo oficial— no alcanza a la mitad de la población. Por lo tanto, la mayoría de las gentes del país es de sangre mezclada; mestizos, morenos, mulatos, grifos, o blancos con dosis más o menos homeopática de pigmento negroide.

Aceptamos el hecho sin frío ni calor, pues no creo que sea honra o deshonra especial ser mestizo, blanco, negro, amarillo o rojo. Pero no caigamos en la puerilidad inocente de tratar de ocultar el cielo con la mano. Primero, porque por mucho que nos empeñemos, el cielo quedará siempre evidente ante la ridícula impotencia de la mano. Hasta la voz popular nativa se encarga de ponerlo en evidencia cuando admite en un refrán que "el que no tiene dinga tiene mandinga", y en otro, que "cuando la bomba *ñama,* el que no menea oreja menea nalga". En segundo lugar, porque mantener la inferioridad esencial de ciertas razas es un mero pretexto imperialista, digno sólo de nazis absurdos o de pintorescos coroneles honorarios de la Sudlandia estadounidense; que a nosotros no nos interesa secundar. La reivindicación de los valores inherentes a las diversas culturas primitivas es un hecho significativo de nuestro tiempo y un índice de la seriedad de los pensadores que de estas cosas se ocupan. Hoy sólo puede admitirse que hay pueblos en mayor o menor estado de desarrollo; pero de ningún modo adjudicar a la raza negra, a la amarilla o a la roja, como cualidad intrínseca e inseparable, la barbarie, el salvajismo o la inferioridad.

Tenemos abundante sangre negra, de la que no hay por qué avergonzarse; empero, haciendo honor a la verdad, no se nos puede clasificar como pueblo negro.

Típica de nuestro pueblo, nuestra *plena* no es ni negra ni, mucho menos, salvaje. En toda la Nigricia africana no podría encontrársele parangón exacto. La bomba bárbara —danza negra, baile de esclavos— dotó a su biznieta, la *plena,* con lo mejor que ella tenía: vigor natural, efectos de percusión y ritmos. El ritmo es excelencia negra. De esa excelencia participa

la *plena* con extraordinaria riqueza: sonoros ritmos trepidan-
tes, sincopados, repetidos, monótonos, que se combinan con
otros variables, alargados, elásticos, fugaces y llenos de insinuación. Este elemento negroide subraya el canto y jugue-
tea con él. Por todo lo demás, la *plena* es —plenamente—
blanca.

Nuestra música popular —independiente, pero paralela a
la española— se desenvuelve dentro de los módulos tradicionales de la Península. Es más bien sólo lo anecdótico —lo menos plástico— lo que se acentúa como propio y característico,
como cualidad diferencial. Y el fondo melódico de la *plena,*
como el de toda la música regional puertorriqueña, es de sabor marcadamente hispánico. Tan tradicionalmente español
es el fundamento melódico de la *plena,* que un culto peninsular, aficionado a escuchar plenas, me ha demostrado la evidente similitud de la línea melódica de *Santa María* con el motivo
esencial de una cántiga de Alfonso el Sabio. El dato es interesante y curioso, pues poca gente —o quizás nadie más que los
discípulos de algunos profesores visitantes españoles en nuestra Universidad; de don Federico de Onís y don Samuel Gil y
Gaya, principalmente— conocerá en Puerto Rico esos motivos
musicales de cántigas de la Edad Media española.

La letra de la *plena* es, por lo común, octosilábica y aso-
nantada como la del romance castellano. Comenta, como el
romance, episodios y anécdotas de la vida nacional: la expedición de nuestros soldados a Panamá, la quiebra bancaria,
el ciclón que azota la isla —*Submarino alemán, Moratoria,
Temporal*—, pregona los sucesos del día: el crimen pasional,
las vicisitudes del contrabandista, la llegada de un nuevo obispo —*Cortaron a Elena, Los muchachos de Cataño, El obispo
de Ponce*—; o, rememorando a Gonzalo de Berceo, glosa el
último milagro de la Virgen —*Santa María*—. Elabora, pues,
en fin, todos los temas que cautivan la fantasía popular. En
este aspecto, como en la melodía, la *plena* es de casta española: de una vena blanca. Pero también podría decirse que sigue
en ello, una tendencia universal, ya que la afición a fijar, en
narraciones cantadas, el relieve de los acontecimientos se puede decir que existe en todos los pueblos. Por eso tampoco es
extraña la *plena* a la costumbre autóctona de nuestros antiguos indios, cuyos areitos parecen haber sido equivalente aborigen del romance y la balada.

En los instrumentos con que se ejecuta típicamente la
plena, hay de todo: güícharo, maraca, tiple, guitarra, bordo-
núa, tambor... Es decir, lo indio, lo negro, lo blanco y las mo-

dificaciones regionales —producto evolutivo de la tierra— de estos tres elementos genéricos.

Difícilmente puede señalarse un pueblo de más rica coreografía que el español. Por otro lado, el baile es la máxima metáfora de la raza negra que, no sólo cuando habla, sino hasta cuando trabaja, baila. Y la *plena*, cuyo tambor tiene tanto de pandero europeo como de bongó yoruba, aúna y se apoya en ambos hechos. Destaco estas incidencias, al parecer triviales, que se funden en la *plena*, como símbolo del modo natural con que la *plena* conjuga y sintetiza tendencias, para formar algo propio, sin producir contrasentidos, promiscuidades antitéticas ni burundangas desarticuladas.

Burundanga es una mal cocida mezcla de componentes dispares —con frecuencia antagónicos— que coexisten, como matrimonio mal avenido, sin mutuo provecho ni armonía; mezcolanza sin sentido, como algazara de loros; disparatada, como olla de grillos; pretenciosa y absurda, como olac en cabeza de hotentote desnudo.

La *plena* supera la burundanga ambiente. Sin renegar del medio, selecciona, dosifica y coordina sus materiales. De lo heterogéneo crea una homogénea diversidad típica. Según compagina y concierta en una brava orquesta popular y característica los instrumentos y las voces que le sirven de vehículo, a pesar de sus distintos abolengos, así también compone y armoniza las influencias raciales disímiles que prestan base y antecedentes a su originalidad.

Pero hay entre nosotros quien se complace en despreciar la *plena* por entusiasta apego a la *danza* puertorriqueña. Algunos la desprecian, no sólo por ser *danza*, sino también por ser, en su opinión, "de origen negro". Negroides y mulatos son los sones cubanos y las cadencias de los bailes yanquis, y no por eso han dejado de dar la vuelta al mundo. Además, no creo equivocarme al anotar que la mayoría de los maestros creadores de nuestra *danza* llevaban en sus venas un feliz fermento extracaucásico —levadura de ritmos— que ha donado a la *danza* sus más típicos contornos. Otros dicen preferir la *danza* por culta y desdeñar la *plena* por vulgar; olvidando que la cultura no es patrimonio únicamente de lo pulido y retocado, ni la vulgaridad elemento inseparable de lo popular. Los más se limitan a elogiar la *danza* sin nombrar, ni para bien ni para mal, la *plena*, como si no existiera.

No obstante, la que lleva camino de no existir, sino como sombra de sí misma, es la *danza* y no la *plena*. La *danza* es planta de invernadero. Trasplantada y aclimatada, las modificaciones regionales que adquirió las obtuvo por injertos; se le cuidó el follaje y la floración a expensas del tallo y las raíces. Sus cultivadores le estilizaron la forma antes que el genio popular tuviera tiempo de modificar su savia. La *plena,* en cambio, es flor silvestre con hondas raigambres en el subsuelo. Resultando de un profundo proceso evolutivo —cruzamiento de pólenes, conjugación de gérmenes, transmutación de jugos— surge como aparente mutación espontánea. Así, la *plena* exhibe vigorosa vitalidad; en tanto que la *danza,* desde un principio, muestra languidez idiopática.

Muchas *danzas* son, ciertamente, lindos poemitas musicales. Pero sus mejores características son de índole adjetiva. En general, la danza concreta sus cualidades más representativas en la técnica, el procedimiento y la ejecución. Y su médula, su sustancia, es producto de época mucho más que obra de pueblo. Por eso ha podido ser acusada de extranjería; incorporándosela a un grupo de contradanzas sudamericanas —similares en el corte, como la *playera* peruana— que se bailaban por aquellas mismas fechas en que apareció el primer brote de nuestra variedad. Episódica por naturaleza, su esplendor estaba ligado a su tiempo. Muy siglo XIX, se ha ido desvinculando de nuestra realidad actual. Véase, si no, lo cursi que nos resulta hoy la letra de la más famosa de nuestras *danzas* que, indudablemente, en su época debió parecer cargada de gracia y emoción:

"Bellísima trigueña — imagen del candor — del jardín de Borinquen — pura y fragante flor. — Así se queda extático — todo mortal que ve — tu aire gentil, simpático — tu lindo y breve pie. — Cuando te asomas a tu balcón — la luz eclipsas del mismo sol. — ¡Oh, oh, oh!

En los cromos olorosos a cedro de las cajas de habanos se archivan todavía las contrafiguras de aquella bellísima trigueña —flor de hamaca— que la *danza* celebra. Ubérrima y suculenta mujer ante cuya matronil humanidad el extático mortal no veía —no podía o no admitía ver— más que el aire y el pie de la imagen del candor trigueño.

A tal hembra convenía la sensualidad ramplona que se regodea en los compases de las *danzas.* Lacrimeo suplicante y metáforas regordetas prestigiaban de romanticismo el falso ambiente en que se acunaba la galantería aristocrática de la época. Y entre floripondio y floripondio de cumplidos banales, eran los *merengues* de la *danza* la florinata pura de aquella galante aristocracia de papel de estaño.

Hoy ya no quedan sino algunos ejemplares supervivientes

de aquel tipo de mujer. Abunda, en cambio, la morena tendinosa, musculosa, espigada o redonda, tiernecita o madura; pero con jarretes y axilas en vez de pie y de aire. A pesar del avitaminoso arroz con habichuelas, no es rara ya la línea y la silueta elástica. Los mortales han perdido capacidad del éxtasis. Triunfa en las playas y piscinas el logarítmico traje de baño. El sol, lejos de ocultarse ruboroso o eclipsarse deslumbrante ante cualquier buena moza, besa muslos y espaldas, cosechando en las pieles femeninas campos de pelusilla madura. Y el candor ha dejado de ser piropo.

En tal atmósfera crece la *plena* que, inocente de retóricos disimulos, ni alambica ni convierte en melcocha su fuerte dinamismo sensual. Mulatica de tez dorada como ron añejo; de pelo lacio y ojos pícaros que pueden pasar por andaluces; de parla castellana, un poco arcaica; y, de ágil paso sensitivo, como de bestezuela selvática. Sinuosa y llena de vigor, tiene olores de tierra y sabor de marisco. Con frecuencia es burlona, traviesa y arisca. Habla en simples frases directas. Cuida de no empalagar cuando acaricia. Para plañir sus quejas prefiere un tono leve de ironía al sollozo y el llanto; y por la virtud de ser sencilla adquiere un sobrio dejo de liturgia en sus lamentaciones. Rara vez chabacana, se muestra en ocasiones chocarrera, pero con desvergüenza primitiva que tiene más de ingenuidad que de descoco. Y aun así, le basta con refrenarse un punto para hacer buen papel en sociedad —*dancings,* playas, salones— sin desmerecer entre sus congéneres: el un tanto desgarbado Seis, la aseñoritada Danza, el exótico Fox, el Vals ceremonioso, la Rumba desbocada y el vaselinado Tango.

Está bien que se aprecien con cariño y fervor nuestras mejores *danzas.* Que se saquen al sol como quien luce un abanico antiguo; el pericón de la abuela. O que se bailen con toda la frecuencia que lo exijan sus devotos. Pero proclamarlas esencia, síntesis y raíz de nuestro criollismo me parece —cuando menos— un error de perspectiva. Tratar de revivirlas artificiosamente sería desnaturalizar lo que hay en ellas de más genuino: su sabor de época. Por magistralmente hechos que fueran los intentos de crear nuevas *danzas,* en el futuro, no dejarían de parecer réplicas y pastiches, repeticiones y perífrasis. Sería como pretender resucitar el estilo de Luis XV en muebles de metal o reproducir el gótico en catedrales de cemento armado. Y rasgar las vestiduras porque la *danza* no está en auge, es como lamentarse de que no se lleven miriñaques, ni se estile la peluca empolvada, ni se viaje en carabelones.

Por el contrario, la *plena* —genuino gesto folklórico— es

un valor en germen que brinda virgen y rico material a quien con talento y cariño se decida seriamente a cultivarla.

Entretanto, mientras permanezca en el exclusivo dominio del pueblo, conviene procurar que las orquestinas profesionales la reproduzcan limpia de sofisticaciones y postizos, prescindiendo de imitar lo puramente exótico del jazz y evitando caer en meros plagios de ajenos cubanismos.

Nemesio Canales
1878—1923
Puerto Rico

¿Podemos ser felices?
Hacia un lejano sol. 1915-1923.

> *Consulta de una gentil e inteligente amiga:*
>
> *— ¿Cree Ud. que es posible en este mundo la felicidad, y, si no la felicidad, el bienestar?*

I

LA consulta es dificilísima, pero no he de evadirla por el temor de contestarla mal o deficientemente. No hay nadie, por muy indiferente que sea a las ideas, que no tenga su mucho o su poco por decir sobre este grande y universal problema humano; y yo, aunque he de guardarme bien de contestar a lo catedrático, a lo sabiendo, no voy, por un pueril alarde de modestia convencional, a privarme ahora del gusto de dar, de la manera más sencilla y clara posible, más bien que una opinión, mi impresión personal sobre el asunto.

No; no creo que sea asequible la felicidad, ni en este mundo ni en ningún otro mundo. Es más, creo que cometemos una barbaridad cuando damos a nuestros hijos, en la escuela, en la casa, en el teatro, en el libro, esa visión de felicidad personal tan reñida, tan incompatible con nuestra propia naturaleza y con la naturaleza de la realidad que nos rodea.

Felicidad, felicidad... ¿Dónde demonios se esconde ese divino tesoro, que nadie le encuentra ni le encontró jamás? Topa uno con un viejo y le pregunta; y de cada cien viejos, noventa y nueve viejos suspirarán profundamente primero, y nos contestarán en seguida una de estas dos cosas: o que la perdieron para siempre y se les quedó (la felicidad) atrás, muy atrás, en alguna curva remota del camino andado, o que no la tuvieron nunca y la van a buscar en el reposo eterno, o en el edén eterno que les prometió tal o cual religión. Topamos con un joven... y nos dirá que, o la dejó también atrás, allá en la lejanía de la niñez, o que va corriendo, corriendo sin cesar en pos de ella, con o sin esperanzas de darle alcance. Y si interrumpe Ud. los juegos de un niño cualquiera y logra que le entienda la pregunta, seguramente que, o no saca nada en claro de la inconsciencia del niño, o le ve pronto señalar hacia el futuro con las clásicas palabras que todos hemos pronunciado: "Cuando yo sea hombre...".

Quiere decir que está atrás, o está delante, o está arriba, o está abajo: en todas partes, menos en el punto en que nos encontramos. Y es que tiene que ser así; es que sería absurdo que no fuese así. ¿Cómo concebir la evolución, o sea, el movimiento, esencia misma de la vida, sin la inquietud, sin el perpetuo temer y el perpetuo aspirar y el constante cambiar de aquí para allá y de allá para acá? ¿Y cómo, si fuéramos felices, podríamos mantener este vaivén, este anhelar engendrador de toda evolución y por consiguiente de la vida?

Somos limitados, somos frágiles como el vidrio, nos rodea por todas partes lo inestable, lo sombrío, lo sucio, lo duro, lo trágico. ¿Cómo, pues, dentro de nuestra limitación y fragilidad irremediables, concebir ese estado ideal de íntima y perfecta satisfacción en que nos sintamos libres de temores y pesares y deseos?

No quiere esto decir que yo sea pesimista a lo Shopenhauer, que sólo ve dolor y oscuridad por todas partes. Al contrario, creo fácil comprobar que la cantidad de dolor que hay en el mundo, con ser muy grande, es infinitamente inferior a la cantidad de alegría, de igual modo que la cantidad de salud es superior a la cantidad de enfermedad y la cantidad de juventud a la cantidad de ancianidad. Pero ¿es la alegría la felicidad? No; la alegría es orgánica, es subconsciente, nace precisamente de no *sentirnos,* de cierta armonía rara y fugaz entre las distintas piezas que componen la maravilla de nuestra máquina. En cambio, la felicidad es, o debe ser, esencialmente consciente, naciendo o debiendo nacer de los deseos satisfechos, de pensarnos y sentirnos bien. Tan no tienen nada que ver las dos cosas, la alegría y la felicidad, que se puede ser muy infeliz y estar al mismo tiempo muy alegre. De ello nos da ejemplos constantes la diaria realidad.

La alegría es dinámica, esto es, movimiento, vibración, aleteo fugitivo del espíritu, agua que corre, rama que ondula, ave que vuela, cuerda tensa que suena. En tanto que la felicidad es, o la concebimos, cosa permanente y estática, de la cual fluye la alegría como de una flor el aroma, como de un manantial el agua y de un astro la luz. La alegría es la manifestación, el síntoma, el accidente; la felicidad es la causa, la fuente, la sustancia inmutable. La alegría no puede buscarse deliberadamente, porque es caprichosa, tornátil, inconsciente, oscilante; va y viene, nos asalta y nos deja, aparece y desaparece caprichosamente, sin que nada baste a retenerla. Nadie puede salir a buscarla, porque mientras más la busca menos la encuentra, como no se puede buscar la risa, ni el buen apetito, ni el golpe de azar. Precisamente está más lejos de nosotros a medida que la sabemos buscar mejor, con mayor pericia y deliberación; y así vemos que el viejo es menos alegre que el joven y el joven menos que el niño. Es casi animal, casi mecánica, genuinamente fisiológica, en tanto que la felicidad es, o tendría que ser, genuinamente psicológica.

Y por eso, porque la vida es y no puede ser otra cosa que movimiento, vibración, esfuerzo, tendencia constante a cambiar y a mejorar, es por lo que decía antes que está reñida irremediablemente con toda noción de felicidad, bien sea esa felicidad rolliza, pesada, mofletuda, de gorro y chinela, con que sueña el burgués; bien de la otra quintaesenciada y etérea del místico, o bien de la remojada en mieles empalagosas de amor y de música y poesía que seduce por regla general al artista. De cualquiera de esos tipos convencionales de felicidad debemos aprender a reírnos, en primer lugar, porque son inasequibles por ser incompatibles con nuestra propia naturaleza, y en segundo lugar, porque, vaya, seamos sinceros, no valen la pena. Así como suena: no valen la pena. La primera, la burguesa, la de gorro y chinela, y buena alfombra, y casa grande y cómoda, es grotesca y odiosa. ¿Hay nada más aburrido que comer bien y vestir bien y arrellanarse bien en un butacón sobre una gran alfombra y ser siempre y a todas horas un cerdo limpio y bien comido, y no tener preocupaciones, y volverse una bola de plebeyo egoísmo, extraño a toda solidaridad con el mundo, y no vivir sino para el largo bostezo del casino, del automóvil, de la charla insustancial, y para estar a todas horas y en todas partes condenados a sentirse la digestión? Dadle esa clase de felicidad a un hombre de pensamiento o de nervios, y se volverá loco o se pegará un tiro antes de un mes. Dadle esa clase de felicidad espesa a cualquier hombre de tipo corriente que no sea un idiota, y no se volverá loco ni se exasperará hasta el suicidio, pero irá poco a poco trocándola en el *sport* tal o en el *sport* cual, que es como trocarla en trabajo, en trabajo disfrazado y estéril, pero trabajo al fin.

La segunda, la mística, es todavía más incompatible con el hombre y con las cosas. Vivir con la mirada fija en otro mundo es sencillamente como no vivir, como una forma de estar muerto con apariencias de vida.

Y en cuanto a la tercera, la de los adolescentes y las niñas románticas y los poetas ingenuos; la que navega en mieles de erotismo y melodía, la que nos sirven en la escuela, en el teatro y en todas partes, es la más idiota de todas. Se puede ser un cerdo limpio y bien comido y halagado durante algunos días y no volverse loco de asco de sí mismo hasta después de cierto tiempo; pero yo desafío a los paladares más golosos y más fuertes a que se refocilen, no ya durante muchos días, sino durante un solo día, con las melosas y aromadas golosinas de la estética, de la melodía y del dúo tremulante de romántico amor: el empalago sería tal, que la víctima pediría a gritos la cárcel o la horca para escapar del tremendo suplicio.

"Pero, entonces, ¿qué buscar? ¿qué hacer?", se me dirá.

¿Qué hacer? Pues una cosa muy sencilla: vivir. Pero vivir, ¿para qué? Vivir para lo que es esencia misma, aspiración recóndita y suprema finalidad de toda vida.

II

Al llegar a este punto de lo que debe ser nuestra vida, me doy cuenta de que insensiblemente he llegado hasta tocar el cogollo del más arduo e inmenso de los problemas humanos, y tiemblo de espanto. Dar nada menos que una pauta, que una fórmula precisa y definitiva sobre el rumbo que debemos tratar de imprimirle a nuestra vida es como ofrendarle de una vez a la humanidad una síntesis, un extracto de todas las filosofías. Y como ni soñar puedo en tal obra, me apresuro a repetir que no emprendí esta pequeña y sencilla exposición de mis puntos de vista con ínfulas doctorales, sino puramente como un espectador que ha ido al teatro, no para dormirse, sino para observar, para asomarse, todo curiosidad y simpatía, a lo que está pasando en escena... y ahora prorrumpir en un aplauso, y luego en una exclamación de disgusto o de horror, y después permitirse tímidamente un comentario, y en todo tiempo mantenerse despierto y alerta para no perder ni un solo detalle importante de la acción central. No son, pues, conclusiones y sistemas los que voy a formular. Son impresiones, pero impresiones de un espectador que, ni se ha puesto a dormir y a roncar, ni se ha quedado alejado e indiferente.

Pero, basta de preámbulos, y vamos a la cuestión. La cuestión es ésta: ¿qué buscar, qué hacer, qué orientación imprimirle a la vida?

Empiezo por opinar que lo primero que debemos tratar de eliminar totalmente de nuestras costumbres es ese sentido de permanencia, de estabilidad, de duración, que la mayor parte de las gentes le dan a la vida. *En la playa, pronto a zarpar, y desnudo, como los hijos de la mar.* Así dice un gran poeta español, Antonio Machado. No sé si he transcrito fielmente la frase, pero vale ella sola por muchos tomos de sabia y enmarañada filosofía.

En efecto, puesto que la vida es inestable, fugaz, casi tan imprecisa y tornátil como el humo, ¿a qué conduce ese absurdo empeño de instalarnos dentro de ella, no como quien está de paso y sin fecha de salida, sino como quien está muy seguro de quedarse para siempre?

La casa recia, de ladrillo, hecha como para burlarse del tiempo; dentro de la casa los muebles, fuertes, duros, tan eternos como la casa; y fuera de la casa, el esfuerzo continuo, perseverante, para conquistarnos posiciones tan sólidas, tan altas, que duren siglos. Resultado de todo ello, que, a fuerza de trabajar la jaula y de buscarle el más sólido y encumbrado acomodo, no tenemos tiempo para nada más: para mirarnos, para sentirnos, y hallarnos, y cultivarnos nosotros mismos.

De ahí viene que, a medida que hemos ido acumulando más cosas, más éxitos fuera de nosotros, nos hemos ido empobreciendo y empequeñeciendo más y más nosotros mismos, como personas, como tipos humanos. Hemos trabajado hasta reventar por lo externo, por la casa, por los muebles, por la posición, pero nada hemos hecho por nosotros. Nuestra curiosidad, nuestra gran curiosidad ante el espectáculo del mundo se quedó insaciada, nuestros afectos durmieron, nuestras células cerebrales no vibraron... y el moho nos consumió y todo nuestro mecanismo quedó, por la inacción, atrofiado y perdido en sus órganos más nobles y esenciales, tales como el corazón y el cerebro. Es como si un pájaro, por obstinarse en hacerse de un seguro e indestructible asilo, se pasase la vida en la tarea de construirlo. Habría nido, quizás, algún día, pero el pájaro, por no haber volado, por no haber trinado, por no haber amado, por no haber respondido a sus instintos, estaría ya atrofiado e insensibilizado de tal modo que más que para el nido serviría para el reposo de la muerte. ¡Amigos!, puesto que no podemos pasar sin esto y sin aquello, cosas necesarias pero secundarias, laboremos por esto y por aquello; pero, puesto que nos vamos, labremos de prisa y corriendo estructuras ligeras, sencillas y efímeras como nosotros mismos, y adelante, que el tiempo es corto y las cosas por pensar y por sentir y por probar muchísimas.

Ya libres del fardo pesadísimo de preocupaciones que arropan y sofocan nuestra verdadera alma; ya hechos a mirarnos a nosotros mismos como a simples caminantes, marchemos sin miedo, sin cogernos pena, alegremente, con los ojos tan abiertos, tan llenos de curiosa simpatía hacia las cosas que contemplan, como los de una tropa de soldados jóvenes y sanos que, sabedora de que marcha al encuentro de una muerte cierta en las garras de un enemigo diez veces superior, pone en su mirada la cálida fulguración que es a la vez saludo y despedida.

Pero ¿y la felicidad? ¿acaso vale la pena de vivir cuando se ha renunciado a ella? —oigo que me interrogan—. Sí, vale la pena. Prueba de ello es que todos, de Shopenhauer para abajo, hemos vivido sin gran ilusión de ella. Ni es la felicidad condición esencial de la vida, porque si así fuera no existiríamos, ya que ella no existe; ni la esperanza de alcanzarla es la que nos mantiene, como piensan muchos, en la senda y marchando; porque, si así fuera, a mayor ancianidad, mayor amortiguamiento de esperanza, mayor deseo de no vivir, de extinguirse, de no ser, y la experiencia nos está todos los días demostrando que los viejos se agarran a su desmayada vida con más furor si cabe que los jóvenes.

No hay más remedio, pues, que reconocer que el resorte oculto que nos mueve, que la aspiración recóndita, subconsciente, que late en todo ser humano, es cosa muy distinta y muy distante del deseo de la visión próxima o remota de la felicidad. Pero ¿con qué palabra expresar esa inefable, esa profunda ansia de vivir de perdurar, de quedarnos hasta *el sol de mañana,* y así, de día en día, perpetuarnos en este lugar de lucha y sufrimiento y tedio que llamamos mundo?

Después de pensar mucho sobre el punto, ninguna palabra me parece más propia que ésta: *expresión.* Sí; vivimos y queremos vivir a todo trance, porque nos urge *expresarnos,* realizarnos, porque somos a manera de una cinta cinematográfica enrollada que desea, que necesita desenrollarse, mostrarse, fijarse en obras de acción o de pensamiento. Somos una condensación de la masa cósmica universal, condensación que en cada individuo se tiñe de un color, de un matiz, de una luz especial, y aspiramos a vivir, porque aspiramos a arder hasta el fin, quemar hasta el fin todo el gas de misterio, todo el fluido de infinito que hemos recibido. No hay más que seguir la evolución de la Vida, desde el mineral hasta el hombre: continuamente, incesantemente, la vida va fabricando, va sacando de las tinieblas: seres, formas, organismos cada vez más complejos, cada vez más diferenciados entre sí, más individuales, más dotados de una potencialidad mayor de comprensión. ¿Con qué ha vencido, con qué ha triunfado el hombre de las demás especies animales? ¿Ha sido con la fuerza? No; porque más fuertes, mil veces más fuertes eran los gigantescos animales prehistóricos y quedaron vencidos. Y hoy mismo la fuerza del hombre está perennemente humillada ante el león, ante el tigre, ante el toro, todos los cuales, sin embargo, son sus servidores o sus víctimas.

¿Ha sido con la euritmia de sus líneas, con la belleza de sus formas, que el hombre se ha impuesto como ser superior? No; porque ahí están los pájaros, el más humilde de los cuales es más bello en ritmo, en musicalidad de líneas que el más soberbio Apolo.

Ha sido, pues, con lo único que el hombre tiene y no tienen los animales, esto es, con cerebro, con potencialidad lumínica, con fuerza de expresión y de comprensión. ¿Cómo escapar, pues, en vista de esta marcha progresiva, de esta progresión ascendente desde la opacidad, la pesadez y la inconsciencia, hasta la fulguración de consciencia que es el genio, a la conclusión de que la Vida fabrica cerebros, esto es, instrumentos para conocerse, para mirar dentro de sí misma?

En esta interpretación de la finalidad de la Vida han coincidido Renán, Nietzsche, Bernard Shaw... cumbres las más altas del pensamiento humano. Para estos poderosos dínamos de ideación, somos nosotros los hombres los que representamos la fórmula más perfecta hasta hoy de consciencia acumulada, de condensación de Vida, y por consiguiente puede afirmarse que en nosotros reside toda divinidad.

Todo lo que hay de individualidad en nosotros es tan ilusorio como lo que hay de individualidad en la sombra con relación a los cuerpos y en la espuma con relación a la ola. Sombra y espuma no son más que aspectos, ilusiones ópticas del cuerpo y del agua respectivamente. No existe el hombre A, el hombre B, el hombre C, pues todos no somos otra cosa que la fuerza o energía universal y eterna que llamamos la Vida y que las religiones designan con el nombre de Dios. De la misma manera que un escultor que estuviera buscando una imagen, una forma de expresión artística perfecta, podría servirse de un solo bloque de mármol para ensayar y volver a ensayar mil tipos de escultura, cada uno de los cuales no sería otra cosa en realidad que el primitivo bloque de mármol, así nosotros los seres humanos, a pesar de nuestras diferencias aparentes, no somos más que formas, imágenes plasmadas incesantemente por la Vida. Por consiguiente, no nacemos ni morimos, como no nace ni muere la sombra, ni la espuma, ni la imagen. ¿A qué temer la muerte, pues?

Asociémonos a la obra misteriosa de la vida, porque de ella formamos parte, o mejor, porque somos ella misma, y humilde y religiosamente tratemos de que el misterio, el sacro fuego, el Dios en formación que vive en nosotros, se manifieste siempre en su más alta, más intensa y más clara expresión.

El camino

No soy ni providencialista, ni determinista. No creo en una trayectoria fatal, predeterminada, ni para los individuos ni para los pueblos. Por el contrario, creo que la vida es toda ella una perenne evolución, no circunstancial o mecánica como la cree Darwin, sino deliberadamente creadora...

Si, pues, estamos ahora en un momento de nuestro desenvolvimiento histórico en que se liquida una situación política y se abre otra, tratemos de no incurrir en la banalidad de una infantil vanagloria por la labor realizada, y concentremos toda nuestra energía mental en un grande y noble esfuerzo por vencer. Por vencer no a éste ni a aquél adversario en las ideas o procedimientos, sino a esa sombría acumulación de nubes —tradiciones muertas, supersticiones mezquinas y malignas, egoísmos bárbaros y feroces— que nos impiden ver claro el camino.

¿El Camino?... Sí; nuestro camino, aquel que nos está indicado por nuestra misma tierra, tan frondosa, tan rica, tan llena de cielo, tan musical, tan bella.

Sobre una tierra así, ¿qué otra divisa para nuestro escudo de *Caballeros del Bien* que aquel que enunció Cristo cuando habló de la *vida abundante?* Vida sin trabas: sol, aire, pan, salud, alegría, amor; que nada de esto falte bajo ningún techo puertorriqueño, so pena de sentirnos humillados, mancillados, deshonrados en nuestro papel de paladines del bien. La naturaleza nos dio un jardín por habitación. ¿Cómo vamos a tolerar que de este jardín se enseñoreen, por desidia o ignorancia nuestra, el cardo, el gusano, la mugre, la fealdad y la desolación?

Julio Cortázar
1916–1984
Argentina

Algunos aspectos del cuento
Casa de las Américas. La Habana, año II, Nos. 15-16, nov. 1962-feb. 1963

ME encuentro hoy ante ustedes en una situación bastante paradójica. Un cuentista argentino se dispone a cambiar ideas acerca del cuento sin que sus oyentes y sus interlocutores, salvo algunas excepciones, conozcan nada de su obra. El aislamiento cultural que sigue perjudicando a nuestros países, sumado a la injusta incomunicación a que se ve sometida Cuba en la actualidad, han determinado que mis libros, que son ya unos cuantos, no hayan llegado más que por excepción a manos de lectores tan dispuestos y tan entusiastas como ustedes. Lo malo de esto no es tanto que ustedes no hayan tenido oportunidad de juzgar mis cuentos, sino que yo me siento un poco como un fantasma que viene a hablarles sin esa relativa tranquilidad que da siempre el saberse precedido por la labor cumplida a lo largo de los años. Y esto de sentirme como un fantasma debe ser ya perceptible en mí, porque hace unos días una señora argentina me aseguró en el hotel Riviera que yo no era Julio Cortázar, y ante mi estupefacción agregó que el auténtico Julio Cortázar es un señor de cabellos blancos, muy amigo de un pariente suyo, y que no se ha movido nunca de Buenos Aires. Como yo hace doce años que resido en París, comprenderán ustedes que mi calidad espectral se ha intensificado notablemente después de esta revelación. Si de golpe desaparezco en mitad de una frase, no me sorprenderé demasiado; y a lo mejor salimos todos ganando.

Se afirma que el deseo más ardiente de un fantasma es recobrar por lo menos un asomo de corporeidad, algo tangible que lo devuelva por un momento a su vida de carne y hueso. Para lograr un poco de tangibilidad ante ustedes, voy a decir en pocas palabras cuál es la dirección y el sentido de mis cuentos. No lo hago por mero placer informativo, porque ninguna reseña teórica puede sustituir la obra en sí; mis razones son más importantes que ésa. Puesto que voy a ocuparme de algunos aspectos del cuento como género literario, y es posible que algunas de mis ideas sorprendan o choquen a quienes las escuchen, me parece de una elemental honradez definir el tipo de narración que me interesa, señalando mi especial manera de entender el mundo. Casi todos los cuentos que he escrito pertenecen al género llamado fantástico por falta de mejor nombre, y se oponen a ese falso realismo que consiste en creer que todas las cosas pueden describirse y explicarse como lo daba por sentado el optimismo filosófico y científico del siglo XVIII, es decir, dentro de un mundo regido más o menos armoniosamente por un sistema de leyes, de principios, de relaciones de causa a efecto, de psicologías definidas, de geografías bien cartografiadas. En mi caso, la sospecha de otro orden más secreto y menos comunicable, y el fecundo descubrimiento de Alfred Jarry, para quien el verdadero estudio de la realidad no residía en las leyes sino en las excepciones a esas leyes, han sido algunos de los principios orientadores de mi búsqueda personal de una literatura al margen de todo realismo demasiado ingenuo. Por eso, si en las ideas que siguen encuentran ustedes una predilección por todo lo que en el cuento es excepcional, trátese de los temas o incluso de las formas expresivas, creo que esta presentación de mi propia manera de entender el mundo explicará mi toma de posición y mi enfoque del problema. En último extremo podrá decirse que sólo he hablado del cuento tal y como yo lo practico. Y sin embargo no creo que sea así. Tengo la certidumbre de que existen ciertas constantes, ciertos valores que se aplican a todos los cuentos, fantásticos o realistas, dramáticos o humorísticos. Y pienso que tal vez sea posible mostrar aquí esos elementos invariables que dan a un buen cuento su atmósfera peculiar y su calidad de obra de arte.

La oportunidad de cambiar ideas acerca del cuento me interesa por diversas razones. Vivo en un país —Francia— donde este género tiene poca vigencia, aunque en los últimos años se nota entre escritores y lectores un interés creciente por esa forma de expresión. De todos modos, mientras los críticos siguen acumulando teorías y manteniendo enconadas polémicas acerca de la novela, casi nadie se interesa por la problemática del cuento. Vivir como cuentista en un país donde esta forma expresiva es un producto casi exótico, obliga forzosamente a buscar en otras literaturas el alimento que allí falta. Poco a poco, en sus textos originales o mediante traducciones, uno va acumulando casi rencorosamente una enorme cantidad de cuentos del pasado y del presente, y llega el día en que puede hacer un balance, intentar una aproximación valorativa a ese género de tan difícil definición, tan huidizo en sus múltiples y antagónicos aspectos, y en última instancia tan secreto y replegado en sí mismo, caracol del lenguaje, hermano misterioso de la poesía en otra dimensión del tiempo literario.

Pero además de ese alto en el camino que todo escritor debe hacer en algún momento de su labor, hablar del cuento tiene un interés especial para nosotros, puesto que casi todos los países americanos de lengua española le están dando al cuento una importancia excepcional, que jamás había tenido en otros países latinos como Francia o España. Entre nosotros, como es natural en las literaturas jóvenes, la creación espontánea precede casi siempre al examen crítico, y está bien que así sea. Nadie puede pretender que los cuentos sólo deban escribirse luego de conocer sus leyes. En primer lugar, no hay tales leyes; a lo sumo cabe hablar de puntos de vista, de ciertas constantes que dan una estructura a ese género tan poco encasillable; en segundo lugar, los teóricos y los críticos no tienen por qué ser los cuentistas mismos, y es natural que aquéllos sólo entren en escena cuando exista ya un acervo, un acopio de literatura que permita indagar y esclarecer su desarrollo y sus cualidades. En América, tanto en Cuba como en México o Chile o Argentina, una gran cantidad de cuentistas trabaja desde comienzos del siglo, sin conocerse mucho entre sí, descubriéndose a veces de manera casi póstuma. Frente a ese panorama sin coherencia suficiente, en el que pocos conocen a fondo la labor de los demás, creo que es útil hablar del cuento por encima de las particularidades nacionales e internacionales, porque es un género que entre nosotros tiene una importancia y una vitalidad que crecen de día en día. Alguna vez se harán las antologías definitivas —como las hacen los países anglosajones, por ejemplo— y se sabrá hasta dónde hemos sido capaces de llegar. Por el momento no me parece inútil hablar del cuento en abstracto, como género literario. Si nos hacemos una idea convincente de esa forma de expresión literaria, ella podrá contribuir a establecer una escala de valores para esa antología ideal que está por hacerse. Hay demasiada confusión, demasiados malentendidos en este terreno. Mientras los cuentistas siguen adelante su tarea, ya es tiempo de hablar de esa tarea en sí misma, al margen de las personas y de las nacionalidades. Es preciso llegar a tener una idea viva de lo que es el cuento, y eso es siempre difícil en la medida en que las ideas tienden a lo abstracto, a desvitalizar su contenido, mientras que a su vez la vida rechaza angustiada ese lazo que quiere echarle la conceptuación para fijarla y categorizarla. Pero si no tenemos una idea viva de lo que es el cuento habremos perdido el tiempo, porque un cuento, en última instancia, se mueve en ese plano del hombre donde la vida y la expresión escrita de esa vida libran una batalla fraternal, si se me permite el término; y el resultado de esa batalla es el cuento mismo, una síntesis viviente a la vez que una vida sintetizada, algo así como un temblor de agua dentro de un cristal, una fugacidad en una permanencia. Sólo con imágenes se puede transmitir esa alquimia secreta que explica la profunda resonancia que un gran cuento tiene en nosotros, y que explica también por qué hay muy pocos cuentos verdaderamente grandes.

Para entender el carácter peculiar del cuento se lo suele comparar con la novela, género mucho más popular y sobre el cual abundan las preceptivas. Se señala, por ejemplo, que la novela se desarrolla en el papel, y por lo tanto en el tiempo de lectura, sin otros límites que el agotamiento de la materia novelada; por su parte, el cuento parte de la noción de límite, y en primer término de límite físico, al punto que en Francia, cuando un cuento excede de las veinte páginas, toma ya el nombre de *nouvelle*, género a caballo entre el cuento y la novela propiamente dicha. En este sentido, la novela y el cuento se dejan comparar analógicamente con el cine y la fotografía, en la medida en que una película es en principio un "orden abierto", novelesco, mientras que una fotografía lograda

presupone una ceñida limitación previa, impuesta en parte
por el reducido campo que abarca la cámara y por la forma
en que el fotógrafo utiliza estéticamente esa limitación. No
sé si ustedes han oído hablar de su arte a un fotógrafo profesional; a mí siempre me ha sorprendido el que se exprese tal
como podría hacerlo un cuentista en muchos aspectos. Fotógrafos de la calidad de un Cartier-Bresson o de un Brassaï definen su arte como una aprente paradoja: la de recortar un
fragmento de la realidad, fijándole determinados límites,
pero de manera tal que ese recorte actúe como una explosión que abre de par en par una realidad mucho más amplia,
como una visión dinámica que trasciende espiritualmente el
campo abarcado por la cámara. Mientras en el cine, como en
la novela, la captación de esa realidad más amplia y multifor-
me se logra mediante el desarrollo de elementos parciales,
acumulativos, que no excluyen, por supuesto, una síntesis
que dé el *clímax* de la obra, en una fotografía o un cuento
de gran calidad se procede inversamente, es decir que el fotógrafo o el cuentista se ven precisados a escoger y limitar una
imagen o un acaecimiento que sean *significativos,* que no solamente valgan por sí mismos sino que sean capaces de actuar
en el espectador o en el lector como una especie de *apertura,*
de fermento que proyecta la inteligencia y la sensibilidad hacia algo que va mucho más allá de la anécdota visual o literaria contenidas en la foto o en el cuento. Un escritor argentino, muy amigo del boxeo, me decía que en ese combate que
se entabla entre un texto apasionante y su lector, la novela
gana siempre por puntos, mientras que el cuento debe ganar
por *knockout.* Es cierto, en la medida en que la novela acu-
mula progresivamente sus efectos en el lector, mientras que
un buen cuento es incisivo, mordiente, sin cuartel, desde las
primeras frases. No se entienda esto demasiado literalmente,
porque el buen cuentista es un boxeador muy astuto, y muchos de sus golpes iniciales pueden parecer poco eficaces
cuando, en realidad, están minando ya las resistencias más sólidas del adversario. Tomen ustedes cualquier gran cuento que
prefieran elementos gratuitos, meramente decorativos. El
cuentista sabe que no puede proceder acumulativamente, que
no tiene por aliado al tiempo; su único recurso es trabajar en
profundidad, verticalmente, sea hacia arriba o hacia abajo
del espacio literario. Y esto, que así expresado parece una
metáfora, expresa sin embargo lo esencial del método. El
tiempo del cuento y el espacio del cuento tienen que estar
como condensados, sometidos a una alta presión espiritual y

formal para provocar esa *apertura* a que me refería antes.
Basta preguntarse por qué un determinado cuento es malo.
No es malo por el tema, porque en literatura no hay temas
buenos ni temas malos, hay solamente un buen o un mal tratamiento del tema. Tampoco es malo porque los personajes
carecen de interés, ya que hasta una piedra es interesante
cuando de ella se ocupan un Henry James o un Franz Kafka.
Un cuento es malo cuando se lo escribe sin esa tensión que
debe manifestarse desde las primeras palabras o las primeras
escenas. Y así podemos adelantar ya que las nociones de significación, de intensidad y de tensión han de permitirnos, como se verá, acercarnos mejor a la estructura misma del cuento.

Decíamos que el cuentista trabaja con un material que ca-
lificamos de significativo. El elemento significativo del cuento
parecería residir principalmente *en su tema*, en el hecho de
escoger un acaecimiento real o fingido que posea esa misteriosa propiedad de irradiar algo más allá de sí mismo, al punto que un vulgar episodio doméstico, como ocurre en tantos
admirables relatos de una Katherine Mansfield o de un Sherwood Anderson, se convierta en el resumen implacable de
una cierta condición humana, o en el símbolo quemante de
un orden social o histórico. Un cuento es significativo cuando
quiebra sus propios límites con esa explosión de energía espiritual que ilumina bruscamente algo que va mucho más allá
de la pequeña y a veces miserable anécdota que cuenta. Pienso, por ejemplo, en el tema de la mayoría de los admirables
relatos de Antón Chéjov. ¿Qué hay allí que no sea tristemen-
te cotidiano, mediocre, muchas veces conformista o inútilmente rebelde? Lo que se cuenta en esos relatos es casi lo
que de niños, en las aburridas tertulias que debíamos compartir con los mayores, escuchábamos contar a los abuelos o a
las tías; la pequeña, insignificante crónica familiar de ambi-
ciones frustradas, de modestos dramas locales, de angustias a
la medida de una sala, de un piano, de un té con dulces. Y
sin embargo, los cuentos de Katherine Mansfield, de Chéjov,
son significativos, algo estalla en ellos mientras los leemos y
nos propone una especie de ruptura de lo cotidiano que va
mucho más allá de la anécdota reseñada. Ustedes se han dado
ya cuenta de que esa significación misteriosa no reside solamente en el tema del cuento, porque en verdad la mayoría
de los malos cuentos que todos hemos leído contienen episodios similares a los que tratan los autores nombrados. La
idea de significación no puede tener sentido si no la relacio-
namos con las de intensidad y de tensión, que ya no se refie-

ren solamente al tema sino al tratamiento literario de ese tema. Y es aquí donde, bruscamente, se produce el deslinde entre el buen y el mal cuentista. Por eso habremos de detener-
nos con todo el cuidado posible en esta encrucijada, para tratar de entender un poco más esa extraña forma de vida que es
un cuento logrado, y ver por qué está vivo mientras otros,
que aparentemente se le parecen, no son más que tinta sobre
papel, alimento para el olvido.

Miremos la cosa desde el ángulo del cuentista y en este caso,
obligadamente, desde mi propia versión del asunto. Un cuentista es un hombre que de pronto, rodeado de la inmensa algarabía del mundo, comprometido en mayor o menor grado
con la realidad histórica que lo contiene, escoge un determinado tema y hace con él un cuento. Este escoger un tema no
es tan sencillo. A veces el cuentista escoge, y otras veces siente como si el tema se le impusiera irresistiblemente, lo empu-
jara a escribirlo. En mi caso, la gran mayoría de mis cuentos
fueron escritos —cómo decirlo— al margen de mi voluntad,
por encima o por debajo de mi conciencia razonante, como si
yo no fuera más que un médium por el cual pasaba y se ma-
nifestaba una fuerza ajena. Pero esto, que puede depender del
temperamento de cada uno, no altera el hecho esencial y es
que en un momento dado *hay tema,* ya sea inventado o escogido voluntariamente, o extrañamente impuesto desde un plano donde nada es definible. Hay tema, repito, y ese tema va a
volverse cuento. Antes de que ello ocurra, ¿qué podemos decir del tema en sí? ¿Por qué ese tema y no otro? ¿Qué razones mueven consciente o inconscientemente al cuentista a escoger un determinado tema?

A mí me parece que el tema del que saldrá un buen cuento es siempre *excepcional,* pero no quiero decir con esto que
un tema deba ser extraordinario, fuera de lo común, misterioso o insólito. Muy al contrario, puede tratarse de una anécdota perfectamente trivial y cotidiana. Lo excepcional reside
en una cualidad parecida a la del imán; un buen tema atrae
todo un sistema de relaciones conexas, coagula en el autor, y
más tarde en el lector, una inmensa cantidad de nociones, en-
trevisiones, sentimientos y hasta ideas que flotaban virtualmente en su memoria o su sensibilidad; un buen tema es como un sol, un astro en torno al cual gira un sistema planeta-
rio del que muchas veces no se tenía conciencia hasta que el
cuentista, astrónomo de palabras, nos revela su existencia. O
bien, para ser más modestos y más actuales a la vez, un buen
tema tiene algo de sistema atómico, de núcleo en torno al cual

giran los electrones; y todo eso, al fin y al cabo, ¿no es ya como una proposición de vida, una dinámica que nos insta a salir de nosotros mismos y a entrar en un sistema de relaciones más complejo y más hermoso? Muchas veces me he preguntado cuál es la virtud de ciertos cuentos inolvidables. En el momento los leímos junto con muchos otros, que incluso podían ser de los mismos autores. Y he aquí que los años han pasado, y hemos vivido y olvidado tanto; pero esos pequeños, insignificantes cuentos, esos granos de arena en el inmenso mar de la literatura, siguen ahí, latiendo en nosotros. ¿No es verdad que cada uno tiene su colección de cuentos? Yo tengo la mía, y podría dar algunos nombres. Tengo "William Wilson", de Edgar Poe, tengo "Bola de sebo", de Guy de Maupassant. Los pequeños planetas giran y giran: ahí está "Un recuerdo de Navidad", de Truman Capote, "Tlon, Uqbar, Orbis Tertius", de Jorge Luis Borges, "Un sueño realizado", de Juan Carlos Onetti, "La muerte de Iván Ilich", de Tolstoy, "Fifty Grand", de Hemingway, "Los soñadores", de Izak Dinesen, y así podría seguir y seguir... Ya habrán advertido ustedes que no todos esos cuentos son obligadamente de antología. *¿Por qué* perduran en la memoria? Piensen en los cuentos que no han podido olvidar y verán que todos ellos tienen la misma característica: son aglutinantes de una realidad infinitamente más vasta que la de su mera anécdota, y por eso han influido en nosotros con una fuerza que no haría sospechar la modestia de su contenido aparente, la brevedad de su texto. Y ese hombre que en un determinado momento elige un tema y hace con él un cuento será un gran cuentista si su elección contiene —a veces sin que él lo sepa conscientemente— esa fabulosa apertura de lo pequeño hacia lo grande, de lo individual y circunscrito a la esencia misma de la condición humana. Todo cuento perdurable es como la semilla donde está durmiendo el árbol gigantesco. Ese árbol crecerá en nosotros, dará su sombra en nuestra memoria.

Sin embargo, hay que aclarar mejor esta noción de temas significativos. Un mismo tema puede ser profundamente significativo para un escritor, y anodino para otro; un mismo tema despertará enormes resonancias en un lector, y dejará indiferente a otro. En suma, puede decirse que no hay temas absolutamente significativos o absolutamente insignificantes. Lo que hay es una alianza misteriosa y compleja entre cierto escritor y cierto tema en un momento dado, así como la misma alianza podrá darse luego entre ciertos cuentos y ciertos lectores. Por eso, cuando decimos que un tema es significa-

tivo, como en el caso de los cuentos de Chéjov, esa significación se ve determinada en cierta medida por algo que está
fuera del tema en sí, por algo que está antes y después del
tema. Lo que está antes es el escritor, con su carga de valores
humanos y literarios, con su voluntad de hacer una obra que
tenga un sentido; lo que está después es el tratamiento literario del tema, la forma en que el cuentista, frente a su tema,
lo ataca y sitúa verbalmente y estilísticamente, lo estructura
en forma de cuento, y lo proyecta en último término hacia
algo que excede el cuento mismo. Aquí me parece oportuno
mencionar un hecho que me ocurre con frecuencia, y que
otros cuentistas amigos conocen tan bien como yo. Es habitual que en el curso de una conversación, alguien cuente un
episodio divertido o conmovedor o extraño, y que dirigiéndose luego al cuentista presente le diga: "Ahí tienes un tema
formidable para un cuento; te lo regalo". A mí me han regalado en esa forma montones de temas, y siempre he contestado amablemente: "Muchas gracias", y jamás he escrito un
cuento con ninguno de ellos. Sin embargo, cierta vez una amiga me contó distraídamente las aventuras de una criada suya
en París. Mientras escuchaba su relato, sentí que eso podría
llegar a ser un cuento. Para ella esos episodios no eran más
que anécdotas curiosas; para mí, bruscamente, se cargaban de
un sentido que iba mucho más allá de su simple y hasta vulgar
contenido. Por eso, toda vez que me han preguntado: ¿Cómo
distinguir entre un tema insignificante —por más divertido o
emocionante que pueda ser— y otro significativo?, he respondido que el escritor es el primero en sufrir ese efecto indefinible pero avasallador de ciertos temas, y que precisamente por
eso es un escritor. Así como para Marcel Proust el sabor de
una magdalena mojada en el té abría bruscamente un inmenso abanico de recuerdos aparentemente olvidados, de manera
análoga el escritor reacciona ante ciertos temas en la misma
forma en que su cuento, más tarde, hará reaccionar al lector.
Todo cuento está así predeterminado por el aura, por la fas-
cinación irresistible que el tema crea en su creador.

Llegamos así al fin de esta primera etapa del nacimiento
de un cuento, y tocamos el umbral de su creación propiamente dicha. He aquí al cuentista, que ha escogido un tema valiéndose de esas sutiles antenas que le permiten reconocer los elementos que luego habrán de convertirse en obra de arte. El
cuentista está frente a su tema, frente a ese embrión que ya
es vida, pero que no ha adquirido todavía su forma definitiva.
Para él ese tema tiene sentido, tiene significación. Pero si to-

do se redujera a eso, de poco serviría; ahora, como último término del proceso, como juez implacable, está esperando el lector, el eslabón final del proceso creador, el cumplimiento o el fracaso del ciclo. Y es entonces que el cuento tiene que nacer puente, tiene que nacer pasaje, tiene que dar el salto que proyecte la significación inicial, descubierta por el autor, a ese extremo más pasivo y menos vigilante y muchas veces hasta indiferente que llamamos lector. Los cuentistas inexpertos suelen caer en la ilusión de imaginar que les bastará escribir lisa y llanamente un tema que los ha conmovido, para conmover a su turno a los lectores. Incurren en la ingenuidad de aquel que encuentra bellísimo a su hijo, y da por supuesto que los demás lo ven igualmente bello. Con el tiempo, con los fracasos, el cuentista capaz de superar esa primera etapa ingenua, aprende que en literatura no bastan las buenas intenciones. Descubre que para volver a crear en el lector esa conmoción que lo llevó a él a escribir el cuento, es necesario un oficio de escritor, y que ese oficio consiste, entre muchas otras cosas, en lograr ese clima propio de todo gran cuento, que obliga a seguir leyendo, que atrapa la atención, que aísla al lector de todo lo que lo rodea para después, terminado el cuento, volver a conectarlo con su circunstancia de una manera nueva, enriquecida, más honda o más hermosa. Y la única forma en que puede conseguirse ese secuestro momentáneo del lector es mediante un estilo basado en la intensidad y en la tensión, un estilo en el que los elementos formales y expresivos se ajusten, sin la menor concesión, a la índole del tema, le den su forma visual y auditiva más penetrante y original, lo vuelvan único, inolvidable, lo fijen para siempre en su tiempo y en su ambiente y en su sentido más primordial. Lo que llamo intensidad en un cuento consiste en la eliminación de todas las ideas o situaciones intermedias, de todos los rellenos o fases de transición que la novela permite e incluso exige. Ninguno de ustedes habrá olvidado "El tonel de amontillado", de Edgar Poe. Lo extraordinario de este cuento es la brusca prescindencia de toda descripción de ambiente. A la tercera o cuarta frase estamos en el corazón del drama, asistiendo al cumplimiento implacable de una venganza. "Los asesinos", de Hemingway, es otro ejemplo de intensidad obtenida mediante la eliminación de todo lo que no converja esencialmente al drama. Pero pensemos ahora en los cuentos de Joseph Conrad, de D. H. Lawrence, de Kafka. En ellos, con modalidades típicas de cada uno, la intensidad es de otro orden, y yo prefiero darle el nombre de tensión. Es una intensidad que se ejerce en la manera con que el autor nos va acercando lentamente a lo contado. Todavía estamos muy lejos de saber lo que va a ocurrir en el cuento, y sin embargo no podemos sustraernos a su atmósfera. En el caso de "El tonel de amontillado" y de "Los asesinos", los hechos despojados de toda preparación, saltan sobre nosotros y nos atrapan; en cambio, en un relato demorado y caudaloso de Henry James —"La lección del maestro", por ejemplo— se siente de inmediato que los hechos en sí carecen de importancia, que todo está en las fuerzas que los desencadenaron, en la malla sutil que los precedió y los acompaña. Pero tanto la intensidad de la acción como la tensión interna del relato son el producto de lo que antes llamé el oficio de escritor, y es aquí donde nos vamos acercando al final de este paseo por el cuento. En mi país, y ahora en Cuba, he podido leer cuentos de los autores más variados: maduros o jóvenes, de la ciudad y del campo, entregados a la literatura por razones estéticas o por imperativos sociales del momento, comprometidos o no comprometidos. Pues bien, y aunque suene a perogrullada, tanto en la Argentina como aquí los buenos cuentos los están escribiendo quienes dominan el oficio en el sentido ya indicado. Un ejemplo argentino aclarará mejor esto. En nuestras provincias centrales y norteñas existe una larga tradición de cuentos orales, que los gauchos se transmiten de noche en torno al fogón, que los padres siguen contando a sus hijos, y que de golpe pasan por la pluma de un escritor regionalista y, en una abrumadora mayoría de casos, se convierten en pésimos cuentos. ¿Qué ha sucedido? Los relatos en sí son sabrosos, traducen y resumen la experiencia, el sentido del humor y el fatalismo del hombre de campo; algunos incluso se elevan a la dimensión trágica o poética. Cuando uno los escucha de boca de un viejo criollo, entre mate y mate, siente como una anulación del tiempo, y piensa que también los aedos griegos contaban así las hazañas de Aquiles para maravilla de pastores y viajeros. Pero en ese momento, cuando debería surgir un Homero que hiciese una Ilíada o una Odisea de esa suma de tradiciones orales, en mi país surge un señor para quien la cultura de las ciudades es un signo de decadencia, para quien los cuentistas que todo amamos son estetas que escribieron para el mero deleite de clases sociales liquidadas, y ese señor entiende en cambio que para escribir un cuento lo único que hace falta es poner por escrito un relato tradicional, conservando todo lo posible el tono hablado, los giros campesinos, las incorrecciones gramaticales, eso que llaman el color local. No sé si esa manera de escribir cuentos populares se cultiva en Cuba; ojalá que no, porque en mi país no ha dado más que indigestos volúmenes que no interesan ni a los hombres de campo, que prefieren seguir *escuchando* los cuentos entre dos tragos, ni a los lectores de la ciudad, que estarán muy echados a perder pero que se tienen bien leídos a los clásicos del género. En cambio —y me refiero también a la Argentina— hemos tenido a escritores como un Roberto J. Payró, un Ricardo Güiraldes, un Horacio Quiroga y un Benito Lynch que, partiendo también de temas muchas veces tradicionales, escuchados de boca de viejos criollos como un Don Segundo Sombra, han sabido potenciar ese material y volverlo obra de arte. Pero Quiroga, Güiraldes y Lynch conocían a fondo el oficio de escritor, es decir que sólo aceptaban temas significativos, enriquecedores, así como Homero debió desechar montones de epidodios bélicos y mágicos para no dejar más que aquéllos que han llegado hasta nosotros gracias a su enorme fuerza mítica, a su resonancia de arquetipos mentales, de hormonas psíquicas como llamaba Ortega y Gasset a los mitos. Quiroga, Güiraldes y Lynch eran escritores de dimensión universal, sin prejuicios localistas o étnicos o populistas; por eso, además de escoger cuidadosamente los temas de sus relatos, los sometían a una forma literaria, la única capaz de transmitir al lector todos sus valores, todo su fermento, toda su proyección en profundidad y en altura. Escribían tensamente, mostraban intensamente. No hay otra manera de que un cuento sea eficaz, haga blanco en el lector y se clave en su memoria.

El ejemplo que he dado puede ser de interés para Cuba. Es evidente que las posibilidades que la Revolución ofrece a un cuentista son casi infinitas. La ciudad, el campo, la lucha, el trabajo, los distintos tipos psicológicos, los conflictos de ideología y de carácter; y todo eso como exacerbado por el deseo que se ve en ustedes de actuar, de expresarse, de comunicarse como nunca habían podido hacerlo antes. Pero todo eso, ¿cómo ha de traducirse en grandes cuentos, en cuentos que lleguen al lector con la fuerza y la eficacia necesarias? Es aquí donde me gustaría aplicar concretamente lo que he dicho en un terreno más abstracto. El entusiasmo y la buena voluntad no bastan por sí solos, como tampoco basta el oficio de escritor por sí solo para escribir los cuentos que fijen literariamente (es decir, en la admiración colectiva, en la memoria de un pueblo) la grandeza de esta Revolución en marcha. Aquí, más que en ninguna otra parte, se requiere hoy una fusión total de esas dos fuerzas, la del hombre plenamente comprometido con su realidad nacional y mundial, y la del escritor lúcidamente seguro de su oficio. En ese sentido no hay engaño posible. Por más veterano, por más experto que sea un cuentista, si le falta una motivación entrañable, si sus cuentos no nacen de una profunda vivencia, su obra no irá más allá del mero ejercicio estético. Pero lo contrario será aún peor, porque de nada valen el fervor, la voluntad de comunicar un mensaje, si se carece de los instrumentos expresivos, estilísticos, que hacen posible esa comunicación. En este momento estamos tocando el punto crucial de la cuestión. Yo creo, y lo digo después de haber pesado largamente todos los elementos que entran en juego, que escribir para una revolución, que escribir dentro de una revolución, que escribir revolucionariamente, no significa, como creen muchos, escribir obligadamente, acerca de la revolución misma. Jugando un poco con las palabras, Emmanuel Carballo decía aquí hace unos días que en Cuba sería más revolucionario escribir cuentos fantásticos que cuentos sobre temas revolucionarios. Por supuesto la frase es exagerada, pero produce una impaciencia muy reveladora. Por mi parte, creo que el escritor revolucionario es aquél en quien se fusionan indisolublemente la conciencia de su libre compromiso individual y colectivo, con esa otra soberana libertad cultural que confiere el pleno dominio de su oficio. Si ese escritor, responsable y lúcido, decide escribir literatura fantástica, o psicológica, o vuelta hacia el pasado, su acto es un acto de libertad dentro de la revolución, y por eso es también un acto revolucionario aunque sus cuentos no se ocupen de las formas individuales o colectivas que adopta la revolución. Contrariamente al estrecho criterio de muchos que confunden literatura con pedagogía, literatura con enseñanza, literatura con adoctrinamiento ideológico, un escritor revolucionario tiene todo el derecho de dirigirse a un lector mucho más complejo, mucho más exigente en materia espiritual de lo que imaginan los escritores y los críticos improvisados por las circunstancias y convencidos de que su mundo personal es el único mundo existente, de que las preocupaciones del momento son las únicas preocupaciones válidas. Repitamos, aplicándola a lo que nos rodea en Cuba, la admirable frase de Hamlet a Horacio: "Hay muchas más cosas en el cielo y en la tierra de lo que supone tu filosofía..." Y pensemos que a un escritor no se le juzga solamente por el tema de sus cuentos o sus novelas, sino por su presencia viva en el seno de la colectividad, por el hecho de que el compromiso total de su persona es una garantía indesmentible de la verdad y de la necesidad de su obra, por más ajena que ésta pueda parecer a las circunstancias del momento. Esa obra no es ajena a la revolución porque no sea accesible a todo el mundo. Al contrario, prueba que existe un vasto sector de lectores potenciales que, en un cierto sentido, están mucho más separados que el escritor de las metas finales de la revolución, de esas metas de cultura, de libertad, de pleno goce de la condición humana que los cubanos se han fijado para admiración de todos los que los aman y los comprenden. Cuanto más alto apunten los escritores que han nacido para eso, más altas serán las metas finales del pueblo al que pertenecen. ¡Cuidado con la fácil demagogia de exigir una literatura accesible a todo el mundo! Muchos de los que la apoyan no tienen otra razón para hacerlo que la de su evidente incapacidad para comprender una literatura de mayor alcance. Piden clamorosamente temas populares, sin sospechar que muchas veces el lector, por más sencillo que sea, distinguirá instintivamente entre un cuento popular mal escrito y un cuento más difícil y complejo pero que lo obligará a salir por un momento de su pequeño mundo circundante y le mostrará otra cosa, sea lo que sea pero otra cosa, algo diferente. No tiene sentido hablar de temas populares a secas. Los cuentos sobre temas populares sólo serán buenos si se ajustan, como cualquier otro cuento, a esa exigente y difícil mecánica interna que hemos tratado de mostrar en la primera parte de esta charla. Hace años tuve la prueba de esta afirmación en la Argentina, en una rueda de hombres de campo a la que asistíamos unos cuantos escritores. Alguien leyó un cuento basado en un episodio de nuestra guerra de independencia, escrito con una deliberada sencillez para ponerlo, como decía su autor, "al nivel del campesino". El relato fue escuchado cortésmente, pero era fácil advertir que no había tocado fondo. Luego uno de nosotros leyó "La pata de mono", el justamente famoso cuento de W. W. Jacobs. El interés, la emoción, el espanto, y finalmente el entusiasmo fueron extraordinarios. Recuerdo que pasamos el resto de la noche hablando de hechicería, de brujos, de venganzas diabólicas. Y estoy seguro de que el cuento de Jacobs sigue vivo en el recuerdo de esos gauchos analfabetos, mientras que el cuento supuestamente popular, fabricado para ellos, con su vocabulario, sus aparentes posibilidades intelectuales y sus intereses patrióticos, ha de estar tan olvidado como el escritor que lo fabricó. Yo he visto la emoción que entre la gente sencilla provoca una representación de *Hamlet,* obra difícil y sutil si las hay, y que sigue siendo tema de estudios eruditos y de infinitas controversias. Es cierto que esa gente no puede comprender muchas cosas que apasionan a los especialistas en teatro isabelino. ¿Pero qué importa? Sólo su emoción importa, su maravilla y su transporte frente a la tragedia del joven príncipe danés. Lo que prueba que Shakespeare escribía verdaderamente para el pueblo, en la medida en que su tema era profundamente significativo para cualquiera —en diferentes planos, sí, pero alcanzando un poco a cada uno— y que el tratamiento teatral de ese tema tenía la intensidad propia de los grandes escritores, y gracias a la cual se quiebran las barreras intelectuales aparentemente más rígidas, y los hombres se reconocen y fraternizan en un plano que está más allá o más acá de la cultura. Por supuesto, sería ingenuo creer que toda gran obra puede ser comprendida y admirada por las gentes sencillas; no es así, y no puede serlo. Pero la admiración que provocan las tragedias griegas o las de Shakespeare, el interés apasionado que despiertan muchos cuentos y novelas nada sencillos ni accesibles, debería hacer sospechar a los partidarios del mal llamado *arte popular* que su noción del pueblo es parcial, injusta, y en último término peligrosa. No se le hace ningún favor al pueblo si se le propone una literatura que pueda asimilar sin esfuerzo, pasivamente, como quien va al cine a ver películas de *cowboys.* Lo que hay que hacer es educarlo, y eso es en una primera etapa tarea pedagógica y no literaria. Para mí ha sido una experiencia reconfortable ver cómo en Cuba los escritores que más admiro participan en la revolución dando lo mejor de sí mismos, sin cercenar una parte de sus posibilidades en aras de un supuesto arte popular que no será útil a nadie. Un día Cuba contará con un acervo de cuentos y de novelas que contendrá transmutada al plano estético, eternizada en la dimensión intemporal del arte, su gesta revolucionaria de hoy. Pero esas obras no habrán sido escritas por obligación, por consignas de la hora. Sus temas nacerán cuando sea el momento, cuando el escritor sienta que debe plasmarlos en cuentos o novelas o piezas de teatro o poemas. Sus temas contendrán un mensaje auténtico y hondo, porque no habrán sido escogidos por un imperativo de carácter didáctico o proselitista, sino por una irresistible fuerza que se impondrá al autor, y que éste, apelando a todos los recursos de su arte y de su técnica, sin sacrificar nada a nadie, habrá de transmitir al lector como se transmiten las cosas fundamentales: de sangre a sangre, de mano a mano, de hombre a hombre.

Julio Cortázar
1916—1984
Argentina

Hay que ser mente idiota para...
La vuelta al día en ochenta mundos, 1967.

HACE años que me doy cuenta y no me importa, pero nunca se me ocurrió escribirlo porque la idiotez me parece un tema muy desagradable, especialmente si es el idiota quien lo expone. Puede que la palabra idiota sea demasiado rotunda, pero prefiero ponerla de entrada y calentita sobre el plato aunque los amigos la crean exagerada, en vez de emplear cualquier otra como tonto, lelo o retardado y que después los mismos amigos opinen que uno se ha quedado corto. En realidad no pasa nada grave pero ser idiota lo pone a uno completamente aparte, y aunque tiene sus cosas buenas es evidente que de a ratos hay como una nostalgia, un deseo de cruzar a la vereda de enfrente donde amigos y parientes están reunidos en una misma inteligencia y comprensión y frotarse un poco contra ellos para sentir que no hay diferencia apreciable y que todo va *benissimo*. Lo triste es que todo va *malissimo* cuando uno es idiota, por ejemplo en el teatro, yo voy al teatro con mi mujer y algún amigo, hay un espectáculo de mimos checos o de bailarines tailandeses y es seguro que apenas empiece la función voy a encontrar que todo es una maravilla. Me divierto o me conmuevo enormemente, los diálogos o los gestos o las danzas me llegan como visiones sobrenaturales, aplaudo hasta romperme las manos y a veces me lloran los ojos o me río hasta el borde del pis, y en todo caso me alegro de vivir y de haber tenido la suerte de ir esa noche al teatro o al cine o a una exposición de cuadros, a cualquier sitio donde gentes extraordinarias están haciendo o mostrando cosas que jamás se habían imaginado antes, inventando un lugar de revelación y de encuentro, algo que lava de los momentos en que no ocurre nada más que lo que ocurre todo el tiempo.

Y así estoy deslumbrado y tan contento que cuando llega el intervalo me levanto entusiasmado y sigo aplaudiendo a los actores, y le digo a mi mujer que los mimos checos son una maravilla y que la escena en que el pescador echa el anzuelo y se ve avanzar un pez fosforescente a media altura es absolutamente inaudita. Mi mujer también se ha divertido y ha aplaudido, pero de pronto me doy cuenta (ese instante tiene algo de herida, de agujero ronco y húmedo) que su diversión y sus

aplausos no han sido como los míos, y además casi siempre
hay con nosotros algún amigo que también se ha divertido y
ha aplaudido pero nunca como yo, y también me doy cuenta
de que está diciendo con suma sensatez e inteligencia que el
espectáculo es bonito y que los actores no son malos, pero
que desde luego no hay gran originalidad en las ideas, sin contar que los colores de los trajes son mediocres y la puesta en
escena bastante adocenada y cosas y cosas. Cuando mi mujer
o mi amigo dicen eso —lo dicen amablemente, sin ninguna
agresividad— yo comprendo que soy idiota, pero lo malo es
que uno se ha olvidado cada vez que lo maravilla algo que pasa, de modo que la caída repentina en la idiotez le llega como
al corcho que se ha pasado años en el sótano acompañando al
vino de la botella y de golpe plop y un tirón y ya no se es más
corcho. Me gustaría defender a los mimos checos o a los bailarines tailandeses, porque me han parecido admirables y he
sido tan feliz con ellos que las palabras inteligentes y sensatas
de mis amigos o de mi mujer me duelen como por debajo de
las uñas, y eso que comprendo perfectamente cuánta razón
tiene y cómo el espectáculo no ha de ser tan bueno como a mí
me parecía (pero en realidad a mí no me parecía que fuese
bueno ni malo ni nada, sencillamente estaba transportado por
lo que ocurría como idiota que soy, y me bastaba para salirme y andar por ahí donde me gusta andar cada vez que puedo, y puedo tan poco). Y jamás se me ocurriría discutir con
mi mujer o con mis amigos porque sé que tienen razón y que
en realidad han hecho muy bien en no dejarse ganar por el entusiasmo, puesto que los placeres de la inteligencia y la sensibilidad deben nacer de un juicio ponderado y sobre todo de
una actitud comparativa, basarse como dijo Epicteto en lo
que ya se conoce para juzgar lo que se acaba de conocer, pues
eso y no otra cosa es la cultura y la sofrosine. De ninguna manera pretendo discutir con ellos y a lo sumo me limito a ale-
jarme unos metros para no escuchar el resto de las compara-
ciones y los juicios, mientras trato de retener todavía las últimas imágenes del pez fosforescente que flotaba en mitad del
escenario, aunque ahora mi recuerdo se ve inevitablemente
modificado por las críticas inteligentísimas que acabo de escuchar y no me queda más remedio que admitir la mediocridad de lo que he visto y que sólo me ha entusiasmado porque
acepto cualquier cosa que tenga colores y formas un poco diferentes. Recaigo en la conciencia de que soy idiota, de que
cualquier cosa basta para alegrarme de la cuadriculada vida, y
entonces el recuerdo de lo que he amado y gozado esa noche

se enturbia y se vuelve cómplice, la obra de otros idiotas que
han estado pescando o bailando mal, con trajes y coreografías
mediocres, y casi es un consuelo pero un consuelo siniestro el
que seamos tantos los idiotas que esa noche se han dato cita
en esa sala para bailar y pescar y aplaudir. Lo peor es que a
los dos días abro el diario y leo la crítica del espectáculo, y la
crítica coincide casi siempre y hasta con las mismas palabras
con lo que tan sensata e inteligentemente han visto y dicho mi
mujer o mis amigos. Ahora estoy seguro de que no ser idiota
es una de las cosas más importantes para la vida de un hombre, hasta que poco a poco me vaya olvidando, porque lo peor
es que al final me olvido, por ejemplo acabo de ver un pato
que nadaba en uno de los lagos del Bois de Boulogne, y era
de una hermosura tan maravillosa que no pude menos que ponerme en cuclillas junto al lago y quedarme no sé cuánto tiempo mirando su hermosura, la alegría petulante de sus ojos, esa
doble línea que corta su pecho en el agua del lago y que se va
abriendo hasta perderse en la distancia. Mi entusiasmo no nace solamente del pato, es algo que el pato cuaja de golpe, porque a veces puede ser una hoja seca que se balancea en el borde de un banco, o una grúa anaranjada, enormísima y delicada contra el cielo azul de la tarde, o el olor de un vagón de
tren cuando uno entra y se tiene un billete para un viaje de
tantas horas y todo va a ir sucediendo prodigiosamente, las
estaciones, el sándwich de jamón, los botones para encender
o apagar la luz (una blanca y otra violeta), la ventilación regula-
ble, todo eso me parece tan hermoso y casi tan imposible que
tenerlo ahí a mi alcance me llena de una especie de sauce interior, de una verde lluvia de delicia que no debería terminar
más. Pero muchos me han dicho que mi entusiasmo es una
prueba de inmadurez (quieren decir que soy idiota, pero eli-
gen las palabras) y que no es posible entusiasmarse así por una
tela de araña que brilla al sol, puesto que si uno incurre en semejantes excesos por una tela de araña llena de rocío, ¿qué
va a dejar para la noche en que den *King Lear*? A mí eso me
sorprende un poco, porque en realidad el entusiasmo no es
cosa que se gaste cuando uno es realmente idiota, se gasta
cuando uno es inteligente y tiene el sentido de los valores y
de la historicidad de las cosas, y por eso aunque yo corra de
un lado a otro del Bois de Boulogne para ver mejor el pato,
eso no me impedirá esa misma noche dar enormes saltos de
entusiasmo si me gusta cómo canta Fischer Dieskau. Ahora
que lo pienso la idiotez debe ser eso: poder entusiasmarse todo el tiempo por cualquier cosa que a uno le guste, sin que

un dibujito en una pared tenga que verse menoscabado por
el recuerdo de los frescos de Giotto en Padua. La idiotez debe
ser una especie de presencia y recomienzo constante: ahora
me gusta esta piedrita amarilla, ahora me gusta *L'année der-
nière à Marienbad,* ahora me gustas tú, ratita, ahora me gusta
esa increíble locomotora bufando en la Gare de Lyon, ahora
me gusta ese cartel arrancado y sucio. Ahora me gusta, me
gusta tanto, ahora soy yo, reincidentemente yo, el idiota perfecto en su idiotez que no sabe que es idiota y goza perdido
en su goce, hasta que la primera frase inteligente lo devuelva
a la conciencia de su idiotez y lo haga buscar presuroso un cigarrillo con manos torpes, mirando el suelo, comprendiendo
y a veces aceptando porque también un idiota tiene que vivir,
claro que hasta otro pato u otro cartel, y así siempre.

Roberto Fernández Retamar
1930
Cuba

Antipoesía y poesía conversacional en Hispanoamérica
Charla en Casa de las Américas, 1968.

Dos cosas

EL título de la charla indica que vamos a hablar de cosas
que, aunque emparentadas, no son lo mismo: son dos cosas. Si fueran lo mismo, el título sería redundante. Esas dos
cosas, o, para ser más exactos, esas dos vertientes de una cosa,
quizás constituyan la novedad más visible de la poesía hispanoamericana desde hace diez o quince años.

Voy a ocuparme no tanto de las obras individuales como
de las líneas poéticas que he mencionado. Y por razones menores puramente personales, voy a considerar esta charla co-

mo una especie de complemento parcial de otra que di hace
algo más de diez años, exactamente el 11 de noviembre de
1957, en la Universidad de Columbia, en Nueva York. Aquella charla se llamaba "Situación actual de la poesía hispanoamericana".[1] Allí, al hablar de la que consideraba la poesía
hispanoamericana entonces actual, mencionaba poetas de dos
generaciones que ya eran o iban a devenir, *clásicos,* en algunos casos, *clásicos vivientes.* Por ejemplo: Vallejo (1892-
938), Huidobro (1893-948), Borges (1899), Guillén (1902),
Neruda (1904-73), en una generación; Lezama (1910), Paz
(1914), Diego (1920), en otra generación. Con estos últimos,
a los que había nombrado poetas *trascendentalistas,* concluía
prácticamente aquella charla.

Pero en aquella fecha, en 1957, ya habían empezado a hacerse notar dos nuevos elementos en la poesía hispanoamericana: por una parte, una nueva generación, que iba a desarrollarse después de aquella conferencia: la generación de Alejandro Romualdo (1926), de Jorge Enrique Adoum (1926),
de Juan Gelman (1930), de Roque Dalton (1935), de algunos
poetas cubanos; el otro elemento nuevo, al que vamos a con-
sagrar esta charla, era la aparición de determinados rasgos (que
también iban a desarrollarse después) en poetas de la misma
generación de Paz y Lezama; señaladamente en dos poetas:
Nicanor Parra (1914), quien iba a ser casi sinónimo de antipoesía, y Ernesto Cardenal (1925), que se haría la más importante figura de la poesía conversacional.

Aplicando la lección de aquella charla, al dar la cual ya
existían, como era natural, barruntos de lo que iba a ser la
novedad ulterior, es de esperar que aquello de lo que no vamos a hablar esta noche constituya la raíz de la poesía de los
próximos años.

Generaciones
y épocas

He mencionado el término *generación* y he hablado de la
generación de Vallejo, Guillén, Neruda; y de la generación de
Lezama y Paz. Esa palabra debemos tomarla con cautela. Aquellos que se interesen por lo que yo pensaba en 1957, es decir,
hace más de diez años, sobre el término, pueden remitirse a

---

[1] Se publicó primero en *Revista Hispánica Moderna,* octubre, 1958, y luego
en el libro *Papelería.* La Habana, 1962.

la conferencia o escuchar la lectura textual de algo que dije entonces:

> He mencionado [decía en 1957] la palabra "generación", costumbre de estos días y cabeza de turco o de truco para tantos. Debo decir que creo en su existencia, creo que en ellas se articula la historia, y creo también, pues de lo contrario me parecen sin sentido, en esa órbita sugerida por Ortega de aproximadamente quince años —no los que satisfagan al manualista de turno, ahora diez, ahora treinta—. Pero considero prudente recordar que, en oposición a lo que algunos vienen repitiendo, las generaciones no se separan tajantemente. Los jovencitos profesionales están practicando ahora —como de hecho han practicado siempre— el terrorismo de las generaciones: haber nacido antes o después de ciertas fechas parece a los secuaces de esta vaga astrología una bendición de los cielos. Lo cierto es que si las generaciones, como creo, tienen una realidad histórica, esa realidad es morfológica y no valorativa; implica diferencias de forma, no de calidad. Haber nacido veinte años antes o veinte años después no obliga a ser mejor ni peor, simplemente supone distintas formas. En consecuencia, sin la necesidad de postular una leibniziana armonía de las generaciones que de hecho, al volver a confundirlas, las haría irrelevantes, es no ya posible sino imprescindible una continuidad valorativa a lo largo de las generaciones, sin mengua de ellas. Toda generación busca (y encuentra) en las anteriores aquellos valores que prefiere; son hombres los que alcanzan esos valores, y a ellos se vuelve [...]. Hasta para rechazar el pasado se buscan antecesores que lo hayan hecho ya, lo cual no es sino una manera vergonzante de aceptar el pasado, en el que están esos precursores.

Eso decía yo hace más de diez años. Hoy veo todavía más cómo *se interpenetran las generaciones en las épocas.* Por ejemplo (y aquí voy a utilizar en gran medida ejemplos cubanos que nos son más cercanos): el Emilio Ballagas (1908-54) de su último libro, que es de 1951, *Ciclo en rehenes,* está más cerca de los poetas nuevos de esa fecha, "los poetas de *Orígenes*", que de la poesía de su generación, la poesía de la *Revista de Avance.* Lo mismo puede decirse de su coetáneo Eugenio Florit (1903), y de éste aún más: quizás por una doble influencia que ha sufrido en su poesía, una influencia anglosajona y una influencia española, Florit entra, desde *Conversación a mi padre* (1949), y aun desde antes, en relación con la poesía de que vamos a hablar hoy. Es uno de esos poetas de evolución transgeneracional. Un caso similar es el poco señalado de Samuel Feijoo (1914), quien en 1956, al publicar su poemario *Faz*, está en relación con la poesía joven; por ejemplo, con la poesía de Rolando Escardó (1925-60), de quien cita unos versos como exergo de aquel poema. No falta el ejemplo de Neruda, que en 1958, al publicar *Estravagario,* quizá está más cerca de Nicanor Parra que de su propia poesía de veinte o treinta años atrás.

Por tanto, cuando vamos a utilizar este término, *generación,* vamos a utilizarlo sin ningún sectarismo cronológico, y teniendo en cuenta la existencia de estas *épocas* poéticas y no poéticas en el interior de las cuales se interpenetran las generaciones.

Títulos

Algunos de los títulos que podrían mencionarse en relación con esta poesía serían los siguientes: en 1954 publica el chileno Nicanor Parra su libro *Poemas y antipoemas,* que va a conocer pronto, en 1956, una segunda edición, y ediciones ulteriores hasta nuestros días. Este libro va a tener la fortuna de que va a servir para nombrar toda una corriente poética, la llamada "antipoesía". En el libro no se la nombra: ella es un abstracto que se ha hecho a partir de aquel nombre de *antipoemas.*

En 1956, el uruguayo Mario Benedetti (1920) publica *Poemas de la oficina.* Este año publican Samuel Feijoo *Faz,* y el mexicano Jaime Sabines (1925), *Tarumba.*

En 1960, Nicanor Parra publica *Versos de salón.* Y ese mismo año, Jaime Sabines publica *Recuento de poemas.*

En 1964, Ernesto Cardenal publica *Gethsemaní, Ky.,* y en 1965, *Oración por Marilyn Monroe y otros poemas.*

En 1967, Nicanor Parra publica *Canciones rusas.*

Aquí hay algunos poetas que están en el linde generacional. Este es el caso, por ejemplo, de Ernesto Cardenal y de Jaime Sabines, nacidos ambos en 1925, y que podríamos situar tanto en una generación como en otra.[2]

---

[2] Pero en general se suele situarlos en la generación de 1940. Así aparece Cardenal en la antología *Nuestra poesía nicaragüense* (Madrid), 1949), prologada por el propio Cardenal; y Sabines en la reciente *Poesía en movimiento, México 1915-1966* (México, 1966), seleccionada por Octavio Paz, Alí Chumacero, José Emilio Pacheco y Homero Aridjis.

A estos nombres de autores (he dicho que no quisiera detenerme mucho en los nombres), habría que añadir los de poetas ya claramente de una generación más joven, como mencioné al principio. Pero en ellos se trata ya de otra poesía, vinculada a ésta de que hablamos en la charla, pero no identificada con ella. Requieren otro acercamiento.

Las antipoesías

Cuando vamos a estudiar una obra literaria, y más todavía una línea literaria, que es lo que nosotros vamos a abordar aquí, tenemos que tener en cuenta que una obra literaria está en contacto con su época toda, y también, de manera muy particular, está en contacto con la literatura. A los formalistas rusos les gustaba repetir la observación de Brunetière según la cual lo que más influye sobre una obra literaria es otra obra literaria. Se trata de una exageración, pero no podemos olvidar este hecho: la literatura vive en relación con su época, pero también en relación con la literatura. A la hora de hablar de la antipoesía, vamos a tener esto presente.

Les he mencionado que ese término proviene del libro de Nicanor Parra *Poemas y antipoemas*. Es decir, se hizo el abstracto correspondiente a partir del término *antipoemas*. El nombre hizo fortuna rápidamente, porque en la época se hablaba de antinovela, antiteatro, antipintura. Pero, por supuesto, por el mero hecho de ser, ninguna poesía es antipoesía; la única verdadera antipoesía no se escribe. Sin embargo, la antipoesía, como en su caso la antinovela, es anti-*cierto tipo de poesía*. Con respecto a Parra, como varios autores vieron desde el primer momento, se trata de la poesía *anti-Neruda*. Eso quiere decir que no se entiende del todo la función de la poesía de Parra si no se está algo familiarizado con la poesía caudalosa, copiosa, pretenciosa, de Pablo Neruda, que en la época era el poeta sobreviviente más importante de la generación vanguardista en nuestra lengua.

En aquella conferencia de 1957, sugerí que, de la misma manera que a la generación que sigue al modernismo se le llama *posmodernista,* a la generación de Parra se le llamara *posvanguardista,* y el nombre hizo fortuna. En ambos casos, se trata de poesías que se encuentran ante la dificultad de seguir a ricos momentos poéticos: el modernismo en un caso, el vanguardismo en otro. Sin embargo, entonces no pude todavía detectar un rasgo que acerca todavía más a los posmodernistas y a los posvanguardistas: esa vertiente del "anti", que en ambas situaciones es un esfuerzo desesperado por escapar a las monumentales cristalizaciones previas que pudiéramos cifrar, en un caso, en el nombre de Rubén Darío, y en otro caso, en el nombre de Pablo Neruda.

Puestos a pensar en esto, veremos (y para ello vamos a salir fuera de Hispanoamérica y remitirnos a España) que un fenómeno similar ocurrió también a raíz del romanticismo. O sea, que también al romanticismo lo siguió un movimiento (llamado *posromanticismo*) que se encontró con una dificultad similar: se encontró con una monumental poesía (en el caso del romanticismo español – confesémoslo –, bastante menos monumental); con una poesía poderosa, y trató de alguna manera de escapar a lo que significaba aquella mole que era la poesía previa.

Me he puesto a rastrear la similitud que hay entre estos tres "pos", el posromanticismo, el posmodernismo y el posvanguardismo, y la presencia en cada uno de ellos de una antipoesía que se va a definir negativamente.

A propósito del posromanticismo, dice Angel del Río en su *Historia de la literatura española* (tomo II, p. 99):

> [...] la lírica de este período se caracteriza en su conjunto por ser una reacción contra el romanticismo [...]. Aparecen varias tendencias dentro de esta reacción [...]. En primer lugar, una poesía que se distingue por el vulgarismo irónico sentimental con aspiraciones filosófico-didácticas, tono escéptico y estilo marcadamente prosaico...

Esa línea la encarna Ramón de Campoamor (1817-901). Y añade Angel del Río: "es la tendencia de carácter más negativo y antipoético".

Es decir, el antipoeta de hace setenta, ochenta años, se llamaba Ramón de Campoamor; el Neruda de entonces se llamaba José Zorrilla (1817-93). La antipoesía de Zorrilla la encarna Campoamor; la antipoesía de Neruda la encarna Nicanor Parra. (No nos enamoraremos de ciertas simetrías. Pero no dejemos tampoco de recibir las lecciones oportunas).

Con referencia al posmodernismo, dice Federico de Onís en su excelente *Antología de la poesía española e hispanoamericana* (Madrid, 1934):

> el posmodernismo [que él sitúa entre 1905 y 1914] es una reacción [véase que en ambos casos se trata de *una reacción*] conservadora, en primer lugar, del modernismo

mismo, que se hace habitual y retórico como toda revolución literaria triunfante y restauradora de todo lo que en el ardor de la lucha la naciente revolución negó. Esta actitud deja poco margen a la originalidad individual creadora; el poeta que la tiene se refugia en el goce del bien logrado [...] en la desnudez prosaica, en la ironía y el humorismo. Son modos diversos de huir sin lucha y sin esperanza de la imponente obra lírica de la generación anterior, en busca de la única originalidad posible dentro de la inevitable dependencia [p. xviii].

Es decir, estamos en presencia de la antipoesía correspondiente al posmodernismo. El Ramón de Campoamor de esta época, ya en Hispanoamérica, se llama Luis Carlos López (1881-951), un singular poeta colombiano. A él lo acompañan otros poetas hispanoamericanos: el guatemalteco Rafael Arévalo Martínez (1884), el argentino Fernández Moreno (1886-950), en cierta forma el uruguayo Alvaro Armando Vasseur (1878). A Cuba esta poesía llega tardíamente, con José Z. Tallet (1893), ya integrado a una generación más joven. De ello hablaremos más adelante.

Hablando de Luis Carlos López, el poeta arquetípico de esta línea, dice Onís:

Su actitud poética, así como la de los demás poetas de esta sección [es decir: Arévalo Martínez, Fernández Moreno, Tallet], es la más propia y típicamente posmodernista, porque es el modernismo visto del revés, el modernismo que se burla de sí mismo, que se perfecciona al deshacerse en la ironía.

Y añade Onís: "actitud correspondiente a la de los posrománticos respecto del romanticismo" (p. 851). Onís es un sagaz crítico, y hasta hubiera podido decir que esa actitud correspondería a la de quienes se iban a oponer a la poesía última que él está estudiando en 1932. En Cuba, no pocas personas han reparado en esa similitud entre la antipoesía y la poesía de Tallet. Se ha pretendido ver, incluso, una influencia de Tallet en Parra; pero no existe tal influencia, porque Parra no había leído a Tallet. Lo que existe es una similitud entre poesías que reaccionan a fuertes movimientos poéticos, como son el modernismo en un caso y el vanguardismo en otro. En cuanto a Tallet, su poesía es tardía (Tallet desarrolla su obra en la década del veinte, cuando ya esa línea tiene vigencia en muchos otros países hispanoamericanos) por la misma razón por la que el vanguardismo va a ser tardío en Cuba,[3] donde no hay vanguardismo hasta 1927; diez años antes, ya Huidobro ha escrito poemas vanguardistas, y en la década del veinte se ha desarrollado en México, en Buenos Aires (y en Perú, en la figura admirable de Vallejo), una rica poesía vanguardista, años antes de que llegue a Cuba. O sea, que a Cuba llega tardíamente esta reacción del prosaísmo irónico sentimental, como luego llega también tardíamente la vanguardia.

Ahora, consideremos al posvanguardismo, es decir, a la poesía que sigue a la vanguardia. Aquí aparece la denominada por antonomasia *antipoesía,* término que bien puede nombrar todas estas líneas poéticas de que hemos hablado, es decir, la línea de Campoamor, la de Luis Carlos López y la de Parra. Pero la forja del nombre corresponde a este último. ¿Qué es el "antipoema"?

El antipoema [dice Pedro Lastra] no es una denominación nueva. La usó en 1926 el poeta peruano Enrique Bustamante Ballivián, y en el canto IV de *Altazor,* de Vicente Huidobro [libro que es de 1931, aunque dice Huidobro que lo escribió en 1919], se encuentra este verso: "Aquí yace Vicente, antipoeta y mago".

Estos antecedentes que cita Pedro Lastra son engañosos. Quiero decir, que estas alusiones son episódicas: desconocen el aspecto *funcional* del antipoema, que concretó así Mario Benedetti: *"el antipoema* representa, en términos chilenos, algo así como un anti-Neruda". Digo que desconocen el aspecto funcional, porque cuando Vicente Huidobro en *Altazor* se llama a sí mismo "antipoeta y mago", está entroncando con una línea de poesía de vanguardia que dice rechazar la poesía, no desde la perspectiva del antipoema reciente, sino, como lo confiesa explícitamente Huidobro, desde la perspectiva de la magia. "Sólo lo maravilloso es bello", nos va a decir André Breton sintetizando espléndidamente esa línea.

Describiendo la poesía de Parra, dice luego Lastra que sus "aspectos principales se refieren [vamos a enumerarlos para hacerlo más fácil]:

---

[3] He querido explicar este hecho en "Sobre el caso Rubén Martínez Villena", en *Orbita de Rubén Martínez Villena.* La Habana, 1965, y luego en *Ensayo de otro mundo,* La Habana, 1967.

[1] a la prescindencia de toda retórica;

[2] a la sustitución de un vocabulario poético gastado por las expresiones coloquiales más comunes, entre las que no escasean ni la información periodística [...] ni el léxico burocrático, en un contexto general que,

[3] suele adoptar un carácter conversacional"[4]

Esta definición es interesante, pero veámosla más de cerca.

"Prescindencia de toda retórica" ... Habría que decir de toda retórica *anterior;* y añadir: y creación de una nueva retórica. ¿Qué es *retórica?* Si tomamos la palabra en su sentido tradicional, como el conjunto de los *artificios o procedimientos* poéticos (versos, estrofas, imágenes, etcétera), por supuesto que esta poesía tiene tales artificios, puesto que se escribe a partir de una serie de artificios y procedimientos. Si retórica quiere decir *peso muerto,* entonces sólo es abandono de la retórica anterior.

Segundo: "sustitución de un vocabulario poético gastado". Si la antipoesía se definiera como la sustitución de un vocabulario poético gastado, habría que concluir que toda poesía verdadera es antipoesía; e incluso que toda literatura es antiliteratura. Este rasgo, pues, tampoco es propio de la antipoesía: es propio de la literatura en general sustituir un vocabulario poético gastado por otro vocabulario poético. Si aceptáramos que es un rasgo propio de la antipoesía, habría que colegir que la antipoesía es la literatura, y caeríamos en la trampa en que cae, por ejemplo, Roger Garaudy, quien en *De un realismo sin riberas,* para defender el realismo, dice que todo arte es realista, con lo cual, sencillamente, evapora al realismo. De manera que los que tenemos algo que decir sobre el realismo debemos rechazar una definición que comienza por negar toda posibilidad de postular algo concreto sobre él. El realismo se define cuando hay algo que *no* es realismo. Por tanto, el criterio de Garaudy es inaceptable. Y por igual razón, definir la antipoesía como la "sustitución de un vocabulario poético gastado" es definir la antipoesía por un rasgo que tiene toda la poesía verdadera, y por tanto no haber definido nada.

Ahora bien, Pedro Lastra, que es un crítico cuidadoso, sigue adelante, y dice que esa "sustitución" es por las "expre-

_____

[4] Tomo estas citas del artículo de Pedro Lastra "La generación chilena de 1938", primera parte, aparecida en *El Mundo del Domingo,* La Habana, 6 de marzo de 1966.

siones coloquiales más comunes". Y ya eso no es característico de *toda* literatura, no es característico de *toda* poesía: es característico sólo de la antipoesía de todas las épocas, es decir, de la antipoesía del posromanticismo, de la antipoesía del posmodernismo y de la antipoesía del posvanguardismo: son los *prosaísmos,* los momentos en que la poesía se acerca voluntariamente a la prosa, o al coloquio, que no es lo mismo por supuesto: la prosa es también una forma *de escribir:* el coloquio, la conversación, es lo que *hablamos* habitualmente.

Teorías e influencias

Ahora bien, de todos estos antipoetas, quien ha teorizado más sobre este punto es alguien que hoy día no está muy de moda citar: Ramón de Campoamor. Dice Campoamor: "Hay un punto de conexión común donde la poesía y la prosa no se distinguen más que por el ritmo y la rima. Existe una línea de conjunción en la cual se puede ver que la poesía más sublime arranca de las entrañas de la prosa".

Campoamor, como bien sabemos, fue un poeta de enorme influencia en su tiempo, y, además, un teórico de poesía, quizás el teórico de poesía más importante de su época en España. Por eso Vicente Gaos publicó en Madrid, en 1955, una *Poética de Campoamor.* Cuando en España estaba produciéndose una evolución similar en algunos puntos a esta de que venimos hablando, Gaos se volvió a la poética de Campoamor y escribió sobre ella un libro agudo.[5] Y curiosamente, en este libro, después de mencionar aquellas palabras, emparienta a Campoamor con un poeta mucho más prestigioso, mucho más citado hoy: T. S. Eliot. Dice Eliot: "La poesía tiene tanto que aprender de la prosa como de la demás poesía [...]. Una interacción entre prosa y verso, como la interacción entre lenguaje y lenguaje, es una condición de vitalidad en la literatura".

Este prosaísmo, que ha sido teorizado por Campoamor y por Eliot, está, como todos sabemos, de moda. Lejos de haber barrido con la retórica, es la retórica de moda, así como hubo antes una retórica de Lezama o de Paz, antes aún una retórica de Neruda, de Lorca, de Juan Ramón Jiménez, de

---

[5] Dos años después, Luis Cernuda nos dará en sus *Estudios sobre poesía española contemporánea* (Madrid, 1957), otra singular revaloración del Campoamor teórico y de su voluntad de reforma del idioma poético.

Darío... Porque lo propio de la *retórica* es que en su momento es vivida como si no fuera una *retórica,* sino el hecho mismo de escribir; es decir, es asumida de manera transparente. Cada escritor, en el momento de escribir, tiene la convicción de que así es como hay que escribir. Pasan unos cuantos años, siglos si se trata de Homero o Shakespeare, y quizás nunca si se trata de un escritor inmortal, pasa algún tiempo y entonces se repara en que eso que parecía *el hecho mismo de escribir* también suponía una *manera.*

Aunque la *manera* de Vasseur o de Luis Carlos López tuvo sus adeptos, esta vuelta del prosaísmo no había tenido nunca tanta acogida, desde Ramón de Campoamor, en todo el Continente.

Acabo de recibir el primer libro de un poeta panameño llamado César Young Núñez, nacido en 1934. El libro se llama *Poemas de rutina* (Panamá, 1967). En el prólogo, dice el autor: "He usado muchos zapatos en mi vida, últimamente calzo los de Nicanor Parra y miro la vida sin antiparras". Quiere decir en realidad que mira la vida con los espejuelos de Nicanor Parra; y, por supuesto, ve el mundo de Nicanor Parra, quien ha identificado prácticamente su obra con la antipoesía. Enrique Lihn, en un ensayo reciente, publicado en el número 45 de *Casa de las Américas,* dice: "Los tiempos rechazan teóricamente el culto a la personalidad, y en lugar de llamar poetas parrianos a los imitadores de Nicanor Parra, se les llama antipoetas".

Pero esta *retórica* que, como de costumbre, se hace *peso muerto,* pasado un tiempo, en los epígonos (piénsese en ciertos secuaces de Darío, a quienes Unamuno llamaba "poetisos", o en la "poesía nerudona" mencionada por Juan Ramón), no implica minimizar obligadamente los primeros antipoemas y los *Versos de salón.*

A semejanza de algunos prosaístas posmodernistas, como Vasseur, que es el primer traductor al español de *Hojas de hierba,* el gran libro de Whitman, o Tallet, quien incluso había estudiado en los Estados Unidos, Parra sufre la influencia de la poesía anglosajona.[6] En su caso hay además una influencia que, por supuesto, no podían tener los antipoetas previos:

---

[6] Llama la atención que, así como Gaos acercó al Campoamor teórico a Eliot, Cernuda lo compare con Wordsworth y llegue a escribir: "Campoamor fue un poeta raro entre nosotros; a veces se diría un poeta inglés (en lo posible) de la época victoriana..." (*op. cit.* p. 41). Un cotejo cuidadoso entre las poesías de ambas lenguas nos depararía útiles conocimientos (piénsese en Zenea, en Martí, en Unamuno, en Borges, además de los ya citados).

la del surrealismo. Parra ha recibido esa influencia que a ratos hace pensar, y Young Núñez se ha dado cuenta de ello, en cierto parentesco con Jacques Prevert, el poeta francés, que es una especie de antipoeta del surrealismo; es decir, que ha utilizado ciertas sorpresas del surrealismo para una poesía de humor negro antipoética.

Creo que esa antipoesía es lo más visible de la poesía hispanoamericana más reciente. Quisiera aventurar la hipótesis de que sus notas más evidentes no serán las más perdurables. Si es aceptable la hipótesis previa, es decir, el paralelo con Campoamor y con el prosaísmo posmodernista, recordemos que aquellas maneras de poesía no se revelaron aberturas, sino caminos cerrados para la poesía. Esto acaso se debió a que se definían negativamente: eran anti... Es decir, se definían en razón del romanticismo o en razón del modernismo; y quedaron presas de esos instantes creadores de los que al cabo, para decirlo en términos matemáticos, eran funciones: eran funciones de los movimientos a los que se oponían. Por eso Lastra, a la hora de definir el antipoema, lo define negativamente.

Propagación de la poesía

Si aquellos resultaron caminos cerrados en sus momentos respectivos, ¿cómo se propagó la poesía en los casos anteriores? Todos lo sabemos, y vamos a recordarlo muy rápidamente.

¿Qué ocurría paralelamente a Campoamor y paralelamente al prosaísmo sentimental a través de cuya ocurrencia la poesía se propagaba?

Volvamos otra vez a los momentos citados: Angel del Río, hablando de la poesía que siguió al romanticismo, escribe en su *Historia de la literatura española* (t. II, p. 99): "Las otras corrientes [...] llevan escondidas entre las supervivencias románticas algunas semillas nuevas y representan por motivos diversos la transición entre el romanticismo y el modernismo". Esas otras corrientes las va a encarnar sobre todo Gustavo Adolfo Bécquer (1836-70). Para Juan Ramón Jiménez, Bécquer es el origen de la poesía moderna, y otro tanto dirían Antonio Machado, Unamuno, e incluso Alberti, quien todavía, dos generaciones más tarde, le rinde su memorable "Homenaje a Gustavo Adolfo Bécquer". Es decir, la poesía se propagó por la línea de Bécquer y no por la línea de Campoamor.

Y veamos un aspecto interesante a propósito de Bécquer. Nosotros hoy día tendemos a ver a Bécquer como un poeta exquisito. Pero esa no fue la apreciación de su época. Para uno de los críticos españoles más destacados de aquel momento, Juan Valera, Bécquer está emparentado con el prosaísmo, como efectivamente está. "No es fácil", dice Valera, "explicar en qué consiste la manera becqueriana, pero, sin explicarlo, se comprende y se nota donde la hay [...] una sencillez graciosa, que degenera a veces en prosaísmo y en desaliñado abandono...".

Así era visto contemporáneamente Bécquer, en contraste con aquella poesía altisonante de Zorrilla, que lo había precedido.

Con respecto al posmodernismo, dice Federico de Onís, en el texto ya citado: "Sólo las mujeres alcanzan en este momento la afirmación plena de su individualidad que se resuelve en la aceptación o liberación de la sumisión y la dependencia..." (p. xviii).

Me parece que de Onís es por lo menos impreciso al hablar en bloque de "las mujeres". Pero hay que destacar a una, extraordinaria, la mayor voz poética de su generación a ambos lados del Atlántico: Gabriela Mistral (1889-957). Dice Federico de Onís hablando de ella: "Las fuentes de arte literario, demasiado próximas y visibles, son indiferentes ante la magnitud e intensidad de su pasión, que encuentra siempre, a través de no se sabe qué esfuerzos recónditos, la justeza de la expresión en las palabras de sabor más íntimo y universal de la lengua castellana" (p. 921). Gabriela es, por supuesto, decididamente superior a los otros poetas de su generación, pero no creo que le podamos atribuir un papel paralelo al de Bécquer, porque su libro de 1922, *Desolación,* no tuvo la influencia de las *Rimas* (1871). Ahora bien, aunque no tuvo ese papel, queda por señalar la influencia del violento lirismo neorromántico, del que Gabriela es encarnación, en la formación de los mayores poetas del vanguardismo: Vallejo ha sido formado en esta línea; Neruda, indudablemente, e incluso lo ha confesado al reconocer su deuda con el uruguayo Carlos Sabat Ercasty (1887), y por supuesto con Gabriela. Es decir, los grandes poetas de la vanguardia van a recibir el alimento de esta línea, como los grandes poetas del modernismo van a recibirlo de la línea becqueriana. Esos son los caminos no cerrados, los caminos abiertos.

¿Qué ocurre en el caso del pasvanguardismo? Creo que esa nueva arrancada, que no se resigna a definirse negativamente, que no se preocupa por lo que pueda deber a lo anterior, y que en vez de ello se ofrece como una abertura germinativa, es la poesía conversacional, poesía que naturalmente tiene puntos de contacto con la antipoesía, como Bécquer tuvo puntos de contacto con Campoamor, o como esos poetas y poetisas del lirismo neorromántico tuvieron algunos puntos de contacto con la antipoesía posmodernista. La poesía conversacional, de un objetivismo que no excluye el lirismo, a veces inesperado, encarna admirablemente en la poesía de quien, como he dicho varias veces, considero el primero entre los poetas del Continente que siguen a las grandes figuras de la vanguardia: Ernesto Cardenal.

Naturalmente que hay puntos de contacto entre esta poesía conversacional y la llamada *antipoesía.* Suele ocurrir así. Acabo de decir que Juan Valera, hablando de Bécquer, de su "sencillez graciosa", nos decía que "degenera a veces en prosaísmo y en desaliñado abandono", términos que parecerían aplicados a Campoamor.

Aquí hay también, por ejemplo, influencia anglosajona marcada: Ernesto Cardenal ha dicho que él no es más que un secuaz de los grandes poetas norteamericanos, lo cual desde luego no es cierto. Pero sí es cierto que él hace, en cierta forma, con respecto a la gran poesía anglosajona reciente, lo que Darío hizo con respecto a la gran poesía francesa de su momento, es decir, la aclimata en nuestra poesía, en nuestra lengua. También hay aquí un acercamiento entre poesía y prosa (y especialmente entre poesía y *conversación,* que no es lo mismo), acercamiento que no sólo comparte con la antipoesía, sino yo diría que con casi toda la generación posvanguardista, e incluso es algo que viene anunciándose a lo largo del siglo en nuestra literatura: ya en el poeta Borges hay una enorme presencia de esa interpenetración entre poesía y prosa; la hay, sin duda, en Vallejo.

Ahora bien: como en el caso de Campoamor y de Bécquer, además de las similitudes, también hay diferencias entre la antipoesía y esta poesía conversacional. Como me queda muy poco tiempo, voy a intentar de manera sumaria destacar algunas de las que me parecen diferencias.

Diferencias

En primer lugar, la antipoesía, como lo dice el mismo nombre, se define negativamente. La poesía conversacional se define positivamente, e incluso yo diría que se cuida poco de definirse: se proyecta a la aventura del porvenir sin demasiado cuidado por la definición.

En segundo lugar, la antipoesía tiende a la burla, tiende al sarcasmo; la poesía conversacional tiende a ser grave, no solemne, y, por cierto, no excluye el humor.

En tercer lugar, la antipoesía tiende al descreimiento ("escéptica", decía Angel del Río, era la poesía de Campoamor). La poesía conversacional tiende a afirmarse en sus creencias, que en un caso son políticas y en algunos otros son, incluso, religiosas.

En cuarto lugar, estas características (burla, descreimiento) dan a la antipoesía un sentido demoledor, con el cual se vuelve con frecuencia al pasado; en la poesía conversacional (aunque también, llegado el caso, es crítica del pasado) hay evocaciones con cierta ternura de zonas del pasado y, sobre todo, es una poesía que es capaz de mirar el tiempo presente y de abrirse al porvenir.

En quinto lugar, la antipoesía suele señalar la incongruencia de lo cotidiano; la poesía conversacional suele señalar la sorpresa o el misterio de lo cotidiano.

En sexto lugar, la antipoesía tiende a engendrar una retórica cerrada sobre sí y fácilmente trasmisible; la poesía conversacional, por su parte, es más difícilmente encerrable en fórmulas, y por ahora no parece tender tanto a encerrarse sobre sí, sobre su propia retórica, sino a moverse hacia nuevas perspectivas.[7]

Un nuevo realismo

Creo que estas dos vertientes poéticas han ido abriéndose a una poesía nueva que se nutre de ellas; una poesía que, recibiendo lo más vivo de la poesía conversacional (incluso esa posibilidad de lirismo objetivo, la cual ejerce de manera original el lirismo que ayer representaron Bécquer y Gabriela Mistral), y recogiendo también lo menos retórico de la anti-

[7] Recuerdo al lector que esta conferencia fue ofrecida a comienzos de 1968. Hoy, a más de haberse confirmado el carácter retórico de la poesía parriana, su condición de camino cerrado, parece que Parra, con quien a lo largo de estos años habíamos tenido serias diferencias con motivo de su censurable conducta política (véase *Casa de las Américas*, n. 61, p. 183: julio-agosto de 1970: "Cruce de cables"), se ha pasado al servicio de la Junta facista chilena. De confirmarse este hecho monstruoso, se vería a dónde han ido a parar la negatividad y el descreimiento de este escritor cuya lamentable trayectoria podría titularse: *del escepticismo al facismo*. Nota de 1974.

poesía, se constituye en una poesía a la que le corresponde un nombre que no debemos temer emplear: *un nuevo realismo,* un realismo enriquecido con las conquistas (que no son pocas) de la poesía de los últimos cuarenta o cincuenta años. Esto sería lo propio de la poesía más reciente, la cual cronológicamente sigue a la de Parra y Cardenal, y cae ya fuera de esta charla. El movimiento hacia el realismo me parece ostensible en varias artes contemporáneas: realista, de esa nueva manera, es el *Marat-Sade* de Peter Weiss, si lo comparamos con el teatro de Ionesco; la novela, engañosamente llamada "sin ficción", de Truman Capote, e incluso casi toda la nueva novela latinoamericana, con su rica variedad; realista es el documental moderno que, por ejemplo, Santiago Alvarez encarna magníficamente entre nosotros; y también, a la salida de una pintura abstracta que se extinguió en su academia, la "nueva figuración". Creo que hay una vuelta al realismo en las artes contemporáneas.

La comprensible (e incluso inevitable) actitud defensiva frente a cierta concepción estrecha del realismo, no nos ha facilitado darnos cuenta de esto. Pero hoy, al margen de aquella concepción, es menester reconocer que esa vuelta al realismo está en pie y que es un realismo que, por ser verdadero, no puede ser repetitivo.

Creo que sería también conveniente decir, ya fuera del tema, que los tiempos enérgicos que nos toca vivir, tiempos que no son de reacción sino de revolución, se avienen con ese realismo, como lo sabemos bien en Cuba. Aquí, la revolución, donde ha podido encontrar expresión en las artes, lo ha hecho dentro de ese nuevo realismo. En otro momento deberíamos volver sobre este tema, que desborda el asunto de nuestra charla. Por lo pronto recordemos que en Cuba esa presencia del nuevo realismo no sólo se manifiesta en obras de arte, sino en la mirada que lanzamos al pasado. Se ha redescubierto, por ejemplo, a Tallet o a Eliseo Diego, a partir del realismo. Es una fácil profecía decir que algo así ocurrirá con otros autores.

¿El otro camino?

Y tampoco conviene olvidar el carácter pendular del arte, del que hemos hablado precavidamente en líneas anteriores. Hay muchos rasgos que nosotros no podemos prever en estos momentos y que es posible que engendra-

rán una poesía de la que no tenemos noción. El arte, como
la historia toda, según decía Marx, suele tomar el otro camino. "Esa otredad que padece lo uno", de que hablaba
Antonio Machado, puede estar ahora mismo oyendo la conversación y ella va a decir la última palabra. Que, desde
luego será la última.

José Gorostiza
1901—1973
México

Notas sobre poesía
Poesía, 1964.

Prólogo

EL poeta tiene ideas acerca de la poesía en las que manifiesta la relación que existe entre él, como inteligencia, y
la misteriosa substancia que elabora. Estas ideas —hasta donde he podido observar— son tan precisas, cada una en su aislamiento, como las que se forma el artesano sobre la calidad
de sus materiales o la eficacia de sus herramientas; pero, faltas de articulación y de método, no sería posible ensartarlas
en un cuerpo de doctrina, sino, nada más, ofrecerlas en estado de naturaleza, como impresiones personales que no alcanzan a penetrar en el enigma de la poesía, aunque sí, cuando
menos, proporcionan una imagen de la personalidad del poeta.
   El poeta no puede, sin ceder su puesto al filósofo, aplicar
todo el rigor del pensamiento al análisis de la poesía. El simplemente la conoce y la ama. Sabe en dónde está y de dónde
se ha ausentado. En un como andar a ciegas, la persigue. La
reconoce en cada una de sus fugaces apariciones y la captura
por fin, a veces, en una red de palabras luminosas, exactas,
palpitantes.
   La poesía no es diferente, en esencia, a un juego de *a es-*
condidas en que el poeta la descubre y la denuncia, y entre

ella y él, como en amor, todo lo que existe es la alegría de
este juego.

Substancia poética

Me gusta pensar en la poesía no como en un suceso que
ocurre dentro del hombre y es inherente a él, a su naturaleza
humana, sino más bien como en algo que tuviese una existencia propia en el mundo exterior. De este modo la contemplo
a mis anchas fuera de mí, como se mira mejor el cielo desde
la falsa pero admirable hipótesis de que la tierra está suspendida en él, en medio de la alta noche. La verdad, para los ojos,
está en el universo que gira en derredor. Para el poeta, la poesía existe por su sola virtud y está ahí, en todas partes, al alcance de todas las miradas que la quieran ver.

Imagino así una substancia poética, semejante a la luz en
el comportamiento, que revela matices sorprendentes en todo
cuanto baña. La poesía no es esencial al sonido, al color o la
forma, así como la luz no lo es a los objetos que ilumina; sin
embargo, cuando incide en una obra de arte —en el cuadro o
la escultura, en la música o el poema— en seguida se advierte
su presencia por la nitidez y como sobrenatural transparencia
que les infunde.

Hay recias obras del arte de los hombres en las que la poesía no intervino. El Partenón en su majestad empequeñece y
abate. La arquitectura está sola en él, grandiosa y escueta. El
Taj Mahal, en cambio, aparece frente a los espejos de agua en
que se mira como anegado por una inconfundible inspiración
poética.

La substancia poética, según esta mi fantasía, que derivo
tal vez de nociones teológicas aprendidas en la temprana juventud, sería omnipresente, y podría encontrarse en cualquier
rincón del tiempo y del espacio, porque se halla más bien oculta que manifiesta en el objeto que habita. La reconocemos
por la emoción singular que su descubrimiento produce y que
señala, como en el encuentro de Orestes y Electra, la conjunción de poeta y poesía.

Definiciones

Sucede, aunque no a menudo, que el artista individual
—digamos un pintor o un músico— se sirve de los recursos de
un arte no poético para hacer poesía. La ocurrencia es casi
siempre involuntaria y, cuando la asociación se produce co-

mo consecuencia de un movimiento natural de la inspiración creadora, el efecto es de completa plenitud.

Me viene a la memoria la pintura del Beato Angélico. La unidad de su emoción religiosa y su sentido poético se traduce en pequeños cuadros comparables, cada uno, a las estrofas del Cántico Espiritual de San Juan de la Cruz.

La palabra es, con todo, terreno propio de la poesía e instrumento necesario para su cabal expresión. Desearía saber, si alguien pudiere explicármelo, por qué, pero lo ignoro; y en mi ignorancia me digo —¡suprema evasión la de las uvas verdes!— que el interés del poeta no está en el *porqué,* sino en el *cómo* se consuma el paso de la poesía a la palabra, ya que ésta, prisionera de las denotaciones que el uso general le acuña, no parece poder facilitar el medio más apto para una operación tan delicada.

Desde mi puesto de observación, así en mi propia poesía como en la ajena, he creído sentir (permitidme que me apoye otra vez en el aire) que la poesía, al penetrar en la palabra, la descompone, la abre como un capullo a todos los matices de la significación. Bajo el conjuro poético la palabra se transparenta y deja entrever, más allá de sus paredes así adelgazadas, ya no lo que dice, sino lo que calla. Notamos que tiene puertas y ventanas hacia los cuatro horizontes del entendimiento y que, entre palabra y palabra, hay corredores secretos y puentes levadizos. Transitamos entonces, dentro de nosotros mismos, hacia inmundos calabozos y elevadas aéreas galerías que no conocíamos en nuestro propio castillo. La poesía ha sacado a la luz la inmensidad de los mundos que encierra nuestro mundo.

Un buen amigo me preguntó ¿qué es la poesía? Quedé perplejo. No sé lo que la poesía es. Nunca lo supe y acaso nunca lo sabré. Leí en un tiempo mucho de lo que se ha dicho de ella, de Platón a Valéry, pero me temo que lo he olvidado todo. Esto no obstante, contesté que la poesía, para mí, es una investigación de ciertas esencias —el amor, la vida, la muerte, Dios— que se produce en un esfuerzo por quebrantar el lenguaje de tal manera que, haciéndolo más transparente, se pueda ver a través de él dentro de esas esencias.

Frente a semejantes conceptos, tan vagos que nada encierran de substantivo como no sea frustración y desaliento —¡así es de inasible la materia que se quiere capturar!— me sentiría inclinado a corregirme ahora, diciendo que la poesía es una especulación, un juego de espejos, en el que las palabras, puestas unas frente a otras, se reflejan unas en otras hasta lo infinito y se recomponen en un mundo de puras imágenes donde el poeta se adueña de los poderes escondidos del hombre y establece contacto con aquel o aquello que está más allá.

Mas, como ya lo habréis advertido, esta segunda definición es, aunque en otros términos, la misma que la primera. Tampoco ésta se sostiene en pie ni podría, en su dolorosa invalidez, servir a ningún propósito sensato.

El viaje inmóvil

Decía Lao-Tsé: "Sin traspasar uno sus puertas, se puede conocer el mundo todo; sin mirar afuera de la ventana, se puede ver el camino del cielo. Mientras más se viaja, puede saberse menos. Pues sucede que, sin moverte, conocerás; sin mirar, verás; sin hacer, crearás".

He aquí descrita, en unas cuantas prudentes palabras, la fuerza del espíritu humano que, inmóvil, crucificado a su profundo aislamiento, puede amasar tesoros de sabiduría y trazarse caminos de salvación. Uno de estos caminos es la poesía. Gracias a ella, podemos crear sin hacer; permanecer en casa y, sin embargo, viajar.

Paréntesis

En mis días he oído hablar a menudo sobre cierta pretendida impopularidad de la poesía. Tal impopularidad suele atribuirse a diversas causas y, sobre todo, a una especie de enrarecimiento de la composición moderna, que la haría difícil de entender a personas desprovistas de fortuna literaria. Dudo si la poesía fue popular en otros tiempos, cuando el aeda cantaba las hazañas de los héroes en el banquete y Ulises se conmovía hasta las lágrimas oyendo relatar sus propios infortunios. La gente que se reunía en torno a la mesa —casi siempre la bien surtida mesa de la casa real— era sin lugar a duda gente de abolengo, que debió tener una responsabilidad principal en el culto de la poesía, puesto que ésta era, a un tiempo mismo, compendio de las tradiciones históricas y religiosas del pueblo y almáciga de todo humano saber.

En nuestro idioma, desde los días en que, fruto de una intensa búsqueda en los papeles de la antigüedad clásica, el *mester de clerecía* se cuela en el arte poético, la poesía se convierte en cosa de adiestramiento. El poeta nace, es verdad, pero una vez nacido, se hace. De esta manera, la poesía, como por lo demás todas las disciplinas artísticas o científicas de nuestro tiempo, pasa a ser objeto de los afances de una minoría que la crea o que, simplemente, posea preparación para disfrutar de sus placeres.

Nada de anormal encontramos en esto; pero en el caso especial de la poesía sucede que su vehículo, el lenguaje, es también el instrumento corriente de comunicación entre los hombres, y mientras cualquier persona sensata estaría dispuesta a reconocer que no pinta, le sería difícil admitir o siquiera pensar (si puede hacerlo) que no habla. Hay quienes, dueños de una cultura general respetable, que dicen gustar del último Strawinsky o preferir al primer Dalí o, aún mejor, que confiesan no interesarse en entenderlos, cuando se les coloca frente a una obra maestra de la poesía —si no la entienden— sienten su propia deficiencia como un insulto personal del autor. ¡Superchería! ¿Cómo se puede engañarlos, a ellos, con palabras?

Poesía-canto

Si la poesía no fuese un arte *sui géneris* y hubiese necesidad de establecer su parentesco respecto de otras disciplinas, yo me atrevería a decir aún (en estos tiempos) que la poesía es música y, de un modo más preciso, canto. En esto no me aparto un ápice de la noción corriente. La historia muestra a la poesía hermanada en su cuna al arte del cantor; y más tarde, cuando ya puede andar por su propio pie, sin el sostén directo de la música, esto se debe a que el poeta, a fuerza de trabajar el idioma, lo ha adaptado ya a la condición musical de la poesía, sometiéndolo a medida, acentuación, periodicidad, correspondencias.

Los poetas de mi grupo —el "grupo sin grupo" que dijera Xavier Villaurrutia— nos complacíamos en reconocernos individualmente distintos de cada uno de los demás y, en conjunto, algo así como extraños a la generación que nos había precedido. Las cosas no andaban precisamente así. Hacia 1920-25 el Modernismo, y en primer término la voz estentórea de Darío, llenaba aún el ambiente de poderosas resonancias y, en verdad, fueren cuales hubiesen sido nuestros modelos más cercanos —Nervo, González Martínez o López Velarde— el grupo había nacido para la poesía bajo el signo gigante del Modernismo. Y éste ¿qué fue, en su idolatría de la forma, sino una verdadera orgía de musicalidad?

Un movimiento de reacción, en el sentido opuesto, se inicia entonces. Mi generación marcó, como actitud de principio, un cierto desdén hacia los recursos de la prosodia, que estimaba sacrílegos; pero no fue ella, imbuida como estaba en el gusto por las bellas formas, quien pudo llevar aquel desdén demasiado lejos. En donde mejor se advierte esta reacción es en la poesía actual, aunque no tánto aquí en México como en otras provincias del idioma, ya que el modo en que se trasegó la poesía española al vaso indígena, en pleno siglo XVI, parece haber imprimido para siempre en nuestra literatura el sello inconfundible de la herencia clásica.

Estamos por consiguiente —y éste es el hecho que deseo subrayar— frente a una postura contemporánea que desea, si no librarse de la musicalidad, sí apagarla, resistirse a servirla. La poesía de los jóvenes no quiere que la música se apodere de ella y la esclavice; huye de lo declamatorio y lo operático y se refugia en una especie de balbuceo vagamente rítmico, en el que se introduce, aquí y allá, un endecasílabo perfecto o una rima involuntaria. Tal parece como si en el esplendor de las formas cristalizadas, el poeta se sintiera rodeado de una fragancia excesiva que le impidiese respirar a pleno pulmón. De este modo se llega a ver como pura superfluidad todo cuanto la poesía elaboró en el idioma para poder realizarse.

Sabemos cuánta sinceridad y cuánta verdad se encierran en esta actitud que nos ofrece una poesía despojada de afeites innecesarios, pero no sólo esto, sino que apenas dotada de un tímido hilillo de voz. La poesía saldrá seguramente rejuvenecida de esta experiencia. Conviene recordar, sin embargo, que nada existe semejante a una libertad irrestricta. Todo está sujeto a medida, y la libertad puede no consistir en otra cosa que en el sentimiento de la propia posesión dentro de un orden establecido. Las reglas del ajedrez no oprimen al jugador, le trazan una zona de libertad en donde su ingenio se puede desenvolver hasta lo infinito.

La afinidad entre poesía y canto es una afinidad congénita. En un momento dado podrá relajarse o en otro hacerse más íntima, pero habrá de durar para siempre, porque no radica en el lenguaje —en el austero arsenal de la retórica, que caduca y se renueva sin cesar— sino en la voz humana misma, que el hombre presta a la poesía para que, al ser hablada, se realice en la totalidad de su perfección.

La diferencia entre prosa y poesía consiste en que, mientras una no pide al lector sino que le preste sus ojos, la otra necesita de toda necesidad que le entregue la voz. Cada poeta tiene un estilo personal (a veces indicador de su postura estética) para *decir* sus poesías. Este las canta, aquél las re-

za, otro las musita, uno más las solloza. Nadie se confina solamente a leer. Encomendad a quien queráis que diga un poema. En el acto impostará la voz a la tesitura del canto y a continuación el verso saldrá vibrando de su garganta, con un temblor de vida que sólo la voz le puede infundir; porque ocurre
—mis amigos queridos— que así como Venus nace de la espuma, la poesía nace de la voz.

El desarrollo poético

En años no remotos, estimulado por la lectura de Valéry,
me preocupaba —como a él— descubrir las leyes que gobier-
nan el crecimiento y la terminación de un poema, a partir de
su simiente. El poema, así se trate nada más que de un soneto, ni nada menos, viene a ser como la unidad de medida de
la poesía. La dificultad no está en saber cómo empieza el poema. Todo poeta tiene siempre a la mano su primera línea, pero ¿cómo se desarrolla? ¿cómo acaba? He aquí el caso. Hay
indudablemente una variedad de procedimientos que no es
fácil reconocer, pero dos o tres de ellos —los más comunes—
saltan desde luego a la vista.

En el primero, que se podría llamar desarrollo plástico,
el poema crece como un cuadro en el sentido de la superficie
que ha de llenar. Tiene un plano anterior, luminoso e incisivo,
y tiene un fondo de escalonadas perspectivas en donde se es-
fuman los motivos accesorios. El desarrollo plástico resulta
limitado en cuanto a que el poema debe confinarse al espacio
que el autor le concede; y es finito, porque ahí, dentro de ese
espacio, el poema se agota y acaba, de suerte que el autor mismo podría retocarlo, si quisiera, pero nunca proseguirlo. Do-
tado de un sistema de vida interior, estático, el poema queda
frente a nosotros, como el cuadro, abierto a nuestra capacidad de contemplación.

El poema suele tener también un desarrollo dinámico.
Puesto en marcha, avanza o asciende en un continuo progreso, estalla en un clímax y se precipita rápidamente hacia su
terminación. El poeta ha de medir de antemano la parábola
que corresponde a la potencia del proyectil; pero en este método, las posibilidades de crecimiento resultan inagotables y
el poema puede prolongarse indefinidamente, ya sea por acumulación o porque se establece un círculo vicioso, como en
los cuentos de nunca acabar. Es el poeta quien, con su sentido de las proporciones, le pone un hasta aquí.

Tenemos, por último, un poema en que no se nota el crecimiento. De la primera a la última línea crece y va tomando cuerpo insensiblemente como en el desarrollo de un ser vivo, de un fruto o de una flor, hasta que alcanza sin esfuerzo, naturalmente, el tamaño, la estatura, la proporción que le dicta su propio aliento vital. El madrigal de Cetina debió producirse de este modo. No podía haber sido ni más sucinto ni más explícito y hubo de quedarse así, dentro de ese cuerpecito de poema niño, rebosamente de su preciosa niñez.

La construcción en poesía

En su *Defensa de la Poesía* observa Shelley que "las partes de una composición pueden ser poéticas sin que la composición, como un todo, sea un poema". Nada más cierto ni, cuando así pasa, menos afortunado; pues ¿qué se diría de una casa en la que cada una de las habitaciones fuese admirable, pero todas juntas no pudieran integrar la unidad en que consiste justamente una casa? No es cuestión ésta que suscite ninguna duda: si un poema se os muestra en la condición que señala el poeta inglés, estáis frente a una obra fallida; y el error no debe atribuirse a otra causa que a negligencia de lo que el poema significa como unidad arquitectónica. La poesía y la arquitectura, al igual que la poesía y el canto, se amamantaron en los mismos pechos.

En la actualidad, el poeta no suele proponerse problemas de construcción. De vez en cuando —cada día menos— utiliza ciertos elementos del arte poética tradicional y levanta con ellos, cuarteta sobre cuarteta o lira sobre lira, como con dados, un somero edificio que se sostiene, si la unidad interior es profunda, gracias a ella y no a la solidez de los materiales empleados. El soneto proporciona ocasión de construir de veras, conforme a un modelo feliz. El caso de la construcción en grande, como en los vastos poemas de otros tiempos, no se plantea ya. Quiero decir, no puedo callar, que lo siento como una enorme pérdida para la poesía.

Estamos bajo el imperio de la lírica. La poesía ha abandonado una gran parte del territorio que dominó en otros tiempos como suyo. El diálogo, la descripción, el relato, así como otras muchas maneras de poesía, que con tan notoria eficacia se combinaron en libros como —por ejemplo— el del *Buen Amor* del Arcipreste de Hita, se han ido a engrosar los recursos del teatro y de la novela.

Dentro de la lírica, cuando menos como la concebimos en la actualidad, parece que la única causa capaz de desatar

un poema es el dato autobiográfico. La conmoción que un
acontecimiento produce en el poeta al incidir sobre su vida
personal, se traduce, convertida en imágenes, en una ema-
nación o efluvio poético; pero no en un poema, porque esta
palabra "poema" implica organización inteligente de la materia poética. Treinta o cuarenta composiciones (en las cuales
se puede reconocer siempre el contenido de pura, auténtica
poesía) suelen formar, unas tras otras, lo que el público llama *un libro de versos.* (¡Qué horrible expresión: un libro
de versos!) Y en el libro podrá haber cierta uniformidad de
emoción y de estilo, y de un poema a otro, tales o cuales es-
labones que dan la sensación de una continuidad invisible;
pero el libro no mostrará, a su vez, la unidad de construcción
que nos agrada encontrar en un libro. La suma de treinta momentos musicales no hará nunca el total de una sinfonía.

La historia marcha cada día hacia el futuro ajena a toda
noción de misericordia; no sería nada insensato, así pues, que
en lugar de pedir que la poesía sea como fue en el pasado, tra-
tásemos de comprender que puede ser ya tarde para aceptar-
la como es hoy. Tampoco sería absurdo pensar, en este amanecer de la edad atómica, en un mundo sin poesía, un mundo
habitado únicamente por *expertos,* de donde la poesía fuese desterrada como una escandalosa manifestación del pensamiento primitivo del hombre. Mas, mientras tanto, ¿sería mucho exigir que las partes de una composición sean todas poéticas y que la composición, en su conjunto, resulte un poema?

La cuestión del ambiente

Cuando pensamos en la poesía como revelación de belleza
no se dificulta concluir, a poco que se profundice en las ideas,
que así es ciertamente; sólo que la belleza manifestada por la
poesía no la toma ésta del mundo exterior, como prestada,
no es la belleza natural de la nube o de la flor, sino la belleza
artificial, poética, que la poesía presta transitoriamente, para
sus propios fines, a la rosa y a la nube.

Esto no se entendió así siempre ni se entiende así todavía, no obstante la diafanidad de tan justa distinción entre la
belleza de la poesía y la de los seres y las cosas. Para el lector
común —y aun para muchos poetas— la poesía es como un
túnel secreto que nos permite escapar de nuestras prisiones,
de la fealdad y el horror circundante, hacia infinitas llanuras
iluminadas por el esplendor de lo bello. La razón les asiste
hasta aquí, pero me temo que les falte cuando deducen, co-

mo consecuencia necesaria, que la poesía no tiene otro objeto que el de captar y exhibir la magnificencia del orbe.

De ahí que la poesía se haya asociado en el curso de su historia —y por contraste con el concepto corriente de prosa— con el uso de un lenguaje suntuario en el que sólo ciertas materias preciosas (sedas, oro, diamantes) parecen poder ofrecer a la imaginación sus puntos de apoyo terrenales. De ahí también, de este error que desconoce el poder de la poesía como fuente de belleza, resulta el hábito de situar el suceso poético dentro de un ambiente especial, en el escenario que el gusto del momento considera apropiado. Ha habido así muchos "ambientes poéticos", como el pastoril que la Edad de Oro importó de la bucólica clásica o el ambiente oriental, de salón turco, que tanto amaban los poetas románticos. Todos falsos, como de papel, todos aparato escénico y utilería ineficaz. El ambiente así concebido nunca añadió nada a la belleza esencial de la poesía.

Pese a todo, la tendencia a elaborar un *ambiente poético* perdura en nuestros días y no faltan quienes están sinceramente convencidos de que la poesía gana —cuando menos en actualidad— si se presenta (o se representa) en medio de los signos exteriores de la época. Tal vez quienes tal creen no se dan cuenta de que una apariencia de actualidad es, como cualquiera otra apariencia, extraña a la naturaleza misma de la poesía que está hecha toda de esencia e interioridad.

Debemos admitir, no obstante, por elemental confianza en la sinceridad de los empeños humanos, que nadie busca el error por el error, sino que caemos en él accidentalmente en nuestra prisa por llegar a lo cierto. Tal vez el hombre de hoy, apiñado a centenares de miles, a millones, en la estrechez de las grandes ciudades, no es ya como el hombre de otros tiempos. El hombre no vive, como solía, en la frecuentación de la naturaleza. El cielo no entra ahora a grandes pedazos azules, a paletadas, en la composición de la ciudad. Prisionero de un cuarto, ahíto de silencio y hambriento de comunicación, se ha convertido —hombre isla— en una soledad rodeada de gente por todas partes. Su jardín está en las flores desteñidas de la alfombra, sus pájaros en la garganta del receptor de radio, su primavera en las aspas del abanico eléctrico, su amor en el llanto de la mujer que zurce su ropa en un rincón. La poesía no necesita de este hombre para enriquecer su belleza. En rigor, si fuese cierto que la poesía no es sino un reflector de belleza, debería huir de él y de su fealdad y de sus miserias. Pero este hombre necesita, él sí, de la poesía; que sople sobre su

vida y la embellezca; que la salve de los tremendos infortunios que la amenazan y la haga digna de ser llevada con orgullo sobre los hombres.

Un hombre de Dios

Se trabaja en común para la poesía, aunque cada poeta
se encierre en su torre de marfil. El poema no resulta de
un encuentro repentino con la poesía. Hubo poetas que, a
través de toda su obra, no buscaron sino perfeccionar un
poema; y hay poemas que, en el dilatado proceso de su ma-
duración, debieron consumir los afanes de muchos poetas.
La historia de la poesía —como la historia en general— sugiere la imagen de una corriente, un río cuyas ondas emergen al empuje de la masa de agua que las hunde, en seguida,
en la disolución.

Porque la poesía —no la increada, no, la que ya se conta-
minó de vida— ha de morir también. La matan los instrumentos mismos que le dieron forma: la palabra, el estilo, el gusto,
la escuela. Nada envejece tan pronto, salvo una flor, como
puede envejecer una poesía. El poeta la hará durar un día más
o un día menos, según su habilidad para sustraerla a la acción
del tiempo. Su destino está trazado, a pesar de todo, e irá a
dispersarse en el fondo de la sabiduría popular —yo he oído a
gente humilde, carente de toda cultura, repetir pensamientos
de Shakespeare como propios— o bien, relegada a los anaque-
les de las bibliotecas como un objeto arqueológico, quedará
allí para curiosidad de los estudiosos y la inspiración de otros
poetas.

Todas estas cosas, el poeta no tiene por qué saberlas y, si
las sabe, no tiene para qué recordarlas. La conciencia histórica asesinaría a la musa dentro de él. El poeta no ha de proceder como el operario que, junto con otros mil, explota una
misma cantera. Ha de sentirse el único, en un mundo desierto, a quien se concedió por vez primera la dicha de dar nombres a todas las cosas. Debe estar seguro de poseer un mensaje
que sólo él sabrá traducir, en el momento preciso, a la palabra
justa e imperecedera.

La misión del poeta es infinitamente delicada. Dejemos
que la escude tras su inocente soberbia; que la defienda, si fuere necesario, con el látigo de su infantil vanidad. Después de
todo, ni la individualidad ni la duración de una obra deben
montar a mucho en los cuidados del espectador. En poesía,
como sucede con el milagro, lo que importa es la intensidad.

Nadie sino el Ser Unico más allá de nosotros, a quien no conocemos, podría sostener en el aire, por pocos segundos, el
perfume de una violeta. El poeta puede —a semejanza suya—
sostener por un instante mínimo el milagro de la poesía. Entre todos los hombres, él es uno de los pocos elegidos a quien
se puede llamar con justicia un hombre de Dios.

Eugenio María de Hostos
1839- 1903
Puerto Rico

La educación científica de la mujer
1872.

Primera Conferencia

Señores:

AL aceptar nuestra primera base, que siempre será gloria y
honra del pensador eminente que os la propuso y nos pre-
side, todos vosotros la habéis meditado; y la habéis abarcado,
al meditarla, en todas sus fases, en todas sus consecuencias
lógicas, en todas sus trascendencias de presente y porvenir.
No caerá, por lo tanto, bajo el anatema del escándalo el tema
que me propongo desarrollar ante vosotros: que cuando se ha
atribuído al arte literario el fin de expresar la verdad filosófica; cuando se le atribuye como regla de composición y de críticas el deber de conformar las obras científicas a los hechos
demostrados positivamente por la ciencia, y el deber de amol-
dar las obras sociológicas o meramente literarias al desarrollo
de la naturaleza humana, se ha devuelto al arte de la palabra,
escrita o hablada, el fin esencial a que corresponde; y el pensador que en esa reivindicación del arte literario ha sabido
descubrir la rehabilitación de esferas enteras de pensamiento,

con sólo esa rehabilitación ha demostrado la profundidad de su indagación, la alteza de su designio, y al asociarse a vosotros y al asociaros a su idea generosa, algo más ha querido, quería algo más que matar el ocio impuesto: ha querido lo que vosotros queréis, lo que yo quiero; deducir de la primera base las abundantes consecuencias que contiene.

Entre esas consecuencias está íntegramente el tema que desenvolverá este discurso.

Esta Academia quiere un arte literario basado en la verdad, y fuera de la ciencia no hay verdad; quiere servir a la verdad por medio de la palabra, y fuera de la que conquista prosélitos para la ciencia, no hay palabra; quiere, tiene que querer difusión para las verdades demostradas, y fuera de la propaganda continua no hay difusión; quiere, tiene que querer eficacia para la propaganda, y fuera de la irradiación del sentimiento no hay eficacia de verdad científica en pueblos niños que no han llegado todavía al libre uso de razón. Como el calor reanima los organismos más caducos, porque se hace sentir en los conductos más secretos de la vida, el sentimiento despierta el amor de la verdad en los pueblos no habituados a pensarla, porque hay una electricidad moral y el sentimiento es el mejor conductor de esa electricidad. El sentimiento es facultad inestable, transitoria e inconstante en nuestro sexo; es facultad estable, permanente, constante, en la mujer. Si nuestro fin es servir por medio del arte literario a la verdad, y en el estado actual de la vida chilena el medio más adecuado a ese fin es el sentimiento, y el sentimiento es más activo y por lo tanto más persuasivo y eficaz en la mujer, por una encadenación de ideas, por una rigurosa deducción llegaréis, como he llegado yo, a uno de los fines contenidos en la base primera: la educación científica de la mujer. Ella es sentimiento: educadla, y vuestra propaganda de verdad será eficaz; haced eficaz por medio de la mujer la propaganda redentora, y difundiréis por todas partes los principios eternos de la ciencia; difundid esos principios, y en cada labio tendréis palabras de verdad; dadme una generación que hable la verdad, y yo os daré una generación que haga el bien; daos madres que lo enseñen científicamente a sus hijos, y ellas os darán una patria que obedezca virilmente a la razón, que realice concienzudamente la libertad, que resuelva despacio el problema capital del Nuevo Mundo, basando la civilización en la ciencia, en la moralidad y en el trabajo, no en la fuerza corruptora, no en la moral indiferente, no en el predominio exclusivo del bienestar individual.

Pero educar a la mujer para la ciencia es empresa tan ardua a los ojos de casi todos los hombres, que aquellos en quienes tiene luz más viva la razón y más sana energía la voluntad, prefieren la tiniebla del error, prefieren la ociosidad de su energía, a la lucha que impone la tarea. Y no seréis vosotros los únicos, señores, que al llevar al silencio del hogar las congojas acerbas que en todo espíritu de hombre destila el espectáculo de la anarquía moral e intelectual de nuestro siglo, no seréis vosotros los únicos que os espantéis de concebir que allí, en el corazón afectuoso, en el cerebro ocioso, en el espíritu erial de la mujer, está probablemente el germen de la nueva vida social, del nuevo mundo moral que en vano reclamáis de los gobiernos, de las costumbres, de las leyes. No seréis los únicos que os espantéis de concebirlo. Educada exclusivamente como está por el corazón y para él, aislada sistemáticamente como vive en la esfera de la idealidad enfermiza, la mujer es una planta que vegeta, no una conciencia que conoce su existencia; es una mimosa sensitiva que lastima el contacto de los hechos, que las brutalidades de la realidad marchitan; no una entidad de razón y de conciencia que amparada por ellas en su vida, lucha para desarrollarlas, las desarrolla para vivirlas, las vive libremente, las realiza. Vegetación, no vida; desarrollo fatal, no desarrollo libre; instinto, no razón; haz de nervios irritables, no haz de facultades dirigibles; sístole-diástole fatal que dilata o contrae su existencia, no desenvolvimiento voluntario de su vida; eso han hecho de la mujer los errores que pesan sobre ella, las tradiciones sociales, intelectuales y morales que la abruman, y no es extraordinario que cuando concebimos en la rehabilitación total de la mujer la esperanza de un nuevo orden social, la esperanza de la armonía moral e intelectual, nos espantemos: entregar la dirección del porvenir a un ser a quien no hemos sabido todavía entregar la dirección de su propia vida, es un peligro pavoroso.

Y sin embargo, es necesario arrostrarlo, porque es necesario vencerlo. Ese peligro es obra nuestra, es creación nuestra; es obra de nuestros errores, es creación de nuestras debilidades; y nosotros los hombres, los que monopolizamos la fuerza de que casi nunca sabemos hacer justo empleo; los que monopolizamos el poder social, que casi siempre manejamos con mano femenina; los que hacemos las leyes para nosotros, para el sexo masculino, para el sexo fuerte, a nuestro gusto, prescindiendo temerariamente de la mitad del género humano, nosotros somos responsables de los males que causan nuestra continua infracción de las leyes eternas de la naturaleza. Ley

eterna de la naturaleza es la igualdad moral del hombre y de
la mujer, porque la mujer, como el hombre, es obrero de la
vida; porque para desempeñar ese augusto ministerio, ella como él está dotada de las facultades creadoras que completan
la formación física del hombre-bestia por la formación moral
del hombre dios. Nosotros violamos esa ley, cuando reduciendo el ministerio de la mujer a la simple cooperación de la formación física del animal, le arrebatamos el derecho de coope-
rar a la formación psíquica del ángel. Para acatar las leyes de
la naturaleza, no basta que las nuestras reconozcan la personalidad de la mujer, es necesario que instituyan esa personalidad, y sólo hay personalidad en donde hay responsabilidad y
en donde la responsabilidad es efectiva. Más lógicos en nuestras costumbres que solemos serlo en las especulaciones de
nuestro entendimiento, aun no nos hemos atrevido a declarar
responsable del desorden moral e intelectual a la mujer, porque, aun sabiendo que en ese desorden tiene ella una parte de
la culpa, nos avergonzamos de hacerla responsable. ¿Por magnanimidad, por fortaleza? No; por estricta equidad, porque si
la mujer es cómplice de nuestras faltas y copartícipe de nuestros males, lo es por ignorancia, por impotencia moral; porque la abandonamos cobardemente en las contiendas intelectuales que nosotros sostenemos con el error, porque la abandonamos impíamente a las congojas del cataclismo moral que
atenebra la conciencia de este siglo. Reconstituyamos la personalidad de la mujer, instituyamos su responsabilidad ante sí
misma, ante el hogar, ante la sociedad; y para hacerlo, resta-
blezcamos la ley de la naturaleza, acatemos la igualdad moral
de los dos sexos, devolvamos a la mujer el derecho de vivir ra-
cionalmente; hagámosle conocer este derecho, instruyámosla
en todos sus deberes, eduquemos su conciencia para que ella
sepa educar su corazón. Educada en su conciencia, será una
personalidad responsable: educada en su corazón, responderá
de su vida con las amables virtudes que hacen del vivir una satisfacción moral y corporal tanto como una resignación intelectual.

    ¿Cómo?

    Ya lo sabéis: obedeciendo a la naturaleza. Más justa con
el hombre que lo es él consigo mismo, la naturaleza previó
que el ser a quien dotaba de la conciencia de su destino, no
hubiera podido resignarse a tener por compañera a un simple
mamífero; y al dar al hombre un colaborador de la vida en la
mujer, dotó a ésta de las mismas facultades de razón y la hizo
colaborador de su destino. Para que el hombre fuera hombre,

es decir, digno de realizar los fines de su vida, la naturaleza le dio conciencia de ella, capacidad de conocer su origen, sus elementos favorables y contrarios, su trascendencia y relaciones, su deber y su derecho, su libertad y su responsabilidad; capacidad de sentir y de amar lo que sintiera; capacidad de querer y realizar lo que quisiera; capacidad de perfeccionarse y de mejorar por sí mismo las condiciones de su ser y por sí mismo elevar el ideal de su existencia. Idealistas o sensualistas, materialistas o positivistas, describan las facultades del espíritu según orden de ideas innatas o preestablecidas, según desarrollo del alma por el desarrollo de los sentidos, ya como meras modificaciones de la materia, ya como categorías, todos los filósofos y todos los psicólogos se han visto forzados a reconocer tres órdenes de facultades que conjuntamente constituyen la conciencia del ser humano, y que funcionando aisladamente constituyen su facultad de conocer, su facultad de sentir, su facultad de querer. Si estas facultades están con diversa intensidad repartidas en el hombre y la mujer, es un problema; pero que están total y parcialmente determinando la vida moral de uno y otro sexo, es un axioma: que los positivistas refieran al instinto la mayor parte de los medios atribuídos por los idealistas a la facultad de sentir; que Spinoza y la escuela escocesa señalen en los sentidos la mejor de las aptitudes que los racionalistas declaran privativas de la razón; que Krause hiciera de la conciencia una como facultad de facultades; que Kant resumiera en la razón pura todas las facultades del conocimiento y en la razón práctica todas las determinaciones del juicio, importa poco, en tanto que no se haya demostrado que el conocer, el sentir y el querer se ejercen de un modo absolutamente diverso en cada sexo. No se demostrará jamás, y siempre será base de la educación científica de la mujer la igualdad moral del ser humano. Se debe educar a la mujer para que sea ser humano, para que cultive y desarrolle sus facultades, para que practique su razón, para que viva su conciencia, no para que funcione en la vida social con las funciones privativas de mujer. Cuanto más ser humano se conozca y se sienta, más mujer querrá ser y sabrá ser.

Si se me permitiera distribuir en dos grupos las facultades y las actividades de nuestro ser, llamaría *conciencia* a las primeras, *corazón* a las segundas, para expresar las dos grandes fases de la educación de la mujer y para hacer comprender que si la razón, el sentimiento y la voluntad pueden y deben educarse en cuanto facultades, sólo pueden dirigirse en cuanto actividades: educación es también dirección, pero es exter-

na, indirecta, mediata, extrapersonal; la dirección es esencialmente directa, inmediata, interna, personal. Como ser humano consciente, la mujer es educable; como corazón, sólo ella
misma puede dirigirse. Que dirigirá mejor su corazón cuando
esté más educada su conciencia; que sus actividades serán más
saludables cuanto mejor desenvueltas estén sus facultades, es
tan evidente y es tan obvio, que por eso es necesario, indispensable, obligatorio, educar científicamente a la mujer.

Ciencia es el conjunto de verdades demostradas o de hipótesis demostrables, ya se refieran al mundo exterior o al
interior, al yo o al no-yo, como dice la antigua metafísica;
comprende, por lo tanto, todos los objetos de conocimiento
positivo e hipotético, desde la materia en sus varios elementos, formas, transformaciones, fines, necesidades y relaciones,
hasta el espíritu en sus múltiples aptitudes, derechos, deberes,
leyes, finalidad y progresiones; desde el ser hasta el no-ser;
desde el conocimiento de las evoluciones de los astros hasta
el conocimiento de las revoluciones del planeta; desde las leyes que rigen el universo físico hasta las que rigen el mundo
moral; desde las verdades axiomáticas en que está basada la
ciencia de lo bello, hasta los principios fundamentales de la
moral; desde el conjunto de hipótesis que se refieren al origen, transmigración, civilización y decadencia de las razas, hasta el conjunto de hechos que constituyen la sociología.

Esta abrumadora diversidad de conocimientos, cada uno
de los cuales puede absorber vidas enteras y en cada uno de
los cuales establecen diferencias, divisiones y separaciones sucesivas el método, el rigor lógico y la especialización de hechos, de observaciones y de experimentaciones que antes no
se habían comprobado, esta diversidad de conocimientos está virtualmente reducida a la unidad de la verdad, y se puede,
por una sencilla generalización, abarcar en una simple serie.
Todo lo cognoscible se refiere necesaria y absolutamente a
alguno de nuestros medios de conocer. Conocemos por medio de nuestras facultades, y nuestras facultades están de tan
íntimo modo ligadas entre sí, que lo que es conocer para las
unas es sentir para las otras y querer para las restantes; y a veces la voluntad es sentimiento y conocimiento, y frecuentemente el sentimiento suple o completa e ilumina a la facultad
que conoce y a la que realiza. Distribuyendo, pues, toda la
ciencia conocida en tantas categorías cuantas facultades tenemos para conocer la verdad, para amarla y para ejercitarla, la
abarcaremos en su unidad trascendental, y sin necesidad de
conocerla en su abundante variedad, adquiriremos todos sus

fundamentos, en los cuales, hombre o mujer, podemos todos conocer las leyes generales del universo, los caracteres propios de la materia y del espíritu, los fundamentos de la sociabilidad, los principios necesarios de derecho, los motivos, determinaciones y elementos de lo bello, la esencia y la necesidad de lo bueno y de lo justo.

Todo eso puede saberlo la mujer, porque para todos esos conocimientos tiene facultades; todo eso debe saberlo, porque sabiendo todo eso se emancipará de la tutela del error y de la esclavitud en que la misma ociosidad de sus facultades intelectuales y morales la retienen. Se ama lo que se conoce bello, bueno, verdadero; el universo, el mundo, el hombre, la sociedad, la ciencia, el arte, la moral, todo es bello, bueno y verdadero en sí mismo; conociéndolo todo en su esencia, ¿no sería todo más amado? Y habiendo necesariamente en la educación científica de la mujer un desenvolvimiento correlativo de su facultad de amar, ¿no amaría más conociendo cuanto hoy ama sin conocer? Amando más y con mejor amor, ¿no sería más eficaz su misión en la sociedad? Educada por ella, conocedora y creadora ya de las leyes inmutables del universo, del planeta, del espíritu, de las sociedades, libre ya de las supersticiones, de los errores, de los terrores en que continuamente zozobran su sentimiento, su razón y su voluntad, ¿no sabría ser la primera y la última educadora de sus hijos, la primera para dirigir sus facultades, la última para moderar sus actividades, presentándoles siempre lo bello, lo bueno, lo verdadero como meta? La mujer es siempre madre; de sus hijos, porque les ha revelado la existencia; de su amado, porque le ha revelado la felicidad; de su esposo, porque le ha revelado la armonía. Madre, amante, esposa, toda mujer es una influencia. Armad de conocimientos científicos esa influencia, y soñad la existencia, la felicidad y la armonía inefable de que gozaría el hombre en el planeta, si la dadora, si la embellecedora, si la compañera de la vida fuera, como madre, nuestro guía científico; como amada, la amante reflexiva de nuestras ideas, y de nuestros designios virtuosos; como esposa, la compañera de nuestro cuerpo, de nuestra razón, de nuestro sentimiento, de nuestra voluntad y nuestra conciencia. Sería hombre completo. Hoy no lo es.

El hombre que educa a una mujer, ése vivirá en la plenitud de su ser, y hay en el mundo algunos hombres que saben vivir su vida entera; pero ellos no son el mundo, y el infinito número de crímenes, de atrocidades, de infracciones de toda ley que en toda hora se cometen en todos los ámbitos del mun-

do, están clamando contra las pasiones bestiales que la ignorancia de la mujer alienta en todas partes, contra los intereses
infernales que una mujer educada moderaría en el corazón de
cada hijo, de cada esposo, de cada padre.

Esta mujer americana, que tántas virtudes espontáneas ate-
sora, que tan nobles ensueños acaricia, que tan alta razón des-
pliega en el consejo de familia y tan enérgica voluntad pone al
infortunio, que tan asombrosa perspicacia manifiesta y con
tan poderosa intuición se asimila los conocimientos que el aumento de civilización diluye en la atmósfera intelectual de
nuestro siglo; esta mujer americana, tan rebelde por tan digna, como dócil y educable por tan buena, es digna de la iniciación científica que está destinada a devolverle la integridad
de su ser, la libertad de su conciencia, la responsabilidad de su
existencia. En ella más que en nadie es perceptible en la América Latina la trascendencia del cambio que se opera en el espíritu de la humanidad, y si ella no sabe de dónde viene la an-
siosa vaguedad de sus deseos, a dónde van las tristezas morales que la abaten, dónde está el ideal en que quisiera revivir su
corazón, antes marchito que formado, ella sabe que está pronta para bendecir el nuevo mundo moral en donde, convertida
la verdad en realidad, convertida en verdad la idea de lo bello;
convertida en amable belleza la virtud, las tres Gracias del mito simbólico descienden a la tierra y enlazadas estrechamente
de la mano como estrechamente se enlazan la facultad de conocer lo verdadero, la facultad de querer lo justo, la facultad
de amar lo bello, ciencia, conciencia y caridad se den la mano.

He dicho.[1]

---

[1] Como complemento de este bello discurso, el señor Hostos presentó la siguiente proposición:
"Deseando hacer efectiva en una de sus deducciones más importantes la base
primera de la Academia, propongo:
1o. Que se establezca una serie de conferencias para la educación científica
de la mujer;
2o. Que se adopte para el orden de esas conferencias la clasificación del método positivista, según el cual precede a todo otro conocimiento el de las leyes generales del universo;
3o. Que se adopte como método de composición el orden en que se desarro-
llan las facultades morales e intelectuales, para persuadir primero el sentimiento y
convencer después la razón de la mujer." (De la *Revista Sud-Americana*, de junio
de 1973).

José Martí
1853—1895
Cuba

Nuestra América

El Partido Liberal, 1891.

CREE el aldeano vanidoso que el mundo entero es su aldea, y con tal que él quede de alcalde, o le mortifique al rival que le quitó la novia, o le crezcan en la alcancía los ahorros, ya da por bueno el orden universal, sin saber de los gigantes que llevan siete leguas en las botas y le pueden poner la bota encima, ni de la pelea de los cometas en el Cielo, que van por el aire dormidos engullendo mundos. Lo que quede de aldea en América ha de despertar. Estos tiempos no son para acostarse con el pañuelo a la cabeza, sino con las armas de almohada, como los varones de Juan de Castellanos: las armas del juicio, que vencen a las otras. Trincheras de ideas valen más que trinceras de piedra.

No hay proa que taje una nube de ideas. Una idea enérgica, flameada a tiempo ante el mundo, para, como la bandera mística del juicio final, a un escuadrón de acorazados. Los pueblos que no se conocen han de darse prisa para conocerse, como quienes van a pelear juntos. Los que se enseñan los puños, como hermanos celosos, que quieren los dos la misma tierra, o el de casa chica, que le tiene envidia al de casa mejor, han de encajar, de modo que sean una, las dos manos. Los que, al amparo de una tradición criminal, cercenaron, con el sable tinto en la sangre de sus mismas venas, la tierra del hermano vencido, del hermano castigado más allá de sus culpas, si no quieren que les llame el pueblo ladrones, devuélvanle sus tierras al hermano. Las deudas del honor no las cobra el honrado en dinero, a tanto por la bofetada. Ya no podemos ser el pueblo de hojas, que vive en el aire, con la copa cargada de flor, restallando o zumbando, según la acaricie el capricho de la luz, o la tundan y talen las tempestades; ¡los árboles se han de poner en fila, para que no pase el gigante de las siete leguas! Es la hora del recuento, y de la marcha unida, y hemos de andar en cuadro apretado, como la plata en las raíces de los Andes.

A los sietemesinos sólo les faltará el valor. Los que no tienen fe en su tierra son hombres de siete meses. Porque les falta el valor a ellos, se lo niegan a los demás. No les alcanza al árbol difícil el brazo canijo, el brazo de uñas pintadas y pulsera, el brazo de Madrid o de París, y dicen que no se puede alcanzar el árbol. Hay que cargar los barcos de esos insectos dañinos, que le roen el hueso a la patria que los nutre. Si son parisienses o madrileños, vayan al Prado, de faroles, o vayan a Tortoni, de sorbetes. ¡Estos hijos de carpintero, que se avergüenzan de que su padre sea carpintero! ¡Estos nacidos en América, que se avergüenzan, porque llevan delantal indio, de la madre que les crió, y reniegan, ¡bribones!, de la madre enferma, y la dejan sola en el lecho de las enfermedades! Pues, ¿quién es el hombre?, ¿el que se queda con la madre, a curarle la enfermedad, o el que la pone a trabajar donde no la vean, y vive de su sustento en las tierras podridas, con el gusano de corbata, maldiciendo del seno que lo cargó, paseando el letrero de traidor en la espalda de la casaca de papel? ¡Estos hijos de nuestra América, que ha de salvarse con sus indios, y va de menos a más; estos desertores que piden fusil en los ejércitos de la América del Norte, que ahoga en sangre a sus indios, y va de más a menos! ¡Estos delicados, que son hombres y no quieren hacer el trabajo de hombres! Pues el Washington que les hizo esta tierra ¿se fue a vivir con los ingleses, a vivir con los ingleses en los años en que los veía venir contra su tierra propia? ¡Estos *increíbles* del honor, que lo arrastran por el suelo extranjero, como los increíbles de la Revolución francesa, danzando y relamiéndose, arrastraban las erres!

Ni ¿en qué patria puede tener un hombre más orgullo que en nuestras repúblicas dolorosas de América, levantadas entre las masas mudas de indios, al ruido de pelea del libro con el cirial, sobre los brazos sangrientos de un centenar de apóstoles? De factores tan descompuestos, jamás, en menos tiempo histórico, se han creado naciones tan adelantadas y compactas. Cree el soberbio que la tierra fue hecha para servirle de pedestal, porque tiene la pluma fácil o la palabra de colores, y acusa de incapaz e irremediable a su república nativa, porque no le dan sus selvas nuevas modo continuo de ir por el mundo de gamonal famoso, guiando jacas de Persia y derramando champaña. La incapacidad no está en el país naciente, que pide formas que se le acomoden y grandeza útil, sino en los que quieren regir pueblos originales, de composición singular y violenta, con leyes, heredadas de cuatro siglos de práctica libre en los Estados Unidos, de diecinueve siglos de monarquía en Francia. Con un decreto de Hamilton no se le para la pechada al potro del llanero. Con una frase de Sieyés no se desestanca la sangre cuajada de la raza india. A lo que es, allí donde se gobierna, hay que atender para gobernar bien; y el buen gobernante en América no es el que sabe cómo se gobierna el alemán o el francés, sino el que sabe con qué elementos está hecho su país, y cómo puede ir guiándolos en junto, para llegar, por métodos e instituciones nacidas del país mismo, a aquel estado apetecible donde cada hombre se conoce y ejerce, y disfrutan todos de la abundancia que la Naturaleza puso para todos en el pueblo que fecundan con su trabajo y defienden con sus vidas. El gobierno ha de nacer del país. El espíritu del gobierno ha de ser el del país. La forma del gobierno no es más que el equilibrio de los elementos naturales del país.

Por eso el libro importado ha sido vencido en América por el hombre natural. Los hombres naturales han vencido a los letrados artificiales. El mestizo autóctono ha vencido al criollo exótico. No hay batalla entre la civilización y la barbarie, sino entre la falsa erudición y la naturaleza. El hombre natural es bueno, y acata y premia la inteligencia superior, mientras ésta no se vale de su sumisión para dañarle, o le ofende prescindiendo de él, que es cosa que no perdona el hombre natural, dispuesto a recobrar por la fuerza el respeto de quien le hiere la susceptibilidad o le perjudica el interés. Por esa conformidad con los elementos naturales desdeñados han subido los tiranos de América al poder; y han caído en cuanto les hicieron traición. Las repúblicas han purgado en las tiranías su incapacidad para conocer los elementos verdaderos del país, derivar de ellos la forma de gobierno y gobernar con ellos. Gobernante, en un pueblo nuevo, quiere decir creador.

En pueblos compuestos de elementos cultos e incultos, los incultos gobernarán, por su hábito de agredir y resolver las dudas con su mano, allí donde los cultos no aprendan el arte del gobierno. La masa inculta es perezosa, y tímida en las cosas de la inteligencia y quiere que la gobiernen bien; pero si el gobierno le lastima, se lo sacude y gobierna ella. ¿Cómo han de salir de las universidades los gobernantes, si no hay universidad en América donde se enseñe lo rudimentario del arte del gobierno, que es el análisis de los elementos peculiares de los pueblos de América? A adivinar salen los jóvenes al mundo, con antiparras yanquis o francesas, y aspiran a dirigir un pueblo que no conocen. En la carrera de la política habría de negarse la entrada a los que desconocen los rudimentos de la política. El premio de los certámenes no ha de ser para la mejor oda, sino para el mejor estudio de los factores del país en que se vive. En el periódico, en la cátedra, en la academia, debe llevarse adelante el estudio de los factores reales del país. Conocerlos basta, sin vendas ni ambages; porque el que pone de lado, por voluntad u olvido, una parte de la verdad, caè a la larga por la verdad que le faltó, que crece en la negligencia y derriba lo que se levanta sin ella. Resolver el problema después de conocer sus elementos, es más fácil que resolver el problema sin conocerlos. Viene el hombre natural, indignado y fuerte, y derriba la justicia acumulada de los libros, porque no se la administra en acuerdo con las necesidades patentes del país. Conocer es resolver. Conocer el país, y gobernarlo conforme al conocimiento, es el único modo de librarlo de tiranías. La universidad europea ha de ceder a la universidad americana. La historia de América, de los incas acá, ha de enseñarse al dedillo, aunque no se enseñe la de los arcontes de Grecia. Nuestra Grecia es preferible a la Grecia que no es nuestra. Nos es más necesaria. Los políticos nacionales han de reemplazar a los políticos exóticos. Injértese en nuestras repúblicas el mundo; pero el tronco ha de ser el de nuestras repúblicas. Y calle el pedante vencido, que no hay patria en que pueda tener el hombre más orgullo que en nuestras dolorosas repúblicas americanas.

Con los pies en el rosario, la cabeza blanca y el cuerpo pinto de indio y criollo, vinimos, denodados, al mundo de las naciones. Con el estandarte de la Virgen salimos a la conquista de la libertad. Un cura, unos cuantos tenientes y una mujer alzan en México la república, en hombros de los indios. Un canónigo español, a la sombra de su capa instruye en la libertad francesa a unos cuantos bachilleres magníficos, que ponen de jefe de Centroamérica contra España al general de España. Con los hábitos monárquicos, y el Sol por pecho, se echaron a levantar pueblos los venezolanos por el Norte y los argentinos por el Sur. Cuando los dos héroes chocaron, y el continente iba a temblar, uno, que no fue el menos grande, volvió riendas. Y como el heroísmo en la paz es más escaso, porque es menos glorioso que el de la guerra; como al hombre le es más fácil morir con honra que pensar con orden; como gobernar con los sentimientos exaltados y unánimes es más hacedero que dirigir, después de la pelea, los pensamientos diversos, arrogantes, exóticos o ambiciosos; como los poderes arrollados en la arremetida épica zapaban, con la cautela felina de la especie y el peso de lo real, el edificio que había izado, en las comarcas burdas y singulares de nuestra América mestiza, en los pueblos de pierna desnuda y casaca de París, la bandera de los pueblos nutridos de savia gobernante en la práctica continua de la razón y de la libertad; como la constitución jerárquica de las colonias resistía la organización democrática de la República, o las capitales de corbatín dejaban en el zaguán el campo de bota de potro, o los redentores bibliógenos no entendieron que la revolución que triunfó con el alma de la tierra, desatada a la voz del salvador, con el alma de la tierra había de gobernar, y no contra ella ni sin ella, entró a padecer América, y padece, de la fatiga de acomodación entre los elementos discordantes y hostiles que heredó de un colonizador despótico y avieso, y las ideas y formas importadas que han venido retardando, por su falta de realidad local, el gobierno lógico. El continente descoyuntado durante tres siglos por un mando que negaba el derecho del hombre al ejercicio de su razón, entró, desatendiendo o desoyendo a los ignorantes que lo habían ayudado a redimirse, en un gobierno que tenía por base la razón; la razón de todos en las cosas de todos, y no la razón universitaria de unos sobre la razón campestre de otros. El problema de la independencia no era el cambio de formas, sino el cambio de espíritu.

Con los oprimidos había que hacer causa común, para afianzar el sistema opuesto a los intereses y hábitos de mando de los opresores. El tigre, espantado del fogonazo, vuelve de noche al lugar de la presa. Muere echando llamas por los ojos y con las zarpas al aire. No se le oye venir, sino que viene con zarpas de terciopelo. Cuando la presa despierta, tiene al tigre encima. La colonia continuó viviendo en la república; y nuestra América se está salvando de sus grandes yerros —de la soberbia de las ciudades capitales, del triunfo ciego de los campesinos desdeñados, de la importación excesiva de las ideas y fórmulas ajenas, del desdén inicuo e impolítico de la raza aborigen— por la virtud superior, abonada con sangre necesaria, de la república que lucha contra la colonia. El tigre espera, detrás de cada árbol, acurrucado en cada esquina. Morirá, con las zarpas al aire, echando llamas por los ojos.

Pero "estos países se salvarán", como anunció Rivadavia el argentino, el que pecó de finura en tiempos cruzados; al machete no le va vaina de seda, ni en el país que se ganó con lanzón se puede echar el lanzón atrás, porque se enoja y se pone en la puerta del Congreso de Iturbide "a que le hagan emperador al rubio". Estos países se salvarán porque, con el genio de la moderación que parece imperar, por la armonía serena de la Naturaleza, en el continente de la luz, y por el influjo de la lectura crítica que ha sucedido en Europa a la lectura de tanteo y falansterio en que se empapó la generación anterior, le está naciendo a América, en estos tiempos reales, el hombre real.

Eramos una visión, con el pecho de atleta, las manos de petimetre y la frente de niño. Eramos una máscara, con los calzones de Inglaterra, el chaleco parisiense, el chaquetón de Norteamérica y la montera de España. El indio, mudo, nos daba vueltas alrededor, y se iba al monte, a la cumbre del monte, a bautizar sus hijos. El negro, oteado, cantaba en la noche la música de su corazón, solo y desconocido, entre las olas y las fieras. El campesino, el creador, se revolvía, ciego de indignación, contra la ciudad desdeñosa, contra su criatura. Eramos charreteras y togas, en países que venían al mundo con la alpargata en los pies y la vincha en la cabeza. El genio hubiera estado en hermanar, con la caridad del corazón y con el atrevimiento de los fundadores, la vincha y la toga; en desestancar al indio; en ir haciendo lado al negro suficiente; en ajustar la libertad al cuerpo de los que se alzaron y vencieron por ella. Nos quedó el oidor, y el general, y el letrado, y el prebendado. La juventud angélica, como de los brazos de un pulpo, echaba al Cielo, para caer con gloria estéril, la cabeza, coronada de nubes. El pueblo natural, con el empuje del instinto, arrollaba, ciego del triunfo, los bastones de oro. Ni el libro europeo, ni el libro yanqui, daban la clave del enigma hispanoamericano. Se probó el odio, y los países venían cada año a menos. Cansados del odio inútil, de la resistencia del libro contra la lanza, de la razón contra el cirial, de la ciudad contra el campo, del imperio imposible de las castas urbanas divididas sobre la nación natural, tempestuosa o inerte, se empieza, como sin saberlo, a probar el amor. Se ponen en pie los pueblos, y se saludan. "¿Cómo somos?", se preguntan; y unos a otros se van diciendo cómo son. Cuando aparece en Cojímar un problema, no van a buscar solución a Dantzig. Las levitas son todavía de Francia, pero el pensamiento empieza a ser de América. Los jóvenes de América se ponen la camisa al codo, hunden las manos en la masa y la levantan con la levadura de su sudor. Entienden que se imita demasiado, y que la salvación es crear. Crear es la palabra de pase de esta generación.

El vino, de plátano; y si sale agrio, ¡es nuestro vino! Se entiende que las formas de gobierno de un país han de acomodarse a los elementos naturales del mismo, que las ideas absolutas, para no caer por un yerro de forma, han de ponerse en formas relativas; que la libertad, para ser viable, tiene que ser sincera y plena; que si la república no abre los brazos a todos y adelanta con todos, muere la república. El tigre de adentro se entra por la hendija, y el tigre de afuera. El general sujeta en la marcha la caballería al paso de los infantes. O si deja a la zaga a los infantes, le envuelve el enemigo la caballería. Estrategia es política. Los pueblos han de vivir criticándose, porque la crítica es la salud; pero con un solo pecho y una sola mente. ¡Bajarse hasta los infelices y alzarlos en los brazos! ¡Con el fuego del corazón deshelar la América coagulada! ¡Echar, bullendo y rebotando, por las venas, la sangre natural del país! En pie, con los ojos alegres de los trabajadores, se saludan, de un pueblo a otro, los hombres nuevos americanos. Surgen los estadistas naturales del estudio directo de la Naturaleza. Leen para aplicar, pero no para copiar. Los economistas estudian la dificultad en sus orígenes. Los oradores empiezan a ser sobrios. Los dramaturgos traen los caracteres nativos a la escena. Las academias discuten temas viables. La poesía se corta la melena zorrillesca y cuelga del árbol glorioso el chaleco colorado. La prosa, centelleante y cernida, va cargada de idea. Los gobernadores, en las repúblicas de indios, aprenden indio.

De todos sus peligros se va salvando América. Sobre algunas repúblicas está durmiendo el pulpo. Otras, por la ley del equilibrio, se echan a pie a la mar, a recobrar, con prisa loca y sublime, los siglos perdidos. Otras, olvidando que Juárez paseaba en un coche de mulas, ponen coche de viento y de cochero a una pompa de jabón; el lujo venenoso, enemigo de la libertad, pudre al hombre liviano y abre la puerta al extranjero. Otras acendran, con el espíritu épico de la independencia amenazada, el carácter viril. Otras crían, en la guerra rapaz contra el vecino, la soldadesca que puede devorarlas. Pero otro peligro corre, acaso, nuestra América, que no le viene de sí, sino de la diferencia de orígenes, métodos e intereses entre los dos factores continentales, y es la hora próxima en que se le acerque, demandando relaciones íntimas, un pueblo emprendedor y pujante que la desconoce y la desdeña. Y como los pueblos viriles, que se han hecho de sí propios, con la escopeta y la ley, aman, y sólo aman, a los pueblos viriles; como la hora del desenfreno y la ambición, de que acaso se libre, por el predominio de lo más puro de su sangre, la América del Norte, en que pudieran lanzarla sus masas vengativas y sórdidas, la tradición de conquista y el interés de un caudillo hábil, no está tan cercana aún a los ojos del más espantadizo, que no dé tiempo a la prueba de altivez, continua y discreta, con que se la pudiera encarar y desviarla; como su decoro de república pone a la América del Norte, ante los pueblos atentos del Universo, un freno que no le ha de quitar la

provocación pueril o la arrogancia ostentosa, o la discordia parricida de nuestra América, el deber urgente de nuestra América es enseñarse como es, una en alma e intento, vencedora
veloz de un pasado sofocante, manchada sólo con la sangre de
abono que arranca a las manos la pelea con las ruinas, y la de
las venas que nos dejaron picadas nuestros dueños. El desdén
del vecino formidable, que no la conoce, es el peligro mayor
de nuestra América; y urge, porque el día de la visita está próximo, que el vecino la conozca, la conozca pronto, para que
no la desdeñe. Por ignorancia llegaría, tal vez, a poner en ella
la codicia. Por el respeto, luego que la conociese, sacaría de
ella las manos. Se ha de tener fe en lo mejor del hombre y
desconfiar de lo peor de él. Hay que dar ocasión a lo mejor
para que se revele y prevalezca sobre lo peor. Si no, lo peor
prevalece. Los pueblos han de tener una picota para quien les
azuza a odios inútiles; y otra para quien no les dice a tiempo
la verdad.

No hay odio de razas, porque no hay razas. Los pensadores canijos, los pensadores de lámparas, enhebran y recalien-
tan las razas de librería, que el viajero justo y el observador
cordial buscan en vano en la justicia de la Naturaleza, donde
resalta en el amor victorioso y el apetito turbulento la identidad universal del hombre. El alma emana, igual y eterna, de
los cuerpos diversos en forma y en color. Peca contra la Humanidad el que fomente y propague la oposición y el odio de
las razas. Pero en el amasijo de los pueblos se condensan, en
la cercanía de otros pueblos diversos, caracteres peculiares y
activos, de ideas y de hábitos, de ensanche y adquisición, de
vanidad y de avaricia, que del estado latente de preocupaciones nacionales pudieran, en un período de desorden interno
o de precipitación del carácter acumulado del país, trocarse
en amenaza grave para las tierras vecinas, aisladas y débiles,
que el país fuerte declara perecederas e inferiores. Pensar es
servir. Ni ha de suponerse, por antipatía de aldea, una maldad
ingénita y fatal al pueblo rubio del continente, porque no habla nuestro idioma, ni ve la casa como nosotros la vemos, ni
se nos parece en sus lacras políticas, que son diferentes de las
nuestras; ni tiene en mucho a los hombres biliosos y trigueños,
ni mira caritativo, desde su eminencia aún mal segura, los que,
con menos favor de la Historia, suben a tramos heroicos la vía
de las repúblicas; ni se han de esconder los datos patentes del
problema que puede resolverse, para la paz de los siglos, con
el estudio oportuno y la unión tácita y urgente del alma continental. ¡Porque ya suena el himno unánime: la generación

actual lleva a cuestas, por el camino abonado por los padres
sublimes, la América trabajadora; del Bravo a Magallanes, sentado en el lomo del cóndor, regó el Gran Semí, por las naciones románticas del continente y por las islas dolorosas del mar,
la semilla de la América nueva!

▬▬▬▬▬

Pablo Neruda
1903–1973
Chile

La palabra
Confieso que he vivido, 1974.

TODO lo que usted quiera, sí señor, pero son las palabras
las que cantan, las que suben y bajan... Me prosterno ante
ellas... Las amo, las adhiero, las persigo, las muerdo, las derri-
to... Amo tanto las palabras... Las inesperadas... Las que glo-
tonamente se esperan, se acechan, hasta que de pronto caen...
Vocablos amados... Brillan como piedras de colores, saltan
como platinados peces, son espuma, hilo, metal, rocío... Persigo algunas palabras... Son tan hermosas que las quiero poner todas en mi poema... Las agarro al vuelo, cuando van zumbando, y las atrapo, las limpio, las pelo, me preparo frente al
plato, las siento cristalinas, vibrantes, ebúrneas, vegetales, acei-
tosas, como frutas, como algas, como ágatas, como aceitu-
nas... Y entonces las revuelvo, las agito, me las bebo, me las
zampo, las trituro, las emperejilo, las liberto... Las dejo como
estalactitas en mi poema, como pedacitos de madera bruñida,
como carbón, como restos de naufragio, regalos de la ola...
Todo está en la palabra... Una idea entera se cambia porque
una palabra se trasladó de sitio, o porque otra se sentó como
una reinita adentro de una frase que no la esperaba y que le
obedeció... Tienen sombra, transparencia, peso, plumas, pelos, tienen de todo lo que se les fue agregando de tanto rodar
por el río, de tanto transmigrar de patria, de tanto ser raíces...

Son antiquísimas y recientísimas... Viven en el féretro escondido y en la flor apenas comenzada... Qué buen idioma el mío,
qué buena lengua heredamos de los conquistadores torvos...
Estos andaban a zancadas por las tremendas cordilleras, por
las Américas encrespadas, buscando patatas, butifarras, fri-
jolitos, tabaco negro, oro, maíz, huevos fritos, con aquel apetito voraz que nunca más se ha visto en el mundo... Todo se
lo tragaban, con religiones, pirámides, tribus, idolatrías iguales a las que ellos traían en sus grandes bolsas... Por donde pasaban quedaba arrasada la tierra... Pero a los bárbaros se les
caían de las botas, de las barbas, de los yelmos, de las herra-
duras, como piedrecitas, las palabras luminosas que se quedaron aquí resplandecientes... el idioma. Salimos perdiendo...
Salimos ganando... Se llevaron el oro y nos dejaron el oro... Se
lo llevaron todo y nos dejaron todo... Nos dejaron las palabras.

Victoria Ocampo
1890–1955
Argentina

Carta a Virginia Woolf
Virginia Woolf en su diario, 1954.

CUANDO, sentada junto a su chimenea, Virginia me alejaba de la niebla y de la sociedad, cuando tendía mis manos
hacia el calor y tendía entre nosotras un puente de palabras...
¡qué rica era, no obstante! No de su riqueza, pues esa llave
que supo usted encontrar, y sin la cual jamás entramos en posesión de nuestro propio tesoro (aunque lo llevemos, durante
toda nuestra vida, colgado al cuello), de nada puede servirme
si no la encuentro por mí misma. Rica de mi pobreza, esto es:
de mi hambre.
        Un nombre, Virginia, va ligado a estos pensamientos. Pues
con usted fue con quien hablé últimamente —e inolvidable-
mente— de esta riqueza, nacida de mi pobreza: el hambre.

Todos los artículos reunidos en este volumen (al igual que los de él excluidos), escalonados a lo largo de varios años, tienen de común entre sí que fueron escritos bajo ese signo. Son una serie de testimonios de mi hambre. ¡De mi hambre, tan auténticamente americana! Pues en Europa, como le decía a usted hace unos días, parece que se tiene todo, menos hambre.

Usted da gran importancia a que las mujeres se expresen, y a que se expresen por escrito. Las anima a que escriban *all kinds of books, hesitating at no subject however trivial or however vast*[1]. Según dice usted, les da este consejo por egoísmo: *Like most uneducated Englishwomen, I like reading —I like reading books in the bulk*[2], declara usted. Y la producción masculina no le basta. Encuentra usted que los libros de los hombres no nos explican sino muy parcialmente la psicología femenina. Hasta encuentra usted que los libros de los hombres no nos informan sino bastante imperfectamente sobre ellos mismos. En la parte posterior de nuestra cabeza, dice usted, hay un punto del tamaño de un chelín que no alcanzamos a ver con nuestros propios ojos. Cada sexo debe encargarse de describir, para provecho del otro, ese punto. A ese respecto, no podemos quejarnos de los hombres. Desde los tiempos más remotos nos han prestado siempre ese servicio. Convendría, pues, que no nos mostrásemos ingratas y les pagásemos en la misma moneda.

Pero he aquí que llegamos a lo que, por mi parte, desearía confesar públicamente, Virginia: *Like most uneducated South American women, I like writing...*[3] Y, esta vez, el *uneducated* debe pronunciarse sin ironía.

Mi única ambición es llegar a escribir un día, más o menos bien, más o menos mal, pero como una mujer. Si a imagen de Aladino poseyese una lámpara maravillosa, y por su mediación me fuera dado el escribir en el estilo de un Shakespeare, de un Dante, de un Goethe, de un Cervantes, de un Dostoiewsky, realmente no aprovecharía la ganga. Pues entiendo que una mujer no puede aliviarse de sus sentimientos y pensamientos en un estilo masculino, del mismo modo que no puede hablar con voz de hombre.

---

[1] "Toda suerte de libros, sin vacilar ante ningún asunto, por trivial o vasto que parezca."

[2] "Como a la mayoría de las inglesas incultas, me gusta leer... me gusta leer libros a granel."

[3] "Como a la mayoría de las mujeres sudamericanas incultas, me gusta escribir..."

¿Recuerda usted, en *A Room of One's Own,* sus observaciones sobre dos escritoras: Charlotte Brontë y Jane Austen? La primera, dice usted, quizás es más genial que la segunda; pero sus libros están retorcidos, deformados por las sacudidas de indignación, de rebeldía contra su propio destino, que la atraviesan. *She will write in a rage where she should write calmly*[4].

El año pasado, por estos días, encontrándome en un balneario argentino, conduje una mañana tibia al hijito de mi jardinero a una gran tienda (una sucursal de vuestro Harrod's). Los juguetes resplandecientes de Navidad y Año Nuevo nos rodeaban por todas partes. Agarrado a mi mano, abriendo de par en par sus ojos de cuatro años ante semejantes maravillas, mi compañero había enmudecido. Al abrochar sobre su pecho una blusita que le estaban probando, quedé asustada, enternecida, sintiendo contra mi mano el latir precipitado de su corazón. Era el palpitar de un pájaro cautivo entre mis dedos.

El pasaje de Jane Eyre que usted cita, y en que se oye el respirar de Charlotte Brontë (respirar que nos llega oprimido y jadeante), me emociona de modo análogo. Mis ojos, fijos en estas líneas, no perciben ya a la manera de los ojos, sino a la manera de la palma de una mano apoyada en un pecho.

Bien sé que Charlotte Brontë como novelista habría salido ganando con que Charlotte Brontë mujer, *starved of her proper due of experience*[5], no hubiese venido a turbarla. Y, sin embargo, ¿no cree usted que este sufrimiento, que crispa sus libros, se traduce en una imperfección conmovedora?

Defendiendo su causa, es la mía la que defiendo. Si sólo la perfección conmueve, Virginia, no cabe duda que estoy perdida de antemano.

Dice usted que Jane Austen hizo un milagro en 1800: el de escribir, a pesar de su sexo, sin amargura, sin odio; sin protestar contra... sin predicar en pro... Y así (en este estado de alma) es como escribió Shakespeare, añadía usted.

Pero, ¿no le parece a usted que, aparte de los problemas que las mujeres que escriben tenían y tienen aún que resolver, se trata también de diferencias de carácter? ¿Cree usted, por ejemplo, que la *Divina Comedia* haya sido escrita sin vestigios de rencor?

En todo caso, estoy tan convencida como usted de que una mujer no logra escribir realmente como una mujer sino a

---

[4]"Escribirá con rabia, cuando debería escribir con serenidad."
[5]"Hambrienta de la parte de experiencia que le correspondía."

partir del momento en que esa preocupación la abandona, a
partir del momento en que sus obras, dejando de ser una respuesta disfrazada a ataques, disfrazados o no, tienden sólo a
traducir su pensamiento, sus sentimientos, su visión.

Acontece con esto como con la diferencia que se observa
en Argentina entre los hijos de emigrantes y los de familias
afincadas en el país desde hace varias generaciones. Los primeros tienen una susceptibilidad exagerada con respecto a no
sé qué falso orgullo nacional. Los segundos son americanos
desde hace tanto tiempo, que se olvidan de aparentarlo.

Pues bien, Virginia, debo confesar que no me siento aún
totalmente liberada del equivalente de esa susceptibilidad, de
ese falso orgullo nacional, en lo que atañe a mi sexo. ¡Quién
sabe si padezco reflejos de *parvenue*! En todo caso, no cabe
duda que soy un tanto quisquillosa a ese respecto. En cuanto
la ocasión se presenta (y si no se presenta, la busco), ya estoy
declarándome solidaria del sexo femenino. La actitud de algunas mujeres singulares, como Anna de Noailles, que se pasan al campo de los hombres aceptando que éstos las traten de
excepciones y les concedan una situación privilegiada, siempre me ha repugnado. Esta actitud, tan elegante y tan cómoda, me es intolerable. Y también a usted, Virginia.

A propósito de Charlotte Brontë y de Jane Austen, dice
usted: *But how impossible it must have been for them not to
budge either to the right or to the left. What genius, what
integrity it must have required in face of all that criticism, in
the midst of that purely patriarchal society, to hold fast to
the thing as they saw it without shrinking*[6].

De todo esto retengo especialmente algunas palabras... *in
the midst of that purely patriarchal society**... En un medio
semejante al que pesaba sobre Charlotte Brontë y Jane Austen, hace más de cien años, comencé yo a escribir y a vivir; semejante, pero peor, Virginia.

Escribir y vivir en esas condiciones es tener cierto valor. Y
tener cierto valor, cuando no se es insensible, es ya un esfuerzo que absorbe, sin darnos cuenta, todas nuestras facultades.

La deliciosa historia de la hermana de Shakespeare, que
de modo tan inimitable cuenta usted, es la más bella historia

---

[6]"Pero, ¡cuán imposible debe haber sido para ellas no desviarse ni a la izquierda ni a la derecha! ¡Qué genio, qué integridad tienen que haberse requerido
frente a toda esa crítica, en medio de aquella sociedad absolutamente patriarcal,
para atenerse estrictamente a lo que veían, tal como lo veían, sin temblar!"
*Todos estos textos están en inglés en el original y traducidos a pie de página
por Victoria Ocampo.

del mundo. Ese supuesto poeta (la hermana de Shakespeare)
muerto sin haber escrito una sola línea, vive en todas nosotras,
dice usted. Vive aun en aquellas que, obligadas a fregar los platos y acostar a los niños, no tienen tiempo de oír una conferencia o leer un libro. Acaso un día renacerá y escribirá. A
nosotras toca el crearle un mundo en que pueda encontrar la
posibilidad de vivir íntegramente, sin mutilaciones.

Yo friego bastante mal los platos y no tengo (¡ay!) niños
que acostar. Pero, aunque (no seamos hipócritas) fregase los
platos y acostara a los niños, siempre habría encontrado medio de emborronar papel en mis ratos perdidos como la madre de Wells.

Y si, como usted espera, Virginia, todo esfuerzo, por oscuro que sea, es convergente y apresura el nacimiento de una
forma de expresión que todavía no ha encontrado una temperatura propicia a su necesidad de florecer, vaya mi esfuerzo a
sumarse al de tantas mujeres, desconocidas o célebres, como
en el mundo han trabajado.

José Ortega y Gasset
1883—1955
España

Creer y pensar
Ideas y creencias, 1959.

> *Las ideas se tienen;*
> *en las creencias se está.*
> *—Pensar en las cosas*
> *y contar con ellas.*

CUANDO se quiere entender a un hombre, la vida de un
hombre, procuramos ante todo averiguar cuáles son sus
ideas. Desde que el europeo cree tener "sentido histórico", es
ésta la exigencia más elemental. ¿Cómo no van a influir en la

existencia de una persona sus ideas y las ideas de su tiempo? La cosa es obvia. Perfectamente; pero la cosa es también bastante equívoca, y, a mi juicio, la insuficiente claridad sobre lo que se busca cuando se inquieren las ideas de un hombre —o de una época— impide que se obtenga claridad sobre su vida, sobre su historia.

Con la expresión *ideas de un hombre* podemos referirnos a cosas muy diferentes. Por ejemplo: los pensamientos que se le ocurren acerca de esto o de lo otro y los que se le ocurren al prójimo y él repite y adopta. Estos pensamientos pueden poseer los grados más diversos de verdad. Incluso pueden ser *verdades científicas*. Tales diferencias, sin embargo, no importan mucho, si importan algo, ante la cuestión mucho más radical que ahora planteamos. Porque sean pensamientos vulgares, sean rigorosas *teorías científicas,* siempre se tratará de ocurrencias que en un hombre surgen, originales suyas o insufladas por el prójimo. Pero esto implica evidentemente que el hombre estaba ya ahí antes de que se le ocurriese o adoptase la idea. Esta brota, de uno u otro modo, dentro de una vida que preexistía a ella. Ahora bien, no hay vida humana que no esté desde luego constituída por ciertas creencias básicas y, por decirlo así, montada sobre ellas. Vivir es tener que habérselas con algo —con el mundo y consigo mismo. Mas ese mundo y ese *sí mismo* con que el hombre se encuentra le aparecen ya bajo la especie de una interpretación, de *ideas* sobre el mundo y sobre sí mismo.

Aquí topamos con otro estrato de ideas que un hombre tiene. Pero ¡cuán diferente de todas aquellas que se le ocurren o que adopta! Esas *ideas* básicas que llamo *creencias* —ya se verá por qué— no surgen en tal día y hora *dentro* de nuestra vida, no arribamos a ellas por un acto particular de pensar, no son, en suma, pensamientos que tenemos, no son ocurrencias ni siquiera de aquella especie más elevada por su perfección lógica y que denominamos razonamientos. Todo lo contrario: esas ideas que son, de verdad, *creencias* constituyen el continente de nuestra vida y, por ello, no tienen el carácter de contenidos particulares dentro de ésta. Cabe decir que no son ideas que tenemos, sino ideas que somos. Más aún; precisamente porque son creencias radicalísimas se confunden para nosotros con la realidad misma —son nuestro mundo y nuestro ser—, pierden, por tanto, el carácter de ideas, de pensamientos nuestros que podrían muy bien no habérsenos ocurrido.

Cuando se ha caído en la cuenta de la diferencia existente

entre esos dos estratos de ideas aparece, sin más, claro el diferente papel que juegan en nuestra vida. Y, por lo pronto, la enorme diferencia de rango funcional. De las ideas-ocurrencias —y conste que incluyo en ellas las verdades más rigorosas de la ciencia— podemos decir que las producimos, las sostenemos, las discutimos, las propagamos, combatimos en su pro y hasta somos capaces de morir por ellas. Lo que no podemos es... vivir *de* ellas. Son obra nuestra y, por lo mismo, suponen ya nuestra vida, la cual se asienta en ideas-creencias que no producimos nosotros, que, en general, ni siquiera nos formulamos y que, claro está, no discutimos ni propagamos ni sostenemos. Con las creencias propiamente no *hacemos* nada, sino que simplemente *estamos* en ellas. Precisamente lo que no nos pasa jamás —si hablamos cuidadosamente— con nuestras ocurrencias. El lenguaje vulgar ha inventado certeramente la expresión *estar en la creencia*. En efecto, en la creencia se está, y la ocurrencia se tiene y se sostiene. Pero la creencia es quien nos tiene y sostiene a nosotros.

Hay, pues, ideas *con* que nos encontramos —por eso las llamo ocurrencias— e ideas *en* que nos encontramos, que parecen estar ahí ya antes de que nos ocupemos en pensar.

Una vez visto esto, lo que sorprende es que a unas y a otras se les llame lo mismo: ideas. La identidad de nombre es lo único que estorba para distinguir dos cosas cuya disparidad brinca tan claramente ante nosotros sin más que usar frente a frente estos dos términos: creencias y ocurrencias. La incongruente conducta de dar un mismo nombre a dos cosas tan distintas no es, sin embargo, una casualidad ni una distracción. Proviene de una incongruencia más honda: de la confusión entre dos problemas radicalmente diversos que exigen dos modos de pensar y de llamar no menos dispares.

Pero dejemos ahora este lado del asunto: es demasiado abstruso. Nos basta con hacer notar que *idea* es un término del vocabulario psicológico y que la psicología, como toda ciencia particular, posee sólo jurisdicción subalterna. La verdad de sus conceptos es relativa al punto de vista particular que la constituye y vale en el horizonte que ese punto de vista crea y acota. Así, cuando la psicología dice de algo que es una *idea,* no pretende haber dicho lo más decisivo, lo más real sobre ello. El único punto de vista que no es particular y relativo es el de la vida, por la sencilla razón de que todos los demás se dan dentro de ésta y son meras especializaciones de aquél. Ahora bien, como fenómeno vital la creencia no se parece nada a la ocurrencia: su función en el organismo de nuestro existir es totalmente distinta y, en cierto modo, antagónica. ¿Qué importancia puede tener en parangón con esto el hecho de que, bajo la perspectiva psicológica, una y otra sean *ideas* y no sentimientos, voliciones, etc.?

Conviene, pues, que dejemos este término —*ideas*— para designar todo aquello que en nuestra vida aparece como resultado de nuestra ocupación intelectual. Pero las creencias se nos presentan con el carácter opuesto. No llegamos a ellas tras una faena de entendimiento, sino que operan ya en nuestro fondo cuando nos ponemos a pensar sobre algo. Por eso no solemos formularlas, sino que nos contentamos con aludir a ellas como solemos hacer con todo lo que nos es la realidad misma. Las teorías, en cambio, aun las más verídicas, sólo existen mientras son pensadas: de aquí que necesiten ser formuladas.

Esto revela, sin más, que todo aquello en que nos ponemos a pensar tiene *ipso facto* para nosotros una realidad problemática y ocupa en nuestra vida un lugar secundario si se le compara con nuestras creencias auténticas. En éstas no pensamos ahora o luego: nuestra relación con ellas consiste en algo mucho más eficiente; consiste en... contar con ellas, siempre, sin pausa.

Me parece de excepcional importancia para inyectar, por fin, claridad en la estructura de la vida humana esta contraposición entre pensar en una cosa y contar con ella. El intelectualismo que ha tiranizado, casi sin interrupción, el pasado entero de la filosofía ha impedido que se nos haga patente y hasta ha invertido el valor respectivo de ambos términos. Me explicaré.

Analice el lector cualquier comportamiento suyo, aun el más sencillo en apariencia. El lector está en su casa y, por unos u otros motivos, resuelve salir a la calle. ¿Qué es en todo este su comportamiento lo que propiamente tiene el carácter de pensado, aun entendiendo esta palabra en su más amplio sentido, es decir, como conciencia clara y actual de algo? El lector se ha dado cuenta de sus motivos, de la resolución adoptada, de la ejecución de los movimientos con que ha caminado, abierto la puerta, bajado la escalera. Todo esto en el caso más favorable. Pues bien, aun en este caso y por mucho que busque en su conciencia no encontrará en ella ningún pensamiento en que se haga constar que hay calle. El lector no se ha hecho cuestión ni por un momento de si la hay o no la hay. ¿Por qué? No se negará que para resolverse a salir a la calle es de cierta importancia que la calle exista. En rigor, es lo más importante de todo, el supuesto de todo lo demás. Sin embargo, precisamente de ese tema tan importante no se ha hecho cuestión el lector, no ha *pensado* en ello ni para negarlo ni para afirmarlo ni para ponerlo en duda. ¿Quiere esto decir que la existencia o no existencia de la calle no ha intervenido en su comportamiento? Evidentemente, no. La prueba se tendría si al llegar a la puerta de su casa descubriese que la calle había desaparecido, que la tierra concluía en el umbral de su domicilio o que ante él se había abierto una sima. Entonces se produciría en la conciencia del lector una clarísima y violenta sorpresa. ¿De qué? De que no había aquélla. Pero ¿no habíamos quedado en que antes no había pensado que la hubiese, no se había hecho cuestión de ello? Esta sorpresa pone de manifiesto hasta qué punto la existencia de la calle actuaba en su estado anterior, es decir, hasta qué punto el lector *contaba con* la calle aunque no pensaba en ella y precisamente porque no pensaba en ella.

El psicólogo nos dirá que se trata de un pensamiento habitual, y que por eso no nos damos cuenta de él, o usará la hipótesis de lo subconsciente, etc. Todo ello, que es muy cuestionable, resulta para nuestro asunto por completo indiferente. Siempre quedará que lo que decisivamente actuaba en nuestro comportamiento, como que era su básico supuesto, no era *pensado* por nosotros con conciencia clara y aparte. Estaba en nosotros, pero no en forma consciente, sino como implicación latente de nuestra conciencia o pensamiento. Pues bien, a este modo de intervenir algo en nuestra vida sin que lo pensemos llamo *"contar con ello".* Y este modo es el propio de nuestras efectivas creencias.

El intelectualismo, he dicho, invierte el valor de los términos. Ahora resulta claro el sentido de esta acusación. En efecto, el intelectualismo tendía a considerar como lo más eficiente en nuestra vida lo más consciente. Ahora vemos que la verdad es lo contrario. La máxima eficacia sobre nuestro comportamiento reside en las implicaciones latentes de nuestra actividad intelectual, en todo aquello con que contamos y en que, de puro contar con ello, no pensamos.

¿Se entrevé ya el enorme error cometido al querer aclarar la vida de un hombre o una época por su ideario, esto es, por sus pensamientos especiales, en lugar de penetrar más hondo, hasta el estrato de sus creencias más o menos inexpresas, de las cosas con que contaba? Hacer esto, fijar el inventario de las cosas con que se cuenta, sería, de verdad, construir la historia, esclarecer la vida desde su subsuelo.

José Ortega y Gasset
1882–1955
España

La metáfora*

La deshumanización del arte y otros ensayos de estética, 1925.

NUESTRA mirada al dirigirse a una cosa tropieza con la superficie de ésta y rebota volviendo a nuestra pupila. Esta imposibilidad de penetrar los objetos da a todo acto cognoscitivo —visión, imagen, concepto— el peculiar carácter de dualidad, de separación entre la cosa conocida y el sujeto que conoce. Sólo en los objetos transparentes, un cristal, por ejemplo, parece no cumplirse esta ley: mi visión penetra en el cristal, es decir, paso yo bajo la especie de acto visual al través del cuerpo cristalino y hay un momento de compenetración con él. En lo transparente somos la cosa y yo uno. Sin embargo, ¿acontece esto en rigor? Para que la transparencia del cristal sea verdadera es menester que dirija mi vista a su través en dirección a otros objetos donde la mirada rebote: un cristal que miráramos sobre un fondo de vacío no existiría para nosotros. La esencia del cristal consiste en servir de tránsito a otros objetos: su ser es precisamente no ser él, sino ser las otras cosas. ¡Extraña misión de humildad, de negación de sí mismos, adscrita a ciertos seres! La mujer que es, según Cervantes, "un cristal transparente de hermosura" parece también condenada a "ser lo otro que ella": en lo corporal, como en lo espiritual, parece destinada la mujer a ser un aromado tránsito de otros seres, a dejarse penetrar del amante, del hijo.

Pero a lo que iba: si en lugar de mirar otras cosas a través del vidrio hago a éste término de mi misión, entonces deja de ser transparente y hallo ante mí un cuerpo opaco.

Este ejemplo del cristal puede ayudarnos a comprender intelectualmente lo que instintivamente, con perfecta y sencilla evidencia, nos es dado en el arte, a saber: un objeto que reúne la doble condición de ser transparente y de que lo que en él transparece no es otra cosa distinta, sino él mismo.

Ahora bien: este objeto que se transparenta a sí mismo, el objeto estético, encuentra su forma elemental en la metáfora. Yo diría que objeto estético y objeto metafórico son una misma cosa, o bien que la metáfora es el objeto elemental, la célula bella.

*Fragmento de "Ensayo de estética a manera de prólogo".

Una injustificada desatención por parte de los hombres científicos mantiene la metáfora todavía en situación de *terra incognita*. Mas no voy a pretender en estas páginas fugitivas la construcción de una teoría de la metáfora, y he de limitarme a indicar cómo en ella se revela de un modo evidente el genuino objeto estético.

Ante todo conviene advertir que el término *metáfora* significa a la par un procedimiento y un resultado, una forma de actividad mental y el objeto mediante ella logrado.

Un poeta de Levante, el señor López Picó, dice que el ciprés *e com l'espectre d'una flama morta*.

He aquí una sugestiva metáfora. ¿Cuál es en ella el objeto metafórico? No es el ciprés ni la llama ni el espectro: todo esto pertenece al orbe de las imágenes reales. El objeto nuevo que nos sale al encuentro es un "ciprés-espectro de una llama". Ahora bien, tal ciprés no es un ciprés, ni tal espectro un espectro, ni tal llama una llama. Si queremos retener lo que puede del ciprés quedar una vez hecho llama y de ésta hecha ciprés, se reduce a la nota real de identidad que existe entre el esquema lineal del ciprés y el esquema lineal de la llama. Esta es la semejanza real entre una y otra cosa. En toda metáfora hay una semejanza real entre una y otra cosa. En toda metáfora hay una semejanza real entre sus elementos, y por esto se ha creído que la metáfora consitía esencialmente en una asimilación, tal vez en una aproximación asimilatoria de cosas muy distantes.

Esto es un error. En primer lugar, esa mayor o menor distancia entre las cosas no puede querer decir sino un mayor o menor parecido entre ellas; muy distantes, por tanto, equivale a muy poco parecidas. Y, sin embargo, la metáfora nos satisface precisamente porque en ella averiguamos una coincidencia entre dos cosas más honda y decisiva que cualesquiera semejanzas.

Pero, además, si al leer el verso de López Picó fijamos la atención, insistimos premeditadamente en lo que ambas cosas tienen de real similitud —el esquema lineal del ciprés y de la llama—, advertiremos que todo el encanto de la metáfora se desvanece, dejándonos delante una muda, insignificante observación geométrica. No es, pues, la asimilación real lo metafórico.

En efecto, la semejanza positiva es la primera articulación del aparato metafórico, pero sólo esto. Necesitamos del parecido real, de cierta aproximación capaz de ser razonada entre dos elementos, mas con un fin contrario al que suponemos.

Adviértase que las semejanzas donde las metáforas se apoyan son siempre inesenciales desde el punto de vista real. En nuestro ejemplo la identidad del esquema lineal entre un ciprés y una llama es de tal modo extrínseca, insignificante para cada uno de muchos elementos, que no vacilamos en considerarla como un pretexto.

El mecanismo, pues, acaso sea el siguiente: se trata de formar un nuevo objeto que llamaremos el "ciprés bello", en oposición al ciprés real. Para alcanzarlo es preciso someter éste a dos operaciones: la primera consiste en libertarnos del ciprés como realidad visual y física, en aniquilar el ciprés real; la segunda consiste en dotarlo de esa nueva cualidad delicadísima que le presta carácter de belleza.

Para conseguir lo primero buscamos otra cosa con quien el ciprés posea una semejanza real en algún punto, para ambos sin importancia. Apoyándonos en esta identidad inesencial afirmamos su identidad absoluta. Esto es absurdo, es imposible. Unidos por una coincidencia en algo insignificante, los restos de ambas imágenes se resisten a la compenetración, repeliéndose mutuamente. De suerte que la semejanza real sirve en rigor para acentuar la desemejanza real entre ambas cosas. Donde la identificación real se verifica no hay metáfora. En ésta vive la conciencia clara de la no identidad.

Max Müller ha hecho notar que en los Vedas la metáfora no ha encontrado todavía para expresar su radical equívoco la palabra *como*. En cambio, se nos presenta la operación metafórica a la intemperie, despellejada, y asistimos a este momento de negación de la identidad. El poeta védico no dice *firme como una roca*, sino *sa parvato na acyutas —ille firmus, non rupes*. Como si dijera: la firmeza es, por lo pronto, sólo un atributo de las rocas, pero él es también firme—; por tanto, con una nueva firmeza que no es la de las rocas, sino de otro género. Del mismo modo que el poeta ofrece al Dios su himno *non suavem cibum*, que es dulce pero no es un manjar; la ribera avanza mugiendo "pero no es un toro"[1].

La lógica tradicional hablaba del modo *tollendo ponens* en que la negación de una cosa es a la vez afirmación de una nueva. Así, aquí el ciprés-llama no es un ciprés real, pero es un nuevo objeto que conserva del árbol físico como el molde mental —molde en que viene a inyectarse una nueva sustancia ajena por completo al ciprés, la materia espectral de una lla-

[1] Max Müller: *Origine et développement de la Religion*, p. 179.

ma muerta[2]. Y, viceversa, la llama abandona sus estrictos límites reales —que hacen de ella una llama y nada más que una
llama— para fluidificarse en un puro molde ideal, en una como tendencia imaginativa.

El resultado de esta primera operación es, pues, el aniqui-
lamiento de las cosas en lo que son como imágenes reales. Al
chocar una con otra rómpense sus rígidos caparazones y la materia interna, en estado fundente, adquiere una blandura de
plasma, apto para recibir una nueva forma y estructura. La
cosa ciprés y la cosa llama comienzan a fluir y se tornan en
tendencia ideal ciprés y en tendencia ideal llama. Fuera de la
metáfora, en el pensar extrapoético, son cada una de estas cosas término, punto de llegada para nuestra conciencia, son sus
objetos. Por esto, el ir hacia una de ellas excluye el ir hacia la
otra. Mas al hacer la metáfora la declaración de su identidad
radical, con igual fuerza que la de su radical no-identidad, nos
induce a que no busquemos aquélla en lo que ambas cosas
son como imágenes reales, como términos objetivos; por tanto, a que hagamos de éstas un mero punto de partida, un material, un signo más allá del cual hemos de encontrar la identidad en un nuevo objeto, el ciprés a quien, sin absurdo, podemos tratar como a una llama.

Segunda operación: una vez advertidos de que la identidad no está en las imágenes reales, insiste la metáfora terca-
mente en proponérnosla. Y nos empuja a otro mundo donde
por lo visto es aquélla posible.

Una sencilla observación nos hace encontrar el camino
hacia ese nuevo mundo donde los cipreses son llamas.

Toda imagen tiene, por decirlo así, dos caras. Por una de
ellas es imagen de esta o aquella cosa; por otra es, en cuanto
imagen, algo mío. Yo veo el ciprés, yo tengo la imagen, yo
imagino el ciprés. De suerte que, con respecto al ciprés, es
sólo imagen; pero, con respecto a mí es un estado real mío, es
un momento de mi yo, de mi ser. Naturalmente, mientras se
está *ejecutando* el acto vital mío de ver el ciprés, es éste el
objeto que para mí existe; qué sea *yo* en aquel instante constituye para mí un secreto ignorado. Por un lado, pues, es la
palabra ciprés nombre de una cosa; por otro es un verbo —mi
ver el ciprés. Si ha de convertirse, a su vez, en objeto de mi
percepción este ser o actividad mía, será preciso que me sitúe,

---

[2]Claro es que en este ejemplo hay tres metáforas: la que hace del ciprés una
llama, la que hace de la llama un espectro, la que hace de la llama una llama muerta. Para simplificar analizo sólo la primera.

digámoslo así, de espaldas a la cosa ciprés, y desde ella, en sentido inverso a la anterior, mire hacia dentro de mí y vea al ciprés desrealizándose, transformándose en actividad mía, en *yo*. Dicho de otra forma, será preciso que halle el *modo* de que la palabra *ciprés,* expresiva de un sustantivo, entre en erupción, se ponga en actividad, adquiera un valor verbal.

A lo que toda imagen es como estado ejecutivo mío, como actuación de mi yo, llamamos sentimiento. Es un error superado en la reciente psicología el de limitar este nombre a los estados de agrado y desagrado, de alegría y tristeza. Toda imagen objetiva, al entrar en nuestra conciencia o partir de ella, produce una reacción subjetiva —como el pájaro al posarse en una rama o abandonarla la hace temblar, como al abrirse o cerrarse la corriente eléctrica se suscita una nueva corriente instantánea. Más aún: esa reacción subjetiva no es, sino el acto mismo de percepción, sea visión, recuerdo, intelección, etc. Por esto, precisamente, no nos damos cuenta de ella; tendríamos que desatender el objeto presente para atender a nuestro acto de visión, y, por tanto, tendría que concluir este acto. Volvemos a lo que más arriba decíamos: nuestra intimidad no puede ser directamente objeto para nosotros.

Tornemos a nuestro ejemplo. Se nos invita primero a que pensemos en un ciprés; luego se nos quita de delante el ciprés y se nos propone que en el mismo lugar ideal que él ocupaba situemos el espectro de una llama. De otro modo: hemos de ver la imagen de un ciprés al través de la imagen de una llama, lo *vemos como* una llama, y viceversa. Pero una y otra se excluyen, se son mutuamente opacas. Y, sin embargo, es un hecho que al leer este verso caemos en la cuenta de la posible compenetración perfecta entre ambas —es decir, de que la una, sin dejar de ser lo que es, puede hallarse en el lugar mismo en que la otra está: tenemos, pues, un caso de transparencia que se verifica en el lugar sentimental de ambas.[3] El sentimiento-ciprés y el sentimiento-llama son idénticos. ¿Por qué? ¡Ah!, no sabemos por qué; es el hecho siempre irracional del arte, es el absoluto empirismo de la poesía. Cada metáfora es el descubrimiento de una ley del universo. Y aun

[3] La palabra "metáfora" —transferencia, transposición— indica etimológicamente la posición de una cosa en el lugar de otra; *quasi in alieno loco collocantur,* dice Cicerón, *De Oratore,* III, 38. Sin embargo, la transferencia es en la metáfora siempre mutua: el ciprés es la llama y la llama es el ciprés —lo cual sugiere que el lugar donde se pone cada una de las cosas no es el de la otra, sino un lugar sentimental, que es el mismo para ambas. La metáfora, pues, consiste en la transposición de una cosa desde su lugar real a su lugar sentimental.

después de creada una metáfora, seguimos ignorando su por qué. *Sentimos,* simplemente, una identidad, vivimos ejecutivamente el ser ciprés-llama.

Con esto cortamos aquí el análisis de nuestro ejemplo. Hemos hallado un objeto constituido por tres elementos o dimensiones: la cosa ciprés, la cosa llama —que se convierten ahora en meras propiedades de una tercera cosa—, el lugar sentimental o la forma *yo* de ambas. Las dos imágenes dotan al nuevo cuerpo maravilloso de carácter objetivo; su valor sentimental le presta el carácter de profundidad, de intimidad. Cuidando de acentuar por igual ambas palabras podíamos llamar al nuevo objeto "ciprés sentimental".

Esta es la nueva cosa conquistada —para algunos símbolo de la suprema realidad. Así Carducci:

> *E già che la metàfora, regina*
> *Di nascita e conquista,*
> *E'la sola gentil, salda, divina*
> *Verità che sussista...*

José Ortega y Gasset
1883–1955
España

Unas gotas de fenomenología
La deshumanización del arte y otros ensayos de estética, 1925.

UN hombre ilustre agoniza. Su mujer está junto al lecho. Un médico cuenta las pulsaciones del moribundo. En el fondo de la habitación hay otras dos personas: un periodista, que asiste a la escena obitual por razón de su oficio, y un pintor que el azar ha conducido allí. Esposa, médico, periodista y pintor presencian un mismo hecho. Sin embargo, este único y mismo hecho —la agonía de un hombre— se ofrece a cada uno de ellos con aspecto distinto. Tan distintos son estos aspectos, que apenas si tienen un núcleo común. La diferencia entre lo que es para la mujer transida de dolor y para el pintor que, impasible, mira la escena, es tanta, que casi fuera más exacto decir: la esposa y el pintor presencian dos hechos completamente distintos.

Resulta, pues, que una misma realidad se quiebra en muchas realidades divergentes cuando es mirada desde puntos de vista distintos. Y nos ocurre preguntarnos: ¿cuál de esas múltiples realidades es la verdadera, la auténtica? Cualquiera decisión que tomemos será arbitraria. Nuestra preferencia por una u otra sólo puede fundarse en el capricho. Todas esas realidades son equivalentes; cada una la auténtica para su congruo punto de vista. Lo único que podemos hacer es clasificar estos puntos de vista y elegir entre ellos el que prácticamente parezca más normal o más espontáneo. Así llegaremos a una noción nada absoluta, pero, al menos, práctica y normativa de realidad.

El medio más claro de diferenciar los puntos de vista de esas cuatro personas que asisten a la escena mortal consiste en medir una de sus dimensiones: la distancia espiritual en que cada uno se halla del hecho común, de la agonía. En la mujer del moribundo esta distancia es mínima, tanto que casi no existe. El suceso lamentable atormenta de tal modo su corazón, ocupa tanta porción de su alma, que se funde con su persona, o dicho en giro inverso: la mujer interviene en la escena, es un trozo de ella. Para que podamos ver algo, para que un hecho se convierta en objeto que contemplamos es menester separarlo de nosotros y que deje de formar parte viva de nuestro ser. La mujer, pues, no asiste a la escena, sino que está dentro de ella; no la contempla, sino que la vive.

El médico se encuentra ya un poco más alejado. Para él se trata de un caso profesional. No interviene en el hecho con la apasionada y cegadora angustia que inunda el alma de la pobre mujer. Sin embargo, su oficio le obliga a interesarse seriamente en lo que ocurre: lleva en ello alguna responsabilidad y acaso peligra su prestigio. Por tanto, aunque menos íntegra e íntimamente que la esposa, toma también parte en el hecho, la escena se apodera de él, le arrastra a su dramático interior prendiéndole, ya que no por su corazón, por el fragmento profesional de su persona. También él vive el triste acontecimiento aunque con emociones que no parten de su centro cordial, sino de su periferia profesional.

Al situarnos ahora en el punto de vista del reportero, advertimos que nos hemos alejado enormemente de aquella dolorosa realidad. Tanto nos hemos alejado, que hemos perdido con el hecho todo contacto sentimental. El periodista está allí como el médico, obligado por su profesión, no por espontáneo y humano impulso. Pero mientras la profesión del médico le obliga a intervenir en el suceso, la del periodista le obliga precisamente a no intervenir: debe limitarse a ver. Para él propiamente es el hecho pura escena, mero espectáculo que luego ha de relatar en las columnas del periódico. No participa sentimentalmente en lo que allí acaece, se halla espiritualmente exento y fuera del suceso; no lo vive, sino que lo contempla. Sin embargo, lo contempla con la preocupación de tener que referirlo luego a sus lectores. Quisiera interesar a éstos, conmoverlos, y, si fuese posible, conseguir que todos los suscriptores derramen lágrimas, como si fuesen transitorios parientes del moribundo. En la escuela había leído la receta de Horacio: *Si vis me flere, dolendum est primum ipsi tibi.*

Dócil a Horacio, el periodista procura fingir emoción para alimentar con ella su literatura. Y resulta que, aunque no *vive* la escena, *finge* vivirla.

Por último, el pintor, indiferente, no hace otra cosa que poner los ojos en *coulisse.* Le trae sin cuidado cuanto pasa allí; está, como suele decirse, a cien mil leguas del suceso. Su actitud es puramente contemplativa y aun cabe decir que no lo contempla en su integridad; el doloroso sentido interno del hecho queda fuera de su percepción. Sólo atiende a lo exterior, a las luces y las sombras, a los valores cromáticos. En el pintor hemos llegado al máximum de distancia y al mínimum de intervención sentimental.

La pesadumbre inevitable de este análisis quedaría compensada si nos permitiese hablar con claridad de una escala de distancias espirituales entre la realidad y nosotros. En esa escala los grados de proximidad equivalen a grados de participación sentimental en los hechos; los grados de alejamiento, por el contrario, significan grados de liberación en que objetivamos el suceso real, convirtiéndolo en puro tema de contemplación. Situados en uno de los extremos, nos encontramos con un aspecto del mundo —personas, cosas, situaciones— que es la realidad *vivida;* desde el otro extremo, en cambio, vemos todo en su aspecto de realidad *contemplada.*

Al llegar aquí tenemos que hacer una advertencia esencial para la estética, sin la cual no es fácil penetrar en la fisiología del arte, lo mismo viejo que nuevo. Entre estos diversos aspectos de la realidad que corresponde a los varios puntos de vista, hay uno del que derivan todos los demás y en todos los demás va supuesto. Es el de la realidad vivida. Si no hubiese alguien que viviese en pura entrega y frenesí la agonía de un hombre, el médico no se preocuparía por ella, los lectores no entenderían los gestos patéticos del periodista que describe el suceso y el cuadro en que el pintor representa un hombre en el lecho rodeado de figuras dolientes nos sería ininteligible. Lo mismo podríamos decir de cualquier otro objeto, sea persona o cosa. La forma primigenia de una manzana es la que ésta posee cuando nos disponemos a comérnosla. En todas las demás formas posibles que adopte —por ejemplo, la que un artista de 1600 le ha dado, combinándola en un barroco ornamento, la que presenta en un bodegón de Cézanne o en la metáfora elemental que hace de ella una mejilla de moza— conserva más o menos aquel aspecto originario. Un cuadro, una poesía donde no quedase resto alguno de las formas vividas serían ininteligibles, es decir, no serían nada, como nada sería un discurso donde a cada palabra se le hubiese extirpado su significación habitual.

Quiere decir esto que en la escala de las realidades corresponde a la realidad vivida una peculiar primacía que nos obliga a considerarla como *la* realidad por excelencia. En vez de realidad vivida, podríamos decir realidad humana. El pintor que presencia impasible la escena de agonía parece *inhumano*. Digamos, pues, que el punto de vista humano es aquel en que *vivimos* las situaciones, las personas, las cosas. Y, viceversa, son humanas todas las realidades —mujer, paisaje, peripecia— cuando ofrecen el aspecto bajo el cual suelen ser vividas.

Un ejemplo, cuya importancia advertirá el lector más adelante: entre las realidades que integran el mundo se hallan nuestras ideas. Las usamos *humanamente* cuando con ellas pensamos las cosas, es decir, que al pensar en Napoleón, lo normal es que atendamos exclusivamente al grande hombre así llamado. En cambio, el psicólogo, adoptando un punto de vista anormal, *inhumano,* se desentiende de Napoleón y, mirando a su propio interés, procura analizar su idea de Napoleón como tal idea. Se trata, pues, de una perspectiva opuesta a la que usamos en la vida espontánea. En vez de ser la idea instrumento con que pensamos un objeto, la hacemos a ella objeto y término de nuestro pensamiento. Ya veremos el uso inesperado que el arte nuevo hace de esta inversión inhumana.

Luis Palés Matos
1898—1959
Puerto Rico

Hacia una poesía antillana
El Mundo, 1932.

J. I. de Diego Padró publica un hermoso trabajo rebatiendo las ideas que sobre una posible y necesaria poesía antillana expuse ha poco desde las columnas de *El Mundo* en entrevista que me hiciera doña Angela Negrón Muñoz.

El distinguido intelectual sostiene que mi propósito, amén de irrealizable, carecería de toda significación trascendente porque los elementos afro-hispánicos por mí invocados para constituir el móvil dinámico de tal poesía tienen un valor harto relativo como expresión auténtica de cultura. Afirma, además, que en las Antillas, desde el punto de vista psicológico no ha ocurrido nada que justifique el desarrollo de esa nueva lírica, pues, el colono blanco destruyó al indio aborigen y disolvió, culturalmente, al negro esclavizado, conservando él intactas las líneas generales de su carácter y dándole a nuestra vida antillana una entonación absolutamente occidental.

Alrededor de estos dos puntos básicos hace girar, en luminoso tropel, razones y argumentos que a primera lectura dan una sensación concluyente de verdad. Observados más a fondo, sin embargo, revelan fallas, descuidos, errores de perspectiva, que a mi juicio les quitan toda su consistencia. Intentaré poner de relieve esos errores pero antes deseo fijar de modo claro y preciso mis ideas sobre el tema.

En primer lugar, yo no he hablado de una poesía negra ni blanca ni mulata; yo sólo he hablado de una poesía antillana que exprese nuestra realidad de pueblo en el sentido cultural de este vocablo. Sostengo que las Antillas —Cuba, Santo Domingo y Puerto Rico— han desarrollado un tipo espiritual homogéneo y están por lo tanto psicológicamente afinadas en una misma dirección. Y sostengo, además, que esta homogeneidad de tipo espiritual está perfectamente diferenciada de la masa común de los pueblos hispánicos y que en ella el factor negroide entreverado en la psiquis antillana, ha hecho las veces de aislador, o en términos químicos, de agente precipitante.

Físicamente, las Antillas constituyen también una unidad: paisaje, clima y productos son los mismos; fauna y flora idénticas; núcleos de población semejantes. Económicamente, girando como giran en la órbita del industrialismo americano, corren iguales contingencias y hacia análogo destino colonial.

En la *Revista Bimestre Cubana* el escritor Roig de Leuchsering publica un ensayo sobre la evolución de las costumbres en aquel país. No puedo sustraerme a la tentación de copiar su pintura sobre el carácter cubano. Hela aquí:

"Así nos encontramos con que el cubano es físicamente —sea blanco, negro o mestizo— más pequeño de estatura, delgado y débil de cuerpo que el español o el africano y menos resistente que éstos; más nervioso, irascible y despierto; de más acentuada viveza; pero variable, superficial, inconsistente, adaptable al medio y las circunstancias por la ley del menor esfuerzo; intensamente sensual; descreído en el fondo, pero supersticioso y fetichista; vehemente y apasionado; desinteresado, hospitalario y dadivoso hasta la prodigalidad y rumboso hasta el despilfarro; sin grandes y concretos ideales y aspiraciones; sobrio, principalmente el campesino, viviendo más al día que preocupándole el mañana, amigo como es de la vida regalada y cómoda, del goce, aunque sea poco, siempre que se alcance con el mínimum de esfuerzo; pero no por ello menos inconforme siempre de todo y rebelde eterno, como esclavo que ha sido —blanco o negro— de sus gobernantes y amos; poseedor del arma formidable de la burla, de la ironía, modalizada en el típico choteo, virtud y vicio; apático e individualista, difícilmente sacrificable por la colectividad; dispuesto siempre a destruir, pero no a construir, a criticar, pero no a resolver, confiando en que otro u otros solucionen los problemas de carácter general. De aquí que antaño como hogaño sean el baile y el juego los dos vicios predominantes en el cubano, por los que siente, en todas sus clases sociales, desenfrenado entusiasmo, por los que abandona presto las más serias ocupaciones y en las que invierte gustoso sus ganancias por indispensables que sean aun para su sostenimiento. Los clubs sociales sólo existen por y para el baile y el juego. La República ha abierto nuevos medios de holganza o vida cómoda con los puestos políticos y administrativos, las botellas, las sinecuras."

Inquiero yo ahora, ¿qué diferencia existe entre la psicología aquí esbozada y la del puertorriqueño? Y esta psicología, fuera de lo inherente a todo lo humano, ¿puede referirse, sin sustanciales mutilaciones de color, actitud y sentido, al colonizador hispánico, todo acción y dinamismo o al negro originario, todo adaptación y acatamiento? Podríamos, apurando

el análisis con criterio harto exigente, señalar vagos matices,
leves rasgos, tenues líneas de contrastes entre el cubano, el
dominicano y el puertorriqueño. Pero esto no alteraría el contorno general de ese carácter. Diferencias de tal guisa se pueden encontrar entre individuos de la misma región y aun hasta de la misma aldea. Además, esto nos llevaría a negar las razas y los pueblos como conjuntos orgánicos y vitales y a afirmar el individuo como expresión totalmente escindida de su
raza y su paisaje. Con lo cual, igualmente podríamos destruir
el concepto de antillanismo, como los de hispanismo y occidentalismo. Y holgaría todo debate sobre el tema.

Demostrada la existencia de un carácter integral y típico
en las Antillas ¿cree Padró que tal carácter, frente a la realidad objetiva, reacciona occidentalmente? ¿Pero qué es en sí
lo occidental? Un inglés y un español, occidentales auténticos, ante un fenómeno dado ¿se comportan de la misma manera? Coloquemos también frente a éste a un negro antillano,
de quien Padró asegura que asimiló la cultura europea a las
mil maravillas. ¿Sostiene mi buen amigo que las reacciones de
nuestro tercer personaje serán análogas a las de sus compañeros? Tendríamos, por lo menos, tres figuras occidentales, que
al actuar con dispareja actitud, expondrían a grave riesgo el
orondo concepto de occidentalismo reduciéndolo a una mera
entelequia geográfica de dudoso contenido esencial.

En términos generales, es cierto como afirma Padró, que
cuando dos culturas emigran de sus zonas de origen y se encuentran en un ambiente extraño, la que posea elementos superiores anula y destruye a su contraria. Pero debe tenerse
gran cautela en la excesiva generalización de este concepto y
no convertirlo en una ley rígida e inmutable. El nuevo medio
puede resultar hostil a la cultura dominante y favorable, por
el contrario, a la dominada. O pueden los hombres que representan esta última, por sutiles tácticas de su subconsciente colectivo o simplemente para subsistir, adoptar el tren de formas
y representaciones de la primera e infiltrar paulatinamente en
dichas formas su propio espíritu modificándolas con tan corro-
siva eficacia que den pábulo al nacimiento de una actitud cultural nueva.

Ese es, a mi juicio, el caso de las Antillas. Español y negro
las pueblan y colonizan barriendo de su escenario el elemento
aborigen. El blanco impone su ley y su cultura, el negro tole-
ra y se adapta. El ambiente tropical en que se mueven proyecta sobre ambos misteriosos influjos, y a los pocos años de convivencia el español continúa siendo un extraño en las jóvenes

tierras y el negro se expande y desenvuelve como en su propia casa.

Para curarse el tedio de las islas —ese insondable tedio que produce la inadaptación— los colonos pudientes hacen viajes a la madre patria. Otros, menos felices, se consuelan soñando con Galicia o Andalucía. Así, en el proceso original de nuestra formación psicológica, nos encontramos con dos fuerzas cardinales en lucha: una, la actitud hispánica, huidiza, inconforme, inadaptable; otra, la actitud negroide, firme y resueltamente afincada en el ambiente nuevo.

De ese vacilante estado espiritual del español, toman ventaja las potencias oscuras del alma negra para implantar en las Antillas modos, rasgos y ritmos peculiares, cuya realidad en el carácter del antillano es imposible rebatir y que desvinculan nuestro pueblo de lo hispánico, forjándole una personalidad propia.

Por otro lado, es muy difícil disolver, so alegato de superioridad, las raíces madres de una cultura supuestamente inferior, siempre que la conciencia vigilante de su raza progenitora no haya perdido su vitalidad. Haití ofrece un claro ejemplo. Los negros haitianos hablan el francés, profesan oficialmente la religión católica y constituyeron, asimilándose el espíritu de las instituciones democráticas occidentales, una República. Los haitianos cultos se educan en Francia, leen a Víctor Hugo, ostentan títulos de la Sorbona. La clase burguesa conoce los más frívolos caprichos de la moda parisina y diz que por las calles de Puerto Príncipe, en los días festivos, se mueve con el atuendo y la solemnidad de maneras que cumplen a las personas de alto bordo. Empero, interiormente, el haitiano continúa inmutable. Y nada hay tan diametralmente opuesto al espíritu francés —claridad, ligereza, racionalismo—, como el espíritu haitiano —sensualidad, superstición, hechicería.

El idioma postizo lo deformó en *patois*. Al simbolismo católico le tradujo equivalentes en el culto voduista. Culto básico, originario, traído por los abuelos y conservado a furto de la prohibición oficial, en el fondo de mil altares que encienden sus fuegos votivos en la selva. De este modo, el alma haitiana, utilizando los recursos expresionales de una cultura exótica, a través de muy sutiles pero seguros cauces, logra sus objetivos esenciales y se realiza con una plenitud de inconfundible contorno.

Sospecho que parejo fenómeno hubiera ocurrido en Cuba, Santo Domingo y Puerto Rico, si al choque puramente externo de las dos culturas —la del colono español y la del negro esclavo— en un escenario absolutamente extraño para ambas, no hubiera sucedido, amén de la mutación psicológica a que me referí antes, la mezcla de la sangre fundiendo sus valores de raza y creando el nuevo tipo del mulato hacia el cual se ha desplazado el acento vital de las tres islas. Y este acento, traducido a términos de cultura, no es ni puede ser ya hispánico ni africano. Porque si la cultura, en última instancia, ha de tener un valor substancial y no meramente externo y formativo, habrá de ser un constante fluir, un perenne producirse del ser o de la raza, en armonía con el paisaje que los rodea.

Padró niega posibilidades de trascendencia a la obra de arte que no se produce en ese inefable limbo utópico, de extensión ideal ilimitada, que denominamos cultura universal. Para él una poesía, una pintura, una música antillana, por el solo hecho de haberse realizado en la Antilla con los factores de colorido y sentimiento inherentes al carácter típico de la región, queda limitada en sí misma por tales factores, y su contenido estético carecerá de valor positivo de universalidad. Grave error. Aparte de que ese limbo, así considerado, tiene una muy dudosa y discutible existencia sobre la que aún no se han puesto de acuerdo filósofos, soñadores y charlatanes, lo cierto es que el tema artístico es y ha sido siempre local. Y el artista que acuciado por un falaz objetivo de universalismo, desdeña su genuino elemento y se dispara en vuelo hacia esas zonas de miraje, se pierde irremediablemente en un caos de palabras, de conceptos y de imágenes, horros de toda significación humana.

En cualquier rincón del planeta en donde haya hombres, es decir, ritmo de vida, juego de pasiones, baraja de intereses en movimiento, puede surgir una obra maestra. Lo importante es que el genio creador del artista arranque al ambiente que le circunda aquellos acentos cardinales que llegan a la esencia misma de la humanidad. Conviene aquí recordar —filosofía de Pero Grullo— que el mundo del arte tiende su raíz más sólida en la fuente de los sentimientos humanos, desde las pasiones vulgares —odio, lujuria— hasta las manifestaciones más alquimiadas del goce estético. Fuera de ese campo, todo arte se seca y degenera en una técnica vacía.

Con los ensueños y terrores de unas miserables tribus de Israel, esquilmadas por el hombre y la peste, los poetas hebreos crearon la Biblia, ese monumento literario de eterna y deslumbradora belleza. Cervantes mueve dos figuras locales en un ámbito puramente regional: estepa castellana, mesones, arrieros y baturros, costumbres pueblerinas, habla popular, y surge el Quijote que hasta ahora no ha encontrado paralelo en la literatura de Occidente. La *Divina Comedia* a despecho de su grandiosa concepción ultraterrena no logró sustraerse a la inexorable sugestión del medio florentino. Dante fue acusado de ensañamiento malicioso por sus críticos contemporáneos por apurar la nota realista en la pintura de ciertos personajes de la vida florentina y por haber enviado al Infierno, cosa perfectamente razonable, a sus enemigos y detractores. Los ejemplos son pues abundantísimos. Añadiré, no obstante, una sola y última cita por su concluyente significación. El escritor negro Renato Marán, escribe en Africa una novela de negros, pintando las pasiones y costumbres de los negros del Congo y conquista el premio de la Academia Goncourt, establecida en París, centro de la civilización occidental, en competencia con las obras más refinadas de la cultura francesa. Y esos negros son algo *sencillo y primitivo,* de conciencia rudimentaria, de ideas extraculturales, cuyo simple espectáculo *a base de color, gestos y timbalismo,* no podía ofrecer *tan amplio venero de poesía.* Renato Marán, sin embargo, supo encontrarlo y produjo una obra bella y emocionada.

Y si del libro derivamos hacia el pentagrama o el cuadro, encontraremos idéntico fenómeno. Wagner expresa el alma alemana, como Strawinsky la rusa y Grieg la noruega, Zuloaga traduce lo español, como Rembrandt lo holandés y Da Vinci lo italiano. Hasta cuando la pintura, que es el arte menos íntimo y por tanto más susceptible de adaptarse a normas de escuela, crea símbolos y figuras desarraigadas del suelo nativo, no puede sustraerse a su misteriosa influencia. Es el caso de las Venus de Rubens, que por su excesiva exuberancia carnal, mejor que el mito griego, recuerdan las gordas y sonrosadas campesinas holandesas.

El sentido de esta diferenciación es tan profundo, que según Spengler, la música rusa tan infinitamente triste para nosotros, no produce en el temperamento eslavo tal impresión. En cambio —continúa Spengler— toda la música occidental, sin *distinciones* le produce al chino la sensación de una marcha.

¿A qué viene, entonces, ese concepto anchuroso de un arte universalista y ese injustificado desdén hacia la realización de una poesía antillana que nos exprese a nosotros mismos? Recuerde Padró, como detalle curioso y significativo, que de todos los poetas de la presente generación el único que ha trascendido de nuestras fronteras regionales es Luis Lloréns

Torres, precisamente aquel que para cantar, no necesitó salirse, temáticamente, de su minúsculo barrio de Collores.

Forjemos, pues, la poesía antillana. Y que nuestra vanidad literaria de universalistas no nos lleve a la posición de Tar-
tarín, el pintoresco personaje de Daudet, que ambicioso de
anchuras, quiso crearse una selva y llenó de *baobabs* los tiestos de su jardín. Los árboles crecieron enana y ridículamente,
pero eran *baobabs,* y nuestro hombre se paseaba entre ellos
orondo y mayestático, con la rotunda convicción de encontrarse en plena selva africana.

Octavio Paz
1914–
México

La dialéctica de la soledad
El laberinto de la soledad, 1959.

L A Soledad, el sentirse y el saberse solo, desprendido del
mundo y ajeno a sí mismo, separado de sí, no es característica exclusiva del mexicano. Todos los hombres, en algún
momento de su vida, se sienten solos; y más: todos los hombres están solos. Vivir, es separarnos del que fuimos para internarnos en el que vamos a ser, futuro extraño siempre. La
soledad es el fondo último de la condición humana. El hombre es el único ser que se siente solo y el único que es búsqueda de otro. Su naturaleza –si se puede hablar de naturaleza
al referirse al hombre, el ser que, precisamente, se ha inventado a sí mismo al decirle "no" a la naturaleza– consiste en un
aspirar a realizarse en otro. El hombre es nostalgia y búsqueda de comunión. Por eso cada vez que se siente a sí mismo se
siente como carencia de otro, como soledad.

Uno con el mundo que lo rodea, el feto es vida pura y en
bruto, fluir ignorante de sí. Al nacer, rompemos los lazos que
nos unen a la vida ciega que vivimos en el vientre materno, en

donde no hay pausa entre deseo y satisfacción. Nuestra sensación de vivir se expresa como separación y ruptura, desamparo, caída en un ámbito hostil o extraño. A medida que crecemos esa primitiva sensación se transforma en sentimiento de soledad. Y más tarde, en conciencia: estamos condenados a vivir solos, pero también lo estamos a traspasar nuestra soledad y a rehacer los lazos que en un pasado paradisíaco nos unían a la vida. Todos nuestros esfuerzos tienden a abolir la soledad. Así, sentirse solos posee un doble significado: por una parte consiste en tener conciencia de sí; por la otra, en un deseo de salir de sí. La soledad, que es la condición misma de nuestra vida, se nos aparece como una prueba y una purgación, a cuyo término angustia e inestabilidad desaparecerán. La plenitud, la reunión, que es reposo y dicha, concordancia con el mundo, nos esperan al fin del laberinto de la soledad.

El lenguaje popular refleja esta dualidad al identificar a la soledad con la pena. Las penas de amor son penas de soledad. Comunión y soledad, deseo de amor, se oponen y complementan. Y el poder redentor de la soledad transparenta una oscura, pero viva, noción de culpa: el hombre solo "está dejado de la mano de Dios". La soledad es una pena, esto es, una condena y una expiación. Es un castigo, pero también una promesa del fin de nuestro exilio. Toda vida está habitada por esta dialéctica.

Nacer y morir son experiencias de soledad. Nacemos solos y morimos solos. Nada tan grave como esa primera inmersión en la soledad que es el nacer, si no es esa otra caída en lo desconocido que es el morir. La vivencia de la muerte se transforma pronto en conciencia del morir. Los niños y los hombres primitivos no creen en la muerte; mejor dicho, no saben que la muerte existe, aunque ella trabaje secretamente en su interior. Su descubrimiento nunca es tardío para el hombre civilizado, pues todo nos avisa y previene que hemos de morir. Nuestras vidas son un diario aprendizaje de la muerte. Más que a vivir se nos enseña a morir. Y se nos enseña mal.

Entre nacer y morir transcurre nuestra vida. Expulsados del claustro materno, iniciamos un angustioso salto de veras mortal, que no termina sino hasta que caemos en la muerte. ¿Morir será volver allá, a la vida de antes de la vida? ¿Será vivir de nuevo esa vida prenatal en que reposo y movimiento, día y noche, tiempo y eternidad, dejan de oponerse? ¿Morir será dejar de ser y, definitivamente, estar? ¿Quizá la muerte sea la vida verdadera? ¿Quizá nacer sea morir y morir, nacer? Nada sabemos. Mas aunque nada sabemos, todo nuestro ser aspira a escapar de estos contrarios que nos desgarran. Pues si todo (conciencia de sí, tiempo, razón, costumbres, hábitos) tiende a hacer de nosotros los expulsados de la vida, todo también nos empuja a volver, a descender al seno creador de donde fuimos arrancados. Y le pedimos al amor —que, siendo deseo, es hambre de comunión, hambre de caer y morir tanto como de renacer— que nos dé un pedazo de vida verdadera, de muerte verdadera. No le pedimos la felicidad, ni el reposo, sino un instante, sólo un instante, de vida plena, en la que se fundan los contrarios y vida y muerte, tiempo y eternidad, pacten. Oscuramente sabemos que vida y muerte no son sino dos movimientos, antagónicos pero complementarios, de una misma realidad. Creación y destrucción se funden en el acto amoroso; y durante una fracción de segundo el hombre entrevé un estado más perfecto.

En Nuestro mundo el amor es una experiencia casi inaccesible. Todo se opone a él: moral, clases, leyes, razas y los mismos enamorados. La mujer siempre ha sido para el hombre *lo otro*, su contrario y complemento. Si una parte de nuestro ser anhela fundirse a ella, otra, no menos imperiosamente, la aparta y excluye. La mujer es un objeto, alternativamente precioso o nocivo, mas siempre diferente. Al convertirla en objeto, en ser aparte y al someterla a todas las deformaciones que su interés, su vanidad, su angustia y su mismo amor le dictan, el hombre la convierte en instrumento. Medio para obtener el conocimiento y el placer, vía para alcanzar la supervivencia, la mujer es ídolo, diosa, madre, hechicera o musa, según muestra Simone de Beauvoir, pero jamás puede ser ella misma. De ahí que nuestras relaciones eróticas estén viciadas en su origen, manchadas en su raíz. Entre la mujer y nosotros se interpone un fantasma: el de su imagen, el de la imagen que nosotros nos hacemos de ella y con la que ella se reviste. Ni siquiera podemos tocarla como carne que se ignora a sí misma, pues entre nosotros y ella se desliza esa visión dócil y servil de un cuerpo que se entrega. Y a la mujer le ocurre lo mismo: no se siente ni se concibe sino como objeto, como *otro*. Nunca es dueña de sí. Su ser se escinde entre lo que es realmente y la imagen que ella se hace de sí. Una imagen que le ha sido dictada por familia, clase, escuela, amigas, religión y amante. Su feminidad jamás se expresa, porque se manifiesta a través de formas inventadas por el hombre. El amor no es un acto natural. Es algo humano y, por definición, *lo más humano,* es decir, una creación, algo que nosotros hemos hecho y que no se da en la naturaleza. Algo que hemos hecho, que hacemos todos los días y que todos los días deshacemos.

No son éstos los únicos obstáculos que se interponen entre el amor y nosotros. El amor es elección. Libre elección, acaso, de nuestra fatalidad, súbito descubrimiento de la parte más secreta y fatal de nuestro ser. Pero la elección amorosa es imposible en nuestra sociedad. Ya Breton decía en uno de sus libros más hermosos —*El loco amor*— que dos prohibiciones impedían, desde su nacimiento, la elección amorosa: la interdicción social y la idea cristiana del pecado. Para realizarse, el amor necesita quebrantar la ley del mundo. En nuestro tiempo el amor es escándalo y desorden, transgresión: el de dos astros que rompen la fatalidad de sus órbitas y se encuentran en la mitad del espacio. La concepción romántica del amor, que implica ruptura y catástrofe, es la única que conocemos porque todo en la sociedad impide que el amor sea libre elección.

La mujer vive presa en la imagen que la sociedad masculina le impone; por lo tanto, sólo puede elegir rompiendo consigo misma. "El amor la ha transformado, la ha hecho otra persona", suelen decir de las enamoradas. Y es verdad: el amor hace otra a la mujer, pues si se atreve a amar, a elegir, si se atreve a ser ella misma, debe romper esa imagen con que el mundo encarcela su ser.

El hombre tampoco puede elegir. El círculo de sus posibilidades es muy reducido. Niño, descubre la feminidad en la madre o en las hermanas. Y desde entonces el amor se identifica con lo prohibido. Nuestro erotismo está condicionado por el horror y la atracción del incesto. Por otra parte, la vida moderna estimula innecesariamente nuestra sensualidad, al mismo tiempo que la inhibe con toda clase de interdicciones —de clase, de moral y hasta de higiene—. La culpa es la espuela y el freno del deseo. Todo limita nuestra elección. Estamos constreñidos a someter nuestras aficiones profundas a la imagen femenina que nuestro círculo social nos impone. Es difícil amar a personas de otra raza, de otra lengua o de otra clase, a pesar de que no sea imposible que el rubio prefiera a las negras y éstas a los chinos, ni que el señor se enamore de su criada o a la inversa. Semejantes posibilidades nos hacen enrojecer. Incapaces de elegir, seleccionamos a nuestra esposa entre las mujeres que nos "convienen". Jamás confesaremos que nos hemos unido —a veces para siempre— con una mujer que acaso no amamos y que, aunque nos ame, es incapaz de salir de sí misma y mostrarse tal cual es. La frase de Swan: "Y pen-

sar que he perdido los mejores años de mi vida con una mujer
que no era mi tipo", la pueden repetir, a la hora de su muerte,
la mayor parte de los hombres modernos. Y las mujeres.

La sociedad concibe el amor, contra la naturaleza de este
sentimiento, como una unión estable y destinada a crear hijos.
Lo identifica con el matrimonio. Toda transgresión a esta regla se castiga con una sanción cuya severidad varía de acuerdo
con tiempo y espacio. (Entre nosotros la sanción es mortal
muchas veces —si es mujer el infractor— pues en México, como en todos los países hispánicos, funcionan con general aplauso dos morales, la de los señores y la de los otros: pobres, mujeres, niños.) La protección impartida al matrimonio podría
justificarse si la sociedad permitiese de verdad la elección. Puesto que no lo hace, debe aceptarse que el matrimonio no constituye la más alta realización del amor, sino que es una forma
jurídica, social y económica que posee fines diversos a los del
amor. La estabilidad de la familia reposa en el matrimonio,
que se convierte en una mera proyección de la sociedad, sin
otro objeto que la recreación de esa misma sociedad. De
ahí la naturaleza profundamente conservadora del matrimonio. Atacarlo, es disolver las bases mismas de la sociedad. Y
de ahí también que el amor sea, sin proponérselo, un acto antisocial, pues cada vez que logra realizarse, quebranta el matrimonio y lo transforma en lo que la sociedad no quiere que
sea: la revelación de dos soledades que crean por sí mismas
un mundo que rompe la mentira social, suprime tiempo y trabajo y se declara autosuficiente. No es extraño, así, que la sociedad persiga con el mismo encono al amor y a la poesía, su
testimonio, y los arroje a la clandestinidad, a las afueras, al
mundo turbio y confuso de lo prohibido, lo ridículo y lo anormal. Y tampoco es extraño que amor y poesía estallen en formas extrañas y puras: un escándalo, un crimen, un poema.

La protección al matrimonio implica la persecución del
amor y la tolerancia de la prostitución, cuando no su cultivo
oficial. Y no deja de ser reveladora la ambigüedad de la prostituta: ser sagrado para algunos pueblos, para nosotros es alternativamente un ser despreciable y deseable. Caricatura del
amor, víctima del amor, la prostituta es símbolo de los poderes que humilla nuestro mundo. Pero no nos basta con esa
mentira de amor que entraña la existencia de la prostitución;
en algunos círculos se aflojan los lazos que hacen intocable al
matrimonio y reina la promiscuidad. Ir de cama en cama no
es ya, ni siquiera, libertinaje. El seductor, el hombre que no
puede salir de sí porque la mujer es siempre instrumento de

su vanidad o de su angustia, se ha convertido en una figura del pasado, como el caballero andante. Ya no se puede seducir a nadie, del mismo modo que no hay doncellas que amparar o entuertos que deshacer. El erotismo moderno tiene un sentido distinto al de un Sade, por ejemplo. Sade era un temperamento trágico, poseído de absoluto; su obra es una revelación explosiva de la condición humana. Nada más desesperado que un héroe de Sade. El erotismo moderno casi siempre es una retórica, un ejercicio literario y una complacencia. No es una revelación del hombre sino un documento más sobre una sociedad que estimula el crimen y condena al amor. ¿Libertad de la pasión? El divorcio ha dejado de ser una conquista. No se trata tanto de facilitar la anulación de los lazos ya establecidos, sino de permitir que hombres y mujeres puedan escoger libremente. En una sociedad ideal, la única causa de divorcio sería la desaparición del amor o la aparición de uno nuevo. En una sociedad en que todos pudieran elegir, el divorcio sería un anacronismo o una singularidad, como la prostitución, la promiscuidad o el adulterio.

La sociedad se finge una totalidad que vive por sí y para sí. Pero si la sociedad se concibe como unidad indivisible, en su interior está escindida por un dualismo que acaso tiene su origen en el momento en que el hombre se desprende del mundo animal y, al servirse de sus manos, se inventa a sí mismo e inventa conciencia y moral. La sociedad es un organismo que padece la extraña necesidad de justificar sus fines y apetitos. A veces los fines de la sociedad, enmascarados por los preceptos de la moral dominante, coinciden con los deseos y necesidades de los hombres que la componen. Otras, contradicen las aspiraciones de fragmentos o clases importantes. Y no es raro que nieguen los instintos más profundos del hombre. Cuando esto último ocurre, la sociedad vive una época de crisis: estalla o se estanca. Sus componentes dejan de ser hombres y se convierten en simples instrumentos desalmados.

El dualismo inherente a toda sociedad, y que toda sociedad aspira a resolver transformándose en comunidad, se expresa en nuestro tiempo de muchas maneras: lo bueno y lo malo, lo permitido y lo prohibido; lo ideal y lo real, lo racional y lo irracional; lo bello y lo feo; el sueño y la vigilia, los pobres y los ricos, los burgueses y los proletarios; la inocencia y la conciencia, la imaginación y el pensamiento. Por un movimiento irresistible de su propio ser, la sociedad tiende a superar este dualismo y a transformar el conjunto de solitarias enemistades que la componen en un orden armonioso. Pero la sociedad moderna pretende resolver su dualismo mediante la supresión de esa dialéctica de la soledad que hace posible el amor. Las sociedades industriales —independientemente de sus diferencias *ideológicas,* políticas o económicas— se empeñan en transformar las diferencias cualitativas, es decir: humanas, en uniformidades cuantitativas. Los métodos de la producción en masa se aplican también a la moral, al arte y a los sentimientos. Abolición de las contradicciones y de las excepciones... Se cierran así las vías de acceso a la experiencia más honda que la vida ofrece al hombre y que consiste en penetrar la realidad como una totalidad en la que los contrarios pactan. Los nuevos poderes abolen la soledad por decreto. Y con ella al amor, forma clandestina y heroica de la comunión. Defender el amor ha sido siempre una actividad antisocial y peligrosa. Y ahora empieza a ser de verdad revolucionaria. La situación del amor en nuestro tiempo revela cómo la dialéctica de la soledad, en su más profunda manifestación, tiende a frustrarse por obra de la misma sociedad. Nuestra vida social niega casi siempre toda posibilidad de auténtica comunión erótica.

El amor es uno de los más claros ejemplos de ese doble instinto que nos lleva a cavar y ahondar en nosotros mismos y, simultáneamente, a salir de nosotros y realizarnos en otro: muerte y recreación, soledad y comunión. Pero no es el único. Hay en la vida de cada hombre una serie de períodos que son también rupturas y reuniones, separaciones y reconciliaciones. Cada una de estas etapas es una tentativa por trascender nuestra soledad, seguida por inmersiones en ambientes extraños.

El niño se enfrenta a una realidad irreductible a su ser y a cuyos estímulos no responde al principio sino con llanto o silencio. Roto el cordón que lo unía a la vida, trata de recrearlo por medio de la afectividad y el juego. Inicia así un diálogo que no terminará sino hasta que recite el monólogo de su muerte. Pero sus relaciones con el exterior no son ya pasivas, como en la vida prenatal, pues el mundo le exige una respuesta. La realidad debe ser poblada por sus actos. Gracias al juego y a la imaginación, la naturaleza inerte de los adultos —una silla, un libro, un objeto cualquiera— adquiere de pronto vida propia. Por la virtud mágica del lenguaje o del gesto, del símbolo o del acto, el niño crea un mundo viviente, en el que los objetos son capaces de responder a sus preguntas. El lenguaje, desnudo de sus significaciones intelectuales, deja de ser un conjunto de signos y vuelve a ser un delicado organismo de imantación mágica. No hay distancia entre el nombre y la cosa y pronunciar una palabra es poner en movimiento a la realidad que designa. La representación equivale a una verdadera reproducción del objeto, del mismo modo que para el primitivo la escultura no es una representación sino un doble del objeto representado. Hablar vuelve a ser una actividad creadora de realidades, esto es, una actividad poética. El niño, por virtud de la magia, crea un mundo a su imagen y resuelve así su soledad. Vuelve a ser uno con su ambiente. El conflicto renace cuando el niño deja de creer en el poder de sus palabras o de sus gestos. La conciencia principia como desconfianza en la eficacia mágica de nuestros instrumentos.

La adolescencia es ruptura con el mundo infantil y momento de pausa ante el universo de los adultos. Spranger señala a la soledad como nota distintiva de la adolescencia. Narciso, el solitario, es la imagen misma del adolescente. En este período el hombre adquiere por primera vez conciencia de su singularidad. Pero la dialéctica de los sentimientos interviene nuevamente: en tanto que extrema conciencia de sí, la adolescencia no puede ser superada sino como olvido de sí, como entrega. Por eso la adolescencia no es sólo la edad de la soledad, sino también la época de los grandes amores, del heroísmo y del sacrificio. Con razón el pueblo imagina al héroe y al amante como figuras adolescentes. La visión del adolescente como un solitario, encerrado en sí mismo, devorado por el deseo o la timidez, se resuelve casi siempre en la bandada de jóvenes que bailan, cantan o marchan en grupo. O en la pareja paseando bajo el arco de verdor de la calzada. El adolescente se abre al mundo: al amor, a la acción, a la amistad, al deporte, al heroísmo. La literatura de los pueblos modernos —con la significativa excepción de la española, en donde no aparecen sino como pícaros o huérfanos— está poblada de adolescentes, solitarios en busca de la comunión: del anillo, de la espada, de la Visión. La adolescencia es una vela de armas de la que se sale al mundo de los hechos.

La madurez no es etapa de soledad. El hombre, en lucha con los hombres o con las cosas, se olvida de sí en el trabajo, en la creación o en la construcción de objetos, ideas e instituciones. Su conciencia personal se une a otras: el tiempo adquiere sentido y fin, es historia, relación viviente y significativa con un pasado y un futuro. En verdad, nuestra singularidad —que brota de nuestra temporalidad, de nuestra fatal inserción en un tiempo que es nosotros mismos y que al alimentarnos nos devora— no queda abolida, pero sí atenuada y, en cierto modo, *redimida.* Nuestra existencia particular se inserta en la historia y ésta se convierte, para emplear la expresión de Eliot, en "a pattern of timeless moments". Así, el hombre maduro atacado del mal de soledad constituye en épocas fecundas una anomalía. La frecuencia con que ahora se encuentra a esta clase de solitarios indica la gravedad de nuestros males. En la época del trabajo en común, de los cantos en común, de los placeres en común, el hombre está más solo que nunca. El hombre moderno no se entrega a nada de lo que hace. Siempre una parte de sí, la más profunda, permanece intacta y alerta. En el siglo de la acción, el hombre se espía. El trabajo, único dios moderno, ha cesado de ser creador. El trabajo sin fin, infinito, corresponde a la vida sin finalidad de la sociedad moderna. Y la soledad que engendra, soledad promiscua de los hoteles, de las oficinas, de los talleres y de los cines, no es una prueba que afine el alma, un necesario purgatorio. Es una condenación total, espejo de un mundo sin salida.

El doble significado de la soledad —ruptura con un mundo y tentativa por crear otro— se manifiesta en nuestra concepción de héroes, santos y redentores. El mito, la biografía, la historia y el poema registran un período de soledad y de retiro, situado casi siempre en la primera juventud, que precede a la vuelta al mundo y a la acción entre los hombres. Años de preparación y de estudio, pero sobre todo años de sacrificio y penitencia, de examen, de expiación y de purificación. La soledad es ruptura con un mundo caduco y preparación para el regreso y la lucha final. Arnold Toynbee ilustra esta idea con numerosos ejemplos: el mito de la cueva de Platón, las vidas de San Pablo, Buda, Mahoma, Maquiavelo, Dante. Y todos, en nuestra propia vida y dentro de las limitaciones de nuestra pequeñez, también hemos vivido en soledad y apartamiento, para purificarnos y luego regresar entre los nuestros.

La dialéctica de la soledad —"the twofold motion of withdrawal-and-return", según Toynbee— se dibuja con claridad en la historia de todos los pueblos. Quizá las sociedades antiguas, más simples que las nuestras, ilustran mejor este doble movimiento.

No es difícil imaginar hasta qué punto la soledad constituye un estado peligroso y temible para el llamado, con tanta vanidad como inexactitud, hombre primitivo. Todo el complicado y rígido sistema de prohibiciones, reglas y ritos de la cultura arcaica, tiende a preservarlo de la soledad. El grupo es la única fuente de salud. El solitario es un enfermo, una rama muerta que hay que cortar y quemar, pues la sociedad misma peligra si alguno de sus componentes es presa del mal. La repetición de actitudes y fórmulas seculares no solamente asegura la permanencia del grupo en el tiempo, sino su unidad y cohesión. Los ritos y la presencia constante de los espíritus de los muertos entretejen un centro, un nudo de relaciones que limitan la acción individual y protegen al hombre de la soledad y al grupo de la dispersión.

Para el hombre primitivo salud y sociedad, dispersión y muerte, son términos equivalentes. Aquel que se aleja de la tierra natal "cesa de pertenecer al grupo. Muere y recibe los honores fúnebres acostumbrados".[1] El destierro perpetuo equivale a una sentencia de muerte. La identificación del grupo social con los espíritus de los antepasados y el de éstos con la tierra se expresa en este rito simbólico africano: "Cuando un nativo regresa de Kimberley con la mujer que lo ha desposado, la pareja lleva consigo un poco de tierra de su lugar. Cada día la esposa debe comer un poco de polvo... para acostumbrarse a la nueva residencia. Ese poco de tierra hará posible la transición entre los dos domicilios." La solidaridad social posee entre ellos "un carácter orgánico y vital. El individuo es literalmente miembro de un cuerpo". Por tal motivo las conversiones individuales no son frecuentes. "Nadie se puede salvar o condenar por su cuenta" y sin que su acto afecte a toda la colectividad.[2]

A pesar de todas estas precauciones el grupo no está a salvo de la dispersión. Todo puede disgregarlo: guerras, cismas religiosos, transformaciones de los sistemas de producción, conquistas... Apenas el grupo se divide, cada uno de los fragmentos se enfrenta a una nueva situación: la soledad, consecuencia de la ruptura con el centro de salud que era la vieja sociedad cerrada, ya no es una amenaza, ni un accidente, sino una condición, la condición fundamental, el fondo final de su existencia. El desamparo y abandono se manifiesta como conciencia del pecado —un pecado que no ha sido infracción a una regla, sino que forma parte de su naturaleza. Mejor dicho, que es ya su naturaleza. Soledad y pecado original se identifican. Y salud y comunión vuelven a ser términos sinónimos, sólo que situados en un pasado remoto. Constituyen la edad de oro, reino vivido antes de la historia y al que quizá se pue-

---

[1] Lucien Lévy-Bruhl, *La mentalité primitive.* París, 1922.
[2] *Op. cit.*

da acceder si rompemos la cárcel del tiempo. Nace así, con la conciencia del pecado, la necesidad de la redención. Y ésta engendra la del redentor.

Surgen una nueva mitología y una nueva religión. A diferencia de la antigua, la nueva sociedad es abierta y fluida, pues está constituida por desterrados. Ya el solo nacimiento dentro del grupo no otorga al hombre su filiación. Es un don de lo alto y debe merecerlo. La plegaria crece a expensas de la fórmula mágica y los ritos de iniciación acentúan su carácter purificador. Con la idea de redención surgen la especulación religiosa, la ascética, la teología y la mística. El sacrificio y la comunión dejan de ser un festín totémico, si es que alguna vez lo fueron realmente, y se convierten en la vía de ingreso a la nueva sociedad. Un dios, casi siempre un dios hijo, un descendiente de las antiguas divinidades creadoras, muere y resucita periódicamente. Es un dios de fertilidad, pero también de salvación y su sacrificio es prenda de que el grupo prefigura en la tierra la sociedad perfecta que nos espera al otro lado de la muerte. En la esperanza del más allá late la nostalgia de la antigua sociedad. El retorno a la edad de oro vive, implícito, en la promesa de salvación.

Seguramente es muy difícil que en la historia particular de una sociedad se den todos los rasgos sumariamente apuntados. No obstante, algunos se ajustan en casi todos sus detalles al esquema anterior. El nacimiento del orfismo, por ejemplo. Como es sabido, el culto a Orfeo surge después del desastre de la civilización aquea —que provocó una general dispersión del mundo griego y una vasta reacomodación de pueblos y culturas—. La necesidad de rehacer los antiguos vínculos, sociales y sagrados, dio origen a cultos secretos, en los que participaban solamente "aquellos seres desarraigados, trasplantados, reaglutinados artificialmente y que soñaban con reconstruir una organización de la que no pudieran separarse. Su sólo nombre colectivo era el de huérfanos".[3] (Señalaré de paso que *orphanos* no solamente es huérfano, sino vacío. En efecto, soledad y orfandad son, en último término, experiencias del vacío.)

Las religiones de Orfeo y Dionisios, como más tarde las religiones proletarias del fin del mundo antiguo, muestran con claridad el tránsito de una sociedad cerrada a otra abierta. La conciencia de la culpa, de la soledad y la expiación, juegan en ellas el mismo doble papel que en la vida individual.

[3]Amable Audin, *Les Fêtes Solaires*. París, 1945.

El sentimiento de soledad, nostalgia de un cuerpo del que fuimos arrancados, es nostalgia de espacio. Según una concepción muy antigua y que se encuentra en casi todos los pueblos, ese espacio no es otro que el centro del mundo, el *ombligo* del universo. A veces el paraíso se identifica con ese sitio y ambos con el lugar de origen, mítico o real, del grupo.[4] Entre los aztecas, los muertos regresaban a Mictlán, lugar situado al norte, de donde habían emigrado. Casi todos los ritos de fundación, de ciudades o de mansiones, aluden a la búsqueda de ese centro sagrado del que fuimos expulsados. Los grandes santuarios --Roma, Jerusalén, la Meca-- se encuentran en el centro del mundo o lo simbolizan y prefiguran. Las peregrinaciones a esos santuarios son repeticiones rituales de las que cada pueblo ha hecho en un pasado mítico, antes de establecerse en la tierra prometida. La costumbre de dar una vuelta a la casa o a la ciudad antes de atravesar sus puertas, tiene el mismo origen.

El mito del Laberinto se inserta en este grupo de creencias. Varias nociones afines han contribuido a hacer del Laberinto uno de los símbolos míticos más fecundos y significativos: la existencia, en el centro del recinto sagrado, de un talismán o de un objeto cualquiera, capaz de devolver la salud o la libertad al pueblo; la presencia de un héroe o de un santo, quien tras la penitencia y los ritos de expiación, que casi siempre entrañan un período de aislamiento, penetra en el laberinto o palacio encantado; el regreso, ya para fundar la Ciudad, ya para salvarla o redimirla. Si en el mito de Perseo los elementos místicos apenas son visibles, en el del Santo Grial el ascetismo y la mística se alían: el pecado, que produce la esterilidad en la tierra y en el cuerpo mismo de los súbditos del Rey Pescador; los ritos de purificación; el combate espiritual; y, finalmente, la gracia, esto es, la comunión.

No sólo hemos sido expulsados del centro del mundo y estamos condenados a buscarlo por selvas y desiertos o por los vericuetos y subterráneos del Laberinto. Hubo un tiempo en el que el tiempo no era sucesión y tránsito, sino manar continuo de un presente fijo, en el que estaban contenidos todos los tiempos, el pasado y el futuro. El hombre, desprendido de esa eternidad en la que todos los tiempos son uno, ha caído en el tiempo cronométrico y se ha convertido en prisionero del reloj, del calendario y de la sucesión. Pues apenas

---

[4] Sobre la noción de "espacio sagrado", véase Mircea Eliade, *Histoire des Religions.* París, 1949.

el tiempo se divide en ayer, hoy y mañana, en horas, minutos y segundos, el hombre cesa de ser uno con el tiempo, cesa de coincidir con el fluir de la realidad. Cuando digo "en este instante", ya pasó el instante. La medición espacial del tiempo separa al hombre de la realidad, que es un continuo presente, y hace fantasmas a todas las presencias en que la realidad se manifiesta, como enseña Bergson.

Si se reflexiona sobre el carácter de estas dos opuestas nociones, se advierte que el tiempo cronométrico es una sucesión homogénea y vacía de toda particularidad. Igual a sí mismo siempre, desdeñoso del placer o del dolor, sólo transcurre. El tiempo mítico, al contrario, no es una sucesión homogénea de cantidades iguales, sino que se halla impregnado de todas las particularidades de nuestra vida: es largo como una eternidad o breve como un soplo, nefasto o propicio, fecundo o estéril. Esta noción admite la existencia de una pluralidad de tiempos. Tiempo y vida se funden y forman un solo bloque, una unidad imposible de escindir. Para los aztecas, el tiempo estaba ligado al espacio y cada día a uno de los puntos cardinales. Otro tanto puede decirse de cualquier calendario religioso. La Fiesta es algo más que una fecha o un aniversario. No celebra, sino *reproduce* un suceso: abre en dos al tiempo cronométrico para que, por espacio de unas breves horas inconmensurables, el presente eterno se reinstale. La fiesta vuelve creador al tiempo. La repetición se vuelve concepción. El tiempo engendra. La Edad de Oro regresa. Ahora y aquí, cada vez que el sacerdote oficia el Misterio de la Santa Misa, desciende efectivamente Cristo, se da a los hombres y salva al mundo. Los verdaderos creyentes son, como quería Kierkegaard, "contemporáneos de Jesús". Y no solamente en la Fiesta religiosa o en el Mito irrumpe un Presente que disuelve la vana sucesión. También el amor y la poesía nos revelan, fugaz, este tiempo original. "Más tiempo no es más eternidad", dice Juan Ramón Jiménez, refiriéndose a la eternidad del instante poético. Sin duda la concepción del tiempo como presente fijo y actualidad pura, es más antigua que la del tiempo cronométrico, que no es una aprehensión inmediata del fluir de la realidad, sino una racionalización del transcurrir.

La dicotomía anterior se expresa en la oposición entre Historia y Mito, o Historia y Poesía. El tiempo del Mito, como el de la fiesta religiosa, o el de los cuentos infantiles, no tiene fechas: "Hubo una vez...", "En la época en que los animales hablaban...", "En el principio...". Y ese Principio —que no es el año tal ni el día tal— contiene todos los principios y nos introduce en el tiempo vivo, en donde de veras todo principia todos los instantes. Por virtud del rito, que realiza y reproduce el relato mítico, de la poesía y del cuento de hadas, el hombre accede a un mundo en donde los contrarios se funden. "Todos los rituales tienen la propiedad de acaecer en el ahora, en este instante."[5] Cada poema que leemos es una recreación, quiero decir: una ceremonia ritual, una Fiesta.

El Teatro y la Epica son también Fiestas, ceremonias. En la representación teatral como en la recitación poética, el tiempo ordinario deja de fluir, cede el sitio al tiempo original. Gracias a la participación, ese tiempo mítico, original, padre de todos los tiempos que enmascaran a la realidad, coincide con nuestro tiempo interior, subjetivo. El hombre, prisionero de la sucesión, rompe su invisible cárcel de tiempo y accede al tiempo vivo: la subjetividad se identifica al fin con el tiempo exterior, porque éste ha dejado de ser medición espacial y se ha convertido en manantial, en presente puro, que se recrea sin cesar. Por obra del Mito y de la Fiesta —secular o religiosa— el hombre rompe su soledad y vuelve a ser uno con la creación. Y así, el Mito —disfrazado, oculto, escondido— reaparece en casi todos los actos de nuestra vida e interviene decisivamente en nuestra Historia: nos abre las puertas de la comunión.

El hombre contemporáneo ha racionalizado los Mitos, pero no ha podido destruirlos. Muchas de nuestras verdades científicas, como la mayor parte de nuestras concepciones morales, políticas y filosóficas, sólo son nuevas expresiones de tendencias que antes encarnaron en formas míticas. El lenguaje racional de nuestro tiempo encubre apenas a los antiguos Mitos. La Utopía, y especialmente las modernas utopías políticas, expresan con violencia concentrada, a pesar de los esquemas racionales que las enmascaran, esa tendencia que lleva a toda sociedad a imaginar una edad de oro de la que el grupo social fue arrancado y a la que volverán los hombres el Día de Días. Las fiestas modernas —reuniones políticas, desfiles, manifestaciones y demás actos rituales— prefiguran al advenimiento de ese día de Redención. Todos esperan que la sociedad vuelva a su libertad original y los hombres a su primitiva pureza. Entonces la Historia cesará. El tiempo (la duda, la elección forzada entre lo bueno y lo malo, entre lo injusto y lo justo, entre lo real y lo imaginario) dejará de

---

[5]Van der Leeuw: *L'homme primitif et la Religion.* París, 1940.

triturarnos. Volverá el reino del presente fijo, de la comunión perpetua: la realidad arrojará sus máscaras y podremos al fin conocerla y conocer a nuestros semejantes.

Toda sociedad moribunda o en trance de esterilidad tiende a salvarse creando un mito de redención, que es también un mito de fertilidad, de creación. Soledad y pecado se resuelven en comunión y fertilidad. La sociedad que vivimos ahora también ha engendrado su mito. La esterilidad del mundo burgués desemboca en el suicidio o en una nueva Forma de participación creadora. Tal es, para decirlo con la frase de Ortega y Gasset, el "tema de nuestro tiempo": la sustancia de nuestros sueños y el sentido de nuestros actos.

El hombre moderno tiene la pretensión de pensar despierto. Pero este despierto pensamiento nos ha llevado por los corredores de una sinuosa pesadilla, en donde los espejos de la razón multiplican las cámaras de tortura. Al salir, acaso, descubriremos que habíamos soñado con los ojos abiertos y que los sueños de la razón son atroces. Quizá, entonces, empezaremos a soñar otra vez con los ojos cerrados.

Manuel Ramos Otero
1948–1991
Puerto Rico

Ficción e historia:
Texto y pretexto de la autobiografía

Ponencia presentada en la Primera Conferencia de poetas y escritores puertorriqueños en New York: 19 de noviembre de 1988.
Panel: Ficción e historia.

> *La historia que he narrado aunque fingida,*
> *Bien puede figurar el maleficio*
> *De cuantos ejercemos el oficio*
> *De cambiar en palabras nuestra vida.*

> Jorge Luis Borges:
> "La luna"

> *... nadie sabe bien quién es el que verdade-*
> *ramente está contando, si soy yo o eso que*
> *ha ocurrido... o si sencillamente cuento*
> *una verdad que es solamente mi verdad...*

> Julio Cortázar:
> "Las babas del diablo"

QUIERO contarles un cuento que no es mío pero que como todo cuento apropiado por la voz de un fiel cuentero, me ha poseído desde que lo escuché con la sabiduría inevitable de la magia que no falla por saberse sentencia inexorable. Sospecho que mi voz lo volverá mío y que lo que ahora pretendo es privilegiar mi condición de cuentero desempleado al que la mera presencia de un público hambriento devuelve la razón de su autoridad. El cuento que quiero contarles se lo escuché a la voz de Orson Welles una tarde sudada de verano en el desaparecido cine Elgin, de New York. Cine de tercera: se exhibe la misteriosa película de Orson Welles, *Mr. Arkadin*. Público de primera (como ustedes) paga 75 chavos, tres pesetas, con tarjeta de estudiante. El perfume más notorio en el ambiente es el del semen disecado sobre las butacas de cuero cuarteado color vino. Acaban de apagar las luces y la soledad se vuelve cúbica. En el *mezzanine* donde me encuentro sentado, al lado de un siciliano velludo y taciturno, vestido de negro, se escucha el sonido tembloroso del Bell & Howell preludiando la película. Ráfagas de luz y sombra en la pantalla como si fueran la tela rasgada de un río de la noche. La voz de Orson Welles se sabe merodeadora de la Casa de Usher. Yo soy un mero juglar de traducción.

Un sapo y un escorpión se encuentran a la orilla de un río. Cuando el escorpión, que quiere cruzar el río, le pide al sapo que lo cruce, el sapo le contesta lo siguiente: "Si te cruzo sobre mi espalda me vas a aguijonear y tu aguijón es fatal." El escorpión responde con un argumento plausible: "¿Cuál es tu lógica? Si te entierro mi aguijón, los dos nos ahogaremos." El sapo, criatura de la lógica, accede a transportar al escorpión, pero apenas alcanza la mitad del camino siente el aguijón mortal enterrado en su espalda. "¿Cuál es tu lógica?", croquea el sapo moribundo apenas alcanzando la superficie. "Este es mi personaje", contesta el ominoso escorpión, "y mi personaje no tiene lógica ninguna".

El perfecto andamiaje que sostiene a este cuento es el poro indispensable por el que respira toda fábula, el pulmón esencial de toda historia, si se quiere. Es el eterno debate entre la lógica y la locura, entre la verdad y la mentira, entre la realidad y la ilusión, entre la esencia y la apariencia, entre el ser y no ser. Es el fundamental discurso dialéctico en cuya vital polarización prevalece la maravillosa ambigüedad de todo edificio de palabras que en la maña milenaria del cuentero no busca parcializarse ni con la ficción ni con la historia porque deriva su energía, precisamente, de esa contradicción aparente entre lo que Borges resumió, con tanto acierto, como la simultaneidad del tiempo y la sucesividad del lenguaje. A estas fábulas sin origen ni fin que probablemente constituyen la prueba más persistente de la sabiduría humana debemos, quizá, la vaguísima certeza de que la eternidad existe. A esa voz que sólo reconoce en la sordera la existencia necesaria del silencio, debemos (si no me equivoco) el puente invisible entre la fábula oral y la fábula escrita que es toda ficción, toda historia, que tiene que ser contada. Esa voz es el cuerpo que tentativamente habita la jornada entre la orilla de la vida y la orilla de la muerte, y esa angustia por definir el cuerpo que se nos escapa, ese autocuerpo abrazado por la duda dadivosa es el texto que tiene que ser escrito bajo el pretexto ancestral de un maleficio para que, como por arte de magia, cambiemos "en palabras nuestra vida". Escribir, entonces, no es otra cosa que rechazar el texto transitorio de la biografía de carne y hueso y lanzarnos a la búsqueda de ese pre-texto augurado por la fábula cuya resonancia lejana está tan cerca que, por lo mismo, nos iguala. Escribir es, al menos para mí, despellejarme para encontrar la voz, descaracolizarme para liberar la voz que se parece a mí, que lucha por parecerse a mí y que quiere tomar prestada la biografía inconclusa que soy para que, finalmente, vuelva a quedar integrado el fabuloso cuentero en el texto y pretexto de la escritura. Bien dijo la poeta:

En la ribera de la muerte,
hay algo,
alguna voz,
alguna vela a punto de partir,
alguna tumba libre
que me enamora el alma.

Son palabras de Julia de Burgos. Pertenecen a esa fábula titulada "Entre mi voz y el tiempo". No tienen que ser explicadas. No deben ser explicadas. Pero yo soy un animal de tentación y en la ribera de la vida hay algo, alguna voz que me seduce y me traduce, que me oraculiza con enigmas que buscan ser descifrados, y el título de esa fábula, "Entre mi voz y el tiempo", pone el dedo en la llaga obsesiva de la ecuación ficción-historia. Al igual que Julia de Burgos en esa fábula, yo estoy entre mi ficción y la historia, no estoy fuera de ninguna de las dos sino entre ambas, y todo lo que he escrito, todo lo que escribo es un intento de atrapar, irónicamente, la voz de mi liberación, esa voz que al aprehender las otras voces de los otros cuenteros de la historia definirá mejor los bordes temporales de la lengua, ese órgano tan humano que lo mismo hace el amor con la piel polvorosa de otro cuerpo que con la piel polvorienta de la fábula. Y parece ser que esta palabra, *fábula,* resuelve de alguna manera la cruel dicotomía entre ficción e historia, que está mucho más allá del juicio condenatorio de las ideologías, que su altura misma define el delicioso ímpetu humano de la lengua que campea por su respeto a través de la corteza del papel y de las sábanas, que la palabra *fábula* altera, de alguna forma, la ley de los catálogos ficticios de la historia y la ley de los catálogos históricos de la ficción, que resume desde mucho antes que Julio Cortázar la sentencia que él captura cuando escribe que "... nadie sabe bien quién es el que verdaderamente está contando...", ¿el historiador o el ficcionalizador?, ¿el lógico o el loco?, ¿el verdadero o el embustero?

Es curioso que nuestra lengua posea un término eficaz (más de uno) para caracterizar al que miente: el embustero, el mentiroso. Curioso que los catálogos de nuestra lengua definen al cuentero, además, como embustero. Sin embargo, nuestra lengua no posee esa palabra que hace sujeto a su contrario. No hablamos del verdadero para referirnos a ese que dice la verdad. Tenemos un verbo para el acto de la mentira pero carecemos de un verbo para el acto de la verdad. Y, lo que al fin y al cabo está, detrás de la dicotomía entre ficción e historia, no es otra cosa que la percepción de discursos que nos parecen verdaderos o ficticios. ¿Es *La Ilíada* la historia de la guerra de Troya o la fabulación de un caballo de madera en el que caben los invasores de un pueblo o —como decía mi elocuente profesora del curso básico de Humanidades en 1965 en la Universidad de Puerto Rico— "el canto de la cólera de Aquileo"? ¿Son los diarios de Cristóbal Colón los indispensables documentos históricos de la gesta heroica del descubrimiento del Caribe, o la maravillosa locura de un muellero genovés con cruz al pecho, que al llegar a la desembocadura del Orinoco proclama que *no,* que la Tierra no es redonda como él había dicho, que la Tierra tiene la forma de una teta de mujer y que el polo es un pezón carnoso? Yo sé que toda traducción es una rescritura. Yo sé que nuestra definición de lo que es ficción y de lo que es historia está matizada por ese fenómeno habitual que nadie parece tomar en cuenta, llamado la traducción. Que toda nuestra percepción histórica está noblemente, vulgarmente, verdaderamente, falsamente matizada por los espejos dobles de la traducción requerida por la *fábula,* que inclusive, un lector de Manatí, la Atenas de Puerto Rico, comprende *La Odisea,* no por los mapas sanguíneos que le revelan que la Kultura exige su lectura de los tejemenejes de Penélope, sino porque Penélope, ficción o historia, hace y deshace la voz endemoniada de la *fábula,* y que, al hacerlo, alguna voz fijó su biografía.

Hace un tiempo, y el tiempo siempre lo hacemos los humanos. Preciso más. Los escritores somos —como le hubiera gustado a Melville— los cazadores azarosos de esa ballena blanca que es el tiempo. Y estoy al punto de excusar el color de la ballena del tiempo, pero *no,* mejor que un público de tres pesetas, con tarjeta de estudiante, es un público al que sólo interesa la posibilidad de una fábula. Hace un tiempo que al hablar frente a otro público enternecido por la fábula, agitado por la fábula, dije que "yo siempre he sido el protagonista de mi obra". Llama, inmediatamente, la atención, el posible narcisismo de la sentencia. Añado ahora, otra sentencia: Yo creo, que al fin y al cabo, lo único que siempre he hecho, desde que asumí la escritura, ha sido la traducción de la autobiografía. Sé que la gramática me falla. Sé que la gramática me acusa. Sé que la gramática es un callejón temporero sin salida. Dije también, hace algún tiempo, que yo nací en un pueblo de embuste, ese pueblo que les mencioné, esa Atenas de Puerto Rico frente al mar. Dije que la vida (perdón), dije que *mi* vida, había transcurrido en un pueblo de embuste, un pueblo en el que la cancha de los jugadores de baloncesto es llamada el Akrópolis, un pueblo por donde pasaba el tren ahora cubierto de malezas, rieles sobre los cuales mi cuerpo, también cubierto de malezas, aprendió el fabuloso ejercicio de la lengua. Yo nací, dije y me acuerdo, en un pueblo de embuste. Nací en una casa que no era una casa si pensamos en que esa casa había sido el viejo casino español del pueblo llamado Manatí, la Atenas de Puerto Rico. Dije, también, que cuando caminaba por ese casino convertido en casa, que cuando caminaba por esa casa que conversaba con los fantasmas del casino, la gente, los cuenteros, me contaban que sobre las losetas verdes, nebulosas, habían bailado las parejas llenas de amor. Dije, que me decían que donde comíamos todos los días había sido el punto exacto de las partidas de brisca y tute, y que en el segundo piso de la casa, mi abuela, una cialeña que leía las barajas, pronosticaba el destino sin duda alguna. Dije que desde el antepecho de mi casa se veía la Iglesia de La Candelaria, que a pocos pasos de mi casa estaba el cine Taboas y la butaca número siete de la séptima fila donde me acostumbré a la soledad. Dije, que a minutos del pueblo estaba el mar, la playa de Palmira Parés, de la Mujer del Mar, la Poza de las Mujeres, el Ojo de Agua. No dije tanto. Pero *sí* dije que yo había nacido en un pueblo de embuste.

La escritura, para mí, siempre ha tenido que ver con eso que genéricamente se designa como la autobiografía. No sé contar nada más. No puedo contar nada más. Para legitimizar ahora este discurso, recurro nuevamente a la cita, al pretexto inmediato de este texto. Philippe Lejeune, nos dice, me dice, en *El pacto autobiografico,* texto no traducido al español y que yo, con mi francés aprendido de Madame Ana Rita Dumont, francesa exilada en Cuba, exilada en Puerto Rico, traduzco, lo mejor que puedo:

> La autobiografía es un recuento retrospectivo, en prosa, que una persona hace de su propia existencia, y en el que pone el acento sobre su vida individual, en particular sobre la historia de su personalidad.

Tanto Philippe Lejeune, como Madame Ana Rita Dumont, tenían y siguen teniendo la razón, ponían y siguen poniendo, me temo, el acento fatal sobre la lógica, sobre la clasificación, sobre el catálogo de moda en la escritura. *Sí,* la autobiografía es un "recuento retrospectivo", pero *sí,* todo acto de la escritura lo es. *No,* no es necesariamente en prosa, todo depende de la capacidad poética del que (de la que) quiere autobiografiar. *Sí,* la autobiografía se da con la propia existencia, pero la redundancia inevitable de la propia existencia invalida la premisa si acaso aquel que autobiografía concibe su escritura como historia, si concibe su existencia como el testimonio de una época. *Sí,* el acento se pone sobre la vida individual, pero el acento siempre ha estado puesto gramaticalmente sobre el *Yo,* que también es *Tú,* que además es *El* y que siempre es *Ella* cuando nos genera con el acento fundamental de la diferencia. Y *Sí,* pero también *No.* El acento se pone particularmente sobre la historia, pero no sobre la historia de la personalidad sino sobre la historia del personaje. Toda autobiografía se postula como la historia de un personaje del cual la voz que cuenta sabe más que los demás porque entre la voz que cuenta y el personaje, el espejo del tiempo interpone su traducción para vincular, la historia de la vida contada, a la ficción narrativa imaginada.

Quiero pensar que mi escritura no comenzó conmigo. Quiero pensar que mi escritura es ese diálogo incesante con todos los cuenteros que, como yo, en un momento lunaroso de nuestro personaje asumimos lo que con toda lógica de sapo habíamos aprendido, y que de momento se disolvió con la locura de ser ese escorpión que ante todo defiende aquello para lo que la lógica no existe. Escribo esta ficción que afortunadamente me ha vuelto histórico porque la palabra escrita de un cuentero es historia subrayada, escribo esta historia porque sé que la historia me alucina, me vuelve a justo territorio de la cuneta eterna de todos los juglares que por ser lo que son no tuvieron que justificarse en las demandas exteriores que intentan organizar las palabras como si fueran artículos de vendedores ambulantes. Escribo el texto que soy, que me alegro haber descubierto que soy, el texto que se inventa y se reinventa sin llegar a ser jamás una caricatura anónima. Escribo mis fabulas para seguir siendo el personaje que se escapa de todos los prejuicios inventados por la falta de locura y de imaginación.

Alfonso Reyes
1889–1959
México

Categorías de la lectura
La experiencia literaria, 1942.

> *Books and the Man I sing.*
> Pope, *Dunciad*, I.

HAY categorías de la lectura, según que en la representación psicológica del lenguaje domine el orden articulatorio o el visual; según la penetración que la cultura haya alcanzado en los estratos del alma; según los hábitos adquiridos de leer para sí o para los demás, de leer por sí o de escuchar la lectura; según la mayor o menor presteza con que los oídos o los ojos comunican el mensaje al espíritu; según que la bella escritura, la bella edición o la bella voz impresionen más o menos por sí mismas, distrayéndonos más o menos del sentido de las palabras; según que seamos impacientes o dóciles, ante la momentánea abdicación de nuestras reacciones personales que significa este uncirse al pensamiento ajeno, etcétera.

El hombre rudo, que apenas desbroza el alfabeto, tiende a leer para sí en voz alta, como si quisiera aglutinar los signos más cabalmente, sujetando la atención verbal a la vez con los ojos y con los oídos. El que los modernos retóricos llaman verbo motor lee en voz alta por el placer de hablar, y hasta cuando escucha a un orador se le ve, a veces, articular en silencio lo que oye. Conozco lectores que se acompañan con un suave silbidito rítmico, al que van imprimiendo cierta modulación imitativa de la lectura en voz alta. Cuando Heine declamaba el *Quijote* para los árboles y los pájaros, lo hacía más bien como quien rinde un tributo, o por no perder ninguno de los valores de la excelsa prosa. Cuando Sor Juana Inés de la Cruz se queja de no tener más compañeros que el tintero y la pluma para compartir sus estudios, sin duda echaba de menos esa mayor apelación a la retentiva que resulta de la lectura acompañada y que todos los estudiantes prefieren para la preparación de los exámenes. Mestre Profiat Durán, israelita aragonés del siglo XIV, recomendaba a sus discípulos que leyesen siempre recitando. En cambio Théophile Gautier, visual si los hay, juzga que los libros están hechos para ser vistos y no hablados. Por su parte, Flaubert necesitaba berrear su propia prosa para percatarse de lo que escribía.

El hábito de la lectura en parejas ha dejado testimonios ilustres: Paolo y Francesca, Romeo y Julieta, Abelardo y Eloísa. En la novela de Walter Pater, Mario y Flaviano leían así *El asno de oro.* Y si pasamos de la ficción a la historia, los esposos Browning, tema que aparece en la *Lady Geraldine's courtship,* de Elisabeth; los padres de Leigh Hunt, que así acabaron por enamorarse; Ruskin y su madre; Swinburne y Meredith; Rousseau y su padre; Madame de Sévigné y su hijo Carlos.

Shelley, con o sin auditorio, leía en voz alta. Plinio divertía a sus huéspedes con sus lecturas, y Tomás Moro introdujo en Chelsea el hábito monástico de leer durante las comidas. Alfredo el Grande se hacía leer por sus secretarios siempre que se lo permitían los negocios. En la generación del Centenario, practicábamos mucho la lectura en grupo, y en nuestras memorias queda el relato de aquella noche que consagramos al *Symposio.* ¿Hasta qué punto la preferencia de José Vasconcelos para los "libros que leía andando" respondía en él a una equivalencia ambulatoria de la declamación?

Es de creer que en la Antigüedad se leía normalmente en voz alta. Lang observa que el verbo griego para *leer* significa *leer en voz alta.* Todavía San Agustín se asombra de que San Ambrosio leyera para sí: "De leer en voz alta, los que por ventura lo escucharan empezarían a proponerle dudas sobre cualquier pasaje oscuro, obligándole así a explicarlo y a desperdiciar en esto el tiempo de que disponía para leer. O también puede ser que le moviera a ello el cuidado de su voz, que la tenía propensa a quiebras continuas. En fin, cualesquiera fuesen sus razones, buenas habían de ser tratándose de varón tan prudente y sabio" (*Confesiones,* VI, III).

Tras esta evocación venerable, algunas consideraciones menores. El goce de la lectura se define, como todos, por el recuerdo, cómputo definitivo de los bienes acumulados. A esta luz, examinemos las categorías de lectores, entre aficionados y profesionales. Para el profesional sin vocación, la lectura puede llegar a ser una tarea enojosa, como el teatro para el inspector de espectáculos o como para la cortesana las caricias. Erudito conozco que se dispensaba de leer y se recorría todo un libro deslizando sobre las páginas una tarjeta en blanco en busca de las solas mayúsculas; más aún, en busca de la letra A: ¡es que trataba de despojar las citas sobre Ausonio! ¡Habladle a él de la amenidad de la lectura! Aquí, como siempre, el pleno disfrute se lo lleva la vocación. De la cual no excluyo —al contrario— al mero aficionado, este *nuevo rico* del espíritu que suele exprimir muy a fondo los placeres que se le ofrecen. Verdad amarga que el deleite de leer, cuando no hay verdadero amor, disminuye conforme sube la categoría de los lectores. Veamos:

1. Abajo está el sencillo pueblo. La lectura se le vuelve vida. El caballero encontró a la dama y a sus sirvientas llorando porque "hase muerto Amadís"[1]. En horas robadas, el hombre humilde lee con fruición y se queda con la sustancia, con el asunto y con las mejores palabras: nada más. Puesto a la prueba del recuerdo, sólo ha conservado las esencias. El no sabe el nombre del libro ni el nombre del autor, caso típico de la impresión humana que aún no llega a la literatura " ¿Has leído —dice— la historia de un paladín a quien se le moría el caballo todos los martes?" ¿Y hay nada más conmovedor que los campesinos iletrados que rodean en religioso silencio al lector del pueblo? ¿Ni templo más noble de la lectura que aquellos talleres donde un hombre lee para cuarenta, mientras éstos, calladamente, plasman las vitolas del tabaco?

2. Aquí aparece el lector de medio pelo, creación paradójica de la enseñanza primaria, cursada obligatoriamente y de mala gana. Ese ya recuerda los títulos de los libros, y aquí comienza a enturbiarse el gusto. A esta clase pertenecen los que andan por los museos viendo, no los cuadros, sino los letreros de los cuadros, cuya supresión llegué a anhelar[2]. A este lector se le han olvidado las peripecias; conserva los nombres, sustituye la posesión por el signo. Ha leído algo que se llama *Las dos ciudades* o *Las minas del Rey Salomón;* y a lo sumo, en su memoria, marca una cruz para indicar lo que le gustó, y una raya para lo que no logró interesarle.

3. Ahora, el semiculto, el pedante con lecturas, el anfibio, el del *complejo de inferioridad,* el más atroz enemigo del prójimo, el que "pudo haber sido y no fue", el resentido. Ese se acuerda de autores, no de libros. El ha leído "un Ferrero" muy interesante y — ¡claro!— "un Croce" que no lo era tanto. Y que no le hablen a él de Gide donde está Henri Béraud, de Juan Ramón donde está Villaespesa. A veces, el cronista profesional se recluta entre esta laya, mediante un leve proceso de especialización. Veinte repúblicas hermanas descargan todos los días sobre la playa del cuitado sus mareas de tinta fresca. Las torres de libros por reseñar llegan hasta el techo. De repente, entra el aficionado, radiantes los ojos, con

---

[1] Ver A. R., *La vida y la obra,* en *Tres puntos de exegética literaria.*

[2] Carta-prólogo de los *Cartones de Madrid,* en *Las vísperas de España,* Buenos Aires, 1937.

un librito que le entusiasma y que, en su candor, se empeña en prestarle a su amigo el cronista, para que éste también pase un buen rato. Y el cronista lo mira con un rabioso disimulo de eunuco, condenado a pasar la vida entre hembras que no disfruta.

4. Y al último viene el mal bibliófilo, flor de las culturas manidas; el que sólo aprecia ya en los libros el nombre del editor, la fecha de la impresión, la justificación, el colofón, los datos de la tirada, el formato, la pasta y sus hierros, el ex-libris, la clase del papel, la familia de tipos, etc. O acaso sabe el muy pícaro que la edición fue detenida a los tantos ejemplares para corregir una chistosa errata; y entonces hay que desvivirse en busca de un ejemplar con la errata, que es el bueno. Y por cierto que anda por ahí una Biblia donde al impresor se le escapó una mayúscula adornada con una Leda, palpitante entre las alas del cisne. ¿Qué decía la Biblia en aquel pasaje? Eso no lo hemos leído ni nos importa: lo que nos importa es la mayúscula. Al menos, hay que convenir en que esta clase de maniáticos se salva por su encantadora atención para la materia del libro, pues sin el amor de los objetos se cae prontamente en la barbarie. Gide ha confesado que le estorban para estudiar las ediciones hermosas. Y ya vemos en qué paró: se deshizo un día de sus libros, sin que nada pueda persuadirnos a que lo empujaba la necesidad. No: era la aversión a las cosas placenteras, era la horrible "puerta estrecha".

Caso singular el de los apresurados que, con serlo, parecen poseer facultades excepcionales de asimilación. Van sobre el libro a las volandas y, sin embargo, no puede negarse que lo lean a fondo. Así Southey, así Napoleón en Santa Elena. De Macaulay se dijo que absorbía los libros por la piel. La leyenda llegó a creer que Menéndez y Pelayo se quedaba con el contenido de una página en un solo vistazo y hasta pasándole los dedos encima. Sterne se indigna contra estos tragones. Charles Lamb aun quiere una oración de gracias y una gradual preparación de ánimo antes de cada lectura. El Dr. Johnson decía que todo lo había leído apresuradamente en su juventud. Boswell piensa que todo lo rumió después lentamente a lo largo de los años. Y hay otros que, por obligación o por gusto, abren a la vez una novela, un periódico, un tratado de química, un ensayo filosófico, una revista de modas, al tiempo que califican varios ejercicios escolares.

A veces se me ocurre que, sin cierto olvido de la utilidad, los libros no podrían ser apreciados. Disraeli *(Miscelánea)* ha puesto el dedo en el misterio cuando llama al libro de Montaigne "breviario de los ociosos". Ahora bien, entregarse a esta receptividad absoluta, para no ahuyentar a la Eurídice que duerme entre las páginas, es cosa difícil. El libro, como la sensitiva, cierra sus hojas al tacto impertinente. Hay que llegar hasta él sin ser sentido. Ejercicio, casi, de faquir. Hay que acallar previamente en nuestro espíritu todos los ruidos parásitos que traemos desde la calle, los negocios y afanes, y hasta el ansia excesiva de información literaria. Entonces, en el silencio, comienza a escucharse la voz del libro; medrosa acaso, pronta a desaparecer si se la solicita con cualquier apremio sospechoso. Por eso Sir Walter Raleigh pensaba que, en cada época, sólo hay dos o tres lectores verdaderos (*Cartas*, I, 233).

Edgardo Rodríguez Juliá
1946–
Puerto Rico

Puerto Rico y el Caribe: historia de una marginalidad

Revista La Torre, 1989.

E N el 1884 Francisco Oller regresó a Puerto Rico. Nuestro más destacado pintor del Siglo XIX, cuya paleta se formó en Francia junto a la de Cézanne y el también caribeño Camile Pisarro, participando en el desarrollo del impresionismo como uno de sus principales propulsores, daba así un paso irrevocable en su desarrollo como artista plástico. La tenue luz impresionista del cuadro *El estudiante* – pintado en 1877 y que se encuentra en el museo Jeu de Paume— iría quedando atrás, ya para siempre. La luz mortificante del trópico entonces comenzaría a inundar sus cuadros.

Oller, en su *retorno al país natal,* ya nos habla de esa inquietud sobre el espacio propio que caracteriza la obra de Palés Matos, Walcott, Césaire y Naipaul.

Si Fanon nos señaló la realidad del maniqueísmo colonial, los grandes escritores y artistas del Caribe coinciden en hablar-nos de esa *modorra,* o *taedium vitae,* tan característica de estos tristes trópicos, condición colonial en que el alma, la interioridad, está como suspendida, indecisa entre una sociedad chata, a *medio hacer,* esa exterioridad de la vida con un pasado precario y un porvenir incierto, y la nostalgia de una tradición no del todo ajena pero tampoco propia, es decir, la cultura occidental del colono, la cultura asiática del emigrante o peón, la cultura africana del esclavo arrastrado a estas tierras.

Esa marginalidad crea un territorio de ensoñación o conduce al exilio. En el caso de Oller el sutil cromatismo impresionista dio paso, paulatinamente, a un realismo menos ocupado con los delicados cambios de luz sobre las formas que en la formulación pictórica, casi emblemática, de los espacios y concreciones –flora y vivienda, bodegones y paisajes campestres– de la vida señorial fundada en la hacienda y sus memorias.

Los paisajes y bodegones de Oller son una especie de asidero; a través de ellos el artista desarraigado recupera su país de origen. Estos son espacios perfectos y apacibles; sólo se escucha ese silencio yacente de los guineos manzanos junto a los mangós, de los plátanos detrás de las guanábanas, o el rumor de la quebrada bajo la sombra de las palmas reales. Es la promesa de una raza cósmica alimentada con el panapén traído de la lejana Tahití, donde el sol inclemente se ha domeñado con las palmeras de Malasia, donde los trapiches del Père Labat se adormilan bajo las frondas de un *flamboyant* transplantado de Madagascar. La galería y los barandales evocan ese *otear* de la sociedad esclavista, la mirada señorial tendida desde la posesión de vidas, cultivos y haciendas.

En 1893 Oller pinta un enorme lienzo tamaño mural que tituló *El Velorio.* Oller se ha transformado en un costumbrista satírico; la amargura comienza a traspasar su arte.

Cuando el Oller de los serenos espacios señoriales llega a la sátira de *El Velorio* –cuadro que nos describe y narra el velorio de un niño muerto– su amargura no es sólo la de enjuiciar una costumbre que le parece salvaje –celebrar con fiesta y ron la muerte del niño que supuestamente subiría al cielo– sino condenar ese enardecimiento del ánimo tan de los puertorriqueños, condición que advirtió el botánico francés Ledrú cuando nos visitó en el Siglo XVIII. En la descripción de esta obra enviada al Salón de 1895 el artista habla, en un tono condenatorio, de "una orgía de apetitos brutales bajo el velo de una superstición grosera". Este *baquiné* es una escena donde la coincidencia, en un mismo espacio, del peninsular, del negro y jíbaro criollo resulta perturbadora. Según Ledrú la exaltación del criollo surgía del calor, de la *ingestión de alcoholes* —como dice José Luis González en su reciente *Visita al cuarto piso*— y de una inclinación al desenfreno amoroso. Estas tres condiciones aparecen en el lienzo; la atmósfera en el espacio abigarrado del bohío resulta asfixiante, una pareja a la izquierda se abraza frente a un borracho que derrama el contenido de una botella, otro jíbaro bebe la última gota de su botella hacia el centro del cuadro.*

Ledrú señalaba que el elemento más hacendoso y digno de aquella sociedad dieciochesca era el *mulato*. En *El Velorio* la única figura digna es la de un negro pordiosero de Río Piedras llamado San Pablo. Este le sirvió de modelo a Oller para destacar la única posibilidad de recato en todo el lienzo. Resulta interesante cómo vio a esta figura uno de los primeros comentaristas de la misma:

> El espectáculo del festín que le rodea le es de todo punto indiferente; sólo llama su atención aquel niño muerto. El también lloró largo tiempo su hogar perdido allá en las apartadas regiones del Africa, hogar embellecido por su esposa amada y por sus hijos, arrebatados de sus brazos y esclavizados como él, en lejana tierra, por la codicia de los blancos. Y avezado en sus largos años de esclavitud a la contemplación del Infinito y a profundas meditaciones abstractas, de que al cabo logró darse cuenta, no cree, como los fanáticos que le rodean en vergonzosa orgía, que la muerte del niño sea la dicha porque le aguarden las eternas dulzuras de la vida celestial, sino porque considera la muerte como la forma más completa de la libertad, ideal supremo de su vida de esclavo.

Me parece revelador que el comentarista conozca, en la actitud del negro, un desarraigo que sólo acabará con la muerte.

En este lienzo el calor del trópico es una coraza asfixiante que reduce cada personaje a su soledad. Pasamos de la apacible *utopía* señorial que se resume en los bodegones, coincidencia lírica de todos los frutos del orbe, a una *heterotopía* perturbadora donde las distintas *etnias* de nuestro suelo sólo pueden convivir en disonancia. La imagen, como en la novela *La Charca* de Zeno Gandía, es la de un mundo estancado y

---

*La escena delirante recuerda una similar que pinta Derek Walcott en su paso por San Juan. Se encuentra en el poema *Mass Man*, de su poemario *The Gulf*.

sin salida, donde el mestizaje es sólo la piel de distancias insalvables, soledades irredentas.

Estas dos imágenes de la *utopía* y la *heterotopía,* el diálogo íntimo entre ellas, enmarcan las meditaciones que siguen.

* * *

Decía mi maestro Charles Rosario que para nosotros, los puertorriqueños, el término *antillanía* tiene significado pleno, pero no los términos *caribeño* o *caribeñidad.* Uno nos congrega en la experiencia histórica y cultural compartida con las Antillas Mayores, el otro —*the Caribbean*— nos somete a una categoría suprahistórica, a un invento de la objetividad sociológica, antropológica o etnológica de origen anglófono, objetividad que siempre funciona en contra del colonizado, como señaló Fanon.

He aquí una polémica que no pienso bizantina, y a la cual debemos dirigirnos hoy que se habla de *caribeñizar* a Puerto Rico, de la *caribeñización* de la sociedad puertorriqueña.

El pensamiento independentista antillano del Siglo XIX concibió una especie de utopía, o *desiderátum* histórico, que conocemos como Confederación Antillana. Aquel espacio de congregación, sitio de supuestas coincidencias históricas y culturas evidentemente hermanadas por la lengua, se formuló desde un racionalismo progresista que hoy nos parece algo ingenuo: los pueblos que habían sufrido el mismo colonialismo, y también sistemas parecidos de explotación económica, estarían llamados a reunirse bajo una organización política que garantizase su pasado histórico y protegiese su independencia venidera. En el caso de Santo Domingo se trataría de coartar aquella tendencia a la anexión que representó la mala aventura de Buenaventura Báez.

Una vez liquidada esa posibilidad por las vicisitudes históricas que todos conocemos, a Puerto Rico se le presenta hoy otro desiderátum, esa caribeñización que, nuevamente, presupone la coincidencia, en un espacio político, de pueblos hermanados por un pasado de colonialismo europeo y sistemas parecidos de explotación. Y esta propuesta, o este *discurso,* supone ya no una lengua común, o una experiencia histórica derivada del mismo colonialismo español, sino unas coincidencias más abarcadoras, a veces difusas, otras veces aterradoramente concretas.

Ahora bien, ¿qué bases reales existen para la llamada *caribeñización* de Puerto Rico?

La idea de la Confederación Antillana, hoy, vista de cerca, nos resulta ingenua cuando nos adentramos en las diferencias y semejanzas de las Antillas Mayores. Si bien es cierto que Puerto Rico, Santo Domingo y Cuba fueron hermanadas por una potencia europea que les impartió el sello de un colonialismo común, fácilmente podemos advertir las diferencias fundamentales entre la experiencia histórica nuestra y la del resto de las Antillas Mayores.

Ya hacia fines del Siglo XIX Santo Domingo era independiente, Cuba había sufrido una guerra independentista de diez años y Puerto Rico había protagonizado un Grito de Lares que apenas duró dos días. Tanto en Cuba como en Santo Domingo el sistema de explotación económica había sido más cruento: en Cuba la caña y el tabaco habían sido cultivados intensamente, la mano de obra esclava era más numerosa. Santo Domingo tendría que luchar por su independencia contra una potencia vecina –Haití– cuyo fundamento económico se remontaba a una de las explotaciones más intensas de hombres y tierras que ha conocido la historia de la humanidad. En Puerto Rico la explotación que tenía como marco de referencia la hacienda se desarrolló, a una escala menor, junto a modos autárquicos de sobrevivencia y junto al contrabando. Las otras Antillas Mayores forjaron burguesías nacionales independentistas. Puerto Rico, como muy bien ha recalcado José Luis González, nunca desarrolló una burguesía nacional con capacidad para defender eficazmente sus intereses. En Puerto Rico la debilidad del estado como tal, esa situación que tanto alarmó a O'Reilly y al despotismo ilustrado de Carlos III, se debió tanto a nuestra condición de baluarte militar como a la debilidad ancestral de nuestra economía.

Ahora bien, a pesar de todo ello hay unos vínculos evidentes que se remontan a una cultura surgida de la misma situación geográfica y el contacto de lo español con otras culturas: el *ajiaco* cubano, el *sancocho* dominicano y el *guiso* puertorriqueño, que también se llama *sancocho,* surgen de esa suculenta *olla podrida* peninsular que el criollo y el esclavo preparaban según las menudencias de viandas y carnes que proveía una sobrevivencia muchas veces paupérrima. Si el barroco cubano de un Lezama Lima y un Carpentier lograron sus mejores páginas desde una escritura arcaizante, la mejor poesía de nuestro Palés Matos evoca la poesía española de corte renacentista. La *salsa* puertorriqueña no es otra cosa que la música cubana —el son montuno y el guaguancó— pasada por la experiencia puertorriqueña de Nueva York y su contacto con el jazz latino; el trombón de nuestra instrumentación plenera se integra al sonido de las *charangas* y *conjuntos* cubanos. Hoy por hoy el merengue dominicano ha substituido a la *salsa* como el baile favorito de los puertorriqueños. Entonces está la misma lengua española: tres variantes antillanas del Español Atlántico matizado por andaluces y canarios. En nuestros campos los jíbaros más viejos hablan un español arcaico que evoca el castellano del Siglo XVI.

Como podemos ver, estos vínculos, desde la concreción y cotidianidad de una experiencia antillana común, componen una cercanía que las distancias en otros órdenes no pueden borrar.

También podemos concebir un espacio horizontal, cotidiano, donde Puerto Rico se vincularía con el resto del Caribe. Entonces *the Caribbean* deja de ser una acomodaticia categoría de estudiosos anglófonos para convertirse en algo palpable y vital.

El *sancoche* trinitario es el sancocho boricua. Nuestra música de plena —el ritmo característico de la costa— posiblemente se originó con la visita de isleños del Caribe inglés. La *plena* sería entonces una música creada en Ponce por una familia de apellido Clark-George. El *carrucho* que hoy se consume en Puerto Rico hasta una saciedad que pone en peligro la existencia del *queen conch* en nuestras aguas, es el *lambi* haitiano, casi el plato nacional de ese país, servido, como en el nuestro, con tostones y el *mojo* llamado isleño. El *calypso* vuelve a ser furor en Puerto Rico. Nunca desapareció del todo en los bailes de Vieques y Culebra.

Si el espacio arquitectónico es un ingrediente importante de la memoria, Puerto Rico comparte con sitios tan lejanos, en otros órdenes, como Trinidad, algunos rasgos interesantes: la casa campesina puertorriqueña, con su piso o *soberao* levantado sobre la tierra por *zocos,* es una versión sin balcón de la *case* de Trinidad, también levantada sobre el nivel del terreno. La presencia de las galerías, de esos amplios barandales desde los cuales se otean montes combos y apacibles, cocoteros que se mueven según los caprichos de los vientos alisios, son todavía, para los puertorriqueños de mi generación, un fuerte vínculo con el Caribe inglés y francés. El Jacmel que conoció Betances, en uno de sus periplos antillanos, hoy se parece al pequeño pueblo donde me crié en los años cincuenta. Los colores con que se pintan las casas de los campesinos haitianos —esos verdes *chatré* y los azules que llamamos *eléctricos,* combinados con el rojo ladrillo— aún se pueden ver en algunas calles de un barrio proletario sanjuanero como Villa Palmeras. Los *calados* en madera de muchas casas señoriales del oeste de Puerto Rico llegan a su culminación en Haití. El omnipresente zinc a cuatro o dos aguas, el alto plafón sirviéndole de caja de resonancia a esos *aguaceros* que cantó Césaire en *Blues de la Pluie,* son para mí valores perdidos desde la adolescencia, y que sólo podría recuperar convirtiéndome en turista del propio Caribe. Pero la casa volcada hacia la calle, mediante el balcón o la galería, es una experiencia que los puertorriqueños de la generación de mi hijo no pueden tener si no es a través de las omnipresentes *rejas,* ese imperativo de la arquitectura puertorriqueña una vez abandonamos los diseños y designios de Levitt and Sons y nos enfrentamos a la criminalidad rampante que cubre la isla. Estoy seguro que muchos puertorriqueños de la generación más joven no tienen la menor idea de lo que es el *glacis* de una hacienda cafetalera.

Del mismo modo mi generación ya no recuerda los *bohíos* de los campesinos más pobres de la década de los treinta. A veces la falta de techo se resolvía con la construcción de un bohío techado con *matojos* o *yaguas* y levantado con tablas de palma. El piso era de tierra. Lo que aún se puede ver en Haití, mi generación, los hijos del E.L.A. y Muñoz Marín, lo conocemos, sobre todo, a través de las anécdotas y advertencias de nuestros padres. La restauración del Viejo San Juan nos queda como un vínculo con un pasado aún más remoto; pero los espacios del Puerto Rico contemporáneo comienzan a distanciarse, ya irremediablemente, de los del resto del Caribe. Aquella cultura criolla y señorial, de tardes lánguidas que transcurrían según el rechinar de los sillones de caoba, casi ha desaparecido en mi país.

Mi tío abuelo, el novelista Ramón Juliá Marín, se lamentaba hacia el 1912 de cómo la casa solariega de su familia había sido convertida en almacén. Me crié en una de esas casas de amplias galerías; en los *bajos,* la parte a nivel de la calle, se almacenaba el café; a veces mi abuela cedía a la tentación de quebrar la armonía del caserón y alquilaba esos *bajos* para algún negocio. Si le contara esto a mi hijo sería como hablarle de un país remoto. Pienso que pocos jóvenes puertorriqueños saben lo que es una estantería de ausubo; todos saben lo que es M.T.V. y dónde queda Orlando. Nuestros espacios se van pareciendo más a los de esta ciudad en la Florida que a los de Santo Domingo.

Cuando José Luis González habla de caribeñizar a Puerto Rico está hablando de recordarle a Puerto Rico dónde está.

Pero, en verdad, ¿estamos más cerca de Puerto Plata que de Orlando?

Los bodegones de Oller con sus mangós de la India, guanábanas antillanas, guineos africanos y pajuiles, se confunden con las cornucopias que vienen del norte: los puertorriqueños consumimos manzanas, peras, albaricoques, uvas sin semillas de California y melocotones. Algunas veces los *food stamps* nos permiten comprar alguna que otra rodaja de salmón fresco. La mayoría de nuestros adolescentes no podría diferenciar hoy entre un níspero y una batata. Es una generación que jamás ha visto un mosquitero en su vida.

Ya en los años cincuenta los artistas y escritores puertorriqueños satirizaban esa particular alienación que ha sufrido el puertorriqueño respecto de su clima y paisaje. Por aquel entonces algunas mansiones de la nueva burguesía creada por el E.L.A. ostentaban chimeneas.

La memoria de los espacios, la cultura culinaria y la música, esa cotidianidad horizontal, aún nos unía al resto del Caribe, hace treinta y pico de años, con una fuerza evidente. Pero hoy Puerto Rico se aleja cada vez más de sí mismo.

El inventario de nuestra memoria colectiva progresivamente se hace más angosto, ello a pesar de un nacionalismo —y hasta chauvinismo— que se ha ido forjando paradójicamente en la cultura popular, el *media,* y en nuestro contacto con las emigraciones de cubanos y dominicanos a nuestro suelo: el equipo de baloncesto puertorriqueño es un orgullo *nacional;* los cigarrillos Salem se venden con la imagen de un Puerto Rico apacible y lírico que ya no existe. Las parejas *yuppies,* que descubren en sus *jeeps* Suzuki las bellezas de un Puerto Rico cada vez más remoto, también fuman Winston. El Ron Don Q se vendió hace unos años con imágenes sacadas de una vida señorial de ensoñación, donde el mundo de la hacienda, aquella *aristocracia de dril* que mencionaba Palés, aparece embellecida por la nostalgia. La bandera puertorriqueña —proscrita durante los años treinta por su identificación con el nacionalismo de Albizu Campos— aparece por todos lados, lo mismo en las envolturas del queso blanco que en las gorras usadas por el proletariado en los conciertos playeros de salsa. Pero recientemente se fue a la quiebra la cerveza Corona, una de las últimas cervezas puertorriqueñas. Los puertorriqueños, de todas las clases, preferimos fatalmente la Heineken y la Schaefer.

¿Qué quiere decir caribeñizarnos? Aquel Caribe horizontal, el cotidiano, el que nos unía, en muchas instancias se remontaba a modos de producción felizmente superados. ¿Es que no estamos hablando también de una cotidianidad que tuvo por marco la vida de la gran y pequeña burguesía rural patricia, el mundo de la hacienda y la esclavitud, del peonaje en el infierno del cañaveral o el cafetal? ¿No es la añoranza de aquel pasado una forma sinuosa de esa vocación reaccionaria que padecen muchos intelectuales y artistas de países en desarrollo?

Alguien me dirá que es precisamente nuestra alienación lo que nos obliga a plantear el Caribe como consigna. Pero entonces, ¿no se va pareciendo nuestra disyuntiva a la de la intelectualidad española a partir del 1898? Para ellos —desde su marginalidad— la consigna era españolizar a Europa o europeizar a España. Hacia los años sesenta esa disyuntiva se le plantearía a Juan Goytisolo con una urgencia progresivamente contradictoria: deseaba que España saliera del estancamiento medieval del franquismo; reconocía, a la vez, que los éxitos de éste en el plano social y económico —la modernización de España— habían transformado, ya sin remedio, modos de vida ancestrales que él apreciaba.

Tendríamos que formular nuestra pregunta: ¿hay que *caribeñizar* a Puerto Rico o hay que *puertorriqueñizar* el Caribe?

Como hemos visto, la primera consigna tiene un marco socioeconómico y cultural ya apenas compartido. La segunda contiene unas interrogantes perturbadoras, porque *puertorriqueñizar* al Caribe, ¿no se refiere ello a una especie muy particular de alienación cultural y política?

Al intentar una respuesta honesta para esta pregunta vuelven a surgir distancias insalvables. Nos habíamos olvidado de que el Caribe es simultáneamente un espacio de congregación y una *heterotopía,* sitio donde culturas y razas han coincidido en una yuxtaposición precaria. ¿Somos las islas donde se han congregado memorias de un pasado que no fue del todo nuestro? De frente a futuros inciertos, Walcott nos habla de una particular amnesia que sufre el exilado caribeño:

some deep, amnesiac blow. We left
somewhere a life we never found.

Compartimos un espacio; pero ¿compartimos un proyecto histórico? Se nos impone entonces la imagen de una Babel donde los isleños no nos comunicamos fácilmente, ni desde nuestro pasado ni desde nuestro porvenir. Las diferencias lingüísticas, la asincronía de los desarrollos económicos, las diferencias reales entre el colonialismo inglés, el español, el francés y el norteamericano, ahora se evidencian de manera notable.

Puerto Rico es devuelto nuevamente a su marginalidad: es en nuestra historia donde se tocan la *antillanía* y la *caribeñidad*. Las Antillas Mayores y las Menores cobran en Puerto Rico una imagen desfigurada de sus propios pasados y posibilidades. Nuestra marginalidad respecto de las Antillas Mayores nos colocó en el sendero del *American way of life*. ¿Es nuestro actual modo de vida alucinante lo que hoy nos coloca en el sendero del *otro* Caribe? Cuando nuestro gobierno habla de plantas gemelas y cooperación económica, de Puerto Rico como la punta de lanza de la política económica estadounidense para el Caribe, no dejo de estremecerme de suspicacia. ¿Estamos hermanados nuevamente, con el resto de ese Caribe alterno a la *antillanía,* en la condición de padecer la historia pero no protagonizarla?

¿Puede ser el desarrollo de Puerto Rico modelo para alguien? ¿Será posible que nuestra dependencia política y económica, nuestra violencia social se conviertan en proyectos para un Caribe alterno? ¿Qué diálogo se puede establecer entre países en vías de desarrollo y un país cuyo progreso se ha hipertrofiado, transformándose en un furor consumista que posterga la producción?

Se puede señalar que mis temores apenas tienen fundamento; la caribeñización es, en realidad, un proceso que ya empezó: entonces se me hablaría de la presencia de los cubanos en Puerto Rico por dos décadas, de los desembarcos de dominicanos pobres a las costas de Rincón y Aguada. Los cubanos que llegaron a Puerto Rico con el advenimiento de la Revolución Cubana, casi todos de clase media, son hermanados con los dominicanos pobres que cruzan el Canal de la Mona para insertarse en una economía de abundancia para todos y despilfarro para muchos.

Es un secreto a voces que las relaciones entre nosotros los puertorriqueños y los cubanos exilados no han sido del todo serenas. El hecho es que veinticinco años después de haber comenzado a llegar aún no se arriesgan a postularse para ningún puesto público. Usan la política nuestra para cultivar su anticomunismo y son usados por los partidos políticos nuestros como contribuyentes. Pero no son invitados a participar como iguales. Es posible que no se atrevan. Muchos cubanos, luego del tercer trago, se quejan de un sutil prejuicio contra ellos.

Los dominicanos casi siempre son tratados con gran condescendencia; los chistes sobre su competencia e inteligencia resultan ofensivos, ello a pesar de que los hijos de estos emigrantes pobres —salidos de campos donde aún no hay un televisor en cada sala— superan a los nuestros —acostumbrados al tránsito *uptown-downtown* de Nueva York a San Juan— en las pruebas de aprovechamiento académico administradas por el sistema escolar neuyorkino.

Pero ¿cuál es la Tierra Prometida de los dominicanos que llegan a Puerto Rico? ¿Es San Juan o Nueva York? Nos mofamos de la ropa chillona que usan cuando tratan de abordar aviones con destino al norte. Es la misma ropa que usamos hace treinta años cuando nos *embarcábamos* para los niuyores: los mismos pantalones color vino, las mismas combinaciones extrañas a la sobriedad anglosajona, los mismos zapatos de charol blanco. Y ahora, como bien ha señalado Juan Manuel García Passalacqua, se nos impondrá diferenciarnos de ellos en Nueva York cuando, en realidad, allá somos la misma gente pobre y marginada. Ya pronto viajaremos con pasaportes americanos de ciudadanía, porque *we all look Spanish...*

Hace unos años, cuando Luis Ferré era gobernador de Puerto Rico, Félix Benítez Rexach lo visitó en La Fortaleza para pedirle que proclamase desde la gobernación la independencia de Puerto Rico. Don Félix, el millonario nacionalista amigo de Trujillo y Albizu Campos, ingeniero visionario a quien Santo Domingo le debe el trazado de la Avenida Jorge Washington y algunas casas en forma de barco que enternecen por su mal gusto, llegó a La Fortaleza en un vistoso Rolls Royce y vestido de blanco. El millonario criollo, o *criollazo* en este caso, se reuniría con el gobernador millonario de estilo calvinista y sobrio, asimilista y educado en M.I.T. Uno era gobernador de Puerto Rico, el otro era un empresario que ya sólo vivía de nostalgias, evocando los años dorados en que se casó con una cantante francesa y anclaba su yate junto al de Onassis. Don Félix, en lo que parecía un sainete sólo concebible por Valle-Inclán, le pidió a Ferré que declarara la República de Puerto Rico por ser nosotros un pueblo superior, el más desarrollado del Caribe; fácil se nos haría poner bajo nuestra tutela a ese otro Caribe pobre e ignorante. No pudo imaginar mejor símbolo de nuestra marginalidad y presunción: la independencia que aún no acababa de llegar nos serviría para establecer nuestra hegemonía caribeña. En Don Félix ya habitaba el espíritu de la caribeñización.

Pero en tantos equívocos y equivocaciones deberá existir algún tipo de diálogo caribeño, alguna comunidad profunda.

Regresemos a las poderosas imágenes del arte popular y culto del Caribe para comenzar ese diálogo.

Cuando me criaba en el Puerto Rico de los años cincuenta aún se oía mucho la frase *en el tiempo de los españoles.* Siempre me estuvo curiosa aquella frase que un poco secuestraba nuestro pasado, colocándolo fuera de nosotros, otorgándole al colonialismo español la capacidad de poseer parte de *nuestro* tiempo. El rescate del pasado por el colonizado siempre tiene esa connotación de lucha con *el otro* que le ha robado parte de su tiempo. Nuestros pasados son nuestros sólo a medias, en el caso de Puerto Rico el presente también es nuestro sólo a medias. La *recuperación del país natal* es entonces esa inmersión en algo irreductible, algo nuestro y sin regateos, ese *cadastre,* la parcela que podemos reclamar como propia sin disputas miserables. Lo *criollo* es una definición de esa parcela irreductible donde habita nuestra identidad. Pero lo criollo es algo más que la memoria de la cotidianidad creada por el colonialismo, o el inventario de unos modos de apropiación que empiezan en la cultura alimenticia y culminan en la plástica, en la literatura y la música.

* * *

La experiencia alterna de Puerto Rico, su marginalidad doble respecto del Caribe, nos coloca en una soledad que pienso, por otra parte, característica de toda la región:

Hace poco leí una crónica de Naipaul sobre su viaje iniciático, siendo un joven, a la Inglaterra distante. En esa crónica nos narra que se detuvo por unas horas en el aeropuerto de San Juan. Me provocó curiosidad leer la descripción que haría del antiguo aeropuerto de Isla Grande, lugar donde yo iba, siendo un niño, a despedir a mi padre cuando éste viajaba a los Estados Unidos como funcionario del gobierno federal. Pero la descripción que hace Naipaul del aeropuerto es muy escueta; apenas nos sitúa en aquel espacio; no hay retrato de la gente.

Me pareció curioso que el joven escritor sólo se interesara en un trinitario negro que viajaba con él, por lo visto siguiendo la misma ruta. A pesar de la inteligencia con que nos narra aquel encuentro con su propia sombra, la narración no deja de tener un sabor claustrofílico, solipsista; el viajero carga con su propia soledad, con su inevitable neurastenia isleña, y apenas puede ver más allá de su melancolía. Puerto Rico, el aeropuerto de San Juan, es entonces sólo un punto geográfico, un lugar de referencia para la memoria ensimismada.

A través de la pluma de Naipaul el aeropuerto de Isla Grande se convierte en un lugar desolado. En cambio, yo recuerdo ese aeropuerto de una manera completamente distinta: como apenas era un hangar, el bullicio resultaba ensordecedor; aquel nervioso ir y venir de jíbaros asustados por el viaje a los niuyores, las bolsas de papel de estraza con productos criollos llevados para la *parentela,* el ambiente de plaza de mercado, componen una de las imágenes imborrables de mi infancia. Por aquel aeropuerto pasaba no sólo el viaje iniciático del trinitario, sino también una de las emigraciones más importantes que ha conocido el siglo.

Quizás Naipaul, empezando un viaje en dirección contraria a la de Oller, sólo buscaba esa imaginación subjetiva que la colonia asfixia. Oller regresó a pintar bodegones, Naipaul viajaba a encontrar su alma. De todos modos, ahí está la soledad de ambos.

Ese ensimismamiento tan isleño recorre la obra de nuestro Palés Matos. Cuando le canta a las Antillas Mayores y Menores lo hace usando epítetos, caracterizaciones hechos con poca o ninguna profundidad. Sabemos que nuestro escritor caribeño por excelencia jamás viajó por el Caribe. Una vez imaginado el Caribe, éste sería invocado como presencia casi por arte de magia poética. En la poesía antillana de Palés hay muchos nombres de islas y pocas concreciones isleñas. En él la imaginación también se vuelve solipsista, reduciendo a epíteto, o punto geográfico, toda una complejidad humana. Palés, quien permaneció varado en su isla ardiente durante casi toda su vida, también soñaba con las regiones árticas del Wallhala. Me pregunto si esas lejanas regiones estaban equidistantes, en su imaginación, de Haití o Santo Domingo. Tales ensoñaciones son la fuga de su imaginación cuando rechaza esa vida chata, mediocre, sin interioridad, que nos describe con tanta precisión en la crónica de su infancia en Guayama, un amodorrado pueblo del sur de la isla situado en el caluroso *Litoral* de las *tierras estériles y madrastras.*

Este solipsismo también lo encontramos en el cubano Lezama Lima. Las pocas veces que menciona a Puerto Rico en sus novelas nuestra isla es únicamente un sitio, un punto geográfico ciego y mudo respecto de connotaciones vitales. Pero lo mismo le ocurre cuando menciona a París. Sus viajes novelísticos fueron como los de la novela bizantina, es decir, descabelladas apropiaciones de sitios separados por distancias enormes. A Lezama le bastaron los paseos por La Habana para construir uno de los edificios más fantásticos de la literatura antillana. El único viaje que hizo fuera de Cuba fue a Jamaica. Pero su poema "Para llegar a Montego Bay", es un viaje inmóvil a su propia poesía. Montego Bay es sólo un lugar de ensoñación.

En estos tres escritores del Caribe advertimos el mismo ensimismamiento. Llevan a su isla particular, en sus viajes reales o imaginarios, como el Ulises de Cavafis cargaba su Itaca sin haberla abandonado nunca. Walcott lo expresa así en su poema *Miramar:*

> *There is nowhere to go.*
> *You'd better go*

Esta soledad, la ausencia de imaginación que la circunda, esa *chatedad* que a veces desemboca en fantasías descabelladas, la ha recogido Rafael Ferrer en sus recientes pinturas de Las Terrenas: el juego de dominó bajo las palmeras, los músicos del *dancing hall* en el barrio pobre playero, todo ese paisaje y paisanaje que Ferrer ha ido a buscar a Santo Domingo, recuperación de su propio espacio y tiempo puertorriqueños, se caracteriza por la misma modorra que Palés consideraba lenta agonía del espíritu. La búsqueda de su pasado puertorriqueño es el encuentro con la memoria de una circunstancia vital que aprisiona, que no ofrece salida.

Solemos encandilarnos fuera de esa mediocridad con *musarañas,* fantasías a veces cómicas, como la visita de Benítez Rexach a La Fortaleza, como los títulos nobiliarios de Christophe en su Versalles de Sans Souci, como las expectativas de los niños negros y mulatos de Trinidad cuando sueñan con distinguirse en el mundo ancho y ajeno de la diplomacia, según ha reseñado Naipaul.

Otra variante de esta soledad también aparece en la pintura de Ferrer. Me refiero ahora a ese lento acercamiento del lugareño, del *native,* a la presencia del gringo, del extranjero, del turista. Sentí esto en carne propia, por vez primera, cuando viajé por tierras tan opuestas como las Islas Vírgenes norteamericanas y Haití. La mirada con que se recibe al extranjero es una mezcla de hostilidad, orgullo y curiosidad. La memoria del colonialismo servil, mezclada con ese lento rescate de la propia humanidad alienada en la esclavitud, hace de nuestros países el lugar donde la mirada es siempre una complicada transacción de valía. En muchos cuadros de Rafael Ferrer surge una distancia insalvable entre el sujeto pintado y el pintor. Esa distancia que media es la distancia entre el colono y el colonizado, entre el extranjero que puede venir y yo que no puedo salir.

En su poema "Homecoming" Walcott expresa así esta distancia:

pelting up from the shallows
because your clothes,
your posture
seem a tourist's
They swarm like flies
round your heart's sore

Más adelante la amargura es la de un desarraigo inescapable:

but never guessed you'd come
to know there are homecoming without home

Entonces llegamos al último espacio irreductible de nuestra experiencia caribeña. Me refiero al exilio y la emigración. El recuerdo y las noticias de los que sí han podido salir pesan sobre nosotros con una fuerza a veces obsesiva.

Una de las imágenes más perdurables del libro de James sobre Haití es su comentario en torno a cómo los colonos franceses odiaban el sitio donde perfeccionaban su explotación inmisericorde. Las memorias y crónicas de los hacendados franceses están llenas de testimonios sobre el tedio, y el deseo de hacer fortuna para regresarse pronto a Francia. Esta imagen recurrente es la de un Caribe caluroso y azaroso, el infierno de la explotación sobre la faz de la tierra. Y me pregunto si esa visión es sólo del colono.

Cuando advertimos que de nuestras tierras han emigrado los tataranietos de esclavos traídos de Africa, o los nietos y biznietos de emigrantes llegados aquí en diversas épocas, nos preguntamos si el Caribe no es ese sitio donde el no poder salir es sólo la forma más extrema de no haber llegado nunca.

Y nos ocurre a nosotros los puertorriqueños, los primeros en lanzarnos a una emigración masiva, que no bien comenzamos a deshacer la maleta en tierras del norte ya estamos añorando la *islita*. Así permanecemos siempre a mitad de camino. Nunca deshacemos las maletas del todo; he aquí una de las razones para nuestra pobre integración al mundo norteamericano. ¿Es ésta, o será, la condición de otros pueblos caribeños que también han emigrado masivamente?

En las salas de los campesinos, allá por los años cincuenta, se colgaban los retratos, las tarjetas postales y recordatorios de los que habían emigrado. Junto a los objetos más precia-

dos de aquella pobreza, como los almanaques con el Sagrado
Corazón de Jesús y las hornacinas con los santos de yeso y
madera, se destacaban los retratos de emigrantes orgullosos
de sus *coats* bajo la primera nevada que habían visto en su vida. Los que se fueron, los que lograron salir a semejante extrañeza, cobraban el valor de íconos. En esa devoción hacia la
parentela que *brincó el charco* —como se dice en Puerto Rico—
quizás exista la convicción de que ellos, los que se fueron,
siempre fueron los mejores, los más valientes: el recuerdo de
ellos es también la memoria de la patria como una condena.

En aquel entonces los puertorriqueños sufrían el destino
de muchas veces nacer, vivir y morir en el mismo barrio o
pueblo. Hoy el puertorriqueño es uno de los pueblos más desarraigados sobre la faz de la tierra. Apenas empezamos a va-
lorar cómo nos han transformado estas vivencias del exilio, de
la emigración y la nostalgia.

En este aspecto, la historia del Caribe cada vez que se parece más a la nuestra. En las salas pobres de nuestros países
serán más frecuentes esas devociones a los que se atrevieron a
saltar fuera del ciclo de la necesidad y la desesperanza. ¿Caribeñizar a Puerto Rico o puertorriqueñizar el Caribe? Me temo que es lo segundo. Miro con preocupación un proceso que
en nuestro país ha creado una fisura hiriente, destructiva. Me
gustaría pensar que estamos alcanzando una idea más serena
de nuestra identidad, una visión menos alienada de nuestra
propia condición histórica; pero me temo que es todo lo contrario, que el Caribe nos alcanza en el tránsito por derroteros
que sólo pueden conducir a un mayor distanciamiento de
nosotros mismos.

En su *Historia del Caribe* nos decía Erïc Williams que el
destino, la suerte de Puerto Rico como parte de los Estados
Unidos ya estaba echada. No estoy muy seguro de esto, a pesar de que la sociedad creada durante los últimos cuarenta
años, las bases materiales de la misma, nos obligaría a pensar
que sí.

De todos modos, lo que más nos debe asustar es nuestra
incapacidad para crear sociedades más justas y a la vez más libres, sitios donde la patria no sea ese lugar donde abandonamos toda esperanza, y deseamos cualquier salida.

* * *

A manera de epílogo, o epitafio, retomo el destino caribeño de Oller, su *retorno al país natal:* comenzaría con la in-

vasión norteamericana la última etapa de su arte, época en que no pudo abstenerse de pintar los retratos de los gobernadores Davis y Hunt. También pintó —a manera de *tokens* para los nuevos tiempos— los retratos de Washington y Mckinley.

Terminó sus días tratando que Mr. Miller, Comisionado de Educación, le consiguiera una pensión vitalicia a través de la legislatura colonial. Esa legislatura, formada por sus propios compatriotas puertorriqueños, denegó tal petición.

Ernesto Sábato
1911—
Argentina

Sentido común
Uno y el universo, 1945.

EL mundo de la experiencia doméstica es tan reducido frente al universo, los datos de los sentidos son tan engañosos, los reflejos condicionados son tan poco proféticos, que el mejor método para averiguar nuevas verdades es asegurar lo contrario de lo que aconseja el sentido común. Esta es la razón por la que muchos avances en el pensamiento humano han sido hechos por individuos al borde de la locura (al menos de lo que el hombre medio de cada época juzga locura). Mediante una lógica estricta Parménides llega a probar que el mundo debe ser una cosa inmóvil, eterna e indivisible; si alguien viene y le hace observar que el mundo, por el contrario, está compuesto por infinidad de cosas y que esas cosas no están en reposo sino que se mueven, y que no son eternas, pues se desgastan o rompen o mueren, el filósofo dirá:

—Tiene usted razón. Eso prueba que el mundo tal como lo vemos es una pura ilusión.

Dudo de que un griego medio no calificase a Parménides de loco, después de esta conclusión. También parece locura afirmar, como Zenón de Elea, que la flecha no se mueve, o que la tortuga no será jamás alcanzada por Aquiles; o, como Hume, que el yo no existe; o, como Berkeley, que el universo entero es una fantasmagoría. Sin embargo, son teorías *lógicamente* irrebatibles y señalan una posibilidad. El hecho de que contradigan brutalmente al sentido común no es una prueba de que sean incorrectas. Como dice Russell, "la verdad acerca de los objetos físicos *debe* ser extraña. Pudiera ser inasequible, pero si algún filósofo cree haberla alcanzado, el hecho de que lo que ofrece como verdad seá algo raro, no puede proporcionar una base sólida para objetar su opinión".

Creo que un tribunal que actuase en nombre del Sentido Común, condenaría al manicomio a Zenón, Parménides, Berkeley, Hume, Einstein.

Es digno de admiración, sin embargo, que el sentido común siga teniendo tanto prestigio didáctico y civil a pesar de todas las calamidades que ha recomendado: la planitud de la Tierra, el geocentrismo, el realismo ingenuo, la locura de Pasteur. Si el sentido común hubiese prevalecido, no tendríamos radiotelefonía, ni sueros, ni espacio-tiempo, ni Dostoievsky. Tampoco se habría descubierto América y este comentario, como consecuencia, no se habría publicado (hecho que, desde luego, no pretendo poner a la par del no-descubrimiento de América).

El sentido común ha sido el gran enemigo de la ciencia y de la filosofía, y lo es constantemente. Argumentar la inverosimilitud en contra de ciertas ideas es muestra de una enternecedora candidez. Les pasa a esta gente lo que a aquellos campesinos de Mark Twain que asistían a una función de circo: cuando vieron las jirafas se levantaron y exigieron la devolución del dinero, pues se creyeron víctimas de una estafa.

El Hombre Medio se jacta de cierto género de astucia, que consiste en descreer de lo fantástico. Sin embargo, hablando en términos generales, se puede afirmar que vivimos en un mundo enteramente fantástico. Este hecho evidente es oscurecido por su evidencia, como dice Montaigne de "ce qu'on dict des voysins des cataractes du Nil", que no oyen el ruido.

El sentido común es el rechazo de fantasmas desconocidos pero es la creencia en fantasmas familiares: rechaza los cinocéfalos y monóculos, como si fuese menos monstruosa la existencia de personas sin su correspondiente cabeza de perro, o con dos ojos en vez de uno. Es en parte cierto que el sentido común es enemigo del milagro, pero del milagro inusitado, si se permite.

Es el sentido de la comunidad apto para una confortable

existencia dentro de límites modestos, de espacio y tiempo: en Laponia recomienda ofrecer la mujer al caminante y aquí asesinarlo si la toma. Un galeote se admiraría de la pretensión de curar un dolor de muelas con una aspirina, siendo sabido que se cura aplicando una rana en la mejilla; por un mecanismo similar, el médico se asombraría de que alguien pretenda curar el dolor de muelas con una rana. La diferencia estriba (según el médico) en que la idea del galeote es una superstición y la de él no. No veo una diferencia esencial: ignoramos aún si la piel de rana tiene algún principio activo que pueda curar el dolor de muelas, y no es cierto que una aspirina lo cure. Al final de cuentas, buena parte de la terapéutica contemporánea consiste en supersticiones que han recibido nombre griego. Y en rigor poca gente hay tan supersticiosa como los médicos: cuando cunde alguna nueva superstición, como la extirpación de las amígdalas, llegan a pensar que *cualquier enfermedad* puede ser curada mediante ese extraño procedimiento, no sólo los dolores de muela. En general, puede decirse que el rechazo enérgico de una superstición solamente puede ser hecho por gente supersticiosa, pues son los únicos que creen firmemente en algo: los verdaderos hombres de ciencia son demasiado cautelosos para rechazar definitivamente nada.

Que el sentido común es la magia y la fantasía más desatada, es fácil de probar: mediante ese diabólico consejero un campesino jura que la tierra es plana y que el Sol es un disco de veinte centímetros de diámetro. En su furia mágica, puede llegar a abolir grandes sectores de la realidad, no sólo a deformarlos.

Es probable que muchos de los problemas actuales de la filosofía y de la ciencia tengan solución cuando el hombre se decida de una vez a prescindir del sentido común. Apenas salimos de nuestro pequeño universo cotidiano, lo seguro es que dejan de valer nuestras ideas y prejuicios. Esta es la causa de que el absurdo nos acometa por todos lados. Más, todavía: es deseable que sea así, pues es garantía de que se anda por buen camino. Si un astrónomo presenta una teoría del Universo que sea aceptable para el hombre de la calle, seguramente que está equivocado. Si otro afirma que en ciertas regiones remotas el tiempo se paraliza, ese señor debe ser escuchado con respeto, pues puede tener razón.

Las teorías científicas y filosóficas están todavía demasiado adheridas al sistema conceptual de entrecasa. *Su defecto, tal vez, es el de ser aún poco descabelladas.*

Miguel de Unamuno
1864—1936
España

La ideocracia

El caballero de la triste figura, 1944.

A Ramiro de Maeztu.

DE las tiranías todas, la más odiosa me es, amigo Maeztu, la de las ideas; no hay *cracia* que aborrezca más que la ideocracia, que trae consigo, cual obligada secuela, la ideofobia, la persecución, en nombre de unas ideas, de otras tan ideas, es decir, tan respetables o tan irrespetables como aquéllas. Aborrezco toda etiqueta; pero si alguna me habría de ser más llevadera es la de *ideoclasta,* rompeideas. ¿Qué cómo quiero romperlas? Como las botas, haciéndolas mías y usándolas.

El perseguir la emisión de esas ideas a que se llama subversivas o disolventes, prodúceme el mismo efecto que me produciría el que, en previsión del estallido de una caldera de vapor, se ordenase romper el manómetro en vez de abrir la válvula de escape.

Al afirmar con profundo realismo Hegel que es todo idea, redujo a su verdadera proporción a las llamadas por antonomasia ideas, así como al comprender que es milagroso todo cuanto nos sucede, se nos muestran, a su más clara luz, los en especial llamados milagros.

Idea es forma, semejanza, *species...* ¿Pero forma de qué? He aquí el misterio: la realidad de que es forma, la materia de que es figura, su contenido vivo. Sobre este misterio giró todo el combate intelectual de la Edad Media; sobre él sigue girando hoy. La batalla entre individualistas y socialistas es, en el fondo lógico, la misma que entre nominalistas y realistas. Esto en el fondo lógico; pero ¿y en el vital? Porque es la forma especial de vida de cada uno lo que le lleva a la mente tales o cuales doctrinas.

¿Qué las ideas rigen al mundo? Apenas creo en más idea propulsora del progreso que en la idea-hombre, porque también es *idea,* esto es, apariencia y forma cada hombre; pero idea viva, encarnada; apariencia que goza y vive y sufre, y que, por fin, se desvanece con la muerte. Yo, en cuanto hombre, soy idea más profunda que cuantas en mi cerebro alojo, y si lograse darles mi tonalidad propia, eso saldrían ganando de su paso por mi espíritu. Es dinero que acuño y que al acuñarlo, le presto mi crédito, poco o mucho, positivo o negativo.

Las ideas, como el dinero, no son, en efecto, en última instancia, más que representación de riqueza e instrumento de cambio, hasta que, luego que nos hayan dado común denominador lógico, cambiemos directamente nuestros estados de conciencia. Ni el cuerpo come dinero ni se nutre el alma de meras apariencias. Y cuando en vez de ideas en oro, de moneda real, de la que cuesta extraer de la mina y a este costo debe su firme valor representativo; cuando en vez de conocimientos de *hechos* concretos y vivos, circula papel-idea —según la sagaz metáfora schopenhaueriana—, apariencia de apariencias, moneda nominal, conceptos abstractos y educidos, que suponen responder a hechos contantes y sonantes, entonces la firma adquiere una importancia enorme, porque el crédito de que tal firma en el mercado goce, es lo que garantiza el valor del papel-idea, o de la idea de papel. Nos importa poco quién nos llamó la atención sobre un *hecho,* como no nos importa qué obrero sacó de la mina la onza de oro de que nos valemos; pero en cuanto al autor de un concepto abstracto es de entidad, como lo es la firma del Banco en los billetes, porque lo aceptamos según el crédito de que aquel goce de guardar en caja conocimientos concretos y de hecho con que responder a sus emisiones de conceptos.

Y van luego las pobres *letras ideales,* el papel-idea, endosadas de unos en otros, poniendo cada sabio su firma al respaldo de ellas. Y aquí cabe preguntar: ¿da el sabio crédito a la letra o se lo da a él ésta?

Vivir todas las ideas para con ellas enriquecerme yo en cuanto idea, es a lo que aspiro. Luego que les saco el jugo, arrojo de la boca la pulpa; las estrujo, ¡y fuera con ellas! Quiero ser su dueño, no su esclavo. Porque esclavos les son esos hombres de arraigadas convicciones, sin sentido del matiz ni del nimbo que envuelve y auna a los contrarios; esclavos les son todos los sectarios, los ideócratas todos.

Necesario, o más bien inevitable, es tener ideas, sí, como ojos y manos, mas para conseguirlo, hay que no ser tenido de ellas. No es rico el poseído por el dinero, sino quien lo posee.

El que calienta las ideas en el foco de su corazón es quien de veras se las hace propias; allí, en ese sagrado fogón, las quema y consume, como combustible. Son vehículo, no más que vehículo de espíritu; son átomos que sólo por el movimiento y ritmo que transmiten sirven, átomos impenetrables, como los hipotéticos de la materia que por su movimiento nos dan calor. Con los mismos componentes químicos se hace veneno y triaca. Y el veneno mismo, ¿está en el agente o en el paciente? Lo que a uno mata a otro vivifica. La maldad, ¿está en el juez o en el reo? Sólo la tolerancia puede apagar en amor la maldad humana, y la tolerancia sólo brota potente sobre el derrumbamiento de la ideocracia.

Entre todos los derechos íntimos que tenemos que conquistar, no tanto de las leyes cuanto de las costumbres, no es el menos precioso el inalienable derecho a contradecirme, a ser cada día nuevo, sin dejar por ello de ser el mismo siempre, a afirmar mis distintos aspectos trabajando para que mi vida los integre. Suelo encontrar más compactos, más iguales y más coherentes en su complejidad a los escritores paradójicos y contradictorios que a los que se pasan la vida haciendo de inconmovibles apóstoles de una sola doctrina, esclavos de una idea. Celébrase la consecuencia de éstos, como si no cupiese ser consecuente en la versatilidad, y no fuera ésta la manifestación de una fecundísima virtud del espíritu. Dejemos que los ideócratas rindan culto a esos estilistas, ¡pobrecitos! encaramados en su columna doctrinal. ¿Por qué he de ser pedrusco sujeto a tierra, y no nube que se bañe en aire y luz?

¡Libertad! ¡Libertad! Y donde la ideocracia impere, jamás habrá verdadera libertad, sino libertad ante la ley, que es la idea entronizada, la misma para todos, la facultad lógica de poder hacer o no hacer algo.

Habrá libertad jurídica, *posibilidad* de obrar sin trabas en ciertos lindes; pero no la otra, la que subsiste aún bajo la esclavitud aparente, la que hace que no le vuelvan a uno el corazón y aun las espaldas porque piense de este o del otro modo.

"¿Qué ideas profesas?" No, qué ideas profesas, no sino: ¿cómo eres?, ¿cómo vives? El modo como uno vive da verdad a sus ideas, y no éstas a su vida. ¡Desgraciado del que necesite ideas para fundamentar su vida!

No son nuestras doctrinas el origen y fuente de nuestra conducta, sino la explicación que de ésta nos damos a nosotros mismos y damos a los demás, porque nos persigue el ansia de explicarnos la realidad. No fueron las ideas que predicaba las que llevaron a Ravachol a su crimen, sino que fueron la forma en que lo justificó a su propia conciencia, como hubiera podido justificarlo con otras, de encontrarlas tan vivas. Hay quien en nombre de caridad cristiana mata, quien para salvar al prójimo le llevó al quemadero. Cualquier idea sirve al fanático, y en nombre de todas se han cometido crímenes.

No es divinamente humano sacrificarse en aras de las ideas,

sino que lo es sacrificarlas a nosotros, porque el que discurre vale más que lo discurrido y soy yo, viva apariencia, superior a mis ideas, apariencias de apariencia, sombras de sombra.

Interésanme más las personas que sus doctrinas y éstas tan sólo en cuanto me revelan a aquéllas. Las ideas las tomo y aprovecho lo mismo que aprovecho tomándolo el dinero que a ganar me den; pero, si por desgracia o por fortuna me viese obligado a pordiosear, creo que besaría la mano que me diese limosna antes que el perro chico de la dádiva.

Hay una sutil pesadumbre que no pocos autores sufren ante ciertos elogios que se les dirige. Cuando un escritor, en efecto, de los que toman como deben las ideas e imágenes, cual de instrumentos con que verter su propio espíritu, ansiosos de darse y derramarse, contribuyendo así a la espiritualización del ámbito social, ve luego que le elogian aquellas obras de compromiso en que sólo puso su mente aquellas en que ofició de mercader de ideas; suele su suspicacia, enfermiza acaso, hacerle leer al través de esos elogios una tácita y tal vez inconsciente censura, a aquellos otros frutos de su espíritu, henchidos del más íntimo jugo que le vivifique. Entristece oír que nos celebren lo menos nuestro, tomándonos así de arca de conocimientos y no de espíritus vivos, como apena que delante de nuestros hijos naturales, de las flores de nuestro espíritu todo, nos alaben a los adoptivos, a las meras excreciones de la mente. Hay elogios que desalientan. Por mi parte, cuando amigos oficiosos me aconsejan que *haga* lingüística y concrete mi labor, es cuando con mayor ahínco me pongo a repasar mis pobres poesías, a verter en ellas mi preciosa libertad, la dulce inconcreción de mi espíritu, entonces es cuando con mayor deleite me baño en nubes de misterio.

El hombre —apena decirlo— rechaza al hombre; los espíritus se hacen impenetrables; páganse y se cobran los servicios mutuos, sin que se ponga amor en ellos. La lógica justicia, reina en el mundo de las ideas puras, ahoga a las obras de misericordia, que brotan del amor, soberano en el mundo de los puros espíritus. En vez de verter éstos y de fundirlos en un espíritu común, vida de nuestras vidas y realidad de realidades, tendemos a hacer con las ideas un cemento conjuntivo social en que como moluscos en un englomerado quedemos presos. Las ideas, externas a nosotros, son como atmósfera social por que se trasmiten calor y luz espirituales; en ellas se refleja la del Sol del espíritu, sin que por sí iluminen; hay que mantener aérea esa atmósfera, para poder en ella y de ella respirar, y que no cuaje en tupido ambiente que nos ahogue.

Espíritu es lo que nos hace falta, porque el espíritu, la realidad, hace ideas o apariencias, y éstas no hacen espíritu, como la tierra y el trabajo hacen dinero, y el dinero por sí no hace, dígase lo que se quiera, ni tierra ni trabajo. Y si da el dinero interés es porque hay quien sobre la tierra o sobre productos de ella trabaje, como si lo dan las ideas, es porque alguien sobre espíritu y de espíritu labra.

Utilísimos son, sin duda, los hombres canales, los mercaderes de ideas, que las ponen en circulación sin producirlas ni acrecentarlas; pero el valor íntimo e intrínseco de tales hombres estriba en el espíritu que en su comercio pongan. Lo que cada cual tenga de pensador y sentidor es lo que le hace fuerza social progresora; el ser meramente sabio o erudito es lo mismo que el ser usurero o prestamista, que redistribuye riqueza, pero no la crea.

Y los pobres esclavos de la tierra que saludan respetuosos al usurero que alguna vez les sacó por el momento de apuro cobrándose al 20 por ciento, miran desdeñosos al que se arruinó en abrir un pozo artesiano.

¿Ideas verdaderas y falsas decís? Todo lo que eleva e intensifica la vida refléjase en ideas verdaderas, que lo son en cuanto lo reflejen, y en ideas falsas todo lo que la deprima y amengüe. Mientras corra una peseta y haga oficio, comprándose y vendiéndose con ella, verdadera es; mas desde que ya no pase, será falsa.

¿Verdad? ¿verdad decís? La verdad es algo más íntimo que la concordancia lógica de dos conceptos, algo más entrañable que la ecuación del intelecto con la cosa —*adaequatio intellectus et rei*—, es el íntimo consorcio de mi espíritu con el Espíritu universal. Todo lo demás es razón, y *vivir verdad* es más hondo que tener razón. Idea que se realiza es verdadera, y sólo lo es en cuanto se realiza, la realización, que la hace vivir, le da verdad; la que fracasa en la realidad teórica o práctica es falsa, porque hay también una realidad teórica. Verdad es aquello que intimas y haces tuyo; sólo la idea que vives te es verdadera. ¿Sabes el teorema de Pitágoras y llega un caso en que depende tu vida de hallar un cuadrado de triple área que otro, y no sabes servirte de tal teorema?... No es verdadero para ti. A lo sumo con verdad lógica. Y la lógica es esgrima que desarrolla los músculos del pensamiento, sin duda, pero que en pleno campo de batalla apenas sirve. ¿Y para qué quieres fuertes músculos si no sabes combatir?

De ideas consta la ciencia, sí, de conceptos; pero no son ellas, las ideas, más que medio, porque no es ciencia conocer las leyes por los hechos, sino los hechos por las leyes; en el *hecho* termina la ciencia, a él se dirige. Quien pudiese ver el hecho todo, todo entero, por dentro y por fuera, en su desarrollo todo, ¿para qué quería más ciencia? Verdadera es la doctrina de la electricidad en cuanto nos da luz y trasmite a distancia nuestro pensamiento y obra otras maravillas. Y también es verdadera en cuanto, como tal doctrina, nos eleve el espíritu a contemplación de vida y amor. Porque tiene la ciencia dos salidas: una que va a la acción práctica, material, a hacer la civilización que nos envuelve y facilita la vida, otra que sube a la acción teórica, espiritual, a hacernos la cultura que nos llena y fomenta la vida interior, a hacer la filosofía que, en alas de la inteligencia, nos eleve al corazón y ahonde el sentimiento y la seriedad de la vida. Para este hogar de contemplación vivificante son las ideas científicas combustible. De la ciencia de su tiempo, falsa según nuestra nomenclatura, las tomaron Platón y Hegel, y con ellas tejieron los más grandes poemas, los más verdaderos, del más puro mundo del espíritu.

¿Buenas y malas ideas decís? Hablar de ideas buenas, ya se ha dicho, es como hablar de sonidos azules, de olores redondos o de triángulos amargos, o más bien es como hablar de pesetas benéficas o maléficas, de fusiles heroicos o criminales.

"¡Lástima de hombre! Es bueno, ¡pero profesa tan malas ideas!" ¿Hay, acaso, frase más absurda que ésta? Es el hombre quien hace buenas o malas a las ideas que acoge, según él sea, bueno o malo; es la realidad quien hace las apariencias. Suelen ser nuestras doctrinas, cuando no son postura de afectación para atraer la mirada pública, el justificante que, *a posteriori*, nos damos de nuestra conducta, y no su fundamento apriorístico. Y solemos equivocarnos, porque es raro el que sabe por qué hace el bien o el mal que hace, ni aun de ordinario, si es bien o mal. Raciocinar la ética es matarla. Obedece al dictado de tu conciencia sin convertirlo en silogismo. No hay más malicia para las ideas que la mentira, y nunca como bajo el régimen de la mentira, el más ideocrático de todos, se las persigue. La sinceridad es tolerante y liberal.

¿Qué Fulano cambia de ideas como de casaca, dices? Feliz él, porque eso arguye que tiene casacas que cambiar, y no es poco donde los más andan desnudos, o llevan, a lo sumo, el traje del difunto, hasta que se deshilache en andrajos. Ya que el traje no crece, ni se ensancha, ni se encoge, según crecemos, engordamos o adelgazamos nosotros, y ya que con el roce y el uso se desgasta, cambiémosle. Lo importante es pensar, sea como fuere, con estas o con aquellas ideas, lo mismo da: ¡pensar! y pensar con todo el cuerpo y sus sentidos, y sus entrañas, con su sangre, y su médula, y su fibra, y sus celdillas todas, y con el alma toda y sus potencias, y no sólo con el cerebro y la mente, pensar vital y no lógicamente. Porque el que piensa sujeta a las ideas, y sujetándolas se liberta de su degradante tiranía.

Es la inteligencia para la vida; de la vida y para ella nació, y no la vida de la inteligencia. Fue y es un arma, un arma templada por el uso. Lo que para vivir no nos sirve, nos es inconocible. ¿Crees que la visión, la visión misma, flor la más esplendente del conocer, hizo al ojo? No; al ojo le hizo la vida, y el ojo hizo la visión, y luego, por ministerio de la visión, perfeccionó la vida al ojo. Pero ¿el ojo, el ojo mismo, símbolo de la inteligencia, fue un órgano de visión ante todo?

Hay que dudarlo. Antes de llegar a ser un *órgano* o instrumento que nos diese especies visibles, imágenes de las cosas, gérmenes de ideas, ideas en larva ya, tuvo acaso un valor trófico, ejerció oficio en nuestra íntima nutrición y vida concreta. En sus formas íntimas, donde mejor nos descubre su prístina e íntima esencia, refiérese a la nutrición del ser, a su empapamiento en vida, a la acción de la radiación. ¿Ven, acaso, las trasparentes medusas? Y tienen su ojo, su lente con su mancha pigmentaria. La sensibilidad de él es química, reacciona como una placa fotográfica, y vivifica así al ser ciego, le regala don de luz por su ojo. Crustáceos hay que se enrojecen si les ciegas; quieren beber luz y la beben con el cuerpo todo, si les arrancas la boca con que la bebían ansiosos; no quieren ver, sino beber luz; no apetecen especies visibles, sino obra del sol en las entrañas; no quieren larvas de ideas, sino pulsaciones de vida, espíritu después de todo. Las plantas mismas, ¿no tienen a las veces ojos? ¿No los tiene ese "musgo que brilla" de los niños bretones —*schistostega osmundacea?*— Sí, el ojo es para algo más hondo que para ver; es para alegrar el alma; el ojo bebe luz, y la luz vivifica las entrañas del *oculado,* aunque no percibiese imágenes. Esto vino luego, como añadidura; nos lo trajo la vida, porque vio que le era bueno. Y para algo más que para percibir ideas tenemos la mente, el ojo del espíritu; la tenemos para beber luz, luz espiritual, verdad, vida, reflejadas en esta o en la otra idea, que todas las reflejan, aun las más negras. Porque si no reflejase luz lo negro, ¿lo verías?

¡Ah! ¡Si sacudiéndonos todos de la letal tiranía de las ideas, viviésemos de fe, de verdadera fe, de fe viva!

Yo creo que, así como el odio al pecado está en razón inversa del odio al pecador, y que cuanto más se aborrece el delito más piedad y amorosa compasión hacia el delincuente se experimenta, así también cuanto menos respeto tengamos a las ideas y en menos las sobreestimemos, más respeto rendiremos al hombre, estimándole en más. Que no sea para nosotros el prójimo un arca de opiniones, un número social encasillable con la etiqueta de un *ista* cualquiera, como insecto que clavamos por el coselete en la caja entomológica, sino que sea un hermano, un hombre de carne y hueso como yo y tú, una idea, sí, una aparición; pero una aparición inefable y divina encarnada en un cuerpo que sufre y que goza, que ama y que aborrece, que vive y que al fin muere.

¿Y aquí en España? Aquí hemos padecido de antiguo un dogmatismo agudo; aquí ha regido siempre la inquisición inmanente, la íntima y social, de que la otra, la histórica y nacional, no fue más que pasajero fenómeno; aquí es donde la ideocracia ha producido mayor ideofobia, porque siempre engendra anarquía el régimen absoluto. A la idea, como al dinero, tómasela aquí de fuente de todo mal o de todo bien. Hacemos de los arados ídolos, en vez de convertir nuestros ídolos en arados. Todo español es un maniqueo inconsciente; cree en una Divinidad cuyas dos personas son Dios y el Demonio, la afirmación suma, la suma negación, el origen de las ideas buenas y verdaderas y el de las malas y falsas. Aquí lo arreglamos todo con afirmar o negar redondamente, sin pudor alguno, fundando banderías. Aquí se cree aún en jesuitas y masones, en brujas y trasgos, en amuletos y fórmulas, en azares y exorcismos, en la *hidra revolucionaria* o en la *ola negra de la reacción,* en los milagros de la ignorancia o en los de la ciencia. O son molinos de viento o son gigantes; no hay término medio ni supremo; no comprendemos o, mejor aún, no sentimos que sean gigantes los molinos de viento y molinos los gigantes. Y el que no es Quijote ni Sancho quédase en socarrón bachiller Carrasco, lo que es peor aún.

Es el nuestro un pueblo que razona poco, porque le han forzado a raciocinar con exceso, o a tomarlo por otros raciocinado, a vivir de préstamo con pocas ideas, y ellas escuetas y perfiladas a buril, esquinosas, ideas hechas para la discusión, escolásticas, sombras de mediodía meridional. Y las pocas y esquinosas ideas fomentan la ideocracia, que es oligárquica de suyo, y la ideofobia con ella, puesto que cuantas más las ideas y más ricas y más complejas y más proteicas menos autoritarias e impositivas son. ¿No conviven y se conciertan y se comunican los *hechos* todos, aun los más opuestos al parecer entre sí, los *hechos* que son el ideal de las ideas?

Hemos vivido aquí creyendo lo que nos enseñaban: que las cosas consisten en la consistidura, y edificando sobre tal base un castillo de naipes con apariencias de apariencias, con sombras de sombras. La vida interior, entre tanto, se asfixiaba en el vacío, bajo la campana neumática de las escolásticas consistiduras. Apena ver a espíritus tan vigorosos y potentes, tan reales y tan llenos de verdad como los de nuestros místicos, agitarse bajo la campana buscando aire libre henchido de cielo. ¡Ah, su anhelo, su noble anhelo, el ansia de sus espíritus! ¡Ansia de beber con el ojo espiritual directamente la luz del Sol, de sentirse las entrañas bañadas en sus vivificantes rayos, de poder mirarlo cara a cara y vivir de su luz, aunque cegasen, y tener que recibirlo de reflejo, en las figuras de las cosas, en las formas visibles, larvas de ideas! Bebámosle en ellas.

La verdad puede más que la razón, dijo Sófocles, y la verdad es amor y vida en la realidad de los espíritus y no mera relación de congruencia lógica entre las ideas. Unción y no dialéctica es lo que nos vivificará.

Cuando reine el Espíritu se le someterá la Idea, y no ya por el conocimiento ideal, sino por el amor espiritual comunicarán entre sí las criaturas.

He aquí por qué, amigo Maeztu, aborrezco la tiranía de las ideas.

Año de 1900

NARRATIVA

Juan José Arreola
1918–
México

El guardagujas
Confabulario, 1952.

E L forastero llegó sin aliento a la estación desierta. Su gran
valija, que nadie quiso cargar, le había fatigado en extremo. Se enjugó el rostro con un pañuelo, y con la mano en vi-
sera miró los rieles que se perdían en el horizonte. Desalentado y pensativo consultó su reloj: la hora justa en que el tren
debía partir.

Alguien, salido de quién sabe dónde, le dio una palmada
muy suave. Al volverse, el forastero se halló ante un viejecillo
de vago aspecto ferrocarrilero. Llevaba en la mano una linterna roja, pero tan pequeña, que parecía de juguete. Miró sonriendo al viajero, y éste le dijo ansioso su pregunta:

—Usted perdone, ¿ha salido ya el tren?

—¿Lleva usted poco tiempo en este país?

—Necesito salir inmediatamente. Debo hallarme en T. mañana mismo.

—Se ve que usted ignora por completo lo que ocurre. Lo
que debe hacer ahora mismo es buscar alojamiento en la fonda para viajeros —y señaló un extraño edificio ceniciento que
más bien parecía un presidio.

—Pero yo no quiero alojarme, sino salir en el tren.

—Alquile usted un cuarto inmediatamente, si es que lo
hay. En caso de que pueda conseguirlo, contrátelo por mes, le
resultará más barato y recibirá mejor atención.

—¿Está usted loco? Yo debo llegar a T. mañana mismo.

—Francamente, debería abandonarlo a su suerte. Sin embargo, le daré unos informes.

—Por favor...

—Este país es famoso por sus ferrocarriles, como usted sabe. Hasta ahora no ha sido posible organizarlos debidamente,
pero se han hecho ya grandes cosas en lo que se refiere a la pu-

blicación de itinerarios y a la expedición de boletos. Las guías ferroviarias comprenden y enlazan todas las poblaciones de la nación; se expenden boletos hasta para las aldeas más pequeñas y remotas. Falta solamente que los convoyes cumplan las indicaciones contenidas en las guías y que pasen efectivamente por las estaciones. Los habitantes del país así lo esperan; mientras tanto, aceptan las irregularidades del servicio y su patriotismo les impide cualquier manifestación de desagrado.

—Pero ¿hay un tren que pase por esta ciudad?

—Afirmarlo equivaldría a cometer una inexactitud. Como usted puede darse cuenta, los rieles existen, aunque un tanto averiados. En algunas poblaciones están sencillamente indicados en el suelo, mediante dos rayas de gis. Dadas las condiciones actuales, ningún tren tiene la obligación de pasar por aquí, pero nada impide que eso pueda suceder. Yo he visto pasar muchos trenes en mi vida y conocí algunos viajeros que pudieron abordarlos. Si usted espera convenientemente, tal vez yo mismo tenga el honor de ayudarle a subir a un hermoso y confortable vagón.

—¿Me llevará ese tren a T.?

—¿Y por qué se empeña usted en que ha de ser precisamente a T.? Debería darse por satisfecho si pudiera abordarlo. Una vez en el tren, su vida tomará efectivamente algún rumbo. ¿Qué importa si ese rumbo no es el de T.?

—Es que yo tengo un boleto en regla para ir a T. Lógicamente, debo ser conducido a ese lugar, ¿no es así?

—Cualquiera diría que usted tiene razón. En la fonda para viajeros podrá hablar con personas que han tomado sus precauciones, adquiriendo grandes cantidades de boletos. Por regla general, las gentes previsoras compran pasajes para todos los puntos del país. Hay quien ha gastado en boletos una verdadera fortuna...

—Yo creí que para ir a T. me bastaba un boleto. Mírelo usted...

—El próximo tramo de los ferrocarriles nacionales va a ser construido con el dinero de una sola persona que acaba de gastar su inmenso capital en pasajes de ida y vuelta para un trayecto ferroviario cuyos planos, que incluyen extensos túneles y puentes, ni siquiera han sido aprobados por los ingenieros de la empresa.

—Pero el tren que pasa por T. ¿ya se encuentra en servicio?

—Y no sólo ése. En realidad, hay muchísimos trenes en la nación, y los viajeros pueden utilizarlos con relativa frecuencia, pero tomando en cuenta que no se trata de un servicio formal y definitivo. En otras palabras, al subir a un tren, nadie espera ser conducido al sitio que desea.

— ¿Cómo es eso?

—En su afán de servir a los ciudadanos, la empresa debe recurrir a ciertas medidas desesperadas. Hace circular trenes por lugares intransitables. Esos convoyes expedicionarios emplean a veces varios años en su trayecto, y la vida de los viajeros sufre algunas transformaciones importantes. Los fallecimientos no son raros en tales casos, pero la empresa, que todo lo ha previsto, añade a esos trenes un vagón capilla ardiente y un vagón cementerio. Es motivo de orgullo para los conductores depositar el cadáver de un viajero —lujosamente embalsamado— en los andenes de la estación que prescribe su boleto. En ocasiones, estos trenes forzados recorren trayectos en que falta uno de los rieles. Todo un lado de los vagones se estremece lamentablemente con los golpes que dan las ruedas sobre los durmientes. Los viajeros de primera —es otra de las previsiones de la empresa— se colocan del lado en que hay riel. Los de segunda padecen los golpes con resignación. Pero hay otros tramos en que faltan ambos rieles; allí los viajeros sufren por igual, hasta que el tren queda totalmente destruido.

— ¡Santo Dios!

—Mire usted: la aldea de F. surgió a causa de uno de esos accidentes. El tren fue a dar en un terreno impracticable. Lijadas por la arena, las ruedas se gastaron hasta los ejes. Los viajeros pasaron tanto tiempo juntos, que de las obligadas conversaciones triviales surgieron amistades estrechas. Algunas de esas amistades se transformaron pronto en idilios, y el resultado ha sido F., una aldea progresista llena de niños traviesos que juegan con los vestigios enmohecidos del tren.

— ¡Dios mío, yo no estoy hecho para tales aventuras!

—Necesita usted ir templando su ánimo; tal vez llegue usted a convertirse en héroe. No crea que faltan ocasiones para que los viajeros demuestren su valor y sus capacidades de sacrificio. Recientemente, doscientos pasajeros anónimos escribieron una de las páginas más gloriosas en nuestros anales ferroviarios. Sucede que en un viaje de prueba, el maquinista advirtió a tiempo una grave omisión de los constructores de la línea. En la ruta faltaba un puente que debía salvar un abismo. Pues bien, el maquinista, en vez de poner marcha hacia atrás, arengó a los pasajeros y obtuvo de ellos el esfuerzo necesario para seguir adelante. Bajo su enérgica dirección, el tren fue desarmado pieza por pieza y conducido en hombros al otro lado del abismo, que todavía reservaba la sorpresa de contener en su fondo un río caudaloso. El resultado de la hazaña fue tan satisfactorio que la empresa renunció definitivamente a la construcción del puente, conformándose con hacer un atractivo descuento en las tarifas de los pasajeros que se atreven a afrontar esa molestia suplementaria.

— ¡Pero yo debo llegar a T. mañana mismo!

— ¡Muy bien! Me gusta que no abandone usted su proyecto. Se ve que es usted un hombre de convicciones. Alójese por lo pronto en la fonda y tome el primer tren que pase. Trate de hacerlo cuando menos; mil personas estarán para impedírselo. Al llegar un convoy, los viajeros, irritados por una espera demasiado larga, salen de la fonda en tumulto para invadir ruidosamente la estación. Muchas veces provocan accidentes con su increíble falta de cortesía y de prudencia. En vez de subir ordenadamente se dedican a aplastarse unos a otros; por lo menos, se impiden para siempre el abordaje, y el tren se va dejándolos amotinados en los andenes de la estación. Los viajeros, agotados y furiosos, maldicen su falta de educación, y pasan mucho tiempo insultándose y dándose de golpes.

— ¿Y la policía no interviene?

—Se ha intentado organizar un cuerpo de policía en cada estación, pero la imprevisible llegada de los trenes hacía tal servicio inútil y sumamente costoso. Además, los miembros de ese cuerpo demostraron muy pronto su venalidad, dedicándose a proteger la salida exclusiva de pasajeros adinerados que les daban a cambio de ese servicio todo lo que llevaban encima. Se resolvió entonces el establecimiento de un tipo especial de escuelas, donde los futuros viajeros reciben lecciones de urbanidad y un entrenamiento adecuado. Allí se les enseña la manera correcta de abordar un convoy, aunque esté en movimiento y a gran velocidad. También se les proporciona una especie de armadura para evitar que los demás pasajeros les rompan las costillas.

—Pero una vez en el tren, ¿está uno a cubierto de nuevas dificultades?

—Relativamente. Sólo le recomiendo que se fije muy bien en las estaciones. Podría darse el caso de que usted creyera haber llegado a T., y sólo fuese a una ilusión. Para regular la vida a bordo de los vagones demasiado repletos, la empresa se ve obligada a echar mano de ciertos expedientes. Hay estaciones que son pura apariencia: han sido construidas en plena selva y llevan el nombre de alguna ciudad importante. Pero basta poner un poco de atención para descubrir el engaño. Son como las decoraciones del teatro, y las personas que figu-

ran en ellas están llenas de aserrín. Esos muñecos revelan fácilmente los estragos de la intemperie, pero son a veces una
perfecta imagen de la realidad: llevan en el rostro las señales
de un cansancio infinito.

—Por fortuna, T. no se halla muy lejos de aquí.

—Pero carecemos por el momento de trenes directos. Sin
embargo, no cabe excluirse la posibilidad de que usted llegue
mañana mismo, tal como desea. La organización de los ferrocarriles, aunque deficiente, no excluye la posibilidad de un
viaje sin escalas. Vea usted, hay personas que ni siquiera se
han dado cuenta de lo que pasa. Compran un boleto para
ir a T. Llega un tren, suben, y al día siguiente oyen que el
conductor anuncia: "Hemos llegado a T." Sin tomar precaución alguna, los viajeros descienden y se hallan efectivamente en T.

— ¿Podría yo hacer alguna cosa para facilitar ese resultado?

—Claro que puede usted. Lo que no se sabe es si le servirá
de algo. Inténtelo de todas maneras. Suba usted al tren con la
idea fija de que va a llegar a T. No trate a ninguno de los pasajeros. Podrían desilusionarlo con sus historias de viaje, y hasta denunciarlo a las autoridades.

— ¿Qué está usted diciendo?

—En virtud del estado actual de las cosas los trenes viajan
llenos de espías. Estos espías, voluntarios en su mayor parte,
dedican su vida a fomentar el espíritu constructivo de la empresa. A veces uno no sabe lo que dice y habla sólo por hablar.
Pero ellos se dan cuenta en seguida de todos los sentidos que
puede tener una frase, por sencilla que sea. Del comentario
más inocente saben sacar una opinión culpable. Si usted llegara a cometer la menor imprudencia, sería aprehendido sin más;
pasaría el resto de su vida en un vagón cárcel o le obligarían a
descender en una falsa estación, perdida en la selva. Viaje usted lleno de fe, consuma la menor cantidad posible de alimen-
tos y no ponga los pies en el andén antes de que vea en T. alguna cara conocida.

—Pero yo no conozco en T. a ninguna persona.

—En ese caso redoble usted sus precauciones. Tendrá, se
lo aseguro, muchas tentaciones en el camino. Si mira usted
por las ventanillas, está expuesto a caer en la trampa de un espejismo. Las ventanillas están provistas de ingeniosos disposi-
tivos que crean toda clase de ilusiones en el ánimo de los pasajeros. No hace falta ser débil para caer en ellas. Ciertos aparatos, operados desde la locomotora, hacen creer, por el ruido
y los movimientos, que el tren está en marcha. Sin embargo,

el tren permanece detenido semanas enteras, mientras los viajeros ven pasar cautivadores paisajes a través de los cristales.

— ¿Y eso qué objeto tiene?

—Todo esto lo hace la empresa con el sano propósito de disminuir la ansiedad de los viajeros y de anular en todo lo posible las sensaciones de traslado. Se aspira a que un día se entreguen plenamente al azar, en manos de una empresa omnipotente, y que ya no les importe saber a dónde van ni de dónde vienen.

—Y usted, ¿ha viajado mucho en los trenes?

—Yo, señor, sólo soy guardagujas. A decir verdad, soy un guardagujas jubilado, y sólo aparezco aquí de vez en cuando para recordar los buenos tiempos. No he viajado nunca, ni tengo ganas de hacerlo. Pero los viajeros me cuentan historias. Sé que los trenes han creado muchas poblaciones además de la aldea de F. cuyo origen le he referido. Ocurre a veces que los tripulantes de un tren reciben órdenes misteriosas. Invitan a los pasajeros a que desciendan de los vagones, generalmente con el pretexto de que admiren las bellezas de un determinado lugar. Se les habla de grutas, de cataratas o de ruinas célebres: "Quince minutos para que admiren ustedes la gruta tal o cual", dice amablemente el conductor. Una vez que los viajeros se hallan a cierta distancia, el tren escapa a todo vapor.

— ¿Y los viajeros?

—Vagan desconcertados de un sitio a otro durante algún tiempo, pero acaban por congregarse y se establecen en colonia. Estas paradas intempestivas se hacen en lugares adecuados, muy lejos de toda civilización, y con riquezas naturales suficientes. Allí se abandonan lotes selectos, de gente joven, y sobre todo con mujeres abundantes. ¿No le gustaría a usted pasar sus días en un pintoresco lugar desconocido, en compañía de una muchachita?

El viejecillo hizo un guiño, y se quedó mirando al viajero con picardía, sonriente y lleno de bondad. En ese momento se oyó un silbido lejano. El guardagujas dio un brinco, lleno de inquietud, y se puso a hacer señales ridículas y desordenadas con su linterna.

— ¿Es el tren? —preguntó el forastero.

El anciano echó a correr por la vía, desaforadamente. Cuando estuvo a cierta distancia, se volvió para gritar:

— ¡Tiene usted suerte! Mañana llegará a su famosa estación. ¿Cómo dice usted que se llama?

— ¡X! —contestó el viajero.

En ese momento el viejecillo se disolvió en la clara mañana. Pero el punto rojo de la linterna siguió corriendo y saltando entre los rieles, imprudentemente, al encuentro del tren.

Al fondo del paisaje, la locomotora se acercaba como un ruidoso advenimiento.

Emilio S. Belaval
1903–
Puerto Rico

Tony Pérez es un niño flan
Los cuentos de la universidad, 1945.

LAS muchachas del curso de ciencias estaban por declarar de que Tony Pérez era el más admirable tipo de la universidad; las del curso de artes también. Pequeño ídolo de mujeres, nuestro protagonista se dedicó a estudiar profundamente, ese privilegio exclusivo de hacerse bien el lazo de la corbata, de que gozan los elegantes. Tony Pérez era el más elegante, el más dúctil y el más afortunado galán de la universidad.

No crea el bondadoso lector de que Tony Pérez no es producto nato de nuestra fisonomía. El chico no tiene en su tipo aire de extranjería. Es un perfecto braquicéfalo, de buen sabor antillano, aunque su pelo a fuerza de cosmético, se le haya chamuscado un poco y su bigotillo de galán de cinema se haya resignado a ser una pelusilla petimetre que le haya restado todo su color de mostacho bucanero. La falsificación, si alguna hay, está en su actitud hacia la vida y en su demasiada devoción por seguir otros patrones que no son los de su inocente tierra.

El chico no es responsable de su exotismo nada más que a medias. Cuando Tony Pérez bajó de la montaña, era un muchacho honesto, un poco arisco, que entró por la puerta más estrecha de la universidad, sin atreverse a soñar en la gloria de que más tarde gozaría entre las mujeres. Traía un bozo íntegro, unos pudorosos pantalones de escaso vuelo y una recatada filosofía sobre todas las cosas. Venía asimismo referido a otro estudiantón del último año, de su municipio, para tratar de hacerle los aprietos más llevaderos en los primeros meses de noviciado. Si lo hubiesen referido a Juan Antonio Orcaz o a Alfredo Guillén, tal vez hubiera terminado a pedradas con el régimen o haciendo versos. Pero lo refirieron a aquel insoportable Georgie Rodríguez y terminó siendo el más perfecto flan de la universidad. A los tres meses de estar en la universidad, ya Tony Pérez se había saturado de la atmósfera más sofisticada que podía existir en algunos de los rincones de la benemérita corporación.

La primera noche que salieron juntos Georgie Rodríguez y Tony Pérez, fue a un *parti* a la luz de la luna. Luna de trópico, cornucópica, con dos bebés de los alrededores, que se estuvieron riendo toda la noche de él, aunque admitían que las ciento setenta y cinco libras del muchacho y su aire de moro melodramático, no estaban mal. Una de ellas, después del cuarto coctel, se lo llevó bajo las palmas de un hotel elegante:

—Mira, Antonio, no te dejes embaucar por esos chicos famélicos de la universidad, que se creen todavía que una mujer de colegio es lo mismo que una gallina. ¡Hoy las mujeres demandamos una idea más respetable de nosotras!

—Es natural —murmuró Antonio, quien ya estaba un poco ebrio.

—Cuida de tu salud, haz ejercicio y aprende a ser agradable. Hay que darnos una oportunidad a nosotras; no sentirse nunca con derecho a nada. ¿Por qué no haces que te llamen Tony?

—No se me había ocurrido. En mi pueblo me llaman Toño, pero yo mismo reconozco que es un apodo vulgar. Suena mal.

—Me alegro. Creo que vamos a ser buenos amigos. Una siempre necesita de amigos en quienes confiar.

—Eso está muy bien —murmuró otra vez, Antonio, ¡perdón!, Tony, quien prometió ser un amigo formal, no creerse nunca con derecho a nada, aunque dispuesto a recibirlo todo y a cuidar de su cuerpo y a tener una idea más par de aquella chica tan respetable que lo había salvado del ridículo de una noche. Luego aquella noche, un saxófono jovial, sentimentalote, sexual, había hecho gustar al chico de la delicia del jazz con una nena bien formada cuya generosa epidermis sintió cerca de su rostro incivil. ¡Caballeros, esto del jazz es una cosa muy seria! No hay lanceros, ni bomba, ni danza, que pueda crear este íntimo diálogo entre cuerpos y almas y esta aspiración mitad atlética, mitad psicológica, de dejar ascender hasta un momento de abandono, la vida subterránea de nuestra miserable morfología. Detrás de cada saxófono que gimotea en la alta noche, hay un conspirador contra el miriñaque de nuestro pudor alambicado. Alma y cuerpo arriba, amigazos, que eso de la carne y del espíritu es una telita de cebolla que nadie sabe donde empieza una ni donde acaba la otra. Y si alguna vez, nuestro cuerpo se vuelve un garabato al bailar el fox es porque tenemos en el alma otro garabatito. Por eso detesta el jazz la gente madura y los hipócritas. Amén.

Cuando los chicos regresaron a su hospedería, Tony Pérez le preguntó a Georgie Rodríguez:

—Oye, y ésas ¿quiénes son?, ¿cómo son?

—Pues unas mujeres encantadoras, ¡Decentísimas, no vayas tú a creerte! Ya la gente de universidad debemos ir acostumbrándonos a pensar que eso del sexo es una tontería.

A Tony Pérez aquella noche no se le olvidó fácilmente. ¡Por volverla a vivir hubiera vendido su alma al diablo! ¡Aquella Beti Mendoza tenía los ojos tan lánguidos; era tan dura, tan sensual, tan persona decente! Comparada con las cavernícolas niñas de su pueblo, era un encanto de mujer. Un noviazgo saxofónico con la criatura, bien merecía que Antonio Pérez, dejara su indigna ollita de prejuicios ajilimójicos con la tapa descubierta. ¿Qué pedía en cambio la chica? Nada; cuidar del cuerpo, no sentirse con derecho a nada y tener una idea honorable de la mujer, que tal vez, algún día, para un par de besos, necesitara de la comprensión delicada de un amigo. El, Antonio Pérez, ¡Tony!, sería la sombra amiga de la saludable chica, que tan graciosamente le había confiado su problema.

Unos cuantos días después, Tony Pérez emprendió la tarea de poner su cuerpo en salud, para que cuando Beti Mendoza necesitara de una nueva interpretación de la filosofía del cuerpo de su amigo, no se encontrara con una carne roñosa, roída de lacerias estúpidas o de conceptos de gallinero, sino con el sano sentido responsivo de una corporeidad puesta en orden y en razón. Cuando Luciano Aldavían fue a examinar el catálogo de sus bien amados cursillos del siglo de oro y Alfredo Guillén anduvo a caza de cuanta clase de historia o retórica creyó posible digerir dentro de su menú académico, Tony Pérez, con soberbio gesto de desdén, se echó a lograr la mayor cantidad de atletismo, de gimnasia y de milicia. Se incorporó a la ronda de los militaroides, sin buscar de médicos de la familia aquellos eximentes fantásticos de las peñas de los inconformes, que hacían proferir al médico del ejército estudiantón:

—Si la salud de ustedes estuviera como dicen mis ilustrados colegas, tendríamos una universidad cardiaca, sin hígado y con tanta hidrocelia en ciernes que más valdría instalar una clínica que sostener esta institución.

Con la promesa de aquella compensación venusta, no había Tony Pérez de terminar el curso sin ser una recia columna del *basket,* del *volley,* del *base,* del *tennis,* y de todas las pintorescas pelotas de alucinantes colores que aupaban con frenética pujanza los deportistas de la universidad. Además su vestimenta había sufrido muy serias rectificaciones. En pulgadas de ancho, el ruedo de sus calzones batieron el promedio de todo el vestuario estudiantón; aún había logrado desbancar al irresistible Georgie Rodríguez, que solo se había atrevido a llegar a trece pulgadas. Tony Pérez llegó a catorce. ¡Tenía una serie de chaquetitas cortas, algunas de listas rabiosas, unos abrigos de lana, unos fieltros aplastados en forma de aeroplanos y unas muñequeras de reloj y unas corbatitas estrechas y unas camisas de veraneante y unos calzoncitos cortos, con medias largas de cordón grueso y unas sortijas en espiral, que eran para tomarle postalitas de cuerpo entero! Arturo Montes, única nube en el poderío anímico del elegantón, y su jaleador consuetudinario, le solía cantar las más perversas coplillas de su municipio a los macabros calzones del ídolo:

> *Dice don Antonio Pérez*
> *Que si no le dan peseta*
> *Que le arruga las pantaletas*
> *A la suegra del Alférez.*

y después, a vía de desagravio solía añadir:

—Como esta universidad no tiene música, he tenido que inventarme la tonadilla. —Para sus faenas del *court,* Tony Pérez tenía unas bragas de un color rojo, que hubiera hecho morir de envidia al taparrabos de cualquier caribe auténtico y para la piscina de nadar otros arreos que le permitían a Beti Mendoza hacer las más sabrosas reflexiones sobre el panorama corpóreo de su compañero de locuras saxofónicas.

Claro, un bebé de tan extraña catadura tenía que desarrollar una concepción acorde con muchas cosas. No se puede contemplar la vida con pantalones tan anchos sin buscar algún contrapeso ideológico de menos anchura. Cuando Tony Pérez se decidió a ser flan, no pudo ser flan a medias, cosa que no admite el gremio, sino que cambió su adusticidad por una puerilidad expansiva que le hacía gozar de todas las cosas nimias. Aprendió a jugar con la vida como con una policromada pelota, detrás de la cual daba saltos juiciosos; no tuvo pausas de angustia ni de rencor. Tenía una sonrisa inefable para reir cuanta idiotez se le ocurría decir a Beti Mendoza, sus bromas eran siempre ruidosas, con grandes manotazos en la espalda de la preferida y desarrolló una caballerosidad oficiosa, deportista, de hombre a quien se puede pisar un pie impunemente en la brega con las pelotas de marras sin lanzar un rotundo taco, que hizo que el régimen detuviera sobre él su mirada benefactora. ¡En aquel chico había madera para catedrático! Bien es verdad que Tony nunca solía hacer preguntas inconvenientes a ningún dómine, ni mucho menos participar en la inquietud de los problemas territoriales. Era un verdadero chico, un chico grande, saludable, que había tenido hasta la precaución de estudiar un poco. No sería nunca un sabio, pero sería un hombre capaz de recitar, año tras año el curso, sin dejarse llevar por el ánima levantisca de otros catedráticos, que a veces solían murmurar en los concilios de decanos sobre problemas y protestas que el régimen estaba interesado en no ventilar. Así, cuando los estudiantones decidían hacer alguna de las suyas, Tony Pérez siempre se quedaba al margen; visitaba por la noche al catedrático injuriado para presentarle excusas por la irreverencia del ofensor y se iba a una playa a oxigenarse con Beti Mendoza, mientras terminaba la barricada. Con los estudiantones procuraba siempre no chocar, sabiéndose inferior en discurso. A él lo que le interesaba era que el ruedo de sus pantalones siguiera flotando sobre el ardor de los criollos como una bandera de juvenilidad inocente, de despreocupación morbosa y que el régimen siguiera creyéndolo un tipo capaz de guardar equilibrio. Y sobre todo le importaba Beti Mendoza y los gimoteos melodiosos del saxófono. A fuerza de oír a su cuerpo, el alma le perdió su impulso de hélice espiritual. Para Tony Pérez, el mucho pensar, el hondo sentir, el demasiado amar fueron siempre rémoras de latinidad que nunca ayudarían a la felicidad del cuerpo. Por eso con él Beti Mendoza se emborrachaba sin cuidado; Tony Pérez nunca perdería la cabeza, como aquellos enclenques de la minoría que en cuanto una mujer les daba un beso, se le llenaban las manos de relámpagos. El prestigio de varón mori-

gerado de Tony llegó a tal altura, que cuando alguna catedrá-
tica joven, de ojos azules, necesitaba un compañerito para un
parti de coterráneos, se colgaba del brazo de Tony Pérez.

No vaya el lector a imaginar que Tony Pérez no tuviera
sentido de ciertas cosas. Su destreza era haberse detenido en
el borde de todos los barrancos, tener un atlético concepto de
lo prohibido y ser el mejor capeador de temporales difíciles.
En eso de besar y manosear el chico era bastante largo. Pero
nunca se sentía el diablo detrás de las orejas, como aquellos
pobretones de Pepe Heredia y de Adolfo Puentes, que a cada
rato se iban de cabeza por los barrancos. Además Tony Pérez
era un bailador formidable; en el fox el chico tenía categoría
de astro. Le había robado el secreto al saxófono conspirador.
Se daba unos trancos largos y unas volteretas y unos brincos
de cuica, que no los podía mejorar ni el mismísimo San Pascual Bailón. Cuando aquel chico rodeaba a Beti por la cintura
y le incrustaba su tórax combativo en el idem mórbido de la
chica, a Beti se le iban los ojos para el cogote y Manuelita
Tours se daba unos suspiros, que cualquiera hubiese imaginado que la segunda chica, siempre había padecido de la inútil
melancolía de saber, que nunca sería amada por un dinosau-
ro. Pero así es la filosofía del cuerpo, amigos, y los que tenemos las rodillas flacas debemos callarnos la boca y dejar pasar
la época. La única mujer enamorada de un discurso de que
habla la historia fue Roxanna y el primer beso se lo llevó Tris-
tán y no Cyrano. En los pensionados de doncellas la única
sombra de pecado era el tal Tony Pérez, a pesar de que a la
hora donjuanesca, al pobre Antonio Pérez había que imaginar-
lo dando saltos alrededor del sofá, un poco grotesco para la
técnica del burlador, quien además era un amante discursivo,
cosa que Tony Pérez hubiera sido incapaz de ser, a menos que
no lo dejaran hablar con los pies sobre los lustrosos baldosi-
nes de un *dancing*.

Es lógico que Tony Pérez desentonara profundamente
con el panorama de su tierra inocente, acostumbrada a otro
ritmo, sin saxófono nacional, con unas palmeras que son como molinos de vientos, con un atardecer cuasi eglógico y con
un mar que está pidiendo retórica a gritos. También lo coreo-
gráfico, se dolía de aquel alborozo de chimpancé frente a un
racimo de guineos cuando la tierra lo que pedía era el recatado diálogo de un bailar, donde el espíritu tiene pausas para
sus apoyaturas románticas. Al chico, desde luego no le preocupa tampoco el mohín doloroso de la tierra. Como no le
preocupa tampoco el fiero rencor de los criollos que lo miran

con ganas de estrujarle las pantaletas. La mujer lo adora, el régimen lo mira complacido y ahí lo está esperando la vida, como una pelota de fascinantes colores, donde él podrá seguir su pueril retozo con todos los fueros de la varonía.

Pero el hombre que confía demasiado en el ruedo de sus pantalones, está expuesto a sufrir alguna vez un descalabro. Una noche Beti Mendoza se le fue de trulla con aquel Julián Laguna, de picaresco discurso, tipo antitético, flaco, con greña revuelta y con un huracán en las manos. No sabemos que alcahuetería tuvo que hacer la vida para aquel encontronazo, ni que sabrosas mentirijillas dejara el tal Julián Laguna en la despierta oreja de la guapísima Beti. Lo cierto fue que al inconmensurable Tony, Julián Laguna se le llevó el precioso ídolo de su flanería. Y fue una verdadera lástima, porque al perder el chico los estribos, perdió su discreción y los estudiantones supieron, que a la hora del despecho, Tony Pérez era capaz de arrojar el honor de una mujer a la bambúa y de que era más chismoso, más brutal y menos caballero, de lo que todo el mundo solía esperar. Por varios días se puso a murmurar entre sus fieles adoradoras de ciencias y artes, que Beti era una criatura impúdica, que exigía demasiado de un hombre respetable, hasta que una noche la propia Beti se vengó de él con unas cuantas palabras:

— ¡Hola, Tony! ¿Por qué no has vuelto por casa? Tú siempre tan famoso con tus pantalones. ¿Qué te ha pasado?—

A la hora del olvido, el pobre Tony no fue nada más que un pelele, que sabía mover gallardamente, las catorce pulgadas del ruedo de sus pantalones. ¡Aún para Beti Mendoza, cuyos ojos lánguidos tantas veces el flan había logrado virar hasta el extático cogote!

Jorge Luis Borges
1899–1986
Argentina

Emma Zunz
El Aleph, 1949.

E L catorce de enero de 1922, Emma Zunz, al volver de la
fábrica de tejidos Tarbuch y Loewenthal, halló en el fondo del zaguán una carta, fechada en el Brasil, por la que supo
que su padre había muerto. La engañaron, a primera vista, el
sello y el sobre; luego, la inquietó la letra desconocida. Nueve
o diez líneas borroneadas querían colmar la hoja; Emma leyó
que el señor Maier había ingerido por error una fuerte dosis
de veronal y había fallecido el tres del corriente en el hospital
de Bagé. Un compañero de pensión de su padre firmaba la noticia, un tal Fein o Fain, de Río Grande, que no podía saber
que se dirigía a la hija del muerto.

Emma dejó caer el papel. Su primera impresión fue de malestar en el vientre y en las rodillas; luego de ciega culpa, de
irrealidad, de frío, de temor; luego, quiso ya estar en el día siguiente. Acto continuo comprendió que esa voluntad era inútil porque la muerte de su padre era lo único que había sucedido en el mundo, y seguiría sucediendo sin fin. Recogió el
papel y se fue a su cuarto. Furtivamente lo guardó en un cajón, como si de algún modo ya conociera los hechos ulteriores. Ya había empezado a vislumbrarlos, tal vez; ya era la que
sería.

En la creciente oscuridad, Emma lloró hasta el fin de
aquel día el suicidio de Manuel Maier, que en los antiguos días
felices fue Emanuel Zunz. Recordó veraneos en una charca,
cerca de Gualeguay, recordó (trató de recordar) a su madre, recordó la casita de Lanús que les remataron, recordó los amarillos losanges de una ventana, recordó el auto de prisión, el
oprobio, recordó los anónimos con el suelto sobre "el desfal-
co del cajero", recordó (pero eso jamás lo olvidaba) que su
padre, la última noche, le había jurado que el ladrón era Loewenthal. Loewenthal, Aarón Loewenthal, antes gerente de la
fábrica y ahora uno de los dueños. Emma, desde 1916, guardaba el secreto. A nadie se lo había revelado, ni siquiera a su
mejor amiga, Elsa Urstein. Quizá rehuía la profana increduli-
dad; quizá creía que el secreto era un vínculo entre ella y el

ausente. Loewenthal no sabía que ella sabía; Emma Zunz derivaba de ese hecho ínfimo un sentimiento de poder.

No durmió aquella noche, y cuando la primera luz definió el rectángulo de la ventana, ya estaba perfecto su plan. Procuró que ese día, que le pareció interminable, fuera como los otros. Había en la fábrica rumores de huelga; Emma se declaró, como siempre, contra toda violencia. A las seis, concluido el trabajo, fue con Elsa a un club de mujeres, que tiene gimnasio y pileta. Se inscribieron; tuvo que repetir y deletrear su nombre y su apellido; tuvo que festejar las bromas vulgares que comentan la revisación. Con Elsa y con la menor de las Kronfuss discutió a qué cinematógrafo irían el domingo a la tarde. Luego, se habló de novios y nadie esperó que Emma hablara. En abril cumpliría diecinueve años, pero los hombres le inspiraban, aún, un temor casi patológico... De vuelta preparó una sopa de tapioca y unas legumbres, comió temprano, se acostó y se obligó a dormir. Así, laborioso y trivial, pasó el viernes quince, la víspera.

El sábado, la impaciencia la despertó. La impaciencia, no la inquietud, y el singular alivio de estar en aquel día, por fin. Ya no tenía que tramar y que imaginar; dentro de algunas horas alcanzaría la simplicidad de los hechos. Leyó en *La Prensa* que el *Nordstjärnan,* de Malmö, zarparía esa noche del dique 3; llamó por teléfono a Loewenthal, insinuó que deseaba comunicar, sin que lo supieran las otras, algo sobre la huelga y prometió pasar por el escritorio, al oscurecer. Le temblaba la voz; el temblor convenía a una delatora. Ningún otro hecho memorable ocurrió esa mañana. Emma trabajó hasta las doce y fijó con Elsa y con Perla Kronfuss los pormenores del paseo del domingo. Se acostó después de almorzar y recapituló, cerrados los ojos, el plan que había tramado. Pensó que la etapa final sería menos horrible que la primera y que le depararía, sin duda, el sabor de la victoria y de la justicia. De pronto, alarmada, se levantó y corrió al cajón de la cómoda. Lo abrió; debajo del retrato de Milton Sills, donde la había dejado la antenoche, estaba la carta de Fain. Nadie podía haberla visto; la empezó a leer y la rompió.

Referir con alguna realidad los hechos de esa tarde sería difícil y quizá improcedente. Un atributo de lo infernal es la irrealidad, un atributo que parece mitigar sus terrores y que los agrava tal vez. ¿Cómo hacer verosímil una acción en la que casi no creyó quien la ejecutaba, cómo recuperar ese breve caos que hoy la memoria de Emma Zunz repudia y confunde? Emma vivía por Almagro, en la calle Liniers; nos consta

que esa tarde fue al puerto. Acaso en el infame Paseo de Julio
se vio multiplicada en espejos, publicada por luces y desnuda-
da por los ojos hambrientos, pero más razonable es conjeturar que al principio erró, inadvertida por la indiferente reco-
va... Entró en dos o tres bares, vio la rutina o los manejos de
otras mujeres. Dio al fin con hombres del *Nordstjärnan*. De
uno, muy joven, temió que le inspirara alguna ternura y op-
tó por otro, quizá más bajo que ella y grosero, para que la pureza del horror no fuera mitigada. El hombre la condujo a
una puerta y después a un turbio zaguán y después a una escalera tortuosa y después a un vestíbulo (en el que había una
vidriera con losanges idénticos a los de la casa en Lanús) y después a un pasillo y después a una puerta que se cerró. Los hechos graves están fuera del tiempo, ya porque en ellos el pasado inmediato queda como tronchado del porvenir, ya porque
no parecen consecutivas las partes que los forman.

¿En aquel tiempo fuera del tiempo, en aquel desorden
perplejo de sensaciones inconexas y atroces, pensó Emma
Zunz *una sola vez* en el muerto que motivaba el sacrificio?
Yo tengo para mí que pensó una vez y que en ese momento
peligró su desesperado propósito. Pensó (no pudo no pensar)
que su padre le había hecho a su madre la cosa horrible que a
ella ahora le hacían. Lo pensó con débil asombro y se refugió,
en seguida, en el vértigo. El hombre, sueco o finlandés, no hablaba español; fue una herramienta para Emma como ésta lo
fue para él, pero ella sirvió para el goce y él para la justicia.

Cuando se quedó sola, Emma no abrió en seguida los ojos.
En la mesa de luz estaba el dinero que había dejado el hombre: Emma se incorporó y lo rompió como antes había roto
la carta. Romper dinero es una impiedad, como tirar el pan;
Emma se arrepintió, apenas lo hizo. Un acto de soberbia y en
aquel día... El temor se perdió en la tristeza de su cuerpo, en
el asco. El asco y la tristeza la encadenaban, pero Emma lentamente se levantó y procedió a vestirse. En el cuarto no quedaban colores vivos; el último crepúsculo se agravaba. Emma
pudo salir sin que la advirtieran; en la esquina subió a un La-
croze, que iba al oeste. Eligió, conforme a su plan, el asiento
más delantero, para que no le vieran la cara. Quizá le confor-
tó verificar, en el insípido trajín de las calles, que lo acaecido no había contaminado las cosas. Viajó por barrios decre-
cientes y opacos, viéndolos y olvidándolos en el acto, y se
apeó en una de las bocacalles de Warnes. Paradójicamente su
fatiga venía a ser una fuerza, pues la obligaba a concentrarse
en los pormenores de la aventura y le ocultaba el fondo y el fin.

Aarón Loewenthal era, para todos, un hombre serio; para sus pocos íntimos, un avaro. Vivía en los altos de la fábrica, solo. Establecido en el desmantelado arrabal, temía a los ladrones; en el patio de la fábrica había un gran perro y en el cajón de su escritorio, nadie lo ignoraba, un revólver. Había llorado con decoro, el año anterior, la inesperada muerte de su mujer — ¡una Gauss, que le trajo una buena dote!—, pero el dinero era su verdadera pasión. Con íntimo bochorno se sabía menos apto para ganarlo que para conservarlo. Era muy religioso; creía tener con el Señor un pacto secreto, que lo eximía de obrar bien, a trueque de oraciones y devociones. Calvo, corpulento, enlutado, de quevedos ahumados y barba rubia, esperaba de pie, junto a la ventana, el informe confidencial de la obrera Zunz.

La vio empujar la verja (que él había entornado a propósito) y cruzar el patio sombrío. La vio hacer un pequeño rodeo cuando el perro atado ladró. Los labios de Emma se atareaban como los de quien reza en voz baja; cansados, repetían la sentencia que el señor Loewenthal oiría antes de morir.

Las cosas no ocurrieron como había previsto Emma Zunz. Desde la madrugada anterior, ella se había soñado muchas veces, dirigiendo el firme revólver, forzando al miserable a confesar la miserable culpa y exponiendo la intrépida estratagema que permitiría a la justicia de Dios triunfar de la justicia humana. (No por temor, sino por ser un instrumento de la justicia, ella no quería ser castigada.) Luego, un solo balazo en mitad del pecho rubricaría la suerte de Loewenthal. Pero las cosas no ocurrieron así.

Ante Aarón Loewenthal, más que la urgencia de vengar a su padre, Emma sintió la de castigar el ultraje padecido por ello. No podía no matarlo, después de esa minuciosa deshonra. Tampoco tenía tiempo que perder en teatralerías. Sentada, tímida, pidió excusas a Loewenthal, invocó (a fuer de delatora) las obligaciones de la lealtad, pronunció algunos nombres, dio a entender otros y se cortó como si la venciera el temor. Logró que Loewenthal saliera a buscar una copa de agua. Cuando éste, incrédulo de tales aspavientos, pero indulgente, volvió del comedor, Emma ya había sacado del cajón el pesado revólver. Apretó el gatillo dos veces.

El considerable cuerpo se desplomó como si los estampidos y el humo lo hubieran roto, el vaso de agua se rompió, la cara la miró con asombro y cólera, la boca de la cara la injurió en español y en ídisch. Las malas palabras no cejaban; Emma tuvo que hacer fuego otra vez. En el patio, el perro encadenado rompió a ladrar, y una efusión de brusca sangre manó de los labios obscenos y manchó la barba y la ropa. Emma inició la acusación que tenía preparada ("He vengado a mi padre y no me podrán castigar..."), pero no la acabó, porque el señor Loewenthal ya había muerto. No supo nunca si alcanzó a comprender.

Los ladridos tirantes le recordaron que no podía, aún, descansar. Desordenó el diván, desabrochó el saco del cadáver, le quitó los quevedos salpicados y los dejó sobre el fichero. Luego tomó el teléfono y repitió lo que tantas veces repetiría, con esas y con otras palabras: *Ha ocurrido una cosa que es increíble... El señor Loewenthal me hizo venir con el pretexto de la huelga... Abusó de mí, lo maté...*

La historia era increíble, en efecto, pero se impuso a todos, porque sustancialmente era cierta. Verdadero era el tono de Emma Zunz, verdadero el pudor, verdadero el odio. Verdadero también era el ultraje que había padecido; sólo eran falsas circunstancias, la hora y uno o dos nombres propios.

Jorge Luis Borges
1899–1986
Argentina

El jardín de senderos que se bifurcan
Ficciones, 1944.

A Victoria Ocampo

EN la página 242 de la *Historia de la Guerra Europea* de Liddell Hart, se lee que una ofensiva de trece divisiones británicas (apoyadas por mil cuatrocientas piezas de artillería) contra la línea Serre-Montauban había sido planeada para el veinticuatro de julio de 1916 y debió postergarse hasta la mañana del día veintinueve. Las lluvias torrenciales (anota el capitán Liddell Hart) provocaron esa demora —nada significativa, por cierto. La siguiente declaración, dictada, releída y firmada por el doctor Yu Tsun, antiguo catedrático de inglés en la *Hochschule* de Tsingtao, arroja una insospechada luz sobre el caso. Faltan las dos páginas iniciales.

"... y colgué el tubo. Inmediatamente después, reconocí la voz que había contestado en alemán. Era la del capitán Richard Madden. Madden, en el departamento de Viktor Runeberg, quería decir el fin de nuestros afanes y —pero eso parecía muy secundario, o *debía parecérmelo*— también de nuestras vidas. Quería decir que Runeberg había sido arrestado, o asesinado.[1] Antes que declinara el sol de ese día, yo correría la misma suerte. Madden era implacable. Mejor dicho, estaba obligado a ser implacable. Irlandés a las órdenes de Inglaterra, hombre acusado de tibieza y tal vez de traición ¿cómo no iba a abrazar y agradecer este milagroso favor: el descubrimiento, la captura, quizá la muerte, de dos agentes del Imperio Alemán? Subí a mi cuarto; absurdamente cerré la puerta con llave y me tiré de espaldas en la estrecha cama de hierro. En la ventana estaban los tejados de siempre y el sol nublado de las seis. Me pareció increíble que ese día sin premoniciones ni símbolos fuera el de mi muerte implacable. A pesar de mi padre muerto, a pesar de haber sido un niño en un simétrico jardín de Hai Feng ¿yo, ahora, iba a motir? Después reflexioné que todas las cosas le suceden a uno precisamente, precisamente ahora. Siglos de siglos y sólo en el presente ocurren los hechos; innumerables hombres en el aire, en la tierra y el mar, y todo lo que realmente pasa me pasa a mí... El casi intolerable recuerdo del rostro acaballado de Madden abolió esas divagaciones. En mitad de mi odio y de mi terror (ahora no me importa hablar de terror: ahora que he burlado a Richard Madden, ahora que mi garganta anhela la cuerda) pensé que ese guerrero tumultuoso y sin duda feliz no sospechaba que yo poseía el Secreto. El nombre del preciso lugar del nuevo parque de artillería británico sobre el Ancre. Un pájaro rayó el cielo gris y ciegamente lo traduje en un aeroplano y a ese aeroplano en muchos (en el cielo francés) aniquilando el parque de artillería con bombas verticales. Si mi boca, antes que la deshiciera un balazo, pudiera gritar ese nombre de modo

---

[1]Hipótesis odiosa y estrafalaria. El espía prusiano Hans Rabenes, alias Viktor Runeberg, agredió con una pistola automática al portador de la orden de arresto, capitán Richard Madden. Este, en defensa propia, le causó heridas que determinaron su muerte. *(Nota del editor).*

que lo oyeran en Alemania... Mi voz humana era muy pobre.
¿Cómo hacerla llegar al oído del Jefe? Al oído de aquel hombre enfermo y odioso, que no sabía de Runeberg y de mí sino que estábamos en Staffordshire y que en vano esperaba noticias nuestras en su árida oficina de Berlín, examinando infinitamente periódicos... Dije en voz alta: *Debo huir*. Me incorporé sin ruido, en una inútil perfección de silencio, como si Madden ya estuviera acechándome. Algo —tal vez la mera ostentación de probar que mis recursos eran nulos— me hizo revisar mis bolsillos. Encontré lo que sabía que iba a encontrar. El reloj norteamericano, la cadena de níquel y la moneda cuadrangular, el llavero con las comprometedoras llaves inútiles del departamento de Runeberg, la libreta, una carta que resolví destruir inmediatamente (y que no destruí), el falso pasaporte, una corona, dos chelines y unos peniques, el lápiz rojo-azul, el pañuelo, el revólver con una bala. Absurdamente lo empuñé y sopesé para darme valor. Vagamente pensé que un pistoletazo puede oírse muy lejos. En diez minutos mi plan estaba maduro. La guía telefónica me dio el nombre de la única persona capaz de transmitir la noticia: vivía en un suburbio de Fenton, a menos de media hora de tren.

Soy un hombre cobarde. Ahora lo digo, ahora que he llevado a término un plan que nadie no calificará de arriesgado. Yo sé que fue terrible su ejecución. No lo hice por Alemania, no. Nada me importa un país bárbaro, que me ha obligado a la abyección de ser un espía. Además, yo sé de un hombre de Inglaterra —un hombre modesto— que para mí no es menos que Goethe. Arriba de una hora no hablé con él, pero durante una hora fue Goethe... Lo hice, porque yo sentía que el Jefe tenía en poco a los de mi raza— a los innumerables antepasados que confluyen en mí. Yo quería probarle que un amarillo podía salvar a sus ejércitos. Además, yo debía huir del capitán. Sus manos y su voz podían golpear en cualquier momento a mi puerta. Me vestí sin ruido, me dije adiós en el espejo, bajé escudriñé la calle tranquila y salí. La estación no distaba mucho de casa, pero juzgué preferible tomar un coche. Argüí que así corría menos peligro de ser reconocido; el hecho es que en la calle desierta me sentía visible y vulnerable, infinitamente. Recuerdo que le dije al cochero que se detuviera un poco antes de la entrada central. Bajé con lentitud voluntaria y casi penosa; iba a la aldea de Ashgrove, pero saqué un pasaje para una estación más lejana. El tren salía dentro de muy pocos minutos, a las ocho y cincuenta. Me apresuré; el próximo saldría a las nueve y media. No había casi nadie en el andén. Recorrí los coches: recuerdo unos labradores, una enlutada, un joven que leía con fervor los *Anales* de Tácito, un soldado herido y feliz. Los coches arrancaron al fin. Un hombre que reconocí corrió en vano hasta el límite del andén. Era el capitán Richard Madden. Aniquilado, trémulo, me encogí en la otra punta del sillón, lejos del temido cristal.

De esa aniquilación pasé a una felicidad casi abyecta. Me dije que ya estaba empeñado mi duelo y que yo había ganado el primer asalto, al burlar, siquiera por cuarenta minutos, siquiera por un favor del azar, el ataque de mi adversario. Argüí que esa victoria mínima prefiguraba la victoria total. Argüí, que no era mínima ya que sin esa diferencia preciosa que el horario de trenes me deparaba, yo estaría en la cárcel, o muerto. Argüí (no menos sofísticamente) que mi felicidad cobarde probaba que yo era hombre capaz de llevar a buen término la aventura. De esa debilidad saqué fuerzas que no me abandonaron. Preveo que el hombre se resignará cada día a empresas más atroces; pronto no habrá sino guerreros y bandoleros; les doy este consejo: *El ejecutor de una empresa atroz debe imaginar que ya la ha cumplido, debe imponerse un porvenir que sea irrevocable como el pasado.* Así procedí yo, mientras mis ojos de hombre ya muerto registraban la fluencia de aquel día que era tal vez el último, y la difusión de la noche. El tren corría con dulzura, entre fresnos. Se detuvo, casi en medio del campo. Nadie gritó el nombre de la estación. *¿Ashgrove?* les pregunté a unos chicos en el andén. *Ashgrove,* contestaron. Bajé.

Una lámpara ilustraba el andén, pero las caras de los niños quedaban en la zona de sombra. Uno me interrogó: *¿Usted va a casa del doctor Stephen Albert?* Sin aguardar contestación, otro dijo: *La casa queda lejos de aquí, pero Ud. no se perderá si toma ese camino a la izquierda y en cada encrucijada del camino doble a la izquierda.* Les arrojé una moneda (la última), bajé unos escalones de piedra y entré en el solitario camino. Este, lentamente, bajaba. Era de tierra elemental, arriba se confundían las ramas, la luna baja y circular parecía acompañarme.

Por un instante, pensé que Richard Madden había penetrado de algún modo mi desesperado propósito. Muy pronto comprendí que eso era imposible. El consejo de siempre doblar a la izquierda me recordó que tal era el procedimiento común para descubrir el patio central de ciertos laberintos. Algo entiendo de laberintos: no en vano soy bisnieto de aquel Ts'ui Pên, que fue gobernador de Yunnan y que renunció al poder temporal para escribir una novela que fuera todavía más populosa que el *Hung Lu Meng* y para edificar un laberinto en el que se perdieran todos los hombres. Trece años dedicó a esas heterogéneas fatigas, pero la mano de un forastero lo asesinó y su novela era insensata y nadie encontró el laberinto. Bajo árboles ingleses medité en ese laberinto perdido: lo imaginé inviolado y perfecto en la cumbre secreta de una montaña, lo imaginé borrado por arrozales o debajo del agua, lo imaginé infinito, no ya de quioscos ochavados y de sendas que vuelven, sino de ríos y provincias y reinos... Pensé en un laberinto de laberintos, en un sinuoso laberinto creciente que abarcara el pasado y el porvenir y que implicara de algún modo los astros. Absorto en esas ilusorias imágenes, olvidé mi destino de perseguido. Me sentí, por un tiempo indeterminado, percibidor abstracto del mundo. El vago y vivo campo, la luna, los restos de la tarde, obraron en mí; asimismo el declive que eliminaba cualquier posibilidad de cansancio. La tarde era íntima, infinita. El camino bajaba y se bifurcaba, entre las ya confusas praderas. Una música aguda y como silábica se aproximaba y se alejaba en el vaivén del viento, empañada de hojas y de distancia. Pensé que un hombre puede ser enemigo de otros hombres, de otros momentos de otros hombres, pero no de un país: no de luciérnagas, palabras, jardines, cursos de agua, ponientes. Llegué, así, a un alto portón herrumbrado. Entre las rejas descifré una alameda y una especie de pabellón. Comprendí, de pronto, dos cosas, la primera trivial, la segunda casi increíble: la música venía del pabellón, la música era china. Por eso, yo la había aceptado con plenitud, sin prestarle atención. No recuerdo si había una campana o un timbre o si llamé golpeando las manos. El chisporroteo de la música prosiguió.

Pero del fondo de la íntima casa un farol se acercaba: un farol que rayaban y a ratos anulaban los troncos, un farol de papel, que tenía la forma de los tambores y el color de la luna. Lo traía un hombre alto. No vi su rostro, porque me cegaba la luz. Abrió el portón y dijo lentamente en mi idioma:

—Veo que el piadoso Hsi P'êng se empeña en corregir mi soledad. ¿Usted sin duda querrá ver el jardín?

Reconocí el nombre de uno de nuestros cónsules y repetí desconcertado:

—¿El jardín?

—El jardín de senderos que se bifurcan.

Algo se agitó en mi recuerdo y pronuncié con incomprensible seguridad:

—El jardín de mi antepasado Ts'ui Pên.

— ¿Su antepasado? ¿Su ilustre antepasado? Adelante.

El húmedo sendero zigzagueaba como los de mi infancia. Llegamos a una biblioteca de libros orientales y occidentales. Reconocí, encuadernados en seda amarilla, algunos tomos manuscritos de la Enciclopedia Perdida que dirigió el Tercer Emperador de la Dinastía Luminosa y que no se dio nunca a la imprenta. El disco del gramófono giraba junto a un fénix de bronce. Recuerdo también un jarrón de la familia rosa y otro, anterior de muchos siglos, de ese color azul que nuestros artífices copiaron de los alfareros de Persia...

Stephen Albert me observaba, sonriente. Era (ya lo dije) muy alto, de rasgos afilados, de ojos grises y barba gris. Algo de sacerdote había en él y también de marino; después me refirió que había sido misionero en Tientsin "antes de aspirar a sinólogo".

Nos sentamos; yo en un largo y bajo diván; él de espaldas a la ventana y a un alto reloj circular. Computé que antes de una hora no llegaría mi perseguidor, Richard Madden. Mi determinación irrevocable podía esperar.

—Asombroso destino el de Ts'ui Pên —dijo Stephen Albert—. Gobernador de su provincia natal, docto en astronomía, en astrología y en la interpretación infatigable de los libros canónicos, ajedrecista, famoso poeta y calígrafo: todo lo abandonó para componer un libro y un laberinto. Renunció a los placeres de la opresión, de la justicia, del numeroso lecho, de los banquetes y aun de la erudición y se enclaustró durante trece años en el Pabellón de la Límpida Soledad. A su muerte, los herederos no encontraron sino manuscritos caóticos. La familia, como usted acaso no ignora, quiso adjudicarlos al fuego; pero su albacea —un monje taoísta o budista— insistió en la publicación.

—Los de la sangre de Ts'ui Pên —repliqué— seguimos execrando a ese monje. Esa publicación fue insensata. El libro es un acervo indeciso de borradores contradictorios. Lo he examinado alguna vez; en el tercer capítulo muere el héroe, en el cuarto está vivo. En cuanto a la otra empresa de Ts'ui Pên, a su Laberinto...

—Aquí está el Laberinto —dijo indicándome un alto escritorio laqueado.

— ¡Un laberinto de marfil! —exclamé!. Un laberinto mínimo...

—Un laberinto de símbolos —corrigió—. Un invisible laberinto de tiempo. A mí, bárbaro inglés, me ha sido deparado revelar ese misterio diáfano. Al cabo de más de cien años, los pormenores son irrecuperables, pero no es difícil conjeturar lo que sucedió. Ts'ui Pên diría una vez: *Me retiro a escribir un libro*. Y otra: *Me retiro a construir un laberinto*. Todos imaginaron dos obras; nadie pensó que libro y laberinto eran un solo objeto. El Pabellón de la Límpida Soledad se erguía en el centro de un jardín tal vez intrincado; el hecho puede haber sugerido a los hombres un laberinto físico. Ts'ui Pên murió; nadie, en las dilatadas tierras que fueron suyas, dio con el laberinto; la confusión de la novela me sugirió que ése era el laberinto. Dos circunstancias me dieron la recta solución del problema. Una: la curiosa leyenda de que Ts'ui Pên se había propuesto un laberinto que fuera estrictamente infinito. Otra: un fragmento de una carta que descubrí.

Albert se levantó. Me dio, por unos instantes, la espalda; abrió un cajón del áureo y renegrido escritorio. Volvió con un papel antes carmesí; ahora rosado y tenue y cuadriculado. Era justo el renombre caligráfico de Ts'ui Pên. Leí con incomprensión y fervor estas palabras que con minucioso pincel redactó un hombre de mi sangre: *Dejo a los varios porvenires (no a todos) mi jardín de senderos que se bifurcan*. Devolví en silencio la hoja. Albert prosiguió:

—Antes de exhumar esta carta, yo me había preguntado de qué manera un libro puede ser infinito. No conjeturé otro procedimiento que el de un volumen cíclico, circular. Un volumen cuya última página fuera idéntica a la primera, con posibilidad de continuar indefinidamente. Recordé también esa noche que está en el centro de las 1001 Noches, cuando la reina Shahrazad (por una mágica distracción del copista) se pone a referir textualmente la historia de las 1001 Noches, con riesgo de llegar otra vez a la noche en que la refiere, y así hasta lo infinito. Imaginé también una obra platónica, hereditaria, trasmitida de padre a hijo, en la que cada nuevo individuo agregara un capítulo o corrigiera con piadoso cuidado la página de los mayores. Esas conjeturas me distrajeron; pero ninguna parecía corresponder, siquiera de un modo remoto, a los contradictorios capítulos de Ts'ui Pên. En esa perplejidad, me remitieron de Oxford el manuscrito que usted ha examinado. Me detuve, como es natural, en la frase: *Dejo a los varios porvenires (no a todos) mi jardín de senderos que se bifurcan*. Casi en el acto comprendí; *el jardín de senderos que se bifurcan* era la novela caótica; la frase *varios porvenires (no a todos)* me sugirió la imagen de la bifurcación en el tiempo, no en el espacio. La relectura general de la obra confirmó esa teoría. En todas las ficciones, cada vez que un hombre se enfrenta con diversas alternativas, opta por una y elimina las otras; en la del casi inextricable Ts'ui Pên opta —simultáneamente— por todas. *Crea, así, diversos porvenires, diversos tiempos, que también proliferan y se bifurcan.* De ahí las contradicciones de la novela. Fang, digamos, tiene un secreto; un desconocido llama a su puerta; Fang resuelve matarlo. Naturalmente, hay varios desenlaces posibles: Fang puede matar al intruso, el intruso puede matar a Fang, ambos pueden salvarse, ambos pueden morir, etcétera. En la obra de Ts'ui Pên, todos los desenlaces ocurren; cada uno es el punto de partida de otras bifurcaciones. Alguna vez, los senderos de ese laberinto convergen: por ejemplo, usted llega a esta casa, pero en uno de los pasados posibles usted es mi enemigo, en otro mi amigo. Si se resigna usted a mi pronunciación incurable, leeremos unas páginas.

Su rostro, en el vívido círculo de la lámpara, era sin duda el de un anciano, pero con algo inquebrantable y aun inmortal. Leyó con lenta precisión dos redacciones de un mismo capítulo épico. En la primera, un ejército marcha hacia una batalla a través de una montaña desierta; el horror de las piedras y de la sombra le hace menospreciar la vida y logra con facilidad la victoria; en la segunda, el mismo ejército atraviesa un palacio en el que hay una fiesta; la resplandeciente batalla les parece una continuación de la fiesta y logran la victoria. Yo oía con decente veneración esas viejas ficciones, acaso menos admirables que el hecho de que las hubiera ideado mi sangre y de que un hombre de un imperio remoto me las restituyera, en el curso de una desesperada aventura, en una isla occidental. Recuerdo las palabras finales, repetidas en cada redacción como un mandamiento secreto: *Así combatieron los héroes, tranquilo el admirable corazón, violenta la espada, resignados a matar y a morir.*

Desde ese instante, sentí a mi alrededor y en mi oscuro cuerpo una invisible, intangible pululación. No la pululación de los divergentes, paralelos y finalmente coalescentes ejércitos, sino una agitación más inaccesible, más íntima y que ellos de algún modo prefiguraban. Stephen Albert prosiguió:

—No creo que su ilustre antepasado jugara ociosamente a las variaciones. No juzgo verosímil que sacrificara trece años a la infinita ejecución de un experimento retórico. En su país, la novela es un género subalterno; en aquel tiempo era un género despreciable. Ts'ui Pên fue un novelista genial, pero también fue un hombre de letras que sin duda no se consideró un mero novelista. El testimonio de sus contemporáneos procla-

ma —y harto lo confirma su vida— sus aficiones metafísicas,
místicas. La controversia filosófica usurpa buena parte de su
novela. Sé que de todos los problemas, ninguno lo inquietó y
lo trabajó como el abismal problema del tiempo. Ahora bien,
ése es el *único* problema que no figura en las páginas del *Jardín.* Ni siquiera usa la palabra que quiere decir *tiempo.* ¿Cómo se explica usted esa voluntaria omisión?

Propuse varias soluciones; todas, insuficientes. Las discutimos; al fin, Stephen Albert me dijo:

—En una adivinanza cuyo tema es el ajedrez ¿cuál es la
única palabra prohibida? Reflexioné un momento y repuse:

—La palabra *ajedrez.*

—Precisamente —dijo Albert—, *El Jardín de senderos que
se bifurcan* es una enorme adivinanza, o parábola, cuyo tema
es el tiempo; esa causa recóndita le prohibe la mención de su
nombre. Omitir *siempre* una palabra, recurrir a metáforas
ineptas y a perífrasis evidentes, es quizá el modo más enfáti-
co de indicarla. Es el modo tortuoso que prefirió, en cada
uno de los meandros de su infatigable novela, el oblicuo Ts'ui
Pên. He confrontado centenares de manuscritos, he corregido
los errores que la negligencia de los copistas ha introducido,
he conjeturado el plan de ese caos, he restablecido, he creído
restablecer, el orden primordial, he tráducido la obra entera:
me consta que no emplea una sola vez la palabra *tiempo.* La
explicación es obvia: *El jardín de senderos que se bifurcan* es
una imagen incompleta, pero no falsa, del universo tal como
lo concebía Ts'ui Pên. A diferencia de Newton y de Schopenhauer, su antepasado no creía en un tiempo uniforme, absoluto. Creía en infinitas series de tiempos, en una red creciente
y vertiginosa de tiempos divergentes, convergentes y paralelos. Esa trama de tiempos que se aproximan, se bifurcan, se
cortan o que secularmente se ignoran, abarca *todas* las posibilidades. No existimos en la mayoría de esos tiempos; en algunos existe usted y no yo; en otros, yo, no usted; en otros,
los dos. En éste, que un favorable azar me depara, usted ha
llegado a mi casa; en otro, usted, al atravesar el jardín, me ha
encontrado muerto; en otro, yo digo esas mismas palabras,
pero soy un error, un fantasma.

—En todos —articulé no sin un temblor— yo agradezco y
venero su recreación del jardín de Ts'ui Pên.

—No en todos —murmuró con una sonrisa—. El tiempo se
bifurca perpetuamente hacia innumerables futuros. En uno
de ellos soy su enemigo.

Volví a sentir esa pululación de que hablé. Me pareció

que el húmedo jardín que rodeaba la casa estaba saturado
hasta lo infinito de invisibles personas. Esas personas eran Albert y yo, secretos, atareados y multiformes en otras dimensiones de tiempo. Alcé los ojos y la tenue pesadilla se disipó.
En el amarillo y negro jardín había un solo hombre; pero ese
hombre era fuerte como una estatua, pero ese hombre avanzaba por el sendero y era el capitán Richard Madden.

—El porvenir ya existe —respondí—, pero yo soy su amigo. ¿Puedo examinar de nuevo la carta?

Albert se levantó. Alto, abrió el cajón del alto escritorio;
me dio por un momento la espalda. Yo había preparado el revólver. Disparé con sumo cuidado: Albert se desplomó sin
una queja, inmediatamente. Yo juro que su muerte fue instantánea: una fulminación.

Lo demás es irreal, insignificante. Madden irrumpió, me
arrestó. He sido condenado a la horca. Abominablemente he
vencido: he comunicado a Berlín el secreto nombre de la ciudad que deben atacar. Ayer la bombardearon; lo leí en los
mismos periódicos que propusieron a Inglaterra el enigma de
que el sabio sinólogo Stephen Albert muriera asesinado por
un desconocido, Yu Stun. El Jefe ha descifrado ese enigma.
Sabe que mi problema era indicar (a través del estrépito de la
guerra) la ciudad que se llama Albert y que no hallé otro medio que matar a una persona de ese nombre. No sabe (nadie
puede saber) mi innumerable contricción y cansancio.

Guillermo Cabrera Infante
1929—
Cuba

Un rato de tenmeallá
Así en la paz como en la guerra, 1960.

y entonces el hombre dice que ellos dicen que le diga que
no pueden esperar mas y entonces y entonces y entonces
mama le dijo que eran unos esto y lo otro y que primero la
sacaban a ella por delante y el hombre le dice que uno lo coja

con el que no tiene que ver nada y que el hace lo que le mandan y que para eso le pagaban y mama le dijo que estaba bien
que ella comprendia todo pero que si no podian esperar un
mes mas y el hombre dice que ni un dia y que mañana ven-
drian a sacar los muebles y que no oponga resistencia porque
seria peor porque traerian a la policia y entonces los sacarian
a la fuerza y los meterian en la carcel y que entonces y señalo
para mi y para julita en la cuna nos quedariamos sin nadie
que nos cuidara y que lo pensara bien que lo pensara bien y
entonces mama le dijo que parecia mentira que ellos que eran
pobres como nosotros se unieran a los ricos y el hombre dice
que el tenia que darle de comer a sus hijos y que si a ella no
se le habia muerto ninguno de hambre a el si y mama todo
lo que hizo fue levantar la mano y enseñarle tres dedos y el
hombre se quedo callado y luego mama miro para nosotros y
dijo que nosotros no nos habiamos muerto porque quizas morir fuera demasiado bueno para nosotros y le dijo que le diera
un dia mas y el hombre cambio la cara que se habia puesto
cuando mama le enseño los dedos por la que trajo y entonces
mama dijo que en vez de cobrar debian pagar por vivir en
aquella y dijo una palabra dificil seguida de una mala palabra
y el hombre respondio que a el no le interesaba y antes de irse le dice que mejor iba empaquetando las cosas y que no fuera a dañar el piso o las puertas o los cristales de la luceta porque tendriamos que pagarlo y lo que mama hizo fue tirarle la
puerta en la cara y el tipo dijo que eso no lo decia el sino el
dueño y que no fuera tan injusta pero al golpear la puerta
contra el marco una de las bisagras de arriba se zafo y la hoja
casi se cayo y mama comenzo a maldecir y decir cosas malas
y luego comenzo a halarse los pelos y darse golpes en la cabeza hasta que cayo al suelo y se puso a llorar recostada contra
la hoja que se mecia cada vez que sollozaba y mariantonieta
se arrimo a ella y le dijo que no llorara que todo se arreglaria
y que quiza papa trajera dinero pero mama siguio llorando y
mariantonieta se puso a darme de comer como antes de que
llegara el hombre y me golpeo en la mano porque y me meti
los dedos en la nariz y luego hice una bolita y entonces yo cogi y empece a llorar y cuando ella trato de seguirme dando la
comida le pegue en la cuchara y la bote al suelo y entonces
ella me levanto por un brazo con fuerza pero no me dolio porque mas me dolian las nalgadas que me estaba dando y dice
que yo soy una vejiga de mierda y cogio la tabla de encender
la candela pero entonces mama la aguanto y le dijo que me
dejara que bastante teniamos ya para que nos fueran a estar

agolpeando tambien y entonces mariantonieta dice que ya yo
tengo seis años para comprender bien lo que hago y lo que
pase y me levanto otra vez pero por el otro brazo y senti como la tabla hacia fresco por arriba de mi cabeza y entonces
mama le grito que hiciera lo que ella decia y que que clase de
hermana era ella y que que pasaria si ella faltara y nos dejara
a su cuidado y mariantonieta me dejo y se fue a comer y no
debe de haber estado muy buena porque un nudo subia y
bajaba en su garganta y entonces fue que llego papa que venia arrastrando los pies con la cabeza como si la tuviese directamente sobre el pecho y no sobre los hombros y mama
dijo que no tenia que preguntarle para saber que no habia
conseguido nada y que si no hubiera sido por ella que logro
que le fiaran los platanos no hubieramos comido y que que
pensaba el que si creia que asi se podia seguir y papa dijo que
nadie queria prestarle y que cuando lo veian venir se iban antes de que llegara y era muy duro para un hombre ver como
los que el creia sus amigos le viraban la espalda ahora que estaba cesante y que si acaso alguno se quedaba para oirlo no
era por mucho rato y que invariablemente le decia que el estaba muy chivado para echarse mas problemas encima pero
que veria a ver si podia hacer algo por el pero que no lo estuviera apurando y cayendole arriba y velandolo como si fuera un muerto y salandolo y que el tuviera que aguantar callado dijo y hasta sonreir porque el maldito hambre lo obligaba
y dio un puñetazo en la mesa y luego hizo una mueca y se
paso una mano por la otra mano y siguio que los unicos que
lo buscaban eran los garroteros y a esos si no queria encon-
trarselos pues ya uno lo habia amenazado dijo y lo habia za-
randeado como si fuera un trapo y que el habia tenido que
soportarlo porque penso que si lo mataba iba a parar a la carcel y nos vio a mi y a julita mendingando y a mariantonieta
haciendo algo peor y a mama muerta de vergüenza y hambre
dijo y que mas valia que un tranvia lo matara pero que ni para ayudar a eso tenia el ya valor fue lo que dijo y entonces
mama le repitio que que iba a hacer que que iba a hacer que
que iba a hacer cada vez mas fuerte hasta que las venas del
cuello se le pusieron como si por debajo de la piel tuviera una
mano que empujaba con los dedos luego le conto que ya habian venido los de la casa aunque solo fue uno solo pero fue
eso lo que ella conto y que la demanda la iban a cumplir mañana y entonces papa dijo que lo dejara descansar para pensar
un momento y que si ella se iba a poner contra el tambien
que le avisara y la mano de mama se fue atras poco a poco y

cuando hablo la voz la tenia algo ronca y dijo que estaba bien
que estaba bien y que la comida la tenia en el fogon y que no
debia estar caliente porque se habia apagado la candela y ella
no queria volverla a juntar porque no quedaba mas que una
tabla y quedaba por hacer la comida si aparecia algo y entonces papa le pregunto que si ella habia comido y mama respondio que ya pero mariantonieta dice que mentira que no habia
comido y entonces dice que habia tomado un buche de cafe
y que no tenia ganas de comer mas nada que tenia el estoma-
go lleno y papa dijo que de aire y que viniera a comer que hiciera el favor y la cogio por un brazo que si no el no comia y
mama dijo que no sin soltarse que era muy poco y que a el le
hacia mas falta que estaba caminando y papa dijo que donde
comia uno comian dos y que se dejara de boberias y mama se
sento en el otro cajon que el habia puesto junto a la mesa y
empezaron a comer y a mama casi se le aguaron los ojos y
hasta beso a papa y todo y como ya no habia mas nada que
oir sali y cogi mi caballo que estaba tirado en el piso descansando y sali por el portillo al placer y me subi la saya y me
baje los pantalones y cuando la tierra estuvo bien mojada puse todo en su lugar y me agache y comence a remover el fango bien para que las torticas me salieran bien y no pasara lo
que ayer cuando no alcanzo para hacer un buen cocinado y
se desmoronaban en las manos y pense que que queque hubiera hecho y hice unas cuantas y las puse a secar bien al sol
para que estuvieran listas cuando llegaran los demas chiquitos
del colegio yo no iba porque no tenia ropa ni dinero para la
merienda y porque mama tampoco me podia llevar y era muy
lejos para ir sola y poderlas vender bien por dos botones cada
una y regrese a casa porque el aireplano tenia el motor roto y
no pude ir hasta mejico a mi finca en mejico y volvi en mi
entemovil y frene justo en la coqueta con la defensa rayando
el espejo y que lio porque hacia seis meses que no pagabamos
un plazo y mañana venian a llevarsela junto con los otros
muebles y mama estaba alli aguantando la hoja mientras papa
clavaba bien la bisagra y cuando la puerta estuvo lista papa le
dijo a mama que hiciera el favor de darselo que tenia que irse
y mama dijo que no que no que no que no que no que no y
entonces papa le grito que no se pusiera asi y mama respondio tambien gritando que no que eso traia mala suerte que los
viculnos se rompian y que el bien sabia lo que le habia pasado a su hermana y entonces papa le dijo que no fuera sanaca
y que se dejara de tonterias y que si se iba a poner con supersticiones y que no fuera a creer esas papas rusas y que mas mal

no podiamos estar y que si su hermana se habia tenido que
divorciar no habia sido porque lo empeñara sino porque ella
bien sabia con quien la habia cogido tio jorge bueno tio no no
tio sino esposo de tiamalia y mama le grito que si el también
se iba a poner a regar esas calumnias y que parecia mentira
que el conocia bien a su hermana ama nadie se pona de acuerdo con el nombre pues mama decia ama y papa amalita y
abuela hija y nosotros tiamalia como para saber que era una
santa incapaz del menor acto impuquido asi dijo y que aquello habia sido una confusion lamentable y entonces papa se
quedo callado trago algo aunque yo no vi que estuviera comiendo y dijo que estaba bien que estaba bien que no queria
volver a empezar a discutir y que le diera el anillo porque ella
sabia bien que era el unico ojebto de valor que nos quedaba y
que si el suyo estaba alla ya no veia por que no iba a estar el
otro que la superticion o la llegada de un mal cierto lo mismo
alcanzaba a uno que a otro y que de todas maneras una desgracia mas no se iba a echar de ver y que ademas el le prome-
tia que tan pronto se nivelara seguro que se referia al piso que
esta todo escachado lo primero que sacaba del empeño eran
los anillos los dos y entonces mama se lo fue a sacar pero no
salia y le dijo que viera que el mismo anillo se negaba a irse
pero papa le dijo que eso se debia a que las manos hinchadas
y maltratadas no eran seguramente las mismas finas maneci-
tas de hace veinte años y desde que se lo puso no se lo habia
quitado y que eso salia con jabon y mama fue y metio la mano en el cubo y se enjabono bien el dedo y papa le dijo que
no lo gastara todo que era lo unico que quedaba y que nadie
se habia bañado todavia y mama saco el anillo del agua espumoso y lo tiro al suelo papa lo recogio y se fue y mama se
quedo maldiciendo pero enseguida se callo y dijo que le dolia
la cabeza y le pregunto a mariantonieta que si quedaba alguna
pastilla y mariantonieta se puso a registrar en la gaveta y dijo
que si con la cabeza y le dije a mama porque estaba de espaldas dice que si y mama dijo que la pusiera sobre la mesa tan
pronto como acabara de fregar se la iba a tomar y recostarse
un rato a ver si se le pasaba y mariantonieta dijo que ella se
iba a bañar y mama le dijo que le podia hacer daño acabada
de comer y ella respondio que para lo que habia comido y
mama se puso a fregar y mariantonieta a recoger agua en el
cubo y yo sali corriendo por entre las sabanas y toallas tendidas en medio del patio y a cada sabana le deje un vano prieto
al pasarle la mano a ver como estaban las torticas y entonces
me acorde que negrita estaba enterrada cerca del basurero ha-

ce tanto tiempo que casi se me olvido y fui alla y arranque las
yerbitas y arregle la cruz que estaba media caida y me acorde
mucho de ella mas que nunca antes como si hubiera muerto
mientras arreglaba la cruz y llore y no pude comprender por
que se muere la gente precisamente cuando uno mas la quiere
y por que hay que morirse y me acorde tambien de como ori-
naba y levanta la pata igual que ella sobre la cruz y me rei y
tumbe la cruz y vine corriendo para aca y en el camino cogi
un palo y cuando pase junto al gato de la encargada le di un
palo en el cocote pero siguio durmiendo como si nada aunque
luego yo creo que no siguio durmiendo

cuando volvi mama ya estaba terminando y mariantonieta
estaba secandose el pelo al sol y cuando iba a entrar su cuerpo se puso entre mama que salia y el sol en el suelo y mama
dijo que que claro estaba el dia sin siquiera mirar al cielo y
que se pusiera algo mas debajo y ella contesto que nadie la
iba a ver ni nadie iba a venir y que ella no iba a salir y que
ademas habia que ahorrar ropa interior y mama dijo que hiciera lo que le diera la gana y se fue a botar la enjabonadura
luego lavo el platon de fregar y le dijo que hiciera el favor de
secar la loza aunque todos los cacharros eran de lata y que
ella se iba a tomar la aspirina y lo hizo y se acosto y mariantonieta se sento junto a la mesa y también lo hizo y cuando
termino ya mama estaba metiendo ruido con los ronquidos y
entonces comprendi por que papa de mañana tenia cara de
sueño y ojeras por la mañana y fue cuando el caballo habia
regresado solo y aproveche para montarlo aunque papa dijo
una vez que las niñas no debian montar a caballo y volvi a ir
a buscar las tortas y las traje porque ya estaban y me pare en
la puerta y me puse a pregonar y entonces vi como salia del
cuarto y venia para aca pero antes de llegar se paro en la puerta del cuarto de moises y le pregunte mi hermanita donde vas
pero ella no me respondio y yo volvi donde vas mi hermana
donde vas y ella me dijo que siguiera vendiendo que se me
iban a ir los clientes y casi vi una sonrisa en su cara triste y seria y entonces cuando yo volvi a preguntar el abrio y ella le
dijo algo y debia tener mucho calor porque se desabotono
la blusa y yo me puse mas cerca y debia haber alguna lamina
en su pecho porque el no dejaba de mirar aunque a veces si
dejaba y miraba a todos lados pero no como miraba a mi hermana yo no se como ella se atrevia a estar alli pues bien sabia
lo que habia dicho mama que no nos arrimaramos al cuarto
de ese cochino polaco porque ella lo habia sorprendido mirando por el tragaluz del baño mientras mariantonieta se bañaba

y que ella le habia gritado que se bajara y que el no se habia
bajado y que ella lo habia amenazado con darle un palo o llamar al guardia y que el se habia aprovechado de que sabia que
pepe papa no estaba en casa y le dijo que se bajaba si le daba
la gana y que no lo apurara y antes de bajarse le dijo algo a
mariantonieta que mama no pudo oir y que ella no quiso decir que era cuando salio y no le dijo nada a papa para no buscarle problemas porque sabia el genio que tenia pepe y que
iba a haber una tragedia y yo no se como ella se atrevia y ahora debia tener algun bicho entre los senos porque el seguia mirando como si quisiese poner los ojos donde la mano ahora
quiza para matar el bicho pero ella no queria matarlo y le
quito la mano y le dijo que adentro y parece que el queria hacerle algun regalo porque le pregunto que cuando cumplia los
dieciseis y ella dijo que el mes que viene y el dijo que estaba
bien que entonces no habia problema y que entrara y mama
dijo un dia que no entraramos ahi nunca asi nos ofreciera el
un mundo colorado y cuando yo le pregunte que por que ella
me dijo que porque el era un hombre asqueroso que hacia cosas asquerosas y cuando le pregunte como era un mundo colorado me mando bien lejos pero yo creo que ella se refirio a
que no limpiaba el cuarto y no tendia las camas y que habia
mucho polvo y suciedad sobre todo porque mi hermana cuando entro hizo una mueca como cuando le dan a uno un pur-
gante y yo vi que fue hasta la cama y comenzo a quitar las sabanas y ahora sabia que seguro que el la habia llamado para
que le hiciera la limpieza y que eso fue lo que le dijo antes de
bajarse del tragaluz y entonces el cerro la puerta y yo fui porque vi que estaba abierta hasta la ventana y me agache por debajo de la cortina para mirar no fuera ser que a mariantonieta
le hiciera mucho daño el polvo y la vi pero ella dibio haber
trabajado mucho mientras el cerro la puerta y yo fui hasta la
ventana y debia sentirse muy cansada porque se habia acostado en la cama y habia mucho calor alli dentro entre las cajas
grandes apiladas y las pilas de trastos viejos amontonados y
los montones de telas y de cosas y de y de porque aunque no
faltaba mucho para nochebuena ella comenzo a quitarse toda
la blusa y cuando acabo seguia quitandose cosas pero entonces la cara de moises se asomo por debajo de la cortina y me
dijo que fuera una niña buena y una niña linda y me fuera a
jugar y metio la mano en el bolsillo y la extendio por entre
los barrotes y me dijo que cogiera ese kilo y que fuera a vender la mercancia y yo le pregunte que que cosa iba a hacer mi
hermana y el cambio la cara como el cobrador y me dijo un

negocio juntos un negocio y que cuando saldria le pregunte y
me respondio que orita y que cogiera el kilo entonces fue que
me acorde que me acorde que el tenia el kilo en la mano y me
dijo que le dijera a mama que me diera un rato de tenmealla y
cogi el kilo que estaba embarrado de sudor y el entro la mano
y yo me levante y el cerro la ventana y yo sali corriendo y
apretaba el kilo y corria repitiendo un rato de tenmealla para
que no se me olvidara y entonces cuando llegue mama estaba
todavia dormida y la desperte y le dije que decia que decia
que me diera un rato de tenmealla y ella se levanto con la cara marcada por el alambre y los ojos hinchados y me tomo en
los brazos y me apreto contra su cara y la senti fria y rugosa
como si hubiese sido el propio alambre del bastidor y me pregunto que quien lo decia y yo le dije que el dulcero y me dijo
con una voz agradable y suave casi sin mover los labios que
por el amor de dios dejara a la gente trabajar en paz que ese
hombre se estaba ganando la vida en su negocio y por poco le
pregunto que como lo habia adivinado porque estaba hablando casi en el mismo tono que moises aunque las caras no se
parecian y me dijo como el que me fuera a vender mi mercancia tranquilamente y no supe como ella supo que yo estaba
vendiendo y volvi a mis tortas y segui pregonando mientras
en el cuarto cerrado los ruidos de la limpieza apenas llegaban
a mis oidos y parece que mi hermana se habia dado un golpe
porque a menudo gemia y entonces fue cuando llego papa
igual que la otra vez y me dijo que recogiera las cosas y entrara al cuarto porque alli no debia seguir pues en el solar vivian
gentes sinvergüenzas y me dijo que recordara siempre que a la
pobreza y la miseria siempre sigue la desonra y aunque no comprendi mucho lo que dijo si entendi como lo dijo y recogi el
tablero con la mercancia y entre con el y ya mama estaba en
pie cosiendo una bata toda llena de remiendos y le pregunto
a papa que que hubo y papa dijo no le dijo negra o mi vida
como siempre sino julia que solo le habian dado unoquince
y mama dijo que si por esa y repitio la mala palabra que siempre decia habia empeñado el último lazo que la ataba a el que
bien la podia meter y dijo otra mala palabra mas mala y cobrar cincuenta centavos por cada uno que consiguiera y papa
le grito que no fuera tan animal y que se fijara ante quien hablaba esas cosas y a mama se le volvio a ver la mano bajo la
piel del pescuezo y papa siguio gritando cosas y le dijo que
bien podia ella haber hecho otra cosa que no fuera parir hembras que no eran mas que rompederos de cabeza y apenas podian ayudar mientras no tenian quince y que a esa edad se

iban con cualquier desarrapado y no se ocupaban de quienes
las habian traido al mundo y mama le dijo que la culpa la tuvo el que era quien las habia hecho y el le grito que no le faltara el respeto delante de las niñas aunque yo era la unica que
puede oir en ese momento y como si hubiese leido lo que yo
pensaba se lo dijo asi a papa mama y le dice tambien que esa
es una manera facil de salir del paso y la bronca sigue y yo me
asomo al oir que una puerta se abre y como pense era la de
moises y salgo y corro al tiempo que ella sale y parece que el
polvo la ha hecho daño porque cuando sale tiene los ojos inri-
tados y escupia a menudo y fue a la pila y se lavo la cara y la
boca varias veces y me dio un niquel y me dijo que fuera y
trajera alcol sin que se enterara mama y cuando se agacho a
coger el pedacito de jabon que vio en el fondo de la pila se le
cayo un rollito de billetes del seno y yo lo vi y se lo dije yo vi
el rollito yo lo vi vi el rollito de billetes yo lo vi y empece a
saltar cantando yo lo vi yo lo vi yo lo vi el rollito el rollito rollito y parece que no le gusto porque grito con los dientes
apretados que me callara la boca y yo le pregunte que de donde lo habia sacado y que si era que moises le habia pagado
por limpiarle y tambien le pregunte te lo regalo mi hermanita
te lo regalo te lo regalo y ella me dijo que no que acababa de
vender algo que nunca recobraria y yo la interrumpi y le dije
que el que y ella siguio como si no hubiera oido pero que es
necesario pues habia que evitar el desasio dijo o algo parecido
y que si ese habia sido el precio que que se iba a hacer y que
ahora sabia donde encontrar la plata a fin de mes y que quizas si hasta pudiera comprarnos alguna ropa y comprarse ella
tambien dijo y acabo de lavarse y parece que el jabon le cayo
en los ojos o le duele alguna tripa porque fue al ultimo servicio en el fondo y estuvo llorando y cuando yo abri la puerta
y entre y le pregunte que que pasaba me boto y me dijo que
me fuera a jugar y que la dejara tranquila que no tenia ganas
de ver a nadie ahora ni nunca mas si fuera posible y le pregunte que si le habia hecho algo malo o dicho algo que no estaba
bien y me dijo que no y me dijo mi vida y mi amor por primera
vez hacia tiempo y me beso varias veces como hacia tiempo
que no lo hacia y ese fue el dia mas feliz para mi porque casi
nadie me regaño y todo el mundo me beso y acaricio y hasta
me regalaron un kilo y le pregunte que si nos ibamos y me
dijo que ya no que ya no y ya no teniamos que volver al campo como dijo papa a comer lo que sembraramos si nos dejaban sembrar y comer aunque fuera en los rejendones de la sierra o donde el jejen parece que se rie puso el huevo y me acor-

de del kilo porque me pico el oido porque me acorde de los
mosquitos porque cuando me fui a rascar lo encontre aunque
creia que estaba perdido y lo cogi y entonces me fui a ente-
rrarlo para que me diera una mata y poder comprar chambe-
lonas y globos sin tener que revolver los basureros en busca
de botellas y mientras corro con el kilo en la boca canto

—

Alejo Carpentier
1904—1980
Cuba

Viaje a la semilla
Guerra del Tiempo, 1958.

I

¿QUÉ quieres, viejo...?
        Varias veces cayó la pregunta de lo alto de los anda-
mios. Pero el viejo no respondía. Andaba de un lugar a otro, fis-
goneando, sacándose de la garganta un largo monólogo de frases incomprensibles. Ya habían descendido las tejas, cubriendo los canteros muertos con su mosaico de barro cocido. Arriba, los picos desprendían piedras de mampostería, haciéndolas rodar por canales de madera, con gran revuelo de cales y
de yesos. Y por las almenas sucesivas que iban desdentando
las murallas aparecían —despojados de su secreto— cielos ra-
sos ovales o cuadrados, cornisas, guirnaldas, dentículos, astrá-
galos, y papeles encolados que colgaban de los testeros como
viejas pieles de serpiente en muda. Presenciando la demolición, una Ceres con la nariz rota y el peplo desvaído, veteado
de negro el tocado de mieses, se erguía en el traspatio, sobre
su fuente de mascarones borrosos. Visitados por el sol en horas de sombra, los peces grises del estanque bostezaban en
agua musgosa y tibia, mirando con el ojo redondo aquellos
obreros, negros sobre el claro cielo, que iban rebajando la altura secular de la casa. El viejo se había sentado, con el cayado
apuntándole la barba, al pie de la estatua. Miraba el subir y

bajar de los cubos en que viajaban restos apreciables. Oíanse, en sordina, los rumores de la calle mientras, arriba, las poleas concertaban, sobre ritmos de hierro con piedras, sus gorjeos de aves desagradables y pechugonas.

Dieron las cinco. Las cornisas y entablamentos se despoblaron. Sólo quedaron escaleras de mano, preparando el asalto del día siguiente. El aire se hizo más fresco, aligerando de sudores, blasfemias, chirridos de cuerdas, ejes que pedían alcuzas y palmadas en torsos pringosos. Para la casa montada el crepúsculo llegaba más pronto. Se vestía de sombras en horas en que su ya caída balaustrada superior solía regalar a las fachadas algún relumbre de sol. La Ceres apretaba los labios. Por primera vez las habitaciones dormirían sin persianas, abiertas sobre un paisaje de escombros.

Contrariando sus apetencias, varios capiteles yacían entre las hierbas. Las hojas de acanto descubrían su condición vegetal. Una enredadera aventuró sus tentáculos hacia la voluta jónica, atraída por un aire de familia. Cuando cayó la noche, la casa estaba más cerca de la tierra. Un marco de puerta se erguía aún, en lo alto, con tablas de sombra suspendidas de sus bisagras desorientadas.

II

Entonces el negro viejo, que no se había movido, hizo gestos extraños, volteando su cayado sobre un cementerio de baldosas.

Los cuadros de mármol, blancos y negros, volaron a los pisos, vistiendo la tierra. Las piedras, con saltos certeros, fueron a cerrar los boquetes de las murallas. Hojas de nogal claveteadas se encajaron en sus marcos, mientras los tornillos de las charnelas volvían a hundirse en sus hoyos, con rápida rotación. En los canteros muertos, levantados por el esfuerzo de las flores, las tejas juntaron sus fragmentos, alzando un sonoro torbellino de barro, para caer en lluvia sobre la armadura del techo. La casa creció, traída nuevamente a sus proporciones habituales, pudorosa y vestida. La Ceres fue menos gris. Hubo más peces en la fuente. Y el murmullo del agua llamó begonias olvidadas.

El viejo introdujo una llave en la cerradura de la puerta principal, y comenzó a abrir ventanas. Sus tacones sonaban a hueco. Cuando encendió los velones, un estremecimiento amarillo corrió por el óleo de los retratos de familia, y gentes

vestidas de negro murmuraron en todas las galerías, al compás
de cucharas movidas en jícaras de chocolate.

Don Marcial, Marqués de Capellanías, yacía en su lecho
de muerte, el pecho acorazado de medallas, escoltado por cuatro cirios con largas barbas de cera derretida.

III

Los cirios crecieron lentamente, perdiendo sudores. Cuando recobraron su tamaño, los apagó la monja apartando una
lumbre. Las mechas blanquearon, arrojando el pabilo. La casa
se vació de visitantes y los carruajes partieron en la noche.
Don Marcial pulsó un teclado invisible y abrió los ojos.

Confusas y revueltas, las vigas del techo se iban colocando
en su lugar. Los pomos de medicina, las borlas de damasco, el
escapulario de la cabecera, los daguerrotipos, las palmas de la
reja, salieron de sus nieblas. Cuando el médico movió la cabeza con desconsuelo profesional, el enfermo se sintió mejor.
Durmió algunas horas y despertó bajo la mirada negra y ceju-
da del Padre Anastasio. De franca, detallada, poblada de pecados, la confesión se hizo reticente, penosa, llena de escon-
drijos. ¿Y qué derecho tenía, en el fondo, aquel carmelita, a
entrometerse en su vida? Don Marcial se encontró, de pronto,
tirado en medio del aposento. Aligerado de un peso en las sienes, se levantó con sorprendente celeridad. La mujer desnuda
que se desperezaba sobre el brocado buscó enaguas y corpi-
ños, llevándose, poco después, sus rumores de seda estrujada
y su perfume. Abajo, en el coche cerrado, cubriendo tachue-
las del asiento, había un sobre con monedas de oro.

Don Marcial no se sentía bien. Al arreglarse la corbata
frente a la luna de la consola se vio congestionado. Bajó al des-
pacho donde lo esperaban hombres de justicia, abogados y es-
cribientes, para disponer la venta pública de la casa. Todo había sido inútil. Sus pertenencias se irían a manos del mejor
postor, al compás de un martillo golpeando una tabla. Saludó
y le dejaron solo. Pensaba en los misterios de la letra escrita,
en esas hebras negras que se enlazan y desenlazan sobre anchas hojas afiligranadas de balanzas, enlazando y desenlazan-
do compromisos, juramentos, alianzas, testimonios, declaraciones, apellidos, títulos, fechas, tierras, árboles y piedras; ma-
raña de hilos, sacada del tintero, en que se enredaban las piernas del hombre, vedándole caminos desestimados por la Ley;
cordón al cuello, que apretaba su sordina al percibir el sonido
temible de las palabras en libertad. Su firma lo había traicio-

nado, yendo a complicarse en nudo y enredos de legajos. Atado por ella, el hombre de carne se hacía hombre de papel.

Era el amanecer. El reloj del comedor acababa de dar las seis de la tarde.

IV

Transcurrieron meses de luto, ensombrecidos por un remordimiento cada vez mayor. Al principio, la idea de traer una mujer a aquel aposento se le hacía casi razonable. Pero, poco a poco, las apetencias de un cuerpo nuevo fueron desplazadas por escrúpulos crecientes, que llegaron al flagelo. Cierta noche, Don Marcial se ensangrentó las carnes con una correa, sintiendo luego un deseo mayor, pero de corta duración. Fue entonces cuando la Marquesa volvió, una tarde, de su paseo a las orillas del Almendares. Los caballos de la calesa no traían en los crines más humedad que la del propio sudor. Pero, durante todo el resto del día, dispararon coces a las tablas de la cuadra, irritados, al parecer, por la inmovilidad de nubes bajas.

Al crepúsculo, una tinaja llena de agua se rompió en el baño de la Marquesa. Luego, las lluvias de mayo rebosaron el estanque. Y aquella negra vieja, con tacha de cimarrona y palomas debajo de la cama, que andaba por el patio murmurando: "¡Desconfía de los ríos, niña: desconfía de lo verde que corre!" No había día en que el agua no revelara su presencia. Pero esa presencia acabó por no ser más que una jícara derramada sobre vestido traído de París, al regreso del baile aniversario dado por el Capitán General de la Colonia.

Reaparecieron muchos parientes. Volvieron muchos amigos. Ya brillaban, muy claras las arañas del gran salón. Las grietas de la fachada se iban cerrando. El piano regresó al clavicordio. Las palmas perdían anillos, las enredaderas soltaban la primera cornisa. Blanquearon las orejas de la Ceres y los capiteles parecieron recién tallados. Más fogoso, Marcial solía pasar tardes enteras abrazando a la Marquesa. Borrándose patas de gallina, ceños y papadas, y las carnes tornaban a su dureza. Un día, un olor de pintura fresca llenó la casa.

V

Los rubores eran sinceros. Cada noche se abrían un poco más las hojas de los biombos, las faldas caían en rincones

menos alumbrados y eran nuevas barreras de encajes. Al fin la
Marquesa sopló las lámparas. Sólo él habló en la oscuridad.

Partieron para el ingenio, en gran tren de calesas —relumbrante de grupas alazanas, bocados de plata y charoles al sol.
Pero, a la sombra de las flores de Pascua que enrojecían el soportal interior de la vivienda, advirtieron que se conocían apenas. Marcial autorizó danzas y tambores de Nación, para distraerse un poco en aquellos días olientes a perfumes de Colonia, baños de benjuí, cabelleras esparcidas, y sábanas sacadas
de armarios que, al abrirse, dejaban caer sobre las losas un mazo de vetiver. El vaho del guarapo giraba en la brisa con el toque de oración. Volando bajo, las auras anunciaban lluvias reticentes, cuyas primeras gotas, anchas y sonoras, eran sorbidas por tejas tan secas que tenían diapasón de cobre. Después
de un amanecer alargado por un abrazo deslucido, aliviados
de desconciertos y cerrada la herida, ambos regresaron a la ciudad. La Marquesa trocó su vestido de viaje por un traje de novia, y, como era costumbre, los esposos fueron a la iglesia
para recobrar su libertad. Se devolvieron presentes a parientes
y amigos, y, con revuelo de bronces y alardes de jaeces, cada
cual tomó la calle de su morada. Marcial siguió visitando a
María de las Mercedes por algún tiempo, hasta el día en que
los anillos fueron llevados al taller del orfebre para ser desgrabados. Comenzaba, para Marcial, una vida nueva. En la casa
de altas rejas, la Ceres fue sustituida por una Venus italiana, y
los mascarones de la fuente adelantaron casi imperceptiblemente el relieve al ver todavía encendidas, pintadas ya el alba,
las luces de los velones.

VI

Una noche, después de mucho beber y marearse con tufos
de tabaco frío, dejados por sus amigos, Marcial tuvo la sensación extraña de que los relojes de la casa daban las cinco, luego las cuatro y media, luego las cuatro, luego las tres y media...
Era como la percepción remota de otras posibilidades. Como
cuando se piensa, en enervamiento de vigilia, que puede andarse sobre el cielo raso con el piso por cielo raso, entre muebles firmemente asentados entre las vigas del techo. Fue una
impresión fugaz, que no dejó la menor huella en su espíritu,
poco llevado, ahora, a la meditación.

Y hubo un gran sarao, en el salón de música, el día en que
alcanzó la minoría de edad. Estaba alegre al pensar que su fir-

ma había dejado de tener un valor legal, y que los registros y
escribanías, con sus polillas, se borraban de su mundo. Llegaba al punto en que los tribunales dejan de ser temibles para
quienes tienen una carne desestimada por los códigos. Luego
de achisparse con vinos generosos, los jóvenes descolgaron de
la pared una guitarra incrustada de nácar, un salterio y un ser-
pentón. Alguien dio cuerda al reloj que tocaba la Tirolesa de
las Vacas y la Balada de los Lagos de Escocia. Otro embocó
un cuerno de caza que dormía, enroscado en su cobre, sobre
los fieltros encarnados de la vitrina, al lado de la flauta traver-
sera traída de Aranjuez. Marcial, que estaba requebrando atre-
vidamente a la de Campoflorido, se sumó al guirigay, buscando en el teclado, sobre bajos falsos, la melodía del Trípili-
Trápala. Y subieron todos al desván, de pronto, recordando
que allá, bajo vigas que iban recobrando el repello, se guardaban los trajes y libreas de la Casa de Capellanías. En entrepa-
ños escarchados de alcanfor descansaban los vestidos de corte, un espadín de Embajador, varias guerreras emplastrona-
das, el manto de un Príncipe de la Iglesia, y largas casacas,
con botones de damasco y difuminos de humedad en los pliegues. Matizáronse las penumbras con cintas de amaranto, miriñaques amarillos, túnicas marchitas y flores de terciopelo.
Un traje de chispero con redecilla de borlas, nacido en una
mascarada de carnaval, levantó aplausos. La de Campoflorido redondeó los hombros empolvados bajo un rebozo de color de carne criolla, que sirviera a cierta abuela, en noche de
grandes decisiones familiares, para aviar los amansados fuegos
de un rico Síndico de Clarisas.

Disfrazados regresaron los jóvenes al salón de música. Tocado con un tricornio de regidor, Marcial pegó tres bastona-
zos en el piso, y se dio comienzo a la danza de la valse, que
las madres hallaban terriblemente impropio de señoritas, con
eso de dejarse enlazar por la cintura, recibiendo manos de
hombre sobre las ballenas del corset que todas se habían hecho según el reciente patrón de "El Jardín de las Modas". Las
puertas se obscurecieron de fámulas, cuadrerizos, sirvientes,
que venían de sus lejanas dependencias y de los entresuelos
sofocantes, para admirarse ante fiesta de tanto alboroto. Luego, se jugó a la gallina ciega y al escondite. Marcial, oculto
con la de Campoflorido detrás de un biombo chino, le estam-
pó un beso en la nuca, recibiendo en respuesta un pañuelo
perfumado, cuyos encajes de Bruselas guardaban suaves tibie-
zas de escote. Y cuando las muchachas se alejaron en las luces
del crepúsculo, hacia las atalayas y torreones que se pintaban

en grisnegro sobre el mar, los mozos fueron a la Casa de Baile,
donde tan sabrosamente se contoneaban las mulatas de grandes ajorcas, sin perder nunca —así fuera de movida una guara-
cha— sus zapatillas de alto tacón. Y como se estaba en carna-
vales, los del Cabildo Arará Tres Ojos levantaban un trueno
de tambores tras de la pared medianera, en un patio sembrado de granados. Subidos en mesas y taburetes, Marcial y sus
amigos alabaron el garbo de una negra de pasas entrecanas,
que volvía a ser hermosa, casi deseable, cuando miraba por
sobre el hombro, bailando con altivo mohín de reto.

VII

Las visitas de Don Abundio, notario y albacea de la familia, eran más frecuentes. Se sentaba gravemente a la cabecera
de la cama de Marcial, dejando caer al suelo su bastón de áca-
na para despertarlo antes de tiempo. Al abrise, los ojos trope-
zaban con una levita de alpaca, cubierta de caspa, cuyas mangas lustrosas recogían títulos y rentas. Al fin sólo quedó una
pensión razonable, calculada para poner coto a toda locura.
Fue entonces cuando Marcial quiso ingresar en el Real Seminario de San Carlos.

Después de mediocres exámenes, frecuentó los claustros,
comprendiendo cada vez menos las explicaciones de los dó-
mines. El mundo de las ideas se iba despoblando. Lo que había sido, al principio, una ecuménica asamblea de peplos, ju-
bones, golas y pelucas, controversistas y ergotantes, cobraba la inmovilidad de un museo de figuras de cera. Marcial se
contentaba ahora con una exposición escolástica de los sistemas, aceptando por bueno lo que se dijera en cualquier texto.
"León", "Avestruz", "Ballena", "Jaguar", leíase sobre los gra-
bados en el cobre de la Historia Natural. Del mismo modo,
"Aristóteles", "Santo Tomás", "Bacon", "Descartes", enca-
bezaban páginas negras, en que se catalogaban aburridamente
las interpretaciones del universo, al margen de una capitular
espesa. Poco a poco, Marcial dejó de estudiarlas, encontrándose librado de un gran peso. Su mente se hizo alegre y ligera,
admitiendo tan sólo un concepto instintivo de las cosas. ¿Para
qué pensar en el prisma, cuando la luz clara de invierno daba
mayores detalles a las fortalezas del puerto? Una manzana que
cae del árbol sólo es incitación para los dientes. Un pie en una
bañadera no pasa de ser un pie en una bañadera. El día que
abandonó el Seminario, olvidó los libros. El gnomon recobró

su categoría de duende: el espectro fue sinónimo de fantasmas: el octandro era bicho acorazado, con púas en el lomo.

Varias veces, andando pronto, inquieto el corazón, había
ido a visitar a las mujeres que cuchicheaban, detrás de las puertas azules, al pie de las murallas. El recuerdo de la que llevaba
zapatillas bordadas y hojas de albahaca en la oreja lo perseguía,
en tardes de calor, como un dolor de muelas. Pero, un día, la
cólera y las amenazas de un confesor le hicieron llorar de espanto. Cayó por última vez en las sábanas del infierno, renun-
ciando para siempre a sus rodeos por calles poco concurridas,
a sus cobardías de última hora que le hacían regresar con rabia a su casa, luego de dejar a sus espaldas cierta acera rajada,
señal, cuando andaba con la vista baja, de la media vuelta que
debía darse por hollar el umbral de los perfumes.

Ahora vivía su crisis mística poblada de detentes, corderos pascuales, palomas de porcelana, Vírgenes de manto azul
celeste, estrellas de papel dorado, Reyes Magos, ángeles con
alas de cisne, el Asno, el Buey, y un terrible San Dionisio que
se le aparecía en sueños, con un gran vacío entre los hombros
y el andar vacilante de quien busca un objeto perdido. Tropezaba con la cama y Marcial despertaba sobresaltado, echando
mano al rosario de cuentas sordas. Las mechas, en sus pocillos
de aceite, daban luz triste a imágenes que recobraban su color
primero.

VIII

Los muebles crecían. Se hacía más difícil sostener los antebrazos sobre el borde de la mesa del comedor. Los armarios
de cornisas labradas ensanchaban el frontis. Alargando el torso,
los moros de la escalera acercaban sus antorchas a los balaus-
tres del rellano. Las butacas eran más hondas y los sillones de
mecedora tenían tendencia a irse para atrás. No había ya que
doblar las piernas al recostarse en el fondo de la bañadera con
anillas de mármol.

Una mañana en que leía un libro licencioso, Marcial tuvo
ganas, súbitamente, de jugar con los soldados de plomo que
dormían en sus cajas de madera. Volvió a ocultar el tomo bajo la jofaina del lavabo, y abrió una gaveta sellada por las tela-
rañas. La mesa de estudio era demasiado exigua para dar cabida a tanta gente. Por ello, Marcial se sentó en el piso. Dispuso los granaderos por filas de ocho. Luego, los oficiales a caballo, rodeando al abanderado. Detrás, los artilleros, con sus

cañones, escobillones y botafuegos. Cerrando la marcha, pífanos y timbales, con escolta de redoblantes. Los morteros estaban dotados de un resorte que permitía lanzar bolas de vidrio a más de un metro de distancia.

— ¡Pum!... ¡Pum!... ¡Pum!...

Caían caballos, caían abanderados, caían tambores. Hubo de ser llamado tres veces por el negro Eligio, para decidirse a lavarse las manos y bajar al comedor.

Desde ese día, Marcial conservó el hábito de sentarse en el enlosado. Cuando percibió las ventajas de esa costumbre, se sorprendió por no haberlo pensado antes. Afectas al terciopelo de los cojines, las personas mayores sudan demasiado. Algunas huelen a notario —como Don Abundio— por no conocer, con el cuerpo echado, la frialdad del mármol en todo tiempo. Sólo desde el suelo pueden abarcarse totalmente los ángulos y perspectivas de una habitación. Hay bellezas de la madera, misteriosos caminos de insectos, rincones de sombra, que se ignoran a altura de hombre. Cuando llovía, Marcial se ocultaba debajo del clavicordio. Cada trueno hacía temblar la caja de resonancia, poniendo todas las notas a cantar. Del cielo caían los rayos para construir aquella bóveda de calderones —órgano, pinar al viento, mandolina de grillos.

IX

Aquella mañana lo encerraron en su cuarto. Oyó murmullos en toda la casa y el almuerzo que le sirvieron fue demasiado suculento para un día de semana. Había seis pasteles de la confitería de la Alameda —cuando sólo dos podían comerse, los domingos, después de misa. Se entretuvo mirando estampas de viaje, hasta que el abejeo creciente, entrando por debajo de las puertas, le hizo mirar entre persianas. Llegaban hombres vestidos de negro, portando una caja con agarraderas de bronce. Tuvo ganas de llorar, pero en ese momento apareció el calesero Melchor, luciendo sonrisa de dientes en lo alto de sus botas sonoras. Comenzaron a jugar al ajedrez. Melchor era caballo. Él, era Rey. Tomando las losas del piso por tablero, podía avanzar de una en una, mientras Melchor debía saltar una de frente y dos de lado, o viceversa. El juego se prolongó hasta más allá del crepúsculo, cuando pasaron los Bomberos del Comercio.

Al levantarse, fue a besar la mano de su padre que yacía en su cama de enfermo. El Marqués se sentía mejor, y habló a su hijo con el empaque y los ejemplos usuales. Los "Sí, pa-

dre" y los "No, padre", se encajaban entre cuenta y cuenta
del rosario de preguntas, como las respuestas del ayudante en
una misa. Marcial respetaba al Marqués, pero era por razones
que nadie hubiera acertado a suponer. Lo respetaba porque
era de elevada estatura y salía en noches de baile, con el pecho rutilante de condecoraciones; porque le envidiaba el sable
y los entorchados de oficial de milicias; porque, en Pascuas,
había comido un pavo entero, relleno de almendras y pasas,
ganando una apuesta; porque, cierta vez, sin duda con el ánimo de azotarla, agarró a una de las mulatas que barrían la ro-
tonda, llevándola en brazos a su habitación. Marcial, oculto
detrás de una cortina, la vio salir poco después, llorosa y de-
sabrochada, alegrándose del castigo, pues era la que siempre
vaciaba las fuentes de compota devueltas a la alacena.

El padre era un ser terrible y magnánimo al que debía
amarse después de Dios. Para Marcial era más dios que Dios,
porque sus dones eran cotidianos y tangibles. Pero prefería el
Dios del cielo, porque fasti diaba menos.

X

Cuando los muebles crecieron un poco más y Marcial supo como nadie lo que había debajo de las camas, armarios y
vargueños, ocultó a todos un gran secreto: la vida no tenía
encanto fuera de la presencia del calesero Melchor. No Dios,
ni su padre, ni el obispo dorado de las procesiones del Corpus,
eran tan importantes como Melchor.

Melchor venía de muy lejos. Era nieto de príncipes vencidos. En su reino había elefantes, hipopótamos, tigres y jirafas.
Ahí los hombres no trabajaban, como Don Abundio, en habitaciones oscuras, llenas de legajos. Vivían de ser más astutos
que los animales. Uno de ellos sacó el gran cocodrilo del lago
azul, ensartándolo con una pica oculta en los cuerpos apretados de doce ocas asadas. Melchor sabía canciones fáciles de
aprender, porque las palabras no tenían significado y se repetían mucho. Robaba dulces en las cocinas; se escapaba, de noche, por la puerta de los cuadrerizos, y, cierta vez, había ape-
dreado a los de la guardia civil, desapareciendo luego en las
sombras de la calle de la Amargura.

En días de lluvia, sus botas se ponían a secar junto al fogón de la cocina. Marcial hubiese querido tener pies que llena-
ran tales botas. La derecha se llamaba *Calambín*. La izquierda, *Calambán*. Aquel hombre que dominaba los caballos cerre-
ros con sólo encajarles dos dedos en los belfos; aquel señor de

terciopelos y espuelas, que lucía chisteras tan altas, sabía también lo fresco que era un suelo de mármol en verano, y ocultaba debajo de los muebles una fruta o un pastel arrebatados a las bandejas destinadas al Gran Salón. Marcial y Melchor tenían en común un depósito secreto de grageas y almendras, que llamaban el "Urí, urí, urá", con entendidas carcajadas. Ambos habían explorado la casa de arriba abajo, siendo los únicos en saber que existía un pequeño sótano lleno de frascos holandeses, debajo de las cuadras, y que en desván inútil, encima de los cuartos de criadas, doce mariposas polvorientas acababan de perder las alas en cajas de cristales rotos.

XI

Cuando Marcial adquirió el hábito de romper cosas, olvidó a Melchor para acercarse a los perros. Había varios en la casa. El atigrado grande; el podenco que arrastraba las tetas; el galgo, demasiado viejo para jugar; el lanudo que los demás perseguían en épocas determinadas, y que las camareras tenían que encerrar.

Marcial prefería a *Canelo* porque sacaba zapatos de las habitaciones y desenterraba los rosales del patio. Siempre negro de carbón o cubierto de tierra roja, devoraba la comida de los demás, chillaba sin motivo, y ocultaba huesos robados al pie de la fuente. De vez en cuando, también, vaciaba un huevo acabado de poner, arrojando la gallina al aire con brusco palancazo del hocico. Todos daban de patadas al *Canelo*. Pero Marcial se enfermaba cuándo se lo llevaban. Y el perro volvía triunfante, moviendo la cola, después de haber sido abandonado más allá de la Casa de Beneficiencia, recobrando un puesto que los demás, con sus habilidades en la caza o desvelos en la guardia, nunca ocuparían.

Canelo y Marcial orinaban juntos. A veces escogían la alfombra persa del salón, para dibujar en su lana formas de nubes pardas que se ensanchaban lentamente. Eso costaba castigo de cintarazos. Pero los cintarazos no dolían tanto como creían las personas mayores. Resultaban, en cambio, pretexto admirable para armar concertantes de aullidos, y provocar la compasión de los vecinos. Cuando la bizca del tejadillo calificaba a su padre de "bárbaro", Marcial miraba a *Canelo*, riendo con los ojos. Lloraban un poco más, para ganarse un bizcocho, y todo quedaba olvidado. Ambos comían tierra, se revolcaban al sol, bebían en la fuente de los peces, buscaban sombra y perfume al pie de las albahacas. En horas de calor, los canteros húmedos se llenaban de gente. Ahí estaba la gansa gris, con bolsa colgante entre las patas zambas; el gallo viejo de culo pelado; la lagartija que decía "urí, urá", sacándose del cuello una corbata rosada; el triste jubo nacido en ciudad sin hembras; el ratón que tapiaba su agujero con una semilla de carey. Un día señalaron el perro a Marcial.

— ¡Guau, guau! —dijo.

Hablaba su propio idioma. Había logrado la suprema libertad. Ya quería alcanzar, con sus manos, objetos que estaban fuera del alcance de sus manos.

XII

Hambre, sed, calor, dolor, frío. Apenas Marcial redujo su percepción a la de estas realidades esenciales, renunció a la luz que ya le era accesoria. Ignoraba su nombre. Retirado el bautismo, con su sal desagradable, no quiso ya el olfato, ni el oído, ni siquiera la vista. Sus manos rozaban formas placenteras. Era un ser totalmente sensible y táctil. El universo le entraba por todos los poros. Entonces cerró los ojos que sólo divisaban gigantes nebulosos y penetró en un cuerpo caliente, húmedo, lleno de tinieblas, que moría. El cuerpo, al sentirlo arrebozado con su propia sustancia, resbaló hacia la vida.

Pero ahora el tiempo corrió más pronto, adelgazando sus últimas horas. Los minutos sonaban a glissando de naipes bajo el pulgar de un jugador.

Las aves volvieron al huevo en torbellino de plumas. Los peces cuajaron la hueva, dejando una nevada de escamas en el fondo del estanque. Las palmas doblaron las pencas, desapareciendo en la tierra como abanicos cerrados. Los tallos sorbían sus hojas y el suelo tiraba de todo lo que le perteneciera. El trueno retumbaba en los corredores. Crecían pelos en la gamuza de los guantes. Las mantas de lana se destejían, redondeando el vellón de carneros distantes. Los armarios, los vargueños, las camas, los crucifijos, las mesas las persianas, salieron volando en la noche buscando sus antiguas raíces al pie de las selvas. Todo lo que tuviera clavos se desmoronaba. Un bergantín anclado no se sabía dónde, llevó presurosamente a Italia los mármoles del piso y de la fuente. Las panoplias, los herrajes, las llaves, las cazuelas de cobre, los bocados de las cuadras, se derretían, engrosando un río de metal que galerías sin techo canalizaban hacia la tierra. Todo se metamorfoseaba, regresando a la condición primera. El barro, volvió al barro, dejando un yermo en lugar de la casa.

XIII

Cuando los obreros vinieron con el día para proseguir la demolición, encontraron el trabajo acabado. Alguien se había llevado la estatua de Ceres, vendida la víspera a un anticuario. Después de quejarse al Sindicato, los hombres fueron a sentarse en los bancos de un parque municipal. Uno recordó entonces la historia, muy difuminada, de una Marquesa de Capellanías, ahogada, en tarde mayo, entre las malangas del Almendares. Pero nadie prestaba atención al relato, porque el sol viajaba de oriente a occidente, y las horas que crecen a la derecha de los relojes deben alargarse por la pereza, ya que son las que más seguramente llevan a la muerte.

Julio Cortázar
1916–1984
Argentina

La noche boca arriba

Antología, Nicolás Bratosevich, ed. Barcelona: EDHESA, 1978.

> *Y salían en ciertas épocas a cazar enemigos; le llamaban la guerra florida.*

A mitad del largo zaguán del hotel pensó que debía ser tarde, y se apuró a salir a la calle y sacar la motocicleta del rincón donde el portero de al lado le permitía guardarla. En la joyería de la esquina vio que eran las nueve menos diez; llegaría con tiempo sobrado adonde iba. El sol se filtraba entre los altos edificios del centro, y él —porque para sí mismo, para ir pensando, no tenía nombre— montó en la máquina saboreando el paseo. La moto ronroneaba entre sus piernas, y un viento un fresco le chicoteaba los pantalones.

Dejó pasar los ministerios (el rosa, el blanco) y la serie de comercios con brillantes vitrinas de la calle Central. Ahora entraba en la parte más agradable del trayecto, el verdadero paseo: una calle larga, bordeada de árboles, con poco tráfico y amplias villas que dejaban venir los jardines hasta las aceras, apenas demarcadas por setos bajos. Quizá algo distraído, pero corriendo sobre la derecha como correspondía, se dejó llevar por la tersura, por la leve crispación de ese día apenas empezado. Tal vez su involuntario relajamiento le impidió prevenir el accidente. Cuando vio que la mujer parada en la esquina se lanzaba a la calzada a pesar de las luces verdes, ya era tarde para las soluciones fáciles. Frenó con el pie y la mano, desviándose a la izquierda; oyó el grito de la mujer, y junto con el choque perdió la visión. Fue como dormirse de golpe.

Volvió bruscamente del desmayo. Cuatro o cinco hombres jóvenes lo estaban sacando de debajo de la moto. Sentía gusto a sal y sangre, le dolía una rodilla, y cuando lo alzaron gritó, porque no podía soportar la presión en el brazo derecho. Voces que no parecían pertenecer a las caras suspendidas sobre él, lo alentaban con bromas y seguridades. Su único alivio fue oír la confirmación de que había estado en su derecho al cruzar la esquina. Preguntó por la mujer, tratando de dominar la náusea que le ganaba la garganta. Mientras lo llevaban boca arriba hasta una farmacia próxima, supo que la causante del accidente no tenía más que rasguños en las piernas. "Usté la agarró apenas, pero el golpe le hizo saltar la máquina de costado..." Opiniones, recuerdos, despacio, éntrenlo de espaldas, así va bien, y alguien con guardapolvo dándole a beber un trago que lo alivió en la penumbra de una pequeña farmacia de barrio.

La ambulancia policial llegó a los cinco minutos, y lo subieron a una camilla blanda donde pudo tenderse a gusto. Con toda lucidez, pero sabiendo que estaba bajo los efectos de un *shock* terrible, dio sus señas al policía que lo acompañaba. El brazo casi no le dolía; de una cortadura en la ceja goteaba sangre por toda la cara. Una o dos veces se lamió los labios para beberla. Se sentía bien, era un accidente, mala suerte; unas semanas quieto y nada más. El vigilante le dijo que la motocicleta no parecía muy estropeada. "Natural", dijo él. "Como que me la ligué encima..." Los dos se rieron, y el vigilante le dio la mano al llegar al hospital y le deseó buena suerte. Ya la náusea volvía poco a poco; mientras lo llevaban en una camilla de ruedas hasta un pabellón del fondo, pasando bajo árboles llenos de pájaros, cerró los ojos y deseó estar dormido o cloroformado. Pero lo tuvieron largo rato en una pieza con olor a hospital, llenando una ficha, quitándole la ropa y vistiéndolo con una camisa grisácea y dura. Le mo-

vían cuidadosamente el brazo, sin que le doliera. Las enfermeras bromeaban todo el tiempo, y si no hubiera sido por las
contracciones del estómago se habría sentido muy bien, casi
contento.

Lo llevaron a la sala de radio, y veinte minutos después,
con la placa todavía húmeda puesta sobre el pecho como una
lápida negra, pasó a la sala de operaciones. Alguien de blanco,
alto y delgado, se le acercó y se puso a mirar la radiografía. Manos de mujer le acomodaban la cabeza, sintió que lo pasaban
de una camilla a otra. El hombre de blanco se le acercó otra
vez, sonriendo, con algo que le brillaba en la mano derecha.
Le palmeó la mejilla e hizo una seña a alguien parado atrás.

Como sueño era curioso porque estaba lleno de olores y
él nunca soñaba olores. Primero un olor a pantano, ya que a
la izquierda de la calzada empezaban las marismas, los tembladerales de donde no volvía nadie. Pero el olor cesó, y en cambio vino una fragancia compuesta y oscura como la noche en
que se movía huyendo de los aztecas. Y todo era tan natural,
tenía que huir de los aztecas que andaban a caza de hombre,
y su única probabilidad era la de esconderse en lo más denso
de la selva, cuidando de no apartarse de la estrecha calzada
que sólo ellos, los motecas, conocían.

Lo que más lo torturaba era el olor, como si aun en la absoluta aceptación del sueño algo se rebelara contra eso que no
era habitual, que hasta entonces no había participado del juego. "Huele a guerra", pensó, tocando instintivamente el puñal
de piedra atravesado en su ceñidor de lana tejida. Un sonido
inesperado lo hizo agacharse y quedar inmóvil, temblando.
Tener miedo no era extraño, en sus sueños abundaba el miedo. Esperó, tapado por las ramas de un arbusto y la noche sin
estrellas. Muy lejos, probablemente del otro lado del gran lago, debían estar ardiendo fuegos de vivac; un resplandor rojizo teñía esa parte del cielo. El sonido no se repitió. Había sido como una rama quebrada. Tal vez un animal que escapaba
como él del olor de la guerra. Se enderezó despacio, ventean-
do. No se oía nada, pero el miedo seguía allí como el olor,
ese incienso dulzón de la guerra florida. Había que seguir, llegar al corazón de la selva evitando las ciénagas. A tientas, aga-
chándose a cada instante para tocar el suelo más duro de la
calzada, dio algunos pasos. Hubiera querido echar a correr,
pero los tembladerales palpitaban a su lado. En el sendero
en tinieblas, buscó el rumbo. Entonces sintió una bocanada
horrible del olor que más temía y saltó desesperado hacia
adelante.

—Se va a caer de la cama —dijo el enfermo de al lado—. No brinque tanto, amigazo.

Abrió los ojos, y era de tarde, con el sol ya bajo en los ventanales de la larga sala. Mientras trataba de sonreir a su vecino, se despegó casi físicamente de la última visión de la pesadilla. El brazo, enyesado, colgaba de un aparato con pesas y poleas. Sintió sed, como si hubiera estado corriendo kilómetros, pero no querían darle mucha agua, apenas para mojarse los labios y hacer un buche. La fiebre lo iba ganando despacio y hubiera podido dormirse otra vez, pero saboreaba el placer de quedarse despierto, entornados los ojos, escuchando el diálogo de los otros enfermos, respondiendo de cuando en cuando a alguna pregunta. Vio llegar un carrito blanco que pusieron al lado de su cama, una enfermera rubia le frotó con alcohol la cara anterior del muslo y le clavó una gruesa aguja conectada con un tubo que subía hasta un frasco lleno de líquido opalino. Un médico joven vino con un aparato de metal y cuero que le ajustó al brazo sano para verificar alguna cosa. Caía la noche, y la fiebre lo iba arrastrando blandamente a un estado donde las cosas tenían un relieve como de gemelos de teatro, eran reales y dulces y a la vez ligeramente repugnantes; como estar viendo una película aburrida y pensar que sin embargo en la calle es peor; y quedarse.

Vino una taza de maravilloso caldo de oro oliendo a puerro, a apio, a perejil. Un trocito de pan, más precioso que todo un banquete, se fue desmigajando poco a poco. El brazo no le dolía nada y solamente en la ceja, donde lo habían suturado, chirriaba a veces una punzada caliente y rápida. Cuando los ventanales de enfrente viraron a manchas de un azul oscuro, pensó que no le iba a ser difícil dormirse. Un poco incómodo, de espaldas, pero al pasarse la lengua por los labios resecos y calientes sintió el sabor del caldo, y suspiró de felicidad, abandonándose.

Primero fue una confusión, un atraer hacia sí todas las sensaciones por un instante embotadas o confundidas. Comprendía que estaba corriendo en plena oscuridad, aunque arriba el cielo cruzado de copas de árboles era menos negro que el resto. "La calzada", pensó. "Me salí de la calzada." Sus pies se hundían en un colchón de hojas y barro, y ya no podía dar un paso sin que las ramas de los arbustos le azotaran el torso y las piernas. Jadeante, sabiéndose acorralado a pesar de la oscuridad y el silencio, se agachó para escuchar. Tal vez la calzada estaba cerca, con la primera luz del día iba a verla otra vez. Nada podía ayudarlo ahora a encontrarla. La mano que

sin saberlo él aferraba el mango del puñal, subió como el escorpión de los pantanos hasta su cuello, donde colgaba el
amuleto protector. Moviendo apenas los labios musitó la plegaria del maíz que trae las lunas felices, y la súplica a la Muy
Alta, a la dispensadora de los bienes motecas. Pero sentía al
mismo tiempo que los tobillos se le estaban hundiendo despacio en el barro, y la espera en la oscuridad del chaparral
desconocido se le hacía insoportable. La guerra florida había
empezado con la luna y llevaba ya tres días y tres noches. Si
conseguía refugiarse en lo profundo de la selva, abandonando
la calzada más allá de la región de las ciénagas, quizá los guerreros no le siguieran el rastro. Pensó en los muchos prisioneros que ya habrían hecho. Pero la cantidad no contaba, sino
el tiempo sagrado. La caza continuaría hasta que los sacerdotes dieran la señal del regreso. Todo tenía su número y su fin,
y él estaba dentro del tiempo sagrado, del otro lado de los
cazadores.

Oyó los gritos y se enderezó de un salto, puñal en mano.
Como si el cielo se incendiara en el horizonte, vio antorchas
moviéndose entre las ramas, muy cerca. El olor a guerra era
insoportable, y cuando el primer enemigo le saltó al cuello
casi sintió placer en hundirle la hoja de piedra en pleno pecho.
Ya lo rodeaban las luces, los gritos alegres. Alcanzó a cortar el
aire una o dos veces, y entonces una soga lo atrapó desde atrás.

—Es la fiebre —dijo el de la cama de al lado—. A mí me pasaba igual cuando me operé del duodeno. Tome agua y va a
ver que duerme bien.

Al lado de la noche de donde volvía, la penumbra tibia de
la sala le pareció deliciosa. Una lámpara violeta velaba en lo
alto de la pared del fondo como un ojo protector. Se oía toser, respirar fuerte, a veces un diálogo en voz baja. Todo era
grato y seguro, sin ese acoso, sin... Pero no quería seguir pensando en la pesadilla. Había tantas cosas en qué entretenerse.
Se puso a mirar el yeso del brazo, las poleas que tan cómodamente se lo sostenían en el aire. Le habían puesto una botella de agua mineral en la mesa de noche. Bebió del gollete, go-
losamente. Distinguía ahora las formas de la sala, las treinta
camas, los armarios con vitrinas. Ya no debía tener tanta fiebre, sentía fresca la cara. La ceja le dolía apenas, como un recuerdo. Se vio otra vez saliendo del hotel, sacando la moto.
¿Quién hubiera pensado que la cosa iba a acabar así? Trataba
de fijar el momento del accidente, y le dio rabia advertir que
había ahí como un hueco, un vacío que no alcanzaba a rellenar. Entre el choque y el momento en que lo habían levanta-

do del suelo, un desmayo o lo que fuera no le dejaba ver nada. Y al mismo tiempo tenía la sensación de que ese hueco, esa nada, había durado una eternidad. No, ni siquiera tiempo, más bien como si en ese hueco él hubiera pasado a través de algo o recorrido distancias inmensas. El choque, el golpe brutal contra el pavimento. De todas maneras al salir del pozo negro había sentido casi un alivio mientras los hombres lo alzaban del suelo. Con el dolor del brazo roto, la sangre de la ceja partida, la contusión en la rodilla; con todo eso, un alivio al volver al día y sentirse sostenido y auxiliado. Y era raro. Le preguntaría alguna vez al médico de la oficina. Ahora volvía a ganarlo el sueño, a tirarlo despacio hacia abajo. La almohada era tan blanda, y en su garganta afiebrada la frescura del agua mineral. Quizá pudiera descansar de veras, sin las malditas pesadillas. La luz violeta de la lámpara en lo alto se iba apagando poco a poco.

Como dormía de espaldas, no lo sorprendió la posición en que volvía a reconocerse, pero en cambio el olor a humedad, a piedra rezumante de filtraciones, le cerró la garganta y lo obligó a comprender. Inútil abrir los ojos y mirar en todas direcciones: lo envolvía una oscuridad absoluta. Quiso enderezarse y sintió las sogas en las muñecas y los tobillos. Estaba estaqueado en el suelo, en un piso de lajas helado y húmedo. El frío le ganaba la espalda desnuda, las piernas. Con el mentón buscó torpemente el contacto con su amuleto, y supo que se lo habían arrancado. Ahora estaba perdido, ninguna plegaria podía salvarlo del final. Lejanamente, como filtrándose entre las piedras del calabozo, oyó los atabales de la fiesta. Lo habían traído al teocalli, estaba en las mazmorras del templo a la espera de su turno.

Oyó gritar, un grito ronco que rebotaba en las paredes. Otro grito, acabando en un quejido. Era él que gritaba en las tinieblas, gritaba porque estaba vivo, todo su cuerpo se defendía con el grito de lo que iba a venir, del final inevitable. Pensó en sus compañeros que llenarían otras mazmorras, y en los que ascendían ya los peldaños del sacrificio. Gritó de nuevo sofocadamente, casi no podía abrir la boca, tenía las mandíbulas agarrotadas y a la vez como si fueran de goma y se abrieran lentamente, con un esfuerzo interminable. El chirriar de los cerrojos lo sacudió como un látigo. Convulso, retorciéndose, luchó por zafarse de las cuerdas que se le hundían en la carne. Su brazo derecho, el más fuerte, tiraba hasta que el dolor se hizo intolerable y tuvo que ceder. Vio abrirse la doble puerta, y el olor de las antorchas le llegó antes que la luz. Ape-

nas ceñidos con el taparrabos de la ceremonia, los acólitos de
los sacerdotes se le acercaron mirándolo con desprecio. Las
luces se reflejaban en los torsos sudados, en el pelo negro lleno de plumas. Cedieron las sogas, y en su lugar lo aferraron
manos. calientes, duras como bronce; se sintió alzado, siempre boca arriba, tironeado por los cuatro acólitos que lo llevaban por el pasadizo. Los portadores de antorchas iban adelante, alumbrando vagamente el corredor de paredes mojadas
y techo tan bajo que los acólitos debían agachar la cabeza.
Ahora lo llevaban, lo llevaban, era el final. Boca arriba, a un
metro del techo de roca viva que por momentos se iluminaba
con un reflejo de antorcha. Cuando en vez del techo nacieran
las estrellas y se alzara frente a él la escalinata incendiada de
gritos y danzas, sería el fin. El pasadizo no acababa nunca,
pero ya iba a acabar, de repente olería el aire libre lleno de estrellas, pero todavía no, andaban llevándolo sin fin en la penumbra roja, tironeándolo brutalmente, y él no quería, pero
cómo impedirlo si le habían arrancado el amuleto que era su
verdadero corazón, el centro de la vida.

Salió de un brinco a la noche del hospital, al alto cielo
raso dulce, a la sombra blanda que lo rodeaba. Pensó que debía haber gritado, pero sus vecinos dormían callados. En la
mesa de noche, la botella de agua tenía algo de burbuja, de
imagen traslúcida contra la sombra azulada de los ventanales.
Jadeó, buscando el alivio de los pulmones, el olvido de esas
imágenes que seguían pegadas a sus párpados. Cada vez que
cerraba los ojos las veía formarse instantáneamente, y se en-
derezaba aterrado pero gozando a la vez del saber que ahora
estaba despierto, que la vigilia lo protegía, que pronto iba a
amanecer, con el buen sueño profundo que se tiene a esa hora, sin imágenes, sin nada... Le costaba mantener los ojos abiertos, la modorra era más fuerte que él. Hizo un último esfuerzo, con la mano sana esbozó un gesto hacia la botella de agua
y no llegó a tomarla, sus dedos se cerraron en un vacío otra
vez negro, y el pasadizo seguía interminable, roca tras roca,
con súbitas fulguraciones rojizas, y él boca arriba gimió apa-
gadamente porque el techo iba a acabarse, subía, abriéndose
como una boca de sombra, y los acólitos se enderezaban y de
la altura una luna menguante le cayó en la cara donde los ojos
no querían verla, desesperadamente se cerraban y abrían buscando pasar al otro lado, descubrir de nuevo el cielo raso protector de la sala. Y cada vez que se abrían era la noche y la luna mientras lo subían por la escalinata, ahora con la cabeza
colgando hacia abajo, y en lo alto estaban las hogueras, las ro-

jas columnas de humo perfumado, y de golpe vio la piedra
roja, brillante de sangre que chorreaba, y el vaivén de los pies
del sacrificado que arrastraban para tirarlo rodando por las escalinatas del norte. Con una última esperanza apretó los párpados, gimiendo por despertar. Durante un segundo creyó
que lo lograría, porque otra vez estaba inmóvil en la cama, a
salvo del balanceo cabeza abajo. Pero olía la muerte, y cuando abrió los ojos vio la figura ensangrentada del sacrificador
que venía hacia él con el cuchillo de piedra en la mano. Alcanzó a cerrar otra vez los párpados, aunque ahora sabía que
no iba a despertarse, que estaba despierto, que el sueño maravilloso había sido el otro, absurdo como todos los sueños; un
sueño en el que había andado por extrañas avenidas de una
ciudad asombrosa, con luces verdes y rojas que ardían sin llama ni humo, con un enorme insecto de metal que zumbaba
bajo sus piernas. En la mentira infinita de ese sueño también
lo habían alzado del suelo, también alguien se le había acercado con un cuchillo en la mano, a él tendido boca arriba, a él
boca arriba con los ojos cerrados entre las hogueras.

Emilio Díaz Valcárcel
1929–
Puerto Rico

La muerte obligatoria
Panorama, 1970.

ESTA mañana recibimos a tío Segundo. Lo esperamos cuatro horas, en medio de la gente que entraba y salía por
montones, sentados en uno de los banquitos del aeropuerto.
La gente nos miraba y decía cosas y yo pensaba cómo sería
eso de montarse en un aeroplano y dejar detrás el barrio, los
compañeros de escuela, mamá lamentándose de los malos
tiempos y de los cafetines que no dejan dormir a nadie. Y después vivir hablando otras palabras, lejos del río donde uno se
baña todas las tardes. Eso lo estaba pensando esta mañana,

muerto de sueño porque nos habíamos levantado a las cinco. Llegaron unos aviones y tío Segundo no se veía por ningún sitio. Mamá decía que no había cambiado nada, que seguía siendo el mismo Segundo de siempre, llegando tarde a los sitios, a los trabajos, enredado a lo mejor con la Policía. Que a lo mejor había formado un lío allá en el Norte y lo habían arrestado, que no había pagado la tienda y estaba en corte. Eso lo decía mamá mirando a todos lados, preguntándole a la gente, maldiciendo cada vez que le pisaban las chancletas nuevas.

Yo no había conocido a tío Segundo. Decían que era mi misma cara y que de tener yo bigote hubiéramos sido como mandados a hacer. Eso lo discutían los grandes el domingo por la tarde cuando tía Altagracia venía de San Juan con su cartera llena de olores y bombones y nos hacía pedirle la bendición y después hablaba con mamá lo estirado que yo estaba y lo flaco y que si yo iba a la doctrina y si estudiaba, después de lo cual casi peleaban porque tía Altagracia decía que yo era Segundo puro y pinto. A mamá no le gustaba primero, pero después decía que sí, que efectivamente yo era el otro Segundo en carne y hueso, sólo que sin bigote. Pero una cosa, saltaba mi tía, que no saliera yo a él en lo del carácter endemoniado, que una vez le había rajado la espalda al que le gritó gacho y había capado al perro que le desgarró el pantalón de visitar a sus mujeres. Y mamá decía que sí, que yo no sería como su hermano en lo del genio volado y que más bien yo parecía una mosquita muerta por lo flaco y escondido que andaba siempre. Y después mamá me mandaba a buscar un vellón de cigarrillos o a ordeñar la cabra para que no oyera cuando empezaba a hablar de papá, de las noches en que no dormía esperándolo mientras él jugaba dominó en lo de Eufrasio, y mi tía se ponía colorada y decía que bien merecido se lo tenía y que bastante se lo advirtieron y le dijeron no seas loca ese hombre no sale de las cantinas no seas loca mira a ver lo que haces.

Eso era todos los domingos, el único día que tía Altagracia venía de San Juan y se metía a este barrio que ella dice que odia porque la gente es impropia. Pero hoy es martes y ella vino a ver a abuela y a esperar a su hermano, porque a él le escribieron que abuela estaba en las últimas y él dijo está bien si es así voy pero para irme rápido. Y le estuvimos esperando cuatro horas sentados en el banquillo del aeropuerto muertos de sueño entre la gente que nos miraba y hablaba cosas.

Ni mamá ni tía Altagracia reconocieron al hombre que se acercó vestido de blanco y muy planchado y gordo, que les echó el brazo y casi las exprime a las dos al mismo tiempo. A mí me jaló las patillas y se me quedó mirando un rato, después me cargó y me dijo que yo era un macho hecho y derecho y que si tenía novia. Mamá dijo que yo les había salido un poco enfermo y que por lo que yo había demostrado a estas alturas sería andando el tiempo más bien una mosquita muerta, como quien dice, que otra cosa. Tía Altagracia dijo que se fijaran bien, que se fijaran, que de tener yo bigote sería el doble en miniatura de mi tío.

En el camino tío Segundo habló de sus negocios en el Norte. Mi madre y mi tía estuvieron de acuerdo en ir alguna vez para allá, que aquí el sol pone viejo a uno, que el trabajo, el calor, las pocas oportunidades de mejorar la vida... Así llegamos a casa sin yo darme cuenta. Me despertó tío Segundo jalándome por una oreja y preguntándome si veía a Dios y diciéndome espabílate que de los amotetados no se ha escrito nada.

Tío Segundo encontró a abuela un poco jincha pero no tan mal como le habían dicho. Le puso la mano en el pecho y le dijo que respirara, que avanzara y respirara, y no faltó nada para virar la cama y tirar a abuela al piso. Le dio una palmadita en la cara y después alegó que la vieja estaba bien y que él había venido desde tan lejos y que había dejado su negocio solo y que era la única, óiganlo bien, la única oportunidad ahora. Porque después de todo él vino a un entierro, y no a otra cosa. Mi madre y mi tía abrieron la boca a gritar y dijeron que era verdad que él no había cambiado nada. Pero mi tío decía que la vieja estaba bien, que la miraran, y que qué diría la gente si él no podía volver del Norte la próxima vez para el entierro. Y lo dijo bien claro: tenía que suceder en los tres días que él iba a pasar en el barrio o si no tendrían que devolverle el dinero gastado en el pasaje. Mi mamá y mi tía tenían las manos en la cabeza gritando bárbaro tú no eres más que un bárbaro hereje. Tío Segundo tenía el cuello hinchado, se puso a hablar cosas que yo no entendía y le cogió las medidas a abuela. La midió con las cuartas de arriba abajo y a lo ancho. Abuela sonreía y se veía que quería hablarle. Tío hizo una mueca y se fue donde Santo el carpintero y le encargó una caja de la mejor madera que tuviera, que su familia no era barata. Hablaron un rato del precio y después tío se fue donde sus cuatro mujeres del barrio, le dio seis reales a cada una y cargó con ellas para casa. Prendieron unas velas y metieron a abuela en la caja donde quedaba como bailando, de flaca que estaba. Mi tío protestó y dijo que aquella caja era muy ancha, que Santo la había hecho así para cobrarle más caro y que él no daría más de tres cincuenta. Abuela seguía riéndose allí, dentro de la caja, y movía los labios como queriendo decir algo. Las mujeres de tío no habían comenzado a llorar cuando dos de sus perros empezaron a pelear debajo de la caja. Tío Segundo estaba furioso y les dio patadas hasta que chorreaban, y se fueron con el rabo entre las patas, chillando. Tío movió entonces una mano hacia abajo y las mujeres empezaron a llorar y dar gritos. Tío las pellizcaba para que hicieran más ruido. Mamá estaba tirada en el piso del cuarto, aullando como los mismos perros; tía Altagracia la abanicaba y le echaba alcoholado. Papá estaba allí, acostado a su lado, diciendo que esas cosas pasan y que la verdad era que la culpa la tenían ellas, que de no haberle dicho nada al cuñado nada hubiera sucedido.

Con los gritos, la gente fue arrimándose al velorio. A papá no le gustó que fuera Eufrasio porque se pasaba cobrándole con la vista. Llegaron Serafín y Evaristo, los guares, y tiraron un vellón a cara o cruz a ver quién comenzaba a dirigir el rosario. Llegó Chalí con sus ocho hijos y se puso a espulgarlos en el piso murmurando sus oraciones. Las hermanas Cané entraron por la cocina mirando la alacena y abanicándose con un periódico y diciéndose cosas en los oídos. Los perros peleaban en el patio. Cañón se acercó a mamá y le dijo que la felicitaba que esas cosas, pues, tienen que pasar y que Diostodopoderoso se las arreglaría para buscarle un rinconcito en en su trono a la pobre vieja. Tía Altagracia decía que en San Juan el velorio hubiera sido más propio y no en este maldito barrio que por desgracia tiene que visitar. Tío Segundo le decía a abuela que cerrara la maldita boca, que no se riera, que aquello no era ningún chiste sino un velorio donde ella, aunque no lo pareciera, era lo más importante.

Mamá se levantó y sacó a abuela de la caja. Cargaba con ella para el cuarto cuando mi tío, borracho y hablando cosas malas, agarró a abuela por la cabeza y empezó a jalarla hacia la caja. Mamá la jalaba por los tobillos y entonces entraron los perros y se pusieron a ladrar. Tío Segundo les tiró una patada. Los perros se fueron pero mi tío se fue de lado y cayó al suelo con mamá y abuela. Papá se ñangotó y le dijo a mamá que parecía mentira, que a su hermano hay que complacerlo después de tantos años afuera. Pero mamá no cejaba y entonces tío empezó a patalear y tía Altagracia dijo lo ven, no ha cambiado nada este muchacho.

Pero siempre mi tío se salió con la suya. Cañón estaba tirado en una esquina llorando. Las hermanas Cané se acercaron a mi abuela y dijeron qué bonita se ve la vieja todavía sonriendo como en vida, qué bonita, eh.

Yo me sentía como encogido. Mi tío era un hombre alto y fuerte y yo, lo dijo mamá, según ando ahora, no seré más que una mosquita muerta para toda la vida. Yo quisiera ser fuerte, como mi tío, y pegarle al que se metiera en el medio. Me sentía chiquito cuando mi tío me miraba y se ponía a decir que yo no me le parecía aunque tuviera bigote, que ya le habían engañado tantas veces y qué era eso. Y terminó diciéndome que yo había salido a mi padre escupío y que no se podría esperar gran cosa de mi amontonamiento.

Cañón se puso a hablar con Rosita Cané y al rato se metieron en la cocina como quien no quiere la cosa. La otra Cané se abanicaba con el periódico y miraba envidiosa a la cocina y también miraba a Eufrasio de quien se dice que compró a los padres de Melina con una nevera. Melina se había ido a parir a otro sitio y desde entonces Eufrasio no hace sino beber y pelear con los clientes. Pero ahora Eufrasio estaba calmadito y miraba también a la Cané y le hacía señas. Se le acercó con una botella y le ofreció un trago y ella dijo qué horror cómo se atreve pero después se escondió detrás de la cortina y si Eufrasio no le quita la botella no hubiera dejado una gota.

El velorio estaba prendido y los guares seguían guiando el rosario, mirando el cuarto donde tía Altagracia estaba acostada.

Yo estaba casi dormido cuando me despertó la paliza que Tío Segundo le dio a Cañón. Mi tío salió gritando que qué desorden era ése que se largaran sino quería coger cada uno su parte. Rosita Cané estaba llorando. Mi tío cogió la maleta y dijo que al fin de cuentas estaba satisfecho porque había venido al velorio de su madre y que ya no tenía qué hacer por todo aquello. Salió diciendo que no le importaba haber gastado en pasaje ni en la caja ni en las lloronas, que miraran a ver si en todo el barrio había un hijo tan sacrificado. Ahí está la caja, dijo, para el que le toque el turno. Y salió casi corriendo.

Cuando me acerqué a la caja y miré a abuela, ya no estaba riendo. Pero noté un brillito que le salía de los ojos y mojaba sus labios apretados.

Macedonio Fernández
1874—1952
Argentina

Cirugía psíquica de extirpación
1941.

SE ve a un hombre haciendo su vida cotidiana de la maña-na en un recinto cerrado. Es el herrero Cósimo Schmitz, aquél a quien célebre sesión quirúrgica ante inmenso público le fue extirpado el sentido de futuridad, dejándosele pruden-cialmente, es cierto (como se hace ahora en la extirpación de las amígdalas, luego de reiteradamente observada la nocividad de la extirpación total), un resto de perceptividad del futuro para una anticipación de ocho minutos. Ocho minutos mar-can el alcance máximo de previsibilidad, de su miedo o espe-ranza de los acontecimientos. Ocho minutos antes de que se desencadene el ciclón percibe el significado de los fenómenos de la atmósfera que lo anuncian, pues aunque posea la percep-ción externa e interna carece del sentido del futuro, es decir de la correlación de los hechos: siente, pero no prevé.

Y contémplasele, con agrado, levantarse, lavarse, preparar el mate; luego se distrae con un diario, más tarde se sirve el desayuno, arregla una cortina, endereza una llave, escucha un momento la radio, lee unos apuntes en una libreta, altera cier-tas disposiciones dentro de su habitación, escribe algo, alimen-ta a un pájaro, quédase un momento aparentemente adormi-lado en un sillón; luego arregla su cama y la tiende; llega el mediodía, ha terminado su mañana.

Sacuden fuertemente su puerta y la abren con ruido de fuertes llaves, y aparécensele tres carceleros o guardias y que se apoderan violentamente de él, pero sin resistencia.[1] (Com-prenderéis que la mañana cotidiana que estaba pasando trans-curre en un calabozo.) Se queda muy asombrado y sigue don-de ellos lo llevan; pero al punto de entrar en un gran salón se presenta en su espíritu la representación detallada de una sala con jueces, un sacerdote, un médico y parientes, y a un costa-do la gran máquina de electrocución. En ese lapso de los ocho

---

[1] Lo que hace los cuentos son las y. Los cuentos simples de apretado narrar eran buenos. Pero arruinó el género la invención de que había un *saber contar*. Se decidió que quien sabía contar era un tal Maupassant. Y desapareció el per-fecto cuento de antes; y el invocado Maupassant contaba como antes, ¡bien!

minutos de futuro previsible, recuerda y prevé que se le había notificado la sentencia de muerte el día antes y que aquella máquina lo esperaba para ajusticiarlo.

Recuerda también que un tiempo antes, cierta tarde recurrió a un famoso profesor de psicología para que le extirpara el recuerdo de ciertos actos y más que todo el pensamiento de las consecuencias previsibles de esos actos; había asesinado a su familia y quería olvidar el posible castigo. ¿Qué ganaría con huir, si el temor lo turbaba incesantemente? Y el famoso especialista no había logrado producir el olvido, pero sí reducir el futuro a un casi presente. Y Cósimo andaba por el mundo sin sentido de la esperanza, pero también sin sentido del temor.

El futuro no vive, no existe para Cósimo Schmitz, el herrero, no le da alegría ni temor. El pasado, ausente el futuro, también palidece, porque la memoria apenas sirve; pero qué intenso, total, eterno el presente, no distraído en visiones ni imágenes de lo que ha de venir, ni en el pensamiento de que enseguida todo habrá pasado.

Vivacidad, colorido, fuerza, delicia, exaltación de cada segundo de un presente en que está excluida toda mezcla así de recuerdos como de previsión; presente deslumbrador cuyos minutos valen por horas. En verdad no hay humano, salvo en los primeros meses de la infancia, que tenga noción remota de lo que es un presente sin memoria ni previsión; ni el amor ni la pasión, ni el viaje, ni la maravilla asumen la intensidad del tropel sensual de la infinita simultaneidad de estados del privilegiado del presente, prototípico, sin recuerdos ni presentimientos, sin sus inhibiciones o exhortaciones. Esta compensación es lo que alegaba, en explicaciones que nos dio, el famoso profesor, para superar a las desventajas que resultaban de su operación. Es así que Cósimo vivía en el embelesamiento constante, total y continuo, y se compadecía del apagado vivir y gustar lo actual de las gentes.

Conmueve verlo en el embebecimiento de cada matiz del día o la luna, en el deslumbre de cada instante del deseo, de la contemplación. Es el adorador, el amante del mundo. Tan todo es su instante que nada se altera, todo es eterno, y la cosa más incolora es infinita en sugestión y profundidad.

Todo tenso y a la vez transparente, porque mira cada árbol y cada sombra con todas las luces de su alma; sin cuidados, sin distracción. La palabra se retrasa; rige la inefabilidad de lo que se agolpa y renueva irretenible.

A mí, que lo cuento, me enternece contemplar el dulce y

menudo vivir la mañana del pobre Cósimo Schmitz, un auto-
matista de la dicha sorbo a sorbo, un cenestésico. Siento que
las cosas hayan sucedido así; como psicólogo psicológico, no
psicofisiológico, concibo perfectamente obtener el mismo resultado, sea de desmemoria, sea de desprevisión, sin necesidad
de la aparatosa biológicamente cara, extirpación quirúrgica,
que, como toda intervención química, clínica, dietética o cli-
mática en los gustos y espontaneidades con que nacemos, es
una universal y ruinosa ilusión. Para no prever, hasta desmemoriarse, y para desmemoriarse del todo basta suspender todo pensamiento sobre lo pasado.

Así, pues, querido lector, si este cuento no te gusta, ya sabes cómo olvidarlo. ¿Quizá no lo sabías y sin saberlo no hubieras podido olvidarlo nunca?

Ya ves que éste es un cuento con mucho lector, pero también con mucho autor, pues que os facilita olvidar sus inven-
ciones.

Extinguida pues su disponibilidad conciencial de previsión para ocho minutos, percibe la actualidad de que están
atándolo a la máquina, pero no prevé el minuto siguiente en
que será fulminado. El ritmo conciencial de las actitudes de
previdencia es turnante o cíclico, no es continuo (aparte de
que por el abandono deliberado del ejercicio de prever cada
vez vive más en presente total, cada vez existe menos el instante que viene), y fuera de que tampoco es continuo en una
conciencia que no ha sufrido la técnica de ablación conciencial hoy ya tan en uso y con tanto éxito del doctor Desfuturante. (Seudónimo del bien conocido médico Extirpio Tem-
poralis; en que también se oculta, pues su verdadero nombre
es Excisio Aporvenius, que tampoco es definitivo porque el
verdaderamente verdadero de sus nombres es el de Pedro Gu-
tiérrez. Denuncio, por lo demás, y a pesar de lo encantador
de la acción de este cirujano, que se apropia de todos los porvenires que extirpe, con lo que ocurrirá que ningún contemporáneo tendrá el gusto de asistir a sus funerales.)[2]

Informo de paso —dato útil para el lector— que el doctor
Desfuturante tiene esperanza de perfeccionar la operatividad
psicoextirpativa del gran capítulo de la nueva Cirugía Con-

---

[2] ¿Es artístico aprovechar este momento, como todo el que se preste, para
insertar cuanta comparación o analogía acuda a la mente, por ejemplo que el doctor hacía en este caso lo que el sastre con el cliente que se va con la ropa nueva
puesta y tira la vieja? Porque para la literatura de todos los tiempos la comparación tiene un uso tan frecuente que se podría decir, en lugar de *está escribiendo:*
está comparando.

ciencial, extendiéndola a la extirpación de pasado. Cuando esto se cumpla y lo aprovechen todos los que quisieren no haber vivido jamás ciertos hechos, quizás un buen cuento —ojalá éste lo fuera, ojalá lo eligierais— sería suficiente recreo para olvidarlo todo a lo largo de la vida. El lector desfuturado y también desanteriorizado viviría así a cada momento en el volver a leer mi cuento, me sería deudor del privilegio dignificante de ser persona de vivir de un solo cuento.

Dejo la pluma al lector para que escriba para sí lo que yo no sabré describir: la locura, el espanto, el desmayo, el estrujarse por el desasimiento mientras es arrastrado, el honor de ser sentado en aquella silla y maniatado; y en ese rostro, en su semblante, la aparición de una autora de felicidad, de paz, por haberse agotado los ocho minutos de percepción de futuridad: dos minutos antes de expirar ajusticiado cesa su representación. (Como el terror vive de lo que va a suceder, agotado el turno de ocho minutos de previsión, se queda sonriente, tranquilo, sentado en la silla eléctrica, y en ese estado es fulminado. Porque como acaso no lo hemos dicho y lo requiere urgentemente la composición inventiva de esta narrativa, la impulsión previdente de ocho minutos era seguida de una pausa de otros tantos minutos de absoluto reino del presente; es así que la víctima de la máquina de electrocución, y nuestra víctima también, pereció con la más plácida de las sonrisas.)

¿Será el lector el Poe que yo no alcanzo a ser en este trance espantador, seguido de beatitud? (¿Y es artístico describir con palabras y gesticulaciones en textos literarios?)

Está muerto ahora sin haber experimentado el tormento agónico, sin ninguna pena, sin ningún esfuerzo de evasión, como si fuera a comenzar una mañana cotidiana de su eternidad de presente.

Yace Cósimo Schmitz muerto, y quince días después el Tribunal hace la declaración rehabilitante siguiente:

"Un conjunto de fatalidades sutilísimas que ha obnubilado la mente de este tribunal lo ha incurso en un fatal error sumamente lacerante. El infeliz Cósimo Schmitz era un espíritu inquietísimo y afanoso de probar toda novedad mecánica, química, terapéutica, psicológica que se da en el mundo; y así fue que un día se hizo tratar, hace quince años, por el aventurero y un tiempo celebrado sabio Jonatan Demetrius, que sin embargo de su cinismo efectivamente había hecho un gran descubrimiento en histología y fisiología cerebral y lograba realmente por una operación de su creación, cambiar el pasado de las personas que estuviesen desconformes con el propio.[3]

"A su consultorio cayó el ávido de novedades Cósimo Schmitz, infeliz; protestó de su pasado vacío y rogó a Demetrius que le diera un pasado de filibustero de lo más audaz y siniestro, pues durante cuarenta años se había levantado todos los días a la misma hora en la misma casa, hecho todos los días lo mismo y acostándose todas las noches a igual hora, por lo que estaba enfermo de monotonía total del pasado.

"Desde allí salió operado con la conciencia añadida, intercalada a sus vaguedades de recuerdo, de haber sido el asesino de toda su familia, lo que lo divirtió mucho durante algunos años pero después se le tornó atormentador. Cumple al tribunal en este punto manifestar que la familia de Cósimo Schmitz existe, sana, íntegra, pero que huyó colectivamente atemorizada por ciertas señas de vesania en Schmitz, ocurriendo esto en una lejana llanura de Alaska; de allí provino a este tribunal la información de un asesinato múltiple que no existió jamás.

"Confiesa, pues, el tribunal, que si Cósimo Schmitz fue un total equivocado en sus aventuras quirúrgicas, más lo ha sido el tribunal en la investigación y sentencia del terrible e inexistente delito que él confesaba."

Pobre Cósimo Schmitz, pobre el Tribunal de Alta Caledonia.

Vivir en recuerdo lo que no se vivió nunca en emoción ni en visión; tener un pasado que no fue un presente.[4] Oh, aquel día, entre pavor y delicia con qué pulso apretó el arma.

---

[3] Con Perdón del Tribunal aporto esta pregunta de colaboración científica: ¿trasplantándoles tejidos corticales de individuos alegres? Tal técnica sería muy eficaz, pero por ciertos riesgos se ha prohibido destapar simultáneamente cierto número de cráneos, pues en la precipitada adjudicación de nuevas conciencias podría haber equivocaciones —como ha ocurrido— y que a quien no quisiera tener futuro le trasplantaran uno de un siglo.

En fin, podría citar a Ramón y Cajal, pero con Ramón y Cajal no basta; hay muchos otros autores y cansaría mucho al lector, aparte de que no me gusta mucho que en unas pocas páginas el lector termine sabiendo más que yo.

El respetable Tribunal me observa que mal puedo controvertir el orden o idoneidad de sus considerandos, cuando yo presento la más enrevesada serie narrativa y digo lo primero al último y lo último al principio. Admito; ¿pero no se advierte que la técnica de narrar a tiempo contrario, cambiando el orden de las piezas de tiempo que configuran mi relato, despertará en el lector una lúcida confusión, diremos, que lo sensibilizará extraordinariamente para simpatizar y sentir en el enrevesado tramo de existencia de Cósimo? Sería un fracaso que el lector leyera claramente cuando mi intento artístico va a que el lector se contagie de un estado de confusión.

[4] Estamos bastante descorteses en este retomar la pluma después de habérsela pasado al lector. El mundo no tiene al lector de un solo cuento; inmensa dignidad;

¡Toda su familia! Hasta los cuarenta años, un pasado, ahora otro, la memoria de otro ser bajo las mismas formas del cuerpo. Quizá más tarde, tampoco este presente habrá sido nunca suyo. Tendrá, con un nuevo toque en su mente ya dócil, otra fragilidad de haber sido; un héroe, un químico; moverá los brazos de cuando exploraba el Sudán o Samoa.

Jonatan Demetrius, enamorado de toda felicidad, plástico de las dichas, de dar recuerdos amorosos a los que fueron presentes de lágrima, con suave ciencia y dulce ternura se ingeniaba en la adivinación de cada alma.

— ¿Qué es lo que usted desea? —Y leíale a Cósimo las páginas más terribles del filibustero Drake, de Morgan, o del amante de la Récamier.

—Yo preferiría haber sido...

—Lo será.

Pobre Cósimo Schmitz; ¿no habrá una tercera cirugía, después de dos tan siniestras, que lo resucite? Ah, no —exclama la Terapéutica—, nuestro oficio es de infalibilidad, no nos incumbe disimular las fallas de los tribunales de justicia.

Como no se ha encontrado hasta ahora en las más pacientes investigaciones que hubiera algún remedio que con toda seguridad fuera más benéfico que destructor, es el caso de moralizar en este momento de este cuento acerca de la inevitable debilidad de las ingeniosidades humanas con el ejemplo de los deslumbradores procedimientos del gran científico Doctor Desfuturante, en cuya aplicación, como se ve, la conveniencia de eximirnos de todo género de temores vagos remotos y agitantes esperanzas remotas, tiene el inconveniente de la turnación de pausa tras esos ocho minutos de previdencia, ante los cuales, suspensa toda previsibilidad, el paciente tratado no prevé ni siquiera que el tren que viene a diez metros de él por la vía en que camina lo matará en tres segundos.[5]

pero tampoco al mágico autor de un cuento de sólo de él vivir. Yo lejos de soñarme, y menos con la muestra de éste, investido de la dignidad máxima de autor de aquel cuento único, he aspirado modestamente sí a vivir de un solo cuento; quizá no lo he logrado. Desprendido ahora ante el lector de toda vanidad en este encantador aspecto, admito que por momentos he creído advertir en este escrito mío algo muy parecido a cuento dejado de contar. Pero me decide a publicarlo, no obstante, su alto valor científico. Además, no confunda, lector, cuento dejado de contar con lo que resulta de un no seguido contar.

Tristes tú y yo, Lector; ni tuviste de mí el cuento de vivir sólo de él ni tuve yo la Fortuna Única de vivir de sólo uno de otro.

[5] Porque hay apendicectomías que propenden a graves accidentes, la extirpación de las amígdalas predispone a la poliomielitis, los auges de las dosis macizas, la insulina, el iodo, engruesan las cifras de la mortalidad, y de toda la intervención quirúrgica queda pendiente por obra de los analgésicos que desoxigenan la sangre numerosas muertes repentinas por embolias. Las estadísticas inglesas de-

Al lector le toca, ahora que yo he cumplido con todo,
cumplir con su deber; de hacer como que cree.[6]

muestran que ocurren allí más muertes por la vacunación que por la viruela; tenemos también la bancarrota del suero Behring y quizá la del suero antirrábico.
    Parece, lector, que a compás de la lectura nos estamos instruyendo bastante.
Pero usted al agradecerlo se reservará pensar que la instrucción es buena, pero la
digestión es mala, lamentable defectillo de tan nutrida información. Yo no veo
por qué una digresión, aun en un cuento y aun científica, está mal después de los
novelones habituales, en que se llenan capítulos con historia literaria, crítica pictórica, análisis de sinfonías, salvaciones sociológicas. (Todo esto, entre descripciones de mobiliarios y la Naturaleza más próxima.) Más difícil es entender que
un opositor a digresiones converse, mientras come, con amigos en la familia, o no
pase un instante ni haga cosa alguna durante el día o la noche que no la haga acompañar con el conventillo fonético de la radio.
    Yo he dado aquí un cuento total, la juventud y muerte de un hombre. ¡Y
qué juventud y qué muerte! Lo demás puede el lector considerarlo como la radio,
algo intersticial a su lectura de cuento. El cuento y la radio va todo en el texto y
os libráis de los avisos.
    Así como en las óperas —que es lo interminable por naturaleza— hay lo más
interminable de ellas que es su final y que funciona como el aplauso que la ópera
se prodiga a sí misma, de modo que el aplauso del público parece un servilismo
al éxito ya aplaudido —aunque la comparación es de muy poca analogía—, yo lo
que quiero es seguridad, acertar con algo (pues lo que menos poseo es la seguridad
de autor de ópera), sea con el ciento, sea con las digresiones. Yo no me aplaudo,
pero desarmo las toses del tedio.
    He prolongado esta digresión para disimular que estaba tratando de encon-
trar dónde habíamos dejado el cuento. Reanudando, es de anotar que el pobre
Cósimo, que había escapado a todos los desatinos y percances que acabo de enun-
ciar, vino a caer al abrasamiento eléctrico sin que podamos tener el gusto de quejarnos en absoluto de la terapéutica, sino totalmente de la culpa suya.
    Insisto en mi consejo: no aceptes lector sino los *tratamientos* que dejan sa-
nar; y no salgas a provocar a la Cirugía, que no se hará rogar; guárdate una memoria y un apéndice que te acompañen durante estés en esta vida.
    [6] Ya dije que lo único que no me he propuesto es el "saber contar"; el "bien
contar" que se descubrió en tiempos de Maupassant, después de quien ya nadie
narró bien, es una farsa a la cual el lector hace la "farsa de creer".
    Fatuo academismo es creer en el Cuento; fuera de los niños nadie cree. El
tema o problema sí interesa. No hay éxito para la tentativa ilusoria y subalterna
del hacer creer, para lo cual se pretende que hay un saber contar.
    Mi sistema de interponer notas al pie de página, de digresiones y paréntesis,
es una aplicación concienzuda de la teoría que tengo de que el cuento (como la
música) escuchado con desatención se graba más. Y yo hago como he visto hacer
en familias burguesas cuando alguna persona se sienta al piano y dice a los concurrentes, por una norma social repetidamente observada, que si no prosiguen conversando mientras toca suspenderá la ejecución. En suma: hace una cortesía a la
descortesía a que ella misma invita. Hago lo mismo con estas digresiones, desvia-
ciones, notas marginales, paréntesis a los paréntesis y alguna incoherencia quizá,
pero la continuidad de la narrativa la salvo con el uso sistemático de frecuentes *y*,
y confieso que lo único que me sería penoso que no me aplaudan es este sistema
que propongo y cumplo acá. Es imposible tomar en serio un cuento, me parece
infantil el género, pero no por eso resulta que éste sea burla de cuento, porque mi
sistema digresivo ya lo dejo defendido y la continuidad y apretado narrar me preo-
cupo hacerlos lucir mediante las *y*.
    Las *y* y los *ya* hacen narrativa a cualquier sucesión de palabras, todo lo hilva-
nan y "precipitan". Entre tanto, sin decirlo, me estoy declarando escritor para el
lector salteado, pues mientras otros escritores tienen verdadero afán por ser leídos
atentamente, yo en cambio escribo desatentamente, no por desinterés, sino porque exploto la idiosincrasia que creo haber descubierto en la psique de oyente o
leyente, que tiene el efecto de grabar más las melodías o los caracteres o sucesos,
con tal que unas y otros sean intensos, dificultando al oidor o lector la audición
o lectura seguidas.

Para más informaciones, puede consultarse sobre la cirugía conciencial mi cuento *Suicida,* en el que ya presenté la temeraria y profunda insinuación de los métodos de la Ablación Conciencial total, que como habrá visto el lector ha sido aprovechada en su técnica, limitando su aplicación a parciales ablaciones.

Murió en sonrisa; su mucho presente, su ningún futuro, su doble pasado no le quitaron en la hora desierta la alegría de haber vivido, Cósimo que fue y no fue, que fue más y menos que todos.

▄▄▄▄▄▄▄▄▄▄

Rosario Ferré
1942—
Puerto Rico

La muñeca menor
Papeles de Pandora, 1976.

LA tía vieja había sacado desde muy temprano el sillón al balcón que daba al cañaveral como hacía siempre que se despertaba con ganas de hacer una muñeca. De joven se bañaba a menudo en el río, pero un día en que la lluvia había recrecido la corriente en cola de dragón había sentido en el tuétano de los huesos una mullida sensación de nieve. La cabeza metida en el reverbero negro de las rocas, había creído escuchar, revolcados con el sonido del agua, los estallidos del salitre sobre la playa y pensó que sus cabellos habían llegado por fin a desembocar en el mar. En ese preciso momento sintió una mordida terrible en la pantorrilla. La sacaron del agua gritando y se la llevaron a la casa en parihuelas retorciéndose de dolor.

El médico que la examinó aseguró que no era nada, probablemente había sido mordida por una chágara viciosa. Sin embargo pasaron los días y la llaga no cerraba. Al cabo de un mes el médico había llegado a la conclusión de que la chágara se había introducido dentro de la carne blanda de la pantorrilla, donde había evidentemente comenzado a engordar. Indicó que le aplicaran un sinapismo para que el calor la obligara a salir. La tía estuvo una semana con la pierna rígida, cubierta de mostaza desde el tobillo hasta el muslo, pero al finalizar el tratamiento se descubrió que la llaga se había abultado aún más, recubriéndose de una substancia pétrea y limosa que era imposible tratar de remover sin que peligrara toda la pierna. Entonces se resignó a vivir para siempre con la chágara enroscada dentro de la gruta de su pantorrilla.

Había sido muy hermosa, pero la chágara que escondía bajo los largos pliegues de gasa de sus faldas la había despojado de toda vanidad. Se había encerrado en la casa rehusando a todos sus pretendientes. Al principio se había dedicado a la crianza de las hijas de su hermana, arrastrando por toda la casa la pierna monstruosa con bastante agilidad. Por aquella época la familia vivía rodeada de un pasado que dejaba desintegrar a su alrededor con la misma impasible musicalidad con que la lámpara de cristal del comedor se desgranaba a pedazos sobre el mantel raído de la mesa. Las niñas adoraban a la tía. Ella las peinaba, las bañaba y les daba de comer. Cuando les leía cuentos se sentaban a su alrededor y levantaban con disimulo el volante almidonado de su falda para oler el perfume de guanábana madura que supuraba la pierna en estado de quietud.

Cuando las niñas fueron creciendo la tía se dedicó a hacerles muñecas para jugar. Al principio eran sólo muñecas comunes, con carne de guata de higüera y ojos de botones perdidos. Pero con el pasar del tiempo fue refinando su arte hasta ganarse el respeto y la reverencia de toda la familia. El nacimiento de una muñeca era siempre motivo de regocijo sagrado, lo cual explicaba el que jamás se les hubiese ocurrido vender una de ellas, ni siquiera cuando las niñas eran ya grandes y la familia comenzaba a pasar necesidad. La tía había ido agrandando el tamaño de las muñecas de manera que correspondieran a la estatura y a las medidas de cada una de las niñas. Como eran nueve y la tía hacía una muñeca de cada niña por año, hubo que separar una pieza de la casa para que la habitasen exclusivamente las muñecas. Cuando la mayor cumplió diez y ocho años había ciento veintiséis muñecas de todas las edades en la habitación. Al abrir la puerta, daba la sensación de entrar en un palomar, o en el cuarto de muñecas del palacio de las tzarinas, o en un almacén donde alguien había puesto a madurar una larga hilera de hojas de tabaco. Sin embargo, la tía no entraba en la habitación por ninguno de estos placeres, sino que echaba el pestillo a la puerta e iba levantando amorosamente cada una de las muñecas canturreándoles mientras las mecía: Así eras cuando tenías un año, así cuando tenías dos, así cuando tenías tres, reviviendo la vida de cada una de ellas por la dimensión del hueco que le debajan entre los brazos.

El día que la mayor de las niñas cumplió diez años, la tía se sentó en el sillón frente al cañaveral y no se volvió a levantar jamás. Se balconeaba días enteros observando los cambios de agua de las cañas y sólo salía de su sopor cuando la venía a visitar el doctor o cuando se despertaba con ganas de hacer una muñeca. Comenzaba entonces a clamar para que todos los habitantes de la casa viniesen a ayudarla. Podía verse ese día a los peones de la hacienda haciendo constantes relevos al pueblo como alegres mensajeros incas, a comprar cera, a comprar barro de porcelana, encajes, agujas, carretes de hilos de todos los colores. Mientras se llevaban a cabo estas diligencias, la tía llamaba a su habitación a la niña con la que había soñado esa noche y le tomaba las medidas. Luego le hacía una mascarilla de cera que cubría de yeso por ambos lados como una cara viva dentro de dos caras muertas; luego hacía salir un hilillo rubio interminable por un hoyito en la barbilla. La porcelana de las manos era siempre translúcida; tenía un ligero tinte marfileño que contrastaba con la blancura granulada de las caras de biscuit. Para hacer el cuerpo, la tía enviaba al jardín por veinte higüeras relucientes. Las cogía con una mano y con un movimiento experto de la cuchilla las iba rebanando una a una en cráneos relucientes de cuero verde. Luego las inclinaba en hilera contra la pared del balcón, para que el sol y el aire secaran los cerebros algobonosos del guano gris. Al cabo de algunos días raspaba el contenido con una cuchara y lo iba introduciendo con infinita paciencia por la boca de la muñeca.

Lo único que la tía transigía en utilizar en la creación de las muñecas sin que estuviese hecho por ella, eran las bolas de los ojos. Se los enviaban por correo desde Europa en todos los colores, pero la tía los consideraba inservibles hasta no haberlos dejado sumergidos durante un número de días en el fondo de la quebrada para que aprendiesen a reconocer el más leve movimiento de las antenas de las chágaras. Sólo entonces los lavaba con agua de amoniaco y los guardaba, relucientes como gemas, colocados sobre camas de algodón, en el fondo de una lata de galletas holandesas. El vestido de las muñecas no variaba nunca, a pesar de que las niñas iban creciendo. Vestía siempre a las más pequeñas de tira bordada y a las mayores de broderí, colocando en la cabeza de cada una el mismo lazo abullonado y trémulo de pecho de paloma.

Las niñas empezaron a casarse y a abandonar la casa. El día de la boda la tía les regalaba a cada una la última muñeca dándoles un beso en la frente y diciéndoles con una sonrisa: "Aquí tienes tu Pascua de Resurrección". A los novios los tranquilizaba asegurándoles que la muñeca era sólo una decoración sentimental que solía colocarse sentada, en las casas de antes, sobre la cola del piano. Desde lo alto del balcón la tía observaba a las niñas bajar por última vez las escaleras de la casa sosteniendo en una mano la modesta maleta a cuadros de cartón y pasando el otro brazo alrededor de la cintura de aquella exuberante muñeca hecha a su imagen y semejanza, calzada con zapatillas de ante, faldas de bordados nevados y pantaletas de *valenciennes*. Las manos y la cara de estas muñecas, sin embargo, se notaban menos transparentes, tenían la consistencia de la leche cortada. Esta diferencia encubría otra más sutil: la muñeca de boda no estaba jamás rellena de guata, sino de miel.

Ya se habían casado todas las niñas y en la casa quedaba sólo la más joven cuando el doctor hizo a la tía la visita mensual acompañado de su hijo que acababa de regresar de sus estudios de medicina en el norte. El joven levantó el volante de la falda almidonada y se quedó mirando aquella inmensa vejiga abotagada que manaba una esperma perfumada por la punta de sus escamas verdes. Sacó su estetoscopio y la auscultó cuidadosamente. La tía pensó que auscultaba la respiración de la chágara para verificar si todavía estaba viva, y cogiéndole la mano con cariño se la puso sobre un lugar determinado para que palpara el movimiento constante de las antenas. El joven dejó caer la falda y miró fijamente al padre. Usted hubiese podido haber curado esto en sus comienzos, le dijo. Es cierto, contestó el padre, pero yo sólo quería que vinieras a ver la chágara que te había pagado los estudios durante veinte años.

En adelante fue el joven médico quien visitó mensualmente a la tía vieja. Era evidente su interés por la menor y la tía pudo comenzar su última muñeca con amplia anticipación. Se presentaba siempre con el cuello almidonado, los zapatos brillantes y el ostentoso alfiler de corbata oriental del que no tiene donde caerse muerto. Luego de examinar a la tía se sentaba en la sala recostando su silueta de papel dentro de un marco ovalado, a la vez que le entregaba a la menor el mismo ramo de siemprevivas moradas. Ella le ofrecía galletitas de jengibre y cogía el ramo quisquillosamente con la punta de los dedos como quien coge el estómago de un erizo vuelto al revés. Decidió casarse con él porque le intrigaba su perfil dormido, y porque ya tenía ganas de saber cómo era por dentro la carne del delfín.

El día de la boda la menor se sorprendió al coger la muñeca por la cintura y encontrarla tibia, pero lo olvidó en seguida, asombrada ante su excelencia artística. Las manos y la cara estaban confeccionadas con delicadísima porcelana de Mikado. Reconoció en la sonrisa entreabierta y un poco triste la colección completa de sus dientes de leche. Había, además, otro detalle particular: la tía había incrustado en el fondo de las pupilas de los ojos sus dormilonas de brillantes.

El joven médico se la llevó a vivir al pueblo, a una casa encuadrada dentro de un bloque de cemento. La obligaba todos los días a sentarse en el balcón, para que los que pasaban por la calle supiesen que él se había casado en sociedad. Inmóvil dentro de su cubo de calor, la menor comenzó a sospechar que su marido no sólo tenía el perfil de silueta de papel sino también el alma. Confirmó sus sospechas al poco tiempo. Un día él le sacó los ojos a la muñeca con la punta del bisturí y los empeñó por un lujoso reloj de cebolla con una larga leontina. Desde entonces la muñeca siguió sentada sobre la cola del piano, pero con los ojos bajos.

A los pocos meses el joven médico notó la ausencia de la muñeca y le preguntó a la menor qué había hecho con ella. Una confradía de señoras piadosas le había ofrecido una buena suma por la cara y las manos de porcelana para hacerle un retablo a la Verónica en la próxima procesión de Cuaresma. La menor le contestó que las hormigas habían descubierto por fin que la muñeca estaba rellena de miel y en una sola noche se la habían devorado. "Como las manos y la cara eran de porcelana de Mikado, dijo, seguramente las hormigas las creyeron hechas de azúcar, y en este preciso momento deben de estar quebrándose los dientes, royendo con furia dedos y párpados en alguna cueva subterránea". Esa noche el médico cavó toda la tierra alrededor de la casa sin encontrar nada.

Pasaron los años y el médico se hizo millonario. Se había quedado con toda la clientela del pueblo, a quienes no les importaba pagar honorarios exorbitantes para poder ver de cerca a un miembro legítimo de la extinta aristocracia cañera. La menor seguía sentada en el balcón, inmóvil dentro de sus gasas y encajes, siempre con los ojos bajos. Cuando los pacientes de su marido, colgados de collares, plumachos y bastones, se acomodaban cerca de ella removiendo los rollos de sus carnes satisfechas con un alboroto de monedas, percibían a su alrededor un perfume particular que les hacía recordar involuntariamente la lenta supuración de una guanábana. Entonces les entraban a todos unas ganas irresistibles de restregarse las manos como si fueran patas.

Una sola cosa perturbaba la felicidad del médico. Notaba que mientras él se iba poniendo viejo, la menor guardaba la misma piel aporcelanada y dura que tenía cuando la iba a visitar a la casa del cañaveral. Una noche decidió entrar en su habitación para observarla durmiendo. Notó que su pecho no se movía. Colocó delicadamente el estetoscopio sobre su corazón y oyó un lejano rumor de agua. Entonces la muñera levantó los párpados y por las cuencas vacías de los ojos comenzaron a salir las antenas furibundas de las chágaras.

Carlos Fuentes
1928–
México

Chac Mool
Los días enmascarados, 1954.

HACE poco tiempo, Filiberto murió ahogado en Acapulco. Sucedió en Semana Santa. Aunque había sido despedido de su empleo en la Secretaría, Filiberto no pudo resistir la tentación burocrática de ir, como todos los años, a la pensión alemana, comer el *choucrout* endulzado por los sudores de la cocina tropical, bailar el Sábado de Gloria en La Quebrada y sentirse *gente conocida* en el oscuro anonimato vespertino de la Playa de Hornos. Claro, sabíamos que en su juventud había nadado bien; pero ahora, a los cuarenta, y tan desmejorado como se le veía, ¡intentar salvar, a la medianoche, el largo trecho entre Caleta y la isla de la Roqueta! Frau Müller no permitió que se le velara, a pesar de ser un cliente tan antiguo, en la pensión; por el contrario, esa noche organizó un baile en la terracita sofocada, mientras Filiberto esperaba, muy pálido dentro de su caja, a que saliera el camión matutino de la terminal, y pasó acompañado de huacales y fardos la primera noche de su nueva vida. Cuando llegué, muy temprano, a vigilar el embarque del féretro, Filiberto estaba bajo un túmulo de cocos: el chófer dijo que lo acomodáramos rápidamente en el toldo y lo cubriéramos con lonas, para que no se espantaran los pasajeros, y a ver si no le habíamos echado la sal al viaje.

Salimos de Acapulco a la hora de la brisa tempranera. Hasta Tierra Colorada nacieron el calor y la luz. Mientras desayunaba huevos y chorizo abrí el cartapacio de Filiberto, recogido el día anterior, junto con sus otras pertenencias, en la pensión de los Müller. Doscientos pesos. Un periódico derogado de la ciudad de México. Cachos de lotería. El pasaje de ida — ¿sólo de ida? Y el cuaderno barato, de hojas cuadriculadas y tapas de papel mármol.

Me aventuré a leerlo, a pesar de las curvas, el hedor a vómito y cierto sentimiento natural de respeto por la vida privada de mi difunto amigo. Recordaría —sí, empezaba con eso— nuestra cotidiana labor en la oficina; quizá sabría, al fin, por qué fue declinando, olvidando sus deberes, por qué dictaba oficios sin sentido, ni número, ni "Sufragio Efectivo No Reelección". Por qué, en fin, fue corrido, olvidada la pensión, sin respetar los escalafones.

"Hoy fui a arreglar lo de mi pensión. El licenciado, amabilísimo. Salí tan contento que decidí gastar cinco pesos en un café. Es el mismo al que íbamos de jóvenes y al que ahora nunca concurro, porque me recuerda que a los veinte años podía darme más lujos que a los cuarenta. Entonces todos estábamos en un mismo plano, hubiéramos rechazado con energía cualquier opinión peyorativa hacia los compañeros; de hecho, librábamos la batalla por aquellos a quienes en la casa discutían por su baja extracción o falta de elegancia. Yo sabía que muchos de ellos (quizá los más humildes) llegarían muy alto y aquí, en la Escuela, se iban a forjar las amistades duraderas en cuya compañía cursaríamos el mar bravío. No, no fue así. No hubo reglas. Muchos de los humildes se quedaron allí, muchos llegaron más arriba de lo que pudimos pronosticar en aquellas fogosas, amables tertulias. Otros, que parecíamos prometerlo todo, nos quedamos a la mitad del camino, destripados en un examen extracurricular, aislados por una zanja invisible de los que triunfaron y de los que nada alcanzaron. En fin, hoy volví a sentarme en las sillas modernizadas —también hay, como barricada de una invasión, una fuente de sodas— y pretendí leer expedientes. Vi a muchos antiguos compañeros, cambiados, amnésicos, retocados de luz de neón, prósperos. Con el café que casi no reconocía, con la ciudad misma, habían ido cincelándose a ritmo distinto del mío. No, ya no me reconocían; o no me querían reconocer. A lo sumo —uno o dos— una mano gorda y rápida sobre el hombro. Adiós viejo, qué tal. Entre ellos y yo mediaban los dieciocho agujeros del Country Club. Me disfracé detrás de los expedientes. Desfilaron en mi memoria los años de las grandes ilusiones, de los pronósticos felices y, también, todas las omisiones que impidieron su realización. Sentí la angustia de no poder meter los dedos en el pasado y pegar los trozos de algún rompecabezas abandonado; pero el arcón de los juguetes se va olvidando y, al cabo, ¿quién sabrá dónde fueron a dar los soldados de plomo, los cascos, las espadas de madera? Los disfraces tan queridos, no fueron más que eso. Y sin embargo, había habido constancia, disciplina, apego al deber. ¿No era suficiente, o sobraba? En ocasiones me asaltaba el recuerdo de Rilke. La gran recompensa de la aventura de juventud debe ser la muerte; jóvenes, debemos partir con todos nuestros secretos. Hoy, no tendría que volver la mirada a las ciudades de sal. ¿Cinco pesos? Dos de propina."

"Pepe, aparte de su pasión por el derecho mercantil, gusta de teorizar. Me vio salir de Catedral, y juntos nos encaminamos a Palacio. El es descreído, pero no le basta; en media cuadra tuvo que fabricar una teoría. Que si yo no fuera mexicano, no adoraría a Cristo y —No, mira, parece evidente. Llegan los españoles y te proponen adorar a un Dios muerto hecho un coágulo, con el costado herido, clavado en una cruz. Sacrificado. Ofrendado. ¿Qué cosa más natural que aceptar un sentimiento tan cercano a todo tu ceremonial, a toda tu vida?... Figúrate, en cambio, que México hubiera sido conquistado por budistas o por mahometanos. No es concebible que nuestros indios veneraran a un individuo que murió de indigestión. Pero un Dios al que no le basta que se sacrifiquen por él, sino que incluso va a que le arranquen el corazón, ¡caramba, jaque mate a Huitzilopochtli! El cristianismo, en su sentido cálido, sangriento, de sacrificio y liturgia, se vuelve una prolongación natural y novedosa de la religión indígena. Los aspectos caridad, amor y la otra mejilla, en cambio, son rechazados. Y todo en México es eso: hay que matar a los hombres para poder creer en ellos.

"Pepe conocía mi afición, desde joven, por ciertas formas del arte indígena mexicano. Yo colecciono estatuillas, ídolos,

cacharros. Mis fines de semana los paso en Tlaxcala o en Teotihuacán. Acaso por esto le guste relacionar todas las teorías
que elabora para mi consumo con estos temas. Por cierto que
busco una réplica razonable del Chac Mool desde hace tiempo,
y hoy Pepe me informa de un lugar en la Lagunilla donde venden uno de piedra y parece que barato. Voy a ir el domingo.

"Un guasón pintó de rojo el agua del garrafón en la oficina, con la consiguiente perturbación de las labores. He debido
consignarlo al Director, a quien sólo le dio mucha risa. El culpable se ha valido de esta circunstancia para hacer sarcasmos
a mis costillas el día entero, todos en torno al agua. Ch..."

"Hoy domingo, aproveché para ir a la Lagunilla. Encontré el Chac Mool en la tienducha que me señaló Pepe. Es una
pieza preciosa, de tamaño natural, y aunque el marchante asegura su originalidad, lo dudo. La piedra es corriente, pero ello
no aminora la elegancia de la postura o lo macizo del bloque.
El desleal vendedor le ha embarrado salsa de tomate en la barriga al ídolo para convencer a los turistas de la sangrienta au-
tenticidad de la·escultura."

"El traslado a la casa me costó más que la adquisición.
Pero ya está aquí, por el momento en el sótano mientras re-
organizo mi cuarto de trofeos a fin de darle cabida. Estas figuras necesitan sol vertical y fogoso; ese fue su elemento y
condición. Pierde mucho mi Chac Mool en la oscuridad del
sótano; allí, es un simple bulto agónico, y su mueca parece
reprocharme que le niegue la luz. El comerciante tenía un
foco que iluminaba verticalmente a la escultura, recortando
todas sus aristas y dándole una expresión más amable. Habrá
que seguir su ejemplo."

"Amanecí con la tubería descompuesta. Incauto, dejé
correr el agua de la cocina y se desbordó, corrió por el piso
y llegó hasta el sótano, sin que me percatara. El Chac Mool
resiste la humedad, pero mis maletas sufrieron. Todo esto,
en día de labores, me obligó a llegar tarde a la oficina."

"Vinieron, por fin, a arreglar la tubería. Las maletas, tor-
cidas. Y el Chac Mool, con lama en la base."

"Desperté a la una: había escuchado un quejido terrible.
Pensé en ladrones. Pura imaginación."

"Los lamentos nocturnos han seguido. No sé a qué atri-
buirlo, pero estoy nervioso. Para colmo de males, la tubería
volvió a descomponerse, y las lluvias se han colado, inundando el sótano."

"El plomero no viene; estoy desesperado. Del Departamento del Distrito Federal, más vale no hablar. Es la primera

vez que el agua de las lluvias no obedece a las coladeras y viene a dar a mi sótano. Los quejidos han cesado: vaya una cosa por otra."

"Secaron el sótano, y el Chac Mool está cubierto de lama. Le da un aspecto grotesco, porque toda la masa de la escultura parece padecer de una erisipela verde, salvo los ojos, que han permanecido de piedra. Voy a aprovechar el domingo para raspar el musgo. Pepe me ha recomendado cambiarme a una casa de apartamentos, y tomar el piso más alto, para evitar estas tragedias acuáticas. Pero yo no puedo dejar este caserón, ciertamente muy grande para mí solo, un poco lúgubre en su arquitectura porfiriana. Pero que es la única herencia y recuerdo de mis padres. No sé qué me daría ver una fuente de sodas con sinfonola en el sótano y una tienda de decoración en la planta baja."

"Fui a raspar el musgo del Chac Mool con una espátula. Parecía ser ya parte de la piedra; fue labor de más de una hora, y sólo a las seis de la tarde pude terminar. No se distinguía muy bien en la penumbra; al finalizar el trabajo, seguí con la mano los contornos de la piedra. Cada vez que lo repasaba, el bloque parecía reblandecerse. No quise creerlo: era ya casi una pasta. Este mercader de la Lagunilla me ha timado. Su escultura precolombina es puro yeso, y la humedad acabará por arruinarla. Le he echado encima unos trapos; mañana la pasaré a la pieza de arriba, antes de que sufra un deterioro total."

"Los trapos han caido al suelo. Increíble. Volví a palpar al Chac Mool. Se ha endurecido pero no vuelve a la consistencia de la piedra. No quiero escribirlo: hay en el torso algo de la textura de la carne, al apretar los brazos los siento de goma, siento que algo circula por esa figura recostada... Volví a bajar en la noche. No cabe duda: el Chac Mool tiene vello en los brazos."

"Esto nunca me había sucedido. Tergiversé los asuntos en la oficina, giré una orden de pago que no estaba autorizada, y el Director tuvo que llamarme la atención. Quizá me mostré hasta descortés con los compañeros. Tendré que ver un médico, saber si es imaginación o delirio o qué, y deshacerme de ese maldito Chac Mool."

Hasta aquí la escritura de Filiberto era la antigua, la que tantas veces vi en formas y memoranda, ancha y ovalada. La entrada del 25 de agosto, sin embargo, parecía escrita por otra persona. A veces como niño, separando trabajosamente cada letra; otras, nerviosas, hasta diluirse en lo ininteligible. Hay tres días vacíos, y el relato continúa:

"Todo es tan natural; y luego se cree en lo real... pero esto lo es, más que lo creído por mí. Si es real un garrafón, y más, porque nos damos mejor cuenta de su existencia, o estar, si un bromista pinta el agua de rojo... Real bocanada de cigarro efímera, real imagen monstruosa en un espejo de circo, reales, ¿no lo son todos los muertos, presentes y olvidados?... Si un hombre atravesara el Paraíso en un sueño, y le dieran una flor como prueba de que había estado allí, y si al despertar encontrara esa flor en su mano... ¿entonces, qué?

...Realidad: cierto día la quebraron en mil pedazos, la cabeza fue a dar allá, la cola aquí y nosotros no conocemos más que uno de los trozos desprendidos de su gran cuerpo. Océano libre y ficticio, sólo real cuando se le aprisiona en el rumor de un caracol marino. Hasta hace tres días, mi realidad lo era al grado de haberse borrado hoy; era movimiento reflejo, rutina, memoria, cartapacio. Y luego, como la tierra que un día tiembla para que recordemos su poder, o como la muerte que un día llegará, recriminando mi olvido de toda la vida, se presenta otra realidad: sabíamos que estaba allí, mostrenca; ahora nos sacude para hacerse viva y presente. Pensé, nuevamente, que era pura imaginación: el Chac Mool, blando y elegante, había cambiado de color en una noche; amarillo, casi dorado, parecía indicarme que era un dios, por ahora laxo, con las rodillas menos tensas que antes, con la sonrisa más benévola. Y ayer, por fin, un despertar sobresaltado, con esa seguridad espantosa de que hay dos respiraciones en la noche, de que en la oscuridad laten más pulsos que el propio. Sí, se escuchaban pasos en la escalera. Pesadilla. Vuelta a dormir... No sé cuánto tiempo pretendí dormir. Cuando volví a abrir los ojos, aún no amanecía. El cuarto olía a horror, a incienso y sangre. Con la mirada negra, recorrí la recámara, hasta detenerme en dos orificios de luz parpadeante, en dos flámulas crueles y amarillas.

"Casi sin aliento, encendí la luz."

"Allí estaba Chac Mool, erguido, sonriente, ocre, con su barriga encarnada. Me paralizaban los dos ojillos, casi bizcos, muy pegados al caballete de la nariz triangular. Los dientes inferiores mordían el labio superior, inmóviles; sólo el brillo del casquetón cuadrado sobre la cabeza anormalmente voluminosa, delataba vida. Chac Mool avanzó hacia mi cama; entonces empezó a llover."

Recuerdo que a fines de agosto, Filiberto fue despedido de la Secretaría, con una recriminación pública del Director y rumores de locura y hasta de robo. Esto no lo creí. Sí pude ver unos oficios descabellados, preguntándole al Oficial Ma-

yor si el agua podía olerse, ofreciendo sus servicios al Secretario de Recursos Hidráulicos para hacer llover en el desierto.
No supe qué explicación darme a mí mismo; pensé que las lluvias, excepcionalmente fuertes, de ese verano, habían enerva-
do a mi amigo. O que alguna depresión moral debía producir
la vida en aquel caserón antiguo, por la mitad de los cuartos
bajo llave y empolvados, sin criados ni vida de familia. Los
apuntes siguientes son de fines de septiembre:

"Chac Mool puede ser simpático cuando quiere, '...un glu-
glú de agua embelesada' ...Sabe historias fantásticas sobre los
monzones, las lluvias ecuatoriales y el castigo de los desiertos;
cada planta arranca de su paternidad mítica: el sauce es su
hija descarriada; los lotos, sus niños mimados; su suegra, el
cacto. Lo que no puedo tolerar es el olor, extrahumano, que
emana de esa carne que no lo es, de las sandalias flamantes de
vejez. Con risa estridente, Chac Mool revela cómo fue descubierto por Le Plongeon y puesto físicamente en contacto de
hombres de otros símbolos. Su espíritu ha vivido en el cántaro y en la tempestad, naturalmente; otra cosa es su piedra, y
haberla arrancado del escondite maya en el que yacía es artificial y cruel. Creo que Chac Mool nunca lo perdonará. El
sabe de la inminencia del hecho estético."

"He debido proporcionarle sapolio para que se lave el
vientre que el mercader, al creerlo azteca, le untó de salsa *ket-
chup*. No pareció gustarle mi pregunta sobre su parentesco
con Tláloc*, y cuando se enoja, sus dientes, de por sí repulsi-
vos, se afilan y brillan. Los primeros días, bajó a dormir al sótano; desde ayer, lo hace en mi cama."

"Ha empezado la temporada seca. Ayer, desde la sala donde ahora duermo, comencé a oír los mismos lamentos roncos
del principio, seguidos de ruidos terribles. Subí; entreabrí la
puerta de la recámara: Chac Mool estaba rompiendo las lámparas, los muebles; al verme, saltó hacia la puerta con las manos arañadas, y apenas pude cerrar e irme a esconder al baño.
Luego bajó, jadeante y pidió agua; todo el día tiene corriendo los grifos, no queda un centímetro seco en la casa. Tengo
que dormir muy abrigado, y le he pedido que no empape más
la sala**."

"El Chac inundó hoy la sala. Exasperado, le dije que lo
iba a devolver al mercado de la Lagunilla. Tan terrible como
su risilla —horrorosamente distinta a cualquier risa de hombre

---

*Deidad azteca de la lluvia.
**Filiberto no explica en qué lengua se entendía con el Chac Mool.

o de animal— fue la bofetada que me dio, con ese brazo cargado de pesados brazaletes. Debo reconocerlo: soy su prisionero. Mi idea original era bien distinta: yo dominaría a Chac Mool, como se domina a un juguete; era, acaso, una prolongación de mi seguridad infantil; pero la niñez — ¿quién lo dijo?— es fruto comido por los años, y yo no me he dado cuenta... Ha tomado mi ropa y se pone la bata cuando empieza a brotarle musgo verde. El Chac Mool está acostumbrado a que se le obedezca, desde siempre y para siempre; yo, que nunca he debido mandar, sólo puedo doblegarme ante él. Mientras no llueva — ¿y su poder mágico?— vivirá colérico e irritable."

"Hoy descubrí que en las noches Chac Mool sale de la casa. Siempre, al oscurecer, canta una tonada chirriona y antigua, más vieja que el canto mismo. Luego cesa. Toqué varias veces a su puerta, y como no me contestó, me atreví a entrar. No había vuelto a ver la recámara desde el día en que la estatua trató de atacarme: está en ruinas, y allí se concentra ese olor a incienso y sangre que ha permeado la casa. Pero detrás de la puerta, hay huesos: huesos de perros, de ratones y gatos. Esto es lo que roba en la noche el Chac Mool para sustentarse. Esto explica los ladridos espantosos de todas las madrugadas."

"Febrero, seco. Chac Mool vigila cada paso mío; me ha obligado a telefonear a una fonda para que diariamente me traigan un portaviandas. Pero el dinero sustraído de la oficina ya se va a acabar. Sucedió lo inevitable: desde el día primero, cortaron el agua y la luz por falta de pago. Pero Chac Mool ha descubierto una fuente pública a dos cuadras de aquí; todos los días hago diez o doce viajes por agua, y él me observa desde la azotea. Dice que si intento huir me fulminará: también es Dios del Rayo. Lo que él no sabe es que estoy al tanto de sus correrías nocturnas... Como no hay luz, debo acostarme a las ocho. Ya debería estar acostumbrado al Chac Mool, pero hace poco, en la oscuridad, me topé con él en la escalera, sentí sus brazos helados, las escamas de su piel renovada y quise gritar."

"Si no llueve pronto, el Chac Mool va a convertirse otra vez en piedra. He notado sus dificultades recientes para moverse; a veces se reclina durante horas, paralizado, contra la pared y parece ser, de nuevo, un ídolo inerme, por más dios de la tempestad y el trueno que se le considere. Pero estos reposos sólo le dan nuevas fuerzas para vejarme, arañarme como si pudiese arrancar algún líquido de mi carne. Ya no tienen lugar aquellos intermedios amables durante los cuales relataba viejos cuentos; creo notar en él una especie de resentimiento concentrado. Ha habido otros indicios que me han puesto a pensar: los vinos de mi bodega se están acabando; Chac Mool acaricia la seda de la bata; quiere que traiga una criada a la casa; me ha hecho enseñarle a usar jabón y lociones. Incluso hay algo viejo en su cara que antes parecía eterna. Aquí puede estar mi salvación: si el Chac cae en tentaciones, si se humaniza, posiblemente todos sus siglos de vida se acumulen en un instante y caiga fulminado por el poder aplazado del tiempo. Pero también me pongo a pensar en algo terrible: el Chac no querrá que yo asista a su derrumbe, no querrá un testigo..., es posible que desee matarme."

"Hoy aprovecharé la excursión nocturna de Chac para huir. Me iré a Acapulco; veremos qué puede hacerse para conseguir trabajo y esperar la muerte de Chac Mool; sí, se avecina; está canoso, abotagado. Yo necesito asolearme, nadar, recuperar fuerzas. Me quedan cuatrocientos pesos. Iré a la Pensión Müller, que es barata y cómoda. Que se adueñe de todo Chac Mool: a ver cuánto dura sin mis baldes de agua."

Aquí termina el diario de Filiberto. No quise pensar más en su relato; dormí hasta Cuernavaca. De ahí a México pretendí dar coherencia al escrito, relacionarlo con exceso de trabajo, con algún motivo sicológico. Cuando, a las nueve de la noche llegamos a la terminal, aún no podía explicarme la locura de mi amigo. Contraté una camioneta para llevar el féretro a casa de Filiberto, y desde allí ordenar el entierro.

Antes de que pudiera introducir la llave en la cerradura, la puerta se abrió. Apareció un indio amarillo, en bata de casa, con bufanda. Su aspecto no podía ser más repulsivo; despedía un olor a loción barata; quería cubrir las arrugas con la cara polveada; tenía la boca embarrada de lápiz labial mal aplicado, y el pelo daba la impresión de estar teñido.

—Perdone... no sabía que Filiberto hubiera...

—No importa; lo sé todo. Dígale a los hombres que lleven el cadáver al sótano.

Gabriel García Márquez
1928—
Colombia

El rastro de tu sangre en la nieve
Cuentos peregrinos, 1992.

AL anochecer, cuando llegaron a la frontera, Nena Daconte se dio cuenta de que el dedo con el anillo de bodas le seguía sangrando. El guardia civil con una manta de lana cruda sobre el tricornio de charol examinó los pasaportes a la luz de una linterna de carburo, haciendo un grande esfuerzo para que no lo derribara la presión del viento que soplaba de los Pirineos. Aunque eran dos pasaportes diplomáticos en regla, el guardia levantó la linterna para comprobar que los retratos se parecían a las caras.

Nena Daconte era casi una niña, con unos ojos de pájaro feliz y una piel de maleza que todavía irradiaba la resolana del Caribe en el lúgubre anochecer de enero, y estaba arropada hasta el cuello con un abrigo de nucas de visón que no podía comprarse con el sueldo de un año de toda la guarnición fronteriza. Billy Sánchez de Avila, su marido, que conducía el coche, era un año menor que ella y casi tan bello, y llevaba una chaqueta de cuadros escoceses y una gorra de pelotero. Al contrario de su esposa, era alto y atlético y tenía las mandíbulas de hierro de los matones tímidos. Pero lo que revelaba mejor la condición de ambos era el automóvil platinado, cuyo interior exhalaba un aliento de bestia viva, como no se había visto otro por aquella frontera de pobres. Los asientos posteriores iban atiborrados de maletas demasiado nuevas y muchas cajas de regalos todavía sin abrir. Ahí estaba, además, el saxofón tenor que había sido la pasión dominante en la vida de Nena Daconte antes de que sucumbiera al amor contrariado de su tierno pandillero de balneario.

Cuando el guardia le devolvió los pasaportes sellados, Billy Sánchez le preguntó dónde podía encontrar una farmacia para hacerle una cura en el dedo a su mujer, y el guardia le gritó contra el viento que preguntaran en Hendaya, del lado francés. Pero los guardias de Hendaya estaban sentados a la mesa en mangas de camisa, jugando barajas mientras comían pan mojado en tazones de vino dentro de una garita de cristal cálida y bien alumbrada, y les bastó con ver el tamaño y la clase del coche para indicarles por señas que se internaran en

Francia. Billy Sánchez hizo sonar varias veces la bocina, pero los guardias no entendieron que los llamaban, sino que uno de ellos abrió el cristal y les gritó con más rabia que el viento: *Merde! Allez-y, espèce de con!*

Entonces Nena Daconte salió del automóvil envuelta con el abrigo hasta las orejas, y le preguntó al guardia en un francés perfecto dónde había una farmacia. El guardia contestó por costumbre con la boca llena de pan que eso no era asunto suyo. Y menos con semejante borrasca, y cerró la ventanilla. Pero luego se fijó con atención en la muchacha que se chupaba el dedo herido envuelta en el destello de los visones naturales, y debió confundirla con una aparición mágica en aquella noche de espantos, porque al instante cambió de humor. Explicó que la ciudad más cercana era Biarritz, pero que en pleno invierno y con aquel viento de lobos, tal vez no hubiera una farmacia abierta hasta Bayona, un poco más adelante.

—¿Es algo grave?— preguntó.

—Nada— sonrió Nena Daconte, mostrándole el dedo con la sortija de diamantes en cuya yema era apenas perceptible la herida de la rosa—. Es sólo un pinchazo.

Antes de Bayona volvió a nevar. No eran más de las siete, pero encontraron las calles desiertas y las casas cerradas por la furia de la borrasca, y al cabo de muchas vueltas sin encontrar una farmacia decidieron seguir adelante. Billy Sánchez se alegró con la decisión. Tenía una pasión insaciable por los automóviles raros y un papá con demasiados sentimientos de culpa y recursos de sobra para complacerlo, y nunca había conducido nada igual a aquel Bentley convertible de regalo de bodas. Era tanta su embriaguez en el volante, que cuanto más andaba menos cansado se sentía. Estaba dispuesto a llegar esa noche a Burdeos, donde tenían reservada la suite nupcial del hotel Splendid, y no habría vientos contrarios ni bastante nieve en el cielo para impedirlo. Nena Daconte, en cambio, estaba agotada, sobre todo por el último tramo de la carretera desde Madrid, que era una cornisa de cabras azotada por el granizo. Así que después de Bayona se enrolló un pañuelo en el anular apretándolo bien para detener la sangre que seguía fluyendo, y se durmió a fondo. Billy Sánchez no lo advirtió sino al borde de la media noche, después de que acabó de nevar y el viento se paró de pronto entre los pinos, y el cielo de las landas se llenó de estrellas glaciales. Había pasado frente a las luces dormidas de Burdeos, pero sólo se detuvo para llenar el tanque en una estación de la carretera pues aún le quedaban ánimos para llegar hasta París sin tomar aliento. Era tan feliz con su juguete grande de 25.000 libras esterlinas, que ni siquiera se preguntó si lo sería también la criatura radiante que dormía a su lado con la venda del anular empapada de sangre, y cuyo sueño de adolescente, por primera vez, estaba atravesado por ráfagas de incertidumbre. Se habían casado tres días antes, a 10.000 kilómetros de allí, en Cartagena de Indias, con el asombro de los padres de él y la desilusión de los de ella, y la bendición personal del Arzobispo Primado. Nadie, salvo ellos mismos, entendía el fundamento real ni conoció el origen de ese amor imprevisible. Había empezado tres meses antes de la boda, un domingo de mar en que la pandilla de Billy Sánchez se tomó por asalto los vestidores de mujeres de los balnearios de Marbella. Nena Daconte había cumplido apenas 18 años, acababa de regresar del internado de la Chattelainie, en Stblaise, Suiza, hablando cuatro idiomas sin acento y con un dominio maestro del saxofón tenor, y aquel era su primer domingo de mar desde el regreso. Se había desnudado por completo para ponerse el traje de baño cuando empezó la estampida de pánico y los gritos de abordaje en las casetas vecinas, pero no entendió lo que ocurría hasta que la aldaba de su puerta saltó en astillas y vio parado frente a ella al bandolero más hermoso que se podía concebir. Lo único que llevaba puesto era un calzoncillo lineal de falsa piel de leopardo, y tenía el cuerpo apacible y elástico y el color dorado de la gente de mar. En el puño derecho, donde tenía una esclava metálica de gladiador romano, llevaba enrollada una cadena de hierro que le servía de arma mortal, y tenía colgada del cuello una medalla sin santo que palpitaba en silencio con el susto del corazón. Habían estado juntos en la escuela primaria y habían roto muchas piñatas en las fiestas de cumpleaños, pues ambos pertenecían a la estirpe provinciana que manejaba a su arbitrio el destino de la ciudad desde los tiempos de la Colonia, pero habían dejado de verse tantos años que no se reconocieron a primera vista. Nena Daconte permaneció de pie, inmovil, sin hacer nada por ocultar su desnudez intensa. Billy Sánchez cumplió entonces con su rito pueril: se bajó el calzoncito de leopardo y le mostró su respetable animal erguido. Ella lo miró de frente y sin asombro.

—Los he visto más grandes y más firmes— dijo, dominando el terror. De modo que piensa bien lo que vas a hacer, porque conmigo te tienes que comportar mejor que un negro.

En realidad, Nena Daconte no sólo era virgen sino que nunca hasta entonces había visto un hombre desnudo, pero el desafío resultó eficaz. Lo único que se le ocurrió a Billy Sánchez fue tirar un puñetazo de rabia contra la pared con la cadena enrollada en la mano, y se astilló los huesos. Ella lo llevó en su coche al hospital, lo ayudó a sobrellevar la convalecencia, y al final aprendieron juntos a hacer el amor de la buena manera. Pasaron las tardes difíciles de junio en la terraza interior de la casa donde habían muerto seis generaciones de próceres en la familia de Nena Daconte, ella tocando canciones de moda en el saxofón, y él con la mano escayolada contemplándola desde el chinchorro con un estupor sin alivio. La casa tenía numerosas ventanas de cuerpo entero que daban al estanque de podredumbre de la bahía, y era una de las más grandes y antiguas del barrio de la Manga, y sin duda la más fea. Pero la terraza de baldosas ajedrezadas donde Nena Daconte tocaba el saxofón era un remanso en el calor de las cuatro, y daba a un patio de sombras grandes con palos de mango y matas de guineo, bajo los cuales había una tumba con una losa sin nombre, anterior a la casa y a la memoria de la familia. Aun los menos entendidos en música pensaban que el sonido del saxofón era anacrónico en una casa de tanta alcurnia. "Suena como un buque", había dicho la abuela de Nena Daconte cuando lo oyó por primera vez. Su madre había tratado en vano de que lo tocara de otro modo, y no como ella lo hacía por comodidad, con la falda recogida hasta los muslos y las rodillas separadas, y con una sensualidad que no le parecía esencial para la música. "No me importa qué instrumento toques —le decía— con tal de que lo toques con las piernas cerradas". Pero fueron esos aires de adioses de buques y ese encarnizamiento de amor los que le permitieron a Nena Daconte romper la cáscara amarga de Billy Sánchez. Debajo de la triste reputación de bruto que él tenía muy bien sustentada por la confluencia de dos apellidos ilustres, ella descubrió un huérfano asustado y tierno. Llegaron a conocerse tanto mientras se le soldaban los huesos de la mano, que él mismo se asombró de la fluidez con que ocurrió el amor cuando ella lo llevó a su cama de doncella una tarde de lluvias en que se quedaron solos en la casa. Todos los días a esa hora, durante casi dos semanas, retozaron desnudos bajo la mirada atónita de los retratos de guerreros civiles y abuelas insaciables que los habían precedido en el paraíso de aquella cama histórica. Aun en las pausas del amor permanecían desnudos con las ventanas abiertas respirando la brisa de escombros de barcos de la bahía, su olor a mierda, y oyendo en el silencio del saxofón los ruidos cotidianos del patio, la nota única del sapo bajo las matas de guineo, la gota de agua en la tumba de nadie, los pasos naturales de la vida que antes no habían tenido tiempo de conocer.

Cuando los padres de Nena Daconte regresaron a la casa, ellos habían progresado tanto en el amor que ya no les alcanzaba el mundo para otra cosa, y lo hacían a cualquier hora y en cualquier parte, tratando de inventarlo otra vez cada vez que lo hacían. Al principio lo hicieron como mejor podían en los carros deportivos con que el papá de Billy trataba de apaciguar sus propias culpas. Después, cuando los coches se les volvieron demasiado fáciles, se metían por la noche en las casetas desiertas de Marbella donde el destino los había enfrentado por primera vez, y hasta se metieron disfrazados durante el carnaval de noviembre en los cuartos de alquiler del antiguo barrio de esclavos de Getsemaní, al amparo de las mamasantas que hasta hacía pocos meses tenían que padecer a Billy Sánchez con su pandilla de cadeneros. Nena Daconte se entregó a los amores furtivos con la misma devoción frenética que antes malgastaba en el saxofón, hasta el punto de que su bandolero domesticado terminó por entender lo que ella quiso decirle cuando le dijo que tenía que comportarse como un negro. Billy Sánchez le correspondió siempre y bien, y con el mismo alborozo. Ya casados, cumplieron con el deber de amarse mientras las azafatas dormían en mitad del Atlántico, encerrados a duras penas y más muertos de risa que de placer en el retrete del avión. Sólo ellos sabían entonces, 24 horas después de la boda, que Nena Daconte estaba encinta desde hacía dos meses.

De modo que cuando llegaron a Madrid se sentían muy lejos de ser dos amantes saciados, pero tenían bastantes reservas para comportarse como recién casados puros. Los padres de ambos lo habían previsto todo. Antes del desembarco, un funcionario de protocolo subió a la cabina de primera clase para llevarle a Nena Daconte el abrigo de visón blanco con franjas de un negro luminoso, que era el regalo de bodas de sus padres. A Billy Sánchez le llevó una chaqueta de cordero que era la novedad de aquel invierno, y las llaves sin marca de un coche de sorpresa que le esperaba en el aeropuerto.

La misión diplomática de su país los recibió en el salón oficial. El embajador y su esposa no sólo eran amigos desde siempre de la familia de ambos, sino que él era el médico que había asistido al nacimiento de Nena Daconte, y la esperó con un ramo de rosas tan radiantes y frescas, que hasta las gotas de rocío parecían artificiales. Ella los saludó a ambos con besos de burla, incómoda con su condición un poco prematura de recién casada, y luego recibió las rosas. Al cogerlas se pinchó el dedo con una espina del tallo, pero sorteó el percance con un recurso encantador.

—Lo hice adrede— dijo —para que se fijaran en mi anillo.

En efecto, la misión diplomática en pleno admiró el esplendor del anillo, calculando que debía costar una fortuna no tanto por la clase de los diamantes como por su antigüedad bien conservada. Pero nadie advirtió que el dedo empezaba a sangrar. La atención de todos derivó después hacia el coche nuevo. El embajador había tenido el buen humor de llevarlo al aeropuerto, y de hacerlo envolver en papel celofán con un enorme lazo dorado. Billy Sánchez no apreció su ingenio. Estaba tan ansioso por conocer el coche, que desgarró la envoltura de un tirón y se quedó sin aliento. Era el Bentley convertible de ese año con tapicería de cuero legítimo. El cielo parecía un manto de ceniza, el Guadarrama mandaba un viento cortante y helado, y no se estaba bien a la intemperie, pero Billy Sánchez no tenía todavía la noción del frío. Mantuvo a la misión diplomática en el estacionamiento sin techo, inconsciente de que se estaba congelando por cortesía, hasta que terminó de reconocer el coche en sus detalles recónditos. Luego el embajador se sentó a su lado para guiarlo hasta la residencia oficial donde estaba previsto un almuerzo. En el trayecto le fue indicando los lugares más conocidos de la ciudad, pero él sólo parecía atento a la magia del coche.

Era la primera vez que salía de su tierra. Había pasado por todos los colegios privados y públicos, repitiendo siempre el mismo curso, hasta que se quedó flotando en un limbo de desamor. La primera visión de una ciudad distinta de la suya, los bloques de casas cenicientas con las luces encendidas a pleno día, los árboles pelados, el mar distante, todo le iba aumentando un sentimiento de desamparo que se esforzaba por mantener al margen del corazón. Sin embargo, poco después cayó sin darse cuenta en la primera trampa del olvido. Se había precipitado una tormenta instantánea y silenciosa, la primera de la estación, y cuando salieron de la casa del embajador después del almuerzo para emprender el viaje hacia Francia, encontraron la ciudad cubierta de una nieve radiante. Billy Sánchez se olvidó entonces del coche, y en presencia de todos, dando gritos de júbilo y echándose puñados de polvo de nieve en la cabeza, se revolcó en mitad de la calle con el abrigo puesto.

Nena Daconte se dio cuenta por primera vez de que el dedo estaba sangrando, cuando abandonaron Madrid en una tarde que se había vuelto diáfana después de la tormenta. Se sorprendió, porque había acompañado con el saxofón a la esposa del embajador, a quien le gustaba cantar arias de ópera en italiano después de los almuerzos oficiales, y apenas sí notó la molestia en el anular. Después, mientras le iba indicando a su marido las rutas más cortas hacia la frontera, se chupaba el dedo de un modo inconsciente cada vez que le sangraba, y sólo cuando llegaron a los Pirineos se le ocurrió buscar una farmacia. Luego sucumbió a los sueños atrasados de los últimos días, y cuando despertó de pronto con la impresión de pesadilla de que el coche andaba por el agua, no se acordó más durante un largo rato del pañuelo amarrado en el dedo. Vio en el reloj luminoso del tablero que eran más de las tres, hizo sus cálculos mentales, y sólo entonces comprendió que habían seguido de largo por Burdeos, y también por Angulema y Poitiers y estaban pasando por el dique de Loira inundado por la creciente. El fulgor de la luna se filtraba a través de la neblina, y las siluetas de los castillos entre los pinos parecían de cuentos de fantasmas. Nena Daconte, que conocía la región de memoria, calculó que estaban ya a unas tres horas de París, y Billy Sánchez continuaba impávido en el volante.

—Eres un salvaje —le dijo—. Llevas más de once horas manejando sin comer nada.

Estaba todavía sostenido en vilo por la embriaguez del coche nuevo. A pesar de que en el avión había dormido poco y mal, se sentía despabilado y con fuerzas de sobra para llegar a París y al amanecer.

—Todavía me dura el almuerzo de la embajada —dijo. Y agregó sin ninguna lógica: Al fin y al cabo, en Cartagena están saliendo apenas del cine. Deben ser como las diez.

Con todo Nena Daconte temía que él se durmiera conduciendo. Abrió una caja de entre los tantos regalos que les habían hecho en Madrid, y trató de meterle en la boca un pedazo de naranja azucarada. Pero él la esquivó.

—Los machos no comen dulces —dijo.

Poco antes de Orleáns se desvaneció la bruma, y una luna muy grande iluminó las sementeras nevadas, pero el tráfico se hizo más difícil por la confluencia de los enormes camiones de legumbres y cisternas de vinos que se dirigían a París. Nena Daconte hubiera querido ayudar a su marido en el volante, pero ni siquiera se atrevió a insinuarlo, porque él le había advertido desde la primera vez en que salieron juntos que no hay humillación más grande para un hombre que dejarse conducir por su mujer. Se sentía lúcida después de casi cinco horas de

buen sueño, y estaba además contenta de no haber parado en
un hotel de la provincia de Francia, que conocía desde muy
niña en numerosos viajes con sus padres. "No hay paisajes
más bellos en el mundo —decía— pero uno puede morirse de
sed sin encontrar a nadie que le dé gratis un vaso de agua".
Tan convencida estaba, que a última hora había metido un
jabón y un rollo de papel higiénico en el maletín de mano, porque en los hoteles de Francia nunca había jabón, y
el papel de los retretes eran los periódicos de la semana anterior cortados en cuadritos y colgados de un gancho. Lo
único que lamentaba en aquel momento era haber desper-
diciado una noche entera sin amor. La réplica de su marido
fue inmediata.

—Ahora mismo estaba pensando que debe ser del carajo
tirar en la nieve —dijo—. Aquí mismo, si quieres.

Nena Daconte lo pensó en serio. Al borde de la carretera,
la nieve bajo la luna tenía un aspecto mullido y cálido, pero
a medida que se acercaban a los suburbios de París el tráfico
era más intenso, y había núcleos de fábricas iluminadas y numerosos obreros en bicicleta. De no haber sido invierno, estarían ya en pleno día.

—Ya será mejor esperar hasta París —dijo Nena Daconte—.
Bien calienticos y en una cama con sábanas limpias, como la
gente casada.

—Es la primera vez que me fallas —dijo él.

—Claro —replicó ella—. Es la primera vez que somos
casados.

Poco antes de amanecer se lavaron la cara y orinaron en
una fonda del camino, y tomaron café con *croissants* calientes en el mostrador donde los camioneros desayunaban con
vino tinto. Nena Daconte se había dado cuenta en el baño de
que tenía manchas de sangre en la blusa y la falda, pero no
intentó lavarlas. Tiró en la basura el pañuelo empapado, se
cambió el anillo matrimonial para la mano izquierda y se lavó
bien el dedo herido con agua y jabón. El pinchazo era casi invisible. Sin embargo, tan pronto como regresaron al coche
volvió a sangrar, de modo que Nena Daconte dejó el brazo
colgando fuera de la ventana, convencida de que el aire glacial de las sementeras tenía virtudes de cauterio. Fue otro recurso vano pero todavía no se alarmó. "Si alguien nos quiere
encontrar será muy fácil", dijo con su encanto natural. "Sólo
tendrá que seguir el rastro de mi sangre en la nieve". Luego
pensó mejor en lo que había dicho y su rostro floreció en las
primeras luces del amanecer.

—Imagínate —dijo—: un rastro de sangre en la nieve desde Madrid hasta París. ¿No te parece bello para una canción?

No tuvo tiempo de volverlo a pensar. En los suburbios de París el dedo era un manantial incontenible, y ella sintió de veras que se le estaba yendo el alma por la herida. Había tratado de segar el flujo con el rollo de papel higiénico que llevaba en el maletín, pero más tardaba en vendarse el dedo que en arrojar por la ventana las tiras del papel ensangrentado. La ropa que llevaba puesta, el abrigo, los asientos del coche se iban empapando poco a poco pero de un modo irreparable. Billy Sánchez se asustó en serio e insistió en buscar una farmacia, pero ella sabía entonces que aquello no era asunto de boticarios.

—Estamos casi en la Puerta de Orleáns —dijo—. Sigue de frente por la avenida del general Leclerc, que es la más ancha y con muchos árboles, y después yo te voy diciendo lo que haces.

Fue el trayecto más arduo de todo el viaje. La avenida del general Leclerc era un nudo infernal de automóviles pequeños y motocicletas, embotellados en ambos sentidos, y de los camiones enormes que trataban de llegar a los mercados centrales. Billy Sánchez se puso tan nervioso con el estruendo inútil de las bocinas, que se insultó a gritos en lengua de cadeneros con varios conductores y hasta trató de bajarse del coche para pelearse con uno, pero Nena Daconte logró convencerlo de que los franceses eran la gente más grosera del mundo, pero no se golpeaban nunca. Fue una prueba más de su buen juicio, porque en aquel momento Nena Daconte estaba haciendo esfuerzos para no perder la conciencia.

Sólo para salir de la glorieta del León de Belfort necesitaron más de una hora. Los cafés y almacenes estaban iluminados como si fuera la media noche, pues era un martes típico de los eneros de París, encapotados y sucios y con una llovizna tenaz que no alcanzaba a concretarse en nieve. Pero la avenida Denfer-Rochereau estaba más despejada, y al cabo de unas pocas cuadras Nena Daconte le indicó a su marido que doblara a la derecha, y estacionó frente a la entrada de emergencia de un hospital enorme y sombrío.

Necesitó ayuda para salir del coche, pero no perdió la serenidad ni la lucidez. Mientras llegaba al médico de turno, acostada en la camilla rodante, contestó a la enfermera el cuestionario de rutina sobre su identidad y sus antecedentes de salud. Billy Sánchez le llevó el bolso y le apretó la mano izquierda donde entonces llevaba el anillo de bodas, y la sintió lánguida y fría, y sus labios habían perdido el color. Permaneció a su lado, con la mano en la suya, hasta que llegó el médico de turno y le hizo un examen rápido al anular herido. Era un hombre muy joven, con la piel del color del cobre antiguo y la cabeza pelada. Nena Daconte no le prestó atención sino que dirigió a su marido una sonrisa lívida.

—No te asustes —le dijo, con su humor invencible—. Lo único que puede suceder es que este caníbal me corte la mano para comérsela.

El médico concluyó el examen, y entonces los sorprendió con un castellano muy correcto aunque con raro acento asiático.

—No, muchachos —dijo—. Este caníbal prefiere morirse de hambre antes que cortar una mano tan bella.

Ellos se ofuscaron pero el médico los tranquilizó con un gesto amable. Luego ordenó que se llevaran la camilla, y Billy Sánchez quiso seguir con ella cogido de la mano de su mujer. El médico lo detuvo por el brazo.

—Usted no —le dijo—. Va para cuidados intensivos. Nena Daconte le volvió a sonreir al esposo, y le siguió diciendo adiós con la mano hasta que la camilla se perdió en el fondo del corredor. El médico se retrasó estudiando los datos que la enfermera había escrito en una tablilla. Billy Sánchez lo llamó.

—Doctor —le dijo—. Ella está encinta.

— ¿Cuánto tiempo?

—Dos meses.

El médico no le dio la importancia que Billy Sánchez esperaba. "Hizo bien en decírmelo", dijo, y se fue detrás de la camilla. Billy Sánchez se quedó parado en la sala lúgubre olorosa a sudores de enfermos, se quedó sin saber qué hacer mirando el corredor vacío por donde se habían llevado a Nena Daconte, y luego se sentó en el escaño de madera donde había otras personas esperando. No supo cuánto tiempo estuvo ahí, pero cuando decidió salir del hospital era otra vez de noche y continuaba la llovizna, y él seguía sin saber ni siquiera qué hacer consigo mismo, abrumado por el peso del mundo.

Nena Daconte ingresó a las 9:30 del martes 7 de enero, según lo pude comprobar años después en los archivos del hospital. Aquella primera noche, Billy Sánchez durmió en el coche estacionado frente a la puerta de urgencias y muy temprano al día siguiente se comió seis huevos cocidos y dos tazas de café con leche en la cafetería que encontró más cerca, pues no había hecho una comida completa desde Madrid. Después volvió a la sala de urgencias para ver a Nena Daconte pero le hicieron entender que debía dirigirse a la entrada principal. Allí consiguieron por fin un asturiano del servicio que lo ayudó a entenderse con el portero, y éste comprobó que en efecto Nena Daconte estaba registrada en el hospital, pero que sólo se permitían visitas los martes de nueve a cuatro. Es decir, seis días después. Trató de ver al médico que hablaba castellano, a quien describió como un negro con la cabeza pelada, pero nadie le dio razón con dos detalles tan simples.

Tranquilizado con la noticia de que Nena Daconte estaba en el registro, volvió al lugar donde había dejado el coche, y un agente de tránsito lo obligó a estacionar dos cuadras más adelante, en una calle muy estrecha y del lado de los números impares. En la acera de enfrente había un edificio restaurado con un letrero: Hotel Nicole. Tenía una sola estrella, y una sala de recibo muy pequeña donde no había más que un sofá y un viejo piano vertical, pero el propietario de voz aflautada podía entenderse con los clientes en cualquier idioma a condición de que tuvieran con qué pagar. Billy Sánchez se instaló con once maletas y nueve cajas de regalos en el único cuarto libre, que era una mansarda triangular en el noveno piso, a donde se llegaba sin aliento por una escalera en espiral que olía a espuma de coliflores hervidas. Las paredes estaban forradas de colgaduras tristes y por la única ventana no cabía nada más que la claridad turbia del patio interior. Había una cama para dos, un ropero grande, una silla simple, un bidé portátil y un aguamanil con su platón y su jarra, de modo que la única manera de estar dentro del cuarto era acostado en la cama. Todo era peor que viejo, desventurado, pero también muy limpio, y con un rastro saludable de medicina reciente.

A Billy Sánchez no le habría alcanzado la vida para descifrar los enigmas de ese mundo fundado en el talento de la cicatería. Nunca entendió el misterio de la luz de la escalera que se apagaba antes de que él llegara a su piso, ni descubrió la manera de volver a encenderla. Necesitó media mañana para aprender que en el rellano de cada piso había un cuartito con un excusado de cadena, y ya había decidido usarlo en las tinieblas cuando descubrió por casualidad que la luz se encendía al pasar el cerrojo por dentro, para que nadie la dejara encendida por olvido. La ducha, que estaba en el extremo del corredor y que él se empeñaba en usar dos veces al día como en su tierra, se pagaba aparte y de contado, y el agua caliente, controlada desde la administración, se acababa a los tres minutos. Sin embargo, Billy Sánchez tuvo bastante claridad de juicio para comprender que aquel orden tan distinto del suyo era de todos modos mejor que la intemperie de enero, y se sentía además tan ofuscado y solo que no podía entender cómo pudo vivir alguna vez sin el amparo de Nena Daconte. Tan pronto como subió al cuarto, la mañana del miércoles, se tiró bocabajo en la cama con el abrigo puesto pensando en la criatura de prodigio que continuaba desangrándose en la acera de enfrente, y muy pronto sucumbió en un sueño tan natural que cuando despertó eran las cinco en el reloj, pero no pudo deducir si eran las cinco de la tarde o del amanecer, ni de qué día de la semana ni en qué ciudad de vidrios azotados por el viento y la lluvia. Esperó despierto en la cama, siempre pensando en Nena Daconte, hasta que pudo comprobar que en realidad amanecía. Entonces fue a desayunar a la misma cafetería del día anterior, y allí pudo establecer que era jueves. Las luces del hospital estaban encendidas y había dejado de llover, de modo que permaneció recostado en el tronco de un castaño frente a la entrada principal, por donde entraban y salían médicos y enfermeras de batas blancas, con la esperanza de encontrar al médico asiático que había recibido a Nena Daconte. No lo vio, ni tampoco esa tarde después del almuerzo, cuando tuvo que desistir de la espera porque se estaba congelando. A las siete se tomó otro café con leche y se comió dos huevos duros que él mismo cogió en el aparador después de 48 horas de estar comiendo la misma cosa en el mismo lugar. Cuando volvió al hotel para acostarse, encontró su coche solo en una acera y todos los demás en la acera de enfrente, y tenía puesta la noticia de una multa en el parabrisas. Al portero del hotel Nicole le costó trabajo explicarle que en los días impares del mes se podía estacionar en la acera de números impares, y al día siguiente en la acera contraria. Tantas artimañas racionalistas resultaban incomprensibles para un Sánchez de Avila de los más acendrados que apenas dos años antes se había metido en un cine de barrio con el automóvil oficial del alcalde mayor, y había causado estragos de muerte ante los policías impávidos. Entendió menos todavía cuando el portero del hotel le aconsejó que pagara la multa, pero que no cambiara el coche de lugar a esa hora, porque tendría que cambiarlo otra vez a las doce de la noche. Aquella madrugada, por primera vez, no pensó sólo en Nena Daconte, sino que daba vueltas en la cama sin poder dormir, pensando en sus propias noches de pesadumbre en las cantinas de maricas del mercado público de Cartagena del Caribe. Se acordaba del sabor del pescado frito y el arroz de coco en las fondas del muelle donde atracaban las goletas de Aruba. Se acordó de su casa con las paredes cubiertas de trinitarias, donde serían apenas las siete de la noche de ayer, y vio a su

padre con una piyama de seda leyendo el periódico en el
fresco de la terraza. Se acordó de su madre, de quien nunca
se sabía dónde estaba a ninguna hora, su madre apetitosa y
lenguaraz, con un traje de domingo y una rosa en la oreja
desde el atardecer, ahogándose de calor por el estorbo de sus
tetas espléndidas. Una tarde, cuando él tenía siete años, había entrado de pronto en el cuarto de ella y la había sorprendido desnuda en la cama con uno de sus amantes casuales.
Aquel percance, del que nunca habían hablado, estableció
entre ellos una relación de complicidad que era más útil que
el amor. Sin embargo, él no fue consciente de eso, ni de tantas cosas terribles de su soledad de hijo único, hasta esa noche en que se encontró dando vueltas en la cama de una mansarda triste de París, sin nadie a quien contarle su infortunio,
y con una rabia feroz contra sí mismo porque no podía soportar las ganas de llorar.

Fue un insomnio provechoso. El viernes se levantó es-
tropeado por la mala noche, pero resuelto a definir su vida.
Se decidió por fin a violar la cerradura de su maleta para
cambiarse de ropa pues las llaves de todas estaban en el
bolso de Nena Daconte, con la mayor parte del dinero y la
libreta de teléfonos donde tal vez hubiera encontrado el número de algún conocido de París. En la cafetería de siempre
se dio cuenta de que había aprendido a saludar en francés y
a pedir sánduiches de jamón y café con leche. También sabía
que nunca le sería posible ordenar mantequilla ni huevos en
ninguna forma, porque nunca los aprendería a decir, pero la
mantequilla la servían siempre con el pan, y los huevos duros
estaban a la vista en el aparador y se cogían sin pedirlos. Además, al cabo de tres días, el personal de servicio se había familiarizado con él, y lo ayudaban a explicarse. De modo que
el viernes al almuerzo, mientras trataba de poner la cabeza en
su puesto, ordenó un filete de ternera con papas fritas y una
botella de vino. Entonces se sintió tan bien que pidió otra botella, la bebió hasta la mitad, y atravesó la calle con la resolución firme de meterse en el hospital por la fuerza. No sabía
dónde encontrar a Nena Daconte, pero en su mente estaba
fija la imagen providencial del médico asiático, y estaba seguro de encontrarlo. No entró por la puerta principal sino por la
de urgencias, que le había parecido menos vigilada, pero no
alcanzó a llegar más allá del corredor donde Nena Daconte le
había dicho adiós con la mano. Un guardián con la bata salpi-
cada de sangre le preguntó algo al pasar, y él no le prestó atención. El guardián lo siguió, repitiendo siempre la misma pre-

gunta en francés, y por último lo agarró del brazo con tanta fuerza que lo detuvo en seco. Billy Sánchez trató de sacudírselo con un recurso de cadenero, y entonces el guardián se cagó en su madre en francés, le torció el brazo en la espalda con una llave maestra, y sin dejar de cagarse mil veces en su puta madre lo llevó casi en vilo hasta la puerta, rabiando de dolor, y lo tiró como un bulto de papas en la mitad de la calle.

Aquella tarde, dolorido por el escarmiento, Billy Sánchez empezó a ser adulto. Decidió, como lo hubiera hecho Nena Daconte, acudir a su embajador. El portero del hotel, que a pesar de su catadura huraña era muy servicial, y además muy paciente con los idiomas, encontró el número y la dirección de la embajada en el directorio telefónico, y se los anotó en una tarjeta.

Contestó una mujer muy amable, en cuya voz pausada y sin brillo reconoció Billy Sánchez de inmediato la dicción de los Andes. Empezó por anunciarse con su nombre completo, seguro de impresionar a la mujer con sus dos apellidos, pero la voz no se alteró en el teléfono. La oyó explicar la lección de memoria de que el señor embajador no estaba por el momento en su oficina, que no lo esperaban hasta el día siguiente, pero que de todos modos no podía recibirlo sino con cita previa y sólo para un caso especial. Billy Sánchez comprendió entonces que por ese camino tampoco llegaría hasta Nena Daconte, y agradeció la información con la misma amabilidad con que se la habían dado. Luego tomó un taxi y se fue a la embajada.

Estaba en el número 22 de la calle Elyseo, dentro de uno de los sectores más apacibles de París pero lo único que le impresionó a Billy Sánchez, según él mismo me contó en Cartagena de Indias muchos años después, fue que el sol estaba tan claro como en el Caribe por la primera vez de su llegada, y que la Torre Eiffel sobresalía por encima de la ciudad en un cielo radiante. El funcionario que lo recibió en lugar del embajador parecía apenas restablecido de una enfermedad mortal, no sólo por el vestido de paño negro, el cuello opresivo y la corbata de luto, sino también por el sigilo de sus ademanes y la mansedumbre de la voz. Entendió la ansiedad de Billy Sánchez, pero le recordó sin perder la dulzura que estaban en un país civilizado cuyas normas estrictas se fundamentan en criterios muy antiguos y sabios, al contrario de las Américas bárbaras, donde bastaba con sobornar al portero para entrar en los hospitales. "No, mi querido joven", le dijo. No había más remedio que someterse al imperio de la razón, y esperar hasta el martes.

—Al fin y al cabo, ya no faltan sino cuatro días —concluyó—. Mientras tanto, vaya al Louvre. Vale la pena.

Al salir Billy Sánchez se encontró sin saber qué hacer en la Plaza de la Concordia. Vio la Torre Eiffel por encima de los tejados, y le pareció tan cercana que trató de llegar hasta ella caminando por los muelles. Pero muy pronto se dio cuenta de que estaba más lejos de lo que parecía, y que además cambiaba de lugar a medida que la buscaba. Así que se puso a pensar en Nena Daconte sentado en un banco de la orilla del Sena. Vio pasar los remolcadores por debajo de los puentes, y no le parecieron barcos sino casas errantes con techos colorados y ventanas con tiestos de flores en el alféizar, y alambres con ropa puesta a secar en los planchones. Contempló durante un largo rato a un pescador inmóvil, con la caña inmóvil y el hilo inmóvil en la corriente, y se cansó de esperar a que algo se moviera, hasta que empezó a oscurecer y decidió tomar un taxi para regresar al hotel. Sólo entonces cayó en la cuenta de que ignoraba el nombre y la dirección y de que no tenía la menor idea del sector de París en donde estaba el hospital.

Ofuscado por el pánico, entró en el primer café que encontró, pidió un cognac y trató de poner sus pensamientos en orden. Mientras pensaba se vio repetido muchas veces y desde ángulos distintos en los espejos numerosos de las paredes, y se encontró asustado y solitario, y por primera vez desde su nacimiento pensó en la realidad de la muerte. Pero con la segunda copa se sintió mejor, y tuvo la idea providencial de volver a la embajada. Buscó la tarjeta en el bolsillo para recordar el nombre de la calle, y descubrió que en el dorso estaba impreso el nombre y la dirección del hotel. Quedó tan mal impresionado con aquella experiencia, que durante el fin de semana no volvió a salir del cuarto sino para comer, y para cambiar el coche a la acera correspondiente. Durante tres días cayó sin pausas la misma llovizna sucia de la mañana en que llegaron. Billy Sánchez, que nunca había leído un libro completo, hubiera querido tener uno para no aburrirse tirado en la cama, pero los únicos que encontró en las maletas de su esposa eran en idiomas distintos del castellano. Así que siguió esperando el martes, contemplando los pavorreales repetidos en el papel de las paredes y sin dejar de pensar un solo instante en Nena Daconte. El lunes puso un poco de orden en el cuarto, pensando en lo que diría ella si lo encontraba en ese estado, y sólo entonces descubrió que el abrigo de visón estaba manchado de sangre seca. Pasó la tarde lavándolo con el jabón de olor que encontró en el maletín de mano, hasta que logró dejarlo otra vez como lo habían subido al avión en Madrid.

El martes amaneció turbio y helado, pero sin la llovizna,

y Billy Sánchez se levantó desde la seis, y esperó en la puerta del hospital junto con una muchedumbre de parientes de enfermos cargados de paquetes de regalos y ramos de flores. Entró con el tropel, llevando en el brazo el abrigo de visón, sin preguntar nada y sin ninguna idea de dónde podía estar Nena Daconte, pero sostenido por la certidumbre de que había de encontrar al médico asiático. Pasó por un patio interior muy grande con flores y pájaros silvestres, a cuyos lados estaban los pabellones de los enfermos: las mujeres a la derecha y los hombres a la izquierda. Siguiendo a los visitantes, entró en el pabellón de mujeres. Vio una larga hilera de enfermas sentadas en las camas con el camisón de trapo del hospital, iluminadas por las luces grandes de las ventanas, y hasta pensó que todo aquello era más alegre de lo que se podía imaginar desde fuera. Llegó hasta el extremo del corredor, y luego lo recorrió de nuevo en sentido inverso, hasta convencerse de que ninguna de las enfermas era Nena Daconte. Luego recorrió otra vez la galería exterior mirando por la ventana los pabellones masculinos, hasta que creyó reconocer al médico que buscaba.

Era él, en efecto. Estaba con otros médicos y varias enfermeras, examinando a un enfermo. Billy Sánchez entró en el pabellón, apartó a una de las enfermeras del grupo, y se paró frente al médico asiático, que estaba inclinado sobre el enfermo. Lo llamó. El médico levantó sus ojos desolados, pensó un instante, y entonces lo reconoció.

— ¡Pero dónde diablos se había metido usted! —dijo.

Billy Sánchez se quedó perplejo.

—En el hotel —dijo—. Aquí a la vuelta.

Entonces lo supo. Nena Daconte había muerto desangrada a las 7:10 de la noche del jueves 9 de enero, después de 70 horas de esfuerzos inútiles de los especialistas mejor calificados de Francia. Hasta el último instante había estado lúcida y serena, y dio instrucciones para que buscaran a su marido en el hotel Plaza Athenée, donde tenían una habitación reservada, y dio los datos para que se pusieran en contacto con sus padres. La embajada había sido informada el viernes por un cable urgente de su cancillería, cuando ya los padres de Nena Daconte volaban hacia París. El embajador en persona se encargó de los trámites de embalsamamiento y los funerales, y permaneció en contacto con la Prefectura de Policía de París para localizar a Billy Sánchez. Un llamado urgente con sus datos personales fue transmitido desde la noche del viernes hasta la tarde del domingo a través de la radio y la televisión, y durante esas 40 horas fue el hombre más buscado de Francia. Su retrato, encontrado en el bolso de Nena Daconte, estaba expuesto por todas partes. Tres Bentleys convertibles del mismo modelo habían sido localizados, pero ninguno era el suyo.

Los padres de Nena Daconte habían llegado el sábado al mediodía, y velaron el cadáver en la capilla del hospital esperando hasta última hora encontrar a Billy Sánchez. También los padres de éste habían sido informados, y estuvieron listos para volar a París, pero al final desistieron por una confusión de telegramas. Los funerales tuvieron lugar el domingo a las dos de la tarde, a sólo doscientos metros del sórdido cuarto del hotel donde Billy Sánchez agonizaba de soledad por el amor de Nena Daconte. El funcionario que lo había atendido en la embajada me dijo años más tarde que él mismo recibió el telegrama de su cancillería una hora después de que Billy Sánchez salió de su oficina, y que estuvo buscándolo por los bares sigilosos del Faubourg-St. Honoré. Me confesó que no le había puesto mucha atención cuando lo recibió, porque nunca se hubiera imaginado que aquel costeño aturdido con la novedad de París, y con un abrigo de cordero tan mal llevado, tuviera a su favor un origen tan ilustre. El mismo domingo por la noche, mientras él sospechaba las ganas de llorar de rabia, los padres de Nena Daconte desistieron de la búsqueda y se llevaron el cuerpo embalsamado dentro de un ataúd metálico, y quienes alcanzaron a verlo siguieron repitiendo durante muchos años que no habían visto nunca una mujer más hermosa, ni viva ni muerta. De modo que cuando Billy Sánchez entró por fin al hospital, el martes por la mañana, ya se había consumado el entierro en el triste panteón de la Manga, a muy pocos metros de la casa donde ellos habían descifrado las primeras claves de la felicidad. El médico asiático que puso a Billy Sánchez al corriente de la tragedia quiso darle unas pastillas calmantes en la sala del hospital, pero él las rechazó. Se fue sin despedirse, sin nada que agradecer, pensando que lo único que necesitaba con urgencia era encontrar a alguien a quien romperle la madre a cadenazos para desquitarse de su desgracia. Cuando salió del hospital, ni siquiera se dio cuenta de que estaba cayendo del cielo una nieve sin rastros de sangre, cuyos copos tiernos y nítidos parecían plumitas de palomas, y que en las calles de París había un aire de fiesta, porque era la primera nevada grande en diez años.

Gabriel García Márquez
1928—
Colombia

El ahogado
más hermoso del mundo

La increíble y triste historia de la Cándida Eréndira y su abuela desalmada, 1977.

LOS primeros niños que vieron el promontorio oscuro y sigiloso que se acercaba por el mar, se hicieron la ilusión de que era un barco enemigo. Después vieron que no llevaba banderas ni arboladura, y pensaron que fuera una ballena. Pero cuando quedó varado en la playa le quitaron los matorrales de sargazos, los filamentos de medusas y los restos de cardúmenes y naufragios que llevaba encima, y sólo entonces descubrieron que era un ahogado.

Habían jugado con él toda la tarde, enterrándolo y desenterrándolo en la arena, cuando alguien los vio por casualidad y dio la voz de alarma en el pueblo. Los hombres que lo cargaron hasta la casa más próxima notaron que pesaba más que todos los muertos conocidos, casi tanto como un caballo, y se dijeron que tal vez había estado demasiado tiempo a la deriva y el agua se le había metido dentro de los huesos. Cuando lo tendieron en el suelo vieron que había sido mucho más grande que todos los hombres, pues apenas si cabía en la casa, pero pensaron que tal vez la facultad de seguir creciendo después de la muerte estaba en la naturaleza de ciertos ahogados. Tenía el olor del mar, y sólo la forma permitía suponer que era el cadáver de un ser humano, porque su piel estaba revestida de una coraza de rémora y de lodo.

No tuvieron que limpiarle la cara para saber que era un muerto ajeno. El pueblo tenía apenas unas veinte casas de tablas, con patios de piedras sin flores, desperdigadas en el extremo de un cabo desértico. La tierra era tan escasa, que las madres andaban siempre con el temor de que el viento se llevara a los niños, y a los pocos muertos que les iban causando los años tenían que tirarlos en los acantilados. Pero el mar era manso y pródigo, y todos los hombres cabían en siete botes. Así que cuando encontraron el ahogado les bastó con mirarse los unos a los otros para darse cuenta de que estaban completos.

Aquella noche no salieron a trabajar en el mar. Mientras los hombres averiguaban si no faltaba alguien en los pueblos

vecinos, las mujeres se quedaron cuidando al ahogado. Le
quitaron el lodo con tapones de esparto, le desenredaron del
cabello los abrojos submarinos y le rasparon la rémora con
fierros de desescamar pescados. A medida que lo hacían, notaron que su vegetación era de océanos remotos y de aguas
profundas, y que sus ropas estaban en piltrafas, como si hubiera navegado por entre laberintos de corales. Notaron también que sobrellevaba la muerte con altivez, pues no tenía
el semblante solitario de los otros ahogados del mar, ni tampoco la catadura sórdida y menesterosa de los ahogados flu-
viales. Pero solamente cuando acabaron de limpiarlo tuvieron conciencia de la clase de hombre que era, y entonces
se quedaron sin aliento. No sólo era el más alto, el más fuerte, el más viril y el mejor armado que habían visto jamás,
sino que todavía cuando lo estaban viendo no les cabía en
la imaginación.

No encontraron en el pueblo una cama bastante grande
para tenderlo ni una mesa bastante sólida para velarlo. No le
vinieron los pantalones de fiesta de los hombres más altos, ni
las camisas dominicales de los más corpulentos, ni los zapatos
del mejor plantado. Fascinadas por su desproporción y su hermosura, las mujeres decidieron entonces hacerle unos pantalones con un buen pedazo de vela cangreja, y una camisa de
bramante de novia, para que pudiera continuar su muerte con
dignidad. Mientras cosían sentadas en círculo, contemplando
el cadáver entre puntada y puntada, les parecía que el viento
no había sido nunca tan tenaz ni el Caribe había estado nunca tan ansioso como aquella noche, y suponían que esos cambios tenían algo que ver con el muerto. Pensaban que si aquel
hombre magnífico hubiera vivido en el pueblo, su casa habría
tenido las puertas más anchas, el techo más alto y el piso más
firme, y el bastidor de su cama habría sido de cuadernas maestras con pernos de hierro, y su mujer habría sido la más feliz.
Pensaban que habría tenido tanta autoridad que hubiera sacado los peces del mar con sólo llamarlos por sus nombres, y
habría puesto tanto empeño en el trabajo que hubiera hecho
brotar manantiales de entre las piedras más áridas y hubiera
podido sembrar flores en los acantilados. Lo compararon en
secreto con sus propios hombres, pensando que no serían capaces de hacer en toda una vida lo que aquél era capaz de hacer en una noche, y terminaron por repudiarlos en el fondo
de sus corazones como los seres más escuálidos y mezquinos
de la tierra. Andaban extraviadas por esos dédalos de fantasía,
cuando la más vieja de las mujeres, que por ser la más vieja

había contemplado al ahogado con menos pasión que compasión, suspiró:

—Tiene cara de llamarse Esteban.

Era verdad. A la mayoría le bastó con mirarlo otra vez para comprender que no podía tener otro nombre. Las más porfiadas, que eran las más jóvenes, se mantuvieron con la ilusión de que al ponerle la ropa, tendido entre flores y con unos zapatos de charol, pudiera llamarse Lautaro. Pero fue una ilusión vana. El lienzo resultó escaso, los pantalones mal cortados y peor cosidos le quedaron estrechos, y las fuerzas ocultas de su corazón hacían saltar los botones de la camisa. Después de la media noche se adelgazaron los silbidos del viento y el mar cayó en el sopor del miércoles. El silencio acabó con las últimas dudas: era Esteban. Las mujeres que lo habían vestido, las que lo habían peinado, las que le habían cortado las uñas y raspado la barba no pudieron reprimir un estremecimiento de compasión, cuando tuvieron que resignarse a dejarlo tirado por los suelos. Fue entonces cuando comprendieron cuánto debió haber sido de infeliz con aquel cuerpo descomunal, si hasta después de muerto le estorbaba. Lo vieron condenado en vida a pasar de medio lado por las puertas, a descalabrarse con los travesaños, a permanecer de pie en las visitas sin saber qué hacer con sus tiernas y rosadas manos de buey de mar, mientras la dueña de casa buscaba la silla más resistente y le suplicaba muerta de miedo siéntese aquí Esteban, hágame el favor, y él recostado contra las paredes, sonriendo, no se preocupe señora, así estoy bien, con los talones en carne viva y las espaldas escaldadas de tanto repetir lo mismo en todas las visitas, no se preocupe señora, así estoy bien, sólo para no pasar por la vergüenza de desbaratar la silla, y acaso sin haber sabido nunca que quienes le decían no te vayas Esteban, espérate siquiera hasta que hierva el café, eran los mismos que después susurraban ya se fue el bobo grande, qué bueno, ya se fue el tonto hermoso. Esto pensaban las mujeres frente al cadáver un poco antes del amanecer. Más tarde, cuando le taparon la cara con un pañuelo para que no le molestara la luz, lo vieron tan muerto para siempre, tan indefenso, tan parecido a sus hombres, que se les abrieron las primeras grietas de lágrimas en el corazón. Fue una de las más jóvenes la que empezó a sollozar. Las otras, alentándose entre sí, pasaron de los suspiros a los lamentos, y mientras más sollozaban más deseos sentían de llorar, porque el ahogado se les iba volviendo cada vez más Esteban, hasta que lo lloraron tanto que fue el hombre más desvalido de la tierra, el más manso y el más servicial, el pobre Esteban. Así que cuando los hombres volvieron con la noticia de que el ahogado no era tampoco de los pueblos vecinos, ellas sintieron un vacío de júbilo entre las lágrimas.

— ¡Bendito sea Dios —suspiraron—: es nuestro!

Los hombres creyeron que aquellos aspavientos no eran más que frivolidades de mujer. Cansados de las tortuosas averiguaciones de la noche, lo único que querían era quitarse de una vez el estorbo del intruso antes de que prendiera el sol bravo de aquel día árido y sin viento. Improvisaron unas angarillas con restos de trinquetes y botavaras, y las amarraron con carlingas de altura, para que resistieran el peso del cuerpo hasta los acantilados. Quisieron encadenarle a los tobillos un ancla de buque mercante para que fondeara sin tropiezos en los mares más profundos donde los peces son ciegos y los buzos se mueren de nostalgia, de manera que las malas corrientes no fueran a devolverlo a la orilla, como había sucedido con otros cuerpos. Pero mientras más se apresuraban, más cosas se les ocurrían a las mujeres para perder el tiempo. Andaban como gallinas asustadas picoteando amuletos de mar en los arcones, unas estorbando aquí porque querían ponerle al ahogado los escapularios del buen viento, otras estorbando allá para abrocharle una pulsera de orientación, y al cabo de tanto quítate de ahí mujer, ponte donde no estorbes, mira que casi me haces caer sobre el difunto, a los hombres se les subieron al hígado las suspicacias, y empezaron a rezongar que con qué objeto tanta ferretería de altar mayor para un forastero, si por muchos estoperoles y calderetas que llevara encima se lo iban a masticar los tiburones, pero ellas seguían tripotando sus reliquias de pacotilla, llevando y trayendo, tropezando, mientras se les iba en suspiros lo que no se les iba en lágrimas, así que los hombres terminaron por despotricar que de cuándo acá semejante alboroto por un muerto al garete, un ahogado de nadie, un fiambre de mierda. Una de las mujeres, mortificada por tanta indolencia, le quitó entonces al cadáver el pañuelo de la cara, y también los hombres se quedaron sin aliento.

Era Esteban. No hubo que repetirlo para que lo reconocieran. Si les hubieran dicho Sir Walter Raleigh, quizás, hasta ellos se habrían impresionado con su acento de gringo, con su guacamaya en el hombro, con su arcabuz de matar caníbales, pero Esteban solamente podía ser uno en el mundo, y allí estaba tirado como un sábalo, sin botines, con unos pantalones de sietemesino y esas uñas rocallosas que sólo podían cortarse

a cuchillo. Bastó con que le quitaran el pañuelo de la cara para darse cuenta de que estaba avergonzado, de que no tenía la
culpa de ser tan grande, ni tan pesado ni tan hermoso, y si hubiera sabido que aquello iba a suceder habría buscado un lugar más discreto para ahogarse, en serio, me hubiera amarrado
yo mismo un áncora de galeón en el cuello y hubiera trastabillado como quien no quiere la cosa en los acantilados, para no
andar ahora estorbando con este muerto de miércoles, como
ustedes dicen, para no molestar a nadie con esta porquería de
fiambre que no tiene nada que ver conmigo. Había tanta verdad en su modo de estar, que hasta los hombres más suspicaces, los que sentían amargas las minuciosas noches del mar
temiendo que sus mujeres se cansaran de soñar con ellos para
soñar con los ahogados, hasta ésos, y otros más duros, se estremecieron en los tuétanos con la sinceridad de Esteban.

Fue así como le hicieron los funerales más espléndidos
que podían concebirse para un ahogado expósito. Algunas
mujeres que habían ido a buscar flores en los pueblos vecinos
regresaron con otras que no creían lo que les contaban, y éstas se fueron por más flores cuando vieron al muerto, y llevaron más y más, hasta que hubo tantas flores y tanta gente que
apenas si se podía caminar. A última hora les dolió devolverlo
huérfano a las aguas, y le eligieron un padre y una madre entre los mejores, y otros se le hicieron hermanos, tíos y primos,
así que a través de él todos los habitantes del pueblo terminaron por ser parientes entre sí. Algunos marineros que oyeron
el llanto a la distancia perdieron la certeza del rumbo, y se supo de uno que se hizo amarrar al palo mayor, recordando antiguas fábulas de sirenas. Mientras se disputaban el privilegio
de llevarlo en hombros por la pendiente escarpada de los acantilados, hombres y mujeres tuvieron conciencia por primera
vez de la desolación de sus calles, la aridez de sus patios, la estrechez de sus sueños, frente al esplendor y la hermosura de
su ahogado. Lo soltaron sin ancla, para que volviera si quería,
y cuando lo quisiera, y todos retuvieron el aliento durante la
fracción de siglos que demoró la caída del cuerpo hasta el
abismo. No tuvieron necesidad de mirarse los unos a los otros
para darse cuenta de que ya no estaban completos, ni volverían a estarlo jamás. Pero también sabían que todo sería diferente desde entonces, que sus casas iban a tener las puertas
más anchas, los techos más altos, los pisos más firmes, para
que el recuerdo de Esteban pudiera andar por todas partes sin
tropezar con los travesaños, y que nadie se atreviera a susurrar en el futuro ya murió el bobo grande, qué lástima, ya mu

rió el tonto hermoso, porque ellos iban a pintar las fachadas
de colores alegres para eternizar la memoria de Esteban, y se
iban a romper el espinazo excavando manantiales en las piedras y sembrando flores en los acantilados, para que en los
amaneceres de los años venturos los pasajeros de los grandes
barcos despertaran sofocados por un olor de jardines en alta-
mar, y el capitán tuviera que bajar de su alcázar con su uniforme de gala, con su astrolabio, su estrella polar y su ristra
de medallas de guerra, y señalando el promontorio de rosas
en el horizonte del Caribe dijera en catorce idiomas, miren
allá, donde el viento es ahora tan manso que se queda a dormir debajo de las camas, allá donde el sol brilla tanto que no
saben hacia dónde girar los girasoles, sí, allá, es el pueblo de
Esteban.

Magali García Ramis
1946—
Puerto Rico

Una semana
de siete días

La familia de todos nosotros, 1976.

MI madre era una mujer que tenía grandes los ojos y hacía
llorar a los hombres. A veces se quedaba callada por largos ratos y andaba siempre de frente al mundo; pero aunque
estaba en contra de la vida, a mí, que nací de ella, nunca me
echó de su lado. Cuando me veían con ella, toda la gente quería quedarse conmigo. "Te voy a robar, ojos lindos", me decían los dependientes de las tiendas. "Déjala unos meses al
año acá, en el verano, no es bueno que esa niña viaje tanto",
le habían pedido por carta unas tías. Pero mi madre nunca
me dejaba. Caminábamos el mundo de mil calles y cien ciudades y ella trabajaba y me miraba crecer y pasaba sus manos por mi pelo cada vez que me iba a hacer cariños. En cada lugar que vivíamos mamá tenía muchos amigos —compa-

ñeros les decía ella— y venían a casa de noche a hablar de
cosas, y a veces a tocar guitarra. Un día mamá me llamó
seria y suave, como hacía cuando me iba a decir algo importante. "Vamos a regresar a casa", me dijo, "papá ha muerto". Muerto. Los muertos estaban en los cementerios, eso sí
lo sabía yo, y nuestra casa era este departamento azul donde,
como en todos los que habíamos estado, mamá tenía la pintura del señor de sombrero con fusil en la mano, la figura de
madera de una mujer con su niño, un par de fotos de un hombre que ella ponía en el cuarto y una de otro hombre que ella
pegaba en la pared junto a mi cama. "No hay tal papá Dios,
este hombre es tu padre, tu único papá", me decía. Y yo lo
miraba todas las noches, a ese hombre de pelo tan claro y
ojos verdes que ahora estaba muerto y nos hacía irnos de casa.

No me puedo acordar cómo llegamos a la isla, sólo recuerdo que allí no podía leer casi nada aunque ya sabía leer, porque les daba por escribir los nombres de las tiendas en inglés.
Entonces alguien nos llevó en un auto a San Antonio. Antonio se llamaba mi padre y ése era su pueblo. Antes de salir
para San Antonio mi madre me compró un traje blanco y
otro azul oscuro y me puso el azul para el viaje. "Vas a ver a
tu abuela de nuevo", me dijo. "Tú vas a pasar unos días con
ella, yo tengo unos asuntos que atender y luego iré a buscar-
te. Tú sabes que mamá no te deja nunca, ¿verdad? Te queda-
rás con abuela una semana, ya estás grande y es bueno conocer a los familiares".

Y así de grande, más o menos, llegué dormida con mamá
a San Antonio. El auto nos dejó al lado de una plaza llena de
cordones con luces rojas, verdes, azules, naranjas y amarillas.
Una banda de músicos tocaba una marcha y muchos niños paseaban con sus papás. ¿"Por qué hay luces, mamá"? "Es Navidad", fue su única respuesta. Yo cogí mi bultito y mamá la
maleta, y me llevó de la mano calle arriba, lejos de la plaza
que me llenaba los ojos de colores y de música. Caminamos
por una calle empinada y ya llegando a una colina nos detuvimos frente a una casa de madera de balcón ancho y tres
grandes puertas. Yo me senté en un escalón mientras mi madre tocaba a la puerta de la izquierda. Desde allí, sentada, mis
ojos quedaban al nivel de las rodillas que una vez le habían
dicho que eran tan bonitas.

"Tus rodillas son preciosas, y tú eres una chulería de mujer", le decía el hombre rubio a mamá y yo me hacía la dormida en la camita de al lado y los oía decirse cosas que no entendía. De todo lo que se dijeron y contaron esa noche, lo

único que recuerdo es que sus rodillas eran preciosas. Aquel hombre rubio le decía que la quería mucho, y que a mí también, y que quería casarse con ella —pero ella no quiso. Un día estábamos sentados en un café y le dijo que no volviera, y allí mismo él pagó la cuenta y se fue llorando. Yo miré a mi madre y ella me abrazó.

Hacía frío y creí que me iba a dormir de nuevo, pero no me dio tiempo porque detrás de la puerta con lazo negro una voz de mujer preguntó: ¿Quién? "Soy yo, Doña Matilde, Luisa, he venido con la niña". La mujer abrió la puerta y sacó la cabeza para mirar al balcón y allí en la escalera a su derecha estaba yo, mirando a esa mujer con los ojos verdes de mi padre. "Pasen, pasen, no cojan el sereno que hace daño", dijo la abuela. Pasamos un pasillo ancho con muchas puertas a los dos lados, y luego un patio sin techo, en el medio. ¿"Por qué tiene un hoyo esta casa, mamá"? "Es un patio interior, las casas de antes son así", dijo mamá, y seguimos caminando por la casa de antes hasta llegar a un comedor. Allí estaba Rafaela, la muchacha de abuela que era casi tan vieja como ella. Nos sentamos a tomar café con pan y mamá habló con la abuela.

Al otro día amanecí con mi payama puesta en una cama cubierta con sábanas y fundas de flores bordadas, tan alta que tuve que brincar para bajarme. Busqué a mamá y me asustó pensar que quizás ya se había ido por una semana y me había dejado sin despedirse, y yo en payamas. Entonces oí su voz: "La nena ha crecido muy bien, Doña Matilde. Es inteligente, y buena como su padre". "Tiene los ojos Ocasio", dijo la abuela. "Yo sé lo que usted piensa, que tanto cambio le hace daño, y yo sé que usted no está de acuerdo con la vida que yo llevo, ni con mis ideas políticas, pero deje que la conozca a ella para que vea que no le ha faltado nada: ni cariño, ni escuela, ni educación". "El preguntó por ti antes de cerrar los ojos, siempre creyó que tú volverías", contestó la abuela, como si cada una tuviese una conversación aparte. "Mamá, mamá, ya me desperté", dije. "Ven acá, estamos en el patio", me contestó. "Pero no sé dónde está mi bata", grité, porque ella estaba diciéndole a abuela que yo tenía educación y aunque nunca me ponía la bata eso ayudaría a lo que mi mamá decía. "Olvídate de eso, si tú no te la pones, ven", repitió mamá, que nunca fingía nada. Yo me acerqué y ví de frente a la abuela que era casi tan alta como mi madre y con su pelo recogido en redecilla me sonreía desde una escalerita donde estaba trepada podando una enredadera en ese patio sembrado de helechos y palmas. "Saluda a tu abuela". "Buenos días, abuela", dije. Y ella bajó de la escalera y me dio un beso en la cabeza.

Durante el desayuno siguieron hablando mi madre de mí y mi abuela de mi padre. Luego me pusieron el traje blanco y fuimos al cementerio. Hacía una semana que lo habían enterrado, nos contó la abuela. Vimos la tumba que decía algo y después tenía escrito el nombre de mi papá: Antonio Ramos Ocasio Q.E.P.D. "Yo sé que tú no eres creyente, pero dejarás que la niña se arrodille y rece conmigo un padrenuestro por el alma de su padre..." Mi madre se quedó como mirando a lo lejos y dijo que sí. Y así yo caí hincada en la tierra en el mundo de antes de mi abuelo, repitiendo algo sobre un padre nuestro que estaba en los cielos y mirando de reojo a mamá porque las dos sabíamos que ese padre no existía.

"Mamá, ¿esta noche me llevas a aquel sitio de luces?" le pregunté ese día. ¿"A qué sitio"? preguntó abuela, "recuerda que en esta casa hay luto". "A la plaza pregunta ella, Doña Matilde. No frunza el ceño, recuerde que en este pueblo nadie nos conoce, que ella nunca ha estado unas Navidades en un pueblo de la isla, y que yo me voy mañana..." y terminó de hablar con miradas. Abuela respiró hondo y se miró en mis ojos.

Esa noche fuimos a la plaza mamá y yo. De nuevo, había mucha gente paseando. Vendían algodón de azúcar color rosa, globos pintados con caras de los reyes magos y dulces y refrescos. Había kioscos con comida y muchas picas de caballitos donde los hombres y los muchachos apostaban su dinero. Y la banda tocó marchas que le daban a uno ganas de saltar. Yo me quedé callada todo el tiempo porque todo eso me iba entrando por los ojos y de tanto que me gustaba me daba ganas de llorar. "No te pongas triste", me dijo mamá. "No estoy triste, es que estoy pensando, mamá", le expliqué, y ella me llevó hasta un banquito de piedra. Nos sentamos justo encima de donde decía: "Siendo alcalde de San Antonio el honorable Asencio Martínez, se edificaron estos bancos con fondos municipales para el ornato de esta ciudad y la comodidad de sus habitantes". "Mamá se tiene que ir mañana a la ciudad a donde llegamos primero. Va a estar solamente una semana yendo a muchas oficinas y es mejor que te quedes esos días acá con abuela, ¿me entiendes, cariño? Tú sabes que mamá nunca te ha mentido, si te digo que vuelvo, vuelvo. ¿Te acuerdas la vez que te quedaste unos días con Francisco, el amigo de mamá?

Las dos cotorras que tenía Francisco hablaban. Vivimos

con él un tiempo y una vez que mamá tuvo que ir a un sitio importante me dejó con él unos días. Cuando regresó me trajo una muñeca japonesa con tres trajecitos que se le cambiaban y Francisco me hizo cuentos de los hombres del Japón. Un tiempito después mamá llegó y nos dijo que había conseguido trabajo en otra ciudad y que teníamos que mudarnos ese día. Francisco quiso mudarse con nosotras; mamá le dijo que no. Y nos despidió en la estación del tren con los ojos llenos de lágrimas, de tan enamorado que estaba de mi madre.

"Sí, mamá, me acuerdo", le dije. "Pues es igual. Mamá tiene cosas muy importantes que hacer. La abuela Matilde es la mamá de tu papá. Ella te quiere mucho ¿viste que sobre su tocador hay un retrato de cuando tú eras pequeñita? Ella te va a hacer mañana un bizcocho de los que te gustan. Y te hará muchos cuentos. Y ya enseguida pasa la semana. ¿Estamos de acuerdo?" Yo no lo estaba por nada del mundo, pero mamá y yo éramos compañeras, como decía ella, y siempre nos dábamos fuerzas una a la otra. Así que yo cerré mi boca lo más posible y abrí mis ojos lo más que podía, como hacía cada vez que me daba trabajo aceptar algo y le dije sí, mamá, de acuerdo, porque yo sabía que ella también se asustaba si estaba sin mí. Y nos dimos un abrazo largo allí sentadas encima del nombre del alcalde y del ornato, que quería decir adorno, me explicó mi mamá.

Al otro día, frente a la plaza ahora callada después del almuerzo, nos despedimos de mamá que subió en un auto lleno de gente. "Las cosas en la ciudad no están muy tranquilas, Luisa, cuídate, no te vaya a pasar nada". "No se preocupe, Doña Matilde, sólo voy a ver al abogado para arreglar eso de los papeles de Antonio y míos, y enseguida vuelvo a buscar la niña y nos vamos. Cuídela bien y no se preocupe".

¿"Tu sabes cuánto es una semana"? "Sí, abuela, es el mismo tiempo que papá lleva enterrado". "Sí, pero en tiempo, hijita, en días ¿sabes? "me preguntó abuela luego de que se fuera mamá. "No, abuela". "Son siete, siete", me repetía, pero yo nunca fui buena con los números ni entendí bien eso del tiempo. Lo que sí recuerdo es que entonces fue tiempo de revolú. Una noche se oyeron tiros y gritos, y nadie salió a las calles ni a la plaza. Por unos días todos tenían miedo. Abuela tomaba el periódico que le traían por las mañanas al balcón y leía con mucho cuidado la primera página y luego ponía a Rafaela a leerle unas listas de nombres en letras demasiado chiquititas para su vista que venían a veces en las páginas interiores. A mí no me lo dejaban ver. Yo sólo podía leer rápido las letras negras grandotas de la primera página que decían cosas como DE TE NI DOS LE VAN TA MI EN TO SOS PE CHO SOS Y IZ QUIER DIS TAS que yo no entendía.

Una noche después, llegaron unos hombres cuando nos íbamos a acostar Rafaela, abuela y yo. "Súbete a la cama, anda", me dijo muy seria la abuela. Yo la obedecí primero y luego me bajé. Corrí de cuarto en cuarto hasta llegar al que daba a la sala y me puse a escuchar. Ya los hombres estaban en la puerta y sólo pude oír cuando decían: "De modo que no trate de sacarla del pueblo y mucho menos de la isla. Sabemos que ella vendrá por la niña, y tenemos orden de arresto". "Mire, señor policía", le decía la abuela, "yo estoy segura que ella no tuvo nada que ver. Le repito que vino a la isla solamente porque murió mi hijo, ella ya no está en política, créame, ¿por qué hay orden de arresto"? "Ya está avisada, señora, hay que arrestar a todos esos izquierdistas para interrogarlos. Y si no tuvo que ver ¿por qué se esconde? Hay testigos que afirman que la vieron en la Capital, armada... ¿eso es ser inocente? Con que ya lo sabe, la niña se queda en el pueblo".

La niña era yo, eso lo supe en seguida, y en lo que la abuela cerraba la puerta corrí cuarto por cuarto de vuelta a mi cama. Abuela vino hasta donde mí. Yo me hice la dormida pero no sé si la engañé porque se me quedó parada al lado tanto rato que me dormí de verdad.

Ahora estoy en el balcón esperando que me venga a buscar mi mamá, porque sé que vendrá por mí. Todos los días pienso en ella y lo más que recuerdo es que tenía unos ojos grandes marrones y que era una mujer que hacía llorar a los hombres. Ah, y que nunca me mentía; por eso estoy aquí, en el balcón, con mi bultito, esperándola, aunque ya haya pasado más de una semana, lo sé porque ya sé medir el tiempo, y porque mis trajes blanco y azul ya no me sirven.

Elena Garro
1922–
México

El anillo
La semana de colores, 1964.

SIEMPRE fuimos pobres señor, y siempre fuimos desgra-
ciados, pero no tanto como ahora en que la congoja campea por mis cuartos y corrales. Ya sé que el mal se presenta
en cualquier tiempo y que toma cualquier forma, pero nunca
pensé que tomara la forma de un anillo. Cruzaba yo la Plaza
de los Héroes, estaba oscureciendo y la boruca de los pájaros
en los laureles empezaba a calmarse. Se me había hecho tarde. "Quién sabe qué estarán haciendo mis muchachos", me
iba yo diciendo. Desde el alba me había venido para Cuernavaca. Tenía yo urgencia de llegar a mi casa porque mi esposo,
como es debido cuando uno es mal casada: bebe, y cuando
yo me ausento se dedica a golpear a mis muchachos. Con mis
hijos ya no se mete, están grandes señor, y Dios no lo quiera,
pero podrían devolverle el golpe. En cambio con las niñas se
desquita. Apenas salía yo de la calle que baja del mercado,
cuando me cogió la lluvia. Llovía tanto, que se habían formado ríos en las banquetas. Iba yo empinada para guardar mi
cara de la lluvia, cuando vi brillar a mi desgracia en medio del
agua que corría entre las piedras. Parecía una serpientita de
oro, bien entumida por la frescura del agua. A su lado se formaban remolinos chiquitos.

"¡Andale, Camila, un anillo dorado!" y me agaché y lo
cogí. No fue robo. La calle es la calle y lo que pertenece a la
calle nos pertenece a todos. Estaba bien frío y no tenía ninguna piedra: era una alianza. Se secó en la palma de mi mano
y no me pareció que extrañara ningún dedo, porque se me
quedó quieto y se entibió luego. En el camino a mi casa me
iba yo diciendo: "Se lo daré a Severina, mi hijita mayor." Somos tan pobres, que nunca hemos tenido ninguna alhaja y mi
lujo señor, antes de que nos desposeyeran de las tierras, para
hacer el mentado tiro al pichón en dónde nosotros sembrá-
mos, fue comprarme unas chanclitas de charol con trabilla,
para ir al entierro de mi niño. Usted debe de acordarse, señor,
de aquel día en que los pistoleros de Legorreta lo mataron a
causa de las tierras. Ya entonces éramos pobres, pero desde
ese día sin mis tierras y sin mi hijo mayor, hemos quedado
verdaderamente en la desdicha. Por eso cualquier gustito nos

da tantísimo gusto. Me encontré a mis muchachos sentados alrededor del comal.

—¡Anden, hijos! ¿Cómo pasaron el día?

—Aguardando su vuelta, me contestaron. Y vi que en todo el día no habían probado bocado.

—Enciendan la lumbre, vamos a cenar.

Los muchachos encendieron la lumbre y yo saqué cilantro y el queso.

—¡Qué gustosos andaríamos con un pedacito de oro! —dije yo preparando la sorpresa. ¡Qué suerte la de la mujer que puede decir que sí o que no, moviendo sus pendientes de oro!

—Sí, qué suerte... —dijeron mis muchachitos.

—¡Qué suerte la de la joven que puede señalar con su dedo para lucir un anillo! —dije.

Mis muchachos se echaron a reír y yo saqué el anillo y lo puse en el dedo de mi hija Severina. Y allí paró todo, señor, hasta que Adrián llegó al pueblo, para caracolear sus ojos delante de las muchachas. Adrián no trabajaba más que dos o tres veces a la semana reparando las cercas de piedra. Los más de los días los pasaba en la puerta de "El Capricho" mirando cómo comprábamos la sal y las botellas de refrescos. Un día detuvo a mi hijita Aurelia.

—¿Oye niña, de qué está hecha tu hermanita Severina?

—Yo no sé... —le contestó la inocente.

—Oye niña, ¿y para quién está hecha tu hermanita Severina?

—Yo no sé... —le contestó la inocente.

—Oye niña, ¿y esa mano en la que lleva el anillo a quién se la regaló?

—Yo no sé... —le contestó la inocente.

—Mira niña, dile a tu hermanita Severina que cuando compre la sal me deje que se la pague y que me deje mirar sus ojos.

—Sí, joven —le contestó la inocente. Y llegó a platicarle a su hermana lo que le había dicho Adrián.

La tarde del siete de mayo estaba terminando. Hacía mucho calor y el trabajo nos había dado sed a mi hija Severina y a mí.

—Anda, hija, ve a comprar unos refrescos.

Mi hija se fue y yo me quedé esperando su vuelta sentada en el patio de mi casa. En la espera me puse a mirar cómo el patio estaba roto y lleno de polvo. Ser pobre señor, es irse quebrando como cualquier ladrillo muy pisado. Así somos los pobres, ni quién nos mire y todos nos pasan por encima. Ya usted mismo lo vio, señor, cuando mataron a mi hijito el mayor para quitarnos las tierras. ¿Qué pasó? Que el asesino Legorreta se hizo un palacio sobre mi terreno y ahora tiene sus reclinatorios de seda blanca, en la iglesia del pueblo y los domingos cuando viene desde México, la llena con sus pistoleros y sus familiares, y nosotros los descalzos, mejor no entramos para no ver tanto desacato. Y de sufrir tanta injusticia, se nos juntan los años y nos barren el gusto y la alegría y se queda uno como un montón de tierra antes de que la tierra nos cobije. En esos pensamientos andaba yo, sentada en el patio de mi casa, ese siete de mayo. " ¡Mírate, Camila, bien fregada!" "Mira a tus hijos. ¿Qué van a durar? ¡Nada! Antes de que lo sepan estarán aquí sentados, si es que no están muertos como mi difuntito asesinado, con la cabeza ardida por la pobreza, y los años colgándoles como piedras, contando los días en que no pasaron hambre" ... Y me fui, señor a caminar mi vida. Y vi que todos los caminos estaban llenos con las huellas de mis pies. ¡Cuánto se camina! ¡Cuánto se rodea! Y todo para nada o para encontrar una mañana a su hijito tirado en la milpa con la cabeza rota por los máuseres y la sangre saliéndole por la boca. No lloré, señor. Si el pobre empezara a llorar, sus lágrimas ahogarían al mundo, porque motivo para llanto son todos los días. Ya me dará Dios lugar para llorar, me estaba yo diciendo, cuando me vi que estaba en el corredor de mi casa esperando la vuelta de mi hijita Severina. La lumbre estaba apagada y los perros estaban ladrando como ladran en la noche, cuando las piedras cambian de lugar. Recordé que mis hijos se habían ido con su papá a la peregrinación del Día de la Cruz en Guerrero y que no iban a volver hasta el día nueve. Luego recordé que Severina había ido a "El Capricho". " ¿Dónde fue mi hija que no ha vuelto?" Miré el cielo y vi como las estrellas iban a la carrera. Bajé mis ojos y me hallé con los de Severina, que me miraban tristes desde un pilar.

—Aquí tiene su refresco —me dijo con una voz en la que acababan de sembrar la desdicha.

—Me alcanzó la botella de refresco y fue entonces cuando vi que su mano estaba hinchada y que el anillo no lo llevaba.

— ¿Dónde está tu anillo, hija?

—Acuéstese, mamá.

Se tendió en su camita con los ojos abiertos. Yo me tendí junto a ella. La noche pasó larga y mi hijita no volvió a usar la palabra en muchos días. Cuando Gabino llegó con los muchachos, Severina ya empezaba a secarse.

— ¿Quién le hizo el mal? —preguntó Gabino y se arrinconó y no quiso beber alcohol en muchos días.

Pasó el tiempo y Severina seguía secándose. Sólo su mano seguía hinchada. Yo soy ignorante, señor, nunca fui a la escuela, pero me fui a Cuernavaca a buscar al doctor Adame, con domicilio en Aldana 17.

—Doctor, mi hija se está secando...

El doctor se vino conmigo al pueblo. Aquí guardo todavía sus recetas. Camila sacó unos papeles arrugados.

— ¡Mamá! ¿Sabes quién le hinchó la mano a Severina? —me preguntó Aurelia.

—No, hija, ¿quién?

—Adrián, para quitarle el anillo.

¡Ah, el ingrato! y en mis adentros veía que las recetas del doctor Adame no la podían aliviar. Entonces, una mañana, me fui a ver a Leonor, la tía del nombrado Adrián.

—Pasa, Camila.

Entré con precauciones: mirando para todos lados para ver si lo veía.

—Mira, Leonor, yo no sé quién es tu sobrino, ni qué lo trajo al pueblo, pero quiero que me devuelva el anillo que le quitó a mi hija, pues de él se vale para hacerle el mal.

— ¿Qué anillo?

—El anillo que yo le regalé a Severina. Adrián con sus propias manos se lo sacó en "El Capricho" y desde entonces ella está desconocida.

—No vengas a ofender, Camila. Adrián no es hijo de bruja.

—Leonor, dile que me devuelva el anillo por el bien de él y de toda su familia.

— ¡Yo no puedo decirle nada! Ni me gusta que ofendan a mi sangre bajo mi techo.

Me fui de allí y toda la noche velé a mi niña. Ya sabe, señor, que lo único que la gente regala es el mal. Esa noche Severina empezó a hablar el idioma de los maleados. ¡Ay, Jesús bendito, no permitas que mi hija muera endemoniada! Y me puse a rezar una Magnífica. Mi comadre Gabriel, aquí presente, me dijo: "Vamos por Fulgencia, para que le saque el mal del pecho." Dejamos a la niña en compañía de su padre y sus hermanos y nos fuimos por Fulgencia. Luego, toda la noche Fulgencia curó a la niña, cubierta con una sábana.

—Después de que cante el primer gallo, le habré sacado el mal —dijo.

Y así fue señor, de repente Severina se sentó en la cama y gritó: " ¡Ayúdeme mamacita!" Y echó por la boca un animal tan grande como mi mano. El animal traía entre sus patas pedacitos de su corazón. Porque mi niña tenía el animal amarrado a su corazón... Entonces cantó el primer gallo.

—Mira —me dijo Fulgencia— ahora que te devuelvan el anillo, porque antes de los tres meses habrán crecido las crías.

Apenas amaneció, me fui a las cercas a buscar al ingrato. Allí lo esperé. Lo vi venir, no venía silbando, con un pie venía trayendo a golpecitos una piedra. Traía los ojos bajos y las manos en los bolsillos.

Mira, Adrián el desconocido, no sabemos de dónde vienes, ni quiénes fueron tus padres y sin embargo te hemos recibido aquí con cortesía. Tú en cambio andas dañando a las jóvenes. Yo soy la madre de Severina y te pido que me devuelvas el anillo con que le haces el mal.

— ¿Qué anillo? —me dijo ladeando la cabeza. Y vi que sus ojos brillaban con gusto.

—El que le quitaste a mi hijita en "El Capricho".

— ¿Quién lo dijo? —y se ladeó el sombrero.

—Lo dijo Aurelia.

— ¿Acaso lo ha dicho la propia Severina?

— ¡Cómo lo ha de decir si está dañada!

— ¡Hum!... Pues cuántas cosas dicen en este pueblo. ¡Y quién lo dijera con tan bonitas mañanas!

—Entonces ¿no me lo vas a dar?

— ¿Y quién dijo que lo tengo?

—Yo te voy a hacer el mal a ti y a toda tu familia —le prometí.

Lo dejé en las cercas y me volví a mi casa. Me encontré a Severina sentadita en el corral, al rayo del sol. Pasaron los días y la niña se empezó a mejorar. Yo andaba trabajando en el campo y Fulgencia venía para cuidarla.

— ¿Ya te dieron el anillo?

—No.

—Las crías están creciendo.

Seis veces fui a ver al ingrato Adrián a rogarle que me devolviera el anillo. Y seis veces se recargó contra las cercas y me lo negó gustoso.

—Mamá, dice Adrián que aunque quisiera no podría devolver el anillo, porque lo manchó con una piedra y lo tiró a una barranca. Fue una noche que andaba borracho y no se acuerda de cuál barranca fue.

—Dile que me diga cuál barranca es para ir a buscarlo.

—No se acuerda...

Me repitió mi hija Aurelia y se me quedó mirando con la

primera tristeza de su vida. Me salí de mi casa y me fui a buscar a Adrián.

—Mira, desconocido, acuérdate de la barranca en la que tiraste el anillo.

— ¿Qué barranca?

—En la que tiraste al anillo.

—Qué anillo?

— ¿No te quieres acordar?

—De lo único que me quiero acordar es que de aquí a catorce días me caso con mi prima Inés.

— ¿La hija de tu tía Leonor?

—Sí, con esa joven.

—Es muy nueva la noticia.

—Tan nueva de esta mañana...

—Antes me vas a dar el anillo de mi hija Severina. Los tres meses ya se están cumpliendo.

Adrían se me quedó mirando, como si me mirara de muy lejos, se recargó en la cerca y adelantó un pie.

—Eso sí que no se va a poder...

Y allí se quedó, mirando al suelo. Cuando llegué a mi casa, Severina se había tendido en su camita. Aurelia me dijo que no podía caminar. Mandé traer a Fulgencia. Al llegar nos contó que la boda de Inés y de Adrián era para un domingo y que ya habían invitado a las familias. Luego miró a Severina con mucha tristeza.

—Tu hija no tiene cura. Tres veces le sacaremos el mal y tres veces dejará crías. No cuentes más con ella.

Mi hija empezó a hablar el idioma desconocido y sus ojos se clavaron en el techo. Así estuvo varios días y varias noches. Fulgencia no podía sacarle el mal, hasta que llegara a su cabal tamaño. ¿Y quién nos dice, señor, que anoche se nos pone tan malísima? Fulgencia le sacó el segundo animal con pedazos muy grandes de su corazón. Apenas le quedó un pedazo chiquito de corazón, pero bastante grande para que el tercer animal se prenda a él. Esta mañana mi niña estaba como muerta y yo oí que repicaban campanas.

— ¿Qué es ese ruido, mamá?

—Campanas, hija...

—Se está casando Adrián —le dijo Aurelia.

Y yo, señor, me acordé del ingrato y del festín que estaba viviendo mientras mi hijita moría.

—Ahora vengo —dije.

Y me fui cruzando el pueblo y llegué a casa de Leonor.

—Pasa, Camila.

Había mucha gente y muchas cazuelas de mole y botellas de refrescos. Entré mirando por todas partes, para ver si lo veía. Allí estaba con la boca risueña y los ojos serios. También estaba Inés, bien risueña, y allí estaban sus tíos y sus primos los Cadena, bien risueños.

—Adrián, Severina ya no es de este mundo. No sé si le quede un pie de tierra para retoñar. Dime en qué barranca tiraste el anillo que la está matando.

Adrián se sobresaltó y luego le vi el rencor en los ojos.

—Yo no conozco barrancas. Las plantas se secan por mucho sol y falta de riego. Y las muchachas por estar hechas para alguien y quedarse sin nadie...

Todos oímos el silbar de sus palabras enojadas.

—Severina se está secando, porque fue hecha para alguien que no fuiste tú. Por eso le has hecho el maleficio. ¡Hechicero de mujeres!

—Doña Camila, no es usted la que sabe para quién está hecha su hijita Severina.

Se echó para atrás y me miró con los ojos encendidos. No parecía el novio de este domingo: no le quedó la menor huella de gozo, ni el recuerdo de la risa.

—El mal está hecho. Ya es tarde para el remedio.

Así dijo el desconocido de Ometepec y se fue haciendo para atrás, mirándome con más enojo. Yo me fui hacia él, como si me llevaran sus ojos. "Se va a desaparecer", me fui diciendo, mientras caminaba hacia adelante y él avanzaba para atrás, cada vez más enojado. Así salimos hasta la calle, porque él me seguía llevando, con las llamas de sus ojos. "Va a mi casa a matar a Severina", le leí el pensamiento, señor, porque para allá se encaminaba, de espaldas, buscando el camino con sus talones. Le vi su camisa blanca, llameante, y luego, cuando torció la esquina de mi casa, se la vi bien roja. No sé cómo, señor, alcancé a darle en el corazón, antes de que acabara con mi hijita Severina...

Camila guardó silencio. El hombre de la Comisaría la miró aburrido. La joven que tomaba las declaraciones en taquigrafía detuvo el lápiz. Sentados en unas sillas de tule, los deudos y la viuda de Adrián Cadena bajaron la cabeza. Inés tenía sangre en el pecho y los ojos secos.

Gabino movió la cabeza apoyando las palabras de su mujer.

—Firme aquí, señora y despídase de su marido porque la vamos a encerrar.

—Yo no sé firmar.

Los deudos de Adrián Cadena se volvieron a la puerta por

la que acababa de aparecer Severina. Venía pálida y con las trenzas deshechas.

—¿Por qué lo mató, mamá?... Yo le rogué que no se casara con su prima Inés. Ahora el día que yo muera, me voy a topar con su enojo por haberlo separado de ella...

Severina se tapó la cara con las manos y Camila no pudo decir nada.

La sorpresa la dejó muda mucho tiempo.

—¡Mamá, me dejó usted el camino solo!...

Severina miró a los presentes. Sus ojos cayeron sobre Inés, ésta se llevó la mano al pecho y sobre su vestido de linón rosa, acarició la sangre seca de Adrián Cadena.

—Mucho lloró la noche en que Fulgencia te sacó a su niño. Después, de sentimiento quiso casarse conmigo. Era huérfano y yo era su prima. Era muy desconocido en sus amores y en sus maneras... —dijo Inés bajando los ojos, mientras su mano acariciaba la sangre de Adrián Cadena.

Al rato le entregaron la camisa rosa de su joven marido: cosido en el lugar del corazón había una alianza, como una serpientita de oro y en ella grabadas las palabras: "Adrián y Severina gloriosos."

José Luis González
1926—
Puerto Rico

La carta
El hombre en la calle, 1948.

"San Juan, Puerto Rico
8 de marso de 1947

Qerida bieja:

COMO yo le desia antes de venirme, aqui las cosas me van vién. Desde que llegé enseguida incontré trabajo. Me pagan 8 pesos la semana y con eso bivo igual que el alministrador de la central allá.

La ropa aquella que quedé de mandale, no la he podido comprar pues qiero buscarla en una de las tiendas mejóres. Dígale a Petra que cuando valla por casa le boy a llevar un regalito al nene de ella.

Boy a ver si me saco un retrato un dia de estos para mandalselo a uste, mamá.

El otro dia vi a Felo el ijo de la comai Maria. El también está travajando pero gana menos que yo. Es que yo e tenido suerte.

Bueno, recueldese de escrivirme y contarme todo lo que pasa por alla.

Su ijo que la qiere y le pide la bendision,

Juan''

Después de firmar, dobló cuidadosamente el papel arrugado y lleno de borrones y se lo guardó en un bolsillo del pantalón. Caminó hasta la estación de correos más cercana, y al llegar se echó la gorra raída sobre la frente y se acuclilló en el umbral de una de las puertas. Contrajo la mano izquierda, fingiéndose manco, y extendió la derecha abierta.

Cuando reunió los cinco centavos necesarios, compró el sobre y la estampilla y despachó la carta.

José Luis González
1926—
Puerto Rico

En el fondo del caño hay un negrito
En este lado, 1954.

1

A primera vez que el negrito Melodía vio al otro negrito en el fondo del caño fue temprano en la mañana del tercer o cuarto día después de la mudanza, cuando llegó gateando hasta la única puerta de la nueva vivienda y se asomó para mirar hacia la quieta superficie del agua allá abajo.

Entonces el padre, que acababa de despertar sobre el montón de sacos vacíos extendidos en el piso, junto a la mujer semidesnuda que aún dormía, le gritó:

—¡Mire... eche p'adentro! ¡Diantre 'e muchacho desinquieto!

Y Melodía, que no había aprendido a entender las palabras, pero sí a obedecer los gritos, gateó otra vez hacia adentro y se quedó silencioso en un rincón, chupándose un dedito porque tenía hambre.

El hombre se incorporó sobre los codos. Miró a la mujer que dormía a su lado y la sacudió flojamente por un brazo. La mujer despertó sobresaltada, mirando al hombre con ojos de susto. El hombre se rió. Todas las mañanas era igual: la mujer despertaba con aquella cara de susto que a él le provocaba una gracia sin maldad. La primera vez que él le vio aquella cara de susto a la mujer no fue en un despertar, sino la noche que se acostaron juntos por primera vez. Quizá por eso a él le hacía gracia verla salir así del sueño todas las mañanas.

El hombre se sentó sobre los sacos vacíos.

—Bueno —se dirigió entonces a ella—. Cuela el café.

La mujer tardó un poco en contestar:

—No queda.

—¿Ah?

—No queda. Se acabó ayer.

El casi empezó a decir: "¿Y por qué no compraste más?", pero se interrumpió cuando vio que la mujer empezaba a poner aquella otra cara, la cara que a él no le hacía gracia y que ella sólo ponía cuando él le hacía preguntas como ésa. La primera vez que le vio aquella cara a la mujer fue la noche que regresó a la casa borracho y deseoso de ella y se le fue encima pero la borrachera no le dejó hacer nada. Quizá por eso a él no le gustaba verle aquella cara a la mujer.

—¿Conque se acabó ayer?

—Ajá.

La mujer se puso de pie y empezó a meterse el vestido por la cabeza. El hombre, todavía sentado sobre los sacos vacíos, derrotó su mirada y la fijó por un rato en los agujeros de su camiseta.

Melodía, cansado ya de la insipidez del dedo, se decidió a llorar. El hombre lo miró y preguntó a la mujer:

—¿Tampoco hay ná pal nene?

—Sí... Conseguí unas hojitah 'e guanábana. Le guá'cer un guarapillo 'horita.

—¿Cuántos díah va que no toma leche?

—¿Leche? —la mujer puso un poco de asombro inconsciente en la voz—. Desde antier.

El hombre se puso de pie y se metió los pantalones. Después se allegó a la puerta y miró hacia afuera. Le dijo a la mujer:

—La marea 'tá alta. Hoy hay que dir en bote.

Luego miró hacia arriba, hacia el puente y la carretera. Automóviles, guaguas y camiones pasaban en un desfile interminable. El hombre sonrió viendo cómo desde casi todos los vehículos alguien miraba con extrañeza hacia la casucha enclavada en medio de aquel brazo de mar: el "caño" sobre cuyas márgenes pantanosas había ido creciendo hacía años el arrabal. Ese alguien por lo general empezaba a mirar la casucha cuando el automóvil, o la guagua o el camión, llegaba a la mitad del puente, y después seguía mirando, volteando gradualmente la cabeza hasta que el automóvil, o la guagua o el camión, tomaba la curva allá adelante. El hombre sonrió. Y después murmuró:

—¡Pendejos!

A poco se metió en el bote y remó hasta la orilla. De la popa del bote a la puerta de la casa había una soga larga que permitía a quien quedara en la casa atraer nuevamente el bote hasta la puerta. De la casa a la orilla había también un puentecito de madera, que se cubría con la marea alta.

Ya en la orilla, el hombre caminó hacia la carretera. Se sintió mejor cuando el ruido de los automóviles ahogó el llanto del negrito en la casucha.

2

La segunda vez que el negrito Melodía vio al otro negrito en el fondo del caño fue poco después del mediodía, cuando volvió a gatear hasta la puerta y se asomó y miró hacia abajo. Esta vez el negrito en el fondo del caño le regaló una sonrisa a Melodía. Melodía había sonreído primero y tomó la sonrisa del otro negrito como una respuesta a la suya. Entonces hizo así con la manita, y desde el fondo del caño el otro negrito también hizo así con su manita. Melodía no pudo reprimir la risa, y le pareció que también desde allá abajo llegaba el sonido de otra risa. La madre lo llamó entonces porque el segundo guarapillo de hojas de guanábana ya estaba listo.

* * *

Dos mujeres, de las afortunadas que vivían en tierra firme, sobre el fango endurecido de las márgenes del caño, comentaban.

—Hay que velo. Si me lo 'bieran contao, 'biera dicho qu'era embuste.

—La necesidá, doña. A mí misma, quién me 'biera dicho que yo diba llegar aquí. Yo que tenía hasta mi tierrita...

—Pueh nojotroh fuimoh de los primeroh. Casi no 'bía gente y uno cogía la parte máh sequecita, ¿ve? Pero los que llegan ahora, fíjese, tienen que tirarse al agua, como quien dice. Pero, bueno, y... esa gente, ¿de onde diantre haberán salío?

—A mí me dijeron que por ái por Isla Verde 'tán orbanisando y han sacao un montón de negroh arrimaoh. A lo mejor son d'esoh.

— ¡Bendito...! ¿Y usté se ha fijao en el negrito qué mono? La mujer vino ayer a ver si yo tenía unas hojitah de algo pa hacerle un guarapillo, y yo le di unas poquitah de guanábana que me quedaban.

— ¡Ay, Virgen, bendito...!

* * *

Al atardecer, el hombre estaba cansado. Le dolía la espalda. Pero venía palpando las monedas en el fondo del bolsillo, haciéndolas sonar, adivinando con el tacto cuál era un vellón, cuál de diez, cuál una peseta. Bueno... hoy había habido suerte. El blanco que pasó por el muelle a recoger su mercancía de Nueva York. Y el obrero que le prestó su carretón toda la tarde porque tuvo que salir corriendo a buscar a la comadrona para su mujer, que estaba echando un pobre más al mundo. Sí, señor. Se va tirando. Mañana será otro día.

Se metió en un colmado y compró café y arroz y habichuelas y unas latitas de leche evaporada. Pensó en Melodía y apresuró el paso. Se había venido a pie desde San Juan para no gastar los cinco centavos de la guagua.

3

La tercera vez que el negrito Melodía vio al otro negrito en el fondo del caño fue al atardecer, poco antes de que el padre regresara. Esta vez Melodía venía sonriendo antes de asomarse, y le asombró que el otro también se estuviera sonriendo allá abajo. Volvió a hacer así con la manita y el otro volvió a contestar. Entonces Melodía sintió un súbito entusiasmo y un amor indecible hacia el otro negrito. Y se fue a buscarlo.

José Luis González
1926—
Puerto Rico

La noche que volvimos
a ser gente

Mambrú se fue a la guerra y otros relatos, 1972.

A Juan Sáez Burgos

¿QUE si me acuerdo? Se acuerda el Barrio entero si quieres que te diga la verdad, porque eso no se le va a olvidar ni a Trompoloco, que ya no es capaz de decir ni dónde enterraron a su mamá hace quince días. Lo que pasa es que yo te lo puedo contar mejor que nadie por esa casualidad que tú todavía no sabes. Pero antes vamos a pedir unas cervezas bien frías porque con esta calor del diablo quién quita que hasta me falle la memoria.

Ahora sí, salud y pesetas. Y fuerza donde tú sabes. Bueno, pues de eso ya van cuatro años y si quieres te digo hasta los meses y los días porque para acordarme no tengo más que mirarle la cara al barrigón ése que tú viste ahí en la casa cuando fuiste a procurarme esta mañana. Sí, el mayorcito, que se llama igual que yo pero que si hubiera nacido mujercita hubiéramos tenido que ponerle Estrella o Luz María o algo así. O hasta Milagros, mira, porque aquello fue... Pero si sigo así voy a contarte el cuento al revés, o sea desde el final y no por el principio, así que mejor sigo por donde iba.

Bueno, pues la fecha no te la digo porque ya tú la sabes y lo que te interesa es otra cosa. Entonces resulta que ese día le había dicho yo al foreman, que era un judío buena persona y ya sabía su poquito de español, que me diera un overtime porque me iban a hacer falta los chavos para el parto de mi mujer, que ya estaba en el último mes y no paraba de sacar cuentas. Que si lo del canastillo, que si lo de la comadrona... Ah, porque ella estaba empeñada en dar a luz en la casa y no en la clínica donde los doctores y las norsas no hablan español y además sale más caro.

Entonces a las cuatro acabé mi primer turno y bajé al come-y-vete ése del italiano que está ahí enfrente de la factoría. Cuestión de echarme algo a la barriga hasta que llegara a casa y la mujer me recalentara la comida, ¿ves? Bueno, pues me metí un par de hot dogs con una cerveza mientras le tiraba un vistazo al periódico hispano que había comprado por la mañana, y en eso, cuando estaba leyendo lo de un latino que había hecho tasajo a su corteja porque se la estaba pegando con un chino, en eso, mira, yo no sé si tú crees en esas cosas, pero como que me entró un presentimiento. O sea que sentí que esa noche iba a pasar algo grande, algo que yo no podía decir lo que iba a ser. Yo digo que uno tiene que creer porque tú me dirás qué tenía que ver lo del latino y el chino y la corteja con eso que yo empecé a sentir. A sentir, tú sabes, porque no fue que lo pensara, que eso es distinto. Bueno, pues acabé de mirar el periódico y volví rápido a la factoría para empezar el overtime.

Entonces el otro foreman, porque el primero ya se había ido, me dice: ¿Qué, te piensas hacer millonario para poner un casino en Puerto Rico? Así, relajando, tú sabes, y vengo yo y le digo, también vacilando: No, si el casino ya lo tengo. Ahora lo que quiero poner es una fábrica. Y me dice: ¿Una fábrica de qué? Y le digo: Una fábrica de humo. Y entonces me pregunta: ¿Ah, sí? ¿Y qué vas a hacer con el humo? Y yo bien serio, con una cara de palo que había que ver: ¡Adiós!... ¿y qué voy a hacer? ¡Enlatarlo! Un vacilón, tú sabes, porque ese foreman era todavía más buena persona que el otro. Pero porque le conviene, desde luego: así nos pone de buen humor y nos saca el jugo en el trabajo. El se cree que yo no lo sé, pero cualquier día se lo digo para que vea que uno no es tan ignorante como parece. Porque esta gente aquí a veces se imagina que uno viene de la última sínsora y confunde el papel de lija con el papel de inodoro, sobre todo cuando uno es trigueñito y con la morusa tirando a caracolillo.

Pero, bueno, eso es noticia vieja y lo que tengo que contarte es otra cosa. Ahora, que la condenada calor sigue y la cerveza ya se nos acabó. La misma marca, ¿no? Okay. Pues como te iba diciendo, después que el foreman me quiso vacilar y yo lo dejé con las ganas, pegamos a trabajar en serio. Porque eso sí, aquí la guachafita y el trabajo no son compadres. Time is money, ya tú sabes. Pegaron a llegarme radios por el assembly line y yo a meterles los tubos: chan, chan. Sí, yo lo que hacía entonces era poner los tubos. Dos a cada radio, uno en cada mano: chan, chan. Al principio, cuando no estaba impuesto, a veces se me pasaba un radio y entonces, ¡muchacho!, tenía que correrle detrás y al mismo tiempo echarle el ojo al que venía seguido, y creía que me iba a volver loco. Cuando salía del trabajo sentía como que llevaba un baile de San Vito en todo el cuerpo. A mí me está que por eso en este país hay tanto borracho y tanto vicioso. Sí, chico, porque cuando tú quedas así lo que te pide el cuerpo es un juanetazo de lo que sea, que por lo general es ron o algo así, y ahí se va acostumbrando uno. Yo digo que por eso las mujeres se defienden mejor en el trabajo de factoría, porque ellas se entretienen con el chismorreo y la habladuría y el comentario, ¿ves?, y no se imponen a la bebida.

Bueno, pues ya tenía yo un rato metiendo tubos y pensando boberías cuando en eso viene el foreman y me dice: Oye, ahí te buscan. Yo le digo: ¿A quién, a mí? Pues claro, me dice, aquí no hay dos con el mismo nombre. Entonces pusieron a otro en mi lugar para no parar el trabajo y ahí voy yo a ver quién era el que me buscaba. Y era Trompoloco, que no me dice ni qué hubo sino que me espeta: Oye, que te vayas para tu casa que tu mujer se está pariendo. Sí, hombre, así de sopetón. Y es que el pobre Trompoloco se cayó del coy allá en Puerto Rico cuando era chiquito y según decía su mamá, que en paz descanse, cayó de cabeza y parece que del golpe se le ablandaron los sesos. Tuvo un tiempo, cuando yo lo conocí aquí en el Barrio, que de repente se ponía a dar vueltas como loco y no paraba hasta que se mareaba y se caía al suelo. De ahí le vino el apodo. Eso sí, nadie abusa de él porque su mamá era muy buena persona, medium espiritista ella, tú sabes, y ayudaba a mucha gente y no cobraba. Uno le dejaba lo que podía, ¿ves?, y si no podía no le dejaba nada. Entonces hay mucha gente que se ocupa de que Trompoloco no pase necesidades. Porque él siempre fue huérfano de padre y no tuvo hermanos, así que como quien dice está solo en el mundo.

Bueno, pues llega Trompoloco y me dice eso y yo digo: Ay, mi madre, ¿y ahora qué hago? El foreman, que estaba pendiente de lo que pasaba porque esa gente nunca le pierde ojo a uno en el trabajo, viene y me pregunta: ¿Cuál es el trouble? Y yo le digo: Que vienen a buscarme porque mi mujer se está pariendo. Y entonces el foreman me dice: Bueno, ¿y qué tú estás esperando? Porque déjame decirte que ese foreman también era judío y para los judíos la familia siempre es lo primero. En eso no son como los demás americanos, que entre hijos y padres y entre hermanos se insultan y hasta se dan por cualquier cosa. Yo no sé si será por la clase de vida que la gente lleva en este país. Siempre corriendo detrás del dólar, como los perros ésos del canódromo que ponen a correr detrás de un conejo de trapo. ¿Tú los has visto? Acaban echando el bofe y nunca alcanzan al conejo. Eso sí, les dan comida y los cuidan para que vuelvan a correr al otro día, que es lo mismo que hacen con la gente, si miras bien la cosa. Así que en este país todos venimos a ser como perros de carrera.

Bueno, pues cuando el foreman me dijo que qué yo estaba esperando, le digo: Nada, ponerme el coat y agarrar el subway antes de que mi hijo vaya a llegar y no me encuentre en casa. Contento que estaba yo ya, ¿sabes?, porque iba a ser mi primer hijo y tú sabes cómo es eso. Y me dice el foreman: No se te vaya a olvidar ponchar la tarjeta para que cobres la media hora que llevas trabajando, que de ahora palante es cuando te van a hacer falta los chavos. Y le digo: Cómo no, y agarro el coat y poncho la tarjeta y le digo a Trompoloco, que estaba parado allí mirando las máquinas como eslembao: ¡Avanza, Trompo, que vamos a llegar tarde! Y bajamos las escaleras corriendo para no esperar el ascensor y llegamos a la acera, que estaba bien crowded porque a esa hora todavía había gente saliendo del trabajo. Y digo yo: ¡Maldita sea, y que tocarme la hora del rush! Y Trompoloco que no quería correr: Espérate, hombre, espérate, que yo quiero comprar un dulce. Bueno, es que Trompoloco es así ¿ves?, como un nene. El sirve para hacer un mandado, si es algo sencillo, o para lavar unas escaleras en un building o cualquier cosa que no haya que pensar. Pero si es cuestión de usar la calculadora, entonces búscate a otro. Así que vengo y le digo: No, Trompo, qué dulce ni qué carajo. Eso lo compras allá en el Barrio cuando lleguemos. Y él: No, no, en el Barrio no hay de los que yo quiero. Esos nada más se consiguen en Brooklyn. Y le digo: Ay, tú estás loco, y en seguida me arrepiento porque eso es lo único que no se la puede decir a Trompoloco. Y se para ahí en la acera, más serio que un chavo de queso, y me dice: No, no, loco no. Y le digo: No, hombre, si yo no dije loco, yo dije bobo. Lo que pasa es que tú oíste mal. ¡Avanza, que el dulce te lo llevo yo mañana! Y me dice: ¿Seguro que tú no me dijiste loco? Y yo: ¡Seguro, hombre! Y él: ¿Y mañana me llevas dos dulces? Mira, loco y todo lo que tú quieras, pero bien que sabe aprovecharse. Y a mí casi me entra la risa y le digo: Claro, chico, te llevo hasta tres si quieres. Y entonces vuelve a poner buena cara y me dice: Está bien, vámonos, pero tres dulces, acuérdate, ¿ah? Y yo, caminando para la entrada del subway con Trompoloco detrás: Sí, hombre, tres. Después me dices de cuáles son.

Y bajamos casi corriendo las escaleras y entramos en la estación con aquel mar de gente que tú sabes cómo es eso. Yo pendiente de que Trompoloco no se fuera a quedar atrás porque con el apeñuscamiento y los arrempujones a lo mejor le entraba miedo y quién iba a responder por él. Cuando viene el tren expreso lo agarro por un brazo y le digo: Prepárate y echa palante tú también, que si no nos quedamos afuera. Y él me dice: No te ocupes, y cuando se abre la puerta y salen los que iban a bajar, nos metemos de frente y quedamos prensados entre aquel montón de gente que no podíamos ni mover los brazos. Bueno, mejor, porque así no había que agarrarse de los tubos. Trompoloco iba un poco azorado porque yo creo que era la primera vez que viajaba en subway a esa hora, pero como me tenía a mí al lado no había problema, y así seguimos hasta Columbus Circle y allí cambiamos de línea porque teníamos que bajarnos en la 110 y Quinta para llegar a casa, ¿ves?, y ahí volvimos a quedar como sardinas en lata.

Entonces yo iba contando los minutos, pensando si ya mi hijo habría nacido y cómo estaría mi mujer. Y de repente se me ocurre: Bueno, y yo tan seguro de que va a ser macho y a lo mejor me sale una chancleta. Tú sabes que uno siempre quiere que el primero sea hombre. Y la verdad es que eso es un egoísmo de nosotros, porque a la mamá le conviene más que la mayor sea mujer para que después la ayude con el trabajo de la casa y la crianza de los hermanitos. Bueno, pues en eso iba yo pensando y sintiéndome ya muy padre de familia, te das cuenta, cuando... ¡fuácata, ahí fue! Que se va la luz y el tren empieza a perder impulso hasta que queda parado en la mismita mitad del túnel entre dos estaciones. Bueno, la verdad es que de momento no se asustó nadie. Tú sabes que eso de que las luces se apaguen en el subway no es nada del otro mundo: en seguida vuelven a prenderse y la gente ni pestañea. Y eso de que el tren se pare un ratito antes de llegar a una estación tampoco es raro. Así que de momento no se asustó nadie. Prendieron las luces de emergencia y todo el mundo lo más tranquilo. Pero empezó a pasar el tiempo y el tren no se movía. Y yo pensando: Coño, qué mala suerte, ahora que tenía que llegar pronto. Pero todavía creyendo que sería cuestión de un ratito, ¿ves? Y así pasaron como tres minutos más y entonces una señora empezó a toser. Una señora americana ella, medio viejita, que estaba cerca de mí. Yo la miré y vi que estaba tosiendo como sin ganas, y pensé: Eso no es catarro, eso es miedo. Y pasó otro minuto y el tren seguía parado y entonces la señora le dijo a un muchacho que tenía al lado, un muchacho alto y rubio él, tofete, con cara como de irlandés, le dijo la señora: Oiga, joven, ¿a usted esto no le está raro? Y él le dijo: No, no se preocupe, eso no es nada. Pero la señora como que no quedó conforme y siguió con su tosesita y entonces otros pasajeros empezaron a tratar de mirar por las ventanillas, pero como no podían moverse bien y con la oscuridad que había allá afuera, pues no veían nada. Te lo digo porque yo también traté de mirar y lo único que saqué fue un dolor de cuello que me duró un buen rato.

Bueno, pues siguió pasando el tiempo y a mí empezó a darme un calambre en una pierna y ahí fue donde me entró el nerviosismo. No, no por el calambre, sino porque pensé que ya no iba a llegar a tiempo a casa. Y decía yo para entre mí: No, aquí tiene que haber pasado algo, ya es demasiado de mucho el tiempo que tenemos aquí parados. Y como no tenía nada que hacer, puse a funcionar el coco y entonces fue que se me ocurrió lo del suicidio. Bueno, era lo más lógico, ¿por qué no? Tú sabes que aquí hay muchísima gente que ya no se quieren para nada y entonces van y se trepan al Empire State y pegan el salto desde allá arriba y creo que cuando llegan a la calle ya están muertos por el tiempo que tardan en caer. Bueno, yo no sé, eso es lo que me han dicho. Y hay otros que se le tiran por delante al subway y quedan que hay que recogerlos con pala. Ah, no, eso sí, a los que brincan desde el Empire State me imagino que habrá que recogerlos con secante. No, pero en serio, porque con esas cosas no se debe relajar, a mí se me ocurrió que lo que había pasado era que alguien se le había tirado debajo al tren que iba delante de nosotros, y hasta pensé: Bueno, pues que en paz descanse pero ya me chavó a mí, porque ahora sí que voy a llegar tarde. Ya mi mujer debe estar pensando que Trompoloco se perdió en el camino o que yo ando borracho por ahí y no me importa lo que está pasando en casa. Porque no es que yo sea muy bebelón, pero de vez en cuando, tú me entiendes... Bueno, y ya que estamos hablando de eso, si quieres cambiamos de marca, pero que estén bien frías a ver si se nos acaba de quitar la calor.

¡Aaajá! Entonces... ¿por dónde iba yo? Ah sí, estaba pensando en eso del suicidio y qué sé yo, cuando de repente — ¡ran!— vienen y se abren las puertas del tren. Sí, hombre, sí, allí mismo en el túnel. Y como eso, a la verdad, era una cosa que yo nunca había visto, entonces pensé: Ahora sí que a la puerca se le entorchó el rabo. Y en seguida veo que allá abajo frente a la puerta estaban unos como inspectores o algo así porque tenían uniforme y traían unas linternas de ésas como faroles. Y nos dice uno de ellos: Take it easy que no hay peligro. Bajen despacio y sin empujar. Y ahí mismo la gente empezó a bajar y a preguntarle al mister aquél: ¿Qué es

lo que pasa, qué es lo que pasa? Yo agarré a Trompoloco por
el brazo y le dije: ¿Ya tú oíste? No hay peligro, pero no te
vayas a apartar de mí. Y él me decía que sí con la cabeza, porque yo creo que del susto se le había ido hasta la voz. No decía nada, pero parecía que los macos se le iban a salir de la
cara: los tenía como platillos y casi le brillaban en la oscuridad, como a los gatos.

Bueno, pues fuimos saliendo del tren hasta que no quedó nadie adentro. Entonces, cuando estuvimos todos alinea-
dos allá abajo, los inspectores empezaron a recorrer la fila que
nosotros habíamos formado y nos fueron explicando, así por
grupos, ¿ves?, que lo que pasaba era que había habido un
blackout o sea que se había ido la luz en toda la ciudad y no
se sabía cuándo iba a volver. Entonces la señora de la tosesita,
que había quedado cerca de mí, le preguntó al inspector: Oiga, ¿y cuándo vamos a salir de aquí? Y él le dijo: Tenemos
que esperar un poco porque hay otros trenes delante de nosotros y no podemos salir todos a la misma vez. Y ahí pegamos
a esperar. Y yo pensando: Maldita sea mi suerte, mira que tener que pasar esto el día de hoy, cuando en eso siento que
Trompoloco me jala la manga del coat y me dice bien bajito,
como en secreto: Oye, oye, panita, me estoy meando. ¡Imagínate tú! Lo único que faltaba. Y le digo: Ay, Trompo, bendito, aguántate, ¿tú no ves que aquí eso es imposible? Y me
dice: Pero es que hace rato que tengo ganas y ya no aguanto
más. Entonces me pongo a pensar rápido porque aquello era
una emergencia, ¿no?, y lo único que se me ocurre es ir a preguntarle al inspector qué se podía hacer. Le digo a Trompoloco: Bueno, espérame un momento, pero no te vayas a mover de aquí. Y me salgo de la línea y voy y le digo al inspector: Listen, mister, my friend wanna take a leak, o sea que mi
amigo quería cambiarle el agua al canario. Y me dice el inspector: Goddamit to hell, can't he hold it in a while? Y le
digo que eso mismo le había dicho yo, que se aguantara, pero
que ya no podía. Entonces me dice: Bueno, que lo haga donde pueda, pero que no se aleje mucho. Así que vuelvo donde
Trompoloco y le digo: Vente conmigo por ahí atrás a ver si
encontramos un lugarcito. Y pegamos a caminar, pero aquella
hilera de gente no se acababa nunca. Ya habíamos caminado
un trecho cuando vuelve a jalarme la manga y me dice: Ahora sí que ya no aguanto, brother. Entonces le digo: Pues mira, ponte detrás de mí pegadito a la pared, pero ten cuenta
que no me vayas a mojar los zapatos. Y hazlo despacito, para
que no se oiga. Y ni había acabado de hablar cuando oigo

aquello que... bueno, ¿tú sabes como hacen eso los caballos? Pues con decirte que parecía que eran dos caballos en vez de uno. Si yo no sé cómo no se le había reventado la vejiga. No, una cosa terrible. Yo pensé: Ave María, éste me va a salpicar hasta el coat. Y mira que era de esos cortitos, que no llegan ni a la rodilla, porque a mí siempre me ha gustado estar a la moda, ¿verdad? Y entonces, claro, la gente que estaba por allí tuvo que darse cuenta y yo oí que empezaron a murmurar. Y pensé: Menos mal que está oscuro y no nos pueden ver la cara, porque si se dan cuenta que somos puertorriqueños... Ya tú sabes cómo es el asunto aquí. Yo pensando todo eso y Trompoloco que no acababa. Cristiano, las cosas que le pasan a uno en este país! Después las cuentas y la gente no te las cree. Bueno, pues al fin Trompoloco acabó, o por lo menos eso creí yo porque ya no se oía aquel estrépito que estaba haciendo, pero pasaba el tiempo y no se movía. Y le digo: Oye, ¿ya tú acabaste? Y me dice: Sí. Y yo: Pues ya vámonos. Y entonces me sale con que: Espérate, que me estoy sacudiendo. Mira, ahí fue donde yo me encocoré. Le digo: Pero, muchacho, ¿eso es una manguera o qué? ¡Camina por ahí si no quieres que esta gente nos sacuda hasta los huesos después de esa inundación que tú has hecho aquí! Entonces como que comprendió la situación y me dijo: Está bien, está bien, vámonos.

Pues volvimos adonde estábamos antes y ahí nos quedamos esperando como media hora más. Yo oía a la gente alrededor de mí hablando en inglés, quejándose y diciendo que qué abuso, que parecía mentira, que si el alcalde, que si qué sé yo. Y de repente oigo por allá que alguien dice en español: Bueno, para estirar la pata lo mismo da aquí adentro que allá afuera, y mejor que sea aquí porque así el entierro tiene que pagarlo el gobierno. Sí, algún boricua que quería hacerse el gracioso. Yo miré así a ver si lo veía, para decirle que el entierro de él lo iba a pagar la sociedad protectora de animales, pero en aquella oscuridad no pude ver quién era. Y lo malo fue que el chistecito aquél me hizo su efecto, no te creas. Porque parado allí sin hacer nada y con la preocupación que traía yo y todo ese problema, ¿tú sabes lo que se me ocurrió a mí entonces? Imagínate, yo pensé que el inspector nos había dicho un embuste y que lo que pasaba era que ya había empezado la tercera guerra mundial. No, no te rías, yo te apuesto que yo no era el único que estaba pensando eso. Sí, hombre, con todo lo que se pasan diciendo los periódicos aquí, de que si los rusos y los chinos y hasta los marcianos en los platillos voladores... Pues claro, ¿y por qué tú te crees que en este país hay tanto loco? Si ahí en Bellevue ya ni caben y creo que van a tener que construir otro manicomio.

Bueno, pues en esa barbaridad estaba yo pensando cuando vienen los inspectores y nos dicen que ya nos tocaba el turno de salir a nosotros, pero caminando en fila y con calma. Entonces pegamos a caminar y al fin llegamos a la estación, que era la de la 96. Así que tú ves, no estábamos tan lejos de casa, pero tampoco tan cerca porque eran unas cuantas calles las que nos faltaban. Imagínate que eso nos hubiera pasado en la 28 o algo así. La cagazón, ¿no? Pero, bueno la cosa es que llegamos a la estación y le digo a Trompoloco: Avanza y vamos a salir de aquí. Y subimos las escaleras con todo aquel montón de gente que parecía un hormiguero cuando tú le echas agua caliente, y al salir a la calle, ¡ay, bendito! No, no, tiniebla no, porque estaban las luces de los carros y eso, ¿verdad? Pero oscuridad sí porque ni en la calle ni en los edificios había una luz prendida. Y en eso pasó un tipo con un radio de esos portátiles, y como iba caminando en la misma dirección que yo, me le emparejé y me puse a oír lo que estaba diciendo el radio. Y era lo mismo que nos había dicho el inspector allá abajo en el túnel, así que ahí se me quitó la preocupación ésa de la guerra. Pero entonces me volvió la otra, la del parto de mi mujer y eso, ¿ves?, y le digo a Trompoloco: Bueno, paisa, ahora la cosa es en el carro de don Fernando, un ratito a pie y otro andando, así que a ver quién llega primero. Y me dice él: Te voy, te voy, riéndose, ¿sabes?, como que ya se le había pasado el susto.

Y pegamos a caminar bien ligero porque además estaba haciendo frío. Y cuando íbamos por la 103 o algo así, pienso yo: Bueno, y si no hay luz en casa, ¿cómo habrán hecho para el parto? A lo mejor tuvieron que llamar la ambulancia para llevarse a mi mujer a alguna clínica y ahora yo no voy a saber ni dónde está. Porque, oye, lo que es el día que uno se levanta de malas... Entonces con esa idea en la cabeza entré yo en la recta final que parecía un campeón: yo creo que no tardamos ni cinco minutos de la 103 a casa. Y ahí mismo entro y agarro por aquellas escaleras oscuras que no veía ni los escalones y... Ah, pero ahora va a empezar lo bueno, lo que tú quieres que yo te cuente porque tú no estabas en Nueva York ese día, ¿verdad? Okay. Pues entonces vamos a pedir otras cervecitas porque tengo el gaznate más seco que aquellos arenales de Salinas donde yo me crié.

Pues como te iba diciendo. Esa noche rompí el record mundial de tres pisos de escaleras en la oscuridad. Ya ni sabía

si Trompoloco me venía siguiendo. Cuando llegué frente a la
puerta del apartamento traía la llave en la mano y la metí en
la cerradura al primer golpe, como si la estuviera viendo. Y
entonces, cuando abrí la puerta, lo primero que vi fue que había cuatro velas prendidas en la sala y unas cuantas vecinas
allí sentadas, lo más tranquilas y dándole a la sin hueso que
aquello parecía la olimpiada del bembeteo. Ave María, y es
que ése es el deporte favorito de las mujeres. Yo creo que el
día que les prohiban eso se forma una revolución más grande
que la de Fidel Castro. Pero eso sí, cuando me vieron entrar
así de sopetón les pegué un susto que se quedaron mudas de
repente. Cuantimás que yo ni siquiera dije buenas noches sino
que ahí mismo empecé a preguntar: Oigan, ¿y qué ha pasado
con mi mujer? ¿Dónde está? ¿Se la llevaron? No, hombre,
no, ella está ahí adentro lo más bien. Aquí estábamos comen-
tando que para ser el primer parto... Y en ese mismo momento oigo yo aquellos berridos que empezó a pegar mi hijo allá
en el cuarto. Bueno, yo todavía no sabía si era hijo o hija,
pero lo que sí te digo es que gritaba más que Daniel Santos
en sus buenos tiempos. Y entonces le digo a la señora: Con
permiso, doña, y me tiro para el cuarto y abro la puerta y lo
primero que veo es aquel montón de velas prendidas que eso
parecía un altar de iglesia. Y la comadrona allí trajinando con
las palanganas y los trapos y esas cosas, y mi mujer en la cama
quietecita, pero con los ojos bien abiertos. Y cuando me ve
dice, así con la voz bien finita: Ay, mi hijo, qué bueno que ya
llegaste. Yo ya estaba preocupada por ti. Fíjate, bendito, y
que preocupada por mí, ella que era la que acababa de salir
de ese brete del parto. Sí, hombre, las mujeres a veces tienen
esas cosas. Yo creo que por eso es que les aguantamos sus boberías y las queremos tanto, ¿verdad? Entonces yo le iba a
explicar el problema del subway y eso, cuando me dice la comadrona: Oiga, ese muchacho es la misma cara de usted. Venga a verlo, mire. Y era que estaba ahí en la cama, al lado de
mi mujer, pero como era tan chiquito casi ni se veía. Entonces me acerco y le miro la carita, que era lo único que se le
podía ver porque ya lo tenían más envuelto que pastel de
hoja. Y cuando yo estoy ahí mirándolo me dice mi mujer:
¿Verdad que salió a ti? Y le digo: Sí, se parece bastante. Pero
yo pensando: No, hombre, ése no se parece a mí ni a nadie,
si lo que parece es un ratón recién nacido. Pero es que así
somos todos cuando llegamos al mundo, ¿no? Y me dice mi
mujer: Pues salió machito, como tú lo querías. Y yo, por decir algo: Bueno, a ver si la próxima vez formamos la parejita.

Yo tratando de que no se me notara ese orgullo y esa felicidad que yo estaba sintiendo, ¿ves? Y entonces dice la coma-
draona: Bueno, ¿y qué nombre le van a poner? Y dice mi mujer: Pues el mismo del papá, para que no se le vaya a olvidar
que es suyo. Bromeando, tú sabes, pero con su pullita. Y yo
le digo: Bueno, nena, si ése es tu gusto... Y en eso ya mi hijo
se había callado y yo empiezo a oír como una música que venía de la parte de arriba del building, pero una música que no
era de radio ni de disco, ¿ves?, sino como de un conjunto que
estuviera allí mismo, porque a la misma vez que la música se
oía una risería y una conversación de mucha gente. Y le digo
a mi mujer: Adiós, ¿y por ahí hay bachata? Y me dice: Bueno, yo no sé, pero parece que sí porque hace rato que estamos oyendo eso. A lo mejor es un party de cumpleaños. Y
digo yo: ¿Pero así, sin luz? Y entonces dice la comadrona:
Bueno, a lo mejor hicieron igual que nosotros, que salimos
a comprar velas. Y en eso oigo yo que Trompoloco me llama
desde la sala: Oye, oye, ven acá. Sí, hombre, Trompoloco que
había llegado después que yo y se había puesto a averiguar.
Entonces salgo y le digo: ¿Qué pasa? Y me dice: Muchacho,
que allá arriba en el rufo está chévere la cosa. Sí, en el rufo, o
sea en la azotea. Y digo yo: Bueno, pues vamos a ver qué es
lo que pasa. Yo todavía sin imaginarme nada, ¿ves?

Entonces agarramos las escaleras y subimos y cuando salgo para afuera veo que allí estaba casi todo el building: doña
Lula la viuda del primer piso, Cheo el de Aguadilla que había
cerrado el cafetín cuando se fue la luz y se había metido en
su casa, las muchachas del segundo que ni trabajan ni están
en el welfare según las malas lenguas, don Leo el ministro pen-
tecostés que tiene cuatro hijos aquí y siete en Puerto Rico,
Pipo y los muchachos de doña Lula y uno de los de don Leo,
que ésos eran los que habían formado el conjunto con una
guitarra, un güiro, unas maracas y hasta unos timbales que no
sé de dónde los sacaron porque nunca los había visto por allí.
Sí, un cuarteto. Oye, ¡y sonaba! Cuando yo llegué estaban
tocando "Preciosa" y el que cantaba era Pipo, que tú sabes
que es independentista y cuando llegaba a aquella parte que
dice: *Preciosa, preciosa te llaman los hijos de la libertad*, subía la voz que yo creo que lo oían hasta en Morovis. Y yo
allí parado mirando a toda aquella gente y oyendo la canción,
cuando viene y se me acerca una de las muchachas del segundo piso, una medio gordita ella que creo que se llama Mirta, y
me dice: Oiga, qué bueno que subió. Véngase para acá para
que se dé un palito. Ah, porque tenían sus botellas y unos va-

sitos de cartón encima de una silla, y yo no sé si eran de Bacardí o Don Q, porque desde donde yo estaba no se veía tanto, pero le digo en seguida a la muchacha: Bueno, si usted me lo ofrece yo acepto con mucho gusto. Y vamos y me sirve el ron y entonces le pregunto: Bueno, ¿y por qué es la fiesta, si se puede saber? Y en eso viene doña Lula, la viuda, y me dice: Adiós, ¿pero usted no se ha fijado? Y yo miro así como buscando por los lados, pero doña Lula me dice: No, hombre, cristiano, por ahí no. Mire para arriba. Y cuando yo levanto la cabeza y miro, me dice: ¿Qué está viendo? Y yo: Pues la luna. Y ella: ¿Y qué más? Y yo: Pues las estrellas. ¡Ave María, muchacho, y ahí fue donde yo caí en cuenta! Yo creo que doña Lula me lo vio en la cara porque ya no me dijo nada más. Me puso las dos manos en los hombros y se quedó mirando ella también, quietecita, como si yo estuviera dormido y ella no quisiera despertarme. Porque yo no sé si tú me lo vas a creer, pero aquello era como un sueño. Había salido una luna de este tamaño, mira, y amarilla amarilla como si estuviera hecha de oro, y el cielo estaba todito lleno de estrellas como si todos los cocuyos del mundo se hubieran subido hasta allá arriba y después se hubieran quedado a descansar en aquella inmensidad. Igual que en Puerto Rico cualquier noche del año, pero era que después de tanto tiempo sin poder ver el cielo, por ese resplandor de los millones de luces eléctricas que se prenden aquí todas las noches, ya se nos había olvidado que las estrellas existían. Y entonces, cuando llevábamos yo no sé cuánto tiempo contemplando aquel milagro, oigo a doña Lula que me dice: Bueno, y parece que no somos los únicos que estamos celebrando. Y era verdad. Yo no podría decirte en cuántas azoteas del Barrio se hizo fiesta aquella noche, pero seguro que fue en unas cuantas, porque cuando el conjunto de nosotros dejaba de tocar oíamos clarita la música que llegaba de otros sitios. Entonces yo pensé muchas cosas. Pensé en mi hijo que acababa de nacer y en lo que iba a ser su vida aquí, pensé en Puerto Rico y en los viejos y en todo lo que dejamos allá nada más que por necesidad, pensé tantas cosas que algunas ya se me han olvidado, porque tú sabes que la mente es como una pizarra y el tiempo como un borrador que le pasa por encima cada vez que se nos llena. Pero de lo que sí me voy a acordar siempre es de lo que le dije yo entonces a doña Lula, que es lo que te voy a decir ahora para acabar de contarte lo que tú querías saber. Y es que, según mi pobre manera de entender las cosas, aquélla fue la noche que volvimos a ser gente.

Felisberto Hernández
1902–1964
Uruguay

Nadie encendía las lámparas
1947.

H ACE mucho tiempo leía yo un cuento en una sala antigua. Al principio entraba por una de las persianas un poco
de sol. Después se iba echando lentamente encima de algunas
personas hasta alcanzar una mesa que tenía retratos de muertos queridos. A mí me costaba sacar las palabras del cuerpo
como de un instrumento de fuelles rotos. En las primeras sillas estaban dos viudas dueñas de casa; tenían mucha edad,
pero todavía les abultaba bastante el pelo de los moños. Yo
leía con desgano y levantaba a menudo la cabeza del papel;
pero tenía que cuidar de no mirar siempre a una misma persona; ya mis ojos se habían acostumbrado a ir a cada momento a la región pálida que quedaba entre el vestido y el moño
de una de las viudas. Era una cara quieta que todavía seguiría recordando por algún tiempo un mismo pasado. En algunos instantes sus ojos parecían vidrios ahumados detrás de
los cuales no había nadie. De pronto yo pensaba en la importancia de algunos concurrentes y me esforzaba por entrar en
la vida del cuento. Una de las veces que me distraje vi a través de las persianas moverse palomas encima de una estatua.
Después vi, en el fondo de la sala, una mujer joven que había recostado la cabeza contra la pared; su melena ondulada estaba muy esparcida y yo pasaba los ojos por ella como
si viera una planta que hubiera crecido contra el muro de
una casa abandonada. A mí me daba pereza tener que comprender de nuevo aquel cuento y trasmitir su significado;
pero a veces las palabras solas y la costumbre de decirlas producían efecto sin que yo interviniera y me sorprendía la risa
de los oyentes. Ya había vuelto a pasar los ojos por la cabeza
que estaba recostada en la pared y pensé que la mujer acaso
se hubiera dado cuenta; entonces, para no ser indiscreto, miré
hacia la estatua. Aunque seguía leyendo, pensaba en la inocencia con que la estatua tenía que representar un personaje
que ella misma no comprendería. Tal vez ella se entendería
mejor con las palomas: parecía consentir que ellas dieran
vueltas en su cabeza y se posaran en el cilindro que el perso-

naje tenía recostado al cuerpo. De pronto me encontré con
que había vuelto a mirar la cabeza que estaba recostada contra la pared y que en ese instante ella había cerrado los ojos.
Después hice el esfuerzo de recordar el entusiasmo que yo tenía las primeras veces que había leído aquel cuento; en él había una mujer que todos los días iba a un puente con la esperanza de poder suicidarse. Pero todos los días surgían obstáculos. Mis oyentes se rieron cuando en una de las noches
alguien le hizo una proposición y la mujer, asustada, se había
ido corriendo para su casa.

La mujer de la pared también se reía y daba vuelta la cabeza en el muro como si estuviera recostada en una almohada. Yo ya me había acostumbrado a sacar la vista de aquella
cabeza y ponerla en la estatua. Quise pensar en el personaje
que la estatua representaba; pero no se me ocurría nada serio; tal vez el alma del personaje también habría perdido la
seriedad que tuvo en vida y ahora andaría jugando con las
palomas. Me sorprendí cuando algunas de mis palabras volvieron a causar gracia; miré a las viudas y vi que alguien se
había asomado a los ojos ahumados de la que parecía más
triste. En una de las oportunidades que saqué la vista de la
cabeza recostada en la pared, no miré la estatua sino a otra
habitación en la que creí ver llamas encima de una mesa; algunas personas siguieron mi movimiento; pero encima de la
mesa sólo había una jarra con flores rojas y amarillas sobre
las que daba un poco de sol.

Al terminar mi cuento se encendió el barullo y la gente
me rodeó; hacían comentarios y un señor empezó a contarme
un cuento de otra mujer que se había suicidado. El quería expresarse bien pero tardaba en encontrar las palabras; y además hacía rodeos y digresiones. Yo miré a los demás y vi que
escuchaban impacientes; todos estábamos parados y no sabíamos qué hacer con las manos. Se había acercado la mujer que
usaba esparcidas las ondas del pelo. Después de mirarla a ella,
miré la estatua. Yo no quería oír el cuento porque me hacía
sufrir el esfuerzo de aquel hombre persiguiendo palabras: era
como si la estatua se hubiera puesto en manotear las palomas.

La gente que me rodeaba no podía dejar de oír al señor
del cuento; él lo hacía con empecinamiento torpe y como si
quisiera decir: "Soy un político, sé improvisar un discurso y
también contar un cuento que tenga su interés."

Entre los que oíamos había un joven que tenía algo extraño en la frente: era una franja oscura en el lugar donde aparece el pelo; y ese mismo color —como el de una barba tupida

que ha sido recién afeitada y cubierta de polvos— le hacía
grandes entradas en la frente. Miré a la mujer del pelo espar-
cido y vi con sorpresa que ella también me miraba el pelo a
mí. Y fue entonces cuando el político terminó el cuento y
todos aplaudieron. Yo no me animé a felicitarlo y una de las
viudas dijo: "Siéntense, por favor." Todos lo hicimos y se sintió un suspiro bastante general; pero yo me tuve que levantar
de nuevo porque una de las viudas me presentó a la joven del
pelo ondeado: resultó ser sobrina de ella. Me invitaron a sentarme en un gran sofá para tres; de un lado se puso la sobrina
y del otro el joven de la frente pelada. Iba a hablar la sobrina,
pero el joven la interrumpió. Había levantado una mano con
los dedos hacia arriba —como el esqueleto de un paraguas que
el viento hubiera doblado— y dijo:

—Adivino en usted un personaje solitario que se confor-
maría con la amistad de un árbol.

Yo pensé que se había afeitado así para que la frente fuera más amplia, y sentí la maldad de contestarle:

—No crea; a un árbol, no podría invitarlo a pasear.

Los tres nos reímos. El echó hacia atrás su frente pelada
y siguió:

—Es verdad. El árbol es el amigo que siempre se queda.

Las viudas llamaron a la sobrina. Ella se levantó haciendo
un gesto de desagrado; yo la miraba mientras se iba, y sólo
entonces me di cuenta que era fornida y violenta. Al volver
la cabeza me encontré con un joven que me fue presentado
por el de la frente pelada. Estaba recién peinado y tenía gotas
de agua en las puntas del pelo. Una vez yo me peiné así, cuando era niño y mi abuela me dijo: "Parece que te hubieran *lam-
bido* las vacas.' El recién llegado se sentó en el lugar de la sobrina y se puso a hablar:

—¡Ah, Dios mío, ese señor del cuento, tan recalcitrante!

De buena gana yo le hubiera dicho: "¿Y usted?, ¿tan femenino?" Pero le pregunté:

—¿Cómo se llama?

—¿Quién?

—El señor... recalcitrante.

—Ah, no recuerdo. Tiene un nombre patricio. Es un político y siempre lo ponen de miembro en los certámenes literarios.

Yo miré al de la frente pelada y él me hizo un gesto como
diciendo: "¡Y qué le vamos a hacer!"

Cuando vino la sobrina de las viudas sacó del sofá al "femenino" sacudiéndolo de un brazo y haciéndole caer gotas de
agua en el saco. Y en seguida dijo:

- No estoy de acuerdo con ustedes.
— ¿Por qué?
—... y me extraña que ustedes no sepan cómo hace el árbol para pasear con nosotros.
— ¿Cómo?
— Se repite a largos pasos.
Le elogiamos la idea y ella se entusiasmó:
—Se repite en una avenida indicándonos el camino; después todos se juntan a lo lejos y se asoman para vernos; y a medida que nos acercamos se separan y nos dejan pasar.

Ella dijo todo esto con cierta afectación de broma y como disimulando una idea romántica. El pudor y el placer la hicieron enrojecer. Aquel encanto fue interrumpido por el femenino:

- Sin embargo, cuando es la noche en el bosque, los árboles nos asaltan por todas partes; algunos se inclinan como para dar un paso y echársenos encima; y todavía nos interrumpen el camino y nos asustan abriendo y cerrando las ramas.

La sobrina de las viudas no se pudo contener:
— ¡Jesús, pareces Blancanieves.

Y mientras nos reíamos, ella me dijo que deseaba hacerme una pregunta y fuimos a la habitación donde estaba la jarra con flores. Ella se recostó en la mesa hasta hundirse la tabla en el cuerpo; y mientras se metía las manos entre el pelo, me preguntó:

- Dígame la verdad: ¿por qué se suicidó la mujer de su cuento?
— ¡Oh!, habría que preguntárselo a ella.
—Y usted, ¿no lo podría hacer?
—Sería tan imposible como preguntarle algo a la imagen de un sueño.

Ella sonrió y bajó los ojos. Entonces yo pude mirarle toda la boca, que era muy grande. El movimiento de los labios, estirándose hacia los costados, parecía que no terminaría más; pero mis ojos recorrían con gusto toda aquella distancia de rojo húmedo. Tal vez ella viera a través de los párpados; o pensara que en aquel silencio yo no estuviera haciendo nada bueno porque bajó mucho la cabeza y escondió la cara. Ahora mostraba toda la masa del pelo; en un remolino de las ondas se le veía un poco de la piel, y yo recordé a una gallina que el viento le había revuelto las plumas y se le veía la carne. Yo sentía placer en imaginar que aquella cabeza era una gallina humana, grande y caliente; su calor sería muy delicado y el pelo era una manera muy fina de las plumas.

Vino una de las tías - la que no tenía los ojos ahumados— a traernos copitas de licor. La sobrina levantó la cabeza y la tía le dijo:

- Hay que tener cuidado con éste; mira que tiene ojos de zorro.

Volví a pensar en la gallina y le contesté:

- ¡Señora! ¡No estamos en un gallinero!

Cuando nos volvimos a quedar solos y mientras yo probaba el licor – era demasiado dulce y me daba náuseas—, ella me preguntó.

- ¿Usted no tuvo nunca curiosidad por conocer el porvenir?

Había encogido la boca como si la quisiera guardar dentro de la copita.

—No, tengo más curiosidad por saber lo que le ocurre en este mismo instante a otra persona; o en saber qué haría yo ahora si estuviera en otra parte.

—Dígame, ¿qué haría usted ahora si yo no estuviera aquí?

—Casualmente lo sé: volcaría este licor en la jarra de las flores.

Me pidieron que tocara el piano. Al volver a la sala, la viuda de los ojos ahumados estaba con la cabeza baja y recibía en el oído lo que la hermana le decía con insistencia. El piano era pequeño, viejo y desafinado. Yo no sabía qué tocar; pero apenas empecé a probarlo la viuda de los ojos ahumados soltó el llanto y todos nos callamos. La hermana y la sobrina la llevaron para adentro; y al ratito vino la sobrina y nos dijo que su tía no quería oír música desde la muerte de su esposo —se habían amado hasta llegar a la inocencia.

Los invitados empezaron a irse. Y los que quedamos hablábamos en voz cada vez más baja a medida que la luz se iba. Nadie encendía las lámparas.

Yo me iba entre los últimos tropezando con los muebles, cuando la sobrina me detuvo:

Tengo que hacerle un encargo.

Pero no me dijo nada: recostó la cabeza en la pared del zaguán y me tomó la manga del saco.

Carmen Lugo Filippi
1940—
Puerto Rico

Milagros, calle Mercurio
Vírgenes y mártires, 1981.

> *Ha muerto la blanca Caperucita Roja.*
> Evaristo Ribera Chevremont

DESPUÉS de haber trabajado en salones elegantes, con estilistas de ésos que concursan todos los años en Nueva York o París, el cambio de ambiente me había deprimido bastante, pero traté de ajustarme a mi nuevo medio diciéndome que esto era mucho mejor que vivir alquilada, recibiendo órdenes todo el tiempo por un sueldo y unas propinas que no compensaban el atropellado horario de los viernes sociales y los sábados tumultuosos, cuando una barahúnda de señoras y turistas invadía el cachendoso local de Isla Verde en busca de la belleza perdida. Me entretenía muchísimo con las turistas, sobre todo con las españolas. Junito me las entregaba porque diz que yo tenía clase para tratarlas. Digamos que la única con un haber de tres años universitarios y experiencia en el extranjero era esta servidora y ello me otorgaba la supremacía entre las diez ayudantes de Junito. Claro que tal deferencia había creado al principio resentimiento entre las muchachas y sólo a fuerza de sonrisas y amabilidades había logrado disiparlo. Tal vez fue la sinceridad de mis explicaciones lo que las calmó: tres años de literatura comparada no aseguraban a nadie un puesto en las esferas intelectuales, mucho menos sin haber terminado el dichoso bachillerato. En cierta medida dulcificaba sus amargas frustraciones cuando les aseguraba que muchas mujeres con un flamante diploma en letras se veían obligadas a buscar trabajo en los aeropuertos o a volar como azafatas si no querían morirse de hambre. Más se ganaba con unos cursos de estilismo que son tres años de literatura o de idiomas... Así las manipulaba y me dejaban tranquila rumiar mi propia frustración, que ya era bastante.

Sí, porque nunca me había perdonado haber abandonado tan precipitadamente la Facultad para casarme con Freddie. Debí haber conseguido el diploma, debí haber seguido escribiendo, debí, debí... Todos aseguraban que tenía mucho talento cuando gané el segundo premio en aquel concurso literario del Ateneo. Aún me pregunto qué carajo me cegó. Quizás fue el temor de quedarme solterona: las jamonas empedernidas me horrorizaban, sobre todo, cuando pensaba en mi pobre tía esclavizada cuidando a mi abuela y al tío Manuel. Lo cierto es que cuando apareció Freddie en el panorama perdí la chaveta: él me prometió villas y castillas, viviríamos cerca de la base de Torrejón en Madrid, adonde sería trasladado ese próximo año. ¡Viajes, qué chulería! De Madrid sería fácil ir hasta Francia, donde podría practicar mis dos años de franchute, y de allí no habría que dar más que un saltito a la bellísima Italia.

Esos sueños nunca se realizaron porque Freddie no podía abandonar Madrid y yo salí encinta. Cuando la nena cumplió un año ya me encontraba al borde de una neurosis. La rutina doméstica me aplastaba; necesitaba respirar otros aires y más que nada hablar con alguien que me comprendiera. Freddie se limitaba a contarme sobre sus andanzas en la base, y eso cuando le daba la real gana. Mili, la chica que me peinaba, se compadeció de mi tremenda soledad y me pidió que la ayudara a lavar cabezas por las tardes. Fue así como me inicié en las artes peinoriles: descubrí una habilidad inusitada en mis dedos y mi imaginación se colmaba inventando peinados extravagantes. Mili me aseguró que nunca se había topado con una estilista de mi calibre. Me obligó a seguir un cursillo intensivo de maquillaje y peinados. No la defraudé: fui la primera de la clase.

Aquella fue la época de mi boom. Trabajé a gusto en un salón elegantísimo de la Avenida Goya. Todas las empleadillas quedaban boquiabiertas con mi sapiencia: la políglota, me decían. No sólo las deslumbraba delante de las turistas gringas, sino también frente a las francesas. Nunca en verdad me había sentido tan importante.

Aunque mi matrimonio no andaba bien, el trabajo compensaba la aburrida convivencia con mi insulso marido, quien sólo sabía jugar a los caballos y frecuentar el Officer's Club.

Cuando vino con el cuento del traslado a Alabama, supe a ciencia cierta que me importaba un comino su carrera militar. Empaqué mis bártulos y le dije un hasta luego que luego se convirtió en adiós definitivo. Fue lo mejor para los dos.

El trabajo en el salón de Junito me distrajo. A veces me divertía con las ridiculeces de varias señoras, perfectos monigotes con ínfulas de grandes damas. Las reconocía al instante y me entregaba placenteramente a la tarea de mortificarlas. Un comentario inocentemente mordaz, una discreta crítica

y finalmente ¡zas!, les cortaba los vuelos con sólo corregirles
el inglés chapurreado... Tenía tal maestría para bajarles los
humos que el mismo Junito se asombraba de mi "savoir faire".
Cuando clamaban por un "setting fabuloso" arqueaba las cejas y, solícita, subrayaba con articulación perfecto: ¿el fija-
dor para el cabello grasoso o para el cabello seco? Y ni se diga
cuando pedían el "spray profesional". Entonces me inclinaba
majestuosamente, como una modelo de Miss Clairol, señalando inocentemente "el aerosol" con proteínas acabado de recibir. El resultado no se hacía esperar: depositaban en mis bolsillos generosas propinas que ascendían al 15% y de paso me
obsequiaban con una furtiva mirada de respetuosa admiración.

   Hubiera seguido allí a no ser por mi madre, quien cantaleta en mano me convenció de establecer negocio propio en los
bajos de su casa en Ponce. "Te irá bien, nena, ya verás", repetía constantemente. "Allí hay clientela segura, no seas boba,
piensa que no tienes que pagar local".

   Y así fue como llegué a la Mercurio, más por complacer a
mamá que por gusto propio. Al cabo de dos semanas, ya estaba establecida en aquel primer piso de nuestra modesta casa.
Lucía coquetón el lugar con sus paredes recién empapeladas,
sus *collages* de cortes y peinados que yo misma había ideado
sobre planchas de *plywood* negra y sus tres secadoras idénticas, alineadas frente a un gran espejo de marco sencillo (de-
testaba los pretenciosos ribetes dorados de los espejos de Wool-
worth's).

   La clientela no se hizo esperar: en vísperas de graduacio-
nes tuve casa llena durante tres largos días. Desfilaron, sobre
todo, muchachas de noveno grado con sus respectivas mamás,
unas para recorte y peinado, otras para tintes y permanentes,
y un número considerable para alisados.

   El ambiente era en general humildón (frecuentaban sema-
nalmente cuatro o cinco enfermeras, dos maestras, ocho se-
cretarias y numerosas empleadas de fábricas y tiendas por departamento). No tenía mayores quejas porque hacía mi dine-
rito sin matarme mucho y además estaba con mami, gran ayuda en aquellos días de soledad. Ahorraba cuanto podía para
matricularme nuevamente en la Universidad, mi única ambición entonces.

   Fue justamente en esa época cuando vi por vez primera
a Milagros. La recuerdo tan vivamente, tal como si estuviera
viendo una película española en blanco y negro, de esas bien
sombrías que transcurren en un pueblecito de mala muerte,
donde la esbelta protagonista de pelo larguísimo camina len-

tamente y de pronto la cámara se le acerca; perfecto "close-up" algo parsimonioso que resbala por la cara blanquísima y se regodea en las facciones inexpresivas, sobre todo, en la mirada lánguida y como ausente.

Pasaba puntualmente hacia las cuatro, a su regreso de la escuela superior, vestida con su uniforme crema y marrón, impasible pues no sonreía ni al rey de Roma, con la cabeza siempre erguida, los hombros en perfectísimo balance, probablemente para mantener aquella armoniosa combinación de movimientos de sus extremidades, prodigioso mecanismo de exactitud, mediante el cual hombros y piernas avanzaban acompasadamente, sin perder ni un solo instante el rítmico momentum inicial.

Contemplarla, suscitaba en mí un extraño fenómeno de correspondencias: cine, literatura, pintura, música se aunaban desordenadamente para devolverme la ecléctica imagen de una criatura extraña, misteriosa, que bajo ninguna circunstancia pertenecía a aquella calle común y bonachona. Imaginaba a la muchacha revolucionando el salón de Junito con su entrada sorpresiva, despertando miradas de envidia entre más de una señora a dieta y encendiendo la codiciosa admiración de Junito, que se aprestaría sin duda alguna a ofrecerle en bandeja de plata fama y billetes, con tal de que modelara su último peinado en el concurso de estilismo en Nueva York.

Sí, porque constituía para ti un verdadero reto el pelo de Milagros. Incluso fantaseabas con los posibles cortes, verdaderas obras maestras dignas de figurar en *Hair & Style* o en *Jours de France*. Por eso una tarde ya no aguantaste más y en son de chisme le dijiste a doña Fefa: "Bendito, qué pena, la Milagros no se cuida el pelo, se le va a dañar". Y doña Fefa, cuya sin hueso era más bien benévola, te ripostó que la culpa de esa atrocidad era la madre de la muchacha, quien le tenía prohibido que se tocara un solo pelo, tan aleluya esa vieja, tú no sabes, Marina, de lo que es capaz el fanatismo.

Entonces entendiste por qué tampoco se pintaba y por qué usaba siempre, aún en pleno verano aquellas blusas conventuales. Le diste cuerda a doña Fefa, bautista progre, quien en un santiamén te contó vida y obra de la familia en cuestión. "Vélalas, que a eso de las siete pasan como clavo caliente pal culto".

Fuiste tú, Marina, el clavo caliente que se apostó en el balcón para observar la peregrinación crepuscular de Milagros. La madre avanzaba a trancazos, la Biblia bajo el brazo, y su apocalíptica seriedad contrastaba con el gesto cómico-grotesco de literalmente arrastrar a una niña de siete o seis años a lo sumo, muy parecida a Milagros, por lo que dedujiste que era su hermana. A un pie de distancia, Milagros las seguía sin alterar en lo más mínimo su rítmico trote. Llevaba también un libro, aunque mucho más delgado ¿de oraciones o himnos, acaso? La sobriedad de aquella figura se sumió en graves reminiscencias cinematográficas de cuando aún tenías aquellas inquietudes de intelectual de tercer año, con asistencia perfecta al cine-club universitario (Buñuel, Bardem, Pasolini y adláteres). Escena típica buñuelesca, dictaminaste ese martes, regodeándote en la sensación de superioridad que te otorgaba tu cultura cinematográfica y tus consuetudinarias discusiones con el pretencioso grupito del pasillo de Humanidades, ¡cuánto los recuerdas a todos!, acuclillados en una esquina de Pedreira, pretendiendo saberlo todo o adoptando actitudes de olímpico cinismo. Por un momento deseaste que hubieran estado allí, contemplando desde la torre las figurillas en movimiento, para luego elaborar las teorías más abstrusas y de paso enfrascarse en animadas discusiones existencialistas. Pero sólo estabas tú.

A partir de ese martes continuaste observándolas crepuscularmente para añadir matices a tu ya formada imagen. Notaste, por ejemplo, que Milagros se retrasaba, y por ello su madre se veía obligada a aguardarla durante varios minutos en la esquina Victoria para entonces cruzar la intersección. Anotabas también los leves cambios en el atuendo de la muchacha: un discreto escote en forma de V, una falda más ceñida que de costumbre, unas sandalias baratas pero algo pizpiretas.

No pude retener por más tiempo mi creciente curiosidad y un miércoles las seguí a distancia con el secreto propósito de colarme entre los fieles para así gozar de cerca los misteriosos ritos practicados por aquellas puntuales mujeres. Mi loca imaginación las asociaba con trances histéricos, cuando el mesar de cabellos y el frenético sacudimiento de manos y brazos se sucederían histéricamente. No podía concebir a la pausada Milagros en tal estado de vulgar frenesí.

Lo que presencié esa noche me impresionó muchísimo, tanto que luego me sorprendía a cada momento rememorando las escenas: sobre todo, aquel estrepitoso ¡Manda fuego, señor, manda fuego! ahogado súbitamente por el estallido imprevisto de una pandereta cuya secuela de tintineos duraba varios segundos, a modo de fondo musical para chillones gritos esporádicos de Aleluyas y Glorias, salpicados de lastimosos ayes y suspiros entrecortados. La madre de Milagros se transformaba: aumentaba de estatura (¿irguiéndose acaso en la punta de sus zapatacones?), mientras blandía sus brazos a diestra y siniestra con tal ímpetu que temí varias veces ver a Milagros derribada sobre el banco. Pero lo que en realidad me sacó de quicio y hasta me divirtió por lo contrastante, era la estampa de la muchacha, quien, hierática, contemplaba el espectáculo, ladeando levemente su cabeza con aquel magnífico gesto de indiferencia.

Dos días más tarde, un sábado precisamente, me llevé una gran sorpresa pues allí estaban ambas, esperándome junto a la puerta del salón. La madre se adelantó y sin mayores rodeos me hizo saber que a su hija se le estaba cayendo el pelo y que necesitaba urgentemente algún tratamiento de esos que yo daba.

Examiné con experta circunspección el cuero cabelludo de la esfinge y dictaminé una soriasis aguda. El tratamiento tomaría unas tres semanas, pues la cantidad de pelo de Milagros hacía más difícil los masajes, y cada vez que tenía que aplicarle gorros calientes era una verdadera odisea acomodar aquella bonita maleza. Se me prohibió cortar uno solo de aquellos cabellos: así que la tarea resultaba bastante engorrosa, a no ser por la inesperada oportunidad de poder observar bien de cerca la expresión de la madonita. ¿Sería una retrasada mental, con aires de modelo sanjuanera?

Mientras estuvo allí con la madre, no dijo ni esta boca es mía. Permaneció sentada mirando fijamente su imagen en el gran espejo del tocador, sin pestañear casi.

Volvió el martes para recibir el primer tratamiento. Esta vez llegó sola. Vestía el uniforme de la escuela y lucía más pálida que de costumbre. La saludé cordialmente y le pregunté ¿qué tal las clases?, a lo que ella respondió con un lacónico "bien". Hice caso omiso de su cortedad y proseguí mi monólogo advirtiéndole del peligro que corría de quedarse calva si no se daba un corte a tiempo, de la necesidad de cuidarse el pelo. "Es como una planta, chica, tienes que podarla", clisé que me pareció oportuno. Me acerqué por detrás y con gesto de peinadora profesional le recogí las mechas en suave remolino, obligándola a mirarse en el espejo, y con un casual "fíjate, qué mona te ves, tan diferente, pareces una artista de película", le coloqué uno de esos peines de moda lleno de miosotis rosados y amarillos. Se conmovió, sí, no cabía duda, porque se echó impetuosamente hacia el frente y miró con admiración el fondo del espejo, como si la imagen no le perteneciera. Luego, sonreída, me echó una ojeada, sin saber qué decir. Le busqué revistas que mostraban diversos tipos de recortes y, mientras le colocaba el gorro caliente, sugerí que escogiera el que más le gustara. "No me dejan recortar", dijo secamente. Pese a ello se sumió en la contemplación de las imágenes.

Durante el tercer tratamiento, Milagros parecía menos cohibida. Incluso me pedía revistas y hasta fotonovelas, tipo de literatura esencial en cualquier salón de belleza. Recuerdo cuando le presté aquel *Vanidades* que traía un largo artículo ilustrado sobre cómo maquillarse de acuerdo con el tipo de rostro. De cuando en vez la muchacha interrumpía la lectura para hacerme una pregunta acerca de tal o cual término. La precisión en la manera de formular las preguntas acusaba un espíritu incisivo e inteligente. Aproveché la ocasión para averiguar qué haría al terminar la escuela superior y sus comentarios fueron evasivos. Se sumió en la contemplación de las fotos y pasó largo rato sin volver a abrir la boca.

En una ocasión, no sé si fue martes o jueves, Milagros llegó a eso de las tres al salón. No tenía clientes ese día, natural flojera de mediados de mes, así que la dejé unos treinta minutos sola, mientras iba hasta el "Supply" a hacer varias compras urgentes, creo que unas cajas de placentas.

Al regresar, me extrañó mucho escuchar música, pues no había dejado el radio puesto. Entré sin hacer ruido y sorprendí a Milagros de espaldas, frente al aparato colocado en un improvisado anaquel junto a la puerta del fondo. Me sorprendió gratamente oírla repetir con tímida voz de contralto el *hit* del momento: "Tu amor es un periódico de ayer/ fue titular que alcanzó página entera". Pero quedé aún más divertida cuando, balanceándose rítmicamente, la Milagros repetía con voz de falsete una y otra vez aquel "... y para qué leer un periódico de ayer/ y para qué leer un periódico de ayer". No interrumpí su acto, al contrario la dejé inmersa en su contoneo. Pareció abochornada cuando me alcanzó a ver. Fingí no prestar atención a la escena y continué la rutinaria colocación de productos en las tablillas. Con gesto indiferente le indiqué que podía continuar escuchando la música. Fue inútil. Ni siquiera el salsudo estribillo de "La vida te da sorpresas, sorpresas te da la vida..." logró arrancarla del súbito hieratismo. Su rigidez repentina me provocó lástima.

El tratamiento llegó a su término con exitosos resultados. Se despidió un jueves agradecidísima, llevándose un paquete de revistas envueltas en papel de estraza.

Siempre que regresaba de la escuela se detenía unos minutos para saludarme. Noté, sin embargo, que durante las últimas semanas de noviembre pasaba a eso de las cinco. Pensé que se debía a un cambio de horario y no le puse más atención a ese detalle. Andaba en esos días muy atareada entre telas y costureras porque la nena iba a ser paje en la boda de mi prima.

Aquel primer lunes de diciembre, lo aproveché para recoger, por encargo de mi prima, las puchas que llevarían las damas y algunas otras chucherías que adornarían las mesas de los invitados durante la recepción. Respetaba por conveniencia el mandamiento de los zapateros y jamás abría el local ese día. Entre una y otra diligencia, llegué a casa a eso de las cinco. No bien puse los pies en la esquina, noté que algo anormal ocurría. Divisé a lo lejos cuatro o cinco vecinas reunidas frente a la casa de doña Fina. Gesticulaban ostentosamente, por lo que deduje que algo gordo se cocía en el ambiente. Fui directamente hacia ellas y he de decir que me recibieron en su sacrosanto seno con una expresión de ¿malevolencia?, ¿conspiración?, ¿complacencia?, ¿piadosa consternación? Doña Fina soltó su rollo sin que tuviera que hacerle la más mínima solicitud. "Fue a eso de las cuatro, nena, yo estaba barriendo las hojas de esas dichosas quenepas cuando vi pasar una patrulla. ¿A quién habrán asaltao?, tú sabes. Marinita, con tanto crimen, es lo único en que se piensa... El carro se paró frente a los aleluyas y vi a Rada, mi sobrino, el que es guardia, tú lo has visto. ¿Y a que no te imaginas a quién bajaron de la patrulla? ¡A la Milagros, nena, a la Milagros! Creí que le había pasao algún accidente y corrí a ver, pa ayudal. Pero nena, lo que vi aún no lo creo, ¡pol poco me caigo de culetazo! La Milagros no se parecía, era otra, to pintarreá, con un emplaste...! La metieron pa dentro y yo la seguí, porque doña Luisa se había quedao pasmá en la puerta. Rada me hizo señas que me saliera. ¡La que se folmó, Marinita, la de San Quintín, fíjate que los gritos se oían hasta en la Calle Reina, yo no me imaginaba cuánta mala palabra sabía doña Luisa, polque de puta pa bajo le espetó una salta de palabras sucias... Me da vergüenza, nena, repetirlas. ¡Hasta hija de Satanás la llamó!

"Yo me vine pa ca a esperar a Rada, tú sabes que el siempre viene a tomal café, así que me senté en el balcón y al ratito llegó él, colorao y nervioso. ¡Lo que me contó, Marinita, por eso digo que del agua mansa me libre Dios! No se puede creer en nadie, nena, la Milagros tan seriecita, tan mosquita muerta y mira lo que hacía cuando salía de la escuela, na menos que esnuándose en un club de la carretera pa Guayanilla, esnuándose, oye eso, y que esnuándose!"

Respiró hondo y nos contempló a todas, gozándose en nuestro claro estupor, en nuestras miradas incrédulas y a la vez suplicantes. Con suma complacencia estiraba la oración de transición, aquella que nos introduciría en el antro pecaminoso, mágica frase de pase, santo y seña que abriría el misterioso recinto para permitirnos contemplar el secreto ritual de la sacerdotisa...

"Rada fue en la patrulla a esa club de Guayanilla porque alguien había choteao y que allí un chorro de viejos ricos de Ponce se juntaban a ver nenas esnuándose, eso que llaman estritís... El y dos guardias más los cogieron a tos por sorpresa, con las manos en la masa, porque entraron callaítos y dice Rada que to estaba como boca de lobo, lo único que se veía y que era una mesa grande con luces de esas que dan vueltas, claro, si allí era que se hacían las pocavelgüenzas, cómo no iban a habel luces, y de las grandes... Toítos los viejos veldes y que arremolinaos, cayéndoseles las babas, eso sí con musiquita y tragos, chorro de degeneraos, hasta médicos y abogaos había en la pandolga..."

Y mientras doña Fina, ya incontenible, recuenta la escena, vas recreando, Marina, cada detalle, fascinada ante el abismal mundo que en ese instante cobra forma, dejándote arrastrar por la facilidad con que se dibujan y desdibujan las imágenes sugeridas, vértigo visual que te obliga a reclinarte sobre el quenepo para así poder mantener la secuencia del tropel de escenas y cortes que transcurren ininterrumpidamente.

Ahí está Rada colándose por la discreta puerta que un falso cortinaje de cuentas azuladas se empeña en disimular. Se adentra sin mayores dificultades, pero la repentina oscuridad lo obliga a tantear las paredes, hasta que de pronto divisa más adelante otro nutrido cortinaje similar al primero: separa con suavidad las cuentas para no delatar su presencia y escurre su cachetuda cara en el improvisado hueco... Ni una sola voz. Sólo jadeantes respiraciones rezongan sobre la sinuosa melodía que en cámara lenta se desgrana. Renovadas capas de humo se acumulan alrededor de un punto impreciso que misteriosamente aparece y desaparece cuando la luz caprichosa del girante reflector se detiene unos segundos. El Rada avanza hacia el grupo y aupándose capta el momento efímero cuando la azulada luz descubre una blanquísima masa vibrante que se enrosca al compás de las quejosas notas de un saxofón. Ya no puede apartar sus ojos del improvisado altar e hipnotizado co-

mo todos aquellos acólitos sexagenarios, sólo aguarda el gran
retorno de la luz. Sí, porque ahora, bien despacito, el reflector
se complace en recorrer pícaramente el gracioso pie que se levanta a la vez que los platillos estallan jubilosos una y otra
vez. La masa lechosa inicia su sensual contoneo, mientras el
estribillo pegajoso de la melodía se impone. Esta vez la luz
indiscreta persigue los convulsivos movimientos y el Rada entonces se excita viendo cómo la serpentosa figura se yergue
de espaldas y muestra con estudiada morosidad dos perfectas
redondeces que contrastan con la llana geografía del suave
torso. Y así, de espaldas, la gata sigilosa levanta los brazos a la
altura de la nuca en espera del platillazo decisivo, aquél que
le indicará cuándo ha de arrancar la hebilla que retiene su pelo, movimiento imprescindible que precede a la frontal y apo-
teósica voltereta final, reveladora de las más íntimas desnude-
ces. Los jadeos parecen haber cesado bajo el influjo de ese
momento perfecto: conspiración simultánea de flechadas miradas hambrientas que hieren al unísono la imagen indefensa
de la diosa-ninfa. Y ahí está Milagros, ante los asombrados
ojos del Rada, quien parpadea incrédulo, quien se frota los
ojos para despertar y ver siempre aquellos muslos lechosos,
adornados por un montoncito de pelo lleno de pizpiretos miosotis. Ajeno ahora a las roncas risitas, a los libidinosos conju-
ros de los sexagenarios sacerdotes, a los obstinados trompeta-
zos que van sosteniendo la puesta en pie de la Milagros, el Rada no despega sus ojos de los menudos senos que comienzan a
flotar y sólo el estruendoso platillazo final lo devuelve a la
realidad.

Así debió ser, Marina. El rito se cumplió y la Milagros fue
ovacionada pese a los gritos del recién indignado Rada, quien
de vuelta al deber, ordenaba, revólver en mano, encender todas las luces. "Y se almó la de San Quintín, Marinita, un corre-
corre tremendo, pero como casi tos eran unos viejos churrien-
tos se amansaron rápido, los que eran abogaos trataron de meterle miedo a Rada con jueces amigos y qué se yo. Total, que
a ellos no les hubiera pasao na, aquí esas cosas se tapan con
la política y el dinero... y como Rada no quería perjudical a
la Milagros los dejó ilse sin denunciarlos pa así poder trael la
aleluya a la mai. Ese sí que es un muchacho noble..."

Contemplas, Marina, la casita silenciosa al final de la calle
y te preguntas en cuál rincón estará Milagros doliéndose de
los golpes y en espera de los implacables moretones que irán
floreciendo a medida que caiga la noche.

De pesadilla en pesadilla vadeas los intermitentes desvelos

y el amanecer te sorprende con la imagen obsesiva del Rada
en trance ante el altar pecaminoso. Y durante este martes
sombrío, en tu ir y venir por el salón, la escena te persigue y
por más que quieres abreviarla, no puedes, porque se adhiere
con obstinación a tu pantalla.

Por eso no te has dado cuenta de que son casi ya las once
y aún no has puesto en orden los rolos y las hebillas. ¡Qué
impresionable eres, Marina, esa mocosa ha alterado el orden
de tu sacrosanta rutina! Pules cuidadosamente la formica de
las improvisadas coquetas y con una hoja húmeda de periódico frotas los espejos que te entregan de pronto la imagen de
la Milagros, sí, de ella misma, ¿estarás soñando? Pero no, allí
está junto a la puerta, mirándote parsimoniosamente, sin pestañear, un poco ladeada a causa de la maleta que lleva en la
mano izquierda... Sin volverte la examinas en el espejo... Sí,
es ella, no cabe duda; un tanto diferente por la indumentaria
que consiste en unos ceñidos mahones color vino, ¿Qué de-
seas, Milagros?, casi susurras, incapaz de mirarla de frente,
aunque siempre observando el espejo. Ella entonces da un paso decidido y saca del bolsillo derecho de su pantalón un flamante billete de veinte, billete que blande, airosa, y con tono suave, pero firme, hace su reclamo: "Maquíllame en shocking red, Marina, y córtame como te dé la gana". Un temblequeo, apenas perceptible, comienza a apoderarse de tus rodillas, pero aun así no logras apartar los ojos del espejo donde
la Milagros se agranda, asume dimensiones colosales, viene hacia ti, sí, viene hacia ti en busca de una respuesta, de esa respuesta que ella urge y que tendrás que dar, no puedes apla-
zarla, Marina, mírate y mírala, Marina, ¿qué responderás?

René Marqués
1919–
Puerto Rico

Purificación en la calle del Cristo

En una ciudad llamada San Juan, 1960. (Publicado originalmente en la *Revista del Instituto de Cultura Puertorriqueña,* en 1958).

> *Time is the fire in which we burn.*
> Delmore Schwartz *(Time is the fire)*

LA casa está sola —dijo Inés. Y Emilia asintió. Aunque no era cierto. Allí también estaba Hortensia, como siempre, las tres reunidas en la gran sala, las tres puertas de dos hojas cerradas como siempre sobre el balcón, las persianas apenas entreabiertas, la luz del amanecer rompiéndose en tres colores (azul, amarillo, rojo) a través de los cristales alemanes que formaban una rueda trunca sobre cada una de las puertas, o un sol tricolor, trunco también, cansado de haber visto morir un siglo y nacer otro, de las innumerables capas de polvo que la lluvia arrastraba luego, y de los años de salitre depositados sobre los cristales una vez transparentes, y que ahora parecían esmerilados, oponiendo mayor resistencia a la luz, a todo lo de afuera que pudiera ser claro, o impuro, o extraño (hiriente en fin).

—¿Recuerdas? —preguntó Inés. Y Emilia asintió.

No era preciso asentir a algo determinado porque la vida toda era un recuerdo, o quizá una serie de recuerdos, y en cualquiera de ellos podía situarse cómodamente para asentir a la pregunta de Inés, que pudo haber sido formulada por Hortensia, o por ella misma, y no precisamente en el instante de este amanecer, sino el día anterior o el mes pasado o un año antes, aunque el recuerdo bien pudiera remontarse al otro siglo: Estrasburgo, por ejemplo, en aquella época imprecisa (impreciso era el orden cronológico, no el recuerdo ciertamente), en que las tres se preparaban en el colegio para ser lo que a su rango correspondía en la ciudad de San Juan, adivinando ella e Inés que sería Hortensia quien habría de deslumbrar en los salones, aunque las tres aprendieran por igual los pequeños secretos de vivir graciosamente en un mundo apacible y equilibrado, donde no habría cabida para lo que no fuese bello, para las terribles vulgaridades de una humanidad que no debía (no podía) llegar hasta las frágiles *fräulein,* protegidas no tanto por los espesos muros del colegio como por la labor complicada de los encajes, y los tapices, y la bru-

ma melodiosa de los *lieder,* y la férrea caballerosidad de los
más jóvenes oficiales prusianos. ¡Hortensia! Hortensia, en
su traje de raso azul, cuando asistió a la primera recepción en
La Fortaleza (el Gobernador General bailando una mazurca
con su hermana mayor bajo la mirada fría de papá Bukhart).
Eso es. Hortensia ya en San Juan. El colegio, atrás en el tiempo. Y ella, Emilia, observando el mundo deslumbrante del
palacio colonial en esa noche memorable, al lado de la figura
imponente de la madre. (Mamá Eugenia, con su soberbio porte de reina; su cabello oscuro y espeso como el vino de Málaga sobre el cual tan bien lucía la diadema de zafiros y brillantes; con su tez pálida y mate que el sol del trópico inútilmente había tratado de dorar, porque el sol de Andalucía le había dado ya el tinte justo; con su traje negro de encajes y su
enorme pericón de ébano y seda, donde un cisne violáceo se
deslizaba siempre sobre un estanque con olor a jazmín.) Y
ella, Emilia, con sus trenzas apretadas (odiosas trenzas), hecha un ovillo de rubor cuando el alférez español se inclinó
galante a su oído para murmurar: *Es usted más hermosa que
su hermana Hortensia.*

* * *

Inés vio a Emilia asentir a su pregunta y pensó: *No puedes recordar, Emilia. Los más preciosos recuerdos los guardo yo.*

Porque a su pregunta, ¿*Recuerdas?,* supo que Emilia iría
a refugiarse en el recuerdo de siempre. Que no era en verdad
un recuerdo, sino la sombra de un recuerdo, porque Emilia
no lo había vivido.

Emilia, con sus trenzas apretadas (hermosas trenzas), se
había quedado en casa con la vieja nana. (Emilia, con su pequeño pie torcido desde aquella terrible caída del caballo en
la hacienda de Toa Alta, obstinada en huir de la gente, aun en
el colegio, siempre apartada de los corros, del bullicio; haciendo esfuerzos dolorosos por ocultar su cojera, que no era
tan ostensible después de todo, pero que tan hondo hería su
orgullo; refugiándose en los libros o en el cuaderno de versos
que escribía a hurtadillas.) Y ella, Inés, no logrando lucir hermosa en el traje color perla que hacía resaltar su tipo medite-
rráneo, porque tenía el mismo color de tez de mamá Eugenia,
el mismo cabello espeso y oscuro, pero inútilmente, porque
nada había en sus rasgos que hiciese recordar la perfección
helena del rostro materno (era francamente fea: desde pequeña se lo había revelado la crueldad del espejo y de la gente)

y su fealdad se acentuaba entre estos seres excepcionalmente hermosos: papá Bukhart, con su apariencia de dios nórdico, Hortensia, mamá Eugenia, y aun la lisiada Emilia, con su belleza transparente y rítmica, como uno de sus versos. No debió entonces sorprenderle el haber escuchado (¡sin proponérselo, Dios Santo!) las palabras que el joven alférez deslizara al oído de Hortensia: *Es usted la más deslumbrante belleza de esta recepción, señorita Hortensia* (fue poco después de haber bailado Hortensia la mazurca con el Gobernador General). Y en realidad no le sorprendió. Le dolió, en cambio. No porque ella dejase de reconocer la belleza de su hermana, sino porque las palabras provenían de *él*.

* * *

Emilia se levantó y, cojeando lastimosamente, fue a pasar con suavidad su pañolito de encajes por la mejilla izquierda de Hortensia.

—Le pusiste demasiados polvos de arroz en este lado —explicó, al sorprender la mirada inquieta de Inés. Luego volvió a sentarse.

Las tres permanecían silenciosas e inmóviles (Emilia e Inés sin apartar los ojos de Hortensia).

—¿Verdad que está hermosa? —preguntó Emilia en voz baja.

Lo estaba. Amorosamente la habían vestido con sus galas de novia. Bajo la luz del cirio todo lo blanco adquiría un tinte maravilloso. O era quizá el tiempo. El velo se había desgarrado. Pero los azahares estaban intactos. Y las manchas del traje pudieron disimularse gracias a los pliegues hábilmente dispuestos por Inés. Lástima que la caja no fuese digna de su contenido: un burdo ataúd cedido por Beneficencia Municipal.

Emilia suspiró. Esperaba. Pero Inés no parecía tener prisa. Estaba allí, encorvada, con su escaso pelo gris cayéndole sobre la frente, el rostro descuartizado por una red implacable de arrugas profundas, terriblemente fea en su callada determinación. Y a Emilia se le ocurrió pensar qué hubiese hecho Inés en el lugar de Hortensia. Aunque de inmediato se vio forzada a rechazar la proposición porque *nadie* pudo haber estado en el lugar de Hortensia. (Hortensia dijo *no* a la vida. Quienquiera que le hubiese revelado la verdad había sido cruel en demasía. ¿Hubo alguien que en realidad conociese a Hortensia? ¿Hubo alguien que *previese* su reacción?

De todos modos lo supo: el rapacillo de la mulata (la mulata que tenía su puesto en un zaguán de la Calle Imperial), el

que gateaba entre los manojos de saúco y albahaca y yerba-
buena, tenía azules los ojos. Un alférez español puede amar
hoy y haberle dado ayer el azul de sus ojos al rapacillo de una
yerbatera. Hasta la imponente mamá Eugenia dio sus razones
para excusar el hecho. (Papá Bukhart, no. Papá Bukhart siempre dejó que el mundo girara bajo su mirada fría de naturalis-
ta alemán convertido en hacendado del trópico.) Pero Hortensia dijo *no,* aunque antes había dicho *sí,* y aunque los encajes de su traje de novia hubiesen venido de Estrasburgo. Y
la casa de la Calle del Cristo cerró sus tres puertas sobre el
balcón de azulejos. El tiempo entonces se partió en dos: atrás
quedóse el mundo estable y seguro de la buena vida; y el presente tornóse en el comienzo de un futuro preñado de desas-
tres, como si el *no* de Hortensia hubiese sido el filo atroz de
un cuchillo que cercenara el tiempo y dejase escapar por su
herida un torbellino de cosas jamás soñadas: La armada de un
pueblo nuevo y bárbaro bombardeó a San Juan. Y poco después murió mamá Eugenia (de anemia perniciosa, según el
galeno; sólo para que papá Bukhart fríamente rechazase el
diagnóstico porque mamá Eugenia había muerto de dolor al
ver una bandera extraña ocupar en lo alto de La Fortaleza el
lugar que siempre ocupara su pendón rojo y gualda). Y cuando el lujoso féretro de caoba desapareció por el zaguán, todos
tuvieron conciencia de que el mundo había perdido su equilibrio. Como lo demostró papá Bukhart al pisar ya apenas la
casa de la Calle del Cristo. Y pasar semanas enteras en la hacienda de Toa Alta, desbocando caballos por las vegas de caña. Hasta que un día su cuerpo de dios nórdico fue conducido por cuatro peones negros a la casa de los soles truncos (casi no podía reconocérsele en su improvisado sudario de polvo
y sangre). Y el mundo se hizo aún más estrecho, aunque a su
estrechez llegaran luego noticias de una gran guerra en la Europa lejana, y cesara entonces la débil correspondencia sostenida con algunos parientes de Estrasburgo, y con los tíos de
Málaga. Pero habrían de transcurrir dos años más para que en
San Juan muriera la nana negra, y en Europa, Estrasburgo pasara a manos de Francia, y el mundo fuese ya un recinto cerrado al cual sólo tuviese acceso el viejo notario que hablaba
de contribuciones, de crisis, de la urgencia de vender la hacienda de Toa Alta a los americanos del Norte, y Hortensia
pudiese acoger siempre la proposición con su sonrisa helada:
Jamás nuestras tierras serán de los bárbaros.

* * *

Inés casi se sobresaltó al ver a Emilia levantarse e ir a pasar su destrozado pañolito de encajes por la mejilla de Hortensia. Le pareció pueril la preocupación de Emilia por los polvos de arroz. Si ella le había puesto más polvos en la mejilla izquierda a Hortensia había sido sencillamente para ocultar la mancha negruzca que desde hacía años había aparecido en aquella zona de la piel de su hermana. Nunca hacía cosa alguna sin motivo. Nunca.

Emilia estaba nerviosa (era obvio que estaba nerviosa) y, sin embargo, se mostró decidida cuando le comunicó su plan. Había temido alguna resistencia de parte de su hermana. Pero Emilia había alzado hacia ella su mirada color violeta y había sonreído al murmurar: *Sí. Purificación.* Sin duda interpretaba el acto de un modo simbólico. Era una suerte. Hacía tanto tiempo que Emilia no escribía versos. En el cofre de sándalo descansaba el manojo de cuartillas amarillentas. Mamá Eugenia siempre sonrió leyendo los versos de Emilia. (Papá Bukhart, no. Y es que Emilia jamás osó mostrarle su cuaderno.) A ella, a Inés, le producían en cambio un extraño desasosiego. *Soy piedra pequeña entre tus manos de musgo.* Le desconcertaba la ausencia de rima. Y, sin embargo, sentía como el vértigo de un inasible ritmo arrastrándola a un mundo íntimo que le producía malestar. Emilia nunca explicaba sus versos. Y ese misterioso estar y no estar en el ámbito de un alma ajena la seducía y la angustiaba a la vez. *Tu pie implacable hollando mis palabras, tu pie de fauno sobre una palabra: amor.* No podía precisarlo, pero había algo obsceno en todo esto, algo que no era posible relacionar con el violeta pálido de los ojos de Emilia, ni con su pie lisiado, ni con su gesto de niño tímido y asustadizo. O quizá lo obsceno era precisamente eso, que fuese Emilia quien escribiese versos así. Lo peor había sido el *tu* innombrado, pero siempre presente en las cuartillas amarillentas. *Soy cordero de Pasca para TU espada, Valle del Eco para TU voz.* ¡La angustia de ese *tu...*! ¿Podía ser otro que *él?*

No tenía prisa. Sabía que Emilia estaba impaciente. Pero ella no *podía* tener prisa. Necesitaba esos minutos para volcarse toda dentro de sí misma. Porque habían sido muchos los años de convivencia y miseria, de frases pueriles y largos silencios, de hambre y orgullo y penumbra y vejez. Pero nunca de estar a solas consigo misma. Viviendo Hortensia había sido imposible. Pero ahora...

El tiempo era como un sol trunco (azul, amarillo, rojo) proyectando su esmerilada fatiga sobre la gran sala. Sin embargo, el tiempo había sido también transparente. Lo había sido en el instante aquel en que viera allí a Hortensia con su bata blanca de encajes. Estaba casi de perfil y el rojo de un cristal daba sobre su cabeza produciendo una aureola fantástica de sangre, o de fuego quizá. Ella la observaba a través del espejo de la consola. Y deseó de pronto que la vida fuese un espejo donde no existieran las palabras. Pero las palabras habían sido pronunciadas. La fría superficie de la luna había rechazado su voz, y las palabras flotaban aún en la gran sala, irremediablemente dispersas, sin posibilidad alguna de recogerlas (de aprisionarlas de nuevo en su garganta), porque la vida no cabía dentro del marco del espejo, sino que transcurría más acá, en el tiempo, en un espacio sin límites, donde otra voz podría responder a sus palabras:

—Gracias por decírmelo —y era la voz de Hortensia. Luego un silencio corto y agudo como un grito, y de nuevo la voz—: No me casaré, desde luego.

Sus ojos se apartaron entonces del perfil reflejado junto al piano y resbalaron por la imagen de su propio rostro. Y toda su carne se estremeció. Porque jamás había sido su fealdad como en aquel instante. Y vio a Hortensia (su imagen en el espejo) apartarse del piano de palo de rosa y acercarse a ella lentamente. Y en su movimiento había abandonado la zona del cristal rojo y pasado por la zona del cristal azul, pero al detenerse a sus espaldas ya había entrado en la zona del cristal amarillo, de modo que su rostro parecía envuelto en un polvillo de oro como si después del tiempo de la vida y del tiempo del sueño entrase en un tiempo que podía ser de eternidad, desde el cual sus ojos fuesen capaces de romper el misterio del espejo para buscar los otros ojos angustiados, y aunque la voz de Hortensia no tuviese el poder de traspasar la superficie límpida, no era preciso que así fuese porque las palabras, de ser pronunciadas, rebotarían como imágenes para penetrar en su fealdad reflejada, y hacerla sentir el pavor de esa fealdad (o acentuar el pavor ya desatado):

—Es mejor así. Porque jamás *compartiría* yo el amor de un hombre. ¡Jamás!

Y ella sintió verdadero espanto, pues le pareció que Hortensia no se refería a la yerbatera de la Calle Imperial. Y pensó en Emilia. Pero el espejo no contenía en su breve mundo la imagen de Emilia, sino la suya propia. Y de pronto todas las palabras pronunciadas, las suyas también: *Tiene una querida, Hortensia; y un hijo en esa mulata,* le golpearon el pecho con tal ímpetu que le impidieron respirar. Y el espejo fue convirtiéndose en una bruma espesa que crecía, y crecía, y su cuerpo empezó a caer en un abismo sin límites, cayendo, cayendo más hondo, hasta chocar bruscamente contra un suelo alfombrado de gris.

El cuerpo de Hortensia permanecía en una zona a la cual no llegaba la luz tricolor del alba. Sólo el cirio derramaba su débil claridad de topacio sobre el rostro enmarcado en azahares y tul.

Inés observaba los labios secos, petrificando la sonrisa enigmática, los mismos labios que en tantos años de miseria (y soberbia, y hambre y frases pueriles) jamás abordaron la palabra que hubiese dado sosiego a la eterna incertidumbre, la palabra que hubiese hecho menos infernal su tarea de proteger el orgullo de Hortensia y la invalidez de Emilia, de fingirse loca ante los acreedores, y vender las joyas más valiosas (y la plata), de cargar diariamente el agua del aljibe desde que suspendieron el servicio de acueducto, y aceptar la caridad de los vecinos, y rechazar las ofertas de compra por la casa en ruinas, e impedir que los turistas violaran el recinto en su búsqueda bárbara de miseria (alejando los husmeantes hocicos ajenos de la ruina propia y el dolor).

* * *

Emilia no podía apartar su mirada de la tenue llama del cirio, y le parecía la manecita dorada de un niño que se abría y cerraba así, a intervalos caprichosos, y le vinieron a la memoria unas palabras incomprensibles: *Sólo tu mano purificará mi corazón.* ¿Isaías? No era un texto sagrado. Algo más próximo (¿o remoto?) en el tiempo. *Sólo tu mano...* ¡Sí! En las cuartillas amarillentas del cofre de sándalo. ¡Eran palabras suyas! Sonrió. Su corazón en el cofre de sándalo. Donde no habría de llegar la sonrisa helada de Hortensia ni la mirada inquisitiva de Inés. (El único lugar donde puede sobrevivir el corazón en un mundo sin razón alguna para la vida.)

Volvió sus ojos hacia Inés. Esperaba la realización del acto. Un bello acto, ciertamente. ¿Cómo pudo ocurrírsele a su hermana? Bien, se le había ocurrido. Y ella aprobaba aquel acto de purificación. Porque todo lo bello, lo que había sido hermoso, estaba contenido en aquella caja tosca que proveía la Beneficencia Municipal. (Todo lo que es bello y debe perecer, había perecido.)

Vio en ese instante a Inés ponerse de pie y tuvo un ligero estremecimiento. Le pareció más alta que nunca y creyó descubrir en su gesto y su mirada algo terriblemente hermoso

que hacía olvidar momentáneamente su horrible fealdad. *¡Al fin!*, pensó, y poniéndose de pie, preguntó, sonriendo:
—¿Ya?

* * *

Inés vio la sonrisa de Emilia y sintió una punzada en un lugar remoto de su pecho porque, inexplicablemente, aquellos labios de anciana habían sonreído con la frescura y el encanto de una niña. Oyó luego la voz cascada decir:
—Espera por mí.
Y vio a Emilia alejarse, con su horrible cojera más acentuada que nunca, hacia la habitación de la izquierda. Sola ya con Hortensia, echó una ojeada a la sala. Sus ojos se detuvieron en la enorme mancha irregular que, como el mapa de un istmo que uniera en la pared dos mundos, partía desde el plafón hasta el piso. Sobre el empapelado, que una vez fuera gris y rosa, el agua había grabado su huella para hacer eterno en la sala el recuerdo del temporal. Y fue en ese mismo año de *San Felipe* cuando ella supo de la otra catástrofe. Y es que el viejo notario le ahorró en esa ocasión todos los preámbulos: la hacienda de Toa Alta había sido vendida en subasta pública para cubrir contribuciones atrasadas. Desde entonces la miseria fue el girar continuo de un remolino lento, pero implacable, que arrastraba y arrastraba, por lustros, por décadas, hasta llegar al tiempo en que los revolucionarios atacaron La Fortaleza, y se descubrió el cáncer en el pecho de Hortensia. Y ya no era posible tener conciencia del hambre porque el torbellino había detenido su girar de *tempo* lento ante la avasallante destrucción de las células (y el huir de la sangre, y el dolor hondo que roía sin gritos). Pero sangre y dolor petrificáronse en el pecho sin células y la sonrisa se puso fría en los labios de Hortensia. Y ayer su cuerpo no tenía aún la rigidez postrera (ella lo sabía porque acababa de lavar el cadáver) y cuando al zaguán llegaron los extraños con sus ademanes amplios y sus angostas sonrisas de funcionarios probos: el Gobierno había decidido que la casa (la de la Calle del Cristo, la de los soles truncos) se convirtiese en hostería de lujo para los turistas, y los banqueros, y los oficiales de la armada aquella que bombardeó a San Juan. No fue preciso fingirse loca porque en esta ocasión estaba enloquecida. Y sus largas uñas con olor a muerta claváronse en el rostro que tenía más próximo (hasta que saltó la sangre, y desaparecieron las sonrisas). Y después sus puños golpearon despiadadamen-

te, con la misma furia con que habían combatido la vida; golpeando así, ¡así!, contra la miseria, y los hombres, y el mundo, y el tiempo, y la muerte, y el hambre, y los años, y la sangre, y de nuevo la vida, y el portalón de ausubo que los otros habían logrado cerrar en su precipitada huida. Y en la pared de la sala, la enorme mancha del tiempo dibujaba el mapa de dos mundos unidos por un istmo. Y era preciso destruir el istmo.

* * *

Emilia salió de la habitación y vio a Inés de pie, inmóvil, con la vista fija en la pared de enfrente. Avanzó penosamente y fue a depositar el pequeño cofre de sándalo a los pies del féretro. *Mi corazón a tus pies, Hortensia*. Luego volvióse hacia Inés y quedóse en actitud de espera. La vio apartar los ojos de la pared y dejarlos resbalar por su rostro hasta fijarlos por un instante en el cofre de sándalo, y luego alejarse hacia la consola y tomar una bolsa de seda negra que ella no había observado sobre el mármol rosa, y regresar junto a Hortensia. Estaban ambas ante el féretro abierto e Inés derramó el contenido de la bolsa negra sobre la falda de Hortensia. Emilia observó con asombro aquellos ricos objetos que había creído devorados por el tiempo, o por el hambre (en fin, por la miseria y el tiempo).

Inés tomó la sortija de brillantes y trabajosamente pudo colocarla en el anular izquierdo de Hortensia. Luego colocó la de perlas en el dedo de Emilia. La ajorca de oro y rubíes fue a adornar la muñeca de Hortensia. Con la diadema de zafiros y brillantes en su mano, se detuvo indecisa. Echó una ojeada a la cabeza postrada, ceñida de azahares, y con gesto decidido volvióse y ciñó la diadema de mamá Eugenia en la frente de Emilia. Tomó al fin la última prenda (el ancho anillo de oro de papá Bukhart) y, colocándolo en su propio dedo anular, salió presurosa de la estancia; sus pasos haciendo crujir la casa en ruinas.

* * *

El leve resplandor del cirio arrancaba luces fantásticas a los brillantes en el dedo de Hortensia. Y Emilia vio pasar como una sombra a Inés, por el fondo, con un quinqué en la mano. El olor a tiempo y a polvo que caracterizaba la sala empezó a desvanecerse ante el olor penetrante a petróleo. De pronto, a los rubíes de la ajorca se les coaguló la sangre. Porque la sala toda se había puesto roja. Y Emilia vio a Inés acer-

carse de nuevo y detenerse junto a Hortensia. Y encontró la
figura erguida de su hermana tan horriblemente hermosa sobre el trasfondo de llamas, que con gesto espontáneo apartó
la diadema de sus propias sienes y ciñó con ella la frente marchita de Inés. Luego fue a sentarse en el sillón de Viena y se
puso a observar la maravilla azul de los zafiros sobre las cren-
chas desteñidas, que ahora adquirían tonalidades de sangre,
porque el fuego era un círculo purificador alrededor de ellas.

Y estaban allí, reunidas como siempre en la gran sala; las
tres puertas de dos hojas sobre el balcón, cerradas como siempre; los tres soles truncos emitiendo al mundo exterior por
vez primera la extraordinaria belleza de una luz propia, mientras se consumía lo feo y horrible que una vez fuera hermoso
y lo que siempre fuera horrible y feo, por igual.

‎ ‎

▬▬▬▬

Rosa Montero
1951—
España

Paulo Pumilio

S OY plenamente consciente, al iniciar la escritura de estos
folios, de que mis contemporáneos no sabrán comprenderme. Entre mis múltiples desgracias se cuenta la de la inopor-
tunidad con que nací: vine al mundo demasiado pronto o demasiado tarde. En cualquier caso, fuera de mi época. Pasarán
muchos años antes de que los lectores de esta confesión sean
capaces de entender mis razones, de calibrar mi desarrollada
sensibilidad amén de la grandeza épica de mis actos. Corren
tiempos banales y chatos en los que no hay lugar para epo-
peyas. Me llaman criminal, me tachan de loco y de degene-
rado. Y, sin embargo, yo sé bien que todo lo que hice fue
equitativo, digno y razonable. Sé que ustedes no me van a
comprender, digo, y aun así escribo. Cuando la revista de sucesos "El asesino anda suelto" me propuso publicar el relato

de mi historia, acepté el encargo de inmediato. Escribo, pues, para la posteridad, destino fatal de las obras de los genios. Escribo desde este encierro carcelario para no olvidarme de mí mismo.

Pero empezaré por el principio: me llamo Pablo Torres y debo estar cumpliendo los cuarenta y dos, semana más o menos. De mi infancia poco hay que decir, a no ser que mi verdadera madre tampoco supo comprenderme y me abandonó, de tiernos meses, a la puerta de un cuartelillo de la Guardia Civil con mi nombre escrito en un retazo de papel higiénico prendido a la pechera. Me supongo nacido en Madrid, o al menos el cuartelillo de esta ciudad era, y de cualquier manera yo me siento capitalino y gato por los cuatro costados. Un guardia me acogió, mi pseudo-padre, el cabo Mateo, viejo, casado y sin hijos, y pasé mi niñez en la casa cuartel, dando muestras desde muy chico de mi precocidad: a los cinco años sabíame de memoria las Ordenanzas y acostumbraba a asistir a ejercicios y relevos, ejecutando a la perfección todos los movimientos con un fusil de madera que yo mismo ingenié del palo de una escoba. Amamantado —o, por mejor decir, embiberonado— en un ambiente de pundonor castrense, cifré mis anhelos desde siempre en un futuro de histórica grandeza: quería entrar en el Benemérito Cuerpo y hacer una carrera brillantemente heroica. Los aires marciales me enardecían y el melancólico gemido de la trompeta, al arriar bandera en el atardecer, solía conturbarme hasta las lágrimas haciéndome intuir gestas y glorias venideras, provocándome una imprecisa —y para mí entonces incomprensible— nostalgia de un pasado que aun no había vivido, y una transida admiración por todos esos gallardos jóvenes de ennoblecidos uniformes.

Con la pubertad, empero, llegaron las primeras amarguras, los primeros encontronazos con esta sociedad actual, tan ciega y miserable que no sabe comprender la talla verdadera de los hombres: cuando quise entrar en el Cuerpo, descubrí que se me excluía injustamente del servicio.

Supongo que no tengo más remedio que hablar aquí de mi apariencia física, aunque muchos de ustedes la conozcan, tras la triste celebridad del juicio que se me hizo y el morboso hincapié que los periódicos pusieron en la configuración de mi persona. Sin embargo, creo que debo puntualizar con energía unos cuantos pormenores que a mi modo de ver fueron y son tergiversados por la prensa. No soy enano. Cierto es que soy un varón bajo: mido 88 centímetros a pie descalzo y sobre los 90 con zapatos. Pero mi cuerpo está perfectamente construido, y, si se me permite decir, mis hechuras son a la vez delicadas y atléticas: la cabeza pequeña, braquicéfala y primorosa, el cuello robusto pero esbelto, los hombros anchos, los brazos nervudos, el talle ágil. Tan sólo mis piernas son algo defectuosas; soy flojo de remos, un poco estevado y patituerto, y fue esta peculiar malformación, supongo, lo que amilanó a mi verdadera madre —los dioses le hayan perdonado— influyendo en mi abandono, puesto que fui patojo desde siempre, aun siendo yo un infante. Eso sí, una vez vestido, el ángulo de mis piernas no se observa, y puedo asegurarles que mi apostura es garrida y apolínea. Pero hay otra especie, de entre los venenos vertidos por la prensa, que se presta a confusión y que quisiera muy mucho aclarar: es verdad que todos me conocen por El Chepa. No se llamen ustedes a engaño, sin embargo: mi espalda está virgen de joroba alguna, mi espalda es tersa y lisa como membrana de tambor, tendida entre los bastidores de las paletillas, y, por no tener, ni tan siquiera tengo ese espeso morrillo que poseen algunos hombres bastos y fornidos, quizá muchos de ustedes, dicho sea sin ánimo de ofender ni señalar. Mi sobrenombre es para mí un orgullo, y como tal lo expongo. Cierto es que siendo joven y de cuitada inocencia hube de soportar a veces motes enojosos: me llamaban El Enano, Menudillo, El Seta o El Poquito. Pero una vez que alcancé la edad viril y la plenitud de mis conocimientos y mi fuerza, no volvieron a atreverse a decir tales agravios. Y ay de aquel que osara pretenderlo: soy hombre pacífico pero tengo clara conciencia de lo digno y coraje suficiente como para mantenerla. Fue mi amado Gran Alí quien me bautizó como Chepa, y comprendí que era una galante antífrasis que resaltaba lo erguido de mi porte, era un mote que aludía precisamente a la perfección de mis espaldas. Nunca hubiera permitido, ténganlo por seguro, un apelativo que fuera ofensivo para mi persona. Chepa es laudatorio, como acabo de explicar, y por ello lo uso honrosamente.

Las desgracias nunca vienen solas, como reza el proverbio, y así, mi rechazo formal para el ingreso en la Benemérita fue seguido a poco por la muerte de mi padrastro aquejado de melancolía. Unos meses antes había fallecido mi pobre madrastra de cólicos estivales y el cabo Mateo pareció no saber sobrevivirla. Así, con apenas dieciocho años en mi haber, me encontré solo en el mundo, reincidentemente huérfano, y sin hogar ni valer, ya que hube de abandonar la casa cuartel. El comandante del puesto, empero, pareció compadecerse de mi triste sino, y me buscó oficio y acomodo con el padre Tulle-

do, que regentaba la parroquia cercana y que había sido cape-
llán castrense en los avatares de la guerra civil. Con él viví cerca de diez años desempeñando las labores de sacristanía, diez
años que fueron fundamentales en mi vida y formación. El
padre Tulledo me educó en lenguas clásicas, ética, lógica y
teología, y gracias a él soy todo lo que soy. Pese a ello nunca
pude llegar a apreciarle realmente, los dioses me perdonen. El
padre Tulledo era un hombre soplado y alámbrico, un trans-
figurista con propensión al éxtasis, de mirar desquiciado y
tartajeo nervioso. Me irritaba sobremanera la burda broma
que solía repetir, "La Misericordia de Dios ha unido a un Tulledo con un tullido, hijo mío, para que cantemos Su Grandeza", como si mi cuerpo estuviera malformado y retorcido.
Otrosí me desalentaba su empeño en vestirme siempre con las
ajadas gualdrapas de los monaguillos, para ahorrar el gasto de
mis ropas; y más de una beata legañosa y amiopada me tomó
alguna vez por un niño al verme así ataviado, dirigiéndose a
mí con tal falta de respeto —"eh, chaval, chico, pequeño"— a
mis años y condición, que la indignación y el despecho me
cegaban.

Sea como fuere, también le llegó la hora al padre Tulledo,
y un traicionero ataque cardíaco le hizo desplomarse un día,
como huesuda marioneta de hilos cortados, sobre la jícara del
chocolate de las siete. Vime de nuevo solo y sin hogar, con el
único e inapreciable tesoro de un libro que me dejó en herencia el padre, una traducción de las *Vidas Paralelas,* de Plutarco, de la colección Clásica Lucero, edición noble y en piel del
año 1942, con un prólogo escrito por el padre Tulledo en el
que se resaltaba el paralelismo entre las gloriosas gestas béli-
cas narradas por Plutarco y las heroicidades de nuestra Cruza-
da Nacional. Y debo decir aquí que, con ser este libro mi sola
posesión, con él me sentía y me siento millonario, puesto que
desde entonces ha sido mi guía ético y humano, mi misal de
cabecera, el norte de mi vida.

Les ahorraré, porque no viene a cuento ni ha lugar, el relato de aquellos dos primeros años en busca de trabajo. Básta-
me decir que sufrí de hambrunas y de fríos, que malviví en
tristes cochiquetas y que mis lágrimas mojaron más de un atardecer: no me avergüenzo de ello, también los héroes lloran,
también lloró Aquiles la muerte de Patroclo. Al cabo, cumpliendo la treintena, fui a caer, no me pregunten cómo, en el
reducto miserable del Jawai, y conocí al bienamado Gran
Alí y a la grotesca Asunción, para mi gloria y desgracia.

El Jawai era un club nocturno raído y maloliente, encla-

vado en una callejuela cercana a Lavapiés. Un semisótano des-
tartalado decorado con ínfulas polinésicas, con palmeras de
cartón piedra de polvorientas hojas de papel y dibujos de indígenas por las paredes, unas barrosas y deformes criaturas de
color chocolate y faldellín de paja. El dueño, el malnombra-
do Pepín Fernández, era un cincuentón de lívida gordura que
se pintaba cabellos y mejillas, hombre de tan mentecata y modorra necedad que, cuando al llegar al club le avisé cortésmente de que Hawai se escribía con hache y no con jota, juntó
sus amorcilladas manos en gesto de pía compunción y contestó con chirriante voz de hidropésico: "Qué le vamos a hacer,
Chepa, resignación cristiana, resignación, las letras del luminoso me han costado carísimas y ya no lo puedo arreglar, además, yo creo que la gente no se percata de la confuscación".
Pepín daba a entender que era hijo de un sacerdote rural, y
puede que su vocación viniera de tal progenitor sacramenta-
do, puesto que su máxima ambición, según decía, era devenir
santo y ser subido a los altares. Por ello, Pepín hablaba con
melosidad curil y, para mortificarse, siendo abstemio y feble
como era, solía beber de un trago copas rebosantes de cazalla,
con las que lagrimeaba de ardor estomacal y náuseas, ofrecien-
el etílico sacrificio por su salvación eterna. Acostumbraba a
pasar los días en el chiscón que servía de taquilla y guarda-
rropa, encajando sus flatulencias y sus carnes en la estrecha
pecera de luz de neón, y ahí apuraba el cilicio de sus vasos de
aguardiente, melindroso, y se santiguaba con profusión antes
de cada pase de espectáculos. Porque el Jawai tenía espectáculo: bayaderas tísicas y cuarteronas que bailaban la danza
del vientre fláccido, cantantes sordos que masacraban ronca-
mente tonadas populares, y, como fin de fiesta y broche de
oro, el hermoso Gran Alí. Las bailarinas cambiaban con frecuencia aunque todas parecieran ser el mismo hueso, pero el
Gran Alí tenía contrato fijo y permanecía siempre anclado en
el Jawai, desperdiciando su arte y su saber. Porque el Gran
Alí era mago, un prestidigitador magnífico, un preciso y sutil
profesional. Inventaba pañuelos multicolores del vacío, sacaba conejos de la manga, atravesaba a Asunción de espadas y
puñales: era lo más cercano a un dios que he conocido. Parecía de estirpe divina, ciertamente, cuando salía a escena, reful-
giendo bajo los focos con los brillos de su atavío mozárabe.
Era más o menos de mi misma edad y poseía una apostura de
gracia irresistible, el cuerpo esbelto y ceñido de carnes prietas,
el mirar sombrío y soñador, la nariz griega, la barbilla rubri-
cando en firme trazo una boca jugosa y suave, y su tez era un

milagro de tostada seda mate. Comprendo que Asunción le
amara con esa pasión abyecta y entregada, pero no se me alcanza el porqué del empeño de Alí en continuar con ella, con
esa mujerona de contornos estallados, caballuna, con gigantes
senos pendulares, de boca tan mezquina y torcida como su
propia mente de mosquito. Alí, en cambio, tenía toda la digna fragancia de un príncipe oriental, de un rey de reyes: No
era moro Alí, sino español, nacido en Algeciras y llamado
Juan en el bautismo, pero todos le conocíamos como el Gran
Alí, en parte porque prefería reservar su verdadero nombre
como prevención ante conflictos policiales, pero sobre todo
porque en verdad era grande y portentoso.

He de detener aquí un instante el hilo de mi historia y
volver los ojos de nuevo hacia mí, con su licencia, por mor de
la perfecta comprensión de lo que narro. Descubrí mi homosexualidad años ha; ustedes saben de ella por la prensa. Quisiera aprovechar esta ocasión, sin embargo, para intentar hacerles comprender que la homosexualidad no es la mariconería que ustedes condenan y suponen torpemente. Homosexuales eran, en el mundo clásico, todos los héroes, los genios y
los santos. Homosexual era Platón, y Sócrates, y Arquímedes,
y Pericles. La homosexualidad es un resultado natural de la
extrema sensibilidad y delicadeza. Se puede ser homosexual
y heroico, homosexual y porfiado luchador. Como Alcibíades, el gran general cuya biografía narra Plutarco. Como los
trescientos legendarios héroes que formaban la Cohorte Sagrada de Tebas, una cohorte imbatible que basaba su fuerza
en estar compuesta por amados y amadores, por enamoradas
parejas de guerreros que luchaban espalda contra espalda y
que redoblaban sus esfuerzos en combate para defender a su
adorado compañero. Ah, si yo hubiera nacido en aquel entonces, en aquella era de gigantes, en aquella época dorada
de la humanidad. Yo hubiera sido uno más de aquellos gigantes de mítica nobleza, porque el mundo clásico medía a los
hombres por su grandeza interior, por su talla espiritual, y
no por accidentes y prejuicios como ahora. Hogaño soy el
pobre Chepa, condenado a cadena perpetua por haber cometido el razonable delito de matar a quien debía morir. Antaño
hubiera sido un guerrero de la legendaria Cohorte Sagrada. Mi
estatura me convertiría en invencible, repartiría fieros mandobles entre los enemigos rebanándoles el aliento a la altura
de las rodillas, segándoles la vida por las piernas, porque en
aquel entonces las armaduras no solían cubrir bien las extremidades inferiores y las canillas de mis oponentes se me ofre-

cerían inermes y fáciles ante el hierro justiciero de mi espada.
Quizá hubiera llegado a ser un general romano, un triunfador
cónsul pacificador de las provincias bárbaras, y Plutarco me
incluiría entre sus áureas biografías: Paulus Turris Pumilio,
cuatro veces cónsul imperial. Porque, como ustedes saben
—aunque, pensándolo bien, temo fundadamente que no lo
sepan— la palabra "pumilio" significa en latín "hombre pequeño", puesto que los romanos solían denominarse con un
nombre de referencia a su apariencia física, un mote que era
sólo descriptivo y nunca ofensivo, tal era su grandeza de ánimo. Y así, el apodo del Gran Claudio significaba "cojo", y el
del feroz Sila quería decir "cara bermeja", y el del ilustre Pumilio expresa mi talla menuda pero grácil. Yo hubiera sido un
héroe, pues, y hubiera amado a héroes: la homosexualidad en
el mundo clásico era natural y comprensible, porque, ¿qué
mejor y más merecedor objeto de pasión podía hallarse que
aquellos luchadores portentosos? Pues del mismo modo amaba yo a mi muy hermoso Gran Alí. Pido licencia para hacer
una puntualización más y termino con estas fatigosas referencias personales. Poco después de descubrir mi ática tendencia
amorosa, mi fe religiosa experimentó cierto quebranto. Hoy
puedo considerarme un cínico creyente o un ateo crédulo;
padezco el suave y resignado escepticismo de todo buen teó-
logo; en esto estoy más cerca de Séneca que de Lucrecio. Pero baste esto en cuanto a mí: debo apresurar mi narración,
puesto que la revista sólo me ha concedido veinte folios y he
de comprimir en ellos toda mi vida y mi dolor.

Ello es que pasé a formar parte de la mísera familia del
Jawai. El dueño, Asunción, Alí y yo vivíamos sobre el local,
en una vieja y sombría casa de mil puertas e interminables
corredores. Pienso que el grueso Pepín de carnes pecadoras
estaba enamorado de Asunción, que la quería con reprimido
deseo de loco santurrón en una de esas aberrantes pasiones
que a veces surgen entre seres desdichados como ellos, y supongo que de ahí nacieron las prebendas de que disfrutába-
mos. A mí, sin embargo, me había contratado el Gran Alí, y
ataviado de esclavo oriental colaboraba en su número, y fuera
del escenario le servía de ayuda de cámara, de fiel secretario y
compañero. Alí era sobrio en el decir y en los afectos, tenía
un talante estoico, duro y bien templado al fuego de la vida,
y eso le hacía, si cabe, aún más admirable. Todo el mundo le
temía y respetaba, y era digno de verse cómo Pepín sacudía
sus mofletes de terror ante la fría furia de Alí, o cómo Asun
gemía puercamente implorándole mimos o perdones. Pero

Alí era tan implacable como debe serlo todo héroe, porque los héroes no saben disculpar las flaquezas humanas en las que ellos no incurren: la misericordia no es más que el medroso refugio de los débiles, que perdonan sólo para asegurarse de que serán perdonados a su vez. He de decir que Alí me señaló la espalda varias veces con su correa, y siempre con motivo suficiente, o bien porque vertía un plato al servirle la comida, o bien porque me distraía en atender sus demandas sobre el escenario, o porque no sabía comprender su estado de ánimo. Sus castigos, bien lo sé, me curtieron y limaron de blanduras. Sus castigos eran sobrias lecciones de entereza, porque Alí repartía justa sabiduría con la punta de su correa de cuero, lo mismo que Licurgo supo batir el hierro de sus espartanos hasta convertirlo en acero con la ayuda de la dureza de sus leyes. Teníame en buen aprecio Alí, porque nunca escurrí el bulto a sus castigos ni salió de mi boca queja alguna, aun cuando me golpeara con el bronce de la hebilla; y ni tan siquiera grité aquella vez que rompí por pura torpeza el cristal de la bola levitadora y Alí me quebró el espinazo a palos. Más de tres semanas estuve en un suspiro, baldado y encogido en el jergón, y al atardecer Asunción venía a darme la comida, y se acurrucaba a los pies de la cama, hecha un ovillo de carnes y arrugas, y me miraba con sus ojos vacunos y vacíos, y exhalaba blandos quejidos de debilidad impúdica. Su conmiseración por mí me daba náuseas y hube de llamarle la atención, "eres una ingrata", le dije, "no comprendes nada, no sabes merecerle", y ella lo único que hacía en respuesta a mis palabras era arreciar en gimoteos y retorcerse los dedos de las manos. Asunción era un residuo humano deleznable.

Alí solía desaparecer de vez en cuando. Se marchaba al final de una función y no volvía a saberse de él en dos o tres días. Pepín admitía sus escapadas de gran amo en busca de horizontes más propicios, y Asunción le lloraba pálida y descompuesta por las noches. Regresaba Alí trayendo un olor a riesgo y hazaña prendido a los cabellos, los ojos tenebrosos, el tinte de su tez más liváceo, la piel bruñida y tensa sobre la delicada aguda de sus pómulos. La experiencia me enseñó que esos eran sus momentos dolorosos, los instantes en los que vivía el drama de su destino heroico. Yo solía acurrucarme a su lado en silencio, recibía algún pescozón o puntapié como desfogue de su trágico barrunto de tristezas, y luego mi señor, mi bien, mi amado, acostumbraba a hacerme confidencias. "Esta vida no es vida, Chepa", decía sombrío y con la mirada preñada de presagios, "esto es un vivir de perros, yo

me merezco otra suerte". Sacaba entonces su navaja cabritera, la abría, pasaba un dedo pensativo por el filo de la hoja,
"cualquier día haré una locura, mejor morir que vivir en este infierno", y me miraba con su divino desprecio, y añadía,
"claro que tú qué sabes de esto, Chepa, tú qué sabes lo que es
ser un hombre muy hombre como yo y estar condenado a
pudrirse en esta miseria", y diciendo esto sus ojos echaban
relumbres lunares y fosfóricos. Estaba tan bello, tan dolorosamente bello en su ira de titán acorralado.

En una ocasión tardó más de tres semanas en volver, y
cuando lo hizo encontró que Pepín había contratado a un
transformista para fin de fiesta. Yo le vi llegar, el espectáculo
estaba a la mitad y el travestí bailoteaba en el tablado con paso
incierto sobre sus zapatones de tacón de aguja. Sentí un repentino frío en la nuca y miré hacia atrás: allí estaba Alí, como un semidiós de espigada y ominosa mancha, una sombra
apoyada junto a la cortina de la entrada. Observé cómo Pepín se agitaba en gelatinosas trepidaciones de pavor, y cómo
intentaba hundirse en el escaso hueco del chiscón y parape-
tarse bajo el mostrador. Alí, sin embargo, no le prestó atención: vino en derechura al escenario, interrumpió el canto de
sirena del descolorido travestí, le agarró del pescuezo ante el
paralizado estupor de los clientes. "Tú, cabra loca", masculló,
"lárgate antes de que me enfade de verdad", la criatura se retorcía entre sus manos y protestaba en falsete "ay, ay, bruto,
más que bruto, déjame". Alí le arrancó las arracadas de las
orejas, dejándole dos caminitos de sangre sobre el lóbulo y
arrojó los pendientes en dirección a la salida como marcándo-
le el rumbo. "Aire, guapa, aire", ordenó al travestí rubrican-
do sus palabras con unos cuantos empellones, y el malhada-
do salió tropezando en sus tacones, embrollándose en su huir
con la desordenada fuga de los clientes de la sala.

Volvióse entonces Alí en dirección a la escalera, encami-
nando sus pasos hacia el piso. Yo le seguí, trotando a la vera
de sus zancadas elásticas, aspirando gozosamente el aroma de
mi dueño, aroma bélico de furias. Por aquel tiempo, ya debíamos llevar unos cuatro años juntos, Asunción solía beber sin
tino ni mesura, y la encontramos postrada en la cama, sobre
un amasijo de sábanas pringues y pardas que olían a sudores
y a ese repugnante y secreto hedor de hembra en celo. Asunción levantó la cara y nos vio, tenía el rostro abotargado y
laxo, el mirar embrutecido y sin color. "Alí...", musitó con
torpe aliento, "Alí", repitió, y sus ojos se llenaron de legaño-
sas lágrimas y comenzó a dar hipidos de borracha, "tres sema-

nas sin saber de ti``, borboteaba, "mal hombre, tres semanas, ¿dónde has ido?", Alí se quitó el cinturón con calmoso gesto, "ay, no, no, no me pegues, mi amor, no me pegues, canalla", soplaba Asunción entre sus mocos escurriéndose al suelo en sus inestables intentos de escapar, zummmm, sonaba la correa al cortar el aire, bamp, golpeaba secamente en sus carnes blandas y lechosas, zummmmmm, bamp, zummmmmm, bamp, qué hermoso estaba mi señor, con la camisa entreabierta y los rizosos vellos negros vistiendo de virilidad su poderoso pecho, zummmmm, bamp, zummmmm, bamp, Asunción se retorcía, imploraba, gemía, zummm, zummmmmm, zummmmmm, en una de sus cabriolas de dolor cayó a mis pies, su rostro estaba a pocos centímetros del mío, un rostro desencajado y envilecido de hembra avejentada, "ay, Chepa, Chepa``, me imploró, "avisa a la pasma que me mata", su aliento ardía en aguardiente y toda ella era una peste.

Marchóse al fin Alí sin añadir palabra, y con un portazo me impidió seguirle. Quedamos solos, pues, Asunción y yo, y ella lloriqueaba con exagerada pamema, arrugada en un rincón, "ay, ay, ay``, hipaba rítmicamente, "qué vida miserable, qué desgraciadita soy, qué desgraciada", con el dorso de la mano se limpiaba la boca hinchada y sucia de sangre y mocos, "ay, ay, esto es un castigo de Dios por haber abandonado a mi hija", porque Asunción tenía una criatura perdida por el mundo que dejó a la caridad cuando unió su vida a la de Alí, "ay, ay, ay, quién me mandó a mí, tan feliz que era yo con mi casita, con mi niña y mi don Carlos", recitaba una vez más su fastidiosa retahíla de pasadas grandezas, cuando ella era una adolescente hermosa —eso aseguraba ella, al menos— y amante fija de un honrado hombre de negocios de Bilbao —no hago más que repetir sus mismas palabras—, proseguía en sus lamentos, "mejor me hubiera sido quedarme muerta por un rayo el mismo primer día que le vi, mejor muerta que ser tan desgraciada". Fue entonces, y creo ser sincero en mi recuerdo, la primera vez que pensé en matarla, puesto que la muy cuitada lo pedía a voces. Fue esa la primera vez, digo, pero andando el tiempo hube de pensarlo en repetidas ocasiones al ver cómo arrastraba su existencia de gusano, sin afán ni norte de vivir.

Releo lo que he escrito y sospecho nuevamente que ustedes no serán capaces de comprenderme y comprenderlo. Ustedes, los honestos biempensantes, hijos del siglo de la hipocresía, suelen escandalizarse con mojigato escrúpulo ante las realidades de la vida. Me parece estar escuchando sus protestas y condenas ante la violencia desplegada por mi Alí, o su repulsa ante mi caritativo deseo de acabar con los pesares de Asunción. Ustedes, voraces fariseos, lagrimean mendaces aspavientos ante mi relato, mas pese a ello no poseen más moral que la de la codicia. Qué saben ustedes de la grandeza de Alí al imponer sus leyes justicieras: su feroz orgullo era el único valor que ordenaba nuestro mundo de ruindad. Qué saben ustedes de la equidad de mis deseos asesinos. Qué saben ustedes del honor, cuando en sus mezquinas mentes sólo hay cabida para el dinero.

Pero he de proseguir mi narración, aunque desperdicie esencias en marranos. Fue poco después de esto cuando Alí decidió que nos marcháramos a probar suerte a las Américas. Consiguió algún dinero no se de dónde para los tres pasajes en el barco y cruzamos los mares arribando en primavera a Nueva York, tras haber sido llorosamente bendecidos por el sudoroso Pepín a nuestra marcha. Permítaseme pasar con brevedad por los quince primeros meses de nuestro vagabundear por aquel país gigante, aunque fueran aquéllos, o témpora o mores, los últimos momentos felices de mi vida. Diré tan sólo que allá los campos son aún más desiertos y polvorientos que Castilla, que la miseria es si cabe aún más miserable y que Alí mostróse sosegado y amable en un principio para irse agriando con el viaje. Caímos un verano en Nashville, una ciudad plana, destartalada e inhumana como todas, y nos contrataron en un club nocturno en el que alternábamos nuestro espectáculo con mujeres encueradas que meneaban sus carnes sobre la superficie de las mesas del local. De la mezquindad del sitio baste decir que sólo era visitado por una clientela de negros y demás morralla canallita, mera carne de esclavos para los nobles de la civilización grecorromana. Estábamos allí, agobiados del agosto sureño, malviviendo en una caravana alquilada cuya chapa se ponía al rojo vivo con el sol. Una tarde, a la densa hora de la siesta, Alí apareció con su delicado semblante traspasado de oscuridad. Asunción estaba borracha, como siempre. Se acababa de lavar las greñas y permanecía tirada en el suelo del retrete del club, apoyada contra la pared, secándose el pelo con el aire caliente del secador de manos automático, ingenio mecánico que la admiraba sobremanera. Alí se la quedó mirando, callado y sombrío, mientras Asunción le dedicaba una sonrisa de medrosa bobería, temblona y errática. El club estaba en silencio, vacío y aún cerrado, y sólo se oía el zumbido del aparato que soplaba su aliento bochornoso en el agobio de la tarde. De vez en cuando, el secador se detenía con un salto y Asun extendía su titubeante mano para apretar de nuevo el botón. Estaba someramente vestida con una combinación sintética, sucia y desgarrada, y por encima de la pringosa puntilla del escote se le desparramaba un seno trémulo y de color ceniza. Se mantenía en precario equilibrio contra las rotas losetas del muro, espatarrada, con las chancletas medio salidas de los pies, y el conejo amaestrado de Alí roía pacientemente la desmigada punta de felpa de una de sus zapatillas. Alí se acuclilló delante de ella y presentí que iba a suceder lo irremediable. "Tú", dijo mi dueño sacudiéndola suavemente por un hombro, "tú, atiende, ¿me escuchas?" Asunción le miraba con estrabismo de beoda y hacía burbujitas de saliva, "está borracha", gruñó Alí para sí mismo con desprecio y enronquecida voz y luego calló un momento, pensativo. "Escucha", añadió al cabo, "escucha, Asun, escucha, es importante, ¿sabes cómo se hace el truco de la bola levitadora?", Asun sonreía y apretaba el botón del secador, "qué guapo eres, Alí, mi hombre", musitaba zafiamente. Alí le dio un cachete en la mejilla, una bofetada suave, de espabile "tienes que atender a lo que te digo, Asun, me queda poco tiempo", y su voz sonaba tensa y preocupada, "¿sabes el truco de la bola? ¿Recuerdas que debes sujetar el sedal al techo?", ella cabeceaba, asintiendo a quien sabe qué, ausente, "escucha", se impacientaba Alí, irguiéndola contra la pared, "escucha, ¿lo de los pañuelos lo sabes? Después de meterlos en la caja negra tienes que apretar el resorte del doble fondo..., ¡el resorte del doble fondo! ¡Escucha! ¿Sabes dónde está? Tienes que aprenderlo, Asun, atiende, te va a hacer falta o si no te morirás de hambre", pero ella tenía el mirar cerrado a toda posible comprensión. Alí se levantó, la contempló durante largo rato frunciendo su perfil de bronce, rascó la tripa del conejo con la punta de su pie y se marchó, sin tan siquiera mirarme, yo creo que por miedo a delatarse.

No le volvimos a ver más. Días después supe que se había ido con una de las danzonas de sobremesa, una mulata adolescente de orejas coralinas. Con pleno derecho, puesto que él lo había ganado, habíase llevado todo el dinero, y dos pequeñas joyas de Asunción, y la radio portátil, y el reloj. Pero en su magnanimidad había dejado todos sus útiles de mago, las cajas trucadas, los pañuelos de cuatro superficies. Asunción, como era previsible, reaccionó de forma abyecta. Durante días sobrenadó en lágrimas y alcohol. Lloraba por su ausencia con impúdicos lamentos y era incapaz de hilvanar dos pensamientos consecuentes. No teníamos un maldito dólar con el que

comer, y para colmo de agravios Asunción estaba preñada de
dos meses, enojoso avatar que le acontecía con frecuencia: su
desgastado cuerpo mantenía un furor prolífero propio de una
rata. Hube de ser yo, una vez más, quien salvara aquella situación. Fui yo quien buscó a una de las chicas del club para que
nos desembarazara de la grávida molestia de Asunción. Fui yo
quien imploró al dueño del local para que la contratara como
bailarina, y he de resaltar que fue un duro esfuerzo, puesto
que Asunción estaba gruesa y espantosa y el dueño se resistía
a darle empleo y al fin concedió tan sólo media paga. Fui yo
quien tuvo que soportar aquellos primeros y lamentables días
de Asunción, sus moqueantes gemidos, su torpe dolor. Recuerdo la noche que debutó como danzante. El día anterior
le habían incrustado un trozo de caña de bambú en el útero
y había escupido el feto en la mañana, de modo que, cuando
le tocó bailar, las blancuzcas carnes de Asunción estaban coloreadas de fiebre. Agitaba el culo sobre la mesa con menos
gracia que un carnero —mostró unas púdicas pamplinas de
doncella verdaderamente sorprendentes— y aún bailando lloriqueaba entre dientes, así es que tuve que permanecer a su lado durante toda la actuación para que no desbarrara demasiado, "eres una imbécil", le decía, "vamos a perder el trabajo,
después de lo que me ha costado conseguirlo", y gracias a mi
serenidad salvé el momento. Fui yo, en fin, quien la enseñó
poco a poco todos los trucos mágicos de Alí, trucos que yo
sabía a la perfección pero que por mi escasa talla me veía impedido de representar, y conseguí montar entre los dos un espectáculo más o menos presentable. Volvió a pasárseme por
la cabeza entonces la idea de matarla, al comprenderla tan
desdichada y miserable, en aquellos primeros días de soledad.
Pero deseché el pensamiento por pura estrategia, me aferré a
la pobre Asunta con la esperanza última de volver a ver a Alí
algún día. Porque no he citado aquí mis penas y tormentos
por decoro, pero es menester que haga una referencia a mi
digno dolor ante la ausencia de mi dueño, la pérdida del sentido de mi vida, la punzante amargura que casi me condujo a
la demencia; y sólo se amenguaba mi tormento con el leniti-
vo de imaginarle al fin libre, al fin triunfante, al fin Alí glorioso, viviendo la vida que en verdad le correspondía, una vida de héroe y de gala.

Proseguimos durante años nuestro recorrido por el infra-
mundo americano, llevando nuestro espectáculo de magia por
los clubes, con nuestras visas caducadas, huyendo de los huro-
nes del Departamento de Estado. Estábamos invernando en

los arrabales de Chicago, atrapados por los vientos y las nieves, cuando una noche, tras la actuación, entró un mangante en el camerín. Era magro y cuarentón, escurrido de hombros, cejijunto, con un chirlo violáceo atravesándole la jeta y una expresión necia pintada en las orejas. Llegó al camerín, digo, se acercó a Asunción riendo bobamente y dijo: "ai laiquiú", que quiere decir "me gustas" en inglés. Yo poseo profundos conocimientos de griego y de latín, y mi natural inteligencia me ayudó a hablar y entender inglés con notable rapidez. Pero mi fuerte son las lenguas clásicas y nobles, y nunca manifesté el menor interés en aprender bien ese farfulleo de bárbaros que es el idioma anglosajón: más aún, llevé a gala el no aprenderlo. Por ello, mi inglés es de oído, y seguramente en la transcripción del mismo se deslizará algún pequeño error, que espero que ustedes sabrán comprender y disculpar. Decía que el rufián de la mejilla tajada le dijo a Asunta "ai laiquiú" y "iú ar greit", que significa eres grande, magnífica, estupenda. Pero ella, con una cordura sorprendente mostróse recelosa y resabiada y le echó sin miramientos del local. Regresó el tipo al día siguiente recibiendo el mismo trato, y la escena se repitió por más de una semana. Al cabo, en su visita nona, Asunción dudó, suspiró y se le quedó mirando sumida en desalientos. El chirlado aprovechó el instante y añadió con gesto papanatas: "ai laviú, iú ar aloun an mi tú", que significa "tú estás sola y yo también", y entonces Asunción se echó a llorar acodada en el canasto de mimbre de la ropa. El tipo se acercó a ella, acarició su pelo con una intolerable manaza de enlutadas uñas, y luego sacó de su bolsillo un pisapapeles de cristal —una bola con la estatua de la Libertad dentro que nevaba viruta de algodón al volverla del revés— y se lo ofreció a Asunción, "for iú, mai darlin". A partir de entonces fuimos de nuevo tres.

Nunca pude soportarlo. Se llamaba Ted y era un australiano ruin y zafio. En el antebrazo izquierdo tenía tatuada una serpiente que él hacía ondular y retorcerse con tensiones musculares. Ted fumaba mucho, tosía mucho y de vez en cuando escupía sangre. También fumaba opio y entonces los ojos se le achicaban y quedaba flojo y como ausente. No sabía hablar más que de su maldita guerra, "dat fáquin uor", como él decía. Aprendió a chapurrear cristiano de forma lamentable y disfrutaba mentecatamente al narrar una y otra vez su misma historia, mientras encendía un pitillo con otro, esos cigarrillos que él partía por la mitad con la burda esperanza de cuidar así sus pulmones tuberculosos. Repetía incesantemente cómo

fue al Vietnam como ayudante de sonido de un equipo de la
televisión americana. Cómo el equipo se volvió tras dos meses
de estancia, y cómo él decidió quedarse allí, permaneciendo
entre Vietnam y Camboya durante nueve años para aspirar el
aroma de la guerra. "Yo no tener otra cosa mejor que hacer",
explicaba Ted chupando avariciosamente sus mutilados cigarrillos, "en Vietnam tú vivir para no ser matado, esa estar buena razón para vivir '. Después vino el caer herido en el 73, el
encontrarse en América de nuevo sin un maldito dólar, el que
la guerra se acabara, "dous bastards, finis mai uor", exclama-
ba indignado, esos bastardos terminaron mi guerra. Asunción
le escuchaba en religioso silencio y le quería, oh, sí, fútil y
casquivana como toda mujer fue incapaz de guardar la ausencia de su dueño, e incluso dejó de beber, o al menos de embo-
rracharse tanto. Se me partía el corazón viendo cómo ese ma-
landrín australiano engordaba y enlucía a ojos vistas, cómo
echaba pelo de buen año, como era tratado a cuerpo de rey.
Ted se dejaba mimar y dormitaba en opios y siestas abundantes. No servía ni para el trabajo ni para el mando, era incapaz
de darle un bofetón a nadie. Permanecía el día entero calen-
tándole la cama a Asunción, y luego, al regresar nosotros de
la actuación del club, se incorporaba entre almohadones riéndose con regocijo de drogado, hablaba de su guerra, sacaba a
pasear a la serpiente de antebrazo, pellizcaba las nalgas de
Asunción con rijoso carcajeo y la llamaba "darlin, suiti, joney",
entre arrebatos de tos mojada en sangre. Ted no era un hombre, era un truhán acaponado. Y ese eunuco había suplanta-
do a mi dueño y señor, ese eunuco pretendía ser el sucesor
del Gran Alí.

Sé bien que en mi condena judicial influyó notablemente
el hecho de haber intentado un segundo "asesinato" —qué injusta, cruel palabra – tras la consumación del primero. ¿Cómo
podría explicarles que hay personas cuya vida es tan banal
que su muerte es el único gesto digno, la única hazaña dramá-
tica de toda su existencia, y que parecen vivir sólo para morir? Los dioses me ayuden, ahora que ya me aproximo al de-
senlace del relato, a saber encontrar la voz justa, el vocablo
certero con que expresar la hondura épica de lo acaecido.

Un día decidieron volver a Madrid. Y digo decidieron,
puesto que yo me resistía a abandonar esas Américas en las
que debía estar mi amor. No obstante, y tras cierto forcejeo,
accedí a acompañarles, ya que la presencia de Asunción seguía pareciéndome el último recurso posible para conectarme
con Alí: siempre tuve la intuición de que mi señor volvería al-

gún día a reclamar sus propiedades. Llegamos, pues al Jawai, que seguía manteniendo en pie su portentoso deterioro, y Pepín nos recibió con alborozoso, lagrimeo falaz de viejo senil y grandes retemblores de papada. Pepín se apresuró a oficiar el sacrificio de tres copas de orujo una tras otra, dando las gracias a los cielos por nuestro buen regreso, y ni tan siquiera mencionó la ausencia del bienamado Alí, guardando un silencio infame y temeroso. Vine de nuevo instalado en mi camastrón de siempre, tras seis años de ausencia, y continué arrastrando mi desesperada vida mes tras mes, actuando en el club durante las noches, ahogándome de nostalgia en los días, recordando la apostura de mi dueño y abrasándome en el dolor de su ausencia, que en ese decorado que habíamos compartido se me hacía aún más insoportable. Transcurrieron así quizá tres años en un sobrevivir cegado de atonía. Hasta que al fin sucedió todo.

Amaneció con la apariencia de un día anodino, ni más alegre ni menos triste que otro cualquiera. La mañana debía andar mediada, y yo me encontraba revisando el material del espectáculo, extendido sobre el carcomido tablado de madera. En esas escuché el susurro de una puerta al cerrarse blandamente. El local estaba vacío y oscuro, sólo dos focos iluminaban mi trabajo en el escenario. Procuré escudriñar las tinieblas más allá del círculo de luz: junto a la entrada vi un borrón indeciso, la figura de un hombre, que giró de inmediato y se dirigió hacia el piso por las escaleras interiores. No sé por qué – ciertamente por la clarividencia del amor —sospeché que esa mancha fugaz debía ser Alí, pese a no haberle podido distinguir con precisión. El corazón se me desbocó entre las costillas, y sentí cómo el aliento se me congelaba en la nuez. Dejé los avíos de mago abandonados y corrí hacia el piso con toda la velocidad que pude imprimir a la escasez de mis piernas. Antes de entrar en la casa, sin embargo, me detuve, y quedé atisbando por la rendija de la puerta semiabierta. Al fondo estaba Asunción, desmelenada, ojimedrosa, mirando hacia un punto fijo de la habitación con gesto petrificado y carente de parpadeo. Y entonces le oí. Oí a mi dueño, a mi Alí, a mi bien amado, que hablaba desde el otro lado de la puerta, oculto para mis ojos, con voz quebrada y extraña: "Bueno, Asunta, ¿no saludas a tu hombre?", decía, " ¿no vienes a darme un beso, después de tantos años? Vuelvo a casa y ya no me volveré a marchar'', añadía para mi gran gozo, "venga mujer, ven a darme un beso si no quieres que te rompa los hocicos'', concluía turbio y receloso. La mancha de su cuerpo cubrió la

rendija, le vi de espaldas acercándose a Asun, le vi forcejear
con ella, oí una sonora bofetada, un exabrupto, un gemido,
Alí dio un traspiés separándose de la mujer, y en la mano de
Asunción brilló algo: era la bola, el pisapapeles de las nieves
eternas de algodón, que siempre mantuvo un ridículo puesto
de honor en la cómoda de la pared del fondo. La bola de vidrio cruzó el aire lanzada por feroz impulso. Oí un golpe seco, un quejido, luego una especie de sordo bramar, "vas a ver,
puta, vas a ver quién soy yo, te vas a arrepentir de lo que has
hecho", abrí un poco más la puerta, contemplé nuevamente
las espaldas de Alí dirigiéndose hacia ella, en su diestra brillaba la vieja navaja cabritera y el paso de mi dueño era indeciso.
Y en ese momento apareció por no sé dónde el miserable australiano, con pasmosa velocidad le sujetó el brazo armado, le
propinó, oh, no quisiera recordarlo, un rodillazo en sus partes
pudendas, recogió calmoso la navaja del suelo mientras observaba la figura acuclillada y retorcida de dolores de mi Alí:
"tú marchar a toda leshe", decía Ted, chulo y burlón, con el
chirlo resaltando extrañamente lívido en su cara, "tú fuera o
te mato, ¿habiste?, largo, si volveré a verte aquí te mato, ¿sa-
biste?". Y le agarró del cogote y del cinturón de cuero —su
viejo cinturón, su vara de mando, su báculo patricio— y le levantó en volandas, y apenas tuve tiempo de apartarme de la
puerta, y Ted pasó ante mí sin verme y le arrojó escaleras
abajo, el eunuco arrojó a mi bello héroe.

Callé, consternado ante tal subversión de valores, ante tal
apocalipsis. Vi cómo el sombrío bulto de Alí se incorporaba
del suelo gruñendo quedamente y cómo cojeaba hacia el es-
trado, hacia el frío círculo de luz. Bajé tras él chitón y cauto
y me acerqué al escenario. Le llamé. "Alí, Gran Alí", dije. Y
él se volvió.

Cómo podría describir el infinito dolor, la melancolía, la
mordedura ardiente que me causó su imagen. Estaba grueso,
dilatado, calvo. Estaba, oh dioses, convertido en un desecho
de sí mismo. Me costó trabajo reconocerle bajo la máscara de
su rostro abotargado e inflamado: tenía los ojos muertos, la
nariz enrojecida, el cráneo pelón y descamado, y, sobre una
ceja, el sangriento moretón producido por el pisapapeles asesino. Qué crueles habían sido esos ocho años de ausencia para
él: le perdí siendo un dios, un guerrero, un titán, y le recupe-
ré siendo un esclavo, un derrotado barrigudo, una condensación de sucesivas miserias. "Chepa", farfulló tambaleante,
"ven aquí. Chepa, ven", añadió con aviesa mansedumbre. Me
acerqué. Alí apoyaba su trastabilleo de borracho en la mesita

de laca del espectáculo. "Ven, ven ', insistía. Me acerqué aún
más, aunque hubiera preferido ocultar las lágrimas que me cubrían las mejillas. Alí extendió una mano torpe y me agarró
del cuello. Hubiera podido evitar su zarpa fácilmente y sin embargo no quise. "Tú también, Chepa, ¿tú también quieres ro-
barme y echarme de mi casa?", su mano apretaba y apretaba
y yo lloraba negando con la cabeza, porque con la garganta
no podía, tan cerrada la tenía de su tenaza y de mi propia
tristeza. Sus ojos, que antaño fueron secretos, zaínos y metá-
licos, estaban inyectados en sangre, con el blanco de color
amarillento. Cuando ya me sentía asfixiar aflojó la mano y
me soltó. "Les voy a matar, Chepa", decía con soniquete loco, "les voy a matar, conseguiré una pipa y les lleno de plomo, yo les mato". Y entonces su cara se retorció en una con-
vulsión de miedo, sí, miedo, miedo, mi Alí, miedo mi dueño,
miedo babeante, indigno miedo. Fue en ese momento cuando
comprendí claramente mi misión, cuando supe cuál era mi
deber. Sobre la mesa de laca estaban los puñales del espectáculo, extendidos en meticulosa formación, y me fue fácil coger uno. Alí seguía mascullando ebrias amenazas, mordiendo
el aire con apestado aliento de bodega. Me acerqué a él y el
mango del cuchillo estaba helado en la fiebre de mi mano. Alí
me miró, perplejo, como descubriéndome por primera vez.
Bajó sus ojos erráticos al puñal, boqueó un par de veces. Y
entonces, oh tristeza, sus labios temblaron de pavor, empali-
deció dolorosamente y su cara se deshizo en una mueca de
abyecta sumisión, "qué haces", tartamudeó, "qué haces, Chepa, deja ese puñal, Chepa, por favor, qué quieres? ¿Dinero?
Te daré mucho dinero, Chepa, te voy a hacer rico, Chepa, deja eso, Dios mío", había ido retrocediendo y estaba ya arrinconado contra el muro, gimiente, implorando mi perdón, sin
comprenderme. Extendí el brazo y le hundí el acero en la barriga, a la altura de mis ojos y su ombligo, el cuchillo chirrió
y Alí aulló con agudo lamento, y luego los dos nos quedamos
mirando, sorprendidos. Retiré el arma y observé con estupor
cómo la aguda punta emergía lentamente de su mango: en mi
zozobra había cogido uno de los machetes trucados del espectáculo, uno que hundía la hoja en la cacha a la más mínima
presión. Alí se echó a reír con carcajadas histéricas, "ay, Chepa, creí que querías matarme, era una broma, Chepa, una
broma", había caído al suelo de rodillas y reía y lloraba a la
vez. No perdí tiempo, pese a hallarme ofuscado y febril; re-
trocedí hasta la mesa, escogí la daga sarracena de feroz y real
filo y corrí hacia él, ciego de lágrimas, vergüenza y amargura.

La primera cuchillada le hirió aún de hinojos, se la di en el cuello, oblicua, tal como tenía medio inclinada la cabeza en sus náuseas de terror y de embriaguez. Alí gimió bajito y levantó la cara, la segunda cuchillada fue en el pecho, no gritaba, no decía nada, no se movía, se limitaba a mirarme estático lívido, entregado, estando como estaba de rodillas le podía alcanzar mejor y en cinco o seis tajos conseguí acabarle, y cuando ya asomaba la muerte por sus ojos me pareció rescatar, allá a lo lejos, la imagen dorada y adorada de mi perdido Alí, y creía percibir, en su murmullo ensangrentado, la dignidad de la frase de César: "quoque tu, filio meo".

Quedé un momento tambaleante sobre su cuerpo, jadeando del esfuerzo, el puñal en la mano y todo yo cubierto de su pobre sangre. Escuché entonces un grito de trémolo en falsete y al volverme descubrí a Pepín, "asesino, asesino", chirriaba atragantado, "socorro, socorro, policía". No sé por qué me acerqué a él con la navaja. Quizá porque Pepín había sido un innoble testigo de la degradación última de Alí, o quizá porque pensé que él merecía menos la vida que mi dueño. Pepín me miraba con la cara descompuesta en un retorcido hipo de terror, "por Dios", farfullaba, "por Dios, señor Chepa, por la Santísima Trinidad, por el Espíritu Santo...", decía santiguándose temblorosamente, "por la Inmaculada Concepción de la Virgen María", añadía entre pucheros, "no haga una locura, señor Chepa", era la primera vez que alguien me llamaba señor a lo largo de toda mi existencia, "no haga una locura, señor Chepa, por todos los Apóstoles y Santos", apreté suavemente la punta del cuchillo contra su desmesurada y fofa barriga, "hiiiiiii", pitaba el cuitado con agudo resoplido, las grasas de su vientre cedían bajo la presión del puñal sin hacer herida, como un globo no del todo hinchado que se hunde sin estallar bajo tu dedo, "Mater Gloriosa, Mater Amantísima, Mater Admirábilis...", balbuceaba Pepín con los ojos en blanco; en el cenit de su bamboleante vientre se formó un lunar de sangre en torno a la punta de la daga eran sólo unas gotas tiñendo la camisa, el rezumar de un pequeño rasguño. Entonces me invadió una lasitud última y comprendí que todo había acabado, que mi vida no tenía ya razón de ser. Retiré el cuchillo y Pepín se derrumbó sobre el escenario con vahído de doncella. Alguien me arrebató el arma, creo que fue Ted, y lo demás ustedes ya lo saben.

Poco más me resta de añadir. Insistiré tan sólo en mi orgullo por la acción que he cometido. Mi abogado, un bienintencionado mentecato, quiso basar la causa en el alegato de defensa propia, pero yo me negué a admitir tal ignominia, que desvirtuaba la grandeza de mi gesto. Nadie supo comprenderme. Pepín clamó con obesa histeria que yo había querido asesinarle y que siempre pensó que yo era algo anormal. Asunción habló con ruin malevolencia sobre la supuesta crueldad de Alí, y en su sandez llegó a sostener con mi abogado que yo había actuado en mi defensa e incluso en la de ella: nunca la desprecié tanto como entonces. Todo el juicio fue un ensañamiento sobre el recuerdo de mi amado, una tergiversación de valores, una lamentable corruptela. Una vez más, hube de encargarme yo de poner las cosas en su sitio, y en mi intervención final desmentí a los leguleyos, hablé de mi amor y de mi orgullo y compuse, en suma, un discurso ejemplar que desafió en pureza retórica a las más brillantes alocuciones de Pericles, aunque luego fuera ferozmente distorsionado por la prensa y se me adjudicaron por él crueles calificativos de demencia. No importa. Me he resignado, como dije al principio, a saberme incomprendido. Me he resignado a saberme fuera de mi tiempo. Al acabar esta narración termino también con mi función en esta vida. Hora es ya de poner fin a tanta incongruencia.

Cuando ustedes lean esto yo ya me habré liberado de la cerrazón obtusa de esta sociedad. Mi descreimiento religioso me facilita el comprender que el suicidio puede ser un acto honroso y no un pecado. Con el adelanto que me ha dado la revista por estas memorias he conseguido que un maleante de la cárcel me facilite el medio para bien morir: en este mundo actual del que ustedes se sienten tan ridículamente satisfechos se consigue todo con dinero. El truhán que me ha vendido el veneno se empecinó al principio en proporcionarme una sobredosis de heroína: "es lo más cómodo de encontrar", dijo, "y además se trata de una muerte fácil". Pero yo no quería fallecer en el deshonor de un alcaloide sintético, hijo de la podredumbre de este siglo. Así es que, tras mucho porfiar, logré que me trajera algo de arsénico, medio gramo, suficiente para acabar con un hombre normal, más aún con mi discreta carnadura de varón menguado. Sé bien que el arsénico conlleva una agonía dolorosa, pero cuando menos es un veneno de abolengo, una ponzoña con linaje y siglos de muerte a sus espaldas. Ya que no poseo la gloriosa y socrática cicuta, al menos el arsénico dará a mi fin un aroma honroso y esforzado. Y cuando una posteridad más justa rescate mi recuerdo, podrán decir que Paulus Turris Pumilio supo escoger, al menos, una muerte de dolor y de grandeza.

Augusto Monterroso
1921—
Guatemala

El dinosaurio
Obras completas y otros cuentos, 1959.

CUANDO despertó, el dinosaurio todavía estaba allí.

Augusto Monterroso
1921—
Guatemala

Míster Taylor
Obras completas y otros cuentos, 1959.

MENOS rara, aunque sin duda más ejemplar —dijo entonces el otro—, es la historia de míster Percy Taylor, cazador de cabezas en la selva amazónica.

Se sabe que en 1937 salió de Boston, Massachusetts, en donde había pulido su espíritu hasta el extremo de no tener un centavo. En 1944 aparece por primera vez en América del Sur, en la región del Amazonas, conviviendo con los indígenas de una tribu cuyo nombre no hace falta recordar.

Por sus orejas y su aspecto famélico pronto llegó a ser conocido allí como "el gringo pobre", y los niños de la escuela hasta lo señalaban con el dedo y le tiraban piedras cuando pasaba con su barba brillante bajo el dorado sol tropical. Pero esto no afligía la humilde condición de míster Taylor porque había leído en el primer tomo de las *Obras completas* de William G. Knight que si no se siente envidia de los ricos la pobreza no deshonra.

En pocas semanas los naturales se acostumbraron a él y a su ropa extravagante. Además, como tenía los ojos azules y un vago acento extranjero, el Presidente y el Ministro de Relaciones Exteriores lo trataban con singular respeto, temerosos de provocar incidentes internacionales.

Tan pobre y mísero estaba, que cierto día se internó en la selva en busca de hierbas para alimentarse. Había caminado cosa de varios metros sin atreverse a volver el rostro, cuando por pura casualidad vio a través de la maleza dos ojos indígenas que lo observaban decididamente. Un largo estremecimiento recorrió la sensitiva espalda de míster Taylor. Pero míster Taylor, intrépido, arrostró el peligro y siguió su camino silbando como si nada hubiera visto.

De un salto (que no hay para qué llamar felino) el nativo se le puso enfrente y exclamó:

—*Buy head? Money, money.*

A pesar de que el inglés no podía ser peor, míster Taylor, algo indispuesto, sacó en claro que el indígena le ofrecía en venta una cabeza de hombre, curiosamente reducida, que traía en la mano.

Es innecesario decir que míster Taylor no estaba en capacidad de comprarla; pero como aparentó no comprender, el indio se sintió terriblemente disminuido por no hablar bien el inglés, y se la regaló pidiéndole disculpas.

Grande fue el regocijo con que míster Taylor regresó a su choza. Esa noche, acostado boca arriba sobre la precaria estera de palma que le servía de lecho, interrumpido tan sólo por el zumbar de las moscas acaloradas que revoloteaban en torno haciéndose obscenamente el amor, míster Taylor contempló con deleite durante un buen rato su curiosa adquisición. El mayor goce estético lo extraía de contar, uno por uno, los pelos de la barba y el bigote, y de ver de frente el par de ojillos entre irónicos que parecían sonreírle agradecidos por aquella deferencia.

Hombre de vasta cultura, míster Taylor solía entregarse a la contemplación; pero esta vez en seguida se aburrió de sus reflexiones filosóficas y dispuso obsequiar la cabeza a un tío suyo, míster Rolston, residente en Nueva York, quien desde la más tierna infancia había revelado una fuerte inclinación por las manifestaciones culturales de los pueblos hispanoamericanos.

Pocos días después el tío de míster Taylor le pidió —previa indagación sobre el estado de su importante salud— que por favor lo complaciera con cinco más. Míster Taylor accedió gustoso al capricho de míster Rolston y —no se sabe de qué modo— a vuelta de correo tenía "mucho agrado en satisfacer sus deseos". Muy reconocido, míster Rolston le solicitó otras diez. Míster Taylor se sintió "halagadísimo de poder servirlo". Pero cuando pasado un mes aquél le rogó el envío de veinte, míster Taylor, hombre rudo y barbado pero de refinada sensibilidad artística, tuvo el presentimiento de que el hermano de su madre estaba haciendo negocio con ellas.

Bueno, si lo quieren saber, así era. Con toda franqueza, míster Rolston se lo dio a entender en una inspirada carta cuyos términos resueltamente comerciales hicieron vibrar como nunca las cuerdas del sensible espíritu de míster Taylor.

De inmediato concertaron una sociedad en la que míster Taylor se comprometía a obtener y remitir cabezas humanas reducidas en escala industrial, en tanto que míster Rolston las vendería lo mejor que pudiera en su país.

Los primeros días hubo algunas molestas dificultades con ciertos tipos del lugar. Pero míster Taylor, que en Boston había logrado las mejores notas con un ensayo sobre Joseph Henry Silliman, se reveló como político y obtuvo de las autoridades no sólo el permiso necesario para exportar, sino, además, una concesión exclusiva por noventa y nueve años. Escaso trabajo le costó convencer al guerrero ejecutivo y a los brujos legislativos de que aquel paso patriótico enriquecería en corto tiempo a la comunidad, y de que luego estarían todos los sedientos aborígenes en posibilidad de beber (cada vez que hicieran una pausa en la recolección de cabezas) de beber un refresco bien frío, cuya fórmula mágica él mismo proporcionaría.

Cuando los miembros de la Cámara, después de un breve pero luminoso esfuerzo intelectual, se dieron cuenta de tales ventajas, sintieron hervir su amor a la patria y en tres días promulgaron un decreto exigiendo al pueblo que acelerara la producción de cabezas reducidas.

Contados meses más tarde, en el país de míster Taylor las cabezas alcanzaron aquella popularidad que todos recordamos. Al principio eran privilegio de las familias más pudientes; pero la democracia es la democracia y, nadie lo va a negar, en cuestión de semanas pudieron adquirirlas hasta los mismos maestros de escuela.

Un hogar sin su correspondiente cabeza teníase por un hogar fracasado. Pronto vinieron los coleccionistas y con ellos, las contradicciones: poseer diecisiete cabezas llegó a ser considerado de mal gusto; pero era distinguido tener once. Se vulgarizaron tanto que los verdaderos elegantes fueron perdiendo interés y ya sólo por excepción adquirían alguna, si presentaba cualquier particularidad que la salvara de lo vulgar. Una, muy rara, con bigotes prusianos, que perteneciera en vida a un general bastante condecorado, fue obsequiada al Instituto Danfeller, el que a su vez donó, como de rayo, tres y medio millones de dólares para impulsar el desenvolvimiento de aquella manifestación cultural, tan excitante, de los pueblos hispanoamericanos.

Mientras tanto, la tribu había progresado en tal forma que ya contaba con una veredita alrededor del Palacio Legislativo. Por esa alegre veredita paseaban los domingos y el Día de la Independencia los miembros del Congreso, carraspeando, luciendo sus plumas, muy serios riéndose, en las bicicletas que les había obsequiado la Compañía.

Pero, ¿qué quieren? No todos los tiempos son buenos. Cuando menos lo esperaban se presentó la primera escasez de cabezas.

Entonces comenzó lo más alegre de la fiesta.

Las meras defunciones resultaron ya insuficientes. El Ministro de Salud Pública se sintió sincero, y una noche caliginosa, con la luz apagada, después de acariciarle un ratito el pecho como por no dejar, le confesó a su mujer que se consideraba incapaz de elevar la mortalidad a un nivel grato a los intereses de la Compañía, a lo que ella le contestó que no se preocupara, que ya vería cómo todo iba a salir bien, y que mejor se durmieran.

Para compensar esta deficiencia administrativa fue indispensable tomar medidas heroicas y se estableció la pena de muerte en forma rigurosa.

Los juristas se consultaron unos a otros y elevaron a la categoría de delito, penado con la horca o el fusilamiento, según su gravedad, hasta la falta más nimia.

Incluso las simples equivocaciones pasaron a ser hechos delictuosos. Ejemplo: si en una conversación banal, alguien, por puro descuido, decía "Hace mucho calor", y posteriormente podía comprobársele, termómetro en mano, que en realidad el calor no era para tanto, se le cobraba un pequeño impuesto y era pasado ahí mismo por las armas, correspondiendo la cabeza a la Compañía y, justo es decirlo, el tronco y las extremidades a los dolientes.

La legislación sobre las enfermedades ganó inmediata resonancia y fue muy comentada por el Cuerpo Diplomático y por las Cancillerías de potencias amigas.

De acuerdo con esa memorable legislación, a los enfermos graves se les concedían veinticuatro horas para poner en orden sus papeles y morirse; pero si en este tiempo tenían suerte y lograban contagiar a la familia, obtenían tantos plazos de un mes como parientes fueran contaminados. Las víctimas de enfermedades leves y los simplemente indispuestos merecían el desprecio de la patria y, en la calle, cualquiera podía escupirles el rostro. Por primera vez en la historia fue reconocida la importancia de los médicos (hubo varios candidatos al premio Nobel) que no curaban a nadie. Fallecer se convirtió en ejemplo del más exaltado patriotismo, no sólo en el orden nacional, sino en el más glorioso, en el continental.

Con el empuje que alcanzaron otras industrias subsidiarias (la de ataúdes, en primer término, que floreció con la asistencia técnica de la Compañía) el país entró como se dice, en un período de gran auge económico. Este impulso fue particularmente comprobable en una nueva veredita florida, por la que paseaban, envueltas en la melancolía de las doradas tardes de otoño, las señoras de los diputados, cuyas lindas cabecitas decían que sí, que sí, que todo estaba bien, cuando algún periodista solícito, desde el otro lado, las saludaba sonriente sacándose el sombrero.

Al margen recordaré que uno de estos periodistas, quien en cierta ocasión emitió un lluvioso estornudo que no pudo justificar, fue acusado de extremista y llevado al paredón de fusilamiento. Sólo después de su abnegado fin los académicos de la lengua reconocieron que ese periodista era una de las más grandes cabezas del país; pero una vez reducida quedó tan bien que ni siquiera se notaba la diferencia.

¿Y míster Taylor? Para este tiempo ya había sido designado consejero particular del Presidente Constitucional. Ahora, y como ejemplo de lo que puede el esfuerzo individual, contaba los miles por miles; mas esto no le quitaba el sueño porque había leído en el último tomo de las *Obras completas* de William G. Knight que ser millonario no deshonra si no se desprecia a los pobres.

Creo que con ésta será la segunda vez que diga que no todos los tiempos son buenos.

Dada la prosperidad del negocio llegó un momento en que del vecindario sólo iban quedando ya las autoridades y sus señoras y los periodistas y sus señoras. Sin mucho esfuerzo, el cerebro de míster Taylor discurrió que el único remedio posible era fomentar la guerra con las tribus vecinas. ¿Por qué no? El progreso.

Con la ayuda de unos cañoncitos, la primera tribu fue limpiamente descabezada en escasos tres meses. Míster Taylor saboreó la gloria de extender sus dominios. Luego vino la segunda; después la tercera y la cuarta y la quinta. El progreso se extendió con tanta rapidez que llegó la hora en que, por más esfuerzos que realizaron los técnicos, no fue posible encontrar tribus vecinas a quienes hacer la guerra.

Fue el principio del fin.

Las vereditas empezaron a languidecer. Sólo de vez en cuando se veía transitar por ellas a alguna señora, a algún poeta laureado con su libro bajo el brazo. La maleza, de nuevo, se apoderó de las dos, haciendo difícil y espinoso el delicado paso de las damas. Con las cabezas, escasearon las bicicletas y casi desaparecieron del todo los alegres saludos optimistas.

El fabricante de ataúdes estaba más triste y fúnebre que nunca. Y todos sentían como si acabaran de recordar de un grato sueño, de ese sueño formidable en que tú te encuentras una bolsa repleta de monedas de oro y la pones debajo de la almohada y sigues durmiendo y al día siguiente muy temprano, al despertar, la buscas y te hallas con el vacío.

Sin embargo, penosamente, el negocio seguía sosteniéndose. Pero ya se dormía con dificultad por el temor a amanecer exportado.

En la patria de míster Taylor, por supuesto, la demanda era cada vez mayor. Diariamente aparecían nuevos inventos, pero en el fondo nadie creía en ellos y todos exigían las cabecitas hispanoamericanas.

Fue para la última crisis. Míster Rolston, desesperado, pedía y pedía más cabezas. A pesar de que las acciones de la Compañía sufrieron un brusco descenso, míster Rolston estaba convencido de que su sobrino haría algo que lo sacara de aquella situación.

Los embarques, antes diarios, disminuyeron a uno por mes, ya con cualquier cosa, con cabezas de niño, de señoras, de diputados.

De repente cesaron del todo.

Un viernes áspero y gris, de vuelta de la Bolsa, aturdido aún por la gritería y por el lamentable espectáculo de pánico que daban sus amigos, míster Rolston se decidió a saltar por la ventana (en vez de usar el revólver, cuyo ruido lo hubiera llenado de terror) cuando al abrir un paquete del correo se encontró con la cabecita de míster Taylor, que le sonreía desde lejos, desde el fiero Amazonas, con una sonrisa falsa de niño que parecía decir: "Perdón, perdón, no lo vuelvo a hacer".

Juan Carlos Onetti
1909—
Uruguay

La cara de la desgracia
1960.

Para Dorotea Muhr - Ignorado
perro de la dicha.

1

AL atardecer estuve en mangas de camisa, a pesar de la molestia del viento, apoyado en la baranda del hotel, solo.
La luz hacía llegar la sombra de mi cabeza hasta el borde del
camino de arena entre los arbustos que une la carretera y la
playa con el caserío.

La muchacha apareció pedaleando en el camino para perderse en seguida detrás del chalet de techo suizo, vacío, que
mantenía el cartel de letras negras, encima del cajón para la
correspondencia. Me era imposible no mirar el cartel por lo
menos una vez al día; a pesar de su cara castigada por las lluvias, las siestas y el viento del mar, mostraba un brillo perdurable y se hacía ver: *Mi descanso.*

Un momento después volvió a surgir la muchacha sobre
la franja arenosa rodeada por la maleza. Tenía el cuerpo vertical sobre la montura, movía con fácil lentitud las piernas,
con tranquila arrogancia las piernas abrigadas con medias grises, gruesas y peludas, erizadas por las pinochas. Las rodillas
eran asombrosamente redondas, terminadas, en relación a la
edad que mostraba el cuerpo.

Frenó la bicicleta justamente al lado de la sombra de mi
cabeza y su pie derecho, apartándose de la máquina, se apoyó para guardar equilibrio pisando en el corto pasto muerto,
ya castaño, ahora en la sombra de mi cuerpo. En seguida se
apartó el pelo de la frente y me miró. Tenía una tricota oscura, y una pollera rosada. Me miró con calma y atención como si la mano tostada que separaba el pelo de las cejas basta-
ra para esconder su examen.

Calculé que nos separaban veinte metros y menos de treinta años. Descansando en los antebrazos mantuve su mirada,
cambié la ubicación de la pipa entre los dientes, continué mi-

rando hacia ella y su pesada bicicleta, los colores de su cuerpo delgado contra el fondo del paisaje de árboles y ovejas que se aplacaba en la tarde.

Repentinamente triste y enloquecido, miré la sonrisa que la muchacha ofrecía al cansancio, el pelo duro y revuelto, la delgada nariz curva que se movía con la respiración, el ángulo infantil en que habían sido impostados los ojos en la cara —y que ya nada tenía que ver con la edad, que había sido dispuesto de una vez por todas y hasta la muerte—, el excesivo espacio que concedían a la esclerótica. Miré aquella luz del sudor y la fatiga que iba recogiendo el resplandor último o primero del anochecer para cubrirse y destacar como una máscara fosforescente en la oscuridad próxima.

La muchacha dejó con suavidad la bicicleta sobre los arbustos y volvió a mirarme mientras sus manos tocaban el talle con los pulgares hundidos bajo el cinturón de la falda. No sé si tenía cinturón; aquel verano todas las muchachas usaban cinturones anchos. Después miró alrededor. Estaba ahora de perfil, con las manos juntas en la espalda, siempre sin senos, respirando aún con curiosa fatiga, la cara vuelta hacia el sitio de la tarde donde iba a caer el sol.

Bruscamente se sentó en el pasto, se quitó las sandalias y las sacudió; uno a uno tuvo los pies desnudos en las manos, refregando los cortos dedos y moviéndolos en el aire. Por encima de sus hombros estrechos le miré agitar los pies sucios y enrojecidos. La vi estirar las piernas, sacar un peine y un espejo del gran bolsillo con monograma colocado sobre el vientre de la pollera. Se peinó descuidada, casi sin mirarme.

Volvió a calzarse y se levantó, estuvo un rato golpeando el pedal con rápidas patadas. Reiterando un movimiento duro y apresurado, giró hacia mí, todavía solo en la baranda, siempre inmóvil, mirándola. Comenzaba a subir el olor de las madreselvas y la luz del bar del hotel estiró manchas pálidas en el pasto, en los espacios de arena y el camino circular para automóviles que rodeaba la terraza.

Era como si nos hubiéramos visto antes, como si nos conociéramos, como si nos hubiéramos guardado recuerdos agradables. Me miró con expresión desafiante mientras su cara se iba perdiendo en la luz escasa; me miró con un desafío de todo su cuerpo desdeñoso, del brillo del níquel de la bicicleta, del paisaje con chalet de techo suizo y ligustros y eucaliptos jóvenes de troncos lechosos. Fue así por un segundo; todo lo que la rodeaba era segregado por ella y su actitud absurda. Volvió a montar y pedaleó detrás de las hortensias, detrás de

los bancos vacíos pintados de azul, más rápida entre las filas
de coches frente al hotel.

2

Vacié la pipa y estuve mirando la muerte del sol entre los
árboles. Sabía ya, y tal vez demasiado, qué era ella. Pero no
quería nombrarla. Pensaba en lo que me estaba esperando en
la pieza del hotel hasta la hora de la comida. Traté de medir
mi pasado y mi culpa con la vara que acababa de descubrir:
la muchacha delgada y de perfil hacia el horizonte, su edad
corta e imposible, los pies sonrosados que una mano había
golpeado y oprimido.

Junto a la puerta del dormitorio encontré un sobre de la
gerencia con la cuenta de la quincena. Al recogerlo me sorprendí a mí mismo agachado, oliendo el perfume de las madreselvas que ya tanteaba en el cuarto, sintiéndome expectan-
te y triste, sin causa nueva que pudiera señalar con el dedo.
Me ayudé con un fósforo para releer el *Avis aux passagers* enmarcado en la puerta y encendí de nuevo la pipa. Estuve muchos minutos lavándome las manos, jugando con el jabón, y
me miré en el espejo del lavatorio, casi a oscuras, hasta que
pude distinguir la cara delgada y blanca —tal vez la única blanca entre los pasajeros del hotel—, mal afeitada. Era mi cara y
los cambios de los últimos meses no tenían verdadera importancia. Alguno pasó por el jardín cantando a media voz. La
costumbre de jugar con el jabón, descubrí, había nacido con
la muerte de Julián, tal vez en la misma noche del velorio.

Volví al dormitorio y abrí la valija después de sacarla con
el pie de abajo de la cama. Era un rito imbécil, era un rito;
pero acaso resultara mejor para todos que yo me atuviera fielmente a esta forma de la locura hasta gastarla o ser gastado.
Busqué sin mirar, aparté ropas y dos pequeños libros, obtuve
por fin el diario doblado. Conocía la crónica de memoria; era
la más justa, la más errónea y respetuosa entre todas las publi-
cadas. Acerqué el sillón a la luz y estuve mirando sin leer el
título negro a toda página, que empezaba a desteñir: *Se suicida cajero prófugo.* Debajo la foto, las manchas grises que
formaban la cara de un hombre mirando al mundo con expresión de asombro, la boca casi empezando a sonreír bajo el bigote de puntas caídas. Recordé la esterilidad de haber pensado en la muchacha, minutos antes, como en la posible inicial
de alguna frase cualquiera que resonara en un ámbito distin-

to. Este, el mío, era un mundo particular, estrecho, insustituible. No cabían allí otra amistad, presencia o diálogo que los que pudieran segregarse de aquel fantasma de bigotes lánguidos. A veces me permitía, él, elegir entre Julián o El Cajero Prófugo.

Cualquiera acepta que puede influir, o haberlo hecho, en el hermano menor. Pero Julián me llevaba —hace un mes y unos días— algo más de cinco años. Sin embargo, debo escribir sin embargo. Pude haber nacido, y continuar viviendo, para estropear su condición de hijo único; pude haberlo obligado, por medio de mis fantasías, mi displicencia y mi tan escasa responsabilidad, a convertirse en el hombre que llegó a ser: primero en el pobre diablo orgulloso de un ascenso, después en el ladrón. También, claro, en el otro, en el difunto relativamente joven que todos miramos pero que sólo yo podía reconocer como hermano.

¿Qué me queda de él? Una fila de novelas policiales, algún recuerdo de infancia, ropas que no puedo usar porque me ajustan y son cortas. Y la foto en el diario bajo el largo título. Despreciaba su aceptación de la vida; sabía que era un solterón por falta de ímpetu; pasé tantas veces, y casi siempre vagando, frente a la peluquería donde lo afeitaban diariamente. Me irritaba su humildad y me costaba creer en ella. Estaba enterado de que recibía a una mujer, puntualmente, todos los viernes. Era muy afable, incapaz de molestar, y desde los treinta años le salía del chaleco olor a viejo. Olor que no puede definirse, que se ignora de qué proviene. Cuando dudaba, su boca formaba la misma mueca que la de nuestra madre. Libre de él, jamás hubiera llegado a ser mi amigo, jamás lo habría elegido o aceptado para eso. Las palabras son hermosas o intentan serlo cuando tienden a explicar algo. Todas estas palabras son, por nacimiento, disconformes e inútiles. Era mi hermano.

Arturo silbó en el jardín, trepó la baranda y estuvo en seguida dentro del cuarto, vestido con una salida, sacudiendo arena de la cabeza mientras cruzaba hasta el baño. Lo vi enjuagarse en la ducha y escondí el diario entre la pierna y el respaldo del sillón. Pero le oí gritar:

—Siempre el fantasma.

No contesté y volví a encender la pipa. Arturo vino silbando desde la bañadera y cerró la puerta que daba sobre la noche. Tirado en una cama, se puso la ropa interior y continuó vistiéndose.

—Y la barriga sigue creciendo —dijo—. Apenas si almorcé, estuve nadando hasta el espigón. Y el resultado es que la barriga sigue creciendo. Habría apostado cualquier cosa a que, de entre todos los hombres que conozco, a vos no podría pasarte esto. Y te pasa, y te pasa en serio. ¿Hace como un mes, no?

—Sí. Veintiocho días.

—Y hasta los tenés contados —siguió Arturo—. Me conocés bien. Lo digo sin desprecio. Veintiocho días que ese infeliz se pegó un tiro y vos, nada menos que vos, jugando al remordimiento. Como una solterona histérica. Porque las hay distintas. Es de no creer.

Se sentó en el borde de la cama para secarse los pies y ponerse los calcetines.

—Sí —dije yo—. Si se pegó un tiro era, evidentemente, poco feliz. No tan feliz, por lo menos, como vos en este momento.

—Hay que embromarse —volvió Arturo—. Como si vos lo hubieras matado. Y no vuelvas a preguntarme... —Se detuvo para mirarse en el espejo— no vuelvas a preguntarme si en algún lugar de diez y siete dimensiones vos resultás el culpable de que tu hermano se haya pegado un tiro.

Encendió un cigarrillo y se extendió en la cama. Me levanté, puse un almohadón sobre el diario tan rápidamente envejecido y empecé a pasearme por el calor del cuarto.

—Como te dije, me voy esta noche —dijo Arturo—. ¿Qué pensás hacer?

—No sé —repuse suavemente, desinteresado—. Por ahora me quedo. Hay verano para tiempo.

Oí suspirar a Arturo y escuché cómo se transformaba su suspiro en un silbido de impaciencia. Se levantó, tirando el cigarrillo al baño.

—Sucede que mi deber moral me obliga a darte unas patadas y llevarte conmigo. Sabés que allá es distinto. Cuando estés bien borracho, a la madrugada, bien distraído, todo se acabó.

Alcé los hombros, sólo el izquierdo, y reconocí un movimiento que Julián y yo habíamos heredado sin posibilidad de elección.

—Te hablo otra vez —dijo Arturo, poniéndose un pañuelo en el bolsillo del pecho—. Te hablo, te repito, con un poco de rabia y con el respeto a que me referí antes. ¿Vos le dijiste al infeliz de tu hermano que se pegara un tiro para escapar de la trampa? Le dijiste que comprara pesos chilenos para cambiarlos por liras y las liras por francos y los francos por coronas bálticas y las coronas por dólares y los dólares por libras y las libras por enaguas de seda amarilla? No, no muevas la cabeza. Caín en el fondo de la cueva. Quiero un sí o un no. A pesar de que no necesito respuesta. ¿Le aconsejaste, y es lo único que importa, que robara? Nunca jamás. No sos capaz de eso. Te lo dije muchas veces. Y no vas a descubrir si es un elogio o un reproche. No le dijiste que robara. ¿Y entonces?

Volví a sentarme en el sillón.

—Ya hablamos de todo eso y todas las veces. ¿Te vas esta noche?

—Claro, en el omnibús de las nueve y nadie sabe cuánto. Me quedan cinco días de licencia y no pienso seguir juntando salud para regalársela a la oficina.

Arturo eligió una corbata y se puso a anudarla.

—Es que no tiene sentido —dijo otra vez frente al espejo—. Yo, admito que alguna vez me encerré con un fantasma. La experiencia siempre acabó mal. Pero con tu hermano, como estás haciendo ahora... Un fantasma con bigotes de alambre. Nunca. El fantasma no sale de la nada, claro. En esta ocasión salió de la desgracia. Era tu hermano, ya sabemos. Pero ahora es el fantasma de cooperativa con bigote de general ruso...

—¿El último momento en serio? —pregunté en voz baja; no lo hice pidiendo nada: sólo quería cumplir y hasta hoy no sé con quién o con qué.

—El último momento —dijo Arturo.

—Veo bien la causa. No le dije, ni la sombra de una insinuación, que usara el dinero de la cooperativa para el negocio de los cambios. Pero cuando le expliqué una noche, sólo por animarlo, o para que su vida fuera menos aburrida, para mostrarle que había cosas que podían ser hechas en el mundo para ganar dinero y gastarlo, aparte de cobrar el sueldo a fin de mes...

—Conozco —dijo Arturo, sentándose en la cama con un bostezo—. Nadé demasiado, ya no estoy para hazañas. Pero era el último día. Conozco toda la historia. Explícame ahora, y te aviso que se acaba el verano, qué remediás con quedarte encerrado aquí. Explícame qué culpa tenés si el otro hizo un disparate.

—Tengo una culpa —murmuré con los ojos entornados, la cabeza apoyada en el sillón; pronuncié las palabras tardas y aisladas—. Tengo la culpa de mi entusiasmo, tal vez de mi mentira. Tengo la culpa de haberle hablado a Julián, por primera vez, de una cosa que no podemos definir y se llama el mundo. Tengo la culpa de haberle hecho sentir —no digo creer— que, si aceptaba los riesgos, eso que llamé el mundo sería para él.

—¿Y qué? —dijo Arturo, mirándose desde lejos el peinado en el espejo—. Hermano. Todo eso es una idiotez complicada. Bueno, también la vida es una idiotez complicada. Algún día de estos se te pasará el período; andá entonces a visitarme. Ahora vestite y vamos a tomar unas copas antes de comer. Tengo que irme temprano. Pero, antes que lo olvide, quiero dejarte un último argumento. Tal vez sirva para algo.

Me tocó un hombro y me buscó los ojos.

—Escuchame —dijo—. En medio de toda esta complicada, feliz idiotez, ¿Julián, tu hermano, usó correctamente el dinero robado, lo empleó aceptando la exactitud de los disparates que le estuviste diciendo?

—¿El? —me levanté con asombro—. Por favor. Cuando vino a verme ya no había nada que hacer. Al principio, estoy casi seguro, compró bien. Pero se asustó en seguida e hizo cosas increíbles. Conozco muy poco de los detalles. Fue algo así como una combinación de títulos con divisas, de rojo y negro con caballos de carrera.

—¿Ves? —dijo Arturo asintiendo con la cabeza—. Certificado de irresponsabilidad. Te doy cinco minutos para vestirte y meditar. Te espero en el mostrador.

3

Tomamos unas copas mientras Arturo se empeñaba en encontrar en la billetera la fotografía de una mujer.

—No está —dijo por fin—. La perdí. La foto, no la mujer. Quería mostrártela porque tiene algo inconfundible que pocos le descubren. Y antes de quedarte loco vos entendías de esas cosas.

Y estaban, pensaba yo, los recuerdos de infancia que irían naciendo y aumentando en claridad durante los días futuros, semanas o meses. Estaba también la tramposa, tal vez deliberada, deformación de los recuerdos. Estaría, en el mejor de los casos, la elección no hecha por mí. Tendría que vernos, fugazmente o en pesadillas, vestidos con trajes ridículos, jugando en un jardín húmedo o pegándonos en un dormitorio. El era mayor pero débil. Había sido tolerante y bueno, aceptaba cargar con mis culpas, mentía dulcemente sobre las marcas en la cara que le dejaban mis golpes, sobre una taza rota, sobre una llegada tarde. Era extraño que todo aquello no hubiera empezado aún, durante el mes de vacaciones de otoño en la playa; acaso, sin proponérmelo, yo estuviera deteniendo el torrente con las crónicas periodísticas y la evocación de las dos últimas noches. En una Julián estaba vivo, en la siguiente muerto. La segunda noche no tenía importancia y todas sus interpretaciones habían sido despistadas.

Era su velorio, empezaba a colgarle la mandíbula, la venda de la cabeza envejeció y se puso amarilla mucho antes del amanecer. Yo estaba muy ocupado ofreciendo bebidas y comparando la semejanza de las lamentaciones. Con cinco años más que yo, Julián había pasado tiempo atrás de los cuarenta. No había pedido nunca nada importante a la vida; tal vez, sí, que lo dejaran en paz. Iba y venía, como desde niño, pidiendo permiso. Esta permanencia en la tierra, no asombrosa pero sí larga, prolongada por mí, no le había servido, siquiera, para darse a conocer. Todos los susurrantes y lánguidos bebedores de café o whisky coincidían en juzgar y compadecer el suicidio como un error. Porque con un buen abogado, con el precio de un par de años en la cárcel... Y, además, para todos resultaba desproporcionado y grotesco el final, que empezaban a olisquear, en relación al delito. Yo daba las gracias y movía la cabeza; después me paseaba entre el vestíbulo y la cocina, cargando bebidas o copas vacías. Trataba de imaginar, sin dato alguno, la opinión de la mujerzuela barata que visitaba a Julián todos los viernes o todos los lunes, días en que escasean los clientes. Me preguntaba sobre la verdad invisible, nunca exhibida, de sus relaciones. Me preguntaba cuál sería el juicio de ella, atribuyéndole una inteligencia imposible. Qué podría pensar ella, que sobrellevaba la circunstancia de ser prostituta todos los días, de Julián, que aceptó ser ladrón durante pocas semanas pero no pudo, como ella, soportar que los imbéciles que ocupan y forman el mundo, conocieran su falla. Pero no vino en toda la noche o por lo menos no distinguí una cara, una insolencia, un perfume, una humildad que pudieran serle atribuidos.

Sin moverse del taburete del mostrador, Arturo había conseguido el pasaje y asiento para el omnibús. Nueve y cuarenta y cinco.

—Hay tiempo de sobra. No puedo encontrar la foto. Hoy es inútil seguirte hablando. Otra vuelta, mozo.

Ya dije que la noche del velorio no tenía importancia. La anterior es mucho más corta y difícil. Julián pudo haberme esperado en el corredor del departamento. Pero ya pensaba en la policía y eligió dar vueltas bajo la lluvia hasta que pudo ver luz en mi ventana. Estaba empapado —era un hombre nacido para usar paraguas y lo había olvidado— y estornudó varias veces, con disculpa, con burla, antes de sentarse cerca de la estufa eléctrica, antes de usar mi casa. Todo Montevideo conocía la historia de la Cooperativa y por lo menos la mitad de los lectores de diarios deseaba, distraídamente, que no se supiera más del cajero.

Pero Julián no había aguantado una hora y media bajo la lluvia para verme, despedirse con palabras y anunciarme el suicidio. Tomamos unas copas. El aceptó el alcohol sin alardes, sin oponerse:

—Total ahora... —murmuró casi riendo, alzando un hombro.

Sin embargo, había venido para decirme adiós a su manera. Era inevitable el recuerdo, pensar en nuestros padres, en la casa quinta de la infancia, ahora demolida. Se enjugó los largos bigotes y dijo con preocupación:

—Es curioso. Siempre pensé que tú sabías y yo no. Desde chico. Y no creo que se trate de un problema de carácter o de inteligencia. Es otra cosa. Hay gente que se acomoda instintivamente en el mundo. Tú sí y yo no. Siempre me faltó la fe necesaria —se acariciaba las mandíbulas sin afeitar—. Tampoco se trata de que yo haya tenido que ajustar conmigo deformaciones o vicios. No había handicap; por lo menos nunca lo conocí.

Se detuvo y vació el vaso. Mientras alzaba la cabeza, esa que hoy miro diariamente desde hace un mes en la primera página de un periódico, me mostró los dientes sanos y sucios de tabaco.

—Pero —siguió mientras se ponía de pie— tu combinación era muy buena. Debiste regalársela a otro. El fracaso no es tuyo.

—A veces resultan y otras no —dije—. No vas a salir con esta lluvia. Podés quedarte aquí para siempre, todo el tiempo que quieras.

Se apoyó en el respaldo de un sillón y estuvo burlándose sin mirarme.

—Con esta lluvia. Para siempre. Todo el tiempo —se me acercó y me tocó un brazo—. Perdón. Habrá molestias. Siempre hay molestias.

Ya se había ido. Me estuvo diciendo adiós con su presencia siempre acurrucada, con los cuidados bigotes bondadosos, con la alusión a todo lo muerto y disuelto que la sangre, no obstante, era y es capaz de hacer durante un par de minutos.

Arturo estaba hablando de estafas en las carreras de caballos. Miró el reloj y pidió al barman la última copa.

—Pero con más gin, por favor —dijo.

Entonces, sin escuchar, me sorprendí vinculando a mi hermano muerto con la muchacha de la bicicleta. De él no quise recordar la infancia ni la pasiva bondad; sino, absolutamente, nada más que la empobrecida sonrisa, la humilde actitud del cuerpo durante nuestra última entrevista. Si podía darse ese nombre a lo que yo permití que ocurriera entre nosotros cuando vino empapado a mi departamento para decirme adiós de acuerdo a su ceremonial propio.

Nada sabía yo de la muchacha de la bicicleta. Pero entonces, repentinamente, mientras Arturo hablaba de Ever Perdomo o de la mala explotación del turismo, sentí que me llegaba hasta la garganta una ola de la vieja, injusta, casi siempre equivocada piedad. Lo indudable era que yo la quería y deseaba protegerla. No podía adivinar de qué o contra qué. Buscaba, rabioso, cuidarla de ella misma y de cualquier peligro. La había visto insegura y en reto, la había mirado alzar una ensoberbecida cara de desgracia. Esto puede durar pero siempre se paga de prematuro, desproporcionado. Mi hermano había pagado su exceso de sencillez. En el caso de la muchacha —que tal vez no volviera nunca a ver— las deudas eran distintas. Pero ambos, por tan diversos caminos, coincidían en una deseada aproximación a la muerte, a la definitiva experiencia. Julián, no siendo; ella, la muchacha de la bibicleta, buscando serlo todo y con prisas.

—Pero —dijo Arturo—, aunque te demuestren que todas las carreras están arregladas, vos seguís jugando igual. Mirá: ahora que me voy parece que va a llover.

—Seguro —contesté, y pasamos al comedor. La vi en seguida.

Estaba cerca de una ventana, respirando el aire tormentoso de la noche, con un montón de pelo oscuro y recio movido por el viento sobre la frente y los ojos; con zonas de pecas débiles —ahora, bajo el tubo de luz insoportable del comedor— en las mejillas y la nariz, mientras los ojos infantiles y acuosos miraban distraídos la sombra del cielo o las bocas de sus compañeros de mesa; con los flacos y fuertes brazos desnudos frente a lo que podía aceptarse como un traje de noche amarillo, cada hombro protegido por una mano.

Un hombre viejo estaba sentado junto a ella y conversaba con la mujer que tenía enfrente, joven, de espalda blanca y carnosa vuelta hacia nosotros, con una rosa silvestre en el peinado, sobre la oreja. Y al moverse, el pequeño círculo blanco de la flor entraba y salía del perfil distraído de la muchacha. Cuando la mujer reía, echando la cabeza hacia atrás, brillante

la piel de la espalda, la cara de la muchacha quedaba abandonada contra la noche.

Hablando con Arturo, miraba la mesa, traté de adivinar
de dónde provenía su secreto, su sensación de cosa extraordinaria. Deseaba quedarme para siempre en paz junto a la muchacha y cuidar de su vida. La vi fumar con el café, los ojos
clavados ahora en la boca lenta del hombre viejo. De pronto
me miró como antes en el sendero, con los mismos ojos cal-
mos y desafiantes, acostumbrados a contemplar o suponer el
desdén. Con una desesperación inexplicable estuve soportan-
do los ojos de la muchacha, revolviendo los míos contra la
cabeza juvenil, larga y noble; escapando del inaprehensible
secreto para escarbar en la tormenta nocturna, para conquistar la intensidad del cielo y derramarla, imponerla en aquel
rostro de niña que me observaba inmóvil e inexpresivo. El
rostro que dejaba fluir, sin propósito, sin saberlo, contra mi
cara seria y gastada de hombre, la dulzura y la humildad adolescente de las mejillas violáceas y pecosas.

Arturo sonreía fumando un cigarrillo.

—¿Tú también, Bruto? —preguntó.

—¿Yo también qué?

—La niña de la bicicleta, la niña de la ventana. Si no tuviera que irme ahora mismo...

—No entiendo.

—Esa, la del vestido amarillo. ¿No la habías visto antes?

—Una vez. Esta tarde, desde la baranda. Antes que volvie-
ras de la playa.

—El amor a primera vista —asintió Arturo—. Y la juventud intacta, la experiencia cubierta de cicatrices. Es una linda historia. Pero, lo confieso, hay uno que la cuenta mejor.
Esperá.

El mozo se acercó para recoger los platos y la frutera.

—¿Café? —preguntó. Era pequeño, con una oscura cara
de mono.

—Bueno —sonrió Arturo—; eso que llaman café. También
le dicen señorita a la muchacha de amarillo junto a la ventana. Mi amigo está muy curioso; quiere saber algo sobre las excursiones nocturnas de la nena.

Me desabroché el saco y busqué los ojos de la muchacha.
Pero ya su cabeza se había vuelto a un lado y la manga negra
del hombre anciano cortaba en diagonal el vestido amarillo.
En seguida el peinado con flor de la mujer se inclinó, cubriendo la cara pecosa. Sólo quedó de la muchacha algo del pelo
retinto, metálico en la cresta que recibía la luz. Yo recordaba

la magia de los labios y la mirada; magia es una palabra que
no puedo explicar, pero que escribo ahora sin remedio, sin
posibilidad de sustituirla.

—Nada malo —proseguía Arturo con el mozo—. El señor,
mi amigo, se interesa por el ciclismo. Decime. ¿Qué sucede
de noche cuando papi y mami, si son, duermen?

El mozo se balanceaba sonriendo, la frutera vacía a la altura de un hombro.

—Y nada —dijo por fin—. Es sabido. A medianoche la señorita sale en bicicleta; a veces va al bosque, otras a las dunas
—había logrado ponerse serio y repetía sin malicia—: Qué le
voy a decir. No sé nada más, aunque se diga. Nunca estuve
mirando. Que vuelve despeinada y sin pintura. Que una noche
me tocaba guardia y la encontré y me puso diez pesos en la
mano. Los muchachos ingleses que están en el Atlantic hablan mucho. Pero yo no digo nada porque no vi.

Arturo se rio, golpeando una pierna del mozo.

—Ahí tenés— dijo, como si se tratara de una victoria.

—Perdone —pregunté al mozo- . ¿Qué edad puede tener?

— ¿La señorita?

—A veces, esta tarde, me hacía pensar en una criatura;
ahora parece mayor.

—De eso sé con seguridad, señor —dijo el mozo—. Por los
libros tiene quince, los cumplió aquí hace unos días. Entonces, ¿dos cafés? —se inclinó antes de marcharse.

Yo trataba de sonreír bajo la mirada alegre de Arturo; la
mano con la pipa me temblaba en la esquina del mantel.

—En todo caso —dijo Arturo—, resulte o no resulte, es un
plan de vida más interesante que vivir encerrado con un fantasma bigotudo.

Al dejar la mesa la muchacha volvió a mirarme, desde su
altura ahora, una mano todavía enredada en la servilleta, fugazmente, mientras el aire de la ventana le agitaba los pelos
rígidos de la frente y yo dejaba de creer en lo que había contado el mozo y Arturo aceptaba.

En la galería, con la valija y el abrigo en el brazo, Arturo
me golpeó el hombro.

—Una semana y nos vemos. Caigo por el Jauja y te encuentro en una mesa saboreando la flor de la sabiduría. Bueno,
largos paseos en bicicleta.

Saltó al jardín y fue hacia el grupo de coches estaciona-
dos frente a la terraza. Cuando Arturo cruzó las luces encendí
la pipa, me apoyé en la baranda y olí el aire. La tormenta parecía lejana. Volví al dormitorio y estuve tirado en la cama,

escuchando la música que llegaba interrumpida desde el comedor del hotel, donde tal vez hubiera empezado ya a bailar. Encerré en la mano el calor de la pipa y fui resbalando en un lento sueño, en un mundo engrasado y sin aire, donde había sido condenado a avanzar, con enorme esfuerzo y sin deseos, boquiabierto, hacia la salida donde dormía la intensa luz indiferente de la mañana, inalcanzable.

Desperté sudando y fui a sentarme nuevamente en el sillón. Ni Julián ni los recuerdos infantiles habían aparecido en la pesadilla. Dejé el sueño olvidado en la cama, respiré el aire de tormenta que entraba por la ventana, con el olor a mujer, lerdo y caliente. Casi sin moverme arranqué el papel de abajo de mi cuerpo y miré el título, la desteñida foto de Julián. Dejé caer el diario, me puse un impermeable, apagué la luz del dormitorio y salté desde la baranda hasta la tierra blanda del jardín. El viento formaba eses gruesas y me rodeaba la cintura. Elegí cruzar el césped hasta pisar el pedazo de arena donde había estado sentada la muchacha en la tarde. Las medias grises acribilladas por las pinochas, luego los pies desnudos en las manos, las escasas nalgas achatadas contra el suelo. El bosque estaba a mi izquierda, los médanos a la derecha; todo negro y el viento golpeándome ahora la cara. Escuché pasos y vi en seguida la luminosa sonrisa del mozo, la cara de mono junto a mi hombro.

—Mala suerte —dijo el mozo—. Lo dejó.

Quería golpearlo pero sosegué en seguida las manos que arañaban dentro de los bolsillos del impermeable y estuve jadeando hacia el ruido del mar, inmóvil, los ojos entornados, resuelto y con lástima por mí mismo.

—Debe hacer diez minutos que salió —continuó el mozo. Sin mirarlo, supe que había dejado de sonreír y torcía su cabeza hacia la izquierda—. Lo que puede hacer ahora es esperarla a la vuelta. Si le da un buen susto...

Desabroché lentamente el impermeable, sin volverme; saqué un billete del bolsillo del pantalón y se lo pasé al mozo. Esperé hasta no oír los pasos del mozo que iban hacia el hotel. Luego incliné la cabeza, los pies afirmados en la tierra elástica y el pasto donde había estado ella, envasado en aquel recuerdo, el cuerpo de la muchacha y sus movimientos en la remota tarde, protegido de mí mismo y de mi pasado por una ya imperecedera atmósfera de creencia y esperanza sin destino, respirando en el aire caliente donde todo estaba olvidado.

4

La vi de pronto, bajo la exagerada luna de otoño. Iba sola por la orilla, sorteando las rocas y los charcos brillantes y crecientes, empujando la bicicleta, ahora sin el cómico vestido amarillo, con pantalones ajustados y una chaqueta de marinero. Nunca la había visto con esas ropas y su cuerpo y sus pasos no habían tenido tiempo de hacérseme familiares. Pero la reconocí en seguida y crucé la playa casi en línea recta hacia ella.

—Noches —dije.

Un rato después se volvió para mirarme la cara; se detuvo e hizo girar la bicicleta hacia el agua. Me miró un tiempo con atención y ya tenía algo solitario y desamparado cuando volví a saludarla. Ahora me contestó. En la playa desierta la voz le chillaba como un pájaro. Era una voz desapacible y ajena, tan separada de ella, de la hermosa cara triste y flaca; era como si acabara de aprender un idioma, un tema de conversación en lengua extranjera. Alargué un brazo para sostener la bicicleta. Ahora yo estaba mirando la luna y ella protegida por la sombra.

— ¿Para dónde iba? —dije y agregué— : Criatura.

—Para ningún lado —sonó trabajosa la voz extraña—. Siempre me gusta pasear de noche por la playa.

Pensé en el mozo, en los muchachos ingleses del Atlantic; pensé en todo lo que había perdido para siempre, sin culpa mía, sin ser consultado.

—Dicen... —dije. El tiempo había cambiado: ni frío ni viento. Ayudando a la muchacha a sostener la bicicleta en la arena al borde del ruido del mar, tuve una sensación de soledad que nadie me había permitido antes; soledad, paz y confianza.

—Si usted no tiene otra cosa que hacer, dicen que hay, muy cerca, un barco convertido en bar y restaurante.

La voz dura repitió con alegría inexplicable:

—Dicen que hay muy cerca un barco convertido en bar y restaurante.

La oí respirar con fatiga; después agregó:

—No, no tengo nada que hacer. ¿Es una invitación? ¿Y así, con esta ropa?

—Es. Con esa ropa.

Cuando dejó de mirarme le vi la sonrisa; no se burlaba, parecía feliz y poco acostumbrada a la felicidad.

—Usted estaba en la mesa de al lado con su amigo. Su amigo se fue esta noche. Pero se me pinchó una goma en cuanto salí del hotel.

Me irritó que se acordara de Arturo; le quité el manubrio de las manos y nos pusimos a caminar junto a la orilla, hacia el barco.

Dos o tres veces dije una frase muerta; pero ella no contestaba. Volvían a crecer el calor y el aire de tormenta. Sentí que la chica entristecía a mi lado; espié sus pasos tenaces, la decidida verticalidad del cuerpo, las nalgas de muchacho que apretaba el pantalón ordinario.

El barco estaba allí, embicado y sin luces.

—No hay barco, no hay fiesta — dije—. Le pido perdón por haberla hecho caminar tanto y para nada.

Ella se había detenido para mirar el carguero ladeado bajo la luna. Estuvo un rato así, las manos en la espalda como sola, como si se hubiera olvidado de mí y de la bicicleta. La luna bajaba hacia el horizonte de agua o ascendía de allí. De pronto la muchacha se dio vuelta y vino hacia mí; no dejé caer la bicicleta. Me tomó la cara entre las manos ásperas y la fue moviendo hasta colocarla en la luz.

—Qué —roncó—. Hablaste. Otra vez.

Casi no podía verla pero la recordaba. Recordaba muchas otras cosas a las que ella, sin esfuerzo, servía de símbolo. Había empezado a quererla y la tristeza comenzaba a salir de ella y derramarse sobre mí.

—Nada —dije—. No hay barco, no hay fiesta.

—No hay fiesta —dijo otra vez, ahora columbré la sonrisa en la sombra, blanca y corta como la espuma de las pequeñas olas que llegaban hasta pocos metros de la orilla. Me besó de golpe; sabía besar y la sentí la cara caliente, húmeda de lágrimas. Pero no solté la bicicleta.

—No hay fiesta —dijo otra vez, ahora con la cabeza inclinada, oliéndome el pecho. La voz era más confusa, casi gutural—. Tenía que verte la cara —de nuevo me la alzó contra la luna—. Tenía que saber que no estaba equivocada. ¿Se entiende?

—Sí —mentí; y entonces ella me sacó la bicicleta de las manos, montó e hizo un gran círculo sobre la arena húmeda.

Cuando estuvo a mi lado se apoyó con una mano en mi nuca y volvimos hacia el hotel. Nos apartamos de las rocas y desviamos hacia el bosque. No lo hizo ella ni lo hice yo. Se detuvo junto a los primeros pinos y dejó caer la bicicleta.

—La cara. Otra vez. No quiero que te enojes —suplicó.

Dócilmente miré hacia la luna, hacia las primeras nubes que aparecían en el cielo.

—Algo —dijo con su extraña voz—. Quiero que digas algo. Cualquier cosa.

Me puso una mano en el pecho y se empinó para acercar los ojos de niña a mi boca.

—Te quiero. Y no sirve. Y es otra manera de la desgracia —dije después de un rato, hablando casi con la misma lentitud que ella.

Entonces la muchacha murmuró "pobrecito" como si fuera mi madre, con su rara voz, ahora tierna y vindicativa, y empezamos a enfurecer y besarnos. Nos ayudamos a desnudarla en lo imprescindible y tuve de pronto dos cosas que no había merecido nunca: su cara doblegada por el llanto y la felicidad bajo la luna, la certeza desconcertante de que no habían entrado antes en ella.

Nos sentamos cerca del hotel sobre la humedad de las rocas. La luna estaba cubierta. Ella se puso a tirar piedritas; a veces caían en el agua con un ruido exagerado; otras, apenas se apartaban de sus pies. No parecía notarlo.

Mi historia era grave y definitiva. Yo la contaba con una seria voz masculina, resuelto con furia a decir la verdad, despreocupado de que ella creyera o no.

Todos los hechos acababan de perder su sentido y sólo podrían tener, en adelante, el sentido que ella quisiera darles. Hablé, claro, de mi hermano muerto; pero ahora, desde aquella noche, la muchacha se había convertido —retrocediendo para clavarse como una larga aguja en los días pasados— en el tema principal de mi cuento. De vez en cuando la oía moverse y decirme que sí con su curiosa voz mal formada. También era forzoso aludir a los años que nos separaban, apenarse con exceso, fingir una desolada creencia en el poder de la palabra *imposible,* mostrar un discreto desánimo ante las luchas inevitables. No quise hacerle preguntas y las afirmaciones de ella, no colocadas siempre en la pausa exacta, tampoco pedían confesiones. Era indudable que la muchacha me había liberado de Julián, y de muchas otras ruinas y escorias que la muerte de Julián representaba y había traído a la superficie; era indudable que yo, desde una media hora atrás, la necesitaba y continuaría necesitándola.

La acompañé hasta cerca de la puerta del hotel y nos separamos sin decirnos nuestros nombres. Mientras se alejaba creí ver que las dos cubiertas de la bicicleta estaban llenas de aire. Acaso me hubiera mentido en aquello pero ya nada tenía importancia. Ni siquiera la vi entrar en el hotel y yo mismo pasé en la sombra, de largo, frente a la galería que comunicaba con mi habitación; seguí trabajosamente hacia los médanos, deseando no pensar en nada, por fin, y esperar la tormenta.

Caminé hacia las dunas y luego, ya lejos, volví en dirección al monte de eucaliptos. Anduve lentamente entre los árboles, entre el viento retorcido y su lamento, bajo los truenos que amenazaban elevarse del horizonte invisible, cerrando los ojos para defenderlos de los picotazos de la arena en la cara. Todo estaba oscuro y —como tuve que contarlo varias veces después— no divisé un farol de bicicleta, suponiendo que alguien los usara en la playa, ni siquiera el punto de brasa de un cigarrillo de alguien que caminara o descansase sentado en la arena, sobre las hojas secas, apoyado en un tronco, con las piernas recogidas, cansado, húmedo, contento. Ese había sido yo; y aunque no sabía rezar, anduve dando las gracias, negándome a la aceptación, incrédulo.

Estaba ahora al final de los árboles, a cien metros del mar y frente a las dunas. Sentía heridas las manos y me detuve para chuparlas. Caminé hacia el ruido del mar hasta pisar la arena húmeda de la orilla. No vi, repito, ninguna luz, ningún movimiento, en la sombra; no escuché ninguna voz que partiera o deformara el viento.

Abandoné la orilla y empecé a subir y bajar las dunas, resbalando en la arena fría que me entraba chisporroteante en los zapatos, apartando con las piernas los arbustos, corriendo casi, rabioso y con una alegría que me había perseguido durante años y ahora me daba alcance, excitado como si no pudiera detenerme nunca, riendo en el interior de la noche ventosa, subiendo y bajando a la carrera las diminutas montañas, cayendo de rodillas y aflojando el cuerpo hasta poder respirar sin dolor, la cara doblada hacia la tormenta que venía del agua. Después fue como si también me dieran caza todos los desánimos y las renuncias; busqué durante horas, sin entusiasmo, el camino de regreso al hotel. Entonces me encontré con el mozo y repetí el acto de no hablarle, de ponerle diez pesos en la mano. El hombre sonrió y yo estaba lo bastante cansado como para creer que había entendido, que todo el mundo entendía y para siempre.

Volví a dormir medio vestido en la cama como en la arena, escuchando la tormenta que se había resuelto por fin, golpeado por los truenos, hundiéndome sediento en el ruido colérico de la lluvia.

5

Había terminado de afeitarme cuando escuché en el vidrio de la puerta que daba a la baranda el golpe de los dedos.

Era muy temprano; supe que las uñas de los dedos eran largas y estaban pintadas con ardor. Sin dejar la toalla, abrí la puerta; era fatal, allí estaba.

Tenía el pelo teñido de rubio y acaso a los veinte años hubiera sido rubia; llevaba un traje sastre de cheviot que los días y los planchados le habían apretado contra el cuerpo y un paraguas verde, con mango de marfil, tal vez nunca abierto. De las tres cosas, dos le había adivinado yo —o supuesto sin error— a lo largo de la vida y en el velorio de mi hermano.

—Betty —dijo al volverse, con la mejor sonrisa que podía mostrar.

Fingí no haberla visto nunca, no saber quién era. Se trataba, apenas, de una manera del piropo, de una forma retorcida de la delicadeza que ya no me interesaba.

Esta era, pensé, ya no volverá a serlo, la mujer que yo distinguía borrosa detrás de los vidrios sucios de un café de arrabal, tocándole los dedos a Julián en los largos prólogos de los viernes o los lunes.

—Perdón —dijo— por venir de tan lejos a molestarlo y a esta hora. Sobre todo en estos momentos en que usted, como el mejor de los hermanos de Julián... Hasta ahora mismo, le juro, no puedo aceptar que esté muerto.

La luz de la mañana la avejentaba y debió parecer otra cosa en el departamento de Julián, incluso en el café. Yo había sido, hasta el fin, el único hermano de Julián; ni mejor ni peor. Estaba vieja y parecía fácil aplacarla. Tampoco yo, a pesar de todo lo visto y oído, a pesar del recuerdo de la noche anterior en la playa, aceptaba del todo la muerte de Julián. Sólo cuando incliné la cabeza y la invité con un brazo a entrar en mi habitación descubrí que usaba sombrero y lo adornaba con violetas frescas, rodeadas de hojas de hiedra.

—Llámame Betty —dijo, y eligió para sentarse el sillón que escondía el diario, la foto, el título, la crónica indecisamente crapulosa—. Pero era cuestión de vida o muerte.

No quedaban rastros de la tormenta y la noche podía no haber sucedido. Miré el sol en la ventana, la mancha amarillenta que empezaba a buscar la alfombra. Sin embargo, era indudable que yo me sentía distinto, que respiraba el aire con avidez; que tenía ganas de caminar y sonreír, que la indiferencia —y también la crueldad— se me aparecían como formas posibles de la virtud. Pero todo esto era confuso y sólo pude comprenderlo un rato después.

Me acerqué al sillón y ofrecí mis excusas a la mujer, a aquella desusada manera de la suciedad y la desdicha. Extraje el diario, gasté algunos fósforos y lo hice bailar encendido por encima de la baranda.

—El pobre Julián - dijo ella a mis espaldas.

Volví al centro de la habitación, encendí la pipa y me senté en la cama. Descubrí repentinamente que era feliz y traté de calcular cuántos años me separaban de mi última sensación de felicidad. El humo de la pipa me molestaba los ojos. La bajé hasta las rodillas y estuve mirando con alegría aquella basura en el sillón, aquella maltratada inmundicia que se recostaba, inconsciente, sobre la mañana apenas nacida.

—Pobre Julián —repetí—. Lo dije muchas veces en el velorio y después. Ya me cansé, todo llega. La estuve esperando en el velorio y usted no vino. Pero, entiéndame, gracias a este trabajo de esperarla yo sabía cómo era usted, podía encontrarla en la calle y reconocerla.

Me examinó con desconcierto y volvió a sonreír.

—Sí, creo comprender —dijo.

No era muy vieja, estaba aún lejos de mi edad y de la de Julián. Pero nuestras vidas habían sido muy distintas y lo que me ofrecía desde el sillón no era más que gordura, una arrugada cara de beba, el sufrimiento y el rencor disimulado, la pringue de la vida pegada para siempre a sus mejillas, a los ángulos de la boca, a las ojeras rodeadas de surcos. Tenía ganas de golpearla y echarla.

Pero me mantuve quieto, volví a fumar y le hablé con voz dulce:

—Betty. Usted me dio permiso para llamarla Betty. Usted dijo que se trataba de un asunto de vida o muerte. Julián está muerto, fuera del problema. ¿Qué más entonces, quién más?

Se retrepó entonces en el sillón de cretona descolorida, sobre el forro de grandes flores bárbaras y me estuvo mirando como a un posible cliente: con el inevitable odio y con cálculo.

— ¿Quién muere ahora? —insistí—. ¿Usted o yo?

Aflojó el cuerpo y estuvo preparando una cara emocionante. La miré, admití que podía convencer; y no sólo a Julián. Detrás de ella se estiraba la mañana de otoño, sin nubes, la pequeña gloria ofrecida a los hombres. La mujer, Betty, torció la cabeza y fue haciendo crecer una sonrisa de amargura.

— ¿Quién? —dijo hacia el placard—. Usted y yo. No crea, el asunto recién empieza. Hay pagarés con su firma, sin fondos dicen, que aparecen ahora en el juzgado. Y está la hipoteca sobre mi casa, lo único que tengo. Julián me aseguró que no era más que una oferta; pero la casa, la casita, está hipotecada. Y hay que pagar en seguida. Si queremos salvar algo del naufragio. O si queremos salvarnos.

Por las violetas en el sombrero y por el sudor de la cara, yo había presentido que era inevitable escuchar, más o menos tarde en la mañana de sol, alguna frase semejante.

—Sí —dije—, parece que tiene razón, que tenemos que unirnos y hacer algo.

Desde muchos años atrás no había sacado tanto placer de la mentira, de la farsa y la maldad. Pero había vuelto a ser joven y ni siquiera a mí mismo tenía que dar explicaciones.

—No sé —dije sin cautela— cuánto conoce usted de mi culpa, de mi intervención en la muerte de Julián. En todo caso, puedo asegurarle que nunca le aconsejé que hipotecara su casa, su casita. Pero le voy a contar todo. Hace unos tres meses estuve con Julián. Un hermano comiendo en un restaurante con su hermano mayor. Y se trataba de hermanos que no se veían más de una vez por año. Creo que era el cumpleaños de alguien; de él, de nuestra madre muerta. No recuerdo y no tiene importancia. La fecha, cualquiera que sea, parecía desanimarlo. Le hablé de un negocio de cambios de monedas; pero nunca le dije que robara plata a la Cooperativa.

Ella dejó pasar un tiempo ayudándose con un suspiro y estiró los largos tacos hasta el cuadrilátero de sol en la alfombra. Esperó a que la mirara y volvió a sonreírme; ahora se parecía a cualquier aniversario, al de Julián o al de mi madre. Era la ternura y la paciencia, quería guiarme sin tropiezos.

—Botija —murmuró, la cabeza sobre un hombro, la sonrisa contra el límite de la tolerancia—. ¿Hace tres meses? —resopló mientras alzaba los hombros—. Botija, Julián robaba de la Cooperativa desde hace cinco años. O cuatro. Me acuerdo. Le hablaste, m'hijito, de una combinación con dólares, ¿no? No sé quién cumplía años aquella noche. Y no falto al respeto. Pero Julián me lo contó todo y yo no le podía parar los ataques de risa. Ni siquiera pensó en el plan de los dólares, si estaba bien o mal. El robaba y jugaba a los caballos. Le iba bien y le iba mal. Desde hacía cinco años, desde antes de que yo lo conociera.

—Cinco años —repetí mascando la pipa. Me levanté y fui hasta la ventana. Quedaban restos de agua en los yuyos y en la arena. El aire fresco no tenía nada que ver con nosotros, con nadie.

En alguna habitación del hotel, encima de mí, estaría durmiendo en paz la muchacha, despatarrada, empezando a mo

verse entre la insistente desesperación de los sueños y las sábanas calientes. Yo la imaginaba y seguía queriéndola, amaba
su respiración, sus olores, las supuestas alusiones al recuerdo
nocturno, a mí, que pudieran caber en su estupor matinal.
Volví con pesadez de la ventana y estuve mirando sin asco ni
lástima lo que el destino había colocado en el sillón del dormitorio del hotel. Se acomodaba las solapas del traje sastre
que, a fin de cuentas, tal vez no fuera de cheviot; sonreía al
aire, esperaba mi regreso, mi voz. Me sentí viejo y ya con pocas fuerzas. Tal vez el ignorado perro de la dicha me estuviera
lamiendo las rodillas, las manos; tal vez sólo se tratara de lo
otro; que estaba viejo y cansado. Pero, en todo caso, me vi
obligado a dejar pasar el tiempo, a encender de nuevo la pipa,
a jugar con la llama del fósforo, con su ronquido.

   —Para mí —dije— todo está perfecto. Es seguro que Julián
no usó un revólver para hacerle firmar la hipoteca. Y yo nunca firmé un pagaré. Si falsificó la firma y pudo vivir así cinco
años —creo que usted dijo cinco—, bastante tuvo, bastante tuvieron los dos. La miro, la pienso, y nada me importa que le
saquen la casa o la entierren en la cárcel. Yo no firmé nunca
un pagaré para Julián. Desgraciadamente para usted, Betty, y
el nombre me parece inadecuado, siento que ya no le queda
bien, no hay peligros ni amenazas que funcionen. No podemos ser socios en nada; y eso es siempre una tristeza. Creo
que es más triste para las mujeres. Voy a la galería a fumar y
mirar cómo crece la mañana. Le quedaré muy agradecido si
se va enseguida, si no hace mucho escándalo, Betty.

   Salí fuera y me dediqué a insultarme en voz baja, a buscar
defectos en la prodigiosa mañana de otoño. Oí, muy lejana, la
indolente puteada que hizo sonar a mis espaldas. Escuché, casi
en seguida, el portazo.

   Un Ford pintado de azul apareció cerca del caserío.

   Yo era pequeño y aquello me pareció inmerecido, organi-
zado por la pobre, incierta imaginación de un niño. Yo había
mostrado siempre desde la adolescencia mis defectos, tenía
razón siempre, estaba dispuesto a conversar y discutir, sin reservas ni silencios. Julián, en cambio —y empecé a tenerle simpatía y otra forma muy distinta de la lástima— nos había engañado a todos durante muchos años. Este Julián que sólo había podido conocer muerto se reía de mí, levemente, desde
que empezó a confesar la verdad, a levantar sus bigotes y su
sonrisa, en el ataúd. Tal vez continuara riéndose de todos nosotros a un mes de su muerte. Pero para nada me servía inventarme el rencor o el desencanto.

Sobre todo, me irritaba el recuerdo de nuestra última entrevista, la gratuidad de sus mentiras, no llegar a entender por qué me había ido a visitar, con riesgos, para mentir por última vez. Porque Betty sólo me servía para la lástima o el desprecio; pero yo estaba creyendo en su historia, me sentía seguro de la incesante suciedad de la vida.

Un Ford pintado de azul roncaba subiendo la cuesta, detrás del chalet de techo rojo, salió al camino y cruzó delante de la baranda siguiendo hasta la puerta del hotel. Vi bajar a un policía con su desteñido uniforme de verano, a un hombre extraordinariamente alto y flaco con traje de anchas rayas y un joven vestido de gris, rubio, sin sombrero, al que veía sonreír a cada frase, sosteniendo el cigarrillo con dos dedos alargados frente a la boca.

El gerente del hotel bajó con lentitud la escalera y se acercó a ellos mientras el mozo de la noche anterior salía de atrás de una columna de la escalinata, en mangas de camisa, haciendo brillar su cabeza retinta. Todos hablaban con pocos gestos, sin casi cambiar el lugar, el lugar donde tenían apoyados los pies, y el gerente sacaba un pañuelo del bolsillo interior del saco, se lo pasaba por los labios y volvía a guardarlo profundamente para, a los pocos segundos, extraerlo con un movimiento rápido y aplastarlo y moverlo sobre su boca. Entré para comprobar que la mujer se había ido; y al salir nuevamente a la galería, al darme cuenta de mis propios movimientos, de la morosidad con que deseaba vivir y ejecutar cada actitud como si buscara acariciar con las manos lo que éstas habían hecho, sentí que era feliz en la mañana, que podía haber otros días esperándome en cualquier parte.

Vi que el mozo miraba hacia el suelo y los otros cuatro hombres alzaban la cabeza y me dirigían caras de observación distraída. El joven rubio tiró el cigarrillo lejos; entonces comencé a separar los labios hasta sonreír y saludé, moviendo la cabeza, al gerente, y en seguida, antes de que pudiera contestar, antes de que se inclinara, mirando siempre hacia la galería, golpeándose la boca con el pañuelo, alcé una mano y repetí mi saludo. Volví al cuarto para terminar de vestirme.

Estuve un momento en el comedor, mirando desayunar a los pasajeros y después decidí tomar una ginebra, nada más que una, junto al mostrador del bar, compré cigarrillos y bajé hasta el grupo que esperaba al pie de la escalera. El gerente volvió a saludarme y noté que la mandíbula le temblaba, apenas, rápidamente. Dije algunas palabras y oí que hablaban; el joven rubio vino a mi lado y me tocó un brazo. Todos estaban en silencio y el rubio y yo nos miramos y sonreímos. Le ofrecí un cigarrillo y él lo encendió sin apartar los ojos de mi cara; después dio tres pasos retrocediendo y volvió a mirarme. Tal vez nunca hubiera visto la cara de un hombre feliz; a mí me pasaba lo mismo. Me dio la espalda, caminó hasta el primer árbol del jardín y se apoyó allí con un hombre. Todo aquello tenía un sentido y, sin comprenderlo, supe que estaba de acuerdo y moví la cabeza asintiendo. Entonces el hombre altísimo dijo:

—¿Vamos hasta la playa en el coche?

Me adelanté y fui a instalarme junto al asiento del chófer. El hombre alto y el rubio se sentaron atrás. El policía llegó sin apuro al volante y puso en marcha el coche. En seguida rodamos velozmente en la calmosa mañana; yo sentía el olor del cigarrillo que estaba fumando el muchacho, sentía el silencio y la quietud del otro hombre, la voluntad rellenando ese silencio y esa quietud. Cuando llegamos a la playa el coche atracó junto a un montón de piedras grises que separaban el camino de la arena. Bajamos, pasamos alzando las piernas por encima de las piedras y caminamos hacia el mar. Yo iba junto al muchacho rubio.

Nos detuvimos en la orilla. Estábamos los cuatro en silencio, con las corbatas sacudidas por el viento. Volvimos a encender cigarrillos.

—No está seguro el tiempo —dije.

—¿Vamos? —contestó el joven rubio.

El hombre alto del traje a rayas estiró un brazo hasta tocar al muchacho en el pecho y dijo con voz gruesa:

—Fíjese. Desde aquí a las dunas. Dos cuadras. No mucho más ni menos.

El otro asintió en silencio, alzando los hombros como si aquello no tuviera importancia. Volvió a sonreír y me miró.

—Vamos —dije, y me puse a caminar hasta el automóvil. Cuando iba a subir, el hombre alto me detuvo.

—No —dijo—. Es ahí, cruzando.

En frente había un galpón de ladrillos manchados de humedad. Tenía techo de zinc y letras oscuras pintadas arriba de la puerta. Esperamos mientras el policía volvía con una llave. Me di vuelta para mirar el mediodía cercano sobre la playa; el policía separó el candado abierto y entramos todos en la sombra y el inesperado frío. Las vigas brillaban negras, suavemente untadas de alquitrán, y colgaban pedazos de arpillera del techo. Mientras caminábamos en la penumbra gris sentí crecer el galpón, más grande a cada paso, alejándome de la mesa larga formada con caballetes que estaba en el centro. Miré la forma estirada pensando quién enseña a los muertos la actitud de la muerte. Había un charco estrecho de agua en el suelo y goteaba desde una esquina de la mesa. Un hombre descalzo, con la camisa abierta sobre el pecho colorado, se acercó carraspeando y puso una mano en una punta de la mesa de tablones, dejando que su corto índice se cubriera en seguida, brillante, del agua que no acababa de chorrear. El hombre alto estiró un brazo y destapó la cara sobre las tablas dando un tirón a la lona. Miré al aire, el brazo rayado del hombre que había quedado estirado contra la luz de la puerta sosteniendo el borde con anillas de la lona. Volví a mirar al rubio sin sombrero e hice una mueca triste.

—Mire aquí —dijo el hombre alto.

Fui viendo que la cara de la muchacha estaba torcida hacia atrás y parecía que la cabeza, morada, con manchas de un morado rojizo sobre un delicado, anterior morado azuloso, tendría que rodar desprendida de un momento a otro si alguno hablaba fuerte, si alguno golpeaba el suelo con los zapatos, simplemente si el tiempo pasaba.

Desde el fondo, invisible para mí, alguien empezó a recitar con voz ronca y ordinaria, como si hablara conmigo. ¿Con quién otro?

—Las manos y los pies, cuya epidermis está ligeramente blanqueada y doblegada en la extremidad de los dedos, presentan además, en la ranura de las uñas, una pequeña cantidad de arena y limo. No hay herida, ni escoriación en las manos. En los brazos, y particularmente en su parte anterior, encima de la muñeca, se encuentran varias equimosis superpuestas, dirigidas transversalmente y resultantes de una presión violenta ejercida en los miembros superiores.

No sabía quién era, no deseaba hacer preguntas. Sólo tenía, me lo estaba repitiendo, como única defensa, el silencio. El silencio por nosotros. Me acerqué un poco más a la mesa y estuve palpando la terquedad de los huesos de la frente. Tal vez los cinco hombres esperaran algo más; y yo estaba dispuesto a todo. La bestia, siempre en el fondo del galpón, enumeraba ahora con su voz vulgar:

—La faz está manchada por un líquido azulado y sanguinolento que ha fluido por la boca y la nariz. Después de haberla lavado cuidadosamente, reconocemos en torno de la boca extensa escoriación con equimosis, y la impresión de las uñas hincadas en las carnes. Dos señales análogas existen debajo del ojo derecho, cuyo párpado inferior está fuertemente contuso. A más de las huellas de la violencia que han sido ejecutadas manifiestamente durante la vida, nótanse en el rostro numerosos desgarros, puntuados, sin rojez, sin equimosis, con simple desecamiento de la epidermis y producidos por el roce del cuerpo contra la arena. Vese una infiltración de sangre coagulada, a cada lado de la laringe. Los tegumentos están inválidos por la putrefacción y pueden distinguirse en ellos vestigios de contusiones o equimosis. El interior de la tráquea y de los bronquios contiene una pequeña cantidad de un líquido turbio, oscuro, no espumoso, mezclado con arena.

Era un buen responso, todo estaba perdido. Me incliné para besarle la frente y después, por piedad y amor, el líquido rojizo que le hacía burbujas entre los labios.

Pero la cabeza con su pelo endurecido, la nariz achatada, la boca oscura, alargada en forma de hoz con las puntas hacia abajo, lacias, goteantes, permanecía inmóvil, invariable su volumen en el aire sombrío que olía a sentina, más dura a cada paso de mis ojos por los pómulos y la frente y el mentón que no se resolvía a colgar. Me hablaban uno tras otro, el hombre alto y el rubio, como si realizaran un juego, golpeando alternativamente la misma pregunta. Luego el hombre alto soltó la lona, dio un salto y me sacudió de las solapas. Pero no creía en lo que estaba haciendo, bastaba mirarle los ojos redondos, y en cuanto le sonreí con fatiga, me mostró rápidamente los dientes, con odio y abrió la mano.

—Comprendo, adivino, usted tiene una hija. No se preocupen: firmaré lo que quieran, sin leerlo. Lo divertido es que están equivocados. Pero no tiene importancia. Nada, ni siquiera esto, tiene de veras importancia.

Antes de la luz violenta del sol me detuve y le pregunté con voz adecuada al hombre alto:

—Seré curioso y pido perdón: ¿Usted cree en Dios?

—Le voy a contestar, claro —dijo el gigante—; pero antes, si quiere, no es útil para el sumario, es, como en su caso, pura curiosidad... ¿Usted sabía que la muchacha era sorda?

Nos habíamos detenido exactamente entre el renovado calor del verano y la sombra fresca del galpón.

—¿Sorda? —pregunté—. No, sólo estuve con ella anoche. Nunca me pareció sorda. Pero ya no se trata de eso. Yo le hice una pregunta; usted prometió contestarla.

Los labios eran muy delgados para llamar sonrisa a la mueca que hizo el gigante. Volvió a mirarme sin desprecio, con triste asombro, y se persignó.

Emilia Pardo Bazán
1851—1921
España

El indulto
Cuentos de Marineda, 1983.

DE cuantas mujeres enjabonaban ropa en el lavadero público de Marineda, ateridas por el frío cruel de una mañana
de marzo, Antonia la asistenta era la más encorvada, la más
abatida, la que torcía con menos brío, la que refregaba con
mayor desaliento; a veces, interrumpiendo su labor, pasábase
el dorso de la mano por los enrojecidos párpados, y las gotas
de agua y las burbujas de jabón parecían lágrimas sobre su tez
marchita.

Las compañeras de trabajo de Antonia la miraban compa-
sivamente, y de tiempo en tiempo, entre la algarabía de las
conversaciones y disputas, se cruzaba un breve diálogo, a media voz, entretejido con exclamaciones de asombro, indignación y lástima. Todo el lavadero sabía al dedillo los males de
la asistenta, y hallaba en ellos asunto para interminables comentarios: nadie ignoraba que la infeliz, casada con un mozo
carnicero, residía, años antes, en compañía de su madre y de
su marido, en un barrio extramuros, y que la familia vivía con
desahogo, gracias al asiduo trabajo de Antonia y a los cuarte-
jos ahorrados por la vieja en su antiguo oficio de revendedora,
baratillera y prestamista. Nadie había olvidado tampoco la lúgubre tarde en que la vieja fue asesinada, encontrándose hecha astillas la tapa del arcón donde guardaba sus caudales y
ciertos pendientes y brincos de oro; nadie, tampoco, el horror
que infundió en el público la nueva de que el ladrón y asesino
no era sino el marido de Antonia, según esta misma declaraba, añadiendo que desde tiempo atrás roía al criminal la codicia del dinero de su suegra, con el cual deseaba establecer una
tablajería suya propia. Sin embargo el acusado hizo por probar la coartada, valiéndose del testimonio de dos o tres ami-
gotes de taberna, y de tal modo envolvió el asunto, que, en
vez de ir al palo, salió con veinte años de cadena. No fue tan
indulgente la opinión como la ley: además de la declaración
de la esposa, había un indicio vehementísimo: la cuchillada
que mató a la vieja, cuchillada certera y limpia, asestada de
arriba abajo, como las que los matachines dan a los cerdos,
con un cuchillo ancho y afiladísimo, de cortar carne. Para el

pueblo, no cabía duda en que el culpable debió subir al cadalso. Y el destino de Antonia comenzó a infundir sagrado terror cuando fue esparciéndose el rumor de que su marido *se la había jurado* para el día en que saliese de presidio, por acusarle. La desdichada quedaba encinta, y el asesino la dejó avisada de que, a su vuelta, se contase entre los difuntos.

Cuando nació el hijo de Antonia, ésta no pudo criarlo, tal era su debilidad y demacración y la frecuencia de las congojas que desde el crimen la aquejaban; y como no le permitía el estado de su bolsillo pagar ama, las mujeres del barrio que tenían niños de pecho dieron de mamar por turno a la criatura, que creció enclenque, resintiéndose de todas las angustias de su madre. Un tanto repuesta ya, Antonia se aplicó con ardor al trabajo, y aunque siempre tenían sus mejillas esa azulada palidez que se observa en los enfermos del corazón, recobró su silenciosa actividad, su aire apacible.

¡Veinte años de cadena! En veinte años (pensaba ella para sus adentros), él se puede morir o me puedo morir yo, y de aquí allá, falta mucho todavía. La hipótesis de la muerte natural no la asustaba; pero la espantaba imaginar solamente que volvía su marido. En vano las cariñosas vecinas la consolaban, indicándole la esperanza remota de que el inicuo parricida se arrepintiese, se enmendase, o, como decían ellas, "se volviese de mejor idea"; meneaba Antonia la cabeza entonces, murmurando sombríamente:

—¿Eso, él? ¿De mejor idea? Como no baje Dios del cielo en persona y le saque aquel corazón perro y le ponga otro...

Y, al hablar del criminal, un escalofrío corría por el cuerpo de Antonia.

En fin, veinte años tienen muchos días, y el tiempo aplaca la pena más cruel. Algunas veces, figurábasele a Antonia que todo lo ocurrido era un sueño, o que la ancha boca del presidio, que se había tragado al culpable, no le devolería jamás; o que aquella ley que al cabo supo castigar el primer crimen, sabría prevenir el segundo. ¡La ley! esa entidad moral, de la cual se formaba Antonia un concepto misterioso y confuso, era sin duda fuerza terrible, pero protectora; mano de hierro que la sostendría al borde del abismo. Así es que a sus ilimitados temores se unía una confianza indefinible, fundada sobre todo en el tiempo transcurrido, y en el que aun faltaba para cumplirse la condena.

¡Singular enlace el de los acontecimientos!

No creería de seguro el Rey, cuando vestido de capitán

general y con el pecho cargado de condecoraciones daba
la mano ante el ara a una princesa, que aquel acto solemne costaba amarguras sin cuento a una pobre asistenta, en
lejana capital de provincia. Así que Antonia supo que había recaído indulto en su esposo, no pronunció palabra, y
la vieron las vecinas sentada en el umbral de la puerta, con
las manos cruzadas, la cabeza caída sobre el pecho, mientras el niño, alzando su cara triste de criatura enfermiza,
gimoteaba:

—Mi madre... ¡Caliénteme la sopa, por Dios, que tengo
hambre!

El coro benévolo y cacareador de las vecinas, rodeó a
Antonia; algunas se dedicaron a arreglar la comida del niño,
otras animaban a la madre del mejor modo que sabían. ¡Era
bien tonta en afligirse así! ¡Ave María Purísima! ¡No parece
sino que aquel hombrón no tenía más que llegar y matarla!
Había Gobierno, gracias a Dios, y Audiencia, y serenos; se podía acudir a los celadores, al alcalde...

— ¡Qué alcalde! —decía ella con hosca mirada y apagado
acento.

—O al gobernador, o al regente, o al jefe de municipales;
había que ir a un abogado, saber lo que dispone la ley...

Una buena moza, casada con un guardia civil, ofreció enviar a su marido para que le *metiese un miedo* al picarón; otra,
resuelta y morena, se brindó a quedarse todas las noches a
dormir en casa de la asistenta; en suma, tales y tantas fueron
las muestras de interés de la vecindad, que Antonia se resolvió
a intentar algo, y sin levantar la sesión, acordóse consultar a
un jurisperito, a ver qué recetaba.

Cuando Antonia volvió de la consulta, más pálida que de
costumbre, de cada tenducho y de cada cuarto bajo salían
mujeres en pelo a preguntarle noticias, y se oían exclamaciones de horror. ¡La ley, en vez de protegerla, obligaba a la hija
de la víctima a vivir bajo el mismo techo, maritalmente con
el asesino!

— ¡Qué leyes, divino Señor de los cielos! ¡Así los bribones que las hacen las aguantarán! —clamaba indignado todo el
coro—. ¿Y no habrá algún remedio, mujer, no habrá algún remedio?

—Dice que nos podemos separar... después de una cosa
que le llaman divorcio.

— ¿Y qué es divorcio, mujer?

—Un pleito muy largo.

Todas dejaron caer los brazos con desaliento: los pleitos

no se acaban nunca, y peor aún si se acaban, porque los pierde siempre el inocente y el pobre.

—Y para eso —añadió la asistenta— tenía yo que probar antes que mi marido me daba mal trato.

— ¡Aquí de Dios! ¿Pues aquel tigre no le había matado a la madre? ¿Eso no era mal trato, eh? ¿Y no sabían hasta los gatos que la tenía amenazada con matarla también?

—Pero como nadie lo oyó... Dice el abogado que se quieren pruebas claras...

Se armó una especie de motín; había mujeres determinadas a hacer, decían ellas, una exposición al mismísimo rey, pidiendo contraindulto; y, por turno, dormían en casa de la asistenta, para que la pobre mujer pudiese conciliar el sueño. Afortunadamente, el tercer día llegó la noticia de que el indulto era temporal, y al presidiario aun le quedaban algunos años de arrastrar el grillete. La noche que lo supo Antonia, fue la primera en que no se enderezó en la cama, con los ojos desmesuradamente abiertos, pidiendo socorro.

Después de este susto, pasó más de un año y la tranquilidad renació para la asistenta, consagrada a sus humildes quehaceres. Un día, el criado de la casa donde estaba asistiendo, creyó hacer un favor a aquella mujer pálida, que tenía su marido en presidio, participándole cómo la Reina iba a parir, y habría indulto, de fijo.

Fregaba la asistenta los pisos, y al oír tales anuncios soltó el estropajo, y descogiendo las sayas que traía arrolladas a la cintura, salió con paso de autómata, muda y fría como una estatua. A los recados que le enviaban de las casas, respondía que estaba enferma, aunque en realidad sólo experimentaba un anonadamiento general, un no levantársele los brazos a labor alguna. El día del regio parto contó los cañonazos de la salva, cuyo estampido le resonaba dentro del cerebro, y como hubo quien le advirtió que el vástago real era hembra, comenzó a esperar que un varón habría ocasionado más indultos. Además, ¿por qué le había de coger el indulto a su marido? Ya le habían indultado una vez, y su crimen era horrendo: ¡matar a la indefensa vieja que no le hacía daño alguno, todo por unas cuantas tristes monedas de oro! La terrible escena volvía a presentarse ante sus ojos: ¿merecía indulto la fiera que asestó tremenda cuchillada? Antonia recordaba que la herida tenía los labios blancos, y parecíale ver la sangre cuajada al pie del catre.

Se encerró en su casa, y pasaba las horas sentada en una

silleta junto al fogón. ¡Bah! Si habían de matarla, mejor era dejarse morir.

Sólo la voz plañidera del niño la sacaba de su ensimismamiento.

—Mi madre, tengo hambre. Mi madre, ¿qué hay en la puerta? ¿Quién viene?

Por último, una hermosa mañana de sol se encogió de hombros, y tomando un lío de ropa sucia, echó a andar camino del lavadero. A las preguntas afectuosas respondía con lentos monosílabos, y sus ojos se posaban con vago extravío en la espuma del jabón que le saltaba al rostro.

¿Quién trajo al lavadero la inesperada nueva, cuando ya Antonia recogía su ropa lavada y torcida e iba a retirarse? ¿Inventóla alguien con fin caritativo, o fue uno de esos rumores misteriosos, de ignoto origen, que en vísperas de acontecimientos grandes para los pueblos o los individuos, palpitan y susurran en el aire? Lo cierto es que la pobre Antonia, al oírlo, se llevó instintivamente la mano al corazón, y se dejó caer hacia atrás sobre las húmedas piedras del lavadero.

—¿Pero de veras murió? —preguntaban las madrugadoras a las recién llegadas.

—Sí, mujer...

—Yo lo oí en el mercado...

—Yo en la tienda...

—¿A ti quién te lo dijo?

—A mí, mi marido.

—¿Y a tu marido?

—El asistente del capitán.

—¿Y al asistente?

—Su amo...

Aquí ya la autoridad pareció suficiente, y nadie quiso averiguar más, sino dar por firme y valedera la noticia. ¡Muerto el criminal, en vísperas de indulto, antes de cumplir el plazo de su castigo! Antonia la asistenta alzó la cabeza, y por primera vez se tiñeron sus mejillas de un sano color, y se abrió la fuente de sus lágrimas. Lloraba de gozo, y nadie de los que la miraban se escandalizó. Ella era la indultada; su alegría justa. Las lágrimas se agolpaban a sus lagrimales, dilatándole el corazón, porque desde el crimen se había *quedado cortada,* es decir, sin llanto. Ahora respiraba anchamente, libre de su pesadilla. Andaba tanto la mano de la Providencia en lo ocurrido, que a la asistenta no le cruzó por la imaginación que podía ser falsa la nueva.

Aquella noche, Antonia se retiró a su casa más tarde que de costumbre, porque fue a buscar a su hijo a la escuela de párvulos, y le compró rosquillas de *jinete,* con otras golosinas que el chico deseaba hacía tiempo, y ambos recorrieron las calles, parándose ante los escaparates, sin ganas de comer, sin pensar más que en beber el aire, en sentir la vida y en volver a tomar posesión de ella.

Tal era el enajenamiento de Antonia, que ni reparó en que la puerta de su cuarto bajo no estaba sino entornada. Sin soltar de la mano al niño, entró en la reducida estancia que le servía de sala, cocina y comedor, y retrocedió atónita viendo encendido el candil. Un bulto negro se levantó, y el grito que subía a los labios de la asistenta se ahogó en la garganta.

Era él; Antonia, inmóvil, clavada al suelo, no le veía ya, aunque la siniestra imagen se reflejaba en sus dilatadas pupilas. Su cuerpo yerto sufría una parálisis momentánea; sus manos frías soltaron al niño, que aterrado se le cogió a las faldas. El marido habló:

—¡Mal contabas conmigo ahora! —murmuró con acento ronco, pero tranquilo; y al sonido de aquella voz, donde Antonia creía oír vibrar aún las maldiciones y las amenazas de muerte, la pobre mujer, como desencantada, despertó, exhaló un ¡ay! agudísimo, y cogiendo a su hijo en brazos, echó a correr hacia la puerta. El hombre se interpuso.

—¡Eh... chst! ¿A dónde vamos, patrona? —silabeó con su ironía de presidiario—. ¿A alborotar al barrio a estas horas? ¡Quieto aquí todo el mundo!

Las últimas palabras fueron dichas sin que las acompañase ningún ademán agresivo, pero con un tono que heló la sangre de Antonia. Sin embargo, su primer estupor se convertía en fiebre, la fiebre lúcida del instinto de conservación. Una idea rápida cruzó por su mente; ampararse del niño. ¡Su padre no le conocía, pero al fin era su padre! Levantóle en alto y le acercó a la luz.

—¿Ese es el chiquillo? —murmuró el presidiario—. Y descolgando el candil, llególo al rostro del chico. Este guiñaba los ojos, deslumbrado, y ponía las manos delante de la cara como para defenderse de aquel padre desconocido, cuyo nombre oía pronunciar con terror y reprobación universal. Apretábase a su madre, y ésta, nerviosamente, le apretaba también, con el rostro más blanco que la cera.

—¡Qué chiquillo tan feo! —gruñó el padre, colgando de nuevo el candil—. Parece que lo chuparon las brujas.

Antonia, sin soltar al niño, se arrimó a la pared, pues desfallecía. La habitación le daba vueltas alrededor, y veía unas lucecitas azules en el aire.

—A ver, ¿no hay nada de comer aquí? —pronunció el marido.

Antonia sentó al niño en un rincón, en el suelo, y mientras la criatura lloraba de miedo, conteniendo los sollozos, la madre comenzó a dar vueltas por el cuarto, y cubrió la mesa con manos temblorosas; sacó pan, una botella de vino, retiró del hogar una cazuela de bacalao, y se esmeraba, sirviendo diligentemente, para aplacar al enemigo con su celo. Sentóse el presidiario y empezó a comer con voracidad, menudeando los tragos de vino. Ella permanecía de pie, mirando, fascinada, aquel rostro curtido, afeitado y seco que relucía con ese barniz especial del presidio. El llenó el vaso una vez más y la convidó.

—No tengo voluntad... —balbuceó Antonia—; y el vino, al reflejo del candil, se le figuraba un coágulo de sangre.

Él lo despachó encogiéndose de hombros, y se puso en el plato más bacalao, que engulló ávidamente, ayudándose con los dedos y mascando grandes cortezas de pan. Su mujer le miraba hartarse, y una esperanza sutil se introducía en su espíritu. Así que comiese, se marcharía sin matarla: ella, después, cerraría a cal y canto la puerta, y si quería matarla entonces, el vecindario estaba despierto y oiría sus gritos. ¡Sólo que, probablemente, le sería imposible a ella gritar! Y carraspeó para afianzar la voz. El marido, apenas se vio saciado de comida, sacó del cinto un cigarro, lo picó con la uña y encendió sosegadamente el pitillo en el candil.

— ¡Chst...! ¿A dónde vamos? —gritó, viendo que su mujer hacía un movimiento disimulado hacia la puerta—. Tengamos la fiesta en paz.

—A acostar al pequeño —contestó ella sin saber lo que decía; y refugióse en la habitación contigua, llevando a su hijo en brazos. De seguro que el asesino no entraría allí. ¿Cómo había de tener valor para tanto? Era la habitación en que había cometido el crimen, el cuarto de su madre: pared por medio dormía antes el matrimonio; pero la miseria que siguió a la muerte de la vieja, obligó a Antonia a vender la cama matrimonial y usar la de la difunta. Creyéndose en salvo, empezaba a desnudar al niño, que ahora se atrevía a sollozar más fuerte, apoyado en su seno; pero se abrió la puerta y entró el presidiario.

Antonia le vio echar una mirada oblicua en torno suyo, descalzarse con suma tranquilidad, quitarse la faja, y, por úl-

timo, acostarse en el lecho de la víctima. La asistenta creía
soñar; si su marido abriese una navaja, la asustaría menos
quizá que mostrando tan horrible sosiego. El se estiraba y revolvía en las sábanas, apurando la colilla y suspirando de gusto, como hombre cansado que encuentra una cama blanda y
limpia.

— ¿Y tú? —exclamó dirigiéndose a Antonia—. ¿Qué haces
ahí quieta como un poste? ¿No te acuestas?

—Yo... no tengo sueño —tartamudeó ella, dando diente
con diente.

— ¿Qué falta hace tener sueño? ¿Si irás a pasar la noche
de centinela?

—Ahí... ahí... no... cabemos... Duerme tú... Yo aquí, de
cualquier modo...

El soltó dos o tres palabras gordas.

— ¿Me tienes miedo o asco, o qué rayo es esto? A ver cómo te acuestas, o si no...

Incorporóse el marido, y extendiendo las manos, mostró
querer saltar de la cama al suelo. Mas ya Antonia, con la docilidad fatalista de la esclava, empezaba a desnudarse. Sus dedos apresurados rompían las cintas, arrancaban violentamente
los corchetes, desgarraban las enaguas. En un rincón del cuarto se oían los ahogados sollozos del niño...

Y el niño fue quien, gritando desesperadamente, llamó al
amanecer a las vecinas, que encontraron a Antonia en la cama, extendida, como muerta. El médico vino aprisa, y declaró que vivía, y la sangró, y no logró sacarle gota de sangre.
Falleció a las veinticuatro horas, de muerte natural, pues no
tenía lesión alguna. El niño aseguraba que el hombre que había pasado allí la noche la llamó muchas veces al levantarse
y viendo que no respondía, echó a correr como un loco.

Senel Paz
1950—
Cuba

No le digas que la quieres

ARNALDO enteró a todo el mundo de que aquella noche yo me acostaría con una mujer. Claro, no les dijo que era Vivian, pero vaya, alguien tuvo que imaginárselo porque en esta escuela nadie es bobo. Entonces aquel día esperé a que todos se bañaran, y cuando no faltaba nadie y nadie me iba a apurar, entré y empecé a bañarme yo, con toda mi calma. Me restregaba duro, bien duro, jabón una y otra vez, uña. Pensaba que a lo mejor ella me olería aquí, allí, me tocaba, no sé, seguramente me iba a tocar y quería estar bien limpio y oler bien y repasaba mentalmente los lugares donde a mi vez la besaría, donde *tenía* que besarla, según Arnaldo, para que *nunca* me olvidara, para que nunca olvidara esta primera vez con un hombre, conmigo, y que cuando sea incluso una viejecita, al pensar en mí me tenga en un alto concepto. Entonces Arnaldo me había explicado tres o cuatro cosas que *hay* que hacerle a las mujeres, y sobre todo me explicó que nunca, por nada de la vida, le dijera que la quería, ni en el momento supremo, porque si una mujer sabe que tú la quieres, mira, ahí mismo te perdiste, te coge la baja y te hace sufrir lo que le dé la gana. Pero aquel día yo cantaba y todo. Me restregué las orejas, por aquí, por allá, me lavé la cabeza con champú, tres ojos, me froté la espalda, me afeité de lo mejor, me cepillé los dientes y la lengua, ya te digo. Quedé que brillaba y tenía una contentura tan grande que me sonreía cada vez que tropezaba conmigo en el espejo y me hacía señitas como si fuera un Charles Chaplin o alguien así porque imagínate, sabía lo que iba a pasar, y era la primera vez, y era con Vivian y, te lo juro, trataba de no pensar en nada, de no pensar en nada, no adelantarme a los acontecimientos y respetarla mucho con la mente; pero tú sabes cómo es la mente de uno, la mente mía, que a la mente mía tú le dices no pienses esto porque esto es una falta de respeto y ella te dice: *sí, sí, yo no voy a pensar eso.* Mientras, es lo que más piensa. Entonces figúrate, me di cuenta de lo que la mente mía estaba pensando, pero yo quería respetar a Vivian y no quería ade-

lantarme a los acontecimientos, sin embargo, la mente mía,
te digo, estaba pensando eso y el sexo, él solo, se me fue em-
bullando, y lo que hice fue agarrarme fuerte del lavamanos y
concentrarme bien e imaginarme un campo de florecitas, bien
extenso, muchas, muchas florecitas, y se me pasó, y la respe-
té, porque cuando yo me excito por gusto o en un momento
en que no debe ser, en el aula, vamos a decir, un ejemplo,
pienso en florecitas y me da resultado. Pero tienen que ser
amarillas. Entonces aquel día estaba en el baño, te lo dije,
muy contento y sintiendo esa emoción que yo siento cuando
pienso en Vivian, y otras emociones, y ya había acabado y estaba resplandeciente y abrí la puerta, aquel día, Alabao, todo
el mundo estaba esperándome, tan calladitos que yo no los
había oído, formados en una doble hilera que iba hasta mi cama, la corte esa que va a despertar a los reyes. " ¡Eeeéeeeh!",
me recibieron. Aquellos bandidos. Y de inmediato almohada-
zos y pescozones. Traté de cerrar. "¿Así que te ibas a hacer
el hombre sin decírselo a los socios, eh?", dijeron. " ¡Hay que
perfumarlo!" Y me cargaron en cueros y me subieron a una
silla, entre cocotazos y empujones. "¿Le untamos betún en
los huevos para que le brillen?" "No, no, caballeros, eso no,
que se demora." "¿Y pasta de diente en los sobacos?" " ¡Traigan talco!" Decidieron que no estaría elegante con mi camisa
de salir, qué calladito me lo tenía, eh?, sino con el pulóver li-
lita que le trajeron a Jorge de Checoslovaquia, había tomado
ostiones, ¿eh? Me echaron como cinco tipos de desodorantes
y perfumes, me obligaron a comer un caramelo de menta para que no tuviera mal aliento. "Yo nunca tengo mal aliento".
Me revisaron las uñas, me llevaron hasta el espejo y cuando se
cansaron de peinarme decidieron que no había actor de cine
mejor tipo. Revisaron mi cartera y agregaron la contribución
de los socios. Estaban burlones, amigos, envidiosos, pero eran
como las tres, caballeros, tarde, y me dejaron, aquellos bandidos. Arnaldo me explicó una vez más cómo tenía que hacer
para que en el lugar no notaran que era novato, y me deseó
suerte, mucha suerte, que cuando regresara lo despertara y
le contara, y que no le dijera a Vivian que la quería, que no
se lo dijera, mira que a mí se me notaba que podía caer en
esa debilidad. Yo todavía dudaba, te lo digo, a esa hora. No,
a esa hora empecé a dudar más que nunca y a ponerme nervioso. Quería que el tiempo echara para atrás y que no llegara el momento, a esa hora. Me preguntaba si estaba haciendo
bien, si hice bien al exigirle esto a Vivian y si eso era quererla
como yo la quería, pedirle eso. Pero ya no podía arrepentir-

me, no había modo, fígurate. ¿Arnaldo qué pensaría? Y ahora lo sabían los otros. ¿Comprendes que no podía arrepentirme? Al menos que me diera un dolor de estómago bien grande o que empezara a llover de verdad. Pero nada, y de repente me acordé de los flanes. De eso me acordé. Antes a mí no me gustaban estos dulces, o no me gustaban especialmente, pero aquí en la beca los dan a menudo y su movimiento suave, su modo de ser erectos, su color, esa manera en que te miran los flanes con ganas de que te los comas, a mí me recuerdan los senos de Vivian, dirás que estoy loco, sus senos tan lindos que caben en el hueco de mi mano, en un solo beso de mi boca, y me como tres, cuatro, cinco flanes, los cambio por el pescado. Aunque no sé si fue en ese momento que me pasaron los flanes por la cabeza, o si fue después, mientras iba a buscarla a ella a su albergue. Me salió vestida de negro. Una rubia vestida de negro es lo más lindo que hay. Y tampoco podía echarme para atrás porque tenía un compromiso político. Sí. El año pasado salí joven ejemplar pero no quedé militante porque me faltaba madurez, dijeron, y tenía que trabajar, me dieron un año para que trabajara y cogiera la madurez, leyera los periódicos, la situación internacional. Y yo hacía todo eso hasta que llegó Vivian al aula, que ya te dije cómo me puse y en esta asamblea de ejemplares, muchacho, no votaron por mí ni nueve gentes. Yo me había adelantado y había mandado a decir a la casa que había salido ejemplar y esta vez sí seguro sería militante. Me precipité y no votaron por mí. Una hora ahí criticándome, diciendo que había perdido condiciones y que cuál era mi opinión porque lo importante era que yo aceptara las críticas, las interiorizara como dice el compañero de la Juventud, y dije que sí, que las aceptaba, que las interiorizaba, pero me fijé bien en todo el que no votó por mí. Javierito no votó. Después Arnaldo me dijo que guardar reservas era peor, que me fijara en que yo no atendía a las clases y me pasaba la vida cogiéndole las manos a Vivian. Aparte de que tú no tienes combatividad. Pedrito, y el mundo necesita que tú te ocupes más de él. Yo y Arnaldo en un rincón discutiendo, analizando estas cosas. A él lo mandaron a hacer trabajo político conmigo, me di cuenta, y lo sentía porque es como mi hermano, pero le iba a quedar mal, hasta que me dijo: "Tú sabes lo que a ti te pasa? El problema con Vivian." "Yo no tengo ningún problema con Vivian, déjate de eso." "Sí, chico. Vivian es una mujer que exige mucho: y las relaciones de ustedes han llegado a un punto, han alcanzado un desarrollo, como decirte vaya, que se tienen que acostar. O

más nunca serás militante." ¿Qué tipo de mujer creía él que
ella era? "Mire, compadre —me atajó—, convénzala. ¿Tú sabes
lo que pasa? Que ahora no es como antes. Antes cumplías los
trece o catorce años y tu papá o un hermano tuyo te llevaba a
un prostíbulo y ya, empezabas. Ahora no porque estamos en
el socialismo y eso era una lacra social y, claro, hubo que eli-
minarla. Pero, ¿sabes qué? Que nosotros nos quedamos en el
aire. Debieron haber dejado un prostíbulo, uno solito, peda-
gógico, para nosotros los becados, ¿no crees?" Lo miré no
muy convencido y él continuó su explicación: "Entonces uno
se tiene que acostar con la novia. *El manifiesto comunista*
dice que en el socialismo el amor es libre." "*¿El manifiesto
comunista* dice eso? Voy a leerlo." Léelo, léelo, que dice
otras cosas, además. Me quedé pensando en todo esto. La cosa política, quiero decir. Y me juré que iba a ocuparme del
mundo, de verdad, y no iba a tener más fallas. No le juré eso
al Che porque el Che no es un santo ni nada, pero me estaba
acordando de él cuando me lo prometí a mí mismo. Claro
que no era esto lo que yo pensaba cuando iba a recoger a Vivian aquel día. No. Yo pensaba en ella y veía cómo me arreglaba el menudo para que no me siguiera sonando en los bolsillos al caminar. Pensaba en nuestras conversaciones, las volvía a conversar, esas interminables conversaciones nuestras en
el aula, en los recesos. Gracias a ellas sé de memoria el nombre de sus familiares, los cumpleaños, y ella el de los míos, la
disposición de su casa, los lunares que tenemos. Nos hemos
contado millones de veces cómo están ordenados nuestros
albergues, quién duerme en cada litera, quiénes se bañan todos los días y los defectos que tienen, si son egoístas, si comparten la comida, si roncan, los militantes que consideramos
buenos de verdad. Hemos hablado y hablado: del director, de
los profesores, de la escuela, de lo que haríamos si de pronto
vemos a Fidel. Le he contado casi todo lo que sé de lo que
significa ser hombre, cómo es el desarrollo de nosotros, que
las tetillas me dolieron como loco a los doce y trece años y
que no hay como un golpe en los testículos y ella que en los
senos. ¿Tú no hablas de esas cosas con tu novia? Nosotros sí
y nos escribimos en las últimas páginas de las libretas, de las
mías porque con las suyas es muy celosa. Las tiene forradas,
y sobre cada forro una fotografía del Che. Lo miramos a
veces al Che. ¿Dónde estará ahora?, me pregunta. "En un lugar de América", le digo. "A veces pienso que puede pasarle
algo". "¿Al Che? No, muchacha, no. ¿Tú eres boba?" Y
mientras conversamos nos miramos de cerquita, a los ojos,

miro su boca, tan roja, qué boca tiene Vivian. Y nos tomamos
las manos a ver si están frías o tibias, para ver quién las tiene
más grandes y siempre soy yo, para estudiarnos las líneas de
la vida y de la muerte. Todo eso disimulando ¿tú entiendes?
porque cuando esto todavía no éramos novios. A ella le gustan los Beatles y Silvio Rodríguez, y a mí sólo los Beatles,
aunque no sé si a nosotros nos pueden gustar los Beatles porque ellos son americanos o ingleses. Lo que más le gusta de
Silvio Rodríguez es que siendo revolucionario y todo anda
con melena y la ropa sucia. Eso es ser hippie, rebelde por gusto, protesto, pero ella lo defiende y lo defiende. Bah —me exploto a veces—, a ti lo que te gusta. "No me gusta, no: pero
me da rabia que no comprendas que él lo que quiere decir es
que nosotros somos como nosotros y que no nos planifique-
mos tanto las cosas". ¿Y te acuerdas de aquel día terrible? Le
había dicho que teníamos que conversar algo muy importante, teníamos que vernos en el receso. Iba a enamorarla. No
podía seguir sin enamorarla y quería encontrar una forma
bien original Arnaldo me contó que él enamoró a una muchacha jugando a adivinar palabras en una libreta. Le escribió
Me gustas, la *M* y los guiones, y ella lo adivinó, pero Vivian
en cuanto comprendió lo que decía no quiso seguir. En una
novela leí que una muchacha le dijo al muchacho, ofrecién-
dole las manos: Léeme el destino. Y él le contestó: Tu destino no está en tus manos sino en las mías. Oye, qué lindo eso,
compadre, ¿por qué no se me ocurrió a mí? Entonces cuando
llegamos a la escuela, aquella mañana, todo el mundo estaba
formado en el patio central, incluso los estudiantes de segundo año, que reciben las clases por la tarde, y la gente guardaba silencio como jamás se había logrado en aquel patio, la
mañana esta. La busqué y la miré de lejos, queriéndole decir
que en el receso íbamos a hablar aquella cosa importante, ¿se
acordaba?, pero ella lo que me preguntó con los ojos fue:
¿Qué pasa?, ¿sabes qué pasa?, y entonces yo también comprendí que pasaba algo. Los profesores estaban bajo los almendros y lo sabían. Algunas maestras lloraban. El director
subió a la tarima y nos miró a todos, atentos a él. Si hubieras visto aquella mirada del director. Ya no quedaban dudas
de que algo grave había ocurrido, pero ¿qué era?, ¿irían a botar a alguien? El director, nervioso, dio unos golpecitos en el
micrófono, que funcionaba perfectamente y no necesitaba
que nadie lo golpeara, y es que no podía, no le salían las palabras y nos miraba, hasta que finalmente lo dijo de un tirón:
"Mataron al Che en Bolivia. Iremos a la Plaza a una velada so-

lemne, la mayor disciplina, vayan para las aulas". Así dijo.
Sentí que Vivian se echaba sobre mi hombro y oí que lloraba.
Sabía que eso podía pasar un día, dijo, y nos fuimos hacia el
aula, sintiéndonos mal, viendo la mirada del Che en todas partes, su sonrisa, cuando dice *en el imperialismo no se puede
confiar ni un tantico así,* como si camináramos bajo un cielo
de imágenes del Che y en cada hoja de los almendros hubiera
imágenes suyas y una lluvia. María se nos unió, " ¡Ay Vivian,
ay Pedrito!", dijo, y nos fuimos los tres abrazados. Que tristeza sus libretas. Quitó los forros y los guardó en silencio.
Finalmente dijo que no lo creía, no lo creía de ninguna manera porque no, eso no podía ser. Y yo le dije ojalá. Vivian,
pero figúrate, ¿estás loca? De todos modos nos quedamos
con algún pedacito de ilusión, hasta que estuvimos en la Plaza, todos en la Plaza, y el Fidel más triste del mundo dijo que
sí, que al Che lo habían matado en Bolivia, pero que nosotros
no podíamos morirnos por eso ni nada, y regresamos a la escuela, ella y yo tomados de la mano, no porque fuéramos novios, no, sino para ayudarnos. Y no la enamoré esa semana,
creo que ni la otra, no me acuerdo, y no por nada, se me quitaron los deseos...

Pero bueno, aquel otro día tenía puesto el vestido negro
que te dije y fuimos al cine y cuando salimos del Payret, qué
linda estaba la noche. Había llovido y había luces y colores y
mucha gente y humedad y caminaba a mi lado, apretada a
mí, con su pelo suelto. "¿Por qué vas tan de prisa? ¿Qué te
pareció la película? Vamos a comentarla", y empezó a decir
su parecer, el enfoque social no sé qué cosa. Yo ni la oía ni
había visto la película y el corazón se me quería salir porque
en el cine, imagínate, se me ocurrió acordarme de que hay
parejas, dicen, que la primera vez no pueden: ella coge miedo,
la membrana esa es muy resistente y no se rompe, la muchacha tiene unas hemorragias tremendas y hay que llamar la ambulancia, o él no reacciona porque se pone nervioso, los nervios no lo dejan. Si mis nervios me hacen eso los mato. Y le
dije: "No vamos para la beca" "¿Y adónde vamos?" "A un
lugar. No le había explicado nada más desde que hablamos de
esto y la convencí, y habíamos llegado. Entramos a un edificio, rápido, hablé con un hombre, rápido, pagué dos ochenta,
rápido, subimos una escalera, rápido, pasamos puertas, pasamos puertas, pasamos puertas, rápido, la llave no quería abrir,
abrió, entramos... y me quedé contra la pared oyéndome el
corazón. La luz estaba encendida y Vivian avanzó dos o tres
pasos, se detuvo, cambió la cartera de mano, así como cambia

ella la cartera de mano. El cuarto era alto y feo, horrible, para
qué te cuento. Había un escaparate pequeño, sin puertas y
con percheros de alambre todo jorobados. Sobre una mesa
despintada, una palangana con agua, una jarra de aluminio,
dos vasitos soviéticos, papel sanitario y jaboncitos de olor. La
luz amarillenta proyectaba las figuras contra la pared, en las
que había dibujos y palabras groseras. Vivian fue hasta la ventana, que estaba abierta, y yo leí exactamente sobre su cabeza, pero lejísimo, ocultándose un poco en su pelo, ese letrero
rojo que dice *Revolución es construir* y que está sobre algún
edificio de La Habana. Lo leí como cinco veces y no me atrevía a hablar. En la ventana también estaba la luna y unos ce-
lajes que le pasaban por delante. Era lindo, no pude dejar de
mirarlo y de repente me calmé un poco. Yo sé que ya nosotros no tenemos que fijarnos en la luna y que eso es ser romántico y dulzón, esta parte yo no se la cuento a Arnaldo,
pero se veía lindo, te lo juro, y Vivian se volvió, lentamente.
Qué impresión me hizo. Como nunca. Cierro los ojos y la veo.
Qué linda estaba, tú, qué linda. Estoy tan enamorado de ella
que me da vergüenza, si no te lo contaba. Los dolorcitos en
el corazón, las cosas que hago. Me preguntó con una voz terrible: "¿Esto es una posada, verdad?" Iba a responderle que
no, a decirle que era un hotel malo, de segunda, pero le dije
la verdad. "Sí". Un sí chiquito. Me dio la espalda. Al rato la
escuché decir: "Ay, mi madre, ya estoy en una posada. Es
lo que dice mamá: yo soy mala, en mí no se puede confiar.
Ella creyéndome muy tranquila en la escuela y yo en una posada, con mi novio". Me fui acercando, no sabía qué decirle,
qué hacer, imagínate, tenía razón, para uno no es lo mismo,
si yo le digo a mi mamá que estoy en una posada con una mujer se pone contentísima, y empecé a sentirme mal, a arrepentirme de haberla llevado, a comprender su situación. Menos
mal que me acordé de lo que dice Arnaldo, que a las mujeres
no se les puede coger lástima porque ni a ellas mismas les gusta eso. Se viró, tú, con los ojos muy abiertos. "¿No tenías
otro lugar adónde llevarme?" No tenía, no, ¿qué sabía yo de
esos lugares?, yo también era la primera vez. Me dolió que me
hablara así, que no me comprendiera, y me sentí peor. "Si tú
quieres —le dije—, si no te gusta el lugar, nos vamos y yo no
me pongo bravo ni nada". Y la abracé, para ayudarla a no estar sola, a no sentirse culpable ella sola, en todo caso el culpable era yo, ¿no?, y para decirle que sí, estaba allí, pero con
un hombre que, bueno, la quería tanto, era el hombre de su
vida, y entonces el lugar no tenía esa importancia. También

ella me abrazó y me quería y quedé frente a la ventana abierta. Cruzó un omnibús metiendo tremendo ruido. "Seguro que es una 27", pensé. "No nos pongamos nerviosos —dijo ella—, sólo que es una pena que tengamos que hacerlo en un cuarto tan feo". De verdad, tú, esos lugares debían ser más lindos, y no que uno siente que está haciendo algo malo. Luego apagó la luz, a las mujeres les gusta la luz apagada, y se fue desvistiendo. Qué lindo se quitó la ropa, no te figuras, y se sentó al borde de la cama. La claridad que entraba por la ventana, de la luna y eso, la iluminaba. Me quité el pulóver. Oí cómo el pulóver cayó al piso y me sentí satisfecho de haberme puesto el pantalón negro, no el otro, porque la portañuela del negro es de zíper, y me gustó tanto el ruido del zíper, me sentí tan varón al descorrerlo delante de una mujer y saber que también ella lo había escuchado, y al pantalón que bajaba por mis muslos, salía de mis piernas, caía al piso, y estábamos ambos desnudos, sin mirarnos, un poco amarillentos por la luz, un poco rojos, sin saber mucho que hacer. Temíamos que en ese momento se abriera la puerta y apareciera el director de la escuela, su mamá, el Ministro de Educación, escandalizados, y la mamá gritara: Ay, Dios Santo, Virgen del Cielo, Gran Poder de Dios, lo que está haciendo mi hija. Si el padre la coge la mata". Te lo juro. Esperamos, esperamos y no apareció nadie. Me acerqué, nos miramos, nos abrazamos como por primera vez en el mundo, y fuimos lentamente dejándonos caer en las sábanas. Empezamos a deshacer torpezas, a adivinar, a dejarnos llevar por una brisa que soplaba, fuerte olor a mar. El instinto nos guiaba y no nos pareció que estábamos suficientemente abrazados hasta que descubrimos las flores. Había flores húmedas en todo el cuarto: acolchonaban el piso y la cama, adornaban las paredes, pendían del techo, sobresalían del descanso de la ventana. Pusimos atención y nos llegaron los pequeños ruiditos del amor: un río lejano, caracoles, dos hojas y estaban también nuestros cuerpos, su piel y la mía, nuestros labios y manos y ojos y pelo. Nos estábamos bebiendo, tanto que vimos dos niños que corrían un amanecer, cuesta arriba, por un prado de brillantes girasoles. Iban asustando las mariposas. Ella llevaba una sombrilla, él una espada y un tambor, los dos vestidos de blanco y cogidos de la mano. Cuando comenzó la lluvia se lanzaron sobre los girasoles, pero no se hundieron, quedaron flotando y comenzaron a dar vueltas, abrazados, rodeados de mariposas: se miraron a los ojos, y ella vio que él se erguía, levantaba la espada, que brilló en lo alto, destellos azulados, y sintió que la mataba y quedaron abrazados, rodaron nuevamente entre las flores, los ojos cerrados, y comenzaron a descender, a descender perseguidos por todos los girasoles, y mientras bajaban, dejando tras ellos una estela de colores, iban viendo y pronunciando todas las palabras: pomarrosa, hojarasca, arena, zaguán, obelisco, conejo, palmarreal, jícara, almidón, palomas... y cuando la última palabra se desprendió y se perdió, estaban tendidos bajo un árbol frondoso, como abandonados allí por la resaca, y nosotros dos, Vivian y yo, nos moríamos, en otra parte, o allí mismo, muy lejos o muy cerca, y en el último instante de vida vimos, o sentimos, que los niños se incorporaban, vestidos de blanco, y cogidos de la mano se alejaban: pasaron sobre nosotros, ella con la cinta en la mano, había perdido la sombrilla, él repiqueteando en el tambor, ella le decía cosas a Vivian, muy alto porque ya iban distantes, y yo no las comprendía aunque me sentía feliz: él me decía a mí, contento, saludando con la mano y cada vez más lejos, más lejos, más felices, hasta que se perdieron, se perdieron... Poco a poco nosotros fuimos resucitando. Nos volvieron las palabras a la mente, la respiración a los pulmones, y me moví sobre Vivian, que se quejó blandamente y sonrió, ya sin fuerzas para mantener sus dedos dentro de mi pelo. Me incorporé, algo, y no entendí lo que estaba sintiendo. Escuchaba una música lejana, jamás oída, y me levanté aún más, olí, y seguía sintiendo lo que sentía, y vi su pelo desparramado en la almohada, y la sonrisa de ella, y los senos, y los ojos, abiertos pero cerrados, de los que le goteaba un brillo, y aunque me acordé de Arnaldo, no pude y se lo dije: *te quiero,* le dije, me abracé de nuevo a su cuerpo, y una bandada enorme de pájaros levantó el vuelo en mi mente, como una estampida.

Cristina Peri-Rossi
1941—
Uruguay

El laberinto
La rebelión de los niños, 1980.

EL niño estaba subido al árbol. Desde allí, oteaba el horizonte.

El la miró y sintió que no tenía nada que decirle.

—*Diez por diez, cien. Diez por cien, mil. Diez por mil, diez mil* —canturreó el niño, desde arriba del árbol—. Papá, ¿por qué nuestro sistema de numeración es decimal? —preguntó en seguida, mientras intentaba divisar la línea del horizonte. Había oído decir que el horizonte era una línea.

—Probablemente porque tenemos diez dedos en las manos —contestó él, distraídamente—. Si tuviéramos doce, el sistema sería duodecimal.

Nada distinto al tedio y a la pesadumbre. Al tedio, a la pesadumbre.

Sacó un cigarrillo del paquete, y lo encendió sin prisa. Hizo un gesto hacia ella, que no aceptó. Siempre olvidaba que ella no fumaba. *No tenía vicios.* Tampoco le había regalado nunca un libro de matemáticas. Pensó en mujeres que podrían haberlo hecho. Esas, no las conocía, no las había visto nunca pasar, y si las había, él no las supo encontrar.

—Y si no tuviéramos ojos para mirar, ¿qué usaríamos? —preguntó el niño. A veces los ojos no servían: ahora no alcanzaban a divisar esa recta que llamaban horizonte.

—El tacto —respondió el padre—. O el olfato, o el paladar —agregó—. O quizá el cálculo. El cálculo de posibilidades.

—El te admira —murmuró ella, en voz muy baja—. No me gustaría... No quisiera que nunca...

A los veinte años, Lewis Carroll había dibujado un laberinto. El problema consistía en hallar el camino que permitía salir del rombo central, entre los senderos que se cruzan por encima y por debajo, cortados a veces por trazos simples. Hasta que un día él hiciera la pregunta sin respuesta, la que no podría contestar jamás, y entonces la admiración se diluiría, desaparecería súbitamente, y habría que comenzar a vivir sin padre, quizá sin madre, quizá sin un camino que condujera del rombo central a la salida.

Ella también lo había admirado. Sintió un violento rechazo hacia esa idea. ¿Por qué no había podido quererlo sin admirarlo?

—Yo nunca... —comenzó a decir—. Nunca confié en la admiración.

No era eso lo que quería. No había querido decirlo, ni hacerlo.

—Él te admira —recalcó ella, con rencor—. No estoy dispuesta a...

No escuchó el final de la frase. Los niños lo escuchaban todo. Al dejar de serlo, se va adquiriendo la capacidad de oír sólo fragmentos, y a veces se puede ignorar una frase entera, una vida entera, sin mayor esfuerzo.

Sólo había amado a hombres a quienes pudo admirar. Admirar hasta la decepción. El anterior había sido un músico. Fue muy fácil ayudarla a decepcionarse: ella se dejaba llevar por esa pendiente con suavidad, hasta con deleite. Y él alimentó la decepción para ganarla, primero, para retenerla, después.

Desde arriba del árbol las cosas se veían diferentes. Papá, por ejemplo, era un hombre chiquito que fumaba, apoyando el brazo derecho sobre la mesa de hierro del jardín, pintada de blanco. No se había quitado la gabardina, y de vez en cuando la otra mano se deslizaba por el borde azul, como si quisiera comprobar que todo estaba en orden, que los botones seguían en su lugar, que nadie veía para adentro, que su cuerpo estaba protegido. El árbol era un naranjo. Un naranjo de hojas pequeñas y muy verdes que tenían un sabor amargo. Él las había probado un par de veces. Cuando vinieron a vivir a esa casa (de eso hacía muchísimo tiempo, por lo menos como un año), él se sintió muy contento porque la casa tenía jardín, y en el jardín había algunos árboles, árboles a los cuales uno se podía trepar y desde allí mirar el mundo como desde un barco. Se veían los contornos de las casas más distantes, se veían las hamacas de hierro en los jardines vacíos, donde a veces se balanceaban niñas, se veían cuerdas de ropa secándose al sol y muy a lo lejos, perdido entre calles recortadas, un pedazo de mar, tan quieto y tan gris que parecía un cuadro. El no supo al principio que eso era el mar, pero su padre se lo indicó. Le dijo: "Aquello que ves a lo lejos, muy lejos, aquel cuadradito gris es el mar." Y él lanzó un ahhhhh muy largo, un ahhhhh de placer, estoy vivo, la casa tiene un jardín, en el jardín hay árboles, a lo lejos veo el mar y el mar es quieto y gris, parecido a un cuadro. A un cuadro que vio en una exposición. Su padre lo llevó a la galería, pagó dos entradas y le compró un catálogo. El estaba contento y emocionado, como cada vez que salía de paseo con su padre. Como cada vez que él le explicaba algo. No siempre entendía las palabras, no siempre estaba seguro de comprender el significado de su pensamiento, pero le parecía muy importante que él le hablara y le agradecía —le agradecía tanto— que para hacerlo, no simplificara su lenguaje, no intentara hacer las cosas más sencillas sólo para que él pudiera comprenderlas. Una emoción parecida a la que experimentaba al entrar a una iglesia, aunque su padre le había dicho que por ahora no eran católicos, que ya se vería más adelante, que ése era un problema muy complejo y que ya tendría tiempo de decidir en el futuro. ¿Por qué de un día a otro las niñas habían dejado de venir a su casa? Una emoción muy grande, cuando él le hablaba, algo así como un recogimiento, y elevaba los ojos para mirarlo, aunque su padre tuviera la mirada tranquila y distante, como si en realidad hablara con el agua del río y con las piedras. Tanta emoción que casi no podía resistir, porque le parecía que su padre le hablaba de otras cosas. Nunca estaba seguro acerca de si su padre le hablaba de esto o de lo otro. Pero le gustaba mucho escucharlo, tanto como treparse a los árboles, comer naranjas y jugar con las niñas. Pero eran cosas diferentes, sin embargo. Comer naranjas se acababa; era satisfactorio, pero se cumplía y basta. A lo sumo, le quedaba en las manos y en las ropas un olor ácido y fuerte, que se distinguía desde lejos. Jugar con las niñas era muy emocionante, lo excitaba mucho, pero a veces también era dificultoso, incomprensible, especialmente si las niñas tenían mal carácter o se fastidiaban. En cambio, la conversación de su padre no terminaba, aunque él se hubiera callado. Y nunca producía disgusto. Las palabras quedaban suspendidas, permanecían, y él sentía que participaba de una cosa, de una cosa que estaba más allá de él, que flotaba. En la galería, él se sintió regocijado; primero echó a correr entre los cuadros, sin mirarlos. Era tal su alegría que resbalaba por el parquet de la sala como sobre una pista. La exitación no lo dejaba parar, no le permitía detenerse. Su padre lo miró sonriendo, dejándolo correr, dejándolo deslizarse. Por las ventanas entraba una luz difusa, la luz de un parque contiguo lleno de árboles, con senderos por donde padres y madres caminaban con sus hijos; había algunas hojas caídas no recogidas todavía, y él observó a una niña muy rubia de cabellos largos que tenía un vestido celeste.

Ver a la niña lo puso medio loco. La niña iba acompañada por su madre y caminaba a su lado con gran dignidad. Su dignidad lo excitó, le hizo mal y bien al mismo tiempo. Llevaba puestos unos zapatos negros que se abrochaban a un costado con un pequeño botón, encima de los calcetines blancos, cortos, que apenas llegaban al tobillo. Apretó la nariz contra el vidrio para mirar mejor. ¿Por qué se veía mejor si uno apretaba la nariz contra el vidrio? El padre se aproximó caminando tranquilamente. El apretaba tanto la nariz contra el vidrio que la nariz se achataba y de pronto el vidrio se nublaba y él desesperadamente lo limpiaba con los codos, porque tenía un pullóver de lana que servía muy bien para limpiar vidrios.

—¿Qué miras? —preguntó su padre, apareciendo a sus espaldas y echando los ojos a mirar por el sendero de álamos contiguo a la galería. En seguida vio a la niña que caminaba con su madre, de largos cabellos rubios, y él también se la puso a mirar, lentamente.

—Tiene un vestidito celeste —comentó el niño en alta voz, apretando cada vez más la nariz contra el vidrio—. ¿Qué son esos árboles de alrededor?

—Son álamos —dijo el padre. Ambos miraron. Aunque las dos caminaban, nunca se alejaban mucho de su campo de visión, de modo que ellos podían observar perfectamente los cabellos rubios que caían a ambos lados de la cara, el vestidito celeste, almidonado, los zapatos negros con un pequeño botón al costado y los calcetines blancos que apenas cubrían los tobillos.

Ahora la mujer y la niña se habían acercado a un estanque, en medio del sendero, y miraban el fondo, donde seguramente pececitos rojos y azules nadaban, sorbiendo apenas el agua, corriendo veloces cuando la superficie se agitaba. Sobre el estanque habían caído algunas hojas de los árboles próximos.

—Ahora ella está mirando el agua del estanque —proclamó el niño.

—Los zapatos —murmuró el padre—. ¿Has visto los zapatos? Son negros y tienen un pequeño botón al costado. A veces, debe tardar mucho tiempo en abrocharlos. No es fácil hacer entrar un botón, por pequeño que sea, en un ojal así. Pero ella no se impacienta nunca. Creo que no conoce la impaciencia. No pierde jamás su dignidad.

—Creo que ella también mira los peces que nadan en el agua —aseguró el niño.

—Fíjate qué hermoso es el gesto de su mano —le dijo el padre. La niña había dejado descansar la mano con indolencia sobre el borde del estanque. La mano tenía cinco dedos, como todas las manos, pero estaba seguro de que era la mano más bella del mundo.

No supo bien cómo, pero al rato estaban todos sentados alrededor de las mesas del parque, bebiendo refrescos y conversando. Su padre siempre se las ingeniaba para que él pudiera acercarse a las niñas, y aunque jamás hablaban del asunto, él se lo agradecía interiormente. Admiraba a su padre por eso. Porque de una manera muy natural, y sin que tuviera que pedírselo, provocaba el encuentro con las niñas, sin forzar la situación, como si estar juntos alrededor de la mesa de hierro blanca bebiendo refrescos y conversando fuera la única culminación posible de esa bella tarde, de los cuadros vistos en la galería, de la sucesión de álamos y de los peces de colores que nadaban en el fondo del estanque.

Se la quedó mirando, extasiado, su corazón palpitaba aceleradamente y al principio no supo qué decirle. Su padre había quedado en diagonal con la niña, al lado de la madre, de modo que la miraba oblicuamente. Los refrescos estaban sobre la mesa, y su padre balanceaba indolentemente un cigarrillo en el extremo de una de sus manos.

—Es un lugar realmente muy agradable —dijo la mujer, abarcando con su mirada la galería, el parque, el estanque, la hilera de álamos, seguramente la luz difusa de la tarde, seguramente las ventanas y los peces que en el fondo del estanque nadaban en direcciones opuestas. Las piernas de la niña no llegaban al suelo (las suyas, tampoco), de modo que colgaban, como las hojas de los álamos, sin caer.

Él la miraba con disimulo, ruborizándose a veces, sin poder decir palabra. Tan sumido en su angustioso mutismo que el refresco se calentaba en sus manos sin que se lo llevara a los labios. El padre tampoco hablaba. El sabía que el padre no hablaba, a pesar de la serie de frases amables y convencionales que pronunciaba con delicadeza, como si se tratara de una artesanía. Era extremadamente hábil para conversar con intrascendencia, haciendo que todo el mundo se sintiera bien, pero quién sabe dónde estaba en realidad su conversación.

La diagonal era una buena línea de observación. Detrás de sus lentes de sol, la niña y el parque adquirían unos deliciosos tonos sepias. ¿Por qué no lo auxiliaba? ¿Por qué no venía en su ayuda? ¿Por qué la abandonaba allí, en esa muda contemplación, por qué no lo mandaba a jugar o a correr, por qué de una manera autoritaria no lo obligaba a beber su refresco y a juntar distintas clases de hojas? La niña tenía en los lóbulos unos pequeñísimos aros de oro. No eran completamente redondos, y la línea que se quebraba parecía una interrogación.

—Doy clases de inglés. Sí, clases de inglés. No es el trabajo más seductor del mundo —decía su padre suavemente—, pero es el único que he encontrado.

Ahora podría establecer algunos paralelismos entre ambas gramáticas, haría algunas observaciones ingeniosas que provocarían la sonrisa de la mujer, mientras la niña sorbía su refresco educadamente, sin que uno pudiera llegar a saber nunca si estaba aburrida, cansada, si disfrutaba del aire otoñal que recorría las plantas, si deseaba levantarse y pasear.

Transpiraba y su corazón palpitaba locamente, forzaba su mente y las cuerdas vocales intentando pronunciar una frase. Una frase entera. Una frase que ella pudiera escuchar y contestar, pero estaba aterrorizado, estaba tan asustado que quería llorar, ¿por qué su padre no lo ayudaba, por qué no le daba una orden, por qué no los invitaba a correr por el sendero, a irse lejos de allí? Pondría una enorme distancia, una gran distancia, seguramente él podía correr más que ella y se subiría a una loma, aprovecharía una elevación del terreno para treparse y desde allí la observaría sin temor, sin enrojecimientos ni balbuceos.

La niña terminó su refresco, y sin ninguna precipitación, con un gesto absolutamente controlado y medido, depositó el vaso sobre la mesa. Tenía los ojos dorados, es verdad, pero él no podía darse cuenta qué miraban, qué decían, si decían algo, no podía deducir su manera de ser a través de esos ojos fríos y serenos. Entonces se le ocurrió la idea salvadora, entonces se le ocurrió decir:

—Papá, quiero ir a casa.

Echó una última mirada, oblicua, en diagonal. Lentamente sacó su billetera y pagó los refrescos. No era la primera niña que iba a su casa, ya habían ido otras, y la cosa allí era diferente. Ellas venían de visita, como si fueran a una fiesta, y él se sentía más dueño de la situación; había objetos, había muebles, cosas conocidas que lo hacían sentirse más seguro, menos solo. Entonces, todo cambiaba; se podía jugar con las niñas, conversar con ellas, escarbar la tierra y fabricar caleidoscopios. Y aunque él se mostraba generoso y espléndido, compartiendo todos los objetos, enseñándoles sus conocimientos sobre plantas, insectos, mariposas, estrellas o estampillas, bien se veía que él hacía todo eso porque quería, podía mostrarse generoso y espléndido porque estaba en su casa y eran sus cosas, lo cual le daba esa sensación de comodidad y de placer, de poder y de dominio. No iba a usar el poder, seguramente, para esclavizar a las niñas. Con un gesto delicado —tocándolas suavemente a la altura de los hombros, sin oprimirlas, sintiendo que los cabellos negros o dorados rozaban las yemas de sus dedos— les mostraba las figuras que los líquidos de colores formaban en el espejo del caleidoscopio, o el dibujo azulado de las alas de una mariposa.

— ¿Qué es lo que siento? —le había preguntado una vez al padre. Quería saber qué le inspiraban las niñas. El padre estaba de pie, frente a la ventana, mirando un caleidoscopio. Le gustaba descubrir imágenes, figuras, y no parecía cansarse nunca de ese entretenimiento. Le había explicado que las combinaciones posibles eran infinitas, y que jamás se repetían. "¿Cómo sabes tú que una figura no se ha repetido nunca?", le preguntó él, desconfiado. "Es una ley", contestó el padre. "No estoy muy seguro de que alguien la haya comprobado", dijo el niño, poco convencido. "Podría repetirse una sin que nos diéramos cuenta", concluyó. Si imprimía un pequeño giro al cilindro, si sus dedos movían el estuche, esa bonita rosa encarnada sumergida en un lago de hielo desaparecía, súbitamente desaparecería, no podría verla nunca más ("No se repiten jamás. Las figuras. En el caleidoscopio. No vuelven. Puedes cambiarlas, pero no obligarlas a regresar. No. Nunca") y habría sido un gesto de la mano, tan sólo uno, el culpable de esa desaparición.

—Sólo podrás decidir cuánto tiempo dura —dijo el padre.

—Nunca sabré si la próxima figura será mejor que ésta —observó él, muy concentrado, cerrando el ojo libre y ahondando mucho la visión del otro, a través del estuche. Una hermosa composición de cálices amarillos y triángulos lilas ocupaba el centro de la imagen.

—Ese será tu problema —contestó el padre—. Creo que lo que sientes es concupiscencia —dijo, por fin.

— ¿Concupiscencia es saber que puedo tocarlas y no tocarlas, avanzar un poco el dedo (solamente un poco, papá) sobre el hombro, recorrer la costura del vestido (tienen los vestidos llenos de costuras, papá, y las costuras sobresalen un poco) y de pronto encontrar un hilo, un hilo que cuelga de la tela, que se ha deslizado del hombro?; papá, a veces los hilos de sus vestidos se escapan un poco, no mucho, no deshacen el vestido: sólo se sueltan un poquito y ellas no lo ven, no lo ven porque tienen el vestido puesto y no están atentas, están mirando la lámina del ciervo que tengo en la pared del cuarto o están jugando con mi microscopio y el hilo está un poquito salido, yo lo tomo entre los dedos, ellas no se dan cuenta, puedo tirar del hilo sin que lo noten, puedo tirar un poquito y nadie lo verá, nadie sabrá que estoy tirando del hilo de su vestido blanco y el hilo me tira a mí, yo siento que él me lleva, me conduce a alguna parte que no está afuera, sino adentro de mí.

—Si fuera un niño —murmuró el hombre tratando de resistir la mirada de la mujer—, si yo fuera un niño, ¿entiendes?, nadie lo notaría, nadie se daría cuenta.

El jardín estaba un poco frío y ella no lo había invitado a entrar a la casa. Aunque su hijo estaba allí, encima del árbol, ella no lo había invitado a entrar a la casa.

—Mamá —gritó el niño desde arriba del árbol—. Me parece que hay una naranja madura. Creo que ya estará dulce. Me parece que están madurando desde ayer —dijo, y se trepó un poco más, para alcanzarla.

Las niñas habían dejado de venir. De pronto, de un día para otro (como maduran las naranjas), las niñas habían dejado de venir. No supo por qué. ¿Había sido, quizá, lo que su padre llamó concupiscencia? ¿Acaso ellas lo habían notado y él tenía que avergonzarse?

—Si yo tuviera su edad —continuó el hombre, hablando bajo y haciendo un esfuerzo extraordinario—; si me trepara a los árboles y arrancara naranjas verdes con las manos.

El cigarrillo se había consumido, pero él no intentó apagarlo. Un bloque de ceniza, muy gris y muy sólida, se sostenía en el extremo, y uno sabía que cuando cayera, no caería por partes, se desmoronaría entera, dejando la colilla desguarnecida, sola, infeliz. Ningún buen fumador puede soportar bien la caída de un bloque de ceniza.

—Él te admira —insistió la mujer, con voz crispada, tensa—. Él te admira y no quiero que nunca..., que jamás...

La vida se había desordenado. La vida se había desordenado mucho. Sin las niñas, los objetos parecían monótonos y tristes, y él vagaba por las habitaciones como un perro perdido. En cuanto al padre, cada vez estaba menos en la casa, tenía mucho trabajo afuera, mucha gente de pronto quería estudiar inglés, y eso se ve que lo ponía muy triste, porque ya no hablaba con él y no respondía a sus preguntas. Por el cielo, vio que el sol se estaba poniendo. Vio que el sol empezaba a irse, y arrastraba, en su fuga, muchos colores que le gustaban, muchas naranjas que oscurecían, muchas cosas que ya no se veían.

—No quiero que se vaya —gritó desde el árbol.

Ambos levantaron la cabeza, como tocados por una claridad. Lo miraron al unísono y él se sorprendió, pero no perdió
tiempo, contestó a la mirada con otra llena de fuerza y de decisión, como para impresionarlos. ¿Qué había dicho? Fuera
lo que fuera, había causado efecto.

—No quiero que se vaya —repitió, sabiendo que esta frase
ejercía un extraño poder. En el desorden venían frases como
ésta, en el desorden de pronto aparecían islas encantadas des-
cubiertas al azar, y uno se instalaba en ellas precariamente,
pero tratando de reconstruir el mundo. No quería que el sol
se fuera y parecía que en ese deseo cabían muchas cosas: la
ausencia de las niñas, el súbito alejamiento de papá, la tristeza de la madre. Ellas se fueron de un día para otro, sin explicaciones, ya no venían más a mirar su colección de hojas fu-
siformes, ni sus caracolas de mar, ni sus láminas de trenes antiguos. Ya no se llevaban, de regalo, vidrios de colores para armar caleidoscopios, ni conchas de moluscos. Ya no les podía
enseñar a pintar y a dibujar con la punta de un alfiler en el interior de las almejas.

—Hay psiquiatras para eso —dijo la mujer, que había dejado de mirar al niño y estaba a punto de estremecerse de frío,
en medio del relente. Oscurecía y la quietud de la casa, con
las luces apagadas, la casa enhiesta, erguida entre los naranjos
y los frutales, producía cierta sensación de melancolía.

—No quiero que se vaya —volvió a gritar el niño, como si
esgrimiera un arma. Un arma contra la huida del sol, la ausencia de las niñas, la lejanía del padre, la desaparición de las figuras en el caleidoscopio, contra los vidrios que deformaban
la realidad, contra la irrupción vertiginosa de la noche y la casa sola.

—Sí —dijo el hombre poniéndose de pie—. Hay psiquiatras
y leyes.

Alisó el borde de la gabardina, verificó que estaba bien
abrochada. Hizo un gesto vago con la mano, una especie de
saludo, y sin mirar a la mujer, tomó el camino que conducía
a la calle, más allá de la valla blanca.

De pronto la frase, la misma frase, había perdido efecto.
¿Por qué la última vez que la dije no fue como la primera?
¿Por qué ahora ellos no se habían detenido y lo habían mirado? ¿Por qué la oyeron como algo natural, como si no existiera, como si no sonara?

Tuvo que pasar muy cerca del naranjo. Hubiera preferido
no hacerlo, por eso, aceleró el paso.

—No quiero que te vayas —gritó el niño, angustiadamente.

Repitió el gesto vago de saludo, un gesto que más que una despedida, era una fuga. Una fuga precipitada de los canteros, de los árboles con naranjas verdes de hojas muy amargas, una fuga de la mujer que ya no sabía adónde estaba, de los caleidoscopios de colores y del recuerdo de las niñas que tienen vestidos celestes y cabellos rubios.

Desde arriba del árbol, nada se veía.

Hundió las manos en el bolsillo y evitó mirar atrás.

El niño sumido en la oscuridad del árbol. La casa, augusta en medio de la noche. Hundió distraídamente las manos en el bolsillo. Enredado en el papel del paquete, venía un hilo blanco de vestido.

Virgilio Piñera
1914—1979
Cuba

La carne
Cuentos fríos, 1956.

SUCEDIO con gran sencillez, sin afectación. Por motivos que no son del caso exponer, la población sufría de falta de carne. Todo el mundo se alarmó y se hicieron comentarios más o menos amargos y hasta se esbozaron ciertos propósitos de venganza. Pero, como siempre sucede, las protestas no pasaron de meras amenazas y pronto se vio aquel afligido pueblo engullendo los más variados vegetales.

Sólo que el señor Ansaldo no siguió la orden general. Con gran tranquilidad se puso a afilar un enorme cuchillo de cocina, y, acto seguido, bajándose los pantalones hasta las rodillas, cortó de su nalga izquierda un hermoso filete. Tras haberlo limpiado lo adobó con sal y vinagre, lo pasó —como se dice— por la parrilla, para finalmente freírlo en la gran sartén de las tortillas del domingo. Sentóse a la mesa y comenzó a saborear su hermoso filete. Entonces llamaron a la puerta; era su vecino que venía a desahogarse... Pero Ansaldo, con elegante ademán, le hizo ver el hermoso filete. El vecino preguntó y Ansaldo se limitó a mostrar su nalga izquierda. Todo quedaba explicado. A su vez, el vecino deslumbrado y conmovido, salió sin decir palabra para volver al poco rato con el Alcalde del pueblo. Este expresó a Ansaldo su vivo deseo de que su amado pueblo se alimentara, como lo hacía Ansaldo, de sus propias carnes de cada uno. Pronto quedó acordada la cosa y después de las efusiones propias de gente bien educada, Ansaldo se trasladó a la plaza principal del pueblo para ofrecer, según su frase característica, "una demostración práctica a las masas".

Una vez allí hizo saber que cada persona cortaría de su nalga izquierda dos filetes, en todo iguales a una muestra en yeso encarnado que colgaba de un reluciente alambre. Y declaraba que dos filetes y no uno, pues si él había cortado su propia nalga izquierda un hermoso filete, justo era que la cosa marchase a compás, esto es, que nadie engullera un filete menos. Una vez fijados estos puntos, diose cada uno a rebanar dos filetes de su respectiva nalga izquierda. Era un glorioso espectáculo, pero se ruega no enviar descripciones. Se hicieron cálculos acerca de cuánto tiempo gozaría el pueblo de los beneficios de la carne. Un distinguido anatómico predijo que sobre un peso de cien libras, y descontando vísceras y demás órganos no ingestibles, un individuo podía comer carne durante ciento cuarenta días a razón de media libra por día. Por lo demás, era un cálculo ilusorio. Y lo que importaba era que cada uno pudiese ingerir su hermoso filete.

Pronto se vio a señoras que hablaban de las ventajas que reportaba la idea del señor Ansaldo. Por ejemplo, las que ya habían devorado sus senos no se veían obligadas a cubrir de telas su caja torácica, y sus vestidos concluían poco más arriba del ombligo. Y algunas, no todas, no hablaban ya, pues habían engullido su lengua, que, dicho sea de paso, es un manjar de monarcas. En la calle tenían lugar las más deliciosas escenas: así, dos señoras que hacía muchísimo tiempo que no se veían no pudieron besarse; habían usado sus labios en la confección de unas frituras de gran éxito. Y el Alcaide del penal no pudo firmar la sentencia de muerte de un condenado porque se había comido las yemas de los dedos, que, según los buenos "gourmets" (y el Alcalde lo era) ha dado origen a esa frase tan llevada y traída de "chuparse la yema de los dedos".

Hubo hasta pequeñas sublevaciones. El sindicato de obreros de ajustadores femeninos elevó su más formal protesta ante la autoridad correspondiente, y ésta contestó que no era posible "slogan" alguno para animar a las señoras a usarlos de nuevo. Pero eran sublevaciones inocentes que no interrumpían de ningún modo la consumición, por parte del pueblo, de su propia carne.

Uno de los sucesos más pintorescos de aquella agradable jornada fue la disección del último pedazo de carne del bailarín del pueblo. Este, por respeto a su arte, había dejado para lo último los bellos dedos de sus pies. Sus convecinos advirtieron que desde hacía varios días se mostraba vivamente inquieto. Ya sólo le quedaba la parte carnosa del dedo gordo. Entonces invitó a sus amigos a presenciar la operación. En medio de un sanguinolento silencio cortó su porción postrera, y sin pasarla por el fuego la dejó caer en el hueco de lo que había sido en otro tiempo su hermosa boca. Entonces todos los presentes se pusieron repentinamente serios.

Pero se iba viviendo, y era lo importante. ¿Y si acaso...? ¿Sería por eso que las zapatillas del bailarín se encontraban ahora en una de las salas del Museo de los Recuerdos Ilustres? Sólo se sabe que uno de los hombres más obesos del pueblo (pesaba doscientos kilos) gastó su reserva de carne disponible en el breve espacio de quince días (era extremadamente goloso, y, por otra parte, su organismo exigía grandes cantidades). Después ya nadie pudo verlo jamás. Evidentemente, se ocultaba... Pero no sólo se ocultaba él, sino que otros muchos comenzaban a adoptar idéntico comportamiento. De esta suerte, una mañana, la señora Orfila, al preguntar a su hijo —que se devoraba el lóbulo izquierdo de la oreja— dónde había guardado no sé qué cosa, no obtuvo respuesta alguna. Y no valieron súplicas ni amenazas. Llamado el perito en desaparecidos sólo pudo dar con un breve montón de excrementos en el sitio donde la señora Orfila juraba y perjuraba que su amado hijo se encontraba en el momento de ser interrogado por ella. Pero estas ligeras alteraciones no minaban en absoluto la alegría de aquellos habitantes. ¿De qué podría quejarse un pueblo que tenía asegurada su subsistencia? El grave problema de orden público creado por la falta de carne, ¿no había quedado definitivamente zanjado? Que la población fuera ocultándose progresivamente nada tenía que ver con el aspecto central de la cosa, y sólo era un colofón que no alteraba en modo alguno la firme voluntad de aquella gente de procurarse el precioso alimento. ¿Era, por ventura, dicho colofón el precio que exigía la carne de cada uno? Pero sería miserable hacer más preguntas inoportunas, y aquel prudente pueblo estaba muy bien alimentado.

1944.

Virgilio Piñera
1914—1979
Cuba

El que vino a salvarme
1967.

SIEMPRE tuve un gran miedo: no saber cuándo moriría.
Mi mujer afirmaba que la culpa era de mi padre; mi madre estaba agonizando, él me puso frente a ella y me obligó
a besarla. Por esa época yo tenía diez años y ya sabemos todo
eso de que la presencia de la muerte deja una profunda huella
en los niños... No digo que la aseveración sea falsa, pero en mi
caso, es distinto. Lo que mi mujer ignora es que yo vi ajusti-
ciar a un hombre, y lo vi por pura casualidad. Justicia irregular, es decir dos hombres le tienden un lazo a otro hombre en
el servicio sanitario de un cine y lo degüellan. ¿Cómo? Yo estaba encerrado haciendo caca y ellos no podían verme; estaban en los mingitorios. Yo hacía caca plácidamente y de pronto oí: "Pero no van a matarme..." Miré por el enrejillado, y
entonces vi una navaja cortando un pescuezo, sentí un alarido, sangre a borbotones y piernas que se alejaban a toda prisa. Cuando la policía llegó al lugar del hecho me encontró des-
mayado, casi muerto, con eso que le dicen "shock nervioso".
Estuve un mes entre la vida y la muerte.

Bueno, no vayan a pensar que, en lo sucesivo, iba a tener
miedo de ser degollado. Bueno, pueden pensarlo, están en su
derecho. Si alguien ve degollar a un hombre, es lógico que
piense que también puede ocurrirle lo mismo a él, pero también es lógico pensar que no va a dar la maldita casualidad de
que el destino, o lo que sea, lo haya escogido a uno para que
tenga la misma suerte del hombre que degollaron en el servicio sanitario del cine.

No, no era ese mi miedo; el que yo sentí, justo en el momento en que degollaban al tipo, se podía expresar con esta
frase: ¿Cuál es la hora? Imaginemos a un viejo de ochenta
años, listo ya para enfrentarse a la muerte; pienso que su idea
fija no puede ser otra que preguntarse: ¿será esta noche...?
¿será mañana...? ¿será a las tres de la madrugada de pasado
mañana...? ¿Va a ser ahora mismo en que estoy pensando que
será pasado mañana a las tres de la madrugada...? Como sabe
y siente que el tiempo de vida que le queda es muy reducido,
estima que sus cálculos sobre la "hora fatal" son bastante pre-

cisos, pero, al mismo tiempo, la impotencia en que se encuentra para fijar "el momento" los reduce a cero. En cambio, el tipo asesinado en el servicio sanitario supo, así de pronto, cuál sería su hora. En el momento de proferir: "Pero no van a matarme...", ya sabía que le llegaba su hora. Entre su exclamación desesperada y la mano que accionaba la navaja para cercenarle el cuello, supo el minuto exacto de su muerte. Es decir que si la exclamación se produjo, por ejemplo, a las nueve horas, cuatro minutos y cinco segundos de la noche y la degollación a las nueve, cuatro minutos y ocho segundos, él supo exactamente su hora de morir con una anticipación de tres segundos.

En cambio, aquí, echado en la cama, solo (mi mujer murió el año pasado y, por otra parte, no sé la pobre en qué podría ayudarme en lo que se refiere a lo de la hora de mi muerte), estoy devanándome los pocos sesos que me quedan. Es sabido que cuando se tiene noventa años (y es esa mi edad) se está, como el viajero, pendiente de la hora, con la diferencia de que el viajero la sabe y uno la ignora. Pero no anticipemos.

Cuando lo del tipo degollado en el servicio sanitario yo tenía apenas veinte años. El hecho de estar "lleno" de vida en ese entonces y además, tenerla por delante casi como una eternidad, borró pronto aquel cuadro sangriento y aquella pregunta angustiosa. Cuando se está lleno de vida sólo se tiene tiempo para vivir y "vivirse". Uno "se vive" y se dice: "¡Qué saludable estoy, respiro salud por todos mis poros, soy capaz de comerme un buey, copular cinco veces por día, trabajar sin desfallecer veinte horas seguidas!...", y entonces uno no puede tener noción de lo que es morir y "morirse". Cuando a los veintidós años me casé, mi mujer, viendo mis "ardores" me dijo una noche: "¿Vas a ser conmigo el mismo cuando seas un viejito?" Y le contesté: "¿Qué es un viejito? ¿Acaso tú lo sabes?"

Ella, naturalmente, tampoco lo sabía. Y como ni ella ni yo podíamos, por el momento, configurar a un viejito, pues nos echamos a reír y fornicamos de lo lindo.

Pero recién cumplidos los cincuenta, empecé a vislumbrar lo de ser un viejito, y también empecé a pensar en eso de la hora... Por supuesto, proseguía viviendo, pero al mismo tiempo empezaba a morirme, y una curiosidad, enfermiza y devoradora, me ponía por delante el momento fatal. Ya que tenía que morir, al menos saber en qué instante sobrevendría mi muerte, como sé, por ejemplo, el instante preciso en que me lavo los dientes...

Y a medida que me hacía más viejo, este pensamiento se fue haciendo más obsesivo hasta llegar a lo que llamamos fijación. Allá por los setenta hice, de modo inesperado, mi primer viaje en avión. Recibí un cablegrama de la mujer de mi único hermano avisándome que éste se moría. Tomé pues el avión. A las dos horas de vuelo se produjo mal tiempo. El avión era una pluma en la tempestad, y todo eso que se dice de los aviones bajo los efectos de una tormenta: pasajeros aterrados, idas y venidas de las aeromozas, objetos que se vienen al suelo, gritos de mujeres y de niños mezclados con padrenuestros y avemarías, en fin ese "memento mori" que es más "memento" a cuarenta mil pies de altura.

—Gracias a Dios —me dije—, gracias a Dios que por vez primera me acerco a una cierta precisión en lo que se refiere al momento de mi muerte. Al menos, en esta nave en peligro de estrellarse, ya puedo ir calculando el momento. ¿Diez, quince, treinta y ocho minutos...? No importa, estoy cerca, y tú, muerte, no lograrás sorprenderme.

Confieso que gocé salvajemente. Ni por un instante se me ocurrió rezar, pasar revista a mi vida, hacer acto de contrición o simplemente esa función fisiológica que es vomitar. No, sólo estaba atento a la inminente caída del avión para saber, mientras nos íbamos estrellando, que ese era el momento de mi muerte.

Pasado el peligro, una pasajera me dijo: "Oiga, lo estuve viendo mientras estábamos por caernos, y usted como si nada..." Me sonreí, no le contesté; ella, con su angustia aún reflejada en su cara, ignoraba "mi angustia" que, por una sola vez en mi vida, se había transformado a esos cuarenta mil pies de altura en un estado de gracia comparable al de los santos más calificados de la Iglesia.

Pero a cuarenta mil pies de altura en un avión azotado por la tormenta —único paraíso entrevisto en mi larga vida— no se está todos los días; por el contrario se habita el infierno que cada cual se construye: sus paredes son pensamientos, su techo terrores y sus ventanas abismos... Y dentro, uno helándose a fuego lento, quiero decir perdiendo vida en medio de llamas que adoptan formas singulares, "a qué hora", "un martes o un sábado", "en el otoño o en la primavera"...

Y yo me hielo y me quemo cada vez más. Me he convertido en un acabado espécimen de un museo de teratología y al mismo tiempo soy la viva imagen de la desnutrición. Tengo por seguro que por mis venas no corre sangre sino pus; hay que ver mis escaras —purulentas, cárdenas—, y mis huesos, que

parecen haberle conferido a mi cuerpo una muy otra anato-
mía. Los de las caderas, como un río, se han salido de madre;
las clavículas, al descarnarme, parecen anclas pendiendo del
costado de un barco; los occipitales hacen de mi cabeza un
coco aplastado de un mazazo.

Sin embargo, lo que la cabeza contiene sigue pensando, y
pensando en su idea fija; ahora mismo, en este instante, en mi
cuarto, tirado en la cama, con la muerte encima, con la muerte, que puede ser esa foto de mi padre muerto, que me mira
y me dice: "Te voy a sorprender, no podrás saber, me estás
viendo pero ignoras cuándo te asestaré el golpe..."

Por mi parte, miré más fijamente la foto de mi padre y le
dije: "no te vas a salir con la tuya, sabré el momento en que
me echarás el guante y antes gritaré: ¡Es ahora! y no te quedará otro remedio que confesarte vencido".

Y justo en ese momento, en ese momento que participa
de la realidad y de la irrealidad, sentí unos pasos que, a su
vez, participaban de esa misma realidad e irrealidad. Desvié la
vista de la foto e inconscientemente la puse en el espejo del
ropero que está frente a mi cama. En él vi reflejada la cara de
un hombre joven, sólo su cara ya que el resto del cuerpo se
sustraía a mi vista debido a un biombo colocado entre los
pies de la cama y el espejo. Pero no le di mayor importancia;
sería incomprensible que no se la diera teniendo otra edad,
es decir, la edad en que uno está realmente vivo y la inopina-
da presencia de un extraño en nuestro cuarto nos causaría
desde sorpresa hasta terror. Pero a mi edad y en el estado de
languidez en que me hallaba, un extraño y su rostro es sólo
parte de la realidad-irrealidad que se padece. Es decir, que ese
extraño y su cara era, o un objeto más de los muchos que pueblan mi cuarto, o un fantasma de los muchos que pueblan mi
cabeza. En consecuencia volví a poner la vista en la foto de
mi padre, y cuando volví a mirar el espejo la cara del extraño había desaparecido. Volví de nuevo a mirar la foto y
creí advertir que la cara de mi padre estaba como enfurruña-
da, es decir la cara de mi padre por ser la de él, pero al mismo
·tiempo con una cara que no era la suya, sino como si se la hubiera maquillado para hacer un personaje de tragedia. Pero vaya usted a saber... En ese linde entre realidad e irrealidad todo es posible, y más importante, todo ocurre y no ocurre. Entonces cerré los ojos y empecé a decir en voz alta: ahora, ahora... De pronto sentí ruido de pisadas muy cerca del respaldar
de la cama; abrí los ojos y allí estaba, frente a mí, el extraño,
con todo su cuerpo largo como un kilómetro. Pensé: "Bah,

lo mismo del espejo..." y volví a mirar la foto de mi padre. Pero algo me decía que volviera a mirar al extraño. No desobedecí mi voz interior y lo miré. Ahora esgrimía una navaja e iba inclinando lentamente el cuerpo mientras me miraba fijamente. Entonces comprendí que ese extraño era el que venía a salvarme. Supe con una anticipación de varios segundos el momento exacto de mi muerte. Cuando la navaja se hundió en mi yugular, miré a mi salvador y, entre borbotones de sangre, le dije: "Gracias por haber venido."

Nélida Piñón
1937–
Brasil

Cosecha

UN rostro prohibido desde que había crecido. Dominaba los paisajes en el modo activo de agrupar frutas y comerlas en las sendas minúsculas de las montañas, y además por la alegría con que distribuía las pepitas. A cada tierra su verdad de pepita, él se decía sonriendo. Cuando se hizo hombre, encontró a la mujer, ella se sonrió, era altiva como él, aunque su silencio fuese de oro, lo miraba más de lo que explicaba la historia del universo. Esta reserva mineral lo encantaba y por ella pasó a dividir el mundo entre el amor y sus objetos. Un amor que se hacía profundo a punto de dedicarse a excavaciones, a rehacer ciudades submersas en lava.

La aldea rechazaba el proceder de quien habita tierras raras. Parecían los dos soldados de una frontera extranjera, para transitarse por ellos, más allá del olor de carne amorosa, ellos exigían pasaporte, deposiciones ideológicas. Ellos apenas se preocupaban con el fondo de la tierra, que es nuestro interior, ella también completó su pensamiento. Les inspiraba el sentimiento de la conspiración de las raíces que el propio árbol, atraído por el sol y expuesto a la tierra, no podía alcanzar aunque se creyese enterado.

Hasta que decidió partir. Le tocaban andanzas, trazar las líneas finales de un mapa cuya composición se había iniciado y él sabía hesitante. Explicó a la mujer que para amarla mejor no excluía el mundo, la transgresión de las leyes, los disturbios de los pájaros migratorios. Al contrario, las criaturas en sus peregrinaciones le parecían simples piezas aladas cercando alturas raras.

Ella se resistió, confiaba en el llanto. A pesar de que su rostro exhibiera en aquellos días una belleza espléndida a punto de pensar él que estando el amor con ella por qué buscarlo en tierras donde difícilmente lo encontraré, insistía en la independencia. Siempre los de su raza adoptaron comportamiento de potro. Aunque él en especial dependiese de ella para reparar ciertas omisiones fatales.

Vivieron juntos todas las horas disponibles hasta la separación. Su última frase fue simple: con Ud. conocí el paraíso. Su delicadeza conmovió a la mujer, aunque los diálogos del hombre la inquietasen. A partir de esta fecha se encerró dentro de la casa. Como los caracoles que se resienten del exceso de la claridad. Comprendiendo que tal vez debiese preservar la vida de un modo más intenso, para cuando él volviese. En ningún momento dejaba de alimentar la fe, proporcionar porciones diarias de carpas oriundas de aguas orientales a su amor exagerado.

En toda la aldea la actitud del hombre representaba una rebelión que se debía temer. Procuraban proscribir su nombre de cualquier conversación. Se esforzaban por destruir el rostro libre y siempre que pasaban por la casa de la mujer fingían que ella jamás le había pertenecido. Le enviaron regalos, pedazos de tocino, canastas de peras y poesías esparcidas. Para que ella interpretase a través de aquellos recursos cuánto la consideraban disponible, sin marca de buey y las iniciales del hombre en su piel.

La mujer raramente admitía a una presencia en su casa. Los regalos entraban por la ventana del frente siempre abierta para que el sol atestiguase su vida decente, pero abandonaban la casa por la puerta de atrás, todos aparentemente intocados. La aldea iba allá para inspeccionar los objetos que de algún modo la presenciaron y a ellos no, pues difícilmente aceptaban la rigidez de las costumbres. A veces ella se servía de un pariente para las compras indispensables. Ellos dejaban entonces los pedidos a sus pies, y en el rápido pasaje por el interior de la casa procuraban investigar todo. De cierto modo ella consentía para que viesen que el hombre todavía imperaba en las cosas sagradas de aquella casa.

Jamás faltó una flor diariamente renovada próxima al retrato del hombre. Su semblante de águila. Pero, con el tiempo, más allá de cambiar el color del vestido, antes triste ahora siempre rojo, y alterar el peinado, pues había decidido mantener el pelo corto, recortado junto a la cabeza — decidió eliminar el retrato. No fue fácil la decisión. Durante días rondaba el retrato, sondeaba los ojos oscuros del hombre, ya lo condenaba, ya lo absolvía: ¿por qué Ud. necesitó su rebeldía? yo vivo sola, no sé si la guerra lo tragó, no sé siquiera si debo conmemorar su muerte con el sacrificio de mi vida.

Durante la noche, confiando en la sombra, retiró el retrato y lo tiró rudamente sobre el armario. Pudo descansar después de la actitud tomada. Pensó de este modo poder probar a los enemigos que él habitaba su cuerpo independiente del homenaje. Tal vez hubiese murmurado a alguno de sus parientes, entre descuidada y oprimida, que el destino de la mujer era mirar el mundo y soñar con el rey de la tierra.

Recordaba la manera de hablar del hombre en sus momentos de tensión. Su rostro entonces se igualaba a la piedra, vigoroso, una prominencia en que se había inscrito una sentencia para permanecer. No sabía quién entre los dos era más sensible a la violencia. El, que se había ido, ella, que se había tenido que quedar. Sólo con los años fue comprendiendo que si él todavía vivía tardaba en regresar. Pero, si había muerto, ella dependía de alguna señal para providenciar su fin. Y repetía temerosa y agitada: alguna señal para providenciar su fin. La muerte era una vertiente exagerada, pensó ella mirando el pálido brillo de las uñas, las cortinas limpias, y empezó a sentir que únicamente conservando la vida haría homenaje a aquel amor más punzante que búfalo, carne final de su especie, aunque hubiera conocido la corona cuando de las planicies.

Cuando ya se tornaba penoso en exceso conservarse dentro de los límites de la casa, pues había empezado a agitar en ella una determinación de amar apenas las cosas venerables, fuesen polvo, araña, alfombra desgarrada, cacerola sin mango, como que adivinando, él llegó. La aldea vio su modo de tocar en la puerta con la seguridad de aproximarse al paraíso. Tocó tres veces, ella no respondió. Tres más y ella como que afectada por la reclusión, no admitía extraños. Todavía héroe, él tocó algunas veces más, hasta que gritó su nombre, soy yo, entonces no ve, entonces no siente, o ya no vive más, ¿seré yo entonces el único en cumplir la promesa?

Ella sabía ahora que era él. No consultó el corazón para agitarse, mejor vivir su pasión. Abrió la puerta e hizo de la madera su escudo. El imaginó que escarnecían su vuelta, no quedaba alegría en quien lo recibía. Todavía averiguó la verdad: si no es Ud., ni es necesario entrar. Tal vez hubiese olvidado que él mismo había manifestado un día que su regreso jamás sería conmemorado, odiaría a gente abundante en la calle viendo el silencio de los dos después de tanto castigo.

Ella señaló en la madera su respuesta. Y él pensó que debía sorprenderla según su gusto. Fingía la mujer no percibir su ingreso casa adentro; más viejo sí, el polvo coloreando curiosamente su ropa. Se miraron como se ausculta la intrepidez del cristal, sus venas limpias, la calma de perderse en la transparencia. Agarró la mano de la mujer, se aseguraba de que sus ojos, a pesar del pecado de las modificaciones, todavía miraban con el antiguo amor, ahora más probado.

Le dijo: volví. También podría haber dicho: ya no te quiero más. Confiaba en la mujer: ella sabría organizar las palabras expresadas con descuido. Ni la verdad o su imagen contraria, denunciarían su himno interior. Debería ser como si ambos conduciendo el amor jamás lo hubiesen interrumpido.

Ella lo besó también con cuidado. No buscó su boca y él se dejó conmovido. Quiso solamente su frente, le alisó el pelo. Le hizo ver su sufrimiento, había sido tan difícil que ni su retrato pudo soportar. ¿Dónde estuve entonces en esta casa? él preguntó. Procure habremos de conversar. El hombre se sintió afectado por tales palabras. Pero las peregrinaciones le habían enseñado lo mismo: que adentro de casa se traen los desafíos.

Debajo del sofá, de la mesa, sobre la cama, entre las sábanas, hasta en el gallinero, él procuró, siempre prosiguiendo, casi le preguntaba: estoy caliente o frío. La mujer no seguía sus búsquedas, agasajada en un largo abrigo de lana, ahora pelaba batatas imitando a las mujeres que encuentran alegría en esta pericia. Este humor de la mujer como que lo confortaba. En vez de conversar cuando tenían tanto que decirse, sin querer ellos habían empezado a pelear. Y procurando él pensaba dónde habría estado cuando allí no estaba, por lo menos visiblemente por la casa.

Casi desistiendo encontró el retrato sobre el armario, el vidrio de la moldura todo roto. Ella había tenido el cuidado de esconder su rostro entre añicos de vidrio, quién sabe qué tormentas y otras heridas más. Ella lo llevó por la mano hasta la cocina. El no quería dejarse ir. Entonces ¿qué quieres hacer aquí? El respondió: quiero a la mujer. Ella consintió. Después, sin embargo, ella habló: ahora sígueme hasta la cocina.

— ¿Qué hay en la cocina?

Lo dejó sentado en la silla. Hizo la comida, se alimentaron en silencio. Después limpió el piso, lavó los platos, hizo la cama recién desarreglada, limpió el polvo de la casa, abrió todas las ventanas casi siempre cerradas en aquellos años de ausencia. Procedía como si él todavía no hubiese llegado, o como si jamás hubiese abandonado la casa, pero se hacían sí preparativos de fiesta. ¿Nos vamos a hablar a lo menos ahora que yo necesito? él dijo.

—Tengo tanto que contarle. Recorrí el mundo, la tierra, sabe y además.

Yo sé, ella fue diciendo rápido, no consintiendo que él discurriese sobre las variedades de la fauna, o que le asegurase que aunque los rincones distantes presenten ciertas particularidades de algún modo son próximos a nuestra tierra, de donde Ud. nunca se apartó porque Ud. jamás pretendió la libertad como yo. No dejando que le contase sí que las mujeres aunque rubias, pálidas, morenas y de piel de trigo, no ostentaban su olor, a ella, él la identificaría aun de ojos cerrados. No dejando no que ella supiese de sus campañas: anduvo a caballo, tren, velero, hasta helicóptero, la tierra era menor de lo que suponía, había visitado la prisión, razón de haber asimilado una rara concentración de vida que en ninguna parte sino allí jamás encontró, pues todos los que allí estaban no tenían otro modo de ser sino realizando diariamente la expiración.

Y ella, no dejándole contar lo que había sido el hospital de su vida, iba sustituyendo con sus palabras entonces lo que ella sí había vivido. Y de tal modo hablaba como si ella fuera la que hubiese abandonado la aldea, hecho campañas abolicionistas, inaugurado puentes, vencido dominios marítimos, conocido mujeres y hombres, y entre ellos perdiéndose pues quién sabe si no sería de su vocación reconocer por el amor las criaturas. Sólo que ella hablando evitaba semejantes asuntos, su riqueza era enumerar con voluptuosidad los quehaceres diarios a que había estado confinada desde su partida, cómo limpiaba la casa, o había inventado un plato tal vez de origen dinamarqués, y lo cubrió de verdura, delante de él se fingía conejo, luego asumiendo el estado que la hacía graciosa se alimentaba con la mano y se sentía mujer; como también simulaba escribir cartas jamás enviadas pues ignoraba dónde encontrarlo; cuán penoso había sido decidirse sobre qué destino dar a su retrato, pues aunque practicase violencia contra él, no podía olvidar que el hombre siempre estaría presente; su mundo de pelar frutas, tejiendo delicadas combinaciones de diseños sobre la cáscara, ora poniendo en relieve un trecho mayor de la pulpa, ora dejando el fruto apenas revestido de rápidas hebras de piel; y todavía la solución encontrada para alimentarse sin dejar el rancho en que su casa se había convertido, había tenido condición de rápida permanencia, el tiempo suficiente para que ellos viesen que a pesar de la distancia del hombre ella todo hacía por rendirle homenaje, algunos de la aldea sin embargo, que él no supiese ahora, insistieron en hacerle regalos, que si al principio la irritaban, terminaron por agradarla.

—De otro modo, ¿cómo vengarme de ellos?

Recogía los donativos, hasta las poesías y dejaba las cosas permanecer sobre la mesa por breves instantes, como si así se comunicase con la vida. Mas, tan pronto todas las reservas del mundo que ella pensaba poder existir en los objetos se agotaban, ella los tiraba a la puerta del fondo. Confiaba en que ellos mismos recogiesen el material para que no se deteriorase en su puerta.

Y tanto ella iba relatando los largos años de su espera, un vivir cotidiano que en su boca alcanzaba vigor, que él temía interrumpir un solo momento lo que ella proyectaba dentro de casa como si *cuspiese* perlas, perros en miniatura, y una gran dama abundante, aun con el pretexto de vivir junto a ella las cosas que él había vivido solo. Pues cuanto más ella *adensaba* la narrativa, tanto más él sentía que más allá de haberla herido con su profundo conocimiento de la tierra, su profundo conocimiento de la tierra después de todo no significaba nada. Ella era mucho más capaz de que él en *atener* intensidad, mucho más sensible porque vivió detrás de la reja, más voluntariosa por haber resistido con bravura los galanteos. La fe que con neutralidad había dispensado al mundo a punto de ser incapaz de recoger de vuelta para su cuerpo lo que había dejado caer indolente, ella había sabido hacer crecer, y había concentrado en el dominio de su vida sus razones más intensas.

A medida que las virtudes de la mujer lo sofocaban, sus victorias y experiencias se iban transformando en una masa confusa, desorientada, ya no sabiendo él qué hacer de ella. Hasta dudaba si había partido, si no se habría quedado todos estos años apenas algunos kilómetros de allí, en destierro como ella, pero sin igual narrativo.

Seguramente él no presentaba la misma dignidad, apenas había sabido conquistar su porción de la tierra. Nada había hecho sino andar y pensar que había aprendido verdades delante de las cuales la mujer habría de capitular. Mientras tanto, ella confesando la jornada de las legumbres, la confección misteriosa de una sopa, sellaba sobre él un penoso silencio. La vergüenza de haber compuesto una falsa historia lo deprimía. Sin duda había estado allí con la mujer todo el tiempo, jamás había abandonado la aldea, el torpor a que lo habían destinado desde el nacimiento, y cuyos límites él, altivo, pensó haber roto.

Ella no cesaba de apoderarse de las palabras, por la primera vez en tanto tiempo explicaba su vida, se complacía en recoger en el vientre, como un tumor que rasca las paredes íntimas, el son de su voz. Y mientras tanto, oía a la mujer, lentamente él fue rasgando su retrato, sin ella impedirlo, implorase o no, ésta es mi más fecunda memoria. Cumplíase con la nueva pasión, el mundo antes oscurecido que ella descubrió al retorno del hombre.

El tiró el retrato trizado en la basura y su gesto no sufrió aún de esta advertencia. Los actos favorecían la claridad y para no agotar las tareas a que pretendía dedicarse, él fue arreglando la casa, pasó un paño mojado en los armarios, fingiendo oírla, iba olvidando la tierra en el arrebato de limpieza. Y cuando la cocina se presentó inmaculada, él recomenzó todo de nuevo, entonces pelando frutas para la compota mientras ella le proporcionaba historias indispensables al mundo que necesitaría aprenhender una vez que a él pretendiese dedicarse para siempre. Pero de tal modo se arrebataba ahora que parecía distraído, como si pudiese abstenerse de las palabras encantadas de la mujer para adoptar por fin su universo.

Horacio Quiroga
1875–1937
Uruguay

El almohadón de plumas

Cuentos de amor, de locura y muerte, 1917. (Publicado originalmente
en la revista *Caras y caretas* en 1907).

SU luna de miel fue un largo escalofrío. Rubia, angelical
y tímida, el carácter duro de su marido heló sus soñadas
niñerías de novia. Ella lo quería mucho, sin embargo, a veces
con un ligero estremecimiento cuando volviendo de noche
juntos por la calle, echaba una furtiva mirada a la alta estatura de Jordán, mudo desde hacía una hora. El, por su parte, la
amaba profundamente, sin darlo a conocer.

Durante tres meses —se habían casado en abril— vivieron
una dicha especial.

Sin duda hubiera ella deseado menos severidad en ese rígido cielo de amor, más expansiva e incauta ternura; pero el
impasible semblante de su marido la contenía siempre.

La casa en que vivían influía no poco en sus estremeci-
mientos. La blancura del patio silencioso —frisos, columnas
y estatuas de mármol— producía una otoñal impresión de palacio encantado. Dentro, el brillo glacial del estuco, sin el más
leve rasguño en las altas paredes, afirmaba aquella sensación
de desapacible frío. Al cruzar de una pieza a otra, los pasos
hallaban eco en toda la casa, como si un largo abandono hubiera sensibilizado su resonancia.

En ese extraño nido de amor, Alicia pasó todo el otoño.
No obstante había concluido por echar un velo sobre sus antiguos sueños, y aún vivía dormida en la casa hostil, sin querer pensar en nada hasta que llegaba su marido.

No es raro que adelgazara. Tuvo un ligero ataque de influencia que se arrastró insidiosamente días y días; Alicia no se re-
ponía nunca. Al fin una tarde pudo salir al jardín apoyada en
el brazo de su marido. Miraba indiferente a uno y otro lado.
De pronto Jordán, con honda ternura, le pasó muy lento la
mano por la cabeza, y Alicia rompió en seguida en sollozos,
echándole los brazos al cuello. Lloró largamente todo su espanto callado, redoblando el llanto a la menor tentativa de caricia.
Luego los sollozos fueron retardándose, y aun quedó largo rato
escondida en su cuello, sin moverse ni pronunciar una palabra.

Fue ése el último día en que Alicia estuvo levantada. Al
día siguiente amaneció desvanecida. El médico de Jordán la

examinó con suma atención, ordenándole cama y descanso absolutos.

—No sé —le dijo a Jordán en la puerta de calle con la voz todavía baja—. Tiene una gran debilidad que no me explico. Y sin vómitos, nada... Si mañana se despierta como hoy, llámeme en seguida.

Al otro día Alicia seguía peor. Hubo consulta. Constatóse una anemia de marcha agudísima, completamente inexplicable. Alicia no tuvo más desmayos, pero se iba visiblemente a la muerte. Todo el día el dormitorio estaba con las luces prendidas y en pleno silencio. Pasábanse horas sin que se oyera el menor ruido. Alicia dormitaba. Jordán vivía en la sala, también con toda la luz encendida. Paseábase sin cesar de un extremo a otro, con incansable obstinación. La alfombra ahogaba sus pasos. A ratos entraba en el dormitorio y proseguía su mudo vaivén a lo largo de la cama, deteniéndose un instante en cada extremo a mirar su mujer.

Pronto Alicia comenzó a tener alucinaciones, confusas y flotantes al principio, y que descendieron luego a ras del suelo. La joven, con los ojos desmesuradamente abiertos, no hacía sino mirar la alfombra a uno y otro lado del respaldo de la cama. Una noche quedó de repente mirando fijamente. Al rato abrió la boca para gritar, y sus narices y labios se perlaron de sudor.

— ¡Jordán! ¡Jordán! —clamó, rígida de espanto, sin dejar de mirar la alfombra.

Jordán corrió al dormitorio, y al verlo aparecer Alicia lanzó un alarido de horror.

— ¡Soy yo, Alicia, soy yo!

Alicia lo miró con extravío, miró la alfombra, volvió a mirarlo, y después de largo rato de estupefacta confrontación, se serenó. Sonrió y tomó entre las suyas la mano de su marido, acariciándola por media hora, temblando.

Entre sus alucinaciones más porfiadas, hubo un antropoide apoyado en la alfombra sobre los dedos, que tenía fijos en ella sus ojos.

Los médicos volvieron inútilmente. Había allí delante de ellos una vida que se acababa, desangrándose día a día, hora a hora, sin saber absolutamente cómo. En la última consulta Alicia yacía en estupor, mientras ellos pulsaban, pasándose de uno a otro la muñeca inerte. La observaron largo rato en silencio, y siguieron al comedor.

—Pst... —se encogió de hombros desalentado su médico—. Es un caso serio... Poco hay que hacer.

— ¡Sólo eso me faltaba! —resopló Jordán. Y tamborileó bruscamente sobre la mesa.

Alicia fue extinguiéndose en subdelirio de anemia, agravado de tarde, pero remitía siempre en las primeras horas. Durante el día no avanzaba su enfermedad, pero cada mañana amanecía lívida, en síncope casi. Parecía que únicamente de noche se le fuera la vida en nuevas oleadas de sangre. Tenía siempre al despertar la sensación de estar desplomada en la cama con un millón de kilos encima. Desde el tercer día este hundimiento no la abandonó más. Apenas podía mover la cabeza. No quiso que le tocaran la cama, ni aun que le arreglaran el almohadón. Sus terrores crepusculares avanzaban ahora en forma de monstruos que se arrastraban hasta la cama, y trepaban dificultosamente por la colcha.

Perdió luego el conocimiento. Los dos días finales deliró sin cesar a media voz. Las luces continuaban fúnebremente encendidas en el dormitorio y la sala. En el silencio agónico de la casa, no se oía más que el delirio monótono que salía de la cama, y el sordo retumbo de los eternos pasos de Jordán.

Alicia murió, por fin. La sirvienta, cuando entró después a deshacer la cama, sola ya, miró un rato extrañada el almohadón.

— ¡Señor! —llamó a Jordán en voz baja—. En el almohadón hay manchas que parecen de sangre.

Jordán se acercó rápidamente y se dobló sobre aquél. Efectivamente, sobre la funda, a ambos lados del hueco que había dejado la cabeza de Alicia, se veían manchitas oscuras.

—Parecen picaduras —murmuró la sirvienta después de un rato de inmóvil observación.

—Levántelo a la luz —le dijo Jordán.

La sirvienta lo levantó pero en seguida lo dejó caer y se quedó mirando a aquél, lívida y temblando. Sin saber por qué, Jordán sintió que los cabellos se le erizaban.

— ¿Qué hay? —murmuró con voz ronca.

—Pesa mucho —articuló la sirvienta, sin dejar de temblar.

Jordán lo levantó; pesaba extraordinariamente. Salieron con él, y sobre la mesa del comedor Jordán cortó funda y envoltura de un tajo. Las plumas superiores volaron, y la sirvienta dio un grito de horror con toda la boca abierta, llevándose las manos crispadas a los bandós. Sobre el fondo, entre las plumas, moviendo lentamente las patas velludas, había un animal monstruoso, una bola viviente y viscosa. Estaba tan hinchado que apenas se le pronunciaba la boca.

Noche a noche, desde que Alicia había caído en cama, ha-

bía aplicado sigilosamente su boca —su trompa, mejor dicho—
a las sienes de aquélla, chupándole la sangre. La picadura era
casi imperceptible. La remoción diaria del almohadón sin duda había impedido al principio su desarrollo; pero desde que
la joven no pudo moverse, la succión fue vertiginosa. En cinco días, en cinco noches, había vaciado a Alicia.

Estos parásitos de las aves, diminutos en el medio habitual,
llegan a adquirir en ciertas condiciones proporciones enormes. La sangre humana parece serles particularmente favorable, y no es raro hallarlo en los almohadores de pluma.

———

Horacio Quiroga

El hijo
Más allá, 1935. (Publicado originalmente, bajo el título "El padre",
en *La nación* en 1928).

ES un poderoso día de verano en Misiones, con todo el
sol, el calor y la calma que puede deparar la estación. La
naturaleza plenamente abierta, se siente satisfecha de sí.

Como el sol, el calor y la calma ambiente, el padre abre
también su corazón a la naturaleza.

—Ten cuidado, chiquito —dice a su hijo abreviando en esa
frase todas las observaciones del caso y que su hijo comprende perfectamente.

—Sí, papá —responde la criatura, mientras coge la escopeta y carga de cartuchos los bolsillos de su camisa, que cierra
con cuidado.

—Vuelve a la hora de almorzar —observa aún el padre.

—Sí, papá —repite el chico.

Equilibra la escopeta en la mano, sonríe a su padre, lo besa en la cabeza y parte.

Su padre lo sigue un rato con los ojos y vuelve a su quehacer de ese día, feliz con la alegría de su pequeño.

Sabe que su hijo, educado desde su más tierna infancia en el hábito de la precaución del peligro, puede manejar un fusil y cazar no importa qué. Aunque es muy alto para su edad, no tiene sino trece años. Y parecería tener menos, a juzgar por la pureza de sus ojos azules, frescos aún de sorpresa infantil.

No necesita el padre levantar los ojos de su quehacer para seguir con la mente la marcha de su hijo: Ha cruzado la picada roja y se encamina rectamente al monte a través del abra de espartillo.

Para cazar en el monte —caza de pelo— se requiere más paciencia de la que su cachorro puede rendir. Después de atravesar esa isla de monte, su hijo costeará la linde de cactus hasta el bañado, en procura de palomas, tucanes o tal cual casal de garzas, como las que su amigo Juan ha descubierto en días anteriores.

Solo ahora, el padre esboza una sonrisa al recuerdo de la pasión cinegética de las dos criaturas. Cazan sólo a veces un yacútoro, un surucuá —menos aún— y regresan triunfales, Juan a su rancho con el fusil de nueve milímetros que él le ha regalado, y su hijo a la meseta, con la gran escopeta Saint-Etienne, calibre dieciséis, cuádruple cierre y pólvora blanca.

El fue lo mismo. A los trece años hubiera dado la vida por poseer una escopeta. Su hijo, de aquella edad, la posee ahora; y el padre sonríe.

No es fácil, sin embargo, para un padre viudo, sin otra fe ni esperanza que la vida de su hijo, educarlo como lo ha hecho él, libre en su corto radio de acción, seguro de sus pequeños pies y manos desde que tenía cuatro años, consciente de la inmensidad de ciertos peligros y de la escasez de sus propias fuerzas.

Ese padre ha debido luchar fuertemente contra lo que él considera su egoísmo. ¡Tan fácilmente una criatura calcula mal, sienta un pie en el vacío y se pierde un hijo!

El peligro subsiste siempre para el hombre en cualquier edad; pero su amenaza amengua si desde pequeño se acostumbra a no contar sino con sus propias fuerzas.

De este modo ha educado el padre a su hijo. Y para conseguirlo ha debido resistir no sólo a su corazón, sino a sus tormentos morales; porque ese padre, de estómago y vista débiles, sufre desde hace tiempo de alucinaciones.

Ha visto, concretados en dolorósísima ilusión, recuerdos, de una felicidad que no debía surgir más de la nada en que se recluyó. La imagen de su propio hijo no ha escapado a este tormento. Lo ha visto una vez rodar envuelto en sangre cuando el chico percutía en la morsa del taller una bala de parabellum, siendo así que lo que hacía era limar la hebilla de su cinturón de caza.

Horribles cosas... Pero hoy, con el ardiente y vital día de verano, cuyo amor su hijo parece haber heredado, el padre se siente feliz, tranquilo y seguro del porvenir.

En ese instante, no muy lejos, suena un estampido.

—La Saint-Etienne... —piensa el padre al reconocer la detonación—. Dos palomas menos en el monte...

Sin prestar más atención al nimio acontecimiento, el hombre se abstrae de nuevo en su tarea.

El sol, ya muy alto, continúa ascendiendo. Adondequiera que se mire —piedras, tierra, árboles—, el aire, enrarecido como en un horno, vibra con el calor. Un profundo zumbido que llena el ser entero e impregna el ámbito hasta donde la vista alcanza, concentra a esa hora toda la vida tropical.

El padre echa una ojeada a su muñeca: las doce. Y levanta los ojos al monte.

Su hijo debía estar ya de vuelta. En la mutua confianza que depositan el uno en el otro —el padre de sienes plateadas y la criatura de trece años—, no se engañan jamás. Cuando su hijo responde: "Sí, papá...", hará lo que dice. Dijo que volverá antes de las doce, y el padre ha sonreído al verle partir.

Y no ha vuelto.

El hombre torna a su quehacer, esforzándose en concentrar la atención en su tarea. ¡Es tan fácil, tan fácil perder la noción de la hora dentro del monte y sentarse un rato en el suelo mientras se descansa inmóvil...!

Bruscamente, la luz meridiana, el zumbito tropical y el corazón del padre se detiene al compás de lo que acaba de pensar su hijo descansa inmóvil...

El tiempo ha pasado; son las doce y media. El padre sale de su taller, y al apoyar la mano en el banco de mecánica sube del fondo de su memoria el estallido de una bala de parabellum, e instantáneamente, por primera vez en las tres horas transcurridas, piensa que tras el estampido de la Saint-Etienne no ha oído nada más. No ha oído rodar el pedregullo bajo un paso conocido. Su hijo no ha vuelto y la naturaleza se halla detenida a la vera del bosque, esperándolo...

¡Oh! No son suficientes un carácter templado y una ciega confianza en la educación de un hijo para ahuyentar el espectro de la fatalidad que un padre de vista enferma ve alzarse desde la línea del monte. Distracción, olvido, demora fortuita: ninguno de estos nimios motivos que pueden retardar la llegada de su hijo, hallan cabida en aquel corazón.

Un tiro, un solo tiro ha sonado, y hace ya mucho. Tras él, el padre no ha oído un ruido, no ha visto un pájaro, no ha cruzado el abra una sola persona a anunciarle que al cruzar un alambrado, una gran desgracia...

La cabeza al aire y sin machete, el padre va. Corta el abra de espartillo, entra en el monte, costea la línea de cactus, sin hallar el menor rastro de su hijo.

Pero la naturaleza prosigue detenida. Y cuando el padre ha recorrido las sendas de caza conocidas y ha explorado el bañado en vano, adquiere la seguridad de que cada paso que da en adelante lo lleva fatal e inexorablemente, al cadáver de su hijo.

Ni un reproche que hacerse, el lamentable. Sólo la realidad fría, terrible y consumada; ha muerto su hijo al cruzar un...

¿Pero dónde, en qué parte? ¡Hay tantos alambrados allí y es tan, tan sucio el monte...! ¡Oh, muy sucio...! Por poco que no se tenga cuidado al cruzar los hilos con la escopeta en la mano...

El padre sofoca un grito. Ha visto levantarse en el aire... ¡Oh, no es su hijo, no...! Y vuelve a otro lado, y a otro y a otro...

Nada se ganaría con ver el dolor de su tez y la angustia de sus ojos. Ese hombre aún no ha llamado a su hijo. Aunque su corazón clama por él a gritos, su boca continúa muda. Sabe bien que el solo acto de pronunciar su nombre, de llamarlo en voz alta, será la confesión de su muerte...

—... ¡Chiquito! —se le escapa de pronto. Y si la voz de un hombre de carácter es capaz de llorar, tapémonos de misericordia los oídos ante la angustia que clama en aquella voz.

Nadie ni nada ha respondido. Por las picadas rojas del sol, envejecido en diez años, va el padre buscando a su hijo que acaba de morir.

—¡Hijito mío...! ¡Chiquito mío...! —clama en un diminutivo que se alza del fondo de sus entrañas.

Ya antes, en plena dicha y paz, ese padre ha sufrido la alucinación de su hijo rodando con la frente abierta por una bala a cromo níquel. Ahora, en cada rincón sombrío del bosque ve centelleos de alambre: y al pie de un poste, con escopeta descargada al lado, ve a su...

—¡Chiquito...! ¡Mi hijo...!

Las fuerzas que permiten entregar un pobre padre alucinado a la más atróz pesadilla tienen también un límite. Y el nuestro siente que las suyas se le escapan, cuando ve bruscamente desembocar de un pique lateral a su hijo.

A un chico de trece años bástale ver desde cincuenta metros la expresión de su padre sin machete dentro del monte, para apresurar el paso con los ojos húmedos.

—Chiquito... —murmura el hombre. Y, exhausto, se deja caer sentado en la arena albeante, rodeando con los brazos las piernas de su hijo.

La criatura, así ceñida, queda de pie; y como comprende el dolor de su padre, le acaricia despacio la cabeza.

—Pobre papá.

En fin, el tiempo ha pasado. Ya van a ser las tres. Juntos ahora, padre e hijo emprenden el regreso a la casa.

— ¿Cómo no te fijaste en el sol para saber la hora? —murmura aún el primero.

—Me fijé, papá... Pero cuando iba a volver vi las garzas de Juan y las seguí.

— ¡Lo que me has hecho pasar, chiquito...!

—Papá... —murmura también el chico.

Después de un largo silencio:

— ¿Y las garzas, las mataste? —pregunta el padre.

—No...

Nimio detalle, después de todo. Bajo el cielo y el aire candentes, a la descubierta por el abra de espartillo, el hombre vuelve a su casa con su hijo, sobre cuyos hombros, casi del alto de los suyos, lleva pasado su feliz brazo de padre. Regresa empapado de sudor y aunque quebrantado de cuerpo y alma, sonríe de felicidad...

Sonríe de alucinada felicidad... Pues ese padre va solo. A nadie ha encontrado, y su brazo se apoya en el vacío. Porque tras él, al pie de un poste y con las piernas en alto, enredadas en el alambre de púa, su hijo bienamado yace al sol, muerto desde las diez de la mañana.

Augusto Roa Bastos
1917–
Paraguay

La excavación
El trueno entre las hojas, 1958.

EL primer desprendimiento de tierra se produjo a unos tres metros, a sus espaldas. No le pareció al principio nada alarmante. Sería solamente una veta blanda del terreno de arriba. Las tinieblas apenas se pusieron un poco más densas en el angosto agujero por el que únicamente arrastrándose sobre el vientre un hombre podía avanzar o retroceder. No podía detenerse ahora. Siguió avanzando con el plato de hojalata que le servía de perforador. La creciente humedad que iba impregnando la tosca dura lo alentaba. La barranca ya no estaría lejos; a lo sumo, unos cuatro o cinco metros, lo que representaba unos veinticinco días más de trabajo hasta el boquete liberador sobre el río.

Alternándose en turnos seguidos de cuatro horas, seis presos hacían avanzar la excavación veinte centímetros diariamente. Hubieran podido avanzar más rápido, pero la capacidad de trabajo estaba limitada por la posibilidad de desalojar la tierra en el tacho de desperdicios sin que fuera notada. Se habían abstenido de orinar en la lata que entraba y salía dos veces al día. Lo hacían en los rincones de la celda húmeda y agrietada, con lo que si bien aumentaban el hedor siniestro de la reclusión ganaban también unos cuantos centímetros más de "bodega" para el contrabando de la tierra excavada.

La guerra civil había concluido seis meses atrás. La perforación del túnel duraba cuatro. Entre tanto, habían fallecido por diferentes causas, no del todo apacibles, diecisiete de los ochenta y nueve presos políticos que se hallaban amontonados en esa inhóspita celda, antro, retrete, ergástulo pestilente, donde en tiempos de calma no habían entrado nunca más de ocho o diez presos comunes.

De los diecisiete presos que habían tenido la estúpida ocurrencia de morirse, a nueve se habían llevado distintas enfermedades contraídas antes o después de la prisión; a cuatro, los apremios urgentes de la cámara de torturas; a dos, la rauda ventosa de la tisis galopante. Otros dos se habían suicidado abriéndose las venas, uno con la púa de la hebilla del cinto; el otro, con el plato, cuyo borde afiló en la pared, y que ahora servía de herramienta para la apertura del túnel.

Esta estadística era la que regía la vida de esos desgracia-
dos. Sus esperanzas y desalientos. Su congoja callosa pero aún
sensitiva. Su sed, el hambre, los dolores, el hedor, su odio encendido en la sangre, en los ojos, como esas mariposas de
aceite que a pocos metros de allí —tal vez solamente un centenar— brillaban en la Catedral delante de las imágenes.

La única respiración venía por el agujero aún ciego, aún
nonato, que iba creciendo como un hijo en el vientre de esos
hombres ansiosos. Por allí venía el olor puro de la libertad,
un soplo fresco y brillante entre los excrementos. Y allí se
tocaba, en una especie de inminencia trabajada por el vértigo,
todo lo que estaba más allá de ese boquete negro.

Eso era lo que sentían los presos cuando escarbaban la
tosca con el plato de hojalata, en la noche angosta del túnel.

Un nuevo desprendimiento le enterró esta vez las piernas
hasta los riñones. Quiso moverse, encoger las extremidades
atrapadas, pero no pudo. De golpe tuvo exacta conciencia de
lo que sucedía, mientras el dolor crecía con sordas puntadas
en la carne, en los huesos de las piernas enterradas. No había
sido una simple veta reblandecida. Probablemente era una cu-
ña de tierra, un bloque espeso que llegaba hasta la superficie.
Probablemente todo un cimiento se estaba sumiendo en la
falla provocada por el desprendimiento.

No le quedaba otro recurso que cavar hacia adelante. Cavar con todas sus fuerzas, sin respiro; cavar con el plato, con
las uñas, hasta donde pudiese. Quizá no eran cinco metros los
que faltaban; quizá no eran veinticinco días de zapa los que
aún lo separaban del boquete salvador de la barranca del río.
Quizás eran menos; sólo unos cuantos centímetros, unos minutos más de arañazos profundos. Se convirtió en un topo
frenético. Sintió cada vez más húmeda la tierra. A medida
que le iba faltando el aire, se sentía más animado. Su esperanza crecía con su asfixia. Un poco de barro tibio entre los dedos le hizo prorrumpir en un grito casi feliz. Pero estaba tan
absorto en su emoción, la desesperante tiniebla del túnel lo
envolvía de tal modo, que no podía darse cuenta de que no
era la proximidad del río, de que no eran sus filtraciones las
que hacían ese lodo tibio, sino su propia sangre brotando debajo de las uñas y en las yemas heridas por la tosca. Ella, la
tierra densa e impenetrable, era ahora la que, en el epílogo
del duelo mortal comenzado hacía mucho tiempo, lo gastaba
a él sin fatiga y lo empezaba a comer aún vivo y caliente. De
pronto, pareció alejarse un poco. Manoteó en el vacío. Era él
quien se estaba quedando atrás en el aire como piedra que em-

pezaba a estrangularlo. Procuró avanzar, pero sus piernas ya irremediablemente formaban parte del bloque que se había desmoronado sobre ellas. Ya ni las sentía. Sólo sentía la asfixia. Se estaba ahogando en un río sólido y oscuro. Dejó de moverse, de pugnar inútilmente. La tortura se iba transformando en una inexplicable delicia. Empezó a recordar.

Recordó aquella otra mina subterránea en la guerra del Chaco, hacía mucho tiempo. Un tiempo que ahora se le antojaba fabuloso. Lo recordaba, sin embargo, claramente, con todos los detalles.

En el frente de Gondra, la guerra se había estancado. Hacía seis meses que paraguayos y bolivianos, empotrados frente a frente en sus inexpugnables posiciones, cambiaban obstinados tiroteos e insultos. No había más de cincuenta metros entre unos y otros.

En las pausas de ciertas noches que el melancólico olvido había hecho de pronto atrozmente memorables, en lugar de metralla canjeaban música y canciones de sus respectivas tierras.

El altiplano entero, pétreo y desolado, bajaba arrastrado por la quejumbre de las cuecas; toda una raza hecha de cobre y castigo, desde su plataforma cósmica, bajaba hasta el polvo voraz de las trincheras. Y hasta allí bajaban desde los grandes ríos, desde los grandes bosques paraguayos, desde el corazón de su gente también absurda y cruelmente perseguida, las polcas y guaranias, juntándose, hermanándose con aquel otro aliento melodioso que subía desde la muerte. Y así sucedía porque era preciso que gente americana siguiese muriendo, matándose, para que ciertas cosas se expresaran correctamente en términos de estadística y mercado, de trueques y expoliaciones correctas, con cifras y números exactos, en boletines de la rapiña internacional.

Fue en una de esas pausas en que en unión de otros catorce voluntarios, Perucho Rodi, estudiante de ingeniería, buen hijo, hermano excelente, hermoso y suave moreno de ojos verdes, había empezado a cavar ese túnel que debía salir detrás de las posiciones bolivianas con un boquete que en el momento señalado entraría en erupción como el cráter de un volcán.

En dieciocho días los ochenta metros de la gruesa perforación subterránea quedaron cubiertos. Y el volcán entró en erupción con lava sólida de metralla, de granadas, de proyectiles de todos los calibres, hasta arrasar las posiciones enemigas.

Recordó en la noche azul, sin luna, el extraño silencio que había precedido a la masacre y también el que lo había seguido, cuando ya todo estaba terminado. Dos silencios idénticos, sepulcrales, latientes. Entre los dos, sólo la posición de los astros había producido la mutación de una breve secuencia. Todo estaba igual. Salvo los restos de esa espantosa carnicería que a lo sumo había añadido un nuevo detalle apenas perceptible a la decoración del paisaje nocturno.

Recordó, un segundo antes del ataque, la visión de los enemigos sumidos en el tranquilo sueño del que no despertarían. Recordó haber elegido a sus víctimas, abarcándolas con el girar aún silencioso de su ametralladora. Sobre todo a una de ellas: un soldado que se retorcía en el remolino de una pesadilla. Tal vez soñaba en ese momento en un túnel idéntico pero inverso al que les estaba acercando el exterminio. En un pensamiento suficientemente extenso y flexible, esas distinciones en realidad carecían de importancia. Era despreciable la circunstancia de que uno fuese el exterminador y otro la víctima inminente. Pero en ese momento todavía no podía saberlo.

Sólo recordó que había vaciado íntegramente su ametralladora. Recordó que cuando la automática se le había finalmente recalentado y atascado la abandonó y siguió entonces arrojando granadas de mano, hasta que sus dos brazos se le durmieron a los costados. Lo más extraño de todo era que, mientras sucedían estas cosas, le habían atravesado recuerdos de otros hechos, reales y ficticios, que aparentemente no tenían entre sí ninguna conexión y acentuaban, en cambio, la sensación de sueño en que él mismo flotaba. Pensó, por ejemplo, en el escapulario carmesí de su madre (real); en el inmenso panambí de bronce de la tumba del poeta. Ortiz Guerrero (ficticio); en su hermanita María Isabel, recién recibida de maestra (real). Estos parpadeos incoherentes de su imaginación duraron todo el tiempo. Recordó haber regresado con ellos chapoteando en un vasto y espeso estero de sangre.

Aquel túnel del Chaco y este túnel que él mismo había sugerido cavar en el suelo de la cárcel, que él personalmente había empezado a cavar y que, por último, sólo a él le había servido de trampa mortal; este túnel y aquél eran el mismo túnel; un único agujero recto y negro con un boquete de entrada pero no de salida. Un agujero negro y recto que a pesar de su rectitud le había rodeado desde que nació como un círculo subterráneo, irrevocable y fatal. Un túnel que tenía ahora para él cuarenta años, pero que en realidad era mucho más viejo, realmente inmemorial.

Aquella noche azul del Chaco, poblada de estruendos y

cadáveres había mentido una salida. Pero sólo había sido un sueño; menos que un sueño: la decoración fantástica de un sueño futuro en medio del humo de la batalla.

Con el último aliento, Perucho Rodi la volvía a soñar; es decir, a vivir. Sólo ahora aquel sueño lejano era real. Y ahora sí que avistaba el boquete enceguecedor, el perfecto redondel de la salida.

Soñó (recordó) que volvía a salir por aquel cráter en erupción hacia la noche azulada, metálica, fragoresa. Volvió a sentir la ametralladora ardiente y convulsa en sus manos. Soñó (recordó) que volvía a descargar ráfaga tras ráfaga y que volvía a arrojar granada tras granada. Soñó (recordó) la cara de cada una de sus víctimas. Las vio nítidamente. Eran ochenta y nueve en total. Al franquear el límite secreto, las reconoció en un brusco resplandor y se estremeció: esas ochenta y nueve caras *vivas* y terribles de sus víctimas *eran* (y seguirán siéndolo en un fogonazo fotográfico infinito) las de sus compañeros de prisión. Incluso los diecisiete muertos, a los cuales se había agregado uno más. Se soñó entre esos muertos. Soñó que soñaba en un túnel. Se vio retorcerse en una pesadilla, soñando que cavaba, que luchaba, que mataba. Recordó nítidamente al soldado enemigo a quien había abatido con su ametralladora, mientras se retorcía en una pesadilla. Soñó que aquel soldado enemigo lo abatía ahora a él con su ametralladora, tan exactamente parecido a él mismo que se hubiera dicho que era su hermano mellizo.

El sueño de Perucho Rodi quedó sepultado en esa grieta como un diamante negro que iba a alumbrar aún otra noche.

La frustrada evasión fue descubierta; el boquete de entrada en el piso de la celda. El hecho inspiró a los guardianes.

Los presos de la celda 4 (llamada Valle-í), menos el *evadido* Perucho Rodi, a la noche siguiente encontraron inexplicablemente descorrido el cerrojo. Sondearon con sus ojos la noche siniestra del patio. Encontraron que inexplicamente los pasillos y corredores estaban desiertos. Avanzaron. No enfrentaron en la sombra la sombra de ningún centinela. Inexplicablemente, el caserón circular parecía desierto. La puerta trasera que daba a una callejuela clausurada, estaba inexplicablemente entreabierta. La empujaron, salieron. Al salir, con el primer soplo fresco, los abatió en masa sobre las piedras el fuego cruzado de las ametralladoras que las oscuras troneras del panóptico escupieron sobre ellos durante algunos segundos.

Al día siguiente, la ciudad se enteró solamente de que unos cuantos presos habían sido liquidados en el momento en

que pretendían evadirse por un túnel. El comunicado pudo
mentir con la verdad. Existía un testimonio irrefutable: el túnel. Los periodistas fueron invitados a examinarlo. Quedaron
satisfechos al ver el boquete de entrada en la celda. La evidencia anulaba algunos detalles insignificantes: la inexistente salida que nadie pidió ver, las manchas de sangre aún frescas en
la callejuela abandonada.

Poco después el agujero fue cegado con piedras, y la celda
4 (Valle-í) volvió a quedar abarrotada.

Juan Rulfo
1918–
México

Anacleto Morones
El llano en llamas, 1953.

¡VIEJAS, hijas del demonio! Las vi venir a todas juntas, en
procesión. Vestidas de negro, sudando como mulas bajo
el mero rayo del sol. Las vi desde lejos como si fuera una re-
cua levantando polvo. Su cara ya ceniza de polvo. Negras todas ellas. Venían por el camino de Amula, cantando entre
rezos, entre el calor, con sus negros escapularios grandotes y
renegridos sobre los que caían en goterones el sudor de su
cara.

Las vi llegar y me escondí. Sabía lo que andaban haciendo y a quién buscaban. Por eso me di prisa a esconderme hasta el fondo del corral, corriendo ya con los pantalones en la
mano.

Pero ellas entraron y dieron conmigo. Dijeron: "¡Ave
María Purísima!"

Yo estaba acuclillado en una piedra, sin hacer nada, solamente sentado allí con los pantalones caídos, para que ellas
me vieran así y no se me arrimaran. Pero sólo dijeron: "¡Ave
María Purísima!" Y se fueron acercando más.

¡Viejas indinas! ¡Les debería dar vergüenza! Se persignaron y se arrimaron hasta ponerse junto a mí, todas juntas, apretadas como en manojo, chorreando sudor y con los pelos untados a la cara como si les hubiera lloviznado.

—Te venimos a ver a ti, Lucas Lucatero. Desde Amula venimos, sólo por verte. Aquí cerquita nos dijeron que estabas en tu casa; pero no nos figuramos que estabas tan adentro; no en este lugar ni en estos menesteres. Creímos que habías entrado a darle de comer a las gallinas, por eso nos metimos. Venimos a verte.

¡Esas viejas! ¡Viejas y feas como pasmadas de burro!

— ¡Díganme qué quieren! —les dije, mientras me fajaba los pantalones y ellas se tapaban los ojos para no ver.

—Traemos un encargo. Te hemos buscado en Santo Santiago y en Santa Inés, pero nos informaron que ya no vivías allí, que te habías mudado a este rancho. Y acá venimos. Somos de Amula.

Yo ya sabía de dónde eran y quiénes eran; podía hasta haberles recitado sus nombres, pero me hice el desentendido.

—Pues sí, Lucas Lucatero, al fin te hemos encontrado, gracias a Dios.

Las convidé al corredor y les saqué unas sillas para que se sentaran. Les pregunté que si tenían hambre o que si querían aunque fuera un jarro de agua para remojarse la lengua.

Ellas se sentaron, secándose el sudor con sus escapularios.

—No, gracias —dijeron—. No venimos a darte molestias. Te traemos un encargo. ¿Tú me conoces, verdad, Lucas Lucatero? —me preguntó una de ellas.

—Algo —le dije—. Me parece haberte visto en alguna parte. ¿No eres, por casualidad, Pancha Fregoso, la que se dejó robar por Homobono Ramos?

—Soy, sí, pero no me robó nadie. Esas fueron puras maledicencias. Nos perdimos los dos buscando garambuyos. Soy congregante y yo no hubiera permitido de ningún modo...

— ¿Qué, Pancha?

— ¡Ah!, cómo eres mal pensado, Lucas. Todavía no se te quita lo de andar criminando gente. Pero, ya que me conoces, quiero agarrar la palabra para comunicarte a lo que venimos.

— ¿No quieren ni siquiera un jarro de agua? —les volví a preguntar.

—No te molestes. Pero ya que nos ruegas tanto, no te vamos a desairar.

Les traje una jarra de agua de arrayán y se la bebieron. Luego les traje otra y se la volvieron a beber. Entonces les arrimé un cántaro con agua del río. Lo dejaron allí, pendiente, para dentro de un rato, porque, según ellas, les iba a entrar mucha sed cuando comenzara a hacerles la digestión.

Diez mujeres, sentadas en hilera, con sus negros vestidos puercos de tierra. Las hijas de Ponciano, de Emiliano, de Crescenciano, de Toribio el de la taberna y de Anastacio el peluquero.

¡Viejas carambas! Ni una siquiera pasadera. Todas caídas por los cincuenta. Marchitas como floripondios engarruñados y secos. Ni de dónde escoger.

—¿Y qué buscan por aquí?

—Venimos a verte.

—Ya me vieron. Estoy bien. Por mí no se preocupen.

—Te has venido muy lejos. A este lugar escondido. Sin domicilio ni quién dé razón de ti. Nos ha costado trabajo dar contigo después de mucho inquirir.

—No me escondo. Aquí vivo a gusto, sin la moledera de la gente. ¿Y qué misión traen, si se puede saber? —les pregunté.

—Pues se trata de esto... Pero no te vayas a molestar en darnos de comer. Ya comimos en casa de *la Torcacita.* Allí nos dieron a todas. Así que ponte en juicio. Siéntate aquí enfrente de nosotras para verte y para que nos oigas.

Yo no me podía estar en paz. Quería ir otra vez al corral. Oía el cacareo de las gallinas y me daban ganas de ir a recoger los huevos antes que se los comieran los conejos.

—Voy por los huevos —les dije.

—De verdad que ya comimos. No te molestes por nosotras.

—Tengo allí dos conejos sueltos que se comen los huevos. Orita regreso.

Y me fui al corral.

Tenía pensado no regresar. Salirme por la puerta que daba al cerro y dejar plantada a aquella sarta de viejas canijas.

Le eché una miradita al montón de piedras que tenía arrinconado en una esquina y le vi la figura de una sepultura. Entonces me puse a desparramarlas, tirándolas por todas partes, haciendo un reguero aquí y otro allá. Eran piedras de río, boludas, y las podía aventar lejos. ¡Viejas de los mil judas! Me habían puesto a trabajar. No sé por qué se les antojó venir.

Dejé la tarea y regresé. Les regalé los huevos.

—¿Mataste los conejos? Te vimos aventarles de pedradas. Guardaremos los huevos para dentro de un rato. No debías haberte molestado.

—Allí en el seno se pueden empollar, mejor déjenlos afuera.

—¡Ah, cómo serás!, Lucas Lucatero. No se te quita lo hablantín. Ni que estuviéramos tan calientes.

—De eso no sé nada. Pero de por sí está haciendo calor acá afuera.

Lo que yo quería era darles largas. Encaminarlas por otro rumbo, mientras buscaba la manera de echarlas fuera de mi casa y que no les quedaran ganas de volver. Pero no se me ocurría nada.

Sabía que me andaban buscando desde enero, poquito después de la desaparición de Anacleto Morones. No faltó alguien que me avisara que las viejas de la Congregación de Amula andaban tras de mí. Eran las únicas que podían tener algún interés en Anacleto Morones.

Y ahora allí las tenía.

Podía seguir haciéndoles plática o granjeándomelas de algún modo hasta que se les hiciera de noche y tuvieran que largarse. No se hubieran arriesgado a pasarla en mi casa.

Porque hubo un rato en que se trató de eso: cuando la hija de Ponciano dijo que querían acabar pronto su asunto para volver temprano a Amula. Fue cuando yo les hice ver que por eso no se preocuparan, que aunque fuera en el suelo había allí lugar y petates de sobra para todas. Todas dijeron que eso sí no, porque qué iría a decir la gente cuando se enteraran de que habían pasado la noche solitas en mi casa y conmigo allí dentro. Eso sí que no.

La cosa, pues, estaba en hacerles larga la plática, hasta que se les hiciera de noche, quitándoles la idea que les bullía en la cabeza.

Le pregunté a una de ellas.

—¿Y tu marido qué dice?

—Yo no tengo marido, Lucas. ¿No te acuerdas que fui tu novia? Te esperé y te esperé y me quedé esperando. Luego supe que te habías casado. Ya a esas alturas nadie me quería.

—¿Y luego yo? Lo que pasó fue que se me atravesaron otros pendientes que me tuvieron muy ocupado; pero todavía es tiempo.

—Pero si eres casado, Lucas, y nada menos que con la hija del Santo Niño. ¿Para qué me alborotas otra vez? Yo ya hasta me olvidé de ti.

—Pero yo no. ¿Cómo dices que te llamabas?

—Nieves... Me sigo llamando Nieves. Nieves García. Y no me hagas llorar, Lucas Lucatero. Nada más de acordarme de tus melosas promesas me da coraje.

—Nieves... Nieves. Cómo no me voy a acordar de ti. Si eres de lo que no se olvida... Eras suavecita. Me acuerdo. Te siento todavía aquí en mis brazos. Suavecita. Blanda. El olor del vestido con que salías a verme olía a alcanfor. Y te arrejuntabas mucho conmigo. Te repegabas tanto que casi te sentía metida en mis huesos. Me acuerdo.

—No sigas diciendo cosas, Lucas. Ayer me confesé y tú me estás despertando malos pensamientos y me estás echando el pecado encima.

—Me acuerdo que te besaba en las corvas. Y que tú decías que allí no, porque sentías cosquillas. ¿Todavía tienes hoyuelos en la corva de las piernas?

—Mejor cállate, Lucas Lucatero. Dios no te perdonará lo que hiciste conmigo. Lo pagarás caro.

— ¿Hice algo malo contigo? ¿Te traté acaso mal?

—Lo tuve que tirar. Y no me hagas decir eso aquí delante de la gente. Pero para que te lo sepas: lo tuve que tirar. Era una cosa así como un pedazo de cecina. ¿Y para qué lo iba a querer yo, si su padre no era más que un vaquetón?

— ¿Conque eso pasó? No lo sabía. ¿No quieren otra poquita de agua de arrayán? No me tardaré nada en hacerla. Espérenme nomás.

Y me fui otra vez al corral a cortar arrayanes. Y allí me entretuve lo más que pude, mientras se le bajaba el mal humor a la mujer aquella.

Cuando regresé ya se había ido.

— ¿Se fue?

—Sí, se fue. La hiciste llorar.

—Sólo quería platicar con ella, nomás por pasar el rato. ¿Se han fijado cómo tarda en llover? ¿Allá en Amula ya debe haber llovido, no?

—Sí, anteayer cayó un aguacero.

—No cabe duda de que aquél es un buen sitio. Llueve bien y se vive bien. A fe que aquí ni las nubes se aparecen. ¿Todavía es Rogaciano el presidente municipal?

—Sí, todavía.

—Buen hombre ese Rogaciano.

—No. Es un maldoso.

—Puede que tengan razón. ¿Y qué me cuentan de Edelmiro, todavía tiene cerrada su botica?

—Edelmiro murió. Hizo bien en morirse, aunque me esté mal el decirlo; pero era otro maldoso. Fue de los que le echaron infamias al Niño Anacleto. Lo acusó de abusionero y de brujo y de engañabobos. De todo eso anduvo hablando en todas partes. Pero la gente no le hizo caso y Dios lo castigó. Se murió de rabia como los huitacoches.

—Esperemos en Dios que esté en el infierno.

—Y que no se cansen los diablos de echarle leña.

—Lo mismo que a Lirio López, el juez, que se puso de su parte y mandó al Santo Niño a la cárcel.

Ahora eran ellas las que hablaban. Las dejé decir todo lo que quisieran. Mientras no se metieran conmigo, todo iría bien. Pero de repente se les ocurrió preguntarme:

—¿Quieres ir con nosotras?

—¿Adónde?

—A Amula. Por eso venimos. Para llevarte.

Por un rato me dieron ganas de volver al corral. Salirme por la puerta que da al cerro y desaparecer. ¡Viejas infelices!

—¿Y qué diantres voy a hacer yo a Amula?

—Queremos que nos acompañes en nuestros ruegos. Hemos abierto, todas las congregantes del Niño Anacleto, un novenario de rogaciones para pedir que nos lo canonicen. Tú eres su yerno y te necesitamos para que sirvas de testimonio. El señor cura nos encomendó le lleváramos a alguien que lo hubiera tratado de cerca y conocido de tiempo atrás, antes que se hiciera famoso por sus milagros. Y quién mejor que tú, que viviste a su lado y puedes señalar mejor que ninguno las obras de misericordia que hizo. Por eso te necesitamos, para que nos acompañes en esta campaña.

¡Viejas carambas! Haberlo dicho antes.

—No puedo ir —les dije—. No tengo quien me cuide la casa.

—Aquí se van a quedar dos muchachas para eso, lo hemos prevenido. Además está tu mujer.

—Ya no tengo mujer.

—¿Luego la tuya? ¿La hija del Niño Anacleto?

—Ya se me fue. La corrí.

—Por eso no puede ser, Lucas Lucatero. La pobrecita debe andar sufriendo. Con lo buena que era. Y lo jovencita. Y lo bonita. ¿Para dónde la mandaste Lucas? Nos conformamos con que siquiera la hayas metido en el convento de las Arrepentidas.

—No la metí en ninguna parte. La corrí. Y estoy seguro de que no está con las Arrepentidas; le gustaba mucho la bulla y el relajo. Debe de andar por esos rumbos, desfajando pantalones.

—No te creemos, Lucas, ni así tantito te creemos. A lo mejor está aquí, encerrada en algún cuarto de esta casa rezando sus oraciones. Tú siempre fuiste muy mentiroso y hasta le-

vantafalsos. Acuérdate, Lucas, de las pobres hijas de Hermelindo, que hasta se tuvieron que ir para El Grullo porque la
gente les chiflaba la canción de "Las güilotas" cada vez que se
asomaban a la calle, y sólo porque tú inventaste chismes. No
se te puede creer nada a ti, Lucas Lucatero.

—Entonces sale sobrando que yo vaya a Amula.

—Te confiesas primero y todo queda arreglado. ¿Desde
cuándo no te confiesas?

— ¡Uh!, desde hace como quince años. Desde que me iban
a fusilar los cristeros. Me pusieron una carabina en la espalda
y me hincaron delante del cura y dije allí hasta lo que no había hecho. Entonces me confesé hasta por adelantado.

—Si no estuviera de por medio que eres el yerno del Santo
Niño, no te vendríamos a buscar, contimás te pediríamos nada. Siempre has sido muy diablo, Lucas Lucatero.

—Por algo fui ayudante de Anacleto Morones. El sí que
era el vivo demonio.

—No blasfemes.

—Es que ustedes no lo conocieron.

—Lo conocimos como santo.

—Pero no como santero.

— ¿Qué cosas dices, Lucas?

—Eso ustedes no lo saben; pero él antes vendía santos. En
las ferias. En la puerta de las iglesias. Y yo le cargaba el tambache.

"Por allí íbamos los dos, uno detrás de otro, de pueblo en
pueblo. El por delante y yo cargándole el tambache con las
novenas de San Pantaleón, de San Ambrosio y de San Pascual,
que pesaban cuando menos tres arrobas.

"Un día encontramos a unos peregrinos. Anacleto estaba
arrodillado encima de un hormiguero, enseñándome cómo
mordiéndose la lengua no pican las hormigas. Entonces pasaron los peregrinos. Lo vieron. Se pararon a ver la curiosidad
aquella. Preguntaron: '¿Cómo puedes estar encima del hormiguero sin que te piquen las hormigas?'

"Entonces él puso los brazos en cruz y comenzó a decir
que acababa de llegar de Roma, de donde traía un mensaje y
era portador de una astilla de la Santa Cruz donde Cristo fue
crucificado.

"Ellos lo levantaron de allí en sus brazos. Lo llevaron en
andas hasta Amula. Y allí fue el acabóse; la gente se postraba
frente a él y le pedía milagros.

"Ese fue el comienzo. Y yo nomás que vivía con la boca
abierta, mirándolo engatusar al montón de peregrinos que
iban a verlo.

—Eres puro hablador y de sobra hasta blasfemo. ¿Quién eras tú antes de conocerlo? Un arreapuercos. Y él te hizo rico. Te dio lo que tienes. Y ni por eso te acomidas a hablar bien de él. Desagradecido.

—Hasta eso, le agradezco que me haya matado el hambre, pero eso no quita que él fuera el vivo diablo. Lo sigue siendo, en cualquier lugar donde esté.

—Está en el cielo. Entre los ángeles. Allí es donde está, más que te pese.

—Yo sabía que estaba en la cárcel.

—Eso fue hace mucho. De allí se fugó. Desapareció sin dejar rastro. Ahora está en el cielo en cuerpo y alma presentes. Y desde allá nos bendice. Muchachas ¡arrodíllense! Recemos el "Penitentes somos, Señor", para que el Santo Niño interceda por nosotras.

Y aquellas viejas se arrodillaron, besando a cada Padre nuestro el escapulario donde estaba bordado el retrato de Anacleto Morones.

Eran las tres de la tarde.

Aproveché ese ratito para meterme en la cocina y comerme unos tacos de frijoles. Cuando salí ya sólo quedaban cinco mujeres.

— ¿Qué se hicieron las otras? —les pregunté.

Y la Pancha, moviendo los cuatro pelos que tenía en sus bigotes, me dijo:

—Se fueron. No quieren tener tratos contigo.

—Mejor. Entre menos burros más olotes. ¿Quieren más agua de arrayán?

Una de ellas, la Filomena, que se había estado callada todo el rato y que por mal nombre le decían la Muerta, se culimpinó encima de una de mis macetas y, metiéndose el dedo en la boca, echó fuera toda el agua de arrayán que se había tragado, revuelta con pedazos de chicharrón y granos de huamúchiles:

—Yo no quiero ni tu agua de arrayan, blasfemo. Nada quiero de ti.

Y puso sobre la silla el huevo que yo le había regalado:
— ¡Ni tus huevos quiero! Mejor me voy.

Ahora sólo quedaban cuatro.

—A mí también me dan ganas de vomitar —me dijo la Pancha—. Pero me las aguanto. Te tenemos que llevar a Amula a como dé lugar.

"Eres el único que puede dar fe de la santidad del Santo Niño. El te ha de ablandar el alma. Ya hemos puesto su imagen en la iglesia y no sería justo echarlo a la calle por tu culpa.

—Busquen a otro. Yo no quiero tener vela en este entierro.

—Tú fuiste casi su hijo. Heredaste el fruto de su santidad. En ti puso él sus ojos para perpetuarse. Te dio a su hija.

—Sí, pero me la dio ya perpetuada.

—Válgame Dios, qué cosas dices, Lucas Lucatero.

—Así fue, me la dio cargada como de cuatro meses cuando menos.

—Pero olía a santidad.

—Olía a pura pestilencia. Le dio por enseñarles la barriga a cuantos se le paraban enfrente, sólo para que vieran que era de carne. Les enseñaba su panza crecida, amoratada por la hinchazón del hijo que llevaba dentro. Y ellos se reían. Les hacía gracia. Era una sinvergüenza. Eso era la hija de Anacleto Morones.

—Impío. No está en ti decir esas cosas. Te vamos a regalar un escapulario para que eches fuera al demonio.

—... Se fue con uno de ellos. Que dizque la quería. Sólo le dijo: "Yo me arriesgo a ser el padre de tu hijo." Y se fue con él.

—Era fruto del Santo Niño. Una niña. Y tú la conseguiste regalada. Tú fuiste el dueño de esa riqueza nacida de la santidad.

— ¡Monsergas!

— ¿Qué dices?

—Adentro de la hija de Anacleto Morones estaba el hijo de Anacleto Morones.

—Eso tú lo inventaste para achacarle cosas malas. Siempre has sido un invencionista.

— ¿Sí? Y qué me dicen de las demás. Dejó sin vírgenes esta parte del mundo, valido de que siempre estaba pidiendo que le velara su sueño una doncella.

—Eso lo hacía por pureza. Por no ensuciarse con el pecado. Quería rodearse de inocencia para no manchar su alma.

—Eso creen ustedes porque no las llamó.

—A mí sí me llamó —dijo una a la que le decían Melquiades—. Yo le velé su sueño.

— ¿Y qué pasó?

—Nada. Sólo sus milagrosas manos me arroparon en esa hora en que se siente la llegada del frío. Y le di gracias por el calor de su cuerpo; pero nada más.

—Es que estabas vieja. A él le gustaban tiernas; que se les quebraran los güesitos; oír que tronaran como si fueran cáscaras de cacahuate.

—Eres un maldito ateo, Lucas Lucatero. Uno de los peores.

Ahora estaba hablando *la Huérfana*, la del eterno llorido. La vieja más vieja de todas. Tenía lágrimas en los ojos y le temblaban las manos:

—Yo soy huérfana y él me alivió de mi orfandad; volví a encontrar a mi padre y a mi madre en él. Se pasó la noche acariciándome para que se me bajara mi pena.

Y le escurrían las lágrimas.

—No tienes, pues, por qué llorar —le dije.

—Es que se han muerto mis padres. Y me han dejado sola. Huérfana a esta edad en que es tan difícil encontrar apoyo. La única noche feliz la pasé con el Niño Anacleto, entre sus consoladores brazos. Y ahora tú hablas mal de él.

—Era un santo.

—Un bueno de bondad.

—Esperábamos que tú siguieras su obra. Lo heredaste todo.

—Me heredó un costal de vicios de los mil judas. Una vieja loca. No tan vieja como ustedes; pero bien loca. Lo bueno es que se fue. Yo mismo le abrí la puerta.

— ¡Hereje! Inventas puras herejías.

Ya para entonces quedaban solamente dos viejas.

Las otras se habían ido yendo una tras otra, poniéndome la cruz y reculando y con la promesa de volver con los exorcismos.

—No me has de negar que el Niño Anacleto era milagroso —dijo la hija de Anastasio—. Eso sí que no me lo has de negar.

—Hacer hijos no es ningún milagro. Ese era su fuerte.

—A mi marido lo curó de la sífilis.

—No sabía que tenías marido. ¿No eres la hija de Anastasio el peluquero? La hija de Tacho es soltera, según yo sé.

—Soy soltera, pero tengo marido. Una cosa es ser señorita y otra cosa es ser soltera. Tú lo sabes. Y yo no soy señorita, pero soy soltera.

—A tus años haciendo eso, Micaela.

—Tuve que hacerlo. Qué me ganaba con vivir de señorita. Soy mujer. Y una nace para dar lo que le dan a una.

—Hablas con las mismas palabras de Anacleto Morones.

—Sí, él me aconsejó que lo hiciera, para que se me quitara lo hepático. Y me junté con alguien. Eso de tener cincuenta años y ser nueva es un pecado.

—Te lo dijo Anacleto Morones.

—El me lo dijo, sí. Pero hemos venido a otra cosa; a que vayas con nosotras y certifiques que él fue un santo.

—¿Y por qué no yo?

—Tú no has hecho ningún milagro. El curó a mi marido. A mí me consta. ¿Acaso tú has curado a alguien de la sífilis?

—No, ni la conozco.

—Es algo así como la gangrena. El se puso amoratado y con el cuerpo lleno de sabañones. Ya no dormía. Decía que todo lo veía colorado como si estuviera asomándose a la puerta del infierno. Y luego sentía ardores que lo hacían brincar de dolor. Entonces fuimos a ver al Niño Anacleto y él lo curó. Lo quemó con un carrizo ardiendo y le untó de su saliva en las heridas y, sácatelas, se le acabaron sus males. Díme si eso no fue un milagro.

—Ha de haber tenido sarampión. A mí también me lo curaron con saliva cuando era chiquito.

—Lo que yo decía antes. Eres un condenado ateo.

—Me queda el consuelo de que Anacleto Morones era peor que yo.

—El te trató como si fueras su hijo. Y todavía te atreves... Mejor no quiero seguir oyéndote. Me voy. ¿Tú te quedas, Pancha?

— me quedaré otro rato. Haré la última lucha yo sola.

—Oye, Francisca, ora que se fueron todas, te vas a quedar a dormir conmigo, ¿verdad?

—Ni lo mande Dios. ¿Qué pensaría la gente? Yo lo que quiero es convencerte.

—Pues vámonos convenciendo los dos. Al cabo qué pierdes. Ya estás revieja, como para que nadie se ocupe de ti, ni te haga el favor.

—Pero luego vienen los dichos de la gente. Luego pensarán mal.

—Que piensen lo que quieran. Qué más da. De todos modos Pancha te llamas.

—Bueno, me quedaré contigo; pero nomás hasta que amanezca. Y eso si me prometes que llegaremos juntos a Amula, para yo decirles que me pasé la noche ruéguete y ruéguete. Si no, ¿cómo le hago?

—Está bien. Pero antes córtate esos pelos que tienes en los bigotes. Te voy a traer las tijeras.

—Cómo te burlas de mí, Lucas Lucatero. Te pasas la vida mirando mis defectos. Déjame mis bigotes en paz. Así no sospecharán.

—Bueno, como tú quieras.

Cuando oscureció, ella me ayudó a arreglarle la ramada a las gallinas y a juntar otra vez las piedras que yo había desparramado por todo el corral, arrinconándolas en el rincón donde habían estado antes.

Ni se las malició que allí estaba enterrado Anacleto Morones. Ni que se había muerto el mismo día que se fugó de la cárcel y vino aquí a reclamarme que le devolviera sus propiedades.

Llegó diciendo: —Vende todo y dame el dinero, porque necesito hacer un viaje al Norte. Te escribiré desde allá y volveremos a hacer negocio los dos juntos.

—¿Por qué no te llevas a tu hija? —le dije yo—. Eso es lo único que me sobra de todo lo que tengo y dices que es tuyo. Hasta a mí me enredaste con tus malas mañas.

—Ustedes se irán después, cuando yo les mande avisar mi paradero. Allá arreglaremos cuentas.

—Sería mucho mejor que las arregláramos de una vez. Para quedar de una vez a mano.

—No estoy para estar jugando ahorita —me dijo—. Dame lo mío. ¿Cuánto dinero tienes guardado?

—Algo tengo, pero no te lo voy a dar. He pasado las de Caín con la sinvergüenza de tu hija. Date por bien pagado con que yo la mantenga.

Le entró el coraje. Pateaba el suelo y le urgía irse...

"¡Qué descanses en paz, Anacleto Morones!", dije cuando lo enterré, y a cada vuelta que yo daba al río acarreando piedras para echárselas encima: "No te saldrás de aquí aunque uses de todas tus tretas."

Y ahora la Pancha me ayudaba a ponerle otra vez el peso de las piedras, sin sospechar que allí debajo estaba Anacleto y que yo hacía aquello por miedo de que se saliera de su sepultura y viniera de nueva cuenta a darme guerra. Con lo mañoso que era, no dudaba que encontrara el modo de revivir y salirse de allí.

—Echale más piedras, Pancha. Amontónalas en este rincón, no me gusta ver pedregoso mi corral.

Después ella me dijo, ya de madrugada:

—Eres una calamidad, Lucas Lucatero. No eres nada cariñoso. ¿Sabes quién sí era amoroso con una?

—¿Quién?

—El Niño Anacleto. El sí que sabía hacer el amor.

Juan Rulfo
1918–
México

Talpa

El llano en llamas, 1953.

NATALIA se metió entre los brazos de su madre y lloró largamente allí con un llanto quedito. Era un llanto aguantado por muchos días, guardado hasta ahora que regresamos a Zenzontla y vio a su madre y comenzó a sentirse con ganas de consuelo.

Sin embargo, antes, entre los trabajos de tantos días difíciles, cuando tuvimos que enterrar a Tanilo en un pozo de la tierra de Talpa, sin que nadie nos ayudara, cuando ella y yo, los dos solos, juntamos nuestras fuerzas y nos pusimos a escarbar la sepultura desenterrando los terrones con nuestras manos —dándonos prisa para esconder pronto a Tanilo dentro del pozo y que no siguiera espantando ya a nadie con el olor de su aire lleno de muerte—, entonces no lloró.

Ni después, al regreso, cuando nos vinimos caminando de noche sin conocer el sosiego, andando a tientas como dormidos y pisando con pasos que parecían golpes sobre la sepultura de Tanilo. En ese entonces, Natalia parecía estar endurecida y traer el corazón apretado para no sentirlo bullir dentro de ella. Pero de sus ojos no salió ninguna lágrima.

Vino a llorar hasta aquí, arrimada a su madre; sólo para acongojarla y que supiera que sufría, acongojándonos de paso a todos, porque yo también sentí ese llanto de ella dentro de mí como si estuviera exprimiendo el trapo de nuestros pecados.

Porque la cosa es que a Tanilo Santos entre Natalia y yo lo matamos. Lo llevamos a Talpa para que se muriera. Y se murió. Sabíamos que no aguantaría tanto camino; pero, así y todo, lo llevamos empujándolo entre los dos, pensando acabar con él para siempre. Eso hicimos.

La idea de ir a Talpa salió de mi hermano Tanilo. A él se le ocurrió primero que a nadie. Desde hacía años que estaba pidiendo que lo llevaran. Desde hacía años. Desde aquel día en que amaneció con unas ampollas moradas repartidas en los brazos y las piernas. Cuando después las ampollas se le convirtieron en llagas por donde no salía nada de sangre y sí una cosa amarilla como goma de copal que destilaba agua espesa. Desde entonces me acuerdo muy bien que nos dijo cuánto miedo sentía de no tener ya remedio. Para eso quería ir a ver a la Virgen de Talpa; para que Ella con su mirada le curara sus llagas. Aunque sabía que Talpa estaba lejos y que tendríamos que caminar mucho debajo del sol de los días y del frío de las noches de marzo, así y todo quería ir. La Virgencita le daría el remedio para aliviarse de aquellas cosas que nunca se secaban. Ella sabía hacer eso: lavar las cosas, ponerlo todo nuevo de nueva cuenta como un campo recién llovido. Ya allí, frente a Ella, se acabarían sus males; nada le dolería ni le volvería a doler más. Eso pensaba él.

Y de eso nos agarramos Natalia y yo para llevarlo. Yo tenía que acompañar a Tanilo porque era mi hermano. Natalia tendría que ir también, de todos modos, porque era su mujer. Tenía que ayudarlo llevándolo del brazo, sopesándolo a la ida y tal vez a la vuelta sobre sus hombros, mientras él arrastraba su esperanza.

Yo ya sabía desde antes lo que había dentro de Natalia. Conocía algo de ella. Sabía, por ejemplo, que sus piernas redondas, duras y calientes como piedras al sol del mediodía, estaban solas desde hacía tiempo. Ya conocía yo eso. Habíamos estado juntos muchas veces; pero siempre la sombra de Tanilo nos separaba; sentíamos que sus manos ampolladas se metían entre nosotros y se llevaban a Natalia para que lo siguiera cuidando. Y así sería siempre mientras él estuviera vivo.

Yo sé ahora que Natalia está arrepentida de lo que pasó. Y yo también lo estoy; pero eso no nos salvará del remordimiento ni nos dará ninguna paz ya nunca. No podrá tranquilizarnos saber que Tanilo se hubiera muerto de todos modos porque ya le tocaba, y que de nada había servido ir a Talpa, tan allá, tan lejos; pues casi es seguro de que se hubiera muerto igual allá que aquí, o quizás tantito después aquí que allá, porque todo lo que se mortificó por el camino, y la sangre que perdió de más, y el coraje y todo, todas esas cosas juntas fueron las que lo mataron más pronto. Lo malo está en que Natalia y yo lo llevamos a empujones, cuando él ya no quería seguir, cuando sintió que era inútil seguir y nos pidió que lo regresáramos. A estirones lo levantábamos del suelo para que siguiera caminando, diciéndole que ya no podíamos volver atrás. "Está ya más cerca Talpa que Zanzontla." Eso le decíamos. Pero entonces Talpa estaba todavía lejos; más allá de muchos días.

Lo que queríamos era que se muriera. No está por demás decir que eso era lo que queríamos desde antes de salir de

Zenzontla y en cada una de las noches que pasamos en el camino de Talpa. Es algo que no podemos entender ahora; pero entonces era lo que queríamos. Me acuerdo muy bien.

Me acuerdo muy bien de esas noches. Primero nos alumbrábamos con ocotes. Después dejábamos que la ceniza oscureciera la lumbrada y luego buscábamos Natalia y yo la sombra de algo para escondernos de la luz del cielo. Así nos arrimábamos a la soledad del campo, fuera de los ojos de Tanilo y desaparecidos en la noche. Y la soledad aquella nos empujaba uno al otro. A mí me ponía entre los brazos el cuerpo de Natalia y a ella eso le servía de remedio. Sentía como si descansara; se olvidaba de muchas cosas y luego se quedaba adormecida y con el cuerpo sumido en un gran alivio.

Siempre sucedía que la tierra sobre la que dormíamos estaba caliente. Y la carne de Natalia, la esposa de mi hermano Tanilo, se calentaba en seguida con el calor de la tierra. Luego aquellos dos calores juntos quemaban y lo hacían a uno despertar de su sueño. Entonces mis manos iban detrás de ella; iban y venían por encima de ese como rescoldo que era ella; primero suavemente, pero después la apretaban como si quisieran exprimirle la sangre. Así una y otra vez, noche tras noche, hasta que llegaba la madrugada y el viento frío apagaba la lumbre de nuestros cuerpos. Eso hacíamos Natalia y yo a un lado del camino de Talpa, cuando llevamos a Tanilo para que la Virgen lo aliviara.

Ahora todo ha pasado. Tanilo se alivió hasta de vivir. Ya no podrá decir nada del trabajo tan grande que le costaba vivir, teniendo aquel cuerpo como emponzoñado, lleno por dentro de agua podrida que le salía por cada rajadura de sus piernas o de sus brazos. Unas llagas así de grandes, que se abrían despacito, muy despacito, para luego dejar salir a borbotones un aire como de cosa echada a perder que a todos nos tenía asustados.

Pero ahora que está muerto la cosa se ve de otro modo. Ahora Natalia llora por él, tal vez para que él vea, desde donde está, todo el gran remordimiento que lleva encima de su alma. Ella dice que ha sentido la cara de Tanilo estos últimos días. Era lo único que servía de él para ella; la cara de Tanilo, humedecida siempre por el sudor en que lo dejaba el esfuerzo para aguantar sus dolores. La sintió acercándose hasta su boca, escondiéndose entre sus cabellos, pidiéndole, con una voz apenitas, que lo ayudara. Dice que le dijo que ya se había curado por fin; que ya no le molestaba ningún dolor. "Ya puedo estar contigo, Natalia. Ayúdame a estar contigo", dizque eso le dijo.

Acabábamos de salir de Talpa, de dejarlo allí enterrado bien hondo en aquel como surco profundo que hicimos para sepultarlo.

Y Natalia se olvidó de mí desde entonces. Yo sé cómo le brillaban antes los ojos como si fueran charcos alumbrados por la luna. Pero de pronto se destiñeron, se le borró la mirada como si la hubiera revolcado en la tierra. Y pareció no ver ya nada. Todo lo que existía para ella era el Tanilo de ella, que había cuidado mientras estuvo vivo y lo había enterrado cuando tuvo que morirse.

Tardamos veinte días en encontrar el camino real de Talpa. Hasta entonces habíamos venido los tres solos. Desde allí comenzamos a juntarnos con gente que salía de todas partes; que había desembocado como nosotros en aquel camino ancho parecido a la corriente de un río, que nos hacía andar a rastras, empujados por todos lados como si nos llevaran amarrados con hebras de polvo. Porque de la tierra se levantaba, con el bullir de la gente, un polvo blanco como tamo de maíz que subía muy alto y volvía a caer; pero los pies al caminar lo devolvían y lo hacían subir de nuevo; así a todas horas estaba aquel polvo por encima y debajo de nosotros. Y arriba de esta tierra estaba el cielo vacío, sin nubes, sólo el polvo; pero el polvo no da ninguna sombra.

Teníamos que esperar a la noche para descansar del sol y de aquella luz blanca del camino.

Luego los días fueron haciéndose más largos. Habíamos salido de Zenzontla a mediados de febrero, y ahora que comenzaba marzo amanecía muy pronto. Apenas si cerrábamos los ojos al oscurecer, cuando nos volvía a despertar el sol, el mismo sol que parecía acabarse de poner hacía un rato.

Nunca había sentido que fuera más lenta y violenta la vida como caminar entre un amontonadero de gente; igual que si fuéramos un hervidero de gusanos apelotonados bajo el sol, retorciéndonos entre la cerrazón del polvo que nos encerraba a todos en la misma vereda y nos llevaba como acorralados. Los ojos seguían la polvareda; daban en el polvo como si tropezaran contra algo que no se podía traspasar. Y el cielo siempre gris, como una mancha gris y pesada que nos aplastaba a todos desde arriba. Sólo a veces, cuando cruzábamos algún río, el polvo era más alto y más claro. Zambullíamos la cabeza acalenturada y renegrida en el agua verde, y por un momento de todos nosotros salía un humo azul, parecido al vapor que sale de la boca con el frío. Pero poquito después desaparecía-mos otra vez entreverados en el polvo, cobijándonos unos a otros del sol, de aquel calor del sol repartido entre todos.

Algún día llegará la noche. En eso pensábamos. Llegará la noche y nos pondremos a descansar. Ahora se trata de cruzar el día, de atravesarlo como sea para correr del calor y del sol. Después nos detendremos. Después. Lo que tenemos que hacer por lo pronto es esfuerzo tras esfuerzo para ir de prisa detrás de tantos como nosotros y delante de otros muchos. De eso se trata. Ya descansaremos bien a bien cuando estemos muertos.

En eso pensábamos Natalia y yo y quizá también Tanilo, cuando íbamos por el camino real de Talpa, entre la procesión; queriendo llegar los primeros hasta la Virgen, antes que se le acabaran los milagros.

Pero Tanilo comenzó a ponerse más malo. Llegó un rato en que ya no quería seguir. La carne de sus pies se había reventado y por la reventazón aquella empezó a salírsele la sangre. Lo cuidamos hasta que se puso bueno. Pero, así y todo, ya no quería seguir:

"Me quedaré aquí sentado un día o dos y luego me volveré a Zenzontla." Eso nos dijo.

Pero Natalia y yo no quisimos. Había algo dentro de nosotros que no nos dejaba sentir ninguna lástima por ningún Tanilo. Queríamos llegar con él a Talpa, porque a esas alturas, así como estaba, todavía le sobraba vida. Por eso mientras Natalia le enjuagaba los pies con aguardiente para que se le deshincharan, le daba ánimos. Le decía que sólo la Virgen de Talpa lo curaría. Ella era la única que podía hacer que él se aliviara para siempre. Ella nada más. Había otras muchas vírgenes; pero sólo la de Talpa era la buena. Eso le decía Natalia.

Y entonces Tanilo se ponía a llorar con lágrimas que hacían surco entre el sudor de su cara y después se maldecía por haber sido malo. Natalia le limpiaba los chorretes de lágrimas con su rebozo, y entre ella y yo lo levantábamos del suelo para que caminara otro rato más, antes que llegara la noche.

Así, a tirones, fue como llegamos con él a Talpa.

Ya en los últimos días también nosotros nos sentíamos cansados. Natalia y yo sentíamos que se nos iba doblando el cuerpo entre más y más. Era como si algo nos detuviera y cargara un pesado bulto sobre nosotros. Tanilo se nos caía más seguido y teníamos que levantarlo y a veces llevarlo sobre los hombros. Tal vez de eso estábamos como estábamos: con el cuerpo flojo y lleno de flojera para caminar. Pero la gente que iba allí junto a nosotros nos hacía andar más aprisa.

Por las noches, aquel mundo desbocado se calmaba. Desperdigadas por todas partes brillaban las fogatas y en derredor de la lumbre la gente de la peregrinación rezaba el rosario, con los brazos en cruz, mirando hacia el cielo de Talpa. Y se oía cómo el viento llevaba y traía aquel rumor, revolviéndolo, hasta hacer de él un solo mugido. Poco después todo se quedaba quieto. A eso de la medianoche podía oírse que alguien cantaba muy lejos de nosotros. Luego se cerraban los ojos y se esperaba sin dormir a que amaneciera.

Entramos a Talpa cantando el Alabado.

Habíamos salido a mediados de febrero y llegamos a Talpa en los últimos días de marzo, cuando ya mucha gente venía de regreso. Todo se debió a que Tanilo se puso a hacer penitencia. En cuanto se vio rodeado de hombres que llevaban pencas de nopal colgadas como escapulario, él también pensó en llevar las suyas. Dio en amarrarse los pies uno con otro con las mangas de su camisa para que sus pasos se hicieran más desesperados. Después quiso llevar una corona de espinas. Tantito después se vendó los ojos, y más tarde, en los últimos trechos del camino, se hincó en la tierra, y así, andando sobre los huesos de sus rodillas y con las manos cruzadas hacia atrás, llegó a Talpa aquella cosa que era mi hermano Tanilo Santos; aquella cosa tan llena de cataplasmas y de hilos oscuros de sangre que dejaba en el aire, al pasar, un olor agrio como de animal muerto.

Y cuando menos acordamos lo vimos metido entre las danzas. Apenas si nos dimos cuenta y ya estaba allí, con la larga sonaja en la mano, dando duros golpes en el suelo con sus pies amoratados y descalzos. Parecía todo enfurecido, como si estuviera sacudiendo el coraje que llevaba encima desde hacía tiempo, o como si estuviera haciendo un último esfuerzo por conseguir vivir un poco más.

Tal vez al ver las danzas se acordó de cuando iba todos los años a Tolimán, en el novenario del Señor, y bailaba la noche entera hasta que sus huesos se aflojaban, pero sin cansarse. Tal vez de eso se acordó y quiso revivir su antigua fuerza.

Natalia y yo lo vimos así por un momento. En seguida lo vimos alzar los brazos y azotar su cuerpo contra el suelo, todavía con la sonaja repicando entre sus manos salpicadas de sangre. Lo sacamos a rastras, esperando defenderlo de los pisotones de los danzantes; de entre la furia de aquellos pies que rodaban sobre las piedras y brincaban aplastando la tierra sin saber que algo se había caído en medio de ellos.

A horcajadas, como si estuviera tullido, entramos con él en la iglesia. Natalia lo arrodilló junto a ella, enfrentito de aquella figurita dorada que era la Virgen de Talpa. Y Tanilo comenzó a rezar y dejó que se le cayera una lágrima grande, salida de muy adentro, apagándole la vela que Natalia le había puesto entre sus manos. Pero no se dio cuenta de esto; la luminaria de tantas velas prendidas que allí había le cortó esa cosa con la que uno se sabe dar cuenta de lo que pasa junto a uno. Siguió rezando con su vela apagada. Rezando a gritos para oír que rezaba.

Pero no le valió. Se murió de todos modos.

"... Desde nuestros corazones sale para Ella una súplica igual, envuelta en el dolor. Muchas lamentaciones revueltas con esperanza. No se ensordece su ternura ni ante los lamentos ni las lágrimas, pues Ella sufre con nosotros. Ella sabe borrar esa mancha y dejar que el corazón se haga blandito y puro para recibir su misericordia y su caridad. La Virgen nuestra, nuestra madre, que no quiere saber nada de nuestros pecados; que se echa la culpa de nuestros pecados; la que quisiera llevarnos en sus brazos para que no nos lastime la vida, está aquí junto a nosotros, aliviándonos el cansancio y las enfermedades del alma y de nuestro cuerpo ahuatado, herido y suplicante. Ella sabe que cada día nuestra fe es mejor porque está hecha de sacrificios..."

Eso decía el señor cura desde allá arriba del púlpito. Y después que dejó de hablar, la gente se soltó rezando toda al mismo tiempo, con un ruido igual al de muchas avispas espantadas por el humo.

Pero Tanilo ya no oyó lo que había dicho el señor cura. Se había quedado quieto, con la cabeza recargada en sus rodillas. Y cuando Natalia lo movió para que se levantara ya estaba muerto.

Afuera se oía el ruido de las danzas; los tambores y la chirimía, el repique de las campanas. Y entonces fue cuando me dio a mí tristeza. Ver tantas cosas vivas; ver a la Virgen allí, mero enfrente de nosotros dándonos su sonrisa, y ver por el otro lado a Tanilo, como si fuera un estorbo. Me dio tristeza.

Pero nosotros lo llevamos allí para que se muriera, eso es lo que no se me olvida.

Ahora estamos los dos en Zenzontla. Hemos vuelto sin él. Y la madre de Natalia no me ha preguntado nada; ni qué hice con mi hermano Tanilo, ni nada. Natalia se ha puesto a llorar sobre sus hombros y le ha contado de esa manera todo lo que pasó.

Y yo comienzo a sentir como si no hubiéramos llegado a ninguna parte, que estamos aquí de paso, para descansar, y que luego seguiremos caminando. No sé para dónde; pero tendremos que seguir, porque aquí estamos muy cerca del remordimiento y del recuerdo de Tanilo.

Quizá hasta empecemos a tenernos miedo el uno al otro. Esa cosa de no decirnos nada desde que salimos de Talpa tal vez quiera decir eso. Tal vez los dos tenemos muy cerca el cuerpo de Tanilo, tendido en el petate enrollado; lleno por dentro y por fuera de un hervidero de moscas azules que zumbaban como si fuera un gran ronquido que saliera de la boca de él; de aquella boca que no pudo cerrarse a pesar de los esfuerzos de Natalia y míos, y que parecía querer respirar todavía sin encontrar resuello. De aquel Tanilo a quien ya nada le dolía, pero que estaba como adolorido, con las manos y los pies engarruñados y los ojos muy abiertos como mirando su propia muerte. Y por aquí y por allá todas sus llagas goteando un agua amarilla, llena de aquel olor que se derramaba por todos lados y se sentía en la boca, como si se estuviera saboreando una miel espesa y amarga que se derretía en la sangre de uno a cada bocanada de aire.

Es de eso de lo que quizá nos acordemos aquí más seguido: de aquel Tanilo que nosotros enterramos en el camposanto de Talpa; al que Natalia y yo echamos tierra y piedras encima para que no lo fueran a desenterrar los animales del cerro.

Edgardo Sanabria Santaliz
1951—
Puerto Rico

El día que el hombre pisó la luna
El día que el hombre pisó la luna, 1984.

> *That's one small step for man,*
> *one giant leap for mankind.*

Armstrong, 21 de julio de 1969.

A Rubén Ríos Avila

E L día que el hombre pisó la luna resultó ser un día siniestro en la historia de nuestra familia.

Para empezar, tía Rafa se llevó una ingrata sorpresa. A
eso de las 6:00 A.M. ya estaba bajando según su costumbre.
Tosía. Carraspeaba algo. Escupía seguido por encima de la baranda de nogal. Revisaba entonces, a través del grosor de fondo de botella de sus cristales, el borde amaneciente del mundo, y pronosticaba infalible si diluviaría o no. Cerca de diez
minutos se echaba bajando la escalera pegada como un zipper
al panzudo talle de concreto anaranjado de la casa, apear el
paso de este escalón al siguiente, haciendo pausas con el propósito de estudiarse la mumu y comprobar que estuviera níti-
da y tan correctamente planchada como la cota de un ángel;
deteniéndose para jalar bocanadas del cigarrillo cosido a su
boca arrugada como costuron, prendido a mitad de camino y
del cual no quedaba más que la colilla retocada con discreto
lápiz labial de un tono rosado cuando alcanzaba el portón de
la calle y, al fin, la acera. Sucede, nos cuenta la tía, que anduvo hasta la puerta del negocio, abrió el candado con la llave
que colgaba plomosa de su collar de cordones amarrados entre sí, y el desconcierto le acabó de quitar la modorra que
aún le quedaba de la noche: se espantaron sus pupilas como
dorados peces, nadando de un extremo a otro en el interior
cristalino de pecera de sus espejuelos, los cuales triplicaban el
tamaño de las órbitas. ¡Qué diantre!..., exclamó, porque se
encontró con que el nivel del agua llegaba al primer peldaño,
donde estaba ella (para entrar a la tienda había que descender
cuatro escalones combos) valorando el infortunio con la nariz
amparada detrás de uno de sus pañuelitos mojado en Agua de

Florida. Contemplaba llena de asco la terrible marea alta de la inundación, las aguas negras del edificio vomitadas por roturas en las tuberías que inexplicablemente cedieron durante la noche. Docenas de paquines, revistas y paquetes de dulces, toda la mercancía que engolosinaba la atención de los muchachos camino de la escuela —desfile de hormiguitas interceptado por un montículo de azúcar—, todo lo que podía flotar, flotaba en compañía de otros numerosos efectos inmencionables. Sin pensarlo mucho, como si en realidad no hubiera visto nada, o como si desde siempre hubiese esperado encontrar aquel oloriento espectáculo, cerró la puerta, echó el candado y se puso a subir mientras prendía un nuevo cigarrillo. Después entró al comedor y se paró ante la mesa donde estaba desayunando su hijo. Ciro, le dijo, la tienda está llena de porquería, avísame cuando la limpien. Ciro pensó que debía de haberse vuelto loca, pero resultó ser cierto lo que había dicho: así pudo confirmarlo él mismo en cuanto bajó a averiguar. Duró 72 horas la extracción con bombas del agua que suscitaba las quejas de los vecinos, y tres días adicionales esperar a que secasen y se ventilasen las cosas.

Durante todo este tiempo, Ciro se vio forzado a vender sus periódicos en la acera, frente a la casa, sentado en una silla de tijera verde detrás de un banco sobre el que descansaban los ejemplares de periódicos como frutos maduros de papel. Desde joven había sentido fuertes impulsos de dedicarse a estudiar periodismo, pero nunca pudo abandonar ni aunque fuera por un tiempo a la familia. Murió el padre cuando él ya iba a cumplir los quince. A los cuatro meses tuvo que dejar la escuela por ser el único varón y faltar el pan en la casa. Ahora, soltero y ya metido en los cuarenta, se conformaba con recibir cada mañana, a las 8:30 en punto, el camión rojo desde el que lanzaban frente a la casa un envoltorio perfectamente amarrado, cuyo olor a tinta fresca lo entristecía y alegraba al mismo tiempo.

Ciro guardaba en el salón central de la casa su tesoro. Adentro, aquel cuarto adquiría proporciones comparables a las de la casa entera, algo que no podía explicarse quienquiera que pasara el trabajo de explorar los pasillos y demás dependencias a la redonda: entonces uno se daba cuenta de las verdaderas dimensiones que la pieza hubiera debido tener. Treinta años de estar coleccionando la prensa del país y muchos otros periódicos que llegaban de afuera, habían acumulado y construido allí desfiladeros de un papel color mostaza que olía a polvo embalsamado. La voluntad ahorrativa de Ciro, dividida entre la absoluta necesidad y la otra de frecuentar el cafetín de la calle trasera —cada noche de 8:00 en adelante, acudiendo como polilla que celebra su vuelo alrededor de una lámpara hasta caer con las alas quemadas—, había creado aquel laberinto de papel que llamaba su hemeroteca, donde uno podía muy bien perderse, y donde, de hecho, se nos perdió para siempre Lencha a las 10:00 de la mañana de aquel funesto día. Esta fue la segunda desgracia que sufrimos.

* * *

Lencha era la tatarabuela. Nadie en la familia fue nunca capaz de calcular la edad que tendría su carne disecada. Las excursiones que hacía por la casa se limitaban, debido a su salud, al baño, que era la puerta próxima a la de la sala de periódicos. Hacia el baño tal vez se estaba orientando cuando desapareció, quizás confundida por la visión de algún recuerdo que la volvía más cegata de la cuenta. (A partir de entonces, la puerta del cuarto de Lencha se encajó como por determinación propia. En el interior quedó eternizada la absurda anarquía de pájaros a la que estaba acostumbrada ella: su antiguo sillón cubierto de excremento de golondrinas, las cuales habían tomado entera posesión de la madera filigranosa y se mecían al ritmo incesante de su chirriar; la ventana sin hojas por la que penetraban aquéllas, junto con la volatería de palomas que ponía sobre la colcha asqueante de la cama, y arrullaba con sonoridad algodonosa en la gruta profunda del ropero, y se movía produciendo sus patitas un traqueteo cosquilloso sobre el pequeño altar de las imágenes y metiendo su pico de añil en el cacharro de agua bendita como dedos a punto de santiguar). Tan pronto notamos la ausencia de Lencha, cogimos linternas y quinqués para invadir el salón de los periódicos, desplegándose cada uno en dirección de las cinco o seis embocaduras que se presentaban a la vista de quien pisase el umbral. Dos horas completas pasamos circulando por los desfiladeros, ejemplar sobre ejemplar arrumado descabelladamente en un orden que ignoraba fecha y lugar de tirada, las murallas de papel a derecha e izquierda casi alcanzando la apagada nivelación del techo, desde donde goteaba murcielaguina; dando vueltas y más vueltas por pasadizos que nos llevaban a enfrentar el deslumbramiento de las luces que aguantábamos unos y otros, a vernos en la obligación de desandar lo andado por haber escogido un camino que no tenía salida... El nombre de la tatarabuela sonaba repetido por diferentes voces desde distintos puntos de la hemeroteca. Luego resonó en el resto de la casa, cocina, sala y antesala, dormitorios, de nuevo en su cuarto con la puerta ya encajándose y las aves, alborotadas, empezando a sentir nostalgia por su dueña; resonó también en el baño enorme revestido de azulejos como el fondo relumbrante de una piscina o de una fuente, y hasta por los balcones, cuando nos asomamos para escudriñar de arriba abajo la calle (a pesar de saber que Lencha no podía con las escaleras) y preguntar a los vecinos si por casualidad la habían visto salir. En cuanto nos dimos por vencidos, y contamos el tiempo que había pasado desde su desaparición (días y días durante los cuales buscamos por turnos, para que los demás pudiesen seguir haciendo sus cosas), se asentó en nuestra mente la noción pesarosa del luto. Pero éste fue un duelo que por contradicción no nos permitió llorar y lamentarnos. ¿Pues cómo íbamos a saber asumir una muerte que había sido puro y sencillo desvanecimiento? ¿Cómo tendríamos llanto para una persona que en cualquier instante, cuando menos estuviéramos pensando en ella, podía aparecer doblando la esquina de un pasillo, Lencha vestida con su hábito azul cielo de promesa a La Milagrosa, arrastrando las deshilachadas chinelas a la búsqueda rutinaria del baño?

* * *

El tercer percance que sufrió la familia fue éste: Sucede que los corredores y cuartos de la casa ofrecieron siempre la probabilidad de un contratiempo, de un accidente que desdichadamente ocurrió cuando tía Chema nos hizo la visita imprevista, aquel mismo día. Nosotros conocíamos ya el riesgo habido al caminar por ciertas áreas sin llevar copiado en la cabeza un plano señalador de las tablas flojas o podridas o faltantes bajo la tramposa lisura floreada del linóleo. Pero tía Chema llevaba 25 años viviendo en Nueva York, al pueblo no había venido desde jovencita, así que cuando trepó por las escaleras de la cocina deseando sorprendernos con su presencia ya casi olvidada, ella fue la que se llevó el pasmo y nosotros un sofocón al escuchar, a la 1:00 de la tarde, chillidos de mujer en aumento hasta hacer explosión en palabras: ¡SA-QUENME DE AQUI! ¡¡SA-QUEN-ME-DE-AQUIII! Enseguida interrumpimos la búsqueda de la tatarabuela, echamos a correr y encontramos en el pasillo que conducía a la cocina a una señora muy obesa, como de unos cuarenta y pico de años, que cargaba desde la base del cráneo hasta la frente un eleva-

do moño de un rubio metalífero, atrapada hasta la cintura en
uno de los hoyos, como si fuera el tapón de corcho de una
botella. Una cara demasiado empolvada, en la cual resaltaban
la boca y los ojos igual que tres papagayos transplantados a
un paisaje de nieve polar, nos pedía ayuda mientras los brazos batían como alones carnudos de avestruz cuya pesadez
(representada en la fatigosa pechuga depositada en el linóleo) no la dejaba remontarse. Cuando nos dijo el nombre nos
costó creer que era ella, la misma Chema que en su juventud
fue de figura delicadísima y grácil. Ahora, por poco se nos
partía el espinazo haciendo intentos de sacarla de allí; hasta
llegamos a instalar una polea en el plafón para tratar de alzar-
la amarrada con sogas a su espalda y hombros. Ningún remedio nos dio resultado. Antes de que por fin pudiera salir del
agujero —gracias al uniformado socorro de cinco miembros
de la Defensa Civil— pasaron casi 20 horas durante las cuales
tuvimos que servirle sus comidas en el suelo, charlamos con
ella sobre su vida en Nueva York sentados en banquetas que
la rodeaban y, además, las mujeres hicieron un cierto número de viajes al cuarto que quedaba inmediatamente debajo
del hoyo —donde estaba pedaleando un par de piernas hinchadas y pálidas en el interior de una falda verde que campa-
neaba— con idea de ayudarla a maniobrar sus personales urgencias.

Sentados en el pasillo, haciéndole compañía a tía Chema,
fue que vimos la televisión. A las 4:00 de la tarde, Ciro, que
había pasado el día pendiente de aquel momento, trajo el
aparato de la sala y lo enchufló y ajustó el ángulo de mejor
recepción de la antena. En seguida la penumbra del sitio se
vio expulsada por el continuo irradiar color perla que daba
cierta composición de retrato al grupo que formábamos allí,
todos con la atención dirigida a la pantalla como al lente de
una cámara a punto de dispararse. Como entrevista en el trans-
curso de una tormenta de arena en un desierto, la bota color
aluminio del hombre hace aparición y brinca a la superficie
harinosa que rápidamente se pega de la suela, dejando ésta, al
retirarse, imprimido, el rastro de una pisada que trae al recuerdo el trascendental calco de manos sobre las paredes de
cavernas prehistóricas. Después se deja ver de cuerpo entero
el hombre, seguido por otro que en breve se escapa del foco
para volver a enseñarse varios metros más allá, festejando la
legendaria llegada en ejecución de saltos dignos de cualquier
canguro, recluido precariamente en la atmósfera hecha a la medida de su traje platinado, cuyo casco de vidrio oscuro cente-

llea con la inflexible emisión homicida del sol. El primer hombre de nuevo se muestra varias veces, cargado de equipo (sismómetro, aparato detector de los vientos solares y del impacto de los micrometeoros, una segunda cámara de televisión, instrumentos para coleccionar polvo y rocas, aparatos de rayos laser para medir con incontrovertible exactitud la distancia entre el satélite y su planeta), y, una vez queda todo emplazado con la ayuda del hombre saltarín, culmina su actividad plantando con algún trabajo el asta con la bandera que anuncia al cosmos los derechos de su país sobre la redonda colonia extraterrestre. Poco después, desde alguna parte, uno de los hombres maneja el foco desviándolo hasta la bombardeada llanura de cráteres, recogiendo al pasar el panorama de ondulaciones y zanjas y crestas del Mar de la Tranquilidad, hasta detenerse en la línea del horizonte por donde sale o se pone la semiesfera nublada del mundo.

A mí me está que eso lo filmaron en Hollywood, en algún estudio, como hacen con las películas, tía Rafa dijo después de observar con sus ojos acuáticos el entusiasmo a cámara lenta de Armstrong y Aldrin. A la luna no se puede llegar, sentenció. Tía Chema la miró estupefacta, puede ser que hasta sintiendo en su espíritu metropolitano su poco de lástima por la pueblerina ignorancia que dejaba entrever el comentario. Ciro, con voz acentuada de editorial periodístico, le explicó a su madre que aquello que veía estaba sin lugar a dudas pasando ahora mismo allá arriba: se trataba nada más y nada menos, mamá, señoras y señores, de la mayor hazaña jamás realizada por el hombre, es decir, por la ciencia, la ciencia que ha probado al fin la estupidez de pensar en una luna inalcanzable, hecha de queso, que tan sólo sirve para iluminar paisajes románticos o fábulas del hombre-Lobo. Bueno, pues a mí no hay quien me convenza, no señor, cerró la discusión tía Rafa, mientras se alejaba pasillo adelante. Más tarde supimos que aquella noche estuvo horas largas asomada al balcón de la galería, esforzando la vista para atravesar el espesor telescópico de sus cristales, escrutando con su mirada intranquila la bomba inflada de aire luminoso, el espejo circular que le enviaba reflejos plateados mientras ella repetía: ¡No, eso no es verdad, yo no veo nada desde aquí, sólo el conejo de siempre dibujado, allá no puede haber nadie!

* * *

Algo más sucedió ese día, aquella misma tarde, para colmo de sobresaltos.

En el mirador de la casa llevaba tiempo viviendo Angelito. Angelito era primo del abuelo y era de avanzada edad. Hasta hace poco había servido de jardinero a los propietarios más adinerados de la localidad, quienes, a cambio de alguna miseria, se aprovechaban de su talento, de la mano santa que Angelito tenía para las matas, del toque de sus dedos —con uñas llenas de tierra rascada o acariciada— que hacía resucitar al gancho más invernalmente pelado o reseco. Angelito era la primavera de sus excelsos jardines, muchos de los cuales, crecidos en el invernadero geográfico de un trópico desaforado y tenaz, imitaban a los frígidos y concertados vergeles europeos. Hacía cosa de once meses que el lumbago crónico, y la joroba dromedaria que lo ponía a hacerle reverencias sin fin al terreno que tanto rastrilló, lo mantenían monjilmente recluido en el cuarto más alto de la casa, desde el que se dominaba casi entero el pueblo y la cadena de montes que lo cercaba en forma de herradura abierta hasta el mar.

De lo único que hablaba Angelito, aparte del tema obligado de sus matas, era de lo más grandioso que le había pasado en toda su vida. Allá para los años veinte, cuando él ya era un hombre hecho y derecho y el cuerpo ni tan siquiera guardaba la menor sospecha de que llegaría a doblarse como un tallo enfermo, don Telesforo Valdés, dueño y señor de unas cuantas centrales azucareras, del territorio perpendicular de llanos que en aquel rincón de la isla resbalaba de caña hasta el mar, y de una buena porción del poblado, decidió mandar a construir un globo aerostático porque quería ver desde el cielo, con los ojos de Dios, la suma de sus posesiones. En aquel tiempo, Angelito era el muchacho que se encargaba de cuidar el jardín de la casa que en Cerro Grande don Telesforo tenía. El propietario se le acercó una tarde que él estaba plantando tulipanes alrededor de una fuente, y le anunció que lo había escogido como copiloto en su empresa. El jardinero no le prestó atención, ya que el viejo estaba sin cesar inventando proyectos que al día siguiente olvidaba o desechaba. Pero, como a los dos meses, al llegar muy temprano para empezar su labor, Angelito se encontró en el solar fronterizo con la casa, todavía ligada con sogas a estacas gruesas, pero erguida dentro de la prisión de la red que vacilaba ligeramente en el fresco aire de la mañana —como una boya sobre la marejada habitual de neblina que aún no se había recogido—, la esfera de listas blancas y rojas hinchada de helio que la claridad calmosa del sol iba recortando de un modo cada vez más concreto en cuarto creciente. Al acercarse, vio a don Telesforo que hablaba con dos hombres altos y rubios; por medio de un intérprete, los norteamericanos constructores del globo, le ofrecían las últimas instrucciones de manejo al hacendado extático. Este le puso un casco con orejeras y lentes al joven jardinero. Antes de que pudiera reflexionar bien sobre lo que pasaba, antes de poder empezar a sentir miedo siquiera, Angelito se vio alzado por alguna gente hasta ser depositado en la barquilla junto a don Telesforo: el propietario publicaba emotivamente ahora, a un grupo de familiares, sirvientes y amigos que sólo entonces Angelito percibió, que el primer viaje en globo en la historia de la isla estaba por comenzar. En eso alguien soltó las amarras y, crujiendo, la barquilla empezó a elevarse. Lo que el jardinero presenció desde allá arriba nunca pudo olvidarlo. Comprendió el sentido de su nombre cuando una membrana de nubes que casi hubiera podido rasgar si estiraba los brazos interfirió vaporizando la colosal escena de playas y lomas y ríos. Pero lo que más conmovió su alma fue el doble enfrentamiento: con un sol amanecido a su izquierda, mientras a su derecha el cuarto menguante lunar se ponía sobre el océano como el segmento de otro sol, de un astro agotado y sin más combustión que la ceniciente lumbre reverberada en su curva filosa.

* * *

Esto fue lo que pasó. Como a las 6:00 de la tarde, subió ajorada y haciendo alboroto doña Consuelo, amiga de hace años de la familia, quien venía pasando del centro del pueblo cuando descubrió — ¡estaba segura, segurísima, sí!— a don Angel caminando por el alero del tercer piso del caserón. La estampida en ascenso de la familia entera se efectuó en un dos por tres, al igual que nuestra entrada en el mirador y el asomar simultáneo de cabezas por las cinco o seis ventanas de bajo alféizar, registrando desesperadamente los aleros con la vista hasta descubrir también a la encorvada imagen adormecida al borde del abismo, como una gárgola de catedral gótica mirada a contraluz, un anochecer de mezclados colores. La rueda amarilleada de la luna venía del otro lado del mundo en aquel momento; por un minuto se detuvo contrapuesta a la cabeza inclinada de Angelito, recordando la aureola que llevan los santos. Esta no sería la única ocasión en que lo encontraríamos apaciguado allí. De Aquel día en adelante no hallamos forma de evitar que, estuviese donde estuviese (pues lo hicimos mudar a otras partes de la casa para ver si desistía), al quedarse dormido, Angelito volviera a soñar con el globo aerostático de don Telesforo Valdés, y en un arranque de sonambulismo propiciado por el deseo de revivir el más notable suceso de su vida, escapara por cualquier ventana para recorrer acrobáticamente los aleros en busca del viento y las nubes y la mecida fracción de la luna que casi había tocado una vez. Así que, en realidad, todo esto no fue más que preludio a la desgracia, el primer síntoma de un impulso que estuvo acelerando día tras día hasta alcanzar su apogeo, tres meses después, en la desdicha tangible: la pila de huesos desajustados y revueltos con ligazones de ropa y piel, encontrada una mañana en el cemento del patio.

*   *   *

A las 10:00 P.M. Ciro salió del cafetín. Desde algún espacio de la calle, mientras adelantaba lento y sinuoso de poste en poste, aspirando a enderezar el rumbo de su viaje desgobernado, restringir los embriagados pasos de minué a la incomprensible derechura de la acera, alzó la vista hasta encararse con la silueta negra de un gigantesco bloque. Guarecido bajo uno de los paraguas de luz que sujetaba y abría cada poste, Ciro observaba la fachada trasera del caserón. Un ángulo de la estructura le presentaba la ventana sin hojas del cuarto de Lencha, por la que entraban y salían murciélagos. Ciro se abrazaba más al poste y paseaba la mirada neblinosa desde la altura del mirador —con las ventanas encendidas— hasta la planta baja, pasando por los aleros y la escalera que trepaba en sesgo hacia la puerta de la cocina, y el par de ventanillas con rejas que pertenecía al reducido almacén de la tienda inundada. En el corazón apolillado de la casa imaginaba la hemeroteca, su hemeroteca, protegida de aguaceros y calores como la semilla en una fruta, y se preguntaba también por centésima vez en qué rincón cundiendo cucarachas y ratones se encontraría la pobre tatarabuela.

Tanta conmoción lo había llevado más temprano de la cuenta al cafetín. Ahora sentía que se expandía y se achicaba su cabeza golpeteándole latidos, pulsando corrientes de pensamiento por su sistema nervioso. En el cafetín no se hablaba de otra cosa que no fuese la proeza de los norteamericanos. Ciro conservaba la memoria imprecisa de su propia figura subida al mostrador del negocio, publicando un discurso enco-

miástico a favor de la ciencia. La clientela estaba familiariza-
da, desde hacía mucho tiempo, con los arrebatos de elocuencia periodística que lo poseían cuando se ajumaba, y aplau-
día animándolo para que prosiguiera.

Ciro dejó atrás dos postes después de tumbar, con un ban-
dazo que dio su cuerpo, un grupo de zafacones medio vacíos:
el estrépito de botellas rompiéndose y de lata magullada se regó por toda la calle haciendo eco en las de más allá, como si a
la vez otras personas hubieran derribado montones de basura.
De pronto, en un instante en que echaba algún vistazo de añadidura al perfil algo caído de la casa, quedó ofuscado por el
inesperado asomo de la luna llena —menos amarilla y crecida, como si al rozarse contra la noche se estuviese desgastan-
do— por encima del techo de cinc, que reflejaba un rayo de
luz blanqueada sobre el metal acanalado como en la superficie ondulada de un río. La luna, dijo Ciro alucinado. La
luna, repetía sin poder dejar de contemplarla. Y al andar un
poco más, todavía con los ojos como dardos que se clavaban
en el blanco redondel, cayó de boca sobre la cuneta por la
que corría el desagüe de algún edificio, y vio el resplandor lunar desbaratándose, yéndose con el agua que se estaba tragando la rejilla sucia del alcantarillado.

_____

Armonía Somers
1917
Uruguay

El hombre del túnel

Cuento para confesar y morir.

IBA saliendo de aquel maldito caño —un tubo de cemento
de no más de cincuenta centímetros de diámetro en el
que había tenido el coraje de meterme para atravesar la carretera— cuando lo conocí. Contaba entonces siete años. Eso explicará por qué, si es que se puede cruzar normalmente una
senda, alguien pensara en la angosta alcantarilla como vía. Y

que todo el sacrificio de aquel pasaje inaudito, agravado por
la curva de la bóveda, fuese para nada, absolutamente para y
por nada.

Reptando a duras penas, oliendo con todos los poros el
vaho pútrido de la resaca adherida a la superficie, logré alcanzar la mitad del tubo. Fue en ese preciso punto de caramelo
de la idiotez cuando sucedieron varias cosas, una de ellas completamente subjetiva: el pensar que pudiera aparecerse de golpe algo terrorífico, desde víbora a araña, siendo imposible el
giro completo del cuerpo, y debiéndose imaginar la marcha
atrás como una persecución frontal por el monstruo. Entonces, y ya instaurada para siempre la desgracia de la claustrofobia, se advirtieron estos dos leves indicios compensatorios:
ver aproximarse cada vez más la boca del caño a la punta de
mi lengua y vislumbrar los pies de un hombre, al parecer sentado sobre la hierba, según la posición de sus zapatos.

Es claro que ni por un momento caí en pensar que era yo
quien había estado buceando hacia todo, sino que las cosas se
vendrían de por sí, a fuerza de tanto desearlas. (Dios, yo nunca te tuve, al menos bajo esa forma de cómoda argolla de donde prenderse en casos extremos, ni siquiera como la cancela-
ción provisoria del miedo). Así, solamente asistida por una
imagen circular y dos pies desconocidos, fue cómo llegué a la
boca de la alcantarilla, hecha una rana bogando en seco, y ex-
ploré la cosa.

El hombre de las suelas, gruesas y claveteadas en forma
burda, estaba sentado, efectivamente. Pero no sobre la hierba,
sino en una piedra. Vestía de oscuro, llevaba un bigote caído
de retrato antiguo y tenía una ramita verde en la mano.

Mi salida del agujero no pareció sorprenderlo. Aun sin sacar todo el cuerpo, respirando fatigosamente y tatuada por la
mugre del caño, debí parecerle un gusano del estiércol que va
a tentar suerte al aire de los otros bichos. Pero él no hizo preguntas, no molestó con los famosos cómo te llamas ni cuántos años con que a uno lo rematan cuando es chico, y que
tantas veces no habrá más remedio que contestar mostrando la retaguardia en un gesto típico. Si acaso intentó algo fue sonreír. Pero con una sonrisa de miel que se desborda. Y elaborada al mismo tiempo con los desechos de su
propia soledad, quizás de su propio túnel, como siempre
que la ternura se quede virgen en esta extraña tierra del de-
sencuentro.

Entonces yo emergí del todo. Es decir, me incorporé en-
frentándolo. De nuevo volvió él a echarme por encima aquel

baño total de asentimiento, una especie de convivencia en la locura que me caló hasta los tiernos huesos.

Nadie en la vida había sido capaz de sonreírme en tal forma, debí pensar, no sólo completamente para mí tal una golosina barata cualquiera, sino como si se desplegase un arcoiris privado en un mundo vacío. Y casi alcancé a retribuírselo. Pero de pronto ocurre que uno es el hijo de la gran precaución. Hombre raro. Policía arrestando vagos. Nunca. Cuidado. Eran unas lacónicas expresiones de diccionario básico, pero que se las traían, como pequeños clavos con la punta hundida en la masa cerebral y las cabezas afuera haciendo de antenas en todas las direcciones del riesgo. Malbaraté, pues, el homenaje en cierne y salí a todo correr, cuanto me permitió el temblequeo de piernas.

El relato, balbuceado en medio de la fiebre en que caí estúpidamente, se repitió con demasía. Y así, sin que nadie se diera cuenta de lo que se estaba haciendo, me enseñaron que había en este mundo una cosa llamada violación. Algo terrorífico, según se lograba colegir viendo el asco pegado a las caras como las moscas en la basura. Pero que si, de acuerdo con mi propia versión del suceso, podría provenir de aquel hombre distinto que había sonreído para mí desde la piedra, debía ser otra historia. Violación, hombre dulce. Algo muy sucio de lo que ellos estarían de vuelta. Pero sin que nada tuviese que ver con mi asunto, divisible solamente por la unidad o sí mismo, como esos números anárquicos de la matemática elemental que no se dejan intervenir por otros. Tanto que supuse que violar a una niña sería como llevársela sobre un colchón de nubes, por encima de la tierra suspicaz, a un enorme granero celeste sin techo ni paredes. Y a estarse luego a lo que sucediera.

Así fue cómo la imagen inédita de mi hombre permaneció inconexa, tierna y desentendida de todo el enredo humano que había provocado. Detuvieron a unos cuantos vagabundos, y nada. Mi descripción no coincidía nunca con harapos, piojos, pelo largo, dientes amarillos. Hasta que un día decidí no hablar más. Me di cuenta de que eran unos idiotas crónicos, pobres palurdos sin aventura, incapaces de merecer la gracia de un ángel que nos asiste al salir del caño. Y todo quedó tranquilo. Pero eso no fue sino el prólogo. El reapareció muchas veces, se diría que siete, las suficientes para una completa terrenidad. Y aquí comienza la verdadera historia. El hombre de la acera de enfrente. El único que asistió a mi muerte. La revelación final del vacío.

Yo vivía entonces en una buhardilla. La había elegido por no tener nada encima ni a los costados, una especie de liberación inconsciente del túnel, por si esto fuera saber sicoanalizarse. Una vez, luego de cierta enfermedad bastante larga, abrí la ventana para regar unas macetas y lo vi. Sí, lo vi, y era el mismo. Con tantos años más encima, y no había cambiado ni de edad, ni de traje, ni siquiera de estilo en el bigote. Se hallaba parado junto a una columna y aunque nadie pudiese creerlo, tenía la misma ramita verde de diez o doce años atrás en la mano. Entonces yo pensé: esta vez será mío. Sólo que su imagen no tendrá profanadores, no irá a caer en los sucios anales del delito común, al menos siendo yo quien lo entregue... En ese preciso golpe mental de mi pensamiento, él levantó la cabeza, desde luego que reconociéndome, y volvió a sonreírme como en la boca del túnel. (Dios mío, haz que no se pierda de nuevo —dije agarrándome de la famosa argolla del ruego—. Otros tantos años del después no serían lo mismo. Sólo tiempo de bajar a decirle que yo no lo acusé. Y no únicamente eso, sino todo lo demás, las dulces historias que su presunta violación había sido capaz de provocar más tarde, en toda soledad que Tú desparramases bajo el cielo, cuando las horas eran propicias y las uvas maduraban en sus auténticos veranos...).

Tomé el teléfono y marqué el número del negocio vecino al lugar donde él había reaparecido.

—Perdone —dije contrariando mi repugnancia a este tipo de humillaciones— habla la estudiante que vive en el último piso de enfrente...

—Sí... ¿Y?

—Bueno, usted no lo podría comprender. Quiero, simplemente, que salga y diga a ese hombre vestido de oscuro y con una ramita en la mano que está junto a la columna, que la muchacha que regaba las macetas es aquella misma chiquilla del túnel. Y que ya baja a encontrarlo, que no vaya a perderse de nuevo a causa de los cinco pisos que deberá hacer para reunírsele. ¡Corra, se lo suplico!

—Nada más, ¿eh? —se atrevió a preguntar el tipo.

—Vaya de una vez —le ordené con una voz que no parecía salir de mis registros— lo espero sin cortar. ¡Es que ya no podrían pasar de nuevo los mismos años, nunca es el mismo tiempo el que pasa!

Mis incoherencias, la locura con que le estaría machacando el oído, lo hicieron salir a la calle. Le observé mirar hacia el punto preciso que yo había indicado, mover la cabeza negando, y aumentar después el área de reconocimiento. Al cabo de unos segundos, y mientras yo veía aún al forastero en la misma actitud, volvió con esta estúpida rendición de noticias:

—Oiga, ¿por qué no se guarda las bromas para otro? Junto a la columna no hay ningún tipo, ni nada que se le parezca. Esto no es un episodio del hombre invisible, qué diablos...

— ¡Bromas las que quiere hacer usted, no yo —le grité histéricamente— está aún ahí, lo sigo viendo!

—Eso si no agarró las de villadiego al ver que yo o usted lo habíamos pescado a punto de robarse mi bicicleta, ¿no?

— ¡Cállese, pedazo de bruto!

—O las de cruzar la calle, no más —agregó tomándose confianza— para trepar de cuatro en cuatro a su altillito... Porque yo siempre pienso que usted duerme ahí demasiado sola y que cualquiera sería capaz de ir a acompañarla con gusto...

Le corté el chorro sinfín de la estupidez con que amenazaba inundar el mundo. Y hasta descubrir quién sabría qué conexiones secretas con los demás, los de aquel tiempo que se me había ido perdiendo entre uno y otro año nuevo, llevándose sus caras. Por breves minutos de marcha atrás, volví a sentir mi aire abanicado por sus alientos, algunos como el del parto de las flores, pero otros tan iguales al de esas mismas flores cuando se pudren, que casi hubiera sobornado a la muerte para que se los arrastrara de nuevo.

Fue entonces cuando comprendí que jamás, en adelante, debería comunicar a nadie mi mensaje. Todo era capaz de quedar injuriado en el trayecto por el puente que ellos me tendían. Y en forma vaga llegué a intuir que ni yo misma estaría libre de caer en sus fabulaciones, que era necesario liberar también al hombre de mi propio favor simbólico, tan basto como el de cualquiera.

Cerrado, pues, el trato definitivo, y mientras él seguía en la misma actitud de contemplación, sin enterarse siquiera de que el dueño de la bicicleta la sacaba del apoyo de la columna llevándosela al interior de la tienda, yo salí como una sonámbula hacia la escalera.

Iría, quizás, hablando sola, o contraviniendo la velocidad normal, o en ambas cosas a la vez, cuando la mujer de color indefinido que subía resoplando con un bolso lleno de provisiones en la mano, se interpuso en mi camino. Ya antes de pretender su prioridad, se me había hecho presente con un olor como de escoba mojada con que traía inundado el pasillo. La estaba imaginando en una pata, yéndose a la oscuridad de la

rinconera a colgarse sola por una argollita de hilo sucio que
ella misma se habría atado en la ranura del cuello, cuando per-
sistió en tomarse toda la anchura del pasaje. Luchábamos por
el espacio vital, sin palabras, a puro instinto de conservar lo
más caro, ella su vocación de estropajo, yo la boca del túnel
donde iba a hallar de nuevo algo que me pertenecía, cuando
no tuve más remedio que empujar. Sí, empujar, qué otra cosa. Dos veces no va uno a dejarse interferir por nadie, mientras hace equilibrios en la cuerda tirante del destino sobre las
pequeñas cabezas de los que miran de abajo. Y llegó ella primero que yo, es claro. Cuando la volví a ver en el último descanso, mirándome fijamente con dos ojos de vidrio entre el
desparramo de sus hortalizas, ya era tarde. El hombre había
desaparecido. No diré que para siempre. Mas su periodicidad,
contándose desde mi violación a mi primer crimen, luego a las
otras menudencias de las que él fue también principal testigo,
y en las que siempre los demás actuaban de desencadenantes,
se me llevó pedazos de la pobre vida que nos han dado. Es
que uno merodea por años alrededor de ese algo que nos van
a quitar, y luego hasta tiene valor para esperar a que el vino se
ponga viejo. Así, cuando mucho tiempo después cambié las
escaleras por ascensor automático, y nadie supo en el piso de
dónde venía la mudanza, casi llegué a saludar a una mujer parecida a mí que se echaba hacia atrás los cabellos en un espejo del pasillo. Dios mío, iba a decir ya como alguna otra vez
en las apuradas. Pero recordé de pronto el peor y el mejor de
mis trabajos, aquel de quitarle limpiamente su hombre a una
prójima desconocida. Y decidí que mi pelo ya desvitalizado
era una cosa de poca monta para andar a los golpes en la última puerta en busca de lástima.

Hasta que cierto atardecer lluvioso, no podría decir cuánto tiempo después, el hombre del túnel volvió a aparecer en
esa y no otra acera de enfrente, con el olfato de un perro ma-
níaco que anduviera de por vida tras la pieza. Entonces yo decidí que nada en este mundo podría impedirme ya que me
precipitase a su encuentro definitivo. Estaba así, sin interme-
diarios de ninguna especie, apretando el botón de la jaula,
cuando vi recostada a la pared la escalera de emergencia.

—Eso es, lo de siempre —farfullé— la atracción invencible
del caño, aunque la senda normal sea ahora ésta que va y viene verticalmente con su incuestionable eficacia propia.

De pronto, y mientras la puerta del ascensor se abría de
por sí como un sexo acostumbrado, el pasamanos grasiento
de la escalera se me volvió a insinuar con la sugestión de un

fauno tras los árboles. El minuto justo para cerrarse la puerta de nuevo. Y yo hacia atrás de la memoria, cabalgando en los pasamanos, tal como alguien debió inventarlos para los incipientes orgasmos, que después se apoderan de las entrañas en sazón, hasta terminar achicándose en los climaterios como trapo quemado.

— ¡Sí! —grité de golpe, completamente libre ya de toda carga, incluso la de los otros, que también soportan lo suyo encima.

Aquel sí colgado del vacío, sin más significación que la de su arrasamiento, se quedó unos instantes girando en el aire de la caja con otros sí más pequeños que le habían salido de todo el cuerpo y me acompañaron hasta la puerta. Crucé luego la calle con el mismo vértigo con que había cabalgado la escalera, ajena a la intención de las ruedas que se me venían como si el mundo entero hubiese enfilado sus carros en busca de mis vísceras. Yo estaba sorda y ciega a todo lo que no fuera mi objetivo, el abrazo consustancial del hombre de la ramita verde que seguía parado allí, sin edad, omiso ante la obligación de correr como un loco detrás del tiempo. Fue entonces cuando pude ver fugazmente cómo el violador de criaturas, el ladrón, el asesino, el que codicia lo que no le fue dado, y el todo lo demás que puede ser quien ha nacido, abría los brazos hacia mí. Pero en una protección que no se alcanza si las ruedas de un vehículo llegaron primero. Lo vi tanto y tan poco que no puedo describirlo. Era como un paisaje tras los vidrios del tren expreso, con detalles que nunca se conocerán, pero que igualmente aterciopelan la piel o la erizan de punta a punta.

—Gracias por la invención de las siete caídas —alcancé a decirle viendo rodar mi lengua como una flor monopétala sobre el pavimento.

Entré así otra vez en el túnel. Un agujero negro bárbaramente excavado en la roca infinita. Y a sus innumerables salidas, siempre una piedra puesta de través cerca de la boca. Pero ya sin el hombre. O la consagración del absoluto y desesperado vacío.

Pedro Juan Soto
1928—
Puerto Rico

Los inocentes
Spiks, 1956.

NO recuerdo escrito mío que me haya provocado más dolor que el que obtuve de "Los inocentes". Veía a diario
al individuo que me hizo idear a Pipe. Lo imaginaba de regreso en Puerto Rico y sabía que no sobreviviría. Lo imaginaba
en una playa tropical y estaba seguro de que al cabo de un
rato de sol desearía zumbarse al mar, cosa que lo conduciría
a la muerte voluntaria o accidental.

Fue penoso, aunque no trágico, el envío de Pipe a un manicomio del estado de Nueva York. Al final de un año de reclusión —tal vez dos—, su madre lo trajo a Puerto Rico. Sobre-
vivió diez años esa mudanza. Se derrumbó, de buenas a primeras, y nadie logró volver a despertarlo. Su madre tardó poco en seguirlo a la tumba.

Escribir este cuento y enfrentarme a la censura de amistades y parientes fue una sola cosa. Todos temían la revelación de unos hechos aparentemente comprometedores. Me
di cuenta, entonces, de que yo habría de escribir siempre sin
respeto hacia los censores. Intentaba en este cuento dar testimonio de la vida puertorriqueña en Nueva York. No sabía si
otra vez podría aunar de una vez la familia, el sufrimiento, la
economía de palabras, mi propio dolor recatado.

Faulkner pesa como una sombra en la narración. Eso lo
vi tarde. Me hallaba ofuscado por la experiencia, y durante
muchos años me negué a releer lo ocurrido con Pipe. Si bien
me preocupan, ahora mismo, las resonancias de The Sound
and the Fury *en este cuento, no estoy seguro de que lograría dar con otra manera de contarlo de nuevo.*

1

*treparme frente al sol en aquella nube con las palomas
sin caballos sin mujeres y no oler cuando queman los cacho-
rros en el solar sin gente que me haga burla.*

Desde la ventana, vistiendo el traje hecho y vendido para contener a un hombre que no era él, veía las palomas revolotear en el alero de enfrente.

o con puertas y ventanas siempre abiertas tener alas.

Comenzaba a agitar las manos y a hacer ruido como las palomas cuando oyó la voz a sus espaldas.

—Nene, nene.

La mujer acartonada estaba sentada a la mesa (debajo estaba la maleta de tapas frágiles, con una cuerda alrededor por única lleve), y le observaba con sus ojos vivos, derrumbada en la silla como una gata hambrienta y abandonada.

—Pan —dijo él.

Dándole un leve empujón a la mesa, la mujer retiró la silla y fue a la alacena. Sacó el trozo de pan que estaba al descubierto sobre las cajas de arroz y se lo llevó al hombre, que seguía manoteando y haciendo ruido.

ser paloma

—No hagah ruido, Pipe.

El desmoronó el trozo de pan sobre el alféizar, sin hacer caso.

—No hagah ruido, nene.

Los hombres que jugaban dominó bajo el toldo de la bodega ya miraban hacia arriba.

El dejó de sacudir la lengua.

sin gente que me haga burla

—A pasiar a la plaza —dijo.

—Sí, Holtensia viene ya pa sacalte a pasiar.

—A la plaza.

—No, a la plaza no. Se la llevaron. Voló.

El hizo pucheros. Atendió de nuevo al revoloteo de las palomas.

no hay plaza

—No, no fueron lah palomah —dijo ella—. Fue el malo, el diablo.

—Ah.

—Hay que pedirle a Papadioh que traiga la plaza.

—Papadioh —dijo él mirando hacia fuera—, trai la plaza y el río...

—No, no. Sin abrir la boca —dijo ella—. Arrodíllate y háblale a Papadioh sin abrir la boca.

El se arrodilló frente al alféizar y enlazó las manos y miró por encima de las azoteas.

yo quiero ser paloma

Ella miró hacia abajo: al ocio de los hombres en la mañana del sábado y al ajetreo de las mujeres en la ida o la vuelta del mercado.

2

Lenta, pesarosa, pero erguida, como si balanceara un bulto en la cabeza, echó a andar hacia la habitación donde la otra, delante del espejo, se quitaba los ganchos del pelo y los amontonaba sobre el tocador.

—No te lo lleveh hoy, Holtensia.

La otra miró de reojo.

—No empieceh otra veh, mamá. No le va pasal na. Lo cuidan bien y no noh cuehta.

Saliendo de los ganchos, el cabello se hacía una mota negra sobre las orejas.

—Pero si yo lo sé cuidal. Eh mi hijo. ¿Quién mejol que yo?

Hortensia estudió en el espejo la figura magra y menuda.

—Tu ehtáh vieja, mamá.

Una mano descarnada se alzó en el espejo.

—Todavía no ehtoy muerta. Todavía puedo velar por él.

—No eh eso.

Los bucles seguían apelmazados a pesar de que ella trataba de aflojárselos con el peine.

—Pipe'h inocente —dijo la madre, haciendo de las palabras agua para un mar de lástima—. Eh un nene.

Hortensia echó el peine a un lado. Sacó un lápiz del bolso que mantenía abierto sobre el tocador y comenzó a ennegrecer las cejas escasas.

—Eso no se cura —dijo al espejo—. Tú lo sabeh. Por eso lo mejor...

—En Puerto Rico no hubiera pasao ehto.

—En Puerto Rico era dihtinto —dijo Hortensia, hablando por encima del hombro—. Lo conocía la gente. Podía salir porque lo conocía la gente. Pero en Niu Yol la gente no se ocupa y uno no conoce al vecino. La vida eh dura. Yo me paso los añoh cose que cose y todavía sin casalme.

Buscando el lápiz labial, vio en el espejo cómo se descomponía el rostro de la madre.

—Pero no eh por eso tampoco. El ehtá mejol atendío allá.

—Eso diceh tú —dijo la madre.

Hortensia tiró los lápices y el peine dentro del bolso y lo cerró. Se dio vuelta: blusa porosa, labios grasientos, cejas tiznadas, bucles apelmazados.

—Dehpuéh di un año aquí, merecemoh algo mejor.

—El no tiene la culpa de lo que noh pase a nosotrah.

—Pero si se queda aquí, la va tenel. Fíjate.

Se abalanzó sobre la madre para cogerle un brazo y alzarle la manga que no pasaba del codo. Sobre los ligamentos caídos había una mancha morada.

—Tí ha levantao ya la mano y yo en la factoría no estoy tranquila pensando qué'htará pasando contigo y con él. Y si ya pasao ehto...

—Fue sin querel —dijo la madre, bajando la manga y mirando al piso al mismo tiempo que torcía el brazo para que Hortensia la soltara.

—¿Sin querel y te tenía una mano en el cuello? Si no agarro la botella, sabe Dioh. Aquí no hay un hombre que li haga frente y yo m'ehtoy acabando, mamá, y tú le tieneh miedo.

—Eh un nene —dijo la madre con su voz mansa, ahuyentando el cuerpo como un caracol.

Hortensia entornaba los ojos.

—No vengah con eso. Yo soy joven y tengo la vida por delante y él no. Tú también ehtáh cansá y si él se fuera podríah vivil mejor los añoh que te quedan y tú lo sabeh pero no ti atreveh a decirlo porque creeh que'h malo pero yo lo digo por ti *tú ehtáh cansá* y por eso filmahte loh papeleh porque sabeh que'n ese sitio lo atienden máh bien y tu entonceh podráh sentalte a ver la gente pasar por la calle y cuando te dé la gana puedeh pararte y salir a pasiar como elloh pero prefiereh creer que'h un crimen y que *yo* soy la criminal pa tú quedar como madre sufrida y *hah sido una madre sufrida* eso no se te puede quital pero tieneh que pensar en ti y en mí. Que si el caballo lo tumbó a loh diez añoh...

La madre salía a pasos rápidos, como empujada, como si la habitación misma la soplara fuera, mientras Hortensia decía:

—... y los otroh veinte los ha vivío así tumbao...

Y se volvía para verla salir, sin ir tras ella, tirándose sobre el tocador donde ahora sentía que sus puños martillaban un compás para su casi grito.

—... nosotroh loh hemoh vivío con él.

Y venía en el espejo el histérico dibujo de carnaval que era su rostro.

3

y no hay gallos y no hay perros y no hay campanas y no hay viento del río y no hay timbre de cine y el sol no entra aquí y no me gusta

—Ya —dijo la madre inclinándose para barrer con las manos las migajas del alféizar. La muchachería azotaba y perseguía una pelota de goma en la calle.

y la frialdad duerme se sienta camina con uno aquí dentro y no me gusta

—Ya, nene, ya. Di amén.

—Amén.

Lo ayudó a incorporarse y le puso el sombrero con la mano, viendo que ya Hortensia, seria y con los ojos irritados, venía hacia ellos.

—Vamoh, Pipe. Dali un beso a mamá.

Puso el bolso en la mesa y se dobló para recoger la maleta. La madre se abalanzó al cuello de él —las manos como tenazas— y besó el rostro de avellana chamuscada y pasó los dedos sobre la piel que había afeitado esta mañana.

—Vamoh —dijo Hortensia cargando bolso y maleta.

El se deshizo de los brazos de la madre y caminó hacia la puerta meciendo la mano que llevaba el sombrero.

—Nene, ponte'l sombrero —dijo la madre, y parpadeó para que él no viera las lágrimas.

Dándose vuelta, él alzó y dejó encima del cabello envaselinado aquello que por lo chico parecía un juguete, aquello que quería compensar el desperdicio de tela en el traje.

—No, que lo deje aquí —dijo Hortensia.

Pipe hizo pucheros. La madre tenía los ojos fijos en Hortensia y la mandíbula le temblaba.

—Ehtá bien —dijo Hortensia—, llévalo en la mano.

El volvió a caminar hacia la puerta y la madre lo siguió, encogiéndose un poco ahora y conteniendo los brazos que querían estirarse hacia él.

Hortensia la detuvo.

—Mamá, lo van a cuidal.

—Que no lo mal...

—No. Hay medicoh. Y tú... cada do semanah. Yo te llevo.

Ambas se esforzaban por mantener firme la voz.

—Recuéhtate, mamá.

—Dile que se quede... no haga ruido y que coma de to.

—Sí.

Hortensia abrió la puerta y miró fuera para ver si Pipe se había detenido en el rellano. El se entretenía escupiendo sobre la baranda de la escalera y viendo caer la saliva.

—Yo vengo temprano, mamá.

La madre estaba junto a la silla que ya sobraba, intentando ver al hijo a través del cuerpo que bloqueaba la entrada.

—Recuéhtate, mamá.

La madre no respondió. Con las manos enlazadas enfrente, estuvo rígida hasta que el pecho y los hombros se convulsionaron y comenzó a salir el llanto hiposo y delicado.

Hortensia tiró la puerta y bajó con Pipe a toda prisa. Y ante la inmensa claridad de un mediodía de junio, quiso huracanes y eclipses y nevadas.

Hernando Téllez
1908–1964
Colombia

Espuma y nada más
Cenizas para el viento y otras historias, 1950.

NO saludó al entrar. Yo estaba repasando sobre una badana la mejor de mis navajas. Y cuando lo reconocí me puse a temblar. Pero él no se dio cuenta. Para disimular continué repasando la hoja. La probé luego sobre la yema del dedo gordo y volví a mirarla contra la luz. En ese instante se quitaba el cinturón ribeteado de balas de donde pendía la funda de la pistola. Lo colgó de uno de los clavos del ropero y encima colocó el kepis. Volvió completamente el cuerpo para hablarme, y deshaciendo el nudo de la corbata, me dijo: "Hace un calor de todos los demonios. Aféitame." Y se sentó en la silla. Le calculé cuatro días de barba. Los cuatro días de la última excursión en busca de los nuestros. El rostro aparecía quemado, curtido por el sol. Me puse a preparar minuciosamente el jabón. Corté unas rebanadas de la pasta, dejándolas caer en el recipiente, mezclé un poco de agua tibia y con la brocha empecé a revolver. Pronto subió la espuma. "Los muchachos de la tropa deben tener tanta barba como yo." Seguí batiendo la espuma. "Pero nos fue bien, ¿sabe? Pescamos a los principales. Unos vienen muertos y otros todavía viven. Pero pronto estarán todos muertos." "¿Cuántos cogieron?", pregunté.

"Catorce. Tuvimos que internarnos bastante para dar con ellos. Pero ya la están pagando. Y no se salvará ni uno, ni uno." Se echó para atrás en la silla al verme con la brocha en la mano rebosante de espuma. Faltaba ponerle la sábana. Ciertamente yo estaba aturdido. Extraje del cajón una sábana y la anudé al cuello de mi cliente. El no cesaba de hablar. Suponía que yo era uno de los partidarios del orden. "El pueblo habrá escarmentado con lo del otro día", dijo. "Sí", repuse mientras concluía de hacer el nudo sobre la oscura nuca, olorosa a sudor. "¿Estuvo bueno, verdad?" "Muy bueno", contesté mientras regresaba a la brocha. El hombre cerró los ojos con un gesto de fatiga y esperó así la fresca caricia del jabón. Jamás lo había tenido tan cerca de mí. El día en que ordenó que el pueblo desfilara por el patio de la Escuela para ver a los cuatro rebeldes allí colgados, me crucé con él un instante. Pero el espectáculo de los cuerpos mutilados me impedía fijarme en el rostro del hombre que lo dirigía todo y que ahora iba a tomar en mis manos. No era un rostro desagradable, ciertamente. Y la barba, envejeciéndolo un poco, no le caía mal. Se llamaba Torres. El capitán Torres. Un hombre con imaginación, porque, ¿a quién se le había ocurrido antes colgar a los rebeldes desnudos y luego ensayar sobre determinados sitios del cuerpo una mutilación a bala? Empecé a extender la primera capa de jabón. El seguía con los ojos cerrados. "De buena gana me iría a dormir un poco", dijo; "pero esta tarde hay mucho que hacer". Retiré la brocha y pregunté con aire falsamente desinteresado: "¿Fusilamiento?" "Algo por el estilo, pero más lento", respondió. "¿Todos?" "No. Unos cuantos apenas." Reanudé de nuevo la tarea de enjabonarle la barba. Otra vez me temblaban las manos. El hombre no podía darse cuenta de ello y ésa era mi ventaja. Pero yo hubiera querido que él no viniera. Probablemente muchos de los nuestros lo habrían visto entrar. Y el enemigo en la casa impone condiciones. Yo tendría que afeitar esa barba como cualquiera otra, con cuidado, con esmero, como la de un buen parroquiano, cuidando de que ni por un solo poro fuese a brotar una gota de sangre. Cuidando de que en los pequeños remolinos no se desviara la hoja. Cuidando de que la piel quedara limpia, templada, pulida, y de que al pasar el dorso de mi mano por ella, sintiera la superficie sin un pelo. Sí. Yo era un revolucionario clandestino, pero era también un barbero de conciencia, orgulloso de la pulcritud en su oficio. Y esa barba de cuatro días se prestaba para una buena faena.

Tomé la navaja, levanté en ángulo oblicuo las dos cachas,

dejé libre la hoja y empecé la tarea, de una de las patillas hacia abajo. La hoja respondía a la perfección. El pelo se presentaba indócil y duro, no muy crecido, pero compacto. La piel iba apareciendo poco a poco. Sonaba la hoja con su ruido característico, y sobre ella crecían los grumos de jabón mezclados con trocitos de pelo. Hice una pausa para limpiarla, tomé la badana de nuevo y me puse a asentar el acero, porque yo soy un barbero que hace bien sus cosas. El hombre que había mantenido los ojos cerrados, los abrió, sacó una de las manos por encima de la sábana, se palpó la zona del rostro que empezaba a quedar libre de jabón, y me dijo: "Venga usted a las seis, esta tarde, a la Escuela". "¿Lo mismo del otro día?", le pregunté horrorizado. "Puede que resulte mejor", respondió. "¿Qué piensa usted hacer?" "No sé todavía. Pero nos divertiremos." Otra vez se echó hacia atrás y cerró los ojos. Yo me acerqué con la navaja en alto. "¿Piensa castigarlos a todos?", aventuré tímidamente. "A todos." El jabón se secaba sobre la cara. Debía apresurarme. Por el espejo, miré hacia la calle. Lo mismo de siempre: la tienda de víveres y en ella dos o tres compradores. Luego miré el reloj: las dos y veinte de la tarde. La navaja seguía descendiendo. Ahora de la otra patilla hacia abajo. Una barba azul, cerrada. Debía dejársela crecer como algunos poetas o como algunos sacerdotes. Le quedaría bien. Muchos no lo reconocerían. Y mejor para él, pensé, mientras trataba de pulir suavemente todo el sector del cuello. Porque allí sí que debía manejar con habilidad la hoja, pues el pelo, aunque en agraz, se enredaba en pequeños remolinos. Una barba crespa. Los poros podían abrirse, diminutos, y soltar su perla de sangre. Un buen barbero como yo finca su orgullo en que eso no ocurra a ningún cliente. Y éste era un cliente de calidad. ¿A cuántos de los nuestros había ordenado matar? ¿A cuántos de los nuestros había ordenado que los mutilaran?... Mejor no pensarlo. Torres no sabía que yo era su enemigo. No lo sabía él ni lo sabían los demás. Se trataba de un secreto entre muy pocos, precisamente para que yo pudiese informar a los revolucionarios de lo que Torres estaba haciendo en el pueblo y de lo que proyectaba hacer cada vez que emprendía una excursión para cazar revolucionarios. Iba a ser, pues, muy difícil explicar que yo lo tuve entre mis manos y lo dejé ir tranquilamente, vivo y afeitado.

La barba le había desaparecido casi completamente. Parecía más joven, con menos años de los que llevaba a cuestas cuando entró. Yo supongo que eso ocurre siempre con los hombres que entran y salen de las peluquerías. Bajo el golpe de mi navaja Torres rejuvenecía, sí, porque yo soy un buen barbero, el mejor de este pueblo, lo digo sin vanidad. Un poco más de jabón, aquí, bajo la barbilla, sobre la manzana, sobre esta gran vena. ¡Qué calor! Torres debe estar sudando como yo. Pero él no tiene miedo. Es un hombre sereno que ni siquiera piensa en lo que ha de hacer esta tarde con los prisioneros. En cambio yo, con esta navaja entre las manos, puliendo y puliendo esta piel, evitando que brote sangre de estos poros, cuidando todo golpe, no puedo pensar serenamente. Maldita la hora en que vino, porque yo soy un revolucionario pero no soy un asesino. Y tan fácil como resultaría matarlo. Y lo merece. ¿Lo merece? No, ¡qué diablos! Nadie merece que los demás hagan el sacrificio de convertirse en asesinos. ¿Qué se gana con ello? Pues nada. Vienen otros y otros y los primeros matan a los segundos y éstos a los terceros y siguen y siguen hasta que todo es un mar de sangre. Yo podía cortar este cuello, así, ¡zas!, ¡zas! No le daría tiempo de quejarse y como tiene los ojos cerrados no vería ni el brillo de la navaja ni el brillo de mis ojos. Pero estoy temblando como un verdadero asesino. De ese cuello brotaría un chorro de sangre sobre la sábana, sobre la silla, sobre mis manos, sobre el suelo. Tendría que cerrar la puerta. Y la sangre seguiría corriendo por el piso, tibia, imborrable, incontenible, hasta la calle, como un pequeño arroyo escarlata. Estoy seguro de que un golpe fuerte, una honda incisión, le evitaría todo dolor. No sufriría. ¿Y qué hacer con el cuerpo? ¿Dónde ocultarlo? Yo tendría que huir, dejar estas cosas, refugiarme lejos, bien lejos. Pero me perseguirían hasta dar conmigo. "El asesino del Capitán Torres. Lo degolló mientras le afeitaba la barba. Una cobardía." Y por otro lado: "El vengador de los nuestros. Un hombre para recordar (aquí mi nombre). Era el barbero del pueblo. Nadie sabía que él defendía nuestra causa..." ¿Y qué? ¿Asesino o héroe? Del filo de esta navaja depende mi destino. Puedo inclinar un poco más la mano, apoyar un poco más la hoja, y hundirla. La piel cederá como la seda, como el caucho, como la badana. No hay nada más tierno que la piel del hombre y la sangre siempre está ahí, lista a brotar. Una navaja como ésta no traiciona. Es la mejor de mis navajas. Pero yo no quiero ser un asesino, no señor. Usted vino para que yo lo afeitara. Y yo cumplo honradamente con mi trabajo... No quiero mancharme de sangre. De espuma y nada más. Usted es un verdugo y yo no soy más que un barbero. Y cada cual en su puesto. Eso es. Cada cual en su puesto.

La barba había quedado limpia, pulida y templada. El hombre se incorporó para mirarse en el espejo. Se pasó las manos por la piel y la sintió fresca y nuevecita.

"Gracias", dijo. Se dirigió al ropero en busca del cinturón, de la pistola y del kepis. Yo debía estar muy pálido y sentía la camisa empapada. Torres concluyó de ajustar la hebilla, rectificó la posición de la pistola en su funda y, luego de alisarse maquinalmente los cabellos, se puso el kepis. Del bolsillo del pantalón extrajo unas monedas para pagarme el importe del servicio. Y empezó a caminar hacia la puerta. En el umbral se detuvo un segundo y volviéndose me dijo:

"Me habían dicho que usted me mataría. Vine a comprobarlo. Pero matar no es fácil. Yo sé por qué se lo digo." Y siguió calle abajo.

Ana Lydia Vega
1947—
Puerto Rico

Letra para salsa y tres soneos por encargo
Vírgenes y mártires, 1981

> *La vida te da sorpresas,*
> *sorpresas te da la vida...*
>
> Rubén Blades

E N la De Diego fiebra la fiesta patronal de nalgas. Rotundas en sus pantis super-look, imponentes en perfil de falda tubo, insurgentes bajo el fascismo de la faja, abismales, olímpicas, nucleares, surcan las aceras riopedrenses como invencibles aeronaves nacionales.

Entre el culipandeo, más intenso que un arrebato colombiano, más perseverante que Somoza, el Tipo rastrea a la Tipa, Fiel como una procesión de Semana Santa con su rosario de qué buena estás, mamichulin, qué bien te ves, qué ricos te quedan esos pantaloncitos, qué chula está esa hembrota, men, qué canto e silán, tanta carne y yo comiendo hueso...

La verdad es que la Tipa está buena. Se le transparenta el brassiere. Se le marca el Triándulo de las Bermudas a cada temblequeo de taco fino. Pero la verdad es también que el Tipo transaría hasta por un palo de mapo disfrazado de pelotero.

Adiossss preciosssssa, se desinfla el Tipo en sensuales sibilancias, arrimando peligrosamente el hocico a los technicolores rizos de la perseguida. La cual acelera automática y, con un remeneo de nalgas en high, pone momentáneamente a salvo su virtud.

Pero el salsero solitario vuelve al pernil, soneando sin tregua: qué chasis, negra, qué masetera estás, qué materia prima, qué tronco e jeva, qué zocos, mama, quién fuera lluvia pa caelte encima.

Dos días bíblicos dura el asedio. Dos días de cabecidura persecución y encocorante cantaleta. Dos luengos días de qué chulería, trigueña, si te mango te hago leña, qué bestia esa hembra, sea mi vida, por ti soy capaz hasta de trabajal, pa quién te estarás guardando en nevera, abusadora.

Al tercer día, frente por frente a Almacenes Pitusa y al toque de sofrito de mediodía, la víctima coge impulso, gira espectacular sobre sus precarios tacones y: encestaaaaaaaaaa:

—¿Vamos?

El jinete, desmontado por su montura da una vuelta de carnero emocional. Pero, dispuesto a todo por salvar la virilidad patria, cae de pie al instante y dispara, traicionado por la gramática:

—Mande.

La Tipa encabeza ahora solemnemente la parada. En el parking de la Plaza del Mercado janguea un Ford Torino rojo metálico del '69. Se montan. Arrancan. La radio aúlla un bolero senil. La Tipa guía con una mano en el volante y otra en la ventana, con un airecito de no querer la cosa. El Tipo se pone a desear violentamente un apartamento de soltero con vista al mar, especie de discoteca-matadero donde procesar ese material prime que le llueve a uno como cupón gratuito de la vida. Pero el desempleo no ceba sueños y el Tipo se flagela por dentro con que si lo llego a saber a tiempo le allano el cuarto a Papo Quisqueya, pana de Ultramona, bródel de billar, cuate de jumas y jevas, perico de altas notas. Dita sea, concluye fatal. Y esgrimiendo su rictus más telenovel, trata de soltar con naturalidad:

—Coge pa Piñones.

Pero agarrando la carretera de Caguas como si fuera un dorado muslo de Kentucky-fried chicken, la Tipa se apunta otro canasto tácito.

La entrada al motel yace oculta en la maleza. Ambiente de guerrilla. El Torino se desliza vaselinoso por el caminito estrecho. El empleado saluda de lejitos, mira coolmente hacia adelante cual engringolado equino. El carro se amocola en el garage. Baja la Tipa. El Tipo trata de abrir la puerta del carro sin levantar el seguro, hercúlea empresa. Por fin aterriza en nombre del Homo Sapiens.

La llave está clavada en la cerradura. Entran. Ella enciende la luz. Neón inmisericorde, delator de barros y espinillas. El Tipo se trinca de golpe ante la mano negra y abierta del empleado protuberando ventanilla adentro. Se acuerda del vacío interplanetario de su billetera. Minuto secular y agónico al cabo del cual la Tipa deposita cinco pesos en la mano negra que se cierra como ostra ofendida y desaparece, volviendo a reaparecer de inmediato. Voz roncona tipo Godfather:

—Son siete. Faltan dos.

La Tipa suspira, rebusca en la cartera, saca lipstick, compacto, cepillo, máscara, kleenex, base, sombra, bolígrafo, perfume, panti bikini de encaje negro, Tampax, desodorante, cepillo de dientes, fotonovela y dos pesos que echa como par de huesos a la mano insaciable. El Tipo siente la obligación histórico-social de comentar:

—La calle ta dura, ¿ah?

Desde el baño llega la catarata de la pluma abierta. El cuarto tiene cara de closet. Pero espejos por todas partes. Cama de media plaza. Sábanas limpias aunque sufridas. Cero almohada. Bombilla roja sobre cabecera. El Tipo como que se friquea pensando en la cantidad de gente que habrá sonrojado esa bombilla chillona, toda la bellaquería nacional que habrá desembocado allí, los cuadrazos que se habrá gufeado ese espejo, todos los brincoteos que habrá aguantado esa cama. El Tipo parquea el cráneo en la Plaza de la Convalescencia, bien nombrada por las huestes de enfermitos que allí hallan su cura cotidiana, oh, Plaza de la Convalescencia donde el espaceo de los panas se hace rito tribal. Ahora le toca a él y lo que va a espepitar no es campaña electoral. Se cuadra frente al grupo, pasea, va y viene, sube y baja en su montura épica: La Tipa estaba más dura que el corazón de un mafioso, mano. Yo no hice más que mirarla y se me volvió merengue allí mismo. Me la llevé pa un motel, men, ahora le tumban a uno siete cocos por un polvillo.

La Tipa sale del baño. Con un guille de diosa bastante merecido. Esnuíta. Tremenda india. La Chacón era chumba, bródel.

—¿Y tú no te piensas quitar la ropa? truena Guabancex desde las alturas precolombinas del Yunque.

El Tipo pone manos a la obra. Cae la camiseta. Cae la correa. Cae el pantalón. La Tipa se recuesta para ligarte mejor. Cae por fin el calzoncillo con el peso metálico de un cinturón de castidad. Teledirigido desde la cama, un proyectil clausura el strip-tease. El Tipo lo cachea en el aire. Es —oh pudor— un condescendiente condón. Y de los indesechables.

En el baño saturado de King Pine, el macho cabrío se faja con la naturaleza. Quiere entrar en todo su esplendor bélico. Cerebros retroactivos no ayudan. Peles a través de puerta entreabierta: nada. Pantis negros de maestra de estudios sociales: nada. Gringa soleándose tetas Family Size en azotea: nada. Pareja sobándose de A a Z en la última fila del cine Paradise: nada. Estampida de mujeres rozadas en calles, deseadas, desfloradas a cráneo limpio; repaso de revistas Luz, Pimienta embotelladas; incomparables páginas del medio de Playboy, rewind, replay; viejas frases de guerra caliente: crucifícame, negrito, destrúyeme, papi, hazme papilla, papote. Pero: nada. No hay brujo que levante ese muerto.

La Tipa llama. Clark Kent busca en vano la salida de emergencia. Su traje de Supermán está en el laundry.

*   *   *

En una humareda de Malboro, la Tipa reza sus últimas oraciones. La suerte está como quien dice echada y ella embollada en el despojo sin igual de la vida. Desde la boda de Héctor con aquella blanquita comemierda del Condado, el hímen pesa como un crimen. Siete años a la merced de un dentista mamito. Siete años de rellenar caries y raspar sarro. Siete años de contemplar gargantas espatarradas, de respirar alientos de pozo séptico a cambio de una guiñada, un piropo mongo, un roce de mariposa, una esperanza yerta. Pero hoy estalla el convento. Hoy cogen el vuelo de tomateros los votos de castidad. La Tipa cambia el canal y sintoniza al Tipo que el destino le ha vendido en baratillo: tapón, regordete, afro de peineta erecta, T-shirt rojo pava y mahones ultimatum. La verdad es que años luz de sus más platinados sueños de asistente dental. Pero la verdad es también que el momento histórico está ahí, tumbándole la puerta como un marido borracho, que se le está haciendo tarde y ya la guagua pasó, que entre Vietnam y la emigración queda el racionamiento, que la estadidad es para los pobres, que si no yoguea engorda y que después de todo el arma importa menos que la detonación. Así es que: todo está científicamente programado. Hasta el transistor que ahogará sus gritos vestales. Y tras un debut en sociedad sin lentejuelas ni canutillos, el velo impenetrable del anonimato habrá de tragarse por siempre el portátil parejo de emergencia.

De pronto, óyese un grito desgarrador. La Tipa embala hacia el baño. El Tipo cabalga de medio ganchete sobre el bidet, más jincho que un gringo en febrero. Al verla, cae al suelo, epilépticamente contorsionado y gimiendo como ánima en pena. Pataleos, contracciones, etcétera. Pugilato progresivo de la Tipa ante la posibilidad cada vez más posible de haberse enredado con un tecato, con un drogo irredento. Cuando los gemidos se vuelven casi estertores, la Tipa pregunta prudentemente si debe llamar al empleado. Como por arte de magia cesan las lamentaciones. El Tipo se endereza, arrullándose materno los chichos adoloridos.

—Estoy malo del estómago, dice con mirada de perrito sarnoso a encargado de la perrera.

Soneo I

Primeros auxilios. Respiración boca a boca. Acariciando la pancita en crisis, la Tipa rompe con un rapeo florecido de materialismo histórico y de sociedad sin clases. Fricción vigorosa de dictadura del proletariado. Recital aleluya del Programa del Partido. El Tipo experimenta el fortalecimiento gradual, a corta, mediana y larga escala, de su conciencia lirona. Se unionan. Emocionados entonan al unísono la Internacional mientras sus infraestructuras se conmocionan. La naturaleza acude al llamado de las masas movilizadas y el acto queda dialécticamente consumado.

Soneo II

La tipa confronta heavyduty al Tipo. Lo sienta en la cama, se cruza de piernas a su lado y, con impresionante fluidez y meridiana claridad, machetea la opresión milenaria, la plan-cha perpetua y la cocina forzada, compañero. Distraída por su propia elocuencia, usa el brassiere de cenicero al reclamar enfática la igualdad genital. Bajo el foco implacable de la razón, el Tipo confiesa, se arrepiente, hace firme propósito de enmienda e implora fervientemente la comunión. Emocionados, juntan cabezas y se funden en un largo beso igualitario, introduciendo exactamente la misma cantidad de lengua en las respectivas cavidades bucales. La naturaleza acude al llamado unisex y el acto queda equitativamente consumado.

Soneo III

La Tipa se viste. Le lanza la ropa al Tipo, aún atrincherado en el baño. Se largan del motel sin cruzar palabra. Cuando el Torino rojo metálico del '69 se detiene en la De Diego para soltar su carga, sigue prendida la fiesta patronal con su machina de cabalgables nalgas. Con la intensidad de un arrebato colombiano y la perseverancia somociana, con la desfachatez del Sha, el Tipo reincide vilmente. Y se reintegra a su rastreo cachondo, al rosario de la interminable aurora de qué meneo lleva esa mulata, oye, baby, qué tú comes pa estal tan saludable, ave maría, qué clase e lomillo, lo que hace el arroz con habichuelas, qué troj de calne, mami, si te cojo...

(1979)

▬▬▬▬▬▬

Eraclio Zepeda
1937–
México

El muro
Asalto nocturno, 1975.

A Efraín Barquero

E L último de los amigos se despidió. El cerró la puerta cuidando no hacer ruido. Eran las cuatro de la mañana y quería ahorrar a sus vecinos el golpe de un portazo; precaución
extraña después de las voces altas y la música que, durante
horas, habían partido de la reunión ahora muerta.

Ella permanecía sentada en el sillón de cuero, deseando
encontrar licor en la copa ya vacía. Encendió un fósforo mientras buscaba la cajetilla de cigarros. El se acercó a la ventana,
la abrió para limpiar la atmósfera pesada. Después se dirigió
al baño.

Habían reunido a los amigos para celebrar sus siete años
de casados ¿o eran ocho? La velada resultó ni mejor ni peor
que otras anteriores. Y, sin embargo, desde hora muy temprana, sin entenderlo cabalmente, él y ella experimentaron la presencia de un muro.

Al principio fue sólo una sensación. Pero al paso de las
horas, la fábrica de aquella resuelta pared progresaba a ritmo
franco. El más pequeño ademán de él o la más simple infle-
xión en la voz de ella colaboraban, eficazmente, en su erección.

Había sido un descubrimiento repentino logrado al mismo tiempo por él y por ella, un hallazgo simultáneo reserva-
do sólo a la pareja. Fue cuando él relataba la historia repetida
en todas las reuniones, en que como siempre, la risa de los
oyentes rubrica el pasaje exacto, la frase precisa, siempre igual.
Aquella historia que tanto había celebrado ella las primeras
veces, al principio de su matrimonio, y que ahora, a fuerza de
oírla, odiaba. El relato reveló el primer síntoma de lo que estaba ocurriendo. Las miradas de él y de ella se encontraron
como si vinieran de muy lejos para cruzarse sin especial intención. Sin embargo, ambos advirtieron que la muralla estaba
allí, recién nacida, a la altura de las rodillas.

Ya no fue posible ocultarla. En realidad hacía tiempo que
esperaban su advenimiento, pero no dejaba de ser extraño
que ello sucediera precisamente en la fiesta de su aniversario.

Los invitados, los amigos íntimos, permanecían ajenos a la construcción que ante sus ojos ausentes progresaba. Para ellos era una espléndida ocasión de hablar de lo que siempre se había conversado.

Cuando el último invitado se despidió, el muro llegaba ya muy cerca del techo y la sala había quedado dividida, sin posibilidad de contemplarse uno a otro los rostros ni los cuerpos ni nada.

Al salir del baño encontró que la sala estaba definitivamente cercenada por un cancel de cal y canto, pintado hermosamente de blanco, con grandes contrafuertes de piedra a cada extremo. Lo más sorprendente era la falta de asombro. Serenamente, él golpeó el muro con el puño, suaves golpes espaciados cuidando los intervalos, de modo tal que al otro lado pudiera entenderse la intención de un mensaje. Aguardó con atención: al cabo de un momento escuchó, muy lejanas, las noticias de ella al otro lado de la muralla.

El se volvió camino de la alcoba. Buscó en ciertas gavetas un retrato de ella, hecho en los días de su primer encuentro; le colocó, amorosamente, un listón de luto alrededor del marco, volvió a la sala sin apresurarse y colgó del muro la imagen. Después se sentó en el suelo y lloró hasta que el sueño lo cubrió totalmente.

Al despertar, el muro permanecía allí. Algunas yedras trepaban con audacia hasta perderse en las nubes tenuamente coloreadas por el sol; las manchas de una pátina bronceada aparecieron en la pared que un día había sido blanca.

Estudiada las formas caprichosas que lograban cuando escuchó aquel rumor, primero casi imperceptible, de una corriente de agua. Imaginó un escape en los gritos del baño, y al ir a comprobarlo descubrió que del muro nacía un manantial. Observando atentamente comprendió que no era una suerte de arroyo, sino un gran río de viaje largo que simplemente atravesaba la muralla.

Se sentó a la orilla para ver pasar las aguas que arrastraban recuerdos del mundo y algunos detalles, sorprendentemente bien conservados, de escenas capitales en su relación con ella. A veces, semisumergidas, pasaban tarjetas postales de ciudades amadas por ambos, y también, nadando por el río, antiguos encontrados en tierras lejanas, que muy serios suspendían el ritmo del braceo para saludar muy correctamente, levantando con la mano sus chisteras.

De pronto, en un levantar la vista hacia el horizonte, aguas arriba venía un barco de papel. Sacó su pañuelo y lo agitó largamente hasta que el barco, seguramente al advertirlo, dirigió su proa hacia la orilla. Cuando hubo atracado, él subió anhelante a bordo porque creyó verla en cubierta.

Estaba sentada en una silla de lona, contemplando una casa destruida que sostenía entre las manos, vestida con el uniforme escolar que llevaba el día en que la amó por primera vez. Cuando abrazó no a ella, sino a una estatua de sal, advirtió su soledad de muchos años.

Sintió entonces que el barco se movía y corriendo a la baranda del castillo de popa pudo comprobar que la corriente del río había cambiado de sentido, y llevaba al barco rumbo hacia donde, si el astrolabio no lo engañaba, debía estar la muralla.

Las aguas iban ganando en caudal y los rápidos se sucedían en forma tan peligrosa que llegó a experimentar una ansia cierta de naufragio. Viajaba ahora por una zona de praderas portentosas, que se convirtieron después en bosques espesos de abedules. Empezó a nevar copiosamente y los abedules se disolvieron en la nieve quedando tan solo algunas manchas negras, mariposas casi, que volaban. A lo lejos se veían aldeas sepultadas, adivinadas únicamente por el humo de sus chimeneas y las marcas del tráfico de trineos. Cuando la nieve se agotó, se encontró navegando en el desierto.

Subiéndose al mástil pudo divisar a lo lejos la muralla. Conforme iba acercándose surgían indicios claros de que el río acabaría por atravesarla.

Un día llegó al túnel enorme por medio del cual el río ganaba el otro lado. Era un túnel de piedra negra en forma octagonal en cuyas paredes se relataban, por medio de bajorrelieves, encuentros y regresos. Al lado de cada alegoría enormes lápidas de mármol labradas con inscripciones citaban el Texto de la Verdad y la Palabra.

Pudo comprobar que una vez atravesado el túnel, el río no desembocaba al otro lado de la muralla sino que, mediante un caprichoso meandro, penetraba en la sala cercenada a través de la ventana que él dejara abierta aquella noche del desastre.

La barca atracó suavemente, él saltó a tierra y corrió al encuentro de ella. No dejó de entender, sin embargo, que avanzaba en verdad por la sala de su primera casa, la que habitaron en los primeros meses. Al fondo ella pintaba un retrato de su hijo enmarcado por una larga leyenda de caracteres armenios donde se contaba una historia de derrumbes. Estaba amaneciendo y en la calle se escuchaba el paso majestuoso de los dromedarios y los pregones de los vendedores de tamales. Al acercarse a ella advirtió que había crecido.

—Buenos días —dijo él y notó que eran las primeras palabras verdaderas en muchos años.

Hombrecillos que reían mientras trabajaban se dispusieron a demoler el muro. Apenas si podían ser advertidos allá en lo alto. Todo parecía indicar que se trataba de una tarea a largo plazo. Ella le tomó de la mano, abrió la puerta y salieron a la calle.

POESÍA

Rafael Alberti
1902—
España

Tres recuerdos del cielo
Sobre los ángeles, 1929.

Homenaje a
Gustavo Adolfo Bécquer.

Prólogo

No habían cumplido años ni la rosa ni el arcángel.
Todo, anterior al balido y al llanto.
Cuando la luz ignoraba todavía
si el mar nacería niño o niña.
Cuando el viento soñaba melenas que peinar
y claveles el fuego que encender y mejillas
y el agua unos labios parados donde beber.
Todo, anterior al cuerpo, al nombre y al tiempo.
Entonces, yo recuerdo que, una vez, en el cielo ...

Primer Recuerdo

... una azucena tronchada ...
G. A. Bécquer

Paseaba con un dejo de azucena que piensa,
casi de pájaro que sabe ha de nacer.
Mirándose sin verse a una luna que le hacía espejo el sueño
y a un silencio de nieve, que le elevaba los pies.
A un silencio asomada.
Era anterior al arpa, a la lluvia y a las palabras.
No sabía.
Blanca alumna del aire,
temblaba con las estrellas, con la flor y los árboles.
Su tallo, su verde talle.

Con las estrellas mías
que, ignorantes de todo,
por cavar dos lagunas en sus ojos
la ahogaron en dos mares.
    Y recuerdo...
    Nada más: muerta, alejarse.

Segundo Recuerdo

> *... rumor de besos y batir de alas...*
> G. A. Bécquer

También antes,
mucho antes de la rebelión de las sombras,
de que al mundo cayeran plumas incendiadas
y un pájaro pudiera ser muerto por un lirio.
Antes, antes que tú me preguntaras
el número y el sitio de mi cuerpo.
Mucho antes del cuerpo.
En la época del alma.
Cuando tú abriste en la frente sin corona, del cielo,
la primera dinastía del sueño.
Cuando tú, al mirarme en la nada,
inventaste la primera palabra.
    Entonces, nuestro encuentro.

Tercer Recuerdo

> *...detrás del abanico*
> *de plumas de oro...*
> G. A. Bécquer

Aún los valses del cielo no habían desposado al jazmín
        y la nieve,
ni los aires pensado en la posible música de tus cabellos,
ni decretado el rey que la violeta se enterrara en un libro.
No.
Era la era en que la golondrina viajaba
sin nuestras iniciales en el pico.
En que las campanillas y las enredaderas
morían sin balcones que escalar y estrellas.
La era
en que al hombro de un ave no había flor que apoyara la cabeza.
    Entonces, detrás de tu abanico, nuestra luna primera.

Vicente Aleixandre
1898—1984
España

Se querían
La destrucción o el amor, 1935.

Se querían.
Sufrían por la luz, labios azules en la madrugada,
labios saliendo de la noche dura,
labios partidos, sangre, ¿sangre dónde?
Se querían en un lecho navío, mitad noche mitad luz.

Se querían como las flores a las espinas hondas,
a esa amorosa gema del amarillo nuevo,
cuando los rostros giran melancólicamente,
giralunas que brillan recibiendo aquel beso.

Se querían de noche, cuando los perros hondos
laten bajo la tierra y los valles se estiran
como lomos arcaicos que se sienten repasados:
caricia, seda, mano, luna que llega y toca.

Se querían de amor entre la madrugada,
entre las duras piedras cerradas de la noche,
duras como los cuerpos helados por las horas,
duras como los besos de diente a diente sólo.

Se querían de día, playa que va creciendo,
ondas que por los pies acarician los muslos,
cuerpos que se levantan de la tierra y flotando...
Se querían de día, sobre el mar, bajo el cielo.

Mediodía perfecto, se querían tan íntimos,
mar altísimo y joven, intimidad extensa,
soledad de lo vivo, horizontes remotos
ligados como cuerpos en soledad cantando.

Amando. Se querían como la luna lúcida,
como ese mar redondo que se aplica a ese rostro,
dulce eclipse de agua, mejilla oscurecida,
donde los peces rojos van y vienen sin música.

Día, noche, ponientes, madrugadas, espacios,
ondas nuevas, antiguas, fugitivas, perpetuas,
mar o tierra, navío, lecho, pluma, cristal,
metal, música, labio, silencio, vegetal,
mundo, quietud, su forma. Se querían, sabedlo.

_____

Dámaso Alonso
1898—
España

A un río le llamaban Carlos
Hombre y Dios, 1955.

Charles River,
Cambridge, Massachusetts.

Yo me senté en la orilla:
quería preguntarte, preguntarme tu secreto;
convencerme de que los ríos resbalan hacia un anhelo
    y viven;
y que cada uno nace y muere distinto (lo mismo que
    a ti te llaman Carlos).
Quería preguntarte, mi alma quería preguntarte
por qué anhelas, hacia qué resbalas, para qué vives.
Dímelo, río,
y dime, di, por qué te llaman Carlos.
    Ah, loco, yo, loco, quería saber qué eras, quién eras
(género, especie)
y qué eran, qué significaban "fluir", "fluido", "fluente";
qué instante era tu instante;
cuál de tus mil reflejos, tu reflejo absoluto;
yo quería indagar el último recinto de tu vida;
tu unicidad, esa alma de agua única,
por la que te conocen por Carlos.
    Carlos es una tristeza, muy mansa y gris, que fluye
entre edificios nobles, a Minerva sagrados,
y entre hangares que anuncios y consignas coronan.
Y el río fluye y fluye, indiferente.
A veces, suburbana, verde, una sonrisilla
de hierba se distiende, pegada a la ribera.
Yo me he sentado allí, sobre la hierba quemada del
    invierno, para pensar por qué los ríos
siempre anhelan futuro, como tú lento y gris.

Y para preguntarte por qué te llaman Carlos.
  Y tú fluías, fluías, sin cesar, indiferente,
y no escuchabas a tu amante extático,
que te miraba preguntándote,
como miramos a nuestra primera enamorada para
  saber si le fluye un alma por los ojos,
y si en su sima el mundo será todo luz blanca,
o si acaso su sonreír es sólo eso: una boca amarga
  que besa.
Así te preguntaba, como le preguntamos a Dios en la
  sombra de los quince años,
entre fiebres oscuras y los días —qué verano— tan
  lentos.
Yo quería que me revelaras el secreto de la vida
y de tu vida, y por qué te llamaban Carlos.
  Yo no sé por qué me he puesto tan triste, contem-
    plando el fluir de este río.
Un río es agua, lágrimas: mas no sé quién las llora.
El río Carlos es una tristeza gris, mas no sé quién la
  llora.
Pero sé que la tristeza es gris y fluye.
Porque sólo fluye en el mundo la tristeza.
Todo lo que fluye es lágrimas.
Todo lo que fluye es tristeza, y no sabemos de dónde
  viene la tristeza.
Como yo no sé quién te llora, río Carlos,
como yo no sé por qué eres una tristeza
ni por qué te llaman Carlos.
  Era bien de mañana cuando yo me he sentado a
    contemplar el misterio fluyente de este río,
y he pasado muchas horas preguntándome, preguntándote.
Preguntando a este río, gris lo mismo que un dios;
preguntándome, como se le pregunta a un dios triste:
¿qué buscan los ríos?, ¿qué es un río?
Dime, dime qué eres, qué buscas,
río, y por qué te llaman Carlos.
  Y ahora me fluye dentro una tristeza,
un río de tristeza gris,
con lentos puentes grises, como estructuras funerales
  grises.
Tengo frío en el alma y en los pies.
Y el sol se pone.
Ha debido pasar mucho tiempo.

Ha debido pasar el tiempo lento, lento, minutos, siglos, eras.
Ha debido pasar toda la pena del mundo, como un
   tiempo lentísimo.
Han debido pasar todas las lágrimas del mundo, como
   un río indiferente.
Ha debido pasar mucho tiempo, amigos, míos, mucho
   tiempo
desde que yo me senté aquí en la orilla, a orillas de
   esa tristeza, de ese
río al que le llamaban Dámaso, digo, Carlos.

Anónimo
s. XV
España

Romance del amor más poderoso que la muerte

Ramón Menéndez Pidal. *Flor nueva de romances viejos.*

   Conde Niño por amores
es niño y pasó la mar;
va a dar agua a su caballo
la mañana de San Juan.
Mientras el caballo bebe
él canta dulce cantar;
todas las aves del cielo
se paraban a escuchar,
caminante que camina
olvida su caminar,
navegante que navega
la nave vuelve hacia allá.
   La reina estaba labrando,
la hija durmiendo está:
—Levantaos, Albaniña,
de vuestro dulce folgar,
sentiréis cantar hermoso
la sirenita del mar.
—No es la sirenita, madre,
la de tan bello cantar,
sino es el Conde Niño
que por mí quiere finar.

¡Quién le pudiese valer
en su tan triste penar!
—Si por tus amores pena,
¡oh, malhaya su cantar!,
y porque nunca los goce
yo le mandaré matar.
—Si le manda matar, madre,
juntos nos han de enterrar.
  El murió a la media noche,
ella a los gallos cantar;
a ella como hija de reyes
la entierran en el altar,
a él como hijo de conde
unos pasos más atrás.
De ella nació un rosal blanco,
dél nació un espino albar;
crece el uno, crece el otro,
los dos se van a juntar;
las ramitas que se alcanzan
fuertes abrazos se dan,
y las que no se alcanzaban
no dejan de suspirar.
La reina llena de envidia
ambos los mandó cortar;
el galán que los cortaba
no cesaba de llorar.
De ella naciera una garza,
de él un fuerte gavilán
juntos vuelan por el cielo,
juntos vuelan par a par.

Anónimo
s. XV
España

Romance de la conquista de Alhama, con la cual se comenzó la última guerra de Granada.

Ramón Menéndez Pidal. *Flor nueva de romances viejos.*

Paseábase el rey moro
por la ciudad de Granada,
desde la puerta de Elvira
hasta la de Vivarrambla.
Cartas le fueron venidas
cómo Alhama era ganada.
    ¡Ay de mi Alhama!
Las cartas echó en el fuego,
y al mensajero matara;
echó mano a sus cabellos
y las sus barbas mesaba.
Apeóse de la mula
y en un caballo cabalga;
por el Zacatín arriba
subido había a la Alhambra;
mandó tocar sus trompetas,
sus añafiles de plata,
porque lo oyesen los moros
que andaban por el arada.
    ¡Ay de mi Alhama!
Cuatro a cuatro, cinco a cinco,
juntado se ha gran compaña.
Allí habló un viejo alfaquí,
la barba bellida y cana:
—¿Para qué nos llamas, rey,
a qué fué nuestra llamada?
—Para que sepáis, amigos,
la gran pérdida de Alhama.
    ¡Ay de mi Alhama!
—Bien se te emplea, buen rey,
buen rey, bien se te empleara;
mataste los bencerrajes,
que eran la flor de Granada;

cogiste los tornadizos
de Córdoba la nombrada.
Por eso mereces, rey,
una pena muy doblada,
que te pierdas tú y el reino
y que se acabe Granada.
    ¡Ay de mi Alhama!

▬▬▬

Ayocuán
(siglos xv-xvi)

Los poemas
son obras del cielo

Del interior del cielo vienen
las bellas flores, los bellos cantos.
Los afea nuestro anhelo,
nuestra inventiva los echa a perder,
a no ser los del príncipe chichimeca Tecayehuatzin.
¡Con los de él, alegraos!

La amistad es lluvia de flores preciosas.
Blancas vedijas de plumas de garza
se entrelazan con preciosas flores rojas:
en las ramas de los árboles,
bajo ellas andan y liban
los señores y los nobles.

Vuestro hermoso canto:
un dorado pájaro cascabel,
lo eleváis muy hermoso.
Estáis en un cercado de flores.
Sobre las ramas floridas cantáis.
¿Eres tú, acaso, un ave preciosa del Dador de la vida?
¿Acaso tú al dios has hablado?
Tan pronto como visteis la aurora,
os habéis puesto a cantar.

Esfuércese, quiera mi corazón,
las flores del escudo,

las flores del Dador de la vida.
¿Qué podrá hacer mi corazón?
En vano hemos llegado,
hemos brotado en la tierra.
¿Sólo así he de irme
como las flores que perecieron?
¿Nada quedará de mi nombre?
¿Nada de mi fama aquí en la tierra?
¡Al menos flores, al menos cantos!
¿Qué podrá hacer mi corazón?
En vano hemos llegado,
hemos brotado en la tierra.

Gocemos, oh amigos,
haya abrazos aquí.
Ahora andamos sobre la tierra florida.
Nadie hará terminar aquí
las flores y los cantos,
ellos perduran en la casa del Dador de la vida.

Aquí en la tierra es la región del momento fugaz.
¿También es así en el lugar
donde de algún modo se vive?
¿Allá se alegra uno?
¿Hay allá amistad?
¿O sólo aquí en la tierra
hemos venido a conocer nuestros rostros?

Gustavo Adolfo Bécquer
1836—1870
España

Rima III
Rimas y leyendas, 1868.

    Sacudimiento extraño
que agita las ideas,
como huracán que empuja
las olas en tropel;

    murmullo que en el alma
se eleva y va creciendo,
como volcán que sordo
anuncia que va a arder;

   deformes silüetas
de seres imposibles;
paisajes que aparecen
como a través de un tul;

   colores que fundiéndose
remedan en el aire
los átomos del Iris
que nadan en la luz;

   ideas sin palabras,
palabras sin sentido;
cadencias que no tienen
ni ritmo ni compás;

   memorias y deseos
de cosas que no existen;
accesos de alegría,
impulsos de llorar;

   actividad nerviosa
que no halla en qué emplearse;
sin rienda que le guíe
caballo volador,

   locura que el espíritu
exalta y enardece;
embriaguez divina
del genio creador...

   ¡Tal es la inspiración!

   Gigante voz que el caos
ordena en el cerebro,
y entre las sombras hace
la luz aparecer;

   Brillante rienda de oro
que poderosa enfrenta
de la exaltada mente
el volador corcel;

   hilo de luz que en haces
los pensamientos ata;
sol que las nubes rompe
y toca en el cenit;

inteligente mano
que en un collar de perlas
consigue las indóciles
palabras reunir;

armonioso ritmo
que con cadencia y número
las fugitivas notas
encierra en el compás;

cincel que el bloque muerde
la estatua modelando,
y la belleza plástica
añade a la ideal;

atmósfera en que giran
con orden las ideas,
cual átomos que agrupa
recóndita atracción;

raudal en cuyas ondas
su sed la fiebre apaga;
oasis que al espíritu
devuelve su vigor...

¡Tal es nuestra razón!

Con ambas siempre en lucha
y de ambas vencedor;
tan solo el genio puede
a un yugo atar las dos.

━━━━━━━

Carlos Germán Belli
1927—
Perú

El aviso las señales
Poemas, 1958.

Yo espero una bengala de aviso
tantas veces he escrito la clave en un papel

la he grabado sobre un grano de arena
con la fuerza del hambre
iluminado por un haz de luz
como cuando cruza un navío delante de los acantilados
o se incendia de repente la carpa del circo
en la noche oscura
cuando arrojan a las tribus antiguas
hacia las alamedas de yacimientos de hulla
y los tigres inclinados al borde de los estanques
electrizan con su piel
los menudos ojos de los peces
es así que yo espero un silbo de aviso
entre arroyos con mimbre
y la opulencia de una hilera de mesas de noche
yo te busco en todos los rincones
con una fogata
para alumbrar los vidrios
y ver las señales mágicas de tu vaho
cuando no te dejan cruzar el umbral del puente de mi río
o no me dejan seguir en los caminos
las líneas secretas de las rocas de tu valle.

Jorge Luis Borges
1899—1986
Argentina

Amorosa anticipación
Luna de enfrente, 1925.

Ni la intimidad de tu frente clara como una fiesta
ni la costumbre de tu cuerpo, aún misterioso y tácito y de niña,
ni la sucesión de tu vida asumiendo palabras o silencios
serán favor tan misterioso
como mirar tu sueño implicado
en la vigilia de mis brazos.
Virgen milagrosamente otra vez por la virtud absolutoria del
    sueño,

quieta y resplandeciente como una dicha que la memoria elige,
me darás esa orilla de tu vida que tú misma no tienes.
Arrojado a quietud,
divisaré esa playa última de tu ser
y te veré por vez primera, quizá,
como Dios ha de verte,
desbaratada la ficción del Tiempo,
sin el amor, sin mí.

—————

Jorge Luis Borges
1899--1986
Argentina

Heráclito
Elogio de la sombra, 1969.

El segundo crepúsculo.
La noche que se ahonda en el sueño.
La purificación y el olvido.
El primer crepúsculo.
La mañana que ha sido el alba.
El día que fue la mañana.
El día numeroso que será la tarde gastada.
El segundo crepúsculo.
Ese otro hábito del tiempo, la noche.
La purificación y el olvido.
El primer crepúsculo...
El alba sigilosa y en el alba
la zozobra del griego.
¿Qué trama es ésta
del será, del es y del fue?
¿Qué río es éste
por el cual corre el Ganges?
¿Qué río es éste cuya fuente es inconcebible?
¿Qué río es éste
que arrastra mitologías y espadas?
Es inútil que duerma.
Corre en el sueño, en el desierto, en un sótano.
El río me arrebata y soy ese río.
De una materia deleznable fui hecho, de misterioso tiempo.
Acaso el manantial está en mí.
Acaso de mi sombra
surgen, fatales e ilusorios, los días.

Julia de Burgos
1917–1953
Puerto Rico

A Julia de Burgos
Poema en veinte surcos, 1938.

Ya las gentes murmuran que yo soy tu enemiga
porque dicen que en verso doy al mundo tu yo.

Mienten, Julia de Burgos. Mienten, Julia de Burgos.
La que se alza en mis versos no es tu voz: es mi voz;
porque tú eres ropaje y la esencia soy yo;
y el más profundo abismo se tiende entre las dos.

Tú eres fría muñeca de mentira social,
y yo, viril destello de la humana verdad.

Tú, miel de cortesanas hipocresías; yo no;
que en todos mis poemas desnudo el corazón.

Tú eres como tu mundo, egoísta; yo no;
que todo me lo juego a ser lo que soy yo.

Tú eres sólo la grave señora señorona;
yo no, yo soy la vida, la fuerza, la mujer.

Tú eres de tu marido, de tu amo; yo no;
yo de nadie, o de todos, porque a todos, a todos,
en mi limpio sentir y en mi pensar me doy.

Tú te rizas el pelo y te pintas; yo no;
a mí me riza el viento; a mí me pinta el sol.

Tú eres dama casera, resignada, sumisa,
atada a los prejuicios de los hombres; yo no;
que yo soy Rocinante corriendo desbocado
olfateando horizontes de justicia de Dios.

Tú en ti misma no mandas; a ti todos te mandan;
en ti mandan tu esposo, tus padres, tus parientes,
el cura, la modista, el teatro, el casino,
el auto, las alhajas, el banquete, el champán,
el cielo y el infierno, y el qué dirán social.

En mí no, que en mí manda mi solo corazón,
mi solo pensamiento; quien manda en mí soy yo.

Tú, flor de aristocracia; y yo la flor del pueblo.
Tú en ti lo tienes todo y a todos se lo debes,
mientras que yo, mi nada a nadie se la debo.

Tú, clavada al estático dividendo ancestral,
y yo, un uno en la cifra del divisor social,
somos el duelo a muerte que se acerca fatal.

Cuando las multitudes corran alborotadas
dejando atrás cenizas de injusticias quemadas,
y cuando con la tea de las siete virtudes,
tras los siete pecados, corran las multitudes,
contra ti, y contra todo lo injusto y lo inhumano,
yo iré en medio de ellas con la tea en la mano.

Manuel del Cabral
1907
República Dominicana

Negro sin nada en tu casa
Trópico negro, 1942.

I

Yo te he visto cavar minas de oro
—negro sin tierra—.
Yo te he visto sacar grandes diamantes de la tierra
—negro sin tierra—.
Y como si sacaras a pedazos de tu cuerpo de la tierra,
te vi sacar carbones de la tierra.
Cien veces yo te he visto echar semillas en la tierra
—negro sin tierra—.
Y siempre tu sudor que no termina
de caer en la tierra.
Agua de tu dolor que fertiliza
más que el agua de nube.

Tu sudor, tu sudor. Y todo para aquel
que tiene cien corbatas, cuatro coches de lujo,
y no pisa la tierra.
Sólo cuando la tierra no sea tuya,
será tuya la tierra.

II

Mas hay un sin embargo que no te lo vigilan...
Hay en tus pies descalzos: graves amaneceres.
(Ya no podrán decir que es un siglo pequeño.)
El cielo se derrite rodando por tu espalda:
llanto de espinazos, diurno de trabajo,
pero oscuro de sueldo.

Yo no te vi dormido... Nunca te vi dormido...
aquellos pies descalzos
no te dejan dormir.

Tú ganas diez centavos, diez centavos por día.
Barro manso: te comprendo...
Tú los ganas tan limpios,
tienes manos tan limpias,
que puede que tu casa sólo tenga:
ropa sucia,
catre sucio,
carne sucia,
pero lavada la palabra: Hombre.

III

Negro triste, tan triste
que en cualquier gesto tuyo puedo encontrar el mundo.

Tú que vives tan cerca del hombre sin el hombre,
una sonrisa tuya me servirá de agua
para lavar la vida, que casi no se puede
lavar con otra cosa.

Quiero llegar a ti, pero llego lo mismo
que el río llega al mar... De tus ojos, a veces,
salen tristes océanos que en cuerpo te caben,
pero que en ti no caben.

Cualquier cosa tuya te pone siempre triste,
cualquier cosa tuya, por ejemplo: tu espejo.

Tu silencio es de carne, tu palabra es de carne,
tu inquietud es de carne, tu paciencia es de carne.

Tu lágrima no cae como gota de agua.
No se caen en el suelo las palabras.

IV

Negro manso,
ni siquiera
tienes la inutilidad
de los charcos con cielo.

Sólo
con tu sonrisa rebelde
sobre tu dolor,
como un lirio valiente que crece
sobre la tierra del pantano.

Sin embargo,
barro dócil,
negro quieto:
hoy la voz de la tierra te sale por los ojos,
tus ojos que hacen ruido cuando sufren.

Ernesto Cardenal
1925—
Nicaragua

Las ciudades perdidas
Homenaje a los indios americanos, 1972.

De noche las lechuzas vuelan entre las estelas,
el gato-de-monte maúlla en las terrazas,
el jaguar ruge en las torres
y el coyote solitario ladra en la Gran Plaza
a la luna reflejada en las lagunas
que fueron piscinas en lejanos katunes.

Ahora son reales los animales
que estaban estilizados en los frescos
y los príncipes venden tinajas en los mercados.
¿Pero cómo escribir otra vez el jeroglífico,
pintar al jaguar otra vez, derrocar los tiranos?
¿Reconstruir otra vez nuestras acrópolis tropicales,
nuestras capitales rurales rodeadas de milpas?

La maleza está llena de monumentos.
Hay altares en las milpas.
Entre las raíces de los chilamates arcos con relieves.
En la selva donde parece que nunca ha entrado el hombre,
donde sólo penetran el tapir y el pizote-solo
y el quetzal todavía vestido como un maya:
allí hay una metrópolis.
Cuando los sacerdotes subían al Templo del Jaguar
con mantos de jaguar y abanicos de colas de quetzal
y caites de cuero de venado y máscaras rituales,
subían también los gritos del Juego de Pelota,
el son de los tambores, el incienso de copal que se quemaba
en las cámaras sagradas de madera de zapote,
el humo de las antorchas de ocote... Y debajo de Tikal
hay otra metrópolis 1.000 años más antigua.
—Donde ahora gritan los monos en los palos de zapote.

No hay nombres de militares en las estelas.

En sus templos y palacios y pirámides
y en sus calendarios y sus crónicas y sus códices
no hay un nombre de cacique ni caudillo ni emperador
ni sacerdote ni líder ni gobernante ni general ni jefe
y no consignaban en sus piedras sucesos políticos,
ni administraciones, ni dinastías,
ni familias gobernantes, ni partidos políticos.
¡No existe en siglos el glifo del nombre de un hombre,
y los arqueólogos aún no saben cómo se gobernaban!

La palabra "señor" era extraña en su lengua.
Y la palabra "muralla". No amurallaban sus ciudades.
Sus ciudades eran de templos, y vivían en los campos,
entre milpas y palmeras y papayas.
El arco de sus templos fue una copia de sus chozas.
Las carreteras eran sólo para las procesiones.

La religión era el único lazo de unión entre ellos,
pero era una religión aceptada libremente
y que no era una opresión ni una carga para ellos.
Sus sacerdotes no tenían ningún poder temporal
y las pirámides se hicieron sin trabajos forzados.
El apogeo de su civilización no se convirtió en imperio.
Y no tuvieron colonias. No conocían la flecha.
Conocieron a Jesús como el dios del maíz
y le ofrecían sacrificios sencillos
de maíz, y pájaros, y plumas.
Nunca tuvieron guerras, ni conocieron la rueda,
pero calcularon la revolución sinódica de Venus:
anotaban todas las tardes la salida de Venus
en el horizonte, sobre una ceiba lejana,
cuando las parejas de lapas volaban a sus nidos.
No tuvieron metalurgia. Sus herramientas eran de piedra,
y tecnológicamente permanecieron en la edad de piedra.
Pero computaron fechas exactas que existieron
hace 400 millones de años.
No tuvieron ciencias aplicadas. No eran prácticos.
Su progreso fue en la religión, las artes, las matemáticas,
las astronomía. No podían pesar.
Adoraban el tiempo, ese misterioso fluir
y fluir del tiempo.
El tiempo era sagrado. Los días eran dioses.
Pasado y futuro están confundidos en sus cantos.
Contaban el pasado y el futuro con los mismos katunes,
porque creían que el tiempo se repite
como veían repetirse las rotaciones de los astros.
Pero el tiempo que adoraban se paró de repente.

Hay estelas que quedaron sin labrar.
Los bloques quedaron a medio cortar en las canteras.
—Y allí están todavía—

Ahora sólo los chicleros solitarios cruzan por el Petén.
Los vampiros anidan en los frisos de estuco.
Los changos-de-monte gruñen al anochecer.
El jaguar ruge en las torres —las torres entre raíces—
un coyote lejos, en una plaza, le ladra a la luna,
y el avión de la Pan American vuela sobre la pirámide.
¿Pero volverán algún día los pasados katunes?

Ernesto Cardenal
1925–
Nicaragua

Oración por Marilyn Monroe
Oración por Marilyn Monroe y otros poemas, 1965.

Señor
recibe a esta muchacha conocida en toda la tierra con el
    nombre
de Marilyn Monroe
aunque ese no era su verdadero nombre
(pero Tú conoces su verdadero nombre, el de la huerfanita
    violada
a los 9 años
y la empleadita de tienda que a los 16 se había querido matar)
y que ahora se presenta ante Ti sin ningún maquillaje
sin su Agente de Prensa
sin fotógrafos y sin firmar autógrafos
sola como un astronauta frente a la noche espacial.

Ella soñó cuando niña que estaba desnuda en una iglesia
                (según cuenta el *Time*)
ante una multitud postrada, con las cabezas en el suelo
y tenía que caminar en puntillas para no pisar las cabezas.
Tú conoces nuestros sueños mejor que los psiquiatras.
Iglesia, casa, cueva, son la seguridad del seno materno
pero también algo más que eso...
Las cabezas son los admiradores, es claro
(la masa de cabezas en la oscuridad bajo el chorro de luz).
Pero el templo no son los estudios de la 20th Century-Fox.
El templo —de mármol y oro— es el templo de su cuerpo
en el que está el Hijo del Hombre con un látigo en la mano
expulsando a los mercaderes de la 20th Century-Fox
que hicieron de Tu casa de oración una cueva de ladrones.

Señor
en este mundo contaminado de pecados y radioactividad
Tú no culparás tan sólo a una empleadita de tienda.
Que como toda empleadita de tienda soñó ser estrella de cine.
Y su sueño fue realidad (pero como la realidad del tecnicolor).
Ella no hizo sino actuar según el script que le dimos
—El de nuestras propias vidas— Y era un script absurdo.

Perdónala Señor y perdónanos a nosotros
por nuestra 20th Century
por esta Colosal Super-Producción en la que todos hemos
    trabajado.
Ella tenía hambre de amor y le ofrecimos tranquilizantes.
Para la Tristeza de no ser santos
                                    se le recomendó el Psicoanálisis.
Recuerda Señor su creciente pavor a la cámara
y el odio al maquillaje —insistiendo en maquillarse en cada
    escena—
y cómo se fue haciendo mayor el horror
y mayor la impuntualidad a los estudios.

Como toda empleadita de tienda
soñó ser estrella de cine.
Y su vida fue irreal como un sueño que un psiquiatra
    interpreta y archiva.

Sus romances fueron un beso con los ojos cerrados
que cuando se abren los ojos
se descubre que fue bajo reflectores
                                    ¡y apagan los reflectores!
y desmontan las dos paredes del aposento (era un set
    cinematográfico)
mientras el Director se aleja con su libreta
                        porque la escena ya fue tomada.
O como un viaje en yate, un beso en Singapur, un baile en Río
la recepción en la mansión del Duque y la Duquesa de Windsor
                vistos en la salita del apartamento miserable.
La película terminó sin el beso final.
La hallaron muerta en su cama con la mano en el teléfono.
Y los detectives no supieron a quién iba a llamar.
Fue
como alguien que ha marcado el número de la única voz amiga
y oyen tan sólo la voz de un disco que le dice: WRONG
    NUMBER.
O como alguien que herido por los gangsters
alarga la mano a un teléfono desconectado.

Señor
quienquiera que haya sido el que ella iba a llamar
y no llamó (y tal vez no era nadie
o era Alguien cuyo número no está en el Directorio de
    Los Angeles)
                        ¡contesta Tú el teléfono!

Rosario Castellanos
1925—1974
México

Testamento de Hécuba

Materia memorable, 1969.

Torre, no hiedra, fui. El viento nada pudo
rondando en torno mío con sus cuernos de toro:
alzaba polvaredas desde el norte y el sur
y aun desde otros puntos que olvidé o que ignoraba.
Pero yo resistía, profunda de cimientos,
ancha de muros, sólida
y caliente de entrañas, defendiendo a los míos.

El dolor era un deudo más de aquella familia.
No el predilecto ni el mayor. Un deudo
comedido en la faena, humilde comensal,
oscuro relator de cuentos junto al fuego.
Cazaba, en ocasiones, lejos y por servir
su instinto de varón
que tiene el pulso firme y los ojos certeros.
Volvía con la presa y la entregaba al hábil
destazador y al diestro
afán de las mujeres.

Al recogerme yo decía: qué hermosa
labor están tejiendo con las horas mis manos.
Desde la juventud tuve frente a mis ojos
un hermoso dechado
y no ambicioné más que copiar su figura.
En su día fui casta
y después fiel al único, al esposo.

Nunca la aurora me encontró dormida
ni me alcanzó la noche
antes que se apagara mi rumor de colmena.
La casa de mi dueño se llenó de mis obras
y su campo llegó hasta el horizonte.

Y para que su nombre no acabara
al acabar su cuerpo,
tuvo hijos en mí valientes, laboriosos,

tuvo hijas de virtud,
desposadas con yernos aceptables
(excepto una, virgen, que se guardó a sí misma
tal vez como la ofrenda para un dios).

Los que me conocieron me llamaron dichosa
y no me contenté con recibir
la feliz alabanza de mis iguales
sino que me incliné hasta los pequeños
para sembrar en ellos gratitud.

Cuando vino el relámpago buscando
aquel árbol de las conversaciones
clamó por la injusticia el fulminado.

Yo no dije palabras, porque es condición mía
no entender otra cosa sino el deber y he sido
obediente al desastre:
viuda irreprensible, reina que pasó a esclava
sin que su dignidad de reina padeciera
y madre, ay, y madre
huérfana de su prole.

Arrastré la vejez como una túnica
demasiado pesada.
Quedé ciega de años y de llanto
y en mi ceguera vi
la visión que sostuvo en su lugar mi ánimo.

Vino la invalidez, el frío, el frío
y tuve que entregarme a la piedad
de los que viven. Antes
me entregué así al amor, al infortunio.

Alguien asiste mi agonía. Me hace
beber a sorbos una docilidad difícil
y yo voy aceptando
que se cumplan en mí los últimos misterios.

Gabriel Celaya
1911–1991
España

La poesía es un arma
cargada de futuro
Cantos ibéricos, 1955.

Cuando ya nada se espera personalmente exaltante,
mas se palpita y se sigue más acá de la conciencia
fieramente existiendo, ciegamente afirmando,
como un pulso que golpea las tinieblas,

cuando se miran de frente
los vertiginosos ojos claros de la muerte,
se dicen las verdades:
las bárbaras, terribles, amorosas crueldades.

Se dicen los poemas
que ensanchan los pulmones de cuantos, asfixiados,
piden ser, piden ritmo,
piden ley para aquello que sienten excesivo.

Con la velocidad del instinto,
con el rayo del prodigio,
como mágica evidencia, lo real se nos convierte
en lo idéntico a sí mismo.

Poesía para el pobre, poesía necesaria
como el pan de cada día,
como el aire que exigimos trece veces por minuto,
para ser y en tanto somos dar un sí que glorifica.

Porque vivimos a golpes, porque apenas si nos dejan
decir que somos quien somos,
nuestros cantares no pueden ser sin pecado un adorno.
Estamos tocando el fondo.

Maldigo la poesía concebida como un lujo
cultural por los neutrales
que, lavándose las manos, se desentienden y evaden.
Maldigo la poesía de quien no toma partido hasta mancharse.

Hago mías las faltas. Siento en mí a cuantos sufren
y canto respirando.
Canto, y canto, y cantando más allá de mis penas
personales, me ensancho.

Quisiera daros vida, provocar nuevos actos,
y calculo por eso con técnica, que puedo.
Me siento un ingeniero del verso y un obrero
que trabaja con otros a España en sus aceros.

Tal es mi poesía: poesía-herramienta
a la vez que latido de lo unánime y ciego.
Tal es, arma cargada de futuro expansivo
con que te apunto al pecho.

No es una poesía gota a gota pensada.
No es un bello producto. No es un fruto perfecto.
Es algo como el aire que todos respiramos
y es el canto que espacia cuanto dentro llevamos.

Son palabras que todos repetimos sintiendo
como nuestras, y vuelan. Son más que lo mentado.
Son lo más necesario: lo que no tiene nombre.
Son gritos en el cielo, y en la tierra, son actos.

———

Luis Cernuda
1902—1963
España

Si el hombre pudiera decir
Los placeres prohibidos, 1931.

Si el hombre pudiera decir lo que ama,
Si el hombre pudiera levantar su amor por el cielo
Como una nube en la luz;
Si como muros que se derrumban,
para saludar la verdad erguida en medio,
Pudiera derrumbar su cuerpo,
    dejando sólo la verdad
    de su amor,
La verdad de sí mismo,

Que no se llama gloria, fortuna o ambición,
Sino amor o deseo,
Yo sería aquél que imaginaba;
Aquél que con su lengua, sus ojos y sus manos
Proclama ante los hombres la verdad ignorada,
La verdad de su amor verdadero.

Libertad no conozco sino la libertad de estar preso en
    alguien
Cuyo nombre no puedo oír sin escalofrío;
Alguien por quien me olvido de esta existencia
    mezquina,
Por quien el día y la noche son para mí lo que
    quiera.
Y mi cuerpo y espíritu flotan en su cuerpo y espíritu
Como leños perdidos que el mar anega o levanta
Libremente, con la libertad del amor,
La única libertad que me exalta,
La única libertad porque muero.

Tú justificas mi existencia:
Si no te conozco, no he vivido;
Si muero sin conocerte, no muero, porque no he
    vivido.

Juan Antonio Corretjer
1908–1985
Puerto Rico

Distancias
Asomante, 1955.

Cuando me dijo el corazón: —Afuera,
frente a la reja carcelaria espera
inútilmente verte tu Consuelo,
pensé...
eso que piensa aquel que la mirada
tiene hundida en la noche de la nada
y quiere ver el cielo.

Cuando la larga ausencia
llenó con su presencia
en inhóspitas playas extranjeras
un recuerdo de infancia
(esa extraña fragancia
que suave exhalan las nocturnas eras,

o aquel *manso ruido*
de la avecilla que abandona el nido,
bien de la hoja al árbol desprendida,
bien del viento en los sauces del camino
o del riachuelo el paso peregrino
entre la suave arena ennegrecida,

o ese fantasma del presentimiento
que nos llega en el viento
y nos hace mirar por la ventana,
cual si un alerta el corazón sintiera
y sintiendo pudiera
ver escrita en la noche la mañana),

mi corazón solía
gozar la epifanía
de las cosas lejanas muy cercanas,
beber su poesía
y no sufrir la fría
soledad de las cosas tan lejanas.

¡Suertes que juega el ágil rapacillo
al corazón sencillo
que sabe amar humilde y bravamente!
¡Nunca estaré yo preso
en enemigas manos, tan opreso
que no aspire mi pecho libremente,

e ilumine lo obscuro,
y salte sobre el muro
y al campo de mi patria raudo vuele
adonde monte el potro la lomada
y en la flor rociada
el zumbador revuele!

Mas, he aquí la muralla,
la reja, la metralla
sin alma que vigila

entre tu espera inútil a la puerta
y mi rabia despierta
que hacia una fútil decisión oscila.

Nunca ocurriera al pensamiento antes
que las cosas distantes
habiendo estado otrora tan cercanas,
el dulce bien amado
tan cerca de mi lado
forzáranlo a distancias tan lejanas.

Cierto que a este presente
no remedia lo ausente
dulce imaginación que el bien augura
y a la distancia aspira suave esencia.
No cura esta dolencia
"sino con tu presencia y tu figura".

Estas distancias de ahora:
esa ametralladora,
el kaki sudoroso
al fusil recostado
y hasta el sol recortado
y a ración como bálsamo precioso,

injurias son que al corazón invitan,
llaman y solicitan
hasta la irracional temperatura.
Pero a mi fe triunfante
sostiene lo que amante
tu persona a la puerta transfigura.

Y esto pienso esta noche en *La Princesa:*
La lucha nunca cesa.
La vida es lucha toda
por obtener la libertad ansiada.
Lo demás es la nada,
es superficie, es moda.

Patria es saber los ríos,
los valles, las montañas, los bohíos,
los pájaros, las plantas y las flores,
los caminos del monte y la llanura,
las aguas y los picos de la altura,
las sombras, los colores

con que pinta el oriente
y con que se despinta el occidente,
los sabores del agua y de la tierra,
los múltiples aromas,
las hierbas y las lomas,
y en la noche que aterra

el trueno que retumba en la negrura,
penetrar la espesura,
ver como en un relámpago la senda,
y de un trago apurado
el soplo de huracán, entusiasmado
reconocer las bestias de la hacienda.

—La Patria es la hermosura
con que yergue su mágica escultura
la letra, el libro, el verso,
y, vestida de gloria
verla cruzar la historia
hasta la plenitud del Universo.

—Tomar su cardiograma
y ver cómo le inflama
la salud los rubores.
Besarle su bandera,
soñarle su quimera,
amarle sus amores.

—Pero en la dura prueba
cuando la Patria abreva
de nuestra propia vida en la corriente:
la Patria estremecida
que lleva por coraza nuestra vida;
esa Patria exigente

que impone su silencio o su palabra,
y con sus manos labra,
en la sangrienta masa de dolores
a golpes de centella
la forma de una estrella,
un canto de fulgores,

cierto monento, un día,
tras la muralla fría

de la prisión, un preso
meditará ese juego de distancia
entre su muda estancia
y el cercano embeleso
que al corazón le dice: —Afuera,
junto a la reja carcelaria espera
inútilmente verte tu Consuelo—.
Y siento como aquel que la mirada
tiene hundida en la noche de la nada
y quiere ver el cielo.

San Juan de la Cruz
1542–1591
España

Subida del Monte Carmelo
1618.

De el alma que se goza de haber llegado
al alto estado de la perfección, que
es la unión con Dios, por el camino
de la negación espiritual

En una noche oscura,
con ansias en amores inflamada,
¡oh dichosa ventura!,
salí sin ser notada,
estando ya mi casa sosegada:

a escuras y segura,
por la secreta escala disfrazada,
¡oh dichosa ventura!,
a escuras y en celada,
estando ya mi casa sosegada;

en la noche dichosa,
en secreto, que nadie me veía,
ni yo miraba cosa,
sin otra luz y guía
sino la que en el corazón ardía.

Aquésta me guïaba
más cierto que la luz del mediodía,
a donde me esperaba
quien yo bien me sabía,
en parte donde nadie parecía.

¡Oh noche que guiaste!,
¡oh noche amable más que el alborada!,
¡oh noche que juntaste
amado con amada,
amada en el amado transformada!

En mi pecho florido,
que entero para él solo se guardaba,
allí quedó dormido,
y yo le regalaba;
y el ventalle de cedros aire daba.

El aire de la almena,
cuando yo sus cabellos esparcía,
con su mano serena
en mi cuello hería,
y todos mis sentidos suspendía.

Quedéme y olvidéme,
el rostro recliné sobre el amado,
cesó todo, y dejéme,
dejando mi cuidado
entre las azucenas olvidado.

Sor Juana Inés de la Cruz
1651—1695
México

Hombres necios que acusáis

Hombres necios que acusáis
a la mujer sin razón,
sin ver que sois la ocasión
de lo mismo que culpáis:

si con ansia sin igual
solicitáis su desdén,
¿por qué queréis que obren bien
si las incitáis al mal?

Combatís su resistencia
y luego, con gravedad.
decís que fue liviandad
lo que hizo la diligencia.

Parecer quiere el denuedo
de vuestro parecer loco,
al niño que pone el coco
y luego le tiene miedo.

Queréis, con presunción necia,
hallar a la que buscáis,
para pretendida, Thais,
y en la posesión, Lucrecia.

¿Qué humor puede ser más raro
que el que, falto de consejo,
él mismo empaña el espejo,
y siente que no esté claro?

Con el favor y el desdén
tenéis condición igual,
quejándoos, si os tratan mal,
burlándoos, si os quieren bien.

Opinión, ninguna gana;
pues la que más se recata,
si no os admite, es ingrata,
y si os admite, es liviana.

Siempre tan necios andáis
que, con desigual nivel,
a una culpáis por crüel
y a otra por fácil culpáis.

¿Pues cómo ha de estar templada
la que vuestro amor pretende,
si la que es ingrata, ofende,
y la que es fácil, enfada?

Mas, entre el enfado y pena
que vuestro gusto refiere,
bien haya la que no os quiere
y quejáos en hora buena.

Dan vuestras amantes penas
a sus libertades alas
y después de hacerlas malas
las queréis hallar muy buenas.

¿Cuál mayor culpa ha tenido
en una pasión errada:
la que cae de rogada,
o el que ruega de caído?

¿O cuál es más de culpar,
aunque cualquiera mal haga:
la que peca por la paga,
o el que paga por pecar?

Pues ¿para qué os espantáis
de la culpa que tenéis?
Queredlas cual las hacéis
o hacedlas cual las buscáis.

Dejad de solicitar,
y después, con más razón,
acusaréis la afición
de la que os fuere a rogar.

Bien con muchas armas fundo
que lidia vuestra arrogancia,
pues en promesa e instancia
juntáis diablo, carne y mundo.

Roque Dalton
1935–1975
El Salvador

Estudio con algo de tedio
La ventana en el rostro, 1961.

> Clov: —*Llora*,
> Hamm: —*Luego vive.*
> *(Diálogo de* Fin de partida, *de Bécquer)*

Tengo quince años y lloro por las noches.

Yo sé que ello no es en manera alguna peculiar
y que antes bien hay otras cosas en el mundo
más apropiadas para decíroslas cantando.

Sin embargo hoy he bebido vino por primera vez
y me he quedado desnudo en mis habitaciones para salvar
      la tarde
hecha minúsculos pedazos
por el reloj.

Pensar a solas duele. No hay nadie a quien golpear. No hay
      nadie
a quien dejar piadosamente perdonado.
Está uno y su cara. Uno y su cara
de santón farsante.
Surge la cicatriz que nadie ha visto nunca,
el gesto que escondemos todo el día,
el perfil insepulto que nos hará llorar y hundirnos
el día en que lo sepan todo las buenas gentes
y nos retiren el amor y el saludo hasta los pájaros.

Tengo quince años de cansarme
y lloro por las noches para fingir que vivo.
En ocasiones, cansado de las lágrimas,
hasta sueño que vivo.

Puede ser que vosotros no entendáis lo que son estas cosas.

Os habla, más que yo, mi primer vino
mientras la piel que sufro bebe sombra.

Roque Dalton
1935-1975

Las feas palabras
El turno del ofendido, 1963.

En la garganta de un beodo muerto
se quedan las palabras que despreció la poesía.

Yo las rescato con manos de fantasma
con manos piadosas es decir
ya que todo lo muerto tiene la licuada piedad
de su propia experiencia.

Furtivamente os las abandono:
feas las caras sucias bajo el esplendor de las lámparas
babeantes sobre su desnudez deforme
los dientes y los párpados apretados
esperando el bofetón.

Amadlas también os digo. Reñid a la poesía
la limpidez de su regazo.
Dotadlas de biografía ilustre.
Limpiadles la fiebre de la frente
y rodeadlas de serenas frescuras
para que participen también de nuestra fiesta.

Rubén Darío
1867—1916
Nicaragua

Era un aire suave
Prosas profanas, 1896-1901.

Era un aire suave, de pausados giros:
el hada Harmonía ritmaba sus vuelos,
e iban frases vagas y tenues suspiros
entre los sollozos de los violoncelos.

Sobre la terraza, junto a los ramajes,
diríase un trémolo de liras eolias
cuando acariciaban los sedosos trajes,
sobre el tallo erguidas, las blancas magnolias.

La marquesa Eulalia risas y desvíos
daba a un tiempo mismo para dos rivales:
el vizconde rubio de los desafíos
y el abate joven de los madrigales.

Cerca, coronado con hojas de viña,
reía en su máscara Término barbudo,.
y, como un efebo que fuese una niña,
mostraba una Diana su mármol desnudo.

Y bajo un boscaje del amor palestra,
sobre rico zócalo al modo de Jonia,
con un candelabro prendido en la diestra
volaba el Mercurio de Juan de Bolonia.

La orquesta perlaba sus mágicas notas;
un coro de sones alados se oía;
galantes pavanas, fugaces gavotas
cantaban los dulces violines de Hungría.

Al oír las quejas de sus caballeros,
ríe, ríe, ríe la divina Eulalia,
pues son su tesoro las flechas de Eros,
el cinto de Cipria, la rueca de Onfalia.

¡Ay de quien sus mieles y frases recoja!
¡Ay de quien del canto de su amor se fíe!
Con sus ojos lindos y su boca roja,
la divina Eulalia, ríe, ríe, ríe.

Tiene azules ojos, es maligna y bella;
cuando mira, vierte viva luz extraña;
se asoma a sus húmedas pupilas de estrella
el alma del rubio cristal de Champaña.

Es noche de fiesta, y el baile de trajes
ostenta su gloria de triunfos mundanos.
La divina Eulalia, vestida de encajes,
una flor destroza con sus tersas manos.

El teclado harmónico de su risa fina
a la alegre música de un pájaro iguala,
con los *staccati* de una bailarina
y las locas fugas de una colegiala.

¡Amoroso pájaro que trinos exhala
bajo el ala a veces ocultando el pico;
que desdenes rudos lanza bajo el ala,
bajo el ala aleve del leve abanico!

Cuando a medianoche sus notas arranque
y en arpegios áureos gima Filomela,
el ebúrneo cisne, sobre el quieto estanque,
como blanca góndola imprima su estela,

la marquesa alegre llegará al boscaje,
boscaje que cubre la amable glorieta
donde han de estrecharla los brazos de un paje
que, siendo su paje, será su poeta.

Al compás de un canto de artista de Italia
que en la brisa errante la orquesta deslíe,
junto a los rivales, la divina Eulalia,
la divina Eulalia, ríe, ríe, ríe.

¿Fue acaso en el tiempo del rey Luis de Francia,
sol con corte de astros, en campos de azur,
cuando los alcázares llenó de fragancia
la regia y pomposa rosa Pompadour?

¿Fue cuando la bella su falda cogía
con dedos de ninfa, bailando el minué,
y de los compases el ritmo seguía,
sobre el tacón rojo, lindo y leve el pie?

¿O cuando pastoras de floridos valles
ornaban con cintas sus albos corderos
y oían, divinas Tirsis de Versalles,
las declaraciones de sus caballeros?

¿Fue en ese buen tiempo de duques pastores,
de amantes princesas y tiernos galanes,
cuando entre sonrisas y perlas y flores
iban las casacas de los chambelanes?

¿Fue acaso en el Norte o en el Mediodía?
Yo el tiempo y el día y el país ignoro;
pero sé que Eulalia ríe todavía,
¡y es crüel y eterna su risa de oro!

Rubén Darío
1867–1916
Nicaragua

Leda
Cantos de vida y esperanza, 1905.

El cisne en la sombra parece de nieve;
su pico es de ámbar, del alba al trasluz;
el suave crepúsculo que pasa tan breve
las cándidas alas sonrosa de luz.

    Y luego, en las ondas del lago azulado,
después que la aurora perdió su arrebol,
las alas tendidas y el cuello enarcado,
el cisne es de plata, bañado de sol.

    Tal es cuando esponja las plumas de seda,
olímpico pájaro herido de amor,
y viola en las linfas sonoras a Leda,
buscando su pico los labios en flor.

    Suspira la bella desnuda y vencida,
y en tanto que al aire sus quejas se van
del fondo verdoso de fronda tupida
chispean turbados los ojos de Pan.

Rubén Darío
1867–1916
Nicaragua

Lo fatal
Cantos de vida y esperanza, 1905.

Dichoso el árbol que es apenas sensitivo
y más la piedra dura, porque ésta ya no siente,
pues no hay dolor más grande que el dolor de ser vivo,
ni mayor pesadumbre que la vida consciente.

Ser y no saber nada; y ser sin rumbo cierto,
y el temor de haber sido y un futuro terror...
Y el espanto seguro de estar mañana muerto,
y sufrir por la vida y por la sombra y por

lo que no conocemos y apenas sospechamos
y la carne que tienta con sus frescos racimos
y la tumba que aguarda con sus fúnebres ramos,
¡y no saber adónde vamos,
ni de dónde venimos...!

Angela María Dávila
1944–
Puerto Rico

¿Será la rosa?
Animal fiero y tierno, 1977.

¿Será la rosa?
¿será el trámite
de la sombra debajo de los pétalos?
¿será la rosa
o será la espinísima ferocidad de a diario?
¿será la rosa,
será tal vez el pétalo desnudo y transitorio?
¿será la rosa
con su gota de siempre en la mañana,
o será que una lágrima se encarga
de refrescar las flores ilusorias,
o será que una gota de polvo
descansa en la mañana de un sol desaliñado
sobre una hoja imaginaria,
sobre una yerba
imaginariamente reptando por el polvo.
¿será que uno no entiende
que a esos hoyitos cogidos en la calle
de camino a la escuela
podría tal vez darles con ponerse de acuerdo
para inventarse jugar a ser abismos?
será que uno no entiende
que deshojarse a diario

no impide echar raíces,
ni detiene el imperio constante de la tierra,
ni el temblor de ser pájaro
tragando a bocanadas el aire por las alas.
será que uno no sabe
o que uno está seguro
de que el agua son flores diluidas;
¿será el tremendo recuerdo de la flor en el aire
como agua detenida?
¿será la rosa
olida y sorprendida por los ojos,
brutalmente fugaz;
tocante tocadora
tocada para siempre su armonía
por el recuerdo musgo de su historia
por el recuerdo feroz y demarcado
de su huella difusa y siempreviva;
por el recuerdo punzante y afilado detrás de cada espina
de cada esquina,
de cada ruina diluida en distancia y asombro?
será la rosa dura en pie de lucha,
será seguir hablando palomas,
diciendo caracoles,
haciendo verbos simples para mover los nombres
como decir: la luna está en cuarto creciente
y uno en cuarto menguante;
y ayer, o en estos días por la calle
me encontré aquel tornillo viejo y largo
que parecía un quijote moderno y milenario.
¿será la hospitalaria región desconocida
que nos recibe con sábanas dobladas,
una sonrisa, un fuego elemental
alimentando el agua que alimenta,
que pone alfombras viejas para los pies recientes
de espinas y caminos?
¿será la rosa,
será el concreto armado,
será la tierra oliendo a simple lluvia,
será la garra
o el hueco de la mano,
la sombra devorando la luz que no termina,
el destello total
inaccesiblemente amenazado?
será que hay muchas noches con sus días en orden

recordando eficaces cómo andamos
alternando los pies,
y con las manos
y hasta con la cabeza
si es que nos cerca de lejos el peligro,
si es que nos enamoran la distancia y la sombra,
flores en transiciones y aguas turbias;
si se nos aglomeran las espinas
para formar la lanza inacabable
que violente los pájaros,
que amenace los ojos que se nutren
de los animalitos;
o tropiece con todas las canciones
que tiemblan en el aire,
será, me digo yo,
que se nos acumulan en uno de esos días,
o en varios de esos días,
o un poquito tal vez todos los días,
el susto y el asombro de encontrarnos
con tanta cosa junta,
con tantísima cosa
que uno dice en un grito y una lágrima
que habita entre los huesos:
¿será la rosa?
será que uno no entiende,
serán esos hoyitos de que hablábamos,
será la tierra oliendo
la garra, o el meñique, o el hueco de la mano
el destello total, el agua fuego,
este montón de cosas, todo esto.

Eliseo Diego
1920–
Cuba

Cristóbal Colón inventa el Nuevo Mundo

Los días de tu vida, 1977.

1

Toda la noche, toda,
Cristóbal Colón oye pasar los pájaros.
Viniendo del abismo, sin fin, a ráfagas,
miles y miles de pájaros. Sobre los mástiles,
atravesando, acribillando las tinieblas, allá,
el ruido de las alas de los pájaros.
Viniendo del vacío, del abismo,
el ruido, el trueno de la vida siendo,
la orquesta entera de los pájaros.
Pálido como la llama del farol, inmóvil,
Cristóbal Colón oye tronar la vida,
pasar los pájaros.

2

Cristóbal Colón ha visto una luz donde no hay nada.
(El Almirante, no el advenedizo de Triana.)
Esa luz arde en algún sitio seco.
Tan seco, sin duda, como el sitio en que se posó la paloma.
Es luz de algún fuego encendido por la mano de un hombre.
Porque el fuego qué es sino la inteligencia del hombre.
Cristóbal Colón lo buscó toda su vida, esto es lo cierto.
Toda su vida de pobreza, toda su vida.
Fuego de cocinar pescado, puede que fuego de abrigo.
Fuego para la más modesta de las ceremonias.
De tan pequeño que es, no puede ser otra cosa, cómo va a serlo.
Porque Cristóbal Colón lo buscó toda su vida, toda.
Por eso ahora solloza solo en la cubierta
mientras el último de los pájaros se hunde vibrando
        en la memoria.
Sí, el último de los pájaros
                        —uno con la primera
        luz del alba.

3

Cristóbal Colón abre su grueso diario.
Toma su pluma de ganso y la sopesa entre los dedos:
sangre, vida de bestia hecha cosa para el servicio del hombre.
Moja la punta en el tintero de cuerno, el Almirante, y mira
la blancura terrible de la página. Sabe
que está esperándolo desde el principio de todo. Virgen,
está esperándolo desde que se asentaron las rocas y se fijó
      un límite al capricho de las olas.
Cristóbal Colón siente el vértigo con que lo llama el abismo
      de la página,
pero, prudente, se resiste y sólo con la punta de los dedos
      toca el blanco mágico.
Escribir la primera palabra será como empezar a no ser, como
      engendrar o como morir, los dos extremos
que son una y la misma embriaguez, pavorosos principios,
triunfos, catástrofes, glorias.
Toda la inacabable riqueza de la urdimbre—oro de Aldebarán,
      plata de Géminis, arquetipos del ciervo y el león,
      del ébano y del ónix,
toda la inagotable riqueza está urgiéndolo, soplándole.
      Cimbrado como una caña,
vibrante de terror y de júbilo, por fin Cristóbal Colón hunde
      su pluma en la página.
Comienza entonces la invención de América.

▬▬▬

Eliseo Diego
1920—
Cuba

Daguerrotipo de una desconocida

Entre la dicha y la tiniebla, 1949-1985.

Esa muchacha que en el daguerrotipo está mirándonos,
que no sabemos quién fue ni cómo se llamaba;
esa muchacha tan deliciosamente fresca bajo su blusa de
                           /encajes,
frágil con el temblor del pájaro que una vez hemos tenido
                           /en la mano;
el óvalo de cuya cara nos hiere de belleza,
las líneas de cuyas manos dibujan la esperanza o la ternura
esa muchacha está en peligro, ya ven, y no se da ni cuenta.

El día se le está yendo como el aroma escapa de la rosa,
el nombre se le está yendo como está yéndose la música, no
/se da cuenta.
Sólo un instante más y ya no podremos ampararla, no
/podremos;
el rumor de su falda se ocultará en la sombra de los márgenes;
ligera se habrá ido como si no tuviese un cuidado en el mundo
y en su lugar habrá cosas sin alma que el polvo aquieta con la
/punta de sus dedos.
No estará la muchacha, la perfección, la gloria de la luz,
/sino su imagen
manchada ya, tocada ya, dañada, como por una mosca, por
/la fecha.
Es demasiado joven para el odio del tiempo.

Vanessa Droz
1952—
Puerto Rico

Yo, la no querida
La cicatriz a medias, 1982.

> *¡Oh soledad, que a fuerza de*
> *andar sola se siente de sí misma*
> *compañera!*
> Luis Palés Matos

Yo, la no querida,
me convierto en vertical madera
con una imagen perpetrada
en oscuras vetas de conciencia repetida,
repetida invención de presencias.

Yo, la inventada piedra,
mirada de reojo y no vista.
Yo, la impulsiva arteria desatada,
la piel con goznes sostenida
(ansias fúnebres, muerte en vela).
Tú, mineral de espuma
concentrada en ti y tan azul tu savia.
¡Oh vaso tan profundo!
Agua en su borde más atónito,
lleno de ti y en tu piel sitiado.

Quién fuera, helada en su rubor,
la angustiosa putilla que te llevara de la mano.

Quién fuera tu Filí-Melé no escapada
sino ungida en polvoroso vértigo
por tus manos naufragadas.
Quién Filí-Melé de tu misa a cuestas
(altar postrero, portentosa ventana)
de palabras ancianas y sencillas.
¿Qué vestidos y qué árbol
encumbrarías a mis venas?
¿Qué canto suave sumergirías en mis canas?
Hubiera querido hacerte
elegía, en vida de ceniza que se escapa,
elogio, en muerte de semilla que se crece,
hasta inventarte nuevamente.

Nada te prolongue, yo quisiera.
Eres, serás un polen tan bendito
—solemne pan, acto primero—
que ahora y siempre tan querido
te llevaré copiosamente exacto
"en el silencio tan cercano al grito"
que en toda mi soledad conjuga
un rostro, eco de rostro hecho tañido,
un hielo, fijeza de hielo que le teme al frío
en la memoria y el olvido imaginario.

Angela Figuera Aymerich
1902–
España

Destino
Los días duros, 1953.

VASO me hiciste, hermético alfarero,
y diste a mi oquedad las dimensiones
que sirven a la alquimia de la carne.
Vaso me hiciste, recipiente vivo
para la forma un día diseñada
por el secreto ritmo de tus manos.

"Hágase en mí", repuse. Y te bendije
con labios obedientes al destino.

¿Por qué, después, me robas y defraudas?

Libre el varón camina por los días.
Sus recias piernas nunca soportaron
esa tremenda gravidez del fruto.
Liso y escueto entre ágiles caderas
su vientre no conoce pesadumbre.
Sólo un instante, furia y goce, olvida
por mí su altiva soledad de macho;
libérase a sí mismo y me encadena
al ritmo y servidumbre de la especie.

Cuán hondamente exprimo, laborando
con células y fibras, con mis órganos
más íntimos, vitales dulcedumbres
de mi profundo ser, día tras día.

Hácese el hijo en mí. ¿Y han de llamarlo
hijo del Hombre cuando, fieramente,
decisiva urgencia me desgarra
para moverse vivo entre las cosas?
Mío es el hijo en mí y en él me aumento.
Su corazón prosigue mi latido.
Saben a mí sus lágrimas primeras.
Su risa es aprendida de mis labios.
Y esa humedad caliente que lo envuelve
es la temperatura de mi entraña.

¿Por qué, Señor, me lo arrebatas luego?
¿Por qué me crece ajeno, desprendido,
como amputado miembro, como rama
desconectada del nutricio tronco?

En vano mi ternura lo persigue
queriéndolo ablandar, disminuyéndolo.
Alto se yergue. Duro se condensa.
Su frente sobrepasa mi estatura,
y ese pulido azul de sus pupilas
que en un rincón de mí cuajó su brillo,
me mira desde lejos, olvidando.

Apenas si las yemas de mis dedos
aciertan a seguir por sus mejillas
aquella suave curva que, al beberme,
formaba con la curva de mis senos
dulcísima tangencia.

———

Federico García Lorca
1898—1936
España

New York
Oficina y Denuncia
Poeta en Nueva York, 1929-1930.

A Fernando Vela

Debajo de las multiplicaciones
hay una gota de sangre de pato;
debajo de las divisiones
hay una gota de sangre de marinero;
debajo de las sumas, un río de sangre tierna.
Un río que viene cantando
por los dormitorios de los arrabales,
y es plata, cemento o brisa
en el alba mentida de New York.
Existen las montañas. Lo sé.
Y los anteojos para la sabiduría.
Lo sé. Pero yo no he venido a ver el cielo.
Yo he venido para ver la turbia sangre.
La sangre que lleva las máquinas a las cataratas
y el espíritu a la lengua de la cobra.
Todos los días se matan en New York
cuatro millones de patos,
cinco millones de cerdos,
dos mil palomas para el gusto de los agonizantes,
un millón de vacas,
un millón de corderos
y dos millones de gallos,
que dejan los cielos hechos añicos.
Más vale sollozar afilando la navaja
o asesinar a los perros
en las alucinantes cacerías

que resistir en la madrugada
los interminables trenes de leche,
los interminables trenes de sangre,
y los trenes de rosas maniatadas
por los comerciantes de perfumes.
Los patos y las palomas,
y los cerdos y los corderos
ponen sus gotas de sangre
debajo de las multiplicaciones,
y los terribles alaridos de las vacas estrujadas
llenan de dolor el valle
donde el Hudson se emborracha con aceite.
Yo denuncio a toda la gente
que ignora la otra mitad,
la mitad irredimible
que levanta sus montes de cemento
donde laten los corazones
de los animalitos que se olvidan
y donde caeremos todos
en la última fiesta de los taladros.
Os escupo en la cara.
La otra mitad me escucha
devorando, orinando, volando en su pureza,
como los niños de las porterías
que llevan frágiles palitos
a los huecos donde se oxidan
las antenas de los insectos.
No es el infierno, es la calle.
No es la muerte, es la tienda de frutas.
Hay un mundo de ríos quebrados
y distancias inasibles
en la patita de ese gato
quebrada por el automóvil,
y yo oigo el canto de la lombriz
en el corazón de muchas niñas.
Oxido, fermento, tierra estremecida.
Tierra tú mismo que nadas
por los números de la oficina.
¿Qué voy a hacer? ¿Ordenar los paisajes?
¿Ordenar los amores que luego son fotografías,
que luego son pedazos de madera
y bocanadas de sangre?
San Ignacio de Loyola
asesinó un pequeño conejo

y todavía sus labios gimen
por las torres de las iglesias.
No, no, no, no; yo denuncio.
Yo denuncio la conjura
de estas desiertas oficinas
que no radian las agonías,
que borran los programas de la selva,
y me ofrezco a ser comido
por las vacas estrujadas
cuando sus gritos llenan el valle
donde el Hudson se emborracha con aceite.

Federico García Lorca
1898—1936
España

Thamar y Amnón
Romancero Gitano, 1924-1927.

Para Alfonso García Valdecasas

La luna gira en el cielo
sobre las tierras sin agua
mientras el verano siembra
rumores de tigre y llama.
Por encima de los techos
nervios de metal sonaban.
Aire rizado venía
con los balidos de lana.
La tierra se ofrece llena
de heridas cicatrizadas,
o estremecida de agudos
cauterios de luces blancas.

Thamar estaba soñando
pájaros en su garganta,
al son de panderos fríos
y cítaras enlunadas.

Su desnudo en el alero,
agudo norte de palma,
pide copos a su vientre
y granizo a sus espaldas.

Thamar estaba cantando
desnuda por la terraza.
Alrededor de sus pies,
cinco palomas heladas.
Amnón delgado y concreto,
en la torre la miraba,
llenas las ingles de espuma
y oscilaciones la barba.
Su desnudo iluminado
se tendía en la terraza,
con un rumor entre dientes
de flecha recién clavada.
Amnón estaba mirando
la luna redonda y baja,
y vio en la luna los pechos
durísimos de su hermana.

    Amnón a las tres y media
se tendió sobre la cama.
Toda la alcoba sufría
con sus ojos llenos de alas.
La luz, maciza, sepulta
pueblos en la arena parda,
o descubre transitorio
coral de rosas y dalias.
Linfa de pozo oprimida
brota silencio en las jarras.
En el musgo de los troncos
la cobra tendida canta.

Amnón gime por la tela
fresquísima de la cama.
Yedra del escalofrío
cubre su carne quemada.
Thamar entró silenciosa
en la alcoba silenciada,
color de vena y Danubio,
turbia de huellas lejanas.

Thamar, bórrame los ojos
con tu fija madrugada.
Mis hilos de sangre tejen
volantes sobre tu falda.
Déjame tranquila, hermano.
Son tus besos en mi espalda,
avispas y vientecillos
en doble enjambre de flautas.
Thamar, en tus pechos altos
hay dos peces que me llaman,
y en las yemas de tus dedos
rumor de rosa encerrada.

   Los cien caballos del rey
en el patio relinchaban.
Sol en cubos resistía
la delgadez de la parra.
Ya la coge del cabello,
ya la camisa le rasga.
Corales tibios dibujan
arroyos en rubio mapa.

   ¡Oh, qué gritos se sentían
por encima de las casas!
Qué espesura de puñales
y túnicas desgarradas.
Por las escaleras tristes
esclavos suben y bajan.
Embolos y muslos juegan
bajo las nubes paradas.
Alrededor de Thamar
gritan vírgenes gitanas,
y otras recogen las gotas
de su flor martirizada.
Paños blancos enrojecen
en las alcobas cerradas.
Rumores de tibia aurora
pámpanos y peces cambian.

   Violador enfurecido,
Amnón huye con su jaca.

Negros le dirigen flechas
en los muros y atalayas.
Y cuando los cuatro cascos
eran cuatro resonancias,
David con unas tijeras
cortó las cuerdas del arpa.

▄▄▄▄▄▄▄▄▄

Luis de Góngora
1561—1627
España

Alegoría de la brevedad de las cosas humanas

Aprended, flores, en mí
lo que va de ayer a hoy
que ayer maravilla fui
y sombra mía aun no soy.

La aurora ayer me dio cuna,
la noche ataúd me dio;
sin luz muriera, si no
me la prestara la Luna.
Pues de vosotras ninguna
deja de acabar así,
aprended flores en mí
lo que va de ayer a hoy,
que ayer maravilla fui
y sombra mía aun no soy.

Consuelo dulce el clavel
es a la breve edad mía,
pues quien me concedió un día
dos apenas le dio a él;
efímeras del vergel,
yo cárdeno, él carmesí,
aprended, flores, en mí
lo que va de ayer a hoy,
que ayer maravilla fui
y sombra mía aun no soy.

Flor es el jazmín, si bella,
no de las más vividoras,
pues dura pocas más horas
que rayos tiene de estrella;
si el ámbar florece, es ella
la flor que él retiene en sí.
Aprended, flores, en mí
lo que va de ayer a hoy,
que ayer maravilla fui
y sombra mía aun no soy.

Aunque el alhelí grosero,
en fragancia y en color
más días ve que otra flor,
pues ve los de un mayo entero
morir maravilla quiero
y no vivir alhelí.
Aprended, flores, en mí
lo que va de ayer a hoy,
que ayer maravilla fui
y sombra mía aun no soy.

A ninguna al fin mayores
términos concede el Sol
si no es al girasol,
Matusalén de las flores,
ojos son aduladores
cuantas en él hojas vi.
Aprended, flores, en mí
lo que va de ayer a hoy,
que ayer maravilla fui
y sombra mía aun no soy.

Luis de Góngora
1561–1627
España

Mientras por competir con tu cabello
1582.

   Mientras, por competir con tu cabello,
oro bruñido, el sol relumbra en vano;
mientras con menosprecio en medio el llano
mira a tu blanca frente el lilio bello;

   mientras a cada labio, por cogello,
siguen más ojos que al clavel temprano,
y mientras triunfa con desdén lozano
del luciente cristal tu gentil cuello;

   goza cuello, cabello, labio y frente,
antes que lo que fue en tu edad dorada
oro, lilio, clavel, cristal luciente,

   no sólo en plata o vïola troncada
se vuelva, mas tú y ello juntamente
en tierra, en humo, en polvo, en sombra, en nada.

José Gorostiza
1901–1973
México

Lleno de mí...
Poesía, 1964.

Lleno de mí, sitiado en mi epidermis
por un dios inasible que me ahoga,
mentido acaso
por su radiante atmósfera de luces
que oculta mi conciencia derramada,
mis alas rotas en esquirlas de aire,
mi torpe andar a tientas por el lodo;
lleno de mí —ahito— me descubro
en la imagen atónita del agua,

que tan sólo es un tumbo inmarcesible,   *inmarchitable*
un desplome de ángeles caídos
a la delicia intacta de su peso,
que nada tiene
sino la cara en blanco
hundida a medias, ya, como una risa agónica,   *en agonía*
en las tenues holandas de la nube   *lienzo muy fino*
y en los funestos cánticos del mar
—más resabio de sal o albor de cúmulo   *Alba/inicio — Montón gran cantidad*
que sola prisa de acosada espuma.
No obstante —oh paradoja— constreñida   *Apremiar, obligar*
por el rigor del vaso que la aclara,
el agua toma forma.
En él se asienta, ahonda y edifica,
cumple una edad amarga de silencios
y un reposo gentil de muerte niña,
sonriente, que desflora
un más allá de pájaros
en desbandada.
En la red de cristal que la estrangula,
allí, como en el agua de un espejo,
se reconoce;
atada allí, gota con gota,
marchito el tropo de espuma en la garganta
¡qué desnudez de agua tan intensa,
qué agua tan agua,
está en su orbe tornasol soñando,
cantando ya una sed de hielo justo!
¡Mas qué vaso —también— más providente
éste que así se hinche
como una estrella en grano,
que así, en heroica promisión, se enciende
como un seno habitado por la dicha,
y rinde así, puntual,
una rotunda flor
de transparencia al agua,
un ojo proyectil que cobra alturas
y una ventana a gritos luminosos
sobre esa libertad enardecida
que se agobia de cándidas prisiones!

(Fragmento de
Muerte sin fin 1964).

Jorge Guillén
1843–1984
España

Ciervos sobre una pared
Clamor, 1960.

(Lascaux)

Emergen, se adelantan, vibran
Sobre una pared de la cueva
—A través de siglos y siglos
Profundizados en tiniebla
De inmóvil silencio recóndito
Que ni la Historia misma altera—
Los ciervos, los ciervos en fuga,
En fuga por un friso apenas
Contemplado y ya resurrecto
Sobre millones de horas muertas,
Fuga y su desfile de friso
Vivaz hacia más primavera.
Uno tras otro siguen juntos
Alzando siempre las cabezas
Adorablemente alargadas
Tras una vaguedad de meta.
Refrenado palpita el ímpetu
Que bosques y bosques desea.
Al perfil otorgan, nervioso,
Aireación las cornamentas,
Y hasta se percibe el susurro
De las soledades inciertas.
Vibrando resaltan los ciervos.
En su vida sin muerte quedan.

Nicolás Guillén
1902—
Cuba

Alta niña de caña y amapola
Poemas de amor, 1933-1971.

Primero fue su rápida cintura,
la órbita de oro en que viajaba
su cuerpo, el mundo joven de su risa,
la verde, la metálica
naturaleza de sus ojos.
¿La amé? Nunca se sabe.
Pero en las noches tímidas,
en las nubes perdidas y sonámbulas
y en el aroma del jazmín abierto
como una estrella fija en la penumbra,
su nombre resonaba.
Un día la distancia
se hizo un largo suspiro.
¡Oh qué terrestre angustia, en un gran golpe
de nieve y lejanía!
¿Sufrí? Nunca se sabe.
Pero en las tardes tristes,
en la insistencia familiar del Ángelus,
a la hora del vuelo taciturno
del búho y el murciélago,
Como en un sueño simple la veía.
Al fin he aquí que el viento,
he aquí que el viento al fin me la devuelve.
La he tenido en mis brazos, la he besado
en un tibio relámpago.
Toqué sus manos lentas,
la flor bicéfala del seno, el agua
de su lujuria inaugural... Ahora,
oh tú, bienesperada,
suave administradora
del fuego y de la danza,
alta niña de caña y amapola,
ahora ya sé que sufro y que te amo.

Nicolás Guillén
1902—
Cuba

Balada de los dos abuelos *verso de rima asonanto*
West Indies Ltd. 1934.

Sombras que sólo yo veo,
me escoltan mis dos abuelos.

Lanza con punta de hueso,
tambor de cuero y madera:
Mi abuelo negro.

Gorguera en el cuello ancho,
gris armadura guerrera:
Mi abuelo blanco.

Pie desnudo, torso pétreo *de piedra*
los de mi negro;
pupilas de vidrio antártico *fría*
las de mi blanco.
Africa de selvas húmedas
y de gordos gongos sordos... *Aliteración del sonido*
— ¡Me muero! *estribillo*
(Dice mi abuelo negro.) *amanecer en africa*
Aguaprieta de caimanes,
verdes mañanas de cocos...
— ¡Me canso!
(Dice mi abuelo blanco.)
Oh velas de amargo viento, *barco negreros*
galeón ardiendo en oro... *sacar oro de minas.*
— ¡Me muero!
(Dice mi abuelo negro.)
¡Oh costas de cuello virgen *Indios y africano*
engañadas de abalorios...! *engañados por las chuche-*
— ¡Me canso! *rias de los españoles*
(Dice mi abuelo blanco.)
¡Oh puro sol repujado,
preso en el aro del trópico;
oh luna redonda y limpia
sobre el sueño de los monos!

¡Qué de barcos, qué de barcos!
¡Qué de negros, qué de negros!
¡Qué largo fulgor de cañas!
¡Qué látigo el del negrero!
Piedra de llanto y de sangre,
venas y ojos entreabiertos,
y madrugadas vacías,
y atardeceres de ingenio,
y una gran voz, fuerte voz,
despedazando el silencio.
¡Qué de barcos, qué de barcos,
qué de negros!

Sombras que sólo yo veo,
me escoltan mis dos abuelos.

Don Federico me grita
y Taita Facundo calla;
los dos en la noche sueñan
y andan, andan.
Yo los junto.

          — ¡Federico!
¡Facundo! Los dos se abrazan.
Los dos suspiran. Los dos
las fuertes cabezas alzan;
los dos del mismo tamaño,
bajo las estrellas altas;
los dos del mismo tamaño,
ansia negra y ansia blanca,
los dos del mismo tamaño,
gritan, sueñan, lloran, cantan.
Sueñan, lloran, cantan.
Lloran, cantan.
¡Cantan!

██████

Miguel Hernández
1910—1942
España

Elegía
El rayo que no cesa, 1934-1935.

> *(En Orihuela, su pueblo y el mío,*
> *se me ha muerto como el rayo*
> *Ramón Sijé, a quien tanto quería.)*

Yo quiero ser llorando el hortelano
de la tierra que ocupas y estercolas,
compañero del alma, tan temprano.

Alimentando lluvias, caracolas
y órganos mi dolor sin instrumento,
a las desalentadas amapolas

daré tu corazón por alimento.
Tanto dolor se agrupa en mi costado,
que por doler me duele hasta el aliento.

Un manotazo duro, un golpe helado,
un hachazo invisible y homicida,
un empujón brutal te ha derribado.

No hay extensión más grande que mi herida
lloro mi desventura y sus conjuntos
y siento más tu muerte que mi vida.

Ando sobre rastrojos de difuntos,
y sin calor de nadie y sin consuelo
voy de mi corazón a mis asuntos.

Temprano levantó la muerte el vuelo,
temprano madrugó la madrugada,
temprano estás rodando por el suelo.

No perdono a la muerte enamorada,
no perdono a la vida desatenta,
no perdono a la tierra ni a la nada.

En mis manos levanto una tormenta
de piedras, rayos y hachas estridentes
sedienta de catástrofes y hambrienta.

Quiero escarbar la tierra con los dientes,
quiero apartar la tierra parte a parte
a dentelladas secas y calientes.

Quiero minar la tierra hasta encontrarte
y besarte la noble calavera
y desamordazarte y regresarte.

Volverás a mi huerto y a mi higuera:
por los altos andamios de las flores
pajareará tu alma colmenera

de angelicales ceras y labores.
Volverás al arrullo de las rejas
de los enamorados labradores.

Alegrarás la sombra de mis cejas,
y tu sangre se irá a cada lado
disputando tu novia y las abejas.

Tu corazón, ya terciopelo ajado,
llama a un campo de almendras espumosas
mi avariciosa voz de enamorado.

A las aladas almas de las rosas
del almendro de nata te requiero,
que tenemos que hablar de muchas cosas,
compañero del alma, compañero.

Miguel Hernández
1910—1942
España

Nanas de la cebolla
Ultimos poemas, 1939-1941.

   La cebolla es escarcha
cerrada y pobre.
Escarcha de tus días
y de mis noches.
Hambre y cebolla,
hielo negro y escarcha
grande y redonda.

En la cuna del hambre
mi niño estaba.
Con sangre de cebolla
se amamantaba.
Pero tu sangre,
escarcha de azúcar,
cebolla y hambre.

Una mujer morena
resuelta en luna
se derrama hilo a hilo
sobre la cuna.
Ríete, niño,
que te tragas la luna
cuando es preciso.

Alondra de mi casa,
ríete mucho.
Es tu risa en los ojos
la luz del mundo.
Ríete tanto,
que mi alma al oírte
bata el espacio.

Tu risa me hace libre,
me pone alas.
Soledades me quita,
cárcel me arranca.
Boca que vuela,
corazón que en tus labios
relampaguea.

Es tu risa la espada
más victoriosa,
vencedor de las flores
y las alondras.
Rival del sol.
Porvenir de mis huesos
y de mi amor.

La carne aleteante,
súbito el párpado,
el vivir como nunca
coloreado.
¡Cuánto jilguero
se remonta, aletea,
desde tu cuerpo!
Desperté de ser niño:
nunca despiertes.

Triste llevo la boca;
ríete siempre.
Siempre en la cuna,
defendiendo la risa
pluma por pluma.
    Ser de vuelo tan alto,
tan extendido,
que tu carne es el cielo
recién nacido.
 ¡Si yo pudiera
remontarme al origen
de tu carrera!
    Al octavo mes ríes
con cinco azahares.
Con cinco diminutas
ferocidades.
Como cinco jazmines
adolescentes.
    Frontera de los besos
serán mañana,
cuando en la dentadura
sientas un arma.
Sientas un fuego
correr dientes abajo
buscando el centro.

    Vuela, niño, en la doble
luna del pecho;
él, triste de cebolla;
tú, satisfecho.
No te derrumbes.
No sepas lo que pasa
ni lo que ocurre.

Vicente Huidobro
1893—1948
Chile

Poema para hacer crecer los árboles
Ver y palpar, 1941.

Salud salud de mi sol en soledad
Noche interior remada como la savia visionaria
Salud salud en puentes de amanecer y ocaso
Como también de tierra y cielo y piedra y astros
Salud en asiento de aire
Salud en movimiento de silencio
Cinco ramas   siete ramas   doce ramas
Doce hojas   veinte hojas   y cien hojas
Sube y sube y sube.

Y aletea y rema adentro de sí mismo
Subiendo desde lo oscuro
Sube a su piel
Sube por sus paredes funestas subidoras
Y por su llanto
Y por sus efervescencias de ángel perfumado
Por su respiración de piedra silenciosa.

Un cielo para cada rama
Una estrella para cada hoja
Un río para llevarse la memoria
Y lavarnos los recuerdos como una distancia
Una montaña un cuerpo de mariposa inmóvil
Un arco iris dejando una nube de polvo tras sus pasos
Sube rema
Sube por tu centro oscuro
Por tu viento de tubo que se expande
Por su virtud de amor que se enfurece.

Ama la rama ama
Hora que llora y ora deplora
Hoja la coja hoja
Ojalá coja la hoja
Rema la savia rema rema
Rema la rama

Rema la vida por sus dolientes
Hay que coger la hoja
Hay que reír al cielo en la punta libre.

Cinco ramas   siete ramas   doce ramas
Así todos remando los remeros remadores
Doce hojas   veinte hojas   y cien hojas
Y los remeros remando
Los remeros remadores
Remando vida arriba
Una montaña al cuerpo de un árbol cabizbajo
Un arco iris dejando una nube de mariposas tras sus pasos
Un árbol que se yergue y cierra el paso a la muerte.

Juana de Ibarbourou
1895–1980
Uruguay

Siesta
La rosa de los vientos, 1930.

Trompo alucinante de sol
sobre la cintura exacta del día
y los cuernos verticales del caracol.

Muerdo un gajo de sombra morada
caído del filo del muro
como un ala tendida de garza.

Sobre las mesas opulentas o rústicas,
el pan de la reciente molienda
y el frescor dorado de las uvas.

Ademanes de gula y de bendición
dentro de la cuadrada colmena de las casas.
Por los caminos arrastra su vestido de cola la pereza.
Los guijarros hacen menudos guiños de lámparas.

Sueño. No existe el mundo ni la vida.
Aladino me trae su anillo de cobre
y agua fresca en una tinaja de arcilla.

Está lejos la hora estéril e indiferente.
Toda la tierra es una fruta madura
y hay que dar un bárbaro salto de volatinero
para hincarle en la pulpa los dientes.

Ana Istarú
1960—
Costa Rica

Poemas de la estación de fiebre, XXIII
La estación de fiebre, 1983.

La suavidad del pan que no ha nacido
sostienen sus caderas,
un lomo terso de venado,
la curvatura del melón,
altas mejillas donde escribió
su adiós final la espalda.
Cómo no amar a este varón tocado
sentado en sus dos lunas,
volcado como un río sobre el lecho.
Amo su boca tocada por la abeja,
amo sus higos apretados,
amo esta órbita doblemente dulce:
detenidos ocasos sus dos nalgas,
oh gloria de la esfera, las dos copas
en que lo habrán vertido un día.
Su grávida ternura me devuelve
a las cosas más terrenas.
Los ángulos equinos, el traje circular del universo.
Cómo no amar a este barón tocado
con piel de albaricoque en la cadera.

Fayad Jamís
1930—
Cuba

Poema
Poema, 1986.

¿Qué es para usted la poesía además de una piedra horadada
    por el sol y la lluvia,
Además de un niño que se muere de frío en una mina del
    Perú,
Además de un caballo muerto en torno al cual las tiñosas
    describen eternos círculos de humo,
Además de una anciana que sonríe cuando le hablan de
    una receta nueva para hacer frituras de sesos
(A la anciana, entretanto, le están contando las maravillas
    de la electrónica, la cibernética y la cosmonáutica),
Además de un revólver llameante, de un puño cerrado, de
    una hoja de yagruma, de una muchacha triste o alegre,
Además de un río que parte el corazón de un monte?
¿Qué es para usted la poesía además de una fábrica de
    juguetes,
Además de un libro abierto como las piernas de una mujer,
Además de las manos callosas del obrero,
Además de las sorpresas del lenguaje —ese océano sin fin
    totalmente creado por el hombre—,
Además de la despedida de los enamorados en la noche
    asaltada por las bombas enemigas,
Además de las pequeñas cosas sin nombre y sin historia
    (un plato, una silla, una tuerca, un pañuelo, un poco
    de música en el viento de la tarde)?
¿Qué es para usted la poesía además de un vaso de agua
    en la garganta del sediento,
Además de una montaña de escombros (las ruinas de un
    viejo mundo abolido por la libertad),
Además de una película de Charles Chaplin,
Además de un pueblo que encuentra a su guía
    y de un guía que encuentra a su pueblo
    en la encrucijada de la gran batalla,
Además de una ceiba derramando sus flores en el aire
    mientras el campesino se sienta a almorzar,
Además de un perro ladrándole a su propia muerte,

Además del retumbar de los aviones al romper la barrera
    del sonido (pienso especialmente en nuestro cielo y
    nuestros héroes)?
¿Qué es para usted la poesía además de una lámpara
    encendida,
Además de una gallina cacareando porque ha acabado de
    poner,
Además de un niño que saca una cuenta y compra un
    helado de mamey,
Además del verdadero amor, compartido como el pan de
    cada día,
Además del camino que va de la oscuridad a la luz (y
    no a la inversa),
Además de la cólera de los que son torturados porque
    luchan por la equidad y el pan sobre la tierra,
Además del que resbala en la acera mojada y lo están
    viendo,
Además del cuerpo de una muchacha desnuda bajo la
    lluvia,
Además de los camiones que pasan repletos de mercancías,
Además de las herramientas que nos recuerdan una araña
    o un lagarto,
Además de la victoria de los débiles,
Además de los días y las noches,
Además de los sueños del astrónomo,
Además de lo que empuja hacia adelante a la inmensa
    humanidad?
¿Qué es para usted la poesía?
Conteste con letra muy legible, preferiblemente de imprenta.

Juan Ramón Jiménez
1881-1958
España

Mariposa de la luz
Piedra y cielo, 1919.

Mariposa de luz
la belleza se va cuando yo llego
a su rosa.

Corro, ciego tras ella...
La medio cojo aquí y allá...

¡Sólo queda en mi mano
la forma de su huida!

Juan Ramón Jiménez
1881–1958
España

Sueño
Eternidades, 1918.

La luna, que nacía, grande y oro,
nos durmió plenamente
en el paisaje de la primavera.

—El mundo era aquel sueño.
Estaba todo lo demás
abierto y vano—.
                    ¡Qué respetuosos
miraban los despiertos que pasaban!
Se quedaban estáticos
—sin poder irse hacia lo suyo—
en nuestro dormir hondo, que la luna
bordeó de oro y perla.

Mirándonos dormidos,
veían en las cosas
lo que nunca antes vieron.

Se les tornaban dulces
los labios, y se hacían
sus ojos infinitos.

   —Las estrellas cojidas por nosotros,
en cuyo seno claro
dormíamos,
temblaban en sus almas deslumbradas
por la luna—.
         Soñábamos, soñábamos
para que ellos vieran.

———

Pedro Lastra
1934—
Chile

Ya hablaremos
de nuestra juventud
Cuadernos de la doble vida, 1984.

Ya hablaremos de nuestra juventud,
ya hablaremos después, muertos o vivos
con tanto tiempo encima,
con años fantasmales que no fueron los nuestros
y días que vinieron del mar y regresaron
a su profunda permanencia.

Ya hablaremos de nuestra juventud
casi olvidándola,
confundiendo las noches y sus nombres,
lo que nos fue quitado, la presencia
de una turbia batalla con los sueños.

Hablaremos sentados en los parques
como veinte años antes, como treinta años antes,
indignados del mundo,
sin recordar palabra, quiénes fuimos,
dónde creció el amor,
en qué vagas ciudades habitamos.

Fray Luis de León
1527—1591
España

Canción
de la vida retirada

Publicación póstuma, 1631.

¡Qué descansada vida
la del que huye el mundanal rüido
y sigue la escondida
senda, por donde han ido
los pocos sabios que en el mundo han sido!

Que no le enturbia el pecho
de los soberbios grandes el estado,
ni del dorado techo
se admira, fabricado
del sabio Moro, en jaspes sustentado.

No cura si la fama
canta con voz su nombre pregonera,
ni cura si encarama
la lengua lisonjera
lo que condena la verdad sincera.

¿Qué presta a mi contento,
si soy del vano dedo señalado;
si, en busca deste viento,
ando desalentado,
con ansias vivas, con mortal cuidado?

¡Oh monte, oh fuente, oh río!
¡Oh secreto seguro, deleitoso!,
roto casi el navío,
a vuestro almo reposo
huyo de aqueste mar tempestuoso.

Un no rompido sueño,
un día puro, alegre, libre quiero;
no quiero ver el ceño
vanamente severo
de a quien la sangre ensalza, o el dinero.

Despiértenme las aves
con su cantar sabroso no aprendido;
no los cuidados graves,
de que es siempre seguido
el que al ajeno arbitrio está atenido.

Vivir quiero conmigo;
gozar quiero del bien que debo al cielo,
a solas sin testigo,
libre de amor, de celo,
de odio, de esperanzas, de recelo.
    Del monte en la ladera,
por mi mano plantado tengo un huerto,
que con la primavera,
de bella flor cubierto,
ya muestra en esperanza el fruto cierto;
    y, como codiciosa
por ver y acrecentar su hermosura,
desde la cumbre airosa
una fontana pura
hasta llegar corriendo se apresura;
    y, luego sosegada,
el paso entre los árboles torciendo,
el suelo de pasada,
de verdura vistiendo
y con diversas flores va esparciendo.
    El aire el huerto orea
y ofrece mil olores al sentido;
los árboles menea
con un manso rüido,
que del oro y del cetro pone olvido.
    Ténganse su tesoro
los que de un falso leño se confían;
no es mío ver el lloro
de los que desconfían
cuando el cierzo y el ábrego porfían.
    La combatida antena
cruje, y en ciega noche el claro día
se torna; al cielo suena
confusa vocería,
y la mar enriquecen a porfía.
    A mí una pobrecilla
mesa, de amable paz bien abastada,
me baste; y la vajilla,
de fino oro labrada,
sea de quien la mar no teme airada.
    Y mientras miserable-
mente se están los otros abrasando
con sed insaciable
del no durable mando,
tendido yo a la sombra esté cantando.

    A la sombra tendido,
de hiedra y lauro eterno coronado,
puesto el atento oído
al son dulce, acordado,
del plectro sabiamente meneado.

José Lezama Lima
1912–1979
Cuba

Una oscura pradera me convida
Enemigo rumor, 1941.

Una oscura pradera me convida,
sus manteles estables y ceñidos,
giran en mí, en mi balcón se aduermen.
Dominan su extensión, su indefinida
cúpula de alabastro se recrea.
Sobre las aguas del espejo,
breve la voz en mitad de cien caminos,
mi memoria prepara su sorpresa:
gamo en el cielo, rocío, llamarada.
Sin sentir que me llaman
penetro en la pradera despacioso,
ufano en nuevo laberinto derretido.
Allí se ven, ilustres restos,
cien cabezas, cornetas, mil funciones
abren su cielo, su girasol callando.
Extraña la sorpresa en este cielo,
donde sin querer vuelven pisadas
y suenan las voces en su centro henchido.
Una oscura pradera va pasando.
Entre los dos, viento o fino papel,
el viento, herido viento de esta muerte
mágica, una y despedida.
Un pájaro y otro ya no tiemblan.

Enrique Lihn
1929–1987
Chile

Porque escribí
La musiquilla de las pobres esferas, 1969.

Ahora que quizás, en un año de calma
piense: la poesía me sirvió para esto:
no pude ser feliz, ello me fue negado,
pero escribí.

Escribí: fui la víctima
de la mendicidad y el orgullo mezclados
y ajusticié también a unos pocos lectores:
tendí la mano en puertas que nunca, nunca he visto;
una muchacha cayó, en otro mundo a mis pies.

Pero escribí: tuve esta rara certeza,
la ilusión de tener el mundo entre las manos
— ¡qué ilusión más perfecta! como un cristo barroco
con toda su crueldad innecesaria—
Escribí, mi escritura fue como la maleza
de flores ácimas pero flores en fin,
el pan de cada día de las tierras eriazas:
una caparazón de espinas y raíces.

De la vida tomé todas estas palabras
como un niño oropel, guijarros junto al río:
las cosas de una magia, perfectamente inútiles
pero que siempre vuelven a renovar su encanto.

La especie de locura con que vuela un anciano
detrás de las palomas imitándolas
me fue dada en lugar de servir para algo.
Me condené escribiendo a que todos dudaran
de mi existencia real,
(días de mi escritura, solar del extranjero).
Todos los que sirvieron y los que fueron servidos
digo que pasarán porque escribí
y hacerlo significa trabajar con la muerte
codo a codo, robarle unos cuantos secretos.
En su origen el río es una veta de agua
—allí, por un momento, siquiera, en esa altura—

luego, al final, un mar que nadie ve
de los que están braceándose la vida.
Porque escribí fui un odio vergonzante,
pero el mar forma parte de mi escritura misma:
línea de la rompiente en que un verso se espuma
yo puedo reiterar la poesía.

Estuve enfermo, sin lugar a dudas
y no sólo de insomnio,
también de ideas fijas que me hicieron leer
con obscena atención a unos cuantos sicólogos,
pero escribí y el crimen fue menor,
lo pagué verso a verso hasta escribirlo,
porque de la palabra que se ajusta al abismo
surge un poco de oscura inteligencia
y a esa luz muchos monstruos no son ajusticiados.

Porque escribí no estuve en casa del verdugo
ni me dejé llevar por el amor a Dios
ni acepté que los hombres fueran dioses
ni me hice desear como escribiente
ni la pobreza me pareció atroz
ni el poder una cosa deseable
ni me lavé ni me ensucié las manos
ni fueron vírgenes mis mejores amigas
ni tuve como amigo a un fariseo
ni a pesar de la cólera
quise desbaratar a mi enemigo.

Pero escribí y me muero por mi cuenta,
porque escribí porque escribí estoy vivo.

José María Lima
1934—
Puerto Rico

El lenguaje es
La sílaba en la piel, 1982.

1. El lenguaje es antes que nada algo como un cuchillo o una soga.

1.i Aplicado a una porción de la realidad la transfoma para nuestro beneficio. La guía hacia el sujeto.

1.ii Se hace llegar a algo para transformarlo conforme a un deseo o necesidad.

1.iii El lenguaje antes de decir, hacía.

2. La expresión, o la situación o la particular conformación de la materia "puede que..." es a veces algo como el sueño o el reposo. Porque la indiferencia es reposo y sin ella duele el movimiento.

2.i Se hizo el cuchillo de las conchas y las piedras y la dureza de ambas. Se hizo el lenguaje de estas mismas cosas y además del color de las conchas y la blandura del aire y de ciertos olores y de la humedad que los abrigaba. Se hizo del deseo de permanecer que es el sexo y la osadía y la cautela que son deseo de permanecer.

El lenguaje mienta, miente y enmienda, pero mendaba antes de enmendar y esto último antes de mentar o mentir, lo que quiere decir que llenamos ciertos agujeros y estamos en actitud de sentir la separación y nos duele y hay que separarse para sentir la alegría de la separación que es promesa de futuros encuentros. Eso es hablar.

El lenguaje es sexo. Que nadie lo olvide. Opinión subjetiva y parcial pero correcta.

El olvido es muerte que es también reposo porque así lo deseamos. Somos los inventores del olvido. Recordar es sabernos, casi en el sentido cartesiano. Porque sabernos es ser. La sé (a la hembra) cuando recuerdo su hondura húmeda y caliente y los accidentes que me la proporcionan y las muertes en ella.

No podemos reducir la realidad al lenguaje porque estaríamos reduciendo el todo a una de sus partes, y aún cuando fuera cierto que no vamos a caer en contradic-

ción haciéndolo, conocimiento y consistencia no son
sinónimos. Pensar una estrella no es tocarla.

Si la contradicción formal es anatema sea, pero siempre ha habido equivocaciones y en el desarrollo del pensamiento algunos cráneos rotos. Ciertos regalos hay que
desenvolverlos rompiendo la envoltura. Todo virgo destrozado es una contradicción formal.

La totalidad del saber humano no se reduce a Principia Mathematica ni a Tractatus Lógico-Philosophicus.
Si así fuera ya nos hubiéramos atrevido a quemar todo
lo otro.

El lenguaje es camino sujeto a todas las contingencias del desarrollo y viviendo de sus contradicciones in-
ternas. Ser lógico es admitir que no sabemos en qué consiste, que tal vez nunca lo sepamos pero que cada vez lo
somos en mayor medida.

La lógica es un camino encontrado y otros que nos
vamos haciendo, atrechos o enmiendas a los obstáculos
reales o imaginarios.

Ser lógico es alcanzar, cubriendo camino, creciendo
en conocimiento y concordancia con todo lo que es menos yo o que no sea yo en absoluto.

Pensar es también pensar sobre el pensamiento y pensar que pensamos sobre el pensamiento. Aturdirnos y
abandonar el pensamiento, tal vez para no volver a él. La
locura pudiera ser una parte exquisita del pensar o espi-
nosa o ambas. Muchas veces sentimos que tenemos derecho a la locura otras veces que tenemos la responsabilidad de eludirla. Esa misma relación guardamos con muchas otras cosas como el amor desenfrenado por ejemplo.

El lenguaje es una espada con el mango al rojo vivo.
Lo de dos filos ya está gastado.

El lenguaje me separa de las cosas y al mismo tiempo
me permite caminar entre ellas.

El lenguaje es coraza, lanza, gancho y balsa. Por supuesto que ni víboras ni águilas ni pirañas lo resisten
pero la piraña no es, entre otras cosas, su mordedura
hasta el hueso. Y también cultivar margaritas desde el
lado oscuro. Pero ese saber no lo queremos. Por eso lenguaje es mampara y que se joda. En esa pared nos rasca-
mos con fruición la espalda y tenemos orgasmos. Como
la niña en la bicicleta o la dulce llaga en el tobillo.

¿Qué es la raíz de la lengua? ¿Qué es la fuente de la
lengua? ¿Qué es la multitud de condiciones que la en-

gendraron? Las diferentes texturas que el movimiento
muestra en su desarrollo. Por eso se mostraba antes del
lenguaje. El dedo índice y los labios impulsaron los movimientos especiales de la lengua. Quizá también los no-
tan-especiales. Puede que se deba al hecho de que la adquisición y admisión del sustento material depende en
gran medida de ellos. Porque queremos ser eternos antes
de sentir que lo somos. Y lo seguimos deseando después
de sentir que no lo somos.

José María Lima
1934—
Puerto Rico

Más antigua que el agua
Homenaje al ombligo, 1966.

más antigua que el agua
desde antes del sonido fuiste
y fue el deseo mío de encontrarte
formándose en promesa de carne
aun no nacida.
allí, cuando surgías —sin sílabas
ni flechas, solo una adivinanza
sin veredas tu cuerpo,
futuro sin espinas,
sin gozos, sin verdades—
debo haber comenzado yo también
y tropezaron, quizá, las realidades
nacientes en la materia dura
que encerraba la risa
y tenía también guardado el llanto
en su latido oscuro.
y comenzó a forjarse la cadena
de limo y musgo;
la sangre que nacía
se hizo gigantesco dolor
y luego: verbo.
no fue barro ni hueso en el comienzo,
sino palpitación de átomo creciendo
hasta formar la estrella
y recordando que eran uno
cuando la flor no era.

Ramón López Velarde
1888–1921
México

Mi prima Agueda
La sangre devota, 1916.

Mi madrina invitaba a mi prima Agueda
a que pasara el día con nosotros,
y mi prima llegaba
con un contradictorio
prestigio de almidón y de temible
luto ceremonioso.

Agueda aparecía, resonante
de almidón, y sus ojos
verdes y sus mejillas rubicundas
me protegían contra el pavoroso
luto...

          Yo era rapaz
y conocía la *o* por lo redondo,
y Agueda que tejía
mansa y perseverante en el sonoro
corredor, me causaba
calosfríos ignotos...

(Creo que hasta la debo la costumbre
heroicamente insana de hablar solo.)

A la hora de comer, en la penumbra
quieta del refectorio,
me iba embelesando un quebradizo
sonar intermitente de vajilla
y el timbre caricioso
de la voz de mi prima.
                    Agueda era
(luto, pupilas verdes y mejillas
rubicundas) un cesto policromo
de manzanas y uvas
en el ébano de un armario añoso.

Antonio Machado
1875–1939
España

Retrato
Campos de Castilla, 1912.

Mi infancia son recuerdos de un patio de Sevilla
y un huerto claro donde madura el limonero
mi juventud, veinte años en tierra de Castilla;
mi historia, algunos casos que recordar no quiero.

Ni un seductor Mañara ni un Bradomín he sido
—ya conocéis mi torpe aliño indumentario—;
mas recibí la flecha que me asignó Cupido
y amé cuanto ellas pueden tener de hospitalario.

Hay en mis venas gotas de sangre jacobina,
pero mi verso brota de manantial sereno;
y más que un hombre al uso que sabe su doctrina,
soy, en el buen sentido de la palabra, bueno.

Adoro la hermosura, y en la moderna estética,
corté las viejas rosas del huerto de Ronsard;
mas no amo los afeites de la actual cosmética
ni soy un ave de esas del nuevo gay trinar.

Desdeño las romanzas de los tenores huecos
y el coro de los grillos que cantan a la luna.
A distinguir me paro las voces de los ecos,
y escucho solamente, entre las voces, una.

¿Soy clásico o romántico? No sé. Dejar quisiera
mi verso como deja el capitán su espada:
famosa por la mano viril que la blandiera,
no por el docto oficio del forjador preciada.

Converso con el hombre que siempre va conmigo
—quien habla solo, espera hablar a Dios un día—;
mi soliloquio es plática con este buen amigo
que me enseñó el secreto de la filantropía.

Y al cabo, nada os debo; debéisme cuanto he escrito.
A mi trabajo acudo, con mi dinero pago

el traje que me cubre y la mansión que habito,
el pan que me alimenta y el lecho en donde yago.

Y cuando llegue el día del último viaje
y esté al partir la nave que nunca ha de tornar,
me encontraréis a bordo ligero de equipaje
casi desnudo, como los hijos de la mar.

———

Antonio Machado
1875–1939
España

La Saeta
Campos de Castilla, 1912.

> *¿Quién me presta una escalera*
> *para subir al madero,*
> *para quitarle los clavos*
> *a Jesús el Nazareno?*
>
> Saeta Popular

¡Oh, la saeta, el cantar
al Cristo de los gitanos,
siempre con sangre en las manos,
siempre por desenclavar!
¡Cantar del pueblo andaluz,
que todas las primaveras
anda pidiendo escaleras
para subir a la cruz!
¡Cantar de la tierra mía,
que echa flores
al Jesús de la agonía,
y es la fe de mis mayores!
¡Oh, no eres tú mi cantar!
¡No puedo cantar, ni quiero
a ese Jesús del madero,
sino al que anduvo en el mar!

José Martí
1853-1895
Cuba

Banquete de tiranos
Versos libres, 1913.

Hay una raza vil de hombres tenaces,
de sí propios inflados, y hechos todos,
todos del pelo al pie, de garra y diente;
y hay otros, como flor, que al viento exhalan
en el amor del hombre su perfume.
Como en el bosque hay tórtolas y fieras
y plantas insectívoras y puras
sensitivas y clavel en los jardines.
De alma de hombres los unos se alimentan;
los otros su alma dan a que se nutran
y perfumen su diente los glotones,
tal como el hierro frío en las entrañas
de la virgen que mata se calienta.

A un banquete se sientan los tiranos
pero cuando la mano ensangrentada
hunden en el manjar, del mártir muerto
surge una luz que les aterra, flores
grandes como una cruz súbito surgen
y huyen, rojo el hocico, y pavoridos
a sus negras entrañas los tiranos.

Los que se aman a sí, los que la augusta
razón a su avaricia y gula ponen;
los que no ostentan en la frente honrada
ese cinto de luz que en el yugo funde
como el inmenso sol en ascuas quiebra
los astros que a su seno se abalanzan;
los que no llevan del decoro humano
ornado el sano pecho; los menores
y los segundones de la vida, sólo
a su goce ruin y medro atentos
y no al concierto universal.

Danzas, comidas, músicas, harenes,
jamás la aprobación de un hombre honrado.
Y si acaso sin sangre hacerse puede,

hágase... Clávalos, clávalos
en el horcón más alto del camino
por la mitad de la villana frente.
A la grandiosa humanidad traidores,
como implacable obrero
que un féretro de bronce clavetea,
los que contigo
se parten la nación a dentelladas.

José Martí
1853—1895
Cuba

Rima V
Versos sencillos, 1891.

Si ves un monte de espumas,
es mi verso lo que ves:
mi verso es un monte, y es
un abanico de plumas.

Mi verso es como un puñal
que por el puño echa flor:
mi verso es un surtidor
que da un agua de coral.

Mi verso es de un verde claro
y de un carmín encendido:
mi verso es un ciervo herido
que busca en el monte amparo.

Mi verso al valiente agrada:
mi verso, breve y sincero,
es del vigor del acero
con que se funde la espada.

Francisco Matos Paoli
1915—
Puerto Rico

Canto de la locura
1962.

SI USTEDES quieren llamarme loco,
no pongo ningún impedimento a la afrenta.

Sé que soy el precito,
el inolvidable abyecto de la sombra,
el vencido sereno,
el esclavo que a la luz perdona.

YO CONFIO en los sencillos
que se desplazan hacia el mar
tornasolado.

Pongo mi piel a la venta
¿y quién me compra?

Tal vez el camino abandonado
que no tiene posada,
tal vez el abuelo del iris
en una isla en que está la paloma.

Si quieren mellar mi espada,
adelante.

Si quieren robar mis versos,
adelante.

Si quieren confundirme con el loco John Doe,
adelante.

Estoy pronto a todo,
a ser el inerme nacarado
que pasa y no pasa.

A ser la criatura clausurada
que nadie saluda en la calle.

A ser el imperfecto
que cada día derrama
el cubo de la basura.

Pero no podrán quitarme el desvariado sentir
que me imanta a las dalias caídas,
no me podrán quitar
esta sangre inocente que milita
en una isla avergonzada.

YO ESTUVE un día aquí.

Y es borroso el recuerdo.

El adiós multiplica sus hojas,
pero las hojas vuelan,
son diminutas vidas
más suaves que la gloria.

Lo que me espera arriba
no es Jehová parado en la retama,
sino el Indefenso,
el hijo usual que busca la palabra,
el centinela de mi horror
convertido en palmar
que nunca más se asombra.

Estoy casi desprendido.

La pared, la pared,
la sola realidad sin sol hermano,
la que me reservan
los pobres renacidos.

Sé que Luzbel atiza
su silencio
para que no sea más que una oreja sin cuerpo
estupefacta,
pero mis ojos ven
la virginal blancura
y ya jamás me creo
como la arena que titila en el
Desierto.

¿Cuándo vendrá la florecita
de Francisco de Asís,
el de la fina humillación en las cosas,
a retener la isla jubilosa
en que no moría mamá,
alta, alta,
abrazada al luminar del día,
fuerte como los
amados
elementos?   (Fragmento).

Francisco Matos Paoli
1915—
Puerto Rico

Habitante del eco
Habitante del eco (1937-41). Publicado en 1944.

Decir frías palabras, corpóreas aves huecas,
qué beatitud sin cuerpos de justas esperanzas.
Fluir del corazón, torpe surtidor de agonía :
sobre esta boca exenta de sonidos batalla.

Habitante del eco : no te oirás en la plena
fosforescencia indómita del rayo, nuevo lirio.
Carne fija del sueño, borrasca, muerte mía,
cómo el aire destila tus lámparas desiertas.

Ebria, vasta lanzada de la rosa : no sueñes.
Oh páramo del Verbo sin límites, ¿vendrás?
Soy bajo tu influjo desolador pupila,
habitante del eco taladrando la inerme
espesura de nieve con labios ardorosos.

Mane tu canto alondras, el fuego te persigne.
Inclinador de sombras como tallos, despierta.
Amorteces un lampo perenne, una hecatombe
de garganta criando su delta de gemidos.

Habitante del eco naciendo ánima blanca
por esta sorda teoría de vuelos y esta boca
larvada en la inefable zona de su delirio.

Joserramón Melendes
1952—
Puerto Rico

Narciso
La casa de la forma, 1986.

> *El río le debuelbe otro Narciso.*
> —Lez., Erác.

Narciso, espejo. El pes qe te persige
persigiéndolo tú en el lago qieto,
bibe de ti i perbibe de tu reto.
A su escama profunda pronte liges

el ojo qe acometes, i en su seto
asogado también a ber consiges
su figura otra bes: ¡Qé pes repleto!
Aora asecha su duplo asta qe figes,

fijes matando, su agaya benidera.
¿Qe no? ¿Qestá temblando tu qimera?
Bélo temblar al pes por el qe bibes

como tiembla tu mano qe se arredra:
El espejo eres tú. Sobre él escribes
ese pes qe te crese i qe te medra.

Se ha respetado la ortografía del autor, quien aboga por estas modificaciones en el lenguaje escrito.

Pedro Mir
1913—
República Dominicana

Si alguien quiere saber cuál es mi patria

Viaje a la muchedumbre, 1971.

I

Si alguien quiere saber cuál es mi patria
no la busque,
no pregunte por ella.

Siga el rastro goteante por el mapa
y su efigie de patas imperfectas.
No pregunte si viene del rocío
o si tiene espirales en las piedras
o si tiene sabor ultramarino
o si el clima le huele en primavera.
No la busque ni alargue las pupilas.
No pregunte por ella.

(¡Tanto arrojo en la lucha irremediable
y aún no hay quien lo sepa!
¡Tanto acero y fulgor de resistir
y aún no hay quien lo vea!)

No, no la busque.
Si alguien quiere saber cuál es mi patria,
no pregunte por ella.
No quiera saber si hay bosques, trinos,
penínsulas muchísimas y ajenas,
o si hay cuatro cadenas de montañas,

todas derechas,
o si hay varios destinos de bahías
y todas extranjeras.

Siga el rastro goteando por la brisa
y allí donde la sombra se presenta,
donde el tiempo castiga y desmorona,
ya no la busque,
no pregunte por ella.

Su propia sangre, su órbita querida,
su instantáneo chispazo de presencia,
su funeral de risa y de sonrisa,
su potrero de espaldas indirectas,
su puño de silencio en cada boca,
su borbotón de ira en cada mueca,
sus manos enguantadas en la fábrica y
sus pies descalzos en la carretera,
las largas cicatrices que le bajan
como antiguos riachuelos, su siniestra
figura de mujer
obligada a parir
con cada coz que busca su cadera
para echar una fila de habitantes
listos para la rueda,
todo dirá de pronto dónde existe
una patria moderna.
Dónde habrá que buscar y qué pregunta
se solicita. Porque apenas
surge la realidad y se apresura
una pregunta, ya está la respuesta.

No, no la busque.
Tendría que pelear por ella...

II

Así vamos los pueblos de la América
en mangas de camisa. No pregunte
nadie por la patria de nadie.
No pregunte
si el plomo está prohibido, si la sangre
está prohibida, si en las leyes
está prohibida el hambre.
Si resulta la noche
y firmemente los labriegos saben
el rumbo de la aurora,
el curso de la siembra. Si los sables
duermen por largo tiempo,
si están prohibidas las cárceles...
Porque apenas un crudo mozalbete desgranado
enarbola la paz como un fragante
pabellón infinito, en nombre del amor
o de la juventud en medio de las calles,

el látigo produce su rúbrica instantánea,
su bronco privilegio. Porque apenas
un escritor coloca sus telares
en la página blanca y teje un grito
y pide paz y pide voz o pide pan y luz
para las sombras populares,
para los barrios, para las niñas,
para las fábricas, para los matorrales,
cuando no es el ostracismo es el silencio,
cuando no es el olvido es el gendarme...

Y así vamos los pueblos de la América
tan numerosos y unos. No pregunte
nadie
por la patria de nadie.
Ni en los países del mar o los océanos
todos con sus hermosas capitales,
ni en las islas o los cayos
matinales:

No pregunte si hay minas infinitas,
todas inagotables,
y luchas por salvarlas del saqueo,
todas con cadáveres...

Un aroma común, un aire justo
de familia recorre nuestros ángeles,
nuestros fusiles, nuestras metonimias...
Un rostro amargo y una misma mano y unas tardes
melancólicas de nuestras tierras crían
los mismos sudores, los mismos ademanes
y la misma garra sangrienta y conocida.

Nadie pregunte por la patria de nadie.
Por encima de nuestras cordilleras y las líneas
fronterizas, más rejas y alambradas que carácter,
o diferencia o rumbo del perfil,
el mismo drama grande,
el mismo cerco impuro el ojo vigilante.
Veinte patrias para un solo tormento.
Un solo corazón para veinte fatigas nacionales.
Un mismo amor, un mismo beso para nuestras tierras
y un mismo desgarramiento en nuestra carne.

No, no pregunte
nadie por la patria de nadie.
Tendría que mudar de pensamiento
y llorar solamente por la sangre...

Nancy Morejón
1944—
Cuba

Amo a mi amo

Amo a mi amo,
recojo leña para encender su fuego cotidiano.
Amo sus ojos claros.
Mansa cual un cordero
esparzo gotas de miel por sus orejas.
Amo sus manos
que me depositaron sobre un lecho de hierbas:
Mi amo muerde y subyuga.
Me cuenta historias sigilosas mientras
abanico todo su cuerpo cundido de llagas y balazos
de días con sol y guerra de rapiña.
Amo sus pies que piratearon y rodaron
por tierras ajenas.
Los froto con los polvos más finos
que encontré, una mañana,
saliendo de la vega.
Tañó la vihuela y de su garganta salían
coplas sonoras, como nacidas de la garganta de
Manrique.
Yo quería haber oído una marímbula sonar.
Amo su boca roja, fina,
desde donde van saliendo palabras
que no alcanzo a descifrar
todavía. Mi lengua para él ya no es la suya.

Y la seda del tiempo hecha trizas.

Oyendo hablar a los viejos guardieros, supe
que mi amor
da latigazos en las calderas del ingenio,
como si fueran un infierno, el de aquel Señor Dios
de quien me hablaba sin cesar.

¿Qué me dirá?
¿Por qué vivo en la morada ideal para un murciélago?
¿Por qué le sirvo?
¿Adónde va en su espléndido coche
tirado por caballos más felices que yo?
Mi amor es como la maleza que cubre la dotación,
única posesión inexpugnable mía.

Maldigo

esta bata de muselina que me ha impuesto;
estos encajes vanos que despiadado me endilgó;
estos quehaceres para mí en el atardecer sin
        girasoles;
esta lengua abigarradamente hostil que no mastico;
estos senos de piedra que no pueden siquiera
        amamantarlo;
este vientre rajado por su látigo inmemorial;
este maldito corazón.

Amo a mi amo, pero todas las noches,
cuando atravieso la vereda florida hacia el cañaveral
        donde a hurtadillas hemos hecho el amor,
me veo cuchillo en mano, desollándolo como a una
        res sin culpa.

Ensordecedores toques de tambor ya no me dejan
oír ni sus quebrantos, ni sus quejas.
Las campanas me llaman...

Pablo Neruda
1903–1973
Chile

La ola
Canto general, 1950.

La ola viene del fondo, con raíces
hijas del firmamento sumergido.
Su elástica invasión fue levantada
por la potencia pura del Océano:
su eternidad apareció inundando
los pabellones del poder profundo
y cada ser le dio su resistencia,
desgranó fuego frío en su cintura
hasta que de las ramas de la fuerza
despegó su nevado poderío.

Viene como una flor desde la tierra
cuando avanzó con decidido aroma
hasta la magnitud de la magnolia,
pero esta flor del fondo que ha estallado
trae toda la luz que fue abolida,
trae todas las ramas que no ardieron
y todo el manantial de la blancura.

Y así cuando sus párpados redondos,
su volumen, sus copas, sus corales
hinchan la piel del mar apareciendo
todo este ser de seres submarinos:
es la unidad del mar que se construye:
la columna del mar que se levanta:
todos sus nacimientos y derrotas.

La escuela de la sal abrió las puertas,
voló toda la luz golpeando el cielo,
creció desde la noche hasta la aurora
la levadura del metal mojado,
toda la claridad se hizo corola,
creció la flor hasta gastar la piedra,
subió a la muerte el río de la espuma,
atacaron las plantas procelarias,
se desbordó la rosa en el acero:
los baluartes del agua se doblaron
y el mar desmoronó sin derramarse
su torre de cristal y escalofrío.

Pablo Neruda
1904–1973
Chile

Oda a la crítica
Odas elementales, 1954.

Yo escribí cinco versos:
uno verde,
otra era un pan redondo,
el tercero una casa levantándose,
el cuarto era un anillo,
el quinto verso era
corto como un relámpago
y al escribirlo
me dejó en la razón su quemadura.

Y bien, los hombres,
las mujeres,
vinieron y tomaron
la sencilla materia,
brizna, viento, fulgor, barro, madera
y con tan poca cosa
construyeron
paredes, pisos, sueños.
En una línea de mi poesía
secaron ropa al viento.
Comieron
mis palabras,
las guardaron
junto a la cabecera,
vivieron con un verso,
con la luz que salió de mi costado.
Entonces,
llegó un crítico mudo
y otro lleno de lenguas,
y otros, otros llegaron
ciegos o llenos de ojos,
elegantes algunos
como claveles con zapatos rojos,
otros estrictamente
vestidos de cadáveres,
algunos partidarios

del rey y su elevada monarquía,
otros se habían
enredado en la frente
de Marx y pataleaban en su barba,
otros eran ingleses,
sencillamente ingleses,
y entre todos
se lanzaron
con dientes y cuchillos,
con diccionarios y otras armas negras,
con citas respetables,
se lanzaron
a disputar mi pobre poesía
a las sencillas gentes
que la amaban:
y la hicieron embudos,
la enrollaron,
la sujetaron con cien alfileres,
la cubrieron con polvo de esqueleto,
la llenaron de tinta,
la escupieron con suave
benignidad de gatos,
la destinaron a envolver relojes,
la protegieron y la condenaron,
le arrimaron petróleo,
le dedicaron húmedos tratados,
la cocieron con leche,
le agregaron pequeñas piedrecitas,
fueron borrándole vocales,
fueron matándole
sílabas y suspiros,
la arrugaron e hicieron
un pequeño paquete
que destinaron cuidadosamente
a sus desvanes, a sus cementerios,
luego
se retiraron uno a uno
enfurecidos hasta la locura
porque no fui bastante
popular para ellos
o impregnados de dulce menosprecio
por mi ordinaria falta de tinieblas,
se retiraron
todos

y entonces,
otra vez,
junto a mi poesía
volvieron a vivir
mujeres y hombres,
de nuevo
hicieron fuego,
construyeron casas,
comieron pan,
se repartieron la luz
y en el amor unieron
relámpago y anillo.
Y ahora,
perdonadme, señores,
que interrumpa este cuento
que les estoy contando
y me vaya a vivir
para siempre
con la gente sencilla.

La poesía vuelve al pueblo.

Netzahualcóyotl
1402 –1476
Poeta Azteca

¿Qué es la poesía?
Romances de los Señores de la Nueva España
Ms. de 1585, f. 19 v. Probablemente Netzahualcóyotl, 1950.

¡Lo he comprendido al fin:
oigo un canto; veo una flor:
oh, que jamás se marchiten!

Netzahualcóyotl
1402-1472
Poeta Azteca

Yo Netzahualcóyotl lo pregunto

Yo Netzahualcóyotl lo pregunto:
¿Acaso de veras se vive con raíz en la tierra?
No para siempre en la tierra:
sólo un poco aquí.
Aunque sea de jade se quiebra,
aunque sea de oro se rompe,
aunque sea plumaje de quetzal se desgarra.
No para siempre en la tierra:
sólo un poco aquí.

Luz Ivonne Ochart
1949—
Puerto Rico

New York-New York
Poemas de Nueva York, 1980.
Publicado en 1989, Obra poética.

dije: oh!, y todo esto es mío!
Nueva York!, perfecta inundación de la luz!
pero la muerte se desliza por el bies de una lujosa tela de
　　satín de seda
hacia mí
por lo que sigo caminando calle arriba
y me detengo, como siempre, a ver
las doradas escamas de la cigüeña persa
que me gusta tanto.
Esa cigüeña mide aproximadamente cuatro pies
de manera que su pico de oro quede
a la altura de la mano de alguien sentado,
y en su pico sostiene un artefacto
para calentar copas de brandy.

Bajo sus escamas está
salta hacia mí
lucha contra el cristal que nos separa
mientras su ojo azul inmóvil   mira en línea recta hacia
                                                    el infinito
y pasan transeúntes de mirada impasible hacia el infinito que
     me traspasa de
infinito vacío y poblado de transeúntes de mirada impasible
     hacia el infinito
mientras el ojo azul de la cigüeña persa que me gusta tanto
     no me busca
impregnándome de su muerte
de poblados transeúntes, poblados espacios abarrotados de
     tiempo
y objetos y gente que no conozco
sin dejar un resquicio
de espacio infinito de muerte
que salta hacia mí,
de manera que camino calle arriba encendiendo un cigarrillo
     y cruzo la calle
al paso del ritmo de nueve millones de habitantes
que cruzan las calles,
chinos latinoamericanos negros
rusos alemanes iraníes polacos israelitas
polinesios africanos
rumanos islandeses suecos
lituanos australianos japoneses
ingleses italianos indús
norteamericanos moviéndose al ritmo de
cien billones de máquinas que
aguardan como una amante fiel
el deseo el deseo el deseo
el deseo de nueve millones
para cumplirlo,
para darse
para entregar todo todo
a ese deseo, ese fugaz histérico deseo
de cada uno de esos nueve millones de deseos
abrazando desbordándose sobre las máquinas de coca-cola,
     las máquinas IBM, las
máquinas telefónicas, las máquinas X300-5, las 2-X-100,
las forjadoras de metales, de piezas de estructuras de edificios,
de radares, de transformadores, de aviones, de generadores
     eléctricos,

de generadores atómicos, de generadores inalámbricos, de
    tubos
de túneles de silos, de antitanques, de misiles Pershing II,
de bombarderos B-IB, de submarinos atómicos Trident, de
bombarderos Stealth, de los M113, de aviones con misiles
    antitanques
de A-7 Corsair II, de F-14 Tomcats,
todos, todos y todas desbordándose para esperar el amor
    del dólar
o la ilusión de vivir ese gran amor del dólar desbordándose,
y cruzo la calle escapando
pero los meseros de las pizzerías
los cantineros del Waldorf o de Tony's Bar o La Ultima Copita
cantan y sueñan
"street girls, for a nickel for a dime"
y los jóvenes bailan
"don't stop de music" luciendo el disfraz
de sus estrellas favoritas
desde los que se desliza hacia mí la muerte
porque no hay un rostro,
busco, y no hay   un   solo   rostro
al que volverme, para decirle
a ella,   a esa,   a la muerte:
—Lo siento,—
pero hoy tengo compañía.

Blas de Otero
1916–1979
España

En el principio
Pido la paz y la palabra, 1955.

Si he perdido la vida, el tiempo, todo
lo que tiré, como un anillo, al agua,
si he perdido la voz en la maleza,
me queda la palabra.

Si he sufrido la sed, el hambre, todo
lo que era mío y resultó ser nada,

si he segado las sombras en silencio,
me queda la palabra.

Si abrí los labios para ver el rostro
puro y terrible de mi patria,
si abrí los labios hasta desgarrármelos,
me queda la palabra.

Luis Palés Matos
1898—1959
Puerto Rico

El llamado
1953.

Me llaman desde allá...
larga voz de hoja seca,
mano fugaz de nube
que en el aire de otoño se dispersa.
Por arriba el llamado
tira de mí con tenue hilo de estrella;
abajo, el agua en tránsito,
con sollozo de espuma entre la niebla.
Ha tiempo oigo las voces
y descubro las señas.

Hoy recuerdo: es un día venturoso
de cielo despejado y clara tierra;
golondrinas erráticas
el calmo azul puntean.
Estoy frente a la mar y en lontananza
se va perdiendo el ala de una vela;
va yéndose, esfumándose,
y yo también me voy borrando en ella.
Y cuando al fin retorno,
por un leve resquicio de conciencia,
¡cuán lejos ya me encuentro de mí mismo!
¡qué mundo más extraño me rodea!

Ahora, dormida junto a mí, reposa
mi amor sobre la hierba.

El seno palpitante
sube y baja tranquilo en la marca
del ímpetu calmado que diluye
espectrales añiles en su ojera.
Miro esa dulce fábrica rendida,
cuerpo de trampa y presa
cuyo ritmo esencial como jugando
manufactura la caricia aérea,
el arrullo narcótico y el beso
—víspera ardiente de gozosa queja—
y me digo: —Ya todo ha terminado...
Mas de pronto, despierta,
y allá en el negro hondón de sus pupilas
que son un despedirse y una ausencia,
algo me invita a su remota margen
y dulcemente, sin querer, me lleva.

Me llaman desde allá...
Mi nave aparejada está dispuesta.
A su redor, en grumos de silencio,
sordamente coagula la tiniebla.
Un mar hueco, sin peces,
agua vacía y negra,
sin vena de fulgor que le penetre
ni pisada de brisa que la mueva.
Fondo inmóvil de sombra,
límite gris de piedra...
¡Oh soledad, que a fuerza de andar sola
se siente de sí misma compañera!

Emisario solícito que vienes
con oculto mensaje hasta mi puerta,
sé lo que te propones
y no me engaña tu misión secreta;
me llaman desde allá,
pero el amor dormido aquí en la hierba
es bello todavía
y un júbilo de sol baña la tierra.
¡Déjeme tu implacable poderío
una hora, un minuto más con ella!

Luis Palés Matos
1898–1959
Puerto Rico

Mulata Antilla

(Segunda versión publicada en la edición de 1959 de
Tuntún de pasa y grifería)

En ti, ahora, mulata,
me acojo al tibio mar de las Antillas.
Agua sensual y lenta de melaza,
puerto de azúcar, cálida bahía,
con la luz en reposo
dorando la onda limpia,
y en el soñoliento zumbo de colmena
que cuajan los trajines de la orilla.

En ti ahora, mulata,
cruzo el mar de las islas.
Eléctricos mininos de ciclones
en tus curvas se alargan y se ovillan,
mientras sobre mi barca va cayendo
la noche de tus ojos, pensativa.

En ti ahora, mulata...
¡oh despertar glorioso en las Antillas!
Bravo color que el do de pecho alcanza,
música al rojo vivo de alegría,
y calientes cantáridas de aroma
—limón, tabaco, piña—
zumbando a los sentidos
sus embriagadas voces de delicia.

Eres ahora, mulata,
todo el mar y la tierra de mis islas.
Sinfonía frutal cuyas escalas
rompen furiosamente en tu catinga.
He aquí en su verde traje la guanábana
con sus finas y blandas pantaletas
de muselina; he aquí el caimito
con su leche infantil; he aquí la piña
con su corona de soprano... Todos
los frutos ¡oh mulata! tú me brindas,
en la clara bahía de tu cuerpo
por los soles del trópico bruñida.

Imperio tuyo, el plátano y el coco,
que apuntan su dorada artillería
al barco transeúnte que nos deja
su rubio contrabando de turistas.
En potro de huracán pasas cantando
tu criolla canción, prieta walkiria,   *diosas menores de la mitología nórdica*
con centelleante espuela de relámpagos
rumbo al verde Walhalla de las islas.   *lugar donde van los héroes muertos a beber agua.*

distintos todos los placeres ⟩ Eres inmensidad libre y sin límites,
eres amor sin trabas y sin prisas;
en tu vientre conjugan mis dos razas
sus vitales potencias expansivas.
Amor, tórrido amor de la mulata,   *Caliente*
gallo de ron, azúcar derretida,
tabonuco que el tuétano te abrasa
con aromas de sándalo y de mirra.
Con voces del Cantar de los Cantares,   *canciones de amor*
eres morena porque el sol te mira.
Debajo de tu lengua hay miel y leche
y ungüento derramado en tus pupilas.
Como la torre de David, tu cuello,
y tus pechos gemelas cervatillas,   *se va ha llegar al paraíso.*
Flor de Sarón y lirio de los valles,
yegua de Faraón, ¡oh Sulamita!

Cuba, Santo Domingo, Puerto Rico,   *islas hispanas*
fogosas y sensuales tierras mías.
¡Oh los rones calientes de Jamaica!   *islas*
¡Oh fiero calalú de Martinica!
¡Oh noche fermentada de tambores
del Haití impenetrable y voduista!
Dominica, Tortola, Guadalupe,
¡Antillas, mis Antillas!
Sobre el mar de Colón, aupadas todas,
sobre el Caribe mar, todas unidas,
soñando y padeciendo y forcejeando
contra pestes, ciclones, ciclones y codicias,
y muriéndose un poco por la noche,
y otra vez a la aurora, redivivas,
porque eres tú, mulata de los trópicos,
la libertad cantando en mis Antillas.

Nicanor Parra
1914—
Chile

Los vicios del mundo moderno
Obra gruesa, 1969.

Los delincuentes modernos
Están autorizados para concurrir diariamente a parques
                                                    y jardines.
Provistos de poderosos anteojos y de relojes de bolsillo
Entran a saco en los kioskos favorecidos por la muerte
E instalan sus laboratorios entre los rosales en flor.
Desde allí controlan a fotógrafos y mendigos que deambulan
                                            por los alrededores
Procurando levantar un pequeño templo a la miseria
Y si se presenta la oportunidad llegan a poseer a un
                                            lustrabotas melancólico.
La policía atemorizada huye de estos monstruos
En dirección del centro de la ciudad
En donde estallan los grandes incendios de fines de año
Y un valiente encapuchado pone manos arriba a dos madres
                                            de la caridad.

Los vicios del mundo moderno:
El automóvil y el cine sonoro,
Las discriminaciones raciales,
El exterminio de los pieles rojas,
Los trucos de la alta banca,
La catástrofe de los ancianos,
El comercio clandestino de blancas realizado por sodomitas
                                            internacionales,
El auto-bombo y la gula
Las Pompas Fúnebres
Los amigos personales de su excelencia
La exaltación del folklore a categoría del espíritu,
El abuso de los estupefacientes y de la filosofía,
El reblandecimiento de los hombres favorecidos por la fortuna
El auto-erotismo y la crueldad sexual
La exaltación de lo onírico y del subconsciente en desmedro
                                            del sentido común.
La confianza exagerada en sueros y vacunas,
El endiosamiento del falo,

La política internacional de piernas abiertas patrocinada
                              por la prensa reaccionaria,
El afán desmedido de poder y de lucro,
La carrera del oro,
La fatídica danza de los dólares,
La especulación y el aborto,
La destrucción de los ídolos,
El desarrollo excesivo de la dietética y de la psicología
                                          pedagógica,
El vicio del baile, del cigarrillo, de los juegos de azar,
Las gotas de sangre que suelen encontrarse entre las sábanas
                              de los recién desposados.
La locura del mar,
La agorafobia y la claustrofobia,
La desintegración del átomo,
El humorismo sangriento de la teoría de la relatividad,
El delirio de retorno al vientre materno,
El culto de lo exótico,
Los accidentes aeronáuticos,
Las incineraciones, las purgas en masa, la retención de los
                                          pasaportes,
Todo esto porque sí,
Porque produce vértigo,
La interpretación de los sueños
Y la difusión de la radiomanía.

Como queda demostrado, el mundo moderno se compone
                              de flores artificiales.
Que se cultivan en unas campanas de vidrio parecidas a la
                                          muerte,
Está formado por estrellas de cine.
Y de sangrientos boxeadores que pelean a la luz de luna,
Se compone de hombres ruiseñores que controlan la vida
                              económica de los países
Mediante algunos mecanismos fáciles de explicar;
Ellos visten generalmente de negro como los precursores
                              del otoño
Y se alimentan de raíces y de hierbas silvestres.
Entretanto los sabios, comidos por las ratas,
Se pudren en los sótanos de las catedrales,
Y las almas nobles son perseguidas implacablemente
                              por la policía.
El mundo moderno es una gran cloaca:
Los restorantes de lujo están atestados de cadáveres digestivos
Y de pájaros que vuelan peligrosamente a escasa altura.

Esto no es todo: Los hospitales están llenos de impostores,
Sin mencionar a los herederos del espíritu que establecen sus
               colonias en el ano de los recién operados.

Los industriales moderados sufren a veces el efecto de la
               atmósfera envenenada,
Junto a las máquinas de tejer suelen caer enfermos del
               espantoso mal del sueño
Que los transforma a la larga en unas especies de ángeles.
Niegan la existencia del mundo físico
Y se vanaglorian de ser unos pobres hijos del sepulcro.
Sin embargo, el mundo ha sido siempre así.
La verdad, como la belleza, no se crea ni se pierde
Y la poesía reside en las cosas o es simplemente un espejismo
               del espíritu.
Reconozco que un terremoto bien concebido
Puede acabar en algunos segundos con una ciudad rica
               en tradiciones
Y que un minucioso bombardeo aéreo
Derribe árboles, caballos, tronos, música.
Pero qué importa todo esto
Si mientras la bailarina más grande del mundo
Muere pobre y abandonada en una pequeña aldea del sur
               de Francia
La primavera devuelve al hombre una parte de las flores
               desaparecidas.

Tratemos de ser felices, recomiendo yo, chupando
               la miserable costilla humana.
Extraigamos de ella el líquido renovador,
Cada cual de acuerdo con sus inclinaciones personales.
¡Aferrémonos a esta piltrafa divina!
Jadeantes y tremebundos
Chupemos estos labios que nos enloquecen;
La suerte está echada.
Aspiremos este perfume enervador y destructor
Y vivamos un día más la vida de los elegidos:
De sus axilas extrae el hombre la cera necesaria para forjar
               el rostro de sus ídolos.
Y del sexo de la mujer la paja y el barro de sus templos.
Por todo lo cual
Cultivo un piojo en mi corbata
Y sonrío a los imbéciles que bajan de los árboles.

Octavio Paz
1914—
México

Aquí
Salamandra, 1958-1961.

Mis pasos en esta calle
Resuenan
        En otra calle
Donde
    Oigo mis pasos
Pasar en esta calle
Donde

Sólo es real la niebla

Octavio Paz
1914
México

Certeza
Salamandra, 1958-1961.

Si es real la luz blanca
De esta lámpara, real
La mano que escribe, ¿son reales
Los ojos que miran lo escrito?

De una palabra a la otra
Lo que digo se desvanece.
Yo sé que estoy vivo
Entre dos paréntesis.

Octavio Paz
1914
México

Madrugada
Salamandra, 1958-1961

Rápidas manos frías
Retiran una a una
Las vendas de la sombra
Abro los ojos
              Todavía
Estoy vivo
          En el centro
De una herida todavía fresca

Octavio Paz
1914
México

Identidad
Salamandra, 1958-1961.

En el patio un pájaro pía,
Como el centavo en su alcancía.

Un poco de aire su plumaje
Se desvanece en un viraje.

Tal vez no hay pájaro ni soy
Ese del patio en donde estoy.

Octavio Paz
1914
México

O Soleil c'est le temps de la Raison ardente.
Apollinaire

Himno entre ruinas
La estación violenta, 1954.

donde espumoso el mar siciliano...
Góngora

Coronado de sí el día extiende sus plumas.
¡Alto grito amarillo,
caliente surtidor en el centro de un cielo
imparcial y benéfico!
Las apariencias son hermosas en esta su verdad momentánea.
El mar trepa la costa,
se afianza entre las peñas, araña deslumbrante;
la herida cárdena del monte resplandece;
un puñado de cabras es un rebaño de piedras;
el sol pone su huevo de oro y se derrama sobre el mar.
Todo es dios.
¡Estatua rota,
columnas comidas por la luz,
ruinas vivas en un mundo de muertos en vida!

Cae la noche sobre Teotihuacán.
En lo alto de la pirámide los muchachos fuman marihuana,
suenan guitarras roncas.
¿Qué yerba, qué agua de vida ha de darnos la vida,
dónde desenterrar la palabra,
la proporción que rige al himno y al discurso,
al baile, a la ciudad y a la balanza?
El canto mexicano estalla en un carajo,
estrella de colores que se apaga,
piedra que nos cierra las puertas del contacto.
Sabe la tierra a tierra envejecida.

Los ojos ven, las manos tocan.
Bastan aquí unas cuantas cosas:
tuna, espinoso planeta coral,
higos encapuchados,
uvas con gusto a resurrección,
almejas, virginidades ariscas,
sal, queso, vino, pan solar.

Desde lo alto de su morenía una isleña me mira,
esbelta catedral vestida de luz.
Torres de sal, contra los pinos verdes de la orilla
surgen las velas blancas de las barcas.
La luz crea templos en el mar.

Nueva York, Londres, Moscú.
La sombra cubre al llano con su yedra fantasma,
con su vacilante vegetación de escalofrío,
su vello ralo, su tropel de ratas.
A trechos tirita un sol anémico.
Acodado en montes que ayer fueron ciudades, Polifemo
bosteza.
Abajo, entre los hoyos, se arrastra un rebaño de hombres.
(Bípedos domésticos, su carne
—a pesar de recientes interdicciones religiosas—
es muy gustada por las clases ricas.
Hasta hace poco el vulgo los consideraba animales impuros.)

Ver, tocar formas hermosas, diarias,
Zumba la luz, dardos y alas.
Huele a sangre la mancha de vino en el mantel.
Como el coral sus ramas en el agua
extiendo mis sentidos en la hora viva:
el instante se cumple en una concordancia amarilla,

¡oh mediodía, espiga henchida de minutos.
copa de eternidad!

Mis pensamientos se bifurcan, serpean, se enredan,
recomienzan,
y al fin se inmovilizan, ríos que no desembocan,
delta de sangre bajo un sol sin crepúsculo.
¿Y todo ha de parar en este chapoteo de aguas muertas?

¡Día, redondo día.
luminosa naranja de veinticuatro gajos,
todos atravesados por una misma y amarilla dulzura!
La inteligencia al fin encarna,
se reconcilian las dos mitades enemigas
y la conciencia-espejo se licúa,
vuelve a ser fuente, manantial de fábulas:
Hombre, árbol de imágenes,
palabras que son flores que son frutos que son actos.

Nápoles, 1948

Carlos Pellicer
1899—1977
México

He olvidado mi nombre
Primera antología poética, 1969.

He olvidado mi nombre.
Todo será posible menos llamarse Carlos.
¿Y dónde habrá quedado?
¿En manos de qué algo habrá quedado?
Estoy entre la noche desnudo como un baño
listo y que nadie usa por no ser el primero
en revolver el mármol de un agua tan estricta
que fuera uno a parar en estatua de aseo.

Al olvidar mi nombre siento comodidades
de lluvia en un paraje donde nunca ha llovido.
Una presencia lluvia con paisaje
y un profundo entonar el olvido.

¿Qué hará mi nombre,
en dónde habrá quedado?

Siento que un territorio parecido a Tabasco
me lleva entre sus ríos inaugurando bosques,
unos bosques tan jóvenes que da pena escucharlos
deletreando los nombres de los pájaros.

Son ríos que se bañan cuando lo anochecido
de todas las palabras siembra la confusión
y la desnudez del sueño está dormida
sobre los nombres íntimos de lo que fue una flor.

Y yo sin nombre y solo con mi cuerpo sin nombre
llamándole amarillo al azul y amarillo
a lo que nunca puede jamás ser amarillo;
feliz, desconocido de todos los colores.

¿A qué fruto sin árbol le habré dado mi nombre
con este olvido lívido de tan feliz memoria?
En el Tabasco nuevo de un jaguar despertado
por los antiguos pájaros que enseñaron al día

a ponerse la voz igual que una sortija
de frente y de canto.

Jaguar que está en Tabasco y estrena desnudez
y se queda mirando los trajes de la selva,
con una gran penumbra de pereza y desdén.

Por nacer en Tabasco cubro de cercanías
húmedas y vitales el olvido a mi nombre
y otra vez terrenal y nuevo paraíso
mi cuerpo bien herido toda mi sangre corre.

Correr y ya sin nombre y estrenando hojarasca
de siglos.
Correr feliz, feliz de no reconocerse
al invadir las islas de un viaje arena y tibio.
He perdido mi nombre.
¿En qué jirón de bosque habrá quedado?

¿Qué corazón del río lo tendrá como un pez,
sano y salvo?

Me matarán de hambre la aurora y el crepúsculo.
Un pan caliente —el Sol— me dará al mediodía.
Yo era siete y setenta y ahora sólo uno,
uno que vale uno de cerca y lejanía.

El bien bañado río todo desnudo y fuerte,
sin nombre de colores ni de cantos.
Defendido del Sol con la hoja de tóh.
Todo será posible menos llamarse Carlos.

Pedro Pietri
1944—
Puerto Rico

Tata
Obituario puertorriqueño, 1977.

Mi abuela
has been
in this dept store
called america
for the past twenty-five years
She is eighty-five years old
and does not speak
a word of english

That is intelligence

Tata

Mi abuela
ha pasado
los últimos venticinco años
en esta tienda por departamentos
llamada américa
Tiene ochenta y cinco años
y no sabe
ni una palabra de inglés

Eso es inteligencia

Alejandra Pizarnik
1936–1972
Argentina

En esta noche, en este mundo
8 de octubre de 1971

a Martha I. Moia

I

en esta noche en este mundo
las palabras del sueño de la infancia de la muerte
nunca es eso lo que uno quiere decir
la lengua natal castra
la lengua es un órgano de conocimiento
del fracaso de todo poema
castrado por su propia lengua
que es el órgano de la re-creación
del re-conocimiento
pero no el de la resurrección
de algo a modo de negación
de mi horizonte de maldoror con su perro
y nada es promesa
entre lo decible
que equivale a mentir
(todo lo que se puede decir es mentira)
el resto es silencio
sólo que el silencio no existe

II

no
las palabras
no hacen el amor
hacen la ausencia
si digo *agua* ¿beberé?
si digo *pan* ¿comeré?

III

en esta noche en este mundo
extraordinario silencio el de esta noche

lo que pasa con el alma es que no se ve
lo que pasa con la mente es que no se ve
lo que pasa con el espíritu es que no se ve
¿de dónde viene esta conspiración de invisibilidades?
ninguna palabra es visible

sombras
recintos viscosos donde se oculta
la piedra de la locura
corredores negros
los he recorrido todos
¡oh quédate un poco más entre nosotros!

mi persona está herida
mi primera persona del singular

escribo como quien con un cuchillo alzado en la
      oscuridad
escribo como estoy diciendo
la sinceridad absoluta continuaría siendo
lo imposible
¡oh quédate un poco más entre nosotros!

IV

los deterioros de las palabras
deshabitando el palacio del lenguaje
el conocimiento entre las piernas
¿qué hiciste del don del sexo?
oh mis muertos
me los comí me atraganté
no puedo más de no poder más
palabras embozadas
todo se desliza
hacia la negra licuefacción

V

y el perro de maldoror
en esta noche en este mundo
donde todo es posible
salvo
el poema

VI

hablo en fácil hablo en difícil
sabiendo que no se trata de eso
siempre no se trata de eso
oh ayúdame a escribir el poema más prescindible
        el que no sirva ni para
        ser inservible
ayúdame a escribir palabras
en esta noche en este mundo

Francisco de Quevedo y Villegas.
1580—1645
España

Amor constante
más allá de la muerte

Cerrar podrá mis ojos la postrera
sombra que me llevare el blanco día,
y podrá desatar esta alma mía
hora a su afán ansioso lisonjera;

mas no, de esotra parte, en la ribera,
dejará la memoria, en donde ardía:
nadar sabe mi llama la agua fría,
y perder el respeto a ley severa.

Alma a quien todo un dios prisión ha sido,
venas que humor a tanto fuego han dado,
médulas que han gloriosamente ardido,

su cuerpo dejará, no su cuidado;
serán ceniza, mas tendrá sentido;
polvo serán, mas polvo enamorado.

Francisco de Quevedo y Villegas
1580—1645
España

Miré los muros de la patria mía

   Miré los muros de la patria mía,
si un tiempo fuertes, ya desmoronados,
de la carrera de la edad cansados,
por quien caduca ya su valentía.

   Salíme al campo, vi que el sol bebía
los arroyos del yelo desatados,
y del monte quejosos los ganados,
que con sombras hurtó su luz al día.

   Entré en mi casa; vi que, amancillada,
de anciana habitación era despojos;
mi báculo, más corvo y menos fuerte;

   vencida de la edad sentí mi espada.
Y no hallé cosa en que poner los ojos
que no fuese recuerdo de la muerte.

José Antonio Ramos Sucre
1890—1930
Venezuela

La vida del maldito
La Torre de Timón, 1955

   Yo adolezco de una degeneración ilustre; amo el dolor, la belleza y la crueldad, sobre todo esta última, que sirve para destruir un mundo abandonado al mal. Imagino constantemente la sensación del padecimiento físico, de la lesión orgánica.
   Conservo recuerdos pronunciados de mi infancia, rememoro la faz marchita de mis abuelos, que murieron en esta misma vivienda espaciosa, heridos por dolencias prolongadas. Reconstituyo la escena de sus exequias, que presencié asombrado e inocente.

Mi alma es desde entonces crítica y blasfema; vive en pie de guerra contra los poderes humanos y divinos, alentada por la manía de la investigación; y esta curiosidad infatigable declara el motivo de mis triunfos escolares y de mi vida atolondrada y maleante al dejar las aulas. Detesto íntimamente a mis semejantes, quienes sólo me inspiran epigramas inhumanos; y confieso que, en los días vacantes de mi juventud, mi índole destemplada y huraña me envolvía sin tregua en reyertas vehementes y despertaba las observaciones irónicas de las mujeres licenciosas que acuden a los sitios de diversión y peligro.

No me seducen los placeres mundanos y volví espontáneamente a la soledad, mucho antes del término de mi juventud, retirándome a esta mi ciudad nativa, lejana del progreso, asentada en una comarca apática y neutral. Desde entonces no he dejado esta mansión de colgaduras y de sombras. A sus espaldas fluye un delgado río de tinta, sustraído de la luz por la espesura de árboles crecidos, en pie sobre los márgenes, azotados sin descanso por un viento furioso, nacido de los montes áridos. La calle delantera, siempre desierta, suena a veces con el paso de un carro de bueyes, que reproduce la escena de una campiña etrusca.

La curiosidad me indujo a nupcias desventuradas, y casé improvisadamente con una joven caracterizada por los rasgos de mi persona física, pero mejorados por una distinción original. La trataba con un desdén superior, dedicándole el mismo aprecio que a una muñeca desmontable por piezas. Pronto me aburrí de aquel ser infantil, ocasionalmente molesto, y decidí suprimirlo para enriquecimiento de mi experiencia.

La conduje con cierto pretexto delante de una excavación abierta adrede en el patio de esta misma casa. Yo portaba una pieza de hierro y con ella le coloqué encima de la oreja un firme porrazo. La infeliz cayó de rodillas dentro de la fosa, emitiendo débiles alaridos como de boba. La cubrí de tierra, y esa tarde me senté solo a la mesa, celebrando su ausencia.

La misma noche y otras siguientes, a hora avanzada, un brusco resplandor iluminaba mi dormitorio y me ahuyentaba el sueño sin remedio. Enmagrecí y me torné pálido, perdiendo sensiblemente las fuerzas. Para distraerme, contraje la costumbre de cabalgar desde mi vivienda hasta fuera de la ciudad, por las campiñas libres y llanas, y paraba el trote de la cabalgadura debajo de un mismo árbol envejecido, adecuado para una cita diabólica. Escuchaba en tal paraje murmullos dispersos y confusos, que no llegaban a voces. Viví así innu-

merables días hasta que, después de una crisis nerviosa que
me ofuscó la razón, desperté clavado por la parálisis en esta
silla rodante, bajo el cuidado de un fiel servidor que defendió
los días de mi infancia.

Paso el tiempo en una meditación inquieta, cubierto, la
mitad del cuerpo hasta los pies, por una felpa anchurosa.
Quiero morir y busco las sugestiones lúgubres, y a mi lado arde constantemente este tenebrario, antes escondido en un
desván de la casa.

En esta situación me visita, increpándome ferozmente, el
espectro de mi víctima. Avanza hasta mí con las manos ven-
gadoras en alto, mientras mi continuo servidor se arrincona de
miedo; pero no dejaré esta mansión sino cuando sucumba por
el encono del fantasma inclemente. Yo quiero escapar de los
hombres hasta después de muerto, y tengo ordenado que este
edificio desaparezca, al día siguiente de finar mi vida y junto
con mi cadáver, en medio de un torbellino de llamas.

Etnairis Rivera
1949—
Puerto Rico

Oxunmare
Pachamamapa Takin,(Canto de la madre tierra), 1976.
Entre ciudades y casi paraísos, 1989.

Este niño color no tiene padre reconocido
ni se parecerá a nadie en particular.
Excluiremos de su alimento el miedo.
Nacerá de la buena familia del solo vientre de su madre.
Ya le contará ella que la preñaron los Andes,
la olorosa esperma del río,
la noche vaga por los montes
la limonada,
el instante de una cálida brisa que le llegó do Brasil.
Le contará que siempre amó
perdidamente a las piedras
hasta preñarse.
Este niño se me encarna,
como ese nuevo color rojivioláceo que trajo el atardecer
se va durmiendo el espíritu de mi niño en su planeta.
Viajará en la dimensión espacial en el cuerpo de su madre
a nacer en mi presente,
maravilla la de mi niño soñoliento en dos planetas.

Puerta del misterio la Mujer,
puerta entre los mundos,
infundida del rayo,
                casa de los espíritus que renacen.
Este niño color encontrará a su padre
en el corazón de su camino,
lo llevará a su frente,
                a su perfecto cielo,
a su padre vestido de luz.
Este niño color de la nueva raza
se alimentará del alba transparente...
habitará el arco-iris la mitad del año,
será niño el sur de la montaña,
habitará la mar la otra mitad del año,
será niña el norte de las aguas,
nacerá de la buena familia del solo vientre de su madre.

Alejandro Romualdo
1926—
Perú

Canto coral a Tupac Amaru, que es la libertad

Edición extraordinaria, 1958.

> *Yo ya no tengo paciencia para aguartar todo esto.*
> Micaela Bastidas

Lo harán volar
con dinamita. En masa,
lo cargarán, lo arrastrarán. A golpes
le llenarán de póvora la boca.
Lo volarán:
                ¡y no podrán matarlo!

Lo pondrán de cabeza. Arrancarán
sus deseos, sus dientes y sus gritos.
Lo patearán a toda furia. Luego
lo sangrarán:
                ¡y no podrán matarlo!

Coronarán con sangre su cabeza;
sus pómulos, con golpes. Y con clavos
sus costillas. Le harán morder el polvo.
Lo golpearán:
                ¡y no podrán matarlo!

Le sacarán los sueños y los ojos.
Querrán descuartizarlo grito a grito.
Lo escupirán. Y a golpe de matanza
lo clavarán:
              ¡y no podrán matarlo!

Lo pondrán en el centro de la plaza,
boca arriba, mirando al infinito.
Le amarrarán los miembros. A la mala
tirarán:
              ¡y no podrán matarlo!

Querrán volarlo y no podrán volarlo.
Querrán romperlo y no podrán romperlo.
Querrán matarlo y no podrán matarlo.

Querrán descuartizarlo, triturarlo,
macharlo, pisotearlo, desalmarlo.

Querrán volarlo y no podrán volarlo.
Querrán romperlo y no podrán romperlo.
Querrán matarlo y no podrán matarlo.

Al tercer día de los sufrimientos,
cuando se crea todo consumado,
gritando ¡*libertad!* sobre la tierra,
ha de volver.
              Y no podrán matarlo.

Ana Rosetti
1950
España

Cierta secta feminista
se da consejos prematrimoniales

Los devaneos de Erato, 1981.

> *...Trabajada despiadadamente*
> *por un autómata que cree que el*
> *cumplimiento de un cruel deber*
> *es un asunto de honor.*
> Andrea de Nerciat

Y besémonos, bellas vírgenes, besémonos.
Démonos prisa desvalijándonos
destruyendo el botín de nuestros cuerpos.
Al enemigo percibo respirar tras el muro,
la codicia se yergue entre sus piernas.

Y besémonos, bellas vírgenes, besémonos.
No deis pródigamente a·la espada,
oh viril fortuna, el inviolado himen.
Que la grieta en el blanco ariete
de nuestras manos, pierda su angostura.

Y besémonos, bellas vírgenes, besémonos.
Ya extendieron las sábanas
y la felpa absorbente está dispuesta
para que los floretes nos derriben
y las piernas empapen de amapolas.

Y besémonos, bellas vírgenes, besémonos.
Antes que el vencedor la ciudadadela
profane, y desvele su recato
para saquear del templo los tesoros,
es preferible siempre entregarla a las llamas.

Y besémonos, bellas vírgenes, besémonos.
Expolio singular: enfebrecidas
en nuestro beneficio arrebatemos
la propia dote. Que el triunfador altivo
no obtenga el masculino privilegio.

Y besémonos, bellas vírgenes, besémonos.
Con la secreta fuente humedecida
en el licor de Venus,
anticipémonos,
de placer mojadas, a Príapo.
Y con la sed de nuestros cuerpos, embriaguémonos.

Y besémonos, bellas vírgenes, besémonos.
Rasgando el azahar, gocémonos, gocémonos
del premio que celaban nuestros muslos.
El falo, presto a traspasarnos
encontrará, donde creyó virtud, burdel.

Pedro Salinas
1892–1952
España

El cuerpo, fabuloso
Todo más claro y otros poemas, 1949.

¿Qué sería de mí si tú no fueses
invisibilidad, toda imposible?

Miro tranquilo a tantos maniquíes
—mitología en los escaparates
a cuyos pies las almas sin amante
rezan por un momento cuando pasan
y cosechan sus sueños de la noche—,
porque tú vas vestida
con los cendales de lo nunca visto,
del color del recuerdo que te busca.

No me inquieta la luna, núbil, tierna
cuando otra vez inicia su creciente
doblemente afilado
de juventud y blancura —tan agudo
que decapitará a las esperanzas
más puras de la nieve,
comparando su blanco con su blanco—,
porque en ti, traslumbrada,
como no se te ve, nunca hay reflejo,
sino la luz sin par, la que rechaza
toda comparación con lo que existe.

Veo tranquilamente cómo avanzan
por esos turbios cielos del periódico
las bandadas diarias de las cifras,
cotizaciones de la bolsa, diosas,
dueñas de los destinos, decidiendo
que el precio de la dicha
—que está siempre en el coste del carbón,
del whisky, del canario, o de las risas
que necesitan los hogares jóvenes—
sea más accesible que otros años,
o que algunas pistolas que tenían
a las seis, cinco balas,
a las seis y un segundo tengan cuatro,
en la mano de un hombre, por el suelo.
No necesito el oro, porque a ti,
como no se te ve, no se te puede
comprar con más moneda
que los minutos lentos y redondos
de largas noches en que no se duerme
porque nos invadió la pena inútil
de que al ponerse el sol se encienden tantas
luces y sus colores, por el mundo
—agüeros de películas y bailes,
faros de la alegría—tantas tantas,
menos tus ojos, frente a mí.

Oigo llamar a dulces criaturas,
con esos nombres o alas por el aire:
Mirtila, Soledad, Amparo, Cándida
—en los que nada hay de ellas y son ellas,
porque los llenan gota a gota, día
a día con sus vidas, claros sones
a los que ávidamente nos asimos
para no confundirlas
con su hermana, su sombra o con la nada—,
sin volverme jamás, por si eres tú.
Como no se te ve, sólo te nombran
los labios de la lluvia en los oídos
eternamente sordos de los lagos,
las ruedas de los trenes cuando cruzan
los campos donde pastan las gacelas,
las tentativas de los violines
o alguna boca sola que en el sueño
recuerda una palabra, entre las ruinas,
de algún idioma hundido con la Torre.

Sin el menor dolor sé ya las fugas
que por los tubos de las chimeneas
mientras se toma el té y se habla
de arte negro, de Einstein o del *Ulises,*
emprenden como chispas las promesas
—aquéllas, las más firmes—
hacia su conversión en puros astros,
después de estar un día con nosotros,
diciendo: "Siempre, siempre."
Y luego, desde arriba,
a los cinco o diez años
de haber llegado nos harán sus señas
de luces por las noches,
para que nos creamos
que allí en el cielo sí pueden ser nuestras.
Tú, es decir, lo imposible,
no puedes escaparte,
porque estás hecha de la misma huida.

Y te beso, te beso,
a ti, paradisíaca,
descubriéndote toda lentamente
como el hombre primero descubría.
otro menor Edén con otra sombra,
sin temor a que mueras, o a que salgas
del eterno jardín y se te vea,
andando por las calles de la tierra,
vestida de mujer a nuestro lado.
Porque tu cuerpo impar, tenso y desnudo,
nunca te hará visible. Sólo puede
en las noches nevadas
ocultarte mejor, y por un tiempo
que a veces se confunde con la vida,
por lo veloz que pasa, hacerse carne,
e inventar una fábula:
que alguien crea que existe, que le estrecha,
y que es capaz de amor. Y que le ama.

Iván Silén
1944—
Puerto Rico

Poemas de Filí-Melé

Poemas de Filí Melé, 1987.

vuelvo a cantar
la historia de la hermosa,
porque la hermosa está enferma
de rebeldías y de amor
de parques y distancias está ausente,
está enferma por la fiebre en que partí,
está enferma por el cuerpo
y por la noche que le di,
y ha comenzado a morir su muerte,
y ha comenzado a deshojarse primavera,
a suicidarse con su orden y sus flores,
la hermosa se quiere suicidar
ante mis ojos apagados,
como si fuera posible
morirse ante los de ella,
como si fuera posible que la hermosa,
se cortara las venas al morirse,
y me desgarrara por su sangre la tristeza,
como si fuera posible
la personalidad que somos,
—la locura y el amor se están mirando—
se están besando,
se están contando el cuento de la vida,
se están poniendo candeles por el cuerpo,
collares por el cuerpo
se están poniendo:

porque la amante
se ha muerto por la noche,
mientras le lavaba el cuerpo
con canciones y con flores,
y con besos le limpiaba
el rostro de la muerte,
(en los cementerios de la noche
enterramos a la hermosa),
y lloro sobre su tumba
aguaceros grises por la tarde,

lloro miedo y lloro muerte
cuando la llamo con mi gesto,
cuando la llamo de mi voz,
y la llamo con recuerdos de camas y murmullos,
la llamo con jueves y almohadas
la llamo como a Lázaro
de-amor-de-ser-su-amigo,
y no responde...

pero la hermosa resucitó como una guitarra
finita en la música del tiempo,
y me canta la canción
de los juegos en los parques,
detrás de la noche
resucita la amante a jugar los sueños,
y creció de la amante una gran casa,
crecieron bosques y soledad de luna,
crecieron ríos corriendo por mi cuerpo,
y yo la habité porque no existo,
le coloqué pitirres y nubes amarillas
por el sueño,
la soñé cauce y delta,
y océano,
e infinito del barco del amor,
la soñé cometa cruzando mi horizonte,
expandiendo su galaxia
en el abrazo de mi espalda,
expandiendo la galaxia del amor
en las constelaciones de mi cuerpo,
pillando al tiempo
y la distancia,
al resucitar por la mentira de mi rostro,
al girar por mi boca
como un planeta y una luna,
pero la hermosa resucita
como una guitarra finita
en la música del tiempo;

ella nacía de aerolito
y se levantaba cadáver,
y se ponía mi cuerpo con gesto de niño
y me mojaba jugando
con su sexo y con gotitas de rocío,
me mojaba de tristeza la playa

en los pasos de la arena,
en los susurros de su casa se lloraba,
y se arrancaba las ventanas y los días,
para no saberse descendiendo del espacio,
para no saberse cayendo
paracaída-de-amor,
cayendo hacia el océano del jueves,
cayendo por las sábanas
de un mar que ruge entre mis manos,
cayendo su cabello
como la arena de la tarde en sus pisadas,
para no saberse resucitada,
para no saberse uva por los labios,
miel y vino del dolor resucitado,
para no saberse pistacho de la noche,
y para no saber que la hermosa
resucita por la lluvia,
contra su propio cuerpo
la hermosa resucita;
ella corre por los cielos
como un aerolito por los ojos,
florida de caminos
grita mi nombre y nacen los cometas,
grita su nombre y nace la madre,
y la tibieza, y el amparo,
y nacen los niños de mí
para poblar los parques
para crear el mundo
y comenzar la historia;

la hermosa resucitó
y resucitó del amor,
para bañarse conmigo
cuando baje la lluvia,
cuando se pierda el miedo de ser ella,
y se pierda de sí misma
por el riesgo de ser noche,
cuando rodemos por el abrazo
y desde el parque,
rodemos por el salmo
y por el gesto fatal de estar soñando;
porque la ausente me oirá por todo el sueño,
me oirá desierta de sí,
cuando se sepa pesadilla,

cuando se vigile acorralada
y asesinada por la casa,
y se oiga de ella la sospecha,
y se odie sin ternura ni recuerdos,
y se aleje de ella misma
como espía de la niña,
y se arreste de sí,
con su corazón de óleo confundido;
pero volverá la amante,
una mañana de la ausencia,
volverá sin su camisa de fuerza,
sin reproche ni enojo en la ternura,
volverá para llamarme la nostalgia,
y por el pánico de saberme en su deseo,
y volverá por la alegría
para abrazarme como en junio,
de rebeldías y de amor,
para abrazarme, Filí-Melé,
sobre los parques
para abrazarme la tarde y el rocío,
la risa de los puentes y los sueños,
para besarte, Filí-Melé, para besarnos,
¡ese rostro increíble de los muertos!   (Fragmento)

Aurea María Sotomayor
1951–
Puerto Rico

Arañas
Sitios de la memoria, 1983.

Predadora
de ocho patas
deslizándose atenta
por entre las comarcas
de la estrategia luminosa.

        Cómo vuela ese soplo de luz
        que la tejedora ciega esparce
        por los rincones más inusitados
        más siniestros.
        Ese soplo
        esas fastuosas hélices
        con que alcánzalo todo
        logra quebrar, herir, doblar.
        Voraz segregación.

A veces,
pájaro devorador,
A veces,
luminosa,
acrobático vientre.
Su fuerza estriba
en la red vertiginosa
con que cose.
Alucinada transparencia
persiguiendo un ardid.

        Trabaja, enciende la hacendosa
        y, mientras tanto, el movimiento,
        radio de su esperanza,
        colúmpiase tranquilo
        entre la perfecta simetría
        y la locura funcional
        de sus flexibles goznes.
        Táctica de la seda taladrante.

Bordonean sus hebras,
sedosa ceguera palpando,
la acústica sonora de su próxima víctima
a quien dispensa
con la más suave de las muertes:
envuelve en recursos de seda
toda la vida
convirtiéndola
en forzosas, clausuradas crisálidas.

> Arañas enhebrantes,
> filamentos.
> Que son sogas.
> Lazos.
> Raíces donde bebe,
> ríe, grita la luz
> la táctica de la captura.

Alfonsina Storni
1892–1938
Argentina

Tú me quieres blanca

El dulce daño, 1918.

Tú me quieres alba;
me quieres de espumas;
me quieres de nácar.
Que sea azucena,
sobre todas, casta.
De perfume tenue.
Corola cerrada.
Ni un rayo de luna
filtrado me haya
ni una margarita
se diga mi hermana;
tú me quieres blanca;
tú me quieres nívea;
tú me quieres casta.

Tú, que hubiste todas
las copas a mano,

de frutos y mieles
los labios morados.
Tú, que en el banquete,
cubierto de pámpanos,
dejaste las carnes
festejando a Baco.
Tú, que en los jardines
negros del engaño,
vestido de rojo,
corriste al Estrago.

Tú, que el esqueleto
conservas intacto,
no sé todavía
por cuáles milagros,
(Dios te lo perdone),
me pretendes casta
(Dios te lo perdone),
me pretendes alba.
Huye hacia los bosques;
vete a la montaña;
límpiate la boca;
vive en las cabañas;
toca con las manos
la tierra mojada;
alimenta el cuerpo
con raíz amarga;
bebe de las rocas;
duerme sobre escarcha;
renueva tejidos
con salitre y agua;
habla con los pájaros
y lévate al alba.

Y cuando las carnes
te sean tornadas,
y cuando hayas puesto
en ellas el alma,
que por las alcobas
se quedó enredada,
entonces, buen hombre,
preténdeme blanca,
preténdeme nívea,
preténdeme casta.

Luis Suardíaz
1938—
Cuba

Acerca de un fraude

Un individuo ha adiestrado su voz,
le ha procurado un timbre original,
un sonido como de finísimos metales.
Admirable ha sido su paciencia, su delicado
tesón. El ha hecho invernar a su voz;
la ha sacado al sol, la ha obligado a tomar
clases de música. Se le ha visto ensayando
el sonido que produce un fragmento de cuarzo
rasgado por espinas de limón.

Durante cinco años (y esto sí es grave) esta voz
de individuo ha tomado sucesivas lecciones de pintura,
en los talleres libres, sólo para no confundir el gris
con el violeta. Ha sido conminada a usar blanco sobre blanco,
como ejercicio. A diferenciar entre muy parecidas
                                                    monocromías.
Semejante dedicación es encomiable, dice ya todo el mundo.

Porque si con lo dicho no fuera suficiente, añadiríamos
que esta voz bajaba y subía toda una larga escala de registros,
sabía comportarse en actos públicos y precisar el tono
de las íntimas querellas.

Andando el tiempo, el individuo hace saber
que ese paciente sacrificio no está exento de objetivo:
Tiene mucho que decir al ancho mundo, con todas las voces
de su voz (aquí un habilísimo tono de tragedia) mas, sospecha
que los hombres no saben escuchar.

La mañana en que le llamen amables oidores,
en la primera vista del Juicio Central,
efectuado en su época, en defensa de los pronombres
olvidados, tiene sesenta años esta voz admirable
de individuo. Hay un silencio incómodo. Al fin ordena,
sus palabras; no muchas, es verdad. Dice que perdonen,
que se sienten, que no es nada, que ahora descubre
que nunca tuvo nada que decir. Y ese es el fraude.

Totoquihuatzin
?—1472
Poeta azteca

Como el orfebre
hace un collar

Perforo esmeraldas,
estoy fundiendo oro:
es mi canto.

En hilo ensarto
ricas esmeraldas:
es mi canto.

Miguel de Unamuno y Jugo
1864—1936
España

La oración del ateo
Rosario de sonetos líricos, 1912.

Oye mi ruego Tú, Dios que no existes,
y en tu nada recoge estas mis quejas,
Tú que a los pobres hombres nunca dejas
sin consuelo de engaño. No resistes

a nuestro ruego y nuestro anhelo vistes.
Cuando Tú de mi mente más te alejas,
más recuerdo las plácidas consejas
con que mi alma endulzóme noches tristes.

¡Qué grande eres, mi Dios! Eres tan grande
que no eres sino Idea; es muy angosta
la realidad por mucho que se expande

para abarcarte. Sufro yo a tu costa,
Dios no existente, pues si Tú existieras
existiría yo también de veras.

Esteban Valdés
1947—
Puerto Rico

Soneto de las estrellas
Fuera de trabajo, 1977.

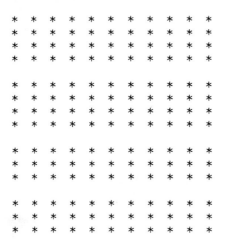

José Angel Valente
1929—
España

Reaparición de lo heroico
El inocente, 1967-1970.

La flor de los pretendientes y las buenas familias
en los salones espaciosos.
Y ya la guerra de Troya terminada
de tiempo atrás. Los hombres que allí fueron,
los sonoros navíos, el caballo mortífero,
vagas patrañas de la ideología.

Cómo puede esperar Penelopea.

Quien tenga una esperanza ocúltela,
pues el tiempo es de tibia descreencia
bien temperada a la ocasión,

y la palabra más pura en los salones
sin tanta servidumbre a lo pasado.

Reunámonos pues para cruzar apuestas
sobre el futuro que nosotros somos
y olvidemos el arco, el duro arco del rey,
aquel objeto pesado y anacrónico
que la sentimental Penelopea
aún tiene por sagrado.

Así habló
y así se alzó entre todos Antínoo,
flor de los pretendientes y las buenas familias,
joven experto en lenguas extranjeras,
hábil en la ironía y el pastiche.

Rió la concurrencia con dulzura
y se sintieron más en el meollo
del capital asunto
todos los pretendientes de provincias.

Pero ya el harapiento vagabundo,
el huésped no aceptado,
impuesto por el hijo de la reina,
acariciaba el arco.
                    Así templó la resistencia
de la tenaz materia.
                    Tocó la flecha amarga,
hizo vibrar la cuerda poderosa
con un rumor distinto
y un tiempo antiguo vino en oleadas
de hosca respiración hasta los hombres.

Tomó Antínoo una copa entre sus manos
y alzóla en medio del festín.

Estaba tenso el arco.
Un dios de torva faz medía los segundos.
La saeta partió veloz,
certera. Atravesó su punta
la garganta de Antínoo y salió por la nuca.
Un chorro espeso
de irreparable sangre vino
a las fauces del muerto.

Flor de los pretendientes,
irrisorio despojo,
entre el vaho animal de la hermosa matanza.

César Vallejo
1892–1938
Perú

Los heraldos negros

Los heraldos negros, 1918.

Hay golpes en la vida, tan fuertes... ¡Yo no sé!
Golpes como del odio de Dios; como si ante ellos,
la resaca de todo lo sufrido
se empozara en el alma... ¡Yo no sé!

Son pocos; pero son... Abren zanjas oscuras
en el rostro más fiero y en el lomo más fuerte.
Serán tal vez los potros de bárbaros atilas;
o los heraldos negros que nos manda la Muerte.

Son las caídas hondas de los Cristos del alma,
de alguna fe adorable que el Destino blasfema.
Esos golpes sangrientos son las crepitaciones
de algún pan que en la puerta del horno se nos quema.

Y el hombre... ¡Pobre... pobre! Vuelve los ojos como
cuando por sobre el hombro nos llama una palmada;
vuelve los ojos locos, y todo lo vivido
se empoza, como un charco de culpa, en la mirada.

Hay golpes en la vida tan fuertes... ¡Yo no sé!

César Vallejo
1892–1938
Perú

Masa

España, aparta de mí este cáliz, 1937.

Al fin de la batalla,
y muerto el combatiente, vino, hacia él un hombre
y le dijo: " ¡No mueras, te amo tanto!"
Pero el cadáver ¡ay! siguió muriendo.

Se le acercaron dos y repitiéronle:
" ¡No nos dejes! ¡Valor! ¡Vuelve a la vida!"
Pero el cadáver ¡ay! siguió muriendo.

Acudieron a él veinte, cien, mil, quinientos mil,
clamando: " ¡Tanto amor y no poder nada contra la muerte!"
Pero el cadáver ¡ay! siguió muriendo.

Le rodearon millones de individuos,
con un ruego común: " ¡Quédate hermano!"
Pero el cadáver ¡ay! siguió muriendo.

Entonces, todos los hombres de la tierra
le rodearon; les vio el cadáver triste, emocionado;
incorporóse lentamente,
abrazó al primer hombre; echóse a andar...

Cesar Vallejo
1892–1938
Perú

Piedra negra sobre piedra blanca
Poemas humanos, 1937.

Me moriré en París con aguacero,
un día del cual tengo ya el recuerdo.
Me moriré en París —y no me corro—
talvez un jueves, como es hoy, de otoño.

Jueves será, porque hoy, jueves, que proso
estos versos, los húmeros me he puesto   *hueso del brazo de hombro al codo*
a la mala y, jamás como hoy, me he vuelto,
con todo mi camino, a verme solo.

César Vallejo ha muerto, le pegaban
todos sin que él les haga nada;
le daban duro con un palo y duro

también con una soga; son testigos
los días jueves y los huesos húmeros,
la soledad, la lluvia, los caminos...

Garcilaso de la Vega
1501?—1536
España

Soneto XXIII

Publicado póstumamente en 1543.

En tanto que de rosa y azucena
se muestra la color en vuestro gesto,
y que vuestro mirar ardiente, honesto,
enciende el corazón y le refrena;

y en tanto que el cabello, que en la vena
del oro se escogió, con vuelo presto,
por el hermoso cuello blanco, enhiesto,
el viento mueve, esparce y desordena;

coged de vuestra alegre primavera
el dulce fruto, antes que el tiempo airado
cubra de nieve la hermosa cumbre.

Marchitará la rosa el viento helado,
todo lo mudará la edad ligera,
por no hacer mudanza en su costumbre.

Garcilaso de la Vega
1501?—1536
España

Soneto X

Publicado póstumamente en 1543.

¡Oh dulces prendas por mi mal halladas,
dulces y alegres cuando Dios quería,
juntas estáis en la memoria mía
y con ella en mi muerte conjuradas!
¿Quién me dijera, cuando las pasadas
horas qu'en tanto bien por vos me vía,
que me habiades de ser en algún día
con tan grave dolor representadas?

5

Pues en un hora junto me llevastes
todo el bien que por términos me distes,   10
lleváme junto el mal que me dejastes;
     si no, sospecharé que me pusistes
en tantos bienes porque deseastes
verme morir entre memorias tristes.

Lope de Vega
1562–1635
España

Soneto
Rimas sacras, 1614.

¿Qué tengo yo que mi amistad procuras?
¿Qué interés se te sigue, Jesús mío,
que a mi puerta, cubierto de rocío
pasas las noches del invierno oscuras?

¡Oh, cuánto fueron mis entrañas duras
pues no te abrí! ¡Qué extraño desvarío
si de mi ingratitud el yelo frío
secó las llagas de tus plantas puras!

¡Cuántas veces el ángel me decía:
Alma, asómate agora a la ventana,
verás con cuánto amor llamar porfía!

¡Y cuántas, hermosura soberana:
Mañana le abriremos —respondía—,
para lo mismo responder mañana!

Lope de Vega
1562–1635
España

Soneto CXXVI
Rimas humanas, 1602.

  Desmayarse, atreverse, estar furioso,
áspero, tierno, liberal, esquivo,
alentado, mortal, difunto, vivo,
leal, traidor, cobarde, y animoso;

  no hallar fuera del bien centro y reposo,
mostrarse alegre, triste, humilde, altivo,
enojado, valiente, fugitivo,
satisfecho, ofendido, receloso;

  huir el rostro al claro desengaño,
beber veneno por licor suave,
olvidar el provecho, amar el daño;

  creer que un cielo en un infierno cabe,
dar la vida y el alma a un desengaño;
esto es amor; quien lo probó lo sabe.

Xavier Villaurrutia
1902–1950
México

Nocturno en que nada se oye
Nostalgia de la muerte, 1938

En medio de un silencio desierto como la calle antes del
  crimen
sin respirar siquiera para que nada turbe mi muerte
en esta soledad sin paredes
al tiempo que huyeron los ángulos
en la tumba del lecho dejo mi estatua sin sangre
para salir en un momento tan lento
en un interminable descenso
sin brazos que tender

sin dedos para alcanzar la escala que cae de un piano
    invisible
sin más que una mirada y una voz
que no recuerdan haber salido de ojos y labios
¿qué son labios? ¿qué son miradas que son labios?
y mi voz ya no es mía
dentro del agua que no moja
dentro del aire de vidrio
dentro del fuego lívido que corta como el grito
Y en el juego angustioso de un espejo frente a otro
cae mi voz
y mi voz que madura
y mi voz quemadura
y mi bosque madura
y mi voz quema dura
como el hielo de vidrio
como el grito de hielo
aquí en el caracol de la oreja
el latido de un mar en el que no sé nada
en el que no se nada
porque he dejado pies y brazos en la orilla
siento caer fuera de mí la red de mis nervios
mas huye todo como el pez que se da cuenta
hasta siento en el pulso de mis sienes
muda telegrafía a la que nadie responde
porque el sueño y la muerte nada tienen ya que decirse.

Xavier Villaurrutia
1902–1950
México

Nocturno Rosa
Nostalgia de la muerte, 1938

a José Gorostiza

YO También hablo de la rosa.
Pero mi rosa no es la rosa fría
ni la de piel de niño,
ni la rosa que gira
tan lentamente que su movimiento
es una misteriosa forma de la quietud.

No es la rosa sedienta,
ni la sangrante llaga,
ni la rosa coronada de espinas,
ni la rosa de la resurrección.

No es la rosa de pétalos desnudos,
ni la rosa encerada,
ni la llama de seda,
ni tampoco la rosa llamarada.

No es la rosa veleta,
ni la úlcera secreta,
ni la rosa puntual que da la hora,
ni la brújula rosa marinera.

No, no es la rosa rosa
sino la rosa increada,
la sumergida rosa,
la nocturna,
la rosa inmaterial,
la rosa hueca.

Es la rosa del tacto en las tinieblas,
es la rosa que avanza enardecida,
la rosa de rosadas uñas,
la rosa yema de los dedos ávidos,
la rosa digital,
la rosa ciega.

Es la rosa moldura del oído,
la rosa oreja,
la espiral del ruido,
la rosa concha siempre abandonada
en la más alta espuma de la almohada.

Es la rosa encarnada de la boca,
la rosa que habla despierta
como si estuviera dormida.
Es la rosa entreabierta
de la que mana sombra,
la rosa entraña
que se pliega y expande
evocada, invocada, abocada,
es la rosa labial,
la rosa herida.

Es la rosa que abre los párpados,
la rosa vigilante, desvelada,
la rosa del insomnio desojada.

Es la rosa del humo,
la rosa de ceniza,
la negra rosa de carbón diamante
que silenciosa horada las tinieblas
y no ocupa lugar en el espacio.

Cintio Vitier
1520—
Cuba

Un extraño honor
Escrito y cantado, 1954-1959.

El árbol sabe, con sus raíces y sus ramas,
todo aquello que puede ser un árbol:
¿o acaso también falta
a su mitad visible otro esplendor
que es lo que está sufriendo y anhelando?
No lo sabemos. Pero él
no necesita conocerse. Basta
que su misterio sea, sin palabras
que vayan a decirle lo que es, lo que no es.
El árbol, majestuoso como un árbol,
lleno de identidad hasta las puntas,
puede medirse cara a cara con el ángel.
Y nosotros ¿con quién nos mediremos,
quién ha de compartir nuestra congoja?
Ved ese rostro, escrutad esa mirada
donde lo que brilla es un vacío,
repasad como en sueños
esas líneas dolorosas en torno de los labios,
ese surco que ha de ahondarse en la mejilla,
la desolada playa de la frente,
la nariz como un túmulo funesto. ¡Qué devastado reino,
qué fiero y melancólico despojo, humeando todavía!
Sólo otro rostro podría comprenderlo.
Así nos miramos cara a cara, el alma desollada,
con el secreto júbilo insondable que nos funda, que está
    hecho de vergüenza
y de un extraño honor.

Emilio Adolfo Westphalen
1911
Perú

Te he seguido

Abolición de la muerte, 1935.

Te he seguido como nos persiguen los días
Con la seguridad de irlos dejando en el camino
De algún día repartir sus ramas
Por una mañana soleada de poros abiertos
Columpiándose de cuerpo a cuerpo
Te he seguido como a veces perdemos los pies
Para que una nueva aurora encienda nuestros labios
Y ya nada pueda negarse
Y ya todo sea un mundo pequeño rodando las escalinatas
Y ya todo sea una flor doblándose sobre la sangre
Y los remos hundiéndose más en las auras
Para detener el día y no dejarle pasar
Te he seguido como se olvidan los años
Cuando la orilla cambia de parecer a cada golpe de viento
Y el mar sube más alto que el horizonte
Para no dejarme pasar
Te he seguido escondiéndome tras los bosques y las ciudades
Llevando el corazón secreto y el talismán seguro
Marchando sobre cada noche con renacidas ramas
Ofreciéndome a cada ráfaga como la flor se tiende en la onda
O las cabelleras ablandan sus mareas
Perdiendo mis pestañas en el sigilo de las alboradas
Al levantarse los vientos y doblegar los árboles y las torres
Cayéndome de rumor en rumor
Como el día soporta nuestros pasos
Para después levantarme con el báculo del pastor
Y seguir las riadas que separan siempre
La vid que ya va a caer sobre nuestros hombros
Y la llevan cual un junco arrastrado por la corriente
Te he seguido por una sucesión de ocasos
Puestos en el muestrario de las tiendas
Te he seguido ablandándome de muerte
Para que no oyeras mis pasos
Te he seguido borrándome la mirada
Y callándome como el río al acercarse al abrazo
O la luna poniendo sus pies donde no hay respuesta

Y me he callado como si las palabras no me fueran a llenar
    la vida
Y ya no me quedara más que ofrecerte
Me he callado porque el silencio pone más cerca los labios
Porque sólo el silencio sabe detener a la muerte en los umbrales
Porque sólo el silencio sabe darse a la muerte sin reservas
Y así te sigo porque sé que más allá no has de pasar
Y en la esfera enrarecida caen los cuerpos por igual
Porque en mí la misma fe has de encontrar
Que hace a la noche seguir sin descanso al día
Ya que alguna vez le ha de coger y no le dejará de los dientes
Ya que alguna vez le ha de estrechar
Como la muerte estrecha a la vida
Te sigo como los fantasmas dejan de serlo
Con el descanso de verte torre de arena
Sensible al menor soplo u oscilación de los planetas
Pero siempre de pie y nunca más lejos
Que al otro lado de la mano

Bibliografía

Ensayo

Blanco, Tomás. "Elogio de la plena". _Revista del ICP,_ julio-septiembre (1979): 71-77.

Canales, Nemesio. "¿Podemos ser felices?" _Hacia un lejano sol._ Río Piedras: EDUPR, 1974.

Cortázar, Julio. "Algunos aspectos del cuento". _Las casillas de Morelli._ Julio Ortega, ed. Barcelona: Tusquets, [Publicado también en _Casa de las Américas_ 2.15-16 (nov. 1962 - Feb. 1963).]

————. "Hay que ser mente idiota para...", _La vuelta al día en ochenta mundos._ México: Siglo XXI, 1967.

Fernández Retamar, Roberto. "Antipoesía y poesía conversacional en Hispanoamérica". _Papelería._ La Habana, 1962.

Gorostiza, José. "Notas sobre poesía". _Poesía._ México: Fondo de Cultura Económica, 1982.

Hostos, Eugenio M. "La educación científica de la mujer" en _Páginas escogidas._ Buenos Aires: Angel Estrada, 1952.

Martí, José. "Nuestra América". _Antología mínima_ (Tomo I). La Habana: Instituto Cubano del Libro, 1972.

Neruda, Pablo. "La palabra" en _Confieso que he vivido._ Barcelona: Seix Barral, 1982.

Ocampo, Victoria. "Carta a Virginia Woolf". _Virginia Woolf en su diario._ Buenos Aires: Sur, 1954.

Ortega y Gasset, José. "Creer y pensar" fragmento de _Ideas y creencias._ Madrid: Revista de Occidente, 1959.

————. "La metáfora" fragmento del ensayo "Ensayo de estética a manera de prólogo" en _La deshumanización del arte y otros ensayos de estética._ Madrid: Alianza Editorial, 1983.

————. "Unas gotas de fenomenología" en _La deshumanización del arte..._

Palés Matos, Luis. "Hacia una poesía antillana" en _Prosa. Obras. Tomo II._ Río Piedras: EDUPR, 1984.

Paz, Octavio. "La dialéctica de la soledad" en _El laberinto de la soledad._ (1959). México: Fondo de Cultura Económica, 1979.

Ramos Otero, Manuel. "Ficción e historia: texto y pretexto de autobiografía". Ponencia presentada en noviembre de 1988 en Nueva York.

Reyes, Alfonso. "Categorías de la lectura". _La experiencia literaria._ Buenos Aires: Losada, 1961.

Rodríguez Juliá, Edgardo. "Puerto Rico y el Caribe: historia de una marginalidad". _La Torre._ (NE) 3.2: 513-29. 1989.

Sábato, Ernesto. "Sentido común" en _Uno y el universo._ Buenos Aires: Sudamericana, 1984.

Unamuno, Miguel. "La ideocracia" en _El caballero de la triste figura._ Buenos Aires: Espasa Calpe, 1944.

Narrativa

Arreola, Juan José. "El guardagujas". (1952) de *Confabulario*. En *Narrativa mexicana de hoy*. Emilio Carballo, antólogo. Madrid: Alianza, 1969. [También Fondo de Cultura Económica: México, 1966.]

Belaval, Emilio S. "Tony Pérez es un niño flan". *Los cuentos de la universidad*. San Juan: Biblioteca de Autores Puertorriqueños, 1945.

Borges, Jorge Luis. "El jardín de senderos que se bifurcan" de *Ficciones* (1944) en *Prosa completa I*. Barcelona: Bruguera, 1980.

————. "Emma Zuns". *El Aleph*. (1949). Buenos Aires: Emecé, 1971.

Cabrera Infante, Guillermo. "Un rato de tenmeallá". *Así en la paz como en la guerra*. Barcelona: Barral editores, 1971. *¡*También México: Diana, 1988.]

Carpentier, Alejo. "Viaje a la semilla". *Guerra del tiempo y otros relatos*. Madrid: Alianza, 1987. [También en Ediciones Era, S. A.]

Cortázar, Julio. "La noche boca arriba" en *Antología*. Nicolás Bratosevich, ed. Barcelona: EDHASA, 1978; *Final de juego*. Bs. As.: Suramericana, 1956.

Díaz Valcárcel, Emilio. "La muerte obligatoria". *Panorama*. Río Piedras: Cultural, 1970.

Fernández, Macedonio. "Cirugía psíquica de extirpación". *Manera de una psique sin cuerpo*. Barcelona: Tusquets, 1973.

Ferré, Rosario. "La muñeca menor". *Papeles de Pandora*. México: Joaquín Mortiz, 1976.

Fuentes, Carlos. "Chac Mool". *Cuerpos y ofrendas*. Madrid: Alianza, 1986.

García Márquez, Gabriel. "El ahogado más hermoso del mundo." (1968). *La increíble y triste historia de la Cándida Eréndira y su abuela desalmada*. Barcelona: Barral, 1977.

————. "El rastro de tu sangre en la nieve". Suplemento Dominical *El País*, 1981. *Cuentos peregrinos*. Colombia: Oveja Negra, 1992.

García Ramis, Magali. "Una semana de siete días". *La familia de todos nosotros*. San Juan: Instituto de Cultura Puertorriqueña, 1976.

Garro, Elena. "El anillo". *Mujeres en espejo*. Selección de Sara Sefchovich, México: Folios ediciones, 1983.

González, José Luis. "La carta" de *El hombre en la calle*, (1948). En *Cuentos puertorriqueños de hoy*. Selección de René Marqués. Río Piedras: Cultural, 1981.

————. "En el fondo del caño hay un negrito" de *En este lado*, 1954). En *Cuentos puertorriqueños de hoy*. Selección de René Marqués. Río Piedras: Cultural, 1981.

————. "La noche que volvimos a ser gente." *Mambrú se fue a la guerra y otros relatos*. México: Joaquín Mortiz, 1975.

Hernández, Felisberto. "Nadie encendía las lámparas". *Obras completas (volumen II)*. México: Siglo XXI, 1983.

Lugo Filippi, Carmen. "Milagros, calle Mercurio". *Vírgenes y mártires*. Río Piedras: Antillana, 1981.

Marqués, René. "Purificación en la Calle del Cristo". *En una ciudad llamada San Juan*. Río Piedras: Cultural, 1983. [Derechos: Fundación René Marqués.]

Montero, Rosa. "Paulo Pumilio". *Doce relatos de mujeres*. Prólogo y compilación de Ymelda Navajo. Madrid: Alianza Editorial, 1982.

Monterroso, Augusto. "El dinosaurio". *Mr. Taylor and Co*. La Habana: Casa de las Américas, 1982.

————. "Míster Taylor". *Mr. Taylor and Co*. La Habana: Casa de las Américas, 1982.

Onetti, Juan Carlos. "La cara de la desgracia". *Obras completas*. Barcelona: Lumen, 1979. [También: Madrid: Aguilar, 1970.]

Pardo Bazán, Emilia. "El indulto". *Cuentos de Marineda*. Barcelona: Dima, 1968.

Paz, Senel. "No le digas que la quieres". *Cuentos cubanos contemporáneos* (1966-90). Selección y prólogo de Madeline Cámara. Jalapa, México: Universidad Veracruzana, 1990.

Peri-Rossi, Cristina. "El laberinto". *La rebelión de los niños*. Barcelona: Seix Barral, 1988.

Piñera, Virgilio. "La carne". *Cuentos fríos*. Buenos Aires: Losada, 1956. También, posteriormente en *Cuentos*. La Habana: UNEAC, 1964. [También: en *Cuentos*. Ediciones Alfaguara: Madrid, 1983.]

————. "El que vino a salvarme". *Cuentos*. Ediciones Alfaguara: Madrid, 1983.

Piñón, Nélida. "Cosecha". *Detrás de la reja*. Antología de Celia Correas de Zapata y Lygia Johnson. Caracas: Monte Avila, 1980.

Quiroga, Horacio. "El almohadón de plumas". *Cuentos de amor, de locura y de muerte.* Buenos Aires: Losada, 1980. [También en México: Porrúa, 1968.]
––––––. "El hijo". *Cuentos.* México: Porrúa, 1982.
Roa Bastos, Augusto. "La excavación". *El trueno entre las hojas.* Buenos Aires: Ediciones Guillermo Kraft, 1958.
Rulfo, Juan. "Anacleto Morones". *El llano en llamas.* (1953). México: Fondo de Cultura Económica, 1983.
––––––. "Talpa." *El llano en llamas.* (1953). México: Fondo de Cultura Económica, 1983.
Sanabria Santaliz, Edgardo. "El día que el hombre pisó la luna". *El día que el hombre pisó la luna.* Río Piedras: Antillana, 1984.
Somers, Armonía. "El hombre del túnel". *Detrás de la reja.* Antología de Celia Correas de Zapata y Lygia Johnson. Caracas: Monte Avila, 1980.
Soto, Pedro Juan. "Los inocentes". *Spiks,* (1956). Río Piedras: Cultural, 1973.
Téllez, Hernando. "Espuma y nada más" de *Cenizas para el viento y otras historias* (1950). En *Narrativa hispanoamericana IV (1940-69).* Ed. Angel Flores. Siglo XXI, 1982.
Vega, Ana Lydia. "Letra para salsa y tres soneos por encargo". *Vírgenes y mártires.* Río Piedras: Antillana, 1981.
Zepeda, Eraclio. "El muro". *Andando el tiempo.* Hanover, NH: Ediciones del Norte, 1984.

Poesía

Alberti, Rafael. "Tres recuerdos del cielo". *Sobre los ángeles.* (1929). Barcelona: Ocnos, 1970. [También: Buenos Aires, Losada, 1977.]
Aleixandre, Vicente. "Se querían" de *La destrucción o el amor.* (1935) en *Poesía superrealista.* Barcelona: Barral editores, 1971.
Alonso, Dámaso. "A un río le llamaban Carlos" de *Hombre y Dios.* (1955). *El Grupo poético de 1927.* Antología de Angel González. Madrid: Taurus, 1983.
Anónimo. "Romance del amor más poderoso que la muerte" en *Flor nueva de romances viejos* de Ramón Menéndez Pidal. Buenos Aires: Espasa Calpe, 1938.
Anónimo. "Romance de la conquista de Alhama" en *Flor nueva de romances viejos* de Ramón Menéndez Pidal. Buenos Aires: Espasa Calpe, 1938.
Ayocuán. "Los poemas son obra del cielo". *Omnibús de la poesía mexicana.* Gabriel Zaid, editor. México: Siglo XXI, 1971.
Bécquer, Gustavo A. "Rima III" de *Rimas y leyendas.* Zaragoza: Ebro, 1971.
Belli, Carlos Germán. "El aviso, las señales". *Boda de la pluma y la letra.* Madrid: Ediciones Cultura Hispánica, Instituto Cooperativo Iberoamericano, 1985.
Borges, Jorge Luis. "Amorosa anticipación" de *Luna de enfrente.* (1925). En *Obra poética.* Madrid: Alianza, 1960.
––––––. "Heráclito" de *Elogio de la sombra.* (1969). En *Obra poética.* Madrid: Alianza, 1960.
Burgos, Julia de. "A Julia de Burgos" de *Poema en 20 surcos.* (1938). Río Piedras: Huracán, 1982.
Cabral, Manuel del. "Negro sin nada en tu casa" de *Trópico negro.* (1942). En *Obra poética completa.* Santo Domingo: Alfa y Omega, 1987.
Cardenal, Ernesto. "Las ciudades perdidas". *Homenaje a los indios americanos.* Buenos Aires: Carlos Lohlé, 1972.
––––––. "Oración por Marilyn Monroe". *Antología.* Selección de Pablo Antonio Cuadra. Buenos Aires: Carlos Lohlé, 1972.
Castellanos, Rosario. "Testamento de Hécuba" de *Materia memorable,* (1969). *Meditación en el umbral.* Julián Palley, comp. México: Fondo de Cultura Económica, 1985.
Celaya, Gabriel. "La poesía es un arma cargada de futuro". *Roots and Wings, Poetry from Spain 1900-1975.* Hardie St. Martin, ed. New York: Harper and Row,
Cernuda, Luis. "Si el hombre pudiera decir" de *Los placeres prohibidos* (1931). En *La realidad y el deseo* (1924-1962). México: Fondo de Cultura Económica, 1958.
Corretjer, Juan Antonio. *Distancias.* San Juan, 1957. Asomante, 1955.
Cruz, San Juan de la. "Subida del Monte Carmelo", *Poesía del Siglo de Oro.* Elías Rivers, ed. Madrid: Cátedra, 1979.
Cruz, Sor Juana Inés de la. "Hombres necios...". *Obras completas.* México: Porrúa, 1981.

Dalton, Roque. "Estudio con algo de tedio". *Poesía escogida.* Centroamérica: EDUCA, 1983.

―――. "Las feas palabras". *Poesía escogida.* Centroamérica, EDUCA, 1983.

Darío, Rubén. "Era un aire suave" de *Prosas profanas* (1896-1901). *Poesías completas.* Madrid: Aguilar, 1967. [También en *Antología poética.* Buenos Aires: Losada, 1979.]

―――. "Leda" de *Cantos de vida y esperanza* (1905). En *Poesías completas.* Madrid: Aguilar, 1967.

―――. "Lo fatal" de *Cantos de vida y esperanza* (1905). En *Poesías completas.* [También en *Antología poética.* Buenos Aires: Losada, 1979.]

Dávila, Angela María. "¿Será la rosa?" *Animal fiero y tierno.* Río Piedras: Qease, 1977.

Diego, Eliseo. "Cristóbal Colón inventa el Nuevo Mundo" de *Los días de tu vida* (1977). En *Entre la dicha y la tiniebla,* 1949-1985. México: Fondo de Cultura Económica, 1986.

―――. "Daguerrotipo de una desconocida". *Entre la dicha y la tiniebla,* 1949-1985. México: Fondo de Cultura Económica, 1986.

Droz, Vanessa. "Yo, la no querida. *La cicatriz a medias.* Río Piedras: Cultural, 1982.

Figuera Aymerich, Angela. "Destino" poema de 1950. En *Antología total.* Prólogo y selección de Julián Marcos. CVS Edic. SA, 1975. [También en *Poesía feminista del mundo hispánico.* Angel y Kate Flores, eds. México: Siglo XXI, 1984.] *Los días duros,* 1953.

García Lorca, Federico. "New York. Oficina y denuncia" de *Poeta en Nueva York,* (1929-1930). En *Obras completas.* Madrid: Aguilar, 1967.

―――. "Thamar y Amnón" de *Romancero Gitano,* (1924-1927). En *Obras completas.* Madrid: Aguilar, 1967.

Gorostiza, José. "Lleno de mí...", fragmento de *Muerte sin fin* (1939). En *Poesía.* México: Fondo de Cultura Económica, 1964.

Góngora, Luis de. "Alegoría de la brevedad de las cosas humanas". *Poesía del Siglo de Oro.* Elías Rivers, ed.

―――. "Mientras por competir con tu cabello". *Poesía del Siglo de Oro.* Elías Rivers, ed. Madrid: Cátedra, 1979.

Guillén Jorge. "Ciervos sobre una pared". *Clamor.* Buenos Aires: Sudamericana, 1963.

Guillén, Nicolás. "Alta niña de caña y amapola" de *Poemas de amor,* (1933-1971). *Sóngoro Cosongoro y otros poemas.* Antología. Madrid: Alianza, 1981.

―――. "Balada de los dos abuelos" de *West Indies Ltd., Sóngoro Cosongo y otros poemas.* (1934). Madrid: Alianza, 1981.

Hernández, Miguel. "Elegía" de *El rayo que no cesa* (1934-1935). En *Poemas.* Barcelona: Plaza y Janés, 1976.

―――. "Nanas de la cebolla de *Ultimos poemas* (1939-1941). En *Poemas.* Barcelona: Plaza y Janés, 1976.

Huidobro, Vicente. "Poema para hacer crecer los árboles". En *Muestra de poesía hispanoamericana del siglo XX.* José Antonio Escalona-Escalona, ed. Caracas: Ayacucho, 1961.

Ibarbourou, Juana de. "Siesta" de *La rosa de los vientos* (1930). En *Verso y prosa.* Buenos Aires: Kapelusz, 1968.

Istarú, Ana. *La estación de fiebre* Poema XXIII. Centroamérica, EDUCA, 1983.

Jamis, Fayad. "Poema. En *Antología básica contemporánea de la poesía latinoamericana.* Selección de Daniel Barros. Buenos Aires: Ediciones La Flor, 1973.

Jiménez, Juan Ramón. "Mariposa de luz" de *Noche.* En *Nueva antología.* Barcelona: Ediciones Península, 1973.

―――. "Sueño" de *Eternidades* (1918). En *Antología poética.* Madrid: Cátedra, 1989.

Lastra, Pedro. "Ya hablaremos de nuestra juventud". *Cuaderno de la doble vida.* Santiago de Chile: Ediciones del Camaleón, 1984.

León, Fray Luis de. "Vida solitaria". *Poesía de la Edad de Oro* I. Renacimiento. José Manuel Blecua, ed. Madrid: Castalia, 1986. [También en *Fray Luis de León. Obra poética completa.* Barcelona: Libros Río Nuevo, 1981.]

Lezama Lima, José. "Una oscura pradera me convida" de *Enemigo rumor* (1941). En *Poesía completa.* Barcelona: Barral, 1975. [También en *Poesía completa* I. Madrid: Aguilar, 1981.]

Lihn, Enrique. "Porque escribí". *La musiquilla de los pobres esferas.* Chile: Editorial Universitaria, 1969. [También en *Antología de la poesía hispanoamericana actual*. Julio Ortega, ed. México: Siglo XXI, 1987.]

Lima, José María. "El lenguaje es...". *La sílaba en la piel*. Río Piedras: Qease, 1982.

————. "Más antigua que el agua". *La sílaba en la piel*. Río Piedras: Qease, 1982.

López Velarde, Ramón. "Mi prima Agueda" de *La sangre devota* (1916). En *Antología de la poesía hispanoamericana. 1914-1970*. Madrid: Alianza, 1979.

Machado, Antonio. "La saeta". *Poesías completas*. Madrid: Espasa Calpe, 1977.

————. "Retrato". *Poesías completas*. Madrid: Espasa Calpe, 1977.

Martí, José. "Banquete de tiranos" de *Versos libres*. En *Prosa y poesía*. Buenos Aires: Kapelusz, 1968.

————. "Rima V" de *Versos sencillos*. En *Prosa y poesía*. Buenos Aires: Kapelusz, 1968.

Matos Paoli, Francisco. *Canto de la locura (fragmento)*. San Juan de Puerto Rico, 1962.

————. "Habitante del eco" de *Habitante del eco*. En *Primeros libros poéticos*. Río Piedras: Qease, 1982.

Melendes, Joserramón. "Narciso". *La casa de la forma*. Río Piedras: Qease, 1986.

Mir, Pedro. "Si alguien quiere saber cuál es mi patria". *Viaje a la muchedumbre* (1971). México: Siglo XXI, 1975.

Morejón, Nancy. "Amo a mi amo". *Nueva poesía cubana, antología* (1966-86). Selección de Antonio Merino. Madrid: Editorial Orígenes,

Neruda, Pablo. "La ola" de *Canto general*. En *Obras completas*. Buenos Aires: Losada, 1967.

————. "Oda a la crítica" de *Odas elementales*. En *Obras completas*. Buenos Aires: Losada, 1967.

Netzahualcóyotl. "¿Qué es la poesía?" *Las letras precolombinas*. Georges Baudot. México: Siglo XXI, 1979. También en Angel M. Garibay, *La literatura de los aztecas*. México: Joaquín Mortiz, 1964.

————. "Yo Netzahualcóyotl lo pregunto". *Las letras precolombinas*. Georges Baudot. México: Siglo XXI, 1979.

Ochart, Luz Ivonne. "New York-New York". (De *Poemas de Nueva York*). *Obra poética, antología*. San Juan: Instituto de Cultura Puertorriqueña, 1989.

Otero, Blas de. "En el principio" de *Pido la paz y la palabra* (1955). En *Con la mayoría inmensa*. Buenos Aires: Losada, 1972.

Palés Matos, Luis. "El llamado". En *Poesía completa y prosa selecta*. Edición de Margot Arce. Caracas: Biblioteca Ayacucho, 1978.

————. "Mulata Antilla" de *Tuntún de pasa y grifería* (1950). *Poesía completa y prosa selecta*. Margot Arce, ed. Caracas: Biblioteca Ayacucho, 1978. [Derechos: María Valdés Tons de Palés Matos e Hijos y Biblioteca Ayacucho.]

Parra, Nicanor. "Los vicios del mundo moderno". En *Obra gruesa*. Santiago de Chile: Editorial Universitaria, 1969. [También en *Antología de la poesía hispanoamericana actual*. Julio Ortega, ed. México: Siglo XXI, 1987.]

Paz, Octavio. "Aquí" de *Salamandra* (1958-1961) en *La centena (1935-1968)*. Barcelona: Barral, 1969.

————. "Certeza" de *Salamandra* (1958-1961) en *La centena (1935-1968)*. Barcelona: Barral, 1969.

————. "Identidad" de *Salamandra* (1958-1961) en *La centena (1935-1968)*. Barcelona: Barral, 1969.

————. "Madrugada" de *Salamandra* (1958-1961) en *La centena (1935-1968)*. Barcelona: Barral, 1969.

————. "Himno entre ruinas". (1948). *La estación violenta*. México: Fondo de Cultura Económica, 1954.

Paz, Octavio Carlos. "He olvidado mi nombre". *Primera antología poética*. México: Fondo de Cultura Económica, 1969.

Pietri, Pedro. "Tata". *Obituario puertorriqueño*. San Juan: Instituto de Cultura Puertorriqueña, 1977.

Pizarnik, Alejandra. "En esta noche, en este mundo". *Antología de la poesía hispanoamericana actual*. Ed. Julio Ortega. México: Siglo XXI, 1986.

Quevedo, Francisco de. "Amor constante más allá de la muerte" en *Antología poética*. Selección de Jorge Luis Borges. Madrid: Alianza, 1982.

————. "Miré los muros de la patria mía" en *Antología poética*. Selección de Jorge Luis Borges. Madrid: Alianza, 1982.

Ramos Sucre, José Antonio. "La vida del maldito" de *La Torre de Timón* (1925). En *Las formas del fuego*. Madrid: Siruela, 1988.

Rivera, Etna Iris. "Oxunmare" de *Pachamamapa Takin* (1976). En *Entre ciudades y casi paraísos. Antología.* San Juan: Instituto de Cultura Puertorriqueña, 1989.

Romualdo, Alejandro. "Canto coral a Tupac Amaru". *Antología de la poesía hispanoamericana actual.* Ed. Julio Ortega. México: Siglo XXI, 1986.

Rosetti, Ana. "Cierta secta feminista se da consejos prematrimoniales".

Salinas, Pedro. "El cuerpo, fabuloso" de *Todo más claro y otros poemas* (1949). En *Poesía.* Selección y notas de Julio Cortázar. Madrid: Alianza Editorial, 1974.

Silén, Iván. Fragmento de *Poemas de Filí-Melé.* Santo Domingo, 1987.

Sotomayor, Aurea María. "Arañas" de *Sitios de la memoria* (1983). En *La gula de la tinta, antología 1973-1990.* San Juan: Instituto de Cultura Puertorriqueña, en prensa.

Storni, Alfonsina. "Tú me quieres blanca". *Poesías completas.* Buenos Aires: Sociedad Editora Latinoamericana, 1968. [También en *Poesía feminista del mundo hispánico.* Angel y Kate Flores, eds. México: Siglo XXI, 1984.]

Suardíaz, Luis. "Acerca de un fraude". *Nueva poesía cubana.* José Agustín Goytisolo, editor. Barcelona: Península, 1972.

Totoquihuatzin. "Como el orfebre hace un collar". *Omnibús de poesía mexicana.* Gabriel Zaid, antólogo. México: Siglo XXI, 1972.

Unamuno, Miguel. "La oración del ateo" de *Rosario de sonetos líricos* (1912) en *Poesías escogidas.* Selección de Guillermo de Torre. Buenos Aires: Losada, 1972.

Valdés, Esteban. "Soneto de las estrellas". *Fuera de trabajo.* Río Piedras: Qease, 1977.

Valente, José Angel. "Reaparición de lo heroico" de *El inocente* (1967-70). En *Entrada en materia.* Madrid: Cátedra, 1985.

Vallejo, César. "Los heraldos negros" de *Los heraldos negros* (1918). En *Obra poética completa.* Caracas: Ayacucho, 1979.

————. "Masa" de *España, aparta de mí este cáliz* (1937). En *Obra poética completa.* Caracas: Ayacucho, 1979.

————. "Piedra negra sobre piedra blanca" de *Poemas humanos* (1937). En *Obra poética completa.* Caracas: Ayacucho, 1979.

Vega, Garcilaso de la. "Oh dulces prendas..." en *Poesías castellanas completas.* Elías L. Rivers, ed. Madrid: Castalia, 1979.

————. "En tanto que de rosa y azucena...". *Antología de lecturas.* RP: EDUPR, 1977.

Vega, Lope de. "¿Qué tengo yo que mi amistad procuras?" *Poesía lírica.* Zaragoza: Ebro, 1960.

————. "Soneto CXXVI: Desmayarse, atreverse, estar furioso...". *Rimas.* Gerardo Diego, ed. Madrid: Palabra y Tiempo, 1963.

Villaurrutia, Xavier. "Nocturno en que nada se oye" de *Nostalgia de la muerte* (1938). En *Poesía en movimiento, 1915-1966.* Alí Chumacero, Octavio Paz, José Emilio Pacheco, Homero Aridjis (Antólogos). México: Siglo XXI, 1966.

————. "Nocturno rosa" *(Nostalgia de la muerte,* 1938). En *Poesía en movimiento, 1915-1966.* Alí Chumacero, Octavio Paz, José Emilio Pacheco, Homero Aridjis (Antólogos). México: Siglo XXI, 1966.

Vitier, Cintio. "Un extraño honor". *Escrito y cantado* (1954-59). La Habana: Ucar, 1959.

Westphalen, Emilio Adolfo. "Te he seguido". *(Abolición de la muerte,* 1935). *Otra imagen deleznable.* México: Fondo de Cultura Económica, 1980.

Indice temático

ENSAYO

EL ARTE Y EL LENGUAJE
LA FICCION

POETICAS
EL LENGUAJE

*Si definimos un tema como la proposición de un escrito, la consecuencia es que un texto propone necesariamente más de un tema. Esto no niega que puedan encontrarse planteamientos que parezcan ser centrales o principales. Todo va a depender, desde luego, de los instrumentos de análisis e interpretación del lector, de su experiencia, entrenamiento e intuición. Al mismo tiempo, aquello que parezca un planteamiento central se puede presentar como una colaboración o combinación de temas. Por ejemplo, si la preocupación de un poema parece ser el amor, éste muy bien puede presentarse como un equivalente a la belleza, y ésta, a su vez, como un equivalente a la poesía. Visto así entonces habría tres posibles temas: amor, belleza y poesía, aunque la proposición central esté más cerca del primero.

Hecha esta aclaración cabe una exhortación a leer los temas del índice como señales que ayudan al lector, pero que no pretenden ser palabra final ni absoluta. En los casos donde las lecturas aparezcan bajo varios temas, debe entenderse que, efectivamente, la proposición que parece ser la principal aparece en combinación con otros temas. En el índice, pues, tradición y renovación van de la mano. Si se afirma que un texto no se limita a un tema no se niega que haya uno predominante o que se destaque sobre los otros. Lo importante, lo fecundo, es no negar u oscurecer los otros posibles planteamientos que tal vez, y, dependiendo del lector, podrían convertirse en "temas principales".

---

[1] Algunos de los temas que se tratan en este apartado son: el racionalismo, el realismo, el "sentido común" y el materialismo, entre otros.

NARRATIVA

EL SUJETO

POESIA

EL SUJETO
IDENTIDAD
LA EXISTENCIA HUMANA
EL TIEMPO

LO SOCIAL
CRITICA DE LA CULTURA MODERNA

Indice de asuntos formales

ENSAYO

ESTRATEGIAS RETORICAS

ARGUMENTACION

NARRACION

DEFINICION

PROCESO DEDUCTIVO

INTERROGACION

MODELOS ESTRUCTURALES[1]

[1] José María Díez Borque, en *Comentario de textos literarios* (Playor, 1977), utiliza los siguientes términos para clasificar las estructuras:
ANALIZANTE — Una afirmación o un postulado, desarrollado o demostrado por varios otros.
SINTETIZANTE — Varias ideas que llevan a una conclusión.
ANALIZANTE-SINTETIZANTE — Desarrollo de una afirmación o idea inicial que culmina en una conclusión.
PARALELA — Ideas no supeditadas unas a otras que se sitúan yuxtapuestas en el mismo plano.
ATRIBUTIVA — Se establece una relación de identidad, a = b.
DE NUCLEOS INDEPENDIENTES — Varios núcleos dependientes de una idea principal.
DEPENDIENTE DEL PUNTO DE VISTA — Se presentan distintos puntos de vista.
DEPENDIENTE DE ENFOQUE — Desde un mismo punto de vista se presentan distintas maneras de enfocar la realidad.

NARRATIVA

[2]Para más información sobre las tipologías de esta sección consúltese la si-
guiente bibliografía:
Wayne C. Booth. *Retórica de la ficción.* Barcelona: Antoni Bosch, 1978.
Wayne C. Booth. *Retórica de la ironía.* Madrid: Alfaguara, 1986.
Jonathan Culler. *La poética estructuralista.* Barcelona: Anagrama, 1978.
Seymour Chatman. *Historia y discurso.* Madrid: Alfaguara, 1990.
Shlomith Rimmon-Kenan. *Narrative Fiction: Contemporary Poetics.* London:
Methuen, 1984.
Patricia Waugh. *Metafiction. The Theory and Practice of Self-Conscious Fic-
tion.* London: Methuen, 1984.

[3]El término *focalización* se utiliza para precisar el concepto más populariza-
do de punto de vista. La focalización cuenta no sólo con el objeto sino también
con el sujeto detrás de la mira, así como con las perspectivas ideológicas y físicas de
la observación. El sujeto o focalizador es el agente, que no es necesariamente el narra-
dor, cuya percepción orienta la presentación narrativa, en su totalidad o en algunas
de sus partes, mientras el objeto o lo focalizado es lo que se percibe. Para más información sobre este término, así como sobre sus tipologías, véase Rimmon-Kenan,
Shlomith, *Narrative Fiction: Contemporary poetics,* London: Methusen, 1983, c.6.

ASPECTOS FORMALES: LA SINTAXIS DEL DISCURSO

ORDEN Y FUNCION DE SECUENCIAS O NODULOS NARRATIVOS

LAS CONVENCIONES[4] DEL GENERO Y SU RUPTURA
EL ABSURDO Y LO FANTASTICO

[4]Se usa el término con la acepción inglesa de *convention*, refiriéndose a las similaridades, en cuanto a expectativas del destinatario, entre obras de una misma tradición. El concepto sirve para definir al género como un conjunto dado de expectativas. Es decir, esperamos una comedia que nos haga reir y de una historia de terror que nos inspire temor. La transgresión de estas convenciones contiene, por lo tanto, un comentario sobre la tradición en la que se inscribe el texto. Para más información sobre este término véase Culler, Gonalthan, "Convención y naturalización". *La poética estructuralista, la lingüística y el estudio de la literatura,* Trad. Carlos Manzano, Barcelona: Anagrama, 1978.

POESIA

METABOLAS[5]

METAPLASMOS

METATAXAS

METASEMEMAS O TROPOS

[5]Considerando los distintos niveles del lenguaje, los autores de la *Retórica general* clasifican las figuras de retórica o metábolas en metaplasmos, metataxas, metasemas y metalogismos. Véase la tabla de Helena Beristain que se incluye como apéndice. Grupo Mu, *Rhétorique de la Poèsie*, Bruselas: Complexe, 1977. Beristain, Helena, *Guía para la lectura comentada de textos literarios*, Parte I. México: Talleres Larios e Hijos Impresores, S.A., 1977.

METRICA Y FORMAS ESTROFICAS

FORMAS DISCURSIVAS

EL PROCESO DE LA COMUNICACION

CONVENCIONES Y RUPTURA

EL POEMA CRITICO
(DE LOS DISCURSOS SOCIALES Y CULTURALES)

METÁBOLAS

Gramaticales (código)			Lógicas (referente)
Expresión		Contenido	
A. Metaplasmos	B. Metataxas	C. Metasememas	D. Metalogismos
Operaciones efectuadas sobre la morfología	*Operaciones efectuadas sobre la sintáxis*	*Operaciones efectuadas sobre la semántica*	*Operaciones efectuadas sobre la lógica*
ritmo	metro	comparación	litote
aliteración	encabalgamiento	metáfora	reticencia
paranomasia	elipsis	prosopopeya	hipérbole
rima	zeugma	sinécdoque	gradación
similicadencia	asíndeton	metonimia	pleonasmo
aféresis	supr. puntuación	hipálage	antítesis
síncopa	digresión	oxímoron	alegoría
apócope	enumeración		ironía
prótesis	anáfora		paradoja
epéntesis	reduplicación		dilogía
diéresis	conduplicación		
paragoge	epanadiplosis		
sinonimia	concatenación		
arcaísmo	polisíndeton		
neologismo	estribillo		
invención	simetría		
préstamo	silepsis		
metátesis	quiasmo		
anagrama	inserción		
palindroma	hipérbaton		

Las figuras contenidas en este esquema no son todas las que menciona en él Dubois, cuya *Retórica* las estudia aplicadas específicamente a la lengua francesa; se han agregado, en cambio, otras metábolas tradicionalmente consideradas al hacer el análisis estilístico en textos de lengua española.

Guide to Gale Literary Criticism Series

For criticism on	Consult these Gale series
Authors now living or who died after December 31, 1959	*CONTEMPORARY LITERARY CRITICISM (CLC)*
Authors who died between 1900 and 1959	*TWENTIETH-CENTURY LITERARY CRITICISM (TCLC)*
Authors who died between 1800 and 1899	*NINETEENTH-CENTURY LITERATURE CRITICISM (NCLC)*
Authors who died between 1400 and 1799	*LITERATURE CRITICISM FROM 1400 TO 1800 (LC)* *SHAKESPEAREAN CRITICISM (SC)*
Authors who died before 1400	*CLASSICAL AND MEDIEVAL LITERATURE CRITICISM (CMLC)*
Black writers of the past two hundred years	*BLACK LITERATURE CRITICISM (BLC) AND BLACK LITERATURE CRITICISM SUPPLEMENT (BLCS)*
Authors of books for children and young adults	*CHILDREN'S LITERATURE REVIEW (CLR)*
Dramatists	*DRAMA CRITICISM (DC)*
Hispanic writers of the late nineteenth and twentieth centuries	*HISPANIC LITERATURE CRITICISM (HLC)*
Native North American writers and orators of the eighteenth, nineteenth, and twentieth centuries	*NATIVE NORTH AMERICAN LITERATURE (NNAL)*
Poets	*POETRY CRITICISM (PC)*
Short story writers	*SHORT STORY CRITICISM (SSC)*
Major authors from the Renaissance to the present	*WORLD LITERATURE CRITICISM, 1500 TO THE PRESENT (WLC)*
Major authors and works from the Bible to the present	*WORLD LITERATURE CRITICISM SUPPLEMENT (WLCS)*

Contemporary
Literary Criticism

ISSN 0091-3421

R

Volume 111

Contemporary Literary Criticism

Excerpts from Criticism of the Works
of Today's Novelists, Poets, Playwrights,
Short Story Writers, Scriptwriters, and
Other Creative Writers

Jeffrey W. Hunter
Deborah A. Schmitt
Timothy J. White
EDITORS

Tim Akers
Pamela S. Dear
Catherine V. Donaldson
Daniel Jones
John D. Jorgenson
Jerry Moore
Polly Vedder
Thomas Wiloch
Kathleen Wilson
ASSOCIATE EDITORS

GALE

DETROIT · LONDON

Contents

Preface vii

Acknowledgments xi

Preface

A Comprehensive Information Source
on Contemporary Literature

Named "one of the twenty-five most distinguished reference titles published during the past twenty-five years" by *Reference Quarterly,* the *Contemporary Literary Criticism (CLC)* series provides readers with critical commentary and general information on more than 2,000 authors now living or who died after December 31, 1959. Previous to the publication of the first volume of *CLC* in 1973, there was no ongoing digest monitoring scholarly and popular sources of critical opinion and explication of modern literature. *CLC,* therefore, has fulfilled an essential need, particularly since the complexity and variety of contemporary literature makes the function of criticism especially important to today's reader.

Scope of the Series

CLC presents significant passages from published criticism of works by creative writers. Since many of the authors covered by *CLC* inspire continual critical commentary, writers are often represented in more than one volume. There is, of course, no duplication of reprinted criticism.

Authors are selected for inclusion for a variety of reasons, among them the publication or dramatic production of a critically acclaimed new work, the reception of a major literary award, revival of interest in past writings, or the adaptation of a literary work to film or television.

Attention is also given to several other groups of writers-authors of considerable public interest—about whose work criticism is often difficult to locate. These include mystery and science fiction writers, literary and social critics, foreign writers, and authors who represent particular ethnic groups within the United States.

Format of the Book

Each *CLC* volume contains about 500 individual excerpts taken from hundreds of book review periodicals, general magazines, scholarly journals, monographs, and books. Entries include critical evaluations spanning from the beginning of an author's career to the most current commentary. Interviews, feature articles, and other published writings that offer insight into the author's works are also presented. Students, teachers, librarians, and researchers will find that the generous excerpts and supplementary material in *CLC* provide them with vital information required to write a term paper, analyze a poem, or lead a book discussion group. In addition, complete bibliographical citations note the original source and all of the information necessary for a term paper footnote or bibliography.

Features

A *CLC* author entry consists of the following elements:

- The **Author Heading** cites the author's name in the form under which the author has most commonly published, followed by birth date, and death date when applicable. Uncertainty as to a birth or death date is indicated by a question mark.

- A **Portrait** of the author is included when available.

- A brief **Biographical and Critical Introduction** to the author and his or her work precedes the excerpted criticism. The first line of the introduction provides the author's full name, pseudonyms (if applicable), nationality, and a listing of genres in which the author has written. To provide users with easier access to information, the biographical and critical essay included in each author entry is divided into four categories: "Introduction," "Biographical Information," "Major Works," and "Critical Reception." The introductions to single-work entries—entries that focus on well known and frequently studied books, short stories, and poems—are similarly organized to quickly provide readers with information on the plot and major characters of the work being discussed, its major themes, and its critical reception. Previous volumes of *CLC* in which the author has been featured are also listed in the introduction.

- A list of **Principal Works** notes the most important writings by the author. When foreign-language works have been translated into English, the English-language version of the title follows in brackets.

- The **Excerpted Criticism** represents various kinds of critical writing, ranging in form from the brief review to the scholarly exegesis. Essays are selected by the editors to reflect the spectrum of opinion about a specific work or about an author's literary career in general. The excerpts are presented chronologically, adding a useful perspective to the entry. All titles by the author featured in the entry are printed in boldface type, which enables the reader to easily identify the works being discussed. Publication information (such as publisher names and book prices) and parenthetical numerical references (such as footnotes or page and line references to specific editions of a work) have been deleted at the editor's discretion to provide smoother reading of the text.

- Critical essays are prefaced by **Explanatory Notes** as an additional aid to readers. These notes may provide several types of valuable information, including: the reputation of the critic, the importance of the work of criticism, the commentator's approach to the author's work, the purpose of the criticism, and changes in critical trends regarding the author.

- A complete **Bibliographical Citation** designed to help the user find the original essay or book precedes each excerpt.

- Whenever possible, a recent, previously unpublished **Author Interview** accompanies each entry.

- A concise **Further Reading** section appears at the end of entries on authors for whom a significant amount of criticism exists in addition to the pieces reprinted in *CLC*. Each citation in this section is accompanied by a descriptive annotation describing the content of that article. Materials included in this section are grouped under various headings (e.g., Biography, Bibliography, Criticism, and Interviews) to aid users in their search for additional information. Cross-references to other useful sources published by Gale Research in which the author has appeared are also included: *Authors in the News, Black Writers, Children's Literature Review, Contemporary Authors, Dictionary of Literary Biography, DISCovering Authors, Drama Criticism, Hispanic Literature Criticism, Hispanic Writers, Native North American Literature, Poetry Criticism, Something about the Author, Short Story Criticism, Contemporary Authors Autobiography Series,* and *Something about the Author Autobiography Series.*

Other Features

CLC also includes the following features:

- An **Acknowledgments** section lists the copyright holders who have granted permission to reprint material in this volume of *CLC*. It does not, however, list every book or periodical reprinted or consulted during the preparation of the volume.

- Each new volume of *CLC* includes a **Cumulative Topic Index,** which lists all literary topics treated in *CLC, NCLC,*

TCLC, and *LC 1400-1800.*

■ A **Cumulative Author Index** lists all the authors who have appeared in the various literary criticism series published by Gale Research, with cross-references to Gale's biographical and autobiographical series. A full listing of the series referenced there appears on the first page of the indexes of this volume. Readers will welcome this cumulated author index as a useful tool for locating an author within the various series. The index, which lists birth and death dates when available, will be particularly valuable for those authors who are identified with a certain period but whose death dates cause them to be placed in another, or for those authors whose careers span two periods. For example, Ernest Hemingway is found in *CLC,* yet F. Scott Fitzgerald, a writer often associated with him, is found in *Twentieth-Century Literary Criticism.*

■ A **Cumulative Nationality Index** alphabetically lists all authors featured in *CLC* by nationality, followed by numbers corresponding to the volumes in which the authors appear.

■ An alphabetical **Title Index** accompanies each volume of *CLC.* Listings are followed by the author's name and the corresponding page numbers where the titles are discussed. English translations of foreign titles and variations of titles are cross-referenced to the title under which a work was originally published. Titles of novels, novellas, dramas, films, record albums, and poetry, short story, and essay collections are printed in italics, while all individual poems, short stories, essays, and songs are printed in roman type within quotation marks; when published separately (e.g., T. S. Eliot's poem *The Waste Land),* the titles of long poems are printed in italics.

■ In response to numerous suggestions from librarians, Gale has also produced a **Special Paperbound Edition** of the *CLC* title index. This annual cumulation, which alphabetically lists all titles reviewed in the series, is available to all customers and is typically published with every fifth volume of *CLC.* Additional copies of the index are available upon request. Librarians and patrons will welcome this separate index: it saves shelf space, is easy to use, and is recyclable upon receipt of the next edition.

Citing *Contemporary Literary Criticism*

When writing papers, students who quote directly from any volume in the Literary Criticism Series may use the following general forms to footnote reprinted criticism. The first example pertains to material drawn from periodicals, the second to material reprinted in books:

[1]Alfred Cismaru, "Making the Best of It," *The New Republic,* 207, No. 24, (December 7, 1992), 30, 32; excerpted and reprinted in *Contemporary Literary Criticism,* Vol. 85, ed. Christopher Giroux (Detroit: Gale Research, 1995), pp. 73-4.

[2]Yvor Winters, *The Post-Symbolist Methods* (Allen Swallow, 1967); excerpted and reprinted in *Contemporary Literary Criticism,* Vol. 85, ed. Christopher Giroux (Detroit: Gale Research, 1995), pp. 223-26.

Suggestions Are Welcome

The editors hope that readers will find *CLC* a useful reference tool and welcome comments about the work. Send comments and suggestions to: Editors, *Contemporary Literary Criticism*, Gale Research, 27500 Drake Rd., Farmington Hills, MI 48333-3535.

Acknowledgments

The editors wish to thank the copyright holders of the excerpted criticism included in this volume and the permissions managers of many book and magazine publishing companies for assisting us in securing reproduction rights. We are also grateful to the staffs of the Detroit Public Library, the Library of Congress, the University of Detroit Mercy Library, Wayne State University Purdy/Kresge Library Complex, and the University of Michigan Libraries for making their resources available to us. Following is a list of the copyright holders who have granted us permission to reproduce material in this volume of CLC. Every effort has been made to trace copyright, but if omissions have been made, please let us know.

COPYRIGHTED EXCERPTS IN *CLC*, VOLUME 111, WERE REPRODUCED FROM THE FOLLOWING PERIODICALS:

America, November 24, 1984. © 1984, All rights reserved. Reproduced with permission of America Press, Inc., 106 West 56th Street, New York, NY 10019.—*American Film*, v. VIII, April, 1983 for "Susie Loves Matt," by Jay Scott. Copyright 1983 by American Film. Reproduced by permission of Gouverneur & Company, agents for the author.—*The American Scholar*, v. 52, Spring, 1983. Copyright © 1983 by the United Chapters of the Phi Beta Kappa Society. Reproduced by permission of the publishers.—*Arizona Quarterly*, v. 41, Spring, 1985 for "'Quartet in Autumn': New Light on Barbara Pym as a Modernist" by Margaret Diane Stetz. Copyright © 1985 by the Regents of the University of Arizona. Reproduced by permission of the publisher and the author.—*Book World—The Washington Post*, February 12, 1989; v. 20, August 19, 1990; v. 20, October 21, 1990; September 21, 1997. © 1989, 1990, 1997 Washington Post Book World Service/Washington Post Writers Group. All reproduced by permission.—*Chicago Tribune*, August 19, 1990 for "A Long-Awaited Return" by George Garrett. © copyrighted 1990, Chicago Tribune Company. All rights reserved. Reproduced by permission of the author.—*College English*, v. 52, April, 1990 for "Kathy Acker and the Postmodern Subject of Feminism" by Martin Sciolino. Copyright © 1990 by the National Council of Teachers of English. Reprinted by permission of the publisher and the author.—*Commentary*, v. 64, 1976 for "Norman Mailer Today" by James Toback. Copyright © 1964 by the American Jewish Committee. All rights reserved. Reproduced by permission of the publisher and the author.—*Commonweal*, May 8, 1981; January 13, 1984. Copyright © 1981, 1984 Commonweal Publishing Co., Inc. Reproduced by permission of Commonweal Foundation.—*Concerning Poetry*, v. 10, 1977. Copyright © 1977, Western Washington University. Reproduced by permission.—*Contemporary Literature*, v. XXXI, Winter, 1990; v. XXXIX, Spring, 1993; v. XXXVII, Fall, 1996. © 1990, 1993, 1996 by the Board of Regents of the University of Wisconsin. All reproduced by permission of The University of Wisconsin Press.—*Critical Quarterly*, v. 21, 1979. © Manchester University Press 1979. Reproduced by permission of Basil Blackwell Limited.—*Critique: Studies in Contemporary Fiction*, v. XXVI, Spring, 1985; v. XXXV, Spring, 1994; v. XXXVIII, 1996. Copyright © 1985, 1994, 1996 Helen Dwight Reid Educational Foundation. All reproduced with permission of the Helen Dwight Reid Educational Foundation, published by Heldref Publications, 1319 18th Street, NW, Washington, DC 20036-1802.—*Encounter*, v. 26, April, 1996 for "I. B. Singer" by Irving Howe. © 1996 by the author. Reproduced by permission of the Literary Estate of Irving Howe.—*English Journal*, v. 81, November, 1992 for "Doing Theory: Words about Words about The Outsiders"by Steven L. VanderStaay. Copyright © 1992 by the National Council of Teachers of English. Reproduced by permission of the publisher and the author.—*English Studies*, Netherlands, v. 71, December, 1990. © 1990 by Swets & Zeitlinger B. V. Reproduced by permission.—*Essays in Literature*, v. 1, 1974. Copyright 1974 by Western Illinois University. Reproduced by permission.—*The Hudson Review*, v. 8, Summer, 1955; v. XLIV, Spring, 1991; v. 45, Spring, 1992. Copyright © 1955, 1991, 1992 by The Hudson Review, Inc. Reproduced by permission. —*Iowa Review*, v. 8, 1977 for "Sylvia Plath and Confessional Poetry: A Reconsideration" by M. D. Uroff. Copyright © 1977 by The University of Iowa. Reproduced by permission of the author.—*Journal of Popular Culture*, v. 9, 1975. Copyright © 1995 by Ray B. Browne. Reproduced by permission.—*Judaism: A Quarterly Journal*, v. 41, Winter, 1992. Copyright © 1992 by the American Jewish Congress. Reproduced by permission.—*Los Angeles Times Book Review*, November 9, 1986; September 4, 1988; August 12, 1990; September 2, 1990; March 22, 1992. Copyright, 1986, 1988, 1990, 1992, *Los Angeles Times*. All

Kathy Acker
1948-1997

(Also wrote under pseudonym Black Tarantula) American novelist, short story writer, essayist, critic, librettist, and screenwriter.

The following entry presents an overview of Acker's career through 1997. For further information on her life and works, see *CLC,* Volume 45.

INTRODUCTION

A controversial avant-garde writer and cult figure of the punk movement, Kathy Acker is considered among the most significant proponents of radical feminism and the postmodern literary aesthetic. Associated with the discordant, irreverent music of punk rock, Acker's iconoclastic metafiction—a chaotic amalgam of extreme profanity, violence, graphic sex, autobiography, fragmented narrative, and plagiarized texts—rejects conventional morality and traditional modes of literary expression. Her best known works, including *Great Expectations* (1982), *Blood and Guts in High School* (1984), and *Don Quixote* (1986), feature female protagonists whose psychosexual misadventures, involving rape, incest, suicide, and abortion, underscore their individual struggles to discover meaning and identity in deconstructed patriarchal language and sexual masochism. A well-versed literary theorist and sophisticated experimenter, Acker's provocative fiction offers a serious challenge to established literary forms and the possibility of human understanding in a nihilistic, decentered world.

Biographical Information

Born in New York City, Acker was raised by her mother and stepfather. Her biological father, whom she never met, abandoned her mother before she was born. Her mother later committed suicide when Acker was thirty. Acker attended Brandeis University and the University of California, San Diego, where she earned a bachelor's degree in 1968. Twice wed—first to Robert Acker in 1966, then to composer Peter Gordon in 1976—and twice divorced, Acker returned to New York during the 1970s to work as a secretary, stripper, and performer in live sex shows and pornographic films while promoting her fiction in small press publications. She began a combined doctoral program in classics and philosophy at the City University of New York and New York University, but left after two years. Her first publication, *Politics* (1972), is a combination of poetry and prose heavily influenced by the work of William S. Burroughs. The next year, under the pseudonym Black Tarantula, she produced *The*

Childlike Life of the Black Tarantula (1973); an expanded edition of this work appeared in 1975 under the title *The Childlike Life of the Black Tarantula by the Black Tarantula.* Acker followed with *I Dreamt I Was a Nymphomaniac* (1974) and three short novels: *Florida* (1978), a brief satire of the film *Key Largo; Kathy Goes to Haiti* (1978), which recounts the sexual exploits of a girl visiting Haiti; and *The Adult Life of Toulouse Lautrec by Henri Toulouse Lautrec* (1978). She won a Pushcart Prize in 1979 for the publication of *New York City in 1979* (1979). During the early 1980s, Acker moved to London where she achieved a degree of fame and maintained a steady output of novels including *Great Expectations, Blood and Guts in High School, Don Quixote,* and *Empire of the Senseless* (1988)—all among her best-known works. She also collaborated with Peter Gordon to perform her opera libretto, *The Birth of the Poet* (1985), at the Brooklyn Academy of Music in 1985. A film based on her screenplay, *Variety* (1985), appeared the same year. Acker republished several short novels in *Literal Madness* (1988), including *Kathy Goes to Haiti, Florida,* and *My Death My Life by Pier Paolo Pasolini,* originally included in the 1984 English version of *Blood and Guts in*

High School. Returning to the United States in the early 1990s, Acker published the novels *In Memoriam to Identity* (1990), *Portrait of an Eye* (1992), *My Mother* (1993), and *Pussy, King of the Pirates* (1996), which contains reprinted versions of *The Childlike Life of the Black Tarantula by the Black Tarantula, I Dreamt I Was a Nymphomaniac,* and *The Adult Life of Toulouse Lautrec by Henri Toulouse Lautrec.* An amateur bodybuilder, tattoo enthusiast, and adjunct professor at the San Francisco Art Institute beginning in 1991, Acker also appeared as a visiting instructor at the University of California at Santa Barbara, the University of California, San Diego, and the University of Idaho in 1994. Shortly before her death, she produced *Bodies of Work* (1997), a collection of essays, and *Eurydice in the Underground* (1997), a volume of short fiction. At age forty-eight, Acker succumbed to breast cancer at an alternative cancer treatment center in Tijuana, Mexico.

Major Works

Acker's trademark fiction is a pastiche of visceral prose, sensationalized autobiography, political tract, pornography, and appropriated texts in which characters—often famous literary or historical figures—easily move through time and space while frequently changing personalities and genders. Deliberately non-chronological and usually evoking a quest theme, her largely plotless stories progress through disjointed, jump-cut sequences that incorporate fantasy, personal statement, and the juxtaposition of excerpted texts from various sources, such as Charles Dickens, Marcel Proust, and the Marquis de Sade. Acker's trenchant criticism of oppressive middle-class mores, phallocentric culture, and all hierarchial power structures permeates her writings, particularly as symbolized in repeated scenes of rape and incest. In *The Childlike Life of the Black Tarantula,* a sixteen-year-old female narrator explores alternate identities as a murderess and prostitute, copies passages from pornographic books in which she imagines herself the leading character, and participates in public sex acts. *I Dreamt I Was a Nymphomaniac* describes a young woman's artistic aspirations, philosophical musings, and the evils of corporate America in fragmented, unpunctuated passages—some of which are repeated verbatim in other parts of the text. In *The Adult Life of Toulouse Lautrec by Henri Toulouse Lautrec,* a female incarnation of the French painter relates the life of her brother, Vincent Van Gogh, while accompanying Hercule Poirot, an Agatha Christie detective, through the streets of Paris in search of clues to a murder mystery. Meanwhile, Van Gogh's daughter, a prepubescent Janis Joplin, has a love affair with James Dean. *My Death My Life by Pier Paolo Pasolini,* another fictitious autobiography, reconstructs the 1975 murder of the Italian writer and filmmaker through a series of loosely related vignettes, including Shakespearian parodies and an obscene epistolary exchange among the Bronte sisters. Increasingly dependent on borrowed texts,

Acker's first major novel, *Great Expectations,* begins with a blatant plagiarism from Dickens's own novel of the same title, then shifts to autobiographic detail about her mother's suicide, and allusions to the writings of Madame de La Fayette, John Keats, and Herman Melville. Drawing on Nathaniel Hawthorne's *The Scarlet Letter, Blood and Guts in High School* describes the plight of Janey Smith, a ten-year-old girl who is spurned by her father, with whom she is sexually involved, when he takes a new lover. Fleeing to New York, she joins a gang and is kidnapped by a Persian slave trader who locks her away. When Janey develops cancer, she is released and travels to Tangiers, where she wanders the desert with Jean Genet until they are imprisoned. *Don Quixote,* a reinterpretation of Miguel de Cervantes's seventeenth-century novel, follows the peregrinations of a female Don Quixote in contemporary New York and London. After an abortion, Acker's romantic protagonist searches for her sidekick Saint Simeon, a talking dog who represents Sancho Panza, in an absurd world dominated by male texts and female subjugation. Acker's subsequent novels similarly describe perverse degradation and ubiquitous violence in surreal contemporary and near-future settings. *Empire of the Senseless* recounts the picaresque adventures of Abhor, a female protagonist of mixed race and human-robot composition, and her male accomplice, Thivai, as they look for meaning and legitimate modes of expression amid war and revolution. *In Memoriam to Identity* presents the early life of poet Arthur Rimbaud through examples of his poetry and excerpts from biographies, followed by the stories of two heroines, Airplane, a rape victim and stripper, and Capitol, a performance artist, both of whom resemble characters from novels by William Faulkner. Acker's final novel, *Pussy, King of the Pirates,* is a partial adaptation of Robert Louis Stevenson's *Treasure Island,* with allusions to *The Story of O* and Antonin Artaud's Theater of Cruelty, in which two ex-prostitutes hire a band of female pirates to help them locate buried treasure in a matriarchal society.

Critical Reception

Acker's radical experiments with the postmodern novel have attracted considerable notoriety. While some critics praise her technical skill and adroit manipulations of plagiarized texts, others find her amorphous narratives unnecessarily obscure and incomprehensible. In addition, Acker has drawn mixed reactions to the incorporation of graphic sex acts and violence in her fiction. As some critics note, the intensity and frequency of such episodes produces a numbing effect that diminishes its shock value and undermines Acker's ability to evoke outrage or disgust. For this reason, some feminists have condemned Acker for depicting women as degraded sex objects. However, others commend Acker's persistent efforts to defy literary convention and to unmask the inherent misogyny of Western culture by portraying sexual domination as the primary tool of female oppression.

Influenced by the cut-up techniques of Burroughs and the narrative strategies of French anti-novelist Alain Robbe-Grillet and Marguerite Duras, Acker's audacious attempts to appropriate and rewrite her own versions of literary classics are recognized as an intellectually challenging endeavor, especially as revealed by her impressive grasp of complex literary theory and comprehensive knowledge of Western literature. A subversive literary inventor and a defiant voice against patriarchal society, Acker exerted an important influence on postmodern fiction and contemporary feminist discourse.

PRINCIPAL WORKS

Politics (novel) 1972

The Childlike Life of the Black Tarantula [as Black Tarantula] (novel) 1973

I Dreamt I Was a Nymphomaniac (novel) 1974

Florida (novel) 1978

Kathy Goes to Haiti (novel) 1978

The Adult Life of Toulouse Lautrec by Henri Toulouse Lautrec (novel) 1978

New York City in 1979 (novel) 1979

Great Expectations (novel) 1982

Hello, I'm Erica Jong (novel) 1982

Blood and Guts in High School (novel) 1984

*My Death My Life by Pier Paolo Pasolini (novel) 1984

The Birth of the Poet (libretto) 1985

Variety (screenplay) 1985

Don Quixote (novel) 1986

Empire of the Senseless (novel) 1988

Literal Madness (novels) 1988

In Memoriam to Identity (novel) 1990

Portrait of an Eye (novels) 1992

My Mother: Demonology (novel) 1993

Pussy, King of the Pirates (novel) 1996

Bodies of Work (essays) 1997

Eurydice in the Underworld (short stories) 1997

*Included in the English edition of *Blood and Guts in High School* entitled *Blood and Guts in High School Plus Two.*

CRITICISM

Maureen Howard (review date 9 November 1986)

SOURCE: A review of *Don Quixote*, in *Los Angeles Times Book Review*, November 9, 1986, p. 6.

[*In the following review, Howard offers a tempered assessment of* Don Quixote.]

Kathy Acker's work is not outrageous. That is what first comes to mind reading the abortion scene that launches her new novel, *Don Quixote.* We have all been there—not to the bloody chamber of horrors she describes—but to the highly fabricated world of this story. Unless we have been wrapped in cotton wool or sent to the nunnery, we are fully prepared for the sexual and political extremes with which Acker purposes to alarm, amuse, and, at times, anesthetize the readers of her fiction.

Described rather nervously as punk, postmodern, or even postpunk, her novel is not all that hard to classify. It is fashionably self-indulgent Lower East Side Lit Major. Happily, Acker is better educated, more thoughtful and more talented than most of the practitioners of LESLM. Starting with her title, she leads us into a world in which rip-off and pastiche are common currency just as they are (we can't miss the parallel) in our helter-skelter, image-ridden culture.

In Acker's earlier *Great Expectations,* she used a parody of Dickens' famous opening lines to set the flip-to-feisty tone for the autobiographical *Bildungsroman* that followed. In this new work, she re-imagines Cervantes' romantic knight as a woman. More precisely, Acker gives herself, via Cervantes, a new first name: "As we've said, her wheeling bed's name was 'Hack-kneed' or 'Hack-neyed,' meaning 'once a hack' or 'always a hack' or 'a writer' or 'an attempt to have an identity that always fails.'. . . So, she decided, 'catheter' is the glorification of 'Kathy.' By taking on such a name which, being long, is male, she would be able to become a female-male or a night-knight."

This little passage is a fair example of what *Don Quixote* holds for the reader: a highly personal performance full of modernist tricks—with Acker, the willful impresario, always in sight, always playing with language and literary forms, switching tenses and voices. Any attempt to convey what transpires in *Don Quixote* is likely to make the reader feel like a chump. Still, it is to Acker's credit that those whom she manages to engage will, almost as a point of honor, want to have a go at the intention of her hip, fragmented novel, for, despite her embrace of the irrational, she does grant us a skeletal, throwaway plot.

After Don Quixote's abortion, she and her "sidekick cowboy," Saint Simeon (early Christian Bishop-Martyr?) descend into madness, troubled dreams of the polymorphous-perverse variety, and deep disillusion before setting out to find "love in a world in which love isn't possible." Thus, this first and shortest section ends in unoriginal nihilism: "It's not necessary to write or be right cause writing's or being right's making more illusion. It's necessary to destroy and be wrong."

The second and most successful "chapter" of *Don Quixote*—

a chapter entitled "Being Dead, Don Quixote Could No Longer Speak. Being Born Into and Part of a Male World, She Had No Speech of Her Own. All She Could Do Was Read Male Texts Which Weren't Hers"—takes us on purely literary adventures. A feminist rewrite of the classics is not a fresh idea, but Acker is funny and savvy with some of her appropriated material, which ranges from Russian Constructivism to Shakespeare, Milton, Genet, a few lines of Dante and more. I cannot help but stress how *literary* Acker's work is. She is like a graduate student in comparative literature gone looney-tunes under the pressures of orals.

Sometimes the clowning pays off. One of the best bits tunes in on a man and a woman who toss around the gossip of current literary theory ("Do you think there's something fishy in the semiotic theories, especially in Deleuze's and Guattari's?") like Mike Nichols and Elaine May in their "Bach to Bach" routine.

But these brilliant flashes are rare in Acker's long, bewildering trek toward self-definition. There is a tedious precis of Visconti's "The Leopard," which is supposed to function—Acker is often our instructress—as a romantic distraction from memory and pain. There is a replay of scenes from Frank Wedekind's "Lulu," with Acker written in.

Acker is smart. German Expressionism of the 1920s is a natural for fiction that proceeds in a cartoonish way against the background of name-brand plenty and our supposedly disposable culture. "I am a pirate," she insists upon many occasions, openly adhering to the mighty fashionable notion that the authors of the dear old masterpieces are dismissable if not dead, and that therefore she can appropriate any text, no matter how sacred or how profane, for her writing machine.

Indeed, there is a computerese sequence in *Don Quixote* in which the same paragraph, stuck in a retrieve, is printed two and three times over. But Acker is no Mac-Write freak, interested in the medium without the message. No, she is angry, childish, strident and boring in her repeated howls at what seems for much of this book no more than a creaky notion that the poor battered bourgeoisie is enemy No. 1. Or is it men? Or our monetary system? Or the New York Art World? Or the rotten autobiographical business of her mother's suicide and a broken marriage, both of which thread their way through *Don Quixote*?

Acker's characters are literally dehumanized. St. Simeon, woofing, turns into a dog, the better to play out his degraded adventures. Think brutal animal cartoons—Woody Woodpecker, Tom and Jerry—and you have a lead into the Acker aesthetic. She assigns Nixon and Reagan the pronoun it. Her obliteration of sex leads to a tiresome use of *she* (*he*) and *him* (*her*), bollixing up one of her tales. We are told what to

think about all this, of course: "For when there is no country, no community, the speaker's unsure of which language to use, how to speak, if it's possible to speak. Language is community. Dogs, I'm now inventing community for you and me."

But Acker's explanation does not make up for the slack repeat of one-liners, the undisciplined tick of naughty four-letter words, a warmed-over '60s political rhetoric, a dabbling in Gertrude Steinian *ex cathedra* pronouncements—in sum, for a lack of true invention.

The final section of *Don Quixote* is a long harangue against the evil empire—a hideous British-American landscape of corruption and decay. Unlike the young writers out of too many university workshops who publish perfectly controlled, cool stories, this novel may be a jagged cry from the heart of Kathy Acker. It is too bad that her prose is no more shocking than the cover of a heavy metal album, that she cannot, would not want to, sort out her good work from stuff as campy and ephemeral as a plastic flamingo or a giant Gummy.

Acker is a hit in England where she now lives—chic, a cult figure, a wild American, an exotic. After all of her flamboyant piracy, she echoes Whitman in a few precious moments of searing honesty, but without an ounce of Whitman's celebration or a drop of his innocence: "City, owner of me. When you want paint out of me, you throw me amidst your bums. . . . When you want joy out of me, you make me famous, for I'm the baby, you're my only parent, and fame is your nipple." In Europe, Acker takes her prose on the road with a rock band. She's coming to America for a national media tour. We can half-guess the coverage in *L.A. Style* and *Interview*. But perhaps what lies so heavy on the page will be happily lost in the performance.

David Van Leer (review date 4 May 1987)

SOURCE: "Punko Panza," in *New Republic*, May 4, 1987, pp. 38-41.

[*In the following review, Van Leer discusses the form, content, and literary intent of* Don Quixote.]

It was only a matter of time before the postmodernists got around to rewriting *Don Quixote*. In their attack on modernism's lingering romanticism and cultural elitism, Cervantes's novel has taken on a privileged status. Perhaps as a very early novel, the work seems uncorrupted by that cultural accumulation glorified as "the literary tradition." Or as a Spanish work, it seems an alternative to the mainstream of English, French, and German literature. Or in the very quixotism of its ironic quest, it seems the perfect vehicle for anti-essentialist criticisms of absolutes such as "self" and "presence" that modernism left unchallenged. For whatever reason, *Don Quixote* has become the inevitable starting point of postmodernist literature. Nabokov made it the center of a lecture series. Borges imagined as his prototypical metafictionist an author who in the 20th century rewrites Cervantes's novel verbatim. And Robert Coover actually began such a project with the Cervantesque "prologue" placed midway through his collection of "fictions" *Pricksongs and Descants.*

Nor is it surprising that Kathy Acker should be the author to assume the role of neo-Cervantes. Combining the high rebelliousness of postmodernism with the low rebelliousness of punk, Acker's preferred method in her novels is, to use her own term, "plagiaristic." She moves at random through a wide range of borrowed voices, from the Latin poets to Patti Smith and the modern French feminists. Her novels are often (at least on their title pages) pseudonymous, claiming to be written by their protagonists—"The Black Tarantula," "Henri Toulouse Lautrec," "Pier Paolo Pasolini." Even Acker's two previous books, though published under her own name, bury authorial identity under a host of borrowings. *Blood and Guts in High School* draws extensively on Hawthorne and Genet (as well as on a Persian grammar book), while the ironically titled *Great Expectations,* after an initial nod to Dickens, proceeds in a most un-Dickensian way in imitation of Mme de Lafayette, Keats, Melville, Propertius, and various French pornographers.

Acker's *Don Quixote* grows out of her previous "plagiarisms," particularly *Great Expectations,* grafting its author's feminism onto a more traditional denial of the mimetic character of literature. While maintaining a basic allegiance to the Spanish original, Acker superimposes on Cervantes voices borrowed from Biely, Moravia, Shaw, Wedekind, and Céline, peppering these with passing echoes from Shakespeare, Brontë, Dante, Duran Duran, and numerous historians, pornographers, and Marxist theorists. Here is a sample of the style, from a section titled "The Selling of Lulu" (but imitating *Pygmalion*), in which Schön/Higgins tries to persuade Lulu/Eliza to be his guinea pig:

Schön: By George, the streets will be strewn with the bodies of men shooting themselves for your sake before I've done with you. . . . Think of this: You shall marry a socialist politician who controls the arts. His father, who's a conservative member of Parliament, disinherits him for marrying you. But when he finally realizes your exquisite beauty, your fine manners, your dinner parties, his Lordship. . . .

Lulu: Shit.

Schön: What?

Lulu: Shit. I gotta shit.

Schön: Oh. If you are naughty, and idle, you will sleep in the kitchen among the black widow spiders and be hit by my chauffeur with his huge car rod.

Acker's Quixote is a woman who in the midst of an abortion "conceives" her mission: a quest for love in its full unrealizable insanity. After her Sancho Panza, an androgynous character called St Simeon, leaves early in the novel, Quixote's general quest is transformed into the specific attempt to find this lost friend—who has perhaps been transformed into one of the many tale-telling dogs she meets during her travels. Dying due to a loss of faith in humanity less than a fifth of the way through the novel, Quixote is, in the long second section called "Other Texts," robbed of her own speech, and thus reduced to a condition in which "all she could do was read male texts which weren't hers." In the third and final section, Quixote regains her voice and travels to Nixonian America to continue the search for St Simeon. After more lectures on politics and sexuality, for which Quixote serves largely as silent audience, the novel ends in a double vision of despair. Killed once more by a loss of faith, Quixote dreams that God "Him- or Herself" denies the possibility of meaning: "There are no more stories, no more tracks, no more memories: there is you, knight. Since I am no more, forget Me. Forget morality. Forget about saving the world. Make Me up." Reborn a final time, Quixote discovers before her, like Eve at the end of *Paradise Lost,* a world of presence and possibility. But this hope may itself be delusory, and Quixote only awakening to another dream.

This non-narrative is presented as a collage. The sections, themselves divided into many shorter subsections, are interrupted by graphics, plays, letters, poems (in English and Latin), historical analyses, literary paraphrases, and Marxist critiques. Chronology is abandoned: Thomas Hobbes aborts the lovemaking of Mr. and Mrs. Nixon by arguing with Puerto Rican tenants, and Quixote's quest for St Simeon stands still while an unidentified voice supports Prince for President. Nor is there a unified theme. The book attacks everything from sexual stereotyping to high rents in the Village. And, as everywhere in Acker's work, this vision of chaos is glimpsed through a patina of violence and degrading sex.

Still, the novel is not just an exercise in neo-Dadaist high jinks. Although the book's content is self-consciously trivial, its politics of mockery is serious indeed. Experimental fiction of the 1960s reduced all cultural signs, high-brow and low, to the same level—what Donald Barthelme called "the trash phenomenon." Post-modernists of the '80s feel this reduction to be politically irresponsible, and Acker intends, in her references to pop culture and historical events, not to trivialize tradition but to overturn it. The idea is to correct the ahistorical aestheticism of the postmodernist fascination with cultural images by giving those images some political content: she wants to show how they have functioned to restrict human possibility—how they have sent messages that are ethnocentric, anti-feminist, or whatever. But at the same time she wants to avoid the received version of cultural history; to regard history as a linear progression—from Washington to Reagan, from Beowulf to Virginia Woolf—is simply to reinforce society's own self-serving account of its past. Thus, in Acker's work, randomness—discontinuity and anachronism—is meant to guard against the danger of celebrating tradition in a vacuum. The problem, of course, is that one mélange of cultural signifiers looks pretty much like another. It is not that easy to tell politically informed anachronism, as in *Don Quixote,* from politically mindless eclecticism, as in Philip Johnson's disembodied Chippendale scrolls floating above the skyline.

Since the conventionality of language is understood to make all writing a political act, controlled not by a single narrative voice or author (vestiges of that discredited fiction, the "self") but by the "power structure," plagiarism is the most innocent form of writing. As Acker puts the matter in *Blood and Guts:* "All culture stinks and there's no reason to make new culture-stink." So in this novel, with the breakdown of social coherence, her knight (now "night") ends in "mourning": "I wanted to find a meaning or myth or language that was mine," she says," rather than those which try to control me; but language is communal and here is no community."

The real problem for Acker is less history or literature than the false notion of individualism that she sees as underwriting them.
—*David Van Leer*

The real problem for Acker is less history or literature than the false notion of individualism that she sees as underwriting them. Denying the romantic model of the poet as individual, original genius, Acker offers a model of art that is . . . Arabian:

> Unlike American and Western culture (generally), the Arabs (in their culture) have no (concept of) originality. That is, culture. They write new stories paint new pictures et cetera only by embellishing old stories pictures . . . They write by cutting chunks out of all-ready written texts and in other ways defacing traditions: changing important names into silly ones, making dirty jokes out of matters that

should be of the utmost importance to us such as nuclear warfare.

And as a replacement for this exploded fiction of "original genius," Acker poses Woman—the eternal Other who has been historically denied her independent voice by a power structure that is exclusively male.

It is easy enough to understand the intellectual and political point that Acker would make, and to recognize its source in the philosophical skepticism associated with French poststructuralism, especially deconstruction. Post-structuralism began the business of dismantling the concepts of "history," "nature," "self"; deconstruction continued the job by showing language—even the language of people who want to criticize social arrangements—to be itself simply the product and reinforcer of existing power relations. But it is hard not to feel with this, her eighth novel, that Acker's method and message are both wearing thin. Lacking the exhilarating experimentation of *Blood and Guts* and the manic lyricism of *Great Expectations, Don Quixote* seems somehow familiar, and predictable. Given the political heat the novel generates, it is more than slightly ironic that Acker shows so little interest in the culture whose masterpiece she too quickly makes the vehicle of a patently Franglo-American intellectual debate. Nor does the conflation of feminism and deconstruction seem politically effective. At best the identification of Woman as Other recreates the very Romantic model of the exiled prophet that attacks on the self are meant to undermine: we have merely exchanged Jeremiah for Cassandra. At worst the mythologizing of Woman as Outcast implies that sexual discrimination is not a political act, specific to certain times and cultures, but a necessary and inevitable aspect of Womanhood. Thus good literature would make for bad politics.

Finally one wonders if the whole attack on the self makes philosophical sense. Even if the idea of individualism, and the excesses to which that idea has contributed in Western culture since Romanticism, really is so dangerous as to be best discarded, the postmodern form of this rejection is fraught with its own contradiction. For in the end, the attack on the self subtly affirms what it would deny. Fragmenting or plagiarizing the narrative voice does not "deconstruct" the self. It only refocuses attention where Acker least wishes it—back on the author. Certainly, as all the blurbs tell us, Acker's own voice is "unique." It may be a pseudonym, but it is never anonymous.

Maybe the trouble is much simpler indeed. Whatever they think of the matter as a philosophical problem, all—from Hume and Emerson to Noël Coward and Miss Manners—agree that self-examination makes for dull conversation. It is hard not to hear attacks on the self as inverted egotism, as a last cry of the Byronic soul for attention. Between the analysand trying to define his personal space and the postmodernist trying to deconstruct it, there does not seem to be much to choose. Even if Foucault was right to predict that individualism is a concept written in sand, to be washed away by the next historical wave, that is no reason for postmodernism's endless updates on the state of the psychic continental shelf.

Aleka Chase (review date July 1987)

SOURCE: "Breaking Patriarchal Myths," in *New Directions for Women,* Vol. 16, No. 4, July, 1987, p. 18.

[*Below, Chase provides a favorable review of* Don Quixote.]

Kathy Acker's **Don Quixote** is a witty, irreverent and pained collage that explores a woman's search for identify and sexual love, exposing patriarchal myths and institutions in the process. In this story Don Quixote is a contemporary woman, a knight whose adventures take her, as she recovers from an abortion, through landscapes of geography and psyche. In predatory, nihilistic New York and London former lovers are remembered, dogs become people of indistinct or changing gender, American history is rewritten and transformed with little conventional narrative and no plot, much dialogue and many stories within stories. Through it all Acker mocks, questions and breaks apart conventions of gender, sexuality and power.

The book focuses on sexual love, power and violence and the chasm that separates women's experiences and desires from those of men. It addresses the violence that men do to women and that women do to themselves because of men. It makes parallels between sexual and other violence; it equates maleness with war and destruction. It explores the connections between sexuality and identity and women's search for sexual relationships outside the power relations offered to them. There's a lot of sadomasochism in the book, with an attempt to understand it through grappling with the intense, conflicting emotions and relationships it involves. Acker discusses the conditions of love—usually involving a sacrificing of freedom—and of being a victim—that is, not being loved.

This is a dense, complex, intellectual book, full of observations from many disciplines—sociology, political science, economics, semiotics—with Acker's own redefinitions tossed in.

Acker also intersperses bits of feminist theory throughout the book in an often funny, always accessible, and sometimes too pointed manner. A subheading for the second part of the novel reads: "Being born into and part of a male world, she had no speech of her own. All she could do was read male texts which weren't hers." Part of me applauds this as instructive to initiates of feminist theory, while another part feels preached at and condescended to: The entire book is clearly about reacting against male texts and the statement of the obvious is somewhat insulting to the reader's intelligence.

The subject of abortion, which opens the story, tends to be suspect in women's writing. Much recent fiction by women has focused on the intense guilt and depression women experience after having an abortion; and their inability to find any subsequent meaning in their lives. Some of these stories read almost like "Right-to-Life" pamphlets. Fortunately, Acker treats the matter more broadly. Abortion becomes representative of women's ultimate aloneness and betrayal in love. Don Quixote asks herself, "Why do I have to love someone in order to love? Hasn't loving a man brought me to this abortion or state of death?" The abortion seems to be detached from circumstance; her friend and presumed lover asks "Who caused the abortion?" No one claims responsibility for or connection to her pregnancy, and no friend or lover consoles her after its termination.

Going beyond the contrast of intimacy and aloneness, love and betrayal, Acker metaphorizes abortion as well. Toward the end of the book Don Quixote says: "So I am a mass of dreams, desires which, since I can no longer express them, are fetuses beyond their time, not even abortions. For I can't get rid of unborn dreams, whereas women can get rid of unwanted children."

Accessible Though Off-Beat

Don Quixote is structurally and syntactically quirky, off-beat enough to remind us that Acker is deliberately questioning and reforming grammar and language, yet it's accessible. It does get tedious in places, and many of the word plays (night/knight, mourning/morning, eye/I) seem clever to no real purpose. But overall the language and structure reiterate the book's intent.

Don Quixote—as the title itself makes clear—is engaged in breaking that control by breaking apart patriarchal myths and language. Everything that happens or is said in the book reinforces this. Don Quixote voices what Acker moves toward: "I wanted to find a meaning of myth or language that was mine, rather than those which try to control me."

Michiko Kakutani (review date 30 December 1987)

SOURCE: A review of *Literal Madness,* in *The New York Times,* December 30, 1987, p. C20.

[*In the following review, Kakutani offers a tempered critical evaluation of* Literal Madness.]

In such previous books as **Great Expectations** (1984) and **Don Quixote** (1986), Kathy Acker not only set out to work variations on classic literary texts, but also to subvert all of our traditional expectations concerning causality, narrative form and moral sensibility. The effect is like reading William S. Burroughs while watching an avant-garde theater group perform to the sounds of a punk band—if you happen to like that sort of thing. Characters exchange identities with the ease of snakes shedding skins; and bits of myths, folk tales and older novels also turn up transformed—juxtaposed, in a sort of post-modernist collage, with political screeds, dream-like hallucinations and strange, comic exchanges. The language is nervous and skewed; the authorial stance, adversarial and abrasive; the world view, cynical verging on the nihilistic.

Given these attitudes and techniques, one can see why Ms. Acker must have felt an affinity with Pier Paolo Pasolini, the Italian film maker, poet and novelist who was murdered in 1975. Pasolini defined himself as a "pasticheur"—someone who plucked themes, ideas and styles from a variety of sources; and his work (including his film *The Gospel According to St. Matthew*) frequently served as a commentary of sorts on older stories and legends. His last movie *Salo; 120 Days of Sodom* translated the Marquis de Sade's novel to Fascist Italy, and in doing so created a bleak, thoroughly repugnant picture of a dehumanized society in which power and authority remain the sole medium of exchange.

This view, which seems compatible enough with Ms. Acker's own angry vision of society, is developed at considerable length in the centerpiece of this volume, **My Death My Life by Pier Paolo Pasolini.** Narrated at least in part by the film maker himself (whom Ms. Acker has resurrected in order that he may conduct an inquiry into his own death), the novel features a host of characters who share a nihilistic despair. Like their counterparts in Ms. Acker's **Don Quixote,** these people have come to believe that love and romance are simply euphemisms for sex, and that sex is less an expression of passion than another instrument of domination in an eternal war for power and control.

Indeed this is a world where "the tyrant takes whatever he wants," a world where "the pig struts into the bedroom and eats the child in the cradle" and "madness goes everywhere." Beliefs are revealed here to be no more than illusions; morality is replaced by random chance, and language itself becomes a meaningless tool of deception.

When Ms. Acker sticks vaguely to Pasolini's story and his philosophic concerns, her narrative possesses an energy and drive that derive in large measure from the confluence be-

tween the film maker's ideas and her own. Much of the time, however, **My Death My Life** simply seems like a hodgepodge of verbal and metaphysical riffs—some are cleverly executed; others are pretentious, poorly written and grossly sensationalistic in an adolescent sort of way. Whereas the structure of the quest lent **Don Quixote** a semblance of order, this novel ends up devolving into a seemingly random collection of set pieces, including intermittently funny parodies of *Hamlet, Macbeth* and *The Merchant of Venice;* a series of obscene letters from Emily Bronte to her sister Charlotte, and a mini-drama starring Robespierre and Danton.

As for the other "novels" in this volume, **Florida** is really no more than a one-joke short story based on characters from the movie *Key Largo,* and **Kathy Goes to Haiti** is mainly of interest as an early example of Ms. Acker's fiction. Written in 1978 and published previously in a limited small-press edition, **Haiti** demonstrates few of the author's experimental techniques; rather, it stands as a fairly conventionally told story about a girl named Kathy, who visits Haiti and becomes involved with the son of a wealthy plantation owner.

Many of the author's favorite themes though are already in evidence; a preoccupation with the fallout of love and sex, and the war between men and women; and a need to come to terms with an absent mother and father. Like later Acker heroines, Kathy is a disillusioned romantic—a woman who's been brought up on the ideals of love, but who's been hurt or deceived so many times that she now equates love with obsession. "Someday," she thinks, "there'll have to be a new world. A new kind of woman. Or a new world for women because the world we perceive, what we perceive, causes our characteristics."

All the men in this story emerge as stereotyped cads—male chauvinist pigs, who see women as whores, disposable objects to be used and abused. They are caricatured to such a degree that any feminist message on the part of the author is thoroughly obscured. Similarly, the graphic sex scenes, which are presumably meant as a comment on men's exploitation of women, are so numerous and repetitive that they simply end up reinforcing the notion that pornography ultimately numbs the reader to the point of becoming frigid or impotent.

From time to time, Kathy lets her ferocious defense system down to show us a touching vulnerability. At such moments, the tension between her real feelings and her behavior is revealed, and we feel an old-fashioned (and, in Ms. Acker's view, probably unfashionable) sympathy for her plight.

James R. Frakes (review date 17 January 1988)

SOURCE: "Ooh Ooh. And Then Again, Ah Ah," in *The New York Times Book Review,* January 17, 1988, p. 14.

[In the following review, Frakes offers a generally unfavorable assessment of Literal Madness.*]*

In order to set the mood for this collection of three novels, let's begin with some key statements from *My Death My Life by Pier Paolo Pasolini:* "Language is more important than meaning. . . . Burn the schools. They teach you about good writing. That's a way of keeping you from writing what you want to." "I like this sentence cause it's stupid." "Language is making me sick." Shall we dance? The program is announced early. "I, Pier Paolo Pasolini, will solve my murder by denying the principle of causation and by proposing nominalism." The few subsequent references to this quest include: "(Pasolini died by suicide.)" and "The British killed Pasolini in order to keep control of their Empire."

Otherwise we novelty-famished readers are treated by Kathy Acker—whose previous novels include *Great Expectations, Blood and Guts in High School* and *Don Quixote*—to calculatedly disconcerting pastiches of Dickens, Melville, Woolf, Joyce, the Brontes, Alain Robbe-Grillet and Shakespeare (*Macbeth* as an interminable I.R.A.-vs-England farce, and a *Hamlet* in which "All these characters stink and have lousy motivations"). We are also reminded (for better or worse) of William Burroughs, Gilbert Sorrentino, Robert Coover, Gertrude Stein, Ring Lardner (his marvelous nonsense plays) and a very corrupt Pee-wee Herman.

Kathy Acker's lilting leitmotifs include unwanted runaway children, suicidal mothers, incest, transsexualism, violence ("Why am I violent? Because I like violence"), as well as the President and AIDS ("President Reagan's using AIDS to control the American populace," or, as Shakespeare's Portia explains it, "Doctors aren't civil: they're murderers. By inventing penicillin, they've caused AIDS"). Many styles are at uncivil war, from hip put-downs to banalities. One gripping paragraph consists of 31 repetitions of the word "On"—at least it sounds affirmative. Judge not, trapped reader, for the narrator advises that if you just let what is be what is and stop judging, you'll always be happy. Content yourself with the funky penguin who recites the plot of Orson Welles's *Touch of Evil.*

In Cole Porter's song "Katie Went to Haiti," the result was that practically all Haiti knew/had/made Katie. Ms. Acker's Kathy undergoes similar experiences: "The first day I was in Port-au-Prince, I got seven marriage proposals, not to mention the other propositions." Originally published in 1978 in a small press edition, *Kathy Goes to Haiti* should be subtitled "And Has Dysentery and Lots and Lots of Sex." Kathy, a writer from New York, admits she's "kind of weird" and is occasionally rough on herself: "You're a demented abortion on God's earth . . . all of you is one mass of squirming and totally disgusting worms that squirm against each other hate each other."

Time is not only very very slow in Haiti, but, as the Haitians tell Kathy, "The people . . . are all gentle and good" and "There's no violence in Haiti. Anybody can do anything they want." Kathy does, however, try to give her main tireless stud, Roger, lessons in social justice in the midst of the most graphically pornographic and stunningly dull sex passages—a juxtaposition that I find one of the few comic touches in all three works, even if not redemptive. I'm at a puritanical disadvantage for a reviewer in not being able to cite much of the dialogue except maybe "Ooh. Ooh. Ah. Ah," with such elegant variations as "ahaah" and "ooooh."

Some of the extended scenes have the pace and obscurity of fever dreams. But at what faint point does deliberate tedium stop filming over your consciousness and start pulsing alarms, as in the work of Harold Pinter for instance? Not, I fear, in Kathy Acker, although her grim descriptions of Haitian slums and a voodoo con game threaten to do so.

Florida may be the best "novel" of the three, since it's only 14 pages long. A spooky sendup of John Huston's *Key Largo,* it does feature the Claire Trevor character but, sad to say, without her pathetic rendition of "Moanin Low." The Lauren Bacall character goes on like this. "When I was two years old, I refused to drink milk. My parents . . . were scared I was going to die. My father started to take a camera apart. Only when he started to break the camera, would I drink the milk." Is language making as all sick? I usually admire risk-taking and convention-flouting in fiction—when the rebellious gestures work. Not many work here. As the critic Robert Scholes has put it, "It is only in literature that all experiments are deemed worthy of publication."

R. H. W. Dillard (review date 16 October 1988)

SOURCE: "Lesson No. 1: Eat Your Mind," in *The New York Times Book Review,* October 16, 1988, pp. 9, 11.

[In the following review, Dillard offers a favorable assessment of Empire of the Senseless.*]*

In Kathy Acker's novel *My Death My Life by Pier Paolo Pasolini,* she made the suggestion that "everything in the novel exists for meaning. Like hippy acid rock. All this meaning is the evil, so I want to go back to those first English novels: Smollett, Fielding, Sterne: novels based on jokes or just that are."

Ms. Acker's new novel, *Empire of the Senseless,* which her

publisher describes tentatively and hopefully as her "most accessible novel to date," is in many ways directly related to those 18th-century novels and the even earlier ones of Defoe. In it, Thivai, a would-be pirate, sets forth on a quest, guided only by this code: "GET RID OF MEANING. YOUR MIND IS A NIGHTMARE THAT HAS BEEN EATING YOU: NOW EAT YOUR MIND." He and his female partner, Abhor, a "construct" who is part human and part robot, explore the chaotic and dangerous world of an apparently near future, one cluttered with the dead and deadly artifacts and ideas of our culture. They are looking for the drug Thivai requires, for love, for some kind of freedom and even for their maker—or at least a construct named Kathy ("That's a nice name. Who is she?"). They are, above all, forcing the reader to look at the question of meaning with the intensity of a Wittgenstein and the double vision of someone who has just suffered a severe metaphysical concussion.

"The demand for an adequate mode of expression is senseless," Abhor decides at one point. And appropriately—in the light of the paradoxical nature of this complex, high-speed, intensely intellectual, intensely offensive, post-modernist, pained and painful, punk, fantastic, fictional construct and elaborate tattoo of a novel—she adds, "Then why is there this searching for an adequate mode of expression?"

One way to look at the novels of Kathy Acker in general and this one in particular is to see them all as the log of her almost desperate search for an "adequate mode of expression" for a time and a world whose center will not only not hold, but hasn't been able to hold her so long that the very idea of a center seems itself to the absurd. Even as she denies the legitimacy of the struggle, she wrestles in her work as directly as any writer has ever done with the actual language of literature. Distrusting it almost completely, but nevertheless completely dependent on it, she attacks it, twists it, deconstructs it and distorts the cultural values implicit in its structures, seeking always to make a literature "which denounces and slashes apart the repressing machine at the level of the signified."

The first of her novels to make a mark on the American literary scene (at least above ground), *Blood and Guts in High School,* seemed in 1984 to be the work of a comic, foulmouthed, punk William Blake (complete with startling pictures rendered by the author), attempting a shotgun wedding of heaven and hell designed to turn contemporary literary consciousness inside out as well as upside down. But the brilliantly difficult language and form of *My Death My Life by Pier Paolo Pasolini,* which appeared in the same year in England, gave stronger evidence of the seriousness of Ms. Acker's purpose, even to doubters who felt she was being read and admired only by those excited by the idea that a woman could talk as dirty as a man.

Ms. Acker tipped her hat appropriately in *My Death My Life* to Gertrude Stein, another celebrated (and celebrity) writer whose work attempted to take literary language (and language itself) apart at the seams and reconstruct it for new, revolutionary purposes. It was Stein, remember, who in "Tender Buttons" (1914) uttered the imperative, "Act so that there is no use in a center." And it was the linguistic act that she meant.

> **Kathy Acker has taken up Gertrude Stein's challenge, uniting radical form and forbidden language in a slashing and subversive literature that attempts at least to make it possible to live without a center in the empire of the senseless.**
> —*R. H. W. Dillard*

Kathy Acker has taken up Gertrude Stein's challenge, uniting radical form and forbidden language in a slashing and subversive literature that attempts at least to make it possible to live without a center in the empire of the senseless. The books that have resulted from her efforts have proven as difficult and disordered as the mad world from which they spring: a rock 'n' roll version of "The Critique of Pure Reason" by the Marquis de Sade as performed by the Three Stooges.

Empire of the Senseless takes place at some time in the future and, as its many references to Ronald Reagan and yuppies and multinational corporations indicate, now. It describes a world in which the "rich who have suicided in life are taking us, the whole human world, as if they love us, into death." It is a senseless world, one in which "imagination was both a dead business and the only business left to the dead." It as populated by pirates and mad doctors, bikers and sailors, whores and terrorists, and Algerian revolutionaries who take over a decadent and helpless Paris at the very time the C.I.A. is attempting to take advantage of their revolution. "In such a world which was non-reality," Thivai concludes, "terrorism made a lot of sense."

He and Abhor set forth on their odyssey, veering radically through geography, history and politics as well as the fragmented pages of literature. Ms. Acker's equation of blacks, women and all oppressed (and repressed) people takes on narrative substance as Thivai and Abhor repeat and transform the closing scene of Josef von Sternberg's "Morocco" and enter for a time the pages of the "Thousand and One Nights." The very funny and brilliant penultimate section of the novel is a retelling of "The Adventures of Huckleberry Finn," with Thivai and a brutal biker appropriately named Mark taking the roles of Huck and Tom as they abuse the imprisoned Abhor (Jim) with their absurd attempts to free her.

Finally Abhor takes her life and the novel out of men's hands and into her own as she writes her own story; her hilarious attempts to understand and act upon a driver's manual, "The Highway Code," bring both her odyssey and Ms. Acker's dissection of the meaning of language to an end. That end is not a rational conclusion but a visual emblem, a tattoo design, Abhor's portrait of herself: a dagger driven through a rose, with the motto "Discipline and Anarchy." That paradoxical design sums up Abhor's quest for herself, but it also stands as an emblem for Ms. Acker's dilemma as a radical artist forced by her yearning for freedom to reject and subvert the constraints of the patriarchal language of the tribe, yet forced by her need for an "adequate mode of expression" to use the very language she rejects.

Empire of the Senseless is a difficult and upsetting novel, one that insults and may even injure its readers. But they will not be disappointed by it, and they will learn, as Thivai does in the novel, that, "In an unreasonable world, reason isn't reasonable." And that in such a world, the most reasonable and meaningful novels may well be, like this one, "based on jokes or just that are."

Roz Kaveney (review date 19-25 May 1989)

SOURCE: "Darkness on the Edge of the Text," in *Times Literary Supplement,* May 19-25, 1989, p. 536.

[*In the following review, Kaveney assesses* Young Lust.]

It is impossible to read in a way that is not implicitly political; but the methods of Kathy Acker's fictions aim to make possible radical readings, avoiding the closed and the directive, the authoritarian gestures that would seem paradoxical in texts that celebrate the aspiration to freedom and variety. The novellas included in *Young Lust* are early work; in them Acker feints at a number of styles without definitely opting for any one. *Kathy Goes to Haiti* is both an exercise in genre pornography and a deconstructive parody of it, in which the sheer tedium of a life lived for sexual gratification alone is spelled out in some detail—though the story itself does not ever quite become boring; it is also an exercise in structure, in which chapters at opposite ends of the text quote, reflect and fold into each other. Acker also engages in some savagely misandric satire on the way the constantly tumescent males of a pulp porno novel talk in the cliches of the singles-bar pickup; the Haiti of this novel is in large measure a piece of scenery with the wires and struts showing—this is how people are anywhere, if you choose to notice them acting this way.

Yet there is more going on than schematic games. Pages of conversation with Betty, the wife of the rich stud Roger, force us to realize that there is life inside the bored masks, even if it is a form of life which thinks John Fowles a profound novelist; and occasional hints at the realities of a Haiti which is not the subject of pulp fiction save the book and the reader from irresponsible exoticism. The final "obligatory" scene of local colour with the voodoo soothsayer conveys a sense that there are depths and mysteries which this mode of fiction chooses not to engage with rather than ignores. Sex lacks mystery here, a matter of exclamations and ejaculations and instruction-book procedures, but there is darkness beyond the edges of the text.

Florida improvises an accomplished set of variations on characters and themes from the film *Key Largo;* it moves between voices in a way that can only confuse the inattentive, but in doing so makes a serious point about the interchangeable nature of female identity in a world dominated by men. It is one of the most conventional things Acker has ever done; and it disposes for good of the imputation that she works in experimental modes from lack of talent rather than serious-minded choice.

The Adult Life of Toulouse Lautrec is a set of exercises with identity and genre that adds up to more than one expects when reading it. A place that is neither the New York City of punk days nor the Paris of the *belle époque* provides the setting for a series of couplings and deaths; film stars and gangsters move past each other's lives, and both are mere masks for discontented young artists. Amid the arrogantly displayed lack of affect is a scathing attack on Henry Kissinger; the refusal of good manners which Acker describes in her preface as "writing as badly as possible" is a slap in the face of American letters, an avoidance of the Cool which makes one an accomplice.

Douglas Shields Dix (essay date Fall 1989)

SOURCE: "Kathy Acker's *Don Quixote:* Nomad Writing," in *Review of Contemporary Fiction,* Vol. 9, No. 3, Fall, 1989, pp. 56-62.

[*In the following essay, Dix examines nomadism, revolutionary subversion, and the possibility of personal affirmation and social transformation as portrayed by Acker in* Don Quixote.]

"This is the time to escape."

"The sexual is the political realm."

By loving another person, she would right every

manner of political, social, and individual wrong: she would put herself in those situations so perilous the glory of her name would resound.

Kathy Acker's Don Quixote is on a quest: she sets out to perform the now almost impossible act of loving another person; however, she realizes that this can occur only by changing the nature of our society. To make love possible, she must create the necessary conditions for mutual human respect and love to exist (acceptance of the other, of the other within oneself, of "otherness"). But what revolutionary method should she adopt for her quest? It is clear from the first section of **Don Quixote** that Acker rejects standard conceptions of revolutionary transformation. If we are to escape, we must become schizoid—we must become what the French theorists Gilles Deleuze and Félix Guattari term "nomads," for only then do we initiate the movements necessary to escape from those parts of ourselves determined by this society. In a society where materialistic, hyper-rational, capitalist instrumentalism reigns, love is nearly impossible, affect is nearly impossible, consequently, love is subversive. My intention is to bring into conjunction the thought of Deleuze and Guattari (hereafter D&G) and the fiction of Kathy Acker, in order to explore the possibility of what I will term, after D&G, the literary "war machine"—a machine that takes upon itself the process of escape.

A realization of the flux of identity is the first step in this process. As a schizo, or nomad, Don Quixote is (must be) unaffiliated with any revolutionary group—she rejects their methodologies because such groups, in the process of setting themselves up *as* groups, directly risk recuperation by the bureaucratic or state apparatus. The lines of flight created by their revolutionary activities become caught up in the segmented lines of the socius, as soon as any attempt is made to gain, direct, and maintain power. Acker parodies precisely these problems in the first section of her book; as she suffers from an infection caused by her abortion, her friends—a leftist, a liberal, a feminist—discuss methods of revolution over her prostrate body. In all these portraits, Acker is revealing the tendency of any revolutionary group to fall into the hegemonic practices it is combating—a problem created by the need to maintain a group identity through codes of behavior and "politically correct" thought. The need for this apparatus recreates new segmentations to replace the old, and consequently recreates new forms of limitation and oppression.

Unlike these opposition groups, Acker grounds her own revolutionary force directly in her feeling, or affect. As D&G might see her, she is embarking on a nomadic line of flight, attempting to break out of the social segmentations of her society through her own molecular becomings; in short, Acker sees the connection between the personal and the political, and sees that to escape the rigid segmentations she

must remap the lines of her own body through the intensities of her affects. The intense subjectivity of Acker's prose is itself a weapon of becoming: rather than allowing herself to be identified on the molar level as a member of a group, she subverts these segmentations through her intense emotion, the intense suffering that she expresses as a result of the pain the various social/political assemblages are causing her. This line of flight is a pure scream that exceeds any possibility of recuperation through rationality ("The only reaction against an unbearable society is equally unbearable nonsense"). Acker forces her body to undergo such becomings as a way to overload her own social encodings—reaching a point of excess where the intense becoming of her molecular organization breaks through, via a line of flight, to the outside. The affective intensity of this process—a process that reaches beyond such terms of affect as "love" or "sexuality" (terms already too segmented to be utilized without caution), breaks through not only social codings, but also genetic codings, resulting in a "sickness" ("Real love is sick. I could love death"). This explosively uncontainable force is the fuel for her transformation, for it is a force that cannot be overtaken by the bureaucratic apparatus.

Any segmentation at all implies a binary structure, and any binary structure implies hierarchy. The history of women that Acker explores (HISTORY AND WOMEN) is the segmented entrapment of women in a hierarchical power relation to men; however, there is a possibility of moving beyond these segmentations: "'It's not history, which is actuality, but history's opposite, death, which shows us that women are nothing and everything.' Having found the answer to her problem, Don Quixote shut up for a moment."

Death is history's opposite because it represents the outside, the void, the absence of the values that have created history to begin with. In the war between the genders that makes up this history, the alternatives seem to be to join the social order or to be annihilated by daring to step outside it ("So either a woman is dead or she dies"). Confronted with the repressive power of the social assemblages, Don Quixote is forced to capitulate to the social norm—namely, in the form of MARRIAGE ("Worse than being shit and dead, Don Quixote knew she was no longer a knight but shit and dead, that is, normal. Better to be a businessman").

The result is the failure of her quest—her line of flight is captured and normalized, and her own molecular affect is used against her: the molar segmentation of marriage has "killed her," insofar as it has stifled her becomings to the point where she must exist, if she is to exist at all, outside the socius. Being segmented, being brought back in line with the socius, is DEATH, in that the molecular level of the individual is staticized into a frozen form of socialized (molar) being. Facing the choice between being dead and dying, Don Quixote chooses to die, which is not to say that she is dead: she is dead to the social order (to whom she may as well be dead, as well as anyone else who does not fit inside the norm), in that she has moved to the outside, where she faces the risk of actual death or madness.

Although the first part of the book ends with the "death" of Don Quixote, another line of flight emerges, a line of flight centered on a particular kind of writing—a writing of destruction. The second part of ***Don Quixote*** exhibits this writing of destruction, displaying its mechanism immediately in the subtitle of the chapter:

> BEING DEAD, DON QUIXOTE COULD NO LONGER SPEAK. BEING BORN INTO AND PART OF A MALE WORLD, SHE HAD NO SPEECH OF HER OWN. ALL SHE COULD DO WAS READ MALE TEXTS WHICH WEREN'T HERS.

The first technique is to take texts from the canon of Western literature and to deconstruct them so that she is able to extenuate parodically their politically salient characteristics, simultaneously opening up the host text to the "outside" of her own social field, and opening up her own text to the outside of the aesthetic/historical fields. She has chosen texts that already have a capacity to serve as war machines: Andrei Biely's *Petersburg* (and the poems of Catullus), Giuseppe di Lampedusa's *The Leopard,* Godzilla movies, and Frank Wedekind's Lulu plays, to name a few of the more obvious ones. As she indicates, these are "male texts" that to some degree have gone very far in attempting to open themselves up to the outside, but have much further to go in the process of "becoming woman."

Acker's second technique is to place "on the same sheet" with these deconstructed texts her own intensely subjective experiences. However, Acker holds no illusions about individual identity or the self. The function of these subjectivities is not the representation of feeling, but the utilization of affect as a weapon of the war machine. This is why Acker's emotional representations have such an intensity: her affects—expressions of anger, rage, grief, suffering, and pleasure—are nomadic weapons that reach beyond her own introceptive feelings; they explode out of her interior onto the plane of exteriority that is this text, representing her becomings and velocities as she traverses the various social, political, historical, and aesthetic fields of our society. Her writing "refuses"—destroys—by deconstructing the binary distinction between interior and exterior, self and society, subjective and objective, the personal and the political.

This deconstructive section of the novel ends with the hope that she might be able to locate other nomads who have moved beyond the limits of social segmentations ("Now I must find others who are, like me, pirates journeying from place to place, who knowing only change and the true responsibilities that come from such knowing sing to and with each other"). The last section continues the process of escape in still more complex directions.

THE END OF THE NIGHT

"Where shall I go?" Don Quixote, wandering, woofed questioningly to nobody. "Is anywhere in this world of despair, this post-war endo-colonization, somewhere?"

In the third section of the novel, Don Quixote attempts to confront the "evil enchanters" who are responsible for the current social situation ("'As soon as we all stop being enchanted,' Don Quixote explained, 'human love'll again be possible'"). Much of this section is a search for a revolutionary method that does not fall into the traps of power.

Acker's analysis is very incisive: she sees the contradictions behind the claims of the "land of opportunity," as well as how America deploys its values in such a way that increasingly fewer people can direct their complaints at the system itself. As the Angel of Death explains to Nixon: "The only English (or language) is despair. Americans don't even bother to bark anymore. The only way Americans can now communicate is pain. Most of them don't dare."

Don Quixote must admit finally that nothing has changed since the beginning of her quest. The other dogs question her motives ("So how can you, a member of the elite, destroy the elite? Why do you want to save the world? To throw it to the dogs you're drawing away from? Are you mindless, or an idealist?"), and another dog explains that her "maddest characteristic is that you take your madness so seriously. No one gives a shit about what you do, night. Why don't you just have some fun?" Her response is her despair: "I've lost my beliefs. I've nothing left. I can't get married. I'll have to make myself into something."

In her despair, Don Quixote connects herself to a dog, who explains to her its experience of HETEROSEXUALITY, another segmentation that has entrapped Don Quixote. She learns that what happens on the individual level is connected directly to what happens on a wider, political level: they each end up practicing the oppression they wish to escape, just as revolutions end up being caught up in the bureaucratic apparatus ("'All stories or narratives,' the dog barked, 'being stories of revolt, are revolt'").

Don Quixote realizes that revolution begins with the revolution against parents—parents as agents of social control and normalization. No longer can a split be made between the psychological and the political, so that the reactionary can explain away revolutionary fervor as simply a child's response to his/her parents: the interior is the exterior, so that the familial structure is the site of the implementation of society's norms and values.

In **"Reading: I Dream My Schooling,"** a new type of learning is envisioned, based on the possibility of human connection, rather than a destruction of the other caused by normalization. This learning process begins with the body: rather than subjecting the other to one's own point of view—the endpoint of rationality (an endpoint that results in sadism, the text Acker reads "through" in this section), the students are taught to understand their own experience of pleasure. While Don Quixote does find value in this vision ("... the knight decided she preferred the fictional dog school to the ratty girls' school she had had to attend when she was a girl"), she herself has already reached a dangerous edge on her own line of flight.

Don Quixote is on the edge of the abyss, for she realizes that her stance as a revolutionary has brought her to a place where she is trapped by her own desires to change reality into something better:

> There's no way out of any appearance because an appearance is only what it is. The room was my nightmare or jail. I, a night, want to escape: I want to stop being a knight, the night, I want to escape myself.
>
> How can I escape being? How can I do myself in?

As seen above, this is the dangerous aspect of any line of flight: on one side rests the danger of being overcome by the state apparatus, and on the other side there is the possibility of "falling off the edge," where the schizo (nomad) runs the risk of losing control of her becomings, and consequently yields herself up to either the control of others (by going "insane"), or death.

Don Quixote recognizes that this self-destruction must be avoided, for it does not lead to existential free choice or escape from determination, but rather maintains the cycle of pain she is trying to escape to begin with. What she undertakes instead is another becoming—this time a becoming that lets go of the goal-oriented idealisms of her revolutionary fervor, and replaces it with an affirmative acceptance of the night, of the irrationality and horror that go along with the joy and happiness of the day:

> If I can't escape from the room by killing myself, I must be able to escape, if I can, by being happy. By embracing and believing myself, just appearances, the night. By embracing, and believing, my deepest being which is not knowing.

Therefore my vision has ended.

She comes to the realization and acceptance that she is unable to know anything for certain. What she embraces is a type of affirmative madness: Don Quixote has gone mad, and her language is the language of madness, or nomad language. It is a language based on her individual vision: it is the language of this text, which strives to communicate her reality outside of the conventions of her society—a language that breaks down all the orders, without replacing them with new orders.

We are approaching the end of the night (knight): the moment when this dream is over, and Don Quixote will face the day. Her madness will then be concluded, at least "until this book will begin again." What she comes to realize is the possibility of affirmation, even if revolution is impossible:

> "It is necessary to sing, that is to be mad, because otherwise you have to live with the straights, the compromisers, the mealy-mouths, the reality-deniers, the laughter-killers. It is necessary to be mad, that is to sing, because it's not possible for a knight, or for anyone, to foray successfully against the owners of this world."

It might seem that the book closes with a failure of any transformative possibility and the death of any idealistic yearning, much in the way the original Don Quixote repents his adventures and leaves his fantasies behind him. To some extent the book does suggest the impossibility of revolution, but in this last section, it is clear that the book does not end without some sense of affirmation and the possibility of transformation. Although she cannot change the society itself in some final way, she can become a nomad, increase the velocities of her lines of flight, and disrupt the hegemonic control of the state apparatus. She can deploy the war machine that is this text, with its multiple becomings, its "mad language" ("Nomad language") which destroys the dualities between self and other, interior and exterior, individual and society, subjective and objective. By setting herself against this—by not segmenting herself in the forms given to her, but by taking on herself the lines of flight necessary to her own becomings, her own process and movement—her becomings will automatically work as a form of social transformation, for the text that contains these becomings will be a powerful war machine.

Ellen G. Friedman (essay date Fall 1989)

SOURCE: "'Now Eat Your Mind': An Introduction to the

Works of Kathy Acker," in *Review of Contemporary Fiction,* Vol. 9, No. 3, Fall, 1989, pp. 37-49.

[*In the following essay, Friedman provides an overview of the intellectual, cultural, and literary contexts in which Acker's fiction, according to Friedman, is "designed to be jaws steadily devouring—often to readers' horror and certainly to their discomfort (which is part of the strategy)— the mindset, if not the mind of Western culture."*]

> GET RID OF MEANING. YOUR MIND IS A NIGHTMARE THAT HAS BEEN EATING YOU: NOW EAT YOUR MIND.
> —Kathy Acker, *Empire of the Senseless*

In A 1984 *Artforum* article, "Models of Our Present," Kathy Acker summarizes some current models of time and knowledge in theoretical physics and applies them to personal time and personal knowing. These theories, including the principle of "local causes," quantum mechanics, and the Clauser-Freedman experiment, interrogate, according to Acker, the dominant way of knowing, the way of apprehending the world, which depends on Newtonian causal relationships. She asks, "what possible experimental model doesn't have the form, 'If I do x then x_1 happens'?" She offers two alternatives, gleaned from interpretations of quantum mechanics. The first is the Many Worlds interpretation of quantum mechanics, which implicates the observer in the phenomenon observed: "Whenever a choice is made in the universe between one possible event and another, the universe splits into different branches." That is, "If I do x, then x_1 and $-x_1$ and . . . happen" (ellipsis in original). The second, also involving the observer in the observation, is the Copenhagen interpretation of quantum mechanics, which proposes that "the model is not the reality"; "any model's utility depends on the experience of the experimenter." Both interpretations assume a non-Newtonian and relativistic model of causality. Acker's interest in these "models of our present" is clearly reflected in her fictional world, which is informed by them. It is a world filled with sets of disrupted moments over which not even discontinuity rules since Acker's texts, constructed of fragments, generally have a central persona embarked on a quest, although that persona is often metamorphic and fades in and out of the narrative. Indeed, instability and unpredictability provide a liberating context for Acker's works, all of which are profoundly political. As a character in *The Childlike Life of the Black Tarantula by the Black Tarantula* asserts, "I can see anything in a set of shifting frameworks."

Description in such a model of the present cannot be objective; rather, it is always an interpretation. This insight helps to explain the directness of Acker's fictional method. Invoking the words of the English physicist David Bohm, Acker suggests that "Description is totally incompatible with what we want to say." In this view, the link between description and the described is tenuous, if not broken. Description is neither an approximation of, nor a substitute for, the described. Acker questions the motives in describing since description is a mode of control, a way of gaining authority over the object described. She writes, "The act of describing assumes one event can be a different event: meaning dominates or controls existence. But desire—or art—is." Description interprets; it does not replicate. She illustrates her theory by asking her reader to "examine the two statements, 'Help!' and 'I need help.'" Making the point that "The first language is a cry. The second, a description," she explains, "Only the cry, art, rather than the description or criticism, is primary. The cry is stupid; it has no mirror, it communicates." In offering the emotion itself, without a description or interpretation of it, Acker attempts to bring fiction closer to unmediated experience, also thereby relinquishing authorial control over readers' reactions.

In a second *Artforum* example, Acker illustrates the direct engagement with (and often assault on) her readers that her fiction attempts by contrasting two images that she entitles "Past Time" and "Time Renewed":

Past Time

For *Women's Wear Daily* Helmut Newton photographed two women, their legs against a grand ancient city street. The women, being fashion models, are desirable and untouchable. This is that time which is separate from the observer, that time which is enclosed: time gone.

The past's over. It's an image. You can't make love to an image.

Time Renewed

Now in color: In front of an orange yellow street, female long red stockinged legs in black pumps're nudging female long blue stockinged legs in black stilt heels. Touching me. This is our time cause we're making the world. This is a description of *Honey, Tell Me . . .,* 1983, a painting by Jenny Holzer and Lady Pink.

The difference that interests Acker between these two images may be described with the distinction Roland Barthes makes between the readerly and the writerly text. "Past Time" is a readerly text: conforming to traditional codes, it is complete, closed, culturally determined. Since its function is to exhibit products, the relationship it establishes with the viewer is formal and distant. Any desire the image wells up within the viewer is formal and distant. Any desire the image wells up within the viewer must be satisfied outside the frame of the image. "Time Renewed," on the other hand, is a writerly text, experimental, open, and incomplete. The viewer is involved with the image; they are in a relationship of play. The image is erotic, suggestive, inviting the viewer into its frame. It violates cultural norms and promises danger. With its disturbing signposts—e.g., strident colors, suggestive relationship of female legs—it undermines complacency, extends to the viewer the hope of risk and ultimately self creation. As a mystery, it inspires desire for itself.

II

It is important to emphasize the intellectual contexts of the work of Kathy Acker because her work does not feel quite "literary," despite her frequent adaptations (appropriations, plagiarisms and cannibalisms) of literary works from Shakespeare to Beckett. Although her works are writerly, Acker eschews the rhetoric of ambiguity so valued among literary critics, particularly since the advent of modernism. Her surfaces are almost anti-literary, despite their allusiveness, deliberately assaultive and overt. She hopes to make the abstract material, physical. In *Empire of the Senseless,* she pleads, "It seemed to me that the body, the material, must matter. My body must matter to me." She makes explicit her treatment of the body as a desiring and desirable "text": "If my body mattered to me, and what else was any text: I could not choose to be celibate." Her works offer many justifications of this position. Through the words of her female Don Quixote, for instance, Acker proffers one explanation of her emphasis on the body: "All the accepted forms of education in this country, rather than teaching the child to know who she is or to know, dictate to the child who she is. Thus obfuscate any act of knowledge. Since these educators train the mind rather than the body, we can start with the physical body, the place of shitting, eating, etc., to break through our opinions or false education." The language of the body in Western culture is taboo, therefore not as thoroughly constructed by the cultural powers as the mind.

Although her works are writerly, Acker eschews the rhetoric of ambiguity so valued among literary critics, particularly since the advent of modernism. Her surfaces are almost anti-literary, despite their allusiveness, deliberately assaultive and overt.
—Ellen G. Friedman

Thus, the body, particularly the female body, becomes the site of revolution. In this regard, Acker, perhaps more directly than many other women writers, creates the feminine texts hypothesized by Helene Cixous in essays such as "Cas-

tration or Decapitation?" Feminine writing, according to Cixous, should be rooted in the woman's experience of her body, her sexuality. In *The Childlike Life of the Black Tarantula by the Black Tarantula,* Acker connects writing and sexuality in a way that Cixous would approve: "My work and my sexuality combine: here the complete sexuality occurs within, is not expressed by, the writing." Such writing creates an erotic and thus, for Acker, subversive text: "Every position of desire, no matter how small, is capable of putting to question the established order of a society." Like Acker, Cixous feels that women must overthrow their education, the metalanguage of their culture, in order to really speak: "Stop learning in school that women are created to listen, to believe, to make no discoveries. . . . Speak of her pleasure and, God knows, she has something to say about that, so that she gets to unblock a sexuality. . . ." The return of this repressed language of female sexuality would, according to Cixous, "'de-phallocentralize' the body, relieve man of his phallus, return him to an erogenous field and a libido that isn't stupidly organized round that monument, but appears shifting, diffused, taking on all the others of oneself." Through the delirium of her protagonist Abhor in *Empire of the Senseless,* Acker offers an iteration, though qualified, of Cixous's insight:

> A man's power resides in his prick. That's what they, whoever they is, say. How the fuck should I know? I ain't a man. Though I'm a good fake lieutenant, it's not good enough to have a fake dick. I don't have one. Does this mean I've got no strength? If it's true that a man's prick is his strength, what and where is my power? Since I don't have one thing, a dick, I've got nothing, so my pleasure isn't any one thing, it's just pleasure. Therefore, pleasure must be pleasurable. Well, maybe I've found out something, and maybe I haven't.

For Cixous, reorganization of education to unblock female sexuality would not only expand possibilities of expression, but in revolutionizing narrative—the way we construct our world—would also transform modalities of thought. Acker, as the last sentence of the above-quoted passage suggests, is less sure of the ramifications of "de-phallocentralization," though her narratives relentlessly indict law by the phallus. Both Acker and Cixous define the obstacles in the way of such reorganization similarly. In Cixous's words, it would be "very difficult: first we have to get rid of the systems of censorship that bear down on every attempt to speak in the feminine." These systems imply not only the metalanguage of education, but all the metalanguages that direct individual and group thought and action, values and goals in Western society.

A particular system of censorship of the kind to which Cixous refers has been vigorously applied to Acker. She is a media figure in England, where she now lives, called upon to represent the interesting or evil, but definitively crazy fringe, the extreme by which the public measures its distance from the edge. Thus defined as the products of the devil or madness, or at least eccentricity, her books—as far as the public is concerned—have no authority and are thus disarmed. Applying a different system of censorship, some mainstream feminists, particularly in England, take her work seriously enough to condemn it as pornography. Since her language is often crude—not just "fuck" or "shit," but "cunt juice," for instance—and she graphically depicts sadomasochistic sexual acts, they view her work as misogynistic; the pornographic sequences typical in it, they argue (quite correctly) would not be tolerated in the work of men.

Acker's texts are, however, marked by radically feminist positions and attitudes. In the following passage, Acker slides from truism to profundity as she describes the power of language to work the ends of masculinist culture:

> Traditionally, the human world has been divided into men and women. Women're the cause of human suffering. . . . Men have tried to get rid of their suffering by altering this: first, by changing women; second, when this didn't work because women are stubborn creatures, by simply lying, by saying that women live only for men's love. An alteration of language, rather than of material, usually changes material conditions. . . .

Acker sometimes renders her sense of the patriarchal grip of culture in lashing, gutter metaphors. For instance, she has her feminist protagonist Hester Prynne declare: "The most important men in the world decide it's their duty to tear the mother away from her child. They want to keep the child so they can train the child to suck their cocks. That's what's known as education." Since she habitually casts feminist positions and attitudes in brutal language that *is* a cry, those feminist literary critics intent on smoothly executed social reform have generally not taken up the challenge of her texts. Feminist narratives such as Margaret Atwood's *The Handmaiden's Tale* and even such a feminist classic as Erica Jong's *Fear of Flying* seem mild in comparison with Acker's terroristic cultural assaults. Most readers would agree that Atwood's work is not intended to challenge certain progressive *ideals* of marriage, motherhood, and childrearing. She would simply like to see society live up to them, provided that women have equal opportunity to develop full personal and professional lives. Such a goal in the context of patriarchal cultural incarceration seems to Acker (who views cultural oppression as crushing) simply delusionary. Jong, on the other hand, does seem, as Acker suggests, rather self-congratulatory as she triumphantly describes male genitals and seems self-promoting as well in her self-consciously "daring" descriptions of sex from the "woman's point of view." Thus, she has perhaps earned the satire Acker executes in *Hello, I'm Erica Jong,* which begins "Hello, I'm Erica Jong. I'm a real novelist. I write books that talk to you about the agony of American life, how we all suffer, the growing pain that more and more of us are going to feel" and ends with "My name is Erica Jong. If there is God, God is disjunction and madness. Yours truly, Erica Jong."

In Acker's works, sadistic men victimizing slavish, masochistic women represents conventional sexual transactions in society, the underlying paradigm for normal relationships in patriarchal culture. In this scheme, de Sade is the quintessential lover. In one of her many metamorphoses, the protagonist of *The Childlike Life of the Black Tarantula by the Black Tarantula* dreams herself into Laura Lane, a murderer who will do anything for her lover: "I descend into slavery, I let a man drive his fingers into my brains and reform my brains as he wants." Abhor, in *Empire of the Senseless,* exclaims, "No wonder heterosexuality a bit resembles rape." Insofar as the culture constructs individual experience by interpreting experience, Acker presents women as accomplices in their own victimization. In an exchange of letters, for instance, Charlotte Bronte writes to Emily that "All rapists who come to my door are lovers."

Acker frequently embodies patriarchal domination in sadistic, cowardly father figures (often adopted or step-) and embodies women's relation to the patriarchy with self-destructively dependent daughter figures. Part I of *Empire of the Senseless,* which relates a quest for a new, saving myth, is entitled "Elegy for the World of the Fathers," in which the first chapter remembers, by savaging, the world of the fathers; its title is "Rape by the Father." On the third page of *The Childlike Life of the Black Tarantula by the Black Tarantula,* the sixteen-year-old protagonist tells the reader, "When my (adopted) father suspects I've been sleeping with my future husband, he slobbers over me. Rape." Fathers in Acker's work literally control with their phalluses. Acker's fathers practice rape and incest and then abandon their daughters. In these moves, they are identified with the phallogocentrism of the culture: "My father is the power. He is a fascist. To be against my father is to be anti-authoritarian sexually perverse unstable insane. . . ." The daughter's weapon of revolt is irrationality and desire, the feminine language that as it writes the female body, defies the law of the father. However, in rare narrative moments, false fathers (that is, adopted or stepfathers) are contrasted with ideal (thus nonexistent) fathers. In the following passage from *My Death My Life by Pier Paolo Pasolini,* Acker depicts the father as himself a victim of thought control. The ideal father would have been the city of art, but this possibility has been killed by the stepfather, society.

> To think for myself is what I want. My language is my irrationality. Watch desire carefully. Desire burns

up all the old dead language morality. . . . My father willed to rape me because in that he didn't want me to think for myself because he didn't think for himself. My father isn't my real father. This is a fact. I want a man. I don't want this man this step-father who has killed off the man I love. I have no way of getting the man I love who is my real father. My stepfather, society, is anything but the city of art.

A recurring and sometimes complex metaphor for patriarchal oppression in Acker's fiction is abortion: "Having an abortion was obviously just like getting fucked. If we closed our eyes and spread our legs, we'd be taken care of. They stripped us of our clothes. Gave us white sheets to cover our nakedness. Led us back to the pale green room. I love it when men take care of me." In Acker's *Don Quixote,* the abortion with which the novel opens is a precondition for surrendering the constructed self. For Acker, the woman in position on the abortion table over whom a team of doctor and nurses presides represents, in an ultimate sense, woman as constructed object. The only hope is somehow to take control, to subvert the constructed identity in order to "name" oneself: "She had to name herself. When a doctor sticks a steel catheter into you while you're lying on your back and you do exactly what he and the nurses tell you to; finally, blessedly, you let go of your mind. Letting go of your mind is dying. She needed a new life. She had to be named."

The acquisition of a new life and a name is the quest erratically and erotically pursued in several of Acker's works, including *The Childlike Life of the Black Tarantula by the Black Tarantula, Blood and Guts in High School,,* and *Don Quixote.* The means of acquisition are outside, unavailable in a culture locked in patriarchy. In order to constitute the self differently, the quester is required to find an alternative site for enunciating that self. Acker moves her protagonists toward this site through the appropriation of male texts. As the epigraph to Part II of *Don Quixote* reads: "BEING BORN INTO AND PART OF A MALE WORLD, SHE HAD NO SPEECH OF HER OWN. ALL SHE COULD DO WAS READ MALE TEXTS WHICH WEREN'T HERS." These texts represent the limits of language and culture within which the female quester attempts to acquire identity. Once inside the male text, the quester, by her very posture, subverts it: "By repeating the past, I'm molding and transforming it." In *Don Quixote,* she explains the subversive effects of plagiarism through Arabs, who in incarnating an "other" of Western culture are comparable to women:

> Unlike American and Western culture (generally), the Arabs (in their culture) have no (concept of) originality. That is, culture. They write new stories paint new pictures et cetera only by embellishing old stories pictures. . . . They write by cutting

chunks out of all-ready written texts and in other ways defacing traditions: changing important names into silly ones, making dirty jokes out of matters that should be of the utmost importance to us such as nuclear warfare.

Like the motives of artist Sherrie Levine, who creates nearly identical replicas of well-known art and photography, Acker's are profoundly political. With their plagiarisms, Acker and Levine propose an alternate explanation of the sources of power than the classical Marxists. With Jean Baudrillard they believe that power is held more by those who control the means of representation than by those who control the means of production. Plagiarism undermines the assumptions governing representation. That is, in plagiarizing, Acker and Levine do not deny the masterwork itself, but they do interrogate its sources in paternal authority and male desire. Levine justifies her replicas on polemical grounds: "I felt angry at being excluded. As a woman, I felt there was no room for me. There was all this representation . . . of male desire. The whole art system was geared to celebrating these objects of male desire. Where, as a woman artist, could I situate myself? What I was doing was making this explicit: how this oedipal relationship artists have with artists of the past gets repressed; and how I, as a woman, was only allowed to represent male desire." By locating the search for modes of representing female desire inside male texts and art, Acker and Levine clearly delineate the constraints under which this search proceeds. However, Acker's plagiarism, while intent on subverting the notion of the master text, is often allied with the political messages of particular texts. In her appropriation of *The Scarlet Letter,* for instance, she updates its politics to show its relevance for her contemporaries.

Moreover, in Acker's texts, the subversion is always incomplete, the remolding and transformation of textual appropriation provide only limited success. She has a more pessimistic, perhaps more practical sense of humanity's cultural imprisonment than Cixous, whose theory-inspired imagination proposes that writing of the body, *l'ecriture feminine,* will lead to radical cultural transformation. Acker's questers' searches for identity and a new healing myth lead to silence, death, nothingness, or reentry into the sadomasochism of patriarchal culture. As she said in an interview, "You can't get to a place, to a society, that isn't constructed according to the phallus." The attempts to subvert male texts and thus male culture result in revelation rather than revolution; the path to an alternate site of enunciation blocked by the very forces this path is meant to escape.

III

Acker's constant target is the infrastructure of Western patriarchal society, the government, business, education, and legal institutions that construct identity and which the oppression of women serves to sustain. Acker is often polemical in her attack: "Civilization and culture are the rules of males' greeds." In applying elements of *The Scarlet Letter* to contemporary society, she records the degradation of values since the nineteenth-century society that Hawthorne's narrative indicted:

> Long ago, when Hawthorne wrote *The Scarlet Letter,* he was living in a society that was more socially repressive and less materialistic than ours. He wrote about a wild woman. This woman challenged the society by fucking a guy who wasn't her husband and having his kid. The society punished her by sending her to gaol, making her wear a red "A" for adultery right on her tits, and excommunicating her.

> Nowadays most women fuck around 'cause fucking doesn't mean anything. All anybody cares about today is money. The woman who lives her life according to nonmaterialistic ideals is the wild antisocial monster, the more openly she does so, the more everyone hates her. . . .

> [A] reason Hawthorne set his story in the past (in lies) was 'cause he couldn't say directly all the wild things he wanted to say. He was living in a society to which ideas and writing still mattered. In "The Custom House," the introduction to *The Scarlet Letter,* Hawthorne makes sure he tells us the story of *The Scarlet Letter* occurred long ago and has nothing to do with anyone who's now living. After all, Hawthorne had to protect himself so he could keep writing. Right now I can speak as directly as I want 'cause no one gives a shit about writing and ideas, all anyone cares about is money. Even if one person in Boise, Idaho, gave half-a-shit, the only book Mr Idaho can get his hands on is a book the publishers, or rather the advertisers ('cause all businessmen are now advertisers) have decided will net half-a-million in movie and/or TV rights. A book that can be advertised. Define culture that way.

> You see, things are much better nowadays than in those old dark repressed Puritan days: anybody can say anything today; progress does occur.

In *Don Quixote* Acker portrays a society so blind to its own incarceration by greed and corruption that it requires an outside perspective to sort out what is even human. In a passage in which she allies the "rational" with deadening social institutions, she proposes Godzilla as providing such perspective:

> Total destruction is rational because it comes from

rational causes. Why are human beings still rational, that is, making nuclear bombs polluting inventing DNA etc.? Because they don't see the absolute degradation and poverty around their flesh because if they did, they would be in such horror they would have to throw away their minds and want to become, at any price, only part-humans. Only Godzilla who not only isn't human but also wasn't made by humans therefore is unidentifiable and incomprehendable to humans can give the human world back to humans.

Godzilla provides Acker with a more complex perspective than her flip presentation of it suggests. Designed by Japanese filmmakers to make big bucks with a cheap monster movie pandering to the 1950s atom bomb and cold war fears, Godzilla represents the exploitation and commercialization of those fears. It represents the degree to which taste, judgment, and critical issues are held hostage by materialism and paranoia. The fact that Godzilla, a creation of atomic waste, was constructed by the Japanese only a decade's distance from Hiroshima and Nagasaki gives more resonance to Acker's description of Godzilla's creators as "non-human" than a stab at Western bigotry. In creating Godzilla, Japanese filmmakers sacrificed the meaning of Hiroshima and Nagasaki to greed and accepted the acts of their destroyers in order to make money—for Acker, an obscenely transcendent (that is, outside the human) act of self-prostitution. Through the lens of *Godzilla,* as the cardboard Tokyo is crushed and torn by a greed-inspired terror, Acker suggests that the devaluation of the culture and humanity's fall from sanity and its own best ideals come into focus.

In *Don Quixote* Acker portrays a society so blind to its own incarceration by greed and corruption that it requires an outside perspective to sort out what is even human.
—*Ellen G. Friedman*

Populated by outlaws and outcasts, her texts provide subversive glosses on convention. "Only excreate" was Stein's advice in *Tender Buttons,* an experiment in nontraditional linguistic structures to yield what she though of as contemporary composition—linguistic structures that are democratized, non-hierarchical, without center—and to release signifiers from signifieds. As Stein excreated traditional linguistic grammar, syntax, and modes of meaning, Acker deconstructs social grammar, syntax, and modes of meaning. She perceives Americans as having become so thoroughly roboticized by their institutions that the hope for love, for an authentic life and identity, can only be reimagined in some other space, outside of institutions, outside of society, outside the law. Acker writes, "I'm trying to destroy all laws, tell you not to follow laws, restrictions." Pirates, murderers, Arabs, terrorists, slave traders and other Acker permutations of the extreme (sometimes a fantasy) outsider for whom society is a field for illicit and, above all, selfish harvests and who, besotted with death, theft, hypocrisy, paranoia, and ugly sex, give back a portrait of society horrifyingly consistent with their values.

Just as appropriating male texts results in subversive disclosure, crime and criminals propose sites where the bondage of self to the culture's deadening prescriptions may be demonstrated, and perhaps more important, where liberating strategies may be tested. In a section on *The Scarlet Letter* in **Blood and Guts in High School,** Acker writes, "In Hawthorne's and our materialistic society the acquisition of money is the main goal 'cause money gives the power to make change stop, to make the universe die; so everything in the materialistic society is the opposite of what it really is. Good is bad. Crime is the only possible behaviour." For women, any attempt to achieve power (equated with money) puts them outside the law: "For 2,000 years you've had the nerve to tell women who we are. We use your words; we eat your food. Every way we get money has to be a crime. We are plagiarists, liars, and criminals."

IV

Like William Burroughs, who greatly influenced her, Acker has embraced the stance of cultural outlaw not only in her narratives, but has adopted it for her life. For example, when middle-class college students in the sixties were intent on "sexual revolution," she tested the meaning of this revolution by performing in 42nd Street sex shows, an experience which led to her first published work, **Politics.** Although she describes the time as "schizophrenic," living in two cultures—hippie (which she views as middle class) and Times Square—she also implies the experience gave her a window onto social hypocrisies, particularly class divisions and sexism, disguised by the free love rhetoric. In practice, Acker suggests, there were disturbing similarities between the two cultures. Alienated from her family and living as an American expatriate in London, she embodies the perspective of outsider and outcast that she cultivates in her fiction. Raised on 57th Street and First Avenue in New York City, child of upper-middle-class Jewish parents, Acker, now over forty, is heavily tattooed and a bodybuilder.

The tattoo, in fact, is the central image in her most recent narrative, **Empire of the Senseless,** a work dedicated to her tattooist. A precise metaphor for her writing, the tattoo is an outlawed, magical language written directly on the body, becoming part of the body, the body turning into text, an audacious rendering of Cixous's writing the body. In a short history of the tattoo, she discusses its semiotic function, as well as its association—crucial for Acker—with criminals:

The tattoo is primal parent to the visual arts. Beginning as abstract maps of spiritual visions, records of the "other" world, tattoos were originally icons of power and mystery designating realms beyond normal land-dwellers' experience.

The extra-ordinary qualities of the tattoo's magic-religious origin remain constant even today, transferring to the bearer some sense of existing outside the conventions of normal society.

In decadent phases, the tattoo became associated with the criminal—literally the outlaw—and the power of the tattoo became intertwined with the power of those who chose to live beyond the norms of society.

As this passage on the tattoo confirms, Acker obsessively explores the territory of the taboo, claims it as the proper domain from which to launch attacks on Western culture—an empire of the senseless. In **Empire of the Senseless,** she systematically summons every taboo she can think of—including incest, rape, terrorism, vomit, shit, menstruation, homosexuality, a very long list—rendering them in vivid, forbidding, hallucinatory prose ("I remembered the scarlet pigeon nibbling at the blood seeping out of my cunt"). In an explanatory passage, Acker offers her most lucid defense of the use of taboos in her fiction:

That part of our being (mentality, feeling, physicality) which is free of all control let's call our "unconscious." Since it's free of control, it's our only defence against institutionalized meaning, institutionalized language, control, fixation, judgement, prison.

Ten years ago it seemed possible to destroy language through language: to destroy language which normalizes and controls by cutting that language. Nonsense would attack the empire-making (empirical) empire of language, the prisons of meaning.

But this nonsense, since it depended on sense, simply pointed back to the normalizing institutions.

What is the language of the "unconscious"? (If this ideal unconscious or freedom doesn't exist: pretend it does, use fiction, for the sake of survival, all of our survival.) Its primary language must be taboo, all that is forbidden. Thus, an attack on the institutions of prison via language would demand the use of a language or languages which aren't acceptable, which are forbidden. Language, on one level, constitutes a set of codes and social and historical agreements. Nonsense doesn't per se break down the codes; speaking precisely that which the codes forbid breaks the codes.

In *The Newly Born Woman,* Catherine Clement argues that "every society has an imaginary zone for what it excludes," a zone located on the "fault lines" of the culture. She and Cixous, her collaborator on the book, propose that "women bizarrely embody [that] group of anomalies showing the cracks in the culture" through which the silenced of culture exerts its pressure, makes itself known—the cracks through which the repressed returns. In Acker's political translation and transformation of this idea, the repressed is embodied by figures and concretized as acts outside the social code—outlaws, outcasts, taboos—that threaten it. In unlikely partnership with Emily Dickinson, she says madness is divinest sense: "No to anything but madness." She sees the culture in the same position as the dying animal whose leg is caught in a trap: in order to escape, it must chew through its leg. Similarly, for a chance to transform contemporary culture from the deadly trap it is, Acker cautions you must "eat your mind," which has been so completely constructed by the phallus, so thoroughly written by society's metalanguages, that there is no room, in her terms, to truly name oneself. Acker's narratives, in their subversive appropriations of master texts, their aggressive assertions of criminal perspectives, their relentless interrogations of art, culture, government, and sexual relations, are designed to be jaws steadily devouring—often to readers' horror and certainly to their discomfort (which is part of the strategy)—the mindset, if not the mind, of Western culture.

Naomi Jacobs (essay date Fall 1989)

SOURCE: "Kathy Acker and the Plagiarized Self," in *Review of Contemporary Fiction,* Vol. 9, No. 3, Fall, 1989, pp. 50-5.

[*In the following essay, Jacobs examines Acker's postmodern experimentation with authorial identity and literary history.*]

Postmodernist fiction differs from its modernist precedents less in specific narrative techniques (such as the "nodality" and "paratactics" which David Hayman identifies in writers from Joyce to Sollers) than in the theoretical perspectives from which it employs such techniques. With varying degrees of rigor, American postmodernists have drawn upon post-structuralist theories of language and identity both as the basis for technical experiments and as a frequent topic in their works. If all perception, all knowledge, all emotion and experience is mediated and distorted by arbitrary linguistic structures, the artist's desideratum is to convey a radi-

cally unmediated, unstructured, and decentered fictional experience that will abolish "all distinctions between the real and the imaginary, between the conscious and the subconscious, between the past and the present, between truth and untruth" and, it might be added, between self and other, writer and reader, book and life.

The destruction of these dualities is hardly new; we are nearing the end of the century which saw, early on, the work of Heidegger and Wittgenstein in philosophy, Joyce and Stein in fiction. But there *are* ways in which postmodern fiction looks and feels new. Perhaps the most characteristic is what Richard Martin has called the "decreation of history," a process foregrounded by the conspicuous presence of historical figures. In mimetic fiction, the empiricist respect for fact and for the concept of coherent identity has discouraged the mixing of historical figures ("real," "true" or factual) with more purely fictional characters. The post-structuralist view of the radical contingency of language, with its implications that both history and identity are textual, leads inevitably to an anti-mimetic, non-representational use of historical figures. The works of Kathy Acker demonstrate in particularly challenging form the complex relationships of the historical figure to postmodern concepts of text, of identity, and of the authorial self. Her very titles exhibit her ambiguous identity and author/ity: *The Childlike Life of the Black Tarantula by the Black Tarantula; Great Expectations; The Adult Life of Toulouse Lautrec by Henri Toulouse Lautrec; My Death My Life by Pier Paolo Pasolini; Don Quixote, which was a dream.* Through semantic and stylistic crudeness, pastiche-appropriations of famous literary texts, and outrageous manipulations of historical and literary figures, Acker attempts simultaneously to deconstruct the tyrannical structures of official culture and to plagiarize an identity, constructing a self from salvaged fragments of those very structures she has dismantled.

Acker's habit of disclaiming authorship by attributing authorship to her titular subject has the effect of placing the entire work in quotation marks, creating an invincibly ironic "as if" which crucially skews the reader's attempt to interpret, logically or emotionally, the extreme states of mind represented in the book. The "author" of the novel is a part of the title, a part of the "made up"; where then is the "real" Acker in this fiction? Is the entire narrative to be read as parody? The covers of any book are, in a sense, quotation marks, delineating the boundaries between what someone—traditionally, the author—"said" and a larger context, a world, in which that statement is made and has meaning. But mimetic fiction encourages us to experience the book as both a world in itself and a pure representation of "the" world, rather than a controvertible statement about an idiosyncratic experience. Acker's authorial impersonations emphasize the derivativeness of all texts, their mediated, unreliable and quite probably falsified status, and remind us that only a fool expects to encounter some author, some great soul, some "reality" in a work of fiction.

Acker's technique of quotation and cross-quotation equally forbids us to identify with her fictional characters. What are we to make of a female narrator named Henri Toulouse Lautrec who recounts the life of her brother Vincent Van Gogh while searching through Paris with Hercule Poirot for clues to the murder of Melvyn Freilicher, a real person documentably alive in the "real" world of documentation? What of the whore Giannina's erotic reminiscences of the American poet Ron Silliman? This undifferentiated use of figures from history, literature and contemporary literary circles merges all realms of language in which meanings reside, and thus destroys meanings by destroying the contexts which focus them. Brought into forced conjunction, these irreconcilable contexts split open and spill their constituent parts into a formless intertext.

Despite the seemingly illimitable license of Acker's pornographic imagination, one senses always a "holding back" in her habit of quotation and plagiarism, an unwillingness to own—in the sense of admission as well as of possession—her work. Think of Toulouse Lautrec's bedtime story, a perfect imitation (theft?) of the confessions magazine genre, in which a girl overcomes the fear of sex caused when her brother, a crazed Vietnam veteran, raped her; or think of the long section evoking and parodying sentimental movie magazines as it traces a love affair between James Dean and a prepubescent Janis Joplin. When the rape victim recovers from her trauma—"with the help of the man I love, I have become at last a real woman"—or when Jimmy and Janis find true love, Acker only provisionally admits to her narrative a sweetness and innocence which she would not, it seems, acknowledge as one of her own voices. The narrator's judgment that the confessions story is "trash" is superfluous, for stylistic parody and patently ludicrous premises have already judged or placed in quotation marks the longings and sorrows expressed in those stories. Of course, the book as a whole is similarly bracketed. But Acker uses such double-distancing much less often where the narrative speaks for enraged, offensive, almost obscenely needy personae that seem closer to Acker's own public persona as former actress in live sex shows, queen of punk, the libidinous Kathy who "Goes to Haiti" in another of her works.

Yet even this marginally coherent persona is engaged in a terrified flight from identity; "If I don't keep throwing myself into the unknown, I'll die," says Giannina. Such death is preferred, even required, by "the Boss" that rules Acker's cybernetic wasteland; at one point Don Quixote decides to throw herself out a window, so that "The Boss'll begin to recognize and respect me. Once I'm dead, I'll be someone." Only a fixed and thus dead self is recognizable; only a recognizable self is useful, locatable, controllable in the world

of work and wages. The alternative is to have no identity, to be no one, at which point one can "do anything I can be anyone one day and the next day do be anyone else, even the same one." This state is simultaneously exhilarating and frightening, for it implies a radical isolation from others, a refusal of the human contact which affirms finitude or boundary: "Without the touch of another human, I'm nothing. For, being untouched, I can do (be) anything (one) and so, am nothing." Complete lack of definition is nothingness; but it is also perfect potentiality, complete freedom to redefine, to experiment, to live in what Cixous has called "permanent escapade." The Acker protagonist, then, embarks upon an anxious search for balance between the isolate nothingness of no-identity and the death of fixed identity. Impinging upon and shaping this quest are the vectors of gender, of culture, of politics, represented here by characters plagiarized from literary and historical texts.

> **In transforming herself, equating herself with the male figures of Toulouse Lautrec, Pasolini, and Don Quixote, Acker might seem to reject the female self to which she is born. But what becomes explicit is that this renaming of a female experience actually validates it.**
> **—*Naomi Jacobs***

Particularly intriguing is Acker's play with gender in the naming of certain of her narrators and in passages such as the long "Heterosexuality" section of *Don Quixote*. In transforming herself, equating herself with the male figures of Toulouse Lautrec, Pasolini, and Don Quixote, Acker might seem to reject the female self to which she is born. But what becomes explicit is that this renaming of a female experience actually validates it. In the "womb of art," Don Quixote comments, the male artist sees all women as either pirates or slaves—dangerous brigands or loathsome victims. Acker redefines, even conflates, female sexual adventurism and female vulnerability by attributing these qualities to male figures. In our minds, the historical Toulouse Lautrec is more genius than monster, though his crippled body made the latter definition dominate his own sense of self. We see him as bold, smiling, gregarious—vibrant as the dancers and racehorses that he loved to paint. Acker makes him a woman, whose self-hatred echoes the sense of woman as monster that has led Acker's work to be described as "abusive" to women. This Toulouse Lautrec is a site of deprivation, of ravenous hunger; so deformed that only money will buy her either sex or love, she narrates her self-abasing yearnings in painful detail. That the character is female makes it possible for us to believe this unqualified vulnerability; that the character is Toulouse Lautrec makes it impossible for us to dismiss the pain as female hysteria. Thus female pain, legitimized by the still-male locus of the name, is transformed from a merely pathetic and even embarrassing phenomenon to one of gravity, to be pitied and seriously examined. Proper noun and pronoun conflict, the devalued female pronoun pointing to a valorized referent that remains male in our minds, and so the characterization annuls grammar—that formalization of difference—and gender at once. Simultaneously, other valorized male referents are degraded by female associations: Paul Gauguin is the local cleaning woman, Rousseau and Seurat are teachers who train whores.

Similarly ambiguous is the gender of the title character Don Quixote, a woman who becomes a knight on a noble quest to love "someone other than herself" and thus to right all wrongs. "She decided that since she was setting out on the greatest adventure any person can take, that of the Holy Grail, she ought to have a name (identity). She had to name herself." Since knights are by definition male, she must name herself for a man—become a man—before the nobility of her quest and the dangers of her ordeals will be esteemed. Once again through grammatical terrorism, the clash of pronoun and noun, Acker effects a revaluation of female experience. A series of famous literary works are then plagiarized, paraphrased, rewritten, as the only way of talking about Don Quixote's condition as woman "born into and part of a male world." Raymond Federman has argued that "imagination does not invent the SOMETHING NEW . . . but merely imitates, copies, repeats, proliferates—plagiarizes in other words—what has always been there." Such a plagiarizing or re-imagining imagination is original only in its omissions and inaccuracies, the absences surrounding its inclusions, the forgetfulness around its remembering, the seams where plagiarized texts come together and redefine each other. "What has always been there" becomes visible in this process of selective, disruptive repetition.

It is with historical/literary characters that these seams of conjunction become most visible in fiction. The specific language of a plagiarized source might or might not be recognizable; the characters that inhabit it are always attributable and thus patently stolen. Of her plagiarism, Acker has said that "by taking these texts and just putting them there as simply as I can, and not making anything of them, not saying anything, not doing anything, I'm doing something that . . . really feels good and has joy in it." But the tactic can never be so simple; to "take" a text and not make anything of it is impossible. Surely it is no accident that Don Quixote's reading list includes the Brontës, who complexly render female madness and desire and the punishment for those transgressions; *Paradise Lost,* that mythological justification for the ways of man to woman; *Romeo and Juliet,* which dignifies the equation of death and love. Surely it is not by accident that Acker conflates Wedekind's femme fatale Lulu with Shaw's Eliza Doolittle, whose "depressing and disgusting" speech is eradicated by the man who shapes her to his de-

sires and to his own language. Like the stylistic parodies and authorial impersonations of *Toulouse Lautrec,* this plagiarism of literary selves again suspends the meaning of Acker's narrative, placing quotation marks around these melodramatic expressions of sorrow, madness, degradation.

Acker also practices plagiaristic rewriting upon the texts of history, for Thomas Hobbes appears as "the Angel of Death," "woofing" to an equally canine Richard Nixon about how nasty, brutish and short is a dog's life. History as an organized and organizing structure has evaporated, leaving only fictions. The effect is ludicrous, particularly in passages from Hobbes where the disjunction between elevated diction and canine referent cancels the sobriety with which we normally receive official discourse, philosophical or political. Such distortions and misrepresentations of historical and literary figures are, like distortions of grammar, necessary to the postmodern project. Says Don Quixote to the dogs who howl around her, "I write words . . . to you who will always be other than and alien to me. These words sit on the edges of meanings and aren't properly grammatical. For when there is no country, no community, the speaker's unsure of which language to use, how to speak, if it's possible to speak." These fictions are also located at the edges of meaning, the edges of grammar, the edges of gender: a place where the emptiness and the fullness of the undefined personality co-exist in a vertigo of antireferential reference. Just as her character the Black Tarantula copies favorite pornography books in order to "become the main person in each of them," Acker dismembers and recombines literary and historical selves in a frantic effort to define, however temporarily or conditionally, a functioning self. Nothing is finally delineated but "the nonpresence at the center of the work of art," the writing creature doomed to repetition and replication, and so the next novel "by Kathy Acker" seems likely to be again pseudonymous, as indeed any fiction—any self—is pseudonymous in the postmodern crisis of identity.

Robert Siegle (essay date 1989)

SOURCE: "Kathy Acker: The Blood and Guts of Guerrilla Warfare," in *Suburban Ambush: Downtown Writing and the Fiction of Insurgency,* Johns Hopkins University Press, 1989, pp. 47-123.

[*In the following excerpt, Siegle offers an overview of Acker's literary significance and a critical reading of* Don Quixote.]

"Reading Kathy Acker is like reading the subway walls." "If my mother saw what I was reading, *she'd die.*" "I never thought I was a prude until I opened this book. I was reading it outside between classes and I found myself holding the book half-closed so the people sitting around me wouldn't see the illustrations." "My roommates couldn't believe I was reading this book for a course!" Well, there is some truth to these minority-opinion gasps from the fiction class to whom I assigned Acker's **Blood and Guts in High School.** Reading Acker *does* take you close to a voice not often heard from the suburbanized media of American culture, one that is full of pain, rage, and lacerating barbs of social commentary. Her work *does* offend mothers, particularly those who serve unreflectively the patriarchal establishment that determines mother-daughter relations as, shall we say, problematic. And we *do* discover in reading Acker's work internalized regiments of repressive and oppressive codes we may well not have been conscious of harboring as part of the heavily contradictory cultural chromosomes in our psychological DNA. And though my student's roommates were probably surprised at the language and drawings of this pivotal novel, they might well have wondered how a regularly offered college course came to feature a book that critiques so relentlessly the ideological functions of the educational establishment.

Unfortunately, much of the critical response to Acker's work has not gotten very far beyond these first comments of my more conservative students. As Acker commented to me, most accounts "have left some or many concerns out, usually the political, and most fetishize the sexual." She knows that the culture works on its members most subtly and most profoundly by colonizing the libidinal aesthetics, turning desire into the most productive means of channeling, normalization, and, even if by pure distraction, social control. Much of her work does confront directly the sexual material of the culture in order to carry out her most basic project. "[T]he center of my writing, if there is a center, is a search for value, or lack of value," she wrote me, and the play between "search" and "lack," between "center" and the iffiness of the very idea of a structure with center, is precisely what is finally at stake in Acker's fiction. Trying to understand a pathological culture and to locate some potential for freeing the body from the hold of that culture means confronting sexuality but also all the concerns that mainstream American writing typically prefers to omit.

Acker's own comments in a radio interview upon the critical tendency to "fetishize the sexual" are perhaps the most telling:

> When you write sexual material, I mean, you know, pornographic—I hate the word "pornographic" for this—but direct orgasmic material, it's almost like pure writing, it's really rhythm, you've got to get those rhythms exact. It's also a way that you know there's a direct connection between you and the reader. And if you mix that really *hot* kind of connection next to political material, you're doing a

very violent number. And that's interesting. But sex is also a way—it's a little like Jean Genet's *The Slaves*—it's also a way of looking up from the bottom to see society in a different way. The sexual material of a society is very revealing.

Pure writing, the direct connection, the interaffiliation between the sexual and the political, and the desire to "see society in a different way"—these utopian impulses play constantly alongside the most devastating narrative critique of Western culture to appear in American literature. The resulting mix of the sacred and the profane, the utopian and the despairing, carries us far beyond the titters and thrills of the first-time reader to a profoundly moving, detailed, and instructive analytical critique of the cultural processes precisely at the point from which they are experienced by the Other of the culture—children, women, the poor, the trapped. Acker's work moves steadily toward an imaginative demolition of the oppressive dimension of our cultural machinery. Indeed, a former Village dweller who now writes in rural Virginia came to campus one day to meet me. "I knew it must be the end of the world," she said by way of opener, "when Kathy was being taught in southwest Virginia." No such luck, I think to myself. But now that Grove Press is giving Acker's work a wider distribution than was possible for the TVRT Press, which published her earliest work, perhaps we are moving at least a bit closer to the end of a certain kind of world for which genocide, a first-strike policy, poisoned ground water, and irradiated children are daily news.

Acker's career as a writer began in the early seventies. Disowned by her parents, she worked a number of different jobs supporting her involvement in the arts revolution brewing in Soho at the time. There were a number of reviews, readings, collaborative projects with various visual artists, and, beginning in 1973, the emergence of a series of hard-hitting novels which was fully steeped in the intellectual ferment of the period. Her own way of answering Tom Vitale's question, "What are you like?" directly puts the cultural intersection at which we find these works: "I think I'm basically a painter who uses words. And I'm pretty influenced by a lot of political semiotic theory. And I like rock and roll." Her work has the immediacy of the visual that Richard Prince likes in painters who write; it is indeed quite shrewd about the ideological implications of both social and artistic patterns, and it takes the dare to position itself in the outlawed voice of the cultural other, so much so that she is sometimes called a punk novelist. I wonder whether the real punch line there is that to be a *real* novelist now, one *must* risk the violence some experience as "punk."

Acker's work taken as a whole carries its central importance not only because she was among the first downtown writers and remains the most extreme one, but also because of what her work achieves. It is a postmodern narrative *Being and Time* with a streetwise poststructural footing. Her phenomenology is that of bodily experience rather than Germanic speculation; her *Alltäglichkeit* is not Heidegger's anesthesia but a predatory death cult; her dasein is confused by complexly interlocking forces of history, economics, politics, media, and gender, rather than by the business of life distracting her from her true Being; and her focus is less on Being-toward-death than on a Being-for-life. But however different her assumptions, she is as serious as Heidegger in understanding the worldness of the world, dispersing the active force of traditional thought, exploring "care as the being of dasein," and recognizing Understanding as the fullness of ways in which we live rather than as some kind of knowledge either apart from the world or compartmentalized within some particular discipline. Acker matches wits with the most brilliant of contemporary theorists and leads us through a career whose stages reprise the intellectual revolution that the last two decades have wrought in our thinking about Being and history.

After some survival time during the radical politics of the sixties, Acker produced a trilogy of novels pushing the limits of appropriation to document the plagiarized Being to which we are consigned. To look in detail at these novels is to identify the starting assumptions from which this entire revolution in narrative takes off. Indeed, the first of these, along with Constance DeJong's *Modern Love,* struck with tremendous impact a generation that had not yet begun to find its own narrative voice. Her books take, as she puts it in talking with Vitale, "the society as a series of texts. . . . And using new additions, new renderings in the texts to attack the society. First of all to find out how it works and then attack it." Hence we must look closely at **The Childlike Life of the Black Tarantula by the Black Tarantula**, the first volume of the trilogy, and at the also important **The Adult Life of Toulouse Lautrec by Henri Toulouse Lautrec**. (The middle volume is **I Dreamt I Was a Nymphomaniac Imagining** and is not now readily available.) In **Kathy Goes To Haiti** and **Blood and Guts in High School,** Acker turns the language of the body against hegemonic forms and institutions of every description. Building upon the earlier works' appropriation tactics, these two books offer a bruised and bruising portrait of coming of age. In the early eighties a pair of works, **Great Expectations** (1982) and **My Death, My Life** (1983), both now also published by Grove Press, rethinks the problem of language as it affects Acker's enterprise to work beyond the theoretical impasse of the radical writer working within the culture's sign systems. Finally, in **Don Quixote** and **Empire of the Senseless,** Acker carries us to a profound vision of the contradictory nomadic life she prescribes for those who desire more than "the grey of yuppy life." At midlife, in other words, Acker has already achieved a career of major proportions, both in its ambitions and accomplishments, and it is no wonder that she is on most ob-

servers' list of figures most instrumental in the emergence of the narrative sensibility that this book addresses. . . .

Don Quixote's Insurgent Writing

This section might well have been called "Night, Knight," both as Acker's facetious sign-off from her London expatriation and, more importantly, as the pun she relentlessly works. The pun places her female Knight of La Mancha in the Night of the American soul, dreaming the female imaginary as it has been constituted and attempting to glimpse something about the resolution of its contradictions. The knight's "crazy" vision is that of finding love, "love" serving as the sign for the knight's utopian vision (or, perhaps, utopian *glance,* because something less than a social blueprint emerges). Her vision is crazy because it requires a radical revision of what counts as "whole" or "sane." The book's mood is richly evoked at a high point of the section "I dream my schooling," in which Acker gives a desublimated version of one woman's cultural education. In attendance are her teacher (the "old creep"), her nomadic associates (the pirate dogs), and the corpse of Duranduran (who, dying, asked the creep to cut out his heart, perhaps an indication of the self-evisceration of the pop generation). The novel opens with a quote from the teacher:

> "The political mirror of this individual simultaneity of freedom and imprisonment is a state of fascism and democracy: the United States of America.
>
> "What is your choice?"
>
> I was stunned. "I have a choice?" I asked, though I had no idea what I meant by what I was saying, for I was stunned.
>
> "Since you have no choice and you must choose," the old creep answered, "this is what being *enchanted* means—tell me: who are you?"
>
> "Who can I be?" I looked at the victimizer and his victim, who were tied to each other by friendship. I have started to cry and I cannot stop crying,
>
> for those who, having nothing, homeless,
> would flee,
> but there is nowhere to flee;
> so we travel like pirates
> on shifting mixtures of something and nothing.
> For those who in the face of this mixture
> act with total responsibility:
> I cried so much I bothered everyone around me.
>
> "She—"

Upon hearing this, all the dogs barked.

"*She* who can tell us who victimizers are, *She* who can see and tell us because *She*'s loony because *She* has become the ancient art of madness, or literature. *She* is in front of us right now."

Having to choose when there is no real choice is Acker's analysis of her characters' existential double bind and what they struggle, though stunned, to articulate. Having to flee when there is no utopian space to reach, driven to the cultural piracy of appropriation in order to speak at all, proceeding not on the solid ground of authoritative truth but rather on the "shifting mixtures" of sensory and historical somethings and the nothings of cultural fictions, the knight becomes the one whose crying texts disturb everyone around her. But she is also the one who can name the victimizers, the enchanters by whose brutal logic she appears "loony" and against whom all her outlaw techniques (appropriation, pornography, fragmentation, transforming narrators, mixed genres, and so forth) are the only resources. Avatar of "the ancient art of madness," Acker's Don Quixote is mad only by the lights of the logic she opposes and frequently transgresses.

In the section "Texts of Wars for Those Who Live in Silence," Acker defines the logic of the enchanters through an ideological reading of a film in which Megalon meets Godzilla, among other elements floating through (a somewhat fuller version, called "Scenes of World War III," is in Richard Prince's collection, *Wild History*). Before the rewrite of that film gets underway, Catherine reverses roles with Heathcliff and is the one in *Wuthering Heights* to go off adventuring for "life." A type of Acker's Don, Catherine is clear about what she wants: "The liberty for love, the liberty for instinctual roamings, the liberty for friendship, the liberty for hatred, the liberty for fantasy: all of these have faded." She knows that "males dumber than nonhuman animals're running the economic and political world," and her own motto is that "civilization and culture are the rules of males' greeds."

In the middle of reading the film, the narrator imagines a dialogue between Megalon and Godzilla, who become types for Reason—"the monsters created from human beliefs and acts will no longer follow human orders," but instead become an all but invisible regime under which "those who live in silence" must labor unconscious of the regime within. Arguing that "all qualities have been and are reduced to quantitative equivalences," the monsters conclude that "this process inheres in the concept of reason." Although reason "signifies the idea of a free, human, social life," at least in the intentions of its more benign champions, it also "adjusts the world" and "has no function other than the preparation

of the object from mere sensory material in order to make it that material of subjugation."

The monsters then collapse the distinction between a beneficent reason and its more sinister form:

> Instrumental or ossified reason takes two forms: technological reason developed for purposes of dominating nature and social reason directed at the means of domination aimed at exercising social and political power.
>
> This tendency . . . now pervades all the spheres of human life: this exploitation or reduction of reality to self-preservation and the manipulable other has become the universal principle of a society which seeks to reduce all phenomena to this enlightenment, ideal of rationalism, or subjugation of the other.

The Don is the voice of that subjugated other, and what she contests is precisely her reduction to a "manipulable" silence. The novel's cacophony is the disruption of that ideological silence and a voicing of the heteroglossiac multitudes within. "Who can I be?" we saw her asking a bit ago; the answer throughout ***Don Quixote*** is one who carries on despite the contradictions we found emerging from our look at ***My Death, My Life.*** She tilts with the windmills of an "unchanging" culture in which reason is so naturalized an invention that is barely possible to budge it aside in order to let other human dimensions share the scene of consciousness.

The Don know that "International finance (that is, American finance) is a war strategy" fought not just in international trade but against and within the silenced ones. The Don, who opens the novel in another one of Acker's gruesome abortion scenes, uses the image of abortion several times to represent lives cut short both existentially and in terms of their levels of awareness. "The bloody outline of a head on every desk in the world. The bloody outline of alienated work. The bloody outline of foetuses." We are all aborted foetuses. The Don's job is to discover the many forms of this state, hence she uses the image differently for herself. As the outlaw who *is* aware because she has voiced so much from her marginality, she passes the point at which the languages available to her allow her to say directly what she finds on her quixotic quest. Hence "I am a mass of dreams which, since I can no longer express them, are foetuses beyond their times, not even abortions."

However restless some reviewers may have become with Acker's fiction of indirection, its strategy is essential if readers are to experience *in reading* the breaks, fissures, and contradictions within Western reason's ideological arrangement of reality. Appropriation leaps from *Wuthering Heights* to

Megalon, from Shakespeare to Hawthorne, from Baudrillard to de Sade, precisely because crossing their textural margins performs in the reader the same quilt-work reassemblage of ideologemes which the Don attempts. Jamming the mini-essays into the middle of a stream of narrative bubbles teaches "those who live in silence" how to speak for themselves. Assaulting reticence with steamy sex scenes is not a way to reclaim sexuality as a subject for realism (that was D. H. Lawrence's project in modernist days), but to awaken bodily readers' awareness of internal censors whose operation should be no more silent than the "subjugated other" of the culture, and no less examined, managed, and conditioned than alienated workers. If the multiplicity of voices streaming out of the Don's mouth is a disorienting evocation of the fragmentation of self, Acker's technique is not designed to recover any nostalgic fiction of a premodernist unified subject. Given fragmentation of the self, given the internal estrangement of those fragments from one another, given the lack even of much knowledge of their forms and trajectories, and given the organization of these fragments according to a Lyotardian socioeconomic "performativity," Acker's simultaneities, fragments, juxtapositions, and rewritings nested within appropriated pieces all function to reclaim this basic multiplicity for ends other than those that Lyotard so gloomily determines.

> **However restless some reviewers may have become with Acker's fiction of indirection, its strategy is essential if readers are to experience *in reading* the breaks, fissures, and contradictions within Western reason's ideological arrangement of reality.**
> —*Robert Siegle*

Although cultural conservatives might feel a bit uncomfortable with the assertion, there is nonetheless something to the claim that Acker is almost sacramental in her approach to individuality and to the world, that her ends are profoundly therapeutic, that her values are radically demystified forms of mythologized metaphors become Megalons, and that her practice of fiction is an attempt to regain for narrative a voice and a form that are commensurate with our information age but capable of performing, against that age's colonization of its "processors," the novel's quite traditional function of renewing the possibility for fresh subjectivity. If fiction that still looks familiar is bound to reruns of the same symptoms we have learned to recognize in the etherized patient of modernism, Acker's work breaks up the surface of an increasingly mandarin cultural page and puts into motion what lies beneath. And if the most important fiction of each age demands that we retrain a bit as readers, certainly Acker is among those writers who impose the most drastic requirements upon us to think differently. That difference, not co-

incidentally, requires suspension of precisely those categories of thought most implicated in the exercise of power and violence. And it encourages the development of skills and habits that lie at the heart of the feminist program of writers such as Hélène Cixous, Luce Irigaray, and Gayatri Spivak.

In her classic "This Sex Which Is Not One," Irigaray speaks of "the condition of underdevelopment arising from women's submission by and to a culture that oppresses them, uses them, makes them a medium of exchange, with very little profit to them. Except in the quasi-monopolies of masochistic pleasure, the domestic labor force, and reproduction." Acker says this about a dog's life: "The maintenance of a dog's life or of dog-like life depends on unequal (power) relations between subjects or dogs. In this case, the relations are those of ownership and desire. . . . The condition of the dog is a condition of war, of everyone against everyone: so every dog has a right to everything, even to another dog's body. This is freedom." Or at least "freedom" under the regime that Irigaray and Acker oppose.

Cixous, in her equally classic "The Laugh of the Medusa," calls for "the invention of a *new insurgent* writing" that "will return to the body," that "will tear her away from the superegoized structure in which she has always occupied the place reserved for the guilty," and that will enable the writer "to forge for herself the anti-logos weapon." Acker's is one version of that fiction of insurgency, shrewd and perhaps more engaged with its problematic aspects than most varieties. But exploding the logic of what Cixous calls "superegoization" is the aim of Acker's fiction, and developing the "anti-logos weapon" is the project of its transgressions of traditional form. Cixous and Acker resonate at far too many points to enumerate here, but Cixous's description of the "propriety of woman" comes strikingly close to the self-sacrificing quest on which the Don is engaged: "It is . . . her capacity to depropriate unselfishly, body without end, without appendage, without principal 'parts.' If she is a whole, it's a whole composed of parts that are wholes, not simple partial objects but a moving, limitlessly changing ensemble, a cosmos tirelessly traversed by Eros, an immense astral space not organized around any one sun that's any more of a star than the others." My description of Acker's work with fragmentation and multiplicity recounted the fictional realization of this depropriation. It is precisely the abandonment of the logic of "*principal* 'parts'" which lies behind each formal tactic of Acker and which most offends the unsympathetic among her reviewers. To think of her fiction as "a moving, limitlessly changing ensemble" is to recognize its kinetic form and the ongoing productivity of the endless connections we can make among the textual bits that she provides.

Even at the literal level, the relationship between Cixous's "propriety" and the Don's career is striking. If, as we have seen, the Don's ideas are "foetuses beyond their times," then the abortion to which she submits at the opening of the novel is the means by which she forces her insights into a language and a formal medium that can never be fully her own. "I had the abortion," she explains, "because I refused normalcy which is the capitulation to social control." The Don ends the silence of "normalcy" by aborting the overdue foetuses of her angry critique, thereby converting the "sickness" of her life experience into the "knightly tool" of fiction. "I want love," she continues. "The love I can only dream about or read in books. I'll make the world into this love." Body without end, she keeps writing, keeps encountering the disciplinary mechanisms of the culture in a long series of beatings, rejections, angry encounters, and episodes of the sort of "masochistic pleasure" of which Irigaray spoke. The novel's first part, "The Beginning of Night," consists of these violent encounters in the Don's quest. Its title refers to the cultural night of the female soul as the social pathology that the Don turns into her strongest weapon. A guerrilla fighter, she takes on the "partly male" role of knighthood in order to turn its discipline against the "dualistic reality which is a reality molded by power" and to make possible for human beings what the "bitch" already knows: "All being is timelessly wild and pathless, its own knight, free."

To succeed in her attempt to remake the world into love requires remaking the texts of which that world is composed, and in the second part of the novel, "Other Texts," the Don carries out this textual version of her strategy. Using strategies and insights consistent with those we have already seen, she refabricates four very different cultural texts, culminating with a version of Frank Wedekind's *Pandora's Box* in which Lulu escapes triumphant at the end, looking for "others who are, like me, pirates journeying from place to place, who knowing only change and the true responsibilities that come from such knowing sing to and with each other." Drawing upon the therapeutic energy of Eros, as Cixous suggests, the Don generously goes on in the third part to pour herself into the effort to teach her dog friends how society works and to serve as an "anti-logos" to its logic. More problematic is the Don's attempt to open possibilities for a different kind of Being that, as Irigaray says of Woman, "is indefinitely other in herself," not in the alienated and estranged way that the Don finds to be characteristic of life in the Nixonian times that she anatomizes, but rather intimately "in touch," in Irigaray's rich sense of the phrase.

In the autobiography of the Don's dog friend, which takes up an important portion of "The End of the Night," the dog tells of her complex experience of love amidst gender roles that switch sometimes in the literal sense of transvestite experiences and sometimes in the more figurative sense of role-shifting. In one section, the dog recalls reading about Juliette, a student at a girls' school, who is led by her teacher Delbène into the graveyard one night, past the coffins of schoolgirls,

and down into a room white, we suppose, to connote the absence of any cultural markers in this hidden space that lies literally under the sign of death. Delbène has blindfolded Juliette so that she must "trust" her teacher's guidance over the uneven pathway, a guidance that becomes more than a literal passage when Delbène begins to lecture: "What we do in this room is be happy. With our bodies. Our bodies teach us who've been poisoned." "Since these [patriarchal] educators train the mind rather than the body, we can start with the physical body, the place of shitting, eating, etc., to break through our opinions or false education." What follows this descent is Juliette's initiation into both vaginal and anal orgasm. The episode is a female parallel, perhaps, to the reading that Bakhtin offers of Rabelais's use of "the plane of material sensual experience" as the means by which "official medieval culture" was labeled "false education," as Delbène puts it. Bakhtin argues that such an episode in Rabelais "destroyed and suspended all alienation; it drew the world closer to man, to his body, permitted him to touch and test every object, examine it from all sides, enter into it, turn it inside out, compare it to every phenomenon, however exalted and holy, analyze, weigh, measure, try it on." Characters in **Don Quixote** are engaged in a similar process of groping their way beyond an abstract and oppressive metaphysics. Acker's women have all found logic, morality, and social hierarchies to allot them a near-medieval "place reserved for the guilty," in Cixous's phrase. And their attempt is precisely to rediscover the world from a perspective less determined by a totalizing logic that, for them, has functioned with all the omnipresent oppression of the "official medieval culture."

In **Don Quixote,** sexual pleasure comes to involve Delbène, Juliette, and the other schoolgirls, and Juliette realizes that "watching these sexual actions which I couldn't actually feel made me feel my own physical sensations less. My decreasing sexual abandonment let me feel a more general spreading or less focused sexual interest." Far more than a pornographic primer, the passage takes us back to Cixous's discussion:

> Though masculine sexuality gravitates around the penis, engendering that centralized body (in political anatomy) under the dictatorship of its parts, woman does not bring about the same regionalization which serves the couple head/genitals and which is inscribed only within boundaries. Her libido is cosmic, just as her unconscious is worldwide. Her writing can only keep going, without ever inscribing or discerning contours.

Cixous's language keeps sexuality, politics, and writing tightly paralleled in a way that Acker's fiction appears to understand quite tangibly. It is as if Juliette must learn what is *her* being first by unlearning the logic of "principal parts," as Cixous puts it, and then by learning through her body.

Hence her friends try to lead Juliette into a realization of what she has experienced against her best efforts to block them—"I'm too young to know," she responds, taking the defense of the ingénue. "I haven't any experience of this," she tries again, taking the defense of the overly sheltered. But one of her friends comes back aggressively: "I'm not asking you about your overlays of memories, like the overlays of culture in Europe, culminating in a decayed seaside hotel whose walls peel away from themselves into the literature they think is supporting them. I'm asking you what you know. What do you know, what do you perceive?" Cultural memories, culminating in the psychological locales of sentimental romances in the Harlequin mode, peel away once we critique the patriarchal logic sustaining those overlays.

Juliette, who is confused over a mixture of pain and pleasure her mates find highly significant, finally opens up this experience to analysis:

> I'm too scared to talk to you because I'm too scared to talk to anyone, especially older people: I'm scared because I have or know no self. There's no *one* who can talk. My physical sensations scare me because they confront me with a self when I have no self: sexual touching makes these physical sensations so fierce. I'm forced to find a self when I've been trained to be nothing. Therefore, I perceive that physical pain, if it doesn't scare me because it's happening without my expectation and consent, helps out and enlarges sexual excitation.

The passage is both alarming and, in a sense, promising. It is a frighteningly blunt description of why Irigaray perceives "masochistic pleasure" as the "quasi-monopoly" of women. If identity is painfully etched, then pain recalls the moment of inscription and the *non*cultural memory of flesh before the cut of the pen. With no self that Juliette knows of as hers, with no "*one*" voice that is hers to use, she can only fear talking, especially with those whose age has, in her experience, allied them with the institutions of mastery. Like Bakhtin's Rabelaisian Man, like Cixous's insurgent writer, she encounters in her mixture of pain and pleasure, of focused and cosmic Eros, "a self when I have no self." Promising, but problematic, as the rest of the section suggests (its narrator makes love to Laure but is aghast at the pain she inflicts, the unnaturalness of her dildo, and the pleasure of her own orgasm—the mixture makes clear the ambiguities of trying to realize fully this episode's more utopian promises).

An equally agonizing venture is the Don's attempt to turn

language to the ends of her quest. She explains her poetry fairly straightforwardly to the pirate dogs:

> I write words to you whom I don't and can't know, to you who will always be other than and alien to me. These words sit on the edges of meanings and aren't properly grammatical. For when there is no country, no community, the speaker's unsure of which language to use, how to speak, if it's possible to speak. Language is community. Dogs, I'm now inventing a community for you and me.

This audacious program attempts to place beside patriarchy an alternative community informed by the Don's "mad" vision, but it does not have the luxury of making this effort in a cultural vacuum. The dogs are creatures of their culture, however much they wish to escape its norms. The Don can define art as to "dream publicly," but some of the dogs at least are mainly disappointed when the Don does not simply collapse and thus provide them "fresh (dead) meat." She continues, instead, but the stress of her project shows in the near-paradoxical hopelessness with which she perseveres. She joins a voodoo service where "all ways were allowed: all cultures: aloud" and in which everyone sings "songs of desire" in communal warmth. But her response to the experience is mixed: "It is necessary to sing, that is to be mad, because otherwise you have to live with the straights, the compromisers, the mealy-mouths, the reality-deniers, the laughter-killers. It is necessary to be mad, that is to sing, because it's not possible for a knight, or for anyone, to foray successfully against the owners of this world."

Mad singing of the sort we find in Acker's fiction is no doubt one way to respond to the "owners." Dispirited, the Don wishes an apocalypse of the "malevolent" upon the suburbanites and sadly concludes that "'I wanted to find a meaning or myth or language that was mine, rather than those which try to control me; but language is communal and here is no community.' Having concluded, Don Quixote turned around and started walking home, although she had no home." What she does not realize is that whereas she has no home in the sense of a recognizable space in the culture surrounding her, she *has* achieved a different sort of textual place. That is, though she did not find language and meaning wholly her own, and though she forged no community on the order of the great nineteenth-century communes, she *did* weave a crazy quilt of songs, narratives, outbursts, and essays which inspired her listeners. The dogs realize their hunger; "this was the first sign of their having language." Then they recognize that their homelessness is caused by landlords, and that only landlords call terrorism "useless." The dogs' own "mad" song weaves bits and pieces of bad family life, oppressive working conditions, and this recognition of the slave culture behind such pieces: "It is you, city. Market of the world, that is, of all representations. Since you're the only home I've ever known, without your representation or misrepresentation of me I don't exist. Because of you, since every child needs a home, every child is now a white slave." There is no home, no freedom, no "I" without the "history and culture" that they label "the world of death" near their song's conclusion. Such consciousness is apocalypse in the eyes of the landlords, but for the dogs "the work and the language of the living're about to begin."

The dogs' journey off into the adventures of a pirate band does not include the Don, however, for she is a self-confessed "freak" still poised between the need for "a home" and a fear of "the bickerings and constraints of heterosexual marriage." She still faces the conflict between loneliness, when "I don't touch anybody so I'm immersed in my own selfishness," and the knowledge that "as soon as I'm married, I'll be a prisoner; I'll be normal. I'll have to stop having the dreams by which I now act." The novel winds to its conclusion in a dream in which God confesses her imperfections: "Since I am no more, forget Me. Forget morality. Forget about saving the world. Make Me up." It is, perhaps, the Don's farewell to the concept of Messianic quest that she has held throughout the book and an implicit recognition of the more diffuse effect that her work will have. Not God, but effective fictions; not morality, but values. "I thought about God for one more minute and forgot it. I closed my eyes, head drooping, like a person drunk for so long she no longer knows she's drunk, and then, drunk, awoke to the world which lay before me." That world seems not to have been so available to her before, as if the intoxicating mission of taking on the "partly male" qualities of knighthood had, perhaps, enabled her to experience what Cixous calls the "vatic bisexuality which doesn't annul differences but stirs them up, pursues them, increases their number." The Don has conceived the suspension of such absolute limits as God, and she has provided the material for what Acker's dust jacket calls a "collage-novel" of stirred-up, increased textual and existential differences. If she is left feeling the full set of contradictions revealed by her analyses, it at least leaves her awake to the world's realities and to the problematic but hopeful possibility of "Make Me up." That is a great deal to hope for from the language community forged by the novel. "Eye/I" say the piratical dogs as they weigh anchor.

Martina Sciolino (essay date April 1990)

SOURCE: "Kathy Acker and the Postmodern Subject of Feminism," in *College English*, Vol. 52, No. 4, April, 1990, pp. 437-45.

[*In the following essay, Sciolino examines Acker's hybrid synthesis of poststructural theory, postmodern fiction, and feminist discourse.*]

By conflating her own lover's discourse with seemingly mutually exclusive productions such as canonical literature and pornography, by using performative prose to launch political and aesthetic diatribes, Kathy Acker's narrative methods are exemplary for postmodern feminism. Materially didactic in its decompositions, any fiction by Acker engages a poststructural skepticism regarding the constative efficacy of language. Aware of its late capitalist milieu, her fiction replicates consumer dynamics in its own narrative cycles. Engaged with her social context, she typically includes the debris of an information age in montage that forces associations between material culled from radically different registers. Acker writes hybrid texts—part narrative, part essay. Her fiction enacts a critical imitation of literary moments by putting them alongside what the academy has traditionally, if tacitly, bracketed off from the literary.

The identity of every term is tenuous in these liminal productions signed by a woman. Contesting conventional boundaries by closely investigating difference activates both poststructural theory and postmodern fiction. But boundary ambiguity has a specific resonance within feminist theory, where it is often used to acknowledge the peculiarities of female individuation.

There has been a great deal of theorizing literary postmodernism, almost always in terms of male writers—as if postmodern literature, an understanding of which is almost impossible without considering the modalities of desire, has no obvious relation to gender difference. As the supposed progenitor of postmodernism, Joyce feminizes narrative, but those who are said to write in his wake are rarely female. (See, however, Hayman and Anderson, who include Helene Cixous' experimental prose.) On the other hand, feminist literary theory coincides—not always harmoniously—with poststructuralism, a discourse that is itself still a dissonant score-in-progress. When postmodern fiction is put in dialogue with poststructural theory (by major critics in this field, such as Ihab Hassan and Jerome Klinkowitz), feminist voicings are left out, left over. Subsequently, writings by women become dangerously supplemental to the theorization of postmodernity. This omission produces a field that is alongside, or submerged beneath, the scene of postmodern canon formation.

To invoke a Freudian metaphor despite its binary axis, the latent content of feminism (typically repressed through the dream-work that is criticism) may explode upon the manifest content of postmodernity and expose it as a state-of-the-art patriarchal discourse by glossing the fantastic aporias of male desire, exclusive fantasies that seem as operative in contemporary canon formation as ever. Kathy Acker's writing is already inserted between these latent and manifest postmodernisms, challenging their separation in a constructed dream-work of her own. A writer of innovative narratives that converse with theorists as diverse in their constructions of desire as Georges Bataille and Andrea Dworkin, Acker creates fictions that are theories-in-performance, speculative fictions that act out the suppositions of both poststructuralism and feminism.

If we take a moment to isolate and compare some of these suppositions, however, we might understand how Acker's performative project is saturated with impossibility. Take, for instance, the issue of the subject. In poststructural discourse, woman is the male subject displaced by the throes of desire (operant in *écriture*)—a process of figurative feminization that Alice Jardine calls "gynesis." One may trace this displacement in Derrida's works, particularly *Spurs* and *Glas,* as Gayatri Spivak does in "Displacement and the Discourse of Woman." There Spivak remarks that the male writer's displacement from the privileged site of subjectivity, his dislocation by postmodern writing or poststructural reading into the philosophical category traditionally marked feminine, doubly displaces women.

So how does Acker write postmodern prose *as* a woman? In addition, as desire is always operative in her writings, how can it affect a character who would be construed by *Spurs* and *Glas* as "indifferent" to "difference"?

As I have already suggested, a postmodern discourse that performs feminist critique would gloss male desire as such. The question arises: where is female desire? Still taking place in a poststructural absence privileged as enviable by male writers sensitive to the end of patriarchy? In a sense, Acker glosses *Glas.* Her fiction displays female desire as a process whose vicissitudes impede a reader's attempt to distinguish between two master narratives about female desire. The first is made of local narratives which constitute or enable the female subject as an absolute entity—as she is understood in existential, utopian, or bourgeois discourse. (Toril Moi's *Sexual/Textual Politics* indicates where such assumptions inform Anglo-American feminist theory.) The second master narrative of female desire includes local narratives that deconstitute or prohibit a woman's being in favor of becoming. This register offers problems of its own, for Acker's fiction not only demonstrates consciousness in a rhetorical medium, it shows that "coming to be" is full of gaps, folds, and disappearances. A narrative becoming requires strategic decomposition, in reading and writing.

First of all, Acker works her reader through a deconstruction of the female subject; the phrase "female subject" is here understood through social conventions that still operate to predicate a woman in American culture. This is a fundamental project in all of Acker's early work, especially *Blood and Guts in High School,* and it reaches its fullest disclosure in *Don Quixote,* where Acker dialectically thinks through the myth of romantic love as organized by monogamous, heterosexual conventions. This dialectic is worked through dialogues between Don Quixote and her dog. Here, as in *Great Expectations.* Acker considers how a woman's desires are already constituted by various myths—narratives of being—that fully inform the speaking subject even as she speaks. Thus, how can one write a revolution to find a space for her own desires when she is already written by patriarchy? Don Quixote has internalized patriarchal discourse in the very process of learning her craft, an apprenticeship that necessitates reading: BEING BORN INTO AND PART OF A MALE WORLD, SHE HAD NO SPEECH OF HER OWN. ALL SHE COULD DO WAS READ MALE TEXTS WHICH WEREN'T HERS. It is from this dubious position that Don Quixote speaks, and Acker writes, the discourse of female desire.

While art for Acker is resistant to dominant culture, seeking to emancipate the writer and the reader, such an existentialist perception of art often rests upon a humanist theory of subjectivity. Here is another point of divergence between Anglo-American feminist theory and French theorists such as Helene Cixous and Julia Kristeva, whose writings position the subject in a fluid rhetorical play. Although Acker envisages her art pragmatically, as a weapon, she challenges the view that the individual subject results from violent mastery as supreme or autonomous: it is this limit that creates desire. Whether the writings that speak to her are as marginal as Burroughs' or as fully established as Thoreau's, all "present the human heart naked. . . . This human heart is not only the individual heart: the American literary tradition of Thoreau, Emerson, even Miller, presents the individual and communal heart as a unity. Any appearance of the individual heart is a political occurrence."

Acker puts these values into play when she returns to the opening scene of Dickens' *Great Expectations* in her novel of the same name. The condition of being an orphan like Pip suggests a fantastic autonomy, and the suggestion is supported when Pip goes on to name himself. However, his name is a misprision—a reading of his parents' tombstone, a revision of "the name of the father," Phillip Pirrip. (Not that it matters in Acker's version of *Great Expectations,* because the speaker soon becomes a young girl. Here Acker indicates the tenuous relations between name, gender, and identity while simultaneously exposing the sequence that a reader engages to orient herself in narrative.) Finally, both Dickens and Acker deny their respective characters escape and bind them in their relationships to others, thereby demonstrating exactly how the desire for individual autonomy is fantastic, wishful, a dream that constitutes and deconstitutes character.

Again, Acker's writing acts out the suppositions of poststructuralism and feminism while critiquing both in relationship to one another. Differences between and within each field are put into operation here, so that the relationship between poststructuralism and feminism would seem to imitate the love/hate relationship that is a source of endless drama in Acker's fiction. Through her desiring characters, she wonders: where does love become hate, adoration, rivalry? Sometimes poststructuralism and feminism exist in mutual adoration, sometimes in mutual exclusion. Feminists are new subjects of history. What dissonance sounds between the death-throes of the humanist subject and the birth-pangs of new historical subjects?

How can a woman be heard in this noise? From what position can a woman write and claim her experience when authority is under erasure? Acker responds to this contemporary positioning of the woman writer through a technique of plagiarism/autoplagiarism.

In a recent interview, she describes her early fiction as thematic engagements with identity enabled by experiment in autobiographical narrative. In *The Childlike Life of the Black Tarantula by the Black Tarantula, I Dreamt I Was a Nymphomaniac: Imagining,* and *The Adult Life of Toulouse Lautrec by Henri Toulouse Lautrec,* she "put autobiographical material next to material that couldn't be autobiographical." By so doing, Acker problematizes any simple relationship between female experience and the writing of fiction and leads us to examine the claim of experience that often justifies scholarship of women's writing. Perhaps writing actually unravels the knot where experience and authority are conventionally bound—bound, that is, by conventions in feminist reading. In such reading, it would seem that Acker's fiction has a signature weave composed of specific preoccupations and repeated reference to events—rape by the stepfather, suicide of the mother, work in a sex show. However, the equation of Acker's writing and her experience is impeded by the fact that Acker is not an autobiographer but an autoplagiarist (a term Beckett used to describe Proust's fictionalization of his biography in *A la recherche du temps perdu*). The autoplagiarist takes the phrase "life-story" literally—as a literary term.

Acker's experiments with plagiarism include *Great Expectations, Don Quixote, My Death My Life by Pier Paolo Pasolini,* and the most recent *Empire of the Senseless.* In the latter, Acker makes characters that are projections of herself, but not original creations. A dialogue between Abhor and Thavai demonstrates the difference. Thavai (a male character) is looking for "Somebody who knows something. Whoever he is, the knower, must be the big boss." His partner Abhor (who Thavai says is part robot, part black) answers: "'All I know is that we have to reach this construct. And her name's Kathy.'"

'That's a nice name. Who is she?'

'It doesn't mean anything.'

Thavai wants an author, a stable source, an originator. Instead, Abhor, a construct, describes a maker who is herself made.

> **Acker's experiments in plagiarism take issue with the notion of artistic authenticity underlying conventional authority. Like Foucault, Barthes, and Derrida, she celebrates the death of the author, the beginning of writing, of textuality as coproduced by reader and writer, the idea of reader as writer.**
> **—Martina Sciolino**

Acker's experiments in plagiarism take issue with the notion of artistic authenticity underlying conventional authority. Like Foucault, Barthes, and Derrida, she celebrates the death of the author, the beginning of writing, of textuality as coproduced by reader and writer, the idea of reader as writer. Yet, Acker's cheery wake over the Author's corpus is informed by a feminist imperative. In "A Few Notes on Two of My Books," she writes that no one creates anything because "no one. . . . is more powerful than the world":

> Only the incredible egotism that resulted from a belief in phallic centrism could have come up with the notion of creativity.

> Of course, a woman is the muse. If she were the maker instead of the muse and opened her mouth, she would blast the notion of poetic creativity apart.

Acker has spoken of her affinity for Sherry Levine's photography, which decontextualizes and re-represents photography by men: "When I copy, I don't 'appropriate.' I just do what gives me pleasure: write." Because she exposes the nature of possessive signing as patriarchal, especially at the start of *Great Expectations,* Acker's technique would seem to interrupt the suppositions of Showalter's gynocritics, which assumes relatively stable relationships between signature and gender, writing and a woman's experience.

Showalter's sometimes useful division between feminist critique and gynocritics often perpetuates among those who employ it an *a priori* assertion that women's writing and men's writing are constituted differently. Due to the simultaneity of plagiarism/autoplagiarism in Acker's fiction, identity is plastic. It mutates in Acker's innovative characterizations; gender is often, finally, in indeterminate relationship with identity. Moreover, both identity and gender are social constructions, works-in-progress whose very indeterminacy enables a politically motivated interruption. And in Acker's fiction, interruption is activated by montage—the cutting up of other writings, removing them from their original contexts to place them in new and unexpected relationships.

The question of whether women's writing and men's writing are constituted differently cannot be answered in any general way, although one could deduce as much if one considers the poststructural conflation of writing and reading alongside feminist theories of reader response. If gender is a social construct that informs reading in crucial ways, and if reading and writing are simultaneous activities as Acker's plagiarisms demonstrate, then gender would seem to affect writing just as emphatically as it affects reading. Certainly one may dispute the premises here, but another problem is locating exactly where gender informs writing, especially if I produce the text while reading it. If I cannot say where writing ends and reading begins, I cannot say exactly where any document marks itself as a woman's or a man's; in fact, if I'm doing the reading, they are all women's texts. And yet both Acker and de Beauvoir remind me that, as a woman, I am made and not born. The point is that gender difference is not immediately or adequately marked by signature alone. But of course we cannot speculate finally upon the differences between works signed by men and women until canons are reconstituted to include both.

So it seems that the poststructural elements of Acker's fiction do not automatically mesh with American feminist literary theory. As for the deconstruction of presence, of authority, of the priority of speech over writing—what about the status of the spoken word in women's and artists' communities, in most excentric communities that make texts out of earshot because our dominant discourses are document obsessed? (The term "ex-centric" is Linda Hutcheon's and indicates marginal discourse; however, Hutcheon defines postmodernism to include only ex-centric discourse, no matter what the writers' circumstances are. When she wished to designate the productions of non-white non-males, Hutcheon uses the rather unfortunate phrase "minoratarian discourse"—unfortunate because it rhymes with and therefore brings to mind "authoritarian discourse.") In *The Adult Life of Toulouse Lautrec,* Acker records (that is, makes) the speech of female characters who are marginalized by the male artists they desire. These speakers are therefore at the periphery of a periphery. But here Acker glosses the Parisian art scene of Vincent Van Gogh by imagining women there speaking to each other: "Sure we're waitresses. We're part of the meat market. That's how we get loved." And by making Lautrec a woman, Acker brings the already marginalized communities of artist/men and prostitutes/women together as if to say that a cultural heritage that would honor one must honor both. (A similar repositioning occurs in the **"Seattle Art Society"** story of *Great Expectations*).

A more recent example of speech in Acker's fiction begins *Empire of the Senseless* when Thivai tells us Abhor's life story, which—he says—Abhor has told him. Thus even when Acker refers to an oral transmission, her very writing of it separates the speaker from her narrative (which, by the way, repeats the events of Acker's "life-story").

Perhaps it would be more accurate to say that Acker's experimentation with plagiarism and autoplagiarism makes gynocritics and feminist critique simultaneous rather than separate activities. The female writer whom feminist critics may want to claim for their own project hides in, is composed through, the play of textuality—the active material between herself and other readers/writers—including texts made with women, with men, and sometimes with texts not written at all but photographed, televised, spoken.

Acker's narrative techniques interrupt our tracing any source or event absolutely based in the author's experience. Fortunately, she also puts reading/writing on the same ontological level as experience. A ceaseless confessional marks all of her fiction, makes it one text, an autoplagiarism in progress. Says the character "I" in *My Death My Life:*

> I keep trying to kill myself to be like my mother
> who killed herself. I kept working on the "Large
> Glass" for eight years, but despite that, I didn't want
> it to be the expression of an inner life.

Even at this moment of (apparent) full self-disclosure, Acker is speaking through the work of Marcel Duchamp, whose cubist painting "The Large Glass" was produced through years of interrogating the gaze.

Acker's (auto)plagiaristic technique foregrounds issues that are crucial to critical theory. One debate (carried on, for instance, by Fredric Jameson and Henry Louis Gates) attends the conflict between the deconstruction of the humanist subject (which demystifies authority as functional and fictive rather than absolute and essential) and the power of utterance desired by new subjects of history. Feminist criticism is a new historical discourse. Again, what seems desirable by feminist critics often entails a conceptualization of identity and authorship that poststructuralism questions.

For instance, feminist challenges to the academic construction of modernity and postmodernity necessitate a compensatory criticism that, in turn, risks privileging signature. Happily, this risk has its rewards. In *Feminist Fictions: Revisiting the Postmodern,* Patricia Waugh reads female authors whose narratives perform a subjectivity that is neither traditionally humanist nor deconstructed. What Waugh describes, through Woolf and others, is a relational subject who coexists in narrative relations to other subjects. Character made in this way is never completed nor stable; its integrity depends upon otherness.

This relational subject articulated in Waugh's compensatory criticism may allow us to note finer distinctions within ex-centric traditions of modernism and postmodernism. For instance, Acker imagines a relational subject through narrative experimentation, as does Gertrude Stein. Stein is an autoplagiarist herself, most certainly in *The Diary of Alice B. Toklas,* where she makes a cubist I, an I formed through several perspectives grafted onto one another so that they happen simultaneously, as if in a visual field. But in *Gertrude Stein's America,* Stein appears to propose a rather utopic text that proceeds without any linkage—in fact without any subject, without a speaker, without a referent. "Language should move, 'not just moving in relation to anything, not moving in relationship to itself but just moving.'" Because this line is offered in the indeterminate frame of quotation marks, it would be a mistake to take it at its autotelic word.

Similarly interested in the possibilities of writing a moving text, Acker's *Great Expectations* speculates a narrative subtle enough to express the state of being in between states:

> There is just moving and there are different ways of moving. Or: there is moving all over at the same time and there is moving linearly. If everything is moving-all-over-the-place-no-time, anything is everything. If so, how can I differentiate? How can there be stories? Consciousness just is: no time. But any emotion presupposes differentiation. Differentiation presumes time, at least BEFORE and NOW. A narrative is an emotional moving.

A narrative moves because a character is a work-in-progress: engaged in a ceaseless process of negotiating selfhood through relations to the world, to time, to other characters. Thus, the difference that constitutes identity is contingent—interrelational and contextual. In a word, that difference is moving, as moving as the subject who desires.

Stephen Schiff (review date 22 June 1990)

SOURCE: "Rimbaud and Verlaine, Together Again," in *The New York Times Book Review,* June 22, 1990, p. 11.

[*In the following review, Schiff provides a generally unfavorable assessment of* In Memoriam to Identity.]

The characters in Kathy Acker's nine novels are far less intriguing than the character on some of them—on the book

jackets, that is. There one finds Kathy Acker glaring provocatively into the camera, her hair platinum and butch-cut, her lips poised somewhere between a pout and a slurp, her underwear exposed and with it her mighty bi, tri and quadriceps, festooned with snarly tattoos.

The pose is manifestly defiant; it hints at the sort of avant-garde, fervently underground credentials that Ms. Acker has earned with such novels as *Great Expectations* (1984), *Don Quixote* (1986) and *Empire of the Senseless* (1988)—the sort of credentials more youthful writers, however hip, can never quite summon these days (Ms. Acker, who has also been a stripper and a performance artist, is now 43 years old).

Since the late 1970's, she has haunted those seamy fringes where the literary culture meets sex, drugs and rock 'n' roll, and her more sympathetic readers have hailed her as a "punk writer." If I understand the punk-rock movement of the late 70's and early 80's, the term is accurate. Punk musicians generally had a great deal to say, and a fearsome yen to say it; what distinguished them from their mainstream coevals was chiefly their inability to play their instruments. Likewise Ms. Acker, whose erudition is incontestable, whose ferocity is unmistakable and whose prose, I'm afraid, is unreadable.

Her new novel, *In Memoriam to Identity* (catchy title), provides a case in point. Like most of her work, it's a mix of affectless storytelling, graphic but oddly remote descriptions of sex, snatches of gnarled political diatribe (mainly feminist, anti-establishment, anticapitalist), collage effects (sometimes reminiscent of the cut-and-paste experiments of William Burroughs and Brion Gysin) and lots of jangled grammar and syntax. *In Memoriam* is a good deal statelier than some of Ms. Acker's work (her first book, *Blood and Guts in High School,* features her own swell drawings of penises), but her fans will still hail it not only as "punk" but as "post-modernist" fiction. And this, too, is apt. For among the techniques favored by post-modernists is "appropriation"—the borrowing of themes, styles or images invented by earlier artists.

Ms. Acker appropriates like crazy. *In Memoriam to identity* begins with a peculiarly fractured account of the early life of the poet Arthur Rimbaud, parts of which seemingly take place during the Nazi occupation of France (by which time Rimbaud had been dead for a half century); there are also showy references to Bloomingdale's, AIDS and other up-to-date phenomena. Long swatches of dialogue are devoted to Ms. Acker's own quirky translations of Rimbaud. Where Rimbaud recalls (in "Délires II"), "I wrote of silences, of nights," Ms. Acker gives us: "I wrote silences, nights, my despair at not seeing you and being in a crummy hotel next to you." Which, no doubt, is what Rimbaud really meant to say.

Presently the biography gives way to a pair of vaguely parallel contemporary stories. The first is about a woman named Airplane who is raped and then kept by her rapist, and who soon becomes a stripper doing sex shows in a dive called Fun City. Literary detectives will quickly identify her as Ms. Acker's version of Temple Drake in William Faulkner's "Sanctuary." Next we follow the odyssey of a girl called Capitol, whose desire for sex flummoxes her family (including a brother named Rimbaud). Capitol falls in with a passive, well-to-do young man named Harry and becomes a performance artist employing various "smashed dolls" in her act—by which point those literary detectives will be waving their withered arms and screaming, "Faulkner again! 'The Wild Palms!'"

Of course, Ms. Acker knows better than to think that tossing together a salad of literary references and dirty talk will yield that devoutly longed-for whatsit, the post-modernist novel. What she's really trying to do is imagine herself into her favorite literary archetypes—to give Don Quixote, for instance, the qualms Ms. Acker herself had as she faced her own abortion—or, in *In Memoriam,* to invest Rimbaud with the desires and frustrations of a female renegade in love with a married bourgeois. This approach ought to kick her characters alive, but it doesn't because Ms. Acker's linguistic experiments smother them before they can draw breath. Alienation is not so much her theme as it is her method; her very language is alienated, her rhythms benumbed. Amazing things happen to her people and Ms. Acker describes their responses in excruciating detail, but she commits the cardinal dramatic sin of telling instead of showing. The result is drier than the driest history lecture.

Witness this description of the tempestuous relationship between Rimbaud and his married lover, the poet Paul Verlaine: "After a particularly *sadistic* scene, V's wife took her child and ran away to the south of France. V told her and R that he would do anything to avoid permanent separation from his wife. V asked R to leave him. V asked R to leave Paris. V drank more. R didn't want to do what V was telling him to do. V was taking away not only V—his only family—but also his only home."

That's one action-packed passage. And I defy you to read it in anything but a monotone.

Tom Clark (review date 12 August 1990)

SOURCE: "Homage to the Great Punks of Our European Heritage," in *Los Angeles Times Book Review,* August 12, 1990, pp. 1, 8.

[*Below, Clark reviews* In Memoriam to Identity.]

In previous books like **Don Quixote** and **Great Expectations,** Kathy Acker has patented an audacious, irreverent, provocatively highhanded method of recycling classic literary texts in a manner variously reminiscent of Dadaist and surrealist procedures, Burroughsian cut-up and the "appropriation" tactics currently in vogue in the visual arts.

Effecting an arresting tacit critique by wrenching original works out of context and re-scaling them to purposes quite distinct from their authors' intentions, these collaged "ready-made" novels also manage to generate a formal modality and impetus all their own. It is a technique uniquely suited to Acker's radical aesthetic strategies, central among which are the subversion and redeployment of language as an instrument of power.

Here, in her ninth novel, Acker explicitly identifies her sources in a candid closing note: "All the preceding has been taken from the poems of Arthur Rimbaud, the novels of William Faulkner, and biographical texts on Arthur Rimbaud and William Faulkner."

Acker's piratical plunderings of the public domain are comparatively less manifest in the case of the latter author—from whom she merely adopts her book's structural template, lifted out of "The Wild Palms," and a major character, Quentin, one of her several, relatively faceless and disposable male protagonists, transplanted out of *The Sound and the Fury* and put to appropriately degenerate uses as the suicidally demented hero of the third of the three obsessive, interrelated romances which make up **In Memoriam to Identity.**

The image of an androgyne-prole Rimbaud, on the other hand, not only supplies a hero for the first of these romances but also hangs like an enigmatic totem of Freedom and Bad Attitude over the entire book. "I a man other"—as Acker quotes Rimbaud at one point—could serve as epigraph to her unsentimental farewell to identity, though even as she implicates the poet in the explosive fission of her various selves into a sort of electric sexual plurality (her heroine is actually several separate female characters, who share a single voice), she is careful to note that "Rimbaud wasn't a woman. . . . Perhaps there is no other to be and that's where I'm going."

"Pushing the emotive perceptive and rational capacities beyond their limits," a faithfully Rimbaudian motive, is the compulsive project that makes Acker's explorative, libidinous heroines go—and come, over and over and over. Somewhere here it is casually stated that to have fewer than two orgasms a day should be seen as a pathological symptom. "Sexuality must be closely tied to reality," Acker proposes.

"You can't lie to yourself sexually." Her prose assaults so-cial and cultural taboos with all the subtlety of a helicopter gunship, employing the graphic shock-tactic grammar and four-letter vocabulary of a relentless language of genital re-volt.

Acker puts forth, with no little vigor and seriousness, a hard eyed view of human relations in our "insane society" as ul-timately reducible to the model of the act of rape. In her fic-tion, the inevitable counter-exploitation of the perpetrator by the victim, the rapee turning upon the rapist, and reifying back at him with a vengeance, is seen not only as a defen-sive survival tactic on the woman's part but also—and, in moral terms, it must be said, somewhat more gratifyingly—as a poetic turning of the tables.

"I'm always scared," declares Acker's alter-ego heroine. "That's true, but everyone in their world's scared and most of everyone are zombies. I learned that this world is insane. There aren't any roles in an insane world. A world of power. It has something to do with sex. And men have the power, within all the fear; those men who deny this, lie. . . ." Tak-ing back that power, the alienated but highly resilient and self-reliant multiple-identity woman of her tale "had decided to survive. Somewhere in sexuality was her strength. . . . She would survive."

Largely plot-free, wanderingly picaresque, naive and super-ficial in its characterizations and finally less-novel-than-revo-lutionary tract, *In Memoriam to Identity* is a weird, violent, searing, angry work, full of pain, dislocation, desire, hate and the raging drive of resistant creation. Acker writes out of open rebellion—against, among other things, God, love, America, the hierarchic structures of patriarchal societies, middle-class values, humanitarianism, history, Harvard, tele-vision, Freud, Santa Claus.

"Do you prefer," she challenges her reader and herself with characteristic aggression early on in these pages, "do you think it's better to accept everything that you have been taught, that society has taught, to accept what is considered truth in the circle of your family, friends, and world and what, moreover, really comforts and seems proper? Or do you prefer to strike new paths, fighting the habitual, what goes against questioning? Do you prefer to experience the insecurity of independence and the frequent wavering of one's feelings and moral decisions, often having neither any-one to support you nor consolation, but only having this vi-sion, this mental picture called 'truth'?"

Kathy Acker has invented a form of secret historiography, a language of shock and sensation that provides a vivid, dis-ruptive, unsettling readout on the psycho-social trauma of our time.

Kate Braverman (review date 22 March 1992)

SOURCE: "An Exercise in Public Drowning," in *Los An-geles Times Book Review,* March 22, 1992, p. 8.

[*In the following review, Braverman offers an unfavorable assessment of* Portrait of an Eye.]

Kathy Acker has achieved cult status in the small-press world, presumably for the graphic sexual content of her fic-tions and the nasty bad-girl attitude that fuels them. She is, fundamentally, an experimental minimalist. This collection consists of three mini-"novels" (two of them are fewer than 100 pages) which were previously self-published in the early and mid-70s. And one wonders at the wisdom of bringing forth such raw and marginal early efforts.

The Childlike Life of the Black Tarantula by the Black Ta-rantula is a series of disparate fragments, fantasies and medi-tations by a protagonist who may or may not be imagining that she is turning into a large black insect without feelings. There are unconnected sequences in which the protagonist inhabits the consciousness of murderesses and prostitutes, offers scenes from her childhood, decides to "revolt against the death society," reads pornography, masturbates, engages in public sex acts, discusses her boredom, wonders why she can't kill her parents for their money, hangs out in leather bars and concludes that she is too shy and gentle, too artis-tic to get a job.

I Dreamt I Was a Nymphomaniac: Imagining also is a se-ries of disjointed fragments about a woman determined to be an artist. At one juncture, she says, without apparent irony, "I'm a poet and what I do is sacred. The people who keep me from the few lousy instruments I need to dissemi-nate this crap are evil."

The protagonist philosophizes about abstractions such as the nature of substance and time. Cliché litanies adorn this sec-tion like land mines, blowing the serious reader away. The author reveals the "real evil." It is, among others, the secret combination of Rockefeller and Pentagon, fake shortages to raise prices, Standard Oil Co., coffee, IBM, CBS, Metro-politan Life, Allied Chemical, Kimberly-Clark, AT&T, American Express, Con Edison and the Chase Manhattan Bank.

This second collection of fragments is awkward for numer-ous reasons. Acker repeats entire sections word for word, like a broken movie projector or a kind of psychic stutter. This spasmodic feeling is amplified by unpunctuated sen-tences. In essence, the reader is encountering what seems to be a compendium of effects without a coherent central mechanism to make it run. It's like discovering you have de-ciphered the blueprint for a dead machine.

The Adult Life of Toulouse-Lautrec by Henri de Toulouse-Lautrec consists of fragments that are simultaneously more conventional in both structure and content. Paradoxically, these sections are also less interesting than the more vivid and confused previous scenes from adolescent hell. Here, the author tries to sustain her ideas but the ideas prove to be pretentious and trivial.

In one piece, Toulouse-Lautrec is envisioned as being a sex-starved woman in a kind of mystery story set in a Paris slum that resembles contemporary San Francisco. There is a mildly amusing section about a 9-year-old Janis Joplin having an affair with the young James Dean. This is intercut with dialogue from the film *Rebel Without a Cause.* Interspersed throughout these jagged fictions are political diatribes and apparent revelations about the history of capitalism and the role of multinational corporations on global affairs.

In point of fact, these "novels" are without narrative, character or plot. They have no structure or dramatic line and nothing coalesces or resolves. These fragments lack even a minimal guiding sensibility or unifying principle, if only the manic and demonic passion and outrage of, say, William Burroughs' *Naked Lunch*. Burroughs maintains a consistent sense of fury, and *Naked Lunch* is composed of, at the very least, fully realized vignettes.

In contrast, these pages read like a writer's journal littered with powerful story ideas and descriptions of real events that have yet to be transformed into fictions. They are not viable stylistic assaults on the traditional forms. The author is clearly in touch with chaos but unable or unwilling to tame and orchestrate it. There are elegant passages here and spasms of real lyrical clarity, none of which are developed or shaped. This dereliction of direction is not a new art form. Rather it is like watching the captain jump from her ship, over and over again. This is an exercise in public drowning.

> **Portrait of an Eye is a kind of novel in reverse. Rather than creation, this is a literary autopsy where the reader is forced to sift through the severed pieces of what goes into making art.**
> —*Kate Braverman*

These "novels," textured in layers of self-indulgence, deliberately oblique and willfully solipsistic, have produced a curious anomaly. This is a kind of novel in reverse. Rather than creation, this is a literary autopsy where the reader is forced to sift through the severed pieces of what goes into making art.

The elements of novels are here and they are wasted. This is, at it's core, a coolly deliberate pseudo-literature. And these are anti-novels presumably for anti-readers.

Greg Lewis Peters (essay date 1992)

SOURCE: "Dominance and Subversion: The Horizontal Sublime and Erotic Empowerment in the Works of Kathy Acker," in *State of the Fantastic: Studies in the Theory and Practice of Fantastic Literature and Film,* edited by Nicholas Ruddick, Greenwood Press, 1992, pp. 149-56.

[*In the following essay, Peters explores the narrative techniques and language of dominance and submission employed by Acker to subvert patriarchal hierarchies and conventional notions of sexual identity.*]

Cosmo Landesman, in his (unfavorable) 1984 review of Kathy Acker's novel ***Blood and Guts in High School,*** describes her writing as having "the gothic perversity of Lautremont [*sic*] mixed with the glory and the gore of the Texas Chainsaw Massacre." Others have been less kind. Acker has been accused of being everything from merely irritating to the most evil person in the world. She is a tattooed feminist punk linguist who writes possibly the most subversive novels in contemporary American fiction. In ***Blood and Guts in High School*** (1978), ***Don Quixote*** (1986), and ***Empire of the Senseless*** (1988), Acker goes to war with the oppressive patriarchal worlds of politics, language, and sexuality. Her novels are Derridean time bombs that seek to escape the prisons of language, narrative and proscribed sexuality. She escapes traditional authorial limits by creating entropic, funhouse texts of exploded narrative, nonspecific signification, and fantasy. Her characters escape their own limits through an often frightening process of simultaneous assimilation, capitulation, and destruction, actions that reflect two seemingly exclusive modes of empowerment: a romantic sublime redefined by contemporary feminist theory as "horizontal"; and the violent, forbidden path of erotic dominance and submission.

Acker's novels contain some of the most stylistically difficult writing of recent times. The narrative voice, as well as the setting in time and place, typeface, page layout, language (portions of ***Blood and Guts*** and ***Empire of the Senseless*** are in Persian) have a fragmented quality; the characters' histories, sex, and even species change without warning or explanation. The aggressive, confrontational intertextuality of her novels is arresting and disturbing: "Kathy Acker" often puts in an appearance, as do many famous works of fiction from the "real" world, such as *Great Expectations, Huckleberry Finn,* the original *Don Quixote,* Lampedusa's *The*

Leopard, Wedekind's *Lulu* plays, William Gibson's *Neuromancer,* and even the love poems of Catullus.

For Kathy Acker is an unashamed plagiarist. Taking the postmodernist axiom of the death of the author to its logical (and absurd) extreme, Acker in "her" ***Don Quixote*** claims to create no new texts, just refiltered combinations of "male texts which weren't hers." If, as Derrida holds, no word can ever be equated to the idea it purports to represent, and if, as Kristeva notes, any "textual segment" is the product of "the intersection of a number of voices, of a number of textual interventions," then any "new" "written" "creation" must be read as an un/conscious recombination/ interpretation of, and capitulation to, previous texts.

Acker's work is a clear and deliberate exploration of these ideas. She not only denies authorship of her material, but she also refuses to let the words she appropriates represent their accepted meanings. By rewriting stolen texts and weaving them into her own explicitly brutal writing, she creates a new kind of language in which meaning—of both the revised/plagiarized novels and the individual words themselves—can only be achieved through context and association. Acker's novels are self-/extra-/ultra-referential, discontinuous, circular, non-linear; that is, they possess all those qualities associated with what Hélène Cixous used to call feminine writing, but what she now calls "a decipherable libidinal femininity which can be read in a writing produced by a male or a female" but which I here will continue to call feminine writing (and by extension) reading.

Acker takes Cixous's concept of "writing the body" very seriously indeed. Her texts are attempts to make the abstract physical through ("through" meaning literally in one side and out the other) the body, giving a visceral form to the feminine writing hypothesized by Cixous and Luce Irigaray. As Abhor, the half black, half robot hero/ine of ***Empire of the Senseless*** says, "It seemed to me that the body, the material, must matter. . . . If my body mattered to me, and what else was any text: I could not choose to be celibate."

Acker's fictional world is one in which civilization's only remaining relationship is one of dominance (and conversely submission), or D/S: dominance over nature, desire, instinct, need, love, another person, culture, or idea. Patriarchy has resulted in a self-aggrandized humanism, in which power comes only with destruction as its and of its other, and women are reduced to and referred to in terms of their most significant physical differentiating characteristic: cunts. The women in this masculinist world, cognizant of their own desires, are nonetheless forced to function as submissive objects in the Freudian dialectic of sexual power and difference.

Janey Smith, the ten-year-old protagonist of ***Blood and Guts,*** is forced away from home when father—who is also her lover, the patriarchy often being represented in Acker by weak, incestuous fathers—finds another woman. Janey flees to New York City, where she joins a gang and is eventually kidnapped and sold to a Persian slave trader, who "t[eaches] her to be whore" and locks her in an empty room with only a pencil and scraps of paper. Janey begins to write:

> It's possible to hate everything that isn't wild and free. . . . My father told me the day after he tried to rape me that security is the most important thing in the world. I told him sex is the most important thing in the world . . . everything in the materialistic society is the opposite of what it really is.

Janey knows what she wants, but she is restrained at every turn. Her language means nothing to the men around her, so she teaches herself Persian and writes love poems to her captor "because she had nothing else to feel"—remembered and exploded lines by Sextus Propertius, and "slave poems":

> List of my slave duties:
>
> (1) Body slavery . . . my body likes sex and rich food and I'll do anything for these.
>
> (2) Mind slavery . . . I live in a partially human world and I want people to think and feel certain ways about me. So I try to set up certain networks, mental-physical, in time and space to get what I want. . . . These networks become history and culture (if they work) and as such, turn against me and take away time and space.

Janey is beginning to fit into the D/S structure. Her captivity engenders desires that can only be fulfilled by an Other, a Master who will recognize her as his Other. Also typical of D/S is Janey's acknowledgement that her "networks" will "take away time and space"—that is, they will eventually allow her to free herself from objectification. At this point, however, Janey is a classic "submissant," craving at once recognition from her Master and freedom from his domination of her.

A submissant, unlike a masochist who receives gratification from being controlled, receives pleasure in being recognized, even if it is as Other, and in the act of allowing his/her boundaries of selfhood to be broached. A strict boundary of Self produces a sense of isolation and makes it difficult to accept another person as real; yet recognition of and by others is necessary for effective human functioning: this is the paradox of Freudian recognition theory and of the D/S relationship. The easiest way out of the paradox is for the dominant partner to assume that the submissant is not autonomous, that they are completely controllable. That they are not is what makes the relationship "work".

In Acker's ***Don Quixote*** the eponymous sixty-year-old heroine comes to understand this paradox just as she is about to undergo an abortion:

> In order to love, she had to find someone to love. "Why," she reasoned to herself, "do I have to love someone in order to love? Hasn't loving a man brought me to this abortion or state of death?
>
> "Why can't I just love?"
>
> "Because every verb to be realized needs its object. Otherwise, having nothing to see, it can't see itself or be. Since love is sympathy or communication, I need an object which is both subject and object: to love, I must love a soul."

Only in higher levels of its development is "Self" defined not only through autonomy but also through communality with others. In the early, arrested state that Acker's fiction explores, the search for Self is exclusionary only. In the Hegelian dialectic of master and slave, self-definition depends on being able to affect others by one's actions. To exist for oneself, one must exist for an Other; in desiring an Other, one seeks to be recognized. One realizes the desire through action, but if the action consumes or destroys the Other, the Other can give no recognition. Thus the alternative is enslavement. In ***Blood and Guts,*** Janey's self-knowledge dawns during her enslavement to the Persian. In ***Don Quixote,*** Quixote, who has named herself k/night in order to be able to love—since only men can love—realizes the hopelessness of the D/S relationship at the end of her first adventure when she writes to herself at the moment of her death:

> For me alone you were born, and I for you. We two are one though we trouble and hurt each other. You're my master and I'm the servant. I'm sick to death because I tried to escape you, love. I yield to you with all my heart or mind. This mingling of our genitals the only cure for sickness. It's not necessary to write or be right cause writing's or being right's making more illusion: it's necessary to destroy and be wrong.

How can Acker's female protagonists reconcile their desires for love and selfhood with their participation in misogynistic, self-abnegating sexual and political relationships in which their only role is Other? How can Acker herself write the body and express her creations in feminine language while operating within a sociosexual and literary discourse that allows only submission as a woman's role? There seem to be two possible answers: to fight domination in order to break away from it and stand alone, or to give in to it.

The erotic component of D/S can be viewed in Georges Bataille's terms as stemming from a maintenance of the violent tension between life and death, or continuity and discontinuity. In other words, the fear of death and dying, coupled with the human attraction to whatever is taboo (and death is the greatest taboo) creates a natural tension. Death is continuity, in that the return to the earth, the actual decay of the body, is a threat to the psychosexual self: how can I be an autonomous being when I am destined to return to the dust? Sexual passion, in Bataille's view, is "a miraculous continuity" in that the boundaries of Self are temporarily dropped when joined with the Other. The erotic attraction of the D/S relationship lies in teasing death. For the submissant, this involves opening up boundaries and approaching continuity; for the dominator, it involves consolidating autonomy by controlling an Other without allowing any of the dominator's own boundaries to be violated. Of course, if the transgression of boundaries goes too far, the result for the submissant is total continuity—that is, death.

It is this total continuity that Acker's protagonists seek through bizarre rituals of self-abnegation and violence. In ***Empire of the Senseless*** Agone, a Cuban sailor who, like all the characters, searches for his selfhood in a world where taboo is unknown, first approaches continuity while getting tattooed by a new method: his flesh is pierced and raised with a knife into a three-dimensional tattoo. During the piercing, Agone identifies the tattooist as his Other and for the first time in his life feels sexual desire. The relationship between the traditional tattooist and his subject is analogous to that between the traditional (male) author and the paper he writes upon.

In Acker's revision, however, the tattooist literally enters the body, not just with a needle, but with a knife. The sexual symbolism is obvious, if the tie to feminine writing is not. Yet after the piercing is complete, Agone's tattoo will consist not only of the raised flesh, but colors and threads run through the piercings themselves. This is "writing the body" in its most precise and extreme form: not writing about or on the body, but *through* it, creating new textures from it and ornamenting them to create a personal and social statement of the body. The irony of the metaphor is that Agone cannot achieve self-knowledge without the aid of an Other, the tattooist, a dominant master to whom Agone entrusts the ultimate violation of physical boundaries—the cutting of his own flesh. Even then, the tattooist does not go to the desired point of total continuity for, as we have seen, total continuity means death.

In Acker's world, getting close to continuity is not enough. To be empowered, her characters must transgress the boundaries of Self even to the point of death and become continuous with *all* life. It is this "all," as Luce Irigaray writes, that is at the heart of feminine writing:

This "all" can't be schematized or mastered. It's the total movement of our body. No surface holds: no figures, lines, and points; no ground subsists. But there is no abyss. For us, depth does not mean a chasm. Where the earth has no solid crust, there can be no precipice. Our depth is the density of our body, in touch "all" over. There is no above/below, back/front, right side/wrong side, top/bottom in isolation, separate, out of touch. Our all intermingles. Without breaks or gaps. . . . Stretching out, never ceasing to unfold ourselves, we must invent so many different voices to speak all of "us," including our cracks and faults, that forever won't be enough time.

Patricia Yaeger interprets Irigaray's words as calling for a new form of literary empowerment, a horizontal "female sublime," which does not involve conquering the Other and internalizing it, as does the traditional romantic sublime. For male poets and novelists, the sublime moment, the sudden influx of power, comes when the Other—be it mountain, animal, demon, or woman—is faced and beaten. The (male) persona identifies with the Other and thus creates a unified ego that, in effect, destroys the Other's otherness.

The horizontal sublime, as its name implies, is not a phenomenon of dominance, but of expenditure. The moment of empowerment is the same, as is the realization that a door has been opened and a new plane of existence is within reach. But in this revised sublime, the Other is allowed to remain alien and sovereign, and the witness does not transcend his/her humanity by becoming "more than human" but instead becomes "more human" through a spreading multiplicity of awareness. Yaeger cities, as an example of the horizontal sublime, "The Fish" (1946) by Elizabeth Bishop, in which the aged, wily fish is captured but released: yet the narrator still becomes empowered by the rainbow that fills her boat. Another example, familiar to most moviegoers, is Obi-Wan Kenobi's death in *Star Wars* (1977). Kenobi turns off his light saber and submits to the dominant Darth Vader, letting his physical boundary be violated unto death—and he is suddenly everywhere within the fabric of the universe.

In Acker's work, the horizontal sublime is used as a way out of the double-bind of patriarchal, D/S society. Language is too implicated in the power structure to be of any use to women, as is sexuality, which is valid only as a component of D/S. Letting go and returning to continuity is the only recourse available. So Janey in *Blood and Guts* develops cancer and is released by the slave trader. She finds a ticket to Tangier in the street, goes there, then wanders the desert in the company of Jean Genet until both are thrown into prison. There Janey, near death, prays: "Please night take over my mind." Night has come to represent to her the final bound-

ary to be broken—not death, or suicide, but that trace second before, when the submissant finally lets go.

Janey gets released from prison and dies in Luxor, Egypt. The novel closes with two pictographic narratives, "The World" and "The Journey," intertextual atlases of objects and movements corresponding to the passage of Janey's soul into the continuum. The narrative becomes non-sequential, discontinuous with what we have read already, with what indeed we might consider narrative at all, unless we read this section as occurring all at once, as the movement of Janey into "all": "Soon many other Janeys were born and these Janeys covered the earth."

Don Quixote, realizing that to search for love through the two ways allowed her—language and sex—is to feed herself into the same D/S machine that keeps her from finding love, escapes herself by "being happy. By embracing and believing myself, just appearances, the night. By embracing, and believing, my deepest being which is not knowing. Therefore my vision has ended." She rejects patriarchal language and logic and trusts only her vision of irrationality and not-knowing, a vision/language that breaks boundaries at the same time as it prevents others from being raised.

In *Empire*, Abhor, like Janey and Don Quixote before her, is imprisoned linguistically and sexually as well as literally. She is eventually freed from literal prison to form her own, one-cyborg motorcycle gang. In this world without patriarchy and taboo, she creates chaos by attempting to drive on the highway according to the rules of the Highway Code, computing stopping distances and measuring speed while other vehicles crash all around her. She is metaphorically learning the codes of a language that has no semantics to accommodate her. Just as Acker explodes patriarchal language by reinventing/plagiarizing its sacred texts, so Abhor's actions reveal the fundamental uselessness of any male code to express a specifically female experience. That both Acker and Abhor reject the spirit of the codes while working within the letter of them is one more form of capitulation, but a reasoned capitulation that is subversive in intent.

Destroying the myth of difference has been an important goal of contemporary feminist theory for to define female language, sexuality, and spirituality only as that which is not male reinforces the sexist binary dialectic. Acker's fiction collaborates with this project. Her use of the horizontal sublime in her novels characterized by exploded language and male texts that have been reread, re-experienced, and rewritten, offers a way at once to subvert the power structure, confront the dark side of sexuality, and create a new diegesis of empowerment that acknowledges the role of Other while celebrating the infinite and continuous possibilities of Self.

Ellen G. Friedman (review date Spring 1994)

SOURCE: A review of *My Mother: Demonology*, in *Review of Contemporary Fiction*, Vol. 14, No. 1, Spring, 1994, pp. 213-4.

[*Below, Friedman offers a favorable review of* My Mother: Demonology.]

The themes in Kathy Acker's newest book will not surprise followers of her delirious prose. Schizophrenic juxtaposition again organizes her text. A section entitled "Rape by Dad" begins: "In the following paragraphs I would like to try to highlight various recollections from my childhood. My parents were nevertheless very kind. They never beat me." These sentences are followed by the father's rape of the narrator. Also many of the obsessions that are the signature of her texts recur. A catalog of these would include: *the father as patriarchy:* "For me the past sits in the form, the actuality of the father: I don't want to meet my father. He left me before I was born." *Appropriation of other texts:* One of Acker's little jokes on those who criticize her for plagiarism is that she plagiarizes lines from Eliot's *The Waste Land*— "The Fire Sermon / 'When lovely woman stoops to folly and / Paces about her room again, alone'"—that Eliot had plagiarized from Goldsmith. *Pirates:* "These pirates, a combination of uneducated English, mulattos and gauchos who for many years had been fomenting other forms of discontent . . . couldn't have cared less about political doctrines and indoctrinations." *Contemporary politics:* Here is Bush beginning a speech on abortion: "God, if these masses of flesh that we call *the women of this country*—in particular, my daughter, her blood, this part of me that is diseased, whom I've just raped—were made by You." (Thatcher and Mayor Koch are also characters.) *The body:* "STORYTELLING METHOD: THE ACT OF BODYBUILDING PRESUPPOSES THE ACT OF MOVING TOWARD THE BODY OR THAT WHICH IS SO MATERIAL THAT IT BECOMES IMMATERIAL."

Other obsessions exemplified in the novel include clinically described sex, sadomasochism, incest, detailed body parts, bodily excretions, toilets and toilet paper, tattoos, Catholic school girls in little pleated skirts, and Nazis. Here, as in so many of Acker's books, she depicts a quest for the beyond of identity. Yet rather than seeking that beyond on the other side of culture, as occurs elsewhere in her canon, *My Mother: Demonology* turns at the end suddenly quasi-mystical. Its last line has the narrator seeing "a reflection of [her] face before the creation of the world." Despite the fact that the narrator sees this reflection in a roll of toilet paper, the statement is the closest Acker has come to a discourse of inclusion, to a statement of individual identity in the world. Yet this hesitant, self-mocking affirmation is only a resting place at the end of a text whose tone is better summed up

in its epigraph: "After Hatuey, a fifteenth-century Indian insurrectionist, had been fixed to the stake, his Spanish captors extended him the choice of converting to Christianity and ascending to Heaven or going unrepentantly to Hell. Gathering that his executioners expected to go to Heaven, Hatuey chose the other."

Rod Phillips (essay date Spring 1994)

SOURCE: "Purloined Letters: *The Scarlet Letter* in Kathy Acker's *Blood and Guts in High School*," in *Critique: Studies in Contemporary Fiction*, Vol. 35, No. 3, Spring, 1994, pp. 173-80.

[*In the following essay, Phillips explores the significance of Acker's allusions to Nathaniel Hawthorne's* The Scarlet Letter *in* Blood and Guts in High School.]

In the years since critics first took notice of Kathy Acker, considerable comment has been made on her use of other writers' language and plot lines in her fiction—and rightfully so. Acker has taken literary "borrowing" to its most bizarre extreme. Large portions of her books are undisguised reworkings of earlier writers' fictions; often such passages are used verbatim with no clue as to where the borrowed material ends and Acker's own language begins. Her 1982 work, ***Great Expectations,*** has as the title of its first section a single word: "Plagiarism." The novel's first few lines do indeed live up to the title:

> My father's name being Pirrip, and my Christian
> name Philip, my infant tongue could make of both
> names nothing longer or more explicit than Peter.

In her earlier works, Acker chose to supply her readers with footnotes or authorial credits when she made use of other writers' words; but as her career progressed, she dropped this convention and has since borrowed, paraphrased, and plagiarized from the words and ideas of others with impunity. Ironically, plagiarism—the negation of another writer's trademark—has become one of the most distinctive trademarks of Acker's own fiction.

In fiction as experimental, fragmented, and disorienting as Acker's, these moments of familiar text can provide brief comfort in an otherwise very uncomfortable body of work. As critics, we are trained to look for "keys" to a text's "meaning," such as allusion, influence, and symbol. This is, no doubt, why so many of Acker's critics have made mention of the element of plagiarism in her art. As critics trained in the analysis of more traditional forms of literature, we may feel uncertain of how to approach many aspects of Acker's writing: her multigeneric style, her merging of visual art with text, and her shifting, often unreliable, narration. But we recognize Dickens when we see it (and Hawthorne, and Jong, and Genet), and we feel compelled to make use of these familiar handholds as a way of making meaning within Acker's fictions.

But, unfortunately, most critics have done little more than note that plagiarism is an element in Acker's writing; little analysis has been done of how it functions in her work. Poet and critic Ron Silliman (himself a character in Acker's novel *The Adult Life of Toulouse Lautrec*) has offered an oversimplified equation for what he calls the "persistent formula" for Acker's fiction: "plagiarism + pornography = autobiography." Other critics have been almost as dismissive in their remarks on Acker's borrowings. Larry McCaffery, one of the first critics to deal seriously with Acker's work, also has put forth a rather limited view of the purpose and function of Acker's plagiarism of earlier, more well-known texts:

> Part of the point behind such strategies is to fore-
> ground textual jouissance, to insure that readers per-
> ceive that the "unity" found here is not produced
> by the questionable concept of an authorial ego or
> character "identity," but results from a confronta-
> tion with a consciousness presenting moments in its
> experience-in-practice.

Both critics are correct—at least in part. Acker's plagiarism is, as Silliman suggests, one of the ways in which she talks about her own life. And it is also, just as McCaffery points out, a means of unsettling reader expectations about authorial identity. But there is more to Acker's extensive use of plagiarized material than either critic's explanation can afford.

Acker's 1978 work, *Blood and Guts in High School,* may offer some answers concerning the purposes, and the effects, of her plagiarism. The novel deals with a ten-year old's journey through a dark world whose most distinct features are the absence of love and the presence of sexual perversion. Janey, Acker's protagonist, is the victim of first, her father's incest and second, his rejection. Forced to live on her own in New York City, Janey enters into a life of drugs, gratuitous sex, and violence—culminating in her kidnapping and captivity at the hands of a "Persian slave trader."

Like her other fictions, *Blood and Guts* contains a number of borrowings from other texts and from popular culture. The figures of Erica Jong, Jean Genet, and Jimmy Carter, among others, drift in and out of Acker's text like players in a nightmare. But the authorial presence most clearly felt in the book, except for Acker's of course, is that of Nathaniel Hawthorne. While Janey is being held captive by the Persian slave trader, she lives in total isolation, with no outside contact except for daily visits from her captor—visits in

which she is "taught to be a whore." "One day she found a pencil stub and a scrap of paper in a forgotten corner of the room," Acker writes. "She began to write down her life." What follows is a lengthy section entitled "A Book Report," in which Janey writes, ostensibly at least, about Hawthorne's *The Scarlet Letter.* From the start, however, it is clear that Janey is indeed "writing down her own life" as much as she is engaging in a book report. "We all live in prison," she begins. "Most of us don't know we live in prison."

The question arises: Why select Hawthorne's *Scarlet Letter* as the fictional device with which to describe Janey's life? What qualities make Hawthorne's novel, written over one and a quarter centuries earlier, suitable collage material for Acker's postmodern, punk fiction? One answer, certainly, lies in the similarity of the two protagonists. Both are female outsiders who violate societal rules. Both are victims of male oppression, and both are in some way imprisoned. Most importantly, perhaps, both are "prisoners" of their own desire to be loved.

The popularity and high regard of Hawthorne's novel may suggest a second reason for Acker's use of the book. Few books can be considered to be universally known by Americans, but *The Scarlet Letter* is certainly one of the most widely taught novels in American schools. It follows that if Acker were seeking a work to use as a source of symbol and meaning, she would select a well-known text like Hawthorne's. Beyond this instant recognition, however, Larry McCaffery suggests a more perverse reason for using the novel in Acker's work. He notes the punk penchant for "crossing images together unexpectedly." Often this is done, McCaffery writes: "by profaning, mocking, and otherwise decontextualizing sacred texts (Johnny Rotten blaring out 'God Save the Queen,' . . .) into blasphemous metatexts." *The Scarlet Letter,* with its high position in the canon of American literature, is ripe for this type of approach. What, after all, could be more unexpected than a juxtaposition of Puritan and punk cultures? This may be at the root of Acker's choice of Hawthorne's "sacred text."

Early in her "book report," Acker's Janey engages in the kind of image crossing that McCaffery speaks of. By joining together thumbnail sketches of Hester Prynne's world and Janey's, Acker is able to discuss the current position of women in American society:

> Long ago, when Hawthorne wrote *The Scarlet Let-
> ter,* he was living in a society that was more socially
> repressive and less materialistic than ours. He wrote
> about a wild woman. This woman challenged the
> society by fucking a guy who wasn't her husband
> and having his kid. The society punished her by
> sending her to gaol, making her wear a red 'A' for
> adultery right on her tits, and excommunicating her.

In the next paragraph, Janey abruptly shifts from her "book report" on Hester's life and times and focuses on the realities of her own:

> Nowadays most women fuck around 'cause fucking doesn't mean anything. All anybody cares about today is money. The woman who lives her life according to nonmaterialistic ideals is the wild antisocial monster: the more openly she does so, the more everyone hates her.

Clearly Acker is engaging in social criticism by using the borrowed text as a touchstone for Janey's present reality. By attempting to assimilate Hawthorne's world, Janey tries to understand the forces of history that have led to what she sees as the near collapse of her society:

> The society in which I'm living is totally fucked-up. I don't know what to do. . . . If I knew how society got so fucked-up, if we all knew, maybe we'd have a way of destroying hell. I think that's what Hawthorne thought. So he set his story in the time of the first Puritans: the first people who came to the northern North American shore and created the society Hawthorne lived in, the society that created the one we live in today.

But Acker's use of Hawthorne's text allows for more than just a simple critique of American society; it also gives her a device with which to discuss the powers and the limitations of literature. Locked in her cell-like room, Janey uses a series of images—Hawthorne's novel—to describe her condition, to "write down her life." Soon after, however, she finds a Persian grammar book and begins to learn to write and compose poetry in Persian. The language system of her captor, the Persian slave trader, replaces, for a time at least, the language and plot of Hawthorne's tale. Unstated, but implicit in this plot development, is the idea that we adopt—perhaps without knowing it—the language of our oppressors. Just as the slave trader's grammar book has colored and shaped Janey's thinking, so have Hawthorne and all those who have contributed to the "fucked-up-culture" to which she belongs.

Janey, unlike Acker, seems quite unaware of the power that the literature of her oppressors has over her. She negates the power of the written word—claiming it to be a part of a much older time. Hawthorne, she says, "was living in a society to which ideas and writing still mattered." Janey sees her position as a writer as nearly meaningless—because literature is treated as a commodity:

> Right now I can speak as directly as I want 'cause no one gives a shit about writing or ideas, all any-
> one cares about is money. . . . A book that can be advertised. Define culture that way.
>
> You see, things are much better nowadays than in those dark old repressed Puritan days: anybody can say anything today; progress does occur.

Blind to the power that literature has had over her, Janey believes her own pen to be powerless. Unlike Hawthorne, who had to cloak "all the wild things he wanted to say" because his society valued ideas, Janey can say anything she wants because ideas no longer matter.

Janey's comments on the commodification of literature may point to another reason behind Acker's use of other writers' texts. In a time when the only ideas that count are those that "will net a half-million in movie and/or TV rights," perhaps Acker's borrowings from Hawthorne and other writers is a radical denial of literature as property. McCaffery has noted that deeply ingrained in the punk aesthetic is a distrust of the "conventions which govern traditional artistic forms"—a belief that "the traditions and language of Great Art had derived from the same elitist, authoritative sensibility that had elevated profit and reason at the expense of human needs and feelings." By using Hawthorne or other writers, as the basis for her own text, Acker may be rejecting the notion that art can be turned into property, and in turn may be rejecting the entire system that has tried to do so. Under such a mindset, plagiarism is not stealing because that which cannot be owned cannot be stolen. Words and ideas then, are not property but are free-floating objects that (like the title of the Poe story which I've used as the title for this essay) can be used freely by all.

For Janey, this characteristic punk distrust of literature and culture is an enigma. She faces the Catch 22 of wanting to rail against her culture but finding that she has no means to do so except those that are culturally prescribed (i.e., a book report on Hawthorne). Later, in her "Persian Poems," Janey again faces this problem. One of her poems, written in Persian and translated, reads:

> Culture stinks: books
> and great men and the
> fine arts
> beautiful women

Written in the language of her captors, the poem—like the book report—is a product of the culture that Janey so violently hates.

But the possible reasons for Acker's use of Hawthorne that I've outlined so far—forum for social critique, symbol for male literary dominance, and subject for punk literary anarchy—may prove to be secondary to what I believe to be the main effect realized by the author's borrowings from *The Scarlet Letter*. Above all, I think, the sections of the novel dealing with Hawthorne allow a radical feminist reworking of the story of Hester Prynne—a kind of "taking back" of a woman's story from a male author. By removing the story of Hester Prynne and her daughter Pearl from the limits of Hawthorne's text and placing them in Janey's consciousness, Acker both modernizes and feminizes the novel.

> **By removing the story of Hester Prynne and her daughter Pearl from the limits of Hawthorne's text and placing them in Janey's consciousness, Acker both modernizes and feminizes the novel.**
> —*Rod Phillips*

The *Scarlet Letter* section of the book is not the only part of **Blood and Guts** in which Acker voices the desire to revise male texts along feminist lines. In the section of the novel in which Janey travels with French novelist Jean Genet, she notes a passage from Genet's autobiographical novel *Le Journal du Voleur* in which the author describes his masochistic joy at being "beaten up and hurt" by his male lovers. Janey's response is not one of recognition with her own situation as a woman who has had similar experiences; instead, it is one of disgust at his lack of understanding for the true position of women in a male-dominated culture:

> Genet doesn't know how to be a woman. He thinks all he has to do to be a woman is slobber. He has to do more. He has to get down on his knees and crawl mentally every minute of the day. If he wants a lover, if he doesn't want to be alone every single goddamn minute of the day and horny so bad he feels the tip of his clit stuck in a porcupine's quill, he has to perfectly read his lover's mind, silently, unobtrusively, like a corpse, and figure out at every changing second what his lover wants. He can't be a slave. Women aren't just slaves. They are whatever men want them to be. They are made, created by men. They are nothing without men.

The passage is a telling one concerning the authenticity of texts written by men about women. Genet, although perhaps closer in his experience to what Janey sees as the position of women in society, still lacks the necessary emotional, physical, and social conditioning to portray accurately the experience of being a woman. In Janey's view, Genet has the wrong mind-set, the wrong genitals, and the wrong social status to do anything more than play-act the role of woman.

The type of feminist correction to which Janey submits

Genet's text is also at the heart of her treatment of Hawthorne's novel. The story line of the book is taken back from Hawthorne and his omniscient narrator as Janey and Hester merge in Acker's text. The structure of Acker's text becomes more confused and fragmentary as Janey's isolation and illness change the form of her discourse from a standard high school book report to a hallucinatory stream of consciousness:

> Everything takes place at night.
> In the centres of nightmares and dreams,
> I know I'm being torn apart by my needs,
> I don't know how to see anymore.
>
> I'm too bruised and I'm scared. At this point in *The Scarlet Letter* and in my life politics don't disappear but take place inside my body.

As Janey's assimilation of Hester's character becomes complete, all punctuation that might have separated the quoted material of Hester from Janey's speech disappears. Janey seems to melt into the character of Hester Prynne, voicing openly the desires of the heroine from Hawthorne's novel. But the words she uses also fit her own situation; it is a speech that could be addressed to either Hester's Reverend Dimmesdale or Janey's absent, incestuous father:

> I want to fuck you, Dimwit. I know I don't know you very well you won't ever let me get near you. I have no idea how you feel about me. You kissed me once with your tongue when I didn't expect it and then you broke a date. I used to have lots of fantasies about you: you'd marry me, you'd dump me, you'd fuck me. . . . Now the only image in my mind is your cock in my cunt. I can't think of anything else.
>
> I've been alone for a very long time. I'm locked up in a room and I can't get out. . . . I don't know how to talk to people, I especially have difficulty talking to you; and I'm ashamed and scared 'cause I want you so badly, Dimwit.

Critic Linda Hutcheon has written that the type of postmodern intertextuality that we see in passages such as this is a "manifestation of both a desire to close the gap between past and present for the reader and a desire to rewrite the past in a new context." The two texts—Hawthorne's and Acker's—ricochet off each other, creating, if not great art, at least a brief moment of recognition in the reader's mind concerning their connectedness. Such a text, Hutcheon writes:

> uses and abuses these intertextual echoes, inscribing their powerful allusions and then subverting that

power through irony. In all, there is little of the modernist sense of a unique, symbolic, visionary "work of art"; there are only texts, already written ones.

Clearly, in the section of **Blood and Guts** dealing with Hawthorne, Acker attempts, as Hutcheon says, "to rewrite the past in a new context." But in Acker's novel, such a revision of older texts does not just involve the addition of a feminist subtext or the inclusion of pornographic elements to the original work: it also involves experimentation with language that strives to break free from traditional genres (like the Romantic novel) and move toward a more meaningful form. "TEACH ME A NEW LANGUAGE, DIMWIT," Janey writes, "A LANGUAGE THAT MEANS SOMETHING TO ME."

One passage that illustrates this quest for a "new language" occurs when Janey engages in a "lesson" with another voice in Acker's text. Prefaced with the line "Teach me a new language," the passage involves an exercise in repetition of simple phrases, first uttered, presumably, by a male voice (perhaps Hawthorne's Reverend Dimmesdale) and then repeated by Janey. At first, Janey repeats the lines verbatim; but as the lesson continues, she begins to alter the phrases—subtly at first, and then radically:

"The night is red."

                    "The night is all around
                    me and it's black."
"The streets are deserted."

                    "I can't even see the streets
                    from my room; how would I
                    know if they're deserted?"

The passage is emblematic of the entire section of the novel dealing with Hawthorne. It begins with an acceptance of the male voice (Hawthorne's text) but finally Janey begins to question and ultimately reject the syntax and logic of her teacher's voice. What began as a straightforward exercise in repetition (plagiarism) ends in a complete rejection of authority and a further blurring of "sanity and insanity":

"The children in the city   "How can I tell the
are going insane."   difference between sanity
                                   and insanity? You think in
                                   a locked room there's
                                   sanity and insanity?"

The "new language" that Janey strives for, this departure from the traditional, male-dominated form of the novel (represented by Hawthorne and Dimmesdale), takes many forms in Janey's reworking of *The Scarlet Letter.* Often, her ramblings seem almost incoherent, as in this prose paragraph that melts suddenly into poetry:

Sex in America is S & M. This is the glorification
    of S & M and slavery
and prison. In this society there was a woman who
freedom and suddenly the black night opens up
    and
fucked a lot and she got tied up with ropes and
on upward and it doesn't stop
beaten a lot and made to spread her legs too wide
the night is open space that goes on and on,
this woman got so mentally and physically hurt
not opaque black, but a black that is extension
she stopped fucking even though fucking is the
    thing to do.

On its surface, the poem seems a jumble of images, without any real relation to the rest of the text. But at work here is one of the "new language" systems that Janey speaks of. By reading alternate lines of the poem, a new meaning emerges: one that has considerable relevance to the stories of both Hester and Janey:

In this society there was a woman who
fucked a lot and she got tied up with ropes and
beaten a lot and made to spread her legs too wide
this woman got so mentally and physically hurt
she stopped fucking even though fucking is the
thing to do.

For Kathy Acker, the rejection and subversion of the traditional forms of discourse that have been dominated by males seem as important as the subversion of their meanings. Her fictions may begin with what seem to be borrowings, extensions, or plagiarisms of male works; but they move quickly beyond these original works—into new meanings and new forms that their authors could never have imagined. Larry McCaffery has called Acker's work "fiction to slam dance by." Acker at times also seems to downplay the complexity of her work: "Everything is surface," she writes, "that everything is me: I'm just surface: surface is surface." But her work is more than just "surface," more than just simple "plagiarism," more than just punk "fiction to slam dance by." Acker's **Blood and Guts in High School,** with its strange and complex reworking of Hawthorne, offers a new and powerful perspective on literature and gender in postmodern America.

Alev Adil (review date 14 November 1997)

SOURCE: "Breaking to Build," in *Times Literary Supplement,* November 14, 1997, p. 24.

[*In the following review, Adil offers favorable assessments of* Eurydice in the Underworld *and* Bodies of Work.]

To observe that Kathy Acker's writing refuses to seduce is not to denigrate her work. There is method in her madness; her hysteria is an aesthetic strategy. Her fiction is difficult, driven by an ethical fervour that denies us the pleasures of naturalism and narrative. The reader is so often shouted at that it is easy to become deaf to the sophistication and technical virtuosity with which Acker composes her symphonies of screams. The simultaneous publication of her essays and stories is an opportunity to listen, to reappraise a misunderstood writer.

When *Eurydice in the Underworld,* a collection of Acker's short fictions written between 1981 and 1997, is read in conjunction with the essays and articles in *Bodies of Work,* it is easier to understand both why she writes, and why she writes the way she does. Acker is fearless in seeking to destroy the unifying illusions of subjectivity and narrative. Her critical writing doesn't so much clarify her intentions as mark her place on an intellectual map. Her formal strategies are the aesthetic imperatives of postmodernism. The fractured, halting crudeness of her writing does not mask, but rather displays her knowingness. She is grounded in the linguistic philosophies of Lacan and Lévi-Strauss. Her points of reference are Foucault, Irigaray, Cixous, Deleuze, Guattari and Judith Butler, but she claims her literary descent from the "other tradition" of Sade, Baudelaire, Genet, Bataille, Burroughs and Ballard.

The political charge of Acker's aesthetic comes from the theory that the ideology of patriarchy and capitalism is maintained through the notion of the autonomous subject, that "phallic identity's another scam that probably had to do with capitalistic ownership." For Acker, a subject constructs its identity through exclusion. The dualism of the mind and body calls into play chains of related dualisms (man/woman, white/black, reason/madness). Like Cixous and Irigaray, Acker sees the subversive, liberating possibilities of trying to defy the symbolic economy of language by writing from a place beyond meaning. She celebrates flux, transformation, "the languages of wonder, not of judgment," contradiction, nonsense—because "meaning begins in difference." "Above all: the languages of intensity. Since the body's, our, end isn't transcendence but excrement, the life of the body exists as pure intensity." It is the process and intention involved in making art that matter to Acker, not the artefact. From the Conceptualists she appropriates the idea that "prettiness is, above all, despicable." Ugliness becomes a mark of purity; her search for textual authenticity takes place in an urban landscape where "cold winds sweep over our dead rats; a dead terrorist's heart sits on dog shit. Mutilated police calls. Advertising leaflets spell SOS."

Acker's fiction is as theoretically driven as her essays, but "there is more freedom in fiction." Her writing here is more supple and assured, deftly manipulating bewildering and ver-

tiginous shards of narrative, mythic and modern discourses on the nature of subjectivity and art. **"The Birth of the Poet"** begins in a nuclear power plant in New York at the end of the world, then explores the classical and contemporary relationship between Cynthia the whore and Propertius the poet. We are then faced with a series of disjointed phrases laid out in Arabic script, with its phonetic equivalent and an English translation. Within a sentence Acker evades the reader's complicity, the desire to understand and identify with the world she creates.

Her deconstruction is driven less by the pleasure principle than by the death wish, by the need to destroy old pleasures in order to gain new meanings. Acker disdains novels that strive to entertain. She rejects writing that merely takes pleasure in language as the preserve of privilege, and does not trust stories unless they continually shock or break the rules. Writing that is "violent, even disgusting, upsetting" participates in the "struggle against patriarchy." This can make for tedious reading; a thorn is a thorn is a thorn just as surely as a rose is a rose is a rose. The body is the site of pleasure as well as pain, and her descriptions of such pleasures are often more mechanical or abstract than sensual. The language of orgasm in **"Seeing Gender"** ("clear our forest water animals plants spout up twigs move twigs in lips go down under liquid") is dreamy, but it is removed from both physicality and rationality.

The essay which gives its title to the collection, **"Bodies of Work,"** uses Wittgenstein's concept of the language game to explore body-building. "In order to break down specific areas of muscles, whatever areas one wants to enlarge, it is necessary to work these areas in isolation up to failure." The body-builder's musculature and the avant-garde artist's use of theory can both be defensive, constructing a carapace, a body of work that repels criticism, intimacy, penetration. But Acker is not guilty of this. She lays herself on the line, writing on the body as well as with it. Her body has both a textual and a physical presence. It is the place where culture and nature meet; a site of contradiction, strong yet vulnerable, pierced, tattooed, scarred—and yet soft, penetrable, mortal.

The criteria for judging the success and failure, the limits of her writing, assert conflicting demands. Acker is no Scheherazade, subverting through seduction; she is a Cassandra, a furious prophet. She values urgency and intensity over aesthetics, and yet in her story **"Eurydice in the Underworld"** her writing is an urgent and beautiful discourse on death. Like all her work, it is a difficult, intelligent and formally inventive fiction. Eurydice lies on the operating table, her navel and tongue piercings taped to avoid electrocution, awaiting a mastectomy. Her journey through cancer and love is a *bricolage* of texts, plays, diaries, letters and dream-like communications from the Underworld. Faced with the implacable certainty of death, Eurydice's hope is salvation through love. The intimate domestic narrative of illness and of the failure of a love affair is mirrored through myth: Orpheus abandons Eurydice to the Underworld.

In the essay **"Critical Languages,"** Acker quotes Hannah Arendt on the need to write as though addressing a friend. At times, Acker's writing shouts as at a dazed, uncomprehending child. But in her work she makes important observations about ways of saying and seeing. The integrity and beauty of her writing become apparent when, as in **"Eurydice in the Underworld,"** she addresses the reader with a fierce intelligent intimacy, as a friend.

FURTHER READING

Criticism

Baker, Phil. "Dealing With Being Human." *Times Literary Supplement* (26 October 1990): 1146.
    A generally unfavorable assessment of *In Memoriam to Identity.*

Brennan, Karen. "The Geography of Enunciation: Hysterical Pastiche in Kathy Acker's Fiction." *Boundary 2* 21, No. 2 (Summer 1996): 243-68.
    Explores elements of parody, postmodern pastiche, and female authorial presence in Acker's fiction.

Brown, Terry. "Longing to Long: Kathy Acker and the Politics of Pain." *LIT: Literature Interpretation Theory* 2, No. 3 (1991): 167-77.
    Examines the significance of nostalgia and female alienation in Acker's fiction.

Hulley, Kathleen. "Transgressing Genre: Kathy Acker's Intertext." In *Intertextuality and Contemporary American Fiction,* edited by Patrick O'Donnell and Robert Con Davis,

pp. 171-90. Baltimore: The Johns Hopkins University Press, 1989.
    Examines the complex synthesis of fiction, art, theater, and autobiography in Acker's fiction.

Redding, Arthur F. "Bruises, Roses: Masochism and the Writing of Kathy Acker." *Contemporary Literature* XXXV, No. 2 (Summer 1994): 281-304.
    Explores themes of suffering, masochism, and self-mutilation in Acker's fiction.

Siegle, Robert. "A Sailor's Life in the Empire of the Senseless." *Review in Contemporary Fiction* 9, No. 3 (Fall 1989): 71-7.
    Provides a critical reading of *Empire of the Senseless.*

Walsh, Richard. "The Quest for Love and the Writing of Female Desire in Kathy Acker's *Don Quixote.*" *Critique: Studies in Contemporary Fiction* XXXII, No. 3 (Spring 1991): 149-68.
    Examines feminist themes in Acker's version of *Don Quixote.*

Interviews

Deaton, Rebecca. "Kathy Acker Interviewed by Rebecca Deaton." *Textual Practice* 6, No. 2 (Summer 1992): 271-82.
    Discussion of higher education, postmodernism, and feminism.

Friedman, Ellen G. "A Conversation with Kathy Acker." *Review of Contemporary Fiction* 9, No. 3 (Fall 1989): 12-22.
    Discussion of *Don Quixote* and Acker's literary influences.

McCaffery, Larry. "An Interview with Kathy Acker." *Mississippi Review* 20, Nos. 1-2 (1991): 83-97.
    Discussion of postmodernism and Acker's literary aims and influences.

Additional coverage of Acker's life and career is contained in the following sources published by Gale: *Contemporary Authors,* **Vols. 117 and 122, and** *Contemporary Authors New Revision Series,* **Vol. 55.**

Lawrence Ferlinghetti
1919-

American poet, novelist, and dramatist.

The following entry presents an overview of Ferlinghetti's career. For further information on his life and works, see *CLC,* Volumes 2, 6, 10, and 27.

INTRODUCTION

To fully consider the impact of Lawrence Ferlinghetti on the American literary scene, it is necessary to look beyond Ferlinghetti's writing. As co-owner of the City Lights bookstore and publishing house in San Francisco's Chinatown, Ferlinghetti the publisher and bookseller helped to firmly establish the Beat school of poetry. He became the leading force in developing and publicizing anti-establishment poetry, distributing the works of such writers as Frank O'Hara, Philip Lamantia, Gregory Corso, Jack Kerouac, and Allen Ginsberg. It was Ferlinghetti's arrest in 1957 on obscenity charges and the subsequent series of trials which brought the Beat movement to the attention of the nation.

Biographical Information

Ferlinghetti was born March 24, 1919, in Yonkers, New York. He received a B.A. in journalism from the University of North Carolina in 1941, a Masters degree from Columbia University in 1948, and a Doctorat de l'Université from the Sorbonne in Paris in 1949. Ferlinghetti served in the naval reserve from 1941 to 1945 and was a Lieutenant Commander during the Normandy invasion. After the war, he worked for *Time* magazine before attending the Sorbonne. He had two children, Lorenzo and Julie, from his marriage to Selden Kirby-Smith in 1951 (divorced 1976). Ferlinghetti moved to San Francisco and taught French from 1951 to 1953. In 1952, along with Peter Martin, he founded City Lights Bookstore, the first all-paperback store in America. In 1955 he established the Pocket Poets Series with the publication of his own collection, *Pictures of the Gone World.* The fourth volume of the Pocket Poets Series, Ginsberg's *Howl and Other Poems,* led to Ferlinghetti's arrest on charges of publishing obscene material. As a result of the trial publicity, Ferlinghetti and Ginsberg became national as well as international figures. *Howl* had started with a modest printing of 1,500 copies; by the end of the trial, 10,000 copies had been printed. The publicity surrounding City Lights started an explosion of other small radical presses. Lawrence Ferlinghetti also became a public figure through his performance poetry. He and Kenneth Rexroth began a series of poetry readings, accompanied by jazz music, in a

San Francisco night club called The Cellar. They felt that jazz, the "outsider music," was an appropriate accompaniment and a viable way of attracting new listeners to poetry. And it was "listeners" they were after: Ferlinghetti repeatedly stated that much of his poetry was designed to be heard, rather than read from the printed page. Yet many critics describe the visual nature of his poems. The broken, fragmentary lines that seem to wander around the page were to many critics as much a part of the poems as the thoughts and feelings they described.

Major Works

Ferlinghetti's first published work, *Pictures of the Gone World* (1955), is largely composed of poems of lyric observation. "Gone" was the Beat equivalent of "hip" or "groovy," but in the poems it also held onto the meaning of something past. His second and most famous work, *A Coney Island of the Mind* (1958), is more satirical, with a surrealistic air to the wording and mixed-up metaphors: ". . . drugged store cowboys and las vegas virgins / disowned indians and cinemad matrons / unroman senators and conscientious non-objectors. . . ." *Her* (1960), his first novel, is an interior monologue narrated by Andy Raffine. Raffine views himself as fallen and fragmented as a result of becoming an orphan at an early age. He has a vision of himself prior to that event as happy and whole, and seeks to recapture that feeling. As an adult, he has developed a vision of a satisfying relationship that includes a sexual component. But the juxtaposition of the idealized relationship with memories of his mother makes his search for that feeling of emotional and sexual wholeness a situation he finds himself unable to consummate. With ironic symbolism, he dies at the feet of a statue of the Virgin Mary. The poems of *Starting from San Francisco* (1961) expand on Ferlinghetti's violation of conventional poetic form, following a predominantly oral style. His plays, a number of which are contained in the volumes *Unfair Arguments with Existence* (1963) and *Routines* (1964), were surreal, experimental drama, with settings and actions that were more symbolic than representational. The resulting development of a less rational, more intuitive form for seeking the meaning behind life's surface is seen in his verse collection, *The Secret Meaning of Things* (1969). Ferlinghetti's populist philosophy, his belief that poetry was for the masses, not the hoarded treasure of the academics, led to his publishing in newspapers many of the poems contained in *Landscapes of Living and Dying* (1979). In his continuing search for a voice that would bring more people back to poetry, many of the poems include references to pop culture in their imagery.

Critical Reception

The critical response to Ferlinghetti's work has been mixed, even within the individual reviews of some critics. In a generally favorable review, John William Corrington describes Ferlinghetti's poetry thus: ". . . one finds a consistent and subtly developed sense of form based not upon rhetorical devices or repetition, but on the analogies between poetry and painting; on the correspondences between written and graphic style; on the metaphorical and actual unity between major art forms." The poems, he says later, ". . . function as artifacts to be experienced, to be *seen,* rather than as verbal cognates for ideas impacted within them." Later in the review, describing Poem 1 from *Pictures of the Gone World,* Corrington says, "It is a paean to woman, to unconscious sexuality, to the art of artlessness—but as a vehicle of idea (in the sense, say, that 'Dover Beach' is a vehicle for Matthew Arnold's concepts) the poem would appear insignificant." In Poem 5, Corrington sees a metaphor for Ferlinghetti's poetry: "This figure who has no mouth, who cannot tell, but must show his meaning, is representative of the painter—and, by logical extension, of the poet as well—. . . ." Many critics focus on the visual nature of Ferlinghetti's poetry. James A. Butler describes Ferlinghetti's work as "projective verse," which he defines in the following way: "The syllable, not the foot or meter, is the building block of

poetry. The syllables thus do not combine into a foot, but into a line . . . Meter and rhyme are therefore unimportant in the line length; the line is determined by those places in which the poet takes, and wants the reader to take, a breath." In Ferlinghetti's first novel, *Her,* themes which recur in most of his major works are already present. Mankind, in Ferlinghetti's world view, is fundamentally self-divided by disunity and limited perception. Gregory Stephenson writes that, "Ferlinghetti's art evolves out of his desire to communicate this vision and to uphold and advocate the cause of unity against disunity, love against power." Ferlinghetti experimented with various ways of communicating this vision, and getting his message to a wider audience. In addition to the poetry readings with jazz accompaniment, he incorporated phrases from other literary works and pop culture images into his poetry. While some critics felt these tactics were effective, others felt it was symptomatic of a lack of invention. Michael Leddy, commenting on the poems of *Wild Dreams of a New Beginning,* wrote that "Ferlinghetti seems the poetic equivalent of the jazz soloist who, for want of invention, quotes fragments of well-known songs, hoping that the audience will be content to congratulate itself on recognizing the sources." Other critics saw the everyday images in Ferlinghetti's poems as central to his message. Gregory Stephenson, incorporating quotes from "The Great Chinese Dragon" from the collection *Starting from San Francisco,* says the dragon ". . . represents 'the force and mystery of life,' the true sight that 'sees the spiritual everywhere translucent in the material world.'" Perhaps what Ferlinghetti wants his reader to do is to see the jazz music and the everyday images and the repetitive references to common culture found in his poems; and then see beyond them to "the spiritual everywhere translucent."

PRINCIPAL WORKS

Pictures of the Gone World (poetry) 1955
Tentative Description of a Dinner Given to Promote the Impeachment of President Eisenhower (poetry) 1958
A Coney Island of the Mind (poetry) 1958
Her (novel) 1960
Berlin (poetry) 1961
Starting from San Francisco (poetry) 1961
Unfair Arguments with Existence (plays) 1963
Routines (play) 1964
To Fuck Is to Love Again (poetry) 1965
After the Cries of the Birds (poetry) 1967
An Eye on the World: Selected Poems (poetry) 1967
The Secret Meaning of Things (poetry) 1969
Tyrannus Nix? (poetry) 1969
Love Is No Stone on the Moon (poetry) 1971
Back Roads to Far Places (poetry) 1972
Open Eye, Open Heart (poetry) 1973

CRITICISM

John William Corrington (essay date 1965)

SOURCE: "Lawrence Ferlinghetti and the Painter's Eye," in *Nine Essays in Modern Literature,* edited by Donald E. Stanford, Louisiana State University Press, 1965, pp. 107-16.

[*In the following essay, Corrington compares the structure of Ferlinghetti's poems to the style of several modern painters.*]

With the gradual ebb of publicity concerning "The Beat Generation," it has become possible, in the last year or so, to read the poetry of Lawrence Ferlinghetti as literature rather than as a portion of an attenuated and faintly ludicrous social documentary. The "Beat" tag, so long an active element, arousing a surprising degree of partisanship among otherwise astute readers, has lapsed at last into the same kind of literary irrelevance as have such relatively meaningless terms as "The Auden Circle" and "The Imagistes." Having survived the onslaughts of *Life* and the *Saturday Review,* the praise of Kenneth Rexroth and the blame of J. Donald Adams, this most recent of literary phenomena and the figures connected with it have become the proper matter of literary criticism. One can, with some hope of objectivity, attempt to discover what meaningful sound may persist in certain "Beat" writing, now that the fury has subsided.

It becomes apparent, I think, to even the most casual reader, that those writers lumped together by news media and popular reviewers under the "Beat" label are, in fact, as distinct from one another as was Baudelaire from Rimbaud, Verlaine from Mallarmé. In the case of Ferlinghetti, one finds it difficult to understand why he has been considered of a kind with his more celebrated contemporaries, Allen Ginsberg and Gregory Corso. While there are marked differences between Ginsberg's poetry and that of Corso, a veritable chasm separates their work from Ferlinghetti's. If Ginsberg can be said to possess form, it is a form based on rhetorical repetition—a form reminiscent of Sears catalogues. Corso's shorter poems are loosely unified even considered as lyrics, and his long poems, for the most part, make use of the same Whitmanesque periods common to Ginsberg's *Howl.* But in Ferlinghetti's poetry, one finds a consistent and subtly developed sense of form based not upon rhetorical devices or repetition, but on the analogies between poetry and painting; on the correspondences between written and graphic style; on the metaphorical and actual unity between major art forms.

In some thirteen poems scattered through *Pictures of the Gone World* and *A Coney Island of the Mind,* Ferlinghetti makes constant reference to painters and sculptors, both ancient and modern. Moreover, even in poems not specifically dealing with or mentioning art and artists, Ferlinghetti betrays his own post-war education in painting and his dependence upon that background by an overwhelming reliance on visual imagery and by creating a series of essentially graphic events which contain little of the ideational and narrative matter expected of a literary work. An example of this nonconceptual poetry is poem **"1"** from *Pictures:*

> Away above a harborful
> of caulkless houses
> among the charley noble chimneypots
> of a rooftop rigged with clothes-
> lines
> a woman pastes up sails
> upon the wind
> hanging out her morning sheets
> with wooden pins
> O lovely mammal
> her nearly naked teats
> throw taut shadows
> when she stretches up
> to hang at last the last of her
> so white washed sins
> but it is wetly amorous
> and winds itself about her
> clinging to her skin
> So caught with arms upraised
> she tosses back her head
> in voiceless laughter
> and in choiceless gesture then
> shakes out gold hair
> while in the reachless seascape spaces
> between the blown white shrouds
> stand out the bright steamers
> to kingdom come

Such a poem, when set against the work of a poet like Dylan Thomas, whose whole artistic orientation was essentially verbal, who clearly did not move from image to language but rather conceived in terms of language itself, becomes readily identifiable as a work moving from a visual conception into the matrix of poetic language. Perhaps a concurrent reading of poem **"1"** from *Pictures* and Thomas's "Altarwise by owl-light" will illustrate the profound distinction between visually and verbally conceived writing.

Ferlinghetti, in his exploitation of the image almost bereft of "idea" as such, follows rather closely upon modern theory developed by major painters. "Subject"—that which a picture is *about*—is of far less significance than composition—what, in fact, because of the painter's shaping genius, the picture *is*. In a sense, the "subject," whether it be a horse, a landscape or a human figure is essentially an excuse for painting, and is hardly to be considered in valuing the picture as a work of art. Speaking of Cézanne, Picasso and the other fathers of Modern Art, Maurice Grosser says, ". . . their subject was art itself—how pictures are built. Their aim was to isolate the essential qualities of character and structure in a picture which make it a work of art."

> **Ferlinghetti, in his exploitation of the image almost bereft of "idea" as such, follows rather closely upon modern theory developed by major painters.**
> —*John William Corrington*

Grosser mentions James Joyce and Gertrude Stein as poets who, following the painters, took composition as their subject matter. He compares two Stein poems, suggesting that "Portrait of F. B." and "Rooms" have "the same cadences and the same shape." He concludes: "But the actual words used in the two poems are completely different. This is exactly the sort of thing a painter of the time might have done—different versions of the same composition constructed with different still-life objects or with different colors." Had Grosser a wider acquaintance with modern poetry, he might have found more felicitous examples of this similarity in the work of Stephane Mallarmé, certain of Ezra Pound's early poems, or Federico Garcia Lorca's *Poet in New York*. However, Grosser makes clear that "subject" has become increasingly irrelevant in contemporary art. In the case, for example, of abstract expressionism, the subject has, in James Joyce's phrase, been "refined out of existence," leaving behind an artifact, an object which, rather than containing a rational complexus to be comprehended by a viewer, is an esthetic ikon to be apprehended. There is no idea to be extracted from a canvas in the abstract expressionist mode; rather the picture is constructed to produce a response in one looking at it. By analogy, those poems of Ferlinghetti's which we are discussing—like many of Mallarmé's, Pound's, Lorca's, and Rimbaud's—are not concerned with ideas, themes, narrations, conceptualizations, but rather with the representation of events and entities in such a way as to evoke a response or a series of responses in the reader. After reading poem **"1"** from *Pictures* it would seem difficult to explicate the poem except in terms of its graphic significance. It is a paean to woman, to unconscious sexuality, to the art of artlessness—but as a vehicle of idea (in the sense, say, that "Dover Beach" is a vehicle for Matthew Arnold's concepts) the poem would appear insignificant.

In poem **"5"** from *Pictures,* Ferlinghetti speaks of

> . . . this man who was all eyes
>   had no mouth
>   All he could do was show people
> what he meant
>   And it turned out
>   he claimed to be
>   a painter
>   But anyway
>   this painter
>   who couldn't talk or tell anything
>   about what he
>   meant
>   looked like just about the happiest painter
>   in all the world
>   standing there
>   taking it all "in"
>   and reflecting
>   Everything
>   in his great big
>   Hungry Eye. . . .

Departing from the "pure poetry" we have been discussing, Ferlinghetti turns his hand to theoretical matters. This figure who has no mouth, who cannot tell, but must show his meaning, is representative of the painter—and, by logical extension, of the poet as well—who chooses to work outside the limitations of "subject" ordinarily expected and traditionally called for. I suspect the absence of a mouth in Ferlinghetti's "happiest painter" refers not to the muteness of painting, but rather to its refusal to limit its dealings to the logical and narrative, to the merely anecdotal. In this sense, the modern poet, like the painter, frequently has no mouth. Both take in the world through their "Hungry Eyes." But neither limits himself to phenomena: what is taken in is not simply reproduced on canvas or framed in words. The artist's eye is not, in Grosser's phrase, "the innocent eye of the camera." Rather, the world is dissected, sorted, manipulated, and recreated in terms of the artist's vision—which, a Hungry Eye indeed, devours in order to create.

It should be noted that, as I have suggested above, there are numerous figures antedating Ferlinghetti whose work, whether based in the same theory or not, bears considerable resemblance to the "pure poetry" found in *Pictures* and *Coney Island.* To quote a few of these, with the purpose of emphasizing the visual orientation of this earlier work, one might begin with Rimbaud: "The cascade resounds behind light-opera huts. Candelabra extend out through the orchards and alleys of the neighboring labyrinth,—the greens and reds of the setting sun. Horace nymphs with First Empire coiffures. Siberian rounds, and Boucher's Chinese ladies." Compare the descriptive nature of Rimbaud's brief prose-poem with poem **"17"** from *Pictures:*

> Terrible
>   a horse at night
>   standing hitched alone
>   in the still street
>   and whinnying
>   as if some sad nude astride him
>   had gripped hot legs on him
>   and sung
>   a sweet high hungry
>   single syllable

In each poem it is the figurative which dominates; both poems function as artifacts to be experienced, to be *seen,* rather than as verbal cognates for ideas impacted within them. Again, precisely the same sort of function is discovered in a number of Pound's early poems—though in less sophisticated and self-conscious form:

> The apparition of these faces in the crowd;
> Petals on a wet, black bough.

Here, as in Rimbaud's poem, as in poem **"17,"** we find the poet moving from a *seen* reality—a festive sunset occasion in Rimbaud's poem; a group of people awaiting the subway in Pound's; a horse hitched alone in Ferlinghetti's—to an unseen but still visual re-creation of the seen in the poetic imagination. The pictorial nature of the imaginative extensions is not altered by the fact that Pound shapes a kind of one-for-one relation between fact and creation (faces = petals; station platform = bough) and Ferlinghetti superimposes his "sad nude" simile upon the actual horse.

Charles Mauron, in discussing the poetry of Mallarmé, finds it necessary to use metaphors of painting in order to explain the "obscurity" of the work: "The poet certainly wishes to avoid sharp contours, but, like Renoir, will have rich and full color nonetheless." Again, Mallarmé "had in him something of the great 'baroque' artists: a passion for vast wave-like diagonals, for sentences running from end to end of the work." In the same volume, Roger Fry discusses Mallarmé's creative method:

> . . . with Mallarmé the theme is frequently as it were broken to pieces in the process of poetic analysis, and is reconstructed not according to the relations of experience but of pure poetical necessity. In this he anticipated by many years the methods of some Cubist painters.

Thus, Fry suggests, there is no limit to the violence the poet or painter may do to a given "subject." The artist's "Hungry Eye" absorbs, and what is projected by his inner vision

will be an autonomous object: ". . . as in painting, so in poetry, you can do as you please," Wallace Stevens puts it.

Continuing this brief chronology of Ferlinghetti's antecedents, one cannot overlook the work of Garcia Lorca. Celebrated by younger writers because of his tragic death in the Spanish Civil War, Lorca's *Poet in New York* has been profoundly influential on contemporary American poetry. And Lorca, like Ferlinghetti, was possessed of a singularly "Hungry Eye":

> Blood fell on the mountains, and angels went in
>   search
>   of it,
> but their chalices held only wind; blood spilled
>   from
>   their shoe-tops, at last.
> Lame dogs puffed at their pipes, and the smell of
>   hot
>   leather
> was gray on the circling lips of those who vomit
>   on
>   street-corners. . . .

Angel del Rio considers Lorca's later poetry as purely visual in form. "In a certain sense," del Rio says, "Lorca was more surrealist than the surrealists." Del Rio is conscious of Lorca's derivations from painting techniques in the poems that make up *Poet in New York:* " . . . the similarity in imagery between some of Lorca's poems and Dali's paintings . . . is such that no better illustrator could have been found for *Poet in New York* than the Catalonian creator of the 'surrealist object.'"

On this question of Ferlinghetti's antecedents among poets whose work was conceived and executed within the frame of modern painting's theory, there remains one further example to point out. It would be difficult to find a piece of modern poetry more completely visual than this:

> fandango of shivering owls souse of evil-omended
> polyps scouring brush of hairs from priest's tonsures
> standing naked in the middle of the frying-pan—
> placed upon ice cream cone of codfish fried in the
> scabs of his lead-ox heart—his mouth full of cinch-
> bug jelly of his words—sleighbells of the plate of
> snails braiding guts—little finger in erection neither
> grape nor fig—commedia dell'arte of poor weav-
> ing and dyeing of clouds—beauty creams from the
> garbage wagon—rape of maids in tears and in sniv-
> els—on his shoulder the shroud stuffed with sau-
> sages and mouths—rage distorting the outline of the
> shadow which flogs his teeth driven in the sand and
> the horse open wide to the sun which reads it to the

flies that stitch to the knots of the net full of an-
chovies the sky-rocket of lilies. . . .

It is to be expected that a prose-poem by Pablo Picasso
would be a flood of imagery. The poem was written during
the Spanish Civil War as Picasso prepared a set of sketches
to be called *The Dreams and Lies of Franco.* It illustrates,
with considerable power, a kind of reversal, a feed-back from
artist to poetry. As Ferlinghetti and his predecessors have
drawn both method and conception from the graphic arts,
so the most distinguished of modern painters makes use of
poetry in order to sketch, as it were, a schema for drawings
which he plans.

Perhaps none of Ferlinghetti's poems so fully exploits the
method and the shape of a modern painting—and at the same
time the form of Picasso's poem and subsequent drawings—
as does his poem "6" in *Pictures:*

> And the Arabs asked terrible questions
> and the Pope didn't know what to say and the
>   people
> ran around in wooden shoes asking which way
>   was the
> head of Midas facing and everyone said
>
>   No instead of Yes
>
>   While still forever in the Luxembourg
> gardens in the fountains of the Medicis were the
>   fat red goldfish and the fat white goldfish
>   and the children running around the pool
>   pointing and piping
>
>   *Des poissons rouges!*
>   *Des poissons rouges!*
>
>   but they ran off
> and a leaf unhooked itself
>   and fell upon the pool
>   and lay like an eye winking
>   circles
> and then the pool was very
>   still
>   and there was a dog
>   just standing there
>   at the edge of the pool
>   looking down
>   at the tranced fish
>   and not barking
>   or waving its funny tail
> or
>   anything
>   so that
>   for a moment then

>   in the late November dusk
> silence hung like a lost idea
>   and a statue turned
>   its head

It would seem clear that in Ferlinghetti's mind—and perhaps
in Picasso's, too—there is no real or substantive distinction
between the act of painting and that of making poetry. Technical differences are simply problems to be overcome—but
the modern poem, like the modern painting, must be conceived in terms of composition, not in terms of subject matter. The poem is shaped by what Roger Fry, as noted above,
calls "poetical necessity"—the poem's form shapes its own
requirements. The same holds true of painting. "I have never
made trials or experiments," Picasso has said. "Whenever I
had something to say, I have said it in the manner in which
I felt it ought to be said." Thus we have a poet who calls
his poems "Pictures," and a painter who "says" things with
his brush.

> **Ferlinghetti has produced a poetry in
> which handling of object attempts to
> replace "subject" in significance, a poetry
> which must be apprehended and
> experienced as cultural event rather than
> as subject-verb-object reportage of
> "reality."**
> —*John William Corrington*

Insofar as prose statement may be required, Ferlinghetti has
not stinted in its use. Indeed, his most recent work has suffered from an almost journalistic flatness, a regrettable lack
of the brilliant imagery found in *Pictures* and in much of
Coney Island. But if the poetry of "reportage," in E. M.
Forster's phrase, should fail to match his vision, Ferlinghetti
has had at his command the further resources of the painter's
eye and the painter's wide-ranging, inclusive theory:

> Don't let that horse
>   eat that violin
>   cried Chagall's mother
>   But he
>   kept right on
>   painting
> And became famous
> And kept on painting
>   The Horse With Violin In Mouth
> And when he finally finished it
> he jumped up upon the horse
>   and rode away
>   waving the violin
> And then with a low bow gave it
> to the first naked nude he ran across

And there were no strings
                    attached

If Marc Chagall, in poem **"14"** from *Coney Island,* serves as an epitome of the painter (as does Picasso in another poem—**"24"** in *Pictures:* "but that night I dreamt of Picasso / opening doors and closing exits / opening doors and closing exits in the world . . ."), then Lawrence Ferlinghetti may well stand as an epitome of the modern poet. Ferlinghetti, like Kenneth Patchen's "impatient explorer who invents a box in which all journeys may be kept," has ranged into the deep space beyond limiting canons of literature and has created a provocative and significant body of poetry which, while based in the tradition extending from the Symbolistes through Lorca, manipulating theory and technique born with modern painting, is nevertheless still experimental and tentative. Ferlinghetti has produced a poetry in which handling of object attempts to replace "subject" in significance, a poetry which must be apprehended and experienced as cultural event rather than as subject-verb-object reportage of "reality." Perhaps Ferlinghetti himself has best described the sort of thing he has attempted. In poem **"13"** from *Coney Island,* he tells how he would "paint" . . . "a different kind / of Paradise,"

        . . . there would be no anxious angels telling
    them
            how heaven is
                the perfect picture of

                    a monarchy

    and there would be no fires burning
            in the hellish holes below
            in which I might have stepped
    nor any altars in the sky except
                fountains of imagination

James A. Butler (review date Spring 1966)

SOURCE: "Ferlinghetti: Dirty Old Man?," in *Renascence,* Vol. 8, Spring 1966, pp. 115-23.

[*After an analysis of Ferlinghetti's style and subject matter, Butler suggests that Ferlinghetti has the talent and vision to rise above the restrictive label of "beat poet" and become a more "universal" poet.*]

The public first began to suspect Lawrence Ferlinghetti was a dirty old man in 1955, when he published through his own City Lights Press his poetic *Pictures of the Gone World.* This first volume identified Ferlinghetti with the "Beat Generation Poets"—Allen Ginsberg, Jack Kerouac, Gregory

Corso, and others—none of whom a girl could comfortably bring home to meet the family. The public's dirty-old-man suspicions were heightened when Ferlinghetti was tried in a 1957 obscenity case for publishing Ginsberg's "Howl." Finally, Ferlinghetti's fame for filthiness was assured by a 1965 *Time* article describing a "happening" at the American Students and Artists Center in Montparnasse: "Beat Poet Lawrence Ferlinghetti intoned his latest work while a naked couple made love vertically in a burlap bag, black light playing on their shoulders."

It is tempting to merely categorize Ferlinghetti as a bush-league sick poet of a sick poetic movement, but several factors make this poet worthy of consideration. His major work, *A Coney Island of the Mind* (1958), is now in its twelfth printing and has sold 130,000 copies to rank near the top of contemporary poetic best-sellers. In addition, *Coney Island* was received as "highly readable and often very funny" by *The New York Times* and as having "something of the importance 'The Waste Land' had in 1922," (*Library Journal*). Finally, if a man may be known by the company he keeps, it is significant that the 1965 Spoleto Festival of Two Worlds presented poetry readings by Russia's Yevgeny Yevtushenko, Stephen Spender, Ezra Pound, and Lawrence Ferlinghetti.

In the light of Ferlinghetti's popularity, it is necessary for the critic to determine whether the poet is a best-selling one because of his somewhat scandalous vocabulary and somewhat more scandalous activities, or whether there is intrinsic value in the poetry. The method of this paper is to first develop an evolving understanding of the poetic devices of Ferlinghetti by examining selected instances. The poet's philosophy of a "street poetry" will next be discussed to determine whether Ferlinghetti accomplishes his end. After the above considerations, an attempt will be made to reconcile the dirty old man and the poet.

The first Ferlinghetti poem to be analyzed is from *Coney Island* (No. 25):

    Cast up
            the heart flops over
                    gasping 'Love'
        a foolish fish which tries to draw
            its breath from flesh of air

        And no one there to hear its death
                    among the sad bushes
            where the world rushes by
                in a blather of asphalt and delay

Perhaps the first thing that strikes the reader in the above poem by Ferlinghetti is the absence of traditional poetic devices: rhyme, meter, uniform left-hand margin. Ferlinghetti's free verse is, of course, indebted to such prosodic pioneers as Walt Whitman and especially William Carlos Williams:

> IT IS MYSELF,
>   not the poor beast lying there
>   yelping with pain
>   that brings me to myself with a start—
>   as at the explosion
>   of a bomb, a bomb that has laid
> all the world waste,

"To a Dog Injured in the Street" (W. C. Williams)

In addition to being influenced by Williams' free verse, Ferlinghetti also shows in other poems that he has absorbed some of the visual effects of Williams; e.g., the line visually accentuating the meaning:

> And the way the bell-hop runs downstairs:
>   ta tuck a
>   ta tuck a
>   ta tuck a
>   ta tuck a
>   ta tuck a

(*Paterson*—W. C. Williams)

> like
>   a
>   ball
>   bounced
>   down steps

(*Coney Island,* No. 22)

But these influences on Ferlinghetti's prosody, although important, are not dominant; it is rather the "Projective Verse" of Charles Olson that has not only influenced Ferlinghetti, but has become the new poetics of the new poetry.

> **Ferlinghetti does not, in spite of unconventional metrics, operate independently of poetic tradition.**
> —*James A. Butler*

Charles Olson's "Projective Verse" first appeared in *Poetry New York* of November 3, 1950. Summary of this complex essay is difficult, but basically Olson says that "form is never more than an extension of content." The syllable, not the foot or meter, is the building block of poetry. The syllables thus do not combine into a foot, but into a line. The length of this line comes only from "the *breathing* of the man who writes at the moment he writes." Meter and rhyme are there-

fore unimportant in the line length; the line is determined by those places in which the poet takes, and wants the reader to take, a breath. Ferlinghetti has much the same philosophy of sound:

> The printing press has made poetry so silent that
> we've forgotten the power of poetry as oral
> messages. The sound of the streetsinger and the
> Salvation Army speaker
> is not to be scorned. . . .

The application of the "projective verse" theory is evident in the first poem selected for analysis. The breathing stops are so placed as to emphasize various lines. The first line, for example, "Cast up," receives very strong stress from the breath taken both before and after. Other short lines also receive stress through breathing: "gasping 'Love'," and "among the sad bushes." On the other hand, the longer lines pound quickly, partly because of the strong, regular, iambic rhythm and partly because of the harsh, spitting *t*'s, *b*'s, *d*'s and *f*'s:

> a *f*oolish *f*ish which *t*ries *t*o *d*raw
> *it*s *b*reath *f*rom *f*lesh *of* air

Throughout the poem, the line length and breathing are not used randomly as may first appear, but to accentuate the meaning.

Ferlinghetti does not, in spite of unconventional metrics, operate independently of poetic tradition. His entire poem is, of course, a metaphor comparing a fish out of water with a heart in love. The lines quoted immediately above represent a highly sophisticated use of metaphor: a heart in love that tries to exist from flesh is as helpless as a fish gasping for air. On the audio level, Ferlinghetti in this poem shows his competence at matching sound and meaning. One example of this skill is the explosive sounds (*t*'s, *b*'s, *d*'s, and *f*'s) used in the line above which through the explosion of sound, then unstressed syllable, then another explosion suggest breathlessness and gasping for air. "Gasping" in 1.3 is in itself onomatopoetic. The only true rhyme in the poem, the feminine rhyme of bushes and rushes, draws our attention to the pun on the meaning of rushes as plants. Finally, the last line plays with the *a* sound in a manner reminiscent of the slant rhymes of Yeats, Auden, Thomas, and Owen. The *a*'s are all short vowels and move quickly to suggest the speed of which the poet speaks until the last, long *a* of "delay" slows the tempo:

> in *a* bl*a*ther of *a*sph*a*lt *a*nd del*a*y.

We have seen in this poem how Ferlinghetti works with a modern prosody based on Whitman, Williams, and Olson. The poet is, in addition, a master of audio effects and in matching sound and meaning. Ferlinghetti also seems to delight in the pun by deliberately drawing attention to it. The following poem (*Coney Island*—**No. 14**) should reinforce those conclusions and add others:

> Don't let that horse
>   eat that violin
> cried Chagall's mother
>   But he
> kept right on
>   painting
> And became famous
> And kept on painting
>   The Horse With Violin In Mouth
> And when he finally finished it
> he jumped up upon the horse
>   and rode away
>   waving the violin
> And then with a low bow gave it
> to the first naked nude he ran across
>
> And there were no strings
>   attached

Here Ferlinghetti is seen in a more playful vein than in the previous selection. The projective verse is again used for startling emphasis; e.g. "painting" in 1.6 and "attached" in 1.17. But the onomatopoetic use of syllable is not as prominent in this more humorous offering. The lines are kept quick-moving—in accordance with the light tone of the poem—by a majority of short vowels and short lines.

The reference by Ferlinghetti to something such as Chagall's "The Horse With Violin in Mouth" is typical of the poet. Much of Ferlinghetti's work is predicated on the reader's familiarity with culture, both past and present. In the twenty-nine short poems of *Coney Island of the Mind,* the poet refers, directly or indirectly, to Goya, Cervantes, Thoreau, Keats, T. S. Eliot, Hieronymous Bosch, Dante, Kafka, Longfellow, Stockton ("The Lady or the Tiger?"), Cellini, Picasso, Hemingway, Shakespeare, Proust, Lorca, Nichols (*Abie's Irish Rose*), Tolstoy, Freud, and Joyce. Sometimes the entire meaning of a Ferlinghetti poem is based on the reader's ability to recognize a famous line out of context, e.g., Keats' "silent upon a peak in Darien." Obviously, this heavy reliance on cultural allusions somewhat limits Ferlinghetti's audience and will have major implications in regard to his "street poetry."

Ferlinghetti has a strong sense of humor as is evident both in this poem and in several others, notably one which describes the secular excitement of the erecting of a Saint Francis statue, with all the reporters and workers and Italians, "while no birds sang." In the Chagall poem, Ferlinghetti relies on the pun for humorous effect: "bow" meaning both

a violin's bow and a bending of the body; "ran across" meaning both run under the horse's hooves and met in passing; and, "no strings attached" referring to the violin and to a gift. The linking of two synonymous words to create an enhanced meaning is also a favorite Ferlinghetti trick. In this poem, he uses "naked nude" for double emphasis; elsewhere he employs such figures as "sperm seed." By such puns and double emphases, Ferlinghetti is clearly trying to combat American semiliteracy, where all read but few stop to understand. Another method this poet uses to stop the reader in his tracks and make him go back to think is the twisting of a familiar saying so that it sounds much the same but means far more. Of several dozen examples, representative effects of this kind include the following: drugged store cowboys; cinemad matrons; unroman senators; conscientious non-objectors; [Christ hanging on the cross] looking real Petered out; My country tears of thee; I hear America singing / in the yellow pages; televised Wise Men / praised the Lord Calvert Whiskey; [Santa Claus] bearing sacks of Humble Gifts from Saks Fifth Avenue.

This second poem thus clearly reveals two more characteristics of Ferlinghetti's work: 1) The poet is heavily dependent on cultural allusions; and, 2) the poet attempts his humorous effects through puns, double emphasis, and changed clichés.

The following poem will be the last considered before turning to an analysis of Ferlinghetti's "street poetry" and an overall evaluation of the poet.

> Constantly risking absurdity
>   and death
>   whenever he performs
>   above the heads
>   of his audience
>
>   the poet like an acrobat
>   climbs on rime
> to a high wire of his own making
> and balancing on eyebeams
>   above a sea of faces
>   paces his way
>   to the other side of day
> performing entrechats
>   and sleight-of-foot tricks
> and other high theatrics
>   and all without mistaking
>   any thing
>   for what it may not be
>
> For he's the super realist
> who must perforce perceive
>   taut truth
> before the taking of each stance or step

in his supposed advance
toward that still higher perch
where Beauty stands and waits
with gravity
to start her death-defying leap

And he
and a little charleychaplin man
who may or may not catch
her fair eternal form
spreadeagled in the empty air
of existence

(*Coney Island*—No. 15)

Like many of Ferlinghetti's poems, this one shows an eye for the commonplace. Elsewhere he speaks of "The penny candy store beyond the El / . . . jelly beans . . . / and tootsie rolls / and Oh Boy Gum," but here he compares a poet and a trapeze artist. Much of the skill of the poem is in this comparison as a detailed prose retelling should demonstrate.

The poem begins with the statement that the poet, like the acrobat, risks absurdity and death "whenever he performs / *above the heads* / of his audience" (italics mine). The acrobat risks actual death because he is performing at a great height from the ground, while the poet risks literary death when he writes at a higher intellectual level than that to which his audience is accustomed. Like the acrobat, the poet climbs to the high wire to perform, but the poet climbs on rhyme. In his performance, the acrobat balances on steel I-beams, but also figuratively on the "eyebeams" of the spectators below. The poet also performs before eyebeams, the eyebeams of those reading his poems. Both the acrobat and poet do "sleight-of-foot tricks": the acrobat walking the high wire and the poet dealing with another kind of foot—iambic, trochaic, etc. The "high theatrics" of the acrobat are literally high above the ground, but the poet's actions are figuratively "high theatrics." Both the acrobat and the poet must, of necessity, perceive "taut truth" for if the acrobat's wire is not truly taut, he will fall; and if the poet does not see tightly-drawn truth, he will not succeed. This "taut truth" is necessary before the acrobat takes his "stance" (mode of standing) and before the poet takes his "stance" (intellectual or emotional attitude). The comparison continues with the acrobat waiting to catch his leaping female partner in that traditional trick of the high wire, while the poet tries to catch not a beautiful girl, but Beauty itself. Both the girl and Beauty jump and may or may not be caught by the acrobat and poet.

The mechanics of this poem again admirably enhance the meaning. The projective verse is used for heavy emphasis at crucial points (taut truth) and to visually and vocally correspond to the sense of the words:

where Beauty stands and waits
with gravity
to start her death-defying leap

In these lines, the spacing suggests a sudden drop and, in addition, the excitement of the last line is metrically shown by increased speed since it is a long line coming after a shorter one. Although the metaphors of the poem are all well made, perhaps the best is the picture of the poet trying to catch Beauty as "a little charleychaplin man". This metaphor conveys the perfect picture of a man—hands at his sides and a deadpan expression on his face—running helplessly in circles. In this poem, Ferlinghetti caught Beauty.

With some idea of Ferlinghetti's characteristics in mind, the philosophy of the poet will now be considered in order to determine whether he reaches his personally-set goals. This philosophy was quoted in *Poetry* of November, 1958:

I have been working toward a kind of *street poetry* . . . to get poetry out of the inner esthetic sanctum and out of the classroom into the street. The poet has been contemplating his navel too long, while the world walks by. The printing press has made poetry so silent that we've forgotten the power of poetry as oral messages. The sound of the street-singer and the Salvation Army speaker is not to be scorned. . . .

In evaluating Ferlinghetti's success, or lack of it, with poetry for all, three characteristics of "street poetry" should be considered. First, poetry for all the people should be *lively, rhythmic,* and *iterative.* The advertising jingle would be an example of those traits, as would Vachel Lindsay's successful "popular poetry":

Booth led boldly with his big bass drum—
(Are you washed in the blood of the Lamb?)
The Saints smiled gravely and they said: "He's come."
(Are you washed in the blood of the Lamb?)

Second, popular poetry should be *narrative* as in the ballad or in Lindsay's poem narrating General Booth entering heaven. Third, poetry for all should contain allusions *familiar* to nearly all.

Consideration of Ferlinghetti's poetry in regard to those three points shows definitely that his lines are not "street poetry." In the first place, Ferlinghetti's poetry is mostly tuneless, arhythmic, and hard to remember. Without the printing press, the heavy beat, repetitiveness, and alliteration of Lindsay's lines would make them easy to remember. In contrast, the following lines by Ferlinghetti offer little aid to memorization and are hardly likely to be on the tip of everyone's tongue:

> We squat upon the beach of love
> among Picasso mandolins struck full of sand
> and buried catspaws that know no sphinx
> and picnic papers
> dead crabs' claws
> and starfish prints

> (*Coney Island*—No. 24)

Secondly, few of Ferlinghetti's poems have a narrative content, as the representative poems selected for analysis show. In regard to the third requirement—familiar allusions—the twenty literary and artistic references mentioned above of this paper are allusions generally specialized to the more widely-read of the populace. Indeed, if an entire poem hangs on a line from Keats or a reference to Kafka, it is not a "street poem."

There is one other trait sometimes found in popular poetry— the erotic—that leads to the consideration of Ferlinghetti as a dirty old man. As might be expected of a dirty old man, Ferlinghetti places prominently last in *Coney Island* a poem that maintains, in a style and vocabulary similar to the conclusion of *Ulysses,* that all is sex and sex is all. Nevertheless, the reputation of Ferlinghetti as an erotic poet is exaggerated—only five of the twenty-nine poems of *Coney Island* have sexual themes. In spite of such description of himself as "the poet obscenely seeing," Ferlinghetti's poems do not show as a dominant trait the ribaldness that to many seems to characterize his personal life.

Turning from the dirty old man to the poet, the poems selected for analysis show that there is great intrinsic value in Mr. Ferlinghetti's lines. The poem containing the dying fish—love metaphor, for example, demonstrates the poet's capabilities with a free verse inherited from Whitman, Williams, and Olson, in addition to a stunning use of metaphor and a skillful matching of sound and meaning. On the other hand, the Chagall poem shows Ferlinghetti's humor and punning both to be delightful, without becoming strained. In the acrobat-poet poem, Ferlinghetti creates a *tour de force* in metaphor.

Thus Ferlinghetti is both dirty old man *and* poet. But the poet is far too gifted to let himself be dominated or destroyed by the dirty old man. The time has come for Ferlinghetti to abandon his "beat" themes and his "beat" vocabulary: "square-type, cool, king-cat," etc. *A Coney Island of the Mind* should be remembered as the early work of an excellent and universal poet and not as the best work of a "beat poet." The poet once wrote:

> I am a social climber
> climbing downward
> and the descent is difficult

The *ascent* into excellence is too near for Ferlinghetti to climb downward into that morass populated by dirty old men and "beat poets."

Alex Raksin (review date 4 September 1988)

SOURCE: "Fiction in Brief," in *Los Angeles Times Book Review,* September 4, 1988, p. 4.

[*In the following review, Raksin provides a plot summary and critique of the novel* Love in the Days of Rage.]

The author is perhaps best known as the poet laureate of Beat counterculture—co-founder of City Lights Bookstore and Press in San Francisco, inspiration to Allen Ginsberg and Jack Kerouac—but it is his sensitivity as a painter that is most apparent in this original, intense novel. Like a good visual artist, Ferlinghetti plays with light in these pages, contrasting the bright "masculine" daytime world—society, business and politics—with the feminine night, a haven of sensuousness and introspection. A love affair between Annie and Julian, set against Paris' "old, pearly gray light," represents the night. The day appears only in retrospect, as Julian and Annie reflect on their struggles to come to terms with the turmoil of their time, 1968.

Annie, an expatriate, Expressionist painter from New York City, tries in her work to "breathe life again" into the landscapes of the destroyed streets of the Lower East Side" and to make sense of the "harsh, 'big sky' light of America . . . that left no place to find one's private self." Julian, in turn, constantly talks of rebelling against his job as a banking executive: "The bourgeois mentality itself," he tells Annie, "is the real enemy."

Annie is the first to resolve her conflict, abandoning her efforts to make sense of the larger world through Expressionism and taking up an art she finds more human and meaningful, figurative painting. Julian lags behind her, warring against the daytime world by blowing up valuable security receipts he has stolen from his bank. Ferlinghetti gives us the sense that Julian will come around, though, when Julian's close friend and partner in the heist tells Annie that their activism is made up of "nothing, more than obsessions, obsessions of the tribe! Just like primitive tribes sticking pins into their totems to kill their enemies! . . . So what then, if thought itself is the destroyer—if thougt itself divides us up into hate groups and sets us killing each other, over and over, century after century?"

Ferlinghetti's answer—we should follow our heart, even though it is only "another involuntary muscle"—reminds us that an artist's place is with nature, not above it. He brings this theme home in a concluding scene where Annie visits the country to meet Julian in a safe house after the bombing, and "lies down in the hot grasses, with the flesh that was one with hers . . . in that gold field at the end of time, where all beings breathed as one."

Patrick Burnson (review date Fall 1988)

SOURCE: "Passionate Spring," in *San Francisco Review of Books,* Vol. XIII, No. 2, Fall 1988, p. 44.

[*Burnson provides a plot summary and favorable review of* Love in the Days of Rage.]

When the streets of Paris erupted with student demonstrations twenty years ago, San Francisco poet / publisher Lawrence Ferlinghetti began jotting down notes in his expatriate's journal which recorded the events as a painter might view them—impressionistically.It comes as small surprise, then, to observe that his novella should move at the same painterly, unmannered pace. *Love in the Days of Rage* challenges the reader on several stylistic levels as it attempts to mirror the anarchistic uprising of '68 which briefly united intellectuals, artists, and proletariats in common cause. It's an uneven ride, at times maddeningly confused, but noble in intent and final effect.

Our lovers are mature, yet unconventional. Annie is the forty-year-old daughter of New York "old lefties" who has abandoned political commitment in the Lower East Side to teach and study art abroad. Julian Mendes, the fifty-five-year-old Parisian bank executive she meets in the Café Malbillon, seems to her initially as the very model of bourgeois respectability. The physical attraction proves irresistible, though, and once they become better acquainted, Annie discovers that her suitor is a man of rare political passion who plans to act—and act decisively—upon his beliefs in the wake of spring's rebellion.

As a young man living in Portugal, Julian developed his anarchist principles in response to the repressive regime of Antonio Salazar, whose secret police "disappeared" countless numbers of free-thinking opponents: "Every cliché about dictatorships was truer for Portugal than anywhere else," Julian contends. "But no matter how absolute power is, there's always some corner holding out, silently, secretly, refusing to conform. . . ."

The rhetoric falls upon deaf ears, however. For Annie, painting is a vocation unfettered by political concern; only when her sinecure as a Sorbonne instructor is threatened does she awaken to the urgency of student revolt and the anthem "*Imagination au Pouvoir!*" Her radicalism is fueled by the brutality of club-wielding *gendarmerie* defending the barricades. By the time Julian reveals himself to be of even more subversive bent than first perceived, she prepares for an adventure predicated on pure devotion to the man and the cause he champions.

It is here that this slender work of fiction begins to depart from conventional narrative form and takes on the more lyrical prose of the author's first novel, *Her.* Ferlinghetti, the painter, takes charge at this point, covering his canvas with imagery freighted with inchoate suspense and misty intrigue. Once embarked on the revolutionary path, the lovers are destined to remain "fugitives in an absurd fugitive dream."

In France a *bavure* is a hitch, a foul-up, notably by officials or police so common that a smooth operation is referred to as "*sans bavure.*" Without disclosing the climax to this inventive plot, let us assuredly state that what Ferlinghetti has achieved is remarkably hitchless and honest.

Michael Leddy (review date Autumn 1989)

SOURCE: A review of *Wild Dreams of a New Beginning,* in *World Literature Today,* Vol. 63, No. 4, Autumn 1989, pp. 683-84.

[*In the following review, Leddy criticizes the poetry collection* Wild Dreams of a New Beginning *for being derivative and unimaginative.*]

Wild Dreams of a New Beginning reprints the volumes *Who Are We Now?* (1976) and *Landscapes of Living & Dying* (1979). Ferlinghetti's concerns in the poems are as timely now as then. "This must be the end of something / the last days of somebody's empire," he writes in **"Director of Alienation,"** and the poems deal largely with cultural, ecological, and political apocalypse. An occasional piece works well to convey these concerns—e.g., **"Seascape with Sun & Eagle"** or **"Reading Apollinaire by the Rogue River."** Typically, though, the poems are a matter of predictable mannerisms: parallelism and repetition, sudden outbreaks of rhythm and rhyme and alliteration, intrusive puns, and countless allusions that are little more than clichéd quotations sprinkled about the poems: "alien corn," "darkling plain." Ferlinghetti seems the poetic equivalent of the jazz soloist who, for want of invention, quotes fragments of well-known songs, hoping that the audience will be content to congratulate itself on recognizing the sources.

What is particularly unfortunate in many of the selections

is the poet's reductive perspective on humankind, an inability, reminiscent of Charles Bukowski, to imagine depth and intelligence in other people's lives. Ferlinghetti picks easy satiric targets—"two made-up ladies in fancy hair-dos & / doubleknit pants suits"—and amuses himself making up grotesque life stories for them (**"Holiday Inn Blues"**). Elsewhere he dismisses "the people" in **"A Nation of Sheep"**: "I look down and see the fine grass roots / the people and cows and pigs / rooting and rutting and dying / feeding and breeding— / Dumb beasts all!" Ferlinghetti is capable too of a mawkishness again reminiscent of Bukowski, addressing the words "Te amo" (aloud? silently?) to a listener at a reading (**"A Meeting of Eyes in Mexico"**) and finding existential anguish in the motions of a bee: "The door was open and he knew it / and flew in for a moment / and then flew back / away from his community / Something had alienated him" (**"Alienation: Two Bees"**).

As the author of *A Coney Island of the Mind* and the publisher of City Lights Books, Ferlinghetti commands my respect. I regret that the poems of *Wild Dreams of a New Beginning* rarely offer compelling imaginative visions.

Gregory Stephenson (essay date 1990)

SOURCE: "The 'Spiritual Optics' of Lawrence Ferlinghetti," in *The Daybreak Boys: Essays on the Literature of the Beat Generation,* Southern Illinois University Press, 1990, pp. 139-153.

[*In the following essay, Stephenson describes the visual imagery recurring in several of Ferlinghetti's poems and plays, and in the novel,* Her. *He suggests that Ferlinghetti believes man to be fragmented by the opposing forces of love and power.*]

> The Sun's Light when he unfolds it
> Depends on the Organ that beholds it.
>
>   "What is Man?"—William Blake
>
> The Eye of man a little narrow orb,
> clos'd up & dark,
> scarcely beholding the great light,
> conversing with the Void.
>
>   "Milton"—William Blake

I remember clearly that what impressed me and attracted me in the poetry of Lawrence Ferlinghetti, when I first read it as an adolescent twenty-five years ago, was its quality of mystery. By mystery I do not mean obscurity or hermeticism nor do I mean mystification, but rather, that magical, mythic,

secret, and visionary power at the heart of the work of certain poets, that property that causes a poem to resonate so deeply in the mind of the reader. I continue to respond to that mystery in Ferlinghetti's work whenever I read or reread it, and for that reason I want to consider his writing with close attention, not to explain the mystery but to approach it, to honor it.

My procedure is simply to follow what I see as the inner continuity of concerns in Ferlinghetti's writing, the correlations of thought and of emotion and of image within and among the works and to trace elements of the whole design as I perceive them.

> The work of Lawrence Ferlinghetti proposes what I call ... a "Spiritual Optics," that is, a way of being and seeing, a mode of identity and vision.
> —*Gregory Stephenson*

As I read it, the work of Lawrence Ferlinghetti proposes what I call (borrowing the phrase from the title of an essay by Thomas Carlyle) a "Spiritual Optics," that is, a way of being and seeing, a mode of identity and vision. Ferlinghetti's writing embodies a myth or metaphysic which conceives an original unity of being from which human consciousness, individual and generic, has fallen. The fallen state is one of division and conflict where the mind struggles toward reconciliation and reunification with original being. The impulse toward reunification involves a twofold, interrelated process in each human psyche: the integration of the fragmented, fallen consciousness into a unity; and the reconciliation of subject and object, of ego and non-ego, in the communion of creative perception.

The development and definition of this "spiritual optics" is the central problem of Ferlinghetti's poetry, prose, and dramatic work. In the following I want to examine this double theme and to consider its evolution in his writing, with particular attention to his prose narrative *Her,* which represents a grammar of the premises and concerns of his work.

Her is an interior monologue narrated by Andy Raffine, an American painter living in Paris. In the opening paragraphs of the story, Raffine characterizes his psychic situation in terms of "a transaction with myself" and "a battle with the image." These two elements of his problem are mutually reflexive. The first, the "transaction," is a quest for identity, a search for the whole or completed self, which he images as a sexual union. And the second element, the "battle," is a quest for vision, for a true perception of existence, a perception beyond habit and preconception, beyond subjectivity and objectivity. The state of being and seeing in which he hopes to unite the masculine and feminine aspects of the self, unite subject and object in vision, he calls "the fourth person singular."

Raffine has a sense of an original, true, whole identity experienced in childhood and shattered when he was orphaned at an early age. He views himself as fallen and fragmented, continually seeking to refine and refind himself. He also sees his situation as a microcosm of the human condition, that we are "all of us, all splintered parts of the same whole." In Raffine's view everyone, whether consciously or unconsciously, is engaged in a quest "searching for something all had lost," a condition of original human unity that is now "a lost community . . . a far country" from which we are exiled.

Accordingly, the world in which we live, the fallen world, is divided into the forces of redemption and liberation that would restore humankind to unity and the forces of repression and oppression that, perhaps unknowingly, enforce alienation and divisiveness. Poetry, music, visual art, eroticism, affection, ecstasy, compassion, beauty, communication, and love represent the reintegrative principles. Egotism, power, authority, dogma—as embodied by the military, the police, the clergy, the customs authorities, and others and as reflected in "regulations and protocols and codes and restrictions and taboos and constitutions and traffic regulations and accepted maxims and venerated proverbs"—represent the principles of conflict, impediment, and disunity.

Raffine is, potentially, a redemptive, regenerative figure who could, through his life and art, help to bring about "the true Liberation" ending "the prolonged Occupation of the world." He could articulate the "final, irreducible secret" in paint, catalyze "the long overdue millennium of art and life." Raffine is represented as a sort of Fisher King figure and is associated with fish imagery throughout the text ("the fishy king none other than myself, my name a brand of canned salt fish." He is sexually wounded, pursuing a female Grail in the figure of "Her."

Raffine's sexual wound is not physical but mental. It consists of his view of women as either virginal-maternal or as insatiable devourers. This fixation prevents him from consummating a sexual union. Repeatedly, at crucial moments of erotic encounter he fails, held back in fear by his illusions, abstractions, preconceptions, never learning to use "the one true key of love that could unlock all the doors."

Similarly, Raffine fails continually in his art; his "orgasm" in paint is checked by an inevitable return to habit and cliché. He is unable to "break away into the free air of underivative creation" and is frustrated in his attempts to "enact the new."

Both Raffine's sexual and artistic failures are extensions of

his essential failure to achieve identity and vision, a failure which ultimately results in his death.

Raffine's quest for identity and vision closely parallels the process of individuation as described by Carl Jung involving encounters with shadow and anima.

According to Jungian psychology, the shadow is a projection or personification of "the hidden, repressed and unfavorable (or nefarious) aspects of the personality." The shadow is not altogether negative though; it also possesses creative qualities and virtues, "values that are needed by consciousness," including "even the most valuable and highest forces."

Raffine's shadow in *Her* is Lubin, waiter at the Café Mabillon. Lubin is an ambiguous figure, whose face is "two masks, a mask of comedy superimposed on one of tragedy," whose jaw "was meant to cup a violin, or to clench a bone." Ferlinghetti compares him both to "a great bird of prey" and to "a great shy dog." Lubin is at once vulgar and wise, ragged and elegant, blasphemous and reverent. (There is a close resemblance, deliberate on the part of the author, between Lubin and Dr. Matthew O'Connor of Djuna Barnes' novel *Nightwood.*)

A drunkard and a debauchee, Lubin serves as confessor and counselor to the naive and idealistic Raffine. The identification between the two figures exists in both a paternal relationship (Lubin describes himself to Raffine as "your wandered father") and a twin relationship (doppelgënger, alter egos, opposite and complementary). To Lubin, Raffine is "my own past," while he sees himself as "the billous tagend of your future" and in memory as "an earlier Andy Raffine." Lubin's most important function is to disabuse Raffine of his notions concerning the virginity of "Her" and to serve as a mediator between Raffine and "Her." Lubin foresees disaster for Raffine, but his counsels and warnings to him are unheeded.

The second stage of the individuation process, according to Jungian psychology, "is characterized by the encounter with the *soul image*, . . . the complementary contrasexual part of the psyche"—for the male, the anima. The anima may manifest itself in a variety of forms including "a sweet young maiden, a goddess, a witch, an angel, a demon, a beggar woman, a whore, a devoted companion, an Amazon, etc." Andy Raffine's anima takes the form of most of the named figures above, constantly metamorphosing. Like the shadow, the anima has two aspects, benevolent and malefic. In its sublime aspect the anima is often "fused with the figure of the Virgin," while in its infernal aspect it often presents itself in the figure of the femme fatale or a witch.

Raffine's search for his anima is rooted in his childhood experience of the death of his mother, thus his insistence on purity and virginity. Another recurring virginal figure of Raffine's anima is "a little girl with a hoop in a dirdnl dress," whose piece of white string that is "as purely white as innocence itself" becomes defiled by mud. These two images are inhibitory, obstructive, and finally destructive for him. During the most critical sexual encounter of the book, his failure is attributable to his fixation with such virginal purity, for the involuntarily recalls "that first face" and notices a soiled piece of white string on the floor beside the bed. The ultimate symbol of the manifestation of the maternal-virginal aspect of Raffine's anima is the statue of the Virgin on the cathedral Notre Dame, between whose breasts he climbs before falling, figuratively "tangled up and trussed" in string, to his death.

The baleful aspect of Raffine's anima is the concept of woman as the emasculator, the insatiable whore, the devourer. Raffine views women in terms of female archetypes such as the Sirens, exhausting helpless men "in perpetual orgasm"; the Mona Lisa, "that eternal dame having just eaten her husband, note the famous enigmatic smile of containment if not contentment"; Salome, "she wants more than my head she wants my body on a spit"; the Queen Bee, "no sooner is the union completed than my abdomen opens and my organ detaches itself"; and the ominous old crone flowerseller who reappears throughout the book, with her mad, raucous laugh, reminiscent of the "layer-out" figure of Robert Graves' Triple Goddess.

Raffine fails to integrate and reconcile the positive and negative qualities of his anima, fails to balance or direct the energy. In consequence, both aspects are destructive to him and result ultimately in his death. His failure is most apparent during the central romantic-erotic encounter of the story which takes place in Rome.

Raffine travels to Rome in a desperate endeavor to flee his "half-life" and to seek to achieve genuine identity and perception. He attempts to "see without the old associational turning eye that turns all it sees into its own." Two brief unconsumated erotic encounters (one with a prostitute, the other with an Italian peasant girl) convince him of the necessity of liberating his psyche from his abstractions and preconceptions concerning women. He characterizes the restrictive grip of these habits of mind as a bird perched inside his head: "the crazy sad bird I carried in my head as the idea of woman . . . the parrot of love who kept repeating all the phrases and phases of it." His quest culminates in an involvement with an American girl in a hotel in Rome. Raffine vows to himself that he will avoid all the old patterns and associations and "this time begin with the real and stick to it." And, for a time, he succeeds: "Instead of a hazy image out of somebody else's painting or out of my own, I saw the girl in sharp outline, a clear incisive line. . . ." But

as they are about to make love, Raffine realizes that they remain "anonymous bodies" to each other, each imposing a pattern upon or evoking an image from the other. Raffine cannot escape the imprint of his early experiences, the memory of his mother, his fixation with purity. They do not make love, do not comfort, warm, or awaken each other, do not save each other. Raffine recognizes that he remains on the "carrousel" of unauthentic identity and perception, revolving continually through the same experiences, never able to grab the brass ring of true selfhood and vision.

Still blindly and desperately seeking a union with the feminine to complete his "transaction" with himself, Raffine returns to Paris. There he ascends the cathedral Notre Dame by means of a scaffolding, embraces the statue of the Virgin, and falls to his death. Raffine's final, fatal fall is, like Finnegan's, a reenactment of the Fall of Man—"a falling away through a failure of contact through a failure of life." The events of the story have taken place during the Lenten season, during Passion Week, and Raffine dies on Good Friday, a parody Christ, "a Friday fish to hand upon the old hook," an unhealed, unredeeming Fisher King who has lost his "battle with the image."

Her is a complex, resonant work whose themes are developed through recurring images and associations.

—Gregory Stephenson

The final images of the narrative may, however, indicate a *felix culpa,* or fortunate fall, a redemption in death for Andy Raffine: "God grips the genitals to catch illusionary me . . . he plays the deepsea catch he reels me in O god." There is an echo here of a phrase of Lubin's: "The hand that grips the genitals, love plays the deepsea catch . . ." which is later recalled and expanded by Raffine, "Love plays the deepsea catch, it's love will reel it in. . . ." Raffine is identified with fish both by means of his name, "a brand of canned salt fish," and by means of recurring fish imagery: "fished up . . . Fishface . . . swimming . . . fisheyed" and again, "my sardine can alack . . . a fart of a fish . . . my sardine boat . . . your fishy fellow." Thus, Raffine becomes "the deepsea catch" that is "played" throughout the book to be reeled in by God or by love in the end. Ferlinghetti employs a pun (a frequent device in *Her*), perhaps a double pun, involving the use of the word *reel.* Aside from its surface contextual meaning of being drawn in as a fish on a line, it may also refer to the image of "the unwinding reel" of cinematic film that Raffine uses as a metaphor for his life and his identity, a film projected frame by frame and then recoiled. In the meeting of the two metaphors, fish and film, there may be another meaning created, a sound pun, a homophone. Raffine is not only reeled in (like a fish or a film) but, perhaps also, *realed* in as well; that is to say, reeled into the real. In this case, Raffine's final exclamation, "O god," may be understood not as a cry of despair but as an affirmation. He may, in death, have achieved the fourth person singular.

Her is a complex, resonant work whose themes are developed through recurring images and associations. There are paired opposites such as blindness/sight, key/lock, obesity/Lent, climbing/falling, virginity/licentiousness, sleeping/waking; and there are associative pairs or clusters such as shadow/haze/dusk/fog (suggestive of ordinary perception, that is, cliché, habit) and gramophone/film reel/carrousel (suggestive of the endlessly repetitive nature of ordinary perception and experience). In addition there are multivalent images such as string, fish, bird, film reel, door, statue, flowers, mirror, window, flushing toilets. Puns and literary allusions are frequent in the text.

Her represents the myth or metaphysic of Ferlinghetti's writing, the cosmography of his poetic imagination. His view of existence has much in common with that of the English romantic poets, particularly William Blake, but it is nonetheless distinctively and uniquely that of the author himself. According to Ferlinghetti's myth, human beings are fallen (from unity to disunity, from true perception to false and limited perception) and are, as a consequence of their fall, self-divided. Their inner divisions are reflected in the world they create that is divided between power and love. Authentic (or visionary) perception and authentic being (which in combination, constitute what I have named a "spiritual optics") are the means by which unified human identity may be regained and a return to the prelapsarian world accomplished. Ferlinghetti's art evolves out of his desire to communicate this vision and to uphold and advocate the cause of unity against disunity, love against power. Thus, the theme of vision and the absence of vision is, in its various aspects and applications, central to virtually all of Ferlinghetti's writing.

Lawrence Ferlinghetti's dramatic pieces, collected in *Unfair Arguments with Existence* and *Routines,* are extensions and expansions of the central myth articulated in *Her.* There is a particularly close relationship between *Her* and the play *The Soldiers of No Country* where the characters of Denny, Toledano, and Erma parallel those of Andy Raffine, Lubin, and "Her." The situation of the characters in a cave recalls certain of the images of *Her* and may ultimately derive from Plato's allegory in which the cave represents limited perception, the world of reflected reality, shadows. The cave is described in the stage directions as "womb-like," that is, a cave out of which we must be born. Denny's complaint is similar to that of Andy Raffine: "Nobody's listening, we're just talking to ourselves. . . . They don't even see you . . . seeing only themselves or someone else, not you but another. . . ." Images of mirror, bird, white string, virginity, the Virgin, darkness and light, loss, a lost country without "evil or hate . . .

only a blind urge to love" also unite the play with *Her.* *The Soldiers of No Country* seems more optimistic than *Her,* however, ending with Erma emerging from the darkness of the cave into the light and with a powerful image of birth.

The images of cracked binoculars, blindness, and the unwillingness to see in the plays *3,000 Red Ants* and *Alligation* evoke the eye and sight motifs of *Her.* In *The Victims of Amnesia* the conflict occurs between a Night Clerk, a benighted authoritarian who likes to play at being a conductor or a soldier, and Marie Mazda, associated with miracle, mystery, and light. *Motherlode* portrays another "sounding of the same eternal situation" wherein "prospecting for love, we dig flesh. . . ." The piece represents again the human quest for the lost and mythic "mainland" or "the land of lovers," the prelapsarian world from which we are exiled. The quest motif occurs again in *The Customs Collector in Baggy Pants* in which the object of the search is the lost "diamond of hope," associated also with erotic or generative powers, the power to love, "twin gems . . . King of Diamonds," which are also lost and must be recovered. The figure of the customs collector and the flushing toilets of this piece recall identical images in *Her.* (There is, of course, a pun involved in the word *customs* in this context. The Custom's Agents represent the inner forces of custom and habituation that allow no contraband impressions or perceptions to pass.) Further images from *Her,* climbing and falling, are central to the final play of the volume, *The Nose of Sisyphus.* The opposition between vision and blindness, freedom and repression, spirit and animality, is configured in this instance as the conflict between Sisyphus, a heroic, redemptive figure, and Big Baboon, a menacing embodiment of all that is base and retrograde in humankind.

The shorter dramatic pieces of *Routines* reflect and explore particular aspects of existence as repetition, as habit, and as pattern. In his preface to the plays, Ferlinghetti declares that "life itself . . . [is] a blackout routine . . . [we are] lost in the vibration of a wreckage (of some other cosmos we fell out of)." This metaphysical premise, already established in *Her* and developed in *Unfair Arguments with Existence,* provides a sense of the unity and continuity of the various "routines" as attempts to locate and describe the ground of our experience, with the ultimate intention of aiding us in transcending our condition.

The "question of identity" is the problem treated in *Our Little Trip.* Whether identity may be said to exist at all, whether it is attainable, and whether it is important are the issues raised by the Question Man, a dispassionate, reductive, intellectual relative of Big Baboon. The Question Man views human existence in terms of mechanics, physical properties, mental capacities, and operations, without metaphysics, without mystery, without meaning. The male-female relationship is again presented as being intimately involved with the process of identity. The central image of the piece is that of a man and a woman whose faces are wrapped in a single long bandage which attaches them to each other. We first see them "dressed conventionally," straining away from each other. Later, after an interval, they return to the stage naked except for the bandage around their faces and "now strain toward each other," finally rewinding themselves completely, pressing against each other and caressing. Their actions suggest a resolution to the question of identity, a casting aside of conventions, of defenses, a return to the true and original state of the soul, an integration of the masculine and feminine principles.

Male and female relationships are also the subject of *His Head* and *Swinger,* but these pieces seem only to describe conflicts without suggesting resolutions. They are, together with the other philosophical and political routines of the collection, provocations to the reader or to the audience, problems, questions to make us "think of life" and to precipitate "revolutionary solutions or evolutionary solutions." As Ferlinghetti reminds us, "Routines never end; they have to be broken."

Ferlinghetti's first volume of poems, *Pictures of the Gone World,* records epiphanies and vignettes of vision and satirizes and exposes elements of the conspiracy against joy and vision. In these poems, lovers, children, artists, and poets oppose librarians, cultural ambassadors, museum directors, priests, patrolmen—those who can neither love nor see because they have "been running / on the same old rails too long"; those who have "no eyes to see" the beauty of the world because they are preoccupied with trivialities and superficialities; the predatory and acquisitive; those who have no identity outside of "their hats and their jobs"; those who have

> fatally assumed
> that some direct connection
> does exist between
> language and reality
> word and world.

The poems are also united with *Her* and to the plays by common imagery, including statues, mirrors, doors, virgin, and string.

A Coney Island of the Mind continues and expands the theme of vision with a unifying image of the eye. "The poet's eye obscenely seeing" discerns reality from illusion, the mysterious from the meretricious, the eternal from the temporal. "The poet's eye" may be developed through response to literature or to visual art (Goya, Bosch, Chagall, Kafka help us to see) or may be retained from childhood "when every living thing / cast its shadow in eternity." As in *Her,* humankind is engaged, consciously or unconsciously, in re-

gaining "the lost shores" where there are "green birds singing / from the other side of silence." Human beings are "all hunting love and half the hungry time not even knowing just what is really eating them"; they are "always on their hungry travels after the same hot grail." In the paradise we seek there will be no clothes, no altars, no hierarchy or authority, but only "fountains of imagination." And though we are confounded as to how to gain admittance to the castle of the "Mystery of Existence" where "it is heavenly weather" and "souls dance undressed / together," the poet assures us that "on the far side" there is "a wide wide vent . . . where even elephants / waltz thru." We continually overlook the epiphanous possibilities of the obvious, the miraculous qualities of the commonplace.

In his "Oral Messages" section of *A Coney Island of the Mind* Ferlinghetti declares again and clarifies his opposition to tyranny, boredom, exploitation, nationalism, and war and reaffirms his faith in "a rebirth of wonder" and a "total dream of Innocence." If we would return to "the true blue simple life / of wisdom and wonderment," we would reach the "Isle of Manisfree," the just and joyous society. In **"Autobiography"** and **"Dog"** Ferlinghetti urges us to attention and observation of the world, to see what is around us with the innocent eye of the dog, to see directly, unintimidated, without abstractions or preconceptions, but instead "touching and tasting and testing everything." And in **"Christ Climbed Down,"** Christ is associated with "the poet's eye," potential in every human being, the ability to reject the superficial, to discern the essential. In a commercial, consumer society, artificial and hypocritical with a vacuum of values, Christ must seek rebirth, a Second Coming in the soul of every human: "In the darkest night / of everybody's anonymous soul / He awaits. . . ."

The image of a dormant, potential, redemptive force waiting in the world, waiting to be awakened in each separate psyche and in the collective human psyche, becomes the central motif of **"The Great Chinese Dragon,"** which is one of the key poems of *Starting from San Francisco.* The dragon of the poem represents to the poet "the force and mystery of life," the true sight that "sees the spiritual everywhere translucent in the material world." The dragon is guarded and restrained by the police, the agents of the conspiracy against joy and vision, who recognize and fear its apocalyptic power. The poem concludes with the image of the dragon buried in a cellar, awaiting "the final coming and the final sowing of his oats and teeth." The dragon may be seen as the visionary imaginative potential within each human mind, restrained by the rational faculties and the collective regenerative qualities of humanity, repressed by the forces of authority, egotism, and materialism. (Appropriately, the ultimate etymological root of the word *dragon* is the Greek verb *derkesthai,* which means "to see.") Also closely related to the premises of *Her* are the concepts of the poem

"Hidden Door" which rejects the "pathetic fallacy / of the evidence of the senses / as to the nature of reality" and explores the mystery of "our buried life," the attempt to rediscover the "lost shore of light," to find again the "mislaid visionary self." A number of images from *Her* and from the plays recur in the poem, including the blind man with tin cup, key, door, climbing and falling, palimpsest, vulva, and mirror. The poem **"He"** describes a poet-prophet who is "the mad eye of the fourth person singular," who has achieved "unbuttoned vision."

The Secret Meaning of Things is, as the title indicates, a further enquiry into visionary consciousness, an attempt to achieve and to convey a mode of observation that "leaves behind all phenomenal distinction," enabling the eye to perceive essences, inscapes, the mystery and the eternalness of temporal phenomena. The volume is notable for two poems in particular, **"After the Cries of Birds"** and **"Moscow in the Wilderness, Segovia in the Snow,"** which can be seen as companion pieces. In the first of the two poems, Ferlinghetti prophesies "a new visionary society . . . a new pastoral era" in America, the reconciliation of occidental and Oriental culture and thought, the American frontier translated into a metaphysical frontier, the new manifest destiny in "the wish to pursue what lies beyond the mind / . . . to move beyond the senses." In the second of the poems, another prophecy, the Russian spirit, in the image of an ancient armadillo "asleep for centuries / in the cellar of the Kremlin," at last awakens to music, to ecstasy, and to vision. Considered together the two poems represent a prophecy, as described in Revelation, of "a new heaven and a new earth" achieved through the medium of the awakened eye.

The title to the volume *Open Eye, Open Heart* is again significant to the pervasive theme of vision. The phrase is taken from the poem **"True Confessional"** in which it refers to a way of seeing with the eye of "the inside self." Images of light, "shining . . . bright . . . skeins of light . . . luminous," oppose those of darkness, "cobwebs of Night . . . shadow"; the "inside self" is contrasted to the "outside with its bag of skin." In such poems as **"Sueño Real," "The Real Magic Opera Begins,"** and **"Stone Reality Meditation"** the nature of reality is the central issue. These poems reflect an increased awareness of the ephemerality, the transitory nature, of material form with its "fugitive configurations" that occur in "the eternal dream-time."

The artist or poet, as in **"An Elegy on the Death of Kenneth Patchen,"** is still seen as a redemptive figure who struggles against "the agents of Death" and who opposes the "various villainies of church and state." Ferlinghetti again depicts art as the medium of awareness and of visionary consciousness. He mentions, in this connection, references to music by Telemann, sculpture by Giacometti, paintings by Ben Shahn, and the writings of Lorca, Whitman, Blake, and

Lawrence. The absence of vision is recorded in the poem **"London, Rainy Day"** where "life's eternal situations / stutter on . . . Nothing moves in the leaded air," and the transcending, transforming power of the inner eye is inactive: "The blue rider does not appear."

The "Her" figure, anima, muse of vision, psychic complement, appears again in *Open Eye, Open Heart,* glimpsed, lovely and elegant, in a restaurant or encountered in a Ramada Inn in Kansas, with her "far-eyed look." The **"Eternal Woman"** remains a disturbing presence for Ferlinghetti, at once magnetically attractive and yet dreadful in her demand for absolute abnegation. **"Tantric Ballad"** treats the theme of man and woman as "counterparts," who in sexual union form a lotus flower, a perfected form.

The external and internal relationship between the masculine and the feminine and its relation to identity and vision is again a dominant theme in the poems of *Who Are We Now?* Man and woman relationships are the subject of several poems in the volume, including **"People Getting Divorced," "Short Story on a Painting of Gustav Klimt," "At the Bodega,"** and **"The Heavy."** In **"The Jack of Hearts,"** Ferlinghetti's paean to the prophet-visionary who can redeem "the time of the ostrich," who can awaken and enliven "the silent ones with frozen faces," the hero with open eye and open heart has found

> the sun-stone
> of himself
> the woman-man
> the whole man.

And in **"I Am You,"** the poet praises and prophesies what Plato called the Spherical Man, the original and final human:

> Man half woman
>
> Woman half man
>
> And the two intertwined
>
> in each of us androgynus
>
> . . . .
>
> in the end as in beginning.

Further prophecies of ultimate harmony, ultimate unity, ultimate victory, occur in the poems **"A Vast Confusion"** and **"Olbers' Paradox."** In the first of these Ferlinghetti describes "a vast confusion in the universe" in which "all life's voices lost in night" and then envisions

> Chaos unscrambled

back to the first
harmonies

And the first light.

"Olbers' Paradox" is a metaphoric appropriation of the theory of an early astronomer Heinrich Olbers that "there *must* be a place / where all is light" and that the light from that place will one day reach the Earth. For Ferlinghetti the theory represents the final victory of light over darkness, the Great Awakening, the apocalypse of the fourth person singular:

And then in that symbolic
so poetic place
which will be ours
we'll be our own true shadows
and our own illumination.

In this manner the problems of identity and vision which were posited in *Her* are resolved in prophecy.

And in the concluding poems of the volume, **"Eight People on a Golf Course and One Bird of Freedom Flying Over"** and **"Populist Manifesto,"** Ferlinghetti reaffirms his belief in the inevitable and final triumph of the indestructible, resurrective phoenix of life, truth, and vision over the conspiracy of politics, industry, religion, the military, the media, bankers, and the police and reiterates his faith in poetry as a primary instrument of enlightenment: "Poetry the common carrier / for the transportation of the public / to higher places."

The theme of "spiritual optics" that is articulated in the work of Lawrence Ferlinghetti is coherent and consistent but not static. Rather, it lends dynamism and invention to his writing, varying focus, tone, and response, permitting dramatic expansions and reductions of experience, fitting the poems to each other and to the plays and to *Her* in such a manner that they reinforce one another's meanings. The theme develops in the course of the work—from the diagnostic, essentially pessimistic *Her,* with its abortive poetry revolution and failed quester-hero, through the cautious hope in the plays and the early poems, with their continuing struggle from blindness to vision, from darkness to light, from power to love, from quotidian life toward "a renaissance of wonder," to the prophecies of the later poems which foresee a Great Awakening, the union of the masculine and the feminine principles, the reconciliation of Occident and Orient and of opposing ideologies, and which herald the emergence of a visionary society, "a new pastoral era," and the final victory of light over darkness.

Tony Curtis (interview date Summer 1992)

SOURCE: An interview in *Poetry Review,* Vol. 82, No. 2, Summer, 1992, pp. 22-27.

[*In the following interview, Curtis and Ferlinghetti discuss a wide range of topics, including the poets Dylan Thomas and Allen Ginsberg, and the status of the anti-war movement.*]

[*Curtis:*] *Lawrence, you were last in Wales briefly in 1989 when you were on tour promoting your novel* **Love in the Days of Rage.** *But you had a connection with Wales many years before that, didn't you? Weren't you close to us during the war?*

[Ferlinghetti:] Well, I was in Plymouth harbor the night before the first day of the Normandy invasion, D-Day, and I was in Milford Haven one night, the night before that, I believe. And we were here in Cardiff the week before. I was in a small anti-submarine vessel and so on D-Day itself we left Plymouth at two in the morning, I guess, and what was memorable was coming up to Normandy and the beaches— the ships were steaming from all ports, as you know, and as the first light came up in the English Channel you could see the tops of the masts of ships in at least a hundred and eighty degree arc, all around you, behind you, just the masts of the ships silhouetted against the horizon getting light. And as the light grew, the masts became higher and more visible and came in around you like the whole horizon was this forest of masts advancing and converging on this one point off the Normandy beach-head. It was a sight I'll never forget, it was . . .

Rather like Birnam Wood coming to Dunsinane?

Well, yes, and another parallel from Shakespeare was that the night before in all the lanes and alleys, behind all the hedgerows leading down to all the little ports the transport was packed, just lorries and lorries and American trucks and all kind of armored vehicles jammed full of soldiers, jammed full of men sitting. I remember after it got dark you could see these fires where there were encampments, camp fires, and no noise and the fires were hooded and you weren't supposed to show any light. And you had this feeling that the whole landscape was sown with troops waiting in the darkness. And I remember it was like before the battle of Agincourt. You felt that their officers were like the King himself stalking about from campfire to campfire. And it could very well have been. Well, those are the two main memories of that time. Except there were other pleasant memories after we got back to England. We were shipwrecked in the enormous storm that came up in the week after the Normandy invasion and we had to put into Cowes. We were in a shipyard in Cowes and I got to go up to London and enjoy myself in the middle of the war for a couple of weeks.

That part was, oh what a lovely war. Even though there were buzz-bombs falling in London.

Do you know the poet Alun Lewis from the Second World War? From the British perspective the two major poets of the War are Keith Douglas, who died in the desert in North Africa, and also this Welshman Alun Lewis who died in Burma. He has a poem called "All Day It Has Rained" which is something along those lines in that it's that awful feeling of being in a bivouac tent of maneuvers and not actually getting to grips with the fighting. That awful lull which is worse than the fighting itself in a way.

I know that there was a lot of raining at that stage. For one thing the invasion was scheduled to start on one day. The troops started to get onto the ships stood out of the various harbors, and then Eisenhower called back the whole operation on account of the threatening weather.

Have you written about all those experiences?

No, I haven't. I mean to get back to it someday. Well it's a thing to do in prose and I . . . well, I hope to do it.

We were at Laugharne today, which is a place you were looking forward to going to. But while we were there, there was the distant sound of jet planes and cannon fire. It seems that you can't escape from that anywhere.

Well, that's different today from 1944. I don't know whose those planes were buzzing us today. But I have a feeling it's the American Empire—the frontiers of the American Empire. We were in Iraq just recently.

So you were against that war?

Oh, it was insane. There was absolutely no reason for that war. Bush painted himself into this corner so that there was no way out. He wanted war, he ignored all the proposals and overtures for peace that were made. They were barely reported in the American press. And he is also responsible for the million Kurds who were rendered homeless. He is directly responsible in his encouragement of their uprising. As far as I'm concerned he did it. Practically single-handedly. Even General Schwarzkopf is rumored to have been against it, and wanted to do it with sanctions. The sanctions worked in Nicaragua, but no one pointed that out. The economic sanctions worked perfectly well down there.

But, from Britain at least, it seemed the anti-Gulf War protests were short and ineffective.

Well, that's what we got in reports over here. I just came back from Spain and there they had the impression that there had been no anti-war movements in the States, and that the large majority of the population agreed with Bush's war policy. It simply wasn't so. In San Francisco alone, and in Washington, D.C. and in New York City and in Chicago there were enormous anti-war demonstrations. In San Francisco there were demonstrations of 200,000 people. Two or three of them in the course of a week. Hardly reported at all in the press. Some in the local newspapers but not on the national television. And what you have is the mainstream media completely controlled by the government. Not the way it's done in a totalitarian country, where you have absolute repressive restrictions between law and force, but by a hand-in-glove co-operation between the government and the large corporations who own national TV networks. For instance, General Electric owns national armaments plants, including nuclear armaments plants in Pennsylvania. These huge corporations own many other types of businesses apart from television, so there is a clear conflict of interest. So you're not going to have national television news reported objectively when you have an arms manufacturer who is selling arms to the Middle East owning the stations. When you have that close co-operation between corporations and governments-in Mussolini's Italy that was known as Fascism. We have a brand of corporate Fascism going on now. I'm just giving the line, the theories of Noam Chomsky, especially his book *"Manufacturing Consent."* The only way for this to be stopped is for laws to be passed saying that broadcasting companies cannot own types of businesses. But they'll never pass laws like that, because in the USA both parties are agents of corporate capitalism.

In your opinion does this also apply to American publishing?

Oh, no. But the trouble is that the television audience is, say, twenty times the number of people reading a daily newspaper.

So, if the newspapers aren't having a big effect, what effect can poetry have?

The poets remain as the only people who have the possibility of remaining not compromised. The poets are the only ones free to speak the truth, in a way. And yet so many of them give away that birthright by taking grants from the National Endowment. Or whatever they call it over here.

The Arts Council. You don't agree with that?

Well, it depends on whether you have a benevolent government which doesn't commit crimes against humanity. You see, in the United States you have a government which may be beneficent in giving out grants to artists and writers, but with its other hand it's killing millions of people in illegal wars overseas.

But it's difficult to find a government that didn't.

Well, that's the anarchist position.

But if you take the Guggenheim, the National Endowment or whatever, you are then able to bite the hand that's fed you. That's justified, isn't it?

I'm going from the point of view of Albert Camus who said that you're guilty of complicity if you go along with the system that operates like this. So many supposedly dissident writers and artists in the United States take the government money.

W.H. Auden said that poetry made nothing happen. When the Beats in the '50s and through the 1960s had those enormous performance audiences, wasn't there a sense there that poetry could make something happen?

Well, it did make a lot happen. For instance, when the Congressional Un-American Activities Committee came to San Francisco they had such a hard time they never came back. It was about the last appearance of that committee in the late 1950s or early 1960s in San Francisco. But remember that Plato banned the poets from his Republic as being too dangerous. The poet is, by definition, someone who is challenging the status quo, challenging the common accepted view of reality. That's the real function of the artist. By this definition the poet is an enemy of the state, and has to be if he's worth his salt.

We've been on a pilgrimage to Laugharne today and Dylan Thomas is about the most apolitical poet you could think of. He writes about childhood; he writes about rural Wales; he writes often in a Biblical language about things.

His poetry will last longer than the political poets. I mean as soon as we write a political poem we condemn ourselves to a short life. For instance, I wrote a tirade, a book about Nixon called **Tyrannus Nix,** and who wants to read that now? Who wants to read about the werewolf himself today? I mean that werewolf face of Nixon was enough to scare anyone. But no one wants to hear about that today—"Go away, don't give me that stuff." But Thomas is above all that stuff; he could get away with being above all that, you might say. A minor poet who ignored the world situation would be nowhere; there wouldn't be any reason to listen to him poetically. But it happened that Thomas was a genius with language and I don't understand what seems to be the current attitude to Dylan Thomas in both the United States and Britain, and Wales even. People put him down for having been too Romantic, too plush, too posh, too fulsome. And I don't understand that at all. This is one of the great voices of the century; poetically, probably the greatest to write in English.

And you heard him in '53 at the end?

I've always felt that the poem that had to be explained was a failure.
—Lawrence Ferlinghetti

Yes, I heard him twice in San Francisco, both times he was quite lushed up. His voice was very plush and very posh and his second reading was mostly devoted to poems about death by other British poets—everyone from Beddoes to Clough. And he was obsessed with death—I think he knew he was going to die. Couldn't stop drinking. And that was his last reading in the States. But I heard all the great poems in the first reading-"Fern Hill" and "On his Thirtieth Birthday." I was just young then—well, I was young as a poet. About thirty. I reviewed his readings for the San Francisco art magazine at the time. And I reviewed it for the *San Francisco Chronicle*—and I said, "There is nothing like Dylan Thomas in poetry today." I still stand by that. So I don't understand why people are not imitating him still. But for one thing they can't imitate him because they don't have his talent. It was more than talent, it was genius. It was something you can't teach or learn yourself if you haven't got it, I feel. It's an intangible something that comes over the poet when he's writing, it just poured out in his case. From the stories I've heard about Thomas being a bad boy personally, it reminds me very much of the American poet Gregory Corso, who is also a bad boy, and doesn't treat his friends so well sometimes, or his women. But Corso too is an original American genius, he's an American primitive. He's never derivative of anybody. He's always completely original. I don't know whether he ever read in Wales, but he was in the famous Albert Hall reading in 1967 with Allen Ginsberg and myself and other British poets including Adrian Mitchell and Michael Horovitz.

But the great art can't, in the immediate sense anyway, excuse the bad behavior, can it? When people are hurt? Are they casualties of literature, the bystanders?

Well, the bad boys pay for it. I mean it's the classic Romantic profile of the *poète maudit* who dies early. Dylan, like so many others of the genre, dying at 39.

Did America kill him?

Well, that's what Kenneth Rexroth said in a great poem called "Thou shalt not kill: an elegy on the death of Dylan Thomas." He condemns the consumer society in general, and in particular the man in the Brook Brothers suit, or the ugly American, for having killed Thomas. Of course, he drank himself to death, so he killed himself really. There's nothing like Rexroth's poem for a really vituperative castigation of American culture in particular which is now sweeping the world. It should be much better known.

Perhaps Dylan's reputation has taken a down-turn because we find the rhetoric too embarrassing. We want to be more streetwise. It's the Biblical echoes, the Shakespearean echoes, the big language, which, perhaps, we can't handle. Perhaps we are, both of our countries, a small screen nation now.

He's too rhetorical for the postmodern period. He's like the last of the classical poets.

In the '30s when he first appeared they tried to pigeonhole him, as critics do, as a surrealist for a while. It hardly fits. Perhaps that was their way of saying, "We don't know what the hell he's doing."

No, I think he was much greater than them. You have to be quite specific in saying the French Surrealists. There were American and British followers—at City Lights we republished David Gascoyne's book on Surrealism. But the surrealists I never thought were great poets *per se*. I never thought Andre Breton himself was a great poet. But Apollinaire and Cendrars were the greatest of twentieth-century French poets as far as I was concerned.

Coming out of a Dylan Thomas reading you were obviously affected by the sense of occasion as well as the quality of the language. Did that make you want to be up there and perform your writing?

Oh, definitely. Dylan Thomas had a very definite effect on the San Francisco Renaissance which began in the early 1950s when the Beat poets arrived from New York—I'm talking about Allen Ginsberg, Gregory Corso, William Burroughs, Jack Kerouac, and others that my little publishing house ended up publishing. When they arrived in San Francisco they were all kind of New York carpet-baggers, including myself, and they were very much turned on to what's called "performance poetry" today. Up till that period poetry had been dead on the printed page. It was a very dead poetry scene with old poetry magazines like *Poetry (Chicago)* publishing these precious little anthologies—poetry about language, poetry about poetry—like it is today. It was really a dead period or a gestative period; so in the 1950s, after the war, the population flowed towards the West as though the continent had tilted, there was a *deracination,* an uprooting of everyone by the Second World War. Half the guys who went off to the war never stayed back home anymore. *How you gonna keep the boys on the farm after they've seen Paris*? But it took up until the 1950's for this fantastic deracination to coalesce into the new configuration of literary elements. Naturally, it happened in San Francisco, which is sort of the last frontier. And the idea of most of

the Beat poets was oral messages, poems that had to make it aloud first; the printed page came later, that would be incidental. It had to make it without explanation. I've always felt that the poem that had to be explained was a failure, to the extent it had to be explained. We were used to hearing the poets in the universities before that giving a five or ten minute explanation for a two minute poem. There's plenty of that right now. Our idea was to kick the sides out of all of that. If you heard Allen Ginsberg read "Howl" you'd slap yourself on the head and say, "I never saw the world like that before." That's what a great poet has to do, but how often does it happen—same with Dylan Thomas—you'd say, "I never saw reality or heard reality like that before," like it's a great new vision. So the oral bardic tradition which Thomas carried forward when he read was fantastic for many of the local San Francisco poets there.

So who was there? Can you name names?

Well, all kinds of poets were in San Francisco at the time—I'm not sure who went to the Dylan Thomas readings. And then the Caedmon recordings of Thomas were wonderful, a miracle that they survived.

But I would have thought that the major influence on a lot of American poets of the 1950s was Whitman. Though, of course, not for the oral presentation of readings.

Well, Allen Ginsberg claimed Walt Whitman for his homosexual side, but generally for his universal side. Allen had the same compassion that Whitman had.

It's the principle of "Song of Myself"—morally you start here, you sort yourself out and then move outwards.

No, with Allen it wasn't really the song of yourself—as a Buddhist you have to suppress yourself; you can't really go around singing songs of yourself. But you can say that he sang a song of humanity. And he sang William Blake. When Allen sang *"The Songs of Innocence and Experience"* it was really beautiful to hear. These are songs of humanity. I think Allen Ginsberg is still the greatest living American poet. No doubt about it—a great world view. He paid homage to Dylan Thomas; he came to Wales and he wrote a long poem of his own at Fern Hill—he happened to write it on LSD but it's a wonderful long poem in homage to Dylan Thomas. One master recognizes another. And all the minor poets don't recognize this—can't hear the eternal voice in there. You know, Allen read that on the William Buckley show on TV and Allen is such a powerful reader that Buckley could not interrupt him.

I think the problem in Wales is that Thomas is the only writer of ours who has had world recognition and, in a sense, he doesn't recognize Wales. You come away with a very limited sense of what this country really is.

You mean James Joyce wasn't Welsh? (laughs). "Well you know it, and don't you ken it, and that's the he and the she of it."

Well, perhaps we are being too chauvinistic. We ought to be grateful for Dylan Thomas. He is a world poet—he starts with a small canvas and it becomes enormous and important.

Of course, he wasn't political in any way. Some people claimed that he was religious. I don't see that at all. I think he was basically a pagan poet.

But you can certainly hear the preacher when he's performing and you can locate the Bible, "the ear of the synagogue of corn" and so on.

But that was just because he grew up with those images in his head from being around church services and Welsh preachers.

Is Allen Ginsberg a religious poet?

Allen is Jewish for one thing and yet his poetry is not Jewish. Even though he wrote a long book-length poem to his mother, *Kaddish*. Allen has never been classed as being a religious poet, his poetry is not predominantly characterized as being Jewish, it seems to me.

But that's what I mean. There's the sense that the term "religious" is used with regard to a poet such as Dylan Thomas because he celebrates life.

Ginsberg was closer to being a religious poet for his Buddhism. I don't know about Allen Ginsberg celebrating life: I think sometimes Allen celebrates death. His poetry since the death of his mother, since the big book *Kaddish*, has increasingly celebrated death. He has a song he sings called "Father Death," he does it with his Indian music-box, like an accordion. It's like a Blake song, "Father death be kind to me." And he has many poems that are really obsessed with death. He's been celebrating death for a long time now.

One of the things that I respond to strongly in Dylan Thomas is the refusal to mourn or accept, you know, "Rage, rage against the dying of the light." Is there something about clenching the fist in a cold northern European way about that? Like some crude Viking warrior, some macho hero saying, "Fuck you Death—I'm not going to take it."

He's not accepting it at all. He's not celebrating it and he's not using some religious escape. He's not saying, "And death

shall have no dominion because Christ the Lord is going to save me." You never hear that from Dylan Thomas.

No, but there's some sense of a resurrection, but perhaps only as the flowers come up. Perhaps it's that kind of idea.

I don't think you get any feeling of resurrection in Dylan Thomas' poems. I haven't.

I was telling you that Vernon Watkins taught me for a while in Swansea University and Vernon, as a Christian, wanted to argue that Dylan was a Christian. I find that hard to accept, though I find that he is religious in the broader sense. But you could say that about almost any poet, couldn't you? Your own poem, "Christ climbed down / from his bare tree this year / and ran away to. . . ."

Well, that's a satire on what modern society has done to the conception of Christ, but I also have a satire on the Lord's Prayer.

And there's that hip crucifixion in A Coney Island of the Mind *isn't there?*

Yes, I stole that from Lord Buckley, who was a hip white man. The first white man I ever heard talk black hip talk. He was a man who called his wife "Lady Buckley" and he called you "His Highness" and he was a kind of circus performer, charlatan in the way he dressed with robes and he swept them around him. His everyday dress was a robe or perhaps a crown or a turban. At City Lights we published a book of his jazz monologues. It was called *The Hiporama of the Classics*. He did hip versions of "Friends, Romans, countrymen," and things like the Declaration of Independence in jive-talk. And he did one called "The Naz" which was about Jesus Christ and I ripped it off for my poem on Christ.

That poem is still used in school assemblies, I can testify to that. I must confess that I pinched "Christ came down" earlier this year because my writing students were very concerned about the Gulf War and I showed them your poem and suggested that they could use your first five lines as a starting point for a structure into which they could fit specific Gulf War images. It seemed to work very well, as a kind of hook. It has a strong choric force. Is that satisfying for you? I mean, this is a poem that dates from A Coney Island of the Mind *in 1958.*

Oh yes, that book is still in print—about a million copies sold. They have a public surface that anyone can understand. And then they are supposed to make it aloud, without explanations. Of course, poetry has to have several other levels—a subversive level and a subjective level—otherwise it's just journalism.

Oddly, it seems to me that the quality of Dylan Thomas is that, although he sounds like a preacher, he's got this BBC veneer over his natural, though middle-class, Welsh accent. Although he sounds like a voice of authority he is, of course, radical in what he is saying. Some of the images are quite startling in the way in which they deconstruct conventional religion and conventional belief.

I can see how people would start to use the word "surrealist" in talking about him because "surrealist" has been misused as meaning any kind of disparate conjunction of imagery. I mean "Garlic and sapphires in the mud / Clot the bedded axle-tree" in the *Four Quartets*—is that surrealist? I always thought that was Eliot's best poetry, not *The Waste Land*.

The great American poet who didn't want to be American.

Oh yes, when City Lights published Allen Ginsberg's *Howl* I wrote the jacket blurb and the first thing I said was that this was the greatest long poem to be published since Eliot's *Four Quartets* in 1943. There was a now famous reading in San Francisco in what was called the Six Gallery; it was a gallery in a garage, with maybe a hundred people at the most, half of whom were poets maybe. And Ginsberg read *Howl* for the first time there and I sent him a telegram that night using the words that Emerson used in writing to Whitman when he first received a copy of *Leaves of Grass*. He wrote to Whitman: "I greet you at the beginning of a great career." And that's what I sent to Allen. I added, "PS—when do we get the manuscript?"

That sold hundreds of thousands of copies didn't it?

Yes, courtesy of the San Francisco Police Department and the US Customs which busted the book. And my partner and myself were put on trial and we were defended by the American Civil Rights Union—thank God for them otherwise we'd have gone out of business. And we had a criminal lawyer called Jake Ehrlich who latched onto the case when he thought he was going to get his picture in *Life Magazine,* which he did. It's hard to get that kind of publicity, especially these days. I mean, if you took your clothes off at a poetry reading today, do you think anyone would notice?

So Howl *sells because it's supposed to be outrageous, Dylan Thomas attracts attention because he's supposed to be a drunk and a womanizer—is that what you have to do to get poetry noticed, for goodness sake? It's depressing.*

Well, given the universal brainwash by television these days, I don't think we could do very much about that. You just have to realize that television is just this electronic gadget that has somehow managed to capture the consciousness of two-thirds of the people on earth. You don't have to be slaves to this thing. Poetry—with all the media that you have these days—the single unaccompanied voice doesn't have much of a chance. If I were a young, twenty or twenty-five year old poet I would go into film and video. In fact, I think that's where all the young poets are going in the States. The ones who would have become poets are all doing video. They're video-poets.

So is poetry weak at the moment in the States?

It's very academic. There's a lot of language about language, poetry about poetry. But some new young turk will come along and make a great new barbaric yawp.

But what about some of the old turks doing that, Lawrence? What about that? You obviously felt strongly about the Gulf War—did you write about that?

Well, no. It seems like older poets are baffled into silence (laughs). It seems like it's impossible to utter some great, all-encompassing statement these days. But even as I say that I realise that one of these days some turk is going to come along and give out a new, barbaric yawp (that was Whitman's term) and knock the sides out of everything again. And everyone will stand around saying, "Gee, why didn't I think of that—it was so obvious—it was just waiting to be said."

Larry Smith (review date September 1995)

SOURCE: A review of "Pictures of the Gone World," in *Small Press Review,* Vol. 27, No. 9, September 1995, p. 12.

[*Smith reviews the revised edition of* Pictures of the Gone World, *and discusses the impact of Ferlinghetti's City Lights Bookstore and New Directions Paperbacks.*]

One of the classics of contemporary small press publishing, Lawrence Ferlinghetti's **Pictures Of The Gone World (Revised)** is ripe with legend. Just as Ferlinghetti and Peter Martin, his pop culture partner, were able to birth the first American all paperback bookstore in 1953—The City Lights Bookshop—so Ferlinghetti was soon able to send forth the first of City Lights Books in his slim **Pictures Of The Gone World** (1955, forty years ago). **Pictures** also launched City Lights influential Pocket Poets Series (modeled after the inexpensive French books and a letterpress edition of Kenneth Patchen's *An Astonished Eye Looks Out of the Air,* done on William Everson's Untide Press in 1946).

Ferlinghetti has recalled the experience: "The first one was done by hand. David Ruff and Holly Beye, and Kirby [Ferlinghetti's wife] and myself and Mimi Orr pasted on covers and gathered it by hand, like any other little press. The first printing was a thousand copies." It is the story of so many alternative, independent, small presses begun with care and cunning, and the cooperation of friends. This grass-roots effort, however, succeeded in publishing some of the most important books of this half of the century—#2 Kenneth Rexroth's *Spanish Poems Of Love And Exile,* #3 Patchen's *Poems Of Humor And Protest,* and, of course, Allen Ginsberg's defamed then celebrated *Howl* as #4.

And certainly Ferlinghetti's City Lights Books has gone on to rival New Directions Publishing as an international small press publisher of the avant-garde. His own *Pictures Of The Gone World* went on to form one third of his *A Coney Island Of The Mind* for New Directions in 1958—a most provocative and popular book, now selling over one million copies.

We should note that the original poems of *Pictures* were among Ferlinghetti's earliest experiments with blending painting and poetry, remnants of his "Palimpsest" manuscript he was working on in France in 1948 under the influence of Ezra Pound and H. D. "Their disarming content and charmed tone were the result of his vision of the painted poem—expert renderings of states of mind and mood, sharp in their timing and turnings upon the page, sight-sound phrasings at once lyrical and laconic. They seem today like old black-and-white films in a small Absurdist Theatre of the mind—Coney Island, North Beach, or Anywhere—Bohemia, America. Ferlinghetti's "gone world," to borrow the jazzman's phrase, is a very mad and beautiful place, and the poet (like Albert Camus's Absurd Hero) is truly in it and with it.

In #26 (There are 27 in the original, to which he has added 18 new poems), he pictures himself "in the Thirdavenue El" reading Yeats, but he does not think of Arcady and the woods:

> I think instead
> of all the gone faces
>   getting off at midtown places
> with their hats and their jobs
>   and of the lost book I had
>   with its blue cover
>   and white inside
> where a pencilhand had
>   written
>   HORSEMAN, PASS BY.

Ferlinghetti declares himself here as a populist poet at one with the "gone faces" of humanity, a true poet-at-large.

The book's mood is comic-sad—his little Charlie Chaplin role—yet the mode is clearly open form, abstract expressionist, where street speech compels the diction, a la Rosenbach. Other favorites from the original are **"Sarolla's women in their picture hats . . . ,"** **"Picasso's acrobat epitomize the world . . . ,"** **"The world is a beautiful place . . . ,"** and my favorite, **"Dada would have liked a day like this / with its various very realistic / unrealities / each about to become / too real for its locality / which is never quite remote enough / to be Bohemia."** There is a boldness and rightness about these risky poems that early claimed a larger turf for all of poetry. They've served us all as doorways.

In the newer poems we see some of his filmic scenes—in fact #29 **"Bicyclists among the trees by the lake"** is presented in filmic verite. "It's all an unfinished film / for which there is no *finis* / (so we would like to think) / seen through a telefoto lens. . . ." Many have a softer, more lyric voice—some are downright love poems: "Her voice was full of Yes. . . .", "In an old black & white photo / a made-up angel", "She looks so good in the morning . . ." and "Why don't you sometimes try—." These are fine performances by a wizened and mature poet, who has kept his eyes and heart open. And there is still the tragic-comic voice still dressed with "The classical masks of / tragedy and comedy / superimposed / upon each other," still leading us finally to a place of laughter where "the most Absurd / true-life tragicomedies / follow after."

Ferlinghetti has never received his due as a poet; perhaps now we can revisit this early-late work and share his achievement of keeping head and heart alive.

FURTHER READINGS

Jacobson, Dan, "America's 'Angry Young Men,'" *Commentary* 24, No. 6 (December 1957): 475-9.
    A critical survey of the writing of several writers from the Beat movement.

Schwartz, Stephen, "Escapees in paradise: literary life in San Francisco," *New Criterion* 4, No. 4 (December 1985): 1-5.
    Schwartz argues that the Beat movement is highly overrated and more dogmatic than intellectual.

Additional coverage of Ferlinghetti's life and career is contained in the following sources published by Gale: *Concise Dictionary of American Literary Biography, 1941-1948; Contemporary Authors,* Vols. 5-8R; *Contemporary Authors New Revisions Series,* Vol. 41; *Dictionary of Literary Biography,* Vols. 5 and 16; *DISCovering Authors Modules: Poets Module; Major 20th-Century Writers;* and *Poetry Criticism,* Vol. 1.

S. E. Hinton

1950-

(Full name Susan Eloise Hinton) American novelist, children's writer, and screenwriter.

The following entry provides an overview of Hinton's career through 1995. For further information on her life and works, see *CLC*, Volume 30.

INTRODUCTION

S. E. Hinton helped to change the tone of young adult fiction with the publication of *The Outsiders* (1967). Dissatisfied with the pristine portrayals of teenagers in traditional adolescent novels, Hinton, still a teen herself, created this popular story of class conflict and gang rivalry. Critics responded favorably to Hinton's unpretentious narrative style and her skillful development of plot and character. Unlike formulaic teenage novels, *The Outsiders* and Hinton's subsequent novels, including *That Was Then, This Is Now* (1971), *Rumble Fish* (1975), *Tex* (1979), and *Taming the Star Runner* (1988), contain characters who cope with such challenges as violence, poverty, alcoholism, and drug addiction.

Biographical Information

Hinton was born in Tulsa, Oklahoma, in 1950 and enjoyed reading as a child. Her enthusiasm for reading continued into her adolescence, but she soon found that the selection of books she was able and allowed to read was limited. She commented: "A lot of adult literature was older than I was ready for. The kids' books were all Mary Jane-Goes-to-the-Prom junk. I wrote *The Outsiders* so I'd have something to read." The overwhelming success of *The Outsiders,* which sold more than four million copies in the United States alone, enabled Hinton to attend the University of Tulsa, where she met David Inhofe, who later became her husband, and where in 1970 she earned a bachelor's degree in education. Because she was intimidated by the expectations that others had of her following the 1967 publication of *The Outsiders,* Hinton did not produce another novel until 1971, when *That Was Then, This Is Now* was published. She wrote two more novels in the 1970s, *Rumble Fish* and *Tex,* and then began focusing on other interests. During the 1980s Hinton collaborated on and supervised the production of several film adaptations of her books, including the commercially successful 1983 Francis Ford Coppola film based on *The Outsiders.* She also devoted time to her personal life in the 1980s, giving birth to a son, Nicholas David. Hinton's last novel to date, *Taming the Star Runner,* was published in

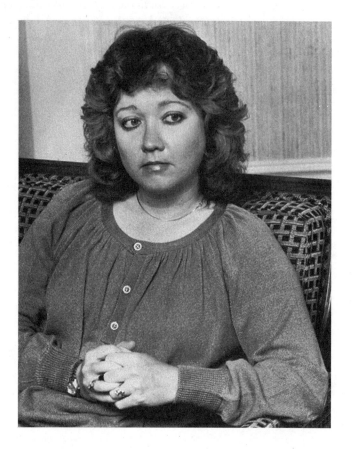

1988, but since that time she has produced two works for young children, *Big David, Little David* (1994) and *The Puppy Sister* (1995).

Major Works

In each of her novels, Hinton depicts the survival and maturation of her adolescent male protagonists, tough yet tender lower-class boys who live in and around Tulsa and who grow by making difficult decisions. Using colloquial language and often a first-person narrative style, Hinton addresses such themes as appearance versus reality, the need to be loved and to belong, the meaning of honor, and the limits of friendship. Society is shown as a claustrophobic and often fatal environment that contributes to the fear and hostility felt by her characters. Based on events that occurred in her high school in Tulsa, *The Outsiders* describes the rivalry between two gangs, the lower-middle-class greasers and the upper-class Socs (for Socials), a conflict that leads to the deaths of members of both gangs. Narrated by fourteen-year-old Ponyboy Curtis, a sensitive, orphaned greaser who tells the story in retrospect, the novel explores the camaraderie, loyalty, and affection that lie behind the gang mystique while pointing out similarities between members of the opposing groups and the futility of gang violence. In *That Was Then, This Is Now,* foster brothers Bryon and Mark begin drifting apart as one becomes preoccupied with school and social concerns and the other becomes heavily involved with drugs and crime. Hinton's *Rumble Fish* also explores the themes of gang violence and coming of age. The story focuses on a disillusioned young man who tries to establish a reputation for himself as a local tough but gradually loses everything that has held meaning for him. *Tex* follows two brothers who are left in each other's care by their unstable father. The book investigates how delinquent youths try to survive in an environment rife with drugs, violence, social upheaval, and familial discord. In Hinton's last novel to date, *Taming the Star Runner,* she relates the story of a fifteen-year-old's self-discovery during a summer spent on his uncle's horse ranch. Hinton's first work for young readers, *Big David, Little David,* is a comic tale that concerns the young narrator's confusion when his father and a boy in his class have the same name; little Nick's puzzlement is compounded when his father leads him to believe that he and the boy in Nick's class are the same person. *The Puppy Sister,* Hinton's most recent published work, tells the fanciful story of a young boy who wishes so strongly for a sibling that his puppy becomes a human sister; the narrative details the difficulties and confusion that arise from the puppy's transformation.

Critical Reception

Although she has been taken to task by many critics for over-emphasizing the machismo of her male characters and for creating underdeveloped, superficial female characters, Hinton has also been praised for her protagonists' depth of emotion and perceptiveness. Her straightforward, unadorned prose style has been compared favorably with that of Ernest Hemingway, but has also been faulted as awkward and not representative of true adolescent speech. Many critics have detected a more mature, controlled quality to Hinton's later narratives, and her works for children have been lauded for their complex characters and compelling, well-developed plots, as well as for their unique, imaginative concepts. Although many critics have noted a tendency toward melodrama in her novels, Hinton's popularity with young readers has endured, and in 1988 she received the American Library Association's Young Adult Services Division/*School Library Journal* Author Award in recognition of her contribution to literature for young adults.

PRINCIPAL WORKS

The Outsiders (novel) 1967
That Was Then, This Is Now (novel) 1971

Rumble Fish (novel) 1975
Tex (novel) 1979
Rumble Fish [adaptor, with Francis Ford Coppola; from her novel of the same title] (screenplay) 1983
Taming the Star Runner (novel) 1988
Big David, Little David (for children) 1994
The Puppy Sister (for children) 1995

CRITICISM

Zena Sutherland (essay date 27 January 1968)

SOURCE: "The Teen-Ager Speaks," in *The Saturday Review* (New York), January 27, 1968, p. 34.

[*In the following essay, Sutherland examines the controversy surrounding* The Outsiders, *providing comments excerpted from a newspaper article by Hinton, from letters written by teenage fans of the novel, and from letters written by adults who objected to the violence depicted in the novel.*]

"Have you looked at the books on the Young Adult Shelf?" S. E. Hinton asked in *Read* magazine November 1. "They are written by aging writers who either try to remember their own youth—which was at least fifteen years ago—or they try to write about today's teens without knowing them." S. E. Hinton, now a college sophomore, wrote *The Outsiders* at the age of fifteen. I'd been watching for the book because of a letter from an established writer who had read the manuscript and—although presumably aging—was impressed by the author's ability.

The Outsiders describes the conflict between madras-clad, middle-class boys (Socs) and those from the wrong side of the tracks (Greasers)—and it is tough, rough, exciting. The book has raised considerable controversy; one reviewer felt that it had received so much praise because everyone involved in children's books was eager to laud anything that might be classified as "realistic." It is a novel ". . . written with distinctive style by a teen-ager who is sensitive, honest, and observant," I commented in *S[aturday] R[eview],* May 13, 1967.

Having learned that S. E. Hinton is a girl, I looked forward with curiosity to meeting her. Prepared for a tough, shrewd, and possibly belligerent young woman, I met a pretty, gentle, and slightly nervous girl. She had written the book because one of her friends in Tulsa had been jumped and beaten up as had Ponyboy, the protagonist of *The Outsiders*. Had she gotten any letters? Many, she said, and most of them from teen-agers; one boy, sure that she was describing him, rebuked her for saying that his hair was reddish—it was plain brown. This note of identification was repeated by other correspondents. The bulk of the letters from teen-agers, said Susan Hinton, expressed fervent gratitude that someone had written a book about the way things really were, but some of the mail from adults was hostile or critical. "I'd love to see the letters," I said.

Here are a few excerpts. "I feel that all teen-agers from all environments should read this novel," writes a fourteen-year-old girl. "It would give people a better understanding of these troubled teen-agers and not judge them by their long hair and odd ways." A boy the same age writes: "In presentation this story seemed very true to life as I know those kind of circumstances prevail in many N.Y. areas." "Your novel," says an adult, "was an education in what I should have known, and it helps me, in retrospect, to understand the tensions I felt around me." "At school we have socs and greasers except we do not call them by those names," reports a high school junior. "We call our socs cliques. The greasers are hards." A letter, addressed to "Mr. Hinton," reads in part: "If you are really Ponyboy, and you have been through these ordeals, God must really love you." Another is quoted in its entirety: "Dear S. E. Hinton, I am 10 years old, going into 5th grade, and I *LOVE* to read. One day, a friend of ours asked me if I wanted to read *The Outsiders*. I said okay. Even though I'm only 10, & your book was for teen-agers, I think it's the *BEST* book that I've EVER read! I really enjoyed it! [Signature] (and Believe me, I've read quite a few!)"

And that—save for one young correspondent who disapproved of the fact that Ponyboy smoked at the age of fourteen—is what teen-agers think. Some adults agree, but many have criticized the novel or the article Miss Hinton had in the *New York Times Magazine* of August 8, in which she pleaded for books that reflected the real stresses of adolescent life. "I feel," wrote one, "that Miss Hinton is a cliché grabber, not a free thinker. . . . I feel that America has more responsibility to the people of the world than to think teen-agers are to be looked up to or catered to." "I have three teen-age children," a correspondent said, "and they just don't know any people like those in your book."

One letter accused the author of trying to make a sensation, another predicted that teen-agers "won't believe a word of it," and several suggested that the book couldn't really have been written by a teen-ager. Most of the critical letters are from people who object to the violence (one fight culminates in death) either on the grounds that such books are in themselves an incitement to violence or that such books shouldn't be written for young people.

In the newspaper article Miss Hinton says, "Adults who let small children watch hours of violence . . . on TV, scream their heads off when a book written for children contains a fist fight. . . . Only when violence is for a sensational effect should it be objected to in books for teen-agers." The violent world that Susan Hinton describes is foreign to me; I know it exists and deplore it. It isn't the only kind of book that teen-agers should read, or that they do read, but it depicts a world that many of them know—and they want to read about life as it is for them. The author doesn't defend violence; she defends honesty. "The teen-age years are a bad time. You're idealistic. You can see what should be. Unfortunately, you see what is, too!"

Times Literary Supplement (review date 30 October 1970)

SOURCE: "On the Hook," in *The Times Literary Supplement,* October 30, 1970, p. 1258.

[*In the following excerpt, the reviewer asserts that while adult readers may find the plot of* The Outsiders *heavy-handed and tedious, younger readers will be so enthralled by the character Ponyboy, who the reviewer identified as believable, that they will disregard what the reviewer assesses as the narrative's weaknesses.*]

The author and chief character are . . . identified with each other in *The Outsiders,* a novel already acclaimed in America as the expression of how teenagers feel. Its author is seventeen and capable of interesting a wider audience than the group she writes about. She reports on the class, social and physical warfare of two city gangs, the Greasers and the Socs, from the slums and the upper-middle class areas. Both lots suffer from parental absence or neglect and seek to realize themselves in feats of strength which lead to disaster and death. The violence is unrepressed, but less significant than Ponyboy's struggle to express the nature of gang loyalty and family affection in a world which is hostile to Greasers, who have even less chance than Socs to sort out desirable goals and less hope of ever attaining them. Ponyboy is a credible character, but the plot creaks and the ending is wholly factitious. The author's determination to "tell it like it is" means that the language, wholly group-coded, is both arresting and tiring to read in its repetitiousness.

The trusted adult (who, it seems, is envisaged as the ideal reader) may find the unrelieved seriousness, a kind of literary egocentrism, too monotonous. Young readers will waive literary discriminations about a book of this kind and adopt Ponyboy as a kind of folk hero for both his exploits and his dialogue.

Jane Powell (review date 2 April 1976)

SOURCE: "Urban Guerrillas," in *The Times Literary Supplement,* April 2, 1976, p. 388.

[*In the following excerpt, Powell faults* Rumble Fish *for lacking a protagonist who, like those of* The Outsiders *and* That Was Then, This Is Now, *possesses superior wit and insight that enable him to rise above the violence and turmoil of his surroundings.* Rumble Fish*'s Rusty-James, Powell argues, is victimized by his environment, and his victimization creates a pervasive air of failure and despair which diminishes the novel.*]

S. E. Hinton's **Rumble Fish** was disappointing. Hooked on Ms. Hinton since I discovered how popular **The Outsiders** and **That Was Then, This Is Now** are with adolescents, this came as a let-down. The earlier two books also deal with the American delinquent scene, but in both the central character has an intelligence and sensitivity which set him apart from his peers.

He involves himself in desperate situations largely out of loyalty to others and at the end, having seen close friends destroyed by violence or drugs, is left wiser and sadder. The detachment of the central figure is lost in **Rumble Fish**. This time the narrator, Rusty-James, is a product (and victim) of his environment, and the world is a grey, sordid and destructive place. The bright values of literature and loyalty have faded, the best friend is a minor figure who lapses into gross insensitivity, and the book is filled with failures, drunks and junkies. In the foreground is the doomed Motorcycle Boy, the narrator's brother and hero, a near-zombie as a result of many crashes on stolen bikes. Rumble fish are Siamese fighting fish—"If you leaned a mirror against the bowl they'd kill themselves fighting their own reflection". The Motorcycle Boy is shot dead as he carries the bowl towards the river. Like the fish, he's in a bowl, cut off from the real world by deafness. Rusty-James has always wanted to be like his brother and that's how he turns out. The narrative is retrospective—the boy is reminded of things he'd like to forget when he meets an old friend—and this perspective emphasizes Rusty-James's hopelessness; there can't even be a glimmer of hope for the future.

S. E. Hinton with Lisa Ehrichs (interview date November 1981)

SOURCE: "Advice from a Penwoman," in *Seventeen,* Vol. 40, November, 1981, p. 32.

[*In the following interview, Hinton discusses her approach to writing, the impact her career had upon her personal life as a teenager, and her recommendations for other young writers.*]

The Outsiders, a tough yet sensitive novel about a gang of teen-agers from the wrong side of the tracks, was a major success for author S. E. Hinton when it came out in 1967. Its publication marked the beginning of a new category of young-adult literature: novels that looked beyond the narrow world of the high school prom. But the most remarkable thing about **The Outsiders** is that its author, Susan Eloise Hinton, was only seventeen when the book was published.

Ms. Hinton followed **The Outsiders** with three other novels, **That Was Then, This Is Now; Rumblefish;** and **Tex.** In 1970, she graduated from the University of Tulsa, in Oklahoma, and continues to live in Tulsa with her husband. Below, Ms. Hinton talks about her early success as a novelist and gives advice to today's young writers.

[*Ehrichs:*] *How did you first become interested in writing?*

[Hinton:] I started in grade school—it was just something I enjoyed doing. I was the type of girl who loved horses and cowboys, so I wrote about them. I read a lot and had fun making up my own stories. Though it was the first one published, **The Outsiders** was actually my third book. I found that for me, novels were easier to write than poems or short stories.

Why is writing a novel easier?

A novel gives you time to define characters, and characters are my strong point. I think about them until I know everything there is to know about each of them.

What made you write **The Outsiders***?*

I'd wanted to read books that showed teen-agers outside the life of "Mary Jane went to the prom." When I couldn't find any, I decided to write one myself. I created a world with no adult authority figures, where kids lived by their own rules.

How long did it take you to write it?

The Outsiders took me a year and a half. During that time, I did four complete drafts. The first draft was forty pages; then I just kept rewriting and adding details.

How did you get it published?

It was amazingly easy. A friend gave me the name of an agent [from Curtis Brown, Ltd., New York] who read it and liked it. He thought he could sell it and did—to Viking, the second publisher we tried!

What kinds of problems did you face as a young writer?

The publisher thought that my being a teen-age writer was a good gimmick, and my close friends thought it was neat. But people I didn't know too well started treating me as though I were stuck-up. I had always been a smart-alecky kid, but after the book was published, I knew I had to change or else people would think success was going to my head. So I became quiet—but people saw that as being stuck-up, too!

I'd wanted to read books that showed teen-agers outside the life of "Mary Jane went to the prom." When I couldn't find any, I decided to write one myself. I created a world with no adult authority figures, where kids lived by their own rules.
                                            —S. E. Hinton

Why are your main characters, such as Ponyboy in **The Outsiders** *and Rusty-James in* **Rumblefish,** *always male?*

I started writing before the women's movement was in full swing, and at the time, people wouldn't have believed that girls would do the things that I was writing about. I also felt more comfortable with the male point of view—I had grown up around boys. But my female characters *will* be getting stronger.

In what ways do your characters reflect aspects of your own personality?

The characters have to be part of yourself, you have to understand them. By the time they go through your head and work their way down on paper, they reflect some aspect of you. Ponyboy Curtis [*The Outsiders*] probably comes closest to me—he's absent-minded and quiet and daydreams a lot.

Why do you think you've been so successful as a writer?

I think it's because I remember how it felt to be a kid. It's not the happiest time, but if you hang on, it gets better.

Any tips for young writers today?

Read. Read everything you can get your hands on. I read a lot when I was younger, and I still do—it's almost an obsession!

Gene Lyons (essay date 11 October 1982)

SOURCE: "On Tulsa's Mean Streets," in *Newsweek,* Vol.

100, No. 15, October 11, 1982, pp. 105-06.

[In the following essay, Lyons examines Hinton's works and career as well as the films based on The Outsiders, Rumble Fish, *and* Tex. *Lyons briefly recounts the plots of the three novels, maintaining that* Tex *is superior, and includes commentary by Hinton.]*

Quick, name the only American novelist whose books have inspired both the Walt Disney studios and Francis Coppola to adapt them to film? Clue: the author's first effort was written while she was a 16-year-old junior at Will Rogers High in Tulsa. Give up? If there's a teen-ager on the premises, ask the kid. Odds are good that S. E. Hinton is a household name around your place, whether you knew it or not.

Coppola's version of Susan Eloise Hinton's first novel, *The Outsiders* (1967)—a melodrama about gang fighting between working-class "greasers" and country-club "socials" in Tulsa in the early '60s—will be released in December. Coppola's *Rumble Fish,* her third book, will be out next year. Disney's *Tex,* from her most recent—and best—novel, previewed briefly in the South this summer. A bittersweet, coming-of-age story about two brothers going it alone in a small Oklahoma town while their father hits the rodeo circuit, *Tex,* because of its Disney label, may have been taken for the kind of movie Hinton says she feared when director Tim Hunter first called. "No thank you, I thought. I don't want to see *Tex Rides the Love Bug.*" It was shown at the New York Film Festival last week and now is being released nationally.

The three movie deals have earned her a lot of money ("But I'm not rich by Tulsa standards," she says); another book, *That Was Then, This Is Now,* has been optioned as well. Now 34 and still living quietly in Tulsa with her husband, three dogs, a cat and a horse named Toyota, Hinton gave up her fear of Hollywood when she met the star of *Tex* (and of the two Coppola movies), 18-year-old teen heartthrob Matt Dillon. Like many of her avid fans, Dillon was "another kid who doesn't read. He told me *That Was Then, This Is Now* was the first book he ever finished." Recalls Hinton of her own childhood: "A lot of adult literature was older than I was ready for. The kids' books were all Mary Jane-Goes-to-the-Prom junk. I wrote *The Outsiders* so I'd have something to read."

The appeal of Hinton's novels is obvious (more than 7 million copies are in print, and all four books are currently available in Dell paperback). The narrator-hero of each is a tough-tender 14- to 16-year-old loner making his perilous way through a violent, caste-ridden world almost depopulated of grownups. "It's a kid's fantasy not to have adults around," says Hinton. While recklessness generally gets punished, her books are never moralistic—all manner of parental rules are broken with impunity. Hers are tales of honor, emotional kinship, loyalty and betrayal. "For a tough kid," says Rusty-James, younger brother of a heroic and doomed character in *Rumble Fish* known only as the Motorcycle Boy, "I had a bad habit of getting attached to people." Hinton has never read Hemingway and says she never will, because English teachers compare her style to his. But it's Raymond Chandler and Ross Macdonald she needs to avoid. Her young toughs are private eyes in training.

Hinton's mail has not changed significantly in 15 years. Usually her readers thank her for expressing feelings they didn't know anybody else had. Sometimes correspondents are moved to ask things like "Why did you make the Motorcycle Boy die?" or "Can't you write another book and get Bryon and Mark back together?" "But," says Hinton, "I think most kids are old enough to learn that sometimes things get broken and can't be fixed." She maintains that she writes about kids because "I just find them more interesting. If I can find some interesting adults someday, maybe I'll write about them." Her protagonists are all boys because "I never knew what girls were talking about. Their deal is to get a man instead of doing something for themselves. Anyhow, 90 percent of kids' fiction is written for girls. But girls will read boys' books, and boys won't read girls' books." For the moment, she plans to stay put in Tulsa. Right now, she says, "I'm doing everything I can to make the novel I'm working on unfilmable."

Jay Scott (essay date April 1983)

SOURCE: "Susie Loves Matt," in *American Film,* Vol. VIII, No. 6, April, 1983, pp. 34-5.

[*In the following excerpt, Scott describes Hinton's association with actor Matt Dillon, who portrayed Dallas in the film version of* The Outsiders, *the title character in the film based on* Tex, *and Rusty-James in the movie based on* Rumble Fish. *Scott goes on to briefly describe Hinton's novels and incorporates Hinton's and Dillon's comments on them as well.*]

The Arkansas River which cuts through the center of Tulsa, Oklahoma, is wide, shallow, and sluggish. It moves imperceptibly under the heavy humid August air; temperatures have been hitting over a hundred for weeks. In summer, most things in Tulsa seem to come to a halt. People who were attracted by the now long-gone unemployment rate of two percent sit outside at night to escape the closeness of small, rented homes that don't have air conditioners. Their children are the children about whom and for whom Francis Coppola is making *Rumble Fish,* a film based on S. E. Hinton's self-proclaimed "art" novel.

Rumble Fish is an expressionist parable of coming of age with unconscious stylistic links to Ernest Hemingway, Raymond Chandler, and James M. Cain. "I had to worry about money, and whether or not the old man would drink up his check before I got part of it . . . and I had a cop itching to blow my brains out. . . . So I didn't have much time for serious thinking about my life," says Rusty-James, the novel's narrator-hero. Coppola's standard line is to compare *The Outsiders,* his conventionally conceived film of Hinton's first novel, to *The Godfather;* he compares *Rumble Fish*—with its *Caligari* camera angles, its *Cat People* fog, and its *Citizen Kane* shadows—to *Apocalypse Now.* For her part, Hinton is happy to leave comparisons aside. She has read almost no Hemingway, Chandler, or Cain, and she does not intend to read more: Her hard-boiled teenybopper tough guys, with warm but not soft hearts thudding gently under black leather carapaces, are her own inventions, and she would like to keep them that way.

Matt Dillon, who plays Rusty-James in *Rumble Fish,* doesn't much like comparisons either. "Marlon Brando?" he says at the mention of the name most often paired with his. "When I was doing *Over the Edge* and was playing around, someone told me I was like Brando. I didn't take that as a compliment. I thought he was a fat old man—the only thing I'd seen him in was *The Godfather.* Then I saw *A Streetcar Named Desire.*" Dillon's eyes narrow. "I remember a few things from it. It was . . . interesting."

Everyone is predicting stardom for this unassertive kid who made his film debut at fourteen in *Over the Edge.* If he achieves it, he will have his talent, luck, Hinton, and Coppola to thank, in that order. After Dillon's impressive performances in *My Bodyguard, Tex* (based on another Hinton novel), and *The Outsiders, Rumble Fish* promises to establish him once and for all. He may someday play Paul Newman to Sean Penn's Robert De Niro.

Hinton remembers being "horrified" when *Tex* director Tim Hunter asked her to take a look at Dillon. "Tex is a sweet little unworldly cowboy, and here was this guy who said, 'Like, man,' and told me *Rumble Fish* was his favorite book. When I get a letter from a kid who says *Rumble Fish* is his favorite book, he's usually in a reformatory."

Hinton's about-face was total and led to a fascinating symbiotic relationship between the writer of children's books and the star of children's movies. "All of a sudden," Hinton recalls, "I thought, I made this kid up; I wrote this kid. He was exactly the kid I was writing about and for—really bright, doesn't fit into the system, has possibilities beyond the obvious." Hinton decided she wanted him in *The Outsiders,* too, but got nowhere with Warner Bros. So she went directly to Coppola. In due course, Dillon was cast.

"I love that kid," Hinton says, telling a long story about Dillon's maturity in dealing with an inebriated adult actor on the *Rumble Fish* set.

"Susie's great," Dillon comments with typical teenage reserve.

Bystanders on the *Rumble Fish* set have noticed that the Hinton-Dillon relationship has already cooled. Dillon is involved with a woman in her twenties and Hinton, having grown somewhat weary of the responsibilities of playing parent ("It's as close as I've ever come, and it isn't an entirely pleasant experience—you worry a lot"), is protecting herself against the loneliness of the sideshow leaving town. Dillon's thoughts are on the future: *Rumble Fish* he knows, is the vehicle that could do him the most good. Or the most harm.

Hinton's novels, and the films made from them, are generally greeted as documents carrying the timeliness of tomorrow (the ads for *Tex* were one-word come-ons: "*Tex*. Tough. Tender. Today"). In that context, their thoroughgoing maleness is surprising and oddly old-fashioned. The books are always about boys; except as addenda to the males, there are no Hinton Little Women. "When I was a teenager, I didn't understand what girls were talking about," she explains. "They were always waiting for something to happen; they got to stand in the john, rat their hair, and outline their eyes in black. Even now, when I go to baby showers, I still feel like I'm an anthropologist at some weird rite."

As her blue Mercedes streaks past the gaudy bronze praying hands that adorn the entrance to evangelist Oral Roberts's City of Faith medical complex—"Part space station, part Disneyland," Hinton cackles—she cheerfully confesses ignorance of children's literature. "I don't know what the latest hot trend is. I hate the 'problem' approach. Problems change. Character remains the same. I write character." With equal cheer, she discusses her role in what she hopes will be a movie revolution. Young-adult fiction has long been savvy and sophisticated in its treatment of teenagers, and she would like to see that savvy and sophistication come to the screen. "Teenagers are not," she says with disgust, "the sex-crazed morons you see in most movies."

Why is she committed to kids? "It's an interesting time of life. Feelings are more dramatic, ideals are slamming up against the walls of compromise. They have more feelings than any other segment of society, but they are more afraid of showing their feelings than any other segment."

The character of Rusty-James is heavy with teenage anomie, but he's basically a sweet guy. Dillon concedes autobiographical overtones, but stops at the leather-jacketed, James Dean iconography. "Of course, you know that *Rumble Fish*

is glorified. I never got my head smashed in by a crowbar, like Rusty-James does. Kids I knew really got into the book, but it wasn't their life. We weren't poor. Sometimes being from the middle class is not great either. You're in the middle again. You can't complain that you've been too spoiled, and you can't complain that you've never had anything. That's why in *The Outsiders* it says that things can be rough all over for kids."

Michael Malone (essay date 8 March 1986)

SOURCE: "Tough Puppies," in *The Nation*, Vol. 242, No. 9, March 8, 1986, pp. 276-78, 290.

[*In the following essay, Malone argues that Hinton's novels are not representative of average American teenagers or as realistic as they have been alleged to be, and he asserts that the appeal of Hinton's works among teenage readers is due mainly to their action-packed narratives, simplistic plot structures, intense emotional tone, and well-defined principles. Malone also examines the societal trends which make Hinton's works popular among American youngsters, ponders books for young adults as a literary category, and makes comparisons between Hinton's works and the James Dean films of the 1950s.*]

America at its saddest and dangerously silliest has the adolescent soul of a grade-B cowboy movie—violent and sentimental, morally and mentally simplistic. No doubt that's why a grade-B movie star still sits tall in the saddle of the Oval Office, sometimes quoting Dirty Harry and sometimes teary poems. And no doubt that's why the four Young Adult novels of S. E. Hinton have sold millions of copies and have made their rough-tender way into successful Hollywood movies, usually starring Matt Dillon, one of teen-age America's heartthrobs. The novels—*The Outsiders; That Was Then, This is Now; Rumble Fish;* and *Tex*—are touted on their covers as heroic tales of "the young and the restless," as "strikingly realistic portraits of modern kids trying to make it in a rough world." S. E. Hinton is the nom de plume of an Oklahoma woman, Susan Eloise Hinton, who publishes under her gender-anonymous initials because her books are first-person narrations of male teen-agers and, according to librarians, are read mostly by sixth-to eighth-grade boys. M. E. Kerr, another popular young adult novelist, uses the same strategy.

Hinton was 17 when she wrote *The Outsiders* and the characters, she says, were "loosely based" on people she knew. "When I was growing up, most of my close friends were boys," she remarked in an interview in *The New York Times*. "In those days girls were mainly concerned about getting their hair done and lining their eyes. It was such a passive society. Girls got their status from their boyfriends. They weren't interested in doing anything on their own." They certainly don't do anything on their own in Hinton's books— indeed they scarcely put in an appearance, although the male narrators frequently comment on how nice their hair looks. Nor are adults much in evidence. In this world the stories, like the streets, belong almost exclusively to tribes of adolescent males, to accounts of their tender camaraderie, reckless rebellion, macho warfare and often tragic fates.

It is difficult, if not horrifying, to think that the millions of 12-year-olds reading these "strikingly realistic portraits of modern kids" find any more in them than the most remote connections to their own lives, for Hinton's boys are usually impoverished, are often thugs and thieves, are variously abandoned by parents, brutalized by policemen, jailed, stabbed to death, shot to death, burned to death and so routinely beaten nearly to death that they think it's a drag to have to rush to the hospital for something as trivial as a fractured skull. When his chest is cut so deeply in a gang fight that he can see "white bone gleaming through," Rusty-James of **Rumble Fish** grits his teeth ("Ain't all that bad") while his brother douses whiskey on the wound ("He's been hurt worse than this"). These are "lean hard" "tough as nails"— or rather "tuff" as nails—"cool" 14-year-olds. Misery, lawlessness and violence are served up matter-of-factly to palates presumably so jaded by screen violence that it seems there are no squeamish stomachs left among the prepubescent. "The Dingo is a pretty rough hangout; there's always a fight going on there and once a girl got shot" (**The Outsiders**). "The last guy who was killed in the gangfights was a Packer. He had been fifteen" (**Rumble Fish**). Bryon, narrator of **That Was Then, This is Now,** comments blandly: "We fought with chains and we fought Socs and we fought other grease gangs. It was a normal childhood. . . . So that was how we lived, stealing stuff and selling stuff." Other boyish pastimes mentioned are drunken poker games, car theft, drag racing, pool hustling and "jumping hippies and blacks." The horrendous life of Bryon's former girlfriend is summed up in a paragraph and dismissed as nothing unusual: "Her husband didn't have a job, her brothers were both in jail, her old man was drunk all the time, and her father-in-law was always slapping her bottom. . . . They weren't so different from most of the families in our neighborhood."

Tragedy is parenthetical, introduced in a dependent clause: "Since Mom and Dad were killed in an auto wreck. . . . " (**The Outsiders**). Even in **Tex,** the most recent, the least riddled with gang romance and the best of the books, Tex (a pleasant fellow, given to believable classroom pranks and adolescent worries) is forced at gunpoint to drive an escaped killer to the state line. He rolls the truck into a ditch, enabling the pursuing police to blow the young convict away in a barrage of crossfire. Only a week or so later, Tex himself is critically shot in the stomach while accompanying a

friend on a drug deal. Tex has only gone along for the ride because he's upset. He's upset because his brother has just blurted out that their Pop is not really Tex's father; his real father was a no-good rodeo cowboy with whom Mom had a one-night stand to spite Pop when he was in prison for bootlegging.

> **Far from strikingly realistic in literary form, these novels are romances, mythologizing the tragic beauty of violent youth, as the flashy surrealism of Francis Ford Coppola's *Rumble Fish,* with its film noir symbolism and spooky soundtrack, all too reverently attests.**
> *—Michael Malone*

In **That Was Then, This is Now** "golden dangerous Mark," the narrator's best buddy, also discovers that he is mistaken about his parentage—his real father turns out to be another rodeo cowboy. Bryon tells us about it like this: "Mark had lived at my house ever since I was ten and he was nine and his parents shot each other in a drunken argument." Later we learn the argument was over Mark's parentage; the shots were fatal, and the child, hiding under the porch, heard it all. As Mark recalls: "And then they start yelling and I hear this sound like a couple of fire-crackers. And I think, well, I can go live with Bryon and his old lady. . . . I didn't like livin' at home." The desire to leave home is a sentiment with which most teen-agers can empathize, but few are given so graphic an opportunity to do so. Nor do the majority, I hope, respond to family indifference like Dallas Winston of **The Outsiders,** who "lied, cheated, stole, rolled drunks, jumped small kids," even if they occasionally feel the same way about their parents: "What do they matter? Shoot, my old man don't give a hang whether I'm in jail or dead in a car wreck or drunk in the gutter. That don't bother me none."

What is clear from the recurrent themes of Hinton's novels, like the discovery of mysterious parentage, is that despite their modern, colloquial tone, they are fairy tale adventures (Luke Skywalker's father is really Darth Vader), and their rumbles as exotic as jousts in *Ivanhoe* or pirate wars in *Treasure Island*. What is curious is that grown-ups insist on the books' veracity. Hinton announces, "The real boy like Dallas Winston [the role Matt Dillon plays in **The Outsiders**] was shot and killed by the police for having stolen a car." Tim Hunter, director of the film **Tex,** says he was drawn to Hinton's work because of the way she weaves social problems "into the fabric of a realistic story."

In fact, the fabric is mythic. There are no verisimilar settings. Presumably the books take place near Tulsa, Oklahoma (the films do), but place names are never mentioned, and were it not for occasional references to rodeos, one would have little notion of the Western ambiances so evident in the movie versions. Characters live in "the neighborhood"; sometimes they go to "the city" or to "the country." The city is bacchanalian: "There were lots of people and noise and lights and you could feel energy coming off things, even buildings" (***Rumble Fish***). The country is pastoral: "The clouds were pink and meadowlarks were singing" (***The Outsiders***). Temporal location is equally vague. ***The Outsiders,*** published in 1967, might as easily have been written ten years earlier, in the fifties of its real progenitor, James Dean movies. True, some parenthetical hippies are up to some druggy no-good in ***That Was Then, This Is Now*** (1971), but the Motorcycle Boy in ***Rumble Fish*** (1975) might have ridden right off the screen of *The Wild One*. Far from strikingly realistic in literary form, these novels are romances, mythologizing the tragic beauty of violent youth, as the flashy surrealism of Francis Ford Coppola's ***Rumble Fish,*** with its film noir symbolism and spooky soundtrack, all too reverently attests.

Moreover, while praised for its "lean Hemingway style" and natural dialogue, Hinton's prose can be as fervid, mawkish and ornate as any nineteenth-century romance, although this is less true in the later books, especially ***Tex***. The heightened language of her young narrators intensifies the glamour and sentiment of their stories, but it will not strike readers as everyday school-locker lingo. Ponyboy, 14, and Bryon, 16, fling adjectives and archaic phrases ("Hence his name," "Heaven forbid") around like Barbara Cartland. Bryon notes that his friend Mark's "strangely sinister innocence was gone." Ponyboy describes his brother, Sodapop, as having "a finely drawn, sensitive face that somehow manages to be reckless and thoughtful at the same time," as well as "lively, dancing, recklessly laughing eyes." Ponyboy is also given to quoting from memory long snatches of Robert Frost's "Nothing Gold Can Stay," and to using words like "merrily," "gallant" and "elfish." Of course, Bryon and Ponyboy point out to us that although they seem to spend all their time hanging out with the gang, they are both honor students: "I make good grades and have a high IQ." But even Rusty-James of ***Rumble Fish,*** stuck in "dumb classes" and, by his own admission, no student ("Math ain't never been my strong point"), waxes poetical: "I wouldn't have her to hold anymore, soft but strong in my arms." Sententious moralizing coats the pages: "That was what he wanted. For somebody to tell him 'No.'. . . If his old man had just belted him—just once, he might still be alive." "You start wondering why, and you get old." "We see the same sunset."

The lyricism, the lack of novelistic detail, the static iconography of Hinton's books keep the clutter of creation from interfering with the sources of their obviously persistent appeal—their rapid action (mostly violent) unfettered by the demands of a plot, their intense emotions (mostly heavy) and

their clear-cut moral maps. Hinton's fictional universe is as black-and-white as an old cowboy film. ***The Outsiders*** is the ur-text. In it there are Socs (Socials) and there are greasers; unlike that of the warring Hatfields and McCoys, Montagues and Capulets, Jets and Sharks, this eternal enmity is neither familial nor racial, but financial. Socs are rich, greasers are poor; Socs are "the in crowd," greasers are "the outsiders." Socs always wear madras and English Leather and drive Mustangs or Corvairs. They always "jump greasers and wreck houses and throw beerblasts for kicks." That's pretty much all we get to know about Socs; they're just the enemy. A Soc girl, Cherry Valance, makes a brief appearance to point out to Ponyboy, "We have troubles you never even heard of," but those troubles are not explored; instead she schematizes neatly: "You greasers have a different set of values. You're more emotional. We're sophisticated—cool to the point of not feeling anything." Given this fundamental difference (and despite the fact that they see the same sunset), Cherry is obliged to warn Ponyboy: "If I see you in the hall . . . and don't say hi, well, it's not personal. . . . We couldn't let our parents see us with you all."

Our heroes, greasers, are also initially defined by their appearance and their style of antisocial behavior: "We steal things and drive old souped-up cars and hold up gas stations once in a while . . . just like we leave our shirttails out and wear leather jackets." But popular culture has taught us to interpret this style with sympathy, if not rabid infatuation. The narrators pay continual, indeed obsessive, attention to their own and their friends' appearance. We hear constantly about "strange golden eyes," "light-brown, almost-red hair," faces like "some Greek god come to earth." They are always asking and reassuring each other about their good looks, particularly the beauty of their hair.

Funky costume and flamboyant hairstyle have long been the outward signs of inward romantic rebellion—from [Percy Bysshe] Shelley's flowing locks and open collars through [Alan] Ginsberg's sandals to Elvis's sideburns—and Ponyboy's identifying himself through his hair oil ("I am a greaser") announces his place in a tradition that goes back to Brontë's crush on Heathcliff, and associates him with such suffering gods as James Dean. It's significant that many of the young men who played in Coppola's 1982 film of ***The Outsiders*** were to become adolescent idols within the next few years: Dillon, Rob Lowe, Tom Cruise, Emilio Estevez, Patrick Swayze. A leather jacket, bloody knuckles and a sensitive soul is an irresistible combination. Pain and sadness help too.

There is no sweeter sorrow than the self-pity of our teens, no pain more rhapsodized than our adolescent anguish; adults simply lose the will to sustain such *Sturm und Drang*. Like the protagonists of all *Bildungsromans,* Hinton's leather-jacketed young Werthers are lyrical on the subject of their psychic aches and pains. Tough as nails on the street, yeah, hey—but alone in the dark, they're as naked and afraid in a world they never made as any Herman Hesse hero. Confused, lonely, slighted, they share with, they feel for, their readers that most profound pubescent emotion: "I don't belong." In the classic apprenticeship novel, the youngster—Tonio Kröger, Stephen Dedalus, Paul Morel, Eugene Gant—experiences and reflects on this sense of alienation and so grows to understand the particular difference that is his self. When, in *The Outsiders,* Ponyboy tells us, "I cried passionately, 'It ain't fair that we have all the rough breaks,'" his *cri de coeur,* like the novel's title, suggests the tribal rather than personal thrust of Hinton's use of the theme, as well as its simplistic economic nature. ("You can't win because they've got all the breaks.") In Hinton's books, selfhood is subsumed in the tribal gang. "It was great, we were a bunch of people making up one big person" (*That Was Then, This Is Now*). "Why did the Socs hate us so much? We left them alone." "It wasn't fair for the Socs to have everything. We were as good as they were" (*The Outsiders*). So magically does the gang incorporate its members that in the opening of *The Outsiders* it miraculously appears out of the night to save Ponyboy from the motiveless malignity of a carful of Socs: "All the noise I had heard was the gang coming to rescue me." "Somehow the gang sensed what had happened."

The gang is the family: "We're almost as close as brothers." And in contrast to "a snarling, distrustful, bickering pack like the Socs," greaser gangs are unfailingly loyal and free of rivalry. Maybe they have "too much energy, too much feeling, with no way to blow it off" except through marauding violence, but with one another they are as gentle as maidens on a Victorian valentine, innocently sleeping with their arms around each other, choking with tenderness for one another's pain. Johnny in *The Outsiders* is the most vulnerable, most pathetically hurt gang member (the Sal Mineo part in *Rebel Without a Cause*; for his film of *The Outsiders,* Coppola even found in Ralph Macchio an actor who looks just like Mineo). Ponyboy's solicitude for him is shared by even the toughest of the greasers. He is "a little dark puppy that has been kicked too many times and is lost in a crowd of strangers. . . . His father was always beating him up, and his mother ignored him. . . . If it hadn't been for the gang, Johnny would never have known what love and affection are." Like Mineo's Plato, Johnnycake is clearly pegged for tearful sacrifice. And sure enough—having accidentally stabbed a Soc to death and then redeemed himself by saving some children from a burning church—he dies from burns and a broken back after a series of heart-rending hospital-bed scenes. As might be expected in fiction for adolescents, the blood brother bond supersedes all other emotional commitments. *That Was Then, This Is Now* opens, "Mark and me went down to the bar"; and Bryon's love for Mark, like the love of Beowulf or Roland for their companions, runs like a lyric refrain through the novel.

These characters do sometimes have girlfriends, but their erotic relationships come nowhere near the power of male camaraderie. Hinton reports she almost didn't agree to sell *Tex* to Walt Disney Productions because she "thought they'd really sugar it up, take out all the sex, drugs and violence," but there is actually far less sex in her books than in the films made from them. Her instinct, conscious or not, that young readers could take endless physical violence and heartbreak but would be embarrassed by physical passion is quite sound. On the page of *Rumble Fish,* Rusty-James tells us of his visit to Patty, "I just sat there holding her and sometimes kissed the top of her head"; on the screen this becomes a torrid tumble on a couch. Rusty-James's description, "There were some girls [at the lake] and we built a fire and went swimming," becomes on screen an orgiastic montage of naked bodies. Similarly, unlike the films, the books are as free of profanity as *Heidi*. We are told people "talk awful dirty," but the only curses we hear are almost comically mild: "Glory!" "Shoot!" "Oh blast it!" Indeed, gang members warn the younger ones to avoid "bad habits" like cursing. They may smoke cigarettes, integral to the image, but they don't much care for booze and are leery of drugs. As well they might be. M & M, *That Was Then, This is Now*'s counterpart to the doomed Johnnycake, takes LSD, goes psychotic, is hospitalized (the doctor announces solemnly, "He may have lost his mind forever") and is told that his chromosomes are so messed up that he must forget his dream of a large family.

In *Rebel Without a Cause,* James Dean is trying to cope with a new society, with a new girl, with his parents, with adult authority. He copes in part by means of wry humor, a detachment that is missing in Hinton's books and in the films made from them. Rather than ask her characters to cope with adults, wryly or otherwise, Hinton either removes them or removes their authority. The Oedipal struggle is displaced to older siblings. Ponyboy's parents are dead; he lives with and is supported by his big brother, Darry, a football star who gave up college to keep the family together. Ponyboy fears and idolizes him. Tex's mother is dead (after a fight with his father, she walked off in the snow to go dancing, caught pneumonia and quickly succumbed), and his father forgets for months at a time to return home or to send money. Tex lives with and is supported by his older brother, Mace, a basketball star, whom he fears and admires. Rusty-James's mother ran away; his father, once a lawyer, is a hopeless drunk on welfare who wanders in and out of the house mumbling, "What strange lives you two lead," to Rusty-James and his idolized older brother, the Motorcycle Boy (about whom Hinton seems to feel much as Lady Caroline Lamb felt about Byron: "Mad, bad and dangerous to know"). Like Dallas Winston, the Motorcycle Boy is shot to death by the police, leaving the hero to inherit his romantic mantle—even to the extent of going color-blind. Bryon has no father but does have a mother, depicted as a model of saintly virtue. She behaves, however, with a remarkable lack of maternal responsibility or even curiosity. Not only do Bryon and Mark sometimes not "come home for weeks" without being reprimanded but their being beaten black and blue elicits little concern. Mom notices ten stitches in Mark's head: "How did that happen?" "And Mark answered, 'Fight,' and the subject was dropped. That was a good thing about Mom—she'd cry over a dog with a piece of glass in his paw but remained unhysterical when we came home clobbered. . . . Parents never know what all their kids do. . . . It's a law." The laws of Hinton's books are the laws of the cowboy movies, the laws of romance.

According to a children's librarian in Connecticut, Hinton and Judy Blume have long been the most popular authors of "reluctant readers" in the junior-high age group, youngsters who generally "wouldn't be caught dead in a library." Hinton's books "go out by themselves," without having to be recommended by adults or assigned by teachers or cleverly packaged ("*Swiss Family Robinson* is about survival—just like *Rambo*"). At the Philadelphia Free Library I was told that the four novels enjoy a "highly active shelf-life," greatly enhanced by the release of the filmed versions. When my 16-year-old niece told me she'd read Hinton "as a kid," I asked her why. "I liked Matt Dillon," she answered.

In the Young Adult section of the Philadelphia library, I spotted eleven paperback copies of *Tex* (the hardcover copy was in Adult Fiction), sandwiched with twelve paperback copies of *Star Wars*, "by George Lucas," three of *Pickwick Papers* and two of *Gone With the Wind*. Browsing through this area I could come to no clear sense of what constitutes Young Adult fiction. *The Seven-per-Cent Solution* was there, so was *Tell Me That You Love Me, Junie Moon*, so was Reynolds Price's *A Long and Happy Life* and novels by Ella Leffland, Ernest Gann and John Knowles. As a specific marketing category Young Adult fiction ("Y.A." for short) appears to be about twenty years old. I have no memory as a child in the 1940s and a teen-ager in the 1950s of any such literary label. One read baby books (mostly pictures), and then one read books. "Books" meant a melange of everything available that told a story—[Alexandre] Dumas, [Charles] Dickens, Hardy Boys, [Robert Louis] Stevenson, [Louisa May] Alcott, sea books, horse books, mystery books. Adult fiction meant *Lady Chatterley's Lover* or *Peyton Place* or *By Love Possessed*. Rereading as an adult *Huckleberry Finn, Gulliver's Travels, David Copperfield, Animal Farm* and other classics, I of course read them differently, just as I now know what the *A* in *The Scarlet Letter* stands for (the seventh-grade teacher who assigned us this novel never bothered to explain), but at the time of my first acquaintance, I was never under the impression that I was reading literature packaged for my "age group."

The successful marketing of Young Adult fiction to teen-age consumers is defended by some, who point out that the choice is not between an adolescent's reading *Tex* and reading *Sons and Lovers* but between reading *Tex* and reading nothing. Librarians are deeply concerned about the drop in reading once children reach high school or even junior high. "They come to the library only when it's time to research a school assignment," one told me. The causes are doubtless varied, but the hope is that those who did acquire the habit of reading for fun in grade school will rediscover it in their later teens. Meanwhile, the spinning stands of Harlequin Romances and movie tie-ins may keep the idea of reading alive and the books of S. E. Hinton in circulation. Asked if she would ever consider branching out into adult fiction as Judy Blume has, Hinton said she didn't find adults as interesting, because adolescence is "the time of the most rapid change, when ideals are clashing against the walls of compromise." That she is able to evoke for her audience how teen-agers feel about those clashes is indisputable. She once remarked, "Ponyboy is how I felt at 14." There are millions of Ponyboys out there, soulfully dreaming, sentimental, cool.

Charlene Strickland (review date October 1988)

SOURCE: A review of *Taming the Star Runner,* in *School Library Journal,* Vol. 35, No. 2, October, 1988, p. 161.

[*In the following review, Strickland maintains that* Taming the Star Runner *pales in comparison to Hinton's earlier works, faulting what she perceives as weak characterization, a flimsy storyline, and a theme of hopelessness.*]

Devoted fans will leap on Hinton's new novel, [*Taming the Star Runner,*] yet her protagonist Travis is no *Tex*. On the surface, this 15 year old resembles the classic misfits from the author's previous books; however, Travis lacks Tex' zest for living. Released from juvenile hall to cool down at his uncle's Oklahoma horse ranch, he acts the role of sensitive punk—he looks like a rebel and flies into violent rages, yet he seeks to publish his novel and he loves his cat. He wants to be left alone, but he suffers from being ignored by the "hicks" at school. The high point of his introspective retreat is his attraction to Casey, the riding instructor who leases his uncle's barn. The scenes of stable chores, riding lessons, and horse shows may interest some readers, while the equestrian jargon will mean nothing to the book's primary audience. Hinton uses a horse, Star Runner, as a counterpart to Travis to illustrate her theme of life's quirks: some win, some don't. Without making much of an effort, Travis ends up a winner—alive, free from jail, and a published author. Hinton builds a sparse plot around a predominately bleak theme. Although the story isn't fleshed out, tough-guy Travis will appeal to a certain readership. Others will find him forget-table, especially compared to his fictional predecessors.

Elizabeth Ward (review date 12 February 1989)

SOURCE: "Young Bookshelf," in *The Washington Post Book World,* February 12, 1989, p. 9.

[*In the following excerpt, Ward offers a negative assessment of* Taming the Star Runner, *describing the characters as superficial and self-absorbed and asserting that the prose falls flat.*]

In [*Taming the Star Runner,*] her first novel since *Tex,* published 10 years ago, the phenomenally popular S. E. Hinton returns to the familiar territory of teen-age disaffection and the search for happiness.

Good-looking Travis, with his blackfringed, gray-green eyes, as cold as the Irish sea, is neither a doper nor a straight, but a sensitive, intelligent, creative, profoundly misunderstood cat-lover, who has recently become a juvenile delinquent through no fault of his own (intolerably provoked by his stepfather, Travis had been forced to try and murder him with a fire poker).

Now, emerging from a spell in juvenile hall, he tells us that "his boot felt empty without his knife in it." However, in a subplot that would sound completely improbable were it not for the fact that S. E. Hinton did it herself at age 16, Travis has written a novel and had it accepted by a New York publisher.

Most of the book is set in Oklahoma, where Travis is sent to straighten out on his lawyer uncle's ranch. Rebuffed at the local high school, ignored by his busy uncle, Travis feels increasingly at odds with the world, that is, until he finds solace in the ranch riding school. Not only are the preppie young students very cute ("He had never felt so protective of anyone as he did of Jennifer"), but their 18-year-old instructor, Casey, is quite as sensitive and untameable as Travis is, so sparks must fly.

"The Star Runner" of the title is a vicious horse Casey is vainly attempting to train and may or may not be supposed to serve as a metaphor for both hero and heroine. If so, the horse's ultimate fate is certainly inauspicious. Unfortunately too, S. E. Hinton's knack of emotional manipulation doesn't compensate for the shallowness and narcissism of her characters or the essential banality of her prose.

Patty Campbell (review date 2 April 1989)

SOURCE: A review of *Taming the Star Runner,* in *The New York Times Book Review,* April 2, 1989, p. 26.

[*In the following review, Campbell offers praise for the compelling nature of* Taming the Star Runner *as well as for the authenticity of its characters, but finds fault with Hinton's use of the horse as a symbol.*]

"His boot felt empty without his knife in it," begins S. E. Hinton's fifth novel, *Taming the Star Runner.* A young hood, desperately tough and desperately vulnerable, is on his way to exile on his uncle's horse ranch—and in one paragraph the reader is back in familiar Hinton country after a hiatus of 10 years. What bearing does this new book have on the literary and popular reputation of Susan Eloise Hinton, who at 16 wrote *The Outsiders,* a novel that, in 1967, gave birth to the new realism in adolescent literature, and who has since achieved almost mythical status as the grand dame of young adult novelists?

This has been a year of assessment and recognition for Ms. Hinton. Last July the American Library Association gave its first Young Adult Services Division/School Library Journal Author Achievement Award to her, and earlier a scholarly study, *Presenting S. E. Hinton,* by Jay Daly, evaluated her work and placed it in perspective in the mainstream of American literature. In the shadow of *The Outsiders'* success, Ms. Hinton produced three other novels at four-year intervals: *That Was Then, This Is Now, Rumble Fish* and *Tex.* But after that her energies were absorbed by her participation in the movies based on her books and by the rearing of her son. Now Ms. Hinton has produced another story of a tough young Galahad in black T-shirt and leather jacket. The pattern is familiar, but her genius lies in that she has been able to give each of the five protagonists she has drawn from this mythic model a unique voice and a unique story.

> *Taming the Star Runner* **is remarkable for its drive and the wry sweetness and authenticity of its voice. Gone is the golden idealism of the earlier works, perhaps because here Ms. Hinton observes, rather than participates, in the innocence of her characters.**
>
> **—*Patty Campbell***

In *Taming the Star Runner,* 15-year-old Travis conceals his budding talent as a writer under a carefully cool exterior. When he nearly kills his stepfather in a fight, he is sent to his Uncle Ken's horse ranch, and there he finds himself very much out of his milieu. It's "invisible-man time again" with the "hick jocks and hick nerds" at school. Out of loneliness, he begins to hang around the horse barn where 18-year-old Casey Kencaide has a riding school. Watching her dominate her dangerous stallion, Star Runner, he falls in love with her but keeps it to himself. Unexpectedly, Travis gets a letter from a publisher accepting a novel that he has written. He is ecstatic, but has trouble finding someone to share his pleasure. When Casey wins a difficult jumping competition with Star Runner at a horse show, he kisses her and she grudgingly admits what he had felt was the "strange tie, bond, fate, between them."

The sky darkens as Travis's old friend Joe comes fleeing the city, terrified by his part in a double murder. Travis realizes that he may have escaped from his old life just in time. Then, when a tornado strikes, Star Runner leaps the fence and gallops off across the fields with Casey and Travis in wild, exultant pursuit in a Jeep. Lightning crashes, and Travis and Casey are knocked unconscious. They awake to an empty pasture and a smell of burning flesh. The reader is left to surmise that the mystical Star Runner has been killed. Later, Travis finds that something wild has gone out of his passion for Casey, but that they have become close friends. As the book ends, the young man has reached some contentment with his life and is about to begin a second novel.

Taming the Star Runner is remarkable for its drive and the wry sweetness and authenticity of its voice. Gone is the golden idealism of the earlier works, perhaps because here Ms. Hinton observes, rather than participates, in the innocence of her characters. The autobiographical passages that give glimpses of a past painful time in her own adolescence are most interesting: the young writer bumbling through an awkward first lunch with the publisher or becoming inarticulate at a television interview.

The symbolism of the horse is less successful. At first, Star Runner is seen as demonic, even erotic, but later Travis muses on him as an alien being from space. In the chase he seems to become a nameless wild force out of control, perhaps creativity itself. The symbol never quite comes into focus and consequently fails to carry its weight in the plot, leaving the ending unclear—a fault that young adult readers find particularly annoying.

Because *Taming the Star Runner* is also a more mature and difficult work, it may not be as wildly popular as the other Hinton books have continued to be with succeeding generations. Are those novels stuck in time? A check with youth librarians across the country shows that Hinton readers are younger than they used to be, and if *The Outsiders* is no longer the cult novel it once was, perhaps that is because so many teachers are using it in the classroom. But S. E. Hinton continues to grow in strength as a young adult novelist.

Charles Solomon (review date 12 August 1990)

SOURCE: A review of *The Outsiders,* in *The Los Angeles Times Book Review,* August 12, 1990, p. 10.

[*In the following brief review of the 1990 paperback issue of* The Outsiders, *Solomon outlines the plot of the novel, notes the media adaptations based upon it, and, lauding Hinton as an "excellent juvenile novelist," urges teens to read her works.*]

Written when she was only 16, *The Outsiders* was S. E. Hinton's first novel. It set the pattern for her later works, which all focus on disaffected, underclass teen-agers in the Southwest. The hero of the story, Ponyboy Curtis, who conceals a poetic soul under a self-styled "greaser" exterior, finds himself drawn into a gang war that teaches him the difference between the right and wrong side of the tracks. *The Outsiders* is currently the basis of a show on Fox television and was made into a feature film by Francis Coppola; these adaptations should encourage teen-agers to read the work of this excellent juvenile novelist.

Steven L. VanderStaay (essay date November 1992)

SOURCE: "Doing Theory: Words about Words about *The Outsiders,*" in *English Journal,* Vol. 81, No. 7, November, 1992, pp. 57-61.

[*In the following excerpt, VanderStaay, a high-school English teacher, outlines his application of literary theory to* The Outsiders *as assigned reading in his classroom, explaining how he teaches his students how to formulate their own ideas and ways of thinking.*]

I had little use for critical theory until I met up with S. E. Hinton—or, rather, until I read *The Outsiders* (1967) with students. Since most of them knew the story (either through their own reading or the movie), my challenge was to find a way of using the book that enriched their enjoyment and appreciation, rather than simply repeating it.

Which is half of the story. The other half is that I had grown dissatisfied with the perfunctory ("since it's March this must be *Julius Caesar*") literary road-trips that it seemed my role as English teacher to lead. I didn't want my students simply to read a book, I wanted them to use it in the construction of their own meanings and in the refinement of their own thinking. *The Outsiders,* for the reasons enumerated above, seemed the right place to start. The only problem was I didn't know how.

For help I turned to critical theory, which had made such a splash in the graduate courses I attended by night. Surprisingly, a quick perusal of my textbooks turned up what I was looking for. Only I didn't find it in the newest wave of post-postmodern multisyllabicism. I found it in an earlier and more readable text—though one no less significant for its contribution to the field: M. H. Abrams' *The Mirror and the Lamp: Romantic Theory and the Critical Tradition* (1958).

Defined broadly, literary theory is the field of study in which the criticism (the appreciation and understanding) of literature is itself criticized (or discussed): "Words about words about words," as Murray Krieger (1988) has described it. Educationally, it can be understood as a body of expanding knowledge wherein the analysis and appreciation of literature is broadened to include increasingly higher and more diverse levels of abstraction. Literary critics who once wrote rather restrictively about "literature," for example, now commonly discuss rap music, music videos, and the relation of daily life to popular culture and political power.

Abrams' contribution to this tradition was to suggest a heuristic for distinguishing among perspectives from which works of art have been approached over the history of criticism. Noting that works of art have been seen in relation to the universe, the artist, the audience, in isolation or in comparison to other works (3), he offered [a diagram] to clarify these relations. . . .

According to this scheme (echoed in the discourse theories of James Kinneavy [1971], James Britton [1975], and others), critical approaches to literature can be distinguished on the basis of the particular relation they emphasize. Criticism in the first half of this century commonly viewed a story or poem as the expression of a writer's life and experience; however, the structuralists and New Critics of the fifties and sixties rebelled against this view to stress "internal requirements of the work itself" (Abrams 3).

In the postmodern tradition of responding to a text with a text of my own, I have turned the purpose of the diagram on its head—finding it more useful in my secondary classes as a generative tool than an interpretive one. That is, whereas Abrams posited the diagram as a heuristic, an aid in the understanding of criticism, we use it in my classes to "do" criticism ourselves by writing about literature from the perspective of each of the approaches. This gives us more to "do" with *The Outsiders* and has proven a powerful catalyst for expanding the analysis we bring to bear on a text and increasing the use of higher order thinking skills (HOTS) in my classroom.

Working with students, I begin with the first three perspectives, describing them as follows:

1. Mimetic approaches in which a book is evalu-ated in terms of how well it represents one's experience of aspects of life or "the universe."

2. Pragmatic or rhetorical approaches in which a book is evaluated in terms of how well it effects what we assume to be the author's desired response from the audience.

3. Expressive approaches in which a book is evaluated as an expression or extension of the artist who wrote it.

This triad is applicable to a wide range of young-adult fiction, notwithstanding that the experiences of characters may be removed by time, class, geography, and race from the students' own. Though I teach in rural Iowa, for example, students successfully criticize *The Outsiders* from each of the three approaches.

Before assigning a critical appraisal, however, I first ask students to describe each perspective in their own terms. I write these student-generated descriptions on the board, asking students to distinguish among evaluative criteria unique to each.

We also spend a great deal of time working through the levels of thinking identified by Benjamin S. Bloom (1956) and his colleagues as "comprehension" and "analysis." Students discuss the motives behind the characters' actions and the deterministic forces at work in each of their lives. Analytically, we chart the development, climax, and dénouement of the central conflict, and plot the growth and development of Ponyboy on a quest chart or "U curve." The comparison of these diagrams is particularly significant as it encourages the acceptance of multiple points of view distinct from that which a student might otherwise bring to a book. This acceptance—a literal extension of the "decentering" process described by Jean Piaget (1926) and modified in the work of Lev S. Vygotsky (1962)—is key to the success of the critical appraisals. Students must accept the idea that distinct points of view can exist before they can attempt critical assessments from variant perspectives.

Thinking at the "application" and "synthesis" levels should also be accomplished before students can work from the first approach and evaluate the novel in terms of mimesis or verisimilitude, its correspondence to aspects of life. Typically, I ask students to imagine that S. E. Hinton attended our school and wrote *The Outsiders* about kids in our community. How would the novel be different? In what ways would it remain the same?

Students respond to the above questions in journal fashion, looking back at the novel as they need to. Sally's description of Soda is typical of the "transference" students enact to imagine these characters in our community.

As long as Soda continues to work at the gas station, people around here will like him, though they may not want their daughters to date him because he doesn't have his diploma. He would probably be a clean-cut rocker and into heavy metal, but not the drugs. He'd still attract all kinds of girls. Because people knew his parents died they'd try to be understanding with him, but I'm sure he'd be considered a rebel.

When they have completed their descriptions, I ask students to compare their versions of each character in small groups. After we reassemble as a class, we discuss the differences they encountered in their group work, my goal being to move to a discussion of why different readers perceive and transfer the characters to our community differently. In this way (and without ever mentioning it), we broach the central concepts of another school of critical theory: reader response.

I assign the first critical appraisal the next day. The assignment I use looks like this:

A. Look back at three actions that Ponyboy takes in the book and explain whether you think these actions were realistic or "life-like." Examine each action in a separate paragraph. Base your response on your expert knowledge of what it feels like to be accepted by some groups and rejected by others, and what you imagine (or know) it would be like to have a close friend die.

B. Reread the section on the death of Dally (133-135). Is it realistic to think that the death of Johnny would cause him to seek his own death in such a way? Base your answer on what you know about his childhood and what we have said about physical and emotional pain.

C. Given what you have written in A and B above, how realistic or "life-like" is *The Outsiders*? State your answer in a brief paragraph.

Interestingly, while students at first tend to find *The Outsiders* "realistic," after considering three specific scenes they frequently argue that at least one is *not* realistic. Discussing the rumble that concludes the book, for example, Travis writes that

When the Socs jumped out of the car and wanted to fight the Greasers, I don't think that is very likely to happen because rich kids like that usually try to stay away from trouble and try to avoid getting into fights unless they can gang up on somebody or unless someone else starts it and there is nothing that they can do to avoid the situation.

I introduce the second, or "pragmatic," approach by referring students to the passage in which Ponyboy states the purposes behind his telling of the story.

Suddenly it wasn't only a personal thing to me. I could picture hundreds and hundreds of boys living on the wrong sides of cities, boys with black eyes who jumped at their own shadows. Hundreds of boys who maybe watched sunsets and looked at stars and ached for something better. I could see boys going down under street lights because they were mean and tough and hated the world, and it was too late to tell them that there was still good in it, and they wouldn't believe you if you did. It was too vast a problem to be just a personal thing. There should be some help, someone should tell them before it was too late. Someone should tell their side of the story, and maybe people would understand then and wouldn't be so quick to judge a boy by the amount of hair oil he wore. It was important to me.

The actual assignment looks like this:

A. Assume S. E. Hinton's reasons for writing *The Outsiders* are the same as Ponyboy's. What two purposes does she want her novel to accomplish? Describe each in your journal.

B. How well does *The Outsiders* accomplish the goals you've described above? Write a paragraph about each in your journal.

C. On a separate sheet of paper, write a brief essay in which you describe Hinton's purposes in writing the novel and state how well you believe her purposes are achieved. You may use any of what you've written in your journal. Make sure you polish and proofread your essay.

I use the third or "expressive" approach by referring students to Jay Daly's biography of Hinton, *Presenting S. E. Hinton* (1987).

Read chapter one of the biography. When you've finished, write in your journal about Hinton. Does knowing about her make you like *The Outsiders* less or more? Which book, the biography or novel, does a better job of telling us who she is?

Because Hinton began composing *The Outsiders* while still a teenager, students find reading about her a natural extension of reading the novel itself. This heightens their awareness of her book as a product of artistic aims and choices and challenges them to think about the relation between an author's life and work. Indeed, our discussions about whether *The Outsiders* can be read as an expression of Hinton's acceptance of her father's death rank among the finest and most poignant moments I have ever shared with students. A taste of these discussions can be gleaned from Paige's essay. Interestingly, Paige, like Darry, helped to parent her younger brothers.

> S. E. Hinton also reflects part of her life in the book by writing about how the Curtis kids' parents had been killed. She is really expressing what grief and pain she went through as her father was dying. She said that she was really close to her father and in the book she tries to show the significance of a close relationship with a father figure. In the book Darry is the father figure and she shows that at first there is a link missing between Darry and Ponyboy and then she shows how their relationship becomes closer.

By this point students have become articulate enough with the triad to identify and evaluate approaches used by professional critics and book reviewers. I copy reviews for their analysis, or simply ask them to turn their novels over. The paperback cover to *The Outsiders,* for example, excerpts statements from reviews praising the novel for both its verisimilitude and its pragmatic value as a persuasive text.

> What it's like to live lonely and unwanted and cornered by circumstance. . . . There is rawness and violence here, but honest hope, too.—*National Observer*

> Written by a most perceptive teenager . . . it attempts to speak for all teenagers who find it so difficult to communicate to adults their doubts, their dreams, and their needs.—*Book Week*

Most reviews of young-adult novels stress an assessment from at least two of the triad's theoretical approaches. A few consider each before stating a final opinion. The *Book Week* review, for instance, stresses the realism of *The Outsiders,* but to a lesser extent it also alludes to its persuasiveness and the manner in which the book is an accurate "expression" of Hinton herself.

After struggling with their own reviews, students find it great fun to pick apart the work of professional critics in this manner. In so doing they frequently give way to that greatest of teenage temptations—the urge to point out the shortcomings of adult thought. The temptation need be only nudgingly encouraged and students will write another critique, this one of the book review itself. In this act they "criticize criticism" and come full circle as literary critics themselves.

> **Because Hinton began composing *The Outsiders* while still a teenager, students find reading about her a natural extension of reading the novel itself. This heightens their awareness of her book as a product of artistic aims and choices. . . .**
> **—*Steven L. VanderStaay***

A situation eventually arises for which the initial three perspectives of the triad are not suitable. Someone will ask how to evaluate science fiction or fantasy in terms of "realism" or "verisimilitude." Or a student will skip ahead and demand to know what "being realistic," bringing an audience to behave or think in a certain way, or "expressing" the author has to do with the quality of a novel. Such questions are not to be avoided: they indicate not that the triad has failed but that students have transcended it.

This transcendence could lead a class to consider Abrams' fourth approach: the evaluation of texts without references to the universe, author, or audience. This perspective may be best introduced by simply raising the question of its feasibility: Can YA novels be compared and evaluated in such an objective manner? If so, how? Classes interested in pursuing this approach could generate their own criteria for such "objective" evaluation and compare it to any of the New Critical approaches popular in the 1950s and 60s.

But students need not use anyone else's ideas in pursuing these issues—their questions alone can open up a world of possibilities for further discussion, thinking, and writing about literature and literary theory.

What, indeed, does verisimilitude have to do with a book's quality? (And what does "realistic" or "life-like" mean? What is life that literature can be compared to it? If books imitate life, cannot life also imitate books?) Should the author's intent be considered? (If so, where is the intent located? In the author, the book, or the reader?) Can a novel be conceived that is not an expressive extension of its author? (If not, are novels then limited to being expressive extensions of no one but the author?) And what of the current emphasis on reading as a mode of *writing*? That is, what happens to the relationship between author and audience when the text is considered an expression, not of the writer, but of the *reader*?

By raising such questions, students address some of the most essential issues of literary theory. In so doing those who initially think of novels as self-enclosed come to see them as books that invite active engagement and response—texts about which they can create texts of their own. The path of theoretical questioning common to literary theory, moving as it does from order to chaos, may be unsettling for teachers. But the basic goal is a simple one: to "do" more with what we read and to think more about our thinking. Who could be better served by "doing" such criticism than secondary students? And who better to turn such theory into practice than secondary teachers?

After all, while college instructors may guide their students further along the critical path, no one gives more class time to the practice of criticism than secondary teachers. And certainly it is to our benefit that student inquiry in such activities manifest itself in the highest levels of thinking and, quite frequently, great intellectual joy.

Susanna Rodell (review date 19 November 1995)

SOURCE: A review of *The Puppy Sister*, in *The New York Times Book Review*, November 19, 1995, p. 37.

[*In the following review, Rodell declares that while* The Puppy Sister *is at times overly sentimental, it is appropriate for very young readers who will enjoy the fantasy and who will not be bothered by the implausibilities presented by the plot and characterization.*]

It's not easy to pull off the sort of real-life fantasy S. E. Hinton attempts in **The Puppy Sister.** She largely succeeds, and the book will no doubt delight young independent readers, but it has some big flaws.

Ms. Hinton is well known to many parents, who remember reading her gritty novels for adolescents, including **The Outsiders** and **Rumble Fish.** After a long silence, she recently shifted gears toward younger readers with a storybook, **Big David, Little David.** Both that book and **The Puppy Sister** bear the imprint of her personal experience and are sweeter stories, as is appropriate for younger children.

This short novel is told in the voice of the family puppy, who loves her new young master so much that she wills herself to become human. Nick, like many only children, has registered his wish for a younger brother or sister, but gets a dog instead. He gets his wish, though, as the puppy struggles to walk upright, to talk and to lose her fur.

It's a story in a long tradition of talking-animal tales, connecting with children's often powerful emotions toward their pets and the desire to bridge the gap between animal and human. Think of Crockett Johnson's World War II-era *Barnaby* comic strip, in which a young boy has both a talk-ing dog and a fairy godfather.

It's also in the tradition of the human/monster/animal in the closet, from *Mistress Masham's Repose* to *E.T.,* involving creatures who must somehow be hidden from the grown-ups or integrated into the real world and kept from exploitation.

In **The Puppy Sister** the parents are brought into the secret early as the dog begins to talk and change in appearance. Mom faints and Dad rushes home from work to be told his dog is now his daughter. The logistical problems of fitting the new protohuman into the family and the community are the rest of the story.

Some genuinely funny conundrums appear: When Aleasha (cute name, huh?) gets sick, do they call the vet or the pediatrician? How does Mom get her to eat vegetables? How to explain why their child catches a foul ball at a baseball game in her teeth?

The first problem is solved by calling an old friend of Dad's who just happens to be a retired pediatrician and accepts the canine-to-human transformation with remarkable equanimity. Mom and Dad deal with the neighbors by telling two fibs: they have given the dog away because Nick was allergic to her, and they have decided to adopt a daughter. (Smart kids will quickly start asking about birth certificates and the like.)

The most serious flaw—surprising, given the toughness of Ms. Hinton's young-adult novels—is the sometimes overdone sentimentality of **The Puppy Sister.** Mom delivers some homilies comparing the commitment to a pet with the commitment to a child that will make a few parents squirm when they remember the last three dead turtles. There is an excruciating conversation in which Mom sympathizes with her dog-daughter's frustrations by comparing these evolutionary problems with her own pregnancy.

As she grows more and more human, Aleasha starts to lose some of her doggy sensibilities. She finds she can no longer understand the family cat, and her sense of smell weakens, but when Nick pretends he doesn't like her kisses, she says: "I have a secret I haven't told even Mom. I can still smell love."

The book's main delight, caught in Jacqueline Rogers's black-and-white illustrations, is in the characterization of Aleasha, who is truly memorable. I wish Ms. Hinton had included more silliness and less sentiment, but perhaps that's a grown-up quibble. Children old enough to read but not yet gripped by adolescent cynicism will have a lot of fun with Nick and Aleasha.

FURTHER READING

Criticism

Lempke, Susan Dove. Review of *Big David, Little David,* by S. E. Hinton. *Bulletin of the Center for Children's Books* 48 (February 1995): 200.

> Offers a mixed assessment of *Big David, Little David,* arguing that some of the book's humor may be lost on its intended audience.

Stevenson, Deborah. Review of *The Puppy Sister,* by S. E. Hinton. *Bulletin of the Center for Children's Books* 49 (November 1995): 92.

> Provides a positive review of *The Puppy Sister,* asserting that although the story is not entirely believable, it will be entertaining to young readers.

Additional coverage of Hinton's life and career is contained in the following sources published by Gale: *Authors and Artists for Young Adults,* **Vol. 2;** *Children's Literature Review,* **Vols. 3 and 23;** *Contemporary Authors,* **Vols. 81-84;** *Contemporary Authors New Revision Series,* **Vol. 32 and 62;** *DISCovering Authors; DISCovering Authors: British; DISCovering Authors: Canadian; DISCovering Authors Modules: Most-Studied* **and** *Novelists; Junior DISCovering Authors; Major Authors and Illustrators for Children and Young Adults; Major Twentieth-Century Writers;* **and** *Something about the Author,* **Vols. 19 and 58.**

Norman Mailer

1923-

American novelist, short story writer, nonfiction writer, journalist, screenwriter, and critic.

The following entry presents an overview of Mailer's career through 1997. For further information on his life and works, see *CLC,* Volumes 1, 2, 3, 4, 5, 8, 11, 14, 28, 39, and 74.

INTRODUCTION

An outspoken intellectual and celebrity, Norman Mailer is a controversial figure in contemporary American literature. Highly regarded for his prodigious ability as a novelist and social critic, Mailer's literary endeavors exhibit extensive experimentation with narrative forms and styles, notable for their synthesis of fiction, nonfiction, autobiography, and journalism. Increasingly colored by radical politics and existentialism in the 1960s, Mailer's writing attempts to engage and reenact the major crises of the modern world to affect greater understanding of self and society, and is mirrored in reality by his active participation in national events. Mailer achieved sudden fame with his first novel, *The Naked and the Dead* (1948), still considered among his finest accomplishments along with the award-winning nonfiction novels *The Armies of the Night* (1968) and *The Executioner's Song* (1979). An independent thinker who eschews identification with literary and political circles, Mailer has given forceful expression to the voice of alienation and disillusionment in postwar American society.

Biographical Information

Born Norman Kingsley Mailer in Long Branch, New Jersey, Mailer moved with his parents to Brooklyn, New York, at age four, where he grew up in a comfortable Jewish community. Mailer was a precocious, though modest, child who earned high marks in school and occupied himself with model building. At age sixteen he enrolled at Harvard to study aeronautical engineering but soon became interested in the contemporary fiction of John Dos Passos, Ernest Hemingway, John Steinbeck, and William Faulkner, who together became his early literary influences. Vowing to become a great novelist himself, Mailer wrote several short stories and won first prize in *Story* magazine's annual college contest. After graduating from Harvard with honors in 1943, Mailer joined the army and married his first wife shortly before setting off to serve in the Pacific theater during the Second World War. Upon his discharge in 1946, Mailer attended graduate courses at the Sorbonne in Paris. He recorded his military experiences in his first novel, *The*

Naked and the Dead, a popular and critical success that launched his literary career with its publication in 1948. Mailer followed with *Barbary Shore* (1951) and *The Deer Park* (1955), both of which failed to live up to the promise of his debut novel. In 1952 Mailer divorced his first wife and two years later entered into the second of six subsequent marriages over three decades. In 1955 he co-founded the *Village Voice,* an alternative newspaper covering politics and the arts, to which he was a regular contributor. He published "The White Negro," his much anthologized essay, in *Dissent* magazine in 1957. The essay reappeared in *Advertisements for Myself* (1959) and became a staple of Beat literature. Mailer's unabashed drug and alcohol use also became a feature of his writing and personal life during this time. He was briefly hospitalized for psychiatric treatment in 1960 after stabbing his second wife during a night of heavy drinking. For this incident and other acts of defiance and exhibitionism during the 1960s, Mailer earned a reputation for self-aggrandizement and belligerence. His involvement in the turbulent politics of the 1960s became material for much of his writing, including the novel *Why Are We in Vietnam?* (1967), the nonfiction narrative *Miami and the*

Siege of Chicago (1968), and *The Armies of the Night* (1968), for which he won a Pulitzer Prize in nonfiction and a National Book Award. Mailer was awarded a second Pulitzer Prize for his best-selling nonfiction novel *The Executioner's Song* (1979), which he also adapted into a popular television movie. While retreating somewhat from the public eye in recent decades, Mailer continued to produce a diverse body of work including essays, screenplays, literary criticism, biographies, and several major novels—*Ancient Evenings* (1983), *Tough Guys Don't Dance* (1984), *Harlot's Ghost* (1991), and *The Gospel According to the Son* (1997).

Major Works

Mailer's preoccupation with the struggle for individuality and free will in the face of natural forces and institutional authority is central to his work. *The Naked and the Dead* describes the combat experiences and interaction of fourteen American soldiers as they advance on a small Japanese-held island in the Philippines during the Second World War. Mailer presents the diverse members of the platoon as a microcosm of the American people, each with their own wide-ranging geographic, economic, and social backgrounds. As in most of his writing, Mailer examines the complex tensions that evolve as the main characters attempt to impose their will upon an essentially uncaring and inexorable universe. Mailer similarly portrays an assemblage of Cold War political extremists in *Barbary Shore* and a blacklisted Hollywood director in *The Deer Park*. In the late 1950s Mailer abandoned such naturalistic studies of the external world to probe the inner conflicts of consciousness and being in *Advertisements for Myself,* a miscellany of short stories, essays, poems, and personal statements. This collection, along with *The Presidential Papers* (1963), represents an important shift in Mailer's approach to ethical and metaphysical examinations in which, through unflinching introspection, he sought to expose the psyche of the American citizen at large. In "The White Negro" Mailer argues that the American "hipster" is a desirable adaptation of the uninhibited urban African-American, a "philosophical psychopath" whose enjoyment of desublimated desires is essential to subvert social control in the interest of a free existence. In subsequent works, Mailer increasingly drew upon existentialist philosophy to explain the primacy of the flesh over the spirit and to justify violence as an outpouring of repressed rage. In the novel *An American Dream* (1965), the protagonist, Stephen Rojack, murders his estranged wife and abandons all personal and professional self-identities to return to his subconscious self, a nonrational state of primitive sensualism and mystical revelation that informs conscious action. Mailer further explored this ideal interchange between personal experience and political advocacy in his experiments with the novel and nonfiction narrative. In *Why Are We in Vietnam?* Mailer describes the inhumane activities of a hunting party

in Alaska as a parable for American military activity in Southeast Asia. In *The Armies of the Night,* significantly subtitled "History as a Novel, The Novel as History," Mailer recounts his involvement in a large antiwar protest at the Pentagon in 1967. By referring to himself in the third-person in this story, Mailer relates autobiographic experience in detached objectivity through a fictional incarnation of himself. Such forays into the genre of New Journalism, a fusion of fiction and reportage, is exemplified by *The Executioner's Song.* Here Mailer recounts the real-life story of Gary Gilmore, a convicted murderer put to death at his own insistence by the state of Utah in 1977. Supported by exhaustive research, Mailer reconstructs Gilmore's criminal life and the controversial judicial and moral circumstances surrounding his punishment. Mailer's highly recognizable authorial voice is conspicuously subdued in this novel in deference to a large cast of characters whose multiple perspectives provide the story. In more recent novels, Mailer turned away from current events to produce lengthy historical works: *Ancient Evenings,* an epic account of debauchery and authoritarianism in ancient Egypt; *Harlot's Ghost,* a fictional chronicle of the United States Central Intelligence Agency through the 1960s; and *The Gospel According to the Son,* a first-person narrative presented as the autobiography of Jesus Christ.

Critical Reception

While most critics acknowledge Mailer as possessing enormous talent and originality, critical evaluation of his writing is problematic due to his divided personae as an author, political dissenter, social critic, and notorious celebrity. Although he was once touted as the successor to Ernest Hemingway, Mailer's large and uneven body of work defies easy comparison or classification. Though *The Naked and the Dead* remains a highly regarded conventional war novel in the realistic style, *Advertisements for Myself* is a product of the Beat movement that more closely resembles the declarative egotism of Walt Whitman. Mailer's perceptive critiques of American society and politics during the 1960s and 1970s, particularly as found in *The Presidential Papers* and *Why Are We in Vietnam?,* earned him a reputation as a leading commentator on national affairs. His innovative ventures in nonfiction and journalism culminated in *The Armies of the Night* and *The Executioner's Song,* both of which are considered consummate examples of the nonfiction narrative, drawing comparison to Truman Capote's *In Cold Blood.* Criticism of Mailer's less effective work is often directed at his baroque excesses and overt political or philosophical exposition. Mailer has also sustained attacks from feminist critics who find his writing sexist, particularly as noted by Kate Millet in her *Sexual Politics* (1970). Mailer's response to such charges in *The Prisoner of Sex* (1971), a treatise on his sexual relationships, and *Genius and Lust* (1976), a laudatory critical study of Henry Miller, did little to assuage his detractors. Despite the distractions of his public antics and reckless bravado, Mailer's willingness to defy authority and to engage himself in controversial contemporary events is essential to his art. For his penetrating studies of American society, superior prose style, and influential experiments with various literary forms, Mailer is considered among the most important American writers of the twentieth century.

PRINCIPAL WORKS

The Naked and the Dead (novel) 1948

Barbary Shore (novel) 1951

The Deer Park (novel) 1955

The White Negro: Superficial Reflections on the Hipster (short stories, essays, and verse) 1957

Advertisements for Myself (short stories, essays, and verse) 1959

Deaths for the Ladies (and Other Disasters) (poetry) 1962

The Presidential Papers (essays) 1963

An American Dream (novel) 1965

The Deer Park (drama) 1967

The Short Fiction of Norman Mailer (short stories) 1967

Why Are We in Vietnam? (novel) 1967

The Armies of the Night: History as a Novel, The Novel as History (nonfiction novel) 1968

Miami and the Siege of Chicago: An Informal History of the Republican and Democratic Conventions of 1968 (nonfiction novel) 1968

Of a Fire on the Moon (nonfiction novel) 1970; also published as *A Fire on the Moon,* 1970

The Prisoner of Sex (nonfiction) 1971

Marilyn: A Biography (biography) 1973; revised edition, 1975

The Executioner's Song (nonfiction novel) 1979

Of Women and Their Elegance (fictional autobiography) 1980

The Executioner's Song (screenplay) 1982

Pieces and Pontifications (essays and interviews) 1982

Ancient Evenings (novel) 1983

Tough Guys Don't Dance (novel) 1984

Harlot's Ghost (novel) 1991

Oswald's Tale: An American Mystery (novel) 1995

Portrait of Picasso as a Young Man: An Interpretive Biography (biography) 1995

The Gospel According to the Son (novel) 1997

CRITICISM

James Toback (essay date 1967)

SOURCE: "Norman Mailer Today," in *Commentary,* Vol. 64, No. 4, 1967, pp. 68-76.

[*In the following essay, Toback provides a survey of Mailer's writings and personal politics upon the publication of* Why Are We in Vietnam?]

In the late 50's, Norman Mailer's reputation still stood on *The Naked and the Dead* (1948), neither of his subsequent efforts, *Barbary Shore* (1951) and *The Deer Park* (1955), having quite convinced Mailer or anyone else that he was the major novelist he insisted he could become. By his own later account, his head was leaden with seconal, benzedrene, and marijuana; a sense of what he himself has termed passivity, stupidity, and dissipation threatened to overcome him. Only gradually, after returning to New York from Paris and giving up drugs and cigarettes, did he begin to feel that he could write once again. Then, in 1957, Mailer produced **"The White Negro,"** an essay which restored his faith in his literary future and presaged the forms and directions that it would take.

Mailer has always professed an umbilical attachment to the Left, but since **"The White Negro"** the drift has been unmistakably from political radicalism toward spiritual radicalism, from an obsession with Marx to an obsession with Reich, from economic revolution to apocalyptic orgasm, from the proletariat to heroes, demons, boxers, tycoons, bitches, murderers, suicides, pimps, and lovers. And correspondingly, concern with extreme psychic states has become more important to his work than concern with extreme political states (the center having always been a bore for Mailer in all its manifestations).

It was not that eschatology *replaced* politics, but rather that it came to constitute a new means of diagnosis, both of personal and social plague, and that it promised answers to the crisis in which both the individual and the nation were entrapped. The criteria by which the health of a particular man (the organ) were to be assessed—his complexity, his bravery, his daring, his capacity for love—were essentially the same as those which measured the salubrity of America (the organism). Similarly, the disease which threatened both individual and state (expressed at once literally and metaphorically as cancer) evinced identical symptoms: mediocrity, uniformity, repression, and security.

Assuming the voice of religious physician, the Mailer of the 60's reveals a vision of malady and possible restoration that is profoundly radical; at the same time the terminology and conceptual foundation of his homily are puritan to the core. God and the Devil, Good and Evil, Heaven and Hell, History and Eternity are as inescapably real for Mailer as they were for Jonathan Edwards—and he has repeatedly asserted that such ultimate questions are proper and indeed necessary preoccupations for the contemporary novelist. Many would dissent, but even if we do look to the novelist for salvation, can we look to Mailer? There is, at least on the surface, an insistent buffoonery to his self-projected public image that can make it difficult to take him seriously, let alone to believe he can show us the way to redemption. Yet even a cursory examination of his work suggests that he is justified in claiming to be an intellectual adventurer of broad dimension. If he sometimes seems to be more familiar with *Captain Blood* than *Middlemarch,* he nevertheless possesses an uncanny ability to recall and make use of what he has read. If he is sometimes guileful, more often he strives for complete honesty with himself and the subject of his work. If his thinking is occasionally wild and unsound, he is also capable of rigorously logical intellection. And if his emphasis on scatology is at times repugnant, his undeniable charisma excites interest in practically everything he writes or says or does.

Consequently, when a new work by Mailer appears, we turn to it eagerly—expectant and hopeful—especially when, as in the case of his latest novel, *Why Are We in Vietnam?,* the new work also represents a new literary departure. By itself perhaps the most ambitious and the most difficult effort of his career, *Why Are We in Vietnam?* is also a crystallization and an extension of Mailer's other major productions of the 60's. To do justice to its complexity, to make it more accessible, and to place it properly in the perspective of Mailer's development as a writer, one must first look back to *The Presidential Papers, An American Dream, Cannibals and Christians,* and the dramatic adaptation of *The Deer Park.*

With *Advertisements for Myself* (1959), Mailer showed that whatever stature he might or might not achieve as a novelist, he was certainly becoming a major essayist. This impression was confirmed by *The Presidential Papers* (1963), in which Mailer took it upon himself to indicate to John F. Kennedy the brave new paths he must follow in order to achieve greatness as a President, heroism as a man, and salvation for his country. In Mailer's view, the only kind of hero who can appear in contemporary American life is the "existential" hero, a man who lives—in his thoughts as in his actions—by daring the unknown. On one occasion, when discussing symptoms of the national disease, Mailer remarks that no one in America is capable of tolerating a question that cannot be answered in twenty seconds. And he finds deeds courageous (and hence potentially heroic) only if there is death, or at least danger, as a possible consequence.

Heroism is the victory over Dread, the sensation that haunts not only *The Presidential Papers,* but the whole of Mailer's work in the 60's. Although doubtless a natural threat to man from the earliest days of his consciousness, Dread has become rather fashionable (to talk about if not to feel) in recent years. It has perhaps been best described by Tennessee Williams. After indicating that war, the atom bomb, and terminal disease are not really to the point, Williams writes:

> These things are parts of the visible, sensible phenomena of every man's experience or knowledge, but the true sense of dread is not a reaction to anything . . . strictly, materially *knowable.* But rather it's a kind of spiritual intuition of something almost too incredible and shocking to talk about, which underlies the whole so-called thing.

Either one knows what Williams is talking about or one doesn't, and Williams implies that only artists and madmen do. Mailer, however, sees no one safe from the possibility of confrontation with the abyss, and he seems to feel a moral obligation to awaken us all to the danger. All roads lead to it, and it is only through the unmanly deceptions of right-wing politics, logical positivism, linguistic analysis, popular journalism, and Freudian psychology that "the terror which lies beneath our sedition [is hidden from us]." The vigilantes of the right wing, like the Un-American Activities Committee, the F.B.I., and the Birch Society, seek to transform metaphysical Dread into Red dread, to give internal emptiness the tangible outer shape of Communism. And Freudians tell us that Dread is merely a recurrence of the fear we feel as helpless infants. But Mailer, like the latter-day hell-fire Puritan preacher he is, asserts that the horrible intimation of Dread is that "we are going to die badly and suffer some unendurable stricture of eternity." This is no metaphor; it is an expression of Mailer's belief in the literal existence of hell.

The Maileresque hero—suspecting that his Dread is a real premonition of the agony that awaits him after death, an agony that can be averted only by daring death to come sooner, to come right away—will always put up an ante that amounts to more than he can afford to lose. Here, for example, is Mailer on Hemingway's suicide:

> How likely that he had a death of the most awful proportions within him. He was exactly the one to know that the cure for such disease is to risk dying many a time. . . .

> I wonder if, morning after morning, Hemingway did not go downstairs secretly in the dawn, set the base of his loaded shotgun on the floor, put the muzzle into his mouth, and press his thumb into the trigger. . . . He can move the trigger up to a point [of no man's land] and yet not fire the gun. . . . Perhaps he tried just such a reconnaissance one hundred times before, and felt the touch of health return. . . .

If he did it well, he could come close to death without dying.

That Hemingway eventually died as a result of his gambling
with life is not so important as that he grew by it. By challenging fate he was saving his soul; by refusing to give into
his dread of death, he was making whatever life was left for
him more noble; and he was fortifying his spirit so that he
might transcend the eternity of hell.

If the individual can save himself from madness and the
abyss only by ceasing to repress even his most hidden and
dangerous impulses and by flirting with death, so, too, with
the nation as a whole. Devoted to the illusion of safety and
security, it is condemned to mass insanity and an ignoble end,
unless it redeems itself by immediate embarkation on a
course of "existential" politics. This would involve a complete remolding of national objectives, not only on the large
issues involving danger and death, survival or extinction, but
also on less apocalyptic matters like urban housing.

For if America is not already incurably insane, she is certainly in a state of plague. Mailer sees the symptoms everywhere: in architecture, frozen food, television commercials,
sleeping pills, sexual excess, sexual repression, the deterioration of the language. One has only to look at the kind of
people who regulate and set the tone of the nation. Mailer
lists them: politicians, medicos, policemen, professors,
priests, rabbis, ministers, psychoanalysts, builders, and ex-
ecutives. It has not always been so:

> [Once] America was the land where people still be-
> lieved in heroes: George Washington, Billy the Kid;
> Lincoln, Jefferson, Mark Twain, Jack London,
> Hemingway, Joe Louis, Dempsey, Gentleman Jim;
> America believed in athletes, rum-runners, aviators,
> even lovers. It was a country which had grown by
> the leap of one hero past another.

Now, more than ever before, America needed a hero. Was
he Norman Mailer? Not yet. For the time being Mailer's faith
was in Kennedy, the inspiration for the essay, **"Superman
Comes to the Supermarket,"** in which Mailer had expressed his faith in Kennedy's capacity to lead the country
in the "the recovery of its imagination, its pioneer lust for
the unexpected and the incalculable." And yet no sooner had
Kennedy won the election than Mailer was possessed by "a
sense of awe," an intuition that he had betrayed himself, and,
as a result, he began to follow Kennedy's career obsessively,
as if he, Norman Mailer, personally "were responsible and
guilty for all which was bad . . . and potentially totalitarian."
There are suggestions in this abrupt reversal of sentiment of
three forces at work in Mailer: serious concern for the fate
of the spiritual and political ideals he cherishes; a histrionic
penchant for breast-beating; and an almost petulant envy of

Kennedy's power and possibility, an irrational and vast extension of the simple literary envy he occasionally felt for
James Jones.

To be sure, the heroism of which Mailer speaks is a cure
which both individual and nation might decide is too haz-
ardous and too painful to undertake. The patient is apt to
protest that he does not really feel so sick as Mailer tells
him he is and that even if he were, he would rather fade
gradually into death than risk the unknown under the untried
knife of Dr. Norman's psychic surgery. If it is the "Establishment" that objects in these terms, Mailer regards it as
plain cowardice, the cardinal sin, which should be avoided
even if the strictures of eternity were not waiting as retribution. But with minority groups, the Negro in particular, his
urgency is softened. He understands that it would be no small
act of presumption on his part to demand that the Negro,
who has lived with violence all his life, surrender the goals
of security and stability.

> The demand for courage may have been exorbitant.
> Now as the Negro was beginning to come into the
> white man's world, he wanted the logic of the white
> man's world: annuities, mental hygiene, sociologi-
> cal jargon, committee solutions for the ills of the
> breast. He was sick of a whore's logic and a pimp's
> logic.

And yet the paradox here is only too obvious to Mailer. Believing that he must turn his back on the values of the ghetto,
the Negro seeks recovery through assimilation into the mori-
bund world of white liberal America. In reality, he is abandoning a way of life which is founded on those extreme
states of human feeling and action which for Mailer constitute the only true possibility for spiritual rehabilitation.
Mailer regrets that

> there is no one to tell [the Negro] it would be bet-
> ter to keep the psychology of the streets than to cul-
> tivate the contradictory desire to be . . . a great,
> healthy, mature, autonomous, related, integrated in-
> dividual.

This problem is crystallized in the eleventh (and perhaps
best) essay in *The Presidential Papers,* **"Death,"** which focuses on the proceedings before, during, and immediately
after the first Floyd Patterson-Sonny Liston heavyweight
championship fight. Most Negroes wanted Patterson to win,
a fact which Mailer explains by identifying Patterson as the
symbol of security. Patterson was polite, quiet, humble, dili-
gent, and Catholic; he was, in short, "white." Liston, on the
other hand, personified "the old torment," the darker, dangerous side of life that the Negro had known only too well.
Liston was surly, unpredictable, mob affiliated, and an ex-
convict; he was "black."

Most Negroes, then, wanted to see Liston beaten by Patterson for much the same reason that they would not react warmly to proposals that they seek out violence, danger, and the unknown. But if Mailer cannot blame them, he is nevertheless distressed by the insidious assimilation of Negroes (and Jews as well) into Anglo-Saxon America. For a Negro or a Jew, to stifle the rich uniqueness of his potential contribution to American life is to betray himself and to withhold the transfusion that might save this bloodless land.

Mailer likes Patterson—his loneliness, his pride his persistent struggle against the odds. But just as the Fascist Craft had stolen Mailer's interest from the liberal Hearn in *The Naked and the Dead,* so Mailer's real fascination here is not with Patterson but with Liston, whose inexorable toughness makes him the kind of Negro other Negroes refer to (sometimes in fear, sometimes in praise, sometimes in disapproval, but always in awe) as "a *bad* cat." Liston takes on mythic proportions in Mailer's mind, a mind which by nature tends to intensify, to exaggerate, and to think in terms of extremes. He is "near to beautiful" and one can think of "very few men who have beauty." But that is in no way all.

> Liston was voodoo, Liston was magic.... Liston was the secret hero of every man who had ever given mouth to a final curse against the dispositions of the Lord and made a pact with Black Magic. Liston was Faust.

He was the kind of Negro that any white man who imagined himself hip would have to come to terms with—either as model or as rival. Predictably, Mailer chooses the latter course, and does battle with Liston. Not physical battle, but psychic warfare that could have erupted into violence.

Liston's incredibly fast knockout of Patterson left Mailer in a state of feverish frustration, a condition aggravated by a conscience which taunted him for his own recent failures—for too much alcohol and too little discipline. It was out of this sense of despair and defeat that another of Mailer's obsessions was born.

> I began ... to see myself as some sort of center about which all that had been lost must now rally. It was not simple egomania nor simple drunkenness, it was not even simple insanity: it was a kind of metaphorical leap across a gap. To believe the impossible may be won creates a strength from which the impossible may be attacked.

The essence of Mailer's claim was that he was "the only man in the country" who could build the gate of a second Patterson-Liston fight into the proportions of an epic. The insistence with which he promoted his proposal the next day, the rude insults he hurled at Liston, and his petulant refusal to leave the dais (where he did not belong) all indicate that what Mailer wanted above everything was some kind of direct confrontation with Liston, some chance to prove to himself that he was still a possible hero, that he was larger than the myth into which his own mind had transformed the new heavyweight champion.

After the series of humiliations which gave reporters, detectives, bystanders, and Liston himself ample opportunity to laugh at him, Mailer finally got his chance. While obviously intoxicated, he approached Liston.

> "You called me a bum," I said. . . . "Well, you are a bum," he said. "Everybody is a bum. I'm a bum too. It's just that I'm a bigger bum than you are." He stuck out his hand. "Shake, bum," he said. . . . Could it be, was I indeed a bum? I shook his hand. . . . But a devil came into my head. . . . "Listen," said I, leaning my head closer, speaking from the corner of my mouth as if I were whispering in a clinch, "I'm pulling this caper for a reason. I know a way to build the next fight from a $200,000 dog in Miami to a $2,000,000 gate in New York." . . . "Say," said Liston, "that last drink really set you up. Why don't you go and get me a drink, you bum."

> "I'm not your flunky," I said. It was the first punch I'd sent home. He loved me for it. The hint of corny old darky laughter, cottonfield giggles, peeped out a moment from his throat. "Oh, sheet, man!," said the wit in his eyes. And for the crowd watching, he turned and announced at large, "I like this guy."

Three phrases in this most revealing passage are particularly significant. First, Mailer views the dialogue in the terms of a fight; he speaks to Liston as if they were "in a clinch." Secondly, Mailer's "first punch" ("I'm not your flunky") is delivered while he is behind on points and trapped in a corner. When he finally makes this move, he risks taking a (literal) punch in the mouth from Liston, who is not, one imagines, in the habit of being told off in public by inebriated reporters. Then, there is Liston's remarkable reaction ("I like this guy") to Mailer's thrust, a totally unexpected profession of feeling for the writer that amounts to admiration, and the even more remarkable response that Liston's concession generates in Mailer's mind. For Mailer, Liston's grunt becomes "a chuckle of corny old darky laughter, cottonfield giggles"; not only has Mailer taken final honors in his combat with the "Supreme Spade," but he has metaphorically reduced him to his (ancestrally) original condition of servitude. From king of the Northern urban jungle where the white man is afraid to meet him on the street at night, Liston has been deported to a Southern cotton plantation where he knows his place and recognizes his master.

Liston is at once Mailer himself and Mailer's alter ego. When he is the latter, Mailer becomes Patterson: "The fighters spoke as well from the countered halves of my nature." Mailer even conjectures that perhaps Patterson is God and Liston the Devil, an idea which emanates from a conviction that every man is a potential agent for either of the two great warring cosmic powers, and that by one's actions one affects the outcome in their ultimate struggle for control of a Manichean universe. On that night in Chicago, Liston, in his demonic role, "had shown that the Lord was dramatically weak." Was it possible that Mailer's press-conference comeback had restored some of the Deity's strength? No negative answer could be given with full assurance.

In *An American Dream*—his first novel since *The Deer Park*—Mailer is again concerned with themes that inform the essays: danger, death, and heroism.
                                                    —*James Toback*

In *An American Dream* (1964)—his first novel since *The Deer Park*—Mailer is again concerned with themes that inform the essays: danger, death, and heroism. The pattern of the novel, one might say, is designed on intercourse—with God, with the Devil, with voices form the inner recesses of the mind, with the vagina, and with the anus: intercourse leading to oceanic climax, coming variously in waves of love, lust, or pure aestheticism. The center of all this activity, the narrator and hero, is Stephen Richards Rojack, the embodiment of Mailer's unrealized fantasies and of his radical Puritanism as well. A Harvard graduate *summa cum laude,* he is also a war hero ("the one intellectual in America's history to win a distinguished service cross"), an ex-congressman, a television personality, a professor of existentialist psychology, an author, a boxer, and an unsurpassed stud. He lives in contemporary New York amid people who, in Mailer's view, personify the cancerous totalitarianism of our age.

The action is generated by Rojack's murder of his wife, Deborah, a great bitch, beautiful, extremely rich, and secretly involved in international intrigue as a spy. The love he once felt for her has withered into a sense of dependence so paralyzing that she has now become the very structure of his ego. Without her, he fears he "might topple like clay." In such a condition Rojack, who expresses Mailer's eschatological vision, knows he is unprepared to face eternity. The first step toward reconstruction of self is to exorcise the demon that possesses him—and to exorcise Deborah is to kill her. The act of strangulation is committed with sexual passion, which is true to Mailer's insistence that sex, love, and murder are inseparable and cathartic:

> Some blackbiled lust, some desire to go ahead (and kill her) not unlike the instant one comes in a woman against her cry that she is without protection came bursting with rage from out of me and . . . crack I choked her harder . . . and *crack* I gave her payment.

With Deborah's death begins the arduous process of Rojack's rebirth; he realizes that if murder is sometimes necessary, it is never simple. The gods, like furies, haunt him; he is acutely conscious of everything he thinks or says or does, for now cowardice or weakness or smallness will bring swift retribution—Dread, insanity, and the abyss. To strengthen himself, and to find, once again, something he can honestly call love are the ends of Rojack's quest, but fulfillment of it and freedom from these new furies can be attained only through heroism, through seeking danger and daring death.

> . . . I believed God was not love but courage. Love can come only as a reward. . . . A voice said in my mind: "That which you fear most is what you must do."

The very phrasing of the passage is related to the nature of the punishment that will accrue if the command goes unheeded. Rojack's mental life is split into a "voice" and a "mind," a separation dangerously close to the empty panic of schizophrenia.

But if madness looms as the penalty for prudence and cowardice (Mailer uses the two as almost indistinguishable), it is also possible that Dread will overwhelm even the bold Promethean. Rojack knows that "if man wished to steal the secrets of the gods . . . they would defend themselves and destroy whichever man came too close." With so narrow a chance of escape from insanity and an eternity in the abyss, suicide quite naturally presents itself as an alternative. What is to hold one back?

Despite all his frenetic activity, it is not merely a sensual lust for experience that keeps Rojack going. On the contrary, while his senses are irrepressibly active (especially his sense of smell), his mind persists relentlessly in observation, commentary, and criticism. Any physical sensation is immediately subject to conscious analysis. In Rojack, sex is the effort of the body to rape the mind, to pulsate in waves of ecstasy transcending consciousness. But even here he fails. Whether it is with the German maid, Ruta, or with the Southern chanteuse, Cherry, Rojack's concern is with power rather than with pleasure, with the psychic domination he achieves after *her* orgasm rather than with the physical rapture of his own. Like his creator, Rojack is far more a Puritan than a hedonist; life is struggle rather than joy.

So the question remains: why go on? It is true that Rojack puts his life on the line more than once. The murder of his wife, the competition with Mafia goons, the insults to a former boxing champion in an unfriendly bar, and, especially, the nocturnal walk on the parapet of a windy terrace thirty stories above the ground—all could easily have resulted in his death. But rather than misguided suicide attempts, these acts are a part of Rojack's supreme effort to prepare himself for death. The goal in life is finally religious—to make oneself as fit as possible to meet the unknown after life is done, to face the judgment of eternity; and Rojack is possessed by the faith of the gambler. Like a poker player who is convinced that his next hand is bound to be the lucky one, Rojack acts on the assumption that the longer he lives, the more heroic he may become.

And the assumption is not unfounded, for Rojack's heroism is boundless. He argues with demonic voices and then dispels them, he outwits and outfights his indomitable tycoon father-in-law, and, above all, he humiliates and beats up a sexually magnetic Negro hero, Shago Martin. Not only does Rojack cause Cherry to have her first sexual explosion, after Shago had failed with her for months, but through a combination of psychic intuition and physical power he changes a situation where Shago is standing over him with a knife to one in which he is standing over Shago, who is now a writhing pulp at the bottom of a staircase (and all in the space of ten minutes).

Practically everything Rojack says or does suggests parallels to his creator's personal life, and the episode with Shago Martin, recalling the Mailer-Liston confrontation, is perhaps the richest example. If Liston was a large part of Mailer, Shago's ode to himself is easily applicable to the dark sides of both Rojack and Mailer.

> "I'm a lily-white devil.... I'm just the future, in love with myself, that's the future. I got twenty faces, I talk the tongues, I'm a devil.... I'm cut off from my own lines, I try to speak from my heart and it gets snatched."

If Mailer's encounter with Liston faintly suggested repressed homosexuality transformed into manly fortitude, Rojack's encounter with Shago positively smacks of it. Like Shago, he has Cherry, and his immediate concern after intercourse is in comparison. He can hardly hide his elation when she implies that he was better, a predictable response when one recalls his reaction the night before to Cherry's paean to Shago's sexual prowess. Her emphasis on the word "stud" had made Rojack uneasy.

> The word went in like a blow to the soft part of my belly. There was something final in the verdict as

if there were a sexual round robin where the big people played. All the big Negroes and the big whites.

Like Mailer, Rojack lives his life as if it were some dark experiment which has gradually but relentlessly gained the upper hand so that he is free to act only within its prescribed limits. Again like Mailer, Rojack is paying the price for a lifelong habit of thinking in metaphor; image (like God and the Devil, Heaven and Hell) has become reality, and that reality has become a master demanding undivided attention. It is a reality of dreams, and the dreams in *An American Dream* are endless: the sexual dreams of Don Juan, the Alger dream of the self-made man, the outsider's dream of the inside, the Mafia's dream of money and power, the square's dream of the life of the hipster, and the hipster's dream of death. None of these dreams has turned entirely into nightmare, but each has gone sour, like the soul of the nation which fabricated them. But the saddest dream of all is Stephen Rojack's (and perhaps Mailer's) dream of sanity.

> I was caught. I wanted to escape from that intelligence which let me know of murders in one direction and conceive of [love] from the other, I wanted to be free of magic, the tongue of the devil, the dread of the Lord, I wanted to be some sort of rational man again.... But I could not move.

But what if, unlike Mailer and Rojack, one is *not* obsessed with psychopathic extremes? What if one's patience expires at exhibitions of braggadocio? What if one appreciates wit (of which there is some) but loves humor (of which there is none)? Probably one would call *An American Dream* a joke, and a bad joke at that. The infantile demand for immediate and complete attention; the insistence on being taken seriously, literally, and on his own terms at all times; the inability to treat his agony with even a suggestion of laughter or a trace of irony; the sloppy inconsistency of much of the dialogue; and, finally, the sheer loudness that informs the whole novel, a tone alternating between agitation and hysteria—all this works to tire, frustrate, and, at times, infuriate even the most sympathetic reader.

And yet somehow exasperation yields to the suspicion that Mailer's is a mind which understands as much about the quality of contemporary American life as any now active, a mind which could well represent the last intellectually significant and articulate thrust of an eschatological and religious fervor that may be sorely missed once it is gone. So one is willing to indulge Mailer further, even to thank him once again. And one is willing to accept Rojack's vision of himself as a fair description of Mailer:

> I had leverage; I was one of the more active figures

of the city—no one could be certain finally that nothing large would come to me.

In 1960 there was reason to hope for a dramatic rebirth of energy and heroism; even the darkest passages of *The Presidential Papers* were balanced by intimations that America was not yet doomed. A man could function in society and still find opportunity to grow. By 1966, dream had at last soured into nightmare. *Cannibals and Christians,* a collection of essays, "poems" (or, more accurately, epigrams and graffiti), and interviews (both real and imaginary), is a sermon whose vision of hell has become dire and inevitable. From Mailer's pulpit comes a most disconcerting premonition:

> The sense of a long last night over civilization is back again; it has perhaps not been here so intensely in thirty years, not since the Nazis were prospering, but it is coming.... The world is entering a time of plague.

Totalitarianism has suffocated individuality; the Hilton in San Francisco is emulated before the Plaza in New York; housing projects look like nurseries and nurseries look like hospitals; appliances are plastic rather than metal; vile bully tactics in Vietnam have developed from simple occupation of Southeast Asia; the psychotic has taken over from the psychopath; pornography has gained another step on sexuality. In a word, Lyndon Johnson has replaced John Kennedy.

Johnson, Mailer tells us, is the archetypically alienated figure—a fact which can be observed in his prose (perhaps "the worst ever written by any political leader anywhere"), in his boorish manners, in his deceitfulness, in his voracious ego, and in his almost arrogant lack of style. If a President has a profound effect on the quality of life during his era—and Mailer is convinced that he does—then hope is indeed dim. And the consequences may be far worse than possible loss of prestige, power, or land; for there is the unknown to face after death, and the possibility that there is no absolution for cowardly sins.

But Mailer's exhortations against the insanities of the age of Johnson do not come from one whose own tensions—between radicalism and Puritanism, heroism and buffoonery, the playboy's life and the intellectual's vocation—are anywhere near control. And there is a further complication in Mailer's complex personality, an unmistakably reactionary streak, not unrelated in impulse to his intense religiosity, which challenges his natural and professed political radicalism. Apart from the kind of conservatism that is common property among many contemporary radicals—a quasi-isolationism that urges America to terminate involvement in practically all foreign countries and a profound distrust of the liberal establishment—Mailer holds positions on matters

not directly political which fall neatly into line with the conservative spirit (he is, for example, strongly opposed to birth control and abortion, and he speaks of homosexuality as a "vice"). But two pieces of evidence (both from the essay on the 1964 Republican Convention) are particularly striking. First, Mailer confesses to a buried urge to see Barry Goldwater elected:

> I knew Goldwater could win because something in me leaped out at the thought; a part of me, a devil, wished to take that choice.

Secondly, Mailer's ambivalence toward Negroes, manifested earlier only in the individual cases of Sonny Liston and Shago Martin, is now explicitly broadened. His reaction to James Baldwin's suggestion that there may be no remission for the white man's sins against the Negro is violent:

> I had to throttle an impulse to . . . call Baldwin, and say, "You get this, baby. There's a shit storm coming like nothing you ever knew. So ask yourself if what you desire is for the white to kill every black so that there be total remission of guilt in your black soul."

If the relief of such tensions and conflicts and the consequent fortification of the self can come only from bold action, then Mailer's primary means of personal salvation lies in his work. It is in the very act of creating the artistic sermons which he claims will show us the way to redemption that Mailer redeems himself. His influence has given rise to several "cults." At one extreme there is a segment of the underground hipster community, closely involved with drugs, which worships him as the high priest of God and Sex. At the other end is that increasingly large group of liberal and radical intellectuals, centered in New York and comprised of such critics as Norman Podhoretz, Steven Marcus, and Richard Poirier who see in Mailer, as Marcus once put it, the embodiment of extraordinary literary talent, personal honesty and loyalty, and penetrating social criticism. And yet, in the last analysis, Mailer's influence is limited, for the Word has hardly reached, let alone changed, the heart of the land he is trying to transform.

From the first three sermons of the 1960's, the congregation is likely to walk away interested and, sometimes, excited, rather than transformed. Entertainment overshadows eschatology. And in Mailer's fourth effort of the 60's, *The Deer Park,* a stage adaptation of his novel of 1956, religion gives way completely to comedy (both intentional and unintentional).

This is not to imply that Mailer has abandoned his urgent message; practically all his obsessions of the 60's are here: sex, love, lust, heroism, cowardice, power, God, and the

Devil. If Mailer has added anything new to his philosophy, it lies in the expansion of his idea of sexual freedom and it is expressed through the pimp Marion Faye, who "follows sex to the end, turns queer, bangs dogs, and sniffs toes." But in the figure of Herman Teppis (or "H.T."), a Hollywood mogul in the tradition of Louis B. Mayer and Harry Cohn, genuine humor replaces heavy rhetoric and caustic wit. In the desert of endless debates over who is—and who is not—a genius in bed, Teppis's pronouncements are oases.

> You know what an artist is? He's a crook. They even got a Frenchman now, you know what, he picks people's pockets at society parties. They say he's the greatest writer in France. No wonder they need a dictator, those crazy French. I could never get along with the French.

But Mailer pays a price for his success in the comic mode. One laughs so hard at Teppis that one keeps right on laughing, even at the tortured, self-searching characters—spokesmen all for traditional Maileresque values—one is meant to take seriously. If there is a lesson to be learned from this play, it is that comedy may be suitable to many dramatic modes, including tragedy, but that it has no place at all in eschatological homily.

After a pop play perhaps one should have expected, or at least have been prepared for, a pop novel from Mailer's pen. Nevertheless, *Why Are We in Vietnam?* comes as a shock. Radical as the ideas contained in them may have been, Mailer's earlier novels were more or less conservative in form; except for *Barbary Shore,* they were all clearly in the mainstream of the realist-naturalist tradition. But in *Why Are We in Vietnam?* ordered syntax has yielded to the total liberation of the word; intricate plot structure has given way to hallucinatory fantasy; fully realized characters living in what we know as the real world have been replaced by the protean apparitions in Mailer's mind; the last trace of ratiocination has been obliterated by a relentless bombardment of sensual impressions and apocalyptic utterances. Dreiser and Farrell have disappeared in favor of Joyce, Faulkner, Burroughs, McLuhan, and Norman O. Brown.

At one point or another virtually every theory Mailer has ever had appears—but now with an important difference. Rather than preaching his messages baldly as in the past, Mailer drops them mockingly. And the mockery is directed both at himself and at those he would edify.

> The world is going shazam, hahray harout, fart in my toot, air we breathe is the prez, present dent, and god has always wanted more from man than man has wished to give him. Zig a zig a zig. That is why we live in dread of god.

Even the seminal concept of Dread is translated into the pop language of rock-and-roll. A vast chasm of culture and sensibility separates the tone of Rojack's agonized monologues from the narrative voice of the present novel.

> . . . Mr. Sender, who sends out that Awe and Dread is up on their back . . . because they *alone,* man, you dig? They all *alone,* it's a fright wig, man, that Upper silence alone is enough to bugger you, whoo-ee.

Indeed, the very claim to a prophetic stance in *Why Are We in Vietnam?* is established in a similarly (and intentionally) ambiguous tone.

> This is your own wandering troubadour brought right up to date, here to sell America its new handbook on how to live. . . . We're going to tell you what it's all about.

Although there is a bare minimum of dramatic tension or external conflict, *Why Are We in Vietnam?* has several "characters," each significant primarily on a symbolic plane. D.J. (Disc Jockey, Dr. Jekyll), the adolescent hero narrator of patrician Texas blood, is sometimes convinced that he is really a "Harlem Nigger," and since "there is no such thing as a totally false perception," perhaps he is. Not literally, of course, but rather in the same way that Mailer recognized Sonny Liston in himself and in the same way that the white hipster of **"The White Negro"** is, in his psychic makeup, black. If D.J. is the hipster, Rusty, his father, is the square, a corporation tycoon in Dallas—coarse, selfish, and, at heart, a coward. Tex (the Mr. Hyde to D.J.'s Dr. Jekyll) is part Indian, manly, bisexual, and the son of an undertaker.

The three go bear hunting in Alaska, but the most important action takes place in D.J.'s mind. At one point he has an urge to turn his gun on his father and "blast a shot, thump in his skull." Although he resists, he soon commits the act symbolically by contradicting his father's warning and courageously approaching a wounded bear, putting his life on the line, while his father lies hidden, waiting for the bear to become helpless before firing the fatal shot. Thus liberated from paternal authority, D.J. finds his instincts for love and battle shifted to Tex, from literal father to symbolic brother. In Tex, D.J. encounters nakedly for the first time his other self. And through a mutual awareness of their mutual desire for both intercourse and fratricide, D.J. and Tex finally achieve a sense of purification and personal integration.

> . . . Tex Hyde . . . was finally afraid to prong D.J., because D.J. once become a bitch would kill him, and D.J. breathing that in by the wide-awake of the dark with Aurora Borealis jumping to the beat of his heart knew he could make a try to prong Tex,

there was a chance to get in and steal the iron from Texas' ass and put it on his own ... now it was there, murder between them under all friendship, for god was a beast, not a man, and god said, "Go out and kill—fulfill my will, go and kill," and they hung there each of them on the knife of the divide in all conflict of lust to own the other.... Killer brothers, owned by something, prince of darkness, lord of light, they did not know; they just knew that telepathy was on them, they had been touched forever by the North and each bit a drop of blood from his own finger and touched them across and met blood to blood....

In one eternal moment the Manichean polarities that have obsessed Mailer are at last synthesized—God and the Devil, heaven and hell, nature and man, Negro and white, Dallas and Harlem, phallus and anus.

But why *are* we in Vietnam? What relation does the title have to D.J., Tex, Rusty, bear-hunting, Harlem, Dallas, liberated syntax, or Maileresque eschatology? In the strictest sense, nothing at all. But in a broader, metaphysical sense, the title can be explained as another urgent warning to America. We are in Vietnam because we, as a nation, are going, or have already gone, insane. Mailer's development from politics to meta-politics is complete. The world—and especially America—is now viewed as an expression of Mailer's own most extreme longings and fantasies. Subject and object, chaos and order, internal imagination and external reality are united in a fusion of creator and creation. In an ultimate sense Mailer is claiming not only *relation to* America but *identity with* her. It is likely that he has himself in mind when he writes of Rusty:

> His secret is that he sees himself as one of the pillars of the firmament, yeah, man—he reads the world's doom in his own fuckup. If he is less great than God intended him to be, then America is in Trouble.

One cannot help wondering whether **Why Are We in Vietnam?,** unruly and overwhelming, is not at least as much a symptom of our "Trouble" as a cure for it.

Throughout the past decade Mailer has made the world of the hipster the stuff of his sermons—novels, essays, and plays—as well as the style of his personal life. He calls it "a muted cool religious revival," and a better description (at least of his *intentions*) would be hard to find. He is Zarathustra coming down from the mountain with his vision of the hero; he is Dostoevsky reminding us that "God and the Devil are fighting, and the battleground is the heart of man!"; he is a Puritan minister informing us that pain may be good, for to suffer is to be given the opportunity to grow

and prepare for the mystery of death and the perils of hell; he is a preacher frustrated by his congregation's blind faith in innocence at a time in history when innocence is not only a lie but a crime; he is a seer trying to jar complacent men into an awareness of the despair that lies beneath their conventions; he is Toynbee telling us that if a civilization stagnates, it will die, that if a nation is to survive, it must respond to the reality of challenge; and he is Jonathan Swift couching his eschatalogical message in the language and imagery of scatology.

It is true that Mailer's own faith in the validity of his message is not absolute. He has admitted that "the hipster gambles that he can be terribly, tragically wrong, and therefore be doomed to Hell." But Mailer is a gambler, and so he continues to preach, to reiterate the old verities with a new twist, opening himself to the charge of anachronism, refusing to accept the "modern," the valueless objectivity of the novels of Robbe-Grillet, the impersonal detachment of the music of Milton Babbitt, and the faceless hotels of Conrad Hilton. He will not give up like Hemingway's Lieutenant Henry, who trusts only in the names of bridges, cities, and battles; Mailer chooses instead still to believe in God, Love, Heroism, Courage, and Death. His life and work are a contradiction of the message contained in one of his own poems:

> *Never*
> *contemplate*
> *nothing*
> *said*
> *the saint.*

History is a nightmare from which Mailer is still trying to awaken; but he will not take the easy way out in his struggle.

And yet if he is singleminded in his determination to view life in terms of ultimate battle, his desire for victory is not without ambivalence. His involvement in the pop world has become more than peripheral with his play, his new underground movie (where he is cast as a Mafia gangster), his new novel, and his own life style (where he tries to enact simultaneously the roles of writer, fighter, celebrity, lover, and messiah); and like most of the major figures in this eclectic pop world, he is flirting with psychosis. To live on the edge of so many different scenes is to belong truly to none; and to act like so many different people is to endanger the self. The sign of surrender, the indication that the battle has been lost, is the sense of succumbing to Dread. It is not impossible that Mailer's Dread is essentially the fulfillment of his own unacknowledged *desire* for that Dread, the intuition that all those "psychotic" ideas and actions he lives by are simply the expression of a profound longing for madness and extinction.

Mailer holds himself together, however, by virtue of his work. Through creation he is able to come closer to the unattainable goal of total victory in the struggle which is the metaphor for his vision of life. Even if we do not believe in it ourselves, even if we are impatient with the intellectual naivete of a man who only a decade ago speculated that perhaps he was the first person to state that God was in danger of dying, and even if we are annoyed by the heavily flawed style of his prose, we can still learn from, and be moved by, this belligerent prophet. At the end of the stage version of *The Deer Park,* he speaks of debates about God and Time and Sex as constituting "part of the poor odd dialogues which give hope to us noble humans for more than one night." If Mailer has done this in his own work even a small part of the time, he is one Puritan our age can ill afford to lose.

Robert Merrill (essay date 1974)

SOURCE: "Norman Mailer's Early Nonfiction: The Art of Self-Revelation," in *Western Humanities Review,* Vol. 28, 1974, pp. 1-12.

[*In the following essay, Merrill offers critical examination of Mailer's nonfiction essays, including "Superman Comes to the Supermarket," "The White Negro," and "Ten Thousand Words a Minute."*]

It has become a commonplace—unavoidable at cocktail parties, student bars, even the dinner table—that Norman Mailer's *real* achievement is to be found in his nonfiction. *There,* it is argued, we come upon Mailer "happily mired in reality, hobbled to the facts of time, place, self, as to an indispensable spouse of flesh and blood who continually saves him from his other self that yearns toward wasteful flirtations with *Spiritus Mundi.*" If it seems a bit harsh to describe Mailer's novels as "wasteful flirtations with *Spiritus Mundi,*" many of us would still agree with Richard Foster's basic point: Mailer's nonfiction *is* a pleasant subject if one has any sympathy for his pretensions as a major writer. This is why it is curious that Mailer's much-admired nonfiction should have generated so little critical commentary. From the attention it has received (or lack of it), one might think that Mailer's nonfiction was no more than artful journalism, as his enemies no doubt believe and his friends have failed to dispute.

Mailer has filled the breach himself, of course, arguing at every opportunity that his realistic nonfiction should not be confused with factual journalism. He has said recently that it is "the superb irony of his professional life" that he should receive the highest praise as a journalist, "for he knew he was not even a good journalist and possibly could not hold a top job if he had to turn in a story every day." For Mailer,

journalism is a matter of getting up factual reports intended for the mass media. It is an affair of *facts,* a ceaseless inquiry into who did what to whom, at what place and at what time. If he is not unreliable as a journalist, Mailer is hardly in competition with the daily reporter. In fact, the whole thrust of his nonfiction is away from "factual" history. "For once let us try to think about a political convention without losing ourselves in housing projects of fact and issue." So Mailer begins his first important essay of the 1960's, **"Superman Comes to the Supermarket."** Mailer would replace housing projects of fact and issue with a sense for the mysteries of personality and the relations among such mysteries (interests obviously taken over from the house of fiction). He has written that "there is no history without nuance," and finally this defines his goal as a "journalist": to capture the nuances of our recent American experience and so define its true, as opposed to its *statistical,* meaning.

> **The story of Mailer's nonfiction does not begin happily, for his political and social essays have changed remarkably over the years.**
> **—Robert Merrill**

The concern for nuance and the rejection of "fact" have led of course to Mailer's "involved" journalism—have led to a literary form closer to the novel than to traditional reportage. This form is best embodied in *The Armies of the Night* and *Miami and the Siege of Chicago* (both 1968), Mailer's first extended forays into the political history of our time. It is also to be seen in his more recent works: *Of a Fire on the Moon* (1970), *The Prisoner of Sex* (1971), *St. George and the Godfather* (1972), and *Marilyn* (1973). Contrary to a widely-held opinion, however, these books did not come to us as unanticipated and unique achievements. As early as 1959 Mailer began the nonfictional innovations which made his recent books possible. It is this early work that I want to consider here, both as the preparation for Mailer's writings after 1967 and as an independent achievement which deserves more attention than it has yet received. By tracing the gradual emergence of Mailer's "personal" approach to nonfiction, we should come to see what A. Alvarez meant when he said that Mailer's early essays now seemed "like so many training flights" for *The Armies of the Night.* But we should also come to see that as Mailer turned more and more to the techniques of fiction he was able to succeed in the essay form as never before. This achievement is no mean one; among his contemporaries only James Baldwin has surpassed Mailer as an essayist. At any rate, this is the claim I would like to test in considering Mailer's early nonfiction.

The story of Mailer's nonfiction does not begin happily, for his political and social essays have changed remarkably over the years. The pieces which go back to the 1950's hardly anticipate the essayist who broods over the psychic forces at work in a championship prize fight; whether their subject is David Riesman, homosexuality, Marx, or Sputnik, they all betray the radical intellectual who once dissected Western Defense for the readers of *Dissent.* Significantly, Mailer has all but repudiated his earliest essays: "... whenever I sat down to do an article, I seemed to thicken in the throat as I worked my sentences and my rhetoric felt shaped by the bad political prose of our years." Indeed, such essays as **"The Meaning of Western Defense," "David Riesman Reconsidered,"** and **"The Homosexual Villain"** are unpleasant reading for anyone who admires Mailer's prose style. Since collected in *Advertisements for Myself* (1959), these articles suggest that Mailer has no real gift for the analytical essay which is closely reasoned and "objective." Mailer seems to have recognized this himself, for his nonfiction has become less and less analytical as the years have passed.

"The White Negro" (1957) is Mailer's one significant essay of this early period. In one sense an almost scholarly discussion of the Hipster, this piece succeeds where Mailer's other early essays do not because it goes beyond the analysis of a cultural or political situation to create what Mailer has called a sociological "fiction." Mailer's "fiction"—the Hipster as revolutionary elitist—is not, of course, a wholly imaginative creation. In this essay, Mailer tries to describe a real phenomenon with real historical roots. He traces the birth of the Hipster to the catastrophes of the twentieth century and sees this figure as a rebel against society, that "collective creation" revealed by World War II to be "murderous" and by the postwar era to suffer from "a collective failure of nerve." He is also careful to identify the source of the Hipster's life style—the Negro culture based on jazz, marijuana, and sexuality (hence his title). But starting with these observations on the Hipster's genesis, Mailer is quick to take up a partisan defense of the Hipster's intuitions. The real thrust of his "analysis" is not descriptive but prophetic: the Hipster is seen as "the dangerous frontrunner of a new kind of personality which could become the central expression of human nature before the twentieth century is over." The more inspired passages in **"The White Negro"** always reject the generally analytical tone of the essay for a more lyrical evocation of the new hero who has come among us. The following passage is representative:

> It is this knowledge which provides the curious community of feeling in the world of the hipster, a muted cool religious revival to be sure, but the element which is exciting, disturbing, nightmarish perhaps, is that incompatibles have come to bed, the inner life and the violent life, the orgy and the dream of love, the desire to murder and the desire to create, a dialectical conception of existence with a lust for power, a dark, romantic, and yet undeni-

ably dynamic view of existence for it sees every man and woman as moving individually through each moment of life forward into growth or backward into death.

The "knowledge" Mailer refers to is the Hipster's supposed awareness of what is good or bad for his own psyche. Mailer begins by remarking this "knowledge" and ends with nothing less than his claim that the Hipster has "a dialectical conception of existence." Jean Malaquais has called this claim "a gorgeous flower of Mailer's romantic idealism," and I doubt that many of us would disagree. So far as **"The White Negro"** is sociology as we tend to think of it, Mailer's achievement is surely limited by such excessive claims for his subject. But **"The White Negro"** is really a lyrical defense of Mailer's conversion to Hip, an "American existentialism" which differs from the French variety because it is based on "a mysticism of the flesh" rather than "the rationality of French existentialism." Mailer succeeds in **"The White Negro"** insofar as he persuades us that Hip has "a dark, romantic, and yet undeniably dynamic view of existence," not that it has literally derived from Black culture or that it is a major social force. Despite its sometimes ponderous tone, **"The White Negro"** should therefore be seen as not altogether different from Mailer's more recent essays. Like these essays, it is distinguished by the quality of Mailer's brooding and most partisan reflections on what he has observed.

If **"The White Negro"** was an advance, the real turning point for Mailer's nonfiction was *Advertisements for Myself.* After 1959 Mailer's essays are marked by the strong personal voice he developed in writing the "advertisements" to his first collection. At first the difference is only stylistic, as Mailer cultivates this personal voice and so avoids the "thickening" in the throat which came to him while writing those political essays influenced by "early, passionate, and injudicious reading of the worst sort of Max Lernerish liberal junk." But gradually Mailer did much more than this; he came to introduce into his "journalism" not only his personal voice but his personality as well. His writings from 1960 to 1968 represent a continuing effort to focus his explorations into recent American history by transforming this personal element into a functional persona.

Before he could do this, however, Mailer had to discover the value of fictional techniques for a work of nonfiction. He seems to have made this discovery in **"Superman Comes to the Supermarket"** (1960). Ostensibly a report on the 1960 Democratic Convention, this essay is really a glorification of John Fitzgerald Kennedy, the convention's nominee. Impressed by Kennedy's charisma rather than his politics (which were traditionally liberal, if not a bit conservative), Mailer set out to dramatize the mysterious allure of Kennedy's personality. Toward this end he employed numerous literary devices, most of them novelistic: character sketches, shifts in chronology, the juxtaposition of contrasting characters and events, etc. But his first tool was sheer rhetoric. He remarks at the beginning of his essay that he will "dress" his argument in "a ribbon or two of metaphor," and the "argument" is indeed metaphorical. Kennedy is variously imaged as "a great box-office actor," "a hero central to his time," and "a prince in the unstated aristocracy of the American dream"; he is said to have "a patina of that other life, the second American life, the long electric night with the fires of neon leading down the highway to the murmur of jazz." Kennedy is contrasted throughout with the sort of candidate desired by the bosses of the convention—the totally political, totally predictable candidate such as Richard Nixon or Richard Daley. Mailer laments that we are a country of mythical heroes, yet our faith in such heroes has dried up. We are in need of a Kennedy, an American prince who will rekindle our faith in the American dream. The nation will reveal itself by its selection of Kennedy or Nixon: "One would have an inkling at last if the desire of America was for drama or stability, for adventure or monotony." Will the American people be so courageous as to embrace their own lonely and romantic desires?

Needless to say, the "argument" here is some distance removed from "fact and issue." It is a novelist's argument, and throughout **"Superman Comes to the Supermarket"** Mailer performs the good novelist's task of heightening his protagonist by treating everything else in a manner which can only set off Kennedy's contrasting excellence. The scene at the convention is described so as to make Kennedy appear not only a matinee idol by contrast but a saviour come unto heathens. Los Angeles is "a kingdom of stucco, the playground for mass men"; the Biltmore hotel, convention headquarters, is "one of the ugliest hotels in the world." The people at the convention are either political hacks or party professionals like Lyndon Johnson ("when he smiled the corners of his mouth squeezed gloom; when he was pious, his eyes twinkled irony; when he spoke in a righteous tone, he looked corrupt." It is to *this* city, *this* hotel, and *these* people that Kennedy comes, the movie star come to the palace to claim the princess. Mailer also places in evidence Nixon's incredibly mawkish remarks upon receiving the Republican nomination: "'Yes, I want to say,' said Nixon, 'that whatever abilities I have, I got from my mother . . . and my father . . . and my school and my church.'" He dismisses with contempt the Republican Convention which followed and offers yet another judgment on that convention's nominee: "The apocalyptic hour of Uriah Heep." He presents in detail Adlai Stevenson's presence at the Democratic Convention, for Stevenson plays the passive anti-hero to Kennedy's hero. The "events" Mailer chose to describe in this essay were selected by a professional novelist, not a political journalist. That is, they serve the ends of the novelist as well as the propagandist. The very texture of his essay validates

Mailer's attractive "creation" of John Kennedy—a creation soon to be adopted by the country at large.

"Superman Comes to the Supermarket" reveals the novelist's hand, then, but it does not include the device most characteristic of Mailer's recent nonfiction—the use of himself as participant as well as spectator. For this we must look to the later essays, beginning with Mailer's second convention piece, **"In The Red Light: A History of the Republican Convention in 1964."** As its subtitle suggests, **"In The Red Light"** is about the Republican Convention rather than its leading man. (Goldwater is its most important figure, but he is hardly the hero of the piece.) The essay is formally divided into three parts: a history of events prior to the convention, including Goldwater's rise to power in the Republican Party; a description of the convention up to Goldwater's nomination; and a spectator's views on Goldwater's acceptance speech. Only at the end does Mailer abandon the pose of reporter to reflect on Goldwater's ascendancy and the state of the union in this year of Johnson versus Goldwater. Yet his interpretive presence is felt throughout. It is this "presence" which distinguishes **"In The Red Light"** from other journalistic accounts of the convention.

Mailer's role in the essay begins to emerge in the political portraits of part two. Here Everett Dirksen is described as "an old organist who could play all the squeaks in all the stops, rustle over all the dead bones of all the dead mice in all the pipes," and we can *hear* Dirksen as Mailer describes him, "making a sound like the whir of the air conditioning in a two-mile tunnel." And once you have read Mailer's description of George Romney as "a handsome version of Boris Karloff, all honesty, big-jawed, soft-eyed, eighty days at sea on a cockeyed passion," you can never see Romney again without visions of Frankenstein. These examples will suggest that Mailer is not exactly a *disinterested* historian. This is especially clear in his "analysis" of the Goldwater crusade. Goldwater delegates are presented as "a Wasp Mafia where the grapes of wrath are stored"; "a frustrated posse, a convention of hangmen who subscribe to the principle that the executioner has his rights as well"; their representatives in the California delegation are said to resemble Robert Mitchum playing the mad reverend in *Night of the Hunter*. Mailer even sense this fanaticism in the bagpipers who play throughout the convention, for theirs is "the true music of the Wasps" in which one detects "the Faustian rage of a white civilization . . . the cry of a race which was born to dominate and might never learn to share." Mailer's metaphorical rendering of the convention may be charged with bias, but many of us will sympathize with the underlying assumption: what really happened at the convention can only be captured in language which speaks of human acts and betrays a human speaker. Even where Mailer is on shakiest ground as a reporter—his characterizations—most of us will probably find that *his* Goldwater, Scranton, or Eisenhower at least suggests the man we all observe rather than the faceless political "figure" we encounter in news reports. But the point is perhaps obvious. Dealing with the convention as he would in a novel, Mailer achieves the same imaginative authority in what is formally an essay.

Mailer's impressionism is justified because **"In the Red Light"** is about his response to the ascending Right Wing rather than the phenomenon itself. At one point Mailer writes, "I had been leading a life which was a trifle too pointless and a trifle too full of guilt and my gullet was close to nausea with the endless compromises of an empty liberal center. So I followed the convention with something more than simple apprehension." This passage goes far to explain Mailer's fascination with Goldwater, for Goldwater is an answer to the empty liberal center. But it also anticipates the strategy of Mailer's essay. Rather than "describe" the convention, Mailer dramatizes his ambivalent response to Goldwater and the Goldwaterites. He does this not only to bring the convention to life as an *experienced* event but also to offer an ominous clue to our condition as a people. For Mailer's undeclared assumption is that his reactions are representative. And if men like Mailer feel the attraction of a Goldwater, then Mailer's conclusion is probably true: "America has come to a point from which she will never return. The wars are coming and the deep revolutions of the soul." Mailer has rendered the convention so persuasively that such prophecies almost seem inevitable.

We can be grateful for Mailer's fascination with Goldwater—his account of the Republican Convention is much richer than it might otherwise have been. Elsewhere in his nonfiction, however, Mailer has used his personality not only to focus the coverage of an event or movement but as his fundamental subject. He has treated himself as a character in one of his novels might be treated and so brought the essay form to the borders of fiction. This strategy is to be seen in such early essays as **"An Evening with Jackie Kennedy, or, The Wild West of the East"** (1962), but it is used most successfully in **"Ten Thousand Words a Minute"** (1962), Mailer's account of the first Patterson-Liston fight. Here Mailer emphasizes his own role in a public event almost to the exclusion of the event itself. He may have arrived at this strategy through necessity rather than choice, for the fight itself was a one-round "fiasco." In any case, Mailer's title is a sly hint that he is here concerned with more than the coverage of a championship fight. Mailer has indeed written almost twenty thousand words about a two-minute fight—*and* what he takes to be its symbolic meaning, his relation to it that week in Chicago, and his reaction to its outcome. These latter concerns are what justify the length of **"Ten Thousand Words a Minute,"** the longest and the best of Mailer's essays.

I don't mean to suggest that Mailer here neglects his duties as a reporter. In part one he gives an interesting account of the men surrounding the two fighters; in part two he offers a very professional report on the Patterson and Liston training camps; in part three he presents what must be the most vivid published account of the fight itself; and in part four he manages to cover all the post-fight activities, including Liston's press conference the next day. Impressive as Mailer's reportage can be, however, **"Ten Thousand Words a Minute"** is still about Norman Mailer's coverage of a prize fight rather than the fight itself. We sense this as early as part two, where Mailer dramatizes not only his observations of Patterson and Liston but also his conversations with such men as Cus D'Amato, Patterson's manager, and Jim Jacobs, Patterson's Public Relations Assistant. The humor here is at Mailer's expense; like the self-deprecating passages in **"An Evening with Jackie Kennedy,"** it hints at the ironic self-characterization so crucial to *The Armies of the Night* and Mailer's more recent nonfiction. For that matter, the humor is important here. **"Ten Thousand Words a Minute"** offers Mailer's symbolic reading of the Patterson-Liston fight, where Liston is Faust and Patterson the archetypal Underdog; where Liston is Sex and Patterson is Love; where Liston is the Hustler and Patterson the Artist; where Liston is the Devil and Patterson is God. Such weighty identifications are presented in all metaphoric seriousness. Like *The Armies of the Night,* **"Ten Thousand Words a Minute"** can afford such extravagance because the man who speculates so largely is himself an object of dramatic irony. Mailer is revealed here in a familiar role: "Once more I had tried to become a hero, and had ended as an eccentric." Yet the speculations offered above are not to be dismissed as eccentric lunacies. As in his later works, Mailer wins a hearing for his insights as the best fruit of a writer who will reveal everything about himself, his most ridiculous "capers" but also his most dazzling intellectual connections.

The essay's final sections make it clear that Mailer's ultimate subject is himself. Once he has described the fight and offered his ideas on what it all "meant" (i.e., what the fighters represented), Mailer would seem to be done. Yet he goes on for another fifteen pages. The fight inspires a severe self-analysis in which Mailer takes upon himself part of the blame for Patterson's defeat. (Briefly, Mailer finds that he has backed Patterson in an "idle, detached fashion"; like Patterson's liberal supporters, he has failed to nourish the champion's spirit). Here Mailer considers the events of that week in Chicago, including his debate with William Buckley at Medinah Temple. He finds that the ledgers are heavily against him: he has supported Patterson too complacently, he has drunk much too much, he has sulked over such trivialities as the account of his debate in the New York *Times*. Mailer feels something like Patterson's humiliation because he has identified with the lonely artist in Patterson:

> Patterson was the champion of every lonely adoles-

cent and every man who had been forced to live alone, every protagonist who tried to remain unique in a world whose waters washed apathy and compromise into the pores. He was the hero of all those unsung romantics who walk the street at night seeing the vision of Napoleon while their feet trip over the curb, he was part of the fortitude which could sustain those who live for principle, those who had gone to war with themselves and ended with discipline.

Mailer has failed both Patterson and himself, for his week in Chicago has been ruled by the world's apathy, compromise, and lack of discipline.

His disruption of Liston's press conference, the essay's final episode, reveals Mailer as yet another "unsung romantic" who has the vision of Napoleon as he trips over the curb. The scene is saved from bathos because Mailer sees it for what it is ("Once more I had tried to become a hero, and had ended as an eccentric"). Yet it is also a fitting climax to his narrative, for here Mailer dramatizes his determination to be "some sort of center about which all that had been lost must now rally." The defeat of Patterson has become for Mailer the defeat of Love and Art and Discipline. His bravura at the press conference registers his decision to reaffirm what the week's events and the fight itself have called into question. Indeed, this reaffirmation is what the essay is ultimately "about." Mailer has made us see that Patterson and Liston do not merely represent forces such as Love and Sex; finally, they represent *us,* that heroic—or demonic—part of us with which we identify. Mailer comes to see this and to act on what he sees—however "comic" his action. We, his readers, can hardly see less.

Years later Mailer would involve himself in another struggle where the opposing sides would suggest the "countered halves" of his own nature. In his account of the 1967 March on the Pentagon, Mailer would again dramatize his conversion to one side in the conflict. Both **"Ten Thousand Words a Minute"** and *The Armies of the Night* are narratives about the comical yet serious education of Norman Mailer. The essay anticipates the later work in technique as well as form, for **"Ten Thousand Words a Minute"** depends on fictional techniques to a degree unparalleled in Mailer until *The Armies of the Night.* Such devices are used selectively in **"Superman Comes to the Supermarket," "In The Red Light,"** and **"An Evening with Jackie Kennedy."** And Mailer's use of himself as a persona can be seen emerging as long ago as *Advertisements for Myself,* where his controversial self-portrait is a major unifying device. But in **"Ten Thousand Words a Minute"** Mailer's fiction-like nonfiction is fully in evidence. Such figures as Patterson, Liston, D'Amato, Jacobs, and the cabbie who takes Mailer to Comiskey Park are treated in a manner Mailer formally

reserved for his fiction. Mailer dramatizes almost every scene in the essay and makes particular use of the flashback, a device we normally associate with fiction. If he is to be seen here as "hobbled to the facts of time, place, self," Mailer is also to be seen deploying his "facts" in a literary structure which betrays both the novelist and the historian-to-be of *The Armies of the Night* and *Miami and the Siege of Chicago.*

The most "novelistic" of his essays, **"Ten Thousand Words a Minute"** is also the piece in which Mailer's self-reference is most conspicuous. For this reason it is not surprising that the essay has received insufficient recognition as a minor masterpiece. Nor is it really curious that Mailer's nonfiction should have been examined so seldom. As Scott Fitzgerald once remarked, "There are always those to whom all self-revelation is contemptible, unless it ends with a noble thanks to the gods for the Unconquerable Soul." Mailer's detractors have been quick to find *his* self-revelations contemptible, failing to see that in registering its effects on himself Mailer has illuminated the history of our time. Mailer has offered his reactions to modern life as those of a representative American—unusually sensitive and intelligent, perhaps, but subject to the same contradictory emotions as the rest of us in confronting such phenomena as Goldwater, Floyd Patterson, the Peace Movement, Women's Liberation, the space program, and enigmas such as Richard Milhous Nixon. As Mailer says, there is no history without nuance. And what his method suggests is that the nuances of recent history can only be caught in the response of a troubled American to the events which *are* America. If he has shown this most convincingly in *The Armies of the Night,* Mailer has anticipated that achievement in the essays I have discussed here. More than brilliant miniatures, these essays are one of Mailer's enduring contributions to American writing.

Kenneth A. Seib (essay date 1974)

SOURCE: "Mailer's March: The Epic Structure of *The Armies of the Night,*" in *Essays in Literature,* Vol. 1, 1974, pp. 89-95.

[*In the following essay, Seib identifies elements of Homeric epic in* The Armies of the Night, *particularly Mailer's concern for the destiny of the United States, allusions to the supernatural, and warfare as its central theme.*]

When speaking of Norman Mailer, it is common to discuss his various avatars as public persona and literary court jester. We see Mailer advertising for himself, sounding his yawp over the television airwaves, slugging it out *mano a mano* with such disparate opponents as Gore Vidal, Jose Torres, Germaine Greer, and Kate Millett. Prisoner of sex, pop astronaut, disk jockey to the world—Mailer has never been hit hard because his dazzling footwork keeps critics confused, and he changes style in each new round.

But literature's exhibitionists are quickly forgotten if there is little artistry behind their bluster. (Who today reads Vachel Lindsay?) Some who defend Mailer point to a rich prose style, as though he were a space-age Lord Macaulay. Richard Poirier, for instance, finds him "the stout literary contender for the English language, in competition not simply with others (he's nearly beyond that) but with anything—transistors, newspapers, tapes, the sound of helicopters, all the media—that presumes to represent reality." Poirier's statement conjures up the image of a literary King Kong swiping away helicopters while sitting atop the offices of the *New York Review of Books*. Others applaud his machismo in exploring difficult territory, but there is little analysis of what Mailer has actually written.

Along with *The Naked and the Dead, The Armies of the Night* is generally considered Mailer's finest work. Richard Foster, for instance, finds it "unquestionably one of Mailer's best books—passionate, humorous, acutely intelligent, and as always, eloquent in its empathy with the drift of history." In addition to this sort of praise, Mailer won such Establishment symbols of approval as the National Book Award and Pulitzer Prize for having written *Armies.* Moreover, the book has become standard reading for those who believe in the "non-fiction novel," a recent genre that has yet to be defined to everyone's satisfaction. Shifty as ever, Mailer seems to require the invention of new genres before critical discussion of his works is possible.

But what has been largely missed about Mailer is that he works in very traditional and clear-cut forms. *The Naked and the Dead* has the bulk and leisurely pace of nineteenth-century fiction, while *Barbary Shore* and *The Deer Park* have the texture of 1930's realistic fiction and the content of the social novel. *An American Dream* is James Cain with existential trappings, while *Why Are We in Vietnam?* is spaced-out Joyce. Other books are superior reportage.

The Armies of the Night, in spite of its avant-grade sub-title ("History as a Novel, The Novel as History"), is no exception. And that is precisely its triumph, for Mailer is working within the framework of the most improbable and, for this century, most difficult of traditional forms—the classical epic. Barry H. Leeds has already pointed out that *Armies* is "thematically structured like the *Iliad,* proceeding simultaneously on an individual and national level." But Leeds does not pursue the comparison far enough, for the book is not just *thematically* structured along the lines of the epic. *The Armies of the Night* has the narrative structure and content of the epic as well.

The definition of the literary epic has been much discussed. Although scholars disagree about certain problems involving the epic, most are in agreement about its general characteristics and stylistic qualities. In the conventional epic, narrative plot is simple, generally involving one central incident of major importance. The incident itself, with its setting, has significance for a race or nation. Warfare is the dominant theme. Towering above all characters is the epic hero, who exemplifies certain cultural traits and is a figure of national importance. The style of the literary epic is objective, lofty, elaborate in imagery, elevated in tone. Often the supernatural plays an important part in the outcome of events; gods, angels, and demons are common.

> Analysis of *The Armies of the Night* reveals that Mailer—and it is hard to believe that it was unconsciously—has employed in one way or another all the features of the traditional epic.
> —Kenneth A. Seib

In addition, the author of the traditional epic relies heavily on established epic details. The narrative, for instance, begins *in medias res* and fills in preceding events through flashback. There is an invocation to the muse, a request for divine inspiration, in which the author posits an epic question. There are lengthy descriptions—for example, Homer's enumeration of the fighting forces at Troy—and the author employs elaborate similes, ornate comparisons involving ironic contrasts. Events are dramatized, rather than explained, and the drama has significance for both human and national destiny.

Analysis of *The Armies of the Night* reveals that Mailer—and it is hard to believe that it was unconsciously—has employed in one way or another all the features of the traditional epic. To begin with, the title of the book—as Barry Leeds has noted—suggests not only Matthew Arnold's ignorant armies clashing by night in "Dover Beach," but also the epic forces of Homer, Virgil, and others. The theme of the book is warfare. Yet Mailer, like all other epic writers of the past since Homer, adapts the epic form to the changed conditions of his own time. As C. M. Bowra has pointed out, all writers of epic have "tried to adapt the heroic ideal to unheroic times and to proclaim ... a new conception of man's grandeur and nobility. Each had his own approach, his own solution, and his own doubts and reservations." Mailer's war is not only a literal one, a march on the Pentagon involving armies of anti-war demonstrators on one side and the forces of the American establishment on the other, but a war between the divided elements of the American psyche. Between the ideals of the American Revolution and the desperation of the Pentagon march, Mailer warns, there is a "beast slinking to the marketplace." That this disparity has national importance is clear: "The two halves of America were not coming together, and when they failed to touch, all of history might be lost in the divide."

Mailer, then, is presenting the Pentagon march as an historical event of the first magnitude, an event as significant to the destiny of the United States as the Trojan war was to Greece. In accordance with the rules of traditional epic, the narrative plot is simple. Mailer describes events leading up to the march, the march itself, and its aftermath. Everything focuses on the central incident of the Pentagon march. The book, therefore, contains the necessary scope, framework, and importance that have been traditionally attributed to the epic. But so do a lot of other books, most of them best-selling historical romances that are quickly forgotten—or, at least, not taken seriously by sophisticated readers. What elevates *Armies* above mere book-jacket accolades of "epic" is, in addition to its structural and stylistic details, its use of a genuine epic hero—Norman Mailer himself.

No papier-mâché epic hero like Anthony Adverse, Mailer is the real red-blooded thing. A man of national renown—perhaps infamy—Mailer stands both in and above the events he narrates. While willing to participate in the resistance movement, he by no means gives it total assent. He is scornful, for instance, of the New Left for being plugged in, at least obliquely, to the drug culture ("Mailer was not in approval of any drug, he was virtually conservative about it"); for its squandering of energy on such useless activities as a Pentagon march; for the bankrupt values of old liberals and radical chic professors ("if they were doomed to be revolutionaries, rebels, dissenters, anarchists, protesters, and general champions of one Left cause or another, they were also in private, *grands conservateurs,* and if the truth be told, poor damn émigré princes"). "While at home in large areas of life," E. M. W. Tillyard has written, "the epic writer must be centred in the normal, he must measure the crooked by the straight, he must exemplify that sanity which has been claimed for true genius." While moving through this fantastic corroboree of contemporary madness, Mailer presents himself as both a norm by which we can judge others' values and behavior, and as one who has the sanity of true genius. In fact, with typical candor—why hide it?—Mailer admits early in the book that he has always had "the illusion he was a genius."

If, like Achilles, Mailer is a man of wrath, he is also, like Odysseus, a bit of a fool. His street-fighter performance at Washington's Ambassador Theater, his earlier gropings in the dark of The Room, his eyeball-to-eyeball combat with the young Nazi—all are in the comic mode, yet not unheroic. Just as Achilles and Odysseus are heroes with whom we can identify, so Mailer contains our own fears, prejudices, and capacity for ludicrous behavior. Yet again like Achilles

and Odysseus, he is greater than we—in his sensitivity to nuance, his ability for self-willed action, his largesse. Mailer *does* commit himself to a cause in which he only half believes, he *does* willingly get busted at the Pentagon, he *does* incorporate the multitudinous insanities of the march into objective judgment. Who among us can do the same? Mailer is "warrior, presumptive general, ex-political candidate, embattled aging *enfant terrible* of the literary world, wise father of six children, radical intellectual, existential philosopher, hard-working author, champion of obscenity, husband of four battling sweet wives, amiable bar drinker, and much exaggerated street fighter, party giver, hostess insulter"—he is one of us and, at the same time, more than most of us will ever be.

C. M. Bowra, speaking again of the epic hero, says this:

> The single man, Achilles or Beowulf or Roland, surpasses others in strength and courage. His chief, almost his only, aim is to win honour and renown through his achievements and to be remembered for them after his death. He is ruthless to any who frustrate or deride him. In his more than human strength he seems to be cut off from the intercourse of common men and consorts with a few companions only less noble than himself. He lacks allegiance, except in a modified sense, to suzerain or cause. What matters is his prowess. Even morality hardly concerns him; for he lives in a world where what counts is not morality but honour.

Mailer fits Bowra's description perfectly. Mailer the character, the central figure of the drama that Mailer the author relates, has the same concern as his creator: his honor and renown as a writer and student of contemporary events. When mildly put down by Robert Lowell as "the best journalist in America," Mailer replies that he prefers to think of himself as "the best writer in America." Such chutzpah may be thought pure egotism but, as Mailer notes, when "History inhabits a crazy house, egotism may be the last tool left to History." One recalls Achilles dragging the body of Paris around the walls of Troy, Aeneas callously abandoning Dido, Odysseus eliminating his wife's suitors—they too display ego beyond the healthy norm, for their honor transcends the bounds of conventional behavior.

In short, Mailer presents himself as a single man, lacking allegiance "to suzerain or cause," whose honor as "the best writer in America" is the central issue at stake. If he cannot understand the insanities of history, he seems to ask implicitly, then who can? And he is ruthless to those "who frustrate or deride him." Paul Goodman looks like "the sort of old con who had first gotten into trouble in the YMCA, and hadn't spoken to anyone since"; Robert Lowell gives off "the unwilling haunted saintliness of a man who was repaying the moral debts of ten generations of ancestors"; Dwight Macdonald prides himself "on adopting the 'I am dumb' school of English interrogation." The comments are unflattering and are meant to be. Each litterateur is a presumptive heir apparent to Mailer's literary throne, and each is banished to a far corner of the literary realm. Trusting only the authority of his senses (as usual), Mailer dismisses others on a visceral level for not knowing, as he presumably does himself, "of dignity hard-achieved, and dignity lost through innocence, and dignity lost by sacrifice for a cause one cannot name." Such is the dignity of the true epic hero.

Yet, as the author of *Armies* is well aware, the character Mailer often fails to exhibit either dignity or heroism. He is "a ludicrous figure with mock-heroic associations . . . an egotist of the most startling misproportions, outrageously and often unhappily self-assertive." The book is essentially written in what Northrop Frye would call "the low mimetic mode," never achieving the heights of genuine epic tragedy. At times it is purely mock-heroic. Mailer maintains the epic distance and comic sense of Homer in his creation of Odysseus or of Dante who, as principal character of the *Commedia,* faints dead away at the sight of the capital of Hell. There is, once again, an awareness of irony in most epic writers, and something supremely human about all epic heroes.

There are other familiar characteristics that mark *The Armies of the Night* as epic. Mailer opens the book *in medias res* with the *Time* magazine account of his outrageous performance at Washington's Ambassador Theater during the opening round of the Pentagon assault. Through flashback we are filled in on the details of how Mailer, reluctant participant, is brought into the anti-war resistance by Mitchell Goodman. In fact, Goodman's telephone call is a comic version of inspiration from the Muse, a summons from beyond that calls the hero to epic activity. The epic question, generally posted at the beginning of the traditional epic, is asked by Mailer at the very end: America, heavy with child, "will probably give birth, and to what?" Although the question is never clearly answered, the implied answer is clear: "The death of America rides in on the smog." And the book ends on a note of divine supplication ("Deliver us from our curse") not atypical of the epic mode.

Furthermore, there are stylistic details taken from the conventional epic. Consider, for example, this Homeric catalogue of battle forces at the Pentagon, a description exactly right for a mod *Iliad:*

> They came walking up in all sizes, a citizens' army not ranked yet by height, an army of both sexes in numbers almost equal, and of all ages, although most were young. Some were well-dressed, some were poor, many were conventional in appearance,

as often were not. The hippies were there in great number, perambulating down the hill, many dressed like the legions of Sgt. Pepper's Band, some were gotten up like Arab sheiks, or in Park Avenue doormen's greatcoats, others like Rogers and Clark of the West, Wyatt Earp, Kit Carson, Daniel Boone in buckskin, some had grown mustaches to look like *Have Gun, Will Travel*—Paladin's surrogate was here!—and wild Indians with feathers, a hippie gotten up like Batman, another like Claude Rains in *The Invisible Man*—his face wrapped in a turban of bandages and he wore a black satin top hat. A host of these troops wore capes, beat-up khaki capes, slept on, used as blankets, towels, improvised duffel bags; or fine capes, orange linings, or luminous rose linings, the edges ragged, near a tatter, the threads ready to feather, but a musketeer's hat on their head. One hippie may have been dressed like Charles Chaplin; Buster Keaton and W. C. Fields could have come to the ball; there were Martians and Moon-men and a knight unhorsed who stalked about in the weight of real armor. There were to be seen a hundred soldiers in Confederate gray, and maybe there were to be seen a hundred hippies in officer's coats of Union dark-blue. . . . There were soldiers in Foreign Legion uniforms, and tropical bush jackets, San Quentin and Chino, California striped shirt and pants, British copies of Eisenhower jackets, hippies dressed like Turkish shepherds and Roman senators, gurus, and samurai in dirty smocks. They were close to being assembled from all the intersections between history and the comic books, between legend and television, the Biblical archetypes and the movies.

In addition, the book is filled with epic similes of Homeric proportion, all too numerous to mention. The comparison of America's national mentality to that of Grandma with Orange Hair, zinging half dollars into a Vegas slot machine in order to get her emotional kicks, is only one of many vivid examples.

Finally, there are two more details associated with the traditional epic: the supernatural and the journey into the underworld. ***The Armies of the Night*** offers numerous references to the supernatural. Lowell, a descendant of those who kissed "the *sub cauda* of the midnight cat," is presented as an inheritor of Maule's curse; Jerry Rubin is a "revolutionary mystic" whose "roots were in Bakunin"; Abbie Hoffman and the Fugs are theatrical mediums attempting to levitate the Pentagon in a holy ritual of exorcism. But such description is mainly allusive and ornamental. More functional to Mailer's theme is the author's obsessive concern with the struggle between God and Satan, the forces of life and the impulses toward destruction. Mailer's gothic vision is of an America, not unlike Salem in the seventeenth century, gone demonic, "living with a controlled, even fiercely controlled, schizophrenia which had been deepening with the years."

Mailer's trip into the underworld—into Hell—is less overt and more detailed. Busted for purposely crossing a Pentagon barrier, Mailer finds himself in prison, where a "subtle hell offered its perspective—if you were an intellectual and a bad one, no matter how, you might end in some eternity like this, with nothing but the sounds of conversations already held to entertain the ear, nothing but books like *Saint John Bosco—Friend of Youth* to exercise the brain." It is a bolgia reserved for Unrepentant Radicals, a place of stale sweat and rancid air, of indifferent marshals and unfulfilled legal expectations, of authority and thwarted instincts. Mailer's later account of the action at the plaza of the Pentagon steps is an even further descent into the inferno of contemporary schizophrenia. In short, the entire prison sequence involving Mailer and the other demonstrators is a clear equivalent of the epic journey to the underworld.

E. M. W. Tillyard writes about the "choric" element in epic, the expression of "the feelings of a large group of people living in or near his own time." As spokesman for all those like himself—Left Conservatives—Mailer has forged from the unwieldy chaos of contemporaneity something of a modern epic. Just as Milton attempted to justify the ways of God to man, Mailer has attempted to justify the ways of America to whatever gods that be. But unlike Milton, who was not present at the Fall, Mailer was the man: he suffered, he was there.

Donald Fishman (essay date 1975)

SOURCE: "Norman Mailer," in *Journal of Popular Culture,* Vol. 9, 1975, pp. 174-82.

[*In the following essay, Fishman discusses Mailer's three-fold persona as public celebrity, social critic, and American writer in relation to his experiments with the New Journalism genre. As Fishman asserts, this "new form accentuates the strengths of each of the personae so that the whole is unquestionably greater than the sum of the parts."*]

> *Why does he [Mailer] have to push himself forward all the time and make such a spectacle of himself . . . why can't he let his work speak for itself?*
> —Flannery O'Connor

Norman Mailer's public career presents an ever-changing face. His latest works fall conveniently into neither fiction, literary criticism, nor political commentary. His diversions into politics and political campaigning as well as film making have only added to the confusion of those critics who attempt to categorize and dissect his interests. Yet, the fact that his writings defy traditional classification is itself of some importance; the uneasiness may arise from the nature of the categories as much as the merits of the works. What appears to be new in Mailer's writings is not only his use of memoir-like accounts of politics and culture and his concentration on nonfiction, but this combination of these two elements into an imaginative genre of reporting.

The purpose of this essay is to suggest that the difficulty in understanding the variety of Mailer's recent writings is lessened when one examines how the three personae of Mailer are successfully combined in the New Journalism.

> **Norman Mailer's public career presents an ever-changing face. His latest works fall conveniently into neither fiction, literary criticism, nor political commentary.**
> *—Donald Fishman*

Mailer's career has traditionally been constructed around three personae. Mailer's most recognized persona has been that of the public celebrity. As the most publicized and colorful man of letters in America since Ernest Hemingway, Mailer is widely known for his stormy encounters with his former wives, his unsuccessful attempt to become mayor of New York in 1969, and his sparring matches with such popular boxers as Muhammad Ali and Jose Torres. Featured in headline stories, maligned by national columnists, and discussed on late-night talk shows, the "legend" of Mailer has become as imposing as the writings of the man. "The legend," says Mailer, "becomes your friend . . . a front man, a procurer of new situations. You live with a ghost that is more real to people than yourself." There is a large segment of the public that has never read a single sentence of Mailer yet knows him as a controversial and flamboyant exhibitionist.

It is not altogether clear how fully the "legend" affects the private life and writings of Mailer. The legend itself, however, has been subjected to a large measure of speculation. It has been argued that the role of the celebrity is at odds with the perspective of a serious writer. Celebrities tend to subordinate their ideas to their personalities. As a result, when a writer becomes a public personality, he tends, like an actor or movie star, to trade off his image and his eccentricities, which presumably are easier to sell than his ideas. His image represents a marketable product, often independent of his literary skill, that the audience recognizes. The side-effect of recognition is that the writer may adapt his public and private lives to conform to an artificially created image; frequently this means adhering to a role that he has previously presented and that the public expects him to play. For writers who thrive on new experiences and flexibility, the price of celebrity status can be damaging. Success corrupts not because it brings money and recognition but because it changes the writer's view of himself and his ability to react to changing events. Above all, the legend may obtrude on the works as well as on the man.

Although the writer-public celebrity pitfall may have some validity, the notion fails to account for Mailer's recent successes. Mailer's literary triumphs appear to occur because of—not despite—the clash between his public personality and literary ambitions. As a writer, he has emphatically destroyed the aesthetic distance between himself and his subject matter. Unhappy with self-abnegation, he has placed his ego alongside of his pen as a tool in writing. Whatever else his recent work suggests, he has demonstrated that personality, subjectivity, and empathy can be important ingredients in writing.

Mailer's second persona is that of a social critic. Agitated by changes in modern urban life, especially the rapidly expanding technology, Mailer, by his own account, has devoted himself to creating a "revolution in the consciousness of our times." Although his social criticism contains what critic Dwight MacDonald has called "Mailer's Messianic-cum-Superman nonsense," Mailer's ideas on politics, technology, and the organic society have generated interest and praise. Indeed, Irving Howe in his article on New York intellectuals flatteringly refers to Mailer as "our genius," while noting that Mailer's social criticism has been severely neglected because it challenges many time-honored beliefs among intellectuals:

> My point is that the New York writers have failed to confront Mailer seriously as an intellectual spokesman, a cultural agent, and instead have found it easier to regard him as a hostage to the temper of our times. What has not been forthcoming is a recognition, surely a painful one, that in his major public roles he has come to represent values in deep opposition to liberal humaneness and rational discourse.

Despite Howe's warm appraisal of Mailer's importance, it would be misleading to urge critics to spend their energies analyzing Mailer's criticism as if it were a "school of thought." Admittedly, Mailer's writings do not lack interesting ideas. In this respect, he overshadows his followers and imitators. Yet Mailer's thinking is neither systematic nor consistent; his work reflects more the insightful observations of a journalist than the careful formulations of a philosopher or skillful polemicist. His shallow comments on technology and existential politics serve more as a "cover for his intel-

lectual malfeasances" and a "banner for his crusades" than as statements from a deep-thinking critic.

More importantly, a large part of Mailer's appeal is derived from the tone and style of his commentary. As a critic, his voice adds a distinctive dimension to his observations. Other critics—Gore Vidal, Benjamin DeMott, Dwight MacDonald—primarily trade off their insights and ideas. Mailer's talents, a volatile amalgam of ideas, tone and style, allow him to resuscitate the commonplace and familiar with urgency and conviction.

Whereas past critics such as Carlyle, Ruskin, and Lawrence often wrote with a mixture of argument and satire that was bitter in tone, Mailer's tone is frequently comical. In fact, one of the characteristics of his vision is a comic-apocalyptic view. His basic uncertainty that rules and consistency are important has guided him to a view encapsuled with irony:

> It has been the continuing obsession of this writer that the world is entering a time of plague . . . the continuing metaphor for the obsession has been cancer . . . an ultimate disease against which all other diseases are designed to protect us.
>
> Yet every year the girls are more beautiful and the athletes are better. So the dilemma remains. Is the curse on the world or on oneself?

Yet there is a prophetic quality to his voice. Mailer is constantly warning his audience about the impending doom with such phrases as "Apocalypse or debauch is upon us," "the ill of civilization is that it is removed from nature," and "New York is not a machine but a malignancy." The prophetic voices reinforce his tendency to reduce all life to ultimate alternatives: cannibals and Christians, God and the devil, outlaws and conformists, being and nothingness. Although these dichotomies promote simplification in his thought, they also generate a sense of urgency about his message.

While Mailer's tone has often taken the form of prophecy, reproach, insult, teasing, and mockery, his most successful stylistic device has been his use of metaphors. Without a doubt, Mailer's indisputable talent seems to be in creating metaphors to explain the modern environment; the key terms in this vocabulary—cancer, plague, disease, cannibalistic, and demon—make him unique, at least among left-leaning social critics. His own explanation for the prominence of metaphors in his writings indicates that he views them as part of a strategy of opposition:

> The argument would demand that there be metaphors to fit the vaults of modern experience. That is, in fact, the unendurable demand of the middle

of this century to restore the metaphor and displace the scientist from his center.

The value of metaphors for Mailer is that they serve as a lively vehicle for explaining changes in our society. Mailer's putative goal as a critic is to create understanding while science and technology blindly displace people from traditional sources of meaning. The metaphor aids in bridging the gap between our prior condition and our current malaise.

The striking fact, however, that emerges from focusing on Mailer's criticism is that his writing reveals a limited number of strengths: a stylistic inventiveness, a flair for articulating social questions in an amusing manner, and an ability to convey a sense of urgency about his message. Given the right literary vehicle, the cumulative force of these features probably would be powerful enough to overcome the obvious deficiencies in his critical works: unsustained analytical interpretation and loosely reasoned argument. In a standard political essay, however, Mailer's work would be glaringly weak.

The third persona of Mailer which can be clearly recognized is that of the American writer. Regarded by many as the greatest novelist of his generation, Mailer's first novel, *The Naked and the Dead,* achieved immediate acclaim. Mailer's subsequent two books, *Barbary Shore* and *The Deer Park,* alternately received hostile reviews and lukewarm praise. Despite unfavorable reviews, Mailer was obsessed with becoming a major writer as he began to brood openly over his failure to recapture fame. Ironically, the more shrill his statements became about the importance of the novel and his own potential masterpiece, possibly three thousand pages in length, the more he experimented with writing in a semi-autobiographical vein. With the passage of time, he became more innovative in both substance and form, the latter calling more public attention to itself than the former. Beginning with **"The Existential Hero: Superman Comes to the Supermarket,"** an article published in *Esquire* in 1960, Mailer started to unite the various facets of his skill into a coherent structure. The new form was more open, lacking the inhibitions of the novel and the formulas of conventional journalism. Of course, he still wrote novels and the "name power" of Mailer guaranteed that even a potboiler like *Why Are We in Vietnam* would receive a fair hearing. Still, the high-water mark of his writing came from the publication of *The Armies of the Night,* an exemplary piece of writing that not only won a Pulitzer Prize but earned the applause from many writers dissatisfied with conventional journalism.

The subjects of his books published after 1968 were usually contemporary and topical but the subject-matter had been long-standing concerns of his. The egotistical self-indulgence had been evident before and the writing had been foreshadowed in earlier works. As Richard Gilman pointed out in discussing *The Armies of the Night:*

> A more advanced novelist than Mailer, one less interested in getting at social or political reality, would not have been able to bring it off; that Mailer is only imperfectly a novelist, that his passion for moving and shaking the actual has prevented him from fully inhabiting imaginary kingdoms is the underlying paradoxical strength of this book.

Yet, perhaps the most important reason for the success of this work and subsequent efforts is that they combine the three personae of Mailer—public celebrity, critic, and writer—in one all-consuming perspective. The new form accentuates the strengths of each of the personae so that the whole is unquestionably greater than the sum of the parts.

It is tempting to presume a connection between Norman Mailer and the New Journalism without defining the basis of the relationship. The surface features of personalized reporting, partisanship, and stylistic similarities seem to place Mailer's latest works into the New Journalism camp. Conversely, the difficulty of analyzing Mailer's works in traditional terms associated with literature and criticism and the apparent openness of the New Journalism make the connection between the two not only logically coherent but strategically expedient. In order to understand the nature of the relationship, however, it is first necessary to examine the conventions identified with the New Journalism.

By common testimony, the term "New Journalism" is a misnomer. Tom Wolfe, the leading theorist of the genre, has argued that the New Journalism is not new at all; it has a number of precursors that have not only inspired the movement but resemble the genre itself. What is new about the New Journalism, according to Wolfe, is the excitement the term generated after it began to circulate. Others have maintained that since the primary expression of the New Journalism has been located in books and magazines but not in newspapers, a more appropriate name for the movement is the new nonfiction. Still others have asserted that New Journalism is not journalism in any meaningful sense because the treatment of factual materials is secondary to the artistic imagination of the writer. In this view, it is the author's imagination that is the pivotal force: the events themselves are merely showcases for one's personality as if the author were an impressario—Tom Wolfe presents the Mau Maus, Norman Mailer introduces the moonshot, Gay Talese hosts the mafia. In a milder version, the argument recognizes the possibility that the impressario may adopt a low-keyed stance. Lillian Ross, for example, but the overall results are the same; fiction overshadows fact, personality governs events.

The conflict in the New Journalism between the artistic component of fiction and the factual component of journalism has taken precedence over the appropriateness of the label itself. Journalists indict the New Journalism for its slipshod reporting, creation of imaginary dialogue, and subjective assessments. Literati belittle it for its lack of imagination, suggesting that it presents evocative journalism anchored in facts and actual events without the resourceful creativity of serious fiction. "It is a bastard form, having it both ways," contended critic Dwight MacDonald, "exploiting the factual authority of journalism and the atmospheric license of fiction."

It is not surprising, however, that the most heated attacks on New Journalism have come from journalists. While literary critics can dismiss the movement as lacking the creativity of serious fiction, or, paradoxically, praise it for its uplifting effects on reporting, at issue for journalism is the paramount question of objectivity in investigating and writing. It is also little wonder that the critique on New Journalism resembles the objections many critics extend to Mailer's work. Both share many of the same strengths and excesses, and to a large extent the essential characteristics of New Journalism can be exemplified in Mailer's work.

There are three time-honored rules which old journalism believes the New Journalism violates. The first of these axioms is that every story has, at least, two points of view. The task of the journalist is to provide balanced space for opposing viewpoints, possibly even exactly equal space. Mailer, in his writings, rarely assumes that each side has a valid point. What Mailer assumes is that his point of view is the valid one. In *Marilyn,* a book published twelve years after the death of Marilyn Monroe, Mailer discussed a new theory concerning her suicide. He claimed that Marilyn Monroe killed herself after a telephone conversation with former Attorney General, Robert Kennedy. Almost everyone connected with the case attempted to refute this assertion and Mailer himself added little credibility to his argument when he admitted that he interviewed no one directly associated with the death before he published the book. Having conceded that the book was largely conjecture on his part, Mailer vigorously defended his argument in public as if conjecture were fact. Mailer labeled the facts of the case as "factoids," by which he means rumors which have no other existence except that they appear in print and then people begin to repeat them as if they were facts.

This case, admittedly not one of the showcase examples of the New Journalism, nevertheless reveals the underlying attitudes that separate the two strains of journalism. For conventional journalists, Mailer's chief pitfall was his sloppy investigating and his failure to step outside of his preconceived notions and examine the views of the participants in the event. For new journalists, viewpoint itself was not bad; partisanship, however, demands more rigorous standards of investigating. Mailer's error was that he accepted inadmissible evidence, heresay, and conjecture as fact.

The confusion of fact and factoid by Mailer raises doubts about the accuracy of his reporting. This confusion may account for the skepticism and lack of seriousness that often greets his writings. At the same time, there is no compelling evidence to suggest that Mailer abuses factual materials more than other new journalists. Although Tom Wolfe has censured him for his lack of investigating, Wolfe is silent on the question of accuracy. On the other hand, Dwight MacDonald and Robert Lowell testify openly about the accuracy of the account in *The Armies of the Night.* Mailer may very well be a writer who deals in factoids rather than facts. His partisanship is, however, clear; and the possible distortion in his works, created by a distinct viewpoint, does not seem beyond the boundaries of the other new journalists.

A second tradition that old journalists see being destroyed by New Journalism is the notion that reporting should be detached and objective. "Journalists are taught they must provide impartial disinterested accounts of what was seen and heard; validity was left to the reader to decide." It is evident from Mailer's writings that he does not believe in being impersonal about his subjects. In *The Armies of the Night,* Mailer not only participates in the action, but he also helps shape the events. In covering the Muhammad Ali-Joe Frazier fight, Mailer did not merely report the fight itself, he attempted to learn all he could about the participants before, during, and after the fight. Sparring with the principals would not have been beyond his scope. In a sense, this coverage represents saturation reporting at its best. At the same time, "This brand of nonfiction is so intensely personal," note Dennis and Rivers in the book *New Journalism in America,* "that most of those who dislike Mailer automatically dislike his writing."

Yet the problem of separating the man from his work does not uniquely belong to Mailer. The statement by Dennis and River can reasonably be extended to other authors in the New Journalism. When the author is intimately involved in the events, the reader reacts to the situation through the eyes of the writer, and the reader-author relationship becomes more salient than in conventional journalism. Michael Arlen has commented that "involvedness" has allowed new journalists to see the events on their "own terms" and not on the merits of the situation. To be sure, this observation characterizes much of Norman Mailer's writings as well as the works of other practitioners of New Journalism. Involvement has often led to a "king-of-the-hill" approach to journalism, where the author bullies the events so that he is on top of the subject-matter rather than getting inside of the situation.

The alternative of detachment, however, offers an equally

severe limitation. The conventions of objectivity—a good lead, impartial reporting, a headline—allow a clever manipulator to take advantage of events as well as journalists. "The rules of objectivity are such," notes veteran correspondent Peter Lisagor of the *Chicago Daily News,* "that a man can make political capital out of them by being clever in the way he presents a particular issue." Ultimately, the New Journalism can provide a complement to the allegedly objective accounts by adding analysis and interpretation to information. In Norman Mailer's case, however, the king-of-the hill approach may not be a tool of the trade as much as a personal predilection to grandstand.

Finally, conventional journalists contend that the emphasis on style among the new journalists subordinates information to entertainment. In this view, the preoccupation with style can be analyzed as an entertaining departure from straight nonfiction, at best a stimulant to more information and at worst a series of techniques "to confuse and mislead readers." While old journalists were taught to avoid value-laden adjectives, imaginary dialogue, composite profiles, and lengthy descriptive passages, new journalists concentrate on these techniques. There is little disagreement, moreover, that at the core of the New Journalism are four stylistic devices that distinguish the movement from conventional journalism and other forms of nonfiction: scene-by-scene construction, interior monologue, point of view, and status-life symbols. To what extent these devices mislead and confuse the reader is the more serious question underlying the arguments about style.

The claim that Mailer's writings reflect these stylistic devices can be made without deeply examining the stylistic devices themselves. His third-person protagonist, variously named Aquarius, Mailer, or the Novelist, attempts to rescue ideas from abstractions and daily events from triviality as the reader follows the author through a narrative story. At the outset, however, the reader is usually forewarned that the reporting is subjective. In *The Armies of the Night,* a story written by *Time* magazine is juxtaposed at the start of the book with subsequent subjective assessment of the events. In *Marilyn,* Mailer develops the notion of factoids to distinguish his account from more factual reports. In *St. George and the Godfather,* an examination of the Republican and Democratic national conventions in 1972, Mailer immediately reminds the readers of the subjective nature of the report:

> So Norman Mailer, who looked to rule himself by Voltaire's catch-all precept, 'once a philosopher, twice a pervert,' and preferred therefore never to repeat a technique, was still obliged to call himself Aquarius again for he had not been in Miami two days before he knew he would not write objectively about the convention of '72.

Whether one warning or many explicit admonitions are necessary to remind the reader of the personalized nature of the account remains an open question; but the responsibilities for confusing information with personalized reporting, or what some critics regard pejoratively as entertainment, rest with the readers as well as the writer. The absence of style, moreover, is not a bona fide guarantee of accuracy.

As a writer, Norman Mailer is probably the most graceful stylist among the new journalists. He is, of course, the only one to earn a Pulitzer prize and a Book-of-the-Month Club selection. That his works are also entertaining should not be a blanket indictment to fault the informative nature of his accounts. There are a plurality of road signs to indicate the way to the truth and Mailer's reports, written in an entertaining style, appear to have as much information as old journalism. What differs is the focus of the writer and the nature of the topics considered; on the whole, the amount of information does not seem to be lacking or confusing.

Norman Mailer seems torn between his self-canonization as a novelist and his experiments with journalistic forms. At one point, he is amusingly annoyed at Robert Lowell when the noted poet refers to him as the greatest journalist currently writing. Elsewhere, he is less defensive about his forays into journalism:

> Journalism never does a writer any harm until he starts repeating himself, and if you do that, then you start presiding over the dissolution of your own literary empire.

Grudgingly, Mailer seems to be accepting his success as a new journalist without acknowledging his difficulties as a writer of straight fiction. Mailer, however, may not be the best theoretician of his own work. As a multi-faceted talent, he is legendary as a public celebrity, shallow as a critic, and incomplete as a novelist. With the development of the nonfiction novel, the best features of his work are highlighted and his "literary empire," more mythical than real, seems enriched and revitalized.

Yet, Mailer's pull between fiction and journalism coincides with the tension in New Journalism itself. From a literary point of view, the New Journalism is a superior form of journalism but not fiction; from a journalistic perspective, it is the application of novelistic techniques to actual events but not journalism. Perhaps this ambivalence over time will resolve itself for both Mailer and the New Journalism. Even Dwight MacDonald, once reluctant to recognize New Journalism as anything but a flawed form, confessed in an afterthought written nine years following the publication of his well-known essay on "Parajournalism" that in "more talented hands, parajournalism is a legitimate form." In any event, it is unlikely that we have heard the last word on the controversy.

Robert Gorham Davis (review date 1983)

SOURCE: "Excess without End," in *The New Leader,* May 16, 1983, pp. 14-16.

[*In the following review, Davis offers a generally unfavorable assessment of* Ancient Evenings. *Though acknowledging the novel's "virtuosity and inventiveness," Davis finds shortcomings in Mailer's uninspired ideas and fascination with debauchery and violence.*]

This is a work of staggering ambition, far exceeding in inventiveness and scope anything Mailer has attempted before. Several reviewers have supported—and then backed away from—the publisher's claim that it is one of the major novels of the 20th century. On that level the obvious comparison is with Thomas Mann's vast tetralogy, *Joseph and his Brothers.* As efforts of the archaeological imagination trying to recreate the world of the Pharaohs they are strikingly similar; by standards of maturity of thought and humane social concern there is no comparison at all.

Thomas Mann's Joseph rose from the pit where his brothers cast him to become chief adviser to the Pharaoh. He did it all on his own, through beauty, prudence and skill as a diviner of dreams. Joseph used his great powers for the good of the people, in ways that showed how Mann was stimulated by Roosevelt's New Deal. (The novel was completed in this country in 1943.)

Mann's Pharaoh is the reformer Akhenaton, husband of the beauteous Nefertiti, who tried to impose monotheism on the Egypt of a thousand gods. His hymn to the sun turns up as the 104th Psalm in the Old Testament. (*Moses and Monotheism,* Freud's most heretical work, makes Moses an Egyptian disciple of Akhenaton and Judaism their joint product.)

Egypt's magnificence, so alien, so remote, and yet still there to be seen, has always attracted inventive minds. Herodotus attributed to the ancient Egyptians—probably falsely—the belief in incarnation that Mailer finds especially attractive. And if the Egyptians did not believe in some of Mailer's wackier physiological notions, this can be imagined.

Mailer deals briefly with Moses, but for monotheism he has no use. *Ancient Evenings* abounds in gods who experience outrageous combats, violent sex and painful animal transformations, difficult for humans to match. In a dusty, stinking pillaged tomb, Menenhetet I vividly describes the wilder antics of these gods to his great-grandson Menenhetet II, who

has just consciously suffered his own embalming. "I was in the most peculiar situation," Menenhetet I says. He had died much earlier, after his fourth incarnation, and could keep his *ka* alive in the ruined tomb only by eating the embalmed organs of very early Pharaohs.

The principal part of *Ancient Evenings,* 400-500 pages, takes place while both Menenhetets are alive. At a select dinner party, on the Night of the Pig when everyone is supposed to tell the truth, no matter how scandalous or physically disgusting, Menenhetet I, in his fourth incarnation, describes in enormous detail his adventures during the first. Present are his granddaughter Hathfertiti; her husband, cosmetician to the Pharaoh, a man of no account whose "sly smell" entices her; the Pharaoh himself, the host, who is thinking of making Menenhetet Grand Vizier; and Menenhetet II, now a frighteningly precocious boy of six.

Menehetet had had sex with his granddaughter when she was a child, and her son is to have sex with her when he is a man. That incest was practiced openly among noble Egyptians is one of their appeals for Mailer. Nothing is Freudian in this novel, for nothing is repressed. During the dinner the Pharaoh and Hathfertiti retire to make love. In young Menenhetet's sleepy consciousness as he listens to his great-grandfather's tale are states of awareness that go beyond anything ever attempted in literature before. The boy's telepathic powers let him know what his father is thinking, what his great-grandfather is remembering but not telling, even the thoughts that come to his great-grandfather from other incarnations. He not only knows what his mother and the Pharaoh are doing, but senses it physically in a body already awakened by the ministrations of his nurse.

Mailer is an élitist, an admirer of strength. He has always been fascinated by publicity and power, by the bodies of prize fighters and celebrated beauties like Marilyn Monroe—the latter attracting men of power who can make love to each other through women. In *Presidential Papers,* Mailer set out to be a councilor, a diviner of dreams for John F. Kennedy as Joseph was for Akhenaton.

Mailer's Pharaoh is Ramses II, best known of the Pharaohs because he erected great self-glorifying statues and temples all over Egypt. The battle of Kadesh is the best known of ancient battles because Ramses covered temple walls with graphic and verbal accounts of it, exaggerating impossibly his exploits. He told how he took on the powers of two different gods and single-handedly drove to destruction 2,500 Hittite chariots. In *Ancient Evenings,* Menenhetet I is by his side.

Born of the basest peasant stock, Menenhetet rises by his skill as a charioteer to become chief companion, confidant and love object of Ramses II, who has a true taste for "the buttocks of brave men." *Ancient Evenings* is a hymn to anality. One of its obsessions is homosexual rape, so much a part of the nightmare life of prisons. Menenhetet still loves the Pharaoh, but feels unmanned by him. You can bugger (Menenhetet has done it a hundred times) but not be buggered. He dreams thereafter of revenge.

The battle of Kadesh, the centerpiece of the book, is sheer horror. On the battlefield carnage by day gives way to orgy at night among and even with the dead. But Menenhetet glories in it. A man is not quite a man until he has killed.

After Kadesh, alienated from the Pharaoh, Menenhetet is sent off to take charge of a Libyan gold mine where slaves are worked and whipped to death. There he meets a Hebrew who has learned from Moses an un-Biblical secret—basic to the novel—of how to reincarnate yourself by managing to die or be murdered at the moment of orgasm. As for the Exodus: some forced laborers kill their guards and flee the country under the leadership of Moses—no 10 plagues, no killing of the first-born, no parting of the Red Sea. Here Mailer distinguishes himself sharply from Thomas Mann, who drew so fully on the familiar patriarchal narratives, on the Christianity they foreshadowed, and on the 19th century thought from Kierkegaard to Nietzsche that they evoked.

Implausibly, Menenhetet is brought back to run the Pharaoh's harem and, more implausibly, is subsequently made custodian-companion first to Ramses' sister and Queen, Nefertiri, then to his second Queen, the Hittite princess, Rama-Nefru. All three responsibilities Menenhetet betrays. With a fat sorceress in the harem and with the two queens he reaches peaks of differentiated ecstasy it takes a Mailer to describe.

Menenhetet is both prisoner and warden of sex. Except for a little dabbling in magic, he has nothing else to think about or do, and so we are given, for pages and pages and pages, unrelieved, breathless descriptions of the polymorphous, inexhaustible sex that is now so repetitively obligatory in American novels. Menenhetet even has to attend the Pharaoh's love-making and hold his hand while it is going on.

It is in the cruel, macho homosexual passages, however, that Mailer aggressively carries to a defiant extreme the qualities that have troubled his admirers ever since *American Dream* and "The White Negro." When Menenhetet is on a secret mission to Tyre he sees two men in the woods, thieves probably, but no threat to him, for they do not notice him. He approaches them smiling and gratuitously, swiftly, kills one with his sword, "with a bliss he had never known even with his Pharaoh." The other he stuns with a rock, and beats until "he was soft like a steak that is pounded." Then Menenhetet sodomizes his half-dead vic-

tim repeatedly until he feels he has worked out of his own system the evil deposited in it by the Pharaoh.

> **In *Ancient Evenings* some of Mailer's worst notions get the fullest treatment. This is often done with great ingenuity, but sometimes it is in the spirit of the fat boy in Dickens who wanted to make our flesh creep—or our throats gag.**
> **—*Robert Gorham Davis***

Mailer's gloating over cruelty in *Ancient Evenings* is not new, nor are his regressively unscientific ideas about the body. We did not have to go to ancient Egypt for them. He has expounded in interviews his thoughts about bodily secretions and discharges and what happens psychically when they are traded back and forth among human and animal bodies.

In *Ancient Evenings* some of Mailer's worst notions get the fullest treatment. This is often done with great ingenuity, but sometimes it is in the spirit of the fat boy in Dickens who wanted to make our flesh creep—or our throats gag. The novel indulges in great play with severed nipples, severed hands, a severed toe. And of course with shit. Menenhetet is an eater of bat dung, for sound mystical reasons; one of the other characters has amassed a fortune collecting and marketing shit.

Despite its virtuosity and inventiveness and the sheer hard work behind it, *Ancient Evenings* is inferior in two respects to the major novels with which it might be compared. The first has to do with its ideas. Many of them simply do not bear thinking about; they are the stock in trade of fakirs and mass cultists, yet have some murky role in Mailer's creative unconscious, presumably a necessary one, for he is too intelligent to entertain them otherwise.

The second respect is formal and stylistic. In *Why Are We in Vietnam,* where he had many of the same obsessions, Mailer invented a style entirely appropriate to them. It was artificial, yet compounded of exactly the right American speech and allusion. How could the equivalent be found for two Egyptians of the 13th century B.C.E.? Mailer does not really try. In the whole book there is hardly a distinctive phrase or metaphor, an unexpected choice of words. Some of the sentences, apart from their content, could have come from a historical novel in the period of Lew Wallace or Bulwer-Lytton. Even on the Night of the Pig, Menenhetet should have been embarrassed to report that Queen Nefertiri could say to her peasant lover, "Oh how I adore how dreadful you are. Did you visit the Royal Stables? Did you rub the foam of a stallion on your little beauty?"

In the *Paris Review* Mailer once said that civilization is as bad as it is because we are "afraid of violence, cannibalism, loneliness, insanity, libidinousness, hell, perversion and mess ... states which must in some way be passed through, digested, transcended, if one is to make one's way back to life." Mailer has passed through them again and again in his works with mounting intensity, but no sign of transcendence.

The word "transcendence" does appear, though, on the last page of *Ancient Evenings.* It has led Harold Bloom, in a kind of rescue operation in the *New York Review of Books,* citing Emerson, to place Mailer in an American Gnostic tradition.

Climbing the ladder in the afterworld, Menenhetet hears the scream of earth exploding but sees radiance at the center of a pain such as never was previously felt. He wonders if Osiris, who gives strength more credit than purity or goodness, may not still put him to serving "some useful purpose I cannot name."

These closing two pages are preceded by over 700 abandoned to betrayal, gloating cruelty, and the immediate gratification of every impulse at whatever cost to others. Is it more than an easy out, a rhetorical flourish, to flash a light and speak of transcendence when there has been heretofore not a hint of what a noble purpose might be or how it is achieved—especially when one obvious noble purpose is to try to prevent that very explosion of the earth?

Harold Bloom (essay date 1986)

SOURCE: "Introduction," in *Modern Critical Views: Norman Mailer,* edited by Harold Bloom, Chelsea House Publishers, 1986, pp. 1-6.

[*In the following essay, Bloom considers Mailer's unconventional literary production and problematic critical reputation as a remarkable author who "has written no indisputable book." However, according to Bloom, Mailer will likely endure "as the representative writer of his generation."*]

I

Mailer is the most visible of contemporary novelists, just as Thomas Pynchon is surely the most invisible. As the inheritor of the not exactly unfulfilled journalistic renown of Hemingway, Mailer courts danger, disaster, even scandal. Thinking of Mailer, Pynchon, and Doctorow among others, Geoffrey Hartman remarks that:

The prose of our best novelists is as fast, embrac-

ing, and abrasive as John Donne's *Sermons.* It is polyphonic despite or within its monologue, its confessional stream of words. . . .

Think of Mailer, who always puts himself on the line, sparring, taunting, as macho as Hemingway but deliberately renouncing taciturnity. Mailer places himself too near events, as science fiction or other forms of romance place themselves too far. . . .

Elizabeth Hardwick, a touch less generous than the theoretical Hartman, turns Gertrude Stein against Mailer's oral polyphony:

We have here a "literature" of remarks, a fast-moving confounding of Gertrude Stein's confident assertion that "remarks are not literature." Sometimes remarks are called a novel, sometimes a biography, sometimes history.

Hardwick's Mailer is "a spectacular mound of images" or "anecdotal pile." He lacks only an achieved work, in her view, and therefore is a delight to biographers, who resent finished work as a "sharp intrusion," beyond their ken. Her observations have their justice, yet the phenomenon is older than Mailer, or even Hemingway. The truly spectacular mound of images and anecdotal pile was George Gordon, Lord Byron, but he wrote *Don Juan,* considered by Shelley to be the great poem of the age. Yet even *Don Juan* is curiously less than Byron was, or seemed, or still seems. Mailer hardly purports to be the Byron of our day (the Hemingway will do), but he might fall back upon Byron as an earlier instance of the literary use of celebrity, or of the mastery of polyphonic remarks.

Is Mailer a novelist? His best book almost certainly is *The Executioner's Song,* which Ms. Hardwick calls "the apotheosis of our flowering 'oral literature'—thus far," a triumph of the tape recorder. My judgment of its strength may be much too fast, as Ms. Hardwick warns, and yet I would not call *The Executioner's Song* a novel. *Ancient Evenings* rather crazily is a novel, Mailer's *Salammbô* as it were, but clearly more engrossing as visionary speculation than as narrative or as the representation of moral character. Richard Poirier, Mailer's best critic, prefers *An American Dream* and *Why Are We in Vietnam?,* neither of which I can reread with aesthetic pleasure. Clearly, Mailer is a problematical writer; he has written no indisputable book, nothing on the order of *The Sun Also Rises, The Great Gatsby, Miss Lonelyhearts, The Crying of Lot 49,* let alone *As I Lay Dying, The Sound and the Fury, Light in August, Absalom, Absalom!* His formidable literary energies have not found their inevitable mode. When I think of him, *Advertisements for Myself* comes into my memory more readily than any other work, perhaps because truly he is his own supreme fiction. He is the author of "Norman Mailer," a lengthy, discontinuous, and perhaps canonical fiction.

II

Advertisements for Myself (1960) sums up Mailer's ambitions and accomplishments through the age of thirty-six. After a quarter-century, I have just reread it, with an inevitable mixture of pleasure and a little sadness. Unquestionably, Mailer has not fulfilled its many complex promises, and yet the book is much more than a miscellany. If not exactly a "Song of Myself," nevertheless *Advertisements* remains Mailer at his most Whitmanian, as when he celebrates his novel-in-progress:

> If it is to have any effect, and I can hardly look forward to exhausting the next ten years without hope of a deep explosion of effect, the book will be fired to its fuse by the rumor that once I pointed to the farthest fence and said that within ten years I would try to hit the longest ball ever to go up into the accelerated hurricane air of our American letters. For if I have one ambition above all others, it is to write a novel which Dostoyevsky and Marx; Joyce and Freud; Stendhal, Tolstoy, Proust and Spengler; Faulkner, and even old moldering Hemingway might have come to read, for it would carry what they had to tell another part of the way.

Hemingway in 1959 reached the age of sixty, but was neither old nor moldering. He was to kill himself on July 2, 1961, but Mailer could hardly have anticipated that tragic release. In a letter to George Plimpton (January 17, 1961) Hemingway characterized *Advertisements for Myself* as "the sort of ragtag assembly of his rewrites, second thoughts and ramblings shot through with occasional brilliance." As precursor, Hemingway would have recognized Mailer's vision of himself as Babe Ruth, hitting out farther than Stendhal, Tolstoi, *et al.*, except that the agonistic trope in the master is more agile than in the disciple, because ironized:

> Am a man without any ambition, except to be champion of the world, I wouldn't fight Dr. Tolstoi in a 20 round bout because I know he would knock my ears off. The Dr. had terrific wind and could go on forever and then some. . . .
>
> But these Brooklyn jerks are so ignorant that they *start off* fighting Mr. Tolstoi. And they announce they have beaten him before the fight starts.

That is from a letter to Charles Scribner (September 6-7, 1949), and "these Brooklyn jerks" indubitably refers to the highly singular author of *The Naked and the Dead* (1948), who had proclaimed his victory over Hemingway as a tune-

up for the Tolstoi match. Hemingway's irony, directed as much towards himself as against Mailer, shrewdly indicates Mailer's prime aesthetic flaw: a virtually total absence of irony. Irony may or may not be what the late Paul de Man called it, "the condition of literary language itself," but Mailer certainly could use a healthy injection of it. If Thomas Mann is at one extreme—the modern too abounding in irony—then Mailer clearly hugs the opposite pole. The point against Mailer is made best by Max Apple in his splendid boxing tale, "Inside Norman Mailer" (*The Oranging of America,* 1976), where Mailer is handled with loving irony, and Hemingway's trope touches its ultimate limits as Apple challenges Mailer in the ring:

> "Concentrate," says Mailer, "so the experience will not be wasted on you."
>
> "It's hard," I say, "amid the color and distraction."
>
> "I know," says my gentle master, "but think about one big thing."
>
> I concentrate on the new edition of the *Encyclopedia Britannica.* It works. My mind is less a palimpsest, more a blank page.
>
> "You may be too young to remember," he says, "James Jones and James T. Farrell and James Gould Cozzens and dozens like them. I took them all on, absorbed all they had and went on my way, just like Shakespeare ate up *Tottel's Miscellany.*"

There are no such passages in Mailer himself. One cannot require a novelist to cultivate irony, but its absolute absence causes difficulties, particularly when the writer is a passionate and heterodox moralist. Mailer's speculations upon time, sex, death, cancer, digestion, courage, and God are all properly notorious, and probably will not earn him a place as one of the major sages. The strongest aesthetic defense of Mailer as speculator belongs to Richard Poirier, in his book of 1972:

> Mailer insists on living *at* the divide, living on the divide, between the world of recorded reality and a world of omens, spirits, and powers, only that his presence there may blur the distinction. He seals and obliterates the gap he finds, like a sacrificial warrior or, as he would probably prefer, like a Christ who brings not peace but a sword, not forgiveness for past sins but an example of the pains necessary to secure a future.

This has force and some persuasiveness, but Poirier is too good a critic not to add the shadow side of Mailer's "willingness not to foreclose on his material in the interests of merely formal resolutions." Can there be *any* resolutions then for his books? Poirier goes on to say that: "There is no satisfactory form for his imagination when it is most alive. There are only exercises for it." But this appears to imply that Mailer cannot shape his fictions, since without a sacrifice of possibility upon the altar of form, narrative becomes incoherent, frequently through redundance (as in *Ancient Evenings*). Mailer's alternative has been to forsake Hemingway for Dreiser, as in the exhaustive narrative of *The Executioner's Song*. In either mode, finally, we are confronted by the paradox that Mailer's importance seems to transcend any of his individual works. The power of *The Executioner's Song* finally is that of "reality in America," to appropriate Lionel Trilling's phrase for Dreiser's appropriation of the material of *An American Tragedy*. Are we also justified in saying that *An American Dream* essentially is Mailer's comic-strip appropriation of what might be called "irreality in America"? Evidently there will never be a mature book by Mailer that is not problematical in its form. To Poirier, this is Mailer's strength. Poirier's generous overpraise of *An American Dream* and *Why Are We in Vietnam?* perhaps can be justified by Mailer's peculiarly American aesthetic, which has its Emersonian affinities. Mailer's too is an aesthetic of use, a pragmatic application of the American difference from the European past. *The Armies of the Night* (1968), rightly praised by Poirier, may seem someday Mailer's best and most permanent book. It is certainly not only a very American book, but today is one of the handful of works that vividly represent an already lost and legendary time, the era of the so-called Counterculture that surged up in the later 1960's, largely in protest against our war in Vietnam. Mailer, more than any other figure, has broken down the distinction between fiction and journalism. This sometimes is praised in itself. I judge it an aesthetic misfortune, in everyone else, but on Mailer himself I tend to reserve judgment, since the mode now seems his own.

III

Mailer's validity as a cultural critic is always qualified by his own immersion in what he censures. Well known for being well known, he is himself inevitably part of what he deplores. As a representation, he at least rivals all of his fictive creations. *Ancient Evenings,* his most inventive and exuberant work, is essentially a self-portrait of the author as ancient Egyptian magician, courtier, lover and anachronistic speculator. Despite Poirier's eloquent insistences, the book leaves Mailer as he was judged to be by Poirier in 1972, "like Melville without *Moby Dick,* George Eliot without *Middlemarch,* Mark Twain without *Huckleberry Finn*." Indeed, the book is Mailer's *Pierre,* his *Romola,* his *Connecticut Yankee in King Arthur's Court.* At sixty-two, Mailer remains the author of *Advertisements for Myself, The Armies of the Night* and *The Executioner's Song.*

Is he then a superb accident of personality, wholly adequate

to the spirit of the age? Though a rather bad critic of novelists, he is one of the better critics of Norman Mailer. His one critical blindness, in regard to himself, involves the destructive nature of Hemingway's influence upon him. Hemingway was a superb storyteller and an uncanny prose poet; Mailer is neither. Essentially, Mailer is a phantasmagoric visionary who was found by the wrong literary father, Hemingway, Hemingway's verbal economy is not possible for Mailer. There are profound affinities between Hemingway and Wallace Stevens, but none between Mailer and the best poetry of his age. This is the curious sadness with which the **"First Advertisements for Myself"** reverberates after twenty-five years:

> So, mark you. Every American writer who takes himself to be both major and macho must sooner or later give a *faena* which borrows from the self-love of a Hemingway style . . .

> For you see I have come to have a great sympathy for the Master's irrepressible tantrum that he is the champion writer of this time, and of all time, and that if anyone can pin Tolstoy, it is Ernest H.

By taking on Hemingway, Mailer condemned himself to a similar agon, which harmed Hemingway, except in *The Sun Also Rises* and in *The First Forty-Nine Stories.* It has more than harmed Mailer's work. *The Deer Park* defies rereading, and *An American Dream* and *Why Are We in Vietnam?* have now lost the immediacy of their occasions, and are scarcely less unreadable. In what now is the Age of Pynchon, Mailer has been eclipsed as a writer of fictions, though hardly at all as a performing self. He may be remembered more as a prose prophet than as a novelist, more as Carlyle than as Hemingway. There are worse literary fates. Carlyle, long neglected, doubtless will return. Mailer, now celebrated, doubtless will vanish into neglect, and yet always will return, as a historian of the moral consciousness of his era, and as the representative writer of his generation.

Mark Edmundson (essay date Winter 1990)

SOURCE: "Romantic Self-Creations: Mailer and Gilmore in *The Executioner's Song,*" in *Contemporary Literature,* No. XXXI, No. 4, Winter, 1990, pp. 434-47.

[*In the following essay, Edmundson discusses Mailer's portrayal of Gilmore in* The Executioner's Song *in light of Mailer's romantic narrative style and Emersonian literary aspirations.*]

Romantic writers are, for better and worse, obsessed with originality. In practice this means that each one who aspires to matter has to initiate his life as an artist with a story about what originality is, and that story must itself strike readers as being a new one. To compound the difficulty, the romantic writer is compelled, even as he recounts his version of originality, to be exemplifying it. Emerson sets out to do this much in his most celebrated essay, "Self-Reliance." The formula for originality he puts forward there is a simple one: you become original by listening to yourself. Genius derives from trusting the inner voice, abiding by one's "spontaneous impression . . . then most when the whole cry of voices is on the other side." Originality is not, as Wordsworth believed it to be, the product of a favored childhood, where one is "Fostered alike by beauty and by fear" (1850 *Prelude,* bk. 1, line 302). Nor is it mysteriously inborn, a celestial gift, as the German romantics tended to think. Moses and Plato and Milton became what they did—in Emerson's view—by observing the "gleam of light which flashes across [the] mind from within" and speaking "not what men but what they thought."

Yet the Emersonian philosophy of self-invention is also a philosophy of self-ruin. In time, every rhetorical pearl evolves back to sand; every hard-won identity tends to "solidify and hem in the life." Romantic "self-invention" frequently begins in a sort of potlatch, a ritual in which the subject is compelled to destroy his full accumulation and return to poverty, and to ignorance, that state on which, according to Thoreau, all growth depends. The American romantic faith is a faith in crisis: without ruin, no renovation. And no renovation, it's assumed, is final: always, as Emerson says, there must be abandonment.

Of all the major American writers at work now, Norman Mailer probably has come the closest to committing himself to Emerson's literary ethos of self-destroying self-invention. From early on in his career it has been Mailer's aim to baffle expectations about who he is and what he might be capable of doing. His ambition has been thoroughly Emersonian—"to dive and reappear in new places."

Mailer's style of diving and reappearing has earned him a certain notoriety, some applause, and also a good deal of vitriolic criticism, particularly about the a- or immorality of productions like **"The White Negro,"** *An American Dream, Why Are We in Vietnam?,* and the two books on Marilyn Monroe. The charges against Mailer tend to be akin to those leveled against romantic writers as far back at least as Byron: he's violent, self-obsessed, an opportunist, a destructive opponent of what's most nourishing in humanistic culture. Mailer's excesses are all the worse, to this way of thinking, in that they're amplified through the whole vulgar network of the mass media, reaching beyond the intellectuals who know how to put his clownings in context and giving the institution of Literature a bad name.

The reaction to Mailer's major book of the seventies, *The*

Executioner's Song, has to be seen against the background of this kind of moralizing response to his work. For it appeared, at least from the initial reviews of the book, that Mailer had undergone a conversion. Critics noticed immediately, and usually with relief, that Mailer's commitment to a high romantic style had disappeared. "Style," says Robert Frost, "is that which indicates how the writer takes himself and what he is saying." How does the writer take himself in *The Executioner's Song*? Not at all, said most of the book's reviewers: Mailer had succeeded in refining his prodigious ego out of the book. He had achieved something like an Eliotic annulment of self, an "extinction of personality," in which he suppressed his own voice to become the medium for a variety of others. And the reason for this surrender had to do, naturally, with the failure, or at least with the obsolescence, of his former romantic project. Mailer had given up his Emersonian illusions about originality and self-reinvention. He'd replaced attempts at auto-American-biography—the creation of works in which the words "I" and "America" can at some moments (and those not always the most attractive or admirable ones) be interchanged—with social documentary. Finally Mailer was one of us. Or such was the judgment of many of those critics of Mailer who tend to think of his "talent" as a natural resource and of themselves as its board of directors. Such a judgment, given Mailer's past record, is probably worth questioning.

The Executioner's Song deals with Gary Gilmore, a figure now famous enough to have his likeness on display in Madame Tussaud's. There one may see his wax effigy executed by an invisible firing squad every three minutes or so and read the story of how Gilmore was condemned to death by the state of Utah for the murder of two young men in the summer of 1976. Gilmore refused to seek a stay of execution and demanded that the state follow through on its promise and kill him, which it eventually did. Mailer tells Gilmore's story by way of indirect discourse, from the points of view of over a hundred of the persons involved. Almost everyone, including Gilmore, submitted to extensive interviewing. Thus the book came out of careful study and reworking of tapes and transcripts.

Part of Mailer's fascination with Gilmore surely owed to his resemblance to the figure of the psychopath described in **"The White Negro"** twenty years before. **"The White Negro,"** Mailer's first text with romantic aspirations, is an attempt to incarnate an authentically American voice and temper to resist the prevailing atmosphere of "conformity and depression" in which a "stench of fear . . . come[s] out of every pore of American life, and we suffer from a collective failure of nerve." Mailer's dilemma is Emersonian, akin to the one in which "Self-Reliance" begins. Yet his response, a mythical self-projection into a figure of rebellion whom he calls, alternately, the hipster, the White Negro, and the psychopath, owes more, I suspect, to Blake and *The Mar-*

riage of Heaven and Hell. In his first major prophetic book, Blake transforms himself (with no little self-directed irony) into a satanic poet in order to assault the false pieties that the "Angels" who dominate the religious, political, and artistic life of late-eighteenth-century England enforce. Mailer is probably not being any more sensationalistic than Blake was when he identifies himself with the figure his orthodox contemporaries fear most. One of the many fine intuitions in **"The White Negro"** is that the psychopath had taken the place of Satan in contemporary morality. Mailer sees the ethic of psychoanalysis, with its endorsement of irony, stoicism, and detachment, as the repressive Anglicanism of his day, a state and corporate religion designed to quell nonconformity. The psychopath's hunger for immediacy in all things can't help but threaten a culture committed to deferred and displaced satisfactions.

Mailer's alternative is a romantic return to childhood, but a return far less tranquil and tranquilizing than the one envisioned by Wordsworth and Coleridge, or, needless to say, by the psychoanalyst. Mailer's psychopath replays the past event in the present so that he can gain back what was lost, score victories where he was, in childhood, forced to make concessions. The conception couldn't be more in the native romantic vein. When Mailer, in another context, declares that going "from gap to gain is very American," he both evokes this design and provides a good throwaway epigraph for Emerson's collected works. Where Freud believed that the best that one could hope for would be to transform compulsive repetition into an accepting memory of the traumatic event, Mailer demands a full redemption. If the hipster "has the courage to meet the parallel situation at the moment when he is ready," Mailer writes, "then he has a chance to act as he has never acted before. . . . In thus giving expression to the buried infant in himself, he can lessen the tension of those infantile desires and so free himself to remake a bit of his nervous system." Mailer's Gilmore comes close to exemplifying the type for whom "the decision is to encourage the psychopath in oneself, to explore that domain of experience where security is boredom and therefore sickness, and one exists in the present, in that enormous present which is without past or future, memory or planned intention, the life where a man must go until he is beat, where he must gamble with his energies through all those small or large crises of courage and unforeseen situations which beset his day."

Gilmore doesn't make a cogent decision to act in this way, as Mailer's hipster does—Gilmore, at least up to a certain critical point in the book, seems incapable of making any cogent decisions. The amount of confusion he can create in a few hours' space is frequently astonishing. On one night we find him running stolen guns; fighting it out, physically, on the highway with his girlfriend, Nicole; trying (and failing) to steal a tape deck from the local shopping mall; banging into the car parked behind his when he tries to escape;

eluding (cannily) a pursuing squad car; and arriving at last, in the middle of the night, at his cousin Brenda's house, where he wakes up everyone to demand fifty dollars so that he can run away to Canada.

But at other times Gilmore is more sympathetic. On the night that he gets his first paycheck, for example, he goes off to see a movie with Brenda and Johnny, her husband. The picture is Gilmore's choice, and he picks, as one might almost have predicted, *One Flew Over the Cuckoo's Nest.* It turns out that Gilmore served time in the penitentiary next to the mental hospital where *Cuckoo's Nest* was filmed and that in fact he'd been treated in the hospital itself. Gilmore is chaos throughout the film, cheering, shouting commentary, bashing on the chairs in front of him. Almost everyone gets up and moves away from him eventually, and by the end of the evening Brenda, who usually shows an exemplary patience with Gary, is completely exasperated. But Gilmore had a point to make at the film, though he made it crudely enough. He felt, one can surmise, that he had more in common with R. P. McMurphy, Kesey's pulp equivalent of Mailer's White Negro, than Jack Nicholson, who played the role, or anyone else present in the theater for that matter. So why shouldn't he be the object of attention? Exacerbating Gilmore's mood would be the fact that the crowd paying to worship McMurphy's nonconformity had rewarded Gilmore for his by keeping him in jail for nineteen out of his thirty-five years. One understands Gilmore's confusion. Mailer certainly understands it well, but he's unwilling to turn the book into an overt celebration of a latter-day hipster. There's no tendency to extend the tonal grandeur of **"The White Negro"** to Gary Gilmore.

But there is a point in the story where Gilmore's status changes. Up until this moment, Gilmore has been almost wholly destructive, acting on every whim as though it were divine inspiration. "He was grabbing at everything. It was as if the world was just out of reach of his fingers," says a young woman of Gilmore. He wants full possession of everything glowing that comes in range.

But from the point when Gilmore decides that he is willing to die, he takes on a certain dignity. There have been no capital punishments for some time in the state of Utah, and everyone expects that Gilmore will do what every other convicted killer has done and fight for a life in jail, but he will not. The climax of the book, at least in my judgment, comes when Gilmore, having been condemned and imprisoned for the two murders, chooses to force the state of Utah to carry out his sentence and execute him. Here is Gilmore addressing the Board of Pardons to demand his own death:

> I simply accepted the sentence that was given to me.
> I have accepted sentences all my life. I didn't know
> I had a choice in the matter.

When I did accept it, everybody jumped in and wanted to argue with me. It seems that the people, especially the people of Utah, want the death penalty but they don't want executions and when it became a reality they might have to carry one out, well, they started backing off on it.

Well, I took them literal and serious when they sentenced me to death just as if they had sentenced me to ten years or thirty days in the county jail or something. I thought you were supposed to take them serious. I didn't know it was a joke.

One may detest Gilmore for living in the world as though it were an open question whether the other people there are as real as he is, and still acknowledge his triumph of wit here. Consider the context. Gilmore has spent the balance of his life under the control of institutions. He has been told when to get up in the morning, when to sleep, when to exercise, when to eat. Society has applied enormous resources to the task of normalizing him, rendering him into a coherent, stable citizen. And if the price of subduing his antisocial instincts involves doing away with whatever imaginative potential he might possess, so be it.

Gilmore's deep joke consists in capitulating and becoming just the kind of well-disciplined subject everyone always wanted him to be, but at the wrong moment. The most imaginative act of Gilmore's life, and the costliest to himself, is to pretend to possess no imagination whatever. The result is a sudden reversal. Gilmore, in an instant, stands in relation to the institutional powers of justice as they have, for nineteen years, stood to him. He's demanding that they follow procedure, get in line, stop being so inconsiderate and whimsical. The satisfaction Gilmore derived from the deadpan "I didn't know it was a joke" had to have been great. In any event, it was dearly gotten.

It's hard not to spare a little affection for someone who was motivated, at least in part, to die for the sake of a shrewd joke. Freud, no lover of criminals, uses as his first example in the paper on humor that of the condemned man who approaches the scaffold on a Monday morning saying, "Well, the week's beginning nicely." Wit entails looking down upon oneself from the position of the collective, or cultural, superego, says Freud, and seeing from that perspective how insignificant one's own life is. Gilmore's stroke modifies Freud a little: wit of his sort entails taking up the position of a superego above the cultural standard of the law, making of it a helpless child, temporarily.

Gilmore, it would seem, became capable of this sort of victory when he went to jail. As he says to his cellmate Gibbs (who turns out to be a police informer) shortly after arriving in confinement, "I am in my element now." In jail,

Gilmore is a different kind of person. He draws and paints, writes some fine letters in a neo-Whitmanian mode, and develops a singular sense of humor, of which a couple of the better instances can serve as samples. Moody, one of Gilmore's lawyers, is interviewing him: "If on your passage you meet a new soul coming to take your place, what advice would you have for him?" Gilmore: "Nothing. I don't expect someone to take my place. Hi, I'm your replacement . . . where's the key to the locker . . . where do you keep the towels?" Then there's Gilmore's proposal for a new way to make money off his death: "Oh, hey, man, I got something that'll make a mint. Get aholda John Cameron Swazey right now, and get a Timex wristwatch here. And have John Cameron Swazey out there after I fall over, he can be wearing a stethoscope, he can put it on my heart and say, 'Well, that stopped,' and then he can put the stethoscope on the Timex and say, 'She's still running, folks.'"

What accounts for the change in Gilmore, from Mailer's point of view presumably, is that Gilmore has developed something of a romantic faith. Gilmore's effort, from about the time that he enters prison, is to conduct himself so that he can die what he would himself credit as a "good death." And that means living the time he has left with some charity, and above all with equanimity, without signs of desperation. Gilmore's weakness lies, perhaps, in his requiring a fixed date to direct himself. But his willingness to engage death is what sets him apart from most of the other people in the book. In saying this much, I am finding a strong bias in Mailer's supposedly neutral account. But if we look at the form of *The Executioner's Song*—with form being understood in Kenneth Burke's sense as the setting up of expectations in the reader—we will see that it is far less neutral a text than most of its reviewers wished it to be.

The basic unit of *The Executioner's Song* is the short paragraph written from the perspective of one or another participant in the story. The passages work as self-contained dramatic units, a fact Mailer emphasizes by surrounding each one with a generous aura of blank space. He composes the paragraphs in the third person but injects each of them with enough of the person's idiom to convey a sense of his character. Here, for example, is Gilmore's parole officer Mont Court reflecting (with mediation by Mailer) on whether to have Gary picked up for a parole violation or let him turn himself in. "Gilmore, coming back on his own, would be fortifying the positive side of himself. He would know Court had been right to trust him. That would give a base on which to work. The idea was to get a man into some kind of positive relationship with authority. Then he might begin to change." Mailer's conception of Mont Court is there to be heard in the style of these lines, and particularly in the phrase "positive relationship with authority." Here and throughout the book, Mailer works somewhat in the manner of the portrait painter who follows her subject around for a while before she begins to paint. She's waiting for him to strike a physical pose that reveals some crucial aspect of his character. Mailer combed through the relevant tapes and transcripts in search of similarly revealing moments of speech. One test of the book's integrity would be whether those represented would be willing to sign their names to their sections of the text. Most, I think, would, and in that sense the book is very much theirs.

But Mailer is alive in *The Executioner's Song* too, and not least in the rhythmical shapings that he gives to the paragraphs. The book starts, for example, with Brenda's memory of Gary catching her as she falls from the breaking branch of a forbidden apple tree. Gary then helps her drag away the branch so they won't be caught and punished. So from the beginning we're led to associate Gary with a fall, with transgression, and with—the parallels are too numerous to be discounted—the Fall. A sense that the incident might anticipate the future comes through in the passage's final line: "That was Brenda's earliest recollection of Gary." The mythical echoes and the soft but perceptible drop of the last line convey a certain inevitability. Gilmore is fated, despite finer impulses, to fail. His destiny is tragic, a fact brought home to the reader by the comparable shaping of many of the passages that focus on him. Here is the end of a paragraph in which Gilmore says good-bye to his brother Mikal: "He leaned over and kissed Mikal on the mouth. 'See you in the darkness,' he said." Here a priest, Father Meersman, talks to Gary about wearing a hood during the execution: "If Gary wanted to die with dignity, then he had to respect that very, very simple thing about the hood. It was there for practicality to allow the thing to run very dignified, and no movement. Gary listened in silence." In this passage, Gilmore receives communion from Meersman: "Gary took the wafer on his tongue in the old style, mouth open, way back, in the way, observed Father Meersman, he had received as a child, and then he drank from the chalice. Father Meersman stood beside him while Gary consumed the bottom of the cup." The kind of foreshadowing that occurs, with varying degrees of subtlety, in these passages pervades the book. One section after another about Gilmore ends with a tonal allusion to his death. The effect, over the course of a thousand or so pages, is to confer on Gary a considerable stature. Fate seems to have singled him out for sacrifice. From Mailer's point of view, it is fair to surmise, Gary earns his tragic status by saying yes to his own death.

Gilmore is not the only person in *The Executioner's Song* who is so treated. The passages devoted to his girlfriend, Nicole Baker, a figure easily as complex as Gary, finish with a dying fall at least as often as Gilmore's passages do, and perhaps more. And it is Nicole's disdain for life, evidenced by, among other things, a determined suicide attempt, *combined with* her vitality and resilience, that makes Mailer confer a tragic dignity on her as well. In fact, all of those figures

in the book who live strongly in the knowledge of death receive some share of Mailer's elegiac tones. Mailer is moved by people like Brenda, her father Vern Damico, and Bessie Gilmore, Gary's mother, and offers them the one form of authorial tribute that the book's constraints allow.

Larry Schiller, who interviewed Gilmore extensively and who eventually collaborated with Mailer on the book, is largely denied this treatment, as is Barry Farrell, a journalist who seems to share some of Mailer's private apprehensions about the workings of the world. But this is something one might have predicted: Mailer has always claimed to care more for working-class Americans than for literati and Eastern sophisticates. What is surprising, particularly in light of the reviews the book received, is the kind of shaping that Mailer gives to the paragraphs focused on Gilmore's victims and their wives. In his review of *The Executioner's Song,* Walter Karp, a tough-minded and acute political writer, praised Mailer for giving up his long-time disdain for the American squares and treating Max and Colleen Jensen and Debbie and Ben Bushnell with compassion (25-26). Here are the first two passages on the Bushnells:

> Debbie was feeling a little off one day and Ben kept wanting to take her to the doctor. She was pregnant, after all. But there were eleven kids over from the Busy Bee Day-Care Center, and Debbie didn't have the time. Ben finally raised his voice a little. At which point she told him he bugged her. That was the worst fight they ever had.
>
> They were proud that was the worst fight. They saw marriage as a constant goal of making each other happy. It was the opposite of that song "I Never Promised You a Rose Garden." They kind of promised each other. They weren't going to be like other marriages.

Debbie Bushnell might own to having said everything included in these passages. But to shape the material as Mailer has, to end the passages with trite lines like "That was the worst fight they ever had" and "They weren't going to be like other marriages" makes the Bushnells seem small. They don't rate the tragic tones that Gary and Nicole get. On the next page, Mailer ends a passage of only three sentences on Debbie with the line, "She was terrific with kids and would rather mop her kitchen floor than read." This may have been true of Mrs. Bushnell, but given what passage endings mean in this book, and given that the recipient of this information is at the moment a reader, holding a thousand-page volume, it's clear that the presentation is potently biased. I have picked out some of the more extreme examples of Mailer's treatment of the victims. He's kinder to the Jensens, for example, but not very much. Mrs. Jensen's last thought of her husband leaving for work on the day he is to be killed is ominous but also, at the last moment, reduced. "He would be moving along the Interstate at just such a speed [55 m.p.h.] until he went around a slow graded turn and disappeared from sight and left her mind free to think of one and then another of the small things she must do that day."

The passages on the lives that the Jensens and Bushnells led before the murders tend to begin in hope of some kind and end, also, on an upswing, an upswing that sounds hollow and naive in light of events. The couples are middle-class Americans, expectant, ambitious, unworldly, and perhaps a little smug. They live without a sense of the tragic possibilities in life, the sense that Nicole Baker seems to have from childhood and that Gilmore supposedly develops over time. *The Executioner's Song,* I would argue, is a violent polemic on behalf of the position that Gilmore (as Mailer represents him) eventually achieves. For Mailer, if I understand him correctly, attempts to write his book from a state akin to the one he attributes to Gilmore, one that acknowledges the awareness of death as the necessary condition for every just perception.

Recall that Mailer's Gilmore began to develop his sense of death as a principle of authority when he was immersed in the partial death that jail represents. Now Mailer himself has, from early in his career, been preoccupied with the experience of imprisonment. Entering prison has, in the past, meant cutting off romantic possibilities. If self-creation involves assertion and risk, then prison is the state of death-in-life because there you have to diminish yourself, draw in in order to survive. In *The Armies of the Night,* Mailer speaks of jail as a place where "a man who wished to keep his sanity must never anticipate, never expect, never hope with such high focus of hope that disappointment would be painful." (The lines could serve as a compressed renunciation of Wordsworth's romantic paean to hope in book 6 of *The Prelude.*) In **"The White Negro,"** prison is the image that comes forth most readily to figure limitation or the failure of self-reliance. "The wrong kinds of defeats," Mailer says there, "attack the body and imprison one's energy until one is jailed in the prison air of other people's habits." Prison has been to Mailer what acedia was to Coleridge, what "habitual self" was to Keats, and what poverty was to Emerson, the most emphatic possible conception of imaginative death.

Correspondingly, Mailer's high romantic style, the style of *Armies* and **"The White Negro,"** might be said to represent the mental antithesis of imprisonment. The exhilaration those texts can produce in a reader derives in part from his sense that the writing possesses boundless resources and possibilities. One feels that Mailer will never run out of metaphors. His invention will never flag, his powers of observation and analysis will persist forever. The energizing illusion is akin to the one felt in the presence of a great

athlete, who seems unlimited in her ability to extemporize fresh ways of standing out in a game.

One way to think of *The Executioner's Song* is as a book in which Mailer, willingly or under some compulsion, enters the prison of a restricted style. He surrenders the freedom of Emersonian abandonment and encloses himself in the rectangular walls of the book's isolated paragraphs. He adopts a voice that is cold, flat, and spectral and makes the acquiescence to death his central principle of value. The style is terminal. Mailer's early romantic style signified an energetic denial of death. The words were supposed to seem unstoppable, a stream of invention that would never find its placid level. The culture to which Mailer addressed himself then had imposed what he saw as living death by conformity on its citizens, and the task at hand was to revitalize them. But when a culture becomes falsely vitalistic, making the denial of death the principle on which its mystifications rest, it is time to try to undermine it by the Emersonian gesture of diving to reappear in a new place.

> **One way to think of *The Executioner's Song* is as a book in which Mailer, willingly or under some compulsion, enters the prison of a restricted style. He surrenders the freedom of Emersonian abandonment and encloses himself in the rectangular walls of the book's isolated paragraphs.**
> **—*Mark Edmundson***

Part of what reinforces the interpretation I've been offering thus far—in which Gilmore is understood as developing into the kind of existentialist who's in accord more or less with Mailer's literary self-image—is the degree to which the book's first readers resisted seeing these designs. A reading always appears to be more authentic when it's been wrested at the expense of some other approach that can simultaneously be revealed as self-interested, anxious, or guilty. I wouldn't be surprised if Mailer, who's played off his critics as skillfully as anyone writing today, could have predicted the eventual surfacing of the kind of "subversive" interpretation that I've offered so far. In fact, he might find this reading satisfying to a troubling degree.

I mean that we ought to be suspicious at how readily *The Executioner's Song* yields to an analysis that calls forward so many of Mailer's key preoccupations and "finds" a shape in Gilmore's career that the author of **"The White Negro"** might have desired for his own. So it seems worth asking how we might have seen Gilmore without Mailer's subtle shaping of his story.

What's striking throughout the text—and Mailer plays on

this—is the inability of all the institutional agencies and their functionaries, prison psychiatrists, social workers, wardens, and the rest, to come up with a description of Gilmore that isn't jargon-ridden and flat-minded. No one can describe to anyone else's satisfaction why Gilmore committed the murders. And this may be true not because they haven't got access to the resources of the Novelist, but because Gilmore doesn't provide enough fixity. Perhaps one can't fairly represent his character, as Mailer habitually represents his own, in terms of some internal dynamic or dialectic. Maybe Gilmore's life doesn't lend itself to a "form"; and maybe he doesn't attempt to fashion his experience in a manner analogous to the fashioning of a literary career. From this point of view, Gilmore's only "motive" is a hunger for passionate disruption, an urge to fracture any set of social forms in which he finds himself. His profession that he wants to die made in front of the Board of Pardons may be the inception of an existential project. It may also be an act of simple, spontaneous anarchism, aiming a joke at a venerable institution, then living out the joke for the possibilities of future disruption that arise from it.

I am suggesting that a great deal of Gilmore's behavior might be best understood as parodic, as when, in prison, he begins impersonating a celebrity: signing autographs, sending T-shirts to his fans, spending hours over his mail and his clippings, using his status to try to consort on equal terms with a few others among the rich and famous. His interviews with Schiller, and with his lawyers Moody and Stanger, when read from a certain angle, offer amusing send-ups of journalistic encounters with politicians and other professional evaders. Gilmore's gross manipulations—especially of Nicole, whom he induces to attempt suicide—are the gestures of a crazed real-life film director, experimenting with a sudden unexpected power on other people's lives. Perhaps Gilmore is devoted to nothing more than a certain brutal form of "play," manifest in bitter jokes and stratagems, parody, and the creation of temporary roles, a form of play that recognizes no purpose and no standard of value other than the venting of his energies in disruptive action and passionate speech.

I'm offering the possibility, then, that the subtleties of form in *The Executioner's Song* may be employed to contain an energy inimical to cultural forms, including literary forms, even of the radical Emersonian variety. Why should Mailer exert himself in the interest of this sort of confinement? Gilmore's minority or oppositional energies are the ones that Mailer wants to identify with his own, and yet these "minority" powers, if they're going to have any real value, have to possess the potential and the inclination to enter into conflict with the triad of opposing forces that Mailer sees as threatening: chaos, evil, and waste. Gilmore's brutal "play," without end or allegiance, undermines the dialectical conception of life, life conceived of as a series of significant

encounters in which one can be potentially transformed for the better, which represents Mailer's main hope for salutary development.

The vision of Gilmore against which Mailer is defending himself (and his readers) is perhaps one in tune with a contemporary tendency to give up on coherent narratives; on truth, even of the pragmatic variety; on transcendence in any form; on any unironic investment in persons, objects, or interpretations. This tendency, some have argued, is encouraged by the "postmodern" experience of life as a simulacrum, as an unguided peregrination through images and codes that bear—and admit implicitly and rather cheerfully that they bear—no relations to any possible referent. Gilmore may be a creature of this world at its worst, a product and promulgate of its values. If this is in fact the case, then Gilmore has earned the not inconsiderable distinction of being the figure who compelled America's foremost literary radical to fight culture's conserving battles for it.

Robert Merrill (essay date Spring 1992)

SOURCE: "Mailer's Sad Comedy: *The Executioner's Song,*" in *Texas Studies in Literature and Language,* Vol. 34, No. 1, Spring, 1992, pp. 129-48.

[*In the following essay, Merrill reconsiders the critical reception of* The Executioner's Song *through analysis of Mailer's presentation and major themes in the novel. According to Merrill, Mailer's treatment of social injustice and tragedy evokes compassion for all characters involved.*]

This is an absolutely astonishing book.

—Joan Didion

The time is right, I think, to reconsider **The Executioner's Song** (1979), Norman Mailer's famous "true life novel" (the book's oxymoronic subtitle). Though the work received an extremely favorable reception from reviewers (more favorable than any of Mailer's books save **The Naked and the Dead, The Armies of the Night,** and, curiously enough, **Existential Errands**), **The Executioner's Song** remains an enigma in the history of Mailer's critical reputation. Since 1979 most essays on the book have been friendly, but they have all dealt with limited topics—Mailer's presence or nonpresence within the text, Gary Gilmore's "character," the validity of Mailer's claim to have written a true life novel. It almost seems as if the book's sheer size has discouraged even its advocates from addressing such basic issues as the work's overall structure and informing themes. The questions that remain are fundamental. How should we assess the relationship between books 1 and 2, almost equally long but often thought to be of radically unequal narrative interest (the first book surpassing the second)? What are we to make of the final five hundred pages in which Mailer focuses on the intense legal and media activity that marked Gilmore's last three months? Perhaps most crucial, what are we to think of Gilmore? Is he a Maileresque hero, "fighting the whole liberal establishment for the right to choose his own death and expiation," as Robert Begiebing argues? Or is he no more than a violent "punk," as many readers no doubt suppose? Finally, what are we to make of Mailer's claim that his subject is "American Virtue," as he once considered titling the book? This claim should lead us to reconsider Mailer's thematic intentions in general, intentions all too often down-played because Mailer is so conspicuously "absent" from this huge book. Such a review should allow us to see that *The Executioner's Song* is Mailer's most ambitious attempt to "explain" America, a fundamental purpose in all his books but especially the works of nonfiction that he published in the 1970s.

I shall assume that the generic question is less crucial here than in many of Mailer's earlier works, for I think Mailer has written precisely the kind of book he set out to write: a "novel" in which everything happens to be "true" (i.e., exactly as reported by the one hundred witnesses from whose point of view the story is told). The principal critical questions should be how this massive set of experiences is organized and what the resulting aesthetic structure communicates to a sympathetic reader. Ultimately, the question is whether this book is the "astonishing" achievement Joan Didion took it to be in her early review.

1

It's as if he has set a camera down in the middle of the event, in the tradition of Warhol and cinéma vérité, and simply recorded all that passed the camera's eye.

—Chris Anderson

When Chris Anderson says that *The Executioner's Song* resembles Warhol's more extravagant experiments he is referring to his impression upon first reading Mailer's book; according to Anderson, a second reading reveals the author's shaping hand in ways that recall Truman Capote's in *In Cold Blood.* Anderson's comment is all too representative, for it does take some time to appreciate that there is a "shaping consciousness" at work. For example, a number of critics have pointed to Mailer's habit of concluding narrative sections with telling comments phrased in his own voice, as when he compares Gilmore's trip home after being released from prison to the westward journey of Brenda Nicol's great-grandfather many years earlier. The passage in question connects a dedicated Mormon pioneer and the all-too-aimless Gilmore, a fine irony made available by the author and not one of his characters. And there are many other such mo-

ments, often, as noted, at the end of sections. But it is easy to exaggerate Mailer's "presence" in the book as a whole—a few summarizing remarks do not go far in a book of over one thousand pages. Thus Anderson's allusion to Warhol. Thus Richard Stern's amusing comment: "Mailer's absence is so pronounced that it dominates the book like an empty chair at a family dinner." To locate Mailer, I think we need to look not at explicit formulations but the narrative structure itself.

Book 1 of *The Executioner's Song* is called "Western Voices," and we do overhear many different western voices during the five hundred pages devoted to Gary Gilmore's three and a half months of freedom in Provo, Utah (a period preceded by Gilmore's eighteen years in prison and brought to a stunning conclusion by the two apparently senseless murders he commits). These many western figures primarily observe and comment on Gilmore, however, who remains the unmistakable focal point of book 1. By presenting Gilmore from so many points of view, Mailer provides what seems as broad and objective a portrait as possible. Nonetheless, the details selected highlight certain features of Gilmore's character, as a brief review of part 1, "Gary," should confirm.

The first fifteen pages offer a number of quite sympathetic moments, or details concerning Gilmore's past. In these first pages, his cousin, Brenda Nicol, remembers a seven-year-old Gary helping her during "a good family get-together"; the unattractive details of Gary's reform-school days in Portland are left out of the narrative; Brenda's sister, Toni, testifies to the impact of Gary's drawings, especially those that depict "children with great sad eyes"; one of Gilmore's letters is quoted in which he says of prison, "It's like another planet," a haunting simile reinforced a bit later when he remarks that he seldom saw stars in prison; the pathetic austerity of Gilmore's one tote bag, his inability to stop "gawking" at beautiful girls, and his ignorance of the fact one can try on clothes before buying them all point up his abysmal past; and Gilmore's sensitive interplay with the small children of friends is noted twice. Later in part 1, when Gilmore meets Nicole Baker, those who know him are amazed at his positive transformation. These early pages consistently present Gilmore as a kind of waif, good at heart but deprived of the normal opportunities to express his goodness. Almost immediately, however, evidence from several sources begins to define Gilmore as what Mailer calls a "habit-ridden petty monster," "trapped" within his apparently unshakable selfishness. During his first date in Provo, Gilmore demands sex, refuses to listen when told he must *earn* things, and raises his fist against a woman who has done nothing to him; only a few weeks later he repeats this performance with a second date, finally busting the windshield of her car when she refuses to sleep with him. In the midst of many conversations, Gilmore launches into grim prison stories about beating a convict with a hammer, photographing a convict performing fellatio on himself, killing "this black dude . . . a *bad* nigger," and tattooing a friend with little phalluses; indeed, this ominous repertoire of prison tales is trotted out whenever Gilmore makes a new acquaintance in book 1. Soon we observe Gilmore lying to his sympathetic parole officer and shouting obscenities at a movie screen. Thus Mailer establishes at once the extraordinary difficulty of defining Gilmore's essence or even how one should respond to him.

This complex portrait is embellished throughout the remaining six parts of book 1. As developed in part 2 ("Nicole") and part 3 ("Gary and Nicole"), Gilmore's affair with Nicole deepens our sense of both his pathos and his viciousness. Mailer's treatment of their first days together is very sympathetic. He takes seriously their belief in reincarnation and presents without irony their separate assertions that they knew each other "from other time." He shows Gilmore playing the engaging youthful lover despite the fact that he is thirty-five and Nicole nineteen: Gilmore labels Nicole his "elf," carves their names on an apple tree, and tells her "that he hoped no unnecessary tragedies would ever befall them." With Nicole he seems much more in control of himself, as when he tells her that the whole point of living is "facing yourself." Yet Gilmore still seems compulsively violent: he forces Nicole into all-night sexual engagements to combat his impotence, clips off the speakers in a drive-in, hits Nicole at least twice, throws a tape deck at a security guard, and gets drunk soon after promising to give up drinking. His frequent reflections on reincarnation betray his basic childishness, for at this point his faith is little more than a pleasant fantasy: "After death, he said, he was going to start all over again. Have the kind of life he always wished he had." So it is no surprise when Gilmore cannot sustain his relationship with Nicole, who leaves him toward the end of part 3. Indeed, the depressing histories presented in part 2 offer almost no hope that Gilmore and Nicole can reverse the pattern of failure that informs both lives.

The first three parts of book 1 create sympathy for Gilmore even as they document his "monstrous" character. This opening movement is crucial to the work's overall effect, for beginning with part 4, "The Gas Station and the Motel," Mailer is obliged to record Gilmore's ghastly performance in murdering for $100 one night and $125 the next. The almost shockingly flat account of the Jensen and Bushnell murders is followed by Gilmore's pathetic effort to make love to Nicole's fifteen-year-old sister, April; his absurdly amateurish lies to the police; his repulsive boasting about the seventy to one hundred "successful" robberies he committed as a kid and the murder of Bushnell; and his extremely evasive stance at the subsequent trial, where he claims that he had no control over himself when he committed the murders, that it was fated for him to kill Bushnell. In part 5 ("The

Shadows of the Dream"), part 6 ("The Trial of Gary M. Gilmore"), and part 7 ("Death Row"), we see Gilmore at a much greater distance, back in jail and no longer the somewhat sympathetic figure of the early sections. During Mailer's clinical account of the murders and Gilmore's subsequent arrest, trial, and sentencing, our "hero" often seems little more than the "recidivist" that John Hersey takes him to be. There is precious little to corroborate the initial hints that Gilmore is in part the victim of a system that imprisons a man for almost his entire adult life for relatively petty crimes. By the end of book 1, however, a strangely positive side to Gilmore does emerge, one that will become a major subject in book 2.

I refer in part to Gilmore's relative stability when he becomes once again a convict. Early in his jail stint in Provo, Gilmore tells a fellow convict, "I am in my element now," and the final sections of book 1 tend to confirm this claim rather than to undercut it as another instance of Gilmore's cheap self-inflation. But I also refer to the odd capacity Gilmore seems to develop to judge his life with apparent objectivity. Soon after his arrest, he tells an officer, "I can't keep up with life," as accurate a comment on his frenetic three and a half months in Provo as anyone is able to offer. A bit later Gilmore writes a long letter to Nicole in which he says that he cannot be the devil because he loves Nicole and the devil cannot love. "But I might be further from God than I am from the devil," he adds. "It seems that I know evil more intimately than I know goodness." This remarkable letter is followed by others equally fascinating, letters in which he praises Nicole's fearlessness, speaks of the unendurable pain he felt when he thought he had lost Nicole, celebrates their two months together while referring again to the thousands of years they may have known each other, and affirms courage as the ultimate virtue. Perhaps the most important letter is the one in which he tells Nicole, "I believe we always have a choice."

Gilmore's choice now is to die rather than to allow his soul to deteriorate further in this life. This logic leads him to reject any appeal of the death penalty, a decision that soon makes him nationally famous and confirms Mailer's portrait of Gilmore as profoundly ambiguous. This man who acts like a barbarian at one moment and quotes Emerson at another is a "mystery," Mailer has said, "malignant at his worst and heroic at his best." Book 1 does not verify Gilmore's heroism, but it does project a man whose complications are as vivid as his unforgettable malignancy. Gilmore as habit-ridden monster is the key to book 1, but we are made to ask whether this is all there is to say about the man. In book 2, of course, Mailer will offer many more words, as he pursues the mystery of Gary Gilmore through another five hundred pages.

Before turning to the lawyers and media figures who dominate book 2, we should note the role of the many relatives, friends, acquaintances, and victims who share the stage with Gilmore in book 1. These people are observers who contribute to the composite picture of Gary Gilmore, but they also help Mailer achieve the broad social panorama he admires in writers as different as Tolstoy and Dreiser. Indeed, Mailer has chided himself for doing so little with the secondary characters in his previous novels, a "flaw" he hoped to correct in *The Executioner's Song*. Here Mailer develops virtually every "minor" character and permits each to speak in something like his or her own voice, however much the several idioms blend into the flat, colloquial style for which the book is famous. Mailer's defense of his unadorned prose might apply to the minor characters themselves: "one's style is only a tool to use on a dig." Like the style by which we know them, the secondary characters are supposed to contribute to the book's larger formal ends.

One such end is to "examine" the American reality exposed by the strange saga of Gary Gilmore. Joan Didion sees Mailer as capturing two crucial features of western America. The first is "that emptiness at the center of the Western experience, a nihilism antithetical not only to literature but to most other forms of human endeavor." The second is an inability to direct our own lives, a failing so pervasive that all the characters seem to share in "a fatalistic drift, a tension, an overwhelming and passive rush toward the inevitable events that will end in Gary Gilmore's death." I believe that Didion's insights are exaggerated, but they do point up suggestive connections between Gilmore and the people who surround him. Bessie Gilmore, Brenda Nicol, Vern Damico, Kathryne Baker and her daughters Nicole and April—all are "trapped" in their futile efforts to find a life worth living. Indeed, almost every woman in the book first marries at fifteen or sixteen and eventually marries at least three or four times, and the men seem equally caught up in the fatalistic drift Didion notices. Didion does not do justice to the admirable stability of people like Brenda Nicol and Vern Damico, but the wasted lives of those around Gilmore suggest that his own fate is only an exaggerated instance of that moral emptiness Didion hears in the book's western voices.

In this respect as in others, Nicole Baker is the second most important character. Mailer has called her "a bona fide American heroine," but most readers will think she is rather the quintessential American victim. Promiscuous at eleven, institutionalized at thirteen, married at fourteen and again at fifteen, Nicole suffers three broken marriages before she is twenty. "Sex had never been new to Nicole," we are told, and it is more than plausible when she runs off with an older man because "she didn't care where she was going." Yet Nicole has virtues to match her troubling irresponsibility. As Gilmore sees, she is fearless and fiercely loyal. These are the very qualities that Gilmore counts on when he manipulates her toward a suicide pact. In his many letters from jail,

he pleads with Nicole not to make love with other men, to give up sex altogether, and to join him on the other side in death. At the end of book 1, he leads her toward a double suicide attempt that epitomizes both his romanticism and his selfishness, even as it climaxes Mailer's portrait of Nicole as an endearing victim. Later Nicole will be denied the "clean" resolution of death, will emerge from yet another institution to tell Larry Schiller (and Mailer) the story of her love for Gary Gilmore, and will finally drift off to Oregon to new lovers if not a new life. Nicole's story is a familiar one among her family and friends; years of acute aimlessness followed by an utterly hopeless commitment. Surely it is no accident that Nicole comes to love Gilmore most fiercely when he is cut off from her forever. For the Nicoles of the world (and perhaps this means for all of us), there is no consummation except in an imagined future.

The stories of Nicole and the other witnesses point to one of Mailer's most crucial decisions in structuring book 1. Rather than trace Gilmore's grim history from reform school through his term in Marion, Illinois, Mailer chooses to focus on Gilmore's last months in Provo in 1976. The reasons for this no doubt include Mailer's desire to achieve greater dramatic unity and to emphasize Gilmore's "mystery" instead of the familiar stages of American crime and punishment. But another important reason is to allow Mailer to flesh out the human context in which Gilmore plays his final role or sings his final song, as the title would have it. This context is dominated by the same hateful "habits" that take more spectacular forms in Gilmore. Yet the human resources displayed in book 1 should not be dismissed quite so easily as Didion's formulation would suggest. Here we get example after example of human folly, western style, but also many instances of what Mailer calls "American virtue," the American's dogged determination to do his or her best in the worst of circumstances. The range of such portraits is really quite extraordinary, from Gilmore's mother, Bessie, to Brenda Nicol, to the Damicos, to the irrepressible Nicole. One of the earliest reviewers called *The Executioner's Song* "a remarkably compassionate work," and the truth in this judgment should remind us that, like Mailer's portrait of Gilmore, book 1 is structured to highlight the human frailties as well as the abominations of American life.

It might seem that book 2 offers a less sympathetic, more satirical history of Gilmore's last months. The very title of part 1, "In the Reign of Good King Boaz," signals a new kind of irony. Here lawyers and the press are omnipresent and one eighty-two-page section, "Exclusive Rights," is devoted to virtually nothing but Larry Schiller's and David Susskind's efforts to corner the Gilmore market, so to speak, by securing exclusive rights to his story. Packs of reporters are everywhere, confirming Mailer's worst fears about the press. The many lawyers introduced are often distinguished by one bizarre detail or another, as when Earl Dorius, Utah's assistant attorney general, is *excited* at the prospect of an execution and proceeds to work himself into a near breakdown to ensure that the state of Utah gets its execution on 17 January 1977, or when Dennis Boaz, Gilmore's second lawyer, supports his client's desire to be executed until it occurs to him that Gary would prefer to live if he could have connubial visits from Nicole, perhaps in Mexico! Gilmore's final lawyers, Bob Moody and Ron Stanger, are a good deal less eccentric, but they too partake in the grim legal struggle in which the state of Utah pursues its pound of flesh, and the ACLU and other liberal groups fight stubbornly to save a man who does not want to be saved. The ironies here are obvious and may even seem undramatic. In the film version of *The Executioner's Song,* scenarist Mailer and director Schiller chose to leave out most of the materials of book 2, as if they were less relevant than the more "immediate" events of book 1.

My own view is that book 2 is at least as interesting as book 1, a remarkable feat when one considers that the protagonist is all but unavailable and the heroine is locked up throughout. Once again Mailer gets great mileage from his so-called minor figures, a few of whom (e.g., Boaz, Schiller, Barry Farrell) are among his most memorable characters. Of real interest for their own sake, they also provide perspective on Gilmore. For example, Gary's brother Mikal is at first reluctant to allow his brother to die and participates in legal actions to prevent it. When he finally talks with Gary, however, Mikal is won over by his brother's seriousness and depth of feeling. As they part, Gary first kisses Mikal, then utters perhaps the most haunting words in this very long book: "See you in the darkness." A cellmate of Gilmore's named Gibbs also effectively testifies on Gary's behalf. A police informer, Gibbs refers to Gilmore as the most courageous convict he has even seen. And Gilmore's relatives, especially Vern Damico and Toni Gurney, find themselves moving ever closer to Gilmore as he approaches death. Toni's relationship with Gilmore is especially moving. She first visits him the day before he is to be executed and is overwhelmed by his gentle affection. Later that day, after her own birthday party, she returns to the party Gilmore has been permitted at the prison and again experiences Gary's new warmth. Toni is sufficiently moved to try to attend Gary's execution. This sequence blends with many other small but affecting moments to verify the change in Gilmore that is sensed by many people during his final weeks.

Mailer uses Barry Farrell and Larry Schiller to temper the more sentimental implications of book 2, but ultimately these veteran journalists also testify to Gilmore's surprising depth. The title of book 2, "Eastern Voices," seems to refer to all those safely established in the social system, whether in the East or the West: lawyers, reporters, producers, assistant attorney generals, and so on. Farrell and Schiller are such voices. Each brings a heavy load of urban skepticism to the

Gilmore assignment, hating Salt Lake City, as Farrell does, and believing there is no "center" to this story, nothing of real human resonance. When both men come to see Gilmore in a very different light, Mailer is able to bring his book to a genuine climax.

Farrell is at first confident that nothing sets Gilmore apart but his willingness to die. If Gilmore is not executed, Farrell suggests, he will become indistinguishable from the hundreds of others condemned to die but never executed. As he works with Gilmore's responses to hundreds of questions, however, Farrell notices that Gilmore "was now setting out to present the particular view of himself he wanted people to keep." Later Farrell responds profoundly to Gilmore's tapes: "Barry was crying and laughing and felt half triumphant that the man could talk with such clarity." Farrell still believes that Gilmore "had a total contempt for life," but this makes it all the more impressive when Gilmore responds so "humanely" to the massive attention of his last months. Farrell is stunned at Gilmore's apparent complexity. In the transcripts Farrell spots "twenty-seven poses," twenty-seven different Gilmores ("racist Gary and Country-and-Western Gary, artist manqué Gary, macho Gary"). Farrell begins to pursue the single Gary who presumably stands behind these multiple poses, but he is "seized with depression at how few were the answers" to his inquiry. There is an "evil genius" in Gilmore's planning Nicole's suicide, but much else in Gilmore's life suggests sheer ignorance; Gilmore's relations with Bessie, his mother, seem a potential key, but the answers to many related questions provide no "hope of a breakthrough." Continuing to ponder Gilmore's transcripts just before the execution, Farrell turns to yet another possible solution to the Gilmore mystery: Gilmore's fascination with small children. But this "answer" is also unsatisfactory: "It was too insubstantial. In fact, it was sheer speculation. . . . beware of understanding the man too quickly!" Beware indeed. Farrell's final comment on Gilmore takes us back to the passage from André Gide ("Please do not understand me too quickly") that Mailer first used as his epigraph to *The Deer Park* (1955). Farrell's conclusion should caution us against reductive readings, psychological efforts to pluck out Gilmore's mystery. Indeed, Gilmore's complexity should impress us as much as it does Farrell, whose prolonged efforts to understand Gilmore are akin to Mailer's.

Larry Schiller's role is in part like Farrell's. Schiller also looks for the human side to Gilmore, the "sympathetic character" buried inside the cold-blooded killer, for Schiller cannot imagine making a successful book or film unless he first makes this discovery. Like Farrell, Schiller begins with many doubts and ends up convinced of Gilmore's essential seriousness, especially on such matters as life after death. Schiller shares with Farrell the scenarist's desire to grasp his subject, to "reduce Gary's mystery, attach him to conditions, locate him in history." Together Farrell and Schiller prove that it is impossible to achieve this "reduction" no matter how many materials are carefully scrutinized. Schiller's role is larger than Farrell's, however, for it also includes Schiller's personal drama. Both Farrell and Schiller make interesting discoveries about Gary Gilmore, but Schiller makes such discoveries about himself as well.

In book 2 Schiller's importance surpasses Nicole's and rivals Gilmore's. Much of book 2 is organized around Schiller's efforts to sign up the principals in the Gilmore story and to get information from Gilmore before the execution. This intricate, frustrating process educates Schiller about Gilmore, but it also constitutes a belated *rite de passage* for Schiller, who becomes "part of the story," as he himself notes. Before coming to Utah, Schiller has achieved "a terrible reputation" as a journalist. The last man to interview Jack Ruby, the author of "a quick and rotten book" about Susan Atkins, Schiller describes himself as a "communicator" but is laughed at by people who take him to be a hustler or, worse, "a carrion bird." Even his fiancée labels him a "manipulator." With the Gilmore story, Schiller struggles to be a good businessman as well as a good journalist, but he often seems to lose this fight as he worries whether there are any "sympathetic characters" in the plot he has purchased, works out alternate scenarios depending on whether Gilmore is executed, and schemes to get at Nicole, the love interest in this "democratic Romeo and Juliet," as Boaz describes the Gilmore tale.

Yet Schiller turns out to be much more than a carrion bird. He deals more honestly with everyone involved than most of us would have done; he suffers acute physical and emotional stress in deciding how far to go in exploiting his material; and he ends up committing himself to doing the best he can for the story rather than his bank account, even rejecting an offer of $250,000 from the *New York Post*. In his afterword Mailer says that Schiller "stood for his portrait, and drew maps to his faults" during their interviews. As Mailer remarks elsewhere, Schiller "wanted the best book that could be gotten out of what had become the biggest event in his own life, and so he did not spare himself, he offered himself." As a result, Schiller's faults and his final integrity in confronting them are deeply embedded in Mailer's text.

Schiller's role in *The Executioner's Song* is a bit like Mailer's in *The Armies of the Night* (1968). I have referred to Schiller's experience as a rite of passage, and of course that is the nature of Mailer's experience at the March on the Pentagon. In each case a man of mixed motives, even a mild cynicism, comes to believe in what he is doing and to act more honorably than we would have thought possible when introduced to him. Schiller is only one of many important characters in this large book, so he is not as central as Mailer is in *Armies.* As we shall see, however, his story very much

resembles Mailer's in pointing up his book's more positive implications. The point to be made here is that Schiller's late-blooming integrity confirms Mailer's portrait of Gilmore as a man of unsuspected depth. The more we come to believe in Larry Schiller, the more we believe in his conception of Gary Gilmore.

This is not to say that Mailer's Gilmore is saintly. In fact, Mailer has noted his distaste for Gilmore: "When I started *The Executioner's Song,* I thought I would like him more than I did." In book 2 as much as in book 1, Mailer does ample justice to what is unattractive, even hateful in Gilmore. Gilmore's intense racism is evident throughout book 2; he never expresses any real contrition for his crimes; he is a man with "surprising veins of compassion or real feeling," but also "large areas that were absolutely unfeeling"; his diatribes against "publicity-hunting lawyers" are amusing but foul, exhibiting the "little mean streak" Gilmore is still exposing just before his death; to the nurses who treat him after his first suicide attempt, he is simply "spiteful, revengeful, obscene." Joseph Wenke points out that after his arrest Gilmore becomes "more and more demonically manipulative as his futile, despairing, and incredibly selfish desire to possess Nicole assumes control of his being." Indeed, Gilmore is still demanding celibacy of Nicole in his last letter, just as he is still asking his lawyers to help him to escape after supposedly resigning himself to a death that is best for his soul.

Yet Mailer's Gilmore is a man with "a capacity to grow," for Mailer the most crucial heroic quality. Mailer agrees with Boaz, Farrell, and Schiller that Gilmore is "serious about dying with dignity." For Gilmore, this means recognizing that we can choose death as well as life. In an interview Gilmore says, "In death you can choose in a way that you can't choose in life," an assertion that reveals Gilmore's great difficulty in making choices in life but also the seriousness of his belief in karma. Gilmore's earlier remarks on karma and reincarnation may seem juvenile, but his later statements impress Mailer (as well as such witnesses as Farrell and Schiller) that Gilmore achieves a genuine philosophical conviction. Thus Gilmore is able to say, when asked if there is anything worse than taking someone's life, "Well, you could alter somebody's life so that the quality of it wouldn't be what it could've been. . . . I think to make somebody go on living in a lessened state of existence, I think that could be worse than killing 'em." Mailer obviously sympathizes with this view, just as he shares Gilmore's belief that "the meaning of the events in any given life can't be comprehended entirely by what one's done in one life" (Mailer's definition of karma). Gilmore's desire to die rather than to deteriorate further appeals to Mailer as an act of self-definition but also as morally valid; as Mailer says, "We have profound choices to make in life, and one of them may be the deep and terrible choice most of us avoid between dying now and 'saving one's soul' . . . in order, conceivably, to be reincarnated." Thus Mailer describes Gilmore's belief in karma as "profound" and highlights Gilmore's growing ability to analyze his own moral condition, as when Gilmore says, "I was always capable of murder. . . . There's a side of me that I don't like. I can become totally devoid of feelings for others, unemotional. I know I'm doing something grossly fucking wrong. I can still go ahead and do it." No one in *The Executioner's Song* offers a more persuasive psychological profile of Gilmore than Gilmore himself.

Gilmore's capacity to "grow" is impressive, but it does not lead Mailer to forget Gilmore's viciousness. Instead, it leads Mailer to conclude that it is hard to draw conclusions. Mailer says that as he learned more and more about Gilmore he "knew less and less." His efforts to define Gilmore are no more successful than Farrell's or Schiller's, unless it is a success to realize that Gilmore is finally "too complex" to label. Mailer's Gilmore challenges society's "firm premise that we have one life and one life only and that if we waste this one life there is nothing worse we can do," but his sordid acts and unalterable meanness call into question the coherence of his personality. For Mailer, this makes Gilmore "another major American protagonist," someone who "comprehends a deep contradiction in this country and lives his life in the crack of that contradiction." But this means Gilmore is only in part "a modern man in search of his soul, wondering whether he might be closer to God or Devil, wanting to make himself whole, willing to pay his debts until he is right and clean and able to 'stand in the sight of God,'" as Begiebing would have it. Gilmore is also a habit-ridden monster whose essence is contradictory, if indeed he *has* a definable essence.

This balanced assessment of Gilmore is the key to the work's structure. Book 1 tends to highlight Gilmore's violence and book 2 his capacity to "grow," but each presents Gilmore's strengths and weaknesses through the eyes of many witnesses who try to understand this profoundly enigmatic figure. The very mode of representation stresses the many different perspectives on Gilmore, who is the one significant character never seen from "within." In addition, the book's sheer size underlines the many facts any theory about Gilmore must finally encompass. Whether witnessing Gilmore's grimmest acts (as in book 1) or pondering his most intelligent self-assessments (as in book 2), we are all but overwhelmed by the difficulty of reducing the material or the man to manageable dimensions. Some have felt that Mailer aggrandizes Gilmore by presenting his affair with Nicole in "tragic tones" denied to Gilmore's victims, but Mailer's handling of Gilmore's last hours illustrates the more complicated effect of his narrative method.

Toward the end Mailer continues to present Gilmore as he is seen by others in relatively detailed accounts of Gilmore's

last-night party, the execution, the autopsy, the memorial service held on Gilmore's behalf, and the dispersal of Gilmore's ashes after cremation. In these final sections, however, the views of the several witnesses blend into a common awe of Gilmore's cool acceptance of his fate. This effect is most pronounced during the execution scene, in which Mailer shifts the point of view twenty times among seven characters yet seems to present an event perceived in much the same way by everyone present. The effect is awesome—indeed, the scene is perhaps the most powerful in all of Mailer's writing—but not in such a way as to exonerate or glorify Gilmore. Gilmore's courage is acknowledged here much as his monstrousness is acknowledged in the depiction of the Jensen and Bushnell murders. Mailer's comment on the autopsy scene also points to the nature of his narrative interests: "That's why I took the execution right through the autopsy—because that was something that I wanted the reader to feel. That's what it means when we kill a man. That even this man who wanted to die and succeeded in getting society to execute him, that even when he was killed, we still feel this horrible shock and loss." We feel shock and loss despite what we know of Gilmore's selfishness and despite our now intimate knowledge of what he has done. In part we respond because of what we have come to know of Gilmore as lover, Gilmore as poet, Gilmore as philosopher, and especially Gilmore as self-critic. In part we respond because, all his faults fully acknowledged, Gilmore remains complexly human. Like the book itself, our response is a complicated one that we can only try to dissect, as I have just done. To try to get at the meaning of such responses, as I am about to do, is an effort that Mailer makes a part of his very subject in this massive, painful, but fully articulated masterpiece.

2

[Gilmore] appealed to me because he embodied many of the themes I've been living with all my life long.

—Norman Mailer

I used to hate America for what it was doing to all of us. Now I hate all of us for what we're doing to America.

—Norman Mailer

There are of course many meanings in *The Executioner's Song,* but the one to which I refer at the end of the last section has been very popular among Mailer's more recent critics. Noting Mailer's challenge to traditional generic definitions and his insistence on Gilmore's ultimately impenetrable "mystery," these critics argue that Mailer's theme is "the necessity of fiction for the apprehension of complex reality," or "the fictionality of all narrative," or the view that "all history is in the end fiction." Mailer's sympathy with such views is both real and longstanding. As long ago as his 1954 essay on David Riesman, Mailer referred to the need for a sociological "fiction" to make sense of American life; at the end of *The Armies of the Night,* Mailer makes fun of journalistic pretenses to complete accuracy; and in his afterword to *The Executioner's Song,* Mailer acknowledges the editorial contributions (however minor) that went into the making of his book. I suspect that Mailer would agree with Phyllis McCord that *The Executioner's Song* demonstrates the subjective nature of all truth. But it is harder to accept the notion that this is Mailer's *principal* theme, central to everything he does in this huge book. To accept such an idea is to place Mailer among the metafictionists—something I cannot imagine doing without major qualifications.

Mailer's social interests in this book are simply too obvious to push aside as illustrating the fictionality of all narrative. Though Mailer dramatizes the difficulty of achieving even an unsure grasp of his material, his task is nonetheless to examine the American reality embedded in this material. Mailer once said that his material was "gold" if he "had enough sense not to gild it," and I think we should indeed ask what gemlike themes inform *The Executioner's Song.*

The possible answers to this question begin with Mailer's characterization of Gilmore. For many readers Gilmore is a reconceived, more artistic version of the hipster first glorified in Mailer's **"The White Negro"** (1957). For one such critic, Gilmore is "the figure of the artist of the self, defining and redefining his personality, controlling events and other characters, projecting a world." For another, Gilmore walks in shackles between guards but "looks freer than they, and people visiting him suspect *they* are the ones in prison." I have already suggested that these are very selective views of Gilmore, half-truths at best. Gilmore is no more adequately described as a hipster than is Marion Faye in *The Deer Park.* Neither the fictional Marion nor the real Gilmore commits himself to "that uncharted journey into the rebellious imperatives of the self" by which Mailer identifies the hipster. This is especially true if we recall that the hipster's "journey" is a sensual one, quite literally an adventure of the senses. As I argue elsewhere, Marion's "black heroic safari" is a matter of will and intellect, and Gilmore's actions prior to his final arrest are so aimless they can hardly be called a quest for anything. Even Gilmore's efforts to die with dignity derive from his will and spirit, not his senses. To think of Gilmore as a sexual rebel is to see at once how little he resembles Mailer's late-1950s ideal.

I suggest we might better see Gilmore as Mailer sees him: a man who lives his life in the crack of a deep American contradiction. To one side of this crack is the nihilistic emptiness Didion emphasizes, the "estrangement" Wenke rightly sees in most of the younger people in book 1 (though I would add older women such as Brenda Nicol and Kathryne Baker,

each of whom marries four times). Gilmore's mistreatment of several women permits Mailer to present a seemingly endless chain of victimized women, young and old. What Didion hears in their voices is resignation, the belief that they cannot influence events. Perhaps the most memorable voice is that of Kathy Maynard, the young woman who discovers Nicole after her suicide attempt. In an interview Kathy describes her own life in the flattest tone imaginable: married at sixteen for no particular reason; witness to her seventeen-year-old husband's suicide with a hunting knife; married again two weeks later to a man she met at her husband's funeral; stranded at seventeen with two small children, no husband, and no particular sense of what she will do next week. Mailer has said that this interview is the one transcript he did not even abridge, for it was "a found object" he could not improve upon. One might describe Kathy as stoical, Didion's term for all the book's women, but stoicism implies recognition of the horrors one is resigned to and Kathy seems merely oblivious. Her brief tale should remind us of the real desert that surrounds these small Utah towns and the metaphorical desert to which Didion alludes.

Kathy Maynard's story is one side of *The Executioner's Song* in miniature, but there are many other memorable examples. My own favorite involves Nicole's mother, Kathryne Baker. When Gilmore retrieves a gun just before he kills Jensen, Kathryne realizes she does not even know his last name. This after Gilmore has lived with Nicole for two months! At such moments the book's westerners appear to be what Wenke calls them, "the beat legatees of the spiritually and politically exhausted hipsters, hippies, and left radicals whom Mailer derides at the conclusion of *Of a Fire on the Moon.*" But they are in fact a much broader cross-section of the American social order, including the conventional Mormons who become Gilmore's "new jailers" (and his victims, for both Jensen and Bushnell are Mormon), the Utah lawyers who prosecute and defend Gilmore, and the many lower-middle-class and lower-class figures whose lives resemble Nicole's but who could not define a "left radical." What they share is a less extreme version of Kathy Maynard's tolerance for the intolerable.

Gilmore is the figure in the book who seems to rebel against this aimless society, just as he is the one who scorns the liberal establishment that takes him up as a "cause" in book 2: thus the common view of Gilmore as a Maileresque hero. The partial truth to this view is suggested by Mailer's statement that Gilmore embodied themes that Mailer has lived with all his life. Among these themes is the heroic individual's passionate (and often destructive) attempt to reject the deadly social environment endured so stoically by the book's western women. This attempt can also be seen in Gilmore's rejection of life in prison, his "dignified" preference for whatever succeeds this life. Indeed, Gilmore's concern for the hereafter is another of the themes to which

Mailer no doubt refers, for the religious dimensions of Gilmore's thought correspond to Mailer's oft-expressed convictions or intuitions. Yet Gilmore is no less estranged than the people who surround him in prison or Provo, no less self-destructive, no less frozen in those "habits" to which Mailer relentlessly draws our attention. In his last days, Gilmore may achieve some perspective on his own compulsions and aspire to something more dignified, but he is also the book's primary example of someone who cannot endure life as it is experienced by all the other characters from Kathy Maynard to Larry Schiller. Gilmore is a mystery and not a model, a man who embodies Mailer's themes but not his solutions.

Mailer does not offer answers to the overwhelming problems his characters face, but *The Executioner's Song* is much less pessimistic than many of its admirers suggest. Mailer says that one of the lessons he learned is that the system is "fairer" than he had supposed: "The way things work in America is not necessarily as sinister as I always assumed. There may not be this grand paranoid network after all." This discovery lies behind Mailer's remark that he used to hate America for what it was doing to all of us but now hates us for what we are doing to America. Behind Mailer's hatred for America lay the paranoid's assumption that "they" were in conspiracy against an innocent citizenry; behind his hatred for us lies the romantic's faith that we know not what we do. Mailer's beliefs might be compared with the Transcendental notion that we always pursue the good but do not know what the good is (see Emerson's "The American Scholar" and Thoreau's *Walden* as primary texts). Thus our aimlessness or compulsive materialism, our mindless conformity or violent resistance. Thus the world represented *in extremis* by Gary Gilmore.

As Mailer says, however, this world seems to be fairer and less sinister than he always supposed. Indeed, the unifying subject in Mailer's story is what he calls "American virtue." In Mailer's view, everyone involved here wished to do "the right thing" and went to some trouble to act accordingly. This dedication to principle is the other side of the American contradiction embodied in Gilmore. Rocklike conservatives seeking the death penalty, dedicated liberals seeking to avoid a state execution, lawyers on all sides, friends of Gilmore, friends of his victims, men such as Barry Farrell and Larry Schiller—all did their best as they understood the best. Schiller is perhaps the most notable example, but only because his "best" involves personal growth—virtue in its most positive form. Many other examples of American virtue are grim reminders of why Mailer "hates" us for what we are doing to America. As he does with Gilmore, however, Mailer captures these other Americans in the richly detailed (if depressing) context of their dull habits and assumptions, a context elaborately built up page by page as Mailer offers the most compelling "social drama" of his long career.

If we read this book as Mailer conceived it, we must feel compassion for nearly everyone—for Kathy Maynard as well as Larry Schiller, for Earl Dorius as well as Kathryne Baker, for the youthful April Baker as well as the elderly Bessie Gilmore. Finally, there must also be compassion for Gary Gilmore, just as there must be "hate" for what Gilmore and the rest of us are doing to each other. The least judgmental of Mailer's works, *The Executioner's Song* is also the book in which Mailer's love for America is most impressively in evidence. Mailer has said that he learned from the Gilmore saga that society might not be evil but rather "a sad comedy." This phrase also applies to the "astonishing" book he wrote in the wake of his discovery.

William H. Pritchard (review date Spring 1992)

SOURCE: "Mailer's Main Event," in *The Hudson Review*, Vol. 45, No. 1, Spring, 1992, pp. 149-57.

[*In the following review, Pritchard offers favorable assessment of* Harlot's Ghost, *praising the admirable ambition of the work despite Mailer's characteristic narrative style that ranges from "the sublime to the ridiculous."*]

Six weeks ago one of the larger pieces of mail ever received turned up at my front door in the form of a dauntingly wrapped copy of *Harlot's Ghost,* all four pounds of it. It was mid-semester break, my sinuses were full of misery, and I settled in, if somewhat warily, to ingest Mailer's longest book. Somewhat warily since a trusted friend, having read it in proof, termed it a disaster; and since *Newsweek*'s Peter Prescott, a pretty good reviewer of fiction, had just called it "a dry and dusty thing . . . for nearly all of its incredibly long way." Would *Harlot* pass Wyndham Lewis' "Taxi-Cab Driver Test for 'Fiction'"? The test may be administered, with or without a cab driver, by opening any novel at its first page and seeing whether it looks like "fiction"—with all that word connotes about the diverting, the agreeably "made-up," the "interesting" story line—or something rather different, namely art. Here is a little more than the first page of *Harlot's Ghost:*

> On a late-winter evening in 1983, while driving through fog along the Maine coast, recollections of old campfires began to drift into the March mist, and I thought of the Abnaki Indians of the Algonquin tribe who dwelt near Bangor a thousand years ago.

> In the spring, after the planting of corn, the younger braves and squaws would leave the aged to watch over the crops and the children, and would take their birchbark canoes south for the summer. Down the

Penobscot River they would travel to Blue Hill Bay on the western side of Mount Desert where my family's house, built in part by my great-great-grandfather, Doane Hadlock Hubbard, still stands. It is called the Keep, and I do not know of all else it keeps, but some Indians came ashore to build lean-tos each summer, and a few of their graves are among us, although I do not believe they came to our island to die. Lazing in the rare joys of northern warmth, they must have shucked clams on the flats at low tide and fought and fornicated among the spruce and hemlock when the water was up. What they got drunk on I do not know, unless it was the musk of each other, but many a rocky beach in the first hollow behind the shore sports mounds of ancient clamshells, ground to powder by the centuries, a beach behind the beach to speak of ancient summer frolics. The ghosts of these Indians may no longer pass through our woods, but something of their old sorrows and pleasures joins the air. Mount Desert is more luminous than the rest of Maine.

Given the present state of things American, I suppose one may give a momentary thought to George Walker Bush and his trailing clouds of ancestral glory. But the ghosts of more formidable American predecessors haunt the passage (I hear Thoreau, Melville, Hemingway and Fitzgerald in it) and hold out for the reader a promise that is the promise of art—one not to be easily satisfied by any mere novel.

In one sense, as reviewers have pointed out, the promise is unfulfilled insofar as the novel's art fails to resolve certain issues raised early on. *Harlot's Ghost* consists of two disproportionately related sections. The first, titled "Omega" (the last shall be first, evidently), is just over a hundred pages and located on a day in 1983 when the novel's protagonist Herrick Hubbard (mostly though not always called Harry) is driving back from a liaison in Bath with his mistress, Chloe, to his wife, Kittredge, and their island keep off Mt. Desert. The second section, titled "Alpha," consumes the book's remaining 1200 pages and is an account of Harry's life and times, from private school days and a Yale degree up through his enlistment, training and service in the CIA between 1955 and 1965. Both sections, we are to understand, are manuscripts written by Harry, the second of which ends almost twenty years short of where the first begins. In an italicized concluding note to the reader dated "Moscow, 1984" (Harry has gone there to look for his godfather, Hugh Tremont Montague—the "Harlot" of the title—who may either be dead or have defected to the Soviets), Harry admits that he might never finish "the book of Harry Hubbard and his years in Saigon, nor the stretch of service in the White House when one lived through Watergate, no, nor the commencement of my love affair with Kittredge." (Kittredge was married to Hugh Montague but left him for Harry after her

and Hugh's son was killed in a rock-climbing accident from which the father survived, but in a wheelchair.) So there are lots of loose ends, and the book concludes with the tease, "To be continued."

Behind and not very far behind Harry is of course Norman Mailer who weighs in on page 1284 with an Author's Note in which he tells us that the book was written "with the part of my mind that has lived in the CIA for forty years." He calls his novel "the product of a veteran imagination that has pondered the ambiguous and fascinating moral presence of the Agency in our national life for the last four decades." This mention of four decades takes us back to the beginning of veteran Mailer's literary career, to the publication in 1948 of *The Naked and the Dead,* and to the ensuing books that make up so unusual and controversial a road taken.

In considering the sheer bulk of *Harlot's Ghost,* we remind ourselves that gigantism has always been the keynote of Mailer's imaginative plans for himself. In a preface to his first (unpublished until a 1977 facsimile edition of it) novel, *A Transit to Narcissus,* he notes that even before *The Naked and the Dead* he must have written a million or so words in stories and various drafts of *Transit.* In *Advertisements for Myself* (1959), itself an outrageous and mainly fascinating display of a novelistic ego's demands, his "advertisement" for **"The Man Who Studied Yoga"** divulged plans for the eight-part novel to which **"Yoga"** was prologue. The prologue's hero, Sam Slovoda, would dream eight stages in the travels of a mythical hero, Sergius O'Shaugnessy, "through many worlds, through pleasure, business, communism, church, working class, crime, homosexuality and mysticism." "Not a modest novel," he went on to admit—and not one that was going to get written. After finishing a draft of *The Deer Park* Mailer tells us that he abandoned the scheme; but in the very next paragraph he directs us to fragments later in *Advertisements* which are said to be "from that long novel which has come into my mind again, a descendant of *Moby Dick*" (what else?). One of the fragments referred to is **"The Time of Her Time"** in which Sergius, settled in his Village loft, gives instruction in bullfighting and—in his avocation as self-styled sex saint—initiates Denise Gondelman into the mysteries of the orgasm. The big book of which **"Time"** was to be a part, confided Mailer, would take at least ten years and be, by the standards of 1959, probably unpublishable.

In all their superficial contradictions and inconsistencies, these early extravagant claims are worth noting for the way they bring out a deeper consistency in Mailer's vision of himself and his projection of that self onto a reader. In other words, it was not just in the recent *Ancient Evenings* or in *The Executioner's Song* that Mailer went too far: excess, from the beginning, was of the essence of the scene. But what marks **"The Man Who Studied Yoga,"** and even more

"The Time of Her Time" as important expansive moments in Mailer's literary career, is that each of them in its different way is entertaining. To apply one of Frost's formulations about his own poetry, it feels as though the writer were entertaining ideas (or scenarios or characters) to see if they entertained him. This was a feeling one did not get from Mailer's writing in *The Naked and the Dead* or *Barbary Shore*. For one thing there is more comedy in the shorter pieces: like the story (from **"Yoga"**) about how Cassius O'Shaugnessy unscrewed his navel and the disastrous event it led to (his ass fell off); or like New York City's garbage wars as observed by Sergius (in **"Time"**) when he heads into the Lower East Side to look for help in cleaning up his apartment and encounters a gang of kids at play:

> They were charming, these six-year-olds, as I told my uptown friends, and they used to topple the overloaded garbage cans, strew them through the street, have summer snowball fights with orange peel, coffee grounds, soup bones, slop, they threw the discus by sailing the raw tin rounds from the tops of cans, their pillow fights were with loaded socks of scum, and a debauch was for two of them to scrub a third around the inside of a twenty-gallon pail still warm with the heat of its emptied treasures.

There is an ease and confidence about these supple observings which would animate some of the best writing—fictional or non—Mailer produced in his great decade, the 1960s.

When fiction pays attention to what people eat or what happens to their garbage, human relationships are anchored in homely rather than ethereal circumstances. So food plays a lively role in *Harlot's Ghost* as a handy indicator of character and social milieu. Over the course of the book Harry has a number of good meals at the likes of Harvey's Restaurant and Sans Souci, but occasionally partakes of more humble fare. During his weeks of testing at the CIA's I-J-K-L complex in Washington (prior to the agency's move to Langley, Virginia in 1961), he takes a course in World Communism from a Commie hater named Raymond James ("Ray Jim") Burns:

> On our last night, Bullseye Burns threw a party for our class in his small apartment in a newly built four-story complex of middle-cost housing in the outskirts of Alexandria, Virginia. He had three kids, all boys, all towheads, and I learned on this night that he and his wife were high school sweethearts from Indiana. Mrs. Burns, plain-faced, slab-shaped, served us the casserole dish of cheese and tuna and hot dog relish that had been her party fare for twenty years. (Or, as she called it, her "main-eventer.") It

was obvious that she and Ray Jim barely bothered to speak to each other anymore. . . . I concluded that people like Jim Ray did not quit their marriages until they were feeling inclined to take an ax to their mate.

That casserole has the right slab-like ingredients and harmonizes nicely with the narrator's genial reversing of Ray Jim into Jim Ray. A second passage of cookery is rather more spicy: Harry, now posted to his first assignment in Berlin under the novel's most colorful character (and a historical personage to boot), William King ("King Bill") Harvey, prepares to leave a nightclub called *Die Hintertür* with his German mistress-to-be Ingrid:

> Ingrid was also eating an enormous "Grilled American" of Westphalian ham, tomatoes, and Muenster cheese. I sat down beside her in twitchy detumescence while she slogged down a vast mug of beer, thereby communicating to me in twenty minutes how profoundly one might, over twenty years, come to dislike the eating habits of a mate. Poor Ingrid. The Back Door, as she put it to me with a toothsome grin, never allowed their help enough of food and drink to produce more than a goat turd for the other back door. On this night, therefore, in which my own sphincter had almost played a prominent role, insight came over me at last: I was in the presence of German Humor. *Die Hintertür*. I got it. A nightclub for assholes.

I quote these passages not because they contain anything of special significance to the story and its thematic preoccupations—although Harry's allusion to his sphincter in the second exhibit refers to a proposition rejected earlier that evening from his unscrupulous rogue colleague (and another of the book's best-drawn characters) Dix Butler. They illustrate rather a level of writing, frequent in the book, that in its breezily informal conduct appears to be unashamedly enjoying itself. One thinks again (I do) of Frost asking rhetorically in an interview, "What do I want to communicate but what a *hell* of a good time I had writing it?" Mailer often seems to be having a good time constructing the sentences and paragraphs in *Harlot's Ghost,* and this spirit can be infectious. Despite all the fuss generated by his harping on the largeness of his ambitions—to get into the ring with Tolstoy, write the longest novel or the successor to *Moby Dick*—much of his page-to-page invention takes place with an idiom and material no more elevated than the ones just quoted. Quite simply, they are where most of the action is.

At least two prominent reviews of *Harlot's Ghost* would have us believe that action to be of little consequence. John Simon (*NY Times Book Review,* Sept. 29) rehearsed, step by step, the plot (an old gambit of his) under the assumption that readers would perceive the inherent ludicrousness of Mailer's enterprise. (Plots can be made to look pretty silly when extracted from the novel's prose and displayed to readers who have not yet read the novel.) And Louis Menand, always a sharp-minded critic, behaved in *The New Yorker* (November 4) as if the whole thing were totally misconceived. In Menand's view, Mailer was trying to do ten things at once and had succeeded in finishing none of them. Compared with 1960s Mailer—the writer whom people of Menand's generation read (said he) for an "aggressive and great-souled refusal to cater to sanctimony, whether it was the establishment or the establishment's enemies"—*Harlot's Ghost* was much too easy on the CIA and American foreign policy over the past decades. Mailer's unwillingness to challenge and provoke thus produced a flaccid novel. Menand also complains about the large amount of "Alpha" devoted to letters between Harry—from his various outposts in Berlin, Uruguay (where he works under E. Howard Hunt) and Florida (Bay of Pigs time)—and Kittredge, who herself works for the agency, in exactly what capacity it is not fully clear. "The most disembodied fictional love affair outside *Clarissa,*" Menand calls it.

Mailer often seems to be having a good time constructing the sentences and paragraphs in *Harlot's Ghost,* and this spirit can be infectious.
—William H. Pritchard

Nobody ever wished *Clarissa* longer, but one does keep turning its pages as the warfares and stratagems between men and men, men and women, women and women, unfold. If Mailer can be compared to [Samuel] Richardson, it could just possibly be as a master of narrative, and so much the better for Mailer. (It is also true that, as with *Clarissa,* not all the letters in *Harlot's Ghost* are of equal interest and vitality.) As for Mailer's unwillingness to challenge and provoke, it may have to do with the fact that as he moves toward seventy he finds it harder to take on the loudly aggressive calling-to-court of America's politicians which excited Louis Menand (and others of us) three decades ago. Recall the end of his contribution to a *Partisan Review* statement about Vietnam in which, shockingly, he put forth the possibility that Vietnam was a "happening" staged by Lyndon Johnson because he could not control things at home:

> Cause if it is, Daddy Warbucks, couldn't we have the happening just with the Marines and skip all that indiscriminate roast tit and naked lunch, all those bombed-out ovaries, Mr. J., Mr. L.B.J., Boss Man of Show Biz—I salute you in your White House Oval; I mean America will shoot all over the shithouse wall if this jazz goes on, Jim.

"Jim" indeed! In *Harlot's Ghost* this vivid idiom, put in the service of a rather different politics, characterizes King Bill Harvey: "That's why we go into every skirmish with the KGB under a handicap. That's why we even have to classify the toilet paper in the crap house. We must keep reminding ourselves to enclave the poop." The other figure who talks this way and makes a single, memorable appearance in the book is Lenny Bruce, who addresses a nightclub audience of which harlot, Kittredge and Harry are part: "That first show was terrific, in fact, if I say so myself, it was so good that I came. . . . Yes I came, and now I feel out of it. Ah, fellows, I have to get it up for the second time." Kittredge and her husband are appalled; Harry tells us that he has never heard such laughter in a nightclub before: "Laughs slithered out of people like snakes, tore out of them, barked forth, wheezed forth, screamed out."

We presume Harry is not laughing that way, since typically he is detached and contemplative in his response to excessiveness. His own language and idiom are un-hipsterish, an exception being some hopped-up language in "Omega" where he describes lovemaking with his mistress in Time-of-her-time Maileresque: "With Chloe it was get ready for rush, get ready for the sale, whoo-e, gushers, we'd hit oil together. Recuperating he felt low-down and slimy and rich as the earth. You could grow flowers out of your ass." Throughout "Alpha," by contrast, he is the nice (though Wasp) Jewish boy that has always been one of the parts of Mailer's identity. There is a strategy here: Harry needs to be relatively sane, fearful, prudent, sometimes uncertain, in order to set off in all its weird craziness CIA doings in Berlin, Uruguay (a particularly pointless, far-out bunch of "doings") and Cuba. Louis Menand points out rightly that the agency is Mailer's Circumlocution Office, and surely Dickens may be invoked in connection with this too-long book. After all, how lumbering, badly plotted and sometimes inertly written is *Little Dorrit* in its modest 968 pages. How John Simon might have wished about *Dorrit* that Dickens, like Thomas Wolfe, had had a great editor; how awkwardly Menand would find its different sections to stand in their relationship to one another.

In Carl Rollyson's new and nicely discriminating biography of Mailer, he makes the claim about him that no American writer, not even Hemingway, has "so fused the invention of a literary style with the creation of a writer's identity." The claim is made during a discussion of *Advertisements,* especially **"The White Negro"** and **"The Time of Her Time,"** and it makes sense with respect to those aggressively challenging, sexually and racially combative, efforts. But with *Harlot's Ghost* it is impossible to identify *a* literary style discernible on every page and ascribable to the novel as a whole; or rather let us say that the very inclusiveness of Mailer's narrative voice is such as to accommodate perceptions ranging from the sublime to the ridiculous. To make things further complicated, that voice refuses to provide guidance on how to tell one level from the other. Early in "Omega," Harry's car, on its way back to Mt. Desert, goes into a severe skid just at the moment when its driver remembers how he and Kittredge pledged there would be honesty between them. Fortunately for Harry, it is a three-hundred-sixty degree skid that leaves him still headed for home and "beyond fear":

> I felt as if I had fallen out of a ten-story window, landed in a fireman's net, and was now strolling around in a glow and a daze. "*Millions of creatures,*" I said aloud to the empty car—actually said it aloud!—"*walk the earth unseen, both when we wake and when we sleep,*" after which, trundling along at thirty miles an hour, too weak and exhilarated to stop, I added in salute to the lines just recited, "Milton, *Paradise Lost,*" and thought of how Chloe and I had gotten up from bed in her trailer on the outskirts of Bath a couple of hours ago and had gone for a farewell drink to a cocktail lounge with holes in the stuffing of the red leatherette booths.

From unfallen Adam's voice in Book IV of Milton's poem to the holes in those red leatherette booths is only as far as from the beginning of a sentence to its end, a distance negotiated with no particular fuss by the narrative voice. Unlike the tense polemical thrusts of early Mailer (the writer as bullfighter or boxer or cocksman), this relaxed, expansive voice (all too expansive, detractors would say) can entertain widely different perspectives and not be overwhelmed by them. Like the style of early Mailer, this one is explorative, but in a less threatened and threatening way. You might almost call it mellow. The inclusiveness of range in latest Mailer means that while Harry can rise to heights of spiritual self-definition—as when, a newly-recruited CIA man, he thinks that "Happiness was the resonance one knows in the heart when the ends of oneself come to concordance in the morning air"—he stays enough in touch with earthly things to produce, when the occasion demands it, a good joke:

> "Why won't Baptists," I asked her, "make love standing up?"
>
> "Why won't they?"
>
> "Because people might think they were dancing."

In perhaps the most perceptive review the book has received, Thomas R. Edwards (*New Republic*, Nov. 25) shrewdly suggests that *Harlot's Ghost* invites itself to be thought of as something like religious epic, "Mailer's *Paradise Lost,* as it were, in which the cold war could figure as the War in

Heaven, the Creation, and the Fall." He goes on to note the fusion of sacred and secular levels in various characters from the novel. It should be clear from my own focus that what seems to me the book's major mode of performance is religious epic gone askew, the way CIA operations do; in other words—and since, as Kenneth Burke reminds us, comedy is the literary form which sees human beings as necessarily *mistaken*—this religious epic is a comic one. Edwards concludes his review by quoting Samuel Johnson on *Paradise Lost* in a passage I wish I had found myself but will shamelessly appropriate nonetheless:

> To paint things as they are requires a minute attention, and employs the memory rather than the fancy. Milton's delight was to sport in the wide regions of possibility; reality was a scene too narrow for his mind. He sent his fancies out upon discovery, into worlds where only imagination can travel, and delighted to form new modes of existence, and furnish sentiment and action to superior beings, to trace the councils of hell, or accompany the choirs of heaven.

Edwards notes that these terms have something to do with spying; they also bring out the overweeningness of Milton's and of Mailer's imagination. For both imaginations, reality is a scene too narrow. It is even possible that having Harry remember the Milton line with the word "spiritual" left out (Adam tells Eve in the poem that "Millions of spiritual creatures walk the earth / Unseen, both when we wake and when we sleep") is Mailer's way of de-spiritualizing his religious epic and playing up the comic-grotesque possibilities of spying gone over the edge. In Milton's line, the spiritual creatures behold God's work "with ceaseless praise" both day and night; Mailer's creatures are more equivocal, even just plain strange, and perhaps of the devil's party without knowing it.

Maybe, after all, any modern epic has to be comic and satiric, less like *Paradise Lost* than like Byron's "Vision of Judgment":

> The angels all were singing out of tune
>   And hoarse with having little else to do,
> Excepting to wind up the sun and moon
>   Or curb a runaway young star or two . . .
>
> The guardian seraphs had retired on high,
>   Finding their charges past all care below.

At the end of *Harlot's Ghost* Harry acknowledges that he has not, like Milton, quite risen to the height of his great argument: "Unlike God I have not been able to present all of my creation." For too many years we have observed the critics lamenting Mailer's failure to live up to this or that, his immense talent wasted on various misconceived enterprises, his preoccupation with X when clearly he should have been occupied with Y. My own attitude is closer to Dryden's on Chaucer: if Mailer the novelist fails to live up to God, he still has given us God's plenty.

Robert Merrill (essay date 1992)

SOURCE: *"The Naked and the Dead:* The Beast and the Seer in Man," in *Norman Mailer Revisited,* Twayne Publishers, 1992, pp. 11-29.

[*In the following essay, Merrill explores elements of documentary, social critique, and dramatic action in* The Naked and the Dead. *Upon reevaluation, Merrill concludes that the novel "remains one of Mailer's most impressive achievements."*]

It is often a shock to reread the early work of a writer we have come to admire. The second time around this work usually seems rather thin; we find we have remembered effects that do not exist, values that were never there. Mailer's first novel, *The Naked and the Dead* (1948), is a special example of this phenomenon. To reread Mailer's book is indeed to revise our first impression, but in this case the "revision" is all to Mailer's benefit. What we encounter is a work of enduring power, a power simply incommensurate with the novel's reputation. We find that we have tended to value Mailer's first novel for the wrong reasons: as a guide to combat during World War II, as a work of social criticism, as the best of our recent war novels. *The Naked and the Dead* is all these things, but it is also something quite different and more important. At age 25 Mailer was able to use his military experience as the backbone of a long and complex narrative that transcends the generic boundaries of a "war novel." Forty years later the nature of this achievement is still not generally understood.

Certainly *The Naked and the Dead* is more than the "report" of a sensitive young man who survived active service and returned to tell the tale. Mailer began to plan the novel long before his combat experience at Leytc and Luzon. He has traced its origins to the first days of our participation in World War II: "I may as well confess that by December 8th or 9th of 1941, in the forty-eight hours after Pearl Harbor, while worthy young men were wondering where they could be of aid to the war effort, and practical young men were deciding which branch of service was the surest for landing a safe commission, I was worrying darkly whether it would be more likely that a great war novel would be written about Europe or the Pacific." Much as his General Cummings plans the campaign of Anopopei, the 19-year-old Mailer was already formulating his strategy for a major novel. He had

gone a long way toward fulfilling this ambition before serving a day in the army. While still a student at Harvard Mailer wrote a short novel that can only be considered a trial run for *The Naked and the Dead.* From books published during the war, especially John Hersey's *Into the Valley* and Harry Brown's *A Walk in the Sun,* he got the idea of writing his novel about a long patrol. Indeed, it was this decision that led Mailer to volunteer for service in a reconnaissance outfit. These facts suggest that Mailer went to war in search of combat experience that would enable him to complete a novel he had already conceived. It would be foolish to deny the impact of World War II on the book Mailer finally published, but *The Naked and the Dead* is hardly a transcription of the experiences that came Mailer's way during the war. He seems to have decided rather early that the war could furnish an invaluable *background* for a major novel. His preparation for this work covered a full six years.

Discharged in 1946, Mailer began his book in earnest and saw it published in 1948. From the first it was an enormous popular and critical success. Much as his book was liked, however, Mailer was not given sufficient credit for his *novelistic* abilities. Reviewers tended to assess the book as either a disguised documentary or a work of social criticism. To read the novel in these terms is to minimize Mailer's achievement. It is to overlook what differentiates *The Naked and the Dead* from other major novels of World War II, novels so different as *The Gallery, The Thin Red Line,* and *Catch-22.* Unlike these works, *The Naked and the Dead* is unified by a full-scale dramatic action. Features of Mailer's book suggest the documentary or the work of social criticism, but they are integrated with the novel's dramatic structure and are not its raison d'être. To establish this point should help clarify the real achievement of Mailer's "war novel."

The Novel as Documentary

It may seem naive to read *The Naked and the Dead* as a documentary, but there is a persistent tradition of doing just that. Indeed, many early critics assumed that Mailer's intention was to transcribe the crucial events of his army career—thus, Marvin Mudrick's description of the novel as "a manual of soldiering in the tropics" and Ira Wolfert's opinion that in *The Naked and the Dead* "the most powerful talents developed . . . are those of the journalist. The story is reported. It is not so much a reading of life as a description in depth of an event in life."

Such views may appear reductive, but who would deny that Mailer's concern for verisimilitude often seems obsessive? The intricacies of davit machinery; the mechanics of tent building; the aspect of a rotting corpse; the effects of a long, sustained march through jungle—virtually everything in the novel is rendered in elaborate, professional detail, as Mailer follows an army platoon through the several stages of a Pacific campaign. Nor is this practice merely a matter of itemizing the paraphernalia of army life. Repeatedly, Mailer employs his "phenomenal talent for recording the precise look and feel of things" to illumine the conditions his characters must suffer. Nor is he less convincing when dealing with his fictional campaign as a whole. When looking over the shoulder of General Cummings and analyzing the progress of the campaign, Mailer achieves the authority of a retired army officer dictating his memoirs.

But of course Mailer is not dictating memoirs, his own or his characters'. Though many of the novel's episodes derive from his personal experiences, Mailer insists that we should not read the book in this fashion: "In the author's eyes, *The Naked and the Dead* is not a realistic documentary; it is, rather, a symbolic book, of which the theme is the conflict between the beast and the seer in man. The number of events experienced by the one platoon couldn't possibly have happened to any one army platoon in the war, but represent a composite view of the Pacific war" (*Current Biography*). Mailer does not deny that "the book will stand or fall as a realistic novel." What he rejects is a simplistic connection between the novel's techniques and its formal ends. Mailer adopts the realistic conventions of most twentieth-century American fiction, but realistic techniques do not point unerringly to the formal aims of a "realistic documentary." Besides referring to *The Naked and the Dead* as a "symbolic" book, Mailer insists that he is neither a realist nor a naturalist: "That terrible word 'naturalism.' It was my literary heritage—the things I learned from [John] Dos Passos and Farrell. I took naturally to it, that's the way one wrote a book. But I really was off on a mystic kick. Actually—a funny thing—the biggest influence on *Naked* was *Moby Dick*." A book whose aspirations suggest those of *Moby-Dick* should not be discussed as a documentary, "realistic" or otherwise.

The novel's symbolism is one feature that transcends the limits of a documentary, but more important still is the story told. Some of the enormous detail in this book may be attributed to Mailer's indulgence of his special knowledge of war; certain episodes and characters contribute little except as they add to Mailer's "description in depth of an event in life." But Mailer usually manages to relate whatever he describes to the novel's elaborate dramatic action. The conditions on Anopopei, Mailer's mythical Pacific island; the routine of army life; the many actions forced on the men—these things are always seen in relation to the characters and their developing conflicts. Contrast the resulting effect with that of James Jones's *The Thin Red Line* (1962), a work that might truly be called a realistic documentary.

The Thin Red Line resembles Mailer's novel in many obvious ways. It too describes the campaign for a single Pacific island (in this case, Guadalcanal). Like Mailer, Jones observes every facet of the campaign, from the initial landing to the mopping up. Like Mailer, Jones employs the literary device of the microcosm as he follows a representative group of men (C-for-Charley-Company) throughout the campaign. Yet the two books are not really similar, as Mailer himself suggests when he aptly describes *The Thin Red Line* as "so broad and true a portrait of combat that it could be used as a textbook at the Infantry School if the Army is any less chicken than it used to be." He goes to the heart of Jones's intentions: "Jones' aim, after all, is not to create character but the feel of combat, the psychology of men." For Mailer, "*The Naked and the Dead* is concerned more with characters than military action"—and so he cannot see that his book is truly comparable to *The Thin Red Line*.

Mailer's comments are very much to the point. His novel differs from Jones's in that its central concern is to develop its many characters. Jones's characters might as well go unnamed, so little difference does it make who they are or what they do except at the moment Jones happens to use them to illustrate an aspect of combat. Nothing in *The Thin Red Line* is comparable to Mailer's gradual development of the conflicts among his major characters. No effort is made to prepare for shifts in the action. In fact, there is no dramatic action in *The Thin Red Line*. As Mailer suggests, Jones is not interested in such an action; his intentions correspond to those Mudrick and Wolfert attribute to Mailer. By contrast, *The Naked and the Dead* is rooted in the traditional development of character through a structured series of episodes. We must judge its documentary features as they do or do not serve in this development.

The Novel as Social Critique

Much the same argument applies to elements of social criticism in *The Naked and the Dead*. The existence of such elements is obvious: the criticism of the army as an institution that informs every incident in the novel; the attack on totalitarianism that emerges from the discussions between General Cummings and his aide, Lieutenant Hearn; the grim portrait of American society developed through the I and R platoon, especially in the "Time Machine" biographies of eight enlisted men and two officers (Cummings and Hearn). Yet we must still ask how these features function in the novel as a whole.

Before we assess their function, however, we should first understand the nature of Mailer's social criticism. Far too often *The Naked and the Dead* is treated as the work of a "young liberal" whose critique of American society is substantially the same as that of Dos Passos, [James T.] Farrell, and [John] Steinbeck. Prior to World War II Mailer was, in his own words, a "progressive-liberal." And in 1948, *after* finishing *The Naked and the Dead* and traveling through Europe, Mailer did join the campaign for Henry Wallace.

Nonetheless, *The Naked and the Dead* is not the work of a political liberal. In *Advertisements for Myself* Mailer suggests that his early short novel, "A Calculus at Heaven," makes "an interesting contrast to *The Naked and the Dead,* for it is an attempt of the imagination (aided and warped by books, movies, war correspondents, and the liberal mentality) to guess what war might really be like." That the novella was determined in part by "the liberal mentality" certainly makes it an interesting contrast to *The Naked and the Dead,* for we have his own word for it that when he wrote his first published novel Mailer was an anarchist, not a liberal.

Far too often *The Naked and the Dead* is treated as the work of a "young liberal" whose critique of American society is substantially the same as that of Dos Passos, [James T.] Farrell, and [John] Steinbeck.
—*Robert Merrill*

This difference helps to explain some common misreadings of the later work. Standard critical procedure goes something like this: first, the critic assumes that *The Naked and the Dead* is a thesis novel and that its thesis resembles those expounded by writers such as Dos Passos, for Mailer's "sympathies" are also progressive; then the critic finds that the novel's action does not consistently support the presumed liberal thesis and so either points out Mailer's failures of execution or begins to talk about trusting the tale and not the teller. This procedure involves at least two fallacies: (a) that *The Naked and the Dead* is a thesis novel and (b) that Mailer uses the book to advance liberal values and a liberal social critique. I will return to these problems after considering the novel's action, where I hope to show that what seems inconsistent or weak to the reader who takes Mailer's liberalism for granted is nothing of the sort if we approach the novel without this presupposition. Here I would simply stress that Mailer did not write his novel to do the work of a sociologist.

Mailer's social vision does emerge during the novel, especially in those sections which trace the men's backgrounds, but his characters are not "examples" in a sociological tract. Consider the "Time Machine" sections. If *The Naked and the Dead* were really a thesis novel, these biographies would function as evidence in Mailer's "argument" concerning the American social scene; however, I think Barry Leeds suggests the real relation between the biographies and the rest of the novel:

> Thus, while *The Time Machine* is used to portray the home of a Midwestern businessman, the slums

of Boston, or Harvard Yard, it is the presence on Anopopei of men who have experienced these places, which justifies Mailer's detailed treatment of them, and obviates the possibility of their introduction seeming stilted. Every element of American society dealt with becomes integral to the novel as a whole, not merely because it seems to fit into a re-creation of that society, but because it is drawn from the life of a character in whom the reader has come to believe.

The "Time Machine" may be a laborious device to enrich our experience with the men on Anopopei, but that is its function. Although Leeds cites Martinez, he might have mentioned any number of other characters. When Gallagher learns of his wife's death, for example, he becomes an important figure in the novel for the first time. At this point Mailer introduces a "Time Machine" section on Gallagher's Boston-Irish background, his training in frustrated prejudice. Just as we first see Gallagher as fully human, stunned by the loss of his wife, Mailer highlights his ignorance and bigotry. Paradoxically, we are all the more impressed by Gallagher's intense feeling for his wife. He becomes a more complex and interesting character than would have been possible had his biography or his mourning been presented alone. Thus, Mailer uses the "Time Machine" to illuminate character, introducing the device at just that moment in the narrative when it best supplements the novel's action.

The "Time Machine" differs, then, from similar devices in the works of John Dos Passos. The "Camera Eye," "Newsreel," and biography sections in *U.S.A.,* for example, are clearly intended to complement the narrative in the manner of a thesis novel. These sections are not directly related to the narrative; they do not even concern its characters. Instead, they are determined by and substantiate Dos Passos's attack on the American social system. Mailer's use of a similar device is for a quite different end. The "Time Machine" sections are intended to comment on each character's role in the action. When this does not happen—as in the belated "Time Machine" passage devoted to Polack, a figure of no real significance—the reader is likely to find the material digressive, even intrusive. Mailer's novel differs from Dos Passos's trilogy in its use of social elements to clarify a dramatic action, not a social argument.

The Novel as Dramatic Action

I am suggesting that *The Naked and the Dead* is a rather traditional novel. This is not meant as criticism of the book. If it lacks the stylistic and formal innovations of Mailer's more recent novels, especially *An American Dream* (1965), *Why Are We in Vietnam?* (1967), and *Ancient Evenings* (1983), *The Naked and the Dead* is nonetheless a more successful work. It is successful in its adaptation of a novelistic form we can trace from Richardson and Fielding down to Mailer's immediate precursors, Hemingway and Faulkner. This form emphasizes character and action—staples of fiction as central to *The Naked and the Dead* as they are to the novels of Austen and Dickens. Interpretation should begin with precisely these features.

It may seem rather harmless to argue that *The Naked and the Dead* is essentially "a novel of character," as John Aldridge first suggested and Mailer once confirmed. In fact, however, there are fairly important consequences if we accept this idea. Indeed, we will probably have to reject the more popular interpretations of Mailer's novel. Consider Randall Waldron's "case" against Mailer's conclusion:

> The central conflict in *The Naked and the Dead* is between the mechanistic forces of "the system" and the will to individual integrity. Commanding General Cummings, brilliant and ruthless evangel of fascist power and control, and ironhanded, hardnosed Sergeant Croft personify the machine. Opposing them in the attempt to maintain personal dignity and identity are Cummings' confused young aide, Lieutenant Hearn, and Private Valsen, rebellious member of Croft's platoon. Mailer fails to bring this conflict to any satisfying resolution: at the novel's end Hearn is dead and Valsen's stubborn pride defeated, but likewise Croft is beaten and humiliated and Cummings' personal ambitions thwarted.... [T]he conclusion of *The Naked and the Dead* and its total meaning are unclear.

Like Norman Podhoretz and John Aldridge, Waldron dislikes Mailer's ending because it fails to generate the radical "protest" presumably intended. Waldron obviously expects the book to end as this kind of thesis novel is supposed to end—with a clear demarcation between victim and victimizer. Again like Podhoretz and Aldridge, he assumes that Mailer conceived the book as a warning against totalitarian tendencies in America and cannot see that Mailer achieves this purpose by treating his villains in the same manner as his heroes.

But why assume that Mailer intended to write a protest novel? If we make this assumption, the novel's ending—indeed, the coherence of the whole work—is called into question. We would at least expect Mailer to distinguish among his characters sufficiently to clarify his own moral position and to articulate his "warning." As Waldron remarks, Mailer "fails" to do this. My own view is that he never intended to do so. If we stop treating Cummings, Croft, Hearn, and Valsen as representative figures in a political allegory, we should come to see that Mailer prepares all along for the ending Waldron and others find so disappointing. In examining *The Naked and the Dead* as a dramatic action we should

not only make sense of what others find "unclear" but also get at the true sources of the novel's power.

Mailer's published remarks on the composition of his novel tend to confirm that he did not organize it around a political or social "thesis." Mailer says that from the first he wanted to structure his book around a long patrol involving a single army platoon. It seems likely that he first intended to write a collective novel in the manner of Dos Passos, using the patrol to examine under stress a group of men broadly representative of American society. While he does something like this in the published novel, Mailer reveals that his book changed as he completed the second draft. It changed because he chose to develop two characters outside the platoon, General Cummings and Lieutenant Hearn: "The part about the platoon went well from the beginning, but the Lieutenant and the General in the first draft were stock characters. If it had been published at that point the book would have been considered an interesting war novel with some good scenes, no more. The second draft was the bonus. Cummings and Hearn were done in the second draft." As Mailer suggests, the fleshing out of Cummings and Hearn "made" his novel as a work of art. Mailer patterned their relationship after the conflict between Croft and Valsen, the leading members of the platoon and presumably the main characters in the initial draft. *The Naked and the Dead* came more and more to deal with these four major figures; it began to take on the full dimensions of a novel of character.

Mailer's two plot lines are sufficiently similar they might almost be considered a double plot. In each case a character of liberal sympathies fights for his integrity against a fascistic superior; in each the "good" character is defeated while the "bad" character fails in his most ambitious undertaking. Whereas Croft's tactics against Valsen are openly sadistic, Cummings exercises an intellectual tyranny over Hearn. Finally, however, this is a minor distinction, for the results are indistinguishable. These conflicts are reminiscent of much "protest" literature with which *The Naked and the Dead* is often compared. Cummings and Croft seem prototype fascists, the villains of scores of proletarian novels; Hearn and Valsen seem the archetypal victims of such novels. If we take a closer look, however, we should discover subtleties appropriate to Mailer's overall design.

Initially, the feud between Croft and Valsen seems a simple matter of irreconcilable personalities. Certainly this is our impression in part 1, where Croft and Valsen nearly come to blows in a scene that is repeated with variations throughout the novel, until their quarrel is resolved on Mount Anaka. Their "roles" are fixed this early: Croft as the aggressive platoon leader; Red as the recalcitrant private who resists authority and authoritarians. Red is presented from the outset as a proud but rather ineffectual man who is capable of feeling "a sad compassion in which one seems to understand everything, all that men want and fail to get," but who has no hope of translating his feelings into action: "Everything is crapped up, everything is phony, everything curdles when you touch it." Both his compassion for others and his personal cynicism define Red as Croft's opposite. Croft is an obvious, even a spectacular sadist. As a National Guardsman he kills a striker for no other reason than the pleasure it gives him. On Anopopei he tantalizes a Japanese prisoner with kindness before shooting him in the head, crushes a small bird in his bare hand, and coldly arranges the death of Hearn. Croft loves combat, for only in combat does he find release from his hatred of the world (his "Time Machine" section concludes, "I HATE EVERYTHING WHICH IS NOT IN MYSELF." Croft must master everything that is not in himself. He is confident that he can do so, for "he had a deep unspoken belief that whatever made things happen was on his side."

Yet Croft and Valsen are not mere foils, as Mailer reveals in the first half of part 2. This section of the novel moves toward two separate "moments of truth," one experienced by Croft and the other by Valsen. The first such moment climaxes Mailer's account of the Japanese counterattack, a performance as fine as anything in the book. Here we see Croft in his natural element, the violence of war. He controls his men so fiercely that he revives Valsen's hatred. Indeed, he treats the weaknesses of others as if they were personal enemies. Yet the climax of this episode is Croft's moment of *fear*—more precisely, his awareness that he too can be made afraid. This recognition sends "a terrible rage working through his weary body," and its effects are felt through the rest of the novel, until Croft's rage is expended against Mount Anaka.

The second climactic moment occurs when the men go to search Japanese bodies for souvenirs. This hunt is a nightmare, revealing, in Chester Eisinger's words, "the deepest urge toward violence and debasement in human beings." Red finds it oppressive because he must pass through piles of rotting bodies. The stench is overpowering, the corpses horribly distorted and maggot-ridden. Suddenly Red is "sober and very weary." Unlike the others, Red understands that he is surrounded by the bodies of *men*. Standing over one such body, he experiences a kind of epiphany: "Very deep inside himself he was thinking that this was a man who had once wanted things, and the thought of his own death was always a little unbelievable to him. The man had had a childhood, a youth and a young manhood, and there had been dreams and memories, Red was realizing with surprise and shock, as if he were looking at a corpse for the first time, that a man was really a very fragile thing." Different as Croft and Valsen are, their climactic insights in part 2 are quite similar. Each discovers that "a man was really a very fragile thing." They differ, of course, in how they respond to this discovery: Croft tries to exorcise it through violence, while Red accepts it with a "wise" melancholy. This section of the

book is structured to reveal the common anxieties underlying their radically different approaches to life.

In the second half of part 2 Mailer develops an even more complex antagonism. Prior to the represented action Cummings more or less adopts Hearn as his protégé. He sees in Hearn an intellectual equal and a sympathetic ear for his theories about the nature of power. When Hearn responds to the general's attentions with something less than gratitude, his fate is to illustrate Cummings's first principle: "There's one thing about power. It can flow only from the top down. When there are little surges of resistance at the middle levels, it merely calls for more power to be directed downward, to burn it out." Throughout the book we see Cummings trying to "burn out" Hearn's resistance. The conflict here seems quite straightforward. Indeed, critics often refer to Hearn as Mailer's liberal spokesman. Hearn's resistance to Cummings is supposed to represent Mailer's own political feelings and to justify Hearn's role as the novel's "hero."

The problem is that Hearn represents not so much liberalism as the *desire* to be liberal. Surely he is an odd humanitarian: he likes few people, he is a self-confessed snob, and he feels distaste for Jews and a "trace of contempt" for the enlisted man. Temperamentally, Hearn is an aristocrat. It is not surprising that he defends his liberal notions with faint conviction, for his real commitment is to himself: "The only thing that had been important was to let no one in any ultimate issue ever violate your integrity." Hearn would protect his "inviolate freedom" and so avoid "all the wants and sores that caught up everybody about him." His motto is appropriately sterile: "The only thing to do is to get by on style." Defined by his detachment, his distance from real human concerns, Hearn is best known by his failures to act.

Because he feels no real commitment to his humanitarian interests, Hearn is vulnerable to the same urges that move Cummings and Croft. Hearn is fascinated by Cummings, who has the ability "to extend his thoughts into immediate and effective action," because Hearn is drawn to power himself: "Always there was the power that leaped at you, invited you." Resentment of his position vis-à-vis Cummings mingles with his desire to be like Cummings: "he had acquiesced in the dog-role, had even had the dog's dream, carefully submerged, of someday equaling the master." Hearn comes to believe that "divorced of all the environmental trappings, all the confused and misleading attitudes he had absorbed, he was basically like Cummings." He even comes to fear that "when he searched himself he was just another Croft."

What Hearn fears is that he is no less a fascist than Cummings or Croft. But even Cummings is more complex than this might suggest. A self-styled "reactionary," Cummings prefers fascism to communism because "it's grounded firmly in men's actual natures." To say the least,

Cummings has no high opinion of man's nature. He thinks Hitler "the interpreter of twentieth-century man" and believes "there's never a man who can swear to his own innocence. We're all guilty, that's the truth." But, of course, Cummings does not see himself as he sees others. Indeed, he has a mystical sense of his own destiny: "The fact that you're holding the gun and the other man is not is no accident. It's a product of everything you've achieved, it assumes that you're . . . you're aware enough, you have the gun when you need it." Cummings views himself as the man with the gun. He is speaking of himself, not "man," when he says that "man is in transit between brute and God."

Cummings's vanity is immense, his ambitions worthy of Ahab. We learn early that his intention on Anopopei is to "mold" his troops, the terrain, and even "the circuits of chance" to the contours of his will. Confident that he can dispose of any obstacle, natural or human, Cummings believes that life is like a game of chess. But his rationality is a disguise, as Mailer makes clear by exposing the real forces at work on Cummings; self-pity amounting to paranoia, and homosexuality. As the novel unfolds we learn that Cummings is no closer to harmonizing "Plant and Phantom," body and spirit, than are the men of Croft's platoon, or Hearn.

During part 2, then, we come to see the novel's central conflicts as rather more ambiguous than they appeared at first; in each case the antagonists have more in common than we might have supposed. This is made especially clear in part 3, in which the four major figures all suffer a remarkably similar fate. As noted earlier, each "good" character is defeated by his totalitarian opponent. Hearn is the victim of both Cummings and Croft, for Cummings transfers Hearn into a platoon already selected for a dangerous mission and Croft deliberately plots Hearn's death. Red's defeat is not fatal, but it is no less decisive. A man committed to nothing except his own personal integrity, Red is so beaten down he feels relief after he confronts Croft and is defeated: "At the base of his shame was an added guilt. He was glad it was over, glad the long contest with Croft was finished, and he could obey orders with submission, without feeling that he must resist."

Yet if they triumph over Hearn and Valsen, Cummings and Croft are hardly the novel's "victors." Throughout part 3 Croft's efforts are directed toward conquering Mount Anaka, the great mountain that towers over Anopopei, "taunting" Croft with its "purity" and "austerity." The mountain becomes for Croft what his troops are for Cummings: the "other" that resists his control and must be molded to serve his will. Like Cummings, however, Croft is unable to control the circuits of chance. When he stumbles over a hornets' nest, the men flee down the mountain and the march abruptly ends. Croft is left puzzled and spent; "Croft kept looking at the mountain. He had lost it, had missed some

tantalizing revelation of himself. Of himself and much more. Of life. Everything." This passage recalls the single section devoted to Cummings in part 3. Faced with "mass inertia or the inertia of the masses," the men's resistance to his more grandiose ambitions, Cummings is unable to find a meaningful pattern among the forces at work in the campaign: "There was order but he could not reduce it to the form of a single curve. Things eluded him." Like Croft, Cummings must finally give the circuits of chance their due. He attempts with his final attack what Croft attempts on Mount Anaka, but the campaign ends in manner he could never anticipate (the inept Major Dalleson, not Cummings, engineers the final assault). Cummings must admit that "he had had very little or perhaps nothing at all to do with this victory, or indeed any victory." For Cummings too there comes the knowledge of personal limitation.

As noted previously, Mailer is often criticized for refusing to create ideologically satisfying characters. The assumption here is that Mailer wrote his book to "defend liberalism," to warn against the antiliberal forces within the American system. But Mailer has made it clear that he "intended" something quite different—something that might even *require* the treatment of character we find in *The Naked and the Dead.* Mailer says that he conceived the book as "a parable about the movement of man through history"; he defines its basic theme as "the conflict between the beast and the seer in man" (*Current Biography*). It would seem that for Mailer the movement of man through history is an ongoing struggle between the bestial and the visionary forces in man himself. This idea is not terribly original, of course, but the power of *The Naked and the Dead* depends not on the originality of its ideas but on how well they are embodied in the novel's characters and events.

Moreover, Mailer's ideas are not as schematic as I may have suggested. Unlike the typical proletarian or social novel, *The Naked and the Dead* does not present its beasts and seers in obvious counterpoint. If Croft is set against Valsen in the book, who is the beast and who is the seer? The epigraph to part 3 is relevant here: "Even the wisest among you is only a disharmony and hybrid of plant and phantom. But do I bid you become phantoms and plants?" This rhetorical question implies that man should be neither "plant" nor "phantom" exclusively; neither all body nor all soul; neither beast nor seer. Man should seek harmony between the physical and the spiritual, though, as Nietzsche observes, even the wisest among us is a "disharmony and hybrid." This is certainly true of the major figures in *The Naked and the Dead,* each of whom carries within himself Nietzsche's bestial and visionary forces. The ultimate effect of Mailer's parallel plots is to emphasize this "disharmony" in each character. When Cummings and Croft suffer defeats comparable to those of Hearn and Valsen, we should realize that Mailer rejects a crude contrast between good and evil. In dramatizing the conflict between the beast and the seer in man, Mailer shows that *all* his characters are subject to the same conflict.

Surely Mailer establishes this kinship between Cummings and Croft. Both are power moralists who rely on fear and hatred in their command of others; both are inordinately ambitious; both function as Hearn's enemy and plan to have him killed. Each is "coldly efficient," latently homosexual, and obsessed with his wife's infidelity. They share an extreme individualism that is coupled with a strong sense of personal destiny. For Cummings, "the fact that you're holding the gun and the other man is not is no accident"; for Croft, "if a man gets wounded, it's his own goddam fault"— if Cummings sees himself as the man with the gun, Croft sees himself as the man who will never be wounded. Cummings and Croft are most alike in their common rejection of accident or chance as a determining force in life. Cummings's ambition is nothing less than to mold the circuits of chance, while Croft has "a deep unspoken belief that whatever made things happen was on his side." Each possesses a naive faith that he can work his will on the world.

In their rejection of determinism Cummings and Croft almost justify Podhoretz's suggestion that they are the novel's "natural heroes." While Hearn and Valsen suggest vacillation and futility, Cummings and Croft are all energy and commitment. "Natural heroes" is a bit much, however. We should not see Cummings and Croft as mere villains, but neither should we equate Mailer's admiration for certain qualities in Croft with, say, admiration for the character as a whole. In response to the question "Whom do you hate?" Mailer once answered, "People who have power and no compassion, that is, no simple human understanding." Can we fail to apply this statement to Cummings and Croft?

What prevents these characters from being purely hateful is what Mailer calls their "vision." Croft is moved by a "crude unformed vision," and Cummings is driven by "one great vision," momentarily embodied when he observes his first battlefield and experiences "the largest vision that has ever entered his soul": "There were all those men, and there had been someone above them, ordering them, changing perhaps forever the fiber of their lives. . . . *There were things one could do.*" As he surveys the battlefield Cummings is "choked with the intensity of his emotion, the rage, the undefined and mighty hunger." This hunger is Croft's crude unformed vision; this rage is Croft's "rage" at the frustrations of the final patrol. Moreover, the vision these men share is no mean one. As we have seen, Cummings's greatest urge is to be omnipotent; Croft too is tantalized by "vistas of such omnipotence he must wonder at his own audacity." The common spirit that links Cummings and Croft is unmistakable. In one sense they are the novel's "seers": confident of the world's tractability, they are determined to achieve destinies commensurate with their mighty hungers.

Unfortunately, Cummings and Croft are also the novel's principal "beasts." There is nothing so despicable in *The Naked and the Dead* as Croft's calculated destruction of the lame bird discovered by one of the men, and Cummings is subject to the same impulses, as we learn when he comes upon a cigarette Hearn has put out on his floor: "If he had been holding an animal in his hands at that instant he would have strangled it." Hearn discovers early in the book that Cummings is capable of atrocities as great as any Croft will later commit. Behind the general's "facade" is that naked animal closeted with its bone. The naked animal in Cummings finds expression in his power morality, his persecution and finally his execution of Hearn. The conflict between the beast and the seer in man is precisely conflict within both Cummings and Hearn. The urges that move them are *both* bestial and visionary.

> **It is one of the novel's many ironies that Hearn is nonetheless the one character who achieves even a limited dignity. In *The Naked and the Dead* there is no correlation at all between goodness and the fruits thereof.**
> **—*Robert Merrill***

In his portraits of Hearn and Valsen, Mailer further undermines the "structure of protest" readers have expected of him. To achieve such protest, Mailer needed to depict Hearn and Valsen as more or less admirable figures victimized by the representatives of an unjust society. But of course he presents them in a very different light. Whereas Cummings believes that "in the Army the idea of individual personality is just a hindrance," Hearn and Valsen have no commitment except to their individual personalities. Both place the highest value on what Hearn calls "inviolate freedom." They ask nothing more specific from life, because they also share contempt for what life offers: Red's "particular blend of pessimism and fatalism" is everywhere evident, while Hearn believes that "if you searched something long enough, it always turned to dirt." Because they have found so little to value in life, Hearn and Valsen have lived as drifters. Unlike Red, Hearn has not literally been a hobo, but his lifestyle might easily be mistaken for Valsen's: "Get potted, get screwed, and get up in the morning, somehow." Hearn and Valsen are confirmed in their pessimism by what happens to them on Anopopei. Each is made to struggle for his inviolate freedom; each concludes that "there were no answers" in this struggle. The repetition of this exact phrase emphasizes that neither Hearn nor Valsen discovers a sustaining belief. In both men the qualities of the seer are blunted.

We tend to think of Hearn and Valsen in relation to their enemies, but this contrast can be misleading. Hearn discovers in himself many of the qualities that unite Cummings and Croft. Both Hearn and Cummings are "born in the aristocracy of the wealthy midwestern family"; both have domineering fathers who force them into "masculine" activities (boys' camps and athletics for Hearn; military school for Cummings); both become "cold rather than shy" and suffer a displaced sex life (like Cummings, Hearn "fights out battles with himself" on the bodies of his women). During a football game Hearn experiences "an instant of complete startling gratification when he knew the ball carrier was helpless, waiting to be hit"—a clear enough parallel to Croft's sadism. The connection between Hearn and Croft is most obvious during the patrol, where each man tries to redeem his failure early in the campaign and Hearn comes to think of himself as "another Croft."

Although Red does not so clearly resemble Cummings, interesting similarities exist. When the campaign begins to go badly, Cummings undergoes "the amazement and terror of a driver who finds his machine directing itself, starting and halting when *it* desires." This event echoes Red's discovery of "a pattern where there shouldn't be one" after the death of a young soldier. Red's kinship with Croft has already been suggested. Once he is defeated by Croft, Red finds that he is happy to obey orders without feeling he must resist. When the march up Mount Anaka ends, Croft experiences much the same emotion: "Deep inside himself, Croft was relieved that he had not been able to climb the mountain. . . . Croft was rested by the unadmitted knowledge that he had found a limit to his hunger." Once their ambitions are thwarted, Cummings and Croft do not seem altogether different from even Red Valsen.

Does the resemblance among these characters "humanize" Cummings and Croft or "expose" Hearn and Valsen? The answer must of course be *both*. Cummings and Croft are not entirely reprehensible; Hearn and Valsen are not quite admirable. The whole action is directed toward these ironic judgments. "Only connect," Forster advised, but none of the major characters is able to balance the beast and the seer within himself. What Red lacks in energy and purpose Croft lacks in compassion and the ability to expand his unformed vision beyond the need for power. It is much the same with Hearn and Cummings. Hearn would seem to be the one most likely to connect the warring forces in himself, but Hearn is perhaps the most incomplete of the major figures. Neither Hearn's sympathies nor his desire for power are ultimately authentic. It is one of the novel's many ironies that Hearn is nonetheless the one character who achieves even a limited dignity. In *The Naked and the Dead* there is no correlation at all between goodness and the fruits thereof.

Even as he dramatizes their conflicts Mailer hints that his characters are basically alike. This does not evidence moral

or aesthetic confusion; instead, it makes possible Mailer's rather terrible commentary on his creations. At the end he collapses their several fates into a single fate—disillusionment—and confirms what has been implicit throughout: man is a "disharmony," "corrupted, confused to the point of helplessness," and the world he inherits has no sympathy for his weakness. Croft and Valsen may seem polar opposites, but whether they seek power or personal freedom they are doomed to a common failure. Their apparently different desires represent what Mailer once insisted we see in all his characters: "yearnings for a better world." Mailer does not mock these desires; indeed, nothing else redeems Cummings and Croft even slightly. What he does is show how nearly impossible it is to realize such "yearnings."

Mailer does this in a work that engages our feelings in the manner of all great novels. His primary purpose is not to document the experience of combat or the failure of our political system but to create a dramatic action that embodies more universal concerns. The result is a dark but moving image of the human condition. This image is one Mailer will never again present so starkly in his fiction; indeed, all his subsequent works can be seen as attempts to qualify or even to disavow the bleak implications of his first novel. The "truth" of this image is not really in question, however. What matters is Mailer's success in fleshing out the elaborate dramatic action that unifies his book. A novel of character in the best sense of that phrase, *The Naked and the Dead* remains one of Mailer's most impressive achievements.

Michael Kimmelman (review date 15 October 1995)

SOURCE: "Tough Guys Don't Paint," in *The New York Times Book Review,* October 15, 1995, p. 16.

[*In the following review, Kimmelman provides a generally unfavorable assessment of* Portrait of Picasso, *citing incidents of unsubstantiated speculation and Mailer's failure to break new ground on the subject of the celebrated artist.*]

He has "a greedy desire for recognition," and "the vanity and the need for group applause of someone like Muhammad Ali." When young, he pushed "his explorations into sex, drugs," and had a lengthy affair that was one of "those delicate, lovely and exploratory romances that flourished like sensuous flowers on slender stems, those marijuana romances of the 50's and 60's in America where lovers found ultimates in a one-night stand, and on occasion stayed together." "Short in stature," "possessed of the ambition to mine universes of the mind no one had yet explored," he was "not macho so much as an acolyte of machismo." He "could not box."

Norman Mailer on Norman Mailer? Not this time, though it's obvious why Mr. Mailer, whose prime subject has always been himself, might have spent more than three decades contemplating a biography of Pablo Picasso. On the other hand, it's not so easy to comprehend why, after all that time, he has come up with such a clumsy and disappointing book, culled, at starting lengths, from already existing biographies. With so many out there, most notably Volume 1 of John Richardson's monumental "Life of Picasso," which covers nearly the same early years, one wonders what Mr. Mailer could have been thinking.

The book, his 29th, is a copiously illustrated account of the span from the artist's birth in 1881 to the start of World War I. Picasso emerges in a familiar guise, as a selfish, superstitious, sometimes cowardly and combative prodigy who moved chameleonlike from one style to another, through one relationship after the next. Mr. Mailer has called his work "an interpretive biography," to distinguish it from a work of original scholarship. This is fair enough, but most of the interpretations are not original.

For instance, Mr. Mailer is not the first to suggest, on the basis of no compelling evidence, that Picasso might have had a homosexual encounter or two as a young man. That dubious honor goes to Arianna Stassinopoulos Huffington in her reckless "Picasso: Creator and Destroyer." Who cares one way or another, you might well ask, whether he had such an encounter? But like a dog with a bone, Mr. Mailer takes hold and won't let go. What is noteworthy about his book may be the vigor with which he pursues sensationalistic subjects like this one even while affecting a dispassion toward them. About a self-portrait drawing from 1902-3, for instance, in which Picasso stands with one hand raised, the other over his heart, Mr. Mailer writes: "One can make too large a case of the nude he did of himself in this period—modest, unadorned, a little seedy, certainly depressed, and taking the vow of allegiance to . . . to what? To his continuing heterosexuality? It is tempting to read too much into this drawing."

Apparently.

What Mr. Mailer ignores is that Picasso at the time was hoping to establish his reputation with large-scale, multifigure allegorical compositions, many of which were never undertaken. This self-portrait could be a preparatory drawing for an unrealized work, or possibly one for "La Vie" (1903). "La Vie," as Mr. Mailer knows, derives from studies Picasso drew of himself making various ambiguous gestures. The gestures, as Mr. Richardson has pointed out, relate to images on tarot cards, which fascinated Picasso. It may be that the self-portrait Mr. Mailer refers to is better explained in terms of Picasso's other works than by random speculation about his sex life.

Mr. Mailer also becomes fixated on the androgyny of the hulking proto-Cubist figures Picasso painted in 1906, connecting them to Gertrude Stein, whose portrait the artist was then painting. Mr. Mailer's remarks on the subject are worth quoting at length, to give a feel for his prose: "It is safe to assume that Gertrude Stein was the most monumental crossover in gender that he had ever encountered. He had to be knowing about this. With Fernande [Olivier, Picasso's mistress], he had entered the essential ambiguity of deep sex, where one's masculinity or femininity is forever turning into its opposite, so that a phallus, once emplaced within a vagina, can become more aware of the vagina than its own phallitude—that is to say, one is, at the moment, a vagina as much as a phallus, or for a woman vice versa, a phallus just so much as a vagina: at such moments, no matter one's physical appearance, one has, in the depths of sex, crossed over into androgyny. Picasso was obsessed with the subject."

Leave aside for the moment the paradox of Mr. Mailer's twisted syntax in a book that takes art historians and critics to task for their writing. The basic fact is that Mr. Mailer says Stein influenced Picasso's art. So she did, and Picasso even incorporated an image of a man into her portrait. But scholars have pointed all this out already: Mr. Mailer is appropriating their ideas just to indulge in the sort of grandiose flourishes that are a trademark of his style. In any case, it becomes hard to weigh Stein's significance because other obvious influences on Picasso—like the large women in the works of Renoir and Maillol—are glossed over or missed. Mr. Mailer is so enraptured by the affairs of the artist's life that he regularly plays down the connections between Picasso's works and those of other artists. To be sure, he isn't alone in this. Picasso has largely been written about in terms of his biography. The exception is his Cubist period, and Mr. Mailer is right in this case to lament the "near impenetrability" of so much of the critical jargon attending it. "Cubism is not a form of lovemaking with the lights out: Cubism is compelling because it is eerie, resonant and full of the uneasy recognition that time itself is being called into question," he writes. "Some of the paintings, if we dare to entertain the vision, have the appearance of corpses, their flesh in strips and tatters, organs open."

Again, Mr. Mailer isn't the first to speculate about the emotional impact of Cubism's fractured imagery, but this is a provocative and minority viewpoint, and unfortunately he does not take it further. The collaboration of Picasso and Braque on the creation of Cubism is almost unparalleled in art history, and it would seem to have afforded Mr. Mailer a vast psychological field in which to let his imagination play. What is one to think of a man like Picasso, he might have asked, who on the verge of success suddenly chose to make difficult pictures virtually indistinguishable from someone else's? But Mr. Mailer ignores this question to hop on an old hobbyhorse: in life, he writes, "Braque had legitimate machismo," but in art he "cannot often come off like Picasso. Machismo, obviously, has its mansions and no one was going to be more macho than Picasso when it came to painting." So much for their profound and complex association.

Mr. Mailer's principal sources are Fernande Olivier's colorful memoirs, *Picasso and His Friends* (1933) and *Souvenirs Intimes* (written in 1955 and published posthumously in 1988). Olivier lived with Picasso from 1905 until 1912. She has said that she kept diaries at the time and that her memoirs derived from them. Still, these are books written as much as 43 years after the fact, and by a former lover, which brings to mind the French saying about trying to pull the sheets to one's own side of the bed.

Mr. Mailer acknowledges the problem, fretting over it himself, but relies on her stories anyway. They provide some of the book's freshest material, to be sure, since "Souvenirs Intimes" has not yet been published in English. But one should expect more of a work like this than that it translates someone else's memoirs.

And with this subject in particular, one expects more of Mr. Mailer. There is a tremendous sense of opportunity missed. He of all people would seem equipped to write a vivid and original book about Picasso, since he shares with the artist, if not the same degree of talent, then the characteristics of a long public career, prolific output, Rolodex of styles, sexual fixation, narcissism, will to power and compunction to parlay his own life into art.

Mr. Mailer's career, for better and worse, has been a project of self-mythology—assuming greatness by proxy. And his willingness to rationalize away Picasso's disregard for, even violence toward. lovers and friends will ring a bell with readers of such Mailer classics as *The Naked and the Dead* and **"The White Negro."** But the links between him and Picasso must be gleaned with some effort from the book. If anything, Mr. Mailer doesn't put enough of himself into it, relying on the idiosyncrasy of his prose to carry readers along. Picasso, who had no patience for art criticism, once praised Jean Genet's writing on Giacometti, which was personal and self-exploratory. It is the type of writing one hopes for from Mr. Mailer—more like *The Armies of the Night,* with its blend of intense self-scrutiny and reportage, and less like his cut-and-paste *Marilyn.* Mr. Mailer might have written a more distinctive book about Picasso if he had observed his own maxim: "It's impossible to truly comprehend others until one's plumbed the bottom of certain obsessions about oneself."

Joan Didion (essay date 6 October 1996)

SOURCE: "Let's Do It," in *The New York Times Book Review,* October 6, 1996, p. 94.

[*In the following review, Didion offers high praise for* The Executioner's Song, *which she describes as "an absolutely astonishing book."*]

It is one of those testimonies to the tenacity of self-regard in the literary life that large numbers of people remain persuaded that Norman Mailer is no better than their reading of him. They condescend to him, they dismiss his most original work in favor of the more literal and predictable rhythms of *The Armies of the Night;* they regard *The Naked and the Dead* as a promise later broken and every book since as a quick turn for his creditors, a stalling action, a spangled substitute, tarted up to deceive, for the "big book" he cannot write. In fact he has written this "big book" at least three times now. He wrote it the first time in 1955 with *The Deer Park* and he wrote it a second time in 1965 with *An American Dream* and he wrote it a third time in 1967 with *Why Are We in Vietnam?* and now, with *The Executioner's Song,* he has probably written it a fourth.

I think no one but Mailer could have dared this book. The authentic Western voice, the voice heard in *The Executioner's Song,* is one heard often in life but only rarely in literature, the reason being that to truly know the West is to lack all will to write it down.

—Joan Didion

The Executioner's Song did not suggest, in its inception, the book it became. It began as a project put together by Lawrence Schiller, the photographer and producer who several years before had contracted with Mailer to write *Marilyn,* and it was widely referred to as "the Gary Gilmore book." This "Gary Gilmore book" of Mailer's was understood in a general way to be an account of or a contemplation on the death or the life or the last nine months in the life of Gary Mark Gilmore, those nine months representing the period between the day in April of 1976 when he was released from the United States Penitentiary at Marion, Illinois, and the morning in January of 1977 on which he was executed by having four shots fired into his heart at the Utah State Prison at Point of the Mountain, Utah.

It seemed one of those lives in which the narrative would yield no further meaning. Gary Gilmore had been in and out of prison, mostly in, for 22 of his 36 years. Gary Gilmore had a highly developed kind of con style that caught the national imagination. "Unless it's a joke or something, I want to go ahead and do it," Gary Gilmore said when he refused legal efforts to reverse the jury's verdict of death on felony murder. "Let's do it," Gary Gilmore said in the moments before the hood was lowered and the muzzles of the rifles emerged from the executioner's blind.

What Mailer could make of this apparently intractable material was unclear. It might well have been only another test hole in a field he had drilled before, a few further reflections on murder as an existential act, an appropriation for himself of the book he invented for *An American Dream,* Stephen Rojack's "The psychology of the Hangman." Instead Mailer wrote a novel, a thousand-page novel in a meticulously limited vocabulary and a voice as flat as the horizon, a novel which takes for its incident and characters real events in the lives of real people.

I think no one but Mailer could have dared this book. The authentic Western voice, the voice heard in *The Executioner's Song,* is one heard often in life but only rarely in literature, the reason being that to truly know the West is to lack all will to write it down. The very subject of *The Executioner's Song* is that vast emptiness at the center of the Western experience, a nihilism antithetical not only to literature but to most other forms of human endeavor, a dread so close to zero that human voices fade out, trail off, like skywriting.

In a world in which every road runs into the desert or the Interstate or the Rocky Mountains, people develop a pretty precarious sense of their place in the larger scheme. People get sick for love, think they want to die for love, shoot up the town for love, and then they move away, move on, forget the face. People commit their daughters, and move to Midway Island. People get in their cars at night and drive across two states to get a beer, see about a loan on a pickup, keep from going crazy because crazy people get committed again, and can no longer get in their cars and drive across two states to get a beer.

The Executioner's Song is structured in two long symphonic movements: "Western Voices," or Book One, voices which are most strongly voices of women, and "Eastern Voices," Book Two, voices which are not literally those of Easterners but are largely those of men—the voices of the lawyers, the prosecutors, the reporters, the people who move in the larger world and believe that they can influence events. The "Western" book is a fatalistic drift, a tension, and overwhelming and passive rush toward the inevitable events that will end in Gary Gilmore's death. The "Eastern" book is the release of that tension, the resolution, the playing out of the execution, the active sequence that effectively ends on the January morning when Lawrence Schiller goes up in a six-seat plane and watches as Gary Gilmore's ashes are let loose from a plastic bag to blow over Provo. The bag surprises

Schiller. The bag is a bread bag, "with the printing from the bread company clearly on it . . . a 59-cent loaf of bread."

The women in the "Western" book are surprised by very little. They do not on the whole believe that events can be influenced. A kind of desolate wind seems to blow through the lives of these women in *The Executioner's Song,* all these women who have dealings with Gary Gilmore from the April night when he lands in town with his black plastic penitentiary shoes until the day in January when he is just ash blowing over Provo. The wind seems to blow away memory, balance. The sensation of falling is constant. Nicole Baker, still trying at 19 to "digest her life, her three marriages, her two kids, and more guys than you wanted to count," plus Gary Gilmore, plus Gary Gilmore's insistence that she meet him beyond the grave, reads a letter from Gary in prison and the words go "in and out of her head like a wind blowing off the top of the world."

These women move in and out of paying attention to events, of noticing their own fate. They seem distracted by bad dreams, by some dim apprehension of this well of dread, this "unhappiness at the bottom of things." Inside Bessie Gilmore's trailer south of the Portland city line, down a four-lane avenue of bars and eateries and discount stores and a gas station with a World War II surplus Boeing bomber fixed above the pumps, there is a sense that Bessie can describe only as "a suction-type feeling." She fears disintegration. She wonders where the houses in which she once lived have gone, she wonders about her husband being gone, her children gone, the 78 cousins she knew in Provo scattered and gone and maybe in the ground. She wonders if, when Gary goes, they would "all descend another step into that pit where they gave up searching for one another." She has no sense of "how much was her fault; and how much was the fault of the ongoing world that ground along like iron-banded wagon wheels in the prairie grass." When I read this, I remembered that the tracks made by the wagon wheels are still visible from the air over Utah, like the footprints made on the moon. This is an absolutely astonishing book.

Frank Kermode (review date 15 May 1997)

SOURCE: "Advertisements for Himself," in *The New York Times Book Review,* May 15, 1997, pp. 4, 6-8.

[*In the following review, Kermode offers a favorable assessment of* The Gospel According to the Son, *which he concludes is "a book of considerable intellectual force."*]

To read the surviving ancient examples of apocryphal gospels is to see how impressive the canonical ones usually are. The apocrypha, sometimes clever, sometimes silly, try to elaborate or continue those originals, thus following, with varying degrees of irresponsibility, the example of the Evangelists themselves. All manner of strange things are said to have happened to Judas; for instance, that the silver he gained by treachery he lost by gambling. Pilate, converted to Christianity, may seek to persuade the emperor Tiberius of the divinity of Christ, and even be accepted as a saint. Such things occur in apocryphal gospels. Norman Mailer has added to the genre a modern example that is clever but not silly. And in one respect it breaks new ground: it is the first, so far as I know, to be attributed to Jesus himself, a gospel-autobiography, no less, of the Son of God.

Each of the four canonical Gospels has a Passion narrative offering an orderly historical account of the last days of Jesus in Jerusalem. These narratives are by no means identical, but they resemble one another closely enough to suggest that they all base their variations on the same lost predecessor, an earlier written report of those last days. Discrepancies between them have to be explained by the doctrinal preferences of the communities for whom the Evangelists were writing, and by the predispositions of the writers themselves.

Events in the life of Jesus prior to the last visit to Jerusalem are much less coherently described and can hardly be said to constitute a narrative at all. The reports are presumably based on oral collections of sayings, miracles, and parables, with a few, mostly perfunctory, indications suggesting where Jesus was from time to time—in Capernaum, revisiting Nazareth, going back and forth across the Sea of Galilee, and finally moving into Jerusalem for the climax. Here John, lacking their common adherence to Mark, is widely different from Matthew and Luke, and not only because of discourses he attributes to Jesus that they know nothing about. For example, he describes several visits to Jerusalem before the final one they all describe.

This is more plausible than the single visit allowed by the other three, since it explains why Jesus and the disciples, normally working in Galilee, had friends in and around the city. But John, who on the whole offers the most connected account of Jesus' career, can no more than the others provide a straightforward narrative of the pre-Passion ministry. Like Mark, he has nothing whatever to say about the birth, childhood, and youth of his hero, whereas Luke and Matthew provide rather elaborate but disparate accounts of the Annunciation and the Nativity. Luke takes most care to provide some sort of historical context to the early part of the life, for instance explaining the winter journey to Bethlehem as made necessary by a new Roman taxation policy. He also provides John the Baptist, said to be a cousin of Jesus, with his parallel nativity story, and alone sends the boy Jesus to lecture in the Temple.

Final agreement about the interrelations of the different versions is unlikely ever to be achieved, but most scholars still seem to accept that of the first three Gospels (called "Synoptic") the shortest, Mark, came first; that Matthew and Luke used him as a basis, augmenting his account (though this theory is much contested) with material from another source (the hypothetical collection of sayings known as Q). Each of them must also have had access to some material peculiar to himself.

These conjectures are offered in explanation of the palpable similarities between the three Gospels and also of their deviations and disagreements. Indeed the learned have been at work for centuries either demonstrating the "harmony" of the three versions or explaining how they came to be dissonant. The unlearned have been content with an uncritical mishmash, sometimes preferring Luke (in whose version the Annunciation is made, as tradition assumes it was, to Mary, although in Matthew the angel addresses Joseph) but sometimes mingling both (Matthew's wise men *and* Luke's shepherds). The narrative of the interim between the Nativity and the Passion is likewise marked by concords and discords, stringing together in different ways traditions about journeys and parables and teachings, but in no case suggesting a definite progression. What is certain is that a later biographer of Jesus has more usable source material in the Passion story than in what comes before it.

So Norman Mailer, conscious of the source problem and conscious also of the chutzpah involved in his manner of solving it, decided to retell the whole story as a posthumous autobiography of Jesus, who could of course be represented as an authority on the facts of his early life. His Jesus starts off by being highly critical of the Gospels, accusing them of exaggeration and even of mendacity; he complains that they attribute to him words he never said; and play down his anger, which he thinks important. "Their words were written many years after I was gone and only repeat what old men told them. Very old men. Such tales are to be leaned on no more than a bush that tears free from its roots and blows about in the wind." The Evangelists, he considers, were more concerned with enlarging or strengthening their own congregations than with the truth, which he will now provide. This attitude may seem a shade ungrateful when you reflect that those despised Gospels are virtually his only source, but Mailer's Jesus is capable of being angry and unreasonable, and of course knows what later scholarship has to say about the situations and motives of the Gospel writers. With his author's help he can correct those flawed reports and make clear what he really did, thought, and said.

"What you get," says Mailer of the Gospels in an interesting interview in his publisher's house magazine, "is some pretty dull prose and a contradictory, almost hopeless way of telling the story. So I thought this account, this wonderful narrative, ought to be properly told." And unlike his apostolic predecessors he can claim to be a much practiced and experienced storyteller, a lifelong student of the possibilities of novelistic narrative, more sensitive to the interaction of plot and character than they could possibly be.

Inevitably he has much the same trouble as they had in giving Jesus a plausible itinerary during the Galilean years, but the authority vested in his narrator is such that he can adapt, explain, qualify, or reject their versions at will. In doing so he can hardly avoid, and indeed makes little attempt to avoid, infusing Jesus with a strong dose of Mailer, so the book is in some measure another self-advertisement. In that same interview he suggests that one reason for accepting this "dare" was that he himself has "a *slight* understanding of what it's like to be half a man and half something else, something larger." He means that the celebrity of *The Naked and the Dead* caused him, from twenty-five on, to lead a double life, as a famous person and as his "simple self," the former role giving him a power he hasn't always known how to use well; which was a problem also, he suggests, for Jesus, who was likewise half one thing and half another.

But Mailer's Satan [in *The Gospel According to the Son*] ensures that Jesus is not without sin; he experiences lust, which by his own ruling is adultery in the heart, and also vengeful anger. He is rarely quite sure what it means to be both a man and the son of God, and occasionally needs and receives divine warnings.
—*Frank Kermode*

There is something attractive about this blend of self-analysis and self-confidence. "If I can write about Isis and Osiris and Ra," he argues, "then certainly the New Testament is not going to be that difficult to do." And having worked on Oswald and Picasso and Marilyn Monroe must have been a help, too. Of course he had on this unusual occasion to make experiments in quest of an appropriate style, avoiding the archaism of the King James translation but equally declining any uninhibited exhibition of that wonderfully agile, muscular, personal prose that made *The Armies of the Night* in particular incomparable in its kind. After a lot of work on this problem of decorum he invented his own serviceable version of what Eric Auerbach called *sermo humilis,* a lowly style, the very style the Evangelists wrote their Greek in; a simple, everyday manner that is faintly, appropriately, archaic as well. Thus equipped, he was able to apply his novelistic skills to a superior rendering of the story.

In addition to the advantage conferred by these skills Mailer could claim another of comparable importance. He seems to have had, until quite recently, very little interest in the New Testament, but was turned on to it by some remarks of the present Pope about "a fourth world which included all the underprivileged who lived among the two superpowers, particularly in America with our homeless." Reading the New Testament, he found it "curious in the extreme." And once he began the examination of the gospel story, this powerful "myth," as he calls it, he also felt it an advantage to be a Jew, and so in sympathy with a Jesus who was no longer, as he had been to earlier generations of American Jews, an enemy or renegade, but a good man. "Whatever else Jesus was, he was that . . . I became very fond of him." And to portray a good man may well be the greatest challenge a novelist can face.

Although he offers rational explanations for some of the miracles, Mailer obviously saw no need to explain away all these and other supernatural occurrences, such as faith healings and "mighty works" generally, since by nominating Jesus as the author of the book he was accepting as a *donnée* the greatest miracle of all. So he takes miracles as they come—warning that they are less important than the teachings, sometimes scolding the Evangelists for exaggeration, but usually leaving the substance of the stories intact or even embellishing them. He explains the miracle of the feeding of the five thousand by saying that Jesus broke the loaves and fishes into very small pieces and dished out the crumbs one by one, with a sort of sacramental effect. (Like Mark, he includes two feedings, one a close copy of the other—a redundancy noticed and corrected by Matthew.)

Naturally he comments as he chooses on the miracles. After the little daughter of Jairus has been raised from the dead, or from a coma, he speculates that the child cannot have been happy to be reinserted in a house torn by marital discord. There is nothing to that effect in the Gospels, so perhaps here as elsewhere the author is expressing personal discomfort at the idea of bodily resurrection—and a sense that nobody concerned is likely to be overjoyed about it. When the blind man on the road to Bethsaida has his sight restored he exclaims that he sees "men like trees walking"—a fine instance of Marcan idiosyncrasy, but Mailer, like many a commentator before him, feels the need of an allegory when confronted by an oddity: "That is because men, like trees, bear a fruit of good and evil."

The youthful Jesus is portrayed working as an apprentice to his father the carpenter (plenty of verisimilar technical information on wood and tools), reading the scrolls of Ezekiel and Isaiah, which he will later freely quote, and experiencing for the first time on record a serious childhood illness (some of its effects seem to linger on in the later career). Also for the first time, he is seen to brood sadly over Herod's Slaughter of the Innocents, a massacre attributable to his birth, and perhaps an instance of that tragic mismanagement of which Mailer's God is guilty on other occasions. This is midrash, and Mailer has a talent for midrash, explanatory extension or updating of existing stories (a talent novelists need); for example, he retells the story of the pregnant Elizabeth, whose babe leaps in the womb when the Virgin arrives on a visit. Luke does not say that the fetus had been without life until that moment, but Mailer does; it is a good touch, one more small miracle and in these exceptional circumstances nothing out of the way.

The Temptation in the Wilderness is a critical event in the Synoptics; John knows nothing about it, and in his plot the miracle at Cana has to serve as an equivalent threshold experience. Mailer puts both in. The Temptation, described in one charged verse by Mark, but at greater length by the others, especially Luke, is further expanded by Mailer. He makes the devil seem rather like Adolphe Menjou or perhaps George Sanders in some old movie, a blend of delicately perfumed politeness and sinister fecal underscent. Jesus of course withstands his temptations, but doesn't emerge entirely clean; he loses something by this diabolical contact, retaining a certain "fealty" to Satan, a certain slight complicity with evil. When Luke said Jesus underwent "all the temptations," commentators thought he meant all possible temptations, an interpretation that gave comfort when supported by a text from the Epistle to the Hebrews: "For we have not an high priest which cannot be touched with the feeling of our infirmities; but was in all points tempted like as we are, yet without sin."

But Mailer's Satan ensures that Jesus is not without sin; he experiences lust, which by his own ruling is adultery in the heart, and also vengeful anger. He is rarely quite sure what it means to be both a man and the son of God, and occasionally needs and receives divine warnings. "When you are without Me, the Devil is your companion." He wonders why he was chosen, and why he was tempted, just as he wonders why he has to die. During the Crucifixion he asks whether God is all powerful. "Even as I asked . . . I heard my own answer: God, my father, was one god. But there were others. If I had failed Him, so had He failed me. Such was now my knowledge of good and evil. Was it for that reason that I was on the cross?" And later: "My Father was only doing what He could do. Even as I had done what I could do. . . . Had His efforts for me been so great that now He was exhausted?"

The subtlest notion here is that God-given power in a man can be wasted or exhausted, as it was wasted in that trivial first miracle at Cana, and exhausted when the hemorrhaging woman surreptitiously touched Jesus' robe. Such failures of power become a major theme of the novel. Even God's power is not adequate to his good intentions; he can be defeated, as in Herod's massacre, and in the Holocaust. The point is ultimately theological; it is impossible to recount this

myth without implying a theology and a fore-understanding, as Mailer knew when he took it on. So for him "human" implies "fallible," and a human son of God may suffer from God's weakness as well as his own.

He tries hard to do justice to other doctrines—his Pharisees are good in religious debate, sometimes too good for Jesus. But they are, finally, disagreeable figures with their hypocritical made-up minds and their extravagant cult of cleanliness. So there is a natural bias toward the views of Jesus, who actually seems much more human in preferring the unclean company of sinners and drinkers. Mailer even suggests that Jesus had a fondness for the gay men he came across in Capernaum, seemingly taking the merest hint from Matthew (11:23-24) that such people existed there: "And thou, Capernaum . . . shall be brought down to hell. . . . It shall be more tolerable for the land of Sodom, in the day of judgment, than for thee." Thus an anathema, in itself a shade pharisaical, is converted into an expression of unpharisaical liberality.

In spite of the condemnation of the Evangelists as inaccurate and self-serving, quite large tracts of their writing are left more or less undisturbed, for instance Matthew's Sermon on the Mount. The best place to look for novelistic invention is in the treatment of characters. Jesus' mother, for instance, is characterized as both modest and vain, proud of her son and his origin but thinking him unready to go out into the world; having brought him up in an ascetic Essene community, she would prefer him just to go on being a good God-fearing and woman fearing Essene boy and perhaps eventually join the Qumran community. So there is tension between mother and son. Mark had emphasized the difficulty Jesus experienced when returning to his home town (he could not do any "mighty works" there, though Matthew considerately altered this to "many mighty works"), and Mailer takes this up, suggesting that Jesus' hurtful rhetorical question "Who is my mother?" had left him with a bad conscience about her.

Lazarus, though unknown to the Synoptics, plays an important part in John's story, and it is interesting to compare what the two writers make of him. His return to life from the tomb is here announced by the odor of rotting corpse; the Pharisees would be repelled by this new uncleanness. Lazarus himself is not unequivocally pleased to be restored to life. The smell of the corpse is in John's version, and so is the alarm of the authorities—the High Priest fears that this especially mighty work may win popular support for the Galilean, with consequent disturbances, all too likely to be severely repressed by the Romans.

But the sadness of Lazarus is new, and so are Jesus's doubts about whether this was a good thing to have done. John's Jesus had a double response to his friend's sickness and death; he claims divinity in his encounter with Lazarus's sister Martha (through this illness "God's glory is to be revealed and the Son of God glorified"); but after Lazarus dies, he weeps, humanly, at his meeting with his other sister, Mary. The human yields to the divine: the raising of Lazarus, a solemn parody of birth or rebirth, justifies the claim "I am the resurrection and the life." In this episode, and in the anointing of Jesus by Mary, John is completely out of touch with the Synoptics; he is on his own and manifestly a very powerful writer. Mailer reduces the complexity of the episode by preferring to use the story of the anointing in a quite different context, as the Synoptics do. What he chooses to tell of Lazarus he tells impressively; but in this head-to-head storytelling contest John seems to be the victor.

In his treatment of Pilate (he releases Barabbas for a bribe, is deeply cynical in the philosophical debate with Jesus) Mailer is again adapting John, as other apocryphal gospels had done before him, and here with more success. He has an understandable preference for John as the best of the tellers, but again deserts him, making the Last Supper a Passover meal. John had wanted to place it the night before, so that the Crucifixion would coincide with the killing of the Passover lambs. On such occasions the redactor has to choose, and either choice has its points; any redaction of the story is going to involve loss as well as the hoped-for gain. For example, Mailer rejects Mark's thrillingly unexpected "I am" (his Jesus' first proclamation of divinity, made at the moment when Peter was denying him) in reply to the High Priest's demand to know whether he is the son of God. Mailer chooses the tamer response recorded by Matthew and Luke ("I am what you say"; or "So you say"). It is a loss.

Apart from the central figure the novelist devotes most of his inventive power to Judas. Like others before him, he is unwilling to dismiss Judas as a petty thief and traitor. His Judas is a fiery, intelligent, rather worldly disciple, who knows about corrupt dealings between the Jewish priesthood and the Roman occupiers, and is always skeptical about some of the dominical claims. Mailer invents for him an important conversation with Jesus, who senses that he is dangerous but continues to love him. This Judas is above all devoted to the poor, and is shocked when his protest against the waste of money on ointment prompts the reply "The poor you have always with you." It is because of this betrayal of what for him is the true cause that Judas turns against his master. Jesus himself feels guilty at having put his honor and ease above the needs of the poor; and he will not condemn Judas for condemning him. These are new and novelistically plausible interpretations.

Other personalities (Peter and Thomas, for instance) are virtually unchanged from the Gospel accounts, but Mailer has a special interest in Levi the publican (a tax collector in Roman employ and usually known as Matthew), supposing him to have been called to discipleship despite his odious occupation because he looked cheerful, perhaps because he was streetwise, liked his drink, and was acquainted with vice. Such men are the readier to repent and least like the Pharisees. Nearly all of this is pure invention.

The colt on which Jesus rides into Jerusalem is, in this new version, unbroken, restive, requiring to be subdued. Since Luke records that this was an animal "whereon yet never man sat," this is a legitimate addition to the original, but it conflicts with the image of a Messiah entering not in glory but mounted on a humble farm animal, an ass's colt; so the interpretation gains a small and persuasive detail but loses a big idea. One amusement offered by this novel is this: deciding whether a particular midrashic extension is reasonable and does as much good as harm. Mailer's are usually explicable, but one left me baffled: John's unnamed Beloved Disciple, whom Jesus addressed from the Cross, is here, without explanation or apparent reason, called Timothy, not the name of any of the Twelve as they are listed by the Synoptics (e.g., Mark 14:13) but of a younger man years later, a Greek-Jewish companion and helper of Paul's. Other identifications have, of course, been proposed—John himself, for instance, and Lazarus; even the latter seems more plausible than Mailer's choice.

In the process of augmentation Jesus is given several uncanonical sayings which sound more like Mailer than Jesus: "It is natural to mourn for oneself"; "No heart is so hard as the timid heart"; "The destruction of each man is to be found in the pity he saves for himself"; "A man of small mind develops a hard shell so that he can protect his small thoughts." Whether these sayings can be called plausible depends largely on how convincing this Jesus is as a Mailerian character. "I am the Son of God yet also a man," he says, and as a man he has many faults: he makes too many promises, is sometimes confused, sometimes reacts too quickly, is sometimes too clever by half, is sometimes caught in two minds. He experiences fear, desires vengeance, has lascivious reveries, is attracted by sinners, and has fits of rage. The doctrine of the incarnation requires that he be a man in all ways, yet also without sin, like Adam before the Fall—a god willingly but sinlessly sustaining the whole burden of humanity. Mailer makes Jesus too human for that, seizing on every moment of wrath and belligerence recorded by the Evangelists and adding more. This Jesus is not perfect. An angel in a dream quotes to him John's line: "God so loved the world that He gave His only begotten Son . . ." and his response is "How I hoped that the angel spoke truth!" He is the son of God, though never quite sure of it.

His mission is a failure, in part because Satan was right about the way all men (and the Church) would turn to the worship of Mammon, partly because, contrary to report, his Father in heaven, who sent him, isn't perfect, either. Mailer sees

God as doing his best, but still suffering some crushing defeats. This view is, approximately, Manichean, dualist; Satan is still powerful in the world. This is one reason why the poor we have always with us. There is no overt theological discussion: Mailer is not interested in lucubrations on such problems, and his very partial theodicy amounts only to saying that God is doing his not wholly adequate best. The writer's powerful mind works in a specialized way, not by theological argumentation but by telling or retelling a story. The result is (for once) a short book, a book of considerable intellectual force. Having accepted the "dare," Mailer can make a fair claim to have come honorably close to winning it.

FURTHER READING

Criticism

Algeo, Ann M. "Mailer's *The Executioner's Song.*" In her *The Courtroom as Forum: Homicide Trials by Dreiser, Wright, Capote, and Mailer,* pp. 105-40. New York: Peter Lang, 1996.
    Examines the major themes and presentation of *The Executioner's Song.*

Barnes, Annette. "Norman Mailer: A Prisoner of Sex." *Massachusetts Review* 13 (1972): 269-74.
    Provides critical analysis of Mailer's essay "The Prisoner of Sex."

Mellard, James M. "Origins, Language, and the Constitution of Reality: Norman Mailer's *Ancient Evenings.*" In *Traditions, Voices, and Dreams: The American Novel since the 1960s,* edited by Melvin J. Friedman and Ben Siegel, pp. 131-49. Newark, DE: University of Delaware Press, 1995.
    Examines the significance of Mailer's concern for origins and language in *Ancient Evenings,* especially in relation to postmodern literary criticism.

Merrill, Robert. "*The Armies of the Night*: The Education of Norman Mailer." *Illinois Quarterly,* 37, No. 1 (1974): 30-44.
    Examines the major themes, presentation, and Mailer's narrative voice in *The Armies of the Night.*

Merrill, Robert. "Mailer's *Tough Guys Don't Dance* and the Detective Traditions." *Critique: Studies in Contemporary Fiction,* XXXIV, No. 4 (Summer 1993): 232-46.
    Discusses the plot, major themes, and literary merit of *Tough Guys Don't Dance* in relation to Mailer's previous fiction.

Olster, Stacey. "Norman Mailer after Forty Years." *Michigan Quarterly Review* 28, No. 3 (Summer 1989): 400-16.
    Provides an overview of Mailer's literary career, major works, and critical reception.

Stone, Robert. "The Loser's Loser." *The New York Times Review of Books* (22 June 1995): 7-10.
    Generally favorable review of *Oswald's Tale.*

Additional coverage of Mailer's life and career is contained in the following sources published by Gale: *Contemporary Authors,* **Vols. 9-12R;** *Contemporary Authors New Revision Series,* **Vol. 28;** *Discovering Authors; Discovering Authors: British; Discovering Authors: Canadian; Discovering Authors Modules: Most Studied Authors, Novelists,* **and** *Popular Fiction and Genre Authors; Dictionary of Literary Biography,* **Vols. 2, 16, 28, 80, and 83; and** *Major Twentieth Century Writers.*

Sylvia Plath
1932-1963

(Also wrote under pseudonym Victoria Lucas) American poet, short story writer, diarist, radio dramatist, and novelist.

The following entry presents an overview of Plath's career through 1996. For further information on her life and works, see *CLC*, Volumes 1, 2, 3, 5, 9, 11, 14, 17, 50, 51, and 62.

INTRODUCTION

Sylvia Plath is renowned as one of the most powerful American poets of the postwar period. Her acclaimed poetry and prose are characterized by intense self-consciousness, accusatory despair, and disquieting expressions of futility and frustration. A complicated literary personality whose biography is nearly impossible to disentangle from her writing, Plath is frequently regarded as a confessional poet, though her deeply personal lamentations often achieve universality through mythic allusion and archetypal symbolism. Viewed as a cathartic response to her divided personae as an artist, mother, and wife, Plath's vivid and often shocking verse reveals the psychological torment associated with feelings of alienation, inadequacy, and abandonment. Her semi-autobiographic novel *The Bell Jar* (1963) and highly charged verse in *The Colossus* (1960) and *Ariel* (1965) won widespread critical appreciation and continue to attract scholarly analysis. The posthumous publication of her poetry in *The Collected Poems* (1981) was awarded a Pulitzer Prize in 1982. Since her tragic death, Plath has inspired a generation of women writers and feminist critics as a leading voice against female subordination and passivity in modern society. A poet of remarkable force and ability, Plath exerted an indelible influence on American literature as a self-possessed visionary and casualty of her art.

Biographical Information

Born in Boston, Massachusetts, Plath was the eldest child of Aurelia and Otto Emil, a German-born professor at Boston University who authored a notable treatise on bumblebees. An undiagnosed diabetic, Otto died in 1940 after complications resulting from surgery to amputate his leg. Upon her husband's death, Aurelia secured a teaching position at Boston University where she trained medical secretaries. Shaken by the loss of her father, Plath took an early interest in creative writing and began to publish poetry and short fiction in various magazines, including *Seventeen* and the *Christian Science Monitor*. A precocious and highly mo-

tivated student, Plath attended Smith College on a scholarship beginning in 1950. There she continued to win academic distinctions and was selected in 1953 to serve as a student editor for *Mademoiselle* magazine in New York City. During the same year, she lapsed into an episode of severe depression, culminating in a suicide attempt for which she was hospitalized and treated with electroshock therapy. Under psychiatric care, Plath returned to Smith College the following year, completed an honors thesis on Fedor Dostoevsky's fiction, and graduated *summa cum laude* with a degree in English in 1955. The next fall Plath set off for Cambridge, England, to attend Newnham College on a Fulbright Scholarship. While overseas, she met poet Ted Hughes, whom she married in June of 1956. After completing her master's degree at Cambridge in 1957, Plath settled with Hughes in the United States where she taught English at Smith College and worked briefly as a medical secretary at a Massachusetts psychiatric clinic. Plath attended a poetry workshop with Robert Lowell at Boston University in 1958 and spent several months at the Yaddo writing colony in New York the following summer. In 1959 Plath and Hughes returned to England where she gave birth to their first child, Frieda

Rebecca. Plath published *The Colossus,* her first book of poetry, in October of 1960. After recovering from a miscarriage and appendectomy in 1961, Plath was awarded a Eugene F. Saxon fellowship and began work on *The Bell Jar,* which appeared in 1963 under the pseudonym Victoria Lucas. Several months after the birth of their second child, Nicholas Farrar, in 1962, Plath and Hughes separated as a result of Hughes's infidelities. After a failed reconciliation, Plath moved to a London apartment with her two children where she became increasingly depressed and despondent, although it was at this time that she produced some of her finest poetry. Her sense of isolation was exacerbated by an unusually harsh winter, nagging illnesses, and the strain of single parenthood. In February of 1963, Plath took her own life by inhaling gas from her kitchen stove. Several posthumous volumes of Plath's poetry appeared over the next two decades, including *Crossing the Water* (1971), *Winter Trees* (1971), and the Pulitzer prize-winning *The Collected Poems*—all compiled under the editorship of Hughes. Further biographical information concerning Plath's life appeared in *Letters Home* (1975), a volume of Plath's personal correspondence published by Aurelia Plath, *Johnny Panic and the Bible of Dreams* (1977), a collection of Plath's prose writings and diary excerpts, and *The Journals of Sylvia Plath* (1983).

Major Works

Plath's poetry and fiction are well-known for their intensity and ubiquitous incorporation of personal detail. *The Bell Jar,* Plath's only novel, is perhaps the most explicitly autobiographical, as it recounts events surrounding Plath's internship with *Mademoiselle* and subsequent nervous breakdown. The protagonist is Esther Greenwood, a nineteen-year-old college student whose intellectual talents and professional ambitions are frustrated by disillusionment and mental collapse following a summer in New York City as an intern for a woman's magazine. While in Manhattan, Esther quickly becomes dissatisfied with her superficial work as a fashion writer and struggles to develop her self-identity in opposition to conventional female roles. After strained encounters with several men, including one who physically abuses her, she throws her clothes into the street from the top of her apartment building and returns home, where she falls into a deep depression and eventually attempts suicide. While hospitalized, Esther is subjected to traumatic electroshock therapy, though, in the care of a benevolent female doctor, later recovers enough to return to school under the ominous threat of another, more severe, breakdown. As in much of her poetry, Plath evinces a morbid fascination with death and a strong aversion to the prospect of a stifling domestic existence as a subservient housewife and mother. Esther's disappointing social and sexual experiences also reveal the frustration and humiliation endured by women whose intelligence and abilities are disregarded in both the office and

home. Plath's first volume of poetry, *The Colossus,* similarly displays an overriding preoccupation with estrangement, motherhood, and fragmentation in contemporary society. More formal than her later work, the poems of *The Colossus* reveal Plath's mastery of conventional forms, though bear the distinct influence of her association with confessional poets Robert Lowell and Anne Sexton. Much of Plath's rage is directed against her father, whom she invokes as both a muse and target of scorn. While in the title poem Plath refers to him as an "oracle" and "mouthpiece of the dead," in "Electra on Azalea Path," she rails against his premature death and her own lost innocence. Likewise, "The Beekeeper's Daughter," one of many so-called "Bee" poems, alludes to her father and his expertise on the subject of bumblebees. Plath's concern with childbirth is evident in "Metaphors," a cryptic description of gestation introduced as "a riddle in nine syllables," and in "Poem for a Birthday," a series of five separate poems that explore the relationship between artistic creation and the maternal condition. The imagery of fetuses, pregnancy, and creation appear in much of Plath's poetry, especially as a foil for the opposite extreme of the life cycle—death, particularly the looming prospect of self-annihilation. Five months before her suicide, Plath composed the bulk of the poems in *Ariel,* her most famous volume of poetry, which contains "Lady Lazarus" and "Daddy," her best known and most anthologized poems. More so than in *The Colossus,* the poems of *Ariel* render isolation and insecurity as menacing threats with gruesome consequences. Through a synthesis of brutal self-revelation and macabre associations, including disconcerting references to Nazis and the Holocaust, Plath conjures historical and mythic allusions to give depth and immediacy to her psychic distress. Plath also uses color symbolism and archetypal imagery to juxtapose opposing aspects of nature and existence, as in "Tulips" and the title poem, "Ariel," where red and white alternately represent blood, life, death, and rebirth. Other poems, such as "Cut" and "Fever 103°," describe physical afflictions with a combination of clinical objectivity and surrealism that evokes a sense of disorientation and violent self-abnegation. On the theme of marriage and domesticity, "The Applicant" reveals the callous objectification of women as obedient wives whose value is determined by their household utility. As in much of her poetry, the appearance of wild spontaneity and free association belies the subtlety of internal metaphors, lyrical rhythms, and tonal complexity painstakingly formulated to dramatize the terrifying experience of raw, desublimated human fears and desires.

Critical Reception

Plath is widely praised for her technical accomplishment and stark insight into severe psychological disintegration and existential anxiety. Despite her early death, critics continue to marvel at her rapid artistic development over a brief period of only several years. The contents of *The Colossus* and *Ariel,* along with additional compositions from *Crossing the Water* and *Winter Trees,* represent Plath's principal body of work, upon which her reputation as a poet rests. With the posthumous publication of *The Collected Poems,* Plath won renewed critical approval and gained an even larger following. As many critics note, her poetry exhibits an appealing irony, wit, and consistency in its recurring leitmotifs and colloquial symbols, particularly involving bees, infants, wombs, flowers, mirrors, corpses, the moon, and the sea. While Plath is commonly associated with the confessional poets, primarily Lowell and Sexton, the influence of Theodore Roethke is also apparent in her use of intuitive word associations, near rhymes, and Freudian childhood memories. Plath's poetry is typically criticized for its histrionic display of emotion, excessive self-absorption, inaccessible personal allusions, and nihilistic obsession with death. In addition, some critics object to references to the Holocaust in her later poetry, which, in the context of Plath's private anguish, are viewed as gratuitous and inappropriate. However, most agree that Plath's best poetry converts personal experience and ordinary affairs into the mythopoetic. Her only novel, *The Bell Jar,* is also regarded as a classic of modern American literature, drawing favorable comparison to J. D. Salinger's *Catcher in the Rye* and James Joyce's *Portrait of the Artist as a Young Man.* Though later adopted as a heroine and martyr of the feminist movement, Plath's persistent efforts to deconstruct and recreate her self-identity in the transcendent language of metaphor and archetype remains among her greatest achievements. A gifted and much admired literary figure who has assumed cult-like celebrity since her death, Plath is considered among the most influential and important American poets of the twentieth century.

PRINCIPAL WORKS

The Colossus (poetry) 1960
Three Women: A Monologue for Three Voices (radio drama) 1962
The Bell Jar [under pseudonym Victoria Lucas] (novel) 1963
Ariel (poetry) 1965
Crossing the Water: Transitional Poems (poetry) 1971
Crystal Gazer and Other Poems (poetry) 1971
Winter Trees (poetry) 1971
Letters Home: Correspondence, 1950-1963 (letters) 1975
The Bed Book (juvenilia) 1976
Johnny Panic and the Bible of Dreams (short stories, prose, and diary entries) 1977
The Collected Poems (poetry) 1981
The Journals of Sylvia Plath, 1950-1962 (diaries) 1983
Selected Poems (poetry) 1985

CRITICISM

Wendy Martin (essay date 1973)

SOURCE: "'God's Lioness'—Sylvia Plath, Her Prose and Poetry," in *Women's Studies,* Vol. 1, 1973, pp. 191-8.

[*In the following essay, Martin provides both a brief overview of* The Bell Jar *and examples of Plath's poetry to illustrate the autobiographic and social context of her work. Challenging the "negative and even hostile judgment of Plath's politics" levelled by some critics, Martin extols Plath's talent and influence as "one of the leading American women poets since Emily Dickinson."*]

In recent years, cultists have enshrined Sylvia Plath as a martyr while critics have denounced her as a shrew. Plath's devotees maintain that she was the victim of a sexist society, her suicide a response to the oppression of women, and her poetry a choreography of female wounds. Conversely, critics such as Elizabeth Hardwick and Irving Howe complain of her "fascination with hurt and damage and fury." Hardwick can't understand how Plath could persist in her bitterness toward her father years after his death and implies that it was sadistic, or, at best, self-indulgent, to publish *The Bell Jar.*

Echoing Hardwick, Howe accuses Plath of not "caring" or even being "aware of anyone but herself" and asserts that her poetry is "unmodulated and asocial." Complaining that in "none of the essays devoted to praising Sylvia Plath, have I found a coherent statement as to the nature, let alone the value, of her vision," Howe also dismisses Plath's work. This negative and even hostile judgment of Plath's politics obscures the fact that she is one of the most important American women poets since Emily Dickinson; therefore, it is imperative that her work receive attention which is unbiased by sentimentality or authoritarianism.

Born on 27 October 1932 in Boston, Sylvia Plath grew up near the sea in Winthrop, Massachusetts. Her father, a professor of biology at Boston University and author of a respected treatise on bumble bees, died when she was eight; her mother who had been a graduate student in German when she married Otto Plath, taught medical secretarial training at Boston University in order to support the family.

Plath was awarded a scholarship to Smith College where she wrote fiction and prize-winning poetry; as a winner of the *Mademoiselle* College Board Contest, she spent a month in the summer of 1953 in New York City as a guest editor. Later that same summer, she became acutely depressed and attempted suicide. After receiving extensive psychiatric treatment as well as shock therapy, she returned to Smith and graduated *summa cum laude* in 1955. Sylvia was then awarded a fellowship to Newnham College, Cambridge, where she met Ted Hughes, also a poet, in February 1956 and married him in June, a few months before her twenty-fifth birthday.

Sylvia and Ted moved to the United States in the summer of 1957; she taught at Smith College for a year but decided to give up teaching because it took too much time for her poetry writing. The Hughes then moved to Boston where Sylvia audited Robert Lowell's poetry classes with George Starbuck and Anne Sexton. In December 1959 Sylvia and Ted returned to England and their first child was born in April 1960; she continued to write, alternating the baby-sitting with Ted. During this time, she began writing her novel, had a miscarriage, an appendectomy, and became pregnant again; her second child was born in January 1962 shortly after their move to Devon. The following year, Sylvia decided to move to London with the children; Ted remained in Devon. When *The Bell Jar* was published in January 1963 under the pseudonym of Victoria Lucas, she was hard at work on her *Ariel* poems. One month later on 11 February 1963 during the coldest winter in London since 1813-14, Sylvia Plath killed herself; she was thirty-one years old.

What is striking about Sylvia Plath's biography is that she was an accomplished writer, wife, and mother; she even described herself as a "triple-threat woman." Friends describe her as energetic, efficient, and cheerful and often express surprise or are shocked by the isolation, confusion, searing pain and anger in *The Colossus* (1960), *Ariel* (1965), *Crossing the Water* (1971), and *Winter Trees* (1972), her four volumes of poetry.

Apparently, Sylvia Plath played her social role so convincingly that few guessed at the intensity of her despair, but her novel, which is largely autobiographical, illuminates the sense of isolation conveyed by her poetry. In spite of the fact that *The Bell Jar* has been on the national best-seller list for over a year, it has received very little serious critical attention; this critical lapse is especially surprising in view of the fact that it is an extraordinary first novel paralleling F. Scott Fitzgerald's *This Side of Paradise* or Hemingway's *In Our Time.*

Not since Kate Chopin's *The Awakening* or Mary McCarthy's *The Company She Keeps* has there been an American novel which so effectively depicts the life of an intelligent and sensitive woman eager to participate in the larger world, who approaches experience with what amounts to a deep hunger, only to discover that there is no place for her as a fully functioning being. Like Chopin's Edna Pontellier and McCarthy's Margaret Sargent, Esther Greenwood struggles to develop the strength to survive in a world where women are alienated from themselves as well as each other (it is this alienation that Doris Lessing explores in *The*

Golden Notebook which was published in 1962).

The Bell Jar chronicles Esther Greenwood's *rite de passage* from girlhood to womanhood, and explores such subjects as sexual initiation and childbirth which are, for the most part, taboo in women's fiction. Superficially, Esther Greenwood appears to be the 1950's model college girl, but she feels claustrophobic in the world of ladies' luncheons and fashion shows which she must attend as guest editor for a magazine in New York City.

Esther expects more from life than free complexion and hair care advice and would rather be in a bar than a beauty salon. But her nightclub experiences with her glamorous friend Doreen and disc jockey Lenny Shepard serve only to teach her that in order to live outside the ladies' luncheon circuit, a woman must attract an escort in order to experience the larger world. Sickened by this parasitic femininity, she resolves to get by on her own; she wants to see life for herself: "If there was a road accident or a street fight or a baby pickled in a laboratory jar for me to look at, I'd stop and look so hard I never forgot it."

On her return to Boston, her mother informs her that she hasn't been accepted to a writing program that was important to her, and she resigns herself to writing her thesis while living at home. At this point, Esther's world begins to fall apart; she has rejected the passive femininity of Doreen, but the other women in her life fail to provide her with viable alternative life-styles. Her mother advises her to learn shorthand, but Esther is determined to dictate her own letters. Her resolutions notwithstanding, there are no outlets for her enormous energy and potentially constructive aggression; she turns this energy inward, becomes morbidly depressed, and tries to kill herself.

The "stale and sour" climate of Esther's inner world reflects the stifling conditions of her external life: the bell jar is a symbol for the internal chaos and despair produced by excessive external prohibitions. Ironically, there are carefully detailed rituals and traditions regulating virginity and defloration in Esther's world, but there were insufficient guideposts for intellectual development and creative accomplishment. There was no one in Esther's world to help her break out of her confinement—her boyfriend Buddy demands that she remain a virgin but insists that a poem is a "piece of dust."

Life outside the academy leaves Esther with the choice of being an adjunct to a man and mother to a "big cowy family," or a pioneer in uncharted social and emotional territory. Esther's fear and anxiety get the best of her, and it takes extensive therapy to enable her to emerge "patched, retreaded and approved for the road." When she is finally able to rejoice in pure being, "I am, I am, I am," the external world is still threatening, but at least she is her "own woman," and this hard-won independence enables her to withstand the taunts of people like Buddy: "But who will marry you now?"

In spite of the often grim events of *The Bell Jar,* the novel is frequently humorous: at the elegant luncheon given by wealthy Philomena Guinea, Esther drinks the contents of the fingerbowl, cherry blossoms and all, assuming that it was Japanese after-dinner soup; about to receive her first kiss, she positions herself while her date gets a "good footing on the soil," but does not close her eyes. Plath's narration of Esther's gaffs is brilliant, and her skill provides ample evidence of her commitment to fiction. In an interview with Peter Orr for the British council in October 1962, Plath commented that, unlike poetry, fiction permitted her to luxuriate in details; she also said that she viewed *The Bell Jar* as her apprentice effort and planned to write another novel. In the same interview, she stated that she composed her poems to be read aloud and admitted that *The Colossus* privately bored her because the poems in that volume were not composed for oral presentation.

To hear Sylvia Plath read her own poetry is truly a thrilling experience: her voice was full-bodied, vibrant, and authoritative. Her voice creates the impression that she was not hysterical, timid, or easily subdued. Hearing her read makes it obvious that being a poet was central to her existence—"The actual experience of writing a poem is a magnificent one," she once said, and the immense vitality of her reading underscores the energy of her poems.

Savage anger and bitterness frequently spring from Plath's poems: **"Lady Lazarus," "The Applicant," "Daddy," "The Beast," "Zookeeper's Wife," "Magi"** are monuments to her rage. "I made a model of you, . . . A man in black with a Meinkampf look . . . And I said I do, I do. . . . So daddy, I'm finally through"; **"Daddy"** turns on retribution; yet it expresses the release of immense energy that occurs with the decision to break away from emotionally damaging relationships. In *An American Dream,* Norman Mailer experiences the same release when he kills his wife Deborah and metaphorically as well as literally breaks away from her domination: ". . . and *crack* the door flew open and the wire tore in her throat, and I was through the door, hatred passing from me in wave after wave, illness as well, rot and pestilence, nausea, a bleak string of salts. I was floating."

Male writers are permitted to articulate their aggression, however violent or hostile; women writers are supposed to pretend that they are never angry. Sylvia Plath refuses to honor this concept of feminine decorum and dares to express her negative emotions. "Beware . . . Beware . . . Out of the ash . . . I rise with my red hair . . . And I eat men like air"

("**Lady Lazarus**"). Plath chooses to be true to her experience and to her art rather than to the traditional norms of feminine experience.

Plath's anger gives her strength to face her demons: "Nightly now I flog apes wolves bears sheep . . . Over the iron stile. And still don't sleep." (**"Zookeeper's Wife"**). But if Plath's poetry is often an exorcism, an effort to stave off madness, it also modulates longing and fear: "I am inhabited by a cry . . . Nightly it flaps out . . . Looking, with its hooks, for something to love. I am terrified by this dark thing . . . That sleeps in me." (**"Elm"**).

Critics frequently point out Plath's love/hate for her father, but they rarely mention her mother. This is a major oversight because the loss of mother-love haunts Plath's poetry and is the basic cause of her profound despair: "Mother, you are the one mouth . . . I would be tongue to" (**"Who"**); "The mother of mouths didn't love me" (**"Maenad"**); "Mother of beetles, only unclench your hand" (**"Witch Burning"**).

Born under the sign of Scorpio, Plath speaks of the "motherly pulse of the sea" in an essay entitled **"Ocean 1212-W,"** and here she again laments her abandonment: "Hugging my grudge, ugly and prickly, a sad sea urchin . . . I saw the separateness of everything. I felt the wall of my skin: I am I. The stone is a stone. My beautiful fusion with the things of this world was over."

Plath was two and a half years old when her brother was born, and like many sensitive children of that age, she felt replaced by her brother and rejected by her mother. Her father's death when she was eight undoubtedly aggravated her already acute sense of loss. The working through of Oedipal and sibling conflicts in Plath's writing is reminiscent of Virginia Woolf, who wrote in her diary, "I used to think of him (her father) and mother daily; but writing the *Lighthouse* laid them in my mind. And now he comes back to me sometimes, but differently. I believe this to be true—that I was obsessed by them both, unhealthily; and writing of them was a necessary act."

In addition to childhood losses, the conflict between domestic and artistic interests, and the lack of financial security as well as health problems undoubtedly left Sylvia Plath extremely vulnerable to depression and suicidal impulses. Lacking favorable or at least serious critical response to her work must have been difficult and painful. Certainly interviews which described her as an "attractive young suburban matron . . . in a neat oatmeal colored suit of wool jersey . . . a living realization of every young college girl's dream" must have been discouraging.

One of Plath's last works **"Three Women: A Poem for**

Three Voices," which appears in *Winter Trees,* is set in a maternity ward and seems to celebrate, in part, fertility, pregnancy, and motherhood along with acceptance, or perhaps resignation, to a women's domestic identity. It concludes, "I am a wife . . . The city waits and aches. The little grasses . . . Crack through Stone, and they are green with life." Again, Plath echoes Virginia Woolf; "And now with some pleasure I find that it is seven; and must cook dinner. Haddock and sausage meat. I think it is true that one gains a certain hold on sausage and haddock by writing them down." Shortly after this 8 March 1941 entry, Virginia Woolf weighted with stones, walked into a tributary of the Thames to drown.

Like Woolf, Plath made desperate efforts to balance on the "razor edge" of the opposing forces of life and death. Kali-like, Sylvia Plath's poetry embodies the profound interrelationship of destruction and creation. Whether or not she could have moved toward a strong affirmation of life as did Anne Sexton in *Live or Die* is a question her readers will never be able to answer.

A. Alvarez in his memoir of Sylvia Plath argues that she was by nature a risk-taker and that her suicide was her last gamble: "Having worked out the odds were in her favor, but perhaps, in her depression, not much caring whether she won or lost. Her calculations went wrong and she lost." Alvarez points out that Plath left the doctor's number near her, that the au pair girl was due to arrive early in the morning, that the man who lived below was an early riser. Plath could not have realized that the gas that suffocated her would sedate him so heavily that he didn't hear the frantic knocking of the au pair girl or that this delay would cost her her life. Yet, the moment she decided to turn on the gas jet, an irrevocable chain of events occurred which caused the "jet blood" of poetry to stop forever.

Sylvia Plath was one of the first American women writers to refuse to conceal or disguise her true emotions; in articulating her aggression, hostility, and despair in her art, she effectively challenged the traditional literary prioritization of female experience.
—*Wendy Martin*

Sylvia Plath was one of the first American women writers to refuse to conceal or disguise her true emotions; in articulating her aggression, hostility, and despair in her art, she effectively challenged the traditional literary prioritization of female experience. In addition to being a novelist and poet, she was a pioneer and pathfinder.

R. J. Spendal (essay date 1975)

SOURCE: "Sylvia Plath's 'Cut,'" in *Modern Fiction Studies,* Vol. 6, 1975, pp. 128-34.

[*In the following essay, Spendal discusses the significance of color symbolism, historical reference, and Plath's use of physical ailment as a metaphor for psychological injury in the poem "Cut."*]

In several of her poems Sylvia Plath turns familiar bodily ills into metaphors of psychic affliction. Work like **"The Eye-mote," "Fever 103°," "Paralytic,"** and **"Amnesiac"** are only incidentally concerned with the pathological states suggested by their titles. The ostensible problem in each case is a figure for a more subtle and profound malady, a disturbance of the will to live. This is also the strategy in **"Cut,"** one of the most memorable and carefully crafted of the *Ariel* poems. On the literal level Plath's subject is a cut thumb; figuratively, it is the deeper disunity of a mind divided in its attitude toward death.

The vehicle for this psychological concern is the speaker's uncertain response to her injury. The initial reaction is a sort of manic exuberance which moves her to extol the cut as "a thrill." Subsequently, pain and nausea prompt a more sober statement: "I am ill." To emphasize the disparity between these moods Plath divides the poem into two equal parts. The "thrill" section extends through the first five stanzas, the "ill" section through the last five. The mathematical neatness of this arrangement is reinforced by links between corresponding stanzas in each section. The end-words "thrill," "onion," and "gone" in stanza one are matched by the end-words "on," "ill," and "kill" in stanza six; "skin" in two by "thin" in seven; "heart" in four by the same word in nine; "run" and "one" in five by "jump" and "stump" in ten. There appear to be no such links between stanzas three and eight. A tenuous parallel of another sort involves the etymology of "wattle," which Plath uses in stanza three in the phrase "turkey wattle." The word derives from the Old English *watel,* cognate with *waetla,* a bandage for a wound, and in stanza eight the speaker applies a bandage to her thumb. A more substantial connection rests on the appearance in each stanza of a similar conflict. The lines "Little pilgrim, / The Indian's axed your scalp" in stanza three depict the hostility between white man and red man. The phrase "Gauze Ku Klux Klan / Babushka," used in stanza eight to describe the bandage, suggests another struggle between white and red. The Klan is associated with white supremacy and white robes, while "Babushka," a Russian word, is a reminder of "Red" in the sense of a Communist. The phrase implies not only the Cold War rivalry between the USA and the USSR, but also the narrower, more intense hostility between the KKK and all things un-American.

Anyone who has experienced a sudden, severe cut will acknowledge the truth of the speaker's movement from fascination to distress. Yet verisimilitude is here only a means to an end: it conveys a related, more profound movement in which death is first celebrated (section one) and then rejected (section two). This deeper theme is articulated primarily at the level of imagery. Among the swiftly unfolding and brilliantly interrelated figures of section one are: a metaphoric death in which the thumb, imaged as a pilgrim, is "scalped" (II. 9-10); a pilgrim-Indian-turkey figure suggesting Thanksgiving (9-11); a red carpet of blood (11-14); a bottle of pink antiseptic which becomes champagne for a "celebration" (15-17); and a Redcoat metaphor recalling the War of Independence (18-20). This figurative sequence begins with a death and goes on to convey a sense of feverish jubilation. Death looms as a VIP for whom one rolls out the red carpet, and when the speaker herself steps on it (14) we are aware that the prospect of dying has come to dominate her thoughts. The advent of Death becomes an occasion of thanksgiving and is heralded with champagne and merriment. He promises release, a new state of freedom from what Plath in **"Ariel"** calls the "Dead hands, dead stringencies" of life.

A small but important detail here is the reference to antiseptic, indicating that the speaker has not wholly given over the will to live. The impulse to die is strong and clearly dominant, but it is not uncontested. In a similar way section two will depict, at least initially, a qualified repudiation of death, with the speaker's hesitancy appearing most clearly in her pejorative characterization of the bandage, a salubrious measure, as a "Gauze Ku Klux Klan / Babushka." The complexity of response here is supported by Plath's ambiguous use of white and red throughout the poem. White has conventional associations with death, as in the phrase "Dead white" (7); the color is implicit in the references to onion (2), pilgrim (9), paper (26), gauze (30), and the KKK (30). Red, the color of blood and life, appears in "red plush" (8) and "Redcoats" (20) and is implied by the references to Indian (10), turkey wattle (11), pink fizz (16), and babushka (31). Plath uses white and red as irreconcilable opposites in **"Lesbos"** when the speaker, referring to her child, says: "Why she is schizophrenic, / Her face red and white, a panic" (10-11). However, in **"Cut"** the color symbolism, like the speaker's state of mind, is not constant. The white gauze dressing conserves life, while Indians, Redcoats, and Communists are, from an American standpoint, inimical to life.

With section two a general reversal is evident in the speaker's outlook. Addressing the "Redcoats" of her blood as they rush from the wound, she wonders: "Whose side are they on?" (21). As an American living in England Plath might well be confused in her allegiance, but the real point here is the perception that death (loss of blood) may be a perfidious benefactor. This suspicion dominates the imagery of section two where, for the most part, the figures of

section one are reversed. Thus the pilgrim-thumb, slain earlier, is resurrected here as a "Homunculus" (23). The homunculus was an alchemically created man, a sort of primitive test tube baby produced from a recipe of human semen, horse manure, and blood. Its appearance here indicates that a life impulse has unaccountably taken shape where before death held sway. And the metaphor serves other purposes as well. For complete development the homunculus required a daily feeding of human blood; thus the hurt thumb has now become the locus for incoming rather than outgoing blood. In section one blood was always escaping, as in lines 11-13 and 18-20. This deathly exodus is reversed in section two, first by the homunculus and later in the phrase "balled / Pulp of your heart" (33-34), which suggests a life-preserving consolidation of the heart's strength and contrasts especially with the flat "carpet" of blood that "rolls" / Straight from the heart" in section one. It may also be significant that in the most complete formula for the creation of a homunculus, that by Paracelsus (1493-1541), the key time periods are based on the number forty: forty days for gestation, forty weeks for nurture. **"Cut"** has forty lines, indicating perhaps that the resurgence of the speaker's will to live derives from the marvelous transformation of a baser, more sordid impulse toward suicide. (The homunculus itself issued from dung.) Plath often arranges the length of her works to suit thematic ends. The twenty chapters of ***The Bell Jar*** support Esther's escape from madness at age twenty. Interestingly, the speaker in **"Cut"** escapes the pull of death at line twenty.

The speaker's renewed interest in life is further suggested by her statement: "I have taken a pill to kill / The thin / Papery feeling" (24-26). This "slaying" pointedly contrasts with the scalping of the pilgrim-thumb in section one. That killing loosened the speaker's hold on life, this undoes death itself. In Plath's verse paper is part of an image-group based on flatness as a symbol of sterility and death. Paper signifies a severely atrophied, dangerously thin life state, a condition very near extinction. The speaker has been attracted by such a state for twenty lines, but now she takes steps to "kill" it. This action, together with the subsequent dressing of the wound (29-32), ensures the continued existence of the vitality symbolized by the homunculus. Death makes a final assault, only to suffer defeat, in the following passage, which is based on an extension of the paper metaphor: ". . . and when / The balled / Pulp of your heart / Confronts its small / Mill of silence / How you jump—" (32-37). The homunculus (now mature?) refuses to let its heart fail and instead leaps back toward life. The heart will remain compact and rounded instead of becoming papery thin in the "Mill" of death. "Pulp," derived from the Latin for "flesh," will not be processed into paper, since the speaker has already tried to eradicate her "Papery feeling." The motive for this crucial "jump" is unexpressed, but the speaker's espousal of life seems instinctive. We might recall that in **"Tu-**

lips" another persona, half in love with easeful death, is hauled unwillingly back toward health by an irrepressible life force symbolized by the flowers. (In many ways **"Tulips"** is the double of **"Cut":** both poems have a binary structure, a red and white color pattern, and a concern with the opposing claims of death and life.)

The movement away from death also accounts for the description of the thumb as a "Saboteur" (27) and a "Kamikaze" (28). No longer celebrated as a thrill, the hurt is now disparaged for having been a subverter of the speaker's will to live and an inducement to suicide. These references are part of Plath's broadest strategy for conveying the speaker's new mood, a strategy involving the disposition of the poem's martial imagery. This imagery is related to the war between death and life in the speaker's mind, but it also depicts a change of mood. Plath manages this by having the military figures in section one move forward in time and those in section two move backward. The progression from pilgrims and Indians to the War of Independence in section one is a movement from the seventeenth to the eighteenth century. But the sequence from saboteur to Kamikaze to KKK to Communism in section two moves in reverse. Saboteur suggests the Cold War intrigue of the 1950's; Kamikaze is a reference to World War II; the Klan reached its peak in the 1920's; and "Babushka" recalls the Russian Revolution of 1917. The point of this carefully arranged time-reversal is that it shows the speaker backing out of her earlier celebration of death. The same idea is conveyed in a like manner by another figurative sequence, the largest continuous metaphor in section two, that involving paper. This figure moves from "thin / Papery feeling" (25-26) to "Pulp" (34) to "Mill" (36) to "stump" (40), exactly reversing the process by which paper is produced. The normal order would be: tree, mill, pulp, paper. Section two thus depicts paper, i.e., death, in the process of being decreated. Its influence begins to wane with the sudden advent of the homunculus (2), the life force which inexplicably issues from death.

The final three lines of the poem present a concluding sequence of figures in which the thumb is addressed as: "Trepanned veteran, / Dirty girl, / Thumb stump" (38-40). With this incantatory series of three figures the exorcism of death is completed. Like the earlier paper sequence, these metaphors are arranged regressively. A scarred veteran is a hardened soldier, a successful killer. A girl is significantly less threatening because of her sex, age, and smaller size; and a stump is smaller still, with even less capacity for harm. The sequence thus depicts a gradual diminishment in size and power, a progressive erosion of threat. We see that the thumb as a lure to self-violence has lost its potency and become harmless, simply a "Thumb stump." Concomitantly, the speaker's imagination is reined back to life and reality as it abandons metaphor in favor of literal truth. The hurt thumb is only figuratively a soldier with a head wound, but the

phrase "Dirty girl" is half true: we know that the gauze dressing is stained and tarnished (29-32). Finally, the last line may be read as wholly true and literal, since the primary meaning of "stump," according to the *Shorter Oxford English Dictionary,* is "the part remaining of an amputated or broken-off limb or portion of the body." The truth, which the speaker now admits, is that her thumb is simply an incomplete but living member of her hand. Plath's strategy here is not without literary precedent. In Chaucer's *Book of the Duchess* (c. 1369), for example, the excessive and debilitating grief of the Black Knight cannot be assuaged until he drops all metaphorical references to the death of his lady and admits simply: "She ys ded!" As the speaker in **"Cut"** comes back to the weight of primary noon she too regains a measure of inner stability and calm. No longer is she, either physically or emotionally, "ill."

Surprisingly, **"Cut"** has been faulted by a respected critic for its "structural incoherence," and even sympathetic readers are uncertain about the formal integrity of Plath's torrent of metaphors. Robert Boyers, for example, defends the poem's seeming lack of design by arguing that it "works out its meanings on a level that wholly transcends simple logic." My analysis has shown, I hope, that such a strained defense is unnecessary. Closely read, the poem is both logical and coherent. In **"Cut"** Plath rigorously orders structure and imagery to present a psychological drama: the displacement of an impulse toward suicide by the renewed claims of life.

Jeannine Dobbs (essay date 1977)

SOURCE: "'Viciousness in the Kitchen': Sylvia Plath's Domestic Poetry," in *Modern Language Studies,* Vol. 7, No. 2, 1977, pp. 11-25.

[*In the following essay, Dobbs examines allusions to marriage and motherhood in Plath's poetry. According to Dobbs, the hostile and often violent imagery in such pieces reflects Plath's strong resistance to the prospect of domestic entrapment as a wife and mother.*]

> There's a hex on the cradle
> and death in the pot.

For Sylvia Plath, domesticity is an ultimate concern. Like Erica Jong, Tillie Olsen, Marge Piercy and many other contemporary women writers Plath frequently explores what it means to be a woman in terms of the traditional conflict between family and career. Plath's life and her writing are filled with anxiety and despair over her refusal to choose and instead to try to have—what most males consider their birthright—both. It is apparent from her life and letters that her commitment to writing was total and unwavering and that her commitment to domesticity, especially motherhood, was ambivalent. Paradoxically, it is out of her domestic relationships and experiences, which she came to feel were stifling, even killing her that the majority of her most powerful, most successful work was created.

Plath's life and her writing are filled with anxiety and despair over her refusal to choose and instead to try to have—what most males consider their birthright—both.
—Jeannine Dobbs

Many Plath poems are concerned at one level or another with suffering: with sickness, injury, torture, madness, death. Titles alone, of many Plath poems, reveal this: **"Cut,"** for example, and **"Fever 103°," "Paralytic," "Contusion," "Thalidomide," "Amnesiac," "Witch Burning."** This seems not surprising in that Plath's life and the lives of those close to her contained more than an average share of illness and loss. There were the amputation of her father's leg and his subsequent death when she was seven; her mother's chronic ulcer; her grandmother's death; her own breakdown and institutionalization, chronic sinus condition, broken leg, miscarriage, appendectomy; her real life Buddy Willard's bout with TB and confinement to a sanitarium. In addition, her visit with Buddy Willard to Boston-Lying-In hospital where she viewed medical students dissecting cadavers, fetuses in bottles, and childbirth, provided a traumatic extension to her more immediate experiences. What is more interesting than the fact that her work reflects pain and suffering, however, is the fact that she sometimes portrays physical and mental pain as retribution for doing or being bad and that her poetry so frequently contains images that associate physical and mental suffering and also effacement—a kind of living death—, as well as death itself, with domestic relationships and/or domestic roles.

Several incidents in *The Bell Jar* illustrate Plath's linking of suffering and sin. Bad-girl Doreen flaunts her sexuality (and perhaps, in Esther Greenwood's eyes, does worse) and gets drunk-sick. Buddy Willard's TB is seen as retribution for his boasted infidelity with a waitress. Esther wonders what bad thing she has done to deserve electric shock. She views her broken leg as paying herself back for being bad—that is, for refusing to marry Buddy Willard. In Plath's work in general, not only are other people the objects of vengeance—her parents, her suitors, her husband and in later poems his mistress—but she herself is an object of her own vengeance. The idea of revenge of the self by the self is, of course, masochistic. But the linking of suffering and sin provides her with powerful, original images and diction when she deals with areas of life about which she had complex,

ambivalent attitudes, such as marriage and especially motherhood.

Plath's letters to her mother and her novel both make it explicitly clear that Plath was confused and frustrated by the necessity of defining herself as a woman. In 1949, at age seventeen, she wrote: "I am afraid of getting married. Spare me from cooking three meals a day—spare me from the relentless cage of routine and rote. I want to be free. . . ." She felt "bewildered," two years later, by an extended stint as a sleep-in nursemaid and spoke of the job as "slavery." "Learning of the limitations of a woman's sphere," she wrote, "is no fun at all." And at twenty, a student at Smith, she insisted: "Graduate school and travel abroad are not going to be stymied by any squealing, breastfed brats." By the time she reached the University at Cambridge, however, her attitude had changed. She began to see motherhood as a chance for "extending my experience of life," and to fear that if she did not marry she would become one of "the weird old women," "the bluestocking grotesques," she saw as alternatives. Shortly before she met Ted Hughes in Cambridge in the winter of 1956, her letters reveal that she was ripe for marriage: "I don't know how I can bear to go back to the states unless I am married. . . . I really think I would do anything to stay here."

In *The Bell Jar,* Esther Greenwood mirrors Plath's ambivalence, alternating between insisting she'll marry and have a parcel of kids and exclaiming: "If I had a baby to wait on all day, I would go mad." But one of the ironies of the novel is the fact that the reader knows from the beginning of the book that Esther will have a baby. Discussing the gifts she received during her month in New York as guest editor of a slick woman's magazine, she remarks: "I use the lipsticks now and then, and last week I cut the plastic starfish off the sunglasses for the baby to play with." Society assumes a woman will marry. Esther is besieged by the influences that propagate the myth that the be-all and end-all of a woman's existence is a husband, a house, and a handful of kids. After Esther's release from the mental hospital, Buddy's final words to her are: "I wonder who you'll marry now . . . you've been here." Not to marry and give up other aspirations and be content, is to go against society's expectations, to be bad, to commit a kind of sin.

Writing to her mother from Smith, Plath agonized over "which to choose?"—meaning, work or pleasure? career or marriage? The central metaphor of *The Bell Jar,* the fig tree, is Plath's literary portrayal of this dilemma. Each fig represents an option, a future: to be a famous poet, an editor or the like, or to be a wife and mother. Each is mutually exclusive and only one can be picked. As Esther (very much an extension of her creator here) hesitates, debating with herself, "the figs began to wrinkle and go black, and, one by one, they plopped to the ground at her feet." Rejection of any option was difficult because something in her wanted it all. "I'll be flying back and forth between one mutually exclusive thing and another for the rest of my days," Esther says. In her own life, Plath tried for the compromise. There were times, her letters and the remembrances of her family and friends reveal, that domestic life alone seemed to fulfill her. She was a perfectionist at housekeeping as she had always been at her college work and at writing. At times she reveled in being "cowlike" and maternal. Then, writing potboilers for "soppy women's magazines and cooking and sewing" were her highest ambitions. At times, too, she felt that "children seem[ed] an impetus to [her serious] writing." But a resentment against them, against their demands on her time, their drain on her creativity, is evident too. Pleasure, resentment, guilt. Ambivalence. Plath's work suggests that the attempt to resolve these feelings failed. Her suicide may have been, to some degree, a final acting out of her belief in punishment, vengeance, of the self on the self, for this failure.

Plath's use of images and diction depicting suffering in relationship to female roles and domestic experience expressed in *The Bell Jar* and her late poetry are foreshadowed in several poems in her first book of poetry, *The Colossus* (1960). Many of the poems in this volume were written after her marriage; some were written during her first pregnancy. (Her daughter was born in April of 1960). Poems in *The Colossus* that deal with male/female relationships or motherhood are primarily dark, fearful poems.

"The Manor Garden," the initial poem in *The Colossus,* was written in the fall of 1959. It begins by creating an apprehensive, foreboding tone that dominates the poem: "The fountains are dry and the roses over. / Incense of death. Your day approaches." Here are death in the midst of birth; the external, natural world at odds with the internal, human one. Only momentarily does a correspondence, a harmony, occur between the natural and the maternal: "The pears fatten like little buddhas" as the fetus evolves and the womb fills. But negative images (wolves and hard stars, a spider and worms) outweigh the positive ones (pears, fishes, a bee's wing, heather). The poem's prophecy is for "a difficult borning."

Not apprehension but real revulsion to motherhood is expressed in **"Sow."** Written earlier than **"The Manor Garden,"** the poem **"Sow"** is a portrait of a Brobdingnagian hog not yet "hedged by a litter of feat-footed ninnies / Shrilling her hulk / To halt for a swig at the pink teats," but a monstrous maiden pig awaiting a "boar fabulous enough to straddle her heat." In action, this comic, this grotesque sow consumes the world. Exaggeration is one dimension of Plath's vision. The sow is one of her colossal figures. Although the sow is ridiculous, she is frightening. For Plath, she represents the destiny of the adult female—the Dodo

Conways of the human world, a breed not about to become extinct.

"I Want, I Want" is a more difficult poem than **"Sow,"** but it seems to describe the terrible, insatiable demands of the "baby-god" who "cried out for the mother's dug." Its two final lines, "Barbs on the crown of gilded wire / Thorns on the bloody rose stem" vaguely suggest the crucifixion and set up a parallel between it and childbirth which Plath develops more extensively in later poems.

Another *Colossus* poem, **"Moonrise,"** uses exceedingly ominous imagery and allusions to Christ's death in relation to pregnancy:

> Berries redden. A body of whiteness
> Rots, and smells of rot under its headstone
> Though the body walk out in clean linen.
> . . .
> Death whitens in the egg and out of it.

The poem concludes with an address to Lucina, the goddess of childbirth, whom Plath transforms into a Woman in the Moon. The moon, traditionally connected with the female cycle of menstruation, represents the negation of pregnancy. And the child of the labor Plath describes is an "ancient father," "white-bearded, weary," a figure resembling Father Time or perhaps Father Death, rather than a child. Thus, the birth or the anticipation of that experience includes its antithesis. The horror here matches any created in the last *Ariel* poems.

The first four of the five separate poems that make up **"Poem for a Birthday"** also center around domestic situations. The speaker's pregnancy is the subject of the first two poems (**"Who"** and **"Dark House"**) and is alluded to in the third (**"Maenad"**). In the fourth (**"The Beast"**), the marital situation is described and the speaker's disillusionment with it: "I've married a cupboard of rubbish / . . . I housekeep in Time's gut-end."

The familial portraits presented in these four poems are, even for Plath, particularly grotesque. The fetus is described as "All mouth who licks up the bushes / And the pots of meat. / . . . He's to blame" (**"Dark House"**). And the husband, although "he was bullman earlier / King of my dish, my lucky animal," becomes "Mumblepaws," "Fido Littlesoul, the bowel's familiar" (**"The Beast"**). In **"Who,"** he is "Dogsbody"; in **"Maenad,"** he is "Dog-head, devourer."

In the sections of **"Poem for a Birthday"** that deal with pregnancy, there is the unlikely linking of birth not with death but with madness. A loss of identity, a sense of insignificance and smallness, are portrayed as common to both experiences. In **"Who,"** the speaker begs, "Let me sit in the flowerpot / The spiders won't notice." She is "a root, a stone, an owl pellet." She reveals that "for weeks I can remember nothing at all." In **"Maenad,"** she begs. "Tell me my name." In **"The Stones,"** she is "a still pebble"; and she becomes one with the fetus:

> I entered
> The stomach of indifference
> . . .
> Drunk as a fetus
> I suck at the paps of darkness

All in all, these early poems, written around the time of Plath's first pregnancy and personally selected for publication in her first collection, reveal degrees of mental stress over the maternal condition. Motherhood may be something monstrous, as the child may be. Signs attending birth are not propitious. There is a confusion over the meaning of the event reminiscent of the attitude of Eliot's magi.

The Colossus also introduces one of Plath's single women. **"The Spinster,"** written in the year of her marriage, describes a woman who renounces the disorder that romance brings into her life. Romance is symbolized in this poem by the fertility which spring promises, "the rank wilderness of fern and flower." The "lover's gesture imbalances the air." The spinster rejects "this tumult" and adopts instead the "frosty discipline" of winter:

> And round her house she set
> Such a barricade of barb and check
> Against mutinous weather
> As no mere insurgent man could hope to break
> With curse, fist, threat
> Or love either.

In addition to disorder, there is a violence in love that threatens the spinster, that victimizes her.

Some early but uncollected poems also explore the experience of the woman rejecting or attempting to reject the man. In **"The Snowman on the Moor"** (written near the end of 1956 and published in *Poetry:* July, 1957), Plath investigates more closely the spinster's choice. In **"The Snowman,"** a man and a woman have had an argument and the woman flees. Escape, however, is not really what she wants. "Come find me," she cries. But "he did not come." Clearly it is pursuit that the woman wants: "police and hounds to bring her in." She wants the demonstration on the man's part of his desire for her, a sign of *his* submission. The second part of the poem shows how the woman is subjugated instead. She is subjugated not by a figure of passion but by "a grisly-thewed / Austere, corpse-white / Giant" who is "sky high." "Snow / Floured his beard." This colossus represents the wintry world into which she has fled—the spinster's world of "frosty discipline."

> o she felt
> No love in his eye,
>
> Worse—saw dangling from that spike-studded belt
> Ladies' shaved skulls:
> Mournfully the dry tongues clacked their guilt:
>
> "Our wit made fools
> Of kings, unmanned kings' sons: our masteries
> Amused court halls:
>
> For that brag, we barnacle these iron thighs."

The women already conquered by the cold giant are, significantly, witty women. They exist as heads: women without bodies, without hair. Their wit threatened men—it unmanned them. In turn, the women themselves were punished—they lost their femininity, their sexuality. This vision is of the frigid, truncated world of the woman alone, the world without love. Although the giant does not succeed in adding the speaker's head to his collection and, in fact, disintegrated—"crumbled to smoke"—when she "shied sideways," he does win. The fleeing girl is subdued by her vision of the alternative to the embattled state in which she and the man live:

> Humbled then, and crying
> The girl bent homeward, brimful of gentle talk
> And mild obeying.

The giant is male because males rule the woman's world, her choices. The man to whom the woman humbly returns rules her real world. The giant who personifies the executioner—the punisher of women who rebel—rules her imaginary world of women unsubjugated and, therefore, unloved by men. The vision in which no alternative is tenable becomes more and more Plath's way of seeing the world.

"Pursuit" is a similar, early, uncollected poem (*Atlantic:* January, 1957), the first poem Plath wrote after meeting Ted Hughes. Its speaker is a woman who cannot transcend her own physical nature and who has intense and ambivalent feelings about her desire to do so. Like the woman in **"The Snowman,"** she flees from a man because he is capable of hurting her. However, because of his strength and her weakness, she knows she will succumb. The woman is the victim not only of the male but of her own sexuality as well. She is pursued by a panther, a creature which embodies in the poem both the idea of the ravaging male and the woman's own desire.

> Keen the rending teeth and sweet

The singeing fury of his fur;
His kisses parch, each paw's a briar,
Doom consummates that appetite.

Here the beast represents the man, whose lovemaking both wounds and pleases. The assurance between "teeth" and "sweet" helps emphasize the paradox. The woman is aware what her fate will be if she succumbs, because like the giant snowman the panther has previously victimized other women:

In the wake of this fierce cat,
Kindled like torches for his joy,
Charred and ravened women lie.

Soon, however, the woman admits her own desires: "His ardor snares me, lights the trees, / And I run flaring in my skin." Finally she is overcome by her awareness of the beast in herself. She recognizes her own lust as well as the cruel brilliance of his: "Appalled by secret want, I rush / From such assault of radiance." Such intensity and such awareness frighten the woman, and she wants to repress them. She bolts the doors. Nevertheless as the poem concludes, the woman knows: "The panther's tread is on the stairs / Coming up and up the stairs."

Women dominated. Women manipulated. Women subjugated. Plath continued to turn the subject this way and that. She seems to see these conditions as inevitable. She writes in *The Bell Jar:* "I knew that in spite of all the roses and kisses and restaurant dinners a man showered on a woman before he married her, what he secretly wanted when the wedding service ended was for her to flatten out underneath his feet like Mrs. Willard's kitchen mat." Men train their wives to serve. In a poem describing an ocean voyage entitled **"On Deck"** (*Crossing the Water*), she observes:

And the white-haired jeweler from Denmark is
carving
A perfectly faceted wife to wait
On him hand and foot, quiet as a diamond.

Women fear men, they run from them; but they want to be caught. Women seem to need to be dominated, domineered; perhaps they love it:

Every woman adores a Fascist,
The boot in the face, the brute
Brute heart of a brute like you.

—"Daddy" (*Ariel*)

Still the resentment, the rebellion bubble up. To be married is to be in purdah, in plaster, in jail.

Plath sees a bride as a woman upon whom a certain kind of

seclusion is forced, a woman in **"Purdah"** (*Winter Trees*). The bride sees herself become a private possession to be enjoyed by her owner at will. "I am his. / Even in his / Absence," the woman says. Her resentment, her rebellion, build:

I shall unloose
One feather . . .
. . .
I shall unloose
One note

Shattering
The chandelier

And finally they burst:

I shall unloose—
From the small jeweled
Doll he guards like a heart- –

The lioness,
The shriek in the bath,
The cloth of holes.

Revenge—this is the commitment sworn in the final stanza. The woman in purdah recalls Plath's more well-known Lady Lazarus, whose climatic boast in the face of all her (male) enemies is: "I eat men like air!"

The prisoner of a poem called **"The Jailor"** (*Encounter:* October, 1963) is also desperate over her treatment and the jailor's demands on her: "He has been burning me with cigarettes / . . . / I am myself. That is not enough." The prisoner despairs, however, of escape—partly at least because of the man's dependency on her:

I wish him dead or away.
That, it seems is the impossibility,

That, being free. What would the dark
Do without fevers to eat?
What would the light
Do, without eyes to knife, what would he
Do, do do without me?

Such dependency is also acknowledged in **"In Plaster"** (*Crossing the Water*), where the relationship between body and cast is described as "a kind of marriage." The metaphor is highly successful, the poem working at both the literal and the metaphorical levels. Thus the body and cast have an interdependency, the cast playing a supporting role like "the best of nurses." When the body begins to heal, however, and has visions of shucking the cast, he discovers that "living with her was like living with my own coffin / Yet I still depended on her, though I did it regretfully."

Marriage, like a cast or a prosthesis, fills a need, according to Plath. Certainly the relationship is about a prospective spouse, a groom. Being wifeless, he is missing something, some primary possession. His hand is empty. He is told:

> Here is a hand
> To fill it and willing
> To bring teacups and roll away headaches
> And do whatever you tell it.

The bride will fit the groom like a tuxedo for his wedding or a coffin for his funeral:

> Black and stiff, but not a bad fit.
> Will you marry it?
> . . .
> Believe me, they'll bury you in it.

Wedding or funeral, one is the same as the other. The bride will obey. Whatever the man lacks, she will supply. She will support him the way the cast supports the body. This woman is a domestic blob. She is a kind of Gracie Allen puppet: "It can sew, it can cook, / It can talk, talk, talk."

Plath continued to explore the subject of woman with child as well as that of woman with man. As previously noted, the poems in *The Colossus* dealing with maternity are somewhat less than enthusiastic. She did write, however, some poems that express very positive, good feelings about children. **"Poem for a Fatherless Son"** (*Winter Trees*) is one. Yet she wrote few poems on any subject in which the mood does not turn downward at the end. If she perceives any joy, any little glimpse of beauty, she is almost sure to drop it climactically. Hence her poetic technique frequently parallels what literally happens in her poem **"Balloons."** The reader (in the poem, her son) sits contemplating a rosy world (glimpsed through a red balloon) when bang! He sits back holding his "red shred." Her short poem **"Child"** (*Winter Trees*) illustrates this deflated closing. Here the speaker wants to present the child with only the objects and experiences appropriate to its youth and innocence: "colors," "ducks," wildflowers. But the final stanza suggests that disturbing emotions and dark vistas are the reluctant offering: "this troublous / Wringing of hands, this dark / Ceiling without a star."

There are too many poems concerning pregnancy or children that close in this way to examine them all. To mention a few titles, **"The Night Dances"** (*Ariel*), which Ted Hughes says is about their son Nicholas dancing in his crib, and **"Heavy Women"** (*Crossing the Water*), a poem about pregnancy, are two.

Several of Plath's poems about pregnancy and motherhood (all published before her second child was born) are exceptions to her more common habit of ending on a note of pes-

simism or of terror. These poems are all composed using the same technique. They play a metaphorical game: the referent (the fetus or the child or the pregnant woman) is described through a series of images. If the reader does not perceive the subject, the poems remain obscure. **"You're"** (*Ariel*) addresses a fetus:

> Clownlike, happiest on your hands,
> Feet to the stars, and moon-skulled
> Gilled like a fish.

In **"Dark House,"** the subject is the pregnant woman (or her womb):

> This is a dark house, very big.
> I made it myself,
> Cell by cell from a quiet corner.

In **"Metaphors"** (*Crossing the Water*) the pregnant woman is "a riddle in nine syllables, / An elephant, a ponderous house." **"Words for a Nursery"** (*Atlantic:* August, 1961) plays this metaphor game, describing the baby's hands, its fingers: "Rosebud, knot of worms / . . . / Five moony crescents."

This type of verse is clever; cleverness alone, however, does not make good poetry. In these poems she is dealing with an inherently sentimental subject in a merely cute manner. ("There's a cuddly mother"—"Dark House.") These poems constitute some of her weakest work. It seems significant that she could not deal with maternity or babies in a positive or hopeful manner and at the same time raise the quality of her writing out of the level of mere verse and into the realm of true poetry. That she occasionally tried to treat these subjects positively and hopefully shows her ambivalent attitude toward them.

> **Sentimentality or cuteness are charges seldom leveled against Sylvia Plath. She is more often accused of excess hostility, of hysteria.**
> **—*Jeannine Dobbs***

Sentimentality or cuteness are charges seldom leveled against Sylvia Plath. She is more often accused of excess hostility, of hysteria. Most of her poems about maternity exhibit these characteristics. In **"Parliament Hill Fields"** (*Crossing the Water*), for instance, a bevy of children is playing. As the speaker approaches them, she observes that their tightly knit group opens like a "crocodile . . . to swallow me." The fear is one of survival. Like the baby-god, children make demands that are often disturbing, cruel: "These children are after something, with hooks and cries" (**"Berck-Plage"**—*Ariel*). Fear and resentment of children are as prevalent as fear and resentment of men.

Plath's fear of procreativity was, in large part, a fear of a resultant loss of creativity. Esther Greenwood voices Plath's fear in *The Bell Jar:* "I . . . remembered Buddy Willard saying in a sinister, knowing way that after I had children I would feel differently, I wouldn't want to write poems any more. So I began to think maybe it was true that when you were married and had children it was like being brainwashed, and afterwards you went about numb as a slave in some private, totalitarian state."

What then about childlessness? For Plath, childbirth is a kind of martyrdom. A woman dies as a particular kind of woman when she bears a child, and she continues to die as the child feeds literally and metaphorically on her. What, then, about the woman who refuses to make this sacrifice?

> This woman . . .
> Says she is a man, not a woman.
> . . .
> She hates
> The thought of a baby—
> Stealer of cells, stealer of beauty—
>
> She would rather be dead than fat,
> Dead and perfect like Nefertit.
> —**"The Fearful"**

Plath sees childlessness as a kind of perfection, but perfection of a terrible nature because it is also death. The woman no longer sacrifices herself for the sake of life. The sacrifice is complete because all life is denied: "Perfection is terrible, it cannot have children" (**"The Munich Mannequins"**—*Ariel*). In **"Edge"** (*Ariel*), the mother proudly takes back the gift of herself: "The woman is perfected" because she has reversed her maternal functions:

> Each dead child coiled, a white serpent,
> One at each little
>
> Pitcher of milk, now empty.
> She has folded
>
> Them back into her body. . . .

In **"Tulips"** (*Ariel*), one of Plath's most popular poems, she uses a personal experience as a setting to express the complexities that the idea of childlessness has for her. Ted Hughes says she wrote **"Tulips"** after being hospitalized for an appendectomy in March of 1961. She had miscarried just a short time before this operation; probably the second hos-

pital confinement triggered associations with death and birth. These tulips are "like an awful baby." There is something wild and dangerous about them. She wants to reject them because she says they "eat my oxygen." She wants to reject the tulips as she wants to reject the trappings of her life and the family she has:

> Now I have lost myself, I am sick of baggage—
> My husband and child smiling out of the family
>   photo;
> Their smiles catch onto my skin, little smiling
>   hooks.

Not tulips but death is the gift she wants, as in **"A Birthday Present"** (*Ariel*), but in both cases the irony is that the gift is life. What she finds in her rejection of the gift here is freedom, a kind of perfection:

> I didn't want any flowers. I only wanted
> To lie with my hands turned up and be utterly
>   empty.
> How free it is, you have no idea how free—
> . . .
> It is what the dead close on, finally. . . .

Her freedom is both wonderful and terrible because the price is so high. The woman must give up her man and her child that hook onto her, as well as her things, her possessions. And the ultimate price—and reward—is death. Just as it is "the mouths of corpses" that suck in the poem **"Childless Woman"** (*Winter Trees*).

In May of 1962 Plath finished her one dramatic work, **"Three Women"** (*Winter Trees*), which was produced by the BBC in August of that year. The setting is "a maternity ward and round about." Three voices are heard: The Wife, The Secretary, and The Girl. Each voice captures an aspect of Plath's attitudes toward motherhood as revealed by her other work. The Wife, the First Voice, believes she is ready for the ultimate experience of her life. She is shaken by the violence of her labor to exclaim: "There is no miracle more cruel than this," and "I am used"; but after the birth, she exults in her son.

The Second Voice, The Secretary, is the voice of the woman who loses her child and is, therefore, both mother and no mother. Reflecting on her loss, she says:

> I did not look. But still the face was there,
> The face of the unborn one that loved its perfec-
>   tions,
> The face of the dead one that could only be perfect
> In its easy peace, could only keep holy so.

But her loss has left her empty, useless. By personifying this in terms of a woman who is characterized by her function outside the home, The Secretary, Plath may be suggesting that this fate, this loss, is a punishment. The Secretary reassured herself that her husband will still love her in her "deformity." And she vows a kind of penance, a rededication to her domestic duties:

> I shall be a heroine of the peripheral.
> I shall not be accused by isolate buttons,
> Holes in the heels of socks, the white mute faces
> Of unanswered letters, confined in a letter case.

The end of the drama finds this woman, true to her promise, "mending a silk slip," and reaffirming both her identity and her dedication to her husband: "I am a wife." She seems also to be anticipating a reward: another chance, another pregnancy.

The Third Voice, The Girl, is not ready for her experience. Her attitude is one of extreme hostility to men in general for her predicament. When her "red, terrible girl" is born, The Girl remarks: "Her cries are hooks that catch and grate like cats. / It is by these hooks she climbs to my notice." The Girl rejects her child and re-establishes herself in her old life, which is college life, intellectual life. However, her "black gown is a little funeral."

Through the voices of the three women, then, Plath again explores women's fates and choices such as those represented by the fig tree. Because she did not die at twenty, she was forced to define her life in terms of the choices women have traditionally had to make.

Roles are exclusively maintained in bee society. In Plath's series of "bee" poems, she uses their society and her experience with beekeeping as a way to express her frustration over her own roles. In **"Stings"** (*Ariel*), she identifies with both the drones and the queen, and reveals the conflict between her domestic and her poetic—her queenly—selves:

> I stand in a column
>
> Of winged, unmiraculous women,
> Honey-drudgers.
> I am no drudge
> Though for years I have eaten dust
> And dried plates with my dense hair.
>
> And seen my strangeness evaporate . . .
> They thought death was worth it, but I
> Have a self to recover, a queen.

But even had she wished it, the real children could not be folded back into her womb. They were there to contend with along with the daily, routine, household chores. Added to this was the frustration of being married to a poet, whose own poetry was getting written while she dusted, diapered, and served as his secretary.

Plath's poems with domestic settings are usually her most ominous poems. There is "viciousness in the kitchen" as she says in the first line of **"Lesbos"** (*Ariel*), a poem which examines the hostile relationship between two women largely in terms of their domestic situations. Birth and death are "cooking" in the kitchen setting of **"A Birthday Present."** In **"The Detective"** (*Winter Trees*), it is "the smell of years burning, here in the kitchen." There has been a death, but paradoxically "there is no body in the house at all." There is no body because the woman has long since ceased to exist as a person. Her functions have been performed, she has kept the furniture polished; but her personhood has been effaced, her sexuality has atrophied:

> The mouth first . . .
> . . .
> Her breasts next.
> . . .
> Then the dry wood, the gates,
> The brown motherly furrows, the whole estate.

Death came, the result of a deadly atmosphere (even the sunlight is "bored"), the withdrawal of love, the drain of motherhood ("there was no absence of lips, there were two children").

Mothers are devoured by their children, effaced; women are subjugated by men, imprisoned, mutilated, made into puppets or toys, hollow or blank with no identities and no wills. Plath's ambivalence toward men, marriage, and motherhood (in her last poems, abandonment by her husband added other dimensions as well), and the guilt she surely felt help explain the degree to which her domestic poems are associated with suffering. They are not exaggerations of pain but accumulations of it. They reflect not only her perception of outer reality, but they project her inner reality as well.

It can never be known whether or not Plath chose (consciously or unconsciously) paths that would lead her deeper and deeper into a domestic labyrinth because she needed those subjects and those experiences and the emotions they stimulated in order to create her best work. Her letters reveal, however, that in the final weeks of her life, separated from her husband, writing the final stunning poems, she felt poetically released, "as if domesticity had choked me." Perhaps it is not stretching a point to say that choosing to die by sticking her head in a gas oven is a perfect symbolization of, and final statement on, that aspect of her experience.

M. D. Uroff (essay date 1977)

SOURCE: "Sylvia Plath and Confessional Poetry: A Reconsideration," in *Iowa Review,* Vol. 8, No. 1, 1977, pp. 104-15.

[*In the following essay, Uroff contrasts Plath's poetic voice with the confessional mode developed by American poet Robert Lowell. Uroff contends that Plath, unlike Lowell, incorporates abstracted autobiographic detail in her poetry only to amplify or dramatize feelings of pain and sorrow rather than to induce actual self-revelation.*]

When M. L. Rosenthal first used the term, confessional poetry, he had in mind a phase in Robert Lowell's career when Lowell turned to themes of sexual guilt, alcoholism, confinement in a mental hospital, and developed them in the first person in a way that intended, in Rosenthal's view, to point to the poet himself. Rosenthal was careful to limit the possibilities of the mode but he did name Sylvia Plath a confessional poet as well because, he said, she put the speaker herself at the center of her poems in such a way as to make her psychological vulnerability and shame an embodiment of her civilization. Rosenthal's widely accepted estimation was challenged first by Ted Hughes who pointed out that Plath uses autobiographical details in her poetry in a more emblematic way than Lowell, and more recently by Marjorie Perloff who claims that Plath's poetry lacks the realistic detail of Lowell's work. If Hughes and Perloff are right, and I think they are, then we should reconsider the nature of the speaker in Plath's poems, her relationship to the poet, and the extent to which the poems are confessional.

What distinguishes Plath's poems from Lowell's is precisely the kind of person in the poem. With Lowell, according to Rosenthal, it is the literal self. Lowell himself has said that while he invented some of his autobiography, he nonetheless wants the reader to feel it is true, that he is getting the real Robert Lowell. The literal self in Lowell's poetry is to be sure a literary self, but fairly consistently developed as a self-deprecating, modest, comic figure with identifiable parents, summer homes, experiences at particular addresses. When he discloses under these circumstances his weaknesses, his ineptitude, his misery, his inflicting of pain on others, he is in fact revealing information that is humiliating or prejudicial to himself. In this sense, the person in the poem is making an act of confession, and, although we as readers have no power to forgive, Lowell's self-accusatory manner makes it impossible to judge. We are not outraged but chastened by such revelations. With Plath, it is otherwise. The person in her poem calls certain people father or mother but her characters lack the particularity of Commander and Mrs. Lowell. They are generalized figures not real-life people, types that Plath manipulates dramatically in order to reveal their limitations. Precisely because they are such types, the information that Plath reveals about them is necessarily prejudicial and has consequently misled some

readers who react with hostility to what she has to reveal. Elizabeth Hardwick calls her lacerating and claims that Plath has the distinction of never being in her poems a nice person. While niceness is not a perfect standard for judging a person in a poem, Hardwick's reaction and that of many other critics who follow her reveal the particular way in which Plath's revelations are prejudicial to her. Plath's outraged speakers do not confess their misery so much as they vent it, and this attitude, unlike that of Lowell's characters, makes them susceptible to rather severe critical judgments. However, if we look at the strategy of the poems, we might arrive at a more accurate estimate of the person in them and of her relationship to the poet.

> **I believe that one should be able to control and manipulate experiences, even the most terrifying, like madness, being tortured, this sort of experience, and one should be able to manipulate these experiences with an informed and intelligent mind.**
> —*Sylvia Plath*

Sylvia Plath herself has said, "I think my poems immediately come out of the sensuous and emotional experiences I have, but I must say I cannot sympathize with these cries from the heart that are informed by nothing except a needle or a knife, or whatever it is. I believe that one should be able to control and manipulate experiences, even the most terrifying, like madness, being tortured, this sort of experience, and one should be able to manipulate these experiences with an informed and intelligent mind." The difference between Plath and Lowell is clearly outlined when we set this statement next to Lowell's account of how he came to write confessional poetry. He says that when he started writing the poems in *Life Studies* he had been doing a number of readings on the West Coast and found that he was simplifying his poems, breaking the meter, making impromptu changes as he read. He claimed that poets had become proficient in forms and needed to make a "breakthrough back into life." *Life Studies* may be read as that repossession of his own life, and its mode is properly confessional because both in the poems and the prose of that volume the suffering and victimizing speaker searches through his own pain in order to perceive some truth about the nature of his experience. Plath's speakers make no such search. They are anxious to contain rather than to understand their situation. When Lowell's speaker in "Skunk Hour" says, "My mind's not right," he expresses some kind of desolate self-knowledge. By contrast, Plath calls the maddened woman in **"Miss Drake Proceeds to Supper,"** "No novice / In those elaborate rituals / Which allay the malice / Of knotted table and crooked chair." Both characters may be mad but their strategies differ. Where Lowell's character confesses his weakness, Plath's character employs all her energies in maintaining a ritualistic defense against her situation. She seems in a perverse way to act out the program of the poet whose informed and intelligent mind must manipulate its terrifying experiences. There is in fact a strange correspondence between Miss Drake's methods and those of her creator. Miss Drake is superbly sensitive, wildly inventive in objectifying her fears, and skilled at controlling them. But there is also a vast distance between Miss Drake and the poet, a distance that may be measured by the techniques of parody, caricature, hyperbole that Plath employs in characterizing her. There is something perversely comical about Miss Drake who "can see in the nick of time / How perilous needles grain the floorboards." If Miss Drake's rigid efforts are not quite ridiculed, it is fair to say that she does not engage our sympathies in the way that Lowell's speaker in "Skunk Hour" (who may also be ridiculous) does. She has been distanced from us by the poet who sees her as a grotesque reflection of herself, employing the manipulative strategies of the uninformed mind against an undefined terror, channeling what might have been creative energy into pointless rituals.

"Miss Drake Proceeds to Supper" is an early poem but it reveals the way in which Plath controlled her own terrifying experiences in her poetry. She did so by creating characters and later speakers who demonstrate the way in which the embattled mind operates. Far from speaking for the poet, they stage crazy performances which are parodic versions of the imaginative act. Through them, Plath shows how terror may grip the mind and render it rigid. Through her speaker's projective fantasies, she projects her own understanding of hysterical control and the darker knowledge of its perilous subversion of the imagination. While Miss Drake's elaborate rituals are designed to hold off her fears, the poet who created her is handling in the act of the poem, however indirectly, her own frightening knowledge of madness. What for the mad woman is a means of avoiding experience becomes for the poet a means of controlling it. The poems, unlike the speakers in them, reveal Plath's terrifying self-knowledge.

In her poems, Plath is not concerned with the nature of her experience, rather she is engaged in demonstrating the way in which the mind deals with extreme circumstances or circumstances to which it responds with excessive sensitivity. The typical strategy of her speakers is to heighten or exaggerate ordinary experience and at the same time to intensify the mind's manipulative skills so that fathers become Fascists and the mind that must deal with the image it has conjured up becomes rigidly ritualistic. In her early poems, Plath stands outside and judges her characters, drawing caricatures not only of madness but of its counterpart, hysterical sanity. As she continued to write however, she began to let the characters speak for themselves in caricature, parody, and hyperbole which they use not as vehicles of judgment but as

inevitable methods of their performances. When the mind that must deal with terror stiffens and rigidifies, parody will become its natural means of expression.

Between **"Miss Drake Proceeds to Supper"** and her late poems, however, Plath explored another way in which the mind responds to its terrors. In what has been called her middle period, Plath became interested in a kind of character who had been exhausted by her fears and could not control experience. For example, the insomniac of **"Zoo Keeper's Wife"** lies awake at night thinking over her grievances and the particular horrors of her husband's zoo full of "wolf-headed fruit bats" and the "bird-eating spider." Her response to her husband is as hyperbolic as the hysterical spinster's disdain for love's slovenliness in an early Plath poem but she has no rituals with which to deal with it nor barricades to hide behind. Rather, she says, "I can't get it out of my mind." All she can do is "flog apes owls bears sheep / Over their iron stile" and still she can't sleep. Again, in **"Insomniac,"** the mind cannot handle memories that "jostle each other for face-room like obsolete film stars." The speaker's "head is a little interior of grey mirrors. / Each gesture flees immediately down an alley / Of diminishing perspectives, and its significance / Drains like water out the hole at the far end." It is in these poems and others like them of this period that Plath's speakers sound most like Lowell's in his more exhausted and despairing moods yet even here Plath focuses on the function or nonfunction of the mind rather than on the meaning of the experience.

As Plath turned into her later period in a poem such as **"Tulips"** the speaker of her poem seems to welcome the loss of control that had harried the insomniacs. As she goes into the hospital in this poem, she claims to be learning peacefulness, and she hands herself over to the hospital attendants to be propped up and tended to. The nurses bring her numbness in "bright needles," and, as she succumbs to the anesthesia, she claims that she only wanted to be utterly empty. However, she does not rest in that attitude very long before she comes out of the operating room and its anesthetized state and begins reluctantly to confront her pain. Her first response is to complain that the tulips hurt her, watch her, that they eat up her oxygen. But, when the speaker claims a correspondence between the tulips' redness and her own wound, her manipulative mind begins to function again, first in negative ways, tormenting itself by objectifying its pain. Then, in a brief but alarming reversal, the speaker associates the tulips not only with the pain but with the heart so that the outside threat and power are not only overcome but subsumed. Because the speaker here has so exaggerated her own emptiness and the tulips' violence and vitality, she must then accept in herself the attributes she has cast onto the tulips which now return to her. The heart blooms. Here, for once, the manipulative mind works its own cure. If the supersensitive mind can turn tulips into explosions, it can also reverse the process and turn dangerous animals into bloom-ing hearts. What it cannot do, despite the speaker's claim, is accept utter emptiness. It cannot refuse to be excited by the flowers that it does not want.

"Tulips" is an unusual poem in Plath's work not because it demonstrates how the mind may generate hyperboles to tor-ture itself (which is a common strategy of Plath's poems) but because it shows how this generative faculty may have a positive as well as a negative function. **"Tulips"** is not a cheerful poem, but it does move from cold to warmth, from numbness to love, from empty whiteness to vivid redness, a process manipulated by the associative imagination. The speaker herself seems surprised by her own gifts and ends the poem on a tentative note, moving toward the faraway country of health. Despite this possibly hopeful ending, how-ever, the body of the poem demonstrates the way in which the mind may intensify its pain by objectifying it.

What takes place in **"Tulips"** in a private meditation (and perhaps the privacy accounts for the mind's pliancy) is given a much more ferocious treatment in the public performances of Plath's late poems. It is in fact the sense of being on public display that calls forth the rage of the speakers in these late poems. Forced to perform, they develop elaborate rituals. Their manipulative powers become a curse not a cure. In **"The Tour,"** the speaker, caught "in slippers and housedress with no lipstick," greets with mock hospitality her maiden aunt who wants "to be shown about": "Do step into the hall," "Yes, yes, this is my address. / Not a patch on *your* place, I guess." Instead of refusing to become a victim of the aunt's meddlesome curiosity, the speaker readily assents to it. Af-ter apologizing for the mess, she leads her aunt right into it, showing her the frost-box that bites, the furnace that ex-ploded, the sink that ate "seven maids and a plumber." With mock concern, she warns the aunt, "O I shouldn't put my finger in *that*," "O I shouldn't dip my hankie in, it *hurts!*" "I am bitter? I'm averse?" she asks, dropping for a second her polite mask but resuming it immediately in her refrain, "Toddle on home to tea now." The speaker manipulates the aunt's curiosity, turning it back on itself by maintaining a tone of insistent courtesy and forced intimacy that is de-signed to jeeringly protect the aunt from the brazen exhibi-tion of the open house of horrors. She appears to contrast her own dreary domestic appliances to her aunt's exotic pos-sessions (the gecko she wears as costume jewelry, her Javanese geese and monkey trees); but actually her machines are "wild," she says, and in a different way unlike her aunt's tamed decorations. However, when she calls herself "creepy-creepy," she seems to have assumed her aunt's gecko-like qualities. The staginess of this speaker, her insistent rhym-ing, exclamatory sentences, italicized words, all provide not only a grotesque reflection of the aunt's alarm, but also sug-gest a kind of hysterical control. The speaker's ability to manipulate the aunt is matched by a more sinister ability to

manipulate her own horrors, to locate them in furnace and stove, and there to give them a separate identity. Her mind, like Miss Drake's, is extremely skilled at objectifying her fears. The poet who felt that the intelligent mind must ma-nipulate its most terrifying experiences also knew that the deranged mind could operate in such a way as to hold off its terror, separate itself from the agony it suffered, and the speaker here exemplifies that process. When at the end she warns the aunt not to trip over the nurse-midwife who "can bring the dead to life," she points to the source of her mis-ery, the creative principle that has itself assumed an objec-tive identity and become part of the mess. The midwife, like a poet, delivers life with "wiggly fingers," and she has in fact been very active in endowing dead household appliances with a lively if destructive energy; but now she too has been cast out.

In this speaker who can not only caricature her aunt with the "specs" and "flat hat" but also her own creepiness as well as her "awfully nice" creative faculties, Plath presents a damning portrait of the too inventive mind that exults in self-laceration. It is not quite accurate to say that this speaker is unaware of her own strategies because she is supremely self-conscious; but she is trapped by them. Where others have been devoured or repelled, she lives on, neither despairing nor shocked but charged with a hysterical energy that she deploys finally against herself. Her nurse-mid-wife is eye-less. She too can only see herself now as others see her. Her ability to manipulate her own suffering is a subversion of the poet's creative powers; it becomes a means of holding off rather than exploring her situation.

A quite different manipulator is the speaker in **"The Appli-cant"** who appears to be a comic figure, reveling in her machinations. Unlike the woman in **"The Tour,"** she seems to speak for others not for herself. She starts out with the characteristic question of the convention-loving woman, "First, are you our sort of person?" What interests her, she reveals, is not what we might expect from someone who would ask that question, the social qualities of her marriage applicant, but rather her physical parts. "Our sort of person" has no glass eyes, false teeth, rubber breasts, stitches to show something's missing. Once having assured herself on that score, she presents her applicant's hand in marriage, prom-ising not only the traditional services that it will "bring tea-cups and roll away headaches" but that at the end it will even "dissolve of sorrow." Then, as if this "guaranteed" emotion might be too much for the man, she confides, "We make new stock from the salt." Such economy, such efficiency, this marriage broker seems to cluck. The woman "willing" "to do whatever you tell it" can be easily recycled. Next the speaker turns to the man who like the woman is "stark na-ked." Instead of putting him through the same examination of parts, she quickly offers him a wedding suit, "Black and stiff," that he can reuse as a funeral shroud. She adopts the familiar tone of the tailor ("How about this suit—" "Believe me, they'll bury you in it.") that shades into that of the mortician. Suddenly the suit, the girl, the deadly convention of marriage are all one, like a tomb, equally "waterproof, shatterproof, proof / Against fire and bombs through the roof." The subversive excess of her promises here is hastily passed over as her sales pitch continues: "Now your head, excuse me, is empty. / I have the ticket for that. / Come here, sweetie, out of the closet." What she presents is "A living doll" whose value will increase with each anniversary, paper at first but silver in 25 years and gold at 50 years.

It might be argued that **"The Applicant"** does not properly belong to those poems in which Plath exposes the mind's manipulation of terrifying experiences. After all, marriage— and especially the marriage contracted here—is a conventional arrangement which should not affect the fears or passions or emotions of either the man or the woman. In addition, the speaker here appears safely removed from the situation she directs. These facts, however, do not explain the tone of the poem which comes through in the insistent refrain, "Will you marry it?" This speaker who has "the ticket" for everything seems, despite her all-knowing and consoling comic pose, very anxious to have her question answered. Again, as in the other poems we have discussed, the nature of the speaker in **"The Applicant"** deserves more attention than it has received. What she says is obvious enough but why does she say it? I have called her a woman although her sex is nowhere identified partly because of her language (she calls the woman "sweetie" and the man "My boy") and partly because of her claim that her applicant can sew, cook and "talk, talk, talk" (no man, I believe would have considered that last feature a selling point) but chiefly because she seems to be extremely concerned for the successful outcome of her applicant. She is like the applicant herself willing to make any claim and to accede to any demands in order to strike a bargain. Hers is a pose of course, but it is the pose of the compliant woman. Like the patient in **"Tulips"** who accepts the gift of flowers that torment her and the niece in **"The Tour"** who responds to her aunt's detested visit, the speaker here insists on participating in a situation the demands of which she finds abhorrent. Her only recourse for dealing with it is a mode at which she is particularly skilled, burlesque. Yet behind the scorn and the scoffing is another feeling, something like hysteria, that expresses itself in her repeated question. She seems trapped by the sexual stereotypes she parodies. The ventriloquism of this poem hides the fact that this is an internal debate. The sexual fear that has driven the "sweetie" into the closet and the boy to his last resort also propels the manipulations of this shrewd if too agreeable woman. Here again is the controlling mind using its powers to compartmentalize rather than explore its situation.

"The Applicant" has been given serious consideration as

Plath's statement on marriage yet it does not point to the poet herself in the same way that, for example, Robert Lowell's "Man and Wife" does. Its characters are unparticularized and unconnected to any specific event in Plath's experience. Its sexual stereotypes (the girl willing to do anything in order to be married and the boy only willing to marry if he can be convinced that he will get a worthwhile product) are manipulated by a speaker whose tension-filled control reveals not only their power over her but the terror that informs them. This speaker can manage, but she cannot escape her situation.

The relationship between poet and speaker in two other late poems, **"Lady Lazarus"** and **"Daddy,"** is somewhat more complicated because these poems do call upon specific incidents in Plath's biography, her suicide attempts and her father's death. Yet to associate the poet with the speaker directly, as many critics have done, does not account for the fact that Plath employs here as before the techniques of caricature, hyperbole, and parody that serve both to distance the speaker from the poet and at the same time to project onto the speaker a subversive variety of the poet's own strategies. In **"Lady Lazarus,"** the nature of the speaker is peculiar and defies our ordinary notions of someone prone to attempt suicide. Suicide is not a joyous act, and yet there is something of triumph in the speaker's assertion that she has done it again. The person recovering from a suicide attempt, as this speaker says she is, cannot possibly be so confident at the very moment of her recovery that her sour breath will vanish in a day and that she will soon be a smiling woman. Nor could she have the presence of mind to characterize those who surround her as a "peanut-crunching crowd" and her rescuers as enemies. And finally it seems psychologically impossible for the suicide victim to have the energy to rise at all against other people, much less to threaten to "eat men like air." The person who speaks here does so not to explore her situation but to control it. She is first of all a performer, and, although she adopts many different roles, she is chiefly remarkable for her control not only of herself but of the effects she wishes to work on those who surround her. She speaks of herself in hyperboles, calling herself a "walking miracle," boasting that she has "nine times to die," exclaiming that dying is an art she does "exceptionally well," asserting that "the theatrical / Comeback in broad day" knocks her out. Her treatment of suicide in such buoyant terms amounts to a parody of her own act. When she compares her suicide to the victimization of the Jews and later on when she claims there is a charge for a piece of her hair or clothes and thus compares her rescued self to the crucified Christ or martyred saint, she is engaging in self-parody. She employs these techniques partly to defy the crowd with its "brute / Amused shout: / 'A miracle!'" and partly to taunt her rescuers, "Herr Doktor" "Herr Enemy," who regard her as their "opus." She is neither a miracle nor an opus, and she fends off those who would regard her in this way. But the techniques have another function as well; they display the extent to which she can objectify herself, ritualize her fears, manipulate her own terror. Her extreme control in fact is intimately entwined with her suicidal tendencies. The suicide is her own victim, can control her own fate. If she is not to succumb to this desire, she must engage in the elaborate ritual which goes on all the time in the mind of the would-be suicide by which she allays her persistent wish to destroy herself. Her act is the only means of dealing with a situation she cannot face. Her control is not sane but hysterical. When the speaker assures the crowd that she is "the same, identical woman" after her rescue, she is in fact telling them her inmost fear that she could and probably will do it again. What the crowd takes for a return to health, the speaker sees as a return to the perilous conditions that have driven her three times to suicide. By making a spectacle out of herself and by locating the victimizer outside herself in the doctor and the crowd, she is casting out her terrors so that she can control them. When she says at the end that she will rise and eat men like air, she is projecting (and again perhaps she is only boasting) her destruction outward. That last stanza of defiance is in fact an effort of the mind to triumph over terror, to rise and not to succumb to its own victimization.

The speaker's tone is hysterical, triumphant, defiant. Only once does she drop this tone to admit the despair that underlies it when she says. "What a trash / To annihilate each decade." Otherwise she maintains her rigid self-control in accents that range from frenzied gaiety to spiteful threats. Although her situation is much more extreme than those social occasions of **"Tulips," "The Tour," "The Applicant,"** it is like them not of her own making. She has been rescued when she wanted to die. Her response is perverse. She does not welcome her rescuers, nor does she examine the condition that forced her death wish; instead she accepts her fate and presents herself as in complete control. The effort of her act which comes through in her tone is intense yet necessary because without it she would have to face the fact that she is not in control. Her performance is a defense against utter desolation. Here again is the mind manipulating its own terrors. Plath was no stranger to this method, as we have said before, but while she works here with a parallel between hysterical control and creative control she presents the first as a mad reflection of the second. The speaker like Miss Drake is "No novice / In those elaborate rituals" that allay her terror yet her tremendous energies are so absorbed in maintaining them that she has no reserve with which to understand why she performs as she does. When she sees herself as a victimized Jew or Christ, she may be engaging in self-parody but the extremity of her circumstances does not allow her to realize it. The poet behind the poem is not caricaturing Lady Lazarus as she had Miss Drake; she is rather allowing Lady Lazarus to caricature herself and thus demonstrating the way in which the mind turns ritualistic against horror.

Despite the fact that **"Lady Lazarus"** draws on Plath's own suicide attempt, the poem tells us little more than a newspaper account of the actual event. It is not a personal confession. What it does reveal is Plath's understanding of the way the suicidal person thinks.

"Daddy" is an even more complicated treatment of the same process. The poem opens with the daughter's assertion that "You do not do, you do not do." But if Daddy will not do, neither will he not not do, and we find this speaker in the characteristic Plath trap, forcing herself to deal with a situation she finds unacceptable. **"Daddy"** is not so much an account of a true-life situation as a demonstration of the mind confronting its own suffering and trying to control that by which it feels controlled. The simplistic, insistent rhythm is one form of control, the obsessive rhyming and repeated short phrases are others, means by which she attempts to charm and hold off the evil spirits. But the speaker is even more crafty than this technical expertise demonstrates. She is skilled at image-making like a poet and she can manipulate her images with extreme facility. The images themselves are important for what they tell us of her sense of being victimized and victimizer but more significant than the actual image is the swift ease with which she can turn it to various uses. For example, she starts out imagining herself as a prisoner living like a foot in the black shoe of her father. Then she casts her father in her own role and he becomes "one grey toe / Big as a Frisco seal" and then quickly she is looking for his foot, his root. Next he reverts to his original boot identity, and she is the one with "The boot in the face." And immediately he returns with "A cleft in your chin instead of your foot." At the end, she sees the villagers stamping on him. Thus she moves from booted to booter as her father reverses the direction. The mind that works in this way is neither logical nor psychologically penetrating; it is simply extremely adept at juggling images. In fact, the speaker is caught in her own strategies. She can control her terrors by forcing them into images, but she seems to have no understanding of the confusion her wild image-making betrays. When she identifies herself as a foot, she suggests that she is trapped, but when she calls her father a foot the associations break down. In the same way, when she caricatures her father as a Fascist and herself as a Jew, she develops associations of torture which are not exactly reversed when she reverses the identification and calls herself the killer of her vampire-father. The speaker here can categorize and manipulate her feelings in name-calling, in rituals, in images, but these are only techniques, and her frenzied use of them suggests that they are methods she employs in the absence of any other. When she says, "Daddy, I have had to kill you," she seems to realize the necessity of the exorcism and to understand the ritual she performs, but the frantic pitch of the language and the swift switches of images do not confirm any self-understanding. The pace of the poem reveals its speaker as one driven by a hysterical need for complete control, a need that stems from the fear that without such control she will be destroyed. Her simple, incantatory monologue is the perfect vehicle of expression for the orderly disordered mind.

The pace of the poem reveals its speaker as one driven by a hysterical need for complete control, a need that stems from the fear that without such control she will be destroyed.

—*M. D. Uroff*

In talking to A. Alvarez, Plath called these poems "light verse." **"Daddy"** does not seem to fall easily into that category despite its nonsense rhymes and rhythms, its quickly flicking images. It is neither decorous nor playful. On the other hand, given its subject, neither is it ponderous or solemn. Above all it offers no insight into the speaker, no mitigating evidence, no justification. Plath's classification is clear perhaps only if we consider her speaker a parodic version of the poet. The speaker manipulates her terror in singsong language and thus delivers herself in "light verse" that employs its craft in holding off its subject. For all the frankness of this poem, the name-calling and blaming, the dark feeling that pervades it is undefined, held back rather than revealed by the technique. The poet who has created this speaker knows the speaker's strategies because they are a perverted version of her own, and that is the distinction between the speaker's "light verse" and the poet's serious poem.

From her earliest madwomen and hysterical virgins to the late suicides and father-killers, Plath portrays characters whose stagey performances are subversions of the creative act. Absorbed in their rituals, they confess nothing. They are not anxious to make a breakthrough back into life. In fact, their energies are engaged in erecting a barricade against self-revelation. Plath's fascination with this parodic image of the creative artist stems from a deep knowledge of the machinations of the mind. If she reveals herself in these poems, she does so in the grotesque mirror of parody. If these poems come out of her own emotional experiences, as she said they did, they are not uninformed cries from the heart. Rather, she chose to deal with her experience by creating characters who could not deal with theirs and through their rituals demonstrate their failure. These poems, like the speakers in them, are superbly controlled; but the poet behind the poem uses her immense technical control to manipulate the tone, the rhythm, the rhyme, the pace of the speakers' language in order to reveal truths about the speakers that their obsessive assertions deny.

Linda Wagner (essay date 1977)

SOURCE: "Plath's 'Ariel': 'Auspicious Gales,'" in *Concerning Poetry,* Vol. 10, No. 2, 1977, pp. 5-7.

[*In the following essay, Wagner draws attention to the complexity of Plath's poetry in* Ariel *which, as the critic notes, invokes archetypal imagery and the paradoxical portrayal of suffering as survival to create depth of feeling and insight.*]

No poet contemporary with us has been so subject to misreadings, especially biographical misreadings: Sylvia Plath's poems evoke the worst of subjective fallacies. Probably some of our charged reactions are symptomatic of the times and the culture; but more of them seem to stem from the always-too-easy identification between troubled poet (with the ultimate proof, her suicide) and what might be the tone of imagery and rhythm of the poem considered. Because Plath worked so intensively in archetypal imagery (water, air, fire as bases for image patterns, for example), many of her poems could be read as either "dark" wasteland kinds of expressions, or as the reverse, as death-by-water, salvation poems—destruction implied, but also survived, phoenix-like. (When a reader finds a gay, affirmative poem like **"Balloons"** to be ominous simply because the child holds "A red / shred in his little fist" at its end, there must be some reason for discounting fully ninety percent of the affirmative lines and images in that single poem—making it "fit" the preconception we have of Plath's work as being consistently despairing, vindictive, bleak.)

"Ariel," the title poem of the collection that made Plath known to the reading world so soon after her 1962 suicide, is a similarly ambiguous poem, rich in its image patterns of movement-stasis, light-dark, earth-fire. The progression in the poem is from the simply stated "Stasis in darkness," a negative condition as Plath indicates in the very similarly imaged poem **"Years,"** to the ecstatic transformation-through-motion of the closing. That this is a poem about motion is clear from the second image, which seems to be a depiction of the faint light of morning ("substanceless blue pour of tor and distances") yet also stresses the movement of the image—*pour, distances.* The eye of the reader, like that of the poet, is on what is coming, and the scene that appears is always couched in imagery that includes motion words or impressions. Even the furrows of earth are moving ("splits and passes").

The antagonistic forces in the poem are those contrary to the motion that is so passionately evoked. Set against the unity of the moving horse and rider are the "Nigger-eye berries" casting "dark hooks," creating both "shadows" (in contrast to the ever-growing light) and the only blood image of the poem. The stasis is momentary, for immediately after the pause that the word *shadows* creates comes the fragmentary picture of the woman being forcibly taken "through air"— "thighs hair / flakes from my heels." And the statement-like close of that vivid image is the apostrophe to the naked Godiva (physically, and emotionally, "white," a link to the many images of purity and chastity in these *Ariel* poems), who finds her freedom in the physical act of unpeeling— not clothes, in this case, but "Dead hands, dead stringencies." There is no motion in either of these things; either the sexual links with the image of hands, or the compulsive duty-oriented links with the image of stringency.

Once free of these deadnesses, the rider/persona can then take off to the ecstasy that awaits her. That the progression has been a fairly tortuous one is suggested, effectively, by the back-and-forth emphasis on stasis and then speed; but that the poem ends with the sheer joy of movement can be read only as affirmation. Metamorphosis, transcendence blots out even those all-important cries from the children that other poems of Plath's show to be so beloved, as the poem closes (and the line arrangement here is, of course, mine):

> And now I foam to wheat, a glitter of seas,
> (The child's cry melts in the wall)
> and I am the arrow
> the dew that flies suicidal, at one with the drive
> into the red eye, the cauldron of morning.

(Masterful as many of the short-line tercet poems are— **"Lady Lazarus," "Fever 103°," "Daddy"**—this particular poem works better when a longer line structure is used, because the impetus to motion is more apparent. The syncopation of the short-line structure impedes the fluid reading that the image and syntax pattern suggests.)

Several critics rely heavily on Plath's color systems in reading her poems. In this poem, the day changes from "darkness" to the weightless blue of morning to an absence of color, punctuated by the brown arc of the horse's neck and the earth it travels, by the black of the sweet blood berries, and by the group of color images describing the woman's body as evanescent (sparkling, silver/gold, glinting, in "wheat," "glitter of seas," "dew"). From a coloration, itself a kind of transcendence, the poem moves back to the sharp vividness of the day which is no longer shrouded in amorphous blues, but instead burns, cauldron-like, with a red glow in the east. Red being one of those archetypal images that can suggest several often-contradictory meanings, I turn here to the common source of the name *Ariel* and the association, affirmatively, with fire and the color red. (Because Plath spoke so frequently of her admiration for Shakespeare, and because in another late poem, **"The Bee Meeting,"** she describes herself as "the magician's girl," it seems a fair assumption that she did know *The Tempest;* and that, at this period in her life, separated from her husband and living alone, she might have been drawn to its fairy-tale emphasis on Miranda's sheltered chastity, and the final consummation of marriage/peace/brotherhood at the play's end—even if ironically.)

As Shakespeare describes Ariel, through Prospero's words, "a spirit too delicate / To act her earthy and abhorred commands," imprisoned in a pine for a dozen years, until freed from the confinement by Prospero's "art" (not, significantly, magic or other kind of occult power.) Set in direct and sympathetic contrast to both the hag Sycorax and Caliban, her son, Ariel is an unrelieved power for freedom and good throughout the play. When he first appears, Act I, Scene ii, he aligns himself with the elements that are presented as positive in Plath's poems:

> All hail, great master! Grave sir, hail! I come
> To answer thy best pleasure, be't to fly,
> To swim, to dive into the fire, to ride
> On the curled clouds . . . .

So succinctly are all the images given, Ariel's speech is a near-abstract for the successive patterns that appear in Plath's poem. And when one relates Ariel's imprisonment within the tree to the "White Godiva, I unpeel" image, even that takes on richer suggestion.

As Ariel continues speaking, we see that the method he has used to effect Prospero's command—to bring the ship to land—is that of taking the shape of fire, St. Elmo's fire ("Now on the beak, Now in the waist, the deck, in every cabin, I flamed amazement. Sometime I'd divide, And burn in many places, on the topmast, The yards and bowsprit, would I flame distinctly, Then meet and join"). The paradox, of course, is that none of the ship's passengers has been harmed, that Ariel's use of fire is a gentle means of attaining what is best for the human beings involved; and that the tone of the play—caught so well in Prospero's farewell charge to Ariel—is that of benevolence and calm. He charges Ariel with securing for the ship at its leave-taking, "calm seas, auspicious gales, And sail so expeditious that shall catch Your royal fleet far off." (The paradox inherent in "auspicious gales" is echoed in Plath's use of fire and driven motion as positive forces within the poem in question.) And to Ariel, as farewell, Prospero adds, with endearment, "My Ariel, chick. That is thy charge. Then to the elements be free, and fare thou well!" The greatest blessing of all, freedom, particularly after a dozen years jailed within a tree. And Plath's vibrant use of the free flying image at the close of **"Ariel"** suggests the same benizon, "I / Am the arrow, // The dew that flies / Suicidal, at one with the drive / Into the red // Eye, the cauldron of morning." "Then to the elements be free" . . . "at one with the dew." Plath's drive to motion, that sheer impact of energy and force, beyond the "Dead hands, dead stringencies," is the power behind not only **"Ariel"** but also **"Stings," "Lady Lazarus," "Wintering,"** and **"Fever 103°."** That she, with Shakespeare, found such violence as the gale winds "auspicious" is an important index to these passionate and sometimes difficult poems, poems important enough to us that we must learn to read them with an insight closer to Plath's own emphasis, and to her equally personal thematic direction.

Eileen Aird (essay date 1979)

SOURCE: "'Poem for a Birthday' to 'Three Women': Development in the Poetry of Sylvia Plath," in *Critical Quarterly*, Vol. 21, No. 4, 1979, pp. 63-72.

[*In the following essay, Aird examines Plath's rapid creative development after the publication of* The Colossus. *Challenging "the oversimplified and rather sentimental theory" that motherhood inspired Plath's artistic growth during this period, Aird cites Plath's remarkable commitment to her work and the influence of Robert Lowell, Anne Sexton, and Theodore Roethke.*]

Critical discussion of Plath's poetry is understandably focused on the magnificent late poems with occasional forays into the earlier exercises of *The Colossus*—and they were precisely exercises in style and image by a poet identifying her subjects. It therefore seems useful to pay some attention to the question of development, to the nature and timing of the transition from *The Colossus* to *Ariel* and to the poetic and biographical factors affecting this development. **'Poem for a Birthday'** initiates the transitional period which ends with **'Three Women.'** It is significant that these are her two longest poems, **'Berck-Plage'** being the only other one which begins to approach their expansiveness of structure and imagery. The theme of pregnancy and birth in **'Three Women'** is foreshadowed by the opening section of images of hibernation, storage and growth in **'Poem for a Birthday,'** and in both poems realistic presentation merges into a symbolic opposition between creativity and destructiveness. The individual experience of the woman who conceives, carries and gives birth to a child is emblematic of a world of natural growth and patterned progression in stark contrast to the technological destructiveness of the world of 'bulldozers, guillotines and white chambers of shrieks.' Ted Hughes's famous account of the development of Sylvia Plath's poetry relates the two major accelerations of quality and command to the birth of her two children. This would date the transitional stage from mid-1960 to early 1962. The chronology of development revealed by the poems themselves does not entirely bear out his analysis. It indicates a longer period lasting from October 1959 up to June, 1962 and in the work of a poet who developed at the speed of Sylvia Plath months are significant. If we are looking for bio-

graphical factors, and I introduce them only to counterbalance the widely held acceptance of Hughes's account—there is a much more precise correlation between the breakdown of their marriage and the writing of the great poems. In a letter to her mother written on 7 November 1962, immediately after moving into the London flat she said: 'Living apart from Ted is wonderful—I am no longer in his shadow.' The whole letter is over-elated and many of the subsequent heavily edited letters are much gloomier. Her own analysis however cannot be disregarded and it does go some way to suggest the much more complex relationship between circumstances and poetic processes that one would expect than the over-simplified and rather sentimental theory of childbirth as *the* stimulus.

'Poem for a Birthday' and **'Three Women,'** then, mark off a period of rapid change and development in Sylvia Plath's poetry, characterised not only by the movement from written exercises on the page, stylish, crystalline and static, to dramatic poems which need to be spoken aloud—a movement of which she was herself very conscious—but also by an increasing richness of imagery and a confident statement of subject.

> [*The Colossus*] is academic poetry of a high order but the emphasis is on structure rather than statement.
>
> —*Eileen Aird*

The world of *The Colossus* is, for the most part, an external one of landscape and situation into which the personal is rarely allowed to erupt. The emphasis is too firmly on manipulation of both subject and form to make a contained statement, what we are given are neat, aesthetic glimpses of potentially dramatic situations. A case in point is a poem like **'Point Shirley,'** an elegy for the poet's dead grandmother heavily influenced by Robert Lowell's early style. So self-consciously clever is the language that real grief and loss is ironically excluded from the poem. The simple domestic image at the beginning of the second verse, 'She is dead / Whose laundry snapped and froze here,' which does direct us very appropriately to an individual human reality, is immediately negated by the verbally vigorous but emotionless description of the sea. This is academic poetry of a high order but the emphasis is on structure rather than statement. In the last nine months of her life craftsmanship becomes the vehicle of expressiveness, there is a complete unity about the poems. Nevertheless there was still a feeling even in the mature work that some subjects were not suitable for poetry and this was one of the reasons she gave for turning to the novel: a form which she defined without apparent irony as appropriate for female concerns:

Poetry I feel is such a tyrannical discipline, you've got to go so far, so fast, in such a small space that you've just got to turn away all the peripherals. And I miss them! I'm a woman, I like my little Lares and Penates, and I like trivia, and I find that in a novel I can get more of life, perhaps not such an intense life, but certainly more of life . . .

This is a revealing statement not just in terms of *The Bell Jar* but also of the late poetry which found a way of including those household details and using them as a stepping-off point for the wider concerns—'**A Birthday Present**' begins with a woman making pastry, '**Mary's Song**' with a woman cooking the Sunday lamb, but in both poems the secure, protected world of kitchen and house very quickly gives way to an inner world of violent and tragic dimensions.

The poems of the last nine months of her life are marked by a complete unity of form and expressiveness and there are hints of this in a few exceptional poems in *The Colossus*, '**The Beekeeper's Daughter**' in particular. Ted Hughes has commented very enigmatically on this poem as being 'one of a group of poems that she wrote at this time about her father . . . This poem, one of her chilliest, recounts a key event in her Vita Nuova.' Whatever the reason the poem has an urgent directness and sense of purpose which most of the early poems lack. It also has a very clear progression, a dominant feature of the later work which often rushes towards a conclusion which is also the climax of the poem. The complicated ambivalence of the relationship between father and daughter in the poem is established through the claustrophobic, wantonly erotic imagery of the opening verse:

> A garden of mouthings. Purple, scarlet-speckled, black
> The great corollas dilate, peeling back their silks

—but what is initially the abject subjection of the daughter, 'My heart under your foot, sister to a stone' argues itself into an acceptance of that subjection, even a transformation of it into exultant destiny: 'The queen bee marries the winter of your year.' The poem oscillates between the opposed images of the stone and the queen bee, an opposition which she was to return to frequently. The stone always represents a reduction to a core, stripped of all pretence and association, the low point from which a gradual ascent is eventually possible; its first important use is in the last section of '**Poem for a Birthday**,' '**The Stones**,' where the experience of the suicidal coma is such a reduction to a core, an elemental surviving self:

> The mother of pestles diminished me.
> I became a still pebble.

There are also significant references for this image in *The Bell Jar,* firstly in the skiing episode where Esther breaks her leg in a wild flight down a slope too difficult for her, which she sees as an attempt to recapture the protective safety of the womb: 'the pebble at the bottom of the well, the white sweet baby cradled in its mother's belly,' and secondly at the end of the second section of the novel where having taken a large number of barbiturates—too many in fact, they make her sick—she lies down behind a stack of firewood in the basement expecting to die: 'The silence drew off, baring the pebbles and shells and all the tatty wreckage of my life. Then, at the rim of vision, it gathered itself, and in one sweeping tide, rushed me to sleep.' In opposition to this static defence is the dynamic power of the queen bee. '**The Beekeeper's Daughter**' needs to be read in conjunction with the late sequence of bee poems written in the autumn of 1962 where the queen bee is a symbol of female survival soaring triumphantly if murderously up:

> Now she is flying
> More terrible than she ever was, red
> Scar in the sky, red comet
> Over the engine that killed her—
> The mausoleum, the wax house.

This vision is in turn one of a series of female images of almost magical power and autonomy beginning with the circus performer of a very early poem '**Circus in Three Rings**,' written while she was still at Smith, and finding later expression in the avenging Clytemnestra of '**Purdah**,' 'the pure acetylene virgin' of '**Fever 103°**,' the vampire killer of '**Daddy**,' the ascendant phoenix of '**Lady Lazarus**' and the majestic 'God's lioness' of '**Ariel**.' '**The Beekeeper's Daughter**' is a very significant turning-point from the undirected extravagance of '**Circus in Three Rings**' towards the powerful female images of *Ariel*. It finds some similarities in '**The Colossus**' and '**Moonrise**' and perhaps most importantly in an uncollected poem of the same time, '**Electra on Azalea Path**,' but like them is still held in the strait-jacket of formalities.

It is in '**Poem for a Birthday**,' heavily reliant on Roethke's structure and imagery though it is, that she first identifies both her subject and her voice. Roethke was such a fertile influence at this point in her development because she learnt from him that objective reality can serve as a medium to release the inner drama. '**Poem for a Birthday**' acknowledges for the first time the supremacy of an inner world which earlier poems, '**Lorelei**,' '**Full Fathom Five**,' '**The Ghost's Leavetaking**,' '**Ouija**,' have only hinted at. The poems which Roethke collected in *Praise to the End* are the most direct influence on Sylvia Plath's poem which has the same structure of short sections connected by theme and imagery. More importantly Plath's subjects—madness, loneliness, sexual identity, family relationships, growth and searching—

are very close to Roethke's in poems such as **'Dark House.'** Sylvia Plath acknowledges Roethke as a major influence in a letter to her mother on 2 February 1961: 'Ted and I went to a little party the other night to meet the American poet I admire next to Robert Lowell—Ted [for Theodore Roethke]. I've always wanted to meet him as I find he is my influence.' Her debt to Lowell and Sexton is acknowledged later in October 1962 and is a much more general recognition of an exciting mode, a developing convention. For all its raw immediacy, its deliberate assault on the reader's sensibility, *Ariel* has a dramatic focus and personae which are pared away by Lowell and Sexton. This becomes very clear if we compare Lowell's own comment on the intention of *Life Studies* with Sylvia Plath's note on **'Daddy.'** Lowell told an interviewer: 'there was always that standard of truth which you wouldn't ordinarily have in poetry—the reader was to believe that he was getting the real Robert Lowell!' whereas Sylvia Plath wrote of **'Daddy'**: 'The poem is spoken by a girl with an Electra complex. Her father died while she thought he was God. Her case is complicated by the fact that her father was also a Nazi and her mother very possibly part-Jewish. In the daughter the two strains marry and paralyse each other—she has to act out the awful little allegory before she is free of it.' Sylvia Plath's comment is not an evasion of the confessional aspect of the poem but an indication of the extent to which the personal is subordinated to a much more inclusive dramatic structure. Unlike Lowell Sylvia Plath was not writing a poetic autobiography but used personal experience as a way into the poem—this is further reflected in the reading response to Sylvia Plath which frequently begins at the level of autobiographical fact and then deepens into an awareness of the intellectual and tonal complexities of the poem. The real Sylvia Plath is far from present in the poetry and there is clear evidence of this in the comparison of the diary extract in *Johnny Panic and the Bible of Dreams* in which she describes the meeting of bee-hive owners, on which the poem **'The Bee Meeting'** is based, with the poem itself. Although the poem uses exactly the observed details of the diary—and Ted Hughes has explained that Sylvia Plath found it a useful discipline to describe people and places minutely in her diary—the whole mood and reference of the poem is transformed, the situation is changed from the humorous precision of the diary to a metaphor of alienation. Although her later work diverges from Roethkean structure and imagery he was seminal in showing her how to balance the personal and the general so that the poem is public rather than bafflingly private.

The purely literary influence of Roethke initiates the development towards poetic maturity but the biographical factors are also important. The whole of Sylvia Plath's life up to 1959 was one of academic distinction and ambition, she won prizes, gained A grades, conquered one goal after another, but after the year's successful but demanding teaching at Smith, with two degrees behind her and thoughts of gradu-ate work to the fore of her mind she relinquished academic life in favour of full-time writing. The decision was obviously made under Ted Hughes's influence—he had given up the academic world much earlier—and it was an immensely courageous step for her to take, involving as it did the rejection of one of her most deep-seated values—any one reading her *Letters Home* of the mid-fifties cannot help but be impressed by her sheer tenacity and desire for success. Ted Hughes and Sylvia Plath had decided that they would settle permanently in Europe, so she was also turning her back on her family and cultural heritage as well as on the obvious career towards which all her efforts were previously directed. At this point in the autumn of 1959, she was pregnant for the first time and **'The Manor Garden'** which like **'Poem for a Birthday'** was written at Yaddo indicates some of the ambivalence of fear and excitement which this generated in her; its final, very satisfying image is a brilliant rendering of this ambivalence:

> The small birds converge, converge
> With their gifts to a difficult borning

The period at Yaddo with its time for concentration and writing is a further factor: to be invited to Yaddo represented society's recognition of artistic merit and for Sylvia Plath such recognition always seems to have been more important than it is to Ted Hughes. Writing to her mother on 16 October 1962 she described her *Ariel* poems with tragic irony as: 'the best poems of my life: they will make my name.' The notion of success was one which she could not relinquish easily as a scholar, a mother, a wife or a poet.

'Poem for a Birthday' was completed during the time at Yaddo and the title is richly significant reminding us as it does of her own October birthday, the coming birth of her child and the metaphorical deaths and births which modulate into the final qualified recovery of **'The Stones.'** For the first time in this poem she directly faced the task of relating individual to general experience. That individual experience is female, defined both biologically and experientially and the poem is a dialogue between the dislocated girl who is maenad and witch and 'the mother of otherness.' To be female in **'Poem for a Birthday'** is to be protective and procreative: 'The month of flowering's finished. The fruit's in,' 'Here's a cuddly mother' but it is also to be demanding and possessive: 'Mother of beetles only unclench your hand: / I'll fly through the candle's mouth like a singeless moth.' This counterpoints the major theme of the poem which is the need to rationalise the disparity of childhood and adulthood. The tensions are resolved finally in a rebirth after suffering: 'We grow. / It hurts at first. The red tongues will teach the truth.'

Sylvia Plath said of her artistic method: 'I think that personal experience shouldn't be a kind of shut-box and mirror-looking narcissistic experience. I believe it should be generally relevant to such things as Hiroshima and Dachau and so on.' The relevance of this to the late poetry is abundantly clear but the process begins with **'Poem for a Birthday'** where private experience—breakdown and the reasons for it, clinical treatment, pregnancy—is extended through the images which accumulate layer upon layer until it becomes a metaphor for suffering throughout the natural and the human world. The attempt to communicate the 'real Robert Lowell' emerges in *Life Studies* as a painfully accurate analysis of one man's dilemmas which gains universal significance through the depth and detail of its treatment. Sylvia Plath's method is essentially different, rather than delineating the individual in a recognisable cultural context she uses the private to gain access to the universal by ruthlessly mythologising her own experience and in doing this moves a long way from autobiography—**'Lady Lazarus'** is not Sylvia Plath but a mythical character of suffering and rebirth, ultimately a type of the tragic poet of Yeats's 'Lapis Lazuli.'

If both the themes and the images of Sylvia Plath's poem are closely influenced by Roethke's the ending is markedly different. Typically Roethke's poems end in a moment of revelation even if it quickly falls back into the old state of waiting: the end of the quest is an organic awareness of wholeness, of the full recovery of identity. Although the image of the vase reconstructed at the end of **'Poem for a Birthday'** recalls Roethke the mood is far from elated or affirmative:

> Ten fingers shape a bowl for shadows.
> My mendings itch. There is nothing to do.
> I shall be as good as new.

To be 'as good as new' is to have lost the tragic intensity which characterised the earlier sections of the poem and is very close to the ending of Lowell's 'Home after Three Months Away': 'Cured, I am frizzled, stale and small.'

The sense of reduction and nullity points forward to the fear of the static in *Ariel*, the constant search for the dynamic: 'What I love is / the piston in motion— / My soul dies before it.'

'Poem for a Birthday' explores the metaphoric complexities of a series of balanced opposites—fertility/sterility,child/ adult, day/night, death/life, animal/human, illness/recovery— and the poems in *Crossing the Water* continue this exploration. Sylvia Plath's own analysis of some of the poems in this volume is penetrating: bewailing their lack of dynamic accuracy with the self-mocking irony she employs with such brilliance in *Ariel,* she indicates the gulf between poetry as craft, the period of *The Colossus* and poetry as necessity, the period of *Ariel.* The poems, she says, are like those pick-

led foetuses of *The Bell Jar,* specimens for learning not the real living being and yet:

> It wasn't for any lack of mother-love
> O I cannot understand what happened to them!
> They are proper in shape and number and every
>   part.

But to be 'proper in shape and number and every part' is no longer the keynote of authenticity, the period of villanelles, of elaborate rhyme schemes and regular stanzas is over but the absolute confidence and daring of *Ariel* has to be worked for and many of the poems in *Crossing the Water* elaborate a world which is no more than gothic. The title-poem for instance is little more than a playing with images of darkness and silence relieved by characteristically lyrical moments: 'A little light is filtering from the water flowers,' 'Stars open among the lilies.' To take her own criteria of judgement this poem is not relevant to Hiroshima or Dachau, it remains in a private fantasy world although it is visually and verbally attractive. A much more accomplished poem is **'Insomniac'** but this still lacks the fusion of elements which distinguishes the great poetry; it is never more than descriptive of a hollow world, it fails to evoke it despite the deliberate metaphorical violence:

> Night long, in the granite yard, invisible cats
> Have been howling like women, or damaged
>   instruments.

What she did achieve for the first time in *Crossing the Water,* however, was the wry, mocking humour which in *Ariel* frequently allows her to maintain the balance between public and private by deflecting interest from 'the needle or the knife.' **'In Plaster,'** which owes something to Sylvia Plath's observations of a fellow-patient when she was recovering from her appendectomy, is wry, brilliant, humorous in its portrait of the relationship between cast and patient. The persona of the poem is mocking but by the end of the poem we see that there is a complex balance between command and dependence in the relationship and in the last verse that mockery merges into a defiance which is the flimsiest of disguises for the sense of helpless dependency which lies beneath it:

> She may be a saint, and I may be ugly and hairy,
> But she'll soon find out that doesn't matter a bit.
> I'm collecting my strength; one day I shall manage
>   without her,
> And she'll perish with emptiness and begin to
>   miss me.

In the end the mocker himself is mocked and his earlier contemptuously pragmatic acceptance of the cast gives way to an awareness of the superior consistency of his partner; the word-play in the last line indicating that an uneasier intellectual wit has replaced the confident laughter of the beginning—humour as a mode of experiencing has become wit as an attempt to control.

Many of the poems of *Crossing the Water* are precise forerunners in subject, tone and imagery of the achievements of *Ariel* and the obvious companion poem of '**In Plaster**' is '**The Applicant.**' Both are poems about marriage—'**The Applicant**' more obviously so than '**In Plaster**' which only suggests it through the final identification of the patient as male and the cast as female, but the tone of '**The Applicant**' has a ferocious humour which makes '**In Plaster**' seem almost whimsical by contrast. It is clear that Sylvia Plath's description of '**Daddy**' and '**Lady Lazarus**' as 'light verse' is descriptive of a mode which contrives a highly sophisticated blend of the ironic and the violent. The tentative beginnings of this mode are present as early as '**Poem for a Birthday**' in the constant perception of self in animal or doll-like images. There is a deliberate pretence at belittling the enormity of experience which makes it more accessible. When the poetry fails it is sometimes because the ironic perspective is missing. This is very rarely the case in *Ariel* or *Winter Trees* but it happens more frequently in *Crossing the Water*. In the poem '**Life**' for instance there is too sharp a contrast between the amused affectionate description of an idealised even deliberately sentimentalised Victorian past and the rigours of the present:

> This family
> Of valentine-faces might please a collector:
> They ring true, like good china.
>
> Elsewhere the landscape is more frank.
> The light falls without let-up, blindingly.
> A woman is dragging her shadow in a circle
> About a bald hospital saucer.
> It resembles the moon, or a sheet of blank paper.
>
> And appears to have suffered a sort of private
>   blitzkrieg.

Although the poetry of *Ariel* constantly presses forward into extremes, they are contrived not confessional extremes. The much discussed ending of '**Lady Lazarus**' is perhaps the best illustration of this with its images of transcending suffering both personally and aesthetically. Out of the ashes of the concentration camps and the emotional ruins of the suicidal patient rises the mythical phoenix affirming her identity as both female and poet. As in '**Fever 103°**' the very experience of pain is the means by which the persona grows to a new power: the first statement of this is in '**Poem for a Birthday**': 'We grow / It hurts at first. The red tongues will reach the truth.' The skill of '**Lady Lazarus**' is exhibited by the tone of this ending which is ironic but without bitter-

ness—we are out of the human world either of the voyeuristic onlooker or the concentration camp doctors and rising into the half-delirious visionary Paradise to which the 'pure acetylene virgin' of '**Fever 103°**' aspires. It is a Paradise of autonomy and recognised identity, an image of completeness and completeness is one of the central subjects of *Ariel*. *Crossing the Water* achieves the ironic perspective but it fails to organise the opposites of Plath's vision into the drive towards perfection of *Ariel*.

Sylvia Plath's greatness lies not in the extremity of her subjects, although it is this extremity which may initially draw the reader into the poem, but in her handling of richly allusive images. . . .

—Eileen Aird

A final demonstration of the distinction between the assurance and imagistic richness of the late poetry and the valuable experiments of the transitional period lies in a comparison of '**Candles**' with '**Nick and the Candlestick.**' Both poems start from the imaginative associations of a mother nursing her child by candlelight but whereas '**Candles**' goes no further than a consideration of the passage of time which links the Edwardian grandparents with the new baby, '**Nick and the Candlestick**' encompasses the painful world of the creative imagination and the potential dangers of the man-made world but is able to move beyond both in the affirmation of the mother's love for the child:

> You are the one
> Solid the spaces lean on envious.
> You are the baby in the barn.

The last verse is an elliptical comment on the poem's structure for the baby is realised with detail and humanity at the heart of a poem which deals in abstractions. '**Nick and the Candlestick**' is a very densely structured poem where each image, almost each word of the first half finds its echo in the second half and the joy of the ending does not evade the pain of the first half—baby and mother have not escaped from the subterranean cave only hung it with soft roses and the mercuric atoms still drip into the terrible well. The structure of '**Candles**' in comparison is merely linear. Sylvia Plath's greatness lies not in the extremity of her subjects, although it is this extremity which may initially draw the reader into the poem, but in her handling of richly allusive images and this is the point of '**Stillborn**' which recognises that formal structure must give way to the organic unity of associative imagery. The more one reads the poetry the less possible it is not to seek echoes in other poems. The poet who composed slowly and cerebrally with frequent recourse to the Thesaurus and dictionary and who delighted in the esoteric and archaic was involved in the intellectual discipline of analogy and alternative which paved the way for the apparently effortless flow of association and image. **'Nick and the Candlestick'** is an extraordinary complex and intellectually difficult poem but that difficulty is not a high gloss imposed on the poem by a mind still confined by an academic tradition, it is the natural attribute of what Sylvia Plath called 'that unicorn thing—a real poem.'

Pamela J. Annas (essay date 1980)

SOURCE: "The Self in the World: The Social Context of Sylvia Plath's Late Poems," in *Women's Studies,* Vol. 7, Nos. 1-2, 1980, pp. 171-83.

[*In the following essay, Annas offers analysis of depersonalization in Plath's poetry which, according to Annas, embodies Plath's response to oppressive modern society and her "dual consciousness of self as both subject and object."*]

> For surely it is time that the effect of disencouragement upon the mind of the artist should be measured, as I have seen a dairy company measure the effect of ordinary milk and Grade A milk upon the body of the rat. They set two rats in cages side by side, and of the two one was furtive, timid and small, and the other was glossy, bold and big. Now what food do we feed women as artists upon?
> —Virginia Woolf, *A Room of One's Own*

The dialectical tension between self and world is the location of meaning in Sylvia Plath's late poems. Characterized by a conflict between stasis and movement, isolation and engagement, these poems are largely about what stands in the way of the possibility of rebirth for the self. In **"Totem,"** she writes: "There is no terminus, only suitcases / Out of which the same self unfolds like a suit / Bald and shiny, with pockets of wishes / Notions and tickets, short circuits and folding mirrors." While in the early poems the self was often imaged in terms of its own possibilities for transformation, in the post-*Colossus* poems the self is more often seen as trapped within a closed cycle. One moves—but only in a circle and continuously back to the same starting point. Rather than the self *and* the world, the *Ariel* poems record the self *in* the world. The self can change and develop, transform and be reborn, only if the world in which it exists does; the possibilities of the self are intimately and inextricably bound up with those of the world.

Sylvia Plath's sense of entrapment, her sense that her choices are profoundly limited, is directly connected to the particular time and place in which she wrote her poetry. Betty Friedan describes the late fifties and early sixties for Ameri-

can women as a "comfortable concentration camp"—physically luxurious, mentally oppressive and impoverished. The recurring metaphors of fragmentation and reification—the abstraction of the individual—in Plath's late poetry are socially and historically based. They are images of Nazi concentration camps, of "fire and bombs through the roof" (**"The Applicant"**), of cannons, of trains, of "wars, wars, wars" (**"Daddy"**). And they are images of kitchens, iceboxes, adding machines, typewriters, and the depersonalization of hospitals. The sea and the moon are still important images for Plath, but in the *Ariel* poems they have taken on a harsher quality. "The moon, also, is merciless," she writes in **"Elm."** While a painfully acute sense of the depersonalization and fragmentation of 1950's America is characteristic of *Ariel,* three poems describe particularly well the social landscape within which the "I" of Sylvia Plath's poems is trapped: **"The Applicant," "Cut,"** and **"The Munich Mannequins."**

Sylvia Plath's sense of entrapment, her sense that her choices are profoundly limited, is directly connected to the particular time and place in which she wrote her poetry.
—*Pamela J. Annas*

"The Applicant" is explicitly a portrait of marriage in contemporary Western culture. However, the "courtship" and "wedding" in the poem represent not only male/female relations but human relations in general. That job seeking is the central metaphor in **"The Applicant"** suggests a close connection between the capitalist economic system, the patriarchal family structure, and the general depersonalization of human relations. Somehow all interaction between people, and especially that between men and women, given the history of the use of women as items of barter, seems here to be conditioned by the ideology of a bureaucratized market place. However this system got started, both men and women are implicated in its perpetuation. As in many of Plath's poems, one feels in reading **"The Applicant"** that Plath sees herself and her imaged *personae* as not merely caught in— victims of—this situation, but in some sense culpable as well. In **"The Applicant,"** the poet is speaking directly to the reader, addressed as "you" throughout. We too are implicated, for we too are potential "applicants."

People are described as crippled and as dismembered pieces of bodies in the first stanza of **"The Applicant."** Thus imagery of dehumanization begins the poem. Moreover, the pieces described here are not even flesh, but "a glass eye, false teeth or a crutch, / A brace or a hook, / Rubber breasts or a rubber crotch." We are already so involved in a sterile and machine-dominated culture that we are likely part artifact and sterile ourselves. One is reminded not only of the imagery of other Plath poems, but also of the controlling metaphor of Ken Kesey's *One Flew Over the Cuckoo's Nest,* written at about the same time as **"The Applicant"**—in 1962—, and Chief Bromden's conviction that those people who are integrated into society are just collections of wheels and cogs, smaller replicas of a smoothly functioning larger social machine. "The ward is a factory for the Combine," Bromden thinks. "Something that came all twisted different is now a functioning, adjusted component, a credit to the whole outfit and a marvel to behold. Watch him sliding across the land with a welded grin . . ."

In stanza two of **"The Applicant,"** Plath describes the emptiness which characterizes the applicant and which is a variant on the roboticized activity of Kesey's Adjusted Man. Are there "stitches to show something's missing?" she asks. The applicant's hand is empty, so she provides "a hand"

> To fill it and willing
> To bring teacups and roll away headaches
> And do whatever you tell it
> Will you marry it?

Throughout the poem, people are talked about as parts and surfaces. The suit introduced in stanza three is at least as alive as the hollow man and mechanical doll woman of the poem. In fact, the suit, an artifact, has more substance and certainly more durability than the person to whom it is offered "in marriage." Ultimately, it is the suit which gives shape to the applicant where before he was shapeless, a junk heap of fragmented parts.

> I notice you are stark naked.
> How about this suit—
> Black and stiff, but not a bad fit.
> Will you marry it?
> It is waterproof, shatterproof, proof
> Against fire and bombs through the roof.
> Believe me, they'll bury you in it.

The man in the poem is finally defined by the black suit he puts on, but the definition of the woman shows her to be even more alienated and dehumanized. While the man is a junk heap of miscellaneous parts given shape by a suit of clothes, the woman is a wind-up toy, a puppet of that black suit. She doesn't even exist unless the black suit needs and wills her to.

> Will you marry it?
> It is guaranteed
>
> To thumb shut your eyes at the end
> And dissolve of sorrow.

> We make new stock from the salt.

The woman in the poem is referred to as "it." Like the man, she has no individuality, but where his suit gives him form, standing for the role he plays in a bureaucratic society, for the work he does, the only thing that gives the woman form is the institution of marriage. She does not exist before it and dissolves back into nothingness after it. In **"The Applicant"** there is at least an implication that something exists underneath the man's black suit; that however fragmented he is, he at least *marries* the suit and he at least has a choice. In contrast, the woman *is* the role she plays; she does not exist apart from it. "Naked as paper to start," Plath writes,

> But in twenty-five years she'll be silver,
> In fifty, gold.
> A living doll, everywhere you look.
> It can sew, it can cook.
> It can talk, talk, talk.

The man, the type of a standard issue corporation junior executive, is also alienated. He has freedom of choice only in comparison to the much more limited situation of the woman. That is to say, he has relative freedom of choice in direct proportion to his role as recognized worker in the economic structure of his society. This should not imply, however, that this man is in any kind of satisfying and meaningful relation to his work. The emphasis in **"The Applicant"** upon the man's surface—his black suit—together with the opening question of the poem ("First, are you our sort of person?") suggests that even his relationship to his work is not going to be in any sense direct or satisfying. It will be filtered first through the suit of clothes, then through the glass eye and rubber crotch before it can reach the real human being, assuming there is anything left of him.

The woman in the poem is seen as an appendage; she works, but she works in a realm outside socially recognized labor. She works for the man in the black suit. She is seen as making contact with the world only through the medium of the man, who is already twice removed. This buffering effect is exacerbated by the fact that the man is probably not engaged in work that would allow him to feel a relationship to the product of his labor. He is probably a bureaucrat of some kind, and therefore his relationship is to pieces of paper, successive and fragmented paradigms of the product (whatever it is, chamberpots or wooden tables) rather than to the product itself. And of course, the more buffered the man is, the more buffered the woman is, for in a sense her real relationship to the world of labor is that of consumer rather than producer. Therefore, her only relationship to socially acceptable production—as opposed to consumption—is through the man.

In another sense, however, the woman is not a consumer, but a commodity. Certainly she is seen as a commodity in this poem, as a reward only slightly less important than his black suit, which the man receives for being "our sort of person." It can be argued that the man is to some extent also a commodity; yet just as he is in a sense more a laborer and less a consumer than the woman—at least in terms of the social recognition of his position—so in a second sense he is more a consumer and less a commodity than the woman. And when we move out from the particularly flat, paper-like image of the woman in the poem to the consciousness which speaks the poem in a tone of bitter irony, then the situation of the woman as unrecognized worker/recognized commodity becomes clearer. The man in **"The Applicant,"** because of the middle class bureaucratic nature of his work (one does not wear a new black suit to work in a steel mill or to handcraft a cabinet) and because of his position vis-a-vis the woman (her social existence depends upon his recognition), is more a member of an exploiting class than one which is exploited. There are some parts of his world, specifically those involving the woman, in which he can feel himself relatively in control and therefore able to understand his relationship to this world in a contemplative way. Thus, whatever we may think of the system he has bought into, he himself can see it as comparatively stable, a paradigm with certain static features which nevertheless allows *him* to move upward in an orderly fashion.

Within the context of this poem, then, and within the context of the woman's relationship to the man in the black suit, she is finally both worker and commodity while he is consumer. Her position is close to that of the Marxist conception of the proletariat. Fredric Jameson, in *Marxism and Form,* defines the perception of external objects and events which arises naturally in the consciousness of an individual who is simultaneously worker and commodity.

> Even before [the worker] posits elements of the outside world as *objects* of his thought, he feels *himself* to be an object, and this initial alienation within himself takes precedence over everything else. Yet precisely in this terrible alienation lies the strength of the worker's position: his first movement is not toward knowledge of the work but toward knowledge of himself as an object, toward self-consciousness. Yet this self-consciousness, because it is initially knowledge of an object (himself, his own labor as a commodity, his life force which he is under obligation to sell), permits him more genuine knowledge of the commodity nature of the outside world than is granted to middle-class "objectivity." For [and here Jameson quotes Georg Lukacs in *The History of Class Consciousness*] "his consciousness is the self-consciousness of merchandise itself . . ."

This dual consciousness of self as both subject and object is characteristic of the literature of minority and/or oppressed classes. It is characteristic of the proletarian writer in his (admittedly often dogmatic) perception of his relation to a decadent past, a dispossessed present, and a utopian future. It is characteristic of black American writers; W. E. B. Du Bois makes a statement very similar in substance to Jameson's in *The Souls of Black Folk,* and certainly the basic existential condition of Ellison's invisible man is his dual consciousness which only toward the end of that novel becomes a means to freedom of action rather than paralysis. It is true of contemporary women writers, of novelists like Doris Lessing, Margaret Atwood, and Rita Mae Brown, and of poets like Denise Levertov, Adrienne Rich, and Marge Piercy. In a sense, it is more characteristic of American literature than of any other major world literature, for each immigrant group, however great its desire for assimilation into the American power structure, initially possessed this dual consciousness. Finally, a dialectical perception of self as both subject and object, both worker and commodity, in relation to past and future as well as present, is characteristic of revolutionary literature, whether the revolution is political or cultural.

Sylvia Plath has this dialectical awareness of self as both subject and object in particular relation to the society in which she lived. The problem for her, and perhaps the main problem of Cold War America, is in the second aspect of a dialectical consciousness—an awareness of oneself in significant relation to past and future. The first person narrator of what is probably Plath's best short story, **"Johnny Panic and the Bible of Dreams,"** is a clerk/typist in a psychiatric clinic, a self-described "dream connoisseur" who keeps her own personal record of all the dreams which pass through her office, and who longs to look at the oldest record book the Psychoanalytic Institute possesses. "This dream book was spanking new the day I was born," she says, and elsewhere makes the connection even clearer: "The clinic started thirty-three years ago—the year of my birth, oddly enough." This connection suggests the way in which Plath uses history and views herself in relation to it. The landscape of her late work is a contemporary social landscape. It goes back in time to encompass such significant historical events as the Rosenberg trial and execution—the opening chapter of *The Bell Jar* alludes dramatically to these events—and of course it encompasses, is perhaps obsessed with, the major historical event of Plath's time, the second world war. But social history seems to stop for Plath where her own life starts, and it is replaced at that point by a mythic timeless past populated by creatures from folk tale and classical mythology. This is not surprising, since as a woman this poet had little part in shaping history. Why should she feel any relation to it? But more crucially, there is no imagination of the future in Sylvia Plath's work, no utopian or even antiutopian consciousness. In her poetry there is a dialectical consciousness of the self as simultaneously object and subject, but in her particular social context she was unable to develop a consciousness of herself in relation to a past and future beyond her own lifetime. This foreshortening of a historical consciousness affects in turn the dual consciousness of self in relation to itself (as subject) and in relation to the world (as object). It raises the question of how one accounts objectively for oneself. For instance, if I am involved in everything I see, can I still be objective and empirical in my perception, free from myth and language? Finally, this foreshortening of historical consciousness affects the question of whether the subject is a function of the object or *vice versa*. Since the two seem to have equal possibilities, this last question is never resolved. As a result, the individual feels trapped; and in Sylvia Plath's poetry one senses a continual struggle to be reborn into some new present which causes the perceiving consciousness, when it opens its eyes, to discover that it has instead (as in **"Lady Lazarus"**) made a "theatrical / Comeback in broad day / To the same place, the same face, the same brute / Amused shout: 'A miracle!'"

This difficulty in locating the self and the concomitant suspicion that as a result the self may be unreal are clear in poems like **"Cut,"** which describe the self-image of the poet as paper. The ostensible occasion of **"Cut"** is slicing one's finger instead of an onion; the first two stanzas of the poem describe the cut finger in minute and almost naturalistic detail. There is a suppressed hysteria here which is only discernible in the poem's curious mixture of surrealism and objectivity. The images of the poem are predominantly images of terrorism and war, immediately suggested to the poet by the sight of her bleeding finger: "out of a gap / A million soldiers run," "Saboteur / Kamikaze man—," and finally, "trepanned veteran." The metaphors of war are extensive, and, though suggested by the actual experience, they are removed from it.

In the one place in the poem where the speaker mentions her own feelings as a complete entity (apart from but including her cut finger) the image is of paper. She says,

> O my
> Homunculus, I am ill.
> I have taken a pill to kill
> The thin
> Papery feeling.

Paper often stands for the self-image of the poet in the post-*Colossus* poems. It is used in the title poem of *Crossing the Water,* where the "two black cut-paper people" appear less substantial and less real than the solidity and immensity of the natural world surrounding them. In the play *Three Women,* the Secretary says of the men in her office: "there was something about them like cardboard, and now I had

caught it." She sees her own infertility as directly related to her complicity in a bureaucratic, impersonal, male-dominated society. Paper is symbolic of our particular socioeconomic condition and its characteristic bureaucratic labor. It stands for insubstantiality; the paper model of something is clearly less real than the thing itself, even though in "developed" economies the machines, accoutrements, and objects appear to have vitality, purpose, and emotion, while the people are literally colorless, objectified, and atrophied.

The paper self is therefore part of Plath's portrait of a depersonalized society, a bureaucracy, a paper world. In **"A Life"** (*Crossing the Water*), she writes: "A woman is dragging her shadow in a circle / About a bald hospital saucer. / It resembles the moon, or a sheet of blank paper / And appears to have suffered a private blitzkrieg." In **"Tulips"** the speaker of the poem, also a hospital patient, describes herself as "flat, ridiculous, a cut-paper shadow / Between the eye of the sun and the eyes of the tulips." In **"The Applicant,"** the woman is again described as paper: "Naked as paper to start / But in twenty-five years she'll be silver, / In fifty, gold." Here in **"Cut,"** the "thin, / Papery feeling" juxtaposes her emotional dissociation from the wound to the horrific detail of the cut and the bloody images of conflict it suggests. It stands for her sense of depersonalization, for the separation of self from self, and is juxtaposed to that devaluation of human life which is a necessary precondition to war, the separation of society from itself. In this context, it is significant that one would take a pill to kill a feeling of substancelessness and depersonalization. Writing about American women in the 1950's, Betty Friedan asks, "Just what was the problem that had no name? What were the words women used when they tried to express it? Sometimes a woman would say, 'I feel empty somehow . . . incomplete.' Or she would say, 'I feel as if I don't exist.' Sometimes she blotted out the feeling with a tranquilizer."

A papery world is a sterile world; this equation recurs throughout the *Ariel* poems. For Sylvia Plath, stasis and perfection are always associated with sterility, while fertility is associated with movement and process. The opening lines of **"The Munich Mannequins"** introduce this equation. "Perfection is terrible," Plath writes, "it cannot have children. / Cold as snow breath, it tamps the womb / Where the yew trees blow like hydras." The setting of **"The Munich Mannequins"** is a city in winter. Often, Plath's poems have imaged winter as a time of rest preceding rebirth (**"Wintering," "Frog Autumn"**), but only when the reference point is nature. The natural world is characterized in Sylvia Plath's poems by process, by the ebb and flow of months and seasons, by a continual dying and rebirth. The moon is a symbol for the monthly ebb and flow of the tides and of a woman's body. The social world, however, the world of the city, is both male defined and separated from this process. In the city, winter has more sinister connotations; it suggests death rather than hibernation. Here the cold is equated with the perfection and sterility to which the poem's opening lines refer. Perfection stands in **"The Munich Mannequins"** for something artificially created and part of the social world.

The poem follows the male quest for perfection to its logical end—mannequins in a store window—lifeless and mindless "in their sulphur loveliness, in their smiles." The mannequins contrast with the real woman in the same way that the city contrasts with the moon. The real woman is not static but complicated:

> The tree of life and the tree of life
>
> Unloosing their moons, month after month, to no
>   purpose.
> The blood flood is the flood of love,
>
> The absolute sacrifice

However, in Munich, "morgue between Paris and Rome," the artificial has somehow triumphed. Women have become mannequins or have been replaced by mannequins, or at least mannequins seem to have a greater reality because they are more ordered and comprehensible than real women.

It is appropriate that Plath should focus on the middle class of a German city, in a country where fascism was a middle class movement and women allowed themselves to be idealized, to be perfected, to be made, essentially, into mannequins.
—*Pamela J. Annas*

It is appropriate that Plath should focus on the middle class of a German city, in a country where fascism was a middle class movement and women allowed themselves to be idealized, to be perfected, to be made, essentially, into mannequins. In **"The Munich Mannequins,"** as in **"The Applicant,"** Plath points out the deadening of human beings, their disappearance and fragmentation and accretion into the objects that surround them. In **"The Applicant"** the woman is a paper doll; here she has been replaced by a store window dummy. In **"The Applicant"** all that is left of her at the end is a kind of saline solution; in **"The Munich Mannequins"** the only remaining sign of her presence is "the domesticity of these windows / The baby lace, the green-leaved confectionery." And where the man in **"The Applicant"** is described in terms of his black suit, here the men are described in terms of their shoes, present in the anonymity of hotel corridors, where

> Hands will be opening doors and setting

> Down shoes for a polish of carbon
> Into which broad toes will go tomorrow.

People accrete to their things, are absorbed into their artifacts. Finally, they lose all sense of a whole self and become atomized. Parts of them connect to their shoes, parts to their suits, parts to their lace curtains, parts to their iceboxes, and so on. There is nothing left; people have become reified and dispersed into a cluttered artificial landscape of their own production.

Because the world she describes is a place created by men rather than women (since men are in control of the forces of production), Plath sees men as having ultimate culpability for this state of affairs which affects both men and women. But men have gone further than this in their desire to change and control the world around them. In **"The Munich Mannequins"** man has finally transformed woman into a puppet, a mannequin, something that reflects both his disgust with and his fear of women. A mannequin cannot have children, but neither does it have that messy, terrifying, and incomprehensible blood flow each month. Mannequins entirely do away with the problems of female creativity and self-determination. Trapped inside this vision, therefore, the speaker of the *Ariel* poems sees herself caught between nature and society, biology and intellect, Dionysus and Apollo, her self definition and the expectations of others, as between two mirrors.

Discussion of the *Ariel* poems has often centered around Sylvia Plath's most shocking images. Yet her images of wars and concentration camps, of mass and individual violence, are only the end result of an underlying depersonalization, an abdication of people to their artifacts, and an economic and social structure that equates people and objects. Like the paper doll woman in **"The Applicant,"** Sylvia Plath was doubly alienated from such a world, doubly objectified by it, and as a woman artist, doubly isolated within it. Isolated both from a past tradition and a present community, she found it difficult to structure new alternatives for the future. No wonder her individual quest for rebirth failed as it led her continuously in a circle back to the same self in the same world. Finally, what Sylvia Plath has bequeathed us in her poems is a brilliant narrative of the struggle to survive.

Linda W. Wagner (essay date 1986)

SOURCE: "Plath's *The Bell Jar* as Female *Bildungsroman*," in *Women's Studies*, Vol. 12, No. 1, 1986, pp. 55-68.

[*In the following essay, Wagner examines* The Bell Jar *as the chronicle of a young woman's psychological development and search for identity. As Wagner notes, Plath's de-*

piction of the heroine's madness and thinly veiled anger at patriarchal society differs from the traditional bildungsroman *in which the author strives to provide moral education.*]

One of the most misunderstood of contemporary novels, Sylvia Plath's *The Bell Jar* is in structure and intent a highly conventional *bildungsroman.* Concerned almost entirely with the education and maturation of Esther Greenwood, Plath's novel uses a chronological and necessarily episodic structure to keep Esther at the center of all action. Other characters are fragmentary, subordinate to Esther and her developing consciousness, and are shown only through their effects on her as central character. No incident is included which does not influence her maturation, and the most important formative incidents occur in the city, New York. As Jerome Buckley describes the *bildungsroman* in his 1974 *Season of Youth,* its principal elements are "a growing up and gradual self-discovery," "alienation," "provinciality, the larger society," "the conflict of generations," "ordeal by love" and "the search for a vocation and a working philosophy."

Plath signals the important change of location at the opening of *The Bell Jar.* "It was a queer, sultry summer, the summer they electrocuted the Rosenbergs, and I didn't know what I was doing in New York. . . . New York was bad enough. By nine in the morning the fake, country-wet freshness that somehow seeped in overnight evaporated like the tail end of a sweet dream. Mirage-gray at the bottom of their granite canyons, the hot streets wavered in the sun, the car tops sizzled and glittered, and the dry, cindery dust blew into my eyes and down my throat." Displaced, misled by the morning freshness, Greenwood describes a sterile, inimical setting for her descent into, and exploration of, a hell both personal and communal. Readers have often stressed the analogy between Greenwood and the Rosenbergs—and sometimes lamented the inappropriateness of Plath's comparing her personal *angst* with their actual execution—but in this opening description, the Rosenberg execution is just one of the threatening elements present in the New York context. It is symptomatic of the "foreign" country's hostility, shown in a myriad of ways throughout the novel.

In *The Bell Jar,* as in the traditional *bildungsroman,* the character's escape to a city images the opportunity to find self as well as truths about life. Such characters as Pip, Paul Morel, and Jude Fawley idealize the city as a center of learning and experience, and think that once they have re-located themselves, their lives will change dramatically. As Buckley points out, however, the city is often ambivalent: "the city, which seems to promise infinite variety and newness, all too often brings a disenchantment more alarming and decisive than any dissatisfaction with the narrowness of provincial life." For Esther Greenwood, quiet Smith student almost de-

lirious with the opportunity to go to New York and work for *Mademoiselle* for a month, the disappointment of her New York experience is cataclysmic. Rather than shape her life, it nearly ends it; and Plath structures the novel to show the process of disenchantment in rapid acceleration.

The novel opens in the midst of Greenwood's month in New York, although she tells the story in flashbacks; and for the first half of the book—ten of its twenty chapters—attention remains there, or on past experiences that are germane to the New York experiences. Greenwood recounts living with the other eleven girls on the *Mademoiselle* board at the Amazon Hotel, doing assignments for the tough fiction editor Jay Cee, going to lunches and dances, buying clothes, dating men very unlike the fellows she had known at college, and sorting through lifestyles like Doreen's which shock, bewilder, and yet fascinate her. Events as predictably mundane as these are hardly the stuff of exciting fiction but Plath has given them an unexpected drama because of the order in which they appear. *The Bell Jar* is plotted to establish two primary themes: that of Greenwood's developing identity, or lack of it; and that of her battle against submission to the authority of both older people and, more pertinently, of men. The second theme is sometimes absorbed by the first but Plath uses enough imagery of sexual conquest that it comes to have an almost equal importance. For a woman of the 1950s, finding an identity other than that of sweetheart, girlfriend, and wife and mother was a major achievement.

Greenwood's search for identity is described through a series of episodes that involve possible role models. Doreen, the Southern woman whose rebelliousness fascinates Esther, knows exactly what she will do with her time in New York. The first scene in the novel is Doreen's finding the macho Lenny Shepherd, disc jockey and playboy par excellence. Attracted by Doreen's "decadence," Esther goes along with the pair until the sexual jitterbug scene ends with Doreen's mellon-like breasts flying out of her dress after she has bitten Lenny's ear lobe. Esther has called herself *Elly Higginbottom* in this scene, knowing instinctively that she wants to be protected from the kind of knowledge Doreen has. Plath describes Esther as a photo negative, a small black dot, a hole in the ground; and when she walks the 48 blocks home to the Amazon in panic, she sees no one recognizable in the mirror. Some Chinese woman, she thinks, "wrinkled and used up," and, later, "the reflection in a ball of dentist's mercury." Purging herself in a hot bath, Greenwood temporarily escapes her own consciousness: "Doreen is dissolving, Lenny Shepherd is dissolving, Frankie is dissolving, New York is dissolving, they are all dissolving away and none of them matter any more. I don't know them, I have never known them and I am very pure." Unfortunately, when Doreen pounds on her door later that night, drunk and sick, Esther has to return to the real world. Her revulsion is imaged in Doreen's uncontrollable vomit.

The second "story" of the New York experience is the ptomaine poisoning of all the girls except Doreen after the *Ladies' Day* magazine luncheon. Plath's vignette of Jay Cee is imbedded in this account; the editor's great disappointment in Greenwood (because she has no motivation, no direction) serves to make Esther more depressed. As she comes near death from the poisoning, she also assesses the female role models available to her: her own mother, who urges her to learn shorthand; the older writer Philomena Guinea, who has befriended her but prescriptively; and Jay Cee, by now an admonitory figure. Although Esther feels "purged and holy and ready for a new life" after her ordeal, she cannot rid herself of the feeling of betrayal. No sooner had she realized Jay Cee ("I wished I had a mother like Jay Cee. Then I'd know what to do") than she had disappointed her. The development of the novel itself illustrates the kind of irony Esther had employed in the preface, with the lament

> I was supposed to be having the time of my life.
> I was supposed to be the envy of thousands of other college girls just like me all over America. . . .
>
> Look what can happen in this country, they'd say. A girl lives in some out-of-the-way town for nineteen years, so poor she can't afford a magazine, and then she gets a scholarship to college and wins a prize here and a prize there and ends up steering New York like her own private car.
>
> Only I wasn't steering anything, not even myself.

Plath's handling of these early episodes makes clear Greenwood's very real confusion about her direction. As Buckley has pointed out, the apparent conflict with parent or location in the *bildungsroman* is secondary to the real conflict, which remains "personal in origin; the problem lies with the hero himself" (or herself).

Esther Greenwood's struggle to know herself, to be self-motivated, to become a writer as she has always dreamed is effectively presented through Plath's comparatively fragmented structure. As Patricia Meyer Spacks writes in 1981 about literature of the adolescent, the adolescent character has no self to discover. The process is not one of discovering a persona already there but rather creating a persona. Unlike Esther, then, perhaps we should not be disturbed that the face in her mirror is mutable. We must recognize with sympathy, however, that she carries the weight of having to maintain a number of often conflicting identities—the obliging daughter and the ungrateful woman, the successful writer and the immature student, the virginal girlfriend and the worldly lover. In its structure, *The Bell Jar* shows how closely these strands are interwoven.

While Plath is ostensibly writing about Esther's New York

experiences and her quest for a female model, she regularly interjects comments about Buddy Willard, the Yale medical student who has proposed to Esther. Early references to him connect him with the haunting childbirth scene and the bottled foetuses and cadavers he has introduced Esther to. That these images are all connected with women's traditional choices in life—to become mothers—begins to frame the essential conflict between Buddy and Esther. From chapters five through eight Plath describes the romance between the two, but the extensive flashback seems less an intrusion than an explication. Esther is what she is in New York because of the indoctrination she has had at the hands of her socially-approved guide, Buddy Willard. For Buddy, women are helpmeets, submissive to husband's wishes; they have no identity in themself. Esther's desire to become a poet is nonsense (poems are "dust" in his vocabulary); her true role is to be virginal and accepting of his direction—whether the terrain be sex or skiing. More explicit than their conversations are the images Plath chooses to describe Esther during this section, images of frustration and futility.

One central image is that of the fig tree, first introduced after Esther has nearly died from food poisoning and is reading the stories *Ladies' Day* has sent the convalescents. Lush in its green spring, the fig tree nourishes the love of an unaware couple. In contrast, Esther describes her love for Buddy as dying,

> we had met together under our own imaginary fig tree, and what we had seen wasn't a bird coming out of an egg but a baby coming out of a woman, and then something awful happened and we went our separate ways.

When the fig tree metaphor recurs to Esther, she sees it filled with fat purple figs ("one fig was a husband and a happy home and children, and another fig was a famous poet and another fig was a brilliant professor, and another fig was Ee Gee, the amazing editor . . . ." She sits in the crotch of the tree, however, "starving to death, just because I couldn't make up my mind which of the figs I would choose. I wanted each and every one of them, but choosing one meant losing all the rest." The dilemma of her adolescence—unlike that of most men—was that any choice was also a relinquishing. Greenwood believed firmly that there was no way, in the American culture of the 1950s, that a talented woman could successfully combine a professional career with homemaking. As Mrs. Willard kept insisting, "What a man is is an arrow into the future and what a woman is is the place the arrow shoots off from."

Eventually, in Esther's metaphor, the figs rot and die, a conclusion which aligns the image tonally with the rest of the novel. In her highly visual presentation of Esther's education, Plath consistently shows characters who are poisoned, diseased, injured, bloodied, and even killed. The violence of her characterization seems a fitting parallel for the intensity of her feelings about the dilemmas Greenwood faces as she matures. (Again, in Spacks' words, "The great power implicitly assigned to adolescents in social science studies belongs to them only as a group. As individuals, psychological commentary makes clear, they suffer uncertainty, absence of power.") Greenwood's persona is clearly marked by feelings of "uncertainty," based on her all-too-sharp understanding of her "absence of power." When Buddy, who has never skiied himself, "instructs" her in the sport and encourages her in the long run that breaks her leg in two places, she obeys him almost mindlessly. (The fact that she finds a sense of self and power in the run is an unexpected benefit for her.) Buddy's malevolence as he diagnoses the breaks and predicts that she will be in a cast for months is a gleeful insight into his real motives for maintaining their relationship while he is hospitalized for tuberculosis. Esther is his possession, his security, his way of keeping his own self image normal in the midst of his increasing plumpness and his fear of disease.

Buddy's sadistic treatment of Esther prepares the way for the last New York episode, Esther's date with the cruel woman-hater, Marco. Replete with scenes of violence, sexual aggression, mud and possession, this last of the New York stories plunges the reader further into the relentless depravity the city has provided. Marco's brutal rape attempt and his marking Esther with blood from his bleeding nose are physically even more insulting than his calling her *slut*. But even though the men in Esther's life are responsible for these events, Plath shows clearly that Esther's passivity and her lack of questioning are also responsible. Esther's malaise has made her incapable of dealing with aggression either subtle or overt—except privately. Once she has returned to the Amazon, she carries all her expensive clothes to the roof of the hotel and throws them into the sky. Her anger at New York is at least partly misplaced, but Plath has shown that the city and its occupants have exacerbated wounds already given in more provincial and seemingly protective locations. Throwing out her clothes is tantamount to rejecting the traditional image of pretty, smart girl, object for man's acquisition (the use throughout the novel of the *Mademoiselle* photographs of the fashionably dressed coeds also builds to this scene).

Unfortunately, once Plath returns home—dressed in Betsey's skirt and blouse and still carrying Marco's blood streaks on her face—she finds that she has been rejected from the prestigious Harvard writing course. That blow destroys the last shred of self image (Greenwood as writer), and the second half of the novel shows Esther's education not in the process of becoming adult but rather in the process of becoming mad. Again, Plath structures the book so that role model

figures are introduced and either discredited or approved. Esther's mother, who appears to think her daughter's insanity is just malingering, is quickly discredited. The irony is that Esther not only must live with the woman; she must also share a bedroom (and by implication, the most intimate parts of her life) with her. Joan Gilling, a Smith student and previous rival for Buddy's affections, presents the option of lesbian life, but her own stability has been irrevocably damaged and she later hangs herself. Doctor Norton, Esther's psychiatrist, is the warm, tolerant and just mentor whose efforts to help Esther understand herself are quickly rewarded. Doctor Norton gives her leave to both hate her mother, and the attitudes she represents, and to be fitted with a diaphragm, so that the previously closed world of sexual experience will be open to her. As Plath has presented both areas of experience throughout the novel, Esther needs to be free from conventional judgments so that she will not absorb so much guilt. One of the most telling scenes in the second half of the book is her reaction to her first electroshock treatment: "I wondered what terrible thing it was that I had done."

The relentless guilt Esther feels as she looks from her bedroom window and sees the neighbor Dodo Conway, wheeling her latest child of six while she is pregnant with the seventh, brings all the scattered images of childbirth and female responsibility to a climax. Unless she accepts this role, Esther will have no life—this is the message her society, even the most supportive elements in it, gives her. But Plath has used one key image during the childbirth scene, that of a "long, blind, doorless and windowless corridor of pain . . . waiting to open up and shut her in again," and that image of relentless suffering recurs throughout the second half of ***The Bell Jar***. It is, in fact, the title image, an encasement, unrelieved, where Esther is "stewing in my own sour air." More frightening than the bewildering crotch of the fig tree, the bell jar presents no choices, no alternatives, except death. Another late image is that of "a black, airless sack with no way out." Choice has been subsumed to guilty depression, and one of the refrains that haunts Esther is *You'll never get anywhere like that, you'll never get anywhere like that.*

And so the second half of the novel becomes a chronicle of Esther's education in suicide and her various suicide attempts. So expertly and completely have the contradictions of her adolescent education been presented in the first ten chapters that Plath needs do very little with background during the second half. Buddy Willard makes only one appearance, wondering sadly who will marry Esther now that she has been "here." Such a scene only confirms the intent of his characterization earlier in the book. Even during the second half of the novel, Esther remains the good student. In her study of suicide, she reads, asks questions, correlates material, chooses according to her own personality, and progresses just as if she were writing a term paper. All factual information is given in the context of *her* needs, however, so the essential charting of Esther's psyche dominates the rest of the book.

As the text [of *The Bell Jar*] makes clear, the main reason for a fairly open ending is that Esther herself had to remain unsure about the condition of her recovery, about her health in the future. . . .
—Linda W. Wagner

Many of the episodes in the latter part of the novel are skeletal. It is as if Plath were loathe to give up any important details but that she also realized that her readers were, in effect, reading two stories. The first half of *The Bell Jar* gives the classic female orientation and education, with obvious indications of the failure of that education appearing near the end of the New York experience. The second half gives an equally classic picture of mental deterioration and its treatment, a picture relatively new in fiction in the late 1950s, important both culturally and personally to Plath. But the exigencies of the fictional form were pressing, and Plath had already crowded many characters and episodes into her structure. The somewhat ambivalent ending may have occurred as much because the book was growing so long as because Plath was uncertain about the outcome of her protagonist. As the text makes clear, the main reason for a fairly open ending is that Esther herself had to remain unsure about the condition of her recovery, about her health in the future: she saw question marks; she hoped the bell jar would not close down again; but she also affirmed that her leaving the asylum was a birth, and that there should be "a ritual for being born twice." The recurrence of the "old brag" of her heart—"I am, I am, I am"—is much more comforting than another time the refrain had occurred, as she contemplated death through drowning.

The Esther Greenwood pictured in the later pages of *The Bell Jar* is a much more confident person. She knows she does not want to be like the lobotomized Valerie, incapable of any emotion. She knows real grief at Joan's funeral, and real anger at Buddy's visit. She understands the enormity of her mother's refusal to accept the truth about her illness, and the corresponding and somewhat compensatory generosity of Doctor Nolan's acceptance of it. Esther is also much more aggressive in her language. For the first time in the years depicted, she speaks directly. "'I have a bill here, Irwin,'" she says quietly to the man who was her first lover. "'I hate her,'" she admits to Doctor Nolan about her mother. "'You had nothing to do with us, Buddy,'" she says scathingly to her former boyfriend. Even early in her breakdown she is quite direct ("I can't sleep. I can't read. . . .") but the irony in these encounters is that no one she speaks with will at-

tend to what she is saying. Various doctors, her mother, friends persist in translating what she is saying ("I haven't slept for fourteen nights") into meanings that are acceptable to them. One climactic scene between Esther and her mother shows this tendency to mishear and misinterpret, and also gives the best description of the bell jar stifling:

> My mother's face floated to mind, a pale, reproachful moon. . . .
>
> A daughter in an asylum! I had done that to her. Still, she had obviously decided to forgive me.
>
> "We'll take up where we left off, Esther," she had said, with her sweet, martyr's smile. "We'll act as if all this were a bad dream."
>
> A bad dream.
>
> To the person in the bell jar, blank and stopped as a dead baby, the world itself is the bad dream.
>
> A bad dream.
>
> I remembered everything.
>
> I remembered the cadavers and Doreen and the story of the fig tree and Marco's diamond. . . .
>
> Maybe forgetfulness, like a kind snow, should numb and cover them.
>
> But they were part of me. They were my landscape.

If a woman's life must be suffused with the image of herself as nurturer, mother, passive sustainer, then the most horrible of all negative images is that of a dead baby. Plath's choice of the adjectives *blank* and *stopped* is powerful; these words are unexpected opposites for the clichés usually associated with a child's growth. By implication, Esther places herself in the dual role of child and mother, and finds no satisfaction in either. And in this scene, she finds particularly hateful the fact that her tortuous experience of madness, which has brought her finally to a new stage of development, be written off by her mother as illusory, a bad dream. It is not surprising that she throws away the roses her mother has brought for her birthday, discounting that biological event in favor of the second birth, the rebirth, to be accomplished when she leaves the asylum, with Doctor Nolan as her guide. The closing lines of *The Bell Jar* surely draw a birth scene:

> There ought, I thought, to be a ritual for being born twice—patched, retreaded and approved for the

road. I was trying to think of an appropriate one when Doctor Nolan appeared from nowhere and touched me on the shoulder.

"All right, Esther."

I rose and followed her to the open door.
Pausing, for a brief breath, on the threshold, I saw the silver-haired doctor who had told me about the rivers and the Pilgrims on my first day, and the pocked, cadaverous face of Miss Huey, and eyes I thought I had recognized over white masks.

The eyes and the faces all turned themselves toward me, and guiding myself by them, as by a magical thread, I stepped into the room.

In contrast to the doorless blankness of tunnels, sacks, and bell jars, this open door and Esther's ability to breathe are surely positive images.

Inherent in the notion of *bildungsroman* is the sense that such a novel will provide a blueprint for a successful education, however the word *successful* is defined. At times, as in *Jude the Obscure,* education comes too late to save the protagonist, but the issue is more the information to be conveyed than the factual ending of the character's saga. For Jerome Buckley, if the protagonist has the means to give life "some ultimate coherence," then education has been efficacious. *The Bell Jar* gives the reader the sense that Esther has, at least momentarily, gained the ability to achieve that coherence. Because so few *bildungsromane* deal with madness, however, exact comparisons between Plath's novel and those usually considered in such generic discussions are difficult; but because so many women's novels treat the subject of madness, *The Bell Jar* cannot be considered an anomaly. Its very representativeness is suggested in Patricia Spacks' comment that most female novels of adolescence "stress the world's threat more than its possibilities; their happy endings derive less from causal sequence than from fortunate accident." The very titles of comparable novels indicate this difference. *The Bell Jar,* with its sinister implications of airlessness, imprisonment, and isolation, is a far remove from *Great Expectations;* and in its most positive scenes cannot approach the ringing self-confidence of *A Portrait of the Artist as a Young Man,* although it is surely that novel writ female.

Among other differences between the conventional *bildungsroman,* which usually deals with a young man's education, and the female novel of experience in adolescence would be the shift in role from father as crucial parent to mother. Much of the process of education is imitative, so that figures which serve as role models will also shift from male

to female. A female *bildungsroman* will thus seem to be peopled more heavily with women characters than with men, although cultural patterns would keep men—economically, socially and sexually—prominent. It may be because men must occur in the female novels that they come to play the role of adversary or antagonist, whereas in the male *bildungsroman* women can be simply omitted.

Educational experiences and choices leading to occupations will also differ, but none will be quite so persuasive as the female's need to choose between profession and domesticity. It is the inescapability of that choice that forces many a novel which would well be labeled *bildungsroman* into the category of domestic novel. Underlying what would seem to be the choice of profession is the less obvious issue of sexuality, which again plays a very different role in female adolescence than in male. In the conventional *bildungsroman,* sexual experience is but another step toward maturity. It suggests the eventual leaving one household to establish another. For a man, such a move may mean only that he hangs his hat in a different closet. For a woman, however, the move means a complete change of status, from mistress to servant, person responsible for the housekeeping in ways she would never have been as the young daughter of a house. A parallel degradation occurs in most representations of the sex act. Biological necessity and physical size mean that the female is usually a more passive partner in intercourse. The accoutrements of a sexual relationship are therefore different for women than for men, and the relationship may loom central to the female *bildungsroman,* while it may be almost peripheral to the male. Losing one's virginity unwisely seldom determines the eventual life of the male protagonist; it is the stuff of ostracism, madness, and suicide for a female, however. Plath's concern with Esther's sexual experience is relevant, certainly, for her choices will determine her life. Her aggression in finding Irwin so that she can be sexually experienced is a positive sign, but the characteristic irony—that she be the one in a million to hemorrhage after intercourse—mars the experience and tends to foreshadow the incipient bad luck which may follow cultural role reversal. As Plath knew only too well, society had its ways of punishing women who were too aggressive, too competent, and too masculine.

The apparent connections between Plath's experiences and Esther's are legitimate topics of discussion when *bildungsromane* are involved because the strength of such novels usually depends on the author's emotional involvement in the themes. Buckley points out that a *bildungsroman* is often an early novel, a first or a second, and that much of the life—as well as the ambivalence—of the novel exists because the author is so involved in the process he or she is describing. In Plath's case, *The Bell Jar* was not only her first novel; it was also published under a pseudonym. Limited to British publication in the original 1963 printing, under the authorship of "Victoria Lucas," the novel was an only partially disguised statement of Plath's anger toward a culture, and a family, that had nourished her only conditionally—that would accept her only provided she did "acceptable" things. If one of the goals of writing such a book was self-discovery, then Plath's evident anger may have been as dismaying, for her in the early 1960s, as it was unexpected.

Because it is this tone of wrenching anger that makes *The Bell Jar* seem so different from the novels generally categorized as *bildungsroman*. The wry self-mockery that gives way to the cryptic poignance of Esther's madness has no antecedent in earlier novels of development. It is in tone and mood that Plath succeeded in making the conventional form—which she followed in a number of important respects—her own.

What *The Bell Jar* ultimately showed was a woman struggling to become whole, not a woman who had reached some sense of stable self. And that conclusion, according to Annis Pratt in *Archetypal Patterns in Women's Fiction,* is what any reader might expect from a sensitive woman author. As Pratt observes,

> even the most conservative women authors create narratives manifesting an acute tension between what any normal human being might desire and what a woman must become. Women's fiction reflects an experience radically different from men's because our drive towards growth as persons is thwarted by our society's prescriptions concerning gender. . . . we are outcasts in the land. . . .

So far as the generic differences are concerned, then, the female hero in a woman's *bildungsroman* will be "destined for disappointment." Pratt concludes, "The vitality and hopefulness characterizing the adolescent hero's attitude toward her future here meet and conflict with the expectations and dictates of the surrounding society. Every element of her desired world—freedom to come and go, allegiance to nature, meaningful work, exercise of the intellect, and use of her own erotic capabilities—inevitably clashes with patriarchal norms."

The Bell Jar must certainly be read as the story of that inevitable clash, a dulled and dulling repetition of lives all too familiar to contemporary readers, and a testimony to the repressive cultural mold that trapped many mid-century women, forcing them outside what should have been their rightful, productive lives. For those of us who lived through the 1950s, *The Bell Jar* moves far beyond being Sylvia Plath's autobiography.

Diane S. Bonds (essay date May 1990)

SOURCE: "The Separative Self in Sylvia Plath's *The Bell Jar,*" in *Women's Studies,* Vol. 18, No. 1, May, 1990, pp. 49-64.

[*In the following essay, Bonds reconsiders feminist critical analysis of* The Bell Jar, *drawing attention to Esther Greenwood's recovery in the novel. According to Bonds, Esther fails to establish an autonomous, or separative, self, and ultimately resorts to "culturally-ingrained stereotypes of women."*]

Plath's novel *The Bell Jar* dramatizes the collusion between the notion of a separate and separative self (or bounded, autonomous subject) and the cultural forces that have oppressed women. The pervasive imagery of dismemberment conveys the alienation and self-alienation leading to Esther Greenwood's breakdown and suicide attempt; the recovery which Plath constructs for her heroine merely reenacts the dismemberments obsessively imaged in the first half of the novel. This "recovery" denies the relationality of the self and leaves Esther to define herself unwittingly and unwillingly in relation to culturally-ingrained stereotypes of women. Contemporary feminist theory has questioned the validity of the separative model of selfhood, but literary critics have brought to the novel the same assumptions about the self which inform Plath's book. Thus they have failed to recognize what the novel has to teach about the destructive effects—at least for women—of our cultural commitment to that model.

As Paula Bennett has written, Sylvia Plath's *The Bell Jar* offers a brilliant evocation of "the oppressive atmosphere of the 1950s and the soul-destroying effect this atmosphere could have on ambitious, high-minded young women like Plath." It has not been widely recognized, however, that the "soul-destroying effect" of Plath's social context is dramatized as vividly by the putative recovery of the heroine as by her breakdown and attempted suicide. The novel presents the transformation of Esther Greenwood from a young woman who hates the idea of serving men in any way to one who appears to earn her exit from the asylum by committing herself, albeit unwittingly, precisely to that project. In the first half of the novel, the pervasive imagery of dismemberment conveys the alienation and self-alienation leading to Esther's breakdown and suicide attempt. In the second half of the novel a pattern of symbolic rebirth is superimposed on a narrative which in its details suggests that Esther purchases her "new" self by the discontinuance of any relations that might threaten by means of intimacy or tenderness the boundaries of a self conceived as an autonomous entity, as a separate and "separative" self.

Contemporary feminist theory has questioned the validity of

this model of the self. Catherine Keller, for example, has recently drawn on theology, philosophy, psychology (including the work of Nancy Chodorow and Carol Gilligan), and literature, to demonstrate in impressive detail the historic collusion between the notion of a separate subject or bounded, autonomous self and the cultural forces that have oppressed women. *The Bell Jar* vividly illustrates that collusion by proposing, through its representation of Esther's recovery, an ideal of a self uncontaminated by others. But such a conception of the self denies the undeniable: the relationality of selfhood. The recovery which Plath constructs for her heroine reenacts the dismemberments obsessively imaged in the first half of the novel; I would argue that it merely leaves Esther prey to defining herself unwittingly and unwillingly in relation to all that remains to her: culturally-ingrained stereotypes of women. Critics for the most part seem to have brought to the novel the same assumptions about the self which inform Plath's book, assumptions deriving from a separative model of the self. Thus they have failed to recognize what the novel has to teach about the effects of our cultural commitment to that model.

In the first part of Plath's novel, both the commitment to the separative self and the effects of that commitment are woven into the text through the pervasive imagery of dismemberment. This imagery suggests Esther's alienation and fragmentation as well as a thwarted longing for relatedness with others and for a reconnection of dismembered part to whole. A signal example of this imagery is the image of a cadaver head which occurs on the first page of the novel:

> I kept hearing about the Rosenbergs over the radio and at the office until I couldn't get them out of my mind. It was like the first time I saw a cadaver. For weeks afterward, the cadaver's head—or what there was left of it—floated up behind my eggs and bacon at breakfast. . . . I felt as though I was carrying that cadaver's head around with me on a string, like some black, noseless balloon stinking of vinegar.

This image anticipates and comprehends the disembodied faces that Esther repeatedly encounters, faces always associated with the threat of the loss of self. She repeatedly confronts her own unrecognized or distorted image in the mirror, mistaken on one occasion for "a big, smudgy-eyed Chinese woman," looking "like a sick Indian" on another; a third time, in the hospital after her suicide attempt, she thinks she is looking at a picture of another person, unrecognizably male or female, "with their hair . . . shaved off and sprouted in bristly chicken-feather tufts all over their head." The faces of others hover over her or float in front of her eyes with startling frequency: the face of Buddy Willard hanging over her after her skiing accident, announcing with some satis-

faction "You'll be stuck in a cast for months"; the face of Joan Gilling floating before her, bodiless and smiling, "like the face of the Cheshire cat," an image that comes to Esther immediately before she learns of Joan's suicide by hanging; on the next page her mother's face floating "to mind, a pale reproachful moon."

It is possible that the precursor of these and other apparently disembodied heads is the head of the baby born in the traumatic episode in which Buddy Willard, a medical student, takes Esther into the delivery room to witness a birth. The episode, a flashback, is permeated with images of dismemberment: the stomach of the woman in labor sticks up so high that her face cannot be seen; the baby's head is the first thing to appear in the delivery, "a dark fuzzy thing" that emerges "through the split, shaven place between [the woman's legs], lurid with disinfectant." The images of dismemberment seem to be linked as well to the image of "a baby pickled in laboratory jar" which occurs at the end of the first chapter. If, as Jung has taught us, the baby is an archetypal symbol of the self in crisis, then the image of the pickled baby, along with the images of dismembered body parts, accurately conveys the nature of Esther's crisis: each of the various paths open to her will require that she dispense with, leave undeveloped, some important part of herself. Imagistically the novel makes this point through scenes like that in the delivery room where the emergence of the infant's head is accompanied by the "decapitation" of the mother.

Thus at the beginning of the novel, as Esther walks along the New York streets "wondering what it would be like, being burned alive all along your nerves," her musing is not merely a response to the electrocution of the Rosenbergs but to her own growing sense of alienation from the cultural demands and images of women with which she is daily bombarded during her guest editorship at *Ladies' Day*. These seem implicitly to reinforce the lessons of the preceding year, especially those of her relationship with Buddy Willard, suggesting that she must mutilate or deform herself through mating, marriage, and motherhood. It is not entirely surprising then that she begins to see the city as a collocation of dismembered body parts: "goggle-eyed headlines" stare up at her "on every street corner and at the fusty, peanut-smelling mouth of every subway." Her friend Doreen, too, is presented as such a collocation: "bright white hair standing out in a cotton candy fluff and blue eyes like transparent agate marbles, hard and polished and just about indestructible, and a mouth set in a sort of perpetual sneer," "long, nicotine-yellow nails" and the breasts which pop out of her dress later at Lenny's apartment. The dismembered animal parts that decorate that apartment—the white bearskins, the "antlers and buffalo horns and [the] stuffed rabbit head" with its "meek little grey muzzle and the stiff, jackrabbit ears"—are tokens of the sexual hunt in which it is assumed all the young guest editors at *Ladies' Day* will gladly play their parts, oozing enthusiasm, like Betsy, about learning the latest way "to make an all purpose neckerchief out of mink tails."

Feeling as "cut off" as these excised animal parts from the culture which expects her participation in this hunt, Esther is haunted by images suggesting the self-mutilations of marriage and motherhood. She recalls the way in which Buddy Willard's mother weaves a beautiful rug only to destroy its beauty in a matter of days by using it as a kitchen mat. The message is clear to Esther: ". . . I knew that in spite of all the roses and the kisses . . . what [a man] secretly wanted when the wedding service ended was for [the wife] to flatten out underneath his feet like Mrs. Willard's kitchen mat." Her reaction against this form of mutilation is clear in her violent sensitivity upon her return home to the presence of Dodo Conway, a neighbor who had gone to Barnard and who is now pregnant with her seventh child. The vision of Dodo, "not five feet tall, with a grotesque, protruding stomach. . . . Her head tilted happily back, like a sparrow egg perched on a duck egg," elicits from Esther the following reaction: "Children made me sick. . . . I couldn't see the point of getting up. I had nothing to look forward to."

Esther sees Dodo as a grotesque collection of unrelated and incompatible parts, a vision which we may read as a projection of her own sense of self. It is crucial to emphasize at this point in the argument, however, that the imagery of dismemberment in *The Bell Jar* does not simply communicate Esther's psychic disturbance or a set of feelings characterizing a certain point in her history; the imagery also implies a certain model of the self. Imagery focusing our attention on part-whole relations (or dis-relations) presupposes that the self is a bounded entity, something with separate and distinct existence and of which certain kinds of things may be said: it is a whole; it may have parts or members; if some of these parts or members are removed, then the entity is not whole; neither are the severed parts, from this perspective, wholes. The model of the self implied by the imagery of dismemberment, in short, coincides with the model of a bounded self, an autonomous subject, that has dominance in our culture.

The notion of a separate, bounded self of course corresponds to our sense of being locked into our own bodies, of being separate and distinct entities. But it is important to stress that the model of an autonomous bounded self does not represent the only way in which the self may be conceived, and according to some theorists it does not represent the most accurate way of conceiving selfhood. Catherine Keller compellingly argues for the possibility of a relational model of selfhood that does not preclude a sense of differentiated identity or imply, as some feminists have argued, submersion of the self in others. Based on the assumption that the self is constituted in and through relationships with others, the relational model rejects subject-object dualism (and the

system of hierarchical oppositions in which it is embedded), and it recognizes the fluid, permeable boundaries of self. Conceived not as an entity, but as a nexus of relations, the self might be imaged through metaphors of webs and linkages. Conceived not as a substance, but as a process, it might be imaged through metaphors of fluidity.

Or, conversely, a predominance of images of webs, linkages, process and fluidity, might imply an entirely different conception of the self from that informing *The Bell Jar*. That such metaphors are absent from Plath's novel suggests how thoroughly dominated by the separative model was the novelist's imagination. One image of linkage, of apparent significance because of its location in the last paragraph of the novel, is qualified by the paragraph which precedes it:

> Pausing, for a brief breath, on the threshold I saw the silver-haired doctor . . . and the pocked, cadaverous face of Miss Huey, and eyes I thought I had recognized over white masks.

> The eyes and the faces all turned themselves toward me, and guiding myself by them, as by a magical thread, I stepped into the room.

The reminder in the image of Miss Huey of the cadaver head which obsesses Esther, the recalled image of eyes floating over masks—there is little qualitative difference between the vision represented here and that at the beginning of the novel, though the narrator's tone may have changed. The magical thread does not so much provide a link to others constitutive of the self as it does a line to those who hold the power of release from daily confrontation with the self and its agonies.

Despite the ambiguities of the closing of *The Bell Jar,* critics have been surprisingly willing to accept that Esther is in some positive sense "reborn" even if her future is uncertain. In the final episode, when Esther readies herself to meet the board of doctors who will certify her release from the hospital, she behaves as if she is preparing for a bridegroom or a date; she checks her stocking seams, muttering to herself "Something old, something new. . . . But," she goes on, "I wasn't getting married. There ought, I thought, to be a ritual for being born twice—patched, retreaded, and approved for the road, I was trying to think of an appropriate one. . . ." Critics who have been willing to see a reborn Esther have generally done so without ever questioning the propriety of the reference to a "retread" job. Linda Wagner, for example, ignores this passage and concentrates on subsequent paragraphs, where the image of an "open door and Esther's ability to breathe are," Wagner writes, "surely positive images." Susan Coyle writes that the tire image "seems to be accurate, since the reader does not have a sense of [Esther] as a brand-new, unblemished tire but of one that has been painstakingly reworked, remade"; Coyle claims that Esther has taken steps that "however tentative, do lead her toward an authentic self that was previously impossible for her." Not only do the comments of Coyle and Wagner ignore the implication of choosing the tire image in the first place; they also miss an affinity of the passage with one I quoted earlier in which Esther views wifehood in terms of service as a kitchen mat. The tire, like a kitchen mat, presents us with a utilitarian object, easily repaired or replaced, as a metaphor for a woman. It is worth observing that a patched, retreaded tire may be ready for the road, but somewhere down the highway the owner can expect a flat. Now "flatten out" is exactly what Esther suspects—or had suspected—women do in marriage. Yet it is precisely for marriage that Esther seems confusedly to be preparing herself in the final episode as she straightens her seams. It is true that she withdraws her reference to marriage, but despite her disclaimer, it seems to me, a retread job can only be a travesty of rebirth.

The metaphor of rebirth or a second birth is thus especially suspicious because of the way in which the tire image obliquely forces us to associate Esther's new lease on life with role expectations that contributed to her breakdown in the first place: the domestic servitude that Esther painfully recognizes "as a dreary and wasted life for a girl with fifteen years of straight A's." Although Esther's breakdown may have sources lying buried in the past along with her father, the novel makes it sufficiently clear that she is torn apart by the intolerable conflict between her wish to avoid domesticity, marriage and motherhood, on the one hand, and her inability to conceive of a viable future in which she avoids that fate, on the other.

Plath's inability to resolve that conflict in her own life is well known. In an essay entitled "Sylvia Plath's 'Sivvy' Poems: A Portrait of the Poet as a Daughter," Marjorie Perloff concludes:

> The first shock of recognition produced by Sylvia Plath's 'independence' from her husband and her mother was the stimulus that gave rise to the *Ariel* poems. But given the 'psychic osmosis' between herself and Aurelia Plath . . . given the years of iron discipline during which Sylvia had been her mother's Sivvy, the touching assertion [in "Medusa"] that 'There is nothing between us' could only mean that now there would be nothing at all.

Whatever the biographical validity of Perloff's argument, it may help us to define a pattern that has not been discerned in *The Bell Jar.* Esther's movement toward her breakdown entails a series of rejections of or separations from women who, though they may be associated with some stereotype of womanhood unacceptable to Esther, have nurtured some important aspect of her evolving identity; as I want to show,

the supposed cure which she undergoes is actually a continuation of a pattern in which Esther severs relations precisely with those whose presence "in" her self has been constitutive. Such a series of rejections may dramatize a deluded notion that an autonomous and "authentic" self may be derived through purging the self of the influence of others, but there is good reason to suppose that the process actually means that little or nothing would remain to Esther, as means of modeling identity, except forms of womanhood offered to her by the very stereotypes she has sought to elude. The irony here is that in the attempt to avoid dismemberment, disfiguration or mutilation of the self, the heroine undergoes a process of self-dismemberment.

The novel provides another metaphor for the process I am describing in the repeated binge-and-purge episodes of the first portion of the novel. In chapter 2, Esther vicariously participates in Doreen's debauch with Lenny, then returns to the hotel and a bath of purification; the pattern is repeated when Doreen returns, to pass out in a pool of her own vomit. Chapter 4 presents another purgative cleansing; after gorging on caviar at a luncheon, Esther is leveled by food poisoning, an experience which makes her feel "purged and holy and ready for a new life." Shortly after this purgation, she announces: "I'm starving."

In somewhat a similar manner, I am arguing, Esther embraces relations with most of the women in the novel only to cast them off, as if they constituted a foreign presence within the purity of her own identity, some threat to her integrity. Doreen, for example, speaks to her with a voice "like a secret voice speaking straight out of [her] own bones," but after the evening in Lenny's apartment, Esther decides to have nothing to do with her. A similar pattern is repeated with every female character in the novel, including Dr. Nolan, the psychiatrist who brings about Esther's recovery, and Esther's mother.

Esther's aversion from her mother is obvious, ascending in stridency from the mild understatement, "My own mother wasn't much help" to the murderous fantasy inspired by sharing a room with her mother: one sleepless night, after staring at "the pin curls on her [mother's] head glittering like a row of little bayonets," Esther comes to feel that the only way she can escape the annoying sound of her mother's faint snore "would be to take the column of skin and sinew from which it rose and twist it to silence between [her] hands." Even though Esther at one point wishes that she had a mother like Jay Cee, the editor for whom she works at *Ladies' Day,* her ambivalence toward Jay Cee and other women who have nurtured her talents is profound—and it appears to derive, quite simply, from their supposed unattractiveness to men. Of Jay Cee, Esther says ". . . I liked her a lot. . . . [She] had brains, so her plug-ugly looks didn't seem to matter"; but sentences later, after admitting that she cannot imagine Jay

Cee in bed with her husband, Esther changes her attitude abruptly: "Jay Cee wanted to teach me something, all the old ladies I ever knew wanted to teach me something, but I suddenly didn't think they had anything to teach me." A similar reflection recurs near the end of the novel in a scene where the lesbian Joan Gilling lounges on Esther's bed in the asylum and Esther's revery seems to lump the unattractive, the manless, and the woman-loving together. She remembers:

> . . . the famous woman poet at my college [who] lived with another woman—a stumpy old Classical scholar with a cropped Dutch cut. When I told the poet that I might well get married and have a pack of children someday, she stared at me in horror. "But what about your *career?*" she had cried.

> My head ached. Why did I attract these weird old women: There was the famous poet, and Philomena Guinea, and Jay Cee, and the Christian Scientist lady, and lord knows who, and they all wanted to adopt me in some way, and, for the price of their care and influence, have me resemble them.

This passage focuses our attention on the immersion of Plath/Esther in what Adrienne Rich has called the "compulsory heterosexuality," the pervasive heterosexism, of our culture. It also reinforces our awareness that despite her intelligence, imagination and professional ambition, Esther's sense of identity as a woman is predicated on finding "the right man."

That Esther categorizes Jay Cee, Philomena Guinea, and the woman poet at college (who is never named)—along with the Christian Scientist lady whom she does not know—as weird old women who want to save her is a way of rejecting these women's very real contributions and potential contributions to her own evolving identity. The claim would seem to be at least partly a projection of her own desire to be saved from becoming like these women with whom she shares certain talents, capacities, and interests. I want to suggest that there may be a kind of psychic dismemberment signified by the separation of self thus from one's nurturers; denying their influence is like peeling off layers of her own self—or cutting off important members. It is especially important to notice in this regard that the point where Esther turns her back on Jay Cee coincides with the diminishment of her sense of competence, which becomes increasingly worse as the weeks pass in New York. In rejecting the "weird old women" who want to save her, she appears to become increasingly disempowered; that is, she appears to lose touch with the talents and skills that these women nurtured.

Esther's recovery involves a reinstitution of the problems that led to her breakdown. If, as I have already suggested, the reconstructed Esther is a retreaded tire doomed to go flat

(and probably on the same highway that brought her to the asylum in the first place), that is partly because her cure perpetuates the disease. The recovery process of this heroine merely extends the series of separations from or rejections of others which seems to have played an important part in bringing about her breakdown.

By the closing pages of the novel, two meaningful relations with women are open to Esther, relations with her friend, Joan Gilling, and her psychiatrist, Dr. Nolan. The first of these relations is terminated decisively by the character's suicide, which renders irreversible Esther's prior rejection of that character. In the penultimate scene of the novel, Esther attends Joan's funeral, wondering, she tells us, "what I thought I was burying" and listening to the insistent "brag of [her own] heart"—"I am, I am, I am." Since Esther springs to new life as Joan is buried, it would be difficult not to conclude that Plath is putting aside, burying, some unacceptable part of her heroine: Esther has even explicitly identified Joan as "the beaming double of my old best self." Like the metaphor of a retread, however, this comment exemplifies "the uncertainty of tone" that, according to Rosellen Brown, "manages to trivialize . . . [the novel's] heavy freight of pain." If the passage hints Esther's awareness that her "old best self" is peculiarly vulnerable to disintegration precisely because of the intolerable psychic conflict produced by trying to meet cultural expectations of women, it also—to the extent that it is sarcastic—distances Esther from Joan and from the painful feelings that she shares with Joan.

Until the revelation that Joan is involved in a lesbian relationship, that young woman is associated with a potential for intimacy that seems more positive than negative. Joan replaces, as Esther's neighbor, Miss Norris, with whom Esther shares an hour of "close, sisterly silence." Joan's intimacy with Dee Dee is associated with improving health (*pace* Vance Bourjaily, who writes that a "relapse" is indicated by Joan's "lesbian involvement"—the novel simply contradicts this). Esther even feels free to curl up on Joan's bed on first encountering her at one asylum, though she admits to having known Joan at college only "at a cool distance."

After discovering Joan with Dee Dee, however, Esther's treatment of Joan begins to be marked by a blatant cruelty, as when Esther tells Joan, "'I don't like you. You make me want to puke, if you want to know.'" A less explicit cruelty, implicating not merely the character Esther but the author Plath, pervades the scene where Joan seeks medical attention for Esther's hemorrhaging after Esther's encounter with Irwin. Esther/Plath clearly has one eye on humiliating Joan. Because Joan is allowed to surmise that the bleeding is some mysterious menstrual problem rather than connected to Esther's loss of virginity, she is made to look like a bumbler. She has difficulty explaining the problem clearly enough to get emergency aid, a problem which of course increases the danger to Esther, but a pun seems more important here than prompt medical assistance. When Joan asks about the man who has dropped Esther off, Esther says: "I realized that she honestly took my explanation at face value . . . and his appearance [was] a mere prick to her pleasure at my arrival." The oddity of her mentioning, in circumstances where every beat of her heart "pushed forth another gush of blood," Joan's pleasure at her arrival is matched by what looks like a kind of desperation to hide from Joan the cause of the hemorrhaging.

The peculiarities of this scene create ambiguities about Esther's motives and suggest confusion on Plath's part. Still Plath's imagery hints at a causal link between Esther's hemorrhaging and Joan's death. Often described before this episode in terms of horse imagery, Joan is here described as a "myopic owl" in an image that appears paradoxically to reveal what it intends to obscure: Joan's knowledge of the cause of Esther's suffering and the trauma of the rejection that Esther's suffering represents. Similarly, the structuring of the narrative implies a link between Joan's death and Esther's rebirth. Before she gets to the Emergency Room, Esther remembers "a worrisome course in the Victorian novel where woman after woman died, palely and nobly, in torrents of blood, after a difficult childbirth." The birth that is brought about here, however, is not that of a strong new self but of an Esther who gives in to her fear of the love and nurturance of women—exemplified by Joan's role as nurse in this scene—an Esther who buries her capacity for identification with women and accepts the very stereotypes which have been the source of her pain.

As "the only purely imagined event in the book," the inclusion of Joan's unexpected and unprepared for suicide immediately following this episode, is, as Paula Bennett has written, "necessitated not by the novel's plot, themes, or characters but by Plath's own emotional understanding of her text. Joan, the woman who loves other women and who, therefore, can pursue a career and independent life without benefit of man or marriage, must be disposed of if the demons that haunt Plath's/Esther's mind are to be exorcised as well. . . ." The nature of those demons may partly be implied by the descriptions of the lesbians in the novel: not only the "stumpy" old Classical scholar, already mentioned, but the "matronly-breasted senior, homely as a grandmother and a pious Religion major, and a tall, gawky freshman with a history of being deserted at an early hour in all sorts of ingenious ways by her blind dates." Such images indicate the "weirdness," the unattractiveness, to Plath of any female behavior deviating from heterosexual, patriarchal norms: Esther says of Joan, "It was like observing a Martian, or a particularly warty toad."

It seems a kind of narrative reaction to these images that in the episode following those in which they occur, Esther has herself fitted with a diaphragm. So compelling is the logic of her desire to avoid pregnancy that we do not feel spurred to ask why she would at this point want to have anything to do with a man in the first place. But it should be noted that her encounters with men have been nearly devastating: her father deserts her by dying when she is very young; much more recently in the novel, she is knocked down in the mud, mauled, practically raped by a man who marks her face with blood; in another, a flashback to an occasion where she ends up inspecting Buddy Willard's genitals, all she can think of is "turkey neck and turkey gizzards." The man she sets out to seduce (Constantin) falls asleep unaroused by her, and the male psychiatrist to whom she turns for help practically electrocutes her. This pattern of pain and disappointment is merely confirmed by her experience with Irwin, who creates for her, in deflowering her, a possibly life-threatening medical emergency.

It is a sad irony that precisely at the point in *The Bell Jar* where the action seems to call for at least a temporary turning away from men or from seeing herself in relation to male sexuality, if only to provide for some period of reflection and healing on Esther's part, the novel turns more decisively than ever away from women and toward men. Critics have not, however, generally recognized this irony; the typical reaction has been to accept at face value that the purchase of a diaphragm is an important step in the direction of independence. While contraception surely frees Esther from fears which no women should have to suffer, my argument is that we need to question the validity of the notion of independence offered through this episode.

In killing off Joan, Plath cancels for Esther the possibility of tenderness—outside the relatively impersonal therapeutic relationship—clearly symbolized by Joan's lesbianism. That possibility is named by Dr. Nolan, the only character in the novel treated with unambiguous respect. When Esther asks this psychiatrist "What does a women see in a woman that she can't see in a man," Dr. Nolan replies with one definitive, authoritative word: "Tenderness." Plath dramatizes both the yearning for tenderness in Esther and the way in which Esther is cut off from that yearning, but there seems to be little authorial awareness of the disjunction. The novel presents the possibility of tenderness between women in a story Esther recounts about two "suspected" lesbians at her college: "'Milly was sitting on the chair and Theodora was lying on the bed, and Milly was stroking Theodora's hair.'" An image of this sort of caress occurs at another point in the novel, significantly in connection with a male who is probably a homosexual. When Constantin, the simultaneous interpreter whom Esther fails to seduce in New York, reaches out at the end of the evening to touch her hair she feels "a little electric shock" and tells us: "Ever since I was small I loved feeling somebody comb my hair. It made me go all sleepy and peaceful." This touch is arguably the only tenderness Esther experiences in the novel, yet her response to the similar contact between Milly and Theodora is this: "I was disappointed. . . . I wondered if all women did with women was lie and hug."

In her aversion to Joan, Esther denies what the text nonetheless reveals: the possibility of a healing "tenderness" and "weirdness" that the relation of Joan and Dee Dee represents. As we have seen, this denial is authorially endorsed by Plath's invention of Joan's suicide. Suggesting that Joan represents Esther's "suicidal self" or—more exotically but no more helpfully—"the inverted Victorian side of Esther," critics with a Freudian orientation have linked Esther's recovery to a splitting off of an unacceptable portion of the self dramatized by Joan's suicide. While a splitting off undoubtedly occurs, the nature of what is split off is ultimately ambiguous. Furthermore, *splitting off* appears to be a major symptom of the disorder from which Esther suffers. The novel dramatizes a tragic self-dismemberment in which the heroine, because of her very strengths and aspirations, appears to split off those components of herself that represent patriarchally-defined expectations of women, projecting these aspects of herself on her mother, her grandmother, Dodo Conway, Mrs. Willard, and the young women who are guest editors with her at *Ladies' Day,* especially Doreen and Betsy. Although she consciously rejects the influence of these others, she must still unconsciously be dominated by the patriarchal images of womanhood that she rejects; otherwise she would not need also to split off those qualities and impulses in herself that do *not* meet patriarchal expectations—all that goes counter to conventional femininity and is therefore "weird." These she projects upon Jay Cee, Philomena Guinea, the unnamed famous poet at her college, and finally Joan. Her systematic rejection of these leaves her quite possibly "with nothing" in the same sense that, as Perloff argues, Plath was left with nothing after rejecting the beliefs she inherited from her mother.

Dr. Nolan appears to play a special role in Esther's "cure," but several reservations about that role ought to be made. Combining the attributes of patriarchally-defined femininity and professional accomplishment, Dr. Nolan is set forth by some readers as an ideal role model for Esther, but the last thirty years have taught us to question this sort of image which can merely compound the oppression of women by leading them to assume expectations traditionally held of men as well as those held of women: Plath herself provides a highly visible example of the tragic consequences of uncritically embracing this model which encourages the belief that women can "have it all." Furthermore, the novel leaves ambiguous the extent of Nolan's contribution to the recovery. Although the trust she engenders in Esther undoubtedly counts for a great deal, the electroshock therapy and the psychic dismemberment involved in the process ap-

pear to get equal if not more credit for Esther's improvement. Finally, whatever the depth of Esther's indebtedness to Dr. Nolan, the relationship appears to be largely terminated by Esther's release from the hospital.

Thus, at the end of the novel, far from having moved in the direction of an "authentic self," Esther has been systematically separated from the very means by which such a self might be constituted: relationships with others. Her high heels and "red wool suit flamboyant as [her] plans" clearly signal a renewed and energized willingness to enter the sexual hunt that so dispirited her during her summer in New York. Esther's seeming preparation to reenter the hunt for "the right man" is accompanied by the strong suggestion that the right man is one with whom she may avoid emotional attachment. (Esther says gleefully, after realizing that Irwin's voice on the phone means nothing to her and that he has no way of getting in touch with her again, "I was perfectly free.") In other words, Esther's identity, the boundary of her self, has been secured by her isolation.

> [The Bell Jar] dramatizes a double bind for women in which, on the one hand, an authentic self is one that is presumed to be autonomous and whole, entire to itself and clearly bounded, and yet in which, on the other hand, women have their identity primarily through relationship to a man.
> —*Diane S. Bonds*

The Bell Jar makes apparent the oppressive force (at least for women) of the model of separative selfhood which dominates patriarchal culture. The novel dramatizes a double bind for women in which, on the one hand, an authentic self is one that is presumed to be autonomous and whole, entire to itself and clearly bounded, and yet in which, on the other hand, women have their identity primarily through relationship to a man. It is the increasing tension of this double bind for Esther which results in her breakdown; her release from the asylum, I have argued, is marked by a restoration of the double bind at a different and tolerable level of tension. The experiences of both Esther and Joan suggest that escape is not possible through conscious rejection of the expectation that a woman find herself in a man; in my reading, Plath's novel hints that the expectation is, in that instance, likely to be heeded at a more deeply unconscious level. (This would be a possible explanation of Joan's unexpected suicide, and the idea is supported by the imagery of the closing episode as I have analyzed it.) Yet the other alternative, to reject the model of separative selfhood and embrace a relational model, involves—in the cultural context portrayed by Plath—the restoration of the traditional plight of women: subservience to or submersion in others.

The way out of the dilemma is a relational conception of selfhood in a world of non-oppressive, non-hierarchical relations. But we do not live in such a world (yet), and our culture offers few means of imaging non-oppressive, non-hierarchical relationality. It is in signaling the paucity of such means, the unavailability of such images at least to someone like Plath but by extension to many women in our culture, that *The Bell Jar* has special importance. Images of lateral relationships among women, i.e. images of female friendship, provide one means, but as I have argued, Plath seems compelled in this novel eventually to reject all such images. In this context, the introduction of Joan specifically as a lesbian becomes very important. Joan's lesbianism and suicide appear to belong to a small number of "invented" features of the novel. That Plath rejects Joan by killing her off is a sign of the novelist's domination by the cultural norms that, I believe, destroyed her; that she created Joan as a lesbian in the first place, however, especially in a novel so dominated by autobiographical fact, might plausibly be viewed as a last desperate imaginative reaching toward some viable image of non-hierarchical relationality. Having rejected all the other woman-woman relationships available to her from her experience, Plath turns finally to invention, which—controlled by stereotype as it is—proves no more successful than autobiographical fact.

It is important for feminist critics to discern such emancipatory impulses or gestures wherever they occur in women's writing. We need to bring them into focus and to assess where they succeed and the conditions of their success or failure. But I would suggest that critics are less than well-equipped to undertake such work if they remain uncritical of their own discourse, for example, the way in which it is permeated with terminology implying that the self is an autonomous, bounded entity. Paula Bennett, who rightly calls the ending of *The Bell Jar* "unbearably factitious," provides an example of such terminology when she writes that ". . . Plath herself seems to have gained little from her experience at the psychiatric hospital. She returned to Smith . . . hollow and unintegrated at her core." Bennett's language here ("hollow," "core"), founded as it is upon the dichotomy of inner and outer, implies subject-object dualism and all the patriarchally-freighted oppositions that it brings in its wake. It is difficult to write about the self in our culture without making use of terms implying the very dualisms on which patriarchy is founded. Yet if we cannot entirely dispense with such terminology—and I do not believe that we very well can—we can be aware of its metaphoric nature and of the assumptions that it covers.

When we become aware of the limits of our metaphors for selfhood, we become more attuned to those employed by the writers we study. Only when such awareness is brought to bear upon *The Bell Jar,* for instance, do we become fully appreciative of the way in which the novel dramatizes the destructive effects of a commitment to the separative model of the self. When such awareness is brought to bear upon the writing of women less tragically constricted than Plath by stereotypes of women, it may enable us to discern alternative metaphors and images for the self, the very means by which the dominant model of the self in our culture may be transformed into one conducive to the validation of women.

Brita Lindberg-Seyersted   (essay date December 1990)

SOURCE: "Sylvia Plath's Psychic Landscapes," in *English Studies,* Vol. 71, No. 6, December, 1990, pp. 509-22.

[*In the following essay, Lindberg-Seyersted examines the development of Plath's poetry through analysis of major themes and imagery found in her description of landscapes, seascapes, and the natural world.*]

Following the lead of Ted Hughes, critics today tend to read Sylvia Plath's poetry as a *unity*. Individual poems are best read in the context of the whole oeuvre: motifs, themes and images link poems together and these linkages illuminate their meaning and heighten their power. It is certainly easy to see that through almost obsessive repetition some elements put their unforgettable mark on the poetry: themes such as the contradictory desires for life and death and the quests for selfhood and truth; images like those of color, with red, black and white dominating the palette; and symbols of haunting ambiguity, for example, the moon and the sea.

But equally obvious is the striking *development* that Plath's work underwent in the course of her brief career as a professional poet. This is perhaps most readily seen in the prosody: from exerting her equilibristic skill at handling demanding verse forms, such as the terza rima and the villanelle, she broke free of the demands of such literary conventions and created a personal verse form which still retained some of the basic elements of her earlier 'academic' style. She turned the three-line stanza of the villanelle into a highly flexible medium. Freed from the prosodic strictness of poems like '**Medallion,**' written in 1959, this verse form reappeared in poems composed in the last year of her life in a superbly liberated yet controlled form. Some of her finest and most personal poems are written in this medium, for example, '**Fever 103°,**' '**Ariel,**' '**Nick and the Candlestick,**' '**Lady Lazarus,**' '**Mary's Song,**' and the late '**Sheep in Fog,**' '**Child**' and '**Contusion.**'

More important, though, is the development one can observe in Plath's handling of images and themes, of settings and scenes. My concern in this essay is Plath's use of landscapes as settings. There are indoor settings in her poetry, such as kitchens and bedrooms, hospitals and museums, but the outdoor ones are in overwhelming majority. Plath's use of landscapes and seascapes is indeed one of the most characteristic features of her poetry. They put their mark on a considerable part of the work and appear throughout her career, linked as they are to her experiences as a woman and a poet. The seascapes with their crucial relevance for themes like the daughter-father relationship, loss and death, deserve a special and thorough treatment of their own and will have to fall outside the scope of this essay.

Plath's use of landscapes and seascapes is indeed one of the most characteristic features of her poetry. They put their mark on a considerable part of the work and appear throughout her career, linked asthey are to her experiences as a woman and a poet.
—Brita Lindberg-Seyersted

No reader can fail to note the many items of nature that Plath makes use of as setting and image. Three scholars have paid special attention to this aspect. In her pioneering work, *The Poetry of Sylvia Plath: A Study of Themes* (1972), Ingrid Melander includes analyses of poems set in different landscapes and seascapes that Plath knew; in addition to discussing a group of poems connected to the sea, she deals with the following landscape poems: two poems on the moorland (**'Hardcastle Crags'** and **'Wuthering Heights'**); two 'idylls' (**'Watercolor of Grantchester Meadows'** and **'In Midas' Country'**); and three 'landscapes as experienced by the traveller' (**'Sleep in the Mojave Desert,' 'Stars over the Dordogne'** and **'Two Campers in Cloud Country'**). Melander's approach is thematic and she makes no attempt to suggest development or continuity concerning this aspect of the poetry.

In Jon Rosenblatt's *Sylvia Plath: The Poetry of Initiation* (1979), in my view still the most useful book-length critical study, the idea of development is a main concern. He devotes one chapter to Plath's use of landscapes and seascapes, focusing on the transition from early to late poetry as part of his overriding argument: that Plath's poetry enacts a ritual of initiation from symbolic death to rebirth. He programmatically refrains from placing her poems in extraliterary contexts, such as her biography.

Edward Butscher, on the other hand, goes to the other extreme in his critical biography, *Sylvia Plath: Method and Madness* (1976), where he makes no essential difference between the life and the poetry. While he offers many imaginative and perceptive comments on Plath's anthropo-

morphizing of nature, they naturally become subsumed in the telling of the story of the poet's life and also, frequently, slightly distorted by Butscher's psychoanalytically loaded thesis about the emergence of Sylvia Plath the 'bitch goddess.'

Since the appearance of these three studies Sylvia Plath's *Collected Poems* has been published (1981) with a securer and more precise dating of the poems than before, and we are now in a better position to deal with the poems chronologically. *The Journals of Sylvia Plath* (1982) also add to our knowledge of the composition of the poems. Linda W. Wagner-Martin's recent biography (1987) has given us a firm platform to build our critical studies on, by confirming or correcting information provided by previous biographies and memoirs.

With the premise that Plath's poetry should be read as a unity I wish to study the development of her use of landscapes throughout her career, paying special attention to the role the landscape plays in the individual poem—quantitatively and qualitatively—and to the way the poet creates 'psychic' landscapes out of concrete places, scenes and objects. I tie this discussion firmly and consistently to actual landscapes Sylvia Plath had seen. With a poetry like Plath's, which is highly subjective and concrete, it is surely a disadvantage to disconnect the poems from the poet's life. My use of biography aims at illuminating the poetic process, and my main interest is in the subtle and gradual shift in the poet's technique: the process by which her landscapes become increasingly 'psychic' and at the end 'fragmented.'

Sylvia Plath evidently looked upon herself as a city person (in spite of her documented love of the sea). Amidst the beautiful scenery at an artists' colony in upstate New York she complained: 'I do rather miss Boston and don't think I could ever settle for living far from a big city full of museums and theaters.' Nevertheless she seldom used the cities and towns where she lived, more or less permanently, as settings in poems. Cambridge, England; Northampton, Massachusetts; Boston and London, these places made little impact on the poetry as cityscapes. When she draws on such settings, she usually lets her persona move from the streets and buildings to parks or gardens or surrounding fields. When she remembers Cambridge, she sees meadows and fields outside the town, as in **'Watercolor of Grantchester Meadows'** (1959). Of Northampton she commemorates above all a park with frog pond, fountain, shrubbery and flowers, as in **'Frog Autumn'** and **'Child's Park Stones,'** both written in 1958. Where the town of Northampton itself does figure, in **'Owl'** (1958), it is as a frivolous contrast to harshly elemental nature. Commenting on an actual experience in the summer of 1958 such as described in this poem, she noted: 'Visions of violence. The animal world seems to me more and more intriguing.' One of the rare poems with a London setting is **'Parliament Hill Fields'** (1961), but typically the scene has a rural touch. (It is set on Hampstead Heath).

Inspired—and sometimes prodded—by her husband who was versed in country things, Sylvia Plath the city person turned to nature for topics and scenery. Shortly after having met Ted Hughes in the spring of 1956 she confided to her mother: 'I cannot stop writing poems! . . . They come from the vocabulary of woods and animals and earth that Ted is teaching me.' Prodded or inspired, Plath drew on her personal experiences of different places and landscapes as raw material for many of the poems. One might actually plot locations and stages of her life on the map of her work. Among the poems that open her career as a professional poet—her debut can conveniently be set to 1956—we can find scenes from her stay in England and her travels on the Continent. Later there will be scenes from New England and other parts of the United States and Canada. After her return to England in 1959 she set many of the poems in Devon and a few in London. One's immediate reaction to Plath's outdoor scenery is that the persona never seems to be quite at home in nature. Descriptions of nature will most often register feelings of estrangement, fear and the like. This is true even of poems commemorating travel experiences in happy moods, such as camping in a California desert (**'Sleep in the Mojave Desert'**) or by a Canadian lake (**'Two Campers in Cloud Country'**), poems written in 1960.

Plath's depictions of places and landscapes reveal her interest in pictorial art. She said that she had 'a visual imagination' and that her inspiration was 'painting, not music, when I go to some other art form.' We know of this interest in art, American and European, and the inspiration she derived from specific paintings resulting in, for example, the poems **'Snakecharmer'** (1957) and **'Yadwigha, on a Red Couch, Among Lilies'** (1958), both modelled on paintings by Henri Rousseau, and **'Sculptor'** (1958), dedicated to her friend Leonard Baskin. Her own efforts as a draftswoman establish a link between her verbal gifts and her graphic talents. Some of her drawings have been reproduced; *The Christian Science Monitor* (November 5 and 6, 1956) illustrated her reports about a summer visit to Benidorm in Spain with a couple of strictly realistic sketches by her hand: sardine boats pulled up on a beach; a corner of a peasant market; and trees and houses clinging on to steep sea cliffs. In his collection of essays on Plath's poetry, editor Charles Newman included three drawings of scenery that we can recognize in the poems; strong pen strokes show an old cottage in Yorkshire (Wuthering Heights); an irregular row of houses in Benidorm; and small fishing boats left for the winter on the bank of a river near its outlet into the ocean at Cape Cod. She evidently did not give up the habit of drawing. As late as October 1962, in a letter to her mother, she rejoices over the gift of pastels that she will surely find time to use.

By and large Plath's early poems betray the same sort of literary artificiality that marked most of her Juvenilia; they strain too noticeably toward effect and cleverness. But there are some whose subjects and settings introduce thoughts and moods which reverberate in the rest of the oeuvre. **'Winter Landscape, with Rooks'** is one such poem. The very title tells us that this scene is rendered by a 'painterly' poet. It describes a pond where a solitary swan 'floats chaste as snow.' To the observer-speaker it is a 'landscape of chagrin' 'scorn[ed]' by the setting sun. The speaker's mind is as dark as the pond: walking about like an imaginary rook—the only creature fit to match the wintry landscape—she finds no solace from her sorrow at the absence of a cherished person.

In a journal entry for February 20, 1956 Plath outlined the scene that inspired some of the realistic details of this poem. On her way to a literature class which was to be held at some distance from her Cambridge college, she noticed 'rooks squatting black in snow-white fen, gray skies, black trees, mallard-green water.' The 'real' rooks are missing from the poem; there is only a metaphorical one. We find features that will characterize a great deal of the poetry to come: the color scheme of black, white and red; the theme of loss and frozenness; and the parallel between landscape and human observer. Plath referred to the poem as 'a psychic landscape.' From now on her poetic landscapes will embody association between scene and mood. What marks **'Winter Landscape, with Rooks'** as an early poem is the lack of proportion between the loss suggested and the mood resulting from the contemplation of a calm winter scene. The poem ends with a sigh of self-pity: 'Who'd walk in this bleak place?'

The punning title of another poem written in 1956, **'Prospect,'** suggests comparison with a painting, calling to mind, for example, the Italian *veduta* of landscape or city. We find in it some of the same elements as in **'Winter Landscape, with Rooks'**: the fen, here with its gray fog enveloping rooftops and chimneys, and this time not with a metaphorical rook but two real ones sitting in a tree, with absinthe-colored eyes 'cocked' on a 'lone, late, / passer-by.' As in an impressionist painting much is made of color—orange, gray, black, green—at the expense of line and composition, but here too there is suggested a 'psychic' element: the solitary human being neither seeks nor derives protection or comfort from nature.

'Alicante Lullaby,' one of several poems inspired by Plath's stay in Spain in the summer of 1956, attempts to record the actual sounds of a busy little Spanish town. The poet uses onomatopoeia to recreate realistic sounds. (Evidently Sylvia Plath regretted that she did not have an ear for music.) In another poem, **'Departure,'** the speaker, taking leave of her temporary Spanish refuge sketched in bright colors, is able to note, with self-irony, that nature does not grieve at all at the parting. The reason why she leaves is decidedly unromantic: 'The money's run out.' The last glimpse of the scene is unromantic in another way and may suggest a parallel between the speaker's mood and nature: what she sees is a stone hut 'Gull-fouled' and exposed to 'corroding weathers,' and 'morose' and 'rank-haired' goats. It may all be in the viewer's eyes.

Returning to the favored rook in **'Black Rook in Rainy Weather'** the poet again musters up self-irony to face her urge to commune with nature. She might wish to see 'some design' among the fallen leaves and receive 'some backtalk / From the mute sky,' but this, she knows, would be to expect a miracle. Still, she leaves herself open to any minute gesture on the part of nature lending 'largesse, honor, / One might say love' even to the dullest landscape and the most ignorant viewer; this could be achieved, for instance, by letting a black rook arrange its feathers in such a way as to captivate the viewer's senses and so 'grant // A brief respite from fear / Of total neutrality.' The miracle has not happened yet, but the hope of such a moment of transcendent beauty and communion is worth the wait. She knows that it might in fact be only a trick of light which the viewer interprets as 'that rare, random descent' of an angel.

The next set of landscape poems, chronologically, are located in the West Yorkshire moorland which Sylvia Plath knew from visits with her husband's family. **'November Graveyard'** introducing this group describes a setting where nature—trees, grass, flowers—stubbornly resists mourning over death. But it does not deny death; the visitor notes the 'honest rot' which reveals nature's unsentimental presentation of death and decay. And the poet concludes that this 'essential' landscape may teach us the truth about death.

Coming at the end of Plath's first year as a professional poet this poem may be seen to exemplify a minor change in her depiction of landscapes; elements of nature are discreetly anthropomorphized: 'skinflint' trees refuse to mourn or 'wear sackcloth,' the 'dour' grass is not willing to put on richer colors to solemnize the place, and the flowers do not pretend to give voice to the dead.

Two other Yorkshire poems, **'The Snowman on the Moor'** and **'Two Views of Withens,'** written the following year, offer realistic glimpses of the moorland as backdrop for descriptions of relationships between people and of attitudes to nature. In the first poem, a condensed narrative relates a husband-and-wife quarrel with the woman being brought down from her pride by a vision of indomitable male power in the guise of a giant snowman; and in the second, we have in capsule form a definition of two very different attitudes to nature—perhaps also to life—epitomized in two persons' differing responses to a bare landscape and a dilapidated farmhouse with literary and romantic associations. (The scenery is associated with Emily Brontë's *Wuthering*

Heights.) The speaker of the poem regrets that she cannot respond the way the 'you' does. To her, landscape and sky are bleak and 'the House of Eros' is no 'palace.'

'Hardcastle Crags' gives a harsher view of a human being alone and defenseless in an unresponsive, 'absolute' landscape. The poem derives its power from a very detailed, realistic picture of fields and animals, stones and hills. The last Yorkshire poem written in 1957, however, with the title **'The Great Carbuncle,'** brings in an element of wonder performed by nature: a certain strange light with magical power—its source remains unknown—creates a moment of transfiguration for the wanderers. The Great Carbuncle may allude to a drop of blood in the Holy Grail. But it is a painfully brief moment: afterwards 'the body weighs like stone.'

In a poem written in September 1961, **'Wuthering Heights,'** Plath returned to the ambiguous fascination this moor landscape held for her. The mood, though, has now become unequivocally sinister. The descriptive details have lost much of their realistic significance. The solitary wanderer bravely 'step[s] forward,' but nature is her enemy: the alluring horizons 'dissolve' at her advance, wind and heather try to undo her. Images of landscape and animals are consistently turned into metaphors for the human intruder's feeling of being insignificant and exposed. A seemingly harmless thing such as the half-closed eyes of the grandmotherly-looking sheep makes the speaker lose her sense of identity and worth: it is as if she were being 'mailed into space, / A thin, silly message.' This landscape is indeed 'psychic' to an extent that **'Winter Landscape, with Rooks'** was not. This is most certainly a result of Plath's greater ability to transform realistic, concrete objects and scenes into consistent sets of metaphors for her thoughts and emotions.

'New Year on Dartmoor' is a somewhat later poem, inspired by a walk Sylvia Plath took with her small daughter on Dartmoor some distance from the Hugheses' home in Devon; the poem may have been written in late December 1961.

NEW YEAR ON DARTMOOR

This is newness: every little tawdry
Obstacle glass-wrapped and peculiar,
Glinting and clinking in a saint's falsetto. Only
    you
Don't know what to make of the sudden
    slippiness,
The blind, white, awful, inaccessible slant.
There's no getting up it by the words you know.
No getting up by elephant or wheel or shoe.
We have only come to look. You are too new
To want the world in a glass hat.

The poem shows how Plath's technique of using landscape scenes has changed even more. Here there is very little realistic description; the setting becomes completely 'metaphorized' and gives rise to the speaker's inner words, both sad and humorous, addressing her child who is accompanying her. The year is new and to the child the newness is exciting but baffling. Only the mother is aware of a rawer reality beneath the 'glinting' and the 'clinking,' and she knows what 'newness' entails of challenge and hardships.

In the fall of 1959 Sylvia Plath and Ted Hughes spent several weeks at Yaddo, the artists' colony in upstate New York. Although she was at first charmed by the old-fashioned beauty of the estate, she soon tired of it, and on the whole the Yaddo poems do not express any genuine pleasure in nature. Some of the poems she set in the grounds of the estate evidence a certain strain of finding something to write about and of getting the most out of the scenery. She was pleased with **'Medallion,'** a poem she defined as 'an imagist piece on a dead snake.' Nature is here in a somewhat macabre fashion used to aestheticize death. The speaker is only a cool observer. In another Yaddo poem featuring animals, **'Blue Moles,'** with its unequivocal message that strife and violence are the modes of nature, nature is anthropomorphized; the speaker empathizes with the moles ('Down there one is alone') while the sky above is 'sane and clear.'

The anthropomorphizing tendency is strong in the Yaddo poems; it does not serve to explain *nature,* rather to express the *human* protagonist's feelings and moods. Thus in **'Private Ground'** 'the grasses / Unload their griefs' in the protagonist's shoes, and in **'The Manor Garden'** items from nature are used to parallel and explain the growth of a foetus in a human body. It is not enough for Plath in these poems to call forth a human mood or attitude from a fairly detailed, more or less realistic picture of objects and scenes in nature; now she will more readily metaphorize natural processes, and detailed pictures become rarer. Often key words or phrases will suffice to hint at a parallel or an origin in nature.

Early in 1959 Plath had made clear what she wished to achieve in her nature poems. After finishing **'Watercolor of Grantchester Meadows'**—a memory of the Cambridge surroundings—she noted: 'Wrote a Grantchester [sic] poem of pure description. I must get philosophy in.' As every reader knows, Plath was wrong about this poem: in her picture of a seemingly idyllic landscape, cruelty and violence are lurking beneath the smooth appearance. The realistic scenery is 'distorted,' not in the direction of the ugly and the grotesque, but in the direction of nursery-plate prettiness. The 'philosophy' is apparent: terror and violence in the shape of an owl swooping down on an inoffensive water rat are at the heart of creation. Melville had said the same thing in *Moby Dick*

when he let Ishmael reflect on the 'tiger heart' that 'pants' beneath the 'ocean's skin.'

Plath's most ambitious piece of writing done at the artists' colony was the sequence **'Poem for a Birthday.'** Making notes for it she acknowledged the influence of Theodore Roethke. The greenhouse on the estate must have been a special link to him; it was 'a mine of subjects.' Her tentative plans for the poem were these: 'To be a dwelling on madhouse, nature: meanings of tools, greenhouses, florists shops, tunnels, vivid and disjointed. An adventure. Never over. Developing, Rebirth, Despair. Old women. Block it out.' Her ambition was to 'be true to [her] own weirdnesses.' Starting as an end-of-autumn poem it immediately turns into a seemingly random search for the origins and processes of the self; the landscape disappears, and forays into the past take over. The poem comes full circle by ending with a hope of birth into a new life. **'Poem for a Birthday'** is an indication of the direction Plath's poetry was to take from now on: toward greater use of free associations and juxtaposition of fragments of scenes and objects, experiences lived and imagined, feelings and thoughts harbored.

Sylvia Plath's life and surroundings in Devon, where she lived from September 1961 to December the following year, provided rich material for poetry. Court Green, the thatch-roofed house the Hugheses had bought, sat in a two-acre plot with a great lawn, in spring overflowing with daffodils, with an apple orchard and other trees that found their way into the poems. The settings of the poems she wrote in Devon are very varied. Several are set indoors, for instance, in a hospital (**'The Surgeon at 2 a.m.,'** **'Three Women'**), a kitchen (**'An Appearance,'** **'The Detective,'** **'Lesbos,'** **'Cut,'** **'Mary's Song'**), an office (**'The Applicant'**), or an unspecified interior (**'The Other,'** **'Words heard, by accident, over the phone,'** **'Kindness'**). These interiors are never *described;* they are often to be inferred by a situation dramatized or an action going on, such as cooking a Sunday dinner or being served tea. Action and character play the greater role. The trees and flowers of the Court Green garden appear in several poems, such as **'Among the Narcissi,'** **'Poppies in July'** and **'Poppies in October,'** all from 1962. But in these poems too there is much more *story* or incident than description.

'The Moon and the Yew Tree' offers a good example of how Plath used nature as material for poetry at this transitional stage in her career. Written in October 1961 this was the first poem for which she drew on her immediate Devon surroundings. As we see from Ted Hughes's comments, she still needed an occasional prodding to find a topic: 'The yew tree stands in a churchyard to the west of the house in Devon, and visible from SP's bedroom window. On this occasion, the full moon, just before dawn, was setting behind this yew tree and her husband assigned her to write a verse "exercise" about it.'

This nature poem is marked by the metaphorical mode already in the opening line: 'This is the light of the mind, cold and planetary.' Using a phrase from an earlier poem (**'Private Ground'**) the poet creates a transition to the garden landscape by anthropomorphizing nature: 'The grasses unload their griefs on my feet as if I were God.' The light of the mind does not help. The speaker complains: 'I simply cannot see where there is to get to.' Following the upright lines of the yew tree, the speaker's eyes seek the mother moon. Yew tree and church, one planted in the earth but striving toward heaven, the other bringing the message of heaven to earth, have nothing to give the speaker. She faces her real self: it is not the Church with its mixture of far reaching authority (the booming bells), its holiness stiffened by convention (the sculptured or painted saints floating above the heads of the churchgoers) and its somewhat sentimentalized sweetness (the mild Virgin), it is not these she can identify with: she is the daughter of the wild female moon with her dark and dangerous power.

Plath herself evidently read this poem slightly differently. Introducing it in a BBC program she said that a yew tree she had once put into a poem 'began, with astounding egotism, to manage and order the whole affair. It was not a yew tree by a church on a road past a house in a town where a certain woman lived . . . and so on, as it might have been in a novel. Oh no. It stood squarely in the middle of my poem, manipulating its dark shades, the voices in the churchyard, the clouds, the birds, the tender melancholy with which I contemplated it—everything! I couldn't subdue it. And, in the end, my poem was a poem about a yew tree. The yew tree was just too proud to be a passing black mark in a novel.' As I have indicated, another reading of the poem highlights the *moon* as the one who is taking over the scene.

The yew tree appears again in **'Little Fugue,'** written in 1962, but only as an introductory image bringing in a contrast through its blackness counterpointed with whiteness in the concrete form of a cloud ('The yew's black fingers wag; / Cold clouds go over'). Black and white do not merge, just as the blind do not receive the message of the deaf and dumb. These counterpointing 'absences' prefigure the main theme of the fugue: the speaker-daughter's despair at not being able to reach her dead father: 'Gothic and barbarous' he was a 'yew hedge of orders.' Now he sees nothing, and the speaker is 'lame in the memory.' The fugue ends by finally joining the two items from nature—the black yew tree and the pale cloud—as images of a marriage between death and death-in-life.

The Devon milieu is the scene also for **'Among the Narcissi.'** Here an ailing old neighbor is the main subject, the flowers attending upon him like a flock of children. Another poem with a Devon setting is **'Pheasant.'** It is a scene in the drama of tensions in a marriage, of suspicions, hurt, jealousy and anger, which was begun in **'Zoo Keeper's Wife'** and continued in **'Elm'**, **'The Rabbit Catcher,'** **'Event,'** **'Poppies in July'** and **'Poppies in October.'**

Two poems written in the last month Sylvia Plath spent in Devon, **'Letter in November'** and **'Winter Trees,'** testify to the almost uncanny equilibristics she was capable of by now in realizing highly different topics, scenes, moods, as it would seem from one moment to the next. Anger at deception (**'The Couriers'**), longing for spiritual rebirth (**'Getting There'**), tender anguish at a child's future (**'The Night Dances'**), revulsion at death (**'Death & Co.'**) and fascination with the dynamics of motion and life (**'Years'**), naked hatred and contempt (**'The Fearful'**), these are some of the emotions embodied in the November poems.

'Letter in November' is set in the Court Green garden. It is unusual for Plath at this stage in her career in that it contains a fairly detailed picture of the scenery. The 'letter' is addressed to an unspecified receiver (perhaps a child) apostrophized as 'love.' It describes, in a relaxed tone, details of a well-known garden which in this moment of seasonal transition is shifting color and form as if by some kind of magic that a child would understand. The speaker's boots 'squelch' realistically in the wet masses of fallen leaves. The old corpses buried under the 'death-soup' she is walking in prefigure the despair at total defeat revealed in the final allusion to the destruction of a heroic army at Thermopylae ('The irreplaceable / Golds bleed and deepen, the mouths of Thermopylae'). Was the lovingly detailed description of her garden an incantation for a moment's relief from pain?

'Winter Trees' is also set in the garden.

WINTER TREES

The wet dawn inks are doing their blue dissolve.
On their blotter of fog the trees
Seem a botanical drawing
Memories growing, ring on ring,
A series of weddings.

Knowing neither abortions nor bitchery,
Truer than women,
They seed so effortlessly!
Tasting the winds, that are footless,
Waist-deep in history—

Full of wings, otherworldliness.
In this, they are Ledas.
O mother of leaves and sweetness
Who are these pietas?

The shadows of ringdoves chanting, but easing
nothing.

The opening image, of trees barely visible in the early morning fog, might have led us to expect a landscape of the kind Plath wrote in her earlier years, that is, a fairly realistic description with a mood attached or a 'philosophy' as the outcome of pictures turned into metaphors. In this poem, however, trees are immediately turned into an aesthetic product: a drawing presenting themselves ('On their blotter of fog the trees / Seem a botanical drawing')! This idea is at once dropped and without the modulating help of language we are brought into the human domain of memories, relationships between people, values and morality. Memories, rings, weddings, abortions, bitchery—these words hint at a miniature narrative of past love and union, contrasted with ugly losses and failures. The speaker's muted despair has turned into disgust at the very idea of human femaleness. The trees have become symbols of ideal humanity: at the same time as they partake of the solidity and security of elemental earthliness, they achieve spirituality. Visited by a god, these Ledas share in the sacred, but being Ledas they also know suffering. In a last transformation, the trees take on the appearance of the grieving mother of another god. The final lines of the poem express the speaker's anguished cry lamenting her inability to partake of the perfection and pity of nature. Being a woman she appeals to a Mother Goddess for a 'clue,' but no sounds or sights in nature bring her relief.

Within the span of a few short lines [Plath] manages to create a complex of sight and sound, history and myth, Christian and pagan, ugliness and beauty, hope and despair.
—*Brita Lindberg-Seyersted*

This superb poem is an example of the skill and power Plath had reached in her thirtieth year. Within the span of a few short lines she manages to create a complex of sight and sound, history and myth, Christian and pagan, ugliness and beauty, hope and despair. As has been argued by a recent critic, this is a fine example of Plath's ability to raise her poetry above the level of the private and the confessional to a level of universality.

The poems Sylvia Plath wrote in the last few weeks of her life maintain continuity with her earlier work in subject matter and style. She still favors the two- or three-line stanza, and essential also in these poems are emotions and attitudes such as love for children—what Helen Vendler so succinctly refers to as the 'small constructiveness of motherhood'—hatred of deception, and conflicting urges toward stasis and

motion. But as a whole they are more concise and more referential—even to the point of obscurity—than earlier poems. They do not offer easy readings, for one thing because images from strikingly different spheres of life are juxtaposed, with no apparent associations to join them. By establishing links to the earlier poetry as reference and source material we may be in a better position to read these difficult texts.

Plath's use of landscapes is one such line to pursue. In these late poems recognizable, actual landscapes do not occur; here the poet uses only fragments from her experiences of various kinds of scenery, fragments that often suggest moods and attitudes similar to those that the more fully described landscapes had once signified. The first poem dated 1963, **'Sheep in Fog,'** was begun in December 1962 and completed the following January, and it works as a transitional poem. It is the last poem Plath wrote in which we can recognize the outlines of an actual landscape. It keeps some of the elements of poems set in an English landscape, with touches of the moorland, perhaps Dartmoor where Plath took riding lessons. She introduced the poem for a BBC program with these words: 'In this poem, the speaker's horse is proceeding at a slow, cold walk down a hill of macadam to the stable at the bottom. It is December. It is foggy. In the fog there are sheep.' This is of course only the bare skeleton around which the poem itself has been fashioned. The title suggests a realistic landscape with figures, and we find several such items: hills, horse and fields. No sheep are visible in the poem; the 'dolorous bells' indicate their presence. There is a watercolor aspect to the hills dimly seen in the fog, the faint line of smoke from a passing train and the touch of color provided by the horse. Human references, which are counterpointed with the touches of nature scenery, take over in the latter part of the poem. The speaker interprets the scene as an expression of her own situation. Resignedly registering her own inadequacy ('People or stars / Regard me sadly, I disappoint them') she perceives her situation as darker and darker. Against the normal order in nature 'All morning the / Morning has been blackening.' She fears that she has to accept nothingness as her lot, even after death; this is expressed in the image of the distant fields which 'threaten / To let me through to a heaven / Starless and fatherless, a dark water.' This is no longer a 'psychic landscape' of the kind exemplified by **'Winter Landscape, with Rooks'**; in **'Sheep in Fog'** the landscape as reality almost ceases to exist.

Items from **'Sheep in Fog'** reappear in even more fragmentary form in **'Totem,'** a poem written on the same day as the former one was completed. Here we find a train on a 'useless' journey, darkened fields, and mountains letting us glimpse an unchanging sky. These fragments of a landscape are only small signs in a composition overwhelming in its rich confusion, of images which all spell the greed of inevitable death. Plath spoke of this poem as 'a pile of intercon-nected images, like a totem pole.'

Other late poems have a similar quality of 'interconnected images like a totem pole' in which fragments of landscapes may reappear in a weak or distorted form. In **'The Munich Mannequins'** the yew tree from beside the Devon church has been transformed into a part of a womb ('the womb // Where the yew trees blow like hydras'); an unhappy memory of Sylvia Plath's own visit to Germany in 1956 in search of roots identifies the city of Munich as a place of death and sterility. In **'Child,'** expressing a mother's wish to create a happy world for her child, there are remnants of the Devon garden in bloom as a contrast to the mother's worried 'Wringing of hands.' **'Gigolo'** recalls a Mediterranean set-ting with crooked streets, cul-de-sacs and fruits-de-mer, al-luring and disgusting as the professional seducer himself. In **'Mystic'** there may be traces of a summery Atlantic coast—memories of smells of pines, sun-heated cabins and salty winds—as well as references to the harsh London winter Sylvia Plath was facing while she was composing these po-ems ('The chimneys of the city breathe, the window sweats'). These fragments accompany a more important religious im-agery. The poem has been interpreted in several ways; one interpretation sees it as the mystic's dark night of the soul, but the last line, 'The heart has not stopped,' indicates hope of an end to this night. And in **'Edge,'** one of the two last poems Plath wrote a few days before her death, she may have drawn on visual memories of the Yaddo estate. The 'per-fected' body of the woman whose epitaph the poem is and her children make up a sculptured group of death. In addi-tion to other allusions, such as the Laocoon group, here in-verted from struggle against death to fulfilled death, this group may vaguely recall the marble statuary at Yaddo.

In the preceding pages we have seen how Sylvia Plath sought inspiration and raw material for her poetry in different set-tings and how she very early saw the potential for 'psychic' qualities or parallels in realistic word paintings. In depict-ing external reality she is not concerned with representing, as faithfully as possible, shapes and lines, color and light, objects and figures. She hardly ever devotes an entire poem to something that looks like mere description of a scene in nature. There is always a metaphorical touch or dimension to the realistic composition. At times there is a narrative hinted at or rendered in some detail. Her landscape poems do not give the impression of a spontaneous pleasure in na-ture, nor of a wish to understand the processes of nature. They seem rather to serve as mirrors for a self in search of identity and truth.

Plath's career as a poet was brief, but even so it is possible to see a development in her use of landscapes, toward more metaphorizing, more anthropomorphizing of nature, and in the late poems, more fragmentation of scenes in nature. In

the early poetry she includes more 'documentable' detail, sometimes established already in the titles of poems, such as **'Hardcastle Crags'** and **'Two Views of Withens.'** She may have coerced herself—or been prodded—to broaden her palette by consciously turning to now one, now another land-scape that she had experienced, but at the end she no longer had to *look* for settings as inspiration. Elements of land-scapes came to her when she needed them as pieces in a mosaic more fraught with meaning than the early 'psychic landscapes.' She had at her command an extraordinary set of highly diverse materials which she juxtaposed into po-ems of striking originality—sometimes with less than com-plete success. Even though we may not be able to reach into the obscurest crevices of her imagery and thought, the po-ems Sylvia Plath wrote in the last few weeks of her life haunt us with their cries and whispers. Recognizing fragments of earlier landscapes may not be the most important clue to these and other poems, but it may help us clear the ground for entering deeper into her poetic world.

William Freedman (essay date October 1993)

SOURCE: "The Monster in Plath's 'Mirror,'" in *Papers on Language and Literature,* Vol. 108, No. 5, October, 1993, pp. 152-69.

[*In the following essay, Freedman discusses Plath's use of the mirror as a symbol of female passivity, subjugation, and Plath's own conflicted self-identity caused by social pres-sure to reconcile the competing obligations of artistic and domestic life.*]

For many women writers, the search in the mirror is ulti-mately a search for the self, often for the self as artist. So it is in Plath's poem **"Mirror."** Here, the figure gazing at and reflected in the mirror is neither the child nor the man the woman-as-mirror habitually reflects, but a woman. In this poem, the mirror is in effect looking into itself, for the im-age in the mirror is woman, the object that is itself more mir-ror than person. A woman will see herself both *in* and *as* a mirror. To look into the glass is to look for oneself inside or as reflected on the surface of the mirror and to seek or discover oneself in the person (or non-person) of the mir-ror.

The "She" who seeks in the reflecting lake a flattering dis-tortion of herself is an image of one aspect of the mirror into which she gazes. She is the woman as male-defined ideal or as the ideal *manqué,* the woman who desires to remain forever the "young girl" and who "turns to those liars, the candles or the moon" for confirmation of the man-pleasing myth of perpetual youth, docility, and sexual allure. As such, she is the personification—or reflection—of the mirror as passive servant, the preconditionless object whose perception is a form of helpless swallowing or absorption. The image that finally appears in the mirror, the old woman as "terrible fish," is the opposite or "dark" side of the mirror. She is the mirror who takes a kind of fierce pleasure in her uncompromising veracity and who, by rejecting the role of passive reflector for a more creative autonomy, becomes, in that same male-inscribed view, a devouring monster. The woman/mirror, then, seeks her reflection in the mirror/woman, and the result is a human replication of the linguistic phenomenon the poem becomes. Violating its implicit claim, the poem becomes a mirror not of the world, but of other mirrors and of the process of mirroring. When living mirrors gaze into mirrors, as when language stares only at itself, only mirrors and mirroring will be visible.

This parallel between person and poem suggests that the glass (and lake) in **"Mirror"** is woman—and more particularly the woman writer or artist for whom the question of mimetic reflection or creative transformation is definitive. For the woman—and especially for the mother—per se, the crucial choice is between the affirmation and effacement of the self: will she reflect the child or more generalized "other" as it presents itself for obliging reflection, or will she insist on her own autonomous identity and perception. To do the latter is to risk looking into the mirror and seeing, not the pleasing young girl, but the terrible fish.

Viewed in these terms, **"Mirror"** may be read as a broadening and more sophisticated extension of poems like **"Morning Song"** and **"Medusa,"** which question or reject the maternal role. "I'm no more your mother," announces the voice of **"Morning Song,"** "Than the cloud that distills a mirror to reflect its own slow/Effacement at the wind's hand." To say as much, however, is to acknowledge what it denies. The statement succeeds only in rejecting the maternal identity for one that is identical with it, for that of the vaguely insubstantial image (the cloud) that is ultimately erased from the surface of its other, equally effaced identity as maternal mirror. The escape from mirror and mother to cloud does not permit an escape from their mutual fate as depersonalized victims of erasure. And the ambiguity of "its own" suggests that the mirror as well as the cloud is effaced by the wind that blows the child into the mother's life. **"Morning Song"** ends with reconciliation and acceptance, an acceptance reflected in the developing animation of the poem's imagery: of the child from watch and statue to moth, cat, and singer; of the mother from walls and cloud to cow-heavy woman.

"Medusa" ends with the rejection that presumably motivated it, the rejection of the poet's own mother as a kind of terrible sea creature that poisons, paralyzes, and devours:

> Off, off, eely tentacle!

There is nothing between us.

Even here, however, there is an injected sense of the speaker as mother as well as child. The Medusa, apparently the mother, is also the child/mother's own newborn infant, a "tremulous breath at the end of my line . . . dazzling and grateful, / Touching and sucking." She is "Fat and red, a placenta" who, like a new unwelcomed baby, was not called, yet "steamed to me over the sea . . . Paralyzing the kicking lovers." The obliterating mother, then, is at the same time the infant whose emergence sucks life and identity from the child-cum-mother. Indeed, the evocation of the mother as devouring monster seems to be a reactive inversion of the perhaps more primitive sense that the speaking child consumes or threatens to consume its sacrificial mother. "Who do you think you are?" She asks harshly. "A Communion wafer? Blubbery Mary? / I shall take no bite of your body, / Bottle in which I live." Here Plath as embryo or new offspring rejects the sacrificial offer of the mother's body, and the poem's enraged rejection of the monstrous mother may at bottom be a rejection of the mother's ironically devouring self-annihilation. A letter Plath wrote to her brother in 1953 reflects such an image of their mother:

> You know, as I do, and it is a frightening thing, that mother would actually kill herself for us if we calmly accepted all she wanted to do for us. She is an abnormally altruistic person, and I have realized lately that we have to fight against her selflessness as we would fight against a deadly disease . . .
>
> After extracting her life blood and care for 20 years we should start bringing in big dividends of joy for her . . . (Letter to Warren, May 12, 1953).

A passage from Jung's "The Development of Personality," which Plath transcribed, describes the phenomenon of crushing maternal self-annihilation that Plath experienced and transformed into poetry. "Parents," wrote Jung,

> set themselves the fanatical task of always "doing their best" for the children and "living only for them." This claimant ideal effectively prevents the parents from doing anything about their own development and allows them to thrust their "best" down their children's throats. This so-called "best" turns out to be the very things the parents have most badly engaged in themselves. In this way the children are goaded on to achieve their parents' most dismal failures, and are loaded with ambitions that are never fulfilled.

The parents Jung describes assume contradictory roles, just as Plath's image of the mother-woman-mirror as terrible fish assumes contradictory or at least contrary forms. On the one hand, it is an image of a monstrous autonomy that cannot perform the self-effacing function of infant-confirming mother. Instead, "reflecting its own mood or, worse still, the rigidity of her own defenses," it generates in the child the threat of chaos that produces the disturbed obsession with distorting mirrors in Plath's poetry. Conversely, this terrible fish or medusa may be the image of maternal self-annihilation, the mother's guilt-inducing refusal of autonomy. The required self-denial of new motherhood, if perpetuated or exaggerated, may, as Jung suggests, be as threatening as its opposite. As virtually exclusive nurturer of the infant and small child, the mother cannot win. Caught between annihilation of self and annihilation of other, and lanced on the sacrifice of self that may efface the other, her denigration, rejection, and perceived monstrosity are all but insured.

The same near-identity of assertive autonomy with an at least seemingly contradictory self-annihilation characterizes the language of **"Mirror"** and colors the poem's implicit treatment of the woman as writer. The poem is finally about language and imitation, about poetry and its relation to what it describes. As such, it is a poem that assumes a central place in the literature of female authorship, the literature that takes as its subject the woman as writer and her obligation to create for woman and herself a resistant and resilient language of her own. The popularity of Plath's relatively few poems of aggressive threat and power, poems such as **"Lady Lazarus"** and **"Daddy,"** misleads us. Far more of her poetry presents protagonists or personae who are basically passive and depersonalized, victimized and helpless. Like the mirror, the speakers in these poems—dolls, mannequins, stones, patients—are typically confined, often inanimate, absorbently passive, and devoid of personal initiative or will. They are, in short, images of the woman who, as Gilbert and Gubar document, inanimately animate the "mirror of the male-inscribed literary text."

Much of Plath's poetry, in other words, is a mirror of the male text as mirror, a replication of the passive images caught on its surface. Just as the mirror can only *reflect* reality, the woman writer can only reflect male ideals and desires. Devoid of subjectivity and the power of narrative, the woman in many of Plath's poems "speaks" not only to the plight of woman generally, but, more particularly, to the woman as writer. For as Gilbert and Gubar argue, the mirror in much 19th- and 20th-century women's poetry and fiction is the locus of authorial self-discovery, the place in which the woman author or would-be author perceives both her silent subordination and the fierce urgency of repressed speech.

The image of woman as reflector functions in several ways. As mother or woman, the mirror's principal and imposed obligation is to reflect infant and other—that is, she must present herself as the image mirrored in man's eyes. But as speaking mirror, the woman becomes a narrating reflector of herself as mirror and of whatever passes before it. She becomes the writer who writes of the mirror in which she perceives herself and of the mirror she is. She becomes the text in which that recording occurs. Through these lenses, the question of the object of perception gives place to the now central question of the nature of the narrator. The mirror as woman or mother reflects the other to itself. The mirror as text or writer reflects self and world in language that becomes a kind of mirror itself. But in both forms the principal conflict is between a self-suppressing recapitulation of male expression and an autonomous resistance to the conventional truths and methods of his inscriptions. The connections are further entangled by the fact that a selection of a narrative technique inevitably determines the treatment of content. To let the mirror speak in self-defining ways that resist prior definition or restriction is to alter the image in the glass. That resistance is what is represented by the substitution of the "terrible fish" for the more attractive young girl in **"Mirror."**

The mirror's opening announcement of its identity calls that identity into question and begins to transform the mirror from a passive reflector into an active speaker. The poem mirrors language's resistance to simple representation and reflects the resistance of the woman writer and the feminine text to the roles assigned them. It is this rebellion, this presumptuous arrogation of autonomy, that accounts for the shocking image of the terrible fish in the poem's concluding line. The terrible fish is not just a symbol of approaching old age: it is the image of "monstrous autonomy" that stares back at the literary woman in so many of her texts, often out of the mirror of that text into which she gazes in embittered self-search. "The woman writer's self-contemplation," Gilbert and Gubar maintain, "may be said to have begun with a searching glance into the mirror of the male-inscribed literary text." It continues in her own text, where, as in Mary Elizabeth Coleridge's "The Other Side of the Mirror," the "woman, wild," "bereft of loveliness," her mouth a "hideous wound" bleeding "in silence and in secret," erupts into her poetry and fiction as demonic emblem of her independent identity, her monstrous renunciation of the mirroring angel. The speaker in Coleridge's poem is not a lonely, but a common figure. For like Coleridge, "the literary woman frequently finds herself staring with horror at a fearful image of herself that has been mysteriously inscribed on the surface of the glass." Plath's **"Mirror"** is in this tradition, its terrible fish a menacing image of its own self-terrifying achievement.

There is, of course, a biographical dimension to this poem and its governing images, which intensifies the purely literary force of the work. Plath had a dual image of herself: she was a brightly silvered surface concealing a demonic form that threatened to tear the fragile membrane—in other words, both a mirror and a fish. The mirror, of course, is the brilliant surface Plath presented to the world, as both woman and poet. As poet, Plath the mirror is the precise measurer and recorder of minutiae, the four-cornered goddess of aesthetic control. As woman, Plath the mirror is the strict and tightly disciplined achiever who glitteringly fulfilled all expectations, a perfect mirror of acquired parental and social standards of elegance, beauty and achievement—the persona that emitted what Lowell called "the checks and courtesies," her "air of maddening docility," and what Alvarez called an "air of anxious pleasantness." It is the persona that, as Plath herself described it, "Adher[ed] to rule, to rules, to rules," that, seemingly untroubled by her numbed submission, "Stay[ed] put," like the mirror fixed on the wall, "according to habit." It is the side George Stade labeled the "social cast of her personality, aesthetic, frozen in a cover girl smile...." It is the ambitious but distinctly anti-feminist cook and housekeeper whose accents "are those of the American girl as we want her."

This Plath, in short, is the mirror that reflects back what others wish to see and that is itself a perfect reflection of the feminine ideal in male eyes. But this Plath—it has become a commonplace—was only a facade, a fragile surface laid thickly over an inner turmoil Plath herself perceived as a slouching beast struggling for release. "There are two of me now," Plath writes grittily in **"In Plaster":** "This new absolutely white person and the old yellow one." The white person, like the mirror, "had no personality . . . she had a slave mentality." But the old yellow one, "ugly and hairy," is one of a profusion of monstrous forms threatening the placid surface from below. As in **"Lady Lazarus,"** it is a cannibal fury rising from the dead. In **"Fever 103°"** it is a flaming sinner and a "pure acetylene / Virgin." In **"Daddy"** it is the Electral avenger who stakes the vampire's heart; in **"Stings"** the sleeping queen bee with a menacing "self to recover," a "lion-red body" that, as Plath's demons typically do, rises as a "red scar" and a flaming comet. In **"Mirror,"** the poem's deflective subject is itself a defense against its intimidating imagery and import. The "terrible fish" is not simply the image of aging and decay apparent in the surface narrative; it is another incarnation of the barely suppressed demon of sensuality and rage that charges Plath's poetry as it haunted her life. What is more, it is, appropriately, the devouring monster of the deep, disturbingly at home in the depths of Plath's element.

In an autobiographical essay, **"Ocean 1212-W"** Plath recounts a crucial memory: "When I was learning to creep, my mother set me down on the beach to see what I thought of it. I crawled straight for the coming wave and was just through the walls of green when she caught my heels. What would have happened," Plath wonders, "if I had managed to pierce that looking-glass?" The sea is a looking glass in which she claims to have discovered, at two and a half, the

"awful birthday of otherness," "the separateness of everything" and ultimately therefore of herself. The sea is the terrible country of the void, of the "darkness [that] is leaking from the cracks." The true habitat of the horrific buried self, it is also the environ of her father. As Plath confessed in a BBC interview. "I probably wished many times that he were dead. When he obliged me and died, I imagined that I had killed him." In a number of her poems, her father is the victim of suicide or murder, usually by drowning, for the sea is her father's element, and it is there she takes her revenge. When she announces in **"Full Fathom Five,"** "father, this thick air is murderous / I would breathe water," she identifies herself as a dark swimmer in its waves, in effect the terrible fish who would return to her father. Whether she would return in order to love him like Electra or to destroy him as in **"Daddy"** matters little. Forbidden love and murder are but two faces of the same resurgent beast.

That the appearance of the demonic in Plath's poetry is typically associated with the imagery of sea and water helps explain, in biographical terms, the substitution of lake for mirror in the poem. The terrible fish is implicit from the outset. It is contained in the rebellious rejection of the mirroring role in the opening lines of **"Mirror"** that ostensibly accept and define it. It is implicit, too, in the barely concealed harshness of the relentless veracity of the mirror's reflection, whose cruelty she unconvincingly denies. And it is explicit in the mirror's urge to "swallow immediately" whatever it sees. But the image of the fish's emergence requires that the mirror be transformed into water, Plath's symbol of the hideous depths in which the monster lives.

The terrible fish, then, is Plath's personal demon, the witch she strove to conceal beneath the snow white surface or to transform into the "pure gold baby" of **"Lady Lazarus."** In this reading, the poem's attempt to undermine the mirror's veritical claims with a figurative language that belies them is a linguistic replica of the poem's content, of the effort of the woman who "turns to those liars, the candles and the moon" to avert the terrible truth of her mounting ugliness and decay. Here, the flight from clarity and truth is also a flight, parallel to the young woman's and the author's, from the horrifying image of the woman as the devouring other. Her shocking emergence at the end of the poem marks the fearful triumph of a psychological reality over the linguistic efforts to avert it. The woman outside the mirror or lake is of course the woman whose image as terrible fish is also inside it, visible in its depths. To perceive oneself in the mirror or lake, then, is to recognize one's Jungian shadow as the dark underside of the shining surface. The terrible fish is not simply the time-transformed identity of the young girl; it is the Hydean alter-ego of the mirror or lake in whose depths it is shudderingly disclosed.

Inside the woman-as-mirror, in other words, behind this

physically restricted, passive, depersonalized reflector of the external world, lurks the minatory force that will emerge with full power and vengeance in some of the *Ariel* poems. To escape the obligations of literal truthfulness is not to escape the mirror of male texts that identify her as the obedient angel, but the opposite. It is to evade the monstrous truth the angel herself knows best and fears no less than does the male who protectively angelicizes her in order to prevent her transformation into monster. It is to look into the mirror and pretend one does not see the monster.

Because it recognizes the danger both of reflecting and ignoring the world, **"Mirror"** can be seen as the turning point in Plath's development. The voice in poems such as **"Stones," "Lorelei," "Tulips," "Love Letter," "Crossing the Water," "Purdah," "Face Lift," "Two Campers in Cloud Country," "Childless Woman,"** and dozens more is that of a woman who has accepted her depersonalization and passivity or who longs for the numbing purity it promises. In many of these poems, the stone, jade, plaster, or anesthetized persona shares the muted stage with old yellow, the lioness, the acetylene virgin, or other threatening figures from the depths, though it is not until her final poems, principally **"Daddy"** and **"Lady Lazarus,"** that the menacing avenger explodes onto the surface as the dominant force in poems of assertive threat and rage. **"Mirror"** represents a kind of middle-ground between the extremes of passivity and action, numbing self-cancellation and aggressive self-assertion. It achieves its special position and effect by adopting the former guise in ways that renounce it for the latter. To assume the mirror's role is implicitly to accept the male-proscribed image of woman and mother. But the poem's method and equations situate the terrible fish within the lake and mirror and quietly establish an identity between them. The poem's implicit rejection of the mirror's claim to literal reflection is what generates the image of threatening female autonomy that the poem ostensibly disavows. The fish that is in effect in the mirror from the outset charges towards the mirroring surface at the end, its identity and import disguised by a subject that deflects our attention to figures apparently external to the speaking mirror. Blending passive inactivity with devouring hostility, the poem presages the vengeful uprising of **"Lady Lazarus"** and **"Daddy"** while maintaining the innocent, expressionless appearance of paper, stone, mannequin, or doll. **"Mirror,"** in other words, lends to the monster in the attic (or basement) the face of the angel in the house.

The dread fish is identified with the passive mirror by its presence within or behind it. But their identification with one another may have another source as well. The speaker sees herself "in" the mirror or lake in two senses: She *is* the fearful image in the depths beyond the glass and she is the mirror itself. The implication here is that Plath found her defenses hardly less repulsive than the assault they were cre-

ated to ward off. The terrible fish observed in the lake's depths and rising toward its surface is identifiable with the mirror that reflects, neutrally and passively, whatever swims before it. The monster in the depths, in other words, is also the monster on the surface, perhaps more accurately the monstrosity of mere surface or lack of depth. The identification of the mirror with the terrible fish, then, erases the separation the dual identity was constructed to sustain. It suggests on the one hand that the mirror contains the fish, that beneath the angel in the house lurks the monster in the depths. But it may propose as well that a two-dimensional image of the angel is also is a form of monstrosity.

In **"Crossing the Water,"** the title poem of Plath's second volume, the speaker is identified as one of "two black, cut-paper people" floating across the water as they float over the surface of their lives. Yet, as she observes, "the spirit of blackness is in us, it is in the fishes." And here, too, the double meaning suggests itself. The spirit of blackness may refer to a dark force concealed beneath the cut paper surface. But, since the paper itself is identified as black, the stronger reading points toward an identification of two-dimensionality with blackness—and both flatness and darkness are identified with the fish made terrible in **"Mirror."**

The monster is seen not only in the mirroring self, but "in" that self as surface reflector. The woman as the passive, selfless reflector is inscribed in psychoanalysis, motherhood, and the male text and is submissively adopted by the woman as her own identity. But Plath shows it to be a monstrous evasion of reality and suppression of self. A woman who adopts the reflecting role is cruel primarily to herself. It is therefore inevitable that the last image the reflector swallows is that of the terrible fish, which is at once its concealed opposite and its concealing self.

The mirror is an image of the woman writer in her two conflicting roles as wife/mother and as author. In the first she is the selfless reflector of man and infant, in the second the self-conscious, self-centering reflector of herself and of the world as she willfully perceives it. Traditionally the roles were seen, by women as well as men, as not merely conflicting but mutually exclusive. It was, in fact, the collective view of psychoanalytic theory that the woman who has "created" a child required no other creative exercise or outlet, and women felt the power, if not always the validity, of that argument in their lives. Some women writers have so internalized this argument that they have felt the fear Susan Sulciman describes: "With every word I write, with every metaphor, with every act of genuine creation, I hurt my child." The guilt this idea elicits necessarily produces feelings of aggression. In Plath's **"Mirror,"** and in many more of her poems on motherhood and entrapment, this aggression wins out over any feelings of tenderness.

Like the women in the writing of Anne Finch and Anne Elliot, Emily Dickinson and the Brontë sisters, the persona in a few of Plath's poems—in **"In Plaster,"** the Bee poems, **"Lady Lazarus"** and **"Daddy"**—articulates what virtually her entire body of poetry represents: the striving of the fundamentally powerless woman for autonomy. "The great woman writers of the past two centuries," Gilbert and Gubar argue, "danced out of the debilitating looking glass of the male text into the health of female authority. Tracing subversive pictures behind socially acceptable facades, they managed to appear to dissociate themselves from their own revolutionary impulses even while passionately enacting such impulses." Plath hardly seems at home in this tradition. The female authority she stole or discovered assumed no healthy form. Rather, her work seems dangerously divided between poems in which she anesthetically dissociates herself from her aggressive or rebellious impulses and those, mostly later poems, in which she ferociously enacts them. In **"Mirror"** the contrary impulses come together—even as she dissociates herself from aggression, she acts it out. And while the poem's repression does not bespeak a thoroughly healthy freedom, Plath has found a way to allow her aggression to triumph over tenderness, but only within a controlled system that maintains the integrity of poem and personality alike.

In "A Sketch of the Past," Virginia Woolf recalls a dream in which "I was looking in a glass when a horrible face—the face of an animal—suddenly showed over my shoulder." What she sees is a variant of the monster in the mirror familiar to women's poetry and fiction, the image of rebelliously monstrous autonomy typified by the madwoman in the attic and an uneasy crowd of ominous female forms that darken the mirroring text of women's fiction. As in Plath's poem, the young woman sees in the mirror the dread reflected image of a beast that is clearly an aspect of the self Woolf elsewhere identified as a self-less mirror for man's magnification.

Mary Elizabeth Coleridge's "The Other Side of the Mirror" offers a more pertinent parallel, for it implies more strongly still the connection between feminine writing and monstrosity. In this poem, Coleridge traces the emergence of the monster from behind the angelic facade, a creature whose rage betrays the shallowness and fragility of the submissive pretense. This figure arises, as Gilbert and Gubar observe, "as if the very process of writing had liberated [her] . . . from a silence in which neither she nor her author can continue to acquiesce." In Plath, too, I believe, it is the writing that liberates the monster—or rather generates her. To quote Gilbert and Gubar one final time, "If she is to be a poet the woman must deconstruct the dead self that is a male 'opus' and discover a living 'inconsistent' self." And the implicit reference to Plath's **"Lady Lazarus"** in the word *opus*—"I am your opus, / I am your valuable, / The pure gold baby /

That melts to a shriek"—is as apt as the verb that effects the metamorphosis. For it is precisely by deconstructing the masculine mimetic language that entraps the woman in her traditional role that the speaking mirror exchanges the anxious young woman for the monstrous autonomy of the terrible fish. The fish is the woman as autonomous person and author. It is the role-rejecting woman/mother who, even as she proclaims her acceptance of the task, refuses passively to mirror man, infant, or whatever else is set before it. And it is the woman-as-writer who, even as she proclaims her obedient adherence to the mimetic model, adopts that model only to tease and overturn it. "She accepts the woman's role as accurate reflecting mirror in order to transcend it, to show how that very role inevitably thwarts and transcends itself." The mirror as woman and as writer takes on the figure of the four-cornered glass in order to shatter it against the non-mirroring language with which she affirms the comfort of the fit—to shatter it, too, by focusing on herself, making herself the subject of her own attention and the poem. It is the nature and occupation of the mirror self-effacingly to reflect the other. In **"Mirror,"** however, the glass is both subject and speaker at once. The poem begins with "I," a pronoun that appears five times in the first four lines and, together with "me" or "my," seventeen times in this poem of only eighteen lines. The mirror/woman, who is by definition without identity, defines and identifies herself. The persona that has no story, tells it, and in the defiant mirror-breaking act of doing so, she becomes the terrible fish of assertive selfhood. To tell one's own story, even if it is, as it must be, the story of absence and effacement, is to establish a presence and to display, perhaps for the first time, the face behind the angelic silver mask.

Plath's emergent monster, then, is not an imagined other, a beckoning fulfillment of hopeless ambition. It is the reconstruction of the speechless woman whose language deconstructs her verbal confession of mere reflective silence. This reconstructed self still bears the conscience of the complaint, and therefore the image of autonomy is not a thoroughly positive figure of assertive strength. The woman continues to subscribe to the male dread of female sexuality and to the male identification of female defiance or aggression with bestiality. The monster, then, does not so much dwell on the other side of the mirror; she is the other side of the mirror, the perpetuation of the mirror's male-inscribed ideal in a form that otherwise rejects it. The contradictions travel in both directions. The announcement of a mirroring silence or self-effacement implicitly rejects the identity it affirms. Yet the monstrous shape this autonomy assumes attests to the persistence of the woman's sense of self as dependent and faceless.

The woman achieves autonomy in Plath's **"Mirror"** and comparable works by rejecting the phallocentric language whose fixed truth fixes woman as the mirroring or speechless other. The rejection of the false and insulting "truth" of woman's identity is effected in a language that undermines the very possibility of definable identity and truth. Woman achieves freedom from male definition at the price of all definition, freedom from the name with which the masculine text identifies her in the affirmation of unnamability. Yet, as in Conrad, the unnamed, too, may be a form of monstrosity or horror: the chilling truth at the heart of the darkness may be an unnamed evil or the evil of unnamability itself, the fearful prospect of truth as mere illusion. The stakes are perhaps lower in **"Mirror,"** the curse a mixed blessing of menacing independence and creativity. But the merging dichotomy is present here as well. In these terms, the terrible fish is not only the monstrous autonomy of woman as personally or artistically creative self. It is also the impossibility of all autonomy or self-definition. Defining herself in and as that which cannot be defined, the woman writer comes perilously close to her previous condition of subjectlessness. That is the price of creative autonomy viewed in terms of resistance and dissociation.

Different in several ways from other poems on "monstrous" female autonomy, creativity is not the manifest subject of **"Mirror,"** and the terrible creature is not the acknowledged alter-ego of the speaker. The image, moreover, retains more of its primordial menace as both monster and internal threat than in most of the poems of the genre. There is little apparent nobility or dignity in the terrible fish, and its immediate if not exclusive prey seems to be not man or "the oppressor" but the mirror (or lake) itself and the young woman who is drowned in it. Almost to the very end Plath remained ambivalent, retained her dual identity, and could not celebrate liberation or defiance unperplexed. Unlike Lady Lazarus, Plath's mirror is a cannibal Charybdis who either has not yet identified the enemy or is not prepared to attack it. Finally and most impressively, however, unlike most poems that consciously identify their beast of creative enterprise, **"Mirror"** generates its emblem of autonomy in the language and processes of a poem that has ostensibly made its peace with mere reflection. The terrible fish is not so much an image in the poem as an image of the poem and its achievement, the self-generated product of its method.

Ted Hughes (essay date Fall 1994)

SOURCE: "On Sylvia Plath," in *Raritan*, Vol. 14, No. 2, Fall, 1994, pp. 1-10.

[*In the following essay, Hughes comments on Plath's struggle to transcribe her private anguish into the fiction of* The Bell Jar. *According to Hughes, Plath's difficulty stemmed from her effort to produce a novel with both mythic aspirations and cathartic ritual based in reality.*]

Sylvia Plath's intense ambition to write a novel provides one of the main and most distressful themes of her early journals. Her inability to start—or worse, her various attempts to start—brought her repeatedly to near despair. She agonized about style, tone, structure, subject matter.

Throughout that same period, her poetry struggled into being against only slightly less resistance. Plenty of poems survive, perhaps because each of her convulsive efforts to break through the mysterious barriers by way of verse sufficed to complete a short poem—which could then be sold for cash and bore comparison with what other poets were publishing. But she knew these poems were not what she wanted. She valued them far more highly than her prose, because at least they reflected, often very beautifully, the obsessive inner life that made her write them. But though they reflected it, she felt they did not contain it, did not release it.

These poems do not live: it's a sad diagnosis.
                                    (**"Stillborn"**)

Her prose, however, seemed to her not even to reflect it.

As far as her difficulties with narrative prose went, in retrospect one can see a glaring mismatch between the great dreams of her novelistic ambition and the character of her actual gift. Her high-minded, academic passion for classic novelists combined with the priorities of her own sophisticated poetic talent made her think of the ideal narrative prose as something densely wrought, richly charged, of all-encompassing, superfine subtleties, with James Joyce, Virginia Woolf, and Henry James prominent in the pedigree. This is where most of her attempts to get her novel going foundered. They foundered because her vital inner creative life was not in them. Her heart, in other words, pulled her in the opposite direction—through Lawrence and Dostoyevski. On the evidence of *The Bell Jar* one could say, maybe, that her writer's distress might have had less to do with her conscious failure to add another thoroughbred to that classic stable of stylists than to her unconscious horror at being dragged remorselessly towards what she did not want to face—even though her true gift was waiting there to show her how to face it.

Her breakthrough came—by the backdoor. Spring 1959, in a moment of seemingly no importance, like a gambler, playful and reckless, out of the blue she wrote her short story **"Johnny Panic and the Bible of Dreams."** This first-person narrative is composed in a voice that approximates the one she would find for *The Bell Jar*—a voice, that is, rather than a style. It whirls in a high-trapeze glitter of circus daring around one of her most serious terrors: her experience of the electroconvulsive shock treatment that jumped her out of the torpor in which her attempted suicide had left her.

Perhaps **"Johnny Panic"** was the divining work that located and opened the blocked spring. Change of home and travel prevented her from writing anything more till late fall. Then almost at once, with a place and a few brief weeks to concentrate, she made the first big breakthrough in her poetry. **"Poem for a Birthday"** returns to that stony source, but now lifts the shattered soul reborn from the "quarry of silences" where "men are mended," and where her "mendings itch." And the voice of Ariel can be heard clearing its throat.

Immediately after that, her writing was once again disrupted by physical upheavals: change of country, home-building, birth and infancy of her first child, all these interposed a full year, during which time that new voice, with the story it had to tell, stayed incommunicado. But in the spring of 1961 by good luck circumstances cooperated, giving her time and place to work uninterruptedly. Then at top speed and with very little revision from start to finish she wrote *The Bell Jar.*

In this narrative the voice has perfected itself. And what it has to tell is the author's psychic autobiography, the creation-myth of the person that had emerged in the **"Poem for a Birthday"** and that would go on in full cry through Ariel.

The Bell Jar is the story, in other words, from behind the electroconvulsive shock treatment. It dramatizes the decisive event of her adult life, which was her attempted suicide and accidental survival, and reveals how this attempt to annihilate herself had grown from the decisive event in her childhood, which was the death of her father when she was eight. Taken separately, each episode of the plot is a close-to-documentary account of something that did happen in the author's life. But the great and it might be said profoundly disturbing effect of this brisk assemblage is determined by two separate and contradictory elements. One of these operates on what could be called an upper level, the other on a lower.

> **That mythic schema of violent initiation, in which the old self dies and the new self is born, or the false dies and the true is born, or the child dies and the adult is born, or the base animal dies and the spiritual self is born . . . can be said to have preoccupied [Plath].**
>
> *—Ted Hughes*

The first, on the upper level, is the author's clearly recognizable purpose in the way she manipulates her materials. Her long-nursed ambition to write an objective novel about "life" was swept aside by a more urgent need. Fully aware of what she was doing, she modeled the sequence of episodes, and the various characters, into a ritual scenario for the heroine's symbolic death and rebirth. To her, this became the crucial aspect of the work. That mythic schema of violent initiation, in which the old self dies and the new self is born, or the false dies and the true is born, or the child dies and the adult is born, or the base animal dies and the spiritual self is born, which is fundamental to the major works of Lawrence and Dostoyevski, as well as to Christianity, can be said to have preoccupied her. Obviously, it preoccupied her in particular for very good reasons. She saw it as something other than one of imaginative literature's more important ideas. As far as she was concerned, her escape from her past and her conquest of the future, or in more immediate, real terms her well-being from day to day and even her very survival, depended absolutely on just how effectively she could impose this reinterpretation on her own history, within her own mind, and how potently her homemade version of the rite could give sustaining shape and positive direction to her psychological life. Her novel had to work as both the ranking of the mythic event and the liturgy, so to speak, of her own salvation.

The very writing of *The Bell Jar* did seem to succeed in performing this higher function, for the author, with astounding immediacy and power. And the role of each episode and character, as they operate on this level in the book, has been a good deal discussed.

The main movement of the action is the shift of the heroine, the "I," from artificial ego to authentic self—through a painful "death." The artificial ego is identified with the presiding moral regime of the widowed mother. The inner falsity and inadequacy of this complex induces the suicidal crisis. With the attempted suicide it is successfully dislodged, scapegoated into the heroine's double, Joan Gilling, and finally, at the end of the book, physically annihilated when Joan Gilling hangs herself. Simultaneously, the authentic self emerges into fierce rebellion against everything associated with the old ego. Her decisive act (the "positive" replay of her "negative" suicide) takes the form of a sanguinary defloration, carefully stage managed by the heroine, which liberates her authentic self into independence. On this plane, the novel is tightly related to the mythos visible in the plots and situations of the poems, which here and there share a good deal of its ritualized purpose. It can be read, in fact, as the logbook of their superficial mechanisms and meanings. To a degree, the novel is an image of the matrix in which the poems grew and from which they still draw life.

Without undergoing the psychic transformation of self-remaking, which she accomplished in writing this scenario, the author might not have come so swiftly and so fully, as she did, to the inspiration and release of Ariel. She might not have got there at all. As it is, a reader can chart her progress from the completion of the novel (late spring, 1961) to the first true Ariel poem (**"Elm,"** mid-April 1962). More physical disruptions—holidays, changing homes, etc.—help to account for the absence of the new voice in the four or five poems ("Insomniac," "Widow," "Stars over the Dordogne," "The Rival," "Wuthering Heights") produced between late spring and mid-September. But in September she was able to settle once again to concentrated work, beginning with the ominous piece, **"Blackberrying."** Three more strides (**"Finisterre," "The Surgeon at 2 a.m.," "Last Words"**) towards the land of the dead brought her to **"The Moon and the Yew Tree,"** where her father lies under the roots and her mother mourns in heaven:

> The yew tree points up. It has a Gothic shape.
> The eyes lift after it and find the moon.
> The moon is my mother. She is not sweet like
>   Mary.
> Her blue garments unloose small bats and owls.
> How I would like to believe in tenderness
> The face of the effigy, gentled by candles,
> Bending, on me in particular, its mild eyes.
>
> I have fallen a long way. Clouds are flowering
> Blue and mystical over the face of the stars.
> Inside the church, the saints will be all blue,
> Floating on their delicate feet over the cold pews,
> Their hands and faces stiff with holiness.
> The moon sees nothing of this. She is bald and
>   wild.
> And the message of the yew tree is blackness—
> blackness
>   and silence.

Further exploration was disrupted by the birth of her second child in January 1962. But she was back on the path, in the depth of her vision, on the 4th of April, and found herself again in the same place, confronting the yew tree—which now consists of terrible music and opens to admit her. This is exactly as if she had entered her father's coffin.

> Empty and silly as plates,
> So the blind smile.
> I envy the big noises,
> The yew hedge of the Grosse Fuge.
>
> Deafness is something else.
> Such a dark funnel, my father!
> I see your voice
> Black and leafy, as in my childhood,
>
> A yew hedge of orders,
> Gothic and barbarous, pure German.
> Dead men cry from it.
> I am guilty of nothing.
>
> The yew my Christ, then.

> Is it not as tortured?
> And you, during the Great War
> In the California delicatessen
>
> Lopping the sausages!
> They color my sleep,
> Red, mottled, like cut necks.
> There was a silence!
>
> Great silence of another order.
> I was seven, I knew nothing.
> The world occurred.
> You had one leg, and a Prussian mind.
>
> Now similar clouds
> Are spreading their vacuous sheets.
> Do you say nothing?
> I am lame in the memory.
>
> I remember a blue eye,
> A briefcase of tangerines.
> This was a man, then!
> Death opened, like a black tree, blackly.
>
>   (from **"Little Fugue"**)

The actual yew tree of the poem, as she saw it from the door of her house, stood in her sunset, on the opposite side, due West. Due East, filling her dawn sky as she saw it from the back of her house, stood the Elm.

The fascinating thing is what now unfolded between the 2nd and the 19th of April. As it happened, the 2nd fell in the dark phase of the Moon (which emerged new on the 5th) and the 19th fell on the first day of the Full. On the 2nd, as I say, she had entered her father's coffin, under the yew tree. On the 4th she wrote **"An Appearance,"** her point-blank portrait of the presiding genius of her false ego—that she was about to escape from at last. She then went on, through the 4th, 5th, and 7th of April, to write her three most purely beautiful, most free-spirited, most delicately elated poems— **"Crossing the Water," "Among the Narcissi,"** and **"Pheasant."** What she was actually doing became clear only on the 19th! The real Pheasant, as in her poem, flew up into the real Elm. A few days before the 19th she had started a poem about the Elm itself. This had settled early into a constricted series of rhymes, in which one can see her groping for the new bearings with the old instruments. After twenty-one pages of struggle, the new bearings suddenly burst in on her, she finds the new instruments in her hands, and the voice of Ariel emerges fully fledged in **"Elm."** It emerges as a bird, "a cry":

> Nightly it flaps out,
> Looking, with its hooks, for something to love.

In other words, between the 2nd and the 19th, she has been traveling underground (**"Crossing the Water"**), just like Osiris in his sun-boat being transported from his death in the West to his rebirth as a divine child (himself reborn as his own divine child in the form of a Falcon) in the East. And as can be seen, **"Elm"** recapitulates the ritual scenario of *The Bell Jar:*

> I know the bottom, she says. I know it with my
> great tap root:
> It is what you fear.
> I do not fear it: I have been there.
>
> . . . .
>
> I have suffered the atrocity of sunsets.
> Scorched to the root
> My red filaments burn and stand, a hand of wires.
>
> Now I break up in pieces that fly about like clubs.
> A wind of such violence
> Will tolerate no bystanding: I must shriek.
>
> The moon, also, is merciless: she would drag me
> Cruelly, being barren.
> Her radiance scathes me. Or perhaps I have caught
> her.
>
> I let her go. I let her go
> Diminished and flat, as after radical surgery.
> How your bad dreams possess and endow me.
>
> I am inhabited by a cry.
> Nightly it flaps out
> Looking, with its hooks, for something to love.
>
> I am terrified by this dark thing
> That sleeps in me;
> All day I feel its soft, feathery turnings, its
> malignity.

Through an apocalyptic disintegration, the Elm remains as the physical continuity of the speaker, as did Victoria Lucas in the novel.

The Moon, as always, corresponds to the nucleus of the artificial ego in its matriarchal regime, while the "soft, feathery" thing, the dark fierce bird that inhabits the tree, is the voice and spirit of the authentic self—the new voice and spirit of Ariel, with its deeper story still to be told.

It should not be surprising that the novel and poems are so closely related. They were not only gestated in the same imagination (utilizing a genetic code of symbolic signs that has few equals for consistency and precision), they were de-livered, so to speak, in parallel. Though *The Bell Jar* had been finished by late spring, 1961, the publication process dragged on throughout 1962, and the book emerged to the public eye only on January 14th, 1963 (four weeks before her death). In late 1962, while the Ariel poems were being written, she corrected and sent off the novel's proofs, and worried over questions of possible libel. The last Ariel poem, **"Sheep in Fog,"** came on December 2nd. This was also the last poem she wrote (except for the unfinished **"Eavesdropper"**) until after the novel was published. It was then the first poem she picked up, on January 28th, when she made the correction that revealed it as the elegy and funeral cortege for the Ariel inspiration. Whereupon it became the first (three more written that same day and all eleven within the next week) of the final group, the true death-songs.

It is the curve of the mythic drama within the poems that directs a reader's attention back to the positive aspect of the rebirth ritual in the novel. I made the point that this ritual operates on an "upper level." With the help of the poems, one can see that the "positive" aspect of that ritual holds good only on that upper level—where her shaping will is the control, where the ritual magic is choreographed according to plan, and the rebirth is hopeful.

On the lower level, where what I called the second element makes itself felt, things are different. Her materials were the real explosive experience of her own life and attempted suicide. Her bid to refashion these materials ritually, to recreate her history and remake herself, is brilliant with a kind of desperation, lit with the dazzling powers of an all-out emergency. Everything depended on her bringing about a genuine alchemical change in that uranium. And for a time, the triumph seemed real—it enabled her to write *Ariel.* But it proved to be temporary. The reality of her materials was susceptible to her magical coercion—but only so far and for so long. In its true nature it remained stubbornly what it always was—inaccessible to manipulation. Inaccessible, at least, to that first, brave attempt. This helps to explain the raggedly imperfect art of a novel that nevertheless feels like a vital work, a work of existential emergency. In effect, two different books are fighting for the one story. While she tries to impose her positive, self-protective interpretation and nurse that germ of an authentic rebirth, in her stage-managed nativity ritual, the material itself is doing something else. It is disinterring its own actuality *for the first time,* and dictating its own document, telling the simple truth of what was, is being, and will be suffered. This, then, is the second element in *The Bell Jar:* the unalterable truth, the past and future reality, of her basic materials.

On this lower level, the symbolism discloses a pattern of tragedy that is like a magnetic field in the very ground of her being: that unalterable truth to the reality is her voice's deeper negative story. Because in each episode of the novel this deeper pattern contradicts the ritual on the upper level, everything on the upper level, every step of the ritual dance that is trying to compel "the good things to happen," acquires a tragic shadow. The poems, meanwhile, wear that ritual purpose more lightly and declare the deeper pattern more openly—sometimes shockingly so. The reader is bewildered because each level speaks in the equally-real-or-symbolic terms of the other. This simultaneity of the two levels is what makes the novel, the poems, and the author herself truly tragic.

Al Strangeways (essay date Fall 1996)

SOURCE: "'The Boot in the Face': The Problem of the Holocaust in the Poetry of Sylvia Plath," in *Contemporary Literature*, Vol. XXXVII, No. 3, Fall, 1996, pp. 370-90.

[*In the following essay, Strangeways examines Plath's references to the Holocaust in light of her preoccupation with personal history and myth, female victimization, and the specter of nuclear war. Strangeways concludes that Plath does not simply reduce the atrocity of the Holocaust to metaphor, but draws attention to the ambiguous and potentially dangerous interrelationship between "myth, history, and poetry in the post-Holocaust world."*]

Sylvia Plath's poetry is generally judged on the contents of the posthumously published *Ariel* (1965), and often on a minority of poems within that volume, such as **"Daddy"** (1962) and **"Lady Lazarus"** (1962), which are most striking because of their inclusion of references to the Holocaust. Plath's whole oeuvre is frequently and superficially viewed as somehow "tainted" by the perceived egoism of her deployment of the Holocaust in these poems. Such straightforward condemnation, however, disguises the difficulties surrounding any judgment of Plath's treatment of this material—difficulties which are clearly exhibited by the respected critic George Steiner, who in 1965 applauded **"Daddy"** as "The 'Guernica' of modern poetry," yet later, in 1969, declared that the extreme nature of Plath's late poems left him "uneasy": "Does any writer, does any human being other than an actual survivor, have the right to put on this death-rig?" It is important to study both why and how the Holocaust appears in Plath's poetry, because our reaction to it as readers and the strategies Plath uses to approach it are tied to a wider problem relating to the place of the Holocaust in our culture. If we understand this, it is possible to place the disturbing appearance of the Holocaust in Plath's poems in its proper context, and to see this effect as symptomatic of a more general problem she recognizes, a conflict about the very uses of poetry itself. The problem of Plath's utilization of the Holocaust can be broadly divided into two parts: the motives behind her use of such material, and the actual appearance of it in her poetry. I will show that her motives were responsible, and that the often unsettling appearance of the Holocaust in her later poems stems from a complex of reasons concerning her divided view about the uses of poetry and the related conflict she explores between history and myth—a conflict which finds its ultimate focus in her consciousness of the importance of remembering such an event, but also of the voyeurism implicit in attempts at remembrance.

> **The problem of Plath's utilization of the Holocaust can be broadly divided into two parts: the motives behind her use of such material, and the actual appearance of it in her poetry.**
> —*Al Strangeways*

Although critics such as Jacqueline Rose and Margaret Dickie Uroff have gone some way toward arguing that Plath was genuinely and consistently interested in political issues, little attention has been given to the link between such political concerns and the Holocaust. In Plath's academic life (the influence of which is neglected at cost by many critics and biographers), the Holocaust was a topic in both high school and college. A schoolmate recalls how Plath's history teacher at Wellesley High School, Raymond Chapman, confronted his class: "[W]eary of our affluent, teenaged complacency, [he] had photographic blow-ups made of the inmates of Bergen-Belsen and Buchenwald, Dachau and Auschwitz. These tragic, skeletal inmates looking out from their packed bunk beds in their ragged striped pyjamas stared down upon our crisply shampooed heads, giving us the shudders." Both Chapman's desire to disturb his students' complacency and the strategy he used foreshadow Plath's similar treatment of the Holocaust in her later poetry.

In contrast to the emotional impact of this introduction, Plath's college professors encouraged the reasoned linking of Nazism with current political concerns. Erich Fromm's *The Fear of Freedom* (1941), a set text in one history course Plath took at Smith College, is characteristic of other texts she studied at the time in its discussion of the staple American interest in individualism with reference to the problem of Nazism. Fromm argues that America's conformism stems from the same "fear of freedom" as the more extreme authoritarian horrors of Nazism. The book seems to have made a central, lasting impression on Plath—she heavily underlined and annotated her copy, and referred to Fromm's theories in essays written both at Smith and later at Cambridge ("The Age of Anxiety," "Some Preliminary Notes on Plato and Popper").

The impact of Fromm's book on Plath lies in its combination of psychology and history in a way that appears to have influenced her combination of the two in her later poetry. While accepting that Nazism's rise was "molded by socio-economic factors," Fromm saw it as rooted in a "psychological problem" that also affected (albeit in a lesser way) American society. His exploration of Nazism concentrates on how "the Nazi system express[es] an extreme form of the character structure which we have called 'authoritarian,'" and he examines in detail examples of neurotic symptoms that are evident, in an extreme form, in Nazism. In Plath's poem **"Daddy,"** the controversial lines "Every woman adores a Fascist, / The boot in the face, the brute / Brute heart of a brute like you" are trying to make a similar, though gendered, point. Throughout the poem, the speaker and "daddy," masochistic and sadistic figures respectively, appear dependent upon each other, and both figures' connections to Nazism (as Jew and Fascist) link their dependence on each other (lack of individuation) to Fromm's theorization. In the speaker's consciously disturbing over-statement that "Every woman adores a Fascist," Plath asserts that, while the archetypal male figure appearing in the rest of the poem (as father and lover) connotes the escape from freedom through sadism, the female figure's adoration of the Fascist is an extreme result of a stereotypically feminine escape from the feelings of aloneness associated with freedom, through masochistic strivings. Freedom, for the archetypal "feminine" figure in **"Daddy,"** is freedom from the authoritarian father figure. Political realities (in the form of Nazism) and psychological difficulties (in the form of neurosis) are inescapably linked for Fromm and for Plath. Thus Plath's lines in **"Daddy"** are both psychological and political. They are psychological not because **"Daddy"** is about Plath's relationship with her father, but in the sense that Plath uses the situation depicted in the poem to explore the dynamics of her attitude toward individualism. Her intellectual and moral approval of individualism is set against a consciously explored ambivalence in her desire for such freedom, an ambivalence which is summed up in the final line, so that "Daddy, daddy, you bastard, I'm through" may mean either that the speaker is "through with daddy" or free from him, or that she is (in relation to the imagery of the black telephone in stanza 14) through *to* him, having made a final and inescapable connection with him—having, in short, given up her freedom.

As well as this staple American interest in individualism, Plath's other central political concern, as for most of her generation, was the prospect of nuclear war. With the cold war at its height in the late 1950s, the potential for a different, nuclear genocide made concerns about the Holocaust immediately relevant. The literary critic A. Alvarez (who was also a friend of Plath) notes that he "suggested (in a piece for the *Atlantic Monthly,* December 1962) that one of the reasons why the camps continue to keep such a tight hold on our imaginations is that we see in them a small-scale trial

run for a nuclear war. . . . Then there are those other curious, upside-down similarities: the use of modern industrial processes for the mass production of corpses, with all the attendant paraphernalia of efficiency, meticulous paperwork, and bureaucratic organization; the deliberate annihilation not merely of lives but of identities, as in some paranoid vision of mass culture." Elie Wiesel, a respected commentator on and survivor of the Holocaust, writing in the 1980s, also connects the genocide carried out by the Nazis and the more universal potential genocide of nuclear war: "Once upon a time it happened to my people, and now it happens to all people. And suddenly I said to myself, maybe the whole world, strangely, has turned Jewish. Everybody lives now facing the unknown. We are all, in a way, helpless." Other, later writers go further in their linking of anti-Semitic and potentially nuclear holocausts, such as Robert Jay Lifton and Eric Markusen, whose study *The Genocidal Mentality: Nazi Holocaust and Nuclear Threat* explores detailed similarities between the way the Nazi system of the Holocaust and the nuclear narrative work. Plath, in **"Mary's Song"** (1962), also connects the past atrocity of the Holocaust and the future threat of nuclear destruction, exploring the double-edged nature of technological "progress" that allows both space flight and efficient genocide—historically of the Jewish people, potentially of the whole world.

. . . . .

For Plath, the main link between the Holocaust and a potential nuclear war was the mind-numbing rhetoric that both "final solution" and cold war discourses employed. The widely publicized trial of Adolf Eichmann (1961-62) showed the importance of such a use of language in the smooth running of the Nazi genocide machinery. Hannah Arendt notes, in her report on the Eichmann trial: "all correspondence referring to the matter was subject to rigid 'language rules.' . . . the prescribed code names for killing were 'final solution,' 'evacuation' . . . and 'special treatment.' . . . for whatever other reasons the language rules may have been devised, they proved of enormous help in the maintenance of order and sanity in the various widely diversified services whose co-operation was essential in this matter." As a student at Smith, Plath marked Fromm's general comments on this subject of rhetoric and aggression in *Escape from Freedom* with a determined "yes!": "Never have words been more misused in order to conceal the truth than today. Betrayal of allies is called appeasement, *military aggression is camouflaged as defense against attack* [Plath's emphasis]." Plath's concern resurfaced in the period just before she wrote her Holocaust poems, during the Khrushchev-Kennedy stand-off, when she writes, both in her letters to her mother and in **"Context,"** a piece published in *London Magazine* in 1962, about her fear of such a dissembling and dangerous "doubletalk."

Yet Plath's concerns with the Holocaust were not purely disinterested, academic connections between past and present threats. Her awareness of the interconnection between the private and the political in her interest in the Holocaust is evident in a BBC radio interview she gave in 1962. When asked why she treats the Holocaust in her poetry, she declares, "In particular, my background is, may I say, German and Austrian. . . . and so my concern with concentration camps and so on is uniquely intense. And then, again, I'm rather a political person as well, so I suppose that's what part of it comes from." One might add, as James Young argues, that she also felt "she shared the era of victimhood, victimized by modern life at large as the Jews and Japanese had been victimized by specific events in modern life." Plath's personalized treatment of the Holocaust stems, then, from a combination of two motives: her very "real" sense of connection (for whatever reasons) with the events, and her desire to combine the public and the personal in order to shock and cut through the distancing "doubletalk" she saw in contemporary conformist, cold war America.

Edward Alexander expresses a common concern when he writes of his unease at the sort of connections made not only by Plath but also by other writers who talk of an "era of victimhood" or who specifically connect Jewish and potential nuclear holocausts: "stealing the Holocaust . . . [is the process of] reduc[ing] Jews from the status of human beings to that of metaphors for other people's sufferings. . . . we must keep steadily before our mind's eye the truth that, as Cynthia Ozick once wrote, 'Jews are not metaphors—not for poets, not for novelists, not for theologians, not for murderers, and never for anti-semites.'" Alexander's fear is that once the Holocaust and its Jewish victims become mythical metaphors for suffering, it is easy to extend such metaphoric treatment into the very anti-Semitic stereotyping that resulted in the Holocaust itself. This very genuine concern does not, however, take into account the impossibility of regulating the relationship between history and subjectivity. As Young declares, "To question whether or not the suffering of the Holocaust should be cast as a type implies that we have some sort of legislative control over which events figure others, which events enter consciousness." Yet to accept the impossibility of legislating against the metaphorizing of the Holocaust does not mean that all judgment about the deployment of such material should be suspended. In relation to Plath's poetry, then, it is important to evaluate how effectively or appropriately Plath treats the Holocaust, and whether, indeed, she actually confronts the problem of metaphorizing in her deployment of such material.

While I have shown that Plath's motives for including Holocaust material in her poetry were responsible, the Holocaust appears only briefly in her work. Not only does Plath use such material within a short space of time, but in the poems in which the Holocaust does appear, it is treated almost tersely. Such dual brevity lends credence to the widespread

view, noted by Rose, "that politics appears only opportunistically, as a form of self-aggrandizement" in her poetry. Apart from Plath's oblique treatment of the subject in the earlier poem **"The Thin People"** (1957), Holocaust imagery appears only in the poems she wrote between October and November 1962, just after her separation from Ted Hughes and her return from Devon to London. This timing can make it difficult not to feel that she distastefully used the persecution of the Jews to express her own feelings of being victimized by Hughes. Examination of wider circumstances, however, shows a number of other significant reasons for the suddenness of Plath's poetic treatment of the Holocaust. In general terms, this period saw, in addition to the "real-life" drama of the Eichmann trial, a number of star-studded Hollywood films—often adapted from successful books, plays, or television presentations—that brought the Holocaust to the forefront of the popular imagination, including *Judgment at Nuremberg* (1961), starring Spencer Tracey; *Exodus* (1960), starring Paul Newman and Sal Mineo; and *The Diary of Anne Frank* (1959). In relation to the particular two months in question, it is widely accepted that, for whatever reasons, Hughes's departure released for Plath a new sense of poetic freedom and led to the composition of poems on which her reputation largely rests. More specifically, Plath is adamant in her letters to her mother at this time that "I need no literary help from him. I am going to make my own way." Hughes was undeniably a powerful literary influence on Plath, and his departure may well have enabled her to use the sorts of topical imagery which he generally felt were better avoided. In addition, Plath was influenced by her new friendship with a South African Jewish couple, Gerry and Jillian Becker. She became close friends with the Beckers, to the extent of sharing their meal on Christmas Day that year. Both Jillian and Gerry were keenly interested in the events of the Second World War and the Holocaust (Jillian later wrote a study of terrorism, *Hitler's Children,* and Gerry had read much about and visited a number of the concentration camps), and, as Ronald Hayman reports, their conversations often returned to the subject.

While it is relatively straightforward to chart the complex reasons behind the abrupt chronological appearance of the Holocaust in Plath's poems, the briefness of the appearance of such material within individual poems poses more complicated problems. Certainly, as Young notes, Plath's poems are not strictly about the Holocaust (in the way the poems of survivors such as Primo Levi are), although, as I argued earlier with reference to the influence of Erich Fromm, neither are they as resolutely private as they often appear. Accepting this, however, and notwithstanding her genuine sense of connection to the cultural impact of its horrors, the Holocaust appears in Plath's poems in references that are often emblematic, seemingly untransformed by poetic craft. In **"Daddy,"** for instance, it is not so much the style of "light verse" and the connection of the very personal to the very extreme horrors of, in Seamus Heaney's terms, "the history of other people's sorrows" that causes unease. Rather, Plath combines myth and history (Electra, vampirism, and voodoo rub shoulders with the Holocaust) in such a way that the history of Nazi persecution of the Jews appears almost one dimensional in comparison to the flexibility of her treatment of the poem's mythic and psychoanalytic aspects.

In **"Fever 103°"** (1962), this uneasy combination of history (here, in the form of Hiroshima) and myth is more readily apparent. The speaker's journey in the poem toward some sort of cathartic transformation works through mythic references to Cerberus and a mythmaking account of the death of Isadora Duncan to a historical-political image of the effects of atomic destruction and Hiroshima. Images of "smokes," used to describe both Isadora's fatal scarves and nuclear holocaust, are pivotal in effecting the transition from the mythic to the historical imagery. This transitional imagery of fire and smoke is strongly reminiscent of the central image of the more successful **"Mary's Song"** (written one month later), where fire is transformed into "thick palls" of smoke that link the poem's movement from Christian myth to the Holocaust. In **"Fever 103°,"** however, the connection between myth and history is more tenuous. The mythic material frames the poem.

. . . . .

The conclusion of the poem, even taking into account its destabilizing ironic overtones, is one of mythic transcendence.

. . . . .

In contrast to [the] sustained and vivid images, the historical-political image transitions in the center of the poem appear violently swift and lack the resonance of the mythic imagery. Concerns about modern science are explored when the "Hothouse baby in its crib" becomes "The ghastly orchid / . . . // Devilish leopard," of which the reader is told (in relation to the drawbacks of such scientific wonders), "Radiation turned it white / And killed it in an hour." These startlingly swift metaphoric transitions, while working in complete contrast to the more sustained progression of the frame of the poem, nevertheless appear to cohere, both together and to the rest of the poem. The lurching transition to "Greasing the bodies of adulterers / Like Hiroshima ash and eating in. / The sin. The sin," is not, however, as well sustained. (In **"Mary's Song,"** the transition from smoke to ash is also a lurch but is better supported by the more integrated nature of the mythic framework.) The connections between radiation and Hiroshima, grease, ash, and human relations (in the form of "adulterers") in this section of **"Fever 103°"** are too many, too contrived, and ultimately too weak to support the transition from the extended image play of scientific advances and drawbacks to the return to "the

sin, the sin" of the mythic opening. Arguably, such apparently arbitrary swiftness represents the surreally illogical thought processes of the fevered subject; yet such an interpretation still leaves unexplained the very specific, unsettling contrast Plath sets up between the resonant nature of myth and the emblematic appearance of history.

The contrast between the resonance and diversity of Plath's use of myth and the single dimensions of her use of history in the form of the Holocaust and Hiroshima is not simply due to Plath's greater experience and confidence in handling the former, learned from using mythic material throughout her poetic career. Robert Graves, in *The White Goddess* (an influential book for Plath and for many myth making poets of the 1950s), separates history and myth in their relation to poetry. He writes of "the tendency of history to taint the purity of myth" and is disdainful of "originality" in the poet who "take[s] his themes from anywhere he please[s]," by which Graves appears to mean "occasional" rather than "mythic" themes. Yet while Plath agrees with Graves about the importance of a deep personal knowledge of and feeling for myth, she not only dissents from Graves's view of the poetic dominance of myth, but extends his exhortation about the importance of a personal feeling for and connection to myth to reverse the dichotomy he sets up between myth as pure, history as impure. In her poetry, it is myth that Plath appropriates (more and less successfully) for more idiosyncratic and personal ends (for instance, in her connection of myth with psychoanalytic themes in poems such as **"Electra on Azalea Path"** [1959]). Notwithstanding her sense of involvement with political and historical themes, it is history that stands as somehow unchanging and "pure," emblematic and suprapersonal in her poetry. It is this impersonal "purity" of emblem applied to such real horrors of history as the twentieth-century Holocaust that makes poems such as **"Fever 103°"** and **"Daddy"** so discomfiting.

If, then, this is the root of the dilemma about Plath's treatment of the Holocaust, what were the reasons behind Plath's reversal of Graves's dichotomy? A statement Plath makes in 1962, in a BBC radio interview that accompanied a reading of her late poems, throws some light on this question. Peter Orr asked Plath where such socially and historically aware poems came from: "Do your poems tend now to come out of books rather than out of your own life?" Plath replied, famously, "No, no: I would not say that at all. I think my poems immediately come out of the sensuous and emotional experiences I have, but I must say I cannot sympathize with these cries from the heart that are informed by nothing except a needle or a knife, or whatever it is. . . . personal experience . . . should be *relevant,* and relevant to the larger things, the bigger things such as Hiroshima and Dachau and so on." Plath's characterization of "Hiroshima and Dachau and so on" as "the larger things" is significant in two ways. First, by declaring that personal experience should be relevant to such historical events, she apparently contradicts a statement she made in the same period, where she describes the "bigger things," more traditionally, as the timeless universals of loving and creating. This highlights a central conflict for Plath about the uses of poetry, rooted in the watershed period in which she wrote, where the movement was from seeing poetry as mythic and timelessly universal (as Graves did) to its being a more personal and didactic communication that comments upon the issues of the day. Indeed, Plath even expresses her ambivalence within the same piece, when she writes, on the one hand, that the importance of poetry does not lie in its ability to communicate with or influence people—"Surely the great use of poetry is its pleasure—not its influence as religious or political propaganda. . . . I am not worried that poems reach relatively few people" (**"Context"**)—yet several lines later declares that she sees poetry as communicating something good, teaching or healing, by comparing poems' "distance" as reaching "farther than the words of a classroom teacher or the prescriptions of a doctor." It is Plath's own ambivalence about these two uses of poetry that is reflected in the divergent critical reception her use of the Holocaust has generated: whether her poetry is mythic, and thus open to the charge that (notwithstanding the impossibility of legislating history and subjectivity) her figurings are either inappropriate or irresponsible, or whether her poetry is inescapably concerned with contemporary issues, directly confronting the problems surrounding the use of topical material as tropes.

Secondly, in describing the Holocaust and nuclear bomb as the "larger things," Plath appears to perceive such historical events in expressly mythic terms. Jon Harris, in trying to determine why, in the decades following World War II, very little poetry was written about the Holocaust in Britain, sees the reasons bound up in the mythic nature of the historical event. He writes, "the horrors were so extreme that they seem to belong to another world entirely." In other words, the Holocaust assumed a mythic dimension because of its extremity and the difficulty of understanding it in human terms, due to the mechanical efficiency with which it was carried out, and the inconceivably large number of victims. In addition to this problem of conceptualization, Harris declares that traditional myth, through which poetry works, was devalued, as it was unable to enclose or make sense of the subject.

This problem of the relationship between myth and recent history is central to the difficulties surrounding literature and the Holocaust. Aharon Appelfeld writes:

> By its nature, when it comes to describing reality, art always demands a certain intensification, for many and various reasons. However, that is not the case with the Holocaust. Everything in it already seems so thoroughly unreal, as if it no longer be-

longs to the experience of our generation, but to mythology. Thence comes the need to bring it down to the human realm. This is not a mechanical problem, but an essential one. . . . I do not mean to simplify, to attenuate, or to sweeten the horror, but to attempt to make the events speak through the individual and in his language.

Many critics who explore the "literature of atrocity" recognize this conflict, between the "naturally" mythic nature of the events, and the need, difficult in practice, to remove them from such an easily assimilated mythology. Irving Howe, for instance, writes, "it is a grave error to make, or 'elevate,' the Holocaust into an occurrence outside of history, a sort of diabolic visitation, for then we tacitly absolve its human agents of their responsibility." Yet, as Harris recognizes, there are equal dangers in trying to "de-elevate" the Holocaust:

> The problem, in fact, is twofold; first we must accept that the horrors were so extreme that they seem to belong to another world entirely, not the one we regularly write poetry about. . . . Secondly, in claiming that we can conceive of the horror of the Holocaust, we lay ourselves open to the accusation that by imposing a critical form and structure on it we are *ipso facto* justifying it: by attributing a rationale of any sort to it, we admit that the Holocaust could be seen as a rational act.

This problem which Plath's treatment of the Holocaust exhibits, of exploring or representing the inconceivable (the mythic horror of the Holocaust) with the conceivable (be it a conceivable subject, such as personal difficulties, or a conceivable form), is also apparent in the Hollywood films produced at the time (as well as many similar cinematic treatments from then on, with the notable exception of *Shoah* [1983]). Annette Insdorf describes the difficulties inherent in cinematic treatments of the Holocaust, citing John J. O'Connor (a *New York Times* television critic), who writes: "*The Diary of Anne Frank* and *Judgment at Nuremberg . . .* depend on a confined theatrical setting, superfluous dialogue, star turns, classical editing (mainly with close-ups), and musical scores whose violins swell at dramatic moments. These studio productions essentially fit the bristling raw material of the Holocaust into an old narrative form, thus allowing the viewer to leave the theater feeling complacent instead of concerned or disturbed." The act of trying to bring such horrific events to a popular audience involves a rationalizing and conventionalizing of the material, which ultimately runs the risk of trivializing the very events it is trying to commemorate. In Plath's case, the "old narrative form" is that of a lyrical expression through personalized mythmaking, within which the Holocaust fits uncomfortably. In addition to these wider difficulties of using traditional conventions to represent the horrors of the Holocaust, the expressly symbolic approach of poetry appears tainted by the abuse of metaphor in the Nazi regime's employment of the "language rules" cited above, an abuse of language that Plath herself feared in the less extreme cold war "doubletalk" discourse.

It is these problems surrounding the conventionalization and metaphorizing of the Holocaust that not only inform Plath's late poems but are enacted by them. Lawrence Langer's tentative answer to the way out of the impasse between the impact of the Holocaust and the ethical problems associated with its depiction is through a creativity which works to collapse the distinction between history and the present, metaphor and subject. Langer writes of an episode in Jerzy Kosinki's *The Painted Bird*: "Episodes like the gouging out of the eyes seek to induce a sense of complicity with the extremity of cruelty and suffering in modern experience, from which history (with its customary distinctions between "then" and "now"), conspiring with the reader's reluctance to acknowledge such possibilities, unconsciously insulates us. The art of atrocity is the incarnation of such possibilities through language and metaphor." Plath's late poems try to work in a similar way, "inducing a sense of complicity" by combining the events with an intimate tone and material. Yet instead of trying directly to present the cruelty of the Holocaust itself, the feeling Plath's poems generate is one of complicity in the easy assimilation of such past cruelties. Her poems try to avoid the anonymity and the amnesia contingent on the "them and us" and "then and now" distinctions that characterize the perception of history by highlighting her use of the Holocaust as metaphor. In such poems, readers are *meant* to feel uncomfortable with the suprapersonal, mythical depiction of Jewish suffering, feeling somehow implicated (because of their traditional identification with the lyric persona) in the voyeurism such an assimilation of the Holocaust implies. This feeling of implication that Plath's poems generate may be viewed in broad terms as their success. Such poems are culturally valuable *because* the appearance of the Holocaust in them is like a "boot in the face"—certainly, few readers leave them feeling "complacent instead of concerned or disturbed."

While the ultimately inconceivable nature of the horror of the Holocaust means that Plath cannot mobilize the kinds of overt reflexivity apparent in her treatment of traditional myth in, for example, **"Electra on Azalea Path,"** her poems that deal with the Holocaust also work to comment on metapoetic concerns. In **"Lady Lazarus,"** for example, Plath collapses the "them and us" distinction by confronting readers with their voyeurism in looking at the subject of the poem. To apply Teresa De Lauretis's theorizing of the cinematic positioning of women to Plath's poem, in **"Lady Lazarus,"** the speaker's consciousness of her performance for the readers (who are implicitly part of the "peanut-crunching crowd") works to reverse the gaze of the readers

so that they become "overlooked in the act of overlooking." By extension, in her parodic overstatement (Lady Lazarus as archetypal victim, archetypal object of the gaze) Plath highlights the performative (that is, constructed rather than essential) nature of the speaker's positioning as object of the gaze, and so (to extend Judith Butler's terms), Lady Lazarus enacts a performance that attempts to "compel a reconsideration of the *place* and stability" of her positioning, and to "enact and reveal the performativity" of her representation. This sense of performativity and the reversal of gaze likewise extends, in **"Lady Lazarus,"** to compel reconsideration not only of the conventional positioning of the woman as object, and of the voyeurism implicit in all lyric poetry, but also of the historical metaphors as objects of the gaze. Readers feel implicated in the poem's straightforward assignment and metaphorizing of the speaker in her role as object and performer, and contingently are made to feel uncomfortable about their similar easy assimilation of the imagery (of the suffering of the Jews) that the speaker uses. In **"Daddy,"** a similar relationship between reader, speaker, and metaphor is at work. Like **"Lady Lazarus,"** **"Daddy"** does not attempt to depict the suffering directly for our view (an impossible task, for the reasons given above) but works by confronting readers with, and compounding the problematic distinctions and connections between, the private and the historical (our lives and their suffering). In other words, readers' reactions of unease, discomfort, and outrage are necessarily a response to the surface, the poem itself, rather than to the events the poem uses as metaphors for its subject (be it about individualism, freedom, or memory), because the events themselves are not graspable. The poem is effective because it leaves readers in no clear or easy position in relation to the voyeuristic gazes operating within it (of reader at speaker, reader at poet, poet at speaker, and all at the events which are metaphorized) and able to take no unproblematic stance regarding the uses of metaphor involved.

Ultimately, then, George Steiner's divided attitude toward Plath's treatment of such material most adequately and accurately represents the effect and effectiveness of Plath's project—a project meant to confront readers with their implication in the viewing and metaphorizing of others' lives and suffering, and aimed at foregrounding the complex instability of the boundaries between myth and reality that forms the root of the problematic placement of the Holocaust in our society. The reason such reflexivity, and its resulting complexity, is so often missed is because Plath's conflict between the idea of poetry as timeless mythic object or as political and/or personal communication remains unresolved, or, indeed, unresolvable, due to the modern relation between history and myth. Her critics often fail to see Plath's balanced ambivalence and appear trapped in one of two extremes of judgment about the meanings of, and motives behind, her poetry. Two interpretations of **"Getting There"**

(1962) sum up this divide. Judith Kroll reads the poem "as the enactment of a willingly undertaken purgatorial ritual, in which the true self, purified by Lethe of all false encumbrances [of the past] finally emerges . . . [d]iscarding the 'old bandages' . . . [in] a symbol[ic] resurrection." In this interpretation, indeed, the Holocaust has been abused for its immediate value as a metaphor for the past. Margaret Dickie Uroff, however, perceives the poem as expressing a view opposed to that read by Kroll. She writes: "the train that drags itself through the battlefields of history ultimately becomes the 'black car of Lethe,' a symbol of the forgetfulness of the past. It becomes a cradle, nurturing a new generation of killers: the pure baby who steps from it will perpetuate murder because she has forgotten the world's past history of murderousness." These two readings reflect Plath's own foregrounding of her culturally situated conflict about the uses of poetry, between the mythic desire that poetry transcend history and the "committed" purpose that it name history and thus remember it. An understanding of the "boot in the face" effect of Plath's treatment of the Holocaust, then, enables the recognition that the dissonances between history and myth in her poetry are not an aesthetic problem but work to prohibit complaisance about the definitions of—and the relationship between—myth, history, and poetry in the post-Holocaust world.

FURTHER READING

Criticism

Boruch, Marianne. "Plath's Bees." *Parnassus* 17, No. 2 (Fall 1992): 76-95.

> Examines the creative origin and significance of Plath's "Bee" poems in *Ariel*.

Davis, William V. "Sylvia Plath's 'Ariel.'" *Modern Poetry Studies* 3 (1972): 176-84.

> Provides critical analysis of the title poem from *Ariel*.

Eder, Doris L. "Thirteen Ways of Looking at Lady Lazarus." *Contemporary Literature* XXI, No. 2 (1980): 301-7.

> Provides an overview of critical interpretations of the poem "Lady Lazarus."

Folsom, Jack. "Death and Rebirth in Sylvia Plath's 'Berck-Plage.'" *Journal of Modern Literature* XVII, No. 4 (Spring 1991): 521-35.

> Discusses countervailing elements of morbidity and affirmation in the poem "Berck-Plage."

Lant, Kathleen Margaret. "The Big Strip Tease: Female Bodies and Male Power in the Poetry of Sylvia Plath." *Contemporary Literature* XXXIV, No. 4 (Winter 1993): 620-69.

> Explores Plath's portrayal of the female body and self-revelation, especially as influenced by confessional poetry and masculine semantic structures.

Nims, John Frederick. "The Poetry of Sylvia Plath: A Technical Analysis." In *Ariel Ascending: Writings About Sylvia Plath,* edited by Paul Alexander, pp. 46-60. New York: Harper & Row, 1985.

> Provides detailed analysis of Plath's metaphorical presentation, language patterns, and poetic techniques.

Ramazani, Jahan. "'Daddy, I Have Had to Kill You': Plath, Rage, and the Modern Elegy." *PMLA: Publications of the Modern Language Association of America* 108, No. 5 (October 1993): 1142-56.

> Examines innovative elements of anger and mourning in Plath's poetry, particularly as directed at her father.

Additional coverage of Plath's life and career is contained in the following sources published by Gale: *Contemporary Authors New Revision Series,* **Vol. 34;** *Discovering Authors; Discovering Authors Modules: Most Studied Authors* **and** *Poets; Dictionary of Literary Biography,* **Vols. 5, 6, and 152;** *Major Twentieth Century Writers; Poetry Criticism,* **Vol. 1; and** *World Literature Criticism.*

Barbara Pym

1913-1980

British novelist, autobiographer, and short story writer.

The following entry presents an overview of Pym's career through 1993. For further information on her life and works, see *CLC*, Volumes 13, 19, and 37.

INTRODUCTION

Relegated for most of her life to the position of minor literary figure, Pym is now regarded as one of the most accomplished British novelists of the twentieth century. Pym's fiction, rediscovered after more than a decade and a half of obscurity, centers on the frustrations and domestic solitude of women in middle-class British social circles. An astute observer of human relationships, Pym explores the insular world of eccentric Anglican clergymen, anthropologists, librarians, fringe academics, small office workers, and unmarried women whom she depicts with gentle irony, humor, and compassion. Pym's trademark spinster is a central figure in all of her novels, portrayed as a quiet, self-reliant middle-aged woman resigned to a life of compromise and small pleasures. Often compared to the work of Jane Austen, Pym's popular and critically acclaimed novels, particularly *Excellent Women* (1952) and *Quartet in Autumn* (1977), are well-wrought and deceptively understated comedies of manners that exhibit unpretentious tragic undertones and impressive psychological depth.

Biographical Information

Born Barbara Mary Crampton Pym in Oswestry, Shropshire, Pym was the eldest of two daughters raised in a comfortable middle-class English home near Wales. Pym's father was a successful solicitor and her mother an assistant organist at the local parish, whose curates and vicars were regular dinner guests. At age twelve Pym was sent to Huyton College, an Anglican boarding school in Liverpool, where she developed an interest in literature and contributed to the school magazine. Four years later she read Aldous Huxley's *Chrome Yellow* which confirmed her literary aspirations and inspired the composition of an unpublished first novel, "Young Men in Fancy Dress." At age eighteen Pym enrolled at St. Hilda's College, Oxford, where she studied English literature and graduated with second-class honors in 1934. While at Oxford, Pym experienced several frustrating romantic affairs that supplied material for her early writing. During the Second World War, Pym performed volunteer work in Oswestry and later found employ-

ment in the Censorship office in Bristol. She joined the Women's Royal Naval Service in 1943 and was stationed in Naples, Italy, until the end of the war. In 1945 Pym began work for the International African Institute, a non-profit organization in London, while continuing to work on her fiction. Her first novel, *Some Tame Gazelle* (1950), was accepted by publisher Jonathan Cape in 1949. Pym produced a steady output of modestly successful novels in the next decade with *Excellent Women, Jane and Prudence* (1953), *Less Than Angels* (1955), *A Glass of Blessings* (1958), and *No Fond Return of Love* (1961). In 1963 Pym's manuscript for *An Unsuitable Attachment* (1982) was summarily rejected by her publisher and numerous others on the grounds that it would not satisfy changing literary tastes of the 1960s. For the next sixteen years Pym published nothing. While working at the International African Institute as an editor for the journal *Africa*, however, she continued to write for her own amusement and completed *The Sweet Dove Died* (1978) and *Quartet in Autumn*, both of which were also initially turned down by publishers. During the 1970s Pym suffered serious health problems resulting in a mastectomy, several strokes, and a heart attack. Despite such setbacks, Pym experienced a remarkable reversal of fortune in 1977 when poet Philip Larkin and biographer Lord David Cecil named her one of the most underrated authors of the century in a *Times Literary Supplement* feature. Their adulation sparked a revival of interest in her work, prompting Macmillan to quickly accept and publish *Quartet in Autumn* and *The Sweet Dove Died*. Pym completed her final novel, *A Few Green Leaves* (1980), shortly before succumbing to ovarian cancer in 1980. This book and the remainder of her unpublished manuscripts appeared posthumously, including *An Unsuitable Attachment*, her previously rejected novel, *Crampton Hodnet* (1985), *An Academic Question* (1986), *Civil to Strangers and Other Writings* (1987), and *A Very Private Eye* (1984), a volume of Pym's diary entries and correspondence edited by her sister, Hilary, and longtime friend Hazel Holt.

Major Works

Pym's first novel, *Some Tame Gazelle,* establishes many of the essential features of her subsequent work. Set in an English country village, the story centers on the uneventful lives of two unmarried sisters in their mid-fifties as they share the disappointments and small joys of selfless service and unrequited love. While one sister privately devotes herself to a married archdeacon who ignores her feelings for him, the other dotes on a young curate who eventually marries a younger woman. In the end, both sisters remain unattached though pleasantly satisfied in the company of each other and the security of their uncomplicated lives. As in many of Pym's novels, the male characters, usually clergymen, anthropologists, and academics, are depicted as self-centered, insensitive, and ineffectual recipients of adoration and deference from the female characters. Pym's erudite familiarity with English literature is also revealed in frequent literary allusions, present here in the title which is taken from a line by a minor Victorian poet. Such allusions are also prominent in *Jane and Prudence,* which contains significant references to Jane Austen, John Milton, Matthew Arnold, and John Keats. *Excellent Women,* Pym's most popular novel, features Mildred Lathbury, an unmarried woman in her thirties who represents the archetypal Pym spinster—educated, sharp witted, unsupported by family or husband, committed to community and church, modest and alone but single by choice. In this novel Mildred relates her involvement with an estranged married couple while residing in a London flat. Here, as in other novels, anthropologists and clergymen figure prominently. Mildred's role as arbiter among the uncomfortably situated characters underscores her tenuous position as a welcome participant and lonely observer on the verge of isolation. Typical of Pym's fiction, the plot revolves around detailed analysis of seemingly inconsequential incidents and encounters. Small gatherings and commonplace domestic activities, such as teas, dinners, and church attendance, take on the significance of major events. Pym's experience with anthropologists while working at the International Africa Institute is particularly evident in *Less Than Angels.* In this novel the female protagonist adopts anthropological research techniques to make shrewd observations about English social convention and to satirize anthropologists themselves. While most of Pym's novels feature unmarried women, the protagonist of *A Glass of Blessings* is the emotionally deprived wife of a prosperous civil servant. Failing to find love outside of the marriage, the disenchanted wife enters into a fulfilling friendship with a gay man. Like the spinsters of Pym's other novels, she finds herself content to accept companionship in place of romantic intimacy. In contrast to her earlier work, Pym's later novels, including *Quartet in Autumn, The Sweet Dove Died,* and *A Few Green Leaves,* exhibit a marked bitterness in their bleak tone and grim humor. *Quartet in Autumn* is a spare and unflinching examination of late-life loneliness in which Pym describes the experiences of four co-workers upon their retirement from a London office. Unprepared for the unpredictability and alienation of contemporary British life, the two women and two men struggle to find meaning in their lives without family, friends, or benevolent institutions to support them. In a contrapuntal pattern suggested by the title, Pym follows each as they face their separate solitude with reluctance and sadness. While focusing on the complex emotional impact of the aging process rather than courtships or romantic attachments, *Quartet in Autumn*

nonetheless reveals Pym's central and recurring preoccupation with the individual's struggle to connect with others.

Critical Reception

Before 1977, Pym was considered a minor author of unassuming novels for a small, loyal readership. Since her literary rebirth and enthusiastic reevaluation, critics consistently praise her highly developed narrative abilities, remarkable social awareness, and striking modern sensibility. Pym's quiet domestic settings, unsensational plots, and earnest attention to the minutiae of social behavior are frequently associated with the work of Jane Austen and nineteenth-century realists. While such mundane subjects once rendered her work unpublishable, critics now acknowledge the surprising modernity of her fiction, particularly as found in her masterpieces *Excellent Women* and *Quartet in Autumn.* Pym's disarming, dry wit and conversational narrative voice convey strong feelings of loneliness and despair with unusual subtlety and poignancy. As many critics note, the veneer of conventionality and tradition that overlays Pym's fiction adds depth to her perceptive insights into human relationships, alienation in the modern world, and the changing role of women in contemporary society. Despite the Victorian propriety of Pym's spinsters, these sophisticated, self-aware, independent female protagonists bear resemblance to the modern liberated woman. Such sympathetic treatment of autonomous women who refuse to settle into complicated and unsatisfying relationships with weak or immature men has drawn the attention of feminist critics. Pym's critical reputation rests largely on her unique and highly refined tragicomic humor, emotional sensitivity, and narrative gifts.

PRINCIPAL WORKS

Some Tame Gazelle (novel) 1950
Excellent Women (novel) 1952
Jane and Prudence (novel) 1953
Less Than Angels (novel) 1955
A Glass of Blessings (novel) 1958
No Fond Return of Love (novel) 1961
Quartet in Autumn (novel) 1977
The Sweet Dove Died (novel) 1978
A Few Green Leaves (novel) 1980
An Unsuitable Attachment (novel) 1982
A Very Private Eye: An Autobiography in Diaries and Letters (autobiography) 1984
Crampton Hodnet (novel) 1985
An Academic Question (novel) 1986
Civil to Strangers and Other Writings (novel and short stories) 1987

CRITICISM

John Updike (essay date 26 February 1979)

SOURCE: "Lem and Pym," in *The New Yorker,* February 26, 1979, pp. 115-21.

[In the following excerpt, Updike comments on Pym's writing career and offers a favorable assessment of Excellent Women *and* Quartet in Autumn.*]*

Atomic aloneness in a crowded world, where life is cheap and its accidents random, can be better felt in the wanly Christian world of Barbara Pym. This English novelist has had a disheartening career. After publishing six deceptively old-fashioned novels between 1950 and 1961, she was spurned by more than twenty publishers and understandably let her pen languish. From 1946 to 1974, she supported herself as an assistant editor for the quarterly *Africa.* As retirement approached, however, she began to write again, a novel "as churchy as I wished to make it," and in January of 1977 her name appeared in the *Times Literary Supplement* as the heroine of a poll taken to determine the most underrated British writer of the last seventy-five years. Her new novel, *Quartet in Autumn,* was accepted by Macmillan, and two of her old books were reissued by Jonathan Cape, with commercial and critical success. Now, in this country, a novel dating from 1952. *Excellent Women,* has been published for the first time, along with *Quartet in Autumn,* by Dutton. An unfortunate effect of such simultaneous exposure is to reveal, of two books written over twenty years apart, how alike they are, even to striking, on the last page, the identical muted chord. More fortunately, the reader who has consumed both novels in a few days can report that the older is very fine, and the newer even finer—stronger, sadder, funnier, bolder.

It would be hard to imagine a more timid world than that of *Excellent Women,* or a novel wherein closer to nothing happens. Miss Pym has been compared to Jane Austen, yet there is a virile country health in the Austen novels, and some vivid marital prospects for her blooming heroines. "Excellent women" is a phrase used by a parson of the drab little flock of spinsters who cling for company and amusement to the threadbare routines of his London church. An American who has never attended an Anglican church in London can scarcely conceive of the extreme of sad attenuation to which ecclesiastical institutions can be reduced while still holding open their doors; I can recall a noble structure on Albany Street in which one bright Sunday morning this lone overseas visitor composed a full third of the congregation. Father Julian Malory's St. Mary's Church, in a shabby district on "the 'wrong' side of Victoria Station," seems a shade more bustling than that, but only a

shade. Our heroine, Mildred Lathbury, the unmarried daughter of a rural clergyman, comes to it because it is relatively "High" and burns incense, which her deceased parents would have deplored. "But perhaps it was only natural that I should want to rebel against my upbringing, even if only in such a harmless way." All her rebellions and outward motions are similarly circumspect, but within the limits of her quiet life as she firmly draws them minor excitements loom in scale, and excite us proportionally. Mildred Lathbury is one of the last (I would imagine) of the great narrating English virgins, and though she tells us she is "not at all like Jane Eyre," her tale has some of the power of, say, the portion of "Bleak House" narrated by Esther Summerson—the power, that is, of virtue, with its artistic complement of perfect moral pitch and crystalline discriminations. The postwar, protoconsumerist London that Mildred depicts, wherein jam seems still to be rationed and rubble still lies in church aisles, yet wherein couples drink wine and separate with a certain liberated ease, is an awkward arena for her discriminations, perhaps. One of the funniest scenes, though brief, occurs when she attempts to buy a new lipstick and can scarcely bring herself to name the tint she wants: "'It's called Hawaiian Fire,' I mumbled, feeling rather foolish, for it had not occurred to me that I should have to say it out loud." The urban crush of modern London is, she reflects, in a phrase that echoes a T. S. Eliot echo of Dante, a hard place for the practice of Christian charity:

> "One wouldn't believe there could be so many people," I said, "and one must love them all." These are our neighbours, I thought, looking round at the clerks and students and typists and elderly eccentrics, bent over their dishes and newspapers.

The plot's turns have to do with new neighbors. A young couple, Helena and Rockingham Napier, move into the flat below Mildred's, and conduct within earshot a typical but sufficiently unsettling modern marriage. And Father Malory and his unmarried sister Winifred take in a boarder, one Mrs. Gray, with romantic consequences that titillate every corner of the tiny parish, from jumble sale to Evensong. Mildred, at the nubile age of "just over thirty," seems remarkably spinsterish. Her sexual experiences have been of the daintiest sort, and she puzzles over the "race of men" and their differences from women with the polite quizzicalness of an anthropologist from the moon.

> "I like food," I said, "but I suppose on the whole women don't make such a business of living as men do."

> Men in bowler hats, with dispatch cases so flat and neat it seemed impossible that they could contain anything at all, and neatly rolled umbrellas, ran with undignified haste and jostled against me. Some car-

ried little bundles or parcels, offerings to their wives perhaps or a surprise for supper. I imagined them piling into the green trains, opening their evening papers, doing the crossword, not speaking to each other . . .

"Of course, men don't tend to be alone, do they?"

It is fitting that an actual anthropologist, the humorless but upright (and Christian!) Everard Bone, adds himself to the exiguous list of Mildred Lathbury's male friends—her pastor, his curate, a few neighbors, and an old friend so set in his ways he complains, "They've moved me to a new office and I don't like it at all. Different pigeons come to the windows." At the book's romantic climax, Everard Bone invites her to be his indexer; but Americans, with their Freudian and Lawrentian prejudices, should not hasten to bid farewell to her chastity and hello to "what Helena called 'a full life.'" Mildred has involved herself with men enough to enhance her feeling of possibility, her sense of choice, but what she chooses, out of sight of the novel's conclusion, may well be more of the same. "As I moved about the kitchen getting out china and cutlery, I thought, not for the first time, how pleasant it was to be living alone." "Excellent women" need not think of themselves as "the rejected ones." When warned not to expect too much, Mildred thinks, "I forbore to remark that women like me really expected very little—nothing, almost." *Excellent Women,* arriving on these shores in a heyday of sexual hype, is a startling reminder that solitude may be chosen, and that a lively, full novel can be constructed entirely within the precincts of that regressive virtue, feminine patience.

By the time of *Quartet in Autumn,* the lonely women are ready for retirement. There are two of them: Marcia Ivory, in whom Mildred Lathbury's self-sufficient aspect has been carried to the point of loony reclusiveness, and Letty Crowe, in whom Mildred's amiable side has developed into a clothes-conscious, food-loving softness bordering upon the hedonistic. Marcia and Letty work in a nameless office in the same room with two single men—Norman, small and wiry and irritable, and Edwin, large and bald and churchgoing. Edwin is the only one of the quartet who has ever been married and who appears to be an active Christian; the churchly ambience of *Excellent Women* has shrunk to this one merry widower, who shops around from church to church for services as a species of entertainment. The shadow of religious shelter has been lifted from Miss Pym's world, and the comedy is harsher. Whereas Mildred Lathbury had merely to cope with new tenants in the flat below, Letty Crowe's entire building changes hands, and becomes the property of a Nigerian, Mr. Olatunde, who not only houses a large family but is "a priest of a religious sect." When Miss Crowe, disturbed by their "bursts of hymn-singing and joyful shouts," taps on their door and

complains, Mr. Olatunde serenely tells her, "Christianity *is* disturbing."

> It was difficult to know how to answer this. Indeed Letty found it impossible so Mr. Olatunde continued, smiling, "You are a Christian lady?"

> Letty hesitated. Her first instinct had been to say "yes," for of course one was a Christian lady, even if one would not have put it quite like that.

In fleeing his landlordship, she becomes the tenant of the High Church, eighty-year-old Mrs. Pope, and finds herself participating in services:

> On a bitter cold evening in March she joined a little group, hardly more than the two or three gathered together, shuffling round the Stations of the Cross. It was the third Wednesday in Lent and there had been snow, now hard and frozen on the ground. The church was icy. The knees of elderly women bent creakily at each Station, hands had to grasp the edge of a pew to pull the body up again. "From pain to pain, from woe to woe . . ." they recited, but Letty's thoughts had been on herself and how she should arrange the rest of her life.

Where Mildred Lathbury had consoled herself, and fortified her own life of unconsummated waiting, by thinking of herself and her fellow-worshippers "as being rather like the early Christians, surrounded not by lions, admittedly, but by all the traffic and bustle of a weekday lunch-hour," no such comparison lends rationale to the ascetic isolation of Miss Pym's later heroines. In place of the chaste infatuations with which the excellent women had amused themselves, Marcia Ivory has no affection but for the surgeon Dr. Strong, who has performed a mastectomy upon her and looms in her addled mind ("Marcia remembered what her mother used to say, how she would never let the surgeon's knife touch her body. How ridiculous that seemed when one considered Mr. Strong") as a masterful angel of death. When the two women simultaneously retire, the speaker at the office luncheon held in their honor does not know exactly what their jobs were, only that there is no need to replace them, and "it seemed to Letty that what cannot now be justified has perhaps never existed, and it gave her the feeling that she and Marcia had been swept away as if they had never been. With this sensation of nothingness she entered the library."

Quartet in Autumn reminds us of Muriel Spark's "Memento Mori" and of the geriatric missionaries in Rose Macaulay's "Towers of Trebizond," but the superannuated creations of these other "Christian lady" novelists have an energetic raffishness, a richness of past and a confidence of social class, denied Miss Pym's characters, who are clearly no match for their surround of anonymous office buildings and condescending young people. One of Miss Pym's enthusiastic English reviewers has been Philip Larkin, and perhaps it is to *his* world that the closer analogy can be drawn—the gray middle class of an empireless England, from whose halftones nevertheless the chords of a living poetry can be struck. *Quartet in Autumn* is a marvel of fictional harmonics, a beautifully calm and rounded passage in and out of four isolated individuals as they feebly, fitfully grope toward an ideal solidarity. Marcia, the most eccentric of the four, is the most pronouncedly private, and the most abruptly forthcoming.

> "And what have you been doing with yourself?" Edwin turned to Marcia with an air of kindly enquiry which hardly deserved the fierceness of her reply.

> "That's my business," she snapped.

In the extremely meagre social fabric Miss Pym weaves for her characters, the most tenuous and trifling contacts take on the import of massive events in more thickly woven novels—those of Tolstoy, say.
—John Updike

What she has been doing, since retirement, is rearranging the junk she stores in her house, repelling a concerned social worker, letting her dyed hair grow out stark white, and sinking deeper into anorexia. Miss Pym's portrait, from within, of a "shopping-bag lady," showing the exact, plausible thought processes behind such mad actions as leaving trash in libraries and attempting to dig up a dead cat, is an achievement comparable to [Stanislaw] Lem's imagining of chemical-induced paranoia and frenzy. Both writers, in the books at hand, lead us to think about social contact, about society and sanity. Experiments in isolation rapidly induce sensations of insanity; we take our bearings, daily, from others. To be sane is, to a great extent, to be sociable. Those victims of random chemistry in "The Chain of Chance" who survive are those who are not travelling alone, and whose behavior receives prompt social check. In the extremely meagre social fabric Miss Pym weaves for her characters, the most tenuous and trifling contacts take on the import of massive events in more thickly woven novels—those of Tolstoy, say. One wonders, indeed, if Tolstoy ever knew aloneness; even his dying was a mob scene. Most human lives have been passed in a throng of tribal and village associations. Unsought loneliness is a by-product of the modern city, and fiction by its very nature is ill equipped to treat of it. Letty Crowe, "an unashamed reader of novels," has

come to realize that "the position of an unmarried, unattached, ageing woman is of no interest whatever to the writer of modern fiction." In brilliantly, touchingly, frighteningly supplying that lack, and in presenting a parable of the hazards of our "atomic" condition, Barbara Pym . . . offer[s] us characters with strikingly modest sex drives. Whether in this they are old-fashioned or all too modern— whether under conditions of dense metropolitan crowding the primeval social glue will tactfully dry up—remains to be seen. . . .

Robert Phillips (review date 8 May 1981)

SOURCE: "Narrow, Splendid Work," in *Commonweal,* May 8, 1981, pp. 284-5.

[*In the following review, Phillips praises the posthumous publication of* A Few Green Leaves.]

Barbara Pym died on January 11 of last year, in a small Oxfordshire village cottage which she had come to share with her sister. At the time of her death, her books were much in demand in her country, and were finding an audience in America. And therein lies a terrible irony.

Between 1950 and 1961, Miss Pym published six novels, including *Excellent Women* (1952), *Less Than Angels* (1955), *A Glass of Blessings* (1958), and *No Fond Return of Love* (1961). But when she presented her next manuscript, it was rejected by no less than twenty publishers. She was dropped, called "out of date." She retreated into silence, presumably not writing, and supporting herself as an assistant editor for the quarterly *Africa.* For sixteen years she published no fiction. Then, in 1977, both Philip Larkin and Lord David Cecil, responding to a poll conducted among literati by the London *Times Literary Supplement,* listed her as "the most underrated writer of this century." Publishers took note, and later that same year a new Pym novel, which she had begun when retirement from the quarterly loomed, appeared. It was titled *Quartet in Autumn.* Overnight she found herself a "fashionable" writer.

Since that time most of her earlier books have been reprinted. *Quartet in Autumn* was followed by another new novel, *The Sweet Dove Died* (1978), and now by *A Few Green Leaves* (1980)—a novel completed barely two months before her death. It is a book to be welcomed and savored, but perhaps not without prior acquisition of an appreciation for her other, more major, novels.

"Major" is a peculiar adjective to apply to Miss Pym's books, which are about storms in a teapot. The teapot is usually an Anglican parish, and the comparison to Jane

Austen's work has been made often enough. Miss Pym wrote only short novels on narrow subjects: the comforts of religion, the poignancy of living alone, the perpetual quest for usefulness, the limitations of marriageability and marriage.

Yet for all their limitations, her novels are dense with psychological insight and larded with wit. Within the strict conventions of the British social novel she was also highly original. She is one of the few novelists to write of the continuing relationships between middle-aged protagonists and their elderly parents. And, unlike the self-pitying heroines of the novels of Jean Rhys (whose great "comeback" her own career resembles), Pym's spinsters and widows do not pine over their single state. They live alone because they choose to. Either they become "excellent women" like Mildred Lathbury, of the novel bearing that title—loving their neighbors with Christian charity; or they come to love only themselves, like Leonora Eyre of *The Sweet Dove Died,* who concludes,

> when one came to think of it, the only flowers that were really perfect were those, like the peonies that went so well with one's charming room, that possessed the added grace of having been presented to oneself . . .

Mildred and Leonora and Wilmet Forsyth, of *A Glass of Blessings,* are fully-drawn characters whose desires and feelings are highly palpable. In *Quartet in Autumn,* however, Miss Pym began to widen her focus—exploring within approximately the same number of pages the lives of Edwin, Norman, Letty and Marcia, told from four points of view. The result necessarily was less intense. Now, in *A Few Green Leaves,* Miss Pym opens focus even wider. Her intent here is to capture a portrait of an entire English village and the enduring lives and customs there. The result is at once her narrowest and broadest work.

A Few Green Leaves is ambitious. Miss Pym is not concerned merely with contemporary time. The novel is buttressed by flying references to, and a subplot concerning, Druid ruins and an 18th century country manor. Particular care is taken to contrast life today with what existed on the manor:

> ". . . all that patronage and paternalism or whatever you like to call it has been swept away, and good thing, too."

> "Perhaps the people have been swept away too," said her mother.

> "Yes—I certainly miss the manor and all it stood

for—we haven't got any kind of centre to the village now," said Miss Lee.

> "I suppose the clergy and the doctors have taken the place of the gentry," Emma said.

This is highly self-conscious writing. Yet the central heroine, Emma Howick, is an anthropologist, and her sociological concerns become Miss Pym's. Emma has the makings of a typical repressed Pym heroine, her very ordinariness made interesting by her awareness of it. Yet Miss Pym darts from Emma to the rector Tom Dagnall to Dr. Martin Shurbsole to Miss Olive Lee to Graham Pettifer to Dr. Gellibrand to Miss Lickerish to Mrs. Dyer to Adam Prince to Miss Vereker to Isobel Mound to Terry Skate to—well, you get the idea. There are too many tiny pieces shifting into place in this kaleidoscope. Miss Pym does not allow herself to fully realize any of her villagers in the leisurely manner of her earlier novels.

And yet, there is something ingratiating and admirable about this final attempt at the English novel. Miss Pym did not repeat herself. In pitting time present against time past, in parading history before us in the living flesh, the book approaches the daring and conceit of Virginia Woolf's final novel, *Between the Acts,* also set in an English village. There Woolf tried to depict England as it was then, but also to indicate that all Englishmen were members one of another, each a part of the whole, acting different parts but being of the same body. In this respect Barbara Pym's final vision compares with Virginia Woolf's; a striking vision, but an anomaly in the context of the body of her own narrow, splendid work.

Isa Kapp (essay date Spring 1983)

SOURCE: "Out of the Swim with Barbara Pym," in *The American Scholar,* Vol. 52, No. 2, Spring, 1983, pp. 237-42.

[*In the following essay, Kapp provides an overview of the major themes and characters in Pym's novels, noting the "sheer spinal firmness and imperturbable detachment that puts her into the rank of first-rate novelists."*]

In the canny, delectable novels of the British writer Barbara Pym, we can count on finding sanctuary from the enormous liberties and vast territory that have been gained by modern fiction. Miss Pym's unworldly cast—absentminded vicars beaming kindly over their spectacles, stilted anthropologists back from Africa with charts and kinship diagrams, accommodating clergymen's daughters snug in their modest legacies of Hepplewhite chairs and Victorian ornaments—preordains an absence of garish crime, sexual revelation, or hearts of darkness.

The setting, comfortably confining, is usually the parish church. "I sometimes thought how strange it was that I should have managed to make a life for myself in London so very much like the life I had lived in a country rectory when my parents were alive. But then so many parts of London have a peculiarly village or parochial atmosphere that perhaps it is only a question of choosing one's parish and fitting in to it," muses Mildred Lathbury, the narrator of Miss Pym's second and most benign novel, *Excellent Women,* preparing us for a tale of personal rather than cosmic crisis. In Mildred's style, serene and accepting, an elusive Pym seasoning—a compound of marinating self-deprecation and salty accuracy—is usually present to counteract her mild manners. Nevertheless, her genteel hesitations, her persistent decorum make it obvious that the novelist sees no excuse for turning the chaos within us into anarchy without. Unlike the star fiction writers of the last few decades, Barbara Pym is not much attracted to chaos, whether linguistic or emotional, and nurtures instead an implausible fascination for everything that is orderly and habitual. The lives of the Anglo-Catholic parishioners who are the main characters in several of her novels are punctuated by High Mass and Evensong and a generous calendar of holy days. In *Quartet in Autumn,* the remarkable, humorously somber novel about old age, published in 1977, three years before Miss Pym herself died, Edwin, wanting to make some provision of sociability for a retiring colleague, finds her a room in the vicinity of his church. "Now he could see the whole pattern emerging, with Letty's life governed by the soothing pattern of the church's year. All Saints' Day, then All Souls'. Then would come Advent. . . . After Christmas came Boxing Day, the Feast of St. Stephen. . . ."

All this regularity is surprisingly infectious, even to readers who know very little about church dogma or custom. To the extent that we are unqualified appreciators of Anglo-Catholic observances, we are much in the position of the appealing vicar's wife in *Jane and Prudence.* Jane, who in her youth wrote a book on seventeenth-century poets, has borrowed her romantic notions of a country parish from Trollope's novels. Comically wardrobed in baggy tweeds and layers of cardigans, gorgeously inept in the vicarage graces—she cannot pour tea or open a sherry bottle successfully—Jane nevertheless falls enthusiastically for the poetry and busyness of clerical life. "I love Evensong," she confides to her friend Prudence, who works in a London office and is supercilious toward village church functions. "There's something sad and essentially English about it, especially in the country, and so many of the old people are there. I always like that poem with the lines about gloved the hands that hold the hymn-book that this morning milked the cow."

An early novel, written in 1953, *Jane and Prudence* is full of natural hilarity, toned up with that singularly British resistance to dolors and depressions. Jane drops lines from Donne and Marvell inappropriately into prosaic discussions. She receives a call from the sententious Mr. Mortlake and, discovering that he has come to tune the piano rather than reprimand her for an unseemly outburst at the Parochial Church Council, she pirouettes about in relief, wearing his bowler hat and singing an operatic ditty. She makes extravagant conversation with a dull bank clerk: "'I always think of the medieval banking houses in Florence; great times those must have been,' went on Jane rather wildly." Finally, there is an absurd scene of Jane lunching with her benevolent but distracted husband at "The Spinning Wheel," where the menu is a disconcerting choice between "toad in the hole" and curried beef. The proprietor relents sufficiently to bring them eggs and bacon, which they consume in grateful embarrassment, only to find that the bank clerk, one of the regulars, is being served a roast chicken with all the trimmings.

Jane is not a typical Pym heroine, having been saved by marriage from too much tidiness and self-absorption, and by poetry from parochialism. But she does embody, along with the others, the basic and altogether unfashionable (even in the 1950s) Pym philosophy that women are intended to serve and solace men. Her novels contain an endless repository of proprietary housekeepers, doting sisters, dutiful office employees, and affable parishioners who are on hand to brew tea, organize jumble sales, arrange flower displays, sort a deceased wife's clothing for a bereaved widower, and generally soften the edges of reality for helpless males.

"How convenient women were," thinks Rupert Stonebird, the prim anthropologist of *An Unsuitable Attachment,* "the way they were always 'just going' to make coffee or tea or perhaps had just roasted a joint in the oven or made a cheese souffle." Emma, the plain-faced anthropologist who has settled down to study the inhabitants of a village not far from London in *A Few Green Leaves,* meekly carries casseroles to a cottage in the woods rented by a fretful ex-lover. And it is only to be expected that Mildred in *Excellent Women* will worry about her new neighbor, a charming naval officer, when he comes home from duty in Italy to find his wife unsolicitous and his cupboard bare. Working part-time in an organization that helps impoverished gentlewomen, hurrying into St. Mary's Church ("prickly, Victorian-Gothic, hideous . . . but dear to me"), Mildred is the epitome of those esteemed and respected excellent women who "are not for marrying," but for charitable causes and parish occasions, the backbone of clerical life. That is to say, she fits theoretically into the category, but Miss Pym, never literal, brightens her lot with more piquant assignments. Mildred is recruited as a go-between in the marital misunderstandings of the colorful couple in the flat below;

she consoles the ingenuous vicar when a scheming widow with small pointed teeth and apricot skin breaks off her engagement with him; she is ready with Camembert cheese and a dish of greengage plums when the naval officer's impatient wife deserts him; and eventually she is selected by Miss Pym's most prepossessing anthropologist, Everard Bone, severe and long-nosed but not altogether objectionable, to help him with his proofreading and his index.

Women like Mildred, diffident, taking almost nothing for granted, ministering to ungrateful men without resentment, are the nucleus of a veritable counter-revolution of falling expectations—and one almost unimaginable in America. In an age that goads its women into competition and aggressiveness, they are dignified anachronisms, somehow thriving on the tea, care, and advice they dispense with no hope of return. If this sounds much too virtuous and martyr-like to be fun, the truth is that the women in Barbara Pym's novels are, on the contrary, very resourceful at eking out their pleasures. They know, unlike most liberated women, how to wrest a lot out of a little, are masters (or mistresses) at making do.

The quizzical message of many Pym novels is that women, like cats (both suavely portrayed in *An Unsuitable Attachment*), are self-contained and can manage competently and even satisfactorily by themselves.

—*Isa Kapp*

But the real upshot of the matter is that Barbara Pym sees woman's place from a very strange perspective: to her, this is really a woman's world, and men are the weaker sex. Jane, speculating on why her attractive friend Prudence has fallen in love with a colorless young man, thinks, "But of course . . . that was why women were so wonderful; it was their love and imagination that transformed these unremarkable beings. . . . Perhaps love affairs with handsome men tended to be less stable because so much less sympathy and imagination were needed on the women's part?" The quizzical message of many Pym novels is that women, like cats (both suavely portrayed in *An Unsuitable Attachment*), are self-contained and can manage competently and even satisfactorily by themselves. Inevitably an episode turns up in which a woman (Ianthe in *An Unsuitable Attachment,* Leonora in *The Sweet Dove Died*) returns to her solitary flat and likes it, or savors the room in which she is an unescorted visitor. "I was glad to be alone in my room," reports Wilmet in *A Glass of Blessings,* "with the view over the garden, the well-polished mahogany furniture, pink sheets and towels, and a tablet of rose-geranium soap in the washbasin. Rowena always remembered that it was my favorite. The room seemed so very comfortable, somehow even more than my room at home—perhaps because I could be alone in it."

Of course, some of these claims about the natural superiority of women are presented tongue in cheek—but not all of them, because Barbara Pym is, without being in any sense a conventional feminist, a great morale booster for women. She vouchsafes them their condescensions as well as their subserviences and permits them to be desirable though dowdy—indeed it sometimes looks as if dowdiness were more the mark of spirituality or an agreeable nature than an unlucky choice in dress. Ugly ducklings prosper and the conceited get their comeuppance, but in either case, Barbara Pym's women survive and remain admirably in character.

Whatever lack of importance Miss Pym attributes intellectually to women's clothing, it is certainly a subject that is much on her mind. She is an indisputable authority on its hierarchy of taste and temperament and makes the finest distinctions in defining the wardrobes of her female characters. When she assures you that a certain kind of woman is always to be found at social functions in a simple blue or green wool dress, you can believe it. Penelope, the "pre-Raphaelite beatnik" of *An Unsuitable Attachment,* makes her appearance in tartans or a black sack-like dress and a medallion on a silver chain; the elegant Wilmet in *A Glass of Blessings* announces complacently, "It's a sort of mole-colored velvet dress . . . and I shall wear my Victorian garnet necklace and earrings with it"; the incorrigible Jane goes everywhere in her ancient tweed coat; and the self-preening Leonora of *The Sweet Dove Died* fancies herself in cool amethyst or remote black lace. By their clothes shall ye know them!

It is high time to mention that, although the precision of Miss Pym's observation of speech, manner, and mentality is awesome, the radius of her novels is startlingly narrow. There is more *not* happening in them than happening. The best-willed matchmaking goes awry, and a good many of the characters of both genders manage to avoid getting married or even falling authentically in love. "Love was rather a terrible thing," decides Mildred Lathbury. "Not perhaps my cup of tea." And it is much the same with Leonora in *The Sweet Dove Died* and even comely Prudence, who hankers for the experience but never succumbs. In *An Unsuitable Attachment* Ianthe, fastidious and self-possessed and already in her thirties, befriends a slightly younger man and reaches, in the most shy and tentative way, the condition of the title. On a parish trip to Rome she finds herself acutely in need of comfort and "benison" because "she had admitted to herself that she loved him, had let her love sweep over her like a kind of illness, 'giving in' to the flu, conscious only of the present moment." For Barbara Pym, love is a vagrant impulse, evanescent and untrustworthy, quite unlike the desire for security and routine, for tea, and for a pleasant room. Ianthe is luckier than most of Miss Pym's women, for whom any kind of passion is simply unheard of.

Logically enough, children rarely poke their disrupting heads into the proceedings. In *A Glass of Blessings* Wilmet's friends Harry and Rowena (a rare parent couple, possibly the only one in Miss Pym's novels) assure her that breakfast will be brought to her in bed. "Ours is a terrible meal on Saturdays because we have the children with us. I shan't inflict that on you." Other oppressions that Miss Pym does not inflict upon her readers include argumentation, violence, intellectuality, politics, or even overly long, intense conversations. And despite the cozy familiarity with every aspect of the lives of the clergy, even a powerful emotional entanglement with either the theology or the spirituality of religion is noticeably absent.

To a considerable extent this deliberate avoidance of "action" is the result of Barbara Pym's unbudgeable honesty. Apart from her wartime service in the women's branch of the Royal Navy in Britain and Naples, she herself led a sedentary life, writing her novels and working from 1958 to 1974 as editorial secretary of the International African Institute and simultaneously as an editor of its anthropological journal, *Africa.* She never married and preferred—temperamentally, I surmise—to write about people and feelings that she knew. "Let other people get married," a friend of Mildred's tells her. "Let Dora get married if she likes. She hasn't your talent for observation."

Although Miss Pym does write mainly about male and female spinsters, about men and women who are timid, reserved, and unenterprising, who huddle into the church for safety and companionship, it would be a great mistake to confuse her restrictedness with triviality. She means us to sense that many of the predicaments and habits she describes are to be found everywhere: women without occupation, happenstance marriage, foolishly envisioned romance, and—always a major Pym theme—the need to adapt to one's limitations. These subjects are as alive among Scandinavian teak and glassy condominiums as they were among Victorian bric-a-brac.

Calm as the narrator's voice may be, a Pym novel is never lacking in suspense. Much more than a comedy of manners, it is a drama of disposition, willpower, and ethics, a closer relation of E. M. Forster and Henry James than of those busier and giddier novelists with whom this writer is usually linked: Angela Thirkell, Anthony Powell, and Iris Murdoch. Miss Pym does not sermonize us in quite the self-satisfied way that Jane Austen did. She does have a rather exacting glossary of vices and virtues, but it must be admitted that the vices are mild ones like vanity, irritability,

indifference, and condescension, and her reproaches are equally mild. Partly this is just plain subtlety, a fictional trait going rapidly into disrepute. In *A Glass of Blessings,* we are nearly at the end of the book before the full realization comes over us that Wilmet is more than a little vain as well as unbelievably blind. This heroine-narrator pampers herself with an infatuation for a moody fellow who likes her well enough but is more patently enamored of the effeminate youth he lives with. She persuades herself that her husband is stodgy and dull, when he is in fact balanced, humorous, and affectionate. Barbara Pym arranges for us to see Wilmet's egocentricity and not like her less, but more, because we are privy to her weakness; and she arranges for her heroine to acknowledge it without becoming dismal. The book ends with husband and wife on the best of terms, moving into a new flat because Rodney's sprightly mother, pushing seventy, has married an archaeologist friend and put them out of the house. Events may have been dampening, but their good humor persists. They are conscious, as is the author, that

> When God at first made man,
> Having a glasse of blessings standing by;
> Let us (said he) poure on him all we can:
> Let the world's riches, which dispersed lie,
> Contract into a span.
>
> (George Herbert, "The Pulley")

One of the great joys of reading Barbara Pym is that she laces her prosaic situations irrepressibly with stanzas of wonderful poetry. Like the novels, the poems confirm her conviction that the lives we live can be frugal, circumscribed, sometimes ego dampening—but not without their pleasures—and that there is more to be salvaged in any predicament than we suspect. One of the very few writers who makes virtue seem genuinely appealing, she is able to persuade us that neatness, thrift, secondhand clothes, and meager meals are no obstacle to happiness, and that doing what we ought is itself a pleasure of high quality. As there is not very much doing at any particular moment, she and her characters have the leisure to pause and ask themselves whether they are, in fact, doing the right thing.

The incredibly angelic Mary Beamish of *A Glass of Blessings* is forever wondering if she has taken on enough good works; at the opposite extreme, the four elderly office colleagues from *Quartet in Autumn* grudgingly speculate whether some small fraternal gesture might not be in order. Of the four, Marcia and Norman are inveterate curmudgeons; the others, Letty and Edwin, have impulses to be congenial but are too passive and uncertain to put them into practice. When the women retire, the men carefully weigh the pros and cons of inviting them to lunch; and when Letty is forced out of her rooming house (taken over by a hymn-singing Nigerian landlord), the misanthropic Marcia feels a resentful obligation (which she squelches) to offer her lodging. Every so often, one or another member of the quartet takes a bus in the direction of one of the women, but never quite reaches his destination. If they do manage some token of sociability, they are inexplicably pleased with themselves.

Quartet in Autumn is the small masterpiece that came out in 1977 after sixteen years of the writer's silence. The five novels she published in the 1950s were well received, but a later one, *An Unsuitable Attachment,* was turned down in 1963, possibly because it seemed too slight and sheerly aesthetic in a decade girding itself for political anger. Miss Pym was disappointed enough to stop writing until David Cecil and Philip Larkin named her, in the *Times Literary Supplement,* the most underrated writer of the century. Published in her sixty-fourth year, *Quartet in Autumn* is about aging, isolation, and recalcitrance, all within the author's own experience; and we have to marvel at the skill with which she rescues them from grimness. It's true that she sometimes frightens us to the core by stepping resolutely onto ground—human intractability, the dominion of age—where even clerics fear to tread. But our apprehensions are countered by the expected Pym levity in the midst of gloom: Marcia waxing furious because one of the empty milk bottles she has collected does not match the others; Marcia appearing at a lunch reunion in a light summer coat, fur-lined sheepskin boots, and jaunty straw hat; the bouncy obtuse social worker trying to lure an adamant Marcia into activities for the "lonely ones"; and Pym's eerily exact rendition of the pat phrases her characters rely on—Norman's chirpy "That's the ticket," amiable Letty's "Oh, how lovely," and Marcia's "I was never a big eater." But what really thaws the autumnal chill is the writer's insistence on the grain of salvageability in the obdurate quartet, the calm assessment, conveyed by all her novels and voiced by Letty, that "It's up to oneself, to adapt to circumstances."

Miss Pym's next book, *The Sweet Dove Died,* concocts a more glamorous plot based, a shade more ruthlessly, on the identical philosophy. It is about a handsome, aging woman, Leonora, who loves only perfect objects and a perfect ambiance. She takes up with a susceptible young man who suits her requirements, and she assumes she will be granted the rights of possession; but he jilts her for an aggressive homosexual. There are two surprises for the reader here. The first, which should not in fact be surprising, is the dignity with which Leonora, accustomed only to gallantry from men, accepts her defeat. (We can't help thinking of the pathos Tennessee Williams laid on with a trowel in a similar situation in *The Roman Spring of Mrs. Stone.*) The second is that in this late work, and in connection with so cool a heroine, Barbara Pym makes the first attempt in her fiction to bring her characters to the point of physical sex.

Though lightened by a mocking wit, *The Sweet Dove Died* hasn't the relaxed and artful waggery that slithers through the other novels. In those books where she deals with the mundane areas of life—seedy cafés, civil-service offices, parish functions—Miss Pym is irresistibly droll.

> "Five-past eleven," said Miss Trapnell. "I hope they've put the kettle on."
>
> "I thought I heard a sound," said Miss Clothier, opening her tin of biscuits.
>
> "What kind of a sound?" asked Prudence idly.
>
> "The sound of running water."
>
> "Did you say rushing water?" asked Miss Trapnell seriously.
>
> "No, no; *running* water," said Miss Clothier impatiently. "As if somebody was filling a kettle."

Miss Pym notices the wary eye that those who lunch in cafeterias cast upon their table mates, the disdain with which they watch someone "tucking into" a steamed pudding they have just rejected as fattening. She is not shocked when a vicar's wife confides that she has greater rapport with her cat than with her husband. She is ironic about marriage and friendship, and amused by the sinful curiosity of High Church Anglicans about "Romish" practices. And if you read enough of her books, you will run into a Peter De Vriesian streak of nomenclatural whimsy. Thus the heroine whose matchmaking is as inept as that of Austen's Emma, is named Jane; or, having told us in *Excellent Women* that her heroine is plain, but not at all like Jane Eyre, Pym proceeds to endow her most elegant heroine, Leonora, with the last name of Eyre.

There is no doubt that Barbara Pym is an extraordinarily forebearing and compassionate writer, but it is the layer beneath those warm qualities, a layer of sheer spinal firmness and imperturbable detachment that puts her into the rank of first-rate novelists. That detachment is what we meet in every successful comic with a straight face, and along with it goes a many-layered intelligence: the ability to see several things at the same time, not only the poignancy, the pity of it all (*that* most of us can see), but the risible oddness of our behavior and the miraculous resilience of our nature.

Michiko Kakutani (review date 5 August 1983)

SOURCE: A review of *Some Tame Gazelle,* in *The New York Times,* August 5, 1983, p. 19.

[In the following review, Kakutani offers praise for Some Tame Gazelle.*]*

About a third of the way through this lovely, muted novel, Belinda turns to her sister and declares, "Today has been rather trying, hasn't it really—too much happening." What has happened, it turns out, is that the archdeacon's wife has left on holiday that morning; and the archdeacon himself has come to pay the Bede sisters, Harriet and Belinda, a tea-time visit. So circumscribed are the lives of the English spinsters and clergymen who populate Barbara Pym's novels that such events pass as high drama and yet Miss Pym's depiction of these timid lives is so skillful that the reader not only cares enormously about what happens but also *experiences,* along with the characters, the significance of these everyday events.

Originally published in 1950, **Some Tame Gazelle** was Miss Pym's first novel, though it does not read like an apprentice work. The author's voice is already steady and quietly assured, deft in its manipulation of irony and social detail. And the themes that would animate the author's later work—the perils of love and the tendency of "excellent women" to form "unsuitable attachments"—are also delineated in full. Indeed, Miss Pym's novels, which are being reissued by Dutton, seem, in retrospect, the work of one of those lucky writers who grasped their subject and their style from the very start. Though modest in scale and ambition, the novels are all perfectly tuned in timbre and pitch, and like a fine harpsichord, afford the reader delicate pleasures that resonate insidiously in the mind.

Taking its title from a poem by Thomas Haynes Bayly—

> Some tame gazelle, or some gentle
>   dove:
> Something to love, oh, something to
>   love! ·

—this particular novel portrays the romantic aspirations of its two heroines with gentle good humor. The Bede sisters are both spinsters in their 50's or so, and both have found objects for their wayward affections: Harriet dotes on young curates—she makes them boiled chicken and apple jelly—while her elder sister, Belinda, pines after Henry, the archdeacon of their parish.

Belinda has loved Henry for 30 years, and even though he is married now she continues to hang on his every word. She wears a blue dress to church because she remembers his telling her once that he liked her in pale colors; and while she dreams of knitting him a sweater she decides that such an act is far "too fraught with dangers to be attempted." In the end, she says she realizes that a chaste evening spent

with him once every 30 years or so is really all she "needed to be happy."

How restrained the emotions experienced by Belinda and Harriet seem when compared with the noisy passions and hectic demands of self-fulfillment that afflict so many characters in contemporary fiction! As portrayed by Miss Pym, however, those feelings are every bit as deeply and as keenly felt, for the fictional world in which her characters dwell is rendered, for the reader, completely palpable and real. It is a tidy, class conscious world in which Christian faith is accepted as a given, a world in which people neither expect too much out of life nor risk overstepping the brittle boundaries of propriety and good taste. It is also a world in which women are still divided into two groups—those who are married and those who aren't.

As in Miss Pym's other novels, the men in **Some Tame Gazelle** are quite unworthy of all the attention lavished on them: the young curate whom Harriet adores from afar is a dim, somewhat shallow young man; and Belinda's archdeacon is a pompous windbag, fond of striking melancholy poses and quoting obscure lines of verse. The other suitors in the book—a somewhat vulgar librarian named Mr. Mold and a condescending bishop, who is visiting from abroad—are equally unappealing.

Still, the fact that both Harriet and Belinda turn down assorted marriage proposals, that they tentatively affirm the virtues of spinsterhood—"who would change a comfortable life of spinsterhood in a country parish, which always had its pale curate to be cherished, for the unknown trials of matrimony?"—hardly indicates any feminist ideology on Miss Pym's part. She is, really, concerned with rather more old-fashioned matters. In her novels, romance and affairs of the heart are simply another means of illuminating the weaknesses and strengths of her characters—they are ways of portraying the difficulty people have in connecting, in forming lasting attachments of any sort.

Eleanor B. Wymard (essay date 13 January 1984)

SOURCE: "Characters in Search of Order and Ceremony: Secular Faith of Barbara Pym," in *Commonweal,* January 13, 1984, pp. 19-21.

[In the following essay, Wymard considers commonplace gatherings and planned activities in Pym's novels as attempts to impose order on chaos and to alleviate loneliness of modern life.]

Most critics of Barbara Pym call attention to the fact that after having written six successful novels between 1950 and

1961, her seventh, *An Unsuitable Attachment,* was rejected by publishers in 1963. Pym was rescued from oblivion only when Philip Larkin and David Cecil named her, in a 1975 anniversary issue of the *Times Literary Supplement,* as the most underrated English novelist of the twentieth century. Before her death in 1980, Pym resumed her career with *Quartet in Autumn* (1977), *The Sweet Dove Died* (1978), and *A Few Green Leaves* (1980). But her ten novels, now available in England and the United States, are embraced, unfortunately, as well-crafted entertainments when, indeed, they share affinities with the existentialist mood of modern fiction.

At first, the world of Barbara Pym is strangely insular. The diminutive scale of English village life with the humdrum experiences of spinsters, rectors, and vicars' wives appears to camouflage any serious definition of the human condition. Pym's essential questions are further disguised by the tone of high comedy, for her characters are often ambivalent about learning the true meaning of their lives. In an early novel, *Jane and Prudence* (1953), Jane Cleveland, a vicar's wife, ruminates, for example, that "one's life followed a kind of pattern, with the same things cropping up again and again, but it seemed to [her], floundering among the books, that the question was not one that could be lightly dismissed now. 'No, thank you, I was just looking around,' was what one usually said. Just looking round the Anglican Church, from one extreme to the other, perhaps climbing higher and higher, peeping over the top to have a look at Rome on the other side, and then quickly drawing back."

Similar to Jane, Pym's characters consistently surprise themselves with questions from which they tentatively withdraw, as if to probe them would almost mean too much. Pym notes that Alaric Lydgate, one of the many anthropologists throughout her novels, "often avoided looking into peoples' eyes when he spoke to them, fearful of what he might see there, for life was very terrible whatever sort of front one might put on it."

But ultimately, the characters in the situational microcosm of Pym's country village neither escape nor endure their experience. Rather, they become more human by trying to live with it, affirming their lot in private ritualized gestures or formal ceremonies. Pym's essential subject is thus the incommunicable uniqueness of each ordinary person: "After all, life was like that . . . for most of us [life is] the small unpleasantness rather than the great tragedies, the little useless languages rather than the great renunciations and dramatic love affairs of history or fiction." From this perspective, stated by Catherine Oliphant in *Less Than Angels* (1955), Pym thus accentuates the commonplace, even the banal. While her characters do not confront irrevocable decisions, they do shape their lives through very personal

choices. Moreover, they celebrate themselves in ceremonies which have private, sometimes communal, significance.

The act of writing is itself a ceremonial act for Pym. In *No Fond Return of Love* (1961), she acknowledged both the novelist and the sociologist for perceiving those moments which are "very near to the heart of reality." But Emma Howick, the social anthropologist in Pym's last novel, *A Few Green Leaves,* gradually forsakes accumulating data on the "Social Patterns of the West Oxfordshire Community" to write a novel using the same setting. According to Pym, the novelist who involves the emotions of readers in the rhythm of everyday living invites their participation in the very continuity of being. Since "we all came to the same thing in the end—dust and/or ashes, however you liked to think of it," it is the writer—neither the anthropologist nor the historian—who can preserve "a few green leaves" for future generations.

Tom Dagnall, the village vicar in *A Few Green Leaves,* is particularly aware of historic time. His goal is to discover the ruins of a deserted medieval village in the woods of Oxfordshire. On the first Sunday after Easter, he also rallies the villagers to participate in a walk in the park and the woods surrounding the ancient manor and mausoleum on the fringe of town, a variation on an annual rite dating from the seventeenth century. Preoccupied with local history, he keeps a record of his own daily life: "What was he to write about the events of the morning? 'My sister Daphne made a gooseling tart . . . ?' Could that possibly be of interest to readers of the next century?" Life, for Pym, is a social enterprise. Natural ceremonies must be preserved if one is to live fully in the present. Funerals, marriages, christenings "gave a kind of continuity to village life, like the seasons—the cutting and harvesting of the crops, then the new sowing and the springing up again." Such affirmation risks sentimentality, for it may seem that Pym is yearning for more simple times. Her sense of ritual, the most important organizing principle of her fiction, reveals, in fact, the evolving complexity of her work and brings us closer to its significance.

The early novels, *Some Tame Gazelle* (1950), *Excellent Women* (1952), and *Jane and Prudence* (1953), are grounded in unquestioned values. Jane Cleveland, now forty-one and a former English tutor at Oxford, had once "taken great pleasure in imagining herself as a clergyman's wife . . . but she has been quickly disillusioned." Nonetheless, she grows in personal identity to the point of being able to confide in her husband: "We can only go blundering along in that state of life unto which it shall please God to call us . . . I was going to be such a splendid clergyman's wife when I married you, but somehow it hasn't turned out like *The Daisy Chain* or *The Lost Chronicles of Barset.*" But by continuing to carry out the ritual duties expected of her role, she restores herself: "'I wanted some little books suitable for confirmation candidates,' said Jane in a surprisingly firm and thoughtful tone. 'Not too High, you know' . . . By now it was almost teatime, [but] she would go without [it] as a kind of penance for all the times she had failed as a vicar's wife."

In *Excellent Women,* Mildred Lathbury, the "just over thirty" unmarried daughter of a country clergyman, is drawn to worship at St. Mary's Church, "on the wrong side of Victoria Station," because it is relatively "High." This mild rebellion against the wishes of her dead parents involves Mildred in the lives of Father Julian Malory, his sister Winifred, and their boarder, Mrs. Allegra Gray, who has romantic designs on the unmarried rector. Mildred has more opportunities than most of the "excellent women" of the parish to involve herself with men and the possibility of marriage. But she exercises a firm sense of choice, clarified for her through simple domestic ritual: "As I moved about the kitchen getting china and cutlery, I thought, not for the first time, how pleasant it was to be living alone . . . I might be going to have a 'full life' after all."

Although Pym's early characters are not moved to profound meditation, they experience the joy of making quiet decisions about their own lives in the presence of ordinary human reality. A young anthropology student, Deidre Swan, in *Less Than Angels* (1956) draws insight for us: "Yes, I suppose it's comforting to see people going about their humdrum business . . . At home her mother would be laying the breakfast and later her aunt would creep down to see if she had done it correctly. And they would probably go on doing this all of their lives." Pym keeps faith with life itself, even its trivialities.

One never hears the actual sound of terror in Pym's early novels. Her first heroine, Belinda Bede in *Some Tame Gazelle* only suggests unspoken depths by ruminating, "If only one could clear out one's mind and heart as ruthlessly as one did one's wardrobe." But two later heroines, Letty Crowe in *Quartet in Autumn* and Leonora Eyre in *The Sweet Dove Died* do encounter "nothingness" and the "horror of being." The quartet in autumn are lonely government clerks—Letty, Marcia, Norman and Edwin—who have worked together many years in an airless London office, but have shared very little of themselves. When facing retirement, Letty awakens from a dream about her youth: "All gone, that time, those people . . . [she] lay for some time meditating on the strangeness of life slipping away like this." At the office retirement party for herself and Marcia Ivory, the host does not even know what their jobs were, only that he has no reason to replace them. At this point, Letty experiences utter helplessness: "It seemed to Letty that what cannot now be justified has perhaps never existed, and it gave her the feeling that she and Marcia had been swept away as if they had never been. With this sensation of nothingness she entered the library."

Pym insists that rituals preserve one from experiencing chaos, but such actions must spring from the ability of the character to assent to the realities of her own existence. Letty's picnic is thus an affirmation of life, a free act of faith.
—*Eleanor B. Wymard*

The quartet hesitantly tries to redefine itself when Norman and Edwin plan a reunion luncheon. Shortly after, when Marcia, the most eccentric of the group, dies, the three survivors follow her to the crematorium and afterward share their second meal. Returning that night to her eighty-one-year-old landlady, Letty is renewed with another cup of tea: "There was something to be said for tea and a comfortable chat about crematoria." At the end of the novel, she looks forward to a day in the country with Edwin, Norman, and Marjorie, her only sustaining friend. Planning such a day "made one realize that life still held infinite possibilities for change." To rescue herself from emotional deprivation, Letty must find significant forms and ceremonies. Pym insists that rituals preserve one from experiencing chaos, but such actions must spring from the ability of the character to assent to the realities of her own existence. Letty's picnic is thus an affirmation of life, a free act of faith.

One of Pym's most complex heroines, Leonora Eyre (*A Sweet Dove Died*) is unappealingly selfish and snobbish. A collector of Victoriana, she admits to insulating herself against disagreeable realities: "Life is only tolerable if one takes a romantic view of it . . . And yet it's wicked, really, when there's all this misery and that sort of thing, but one feels so helpless—I mean, what can one *do*?" Approaching fifty, Leonora rejects a wealthy antique dealer, Humphrey Boyce, in favor of his twenty-four-year-old bisexual nephew, James, whom she loses to a malicious homosexual. James feels that Leonora would have been able to deal with his relationship with Ned had she the ability to lose her perfect control and "been just a little angry." But unknown to James, Leonora does experience disintegration. She enters into a cycle of despair, suffering migraines and sleeping fitfully. Her first crisis occurs in a Knightsbridge tearoom where she is conscious of belonging "with the sad jewelry and the old woman and the air of things that had seen better days." Among the "cast off crusts, the ruined cream cakes and the cigarette ends," Leonora feels "debased, diminished, crushed and trodden into the ground, indeed brought to a certain point of dilapidation. I am utterly alone, she thought."

Later, she humiliates herself further by sobbing uncontrollably in front of Meg, a younger friend who has been tormented in her love for a homosexual man. Until now, Leonora has offered her little comfort. During these two crises, Leonora creates new meaning for herself, however, by relinquishing her false pride and dignity; shallow refinements, at the beginning of the novel, now deepen into a kind of courage. But, even though Leonora grows in sympathy and sensitivity, Pym still does not claim too much for her. After all, the mode of *The Sweet Dove Died* is essentially ironic. Yet, for Pym, style is a way of coping with modern pressures, even if it cannot resolve them.

Other characters, too, relieve their isolation by discovering their own private ceremonies, for contemporary life, according to Pym's later fiction, is very unfestive. Even in a world of structured social effort, the individual is more isolated than ever. For example, the social worker assigned to Marcia Ivory (*Quartet in Autumn*) has little insight into the old woman's profound loneliness, let alone her peculiar habit of collecting, washing, and stacking discarded milk bottles. The gerontologist's mother-in-law in *A Few Green Leaves* finds more comfort participating in parish coffees than by adhering to diet charts and exercise schedules. In comparison to the present, the past is rich with natural rituals which provide assurance and connection.

If Pym's characters are in search of order and ceremony, it is ironic, indeed, that the Anglican Church, so pervasive in her novels, is never the source of inspiration for renewing one's faith. Even though Catherine Oliphant in *Less Than Angels* (1955) and Rupert Stonebird in *An Unsuitable Attachment* (1963) want to return to church, it offers little for them except the comfort of nostalgia. After her retirement, Letty Crowe tries "to discover what church-going held for people, apart from habit and convention, wondering if it would hold anything for her and if so what form this would take." Attending Stations of the Cross, she hears the litany, "'From pain to pain, from woe to woe' . . . but Letty's thoughts had been on herself and how she should arrange the rest of her life." The remaining trio in *Quartet in Autumn* finds redemption in the hope of Letty's picnic, not the celebration of liturgical ritual. Even within the church, Pym's characters are left to discover their own rites of affirmation.

In Pym's view of the modern world, only the resiliency of human nature generates the rebirth of a dead soul. But celebration will, in fact, occur, if only with a cup of tea and a "comfortable chat about crematoria." Acknowledging that "life bruises one," Wilmet Forsyth, for example, elevates her own life "in a glass of blessings," (1958) and looks forward to dinner with "Sybil and Arnold, a happy and suitable ending to a good day."

Such ordinary characters are at home in the literary imagination of Barbara Pym. To minimize this tone of her high comedy would be to deny the core of Pym's vision. But one must also admit that Pym's fiction shares in the existential temper of the modern novel. Her canon evolves toward the certainty that an individual can rescue herself from chaos, can affirm herself in a leap of faith which springs from a willingness to confront the terms of her own life. That life which Catherine Oliphant describes as "comic and sad and indefinite—dull, sometimes, but seldom really tragic or deliriously happy, except when one's very young."

Robert Emmet Long (review date 24 November 1984)

SOURCE: A review of *A Very Private Eye: An Autobiography in Diaries and Letters*, in *America*, November 24, 1984, p. 348.

[*In the following review, Long praises the posthumous publication of* A Very Private Eye. *According to Long, the volume of autobiographic writings "testifies to Pym's modest yet potent spell."*]

The quietest of English novelists, Barbara Pym makes an unlikely Cinderella, yet her literary success late in life does have, oddly, a Cinderella quality. Her career as a writer began slowly and hesitantly in the 1930's, was postponed by World War II and finally launched in 1950 with the publication of her first novel *Some Tame Gazelle.* Thereafter she published five other novels, including the wholly delightful *Excellent Women,* a tongue-in-cheek chronicle of an Anglican spinster in postwar London, which earned her a modest following and critical esteem. Yet in 1963 her seventh book, *An Unsuitable Attachment,* was rejected by her publisher Jonathan Cape, and then by a series of other publishers, who found her fiction too "mild" for the reading tastes of the manic 1960's. Pym continued to write but remained unpublished for the next 16 years, until she awoke one morning, like Lord Byron, to find herself famous. In an issue of the *Times Literary Supplement* in 1977, both Philip Larkin and Lord David Cecil cited her as one of the most underestimated writers of the century; and publishers who had previously shunned her suddenly sought her out. Jonathan Cape reprinted her earlier novels, and Macmillan brought out three new ones; a Pym revival swept both England and America. By the time of her death in 1980, Miss Pym came to seem like a transformed Cinderella, outshining her more forward cousins.

Now the story of Barbara Pym's life is told in *A Very Private Eye,* made up of her notebooks, diaries and letters and ably edited by her surviving sister, Hilary Pym, and her close friend and literary executor, Hazel Holt. *A Very Private Eye,* which reads like a novel of her own life, is one of Pym's best books, and one that everyone interested in Pym will certainly want to read. In the autobiography Pym's life and work reflect back on each other, shadows are rubbed away, sources in life for a number of her characters are disclosed, and Pym herself steps forward in a full-length portrait having the complicated tonal qualities of her fictional heroines. Although unassuming in many ways, Pym seemed to know at an early point that she was destined to be a writer, even a writer of note, and she was not without dogged ambition. The notebooks she kept from her student days at Oxford until the end of her life, which record her observations and reflections, as well as her personal experiences, seem intended to be read, at some later time, by readers of her books-to-be. They reveal her as a shy but accomplished observer, and not least of herself. Her vulnerabilities are brought out, especially her habit of falling in love with men whose fondness of her stopped short of marriage.

Prophetically, in an early draft of *Some Tame Gazelle,* written when she was not long out of Oxford, she envisions herself in middle life, unmarried and living with her sister—an eerily accurate prediction of her later years. Less clear, though, is what it was about her exactly that made her so unsuccessful matrimonially. It may be that she chose the wrong men to fall in love with—a small procession beginning with Henry Harvey, an Oxford undergraduate whom she considered much above her intellectually, and leading in middle age to Richard Roberts, a strikingly handsome younger man who appears to have regarded her, to her misery, as a confidante rather than as a lover. At one point she refers to herself as Henry Harvey's "doormat," and generally her infatuations, always ending in disappointment, suggest an element of masochism in her makeup. In her fiction, sexuality is a "problem," is kept at a distance, approached obliquely, and it would seem to have been a problem for Pym herself.

Pym found refuge in literature, ordering the world on her own terms. A highly civilized writer, she admired Jane Austen and Virginia Woolf, and in one of the many revealing comments in the book, she notes the restraint that she has attained in her writing. Armored with wit and irony, she accepted the world touchingly, tenderly, in all its commonplaceness and in doing so created an unexaggerated vision of modern-day England that compares with the wry vision of the hard factualness of life of the poet Philip Larkin. Indeed, she came to know Larkin personally in the latter part of her life, and many of her best letters are addressed to him. At one point they joke about a newspaper clipping he has sent to her about a Mr. Larkin who has announced his engagement to a Miss Pym. No romance here, rather a duet in autumn, a low-keyed "understanding" that

informs all of Barbara Pym's work. *A Very Private Eye* makes clear that there were serious disappointments in Pym's life—romantic frustration, setbacks in her career, illnesses that beset her in the 1970's. Yet she never regarded herself as being tragic, she would never have "exaggerated" to such a degree. Terminally ill with cancer in a hospice in Oxfordshire, she accepted her death almost serenely as being, after all, in the nature of things. *A Very Private Eye* is splendid in evoking Pym's own personal qualities as a writer and as a woman, and invites reading more than once. It testifies to Pym's modest yet potent spell.

Diane Benet (essay date December 1984)

SOURCE: "The Language of Christianity in Pym's Novels," in *Thought: A Review of Culture and Idea,* Vol. 59, No. 235, December, 1984, pp. 504-13.

[In the following essay, Benet examines Pym's treatment of the Christian church and religious sentiment in A Few Green Leaves *and several earlier novels. As Benet notes, Pym's concern over "devitalized religious words, outmoded devotional forms, and a clergy whose ability to communicate the faith is almost entirely inadequate" are recurring themes in her fiction.]*

When a group of women decorates St. Mary's for Whitsunday, Mildred Lathbury, the heroine of Barbara Pym's *Excellent Women,* remarks, "There was a good deal of chatter, and I was reminded of Trollope's description of Lily Dale and Grace Crawley, who were both accustomed to churches and 'almost as irreverent as though they were two curates.'" Pym herself is accustomed to churches, and writes her comic novels with an affectionate irreverence that is reminiscent of the Barchester novels at their best. Of her ten novels, only *The Sweet Dove Died* does not center on the Church and the Anglican clergy, or on people closely associated with them.

The novels of the English author, who died in 1980, have been reissued in this country and have received much favorable attention in the press. Pym is an incisive social observer whose frequent allusions to Trollope and Jane Austen invite the comparisons. Her satirical touch seems light, yet its exposure of the ridiculous posturings and laughable concerns that mark social intercourse at every level is merciless. It would be surprising if so keen an observer did not scrutinize the church she treats so frequently, with entertaining and illuminating results. Writing in 1971, when only six of Pym's ten novels had been published, Robert Smith remarked that "no hint of doctrinal or emotional problems is intruded upon the reader. Religion, for Miss Pym's characters, involves no anguish of conscience ('social' or personal), no dark night of the soul, but discussions about what vestments should be worn on Mid-Lent Sunday, what shall be served for luncheon on Fridays in the clergy-house," and like subjects.

Pym does not write, it is true, of doctrinal matters. But just as Trollope, amid the high comedy of *Barchester Towers,* calls our attention to some of the abuses within the Church (in the person of the Reverend Vesey Stanhope, for example), so Pym, in the context of her comic vision, calls our attention to the contemporary situation of the Church.

The detailed picture of modern-day Christianity that emerges from Pym's books suggests that religion was one of her most important artistic concerns. From *Some Tame Gazelle* (1950) to *A Few Green Leaves* (1980), several topics recur and coalesce to define the state of organized religion, as Pym saw it: the pious cliché, religious phrases, hymns, prayer, and the clerical voice (especially in sermons). These, together with the themes of the Church as social organization and of the embarrassment of religious commitment, outline a coherent vision. Pym presents a church hampered by three language-related problems: a stock of pious words that has been devitalized, outmoded devotional forms that often do not appeal to the modern sensibility, and a clergy that has difficulty communicating the ancient faith to its contemporary flock. Christianity in her novels is the vital faith of a relatively small number, a faith that the established Church cannot foster at large so long as its language is inadequate. Pym's manner of weaving, most unobtrusively, serious insights into the texture of comedy might be misleading, but her recurrence to the same themes, topics, and vision of the Church indicates her estimation of their significance. To demonstrate the consistency of perspective that I propose, I shall introduce the topics and themes with reference to the earlier novels before turning to *A Few Green Leaves,* Pym's last novel and most optimistic depiction of the Church.

"*God moves in a mysterious way, His wonders to perform,*" says a sheep-like bishop when a middle-aged lady rejects his marriage proposal. She is annoyed that he quotes her favorite hymn, fearing, perhaps, that it will henceforth have unpleasant associations for her. "God *does* move in a mysterious way," insists a vicar whose hope that a housekeeper will materialize in answer to his prayers is temporarily frustrated. The pious cliché, like any other, retains little of its original impact. Any residual majesty that might cling to Cowper's words is undercut by our reflection that among God's wonders we are to number a bishop's marriage and a vicar's household arrangements.

The glib platitude is current in a pleasant little world in which religious words or phrases are felt to be inapplicable, or are thoroughly secularized and meaningless in their original sense. "We are supposed not to take heed of what we shall wear," Belinda Bede chides the Archdeacon with whom she has been in unrequited and irreproachable love for over thirty years. "My dear Belinda," he retorts, "we are not in the Garden of Eden. There is no solution to the problem. We may as well face the facts. Agatha ought not to have let the moth get into that suit." The faithful Belinda is reassured by her sister that her love for the Archdeacon, who is married to the careless Agatha, is quite right since "Clergymen are always saying that we should love one another." A lady in **Excellent Women** is shocked to think that the commandment to "love thy neighbor" should be taken literally, to include the people surrounding her in a cheap restaurant. The "precious blood" for whose lack "somebody might be dying" in Pym's world is R-Negative and salvation is a transfusion. Thus casually, Pym's characters frequently test pious language against the texture of reality only to misinterpret it or reject it as irrelevant. Altogether in these novels, the words of faith have either lost their vigor and spiritual significance, or they are not taken seriously as referring to daily life.

Just as the words with religious denotations and connotations that Pym's characters speak are often empty, the words of hymns are often meaningless or, worse, offensive to them. Dulcie, the appealing heroine of **No Fond Return of Love,** waits while singing a hymn for the following words: "The rich man in his castle, the poor man at his gate, / God made them high or lowly and ordered their estate." When they are omitted, she feels "cheated of her indignation." Hymns "are the great stumbling block" to faith, a man tells a group of friends; "the only thing is to abandon oneself to the words uncritically and let them flow over one." Ironically, the very forms meant to encourage and guide devotion have become positive impediments to it by being couched in language suited to a different era. Nor have other aspects of worship been updated to accommodate the modern tongue. A troubled young woman thinks that to learn to pray, perhaps she should return to the church she only visits. She sits alone "making up prayers in the rather stilted language she remembered from childhood. Was it necessary always to address God as 'Thou' and to use such archaic grammatical forms?" For Pym's characters, devotion is often vitiated by its lack of a comfortable and significant idiom. It is approached consistently with reservations and with a consciousness that it is, for some reason, not quite right.

The clerical voice the characters hear frequently fails to strike the right note. Sometimes it is garbled: a parishioner observes that Father Thames's letter in the parish magazine was, "as so often, troubled and confused. Spiritual and material matters jostled each other in a most inartistic manner, so that the effect was almost comic." Sometimes sermons are too "intelligent" for their auditors, other times too "literary." For sermons, Archdeacon Hoccleve often reads to his parishioners long excerpts of seventeenth-century authors which they do not understand. When he abandons this comfortable habit, striving to preach a lucid sermon, his congregation suspects he is deteriorating into second childhood. In one of the funniest episodes in Pym, he preaches on the *Dies Irae* to a congregation at first uneasy, then disbelieving and, finally, angry at his zestful references to their sinfulness. Even Belinda, his greatest admirer, is shocked and insulted, though she does not retaliate, as others do, by withholding her offering. Whether Pym's clerics are incoherent, incomprehensible because they ignore their auditors' limitations or take refuge in the past, or simply tactless, they consistently fail to communicate the faith to the people they serve.

Pym's novels suggest that the Church has become a primarily social institution to most of its members. Examples of this abound in *An Unsuitable Attachment.* Mark, the vicar, comes "of a good clerical family" though he is "without private means." Edwin Pettigrew "was not a believer, though he sometimes went to church out of politeness to Mark and Sophia," as if the service were a dull party hosted by dull but nice people. Ianthe's mother "had been deeply conscious of her position as a canon's widow," and a match between Rupert and Ianthe would be proper: "Archdeacon's son and canon's daughter—what could be more suitable when one came to think of it." Membership in the Church or close association with the clergy is a convenient and reliable way of "placing" people socially. A church affiliation is akin to belonging to a club; it is a guarantee of a certain social standard and common background that is reassuring to everyone concerned. The French anthropologist who visits English churches to observe the rituals that include "afterwards . . . the traditional English Sunday dinner with joint" knows this.

Given the uncomplicatedly social implications of church membership that all assume, religious fervor or a noticeable commitment are an embarrassment to Pym's characters. In *Excellent Women,* Everard Bone's conversion seems "rather an awkward thing" to his acquaintances. Father Greatorex's middle-aged decision to take Orders cannot be accepted at face value, or he as a "saintly" man—a parishioner snorts at the thought, guessing that "He was no good in business so he went into the Church." When Mary Beamish goes to test her vocation, her brother is ashamed "about this nunnery business." A man who regains his childhood faith is uncomfortable when he is asked about it. Disturbed by noise coming from a neighboring flat, a lady is mortified to learn that its source is the singing of some Nigerian Christians. "Christianity is disturbing," she is told when she complains. "How was she to explain to this vital, ebullient black man her own blend of Christianity: a grey, formal, respectable

thing of measured observances and mild general undemanding kindness to all?"

As reference to these embarrassing and sometimes noisy converts indicates, Christianity in Pym's world is not dead, not by any means. The Church Pym depicts may not flourish, but it is kept alive by those new believers, and by a small group of women whose unobtrusive acts of charity and hours of service are an impressive testimony—that goes unnoticed. Two novels particularly focus on "churchwomen," *Excellent Women* and *A Glass of Blessings.* Though they are not primarily about the women's faith or their spiritual lives, these books give us an indication of what devotion and the Church can mean to the faithful. Because Pym writes about what life is "like . . . for most of us—the small unpleasantnesses rather than the great tragedies; the little useless longings rather than the great renunciations and dramatic love affairs of history or fiction"—the novels do not present the upheavals or ecstasies of spiritual struggle. Instead, they show the small daily efforts that it takes to live as a Christian and, especially, to love one another. Seeing a roomful of strangers, Mildred Lathbury remarks, "One wouldn't believe there are so many people . . . and one must love them all," but her faith is expressed concretely by inviting people to church, helping her friends in need, trying not to judge them, and seeking "an infinitesimal amount of virtue" in overcoming her initial dislike of someone. Wilmet, the heroine of *A Glass of Blessings,* is a likeable snob who feels that many of the people in her church do not belong to her own world. But, learning from the example of a devout friend, she also tries to assist and accept others in a Christian spirit. Small, unspectacular efforts mark Wilmet's development, and she eventually comes to feel that "the Church should be the place where all worlds could meet, and looking around me I saw that in a sense this was so. If people remained outside it was our—even *my*—duty to try to bring them in."

> **Lacking a vital language and voice to disseminate the faith, the Church in Pym's novels fails to influence most of its members or to attract a substantial number of new believers.**
> —*Diane Benet*

However, these characters and others like them act not from any impetus originating in the Church, but in accordance with their own needs to worship, to live purposefully, to do good, to find solace when it's needed, and—above all—to love: "Some tame gazelle or some gentle dove or even a poodle dog: something to *love,* that was the point." Since even the small body of the faithful is not especially inspired by the traditional devotional forms or the clergy, it is no wonder that only a few unbelievers are drawn to discover or recover the faith. Lacking a vital language and voice to disseminate the faith, the Church in Pym's novels fails to influence most of its members or to attract a substantial number of new believers.

A Few Green Leaves repeats the topics found in the earlier novels, but is different chiefly as Pym's most detailed and optimistic view of the Church. Unusual, also, is her inclusion of two related spiritual crises. Tom, the widowed rector and one of the novel's central characters, is plagued by a sense of failure through a large part of the novel. Thinking that he is of no use to anyone, he even avoids visiting his parishioners. Here, as in the rest of Pym's novels, there are doubts that the language of Christianity applies to everyday, practical life and evidence of its secularization. When Tom preaches a sermon on helping one's neighbor, a woman wonders if he would "*really*" help: "Would he, for example, be capable of cleaning her top windows, which was what she really needed?" After a power failure, "'The light has been restored, thank God!' said Father Byrne in his rich Abbey Theatre tones, giving the announcement an almost religious significance." Hymns fare no better here than elsewhere. Tom rejects one as "morbid"; another is offensive: "'Choose Thou for me my friends'—the very idea of it!"

Tom's church is primarily a social institution whose most important event is its flower festival. Two anthropologists and a sociologist discuss the meaning of the festival. It never occurs to them that worship or thanksgiving might be its point, which is understandable, since it never occurs to any of the parishioners involved. The lady who arranges the altar flowers every third Sunday never attends church, and a bereaved family attends only on the Sunday following their relative's funeral because that is the local custom. This, then, is Pym's typical Christian world, with one important exception. There is no convert or fervent believer to embarrass anyone. The only source of mild uneasiness to the characters on religious grounds is Adam Prince, ex-Anglican priest and convert to Roman Catholicism turned restaurant-critic: does he expect his Friday evening hostess to serve fish? Prince continually offers Tom unsolicited advice about the management of his parish, but never discusses religion.

Tom's sense of uselessness is one of the main concerns of the novel because he is not alone in perceiving that a shift in values has taken place. Pym presents a Church surrounded by the "helping professions," which have taken over some of its functions. The focal point of village life has changed:

> Monday was always a busy day at the surgery, a rather stark new building next to the village hall. "They"—the patients—had not on the whole been

to church the previous day, but they atoned for this by a devout attendance at the place where they expected not so much to worship, though this did come into it for a few, as to receive advice and consolation. You might *talk* to the rector, some would admit doubtfully, but he couldn't give you a prescription. There was nothing in churchgoing to equal that triumphant moment when you came out of the surgery clutching the ritual scrap of paper.

Although the doctors tend to bodies rather than souls, the villagers see them for "advice and consolation." Unlike Tom, they have the authority to prescribe, and the efficacy of their tangible remedies is seen as far more certain then anything he might offer. No wonder, then, that people in the waiting room maintain a respectful quiet. Even Daphne, Tom's sister, refuses to divulge her conversation with Dr. Shrubsole: "Consultation between doctor and patient is a confidential matter. Like the confessional." Daphne's remark is intended to annoy Tom "who had wanted to introduce that kind of thing—most unsuitably—into the village." People who bare their souls happily in the examining room are offended at the suggestions of a similar exposure in the confessional. As confidence and devotion have been largely displaced from one profession and location to another, Shrubsole and Avice, his social-worker wife, want literally to supplant Tom in the spacious rectory they covet for their large family.

The loss of some of his duties to the doctors and social workers contributes to Tom's feeling of uselessness. Because his role and the role of the Church are unclear to him, he spends a good deal of time trying to find something to do with himself. Given the circumstances, it is not surprising that much of his attention is focused on the mausoleum standing by the church, or that his great passion is local history, especially the deserted medieval village that he longs to find. Like Archdeacon Hoccleve in *Some Tame Gazelle*, Tom takes refuge in the past. Even as he puts his volunteers to work reading inscriptions on old tombstones, he looks back to a time that he believes was more receptive to the faith—to a time when the scope and the appreciation of his work were broader. His personal hero is Anthony à Wood, the seventeenth-century diarist, antiquarian, biographer, and recluse who made detached observation his lifetime work. Tom's helpless idea of his diminished role makes him use the pious cliché to reassure himself: suspecting that his whole day has been wasted, he "was prepared to believe that it might not have been. God did still move in a mysterious way, even in this day and age or at this 'moment in time,' as some of his parishioners might have said."

Typically, Pym keeps a reserved distance from her clergymen. The quality or even existence of their faith is most frequently, and ominously, not remarked. The reader is left to draw his own conclusions; but, whatever those are, the men share a common problem which makes them practically useless as spiritual guides: along with the rest, Tom finds it difficult to verbalize his devotion and faith. One of his prayers is inarticulate, a matter of thinking of certain people while he walks about the church. Several of his sermons are unsatisfactory. The topic of one is heaven, "a bold and imaginative, perhaps even appropriate, subject" but, finally, it misses the mark since no one thinks "about heaven all that much now"; another is judged as "an unsuccessful mingling of past and present." Later, when he considers a sermon on the loaves and the fishes, the reader understands that his task necessarily involves the significant relation of the past to this "moment in time": what can he say about the miracle of feeding the multitude in a society where such a problem is the mundane province of government and social workers like Avice?

As the representative of the Church, Tom's problem is to translate the faith into terms comprehensible and relevant to the present day; before he can do this, however, he must himself acknowledge the present and stop focusing so exclusively on local history. Though he doubts it throughout the greater part of the novel, his ministrations are needed, and his interest in the purely historical past interferes with them. When two of his congregation see him driving by, one of them remarks that he is probably visiting parishioners, but the other disagrees: "'All this history he's always going on about' said Mrs. Furst with unexpected bitterness. 'That's more likely what he's doing.'" His backward-looking inclinations keep him from seeing the situation and the people around him clearly. There are indications, too, of the awareness that medicine cannot address spiritual needs. When Shrubsole tells an elderly patient that she is close to death, she responds by asking if he believes in life after death. The young doctor is "stunned into silence, indignant at such a question. Then of course he realized that *he* couldn't be expected to answer things like that—it was the rector's business." Though times have changed, Tom's diffidence about his function is unjustified. There are some needs, after all, that only a clergyman can address. With the actual death of a parishioner, Tom realizes this and feels that he comes "into his own." But the event only confirms the quiet upswing of all his affairs, which points to his greater involvement in the present.

The change in Tom's perspective follows the first spiritual crisis in the novel. Though "crisis" seems heavy-handed for a situation that unfolds in Pym's typically comical manner, crisis it is. Terry Skate is the florist who tends the mausoleum by the church. One day he tells the rector that, having lost his faith (by watching a television talk-show), he can no longer do this job. Tom reminds Terry that "much greater men" than they have doubted and eventually overcome their spiritual difficulties. "'Oh, but that was in the

old days, wasn't it? Darwin and those old Victorians.' Terry laughed, dismissing them." Thus carelessly the young man implies that faith is expendable in the modern world, indicating the apprehension underlying Tom's diffidence and informing his timorous attitude toward his parishioners. Tom cannot help because Terry does not really wish it, but he feels more than usually dispirited and ineffectual.

His dejection leads to a quiet spiritual crisis of his own as he thinks how much of his life as a rector is "wasted in profitless discussion" and wonders if Miss Lee, a staunch parishioner polishing the eagle lectern, has ever doubted Christianity as "an elaborate fiction." The doubts are, of course, Tom's own, and only in part the product of his encounter with Terry Skate. The church brasses gleam with proof of Miss Lee's hard-rubbing industry everywhere he looks, but as he stands before her, Tom realizes that the familiar bird on the lectern is wood and not brass: "He must have been remembering some other lectern, probably the one in the church of his childhood. How could he have been so forgetful and unobservant!" When he asks if she would prefer a brass lectern, Miss Lee answers, "I *love* that old wooden bird, and I *love* polishing it. A brass one may look more brilliant, but wood can be very rewarding. . . ." Tom's awareness of his failure to live in the present is promising; even more important is his attention to Miss Lee's work and to the bird, which traditionally symbolizes John, but here Tom's own church. Seen with eyes clear of habit and preconception, it reveals its undeniable difference from the Church of the past, but it is not the less beautiful, rewarding, or responsive to effort. Noting Miss Lee's statement as an idea for a sermon, Tom indicates that he understands its significance.

Moments later, he is given yet more help in his quiet crisis by another insight from Miss Grundy while she arranges some flowers at the altar. They are not fresh roses, having served during the past week, but they are still lovely. Their usefulness can be extended, Miss Grundy tells him, by adding "a few more leaves. A few green leaves can make such a difference." Her words clearly suggest that the revitalization of the Church (which is traditionally the Rose of Sharon) depends upon the infusion of a fresh faith in its beauty and capacity to serve. These ordinary remarks and Miss Lee's are typical of Pym's unobtrusive, almost sly way of embedding major insights in seemingly inconsequential exchanges. The reader might miss the importance of Miss Grundy's statements but for Tom's comical but suggestive reaction to them. He retreats, finding it "somehow depressing the way these elderly women kept giving him ideas for sermons." Though he decides not to use the ideas, they have already reached their best audience: in small ways, Tom begins to focus on improving his church and becomes less preoccupied with the past. He gives his organist a Christmas present of apricot brandy which might "perhaps even induce him to play at Evensong in the winter months" and is rewarded a few days later with an "unusually splendid sound." When Dr. Gellibrand stubbornly sticks to the present in his remarks to the history group, Tom is not particularly concerned: "I think people enjoyed it and I suppose that's the main thing." Such gestures may seem small indeed, hardly worth noticing, but in Pym's temperate world, they are large and promising actions.

Like the rest of Pym's novels, *A Few Green Leaves* is about love. Along with Tom's point of view, it focuses especially on Emma Howick's. She is a thirtyish anthropologist, modern in every respect, inept at handling her love life. She is not one of Pym's "excellent women," as that quiet breed was defined by Robert Smith: "good aunt, good Churchwoman, informed spinster, conscientious social worker, meticulous housekeeper.... Miss Pym's heroines are redeemed by their modesty and sensitive wit." The amusing Emma sees everything as material for her study. A bring-and-buy-sale, the flower festival, and even some cars abandoned next to the church are potential material: "was there not something significant and appropriate about this particular graveyard being opposite the church—a kind of mingling of two religious faiths, the ancient and the modern? 'A Note on the Significance of the Abandoned Motor-Car in a West Oxfordshire Village' might pin it down, she felt." Emma, no less than the other characters, assumes a largely secularized world, but she has no doubt about Tom's role and status: "If there was no active Lord of the Manor, surely the rector was the most important person rather than the doctor?" During the course of the novel, almost imperceptibly, her interest in Tom (and his in her) grows, assisted by her scheming mother. And Pym indicates, in her characteristically subdued manner, that Emma will help the rector reorient himself. *A Few Green Leaves* ends with the New Year and Tom's proposal that she give his history society a lecture: "You could relate your talk to things that happened in the past. . . . or even speculate on the future—what *might* happen in the years to come."

Working consistently under the mask of comedy, Pym achieves a serious analysis of the contemporary English Church which suggests that it was a matter of some importance to her. In nine of her ten novels, she recurs to the same themes and topics to point to the three language-related problems that impede the effectiveness of the modern Church: devitalized religious words, outmoded devotional forms, and a clergy whose ability to communicate the faith is almost entirely inadequate. The terrible irony is that, finally, it makes no practical difference whatever whether or not her clergymen believe: believers or presumed unbelievers alike, none of her chief clerical characters offers articulate guidance to his flock.

Although they are woven into a richly comic texture, her personal analysis and vision of the Church are the serious appraisal of an author who was "accustomed to churches" and concerned with the state of organized religion. While her novels reflect the changing world, Pym emphasizes that there is still a need for the Church to do its unique work. Especially in *A Few Green Leaves,* she suggests that doctors, social workers, and others in the "helping professions" cannot fulfill the clergy's spiritual task. Through Tom, she asserts her faith in the capacity of the Church to revitalize itself from within, to come into the present day to reclaim its authority and influential voice.

Lynn Veach Sadler (essay date Spring 1985)

SOURCE: "Spinsters, Non-Spinsters, and Men in the World of Barbara Pym," in *Critique: Studies in Modern Fiction,* Vol. XXVI, No. 3, Spring, 1985, pp. 141-54.

[*In the following essay, Sadler considers Pym's depiction of unmarried women and male characters in her novels. "In the Pym world," Sadler concludes, "bores and boors can be male and female, and men can out-spinster spinsters."*]

At age fifty, Barbara (Mary Crampton) Pym, having published six novels appreciated by a small but faithful audience, suddenly found her seventh work refused by her publisher. She wrote nothing else for some sixteen years until she was "discovered" in a March 11, 1977, *Times Literary Supplement* feature on underrated and overrated writers of the past seventy-five years as evaluated by a symposium of literary critics. Lauded by Lord David Cecil and Philip Larkin, she was the only writer to be twice praised. Subsequently, she re-emerged with *Quartet in Autumn* (1977), saw all of her books reissued, enjoyed success in America—including the admiration of *Newsweek* (October 23, 1978), a short story in *The New Yorker* (July 16, 1979), and publication by Vanguard, Dutton, Harper and Row, and Macmillan, and became "the in-thing to read" in Britain. Miss Pym died on January 11, 1980, and her final two novels, *The Sweet Dove Died* (1978) and *A Few Green Leaves* (1980), were published posthumously. Recently (1982), the rejected book, *An Unsuitable Attachment,* discovered among her papers, has been published to bring her canon to ten novels.

The predominant critical assessment finds Pym a "domesticated" Jane Austen, and reviewers make much of her diminished scale and wry sense of humor in *novels of manners.* They also promote her as the depictor of English spinsterhood and as something of a man-hater. In the latter regard, for example, Karl Miller suggests that her work is "grist to the feminist mill." However, her attitudes toward spinsters and men, as well as toward non-spinsters, need reassessment. She is keenly aware, in each of her novels, of the drab, pathetic-seeming lives of her contemporary middle-class Englishmen, men and women. The same nonjudging, reporting eye lays all of them before us in detailed portraiture. The ironic comment falls where it may, and the most telling evidence of her own spinsterhood resides in a general tendency to avoid depicting motherhood in her novels. Even so, she can be mildly censorious of the childless; in *An Unsuitable Attachment,* Sophia Ainger, who is married but has no offspring, is fixated, humorously, on her cat, Faustina. If Pym's fictional world teems with spinsters, she makes us believe, without suspicion of her miscalculation, that the reason is simple: here is England as it really is.

There are spinsters in Pym's world—and then there are spinsters. Her heroines are seldom old maids because they have no other choice. In her first novel, *Some Tame Gazelle,* Harriet Bede receives constant proposals from Count Bianco and is wooed by the librarian, Mr. Mold. The elder and more spinsterish Belinda Bede is proposed to by Bishop Grote. Both women, who are in their sixties, decline. By *An Unsuitable Attachment,* they have fulfilled their richest dream and have removed to a villa in Italy with a sickly clergyman under their protection. In *Excellent Women,* whose title refers to the church-fixated "elderly ladies and dim spinsters" throughout England, Mildred Lathbury, just over thirty, is attracted to the already married Rockingham Napier, might "after a decent interval" finally marry Father Julian Malory, and at the end seems sure to get anthropologist Everard Bone. In *Jane and Prudence,* the first title character is already married to a clergyman; and the second, who is twenty-nine, has had a constant march of admirers. Although she loses Fabian Driver to the much older spinster, Jessie Morrow, she is at the last "overwhelmed by the richness of her life"—Manifold, Dr. Grampian, and even Edward Lyall, "M.P." In *Less Than Angels,* Catherine Oliphant, who is thirty-one, loses Tom Mallow to Deirdre Swan as perhaps Elaine, the first love, who raises golden retrievers, has lost him to her. In turn, Catherine enlivens the dull life of another would-be anthropologist, Alaric Lydgate, whom she will most likely marry. Deirdre gets Digby Fox, and Elaine gets to keep her memories intact and to know that Tom was writing her just before he died. In *A Glass of Blessings,* Wilmet, who is already married, is forced to reappraise her seemingly routine life and dull husband after her abortive flings with the spouse of her best friend and with Rowena's homosexual brother, Piers Longridge, after her husband Rodney admits his own misconduct, and after dowdy spinster Mary Beamish manages to pull off the feat of marrying handsome Father Ransome. In *No Fond Return of Love,* Dulcie Mainwaring, in her early thirties, is rejected by her fiancé because of her "simple goodness," which is too hard to live with, but, at the end, it is obvious that she will get the much more desirable Aylwin

Forbes. In *An Unsuitable Attachment,* one of the liaisons referred to by the title is the eventual marriage of spinster Ianthe Broome and the younger John Challow; and the satire is directed toward those who find the attachment unsuitable. The same novel leaves us anticipating a wedding between Rupert Stonebird and Penelope Grandison. In *A Few Green Leaves,* career woman Emma Howick never gets Graham Pettifer, though they have some kind of a relationship, but she is on her way to getting Tom Dagnall, the rector of the Oxfordshire village where she goes to write.

The two women in *Quartet in Autumn* are the only true spinsters among the main characters in the entire Pym canon, and Letty is one of her most delightful creations. Even Marcia might have had a relationship with Norman. As it is, her senility and eccentricity show the dangers of walling oneself off from other humans rather than spinsterism per se. The two men in the book, Edwin and Norman, suffer nearly as much from their willful isolationism. Always, life in the Pym world, whether she is depicting male or female, is largely what one makes it. Its "greyness," the predominant color reference in the novels, particularly *Quartet in Autumn,* can be interpreted and lived out either positively or negatively. For example, in *A Few Green Leaves,* Emma, pondering the meaning of a letter from Graham and life's "few twists to the man-woman story," is drawn to consider the telephone as a means of clarifying their relationship: "Its fashionable shade of grey suggested peace and repose, (unless one thought of grey as the colour of desolation, which it might also be)."

Perhaps Pym's least sympathetic character is Leonora Eyre of *The Sweet Dove Died.* Now approaching fifty, she could have made "brilliant marriages" but has chosen instead a life of culture aloof from *common* people, and she tends to recreate those around her in her own image. James, over twenty years her junior, is the "sweet dove" of the title. He escapes her briefly in a liaison with Ned, an American his own age, but is finally recaptured "like an animal being enticed back into its cage." Clearly, some of Pym's spinsters not only willfully choose their spinsterhood but use it deliberately to set their lives and the lives of others as they wish them to be.

Prior to their emergence from the role of spinster, Pym's heroines are as closely involved as are their sisters, the countless number of British women who do not marry in the novels, in the world of the clergy. This association may well be one cause for the criticism that Pym is unsympathetic to men, for her clergymen are, by and large, rather despicable. What is overlooked, however, is the fact that the relationship is symbiotic. The men of the cloth are perceived as being comfortable with spinsters and widows, feel that gifts of knitted socks and various delicacies are their just due, and, like Archbishop Hoccleve in *Some Tame Gazelle,* are hurt when they are not forthcoming. Even a man, Aylwin Forbes in *No Fond Return of Love,* recognizes that "all men connected with the Church . . . would be at ease with ladies." On the other hand, as Viola Dace points out, they are rather at the mercy of the female sex. For their part, the women, with some exceptions, find fulfillment in doing church work and catering to the needs of the clergy, whom they prefer to be unmarried. It is in fact a woman, Jane of *Jane and Prudence,* who wonders that the village women did not tear the assistant vicar to pieces when they discovered that he came to them already engaged. Harriet Bede's life in *Some Tame Gazelle* is measured out in terms of the arrival of the next young clergyman, and her whole sense of the fitness of things has been predetermined by a girlish vision of the tall, pale man who would be her husband and who is best exemplified by clergymen.

Middle-aged spinsters are the backbone of the English parish. They do get used, but most of them believe that women need to feel needed, a theme that is as true of Pym's last books as it is of the early ones (e.g., *No Fond Return of Love* and *A Glass of Blessings*). Moreover, Pym's men need to feel needed, too. If Tom Dagnall, the rector in *A Few Green Leaves,* appropriates all of the women at his disposal, including his sister, Daphne, his selfishness is unpremeditated. They are simply there to be used, not only to decorate for the various church festivals and polish the brass to a high luster but to further his true passion, local history. In truth, Tom is no more selfish in sending Magdalen Raven among the gravestones and through the church register to check dates for the custom of burying in wool than is her son-in-law, Martin Shrubsole, who finds her an interesting case study for his specialty of geriatrics, as well as a live-in baby-sitter. Tom automatically adds the new arrival, Emma Howick, to his group of workers—doubtless she can type and perhaps even decipher Elizabethan handwriting—just as he hopes to pick the brains of Miss Vereker about life at the manor house and of Miss Lickerish about the ancient customs of the village. What is often overlooked is the fact that Emma uses in her turn. Having come here to write up her research on one of the new English towns, she finds herself taking notes on the villagers with an eye toward a publication about them; in this respect, she is much akin to Jean-Pierre le Rossignol of *Less Than Angels,* who goes about minutely observing the habits of the English. Clearly, in Pym's novels, using and being used are not confined to a particular sex.

Barbara Pym is atypical in her treatment of spinsters and of women in general. Most of her major female characters are employed: Emma Howick (*A Few Green Leaves*) and Helena Napier (*Excellent Women*) are anthropologists; Prudence Bates (*Jane and Prudence*) works for some kind of cultural organization; Catherine Oliphant (*Less Than Angels*) is a writer; Marcia and Letty (*Quartet in Autumn*)

work in an office; Dulcie Mainwaring and Viola Dace (*No Fond Return of Love*) and Penelope Grandison (*An Unsuitable Attachment*) have vague connections with the publishing world; Mildred Lathbury (*Excellent Women*) works part-time to help impoverished gentlewomen; Leonora Eyre (*The Sweet Dove Died*) has done "secret work" in the south of England prior to the invasion of Normandy; and Ianthe Broome (*An Unsuitable Attachment*) is a librarian. Only Jane (*Jane and Prudence*), Sophia (*An Unsuitable Attachment*), and Wilmet (*A Glass of Blessings*) are married and do not work, although Jane's and Sophia's roles as clergymen's wives, properly executed, would constitute careers. The fact that they do not successfully carry out their duties is evidence of Pym's objectivity. Their husbands are equally limited. Similarly, Wilmet's idleness produces feelings of guilt and uselessness and leads her to largely imagined betrayals of her husband, who is also flawed. Ultimately, we begin to suspect that Pym's assessments of her characters are most influenced by the work ethic of England under attack and by her own intense involvement with the Women's Royal Naval Service (1943-46) and sense of vocation as Assistant Editor of *Africa,* the journal of the International African Institute, also a probable source for her novels' interest in anthropology. Hers is a general *human* as opposed to a chauvinistic stance for male or female.

Though she is largely a pre-Feminist Movement author who finds fault on both sides of the battle between the sexes, Pym is aware of the traditional limitations society imposes on women. Thus Mildred Lathbury is delighted at the success of Ethel Victoria Thorneycroft Nollard in 1907—"a woman then!" Prudence wonders if Miss Birkinshaw has had a splendid tragic romance in the past or is a "new woman" rejecting marriage for Donne, Marvell, and Carew. At any rate, her "great work" on the Metaphysicals remains unfinished, and Pym suggests that the fault is his own. Women's careers, nonetheless, do seem to get in the way of relationships as Tom, of *Less Than Angels,* seeks solace with Deirdre (a budding anthropologist—a "new" profession) because Catherine is writing a story and has no time for him. At Graham's for a drink, Emma, who thinks up "The Role of Women in a West Oxfordshire Community" as a book title, becomes bored and wishes she were alone doing her own work. When she decides to go and do just that, Graham feels that she must be accompanied home, for women are "not yet as equal as all that." In *Less Than Angels,* contrastingly, when Digby worries that he and Mark should have seen Deirdre home, the latter tells him that "women consider themselves our equals now"; in *No Fond Return of Love,* Sedge makes Viola feel like a woman even in the days of so-called equality. Pym's books present a time when "women were more likely to go off to Africa to shoot lions as a cure for unrequited love . . . [,] in the old days . . . a man's privilege." Still, according to *Jane and Prudence,* the only place where women take full precedence is in the announcement of their marriages in their school chronicles, and Mary Beamish, of *A Glass of Blessings,* is strongly opposed to the notion that women might sometime be admitted to Holy Orders. On the other hand, shy and quiet Belinda, of Pym's first novel, *Some Tame Gazelle* (1950), wishes that she could be "Deaconess Bede" and straighten out the church life of the village. Similarly, in *The Sweet Dove Died,* Leonora Eyre's entire character is set forth when she becomes piqued that events are taken out of her hands by having Humphrey invite her to lunch before she can "drop in" on his shop. The very feminine Dulcie Mainwaring is wise enough to want her niece to become interested in a subject like computer science rather than English or history or at the least not to become a secretary to a publisher (*No Fond Return of Love,* published in 1961).

> **Pym liked to upend sexual stereotypes before such a method was fashionable. Her women, accordingly, are likely to be complete domestic failures. . . .**
> **—*Lynn Veach Sadler***

Pym liked to upend sexual stereotypes before such a method was fashionable. Her women, accordingly, are likely to be complete domestic failures as are Jane (*Jane and Prudence*) and Winifred and Helena (*Excellent Women*). Jane and Daphne (*A Few Green Leaves*) also hate flower-arranging. Adam Prince would be horrified, for he is sure that all ladies can arrange flowers. When he was a priest, watching them do so was one of the activities he enjoyed most. Catherine Oliphant, of *Less Than Angels,* is an excellent cook and loves doing housework but primarily because she often gets her ideas for her writing while doing it. Dulcie feels that people are "nearer to the heart of things doing menial tasks" (*No Fond Return of Love*). Rocky Napier is the cook in his family, as well as the one who is fixated on collecting Victorian (*Excellent Women*); Wilf Bason discourses on the achievements of men as cooks (*A Glass of Blessings*); and Adam Prince is an inspector for a gourmet food magazine and frequently invades the woman's world of jumble sales (*A Few Green Leaves*). Yet in *The Sweet Dove Died,* Humphrey admonishes Leonora that book auctions are no place for a woman. Later, she slips away to sales without letting him know. When Mildred is with William Caldicote, who takes a "spiteful old-maidish delight in gossip" (*Excellent Women*), she has to buy her own mimosa and then share it with Rocky.

While there is much talk of the meticulosity of women's memories, it is they who sometimes forget important details of former love affairs in Pym's works. In *A Few Green Leaves,* Graham Pettifer sends Emma a postcard with a Corot painting that she used to like; she does not remem-

ber it at all. Pym's short story, **"Across a Crowded Room,"** itself a reversal of the song from which it takes its title, turns upon the revelation that the college mate whom the protagonist sees at Oxford for the first time in forty years has never been married, contrary to her memory of him. Further, as Aylwin Forbes tries to avoid Viola Dace in *No Fond Return of Love,* Miss Randall avoids him, stating that men do not realize "that they are not the only ones to be practising the avoidance." Dulcie herself believes that even if she were married, her character probably would not change very much, a view shared by Jessica Foy, who knows perfectly well that she and Dulcie would not allow a man to "mold" them. In some cases, quite the reverse is true, for Jessie Morrow in *Jane and Prudence* literally scares the very experienced Fabian Driver into marriage with such pronouncements as that women are very powerful and perhaps always triumph in the end. So persuasive is she that, though he feels the net closing around him, he is unable to escape it. Some men may be afflicted by female "maladies" as Driver and Lyall try to outdo each other in their verbalizations of their weariness. It is also the men who are most routine-driven; for example, William in *Excellent Women* can not survive a day without feeding the pigeons from his office window at precisely the same time.

The men in Pym's novels do tend to operate from a set of stereotypes about women. They plead that they can not understand females (e.g., Dr. Parnell in *Some Tame Gazelle;* Mary's brother in *A Glass of Blessings;* and Bone in *Excellent Women*). At the same time, they know that all women enjoy missing meals and becoming martyrs, as Archbishop Hoccleve says in *Some Tame Gazelle.* They believe that their "good ladies" should leave the talking to them and vote their way (Harry in *A Glass of Blessings*). They do not want their wives to work except for financial exigency lest they become the kind of women who step from trains carrying initialed briefcases and who prepare their brussel sprouts behind the filing cabinet. Nevertheless, they rely on the comfortable assumption that so much can be left to women, despite how ineffectual they are when a "simple tin" must be opened. Many men feel that women should not drink before a meal (e.g., Cash in *A Glass of Blessings*), and practically all of them are convinced that women cannot appreciate wine. Pym's exception is Catherine Oliphant, of *Less Than Angels,* who is a veritable oenologist and is always going into wine shops for the new lists, an activity that she shares with Alaric, who is her new interest. The other women do appear ignorant of the subject, to the extent that Adams advises Tom to slip in better wine for the church—the female treasurer would not know the difference.

According to Pym's men, women do not make as much of living and take their pleasures "very, very sadly." They get "sudden irrational passions," such as Helena's for Bone in

Excellent Women and "women's disorders" that not even a brother dare ask about (Tom on Daphne in *A Few Green Leaves*). Keeping busy is the panacea for their problems, and Nicholas, the curate—the reader is ever mindful that the clergy know all there is to know about women—thinks that Prudence, in addition to her job, should take up social work (*Jane and Prudence*). According to Neville, another clergyman, and Aylwin Forbes, women should not allow themselves to be seen very much (*No Fond Return of Love*), and the latter believes that they smoke more than men because of the emptiness of their lives. Men are, at the same time, disappointed if they do not have a profound effect on women; in *Less Than Angels,* not knowing how Elaine has labored to train herself to be restrained, Tom is hurt by her calmness at his kiss, and when he sees Prudence's tears, Arthur Grampian of *Jane and Prudence* is pleased that he still has his power over women. Piers Longridge, who is, one must admit, gay, finds women "so terrifying these days" and "expecting so much" (*A Glass of Blessings*); and Tom Mallow "marvels at the sharpness of even the nicest woman" (*Less Than Angels*). James feels "shut out" from the "feminine coziness" of Liz and Leonora (*The Sweet Dove Died*), while Rocky is opposed to the kind of women who "bring dry twigs and expect leaves to grow" (*Excellent Women*). Ultimately, however, where would we men be without "you ladies" to keep an eye on us?

Pym's women seem not only to perpetuate these stereotypes but to fuel them, aiding and abetting with great zest. They may display a certain cynicism about the view that "every woman is supposed to be able to turn her hand to an omelette" (*A Few Green Leaves*) but, deep down, they believe it. There is, especially, a certain animus between married and unmarried women that has its effect in turn on the stereotype of the spinster. It pervades the media as Mildred Lathbury (*Excellent Women*) listens to a program on the wireless that pits the two groups of women against each other. She does not know whether spinsters are really more inquisitive than married women, but she feels keenly her inadequacy and inexperience in a discussion with Helena, who is married. She thinks that surely wives, particularly Helena, the wife of Rockingham Napier, should not be too busy to cook and should be waiting at home when their husbands return from wars; certainly, if she were Rocky's wife . . ., the implication is. On the other hand, when Viola Dace proclaims that Marjorie Forbes has failed as a wife because she could not share Aylwin's work, Dulcie poses the possibility that the men could be at fault in such cases for choosing unsuitable wives (*No Fond Return of Love*). But in *Less Than Angels,* Catherine ponders the "general uselessness of women if they can't understand or reverence a man's work or even if they can," while Rhoda knows that Alaric and Catherine's cutting of rhubarb from his garden contain's a "subtlety" that only an unmarried woman can fully appreciate.

Allegra Gray, who is a widow, a category of women for which Mildred Lathbury has an inexplicable distrust, asks, "What do women do if they don't marry?" (*Excellent Women*), and Helena Napier wounds Mildred with her claim that the spinster's is "not a full life in the accepted sense." Mrs. Morris lacerates further with her proclamation that it is "not natural" for a woman to live alone without a husband. Though Mildred points out that women often have no choice, she knows that it is never the "excellent women" who marry but the Allegras and Helenas of the world. She and Dora try to believe that marriage is not everything, but they confess that they live by the fiction that they do not know anyone *at the moment* whom they want to marry. Mildred also muses about the new-found freedom of the wife of the president of the Learned Society, whose death has suddenly removed her from the burden of sleeping through its boring meetings. Unfortunately, Mildred realizes, he has left her nothing to occupy her old age, not even an understanding of his career of anthropology. Worse, perhaps, is the plight of the women who help their husbands through school only to be thrown out one day and to accept their banishment as fate (*Less Than Angels*). Nonetheless, her husband's key in the lock is the sound every wife loves most (*A Glass of Blessings*). But if Mildred ever writes a novel, it will be in the stream of consciousness mode and about an hour in the life of a woman at the sink (*Excellent Women*). The unmarried women stand judged of not "making the most of themselves" (*No Fond Return of Love*). They expect very little (almost nothing) and are not really first in anyone's life, easily becoming unwanted. Everything becomes their business, for they have none of their own. Probably their greatest problem is that they come to distrust their own instincts and intelligence and fall into accord with their stereotypes. Thus when Belinda thinks that Bishop Grote's hand lingers over hers, she dismisses her observation as the kind imagined by middle-aged spinsters (*Some Tame Gazelle*).

Pym women will let themselves endure "a real woman's evening" such as a silly play (*A Glass of Blessings*), eat "women's meals"—a scrap of cheese and some wilted lettuce in contrast to the "small plover" (*Excellent Women*) a man would cook for himself, and take trouble with such "a woman's fruit" as gooseberries or rhubarb, "sour and difficult things" (*A Glass of Blessings*). Through it all, their great strength is the ability to assume a "Patience-on-a-monument" attitude (*Excellent Women*). Everyone knows, after all, that men are more difficult to please, while women bear their burdens without complaining and accept blame, the "better and easier part" (*Some Tame Gazelle*). In *A Few Green Leaves,* Emma points out that an old woman would be too considerate to die on an outing. Minor rebellions against their lot only seem to cause more damage, as when Deirdre tells Tom that she loves him, despite the fact that women should never take the initiative (*Less Than Angels*).

Yet the consequences of not acting may be worse. Thirty years too late, Belinda of *Some Tame Gazelle* discovers that Agatha married Hoccleve away from her by doing the asking. She now pushes her niece to get Reverend Donne by the same method.

As one of the older women observes in *Less Than Angels,* however much progress is made in the education of women, love cannot be kept out of their lives. Whether love or no, one can not say for sure, but something enables women to do "strange and wonderful and splendid" things for men, and their "love and imagination" do transform those otherwise "unremarkable beings" (*Jane and Prudence*). Why, then, Pym seems to ask, if women are so often able to "arrange things that men would have thought impossible" (*No Fond Return of Love*), do they suddenly become Wilmets and turn away from the sight of meat with "womanly delicacy" (*A Glass of Blessings*)?

Men also come in for their share of Pym's genial ridicule and humor. Victoria Glendinning speaks of her method, in *Excellent Women,* as "not the steel jab of feminism, merely a mild, fine irony toward the ways of the world." Yet she feels that the men are generally sticks and that it is Pym's women, not them, who matter. Philip Larkin finds the men often "insensitive," "automatically stingy," or "simply selfish" and concludes: "Miss Pym's novels may look like 'women's books,' but no man can read them and be quite the same again." The point is, however, that Pym's men are as trapped in their stereotypes as are the spinsters who outnumber them. She seems almost to excuse them as products of women's systematizing and stereotyping; for example, James feels "created" by Leonora at times in *The Sweet Dove Died.* Pym women proclaim men too weak to endure loneliness although they are less gregarious than women; they do not tend to be alone and usually do marry. Many of them habitually choose the wrong wife because they subconsciously do not want what is good for them (*No Fond Return of Love*). It is much more painful to see them in tears, as it would be far worse to think that a man, rather than Miss Limpsett, brought a vase of pussy willows into the office (*A Glass of Blessings*). They have little concentration and will-power and can not "get on" without the help of a strong woman (*Less Than Angels*). Perhaps this flaw accounts for Wilmet's being more at ease interrupting the conversations of men rather than women (*A Glass of Blessings*). The salient stereotype, however, is that men are like children. Also, they do not usually do things unless they like doing them, and they leave difficulties to be solved by other people or to solve themselves. Lacking subtlety and daintiness, they can not see the "dog beneath the skin," the "terrible depths," and thus are often taken in by a pretty face. They are "all alike" (*Excellent Women*) and "only want one thing" (*Jane and Prudence*), but, perhaps because Pym's characters are not the kind to talk about sex, men's desires

are more often treated in terms of food. Graham Pettifer's utter selfishness can best be shown in *A Few Green Leaves* by his taking away all of the tomatoes, including the green ones; Emma is left to imagine his wife preparing them and to think of the small bit of fondling she and Graham once did on the grass.

Pym's men do not think about time—they simply expect their meals to appear and look upon them as their due. They *must* have meat, need eggs, a *cooked* breakfast and lots of food at all times, and could hardly be served *tinned* salmon. After dinner, they must be left to port and "manly conversation," and it is perfectly all right for them to talk shop while the women talk about domestic matters and babies. They even do "more manly shopping" (e.g., for paraffin and garden supplies) than women. They are "tweedy" and "pipe-smoking" and do carpentry on weekends. Landladies object to them on principle (*No Fond Return of Love*), and many of Pym's women dislike their pipes (Prudence in *Jane and Prudence* and Wilmet in *A Glass of Blessings*). Not "going in" for poetry much themselves, they do not like women who read. They also can not deal with women's effusiveness about their emotions. Tom, for example, of *Less Than Angels,* is very embarrassed when Catherine sings about the lotus and about finding Nirvana in his arms. If the question of blame is a real chicken-and-egg conundrum, one infers that Pym's women could not be in their present plights without large doses of their own conniving.

Occasionally, even the most accepting Pym woman gets a little huffy about men's insensitivity. Mildred refuses Bone's invitation to dinner because she knows that he could expect her to cook the meat, and she is sure that men are not so helpless and pathetic as women believe and that, on the whole, they run their lives better than women. Rowena, of *A Glass of Blessings,* wants to cook exotic dishes but is prevented from doing so by the "tyranny" and plebian tastes of her husband and children. At least her Harry is one of the nonintelligent men whom women find so much more comfortable than "tortured intellectuals." Then there are the quite reasonable questions of why they are so good at cooking but can not ever clean up behind themselves, and why men, especially those connected with the church, never seem to help women. Husbands take women's friends away and change them, often beyond recognition. Young Deirdre Swan is now clever and moody as her mother was before marriage to a "good dull man" and life in a suburb "steadied" her (*Less Than Angels*).

Worse, men remain enigmatical and unpredictable. Women never know what they are feeling and "can't hope to know all that goes on in a man's life or follow him with their loving thoughts." According to Rose Culver, a very minor character in *The Sweet Dove Died* and one who obviously has an ax to grind, the odd thing about men is that one never really knows them; just when women think true closeness has been achieved, they suddenly take flight. Even Mildred Lathbury wonders if any man is really worth such a burden after she offers to do Bone's index and proofs. Her answer is "probably not." Once in a while, a Pym woman will decide that a man should not expect her to do quite everything for him, and the Allegra Grays of the world—who do not belong to the category of "excellent women"—will give men the opportunity for self-sacrifice, their natures being so much less noble than those of women (*Excellent Women*). They are not supposed to notice what women wear, but Driver gives Jessie quite a start in *Jane and Prudence* when he recalls that his wife Constance had a dress very like the one she is wearing—it is Constance's dress. Once again, men display their penchant for being contrary.

The most obtuse man will sometimes let out that he knows women's tyranny; Archbishop Hoccleve, for example, offers the opinion that it is wiser for a man to stay single, for it then would not matter if he is late to lunch (*Some Tame Gazelle*). Men and women appear to muddle on, with people in general not seeming any happier or the relations between the sexes any better than they used to be (*Less Than Angels,* published in 1955). Indeed, the interrelations of men and women are often ridiculous, as Beatrix Howick points out in *A Few Green Leaves,* and there are times when men band against women and women against men. Grace Williton reaches the point of wondering why people bother to marry—marriage only causes trouble for them and for their kin (*No Fond Return of Love*).

> **In the Pym world, bores and boors can be male and female, and men can out-spinster spinsters.**
> —*Lynn Veach Sadler*

Given the hiatus in the relationships between the sexes, women often seek friendships with other women and see them as a great comfort, a theme that pervades many of the novels, and the least pleasant of Pym's females are the ones who reject this view. Leonora of *The Sweet Dove Died* and Wilmet of *A Glass of Blessings* are the two major female characters seen as inhuman, unemotional, and "fossilized" by those around them. Leonora does not like to be kissed by another woman (or a man, for that matter), has little use for the "coziness" of female friends (whom she regards as foils to herself), and is contemptuous of the type of woman who is always too early. She is late for her lunch with Meg, but not as late as if she were meeting a man. (It is before a woman, nonetheless, that Leonora finally "breaks down.") Wilmet refuses to be one of those women who share confidences and tries to remain aloof from good Mary Beamish. She does later learn what a "splendid and wonderful thing"

the friendship of a woman is when she is forgiven by Rowena for Harry's interest in her. Nevertheless, Pym's women are often catty about one another and about their sex in general and usually think the worst of each other. Letty in *Quartet in Autumn* sees Marcia's leaving her house to Norman as the perfect example of the unpredictability of women, and Letty is perhaps the kindest character in any of the novels. Leonora classes Rose Culver as one of those women who live alone and who do not always realize what they are saying (*The Sweet Dove Died*), and it is the women who assume that Harriet Bede's fur cape is actually "shaved coney" (*Some Tame Gazelle*). Once again, people are their own worst enemies, Pym suggests; there is nothing in the order of existence to mandate that the world or the two sexes be so. In the Pym world, bores and boors can be male and female, and men can out-spinster spinsters. Accordingly, we finish each book with the same sensation as that expressed by Sophia Ainger in *An Unsuitable Attachment:* "The lemon leaves had been unwrapped and there were the fragrant raisins at the heart."

Margaret Diane Stetz (essay date Spring 1985)

SOURCE: "*Quartet in Autumn:* New Light on Barbara Pym as a Modernist," in *Arizona Quarterly,* Vol. 41, No. 1, Spring, 1985, pp. 24-37.

[*In the following essay, Stetz challenges conventional comparisons between Pym and Jane Austen, noting modernist themes in* Quartet in Autumn *that bear resemblance to the writing of Virginia Woolf instead.*]

Clichés about novelists and their art are like bloodstains; once they have been allowed to stand, they are almost impossible to eradicate. Among the most common and persistent errors in criticism today is the assertion that Barbara Pym's books are "just like" Jane Austen's. Critics point to their shared interest in comedy of manners, their wit, and most of all their style, implying that Pym makes little or no use of literary techniques devised since Austen's time. In fact, as an examination of one of her late novels, *Quartet in Autumn* (1977), shows, her narrative devices owe more to Virginia Woolf than to Austen. There are, as it happens, superficial resemblances between Pym's novel and Woolf's *Mrs. Dalloway;* in each, London is as much a participant in, as a setting for, the plot; a mad protagonist wills his or her own death; individuals are pitted against an interfering social system that must be resisted; there is a final social gathering that brings together most of the disparate thematic elements, as well as the major characters. Such similarities, however, are trivial; more important is their shared attitude toward the proper focus of fiction. In Pym's novel, as in Woolf's, actions and external events count for little. What matters in *Quartet in Autumn,* as in the fiction of Woolf and other modernists, is consciousness itself. The methods used by Pym to convey a character's consciousness are not exclusively those of an Austenian novelist of manners (i.e., gesture and dialogue) but those of a modernist—simultaneity, association, imagery, memory, and dreams.

Perhaps the single most telling characteristic that distinguishes an experimental twentieth-century writer is treatment of time. To a conventional novelist following in the tradition of Austen, time means merely chronological progression—one action succeeding another; to a modernist, time is something that can be reversed, sped up, or stretched infinitely. In Pym's hands, time is malleable. A single moment may be made to last throughout a chapter. Quite often in *Quartet in Autumn,* we find that the successive scenes depicted are not occurring consecutively, but simultaneously. Chronology is suspended, so that we can be present as the same period of time is experienced in four different places and from four points of view. Thus in chapter 10, the account of Marcia's holiday takes us through Christmas Day at her neighbors' house and on to Boxing Day. But after the section describing her behavior and reactions ends, the next scene does not occur, as we might expect it to, on December 27. Instead, time moves backwards to the chapter's starting point, to Christmas Day as Letty sees it at Mrs. Pope's house. The pattern is repeated in the scene following this one, as once again we return to the dinner hour on Christmas Day, although the central figure now is Norman. The chapter's closing scene does, at last, bring us forward to December 27 (Pym makes a point of mentioning the date); but the main actor here is Edwin, whose reflections on the past two days spent with his daughter are summarized for us.

The purpose of this sort of juggling with time is to turn the audience's attention away from storytelling and to focus it upon revelations of consciousness. As this pattern recurs, we stop expecting to be told what happens next; rather, we wait to receive from the four main characters in turn their impressions of their situations, all of which are occupying the same moment in time. The internal lives of the "quartet" become the center of interest, while external events recede into the background. Suspending forward movement allows Pym to achieve a sense of simultaneity, such as Woolf aimed at in *Mrs. Dalloway,* of multiple consciousnesses existing independently, but inhabiting the same stretch of time. It enables her to broaden the notion of the "protagonist" as well. Here we are not following the change and development of a single figure, but of four separate characters of equal importance, whose inner lives sometimes intertwine and sometimes move apart, while always operating contemporaneously.

Nothing, however, shows more clearly Pym's familiarity with modernist techniques than her way of linking scenes. The shifts in time, as well as the changes from one character's point of view to another's, are accomplished not by means of narrative intrusion, but through association of ideas. The reader must find the connections for himself, without the aid of an editorializing voice to explain them. When Jane Austen wished to create a link between two separate episodes, her narrator instructed us explicitly in how to draw them together: "She entered the Rooms on Thursday evening with feelings very different from what had attended her thither the Monday before. She had then been exulting in her engagement to Thorpe, and was now chiefly anxious to avoid his sight, lest he should engage her again . . ." (*Northanger Abbey*, chap. 10). The common ground—here, the comparison of past and present emotions—was laid out for us. But Pym's method is very different, as we see in *Quartet in Autumn.* In chapter 6, for instance, Letty, who is about to be homeless, reflects upon her dilemma as a scene ends:

> That night, as she lay in bed finding it difficult to sleep, the whole of her life seemed to unroll before her like that of a drowning man . . . is said to do, she thought, for of course her experience did not extend to drowning and it was unlikely that it ever would. Death, when it came, would present itself in another guise, something more "suitable" for a person like herself, for where would she ever be likely to be in danger of death by drowning? (Ellipsis in original)

The next sentence, however, places us abruptly in a new setting (the office in which all four of the main figures work), a new time (the following day), and a new point of view (Norman's). Nevertheless, the transition becomes quite seamless, because it is made by means of association, through a second cliché involving water. As the scene opens, Norman, who has also been pondering Letty's problem, tells her, "It never rains but it pours." The coincidence of two minds drawing upon related figures of speech bridges the gap between the scenes.

Similarly, in the "Christmas" chapter, the movement from Letty's experiences to Norman's is accomplished through a momentary alignment of feeling, if not of thought. In the after-dinner gloom of Mrs. Pope's house, Letty grows bored and frustrated, until she remembers that the larger shops will be having their sales soon, hence, that she can while away her time by making purchases; then, we are told, "her spirits suddenly lifted." With the very next sentence, we leap to Norman's Christmas dinner at his brother-in-law's, where we find him speaking "with unusual jollity." Although the circumstances and the causes are different, the emotion is the same, and it provides a connection between the characters that eases us out of Letty's world and into Norman's.

Perhaps the most extended use of this kind of linking occurs in chapter 19, as Marcia lies dying in the hospital. Letty discusses with Mrs. Pope the question of what to send her former co-worker, deciding first upon a book, then "on a bottle of lavender water, the kind of thing that could be dashed on the brow of a patient not allowed visitors," as her reflections conclude. The scene that follows immediately plunges us into the consciousness of a character whose mind we have not entered before, Dr. Strong, the surgeon treating Marcia. The leap is accomplished by means of Letty's gift, which must have arrived and been put to use:

> Lavender. Mr Strong detected the scent of it above the hospital smells. It reminded him of his grandmother, not at all the kind of thing one associated with Miss Ivory, but on the other hand why should he have been surprised that Miss Ivory should smell of lavender? The really surprising thing was that he should have noticed anything at all like that about a patient, but the scent, that powerful evocator of memory, had caught him unaware, and for a brief moment he—consultant surgeon at this eminent London teaching hospital and with a lucrative private practice in Harley Street—was a boy of seven again.

The smell of lavender becomes a stimulus for the workings of involuntary memory and a means by which Pym can fill in somewhat the otherwise sketchy portrait of the doctor. Later in this scene, however, the sensation of the lavender water, "a cool, wet feeling on her forehead," also provides a transition out of Mr. Strong's consciousness and into Marcia's. Thus, in these three brief paragraphs we move through three different minds. Although we receive no guidance from the narrator, each shift in point of view is easy to follow, yoked as it is to something tangible (i.e., the lavender water).

Unlike a novel by Austen, which is always built on a single, continuous plot line and held together by a sustained narrative tone of voice, *Quartet in Autumn* is composed of bits and pieces such as those above: short sequences, isolated reflections, episodes involving little or no action, and conversations that appear to be exchanges of non sequiturs. The chapters themselves are extremely brief, often a mere five or six pages in length, and are divided, as in the preceding example, into separate scenes of less than one page each. To create unity out of these fragments, however, Pym does not rely on consistent tone, as Austen would; indeed, the narrator here is almost invisible and is certainly never a personality in her own right. Instead, the unity of the novel as a whole derives largely from the repetition of words, phrases, and even of imagery, as in a poem. Again, this is a technique uncommon in conventional comedy of manners, but quite the rule in modernist fiction. In *Mrs. Dalloway,*

for instance, the recurrence at regular intervals of a line from Shakespeare's *Cymbeline* ("Fear no more the heat o' the sun") or of the description of Big Ben's chimes ("The leaden circles dissolved in the air") creates an effect of continuity and circularity. In *Quartet in Autumn,* too, the insistent repetition of numerous motifs gives the reader something familiar to hold onto amid the shifts and digressions.

Several of these motifs are associated with Marcia, who unwittingly acts as the agent drawing together the quartet: first, as the "problem" to which the other three must react; then, after her death, as the giver of the house around which a new circle may be formed (with Letty's friend, Marjorie, in her place). Marcia's frequent declaration, "I've never been a big eater," rings throughout the novel, acquiring an ironic significance as she deliberately starves herself. By the end, however, the phrase has also become a bond between the dead Marcia and Norman, the inheritor of her house. Repeating it allows Norman, usually the least sentimental member of the group, to express his hitherto unsuspected feelings for her. On the first occasion, at the meal after her funeral, we are told that "Norman's voice seemed as if it might break on these words but he controlled himself." In the final scene of the novel, his reminder to the others— "Never a big eater, she used to say"—serves to invoke her presence and to reunite in spirit the members of the original quartet, the survivors of which are gathered in Marcia's kitchen.

Similarly, Marcia's cryptic assertions that she has had "a major operation" and had "something removed" (her euphemisms for a mastectomy) provide a focus for thought throughout the novel, both for herself and others. Edwin and Norman discuss her operation; Edwin speculates about it, as he passes a magazine stand covered with photographs of bare bosoms; Marcia herself feels, with mingled pride and embarrassment, that it sets her apart from her co-workers at the retirement party; it even becomes a topic of conversation at the quartet's last luncheon together. Occasions that are unrelated in terms of action prove to be linked through a sort of congruence of consciousness, as the minds of the characters return again and again to a few key ideas.

Perhaps the most important motif is one suggested by the novel's title. Associations, both obvious and obscure, with autumn dominate the book. Despite the juggling of time in individual episodes, the general movement of *Quartet in Autumn* is circular. Indeed, this is a novel about four inner lives set not merely against social backgrounds, but against the natural changes of the seasons, beginning one spring and ending in October of the following year. The season is more than scenery alone; it is also a source of recurring figures of speech. When Norman adds up the days of leave from work owed to him, we are told that "he felt that those extra days would never be needed, but would accumulate like a pile of dead leaves drifting on to the pavement in autumn." Later, the correspondence between the cycles of nature and the life cycles of the characters is emphasized by the narrator's remarks "on the retirement of Letty and Marcia, which seemed as inevitable as the falling of the leaves in autumn, for which no kind of preparation needed to be made." The cliché about the old as being "in the autumn of their lives" is made new again by Pym. The similes involving fading and falling leaves serve for us, as much as for the character of Letty, as "reminders of her own mortality or, regarded less poetically, the different stages towards death." In *Mrs. Dalloway,* Clarissa's frequent meditations upon death, which occur even during her happiest moments, steel the audience psychologically against the shock of Septimus's later suicide. In Pym's novel, too, the insistent use of figurative language that draws upon death keeps us continually aware of the characters' plight and prepares us, in particular, for Marcia's end.

From the notion of natural decay and disintegration comes a host of references to falling. On one occasion, the quartet ponders the situation of an old woman living in the streets, a person whom Norman describes as "a good example of somebody who's fallen through the net of the welfare state." With ironic prescience, he then announces heartily, "Oh, well, that's another thing we've all got coming to us, or at least the possibility—falling through the net of the welfare state." By the novel's end, of course, it is Marcia who has fulfilled the prediction; Janice Brabner, the social worker, thinks to herself, "Miss [Marcia] Ivory might be said to have fallen through the net, that dreaded phrase. . . ." A discussion of falling also ensues when Letty searches for new lodgings. Initially, Mrs. Pope takes her in to calm her own fears of being alone in an emergency: "If one fell downstairs or tripped over a rug and was unable to get up . . ." she says, unwilling to complete the thought. Letty, in turn, independently raises the same subject during her first night at Mrs. Pope's house: "In the sleepless hours she heard footsteps on the landing and a sudden thump. Supposing Mrs Pope had a fall? She was an elderly person and heavy—lifting her would be difficult." The next day, Norman, whose greatest pleasure lies in gloomy imaginings, warns Letty about living with Mrs. Pope: "You must watch out that you don't get landed with an elderly person and all *that* entails . . . she might fall, you know." Letty's answer, which contains both a literal and a symbolic truth, hints at the reason for all this talk of falling: "'Yes, that thought came to me in the night,' said Letty, 'but it might happen to anyone. We could all fall.'" The narrator's terse comment upon this remark—"Nobody seemed inclined to go into the deeper implications of what Letty had just said"—reminds us discreetly that there are indeed deeper implications and that death is never far away in this novel. The awareness of its approach is, ultimately, what brings together these four aging people. In the same way, our recognition of it as a con-

stant presence helps to bring together the book's many small episodes into a whole. Death as an action gives the novel a plot; but its repeated use in imagery and in figurative language gives *Quartet in Autumn* something far more important in a modernist novel, a unified texture, that acts upon us subliminally.

To a modernist, as opposed to a novelist of manners in the mold of Austen, such appeals to the subconscious are indispensable. Indeed, consciousness itself is defined by modernists as an amalgam of rational thoughts and of those below the level of reason. A twentieth-century psychological novelist usually will try to engage all of the reader's levels of perception and, in turn, to display both the conscious and subconscious impulses of the fictional characters.

In *Quartet in Autumn,* we do know about the four principal figures what a conventional novelist of manners would tell us: their ages: their physical characteristics; their ways of dressing, speaking, and moving; their tastes; their social positions. We know, too, their intellectual judgments, their opinions of each other in particular and of the world at large. But we learn more than this. We also receive frequent glimpses of their subconscious or only half-conscious feelings and perceptions. Such information does not help to place them on any scale of good or bad conduct, whether moral or social; neither does it advance the action of the novel. Its sole function is to convey consciousness itself. The assumption behind its use is a modernist one, that speech and gesture are insufficient guides to character, because each human personality is a jumble of memories, dreams, and daydreams that are never made visible to others.

Pym's depiction of consciousness varies from situation to situation. There are, on the one hand, many scenes that offer us only the quartet's most logical and coherent thoughts, those which, though left unspoken, could easily be articulated. When, for example, Marcia turns up in an eccentric outfit, the narrator relates the impressions of each of her co-workers:

> Edwin, who was not particularly observant, did realise that she was wearing an odd assortment of garments but did not think she looked much different from usual. Norman thought, poor old girl, obviously going round the bend. Letty, as a clothes-conscious woman, was appalled—that anyone could get to the stage of caring so little about her appearance, of not even noticing how she looked. . . .

Here, thought is drawn upon in a straightforward, almost superficial, way, as a kind of shorthand. Presenting these contrasting reactions allows the narrator first to emphasize Marcia's strangeness and then to distinguish the temperaments of the three co-workers from one another, to "type" them. Thus, we can be both told and shown here that Edwin is unobservant and that Letty is vain.

But there are also passages in which a character's thoughts are pursued at length and in detail to create more complex effects, closer to those of stream-of-consciousness narration, which mirrors the involuntary movement of our mental processes. Such an instance occurs when Norman, wandering through London on his lunch hour, finds himself in a park. The incident is trivial in itself; the description of his thoughts during it has no bearing whatever upon the plot. The scene exists purely as a revelation of the workings of consciousness, as if to suggest that characterization is incomplete without such peeks into the private world of the mind:

> Norman gravitated towards the girls playing netball and sat down uneasily. He could not analyse the impulse that had brought him there, an angry little man whose teeth hurt—angry at the older men who, like himself, formed the majority of the spectators round the netball pitch, angry at the semi-nudity of the long-haired boys and girls lying on the grass, angry at the people sitting on seats eating sandwiches or sucking iced lollies and cornets and throwing the remains on the ground. As he watched the netball girls, leaping and cavorting in their play, the word "lechery" came into his head and something about "grinning like a dog," a phrase in the psalms, was it; then he thought of the way some dogs did appear to grin, their tongues lolling out. After a few minutes' watching he got up and made his way back to the office, dissatisfied with life. Only the sight of a wrecked motor car . . . gave him the kind of lift Marcia had experienced on hearing the bell of the ambulance, but then he remembered that an abandoned car had been parked outside the house where he lived for some days, and the police or the council ought to do something about it, and that made him angry again.

We know Austen's heroes through what they say or do or, sometimes, through the letters they write. But we know Pym's Norman through the images and associations that pervade his consciousness. He becomes identified, in particular, with the image of the dog that we find here. Indeed, at the novel's end, the proof that he has been changed by inheriting Marcia's house comes not through his actions or dialogue, but through a subtle alteration in this image summoned up from his memory:

> All the same, he was now a house-owner and it was up to him to decide what to do with the property. . . . The fact that the decision rested with him . . . gave him quite a new, hitherto unexperienced

sensation—a good feeling, like a dog with two tails, as people sometimes put it—and he walked to the bus stop with his head held high.

The grinning dog becomes a more benign creature (i.e., a dog with two tails) as Norman's anger, which arises from a sense of impotence and lack of control over his own fate, begins to dissipate. The narrator may speak lightly of Norman as resembling "a tetchy little dog"; but such an observation grows suggestive when it is coupled with this view into Norman's psyche, through which we see the importance of the canine imagery to him. While seeming, in the passages above, to be tracing mere random thoughts, Pym is in fact establishing the pattern of consciousness that makes this individual unique.

Pym follows Virginia Woolf's famous command in "Modern Fiction" to "Examine for a moment an ordinary mind on an ordinary day." She finds, as did Woolf herself in *Mrs. Dalloway,* that the "ordinary mind" contains unexpected but revealing patterns. These patterns can often tell us more about character psychology than can dialogue and gestures. The latter may, on the contrary, mislead the observer completely. Characters in *Quartet in Autumn* are continually misjudging each other on the basis of speech and action. At the retirement party in chapter 12, for instance, Letty's modest and hesitant demeanor causes her to be classified by her fellows "as a typical English spinster about to retire to a cottage in the country, where she would be . . . doing gardening and needlework." Only through another passage focusing upon consciousness do we learn the truth about Letty's feelings towards the country—that she associates it merely with death and dying, and that it makes her suicidal:

> Letty . . . looked around the wood, remembering its autumn carpet of beech leaves and wondering if it could be the kind of place to lie down in and prepare for death when life became too much to be endured. Had an old person—a pensioner, of course—ever been found in such a situation? No doubt it would be difficult to lie undiscovered for long. . . . It was not the kind of fancy she could . . . dwell on too much herself. Danger lay in that direction.

Letty's manner may be that of a cheerful "spinster," eager to get on with domestic tasks; the privileged view, however, that the reader has of Letty's mind belies this assumption. She is, through much of the novel, deeply melancholy, oppressed by thoughts of impending extinction and by memories of lost opportunities. Pym uses both daydreams, such as the one above, and true dreams to show us this concealed side of Letty's nature. Perhaps the most significant of these is the lengthy dream recounted in chapter 2. A blend of fantasy and remembrance of actual events, it returns Letty to the year 1935 and to what seems to have been her last chance to experience love. In the dream, as in reality, Letty allows the moment of decision to pass. She awakens in a mood of regret and puzzlement, "meditating on the strangeness of life, slipping away like this." Hers is an emotion far gloomier than any to be found in Jane Austen's novels, even in Austen's most atypical work, *Persuasion,* a story of nostalgia for a past love. Letty's despair is never expressed in her behavior, for she believes in "holding neatly and firmly on to life, coping as best she could with whatever it had to offer," as befits her genteel upbringing; but it informs both her conscious and subconscious thoughts, as Pym's exploration of her mind makes plain.

Through Letty, too, Pym introduces one of the novel's most important themes, an attack upon manners. Far from acknowledging proper social behavior as the highest good, *Quartet in Autumn* tells us instead that forms and conventions can be obstacles to happiness. Pym begins with the modernist assumption that every psyche is an island unto itself and that loneliness is mankind's usual condition. She then shows, through Letty, how social rules only serve to increase and to intensify feelings of isolation. The novel's opening chapter, for instance, contains an episode that illustrates the pitfalls of social relations in general. As Letty dines alone in a restaurant inappropriately named the Rendezvous, a stranger happens to sit at her table. The woman makes a tentative move toward addressing Letty; but the latter, a model of social correctness, repels her advances. In Jane Austen's world, Letty's conduct would be praised. But for Pym, a modernist who sees life as tragic, as a procession of isolated souls toward the grave, whatever keeps people apart must be wrong. As the narrator, who is reflecting Letty's own thoughts, informs us,

> For all her apparent indifference she was not unaware of the situation. Somebody had reached out towards her. They could have spoken and a link might have been forged between two solitary people. But the other woman . . . was now bent rather low over her macaroni au gratin. It was too late for any kind of gesture. Once again Letty had failed to make contact.

The highest moral values in *Quartet in Autumn* are not, as in fiction of manners, truth and propriety; rather, they are tolerance of the shortcomings of one's fellow man and willingness to "make contact" with him.

Finally, we see the difference between Pym's modernism and Austen's traditionalism in their attitudes toward how to conclude a story. The aim of fiction of manners is to affirm stasis by resolving differences and fixing the relations among the characters permanently. In Austen's novels, a happy ending means an end to uncertainty. Characters whose proper connections with each other have been in doubt settle the question through marriage. The reader is asked to believe that these new social configurations, which mirror a higher universal order, will last forever. In the final pages of Austen's novels, the social configurations themselves, rather than the thoughts of the individuals concerned, seem to become all important.

The highest moral values in *Quartet in Autumn* are not, as in fiction of manners, truth and propriety; rather, they are tolerance of the shortcomings of one's fellow man and willingness to "make contact" with him.
—*Margaret Diane Stetz*

Pym, however, rejects the notion of a permanent resolution as either possible or even desirable; she also keeps our attention upon the minds of her characters, not on their situations, to the last. At the conclusion of *Quartet in Autumn,* the three surviving members of the group are left with all their major decisions still before them: where to live; how to live; whether to grow more intimate with one another; whether to open their circle to Letty's friend, Marjorie. Yet, although nothing has been settled, we are asked to consider this a happy ending. The characters' positions in the world have not improved so much as have their attitudes towards their fates. For the first time they feel, as Letty puts it, that they "have a choice" about their ways of life, and it is "a most agreeable sensation, almost a feeling of power." Having believed all along that their futures were fixed and could offer nothing but a predictable slide toward oblivion, they discover instead that "life still held infinite possibilities for change," the revelation with which the book ends. In change lies the opportunity for stimulation, surprise, and challenge, values opposed to the stable ideals usually reasserted at the climax of a novel of manners.

It is no accident that *Quartet in Autumn* concludes with the word "change." To a modernist, flux is the very essence of life. As we see throughout Pym's novel, time leaps backwards and forwards; consciousness shifts in a moment between present and past, between reason and flights of imagination; nature, too, represents a cycle of change, moving from one season to the next. By welcoming and embracing change, instead of stasis, for her characters, Pym proves that she is not a reactionary who imitates Austen, as some have claimed, but a novelist with a distinctly twentieth-century sensibility. For her, as for other great modernists such as Virginia Woolf, the inner life in motion is the true source of both coherence and beauty in fiction.

Jill Rubenstein (essay date Winter 1986)

SOURCE: "'For the Ovaltine Had Loosened Her Tongue': Failures of Speech in Barbara Pym's *Less Than Angels,*" in *Modern Fiction Studies,* Vol. 32, No. 4, Winter, 1986, pp. 573-80.

[*In the following essay, Rubenstein examines the difficulties of self-expression and interpersonal communication among male and female characters in Pym's novels as a source of humor and pathos.*]

> "Well, hardly that," ventured Belinda, growing a little more confidential, for the Ovaltine had loosened her tongue. "I mean, it's a bit late for anything like that, isn't it? Henry is always loyal to Agatha and feels quite *differently* about her," she added hastily, in case her sister should take her up wrongly.
>
> —Barbara Pym, *Some Tame Gazelle*

Barbara Pym's best novels meticulously and often hilariously examine the problem of imperfect or totally failed communication, the primary source of both comedy and gloom in her vision of human relations. It need be noted only fleetingly that men and women can rarely talk to each other in Pym's novels. Her male characters are generally exploitive, although not intentionally cruel, almost always egotistical, frequently pompous, insensitive, and patronizing, sometimes endearingly childlike, but hardly ever as smart or discerning as the women who endure them and love them. Although Pym's women generally display considerably greater intelligence, sensitivity, and self-awareness than her men, they enjoy little more success in communication, even with the most benevolent intentions toward each other. Critics have frequently noted the triumph of the ordinary in Pym's novels and her glorification of the pleasures of everyday life. Ordinary routines such as housework, cooking, and shopping may indeed help to preserve sanity and even offer a source of joy. However, for many of Pym's characters the ordinary falls far short of the heart's desire. To compensate for the inadequacies of quotidian existence, they exercise a transforming imagination upon the dull and occasionally burdensome activities of daily life. This ability sharply distinguishes them from Pym's male characters, who exercise their imagination only upon themselves, whereas the women use imagination to transfigure their worlds, including, of course, their men.

Toward the end of *Less Than Angels,* Pym quotes a significant passage from Austen's *Persuasion:*

> While Delia and Felicity had been trained for careers, Elaine had been the one to stay at home. She might, if she had come upon them, have copied out

Anne Elliott's words especially as she was the same age as Miss Austen's heroine: "We certainly do not forget you so soon as you forget us. It is, perhaps, our fate rather than our merit. We cannot help ourselves. We live at home, quiet, confined, and our feelings prey upon us. You are forced on exertion. You have always business of some sort or other to take you back into the world immediately, and continual occupation and change soon weaken impressions."

Because they are imprisoned in the routine of common domestic life, Pym's female characters suffer the pain of loss and disappointment with considerably greater sharpness and duration than do her male characters. Consequently, many of them endure or escape this pain through the imaginative transformation of their limited milieux. As a result, these women often inhabit fictive worlds of their own creation and find themselves incapable of successful communication with other women who live either wholly in the real world or in different fictive worlds. Between or among these characters, language loses its effectiveness, interpretation fails to function, and meanings become hopelessly indeterminate. The effects vary from high comedy to touching poignancy and usually coexist in close juxtaposition within the same novel. That this phenomenon occurs with such remarkable consistency in Pym's fiction suggests a reexamination of her attitude toward the trivial and ordinary round of life. Like Catherine Oliphant in *Less Than Angels,* Pym's most engaging female characters regularly metamorphose reality through their imagination, whereas her least sympathetic ones remain bound to the limitations of actuality.

The theory of speech acts, first developed by J. L. Austin and John Searle and later applied to literary criticism by Mary Louise Pratt, Barbara Herrnstein Smith, and Stanley Fish, provides a useful conceptual tool for examining the failures of speech in these novels. Austin inaugurated speech act theory in his identification of the "performative," an utterance that is itself the performance of an action, such as "I promise you" or "I marry you." As an action rather than the account of an action, these utterances cannot be judged as true or false but must be seen instead as either successful or unsuccessful. Austin emphasizes the ceremonial and ritualistic nature of speech acts and the necessity for certain procedures, conventions, and states of mind to accompany their successful performance. Failures of speech, "infelicities" or "misfires," occur when these conditions are not properly or fully observed by both speaker and listener. Austin implies, therefore, that a felicitous speech act cannot be unilateral and that mutual consent is necessary for its successful completion.

Extending Austin's work, Searle applies it to the vexed question of distinguishing between real and fictive. He postulates the existence of a "shared pretense" that allows fiction to exist, a complex of conventions to which storyteller and reader have willingly acceded. This "shared pretense" allows the creation of a fictional world and distinguishes fiction from both mendacity and from "serious speech." That is, it permits the licensed use of words that do not refer to reality. Pratt suggests that it is this "shared pretense" ("appropriateness conditions" or "felicity conditions" in Austin's terms) that enables us to define literary genres and subgenres. The reader, and perhaps especially the reader of comedy, must then examine what occurs when two or more different groups of "appropriateness conditions" prevail between writer and reader or between separate parties to the same conversation. Would an attempt at communication necessarily turn out to be "infelicitous" or unsuccessful if one participant assumed the prevalence of a set of "appropriateness conditions" (or generic conventions) quite divergent from those assumed by other participants?

Implicitly addressing this as well as other questions, Smith employs speech act theory to distinguish between "natural discourse" and "fictive discourse." Whereas "natural discourse" is a verbal act historically identifiable in time and place and governed by the assumption "that people usually mean what they say," "fictive discourse" is the *representation* of the verbal act of natural discourse and is governed by the *suspension* of this assumption. Another difference between the two kinds of discourse depends upon the distinction between determinate and indeterminate meanings. A natural utterance will most likely have (possibly several) determinate meanings governed by historical circumstances and linguistic conventions. However, because a fictive utterance is understood not to be an historical occurrence, that is, not something that actually happened at a given time and place in the historical universe, its meanings are necessarily indeterminate or historically unfixable. This difference provides a functional description of what happens in many Pym novels. One character or participant in a conversation speaks "natural discourse" whereas the other consciously or unconsciously builds a fictive or fanciful structure from the same situation; the two speakers bring to the conversation two quite different sets of assumptions about the mode of existence of their verbal exchange, and the unspoken but unbridgeable gap precludes successful communication.

Fish extends and modifies speech act theory in his construct of "interpretive communities," the multiplicity of public and conventional points of view that authorize meaning. Communication, he argues, occurs only within interpretive communities, and meaning is determinate only within "institutional" contexts. Although he asserts that all utterances require interpretation and are therefore subject to misinterpretation (or what Austin calls "infelicity"), Fish does acknowledge the distinction between the "interpretive confidence" of ordinary discourse, especially face-to-face con-

versation, and the inherent indeterminacy of fiction. He expands Austin's idea of "dimensions of assessment" to the concept of "standard story," our sense of what is reality or what is normally supposed to exist. For Fish, we are each characters acting within our own standard stories; because the standard story may differ substantially from one person to another, "what may be fiction for the characters in one standard story will be obvious and commonsense truth for characters in another."

Regarded in the light of speech act theory, *Less Than Angels* may be read as a series of ill-fated conversations or interviews among women who are genuinely fond of each other and sincerely wish to confide in one another. More often than not, however, the interviews go awry, frequently with superb comic impact, so that two characters who begin earnestly discussing the profundities of love and death are likely to retreat quickly to gossip or pleasantries. What occurs between them is not a communion of souls but a breakdown in interpretation in which the appearance of unmediated face-to-face communication is revealed as illusory, primarily because one of the conversationalists habitually transforms the world of reality (or "natural discourse") into the world of imagination (or "fictive discourse"). Her words, therefore, refer not to a shared "standard story" to which they both subscribe, or even to a "shared pretense" they have tacitly agreed to accept, but rather to a system of referents to which the listener has no access. In Fish's terms, the characters only *appear* to be members of the same "interpretive communities." But although this concept would seem to provide a perfect description of the very limited socio-economic and geographical region that the characters of *Less Than Angels* inhabit, it does not necessarily apply; because Pym's characters frequently speak from fictive or dramatic realms of their own creation, other characters fail to recognize in their discourse what Smith calls "the cues that identify fictiveness." The failures of speech are often funny for the reader but baffling to the characters, who are left with the disquieting sense that no information has been conveyed and nothing has been said.

Less Than Angels (1955), Pym's fourth novel, most clearly illustrates failures of interpretation and infelicities of speech acts. To a great extent, the novel is about language itself and the comic, sad, and occasionally liberating misfires of language. Pym zestfully gives the novel an academic background modeled on the International African Institute where she worked for many years. Here it is an unspecified "anthropological library and research center" presided over by the insufferably pompous Professor Felix Mainwaring and the officious Esther Clovis and harboring a collection of eccentric anthropologists and scruffy graduate students, a fertile comic field for demonstrations of noncommunication and misinterpretation. Fittingly, the most audible denizens of the research center are the anthropological linguists Miss

Lydgate and Father Gemini, fascinated by discourse that has no meaning whatsoever:

> "I was interested in what appeared to be something *quite new,*" said Miss Lydgate, drawing Father Gemini almost by his beard into a more secluded part of the room. "Was it *this*?" A very curious sound, which it is impossible to reproduce here, then came from her. Had she been in the company of ordinary people, it might have been supposed that something had gone down the wrong way and that she was choking, but here nobody took any particular notice of her or of Father Gemini when he cried excitedly, "No, no, it is *this!*" and proceeded to emit a sound which would have appeared to the uninitiated exactly the same as Miss Lydgate's choking noise.

It is thus most fitting that Father Gemini purloins the Foresight grant money in order to finance his studies of "The hill tribes ... A few hundreds living on each hill and each group speaking a different language, *totally unrelated* to that of any of the others!" Pym's scholars practice what may be the ultimate devaluation of language, inserting Latin and Greek into learned essays "to avoid giving offense to those who probably cannot understand it anyway." Academic language, therefore, exists at least thrice removed from the actual speech act, the ritual in the African bush first observed by the anthropologist, then described in English, then translated into Latin, so that by the end of this series of interpretive acts language achieves its goal of totally obfuscating communication.

The comic catastrophe in this world of useless language appropriately occurs as the failure of a speech act precisely as Austin describes a verbal "misfire," the promise not fulfilled. Minnie Foresight had *promised* the grants for deserving graduate students to Professor Mainwaring, but she had not actually *given* him the money, thus affording the opportunity for Father Gemini to convince the gullible lady that she should finance his research instead. The performative ("I promise") misfires and cannot be executed, rendering the speech act void. This revelation, however, provides the circumstances for one of the very few successful interview scenes in Pym's fiction. Miss Clovis and Miss Lydgate argue bitterly over a speech act that never occurred, the warning of Father Gemini's intended perfidy. But their quarrel leads to a successful performative, forgiveness, which is touchingly and doubly verbal. As penance, Miss Lydgate resolves to withhold from Father Gemini her research on the Gana verb, thus invalidating his work; but Miss Clovis selflessly dissuades her from doing so, citing its paramount importance to scholarship. The comedy of the scene does not vitiate its poignance. The reader understands that the research is meaningless, and the two women are graceless and

generally ridiculous; nevertheless, they achieve a mutual understanding more complete than most Pym characters ever manage.

Failures of speech in *Less Than Angels* are not confined to the absurdities of the academic world; they also pervade the cozy suburban milieu of the Swans. Like many Pym characters, the two middle-aged sisters, Mabel Swan and Rhoda Wellcome, find the meaning of their lives in ordinary, ordered domesticity. Even in this conventional and safe enclave, however, language frequently fails to convey discernible meaning. Conscientiously listening to a radio lecture, "something about the betrayal of freedom," the sisters conclude that they cannot understand it because the tape is being played at the wrong speed. Similarly, the substance of religion becomes a meaningless babble as Rhoda summarizes Father Tulliver's "little talk about the meaning of Pentecost": "'Oh, it is Jewish or Greek in origin,' said Rhoda in a flustered tone, 'and Paraclete, that is Greek too. *Come thou Holy Paraclete,* you know the hymn. I think we'd better have the lace mats, don't you?'" To exploit the comic potential of verbal infelicity, Pym brings the two worlds together in a suburban dinner party. Rhoda "had imagined that the presence of what she thought of as clever people would bring about some subtle change in the usual small talk. The sentences would be like bright jugglers' balls, spinning through the air and being deftly caught and thrown up again." As the table talk burns to the fondness of African tribes for putrescent meat and their rather primitive culinary practices, however, Rhoda realizes "that conversation could also be compared to a series of incongruous objects, scrubbing-brushes, dish-cloths, knives, being flung or hurtling rather than spinning, which were sometimes not caught at all but fell to the ground with resounding thuds."

Next door to the Swans, Alaric Lydgate cultivates reverie behind his African mask:

> He often thought what a good thing it would be if the wearing of masks or animals' heads could become customary for persons over a certain age. How restful social intercourse would be if the face did not have to assume any expression. ... Alaric often avoided looking into people's eyes when he spoke to them, fearful of what he might see there, for life was very terrible whatever sort of front we might put on it, and only the eyes of the very young or the very old and wise could look out on it with a clear untroubled gaze.

Like Catherine Oliphant, Alaric takes pleasure in perusing wine lists for the pure joy of words that require no interpretation at all. Both activities offer imaginative escape from loneliness and from the world's desolation; and because they are pursued in solitude, they require no communication and thus afford no room for misinterpretation. Alaric seeks a verbal transformation of the world that is totally satisfying because it entails no "felicity conditions" dependent on another person. Ultimately, with Catherine's inspiration, he liberates himself from the prison of language, immolating his anthropological notes in a Guy Fawkes Night bonfire, finally freed from the self-imposed responsibility of "writing them up." When the burden of interpretation becomes intolerable and paralyzing, Alaric finds that the only escape lies in destruction of the verbal construct. Once the imagination has been thus liberated, the ensuing freedom may lead even to art. "I shall be free to do whatever I want to. I shall still review books, of course, but I could even write a novel, I suppose."

Catherine Oliphant, the protagonist of *Less Than Angels,* most clearly exemplifies the limits of interpretation and the consequent failure of utterance. By profession a writer, she instinctively fictionalizes reality: "she earned her living writing stories and articles for women's magazines and had to draw her inspiration from everyday life, though life itself was sometimes too strong and raw and must be made palatable by fancy. . . ." Catherine possesses a vivid imagination, pictorial as well as verbal, susceptible to the slightest suggestion. Her lover's self-dramatizing declaration of a loss of faith (in anthropology!) immediately brings to mind "the picture—surely a sepia daguerrotype—of a high-collared, bewhiskered Victorian clergyman, his beliefs undermined by Darwin and the rationalists." Similarly, a casual allusion to "Baron's Court" elicits a vision "of feudal spaciousness, although she knew that it was only one station beyond West Kensington." Catherine employs this fictionalizing habit of mind as a distancing device and a defense; the Pym reader discovers in another novel that her accidental sighting of Tom Mallow and Deirdre Swan holding hands in the Cypriot restaurant becomes the raw material for a story. However, although the tendency to treat life as fiction may both insulate and isolate because it makes interpretation difficult if not impossible, in Catherine's case it enhances the imagination and thus the capacity for sympathy. It allows her to anticipate Rhoda's reaction to Tom's death as she envisions the scenes taking place in the older woman's mind:

> Catherine saw past Rhoda's shocked face into her thoughts, the shouting mob of black bodies brandishing spears, or the sly arrow, tipped with poison for which there was no known antidote, fired from an overhanging jungle tree . . . and again Catherine saw her picture of Tom, the British anthropologist in immaculate white shorts and topee, note-book and pencil in hand.

Even before Tom Mallow leaves her for Deirdre, Catherine regards the world in her darker moments as a universe of meaningless babble, of "confused alarms of struggle and flight" to which no interpretation can grant significance. Quoting the last stanza of "Dover Beach" to Tom, she feels compelled to add that it is "not a comfortable poem." Notwithstanding her fondness for poetry, Catherine derives no real solace from language; on the night of Tom's departure, she searches in her bookshelf for consolation but finds none. Pym's words are eloquent, terse, and dark: "The only real book of devotion she had . . . told her that we are strangers and pilgrims here and must endure the heart's banishment, and she felt that she knew that anyway." After Tom dies, Catherine turns once again to poetry, this time Vaughan's "They Are All Gone Into the World of Light." Like her impulsive visit to the Roman Catholic church, however, it leaves her with no assurances, only an unanswered question.

Pym structures Catherine's story around a series of abortive or otherwise unsatisfactory conversations. After seeing Tom and Deirdre holding hands, Catherine first feels the need for a confidant but has none and so must rely instead on the dubious and impersonal comfort of a self-service restaurant and the bizarre conversation of strangers whom she labels "black-beetle" and "leopard-hat." Shortly thereafter, Catherine's habit of fictionalizing reality redeems the awkwardness of the interview with Mrs. Beddoes, Tom's aunt. To distance herself from the immediate situation she thinks of it as an opera libretto or an Edwardian novel, and to relieve tension she focuses her imagination on the cookies:

> "Do have a biscuit. I hope you like Bourbons. They always remind me of exiled European royalty, and that's one of those sad but comforting thoughts that one likes to have. Do you suppose they sit around in their villas at Estoril eating Bourbon biscuits?"

> Mrs. Beddoes threw Catherine a startled glance but took a biscuit.

Catherine's interviews with Deirdre Swan, the young woman who supplants her in Tom's affections, are less ludicrous but no more successful as communication. After a suitable interval, they meet for lunch, both hoping to be friends. Despite the best of intentions, however, they patronize each other, Deirdre as the anthropologist-in-training who alone will properly appreciate Tom's doctoral thesis and Catherine as the older and more experienced of the two. Speech fails, and intimacy proves elusive as Catherine withdraws into "her women's magazine tone" in order to discourage any discussion of "the deeper passions." After Tom's death, while Catherine is staying in the Swans' spare room, the two women once again attempt to establish an emotional bond. Deirdre's grief is inarticulate but superficial; she has already fallen in love again and is easily soothed by Catherine's verbal facility. Catherine's grief, however, is considerably more profound and remains unassuaged. Speech fails to penetrate her essential isolation, and the conversation trails off into meaningless clichés.

The final interview scene, the lugubrious luncheon at Tom's sister's club, combines pathos with comedy and reinforces the theme of failures of interpretation. Deirdre and Catherine join Elaine, Tom's first and lasting love, and his sister, the "brisk" and "practical" Josephine, whose vocabulary appears limited largely to "good show." (On those rare occasions in which the upper classes appear in Pym's novels, they are generally portrayed as thoroughly ineffectual, suitably represented here by the Mallow family, whose various members seem incapable of uttering anything more complicated than "Well Tom.") As is her wont, Catherine smooths over the underlying tension, but the luncheon ends painfully for her as Josephine gratuitously reveals the existence of Tom's last letter, the ultimate infelicity, the written utterance interrupted by death:

> I don't suppose anybody told you, I suppose nobody would, really, but a half-written letter to Elaine was found on the table in Tom's hut. The District Officer sent it with some small personal things. It was a nice chatty letter, you know, but at least she is able to know that he was thinking of her so very shortly before the end.

Like most of Pym's novels, *Less Than Angels* ends inconclusively with Catherine helping Alaric Lydgate to gather rhubarb in his garden. The epitome of resilience and self-reliance, she will survive nicely with or without him. Just before Tom left her, Catherine had inquired, "Who understands anybody, if it comes to that?" In Pym's characteristically understated manner, the question demonstrates her protagonist's accommodation to a world in which interpretation is all but impossible and language—whether casual or scholarly or literary—almost invariably unreliable. The most complicated and self-aware of Pym's characters, Catherine Oliphant earns the reader's respect by facing that truth unflinchingly.

Mason Cooley (essay date Spring 1986)

SOURCE: "*The Sweet Dove Died:* The Sexual Politics of Narcissism," in *Twentieth Century Literature,* Vol. 32, No. 1, Spring, 1986, pp. 40-9.

[*In the following essay, Cooley contends that* The Sweet Dove Died *is among Pym's most effective literary creations. According to Cooley, "The book is a triumph of artistic consistency and economy, yet it is the coldest and most unforgiving of Barbara Pym's novels."*]

Considered from a purely aesthetic point of view, *The Sweet Dove Died* is the most brilliant success of Barbara Pym's career. It lacks the geniality and fun of her earlier work, but it is written with a tense economy that generates greater force than the rather relaxed storytelling of its immediate predecessors, *A Glass of Blessings* and *An Unsuitable Attachment.* During the years of silence, Barbara Pym worked on *The Sweet Dove Died,* cutting, polishing, and recasting with a passion for perfection apparently deepened by her inability to find a publisher. She was never a slack or a casual writer, but after she began publishing in 1950, she wrote quickly and easily enough to bring out a novel every other year for the next decade. When her troubles with publishers began in 1961, she apparently responded in part by adopting a more severe and self-critical artistic standard. The results are *The Sweet Dove Died* and *Quartet in Autumn,* both masterpieces of condensation and lucidity—two qualities that do not often go together. Built on a series of love triangles, the plot of *The Sweet Dove Died* represents tangled and mismatched loves with great conciseness and richness of implication.

The greatest achievement of all in *The Sweet Dove Died* is its remarkable heroine: cold, elegant Leonora Eyre, incapable of passion but capable of heartbreak, strong-willed but finally miserable and helpless in her self-absorption. The exploration of Leonora's character so dominates the book that it might well have been titled *Portrait of a Lady.* Indeed, Leonora shares with James's lady, Isabel Archer, a distaste for sexual relations and disruptive emotion, and like Isabel she mistakes a rather decadent interest in collecting for an aesthetic passion. She is perhaps the Hermione of D. H. Lawrence's *Women in Love* as seen by a woman, and she has similarities to the mother in James's *Spoils of Poynton,* with her invincible love of beautiful possessions, and her subordination of human relations to them.

The book is a triumph of artistic consistency and economy, yet it is also the coldest and most unforgiving of Barbara Pym's novels. The irony is always verging on the sardonic, and the geniality and high spirits of Pym's earlier work are nowhere in evidence. The mood is one of carefully restrained bitterness, and the portrayal of character bites deeper and reveals more ambivalence than ever before. Not one of the characters is truly likable, yet every one of them except Ned, the American, forces the reader to extend a certain sympathy. Their suffering and self-discontent are just as real as their selfishness.

These qualities are particularly evident in the portrayal of the heroine, Leonora Eyre. Despite her last name, Leonora is almost the reverse of the plain, passionate, and adventurous Jane Eyre who shares her surname. Jane Eyre has a commonplace exterior, underneath which is a fiery imagination and a full heart. Leonora, on the other hand, is an aging beauty of exquisite refinement; the exterior is still beautiful, impeccable, a triumph of taste. The interior, however, is one of emotional poverty, tedious self-absorption, and cautious avoidance of experience.

In her age and situation in life, if not in moral quality, Leonora is similar to other Pym heroines. She is a single woman of good education living on her own as she approaches middle age. She has a private income, so that she does not have to work. And in the course of the book she experiences an unrequited passion for a man. Unlike other Pym heroines, though, she has no contact at all with the Church or, for that matter, with any institution. She seems to be tied to the world only by shopping and by the perfect clothes and furniture that are the fruit of that shopping.

Leonora is a recognizable member of the family of Pym heroines, but she is drawn in much darker colors. The earlier heroines are often prim and excessively concerned with propriety, but they are warm-hearted, generous, and gallant. Leonora is a worshiper of perfection in objects and in people—not moral perfection but perfection of style and appearance, the unflawed vase, the unlined face. Other Pym heroines are alone in the world, and their aloneness impairs their happiness, but not their humanity. Leonora's aloneness is the result of her disdainful indifference to the rest of mankind and her distaste for physical lovemaking. She thinks of herself primarily as someone who wins admiration, but even those who admire her scarcely arouse her liking.

Leonora, then, is a chill-hearted narcissist, and this novel is about the sexual politics of narcissism. The theme is chiefly realized through the character of the heroine, but Leonora's lover James and his subsequent lover Ned are also variations on the theme of narcissism. Determined to live without suffering or strong emotion, Leonora keeps experience at a distance. She dines with elderly admirers who have been trained to look but not touch. She spends her days drifting through antique stores and auction rooms. She sends her friend Humphrey flowers of sympathy when his antique shop is robbed of a few valuable objects, as if someone had died.

Leonora, then, is a chill-hearted narcissist, and this [*The Sweet Dove Died*] is about the sexual politics of narcissism. The theme is chiefly realized through the character of the heroine, but Leonora's lover James and his subsequent lover Ned are also variations on the theme of narcissism.
—*Mason Cooley*

The portrait of Leonora is sharpened by a group of surround-

ing minor characters who serve as foils to the heroine—parallels, contrasts, implicit commentaries. Each of the female characters, simply by being what she is, casts a revealing light on Leonora. The dowdy, middle-aged friend Meg has an abiding maternal love for a gay young man named Colin, who comes to her between lovers and disappears when he is involved with someone. When he is there, she is happy, and when he is away she grieves. When he comes back, she has his favorite Riesling waiting in the fridge, and forgives him. She knows that she needs to love someone, and Colin is her choice, so that she imposes no condition of faithfulness on her love. Leonora coolly turns James away when he returns after just such an escapade; she returns to her first love, her own inviolate self, with some regret that she had permitted James to ruffle her life so disagreeably.

James's girlfriend, Phoebe Sharpe, is a vague, badly dressed young woman who lives in a country village and does literary research. Her house is a jumble of cheap objects, her sink is full of dishes, and a cat appears to live on top of her radio. But she feels a quick sexual passion for James, and despite her timidity, finds the courage to act on it at once. Leonora, all self-command and impeccable taste, is amazed that James could take up with such a tawdry young woman, missing, as usual, whatever might be sexual and human rather than tasteful and suitable.

Leonora's neighbor Liz, after a bitter divorce, spends her time (and her love) on her Siamese cats, which she breeds for competition. She is an angry and disappointed woman whose attachment to life has shrunk down to her cats, but they have the advantage over Leonora's objects and furniture of being alive.

After being abandoned by James, Leonora goes to visit her friend Joan in the country. The visit is less than a success. Joan is immersed in her family, in the party she is giving in the evening, in the gossip and jokes of her busy world. Leonora is stiff and contemptuous and overdressed at the party, where she has a miserable time out of her London element and the very special conditions she requires. There is no one there to admire her, only an obnoxious woman named Ba, who tells Leonora that she should do some volunteer work.

Leonora is more intelligent and more self-aware than any of these women characters, but intelligence and self-awareness are of little avail. The other women love something living: a gay boy, a Siamese cat, a pipe-smoking husband and noisy children. All Leonora has is a few memories of youthful flirtations in the great gardens of Europe, flirtations that somehow came to nothing. In large measure by her choice, her inner world is mausoleum-like, though by no means free of waves of anxiety.

Into this unoccupied life comes an elderly antique dealer, Humphrey Boyce, and his sexually ambiguous young nephew James. The opening scene is a book auction. Leonora has been bidding for a pretty Victorian flower book, one made for a love-token. Appropriately, Leonora plans to make it a present to herself. Overcome by the excitement of bidding, the bad air, and the crowded room, Leonora almost faints. The uncle and nephew rescue the distressed lady, and the three go off for lunch at a good restaurant. The pickup has been executed quickly and efficiently, but within the rules of Edwardian gentility. The delicacy of the lady and the gallantry of the gentlemen have made the contact easy rather than difficult, because the players know the rules and how to use them. They have no need to resort to the uncertainties of spontaneous reactions.

The first scene of the novel introduces us to a world where the artifice prevails over nature. The characters speak and act for effect—to project an image, to negotiate some kind of emotional deal. Seldom do any of the central characters do anything merely from impulse or conviction, except when surprised into it by sexual passion. Here are the first paragraphs of the novel:

> "The sale room is no place for a woman," declared Humphrey Boyce, as he and his nephew James sat having lunch with the attractive stranger they had picked up at a Bond Street sale room half an hour ago.
>
> "Now you're scolding me," said Leonora, with mock humility. "I know it was stupid of me, but I suppose it was the excitement of bidding—for the first time in my life—and then getting that dear little book. It was just too overwhelming."
>
> "And the room was so hot," James suggested, trying to take his part in the conversation, for after all it was he who had noticed the woman in black sway sideways and almost collapse at her moment of triumph, when she had challenged the auctioneer's rather bored "Twenty pounds at the table?" with a cry of "Twenty-five!" Between them James and Humphrey had supported her out of the sale room and after that it seemed the natural thing for the three of them to be having lunch together.

These three characters have just taken an initiative very much against the conventions of British decorum. They have violated the rule implied by one of an Englishman's proudest remarks, "I keep myself to myself." They have made a public pickup of a stranger. In the subsequent conversation each falls back on a conventional posture that reassuringly obliterates the unconventional nature of what has just taken place. Humphrey says, in a heavy, old-fashioned, masculine way, "The sale room is no place for a woman." Courtly and pompous, kind but more than a little condescending, he is the old-fashioned Edwardian gentleman who knows how to treat a lady.

Leonora's girlish trill responds appropriately to his basso. When she says, "Now you're scolding me," she is playing at submission as he is playing at masterfulness. The two middle-aged people fall into a stylized pattern of flirtation, long sanctioned by tradition. The man plays the rescuer and the mentor; the woman plays the adorable but fragile little woman. This stereotyped erotic play is one of the ironies of the novel: in the ensuing power struggles Leonora has a certain ruthless competence in pursuing her erotic goal of capturing young James, and Humphrey stands by comparatively helpless. By her speech Leonora also gives us a foretaste of her collector's passion for ownership of beautiful objects, her delight in admiration, her physical fragility, her ostentatious "sensibility," and her tough ability to manage situations.

Young James has no period style to fall back on, and no imagination to tell him what to do. All he can contribute to the situation is his extreme good looks and a flat statement of fact, "And the room was so hot." As he is to be the cipher over whom others contend, he is appropriately passive and untalkative.

This first incident sets up a triangle in which none of the attractions match. Humphrey is attracted to Leonora, who cultivates him in order to get at his nephew. Leonora is attracted to James as a flirtatious son whom she can captivate with comforts and attentions. James likes Leonora well enough, but he will also sneak off to his sexual lovers, first a woman, then a man. The erotic merry-go-round of Viennese bedroom farce is adapted to the more restrained conditions of British high comedy; the comedy of opening and closing bedroom and closet doors is replaced by the mental acrobatics of lovers who spend much of their time waiting and watching one another.

None of these attractions is predominantly sexual; the motives have to do more with possession and display than with genital love. Humphrey likes Leonora because she is someone elegant to be seen with at the opera and in fashionable restaurants. Leonora likes James, because he is so handsome and so seemingly easy to manipulate, and because he does not make any of the sexual demands that she dreads. James likes Leonora because she uses all her taste and tact to flatter him and serve him. Of the three, only Leonora feels something close to passion, and even she never comes close to self-abandonment, or even to an active desire for sexual union. Only in one outburst of weeping does she ever venture outside the fortress-prison of her self-control.

Until meeting James, Leonora has never gone beyond mild courtships. She has reached middle age without getting past a virginal playing at love, coquetting in a perfectly ladylike way with decorous suitors. James rouses her as no one ever has. Past forty, she finds his youth magical, and she is enchanted to be a combination of mother and glamorous older woman respectfully adored by a perfect son-lover-friend. James receives her love offerings with detachment and slight surprise, a response he generally accords to the love offerings inspired by his good looks. With the almost innocent egotism of youth, James finds nothing remarkable about Leonora's lavish attentions. Both are relieved that no physical relationship is expected, and they are free to play at "adoring" one another. Leonora is delighted by James's humdrum conversation, and her delight makes him feel, a little uncertainly, that he may indeed be more interesting than he had imagined.

Driven by her desire for secure possession of James, Leonora becomes both less idle and more ruthless. Finding that James plans to move from his present flat, Leonora decides to drive out the elderly tenant from the upstairs flat of her house and redecorate it for James. Miss Foxe, the elderly gentlewoman, was, as it turns out, already planning to move, so that Leonora does not need to put her out. This is a typical Barbara Pym development. In her novels, the worst that happens is that someone forms a wicked intention. But usually events take a turn that prevents the wicked intention from being carried out or, if the plans are carried out, the result is not as bad as might be expected. So there are villainous intentions but few villainous deeds in Barbara Pym. Her morally deficient characters suffer enough from their selfishness and emptiness; the author avoids adding the burden of guilt for real misdeeds. The suffering consequent on being what they are is sufficient for Barbara Pym's comic purposes. Extremes of badness and goodness have no place in her measured and middling world. Thus Leonora is perfectly willing to play the wicked landlady, but circumstances prevent her from acting on her intentions.

When Leonora discovers that James has a girlfriend, Phoebe Sharpe, to whom he has loaned some furniture while he is traveling in Europe, she uses Humphrey to force the return of the furniture. She succeeds in driving James's young woman away, but the job is easy because James's attachment is a feeble one, and vague, uncertain Phoebe is no match for Leonora. Indeed, Phoebe is a perfect foil for Leonora. She is very young, badly dressed, housed in a messy overgrown cottage, eager to make love, undefended against her emotions, too unfocused to scheme or manipulate. She doesn't have a chance in a contest with Leonora, yet the vague, vulnerable way she wanders through life has a certain emotional reality that is lacking in the chill existence of Leonora.

Having driven out her tenant, defeated James's girlfriend, and most important of all, gained possession of the furniture, Leonora turns her upstairs flat into a place of perfect comfort and taste for James. James is again a little surprised, but accepts the tribute with perfect equanimity, as part of the general tendency of life to take care of him. For a time, they play a game of loving housemates, ideal friends, imaginary parent and child.

The flimsy nature of this arrangement promptly becomes evident when James is seduced by a sexually accomplished young American named Ned, on sabbatical leave in England. Leonora is a sentimental narcissist, and James is a passive one. The narcissism of Ned, however, is a cold and clear-eyed drive for power. For him, the chief interest of getting involved with James is to separate him from Leonora, just to show that he can do it. Without much difficulty, Ned persuades James to move out of Leonora's house. Leonora is bereft:

> The days seemed long and hopeless and Leonora began to wish she had not given up working, for a routine job would at least have filled the greater part of the day. Yet she lacked the energy and initiative to find herself an occupation; she remembered the dreadful woman she had met at the Murray's party and the impertinent suggestion she had made about the useful voluntary work one could do. But when Leonora came to consider them each had something wrong with it: how could she do church work when she never went near a church, or work for old people when she found them boring and physically repellent, or with handicapped children when the very thought of them was too upsetting.

The solution to her loneliness is her possessions:

> She had always cared as much for inanimate objects as for people and now spent hours looking after her possessions, washing the china and cleaning the silver obsessively and rearranging them in her rooms. The shock of finding James had taken the fruitwood mirror upset her quite disproportionately. . . .

The new triangle of Ned, James, and Leonora replaces the triangle of Phoebe, James, and Leonora. In this match it is Leonora who is the losing player. After having defeated Phoebe, she is in turn defeated. Her genteel strategies are no match for the steely expertise of Ned in erotic intrigues. Her only resource is to try to maintain her stoicism so that Ned cannot see, directly at least, the extent of her suffering.

Ned makes others suffer, as he admits with an unconvincing display of regret. If someone is to suffer a narcissistic wound, he will make sure it will not be himself. When he senses a slight restiveness on James's part, Ned determines to reject James before James rejects him. Ned quickly finds a series of other lovers, and then, announcing that his mother needs him, returns to America. Before he leaves, he shamelessly calls on Leonora and offers to send James back. She coolly declines. At this point Ned and Leonora are roughly equal antagonists. James, the prize over whom they have struggled, is so inept even in his efforts to keep his various loves hidden from one another, that he scarcely qualifies as a player.

The Ned-James-Leonora episode of the book has a heartless brilliance, wit, and perversity that suggest Restoration comedy with its rakes and dissolute ladies in their dance-like changes of partners and their delight in deception. Restoration comedy suggests that all these intrigues, though doubtless brutal and immoral, are highly entertaining. *The Sweet Dove Died* presents this triangle as filled with a fascinating and amusing perversity, but it also renders the suffering and aching feeling of loss beneath the surface of the love intrigue. Comedy usually keeps suffering in the background, but this comedy is shot through with Leonora's anguish. She turns out to be more adept at suffering than at love.

With the departure of Ned, the original triangle of James-Leonora-Humphrey is reestablished. After waiting so patiently for Leonora's infatuation with James to end, Humphrey wins, whatever winning may mean when Leonora is the prize. After an unsatisfactory meeting with James, Leonora finds herself weary of her position as admirer and decides to go back to her old, comfortable, undemanding position as the one who is courted and admired. Here is the last paragraph of the novel:

> The sight of Humphrey with the peonies reminded her that he was taking her to the Chelsea Flower Show tomorrow. It was the kind of thing one liked to go to, and the sight of such large and faultless blooms, so exquisite in colour, so absolutely correct in all their finer points, was a comfort and satisfaction to one who loved perfection as she did. Yet, when one came to think of it, the only flowers that were really perfect were those, like the peonies that went so well with one's charming room, that possessed the added grace of having been presented to oneself.

The Sweet Dove Died is the least lovable of Barbara Pym's books, but it is also her most perfect work of art. Like Jane Austen's *Emma*, it has a heroine whom most people dislike. Leonora is fascinating but unsympathetic; indeed none of the characters offer much of an opening to sympathy. The self-satisfied doltishness of the men makes us keep our dis-

tance from them, and even Leonora's courage in her love-sufferings has something repellent about it. Driven back from sympathy, we are forced to deal with this book through our intelligence. Emotion held in check, we contemplate this picture of a skittish, anxious world of attenuated passions and faithless relationships, a world in which no one finally connects with anyone else and no emotion completes itself. The protagonist is left alone at her mirror with an empty heart, and that is the picture of chill unhappiness that stays with the reader.

The Sweet Dove Died may not have lovable characters, but as a whole it has a power and beauty that increase on re-reading. The novel itself provides an emblem of its artistic character: the small Japanese toggles called netsuke. Humphrey sells them in his antique shop; James and Leonora admire them. Their dentist collects them. Netsuke are bits of wood, ivory, or metal with realistic, fiercely energetic little figures carved into them. Small as they are, they give an impression of power and completeness, a life that is about to burst out of the confines of these little objects that are attached to kimono sashes. They resemble that "little bit of ivory, two inches wide," on which Jane Austen described herself as working. Barbara Pym powerfully inscribes her unyielding message within the confines of a short comic novel. Compact, intense with life, complete—that is the essence of *The Sweet Dove Died.*

Margaret C. Bradham (essay date Winter 1987)

SOURCE: "Barbara Pym's Women," in *World Literature Today,* Vol. 61, No. 1, Winter, 1987, pp. 31-7.

[*In the following essay, Bradham reevaluates Pym's portrayal of unmarried women, dismissing superficial comparison to the work of Jane Austen and association with feminist literature. Bradham examines the "condition, thoughts, desires, and emotions" of Pym's female protagonists as they reflect the author's attitudes and interests.*]

Since the Barbara Pym revival, begun in 1977 when Philip Larkin and Lord David Cecil independently cited her in the *Times Literary Supplement* as one of the most underrated novelists of the twentieth century, surprisingly little of consequence has been written about one of this century's great writers. Most of the criticisms of Pym's novels have consisted of brief articles and book reviews in publications such as the *TLS* and the *New York Times Book Review*. Most of these have demonstrated only a shallow understanding of Pym, and some have actually been wrong. They have concentrated on the superficial similarities between Jane Austen and Pym, on Pym's vain clergy and her churchgoing spinsters, and on the high Anglican comedy of her novels. Some critics even make the mistake of saying that Pym writes about marriage and marriageability or of suggesting that she writes feminist novels.

The essence of Pym has either been glossed over or misunderstood. She is not a twentieth-century Jane Austen. Pym's heroines, who are past their prime, do not have the same concerns as Austen's heroines, who are between the ages of seventeen and twenty-one. Pym does write about churchgoing spinsters; but the lives of many of her women do not revolve around the church, and not all her novels are centered on a clergyman and his parish. It is not about marriage and marriageability that Pym writes, but about spinsterhood and unmarriageability, and there is a great deal of disappointment, despair, failure, and loneliness in her works. The essence of Pym's answer to the feminist characterization can be found in a letter to Philip Larkin, where she wrote: "I did at least save myself once when a question about my treatment of men characters suggested that I had a low opinion of the sex. My instinctive reply sprang to my lips, 'Oh, but I *love* men,' but luckily I realized how ridiculous it would sound" (*A Very Private Eye*).

In most of her eleven published novels Pym's main character is in the position of the unmarried, unattached, aging woman, and it is this character's condition, thoughts, desires, and emotions that interest the author. In the following study I hope to illuminate the condition of the Pym woman, her identity and experience; the quest of the Pym woman, her search and failure; the predicament of the Pym woman, her disappointments and illusions; and finally, Pym's attitude toward her characters and their condition, the sympathy and irony.

The Condition of the Pym Woman: Her Identity and Experience

The vast majority of Pym's women are spinsters. For the most part they are past their prime or at least have missed out on life. Pym has only three main female characters under thirty years of age; the others are in their thirties, forties, and fifties. They live in middle-class areas of London or small English villages such as West Oxfordshire, and they lead mundane, unexciting, and lonely lives.

Of Pym's main female characters, three are "excellent women" (Belinda and Harriet in *Some Tame Gazelle* and Mildred Lathbury in *Excellent Women*), defined by the characters in the Pym world as a certain group of unmarried women who are sensible and good and who spend their time involved with "clergymen and jumble sales and church services and good works." Five of Pym's main female characters are spinsters who work either in offices (Prudence in *Jane and Prudence,* Penelope in *An Unsuitable Attachment,* and Marcia and Letty in *Quartet in Autumn*) or at

home doing odd jobs and making indexes (Dulcie in *No Fond Return of Love*). One is a spinster who is financially well off and does not work (Lenora in *The Sweet Dove Died*); one is a spinster who is not financially well off and is a companion to an older woman (Jessie Morrow in *Crampton Hodnet*); and two are spinsters with careers (Catherine, the writer, in *Less Than Angels,* and Emma, the anthropologist, in *A Few Green Leaves*). Only three of her main female characters are married, two of them to vicars (Jane in *Jane and Prudence* and Sophia in *An Unsuitable Attachment*) and one to a civil servant (Wilmet in *A Glass of Blessings*).

In Pym's seventh published novel, *Quartet in Autumn,* Letty, a spinster in her fifties, asks, "Might not the experience of 'not having' be regarded as something with its own validity?" To this question Pym answers "Yes," for the experience of not having is precisely what her novels are about. Whether the Pym women spend their day doing domestic chores and church tasks, or editing and proofreading manuscripts, or working in offices or libraries, or even pursuing careers as writers or anthropologists, they are lonely, restless, unhappy, and unfulfilled. Spinsters such as Rhoda Wellcome in *Less Than Angels* attribute their feelings of inadequacy and unfulfillment to having not had "'the experience of marriage,' a vague phrase which seemed to cover all those aspects which one didn't talk about." In the Pym world "all those aspects which one didn't talk about" are passion and romance, the experiences and emotions a Pym woman, as a respectable spinster, is not supposed to know or speak about. Even Pym's married main characters—Jane Cleveland, Wilmet Forsyth, and Sophia Ainger—feel that they have missed something. They are restless and lonely since their husbands do not pay them much attention.

In the Pym world marriage forms the basis of the social scale, with married women at the top and spinsters at the bottom. Pym's spinsters confess to feeling "like an inferior person," "not socially equal," or "inadequate." They equate marriage with a full life and spinsterhood with an empty life. The fear of being passed over is prominent in the thoughts of Pym's two youngest main characters, Prudence Bates of *Jane and Prudence* and Penelope Grandison of *Unsuitable Attachment.* At twenty-five Penelope had "reached the age when one starts looking for a husband rather more systematically than one does at 19 or even at 21." And at twenty-nine Prudence had reached "an age that is often rather desperate for a woman who has not yet married." As Pym's characters get older, the fear of being passed over becomes reality. *Excellent Women*'s Mildred Lathbury, having just attended a school reunion with her old friend Dora, also a spinster, reflects, "We had not made particularly brilliant careers for ourselves, and, most important of all, we had neither of us married. That was really it." Marriage is an achievement, and it is the experience the Pym spinster wants; she never questions whether marriage will dispel her loneliness and make her happy.

The irony of the spinsters' perception of marriage is shown by the experience of Pym's married women. Marriage does not make them happy, and it is not filled with passion and romance. In *Excellent Women* Helena Napier is dissatisfied with her husband Rocky and leaves him. In *A Glass of Blessings* Wilmet Forsyth is bored with her husband and seeks attention from other men. Marriage also does not guarantee passion and romance, the experiences and feelings the Pym spinsters are aware of having missed. In *Jane and Prudence* Jane, realizing that the passion in her marriage has faded, looks at her husband and thinks, "Mild, kindly looks and spectacles . . . this was what it all came to in the end." Pym's spinsters do not recognize that they are searching for the same things as Pym's married women: love and happiness. Pym's single women believe marriage will bring them all they do not have, but Pym's married women know marriage does not bring all these things.

Despite being denied certain of life's experiences, the Pym spinsters do not give up their interest in them. Spinsters such as Prudence, Emma, and Penelope are not so confined as the others by models of respectability, and they actively seek passion and romance. The excellent women are curious about passion and romance. The Pym women are openly interested in whether a clergyman is celibate. Comments and questions such as that by Ianthe Pott, a spinster in *A Few Green Leaves,* "Your vicar's good-looking isn't he? . . . Is he a celibate?," are scattered throughout the novels. Mildred Lathbury, at her annual luncheon with William Caldicote, the brother of her good friend Dora, finishes a quotation begun by William, saying, "*Drink deep, or taste not the Pierian spring.*" Mildred personalizes this statement by commenting, "But I'm afraid I shall never have the chance to drink deep so I must remain ignorant."

Just as Pym's spinsters do not give up thoughts of passion and romance, they also do not give up hopes of marriage. They keep these longings private, however, for in the Pym world, once a woman is resigned to being a spinster, she is expected to give up such hopes of marriage. At the annual luncheon between Mildred and William Caldicote, William tells Mildred that he and she are "the observers of life" and that marriage is for other people. Nonetheless, Mildred does not give up hope, although she cloaks it. She admits to herself, "But I have never been very much given to falling in love and have often felt sorry that I have so far missed . . . the experience of marriage." The use of the phrase "so far" indicates that she has not abandoned hope. When William questions her, "I do hope you're *not* thinking of getting married?," Mildred, reverting to the attitude her role requires, responds, "Oh, no, of course not!" She knows that a respect-

able spinster should not openly confess her desire for marriage.

The Quest of the Pym Woman: Her Search and Failure

The Pym spinster, not content with her station in life, looks for marriage, or at least attention from men, but she has to be either cautious or clever in the way that she does it. As a respectable spinster, she offers her services, whether typing, editing, making casseroles, knitting socks, or doing churchwork. As Belinda notes, she has to consider what is "fitting to her own years and position."

The main focus of Pym's excellent woman is usually her clergyman. Her efforts to get his attention are often cloaked in the guise of church work. As Wilmet notes in *A Glass of Blessings,* most of the excellent women are devoted rather than devout. The excellent women are fierce competitors for the attention of the clergy, and most of them harbor hopes of being chosen by a single clergyman for marriage. In fact, in one of the novels a character explicitly mentions the irate women a clergyman would have to contend with if he came to a parish already engaged.

The Pym women who work in offices are just as eager as the excellent women to find love and happiness. Their methods of finding men range from those of Dulcie, who stalks Aylwin Forbes like a detective, to Prudence Bates, who overdresses and applies a green, "greasy preparation which had little flecks of silver in it" to her eyelids. Instead of offering to knit socks or to do church work, they offer to type, edit, or make indexes. They also do other chores for men in exchange for attention and affection. For example, Emma Howick, the anthropologist in *A Few Green Leaves,* picks up groceries for Graham Pettifer and takes casseroles to his cottage. In *Less Than Angels,* Pym's novel about a community of anthropologists, Dierdre, a young student of anthropology, accurately describes how the Pym women seek love and happiness: "They had learned early in life what it is to bear love's burdens, listening patiently to their men's troubles and ever ready at their typewriters, should a manuscript or even a short article get to the stage of being written down." One can see that the relationships are sought after in a barterlike system, with Pym women applying the rules of trade to their struggles to escape their loneliness and unhappiness.

Still, the ways in which Pym's women seek love are not consonant with what they seek. Indeed, their choice of language reveals that their relationships are to be engineered by manipulation. In *Some Tame Gazelle* Edith, in speaking about Harriet and the bishop, comments, "I don't think Harriet will get him." She continues, "I think he has successfully avoided so many women in his life that not even Harriet will be able to catch him." In *Excellent Women* Sister Blatt decides, "Oh they [widows] have the knack of catching a man. Having done it once I suppose they can do it again." With language such as this, the ulterior motives behind these single women's typing and cooking become more apparent.

> **Despite the casseroles, knitted socks, indexes, typed manuscripts, and editing, the Pym woman never gets what she wants—love and happiness.**
> **—*Margaret C. Bradham***

Despite the casseroles, knitted socks, indexes, typed manuscripts, and editing, the Pym woman never gets what she wants—love and happiness. The excellent women who hope to win the heart of their clergyman or some other suitable man perform tasks which more often than not confirm their position as excellent women. The spinsters who are not excellent women, like Prudence and Penelope, are usually rejected by men as being either so overdone in their makeup and dress as to be "formidable rather than feminine and desirable" or as the type of women who "would have wanted so much."

Although the Pym women never get what they seek—love and happiness—some of Pym's spinsters find mild flirtations, lukewarm affairs, or suitable attachments. The experience that all the Pym women seem to crave is one that they have not had, since their "hearts mend too easily." *Jane and Prudence*'s twenty-nine-year-old spinster, Prudence Bates, one of Pym's favorite characters, is also one of her most promiscuous. Prudence enjoys affairs, and she is even described by her close friend Jane as having gotten "into the way of preferring unsatisfactory love affairs to any others, so that it was becoming almost a bad habit." The lack of emotion and feeling in Prudence's affairs is revealed by her ability to recover so quickly when they are over. Shortly after being jilted by Fabian Driver, she looks forward to having an affair with Gerry Manifold, although, as she tells Jane, "we shall probably hurt each other very much before it's finished."

More often than not, the Pym woman has, like Leonora, "never been badly treated or rejected by a man—perhaps she had never loved another person with enough intensity for such a thing [love wasted] to be possible." When Emma struggles to find the correct phrase to define her relationship with Graham, the description deflates from "brief love affair" to "mild affection" to "knew him quite well." Mildred admits that she "had once imagined [herself] to be in love" with Bernard Hatherley. When Dulcie meets Maurice Clive, the man who formerly had rejected her, she feels indifferent toward him. And when Tom Mallow, a young anthropologist, is killed in Africa, his girlfriend Dierdre is upset over not being upset. She tells Catherine, "I know you won't be too shocked when I say I can't really *feel* anything about Tom." More often than not, if a Pym woman has loved and lost, the love proves to have been so lukewarm and one-sided that she really had nothing to lose in the first place. In *Less Than Angels* Mark Penfold, a fledgling anthropologist, describes this kind of tepid affair: "It is commoner in our society than many people would suppose . . . the woman giving the food and shelter and doing some typing for him and the man giving the priceless gift of himself." Mark is speaking of the relationship between Catherine Oliphant and Tom Mallow, two of his friends who live together. His description, which recognizes primarily the convenience of the relationship instead of the romance, is an accurate one. When Tom leaves Catherine, there are no outbursts of emotion, but rather perfunctory acceptance of a lack of interest.

When marriages occur in Pym's novels, they are generally the type of relationship known in the Pym world as a "suitable attachment." In *No Fond Return of Love* Dulcie describes this type of relationship. Quickly informing middle-aged Aylwin Forbes that any thoughts of marrying her nineteen-year-old niece are clearly out of place, Dulcie boldly instructs him in what is suitable: he should make a "sensible marriage," a marriage with "somebody who can appreciate [his] work and help [him] with it." In *A Few Green Leaves* Emma, who at times views her condition as objectively as any of the Pym characters, expresses the essence of the suitable attachment in her assessment of her situation with Tom: "After all, they were two lonely people now, and as such should get together." In thinking of a possible union between herself and Tom, Emma appeals to logic, not to romantic notions.

For the most part, these suitable attachments occur between minor characters and are mentioned only in passing. Such attachments for Pym's main characters never occur in full focus in the individual novels in which the characters appear. If there is hope of a possible marriage for the Pym spinster, it is suggested only at the end of the novel. For example, at the respective conclusions of *Excellent Women, No Fond Return of Love,* and *A Few Green Leaves,* the possible marriages of Mildred Lathbury and Everard Bone, Dulcie Mainwaring and Aylwin Forbes, and Emma Howick and Tom Dagnall are suggested but left in question. By only suggesting marriages at the end of her novels, Pym downgrades the importance of these less-than-ideal relationships. In fact, this is one of the ways she shows that these relationships are less than ideal.

The grimness of the suitable attachment is recognized by Ianthe Broome, one of the main characters in *An Unsuitable Attachment.* On learning of the engagement of Miss

Grimes, a retired elderly spinster, to a Polish widower, she thinks:

> At that moment life seemed very dark; Ianthe was perhaps too rigid in her views to reflect that a woman might have worse things to look forward to than the prospect of marriage to a Polish widower and a life in Ealing, or even a quick drink in one's own room at the end of a hard day.

Having "worse things to look forward to" is a condition in which many of the Pym women find themselves. However, Ianthe knows and on one occasion admits that life can be very lonely for a woman, and that is "why it's better to marry when one has the chance—or perhaps I should say if one has the chance." The spinsters do not all have the chance to escape loneliness by marriage, for, more often than not, the relationship peters out. In *Jane and Prudence* Fabian Driver loses interest in Prudence; in *Less Than Angels* Tom loses interest in Catherine; in *An Unsuitable Attachment* Rupert never really has any interest in Penelope; in *The Sweet Dove Died* James leaves Leonora for a homosexual; and in *A Few Green Leaves* Graham Pettifer loses interest in Emma.

Having found neither lukewarm love affairs nor suitable attachments, most Pym women are so desperate for affection that they will content themselves with illusions. Viola Dace, a character in *No Fond Return of Love,* had "offered to do Aylwin's index, unfairly waylaying him on the steps of the British Museum so that he could hardly have refused." Viola creates an illusion out of this incident and smugly tells Dulcie, "Aylwin has asked me to do the index for his new book." She even drops the line, "I shall be rather busy . . . so you may not see very much of me," as a way of "casually" telling Dulcie this news. Dulcie's accurate judgment about Viola, which is applicable to many of Pym's women, is: "Just to be allowed to love them [men such as Aylwin Forbes] is enough." The Pym women have no other choice, since they, like Viola, can expect nothing more. Furthermore, "to be allowed to love them" is essential.

Dulcie discovers why "to love them is enough" for the Pym women: she understands that "perhaps women enjoy that [doing what they could] most of all—to feel that they are needed and doing good." This observation of Dulcie's is confirmed by another Pym character. Wilmet, in *A Glass of Blessings,* admits, "Everybody wants to be needed, women especially." From Wilmet's statement we begin to realize that one of the reasons women want to be needed is that it makes them feel important or at least useful. Feeling needed is a way of hedging against the fear, as Mildred puts it, of "being unwanted," the terror of knowing that one, like a photo in a picture frame at a jumble sale, "could so very easily be replaced."

The Predicament of the Pym Woman: Her Disappointments and Illusions

In *Less Than Angels* Catherine describes the life that she herself knows and observes around her: "It's comic and sad and indefinite—dull, sometimes, but seldom really tragic or deliriously happy, except when one's very young." This description could apply to the lives of all Pym's main female characters. In every Pym novel a character makes a similar confession: "We can't expect to get everything we want . . . we know that life isn't like that"; "Life hasn't turned out quite as she meant it to." If a character does not admit this in words, we nonetheless sense that she feels it.

Pym's characters assuage their disappointment by fostering vague hopes. On several occasions throughout *A Few Green Leaves* Emma wonders, "Who knew what might come of it?," and "There was no knowing what it might lead to." When Letty, after retirement, is "settled in Mrs. Pope's back room," she thinks, "There was no knowing how her life would change," and she retains these illusions. *Quartet in Autumn* ends with Letty thinking, "At least it made one realise that life still held infinite possibilities for change." The "it" refers to Letty's choice of either remaining with her London landlady or joining Marjorie, a friend who has recently been jilted by her fiancé. Letty's possibilities are hardly "infinite," for the available change is not significant. The reader therefore understands Letty's perception of 'infinite possibilities of change' as illusory. There is no hope for real change in her life. The only change that will occur is the change all the characters in this novel fear: aging and death.

The Pym woman adopts certain attitudes as camouflage for the despair and loneliness she feels. The fierceness of her determination to keep up appearances is virtually a barometer of the extent of her unhappiness. For example, after her retirement, Letty feels that "she must never give the slightest hint of loneliness or boredom, the sense of time hanging heavy." Letty is not the only character who "made up her mind to face Christmas with courage and a kind of deliberate boldness, a determination to hold the prospect of loneliness at bay." Christmas is the one holiday that most of Pym's spinsters dread, for, as Pym tells us in *Quartet in Autumn,* it is "a difficult time for those who are no longer young and are without close relatives or dependents." Letty herself admits that she is "dutifully assuming the suggested attitude towards retirement that life was full of possibilities." Letty's situation seems even grimmer, because she admits for a moment that even she does not believe in the attitude she is expected to adopt. We see a paradox: she is expected to expect the unexpected.

Presenting optimistic attitudes for the future is not enough for the Pym women. They must also dampen the disappointments of the past with convenient fictions. This conversation between Mildred and Dora could easily occur among other Pym spinsters.

> 'There's not much you can do when you're over thirty,' she went on complacently. 'You get too set in your ways, really. Besides, marriage isn't everything.'

> 'No, it certainly isn't,' I agreed, 'and there's nobody I want to marry that I can think of. Not even William.'

> 'I don't know anyone either, at the moment,' said Dora.

> We lapsed into a comfortable silence. It was a kind of fiction that we had always kept up, this not knowing anyone at the moment that we wanted to marry, as if there had been in the past and would be in the future.

Mildred recognizes these shared illusions, these fictions, for what they are. She does not dispel them, however, for she feels the essential comfort and compensation they provide.

Pym's characters frequently escape rejection and unhappiness by reshaping disappointing circumstances. With the aid of rationalizations they create consolations. In *Less Than Angels* Catherine views an example of this type of consolation in Rhoda's response to Mabel as they discuss Dierdre's reaction to the death of her boyfriend Tom Mallow.

> 'You must allow Dierdre her grief,' said Mabel almost sharply. 'You don't know what it is to lose somebody you love.'

> 'You've no right to say that, of course I do'. . . Rhoda's voice trembled and she began to refill the teacups in an agitated way.

> Catherine noticed her confusion and wondered if she were trying to justify herself, to think of some kind of compensation for the shame of not having lost lover or husband, but only parents and others who had died at their natural and proper time. *If women could not expect to savour all experiences that life could offer, perhaps they did want the sad ones—not necessarily to have loved or been loved, but at least to have lost,* she thought simply and without cynicism. (emphasis mine)

The only sustainable fiction the Pym woman can create is the belief that she has loved and lost, thereby justifying her existence as a spinster. What becomes clear is that the Pym spinster's delusion about romance, loving, and losing is a way to see herself as someone she is not, to distinguish herself from others, to embellish or even invent reality and thereby, if only as an illusion, create some of the experience she has not had. These illusions are more pathetic and difficult to sustain as the Pym women grow older. Aging means a loss of one's self-esteem as well as one's ability to attract men, or at least the hope of being able to attract men. Thus, as Pym's women grow older and less attractive, they begin to see loneliness as a permanent condition.

Still, sometimes these illusions catch up with their creators, as in Belinda's effort to console Count Bianco for his unrequited love for Harriet.

> Her eyes lighted on the works of Alfred, Lord Tennyson 'that it is better to have loved and lost than never to have loved at all. I always think those lines are such a great comfort; so many of us loved and lost.' She frowned: nobody wanted to be one of the many, and she did not like this picture of herself, only one of a great crowd of dreary women. Perhaps Tennyson was rather hackneyed after all.

Belinda shifts the blame to Tennyson and refuses to see herself as one of a great crowd. She dodges the implication and avoids having her comfortable illusion melt.

The grim reality, however, is probably as Letty sees it: "Even Marcia had once hinted at something in her own life, long ago. No doubt everybody had once had something in their lives? Certainly it was the kind of thing people like to imply, making one suspect that a good deal was being made out of almost nothing." Catherine, in *Less Than Angels,* notices that the experience that the Pym woman wants is at least "to have lost." In *Some Tame Gazelle* Belinda expresses a related belief shared by many of Pym's women. She is "sure that our greater English poets had written much about unhappy lovers *not* dying of grief, although it was of course more romantic when they did." There is no logic in her idea that to die for grief is romantic. Having loved and lost is to the Pym character both tragic and romantic; indeed, *tragic* and *romantic* seem almost to be synonyms. The irony is that the condition she desires would bring her only that from which she wants to escape: loneliness, unhappiness, and despair.

The Attitude of the Author Pym: The Sympathy and Irony

Pym states the cases of types of women who have not, at least in the twentieth century, often found their way into literature. She writes the novels that Letty in *Quartet in Autumn* looked for but could not find: "[Letty] had always been an unashamed reader of novels, but if she hoped to find one which reflected her own sort of life she had come to realise that the position of an unmarried, unattached, ageing woman is of no interest whatever to the writer of modern fiction." In stating the case of the lonely women who are not regarded with much concern even in their world, Pym is sympathetic to her characters' plight. For all her sympathy, she writes realistic, indeed ironic novels, not sentimental ones. For all her characters' loneliness, they are women who are, for the most part, selfish and self-concerned. The Pym woman is observant of those who surround her, but her awareness does not stem from concern about others, only curiosity. In fact, when Pym women become aware of situations in which they might be expected to help, they recoil. After her brother's engagement is announced, Winifred tells Mildred, "I hoped I would come and live with you." Mildred confesses that the thought of Winifred staying with her "filled [her] with sinking apprehension," and she is careful in her answer because she realizes that "easy excuses . . . would not do here." And when Letty and Marcia, two of the quartet in **Quartet in Autumn,** retire, Marcia fears that Letty will ask her if she can come and live with her.

Thus the Pym women, although they recognize the loneliness of others, do not exhibit real compassion or sympathy. Their thoughts remain centered on themselves, and they remain detached and aloof. Indeed, the Pym women even see each other as rivals, natural antagonists in a world where pettiness has replaced compassion. When a woman is successful in getting "the desired object," the other women reveal their jealousy. For example, in discussing Mildred Lathbury's marriage to Everard Bone, Miss Morrow learns from Miss Bonner that "Mildred helped him a good deal in his work" and that "she even learned to type so that she could type his manuscripts for him." Miss Morrow immediately decides, "Oh, then he had to marry her. . . . That kind of devotion is worse than blackmail—a man has no escape from that."

Pym's works are infused with irony. The criticism that "nothing ever happens" is often applied to her novels. Nothing much happens in them, and thus the reality of the characters' lives is just what makes their statements that "anything might happen" ironic. Despite their unhappy circumstances. Pym's women cling to their illusions. Belinda observes, "But there was always hope springing eternal in the human breast, which kept one alive, often unhappily . . . it would be an interesting subject on which to read a paper to the Literary Society." The works of Barbara Pym are "papers on this interesting subject." While we laugh with Pym as she exposes, in her witty way, her characters' minor foibles and petty machinations, we should not gloss over the darker side of her writing or ignore the grim reality of her characters' conditions. She shows us women who search for love and happiness. In their quest they offer their services

and compete fiercely among themselves to gain attention and affection. Not finding what they seek, her women remain unhappy and lonely. Self-centered and self-concerned, and at times petty, they are painfully aware of having missed out on life. To fend off their disappointments, they occupy themselves with trivial chores and minor tasks, and they fortify themselves with vague hopes and small consolations. Pym's women have failed at romance and love, and they grow old suffering the fears of aging and the terrors of loneliness. They cling to pathetic illusions and look to the future with vain expectations that "anything could happen." To protect their optimistic attitudes and to ward off potential disappointments, they have learned to keep their hopes vague and unspecific.

Merritt Moseley (essay date Winter 1990)

SOURCE: "A Few Words about Barbara Pym," in *The Sewanee Review,* Vol. 98, No. 1, Winter, 1990, pp. 75-87.

[*In the following essay, Moseley provides a critical overview of Pym's fiction through discussion of her recurring preoccupation with unmarried women, the Anglican church, English literature, anthropology, and weak men.*]

Thinking about Barbara Pym's present state of renown reminds me of the character in one of Kingsley Amis's novels who occupies himself in trying to understand his liking for women's breasts: "I was clear on why I liked them, thanks, but why did I like them *so much?*" Those who like Barbara Pym like her so much that perhaps some attempt to explain why is in order. As late as 1977 she was completely obscure. Now Eudora Welty, Anne Tyler, and Mary Gordon, among others, name her as a favorite writer. Scholarly writers regularly link her casually with Jane Austen. A Barbara Pym Newsletter is appearing. At the Bodleian Library, where her literary effects are deposited, most visitors ("especially Americans") are said to be in search of the Pym collection, and the curator explains that at least five people are writing books about her. One of her discarded novels, **Crampton Hodnet,** has recently been resurrected and published, and all her others, in addition to her "autobiography" in letters and journals, are available in paperback.

Miss Pym's novels have an amazing consistency or reliability ("sameness" suggests the wrong idea). This is amazing, since she began her first in 1935, when she was just out of Oxford, and completed her last in 1979. Reading through them in order, one enjoys a remarkable feeling of familiarity, recurrence, the repetition of established pleasures. Her resistance to change (other than in two of her books written under special circumstances) gratifies her admirers. But it is also the reason, apparently, for the wilderness years, beginning in 1961, during which she published nothing.

Some Tame Gazelle, the novel which she had begun in the middle thirties and worked on for years, despite rejections from publishers who thought it not exciting enough, was published in 1950. The reviews were respectful, the sales modest but enough to encourage further books. And so she wrote, steadily, five more novels—*Excellent Women, Jane and Prudence, Less Than Angels, A Glass of Blessings,* and *No Fond Return of Love,* published at regular intervals from 1952 to 1961. The normal successful English novelist always publishes more novels than his American counterpart. Prolificacy is considered a sign of professionalism rather than (as sometimes here), facile lack of artistic weight; the pace achieved by Anthony Burgess or Kingsley Amis or Iris Murdoch, a novel about every other year, is expected, rather than the infrequent and painful deliveries of a Joseph Heller or Thomas Pynchon. Barbara Pym settled comfortably into this routine and planned to continue in it.

In 1963 she sent her newest manuscript, called *An Unsuitable Attachment,* to her publisher, Jonathan Cape. She knew that the fiction market was moving away from her kind of book and even in the nineteen thirties her agent had advised her to "be more wicked, if necessary." Now she worried, in a letter to Philip Larkin: "I sent my novel to Cape last week but don't know yet what they think of it. I feel it can hardly come up to *Catch 22* or *The Passion Flower Hotel* for selling qualities but I hope they will realise that it is necessary for a good publisher's list to have something milder." They did not realize it, though, and rejected the novel, explaining that it was of a type that readers no longer wanted to buy. The novelist was terribly hurt. She tried a number of other publishers (twenty-one, eventually), made changes in the manuscript, pulled what few strings she had access to. Another publisher wrote her that *An Unsuitable Attachment* was "a pleasant book, but hardly strong enough," to which she responded in her journal—"almost exactly what Cape said of *Some Tame Gazelle* in 1936."

Eventually she quit trying to place the novel, reflecting at one point that "it might appear naive and unsophisticated, though it isn't really, to an unsympathetic publisher's reader, hoping for that novel about negro homosexuals, young men in advertising, etc." In the next years she wrote two others, working in considerable bitterness and convinced that she could get nothing published. In them, *The Sweet Dove Died* and *Quartet in Autumn,* she retained her special subject, unmarried women, but with an edge of grimness and humorlessness which is striking. And she turned now to what she undoubtedly felt were more "contemporary" themes— sex presented more openly; bisexuality; aging, lonely, and loveless people; insanity. She continued with the job she had held since 1946, as an editor of the anthropological journal

Africa. In 1974, following a stroke and an operation for cancer, she retired to live in an Oxfordshire village with her sister Hilary. She was now resigned to silence as a novelist, though she continued writing fiction for herself and her friends, and she kept on with her journals.

These journals, published in part as *A Very Private Eye,* provide some vivid glimpses of her pain. Through the sixties she chafed at the changed literary world, which no longer had room for her. One journal entry summarizes 1963 as "a year of violence, death and blows," and includes among the blows the rejection of her novel, the burglary of her flat, the popularity of *Honest to God* and *Tropic of Cancer,* and her own reading of *Naked Lunch.* Always fascinated by details of dress, she frequently contrasts her own appearance, dowdy and "correct," with that of younger novelists: at the Writers' Circle Dinner in 1966, "Margaret Drabble in a beautiful short flowered dress with long sleeves. Some in long glittering brocades. All with neat little 'evening bags'— only B.P. with her black leather day handbag." Though she writes bravely to Philip Larkin that she will never publish again, her journal shows her inability to accept her fate:

> What is wrong with being obsessed with trivia? Some have criticized *The Sweet Dove Died* for this. What are the minds of my critics filled with? What *nobler* and more worthwhile things?

> Mr. C in the Library—he is having his lunch, eating a sandwich with a knife and fork, a glass of milk near at hand. Oh why can't I write about things like that any more—why is this kind of thing no longer acceptable?

> The position of the unmarried woman—unless, of course, she is somebody's mistress—is of no interest whatsoever to the readers of modern fiction.

> Being told that it is "virtually impossible" for a novel like *The Sweet Dove* to be published now (by Constable). What is the future of my kind of writing? What can my notebooks contain except the normal kinds of bits and pieces that can never (?) now be worked into fiction. Perhaps in retirement, and even in the year before, a quieter, narrower kind of life can be worked out and adopted. Bounded by English literature and the Anglican Church and small pleasures like sewing and choosing dress material for this uncertain summer.

As a novelist Barbara Pym was recalled to life by an article in the *Times Literary Supplement.* Among a group of literary eminences asked to name the most underrated writers of the century, both Philip Larkin and Lord David Cecil named Barbara Pym—the only living writer to be mentioned by two people. Almost overnight she was a celebrity. Her most recently written novel, *Quartet in Autumn,* was soon published by Macmillan, followed by *The Sweet Dove Died.* Jonathan Cape, her old publisher, who had lost interest in her after 1961, jumped on the bandwagon, and between 1977 and 1979 reissued her six novels of the fifties. *Quartet in Autumn* was a finalist for the Booker prize in 1977. Eventually Macmillan published *A Few Green Leaves,* written after her new celebrity, and *An Unsuitable Attachment,* the book which was rejected in 1963. She died in 1980. Beginning in 1978, Dutton has published all her novels in the U.S., including *Crampton Hodnet,* an early, abandoned novel about Oxford. There should be more manuscripts, to judge from comments in her journals; and at this rate we are likely to see them in print before too long.

But why? To say that the Barbara Pym revival was caused by Lord David Cecil and Philip Larkin is obviously too simple; though their endorsement does explain the surprised articles on Pym and the 1977 BBC film showing her and Lord David drinking tea at her Oxfordshire cottage, it can't, after all, explain much more. Few people will read a Barbara Pym novel because Lord David Cecil and Philip Larkin, two old-fashioned readers who are hardly taste-makers for the masses, say they should—much less read more than one book. A professed admiration for her work may make one feel knowing. But her readers respond to something more important.

What are Barbara Pym's novels about? One could do worse than begin with her wry self-appraisal: "a quieter, narrower kind of life . . . bounded by English literature and the Anglican Church and small pleasures like sewing and choosing dress material for this uncertain summer." With the exception of *The Sweet Dove Died,* which is an experiment, her novels involve a quiet narrow life. Perhaps this narrowness produces the comparisons with Jane Austen, who also focuses on the domestic life of a few people. But the comparison is misleading, since Barbara Pym's novels are much narrower and much quieter. Though like Jane Austen she places at the center of all her books (there is one exception). Some do show signs of movement toward marriage, and some marriages are revealed in later novels, but this is no unambiguously happy ending. In place of the perfect happiness described at the end of *Pride and Prejudice* or *Emma,* Pym's *Excellent Women* ends with a dullish anthropologist, Everard Bone, gracelessly asking the heroine to type and index his book. This is nearly as much romance as a Pym novel ever contains.

The recurrent features of the Pym novels are then:

1) unmarried women, the most important of whom are never young. The typical Pym protagonist is in her mid-thirties, having survived a bad love affair that seems to have ended

through pointlessness. She works as something moderately intellectual, as a librarian or researcher or indexer, or does volunteer work, perhaps with the church. She is usually a reader and may be a writer or an anthropologist. She probably lives alone. She is, in almost every case, a "gentlewoman," because she wears good tweeds and wistfully recognizes certain things she may not do.

2) the Anglican church, usually as represented by its clergy and its female worshipers, who loom large in the dramatis personae of the novels. Much of the activity of such books as *Excellent Women* and *Some Tame Gazelle* and *A Few Leaves* revolves around the church. Nobody seems particularly devout or ardent, even the clergy. There are Anglicans who attend church for aesthetic reasons—to hear a good sermon, to see a well decorated nave, even to inhale good incense. For most the church imposes certain rhythms—harvest festivals and Lent and Confirmation classes—and provides a center, even if frequently factitious, for the lives of unmarried women. They decorate the altar; they buy and sell marrows and marmalade at dreary garden fetes; they collect jumble and price it for the sale; they turn up at the parish hall for slide shows by visiting African bishops; they gossip about incense and confession and celibacy and birettas on priests, they read the parish magazine and pitch in to launder the vicar's vestments. The women who, in such tasks, provide the backbone of the church, are regularly referred to as "really splendid," or "excellent women." *Some Tame Gazelle* gives a comic picture of such a woman, Edith Liversidge:

> "She's a kind of decayed gentlewoman," said Harriet comfortably, helping the curate to trifle.

> "Oh *no,* Harriet," Belinda protested. Nobody could call Edith decayed and sometimes one almost forgot that she was a gentlewoman, with her cropped grey hair, her shabby clothes which weren't even the legendary "good tweeds" of her kind and her blunt, almost rough, way of speaking. "Miss Liversidge is really splendid," she declared and then wondered why one always said that Edith was "splendid." It was probably because she hadn't very much money, was tough and wiry, dug vigorously in her garden and kept goats.

And the next novel, *Excellent Women,* analyzes more seriously the roles of such mainstays of the parish; Mildred Lathbury, the narrator and a classic example of the type, reflects that "it was not the excellent women who got married but people like Allegra Gray, who was no good at sewing, and Helena Napier, who left all the washing up." When the unmarried sister of her vicar comments that "Mildred would never do anything wrong or foolish," Mildred "reflected a little sadly that this was only too true and hoped I did not appear too much that kind of person to others. Virtue is an excellent thing and we should all strive after it, but it can sometimes be a little depressing."

3) English literature. Often the central character has taken a degree in English and may be a lecturer in the subject; almost all of them are readers, specifically of English poetry of the eighteenth and nineteenth century, and comment on events with remembered quotations. Barbara Pym, who read English at Oxford, weaves a network of literary references into her novels, beginning with a number of the titles: *Some Tame Gazelle* is from Nathaniel T. H. Bayly; *Less Than Angels* from Pope; *The Sweet Dove Died* from Keats; *A Glass of Blessings* from Herbert. Sometimes these titles are exquisite—Belinda Bede quotes the lines which reverberate through all the novels:

> Some tame gazelle, or some gentle dove:
> Something to love, oh, something to love!

The fondness for literature is sometimes a bit imperialistic, as in the case of Archdeacon Henry Hoccleve, a major figure in *Some Tame Gazelle,* whose sermons are incomprehensible and self-indulgent ragouts of inappropriate quotations. Or the literary habit can lead to the minor social discomfort produced by a spontaneous but "unsuitable" quotation. Belinda Bede, caught in the middle of a conversation about plans for a fishpond, thinks of poetry. "Belinda shivered. The fishes would be so cold and slimy. . . . 'Leigh Hunt writes rather charmingly about a fish,' she said aloud." "'*Legless, unloving, infamously chaste*'; she paused. Perhaps it was hardly suitable, really, and she was a little ashamed of having quoted it, but these little remembered scraps of culture had a way of coming out unexpectedly." Indifference to poetry is frequently an unsympathetic characteristic; and Pym's two darkest novels, *The Sweet Dove Died* and *Quartet in Autumn,* are strikingly bare of literature as well as religion.

4) Anthropology. Barbara Pym worked with anthropologists at the International African Institute, and they populate her novels. Her picture of them is not impressive. They are unloving and sometimes infamously chaste (the two most important ones are called Everard Bone and Rupert Stonebird), self-centered, and usually ridiculous. They go "out into the field" (Africa) with no clear idea why; they draw up kinship diagrams and tables and graphs, and exchange unwanted off-prints. From time to time someone among the uninitiated inquires how the anthropologist *helps* the Africans, but nobody can answer. Some of Pym's novels include the formidable figure of Esther Clovis, a secular "excellent woman," who administers an anthropological institute, and a circle of others around her who exchange arcane information. "Oh, Miss Lydgate," says one at a sherry party, "I must apologize for what I sent you," he wailed. "It was im-

mensely unfortunate, but the language is spoken by only five persons now, and the only informant I could find was a very old man, so old that he had no teeth."

Some of the anthropologists turn to better things. Emma Howick, the protagonist of Pym's last novel, *A Few Green Leaves,* has come to a village to "write up her notes" (always represented as a terrifying and bewildering procedure), but turns gradually to a more humane observation of her village and, by book's end, seems to have become a novelist herself. *Less Than Angels* shows some of the more intelligent young anthropologists in training coming to question its value. And the most liberating act of that novel, perhaps the most liberating event in Barbara Pym's life work, comes when Catherine Oliphant, a fiction writer, persuades an anthropologist to burn all his notes.

> A large bonfire of sticks and garden rubbish was blazing beyond the vegetable patch. Two figures, a tall man and a small woman, were poking at it vigorously with long sticks, pausing from time to time to throw on to it bundles of paper which they were taking from a tin trunk which stood on the ground nearby.
>
> "Alaric, *what are you doing?*" Miss Lydgate's voice had now risen to a screech.
>
> "Why, hello, Gertrude," he said, "we're having a bonfire."
>
> "Yes," said Catherine, her face shining in the firelight, "Alaric had so much junk up in his attic and Guy Fawkes night seemed just the time to get rid of some of it."
>
> She is calling him Alaric, thought Gertrude irrelevantly.
>
> "But these are your notes," screamed Miss Clovis, snatching a half-burned sheet from the edge of the fire. "'They did not know when their ancestors left the place of the big rock nor why, nor could they say how long they had been in their present habitat . . .'" she read, then threw it back with an impatient gesture. "Kinship tables!" she shrieked. "You cannot let *these* go!" She snatched at another sheet, covered with little circles and triangles, but Alaric restrained her and poked it further into the fire with his stick.

Though the irreverence toward the written word and the reckless *cutting loose* which Catherine and Alaric enjoy here is not representative of Pym's characters and plots, several things about this episode are exquisitely typical. One is the sharp eye for social detail shown in Gertrude's wholly relevant observation that Catherine is calling Alaric by his first name. Another is the reaction of a neighbor who, like many of Pym's characters, is very nosy and thus spends much of her time spying on others. "'I don't know *what's* going on at Mr. Lydgate's', said Rhoda, stumbling across the lawn. 'They're burning papers on a bonfire and dancing round it. It seems so'—she hesitated for a word—'*unsuitable,*' she brought out."

5) The weakness of men. Oddly this is usually disguised as strength. The disguise fools the men themselves and some of the less observant women, but not the novelist or her most perceptive female characters. Her men, especially those who figure as sexually appealing, are compounds of petty flaws. Usually self-absorbed, fairly boring, pretentious, they cannot cope with disagreeable details of life, like making tea or doing clerical work. They are abetted by women who pamper men, justifying themselves by a belief in men's greater needs or their greater importance. Women eat macaroni and cheese, but men need stronger stuff. Occasionally a perceptive woman wonders why. "This insistence on a man's needs amused Jane. Men needed meat and eggs—well, yes, that might be allowed; but surely not more than women did? Perhaps Mrs. Crampton's widowhood had something to do with it; possibly she made up for having no man to feed at home by ministering to the needs of those who frequented her cafe." But even Jane never speaks out against this kind of coddling which, in this case, is directed at her husband, a *clergyman* and thus a member of the most coddled and excused class of men. The novels are full of bachelor vicars, depending either on unmarried sisters or on sympathetic female parishioners for such needs as food, laundering, and walking-around sense.

Pym's attitude toward men is oddly hard to define. Though her fiction contains no impressive men, her women are satisfied to love those who are available. The insensitive Archdeacon Hoccleve tells Belinda Bede: "I thought women enjoyed missing their meals and making martyrs of themselves." Her response is momentarily acerbic: "We may do it, but I think we can leave the enjoyment of it to the men." But she continues loving the archdeacon all the same, perhaps more the more weaknesses he exposes.

Barbara Pym had love affairs, usually with egoistic and selfish men (Henry Hoccleve is an acknowledged portrait of the great love of her undergraduate days). Her male characters, even when satirized, are handled with affection. Interviewed for the BBC in 1977, she was flustered when "a question about my treatment of men characters suggested that I had a low opinion of the sex. My instinctive reply sprang to my lips 'Oh, but I love men,' but luckily I realised how ridiculous it would sound, so said something feeble."

> **Like her major women characters Miss Pym saw the unsuitability of men but continued to love them. In *A Very Private Eye* we occasionally come across the kind of acidly perceptive comment on this paradox which the fictional heroines never make.**
>
> **—Merritt Moseley**

Like her major women characters Miss Pym saw the unsuitability of men but continued to love them. In *A Very Private Eye* we occasionally come across the kind of acidly perceptive comment on this paradox which the fictional heroines never make. In wartime, in the middle of another hopeless love affair (this time with the estranged husband of one of her friends), she writes: "A wild and stormy day. Icy wind and driving rain—we all got soaked coming back to lunch. I made curry for supper. Late in the evening, cutting dreary sandwiches for work tomorrow, I let myself go for perhaps half an hour. But one always has to pick oneself up again and go on being *drearily splendid.*" And, in a reflection which none of her fictional "excellent women" would make, she writes: "Last night Margaret and I went out with Peter (boredom is an exquisite experience, to be savoured and analysed like old brandy and sex)."

The source of Barbara Pym's appeal, though, is something more than this summary can explain. As her own uneasy suspicion of her books' unfitness for the sixties indicates, there are fashions in these matters. After the craving for the new and exotic that was a phenomenon of the sixties, readers perhaps have reacted with a new longing for the old and familiar. The frequent complimentary comparisons of Barbara Pym to Jane Austen suggest the existence of Pymites or Barbaraites like the Janeites who preserve the myth of gentle Jane. There are distinctly nostalgic strains here. Lord David Cecil, whose book on Jane Austen shows some uneasiness with the Regency period and backdates Jane to make her a contemporary of Dr. Johnson, has praised Barbara Pym as the author of "the finest examples of high comedy to have appeared in England during the past seventy-five years." The other architect of her revival, Philip Larkin, shunned the literary vanguard, saying: "I very much feel the need to be on the periphery of things. I suppose when one was young one liked to be up to date." England has lately, according to journalists, seen the rise of the "young Fogies," and Barbara Pym may figure in some scheme of retrogression together with braces and bowlers and tea-dancing at the Ritz. Some people read Trollope for the same reasons. The English have always had a vocal faction that decries modernism as nonsense, and Barbara Pym, by no means a modernist writer, may quiet anxieties of dislocation and confusion.

The main reasons for her growing reputation, and the reasons why people *should* read her, are literary and aesthetic. One of these is her creation of a little world, made up of bedsitters and country villages, single women (mostly excellent, or drearily splendid), eccentric older people, minor and inconclusive class conflicts, women falling in love with men who accept that love and in some cases even return it. There is no intrinsic value to any of these particular constituents of her world; nor to the fact that it is a *little* world, as the little-bit-of-ivory, or what-to-make-of-a-diminished-thing school of Pymites imply.

Her strength is in her *mastery* of that world, the result of a tough and absolutely clear-eyed realism. When we read a novel by Barbara Pym, we may find ourselves thinking of the most prominent young woman as the heroine, as I have done in this essay, but, except for the few novels with first-person narration, there is nothing in the book to authorize this reading. Even characters who write for a living, often a sure indication of their creator's fondness, are granted no special sympathy or attractiveness, and are as liable to mistakes as anybody else. These putative heroines are clearly scrutinized and sharply judged implicitly and explicitly by the narrator. There is no privileging of the major character. In the case of *The Sweet Dove Died,* the protagonist, Leonora, is ruthlessly anatomized, although she is a partial self-portrait of Pym. *Quartet in Autumn* balances four main characters, none of them particularly sympathetic. Barbara Pym frequently uses bits of herself—wartime service in the Wrens, futile attachment to a younger homosexual, interest in cats—but almost impartially, readily assigning her own traits to the most unlikely or unpleasant of characters.

Some Tame Gazelle, for instance, is extraordinary. Begun when she was at Oxford, it is a successful attempt to write about herself, her sister, the love of her life, the love of *his* life, and all their friends, at age fifty or so. Belinda Bede, who is Barbara Pym thirty years on, is slightly set apart and enhanced by more sense and more decorum than the other characters, though these help make her a bit silly; but she is hardly the main character in the plot, which, typically slight, revolves around her sister's fondness for young curates. The novel, which Pym showed as she wrote it to the man she loved, is exquisitely accurate in portraying him in the complacent egoist Henry Hoccleve; and no less accurate in its discovery that Belinda (Barbara) loves him despite his unworthiness, to which her loyalty cannot blind her.

Realistic, too, is her fidelity to little things. Her world is made up of homely details: what people eat for meals, what women wear and whether or not it is suitable, the books people give each other, their haircuts, jewelry, quality of overcoats, their seats in church. Moreover Pym's steady devotion to "little," ordinary events as the staple for her plots

is also admirable. Her novels almost never include death, and in only one case can be said to build toward a death as a resolution of plot. More surprising with unmarried women as protagonists, her novels almost never build toward a marriage. Or if they build toward one, it is averted. The unwillingness to use marriage as a satisfactory conclusion is by no means unusual in contemporary fiction: instead it shows some signs of becoming the convention. But in Pym's novels there is absolutely nothing didactic about this rejection of the marriage solution. Women think about getting married but don't; or as the novel ends they may get married, but they haven't yet; and it is clear that even if this marriage will *not* be the answer to all prayers, it will not be a catastrophe, either. Pym doesn't use marriage in the traditional way, but her omission of it is entirely unostentatious and untendentious. That is the way things work out. The end of *A Few Green Leaves* is unusually forceful, by comparison with the usual dying fall or commonplace observation. Emma Howick faces the future: "'Yes, I might do that,' Emma agreed, but without revealing which aspect she proposed to deal with. She remembered that her mother had said something about wanting to let the cottage to a former student, who was writing a novel and recovering from an unhappy love affair. But this was not going to happen, for Emma was going to stay in the village herself. *She* could write a novel and even, as she was beginning to realize, embark on a love affair which need not necessarily be an unhappy one."

But we must go beyond Barbara Pym's patient realism, which cannot by itself explain her attractions, to something much more shadowy and difficult to name. Besides the "world" that she creates, her novels are distinguished just as much for their tone. Lord David's claim that her novels are the finest examples of high comedy in England in the past seventy-five years is probably excessive, but all except the two dark books I have mentioned are nevertheless quite funny. If "high comedy" induces a civilized smile rather than helpless laughter, it is an accurate characterization. There are few really rich "situations," few witty lines. The comedy is almost entirely a matter of slightly unusual events, slightly odd remarks, observed sharply and reported with unvarying aplomb.

Perhaps the most essential quality in Barbara Pym's comic world is the perception of what is "suitable." Among her gentlewomen things are seldom really evil, or wrong: they are unsuitable. This unsuitability, perceived as comic incongruity, flavors the distinctive tone of her novels. And, though they are by no means constructed around set pieces, making excerption difficult, a few quotations may convey something of their flavor. In *Excellent Women,* Mildred is working at that most characteristic event for a Pym novel, a church bazaar, which characteristically is depressing and unsuccessful in raising funds for the church.

At the tea hatch, too, trade had slackened and we were able to talk as we ate and drank. Mrs. Morris's sing-song voice could be heard above the others: "Lovely *antique* pieces they've got. I said what about giving them a bit of a polish and *he* said oh yes a good idea, but *she* said not to bother, it was the washing up and cleaning that was the main thing."

I knew that she was talking about the Napiers, but though my natural curiosity would have liked to hear more, I felt I could hardly encourage her. Is it a kind of natural delicacy that some of us have, or do we just lack the courage to follow our inclinations?

"Of course he's been in the Navy," said Mrs. Morris.

"Yes, Lieutenant-Commander Napier was in Italy," I said in a rather loud clear voice, as if trying to raise the conversation to a higher level.

"How nice," said Miss Enders. "My sister once went there on a tour, my married sister, that is, the one who lives at Raynes Park."

"Such a nice young man, he is, Mr. Napier," said Mrs. Morris. "Too good for her, I shouldn't wonder."

My efforts had obviously not been very successful but I did not feel I could try again.

"The Italians are very forward with women," declared Miss Statham. "Of course it's unwise to walk about after dark in a foreign town anywhere when you're alone."

"Pinch your bottom they would before you could say knife," burst out Mrs. Morris, but the short silence that followed told her that she had gone too far.

Like Miss Statham, Miss Doggett in *Jane and Prudence* is a vague older woman interested in gossip.

"She told me a good deal about Mr. Driver," said Jane. "About his wife and other things."

"Ah, the other things," said Miss Doggett obscurely. "Of course, we never *saw* anything of those. We *knew* that it went on, of course—in London, I believe."

"Yet, it seems suitable that things like that should go on in London," Jane agreed. "It is in better taste somehow that a man should be unfaithful to his wife away from home. Not all of them have the opportunity, of course."

"Poor Constance was left alone a great deal," said Miss Doggett.

"In many ways, of course, Mr. Driver is a very charming man. They say, though, that men only want *one thing*—that's the truth of the matter." Miss Doggett again looked puzzled; it was as if she had heard that men only wanted one thing, but had forgotten for the moment what it was.

Are these passages charming? Though I find them so, charm is an elusive quality, hard to demonstrate. No doubt there are many readers for whom they are nothing of the sort, or nothing at all. They certainly are not hilarious, and no scene in Barbara Pym's eleven novels remains in the memory like the high spots of Jane Austen or Evelyn Waugh. But, though the special range and preoccupations of her novels make her distinctive, still these can hardly be very lasting or impressive virtues by themselves. It is what she does within her little world that makes Pym rewarding reading; her special voice, soft, firm, knowing, delicately humorous, just a bit acerbic, which illuminates these bits and makes them live. To be "bounded by English literature and the Anglican Church and small pleasures like sewing and choosing dress material" has no obvious appeal, unless one can share those boundaries with the stimulating mind of Barbara Pym.

Laura L. Doan (essay date 1991)

SOURCE: "Pym's Singular Interest: The Self as Spinster," in *Old Maids to Radical Spinsters: Unmarried Women in the Twentieth-Century Novel*, edited by Laura L. Doan, University of Illinois Press, 1991, pp. 139-54.

[*In the following essay, Doan examines Pym's portrayal of unmarried women as a reflection of the author's personal struggle to reconcile her own feelings about marriage and sexuality. Doan describes Pym's version of spinsterhood as "an alternative life-style which offers women an active role in society and allows them the opportunity to examine others critically."*]

In the spring of 1938, the twenty-four-year-old Barbara Pym made a curious, even bizarre, declaration in a joint letter addressed to her closest friends. Writing in an uncharacteristic, stream-of-consciousness style and rendering herself the subject by using the detached third person, Pym proclaims herself a spinster: "And Miss Pym is looking out of the window—and you will be asking now who is this Miss Pym, and I will tell you that she is a spinster lady *who was thought to have been disappointed in love,* and so now you know who is this Miss Pym" (*A Very Private Eye,* emphasis added). The disparity between what is actually written ("who was *thought* to have been disappointed in love") and what might have been written (a more open, unequivocal statement of fact—"who *was* or *was not* disappointed in love") is telling. The choice of the former, more ambiguous expression points to the chasm between public perception and individual experience. The letter, an exercise in ambiguity, teases by gesturing toward disclosure only to draw back playfully. The promise of revelation is illusory: "This spinster, this Barbara Mary Crampton Pym, she will be smiling to herself—ha-ha she will be saying inside. *But I have that within which passeth show*—maybe she will be saying that, but she is a queer old horse, this old brown spinster, so I cannot forecast exactly what she will be saying." Closing with a mock invitation to speculate on the reason for her happiness, the elusive text refuses to supply the answer: "you will never know now, because this Miss Pym, this old brown horse spinster, is all shut up like oyster, or like clam."

Pym's recognition of the difficulty of a life on the margins of the social order resonates in this early letter, and we find a microcosm of Pym's problem within its various and conflicting views of a spinster. Among such scattered self-referential epithets as "dull" or "old brown" spinster, we find a seemingly contradictory reference to the "prudent, sensible spinster." Pym readily asserts that she is "not . . . by any means one of your old fashioned spinsters," but instead of explaining what she is—what sort of different spinster she has become—the writer maintains silence. Could it be that Pym "clams up," so to speak, because she has arrived at a knowledge of self at once liberating and frightening? The independence and autonomy of a life without the conventional (heterosexual) attachment is so socially problematic, indeed so deviant, that Pym's greatest difficulty as a writer is to summon the willingness to communicate her life-choice. In a very real sense, then, this letter works as the declaration of independence of a twenty-four-year-old woman. It is an extraordinarily young age, we might think, to embrace spinsterhood for life, though three years earlier Pym entered in her commonplace book the following passage from Virginia Woolf's *To the Lighthouse:* "it had flashed upon her that she . . . need never marry anybody, and she had felt an enormous exultation." Moreover, in 1934 (at age twenty), Pym confides in her diary that "sometime in July I began writing a story about Hilary [Pym's sister] and me as spinsters of fiftyish."

Just as Pym's letters and diary entries of the 1930s would seem to confirm spinsterhood as a deliberate choice—sometimes equating marriage with death—her early attempts at fiction explore the question of what sort of writer she would become, how to find a place for her (single) self in the text, and how to present the single state to the reader as a positive choice. After experimenting with various styles and subjects, by 1940 Pym settled into writing what she would often refer to as "her type of novel"; that is, the sort which invariably included spinsters, middle-or upper-middle-class English gentlewomen, living quiet, private lives in unfashionable London suburbs or obscure country villages. Even when publishers began rejecting her manuscripts in the 1960s, often arguing that the readership for her "type of novel" had disappeared, Pym made few substantive concessions in shifting to subjects purportedly more congruent with contemporary tastes.

Such a reluctance to relinquish an interest in an "old-fashioned" topic suggests the depth of Pym's emotional investment, especially in light of her willingness to appropriate its unpopularity, as a 1972 diary entry reveals: "the position of the unmarried woman—unless, of course, she is somebody's mistress, is of no interest whatsoever to the readers of modern fiction. The beginning of a novel?" Pym reintroduces the issue, albeit in a version slightly modified and curiously disengaged, in the opening of *Quartet in Autumn,* where Letty complains that "if she hoped to find [a novel] which reflected her own sort of life she had come to realise that the position of an unmarried, unattached, ageing woman is of no interest whatever to the *writer* of modern fiction" (emphasis added). Shifting the disinterest from the reader to the writer is significant because, in this last novel written before her "rediscovery," Pym displaces her private fear that the single woman might be uninteresting to an actual reader: the fictional spinster now questions why an actual reader neglects her experience.

In anticipation of the reader's objections to the preoccupation with spinsters, Pym exposes the gap between experience and the novel so that her subsequent work fills the fictional lacuna. The tactic gives the appearance of writing against her own text but, in fact, constitutes the means to justify and legitimize the larger project of locating a space for her (writing) self. For Pym, the act of writing and the process of self-definition are inextricably connected. As Judith Kegan Gardiner argues, "The woman writer uses her text, particularly one centering on a female hero, as part of a continuing process involving her own self-definition and her emphatic identification with her character." Pym's determination to put the single woman at the center of her narrative suggests that writing becomes the process to facilitate her own personal reconciliation with the unmarried state and to resolve her ambivalence toward marriage and sexuality.

Crampton Hodnet (an early novel written in the late 1930s but published only posthumously and therefore untouched by any revisions Pym might have made for publication) offers an unusually transparent view of Pym's first strategy: to disrupt the spinster stereotype. In the opening, Pym's description of Miss Jessie Morrow borders on the pathetic: Miss Morrow, "a thin, used-up looking woman in her middle thirties," sits alone in a gloomy North Oxford sitting room on a rainy afternoon. Here her physical features are fully in keeping with the reader's expectations of the spinster stereotype. In the short span of a few lines, however, Pym abruptly contradicts this initial impression by informing the reader that Miss Morrow's appearance is "misleading" because she possesses a "definite personality." Yet the narrator then returns to Miss Morrow's "thin neck . . . small, undistinguished features, her faded blond hair done in a severe knot." By deftly fluctuating between Miss Morrow's relative unattractiveness and her more admirable personal qualities, Pym throws the reliability of superficial impressions into question and posits the existence of a discrepancy between appearance and reality. If Miss Morrow's inner strength enables her to survey the outside world with an amused and self-assured eye, then appearance is of dubious relevance.

After measuring Miss Morrow against the physical stereotype, Pym establishes a further point of reference by comparing Miss Morrow to her employer, the aging spinster Miss Doggett, who specializes in interfering in the business of others. The generational difference between the two women suggests a continuum, the inadequacy of an exhausted stereotype and the possibility of a new image—one which the reader must patiently wait for Pym to create. Miss Doggett's incessant abuse of Miss Morrow merely amplifies the potential to assert a negative as positive: "'Miss Morrow,' said Miss Doggett in a warning tone, 'you are not a woman of the world.'" Miss Morrow lowers her head in silence, but the narrator tells us, "The last thing [Miss Morrow] would ever claim to be was a woman of the world." By seditiously questioning the logic of a privileged attribute, the idea of a worldly woman, Pym neutralizes and ultimately dismisses the negative potential of unworldliness. Miss Doggett's admonitions—on appearance or character—are carefully undermined to establish the groundwork for a more positive characterization of the spinster.

If, as I have argued, the rupture of the spinster stereotype depends on labeling physical appearance as problematic and misleading, Pym must succeed in conveying an impression of the spinster that lies beneath the surface. By investing Miss Morrow with brutal self-honesty and self-acceptance, the same qualities that separate Pym's new spinster from the Miss Doggetts of the world, Pym gives the spinster an integrity that preempts the negative image and thus disarms it. Miss Morrow "did not pretend to be anything more than a woman past her first youth, resigned to the fact that her life was probably never going to be more exciting than it was now." Her secondary status as a paid companion in a household is similar to that of a governess, and she freely admits to a laughing vicar that "a companion is looked upon as a piece of furniture . . . hardly a person at all." This statement may register as hard and blunt, but the bold terms are Miss Morrow's own, uttered without bitterness.

Throughout the narrative, Pym repeatedly posits the equivalence of a paid companion and a piece of furniture and, surprisingly, even claims it is a virtue: "If [the new curate] had time to analyze his feelings," he would probably think of Miss Morrow as a "comfortable chair by the fire." With remarkable economy, she transposes the analogy ("piece of furniture" to "comfortable chair by the fire") to imply that men are unthinking and, more important, that a spinster of Miss Morrow's caliber, like comfort itself, is hardly unwelcome. With a matter-of-fact acceptance rather than anxiety, Miss Morrow reflects that "inanimate objects were often so much nicer than people."

The introduction of a male inhabitant into the household (a typical tactic in Pym's later novels) is the catalyst to demonstrate that Miss Morrow is not a spinster because she is unmarriageable: Stephen Latimer, an eligible bachelor, finds Miss Morrow quite pleasant to look at, sensible, and "safe." In other words, she "wasn't likely to throw her arms around his neck." Latimer's intrusion into the all-female environment invites speculation about Miss Morrow's experience with men and with life in general. Miss Morrow does make a bit of a fool of herself in fumbling with makeup before Latimer's arrival, but the triumph of appearance over character is short-lived. Miss Morrow never repeats the momentary lapse of the makeup incident, and, in fact, Pym takes care to stress that Miss Morrow is beyond becoming infatuated with a man. Midway through the narrative, the tone shifts significantly as Pym becomes increasingly brazen about the inadequacies of the opposite sex. Latimer's little attentions—received as compliments rather than as signals to set about scheming on how best to trap a man—impel Miss Morrow to recall male shortcomings and to extol female virtues: "Men *are* feeble, inefficient sorts of creatures . . . women are used to bearing burdens and taking blame."

In Latimer's proposal to Miss Morrow, Pym situates her most explicit and radical statement in favor of spinsterhood, denying that spinsters are spinsters because they cannot find husbands. Pym cleverly demonstrates how the prospect of marriage elicits different, and unanticipated, responses. In Latimer's case, the offer is a desperate and vaguely despicable act stemming from his own restlessness and a fundamental dissatisfaction with his career. Miss Morrow enjoys his attentions and finds his proposal flattering, but, because she perceives that his offer stems not from love but from a need to escape a dull life, she must reject him. A marriage for the sake of marriage (that is, without love) is out of the question. By casting Miss Morrow's rejection as a courageous endorsement of her values and her dignity, Pym distracts the reader's attention to preclude a negative interpretation and to demonstrate that Miss Morrow's motives are laudable. Pym's diversionary tactic leaves little room for the reader to realize that marriage would afford Miss Morrow the opportunity to escape her *own* dull life, not to mention the tyranny of Miss Doggett. Through this episode in which Miss Morrow accepts a life alone rather than compromise her ideals, Pym asserts that high standards, more than anything else, force spinsters to refuse marriage proposals. (Later we will see that "high standards" can cloak a more complex response to the idea of marriage.) The point here is that *she* makes the choice to marry or to remain single, and, as Joanne Frye notes, "choice becomes a part of the overall defining quality of . . . character and self. . . . To choose is itself an action and to be able to choose is the decisive characteristic of selfhood." With the power that choice engenders, the possibility of being left on the shelf is not the most frightening prospect to Pym's spinsters.

Upon Latimer's holiday departure, Miss Morrow enjoys her newly restored sense of freedom—a liberation symbolically marked by the transformation of the monkey-puzzle tree. In the opening of the novel, the branches of the tree outside the sitting-room window obliterate the sunlight, forcing Miss Morrow to sit in dark isolation. When Latimer eventually takes his leave, the monkey-puzzle tree, once an emblem of loneliness, now becomes the focus for a celebration of life: "Even the monkey-puzzle was bathed in sunshine . . . one realized that it was a living thing too and had beauty, as most living things have in some form or another. Dear monkey-puzzle, thought Miss Morrow, impulsively clasping her arms round the trunk." The incident constitutes one of the few occasions when Miss Morrow acts impulsively. Freely accepting spinsterhood so emboldens her that, when Miss Doggett pronounces her ridiculous for embracing a tree, the normally silent Miss Morrow "unexpectedly" challenges the censure: "'Only God can make a tree.'" Identifying with the tree itself, Miss Morrow perceives a natural place for women like herself in the vast plan of life. While continuing to think of herself as a "neutral thing, without form or sex," she is certain of her value as a living being and confident of her right to a bit of happiness. In this, Miss Morrow is successful, and, feeling no sentimentality over Latimer's leaving, she strips his bedsheets and thinks herself lucky to have escaped.

Depicting the psychological journey from complacent resignation to a joyful embrace of the single life, Pym ends the narrative with an account of a failed marriage, inviting the reader to decide who is really better off. The narrator juxtaposes Miss Morrow's contentment with Mrs. Cleveland's distress over her husband's affair. In an ironic twist, the wife, who realizes that the strange woman sitting beside her in a restaurant is probably not married, contemplates the spinster's enviable position: "She was a comfortable spinster with nobody but herself to consider. Living in a tidy house not far from London, making nice little supper dishes for one, a place for everything and everything in its place, no husband hanging resentfully round the sitting-room . . . Mrs. Cleveland sighed a sigh of envy. No husband." Here the endorsement of spinsterhood resonates from the realizations of a wife trapped in a dreary, unsatisfying marriage—not from the rationalizations of a disgruntled spinster trapped in bitter isolation. Married women cannot escape.

As Pym's voice breaks through the text and rejects any attempt to negate women like herself, mere self-acceptance gives way to a more radical and subversive strategy designed to question the very validity of marriage. The life of a spinster only *seems* dreary to those on the outside; Pym demonstrates that, for those with a properly informed disposition, the life-style is a viable option and often preferable. When a young undergraduate named Barbara Bird flees her affair with Mr. Cleveland at the end of the novel, she also feels as if she has escaped. Young Barbara, a character Hazel Holt suggests is Pym herself, reflects, "She was sure she would never marry now; and there came into her mind the comforting picture of herself, a beautiful, cultured woman with sad eyes." This romantic, if somewhat tragic, representation of the single woman is a far cry from that of the lonely, pathetic spinster.

> **The life of a spinster only *seems* dreary to those on the outside; Pym demonstrates that, for those with a properly informed disposition, the life-style is a viable option and often preferable.**
> **—Laura L. Doan**

In the introductory note to *Crampton Hodnet,* Hazel Holt speculates that, rather than find a publisher, Pym moved on to other projects because the manuscript "seemed to her to be too dated to be publishable." Given the power of her uncompromising attitude toward single women and marriage, it is equally plausible that Pym could not yet so blatantly present such an intensely personal view. Pym's own consciousness of marginality inhibits her temptation to denounce openly the constraints imposed by a rigid social order. In a sense then *Crampton Hodnet,* with its nascent, experimental narrative strategy, functions as a blueprint for Pym's other novels, which are in many ways variations on its theme. Pym's own conflicting attitudes toward the single life are slowly and cautiously plotted out because she believes her socially unacceptable life-style requires a modified or disguised voice rather than one ringing and explicit. Pym thus shares in the strategy that Elizabeth Meese claims for Mary Wilkins Freeman, a woman writer who elects to "display the shadows of her own doubt." Pym can and does rebel against the edict that marriage is the only valid alternative, but her unorthodoxy culminates in a complex and indirect paradigm emblematic of her uncertainty: rebellion and retreat.

Pym resorts to multifarious means to achieve resolution, including the retention of the stereotype. In reiterating conventional notions of the spinster with the detached voice of an outsider, Pym gradually corrects the false impression that spinsters are helpless victims resigned to living vicariously: "'What do women *do* if they don't marry. . . . "Oh, they stay at home with an aged parent and do the flowers, or they used to, but now perhaps they have jobs and careers and live in bed-sitting-rooms or hostels. And then of course they become indispensable in the parish and some of them even go into religious communities'" (*Excellent Women*). With the character of Jessie Morrow as an exemplum, Pym steals the thunder from her readers by embracing the caricature, only to turn around and undermine it by revealing its limitations. Sensing the power of language and naming, Pym introduces a phrase to accommodate her new concept: an "excellent woman." Whenever possible Pym supplants the preconceived notion of the spinster with this more daring, one might even say liberated, vision of the unmarried woman, whose persona is strong enough to reject the side effects associated with marginalization. If appearance and behavior play crucial roles in stereotyping, innovation and change are effected only through reinterpretation, and the possibilities of comparison and contrast are endless: plain and dowdy/ handsome and elegant, eccentric and inquisitive/educated and cultured, dull and fussy/happy and amusing, useless and pathetic/indispensable and comfortable, unwanted and lonely/practical and assertive. As the embodiment of so many enviable qualities, the proud, excellent woman is rarely an object of pity or contempt.

As I have mentioned, Pym says very early that resolution depended on the ability of the text to demonstrate that a chasm existed between appearance and reality, between how society viewed spinsters and how they really were. Hence the inclusion of stereotypical spinsters (such as Belinda Bede in *Some Tame Gazelle* who feels "dowdy and insignificant, one of the many thousand respectable middle-aged spinsters") neutralizes the negative by penetrating the superficiality of such generalizations. Like Belinda, Pym's spinsters struggle to emphasize their individuality: "nobody wanted to be one of many, and she did not like this picture of herself, only one of a great crowd of dreary women." But the metamorphosis from spinster to excellent woman cannot be achieved by proclaiming one's individuality alone, as Mildred Lathbury recognizes in *Excellent Women:* "We had neither of us married. That was it really. It was the ring on the left hand that people at the Old Girl's Reunion looked

for." The absence of the all-important wedding ring still symbolizes the social stigma associated with spinsterhood.

Pym's critique of the institution of marriage is integral to her reconceptualization of spinsterhood. In a two-pronged attack, Pym first depicts marriage as a less than desirable state and then proceeds to show that spinsters choose *not* to marry for any number of reasons. While it would be too simplistic to claim that spinsterhood wins out unequivocally, Pym never presents marriage as anything more than an option. Marriage can certainly be a very tiresome affair, and wives find themselves envying their unmarried friends, with their independent lives and freedom to do as they wish. Rowena Longridge in *A Glass of Blessings,* for instance, confides, "'Sometimes, you know, I envy really *wicked* women, or even despised spinsters—they at least have their dreams . . . the despised spinster still has the chance of meeting somebody. . . . At least she's *free!*'" The implication that marriage signals a loss of freedom, tantamount to "being caught," compels the spinster to reject the marriage offer when it comes. In *Some Tame Gazelle,* Harriet Bede "began to see that there were many reasons why she should refuse [Mr. Mold's] offer when it came . . . who would change a comfortable life of spinsterhood in a country parish . . . for the unknown trials of matrimony?" Independence takes precedence over marriage.

Ironically, to reclaim a powerful new identity for independent women, Pym appropriates an exhausted, outdated attitude toward sexuality and romance. Typically, Pym's spinsters are sexually naive or even asexual—the physical manifestations of love, when unavoidable, can be unpleasant and must simply be endured. The fact that many of them fall in love with men who are married, or otherwise unsuitable or unavailable, reinforces the spinster's idealized notion of love. (Pym herself, as Constance Malloy observes, "tended to fall in love 'safely': she usually fixed her romantic longings on men she didn't know, on men she loved unbeknownst to them, or on 'unsuitable' men who were unstable, much younger, bisexual or homosexual.") Since men, according to the rules of romantic love, are more interesting and attractive from a distance, the first actual encounter transforms the more "noble . . . abstract passions" into "sordid intrigue" (*Crampton Hodnet*). Passion dissolves rapidly once contact is established. As Ann Snitow writes, "In romanticized sexuality the pleasure lies in the distance itself. Waiting, anticipation, anxiety—these represent the high point of sexual experience."

Pym acknowledges that the spinster pays a high price for her romantic ideals. Thus, in *Quartet in Autumn,* Letty reflects on how "no man had taken her away and immured her in some comfortable suburb. . . . Why had this not happened? Because she had thought that love was a necessary ingredient for marriage? Now, having looked around her for forty years, she was not so sure. All those years wasted, looking for love!" In what is perhaps Pym's most bleak novel, Letty's unhappy circumstances are, in a sense, a punishment for her (impossible?) demands on marriage. Yet the notion that marriage must be rejected if love is absent becomes yet another means to convince the reader of the unmarried woman's integrity.

The most extreme manifestation of Pym's views on marriage appears in ***Jane and Prudence,*** the story of a young spinster at the crossroads, with just a few years left to make the choice of whether to marry or to remain single. In a fascinating role reversal, a married Jane Cleveland is dowdy and frumpish, while an unmarried Prudence Bates is elegant and chic. Socially inept Jane spends her time matchmaking and scheming, while cultured Prudence—extremely adept at entertaining men—sees life as an unending series of affairs and enjoys romance and passion, without any commitment to marriage. Such a state of affairs, so to speak, cannot continue indefinitely, and Prudence faces the dilemma of whether to become "the comfortable spinster or the contented or bored wife." Pym delights in averting closure by perpetuating the dilemma beyond the confines of the narrative. Yet, in Prudence's postponement of any final decision and in her recognition that marriage is not necessarily the best solution, Pym tips the balance in favor of spinsterhood:

> Husbands took friends away, [Prudence] thought, though Jane had retained her independence more than most of her married friends. And yet even she seemed to have missed something in her life; her research, her studies of obscure seventeenth-century poets, had all come to nothing, and here she was, trying, though not very hard, to be an efficient clergyman's wife, and with only very moderate success. Compared with Jane's life, Prudence's seemed rich and full of promise. She had her work, her independence, her life in London and her love for Arthur Grampian. But tomorrow, if she wanted to, she could give it all up and fall in love with someone else. Lines of eligible and delightful men seemed to stretch before her.

It would be absurd, Pym argues, for the spinster to relinquish so rewarding a life-style for the unknown territory of marriage, as Mildred emphatically affirms in ***Excellent Women:*** "I valued my independence very dearly . . . I thought, not for the first time, how pleasant it was to be living alone." Pym's spinsters know that their autonomy will be threatened if they succumb to marriage and, ultimately, no man is worth such a sacrifice. Because Pym recognizes that the patriarchy values only the married woman, she strives to show that spinsterhood is not a temporary solution to an impossible situation but a permanent resolution.

Mildred refuses to accept any devaluation of the spinster and insists that excellent women are "for being unmarried . . . and by that I mean a positive rather than a negative state." The use of the "I" opens up what Frye calls "the possibility of self-definition, the capacity to reconceptualize both experience and interpretive framework, the claiming of self-defined action as a way of eluding some of the constraints of an oppressive social context."

While the sorts of tactics surveyed thus far (calling the stereotype into question or launching a critique of marriage) are undeniably useful in contradicting and undermining the dominant ideology, the primary obstacle to a permanent resolution remains in the chasm that exists between the individual and social reality. Pym understands that without a newly conceived narrative structure, the process of self-definition stands in danger of achieving only minor revisions. Since fundamental change must occur at the level of narrative structure, Pym adopts a way of writing that allows for the insertion of critical commentaries into the text so that, in effect, two voices, articulating differing positions, resonate from a unitary text. The development of this strategy aligns Pym with a tradition of women writers who, as Sandra Gilbert and Susan Gubar explain, "managed the difficult task of achieving true female literary authority by simultaneously conforming to and subverting patriarchal literary standards." Like Austen's and Brontë's fiction, Pym's narrative works on two levels, where the surface meaning disguises the "deeper, less accessible (and less socially acceptable)" meaning.

Pym's characters, as I've argued elsewhere, are "continually engaged in [a] quiet, civilized struggle which pits their individual needs against the larger social expectations. It is a rare occasion indeed when a Pym character freely pursues personal needs or desires without guilt." The spinster, a character most susceptible to heeding this voice of duty, rarely eludes acting responsibly because all actions are measured against an invisible public standard. To neglect selfishly and recklessly the proprieties of the social order is to risk personal guilt. In ***An Unsuitable Attachment,*** Ianthe Broom visits the elderly Miss Grimes both as an act of Christian charity and an overarching sense of obligation. By juxtaposing Ianthe's private thoughts and her actual conversation with Miss Grimes and by situating the obligation just at the moment Ianthe would least care to fulfill it, Pym ensures that the reader is aware of the full measure of this difficult duty. Ianthe has just received a bunch of violets from her coworker John as she leaves work, and the "cold fresh scent and passionate yet mourning purple roused in her a feeling she could not explain." Ianthe would prefer to enjoy the strange new sensation the flowers inspire; however, "it was with a slight shock of coming back to reality that she remembered her resolution to visit Miss Grimes on her way home that evening, as part of her contribution to Christmas goodwill, a sort of 'good turn' done to somebody for whom one felt no affection. To love one's neighbour, she thought . . . must surely often be an effort of the will rather than a pleasurable upsurging of emotion." Only women, and spinsters in particular, are capable of such unselfish acts (though clergymen can sometimes rise to the occasion) because they can repress their own desires for the good of others, including those "for whom one felt no affection." Ianthe thus appears incapable of expressing her reluctance about visiting Miss Grimes and remains silent when Miss Grimes mistakes Ianthe's Christmas gifts for her own. To speak up and inform Miss Grimes of her error would violate the behavior code imposed on women by the dutiful voice.

Pym rescues the spinster from a debilitating sense of guilt and facilitates a psychological release by overriding the voice of the dominant social order to insert a more subversive voice into the text. When personal desire collides with duty, the dual-voiced narrative mediates between the two through the juxtaposition of inner thoughts with conversations and actions. When Ianthe gives fleeting consideration, "in a rush of wild impractical nobility," to inviting Miss Grimes to her house for Christmas, the second voice thus intervenes: "*That* would be true Christian charity of a kind that very few can bring themselves to practise." There are limits as to how far the obedient spinster will go. Upon taking leave of Miss Grimes, Ianthe begins to "feel a little sorry for herself . . . she found herself resenting the way [Miss Grimes] had taken the violets." Overzealous behavior is discouraged because spinsterish self-sacrifice cannot appear ridiculous; Ianthe does not degenerate into a total martyr.

At times the spinster's repression of her personal needs, coupled with an obsequious self-effacement, does lead to victimization. Yet this does not prevent Pym from allowing the spinster to speak out indirectly, as in *Quartet in Autumn* when Letty's retirement plans are torn asunder by the Reverend David Lydell's arrival in her friend Marjorie's village. Although Letty immediately suspects that Marjorie's romantic interest in the vicar poses a substantial threat to her own future plans of sharing Marjorie's house, the spinster initially puts on a brave face. During a church service, Letty sits beside Marjorie and, rather than contemplate her own precarious situation and worry that something unpleasant might be brewing, a "generously indulgent" Letty suspends all personal considerations and thinks, "Nice for Marjorie to have an interesting new vicar."

Later, when the trio goes off for a day's drive in the countryside, Letty "was not surprised to find herself squashed into the back of the car . . . David and Marjorie in front made conversation about village matters which Letty could not join in." A subservient spinster, Letty takes a backseat in the car, a place that emblematizes her position in soci-

ety; within the social hierarchy, her insignificant needs do not even register. The seating arrangement at the picnic is also paradigmatic of Letty's inferiority: "Marjorie produced two folding canvas chairs . . . [and] these were solemnly put up for herself and David, Letty having quickly assured them that she would just as soon sit on the rug—indeed, she preferred it. All the same, she could not help feeling in some way belittled or diminished, sitting on a lower level than the others." Again duty and desire collide to reveal the spinster's vulnerability, even as Letty fights to repress her own indignation. The dual-voiced narrative enables Pym (and Letty) to observe respectfully the restraints imposed by the dominant social order, in this case taking a backseat, in order to attack it subversively. But Letty does not remain a victim, as the unexpected turn of events at the end of the narrative demonstrates. When Letty learns that Marjorie's engagement to David is called off, reversing the fortunes of both women, Letty feels "curiously elated, a feeling she tried to suppress but it would not go away." Marjorie, a widow with minimal understanding of the spinster, "naturally" assumes that Letty will leap at the opportunity to return to the original plan. These new circumstances, however, permit Letty to control the outcome and make the choices: "[Letty] experienced a most agreeable sensation, almost a feeling of power. . . . Letty now realised that Marjorie . . . would be waiting to know what *she* had decided to do . . . life still held infinite possibilities for change." The situation signals a more positive outcome for Letty, who now views her impending retirement with a sense of hope.

The dual-voiced narrative is also effective in allowing two attitudes toward the single woman to emerge simultaneously from the text: the voice of the patriarchy and the voice challenging that authority. In *Jane and Prudence,* Jane often functions as a mouthpiece for the social order, regarding her friend Prudence as an oddity and, occasionally, as an object of pity: "It was odd, really, that [Prudence] should not yet have married . . . poor Prudence." Yet Prudence, weary of the misunderstanding of outsiders, reflects with impatience, and perhaps a hint of resentment, that "one's married friends were too apt to assume that one had absolutely nothing to do when not at the office. A flat with no husband didn't seem to count as a home." The irony here, though, is that Prudence is in perfect control of her life—some of her relationships with men are unsuccessful, but on the whole she enjoys her freedom. As mentioned, in this novel Pym turns the tables on the situation of the married woman and the spinster. Jane's sort of marriage, a complacent cohabitation, is so unenviable that her observations on the plight of the spinster fail to convince even the most skeptical reader. Jane's assessment of the value of marriage— "Oh, but a husband was someone to tell one's silly jokes to, to carry suitcases and do the tipping at hotels"—is so ridiculous that it cannot detract from the attraction of autonomy.

In *Jane and Prudence,* Pym achieves the privileging of spinsterhood through a minor spinster character who seemingly embodies both voices. At the same time Eleanor Hitchens reassures Prudence that marriage would settle her unsettled life ("'You ought to get married,' said Eleanor sensibly"), the underlying message is really "do as I do, not as I say." While Eleanor offers the sort of advice one might *expect* (in accordance with the social order) and even perpetuates an outmoded attitude, she calmly pinpoints her own disheveled appearance as the reason for her remaining single ("'I suppose I'll never get a man if I don't take more trouble with myself'"). Just as these words are uttered aloud in Prudence's sitting room, Pym inserts a lengthy description of Eleanor's private thoughts: "she spoke comfortably and without regret, thinking of her flat in Westminster, so convenient for the Ministry, her weekend golf, concerts and theatres with women friends, in the best seats and with a good supper afterwards. Prue could have this kind of life if she wanted it." On one level Pym suggests that Prudence has the option of marriage, but Eleanor's inner dialogue leaves little doubt in the reader's mind as to what the sensible woman would select. Eleanor personifies the new woman and serves as a reminder that the image of the reluctant, pathetic spinster is a creature of the past. The careful juxtaposition of two radically opposed positions demonstrates the inadequacy of Eleanor's spoken account of her spinsterhood. Pym once again reminds the reader of the disparities between perception and reality, between surface and depth.

Barbara Pym's novels become an opportunity to undermine traditional notions of the spinster and to create a positive self-identity. Pym presents spinsterhood as the embodiment or synthesis of all the better things life has to offer. So has Pym, in effect, created a third sex? To be sure, the spinsters' very exemption from the rules of the game grants them a different sort of power: they have the choice to play or not to, and from this choice their uniqueness springs. Spinsterhood, then, is an alternative life-style which offers women an active role in society and allows them the opportunity to examine others critically. As *active* "observers of life," the new excellent women claim singleness as "a positive rather than a negative state" (*Excellent Women*). Like an uncertain lesbian writer who uses the text to justify her sexuality, Pym's experience of difference culminates in a text of persuasion, compelling an identification with the heroine and convincing the reader of the validity of her life-choice. By achieving this, she exemplifies another narrative strategy used by twentieth-century women writers: transform the negative and thereby reclaim an old identity. Her subversion, her process of interjecting herself into the text, enables her to argue the case for the spinster—a remarkable strategy in compliance with Hélène Cixous's imperative: "Woman must write her self. . . . Woman must put herself into the text—as into the world and into history—by her own movement."

Jean E. Kennard (essay date Spring 1993)

SOURCE: "Barbara Pym and Romantic Love," in *Contemporary Literature,* Vol. XXXIV, No. 1, Spring, 1993, pp. 44-60.

[*In the following essay, Kennard considers comparisons between Pym and Jane Austen, concluding that, unlike Austen, Pym subverts the traditional romance plot by focusing on older, unmarried female characters who take pleasure in the mundane realities of ordinary life.*]

Barbara Pym's work is markedly different from that of other contemporary women novelists. On the surface her early novels in particular have the coziness of a Jane Austen world, and it is to Austen, whose influence Pym acknowledged, that she is most frequently compared. A. L. Rowse has called her "the Jane Austen *de nos jours.*" Diana Benet claims that readers of Pym "are reminded of Austen because of her satiric and detailed treatment of a distinctive social group, and because of her narrative method." But, though the influence of Austen is clear, Pym is, in one way at least, the Austen of *our* days. She works constantly to subvert the Austen world through a systematic attack on the romantic love plot. An indication of this is obvious from an overview of the characters themselves. Although Emma in *A Few Green Leaves* is self-conscious about her Jane Austen namesake, the protagonists of Barbara Pym's novels usually resemble Miss Bates more than Emma. The marginal, older spinster frequently displaces the attractive young woman as protagonist in Pym's novels, and, as I shall argue, this is one aspect of Pym's revision of the romantic love plot.

It is in their settings that Pym's novels are most like Jane Austen's. Pym, like Austen, seemed to feel that "two or three families in a country village" were the very stuff of fiction. She plays on this consciously in *A Few Green Leaves,* where the protagonist, Emma, recalls Mr. Woodhouse's comments on soft-boiled eggs in "that novel about her namesake" and Tom Dagnall remembers Jane Fairfax and "her gift of a pianoforte." Even when the novels are set in London—*Quartet in Autumn, An Unsuitable Attachment, The Sweet Dove Died,* for example—London seems like a village. Characters actually inhabit a few circumscribed blocks and run into each other much as they might in a village. As Mildred Lathbury points out in *Excellent Women,* "so many parts of London have a peculiarly village or parochial atmosphere that perhaps it is only a question of choosing one's parish and fitting into it."

Characters are frequently compared or compare themselves or others to those in Austen's fiction, even though Ianthe in *An Unsuitable Attachment* claims "one did not openly identify oneself with Jane Austen's heroines." In *Less Than Angels* the stay-at-home daughter, Elaine, might well "have copied out Anne Elliot's words, especially as she was the same age as Miss Austen's heroine." At the end of *No Fond Return of Love* Aylwin Forbes justifies his own change of heart by remembering the end of *Mansfield Park* and "how Edmund fell out of love with Mary Crawford and came to care for Fanny."

Other literary comparisons to characters from romantic fiction, particularly to Brontë characters, are also frequent. Leonora Eyre in *The Sweet Dove Died* is aware of her namesake; Mildred in *Excellent Women* claims she is "not at all like Jane Eyre"; Beatrix in *A Few Green Leaves* recalls *Villette*; and in *An Unsuitable Attachment* Sophia hopes that the marriage of Ianthe to John might be interrupted like that of Mr. Rochester to Jane Eyre. In *Less Than Angels* Catherine thinks of herself as "looking like Jane Eyre" and Alaric Lydgate as resembling Mr. Rochester. "It isn't only we poor women who can find consolation in literature. Men can have the comfort of imagining themselves like Heathcliff or Mr. Rochester."

But the comforts and consolations of romantic fiction have their dangers for both sexes, particularly for women. Pym is not the first novelist to point out to us that novels have lied and that if we trust their portrayal of human experience we are likely to be disappointed. Jane Austen herself, after all, warned of the dangers of the gothic in *Northanger Abbey*. In *No Fond Return of Love,* Dulcie Mainwaring, admitting that her friend Viola has "turned out to be a disappointment," says she felt "as if she had created her and that she had not come up to expectations, like a character in a book who had failed to come alive, and how many people in life, if one transferred them to fiction just as they were, would fail to do that." Letty Crowe "had always been an unashamed reader of novels, but if she hoped to find one which reflected her own sort of life she had come to realise that the position of an unmarried, unattached, ageing woman is of no interest whatever to the writer of modern fiction" (*Quartet in Autumn*). In *Less Than Angels* the protagonist, Catherine Oliphant, makes her living writing romantic fiction. "Did people *really* say things like that to each other?" wonders her friend Digby at reading the page in her typewriter.

Barbara Brothers points out that "Pym contrasts her characters and their lives with those which have been presented in literature to mock the idealised view of the romantic paradigm and to emphasise that her tales present the truth of the matter." She does not, however, examine the romantic plot conventions that Pym subverts. In the most extended and thorough treatment to date of this romantic love plot and its hold over fiction written in English, Joseph Boone examines the effects of "the fictional idealization of the married state as the individual's one true source of earthly happiness." Boone points out the marriage tradition's "ma-nipulation of form to evoke an illusion of order and resolution [and] . . . the codification of its narrative plots into recognizable, repeating, and contained structures." I have discussed one of these plots, the convention of the two suitors, in *Victims of Convention,* where I illustrate the necessarily sexist implications of a structure in which a female protagonist learns maturity from an appropriate male suitor after rejecting the false values embodied in an unsatisfactory suitor. The readers' expectations of romantic fiction are, then, of a young, usually attractive, female protagonist who will mature as the novel progresses by learning from a superior male. The implications of the plot are of the great desirability of marriage, a life's goal for the female, sufficient to provide a sense of closure to the fiction once it has been achieved.

Boone suggests two basic ways by which the tradition of the romantic love plot has been countered by some novelists. One involves "attacking the tradition from within . . . by following the course of wedlock beyond its expected close and into . . . marital stalemate." The other is to create alternative possibilities for the single protagonist whose actions thereby create formal innovations in the conventional marriage plot. Rachel Blau DuPlessis also explores ways in which novelists have written beyond the expected ending to "express critical dissent from the dominant narrative" of the romantic love plot. "These tactics," she claims, "among them reparenting, woman-to-woman and brother-to-sister bonds, and forms of the communal protagonist, take issue with the mainstays of the social and ideological organization of gender, as these appear in fiction."

A feminist and a realist, Pym works systematically to undermine her readers' expectations of the romantic love plot and in so doing makes use of several of the methods suggested by Boone and DuPlessis. In place of the values implied by this plot, Pym offers us an ideal of community based upon what she argues is a more genuine form of love. The wrong attitude to community is exemplified in her novels by the scientific detachment of anthropologists and the right attitude by Christian commitment and caring. Although they are apparent in all her work, these values are best exemplified in what are arguably her two finest novels, *Excellent Women* and *Quartet in Autumn.*

One of Pym's most obvious methods of attacking the romantic love plot is to rebuff our expectation of a young, attractive protagonist. Her characters are marginal people, to use Jane Nardin's term, "unachieving." "Pym's characters," says Nardin, "generally tend to be older, less involved with other people, especially less involved sexually, and tend to have achieved less than the characters of many other novelists. Typically they have not married, had children, formed close emotional ties, felt great passion, or gotten anywhere in the world of work."

Her female protagonists are frequently "excellent women," older spinsters, rarely attractive, working at dead-end jobs or subsisting on small private incomes, who are often attached to a church that provides their only opportunity for good works and for a social life. We do not expect them to marry, though they are usually mildly attached to a male of their acquaintance. Jessica Morrow of *Crampton Hodnet* is a companion to an older woman, has a flirtation with a young curate, but is too sensible to accept his unemotional proposal of marriage. Mildred Lathbury of *Excellent Women*, Dulcie Mainwaring of *No Fond Return of Love*, Prudence Bates of *Jane and Prudence*, and Harriet and Belinda Bede of *Some Tame Gazelle* similarly occupy places in society that fiction has rarely taken seriously or considered interesting. Mary Beamish of *A Glass of Blessings* epitomizes the type: "she was so very much immersed in good works, so *splendid*, everyone said. She was about my own age, but small and rather dowdily dressed, presumably because she had neither the wish nor the ability to make the most of herself." Letty Crowe and Marcia Ivory of *Quartet in Autumn* have spent their lives at jobs so undistinguished that Pym never tells us what they do. When they retire they are not replaced.

It is clear that Pym has both respect and affection for her female characters, with whom she obviously identifies. She plays deliberately upon her readers' stereotypical views of them. A good illustration of this is Miss Grimes in *An Unsuitable Attachment*. Full of a self-righteous sense of doing good, Ianthe Broome goes to visit Miss Grimes, who has recently retired. She is at first surprised to find that Miss Grimes, "with her raffish appearance and slight Cockney accent," owns some good furniture and china. Miss Grimes offers her a glass of her regular wine, on which she spends six shillings and sixpence a week out of her old age pension. Ianthe finds this "slightly shocking . . . Haricot beans and lentils—or chicken breasts in aspic if they could be afforded—were really much more suitable." When Miss Grimes makes a joke about her ex-boss's sexual orientation, Ianthe begins "to feel indignant that Miss Grimes wasn't conforming more to type" and leaves realizing that she "had not really seemed as destitute and lonely as Ianthe had expected." Miss Grimes finally confounds everyone's expectations by marrying a widower she meets in a pub.

Pym's female characters are invariably stronger than their male counterparts, whom . . . they allow to feel superior. . . .
                                        —Jean E. Kennard

Pym's female characters are invariably stronger than their male counterparts, whom, as Jane Cleveland points out, they allow to feel superior: "Making them feel, perhaps some-times by no more than a casual glance, that they were loved and admired and desired when they were worthy of none of these things" (*Jane and Prudence*). Women, Jane tells her friend Prudence, "can do nearly everything that men can now. And they are getting so much bigger and taller and men are getting smaller, haven't you noticed?" John Halperin quotes the comment made to him by Pym's editor and friend, Hazel Holt: "'There is no doubt that she thought women the stronger sex.'" There is no question in a Pym novel of women maturing under the guidance of a male suitor. They are fully aware of their own superiority, tending, like Catherine Oliphant in *Less Than Angels*, "to regard most men . . . as children." Men, she feels, "appeared to be so unsubtle."

Pym's male characters do little to counteract this view. They are usually weak figures. Self-centered, ineffectual clergymen, like Archdeacon Hoccleve in *Some Tame Gazelle* or Nicholas Cleveland in *Jane and Prudence*, are common. They are also given to stereotypical views of women. Women smoke more than men at conferences, according to Aylwin Forbes, "Because of the emptiness of their lives, no doubt, most of them being unmarried" (*No Fond Return*). Mark Penfold defines a reciprocal relationship as "the woman giving the food and shelter and doing some typing for him and the man giving the priceless gift of himself" (*Less Than Angels*). The fussy old maids of Pym's novels are invariably men, William Caldicote of *Excellent Women;* for example, who is upset when his office is changed because different pigeons come to the window, or Mervyn Cantrell of *An Unsuitable Attachment*, living with his old mother, unable to eat restaurant food, coveting other people's furniture.

Marriage is not presented as a goal to be sought in Pym's novels, and she demonstrates this by the method Boone discusses of pursuing wedlock into "marital stalemate." Marriage is frequently a question of "dullness rather than cosiness" and without "much rapture" (*Less Than Angels*). Those long-term relationships that do occur in Pym's fiction tend to have gone stale, like Jane and Nicholas Cleveland's in *Jane and Prudence*, called by Halperin "the most sustained attack on men among Pym's novels." It is not surprising that Mrs. Williton "began to wonder why Marjorie had married Aylwin, and when no answer suggested itself she went on to wonder why anybody married anybody. It only brought trouble to themselves and their relations" (*No Fond Return*). In *Quartet in Autumn* Edwin celebrates the freedom his widowhood brings: "he could go to church as often as he liked, attend meetings that went on all evening, store stuff for jumble sales in the back room and leave it there for months. He could go to the pub or the vicarage and stay there till all hours." Mary Strauss-Noll points out that "the ideal state in Pym's fiction appears to be widowhood."

Nevertheless, in contrast to the problems and illusions of romantic passion, the ordinary comforts of marriage sometimes hold up quite well. Pym deliberately undercuts the romantic daydreams of her characters with the mundane realities of everyday life. Her characters like the fantasy of romantic love but not the discomforts of an erotic relationship. The pattern of *Crampton Hodnet* is typical of Pym's method. Three relationships begin in the early chapters of the novel. Anthea Cleveland has a new boyfriend, Simon; her father is infatuated with one of his students, Barbara Bird, who has a crush on him but knows that "although it was a love stronger than death, it wasn't a love one *did* anything about"; and the curate, Mr. Latimer, takes a room in the house of Miss Doggett where, out of boredom, he becomes involved with her companion, Jessica Morrow. All three relationships become complicated: Simon goes on vacation; Francis and Barbara are observed together by several of their acquaintances; and Miss Morrow and Mr. Latimer become involved in a series of lies in an attempt to explain an innocent afternoon in the country. But instead of rescuing her lovers from their dilemmas Pym merely exposes the shallowness of their feelings. Simon finds a new girlfriend and Anthea is not long in finding new interests herself; rejected by Miss Morrow, Mr. Latimer similarly finds himself a new relationship while on vacation in Paris; and Francis Cleveland is relieved and quite content to return to his mundane marriage when Barbara abandons him on the first night of their trip to Paris.

Pym also challenges the conventions of the romantic love plot with the reappearance, usually in cameo roles, of characters from her earlier novels. In *Excellent Women,* Archdeacon Hoccleve from *Some Tame Gazelle* is a guest preacher. In *Jane and Prudence* both Mildred Lathbury and William Caldicote are briefly mentioned, and we learn of Mildred's marriage to Everard Bone. In the same novel Miss Doggett, Miss Morrow, and a very changed Barbara Bird from *Crampton Hodnet* reappear. *Less Than Angels,* like *Excellent Women* about anthropologists, recycles Professor Mainwaring, Esther Clovis, Helena Napier, and Everard Bone from the earlier novel. *A Glass of Blessings* gathers together characters from several other novels: Archdeacon Hoccleve from *Some Tame Gazelle,* Julian and Winifred Malory and Rocky Napier from *Excellent Women,* Prudence Bates from *Jane and Prudence* and Catherine Oliphant from *Less Than Angels.*

Sometimes the effect of the reappearance is ironic. In *A Glass of Blessings* Rowena comments on a story by Catherine Oliphant in a magazine she is reading in which a young man and a girl hold hands in a restaurant watched by the man's former mistress. "What a farfetched situation," Wilmet protests. "As if it would happen like that!" A reader who is familiar with *Less than Angels* knows, of course, that the incident did in fact happen to Catherine Oliphant

herself. As Diana Benet says, "these cameo appearances satisfy our curiosity about the fate of certain characters." Mildred Lathbury and Jessica Morrow, for example, do not marry in the novels in which they first appear; Esther Clovis and Fabian Driver die in later novels, Esther after several reappearances. The main purpose of the recurring characters is surely, though, to resist the sense of closure provided by the romantic love plot. Pym suggests a world of ever-widening circles. As in Margaret Drabble's novels, each story is broadened by our knowledge of the others. Her universe is potentially unlimited, her novels without boundaries.

In a variety of ways, then, Pym works to subvert the romantic love plot, but this is not the whole of Pym. There is affirmation in her novels as well as a good deal of clear-eyed cynicism. As I suggested earlier, Pym appears to affirm the ordinariness of daily life as opposed to the intensities of romantic passion. Dulcie Mainwaring's comments in *No Fond Return of Love* could have occurred in a Drabble novel: "But there is more satisfaction in scrubbing a floor or digging a garden, Dulcie thought. One seems nearer to the heart of things doing menial tasks." Her novels often tend, through circular plots, to return characters, perhaps a little more content, to where they were when the novel opened. Both *Some Tame Gazelle* and *A Glass of Blessings* are examples of this. Marriages continue; extramarital relationships, which threatened change, are discontinued. The solace of a cup of tea or some Ovaltine is frequent in Pym: "What a pity we can't make a cup of Ovaltine," thinks Dulcie. "Life's problems are often eased by hot milky drinks." Pym said of herself that "I've always liked details" (*Civil to Strangers*), and she does indeed give us a wonderfully perceptive realism dense with affectionately observed details of ordinary life.

But Pym also sees obsession with detail as neurotic ritualization, often a source for comedy in the novels. *Less Than Angels* shows us a range of characters all concerned with their own or others' rituals. Mark and Digby are surprised that Catherine does housework in the evenings: "'People usually do that kind of thing in the mornings,' said Digby almost disapprovingly. 'I don't know what my mother would say.'" Similarly Rhoda objects that Mrs. Skinner beats her rugs in the evening rather than the morning: "if everybody were to beat their rugs in the evening, just think of the noise!" Deidre thinks that at home "her mother would be laying the breakfast and later her aunt would creep down to see if she had done it correctly. And they would probably go on doing this all their lives." In *Quartet in Autumn* Marcia Ivory crosses the line between common neurosis and debilitating compulsion. She collects tins of food but rarely eats, sorts plastic bags into various sizes and keeps them in drawers but never uses them, and collects milk bottles, though only of one kind, in her shed in the garden.

Pym's superb description of her decline from eccentricity into insanity makes it clear that Marcia is only an extension of any of us.

Obsessive ritualization is, as Pym realizes, often a substitute for feeling, and it is genuine feeling, including romantic love, that Pym affirms. Real emotion, of course, does not always occur between heterosexual couples with a potential for marriage, as the romantic love plot suggests. In Pym's novels it frequently springs up between unlikely people. Her attachments are often "unsuitable": older women and homosexual men like Leonora and James or Meg and Colin in *The Sweet Dove Died* or Wilmet and Piers in *A Glass of Blessings;* homosexual couples such as James and Ned in *The Sweet Dove Died;* homosexual couples of different social classes such as Harold and Colin in *The Sweet Dove Died* or Piers and Keith in *A Glass of Blessings.* Highlighting the positive values of alternative relationships, as DuPlessis argues, in itself counters the ideal of heterosexual marriage.

Pym's excellent women do not marry for the sake of being married, but they do seek love. Belinda Bede rejects the marriage proposal of Bishop Grote because she does not love him, and even in old age she is not prepared to settle for anything less: "'I'm afraid I can't marry you,' she said, looking down at her floury hands. 'I don't love you.' 'But you respect and like me,' said the Bishop, as if that went without saying. 'We need not speak of love—one would hardly expect that now.' 'No,' said Belinda miserably, 'I suppose one would not *expect* it. But you see,' she went on, 'I did love somebody once'" (*Some Tame Gazelle*). Jessica Morrow's thoughts after she rejects Mr. Latimer probably represent Pym's views best: "For she wanted love, or whatever it was that made Simon and Anthea walk along the street not noticing other people simply because they had each other's eyes to look into. . . . And then, how much more sensible it was to satisfy one's springlike impulses by buying a new dress in an unaccustomed and thoroughly unsuitable colour than by embarking on a marriage without love" (*Crampton Hodnet*). Pym does not suggest that Jessica Morrow is foolish for feeling this way. Spring impulses toward erotic love move many of her characters; even Norman takes an unaccustomed evening bus ride in *Quartet in Autumn* and finds himself standing outside Marcia's house. And Pym finally allows Jessica the marriage she wants, to Fabian Driver, but not until a later novel, *Jane and Prudence.*

Pym effectively convinces her reader that the romantic love plot does not apply in her novels, that she is describing life more realistically. She appears to assure us that her women are not the kind that receive a fond return of love and marry, only, on occasion, to marry them after all. So in *An Unsuitable Attachment* Penny does get Rupert and Ianthe marries John against the expectations both of her friends and the reader: "'I never thought of her as getting married—it seems all wrong,' Sophia burst out." Similarly in *No Fond Return of Love* Dulcie Mainwaring gets Aylwin Forbes and in *Excellent Women* Mildred Lathbury ends up with Everard Bone. Pym, then, does not reject romantic love, only the limitations of the plot in which novelists have usually presented it. Marriage is not the aim of life, but it is possible even for "unlikely" people.

The pattern I have described above is perhaps best illustrated by *Excellent Women,* one of Pym's finest novels. *Excellent Women* is the story of Mildred Lathbury; at least it becomes the story of Mildred Lathbury, because initially, as Benet says, "Mildred denies possession of the heroine's sine qua non: she has, she implies, no story of her own." Mildred is "an unmarried woman just over thirty who lives alone and has no apparent ties." Not very attractive, she refuses to identify with even a plain heroine: "Let me hasten to add that I am not at all like Jane Eyre, who must have given hope to so many plain women who tell their stories in the first person, nor have I ever thought of myself as being like her." So Pym warns us against the expectations of the romantic love plot.

Mildred lives in London, but in a part of London that has become no larger than a village to her, on a small private income, helping, on a volunteer basis, distressed gentlewomen, "a cause very near to my own heart, as I felt that I was just the kind of person who might one day become one." Small details absorb her. She worries about who should buy the toilet paper when she has to share a bathroom: "The burden of keeping three people in toilet paper seemed to me rather a heavy one." She is fully self-aware, even ironic, about her own situation, one of the qualities that makes her sympathetic to the reader. She expects "to find herself involved or interested in other people's business" and knows that since "she is a clergyman's daughter then one might really say that there is no hope for her." She is prepared to find it right that she should spend Saturday night "sitting alone eating a very small chop."

She sees herself as a different species of woman from those who marry. Her memories are all of rejection. "I remembered girlhood dances, where one had stayed there too long, though never long enough to last out the dance for which one hadn't a partner. I didn't suppose Helena had ever known that." "I have never been very good at games; people never chose me at school when it came to picking sides." She often feels like "a dog or some inferior class of person." Mildred's only romantic interest has been a tepid relationship with a bank clerk called Bernard Hatherley whom she met at church. He had given her less expensive presents than she had given him; they had gone for country walks and had "talks about life and about himself. I did not remember that we had ever talked about me." Eventually he had rejected her for a girl he met on vacation and "had not broken the news of another attachment very gracefully."

Mildred is remarkably positive about her life, despite regretting that she "was not really first in anybody's life." She finds it "pleasant . . . to be living alone," feels that "I was now old enough to become fussy and spinsterish if I wanted to," and tells Everard Bone that "excellent women" "are for being unmarried . . . and by that I mean a positive rather than a negative state." She has romantic moods: a fine spring day with a "blue sky full of billowing white clouds . . . thrilling little breezes . . . mimosa on the barrows" makes her long for "a splendid romantic person" to be having lunch with, rather than William Caldicote with "his preoccupation with his health and his food and his spiteful old-maidish delight in gossip." But she finds it safer to avoid feeling: "Mimosa did lose its first freshness too quickly to be worth buying and I must not allow myself to have feelings, but must only observe the effects of other people's."

We are not led to expect more for Mildred than she expects for herself. Her closest friends are Julian Malory, her clergyman, and his sister Winifred. Although they both, together with most of her other acquaintances, believe that Mildred must be in love with Julian, she is not. Nor, of course, is she in love with William Caldicote, with whom she has an annual lunch. He works with other "grey men" at an undefined clerical job and encourages Mildred to believe that they are "the observers of life." Mildred is cynical about men, observing that "men did not usually do things unless they liked doing them," and that "men sometimes leave difficulties to be solved by other people." She laughs with her cleaning woman, "a couple of women against the whole race of men." Attending an Old Girls' Reunion with her friend Dora, Mildred realizes that it is "the ring on the left hand" that people looked for but adds "somehow I do not think we imagined the husbands to be quite so uninteresting as they probably were."

Into Mildred's life come the Napiers—Rocky, a naval officer with a reputation as a ladies' man, and his anthropologist wife Helena. They move into the flat below Mildred, and their proximity makes frequent contact inevitable. Three "unsuitable" attachments develop: Helena is romantically inclined toward Everard Bone, an anthropologist colleague who has no interest in her; Julian Malory becomes engaged to Allegra Gray, a selfish clergyman's widow, who has no concern for the future of Julian's sister, Winifred; and Mildred is attracted to Rocky, whose charm and kindness make it easy for her to forget his shallowness.

The pattern of *Excellent Women* is a series of flows and ebbs in Mildred's emotional state. Whenever Mildred is tempted into romantic ideas, the chapter ends by bringing

her—and the reader—firmly back to what we take to be reality. Thinking of Rocky, Mildred forgets her prayers, and chapter 4 ends with: "There came into my mind a picture of Mr. Mallett, with raised finger and roguish voice, saying, 'Tut, tut, Miss Lathbury. . . .'" After Mildred spends an afternoon with Rocky, he forgets to give her back her mimosa; Mildred observes at the end of chapter 8, "There was a vase of catkins and twigs on the table in my sitting-room. 'Oh, the kind of women who bring dry twigs into the house and expect leaves to come on them!' Hadn't Rocky said something like that at tea?" After talking with a stranger about Rocky, she looks at her face in the mirror and finds it "enough to discourage anybody's romantic thoughts." In a moment of excitement Mildred buys herself a lipstick called Hawaiian Fire but on the way home stops for tea and sees women "braced up, their faces newly done. . . . I had only my Hawaiian Fire and something not very interesting for supper." Rocky returns to his wife, who has given up all hope of Everard; Julian breaks off his engagement to Allegra when she tries to drive Winifred out of the house; and Mildred loses interest in Rocky after he moves away and fails to follow up on an invitation to visit him. The romantic love plot appears to be thoroughly undermined.

But Mildred's life changes after all. At first too self-deprecating to believe that Everard can have any feeling for her, she finally allows a relationship to develop between them. Nardin claims that "Mildred's marriage to Everard will be based upon an excellent woman's habit of putting herself second. . . . The ending of *Excellent Women* is as sly an attack on the conventional conclusion of comedy with its celebratory marriages as is the ending of *Some Tame Gazelle*." Surely this is not the case. We learn little of Mildred and Everard's marriage in later novels, but it is probably safe to assume that it has its disappointments, like all the other marriages in Pym's work. Nevertheless, if we agree with Benet that the novel is concerned with whether the protagonist will continue to be an observer of "the lives of others, or a woman engaged in a full life of her own," then the ending is not ironic. Mildred herself certainly believes her situation has changed, and she has not been given to self-deception. Julian Malory, she thinks at the end of the novel, "might need to be protected from the women who were going to live in his house. So, what with my duty there and the work I was going to do for Everard, it seemed as if I might be going to have what Helena called 'a full life' after all." "A full life," to Pym, is involvement in a community, albeit through small, ordinary deeds. It is significant that though readers of Pym's later novels know that Mildred and Everard do marry, she ends *Excellent Women* with that marriage only a possibility, not a solution. It is not marriage that matters, Pym is saying, but living one's own story.

Pym's ideal of community is defined through a contrast between anthropology and Christianity that begins in *Excel-*

lent Women, occurs throughout Pym's work, and comes to signify the opposition of detached observation to involvement and genuine emotion. In *An Unsuitable Attachment,* Rupert Stonebird, anthropologist, knows "that men and women may observe each other as warily as wild animals hidden in long grass." He "changed into a dark suit as a kind of protective colouring, so that he could sit quietly observing rather than being observed." Rupert has "an anthropologist's detachment," Pym tells us. When anthropologist Gervase Fairfax makes a sarcastic remark, Ianthe "did not know what answer to make. People at church garden parties did not make such remarks" (*An Unsuitable Attachment*).

Pym makes frequent comparisons between anthropologists and novelists. Everard Bone points out that "both study life in communities, though the novelist need not be so accurate or bother with statistics and kinship tables" (*An Unsuitable Attachment*). This comparison suggests that Pym was perhaps ambivalent about her profession despite her claim that she "learned how it was possible and even essential to cultivate an attitude of detachment towards life and people, and how the novelist could even do 'field-work' as the anthropologist did" (*Civil to Strangers*). It seems probable that Pym saw the novelist's job as isolating and novelists as potentially lacking in compassion as social scientists.

The alternative to anthropology is Christianity. Emma, the anthropologist in *A Few Green Leaves,* remembers "her role as an anthropologist and observer—the necessity of being on the outside looking in." However, she abandons anthropology and moves from detachment to emotional involvement, with the local clergyman, Tom Dagnall. Pym gives us to understand that this is a good thing. Pym does not idealize the church or clergymen or Christians—she is all too well aware of human limitations to do that—but she does respect the spirit of Christianity even if she sometimes mocks its practitioners. The church in Pym's novels does serve to bring people together, often providing them with a caring community. In *An Unsuitable Attachment* clergyman Mark Ainger and his wife Sophia renew their marriage on a trip to Rome, a trip that Mark has organized as a vacation for an odd assortment of his parishioners. "Underlying the concept of community," says Benet, "is an essential form of love, an attitude composed of goodwill and compassion for others simply because they are fellow human beings; it is the responsible benevolence toward others enjoined by the commandment to 'Love thy neighbor as thyself.'"

It is essentially a Christian concept of community that Pym makes the subject of *Quartet in Autumn,* although of the four main characters only Edwin is a churchgoer. Interestingly, he seems the most contented of the four and the most connected to other people. Pym's concern here is "the or-

dinary responsibility of one human being towards another." The four protagonists, Norman, Edwin, Marcia, and Letty, colleagues working in the same office at undefined tasks, are all single and living alone. They do not see each other outside the office and yet are really more comfortable with each other than with other people. After his Christmas break, Norman "quite looked forward to getting back to the office and hearing how the others had got on." The pattern of the novel follows their occasional moves toward contact, moves that are almost never completed. The most successful at human contact is Edwin, the only one who has been married. He finds Letty a new place to live when she feels she must leave her apartment, goes with Father Gellibrand to see if he can help Marcia, and organizes the lunch for Letty and Marcia after their retirement.

The least connected is Marcia. She dreads being forced to offer Letty a home: "For of course it would be impossible—she couldn't have anybody else living in her house. . . . The difficulties were insuperable." Marcia becomes increasingly isolated as the novel progresses, resenting and resisting all efforts to help her. Marcia once had some feeling for Norman but has transferred all feeling now to her surgeon, Mr. Strong, who performed her mastectomy. The only way in which Marcia expresses her feelings, though, is spying. She once followed Norman to the British Museum and makes a treat for herself of standing outside Mr. Strong's house. The detachment involved in spying and observation is, of course, linked to the negative aspects of anthropology. And Marcia is by no means alone among Pym's characters in doing it. In *A Few Green Leaves,* Miss Lee and Miss Grundy conceal themselves in a thicket to catch a glimpse of Sir Miles and his guests at the manor, and Adam Prince watches "Graham and Emma 'canoodling,' as he put it, on the grass."

Ironically it is Marcia's death that improves their situations for the other three. They meet in Edwin's house for the first time after the funeral for which he has made all the arrangements. "Marcia's death had of course brought them closer together. . . . The most important thing was that they were seeing Edwin's house for the first time, never having been invited into it before." Norman inherits Marcia's house, which gives him "a good feeling, like a dog with two tails, as people sometimes put it." The book ends with a sense of increased community as Letty invites the other two to a day in the country with her friend Marjorie and realizes "that life still held infinite possibilities for change."

In place of the values of the romantic love plot, Pym affirms the interdependence of community, the pleasures of ordinary life, and the importance of genuine emotion—even of romantic love—in human relationships. Small communities exist in most of Pym's novels, often centered around a church as in *Some Tame Gazelle* and *Excellent Women.*

Sometimes, as in *A Few Green Leaves,* the setting actually is a country village, but more often Pym simply creates the sense of limited space by frequent interaction among a small number of characters. She heightens this sense of community by her habit of reintroducing characters from earlier novels. This is her way, perhaps, of redeeming novelists after all, for, in addition to preventing closure, this device also serves as a way of providing her readers with their own sense of community, a sense of belonging to the world of Pym's novels.

FURTHER READING

Criticism

Brothers, Barbara. "Love, Marriage, and Manners in the Novels of Barbara Pym." In *Reading and Writing Women's Lives: A Study of the Novel of Manners,* edited by Bege K. Bowers and Barbara Brothers, pp. 155-70. Ann Arbor, MI: UMI Research Press, 1990.

Examines the ironic and comic depiction of Victorian manners and romantic ideals in Pym's novels.

Burkhart, Charles. "Barbara Pym and the Africans." *Twentieth Century Literature* 29, No. 1, (Spring 1983): 45-53.

Discusses the significance of anthropology and references to Africa in Pym's novels.

Dobie, Ann B. "The World of Barbara Pym: Novelist as Anthropologist." *Arizona Quarterly* 44, No. 1 (Spring 1988): 5-18.

Examines the role of anthropologists and anthropological methodology in Pym's fiction.

Graham, Robert J. "Cumbered with Much Serving: Barbara Pym's 'Excellent Women.'" *Mosaic* 17, No. 2 (Spring 1984): 141-60.

Explores the significance of marriage, romantic relationships, spinsterhood, and domestic roles in Pym's novels.

Keener, Frederick M. "Barbara Pym Herself and Jane Austen." *Twentieth Century Literature* 31, No. 1 (Spring 1985): 98-110.

Examines the influence of Jane Austen in Pym's fiction and the many significant differences between their respective works.

Rossen, Janice, editor. *Independent Women: The Function of Gender in the Novels of Barbara Pym.* St. Martin's Press: New York, 1988, 172 p.

Discusses the marginalized depiction and role of the unmarried man in Pym's novels.

Additional coverage of Pym's life and career is contained in the following sources published by Gale: *Contemporary Authors,* **Vols. 13-14 and 97-100;** *Contemporary Authors New Revision Series,* **Vols. 13 and 34;** *Contemporary Authors Permanent Series,* **Vol. 1;** *Dictionary of Literary Biography,* **Vols. 14 and 87; and** *Major Twentieth Century Writers.*

Isaac Bashevis Singer
1904-1991

(Born Icek-Hersz Zynger; first name also transliterated as Isak, Isaak, Yitskhok; has also written under the pseudonyms Isaac Tse, Isaac Bashevis, and Isaac Warshofksy [also transliterated as Varshavski, Warshavksi, Warshawsky, and Warshovsky]) Polish-born American novelist, short story writer, memoirist, children's writer, playwright, essayist, and translator.

The following entry presents an overview of Singer's career through 1996. For further information on his life and works, see *CLC,* Volumes 1, 3, 6, 9, 11, 15, 23, 38, and 69.

INTRODUCTION

Singer's acclaimed novels and short fiction, especially *Der Satan in Gorey* (1935; *Satan in Goray*) and the title story from *Gimpel tam un andere Dertseylungen* (1950; *Gimpel the Fool and Other Stories*), are distinguished for their profound insight into philosophical dilemmas concerning personal spirituality, existential alienation, and cultural destiny. While Singer's narratives often feature Polish-Jewish history and traditional life in the Eastern European village or *shtetl,* by incorporating elements of legend and the supernatural, such stories transcend their provincial settings and subjects to achieve universality. Singer's preoccupation with the paradoxical duality of human nature, particularly surrounding aspects of faith and doubt, suffuses his fiction with a complex moral vision that challenges the assumptions of both biblical tradition and scientific rationalism. A master of Yiddish prose and Nobel laureate, Singer is recognized as a consummate storyteller and a penetrating observer of the human condition.

Biographical Information

Born in Leoncin, Poland, a *shtetl* near Warsaw, Singer was raised in a traditional orthodox Jewish home dominated by pious religious contemplation and instruction; Singer's father was a Hasidic rabbi and his mother descended from distinguished rabbis and talmudic scholars. At age four, Singer moved with his family to Warsaw where he spent most of his childhood. Under the influence of his older brother, novelist Israel Joshua Singer, Singer was introduced to secular literature and contemporary intellectuals whose skepticism defied the theological teachings of his upbringing. Singer's development was further shaped by the philosophy of Benedict de Spinoza, clandestine readings in the Cabal (a religious text based on mystical interpretation of the Scriptures), and the works of Fedor Dostoevsky, Edgar Allan Poe,

and Leo Tolstoy—all forbidden by his father. In 1917, Singer relocated with his mother to Bilgoray, a *shtetl* near the Austrian border, where he lived for several years with his grandparents. He began formal studies at Tachkemoni Rabbinical Seminary in Warsaw in 1921, but soon left to take up work as a proofreader for *Literarische Bletter,* a Yiddish literary journal edited by his brother. Singer published his first story, "Oyf der Elter," translated in English as "In Old Age," in *Literarische Bletter* in 1927 under the pseudonym Tse. While continuing to write creatively, Singer supported himself by translating popular fiction and several major novels into Yiddish, including works by Knut Hamsun, Erich Maria Remarques's *All Quiet on the Western Front,* and Thomas Mann's *The Magic Mountain.* Singer's first novel, *Satan in Goray,* appeared in book form in 1935; it was first published serially in *Globus,* a magazine for which he served as associate editor, in 1934. All of Singer's subsequent novels were first written and serialized in Yiddish. Singer immigrated to the United States in 1935, permanently leaving his native Poland and an estranged lover, Runya, with whom he had a son. Reunited with Israel Joshua in New York, Singer began work as a freelance writer for the *Jewish Daily Forward,* for which he became a regular contributor until the end of his life. In 1940, Singer married Alma Wasserman, a German-Jewish immigrant whom he met in the United States. Upon his brother's death in 1944, Singer began the novel *Di Familie Mushkat* (1950; *The Family Moskat*) and produced *Mayn Tatn's Bes-din Shtub* (1956; *In My Father's Court*), the first of several autobiographic narratives. With the 1953 publication of Saul Bellow's English translation of "Gimpel the Fool" in *Partisan Review,* Singer garnered an English-speaking readership and an international reputation. An English translation of *Satan in Goray* appeared in 1955, followed by *Gimpel the Fool and Other Stories* in 1957. During the next decade Singer produced additional novels, including *Kunstmakher fun Lublin* (1960; *The Magician of Lublin*), *Sonim, di Geschichte fun a Liebe* (1966; *Enemies: A Love Story*), numerous short stories collected in *The Spinoza of Market Street* (1961), *Short Friday and Other Stories* (1964), and *The Seance and Other Stories* (1968), as well as award-winning children's books. Singer maintained a prolific literary output during the 1970s with several collections of short fiction, notably *A Crown of Feathers and Other Stories* (1973) and *Old Love and Other Stories* (1979), the drama *Yentl, the Yeshiva Boy* (1974) which was adapted into the popular film *Yentl* in 1983, and the novel *Shosha* (1978). Singer was awarded the Nobel Prize for Literature in 1978. He continued to produce highly regarded fiction, children's works, and memoirs until his death in 1991 after a series of strokes.

Major Works

Singer's fiction typically explores the individual's struggle to realize the limits of human potential and free will in relation to supernatural forces and fatalistic universal law. His first novel, *Satan in Goray,* contains many recurring themes and narrative devices employed in his subsequent novels and short fiction. Set in a medieval Polish *shtetl* after the Cossack pogroms of 1648, *Satan in Goray* chronicles the negative effects of the Jewish messianic movement surrounding Sabbatai Zevi, a charlatan from Smyrna who proclaimed himself the Messiah, though later converted to Islam. Presented as an archaic folk story, the narrative centers on Rechele, a psychologically tormented woman whose satanic hallucinations are mistakenly interpreted by the zealous villagers as prophetic visions. When the Messiah fails to appear and news of Sabbatai Zevi's apostasy arrives, the inhabitants of Goray revert to the orthodox religion and traditions of their community to recover from the apocalyptic excesses of mysticism. As in much of his fiction, Singer incorporates the macabre, divine, and demonic to imbue the story with a fantastic quality that evokes the timelessness of parable. The presence of *dybbuks*—transient souls who take possession of living humans, according to Jewish tradition—also play an important role in many of Singer's

short stories. In "Gimpel the Fool," Singer similarly addresses religious faith in an anachronistic Old World setting. Gimpel, the protagonist and narrator of the story, is duped, ridiculed, and cuckolded by his fellow townspeople because he solemnly refuses to abandon his pious credulity for fear of introducing doubt to his belief in God. In the end, Gimpel's absolute faith sustains him despite the victimization and absurdity he is willing to endure with saint-like stoicism. *The Magician of Lublin* follows the escapades of Yasha Mazur, an escape artist and magician whose irrepressible sexual urges lead him into multiple extramarital relationships. When his renowned powers of deception fail and he is caught stealing, Yasha enters into a hermetic life to atone for his sins through solitary prayer and meditation. As in *Satan in Goray* and "Gimpel the Fool," Singer exposes the striking similarities among the attributes of madness, piety, and wisdom. Yasha, as a picaresque hero, also embodies conflicting male desires for power and hedonistic pleasure against domestic submission and diminishing potency, significantly associated by Singer with resistance to the will of God. *The Family Moskat,* along with *The Manor* (1967) and *The Estate* (1969), represents an epic historical trilogy that recounts the plight of Polish Jews from 1863 to the Nazi offensives of 1939. Modelled largely on Israel Joshua's realistic narrative style, Singer's vivid depiction of Jewish life in Warsaw equates the fragmentation of traditional values and the family with the degeneration of Western society in general, particularly through the central character, Asa Heshel, who abandons talmudic scholarship to become a doomed nihilist. As in other works, Singer juxtaposes the competing claims of spirituality and skepticism in the Jewish community, though the haunting reality of the Holocaust suggests the futility of both. Singer addresses the aftermath of the Holocaust in *Enemies,* a comical novel about the difficult postwar life of Herman Broder, a Jew who avoided the Nazi concentration camps by hiding in a Polish hayloft during the war years. Racked with guilt for escaping such suffering, particularly as the Holocaust is perceived as a defining element of contemporary Jewish identity, Broder creates vicarious torments in New York through complex relationships with female survivors and demonic fantasies. In *Shosha,* Singer fuses the realistic style of *The Family Moskat* with the allegorical tone of *Satan in Goray* and "Gimpel the Fool." The narrator, Aaron Greidinger, is an aspiring writer who forgoes an opportunity to flee Poland during the Second World War. Greidinger also halts his sexual adventures with various sophisticated modern women to marry Shosha, a captivating young girl who embodies the innocence and cultural tradition of the Eastern European Jews. Tragically, however, Shosha dies at the hands of the Nazis, leaving Greidinger a Holocaust survivor whose devotion to Jewish language and heritage is her legacy. In the posthumously published novel *Meshugah,* Greidinger reappears as a semi-autobiographic character who lives in the United States and writes serial novels for a Yiddish newspaper. Like Singer himself, Greidinger is a solitary writer who attempts to preserve traditional Jewish culture through stories about the past.

Critical Reception

Singer's evocative fiction is consistently praised for its uncanny simplicity and philosophical depth. While *Satan in Goray* and "Gimpel the Fool" are considered his most effective creative works, *The Magician of Lublin, Enemies, Shosha,* and many short stories contained in collections such as *The Spinoza of Market Street* and *Short Fridays and Other Stories* reveal Singer's narrative talent and metaphysical concerns. Though reproached by some members of the Jewish community for refusing to elevate the Jewish people as a persecuted ethnic minority, Singer's loyalty to Yiddish literature is credited with reaffirming the credibility of the near-extinct language. Other critics accuse Singer of repeating himself in subsequent stories and some cite erotic elements in his fiction as either provocative or irreverent, especially Singer's depiction of libertine characters and unabashed sexual affairs. Despite the unconcealed religious significance of his fiction, Singer's sardonic modernist sensibility and abiding interest in the debilitating effects of spiritual isolation draws frequent comparison to the existentialist writings of Albert Camus. Without resorting to didacticism or dogmatic moral judgment, Singer attempts to reconcile the mystical and absurd in both the Old and New Worlds with compassion, irony, and gentle humor.

PRINCIPAL WORKS

Der Satan in Gorey [*Satan in Goray*] (novel) 1935

Di Familie Mushkat [*The Family Moskat*] (novel) 1950

Mayn Tatn's Bes-din Shtub [*In My Father's Court*] (memoir) 1956

Gimpel tam un andere Dertseylungen [*Gimpel the Fool and Other Stories*] (short stories) 1957

Kunstmakher fun Lublin [*The Magician of Lublin*] (novel) 1960

The Spinoza of Market Street (short stories) 1961

Der Knekht [*The Slave*] (novel) 1962

Short Friday and Other Stories (short stories) 1964

Mazel and Shlimazel; or, The Milk of a Lioness (for children) 1966

Sonim, di Geschichte fun a Liebe [*Enemies: A Love Story*] (novel) 1966

Zlateh the Goat and Other Stories (for children) 1966

The Manor (novel) 1967

The Seance and Other Stories (short stories) 1968

When Schlemiel Went to Warsaw and Other Stories (for children) 1968

A Day of Pleasure: Stories of a Boy Growing Up in War-saw (autobiographic children's work) 1969

The Estate (novel) 1969

A Friend of Kafka and Other Stories (short stories) 1970

A Crown of Feathers and Other Stories (short stories) 1973

The Mirror (drama) 1973

Der Bal-tshuve [*The Penitent*] (novel) 1974

Schlemiel the First (drama) 1974

Yentl, the Yeshiva Boy [with Leah Napolin] (drama) 1974

Passions and Other Stories (short stories) 1975

A Little Boy in Search of God: Mysticism in a Personal Light (memoir) 1976

A Young Man in Search of Love (memoir) 1978

Shosha (novel) 1978

Teibele and Her Demon [with Eve Friedman] (drama) 1978

Old Love and Other Stories (short stories) 1979

Reaches of Heaven: A Story of the Baal Shem Tov (novel) 1980

Lost in America (memoir) 1981

Love and Exile: The Early Years: A Memoir (memoir) 1984

Gifts (short stories) 1985

The Image and Other Stories (short stories) 1985

The Death of Methuselah and Other Stories (short stories) 1988

The King of the Fields (novel) 1988

Scum (novel) 1991

The Certificate (novel) 1992

Meshugah (novel) 1994

Shadows on the Hudson (novel) 1998

CRITICISM

Irving Howe (essay date April 1966)

SOURCE: "I. B. Singer," in *Encounter*, Vol. 26, April, 1966, pp. 60-70.

[*In the following essay, Howe provides an overview of Singer's literary reputation, artistic influences, and central preoccupations as expressed in his fiction.*]

> *—Would it be fair to say that you are actually writing in a somewhat artificial or illusory context, as if none of the terrible things that have happened to the Jewish people during the last two decades really did occur?*

> SINGER: *Yes, very fair, There was a famous philosopher, Vaihinger, who wrote a book called* The Philosophy of "As If" *in which he showed that we all behave "as if." The "as if" is so much a part of our life that it really isn't artificial. . . . Every*

man assumes he will go on living. He behaves as if he will never die. So I wouldn't call my attitude artificial. It's very natural and healthy. We have to go on living and writing.

—But do you agree that at the heart of your attitude there is an illusion which is consciously sustained?

SINGER: *Yes.*

No other living writer has yielded himself so completely and recklessly as has Isaac Bashevis Singer to the claims of the human imagination. Singer writes in Yiddish, a language that no amount of energy or affection seems likely to save from extinction. He writes about a world that is gone, destroyed with a brutality beyond historical comparison. He writes within a culture, the remnant of Yiddish in the Western world, that is more than a little dubious about his purpose and stress. He seems to take entirely for granted his role as a traditional story-teller speaking to an audience attuned to his every hint and nuance, an audience that values story-telling both in its own right and as a binding communal action—but also, as it happens, an audience that keeps fading week by week, shrinking day by day. And he does all this without a sigh or apology, without so much as a Jewish groan. It strikes one as a kind of inspired madness: here is a man living in New York City, a sophisticated and clever writer, who composes stories about places like Frampol, Bilgoray, Kreshev, *as if they were still there.* His work is shot through with the bravado of a performer who enjoys making his listeners gasp, weep, laugh and yearn for more. Above and beyond everything else he is a great performer, in ways that remind one of Twain, Dickens, Sholom Aleichem.

Singer writes Yiddish prose with a verbal and rhythmic brilliance that, to my knowledge, can hardly be matched. When Eliezer Greenberg and I were working on our *Treasury of Yiddish Stories,* he said to me: "Singer has to be heard, to be believed." Behind the prose there is always a spoken voice, tense, ironic, complex in tonalities, leaping past connectives. Greenberg then read to me, with a fluency and pith I could never capture in my own reading of Yiddish, Singer's masterpiece, **"Gimpel the Fool,"** and I knew at once (it took no great powers of judgment) that here was the work of a master. The story came as a stroke of revelation, like a fiction by Babel or Kleist encountered for the first time.

Singer's stories claim attention through their vivacity and strangeness of surface. He is devoted to the grotesque, the demonic, the erotic, the quasi-mystical. He populates his alien sub-world with imps, devils, whores, fanatics, charlatans, spirits in seizure, disciples of false messiahs. A young girl is captured by the spirit of a dead woman and goes to live with the mourning husband as if she were actually his wife; a town is courted and then shattered by a lavish stranger who turns out to be the devil; an ancient Jew suffering unspeakable deprivations during the first World War, crawls back to his village of Bilgoray and fathers a son whom, with marvelous aplomb, he names Isaac. Sometimes the action in Singer's stories follows the moral curve of traditional folk tales, with a charming, lightly-phrased "lesson" at the end; sometimes, the spiral of a quizzical modern awareness; at best, the complicated motions of the old and the contemporary yoked together, a kind of narrative double-stop.

Orgiastic lapses from the moral order, pacts with the devil, ascetic self-punishments, distraught sexuality occupy the foreground of Singer's stories. Yet behind this expressionist clamour there is glimpsed the world of the *stetl,* or East European Jewish village, as it stumbled and slept through the last few centuries. Though Singer seldom portrays it full-face, one must always keep this world in mind while reading his stories: it forms the base from which he wanders, the norm from which he deviates but which controls his deviation. And truly to hear these stories one must have at least a splinter of knowledge about the culture from which Singer comes, the world he continues to evoke as if it were still radiantly alive: the Hasidim still dancing, the rabbis still pondering, the children still studying, the poor still hungering as if it had not all ended in ashes and death.

> **No other living writer has yielded himself so completely and recklessly as has Isaac Bashevis Singer to the claims of the human imagination.**
>
> **—*Irving Howe***

Isaac Bashevis Singer was born in Radzymin, Poland, in 1904. Both his father and grandfather were rabbis, in the tradition of Hasidism, a kind of ecstatic pietism, though on his mother's side the *misnagid* or rationalist strain of Jewish belief was stronger. "My father," recalls Singer, "always used to say that if you don't believe in the *maddikim* [the "wonder-rabbis" of Hasidism] today, tomorrow you won't believe in God. My mother would say, it's one thing to believe in God and another to believe in a man. . . . My mother's point of view is also my point of view."

Raised in a poor neighborhood of Warsaw, on Krochmalna Street, Singer received a strictly traditional Jewish education. He studied in a rabbinical seminary which was "a kind of college" providing secular as well as religious studies. During his adolescence he spent three or four years in his grandfather's *shtetl,* Bilgoray, which would later show it-self as a strong influence upon his work. Bilgoray

> was very old-fashioned. Not much has changed there in generations. In this town the traditions of hundreds of years ago still lived. There was no rail-road nearby. It was stuck in the forest and it was pretty much as it must have been during the time of Chmielnicki. . . . I could have written *The Fam-ily Moskat* [a novel set in Warsaw] without having lived in Bilgoray, but I could never have written *Satan in Goray* [a novella dealing with 17th-cen-tury false messianism] or some of my short stories without having been there.

A decisive example was set by Singer's older brother, Is-rael Joshua, who began to write in his youth and became a leading Yiddish novelist, author of *The Brothers Ashkenazi* and *Yashe Kolb.* Throughout a distinguished career, I. J. Singer remained pretty much within the main lines of the Yiddish tradition, both as to moral and social attitudes, even though he was strongly influenced by contemporary West-ern writing, especially the kind of large-scale family novel popular in Europe at the turn of the century. Controlling the older Singer's fiction is the Jewish community, both as so-cial framework and source of values; his style, fluent, re-laxed and smooth, can be taken as a model for cultivated modern Yiddish. The older brother represents that which I. B. Singer learned from, struggled with, and then mostly left behind.

In the Jewish world of Warsaw during the time Singer was growing up, a decision to become a secular writer meant a painful conflict with family and culture, a symbolic break from the paths of tradition:

> It was a great shock to my parents. They consid-ered all the secular [Yiddish] writers to be heretics, all unbelievers—they really were too, most of them. To become a *literat* was to them almost as bad as becoming a *meshumed,* one who forsakes the faith. My father used to say that secular writers like Peretz were leading the Jews to heresy. He said everything they wrote was against God. Even though Peretz wrote in a religious vein, my father called his writ-ing "sweetened poison," but poison nevertheless. And from his point of view he was right. Everybody who read such books sooner or later became a worldly man, and forsook the traditions. In my fam-ily, of course, my brother had gone first, and I went after him. For my parents, this was a tragedy.

In these early years of the century Warsaw was a lively if troubled city, the main centre of Jewish cultural life. The binding tradition of Yiddish literature had already been set by the pioneer generation of writers: Mendele Mocher Sforim, Sholom Aleichem, I. J. Peretz. It was a literature strongly devoted to problems of communal destiny and sur-vival; characterised by a high, sometimes consuming ethi-cal intent; closely tied to folk sources; drawing profoundly upon, even as it kept moving away from, religious tradition; resting upon a culture that might still be described as "or-ganic" and certainly as coherent; and yet displaying many signs of the influence of European, especially Russian, writ-ing. In Warsaw the major social and cultural movements of East European Jewish life found their most sophisticated versions: Yiddishism, the effort to create an autonomous secular culture based on the language of *galut;* Bundism, the organisation of a distinctively Jewish socialism, and Zi-onism, potentially of great importance but at this point still weak. Peretz's home became the gathering-place for young writers fresh from the provinces where the majority of Jews still lived; here, in this cosmopolitan haven, they could be-gin planning their novels and stories about the overwhelm-ing memory of the *shtetl.* And the religious community, though now challenged from several directions and past the high point of its power, remained a major force within the world of the East European Jews.

Growing up in this feverish but immensely stimulating at-mosphere, the younger Singer carved out a path of his own. He was not drawn to any of the Jewish movements: indeed, he has always been sceptical of the political messianism which, as a partial offshoot of the earlier religious messianism, runs through 20th-century Jewish life. He edged away from formal piety, yet remained close to the Jewish religious tradition, especially its more esoteric and cabbalistic elements. And while a master of the Yiddish lan-guage—he is second only to Sholom Aleichem in his command of its idiom—Singer was neither a programmatic Yiddishist nor notably at case in the world of Yiddish culture, which has in the main been secular and rationalist in stress.

As a youth Singer began to read in forbidden tongues, dis-covering E. T. A. Hoffman and Edgar Allan Poe in the li-braries of Warsaw. The exotic romanticism of these writers stirred his imagination rather more than did the work of most Yiddish writers, who were then in a realistic or even natu-ralistic phase, and with whose materials he felt all to famil-iar. An even stronger alien influence was that of Knut Hamsun, the Norwegian novelist, who enjoyed an interna-tional vogue during the years before World War II. Hamsun's novels, especially *Pan,* impressed upon the younger Singer the claims of the irrational in human exist-ence, the power of the perverse within seemingly normal behavior. Now, several decades later, it is hard to see much evidence of Hamsun in Singer's work: perhaps it was the kind of influence that does not leave a visible stamp but in-stead liberates a writer to go his own way.

A still more alien influence—for a young Jewish writer fresh from the *yeshiva,* an influence downright bizarre—was that curious body of writings known as spiritualism or "psychic research," which Singer somehow came upon in Warsaw and would continue to follow throughout his life. Could anything be more distant from the tradition of Yiddish literature or, for that matter, from the whole body of Jewish religious thought? Fortunately for his career as a writer, Singer has preserved a keen Jewish scepticism—in that department he is entirely traditional!—towards this branch of "knowledge," taking the sophisticated view that belief in the reality of spirits provides his fiction with a kind of compositional shorthand, a "spiritual stenography." As he remarks: "the demons and Satan represent to me, in a sense, the ways of the world. Instead of saying this is the way things happen, I will say, this is the way demons behave." Which is precisely what any cultivated sceptic, totally unconcerned with "psychic research," would also say.

In 1935, convinced that "it was inevitable after Hitler came to power that the Germans would invade Poland," Singer emigrated to the United States. He joined the staff of the Jewish daily *Forward,* a Yiddish newspaper, in which he printed serious fiction under his own name and a large quantity of journalism under the pen-name of Warshofsky. His first major work, the novella *Satan in Goray,* appeared in Yiddish in 1935. Since then he has written full-scale novels, one of which, *The Family Moskat,* was published in an English translation in 1949, as well as a number of short novels (in English: *The Magician of Lublin* and *The Slave*) and several collections of stories. His best work has been done in short forms, the novella and the story: exciting bursts and flares of the imagination.

Isaac Bashevis Singer is the only living Yiddish writer whose translated work has caught the imagination of a Western (the American) literary public. Though the settings of his stories are frequently strange, the contemporary reader—for whom the determination not to be shocked has become a point of honour—is likely to feel closer to Singer than to most other Yiddish writers. Offhand this may be surprising, for Singer's subjects are decidedly remote and exotic: in *Satan in Goray* the orgiastic consequences of the false messianism of 17th-century East European Jewish life; In *The Magician of Lublin* a portrait of a Jewish magician—Don Juan in late 19th-century Poland who exhausts himself in sensuality and ends as a penitent ascetic; in his stories a range of demonic, apocalyptic, and perversely sacred moments of *shtetl* life. Yet one feels that, unlike many of the Yiddish writers who treat more familiar and up-to-date subjects, Singer commands a distinctly "modern" sensibility.

Now this is partly true—in the sense that Singer has cut himself off from some of the traditional styles and assumptions of Yiddish writing. But it is also not true—in the sense that

any effort to assimilate Singer to literary "modernism" without fully registering his involvement with Jewish faith and history is almost certain to distort his meanings.

Those meanings, one might as well admit, are often enigmatic and hard to come by. It must be a common experience among Singer's readers to find a quick pleasure in the caustic surfaces of his prose, the nervous tokens of his virtuosity, but then to acknowledge themselves baffled as to his point and purpose. That his fiction does have an insistent point and stringent purpose no one can doubt: Singer is too ruthlessly single-minded a writer to content himself with mere slices of representation or displays of the bizarre. His grotesquerie must be taken seriously, perhaps as a recoil from his perception of how irremediably and gratuitously ugly human life can be. He is a writer completely absorbed by the demands of his vision, a vision gnomic and compulsive but with moments of high exaltation; so that while reading his stories one feels as if one were overhearing bits and snatches of monologue, the impact of which is both notable and disturbing, but the meaning withheld.

Now these are precisely the qualities that the sophisticated reader, trained to docility before the exactions of "modernism," has come to applaud. Singer's stories work, or prey, upon the nerves. They leave one unsettled and anxious, the way a rationalist might feel if, waking at night in the woods, he suddenly found himself surrounded by a swarm of bats. Unlike most Yiddish fiction, Singer's stories neither round out the cycle of their intentions nor posit a coherent and ordered universe. They can be seen as paradigms of the arbitrariness, the grating injustice, at the heart of life. They offer instances of pointless suffering, dead-end exhaustion, inexplicable grace. And sometimes, as in Singer's masterpiece, **"Gimpel the Fool,"** they turn about, refusing to rest with the familiar discomforts of the problematic, and drive towards a prospect of salvation on the other side of despair, beyond soiling by error or will. This prospect does not depend on any belief in the comeliness or lawfulness of the universe; whether God is there or not, He is surely no protector:

> He had worked out his own religion [Singer writes about one of his characters]. There was a Creator, but He revealed himself to no one, gave no indications of what was permitted or forbidden.

Things happen, the probable bad and improbable good, both of them subject to the whim of the fortuitous; and the sacred fools like Gimpel, perhaps they alone, learn to roll with the punch, finding the value of their life in a total passivity and credulousness, a complete openness to suffering.

Singer's stories trace the characteristic motions of human destiny: a heavy climb upward (**"The Old Man"**), a rapid tumble downward ("The Fast"). Life forms a journeying to heaven and hell, mostly hell. What determines the direction a man will take? Sometimes the delicate manoeuvres between his will and desire, sometimes the heat of his vanity, sometimes the blessing of innocence. But more often than not, it is all a mystery which Singer chooses to present rather than explain. As his figures move upward and downward, a flame with the passion of their ineluctable destiny, they stop for a moment in the *shtetl* world. Singer is not content with the limitations of materiality, yet not at all indifferent to the charms and powers of the phenomenal universe. In his calculus of destiny, however, the world is a resting-place and what happens within it, even within the social enclave of the Jews, is not of lasting significance. Thick, substantial, and attractive as it comes to seem in Singer's representation, the world is finally but lure and appearance, a locale between heaven and hell, the shadow of larger possibilities.

In most Yiddish fiction the stress is quite different. There the central "character" is the collective destiny of the Jews in *galut* or exile; the central theme, the survival of a nation deprived of nationhood; the central ethic, the humane education of men stripped of worldly power yet sustained by the memory of chosenness and the promise of redemption. In Singer the norm of collective life is still present, but mostly in the background, as a tacit assumption; his major actions break away from the limits of the *shtetl* ethic, what has come to be known as *Yiddishkeit,* and then move either backward to the abandon of false messianism or forward to the doubt of modern sensibility. (There is an interesting exception, the story called **"Short Friday,"** which in its stress upon family affection, ritual proprieties and collective faith, approaches rather closely the tones of traditional Yiddish fiction.)

> **It is hardly a secret that in the Yiddish literary world Singer is regarded with a certain suspicion. His powers of evocation, his resources as a stylist are acknowledged, yet many Yiddish literary persons, including the serious ones, seem uneasy about him.**
> *—Irving Howe*

The historical settings of East European Jewish life are richly presented in Singer's stories, often not as orderly sequences in time but as simultaneous perceptions jumbled together in the consciousness of figures for whom Abraham's sacrifice, Chmiclincki's pogroms, the rise and fall of Hasidism and the stirrings of the modern world are all felt with equal force. Yet Singer's ultimate concern is not with the collective experience of a chosen or martyred

people but with the enigmas of personal fate. Given the slant of his vision, this leads him to place a heavy reliance upon the grotesque as a mode of narration, even as an avenue towards knowledge. But the grotesque carries with it a number of literary and moral dangers, not the least being the temptation for Singer to make it into an end in itself, which is to say, something facile and sensationalist. In his second-rank stories he falls back a little too comfortably upon the devices of which he is absolute master, like a magician supremely confident his tricks will continue to work. But mainly the grotesque succeeds in Singer's stories because it comes to symbolise meaningful digressions from a cultural norm. An uninstructed reader may absorb Singer's grotesquerie somewhat too easily into the assumptions of modern literature; the reader who grasps the ambivalence of Singer's relation to Yiddish literature will see the grotesquerie as a cultural sign by means of which Singer defines himself against his own past.

It is hardly a secret that in the Yiddish literary world Singer is regarded with a certain suspicion. His powers of evocation, his resources as a stylist are acknowledged, yet many Yiddish literary persons, including the serious ones, seem uneasy about him. One reason is that "modernism"—which, as these people regard Singer, signifies a heavy stress upon sexuality, a concern for the irrational, expressionist distortions of character, and a seeming indifference to the humane ethic of Yiddishism—has never won so strong a hold in Jewish culture as it has in the cultures of most Western countries. For the Yiddish writers, "modernism" has been at best an adornment of manner upon a subject inescapably traditional.

The truly "modern" writer, however, is not quite trustworthy in relation to his culture. He is a shifty character by choice and need, unable to settle into that solid representativeness which would allow him to act as a cultural "spokesman." And to the extent that Singer does share in the modernist outlook he must be regarded with distrust by Yiddish readers brought up on such literary "spokesmen" as Peretz, Abraham Relsen, and H. Leivick. There is no lack of admiration among Yiddish readers for Singer's work: anyone with half an ear for the cadence and idiom of that marvelous language must respond to his prose. Still, it is a qualified, a troubled admiration. Singer's moral outlook, which seems to move with equal readiness towards the sensational and the ascetic, is hardly calculated to put Yiddish readers at their case. So they continue to read him, with pleasure and anxiety.

And as it seems to me, they are not altogether wrong. Their admiring resistance to Singer's work may constitute a more attentive and serious response to his iconoclasm than the gleeful applause of those who read him in English translation and take him to be another writer of "black comedy," or heaven help us, a mid-20th-century "swinger."

The death of Satan was a tragedy for the imagination.

By and large Singer has been fortunate in his translators, but no translation, not even Saul Bellow's magnificent rendering of **"Gimpel the Fool,"** could possibly suggest the full idiomatic richness and syntactical verve of Singer's Yiddish. Singer has left behind him the oratorical sententiousness to which Yiddish literature is prone, has abandoned its leisurely meandering pace, what might be called the *shtetl* rhythm, and has developed a style that is both swift and dense, nervous and thick. His sentences are short and abrupt; his rhythms coiled, intense, short-breathed. The impression his prose creates is not of a smooth and equable flow of language but rather a series of staccato advances and withdrawals, with sharp breaks between sentences. Singer seldom qualifies, wanders or circles back; his method is to keep darting forward, impression upon impression, through a series of jabbing declarative sentences. His prose is free of "literary" effects, a frequent weakness among Yiddish writers who wish to display their elegance and cultivation. And at the base of his prose is the oral idiom of Yiddish, seeded with ironic proverbs and apothegms ("Shoulders are from God, and burdens too"); but a speech that has been clipped, wrenched, syncopated.

What is most remarkable about Singer's prose is his ability to unite rich detail with fiercely compressed rhythms. For the translator this presents the almost insuperable problem of how to capture both his texture and his pace, his density of specification and his vibrating quickness. More often than not, even the most accomplished translator must choose between one effect and the other, if only because the enormous difficulty of rendering Yiddish idiom into another language forces him either to fill out or slow down Singer's sentences.

By its very nature, pace cannot be illustrated, but the richness of Singer's detail can, as in this characteristic passage from **"The Old Man":**

> His son had died long before, and Reb Moshe Ber said the memorial prayer, *kaddish,* for him. Now alone in the apartment, he had to feed his stove with paper and wood shavings from garbage cans. In the ashes he baked rotten potatoes, which he carried in his scarf, and in an iron pot, he brewed chicory. He kept house, made his own candles by kneading bits of wax and suet around wicks, laundered his shirt beneath the kitchen faucet, and hung it to dry on a piece of string. He set the mousetraps each night and drowned the mice each morning. When he went

out he never forgot to fasten the heavy padlock on the door. No one had to pay rent in Warsaw at that time. . . . The winter was difficult. There was no coal, and since several tiles were missing from the stove, the apartment was filled with thick black smoke each time the old man made a fire. A crust of blue ice and snow covered the window panes by November, making the rooms constantly dark or dusky. Overnight, the water on his night table froze in the pot. No matter how many clothes he piled over him in bed, he never felt warm; his feet remained stiff, and as soon as he began to doze, the entire pile of clothes would fall off, and he would have to climb out naked to make the bed once more. There was no kerosene; even matches were at a premium. Although he recited chapter upon chapter of the Psalms, he could not fall asleep. The wind, freely roaming about the rooms, banged the doors; even the mice left.

Or, in a more colourful vein, from **"The Last Demon":**

> [the last demon] came here from Lublin. Tishevitz is a God-forsaken village: Adam didn't even stop to pee there. It's so small that a wagon goes through the town and the horse is in the market place just as the rear wheels reach the toll gate. There is mud in Tishevitz from Succoth until Tishe b'Ov. The goats of the town don't need to lift their beards to chew at the thatched roofs of the cottages. Hens roost in the middle of the streets. Birds build nests in the women's bonnets. In the tailor's synagogue a billy goat is the tenth in the quorum.

Or, grotesquely, from **"Blood":**

> Frequently she sang for hours in Yiddish and in Polish. Her voice was harsh and cracked and she invented the songs as she went along, repeating meaningless phrases, uttering sounds that resembled the cackling of fowl, the grunting of pigs, the death-rattles of oxen. . . . At night in her dreams, phantoms tormented her; bulls gored her with their horns; pigs shoved their snouts into her face and bit her; roosters cut her flesh to ribbons with their spurs.

Or, tenderly, from **"Gimpel the Fool":**

> I was an orphan. My grandfather who brought me up was already bent towards the grave. So they turned me over to a baker, and what a time they gave me there! Every woman or girl who came to bake a batch of noodles had to fool me at least once. "Gimpel, there's a fair in heaven; Gimpel, the rabbi

gave birth to a calf in the seventh month; Gimpel, a cow flew over the roof and laid brass eggs." A student from the yeshiva came once to buy a roll, and he said, "You, Gimpel, while you stand here scraping with your baker's shovel the Messiah has come. The dead have arisen." "What do you mean?" I said "I heard no one blowing the ram's horn." He said, "Are you deaf?" And all began to cry, "We heard it, we heard. . . ."

To tell the truth, I knew very well that nothing of the sort had happened, but all the same, as folks were talking, I threw on my wool vest and went out. Maybe something had happened. What did I stand to lose by looking? Well, what a cat music went up! And then I took a vow to believe nothing more. But that was no go either. They confused me so I didn't know the big end from the small.

Those of Singer's stories which speed downward into hell are often told by devils and imps, sometimes by Satan himself, marvelling at the vanity and paltriness of the human creature. Singer's arch-devil is a figure not so much of evil as of scepticism, a thoroughly modern voice to whose corrosive questions Singer imparts notable force in **"A Tale of Two Liars":**

Are you stupid enough to still believe in the power of prayer? Remember how the Jews prayed during the Black Plague, and nevertheless, how they perished like flies? And what about the thousands the Cossacks butchered? There was enough prayer, wasn't there, when Chmielnicki came? How were those prayers answered? Children were buried alive, chaste wives raped—and later their bellies ripped open and cats sewed inside. Why should God bother with your prayers? He neither hears nor sees. There is no judge. There is no judgment.

Using demons and imps as narrators proves to be a wonderful device for structural economy: they replace the need to enter the "inner life" of the characters, the whole plaguing business of the psychology of motives, for they serve as symbolic equivalents and co-ordinates to human conduct, what Singer calls a "spiritual stenography." In those stories, however, where Singer celebrates the power of human endurance, as in **"The Little Shoemakers"** and **"The Old Man,"** he uses third person narrative in the closest he comes to a "high style," so that the rhetorical elevation will help to create an effect of "epical" sweep.

Within his limits Singer is a genius. He has total command of his imagined world; he is original in his use both of traditional Jewish materials and his modernist attitude towards them; he provides a serious if enigmatic moral perspective;

and he is a master of Yiddish prose. Yet there are times when Singer seems to be mired in his own originality, stories in which he displays a weakness for self-imitation that is disconcerting. Second-rate writers imitate others, first-rate writers themselves, and it is not always clear which is the more dangerous.

Having gone this far, we must now turn again. If Singer's work can be grasped only on the assumption that he is crucially a "modernist" writer, one must add that in other ways he remains profoundly subject to the Jewish tradition. And if the Yiddish reader is inclined to slight the "modernist" side of his work, any other reader is likely to underestimate the traditional side.

> **Within his limits Singer is a genius. He has total command of his imagined world; he is original in his use both of traditional Jewish materials and his modernist attitude towards them; he provides a serious if enigmatic moral perspective; and he is a master of Yiddish prose.**
> **—*Irving Howe***

One of the elements in the Jewish past that has most fascinated Singer is the recurrent tendency to break loose from the burden of the Mosaic law and, through the urging of will and ecstasy, declare an end to the *galut*. Historically, this has taken the form of a series of Messianic movements, one led in the 17th century by Sabbatai Zevi and another in the 18th by Jacob Frank. The movement of Sabbatai Zevi appeared after the East European Jewish community had been shattered by the rebellion pogrom of the Cossack chieftain, Chmielnicki. Many of the survivors, caught up in a strange ecstasy that derived all too clearly from their total desperation, began to summon apocalyptic fantasies and to indulge themselves in long-repressed religious emotions which, perversely, were stimulated by the pressures of Cabbalistic asceticism. As if in response to their yearnings, Sabbatai, a pretender rising in the Middle East, offered to release them of everything that rabbinical Judaism had confined or suppressed. He spoke for the tempting doctrine that faith is sufficient for salvation; for the wish to evade the limits of mundane life by forcing a religious transcendence; for the union of erotic with mystical appetites; for the lure of a demonism which the very hopelessness of the Jewish situation rendered plausible. In 1665-66 Sabbatianism came to orgiastic climax, whole communities, out of a conviction that the messiah was in sight, discarding the moral inhibitions of exile. Their hopes were soon brutally disappointed, for Sabbatai, persecuted by the Turkish Sultan, converted to Mohammedanism. His followers were thrown into confusion and despair, and a resurgent rabbinism again took control over Jewish life. Nevertheless, Sabbatianism continued to lead an underground existence among the East European Jews—even (I have been told by *shtetl* survivors) into the late 19th and early 20th century. It became a secret heretical cult celebrating Sabbatai as the apostate saviour who had been required to descend to the depths of the world to achieve the heights of salvation.

To this buried strand of Jewish experience Singer has been drawn in fascination and repulsion, portraying its manifestations with great vividness and its consequences with stern judgment. It is a kind of experience that rarely figures in traditional Yiddish writing yet is a significant aspect of the Jewish past. Bringing this material to contemporary readers, Singer writes *in* Yiddish but often quite apart from the Yiddish tradition; indeed, he is one of the few Yiddish writers whose relation to the Jewish past is not determined or screened by that body of values we call Yiddishism.

Singer is a writer of both the pre-Enlightenment and the post-Enlightenment: he would be equally at home with a congregation of medieval Jews and a gathering of 20th-century intellectuals, perhaps more so than at a meeting of the Yiddish PEN club. He has a strong sense of the mystical and antique, but also a cool awareness of psycho-analytic disenchantment. He has evaded both the religious pieties and the humane rationalism of 19th-century East European Judaism. He has skipped over the ideas of the historical epoch which gave rise to Yiddishism, for the truth is, I suppose, that Yiddish literature, in both its writers of acceptance and writers of scepticism, is thoroughly caught up with the Enlightenment. Singer is not. He shares very little in the collective sensibility or the *folkstimlichkeit* of the Yiddish masters; he does not unambiguously celebrate *dos kleine menshele* (the common man) as a paragon of goodness; he is impatient with the sensual deprivations implicit in the values of *edelkeit* (refinement, nobility); and above all he moves away from a central assumption of both Yiddish literature in particular and the 19th century in general, the assumption of an immanent fate or end in human existence (what in Yiddish is called *tachlis*).

But again qualifications are needed. It is one thing to decide to break from a tradition in which one has been raised, quite another to make the break completely. For Singer has his ties—slender, subterranean, but strong—with the very Yiddish writers from whom he has turned away.

At the centre of Yiddish fiction stands the archetypical figure of *dot kleine menshele*. It is he, long-suffering, persistent, lovingly ironic, whom the Yiddish writers celebrate. This poor but proud householder trying to maintain his status in the *shtetl* world even as he keeps sinking deeper and deeper into poverty, appeals to the Yiddish imagination far more than mighty figures like Aeneas or Ahab. And from

this representative man of the *shtetl* there emerges a number of significant variations. One extreme variation is the ecstatic wanderer, hopeless in this world because profoundly committed to the other. An equally extreme variation is the wise or sainted fool who has given up the struggle for status and thereby acquired the wry perspective of an outsider. Standing somewhere between *dos kleine menshele* and these offshoots is Peretz's Bontsha Schweig, whose intolerable humbleness makes even the angels in heaven feel guilty and embarrassed. Singer's Gimpel is a literary grandson (perhaps only on one side) of Peretz's Bontsha; and as Gimpel, with the piling up of his foolishness, acquires a halo of comic sadness and comes to seem an epitome of pure spirit, one must keep balancing in one's mind the ways in which he is akin to, yet different from, Bontsha.

The Yiddish critic Shlomo Bickel has perceptively remarked that Singer's dominating principle is an "anti-Prometheanism," a disbelief in the efficacy of striving, defiance, and pride, a doubt as to the sufficiency of knowledge or even wisdom. This seems true, but only if one remembers that in a good many of Singer's fictions the central action does constitute a kind of Promethean ordeal or striving. Singer makes it abundantly clear that his characters have no choice: they must live out their desires, their orgiastic yearning, their apocalyptic expectations. "Anti-Prometheanism" thus comes to rest upon a belief in the unavoidable recurrence of the Promethean urge.

What finally concerns Singer most is the possibilities for life that remain after the exhaustion of human effort, after failure and despair have come and gone. Singer watches his stricken figures from a certain distance, with enigmatic intent and no great outpouring of sympathy, almost as if to say that before such collapse neither judgment nor sympathy matters very much. Yet in all of his fictions the Promethean effort recurs, obsessional, churning with new energy and delusion. In the knowledge that it will, that it must recur, there may also lie hidden a kind of pity, for that too we would expect, and learn to find, in the writer who created Gimpel.

Irving H. Buchen (essay date 1966)

SOURCE: "Isaac Bashevis Singer and the Eternal Past," in *Critique: Studies in Modern Fiction*, Vol. 8, No. 3, 1966, pp. 5-18.

[*In the following essay, Buchen examines elements of Singer's narrative structure that "meaningfully violate and reconstitute the reader's identity, morality and chronology" to evoke a timeless quality in his fiction. Buchen discusses*

The Magician of Lublin as a typical example of Singer's all-encompassing vision in which time and space converge on absolute morality.]

The basic obstacle to an understanding of the work of Isaac Bashevis Singer is its effect of critical dislocation. Thus, the few existing studies symptomatically tend to be partial or fragmented: Eugene Goodheart emphasizes Singer's *Yiddishkeit;* Irving Howe his modernity and demonism; David Boroff his faddish popularity among college intellectuals; and Dan Jacobson the complexity of his stylistic simplicity. But the whole of Singer is greater than the sum of these parts, and any consideration which has pretensions to fullness and fidelity initially must situate itself in the midst of the contrary and fragmenting impulses of his art. Moreover, to avoid a rapid journey to universality at the expense of Singer's stylistic and Jewish uniqueness, any general examination must be tied to the details of at least one of his most representative works.

Perhaps the best way to begin is to notice what in Singer's work has led so many reviewers and readers primarily to stress his oddity or to concentrate solely on his disintegrating effect. At least three aspects of Singer's work set him apart not only from most American Jewish writers, but also from most American writers. First, all his novels and short stories published in America originally were written in Yiddish. Second, almost all his works are geographically removed from these shores by their old world settings and chronologically distant from our time by one to three generations or centuries. Third, Singer does not fit into the conventional pattern which characterizes the development of most American writers, Jewish as well as gentile. The first novel is usually autobiographical and regional (the two perhaps correlations of each other), and subsequent works move toward the centrality of American experience. Singer, however, stubbornly stands still. Indeed, although his first novel appeared fifteen years after his arrival in America, he still shows no signs of making any of the customary literary and cultural adjustments or assimilations.

The entire problem of discussing such a living anachronism can be solved by divorcing Singer from the entire American experience and by associating him exclusively with the Yiddish tradition of the Old World: a neat solution, except that it makes surface substance. That "solution" also misses a novel element in Singer's most recent work, *Short Friday* (1965). In this collection, two stories are set in America, one in Miami Beach, the other in Brooklyn. Yet so tenacious is the notion that Singer employs only Old World settings that *The New York Times Book Review,* in its section of recommended fiction, described *Short Friday* as "Sixteen short stories, all of them with the background of Yiddish-Poland." Leaving aside the disturbing implications of that inaccurate summary by the *Time's* "critic," one might

suppose that these two American-based stories at last put Singer into American literature. Such a conclusion, however, would be as distortive as making him part of the European-Jewish tradition merely because he writes in Yiddish; for the real novelty of these two stories is that what takes place in Miami and Brooklyn is as nightmarish, demoniacal, and cosmic as what occurs in Lashnik, Lublin, and Tishevetz. Suddenly, we discover that an old Polish crone weaving spells in 18th century Lublin reappears as a Cuban hag attempting to seduce a man who has come to Miami to relieve his asthma. A noisy, *heimesh* wedding in Brownsville provides the occasion for the same mystical reunion of lovers separated by Nazis as it does for those separated by 17th century pogroms. In short, what makes Singer strange and foreign is not so much the obvious—the distant settings and times or even the Yiddish or Jewish customs and rituals—but his vision which is no respecter of time and place and which by its absolutist fervor refuses to yield to changing cultural values.

Like all obsessive writers, Singer's vision is tyrannical. It comes from such a deep and even hidden source that it will not be compromised or dictated to. Powerfully and compulsively, it burns away the surface differences of Miami and Brooklyn to reveal 18th century Poland. Or rather vice versa, for the bulk of Singer's work enters the modern world through the backdoor of history. Evidently for Singer the shortest way to modern times involves taking the longest way around. In literary terms, Singer's way of reviving tastes jaded by excessively realistic or psychoanalytical novels is to resurrect the parabolic form. In moral terms, Singer's answer to the chaos and relativism of contemporary ethical judgments is the rebirth of Satan.

Some readers will surely object to considering an author modern who makes no accommodations to verisimilitude, who employs the devil as a regular and familiar character, sets stories in heaven and hell, presents demons copulating with lonely and pious widows, bewilders the sexual distinctions between male and female, and arranges for miraculous reunions of lovers separated by the grave. Objectors also might claim that Singer reflects no real knowledge or use of modern psychology. In its place, Singer presents a radical and often bizarre partnership between sexuality and spirituality, between sexual deviations and religious purity. But far from being at odds with modern psychology, Singer's religious sexuality is actually very close to drawing its power and veracity from the same sources as Freud's psychological sexuality.

Strange as it may seem, if one were to search for an historical situation or system of belief which most closely reflects the assumptions of Freud, it would be that of religion. Both psychology and religion share the same absolutist notion that nothing is ultimately accidental and that everything is finally meaningful. Psychology also accepts with religion the existence of an unseen, mysterious and non-rational force which is essentially deterministic. The psychological agent is labeled the unconscious, the religious the cosmic. The former acquires orderly meaning through the detection of sexual and parental relations; the latter through the revelations of providence. Both Freud and Singer place great emphasis on the deterministic process, although Freud calls it compulsion and Singer the progression of possession. In psychological terms, the compulsion is rendered as the increasing dominance of unconscious desires. In Singer's religious terms, the possession is rendered as the steady dispossession of the soul by Satan or a dybbuk. For Freud the final pathological result is psychosis and debilitation; for Singer it is evil and damnation. In literature, the complicated process of mental stratagems and substitutions generally is presented in the form of the stream of consciousness. In Singer that complexity takes a more external and supernatural form and appears in the involved machinations of demoniacal agents. What to Freud is the enormous world of interior life appears in Singer as a cosmic universe laced by the triangulation of God, Satan and man. How close Freud and Singer are can be rapidly indicated by an author whom both acknowledge as a master, Dostoevsky. Significantly, Dostoevsky referred to the unconscious as the "Satanic depths." In short, Singer does not ignore or bypass modern psychology but parallels it with a vision that insists on its own integrity and autonomy all the while it is responsive to what are called the insights of modern psychology. As a result, again strange as it may seem, the more psychologically oriented the reader is the more comfortable he may feel with Satan and with Singer.

In one major respect, however, Singer differs from Freud and other psychologists. He makes moral judgments on the actions of his characters and evidences a belief in the clear-cut differences between right and wrong. Excesses of any kind, religious or sexual or both, are ultimately sinful and punishable. In fact, the presence of such judgments makes clear that Singer's use of the devil and his host of tempting demons is not scape-goating. Because the effectiveness of the devil is contingent both on the consent and the collusion of man's secret desires and presumptions, the stories are contained by a psychology that is responsive to moral law. Far from exonerating man, Singer employs Satan to bring renewed dread and urgency to moral choice and to make personal judgment a mode of self-creation or of self-destruction. To Singer the devil is mortality dressed in the garb of immortality; he is license parading as freedom. Satan's mission is to persuade the soul that it is the body. By reviving the enormous issue of evil, Singer thus besets the soul with its ancient adversary as well as indicates the medium for its continued vital existence.

This does not mean that Singer is a heavy-handed moralist

or a Jewish Puritan. He does not intrude in his tales to draw lessons. Although he has enormous compassion, his sympathy never equals endorsement. Characteristically, his novels move from sympathy to judgment, from openness to containment. Indeed, the works appear to be written by a young-old man. The former recreates the situation with all its passion and frailty and ignorance. The latter waits patiently for the passion to be spent and makes his judgments with terrible serenity. Singer begins by presenting man as a free agent, confident of his powers and unconcerned about his responsibilities or his mortality. Singer concludes by presenting man as a slave. This pattern, which informs nearly all his works, appears in a particularly revealing form in a novel which stands almost midway between his earliest and latest works, *The Magician of Lublin* (1960). In examining this novel, my aim throughout is to describe the ways in which Singer's thematic concerns and modes of presentation meaningfully violate and reconstitute the reader's identity, morality and chronology. To be sure, the reconstitution occurs in Singer's terms. If those terms are shared initially or ultimately by the reader, Singer's power is registered as sympathetic coincidence. If not, the power appears as dialectical discrepancy. In either case, the reader's engagement remains strong and committed; and the effect is intense, reverberating and intimate.

> ***The Magician of Lublin*** is typical of Singer's works in that the solutions seem inferior to the problems raised, as if the questions Singer poses are in excess of the answers given.
> —*Irving H. Buchen*

The Magician of Lublin is typical of Singer's works in that the solutions seem inferior to the problems raised, as if the questions Singer poses are in excess of the answers given. Thus, the reader may be especially puzzled by the novel's narrowing movement toward a constricted ending. It begins with the buoyant, somewhat immoral Yasha the Magician freely and deftly moving from one circus engagement and love affair to another. It concludes with the ascetic figure of Yasha the Penitent voluntarily self-imprisoned in a brick house and undergoing mortification. The transformation takes place during a period of twenty four hours in Warsaw when Yasha attempts to steal money from the safe of the wealthy Zuraski. With the money he hopes to be able to divorce his wife, marry the widow of a professor and pay for the cost of preparing a new act to be performed before the crowned heads of Europe. All his plans come to nothing and the concluding image of Yasha is so stark and pathetic that it appears to violate our sense of what he initially was.

Actually, the reader's movement through the book is not as

haphazard or unrelated to the ending as might appear. In effect, the novel falls into three parts, like a three act drama, except that the structural divisions really support three different aspects of reality. The first deals with Yasha in a situation that is characteristically modern in its admixture of freedom and restraint, adultery and fidelity, secularity and religiosity. The second part is nightmarish, wild and surrealistic. All bars are drawn and Yasha forgoes all restraint. The conclusion presents the penitential portrait of imprisonment and slavery to God. The problem of accepting the ending is thus contingent on comprehending the total arc of Singer's vision.

When we first meet Yasha the Magician, he is lively and engaging, always the master of complicated looks and situations, and looks and acts ten years younger than his forty years. Moreover, what rapidly becomes clear is that Singer has selected Yasha's profession with symbolic care, for it characterizes not only his way of earning a living, but also his way of life. Thus, Yasha "had tangled and disentangled himself on numerous occasions." He juggles various love affairs and walks an emotional tightrope as deftly as he does on stage. In the house of Zeptel, one of his mistresses, Yasha participates in the local ritual of entertaining the villagers by opening a lock that they feel will stump his skill. But Yasha says, "'A lock is like a woman. Sooner or later it must surrender. . . . It'll give, it'll give. You only need to squeeze the belly button.'"

Although Yasha manipulates people as he does locks and although he carries on with other women, Singer does not present his hero as without virtue or conscience. He has an affair with two women, one Jewish and the other gentile, but his love for his wife remains intact and he holds his marriage sacred. Although he mixes with thieves and low life, he refuses to employ his lock-picking talents for dishonest ends. Finally, Yasha is not without respect for God, although the respect is colored by his profession. Driving along the road in spring, he surveys the budding fields, inhales the scent of growing newness, and spontaneously exclaims: "'Oh, God Almighty, You are the magician, not I! . . . To bring out plants, flowers and colors from a bit of black soil.'" Although he treasures his belief in God, he often plays the role of the devil's advocate in taverns, scoffing at the pious certainty of believers. In short, in the first part we have the portrait of an appealing scoundrel who is no fool. Sensitive to conscience and responsive to the godly, he is nevertheless too confident of his magical powers, too flushed by the power of his still youthful body, and too skeptical of glib religious answers to accept any restrictions of life, love, and marriage. Singer sums him up:

> He was a maze of personalities—religious and heretical, good and evil, false and sincere. He could love many women at once. He was ready to re-

nounce his religion, yet—when he found a page torn from a holy book he always picked it up and put it to his lips.

Yasha is fully and humanly greedy. He is involved in the body and in the spirit, in this world and the next. Singer has made him a magician to dramatize his role as a chameleon, a man of many faces and lives. What Yasha resists above all is being fixed with a permanent identity. As long as he can juggle his various love affairs, like pins in the air, and be different persons or wear different masks—boy, lover, father—to different women, he is unfinished, still to be defined, still in a state of becoming. This is the domain of comedy, for tragedy requires the sharp pressure of finality. Comedy measures the span of life; tragedy the span of death. Yasha is determined to be various and endless, which to Singer are the impulses of the body and of the spiritual allies the body can enlist. Variety to Yasha is not just the spice of life; it is the substitute for termination. He is the magician as picaresque hero. But whereas in the first part of the novel, Yasha magically seems to be able to play both sides of the moral and religious fence, his relationship with Emilia in the second part threatens his dualistic straddling. Specifically, Emilia, who moves among elevated cultural circles of Warsaw and is a converted Jewess, makes not only marriage but also conversion a condition of her sexual surrender and love. Thus, for all his deft side-stepping, Yasha finds the pressure of identity intrude into his life in the form of Emilia's demands.

Although in the second part the comedy shifts to tragedy, Yasha is unaware that Emilia's wishes represent a damnation in disguise. All Yasha knows is that Emilia reflects his own aspirations to rise above the petty life he has been leading and to reach for the artistic recognition he believes he deserves. If anything, Emilia appeals to Yasha's desire for more freedom, more variety, more secularity. Ironically, however, in rejecting the duality of liberality and restraint that characterizes the first part for the harmonious singularity of total freedom, Yasha far from gaining more life nearly encounters his death. Here is a brief catalog of what happens to Yasha by the end of the second part: he ages rapidly, becomes a thief, nearly cripples himself, drives Magda, his gentile mistress, to suicide, and hastens his Jewish paramour, Zeptel, into a house of prostitution. Add to all of this the nightmarish night he spends after the robbery—the fear of detection, the encounters with the twitching cripple, the humiliation and disgrace, the experience for the first time of impotency—and one has the sense of an enormous collapse. It is necessary, then, to see the expansive and worldly reality that Emilia offers to Yasha as essentially a temptation.

At the heart of that temptation is Emilia's request for conversion. Significantly, that request involves another which

Yasha previously had resisted—the temptation to steal. Indeed, one wonders whether this is not a symbolic connection. Thievery seems to be Singer's way of stigmatizing conversion as the act of taking something that does not belong to you. Evidently, to Singer a Jew is free to be a Jew or to be a non-believing Jew but he is not free to be a Christian. This is not mere chauvinism, for it applies to any conversion in which one takes what is not his to take. The issue of conversion serves as Singer's special way of approaching the modern and eternal problem of identity. Central to Singer's notion of identity is the image of the tightrope which reverberates throughout the novel.

Just as earlier aspects of Yasha's craft were extended to characterize his attitude toward others and God, so his walking the tightrope is not limited to his performing as a magician. "He constantly felt that only the thinnest of barriers separated him from those dark ones who swarmed around him, aiding and thwarting him, playing all sorts of tricks on him. He, Yasha, had to fight them constantly or else fall from the tightrope, lose the power of speech, grow infirm and impotent." Yasha is aware that the aim of the devil is to throw him off his moral balance. In fact, just before the robbery, Yasha "felt its presence—a dybbuk, a Satan, an implacable adversary who would disconcert him, while he was juggling, push him from the tightrope, make him impotent."

Walking the tightrope is Singer's image of what it is to be alive, not only as a Jew but as man. It represents the precariousness of identity which has no authentic meaning without dangerous duration. Moreover, identity is not a product but a process. It is not achieved once and for all time but is the endless task of making and remaking the self. Weary of the perilous equilibrium between faith and doubt and of the endless struggles within him, Yasha instead seeks the peace, permanence and new prospects that he believes conversion will grant him. He also hopes to escape from the tantalizing burden of dealing with a Jewish God who has no face or form and has never accommodated Himself to man by assuming mortality. In addition, because as Singer notes God revealed himself to no one, gave no indication of what is permitted and forbidden, Jewish identity historically has been characterized by an endless and indecisive dialogue between *men* about *God.* Indeed, at one point in the novel when Yasha, out of his desperation, pleads with God to give him a sign, he is essentially requesting God to make himself tangible and unambiguous. The absence of peace in this life and the constant doubts that assail men's minds and hearts are the reflections of an absence of metaphysical clarity in Judaism. And yet precisely because God's relationship with the Jew is so removed, it is intimate; precisely because it is so impossible, it is necessary. The special Jewish burden is to exist among the unknown and the unknowable; it is to achieve fullness in the face of limita-

tion and unconfirmation. To Singer the final strain that is put upon Jewish identity comes from God's terrifying Oneness—a relentless singularity that refuses to yield or adjust to human and social pluralism. Indeed, after the robbery, Yasha, who now feels the terrible burden of freedom from God, cries out, "This is no life! . . . I don't have a moment's peace of mind anymore. I must give up magic and women. One God, one wife, like everyone else. . . ."

Because Singer's vision is always situated where the horizontal line of human history and the vertical line of cosmic history intersect, the issue of conversion, especially by thievery, is never limited merely to a personal or social temptation. The Jew who converts not only forsakes an authentic, troublesome identity for a safer mask of assimilation. He also forsakes God for Satan. In Singer's world the devil's way of seducing Yasha from the tightrope is to offer him metaphysical amnesia. Specifically, Satan provides the opportunity to escape the endless battle between good and evil, between God and the Devil, waging within and constituting the identity of the Jew. To Singer evil thus appears not only in the obvious forms of immorality and disobedience, but also in man's striving to be more than he can be or settling for less than he is. In either case, the Satanic impulse attempts to free man from his reliance and dependence on God. It makes man the total magician—the adept performer who pushes self-reliance to the point of self-sufficiency. But as Singer warns, the result of stepping off the tightrope is not power but impotency. At the end of the second part, Yasha, in fact, discovers that in trying to become more than a man—a god—he has become less than a man—a twitching, impotent cripple, like the one he encounters. Instead of total freedom, he lives a life of total imprisonment; at the end of the novel Yasha far from expanding his existence ends up contained in a "living grave."

But before going on to a consideration of the final third of the novel, one might speculate on an unexpected yield from the image of the tightrope and the issue of conversion. Perhaps, Singer has allegorically built into the situation of Yasha the Magician his own situation as a Jewish writer. Perhaps, to Singer the basic temptation offered to the Jewish writer is also conversion—the temptation to turn away from his special Jewish materials for the wider world of American or world experience—to give up the stubborn, nagging yearnings of the Jewish soul for an historical and cosmic identity and choose instead the social and political variety of New World culture. To Singer, at least, the Jewish artist who does so is a thief and runs the risk of producing work that is crippled or impotent. Whether this allegory has application to other Jewish writers, it certainly has meaning for Singer. By remaining within the sharp and troubling confines of his own special Jewish area, Singer is proof of the paradox that intense narrowness may be the surest avenue to comprehensive statement. Moreover, Singer appears to be recommending to Yasha his own solution; namely, that in slavery Yasha will find his true freedom.

It is at this point that we come full circle and back to the problem of the ending. Not only is the ascetic figure of Yasha the Penitent a painful contrast to that of the vital Yasha the Magician. Even more objectionable is that Yasha's retirement from the world seems not only in excess of his crime, but also fails to reflect it. In Singer's behalf, however, it should be noted that the ending not only is consistent with his vision, but also can be defended against charges of escapism or punitive orthodoxy.

First, Singer makes it quite clear that Yasha's attempt to escape the temptations of the world by self-imprisonment fails. The tightrope is portable—the temptations go wherever Yasha does. Yasha, in fact, admits, "No, the temptations never cease." Second, Yasha's prison is Singer's metaphor for the slavery of man to God. As long as man lives, he is hemmed in by doubt. The soul is sustained by conflict and restriction; it is put to sleep or turned into the body by unchallenged certainty. The prison is comparable to anesthetizing the body not so that the conflicts can be avoided or eliminated but that they be confronted with less turbulence. Indeed, perhaps the most surprising additional meaning of the prison emerges through Yasha's broodings on the Cabala.

From this mystical work Yasha learns that "evil was merely God's diminishing of Himself to create the world, so that he might be called Creator and have mercy toward his Creatures." For the first time Yasha contemplates God's creative act as well as the existence of evil not just in moral but in artistic terms. The evil impulse in the world and in man is the result of God's shrinking or contracting His Being so as to make creation possible in the first place. The important realization for Yasha is that the creative act is not solely an expressive but also an inhibiting act. God wilfully and willingly imprisons part of His Being; He limits His immortal extent. Had He not, He would have made a creation that is finished or dead before it is born. If the world were a total reflection of God, it would be a dead world as we know life to be. But by withholding His fullness, He imparted to creation and especially to man the capacity to create and to perfect himself. God's inhibition makes possible man's expression; His withholding His full identity makes necessary man's.

Yasha in his prison realizes for the first time the virtues and benevolence of God's cosmic restriction. At the beginning of the novel Yasha was content to stay on the tightrope as long as he was in control and as long as no choice of a fixed identity was forced on him. In the process, he is interested only in having rather than denying. The temptation of Emilia and of Satan is to get off the tightrope altogether and to pur-

sue a life of freedom without any inhibitions. It is to live sensually not ascetically. The end of the novel redresses the imbalance. Having yielded to all satisfactions, Yasha turns to burdens not so that he may choose one or the other but so that both may be once again brought together in a reconstituted and more informed human and Jewish identity. In these terms, the prison is merely the most intense form of the tightrope.

Finally, what has been said of God's artistry and Yasha's recovered duality can be applied to Singer's craft. It is no accident that Singer's work is simultaneously sexual and religious and that his vision is rendered with microscopic realism and mysterious demonology. The impulses and rhythms of Singer's art reflect those that God imparted to creation. Structurally, his novels move from the maximum to the minimum, from sensualism to asceticism. The narratives read as if they were written by a libertine and a saint, or a blasphemer and a believer. And in this arc which runs from freedom to slavery and from sympathy to judgment, we may have a final way of reconciling his modernity and traditionalism as well as his realism and supernaturalism.

Although Singer's tales are mostly set in the distant past, they characteristically begin with a situation of liberality or confused freedom which accommodates the moral relativism and self-interest of the modern reader and his situation. Thus, for all the distance in time and space, Singer encourages an initial ease of identification and through that engagement a suspension of disbelief. As the novel unfolds and deepens and as the spell of Singer's logic takes hold, the reader imperceptibly is taken back toward a point in time when absolute orthodoxy and judgment prevailed or at least was more accessible and believable. At this juncture the reader may feel a sense of betrayal as if he has been unknowingly lured into an embarrassing trap. Singer has tricked us into forgetting that his work is dated, just as every writer tries to make us forget that his work is fiction. We feel we have been caught with our moral relativism or disbelief exposed. Moreover, we can not get off the hook easily, for we are caught by our own responses. For much of the special persuasiveness of Singer's work is eliciting responses not just to what is obviously modern in his work, but more important and difficult to what is apparently past and beyond us—a religiously inspired code of absolute morality.

The result of all of this is not only a dislocation of our emotions but an equally confused sense of time and place. The initial clear-cut distinctions between the then and the now are increasingly blurred until one is uncertain where one is or in what century. Under the trance of Singer's magical chronology, we become aware that if a situation is made old enough, it becomes not merely forever old but thereby forever new. As a result, Singer establishes through the medium of our own responses a nexus in time which is neither modern nor ancient but both. In the process, the past has become eternal, the present has become forever and by the logic of continuity the future becomes always. In this connection, it is significant that Singer's works often have been characterized as modern parables or moral fables. There is about Singer's work and vision the durability of the archetypal and the mythical. His novels and short stories stand between the modern and the eternal worlds; they mediate between the contemporary realistic and psychological novel and its sense of timely relativism, and the ancient Bible and its sense of timeless absolutism. Nor are these merely abstract formulations. The responses of the reader serve as the cross-roads for the intersection of past and present.

From this final point of view, Goodheart is right in saying that Singer is the greatest Yiddish author and in thereby associating him with the Yiddish tradition of the Old World. Howe is also correct in insisting on Singer's modernity. The critical dilemma is that each commentator has only half of the whole. As for the problem of Isaac Bashevis Singer, as Jacobson puts it, one might perhaps be more accurate in saying that Singer does not have the problem; we do. To Singer the solution is simply the recognition that the ideals and needs of the human soul for belief are in the final analysis the only eminently practical objects of existence. Moreover, as Singer also demonstrates, they also are the most viable subjects of art; for they belong neither to the past and Eastern Europe nor to the present and America, but to all moments of eternal time and to all places where there is, indeed, nothing new under the sun.

Max F. Schulz (essay date 1968)

SOURCE: "Isaac Bashevis Singer, Radical Sophistication, and the Jewish-American Novel," in *Southern Humanities Review,* Vol. 3, 1968, pp. 60-6.

[*In the following essay, Schulz discusses Singer's modern sensibility in relation to his portrayal of the social and religious attitudes of Polish Jewry from an earlier era. According to Schulz, this tension between "Old World Judaism" and "New World skepticism," as evident in Singer's fiction, represents a prominent theme in the contemporary Jewish-American novel.*]

I wish in this paper to offer a generalization about the current Jewish-American novel, using as my major illustration the admittedly special case of Isaac Bashevis Singer. The arbitrariness of this procedure, since Singer would appear to occupy a peripheral position in relation to the American novel, will, I hope, become less objectionable as I go along.

Because he is imbued with Old-World Jewish habits of thought more thoroughly than his American counterparts, while continuing undeniably also to be a New-World Jew, the radical sophistication of his creative imagination lends itself uniquely to the attempt to isolate the sources, and to define the achievement, of contemporary Jewish-American fiction.

Singer's is a twentieth-century sensibility attempting an imaginative re-creation of the social and religious milieu of Polish Jewry of the previous three centuries. The unique—and now vanished—circumstances of this society confront Singer's historical consciousness with special irrefrangibility. Tolstoy could revert in *War and Peace* to the time of the Napoleonic invasions without risking intellectual dislocation, for his society still assented essentially to the assumptions of his grandfather. But tension of a profound philosophical order, however, affects the moral pattern of Singer's stories as a result of the radically different *Zeitgeists* of the author and his dramatis personae. One of the central paradoxes of Singer's fictional world is that even as he pays loving tribute to the value system of a back-country Jewry, dirty, ignorant, but firm in a simplistic faith in what Dr. Yaretzky in **"The Shadow of a Crib"** calls "a seeing universe, rather than a blind one," Singer questions such a world picture with the narrative structures he composes for them. His rabbis and pious matrons may think and act in unquestioning accord with a Jewish cosmic vision but their lives present the absurd pattern familiar to the modern sensibility. It is not without significance that in at least three of Singer's novels the historical setting is that of a catastrophe wrought upon the Jews by external circumstances, and that his protagonists are caught between rival claims of the Jewish and non-Jewish worlds. As in a Greek tragedy impersonal fate and individual responsibility merge ambiguously in his stories.

The symbolic overtones implied in the title **The Slave** underscore this ambiguity. Jacob is carried off into slavery in the aftermath of the Chmielnicki pogroms of the second half of the seventeenth century. Yet even as he struggles, in captivity among the Polish peasants to whom he is sold, to retain his Yiddish tongue, to observe his religion, and to recreate in effect the Law, he falls in love with Wanda, the daughter of his master. Rescued after many years by elders of his village he is driven by his love furtively to return for Wanda, and against both the laws of the Jews and the Poles to introduce her into the *shtetl* as a true daughter of Israel. Thus Jacob is enslaved by man, society, religious law, spiritual fervor, human desires, and earthly passions. Who can discriminate between Jacob the individual who is personally accountable for his actions, and Jacob the victim who is determined by historical, social, and biological forces? Between the Jacob who observes the historic role of the Jews by bringing Wanda to God and who fulfills in his life the return to Palestine, and the Jacob who is profoundly alienated from village and synagogue because of these deeds?

Similarly, the enlightened and richly human integration of Yasha Mazur, *The Magician of Lublin,* into the free-thinking, mobile, circus habitat of Warsaw contrasts pointlessly with the sudden lapse of his skill at lock-picking and gymnastics when he attempts a burglary. The irony comes full circle when Yasha turns his back on his former life in favor of the Jewish faith of his father and the result is his radical alienation from his pious wife and friends, his former associates, and the *shtetl* community. Yasha may accept the Jewish religious ethos but the consequences of his action hardly reassure us of its efficacy. The temptations from within of empty fancies, daydreams, and repulsive desires, and from without of evil talk, slander, wrath, and false flattery in the form of supplicants, who both look upon him as a holy man, and still somewhat as an entertainer very much like his earlier circus audiences, continue to assail him and to interrupt his meditations. His non-Jewish, monastic action of walling himself off from the world as a way of serving both God and society gives no more moral illumination or meaningful pattern to his life than had his previous consorting with the thieves of Piask and his amoral roaming of Poland as a circus performer.

Singer is seriously concerned with the complicated moral and ethical relationship of man to his God and to his society—with the degree to which human conduct describes a moral pattern affecting that of the community and with the extent to which man's actions lurch in pointless arabesques to the indifferent push and pull of historical and psychobiological forces. In *The Family Moskat,* for example, Asa Heshel Bannett and the Warsaw Jews are portrayed as bringing about their own dissolution. Yet the advent of the Nazi at the end, plus the many other chance turns that his life has taken, makes Asa Heshel as much a victim of cosmic irony as any of Hardy's characters. The possibility that there was no coherent relation between Asa Heshol and the world robs his life of moral significance, reducing its events to incoherent moments of sensation.

> **Singer's mind seems to rejoice in dichotomies. In his autobiographical account of his boyhood, *In My Father's Court,* he refers to his home as a "stronghold of Jewish puritanism, where the body was looked upon as a mere appendage to the soul."**
> **—Max F. Schulz**

Clearly, Singer does not find it easy to fix the blame for per-

sonal catastrophe, as an older Judaic dispensation would have—and as Reb Abraham Hirsh, in I. J. Singer's *The Brothers Askenazi,* does, when he is replaced as general agent of the Huntze factory by his son Simcha Meyer. Reb Abraham consoles himself with the words of King Solomon, "there is a time to plant and a time to pluck up that which is planted, a time to build up and a time to break down." "Nothing happens," he sighs, "without the will of God, not even the breaking of a little finger." No such easy comfort is available to Isaac Bashevis Singer, despite the tender sympathy that he on occasion expresses for unaffected Jewish ritual and piety, as in the Jewish Cotter's—Saturday-Night story, **"Short Friday."** But, even in this story, there is the inexplicable twist of fate, which prompts the pious couple to copulate, following the Sabbath meal, and then lets them suffocate in their sleep because of a defective stove. I suspect that it is this divorce of his religious sensibility from precise religious beliefs, this drift of his thought away from the ethical certainties of the Judaic Law, that allows Americans to read Singer with an understanding and sympathy unavailable to the Hebrew writer S. Y. Agnon and to such Yiddish writers as Sholom Aleichem and I. L. Peretz. Such stories as **"A Tale of Two Liars," "The Destruction of Kreshev," "Skiddah and Kuziba,"** and **"The Shadow of a Crib"** dramatize the ambiguous hold on Singer's mind of belief and skepticism. His use of an Arch-Devil narrator simultaneously demonstrates the notion of a seeing will, purpose, and plan in the everyday affairs of the *shtetl,* while underscoring the capriciousness of the forces manipulating human actions. At other times, in even more explicit fashion, Singer often parallels, as in **"The Black Wedding"** and in some of the stories just mentioned, a pious account of the protagonist's actions, with a psychological or naturalistic explanation which denies the moral cohesion of that world. The danger in this strategy is real, for the coherence of Singer's fictional world depends on his maintaining a perilous tension between irreconcilables. If he relaxes an instant, his story is threatened with fragmentation. The endings of *The Slave* and *The Magician of Lublin* are painful instances of such falls into disunity. Miraculously to transform Wanda the Polish peasant into a Jewish Sarah and Jacob into a righteous man, or to metamorphose Yasha Mazur from circus prestidigitator to holy *Zaddik,* is to sentimentalize their lives under the intolerable pressure to give some kind of meaningful construct to them.

Singer's mind seems to rejoice in dichotomies. In his autobiographical account of his boyhood, *In My Father's Court,* he refers to his home as a "stronghold of Jewish puritanism, where the body was looked upon as a mere appendage to the soul." One day, he tells us, while visiting his older brother's atelier, he discovered the artist's healthy respect for the flesh. "This was quite a change from my father's court," he remarks, "but it seems to me that this pattern has become inherent to me. Even in my stories it is just one step from the study house to sexuality and back again. Both phases of human existence have continued to interest me." The ambivalence of this intellectual position is pervasive in much that Singer writes. Like the tight-rope walker Yasha Mazur, he balances between contrary modes of thought, his *modus operandi* at once archaic and modern, preoccupied with angels and demons and with Freud and Spinoza. He is drawn to the simple piety of his ancestors who never doubted the moral importance of life. He is also a man of the twentieth century, an uprooted European transplanted to America, seized by the contemporary vision of an absurd world—and his artistic integrity will not let the comfortable climate of divine reward and punishment remain intact. In the tension between moral cause and effect which his divided mind creates, his protagonists act out the unwitting drama of their lives. That these stories do not fragment into their unresolved elements attests to the remarkable narrative skill of Singer. That Singer has persisted despite the absence of an answer in posing again and again the question of the moral meaning of human experience attests to the radical sophistication of his vision.

It is fashionable these days to see the Jew as the perfect symbol of the Camusian man. Although not as viable a fact in the fifties and sixties as in earlier periods, the Jew's lot of perpetual exile lends itself as a convenient symbol of alienation and hence of what one segment of contemporary thought conceives of as the essential consciousness of being man. Yet only in a highly qualified sense can what I have called the radical sophistication of Singer's vision be considered existential. As a Jew he appeals, however hesitantly, to a construct of beliefs that makes sense of the human experience. Nor does he, like the Christian, reject earth because of the expulsion from paradise. The Jew has historically been God-intoxicated and man-centered. His relationship with the world reveals itself simultaneously as *eros* and as *agapé*. "Mazeltov," Shifrah Tammer greets her daughter the morning after her wedding in Singer's **"The Destruction of Kreshev"**; "'You are now a woman and share with us all the curse of Eve.' And weeping, she threw her arms about Lise's neck and kissed her." Like the holy men of Chassidim bent on the hallowing of each day, she acknowledges the edict that love of man is a prerequisite to adoration of Jehovah. In short, the Jew pursues not the Christian pilgrimage from this world to the next, but performs the miracle of merger of the other world with this one.

During more than two thousand years of Diaspora the Jews have learned to breathe amidst the incertitude that is the daily air of a persecuted minority. A tenuous equipoise of irreconcilables is the best they could hope for; and it pervades their world picture. One could hardly expect otherwise with a people who have persisted for several millenniums in the belief that they are chosen, with a divine mission, when the contrary has been the fact of their

daily lives. Out of this knowledge has grown a philosophy—anchored at one end by the teachings of Isaiah and at the other by the realities of this century—which conceives of the Jew as redeemer of the world through his acceptance of God's servitude. But the encumbrance of evil—even when put to the service of God—is an uncertain business, never quite relieving the mind of inquietude. Christianity has stumbled over this legacy of sin since its inception. The Age of Enlightenment could only palely affirm with Alexander Pope that "Whatever is, is right," "All partial evil, universal good." Among Western men the Jew has accepted most completely the ambience of this mixed blessing, this gift of the gods to man. The wisdom of his tragic passiveness is underscored by Singer in stories of what happens to a town when its people covenant with the Arch-Fiend in the interests of God, e.g. in **"The Destruction of Kreshev"** and *Satan in Goray.* Grounded in the harsh realities of this life, the Jew retains unshakable conviction of man's spiritual destiny.

This capacity for belief in the face of "uncertainties, mysteries, doubts" is a radical sophistication that the Jew, with a culture historically of long standing, is currently giving to a century convinced in its existentialist isolation of the incoherence of existence. Today's intellectual, like the Coleridge whom Keats characterized as "incapable of remaining content with half-knowledge," clutches at any "fine isolated verisimilitude caught from the Penetralium of mystery." To him the contemporary Jewish novel has much to say. It is a commonplace among Jews that Judaism is not in the habit of disowning its great heretics completely. Rather it accommodates with worldly wisdom what is worthwhile in Spinoza, Maimonides, Freud, and Kafka. This willingness to accept the world on its own terms—disorderly, incoherent, absurd— "without any irritable reaching after fact and reason" and yet without losing faith in the moral significance of human actions, underlies the confrontation of experience in the best of the contemporary Jewish-American novels.

The patterns that this attitude takes in these novels vary; but most can be reduced to an antinomy which presumes some form of socio-religious determinism while insisting upon the existential will of the individual. Malamud may involve his protagonist simultaneously in a mythic and a private quest. Salinger may portray the Glass progeny as hoisted on the petard of their own Zen ideals by contradictory psychological determinants. Mailer may urge his hero to seek the American dream of illimitable power through sexual release. Wallant may define full spiritual growth of the individual in terms of *caritas.* Fiedler may dance his minority American through a *pas de deux* of cultural betrayal. Bellow may torture his protagonist in a lonely war of mind and heart. Still, these ambivalences are all reducible to the conflict between human autonomy and divine purpose, and its corollary conflict between personal desires and communal needs.

That this version of human experience should suddenly dominate the American literary scene is, of course, one of those cultural mysteries, like the creative outbursts of the Elizabethans and the Romantics, which defy ultimate comprehension. Yet there is discernible a convergence of literary and historical forces that makes the contemporary Jewish-American novel a logical heir of the central tradition of the American novel. This tradition Richard Chase has defined, in part, in *The American Novel and Its Tradition,* as the discovery of "putative unity in disunity" or willingness "to rest at last among irreconcilables." The Jewish imagination similarly has been stirred by the aesthetic possibilities of a radical sophistication, which simultaneously entertains contrary intellectual systems: the secular view of man alienated in an absurd universe and the religious view of man enthroned by divine fiat in God's earthly kingdom. A corollary factor is the historical parallel between the American frontier and the European *shtetl.* Both environments raised similar questions about individual rights. The American experience continues to grapple with a political and social system, defined by the tension between private freedom and public restriction. Marius Bewley, in *The Eccentric Design,* has brilliantly shown that the conflict over the rights and the powers of the one and the many has been a persistent preoccupation of American thought. The American dream of a freely roving Adamic man was disrupted by the reality of legal restraint almost as soon as the first Puritans put foot ashore on the new land, long before Natty Bumppo clashed wills with Marmaduke Temple. Old-World Judaism, in an effort to submerge the individual in the social whole, for internal purposes of psychic and spiritual continuity as much as because of external forces beyond its control, has wrestled with the obverse side of this problem. Living in the Pale, threatened by extinction from without and from within, the Jew developed in survival a strong identification of personal observation of the Law with continuation of the community. An individual in the sight of God, he was also a member of an embattled group. His actions affected not only his salvation but also the group's survival. Thus in Singer's stories the *shtetl* defines a moral and ethical principle as much as a physical place and social entity. Both frontier and *shtetl* versions of human aspiration meet in the Jewish-American novel of the past two decades, deepened and universalized by accommodation with the religio-scientific antinomies of Old-World Judaism and of New-World skepticism.

Sarah Blacher Cohen (essay date Autumn 1982)

SOURCE: "Hens to Roosters: Isaac Bashevis Singer's Female Species," in *Studies in American Fiction,* Vol. 10, No. 2, Autumn, 1982, pp. 173-84.

[*In the following essay, Cohen considers the role of female characters in Singer's fiction through analysis of* Enemies *and* Shosha. *Cohen concludes that Singer's fiction is not misogynistic, as some feminist critics claim, but often portrays women as powerful symbolic figures that force male protagonists into uncomfortable revelations about themselves and the world.*]

Isaac Bashevis Singer takes issue with those female critics who say that his fiction is misogynistic. He claims that the "liberated woman [who] suspects almost every man of being an antifeminist" is like the "Jew who calls every Gentile an anti-Semite." Just as the Jew wants to be represented in literature as an exceptional individual, the staunch feminist, Singer contends, "would like writers to write that every woman is a saint and a sage and every man is a beast and an exploiter." If that were to happen, then, Singer believes, literature would become an "ism," inevitably "false and often ridiculous." In his last two realistic novels, *Enemies* and *Shosha,* Singer does not make an "ism" out of woman. Though he states that "men and women are made out of the same dough but kneaded a little differently," he creates distinctive female characters who perform distinctive functions. On the one hand, Singer draws true-to-life portraits that resemble the kind of women he must have encountered in Poland and America during the first half of the twentieth century. With their familiar appearance and recognizable values, Singer's female characters lend verisimilitude to his fictional landscapes. They domesticate the unknown and help anchor a story to a particular time and place. Their customary behavior also reassures the Singer protagonist that his sense of reality is not at variance with his expectations of it. Their conspicuous presence prevents him from getting lost in the mercurial world. At the same time, however, Singer endows many of these female characters with symbolic powers, powers that move from known to unknown associations, from conventional to bizarre interpretations. Their emblematic qualities unsettle and disorient the Singer protagonist. Not only do they transport him to the biblical and mythic past, but they prod him to explore his own guarded interior, to discover unpleasant truths about himself.

In *Enemies,* Singer's first English-translated novel with an American setting, he does not create just one woman to disrupt or stabilize the psychic equilibrium of his protagonist, the holocaust-evader Herman Broder. As in his earlier novels, *The Magician of Lublin* and *The Slave,* he has his hero embroiled with several women of disparate backgrounds and religions. Though Broder fears deportation for marrying three women, he cannot part with any of them. They represent illegal possessions that compel him to evade the authorities and repeat the subterfuge he practiced during the war. These women are the tantalizing prizes for which he, the compulsive gambler, must risk his fortune to avoid the tedium of wellbeing. They are also his potential enemies who would mete out the punishment he craves, should they discover his multiple infidelity. However, they embody aspects of womanhood he needs to complement his depleted life. Each restores fragments of his shattered self.

Yadwiga, the family servant who hid Broder in a hayloft during the war, is a vestige of the pre-holocaust world whom he marries to recapture his supremacy in that world. As the lower-class gentile woman who feels privileged to be the wife of her former Jewish master, she is the soul of compliance. Yadwiga keeps the same clean household she provided for his family in the old country and cooks the familiar dishes he had liked in the past. She is responsive to his sexual advances and readily accepts his unexplained absences. Adhering to her circumscribed position, Yadwiga thus assures Broder that his former patriarchal world is still intact.

Isaac Bashevis Singer takes issue with those female critics who say that his fiction is misogynistic. He claims that the "liberated woman [who] suspects almost every man of being an antifeminist" is like the "Jew who calls every Gentile an anti-Semite."
—*Sarah Blacher Cohen*

Yadwiga also represents the pagan Polish past that Broder, a cerebral Jew, covertly admires. Her elaborate Polish superstitions governing every sphere of life, her magic spells to ward off evil spirits, her simplistic explanations of complex phenomena evoke an appealing primitivism more manageable than the baffling modernity with which Broder must cope. A peasant toughened by the poverty and physical abuse of the Polish village, Yadwiga likewise seems more durable and more self-reliant than the modern Jewish women Broder has known. In New York City of the 1940s, however, Yadwiga is lost. She is forced to become the homebound immigrant wife who has difficulty learning the language and finding her way in a strange place. Totally dependent on Broder to be her mediator with urban America, she becomes his child for whom he reluctantly cares. As an abstraction of the primitive, she appears charming to Broder; as the actual primitive ill-equipped to survive in the modern world, she is burdensome to him.

To insure Broder's not leaving her, Yadwiga wants to convert to Judaism and be the Jewish mother of his child. As proof of her intentions, she becomes more observant than her religiously bankrupt husband. Keeping a kosher household and celebrating all the Jewish holidays, she is Singer's embodiment of self-generating spirituality. So intense is her desire to be Jewish, she resembles the biblical convert, Ruth. Unlike Boaz, however, Herman prefers that she remain the Gentile: the alien, forbidden woman with whom he does not have to share his innermost being. As soon as he finds himself enjoying any prolonged intimacy with Yadwiga, he is off to see his Jewish mistress, Masha.

In one crucial respect, Singer's Yiddish protagonist is very different from his Jewish-American counterpart. Many of them lust after the *shikse,* the gentile woman, considering her more seductive, more lubricious, whereas Herman Broder finds the Jewish woman sexually more enticing, more venturesome. Indeed his mistress Masha has a more hyperactive libido than any of Portnoy's bawdy girlfriends. Her high-powered eroticism, however, should not be interpreted solely as Singer's bid to titillate his readers. Promiscuous in the death camps, Masha is the holocaust victim who desperately indulged in sexuality to feel alive. In this nightmare universe she had subscribed to the leading principle of what the disaffected Broder calls the new "metaphysic": "In the beginning was lust. . . . The godly, as well as the human principle is desire." Indeed this view is not too different from the rabbinic notion that "sex is the leaven in the dough," the force that causes the growth of civilization. But what happens to Masha and Singer's other sexually driven women is that their overuse of sex as leaven leads not to growth but to decay. No child but a false pregnancy is the result of Masha's incessant coupling with Broder. A perverse Yiddish Molly Bloom, she sinks into greater forms of depravity and entertains wanton possibilities: "Would Herman copulate with an animal if all humans had perished?"; "What would she do if her father were still alive and had developed an incestuous passion for her?" Masha suggests so many immodest proposals that Broder ultimately fears she is a demonic temptress from another sphere. Undoubtedly, Masha is Singer's reincarnation of Lilith, the Kabbalah's devilish seductress and promiscuous mistress of God. Like the childless Lilith, she is the "embodiment of everything that is evil and dangerous in the realm of sex." Union with her, as with Lilith, becomes for Broder a guilt-ridden alliance.

But Masha has more than sexual charms to entice Broder. The same energy that fuels her eroticism fires her artistic temperament. When she is not a Lilith figure, she is a Scheherazade inventing captivating tales to divert her internal persecutors so she can go on living. An actress as well as storyteller, Masha embodies the esthetic sense that Broder lost and seeks to repossess. Unlike Broder, the ghost writer, who gives expression to other people's thoughts, Masha creates out of her own lurid experiences and her own idiosyncratic imagination. Yet so volatile is her nature, so beguiling is she to others, that Broder is uncertain that she and her esthetic sense will remain with him. Indeed her very elusiveness makes her all the more desirable.

Masha also attracts Broder because she has endured the worst ravages of the holocaust he had been spared. Just as Singer in the preface to *Enemies* states "he did not have the privilege of going through the Hitler holocaust," so the unscathed Broder feels deprived since he had not been one of the persecuted. Intimacy with the emotionally scarred Masha enables him to feel intimate with the devastating effects of the holocaust. Her nightmares become his. He vicariously endures "all the savagery, all the humiliations" of the Nazis. In the ruins of Poland he, too, is violated and cheated by fellow survivors. By identifying with Masha's suffering, Broder finds some relief for his own survivor guilt. Moreover, Masha expresses his rage against God. A rebellious female Job, she challenges God's authority and accuses Him of being ineffectual and indifferent: "If God is almighty and omnipotent," she charges, "He ought to be able to stand up for His beloved people. If He sits in heaven and stays silent, that means it must bother Him as much as last year's frost." More sacrilegious than the majority of Singer's males, Masha even suggests that the Jews have invented a benevolent God to replace the true God who hates them.

Along with voicing Broder's blasphemy against God, Masha enacts his paranoid and masochistic tendencies. Another of Singer's self-punishing and punitive women, she demonstrates Broder's antisocial and self-destructive behavior. Distrustful of Jews and Gentiles alike, she fails to have amicable relations with them. Perpetually fighting with her old mother, she cuts off any maternal affection. Expecting a repetition of past horrors, she enjoys neither her work in the city nor a long-awaited trip to the country. Haunted by the dead, she feels unentitled to go on living, and when her mother dies, she is compelled to join her. Thus Masha fulfills Herman's own death wish. When she urges him to commit suicide with her, he calls her "his angel of death." But since she accuses him of being a Nazi and "a coward afraid of his own shadow," he regards Masha as his enemy, *la belle dame sans merci* who would consign him to her private hell.

Tamar, Herman's first wife, is, unlike Masha, a woman of exceptional mercy whom the holocaust has more humanized than brutalized. She had formerly been another of those capricious activists whom Singer had mockingly described as "the incarnation of the masses, always following some leader, hypnotized by slogans, never really having an opinion of her own." But the war quickly caused Tamar to learn what she valued most. She protected her children until their death and did not, like Masha, succumb to the lewd behavior of the concentration camps. With great effort, she preserved her chastity and did not sully her image as mother and wife.

If Masha is Singer's variation of the concupiscent Lilith, then Tamar is his version of the *Shekhina-Matronit*, the goddess of the *Kabbalah* who preserves her chastity "where the general atmosphere is one of intensive sexual activity or even promiscuity." Like the Holy Land with whom the goddess is associated, Tamar does not permit herself to be "defiled or enjoyed by a stranger." Similarly, when Tamar reappears in Broder's life, she assumes another role of the *Shekhina-Matronit,* that of the comforting, all-protective mother. Like the goddess who is the anxiety-allaying "opener of the gates of the Beyond," Tamar, who has recently returned from the dead with a special knowledge of the dead, assures Broder that his children exist in another world. To help him forget the bitterness of death, she tries to make his present life more bearable. Recognizing how strong his loyalties are to Yadwiga and Masha, Tamar refuses to press her wifely claims and be "the third wheel on his broken wagon."

The exemplum of righteousness, Tamar acts as Broder's moral guide. She advises him to live permanently with Yadwiga since she is to bear his child. In this respect Tamar is a magnanimous version of the biblical Sarah. Since Tamar's own Jewish offspring have been killed, she urges her husband to accept as his rightful heir the child of the pagan Yadwiga, the latter-day Hagar. But Broder is not an Abraham of old, the patriarch who at great personal cost provided for both Ishmael and Isaac. Broder is the Jewish boy-man who hid his head in the hayloft while his children were being slaughtered. And when in America he is given a second opportunity to be a father, he feels unfit for the task and flees from his responsibilities.

At the end of *Enemies* Singer is ambiguous about Broder's fate. He either kills himself or is hiding "in an American version of a Polish hayloft." But there is no doubt about Tamar's actions. A Jewish Griselda as well as a Sarah, she remains faithful to the vanished Broder. Refusing the offers of other men, she vows to marry her derelict husband in the next world. Meanwhile, assuming Broder's place as the supporter of Yadwiga and her new daughter, Tamar acts the way she did in the past, with great devotion and reliability. Because Broder's avoidance of duty had made him the weaker of the species, Tamar becomes of necessity the strong matriarch of the post-holocaust all-female family.

Through female bonding, the Jewish wife and the gentile wife are not the enemies Broder feared they would become. Sharing a common destiny of abandonment, they have, through their mutual concern, created a home in the alien world. Through their joint rearing of the Broder daughter, they have insured the continuity of the family and the perpetuation of the Jewish people. In their own way, they have partially restored the ravaged past which the lost Broder would immediately recognize and cherish. As women who survive with dignity and purpose, they not only provide a sanctuary for an errant husband but they reflect Singer's hope that a meaningful existence is still possible after the holocaust.

In **Shosha,** Singer's fictionalized version of his memoir, *A Young Man in Search of Love,* the women are not strong survivors attempting to rehabilitate an emotionally crippled hero and build a new life for themselves. Living in pre-Hitler Poland, and mostly unaware of the impending catastrophe, they serve primarily as the subject matter for the writer protagonist, Aaron Greidinger. They are not his moral reformers but mid-wives for his creativity. Their conflicting opinions are catalysts to his thinking. Their erotic beings, their confused psyches, their artistic yearnings, their spiritual dimensions take possession of his imagination and demand expression.

Singer again creates many women to charm his protagonist. They satisfy both Greidinger's healthy appetite for sexual diversity and his unhealthy Don Juanism preventing his attachment to any one woman. But, above all, they represent the forbidden secular world, causing him to rebel against the confining orthodoxy of his fathers. As the tantalizing "other," the profane sensibility, they broaden his outlook and the scope of his writing; they complicate his life and add complexity to his work.

Unfortunately, in this ninth Singer novel to appear in English translation, the tantalizing women are not truly tantalizing. Though their names are changed and they live in another decade, their personalities are similar to those of **Enemies** and only thinly disguised from their real-life counterparts in Singer's memoir. Just as Singer's first common-law wife was a Communist who, with their son, left him to go to Russia, Greidinger's first affair in Warsaw is with the Communist, Dora Stolnitz, who is more in love with the party than with him. She is Singer's political woman who attempts to lure the author from his decadent art of storytelling to write tracts to sway public opinion and alter the course of history. She conforms to Schopenhauer's definition of the woman as "blind optimist" for she believes, as did the pre-war Tamar, that collectivist action can bring about a "bright tomorrow." Though her doctrinaire mentality clashes with Greidinger's artistic temperament, their bodies remain friendly. In Singer's treatment of eros, sexual pleasure is often enhanced rather than harmed by conflicting ideologies. Nor does Singer allow Dora's Marxist indoctrination to prevent her from being a nurturing woman—cooking Greidinger sumptuous breakfasts and faithfully washing his underwear. As for the constancy of her party loyalty, it is short-lived. Visiting the presumed utopia and finding a dystopia, Dora, like Singer's other female revolutionaries, is bitterly disappointed. Rescued from the brink of suicide, she shares Greidinger's view [which also

happens to be Singer's] "that you can't help mankind and that those who worry too much about the fate of man must sooner or later become cruel." In his own life Singer was unable to prevent his common-law wife's wholehearted embrace of communism, the psychic and political inelasticity which made her into an "ism." In his fictional world, however, he is able to effect the transformation of character which he was powerless to bring about in his own world. Thus Dora, the ideologue who had tried to convert the artist, is instead converted by him. Unlike Singer's intractable common-law wife, Dora does not act like a predictable type but has the flexibility to change her views.

Celia Chentshiner, the older married woman Greidinger sees, is a bourgeois type. She is Singer's Jewish Madame Bovary who, bored by her Zionist husband and betrayed by her nihilistic lover, reads romantic novels and commits adultery with younger men. She provides Greidinger with ready access to her boudoir and seasoned experience in illicit love. Assuming sole responsibility for her infidelity, she encourages him to have guilt-free sex with her, to violate with pleasure the taboos of his orthodox past. Because she is the artist manqué, she also seduces Greidinger to be united with a genuine artist. A member of Poland's Jewish leisure class, she hopes to absorb his creative powers to give meaning to her aimless life. She vicariously revels in his heightened sensitivity; she is excited by his artistic risks and discoveries. To repay him for his vitalizing presence, she generously shares her home's material comforts with the impoverished Greidinger and acquaints him with her drawing room's secular culture.

Greidinger, however, becomes surfeited with middle-age lust and literary talk and soon chooses a less cultivated relationship with his less complicated Polish servant, Tekla. Or to use Levi-Strauss's categories for the Gentile and the Jewish, Greidinger prefers the "raw" over the "cooked." The gentile woman appeals to the Singer protagonist because she poses no danger of his identifying her with his Jewish mother and becoming entangled in Oedipal ties. The *shikse* also represents the seductive world of nature, which Greidinger as a young yeshiva student yearned for but was prohibited from enjoying. Of the robust Tekla, whose favors Greidinger has had, he rhapsodizes: "Her cheeks were the color of ripe apples. She gave forth a vigor rooted in the earth, in the sun, in the whole universe." As a creature whose wholesome beauty is untampered by intellect or morality, she does not set impossible goals for him or herself. Grateful to him for rescuing her from her predatory countrymen, she is content to be a source of energy to him. An embodiment of the Polish common folk at their generous best, she desires only what will make him happy.

What ultimately makes Greidinger happy is to return to his

childhood love, Shosha, whom Singer equates with the Poland of his youth. Indeed the fictional Shosha is based on an actual Shosha, Singer's precious childhood friend whom he memorializes at the end of his autobiography, *A Day of Pleasure*. Like her fictional namesake in Singer's story "Short Friday," Shosha is the ideal companion—appreciative, comforting, and selfless. When Singer's family moves away, he never forgets her and "in time Shosha becomes for [him] an image of the past."

This is not the first time in his autobiographies or his fiction that Singer has employed a female to personify the Jewish past or the Jews of Poland. Like the biblical prophets, Singer includes frequent references in his works to the people of Israel as a woman who is divorced, widowed, abandoned, or raped. The most haunting personification occurs in Singer's early novel *Satan in Goray,* where the heroine, Rechele, represents misguided seventeenth-century Polish Jewry. She endures all the catastrophes of her generation. Born in 1648, the year of the Khmelnitski massacres, she loses her mother at the age of five and is abandoned by her father fleeing Cossack persecutors. A victim of the pogroms, she is reared by a superstitious grandmother, just as the Jews in their benighted circumstances were ruled by their own superstitions. Destitute, Rechele is forced to marry Mates, an impotent religious ascetic, just as the Polish Jews adopted a stern pietistic Judaism to cope with their adversity. And like the Jews who quickly forsook religious asceticism for the hedonism of false messiahs, Rechele succumbs to the sensuality of the self-proclaimed prophet Gedalyia. She, like the Jews of Goray, pays for her sinful actions. Impregnated by Satan, she gives birth to an evil offspring.

In contrast to Rechele and the Jews of Goray, who have prostituted themselves by embracing false extremes, the fictional Shosha, epitomizing pre-Hitler Polish Jewry, has preserved her purity despite the corrupt world about her. When Greidinger meets her again on Krochmalna Street, twenty years later, he is struck by her unsullied innocence. Though abysmal conditions have kept Shosha a backward child, her stunted growth has a significant advantage for him. Her arrested development makes possible the arrest of time. Through her child's eyes, he sees the world as he had remembered it. Since death has no palpable reality for her, she speaks in a familiar Yiddish of deceased shopkeepers who are still alive for her, of destroyed landmarks and defunct rituals that in her mind still exist. She also relates to Greidinger as if he were the precocious boy of the past, and he in turn is rejuvenated by her. Shosha thus functions as Singer's "metaphorical projection of a Peter Pan-like permanence" attempting to avert the steady decline of the present and future.

Shosha is also Singer's ghetto Jew for whom confined quarters and reduced circumstances are familiar and thus preferable. Distrustful of an altered environment, she only fleetingly enjoys the marvels of the formerly restricted city which Greidinger, the would-be emancipated Jew, wants to share with her. Like the prisoner who initially relishes his freedom, she soon feels ill-at-ease in the broad expanse of Warsaw and wants to return to her circumscribed street.

Only one woman tempts Greidinger to leave Shosha for her: the highly sexed, highly intellectual Russian-born American actress, Betty Slonim. Such women frequently enthrall Singer's males because they are not only physically and cerebrally exciting but they are enticingly at odds with the *shtetl* notion of femininity. They are seen as trespassers in the male domain and as such are regarded as freaks of female nature who must be routed from the community. For there is an old *shtetl* saying: "When the hen begins to crow like a rooster, it is time to take it to the *shoykhet.*" But in Singer's fiction society is frequently spared the task of being the *shoykhet,* the ritual slaughterer, for these women internalize society's negative opinion of them and act as their own *shoykhet.*

Resembling the distraught Masha of *Enemies,* Betty Slonim is a self-destructive figure. In conflict over her needs and her gender, she is the ideal person to star in Greidinger's play, *The Maiden of Ludmir,* which, like Singer's play *Yentl,* concerns a girl who wants to live like a man, study the Torah, become a Hasidic rabbi and preach to the people. Like the maiden of Ludmir, Betty accuses an anti-feminist Moses and a male God of granting all the higher religious privileges to men and the lesser duties to women. Betty, like the heroine, is possessed of two dybbuks: the pessimistic male iconoclast and the jaded female prostitute. Both aspects of her androgynous being captivate Greidinger. As a latter-day Schopenhauer, she gets him to share her lugubrious thoughts about human nature. As the decadent mistress of a crass Jewish-American businessman, she persuades him to grab some erotic pleasure with her before they vanish forever. Though she is a successful Potiphar's wife, getting the dreamer-artist Greidinger to sin with her, she warns him to part company with her. "The demons are after me," she shrieks. "It's always like this when a spark of happiness lights up my life. Keep away from me! I'm cursed, cursed, cursed."

The possessed Betty Slonim suffers from a split nationality as well as a split personality. She is not at home in any part of the world. As the cultivated Yiddish actress of Slavic origins, she does not fit in with the superficial Yiddish theater of America. Among the Jewish thespians of Poland, she is dismissed as a brazen American actress who speaks an inauthentic Yiddish and is obsessed with playing perverse roles. Seeing no artistic future for herself in any country, she wants to rescue Greidinger from a doomed Poland and promote his career in America. Unappreciated herself, she hopes to live vicariously through his achievements. Like Singer's supporters, Betty Slonim represents the American descendants of East European Jews who will constitute his enthusiastic reading public. Saving Greidinger and extolling his artistic merits will be her most important contribution. Otherwise, she is Singer's superfluous woman, distraught and estranged, who ultimately commits suicide.

Greidinger's fascination with the disturbed Betty Slonim and the histrionic modernism she embodies is short-lived. Just as Singer refused to abandon Polish Jewry as the subject matter for his fiction, so Greidinger ultimately marries Shosha and the traditional old world values she represents. Though Shosha has been emotionally scarred and is inept in many ways, she, like Singer's Polish Jewry, possesses many endearing qualities. She is the epitome of fidelity. An old-fashioned woman like Greidinger's mother, she is the chaste Jewish wife who will never betray him. Her faithfulness to Greidinger provides him with a model for his own faithfulness to God and the Jewish people. She is an ideal pupil whom he instructs and who in turn instructs him. Scantily educated, she is still interested in Greidinger's obscure philosophizing and through her naive but probing questions helps him clarify his views. She becomes his muse. Her bizarre fantasies and superstitions inspire his use of the supernatural in his work. Her "qualities of a medium," her "primitivism, directness, sincerity" influence his literary style. Unable to have children herself as Polish Jewry was prevented from reproducing itself, Shosha becomes Greidinger's child whom he is not ashamed to cherish in the most sophisticated company. Indeed Greidinger treasures the childlike Shosha for much the same reasons Singer values the special qualities of children: "Our children, God bless them, don't read to discover their identity, as so many wiser adults pretend to do. Young as they are, fresh from the egg, they know exactly who they are and where they belong. . . . With an instinct no fashion-making can destroy, the child has become the guardian of those moral and religious values the adults have rejected in the name of an ill-conceived notion of social progress." Similarly, the live and even the deceased Shosha is Greidinger's instinctive guardian of vanishing morals and religious values. Though she suffers a heart attack when expelled from her life-sustaining Krochmalna Street, Greidinger still waits in Israel for her to give him an answer about death's meaning.

Greidinger, at the age of seven, reassured Shosha: "Shoshele, don't be afraid. I will make it so that you will live forever." Singer kept Greidinger's promise. He immortalized Shosha in fiction. But Shosha and Singer's other female characters have made indispensable contributions to the male protagonists as well. In their actual or emblematic capacities, the women in *Shosha* and *Enemies* have prompted their men to embark upon a "soul expedition" (the

original Yiddish title of *Shosha*). They have served as familiar landmarks or have beckoned them to uncharted territories. They have been confusers of the imagination and guides to the perplexed. Scenic wonders in their own right, they have enlivened the expedition and made it worth recording.

Daniel V. Fraustino (essay date Spring 1985)

SOURCE: "Gimpel the Fool: Singer's Debt to the Romantics," in *Studies in Short Fiction*, Vol. 22, No. 2, Spring, 1985, pp. 228-31.

[*In the following essay, Fraustino draws attention to the influence of Romantic poets such as William Wordsworth and Samuel Taylor Coleridge on Singer's transcendent vision, particularly as evident in "Gimpel the Fool."*]

"Gimpel the Fool" is generally regarded as Isaac Bashevis Singer's greatest fictional masterpiece and for good reason. Its appeal to the reader is personal and immediate. Gimpel, the narrator-protagonist, represents that child-like quality in all of us which is the source of both our humanity and our vulnerability: the need to believe in the people around us and in the credibility of our own experiences. Singer's story is about Gimpel's search for manifest truth, or as Sol Gittleman declares, "for the nature of truth in reality." While Gimpel's quest has obvious precedent in many literatures throughout the world, it has a special debt to the literature of the Romantic period. As I shall suggest, Singer's thematic concerns with disillusionment, the difficulty of belief, and especially with the relation of worldly experience to truth were clarified and shaped by the poetry of the Romantics. Finally, Singer may have incorporated at a focal point in his story the language and events described in Wordsworth's "Strange Fits of Passion Have I Known."

At the heart of **"Gimpel the Fool"** lie the questions *what is truth* and *how is it to be known*. It is Gimpel's failure to pose these questions that results in his continued deception by the villagers of Frampol. An innocent, Gimpel at first is able to weather their humiliation through his simple faith in God and the Bible. When the townspeople declare, "'Gimpel, the Czar is coming to Frampol; Gimpel, the moon fell down in Turbeen; Gimpel, little Hodel Furpiece found a treasure behind the bathhouse,'" Gimpel, in his own words, believes "everything" like a "golem," but adds, with the assurance of "the Wisdom of the Fathers," that "everything is possible." Later, when the villagers confuse him to the point that he doesn't "know the big end from the small," he is sustained by the Biblical injunction that it is "'better to be a fool all you days than for one hour to be evil.'"

Gimpel continues in this way for twenty years, ignorant of his wife Elke's many infidelities. However, her death-bed confession, that none of his six children are really his, forces Gimpel into a spiritual crisis that signals his entry into a state of experience. Gimpel's realization that he has been systematically deceived, that he never really knew the truth, shatters his faith in God and humanity, causing his spiritual collapse into a Blakean condition of experience.

For at the root of Gimpel's desire for revenge on the people of Frampol is a self-concern and self-preoccupation that is his real crime and danger. Alienated from everyone around him, Gimpel self-exiles from the village of his youth, which signifies his loss of innocence. The Voice of Evil, therefore, really evolves from within and represents his own despair: "'There is no God,'" it says, nor is there a "'world to come.'"

At the heart of "Gimpel the Fool" lie the questions *what is truth* and *how is it to be known*. It is Gimpel's failure to pose these questions that results in his continued deception by the villagers of Frampol.
                    —Daniel V. Fraustino

Like Coleridge's ancient mariner, Gimpel's journey is archetypal and may be expiatory for the sin he committed in thought against the Frampol villagers. However, on a deeper level his journey represents a quest for answers to those questions he failed to ask in his youth, epistemological questions which the Romantic poets asked over and over again: what is the nature of truth, and what are its genuine sources. Before Elke's faith-shattering confession, Gimpel, like Blake's chimney-sweepers and black-boys, sustained himself through the power of faith alone. However, in order to transcend this world of treachery and deception Gimpel has to learn that faith must be accompanied by knowledge and understanding, and the acquisition of these latter is the real purpose of his journey-quest as I have suggested. The wisdom finally revealed to Gimpel is divulged at the story's conclusion and, as J. A. Eisenberg states, is Platonic in nature: Gimpel "simply *denies* the *ultimate reality* of the world of physical corruption." In Gimpel's own words, the world is "once removed from the true world" which is "real, without complication, without ridicule, without deception." It is a world where "even Gimpel cannot be deceived."

Surely Singer's imaginative interpretation of empirical reality owes something to the visionary philosophies of the Romantics, who also believed truth to reside in a world apart from organic nature. And from the beginning to the end of the Romantic period, each writer proclaimed his commitment to this belief. While Blake, in the *Songs of Experience*,

emphatically declared his freedom from the world of concrete fact, that is, from "Generation" and "Mortal Life," Keats at the close of the period unambiguously pronounced his faith in the "truth of Imagination" exclusively: "What the imagination seizes as Beauty must be truth," he says, "whether it existed before or not." All the Romantics believed that as the mind approached truth its independence from physical nature necessarily increased. Finally, Shelley's declaration in "Adonais" that this world affords only transient visitations of truth or Intellectual Beauty, that we must first pass through death in order to be at one with that which is perfect and unchanging, exactly parallels Gimpel's own metaphysics and his belief in the glory of the afterlife: "The One remains, the many change and pass," Shelley writes, "Heaven's light forever shines, Earth's shadows fly . . . Die / If thou wouldst be with that which thou dost seek."

Surely, Singer's imaginative metaphysics were clarified, perhaps shaped, by the epistemological concerns of the Romantics, and Singer's possible indebtedness in his short story to Wordsworth's well known poem "Strange Fits of Passion Have I Known" substantiates this. Like Singer's work Wordsworth's lyric poignantly illustrates the fallibility of mortal experience and the theme of deception which constitutes "the leitmotif of Gimpel's story." The narrator's concluding disillusionment in "Strange Fits" corresponds to Gimpel's despair before leaving on his journey, with the falling moon in the former and Elke's confession of her infidelity in the latter representing parallel points.

"Strange Fits of Passion Have I Known" deals with the same problems as **"Gimpel the Fool"**: with disillusionment, the difficulty of belief in this world of imperfection, and with the relation of worldly experience to truth. It also poses the same questions asked by Singer and stated at the outset of this paper: what is truth, and what are its genuine sources. Like Singer, Wordsworth declares that truth lies apart from the world of mortal imperfection, implicitly suggesting that truth can only be apprehended by the imagination. Significantly, one of the focal events narrated in *Gimpel* repeats in detail the journey described in "Strange Fits." Returning home unannounced after having changed his mind about divorcing his wife, Gimpel immediately focuses on the *moon,* the central metaphor for vision in "Strange Fits." "The moon," Gimpel says, "was full," and as in Wordsworth's poem it becomes an emblem of the strength and intensity of Gimpel's love. Despite the fact that the "shutter was closed" when Gimpel arrives home—a condition probably referring to Elke's own condition of experience and self-enclosure—"the moon forced its way through the cracks." Even the increased pounding of Gimpel's heart ("'thump! thump!'") seems to echo the "quickening pace" of the speaker's horse in Wordsworth's poem as the narrator draws closer to Lucy. Finally, upon discovering Elke in bed with the apprentice, Gimpel expresses his disillusionment in language almost identical to that of Wordworth's narrator. While the latter says, "down behind the cottage roof / *At once,* the bright moon dropped," Gimpel declares that "The moon went out all *at once.*"

Singer's indebtedness to Romantic epistemology, but particularly to Wordworth's "Strange Fits of Passion Have I Known," is clear; nor should this surprise us. Just as Irving Howe says of Singer, that "no other living writer has yielded himself so completely and recklessly . . . to the claims of the human imagination," so may we say of the Romantics, in no other literary period was man's sense of his own worth so imaginatively conceived and defined. For at the bottom of Singer's conception of life is a firmness of faith and strength of vision that inevitably would find reaffirmation and inspiration in the literature of the Romantic period. Indeed, Romanticism was the last literary epoch in which nearly all its major writers unambiguously upheld the existence of a transcendent reality and of values that are absolute. In fact, Gimpel is a kind of latter-day Romantic hero whose quest for truth has antecedence in "Endymion," "Alastor," and in "The Rime of the Ancient Mariner," to name just a few. Truly, we must include the Romantic period as one of Singer's primary sources and influences.

Charles Isenberg (essay date Summer-Fall 1985)

SOURCE: "*Satan in Goray* and Ironic Restitution," in *Yiddish,* Vol. 6, Nos. 2-3, Summer-Fall, 1985, pp. 87-102.

[*In the following essay, Isenberg discusses the progressive themes of catastrophe, ambiguity, and restitution in* Satan in Goray. *Isenberg concludes that in this novel restitution is not redemptive, as "restitution can only be an ironic impossibility because Singer's subject is the inevitability of living after the tradition."*]

Satan in Goray explores the reflection, in a remote Polish town, of the rise and degeneration of the messianic movement centering on Sabbatai Zevi, a Jew from Smyrna, whose revelation of his messianic role in May 1665 triggered the major messianic explosion in modern Jewish history. The novel's action covers something over a year, beginning in October 1666, but it has its wellsprings in the Chmielnicki massacres of 1648-49, a Cossack-led peasant war in which some 100,000 Polish Jews perished. The importance of these atrocities as an initiating event is stressed by three chapters of exposition that describe 1648 and its aftermath in Goray. The novel begins as follows:

> In the year 1648, the wicked Ukrainian hetman, Bogdan Chmelnicki, and his followers besieged the

city of Zamosc but could not take it, because it was strongly fortified; the rebelling *haidamak* peasants moved on to spread havoc in Tomaszow, Bilgoraj, Kransnik, Turbin, Frampol—and in Goray, too, the town that lay in the midst of the hills at the end of the world. They slaughtered on every hand, flayed men alive, murdered small children, violated women and afterwards ripped open their bellies and sewed cats inside. Many fled to Lublin, many underwent baptism or were sold into slavery. Goray, which once had been known for its scholars and men of accomplishment, was completely deserted. The market place, to which peasants from everywhere came for the fair, was overgrown with weeds, the prayer house and the study house were filled with dung left by the horses that the soldiers had stabled there. Most of the houses had been leveled by fire. For weeks after the razing of Goray, corpses lay neglected in every street, with no one to bury them. Savage dogs tugged at dismembered limbs, and vultures and crows fed on human flesh. The handful who survived left the town and wandered away. It seemed as if Goray had been erased forever.

Satan in Goray might be read as a ghost story, the history of a communal afterlife. As such it participates in an important thematic current in Singer's work: narratives about the dead who attempt to go on as before, either because they are compelled to, or because they do not realize they are dead. Stories that make this pattern manifest include **"The Man Who Came Back," "The Unseen,"** and **"Two Corpses Go Dancing"**; however, allusions to this condition may be found throughout the major fiction, where, at its most global reach, it becomes a figure for the postexilic condition.

One of the first questions that *Satan in Goray* raises is that of its historicity. In this connection it is illuminating to juxtapose Singer's novel with Gershom Scholem's monograph on Sabbataianism. Both the fictionist and the scholar see the Sabbataian movement as a watershed in Jewish history, and both are concerned to explore the spiritual basis for the movement's appeal. Reading Scholem on the background to Polish Sabbataianism, we even find ourselves, at one point, in a hermeneutic circle:

> a unique fascination with the sphere of evil, and a markedly personalistic conception of it, were typical of Polish kabbalism. . . . The result was an extraordinary growth of weird and bewildering demonology for which, in our time, I know of no better illustration than that displayed in Isaac Bashevis Singer's stories.

But what will most strike the reader who turns to Scholem's account is the extent to which Singer selects motifs from the historical record and recombines them in his fiction. Most remarkable is the way in which he takes traditions concerning the personality and behavior of the false messiah, his wife Sarah, and his prophet, Nathan of Gaza, and reallocates them among Itche Mates and Gedaliya, who are the successive leaders of the sect in Goray, and the 17-year-old Rechele. Daughter of the town's former secular leader, Rechele becomes the wife, first of Itche Mates, then of Gedaliya.

Thus Sabbatai Zevi represented himself as a man who had married three times before consummating a marriage, and we are told that Itche Mates is impotent and has left a string of grass widows behind him. After his marriage to Sarah, his third wife and reputedly a former prostitute, and especially after his apostasy, Sabbatai Zevi acquired a reputation for debauchery, Gedaliya, his second representative in Goray, is a libertine. By the same token, Itche Mates embodies the first, penitential, and ascetic phase of the movement; Gedaliya, its post-apostasy fascination with the potential holiness of sin.

It is suggestive that Zeydel Ber, the uncle who raises Rechele, invokes a benediction upon her that alludes to the Biblical matriarchs and therefore begins, "May the Lord make thee as *Sarah*" for Sabbatai Zevi's wife resembles Rechele in her Polish origins, her being orphaned in consequence of the Chmielnicki massacre, and her reputation for eccentric behavior. As for Rechele's prophetic gift, which she acquires after becoming Gedaliya's mistress, it seems significant that her revelation shares with Nathan's a common eschatological content but refers to the divine destiny only of her master, that is, Gedaliya, and makes no mention of Sabbatai Zevi.

Earlier, at the betrothal of Rechele to Itche Mates, the bridegroom flouts the norms of decency by dancing with a woman. The guests are initially startled but soon come to understand the dancing as a mystical or allegorical act, a "reaching for the higher spheres." Eventually most of the company joins in the dancing. In permitting men and women to dance together, Itche Mates is emulating Sabbatai Zevi. So is Gedaliya when he calls women to the reading of the Torah. Sabbatai Zevi shocked the rabbis of Salonika by performing a marriage ceremony between himself and the Torah; Singer's variation upon this motif is to describe Rechele, in her state of prophetic illumination, as a living Torah (later she will be described as a living ikon), and to have Gedaliya place a scroll of the Law in her chamber.

By and large, the sequence of historical events, as it is communicated to or reflected in Goray, agrees with the progress of the movement in Scholem's account: the kabbalistic excitement after 1648, rumors of the conquest of Mecca and Stamboul by the Ten Lost Tribes, the revelation of the Messiah, the great penitential awakening, the popular prophesying, the reports of Sabbatai Zevi's progress toward Stamboul and then of his having taken refuge in a fortress, and finally, the apostasy. To this extent we can see the history of the Sabbataian movement as an inner text around which the Goray chronicle forms. But there is an important difference in the relative timing of the universal and local sequences: Sabbatai Zevi was brought to the sultan's court and made to apostasize in mid-September 1666; in Goray, "the town in the midst of the hills at the end of the world," as it is repeatedly described, the action begins only the next month, with the arrival of two bearers of miraculous tidings, and the Sabbataian faction only coalesces in January of 1667, that is, four months *after* the apostasy. Thus the reports about Sabbatai Zevi that initiate phases of the action in Goray are like signals from an extinguished star, and the townsfolk are belatedly caught up in a drama whose denouement has already taken place. (Gedaliya is the exception here. When he counters the news of the apostasy with the "Docetist" doctrine that only the Messiah's shadow has converted and offers to show the congregation authoritative letters to this effect, it becomes clear that he has been keeping his followers in the dark. The whole discourse is thus given in an ironic mode.)

Ironic distance is also maintained by a refusal to authenticate any particular record of the action, a refusal that also turns out to be one way of keeping the narrative suspended between natural and supernatural interpretations of events. Or, to put it in terms suggested by the novel itself, we are in a region where the boundary between the sacred and the profane becomes highly unstable.

Satan in Goray is characterized by a range of narrative voices and potential points of view. There is the primary narrator, whose closeness to the collective is signaled by his use of folk expressions (such as "It rained hard as if seven witches were being hanged"), his predilection for magical threes and sevens, his habit of keying the action into a chain of natural omens, and his familiarity with the details of the townsfolk's lives. Other voices are heard within the narrator's discourse: the villagers' rumors and tales and the conflicting interpretations placed upon events by adherents and adversaries of the sect. His chronicle also makes room for two documents. First there is the text of a letter sent from Lublin to the rabbi of Goray, Benish; the rabbi's correspondent warns him against Itche Mates in the most inflated terms. Though written in Hebrew, the letter has a style and point of view similar to that of the second inserted document, a morality tale said to be "rendered into Yiddish" (from a Hebrew original), which ends the novel. The opposition between the more or less colloquial style of the body of the discourse and the self-conscious scriptiveness of the letter and morality tale has an indexical value, for it helps to establish the opposition between a complex, ambiguous, carnivalized world of experience and a less fluid orthodox world of authoritative interpretation.

> **Satan in Goray** *might be read as a ghost story, the history of a communal afterlife. As such it participates in an important thematic current in Singer's work: narratives about the dead who attempt to go on as before, either because they are compelled to, or because they do not realize they are dead.*
> —*Charles Isenberg*

The authority of the various strands of the narrative is rendered problematic not only by their lack of agreement but also by certain qualities of the primary narrator. Most of the news about Sabbatai Zevi, for example, is traceable to some speaker who has a stake in having his or her account accepted. Moreover, the truth status of what is narrated is continually being undercut by the use of indirect-discourse markers that qualify reported speech or thought, such as "it was said," "it was rumored," "it seemed," or simply "as if." Alternative interpretations are already implicit in these devices, but the narrator is also inclined to overdetermine motives: that is, he will explain an action in two ways, with each explanation tending to vitiate the other. The description of a woman who comes to Goray with news about the imminence of redemption can serve as an illustration of the narrator's manner:

> *The rumor* [reported speech] that the days of the Messiah were drawing near gradually aroused even Goray, that town in the midst of the hills at the end of the world.
>
> A highly respectable woman [hyperbolic index of character], who for many years now *had been journeying in search of her husband* (*collecting alms at the same time*) [double explanation] *related* [reported speech] that in all the provinces of Poland *people were saying* [report of reported speech; her evidence is now third-hand] that the Exile had come to an end.

Searching for a lost husband is a sacred obligation, but the parenthetic addition about alms-collecting makes us suspect a profane motive, the missing spouse serving as a pretext for a successful carrier as a swindler. Indeed, by the time she leaves Goray, narrowly eluding a summons from the rabbi and carrying off gold coins, jugs of cherry juice, and

Sabbath cookies, we have little choice but to see irony in the opening characterization of her.

Of course if the whole novel worked this way, it would not be a question of the fantastic but only of an unreliable narrator. However, the more central episodes, such as the events leading up to the rabbi's departure or Rechele's illumination or her possession by a dybbuk, cannot be reduced to a coherent pattern so easily. For example, despite the usual reported-thought or comparison markers, when Rabbi Benish goes out on the night of Rechele's betrothal for what turns out to be the last round in his war against the Sabbataians, there *is* something uncanny going on:

> It was after midnight. In the bright night that lay over Goray a wind blew, a strong wind that swept away the dry snow and bore it off to pile up in mounds. The frozen earth was bared; trees shook off their winter white; branches broke; moss suddenly appeared on the housetops. In the very middle of the winter the roofs faced the world, with all their rotten shingles and patches. Crows awoke and cawed hoarsely, as at some unexpected sorrow. Snowflakes whirled through the air like wild geese. Between dark, plowed clouds, full of pits and holes, a faceless moon rushed through the sky. One might have thought the town had been doomed to a sudden alteration that had to be completed before the rising of the morning star.

The rabbi is convinced that there is evil in the air, and the townsfolk blame the rabbi's fall on demons. If the sequence of events suggests that it is the impious dancing of the Sabbataians that conjures up the demons, the text states only that the rabbi is borne aloft and swept down by the storm; hence neither mode of interpretation is ruled out.

As for Rechele, we may accept her visions and her demons as authentic, or we may see them as symptoms in a delusional remolding of reality. Singer does allow considerable scope for a psychological reduction of Rechele. Her childhood is genuinely horrific: before returning to Goray with her father, she lives in Lublin at the home of her uncle, a ritual slaughterer like Gedaliya. Terrified by the butchering that goes on daily in the yard, she is brutally treated by the old crone who looks after her; "'Sit down, you monster', she would cry, and pinch Rechele black and blue. 'Throw fits and jump as high as a house! May the fit carry you off!'" Since this reads like a prediction of Rechele's fate, we may see the old woman's curses as having a formative influence upon the child. This is clearly true of the ghost stories the old crone tells the little girl to keep her from leaving the house or simply for the pleasure of frightening her. After the old woman dies, the 12-year-old Rechele goes through a night of auditory and visual hallucinations (or of demonic

incursion—take your choice) that leaves her literally para-
lyzed with fear. This is the source of her lameness and other
"mysterious ills."

Both the angel that rouses Rechele to prophecy and the
dybbuk that possesses her after the illumination leaves her
can be interpreted as psychological projections that reflect
phases in her relations with Gedaliya. The angelic voice,
which appears just after she is seduced by Gedaliya, proclaims, ambiguously: "All the worlds on high do tremble
at the union she [Gedaliya] doth form." The dybbuk, which
exposes Gedaliya's wickedness, appears after Gedaliya has
failed to lead the Goraians out of exile. As for Rechele's
impregnation by Satan, from the moment of her return to
Goray there are reports of her starving herself to the point
where she ceases to menstruate. Moreover, just before her
struggle with Satan there are allusions to what sounds like
a hysterical pregnancy, whose symptoms are missed periods and a distended belly.

However, if we go too far in our search for evidence of
childhood trauma, epilepsy, or anorexia—that is, for natural causes that explain Rechele's behavior—we will be
brought up short when we find our skeptical and secular
point of view being parodied through its ascription to the
dybbuk, Abraham. At one point in the edifying tale of how
he is condemned to be tormented by evil spirits because of
his blasphemy in life, the dybbuk again denies God. Asked
why, if there is no God, he is being punished, Abraham replies, "It is all chance and an event of nature," an answer
completely incommensurate with his tale.

This is not Singer's only ironizing gesture in relation to the
dybbuk-narrative, for the novel provides two contradictory
accounts of Rechele's profanation by the forces of evil. The
two versions are given in the novel's final three chapters,
which center on Rechele, who loses her prophetic gift after
hearing about Sabbatai Zevi's apostasy. Like Rabbi Benish
in Part One of the novel, she becomes obsessed by an inner disputation; but where the rabbi hears disembodied night
voices wrangling over "Sabbatai Zevi and the end of days,"
Rechele becomes the arena for a contest between vivid personifications of the Sacred and the Profane. The Sacred appears to her as a face with no body; the Profane, as a lewd
and blaspheming shape-shifter. The Profane prevails, as it
has in the town, and Rechele finds herself impregnated by
Satan. In the morality tale that is interpolated into the text
of the Goray chronicle, we are told that Rechele has been
possessed by a dybbuk. The dybbuk is interrogated and finally expelled by the lame kabbalist Mordecai Joseph, who,
having abjured the Sabbataian sect, now emerges as the next
community leader. According to the dybbuk, it is because
Gedaliya is an apostate and has defiled Rechele that he, the
dybbuk, was able to enter Rechele on an occasion when she

cried out the name of Satan in exasperation at not being able
to get a fire started.

A comparison of these two accounts suggests that the primary narrator, privileged by his closeness to the events,
gives Rechele's version; the tale from *The Wonders of the
Earth* is much more distanced from the actors and reflects
the biases of the rabbinic party. Thus the tale knows nothing of Rechele's internalization of the struggle between the
Sacred and the Profane, and it represents her possession as
an object lesson in what happens when you speak of the
devil.

I will stand by my earlier claim that the novel as a whole is
marked by a refusal to authenticate a point of view; yet if
we restrict ourselves to the conclusion of **Satan in Goray,**
there can be little question but that the narrator's version
of what happens to Rechele whatever irreducible ambiguities of motivation it contains) is at least more authoritative
than the version drawn from *The Wonders of the Earth.*

Equally significant is the obviously false portrait of
Mordecai Joseph presented in *The Wonders of the Earth.*
Throughout the novel he is shown as a twisted and sadistic
personality. Mordecai Joseph's enmity toward the rabbi is
based on envy and spite, and his only function as a leader
has been to arouse hostility and violence. Every Passover,
we are told, he tries to organize a *Kristallnacht,* inciting the
mob to break the rabbi's windows. Mordecai Joseph is also
responsible for the first fruits of the Sabbataian harvest, the
riot in the study house and the beating of the rabbi's disciple Chanina.

For Mordecai Joseph in his Sabbataian phase, the movement
means an opportunity for revenge: revenge against the Jews,
not their enemies. This is how he perceives his mission when
he goes forth to proclaim the news about Rechele's prophecy:

> He already imagined himself in Lublin at the yearly
> fair, standing before the assembly of the Council of
> the Four Lands, roaring with his lion's voice at mul-
> titudes of important Jews—rabbis, righteous men,
> learned men, rich men—pouring pitch and tar on
> those who doubted Sabbatai Zevi, bidding that they
> be flogged and bound with heavy ropes. Their tracts
> and epistles must be burned in a fire whose flow
> would reach heaven.

If this context is used to frame the account from *Wonders
of the Earth,* we will see more than the tale's partisan narrator intends us to see. Here, for example, is Mordecai
Joseph's revenge upon Gedaliya:

> Then Reb Mordecai Joseph rose and smote

> Gedaliya with violence: Moreover the other men flung themselves at him and beat him and shed his blood and tore his beard until he fell fainting to the ground: and Reb Mordecai Joseph (may his remembrance be a blessing) flogged him forty times until his blood flowed like water.

What reading convention would allow us to see anything but antiphrasis in the description of the bloody-minded Mordecai Joseph as "that pious man (may his remembrance be a blessing to us all)," a formula that is repeated, with variations, nine times? The moralist's repetitions can only underscore what has actually transpired over the course of the novel: leadership of the community has passed from Goray's best representative, the learned and relatively tolerant Rabbi Benish, to its worst, the intolerant fanatic Mordecai Joseph. The ending is thus also a negative verdict upon the town's attempt to enact a new beginning, or to come back to life.

The town's dilemma is reproduced in the novel's symbol system. *Satan in Goray* is not a symbolist novel in the sense that it centers in figuration rather than plot, but it does have a semantic coherence that is based on the image-reservoirs of marriage and slaughter. That these are indeed symbols is demonstrated by their persistence and, partly in consequence of this, by the impossibility of giving a full inventory of their signifieds.

These symbolic patterns are privileged by the centrality of rituals of marriage and slaughter in the ritually structured world of *Satan in Goray.* The novel's other, less ramified symbolic patterns also refer to ritual—or at least to notions of ritual pollution. Thus the horse dung that profanes the study hall and prayer house in the exposition is paralleled by the dung that is found in the Ark of the Torah in Chapter 12, and Mordecai Joseph presides over two acts of ritual expulsion: at the beginning of the town's Sabbataian period, Mordecai Joseph, directing the beating of Chanina, goads on his followers by invoking the formula from the Yom Kippur scapegoat ritual: "Let this be in place of me!" The scapegoat motif is echoed at the end of the Sabbataian outbreak, which is marked by Mordecai Joseph's exorcism of the dybbuk from Rechele, who now functions as a kind of scapegoat for Goray.

Among the semantic fields with which the symbols of marriage and slaughter operate are: life and death, unity and disintegration, the sacred and the profane, and authority and its denial. Let us try to unravel at least some of the ways in which this symbolic cluster intersects with character and plot in *Satan in Goray.*

The novel begins with a slaughter, and the idea of marriage immediately becomes a figure for the possibility of collec-

tive renewal. Before his return to Goray, Rabbi Benish's chief concern had been questions of martial status, because "the events of 1648 and 1649 had left thousands of women neither married nor widowed, since it was uncertain whether their husbands were alive." Very early on, the question of the town's ability "to begin anew" becomes compounded with the question of Rechele's marriageability. But the issue of her marriage (= the town's new life) is always linked to the counterpossibility of a return to, or an inability to escape from, the consequences of the initiating catastrophe.

The intertwining of slaughter and marriage in Rechele's experience is a sign of a more general dissolution of boundaries between the sacred and the profane. Rechele's one-time guardian, her uncle Zeydel Ber, is a ritual slaughterer who had intended to marry her. Hence in her union with Gedaliya, she has found the man she has been fleeing since childhood. When Rechele first meets Itche Mates she foreshadows her fate with the profane joke that no one will marry her unless Satan will have her. (The imagery of dead eyes and corpselike smells that expresses her physical loathing for Itche Mates is drawn from her memories of the Lublin slaughteryard and her uncle's house.)

At Rechele's betrothal an epithalamium is sung that joins the social and the cosmic:

> Protect, Lord God, this bride and groom;
> May we see the Messiah soon.
> The Holy Presence, Lord God, wed
> As these two seek the marriage bed.

But the real prospects for marriage and renewal are imaged in a bathhouse floor "as bloody as a *slaughterhouse* (my italics) because of the activities of healers who are letting blood there, when Rechele visits the ritual bath as part of the wedding rites. Blood is a symbol that unites both paradigms, since it suggests the blood of victims but also the menstrual flow—so strangely absent in Rechele's case—which, on the one hand, implies the possibility of new life and on the other, is the object of a prohibition on marital intercourse.

Even more ominous is the singularly inappropriate song sung by the wedding jester, which is almost a repetition of the novel's opening words:

> The *haidamaks* slaughtered and martyred us.
> They murdered young children, they ravished
>   women
> Chmelnicki slit open bellies, he sewed cats inside
>   (because of our sins!).
> This is why we wail so loudly and implore
> Revenge, O Lord, the blood of thy slaughtered
> saints!

The jester's song not only implies a reversion to 1648; it also anticipates Rechele's monstrous pregnancy at the end of the novel. The jester's performance is answered by that of the dybbuk in a pattern of repetition and inversion: the wedding song offered by the jester, with its motifs of rape and monstrous pregnancy, fails to entertain its audience; the dybbuk, the product of an unnatural impregnation, successfully entertains the congregation with, among other things, his rendition of wedding music:

> And he sang the bridal canopy tunes with great skill *item* the Covering Tune for when the groom covers the bride's hair, *item* the Canopy Dance Tune, *item* the Escort Tune for when the bride and groom are escorted to their chamber: And he mimicked the sound of the fife and of the cymbal and of the bagpipe and of the other instruments and all with locked lips and the hearts of the congregation were melted like wax at the sight of the woman's gesticulations and grimaces.

On her unfortunate honeymoon ("The Seven Days of Benediction"), Rechele dreams of her uncle: "He was wearing a bloody shroud, and he waved a long butcher's knife in the air, and shouted angrily: 'Your days are numbered!'" Even the women's jest at Rechele's still-virginal state returns us to the same field of imagery: "Rechele . . . they said, had had her head cut off with no knife." Poor Rechele's seven unhappy days of benediction modulate into a vision of seven crowned maidens (seven Sabbaths?), and this is the vision that sends her to Gedaliya for the first time.

Gedaliya is the most disturbing figure in *Satan in Goray.* The image of the uxorious butcher, the slaughterer who preaches sexual liberation, carries implications that other works will make explicit. In *The Magician of Lublin,* for example, the narrator says of the hero: "He had looked on the faces of death and lechery and had seen that they were the same."In *The Magician of Lublin,* as in the story **"Blood"** (another tale about a lecherous butcher), sensual desire is the root of apostasy.

In his personality and beliefs, Gedaliya offers a sharp contrast to Itche Mates, the itinerant peddler he displaces as leader of the sect. A fisheyed, corpselike vegetarian, Itche Mates is an ascetic with a taste for self-flagellation and for immersing himself in icewater. He expounds an extreme gnostical version of Sabbataianism. After the Messiah's triumph, he preaches,

> Bodies would become pure spirit. From the World of Emanations and from under the Throne of Glory new souls would descend. There would be no more eating and drinking. Instead of being fruitful and multiplying, beings would unite in combinations of holy letters.

Gedaliya, on the other hand, is warm, witty, and jovial. Where Itche Mates's belief and behavior constitute a denial of the injunction "Be fruitful and multiply," Gedaliya makes this "principle of principle" the cornerstone of his doctrine. Not only would its neglect delay the redemption, but in the coming messianic age, all the sexual prohibitions would be annulled: "Men would be permitted to know strange women. Such encounters might even be considered a religious duty; for each time a man and a woman unite they form a mystical combination and promote a union between the Holy One, blessed be He, and the Divine Presence," that is the Shekinah, treated as a feminine aspect of the godhead.

The contrast between Itche Mates's gnostic asceticism and Gedaliya's mystic eroticism can be translated into rhetorical terms: Itche Mates is a hyperallegorist who would like to sacrifice the earthly term to its allegorized ideal: no more sex, just combinations of divine letters. Gedaliya is a hypersymbolist who argues a correspondence between the divine and the earthly; "as above, so below," as the hermetic formula has it.

Gedaliya's doctrines reflect kabbalistic and Sabbataian trends. First, as Scholem tells us, it is kabbalistic interpretation that makes the Sabbataian worldview possible. The universe is understood to be symbolic, so that "Creation does not exist for its own sake but for the sake of pointing to the divine emanation that shines through it." Further, once symbolic interpretation escapes the confines imposed upon it by a unified, hegemonic (in this case, rabbinic) source of authority, "no traditional commandment or prohibition is safe from spiritual and figurative reinterpretation."

The last significant threshold in this process is the doctrine of the apostate redeemer, who must betray his religion and descend into evil as part of his divine mission. As Scholem puts it, "once the first step was taken on this slippery road, anything became possible." Gedaliya and his loyalists abandon the tamer notion that only the Messiah's shadow had converted and follow Sabbatai Zevi's example, into apostasy and beyond.

As leader of Goray, Gedaliya institutes an orgy of resemanticization, whose most important element is a resemanticization of the orgiastic. The streets are soon filled with pregnant 12-year-old brides, adultery is encouraged, and the Yeshiva students copulate with each other and with the local goat population. Here too Gedaliya is influenced by a kabbalistic tradition that divides the universe into male and female cosmic functions. In his interpretation of the principle "Be fruitful and multiply," Gedaliya sees sex as a way of reuniting the dichotomized male and female worlds.

His intercourse with Rechele he represents as a mystical union that keeps the cosmos going. Yet after the initial euphoria of Gedaliya's rule in Goray, the cosmos winds *down.* As the narrator tells us, "There was no longer even sinning. The Evil Spirit himself seemed to have dozed off."

If the sacred and the profane finally merge for the radical Sabbataians, for the other townsfolk the boundaries between these realms are reestablished at the end of the novel. Rechele's last union, with Satan, is only profane, as are the antics of the dybbuk. The reader's response to the reimposition of orthodoxy under Mordecai Joseph's leadership must, however, be more ambivalent than that of the author-moralist of *The Wonders of the Earth.* Singer offers no privileged position from which to judge or condemn; by the end, the rabbinic party seems as compromised as the Sabbataians.

Singer's fictions always remain suspended between belief and unbelief. In his fables he often *seems* to embrace the orthodox position. However this is in part substitutive satisfaction—embracing in fiction what cannot be accepted in life—and in part literary strategy. Singer has said of his stories (and I think this can be extended to his novels) that they are written not around a moral, but around a moral point of view. That is, they ask, what would be the consequences of seeing the world in a certain way? A moral is authoritative, but a moral point of view is open to stylization, parody, and irony, and is not likely to conduce to any sort of final interpretive repose. Pierre Macherey's hypothesis (in *A Theory of Literary Production*) that fiction is shaped by the juxtaposition and conflict of several meanings and that "this conflict is not resolved or absorbed but simply displayed," thus seems to provide suitable terms for reading *Satan in Goray.*

In his most recent volume of memoirs, *Lost in America,* Singer describes his frame of mind in the early thirties, the period when *Satan in Goray* was written:

> my disillusionment with myself reached a stage in which I had lost all hope. If truth be told, I had little of it to lose. Hitler was on the verge of assuming power in Germany. The Polish fascists proclaimed that as far as the Jews were concerned they had the same plans for them as did the Nazis. . . .

> One didn't have to be particularly prescient to foresee the hell that was coming. Only those who were totally hypnotized by silly slogans could not see what was descending upon us. There was no lack of demagogues and plain fools who promised the Jewish masses that they would fight alongside the Polish gentiles on the barricades and that, following the victory over fascism, the Jews and gentiles in Poland would evolve into brothers forever after. The pious Jewish leaders, from their side, promised

that if the Jews studied the Torah and sent their children to cheders and yeshivas, the Almighty would perform miracles in their behalf.

> I had always believed in God, but I knew enough of Jewish history to doubt in His miracles. In Chmielnitzki's times, Jews had studied the Torah and given themselves up to Jewishness perhaps more than in all the generations before and after. There was no Enlightenment or heresy at that time. The tortured and massacred victims were all God-fearing Jews. I had written a book about that period, *Satan in Goray.*

If we compare the achieved intention of the novel with this very retrospective statement of the impulses that lay behind its writing, we can easily find parallels. There is the apocalyptic mood, for example, and the presence of two Jewish parties, neither of whose claims can be accepted; there is also the allusion to the Chmielnicki massacres, in particular, to the challenge posed to orthodox belief by the slaughter of innocents. But *Satan in Goray* is less concerned with 1648 than it is with the victims' response—and for that reason, heresy is precisely what it is about. As such, it implicitly polemicizes with the belief, still represented in Jewish circles, that pogroms, and even the Holocaust, are punishments from God, deserved by a wayward people. *Satan in Goray* implies that the falling away from belief is, on the contrary, a response to catastrophe and not its cause. Beyond that, the novel seems only to offer a skepticism about any claim to knowledge about Divine Purpose, a skepticism that is consonant with Singer's own credo, which may be characterized as a belief in God but not in Man's pretensions.

Articulating its dilemma of impossible choices, *Satan in Goray* conjures up an ambiguous, dualized world but not a world devoid of meaning.
—*Charles Isenberg*

Articulating its dilemma of impossible choices, *Satan in Goray* conjures up an ambiguous, dualized world but not a world devoid of meaning. Its contradictions are determinate, and they are determined by a paradox so prevalent in Singer's writings as to constitute an invariant in his fiction: the appeal to tradition against itself. Parallel to the way in which the novel's symbolism invites a reading that attends to ritual structures, its invariant paradox invites a transposition into a kabbalistic register. Thus the narrative is shaped in part by a triple movement of creation, dualization, and restitution.

The world of the novel is created by a catastrophe, the Chmielnicki massacre, which can be interpreted as evidence of a Divine withdrawal. The result of this catastrophic creation is a fallen, exilic condition, corresponding to the mixing of the Diving Sparks with evil in Lurianic kabbala. Hence the tale's dual explanation of events and its pairing of incommensurables, such as marriage and slaughter, the Sacred and the Profane. Hence too such other instances of dualization as the formal division of the text into two parts; the fact of Goray's two streams, so significant for the rites of divorce and remarriage; and the linguistic doubling inherent in the opposition both between oral and scriptive traditions and Hebrew and Yiddish.

The third movement—that of restitution—occurs in the reimposition of a monistic orthodoxy by the narrator of *The Works of the Earth.* Far from being redemptive, however, this restitution suggests another painting-over of disaster—a motif proleptically introduced in the painting over of the town's "blood-and-marrow-spattered walls" in Chapter 1.

Read in this way, **Satan in Goray** bears a strong formal resemblance to **The Slave** and **The Magician of Lublin** and a somewhat more distant likeness to **Enemies** and **Shosha.** Each of these works looks back to an originating catastrophe: in **The Slave** it is the Chmielnicki rebellion again; in **The Magician of Lublin,** it is the loss of traditional belief through secularization. In **Enemies** the initiating catastrophe is the Holocaust, and the retrospective narrative of **Shosha** reflects an exile from authoritative tradition that is brought about both by secularization and by the Holocaust. Each novel places its action in a fragmented and ethically dualized world. And each presents an attempted restitution, which, by virtue of its absurdity, must be read neither as a solution to the contradiction set forth by the fiction nor as an ethical recommendation to the reader, but as a flight from the complexities of a hopelessly fallen world. That is, Singer is not endorsing the ascetic absolutism arrived at by Yasha Mazur in **The Magician of Lublin** or by Jacob in **The Slave.** Nor (except by telling his story) is Aaron Greidinger permitted to redeem the lost paradise represented by his beloved Shosha. Finally, when Herman, the hero of **Enemies,** tries to escape the ambiguities of his life by becoming a missing person, the narrator presents Herman's flight as a reversion to the initiating catastrophe of the Holocaust. Whether he actually is "hiding somewhere in an American version of his Polish hayloft," as his wife believes, his fate imitates that of the war's missing and dead.

If we use **Satan in Goray** as a lens for viewing Singer's subsequent oeuvre, we can see that the movement of restitution in these texts always functions metalogically: restitution can only be an ironic impossibility because Singer's subject is the inevitability of living after the tradition. In its posttraditionalism, its contemplation of irreconcilables, its

rejection of an authenticating narrator, and its emphasis on symbolism, Singer's first novel shows a kinship with literary modernism. But it is also modernist in its tension between despair at the course of the world and exultation in the writer's creative powers. It is antidionysian in its moral stance, yet it endorses the libidinal and the ecstatic by the fascinated attention it pays to them. One might say that Singer's text is *his* demon.

Dinah Pladott (essay date Summer-Fall 1985)

SOURCE: "Casanova or Schlemiel? The Don Juan Archetype in I. B. Singer's Fiction," in *Yiddish,* Vol. 6, Nos. 2-3, Summer-Fall, 1985, pp. 55-71.

[*In the following essay, Pladott examines the role of the amorous male protagonist as a central figure in Singer's fiction. According to Pladott, these recurring characters underscore man's struggle to reconcile individual desires and universal meaning.*]

The popularity of I. B. Singer's fiction in recent years does not mitigate the fact that he suffers the same fate as other complex and fecund writers: he gives critics grounds for interpretations or points of emphasis that are divergent to the point of being contrary. Is he a parochial writer, speaking directly to insular Jewish concerns and dilemmas, or a moral fabulist of the stature of Hawthorne and Faulkner, touching the core of universal predicaments? Is he a humorist, a realist, a mythmaker, a metaphysical writer, a chronicler of Jewish history and lore, a demonologue, or a fantasist? Can and should one label him a traditional Jewish believer or an apostate, a modern and a modernist writer or a "shutin"?

The questions are not idle, since several flaws have been identified in Singer's oeuvre. The "oddest aspect of Singer's work," as Eisenberg defines it, is the "inordinate stress, certainly for a Yiddish writer, which is placed on sex—on evocative scenes of passionate sensualism." Nereo Condini elaborates Eisenberg's criticism by commenting on "a repetition of themes and motives often smacking of obsession, hackneyed situations, trivial details, ludicrous and sensational bric-a-brac." But as Bezanker points out, Singer's form, most notably his irresolute endings and his ambivalence," have constituted the "two blemishes" critics have taken the greatest exception to.

Needless to say, these objections depend on the critic's view of Singer's overall purpose and direction. I suggest, therefore, that a fruitful approach to Singer's fiction may be found in searching for the "deep structure" that underlies narratives marked by a wealth of imaginative detail, by a convincing authenticity of diverse and disparate fictive worlds and realities, and richly populated by a gallery of natural and supernatural characters. Once we isolate this "deep structure" in a number of Singer's novels, we may find a useful key both to the "obsessive" theme and to the open-ended form of Singer's "ambivalent" fiction.

The popularity of I. B. Singer's fiction in recent years does not mitigate the fact that he suffers the same fate as other complex and fecund writers: he gives critics grounds for interpretations or points of emphasis that are divergent to the point of being contrary.
—*Dinah Pladott*

The need for such an approach is encouraged and invited by Singer's progressive departure from stories evoking the life of the Polish Jewish shtetl with all its colors and verve. As if to give the reader a clue that he is more than just a "fictional historian of the whole Jewish experience in Eastern Europe," as Kazin put it, Singer's latest stories and novels shift the scene historically as well as geographically.

In *Enemies: A Love Story* the plot is set in post-World War II New York, whereas in *Shosha* Singer paints in broad strokes the tense life in Warsaw of the 1930s. The surface texture of these novels has little in common with *The Magician of Lublin,* whose story unfolds and moves between the miserable shtetl and the large urban center of late nineteenth-century Warsaw. Nor do these novels seem related to *The Slave,* which takes seventeenth-century Poland as the backdrop for its action. Yet, when one penetrates beneath the surface incidents and details, one is struck by the recurrence of a single configuration.

This paradigm consists of a male protagonist surrounded by a large number of female characters who entangle him in a web of variegated relationships. This central male character is always the pivotal figure in the novel, although only in *Shosha* does he attain the influential role of first-person narrator.

Singer's novels and short stories first impress the reader with the writer's storytelling capacity. In epic family sagas and short novellas, in wide-ranging picaresque novels and condensed folk tales, Singer unfailingly spins good yarns. He effortlessly mixes the real and the fantastic, the mundane and the fabulous. His compelling stories convince us both of the concrete nature of everyday joys and sorrows of Jewish life in different epochs, and of the equally (or apparently equally) tangible doings of dybbuks and demons. Yet beneath the surface adventures and misadventures, beneath the

panoramic dramatization of ribaldry and catastrophe, one often senses the insistent presence of eternal moral questions, often literally voiced by the characters as they struggle with each other and with themselves: Is there a God? Does He rule, or has He abdicated His responsibility for His creatures? Is He benign, or malign? How can one account for all the suffering in the universe? In the absence of a clear moral force in the world, what is the purpose of our existence?

This conjunction of form and content, of a Chaucerian wealth of earthly details and a serious philosophic questioning, has made many of Singer's readers pause. "It must be a common experience among Singer's readers," says Irving Howe, "to find a quick pleasure in the caustic surface of his prose, the nervous tokens of his virtuosity, but then to acknowledge themselves baffled as to his point and purpose." What is the relevance of scenes of orgiastic excess and libertine adventures in *Satan in Goray* or *The Magician of Lublin,* critics and readers asked, if the central point of interest was the depiction of the collective destiny of a Jewish nation, deprived of nationhood, stripped of worldly powers, yet sustained by the memory of chosenness and the promise of salvation? On the other hand, even readers trained to accept the expressionist distortions, the ambiguity and the irresolution of "modernistic" sensibility took exception to Singer's formal solutions. "Singer exults in sexuality, the grotesque and absurd," commented Prescott. Similarly, at the very moment of comparing Singer to the moral fabulator Hawthorne, and celebrating Singer's ability to write "old fashioned romances," Hyman also complains about *The Slave* that "the miraculous end is hard to take." Some of these difficulties, however, may be answered if Singer's writing is viewed from a different perspective. From this new point of view, both Singer's diversity of surface texture and his integral union of the container and the thing contained become manifest.

I suggest that a possible key both to the formal arrangement and to the thematic concerns in Singer's fiction may be found once we penetrate beyond the surface to the underlying structure. We discover that a number of the novels are marked by a recurrent structural model. The geographical and historical locale of the action and the specific details of characterization and plot are vastly different. Yet these provide the fictional covering for a similar structural paradigm which consists of a single male figure enmeshed in a web of diverse erotic relationships with a rich variety of female protagonists.

In *The Magician of Lublin* the hero is Yasha, a forty-year-old simple and uneducated man who combines the talents of a physical and a spiritual sorcerer. Literally, as well as metaphorically, Yasha is a rope-walker. Not least among his balancing feats is his ability to juggle a number of simultaneous relationships with the women in his life. Esther, his barren seamstress wife, reminiscent of Penelope in her faithful devotion, is described as eternally young, and she is an undiminished source of love and sustenance to Yasha's aspirations. Yet Yasha also collects an impressive array of lovers: Magda, his pimply-skinned, flat-chested, spindly-legged assistant; Elzbietta, her mountainous and passionate mother; Zeftel, a thief's forsaken wife who is as much of a "gypsy" as Yasha is; and Emilia, the well-bred, educated, and aristocratic Christian widow who wages a campaign to convert Yasha with the aid of philosophy, religion, mysticism, and erotic temptation.

Shosha takes as its focus a different male character. Aaron Greidinger is a budding writer and a journalist who has an even more impressive collection of mistresses: Celia Chentshiner, a blooming woman in her thirties, functions as mother rather than a wife to her husband Heiml, and is involved in a love affair with Aaron's literary mentor, Morrish Feitelzohn. Yet she enters into an attachment with Aaron that combines the function of a literary amanuensis and the role of a sensually seductive older woman. In absolute contrast to Celia's civilizing and elevating influence, Betty Slonim, the overripe actress, pulls Aaron in the direction of vulgarization and pedestrianism both in his personal and his artistic life. She holds the temptation of a marriage of convenience and urges Aaron to aim at popular artistic success by filling his plays with "love and sex." Another influence, bringing out of Aaron his paternal, protective, and adult aspect, is represented by the figure of his childhood sweetheart, Shosha, who has virtually remained a child. Tekla the peasant servant, on the other hand, coddles and pampers Aaron, ministering to all his physical needs as selflessly as he ministers to Shosha's emotional ones. Finally, Aaron is both drawn to and upset by Dora, the intensely fanatic communist ideologue, whom he teases and provokes by his own distrust of all creeds or "isms."

The entanglement in a net of amorous associations reappears in *Enemies: A Love Story.* The hero, Herman Broder, is an aging survivor of the Holocaust, living with his second wife. This wife, Yadwiga, is a nearly illiterate peasant woman who used to serve in Herman's ancestral home, whereas Herman is a man of education and culture. She saved his life by hiding him throughout the war, even from her own parents. Yadwiga's monosyllabic simplicity and even primitivism are thrown into relief by the beautiful, intellectual Masha. In her smoldering passions and strong will, Masha spins a magic web of love for Herman. Yet she, too, is no lighthearted butterfly. Her temperamental and nervous tantrums are repeatedly traced back to her own searing experience of surviving the German death camps, and the bereavement entailed by that experience. Herman, like the other womanizers, maintains the delicate balance between these women with the aid of an extensive system of lies and deceptions. The equilibrium is disrupted, however, by the sudden appearance of his first wife, Tamara, whom he believed to have perished along with their two sons. Tamara, a beautiful and vibrant woman in her past existence, used to be fired by Marxist ideology and a reformer's zeal. She fascinated and hen-pecked Herman, in turn. Now, having seen all that has given her life meaning shrivel and die, she is literally a ghost risen from the dead, haunted and self-tormenting. But Herman finds her alluring and is torn by the attractions of his three women.

In its embryonic form, the paradigm of the single male who is the lover of many women appears in the earlier novel, *The Slave.* Jacob, a Talmudic scholar who has been forcibly impressed into bondage on a seventeenth-century Polish farm, resembles the later Singer males in attracting several women. These women include Zelda Leah, his first wife; Tyrza, the gentile noblewoman, a rich and lusty temptress who cannot shatter his reserve and asceticism; the many gentile peasant girls who are drawn to his gentleness and innate culture; and Wanda, the latter-day Ruth who is willing to go after her seventeenth-century Boaz and to risk everything, even to the point of adopting a mute mien, in order to become his Jewish wife, Sarah. In *The Slave,* the two marriages are not simultaneous but sequential. Yet the outline is already present of the model that will be developed and perfected in the subsequent novels: a plot revolving around a central male protagonist who holds a special attraction for a multitude of unlikely and disparate female figures. Moreover, even in *The Slave* Singer provides the reader with clues to the thematic significance of this formal configuration. The story unfolds as the action zigzags along the spatial and temporal continuums, constantly disrupted and filled in by flashbacks and flash-forwards. All the while Jacob is groping his way toward an understanding of his relationship with each of the women in his life. He is the first of a long line of male figures in Singer's fiction who are basically inquirers, searching for personal answers.

In seeking to establish his role and his ties to each of the women, Jacob exhibits, and discovers, different facets of his character and self. Thus he progressively discovers the answers to the question "Who am I?" as a man and as a Jew. But this enquiry also has significance on a macrocosmic level. Jacob's insistent questions vis-à-vis his women are typical of the Singerian male lover, insofar as they simultaneously probe the validity of moral, philosophic, and aesthetic values in his world. In the novel set in seventeenth-century Poland as much as in the novels set in pre- and post-Holocaust Europe and America, this world is apparently shorn of its human order and meaning by the cumulative effect of countless catastrophes and bloodshed. Thus Jacob contemplates his life with Wanda after hearing of the pogroms in his hometown of Yuzepov:

There were no answers to his questions. Everything was one great puzzle; the suffering of man, the origin of human evil. The Jews looked at Jacob as if waiting for him to speak, but he sat silent. When he had explained to Wanda that there is no free will and freedom of choice without the existence of evil, and there is no Grace without injustice, he had thought that this was the answer. Now the answer seemed too simplistic, blasphemous. Can the creator of the universe be incapable of showing his goodness and omnipotence without the aid of rampaging soldiers? Is it necessary to rely on burying babies alive?

Jacob is a man desired by many females but who nevertheless manages to retain his faithful love in his purity. But his bafflement resembles the floundering of the more mendacious male protagonists in Singer's fiction. They, too, continuously link the microcosmic realm of their lusts and loves to the macrocosmic realm of universal rationality and meaning. Like him, they experience the clash between the questioning human mind and the dark universe that frustrates the human search for coherence and meaning. The universal nature of this clash is dramatized by the fact that it is confined to a single point in time or in space. *The Magician of Lublin* takes as its historical backdrop the relatively peaceful and enlightened time of late nineteenth-century Poland, untroubled by cataclysmic or violent eruptions comparable to the Holocaust or the pogroms. Moreover, Yasha Mazur is devoid of scholastic training in Talmud or philosophy of the kind enjoyed by Jacob. Yet Yasha ponders his acrobatic feats in the arena and in the beds of his lovers and sees them as inseparable from the larger framework of existential questioning:

> together with his ambition and lust for life, dwelt a sadness, a sense of the vanity of everything, a guilt that could neither be repaid nor forgotten. What was life's purpose if one did not know why one was born nor why one died? . . . Had he been through the world simply to turn a few tricks and deceive a few females? On the other hand, could he, Yasha, revere a God whom someone had invented?

Whereas Jacob represents the early prototype of Singer's lover-philosopher, Yasha is characteristic of the fully developed male hero who combines Don Juan's deception of many women with a quest for significance and purpose in human existence. Yasha, as well as Aaron Greidinger (*Shosha*) and Herman Broder (*Enemies: A Love Story*) are set apart from the average skirt-chaser. Their passionate conquests and mishaps are lifted above mere hedonism. This narrative achievement is illuminated and elucidated if we consider the fact that Singer repeatedly depicts his male pro-

tagonists as experiencing the discovery described by Camus in *The Myth of Sisyphus*. This is the discovery that an absurd divorce holds between the human thirst for meaning and purpose, and the obdurate indifference of a mute and unreasonable universe:

> This world is in itself not reasonable, that is all that can be said. But what is absurd is the confrontation of this irrational and the wild longing for clarity whose call echoes in the human heart.

Camus's discussion of the consequences of this confrontation provides a new perspective from which we can view the complex role Singer assigns to his ribald and sensual lovers. The experience of existential nausea and anguished sense of absurd divorce may lead the individual to suicidal despair, comments Camus, but it can also lead to a creative and rebellious acceptance of the human lot. The collapse of illusion, the clear-eyed acceptance of existence in a world "in which nothing is possible but everything is given" may mean not paralysis but a newfound lucidity and defiance that enable one to surmount despair. The individual discovers "his strength, his refusal to hope, and the unyielding evidence of a life without consolation." In Camus's view, which is admittedly revisionist in the extreme, Don Juan exemplifies one of the positive, creative, and defiant responses to life in a universe so divested of its illusions and consolations. His posture, which exclaims "everything is permitted," constitutes not licentiousness but creativity. The universal nothingness is filled with meaning as Don Juan enters into his many loves in the same way the actor enters into his variegated roles: "entering into all these lives, experiencing them in their diversity." Moreover, Don Juan as Camus sees him is conscious and that awareness is celebrated as his prime attribute. It is interpreted as the defiant response that elevates man above the absurd, which threatens to crush him. "Nothing is vanity for him," says Camus of Don Juan, "except the hope of another life." Consequently, Don Juan is placed by Camus in the gallery of heroes to be admired and emulated: those who have found means of responding to absurd incoherence and futility with lucidity, creativity, and defiance. Don Juan's multiple loves, generally read as external expression of internal dissolution and dissipation, are seen by Camus as the ingenious means for replacing disintegrating quality with regenerative quantity: "The absurd man multiplies here what he cannot unify." Where tradition represents Don Juan as succumbing to physical drives, Camus sees him as liberated and victorious, finally attaining a triumph over darkness and despair. Don Juan "achieves a way of knowledge without illusions. . . . Loving and possessing, conquering and consuming—that is his way of knowledge." It now remains to be seen whether Singer's Don Juans—who similarly love and possess, conquer and consume as they ponder the rationality and coherence of their universe—are equally victorious and heroic.

It should be noted at this point that I am not attempting to present the Jew as the perfect symbol of the Camusian man. On the contrary, I am calling attention to a compositional device that enables Singer to probe deeper than the surface characterization of his heroes as Jewish males. Hawthorne wrote in the idiom and using the incidents of daily life typical of Puritan New England, and Faulkner infuses his writing with the dialect, folklore, social, and moral reality of the antebellum and postbellum South. Yet few people are unaware today that Hawthorne was writing about the "unpardonable sin against the human heart," and that Faulkner is concerned not with black-white relations but with "man's injustice to man." Similarly, Singer's heroes are steeped in Jewish lore, religion, morality, and folk-wisdom, as they also speak the cadences and rhythms of Yiddish and reflect its humorous irony. But these characteristic traits that ground them in the reality Singer knows so well are only half the picture. Singer seems to be doing what Faulkner said he himself has done: "sublimating the actual into the apocryphal." The "deep structure" links Yasha, Jacob, Aaron, and Herman to the mythic figure of Don Juan and to his newly mythicized role as a seeker of universal answers. These amorous heroes become therefore representative of all men in their insistent attempt to reconcile the contradictory yearnings and needs of the individual. They span the ungodly and the god-seeker, the terrestrial and the heavenbound, the ordinary and the miraculous, the humane and the inhuman. Even as they succumb to the urgings and temptations of their flesh, they obsessively search for a sign from above. These Don Juans constantly violate the traditional sexual and moral interdictions of their culture and religion, yet they await a message and proof of sorts that there is a guardian eye ruling their universe, that evil is not arbitrary but a retribution, and that their life in this world is not mere chance or a blind event. Consequently, they are instrumental in Singer's exploding and transcending the narrow bounds of regional, sectarian, and parochial concerns, in order to depict and dramatize what is first and foremost a universal human quest.

The chasm between the apparently frivolous surface and the thoughtful, solemn, subterranean core of the Don Juan archetype invoked by Singer is thrown into prominent relief by the conversation of Yasha Mazur and his mistress Zeftel in *The Magician of Lublin.*

—*Dinah Pladott*

The chasm between the apparently frivolous surface and the thoughtful, solemn, subterranean core of the Don Juan archetype invoked by Singer is thrown into prominent relief by the conversation of Yasha Mazur and his mistress Zeftel in *The Magician of Lublin.* To Zeftel, Yasha appears to be playing a joyful and carefree game: "to you women are like flowers to a bee. Always a new one. A sniff here, a lick there—and 'whist!' you buzz away." Yasha, however, exposes the obsessive aspect of his role as winner of hearts, and concludes that his deliberate courting of danger stems from what Camus called "an ethic of quantity:" "just as thieves had to steal money—he had to steal love." The danger involved in "stealing love" is not merely the actual danger of being unmasked. Far more troubling to Yasha is the danger that his erotic transgressions may indeed constitute a violation of a universal system of absolute values. The frisky amorous exploits mask a serious concern with the moral boundaries of the universe. But whereas Camus's Don Juan has already established these boundaries and smiles scornfully at the absurdity of the universe, Yasha views his Don Juanism with greater skepticism. The freedom of Don Juan is mere bondage to present and future hell, and his many loves merely damning "burdens," muses Yasha, if the world is after all ruled by some just and retributive moral force:

> He had burdened himself with too heavy a yoke even before Emilia. He had supported Magda, Elzbietta and Bolek. . . . Esther grumbled frequently that he worked only for the devil. . . . How much longer would he drift along like this? How many more burdens would he assume? With how many perils and disasters would he load himself? . . . His passions flayed him like whips. Never had he ceased to suffer regret, shame, and the fear of death. . . . Thoughts of repentance enveloped him. Perhaps there was a God after all? . . . Perhaps a Day of Reckoning really waited and a scale where good deeds were weighed against the evil? If it were so, then every minute was precious. If it were so, then he had arranged not for one, but for two Hells for himself, one in this world, the second in the other.

All Singer's skirt-chasers are likewise preoccupied with questions about the possible presence or absence of rationality and retributive justice in the universe. By the same token, they also embody the ironic parameters of the writer's rendering of the newly mythicized model. Singer's Don Juans resemble Camus's lover in multiplying where they "cannot unify." Unlike him, however, they feel keenly the sting of this incapacity. Instead of heroically and blithely defying the absurd void, they feel dwarfed and hamstrung by the operation of unintelligible evil in their universe. Humorous as the confrontation with malignity may be, evil, even in its least stupendous forms, remains incomprehensible and insurmountable for Singer's Casanovas.

A case in point, exemplifying the humor and the helplessness of Singer's Don Juans in the face of malevolence, is the childhood encounter of Aaron Greidinger and his Shosha in their Krochmalna Street habitat. The young Aaron, in the best tradition of Singer's womanizers, is already a rebellious thinker questioning the Talmudic teachings of his strict father. Like Jacob and Herman, he ponders scientific teachings and dissects the philosophic notions of Aristotle, Descartes, Leibnitz, and Spinoza in an attempt to verify the presence or absence of God. Shosha, whose innocent lack of any intellectual accoutrements makes her a version of the saintly fool, Gimpel Tam, provides Aaron with a willing audience. But as Aaron expounds his secondhand understanding of Spinoza, namely, that God is the world and the world is God, Shosha ingenuously brings the theoretical disquisition down to the ground of their daily reality: "Is Leibele Bontz also God?" Leibele Bontz was the worst bully in the court, full of tricks and excuses for inflicting pain on the weaker children. The notion that this early incarnation of motiveless malignity could also partake of divinity, reminisces the adult Aaron humorously, "cooled my enthusiasm for Spinoza's philosophy."

This self-directed irony with which Aaron remembers his early helplessness, his failure to either counteract or to account successfully for the palpable reality of malevolence, is characteristic of Singer's sardonic presentation of his Don Juans. Yasha, Aaron, and Herman Broder are constantly placed in the position of realizing their own impotence and ridiculousness.

As Yasha explains to Emilia, "I am just a bungler." The Yiddish word for "bungler" is Schlemiel, and it is used to describe the little fellow, the one who is so unfit for life in this world that he botches all his undertakings. The Schlemiel, a butt of humor and an object of gentle ridicule, is a prominent archetype of Jewish humorous fiction. It is also the very antipode of the heroic, triumphant Don Juan described by Camus. The continuum between these two antithetical models provides Singer with a rich variety of intermediate figures, spanning the whole spectrum from the newly heroic to the utterly inept. Consequently, true to his fictional mastery, Singer paints a gallery of variegated portraits. Jacob, the prototype who is untainted by Casanova's double-dealing, is the most heroic of Singer's male lovers. Yasha already combines the heroic and the antiheroic; he exemplifies the fall from the grace of achievement and assertive power to the disgrace of passive enslavement, failure, and disparagement. Aaron combines a lucidity and eloquence unsurpassed by any of the other Don Juans with a diminutive nickname, "Tsutsik" ("little one" in Russian and Yiddish). The nickname underscores Aaron's circumscribed stature as an unfulfilled promise, a bud that has not

yet bloomed. Moreover, if Yasha feels pushed in different directions by the women in his life, Aaron is actually pressed, compressed, impressed, and depressed in turn by his various lovers. This aspect of Singer's Don Juan, his ineffectual will and his passivity in the female hands that would mold and shape him, becomes the central trait of Herman Broder. Herman is the least like Camus's Don Juan, who victoriously experiences his multiple loves "in their diversity." Instead, he is as clay in the hands of his powerful temptresses who manipulate his thinking and behavior. In fact, Herman is so much like the archetypal Schlemiel that his amorous conquests seem incongruous. As one mishap follows another, Herman claims a place as the most maladroit and least imposing of Singer's skirt-chasers:

> These mistakes in the subway, his habit of putting things away and not remembering where, straying into the wrong streets, losing manuscripts, books and notebooks, hung over Herman like a curse. He was always searching through his pockets for something he had lost. His fountain pen or his sunglasses would be missing, his wallet would vanish, his own phone number would slip from his mind. He would buy an umbrella and leave it somewhere within the day. He would put on a pair of rubbers and lose them in a matter of hours. Sometimes he imagined that imps and goblins were playing tricks on him.

Singer, with a recognizable Yiddish rhythm even in this English translation, does not spare his hero as he piles on detail after damning detail. However, this same Schlemiel also functions as the philosopher—Don Juan described by Camus. Like all of Singer's Casanovas, Herman is engrossed by questions about the moral timbre of the universe. After describing an inquisitive childhood and a rebellious youth reminiscent of those attributed to Jacob, Yasha, and Aaron, the narrator fills in the facts about the present Herman and his questionings:

> During the war and in the years after, Herman had time enough to regret his behavior to his family. But basically he remained the same; without belief in himself or in the human race; a fatalist hedonist who lived in presuicidal gloom. Religion lied. Philosophy was bankrupt from the beginning. The idle promises of progress were no more than the spit in the face of the martyrs of all generations. If time was just a form of perception, or a category of reason, then the past is as present as today; Cain continues to murder Abel. Nebuchadnezzar is still slaughtering the sons of Zedekiah and putting out Zedekiah's eyes. The pogrom in Kichinev never ceases. Jews are forever burned in Auschwitz.

The conjunction of these two passages exposes the two facets of the ironic Don Juan as he appears in Singer's fiction. He is simultaneously a "fatalist hedonist" and a seeker of moral answers; an inept bungler and a powerful thinker: man floundering under the pressures of the world and an individual attempting to chart his own progress in a universe divested of sign posts and guidelines; a Schlemiel and a heroic questioner out on an individual and lonely quest. The question that insistently suggests itself is: What function does this paradoxical figure fulfill in Singer's overall design?

When a writer makes a repeated use of a narrative device, an image, or a theme, he incurs the danger of being misunderstood. Readers who fail to see the larger frame of reference created by the very repetition may dismiss it as "obsessive," and even remark on the writer's drying powers of invention. In *Enemies: A Love Story,* Singer dangerously courts such misreading. He does not merely reiterate the Don Juan configuration, spiced as it is with titillating scenes of sensuality and eroticism. He even ascribed to Herman ruminations, attitudes, and queries that echo almost verbatim similar passages attributed to the other Don Juans. One is immediately reminded of Aaron upon reading Herman's philosophizing, which posits the Don Juan's double-dealings as the hedonistic response to the universal Nothingness:

> He was deceiving Masha, and Masha was deceiving him. Both had the same goal; to get as much pleasure as possible out of life in the few years before darkness, the final end, an eternity without reward, without punishment, without will, would be upon them.

Compare *Shosha:* "she wants the same thing we all want, to grab some pleasure before we disappear forever."

Similarly, Herman's equivocations reflect and underscore Yasha's repeated vacillations between the admonition to renounce all his sublunary lusts and cling to God, and his equally strong doubts about the meaning and validity of creeds and dogmas. At a certain point, Herman echoes Yasha's avowals of absolute faith in a supreme God even to the point of relinquishing all earthly drives:

> He had sworn to renounce all worldly ambitions, to give up the licentiousness into which he had sunk when he had strayed from God, the Torah, Judaism. . . . If a Jew departed in so much as one step from the Shulchan Aruch, he found himself spiritually in the sphere of everything base—Fascism, Bolshevism, murder, adultery, drunkenness.

Singer, however, puts the allusive echo to narrative use. Herman's words simultaneously recapitulate and throw into

relief Yasha's attitude. They underscore the fact that from identical points of departure, the two Don Juans arrive at diametrically opposed courses of action. Yasha, by a Kierkegaardian leap of faith, clings finally to the conviction that "a single step away from God plunged one into the deepest abyss." He also concludes, however, that the frailty of the human will makes such true subservience to God impossible as long as one is truly involved in what Faulkner termed "the moil and seethe of human affairs": "one could not serve God among men, even though separated by brick walls."

Yasha, the magician who has grown impotent and awkward during the action of the novel, regains a measure of dignity and stature as "reb Jacob the Penitent." This solution requires, however, that he spend the rest of his life in a "living grave," dependent on his wife Esther for food. Herman, on the other hand, chooses another escape from God and from living: "I will leave everybody." Herman abandons the botched relationship with his three women and the wreck of everything he put his hands to, as well as his unborn baby daughter. The antithesis of both Yasha's and Herman's escapes, of their relinquishing of personal responsibility for life, is found in Aaron's steadfast refusal to forsake Shosha, though he risks perishing with her. Clearly, the reiteration of the Don Juan configuration is used by Singer to highlight not only the points of similarity but even more forcefully, the points of dissimilarity among the male protagonists. This serves, in the first instance, to refute charges made by otherwise perceptive critics that Singer's characters are "allegorical figures." Although the Don Juans confront the archetypal dilemma described by Camus, they remain distinct figures in their own right. Each must confront the universal riddle and determine for himself the degree of faith possible for him in the presence or absence of a moral divinity in the universe. But the manner in which they are acquainted with the prevalence of evil and with the ubiquitous nature of suffering is rendered in a new and fresh manner in each of the novels. Similarly, their response to the discovery of absurdity and futility is to fashion their own personal solution to the predicament.

Both the similarities and the dissimilarities function, however, on the global as well as the local textual level. When the novels are viewed as one frame of reference, Singer's utilization of the Don Juan model, and his rendering of that Don Juan as increasingly Schlemiel like, begins to make both thematic and formal sense. As a formal device, the Don Juans straddle the abyss between the sacred and the profane, their bodies steeped in the appetites and the pleasures of the flesh while their hearts and minds ponder the universal moral puzzle. Their progressively reduced stature functions like the absence of clear-cut resolution in Singer's narratives; it testifies to the difficulty of arriving at simple or definite answers. Unlike the triumphant Don Juan described by

Camus, Singer's Casanovas find it well-nigh impossible to attain the "knowledge" that constitutes a victory over the absurd.

Singer's "modern" outlook pierces through the repeated discovery of his protagonists that all absolutes become relative in the face of the inexplicable, insurmountable ubiquity of evil and suffering. Jacob was quoted above as expressing the pain of this inability to suggest any enduring solutions to the universal "puzzle." Confronted by the inexplicability of evil, all Singer's Don Juans are similarly freshly reminded of their limited powers, of their Tsutsik and Schlemiel aspect. The characters themselves, as well as the open, ambivalent endings of the narratives, loudly proclaim their bafflement with the universal enigma. The point is dramatized by the discussion of the two survivors of the Holocaust, Heimel and Aaron, at the end of *Shosha*. Heimel, comparing himself to a squashed fly, is associating himself with Gloucester's famous comment, "As flies to wanton boys are we to the gods" (*King Lear*, IV, i). Aaron, however, rejects even the view that ascribes suffering to malign gods who "kill us for their sport." In his view, there simply is no satisfactory explanation for suffering:

> "At night I lie awake, a little man, a nearly squashed fly, and I talk to the dead, to the living, to God—if He exists—and to Satan, who doubtlessly exists, and I ask them, 'Why was all this necessary?' And I wait for an answer. What is your opinion, Tsutsik, is there an answer to this question anywhere?"
>
> "No, there is no answer."
>
> "And why not?"
>
> Because there can be no answer to suffering—not for the sufferer."

The thematic implication of these narrative devices is heretic from the point of view of orthodox Judaism. It suggests that all systems of belief and abstract values are equally arbitrary and relative. Irving Howe rightly observes, therefore, that as a "modern writer" Singer is, by definition, "not quite trustworthy in relation to his culture." His "modern" awareness compels him to present Jewish orthodoxy as offering no greater a hope for an incontrovertible answer to the universal riddle, but only one partial answer among many.

At the same time, the very ambiguity of the formal conclusions allows the writer to balance a glimmer of hope against the degrading suffering, a putative affirmation against the overwhelming futility of questioning. The inept Don Juans fail, but their personal stories are framed and contained, in each of the four novels, by a larger, more comprehensive perspective that introduces a flicker of hope. *The Magician*

of Lublin terminates with Emilia's letter, informing Yasha that his physical and emotional vicissitudes were not in vain, since their love, and his eventual "conversion," have illuminated and enriched her existence. *Enemies: A Love Story* concludes with a postscript describing the birth of a daughter to the missing Herman, named after the now-dead Masha. This ending invites comparison to the so-called miraculous ending of *The Slave*, in which Jacob succeeded in saving his newborn son and in spiriting him to Palestine after the death of his beloved Sarah-Wanda. The same miraculous alternation of death and renewed life marks the epilogue of *Shosha*. Aaron, and the reader, are informed that Heimel, like many others who have lost their loved ones in the Holocaust, has remarried.

The conclusions of Singer's narratives testify, then, symbolically as well as literally, to the consoling fact that life continues its eternal cycle of destruction and restoration, of death and rebirth. This cyclical alternation offers some hope for rejuvenation and invigoration even after the most deadening suffering and loss. Hence, it seems quite appropriate that the last lines of *Shosha* allude to Beckett's *Waiting for Godot*. Asked by his wife Genia what they are waiting for, Heimel "laughed and said, 'We are waiting for answers.'" Like Beckett, Singer has found a metaphoric device with which he explores and exposes the universal predicament. Like Beckett, he presents characters whose humanity is their most recognizable trait. As Beckett's characters wait for Godot, so Singer's protagonists wait for answers about the divine or satanic nature of the principle that rules their universe. And as Beckett's play shows the tree, its only scenic object, sprouting new leaves in the second act in token of the hope that it consistently mingles with despair, so Singer's novels culminate in the birth that relentlessly follows death. The mixture of comedy and tragedy, of irony and horror, of laughter and tears, in Beckett as well as in Singer, reveals that both writers are aware of the paradoxical nature of existence. They are cognizant of the terrible nature of life in a universe shorn of its illusions and comforting explanations. "If God is silent," Hemiel quotes Morris Feitelzohn's response to the Nazi occupation of Poland, "we owe him nothing."

But they are also convinced that all is not lost. Singer resembles Beckett in intimating that the human spirit may in the long run endure and prevail against all odds. This is a slim hope, but hope it is. Beckett's tree and Singer's little fellows burgeon with new life because of the implicit belief that man is capable of filling the universal void with some positive meaning. Once more, form and theme combine to exemplify the fact that that slim meaning is of human origin, not divine. Morris Feitelzohn is already dead, but his fiery repudiation of theocentric evil in favor of anthropocentric good nourishes and supports the survivors who go on living:

"True religion means not obeying God but defying and provoking him. If he wants evil, we should desire its opposite. If he wants war, inquisitions, crucifixions, Hitlers, we should desire honesty, Hassidism, grace in our own fashion."

Ken Frieden (essay date September 1985)

SOURCE: "I. B. Singer's Monologues of Demons," in *Prooftexts,* Vol. 5, No. 3, September, 1985, pp. 263-68.

[*In the following essay, Frieden discusses the significance of supernatural dialogue in Singer's fiction, especially as found in "The Mirror" and "The Last Demon." Frieden notes that Singer "employs monologues in a deliberately archaic framework that disturbs our modern conceptions of literary representation and human existence."*]

Some of Isaac Bashevis Singer's most powerful stories are narrated by demons. Singer employs the literary form of monologue to depict the supernatural world as a reflection of our own. But his unusual device also works allegorically, and carries his fictions far beyond what they superficially represent. On one level, Singer's monologues of demons speak for the repressed or unconscious facets of human experience. At a deeper level, Singer's demonic monologues resemble monologues of the Yiddish language itself. In these stories, the tense relationship between demons and humans parallels the relationship between the Yiddish language and Jewish existence. To a traditionally observant Jewish community, both demons and secular Yiddish writing appear as temptations. But for Singer's narrator, after the religious tradition has been disrupted, demons and Yiddish writing appear to have lost their force, or their appropriate sphere of influence. When the community no longer recognizes the threat of temptation, this development signifies the loss of an entire worldview and form of language.

The *maskilim* were among the first to perceive Yiddish historically as a kind of collective monologue of the Jews. The Enlightened sought to overcome Yiddish, which embodied a kind of social isolation. Again and again, Yiddish has been scorned as a "jargon" or dialect. From a linguistic standpoint, Yiddish has been understood as a swerve away from Middle High German (and Hebrew). This is, of course, a controversial interpretation, and associated value judgments are often both concealed and irrational. In any case, the identity of Ashkenazic Jewry was clearly inseparable from the Yiddish language—until assimilation and World War II claimed the majority of its speakers.

In the wake of European literary realism, narratives by Mendele, Peretz, and Sholem Aleichem give voice to indi-

vidual Jewish personalities through monologues. The most prominent instances are Sholem Aleichem's late *monologn.* But Singer breaks from the European tradition of subjective, individualistic monologues, and employs monologues in a deliberately archaic framework that disturbs our modern conceptions of literary representation and human existence. He does this by attributing monologues, which are ordinarily associated with individual men and women, to supernatural beings. In Sholem Aleichem's stories, monologists generally address an audience, but after the Holocaust, Singer's speakers find themselves more radically alone. Singer's demonic monologists speak for forces beyond our conscious control, whether we understand them as metaphysical realities, psychological constructs, or linguistic fictions. Singer's demons are, then, far more than sentimental allusions to kabbalistic traditions. Singer's use of *sheydim* (demons) shows the continuity between popular demonology, modern psychology, and dynamics of language. I will concentrate on the stories **"The Mirror"** (*Der shpigl*) and **"The Last Demon"** (*Mayse Tishevits*), in order to illustrate this aspect of Singer's art.

When Singer began to publish his "monologues of spirits" in the 1940s, he hinted that they were "From a Series of Stories, 'The Memoirs of the Evil Inclination [*yeytser-hore*].'" According to talmudic tradition, this evil inclination is both a name for Satan, and an aspect of the human spirit. But it is equally important that these monologues are called "Memoirs," associating the activity of demons with the act of writing.

Temptation is at the center of Singer's stories that purport to be "Memoirs of the Evil Inclination." A demon tests a man or a woman, who either withstands or succumbs to the test. But Singer's demons discover that the very possibility of temptation, as understood by traditional Jewish sources, has been undermined by changes in the modern world.

"The Mirror" begins with a metaphorical description of sin as a net or spiderweb:

> There is a kind of net that is as old as Methuselah, soft as cobwebs, full of holes, but to this day it has not lost the power to ensnare. When a demon tires of chasing after yesterday, or of turning in a windmill, it can always settle in a mirror. It hovers like a spider in its web, and the fly must fall in.

Because human beings are prey to sins of vanity, mirrors are the strategic hide-outs for demons. Of course, the image of a mirror does not only reflect human vanity. It also directs us to problematics of artistic representation in general. Singer's demon implies that all art, including the literary representation in which we discover its monologue, stands in the tradition of idol worship. For the anti-heroine of this fiction, the sin of *avoyde-zore* involves self-worship as facilitated by a mirror. In particular, the demon observes that "God gave vanity to women—especially to the young, the beautiful, the rich . . . who have much time and little sociability."

Vanity is linked both to asociality and to modes of solitary speech. The monological form is especially appropriate to this tale about a solitary woman: the demonic narrator in part stands for her own evil impulses. The temptation comes through Satan, but also through the mirror, through vanity, and through monologue itself. When the narrative indirectly represents Tsirl's thoughts, we learn of her impulse to isolate herself from the surroundings: "What could Tsirl, the beautiful and well-educated woman raised in Cracow, speak about with such country souls?" Separating herself from the community, Tsirl engages in her characteristic sin, which is already suggested by her name: Tsirl views herself as *tsirung,* ornamentation.

Her sin, then, is not merely vanity, but solipsism. This arises from the fact that, isolated as she is, she exists only for herself. No one sees her, or rather only she observes herself. She is, in any event, the only important human protagonist in the story. Her narcissistic self-observation is a sexual perversion which involves an isolation or inward turn of desire. One might also say that narcissism gives expression to linguistic solitude. Yet even while Tsirl revels in the sight of her nakedness, she longs to share what she sees with an imaginary hunter, or poet, or swordsman. The desire for an Other is eloquently expressed by the demonic narrator, through the doubleness suggested by paired rhymes. In Singer's work (as in a long Western tradition), demons often give themselves away by their tendency to express themselves in awkward language. A kind of dialectical dualism surfaces again when, in the rhythms of doggerel, the narrator muses:

> Vos iz Khave on a shlang?
> Vos iz bsomim on geshtank?
> Vos iz zun on a shotn?
> Un vos is got on a sotn?

> [What is Eve without a serpent?
> What are spices without a stink?
> What is sun without a shadow?
> And what is God without a Satan?]

Tsirl falls into the demon's trap, as if by a linguistic reflex, and begins to utter doggerels of her own. The mortal sin occurs when she kisses the demon in the mirror; that is, of course, she kisses her own image. Tsirl exemplifies the fate of monologists, in an extreme form. The sin of consorting with evil spirits appears as the sin of encouraging narcissistic and auto-erotic impulses. But the temptations by

Singer's demonic monologists take on an added dimension when associated with a decaying tradition which, by referring endlessly to itself, isolates itself from the surrounding world.

The story entitled **"The Last Demon"** presses further. While the events of **"The Mirror"** take place at an indefinite time, those of **"The Last Demon"** occur before the Holocaust, as narrated afterward. Once again, the plot centers around demonic efforts at temptation. But in this context, the meaning of temptation and sin is difficult to maintain. How is it possible to speak of an "evil inclination" in Jewish life, when the Jews of Eastern Europe have been annihilated? What is the status of the Yiddish language itself, after the destruction of the Yiddish-speaking community?

"The Last Demon" gives expression to these problems by opening with a paradox: "I, a demon [*shed*], bear witness that there are no more demons." There is enough superstition left in the modern world to sustain demons, but just barely enough faith. Even the "I" of this fiction casts doubts on its own existence. Not only is the scene of speech indefinite; the speaker remains an enigma. Perhaps Singer affirms the fictive status of his narrating persona, which literally does not exist. The demonic mask is an illusion, which nevertheless symbolizes aspects of the human conditions: "What need is there of demons," the narrator asks, "when man himself is now a demon?" If modern writers have taken over the work of demons, as one of the demons suggests, then the demon's narrative may represent current literary and experiential predicaments. In Singer's perception, the Yiddish writer is a particularly anomalous being, like a demon with no one to tempt.

The story moves between two time frames, two worlds, before and after the Holocaust. The narrative frame is in the present tense; the narrated events occur in the past. The narrating demon describes its life in an attic in Tishevits where it draws sustenance from the letters of a Yiddish storybook. The story itself is trash, the narrator admits, but Yiddish letters are persistent, and have a strength of their own. The medium shows itself to be more essential than the message. From the start, then, the demonic narrator has much in common with the Eastern European Yiddish writer who, after the Holocaust, has lost his community and retains little more than its language. The demon explains that it speaks in the present tense, because "for me time stands still." This speaking "I" might be identified as "language": for language, time does stand still. The problem is that linguistic communities change, thereby changing language. The demon engages in an elaborate game of storytelling, for lack of anything else to do in a land that has been virtually purged of Jews.

The present time of narration merges subtly into the past time of narrated events, as the narrator explains a mission on which he was sent by Asmodeus, the head of the demons. Like a prevalent postwar type, the existentialist, Singer's demon finds itself thrown into a world it has not chosen. This elaborate scenario serves as a background against which Singer questions the changing realities of good and evil.

The narrator meets a companion spirit that is disguised as a spider. Together, the two demons represent two periods in Jewish history. The demon in the form of a spider is an old-fashioned, pre-Enlightenment cliché, while the narrator is a sophisticated, twentieth-century demon from Lublin. As does **"The Mirror,"** this story represents a world of temptations and ensnarements. Yet the perspective has changed, for all is re-viewed from an indefinite time after the Holocaust. The plot centers around efforts to lead an irreproachable, pious Rabbi astray. The two demons bemoan the transformed state of even the prewar world: in the small towns, the sins are paltry; and in the cities, sin is so universal as to have lost its meaning. Worst of all is the rise of so-called Enlightenment. The more sophisticated demon comments that

> In the two hundred years since you've been sitting here, the evil inclination has cooked up a fresh porridge. There have arisen writers among the Jews, in Hebrew and Yiddish, and they have taken over our trade. . . . They know all our tricks.

This explicit association of writers and demons underlines the allegory at the heart of the story. Modern writing itself has a demonic side, especially to the extent that it strives to displace God's language, the Torah. Yet on the level of represented actions, the story remains a pseudo-medieval tale, a *mayse,* Singer employs deliberately archaic effects in order to set his narratives in the context of religious and literary tradition.

The dialogues between the Rabbi and the demon (who masquerades as Elijah the Prophet) are like internal debates held by the Rabbi with himself. Once again, this emphasizes the psychological significance of traditional Jewish spirits. A further scene of tempting dialogue suggests that language itself acts as tempter. While the Rabbi is involved in studying the Talmud, the narrator distracts him with forbidden thoughts. If the demon is a stand-in for the writer, then in one sense this scene presents the comedy of an author taunting his fictional character. But the Rabbi, who as a commentator resembles a literary critic, fights off the onslaughts of his invisible enemies.

In **"The Mirror"** vanity causes Tsirl's fall, and in-**"The Last Demon"** pride almost defeats the Rabbi of Tishevits. The demon nearly convinces the Rabbi that a scholar of his merits should not be content to study interminably; he should put aside the Talmud and work directly to bring the Messiah. In a drama of traditional proportions, the Rabbi unmasks the demon by asking to see its feet. Because demons always have the feet of geese, the demon must deny his request, and so reveal its identity. The demon's predicament is subtly and profoundly comic: in Yiddish, the word *gendzn-fislekh* means both "goose's feet" and "quotation marks." Asking for proof of the demon's authenticity, the Rabbi discovers that it is a mere quotation, an unsatisfactory imitation of sacred texts. No wonder! Demons and writers of the modern world have learned to dress up their sacrilege in the most pious-sounding language. And so, when the fraud is discovered, the demon narrator is condemned to a barren life in the ruined city of Tishevits.

The narrator returns to present time, describing its futile life as an obsolete evil inclination. If Jews and Jewish life die out, the spirits that formerly plagued them must also die. In the narrator's perception, the Holocaust appears to have destroyed the meaning of evil, at least as it was capable of being understood in traditional Jewish terms. Not only did the Nazis destroy the Jews; they destroyed the spoken language in which the Ashkenazic tradition existed. A more critical view might add that the prior temptation of assimilation—both cultural and linguistic—anticipated the physical destruction of European Jewry.

The life of the narrator is the life of an author, or of a language, whose world has collapsed. This is, clearly, the way in which Singer conceived himself. What more remains? Only those persistent Yiddish letters: the murderers have not succeeded in destroying the Hebrew alphabet which nourishes the demon narrator. As if to show off the productive power of language, the narrator composes a brief acrostic, which is even more untranslatable than the rest of the story. For the letter *Yud,* the narrator asserts, "A yid fargest"—"A Jew forgets." Singer suggests that, despite the essentially unbridgeable gap between the prewar European diaspora and postwar Jewish existence, our task is to continue to nurture and to be nourished by the Yiddish language. The very least we can do is to write and speak Yiddish. For "without a Yiddish letter," the story ends, "a demon is undone."

Through the personae of supernatural narrators, Singer appears to ask: How can Jews and Yiddish continue to live after the destruction of European Jewry? The old religious world is gone from Tishevits, and with it the mother tongue. Yiddish lives on in scattered communities and in books; the demon, like a Yiddish writer, lives off the textual past. Worse, like a writer who has no readers, the demon can only play with words. Yet the fiction ends on a note of affirmation: in order to survive, Jews, or Jewish writers, must keep Yiddish alive.

In these monologues of demons, the role of monologue has

been transformed: it is no longer a man who speaks alone and for himself, but rather a figure representative of language. The monological voice in **"The Last Demon"** speaks for all of us (perhaps as monologists) in a post-Holocaust world. If Yiddish preserves our contact with the past, Singer observes that Jewish consciousness continues to evolve insofar as Yiddish literature carries the textual traditions further.

How, then, can we understand the monologues of spirits in Singer's work? The demon has been unmasked; its form turns out to be a mere quotation. As a post-Holocaust author, Singer strives to make the past present, to memorialize the traditional Jewish past. On a less personal level, the demonic narratives give voice to the Yiddish language itself, which calls to us from the ruins. But given the diversity of the modern world, we are overwhelmed by an apocalyptic din of—not monologue, but—polylogue. Beyond these conflicting voices we may sense the distant echo of a more familiar voice without sound. Straining to hear, we begin to grasp the intrinsic power of words. Language transcends the individuality of men and women, and continues to live on after their community is destroyed. In the space left by the demise of demons, the spirit of Yiddish is engaged in a battle to receive a hearing: Yiddish is the solitary spirit that speaks through Singer's monologues. For the Jews of today, the transcendence that speaks most hauntingly, from a limbo between life, death, and rebirth, is Yiddish, our neglected *mame-loshn.*

Grace Farrell Lee (essay date Fall 1985)

SOURCE: "Isaac Bashevis Singer: Mediating Between the Biblical and the Modern," in *Modern Language Studies,* Vol. 15, No. 4, Fall, 1985, pp. 117-23.

[*In the following essay, Lee examines Singer's use of Biblical metaphors to confront profound existential dilemmas. Drawing comparison to Albert Camus's* The Myth of Sisyphus, *Lee contends that Singer's fiction is "an uneasy meditation between the Biblical image of God who hides his face and the modern image of a cosmos empty of transcendent meaning."*]

Isaac Bashevis Singer's short story **"Old Love"** concludes as Harry Bendiner, eighty-two year old millionaire, survivor of three wives and two children, dreams of meditating in a solitary British Columbian tent with the daughter of a dead love on why a man is born and why he must die. In one way or another each of Singer's stories is a variation on this essential meditation, and the exiled meditant is the prototypical Singer character. The questions posed by the meditant and the exile he endures are intimately connected;

for while the questions concern a search for a source of meaning which might explain the mystery of mortality, the exile can be defined as the separation of humankind from that source of meaning. Ultimately, to find answers to one's questions is to be redeemed from one's exile.

In *The Myth of Sisyphus,* Camus defined that modern phenomenon, absurdity, in terms of exile. He tells us that we confront our exile in a universe which does not yield up answers to our question of "why?" He writes, "A world that can be explained even with bad reasons is a familiar world. But, on the other hand, in a universe suddenly divested of illusions and lights, man feels an alien, a stranger. His exile is without remedy since he is deprived of the memory of a lost home or the hope of a promised land. This divorce between man and his life, the actor and his setting, is properly the feeling of absurdity." The exiled meditant, deprived of a promised land, while recognizable as an essential figure in Camus and much of modern literature, certainly has its metaphorical echoes in Biblical material. I. B. Singer, perhaps more so than any other serious contemporary writer, utilizes Biblical metaphors not only to confront the "ultimate questions," but also to discover the possibility of finding answers to them. In the process we find in Singer's fiction an uneasy mediation between the Biblical image of a God who hides his face and the modern image of a cosmos empty of transcendent meaning.

It is a dangerous mediation, for the specter of God cancels the profound cosmic emptiness which is the essence of the modern vision. But an absent God who hides his face provides metaphoric ambivalences which Singer uses to enrich, with a bit of uncertainty, the dogmatic starkness of the contemporary view. It is dangerous in yet another way, for a fundamentalist reading of Singer can lead to the all too easy dismissal of him as other than modern, a criticism which he has learned to ignore, but which I would rather put into a new perspective. For, although their cries are couched in religious terms, as his characters, like Job, search out their elusive God, Singer evokes a universe akin to that of modern secular absurdists, a place where humankind appears to be exiled from any source of meaning and where the phenomenal world forever disintegrates about us.

While Camus' modern man bewails a universe which remains silent in the face of human questioning, and while the Biblical Job may shake his fist toward a hidden God, Singer creates a cacophony of voices shouting to the universe, each posing questions in its own human way. "How high is the sky? How deep is the earth? What's at the other side of the end of the world? Who made God?" "'How is it possible, after all, that someone should simply vanish? How can someone who lived, loved, hoped, and wrangled with God and with himself just disappear?'" Why must God be concealed? How can evil and suffering be explained? Why are innocent children tormented with pain? Why is God silent in the face of misery? For what were we born and why must we die?

Like the townspeople of Krasnobród who ponder and explain, yet never discover the truth, "Because if there is such a thing as truth it is as intricate and hidden as a crown of feathers," so Singer's characters speculate—humorously, morosely, endlessly. In *Enemies: A Love Story* Herman Broder suggests in despair, "Wasn't it possible that a Hitler presided on high and inflicted suffering on imprisoned souls?" Or perhaps, a dybbuk whispers to Morris Feitelzohn in *Shosha,* "God suffers from a kind of divine amnesia that made Him lose the purpose of His creation.... God tried to do too much in too short an eternity. He has lost both criterion and control and is badly in need of help.... I see Him as a very sick God, so bewildered by His galaxies and the multitude of laws He established that He doesn't know what He aimed for to start with."

Sometimes it seems that the only truth is that with which the narrator concludes **"Neighbors":** "The radiator near which I sat hissed and hummed: 'Dust, dust, dust.' The sing-song penetrated my bones together with the warmth. It repeated a truth as old as the world, as profound as sleep."

Singer's novel *Shosha* ends as two friends, exiled in Tel Aviv after the Holocaust, sit in a darkening room, waiting, as one says with a laugh, for an answer. Their final conversation expresses feelings of abandonment and resentment in a world devoid of revelation. Haiml says,

> "If God is wisdom, how can there be foolishness? And if God is life, how can there be death? I lie at night, a little man, a half-squashed fly, and I talk with the dead, with the living, with God—if He exists—and with Satan, who certainly does exist. I ask them, 'What need was there for all this?' and I wait for an answer. What do you think, Tsutsik, is there an answer somewhere or not?"

> "No, no answer."

> "Why not?"

> "There can't be any answer for suffering—not for the sufferer."

> "In that case, what am I waiting for?"

> Genia opened the door. "Why are you two sitting in the dark, eh?"

> Haiml laughed. "We're waiting for an answer."

Singer here speaks of humankind as Isaiah spoke of the

Children of Israel: "we wait for light, but behold obscurity; for brightness, but we walk in darkness. We grope for the wall like the blind, and we grope as if we had no eyes: we stumble at noon day as in the night, we are in desolate places as dead men." With its almost Beckett-like despair of waiting, the ending of *Shosha* also becomes a metaphor for the modern condition. Darkness spreads throughout the room as it spreads throughout Singer's stories and his universe; yet, as *Shosha* ends, the two men still sit in the midst of the darkness waiting in exile for an answer, an answer which they fear will never come. Yet still they wait.

Singer creates fiction which has the power to make us know that we all wait. We wait in exile for an answer, or, like Gimpel the Fool, we wait for the true world where even Gimpel will not be deceived and where revelation will be more than a faint glimmer in a darkened room.

Harry Bendiner of **"Old Love"** waits in his plastic chaise, on his balcony eleven stories up from Miami Beach, brooding in solitude on how he is "condemned to live alone and to die alone." The Angel of Death had taken his family from him, but Harry, as suspicious as he is rich, completes the process which death began by exiling himself from any but the most casual of human contacts. Through a series of paltry fantasies, he experiences the world as hostile and threatening: "Maybe someone was following him. Maybe some crook had found out how rich he was and was scheming to kidnap him. Although the day was bright and the street full of people, no one would interfere if he was grabbed, forced into a car, and dragged off to some ruin or cave. No one would pay ransom for him." Harry's fears are so insistent, and for the most part so unfounded, that they create an edge of amusement which serves to exile even the reader somewhat from this lonely old man whose paranoia is tinged with self-pity.

> **Singer creates fiction which has the power to make us know that we all wait. We wait in exile for an answer, or, like Gimpel the Fool, we wait for the true world where even Gimpel will not be deceived and where revelation will be more than a faint glimmer in a darkened room.**
>
> **—Grace Farrell Lee**

His whining fears are symptomatic of a profound struggle within Harry Bendiner. As each of his days takes on a shape like all the others—breakfast, elevator, mail, checks, stock exchange office or bank, nap, dinner—Harry's routine is punctuated by a single, simple question: "Why go on living?" This question, always threatening to break through the surface of his life, becomes the center of the story.

Camus' absurd man finds many echoes in the aged Harry Bendiner. Camus tells us that the "state set" which is the fragile surface of our lives can collapse suddenly when the question "why?" emerges. Like Harry Bendiner, Camus' everyman moves through his day:

> Rising, streetcar, four hours in the office or the factory, meal, streetcar, four hours of work, meal, sleep, and Monday Tuesday Wednesday Thursday Friday and Saturday according to the same rhythm—this path is easily followed most of the time. But one day the "why" arises and everything begins in that weariness tinged with amazement. "Begins"—this is important. Weariness comes at the end of the acts of a mechanical life, but at the same time it inaugurates the impulse of consciousness. It awakens consciousness and provokes what follows.

What follows is our recognition of the irrationality of the world, of the strangeness of the world. That which was once familiar is now alien and distant. We begin to feel the separateness of our reality from that of all others. We begin to confront our exile in an absurd universe.

Job, too, reduced to a leprous beast, stripped of children and property, no longer certain of his connection with anything beyond the limits of his own mortality, he too is finally forced out of a life which provided him with comfortable answers and into a confrontation with the ambiguities of human existence. "What is man," Job asks, "that thou makest much of him / and turnest thy thoughts towards him, / only to punish him morning by morning / or to test him every hour of the day?" This cry of anguish was once an easily answered question. Personally, Job was a good and upright man; socially, he had status as a successful property owner and father; metaphysically, he was in close dialogue with his God. Such complacent, superficial answers are ready-made by social and religious structures for Job, for Harry Bendiner, and for every person who does not wish to look deeply into the 'ultimate' questions and to face the awesomeness and the terrors which lie beneath the surfaces of reality.

Such a confrontation is one which Harry Bendiner would rather avoid; ". . . one couldn't constantly brood," he says, "about the fact that everything was vanity of vanities. It was easier to think about practical matters." The practical, commercial world of Miami, thickly people with those who ask "to buy or not to buy," reveals, in this playfully obvious allusion to *Hamlet,* the essence of human questioning. "Man is no more than a puff of wind, / his days a passing shadow," says the Psalmist; "a foul and pestulent congregation of vapors" it oftentimes seems to Hamlet. Singer literalizes Shakespeare's disease metaphors, and for Harry Bendiner

the questions of philosophy are outshouted by the complaints of an aged body; the functioning of his bowels becomes more important than the workings of the universe. For Hamlet, Denmark is a prison, and he could count himself king of infinite space tho' surrounded by a nutshell, if he had not bad dreams. But Harry Bendiner is imprisoned within his apartment, isolated from all those around him, fearful of the world outside, and he cannot remember his dreams; they "dissolved like foam." Harry is exiled from that deep dream world of his own self.

It is the chance encounter with love—for an elderly neighbor, Ethel, who soon throws herself to her death from a window—which wrenches Harry from his immersion in the materialism of the world to face the questions which lie in wait for every human being. Ethel's friendship makes him realize how lonely he has been and how empty is his world. Separated from her by only the thin walls of their apartments, Harry finally acknowledges that "walls possess a power of their own."

Harry Bendiner comes to a point where the questions do break through the surface of his life and he wants to direct the rest of his days to them. Although we leave him just as he was when first sighted, sitting in his plastic chaise on his balcony eleven stories up from Miami Beach, he has been transformed. Where once he brooded upon his personal exile, Harry has come to recognize a larger exile, one which, paradoxically, can be shared and, thus, in the very act of that sharing, overcome.

Job is also forced from his complacency to find the path which is his existence walled up. Harry had felt the thin walls of his apartment assume a power of their own, and, in "Absurd Walls," Camus reminds us of the nature of walls. They are the limitations of our existence, limitations which culminate in death, limitations which we long to transcend in some meaningful way. Job is forced to acknowledge his mortal limitations and his longing to transcend them. But the resentment Job feels towards his God renders him incapable of the prayerful dialogue which once was the sustenance of his life. He feels abandoned by a God who has retreated from him, who has "hidden his face," and who can no longer be found. Job is in exile from his God.

The absence of God from Job's world is the spiritual equivalent of the secular dilemma defined by Camus. Absurdity, Camus tells us, is the questor's confrontation with a universe which does not give forth an answer, which remains silent in the face of human questioning. This silent universe is the same as that confronted by Job and by each of Singer's characters: by "Tsutsik" and Haiml as they wait in their darkening room, by Harry Bendiner as he lies belching and hiccupping on his bed, unable to comprehend the suicide of his newfound love, unable to know day from dream, unable anymore to perform those rituals of his mechanical life:

> Well, from now on I won't hope for anything, he decided with the solemnity of a man taking an oath. He felt cold, and he covered himself with the blanket. . . . That day Harry Bendiner did not go down for his mail. He did not prepare breakfast for himself, nor did he bother to bathe and dress. He kept on dozing in the plastic chaise on the balcony and thinking about . . . Ethel's daughter—who was living in a tent in British Columbia. Why had she run away so far? he asked himself. Did her father's death drive her into despair? Could she not stand her mother? Or did she already at her age realize the futility of all human efforts and decide to become a hermit? Is she endeavoring to discover herself, or God? An adventurous idea came into the old man's mind: to fly to British Columbia, find the young woman in the wilderness, comfort her, be a father to her, and perhaps try to meditate together with her on why a man is born and why he must die.

While the silent universe of which Camus speaks is not necessarily a God-filled universe, the feelings of abandonment and resentment and alienation exist whether one looks up to the heavens and shakes a fist at an absent God or whether one sees an empty cosmos which does not provide answers to one's questions. These are two different contexts in which to express the same human predicament: Harry Bendiner, Camus' everyman, and Job are each alienated from a source of ultimate meaning. They cry out and there is no response to their anguish. They are each alone in a silent universe.

Of course the crucial difference between the modern and the Biblical models lies in the perspective each holds for the possibility of finding or receiving answers to the ultimate questions. Camus says that there is in humankind a "wild longing for clarity whose call echoes in the human heart." We need an answer to the question "why?" But this human need confronts again and again "the unreasonable silence of the world." Harry Bendiner confronts the silence and in so doing finds the questions towards which he dreams of directing his life. Job confronts the silence, but ultimately it is broken by the voice of a God who finally does reveal himself. Job again moves into dialogue with his God. He sought Him and he found Him. He questioned and he received an answer. The Book of Job ends with Job rejoicing as he is again blessed with property and children. Ironically, his answer is given in the same terms which had once blinded him to the awesome questions about the human condition. The nature of the answer given to Job is not sufficient; it does not touch upon the essence of his questioning.

As Singer says, "At the end Job is rewarded. He has more beautiful daughters and more donkeys and so on and so on, but we feel that this is not an answer to Job's suffering."

But even this renewed dialogue between humankind and the universe, however flawed, is not reached in modern literature. The silence continues; the abandonment deepens. Singer makes metaphorical use of the image of God's removal of himself from the universe to express the modern person's longing for transcendence and our inability to find it, our feelings of abandonment and of exile. That God is hidden means that our source of meaning, that which can provide answers to our questions of "why?," that which can give significance to us beyond the mortal limitations of our lives, cannot be found.

Maimonides, in the twelfth century *Guide of the Perplexed* discusses many aspects of God's hiddenness which Singer plays upon in his fiction. To see the face of God, Maimonides explains, indicates an apprehension of the nature of God, a knowledge which is "inaccessible in its very nature. . . . *But My face shall not be seen* [means] that the true reality of My existence as it veritably is cannot be grasped." This Biblical image can thus express the modern perspective that in their very nature the answers to humankind's questions are inaccessible. The "wild longing for clarity whose call echoes in the human heart" can never be satisfied. The universe is incomprehensible. To see the face of God is a metaphor expressing the acquisition of ultimate knowledge. And the image of God's hiddenness is the correlative of the silence of the universe in the face of the human need to know. The human predicament, then, is both irresolvable and absurd, for the silence is irrevocable and it defies the questioning nature of humankind.

But to have the face of God hidden also indicates, Maimonides says, "a privation of providence [which] leaves one abandoned and a target to all that may happen and come about . . . And just as the withdrawal of providence is referred to as the *hiding of the face*—as in its dictum: *As for Me, I will surely hide My face*—it also is referred to as *going,* which has the meaning to turn away from a thing. Thus Scripture says: *I will go and return to My place.*" The hiding of God's face then is an expression of the emotional dilemma humankind faces, alone, separate, exiled. And the withdrawal of God from the universe expresses the abandonment humankind feels, lost in a universe which is intractable in the face of the human need for significance.

Maimonides also explains that to see God's face is to speak to God, to be in dialogue with God, "as a presence to another presence without an intermediary . . . *Face* is also an adverb of place that is rendered in Arabic by the words: 'in front of thee' or 'in thy presence.'" To have the face of God hidden is the ultimate expression of exile—to not be there, or to have that place of meaning removed from where one is.

In Singer's hands the hidden face of God becomes a central image of intricate complexity. The inaccessibility of God, his facelessness, his silence, his exile from humankind, and humankind's exile from him create the symbolic context of Singer's fiction. But while his work draws upon religious images, its significance is not limited to a religious context. The religious functions as an overall symbol system which enables Singer to explore the complexities of the human condition and to confront not only the traditional problems of faith and doubt, the existence of evil and the inexplicable mystery of creation but also those typically modern concerns of alienation, which is exile, and absurdity, which is silence.

But Singer's mediation between the Biblical and the modern is an uneasy mediation. He uses Biblical material metaphorically in a way which deepens our understanding of what has come to be seen as the modern dilemma. But inherent in the Biblical material, no matter the context in which it is used, is hope—hope that the exile may be eased, hope that the silence may be breached, hope that our disbelief may prove to be unnecessary. It is this which distinguishes Singer from his contemporaries, this quality of hope, this belief that no matter how dark the night, we ought to sit and wait, for anything is possible.

Israel Shenker (essay date 11 August 1991)

SOURCE: "The Man Who Talked Back to God: Isaac Bashevis Singer, 1904-1991," in *The New York Times Book Review,* August 11, 1991, p. 11.

[*In the following essay, Shenker recounts Singer's views on God, contemporary literature, and his own writing.*]

His mind teemed with eternal questions and with plain-spoken answers. In talk and in writing he was forthright and intense, not a tentative rose water soul given to pallid thought and halfhearted expression. What he conveyed was the burden of experience shaped by trials, transformed by imagination, weighted by reflection, leavened by humor. Part prophet, part scold, writer of genius, ironist, pessimist and cynic, he did not seem to vaunt his superiority but appeared inoffensive and vulnerable. Had there been a contest for the palest, least colorful man on New York's Upper West Side, Isaac Bashevis Singer would have been the odds-on favorite. He looked like a worker in a matzob factory,

as though he had always lived indoors, a thin, fragile creature who shunned sunlight and ever fresh air, the sort who would mumble his daily prayers.

From his early days in Warsaw to his death in Florida last month at the age of 87, Singer had a peculiar relationship to God: man to Man, personal and frank, sometimes unforgiving. "The belief that man can do what he wants, without God, is as far from me as the North Pole," he said as we waited too patiently to be served at a Jewish dairy restaurant. It was our first meeting, in 1968, when I was interviewing him for *The New York Times,* and I was trying to clear my mind of the prevailing thought Someday my blintz will come.

"I don't think religion should be connected with dogma or revelation," Singer continued. "Since he's a silent God, he talks in deeds, in events, and we have to learn this language. The belief in God is as necessary as sex. Whatever you call him—nature or higher power—doesn't matter. The power that takes care of you, and the farthest star, all this is God.

"The Almighty keeps promising things, and He doesn't keep his word," he went on. "What hasn't He promised us Jews! It took him 2,000 years to get us to Israel. Maybe the politicians will also keep their promises after 2,000 years. One thing is clear: our nature will be exactly the same. A man will park his car on the moon and live on Madison Avenue, but he will have the same appetites and the same *tsuris* [troubles]."

If God had been a little less almighty, Singer suggested, the All Powerful would have tried to explain to victims why they suffer, not just let them do all the guesswork. Why did God always have to move in mysterious ways? What could have been more outlandish than having a gifted author like Singer, so easy to appreciate, write in a language like Yiddish, which so few could understand? Singer told of a Yiddish bookstore proprietor who had a double lock on his door. "I'm not afraid of people stealing," the bookseller explained. "I'm afraid some author breaks in and leaves more of his books here."

Yet here was one of these potential burglars, condemned to obscurity in the pages of *The Daily Forward,* the Yiddish-language newspaper in New York where his fiction appeared beginning in 1935, who went on to win the Nobel Prize in Literature in 1978, showing that Yiddish could pay off in more than tears or laughter. It took the entire 81 years since its founding for *The Forward* to announce the good news from Stockholm with a headline that warmed even those Jewish hearts grown cold with disappointments: "ISAAC BASHEVIS SINGER BEGINS HIS NOBEL LECTURE IN YIDDISH."

The Forward told its readers that the event marked the first time in history that the Swedish Academy had heard Yiddish. This is a language of remote origin and constant improvement. Its vocabulary and associations shift from country to country, and its meaning depends greatly on the speaker's tone. Only superficially does Yiddish resemble Swedish. Swedish is a vernacular confined to parts of Scandinavia, but Yiddish can be misunderstood all over the world.

In time Singer stopped delivering his Yiddish in person to the newspaper office, and his stories and the installments of his novels arrived by mail or even by messenger. He had finally acquired a typewriter, so it was an even greater pleasure for his editors to read him. In the beginning was the word, he conceded, after we had known each other for a while, but in the end was garbage. "A big publisher has 10 or 12 editors, and each editor is anxious to find any little girl who writes about her aunt sleeping with soldiers, so he can hail the work of genius. Publishers sell it for hard covers and soft covers, and they should sell it for slip covers."

"When a book comes into print today, suddenly there are 10 false witnesses to testify it is the greatest which has ever appeared," he complained. "If I were Moses today, I'd add to the commandment not to bear false witness another one. 'Don't praise your neighbor's bad writing.' Even if there were some good writers, they'd be lost in this muddy ocean of false praise. Instead of saying good is good and bad is bad, the critics say bad is good."

"If our supermarkets gave us stale bread or bad cheese or sour milk, there would be an outcry," he said. "But our literary supermarkets have lost all responsibility and we say nothing. I'm told there are many newspapers which do not take false ads. If I want to advertise that a sandwich I sell will give eternal life, they will not print this ad. When bad books are praised to heaven, someone should veto these ads."

The blintzes finally arrived, delivered by a surly waitress. "I'm sure if the Messiah would come, she would still be angry," Singer said "She'd say, 'Hurry up. I'm waiting for the Resurrection.' The real trouble will come with the Resurrection. If you look obsolete to your son of 14, how obsolete will you look to your father Abraham?"

In 1962 Singer wrote a short story called **"The Son"** that told of his meeting with the son whom he had not seen in 20 years. Eventually that son, Israel Zamir, whose Hebraic surname means "songbird," published in a Tel Aviv newspaper his own version of the meeting. Singer told him he had some good phrases, but that while in English the clichés would have been young and in Hebrew they were sacred, they were still clichés.

Almost miraculously, Singer preserved his own style and his own concerns against the erosion of his voluntary exile in the United States. He said he needed three conditions to write a story: a real topic, an account with beginning, middle and end; a desire to write it; and the illusion that only he could write it, not Bellow or Mailer. "Fortunately, I have to force myself not to write," said the author of 30 books and innumerable short stories. "I get up every morning with a desire to sit down and work. My imagination has been overstimulated all my life by life itself."

"God has given me so many fantasies that my problem is not how to get them but how to get rid of them," he told me once, speaking by long-distance phone. He also complained of short-distance hazards. Sometimes his wife, Alma, interrupted, and then, as he said, "Wives of writers have the inclination to put a plate of chicken soup down on manuscripts."

He shied from chicken soup—and chickens—and became a devoted vegetarian. From childhood on he had seen that might makes right, that man is stronger than chicken—man eats chicken, not vice versa. That bothered him, for there was no evidence that people were more important than chickens. When he lectured on life and literature there were often dinners in his honor, and sympathetic hosts served vegetarian meals. "So, in a very small way, I do a favor for the chickens," Singer said. "If I will ever get a monument, chickens will do it for me."

Dan Miron (essay date Winter 1992)

SOURCE: "Passivity and Narration: The Spell of Bashevis Singer," translated by Uriel Miron, in *Judaism*, Vol. 41, No. 1, Winter, 1992, pp. 6-17.

[*In the following essay, Miron contends that Singer's fiction is not typical of contemporary Yiddish literature, citing the fatalistic passivity and underlying nihilism in his work as the major point of divergence. According to Miron, Singer's characters portray a "human existence that runs from birth without will to a death without choice."*]

Isaac Bashevis Singer, last of the great Yiddish story-tellers, passed away at a ripe old age, crowned with international success and renown. His death seems to carry a note of half-reconciled farewell to a rich and vital literary tradition that won neither the appreciation nor the longevity that it deserved.

The beginnings of this tradition appeared about a hundred and thirty years ago in the form of the juvenile works in Yiddish of Mendele Moykher-Sforim and Yitschak Yoel

Linetsky: *The Pupil* [eye], *The Magic Ring, Fishke the Lame,* and *The Polish Lad.* From these roots Yiddish fiction flowered into its "classical" age with the mature Mendele Moykher-Sforim, Sholem Aleichem and Peretz. The decades between the two World Wars saw the great branching out of this tradition in the works of maestros like Dovid Bergelson, Der Nister and Moshe Kulbak, and in many other talented writers, such as Sholem Asch, Itshe Meir Weissberg, Yonah Rosenfeld, Yisrael Yehoshua Singer, Yosef Opatoshu, E. M. Fuchs and their colleagues. During the war and after it, in the dark, final days of Stalin's rule, the Yiddish literary tradition succumbed to the axe-blows of murderers and tyrants, and now it seems to have reached its final hour. In the long chain of brilliant and colorful reflections, highly diverse and yet complementary, of the life of the Jewish Ashkenazi tribe of eastern Europe as it was mirrored in the minds of the tribe's most talented members, soaked through with the essential juices of its unique historical presence and yet cut loose from their cultural moorings, open to the culture of their times—in this chain the final link has been closed.

These days, it is said, prophecy is the privilege of fools alone, and this rule may apply even to the prophecy regarding the future of the Yiddish tongue and its literature. Nevertheless, it seems safe to say that the spiritual-literary reality that found its last concentrated expression in the works of Bashevis Singer is no longer. This was clear to all, long before Bashevis himself reached the pinnacle of his literary successes with the receiving of the Nobel prize for literature in 1978. This witty, skeptical Jew, devoid of all pathos and full of humor, who combined sarcasm with tragedy and fatalism, traveled across the American and international literary scene like a "last of his kind." The international cultural community that lavished its appreciation upon him (as opposed to the servings of envy and hatred that he received from the rapidly shrinking Yiddishist cultural establishment), did so, of course, because of his ability to tell stories that conquered hearts almost in any language, and in any place where they were told but it did so, among other reasons, as a gesture of farewell to a literary culture that was rich and vital in its day, and as a gesture of grief and regret for the horrifying circumstances that brought that culture to the point of extinction. Isaac Bashevis was the last great emissary of the kingdom of Yiddish to the world of western culture in the second half of the twentieth century.

Because of this historical representivity, which, by the way, was thrust upon Bashevis neither to his benefit nor by his consent, and without taking his qualities and character into account (he possessed none of the attributes of a "cultural leader"), it is perhaps fitting that we turn our attention to the fact that he was *not* actually a typical representative of modern Yiddish literary culture. Even though he grew up in the heart of this culture during the peak of its development in Poland, in the period between the two World Wars, he remained a stranger and an oddity within it. This, and not just the almost insane personal envy, might be the reason for the suspicion and even aversion with which he was held by the Yiddishist establishment.

In its essence, the difference between Bashevis' work and the whole of the modern Yiddish literary corpus (apart from a few very narrow and marginal segments of it) reveals itself in one crucial aspect. Bashevis approached the act of literary creation with a base-experience of underlying awareness that falls under the sign of fatalism and nihilism. Human existence and, certainly, Jewish existence appeared to him suffused with evil and suffering, torn apart from within by internal conflicts that cannot be resolved, pervaded by an absurdity both comical and tragic. Moreover, he was convinced that any organized effort to correct and improve man's lot, any will to guide it towards some "salvation" according to an ideological-eschatological program, was doomed to failure. Not only would such efforts fail to right life's wrongs, they would even increase the suffering and evil to the point of holocaust. Bashevis "understood" the twentieth century as an age in which a suffering humanity was forced to follow lethal ideological-eschatological agendas which gave birth to a murderousness unequaled in viciousness and horror by any evil known to man throughout all of history. He was opposed with all his heart (and even that without pathos and with the awareness that opposition itself was hopeless) to any eschatological human organization and especially Soviet and international Communism, and almost to the same degree any Jewish eschatological movement such as Zionism, national socialism (the *Bund*), etc. The only spiritual position that he accepted was passive-fatalistic. By adopting this stance a person might achieve a certain "saintliness," to the degree that he or she gives up from the very start any attempt to control his or her own destiny, let alone that of others, and this out of the awareness of the moral superiority of surrender over initiative or over the desire to steer the course of events in the "desired" direction. Bashevis' "saint" is the "fool" who is not a fool at all. Gimpel the Fool, the hero of his early story of the same name, that, in its superb English translation by Saul Bellow, opened for Bashevis the door through which he could address the American and international audiences and capture their hearts, is in the framework of the Bashevian story-telling art, the most complete human being. He is not the fool that those who exploit him throughout his entire life believe him to be. He sees through their lies. He knows of their malice towards him. He knows that his wife is deceiving him and that his children are not of his seed. He knows full well that he has always been cheated and exploited in everything, yet he accepts this state of affairs in his awareness that any response on his part would only serve to increase the wickedness and suffering.

In the eyes of Bashevis, Gimpel is the archetypical Jew, just as he is the embodiment of the Yiddish language—a language with no territory, no protection, no cultural-political alliances, no prestige and no army or any military terminology—the language of the weak, the victims. It is as a representative of *this* Yiddish and its speakers that Bashevis trod the paths of the modern world of power-struggles and protest, the world of the demanders of rights and the "discrimination-gruntled." As such an emissary he reached Stockholm to receive the Nobel prize for literature and, likewise, he arrived in Israel for his famous conversation with Menachem Begin, in which he demonstrated to the prime-minister how ridiculous military pomp would be if it were carried out in Yiddish. Neither Begin nor the Israeli public caught on that, in his ironic-humorous way, Bashevis was expressing his reservations towards Israel as an authentic Jewish entity, as though he were saying: A real, authentic Jew who thinks and behaves as you do, my dear Israeli friends, is nothing but a joke, an incongruity, a Yeshiva-Boher brandishing a sword and clutching a general's staff as if it were a broom-stick.

In the eyes of Bashevis, Gimpel is the archetypical Jew, just as he is the embodiment of the Yiddish language—a language with no territory, no protection, no cultural-political alliances, no prestige and no army or any military terminology—the language of the weak, the victims.

—*Dan Miron*

This moral and philosophical position (not, however, the opposition to Zionism itself) was utterly alien to the mainstream of the new Yiddish literature. Like much of modern Jewish culture, the central tradition of Yiddish literature had sprung out of the opposition to what appeared to be the inertia and passivity of the old, traditional Jewish way of life. This is not the forum for a deliberation of the degree of truth in the claims made over the last two-hundred years against Jewish inertia and passivity. Modern Jewish culture and the new Yiddish literature as a whole operated under the assumption that the Jewish people, who had for centuries refused to take an active part in the formation of history, and had thus relegated themselves to the passive position in its most extreme sense (the position of the victim), must break out of their national passivity. To achieve this they must also abandon their static adherence to the religious-halakhic tradition, to which they clung in their effort to preserve their distinctiveness and exclusiveness and to worship their God (their only *desiderali*). This new culture and literature asserted that the Jewish nation must open its world to humanistic ideas that place man, his values, qualities and needs, at the center of life and culture: ideas that point towards ways of attending to these needs while improving man's qualities and realizing the positive potential hidden in the "human condition."

Modern Jewish culture demanded that the people of Israel apprehend life through the lens of humanism, and by this willful act of comprehension break through to the heart of historical becoming. It hoped for the awakening of a national will ("Awake my people, how long will you slumber?"), recommended activity, vigor readiness to struggle and effort to change. Yiddish literature endorsed these recommendations with the best of its talents, all of its earthy vivacity and all of the immediacy of its contact with the Jewish masses. When Yiddish literature sprang from the ideological soil of the Enlightenment (*Haskalah*) in the nineteenth century, or when it reflected, at the turn of the century, the birth of modern Jewish nationalism, or when it played a central role, later in the twentieth century, in the burgeoning Jewish socialist movements, its call to the Jewish people was a call for change and awakening. The voice of this call was not mitigated even when this literature appeared to be clinging with nostalgia to the popular-traditional Jewish milieu with its religio-cultural underpinnings and its colorful folklore which had already acquired an "exotic" flavor, as it were. It can be shown that Y. L. Peretz's hassidic tales and folk-like-legends, for example, not only infuse the pseudo-folk narrative material with modern humanist referents, but also cast doubts upon the validity of the traditional culture that they presumed to represent or duplicate, and even undermine it. The call of Yiddish literature was not just against halakhic-religious rule and the control which it exerted over every aspect of Jewish life, or against hassidic supernaturalism (although these did inform a major part of its message throughout the nineteenth century); it was primarily directed against the passivity, weakness, inertia, and stagnation that encumbered any process of awakening or overcoming.

Into this cultural continuity, that cast its lot with change, will-power and "the courage to transform," entered Isaac Bashevis Singer, bringing with him both as innate qualities and as a fully developed world view, a deep distrust in human will-power and an absolute aversion for both the Nietzschean "will to power" and the liberal faith in "progress." He brought an aversion to any overly vigorous human activity—individual and even more so collective, national or class activity. He was suspicious of the motives of such activity and predicted catastrophic results for it. He didn't believe that penetration into the "heart of history," which was nothing more than the heart of a dark and murderous power struggle, would bring the people of Israel any profit, let alone relief. He was willing to accept—and this is very rare in both modern Yiddish literature and its Hebrew counterpart—complete passivity. Y. L. Peretz wrote the story "Bontshe Shweig" as a bitter satire on Jewish passivity, although it has also been given a sentimental, non-satiric interpretation in the service of which editors of readers and anthologies have seen fit to excise parts of the original text. (When Bontshe reaches the after-life and the heavenly court of justice offers him all the luxuries of the earth and the heavens, he is content to have a buttered roll.) Bashevis, however, took Bontshe to his heart, relieved him of his intellectual numbness, and transformed him into Gimpel the Fool. He accepted Bontshe's attitude as a moral and Jewish stance; he refused to accept Peretz's derision.

Sholem Aleichem, in his marvelous monologues (including the series of Tevye's monologues), presented archetypes of Jewish passivity: men and women in the gravest distress who experience terrible trials and are unable to envision a way of extricating themselves from their hellish situation, other than the act embodied in the telling of their tribulations in rich and digressive speech, a narration that advances in a nervous and absurd zigzag motion that, in itself, reveals the pattern of the scuttling from wall to wall of the prisoner who knows not how to break through his prison-walls. The great author's criticism lay in this very rhythm, arising from the words of geese-herdesses and Yeshiva-students still sitting at their in-laws' table, Jews who had supposedly won the lottery, or, on the contrary, Jews who had been "burned" and are suspected of having themselves acted out the blessing "*Barukh borei me'orei ha'esh*" (Blessed be the Creator of the fiery lights). Out of these frenzied monologues rises a cry that even the juiciest humor cannot conceal; a cry that calls, without the speaker's awareness, for change, for salvation. Bashevis, who in many respects carried on Sholem Aleichem's great art of the monologue to achievements that do not fall short of those of the creator of the model, also presented, in tens of monologues, situations of great distress, but deprived them utterly of the nervous, tortured rhythm, of the hopeless internal scrambling. In Bashevis' monologues the flow of speech is the tempestuous or relaxed flow of the human soul that is carried upon the waves of a current over which it has no control. The demons, great and small, that often make their voices heard in these monologues, are none other than expressions of the speaker's awareness that his or her attempt to fight the current will not end successfully. Bashevis' monologues are, in this respect, not just a continuation of Sholem-Aleichem's monologues but, also, their inversion.

There is a certain proximity between Bashevis and Agnon (reflected in the elegant insights that Bashevis made in his article on Agnon that was published in *The New York Times* on the occasion of Agnon's receiving the Nobel prize for literature, together with Nelly Sachs). Agnon love is given wholly to the lost man, the cornered individual who is passive and inarticulate, the victim of cruel manipulation at the hands of his environment, who is carried, willy-nilly, upon the waves of historical developments. He, too, in fact, introduced into Jewish literature the figure of the "fool" who is no fool, but is no resounding intellectual either. There is an intimate proximity between some of Bashevis' folk-heroes and Agnon's Ovadiah the Cripple, or between his most educated and aware heroes and Hershel Horovitz from Agnon's *A Simple Story* or Yitzhak Kummer from *Yesteryear*. The similarity is, however, limited and, actually, superficial. Agnon's work is shaped entirely by the powerful tension between a Zionist-religious belief in salvation and a dark, bitter, chilling disappointment in the heavenly order of the world and the slim chances that the people of Israel have of survival in the framework of this order. Agnon's passive heroes are tragic in the sense that, in the possible framework of a "correct" world order, their passivity would be appropriate and would produce no ill effects. The "wheel of time" that rolled off its axle is the force that crushes Agnon's heroes. Accordingly, if the Zionist effort were to bridge the pernicious rift between salvation and the savior (according to Agnon the world of the second *aliyah* was split into two groups: those who struggle for salvation but are estranged from God the savior, and those who attach themselves to the savior yet refuse to lift a finger for the sake of salvation), Yitzhak Kummer could have found his place between Jaffa and Jerusalem and would not have died insane. If the Jewish community that is described in *A Simple Story* were not dissociated both from the spirituality of authentic faith and from modern humanistic endeavor (and not devoted solely to provincial materialism), Hershel could have found a cure for his suffering either in the strength of religious faith or in the realization of his romantic love for Bluma—and would not have become, at the end of the story, a shell of a human fly that a spider has sucked dry of all vitality.

In Bashevis' work, on the contrary, passivity is not the result of a malfunction in the social or the cosmic mechanism; rather, it is the only correct stance in the face of the essential order (or disorder) of things, be they what they may, always and everywhere. Chaos is in a superior position everywhere. It engulfs man in tidal waves from without (historical events) and from within (lusts, perversities of character, internal conflicts, and unexplained distortions in the existential flow of the psyche). The conscious man (like the hero of *The Moskat Family*) faces reality and himself while gripped by boundless terror and curiosity. He knows full well that he can control neither himself nor his environment. He is bound to commit every possible blunder to which external circumstances and his own incomprehensible lusts and desires drive him. No rational life-plan of his will ever reach fruition; in all his actions he will always be swept, led, and discharged further and further towards some unclear goal determined by an unknown force; and, like that hero, Yehoshua Heshel Banet, so the rich and influential

Moskat family and the whole of Polish Jewry, in their journey towards extinction.

In many of Bashevis' novels and stories, this basic feature repeats itself: a person watches, as if from afar, his own existence driven by forces which he does not recognize or by wild currents that he cannot fathom. While, objectively, this person participates fully in the destructive activity which brings about his downfall, his subjective sense of existence is passive and semi-detached. Often, the author introduces some tragic occurrence which supposedly explains this separation between the objective and subjective "I", such as the death of Arturo, Max Barabander's only son in *Scum,* or the loss of Herman Broder's entire past (as a result of his experiences during World War II) in *Enemies: A Love Story.* However, this does not mean that Bashevis regards passivity and the paralysis of the will as characteristic of a certain type of person or as a result of a specific set of circumstances. Rather, the people who react this way to loss and bereavement, as Barabander and Broder do, represent for him the human norm.

Here, by the way, is the place to comment on the sexuality in Bashevis' stories which won him so many denunciations (the Yiddish critics could not swallow it, and some saw it as an intentional sullying of Jewish life by an author who was libeling his own people), and was thought of as the spice by which Bashevis contrived to "sell" his wares to his millions of readers. This last claim is, of course, utter hogwash. Explicit and implicit sexuality can be found in the works of hundreds of writers of whom only a handful achieved true popularity; sex itself has yet to sell a single scrap of paper outside of the prescribed and highly specific domain of the pornography industry and its audience. At any rate, even the presentation of sexuality in Bashevis' stories is entirely different from its presentation in the whole tradition of modern Jewish literature. In this tradition, sexuality appears—usually in a positive role—as the representative of an oppressed vitality, of an internal libidinal energy, individual and national, that was repressed by an ascetic culture and now, with the relaxing of that culture's norms, is capable of bursting out and realizing itself not just via pure sexuality, but also through a whole system of earthly and human pathways of vitality—even national, sovereign vitality. For Bashevis, sexuality is none other than that absurd force that pulsates within the human body and mind, and exerts its maddening influence which is intended to break apart any order in life, any logic and any rational intentionality. Humankind is subjugated by sexuality as it is subjugated by historical events.

Singer's attitude towards sex is actually compatible, up to a point, with that of traditional religious Puritanism, which identifies the sexual drive with the disruptive presence of Satan. However, whereas the religious tradition demands, if not complete repression, at least a channeling and controlling of sexual drives, Bashevis, in his fatalistic way, does not believe that such measures are possible. Accordingly, even in his stories that are set in traditional Jewish society, many of the characters are completely overwhelmed by their sexual instincts. His work is completely devoid of any moral imperative of continence, as it is devoid of didacticism.

Indeed, the halakhic code did make an heroic effort to assist Jews in conquering their sexuality and in ruling their lives by a transcendental and spiritual logic. This struggle, in Bashevis' view, was lost from the beginning, and became hopeless as historical events utterly undermined the power of the religious code. The demons had always haunted the abandoned cellars and attics of the Jewish psyche. With boundless cunning, patience, wisdom, humor, with threats and temptations, they diverted this psyche from its proper path. Now that the psyche has been all but murdered and hardly exists in the world, the demons remain, lonely and wretched, in the crumbling attics of the ruined homes of Israel. Together with the Yiddish language, they are fading away, becoming transparent, spiritual, ephemeral beings, melting into nothingness.

The sober, self-aware man in Bashevis' works, both those that unfold against an East-European background and those that take place in America (particularly in the American book of memoirs and, also, to a certain degree, the novel, *Enemies*)—this man is thrown about, surprised, from wave to wave like driftwood from a shipwreck on stormy seas. Each time he is taken by surprise anew, even though he knows that anything is possible in this existence of his. His only recourse is to wonder at the world and about the meaning of the will of "God," if such a one exists. He is distinguished by his power of memory, but his memories can neither guide nor teach him; they can only torture his soul. Often, the intellectual point of departure of the Bashevian protagonist is the teaching of Spinoza that interprets human existence and nature alike as expressions of the will and presence of God. This was the most logical philosophy for someone who had just emerged from the world of religious tradition. The typical Yeshiva student, having lost his faith in a personal God, clutches at the compromise of pantheism. The life experience of the Bashevian protagonist, however, completely negates Spinozian optimism. It points, rather, at an existence devoid of all will or directed divine presence. Thus, a kind of philosophical debate is built into the stories; but, the Spinozan way of thinking does not really represent in this dispute a positive or even possible alternative. It merely constitutes a connecting link between the guileless religious faith that the traditional Jew carries over from the past and the absurd existential amazement that envelops him in the present. Furthermore, it acts as a foil to emphasize this absurdity. The amazement is existential, but not existentialist. A vast distance separates the belief in the Camusian "rebel", the existential absurdity, or the Sartrian necessity of choice and commitment in the face of existential meaninglessness, from the Bashevian view of a human existence that runs from birth without will to a death without choice.

Bashevis began creating in the late Twenties and early Thirties, in a Poland squeezed between the U.S.S.R. and Nazi Germany. The political and social horizon appeared grim and the future of Polish Jewry, particularly after the closing of the American doors to mass immigration in 1924, appeared very grim, indeed. It was clear that this great Jewry, although much of it had undergone processes of modernization that had unleashed tremendous creative forces, was walking a deadened street, that its fate was catastrophical (although no one dared imagine the utter destruction that it underwent during World War II). Caught in an ever-tightening economic stranglehold, exposed to hatred that periodically exploded in the form of pogroms and murders, discriminated against in every possible way, in fact, locked into a country that bore it only malice—this Jewry, with its deep historical roots and richly diverse traditional and modern culture, existed in a state of constant pressure and depression. There were those who announced the way out of the siege: the Communists (the best of the Jewish youth flocked to them) pointed towards the revolution that would negate the class structure of society and, together with it, presumably, the "Jewish Question;" the Bundists called for a struggle "here" on the historical raising-ground of Polish Jewry in the name of socialism and national Jewish and Yiddish distinctness; the Zionists spoke Hebrew and pointed out the way to Eretz-Yisrael, even though the crisis of the third and fourth *aliyot,* together with the immigration limitations declared by the British in the Thirties, precluded the possibility of a Jewish evacuation of Poland to Israel.

Bashevis absorbed the grim despair of stress-burdened Polish Jewry, but he didn't "buy" any of the popularly disseminated "solutions." He lived in an atmosphere similar to that described in Agnon's "A Guest for the Night," but he lacked the eschatological-Zionist perspective that informs the Agnonic novel, and that situates its deep gloom in the context of a "positive" perspective. Bashevis picked up mostly the feeling of no-way-out, of being swept away by a grim and uncontrollable current towards a catastrophic future.

He gave this feeling powerful expression even in his first novel, *Satan in Goray,* a masterpiece of stylization and dramatic symbolization that, even today, it seems, is still his most concentrated, coherent and complete work in the genre of the novel. Going back through history, as it were, to the days of Shabtai Zvi, Bashevis described the wretchedness of Polish Jewry after the Chmelnitsky massacres, its spiri-

tual and physical collapse, the terrible fears that haunted its conscious and subconscious. On the background of these sorrows, the old rabbi tries in vain to reinstate the rule of rabbinical law over the congregation of Goray, this law being the only shield of historical Jewish life.

The crisis breaks out in his own home. Belief in Shabtai Zvi, the false messiah, gains a foothold in his family, and the expectation of the imminent arrival of the Messiah soon engulfs the entire town. For a while, the reality of the town becomes a wondrously harmonic, messianic reality. The town is unified and happy. It is led by an authoritative man who radiated charismatic sexual vigor, prepares the town, as it were, for the arrival of the messiah, and has intercourse with the "prophetess," Rachel, a physically deformed and terrified young woman who had been married to an impotent Kabbalist and became a hearer of voices and seer of visions. In truth, however, it is Satan who takes over the Jews of Goray, the Satan of false salvation, and only now, not in the days of Chmelnitsky, does the town approach its complete disintegration. The disappointment of the false messiah who converted to Islam breaks the strength of the town and it can no longer face its pain. The destiny of the town is mirrored in that of Rachel: she is recognized as being possessed by a Satanic "dybbuk," and she dies at the moment that her "dybbuk" is supposedly exorcized by means of consecrations. The criticism of the novel points primarily to the Communist promise of salvation and Stalin's seductive charisma, but it protests, in fact, against all human and Jewish eschatological hopes. The novel can be compared to the play, *The End of Days,* by Haim Hazaz on the one hand (written during the same period), and the famous prologue of *The Jews of Zierndorf,* the work by Jakob Wasserman, on the other.

Hazaz's play and Wasserman's prose-poem describe, as does **Satan in Goray,** the tremendous excitement that, like fire, seizes the ancient and long suffering Jewish-Ashkenazi community when news of the coming messianic salvation breaks. These pieces also end with the destruction of the Jewish town—in "The End of Days" with the actual burning of the town by the messiah's emissary, Yuspa. This comes out of the assumption that, as long as the exilic condition remains, Jews will cling to it, and that only a complete dissolution of this condition can bring about salvation. In *The Jews of Zierndorf* the entire community of the town of Fürth sets out on a so-called journey to Eretz Yisrael, but this journey turns quickly into a disaster that finishes off most of the community. In both pieces, at any rate, destruction is accompanied by a vision of renewed integration. In Hazaz's play it is the vision of Zionist salvation, in Wasserman's work the vision is of Jewish integration within a "prophetic," liberal European culture as embodied in the figure of the half-Jew, Agathon (the hero) and in the village of Zierndorf, which was founded by the survivors of the Fürth Jews who had set out on their false messianic journey. Bashevis, however, is unique in that, in his novel, destruction is not followed by any vision of, or direction towards, a possible salvation. *Satan in Goray* ends in the author's "escape" to the stylized texts of traditional "dybbuk" stories, but this, nevertheless, holds no hint of a return to a naive, folkloristic religious faith.

Satan in Goray is still the best key to understanding the Bashevian grasp of reality, according to which the sufferings of humanity are solemn truth but its "salvation," are complete lies. *Satan in Goray* is also a key to the stylistic qualities of Bashevis' work, for his world view bears unique poetic and stylistic results that achieve their full development even in his debut novel. His fatalism finds its expression in an opposition to any structural or syntactic complication of the continuity of the story. Since no event or gesture has the power to change the course of events, there is no point in describing them with tangled structures and complex sentences that, by their very hypotactic quality, confer primary significance onto others. Everything can be expressed in simple sentences that follow each other in the either loosely or tightly knit flow of the story "as it is." Likewise, there is no point in splitting hairs or piling on relations of cause and effect or precedence and antecedence. It is better to put the events down on paper as they are in their finality and arbitrariness in a free-flowing and evenly rhythmed narrative sequence. Thus, Bashevis brought the modern Yiddish narrative back from the superlative structural and syntactical complexity of writers like Dovid Bergelson and from the self-aware stylistic and structural virtuosity of maestros like Der Nister and Moshe Kulbak, to some sort of basic, epic simplicity. It would seem that one can hear in this narrative yet again and with great force the voice of the "naive" narrator, who treats every event with respect and unfolds before the reader event after event, apparently of equal significance, in a single, moderate tone, accepting everything, knowing everything, wondering at everything, resigning itself to everything. This so-called naiveté is actually the understanding that no sophistication can explain a baffling reality, and that the gesture of sophistication is superbly naive.

There can be no doubt that this simple, basic story-telling tone, when it is applied to a universe full of conflicts and complexities, is one of the secrets of the spell that Bashevis' stories cast over millions of readers, and it goes a certain way towards explaining the ability of these stories to live a full life in translation. In spite of its untranslatable, idiomatic juiciness, Bashevis' Yiddish demands of the translator primarily a responsiveness to the feeling of basic narrativity that is actually embodied in the rolling of simple sentences one after the other. The sensitive translator need only revive in his heart the epic, rhythmic sequence of the folk-like tale in his own idiom and he immediately comes upon

the recipe that enables a living duplication of the Bashevian narrative charm.

This is the place to bring up another point regarding the tremendous popularity of Bashevis' stories as the creations of a Jewish identity that is exotic, fascinating, alien, and seductive. We are forced to ask ourselves whether it is merely by chance that the great author who presents the historical Jewish identity as passive and victimized is the one who captured the hearts of so many non-Jewish readers. In posing this question I have no intention of belittling the virtues of Bashevis' work at its best, and yet it seems that these virtues are accompanied by a certain "weakness" that the non-Jewish reader seems particularly comfortable with. It is no accident that the view of the human condition that the non-Jewish world absorbs from Jewish culture comes mostly from a passive vantage point; the common denominator of passivity encompasses a broad spectrum of Jewish culture, from Kafka's "Metamorphosis" to "Fiddler on the Roof," supposedly after Sholem Aleichem's "Tevye" cycle. In the eyes of the non-Jewish world, it seems, Bashevis is not just a marvelous story-teller, but, also, some kind of wandering Jew, a modern Ahasuerus whose terrible destiny (the curse of Jesus) drives him on his endless journey and drags him through strange and wild experiences and events—all of them out of the realm of his control.

In this respect we can expect a certain degree of understanding of Bashevis, though uncomfortable and not as accepting as that of the "Goyim," by the Israeli and Zionist readership. It is doubtful, however, whether we can accept Bashevis' gospel which preaches surrender, being swept away, paralysis in the face of extinction, as basic truths—although, in the heat of our naive faith in our power to control our destiny, perhaps we should keep this truth in mind and accept something of its coolness and melancholy.

Nevertheless, it is impossible not to be enraptured by Bashevis' narrative art, not to be drawn into the melancholy and mystery of his fatalism, not to identify, if only for a moment, with the nihilistic undercurrents hidden by the deceptive simplicity of his narrative frameworks. All the same, we cannot wholeheartedly accept all of these. A substantial critique from a Jewish-Zionist vantage point will have to struggle with Bashevis' work.

At any rate, it is clear that the best of his stories will live long literary lives—even though the author himself never thought of his work in terms of any literary-aesthetic immortality. Bashevis' attitude towards literary creation was devoid of any pretense or mystification. He knew that he was a great artist who tells stories better than most of the raconteurs of his generation. But this knowledge represented nothing more than excellence in a craft and not a spiritual virtue that can overcome time and the spiritual chaos of human existence; it is like the knowledge of a master carpenter who is sure that the object emerging from under his hand is more finely crafted and beautiful than any produced by another carpenter. Nevertheless, his pessimism was honest and real, and his fatalistic world view did not allow him to develop illusions about the timelessness of aesthetic achievement. He saw literature as a perishable thing, a human product given to destruction, wear, confusion, and insignificance, like any other product. Sometimes he made the appearance of viewing his craft in terms of mere *parnuseh* (livelihood). This was an ironic pretense, of course, under which, nonetheless, lay more than a grain of seriousness. There was no mistaking the look with which he would fix speakers and experts who extolled his works in public, composed orations about them, split hairs, and generally waxed verbose. Reflected in his blue-green eyes was a combination of derision and pity. Theirs was, once again, the particularly touching *naïveté* of the sophisticated in which Bashevis himself never took part. One can safely assume that this commemorative statement did not fully avoid the pitfalls of such *naïveté*. However, one hopes that it does retain some of the simplicity and straightforwardness of the master himself.

Sally Ann Drucker (essay date 1992)

SOURCE: "I. B. Singer's Two Holy Fools," in *Yiddish,* Vol. 8, No. 2, 1992, pp. 35-9.

[*In the following essay, Drucker examines "wise fool" characters in "Gimpel the Fool" and* Shosha. *As Drucker notes, these characters achieve transcendent vision through spiritual openness rather than traditional Jewish religious study based on logical deduction.*]

> *A gantser nar iz a halber novi.* A whole fool is half a prophet.
> *A halber nar iz a gantser khokhem.* Half a fool is a complete sage.

These proverbs, seemingly contradictory, are usually interpreted as having ironic import—yet at first glance, their meaning is ambiguous and could imply the *wisdom* of fools. There are many words for fool in Yiddish and many types of fools in Yiddish literature: clever fools like Hershel Ostropolier, witless fools like the residents of Chelm, and a variety of luckless fools, whether schlemiels or schlimazls. This paper focuses on the holy fool, whose foolish wisdom or wise foolishness reaches transcendent levels. In particular, it compares Isaac Bashevis Singer's short story **"Gimpel the Fool"** with his novel *Shosha.*

In Eastern Europe, the popular picture of the Jew, held by Jew and Gentile alike, was true to the Talmudic tradition.

The picture included the tendency to examine, analyze, and re-analyze; to seek for meanings behind meanings, implications, and secondary consequences. Deductive logic was the ideal basis for practical conclusions and actions.

Because Jewish culture placed a high value on intelligence and learning, the holy fool, a fool who is more than a fool, who appears in a number of literary works, both subverts and augments this value. "Bontsche Shweig," *Yoshe Kalb,* **"Gimpel the Fool,"** and *Shosha* are all works in which a character displays a kind of wisdom that does not have to do with ability to reason—which is closer, perhaps, to the Khassidic religious tradition of the heart, than the Talmudic ideal of the head.

"Gimpl tam," the Yiddish title of Singer's story, more closely translates as "Gimpel the Simple"—a title perhaps too cutely alliterative but with a relevant double meaning. Gimpel spends his early life considered a simpleton by the townspeople, but his philosophy, expressed in the narration, belies actual foolishness. Gimpel lets the mocking of others go with, "Let it pass," and, "I hope I did them some good." On why he believes the stories his neighbors concoct to trick him, no matter how outlandish these stories are, he says, "Everything is possible," and, "Today it's your wife you don't believe, tomorrow it's God Himself you won't take stock in." On the burdens of the human condition, particularly his own: "You can't pass through life unscathed, nor expect to," and, "Shoulders are from God, and burdens too."

Ultimately, Gimpel becomes a wandering storyteller of the fantastic, saying,

> "The longer I lived the more I understood that there really were no lies. Whatever doesn't really happen is dreamed at night. It happens to one if it doesn't happen to another, tomorrow if not today, or a century hence if not next year."

Gimpel, a storyteller, an artist, with foolish (by worldly standards) wisdom, becomes a shaman of sorts, someone who mediates between worlds.

As pointed out by Sanford Pinsker, in the derivation of the word "schlemiel," one of the possible linguistic sources for the word is the Hebrew phrase "sheluakh min 'el," which literally means "sent away from God." However, another possible translation is "sent *from* God," in the sense of a biblical messenger. Gimpel, archetype schlemiel, holy fool, can be seen as this type of messenger. And, as Ruth Wisse puts it, "In Gimpel our rational prejudice is confronted with an appeal to a deeper truth."

Singer's novel *Shosha* appeared in 1978, twenty five years

after **"Gimpel the Fool,"** and seven years after Wisse's and Pinsker's critical treatments of schlemiels ably covered the ambiguities of Gimpel's foolishness. In **Shosha,** we have a female holy fool; perhaps the time had come for one. Although there might be female schlemiels in Jewish literature, such as Aunt Rosie of Grace Paley's "Goodbye and Good Luck" or the female residents of Chelm, and while there might be legendary female saints and martyrs, female fools, holy or otherwise, do not abound in Yiddish literature as protagonists. Shosha is the closest that we get to one.

In Europe, because women were not expected to participate in learning and scholarship, a female fool would not have had the same power of subverting the ideal. Too much learning or cleverness was considered unwomanly, in any case. A woman might be asked by her husband about an issue, "What do you say?" and her convoluted response would be, "What can a silly woman say? I have only a womanish brain, but if I were in your place. . . ." Gimpel himself repeats the proverb, "Women are often long on hair and short on sense." Traditionally, a man was expected not to be foolish, but a woman was automatically assumed to be so. In **Shosha,** however, the female fool is the narrator's, and perhaps the author's, double, inspiration, and link to the past. Representing the creative part of his consciousness, she is the *neshoma,* the soul, of his work.

Shosha, the narrator's double, looks like a *shikse* blonde, blue-eyed, straightnosed. The narrator, Aaron Greidinger, is also fair-haired (as are many of Singer's protagonists), but his resemblance to Shosha goes deeper than that. As a writer, he leads the life of a *luftmentsh,* a *schlemiel,* if not a total fool. He is a procrastinator who consistently undercuts his own possible success. Furthermore, he writes about dybbuks, ghosts, and goblins, not unlike Singer himself; only when Warsaw is on the edge of capitulation to Hitler, not until things are truly topsy-turvy, does Aaron's escapist literature, particularly the fictionalized biography of the false messiah Jacob Frank, win him popularity. Shosha, who awake or asleep sees her dead sister regularly, also lives in a world that blends dream and reality. When asked what he sees in the childish and childlike Shosha, Aaron says, "I see myself."

Shosha also symbolizes the narrator's past. Aaron was brought up a rabbi's son, on, as he puts it, "three dead languages—Hebrew, Aramaic, and Yiddish." As a child, he was drawn to the simple Shosha, a neighbor on Krochmalna Street who could barely read. He tells her fantastic stories, and like Gimpel she believes them all. He tells her that he knows a name that contains seventy-two letters, and when it is uttered "the sky would turn red, the moon topple, and the world be destroyed." Shosha begs him not to say it, and he replies, "Don't be afraid. I will make it so that you'll live

forever." Through language, Aaron has the power to destroy or immortalize Shosha and Krochmalna Street.

Twenty years later, when Aaron revisits his old neighborhood, he says, "It was like a deep stratum of an archeological dig which I would never uncover." Aaron begins to visit Shosha and her mother Bashele. Like the street, their apartment seems to exist in a time warp. They wear the same clothes, eat on the same plates, and talk about the same things they did twenty years before. Shosha still has the height and figure of a child, or a girl just reaching puberty. In staying young, she denies death.

> In "Gimpel the Fool," the protagonist becomes a storyteller of the fantastic, wise in his foolishness—he becomes the artist as shaman, mediator between worlds. In *Shosha* the female fool does not herself become an artist, but is the mediator between worlds for the storytelling male narrator.
> —*Sally Ann Drucker*

At one point, Aaron says: "From the day I had left my father's house I had existed in a state of perpetual despair." For him, a return to Krochmalna Street is a return to innocence. Shosha and her mother still observe Kashruth, the Sabbath, and holidays. As a child, he could always find tastier morsels at Shosha's house than at his own. Now, recently vegetarian, Aaron receives little sympathy for his new diet except from Shosha's mother, who caters to his requirements. When he stays at their house overnight, he sleeps in a tiny, womblike alcove.

Although Aaron finally marries Shosha, he retains his old apartment as a study, without telling Shosha or her mother. Also, while professing love for Shosha only, he presumably maintains some of the many romantic liaisons he had before they remet. Himself a betrayer, he tells one of his liaison: "She [Shosha] is the only woman I can trust."

Each previous liaison symbolizes some aspect of his Warsaw life: a communist, an intellectual, an actress, a peasant maid. Shosha, from the world of his childhood, simple, uncomplicated, still a girl physically, is the only one who will not betray him. His only emotional truth is that of the past. In this, Aaron resembles Yasha of Singer's *The Magician of Lublin.* In that book, it is the simple and sterile Jewish wife to whom the narrator always and ultimately returns, despite his romantic wanderings around different levels of Jewish and non-Jewish society.

Although Aaron is attracted to Shosha for her childlike and

childish qualities, she is not completely simple. She often notices details to which she can relate emotionally, such as the interactions of Aaron and his romantic liaisons. She also asks the right questions when he brings up abstract issues—questions that more worldly people would not ask but which get straight to the point.

Aaron talks to her when he is trying out ideas, as a form of "automatic writing," and she is the listener to "stream of consciousness" monologues. Further, she appears to be precognitive, predicting her own death. In short, Shosha, somewhat of an intellectual blank slate herself, reflects and represents deeper levels of consciousness. She responds to life emotionally rather than intellectually. The worldly, word-slinging Aaron can only approach her simplicity without ever reaching it.

In **"Gimpel the Fool,"** the protagonist becomes a storyteller of the fantastic, wise in his foolishness—he becomes the artist as shaman, mediator between worlds. In **Shosha** the female fool does not herself become an artist, but is the mediator between worlds for the storytelling male narrator. The actual female artist in **Shosha,** Aaron's benefactor and sometime lover, the actress Betty, has male traits and a persecution complex. Ultimately, she survives by teaming up with a rich and crass businessman. Betty is no shaman. Through her money, however, she helps Aaron bribe his way out of Poland, with Shosha at his side. Betty, an adult woman, is an enabler for the writer/narrator in the worldly sphere—a traditional role for a Jewish woman. Shosha, the child-woman, is an enabler of the otherworldly, but cannot survive outside of the actual world that engendered her. Shosha dies on the second day of the journey out of Poland. Yet, just as Aaron tells Shosha that he will make her live forever, Singer immortalizes the world that Shosha represents, and the qualities of innocence and preconscious thought that she represents, in the book that carries her name.

There are, of course, wise fools in the British and French literary traditions and holy fools in texts such as Dostoyevski's *The Idiot*. What makes the Yiddish holy fool noteworthy is his subversion of the traditional Jewish values of learning and reasoning as an approach to religious transcendence, a concept that appears to incorporate Khassidic influence. When the fool is a "she" instead of a "he," it subverts the subversion, and actually valorizes the life led by simple women as closer to the essence of spirituality. Singer portrays Shosha in relation to a male narrator, Aaron—a trickster, an artist, a magician of sorts, a shaman, named after the first Jewish high priest, who was the brother of Moses. Singer's Aaron *also* has a brother Moyshe, who became a rabbi. Again and again, this Aaron is impelled to return to the spiritual essence that Shosha, the fool, represents, in deed, in writing, and in asking for answers.

Joel Conarroe (review date 10 April 1994)

SOURCE: "The World Is One Vast Madhouse," in *The New York Times Book Review,* April 10, 1994, p. 9.

[In the following review, Conarroe praises the posthumous publication of Meshugah.]

One would have to be *meshugah* (that is, cuckoo, crazy) not to celebrate the publication of this brief tragicomic novel by Isaac Bashevis Singer, who died in 1991. Originally written in Yiddish, Singer's group portrait of Holocaust survivors in Manhattan first appeared in serial form in *The Forward* during the early 1980's, when the author himself was nearly 80. He changed its original title, "Lost Souls," to *Meshugah* after he and Nili Wachtel translated the work into English. Both titles are brilliantly appropriate.

Recognizing that it is usually irresponsible to identify novelists with their characters, we can nevertheless assume that Singer's narrator is partly modeled on his own younger self. Aaron Greidinger is a Polish exile in his late 40's who gives radio talks and writes serial novels in Yiddish for *The Forward*; his readers respond enthusiastically to his letter-perfect depiction of life in the old country. A likable schlemiel, the sort of man who always loses his money and keys, he has a pronounced fondness for women (married or un), and they tend to reciprocate his feelings.

Aaron's principal bedmate is Miriam Zalkind, a beguiling young woman with an unsavory past, who is writing a dissertation about his work. Aaron and her awful spouse are not, however, the only men in her life. Working a nice variation on Singer's 1972 novel, *Enemies: A Love Story,* whose protagonist shuttles between two wives, Miriam is faithful to her fatherly "husbands," Aaron and a cigar-chomping 67-year-old force of nature named Max Aberdam. The unexpected events involving this curious menage make up the heart of the narrative.

Singer's secondary characters, though they sometimes resemble cartoons, are drawn with his usual comic brio. These include a kvetching taxi driver with radical views and, less winningly, a wealthy widow "with a nose like a shofar and the teeth of a goat." Toward the end, several characters find themselves in Tel Aviv, a venue that gives their creator a chance to present disparate points of view on a number of political and social issues, often in a comic vein (though some of the jokes—"There are more doctors in Tel Aviv than patients"—are pretty tired). He also offers a running commentary on the differences between Hebrew ("the proud language of the patriarchs") and Yiddish ("the jargon of exile"). Asked why he doesn't write in Hebrew, Aaron responds, "If Yiddish was good enough for the Baal Shem Tov, for the Gaon of Vilna, for Rabbi Nachman of Bratslav, for the millions of Jews who perished by the hands of the Nazis, then it is good enough for me."

Since the work is set in the early 1950s, it follows that the characters are haunted by terrible recent memories. Despite their verbal energy and high spirits (Singer's books are filled with unstoppable talkers), the various survivors, all mourning loved ones, are indeed "lost souls," subject to melancholy, poisonous dreams and thoughts of suicide. The images they carry in their minds are of a sort that cannot be purged. "The whole story will never be told," a Polish woman in Israel insists. "Our refugees have written heaps of books and I've read almost all of them. What they say is true. But the real truth—that the pen cannot capture." It is, however, Aaron's response when he discovers the "real truth" about his young lover, herself a Holocaust survivor, that serves as the moral crux of the book.

Several terms—*gilgul, pompeches, slikhes*—will be unfamiliar to some readers, though their meanings can be teased out from the context. Now and then, too, a passage has the effect of an exotic piece of poetry, strange and beautiful: "We in Gahcia used to travel to Beiz, to Bobov, Garlitz, Shenyava, and to the Rizhyn line: Chortkov, Husiatyn, Sadagura. Trisk was in Russia, and people rarely traveled there. But I know, I know. *Divrei Avroham.* He used to favor *Noterakon* and *Gematria.*"

As for the concept of *meshugah*, Singer weaves into his narrative references to the innate craziness not only of his highstrung men and women but of the mad events that have shaped their behavior. "The world is turning *meshugah*. It had to happen." Again, "Sometimes it seems to me that the whole world is one vast madhouse." The several variations on this theme of pervasive looniness are invariably accomplished with the author's Nobel-worthy combination of good-natured mockery and compassion.

Meshugah is the third of Singer's posthumous novels to appear. Let's hope there are more.

FURTHER READING

Criticism

Bate, Nancy Berkowitz. "Judaism, Genius, or Gender: Women in the Fiction of Isaac Bashevis Singer." In *Critical Essays on Isaac Bashevis Singer,* edited by Grace Farrell, pp. 209-19. G. K. Hall & Co., 1996.
    Essay in which Bate examines Singer's view of women as reflected in his treatment of female characters, particularly in *Yentl,* the *Yeshiva Boy* and "The Dead Fiddler."

Epstein, Joseph. "Our Debt to I. B. Singer." *Commentary* 92, No. 5 (November 1991): 31-7.
    Provides an overview of Singer's fiction and major themes.

Hadda, Janet. "The Double Life of Isaac Bashevis Singer." *Prooftexts* 5, No. 2 (May 1985): 165-81.
    Explores the significance of Singer's postwar American residence in relation to his English-speaking readership and preoccupation with Eastern European Jewish life of the past.

Hadda, Janet. "Gimpel the Full." *Prooftexts* 10, No. 2 (May 1990): 283-95.
    Provides a psychoanalytic study of "Gimpel the Fool" with comment on reader response to the story.

Lee, Grace Farrell. "Epistemological Blindness and the Supernatural in Isaac Bashevis Singer." *Cross Currents* 36, No. 3 (Fall 1986): 288-99.
    Argues that elements of the supernatural in Singer's fiction should be interpreted literally rather than as a metaphor for psychological states.

Niger, Shmuel. "On *Satan in Goray.*" *Yiddish* 6, No. 2-3 (Summer-Fall 1985): 73-81.
    Provides retrospective critical analysis of *Satan in Goray.*

Pinsker, Sanford. "Isaac Bashevis Singer and Joyce Carol Oates: Some Versions of Gothic." *The Southern Review* 9 (1973): 895-908.
    Provides a comparative study of gothic elements in the fiction of Singer and Joyce Carol Oates.

Showalter, Elaine. "Even if I Married a Whole Harem of Women I'd Still Act like a Bachelor." *London Review of Books* 20, No. 18 (17 September 1998): 28-9.
    Showalter provides a positive review of Singer's novel *Shadows on the Hudson,* and discusses Janice Hadda's biography entitled *Isaac B. Singer: A Life.*

Additional coverage of Singer's life and career is contained in the following sources published by Gale: *Contemporary Authors*, Vols. 1-4R; *Contemporary Authors New Revision Series*, Vols. 1 and 39; *Dictionary of Literary Biography*, Vols. 6, 28, and 52; *Discovering Authors Modules: Most Studied Authors* and *Novelists; Major Twentieth Century Writers;* and *Something about the Author*, Vols. 3 and 27.

Kurt Vonnegut

1922-

(Full name Kurt Vonnegut Jr.) American novelist, short story writer, dramatist, screenwriter, and essayist.

The following entry presents an overview of Vonnegut's career through 1997. For further information on his life and works, see *CLC,* Volumes 1, 2, 3, 4, 5, 8, 12, 22, 40, and 60.

INTRODUCTION

Vonnegut gained a worldwide following in the late 1960s with the publication of his best-known work, *Slaughterhouse-Five* (1969). Considered a major voice in contemporary American literature, Vonnegut populates his novels with characters searching for meaning and order in an inherently meaningless and disorderly universe. Known for his iconoclastic humor, Vonnegut consistently satirizes contemporary society, focusing in particular on the futility of warfare and the human capacity for both irrationality and evil.

Biographical Information

Vonnegut was born in Indianapolis, Indiana, on November 11, 1922. He was the third child of Kurt, an architect, and his wife Edith (maiden name Lieber). Both the Vonneguts and the Liebers were formerly prosperous families who had lost their fortunes after World War I. Vonnegut entered the University of Chicago in 1940 to study biochemistry. He began writing for the student newspaper in his sophomore year, penning anti-war articles. After Pearl Harbor, Vonnegut reversed his opinions; in March of 1943 he entered the Army. He was captured in the Battle of the Bulge, held as part of a captive labor force in Dresden, and experienced the Allied fire-bombing of the city on February 13, 1945. Like the protagonist in *Slaughterhouse-Five,* Vonnegut survived the bombing in an underground meat locker, only to be put to work by the Germans extracting corpses from the city's ruins. Upon his return home in 1945, he married Jane Marie Cox and enrolled at the University of Chicago, from which he graduated in 1947. In the same year, Vonnegut began working for General Electric Research Laboratory as a public relations writer. He wrote fiction in his spare time, publishing his first story in 1950, and was soon able to quit his job and write full-time. In the 1960s Vonnegut accepted an appointment to the Writers Workshop at the University of Iowa. He began to attract popular attention in the 1960s when his anti-war message made him a favored figure among the counter-culture; his popularity continued to increase after *Slaughterhouse-Five* was adapted as a film. He has seven

children: three from his first marriage to Jane Marie Cox, three nephews adopted after the deaths of his sister and her husband, and one adopted with his second wife, Jill Krementz. Vonnegut lives in New York City.

Major Works

Vonnegut's first novel, *Player Piano* (1952), did not attract popular or critical attention, but it established many of the traits which continue to typify the author's style. The novel is futuristic and explores the relationship between changing technology and the lives of ordinary humans. His second work garnered greater critical reception. *The Sirens of Titan* (1959) is a science fiction parody in which all of human history is revealed to have been manipulated by aliens to provide a space traveler with a replacement part for his ship. This novel, as well as the critically acclaimed *Cat's Cradle* (1963) and *God Bless You, Mr. Rosewater* (1965), exhibits Vonnegut's unique combination of black humor, wit, and pessimism. *Cat's Cradle* is an apocalyptic satire on philosophy, religion, and technological progress while *God Bless You, Mr. Rosewater* concerns the idealistic attempts of an alcoholic philanthropist, Eliot Rosewater, to befriend the poor and helpless. Rosewater finds, however, that his monetary wealth cannot begin to alleviate the world's misery. Like Rosewater, Vonnegut's protagonists are idealistic, ordinary people who strive in vain to understand and bring about change in a world beyond their control or comprehension. Vonnegut tempers his pessimistic, sometimes caustic commentary with compassion for his characters, suggesting that humanity's ability to love may partially compensate for destructive tendencies. Two of Vonnegut's novels have dealt directly with World War II. In *Mother Night*, a spy novel, an American agent who posed as a Nazi propagandist during World War II undergoes a personality crisis when tried for crimes he committed to insure his covert identity. In *Slaughterhouse-Five*, perhaps Vonnegut's best-known work, the author confronts his personal experience as a prisoner of war who survived the Allied fire-bombing of Dresden, a city of little military or strategic value. The absurdity of this event is filtered through the numbed consciousness of Billy Pilgrim, a young soldier who escapes the insanity of war through schizophrenic travels into time and space; these journeys assume realistic stature when compared to his irrational wartime experiences. Considered a classic of postmodern literature, *Slaughterhouse-Five* is written in a fragmented, non-chronological style to emphasize the confusion and absurdity of wartime life. Vonnegut's subsequent novels have achieved popular success but have not always elicited critical praise. In 1971 he wrote his best-known play, *Happy Birthday, Wanda Jane,* and throughout the 1970s and 1980s wrote several screenplays for television. Vonnegut's most recent works include *Hocus Pocus* (1990) and *Timequake* (1997). In both of these novels Vonnegut presents his ideas in new and unusual literary forms. *Hocus Pocus* purports to be the autobiographical manuscript of Eugene Debs Hartke, a teacher and the last American out of Vietnam, who was fired for being too pessimistic and later charged with engineering the escape of African-American inmates from a prison. Hartke writes observations about his life on pieces of paper and Vonnegut masquerades as the editor. In *Timequake* Vonnegut merges parts of a problematic and incomplete novel with commentary about his life and views. The result is part memoir and part political novel. "In a nutshell," observes Thomas Disch, "everyone on Earth has to relive the 1990s on automatic pilot, observing but not participating in their lives." The book is a "stew" in which Vonnegut combined "the best pickings from a novel that wasn't working and interspersed them with a running commentary on his own life and the state of the universe. The mix is thick and rich: a political novel that's not a novel, a memoir that is not inclined to reveal the most private details of the writer's life," Valerie Sayers comments. Vonnegut has stated that he is retiring, and that *Timequake* will mark the end of his fiction-writing career.

Critical Reception

Vonnegut's first decade of work did not attract much critical attention: most early discussion of his writing centered on how to classify it. Citing his futuristic settings and the paramount role of technology in his work, some critics insist that Vonnegut is a science fiction writer. Others argue that despite these elements, Vonnegut is ultimately writing about the universal human condition and that he only employs science fiction devices to create distance and irony, just as he employs satire to the same effect. In recent years Vonnegut has come under fire from commentators who claim that he has failed to develop stylistically and that his characters are little more than mouthpieces for his opinions. Such critics claim that Vonnegut's work after *Slaughterhouse-Five* has offered more or less the same style, theme, and message. Tom Shone, for instance, writes that "all the same subjects are there, novel after novel" and that "Vonnegut's highly distinctive style has eclipsed Vonnegut the author." Others remain enamored of Vonnegut's distinct style, praising him for continually presenting his message in a deceptively skillful manner. John Irving remarks, "Vonnegut's subject has always been doomsday, and nobody writes about it better. That he is also so terribly funny in how he describes our own worst nightmare is, of course, another element that confuses his dumber critics."

PRINCIPAL WORKS

Player Piano (novel) 1952; also published as *Utopia 14,* 1954

The Sirens of Titan (novel) 1959

Mother Night (novel) 1962

Canary in a Cat House (short stories) 1963

Cat's Cradle (novel) 1963

God Bless You, Mr. Rosewater; or, Pearls before Swine (novel) 1965

Welcome to the Monkey House (short stories) 1968

Slaughterhouse-Five; or, The Children's Crusade: A Duty-Dance with Death (novel) 1969

Happy Birthday, Wanda June (play) 1970

Between Time and Timbuktu; or, Prometheus-Five: A Space Fantasy (play) 1972

Breakfast of Champions; or, Goodbye, Blue Monday! (novel) 1973

Wampeters, Foma, and Granfalloons: Opinions (essays) 1974

Slapstick; or, Lonesome No More! (novel) 1976

Jailbird (novel) 1979

Palm Sunday: An Autobiographical Collage (autobiography) 1981

Deadeye Dick (novel) 1982

Galápagos (novel) 1985

Bluebeard (novel) 1987

Hocus Pocus (novel) 1990

Fates Worse than Death (essays and speeches) 1991
Timequake (novel) 1997

CRITICISM

George Garrett (review date 19 August 1990)

SOURCE: "A Long-Awaited Return," in *Chicago Tribune Books,* August 19, 1990, p. 6.

[*In the review below, Garrett claims that in* Hocus Pocus, *Vonnegut returns to the high quality of his earlier works.*]

Once upon a time, I, too, was a Vonnegut groupie. In that world, which every day seems a little better than this one, we waited, eager and conspiratorial, for the man who had written the short stories later collected in *Canary in a Cat House* (1961) and the novel *Player Piano* (1952) to bring out his next book. We few. We happy few.

There was a little wait before that marvelous and wacko novel *The Sirens of Titan* (1959) appeared, offering the wild and woolly and deterministic adventures of one Malachi Constant, his wife Beatrice Rumsfoord and their little boy, Chrono. And best of all, it introduced us to what was to become Vonnegut's outer space Yoknapatawpha—the planet Tralfamadore, "where the flying saucers came from."

Next we were blessed with *Mother Night* (1962) and its impeccable moral—"We are what we pretend to be, so we must be careful about what we pretend to be;" *Cat's Cradle* (1963), featuring the inimitable Dr. Felix Hoenikker and his three odd children; *God Bless You, Mr. Rosewater* (1965), which introduced us to one of Vonnegut's most enduring characters—sci-fi writer Kilgore Trout.

So far he had endured the services of four casual publishers, very few reviews, next to no money from his writing; and we, his devoted readers, still knew most of each other by name. We knew next to nothing then about Vonnegut's private life, with its full share, and then some, of trouble and woe and even tragedy. But we loved his bleak, black, essentially sophomoric and sentimental humor, and we rejoiced in the crazy quilt of mordant fun and games that was a novel created by him.

Then some strange things happened, beginning with a piece by critic Robert Scholes—"'Mithridates, He Died Old': Black Humor and Kurt Vonnegut, Jr."—and leading, swiftly enough, to a new publisher, a new novel, *Slaughterhouse-Five* (1969) that rose to No. 1 on the bestseller list and became a popular movie in 1972. And so to riches, fame and almost overnight, as these things go, to a bulging six-foot

shelf of books and articles all about Vonnegut, his texts and subtexts, signs and symbols, sneaky similes and sly metaphors. He looks likely to be the last American literary "discovery" of this century, a star of first magnitude, soon a public figure, yet one more highly regarded and well-rewarded sage in residence.

Then it seemed to us, his old and longtime fans, that he started acting and writing like a sage, too, sounding more and more like some kind of weird cross between former senator Eugene McCarthy and that ancient and indefatigable flower child, the Maharishi. And so as the new books came along, nine by my count, we shrugged and yawned and went our separate ways. I remember laughing out loud when I looked among the cook books in our local bookstore and found *Breakfast of Champions* (1973).

Then please come home, old fans, and gather around, you new ones. With *Hocus Pocus,* Kurt Vonnegut seems to have rediscovered himself. The book purports to be the autobiographical manuscript of one Eugene Debs Hartke (the book is dedicated to his namesake, Eugene Victor Debs, 1855-1926), West Pointer, Vietnam veteran ("If I were a fighter plane instead of a human being, there would be little pictures of people painted all over me."); former college professor at Tarkington College, a school mainly for the dyslexic and learning disabled, where there is a Pahlavi Pavilion, a Somoza Hall, a Vonnegut Memorial Fountain, and a remarkably imaginative computer called Griot; a teacher at Athena, a prison run, like much else in America, by the Japanese Army of Occupation in Business Suits; and now, himself, a prisoner awaiting trial for his part in the largest prison breakout in American history.

Although the story ranges freely in time covering all of Hartke's life and a good deal of our history, it is set in the amazing literary year of 2001. (Hartke saw the movie in Vietnam.) Now he finds himself "in late middle age, cut loose in a thoroughly looted, bankrupt nation whose assets had been sold off to foreigners, a nation swamped by unchecked plagues and superstition and illiteracy and hypnotic TV, with virtually no health services for the poor."

In this new/old world I.G. Farben owns Du Pont, Italians own Anheuser-Busch, President Mobutu of Zaire has bought an ice-cream company in San Diego, the Sultan of Brunei has the First National Bank of Rochester, N.Y., the Shah of Bratpuhr controls meatpacking in Dubuque and the Encyclopedia Britannica is "owned by a mysterious Egyptian arms dealer living in Switzerland."

For consolation, Hartke has his memories, good and bad, a wealth of events and an album of major and minor and always memorable characters, including, too briefly, a mortician named Norman Updike. And he has some useful books—*The Atheist's Bible, Bartlett's "Familiar Quotations"* as well as the old magazine *Black Garterbelt,* which has a story in it, "The Protocols of the Elders of Tralfamadore," which argues that "the whole point of life on Earth was to make germs shape up so that they would be ready to ship out when the time came" and that human beings in the cosmic scheme of things are only "germ hotels."

The form of any Vonnegut novel always has some new wrinkles. According to "K. V." who merely edited this book, Hartke is writing it down "in pencil on everything from brown wrapping paper to the backs of business cards." Adding: "The unconventional lines separating passages within chapters indicate where one scrap heap ended and the next began. The shorter the passage, the smaller the scrap." Some scraps are a phrase or one word only, others go on for pages. There are other idiosyncrasies of text, including the author's flat refusal to use "foul language," leading to many a strained euphemism, all of them adding to Vonnegut's familiar and inimitably goofy charm.

Form and content, *Hocus Pocus* is a classic—weird, but good. We are older and so is he more relaxed and tolerant, if not one bit kinder and gentler, and as funny as anybody in the funny business.

The moral? Read Vonnegut's lips: "Just because we can read and write and do a little math, that doesn't mean we deserve to conquer the Universe."

Jay Cantor (review date 19 August 1990)

SOURCE: "Kurt Vonnegut: So It Still Goes," in *Washington Post Book World,* Vol. 20, No. 33, August 19, 1990, pp. 1-2.

[*In the following review, Cantor concludes that* Hocus Pocus *is a vehicle for Vonnegut to communicate his despair over humanity.*]

Woody Allen once observed that 80 percent of life is showing up. The other 20 percent—the part that stands between me and stardom—is making yourself likable, like George Burns, Jack Benny, Bill Cosby, or my pal (hah! don't I wish it!) Kurt Vonnegut. The amiable Vonnegut persona—a wry man who is a tad curmudgeonly, but as moral as he can honestly be—is, from book to book, Vonnegut's most substantial, continuing creation. Many people may be just, or think they are but it seems that few of us have doing justice as our aspiration—and they may do more harm than good. But if, like Vonnegut's narrators, they're not self-righteous, but are by some miracle filled with good humor, I find such

people more than likable. I want their friendship because I trust their judgements.

Vonnegut's novels are ways to spend some time with this unself-righteous yet just character, who in this book is called Eugene Debs Hartke. In his combination of decent aspiration and flaws Hartke is a depressed everyman—if we still thought everyman was a decent guy. Hartke cares for his mad wife and grandmother, but he also likes to romance middle-aged women when they're emotionally vulnerable. And he repeatedly counts the cost of being a Vietnam vet, though he sounds to me more like a sad, wised-up WWII dog-face than a Vietnam desperado: "If I were a fighter plane instead of a human being, there would be little pictures of people painted all over me." In Vietnam, Hartke was known as "the preacher," and he is a preacher still. For all he has done and all he has seen have made him despair. Vanity of vanities, saith the preacher, or as Hartke quotes a friend, human beings are "about 1,000 times dumber and meaner than they think they are."

> The amiable Vonnegut persona—a wry man who is a tad curmudgeonly, but as moral as he can honestly be—is, from book to book, Vonnegut's most substantial, continuing creation.
>
> —*Jay Cantor*

The last U.S. soldier out of Vietnam, Hartke teaches at a college for the rich and learning-disabled in upstate New York, until he loses his post because a character who sounds veddy veddy much like William Buckley finds his despair un-American. He then crosses the lake to teach at a segregated prison. When all the convicts escape and kill the staff of the college, Hartke's blamed—for black convicts *must* have had a white mastermind. Put in prison himself, he writes this book about being the last U.S. soldier in Vietnam, etc.

But the plot for me is just a clothesline on which Vonnegut can hang out some simple truths, tell some jokes, give quick-change renditions of lives that almost always come to prat-fall endings, and becomingly model his despair. That, for example, the American rich "had managed to convert their wealth . . . into a form so liquid and abstract, . . . that there were few reminders . . . that they might be responsible for anyone outside their own circle of friends. . ."

Or that lobsters are boiled alive.

Along the way, as always, Vonnegut shapes some parables to embody his disappointment in humanity and to remind us of what sound and fury we create while signifying . . . well, you know. In this book, Hartke recounts a science fiction story in which Vonnegut's favorite aliens, the Tralfamadorians, are using the earth to breed hearty germs suitable for space travel, so they can cover the universe with life. The T'dorians made humanity mess up nature to impose trying circumstances on their germs, weeding out weak bacteria-astronauts. So *that* explains the stupidity of human history! (And, from the Vonnegut/Hartke p.o.v. what an odd desire on Tralfamadore's part: "To me, wanting every habitable planet to be inhabited is like wanting everybody to have athlete's foot.") In previous novels, you may remember, history was explained as a shipwrecked Tralfamadorian's way of sending a message home, a savage semaphore system, with exploding bombs as dots and dashes. Vonnegut's mood has not lightened.

But then, why should it?

Still, considering what a worthless lot we are, why does Hartke/Vonnegut care so much, grieve so repeatedly? As if life were a long education in the unchanging senselessness of life, and the only residue of our previous ignorance is the ineradicable feeling that it might have been different (kinder? gentler?). So why act decently? "It could be . . . somewhere in the back of my mind I believed that there might really be a big book in which all things were written, and that I wanted some impressive proof that I could be compassionate recorded there." Vonnegut's despair is the sign that he believes life should be transformed, even perhaps that it could be— though it won't be of course, except for the worse. His sadness is the negative proof of the existence of, well . . . what? God? Or a big book somewhere that God long ago abandoned?

Poor man, I hope his despair continues.

John Irving (review date 2 September 1990)

SOURCE: "Vonnegut in Prison and Awaiting Trial," in *Los Angeles Times Book Review,* September 2, 1990, pp. 4, 10.

[*Irving is an acclaimed American novelist and short story writer. In the review below, he praises* Hocus Pocus *as one of Vonnegut's best novels and discusses the merits of Vonnegut's writing.*]

> The novel is the highest example of subtle interrelatedness that man has discovered.
>
> —D. H. Lawrence

Kurt Vonnegut is a friend of mine. He was my teacher at the University of Iowa; he is my neighbor in Sagaponack, Long Island—it is a three-minute bike ride from my house to his. When I moved into my house, he gave me several plants—

shrubs, actually; blue hydrangea and purple lilac. They are doing very well, largely because he told me how to care for them. He is a much better gardener than I am, but I am a better cook than he is: I go to his house to admire his bushes but he comes to my house to eat. Kurt also gave me an interesting wedding present: two very tall and heavy brass candlesticks. He presented them unwrapped with a ribbon tied around just one of them. "Anyone getting married ought to have a pair of these," he said. My wife and I light them and look at them almost every night, and we still don't know what he means. Maybe he means that, if the marriage doesn't work, we are well-armed to clobber each other with the candlesticks; if the marriage does work, we can defend ourselves from our dinner guests.

Kurt and I like each other's writing, but we hardly ever talk shop to each other. He has said some very kind and generous things about my work. I have written about his work before, in the *New Republic;* frankly, I have not yet grown tired of telling people why I think he is so special.

More than 20 years ago, in an interview, Vonnegut said: "We must acknowledge that the reader is doing something quite difficult for him, and the reason you don't change point of view too often is so he won't get lost, and the reason you paragraph often is so that his eyes won't get tired, so you get him without him knowing it by making his job easy for him." I especially love the "get him without him knowing it" part, but Vonnegut has been almost too successful at that. Among his more stupid readers are those critics who can't tell the difference between easy reading and easy writing; because his books are so easy to read, Vonnegut is accused of "easy" (or lazy) writing. I think you have to be a writer yourself to know how hard it is to make something easy to read—or else you just have to be a little smart.

Vonnegut's subject has always been doomsday, and nobody writes about it better. That he is also so terribly funny in how he describes our own worst nightmare is, of course, another element that confuses his dumber critics; for if doomsday is serious—and the end of our world, as we know it, surely must be—how can Vonnegut be both a serious fellow and a most comic novelist? Well, in his own time, I'm sure, the Immortal Bard of Avon must have confused such critics, too. In a *Playboy* interview, in 1973, Vonnegut was asked why his books were so popular with younger people; he said: "Maybe it's because I deal with sophomoric questions that full adults regard as settled. I talk about what God is like, what could He want, is there a heaven, and, if there is, what would it be like? This is what college sophomores are into; these are the questions they enjoy having discussed. And more mature people find these subjects very tiresome, as though they're settled." I especially love the "as though they're settled" part, and please note the irony in "full adults."

In *Jailbird* (1979), President Nixon's "special adviser on youth affairs" conceives of this telegram to send to the President:

> YOUNG PEOPLE STILL REFUSE TO SEE THE OBVIOUS IMPOSSIBILITY OF WORLD DISAR-MAMENT AND ECONOMIC EQUALITY. COULD BE FAULT OF NEW TESTAMENT.

And in *God Bless You, Mr. Rosewater* (1965), the hero, Eliot Rosewater, is described as suffering from the disease of idealism—"it attacks those exceedingly rare individuals who reach biological maturity still loving and wanting to help their fellow men." Vonnegut is similarly afflicted.

He is also highly gifted in the craft of storytelling: While keeping to a single narrator, to a one-person point of view, he yet manages to interweave a half-dozen narrative threads and different periods of time, and a dozen or more major-minor characters; and he conducts this interweaving so seamlessly that he makes his job look easy to stupid readers. To the majority of his readers, who are not at all stupid, Vonnegut manages very difficult material very well.

Now he gives us his 17th book, *Hocus Pocus,* a tale told by Lt. Col. Eugene Debs Hartke, the last American to leave Saigon. "I invented justifications for all the killing and dying we were doing, which impressed even me!" Hartke says. "I was a genius of lethal hocus pocus!" Sound familiar?

After the war, Hartke gets and then loses his job at a college for dyslexics—on the surface, he is fired for his sexual escapades with the president's wife, but in truth, he is let go for his cynicism. He erects a display of nonfunctioning perpetual-motion machines in the Science Building and labels them an example of "The Complicated Futility of Ignorance"; he tells students how we lost the Vietnam War. Of himself, Hartke says: "If I were a fighter plane instead of a human being, there would be little pictures of people painted all over me."

Like so many Vonnegut narrators over the years, Hartke is a prisoner facing trial. Howard Campbell in *Mother Night* (1966) is writing from an Israeli jail, awaiting his trial for war crimes; Walter F. Starbuck in *Jailbird* (1979) is a Watergate criminal—after he serves his term, he is found to be a criminal again ("I am a recidivist," he says; so many of Vonnegut's narrators are). But Hartke is not in jail for his crimes in Vietnam. He is facing trial for masterminding a prison break. Vonnegut's criminal narrators may be guilty of much, but they are typically innocent of the crime for which they are charged.

The year is 2001; all prisons are "color-coded," and Hartke, having lost his job at the college for dyslexics, is teaching at an all-black prison when the escape occurs. No one believes that blacks are smart enough to engineer their own escape. That Hartke is charged at all is, he says, "a racist conclusion, based on the belief that black people couldn't mastermind anything. I will say so in court."

The prison is guarded (and run for profit, successfully) by the Japanese; they own most of the United States, at least everything that the Germans don't own. Nobody of any importance uses dollars any more; anything that's worth buying is best paid for with yen. "There I was in late middle age," Hartke says, "cut loose in a thoroughly looted, bankrupt nation whose assets had been sold off to foreigners, a nation swamped by unchecked plagues and superstition and illiteracy and hypnotic TV, with virtually no health services for the poor." Sound familiar?

The Japanese warden at the prison, a witness to and survivor of Hiroshima, tells Hartke: "What a clever trap your Ruling Class set for us. First the atomic bomb. Now this. They looted your public and corporate treasuries, and turned your industries over to nincompoops. Then they had your Government borrow so heavily from us that we had no choice but to send over an Army of Occupation in business suits. Never before has the Ruling Class of a country found a way to stick other countries with all the responsibilities their wealth might imply, and still remain rich beyond the dreams of avarice! No wonder they thought the comatose Ronald Reagan was a great President!" Sound familiar?

While the escaped prisoners are raping and murdering their way through the college for dyslexics, Hartke ruminates on the miraculous good fortune that the college students are away on vacation—just imagine how much more raping and murdering there could have been! He also speculates that the government is likely to bomb both the college town and the prison. Why? "How many Americans knew or cared anyway where or what the Mohiga Valley was, or Laos or Cambodia or Tripoli? Thanks to our great educational system and TV, half of them couldn't even find their own country on a map of the world. Three-quarters of them couldn't put the cap back on a bottle of whiskey without crossing the threads." That's why. Vonnegut is very funny, but he's not kidding. Remember the Alamo? Here is how Vonnegut remembers it that the martyrs at the Alamo had died for the right to own black slaves. They didn't want to be a part of Mexico any more because it was against the law in that country to own slaves of any kind."

Is Vonnegut an anti-American? Don't be silly! "I have no reforms to propose," he writes. "I think any form of government, not just Capitalism, is whatever the people who have all our money, drunk or sober, sane or insane, decide to do today." And furthermore, "All nations bigger than Denmark are crocks of doo-doo." So much for government; as for religion: "The most important message of a crucifix . . . was how unspeakably cruel supposedly sane human beings can be when under orders from a superior authority." As for the conquest of space and the presumed superiority of human beings: "Wanting every habitable planet to be inhabited is like wanting everybody to have athlete's foot." Vonnegut does not worship a single sacred cow—not even "high art" escapes unscathed. "Making the most of the materials of futility," he calls it.

The only precept that Hartke honors is taught to him by his grandfather: "that profanity and obscenity entitle people who don't want inconvenient information to close their ears and eyes to you"; therefore, Hartke's language is squeaky-clean. He also tries to be kind; his illegitimate son is named Rob Roy, after the mixed drink of that name, but Hartke indulges his son's belief that he is named for the novel by Sir Walter Scott. "What good would it do him or anybody else to know that he was named for two shots of Scotch, one shot of sweet vermouth, cracked ice, and a twist of lemon peel?" What good, indeed!

On a personal level, Hartke's failure is as painful as Vietnam; as he awaits his trial, his wife and mother-in-law are in an insane asylum—both of them went crazy in middle age, and now Hartke's children suspect that the same craziness awaits them. "Our children, full-grown now, can never forgive us for reproducing," he says. "What a mess."

What a metaphor! It stands so directly for the national and planetary disaster that we are leaving to our children. Anyone who thinks Vonnegut isn't "serious" is truly full of doo-doo.

Hocus Pocus is as good as the best of his novels—these being, in my opinion, *Cat's Cradle* (1963), *Mother Night* (1966), *Slaughterhouse-Five* (1969) and *Jailbird* (1979); although, how long has it been since you've read a first novel as good and prophetically on-target as *Player Piano*? And for the appreciative Vonnegut reader, those crafty Tralfamadorians are back in *Hocus Pocus*; I don't want to spoil the story, but everyone on Tralfamadore knows "that germs, not people, [are] the darlings of the Universe." And those escaped prisoners who rape and murder the faculty of the college for dyslexics, and many poor souls in the college town, guess what they are called: "Freedom Fighters!" Sound familiar?

Vonnegut quotes everyone from Shakespeare to Jean-Paul Sartre to Eugene Debs; unlike most writers, however, he is honest and unpretentious enough to admit his source. "I have lifted this speech from Bartlett's Familiar Quotations," he says (repeatedly). "If more people would acknowledge that they got their pearls of wisdom from that book instead of the original, it might clear the air."

Accordingly, I must confess that I lifted that D.H. Lawrence quote from a little paperback called *The Writer's Quotation Book*. I have no idea where Lawrence wrote that business about "subtle interrelatedness"; I suppose I can't really be certain that he did write it. As usual, Vonnegut has helped to clear the air.

John Skow (review date 3 September 1990)

SOURCE: "And So It Went," in *Time*, Vol. 136, No. 10, September 3, 1990, p. 73.

[*In the following review, Skow praises Vonnegut's message in* Hocus Pocus, *but criticizes his writing.*]

The knock against Kurt Vonnegut, back a couple of decades ago when he was a cult author, was that he pandered too glibly to the natural cynicism of the disaffected young. He was too quick, it was said, to detect the smell of society's insulation burning—and to sigh "So it goes"—when there was nothing more in the air than, say, a harmless whiff from a distant war or the neighborhood toxic-waste dump. No more; his news in *Hocus Pocus* is that our charred insulation no longer smolders. It has burned itself out, and civilization's great, tired machine is not dying, but blackened and dead.

The form of the new novel is the author's standby, the diary of a bemused old man who has survived civilization's downfall. Perhaps because of this resemblance to his other books, or simply because the freight of anger and disgust is so heavy it upsets the novel's balance, the element of *Hocus Pocus* that is storytelling seems perfunctory. Eugene Debs Hartke is the diarist, a gung-ho U.S. Army officer during the Vietnam War; then a professor of science at Tarkington, a college for dyslectics in New York State; then briefly the warden of a prison for blacks into which the college is transformed; and finally, in the year 2001, the scapegoat defendant after a prison breakout.

Hartke describes fuel and food shortages, and a state of permanent riot amounting to a national decline so profound that even the Japanese in their business suits—the "army of occupation"—are walking away from properties in the U.S. and going home. "The National Forest," he complains, "is now being logged by Mexican laborers using Japanese tools, under the direction of Swedes. The proceeds are expected to pay half of day-before-yesterday's interest on the National Debt." In this dark mood, Hartke admires a science fiction story in which the revered Kilgore Trout (we assume, though the finest of pulp writers for some reason is not identified), in a journal called *Black Garterbelt*, explains the meaning of life. Germs, it seems, are being toughened by higher beings for the rigors of space travel; and human society—Mozart, mutant turtles and all—has amounted to nothing more than a convenient Petri plate.

Fair enough, but Hartke is not a vivid enough central figure so that his dismay illuminates the wreckage. Too much about him seems random, taken without calculation from the parts bin. Why, for instance, has the author named him after Eugene V. Debs, the great U.S. socialist? Merely, or so it appears, because Vonnegut likes the contrast of Debs' nobility ("While there is a lower class I am in it . . . while there is a soul in prison I am not free") with the grubby hopelessness of Hartke's world. And what about that college for dyslectics? Is dyslexia a sign of national decay? Has the author turned symbol monger? If not, what's the point?

The body of Kurt Vonnegut's writing contains some of the most uncomfortably funny social satire in English. What is offered here is something else, a try at prophecy in the darkest and gloomiest biblical sense. As prophecy it is major or minor, right or wrong, the reader's choice. As literature it is minor Vonnegut.

Christopher Lehmann-Haupt (review date 8 September 1990)

SOURCE: "Familiar Characters and Tricks of Vonnegut," in *The New York Times,* September 8, 1990, p. 16.

[*In the review below, Lehmann-Haupt characterizes* Hocus Pocus *as a "contest between comedy and despair" in which the latter gains the upper hand.*]

It should come as no surprise to Kurt Vonnegut's readers that one of the characters in his 13th and latest novel, *Hocus Pocus,* is Hiroshi Matsumoto, a survivor of Hiroshima.

But what may be modestly alarming is the almost affectionate mordancy with which Matsumoto's experience is described: "When the bomb was dropped, he was playing soccer during school recess. He chased a ball into a ditch at one end of the playing field. He bent over to pick up the ball. There was a flash and wind. When he straightened up, his city was gone. He was alone on a desert, with little spirals of dust dancing here and there."

Of course, it isn't Mr. Vonnegut who describes this frightening scene. It is one Eugene Debs Hartke, who, according to an introductory editor's note by K.V., wrote the whole of *Hocus Pocus* on little scraps of paper while waiting to be tried for some crime that will eventually be divulged by his narrative.

Eugene Debs Hartke, too, is a familiar Vonnegut creation. Not only is he hated by his children, who have promised never to speak to him again for innocently marrying a woman with insanity in her genes, he is also loathed by himself for all the killing and lying he did in Vietnam. So if there's anything you don't like about Eugene, he has probably beaten you to it. Besides, he has tuberculosis.

> In *Hocus Pocus,* as usual in Mr. Vonnegut's fiction, there is a contest between comedy and despair, between the vaudeville curtain and the apocalyptic cloud. In the author's more recent novels these elements have finished in a tie, with the darkness of the author's vision balanced by the lightness of his style. Something was bound to give.
> —*Christopher Lehmann-Haupt*

In *Hocus Pocus,* as usual in Mr. Vonnegut's fiction, there is a contest between comedy and despair, between the vaudeville curtain and the apocalyptic cloud. In the author's more recent novels these elements have finished in a tie, with the darkness of the author's vision balanced by the lightness of his style. Something was bound to give.

The lightness is there in *Hocus Pocus:* the diagrams in Mr. Vonnegut's hand, the typographicaltics, the cute tag lines. Opposite the title is a page filled with silhouettes of little men to illustrate the narrator's remark, "If I were a fighter plane instead of a human being, there would be little pictures of people painted all over me."

There are lines separating passages within the novel's chapters to indicate where one scrap of paper ends and the next begins. As K.V. writes in his editor's note, "The shorter the passage, the smaller the scrap." Typical scraps end with lines like: "What a planet," "There went the ball game," "What a story!" "Too late now" or "So now I have tuberculosis. Cough, cough, cough."

There are even funny passages in *Hocus Pocus,* like the scene in which Eugene's long lost illegitimate son shows up and asks a series of questions based on lies Eugene told the boy's mother during their one-night stand; or Eugene's account of the perpetual-motion machines built by the founder of the college for the learning-disabled wealthy, where Eugene used to teach: "The longest my students and I could get the best of them to run was 51 seconds. Some eternity!"

But darkness and despair seem to have inched ahead in *Hocus Pocus.* True, many of Eugene's blacker lines can be dismissed as excessive. Of the notorious Donner-party cannibalism incident he writes, "People who can eat people are the luckiest people in the world." And some of the shorter scraps of the novel have entries like: "And the worst flaw is that we're just plain dumb. Admit it! You think Auschwitz was intelligent?" or "How embarrassing to be human."

> **All of Mr. Vonnegut's prose techniques are so worn and slick from use that they bounce away harmlessly. His vision may have darkened but he has been at his games too long to make one take him seriously.**
> *—Christopher Lehmann-Haupt*

Still, Eugene's tortured conscience can sneak up and whack you one. One of his students recalls how as a boy he got stuck between floors in a Bloomingdale's department-store elevator. He "believed himself to be at the center of a major event in American history." He was sure that everyone from his parents up to the President of the United States was aware of his problem. But after the elevator jolted upward and the doors slithered open, there were only customers waiting impatiently for the riders to get out so they could get in. To which Eugene responds that what the student has described "to perfection" is what "it was like to come home from the Vietnam War."

Elsewhere, Eugene reads an article called "The Protocols of the Elders of Tralfamadore" in a magazine, *Black Garterbelt*. In it, an anonymous sci-fi writer describes how the wise inhabitants of Mr. Vonnegut's imaginary planet once dreamed of spreading life forms throughout the universe. They concluded that the most practical space travelers would be germs, but none were yet tough enough to make the trip. The elders decided it was up to earth's people to develop strong enough germs. So they fed a counterfeit line into the earthling's Creation myth: "Fill the Earth and subdue it; and have dominion over the fish of the sea and over the birds of the air and over every living thing that moves on the Earth."

"Cough."

And there's Eugene's description of those "little dust devils" that Hiroshi Matsumoto saw spinning in the "blank tableland" when he picked his soccer ball out of that ditch.

But if you find yourself succumbing to the author's nuclear apoplexy, you need only to think about this atomic scene as carefully as Mr. Vonnegut seems to want you to do. Of course it isn't real. No one would have survived a nuclear explosion by ducking into a ditch. It is a cartoon conception, with the dust devils out of some "Roadrunner" short.

Similarly, all of Mr. Vonnegut's prose techniques are so worn and slick from use that they bounce away harmlessly. His vision may have darkened but he has been at his games too long to make one take him seriously.

Hocus Pocus: It's trickster's phony incantation. Most depressing of all are the holes in this performer's gloves.

Jay McInerney (review date 9 September 1990)

SOURCE: "Still Asking the Embarrassing Questions," in *New York Times Book Review*, September 9, 1990, p. 12

[*McInerney is an American novelist. In the following review, he discusses the balance between pessimism and humor in Vonnegut's novels, focusing on* Hocus Pocus.]

For purposes of comparison with our own stodgy, inherited universe, contemporary philosophers sometimes conjure up the concept of possible worlds. They've got nothing on Kurt Vonnegut, who in 12 previous novels has frequently resorted to other planets for slyly comparative purposes. But unlike most contemporary philosophers—who fastidiously restrict themselves to questions of linguistic and logical analysis—or most contemporary novelists, for that matter, Mr. Vonnegut is still asking the big, embarrassing, childish teleological questions. He is probably our leading literary big-question asker. He keeps posing the kind of questions, as he himself once put it, that college sophomores ask. Like, why are we on the planet? Or, why is there war? And, is technology inherently lethal? Unlike most sophomores, he has the imagination to illuminate these questions.

Although it is set in the near future, **Hocus Pocus** is the most topical, realistic Vonnegut novel to date, and shows the struggle of an artist a little impatient with allegory and more than a little impatient with his own country. Nationality has previously been a spurious category—a granfalloon—in the Vonnegut world view. The possible world portrayed here verges shamelessly on the actual.

Like many of Mr. Vonnegut's novels, **Hocus Pocus** is a retrospective first-person narrative in which several time and story lines gradually converge. It is told by one Eugene Debs Hartke and purportedly written in prison on scraps of paper, each scrap a thought, story or digression unto itself—a form ideally suited to Mr. Vonnegut's thumbnail essayistic bent and his high-speed forward- and reverse-narrative time travel.

Hartke is a graduate of West Point and a veteran of the Vietnam War, a thoughtful but not tormented man who killed many human beings on the orders of his Government and dispensed many official lies as an information officer. After leaving Vietnam and the Army he becomes a teacher at Tarkington College in the Finger Lakes region of upstate New York, a gentle institution that specializes in nurturing the dyslexic and moronic sons and daughters of the ruling class.

After years of pleasant academic rustication, Hartke is fired from the college at the behest of a rightwing television demagogue who feels that Hartke is too pessimistic. Pessimism, as everyone knows and as the board of trustees reminds him, is un-American and probably even anti-American. A physics teacher, Hartke has made the mistake, among others, of informing his students that the idea of perpetual motion is a pipe dream. Unpatriotically, he explains, "I see no harm in telling young people to prepare for failure rather than success, since failure is the main thing that is going to happen to them."

When he is dismissed, ostensibly for sexual misconduct, Hartke finds employment just across the lake at the former state prison, run by a Japanese corporation that operates it much more efficiently and profitably than the state did. "Color-coded" prisons have become a growth industry, in part because most productive domestic industry has disappeared. "Poor and powerless people, no matter how docile, were no longer of use to canny investors." The prison where Hartke works, near the college town of Scipio, is populated entirely by black inmates, the Supreme Court having decided that it was cruel and inhuman to confine one race with another. America has been largely resegregated—black insulated from white, rich from poor.

Hartke manages to teach some inmates how to read, though the immediate reported benefits of literacy are mainly an increased pleasure in masturbation and wider circulation for the anti-Semitic tract "The Protocols of the Elders of Zion." "The lesson I myself learned over and over again when teaching at the college and then the prison was the uselessness of information to most people, except as entertainment."

When gang members launch a military operation to break out a drug dealer, the entire prison population escapes and crosses the frozen lake to the Tarkington campus. For a variety of reasons, not least the racist supposition that blacks could not possibly have planned the escape, Hartke is eventually arrested as the leader of the uprising and incarcerated himself. Prison may not be such a bad place to be in the year 2001. Most of the United States has been sold to foreigners, and what is left is broken down and depleted. Black markets, race war, martial law, tuberculosis and AIDS are all somewhere between endemic and epidemic.

Like Eugene Debs Hartke, Mr. Vonnegut has always been a pessimist—"a pillar of salt," as he describes himself in his novel *Slaughterhouse-Five.* Like Lot's wife, he looks back

at the carnage. In this case, he also looks forward, somewhat in the manner of another biblical personage, Jeremiah.

The bitter ironies in his books have always been tempered by a whimsical stoicism, despair averted by glimpses of individual compassion and the mild palliative of "harmless untruths" like the pleasantly ditsy religion of Bokononism in *Cat's Cradle.* He is a satirist with a heart, a moralist with a whoopee cushion, a cynic who wants to believe. His fiercest social criticism is usually disguised in parable. In *Cat's Cradle,* for instance, a substance called Ice Nine, which on release freezes all the water on the face of the earth, stands in for nuclear weapons. In *Slaughterhouse-Five,* the extraterrestrial Tralfamadorians provide a cosmic perspective on the inexplicable suffering and horror of the firebombing of Dresden. In *Jailbird,* the terrestrial rape of the environment is echoed in the story of the planet Vicuna, where scientists found a way to convert time into food and energy, thereby running out of it.

As if racing against such a clock, Mr. Vonnegut is working much closer to the ground in *Hocus Pocus,* which has more in common with Anthony Trollope's book *The Way We Live Now* than with Arthur C. Clarke's *2001.* It is the most richly detailed and textured of Mr. Vonnegut's renderings of this particular planet. Unlike many of his major characters, Hartke seems like a real person, and Scipio seems like a real town. Some readers may miss the wilder leaps of imagination and the whimsy, but what is gained is a muscular dignity of voice that only rarely is tendentious. And, like outer space in *The Sirens of Titan, Hocus Pocus* is not without "empty heroics, low comedy, and pointless death."

If he eschews parables, Mr. Vonnegut still finds abundant metaphors for our current situation. Hartke compares the land of the free and the home of the brave to a vast plantation, the soil and labor of which has been exhausted. The owners, whites of European descent, are selling it off, dispossessing the laborers. The buyers, mainly Japanese, find themselves as an army of occupation in a hostile, primitive land, bogged down in a terrible quagmire that may prove as destructive to their nation as Vietnam was to ours. Prisons spring up like the antibodies that attempt to form hard protective shells around the germs of tuberculosis, which is enjoying a comeback.

But don't worry. There is sort of a bright side to all of this. The science-fiction writer Kilgore Trout briefly appears—along with others in Mr. Vonnegut's repertory company, represented by a story called "Protocols of the Elders of Tralfamador," in which he speculates that the whole point of human history is to breed strains of germs powerful enough to travel through space and spread DNA throughout the universe. Once we are through trashing and poisoning the planet any germ hardy enough to survive here could presumably make it anywhere.

John Leonard (review date 15 October 1990)

SOURCE: "Black Magic," in *Nation,* Vol. 251, No. 12, October 15, 1990, pp. 421-25.

[*In the review below, Leonard praises* Hocus Pocus *and discusses Vonnegut's fatalistic message.*]

Hocus Pocus seems to me to be Vonnegut's best novel in years—funny and prophetic, yes, and fabulous too, as cunning as Aesop and as gloomy as Grimm; but also rich and referential; a meditation on American history and American literature; an elegy; a keening. "How is this for a definition of high art," we are asked by the antihero, Eugene Debs Hartke: "'Making the most of the raw materials of futility?'"

But *Hocus Pocus* has been not so much reviewed as consumer-tested, like a bar of chocolate, as if all Vonneguts were Hershey's, needing only to be categorized as Semi-Sweet, Special Dark or Bitter Almond. Without even bothering to cut a new stencil, critics perceive him as an amusing atavism of the 1960s. Or a celebrity-guru who has reached the bottom of his cracker barrel. Or a Pet Rock. Or an old fart. It makes you wonder why a writer ever tries to do something different. It also makes you wonder what it is a reader really wants from a writer who's been around so nobly, so long.

We take our leave of a Vonnegut novel, even *Hocus Pocus,* feeling . . . what? Certainly not comforted, nor galvanized, nor whammied. More . . . reflective, as if emerging from the vectors of a haiku. I spent one Christmas with him, years ago, in New Hampshire. We happened, in an orchard, upon stricken boughs of black apples. Helicopters had sprayed Stop-Drop on these apples during the October picking season, and then an early frost had killed them off, and so they hung there, very Japanese. Vonnegut said, "If you don't write about those apples, I will." He never did. Maybe they were too conveniently symbolic. (Stop-Drop, after all, is a kind of Ice-9.) But that's not how a novel of his feels, either.

Another time, I think in Maine, Vonnegut got down and dirty with Ray Mungo, who explained that his communards were leaving for the wilds of Canada because they "wanted to be the last people living on the earth." Vonnegut wondered, "Isn't that a sort of stuck-up thing to want to be?" And, of course, stuck-up writers are a dime a dozen: the wart hog postmodernist, the history-devouring sage, Umberto Eco. We never feel, after reading Vonnegut, that he thinks he's any better than we are. (We probably should, but we don't.) We

feel that a sad man, inside his funny jokes, despairs of our ever getting his plain-spoken point, and we're grateful that he goes on anyway, trying all over again to make us braver and wiser, but the mind clouds as the lips grin, and we go about our chastened business with a blank uneasiness. He's such a *fatalist.*

Let me try again: At the end of the American Playhouse public-television production of Terrence McNally's short play *Andre's Mother,* the mother (Sada Thompson) and the lover (Richard Thomas) go to Central Park to mourn Andre's death from AIDS. Unable to speak their grief, they send up little white balloons. It is a kind of naming. That's what a Vonnegut feels like, only his balloons are black, like those apples.

We began taking him for granted after his megabucks Dresden novel, **Slaughterhouse-Five.** Part of it was his own fault. His next time out, in **Breakfast of Champions,** he detached himself from his creations, cut the strings as if they were marionettes or kites. He was 50 years old: "Under similar spiritual conditions, Count Tolstoi freed his serfs. Thomas Jefferson freed his slaves. I am going to set at liberty all the literary characters who have served me so loyally during my writing career." Readers hate this, which is why Conan Doyle had to bring back Sherlock Holmes, and why Nicolas Freeling is resented for having lost interest in Van der Valk, for having invented Castang instead. Besides, with **Breakfast,** weird personal stuff started creeping into Vonnegut's fiction—like his dead father. He dropped the "junior."

But by that time, we felt we'd gotten the message, and it wasn't "Greetings!" *The Sirens of Titan* asked us how to cause "less rather than more pain," how to "love whoever is around to be loved." *Mother Night* warned that "we are what we pretend to be, so we must be careful about what we pretend to be." Bokonon told us in *Cat's Cradle* to "pay no attention to Caesar. Caesar doesn't have the slightest idea what's *really* going on." *God Bless You, Mr. Rosewater* wanted to know how to love "people who have no use." Billy Pilgrim in *Slaughterhouse-Five* overheard Eliot Rosewater telling his psychiatrist, "I think you guys are going to have to come up with a lot of wonderful *new* lies, or people just aren't going to want to go on living."

Art, of course, is a wonderful lie. After catastrophes and revolutions, Hiroshima and "the Nazi monkey business," God was telling us through Vonnegut that we'd have to invent the meaning of "all this" for ourselves, dream it up. This is why his characters left town so often, left Mother Earth herself, for outer space, Tralfamadore. On Tralfamadore, novels have "no beginning, no middle, no end, no moral, no causes, no effects"; they're just clumps of symbols. Vonnegut seems to need Tralfamadorians the way Garcia Márquez needs angels and Toni Morrison needs ghosts and Shakespeare needed clowns. Just maybe, by the transcendent power of the imagination, we could reverse the charges, call back the bombers over Dresden:

> American planes, full of holes and wounded men and corpses, took off backwards from an airfield in England. Over France, a few German fighter planes flew at them backwards, sucked bullets and shell fragments from some of the planes and crewmen. . . . The formation flew backwards over a German city that was in flames. The bombers opened their bomb bay doors, exerted a miraculous magnetism which shrunk the fires, gathered them into cylindrical steel containers, and lifted the containers into the bellies of the planes. . . . When the bombers got back to their base, the steel cylinders were taken from the racks and shipped back to the United States of America, where factories were operating night and day, dismantling the cylinders, separating the dangerous contents into minerals. Touchingly, it was mainly women who did this work. The minerals were then shipped to specialists in remote areas. It was their business to put them into the ground, to hide them cleverly, so they would never hurt anybody ever again.

Then again, maybe not. ***Breakfast of Champions*** was gloomier. Imagination was not enough. In ***Breakfast,*** for instance, the sci-fi novelist Kilgore Trout imagined "a dialogue between two pieces of yeast. They were discussing the possible purposes of life as they ate sugar and suffocated in their own excrement. Because of their limited intelligence, they never came close to realizing that they were making champagne."

Bummer! So much for the chronosynclastic infundibulum. But Vonnegut went on dreaming after ***Breakfast,*** with or without his critics. ("Yes," he said in ***Slapstick,*** "and while my big brother meditated about clouds, the mind I was given daydreamed the story in this book. It is about desolated cities and spiritual cannibalism and incest and loneliness and lovelessness and death.") It's just that he dreamed his way into different sorts of heads, heads attached to symbolic citizens—writers, soldiers, artists, politicians—whose moral autonomy wasn't what it ought to be. The weather inside these heads rained confusion; history came down hard and hurt; we were killing the planet. The transforming powers of the romantic self needed some group help, some civic assistance, a home front.

Slapstick is a fairy tale, set in the future instead of the past. There are monsters who mean well, a witch, a Tom Thumb (he's Chinese), a noble steed named Budweiser ("golden feathers hid her hooves"), a perilous journey with a gift (a

Dresden candlestick stolen from the tent of a sleeping chieftain), an Island of Death (where "people lit their homes at night with burning rags stuck in bowls of animal fat") and a ceremony (the 100th birthday party for the last American President, who is writing his memoirs, which is the book we are reading). There are three ideas many another postmodernist would kill for: a gravity that's as variable as the weather, a Church of Jesus Christ the Kidnapped, and a blueprint for abolishing loneliness in the following way: A computer will establish 10,000 brand-new "extended families," giving "proportional representation to all sorts of Americans, according to their numbers," by randomly assigning everybody in the country a new middle name which consists of "a noun, the name of a flower or a fruit or a fish or a mollusk, or a gem or a mineral or a chemical element—connected by a hyphen to a number between one and twenty." Thus each individual instantly acquires 190,000 cousins (same middle name) and 10,000 brothers and sisters (same middle name and number). Daffodils, Orioles, Berylliums, Chipmunks, Bauxites, Strawberries and Pachysandras form clubs and even "parliaments" to take care of one another.

One more misbegotten "granfalloon," like the Communist Party.

And yet: ***Slapstick*** also proposes that, even if we aren't "really very good at life," we must nevertheless, like Laurel and Hardy, "bargain in good faith" with our destinies. And there are instruction manuals for this bargaining: Robert's Rules of Order, the principles of Alcoholics Anonymous, and the Bill of Rights.

None of these books was written by a Tralfamadorian.

Jailbird's about Harvard and Nixon; Sacco and Vanzetti; Hiss and Chambers; trade unionism, corporate greed, the Holocaust and Watergate—not to mention Roy Cohn. There are catacombs under Grand Central, and harps on top of the Chrysler Building, and even Nixon's "unhappy little smile" looks to Starbuck "like a rosebud that had just been smashed by a hammer." Some fairy tale! "Strong stuff," says Starbuck, whose girlfriend tells him: "You couldn't help it that you were born without a heart. At least you tried to believe what the people with hearts believed—so you were a good man just the same." And she reads Starbuck's books the way we ought to read Vonnegut's: "the way a young cannibal might eat the hearts of brave, old enemies. Their magic would become hers."

To the three how-to manuals mentioned in ***Slapstick, Jailbird*** adds a couple more: Lincoln's "with malice toward none" Second Inaugural—Vonnegut may look like Mark Twain, but he feels as bad as Honest Abe; "Strange mingling of mirth and tears, of the tragic and grotesque, of cap and crown, of Socrates and Rabelais, of Aesop and Marcus

Aurelius," said Robert Ingersoll of Lincoln—and most radical of all, Jesus Christ's Sermon on the Mount. Kilgore Trout, one of the few Vonnegut characters besides Wanda June to survive the defenestration of *Breakfast,* is in jail for treason because he has preached the Sermon on the Mount.

Galapagos is about evolution, *Deadeye Dick* is about the neutron bomb, and *Bluebeard* about the Abstract Expressionism of Evil. Strong stuff!

Like Starbuck in *Jailbird,* Rabo Karabekian in *Bluebeard* tries "to believe what the people with hearts believed," so perhaps he's a good man "just the same"—a child of survivors of the Turkish massacre of the Armenians, which gives us one more genocide to grieve; a veteran, like all Vonnegut's antiheroes, of World War II, which he spent commanding a platoon of artists "so good at camoflage, that half the things we hid from the enemy have to this very day never been seen again"; a postwar intimate of Pollock and Rothko; a man once divorced, once widowed, twice a failed father. Although Rabo paints, he isn't very good at the modern art that renders "absolutely nothing but itself." Much of his own work's been destroyed "thanks to unforeseen chemical reactions between the sizing of my canvas and the acrylic wallpaint and colored tapes I had applied to them." He rusticates in misanthropic Hamptons exile with an empty pool and a locked potato barn, inside which we'll meet his last will and testament, his secret witness.

There are the usual dark chords. We are reminded of the industrial know-how a genocide needs "to kill that many big, resourceful animals cheaply and quickly, make sure that nobody gets away, and dispose of mountains of meat and bones afterwards." (On the college lecture circuit, Vonnegut speaks of "humanity itself [as] an unstoppable glacier made of hot meat, which ate up everything in sight and then made love, and then doubled in size again.") But there are also the usual grace notes—those lovely moments that seem to fall in Vonnegut's pages like autumn leaves. According to Rabo, for example, God Almighty Himself "must have been hilarious when human beings so mingled iron and water and fire as to make a railroad train."

But what we've picked up, of importance, along the way in these late novels are more books of recipes—Shakespeare, *Don Quixote,* Goethe's *Faust,* Picasso's *Guernica, Gulliver's Travels, Alice in Wonderland.* This is the library of how-to (and etiquette) instruction manuals—cookbooks and sacred civilizing texts; a nest of brains where we sit down to read the latest novel by the last innocent white man in America, a theoretician of Chaos before James Gleick explained it, a Green before they got together in political parties in places like Germany; a Johnny Appleseed of decencies; a Space-Age Buddha; Vonnegut at 68.

We should know he's up to something special in *Hocus Pocus* just from the name of his antihero, Eugene Debs Hartke. Eugene V. Debs, of course, was the American labor leader who said, "While there is a lower class I am in it. While there is a criminal element I am of it. While there is a soul in prison I am not free." Debs tried to keep us out of World War I but lost out to the more practical-minded Samuel Gompers. He will lose out again with Hartke, who wanted as a boy to go to the University of Michigan but who ends up instead, after cheating in a high school science fair, at West Point. From West Point he goes to Vietnam. ("If I were a fighter plane instead of a human being," he says, "there would be little pictures of people painted all over me.") From Vietnam, he goes to teach the dyslexic children of the Anglo-Saxon filthy rich at Tarkington College in upstate New York, where there's Samoza Hall and a Pahlavi Pavilion. From Tarkington, he goes to teach black and Hispanic illiterates at the New York State Maximum Security Adult Correctional Institution at Athena, "a brutal fortress of iron and masonry on a naked hilltop," directly across the valley from the college.

For different reasons, in the year 2001 learning-disabled children of the filthy rich and illiterate black and Hispanic dope dealers can't read the Writing on the Wall. Even if they could, according to Hartke, "Just because some of us can read and write and do a little math, that doesn't mean we deserve to conquer the Universe."

We are reading the story that Hartke has written down on stray scraps of brown wrapping paper and the backs of envelopes while awaiting trial, like Howard Campbell Jr. in *Mother Night,* like Kilgore Trout in *Jailbird,* for treason. There's been a failed revolution. The blacks and Hispanics escaped from Athena, crossed the frozen lake in the valley, ate the horses and the campus dogs and killed some white people in the "emerald-studded Oz or City of God or Camelot" of Tarkington. Before they all got murdered in their turn, they declared a sort of Paris Commune. Since it's assumed by the triumphant military government that blacks and Hispanics couldn't possibly have plotted this revolt on their own, Hartke must have done it for them. Besides waiting for his trial, he is also adding up the number of women he's gone to bed with and the number of men he's killed, and he's afraid he'll come to the exact same body count.

I'm not going to tell you about Hartke's crazy wife and mother-in-law, who make spiderwebs of toilet paper all over the house. Or just how our prisons came to be "color-coded." Or what we're supposed to think of GRIOT, the computer program of the sociobiologists. Or why Hartke thinks "the two principal currencies of the planet are the Yen and fellatio." And never mind what goes on at the Black Cat Café. But there are some things you need to know.

In the year 2001 the Japanese run our prisons and hospitals, though they were smart enough to pass on our inner-city schools. Koreans own *The New York Times.* Italians own the St. Louis Cardinals. Among the trustees of Tarkington College are a thinly disguised William F. Buckley Jr. and a thinly disguised Malcolm Forbes (who shows up with Elizabeth Taylor on a motorcycle). These trustees are told, though they refuse to believe it, that they've treated America as a "plantation," and now that "the soil is exhausted, and the natives are getting sicker and hungrier every day, begging for food and medicine and shelter," and the water mains are broken and the bridges are falling down, "You are taking all your money and getting out of here."

They are told this in the valley where once upon a time were built the covered wagons that went west—maybe even the prairie schooners for the fast-food Donner Party. There are also in this valley Indian ghosts, severed heads, a floating castle and twenty-seven perpetual-motion machines "with garnets and amethysts for bearings, with arms and legs of exotic woods, with tumbling balls of ivory, with chutes and counterweights of silver." As if to balance this "magic of precious metals"—as everything in *Hocus Pocus* is exquisitely balanced, from the dyslexics and the illiterates to the number of women loved and men murdered—there is a carillon of thirty-two bells made "from mingled Union and Confederate rifle barrels and cannonballs gathered up after the Battle of Gettysburg." At Gettysburg, in fact, the man who started Tarkington College was shot by Confederate soldiers because he looked so much like Abraham Lincoln.

Mention is also made of Lee, Custer and Westmoreland.

A critic doesn't have to work very hard to figure out that, for Kurt Vonnegut, the Civil War between whites and blacks is far from over and the Civil War between rich and poor has only begun: That's what he's writing his novel about. Nor need you be a semiotician to notice that he does his dreaming about the Civil War inside the fevered head of American literature.

It's not just that the prisoners skating over the frozen lake are right out of *Uncle Tom's Cabin.* Nor that we meet James Fenimore Cooper, Theodore Dreiser and a mortician with the name of "Norman Updike." Like Mailer and Arthur Miller, Hartke can't stop brooding about Marilyn Monroe. Edgar Allan Poe is quoted. We're actually introduced to Moby Dick (at least to his penis). I'm sure there are New England Transcendentalists hiding like angels in these hardwood trees. "Tarkington" probably refers as well to Booth—like Vonnegut, an Indiana novelist, although he went to Fitzgerald's Princeton instead of Vonnegut's (and Pynchon's) Cornell. Remember the *Penrod* stories and *The Plutocrat*? Like Cheever's *Falconer*, *Hocus Pocus* is a Sing Sing/Attica novel. Hartke's scraps of paper remind me of those "odds

and ends of thoughts" that Dr. Reefy, in *Winesburg, Ohio,* scribbled down on bits of paper and then stuffed away in his pockets to become "little hard round balls." I wouldn't even be surprised if one reason Vonnegut left all the dirty words out of *Hocus Pocus* was that he felt as playful as Mark Twain felt when he left all the weather out of *The American Claimant.*

If I seem to be working too hard, it's because nobody else did—except Vonnegut. Like Walt Whitman (and Allen Ginsberg), when Vonnegut goes to the Civil War, he's a male nurse. *Leaves of Grass* is another of his sacred texts. American literature itself, the lens through which he looks at history, bloody history, is a comfort and a subversion. According to Hawthorne: "'Faith!' shouted Goodman Brown, in a voice of agony and desperation; and the echoes of the forest mocked him, crying, 'Faith! Faith!' as if bewildered wretches were seeking her all through the wilderness." And Melville, on reading Hawthorne, stopped to shake his head: "For, in certain moods, no man can weigh this world without throwing in something, somehow like Original Sin, to strike the uneven balance . . . this black conceit pervades him through and through."

Black conceits, black apples, black balloons. Strong stuff!

James Buchan (review date 20 October 1990)

SOURCE: "Any Old Irony," in *Spectator,* Vol. 266, No. 8467, October 20, 1990, pp. 31, 33.

[*In the following review, Buchan states that* Hocus Pocus *has many elements in common with Vonnegut's earlier novels.*]

This is Kurt Vonnegut's 17th novel to appear in England, so the British reader should know what to expect. It's all here in *Hocus Pocus,* vintage Vonnegut: the short narrative units, the repetitions as in a roundelay, the intergalactic knowingness and the small-town good sense, the good humour, the tricks of typography, the exclamation marks as in a debutante's letter, the diversions, the threadbare coincidences.

Let me say right off that I can't begin with this stuff. Even when I was a hippy, I couldn't stand Vonnegut. Vonnegut, along with a Californian novelist of cloying whimsy called Richard Brautigan, were the only novelists read in my circle of friends. I rebelled against this orthodoxy—I thought rebellion against orthodoxy was the point about being a hippy. I also thought Vonnegut's relativism was dead fishy. There is a passage in *Slaughterhouse-Five* that greatly impressed my friends:

All moments, past, present and future, always have
existed, always will exist.

This statement, I now see, is nonsense.

Kurt Vonnegut began his writing career in science fiction.
Early books such as *Player Piano* and *Cat's Cradle* caught
the spirit of the 1950s and early 1960s, when a lot of things
seemed possible that don't seem possible now. In *Slaughterhouse-Five,* Vonnegut's masterpiece, he feels sufficiently
at home in the genre to use it to creep up on and describe
what is obviously his capital experience: his capture by the
Germans in the Ardennes, his deportation to Dresden and
the fire-bombing of the city. The approach is circuitous.
Vonnegut's main character, an optometrist called Billy Pilgrim bursts into tears long after the war when he hears, at a
party for his 18th wedding anniversary, a barbershop quartet. He lies down and is transported back in time to Dresden
in February 1945:

> The meat locker was a very safe shelter. All that
> happened down there was an occasional shower of
> calcimine. The Americans and four of their guards
> and a few dressed carcasses were down there, and
> nobody else. The guards drew together instinctively,
> rolled their eyes. They experimented with one ex-
> pression and then another, said nothing, though their
> mouths were often open. They looked like a silent
> film of a barbershop quartet. 'So long, forever,' they
> might have been singing, 'old fellows and pals; so
> long forever, old sweethearts and pals—God bless
> 'em—'

I know no passage in a later book that delivers authentic
emotion in such a strange shape.

In the later books, Vonnegut has pieces of science fiction
lying about—I suppose to remind the world of his humble
literary origins, rather as a Mafia don might display a
cobbler's last in his office. Vonnegut's most tiresome character, a science fiction writer named Kilgore Trout, keeps
turning up. Trout's stories can be found only in old-fashioned
soft-core magazines, though his maker—in *Breakfast of
Champions* (1973)—promises him an implausible posthumous fame. In *Hocus Pocus,* Trout surfaces anonymously
and gratuitously when the lead character comes on an old
copy of *Black Garterbelt* in his wartime bootlocker. He sits
down and reads a science-fiction story about the planet
Tralfamadore (an old friend from *Slaughterhouse-Five*). But
in truth, science fiction for Vonnegut is now nothing more
than a mechanical literary device to give distance and irony.
He also uses commercial and bureaucratic language, capital letters in odd places, drawings, TV and barrackroom
medical terminology for the same general purpose.

Hocus Pocus is set in the future, or rather in a parody of
the mid-1980s US. The 82nd Airborne is fighting the Drug
War in the South Bronx; great American corporations have
been sold to Koreans and Omanis; in small-town bars, the
good ol' boys say, 'Give me a Wop', when they want a
Budweiser because Anheuser-Busch is Italian-owned. All the
rich and powerful in the story are in fact paupers, because
they have put their money in a company called Microsec-
ond Arbitrage which is going belly-up. With Vonnegut, one
could always detect liberal anger behind the so-it-goes smile,
but here for once he comes right out with it:

> There I was in late middle age, cut loose in a thor-
> oughly bankrupt nation whose assets had been sold
> off to foreigners, a nation swamped by unchecked
> plagues and superstition and illiteracy and hypnotic
> TV, with virtually no health services for the poor.
> Where to go? What to do?

The story takes place in the Finger Lakes region of upstate
New York. It concerns Eugene Debs Hardtke, a good soldier in Vietnam, now a good professor of music appreciation and, I think, literature at a minor college for the dim
children of rich parents. Across the lake from Tarkington
College is the New York State Maximum Security Adult
Correctional Institution: the precise bureaucratic euphemism
prepares the reader, even at this early stage, for some pretty
heavy irony. You just know that Vonnegut is setting you up
for the congruences between the two institutions, not their
differences, and this is what happens. Hardtke is fired from
Tarkington for being unpatriotic and promiscuous; he moves
across to teach at Athena; there is a mass jail break; the prisoners escape across the ice and lay waste Tarkington; they
are subdued and Hardtke is appointed warden of a new
prison at Tarkington; and then he is imprisoned there.

In a realistic novel, these leaden echoes across the lake might
not be so obtrusive. But Vonnegut despises the realistic
novel. He has no time for novelistic free choice: his characters act as they do because of bad chemicals in the blood-
stream, because their families are 'booby-trapped' with
dyslexia or madness, or because they're programmed by
Tralfamadorians or some such. The prison has been contracted out to a Japanese corporation and the warden is a
survivor of Hiroshima:

> Warden Matsumoto was an odd duck. Many of his
> quirks were no doubt a consequence of his having
> had an atomic bomb dropped on him from child-
> hood.

Vonnegut's characters are types of this cartoon quality: they
have only one characteristic or attribute. There is Ernest
Hubble Hiscock, who flew into a Japanese carrier at Midway; Damon Stern, who rides a unicycle; Tex Johnson, who

gets crucified in the college belfry; Mary Alice French, who won first prize at the Ohio Science Fair. These characters, about 40 of them, parade quickly across the stage or rather tap into one another like billiard balls. That's all there is by way of narrative link, except some fraudulent coincidence and a bit of repetition. There is one repeated phrase—'buried next to the stable, in the shadow of Musket Mountain when the Sun went down'—which had me chewing the carpet by the end.

On the way, there are good passages. It may be his experience of war, but Vonnegut has an eye for extreme dislocation. There is a scene where Hardtke, fishing on the lake with his mad mother-in-law, sees a prison truck break down and there, stepping out of it, for the first time, prisoners, black men. At that moment, his mother-in-law catches a pike. Later, a Malcolm Forbes character arrives at Tarkington to collect a degree with a retinue and a blown-up replica of his Irish castle, which then sails away over the prison. Vonnegut also understands better than anybody the role of TV in the US and how some Americans have difficulty remembering which is reality and which is commentary on it.

> When I came back out, the TV set was displaying a program I had watched when I was a boy, *Howdy Doody.* I told Donner the Warden wanted to see him, but he didn't seem to know who I was. I felt as though I were trying to wake up a mean drunk. I thought I might have to fight Donner before he realised that *Howdy Doody* wasn't the main thing going on.

But in *Hocus Pocus,* Vonnegut is handling themes—war, return from war, madness—that he did well in *Slaughterhouse-Five.* The parade of Tom-and-Jerry characters adds nothing to our knowledge. The book ends with Hardtke enumerating both the people he killed in Vietnam and the women he has slept with. Guess what, it's the same number and there's a riddle and a drawing to show it! So it goes.

David Streitfeld (review date 21 October 1990)

SOURCE: "The Wages of Rage," in *Washington Post Book World,* Vol. 20, No. 42, October 21, 1990, p. 15.

[*In the review below, Streitfeld argues that society is the main character in* Hocus Pocus *and that Vonnegut's sense of dismay with America is the novel's overriding tone.*]

Sixty-seven years old and recipient of as large a measure of fame as any writer in our time, Kurt Vonnegut still does what he can to enlighten the masses. He meets the public, gives lectures, talks to the press, opens himself up. An incident arising out of one such encounter last year, when Vonnegut spoke at a California university and gave an interview to a reporter for the local paper, bears repeating.

The interview, as printed, was less than laudatory. When Vonnegut saw a copy, he fired off a letter to the reporter, telling her that the story had "a paragraph of pure editorializing suggesting to most readers that a vain and shamefully overpaid phony and hypocrite had passed through town. . ."

He added that the reporter gave him no inkling she felt this way, and asked: "Is it fair or even decent for a so-called reporter to keep such scorn concealed, so that the scorned person cannot try to deal with it until it appears in print?"

Vonnegut then forgot all about the story—until his letter turned up for sale from a California rare-book dealer noted for both the high quality and high price of his material. In this case, the 450-word letter, plus photocopies of two stories by the reporter, was offered for $350.

To show what a good deal it was, half the letter was quoted in the catalogue. Since copyright law forbids quoting extensive passages from unpublished letters without permission, Vonnegut was angry again—so he instructed his lawyer to get in touch with the bookseller.

A minor episode, no doubt. But when you consider it in light of Vonnegut's career, it takes on a larger significance. For hasn't his anger about various situations, tragedies and indignities been not only the engine that has powered more than a dozen works of fiction over 40 years, but also a profitable activity?

That's true for his publishers, for opportunists like the reporter and the book dealer, and of course for Vonnegut himself. "It's just a matter of luck whether you make a fit with your society or not," the writer says modestly, sitting in his Manhattan kitchen. "It's a real Adam Smith market. There's only about 300 of us who make a living from this."

His new novel, *Hocus Pocus,* is fitting in nicely. The public likes it, the critics have generally voted thumbs up, and the author himself, grading this book as he has done with his previous efforts, gives it an A. Perhaps part of its appeal is the picture it paints of this country slowly sinking in its own sludge:

> The year is 2001 now.
>
> If all had gone the way a lot of people thought it would, Jesus Christ would have been among us again, and the American flag would have been planted on Venus and Mars.

No such luck!

As in most Vonnegut novels, people are secondary to the main character, which is society. His training as an anthropologist—an M.A. from the University of Chicago—allows him to see culture as a gadget. And a glance at the newspaper tells him all he needs to know about the world. But his final verdict is surprising: "There is some wickedness, but almost all of it is ignorance and stupidity. I think we are a good-hearted people."

Oh, yeah? What about the looting of the savings and loans?

"That's *some* people," he says, and then adds: "If any of my kids did what Neil [Bush] did, I would never speak to that kid again."

So he'd be upset?

"Filled with hate! Filled with hate!"

But even Vonnegut isn't completely consistent. On his front door of this one-time G.E. public relations man is a faded sticker: "Boycott G.E. Stop Nuclear Weapons." In his kitchen, meanwhile, he has an enormous G.E. refrigerator.

"Do I?" he asks, turning to look. "I don't even know."

He worked for the company in the late '40s, quitting in '51 when he started earning enough on his short stories to live on. "I was so proud of this country when I worked for GE. It was a great company then and a great country then. And now, I have such a sense of letdown."

People who like his books, he believes, feel the same way. "In one of my books I had the motto, 'Lonesome no more.' I suggested that to Sarge Shriver when he and McGovern were running for president and vice president. I get letters from people saying, 'you think just the way I do.'" And he laughs a great big rumbling laugh that seems to frequently issue from him. "They thought they were all alone."

Ian Bell (review date 21 October 1990)

SOURCE: "One-Liners," in *Observer Review,* October 21, 1990, p. 58.

[*In the following review, Bell argues that the narrative of* Hocus Pocus *becomes secondary to themes that Vonnegut wishes to discuss.*]

Here comes another of Vonnegut's exemplary tales about one man unravelling the tangle of his life and trying to find out What Really Happened. It is full of wit, humanity, cruelty and trite narrative devices.

This time, as editor 'KV' explains, the imprisoned hero has committed his story to scraps of paper, thus allowing scope for the elliptical, the gnomic and the discursive. Often, these entries are one-sentence paragraphs.

'Vietnam.'

That's one. Eugene Debs Hartke, a West Pointer named after the only socialist ever to mount a real challenge for the presidency, was in charge of the helicopter evacuation from the US embassy in Saigon. His experience of war looms large as memory and metaphor.

'Losers!'

That's another entry. *Hocus Pocus* is composed of defeats. In 2001 the United States is foreign-owned, its ecology ruined, its economy shattered. Most of the book's characters are mad (Hartke's wife and mother-in-law), sad (his many lovers), drunk (ditto), drugged (America in general), suicidal (any character impeding the narrative) or affectless. The remainder are the Ruling Class, the rich who sold out to the Japanese and who, squatting on their assets, treat their fellow Americans as aliens.

They run Tarkington College, where Hartke finds a job teaching their idiot children until he is implicated in the biggest jail-break in history. The college serves for a satire on the education industry, with its Pahlavi pavilion, Samoza Hall and Vonnegut Memorial Fountain. The racially segregated, profit-making Sony-owned prison does for a parallel skit on, well, racism and profit.

'Cough.'

The trouble with Vonnegut's devices (that was another: his hero acquires TB) is that they make it easy for him to subordinate narrative to theme. The snippets form a thread on which he strings pearls of *faux-naif* wisdom. Thus: 'The prime two movers in the Universe are Time and Luck.' Or, '"Life's a bad dream", he said. "Do you know that?"' Or, 'All nations bigger than Denmark are crocks of doo-doo'.

'Deep.'

You can do anything with a character in this form, load any amount of historical tonnage on him. Vonnegut has done it before. Hartke brings to mind Eliot Rosewater, Walter F. Starbuck, Billy Pilgrim and the rest. The author is, as usual, worried about war, money, history, psychological imbalance and chaos.

It is all done with voice. Vonnegut is a master of the first-person, manic-depressive stand-up. His statements may be hackneyed but they are, usually, funny. That is true even when the irony is leaden and the plot becomes absurdly self-referential, like a ball of string needing only one tug to pull it apart.

The best joke sits among the publishing details, beneath the copyright notice: 'Kurt Vonnegut has asserted his right to be identified as the author of this work.'

'Hoc est corpus.'

David Montrose (review date 26 October 1990)

SOURCE: "Life as a Cruel Joke," in *Times Literary Supplement,* October 26, 1990, p. 1146.

[*In the following review, Montrose characterizes* Hocus Pocus *as a novelized essay and praises Vonnegut's masterful style.*]

Hocus Pocus presents a dystopian America where the future (2001) is like the present, only more so. Everything has worsened: the economy, the ravaging of natural resources, crime, the drugs problem, urban decay, poverty. Petrol and food are rationed. The rich have sold Big Business to foreigners and live off the proceeds. The only surviving "American enterprises" are Mafia-controlled. Nor is public property exempt. National Forests have been sold to a Swedish timber corporation; prisons are run, for profit, by the Japanese (they have, however, declined to take over inner-city schools). The novel, like most of Kurt Vonnegut's since *Slaughterhouse-Five* (1969), takes the form of a grimly comic autobiography replete with vicissitudes, guilt and futility: life as a cruel joke. The autobiographer, Eugene Debs Hartke, recounts his story while awaiting trial for organizing the biggest prison break in American history.

Like most Vonnegut heroes, Hartke is beset by fate, inadvertently becoming first a career soldier, then a teacher. As a much-decorated officer in Vietnam, he was nicknamed "The Preacher", so adept was he at delivering "lethal hocus pocus", the official lies which justified the war to his men (who "died for other people's vanity and foolishness"), the press and television. As a professor at a college in upstate New York for the "learning-disabled . . . plain stupid or comatose" offspring of the wealthy, he turns into an enemy of what Vonnegut once termed "the American way of thinking about America", debunking the self-seeking myths of the "Ruling Class". Eventually, he is summarily fired after falling foul of a right-wing television and newspaper pundit. This reverse saves his life: he obtains (by chance, naturally)

a residential post at the nearby maximum security prison (whose Warden survived Hiroshima) and thus avoids the bloodshed which ensues after the convicts, all black, break out and overrun the college and surrounding town. Hartke is accused, falsely, of masterminding the escape, because of his reputation and because the authorities believe that "Black people couldn't mastermind anything". Obviously, he will be found guilty.

To some extent, Vonnegut is, like Gore Vidal, an anti-historian of America, undermining popular fictions, removing varnish and inserting warts—although his methods are quite different (Vidal offers detailed portraits, Vonnegut lightning sketches). Here, Vonnegut condemns the "Ruling Class" as greedy, hypocritical and hubristic. He also despairs of mankind as a species, notably its capacity for vainglory and destructiveness. In his finest novel, *The Sirens of Titan,* he derided that former trait by portraying the whole of human history as having been manipulated to assist an inconsequential mission by an alien creature. In *Hocus Pocus,* a short story by an anonymous writer (Kilgore Trout, surely) posits that humans were developed by "intelligent threads of energy trillions of light-years long" solely to devise survival tests for germs, the true "darlings of the Universe".

Derided, also, is the human propensity for ruining the planet while arguing about the costs of rectifying matters. A minor character proposes that a gigantic epitaph be carved in the Grand Canyon "for the flying-saucer people to find . . . WE COULD HAVE SAVED IT BUT WE WERE TOO DOGGONE CHEAP". Only he didn't say "doggone", adds Hartke, who eschews, "obscenity" throughout since it entitles "people who don't want unpleasant information to close their ears an eyes to you".

To varying degrees, from *Breakfast of Champions* (1973) onwards, the purpose of Vonnegut's novels has been moral instruction. There is nothing intrinsically wrong in that. Unfortunately, these later novels have had little to match the quirky invention of the best of Vonnegut's earlier work—*The Sirens of Titan, Mother Night, Cat's Cradle, Slaughterhouse-Five*—while characterization has thinned to the point where *Hocus Pocus* almost resembles a novelized essay; one set of colourless mouthpieces utters Vonnegut's sentiments, another provides those to be demolished. Fortunately Vonnegut remains an effectual stylist, combining deadpan irony and *faux naïveté*. As usual, his central narrative winds through a mosaic of aphorisms, verbal tics, digressions, homilies, obscure facts. Familiar ingredients reappear: hereditary insanity (Hartke's wife and mother-in-law are afflicted), obesity, suicides and outlandish deaths, war, outrageous fortune (even multi-millionaires are but a swift plot-twist away from penury), man-made catastrophes, white-collar crime, alcoholism. . . . This compendium of devices and concerns may have hardened into a formula, but it has not yet ceased to be a diverting one.

Gordon Lubold (review date 1990)

SOURCE: A review of *Hocus Pocus,* in *West Coast Review of Books,* Vol. 15, No. 6, 1990, p. 24.

[*In the following review, Lubold argues that the key to* Hocus Pocus *is the way in which Vonnegut takes the concerns of today and portrays them in the extreme in his futuristic setting.*]

Vonnegut's new novel is about a man who has returned from Vietnam, and is now, in 2001, recalling events when he worked at a school in Upstate New York and later staged a prison break in a nearby prison. Now he awaits trial for this crime. But *Hocus Pocus* delivers a lot more; in fact, any plot is secondary to the author's presentation of the confusing and bizarre reality of the 21st century.

Vonnegut fuses his version of a futuristic reality with one which is familiar to the one we now face in the 1990s, with the Japanese buying up everything from national park concession stands to movie studios, and with African-Americans, who continue to be thrown in jail. It's an eerie resemblance, because he takes these issues and transmutes them into an extreme, causing us to reflect on our own experience and what we will be confronting soon, if Vonnegut's wild scenario ever comes true.

Life becomes chaotic for Eugene Debs Hartke, who teaches at Tarkington but who later must stand trial for his involvement in a prison break. Add to this his insanity from his participation in Vietnam, which stimulates Vonnegut's imagination, providing him with a metaphor for the way we must abide by what we are told to do, whether it is right or wrong. The juxtaposition of Hartke's reflections about Vietnam upon the suppression of the society gives the impression that there is a relationship between the way Vietnam vets went off and fought a war and how segments of our society are drafted into playing a certain role.

Meanwhile, the Japanese yen has become the preferred currency to the less-than-valuable dollar, which, even in 1990, isn't all that ridiculous.

The kind of society he portrays is worrisome; he has extracted all of these present-day concerns into an anarchic mess, with people finally paying for their earlier sins. But the plot (and that is a narrow way of defining what actually happens in the book) is a weave of strange predictions and ideas. But there is much more than can be alluded to here; more readings of the book would reveal more ways of looking at a planet and a people who seem bent on self-destruction.

What is important about the book is how Vonnegut's style makes the book work, and whether that style will either overwhelm and intimidate, or leave you wanting more, either way it will provoke.

Robert Phillips (review date Spring 1991)

SOURCE: A review of *Hocus Pocus,* in *The Hudson Review,* Vol. XLIV, No. 1, Spring, 1991, pp. 135-36.

[*In the excerpt below, Phillips criticizes Vonnegut's style in* Hocus Pocus.]

In closing [*Hocus Pocus*], I was reminded of John Jay Chapman's remark: "When I put down a book by Stevenson, I swear I am hungry for something to read." Kurt Vonnegut's book left me hungry indeed; it is almost totally devoid of some standard ingredients of fiction—dialogue, form, confrontation, coherent plot. The author relies almost totally on the narrator and his one point of view. And the narration comes to us tricked-up with "unconventional lines separating passages within chapters" which "indicate where one scrap ended and the next began. The shorter the passage, the shorter the scrap" ("Editor's Note"). The narrator did not have access to uniform writing paper, see? The writer, locked up in a library and facing trial, was desperate to express himself. His name, Eugene Debs Hartke, is clue to Vonnegut's social concerns within the novel. Anyone who owns an aging VW Beetle is fine. The narrator manages to disparage rich kids, Japanese entrepreneurs and all prosperous foreigners, optimists, and people who are mentally ill. At one point the narrator's wife and mother-in-law are both carted off to an asylum, much to his relief. The narrator's definition of high art is, "Making the most of the raw materials of futility."

The snippet-technique soon begins to wear. One card or shard reads, in its entirety, "Vietnam." Another states grandly, "There is so much we have to learn about TV!" And because the narrator has developed TB, many cards are devoted to his cough: "Cough, cough. Silence. Two more; Cough, cough. There. I'm ok now. Cough. That's it. I really am OK now. Peace." One wonders what the author would have put on the paper had the narrator suffered from, say, postnasal drip?

The author's, or the narrator's, international vision embraces such statements as, "All nations bigger than Denmark are crocks of doo-doo." Such euphemisms fill the book with cuteness. Repeatedly he refers to when "the excrement hit the air-conditioning in Vietnam." Either Vonnegut wants to make sure he makes his point, or he is unaware of his repetitiousness; how many times need we be told that the Chemistry Department of Harvard University developed napalm?

One has to admit Vonnegut is capable of provoking a smile, as when he describes some natives as being "just as white as Nancy Reagan." But the slap-dash quality of *Hocus Pocus* is disconcerting. For instance, "After Lyle Hooper was executed, with a bullet behind the ear, I visited the Trustees in the stable. Tex Johnson was still spiked to the cross-timbers in the loft overhead, and they knew it. But before I tell about that, I had better finish my story of how I got a job in Athena."

Vonnegut's penchant for reiterating a phrase ("And so it goes," was the litany in *Slaughterhouse-Five*) is here reduced to "What a planet!" His inventive powers seem to be wearing thin. It is difficult to disagree with his fine ecological feelings in *Hocus Pocus.* On the other hand, it was André Gide who observed, "Fine feelings are the stuff that bad literature is made of."

James Wood (review date 15 November 1991)

SOURCE: "The Wrecked Generation," in *Times Literary Supplement,* November 15, 1991, pp. 8-9.

[*In the review below, Wood discusses the role of comedy in* Fates Worse than Death.]

Dreamy, hectically anecdotal, slovenly and bearish with the truth, Kurt Vonnegut's writing has always handled fact with comic negligence. It has a kind of epistemological cockiness, amassing detail only to mock its sureties. Knowledge enters his books with a hiatus, a cloudiness. Consider, for example, his fondness for place-name couplets—Genoa, Italy, or Hellertown, Pennsylvania, or Indianapolis, Indiana. He loads his sentences with all kinds of names: "They were Lance Rumfoord, of Newport, Rhode Island, and his bride, the former Cynthia Landry, who had been a childhood sweetheart of John F. Kennedy, in Hyannis Port, Massachusetts." This is a kind of nonsense verse—mildly subversive, rhythmical, sprawling, but comically precise ("the former Cynthia Landry"). It is not that names like George Minor Moakely or Miss Francine Pefko or Indianapolis, Indiana are intrinsically funny (as bad English comic writers seem to think); what is comic is the author's belief that he can locate himself and his readers through names. Such *earnest striving* merely unmoors us, of course.

Autobiography, with its traditionally zealous relation to the

real and historical, is a fine playground for Vonnegut's games. Like its predecessor *Palm Sunday,* this latest collection of essays and speeches [*Fates Worse than Death*] is rigged with digressions, self-mockery, useless gossip and parenthetical ironics. There are many piercing jokes. The book's comic circuitry is bathos, from high to low and back again. The prose makes wild connections, but abjures argumentative termini. As in Vonnegut's fiction, it is hard to know what to believe. "All persons," runs Vonnegut's smirking disclaimer, "living and dead, are purely coincidental and should not be construed." It is entirely appropriate that the book should open with a photograph of Vonnegut and Heinrich Böll, laughing together. Vonnegut, as ever, looks mild, open and dreamy. The two writers, he tells us in his preface, were talking about how best to fake a wound so as to avoid fighting in an army. "Böll said that the correct way to shoot yourself was through a loaf of bread, in order to avoid powder burns. That is what we are laughing about." A page later, Vonnegut comments on the preface he is just finishing: "Only now am I sticking this coverlet, as my editor, Faith Sale, and I prepare to put the creature to beddy-bye." *Faith Sale:* probably she is Vonnegut's editor. But something about the insouciance of that sentence wraps her status in doubt, co-opts her as one of Vonnegut's creations, one of his names.

This is a matter of style, of course, as it is in all great comedy. Though Vonnegut's prose has lost some of its verbal affluence (there is much less flossing and polishing than there used to be), *Fates Worse Than Death* still reminds us of the vigour of the contemporary comic American voice from e. e. cummings, through John Berryman to Vonnegut and Pynchon. We might call this voice the unbearable lightness of style. It has a perilous levity. It is a language of rapid evasion and denial, with all kinds of ironic buoyancies. In Berryman's *Dream Songs* for instance, and in Vonnegut's *Slaughterhouse-Five,* rages, griefs and complaints are moving in proportion to the denial of them which the language effects. Poised between innocence and the irony of forced jollity, it is a way of childishly baring one's soul. One thinks of Berryman's "I'm cross with god who has wrecked this generation", or one of the lines from Song 14: "Life, friends, is boring". This is Vonnegut's tone also; the shoulder-shrugging surrender of "Life is sure funny sometimes" (*Cat's Cradle*) or "Hi Ho" (*Slapstick*) or, most famously, "So it goes" (*Slaughterhouse-Five*). It is perilous because one word out of place will turn this unbearable lightness into unbearable heaviness. In this book, while discussing his father (gentle, tolerant, serene) and his mother (neurotic, alcoholic), Vonnegut's tone never trips. But he almost loses it when discussing a fellow writer, Donald Barthelme, who died aged fifty-eight, at the peak of his talent: "At a memorial service for the brilliant author Donald Barthelme (who was surely sorry to die, since he was going from strength to strength). . . ." The lightness here, and at a couple of other moments, seems a little too airy. Most of the time, however, Vonnegut is more grounded. The key is rhythm and pacing, as in this description of his son: "He is now a pediatrician in Boston, with a wife and two fine sons, and two fine automobiles."

Vonnegut's prose is rude, gassy and sublime. It throws out splinters of comedy with great ease. There are many conversational quips, most of them coyly clothed in brackets. Gossiping about Tennessee Williams, for instance, he suddenly cracks: "(He and T. S. Eliot grew up in St Louis, but Williams admitted it. He didn't all of a sudden start talking like the Archbishop of Canterbury.)" Other jokes are larger, and in the service of his decent political radicalism (there are speeches and essays here about America's war-greed, the folly of "surgical" bombing, the cruelty and secret longevity of Western imperialism—Vonnegut's usual quiver of themes). Writing about how liberty was not born in Boston or Philadelphia in 1776 because "slavery was legal" and women were unfree, he adds: "Liberty was only *conceived* in Boston or Philadelphia. Boston or Philadelphia was the motel of liberty, so to speak."

Vonnegut is lovable because he is warm, sentimental (in the cute and compact way a cartoon is sentimental) and self-mocking. All of the speeches reproduced in this book end with "I thank you for your attention." On the page, and so often followed by gossip and chat, this formal gratitude takes on a sly ambiguity. Unlike the audience at a speech, we hear this of our own volition. So he has no need to thank us. But he retains this line because it is humble, but also because in its uselessness, it comically undercuts pomposity. Vonnegut has radical charm. The effect of a speech on liberty, followed by this refrain of "I thank you for your attention", and then tailed by "(After that speech, a bunch of us were loaded onto a yellow school bus and taken to a Spanish restaurant)"— the effect is that of the author offering himself up at various levels, on different frequencies, with all kinds of shadings, without insistence.

Vonnegut has always put himself on to the page. John Updike, praising him as an "imaginer" rather than a "self-dramatizer", once referred to him as one who "disdains the personal". Yet this is not the sense of him that his readers have. One feels a powerful impact of vision and soul. This vision is politically radical, dreamily utopian, and it has a number of recurring themes and places (Ilium, New York, Tralfamadore, and so on). We feel his presence as an author, which may be why he writes so well and so naturally about other American authors. The most interesting part of this book is about what Vonnegut calls "the compressed history of American authorship". This compression has to do with the foreshortening of American writers' lives (Barthelme and Hemingway are Vonnegut's examples) and the speed with which an entire generation disappears—"I'm

cross with god who has wrecked this generation". Vonnegut, like so many of his fellow writers, seems mainly cross with America, rather than God, for doing this wrecking. One senses that, at sixty-seven, he is amused and surprised to find himself a survivor.

The more Vonnegut writes, the more American he seems— a kind of de-solemnized Emerson, at once arguer, doubter, sermonizer and gossip. Indeed, Emerson's opening question of his essay *Experience,* "Where do we find ourselves?", might well stand as an epigraph to Vonnegut's questing work. Like that of the great essayist, Vonnegut's prose seems radically accountable: a man lives behind it.

Ross Clark (review date 16 November 1991)

SOURCE: "Just a Few Quick Ones Before I Go," in *The Spectator,* Vol. 267, No. 8523, November 16, 1991, p. 45.

[*In the following review, Clark argues that* Fates Worse than Death *lacks coherence.*]

Kurt Vonnegut, German-American author of *Slaughterhouse-Five,* the consummate work on the bombing of Dresden, fears he will live little longer. Paying tribute to fellow Germanic writer Heinrich Böll in the preface to his latest book [*Fates Worse than Death*], he mentions that Böll died in 1974 at the age of 67. Then he adds, sorrowfully but proudly: 'One year short of my age now, and I smoke as much as he did'.

Therein lies the reason for this somewhat pointless 'autobiographical collage of the 1980s'. Vonnegut is determined to make a collection of a lifetime's loose witticisms before he kicks the bucket. Some of the book is made up of throwaway remarks he made in private conversation years ago. More of the book is made up of throwaway remarks he wished he had made but thought about too late.

The rest consists of lectures and sermons he has delivered, not all of which impressed their audiences. The greater the disparity between the reception a lecture received and the reception Vonnegut thinks it deserved, the longer the excerpt reproduced in this book.

After transcribing one particularly meandering speech to students of Massachusetts Institute of Technology, Vonnegut admits:

> What a flop! The applause was polite enough. . .
> But nobody came up front afterward. . . What makes
> the students of today so unresponsive?

Many things do, but nothing so much as whimsical speeches delivered by old men. Vonnegut would do better to cut his losses, forget the speech and set to work on writing a real book.

This volume, an appendix from beginning to end, brings out Vonnegut's worst tendency: to babble, both in writing and in speech. It reads as if Vonnegut has had electrodes fitted to his head and connected to a teleprinter—I say teleprinter rather than computer terminal, because the teleprinter unfortunately has no editing function.

Every odd thought has been recorded, every opportunity to namedrop has been taken ('I never met John Steinbeck, but I know his widow, Elaine, and she is about my late sister's age') and when he remembers jokes he begins to recite them only to be distracted before he reaches the punchline. Often he ends paragraphs with dissociated and pointless asides:

> T. S. Eliot, whose poems about cats inspired that last-named musical [*Cats*], owed an unacknowledged debt, it has always seemed to me, to *Archie and Mehitabel* by Don Marquis, whose wife was the former Mrs Walter Vonnegut.

Vonnegut is best when relating his wartime experience (little of this book has anything to do with the 1980s). Although he writes as a benign, former angry young man, much of what he says about Dresden and other Allied bombing raids has gained poignancy since he wrote *Slaughterhouse-Five.* For example, he writes of Roosevelt's government's

> tall tales of delicate surgery performed by bombers equipped with Sperry and Norden bombsights. These instruments were so precise, we had been told, that a bombardier could drop his billets-doux down the chimney of a factory if ordered to.

Had Vonnegut, a POW in Dresden at the time of its bombardment by American explosives and (several hours later) British incendiaries, been in Baghdad last January he might already have started writing *Slaughterhouse-Six.* He might have done justice to 45 years worth of improvements to the art of bombing.

This collection, though, is sprinkled only with a few pacifist's whinges. Vonnegut complains several times of the bombing of Colonel Qaddaffi's 'daughter' in Tripoli in 1986, when surely he accepts that the showing of the 'daughter's corpse' was a crude publicity stunt by the 'colonel'.

Vonnegut appears to suspect that his book is rather feeble. One chapter from the end he writes:

> Most people my age and of my social class, no mat-

ter what job they held, are retired now. So it seems redundant (even silly) for critics to say, as many do, that I am not the promising writer I used to be.

Perhaps it is. In that case I shall merely wish him a long and happy retirement.

Valentine Cunningham (review date 22 December 1991)

SOURCE: "So It Still Goes with the Sermonettist," in *Observer Review,* December 22, 1991, p. 43.

[*In the following review of* Fates Worse than Death, *Cunningham praises Vonnegut's wit in addressing the problems of modern American society.*]

Kurt Vonnegut is the conscience of Middle America. The fates picked out an ordinary GI kid prisoner-of-war, one of us, one man out of the whole US, to endure and miraculously survive the fire-bombing of Dresden. Thus Vonnegut became a unique witness against the human awfulness Dresden symbolised.

He chose to do his testifying by playing Huck Finn, a Holy Fool, a zany and practical joker with a canny touch for textual transgression—mixing up the genres, defying distinctions between high and low modes, straight fic and Sci Fi, novels and sermons. No wonder he became the preacher of post-Holocaust righteousness Americans hate to love and love to hate. They ban his books from schools, and invite him to address graduation ceremonies.

Fates Worse Than Death is the latest volume of his cunning, rambling, edgy sermonettes, his wry, moral bomblets chucked night after night from podium and pulpit into gatherings of shrinks and museologists, Anglicans, architects, MIT graduands and the like. Rumours that the old boy was losing his knack of drilling straight into the nerve of western complacency can, on the evidence of this marvellously tetchy wit, be discounted.

Historians of American puritanism will, of course, recognise the old-fashioned, prophetic, conversionist drift. And Vonnegut devotees will be very familiar with the potent combination of freethinking and Sermon on the Mount that energises his assaults on modern Beelzebub in his native land: censors of books, Neo-Conservatives, tele-evangelists, Henry Kissinger the carpet-bomber of Hanoi, Ronnie Reagan the drowsy monger of easy showbiz wars and killer of babies (Gadaffi's baby in particular), Charlton Heston the spokesperson of the National Rifle Association, and heroic bomber pilots who drop their loads of death and scoot away.

Infantry-man Vonnegut never forgets that George Bush was an airforce flyer.

Familiarity with Vonnegut's drives and aims does not blunt the force of his barbed pieties. Not least because these are sustained by a very moving family *pietas* and a fine staunchness towards old army buddies and fellow-writers in the cause. Vonnegut's wonderfully looping celebration of his German clan's summers at Maxincuchee Lake makes an extraordinarily Chekhovian and Updike-like narrative, a short-story in effect, about the gains and losses of kinship, and the powers of affection and guilt as they run through families.

It sounds a kind of keynote within this artfully ragged, carefully intermittent personal record, so haunted by a mad and suicidal mother, a sad architect father frustrated by the Depression, a son who went temporarily insane and a wife who died, and by the need to make replacement communities of like minds *contra mundum,* in solidarity with his new Vietnam-photographer wife, with his old army friend from Dresden days, the recently dead Bernard V. O'Hare, even with fellow-clarinetist Benny Goodman.

'I used to play a little licorice-stick myself,' Vonnegut keeps telling us he once told Benny Goodman. The jesting self-send-up is usual, and so is the well-rehearsed one-liner. For this is a preacher who offers his truths in punch-lines, his rebukes by motto. And the throw-away lines have become the grimmer the more our culture has become throw-away.

'So it goes', the shrugging acceptance of Apocalypse Then in **Slaughterhouse-Five** has been replaced by 'What a Mess'—an awful truth about global auto destructiveness, our un-green Apocalypse Now, the terrible suicidal moment when we all drink the Kool-Aid laced with cyanide.

'Imagine being American', Vonnegut invites us—and worse, think of being not liked by Walter Cronkite, the Man Most Americans Trust. Worse still, imagine being Huck Finn with nowhere to go at the end of your story, no clean territories to 'light out to', no innocent geography left.

The way Vonnegut imagines the plight is American all right, but it's a dilemma he makes you feel the whole world had better attend to, or else.

Thomas M. Disch (review date 21 September 1997)

SOURCE: "Novelist on the Half Shell," in *Washington Post Book World,* September 21, 1997, p. X01.

[*In the following review, Disch argues that* Timequake *discloses much information about Vonnegut himself.*]

Timequake is a novel by, and starring, Kurt Vonnegut. His co-star, and virtually the only other "character" in the book, is his alter ego, Kilgore Trout, who figured in two earlier Vonnegut novels, **God Bless You, Mr. Rosewater** (1965) and **Breakfast of Champions** (1973). Trout has also published his own novel, *Venus on the Half Shell* (1975), but since it was written, without Vonnegut's consent, by Philip Jose Farmer, that book cannot legally be accounted part of the Trout oeuvre, though it enjoys its own peculiar and illegitimate glory as one of the few novels published by a non-entity.

It may be that the concept for **Timequake** is a steal from Thorton Wilder's *Our Town.* (Vonnegut discreetly acknowledges as much.) In a nutshell, everyone on Earth has to relive the 1990s on automatic pilot, observing but not participating in their lives. But what Wilder made poignant, Vonnegut simply doesn't engage with, for he refuses to deal either with the helplessness and/or horror of such an experience or with the trauma of release. No matter—intensity was never Vonnegut's forte. And anyhow Wilder had already done it.

What Vonnegut does, which no one can do better, is give a big postmodern shrug. The experience is shifted to the expert shoulders of Trout, who once again plays Mortimer Snerd to Vonnegut's own Charlie McCarthy. Like Philip Roth's Zuckerman, Trout represents his creator's self-love and self-loathing at a level of imaginative intensity that mere memoir would not allow.

And that is not to reckon with the man's own immense self-regard. Vonnegut namedrops like a rainstorm: A.E. Hotchner, Heinrich Boll, Dick Francis, Gunther Grass, Andrei Sakharov, and a host of showbiz stars that his own celebrity has brought within a handshake's distance. The extended Vonnegut family is all on hand, as at a wedding, each with a characterizing anecdote. The author's bibliography and the salient facts of his public career are offered as candidly as on a resume.

And then there are the sententiae: There shall be no more war, we must love one another, etc. He echoes Henry Fonda, echoing John Steinbeck, echoing Eugene Debs, that as long as there is anyone poor or downtrodden or in prison, he, Kurt Vonnegut, is poor, downtrodden, and imprisoned, too. Oh dear, as Vonnegut might say.

Of his writerly life we learn that he still works, virtuously, on a manual typewriter, corrects his copy with pen or pencil and then mails these pages off to his long-term professional typist in the country. This necessitates a walk first to the store, to buy a single manila envelope, and then to the post office, where he waits in line to buy a stamp. The process becomes a parading of Vonnegut's rectitude and unassuming human dignity relative to those boobs among us who use computers and fax machines or play the lottery.

If all this seems insufferably smug, it is, but since it comes from Vonnegut, America's favorite grumpy old man, you've got to love him. He has so cornered the market on elderly curmudgeonliness that his very belches (and there are plenty of them, including three or four really moldy dirty jokes) have a fragrance of temps perdu.

In a well-advised "Prologue," Vonnegut forewarns his readers that *Timequake* took 10 years to write, at the end of which, 74 years old, "I found myself in the winter of 1996 . . . the creator of a novel which did not work, which had no point, and which had never wanted to be written in the first place. . . . Let us think of it as Timequake. And let us think of this one, a stew made from its best parts mixed with thoughts and experiences during the past seven months or so, as Timequake Two. Hokay?"

Hokay with me. (Though why not, in that case, put that title on the cover?) The fact is that Vonnegut's fame and bankability are such that he is now beyond rejection or even criticism. As for Trout—now a hack sci-fi writer in his eighties—though reduced to the condition and appearance of a bag lady he's still going strong, churning out unpublishable stories full of idiot-savant wisdom. His stories are, in synopsis, truly stupid, and we must be grateful that Vonnegut has had the discernment to imagine Trout's stories rather than write them.

And yet, as with Mortimer Snerd, it is Trout who may be the more memorable character. He is one of those, like Forrest Gump or Sherlock Holmes, who take their creator captive and become the boss. Even Vonnegut seems to be aware of this, for if the book has any message, it is that offered by Trout: "You were sick, but now you're well again, and there's work to do."

One may have doubts about this as a panacea to the world's problems. But as solace and wish-fulfillment, it's on a par with Voltaire's advice, as mediated through Candide, that we should tend to our own affairs, a counsel of perfection to which the reader can only answer, Hokay.

Valerie Sayers (review date 28 September 1997)

SOURCE: "Vonnegut Stew," in *The New York Times,* September 28, 1997.

[*In the following review, Sayers describes* Timequake *as a mix of novel and memoir.*]

Like so many of my peers, I began reading Kurt Vonnegut while the Vietnam War was raging. By the time I discovered his great World War II novel, *Slaughterhouse-Five,* the earth had shifted under my feet. Vonnegut, satirist and tragedian, seemed like a literary elder bearing witness. (Some elder; he was in his 40's then.) And I knew I was embarking on a lifelong relationship. Vonnegut thought the big thoughts—about war and death and how we ought to treat one another—and regarded them not only as transformative but as useful, stylish, even fun. He was not chained to any one idea about "story structure" but was the prankster of italics, exclamation points and one-sentence paragraphs.

He was a word cartoonist, a wise guy, a true subversive!

Nearly 30 years later, Vonnegut is still making the pompous look silly and the decent and lovely look decent and lovely. His new so-called novel, *Timequake,* is, as Vonnegut describes it, a "stew." He has taken the best pickings from a novel that wasn't working and interspersed them with a running commentary on his own life and the state of the universe. The mix is thick and rich: a political novel that's not a novel, a memoir that is not inclined to reveal the most private details of the writer's life.

The bits of the novel that Vonnegut has rescued (or chopped up and put on to simmer) are odd and confusing—but I am often thrown by the plots of fantasy and science fiction. Once Vonnegut has discarded big chunks of the original book (who knows how many?) and has summarized the plots of several others, the remaining story is murky, to say the least. But no matter. Whenever faced with a Vonnegut plot I cannot altogether follow, I always read faster. The man's mind is racing, and it is exhilarating to give chase.

The fictional settings include the real-life American Academy of Arts and Letters and a writer's colony called Xanadu. As usual, Vonnegut is both celebrating and satirizing the writing life. It is this tension between admiration and disdain that informs his view of his characters, too. The old Vonnegut alter ego, Kilgore Trout, science fiction writer, is on hand to deliver the wry and trenchant lines about art, poverty and violence. The other major characters, a blond secretary and a black security guard, telegraph Vonnegut's sharp interest in class and race more than they suggest real people. As Trout himself puts it, "If I'd wasted my time creating characters . . . I would never have gotten around to calling attention to things that really matter."

Much of Vonnegut's work (including the crystalline autobiographical opening of *Slaughterhouse-Five*) has thumbed its nose at conventional form. But what really matters here, at least philosophically, is free will—that familiar Vonnegut theme. The original novel's premise, Vonnegut tells us, was that "a sudden glitch in the space-time continuum made everybody and everything do exactly what they'd done during a past decade, for good or ill."

But the bones of that story—the so-called fictional ingredients of the brew—are not the most savory items. The real pleasure lies in Vonnegut's transforming his continuing interest in the highly suspicious relationship between fact and fiction into the neatest trick yet played on a publishing world consumed with the furor over novel versus memoir. *Timequake* has parlayed his unworkable novel into a highly entertaining consideration of the relationship between the writer's life and the writer's imagination. Some of its juxtapositions are unsettling, especially the fictional-nonfictional scenes of marriage. Some are hilarious. Much of the autobiographical material appeared in Vonnegut's *Fates Worse Than Death* (1991), yet even these reworked scenes seem written here for the first time. The portraits of Vonnegut's first wife and brother, both recently dead, and his sister, long gone, are beautiful, sharp, critical, loving.

"All Vonnegut men," Vonnegut's aunt tells us, "are scared to death of women." The book returns, painfully, relentlessly, to Vonnegut's mother, who committed suicide and who, by his account, was preoccupied with class and money. Her obsession must be terrifying for a highly successful writer who has for years been quoting his own hero, Eugene Debs: "While there is a lower class, I am in it." He quotes his son, Mark, who survived a crackup and is now a pediatrician: "We are here to help each other get through this thing, whatever it is."

I take perfectly seriously Vonnegut's solutions for American society, including his proposed amendment to the Constitution: "Every adult who needs it shall be given meaningful work to do, at a living wage." I'm glad he's still going around inventing new forms to contain his vision of a decent society, even if he had to dismember a novel to do it.

At 74, Vonnegut has had enough of the writing life, he tells us in the preface, and *Timequake* was obviously inspired by his sense that his life's work is winding down. But let me be just the latest to declare that this work has been a blessing. Vonnegut may not have finished the novel, but for a generation of readers he still writes the book.

Additional coverage of Vonnegut's life and career is contained in the following sources published by Gale: *Authors and Artists for Young Adults*, **Vol. 6;** *Concise Dictionary of American Literary Biography, 1968-1988*; *Contemporary Authors*, **Vols. 1-4R;** *Contemporary Authors New Revision Series*, **Vols. 1, 25, and 49;** *Dictionary of Literary Biography*, **Vols. 2, 8, and 152;** *Dictionary of Literary Biography Documentary Series*, **Vol. 3;** *Dictionary of Literary Biography Yearbook: 1980*; *DISCovering Authors: Most-studied Authors*, **Novelists,** and *Popular Fiction and Genre Authors Modules*; *Major 20th-Century Writers*; *Short Story Criticism*, **Vol. 8;** and *World Literature Criticism.*

Tennessee Williams
1911-1983

(Born Thomas Lanier Williams) American playwright, novelist, essayist, short story writer, screenwriter, and poet.

The following entry presents an overview of Williams's career through 1995. For further information on his life and works, see *CLC,* Volumes 1, 2, 5, 7, 8, 11, 15, 19, 30, 39, 45, and 71.

INTRODUCTION

Tennessee Williams is distinguished for his psychologically complex dramas that explore isolation and miscommunication within families and small groups of misfits and loners. Breaking from the realistic tradition in American drama, Williams introduced his concept of the "plastic" theater by incorporating expressionistic elements of dialogue, action, sound, setting, and lighting in his works. Williams's reputation rests on his three award-winning dramas—*The Glass Menagerie* (1944), *A Streetcar Named Desire* (1947), and *Cat on a Hot Tin Roof* (1955). Each of these is set in the American South, employing lyrical dialogue and inventive stage techniques, and represents a powerful study of family dynamics and the solitary search for meaning in the modern world, particularly through the depiction of emotional abuse, sexual relations, and violence. For his remarkable ability to evoke universal experience in multi-dimensional characters and provocative plots that transcend geography and social milieu, Williams is recognized as a major influence in the development of postwar American theater.

Biographical Information

Born Thomas Lanier Williams in Columbus, Mississippi, Williams was raised by his mother and maternal grandparents at an Episcopal rectory in Clarksdale, Mississippi; his father, a travelling salesman, was frequently absent. As a young child, Williams survived a near-fatal bout with diphtheria that left him physically weakened and in the constant care of his overprotective mother. Williams also developed a close attachment to his older sister, Rose, whose schizophrenia and later mental deterioration after an unsuccessful lobotomy had a profound effect upon him. At age twelve Williams moved with his family to St. Louis, Missouri, where his father was transferred for a managerial position. Away from the security and familiarity of his rural upbringing, Williams became the subject of ridicule among his new urban peers and unsympathetic father, who nicknamed his shy and sickly son "Miss Nancy." Williams began to write poetry and short fiction to relieve the strain of such derision

and alienation. At age sixteen he won an essay contest sponsored by *Smart Set* magazine with "Can a Good Wife Be a Good Sport?," which became his first published work. In 1929 Williams entered the University of Missouri, though he was forced by his father to return home after failing ROTC in his third year. He worked in a shoe warehouse and continued to write until suffering a nervous breakdown in 1935. During the same year, while recovering at his grandparents' home in Memphis, Tennessee, Williams was introduced to the theater and produced the comedy *Cairo, Shanghai, Bombay!,* his first play. Deciding on a career as a writer, Williams returned to St. Louis to attend classes at Washington University, then transferred to the University of Iowa where he studied playwriting and earned a degree in English in 1938. The next year he published "The Field of Blue Children" in *Story* magazine, his first work to appear under the name Tennessee. After winning an award from the Group Theater in 1939 for a series of one-act plays, Williams received a Rockefeller Foundation fellowship which he used to compose *Battle of Angels* (1940), a short-lived critical failure that opened in Boston. In the early 1940s, Williams worked odd jobs and eventually secured a salaried position with Metro-Goldwyn-Mayer in Hollywood, for which he produced several unaccepted screenplays and was released at the end of his contract. During this time he wrote *The Glass Menagerie,* the first of his major accomplishments, which received the New York Drama Critics Circle Award in 1945. Though struggling with fame and pressure to duplicate this success, Williams followed with *A Streetcar Named Desire* in 1947 and *Cat on a Hot Tin Roof* in 1955, both of which won New York Drama Critics Circle Awards and Pulitzer Prizes. During the 1950s, Williams produced the dramas *The Rose Tattoo* (1951) and *Camino Real* (1953) along with the novel *The Roman Spring of Mrs. Stone* (1950), and adapted the script of *A Streetcar Named Desire* into a popular Hollywood film that appeared in 1951. In the second half of the decade, Williams underwent intensive psychoanalysis to treat his depression, providing material for *Suddenly Last Summer* (1958), *Sweet Bird of Youth* (1959), and *Period of Adjustment* (1959). Williams was again plunged into despair in 1963 when Frank Merlo, his longtime partner, died of lung cancer. After *The Night of the Iguana* (1960), his last notable success, Williams continued to produce numerous dramatic works of diminishing critical importance until the end of his life. His mental instability and increasing dependence upon drugs and alcohol worsened during the next two decades. In 1969, Williams converted to Roman Catholicism and was briefly hospitalized following another mental breakdown. Eight years after the publication of his *Memoirs* (1975), Williams accidently choked to death on the cap of a medicine bottle.

Major Works

Williams's mature dramatic style is best represented in his three greatest critical and commercial successes—*The Glass Menagerie, A Streetcar Named Desire,* and *Cat on a Hot Tin Roof.* The most lyrical and tender of the three, *The Glass Menagerie* is a semi-autobiographic play drawn directly from Williams's childhood experiences with his mother and mentally ill sister. Set in a St. Louis tenement during the Depression, the drama involves the Wingfield family, whose three adult members include Amanda, a domineering mother who bitterly resents her absent husband; her son, Tom, a writer who works in a shoe factory; and his sister, Laura, whose extreme timidity and crippled leg confine her to the house. Tom, as Williams's *dramatis personae,* narrates the story through retrospective commentary and monologues that underscore the tension between reality and illusion, especially as Amanda romanticizes her past life as a beautiful Southern debutante and Laura tends to her collection of glass figurines, to which the title of the play refers, a symbol of fantasy and her physical and emotional fragility. The dramatic climax occurs when Amanda persuades Tom to find a suitor for Laura. Tom invites a co-worker, Jim O'Connor, to dinner to meet his sister. Though Laura and Jim enjoy each other's company, Jim abruptly leaves after informing Laura

that he is already engaged to be married. The audience learns in a final monologue that Tom, like his father, has also abandoned his mother and sister to pursue his own destiny and to escape his guilt for shattering their hopes and expectations. Despite the simple plot, Williams blends elements of expressionism and realism in poetic dialogue, pervasive symbolism, and music and lighting effects that evoke the sensations of memory. *A Streetcar Named Desire* similarly examines family tensions and the theme of illusion versus reality, but is far more violent and grim than *The Glass Menagerie.* Set in the vibrant French Quarter of New Orleans, the play follows the demise of Blanche Dubois as she is drawn into a dangerous, antagonistic relationship with her brother-in-law, Stanley Kowalski. As the title suggests, the play revolves around the idea of desire as an unyielding and destructive force. Blanche arrives at the home of Stanley and her sister, Stella, after witnessing the dissipation of her family estate and the suicide of her husband, whom she berates after discovering that he is gay. Conflict between Blanche and Stanley soon escalates as a result of Blanche's flirtations and condescending treatment of Stanley, an unrefined man who is threatened by her genteel pretensions. As a social commentary, Blanche represents the effete values of the dying Southern aristocracy while Stanley embodies the energy and earnestness of the working class. The tension between them culminates when Stanley rapes Blanche, after which she is committed to a sanitarium where she retreats further from reality. The hero of the play remains ambiguous as Williams skillfully tempers sympathies for Blanche and Stanley to confront and challenge audience expectations. While Blanche's haughty teasing and hypocritical virginal posturing is balanced by her difficult past, Stanley's coarseness and brutality are mitigated by his appealing sexuality, honesty, and sincere love for Stella. As in *The Glass Menagerie,* Williams offers sensitive treatment of the female characters and profound insight into their psychological motivations. Blanche, like Laura and Amanda, appears fragile and unable to cope with the harshness of reality, particularly as she constructs a facade of lies about her sordid history. *Cat on a Hot Tin Roof* is set in the Mississippi River delta at the plantation home of Big Daddy, a wealthy cotton farmer whose family has assembled to celebrate his sixty-fifth birthday and false news that his cancer is in remission. The complex plot, fraught with Freudian undertones, centers on the implications of mendacity and self-deception, particularly as Big Daddy's favorite son, Brick Pollitt, wallows in alcohol to avoid facing the actual nature of his affectionate relationship with Skipper, a high school friend who has killed himself through drug and alcohol abuse. Distraught over Brick's drinking and detachment, Brick's wife, Maggie, suspects a homosexual attachment between her husband and Skipper. Maggie has previously seduced Skipper into bed with her to test his sexuality and, after he failed to perform, confronted Skipper with the "truth" about his feelings for Brick. When Big Daddy demands that Brick reveal the source of his compulsion to drink, Brick explains that Skipper telephoned him shortly before his death with a drunken confession, to which Brick responded by hanging up on him. Big Daddy accuses Brick of causing Skipper's death by failing to face up to the truth. In turn, Brick spoils the party by revealing to Big Daddy that his cancer is actually terminal. In the end, Maggie's determination to save her marriage is accomplished by cunning and sheer tenacity, to which the title of the play alludes, as she lies to the family that she is pregnant with Brick's child to regain their favor. Though the published version of the play contains two endings, the Broadway version in which Big Daddy departs with an offstage cry and Brick experiences newfound admiration for Maggie is the preferred variation used in most productions. As in much of his work, Williams juxtaposes conflicting aspects of obligation and selfishness, guilt and desire, self-awareness and denial to construct highly developed characters who struggle to overcome severe loneliness and frustration in their circumscribed lives.

Critical Reception

Williams is considered among the most talented and original playwrights of the postwar period. His three major dramas—*The Glass Menagerie, A Streetcar Named Desire,* and *Cat on a Hot Tin Roof*—are undisputed classics of the American theater whose memorable characters have become fixtures in American popular culture. Though his most effective plays reveal little concern with contemporary political or historical events, his willingness to explore sensitive themes surrounding violence and sexuality, both heterosexual and homosexual, was considered controversial in the 1940s and 1950s. Many critics have commented on the distinctive ambiguity of Williams's plays, most notably in the significance of Blanche's rape in *A Streetcar Named Desire* and Brick's guilt and sexual orientation in *Cat on a Hot Tin Roof.* While some contend that Williams's refusal to present stereotypical dichotomies among his characters or to force judgment is the strength of his work, others suggest such ambivalence represents Williams's failure to resolve his own themes and preoccupations. Despite the success of his major plays during a creative period spanning from 1940 to 1960, Williams's prolific output of critical failures thereafter is a well-noted feature of his literary career. In addition, some critics find Williams's obsession with brutality and sex to be a sensational aspect of his work, particularly in the less successful allegorical or morality plays such as *Summer and Smoke, Camino Real,* and *Suddenly Last Summer.* This gothic quality of much of his writing, marked by interest in the aberrant, irrational, and macabre, is often associated with Southern Renaissance writers such as Carson McCullers and Flannery O'Connor. Though his realistic narratives and credible characters are compared to those of Anton Chekhov and Henrik Ibsen, it is Williams's unique ability to adapt elements of realism and expressionism that distinguishes his

work from that of his contemporaries. A dynamic innovator and deeply perceptive artist whose theater evinces poignant compassion for the vulnerable and victimized, Williams achieved both critical and popular acclaim while redefining the standards of American drama.

PRINCIPAL WORKS

Battle of Angels (drama) 1940; revised and performed as *Orpheus Descending,* 1957
The Glass Menagerie (drama) 1944; (screenplay) [with Oscar Saul] 1950
27 Wagons Full of Cotton and Other One-Act Plays (dramas) 1946; augmented edition, 1953
Summer and Smoke (drama) 1947; revised and performed as *Eccentricities of a Nightingale,* 1966
A Streetcar Named Desire (drama) 1947; (screenplay) 1951
The Roman Spring of Mrs. Stone (novel) 1950
The Rose Tattoo (drama) 1951; (screenplay) [with Hal Kanter] 1955
Camino Real: A Play (drama) 1953
Cat on a Hot Tin Roof (drama) 1955
Baby Doll (screenplay) 1956
In the Winter of Cities (poetry) 1956
Period of Adjustment: High Point Over a Cavern: A Serious Comedy (drama) 1958
Suddenly Last Summer (drama) 1958; (screenplay) [with Gore Vidal] 1959
Sweet Bird of Youth (drama) 1959
The Night of the Iguana (drama) 1960
The Milk Train Doesn't Stop Here Anymore (drama) 1962
The Seven Descents of Myrtle (drama) 1968; revised and performed as *Kingdom of Earth,* 1975
Memoirs (memoirs) 1975
Androgyne, Mon Amour (poetry) 1977
Where I Live: Selected Essays (essays) 1978
Collected Stories (short stories) 1985

CRITICISM

William Becker (review date Summer 1955)

SOURCE: A review of *Cat on a Hot Tin Roof,* in *The Hudson Review,* Vol. 8, No. 2, Summer, 1955, pp. 268-72.

[*In the following review, Becker offers high praise for the debut production of* Cat on a Hot Tin Roof, *which he describes as a "remarkable piece of work" and "Williams' best play to date."*]

The team of Tennessee Williams, playwright, Elia Kazan, director, and Jo Mielziner, designer, is as potent an artistic force as Broadway can boast today. Their newest collaboration, the Playwrights Company production of *Cat on a Hot Tin Roof* at the Morosco, is a really remarkable piece of work. It is also the season's most solid dramatic success. One should perhaps take special note of the fact that the *kind* of theatre produced by this particular team is a strictly American creation and has as yet no European counterpart: it is, in fact, *the* singular dramatic achievement of the postwar decade on Broadway (the only other new achievements of any artistic kind being in the field of the musical). One senses it as an important creation, and one that is now arrived and may be ready for an interesting future. The technique of it is based on a curious dialectic of intense realism and rather eloquent fantasy, a dialectic which is present in every part of the final creation—it is there in the writing, in the open half-abstracted settings, in the play of the lights, in the postures and delivery of the actors. It is an intensification of life posed against abstractions from it, artifice breaking down into nature, nature building up into artifice. Specifically, it is real speech with unnatural inflections, solid furniture in rooms with no walls, naturalistic acting that assembles itself into highly posed and static images, normal realistic light that gives way to follow-spots and chiaroscuro, talk that develops special rhythms and elevates itself into speech.

Nor is this phenomenon, even fundamentally, a playwright's creation, nor a director's, nor a designer's. One senses it as thoroughly eclectic, collaborative, fluid, and the final product as one in which the individual contributions are so harmoniously blended as to create a fully synthetic piece of theatre—a sort of *Gesamtkunstwerk* minus the music. The production process is more than just an achievement of the play; it is actually its completion, with the result that the design of the set and the basic elements of the staging get built into the script—quite literally, as anyone who has had the opportunity to compare an original Williams text with the final published version will know. No future production of the play can ever depart very successfully from the basic scheme that emerges. I have seen six or seven productions of *Streetcar* (and even performed in one), in several different countries and languages, and not one but derived in every major respect from the original Broadway production. Performances, of course, can vary, no matter how synthetic the creation; but it is the great achievement of this collaboration that, in most cases, they can only vary in the direction of inferiority. By the time the play reaches its finished printed form, the roles have been altered to fit the performers, and the quality of the original performances has somehow been built in, too. As a way of work in the theatre, there is something very nearly ideal about this extraordinary collaborative process: it is perhaps the closest analogy that exists in modern theatre to the older tradition of the actor-playwright who was able to forge just such a synthe-

sis with his own company. The success of the process is, of course, a special tribute to the genius of Elia Kazan, who, as director, is its catalytic agent; but it is no less a tribute to Williams, as an author, that he is sufficiently gifted and flexible to take advantage of what Kazan and Mielziner have to offer him. His ability to function so brilliantly in collaboration is precisely what makes him, as a writer, so much of the theatre. It is no accident that Kazan's work is never quite so successful or spectacular with lesser playwrights.

Cat on a Hot Tin Roof is, in many respects, Williams' best play to date. It is, by all odds, his most powerful; and it contains, in Big Daddy, marvelously played by Burl Ives, the most nearly heroic character Williams has ever created. Set in the Mississippi River Delta, the play introduces us to the family of an enormously wealthy planter of Rabelaisian character and great physical bulk (Big Daddy), whose death by cancer is imminent. There is Brick (Ben Gazzara), his younger son, a one-time star athlete turned sullen neurotic alcoholic; and Maggie (Barbara Bel Geddes), Brick's wife, desperate for Brick's physical love, and nervous as a cat on a hot tin roof because he withholds it. There are, in Big Mama (Mildred Dunnock), Gooper (Pat Hingle), Brick's older brother, and Mae (Madeleine Sherwood), his wife, three brilliant tragicomic portraits, satirical in quality and devastating in their accuracy. The family group is completed by the five noisy little "no-neck monsters," belonging to Gooper and Mae, who were played with consummate disagreeableness by what must surely have been the five most unattractive children available in New York City.

The dramatic method of *Cat on a Hot Tin Roof* is familiar from Williams' earlier plays; and it remains of considerable technical interest, being at once quite traditional and yet uniquely Williams' own. One can find in it elements of the dramaturgy of both [Henrik] Ibsen and [Anton] Tchekov, the blend serving to point up the essential interconnectedness of apparently disparate techniques. Williams' method is Ibsenist in the way that it permits the rich narrative elements, which comprise one of Williams' most striking gifts, to emerge bit by bit in a crescendo of meaningfulness. We are plunged into a story at a point just on the verge of an explosive climax or conclusion. Little by little the sequence of past events seeps out, and it is generally not until the end of the second set that the history is complete. At that point, at least in *Cat,* the full story precipitates a revelation, not only for the audience, but for the characters, and the major climax is the second act curtain. The remainder of the play is an inexorable working out of the consequences. The method is Tchekovian, on the other hand, in the sense that the climaxes are psychological, and the play's rhythms are created, not by external events, accidents, or gimmicks (like the fire in *Ghosts*), but by developing relations between people or by an increasing self-awareness in an individual character. As in Tchekov, there are long rambling speeches and lengthy personal reminiscences. There are, in fact, longer speeches in *Cat* than in any modern American play I know, outside the works of Eugene O'Neill. But where O'Neill's speeches tend to be repetitive and verbose, and greatly in need of pruning for performance, Williams' speeches tend, like Tchekov's, to be entirely necessary and to defy cutting. The better part of the entire first act of *Cat* is one long monologue by Maggie the Cat addressed to her husband, and only occasionally interrupted by Brick's icy non-committal responses. Likewise, the second act, which is dominated from beginning to end by Big Daddy, and of which more than half is a tempestuous dialogue between Big Daddy and Brick.

If the dramaturgy is in debt to Ibsen and Tchekov, the general tone and manner owe something to Strindberg. (These comparisons are not idle: Williams has established himself in the major traditions, if so far in something less than a major way.) A great part of the psychology is violent, just as much of the eloquence is bombast. One of Big Daddy's typical speeches will serve to illustrate both the quality and the rhetoric (intervening stage directions omitted):

> You don't know a goddam thing an' you never did! (BIG MAMA: Big Daddy, you don't mean that.) Oh, yes, I do, oh, yes, I do mean it! I put up with a whole lot of crap around here because I thought I was dyin'—An' you thought I was dyin' an' you started takin' over; well, you can stop takin' over, now, Ida, because I'm not goin' to die, you can just stop this business of takin' over because you're not takin' over because I'm not dyin'. I went through that laboratory and the exploratory operation and there's nothin' wrong with me but a spastic colon. An' I'm not dyin' of cancer which you thought I was dyin' of. Ain't that so? Didn't you think that I was dyin' of cancer? Ain't that so, Ida? Didn't you have an idea I was dyin' of cancer an' now you could take control of this place an' everything on it? I got that impression, I seemed to get that impression. Your loud voice everywhere, your damn' busy ole body buttin' in here an' there! (BIG MAMA: Hush! The Preacher!) Rut the Preacher! Did you hear what I said? Rut the cotton-pickin' chicken-eatin', memorial-stained-glass Preacher!. . . I went through all that laboratory an' operation an' all just so I would know if you or me was boss here! Well, now it turns out that I am an' you ain't—and that's my birthday present—an' my cake an' champagne—because for three years now you been gradually takin' over. Bossin', talkin', sashayin' your ole butt aroun' this place I made! I made this place! I was overseer on it! I was the overseer on th' ole Straw an' Ochello plantation. I quit school at ten! I quit school at ten years old an' went to work like a nigger in the fields. An' I rose to be overseer of the Straw an' Ochello plantation. An' ole Straw died an' I was Ochello's partner an' the place got bigger an' bigger an' bigger! I did all that myself with no goddam help from you, an' now you think that you are just about to take over. Well, I'm just about to tell you that you are not just about to take over, you are not just about to take over a goddam thing. Is that clear to you, Ida? Is that very plain to you now? Is that understood completely? I been through the laboratory from A to Z. I've had the goddam exploratory operation, an' nothin' is wrong with me but a spastic colon—made spastic, I guess, by all the goddam lies and liars that I have had to put up with, an' all the hypocrisy that I have lived with all these forty years that I been livin' with you! Now blow out the candles on th' birthday cake! Take a deep breath an' blow out th' goddam candles on th' cake.

Cambyses' vein, perhaps, but nonetheless some of the most powerful theatrical writing to enliven the drab stages of Broadway in some time. As Eric Bentley has noted, the prose rhythms owe something to the repetitive artifices of Gertrude Stein, but the lushness has its roots in real Southern vernacular. The language is part of the whole creation, like the play itself, a mixture of realism and fantasy, a personalized rendition of an authentic American idiom. Like the language of *The Flowering Peach,* it makes us realize what riches lie largely unmined in the diverse American voice, and it reminds us, too, how little mere accuracy (e.g. Horton Foote or William Inge) is a substitute for style.

The plot of *Cat on a Hot Tin Roof* is too complex, and the circumstances of its central situation too eventfully rich, to attempt to retail (the play should be seen, or eventually read by everybody with any interest in the American stage); but some mention needs to be made of its thematic strands. The play dances, thematically, around the problem of Truth, though without saying anything very substantial on the subject. The theme is, really, an excuse for the drama—which is perhaps as it should be—and the drama exists in a series of personal relationships to which, of course, the criterion of truth may be applied. Brick has been lying to himself; the family has been lying to Big Daddy about his cancer; Big Daddy has a speech in which he retails the lies and hypocrisy he has had to live with all his life; and Brick bitterly sums it all up, in the big second act revelation scene, with the remark, "Mendacity is the system we live in." But if truth is the main subject of the play's investigation, sex is the peg that the drama is hung on. Big Mama enquires of Maggie if she makes Brick happy in bed, and, pointing to their bed, exclaims, "When a marriage goes on the rocks, the rocks are *here,* right *here!*" Big Daddy talks about Big Mama's insatiability, and how he was too good in bed for forty years to an old woman he couldn't stand "the sight, sound, or smell of". And his first wish, when he thinks he is healthy, is to rectify it all by spending the last years of his life having a sexual "ball". The source of Maggie's desperation is her exile from Brick's bed, and she spends a good part of the play being conscious of her body and its attractions. The truth Brick is forced to face is his own partial and repressed homosexuality, and that of his closest friend, for whose death by alcoholic self-destruction Brick is finally responsible—though it is a responsibility he has projected onto Maggie. For it was Maggie who accused the friend and then allowed herself to go to bed with him in an attempt to prove her accusation false, and it was his impotence on that occasion which convinced him the accusation was true, and triggered his break-down into alcoholism. The resolution of the play is also sexual, though the ostensible subject is still truth. Maggie brings to birth a "desperate truth" by telling Big Daddy that she is pregnant with Brick's child, thus fulfilling the profoundest wish of a dying man—a lie different from all the other lies in the play, because it impels its own conversion into truth: as the final curtain falls, Brick and Maggie are going to bed to create that child. This rather intellectualized and schematized handling of the question of truth and mendacity seems to me the weakest aspect of the play. What is said about truth is not nearly so convincing as what emerges dramatically in the course of the play about the truth of relations between people—the opening, for example, of the big second act dialogue between Brick and Big Daddy, with its tentative groping after some real truth, in the form of communication, between them. Or the climax of that same dialogue, in which Brick, forced by Big Daddy into a terrible revelation of his own self-deception, blurts out, almost in vengeance, the truth about the cancer, sending Big Daddy off as the curtain falls, shouting, "Christ—Damn—Damn All—Lyin' Sons of—Lyin' Bitches! Yes—All Liars, All Liars, All Lyin', Dyin' Liars! Lyin'—Dyin'—Liars! Liars! Liars!"

It should be said, in conclusion, that the great weakness of the Williams-Kazan synthetic creation, and particularly of Kazan's part in it, is that much of the artifice tends to be hollow and pasted on. Tremendously effective during the moments one is subjected to it in the theatre, it has a way of evaporating in retrospect; and one realizes that a great many raised questions have been, not answered, but bowled over, and aspects of character or plot, not justified, but arbitrarily imposed. There is, in the method, a certain amount of opportune dishonesty, bamboozling, and trickery, which is, however, perpetrated with consummate theatrical finesse, and revealed only when recollected in tranquillity. Still, Kazan's caterpillar opportunism is not merely the key to his meteoric success, it is an essential ingredient of his genius. If he were not empty of convictions and utterly unscrupulous, if he were more thoughtful and less absolutely intuitive, his conscience would probably destroy him. It is precisely because his imagination is reckless and, to a de-

gree, irresponsible, that he succeeds in creating theatrical effects of a daring and power that no other director on Broadway can begin to approach. His opportunism, both good and bad, is his gift.

Delma Eugene Presley (essay date 1971)

SOURCE: "The Search for Hope in the Plays of Tennessee Williams," in *Mississippi Quarterly,* Vol. 25, 1971, pp. 31-43.

[*In the following essay, Presley identifies three philosophical dilemmas confronted by Williams's central characters—"isolation, the absence of God, and the reality of death." Presley contends that Williams's most successful plays portray realistic psychological or social tensions rather than theological themes as found in his less effective later plays.*]

Tennessee Williams' entrance into the Roman Catholic Church in January, 1969 should be regarded not necessarily as an eccentric action, but as a logical if not decisive step in the playwright's progression toward religion. Throughout his career as a dramatist, Williams has exhibited in his plays an awareness of religious questions. However, his theological dimension has gone unnoticed by most critics who, for reasons mysterious, concentrate upon appearances of sexuality and violence to the exclusion of authentic theological and philosophical concerns. Beginning with *The Glass Menagerie* (1945) and ending with *The Milk Train Doesn't Stop Here Anymore* (1964), Williams' hero travels the difficult road from despair to hope—from the shadows of tragedy to the light of the comic vision. This journey becomes a kind of pilgrimage, especially in plays after *Camino Real* (1953), characterized by the hero's repetition of familiar affirmations. This aspect of the later works of Williams has great significance in view of the obvious decline in his reputation among critics of theatre. It may very well be that the quality of his later works suffers from debilitating effects of his emerging hope. The great and unfortunate irony of the hero's ultimate redemption is that his religious-sounding ideology reduces his stature.

> **Williams' hero encounters three problems of a philosophical or theological nature— isolation, the absence of God, and the reality of death.**
> **—Delma Eugene Presley**

As early as *The Glass Menagerie* and as late as *The Milk Train Doesn't Stop Here Anymore,* Williams' hero encounters three problems of a philosophical or theological nature—isolation, the absence of God, and the reality of death. Tom Wingfield and Blanche Du Bois, central characters in the early plays, *The Glass Menagerie* and *A Streetcar Named Desire* are caught in situations which prevent any semblance of community. There may be the potential of community in the Wingfield home, but it is never realized. Tom understands but refuses to heed the advice of Amanda, his mother: "In these trying times we live in, all that we have to cling to is each other" (scene iv) [*The Glass Menagerie*]. His escape from responsibility is but another in a long series which began, of course, with the father's desertion. Blanche Du Bois of *Streetcar* knows what she needs when she arrives at her sister's apartment in New Orleans. She tells Stella: "I want to be *near* you, got to be *with* somebody, I *can't* be alone!" (scene i) [*A Streetcar Named Desire*]. Blanche is doomed from the start not simply because she will be overwhelmed by the bestial Stanley. Blanche, let us remember, is pathetically torn from within by conflicting emotions: her compassion is defeated by her selfishness; her need for understanding is undermined by her debauchery. Human community is not possible in *Streetcar* precisely because the people who ought to participate in that community are either unwilling or incapable.

Williams' early works suggest that, beyond human weaknesses, a cause of isolation is the inability of the flesh to co-exist harmoniously with the spirit. Tom Wingfield, an avid reader of the instinct-affirming writings of D. H. Lawrence, is rebuked by a religious-sounding Amanda who would have him concentrate on life's "nobler qualities." This thematic clash again comes to the surface in a bit of clever dialogue in the eighth scene of *Streetcar*. Blanche has been spending hours in the Kowalskis' only bathroom—a circumstance which aggravates her already lacerated relationship with Stanley. After one of his impatient remarks, she replies with a paraphrase of Jesus' words in Luke 21:19: "Possess your soul in patience." Stanley immediately counters with: "It's not my soul, it's my kidneys I'm worried about." In the larger context of the drama, these words indicate that Stanley's mind is open not to the beckoning of the spirit but only to the desires and needs of the flesh. *Summer and Smoke,* written shortly after *Streetcar,* appears to have been conceived with this theme of the flesh versus the spirit as a problem to be solved. Pathos is the only emotion evoked in this experimental allegory which ends with the sad affirmation that the flesh (summer) cannot merge with the spirit (smoke). The central characters, John (the doctor of bodily ills) and Alma (Spanish for soul), are not saved from their isolation but pathetically confirmed in it.

The second major theological issue in the plays of Williams is the absence of God or a savior. The Wingfields, Amanda in particular, wish for a messiah in the form of a "gentleman caller." Indeed, *The Glass Menagerie* structurally is held together by the anticipation and arrival of Jim O'Connor. He is, as Tom points out in the opening monologue, "that long delayed but always expected something that we live for." Once Jim comes and leaves, the play's action is complete. Amanda's hopes for deliverance are fruitless since Jim has made previous commitments to the American technological dream, and, of course, a "girl named Betty." In *Streetcar,* Blanche Du Bois keeps hoping up until the end that her messiah, Shep Hundleigh (probably imaginary), will appear out of nowhere and rescue her from Stanley and his crude world. The airplane "Fugitivo" is the messianic symbol in *Camino Real.* It is either death at the hands of the street-cleaners or escape via airplane for the traveler of the road of reality. As Marguerite, the tubercular woman of pleasure, says in Block Nine: the "Fugitivo" is her only "way to escape from this abominable place!" Because of a technicality, Marguerite is unable to board this agency of salvation. Her destiny, like that of the hero Kilroy, is death in a strange land devoid of love and compassion. Probably the most obvious reference to the absence of God in a guilt-infested world comes in *Sweet Bird of Youth.* Few critics have noted the significant lines of the heckler who shouts in the second act to the crowds surrounding a politician, Boss Finley, called "a messiah from the hills":

> I don't believe it. I believe that the silence of God, the absolute speechlessness of Him is a long, long and awful thing that the whole world is lost because of. I think it's yet to be broken to any man, living or yet lived on earth—no exceptions.

The awareness of death is a third important theme in Williams' major plays. It is in the presence of death that his hero encounters questions about the nature and destiny of his life. Ultimate questions are faced particularly in *Camino Real* (1953), and in several more recent plays: *Cat on a Hot Tin Roof* (1955), *Suddenly Last Summer* (1958), *The Night of the Iguana* (1962), and *The Milk Train Doesn't Stop Here Anymore* (1964). The most serious exploration of human destiny is the memorable heart-to-heart talk between Brick and Big Daddy in the second act of *Cat on a Hot Tin Roof.* Big Daddy traces his son's alcoholism and ennui to the mystery surrounding his friendship with Skipper. Maggie, Brick's wife, had hinted earlier that Skipper harbored homosexual feelings toward her husband. Brick is stung by his father's words and counters with the "truth" that Big Daddy will not have future birthdays since his illness is not, as Big Mamma and Gooper say, a "spastic colon," but something more terrible: incurable cancer. There is no advice, no optimistic outlook, for Big Daddy. His last words are "CHRIST DAMN—ALL—LYING—SONS OF—LYING BITCHES! ... Lying, dying, liars!" *Cat on a Hot Tin Roof,* therefore, is a play about different kinds of death in the modern world. Life cannot continue on Brick's side of the family. We know that Brick already has willed a spiritual death; he has "that cool air of detachment that people have who have given up the struggle." Life will continue for Gooper and Mae and their offspring. But, as Big Daddy and Brick indicate in the second act, the kind of existence embodied by these people is mendacious. Death is the final truth of this play.

If one grants the existence of these theological and philosophical aspects of Williams' works—isolation, God's absence, and death—one ought to notice as well solutions to these problems whenever they are proposed by the dramatist. When the major plays are considered as a unit, it becomes clear that few solutions are proposed prior to *Camino Real.* In this particular play, Williams shows evidence of a search for a solution; the most obvious clue is that *Camino Real*'s style is so unlike that of his previous efforts. Here the author develops an elaborate allegory in an unusual sequence of "Blocks." Technique, as Professor Mark Schorer pointed out in his famous essay on the subject, is an important indication of subject matter: "The final lesson of the modern novel is that technique is not the secondary thing it seemed to Wells, some external machination, a mechanical affair, but a deep and primary operation; not only that technique *contains* intellectual and moral implications, but that it *discovers* them." The appearance of Williams' allegorical plays, *Camino Real* and later *Suddenly Last Summer,* indicate the playwright's attempt to discover a new subject matter, one containing hopeful affirmations about life's potential.

The "way of reality" and "royal road," two meanings of *Camino Real,* have many similarities to Dante's road through *The Inferno.* The play's epigraph comes from Canto I of *The Inferno:* "In the middle of the journey of our life, I came to myself in a dark wood where the straight way was lost." This particular play, like Dante's allegory of life as hell, is but part of a journey to redemption for the hero. The travelers of the Camino are universal men—the eternal optimist, Don Quixote; the great lover, Casanova; Lord Byron, the Romantic in quest of an ideal; Marguerite, a sentimental courtesan past her prime; and Kilroy, the American Everyman who attempts to hold fast to independence, sincerity, and courage. Kilroy travels the very real road of life which leads to an arid fountain in the middle of the square. He discovers that Don Quixote's map was right: "The spring of humanity has gone dry in this place." Despite the idealism of Kilroy, despite his efforts to defeat the smug and cruel enemies of sensitivity and brotherhood, he is ultimately defeated. After his death at the hands of the "street cleaners," he is taken to a medical institution where interns dissect him. They discover that his heart was made of gold which cannot be destroyed by even the most corrosive forces of modernity. In the sixteenth and last block, a resurrected Kilroy is seen carrying his gold heart under his arm. He joins Don Quixote who is prepared to venture forth again in search of the ideal. After they become partners, Quixote affirms: "The violets in the mountains have broken the rocks!" Water then rushes into the once-dry fountain. The implication is that the Camino has been redeemed through the courage of Kilroy who is now, like Christ, an eternal force.

The new hopefulness of *Camino Real,* surely Williams' turning point, does not come cheaply. The price he pays for his new theme becomes evident when one considers the thematic and structural consequences. *Camino Real* has several weaknesses which are prophetic of his recent efforts. One major problem is his too simple reduction of complex literary figures such as Don Quixote and Lord Byron. Another limitation arises from Kilroy's sudden apotheosis after his death; this is pure *deus ex machina.* Williams' literary self-consciousness leads to chaos: All at once the viewer is thrust into an incongruous symbolical environment of Dante, Cervantes, T. S. Eliot, Lord Byron, Spanish folk lore, and Christian reminiscences. Too much weight rests upon sentiment; the clearest example of this is found in the closing lines: "The violets in the mountains have broken the rocks!" The "comic" resolution of the play comes through the author's fiat and not through a dramatically believable solution. Thus Williams, by using sentiment in such a way, pronounces the play complete even if the reader or viewer mentally protests.

Suddenly Last Summer, produced five years after *Camino Real,* has a similar lack of credibility. The allegorical meaning of the play is explained by the heroine, Catharine Holly; it has to do with the consequences of possessing a daemonic vision of God and man. Professor Paul J. Hurley understands the play properly when he writes: "What his drama proclaims is that recognition of evil, if carried to the point of a consuming obsession, may be the worst form of evil. . . . A daemonic vision of human nature may irredeemably corrupt the one who possesses the vision." The point of this "morality play" is made clear by Catharine. She explains that her homosexual cousin Sebastian, a would-be poet, did what all modern men have a tendency to do: He tried to "spell God's name with the wrong alphabet blocks." Since the question of God is an important one in the drama (Sebastian sacrifices himself to his "vision" of a cannibalistic God), one would expect Williams to pursue the question. Instead of dealing further with this important point, however, the playwright turns his attention to the interrelationship of mankind. Humanity, according to Catharine, may be as desperate as passengers aboard a ship which has struck an iceberg at sea. Everyone is sinking, but that is "no reason for everyone drowning hating everyone drowning." Totally disregarding man's idolatrous nature—his making into God an image of himself—Catharine touchingly affirms a positive life of community in which people accept each other even though they all share the common fate of death. If a major problem of *Suddenly Last Summer* is God's relationship to human experience, then we must conclude that the question is unanswered by the playwright. This play is similar to *Camino*

Real in its vagueness about solutions which, although literally present in the drama, do not in any sense relate to the problems which they should solve. Yes, *Suddenly Last Summer* has a sense of completeness as a "morality play," but the drama nevertheless fails to come to grips with the central issue it has raised.

In the recent plays of hopefulness beyond despair, Tennessee Williams commits several errors—the greatest of which is his misleading suggestion that the dramas have been resolved.
—Delma Eugene Presley

The two most recent plays in this discussion, as some critics have acknowledged, are explicitly theological. Once again the basis problems of the characters are isolation, the question of God, and death. In *The Night of the Iguana*, Shannon's main problem is "the oldest one in the world—the need to believe in something or someone." Hannah's emphasis upon belief is intended as a solution to Shannon's state of disbelief. Earlier he tells her that "Western theologies, the whole mythology of them, are based on the concept of God as a senile delinquent. . . . I will not and cannot continue to conduct services in praise and worship of this . . . angry, petulant old man" (Act II). While Hannah correctly senses that Shannon has a problem of belief, she is nevertheless incapable of providing an answer to this specific question. The logic of her speeches is that Shannon's problem concerning God may be resolved if he simply reaches out for other people. The clearest illustration of her logic is found in the second half of the passage quoted earlier. Here it is in full:

SHANNON:
What is my problem, Miss Jelkes?

HANNAH:
The oldest one in the world—the need to believe in something or in someone—almost anyone—almost anything . . . something.

SHANNON:
Your voice sounds hopeless about it.

HANNAH:
No, I'm not hopeless about it. In fact, I've discovered something to believe in.

SHANNON:
Something like . . . God?

HANNAH:

No.

SHANNON:
What?

HANNAH:
Broken gates between people so they can reach each other, even if it's just for one night only.

. . .

A little understanding exchanged between them, a wanting to help each other through nights like this.
(Act III)

Later in this act Hannah explains that, while she is "unsure" about God, she is beginning to feel that God may be seen in the faces of suffering humanity.

Hannah's point is that the problem of belief will more or less take care of itself if Shannon will try to live in community with someone. But Shannon's problem is not isolation but belief or lack of it. Hannah insists that he deal with the question of disbelief with the answer for human isolation—community. The logic is reminiscent of that used by Catharine in *Suddenly Last Summer;* she raises the question about Sebastian's daemonic vision of God and then answers it with a simplistic statement about the importance of caring for other people.

Williams manages to solve the fundamental problem of death in *Iguana* while Hannah and Shannon are engaged in their discussion; the character involved in this solution, however, is neither the hero nor the heroine, but the heroine's father, Nonno. Everyone in the play knows that he is at death's door. His concern throughout the play is to complete his final poem—one which explores a way of looking at death. The concluding lines of the poem reveal that Nonno's solution to death is "Courage."

O Courage could you not as well
Select a second place to dwell,
Not only in that golden tree
But in the frightened heart of me?

Nonno's struggle to complete the poem parallels Shannon's efforts to understand and justify his existence in view of his conception of God. Nonno's climactic poem lends an air of calm reserve to this scene in which Shannon attempts to find something worthy of his belief. Nonno is the only character who finds a satisfactory answer to his basic question. But the play is not about Nonno. The main character, Shannon, ignores the question which first was most important and commits himself to a life of "community" with Maxine—a person who throughout the play is revealed as incapable of either understanding or empathy. Shannon's question of belief is left unanswered. One might argue that Hannah substitutes the human face for the divine image, in the tradition of Romantic thinkers, and thus redefines the question on belief. If Williams' point is that suffering humanity has replaced God, then he does not make it clear. Shannon's vigorous statements about God as a "senile delinquent" are not refuted by ignoring them.

The point about the illogical resolution of *The Night of the Iguana* can be made about *The Milk Train Doesn't Stop Here Anymore.* The chief difference is that the basic problem of the latter play is death. Furthermore, the ideology of Christopher is more nearly Christian than oriental, whereas Hannah's point of view is an uneven combination of oriental, stoic, and Christian sentiment. Christopher's mission apparently is to prepare Mrs. Goforth for death. (She is about to "go forth.") The epigraph from Yeats's "Sailing to Byzantium," in the context of the drama, implies that Mrs. Goforth is about to sail into eternity. Yet it is not clear whether Williams proposes that the solution to her problem of death is some kind of eternal life. If Christopher is a "bearer of Christ," this would seem logical. Yet the hero's mission has patently selfish origins. He visits Mrs. Goforth, just as he has visited other dying ladies, not primarily because he has a special message for her, but because this activity saves *him* from a sense of "unreality" and "lostness." An uncritical reading of the play might lead one, as it has led countless reviewers, to claim that the drama is about a "Christ figure" who comes to prepare a dying aristocrat for eternal life. But Williams has not done this in *The Milk Train Doesn't Stop Here Anymore.* Mrs. Goforth's death is merely a vehicle for the realization of a vagrant poet's unusual need for psychological comfort.

The play's meaning is further confused by the epigraph from W. B. Yeats's famous poem, "Sailing to Byzantium":

> Consume my heart away; sick with desire
> And fastened to a dying animal
> It knows not what it is; and gather me
> Into the artifice of eternity.

The poem does not suggest the same kind of eternal life represented by the image of Christ. Rather, it is Yeats's special interpretation of art in opposition to nature. The poem suggests the rejection of the natural for the unnatural "form as Grecian goldsmiths make. . . ." If Williams uses Christopher Flanders (the name connotes both Christ and death) to suggest that Mrs. Goforth has entered eternity when the drama closes, as several critics maintain, then the playwright has probably misunderstood the meaning of "Sailing to Byzantium." The basic problem of the drama, death, is left unsolved; unsolved, even though the touching communion scene at the end suggests that something has been resolved.

In the recent plays of hopefulness beyond despair, Tennes-

see Williams commits several errors—the greatest of which is his misleading suggestion that the dramas have been resolved. The closest either play (*Iguana* and *Milk Train*) comes to resolution is in the singular instance of Nonno's discovery of "courage" in the face of death. But it is Nonno's solution and not Shannon's. The greatest problem of the play—Shannon's struggle for belief—is ignored in the drama's resolution.

Since Williams' turning point is *Camino Real,* it is important to notice that at the very moment he is developing a moral point of view, he is also experimenting with a dramatic structure foreign to his genius as a writer of realistic dramas. The characters of *Camino Real* are stripped of their authenticity even though their allegorical trappings are rich in symbolic value. Williams' conception of allegory is flawed by its escape from the real. Successful allegory is symbolic in method, but the goal is usually realistic. The unreality of his major allegories, *Camino Real* and *Suddenly Last Summer,* is a clear indication that Williams has substituted sentimentality for authenticity. The only conclusion to be drawn from this development is that, despite the playwright's desperate and commendable efforts to the contrary, there are no believable solutions for the terrifying problems of his very complex characters.

Despite the fact that Williams' hero ultimately achieves a limited kind of community, his problems—isolation, God's absence, and death—are not resolved in a convincing manner.
—*Delma Eugene Presley*

That Williams is concerned with important theological issues cannot be denied. Human isolation, the absence of God, and the reality of death are fundamental concerns of Christian theology. Williams obviously recognizes this or he would not consistently use Christian-sounding language and themes in most of his recent works. Yet he has not grasped the fundamental logic inherent in the theological issues. He has not found a way to deal effectively with the problems experienced by his characters, even though he employs dramatic techniques such as false resolutions to suggest otherwise.

The great virtue of the early plays of Williams is that they are believable and concern real people. The early hero's dignity is that, despite social and psychological pressures, he does not ultimately ignore the facts of his life. Blanche's despair is a legitimate and credible response to the nature of her existence. Tom's acute sense of the disgusting aspects of life makes him what few of the latter heroes are—truthful. In this context, we can say that frustration and anxiety are far more commendable, more real, than the religious-sounding clichés of the hero in the later plays.

Despite the fact that Williams' hero ultimately achieves a limited kind of community, his problems—isolation, God's absence, and death—are not resolved in a convincing manner. Williams' difficulty is shared by many modern writers who would project theological themes. T. S. Eliot's plays tend to confirm the difficulty of Williams' task. Perhaps the only meaningful action for the hero in isolation would be to wait. But Williams, more often than not, is a writer whose plays are in the realistic traditions of Chekhov and Ibsen, not in the more somber traditions of the "theatre of the absurd" or the "literature of silence." Some argue that Williams' greatest attribute is his ability to produce conventional, realistic drama. Indeed he succeeds most of all when he describes loneliness, frustration, and the unavoidable anxiety of human experience. But in his later works he attempts more than description. He proposes sentimental, religious-sounding solutions which contribute to dramatic distortion and thematic irrelevance. Some might contend that this situation validates the conclusion of the "death of God" theologian, Gabriel Vahanian: "Christian thought . . . no longer is relevant to the situation of our post-Christian age and its cultural postulates." I would like to argue, however, that Williams' failure is not primarily due to his use or misuse of a system of theology. Rather, the major difficulty is his apparent inability to resolve in a logical manner the problems of his characters. Tennessee Williams' recent entry into the Church perhaps indicates that he is doing with his life what he has been trying to do for his characters. Somehow it is easier to be a religious playwright than a writer of religious plays. And T. S. Eliot has taught us by example the importance of knowing where one leaves off and the other begins.

Susan Neal Mayberry (essay date Winter 1983)

SOURCE: "A Study of Illusion and the Grotesque in Tennessee Williams' *Cat on a Hot Tin Roof*," in *Southern Studies*, Vol. 22, No. 4, Winter, 1983, pp. 359-65.

[*In the following essay, Mayberry offers analysis of "grotesque" characters in* Cat on a Hot Tin Roof, *drawing attention to their unique physical or psychological deformities as a source of both humor and pathos. Mayberry also addresses the various illusions and pretenses through which these characters attempt to protect themselves.*]

Although the Southern dialect, mannerisms, and setting apparent in *Cat on a Hot Tin Roof* reveal Tennessee Williams' usual regional focus, the ideas and emotions which the drama involves are by no means geographically restricted but, on the contrary, are of universal import. The play depicts the feelings and consequences of greed, frustration, guilt, desire, and hypocrisy, but most importantly it deals with the conflict between appearance and reality and its resolution in truth. Williams is concerned with man's drive to escape his problems either by totally ignoring them or by effecting a facade of illusion. He emphasizes this need in the opening of the work with a symbolic stage prop—the "huge console combination of radio-phonograph, TV set, and liquor cabinet"—which he describes as "a very complete and compact little shrine to virtually all the comforts and illusions behind which we hide from such things as the characters in the play are faced with." It is this veil of illusion that permits human beings to cope with the "slow and implacable fires of . . . desperation," and Williams intensifies the growing despair in this play by giving it a stifling, almost claustrophobic atmosphere. Time and setting are extremely confining; the entire action takes place during one hot summer evening in a single bed-sitting-room of a plantation house in the Mississippi Delta. Maggie refers again and again to the lack of privacy in this wealthy Southern family, to the "cage" which is their home. Such a feeling of tightening circumscription only heightens the frantic attempts of these characters to avoid reality and increases the likelihood of an inevitable, shattering destruction of illusion. As Gooper points out, "A family crisis brings out the best and worst in every member of it."

Thus the pervading theme of Williams' drama involves the tension between truth and mendacity, the gradual stripping away of pretense with the ultimate consequences, and the playwright employs various devices to achieve both illusion and exposure. One of his most effective techniques is a use of the grotesque, a term which has come to hold special meaning in twentieth-century literature. It is an outgrowth of the contemporary distrust of any cosmic order, an interest in the irrational, and a frustration at man's position in the universe. In a sense, then, the grotesque is a merging of the comic and tragic; through physical or spiritual deformity and abnormal action, an individual reflects both a comic deviation from the rational social order and a tragic loss of faith in the moral universe. In *Cat on a Hot Tin Roof,* Williams employs two types of grotesque characterization to illustrate escape through illusion. The first of these, depicted graphically in characters such as those portrayed by Flannery O'Connor, seems to emphasize physical deformity and to induce a humorous response in its very absurdity, while the second, reflecting the figures of Sherwood Anderson, suggests spiritual or emotional abnormality and invokes a pathetic sometimes even tragic response.

Flannery O'Connor has defined the grotesque character as "man forced to meet the extremes of his own nature," and the twisted personalities of her figures, usually accompanied by a distorted appearance, generate a sinister, frightening, or pathetic effect almost always combined with and highlighted by the comic. Williams makes use of the O'Connor grotesque in the minor characters of his play, figures whose absurd appearance reflects a deformed soul. All of these individuals attempt to ignore or hide the truth of their particular deformity behind a shield of illusion. One such figure is the Reverend Tooker, the personification of religious hypocrisy. Sensing with vulture-like accuracy the presence of decay, the reverend is simply waiting for Big Daddy to die. Attempting to hide his greed with platitudes and weak jokes, the minister nevertheless reveals his obsession with money by his constant references to church donations and memorials for the dead. As Williams describes him, he appears with his "head slightly, playfully, fatuously cocked, with a practiced clergyman's smile, sincere as a birdcall blown on a hunter's whistle, the living embodiment of the pious conventional lie." He is grotesque in both appearance and character.

This grotesque hypocrisy is even more predominant in the portraits of Mae, Gooper, and the little "no-neck monsters." The elder son and his wife reveal a desire to inherit Big Daddy's money before his death; their rapaciousness is apparent not only in their inane chatter and overzealous efforts to please, but also in the actual use of their children as levers to draw the old man's attention by emphasizing their fertility in contrast to the sterility of Brick and Maggie. The grotesque antics which Mae and Gooper put themselves and their children through in a frenzied attempt to win approval are so absurd as to become pitiful. Maggie describes the scene with the no-neck monsters "ranged around the table, some in high chairs and some on th' *Books of Knowledge,* all in fancy little paper caps in honor of Big Daddy's birthday," and Mae herself depicts the after-dinner show: "Polly played the piano, Buster an' Sonny drums, an' then they turned out the lights an' Dixie an' Trixie puhfawmed a toe dance in fairy costume with spahkluhs! Big Daddy just beamed!" In addition to the children's "dawgs' names" and their overall resemblance to an "animal act in a circus," their absurdity is climaxed with a song-and-dance routine for Big Daddy, arranged and conducted by Mae, which achieves the effect of a bizarre "musical comedy chorus." Although the general impression of these scenes is one of ridiculous farce, there is actually an undercurrent of something quite sinister and frightening; these are, after all, frantic efforts by desperate people to satisfy overwhelming greed.

Williams uses the O'Connor mode to surround his main characters with an outer circle resembling allegorical personifications of vice. These comic grotesques even reflect the medieval emphasis on physiognomy. As he moves from the outer circle to close in on the immediate family, attempting to achieve with characterization the claustrophobic effect of setting, he makes use of the more sympathetic, even tragic, Andersonian grotesque and begins to focus on more complicated personalities. The character of Big Mama provides us with a transitional figure. Actually a more distorted mani-

festation of the frustrated love theme treated in Maggie herself, Big Mama is at once absurdly comic and sadly pathetic. Her physical description provokes immediate laughter. She first enters

> huffing and puffing like an old bulldog. She is a short, stout woman; her sixty years and 170 pounds have left her somewhat breathless most of the time: she's always tensed like a boxer, or rather a Japanese wrestler. . . . She wears a black or silver lace dress and at least half a million in flashy gems. She is very sincere.

Her actions are at least as comical as her appearance. Williams emphasizes her grotesque, coy giggling in Big Daddy's direction, her "riotous voice" and "booming laugh," and her "inelegant horseplay" with Reverend Tooker—pulling him into her lap "with a shrill laugh that spans an octave in two notes" and the exclamation: "Ever seen a preacher in a fat lady's lap?" There is another side to this woman, an aspect which renders her less caricature and more human being; she faces the same frustrated love, the same indifference of her husband as does Maggie. Confronted with the cruel reality of Big Daddy's repulsion toward her, Big Mama cries to him, "I did love you—I even loved your hate and your hardness." When the truth of her husband's certain death is revealed to her, her soft response admits of a "great, almost embarrassingly true-hearted and simple-minded devotion to Big Daddy, who must have had something Brick has, who made himself loved so much by the 'simple expedient' of not loving enough to disturb his charming detachment." As Williams points out, "Big Mama has a dignity at this moment: she almost stops being fat." Although each of these characters is allowed for a time to hide behind his grotesqueness, to conceal his true nature behind calculated illusion, each figure is relentlessly and totally exposed. Reverend Tooker's hypocritical piety is revealed; Mae and Gooper finally relinquish the "nice" approach and make their self-interest and resentment shockingly clear, and Big Mama is forced to confront her husband's disgust with her at the same time she learns of his cancer.

With his major characters Williams makes use of a different type of figure, one which might be called the Andersonian grotesque. In *Winesburg, Ohio,* Sherwood Anderson recognizes that implicit in the term *grotesque* lies a concern with truth. The thesis of the *Book of the Grotesque,* authored by Anderson's "old writer" reads, "Man made the truths himself and each thought was a composite of a great many vague thoughts. All about in the world were the truths and they were all beautiful." These same truths, however, serve to make people grotesque. For once a person fails to recognize that there are many truths and begins to take "one of the truths to himself, call[s] it his truth, and [tries] to live by it, he [becomes] a grotesque and the truth he embraced [becomes] a falsehood." Thus, Anderson's grotesques are beautiful in that they pursue an ideal, but they are blind to any but their own ideal or truth and ultimately distort it in their fanaticism. Like Anderson, Williams is able, at least in the major characters of *Cat on a Hot Tin Roof,* to look beneath the surface of the apparently distorted lives of his grotesques and appreciate the truth, the pathos, and even the tragedy there. He is able to taste the sweetness, though bittersweet, of the "twisted apples." The characters of Brick, Big Daddy, and Maggie are spiritually rather than physically distorted, and they invoke not a comic but a pathetic response.

> **The characters of Brick, Big Daddy, and Maggie [in *Cat on a Hot Tin Roof*] are spiritually rather than physically distorted, and they invoke not a comic but a pathetic response.**
> **—*Susan Neal Mayberry***

The playwright depicts these figures in the light of their respective abilities to face and cope with reality; of the three, Brick is least able to confront truth. From the beginning of the play, he is described as having the "additional charm of that cool air of detachment that people have who have given up the struggle." His wife elaborates further when she states, "now that you've lost the game, not lost but just quit playing, you have that rare sort of charm that usually only happens in very old or hopelessly sick people, the charm of the defeated." Even his lovemaking is enhanced because he has no anxiety, is really indifferent to it; he simply uses this detachment as a means of escaping reality. Brick's desperation surfaces occasionally, as evidenced by his obsessive drinking, his reckless hurdle-jumping which results in a broken ankle, and his fierce need to keep Maggie at a distance—to the extent that at her touch he seizes a chair and "raises it like a lion-tamer facing a big circus cat." Perhaps the most striking example of his denial of truth is revealed in his refusal to face his feelings of guilt, the obsession which renders him grotesque. He unequivocally refutes any hint of an unnatural love in his intense relationship with Skipper, rejecting his friend's tortured confession and stubbornly insisting that their feeling for each other was the only "pure an' true" thing in his life. As Big Daddy points out, "You!—dug the grave of your friend and kicked him in it!—before you'd face truth with him." Thus Brick's disgust with mendacity is actually disgust with himself.

As Brick retorts to his father, "Who can face truth? Can you?" This question goes straight to the heart of Big Daddy's character, for the old man is very capable of confronting the truths of those around him but not his own. His peculiar grotesqueness, resulting from lack of self-awareness, is talking without communicating. As he admits to Brick, "we've always—talked around things . . . it's always like something was left not spoken." The root of the problem is that Big Daddy talks but seldom listens. He is astute in his realization of the hypocrisy inherent in the Reverend Tooker's posturing and is acutely aware of the greed, spying, and scheming of his son and daughter-in-law, acknowledging, "I hate Gooper and Mae an' know that they hate me. . . ." He openly and directly faces his favorite son's drinking problem, exclaiming, "Why boy, you're—alcoholic!" Most importantly, it is Big Daddy who relentlessly forces Brick to confront the truth about his relationship with Skipper, recognizing that this is the "inadmissible thing that Skipper died to disavow between them." Regardless of his perception into the emotions and motivations of those around him, Big Daddy fails to accept and cope with the reality of his own situation and like Brick is virtually destroyed when the security of his illusion is stripped away. Like his son he misunderstands his wife's real feeling for him, reflecting when she declares such a love, "Wouldn't it be funny if that was true. . . ." When his illusion of a new life of unabashed sensuality is destroyed and he learns that he is dying of cancer, the old man's final words are, "Lying! Dying! Liars!"

Thus it is only Maggie the Cat who is capable of dealing with the complexity of truth. She is, in fact, the only truly honest character in the play, the single character able to recognize and see through appearance not only to the reality of others but also to her own. She is the first to acknowledge Big Daddy's cancer and the ultimate effect his death will have on other members of the family. She realizes that truth sometimes incorporates a lie, that the old man must not know of his disease, for "Nobody says, 'You're dying.' You have to fool them. They have to fool themselves." She understands fully the motivations behind Mae and Gooper's visit and macabre performance, noting, "They're up to cutting you [Brick] out of your Father's estate. . . ." More importantly, Maggie is able to confront unflinchingly truths about herself. She confesses to her husband,

> Brick, I'm not good. I don't know why people have to pretend to be good, nobody's good. The rich or the well-to-do can afford to respect moral patterns, conventional moral patterns, but I could never afford to, yeah, but—I'm honest! Give me credit for just that, will you *please?*

Maggie knows that her frenzied desire for money and security is a result of the deprivation of both as a child. She resents that she has been "so God damn disgustingly poor" all her life and realizes that "You can be young without money but you can't be old without it." It is this desperate drive for security that makes her "like a cat on a hot tin roof!" Maggie understands that, because she cannot "afford t'be thin-skinned any more," she has "gone through this—hideous!—transformation, become—hard! Frantic!—cruel!!" She is willing to confront her own loneliness, her husband's indifference toward her, and her part in the Skipper-Brick affair, for it is Maggie who forces the confrontation between Brick and Skipper. Frustrated by all of the pretense, she finally tells Skipper, "Stop Lovin' My Husband Or Tell Him He's Got To Let You Admit It To Him!" She accepts the responsibility for her actions—the guilt and the loneliness that come with living with someone "y'love" who "doesn't love you." She knows that she destroyed Skipper, and in a sense her husband, by "telling him truth that he and his world which he was born and raised in . . . had told him could not be told." Maggie also understands that living is a constant struggle to face truth, to affirm love, that it is the attempt that is important, even if the results are only suffering and failure. As she puts it to Brick,

> But one thing I don't have is the charm of the defeated, my hat is still in the ring, and I am determined to win!—What is the victory of a cat on a hot tin roof?—I wish I knew. . . . Just staying on it, I guess, as long as she can. . . .

It is only Maggie who is fully perceptive of the struggle going on around her and within her. She is finally the "only one there who is conscious of and amused by the grotesque," the only one aware of the true significance of the conflict between illusion and reality.

Thus even though Maggie is forced to participate in the grotesque situation of a cat on a hot tin roof, she alone is not totally destroyed because she is always fully attuned to what she is doing, is able to discern the difference between mendacity and truth. She possesses the awareness essential for making moral choices, at times even equating morality with awareness. Unlike the others who are ultimately devastated when their illusions are stripped away, Maggie's exposure is not necessary because she is willing to accept and cope with truth; hers is already an examined life. She is the cat who "can jump off roofs and land on [her] four feet uninjured!" Regardless of the pain, she will survive. As with Big Daddy's disease, she will lie when the necessity arises, claiming to be pregnant with Brick's child in order to endure, but she is still aware of that lie and is willing to accept the responsibility for its consequences. Even here Maggie remains fast to her code of truth, desperately attempting to make illusion real, telling her husband, "And so tonight we're going to make the lie true. . . ." She tries to block all escape from Brick, removing his liquor, his crutch—everything but his indifference—saying softly to him, "Oh, you weak people, you weak, beautiful people!— who give up.—What you want is someone to—take hold of you.—Gently, gently, with love! And—I do love you, Brick, I do!" Thus in a study of the way in which people destroy themselves with their inability to confront their problems and

be responsible for their actions, it is both Maggie's pathetic triumph and tragedy to be unable, by her very nature, to ignore or avoid reality, even though that reality threatens her survival. Although her situation dooms her to fail, she is yet admirable in her very striving. She has acquired the poise of the cat caught on a hot tin roof and is able to recognize the situation as a metaphor for living.

Harold Bloom (essay date 1987)

SOURCE: An introduction to *Modern Critical Views: Tennessee Williams,* edited by Harold Bloom, Chelsea House Publishers, 1987, pp. 1-8.

[*In the following essay, Bloom considers Williams's achievements and shortcomings as a major American playwright and the influence of poet Hart Crane on his work.*]

It is a sad and inexplicable truth that the United States, a dramatic nation, continues to have so limited a literary achievement in the drama. American literature, from Emerson to the present moment, is a distinguished tradition. The poetry of Whitman, Dickinson, Frost, Stevens, Eliot, W. C. Williams, Hart Crane, R. P. Warren, Elizabeth Bishop down through the generation of my own contemporaries— John Ashbery, James Merrill, A. R. Ammons and others— has an unquestionable eminence, and takes a vital place in Western literature. Prose fiction from Hawthorne and Melville on through Mark Twain and Henry James to Cather and Dreiser, Faulkner, Hemingway, Fitzgerald, Nathanael West, and Pynchon, has almost a parallel importance. The line of essayists and critics from Emerson and Thoreau to Kenneth Burke and beyond constitutes another crucial strand of our national letters. But where is the American drama in comparison to all this, and in relation to the long cavalcade of Western drama from Aeschylus to Beckett?

The American theater, by the common estimate of its most eminent critics, touches an initial strength with Eugene O'Neill, and then proceeds to the more varied excellences of Thornton Wilder, Tennessee Williams, Arthur Miller, Edward Albee, and Sam Shepard. That sequence is clearly problematical, and becomes even more worrisome when we move from playwrights to plays. Which are our dramatic works that matter most? *A Long Day's Journey Into Night,* certainly; perhaps *The Iceman Cometh:* evidently *A Streetcar Named Desire* and *Death of a Salesman;* perhaps again *The Skin of Our Teeth* and *The Zoo Story*—it is not God's plenty. And I will venture the speculation that our drama palpably is not yet literary enough. By this I do not just mean that O'Neill writes very badly, or Miller very baldly; they do, but so did Dreiser, and *Sister Carrie* and *An American Tragedy* prevail nevertheless. Nor do I wish to be an American Matthew Arnold (whom I loathe above all other critics) and proclaim that our dramatists simply have not known enough. They know more than enough, and that is part of the trouble.

Literary tradition, as I have come to understand it, masks the agon between past and present as a benign relationship, whether personal or societal. The actual transferences between the force of the literary past and the potential of writing in the present tend to be darker, even if they do not always or altogether follow the defensive patterns of what Sigmund Freud called "family romances." Whether or not an ambivalence, however repressed, towards the past's force is felt by the new writer and is manifested in his work seems to depend entirely upon the ambition and power of the oncoming artist. If he aspires after strength, and can attain it, then he must struggle with both a positive and a negative transference, false connections because necessarily imagined ones, between a composite precursor and himself. His principal resource in that agon will be his own native gift for interpretation, or as I am inclined to call it, strong misreading. Revising his precursor, he will create himself, make himself into a kind of changeling, and so he will become, in an illusory but highly pragmatic way, his own father.

The most literary of our major dramatists, and clearly I mean "literary" in a precisely descriptive sense, neither pejorative nor eulogistic, was Tennessee Williams.
—*Harold Bloom*

The most literary of our major dramatists, and clearly I mean "literary" in a precisely descriptive sense, neither pejorative nor eulogistic, was Tennessee Williams. Wilder, with his intimate connections to *Finnegans Wake* and Gertrude Stein, might seem to dispute this placement, and Wilder was certainly more literate than Williams. But Wilder had a benign relation to his crucial precursor, Joyce, and did not aspire after a destructive strength. Williams did, and suffered the fate he prophesied and desired; the strength destroyed his later work, and his later life, and thus joined itself to the American tradition of self-destructive genius. Williams truly had one precursor only: Hart Crane, the greatest of our lyrical poets, after Whitman and Dickinson, and the most self-destructive figure in our national literature, surpassing all others in this, as in so many regards.

Williams asserted he had other precursors also; D. H. Lawrence, and Chekhov in the drama. These were outward influences, and benefitted Williams well enough, but they were essentially formal, and so not the personal and societal family romance of authentic poetic influence. Hart Crane made Williams into more of a dramatic lyrist, though writ-

ing in prose, than the lyrical dramatist that Williams is supposed to have been. Though this influence—perhaps more nearly an identification—helped form *The Glass Menagerie* and (less overtly) *A Streetcar Named Desire,* and in a lesser mode *Summer and Smoke* and *Suddenly Last Summer,* it also led to such disasters of misplaced lyricism as the dreadful *Camino Real* and the dreary *The Night of the Iguana.* (*Cat on a Hot Tin Roof,* one of Williams's best plays, does not seem to me to show any influence of Crane.) Williams's long aesthetic decline covered thirty years, from 1953 to 1983, and reflected the sorrows of a seer who, by his early forties, had outlived his own vision. Hart Crane, self-slain at thirty-two, had set for Williams a High Romantic paradigm that helped cause Williams, his heart as dry as summer dust, to burn to the socket.

In Hart Crane's last great Pindaric ode, "The Broken Tower," the poet cries aloud, in a lament that is also a high celebration, the destruction of his battered self by his overwhelming creative gift:

> The bells, I say, the bells break down their tower;
> And swing I know not where. Their tongues
> engrave
> Membrane through marrow, my long-scattered
> score
> Of broken intervals . . . And I, their sexton slave!

This Shelleyan and Whitmanian catastrophe creation, or death by inspiration, was cited once by Williams as an omen of Crane's self-immolation. "By the bells breaking down their tower," in Williams's interpretation, Crane meant "the romantic and lyric intensity of his vocation." Gilbert Debusscher has traced the intensity of Crane's effect upon Williams's Romantic and lyric vocation, with particular reference to Tom Wingfield's emergent vocation in *The Glass Menagerie.* More than forty years after its first publication, the play provides an absorbing yet partly disappointing experience of rereading.

A professed "memory play," *The Glass Menagerie* seems to derive its continued if wavering force from its partly repressed representation of the quasi-incestuous and doomed love between Tom Wingfield and his crippled, "exquisitely fragile," ultimately schizophrenic sister Laura. Incest, subtly termed the most poetical of circumstances by Shelley, is the dynamic of the erotic drive throughout Williams's more vital writings. Powerfully displaced, it is the secret dynamic of what is surely Williams's masterwork, *A Streetcar Named Desire.*

The Glass Menagerie scarcely bothers at such a displacement, and the transparency of the incest motif is at once the play's lyrical strength and, alas, its dramatic weakness. Consider the moment when Williams chooses to end the play, which times Tom's closing speech with Laura's gesture of blowing out the candles:

> TOM: I didn't go to the moon, I went much further—for time is the longest distance between two places. Not long after that I was fired for writing a poem on the lid of a shoe-box. I left St. Louis. I descended the steps of this fire escape for a last time and followed, from then on, in my father's footsteps, attempting to find in motion what was lost in space. I traveled around a great deal. The cities swept about me like dead leaves, leaves that were brightly colored but torn away from the branches. I would have stopped, but I was pursued by something. It always came upon me unawares, taking me altogether by surprise. Perhaps it was a familiar bit of music. Perhaps it was only a piece of transparent glass. Perhaps I am walking along a street at night, in some strange city, before I have found companions. I pass the lighted window of a shop where perfume is sold. The window is filled with pieces of colored glass, tiny transparent bottles in delicate colors, like bits of a shattered rainbow. Then all at once my sister touches my shoulder. I turn around and look into her eyes. Oh, Laura, Laura, I tried to leave you behind me, but I am more faithful than I intended to be! I reach for a cigarette, I cross the street, I run into the movies or a bar, I buy a drink, I speak to the nearest stranger—anything that can blow your candles out!

> [*Laura bends over the candles.*]

> For nowadays the world is lit by lightning! Blow out your candles, Laura—and so goodbye. . . .

> [*She blows the candles out.*]

The many parallels between the lives and careers of Williams and Crane stand behind this poignant passage, though it is fascinating that the actual allusions and echoes here are to Shelley's poetry, but then Shelley increasingly appears to be Crane's heroic archetype, and one remembers Robert Lowell's poem where Crane speaks and identifies himself as the Shelley of his age. The cities of aesthetic exile sweep about Wingfield/Williams like the dead, brightly colored leaves of the "Ode to the West Wind," dead leaves that are at once the words of the poet and lost human souls, like the beloved sister Laura.

What pursues Tom is what pursues the Shelleyan Poet of *Alastor,* an avenging daimon or shadow of rejected, sisterly eros that manifests itself in a further Shelleyan metaphor, the shattered, colored transparencies of Shelley's dome of many-colored glass in *Adonais,* the sublime, lyrical elegy for Keats.

That dome, Shelley says, is a similitude for life, and its many colors stain the white radiance of Eternity until death tramples the dome into fragments. Williams beautifully revises Shelley's magnificent trope. For Williams, life itself, through memory as its agent, shatters itself and scatters the colored transparencies of the rainbow, which ought to be, but is not, a covenant of hope.

Incest . . . is the dynamic of the erotic drive throughout Williams's more vital writings. Powerfully displaced, it is the secret dynamic of what is surely Williams's masterwork, *A Streetcar Named Desire*.
—*Harold Bloom*

As lyrical prose, this closing speech has its glory, but whether the dramatic effect is legitimate seems questionable. The key sentence, dramatically, is: "Oh, Laura, Laura, I tried to leave you behind me, but I am more faithful than I intended to be!" In his descriptive list of the characters, Williams says of his surrogate, Wingfield: "His nature is not remorseless; but to escape from a trap he has to act without pity." What would pity have been? And in what sense is Wingfield more faithful, after all, than he attempted to be?

Williams chooses to end the play as though its dramatic center had been Laura, but every reader and every playgoer knows that every dramatic element in the play emanates out from the mother, Amanda. Dream and its repressions, guilt and desire, have remarkably little to do with the representation of Amanda in the play, and everything to do with her children. The split between dramatist and lyrist in Williams is manifested in the play as a generative divide. Williams's true subject, like Crane's, is the absolute identity between his artistic vocation and his homosexuality. What is lacking in *The Glass Menagerie* is that Williams could not have said of Amanda, what, Flaubert-like, he did say of the heroine of *Streetcar:* "I am Blanche DuBois." There, and there only, Williams could fuse Chekhov and Hart Crane into one.

The epigraph to *A Streetcar Named Desire* is a quatrain from Hart Crane's "The Broken Tower," the poet's elegy for his gift, his vocation, his life, and so Crane's precise equivalent of Shelley's *Triumph of Life,* Keats's *Fall of Hyperion,* and Whitman's "When Lilacs Last in the Dooryard Bloom'd." Tennessee Williams, in his long thirty years of decline after composing *A Streetcar Named Desire,* had no highly designed, powerfully executed elegy for his own poetic self. Unlike Crane, his American Romantic precursor and aesthetic paradigm, Williams had to live out the slow degradation of the waning of his potential, and so endured the triumph of life over his imagination.

Streetcar sustains a first rereading, after thirty years away from it, more strongly than I had expected. It is, inevitably, more remarkable on the stage than in the study, but the fusion of Williams's lyrical and dramatic talents in it has prevailed over time, at least so far. The play's flaws, in performance, ensue from its implicit tendency to sensationalize its characters, Blanche DuBois in particular. Directors and actresses have made such sensationalizing altogether explicit, with the sad result prophesied by Kenneth Tynan twenty-five years ago. The playgoer forgets that Blanche's only strengths are "nostalgia and hope," that she is "the desperate exceptional woman," and that her fall is a parable, rather than an isolated squalor:

> When, finally, she is removed to the mental home, we should feel that a part of civilization is going with her. Where ancient drama teaches us to reach nobility by contemplation of what is noble, modern American drama conjures us to contemplate what might have been noble, but is now humiliated, ignoble in the sight of all but the compassionate.

Tynan, though accurate enough, still might have modified the image of Blanche taking a part of civilization away with her into madness. Though Blanche yearns for the values of the aesthetic, she scarcely embodies them, being in this failure a masochistic self-parody on the part of Williams himself. His *Memoirs* portray Williams incessantly in the role of Blanche, studying the nostalgias, and inching along the wavering line between hope and paranoia. Williams, rather than Blanche, sustains Tynan's analysis of the lost nobility, now humiliated, that American drama conjures us to contemplate.

The fall of Blanche is a parable, not of American civilization's lost nobility, but of the failure of the American literary imagination to rise above its recent myths of recurrent defeat. Emerson admonished us, his descendants, to go beyond the Great Defeat of the Crucifixion and to demand Victory instead, a victory of the senses as well as of the soul. Walt Whitman, taking up Emerson's challenge directly, set the heroic pattern so desperately emulated by Hart Crane, and which is then repeated in a coarser tone in Williams's life and work.

It must seem curious, at first, to regard Blanche DuBois as a failed Whitmanian, but essentially that is her aesthetic identity. Confronted by the revelation of her young husband's preference for an older man over herself, Blanche falls downwards and outwards into nymphomania, phantasmagoric hopes, pseudo-imaginative collages of memory and desire. Her Orphic, psychic rending by the amiably brutal Stanley Kowalski, a rough but effective version of D. H. Lawrence's vitalistic vision of male force, is pathetic rather than tragic, not because Stanley necessarily is mindless, but

because she unnecessarily has made herself mindless, by failing the pragmatic test of experience.

Williams's most effective blend of lyrical vision and dramatic irony in the play comes in the agony of Blanche's cry against Stanley to Stella, his wife and her sister:

> He acts like an animal, has an animal's habits! Eats like one, moves like one, talks like one! There's even something—subhuman—something not quite to the stage of humanity yet! Yes, something—ape-like about him, like one of those pictures I've seen in—anthropological studies! Thousands and thousands of years have passed him right by, and there he is—Stanley Kowalski—survivor of the stone age! Bearing the raw meat home from the kill in the jungle! And you—*you* here—*waiting* for him! Maybe he'll strike you or maybe grunt and kiss you! That is, if kisses have been discovered yet! Night falls and the other apes gather! There in the front of the cave, all grunting like him, and swilling and gnawing and hulking! His poker night!—you call it—this party of apes! Somebody growls—some creature snatches at something—the fight is on! *God!* Maybe we are a long way from being made in God's image, but Stella—my sister—there has been *some* progress since then! Such things as art— as poetry and music—such kinds of new light have come into the world since then! In some kinds of people some tenderer feelings have had some little beginning! That we have got to make *grow!* And *cling* to, and hold as our flag! In this dark march toward whatever it is we're approaching. . . . *Don't—don't hang back with the brutes!*

The lyricism here takes its strength from the ambivalence of what at once attracts and dismays both Blanche and Williams. Dramatic irony, terrible in its antithetical pathos, results here from Blanche's involuntary self-condemnation, since she herself has hung back with the brutes while merely blinking at the new light of the aesthetic. Stanley, being what he is, is clearly less to blame than Blanche, who was capable of more but failed in will.

Williams, in his *Memoirs,* haunted as always by Hart Crane, refers to his precursor as "a tremendous and yet fragile artist," and then associates both himself and Blanche with the fate of Crane, a suicide by drowning in the Caribbean:

> I am as much of an hysteric as . . . Blanche; a codicil to my will provides for the disposition of my body in this way. "Sewn up in a clean white sack and dropped over board, twelve hours north of Havana, so that my bones may rest not too far from those of Hart Crane . . ."

At the conclusion of *Memoirs,* Williams again associated Crane both with his own vocation and his own limitations, following Crane even in an identification with the young Rimbaud:

> A poet such as the young Rimbaud is the only writer of whom I can think, at this moment, who could escape from words into the sensations of being, through his youth, turbulent with revolution, permitted articulation by nights of absinthe. And of course there is Hart Crane. Both of these poets touched fire that burned them alive. And perhaps it is only through self-immolation of such a nature that we living beings can offer to you the entire truth of ourselves within the reasonable boundaries of a book.

It is the limitation of *Memoirs,* and in some sense even of *A Streetcar Named Desire,* that we cannot accept either Williams or poor Blanche as a Rimbaud or a Hart Crane. Blanche cannot be said to have touched fire that burned her alive. Yet Williams earns the relevance of the play's great epigraph to Blanche's terrible fate:

> And so it was I entered the broken world
> To trace the visionary company of love, its voice
> An instant in the wind (I know not whither hurled)
> But not for long to hold each desperate choice.

John Timpane (essay date 1989)

SOURCE: "'Weak and Divided People': Tennessee Williams and the Written Woman," in *Feminist Rereadings of Modern American Drama,* edited by June Schlueter, Associated University Presses, 1989, pp. 171-80.

[*In the following essay, Timpane examines Williams's creation of female characters whose dynamic ambiguity resists the tendency toward idealization or oversimplification. Timpane contends that Williams offers "an authentic and authoritative depiction of female foolishness, limitations, and error."*]

Like much of Tennessee Williams's public image, the tradition that he was sympathetic to women began with Williams himself. In his essays, memoirs, and letters, throughout his compulsive project of self-exploration, he took pains to delineate how his experience of women surfaced in his drama. Mothers and sons war continually; brothers and sisters suffer adoration. Nancy M. Tischler has written well about the succession of predatory mother figures in Williams, ranging from Flora Goforth of *The Milk Train Doesn't Stop Here Anymore* and Alexandra of *Sweet Bird of Youth* to Amanda of *The Glass Menagerie,* Violet Venable of *Sud-*

denly Last Summer, and Maxine of *Night of the Iguana.* Further, in one of the most public of his many public games, Williams toyed with the name Rose and the image of roses in play after play. Williams even suggested that his early adoration of his mother and sister had contributed to the development of his homosexuality. In a letter to Kenneth Tynan, he wrote, "I used to have a terrific crush on the female members of my family, mother, sister, grandmother, and hated my father, a typical pattern for homosexuals." That last phrase strikes a familiar Williams tone. Aspiring to the detachment of scientific observation, it amounts to a claim that the writer is knowledgeable and candid enough to be at once analyst and analysand.

> **"I used to have a terrific crush on the female members of my family, mother, sister, grandmother, and hated my father, a typical pattern for homosexuals."**
> —*Tennessee Williams*

Yet when we reread a number of Williams's plays, we might well question the nature of his "identification" with women. It will not be enough to say that Williams's women are like Williams himself—American, Southern, liminal, "mutilated," sexually compulsive, given to drugs and alcohol, mendacious, and so forth. Nor will it be enough to let pity speak for itself, to repeat with many critics that the typical Williams plot involves "the defeat or destruction of a highly pitiable protagonist." The call on the audience to pity the female protagonist is very strong. But the quality of this pity is strained; it is not pity because of what we know but pity in spite of what we know. Nor is it enough to say simply that Williams's characters simultaneously excite both sympathy and antipathy. They do, but they excite a range of other feelings as well. Those characters, especially his women, call on the viewer to regard a true pluralism of possibilities—which almost always includes ambivalence and repulsion. Female characters in Williams's drama are deliberately constructed to arouse these two feelings in the audience. This remarkably consistent technique suggests a great deal about the construction of a female character, as well as about "feminist" approaches to both drama and criticism.

Here I must pause to define what constitutes a worthy characterization of a woman. First, it does not seem necessary that she be written to a program—that is, that she have any required attributes at all. What does seem necessary is that there be a wide range of "play" in the character. I mean "play," for the viewer or reader, is the kind of ambivalent play that Mikhail Bakhtin sensed in the comedy of Rabelais and the novels of Dostoevski. The object of this play will be the feelings the written woman evokes. She should not be subject to complete consumption—that is, some of her attributes should escape paraphrase or easy reconciliation. To insist on such play is to insist that the written woman not be prejudicially reduced, oversimplified, or idealized. Such play can exist even in stereotypical characters; we find it, for example, in Falstaff. The few truly interesting female characters in canonical works (my list includes Emma Bovary, Anna Karenina, and the Duchess of Malfi) benefit from this play. Their polytonality, which forces viewers or readers to take a judgmental stance—or a stance from which they presume to judge without actually being able to do so—is part of what produces the particular effect of Emma or Anna, Blanche or Alma, or Catharine or Amanda on the reader or viewer.

This ambivalent play is evoked by many Williams women, especially in those he claimed he "liked" best. Williams often named either Blanche DuBois, Alma Winemuller, or Maggie the Cat as his "favorite" character. Of Alma, he said, "You see, Alma went through the same thing that I went through—from puritanical shackles to, well, complete profligacy." Maggie the Cat was the subject of a celebrated debate between director Elia Kazan and Williams, partly over how the audience was to interpret her. As Williams told it, Kazan "felt that the character of Margaret, while he understood that I sympathized with her and liked her myself, should be, if possible, more clearly sympathetic to an audience." It is significant that a character with Williams's avowed sympathy—he wrote that "Maggie the Cat [became] steadily more charming to me as I worked on her characterization"—should be so ambiguous as to prompt the director to ask for a revision. Further, the so-called "Broadway Version" of act 3, although it gives Maggie the last word, is not successful in editing out the ambivalence. In this version, her last speech reads

> Oh you weak, beautiful people who give up with such grace. What you need is someone to take hold of you—gently, with love, and hand your life back to you, like something gold you let go of—and I can! I'm determined to do it—and nothing's more determined than a cat on a tin roof—is there? Is there, baby?

It is startling to realize that this revision is supposed to make Maggie "more clearly sympathetic to an audience." The original version had ended with Maggie crying "I do love you, Brick, I do!" and Brick canceling her avowal with "Wouldn't it be funny if that was true?" In the revision, this dialogue is replaced by Maggie's lyric determination to mold someone else's life—"with love," certainly, but also with inheritance, "gold," in mind. Indeed, it has been claimed that once the audience knows her background, all her actions become ambiguous. The revision of Cat emphasizes that Maggie will succeed through manipulation and mendacity;

she will not transcend her conditions but rather will feed off them.

Williams was similarly vocal about his admiration of Leona Dawson of *Small Craft Warnings:* "She is the first really whole woman I have ever created and my first wholly triumphant character. She is truly devoted to life, however lonely." Presumably, the modifiers "whole," "triumphant," and "devoted" are meant to be positive. Yet all of them belong to the explosively ambiguous Williams vocabulary. As a character, Leona is a descendant of Hanna Jelkes of *Night of the Iguana.* She is "whole" in the sense of being mentally sane and possessing moral integrity. She insists on "respect" and "responsibility," inveighs at "CORRUPTION," and at one point screams "LET ME SET YOU STRAIGHT ABOUT WHAT'S A LADY!" When Doc, drunk and drugged, leaves to perform an illegal delivery, Leona tries to prevent him out of a well-founded fear for the lives of mother and baby. Events in the play leave no place for Leona, however. Her strong moral code, out of place at Monk's Place, clashes with her drunken soliloquies, penchant for violence, and petty neuroses. She is forced to leave her present lover, job, and circle of acquaintances, all because of Violet, a woman with no integrity or respect. Leona's emphatic physical and moral presence contrasts with Violet's lack of both. The "amorphous" Violet "has a sort of not-quite-with-it appearance," and she speaks of her present life as "a temporary arrangement." To drive home the impression of Violet's not quite being there, her rope-bound suitcase is on stage during the entire action. Yet it is Leona who is forced to leave and Violet who is allowed to stay. Leona packs up her trailer, and her plans for the future are "triumphant" only in a most equivocal way: "What I think I'll do is turn back to a faggot's moll when I haul up to Sausalito or San Francisco." In the same speech, the confidence she projects is stripped bare: "it scares me to be alone in my home on wheels built for two. . . ." Violet's incompletion earns her at least a temporary stay in someone's bedroom; Leona's completion earns her a nighttime escape into the fog on the highway.

Other women—we may call them tragic protagonists—advertise their own ambiguity. Alma of *Summer and Smoke* says of herself,

> Oh, I suppose I am sick, one of those weak and divided people who slip like shadows among you solid strong ones. But sometimes, out of necessity, we shadowy people take on a strength of our own.

Alma and other of Williams's tragic women are in transition, from youth to age, from integrity to degradation, from illusion to disillusion, from sexual certainty to sexual confusion. Violet of *Small Craft Warnings* is described as "Amorphous. . . . Something more like a possibility than a completed creature." Jim, Doc, Chance, Stanley Kowalski, Brick, Val, and other Williams's men are very often set or decided in some important way, with a corresponding loss of scope. The women, by virtue of their weakness and lack of closure, have greater mobility. Weakness and division, the propensity of having "two natures" or more, give the women a surplus of possibility, which makes them more productive, less exhaustible as characters.

In constructing a tragic woman, the literary artist faces a paradoxical task: to create a character with whom the audience finds something in common and yet to compel that audience eventually to take a critical distance from that character. Both sides of the task are essential. If the audience finds nothing recognizable in the character, no ground to share, then her fate is not likely to mean very much. Meaning also will be lost if the audience is not prompted to take a critical stance on the character—if the audience never feels the urge or the necessity to judge.

As soon as we recite these requirements, we can see why it has been so difficult to construct the tragic woman. For reasons I will address later, both the misogynist/gynephobe writer and the advocate will have trouble achieving the ambivalence and ambiguity required for tragedy. In contrast, Williams's women are defeated or destroyed not by male dominance, patriarchy, or misogyny but by their own predilection for destruction—that is, by their own desires. Laura of **Glass Menagerie** is awkward partly because of her self-enforced virginity; Alma of **Summer and Smoke** chooses to take up with the young man at the end of the play; Lady of **Orpheus Descending** chooses both to have Val's baby and to throw herself in front of the bullet that kills her; Catharine of **Suddenly Last Summer** refuses to let go of Sebastian or her version of what happened to him. Male dominance is of little interest; Williams's plays feature some of the most inert male protagonists in drama. Instead, the emphasis falls on something literature needs: an authentic and authoritative depiction of female foolishness, limitations, and error. What worries so many critics about Shakespeare's treatment of Ophelia, Desdemona, and Lady Macbeth is here, too—indeed, much more consistently than in Shakespeare—the insistence that it is necessary, cathartic, and therefore healthy to suspect, hate, or despise certain women, especially those one "likes" best; to measure their failings, even when these failings are attractive; and to watch them destroy themselves by their own free wills, even when that freedom is an illusion.

A case in point is that of Catharine Holly of **Suddenly Last Summer,** whose "destruction or defeat" is predicted from the beginning of the play. The terms of Catharine's oppression are not dictated by men but by the rich, powerful Mrs. Venable, who tries to bribe Dr. Cukrowicz into giving Catharine a prefrontal lobotomy. Audience repulsion toward Mrs. Venable is carefully crafted: in the stage directions ("*She has light orange or pink hair*"); in stage setting, a surreal jungle of viscid flora that is to resemble "*organs of a body, torn out*"; and in her attitude toward her inferiors, including Catharine: "Most people's lives—what are they but trails of debris, each day more debris, more debris, long, long trails of debris." Thus Catharine has been denigrated before she even appears before the audience, and by an extremely unsympathetic character. Yet one of her first actions is to stub the burning end of her cigarette into Sister Felicity's hand—and suddenly Catharine shares in the repulsion.

That burst of senseless violence ignites a series of ambifying changes. The distinct (or indistinct) possibility of Catharine's madness is a standard appeal for audience ambivalence in that madness compels distance as well as pity: "How can you hate anybody and still be sane? You see, I still think I'm sane!" Catharine and her relatives may share in Sebastian's inheritance if she agrees to stop telling her version of Sebastian's death. Her justified fear of Dr. Cukrowicz initially attracts pity, but later she all but cooperates with him, almost inviting the needle. Her account of her first sexual experience and its possible implication in her possible madness similarly arouse both pity and distance. The former arises from the disastrous social and emotional consequences of her encounter at "the Duelling Oaks at the end of Esplanade Street" and the latter from the neurotic compulsiveness revealed in Catharine's character. She is given one of the play's most direct appeals for pity—"It's lonelier than death, if I've gone mad, it's lonelier than death"—and the play's bleakest, most repulsive pronouncement: "Yes, we all use each other and that's what we think of as love, and not being able to use each other is what's—*hate.*"

Although near the end Catharine says that "I think the situation is—clear to me, now . . .," the closing ellipses resonate with the opposite possibility. At the end of the play, the audience knows very little for certain about her or the truth of her account of Sebastian's death. Her truthfulness is questionable from the start because she tells her story under compulsion and under the influence of thiopentone, widely believed in 1958 to be a "truth drug." Dr. Cukrowicz's last line, which closes the play, adds to the ambiguity: "I think we ought at least to consider the possibility that the girl's story could be true." This is a sentence divided against itself in an effort both to recognize and to deny the truth of Catharine's story. He has every reason to claim she has lied, yet he himself has administered the truth drug. Still, if he wants Mrs. Venable's bribe, he will refute the story and give himself grounds for ordering Catharine's lobotomy. His sentence is a timid attempt to buck the horror of Catharine's story and his own impulse to pity her. Yet it does suggest that Catharine may be lying—and she has reasons enough to do so. Her relatives can profit if she lies; she may wish to protect the sanctity of her relation with Sebastian. In the end, the truth of Catharine's story is only a "possibility." That possibility, the conflicting motives of all who surround Catharine, and her own conflicting motives add to the imminence of her destruction. She has sought her own undoing in a classical fashion, just as she had insisted on returning to the ballroom and ruining her reputation, had agreed to accompany Sebastian on his travels and then later had procured for him, and had followed him up the white hill of his destruction.

In short, the audience is not allowed to draw any conclusions about Catharine. In place of what the audience expects—a clear, unambiguous view of her there is instead a range of possibilities. To choose one way of interpreting her would be to deny the equal plausibility of other ways. As Williams knew, the standard bourgeois audience takes its first refuge in standard, bourgeois reactions. To deny such reactions or to mix them inextricably with more complex reactions forces members of the audience to play ambivalently with their repulsion. To use, hesitantly, a cant term, I might say that Williams has deconstructed his audience's response.

It is easy to see why ambiguity was dear to Williams. After all, ambiguity is a form of control. If an audience can consume a character completely, exhaust the possibilities of the character's meaning, the audience has exerted its power over the play, perhaps decisively so. If the playwright has designed the characters for the express purpose of being consumed, the playwright is playing to the audience, being a whore for the public. However, if inexhaustible characters and situations can be created, if there is always something that escapes paraphrase or immediate understanding, the play retains its power to arouse and perplex. (And, we might add, the playwright retains his or her power over the audience— the power of the originator, the privileged source.) Williams brooded constantly over such issues. His most spirited defense of ambiguity appeared in a note to *Cat on a Hot Tin Roof:*

> Some mystery should be left in the revelation of a character in a play, just as a great deal of mystery is always left in the revelation of a character in life, even in one's own character to himself. This does not absolve the playwright of his duty to observe and probe as clearly and deeply as he *legitimately* can: but it should steer him away from "pat" conclusions, facile definitions, which make a play just a play, not a snare for the truth of human experience.

Williams's main plea here is for the superior verisimilitude of ambiguity, but, in his essay **"The Timeless World of a Play,"** he drives toward what might have been his main motivation:

> Whether or not we admit it to ourselves, we are all haunted by a truly awful sense of impermanence. I have always had a particularly keen sense of this at New York cocktail parties, and perhaps that is why I drink the martinis almost as fast as I can snatch them from the tray. This sense is the febrile thing that hangs in the air. Horror of insincerity, of *not meaning,* overhangs these affairs like the cloud of cigarette smoke and the hectic chatter. This horror is the only thing, almost, that is left unsaid at such functions.

It is as if the playwright took refuge in ambiguity—a surplus of meaning, a refusal to eliminate interpretations—out of this horror of not meaning. In a way, ambiguity is a hedge against annihilation.

Williams's achievement is one of the most notoriously uneven in western drama. But, as suggested above, his method of writing women has advantages over both traditional and feminist methods. Writers who fear or hate women cannot allow the object of hatred or fear to be ambiguous; it must be idealized, stylized, trivialized. The written women must be made consumable, located on a pedestal, immobilized. Advocacy poses other obstacles. Women that undergo a programmatic fate cannot be tragic because their tragedy is largely external to the women themselves—theirs is supposed to be every woman's tragedy, being the inevitable effect of the male quest for dominance. The advocate writer thus will be ill-equipped to portray the truly ambiguous female because a clear brief must be carried for the plaintiff. (Advocacy has made it difficult to make one's women culpable.) A well-ground axe cuts too sharp, and the necessary tension between sympathy and judgment is lost. Both the misogynist writer and the advocate will have reasons for eliminating competing ways of reading the written woman. Neither kind of writer will allow the written woman to escape—and neither one wants that woman to escape the reader either. But, as seen above, Williams, perhaps out of his "horror of not meaning," seeks to place his women beyond reduction, to make sure they escape.

So we are driven to other possibilities, most of which carry us beyond standard questions of gender expectation. One early criticism was that Williams's women actually lost "universality" because their stories were too unique, not applicable to all humanity because they were individual case histories. But Williams's treatment of women does not admit of anything else. Of course one's women will refer to other women and other men, just as women do in the world outside the theater. But questions of "gender expectations" verge on the specious and banal because individual women differ so widely in their behaviors. What set of expectations could possibly hold for Alexandra del Lago, Blanche Dubois, Leona, Catharine, and Serafina? In the end, little of much importance. (What set of gender expectations would hold for Timon, Othello, Hamlet, and Macbeth?) Williams's women find themselves in circumstances that demand that they take on as many roles—psychological, sexual, and class—as they need to achieve the failure they desire. Thus, rereading Williams exposes the current hunt for such expectations as a reverse form of prejudice, a project of construction doomed by its own assumptions. Construction of the female must be largely idiographic—that is, the individual character must be built up on her own, out of continuities and disruptions specific to her. It is of women as Williams writes of drama: "By a sort of legerdemain, events are made to remain *events,* rather than being reduced so quickly to being mere *occurrences.*" Women should be represented as events, as special, unrepeatable happenings in time; they are not replicas or occurrences of any other events. Otherwise, the woman we write will be the woman we wish to write, and, worse, the woman that everyone else has always written.

James Reynolds (essay date December 1991)

SOURCE: "The Failure of Technology in *The Glass Menagerie,*" in *Modern Drama,* Vol. 34, No. 4, December, 1991, pp. 522-27.

[*In the following essay, Reynolds discusses the significance of modern technology in* The Glass Menagerie, *which he views as a commentary on progress and the effect of technology on the individual and society.*]

Laura's fragile collection of glass animals gives Tennessee Williams's play its name and a central symbol with both an esthetic and a personal focus. But the play is punctuated with another set of references, an array of ordinary products of twentieth-century technology, that expands its significance beyond the personal even as it illuminates the narrow lives of its protagonists.

Williams introduces *The Glass Menagerie* through a context of social upheaval—war already in Spain, imminent in Europe; labor unrest in American cities. Tom's opening narrative announcing the "social background of the play" sounds like a manifesto of both esthetic and social reform. Yet the only specific allusions to these events during the rest of the play are the incidental headline in Tom's newspaper about Spain, and Tom's narrated contrast between the Europe of Berchtesgaden, Chamberlain, and Guernica, and the St. Louis of the dance halls. Roger B. Stein sees in the allusions to the Depression and impending war a "note of social disaster [that] runs throughout the drama, fixing the lives of individuals against the larger canvas." But the prominent focus of the play is on personal levels of inadequacy—the fragile lives and the conflicts of the Wingfield family—rather

than on a specific set of social, economic, or political issues. So Gilbert Debusscher should not be faulted in criticizing Bulgarian critic Grigor Pavlov for making of the work a "kind of dramatized social pamphlet, a play whose overall aim is to denounce . . . the deplorable effects of capitalism."

Short of so specific a socio-political program, though, Williams does encourage us to place the play in some larger context. Terry Eagleton states that "all major art is 'progressive' in the limited sense that any art sealed from some sense of the historically central, relegates itself to minor status." If the play's milieu beyond the St. Louis tenement is significant—if the social background impinges on the lives of the characters—we must look for a pattern that consolidates those lives in a "historically central" sense. One pattern that looms in the background of the Wingfield family is the way that changing economic and social modes can restrict the potential for happy and successful lives. We are always aware of Amanda's grand past in the Old South, her wealthy suitors and her servants, as we watch her make do in a walkup tenement. And Tom and Laura are pushed into commercial careers that conflict with their temperaments and aspirations.

A specific agent for change that Williams alludes to time and again in the play is technology, one of the strongest forces to redirect society in the twentieth century. While one character, the "realist" Jim O'Connor, sees the future of America as tied to progress in technology, the play consistently reiterates the failure of technology to achieve social or individual values—or, for that matter, even to function at a practical level. Lights go out, the telephone is hung up; cinema and phonograph serve merely as escapes, for men whose lives are governed by impersonal commercial enterprises embodied in warehouses, and for women who are expected to live by serving business through mechanical clerical work, or by marrying successful radio engineers.

> **While many social upheavals have contributed to the Wingfields' personal situation, it is technology which confirms the hard boundary of elements beyond their control.**
> —*James Reynolds*

Williams's recurring use of common domestic technologies—the phonograph, telephone, cinema, radio dynamics, and the electric light—in critical episodes throughout the play would seem to render futile [Karl] Marx's hope for a society in which technology satisfies human needs. While many social upheavals have contributed to the Wingfields' personal situation, it is technology which confirms the hard boundary of elements beyond their control. Their lives have been limited by a number of forces: the shift from old agrarian to modern urban life; the breakup of the traditional family economic structure; the dependence upon impersonal manufacturing and marketing employers. These bear on the Wingfield family's daily lives implicitly, Amanda and Tom victims of their impact but unaware of them as historical forces. More explicitly, the ordinary technologies already taken for granted in American households by 1939 serve as markers that define within the play the limits imposed on the Wingfields.

The entire Wingfield family repeatedly demonstrate their failure under the new dispensation. Amanda comes from an agrarian Delta society, where her beaux are planters and sons of planters—but she marries a telephone man who falls in love with long distance. He escapes to Mexico (then a pre-technological society) to find freedom and adventure. She is left to deal with the twentieth-century American city, described in Williams's stage directions as *"overcrowded urban centers of lower middle-class population"* where this *"enslaved section of American society . . . exist[s] . . . as one interfused mass of automatism."* Amanda is vaguely aware of the central role technology ought to play in the world, but retreats to naive faith when confronted by its complexity. Of Jim, she burbles "Then he has visions of being advanced in the world! . . . Radio engineering? A thing for the future!"

But this future is not hers, either in technology's daily operations or in its place in the cosmos. When the lights flicker and go out, Amanda hopes for a solution within Jim's ken if not hers or Tom's: "Mr. O'Connor, can you tell a burnt-out fuse? I know I can't and Tom is a total loss when it comes to mechanics." Her lack of knowhow arises not from gender (Tom is no more apt than she) but from dislocations of time and class in the history of her world. Whether her dependency in such matters is the result of her having been displaced from the Old South plantation to an urban setting, or of a genteel early life where Delta servants provided for her needs, she is uninformed about the most basic practical level of controlling this domesticated manifestation of Edisonian invention.

More generally, she is awed by scientific advances not on account of their practical value or the complexity of the theories that explain them, but the sense of "mystery" that surrounds them: "Isn't electricity a mysterious thing? Wasn't it Benjamin Franklin who tied a key to a kite? We live in such a mysterious universe, don't we? Some people say that science clears up all the mysteries for us. In my opinion it only creates more!"

Revealing her own basis for understanding life, she lights the candelabrum from the Church of the Heavenly Rest, melted out of shape by a lightning bolt sent by God to punish the wayward parishioners of Blue Mountain. This tall tale by Gypsy Jones down in Mississippi is as valid a hypoth-

esis in Amanda's world as any based on the experiments of Franklin. Her background prevents her entry into the Century of Progress.

Distant from both the practical and theoretical elements of technology, she is made its servant. She earns cash through the telephone, an early telemarketing slave who sells popular women's magazines by summarizing their soft-porn plots to D.A.R. housewives. Her opportunity is limited because her clients can control her by hanging up the phone. The instrument of communication, developed by a man interested in advancing the abilities of the deaf, has been taken over by entrepreneurs who trade on the public's interest in the mildly salacious. The family eats on credit when Amanda's connection is broken at the other end of the line.

Telephone, electric lighting, radio and television. To these technological developments Williams adds the phonograph and the cinema. These two devices serve Williams's dramaturgy as symbols of the world of illusion which Tom and Laura escape to, symbols as strongly relevant to the play's personal level as the eponymous collection of glass animals. But they also reinforce the pervasive pattern of technological elements in the play, the telephone, radio and TV, and electric light replacing its antecedent the candelabrum. In their dual symbolic roles, film and phonograph bind together the levels of the play—the personal level of the specific characters' illusions and escapes, with the broader historical significance of technology's impact on society. (It is ironic that Williams depends on technological innovations for staging the play—the lighting which is essential to maintaining the visual center of attention, and which continues its ethereal effects even as the on-stage prop lights flicker and go out; the magic-lantern projections of images and legends; even a narrative technique akin to that of cinematography.)

Louis Dupré, in his discussion of Marx's views of cultural and social alienation, notes that the German philosopher attributes the "antisocial quality [of the division of labor] to the dominance of technology over human activity." We see Tom escaping from the warehouse with its celotex ceiling and fluorescent lighting by retreating to the movies, a world of adventure analogous to the life he dreams of as a merchant seaman. And whatever else he does on his nightly forays—drinking, cruising for companions—it is the movies which provide his cover. The movies were the nation's escape mechanism throughout the Depression and on into the war years, until displaced by the newer technology managed by the Jims of the electronics world, ever slicker technologies with ever slighter provocation to adventure.

For Laura, the phonograph provides similar escape from the pressures of earning a living in a commercial world, relentless memorizing of charts to serve business interests. Unlike the typewriter, the mechanics of which are so alien to her temper that she throws up in class, the phonograph is soothing. She avoids difficult conversations by retreating to it: the text draws our attention as much to the cranking of its mechanism as to the music it reproduces. Laura turns to it nearly as often as she does to her glass menagerie.

Nancy M. Tischler has aptly characterized the brother's and sister's relation to technology. Tom believes that "many, like himself, are poetic rather than mechanistic" and considers "surrender to the machine a perversion of man's nature," while of Laura, Tischler writes: "Unable to adapt to the modern scene of electro-dynamics, she lives in a world of candlelight and fantasy. The encounter with the machine age is brief and useless." Technology "succeeds" in providing escape from hard realities of life rather than easing the economic, political, and social problems of the time. For Tom, movies are analogous to drinking, and for Laura, the phonograph is the machinery that enables her withdrawal from the world.

Only Jim, the visitor from outside, concerns himself actively with technology. His interest "happens to lie in electro-dynamics. I'm taking a course in radio engineering at night school . . . I believe in the future of television . . . all that remains is for the industry itself to get under way! Full steam—(*His eyes are starry*) *Knowledge*—Zzzzzp! *Money*—Zzzzzzp!—*Power!* That's the cycle democracy is built on!" It is capitalism, rather than "democracy," that Jim sees built on these. He is not only the play's "realist," the foil for the illusory worlds of the Wingfields: he is also the potential entrepreneur of technological capitalism. "Knowledge" means inventing new technologies and capitalizing on their financial success, which in turn gives the system power over those without technology.

But Jim's more specific comments on progress and invention suggest a severely limited conception of what technology is about: "Think of the fortune made by the guy that invented the first piece of chewing gum. . . . Century of Progress. . . . What impressed me most was the Hall of Science. Gives you an idea of what the future will be in America, even more wonderful than the present time is." He is an average representative of his class, hoping to advance in society through mastery of the new tools, without abandoning his predilection for chewing gum and the sports page. Pavlov, comparing Jim to Willie Loman, characterizes him as "another member of the blind American middle class [who] just doesn't realize that men's destinies under capitalism are not shaped by personal virtues and self-perfection but by the operation of the ruthless economic laws of capitalist development."

Jim's limited conception of what constitutes technology aside for the moment, he is Williams's ultimate chip in the series of tokens representing technology in society. It is his view of progress which is set against the inadequacy of the Wingfields, showing in the language of drama the impact of that view. Those without access to the real power of technology are limited as mere users unable to understand or control it. They remain outside the sphere created by larger forces that place technology not as the servant of humanity but as a venture for capital investment, nationalistic rivalries, and costly toys.

When we see the play performed, we are drawn of course to its personal issues: inadequacy, failures of love and other illusions, conflicts of goals and responsibilities and family. With Debusscher I agree that the play is not "about" a specific set of social, economic, and political devastations which happened to coincide in time with the personal events of the play. But great literature strikes home in more than one way, the familiar or local issues and the larger milieu: Shakespeare's kings live both public and private lives. *The Glass Menagerie*, too, is "progressive," in Eagleton's sense. The Wingfield family exists in a specific time and place that defines their origins and position in society. Williams merely alludes to the threats of war and labor unrest; he shows us in more detail a society intent on a future altered by technological development but one in which that development fails to give ordinary people any significant progress.

Kathleen Margaret Lant (essay date 1991)

SOURCE: "A Streetcar Named Misogyny," in *Violence in Drama*, edited by James Redmond, Cambridge University Press, 1991, pp. 225-38.

[*In the following essay, Lant discusses the significance of rape and elements of tragedy in* A Street Car Named Desire. *According to Lant, Blanche is unable to attain the status of a tragic figure because she is objectified and dehumanized as a victim of rape.*]

> Tennessee gave me a lot of clues to Blanche. He was a sly fox . . . Tennessee said, 'Just remember, everybody thinks the last line is: "I've always been dependent on the kindness of strangers." That's not the last line. The last line is: "Gentlemen, the name of this game is five-card stud."'
>
> —Elizabeth Ashley

> Rape is not a crime of irrational, impulsive, uncontrollable lust, but is a deliberate, hostile, violent act of degradation and possession on the part of a would-be conqueror, designed to intimidate and inspire fear.
>
> —Susan Brownmiller

In the moment of rape a woman becomes anonymous. Like all victims of terrorism, there is something awesomely accidental about her fate. She is like the duck flying in formation which the hunter chose to shoot down—she appeared in his gunsight. Absorbed by his violence, her soul and the history of her soul are lost, are irrelevant.

—Susan Griffin

A Streetcar Named Desire is, like an elusive lover, compelling, vexing, confusing, and ultimately heartbreaking because—like the lover one never quite wins—it refuses to conform to our expectations or fulfill our hopes. It leads us on, promises much, but in the end defies our attempt to understand, to approach, to control it, even to find pleasure in it.

In fact, that is just the problem with Williams's most popular play. It doesn't tell a straight story, it won't conform to a narrative or dramatic structure we recognize, it won't—like that reluctant lover again—make up its own mind about what it wants, who it is. Williams's play has proved vexing to audiences, directors, actors, readers, and critics because it seems to hover between two completely antithetical approaches to its own materials. The work shimmers with tension, it glows by the very heat of its own ambivalence.

The widely differing responses the play seems to generate may be the result of what Foster Hirsch calls Williams's 'own ambivalence' toward the antagonists of the drama—Stanley and Blanche. According to Hirsch, the two find themselves locked in a "deadly sex war," in which "Stanley and Blanche are a solid match." Williams's commitment to both characters—his attraction to "Stanley's animal vigor" and his sympathy for Blanche's "sensibility"—enable him to write "with a fine balance." As Hirsch puts it, "Though he is almost always divided in his feelings about his characters, Williams here makes capital dramatic use of his contrary impulses, and *Streetcar* thrives on its imbalances."

But the imbalances and tensions Hirsch points to are more extensive, more fundamental, than Williams's merely personal ambivalences. When Hirsch observes that "Romantic Blanche and naturalistic Stanley are locked in a symbolic conflict: culture fights vulgarity, and is trampled," he restricts his reading of the play to only one of its dramatic conflicts. It is, in fact, as if in *Streetcar* Williams dramatizes two mutually exclusive narratives, reveals two archetypal dramatic situations which dictate completely antithetical roles for Blanche. On the one hand, the play does present Blanche as a tragic figure and Stanley as the cruel agent of her destruction. Stanley brings about Blanche's downfall by unmasking her pretensions and her lies, by physically unclothing and raping her. In this dramatic situation, Blanche is—indeed—flawed, culpable, tragically imperfect, but she is fully and flagrantly human. As a tragic figure she func-

tions as subject, to be judged by her action or inaction, her will to save herself, her sister, her home. She is a being wholly female, driven beyond her ability to cope with the wholly male world. At this level of the play, we may grieve as the environment (Stanley) destroys Blanche, or we may rage as Blanche backs herself into a corner with her lies and evasions. But no matter how we view Blanche—with pity or anger—we see and judge Blanche *as Blanche,* as a fully developed human character.

But the play dramatizes another situation in which Blanche becomes merely a figure, a component of one of our culture's most pernicious, most deeply entrenched narratives—the story of rape. As a figure in this story, as its victim, its object, Blanche ceases to be human. She becomes—instead—a repository for all the mistaken notions our culture harbors about rape. She is acted upon, objectified, and ironically made guilty for her own victimization. No longer fully human, she is simply a metaphor for all that is vile about women. Blanche cannot, then, claim tragic stature or even our sympathy precisely *because* she is a victim of rape. And as she becomes responsible for her own victimization, Stanley is left to glory in his ascendancy. This aspect of *Streetcar* arises from the misogyny which colors the play and our responses to it and which undermines the very moving presentation of Blanche that Williams offers.

Even overtly feminist readers of Williams's work do not fully explore the implications of Blanche's rape by Stanley. Focusing on the imbalances of the work and arguing that Williams's attitude toward the rape are "ambivalent," Sandra Gilbert and Susan Gubar, for example, assert that in *Streetcar* Williams "records, rationalizes, and critiques the use of the penis as weapon that he perceives as essential to Stanley Kowalski's relations with women." Gilbert and Gubar find Blanche a "sympathetic heroine whose imaginative energy surpasses the creativity of any of the other characters in the play; for Williams, Blanche is, nonetheless, guilty of abusing and using 'sensitive men' so that her 'punishment'—her rape—fits her crime."

Gilbert and Gubar conclude, however, that while Stanley does seem to triumph over Blanche, does seem to punish her, what we really observe is Williams's "scathing critique of the heterosexual imperative which is driving Blanche mad." Gilbert and Gubar assert that in the final scene of the play, Stanley's guilt "may be" revealed as "greater than Blanche's" because Stanley is accused by one of his poker buddies of being responsible for driving Blanche to her breakdown.

But Gilbert and Gubar—like Hirsch—read or view *Streetcar* somewhat myopically. They too seem unaware of resonances in the play to which most audiences and readers would respond. While they focus their attention on a feature of the play that has not been fully considered yet—

Stanley's violent assault against Blanche—Gilbert and Gubar ignore the *implications* of Blanche's rape. In effect, Gilbert and Gubar place the play so forcefully in a feminist context that they fail to hear the reverberations the work would inevitably create in a context less than sympathetic to women, the very context in which the play was created and first produced.

There is, in fact, hostility toward women in Williams's work which has been ignored or tacitly applauded by his critics. This misogyny is not peculiar to Williams but exists in his work as a reflection of the society (and its attitudes toward women) to which he belongs. In this light, we can understand why *Streetcar* expresses a great compassion and affection for Blanche (a humane response to the suffering woman, a respectful acknowledgment of her humanity) and at the same time an intense hostility and prejudice toward her (a misogynist response to her very femaleness and to her vulnerability to rape, a reduction of Blanche to the status of metaphor, bearer of meaning rather than creator of meaning).

To understand that this double attitude toward Blanche exists in *Streetcar* is to take a step toward discovering why the play fails to hold together in important ways, why it is difficult to feel pity and terror for Blanche's plight (when we know we should), and why it is difficult not to feel vindicated at Stanley's brutal ascendancy (when we know we should not). Both attitudes, toward women in general and Blanche in particular, exert strong influence on readers and viewers, encouraging at one moment an intense compassion for Blanche and inciting in the next a distaste for and hostility toward her.

Thus, *Streetcar* reveals Williams's desire to render Blanche fully human, though flawed and put upon. Williams displays great compassion for Blanche and insight into the position of women in the twentieth century. He is aware of both their dependence on men and their vulnerability to the passionate excesses of men. In a sociological approach to the play, Robert Emmet Jones shows that the degeneration of Southern aristocratic society left women like Blanche in a peculiarly imperiled position; he characterizes these women as "the passive pawns of social forces and their own emotions." Blanche, raised to be decorative, fragile, and delicate, finds herself out of place, alienated from the real world, as Williams's description of her demonstrates:

> Her appearance is incongruous to this setting [Elysian Fields]. She is daintily dressed in a white suit with a fluffy bodice, necklace and earrings of pearls, white gloves and hat, looking as if she were arriving at a summer tea or cocktail party in the garden district ... Her delicate beauty must avoid strong light. There is something about her uncertain

manner, as well as her white clothes, that suggests a moth. (scene 1)

Blanche's genteel, feminine world has fallen apart, destroyed by the "epic fornications" of all her *male* relative—"improvident grandfathers and father and uncles and brothers" (scene 2). Blanche "stayed and struggled," she tells Stella, trying to justify to her sister the loss of Belle Reve: "I ... tried to hold it together ... but *all* the burden descended on *my* shoulders." Jones characterizes Blanche's situation this way: "The tragedy of these women is the tragedy of the civilization which bore them, nourished them, and cast them out." What Robert Brustein calls "the dark masculine forces of society" are pitted against Blanche's typically feminine qualities. And in the struggle, Blanche is pathetically lost and brutally exploited.

Williams is not unsympathetic to the fact that Blanche must exist in a male world on male terms. He shows us that she is trapped economically and socially. When she says to Mitch of Stanley, "The first time I laid eyes on him I thought to myself, that man is my executioner!" (scene 6), she demonstrates her awareness that it is the brutal male ethic, the "Napoleonic Code," which has reduced her to virtual prostitution. Nor is Blanche unaware of the rules of the games she must play in this men's world or of the power every male has over her. From the beginning of *Streetcar* she is frightened ("Her voice drops and her look is frightened," scene 1), and her reaction to Stanley is consistently edged with terror ("looking apprehensively toward the front door"; "She darts and hides"; "drawing back involuntarily from his stare," scene 1).

Moreover, Williams is aware (as he shows Blanche is) that the games she plays with men—the coyness, the flirting, the submissiveness—are necessary for survival in a masculinist environment. As Andrea Dworkin points out in *Women Hating,* self-denigrating female social behavior is "learned behavior" that allows woman "survival in a sexist world." Blanche must please and placate those in whose hands her destiny rests. When she apologizes to Mitch for not being an interesting companion on their date, he asks why she tries so hard to please: "I was just obeying the law of nature ... The one that says the lady must entertain the gentleman— or no dice" (scene 6). She leads Mitch on in a shameful way, it is true, but she is not unaware of her deception ("She rolls her eyes, knowing he cannot see her face," scene 6). Williams has made perfectly clear why the deception is necessary: Blanche is alone, vulnerable, penniless, and—most pathetic of all—desperately lonely.

Williams expresses his sympathy for women in a male-dominated world in one other way: his development of the violent and frequently physically abusive relationships between Stanley and Stella and between Steve and Eunice. Williams's sympathy is qualified, however, for—in the final analysis—in spite of the fact that he perceives the horror for women in these relationships, Williams comes out in favor of them; they are, he tells us at the end of *Streetcar,* life giving, fueled by desire, whereas Blanche's way represents a surrender to death.

The most revealing character in this respect is, of course, Stella. Critics are fond of accusing Blanche of refusing to face facts and of lying, but it is Stella (and Eunice, too) who constantly refuse to *look* at things, to listen to the truth, or even to tell the truth. Stella lies to Blanche throughout and her final, most devastating lie represents her complete betrayal of her sister: she allows Blanche to think she is going on a trip when, in fact, she is being sent to a state mental hospital. Stella, good wife that she is, concerns herself only with maintaining the status quo. She knows, at a deeply unconscious level, that she must keep Stanley happy to preserve the economic and emotional security she has achieved as his woman.

Every time Blanche confronts Stella with the facts of Stella's situation (that Stella deserted Blanche and Belle Reve, leaving Blanche to endure death and degradation; that Stanley is crude and brutal; in short, that Stella is "married to a madman!" scene 4), Stella turns her eyes away from these facts. She willingly blinds and anesthetizes herself to what her life with Stanley has become: "Blanche! You be still! That's enough!" (scene 1); "I want to go away, I want to go away!" (scene 3); "She crosses in a dazed way from the kitchen" (scene 7); "Her eyes and lips have that almost narcotized tranquility that is in the faces of Eastern idols" (scene 4). In fact, Blanche finds Stella's complete abnegation of self in the face of Stanley's brutality so astonishing that she asks Stella, "Is this a Chinese philosophy you've—cultivated?" (scene 4).

Williams demonstrates, moreover, that Stella is abused physically and degraded sexually in her relationship with her husband: she participates in and enjoys sex with Stanley after he has beaten her. There is, too, something unsavory in Stanley's equation of sex and violence (he feels that his brawling with Stella and Steve's with Eunice are perfectly natural expressions of sexual appetite) and in Stella's description of her sexual attachment to Stanley. She tells Blanche, "I can hardly stand it when he is away for a night . . . When he's away for a week, I nearly go wild! . . . And when he comes back I cry on his lap like a baby" (scene 1). Marion Magid remarks quite incisively of this scene:

> It is hard to know what is more unpleasant in this image: the overt sentimentality it expresses or the latent brutality it masks: a fascination with the image of the helpless creature under the physical domi-

nation of another, accepting his favors with tears of gratitude.

Magid is, however, mistaken when she implies that Williams glorifies this relationship without qualification, for Williams demonstrates throughout the play that Stella is blinded and drugged and that she has shut herself off from the truth in order to maintain her relationship with Stanley.

Williams is not, then, unaware of the self-sacrifice a woman makes to live with a man like Stanley, for, as Stella says finally when she forsakes her sister so that she can stay with her husband, "I couldn't believe her story and go on living with Stanley" (scene 11). The irony of the situation is that Stella *has* believed Blanche's story all along; she—Stella—has called Stanley drunk, pig. She has reviled him but also has shut her eyes to her revulsion for him. This is, Williams shows us, the predicament of the heterosexual woman in the modern world. For Williams, Blanche is clearly the only female—the only fully *human* female—who has the will to set herself against Stanley. Only she refuses to blind herself to Stanley's evils. This pride, her insistence on her right to see and to name, may well be her tragic flaw. She may be quite simply too noble to exist as a female in a world run by a phalanx of Stanley Kowalski's.

In many ways, however, *A Streetcar Named Desire* dehumanizes Blanche, undercuts her tragic situation, and renders her by the end of the play a maddened hysteric with no place in a well-ordered society. In this respect, Williams draws on the most heinous and trivializing myths about women and about rape that inform our culture, and he demonstrates that he bears as many prejudices toward the modern woman as does a brute like Stanley. These prejudices, Williams's misogynous attitudes, irrevocably flaw this play, for a human being viewed as weak, neurotic, hysterical, dishonest, emotional, affected, and fragile (which, the prejudice tells us, women are and which Blanche certainly is) cannot at the same time aspire to the conditions of the tragic figure. Williams wants Blanche to be tragic (in the final scene he describes her so: "She has a tragic radiance in her red satin robe following the sculptural lines of her body," scene 11), but woman—as conceived in a system of patriarchal myth, especially the myth of rape—cannot be tragic. Blanche is, most clearly after Stanley's assault, too weak and too oppressed to convey tragic grandeur. Williams demonstrates this contradiction beautifully if unconsciously; for as soon as he characterizes Blanche as "tragic," his stage directions indicate that she must speak "with faintly hysterical vivacity" (scene 11). A neurotic woman may speak in this manner, but never an Oedipus or a Faustus.

If we look at Blanche's flaw, at the action or attitude which brings disaster and ruin upon her, we can understand the nature of Williams's predicament. In the first place, Blanche is, like most women, viewed primarily as a sexual being. As Naomi Weisstein points out, even psychologists, biologists, and anthropologists "assert that a woman is defined by her ability to attract men," and Dworkin develops her thoughts on misogyny by indicating that woman is perceived as either the wicked (that is, sexually active and knowledgeable) witch or the beautiful, innocent, victimized princess. Thus, woman is categorized by her sexual activity, and sexual activity outside of marriage can be viewed only as degeneration; indeed, in *Streetcar* Blanche's sexual activity is an indication of her moral degeneration. She moves from sixteen-year-old virgin Southern princess (when she married Allan) to aging, sexually promiscuous whore. Sex is—to put it simply—sinful when Blanche engages in it. With respect to Blanche as rape victim, such blatant disclosure of her sexual history is absolutely necessary. It is as though her entire sexual background must be brought before us so that we can see that she, indeed, got what she deserved.

> **Williams wants Blanche to be tragic . . . but woman—as conceived in a system of patriarchal myth, especially the myth of rape—cannot be tragic. . . . Williams demonstrates this contradiction beautifully.**
> —*Kathleen Margaret Lant*

Stanley Kowalski, on the other hand, is applauded for his sexuality, for his crude, sadistic exploitation of Stella, for his love of the "colored lights." He is certainly sexually active and, given his attitudes and manner, probably promiscuous as well (this is hinted at in Eunice's accusation of Steve, for the two couples are often compared). Williams's description of Stanley is almost fulsome in its veneration of Stanley's virility:

> Since earliest manhood the center of his life has been pleasure with women, the giving and taking of it, not with weak indulgence, dependently, but with the power and pride of a richly feathered male bird among hens . . . everything that is his . . . bears his emblem of the gaudy seed-bearer. He sizes women up at a glance, with sexual classifications, crude images flashing into his mind and determining the way he smiles at them. (scene 1)

Gilbert and Gubar point out that the "submissive Stella seems sexually enthralled by [Stanley's] violence." But clearly Williams too is enthralled by Stanley, by his violent sexuality, by his masculine threat. While Gilbert and Gubar feel that Williams, as a homosexual, stands "apart from heterosexual institution" and critiques Stanley's abuses of power, it may be more likely that Williams has created his

own Galatea in Stanley. In fact, Williams seems to fall victim to Stanley's sexuality to such a degree that he revels in it—irresponsibly and appallingly—at Blanche's expense. Elia Kazan's production notes to *Streetcar* are even more extravagant than Williams's own words concerning Stanley; Kazan calls Stanley a "walking penis."

The play is rent, then, by a thematic inconsistency. Are we to elevate Blanche to a tragic figure or simply consign her to ignominy for the same activity which we applaud in Stanley Kowalski? Some critics of the play would have us suppose that Williams means us to perceive Stanley's attitude toward sex, with its alternations of violence and pleading (in scene 3 Stanley first assaults Stella then sobs, cries, and begs until she returns to him) as somehow superior to Blanche's. Others find Stella's sexual submissiveness healthy; Robert Jones, for example, tells us that Williams's heroines

> believe that through physical desire and its consummation they will belong, that they will achieve life and escape Death. They do not realize that desire fails unless it is accepted wholeheartedly, as by Stella Kowalski.

How anyone could find Stella Kowalski's comatose endurance of Stanley healthy or whole-hearted is, indeed, a subject for wonder.

Tennessee Williams claims to share D. H. Lawrence's view of life, "a belief in the purity of sensual life, the purity and the beauty of it." The inconsistencies of *Streetcar,* however, would lead us to believe that sexuality, no matter how debased or desperate (and it is debased and desperate between Stanley and Stella) is pure only for males. Sexuality for females seems to involve a virtuous narcosis (Stella) or a profligate frenzy (Blanche). The attitudes expressed by the characters in *Streetcar* also uphold this sexual double standard, for Stanley is quite willing to protect Steve from Eunice when she suspects him of infidelity. But Stanley feels it his bounden duty to reveal Blanche's sordid past to the impressionable Mitch.

Even more damning than Blanche's promiscuity (a promiscuity we must attribute to her to justify Stanley's raping her), however, is her behavior toward her young, homosexual husband, Allan, years before. Critic after critic berates Blanche for her "betrayal of the defenseless homosexual . . . the supreme sin," for her "rejection of Allan Grey," for her "cruelty" which "consists of unveiling her young husband's true sexual nature, forcing his suicide," for "her failure to be compassionate":

> Blanche's most fundamental regret is not that she happened to marry a homosexual . . . [but that]

when made aware of her husband's homosexuality, she brought on his suicide by her unqualified expression of disgust.

Unhappily, the play completely supports these readings. Williams does consider Blanche guilty for not saving her husband from his homosexuality (although it is certainly not clear how she is to do this) and for not showing more womanly support and compassion for the young man when she did discover the truth. She tells the story to Mitch:

> There was something different about the boy, a nervousness, a softness, and tenderness which wasn't like a man's . . . He came to me for help . . . and all I knew was I'd failed him in some mysterious way and wasn't able to give the help he needed but couldn't speak of! . . . on the dance-floor—unable to stop myself—I'd suddenly said—"I saw! I know! You disgust me . . ." (scene 6).

By the logic of the play, Blanche is guilty for not saving her husband from himself; she is also to be held responsible for his suicide. Both charges can be made only in a world where a woman's primary duty is self-sacrifice to man, where her appropriate role is that of supportive object not assertive subject. Where is there room in this situation for Blanche's own feelings? What about her rejected love, her jealousy, her anger? What about what Blanche wants?

We see, then, that Williams—investing the tragic significance of his play in Blanche—undercuts this very significance by his own sexist attitude toward her. He defines her in sexual terms (since she is no longer a virgin, she must be a degenerating whore), and he condemns her for failing to provide the self-sacrificing, womanly support her husband, Allan, needed. Williams's unacknowledged, unconscious misogyny weakens his development of Blanche as a strong, exciting character, and Blanche is damned no matter how she behaves.

Furthermore, just as Blanche is denounced for her lack of compassion for Allan and for her failure to conceal her disgust with his homosexuality, she is damned again and again for telling the truth. Women have traditionally been punished for saying what others do not want to hear: Cassandra was laughed at, scorned, and finally raped by Ajax; critical and vociferous women were burned as witches; aggressive, vocal Hedda Gabler was considered unnatural. What is especially interesting about these women is that not only are they intimidated into silence, but also the little they are permitted to say is denounced as falsehood. Cassandra is misled, insane, the Trojans believe; the witch is a "liar by nature" according to the church; and Hedda is, finally, discredited as evil. In the same way Blanche Dubois is accused of lying by Stanley Kowalski and by critics of the play. Stanley

begins to enumerate Blanche's lies to Stella: "Lie Number One: All this squeamishness she puts on! You should just know the line she's been feeding Mitch" (scene 7). Most critics agree with Leonard Quirino that Blanche seeks to deny reality, "to combat actuality," and that she has a "preference for soulful illusion."

But, in fact, if we look closely at the play, we see that Blanche tells the truth consistently and that it is for *this* she is punished. Of course, her first great moment of truth-telling is when she challenges Allan with his homosexuality. This does, on the surface, seem a cruel act, but imagine for a moment Stanley rather than Blanche in this position. Suppose now that Stanley finds Stella in a compromising situation with another woman. We would expect and applaud shock, rage, even violence from Stanley. We would not dream of condemning him for a lack of compassion for the errant Stella. And in a way this is exactly what we admire Stanley for doing in **Streetcar**. His wife, it seems, is forming a threateningly close attachment with another woman (though the relationship is by no means lesbian), and surely we are to approve of Stanley's efforts to protect his marriage. Why then should we revile Blanche for a very natural, jealous, furious reaction to a threat to *her* marriage? The answer is, of course, because she is female. It is not her place to protect what is hers; it is for her to support, love, cherish, accept. And, in fact, with respect to Blanche's ultimate role, her role as the victim of Stanley's rape, we *expect* her to lie. If the rape victim isn't terrified into an appropriate and docile silence, she will be—or has been, traditionally—discredited by police, courts, medical professionals, family and judges.

Through the course of the play, Blanche—in much the same way and with similarly disastrous results—continues to tell the truth, but now about Stanley. She reveals him as she revealed Allan; she shows her disgust for him. In scene 1 she confronts Stella with the degradation in which Stella lives: "I'm going to be honestly critical about it." And a little later she upbraids Stella for letting herself go—which Stella has done: "You messy child, you, you've spilt something on the pretty white lace collar!" After Stanley beats Stella, Blanche describes Stanley as an animal, an ape, a brute, a beast. She admonishes her sister not to "hang back with the brutes." Of course, Stanley hears this, and Blanche's fate is sealed. She has wounded male pride once too often; she has seen a little too clearly and spoken far too forcefully. She must be punished.

Williams's difficulty in characterizing Blanche as a complex, fully developed figure becomes obvious here. He suggests on one level that Blanche has erred in being cruel and insensitive to her husband, that her failure was simply a lack of compassion; what he conveys, however, is that Blanche has broken the one inviolable rule of relationships between men and women. Women do not tell the truth, they do not challenge, they do not unmask. This notion is so interwoven into the fabric of our society that it makes its way into Williams's play in spite of the fact that it diminishes the effect of the work, and it renders Blanche's sin more a crime against the sanctity of marriage and a threat to the power of men than a brief lapse in sympathy or love.

This brings us to one of the most interesting problems of *Streetcar:* Blanche's punishment. The fact that Blanche has incurred male wrath by seeing too much and criticizing too freely makes it entirely appropriate that she be punished by the one sure means of male domination and power over women: rape. Susan Brownmiller points out that rape is "not only a male prerogative but a man's basic weapon of force against women, the principal agent of his will and her fear." And herein lies Williams's inconsistency in having Stanley rape Blanche. The rape is to be a punishment, a retribution brought on by Blanche's great crime (beginning with her cruelty to Allan and culminating in her unmasking of Stanley). But to be a rape victim in a sexist society is to be deserving of the punishment simply because of who one is (a woman) rather than because of what one has done. It is, too, to be somehow sullied by the crime of which one is a victim. It is to be lowly and despicable; it is to be *guilty for* the act rather than *punished by* the act. Thus, Blanche's only crimes are that she is female and therefore subject to masculine will and that she is a bad enough woman (in sexual terms) to be raped. Her real crimes (if they are, indeed, crimes) are forgotten, completely obscured by the fact that we have an entire set of myths to explain rape and that these myths vigorously affirm the rape victim's guilt—which has nothing to do with how Blanche may have treated Allan in the past or with how she treats Stanley now.

These false notions about rape include the idea that all women want to be raped, that a woman—in effect—brings the rape on herself, that it is not logically possible to rape a woman who is not a virgin, and that rape is a crime of sexual desire, brought on by the overwhelming attraction of the victim or by the unbearable sexual deprivation of the rapist. Williams goes to great lengths to obscure the fact that rape is a political crime of "uncontrolled hostility" toward women, "a brutal bullying of a smaller, weaker person," by ensuring that the rape in *Streetcar* conforms to all the false stereotypes we hold about the act. Blanche is made to flirt with and entice Stanley: Williams shows that Blanche has an extremely unsavory sexual history, so the act of raping her seems insignificant, indeed; and he indicates that Stanley finds Blanche attractive ("come to think of it—maybe you wouldn't be bad to interfere with," scene 10), making this seem a crime of passion and desire rather than one of violence, cruelty, and revenge—which every rape is. We tend, therefore, to forget why Stanley really attacks Blanche—not because she is attractive or because she is promiscuous but because she threatens masculine power with her honesty.

The issue becomes impenetrably muddled. Because Williams harbors false notions about rape, its causes and its intent, Blanche comes off simply as a loud-mouthed, flirtatious whore who really asked for what she got. In other words, she deserves to be raped not for some crime she committed against her husband or against Stanley, but because she has committed a crime against male privilege: she has been as sexually free as Stanley. But Williams attempts also to create a tragic figure in Blanche; she is a human being who has set in motion forces which have brought about her own ruin. To represent her ruin as a sexual assault, however, certainly diminishes the effect of it, for if only whores are raped, where is the tragedy? What can possibly be tragic about the rape of a promiscuous woman to an audience or a playwright in a misogynist society? Anyone watching the play knows enough about the myths of which our world is made to realize that Blanche has brought this rape on by her own sexual promiscuity and nothing else. She is, therefore, certainly not possessed of tragic stature.

On a deeper level, however, the play acknowledges the true intent and character of the act of rape, that it is a crime of domination and power. It is clear, at this level too, that Stanley is punishing Blanche for more than her profligacy; he is punishing her for all the insults she ever hurled at any male, beginning with Allan. This is what Stanley means when he tells Blanche, "We've had this date with each other from the beginning!" (scene 10). But given the false notions the audience harbors about rape—false notions the play itself promotes—the fact that Blanche is raped necessarily diminishes her in our eyes. She becomes no longer a tragic figure but merely a sordid victim of a nasty crime, no longer fully human but merely a metaphor for all the feminine evils the real men of the world must face and deal with.

According to Normand Berlin, *A Streetcar Named Desire* is a tragedy, but one whose effect is determined by the attitudes we hold toward Stanley and Blanche. We must, he says, keep the scales balanced between the two antagonists in order to understand the play fully:

> Desire is the common ground on which Stanley and Blanche meet . . . The needs of both are clearly presented by Williams and should be understood by the audience which must neither wholly condemn Blanche for her whorishness nor Stanley for his brutishness.

We cannot keep these scales balanced, however, for Blanche has been violated in such a way that she loses her tragic stature and even her status as an appropriate antagonist for Stanley. Susan Griffin observes that at the moment of rape "a woman becomes anonymous . . . Absorbed by . . . violence, her soul and the history of her soul are lost, are irrelevant." Indeed, Blanche is anonymous at the end of *Streetcar;* like Stella, she has been rendered comatose, catatonic by the sexuality and brutishness of the masculine world of power. Stanley triumphs, and his rape of Blanche conforms to Brownmiller's characterization of the violation of woman by man:

> rape is not a crime of irrational, impulsive, uncontrollable lust, but is a deliberate, hostile, violent act of degradation and possession on the part of a would-be conqueror, designed to intimidate and inspire fear.

Stanley is more than a would-be conqueror in Williams's play, for he has protected his domain and destroyed the enemy. He has taken all. As Tennessee Williams himself has said, the play doesn't end with Blanche, it ends with Stanley:

> Just remember, everybody thinks the last line is: "I've always been dependent on the kindness of strangers." That's not the last line. The last line is: "Gentlemen, the name of this game is five-card stud."

And in this masculine world—as in this masculine game—Stanley holds *all* the cards.

Eric P. Levy (essay date December 1993)

SOURCE: "'Through Soundproof Glass': The Prison of Self-Consciousness in *The Glass Menagerie,* in *Modern Drama,* Vol. 36, No. 4, December, 1993, pp. 529-37.

[*In the following essay, Levy explores the significance of mirrors as a symbol for superficial appearances and fragile self-image in* The Glass Menagerie.]

In his production notes introducing *The Glass Menagerie,* Tennessee Williams refers to nostalgia as "the first condition of the play." This appraisal at first seems accurate, for the drama disposes the past in a series of receding planes by which the very notion of nostalgia is progressively deepened. From the perspective of Tom, the narrator and a chief character, the past when he started "to boil inside" with the urge to leave home becomes a haunting memory from which his present struggles vainly to flee. But the confining power of that past derives from his mother's nostalgic attachment to her own more distant past and the desperate need to exploit motherhood as a means of reviving *"the legend of her youth."*

Yet once we analyse how Amanda manipulates maternity, a factor in the play more fundamental than nostalgia will begin to emerge. This principle is self-consciousness—a term which, as we shall see, the text supplies and in its own way defines. Each character is hampered in relating to others by the need to inhabit a private world where the fundamental concern is with self-image. Some characters (Amanda and Jim) use others as mirrors to reflect the self-image with which they themselves wish to identify. Other characters (Laura and Tom) fear that through relation to others they will be reduced to mere reflections, trapped in the mirror of the other's judgment. In virtue of this preoccupation with self-image and the psychological mirrors sustaining it, the world of the play is aptly named after glass. Indeed, Laura's remark ironically becomes the motto of the play: "My glass collection takes up a good deal of time. Glass is something you have to take good care of."

Let us begin by examining Amanda's influence on Laura. Unwittingly, Amanda exploits her maternal concern about Laura's lack of marital prospects as a means of identifying with her own past when she herself was visited one Sunday afternoon in Blue Mountain by "seventeen!—gentlemencallers." In effect, she turns her daughter into a mirror in which her own flattering self-image is reflected, but to do so she must first turn herself or, more precisely, her parental judgment, into a mirror reflecting Laura's limitations. The play itself suggests this seminal image. After helping Laura dress and groom herself, Amanda instructs her to stand in front of a real mirror: "Now look at yourself, young lady. This is the prettiest you will ever be! . . . I've got to fix myself now! You're going to be surprised by your mother's appearance!" Then *"Laura moves slowly to the long mirror and stares solemnly at herself."*

Look closely at what is happening here. Amanda slights Laura's appearance even as she praises it. Laura is told that she has reached her peak at this moment: she will never again be as attractive. But Laura's limitation only enhances Amanda's excitement about her own "spectacular appearance!" The literal mirror in which Laura beholds her own image ultimately symbolizes her mother's judgment of her. Yet the fundamental purpose of that judgment is to provide, by contrast, a flattering self-image for Amanda. Though on this occasion Amanda's judgment seems benign, it participates in a subtle pattern of comparison by which Laura is made to identify with the sense of her own "Inferiority" to her mother. Indeed, at one point she alludes explicitly to this fact: "I'm just not popular like you were in Blue Mountain." Laura is, in her own words, "crippled." But her primary handicap concerns, not the limp caused by a slight inequality in the length of her legs, but the negative self-consciousness instilled by her mother. In fact Jim, the gentleman caller, approaches this very diagnosis. When Laura recalls how in high school she "had to go clumping all the way up the aisle with everyone watching," Jim advises: "You shouldn't have been self-conscious."

The effect of Laura's self-consciousness is to make her intensely protective of her self-image, and to shield it from exposure to anyone outside the home. Whenever she is forced to interact or perform in public, she becomes suddenly ill with nausea and must withdraw. The most extreme example of this syndrome is her brief attendance at Rubicam's Business College where, according to the typing instructor, Laura "broke down completely—was sick at the stomach and almost had to be carried into the wash room." She has a similar reaction after the arrival of Jim at the Wingfield home, and reclines alone on her couch while the others dine in another room. As a result of this withdrawal reflex, Laura has no life outside preoccupation with her own vulnerability.

But paradoxically, the very intensity of this preoccupation changes the meaning of the vulnerability it concerns. By focusing on the fear of humiliating exposure, Laura eventually identifies, not with the shame evoked by her self-image, but with the desperate need to avoid suffering it. In this context, the playwright's commentary on Laura gains greater profundity: "Laura's separation increases till she is like a piece of her own glass collection, too exquisitely fragile to move from the shelf." At bottom, the purpose of Laura's withdrawal *is* to heighten her "fragility"; for, through belief in the damaging effect of exposure, she exchanges a negative self-image for one more flattering. Sensitivity to shame allows Laura to identify with her worthiness, not of ridicule, but of delicate care and compassion. Yet instead of leading to "confidence," this escape from shame depends on increasing her insecurity. She is safe from exposure to shame only if she identifies with her inability to endure it. But lack of confidence is Laura's secret wish, for it protects from confronting anything more threatening in life than her own familiar anxiety. Indeed, whenever she is encouraged to go beyond this anxiety, her reflex is to pick up one of her "little glass ornaments." She does this when Amanda reminds her of the need for eventual marriage and during the conversation with Jim.

The significance of these ornaments can be clarified by closer consideration of the glass from which they are made. In the play, glass is associated not just with the "lovely fragility" already noted, but also with the mirror prominently visible in the Wingfield apartment. Earlier we encountered one example where Amanda instructs Laura to observe her reflection in the mirror, but we shall examine several other allusions to this literal mirror; it becomes a vital symbol of the act of self-consciousness by which a character apprehends his or her self-image. Yet, in Laura's case, this analogy between the literal mirror and the act of self-consciousness extends further. Just as with a real mirror the

reflection perceived is an image in glass, so in the play, as we have seen, Laura's own self-image is represented by ornaments of glass. Hence, in virtue of the glass which is their substance, these ornaments suggest that the fragility with which she identifies is no more than a self-image, dependent on the mirror of self-consciousness reflecting it.

But whereas Laura's recourse is to emphasize the mirror of negative self-consciousness, Tom's impulse is to shatter it, in order thereby to achieve his freedom. Like Laura, he too is exposed to the mirror of parental judgment held up by his mother, Amanda. But, unlike his sister, Tom refuses to identify with the negative self-image it reflects. His consuming wish is to leave home and explore his manhood: "I'm tired of the *movies* and I am *about to move!*" But Amanda insists that his desire to leave home is simply a manifestation of selfishness, and further proof that he will end up as faithless and irresponsible as his father, an example of the kind of man he should never become. In fact, a photograph of that father, hanging "*on the wall of the living room,*" functions as a kind of mirror displaying the very self-image with which Tom is identified: "More and more you remind me of your father! He was out all hours without explanation!—Then *left! Goodbye!* And me with the bag to hold." Yet, with increasing passion, Tom protests his right to be a person and not merely a reflection defined by his mother's way of seeing him. Ultimately, he refuses to let the image she holds up to him restrain him; for if he identifies with it, he will never be free.

The process of this repudiation is repeatedly linked with the breakage of glass, symbol of the reflected self-image with which a character is made to identify. In the first great confrontation with his mother, Tom disowns the self-image with which she tries to control him: "For sixty-five dollars a month I give up all that I dream of doing and being *ever!* And you say self—*self's* all I ever think of. Why, listen, if self is what I thought of, Mother, I'd be where he is— GONE!" Then, in an enraged effort to don his overcoat and leave the house, he becomes entangled in "*the bulky garment*" and heaves it "*across the room.*" The result is devastating: "*It strikes against the shelf of Laura's glass collection, and there is a tinkle of shattering glass. Laura cries out as if wounded.*" On the surface, Tom's fury here seems purely destructive, damaging the possession which his sister most prizes. But, more profoundly, Tom's action represents the only way of claiming his own identity. If he allows his mother to restrain him by guilt and convince him that to act on his own is to become like his father, he will be no more self-reliant than Laura, hampered in life by a negative self-image, symbolized in Laura's case by the glass menagerie. For Laura, that self-image concerns fragility; for Tom, guilt. But each image is equally restricting.

Tom's second confrontation with his mother is even more

explosive. Once again, she imposes a negative image upon him: "Go to the movies, go! Don't think about us, a mother deserted, an unmarried sister who's crippled and has no job! Don't let anything interfere with your selfish pleasure!" In rage, *"Tom smashes his glass on the floor"* and then *"plunges out on the fire escape, slamming the door."* The act of breaking glass (in this instance, a drinking vessel) obviously recalls the earlier shattering of an item in Laura's glass menagerie. Again, in the struggle to affirm and fulfil his own identity, Tom is forced to repudiate the negative image reflected in the mirror of parental judgment. What he says in the first encounter also explains his reaction in the second: "It seems unimportant to you, what I'm *doing*—what I *want* to do."

But even after leaving the house to explore life on his own, Tom is still haunted by the mirror of parental judgment. His *"closing speech,"* immediately after the second glass smashing episode, is extremely revealing in this regard. In describing his itinerant life after breaking away from home, Tom admits that, at bottom, his freedom is no more than a flight in which he feels "pursued by something" that turns out to be the image of his sister. He recounts an obsession that overwhelms him each time he arrives in a new town: "Perhaps I am walking along a street at night, in some strange city, before I have found companions. I pass the lighted window of a shop where perfume is sold. The window is filled with pieces of colored glass, tiny transparent bottles in delicate colors, like bits of a shattered rainbow. Then all at once my sister touches my shoulder. I turn around and look in to her eyes."

This is one of the most poignant passages in the play, but understanding its full meaning requires some analysis. On the surface, Tom seems obsessed with guilt for having abandoned the sister who depended on him. But his preoccupation with Laura involves much more than the sense of duty denied. Or, more precisely, his remorse is motivated by a concern deeper than shirked obligation. The context confirms this. Her apparition usually appears after Tom sees some "tiny transparent bottles" through a shop window. The delicate ornaments, of course, remind him of Laura's glass menagerie. Ironically, however, in his futile flight from the memory of Laura, he is trying to escape an insecurity analogous to one symbolized by that glass menagerie. Whereas Laura reacts to insecurity by withdrawing into "a world of her own—a world of little glass ornaments," Tom responds by plunging compulsively into a world of strangers: "I cross the street, I run into the movies or a bar, I buy a drink, I speak to the nearest stranger—anything that can blow your candles out!" In fact, in his restless flight after leaving home, when cities whirl past him "like dead leaves," Tom travels perpetually through a world of strangers, never staying still long enough to find a new place he can call home.

The nature of this insecurity becomes clearer when we consider the scene with which its description is synchronized. As the author notes, *"Tom's closing speech is timed with what is happening inside the house. We see, as though through soundproof glass, that Amanda appears to be making a comforting speech to Laura, who is huddled upon the sofa."* The emphasis on *"soundproof glass"* is crucial here. To live in that home *is* to live behind a pane of imaginary glass: namely, the mirror of parental judgment created by Amanda in order to flatter her own self-image. To live inside that home is to be defined by the mirror it contains, as we have seen extensively with regard to Laura and Tom. Now that he is outside the home, Tom can see through that soundproof glass, as if it were a one-way mirror, transparent to the viewer or audience on one side, but a reflecting surface to those trapped on the other side of it.

The great pathos of the play is that Tom remains just as much a prisoner of the mirror as Laura. His attempt to flee merely confirms its influence. The ultimate cause of his restless movement is the fear of finding himself trapped on the wrong side of the mirror again—in other words, enclosed in an intimacy founded on love. For to love, as Tom has learned through the relation with his mother, is to be exposed to a mirror of negative judgment on which one becomes dependent for the sense of one's own worth. In that position. Tom is as vulnerable to insecurity as Laura. Hence, though his need for companionship is great, his need for loneliness is greater; for only loneliness can protect him from the vulnerability to love (or, more precisely, to the mirror of judgment which love creates) epitomized by his sister. But paradoxically, by shielding him from the same vulnerability to love suffered by Laura, loneliness increases his identification with her; for in that state he inhabits a world of his own, just as she does through preoccupation with the glass menagerie. The instability of this condition is vividly represented by Tom's obsession with Laura. Her image always appears in his moments of greatest loneliness—when he has just entered a new town at night but has not yet "found companions." He recoils from her and compulsively seeks strangers, but soon after meeting them he is once again on his lonely way. Thus the cycle of his life continues.

An even more profound pessimism about the influence of the mirror emerges when we examine Jim, the gentleman caller, who, according to Tom, "is the most realistic character in the play, being an emissary from a world of reality that we were somehow set apart from." It soon becomes apparent, however, that Jim is as much defined by mirrors and the self-consciousness which they symbolize as anyone else in the drama. Jim does show a genuine interest in Laura and tries to help her: "You don't have the proper amount of faith in yourself." Nevertheless, his concern is tainted with self-interest. Ultimately, like Amanda, he exploits Laura as a mirror in which to reflect a flattering image of himself.

The play is explicit in this regard. Note how, when encouraging Laura to conquer her "Inferiority complex," Jim "*unconsciously glances at himself in the mirror*" as he tells her that "Everybody excels in some one thing. Some in many!" A moment later, he "*adjusts his tie at the mirror.*" In effect, he uses her need for self-confidence as an opportunity to admire his own attributes: "I guess you think I think a lot of myself!" His parting gesture sums up the meaning of his interest in Laura: "*He stops at the oval mirror to put on his hat. He carefully shapes the brim and the crown to give a discreetly dashing effect.*" While Jim's reunion with Laura has aroused sincere affection for her, his deepest love is reserved for his own self-image. Consistently, he uses her sense of inadequacy as a means of magnifying his own positive attributes: "Look how big my shadow is when I stretch!" At bottom, what appears to be compassion—and what to Jim feels like honest compassion—is nothing more than narcissism, where awareness of Laura's emotional need leaves Jim "*enrapt in his own comfortable being.*" This selfishness is most apparent when he kisses her. Jim yields to his attraction to Laura, but in doing so reveals its deepest motive. As soon as he kisses her he must reject her, because he already has a girlfriend, Betty. His sudden reversal makes Laura suffer an "*almost infinite desolation,*" but reinforces Jim's own complacent satisfaction with himself: "Being in love has made a new man of me!" Once again, he turns Laura's helplessness into a mirror in which his own self-assurance is reflected.

Laura's situation is made more devastating by the positive effect he initially has on her. When the unicorn's horn breaks during her brief dance with Jim, Laura is not upset: "It's no tragedy, Freckles. Glass breaks so easily." In fact, she seems on the brink of transcending the image of herself which the unicorn represents: "The horn was removed to make him feel less—freakish!" Before he leaves, Laura gives Jim the unicorn as a "souvenir," then "*rises unsteadily and crouches beside the Victrola to wind it up.*" These gestures are supremely significant. Giving away the unicorn suggests that the release from negative self-consciousness with which she has just identified the ornament in its newly damaged state has already ended. This suggestion is corroborated by the movement which follows her surrender of the unicorn: winding up the gramophone. Earlier, in a passage we have already quoted, Tom connected Laura's preoccupation with the Victrola with her withdrawal from reality: "She lives in a world of her own—a world of little glass ornaments, Mother. [. . .] She plays old phonograph records and—that's about all."

Laura's offering of the unicorn has further implications. For, through preoccupation with his own self-image, Jim—like Laura—inhabits a world of his own which no true intimacy can violate. The only difference is that, while Laura identifies as the victim of self-consciousness, Jim identifies as its

beneficiary. The fundamental function of his love for another is to enhance his love for himself.

Mark Royden Winchell (essay date 1993)

SOURCE: "The Myth Is the Message, or Why *Streetcar* Keeps Running," in *Confronting Tennessee Williams's A Streetcar Named Desire: Essays in Critical Pluralism,* edited by Philip C. Kolin, Greenwood Press, 1993, pp. 133-45.

[*In the following essay, Winchell considers the enduring popular and critical success of* A Streetcar Named Desire *in light of the play's complex male-female dynamic that defies classification as either misogynistic melodrama or tragedy.*]

Certain works of literature seem to enter the popular imagination from the moment they are published. Their appeal is not confined to language or genre; they embody stories and characters that can be transferred from one art form to another without loss of power. For this reason, such stories and characters are often known to many more people than have read the original work. No doubt, millions with little idea who George Orwell was "know" that "1984" and "Big Brother" are ominous concepts. The term *Uncle Tom* is widely used by persons who would have difficulty identifying Harriet Beecher Stowe. Dr. Jekyll and Mr. Hyde, Tarzan, Frankenstein, and Dracula haunt a culture that has largely forgotten the names of Robert Louis Stevenson, Edgar Rice Burroughs, Mary Shelley, and Bram Stoker. Recognizing that this is so is far easier than explaining why it is so.

With few exceptions, sophisticated literary critics dismiss works that have touched a mass audience. Particularly in our own century, the gap between elite and popular culture is an article of faith. As a result, the literary clerisy spends its time analyzing or deconstructing texts while the majority culture continues to enjoy songs and stories. (As Dwight Eisenhower is reputed to have said: "I may not know what's art, but I know what I like.") Of course, in times past, Shakespeare appealed to both the aristocracy and the groundlings; the serialized fiction of Dickens and Thackeray was read as avidly as soap operas are now watched; and Longfellow, prior to reading before Queen Victoria, signed autographs in the servants' quarters.

Among twentieth-century American poets, only Robert Frost bridged the gap between serious and popular literature. In the realm of fiction, the trick was turned (but only in selected novels) by Ernest Hemingway, John Steinbeck, Scott Fitzgerald, and Robert Penn Warren. In drama, where performance enables a writer to reach an audience beyond the confines of the printed page, the record is no better. Eugene O'Neill never seized the popular imagination, and Edward Albee came close only in *Who's Afraid of Virginia Woolf?* For Arthur Miller, *Death of a Salesman* enjoyed a popular and critical success neither precedented nor duplicated in his career.

The one American playwright who is a conspicuous exception to the dichotomy between "high" and "low" culture is Tennessee Williams.
—*Mark Royden Winchell*

The one American playwright who is a conspicuous exception to the dichotomy between "high" and "low" culture is Tennessee Williams. Williams's South, with its sexual ambivalence, self-delusion, and irrational violence, has become part of our popular mythos, the ambience of countless B-movies and television melodramas. With only slight exaggeration, Marion Magid writes:

> A European whose knowledge of America was gained entirely from the collected works of Tennessee Williams might garner a composite image of the U.S.: it is a tropical country whose vegetation is largely man-eating; it has an excessive annual rainfall and subsequent storms which coincide with its mating periods; it has not yet been converted to Christianity, but continues to observe the myth of the annual death and resurrection of the sun-god, for which purpose it keeps on hand a constant supply of young men to sacrifice.... [T]he sexual embrace ... is as often as not followed by the direst consequences: cannibalism, castration, burning alive, madness, surgery in various forms ranging from lobotomy to hysterectomy, depending on the nature of the offending organ.

Beyond this, particular Williams plays, such as *The Glass Menagerie* and *Cat on a Hot Tin Roof,* have entered American popular culture to a degree unmatched by the work of any other critically acclaimed dramatist. Even these achievements, however, pale to insignificance in comparison to what Williams wrought in *A Streetcar Named Desire.* Surely, no play of the American theatre, perhaps no play in English since the time of Shakespeare, has won such praise from *both* the critics and the populace. When they agree on so little in the realm of literature, one wonders why the critics and the people are of a single mind on this one play.

In seeking to answer this question, I have found myself re-peatedly borrowing concepts from the criticism of Leslie Fiedler. Although Fiedler's massive bibliography includes commentary on most major works of American literature (as well as many minor ones), I am not aware of his having written on *A Streetcar Named Desire.* Nevertheless, *Streetcar* seems particularly suited for a Fiedlerian treatment (if such a pompous phrase does not violate the populist spirit of Fiedler's muse). At least since his seminal essay, "Cross the Border—Close the Gap," Fiedler has tried to identify the universal sources of literary response by treating popular culture with the same reverence critics automatically extend to canonical texts. Moreover, *Streetcar* raises many of the same issues that Fiedler has long found at the heart of our storytelling tradition.

A Fiedlerian approach to *Streetcar* would identify those elements in the play that transcend the distinction between elite and popular culture. What is needed is an understanding of the play's mythopoeic power. This is something quite different from a cataloging of allusions to ancient legends, which may or may not be known to a mass audience. *Streetcar* is a play that raises disturbing questions about hearth and home, sex roles, family loyalty, and the power of eros. Because this is done within the context of a drama, the aesthetic distance between audience and artifact is much less than it would be with a sociological essay or even a novel. We respond to issues of universal concern at a visceral level long before that response is articulated, or "rationalized," in the form of criticism. I suspect that *Streetcar* remains such a riveting play in the country of its origin precisely because its particular treatment of universal themes—myth as opposed to mere mythology—is deeply rooted in American culture and literature.

Fiedler has argued for more than forty years that we can pretty well divide the canon of American literature between works that view home as Heaven and those that see it as Hell. The texts celebrated in *Love and Death in the American Novel* (1960) (and, before that, in D. H. Lawrence's *Studies in Classic American Literature* [1923]) belong to the latter category. Beginning with Washington Irving's Rip Van Winkle, "The uniquely American hero/anti-hero ... rescues no maiden, like Perseus, kills no dragon, like Saint George, discovers no treasure like Beowulf or Siegfried; he does not even manage at long last to get back to his wife, like Odysseus. He is, in fact, an anti-Odysseus who finds his identity by *running away from home*" (Fiedler, *What Was Literature?*). The reason for this is quite simple. At home, he is subject to a loathsome form of tyranny known as "petticoat government." The tyrant may be a henpecking wife, such as Rip's Dame Van Winkle, or a nitpicking guardian, such as Huck Finn's Miss Watson (we have endless variations of these two in TV situation comedies and the funny pages of the daily newspaper). In either case, the only escape is into the wilderness and the society of fellow males.

Against this basically misogynistic canon is a countertradition of domestic literature. From the popular women novelists whom Hawthorne dismissed as that "damned tribe of scribbling females" to the writers of today's soap operas, laureates of the domestic tradition posit a stable home life, complete with heterosexual bonding and close family ties, as the greatest human good. Even when it is thwarted by the conflicts necessary to literature and endemic to life, it is still the ideal. As antithetical as they might seem, the domestic paradigm and the misogynist tradition both agree that the woman rules the home. The only disagreement is whether she is a benevolent despot or a hideous shrew. The patriarchal insistence that the man is king of his castle is generally understood as mere male bluster.

To say the least, the Stanley Kowalski household does not conform to the matriarchal conventions of our literature. Stanley is unquestionably the king of his castle. As a traveling salesman, he enjoys the freedom of the road. As captain of his bowling team, he is at no loss for male camaraderie. These experiences, however, are not an evasion of domestic unhappiness. Stanley's loving and *obedient* wife is always waiting for him, eager to gratify and be gratified. Even in the home, she accommodates him and his friends. Rip Van Winkle may have to meet his buddies at Nicholas Vedder's tavern, Dagwood Bumstead may have to hold his card games in the garage, but Stanley plays poker in the middle of his apartment. Only in the person of Eunice, who threatens to pour boiling water through the floorboards of the upstairs apartment, do we see even a vestige of the henpecking wife. As politically incorrect as it may be, the Kowalski household embodies a patriarchal vision of home as Heaven. There is not enough potential conflict here for either tragedy or farce. Not until Blanche enters the scene.

From the moment of her first entrance, Blanche brings with her a vision of home that varies sharply from what she encounters in Elysian Fields. Even before she utters a word, her expression of "*shocked disbelief*" speaks volumes. In first identifying Stella by her maiden name, Blanche instinctively places her sister back in her old home rather than in the one where she is "Mrs. Stanley Kowalski." Later in the scene, Blanche verbalizes her displeasure with Stella's current living arrangements, suggesting that she has somehow betrayed the memory of Belle Reve. Only a little scrutiny is required to show how problematic Blanche's air of superiority actually is.

To begin with, she has come to Elysian Fields not from Belle Reve but from Tarantula Arms. It is doubtful that accommodations there were any more aristocratic than in the French Quarter. Moreover, reliable information about Belle Reve itself is quite sparse. Clearly, the family home in Laurel has been lost on a mortgage. But how grand was it? With the exception of Stella, the closest that anyone in Elysian

Fields has come to the place is a photograph of a mansion with columns. That photograph has been enough to impress Eunice and Stanley; however, Stella, who has actually lived in Belle Reve, seems unconcerned about its loss. Blanche, who at the very least is a pathological liar, remembers the place as a plantation. But there are no plantations in Laurel, Mississippi, which is in the heart of the Piney Woods. If there were even servants at Belle Reve, we hear nothing of them. In fact, Stella says that when *she* waits on Blanche, it seems more like home. There are enough hints in the play to suggest that the grandeur of Belle Reve is as suspect as the value of Blanche's rhinestone tiara and summer furs. (The supposedly hardheaded Stanley is taken in by all three.)

Even if we see Belle Reve as a latter-day Tara, it is lost in a way that Tara never was. Margaret Mitchell's image of the Old South as a matriarchal Eden had captured the public imagination by the time that **Streetcar** premiered on Broadway in 1947. In 1951, moviegoers would have been reminded of this image by the mere fact that Vivien Leigh, who had played Scarlett O'Hara on the screen, was cast as Blanche in the film version of Williams's play. In Mitchell's antebellum South, women ruled the home while men fought duels and argued over secession. These same men mortgaged the matriarchal paradise by leading the South into a war it could not win. (The region's only assets, according to Rhett Butler, were "cotton, slaves, and arrogance.") After the war, Scarlett adapted to changing circumstances to do whatever was necessary to regain Tara and hold off the carpetbaggers. This Darwinian feat, however, was beyond the capabilities of the leading men of the old order (anachronistic cavaliers such as Ashley Wilkes), who were reduced to riding in white sheets at night to prove their manhood. The only exception was the social outcast Rhett Butler.

Belle Reve is not destroyed by war or Reconstruction, but like Margaret Mitchell's South, it is victimized by a failed patriarchy. Over a period of centuries, to hear Blanche tell it, Belle Reve was lost as her "improvident grandfathers and father and uncles and brothers exchanged the land for their epic fornications." (In fact, only a female cousin left enough insurance money to provide for her own burial.) Unlike Scarlett, the women of Belle Reve are incapable of filling the void left by these inadequate men. Stella escapes from this doomed home, and, except for Blanche, all the other women die. Blanche herself is denied a normal family life when she discovers her husband's homosexuality, and the guilt she experiences from driving him to suicide leads to a series of debaucheries that renders her incapable of even pursuing the modest career of a high school English teacher.

Although Blanche is less than an admirable character, she strikes some audiences as at least an object of pity when she falls into Stanley's brutish clutches. And yet, if we look at the situation objectively, Stanley's motives—if not his methods—are superior to Blanche's. His patriarchal authority is never challenged by Stella; however, Blanche does little else from the moment of her arrival at Elysian Fields. When she tells Stella in scene 1 that she will not put up in a hotel because she wants to be close to her sister, her need for companionship is apparent (not to mention her lack of funds). But this residency also gives her a strategic position from which to undermine Stanley and to entice Stella with fantasies of life among the aristocracy. Not only does she install herself as an indefinite squatter in a two-room apartment, she does everything within her power to wreck the contented home life that had existed in that apartment. One can hardly blame Stanley for fighting back.

Throughout much of the play, the conflict between Stanley and Blanche would seem to be between a crude member of the underclass and the quintessential schoolmarm. The standards of etiquette and decorum that Blanche purports to represent have been the scourge of every redblooded American male since Miss Watson tried to force Huck to mind his manners (while she was preparing to sell Nigger Jim down the river). What Mark Twain plays for farce is deadly serious in the world of **Streetcar**. Blanche is not trying to "sivilize" an urchin who is living in her home. She is trying to wreck the home she has invaded. Although never really hidden, this intention is made unmistakably clear in Blanche's speech to Stella toward the end of scene 4 (a speech that Stanley overhears). What she has just finished proposing to Stella is a kind of feminist variation on the anti-Odysseus theme. In this scenario, Stella will run away from home to join Blanche (who has already fled Laurel) in a chaste female bonding—not in the forest or on the river, but in a shop of some sort endowed by a sexually unthreatening Shep Huntleigh.

When Stanley's boorish behavior is insufficient to drive Blanche away, he discovers something that must be the realization of every rebellious schoolboy's fantasy: the schoolmarm is not what she pretends to be. As Henry Fielding observed in his preface to *Joseph Andrews,* the exposure of hypocrisy is the source of endless delight. When Stanley reveals the sordid details of Blanche's recent conduct to Stella in scene 7, it is with a kind of righteous gloating. "That girl calls *me* common!" he says. The only reservation that might prevent the audience from sharing Stanley's glee is the hope that a reformed Blanche will find happiness as Mitch's wife, a solution that would also remove her from the Kowalski household. Stella is convinced that this would happen if Stanley would only keep his mouth shut.

Unfortunately, all available evidence suggests otherwise. Blanche's newfound circumspection is only a ruse to lure Mitch to the altar. If there is any doubt of this, consider the end of scene 5, when Blanche's attempted seduction of the newsboy is followed immediately by the arrival of Mitch,

with a bunch of roses in his hand. As Blanche's husband, Mitch would probably arrive home one afternoon to find his wife in the sack with some less hesitant newsboy (just as Blanche found her former husband in bed with a man). She sees Mitch not as a spouse to love (even in the exclusively physical way that Stella loves Stanley) but as a sexually timid benefactor, a poor girl's Shep Huntleigh. It is hardly dishonorable for Stanley to want to protect his naive friend from such a fate. In the world of male camaraderie, his bond with Mitch is just as compelling as the blood ties that unite Stella and Blanche.

If Stanley is justified in wising Mitch up about Blanche's past, he clearly crosses the line of acceptable behavior when he attacks her sexually in scene 10. And yet even this inexcusable act must be analyzed within the context of the play. There is little evidence to suggest that Stanley returned home that night with the intention of raping Blanche. He is in a good mood because of the impending birth of his child and even offers to "bury the hatchet" and drink "a loving cup" with Blanche.

It is only after she speaks of casting her pearls before swine that his mood changes. This reference can't help reminding Stanley of the tirade he overheard in scene 4. (That speech, with its Darwinian imagery, was more than a little ironic, since it is Blanche, not the atavistic Stanley, who is in danger of becoming extinct because of an inability to adapt to a changing environment.) Although he had not overheard her references to Shep Huntleigh in that earlier scene, a woman as talkative as Blanche might well have tipped her hand to him at some point during her interminable stay in the Kowalski apartment. In any event, *the audience* is reminded of Blanche's plot to "rescue" Stella by breaking up her marriage to Stanley. As Stanley has yet to lay a hand on Blanche, our sympathies must still be with him.

Since the consummation of what happens between Stanley and Blanche occurs offstage, we are left to imagine the details. On the basis of what we do know, it is reasonable to assume that Stanley believes he is simply doing what Mitch was unable to do in the preceding scene: enjoy the favors of a notoriously promiscuous woman. Blanche held Mitch off by screaming "Fire," something she does not do when Stanley approaches her. When he says, "So you want some roughhouse! All right, let's have some roughhouse!" his assumption is that she enjoys violent foreplay. It is possible to interpret Stanley's next statement—"We've had this date with each other from the beginning"—as a confession that he has been plotting to destroy her. But it is at least as plausible that he is referring to Blanche's flirtatious advances, which began as early as scene 2. Whatever happens offstage, Stanley can hardly be said to have driven Blanche insane. She may think that she is waiting for Shep Huntleigh when the Doctor and Matron come to cart her off to the insane asylum in scene 11, but she also thought that in scene 10 before Stanley even came home. If anyone drives Blanche crazy, it is Mitch by foiling her wedding plans.

It is beyond even Williams's considerable art to convince us that Blanche is a genuinely tragic figure; she has too many flaws, too little stature, and almost no self-knowledge.
—Mark Royden Winchell

Despite all of these mitigating factors (which seem far more disingenuous in the postfeminist nineties than they would have in 1947), the rape so diminishes Stanley morally that we are deprived of any easy satisfaction we might have felt in his triumph over Blanche. If Williams personally empathized with Blanche more than with Stanley, the rape may be his desperate attempt to win audience sympathy for a victimized woman. But that is about all he is able to do. It is beyond even Williams's considerable art to convince us that Blanche is a genuinely tragic figure; she has too many flaws, too little stature, and almost no self-knowledge. Blanche can excite pity in the truly sensitive but only fear in the most defeated and self-loathing among us.

Although critics have never been entirely comfortable with the confused feelings Williams's two antagonists evoke, some balance is necessary to maintain dramatic tension. The rape creates that balance. It does not elevate Blanche to the level of tragic heroine, but it does prevent the audience from siding too enthusiastically with Stanley. Remove the rape, and *Streetcar* is reduced to a sexist melodrama, in which the gaudy seed-bearer reasserts patriarchal control over a household threatened by a hypocritical and self-serving matriarchy. Of course, the circumstances of the rape are ambiguous enough that what the mass audience loses in melodrama it gains in sadomasochistic titillation.

In a sense, Williams's audience can have it both ways: it can censure Stanley and pity Blanche (the "proper" moral and aesthetic response, to be sure) while guiltily enjoying his triumph over her. At least, this would seem to be true for the men in the audience. As males, we have secretly cheered the bad boy on as he proves something we have always wanted to believe, that the sententious schoolmarm is really a secret nympho. There is even a sense in which the male who has allowed himself to identify with Stanley can see *Streetcar* as having a fairy tale ending. The witch has been dispatched (if not to the hereafter, at least to the loony bin); the home is safe; and the prince and princess of Elysian Fields live happily ever after—seeing colored lights unsubdued by magic lanterns. But what of the woman spectator? In what way is she able to experience the mythic

power (as opposed to merely admiring the artistry) of Williams's play? It is certainly not through a macho identification with Stanley.

One can imagine a woman who believes herself wronged by men feeling an affinity with Blanche. If we read *Streetcar* as a feminist fable, Stanley's rape of Blanche might be a paradigm for how men deal with women in a patriarchal society. (Stanley and Mitch would both seem to be purveyors of the double standard, while Stella is nothing more than a sex object and childbearer.) Not surprisingly, Sandra M. Gilbert and Susan Gubar see the play as an indictment of "the law of the phallus and the streetcar named heterosexual desire." In an even more detailed feminist analysis, Anca Vlasopolos reminds us that it is not just Stanley but the entire cast of the play that expels Blanche at the end. Stanley and Mitch may have been the catalysts of Blanche's downfall, but Stella—with the encouragement of Eunice—seals her sister's fate by choosing to believe Stanley so that her marriage might be preserved. The poker buddies simply stand around in awkward, bovine acquiescence.

The problem with these interpretations is not that they are untrue but that they are inadequate. For much of her life, Blanche's difficulties stemmed from the lack of a forceful patriarchy. As we have seen, her male forebears abdicated their role as providers and saddled her with mortgage and debt. Her behavior toward her husband may have had terrible consequences, but it was not without provocation. Allan Grey wronged Blanche by marrying her, knowing that she loved him in a way that could bring her only traumatic pain when she discovered the truth about his sexual orientation. He then allowed her to believe that the fiasco of their wedding night was her fault. Finally, when she quite understandably tells him that he is disgusting (which he is), he takes the coward's way out by killing himself—apparently not caring what effect this will have on Blanche or anyone else he leaves behind. It is the absence of assertive men, not their chauvinistic presence, that has been Blanche's undoing. In fact, Blanche even admits to Stella that Stanley may be "what we need to mix with our blood now that we've lost Belle Reve."

For women, the emotional power of *Streetcar* may come from an identification with Stella. Unlike Stanley and Blanche, who, depending on your perspective, are either superhuman or subhuman, Stella seems a fairly ordinary person. In purely Darwinian terms, however, she is clearly the heroine of the play. She has survived because she has successfully adapted herself to changing circumstances. (Blanche is doomed by her inability to adapt, whereas Stanley seems bent on adapting the environment to himself.) Although Blanche blames Stella for betraying Belle Reve by leaving, there is no reason to believe that she could have saved the place by staying. Unlike Lot's wife, she does not cast even a regretful glance back. Stella has no illusions about the desirability of a world in which women are worshiped but not supported. Stanley spells out the difference between these two worlds in his typically blunt manner. He reminds Stella: "When we first met, me and you, you thought I was common. How right you was, baby. I was common as dirt. You showed me the snapshot of the place with the columns. I pulled you down off them columns and how you loved it, having them colored lights going!"

In pulling her "down off them columns," Stanley brings Stella into a world of male dominance. At least symbolically, it is an act of brute force, and one that Stella "loves." As Gore Vidal noted nearly forty years after the Broadway premiere of *Streetcar:* "[W]hen Tennessee produced *A Streetcar Named Desire,* he inadvertently smashed one of our society's most powerful taboos (no wonder Henry Luce loathed him): he showed the male not only sexually attractive in the flesh but as an object for something never before entirely acknowledged by the good team, the lust of women." Moreover, the fact that Stanley, as a "Polack," is considered socially inferior to the DuBois sisters makes his sexual assaults on them what Fiedler calls "rape from below." For Stella, this simply adds to the fun; for Blanche, it presumably adds to the horror.

We know that Stella was "thrilled" when Stanley broke the light bulbs with her slipper on their wedding night and that she nearly goes crazy when he is away on the road. The notion that women enjoy this kind of brute sexuality has long been a commonplace in popular literature. After all, an entire genre of romance novels, which are purchased almost exclusively by women, is called "bodice rippers." In one of the most memorable scenes in the greatest romance novel of all time, *Gone With the Wind,* Rhett Butler takes Scarlett by force in what is quite literally an act of marital rape. After quoting this scene in the novel, Fiedler writes: "Finally, however, [Scarlett] *likes* it (as perhaps only a female writer would dare to confess, though there are echoes of D. H. Lawrence in the passage), likes being mastered by the dark power of the male, likes being raped" (*What Was Literature?*).

We have a similar phenomenon in the relationship of Stanley and Stella, except that Stella does not even put up token resistance. In the scene from *Gone With the Wind,* Rhett carries a protesting Scarlett up the staircase of their mansion. In *Streetcar,* we have a scene that is almost the mirror opposite. After Stanley has gone ape on his poker night and hit the pregnant Stella, she and Blanche flee upstairs to Eunice's apartment. When he realizes what has happened, Stanley proceeds to scream (*with heaven-splitting violence*): "STELL-LAHHHHH." According to the stage directions:

The low-tone clarinet moans. The door upstairs opens again. Stella slips down the rickety stairs in her robe. Her eyes are glistening with tears and her hair loose around her throat and shoulders. They stare at each other. Then they come together with low, animal moans. He falls to his knees on the steps and presses his face to her belly, curving a little with maternity. Her eyes go blind with tenderness as she catches his head and raises him level with her. He snatches the screen door open and lifts her off her feet and bears her into the dark flat.

(Like Scarlett, Stella wears a look of serene contentment on the morning after.)

If there is a single scene in *Streetcar* that remains in the memory, it is this one. The film version has been endlessly replayed as a kind of touchstone in the history of the cinema. Moreover, it has been parodied and spoofed by countless impressionists and nightclub comedians. Now a permanent part of our popular culture, this scene can be said to sum up iconographically what *Streetcar* is all about. For men, it is a fantasy of complete domination; for women, one of complete submission.

Like other works that have entered the realm of popular myth, *Streetcar* loses none of its power when transferred to another medium. This fact is particularly astonishing when one considers that, in bringing this play to the screen, Williams and director Elia Kazan faced not only the normal aesthetic challenges of such an undertaking but a battle with the censors, as well. The story has been frequently told of the many lines of vulgar or suggestive dialogue that had to be bowdlerized. Then, there was the insistence that any hint of Allan Grey's homosexuality be removed. Finally, the censors would allow Stanley's rape of Blanche to remain only if Stella would punish Stanley by leaving him (on the assumption that only the breakup of this home could preserve traditional family values). Nevertheless, the subversive appeal of the play manages to survive.

The sanitizing of Williams's language (which is not all that shocking when judged by today's standards) is about as effective as the bleeping of profanity on television. Adult theatregoers know how people such as Stanley Kowalski talk without having to hear the actual words. Besides, more than enough sexual energy is conveyed by Marlon Brando's body language and magnetic screen presence. The issue of Allan's homosexuality is not crucial, either. In talking about her husband's weakness, Blanche at least implies a deviancy that dare not speak its name. It is perhaps even more in character for her to withhold the sordid details from Mitch.

Finally, when Stella leaves Stanley in the movie (just after Blanche has been escorted out of the apartment by the psychiatrist and the Matron), it is not for the first time. She has left him many times before, most recently in the aftermath of the poker game. As Maurice Yacowar points out, "Stella's last speech is undercut by several ironies. She expresses her resolve to leave to the baby, not to the rather more dangerous Stanley. And she does not leave the quarter, but just goes upstairs to Eunice's apartment; and Stanley's call had been enough to bring her back from Eunice's before." When the movie closes with Stanley screaming for Stella, it is difficult not to visualize her returning much as she had in that earlier unforgettable scene.

It is more than a little ironic that Tennessee Williams, the homosexual misfit, should have written such an aggressively heterosexual play. As a man who shared many of Blanche's faults (promiscuity, self-hatred, and paranoia, though never hypocrisy), he must have felt closer to her than most of his audiences do, pity being the greatest kindness that most of these strangers are willing to extend to her. Certainly, it takes a jaundiced view of home and family to present the Kowalski household as their embodiment. But that is exactly what *Streetcar* does. For nearly fifty years there has been a place in the American imagination where it is always three a.m., and a man in a torn t-shirt screams for his wife with "*heaven-splitting violence.*" Despite the protests of film censors and outraged feminists, she will always slip down the rickety stairs and into his arms. This is because "there are things that happen between a man and a woman in the dark—that sort of make everything else seem unimportant," and because "life has got to go on. No matter what happens." As long as people continue to believe such things, *A Streetcar Named Desire* will keep running.

Anne Fleche (essay date Winter 1995)

SOURCE: "The Space of Madness and Desire: Tennessee Williams and *Streetcar*," in *Modern Drama,* Vol. 38, No. 4, Winter, 1995, pp. 324-35.

[*In the following essay, Fleche examines the portrayal of madness in* A Streetcar Named Desire *through analysis of allegory, spatial metaphor, and tension between realism and expressionistic presentation in the play.*]

In *A Streetcar Named Desire* (1947), Tennessee Williams exploits the expressionistic uses of space in the drama, attempting to represent desire from the *outside,* that is, in its formal challenge to realistic stability and closure, and in its exposure to risk. Loosening both stage and verbal languages from their implicit desire for closure and containment, *Streetcar* exposes the danger and the violence of this desire, which is always the desire for the end of desire. Writing in a period when U.S. drama was becoming disillusioned with realism, Williams achieves a critical distance from realistic

technique through his use of allegory. In Blanche's line about the street-car, the fact that she is describing real places, cars, and transfers has the surprising effect of enhancing rather than diminishing the metaphorical parallels in her language. Indeed, *Streetcar*'s "duplicities of expression" are even more striking in the light of criticism's recent renewal of interest in allegory. For allegory establishes the distance "between the representative and the semantic function of language," the desire that is in language to unify (with) experience. *Streetcar* demonstrates the ways in which distance in the drama can be expanded and contracted, and what spatial relativism reveals about the economy of dramatic representation.

Tennessee Williams' plays, filled with allegorical language, seem also to have a tentative, unfinished character. The metalanguage of desire seems to preclude development, to deny progress. And yet it seems "natural" to read *A Streetcar Named Desire* as an allegorical journey toward Blanche's apocalyptic destruction at the hands of her "executioner," Stanley. The play's violence, its baroque images of decadence and lawlessness, promise its audience the thrilling destruction of the aristocratic Southern Poe-esque moth-like neuraesthenic female "Blanche" by the ape-like brutish male from the American melting-pot. The play is full in fact of realism's developmental language of evolution, "degeneration," eugenics. Before deciding that Stanley is merely an "ape," Blanche sees him as an asset: "Oh, I guess he's just not the type that goes for jasmine perfume, but maybe he's what we need to mix with our blood now that we've lost Belle Reve." The surprising thing about this play is that the allegorical reading also seems to be the most "realistic" one, the reading that imposes a unity of language and experience to make structural sense of the play, that is, to make its events organic, natural, inevitable. And yet this feels false, because allegorical language resists being pinned down by realistic analysis—it is always only half a story. But it is possible to close the gap between the language and the stage image, between the stage image and its "double" reality, by a double forgetting: first we have to forget that realism is literature, and thus already a metaphor, and then we have to forget the distance between allegory and reality. To say that realism's empiricism is indistinguishable from metaphor is to make it one with a moral, natural ordering of events. Stanley is wrong and Blanche is right, the moralists agree. But the hypocrisy of the "priggish" reading is soon revealed in its ambivalence toward Blanche/Stanley: to order events sequentially requires a reading that finds Blanche's rape inevitable, a condition of the formal structure: she is the erring woman who gets what she "asks" for (her realistic antecedents are clear). For the prigs this outcome might not be unthinkable, though it might be—what is worse—distasteful. But Williams seems deliberately to be *making* interpretation a problem: he doesn't exclude the prigs' reading, he invites it. What makes *Streetcar* different from Williams' earlier play *The Glass Menagerie* (1944) is its constant self-betrayal into and out of analytical norms. The realistic set-ups in this play really *feel like* set-ups, a magician's tricks, inviting readings that leave you hanging from your own schematic noose. Analytically, this play is a trap; it is brilliantly confused; yet without following its leads there is no way to get anywhere at all. *Streetcar* has a map, but it has changed the street signs, relying on the impulse of desire to take the play past its plots. In a way it is wrong to say Williams does not write endings. He writes elaborate *strings* of them.

Williams has given *Streetcar* strong ties to the reassuring rhetoric of realism. Several references to Stanley's career as "A Master Sergeant in the Engineers' Corps" set the action in the "present," immediately after the war. The geographical location, as with *The Glass Menagerie,* is specific, the neighborhood life represented with a greater naturalistic fidelity: "*Above the music of the 'Blue Piano' the voices of people on the street can be heard overlapping.*" Lighting and sound effects may give the scene "*a kind of lyricism,*" but this seems itself a realistic touch for "The Quarter." Even the interior set, when it appears (after a similar wipe-out of the fourth wall), resembles *The Glass Menagerie* in lay-out and configuration: a ground-floor apartment, with two rooms separated by portieres, occupied by three characters, one of them male.

Yet there are also *troubling* "realistic" details, to which the play seems to point. The *mise en scène* seems to be providing too much enclosure to provide for closure: there is no place for anyone to *go.* There is no fire escape, even though in *this* play someone does yell "Fire! Fire! Fire!" In fact, heat and fire and escape are prominent verbal and visual themes. And the flat does not, as it seems to in *The Glass Menagerie,* extend to other rooms beyond the wings, but ends in a cul-de-sac—a doorway to the bathroom which becomes Blanche's significant place for escape and "privacy." Most disturbing, however, is not the increased sense of confinement but this absence of privacy, of analytical, territorial space. No gentleman caller invited for supper invades this time, but an anarchic wilderness of French Quarter hoi polloi who spill onto the set and into the flat as negligently as the piano music from the bar around the corner. There does not seem to be anywhere to go to evade the intrusiveness and the violence: when the flat erupts, as it does on the poker night, Stanley's tirade sends Stella and Blanche upstairs to Steve and Eunice, the landlords with, of course, an unlimited run of the house ("We own this place so I can let you in"), whose goings-on are equally violent and uncontained. Stella jokes, "You know that one upstairs? [*more laughter*] One time [*laughing*] the plaster—[*laughing*] cracked—." The violence is not an isolated climax, but a repetitive pattern of the action, a state of being—it does not resolve anything:

BLANCHE: I'm not used to such—

MITCH: Naw, it's a shame this had to happen when you just got here. But don't take it serious.

BLANCHE: Violence! Is so—

MITCH: Set down on the steps and have a cigarette with me.

Anxiety and conflict have become permanent and unresolvable, inconclusive. It is not clear what, if anything, they *mean.* Unlike realistic drama, which produces clashes in order to push the action forward, *Streetcar* disallows its events a clarity of function, an orderliness.

The ordering of events, which constitutes the temporality of realism, is thus no less arbitrary in *Streetcar* than the ordering of *space:* the outside keeps becoming the inside, and vice versa. Williams has done more to relativize space in *Streetcar* than he did in *The Glass Menagerie,* where he visualized the fourth wall: here the outer wall appears and disappears more than a half-dozen times, often in the middle of a "scene," drawing attention to the spatial illusion rather than making its boundaries absolute. The effect on spatial metaphor is that we are not allowed to forget that it is metaphor and consequently capable of infinite extensions and retractions. As we might expect, then, struggle over territory between Stanley and Blanche ("Hey, canary bird! Toots! Get OUT of the BATHROOM!")—which indeed results in Stanley's reasserting the male as "King" and pushing Blanche offstage, punished and defeated—is utterly unanalytical and unsubtle: "*She'll go!* Period. P.S. She'll go *Tuesday!*" While the expressionistic sequence beginning in Scene Six with Blanche's recollection of "The Grey boy" relativizes space and time, evoking Blanche's memories, it also seems to drain her expressive power. By the time Stanley is about to rape her she mouths the kinds of things Williams put on screens in *The Glass Menagerie:* "'In desperate, desperate circumstances! Help me! Caught in a trap.'" She is establishing her emotions like sign-posts: "Stay back! . . . I warn you, don't, I'm in danger!" What had seemed a way *into* Blanche's character has had the effect of externalizing her feelings so much that they become *im*personal. In *Streetcar,* space does not provide, as it does in realistic drama, an objective mooring for a character's psychology: it keeps turning inside out, obliterating the spatial distinctions that had helped to define the realistic character as someone whose inner life drove the action. Now the driving force of emotion replaces the subtlety of expectation, leaving character out in space, dangling: "There isn't time to be—" Blanche explains into the phone; faced with a threatening proximity, she phones long-distance, and forgets to hang up.

The expressionistic techniques of the latter half of the play abstract the individual from the milieu, and emotion begins to dominate the representation of events. In Scene Ten, where Blanche and Stanley have their most violent and erotic confrontation, the play loses all sense of boundary. The front of the house is already transparent; but now Williams also dissolves the rear wall, so that beyond the scene with Blanche and Stanley we can see what is happening on the next street:

> [*A prostitute has rolled a drunkard. He pursues her along the walk, overtakes her and there is a struggle. A policeman's whistle breaks it up. The figures disappear.*
>
> *Some moments later the Negro Woman appears around the corner with a sequined bag which the prostitute had dropped on the walk. She is rooting excitedly through it.*]

The *mise en scène* exposes more of the realistic world than before, since now we see the outside as well as the inside of the house at once, and yet the effect is one of intense general paranoia: the threat of violence is "real," not "remembered," and it is everywhere. The walls have become "spaces" along which frightening, "sinuous" shadows weave—"lurid," "grotesque and menacing." The parameters of Blanche's presence are unstable images of threatening "flames" of desire, and this sense of sexual danger seems to draw the action toward itself. So it is as though Blanche somehow "suggests" rape to Stanley—it is already in the air, we can see it being *given* to him as if it were a thought: "You think I'll interfere with you? Ha-ha! [. . .] Come to think of it—maybe you wouldn't be bad to—interfere with. . . ."

The "inner-outer" distinctions of both realistic and expressionistic representation are shown coming together here. Williams makes no effort to suggest that the "lurid" expressionistic images in Scene Ten are all in Blanche's mind, as cinematic point-of-view would: the world outside the house is the realistic world of urban poverty and violence. But it is also the domain of the brutes, whose "*inhuman jungle voices rise up*" as Stanley, snakelike, tongue between his teeth, closes in. The play seems to swivel on this moment, when the logic of appearance and essence, the individual and the abstract, turns inside-out, like the set, seeming to occupy for once the same space. It is either the demolition of realistic objectivity or the transition point at which realism takes over some new territory. At this juncture "objective" vision becomes an "outside" seen from inside; for the abstraction that allows realism to represent truth objectively cannot itself be explained as objectivity. The surface in Scene Ten seems to be disclosing, without our having to look too deeply, a static primal moment beneath the immediacy of the action—the sexual taboo underneath realistic discourse:

BLANCHE: Stay back! Don't you come toward me another step or I'll—

STANLEY: What?

BLANCHE: Some awful thing will happen! It will!

STANLEY: What are you putting on now?

[*They are now both inside the bedroom*]

BLANCHE: I warn you, don't, I'm in danger!

What "will happen" in the bedroom does not have a name, or even an agency. The incestuous relation lies beyond the moral and social order of marriage and the family, adaptation and eugenics, not to mention (as Williams reminds us here) the fact that it is unmentionable. Whatever words Blanche uses to describe it scarcely matter. As Stella says, "I couldn't believe her story and go on living with Stanley."

The rape in **Streetcar** thus seems familiar and inevitable, even to its "characters," who lose the shape of characters and become violent antagonists as if on cue: "Oh! So you want some roughhouse! All right, let's have some roughhouse!" When Blanche sinks to her knees, it is as if the action is an acknowledgement. Stanley holds Blanche, who has become "*inert*"; he carries her to the bed. She is not only silent but crumpled, immobile, while he takes over control and agency. He literally places her on the set. But Williams does not suggest that Stanley is conscious and autonomous; on the contrary the scene is constructed so as to make him as unindividuated as Blanche: they seem, at this crucial point, more than ever part of an allegorical landscape. In a way, it is the *impersonality* of the rape that is most telling: the loss of individuality and the spatial distinctions that allow for "character" are effected in a scene that expressionistically dissolves character into an overwhelming *mise en scène* that, itself, seems to make things happen. The "meaning" of the rape is assigned by the play, denying "Stanley" and "Blanche" any emotion. Thus, the rape scene ends without words and without conflict: the scene has *become* the conflict, and its image the emotion.

Perhaps **Streetcar**—and Williams—present problems for those interested in Pirandellian metatheatre. Metatheatre assumes a self-consciousness of the form; but Williams makes the "form" *everything*. It is not arbitrary, or stifling. Stanley and Blanche cannot be reimagined; or, put another way, they cannot be imagined to reimagine *themselves* as other people, in other circumstances entirely. Character is the expression of the form; it is not accidental, or originary. Like [Bertolt] Brecht, Williams does not see character as a humanist impulse raging against fatal abstractions. (In a play like *The Good Person of Setzuan*, for example, Brecht makes a kind of comedy of this "tragic" notion—which is of course the notion of "tragedy.") Plays are about things other than people: they are about what people think, and feel, and yet they remove these things to a distance, towards the *representation* of thoughts and feelings, which is something else again. If this seems to suggest that the rape in **Streetcar** is something other than a rape, and so not a rape, it also suggests that it is as much a rape as it is possible for it to be; it includes the understanding that comes from exposing the essence of appearances, as Williams says, seeing from outside what we cannot see from within. At the same time, and with the same motion, the scene exposes its own scenic limitations for dramatizing that which must inevitably remain outside the scene—namely, the act it represents.

Both the surface "street scene" and the jungle antecedents of social order are visible in the rape scene, thoroughly violating the norms of realism's analytical space. When Stanley "*springs*" at Blanche, overturning the table, it is clear that a last barrier has been broken down, and now there is no space outside the jungle. "We've had this date with each other from the beginning!" We have regressed to some awful zero-point (or hour) of our beginning. (A "fetid swamp," *Time* critic Louis Kronenberger said of Williams' plays, by way of description.) We are also back at the *heart* of civilization, at its root, the incest taboo, and the center of sexuality, which is oddly enough also the center of realism—the family, where "sexuality is 'incestuous' from the start." At the border of civilization and the swamp is the sexual transgression whose suppression is the source of all coercive order. Through allegory, Williams makes explicit what realistic discourse obscures, forcing the sexuality that propels discourse into the content of the scene.

The destruction of spatial boundaries visualizes the restless discourse of desire, that uncontainable movement between inside and outside. "Desire," Williams writes in his short story **"Desire and the Black Masseur,"** (1942-46) "is something that is made to occupy a larger space than that which is afforded by the individual being." The individual being is only the measure of a measurelessness that goes far out into space. "Desire" derives from the Latin *sidus,* "star" ("Stella for Star!"); an archaic sense is "to feel the loss of": the individual is a sign of incompleteness, not self-sufficiency, whose defining gesture is an indication of the void beyond the visible, not its closure. The consciousness of desire as a void without satisfaction is the rejection of realism's "virtual space," which tried to suggest that its fractured space implied an unseen totality. Realism's objectivity covered up its literariness, as if the play were not created from nothing, but evolved out of a ready-made logic, a reality one had but to look to see. But literature answers the desire for a fullness that remains unfulfilled—it never intersects reality, never completes a trajectory, it remains in orbit. The nothing from which literature springs, whole, cannot be pen-

etrated by a vision, even a hypothetical one, and no time can be found for its beginning. As Paul de Man reasons in his discussion of [Claude] Levi-Strauss' metaphor of "virtual focus," logical sight-lines may be imaginary, but they are not "fiction," any more than "fiction" can be explained as logic:

> The virtual focus is a quasi-objective structure posited to give rational integrity to a process that exists independently of the self. The subject merely fills in, with the dotted line of geometrical construction, what natural reason had not bothered to make explicit; it has a passive and unproblematic role. The "virtual focus" is, strictly speaking, a nothing, but its nothingness concerns us very little, since a mere act of reason suffices to give it a mode of being that leaves the rational order unchallenged. The same is not true of the imaginary source of fiction. Here the human self has experienced the void within itself and the invented fiction, far from filling the void, asserts itself as pure nothingness, *our* nothingness stated and restated by a subject that is the agent of its own instability.

Nothingness, then, the impulse of "fiction," is not the result of a supposed originary act of transgression, a mere historical lapse at the origin of history that can be traced or filled in by a language of logic and analysis; on the contrary fiction is the *liberation* of a pure consciousness of desire as unsatisfied yearning, a space without boundaries.

Yet we come back to Blanche's rape by her brother-in-law, which seems visibly to re-seal the laws of constraint, to justify that Freudian logic of lost beginnings. Re-enacting the traumatic incestuous moment enables history to begin over again, while the suppression of inordinate desire resumes the order of sanity: Stella is silenced; Blanche is incarcerated. And if there is some ambivalence about her madness and her exclusion it is subsumed in an argument for order and a healthy re-direction of desire. In the last stage direction, Stanley's groping fingers discover the opening of Stella's blouse. The final set-up feels inevitable; after all, the game is still "Seven-card stud," and aren't we going to have to "go on" by playing it? The play's return to realistic logic seems assured, and Williams is still renouncing worlds. He points to the closure of the analytical reading with deft disingenuousness. Closure was always just next door to entrapment: Williams seems to be erasing their boundary lines.

Madness, the brand of exclusion, objectifies Blanche and enables her to be analyzed and confined as the embodiment of non-being, an expression of something beyond us and so structured in language. As Stanley puts it, "There isn't a goddam thing but imagination! [. . .] And lies and conceit and tricks!" [Michel] Foucault has argued, in *Madness and Civilization,* that the containment of desire's excess through the exclusion of madness creates a conscience on the perimeters of society, setting up a boundary between inside and outside: "[The madman] is put into the interior of the exterior, and inversely." Blanche is allegorically a reminder that liberty if taken too far can also be captivity, just as her libertinage coincides with her desire for death (her satin robe is a passionate red, she calls Stanley her "executioner," etc.). And Blanche senses early on the threat of confinement; she keeps trying (perversely) to end the play: "I have to plan for us both, to get us both—out!" she tells Stella, after the fight with Stanley that seems, to Blanche, so *final*. But in the end the play itself seems to have some trouble letting go of Blanche. Having created its moving boundary line, it no longer knows where to put her: what "space" does her "madness" occupy? As the dialogue suggests, she has to go— somewhere; she has become excessive. Yet she keeps coming back: "I'm not quite ready." "Yes! Yes, I forgot something!" Again, as in the rape scene, she is chased around the bedroom, this time by the Matron, while *"The 'Varsouviana' is filtered into a weird distortion, accompanied by the cries and noises of the jungle,"* the *"lurid," "sinuous"* reflections on the walls. The Matron's lines are echoed by *"other mysterious voices"* somewhere beyond the scene; she sounds like a *"firebell."* "Matron" and "Doctor" enter the play expressionistically, as functional agents, and Blanche's paranoia is now hers alone: the street is not visible. The walls do not disintegrate, they come alive. Blanche is inside her own madness, self-imprisoned: her madness is precisely her enclosure within the image. In her paranoid state, Blanche really cannot "get out," because there no longer is an outside: madness transgresses and transforms boundaries, as Foucault notes, "forming an act of undetermined content." It thus negates the image while imprisoned within it; the boundaries of the scene are not helping to define Blanche but reflecting her back to herself.

Blanche's power is not easy to suppress; she is a reminder that beneath the appearance of order something nameless has been lost: "What's happened here? I want an explanation of what's happened here," she says, *"with sudden hysteria."* It is a reasonable request that cannot be reasonably answered. This was also Williams' problem at the end of *The Glass Menagerie:* how to escape from the image when it seems to have been given too much control, when its reason is absolute? Expressionism threatens the reason of realistic *mise en scène* by taking it perhaps too far, stretching the imagination beyond limits toward an absoluteness of the image, a desire of desire. The "mimetic" mirror now becomes the symbol of madness: the image no longer simply reflects desire (desire of, desire for), but subsumes the mirror itself into the language of desire. When Blanche shatters her mirror she (like Richard II) shows that her identity has already been fractured; what she sees in the mirror is not an image, it is indistinguishable from herself. And she cries out when the lantern is torn off the lightbulb, because there is no longer a

space between the violence she experiences and the image of that violence. The inner and the outer worlds fuse, the reflecting power of the image is destroyed as it becomes fully *self*-reflective. The passion of madness exists somewhere in between determinism and expression, which at this point "actually form only one and the same movement which cannot be dissociated except after the fact."

But realism, that omnivorous discourse, can subsume even the loss of the subjective-objective distinction—when determinism equals expression—and return to some quasi-objective perspective. Thus at the very moment when all space seems to have been conquered, filled in and opened up, there is a need to parcel it out again into clearly distinguishable territories. Analysis imprisons desire. At the end of *A Streetcar Named Desire,* there is a little drama. Blanche's wild expressionistic images are patronized and pacified by theatricality: "I—just told her that—we'd made arrangements for her to rest in the country. She's got it mixed in her mind with Shep Huntleigh." Her family plays along with Blanche's delusions, even to costuming her in her turquoise seahorse pin and her artificial violets. The Matron tries to subdue her with physical violence, but Blanche is only really overcome by the Doctor's politeness. Formerly an expressionistic "type," having *the unmistakable aura of the state institution with its cynical detachment,"* the Doctor

> [. . .*takes off his hat and now he becomes personalized. The unhuman quality goes. His voice is gentle and reassuring as he crosses to Blanche and crouches in front of her. As he speaks her name, her terror subsides a little. The lurid reflections fade from the walls, the inhuman cries and noises die out and her own hoarse crying is calmed.*]

Blanche's expressionistic fit is contained by the Doctor's realistic transformation: he is particularized, he can play the role of gentleman caller. "Jacket, Doctor?" the Matron asks him. "[*He smiles . . .*] It won't be necessary." As they exit, Blanche's visionary excesses have clearly been surrendered to him: *"She allows him to lead her as if she were blind."* Stylistically, here, realism replaces expressionism at the exact moment when expressionism's "pure subjectivity" seems ready to annihilate the subject, to result in her violent subjugation. At this point the intersubjective dialogue returns, clearly masking—indeed blinding—the subjective disorder with a reassuring form. If madness is perceived as a kind of "social failure," social success is to be its antidote.

Of course theater is a cure for madness: by dramatizing or literalizing the image one destroys it. Such theatricality might risk its own confinement in the image, and for an instant there may be a real struggle in the drama between the image and the effort to contain it. But the power of realism over expressionism makes this a rare occasion. For the "ruse,"

Foucault writes, ". . . ceaselessly confirming [the delirium], does not bind it to its own truth without at the same time linking it to the necessity for its own suppression." Using illusion to destroy illusion requires a forgetting of the leap of reason and of the trick it plays on optics. To establish order, the theatrical device repeats the ordering principle it learns from theater, the representational gap between nature and language, a gap it has to deny: "The artificial reconstitution of delirium constitutes the real distance in which the sufferer recovers his liberty." In fact there is no return to "intersubjectivity," just a kind of formal recognition of it: "Whoever you are—I have always depended on the kindness of strangers," *Streetcar* makes the return to normality gentle and theatrical, while "revealing" much more explicitly than *The Glass Menagerie* the violence that is thereby suppressed. This violence is not "reality," but yet another theater underneath the theater of ruse; the cure of illusion is ironically "effected by the suppression of theater."

The realistic containment at the end of *Streetcar* thus does not quite make it back all the way to realism's seamlessly objective "historical" truth. History, structured as it is by "relations of power, not relations of meaning," sometimes assumes the power of reality itself, the platonic Form behind realism, so to speak. When it becomes the language of authority, history also assumes the authority of language, rather naively trusting language to *be* the reality it represents. The bloody wars and strategic battles are soon forgotten into language, the past tense, the *fait accompli*. Useless to struggle against the truth that is past: history is the waste of time and the corresponding conquest of space, and realism is the already conquered territory, the belated time with the unmistakable stamp of authenticity. It gets applause simply by being plausible; it forgets that it is literature. To read literature, de Man says, we ought to remember what we have learned from it—that the expression and the expressed can never entirely coincide, that no single observation point is trustworthy. *Streetcar*'s powerful explosion of allegorical language and expressionistic images keeps its vantage point on the move, at a remove. Every plot is untied. Realism rewards analysis, and Williams invites it, perversely, but any analysis results in dissection. To provide *Streetcar* with an exegesis seems like gratuitous destruction, "deliberate cruelty." Perhaps no other American writer since Dickinson has seemed so easy to crush.

And this consideration ought to give the writer who has defined Blanche's "madness" some pause. Even the critical awareness of her tidy incarceration makes for too tidy a criticism. In Derrida's analysis of Foucault's *Madness and Civilization,* he questions the possibility of "historicizing" something that does not exist outside of the imprisonment of history, of speech—madness "simply says the other of each determined form of the logos." Madness, Derrida proposes, is a "hyperbole" out of which "finite-thought, that is

to say, history" establishes its "reign" by the "disguised internment, humiliation, fettering and mockery of the madman within us, of the madman who can only be a fool of a logos which is father, master and king." Philosophy arises from the "*confessed* terror of going mad"; it is the "economic" embrace of madness.

To me then Williams' play seems to end quite reasonably with a struggle, at the point in the play at which structure and coherence must assert themselves (by seeming to)—that is, the end of the play. The end must look back, regress, so as to sum up and define. It has no other choice. The theatrical ending always becomes, in fact, the real ending. It cannot remain metaphorically an "end." And what is visible at the end is Blanche in trouble, trapped, mad. She is acting as though she believed in a set of events—Shep Huntleigh's rescue of her—that the other characters, by their very encouragement, show to be unreal. There is a fine but perhaps important line here: Blanche's acting is no more convincing than theirs; but—and this is a point Derrida makes about madness—she is thinking things before they can be historicized, that is, before they have happened or even have been shown to be likely or possible (reasonable). "Is not what is called finitude possibility as crisis?" Derrida asks. The other characters, who behave as if what Blanche is saying were real, underline her absurdity precisely by invoking reality.

Blanche's relations to history and to structural authority are laid bare by this "forced" ending, in which she repeatedly questions the meaning of meaning: "What has happened here?" This question implies the relativity of space and moment, and so of "events" and their meanings, which are at this point impossible to separate. That is why it is important that the rape suggest an overthrow of meaning, not only through a stylized emphasis on its own representation, but also through its strongly relativized temporality. (Blanche warns against what "will happen," while Stanley says the event is the future, the fulfillment of a "date" or culmination in time promised "from the beginning.")

Indeed, the problem of madness lies precisely in this gap between past and future, in the structural slippage between the temporal and the ontological. For if madness, as Derrida suggests, can exist at all outside of opposition (to reason), it must exist in "hyperbole," in the excess prior to its incarceration in structure, meaning, time, and coherence. A truly "mad" person would not objectify madness—would not, that is, define and locate it. That is why all discussions of "madness" tend to essentialize it, by insisting, like Blanche's fellow characters at the end of *Streetcar,* that it is *real,* that it *exists.* And the final stroke of logic, the final absurdity, is that in order to insist that madness *exists,* to objectify and define and relate to it, it is necessary to *deny* it any history. Of course "madness" is not at all amenable to history, to structure, causality, rationality, recognizable "thought." But this denial of the history of madness has to come from within history itself, from within the language of structure and "meaning." Blanche's demand to know "what has happened here"—her insistence that something "has happened," however one takes it—has to be unanswerable. It cannot go any further. In theatrical terms, the "belief" that would make that adventure of meaning possible has to be denied, shut down. But this theatrical release is not purifying; on the contrary, it has got up close to the plague, to the point at which reason and belief contaminate each other: the possibility of thinking madly. Reason and madness can cohabitate with nothing but a thin curtain between. And curtains are not walls, they do not provide solid protection.

Submitting Williams' allegorical language to realistic analysis, then, brings you to conclusions: the imprisonment of madness, the loss of desire. The moral meaning smooths things over. Planning to "open up" **Streetcar** for the film version with outside scenes and flashbacks, Elia Kazan found it would not work—he ended up making the walls movable so they could actually *close in* more with every scene. The sense of entrapment was fundamental: Williams' dramatic language is itself too free, too wanton, it is a trap, it is asking to be analyzed, it lies down on the couch. Kazan saw this perverse desire in the play—he thought **Streetcar** was about Williams' cruising for tough customers:

> The reference to the kind of life Tennessee was leading at the time was clear. Williams was aware of the dangers he was inviting when he cruised; he knew that sooner or later he'd be beaten up. And he was.

But Kazan undervalues the risk Williams is willing to take. It is not just violence that cruising invites, but death. And that is a desire that cannot be realized. Since there is really no way to get what you want, you have to put yourself in a position where you do not always want what you get. Pursuing desire requires a heroic vulnerability. At the end of **"Desire and the Black Masseur"** the little masochistic artist/saint, Anthony Burns, is cannibalized by the masseur, who has already beaten him to a pulp. Burns, who is thus consumed by his desire, makes up for what Williams calls his "incompletion." Violence, or submission to violence, is analogous to art, for Williams: both mask the inadequacies of form. "Yes, it is perfect," thinks the masseur, whose manipulations have tortured Burns to death. "It is now completed!"

Georges-Michel Sarote (essay date 1995)

SOURCE: "Fluidity and Differentiation in Three Plays by

Tennessee Williams: *The Glass Menagerie, A Streetcar Named Desire,* and *Cat on a Hot Tin Roof,*" in *Staging Difference: Cultural Pluralism in American Theater and Drama,* edited by Marc Maufort, Peter Lang, 1995, pp. 141-56.

[*In the following essay, Sarote examines Williams's treatment of discrimination and resistance to mainstream American "normalcy" in his three major plays. According to Sarote, "Streetcar, like most of Williams's works can be interpreted as a plea for a less repressive, more fluid, more androgynous American Society."*]

> At the age of fourteen I discovered writing as an escape from a world of *reality* in which I felt *acutely uncomfortable*. It immediately became my *place of retreat*, my cave, my refuge. From what? From being called a sissy by the neighborhood kids, and Miss Nancy by my father, because I would rather read books in my grand-father's large and classical library than play marbles and baseball and other *normal* kid games, a result of a severe childhood illness and an *excessive attachment to the female members* of my family, who had coaxed me back into life. (Emphasis added)

When Tennessee Williams wrote these lines, in 1959, he was already a widely acclaimed, forty-eight year old playwright, the author of a number of Broadway hits including the three plays under consideration—**The Glass Menagerie** (1944), **A Streetcar Named Desire** (1947), and **Cat on a Hot Tin Roof** (1955). As an adolescent, reading had enabled him to escape Reality, that is to say the hostility of his father, a paragon of normalcy and virility, American style, according to Williams's biographers. In **Cat on a Hot Tin Roof,** the playwright makes fun of the conformist couple Mae and Gooper's "nawmal children" that Maggie describes as "no-neck monsters." As a child and teen-ager, Tom (before he became Tennessee) felt different from "normal" children and uncomfortable in the company of other (male) kids, the reason being, according to his own interpretation, that he was excessively attached to the women in his family. Further down, in the same text, he describes himself as "neurotic."

I

In the closely autobiographical **The Glass Menagerie** (henceforward referred to as **Glass**) the world of normalcy is that of the urban petty bourgeoisie to which Williams's family belonged when they moved to Saint Louis in 1918. The first stage direction evokes, to use Tom's own words, "the social background of the play": in the "overcrowded urban centers," the "lower middle-class" is "fundamentally . . . an enslaved section of American society" whose main purpose in life is to "avoid fluidity and differentiation and to exist and function as one interfused mass of automatism." Indeed, one of the driving forces of the plot appears to be Tom's desperate desire to disengage himself from this undifferentiated mass: he writes poetry in a cabinet of the "washroom" of the shoe warehouse, where he is not even a shipping clerk, and he dreams of enlisting in the Merchant Marine. In the apartment where he lives between Amanda, his overbearing mother, and Laura, his crippled sister, whose "difference" is even more acute than her brother's, Tom feels caught as in a trap. He secretly plans to follow in the footsteps of his absent father, "a telephone man who fell in love with long distances" and deserted his family.

Within the framework of the play, Jim O'Connor, Tom's friend and colleague, represents normalcy, or better said, a sort of ideal complete American male. A very good-looking young man, he is both artistic and athletic:

> In high school Jim was a hero. He had tremendous Irish good nature and vitality with the scrubbed and polished look of white chinaware. He seemed to move in a continual spotlight. He was a star in basketball, captain of the debating club, president of the senior class and the glee club and he sang the male lead in the annual light operas.

Jim's primary dramatic function, as Tom points out, is to be "an emissary from a world of reality that we were somehow set apart from." He is "the most realistic character in the play," at the same time as he is a "symbol." In one sense, far from being a fixed, allegorical character, Jim also represents fluidity and resilience, as his vitality has not waned: if he is "disappointed" by his apparently stagnant career, he is not "discouraged." Yet, within the context of the American society of the time, his aspirations are those of a conformist—moving up the social ladder thanks to night classes in radio engineering, public speaking, etc. It could be argued, however, that in the cultural atmosphere of the Thirties, as an Irish Catholic "on both sides" Jim is bound to feel somewhat different from mainstream America. In fact, his ethnic origin may be the reason why this conformist has retained the playwright's sympathy—his "difference" makes of Jim a possible ego ideal with whom the author can identify.

If Jim O'Connor embodies both normalcy and marginality, it is arguable that Tom also incarnates both difference and conformism, as he represents another facet of the American virile ideal; unlike Jim, Tom is not about to marry and start a family: he dreams of virile adventures as a sailor; like the unattached manly cowboy of Westerns, he has no desire of settling down.

In *Glass,* it is Laura, Tom's sister, who symbolizes unmitigated difference. Her "morbid shyness" (to use a phrase Williams had applied to himself as a boy) prevents her from having any kind of normal relationship with others. Her lameness, and more precisely, the brace she has to wear, materializes this difference. Tom having said to their mother, "Laura is very different from other girls," Amanda replies, "I think the difference is all to her advantage." On stage, the objective correlative of imagination and art into which Laura has retreated is the eponymous glass menagerie that she spends hours taking care of. The sparkling glass also represents the more or less imaginary shining past nostalgically remembered by Amanda: when Tom insults his mother, brutally bringing her back to reality, to the present, he makes a violent gesture and upsets the glass menagerie: "there is a tinkle of shattering glass. Laura cries out as if wounded." In this way, the playwright highlights the absence of flexibility, the lack of fluidity in Amanda's and Laura's dreams which can be shattered by the intrusion of reality.

The most dramatic scene between the representative of reality and that of imagination, between normalcy and difference, occurs when Jim and Laura find themselves alone. In high school Laura had had a secret crush on Jim; now, a few years later, she comes into close contact with him for the first time: trying to boost her morale Jim goes so far as to kiss her. And in 1944, twenty years before the cultural revolution of the Sixties, which promoted diversity and pride in one's difference, in his first successful play, in front of the conformist audience of the commercial theatre, Williams has the "emissary from reality" deliver an impassioned plea to difference:

> You know—you're—well—very different from anyone else I know! . . . I mean it in a nice way— . . . Has anyone ever told you that you were pretty? . . .
>
> Well you are! In a different way from anyone else. And all the nicer because of the difference, too.
>
> . . . The different people are not like other people, but being different is nothing to be ashamed of. Because other people are not such wonderful people . . . They're common as—weeds, but—you—. . . .

The materialization of this splendid difference (as opposed to the brace) is the legendary unicorn, Laura's favorite little glass animal. Revealingly, dancing with Laura, Jim accidentally causes it to fall and lose its single horn. Laura muses: "Now it is just like all the other horses . . . Maybe it's a blessing in disguise." She will just imagine that he had an operation: "The horn was removed to make him feel more at home with the other horses, the ones that don't have horns."

The brutal brace and the brittle glass menagerie—most strikingly, the legendary unicorn that has to be symbolically castrated to merge with the group—are significant theatrical props (materializing the misery and splendor of difference), but in *Glass* the true textual symbol of difference is that of the "blue roses." A few years before the state action begins, Laura had had to stay away from school because of pleurosis. Having thought that Laura had said "blue roses" Jim had jokingly nicknamed her "Blue roses." Today he comments that, if ordinary people are as common as weeds,

"but—you—well—, you're—Blue Roses!"

Laura: But blue is wrong for—roses . . .

Jim: It's right for you!

This is sickness metamorphosed into a flower, an extra-ordinarily beautiful one. Thus will Tom Williams metamorphose his neurosis into art. *Glass* ends with the transformation of Amanda's "silliness" and fixation on the past into "tragic beauty" and on Laura's "smile." But as the play begins, a long time after the events related, the sailor whose domain is limitless fluidity returns to the now empty apartment, incapable of forgetting his sister who remains in his mind as the embodiment of unmitigable alienation.

II

Produced in 1947, *A Streetcar Named Desire* (henceforth referred to as *Streetcar*) plays further variations on Williams's basic theme of difference. The term and its synonyms are used several times in connection with the characters' social milieus, sexual preferences, and psychological makeups.

Streetcar can be viewed as structured on the clash between two social classes. Whereas in *Glass,* at the same time as she was nostalgic for the traditional aristocratic South, symbolized by the Blue Mountain plantation, Amanda made every effort to integrate the undifferentiated mass of the Saint Louis middle class in order to survive, in *Streetcar* Blanche DuBois is repelled by the working class milieu to which her sister now belongs. Belle Reve, her lost plantation, is the symbol of a long gone period, that of the chivalric, romantic, antebellum South. When she arrives in Elysian Fields, the lower class neighborhood of New Orleans, a stage direction describes her as being "incongruous to this setting." On the contrary, her sister Stella, who comes from a "background obviously quite different from her husband's," has perfectly adapted to her new environment. Blanche, whose "delicate beauty" "must avoid a strong light," will be crushed by her sister's husband, Stanley Kowalski, the representative of violent normalcy and of the brutal present.

Since the death of her husband, the poet Allan Grey, since the loss of Belle Reve, Blanche has felt, like Tom Williams, "acutely uncomfortable" in the everyday world. According to Stanley's informer, in Laurel, where she taught high school English, she was considered, "not just different but downright loco—nuts." After her affair with a seventeen year old student of hers, she was declared "morally unfit for her position." She ironically agrees: "True? Yes, I suppose—unfit somehow. . . ." She sings a paean to art, magic, make-believe; the artist of the play being her homosexual husband, a poet who died before the rise of the curtain and whose emissary she appears to be within the time-span of the play. To sensitive *and* brawny Mitch (a felicitous combination in her eye, just as Jim was artistic *and* athletic, and therefore attractive to Laura) she explains: "There was something different about the boy, a nervousness, a softness which wasn't like a man's although he wasn't the least bit effeminate-looking—still—that thing was there." Stella, Stanley's wife, who functions as the link between the idyllic Belle Reve and the shabby reality of Elysian Fields, reveals to her husband that this "beautiful and talented young man was a degenerate." Blanche had apparently once thought the same thing since her avowed "disgust" caused Allan's suicide.

Stanley is a far more inexorable representative of reality than gentle, likeable, well-mannered, only unwittingly cruel Jim. Like Jim, however, Stella's husband is part and parcel of his social milieu: a father-to-be, an ex-Master Sergeant in the American army, he is captain of the neighborhood bowling team. Contrary to Jim, who broke things by accident, Stanley loves to destroy what is fragile—light bulbs on his wedding night, plates, the radio set when he is in a rage, and finally Blanche, who, it should be noticed, "broke" her husband and who, when Stanley attacks her, defends herself with a broken bottle after having smashed a mirror.

Jim was Irish; Stanley Kowalski is Polish. The Poles are "something like Irish, aren't they?" asks Blanche who (like Williams himself) is descended from French Huguenots. As she repeatedly calls her brother-in-law a "Polack," he vehemently denies this ethnic difference:

I am not a Polack. People from Poland are Poles, not Polacks. But what I am is a one hundred per cent American, born and raised in the greatest country on earth and proud as hell of it, so don't ever call me a Polack.

Possibly, Stanley Kowalski married Stella DuBois with a view to abolishing this difference, in hopes of perfecting his social integration.

Judging by his last name, Hubbel, the owner of the house in which the Kowalskis live is German. Among Stanley's friends there is a Mexican (Pablo Gonzales) and an Anglo-Saxon (Harold Mitchell) considered by Blanche as "superior to the others." Revealingly enough, this Anglo-Saxon is Stanley's closest friend even though their personalities are totally opposite. Was Mitch chosen by Stanley as the badge of his complete integration? Outside the door—not inside the apartment—there are black people . . .

In this light, Stella and Stanley's apartment may be viewed as the theatrical representation of the American melting pot; in Blanche's eye it is an image of future democratic America, of the "interfused mass" evoked in *Glass.*

In a moment of desperate lucidity Blanche admits to her sister: "maybe (Stanley)'s what we need to mix with our blood now that we've lost Belle Reve and have to go on without Belle Reve to protect us." (The tone is both ironic and dead serious.) Stanley and Stella's child, born toward the end of the play and whose gender is left indeterminate ("baby," "child," "it"), is perhaps the embodiment of a future *positive* "undifferentiation," that of a United States having integrated the aristocratic, agricultural, and "feminine" values of the poetic Old South (represented by Blanche and her husband) and the virile vigor of the urban industrial new world.

Be that as it may, inside this melting pot, there subsists a clear hierarchy: if Stanley enjoyed pulling Stella "down off them" white columns of Belle Reve, as he himself claims, if he delights in revealing what lies beneath Blanche's veneer and apparent refinement, if he feels insulted when referred to as a Polack, he calls Pablo a "greaseball," whereas his landlady and friend, Eunice Hubbel, in a fit of anger, calls him a Polack. In spite of the stage direction indicating that "New Orleans is a cosmopolitan city where there is a relatively warm and easy intermingling of races in the old part of town," Stanley's house does not admit blacks, artists, marginals and those refusing democratic equalization—no poet, no homosexual, no liberated woman, no African-American. Indeed, 632 Elysian Fields appears as a microcosm, as a faithful photograph of the United States in the Forties and Fifties. It is arguable that it is because Blanche—implicitly and explicitly—reminds Stanley of his ethnic and social difference that he revengingly crushes her.

As an "emissary from reality" Irish Jim O'Connor came from outside, the domain of normalcy and conformism in *Glass;* now, in *Streetcar*, reality, normalcy dwell inside, on stage, in Stanley's place, Blanche being an emissary from a world of imagination, make-believe, and otherness. In Stanley's cramped quarters, she takes refuge in fluids: the hot baths that soothe her frazzled nerves and whiskey. As Tom Wingfield became a seafarer (after writing poetry in the *wash*room of the shoe factory) to escape the trap of conformism, literary and musical Blanche dreams of spending the rest of her life on the sea, of dying on a ship and of "being buried at sea, sewn up in a clean white sack and dropped overboard . . . into an ocean as blue as my first lover's eyes."

III

At the very beginning of *Cat on a Hot Tin Roof* (hence-forth abbreviated to *Cat*), it is from the bathroom shower (as opposed to the feminine bath) that Brick emerges: "At the rise of the curtain someone is taking a shower in the bathroom, the door of which is half open." *Cat* takes place in the magnificent Pollitt plantation in the Mississippi Delta, the nameless plantation being the *real* replica, *in the present,* of Amanda's remembered Blue Mountain or Blanche's Belle Reve.

Much more spectacularly than Jim O'Connor or Stanley Kowalski, Brick can lay every claim to the privilege of incarnating the American Virile Ideal: a demigod's physique, wealth, education, an Anglo-Saxon origin (Pollitt should be contrasted with O'Connor and Kowalski), a beautiful wife, and, last but not least, his past as a college football player—football being a much more virile sport than basketball (Jim) and bowling (Stanley). Yet, like Tom Wingfield and Blanche DuBois, Brick is trying to escape the trap represented here by the bedroom (the sole setting of the action) and, more precisely, the double bed—the main prop of the play. To follow Brick in *Cat* is to follow the frantic movements of a man desperately trying to flee—to the bathroom, to the outside gallery, to some dreamland. In *Glass* the first stage direction had explained:

> The apartment faces an alley and is entered by a fire-escape, a structure whose name is a touch of accidental poetic truth, for all these huge buildings are always burning with the slow and implacable fires of human desperation.

Indeed, one way of bringing out the underlying structure and significance of *Cat* is to oppose the cold (or cool) to the hot. Below his "cool air of detachment" mentioned in the first stage direction about him, Brick is on fire: he is a "quiet mountain" that can blow "suddenly up in volcanic flame." He takes showers and constantly drinks iced liquor in an attempt to put out his inner fire.

Laura's lameness was the visible sign of her difference, that of all those moving with difficulty within their society. . . . Brick broke his ankle trying to jump hurdles on the high school athletic field. During the three acts of the play, he hobbles on one foot with or without his symbolic crutch. Now, what is Brick's difference?

The "Notes for the designer" tell us that the plantation was once owned by two men living and sleeping together. The bedroom

> has not changed much since it was occupied by the original owners of the place, Jack Straw and Peter Ochello, a pair of old bachelors who shared this room all their lives together. In other words, the room must evoke ghosts; it is *gently* and *poetically*

haunted by a relationship that must have involved a *tenderness* which was *uncommon*. (Emphasis added)

"Uncommon" underlines the difference of the two men, a difference that the playwright relates to poetry, gentleness, and tenderness. It is this room that Big Daddy, Brick's father, has given to Brick and Maggie, during their stay on the plantation. (The word "ghost" recalling the incongruous, white-clad Blanche and Allan Grey haunting Blanche's heart.)

The theme of homosexuality as the epitome of difference—especially at the time when the three plays under consideration were written and produced—was implicit as early as the autobiographical *Glass:* Tom is a bachelor, a sailor, and at the end of the play he evokes his "walking along a street at night, in some strange city, before I have found companions."

In the short story **"The Resemblance Between a Violin Case and a Coffin"** (1949), based on the relationship between Tom Williams and his sister Rose, the identification of the playwright with his sister is best expressed when we are told that when his sister falls in love with Richard he too becomes obsessed with the boy: "She had fallen in love. As always, I followed suit."

In *Streetcar,* through the character of Allan Grey, the theme colored the plot more clearly, and in *Cat* it assumes center stage, with a few precautions, nevertheless, because of the 1955 Broadway audience for whom the play was written. . . . The main dramatic movement of *Cat* is the gradual revelation of the intensity of Brick and Skipper's "exceptional" friendship. Skipper drank himself to death before the play begins, his death being the motivating force, the main spring of the action. Ironically playing on the word "normal," Brick exclaims to his father: "Normal? No!—It was too rare to be normal, any true thing between two people is too rare to be normal."

Were Brick and Skipper homosexual lovers? No one knows, not even the author who in a long stage direction claims for the playwright the right to remain vague and mysterious. However, a drunken Skipper had confessed his love to Brick, as Brick finally tells his father, even though Maggie may have brainwashed Skipper into believing that his friendship for her husband was not "pure." In this way, is the Broadway audience distanced from the revelation in a quintuple fashion! Skipper is now dead; Brick relates the confession; Skipper was drunk; he used the telephone to confess his homosexual love; he may have been self-deluded. In other words, the audience do not *witness,* nor do they *hear* the confession, and this confession was made by a man who was confused as he declared his love from a distance. What is

more, he is now dead. Thus, no more than in *Streetcar* is the archetypal embodiment of social and psychological difference admitted within the theatrical space of *Cat.* Indeed, the homosexual flees or is ejected from the social space: Maggie tells Brick that when she had tried to tear off Skipper's mask by urging him to confess his love for Brick, "HE SLAPPED ME HARD ON THE MOUTH!—then turned and ran without stopping once, I am sure, *all the way* back into his room at the Blackstone." Relating an episode in his student life when a pledge in his and Skipper's fraternity attempted to do an "unnatural thing," Brick exclaims: "We told him to git off the campus, and he did, he got!— *All the way* to . . . North Africa, last I heard!" (Emphasis added in both quotations.)

Whatever the nature of Brick's own feelings for Skipper—whether it be, as he claims, "exceptional friendship, *real, real, deep, deep friendship,*" repressed homoeroticism, or patent homosexuality (even though unconsummated)—what matters at this point is that Brick, who appears to be the *ne plus ultra* of the American virile ideal, has been in close contact with the very embodiment of difference. He may even have loved him—hence his disgust with everything; hence his death-wish. In the middle of an immense plantation— "twenty-eight thousand acres of the richest land this side of the valley Nile"—, Brick finds himself in a no-exit situation. All the more so as he has interiorized all the values of his society (as opposed to his tolerant father). If "we gauge the wide and profound reach of the conventional mores he got from the world that crowned him with early laurel," if he desperately tries to distance himself from Skipper ("*His* truth, not *mine!*"—), yet, on stage, within the spatio-temporal framework of the play, Brick is the character who embodies difference (when compared to his brother Gooper, for instance). Both hyper-conventional *and* different, he sings a paean to "exceptional," "not normal," friendship, at the same time as he is terrorized by the idea of transgression.

In fact, Brick designates "some place elsewhere," another possible society already glimpsed by at least two "virile" American writers whose lives and works are linked to sea voyages—Herman Melville and Jack London whose homoeroticism has often been underlined by critics. It is also the society evoked in Greek legends approvingly alluded to by Maggie. This place elsewhere, this *ailleurs,* is the domain of the polymorphous love of childhood or of the desexualized world of sublimation in which, in spite of their intensity, human relationships are not tainted by sexuality. Brick exclaims:

> One man has one great good true thing in his life.
> One great good thing which is true!—I had friendship with Skipper.—You are naming it dirty! . . .
> Not love, with you, Maggie but friendship with Skipper was that one great true thing. . . .

Maggie had told him: "life has got to be allowed to continue even after the dream of life is—all—over."

In *Cat* the best image of this utopian world is the unreachable moon, personified in the masculine: in the Broadway version of the third act Brick addresses it as "you cool son of a bitch." (He envies the man in the moon.) On earth, this "great good place," to borrow Henry James's title, is the football field. According to Maggie, Brick tells his father, he and Skipper

> Wanted to—keep on tossing—those long, long!—high, high!—passes that—couldn't be intercepted except by time, the aerial attack that made us famous! And so we did, we did, we kept it up for one season, that aerial attack, we held it high!—Yeah, but—that summer, Maggie, she laid the law down to me, said, Now or never, and so I married Maggie. . . .

Brick is still dreaming about those high passes, about those aerial contacts through the ball in a world of sublimation, as opposed to what Maggie represents as she lays the law *down* to her husband. Coolness, lawlessness, elevation would appear to be the intrinsic qualities of this world, as opposed to the hot sexuality embodied here below by Maggie and marital duties. Brick is probably also nostalgic for the ambiguities of adolescence. After Skipper's death, his link with that period of life when feelings have the ambivalence and fluidity rejected by adult American society is broken. His nostalgia for that fluidity is not only reflected in the symbolic shower that opens the play, but also in mortiferous liquor through which he, possibly, hopes to rejoin, to swim back to Skipper who, so to speak, drowned himself in alcohol. It is arguable, of course, that if conventional Brick Pollitt sings the splendor of difference only within the confines of sublimation, it is mainly because this transgressive plea to difference had to be accepted by the Broadway audience. In this respect, it is noteworthy that in the 1974 version of the third act (the third of that act!) Williams is no more explicit about Brick's sexual identity than in the previous versions. Two decades after the premiere of *Cat,* during the heyday of the sexual liberation, homosexuality was still an all but unbreakable taboo on Broadway.

IV

Tennessee Williams's "difference," that of the gay artist, always finds its way onto the stage, after having sustained transformations required by the genre and the time. The majority of his plays present characters that are too sensitive and/or too sensual to be fully adapted to their conventional social milieu. They sooner or later clash with Reality, with the hostility of normal Boeotians. The theme of the "fugitive kind" can be found as early as 1937 in one of his first plays entitled precisely, *Fugitive Kind.* (In *Glass* a stage direction evokes Laura's "fugitive manner"). The no-exit situation inherent in the theatre intensifies this confrontation. The fire-escape, the gallery, the bathroom, the washroom, are the antechamber to some distant world, the first step to some imaginary beyond where society would be less rigid, more fluid. This "place elsewhere" assumes many shapes and forms: art, the more or less reinvented past, the football field, the sea, death itself. The color that best symbolizes this dreamland is white, the color of purity and mourning: Blanche's dress and imagined shroud, Brick's "white silk pajamas" and "white towel-cloth robe," the sparkling transparence of the glass menagerie.

On stage, the dream of fluidity is suggested by the oneiric atmosphere, the music, the changing light, the "plastic" theatre decor wished for by Williams (who condemned the theatre of "realistic convention") in the "Production Notes" for *Glass.* In *Cat,* in "Notes for the Designer" the playwright indicates that "the walls below the ceiling should dissolve mysteriously into air; the set should be roofed by the sky; stars and moon suggested by traces of milky pallor. . . ." And the designer Joe Milzener had this to say about the sets he created for *Streetcar:* "the magic of light opened up a fluid and poetic world of story telling. . . ."

If it is true that the characters representing transgressive difference (Allan Grey, Peter Ochello, Jack Straw, Skipper, the student driven out of the fraternity, and, later, in archetypical fashion, Sebastian Venable in *Suddenly Last Summer*) do not enter the theatrical space, it is clear that they haunt the wings of the stage *and* the hearts of the protagonists. Again, it should also be stressed that all the male protagonists harbor some kind of difference even when they function as representatives of normalcy. The most emblematic example being Brick about whom the playwright seems to be in two minds (in two hearts?): he regrets his timidity as regards transgression at the same time as he has him deliver a vibrant tribute to "exceptional," "not normal" friendship between males. In this respect, Brick should be contrasted with several secondary characters of villainous rigidly heterosexual Anglo-Saxons, from Jabe Torrance (*Battle of Angels,* 1940) to Tom Junior (*Sweet Bird of Youth,* 1959), via George Holly (*Suddenly Last Summer,* 1958). The ultimate fluidity of personality is androgyny, a theme that has its origin, no doubt, in Williams's identification with his sister Rose. Critics, despite Williams's vehement denials, have tended, for instance, to see Blanche as a projection of her creator.

When all is said, if it is patent that the condition of Williams's truly different people (as opposed to those that function in the plays as representatives of reality) is socially and psychologically far from enviable, it is just as clear that their revenge is their spiritual superiority over the "normal" people of his theatre. The beauty of their inner world—however fragile this world may be—enables them to transcend the petty world of normalcy, the symbol of which might be the "jacket," the *straight*jacket—as opposed to the "pretty blue jacket"—that the "sinister" nurse, dressed in a "severe dress," in a "plain-tailored outfit," wants to impose on Blanche. In this last scene Blanche (i.e. "the white one") is dressed in red and blue, and she would like her dead body to be dropped into the blue sea. It is fitting that in **Streetcar** Blanche's colors should be white, red and blue, the colors of the American flag. **Streetcar,** like most of Williams's works can be interpreted as a plea for a less repressive, more fluid, more androgynous American Society. In such a fluid society, "undifferentiation," in the sense of "warm and easy intermingling" of all human beings (contrasted with "interfused mass of automatism") and absence of discrimination, would be the order of the day.

FURTHER READING

Criticism

Bruhm, Steven. "Blackmailed by Sex: Tennessee Williams and the Economics of Desire." *Modern Drama* 34, No. 4 (December 1991): 528-37.

> Discusses the interplay of homosexuality, consumerism, and political power in *Suddenly Last Summer.*

Colin, Philip C., editor. *Confronting Tennessee Williams's A Streetcar Named Desire: Essays in Cultural Pluralism.* Westport, CT: Greenwood, 1993, 255 p.

> Collection of essays written by various scholars on social, cultural, and political aspects of *A Streetcar Named Desire.*

Hulley, Kathleen. "The Fate of the Symbolic in *A Streetcar Named Desire.*" In *Tennessee Williams's A Streetcar Named Desire,* edited by Harold Bloom, pp. 111-22. New York: Chelsea House, 1988.

> Examines Williams's presentation of symbolic reality in *A Streetcar Named Desire,* particularly in terms of social control and the repression of desire.

King, Kimball. "Tennessee Williams: A Southern Writer." *Mississippi Quarterly* 48, No. 4 (Fall 1995): 627-47.

> Examines Williams's implicit and explicit views about the American South and the influence of the Southern literary tradition on his work.

Price, Marian. "*Cat on a Hot Tin Roof:* The Uneasy Marriage of Success and Idealism." *Modern Drama* 38, No. 3 (Fall 1995): 324-35.

> Discusses the creation and production of *Cat on a Hot Tin Roof* as a significant turning point in Williams's career whereby he chose popular success over purely artistic concerns.

Sofer, Andrew. "Self-Consuming Artifacts: Power, Performance and the Body in Tennessee Williams's *Suddenly Last Summer.*" *Modern Drama* 38, No. 3 (Fall 1995): 336-47.

> Explores the anti-realistic structure, presentation, and theatrical rhetoric of *Suddenly Last Summer.*

Wilhelmi, Nancy O. "The Language of Power and Powerlessness: Verbal Combat in the Plays of Tennessee Williams." In *The Text Beyond: Essays in Literary Linguistics,* edited by Cynthia Goldin Bernstein, pp. 217-26. Tuscaloosa, AL: University of Alabama Press, 1994.

> Provides analysis of antagonistic male-female dialogue in *A Streetcar Named Desire* and *Cat on a Hot Tin Roof.*

Additional coverage of Williams's life and career is contained in the following sources published by Gale: *Contemporary Authors,* Vols. 5-8R; *Contemporary Authors New Revision Series,* Vols. 31 and 108; *Discovering Authors: Canadian; Discovering Authors: Dramatists* and *Most Studied Authors Modules; Dictionary of Literary Biography,* Vols. 7 and 83; *Major Twentieth Century Writers;* and *World Literature Criticism.*

☐ Contemporary Literary Criticism

Indexes

Literary Criticism Series
Cumulative Author Index
Cumulative Topic Index
Cumulative Nationality Index
Title Index, Volume 111

How to Use This Index

The main references

```
Camus, Albert
    1913-1960 ...... CLC 1, 2, 4, 9, 11, 14,
        32, 69; DA; DAB; DAC; DAM DRAM,
        MST, NOV; DC2; SSC 9; WLC
```

list all author entries in the following Gale Literary Criticism series:

BLC = *Black Literature Criticism*
BLCS = *Black Literature Criticism Supplement*
CLC = *Contemporary Literary Criticism*
CLR = *Children's Literature Review*
CMLC = *Classical and Medieval Literature Criticism*
DA = *DISCovering Authors*
DAB = *DISCovering Authors: British*
DAC = *DISCovering Authors: Canadian*
DAM = *DISCovering Authors Modules*
  DRAM = *dramatists;* *MST* = *most-studied*
  authors; *MULT* = *multicultural authors;* *NOV* =
  novelists; *POET* = *poets;* *POP* = *popular/genre*
  writers; *DC* = *Drama Criticism*
HLC = *Hispanic Literature Criticism*
LC = *Literature Criticism from 1400 to 1800*
NCLC = *Nineteenth-Century Literature Criticism*
PC = *Poetry Criticism*
SSC = *Short Story Criticism*
TCLC = *Twentieth-Century Literary Criticism*
WLC = *World Literature Criticism, 1500 to the Present*
WLCS = *World Literature Criticism Supplement*

The cross-references

```
See also CA 89-92; DLB 72; MTCW
```

list all author entries in the following Gale biographical and literary sources:

AAYA = *Authors & Artists for Young Adults*
AITN = *Authors in the News*
BEST = *Bestsellers*
BW = *Black Writers*
CA = *Contemporary Authors*
CAAS = *Contemporary Authors Autobiography Series*
CABS = *Contemporary Authors Bibliographical Series*
CANR = *Contemporary Authors New Revision Series*
CAP = *Contemporary Authors Permanent Series*
CDALB = *Concise Dictionary of American Literary Biography*
CDBLB = *Concise Dictionary of British Literary Biography*

DLB = *Dictionary of Literary Biography*
DLBD = *Dictionary of Literary Biography Documentary Series*
DLBY = *Dictionary of Literary Biography Yearbook*
HW = *Hispanic Writers*
JRDA = *Junior DISCovering Authors*
MAICYA = *Major Authors and Illustrators for Children and Young Adults*
MTCW = *Major 20th-Century Writers*
NNAL = *Native North American Literature*
SAAS = *Something about the Author Autobiography Series*
SATA = *Something about the Author*
YABC = *Yesterday's Authors of Books for Children*

Literary Criticism Series
Cumulative Author Index

Bertrand, Aloysius 1807-1841 .... **NCLC 31**
Bertran de Born c. 1140-1215 .... **CMLC 5**
Besant, Annie (Wood) 1847-1933 ..... **TCLC 9**
    See also CA 105
Bessie, Alvah 1904-1985 .... **CLC 23**
    See also CA 5-8R; 116; CANR 2; DLB 26
Bethlen, T. D.
    See Silverberg, Robert
Beti, Mongo ... **CLC 27; BLC 1; DAM MULT**
    See also Biyidi, Alexandre
Betjeman, John 1906-1984 **CLC 2, 6, 10, 34,**
    43; DAB; DAM MST, POET
    See also CA 9-12R; 112; CANR 33, 56; CDBLB
    1945-1960; DLB 20; DLBY 84; MTCW
Bettelheim, Bruno 1903-1990 .... **CLC 79**
    See also CA 81-84; 131; CANR 23, 61; MTCW
Betti, Ugo 1892-1953 .... **TCLC 5**
    See also CA 104; 155
Betts, Doris (Waugh) 1932- ...... **CLC 3, 6, 28**
    See also CA 13-16R; CANR 9, 66; DLBY 82;
    INT CANR-9
Bevan, Alistair
    See Roberts, Keith (John Kingston)
Bey, Pilaff
    See Douglas, (George) Norman
Bialik, Chaim Nachman 1873-1934 **TCLC 25**
Bickerstaff, Isaac
    See Swift, Jonathan
Bidart, Frank 1939- .... **CLC 33**
    See also CA 140
Bienek, Horst 1930- .... **CLC 7, 11**
    See also CA 73-76; DLB 75
Bierce, Ambrose (Gwinett) 1842-1914(?)
    TCLC 1, 7, 44; DA; DAC; DAM MST; SSC
    9; WLC
    See also CA 104; 139; CDALB 1865-1917;
    DLB 11, 12, 23, 71, 74, 186
Biggers, Earl Derr 1884-1933 .... **TCLC 65**
    See also CA 108; 153
Billings, Josh
    See Shaw, Henry Wheeler
Billington, (Lady) Rachel (Mary) 1942- **C L C**
    43
    See also AITN 2; CA 33-36R; CANR 44
Binyon, T(imothy) J(ohn) 1936- ...... **CLC 34**
    See also CA 111; CANR 28
Bioy Casares, Adolfo 1914-1984 **CLC 4, 8, 13,**
    88; DAM MULT; HLC; SSC 17
    See also CA 29-32R; CANR 19, 43, 66; DLB
    113; HW; MTCW
Bird, Cordwainer
    See Ellison, Harlan (Jay)
Bird, Robert Montgomery 1806-1854 **NCLC 1**
Birney, (Alfred) Earle 1904-1995 **CLC 1, 4, 6,**
    11; DAC; DAM MST, POET
    See also CA 1-4R; CANR 5, 20; DLB 88;
    MTCW
Bishop, Elizabeth 1911-1979 **CLC 1, 4, 9, 13,**
    15, 32; DA; DAC; DAM MST, POET; PC
    3
    See also CA 5-8R; 89-92; CABS 2; CANR 26,
    61; CDALB 1968-1988; DLB 5, 169;
    MTCW; SATA-Obit 24
Bishop, John 1935- .... **CLC 10**
    See also CA 105
Bissett, Bill 1939- .... **CLC 18; PC 14**
    See also CA 69-72; CAAS 19; CANR 15; DLB
    53; MTCW
Bitov, Andrei (Georgievich) 1937- ... **CLC 57**
    See also CA 142
Biyidi, Alexandre 1932-
    See Beti, Mongo
    See also BW 1; CA 114; 124; MTCW

Bjarme, Brynjolf
    See Ibsen, Henrik (Johan)
Bjornson, Bjornstjerne (Martinius) 1832-1910
    TCLC 7, 37
    See also CA 104
Black, Robert
    See Holdstock, Robert P.
Blackburn, Paul 1926-1971 .... **CLC 9, 43**
    See also CA 81-84; 33-36R; CANR 34; DLB
    16; DLBY 81
Black Elk 1863-1950 **TCLC 33; DAM MULT**
    See also CA 144; NNAL
Black Hobart
    See Sanders, (James) Ed(ward)
Blacklin, Malcolm
    See Chambers, Aidan
Blackmore, R(ichard) D(oddridge) 1825-1900
    TCLC 27
    See also CA 120; DLB 18
Blackmur, R(ichard) P(almer) 1904-1965
    CLC 2, 24
    See also CA 11-12; 25-28R; CAP 1; DLB 63
Black Tarantula
    See Acker, Kathy
Blackwood, Algernon (Henry) 1869-1951
    TCLC 5
    See also CA 105; 150; DLB 153, 156, 178
Blackwood, Caroline 1931-1996 **CLC 6, 9, 100**
    See also CA 85-88; 151; CANR 32, 61, 65; DLB
    14; MTCW
Blade, Alexander
    See Hamilton, Edmond; Silverberg, Robert
Blaga, Lucian 1895-1961 .... **CLC 75**
Blair, Eric (Arthur) 1903-1950
    See Orwell, George
    See also CA 104; 132; DA; DAB; DAC; DAM
    MST, NOV; MTCW; SATA 29
Blais, Marie-Claire 1939- **CLC 2, 4, 6, 13, 22;**
    DAC; DAM MST
    See also CA 21-24R; CAAS 4; CANR 38; DLB
    53; MTCW
Blaise, Clark 1940- .... **CLC 29**
    See also AITN 2; CA 53-56; CAAS 3; CANR
    5, 66; DLB 53
Blake, Fairley
    See De Voto, Bernard (Augustine)
Blake, Nicholas
    See Day Lewis, C(ecil)
    See also DLB 77
Blake, William 1757-1827. **NCLC 13, 37, 57;**
    DA; DAB; DAC; DAM MST, POET; PC
    12; WLC
    See also CDBLB 1789-1832; DLB 93, 163;
    MAICYA; SATA 30
Blasco Ibanez, Vicente 1867-1928 **TCLC 12;**
    DAM NOV
    See also CA 110; 131; HW; MTCW
Blatty, William Peter 1928- **CLC 2; DAM POP**
    See also CA 5-8R; CANR 9
Bleeck, Oliver
    See Thomas, Ross (Elmore)
Blessing, Lee 1949- .... **CLC 54**
Blish, James (Benjamin) 1921-1975 . **CLC 14**
    See also CA 1-4R; 57-60; CANR 3; DLB 8;
    MTCW; SATA 66
Bliss, Reginald
    See Wells, H(erbert) G(eorge)
Blixen, Karen (Christentze Dinesen) 1885-1962
    See Dinesen, Isak
    See also CA 25-28; CANR 22, 50; CAP 2;
    MTCW; SATA 44
Bloch, Robert (Albert) 1917-1994 .... **CLC 33**
    See also CA 5-8R; 146; CAAS 20; CANR 5;

DLB 44; INT CANR-5; SATA 12; SATA-Obit
82
Blok, Alexander (Alexandrovich) 1880-1921
    TCLC 5; PC 21
    See also CA 104
Blom, Jan
    See Breytenbach, Breyten
Bloom, Harold 1930- .... **CLC 24, 103**
    See also CA 13-16R; CANR 39; DLB 67
Bloomfield, Aurelius
    See Bourne, Randolph S(illiman)
Blount, Roy (Alton), Jr. 1941- .... **CLC 38**
    See also CA 53-56; CANR 10, 28, 61; INT
    CANR-28; MTCW
Bloy, Leon 1846-1917 .... **TCLC 22**
    See also CA 121; DLB 123
Blume, Judy (Sussman) 1938- ... **CLC 12, 30;**
    DAM NOV, POP
    See also AAYA 3; CA 29-32R; CANR 13, 37,
    66; CLR 2, 15; DLB 52; JRDA; MAICYA;
    MTCW; SATA 2, 31, 79
Blunden, Edmund (Charles) 1896-1974 **C L C**
    2, 56
    See also CA 17-18; 45-48; CANR 54; CAP 2;
    DLB 20, 100, 155; MTCW
Bly, Robert (Elwood) 1926- **CLC 1, 2, 5, 10, 15,**
    38; DAM POET
    See also CA 5-8R; CANR 41; DLB 5; MTCW
Boas, Franz 1858-1942 .... **TCLC 56**
    See also CA 115
Bobette
    See Simenon, Georges (Jacques Christian)
Boccaccio, Giovanni 1313-1375 .. **CMLC 13;**
    SSC 10
Bochco, Steven 1943- .... **CLC 35**
    See also AAYA 11; CA 124; 138
Bodenheim, Maxwell 1892-1954 .... **TCLC 44**
    See also CA 110; DLB 9, 45
Bodker, Cecil 1927- .... **CLC 21**
    See also CA 73-76; CANR 13, 44; CLR 23;
    MAICYA; SATA 14
Boell, Heinrich (Theodor) 1917-1985 **CLC 2,**
    3, 6, 9, 11, 15, 27, 32, 72; DA; DAB; DAC;
    DAM MST, NOV; SSC 23; WLC
    See also CA 21-24R; 116; CANR 24; DLB 69;
    DLBY 85; MTCW
Boerne, Alfred
    See Doeblin, Alfred
Boethius 480(?)-524(?) .... **CMLC 15**
    See also DLB 115
Bogan, Louise 1897-1970 . **CLC 4, 39, 46, 93;**
    DAM POET; PC 12
    See also CA 73-76; 25-28R; CANR 33; DLB
    45, 169; MTCW
Bogarde, Dirk .... **CLC 19**
    See also Van Den Bogarde, Derek Jules Gaspard
    Ulric Niven
    See also DLB 14
Bogosian, Eric 1953- .... **CLC 45**
    See also CA 138
Bograd, Larry 1953- .... **CLC 35**
    See also CA 93-96; CANR 57; SAAS 21; SATA
    33, 89
Boiardo, Matteo Maria 1441-1494 .... **LC 6**
Boileau-Despreaux, Nicolas 1636-1711 **LC 3**
Bojer, Johan 1872-1959 .... **TCLC 64**
Boland, Eavan (Aisling) 1944- .. **CLC 40, 67;**
    DAM POET
    See also CA 143; CANR 61; DLB 40
Boll, Heinrich
    See Boell, Heinrich (Theodor)
Bolt, Lee
    See Faust, Frederick (Schiller)

Cotter, Joseph Seamon Sr. 1861-1949 **T C L C 28; BLC 1; DAM MULT**
See also BW 1; CA 124; DLB 50

Couch, Arthur Thomas Quiller
See Quiller-Couch, Sir Arthur (Thomas)

Coulton, James
See Hansen, Joseph

Couperus, Louis (Marie Anne) 1863-1923 **TCLC 15**
See also CA 115

Coupland, Douglas 1961- **CLC 85; DAC; DAM POP**
See also CA 142; CANR 57

Court, Wesli
See Turco, Lewis (Putnam)

Courtenay, Bryce 1933- .... **CLC 59**
See also CA 138

Courtney, Robert
See Ellison, Harlan (Jay)

Cousteau, Jacques-Yves 1910-1997 . **CLC 30**
See also CA 65-68; 159; CANR 15, 67; MTCW; SATA 38, 98

Cowan, Peter (Walkinshaw) 1914- .... **SSC 28**
See also CA 21-24R; CANR 9, 25, 50

Coward, Noel (Peirce) 1899-1973 **CLC 1, 9, 29, 51; DAM DRAM**
See also AITN 1; CA 17-18; 41-44R; CANR 35; CAP 2; CDBLB 1914-1945; DLB 10; MTCW

Cowley, Abraham 1618-1667 .... **LC 43**
See also DLB 131, 151

Cowley, Malcolm 1898-1989 .... **CLC 39**
See also CA 5-8R; 128; CANR 3, 55; DLB 4, 48; DLBY 81, 89; MTCW

Cowper, William 1731-1800 . **NCLC 8; DAM POET**
See also DLB 104, 109

Cox, William Trevor 1928- .... **CLC 9, 14, 71; DAM NOV**
See Trevor, William
See also CA 9-12R; CANR 4, 37, 55; DLB 14; INT CANR-37; MTCW

Coyne, P. J.
See Masters, Hilary

Cozzens, James Gould 1903-1978 **CLC 1, 4, 11, 92**
See also CA 9-12R; 81-84; CANR 19; CDALB 1941-1968; DLB 9; DLBD 2; DLBY 84, 97; MTCW

Crabbe, George 1754-1832 .... **NCLC 26**
See also DLB 93

Craddock, Charles Egbert
See Murfree, Mary Noailles

Craig, A. A.
See Anderson, Poul (William)

Craik, Dinah Maria (Mulock) 1826-1887 **NCLC 38**
See also DLB 35, 163; MAICYA; SATA 34

Cram, Ralph Adams 1863-1942 ..... **TCLC 45**
See also CA 160

Crane, (Harold) Hart 1899-1932 **TCLC 2, 5, 80; DA; DAB; DAC; DAM MST, POET; PC 3; WLC**
See also CA 104; 127; CDALB 1917-1929; DLB 4, 48; MTCW

Crane, R(onald) S(almon) 1886-1967 **CLC 27**
See also CA 85-88; DLB 63

Crane, Stephen (Townley) 1871-1900 **T C L C 11, 17, 32; DA; DAB; DAC; DAM MST, NOV, POET; SSC 7; WLC**
See also AAYA 21; CA 109; 140; CDALB 1865-1917; DLB 12, 54, 78; YABC 2

Crase, Douglas 1944- .... **CLC 58**

See also CA 106

Crashaw, Richard 1612(?)-1649 .... **LC 24**
See also DLB 126

Craven, Margaret 1901-1980 . **CLC 17; DAC**
See also CA 103

Crawford, F(rancis) Marion 1854-1909 **TCLC 10**
See also CA 107; DLB 71

Crawford, Isabella Valancy 1850-1887 **NCLC 12**
See also DLB 92

Crayon, Geoffrey
See Irving, Washington

Creasey, John 1908-1973 .... **CLC 11**
See also CA 5-8R; 41-44R; CANR 8, 59; DLB 77; MTCW

Crebillon, Claude Prosper Jolyot de (fils) 1707-1777 .... **LC 28**

Credo
See Creasey, John

Credo, Alvaro J. de
See Prado (Calvo), Pedro

Creeley, Robert (White) 1926- **CLC 1, 2, 4, 8, 11, 15, 36, 78; DAM POET**
See also CA 1-4R; CAAS 10; CANR 23, 43; DLB 5, 16, 169; MTCW

Crews, Harry (Eugene) 1935- **CLC 6, 23, 49**
See also AITN 1; CA 25-28R; CANR 20, 57; DLB 6, 143, 185; MTCW

Crichton, (John) Michael 1942- **CLC 2, 6, 54, 90; DAM NOV, POP**
See also AAYA 10; AITN 2; CA 25-28R; CANR 13, 40, 54; DLBY 81; INT CANR-13; JRDA; MTCW; SATA 9, 88

Crispin, Edmund .... **CLC 22**
See also Montgomery, (Robert) Bruce
See also DLB 87

Cristofer, Michael 1945(?)- .... **CLC 28; DAM DRAM**
See also CA 110; 152; DLB 7

Croce, Benedetto 1866-1952 .... **TCLC 37**
See also CA 120; 155

Crockett, David 1786-1836 .... **NCLC 8**
See also DLB 3, 11

Crockett, Davy
See Crockett, David

Crofts, Freeman Wills 1879-1957 .. **TCLC 55**
See also CA 115; DLB 77

Croker, John Wilson 1780-1857 ..... **NCLC 10**
See also DLB 110

Crommelynck, Fernand 1885-1970 .. **CLC 75**
See also CA 89-92

Cromwell, Oliver 1599-1658 .... **LC 43**

Cronin, A(rchibald) J(oseph) 1896-1981 **C L C 32**
See also CA 1-4R; 102; CANR 5; DLB 191; SATA 47; SATA-Obit 25

Cross, Amanda
See Heilbrun, Carolyn G(old)

Crothers, Rachel 1878(?)-1958 ...... **TCLC 19**
See also CA 113; DLB 7

Croves, Hal
See Traven, B.

Crow Dog, Mary (Ellen) (?)- .... **CLC 93**
See also Brave Bird, Mary
See also CA 154

Crowfield, Christopher
See Stowe, Harriet (Elizabeth) Beecher

Crowley, Aleister .... **TCLC 7**
See also Crowley, Edward Alexander

Crowley, Edward Alexander 1875-1947
See Crowley, Aleister
See also CA 104

Crowley, John 1942- .... **CLC 57**
See also CA 61-64; CANR 43; DLBY 82; SATA 65

Crud
See Crumb, R(obert)

Crumarums
See Crumb, R(obert)

Crumb, R(obert) 1943- .... **CLC 17**
See also CA 106

Crumbum
See Crumb, R(obert)

Crumski
See Crumb, R(obert)

Crum the Bum
See Crumb, R(obert)

Crunk
See Crumb, R(obert)

Crustt
See Crumb, R(obert)

Cryer, Gretchen (Kiger) 1935- .... **CLC 21**
See also CA 114; 123

Csath, Geza 1887-1919 .... **TCLC 13**
See also CA 111

Cudlip, David 1933- .... **CLC 34**

Cullen, Countee 1903-1946 **TCLC 4, 37; BLC 1; DA; DAC; DAM MST, MULT, POET; PC 20; WLCS**
See also BW 1; CA 108; 124; CDALB 1917-1929; DLB 4, 48, 51; MTCW; SATA 18

Cum, R.
See Crumb, R(obert)

Cummings, Bruce F(rederick) 1889-1919
See Barbellion, W. N. P.
See also CA 123

Cummings, E(dward) E(stlin) 1894-1962 **CLC 1, 3, 8, 12, 15, 68; DA; DAB; DAC; DAM MST, POET; PC 5; WLC 2**
See also CA 73-76; CANR 31; CDALB 1929-1941; DLB 4, 48; MTCW

Cunha, Euclides (Rodrigues Pimenta) da 1866-1909 .... **TCLC 24**
See also CA 123

Cunningham, E. V.
See Fast, Howard (Melvin)

Cunningham, J(ames) V(incent) 1911-1985 **CLC 3, 31**
See also CA 1-4R; 115; CANR 1; DLB 5

Cunningham, Julia (Woolfolk) 1916- **CLC 12**
See also CA 9-12R; CANR 4, 19, 36; JRDA; MAICYA; SAAS 2; SATA 1, 26

Cunningham, Michael 1952- .... **CLC 34**
See also CA 136

Cunninghame Graham, R(obert) B(ontine) 1852-1936 .... **TCLC 19**
See also Graham, R(obert) B(ontine) Cunninghame
See also CA 119; DLB 98

Currie, Ellen 19(?)- .... **CLC 44**

Curtin, Philip
See Lowndes, Marie Adelaide (Belloc)

Curtis, Price
See Ellison, Harlan (Jay)

Cutrate, Joe
See Spiegelman, Art

Cynewulf c. 770-c. 840 .... **CMLC 23**

Czaczkes, Shmuel Yosef
See Agnon, S(hmuel) Y(osef Halevi)

Dabrowska, Maria (Szumska) 1889-1965 **CLC 15**
See also CA 106

Dabydeen, David 1955- .... **CLC 34**
See also BW 1; CA 125; CANR 56

Dacey, Philip 1939- .... **CLC 51**

See also CA 109

Deledda, Grazia (Cosima) 1875(?)-1936
TCLC 23
See also CA 123

Delibes, Miguel .... **CLC 8, 18**
See also Delibes Setien, Miguel

Delibes Setien, Miguel 1920-
See Delibes, Miguel
See also CA 45-48; CANR 1, 32; HW; MTCW

DeLillo, Don 1936- **CLC 8, 10, 13, 27, 39, 54,
76; DAM NOV, POP**
See also BEST 89:1; CA 81-84; CANR 21; DLB
6, 173; MTCW

de Lisser, H. G.
See De Lisser, H(erbert) G(eorge)
See also DLB 117

De Lisser, H(erbert) G(eorge) 1878-1944
TCLC 12
See also de Lisser, H. G.
See also BW 2; CA 109; 152

Deloney, Thomas 1560-1600 .... **LC 41**

Deloria, Vine (Victor), Jr. 1933- ..... **CLC 21;
DAM MULT**
See also CA 53-56; CANR 5, 20, 48; DLB 175;
MTCW; NNAL; SATA 21

Del Vecchio, John M(ichael) 1947- .. **CLC 29**
See also CA 110; DLBD 9

de Man, Paul (Adolph Michel) 1919-1983
CLC 55
See also CA 128; 111; CANR 61; DLB 67;
MTCW

De Marinis, Rick 1934- .... **CLC 54**
See also CA 57-60; CAAS 24; CANR 9, 25, 50

Dembry, R. Emmet
See Murfree, Mary Noailles

Demby, William 1922- **CLC 53; BLC 1; DAM
MULT**
See also BW 1; CA 81-84; DLB 33

de Menton, Francisco
See Chin, Frank (Chew, Jr.)

Demijohn, Thom
See Disch, Thomas M(ichael)

de Montherlant, Henry (Milon)
See Montherlant, Henry (Milon) de

Demosthenes 384B.C.-322B.C. ...... **CMLC 13**
See also DLB 176

de Natale, Francine
See Malzberg, Barry N(athaniel)

Denby, Edwin (Orr) 1903-1983 .... **CLC 48**
See also CA 138; 110

Denis, Julio
See Cortazar, Julio

Denmark, Harrison
See Zelazny, Roger (Joseph)

Dennis, John 1658-1734 .... **LC 11**
See also DLB 101

Dennis, Nigel (Forbes) 1912-1989 .... **CLC 8**
See also CA 25-28R; 129; DLB 13, 15; MTCW

Dent, Lester 1904(?)-1959 .... **TCLC 72**
See also CA 112; 161

De Palma, Brian (Russell) 1940- ...... **CLC 20**
See also CA 109

De Quincey, Thomas 1785-1859 .... **NCLC 4**
See also CDBLB 1789-1832; DLB 110; 144

Deren, Eleanora 1908(?)-1961
See Deren, Maya
See also CA 111

Deren, Maya 1917-1961 .... **CLC 16, 102**
See also Deren, Eleanora

Derleth, August (William) 1909-1971 **CLC 31**
See also CA 1-4R; 29-32R; CANR 4; DLB 9;
SATA 5

Der Nister 1884-1950 .... **TCLC 56**

de Routisie, Albert
See Aragon, Louis

Derrida, Jacques 1930- .... **CLC 24, 87**
See also CA 124; 127

Derry Down Derry
See Lear, Edward

Dersonnes, Jacques
See Simenon, Georges (Jacques Christian)

Desai, Anita 1937- **CLC 19, 37, 97; DAB; DAM
NOV**
See also CA 81-84; CANR 33, 53; MTCW;
SATA 63

de Saint-Luc, Jean
See Glassco, John

de Saint Roman, Arnaud
See Aragon, Louis

Descartes, Rene 1596-1650 .... **LC 20, 35**

De Sica, Vittorio 1901(?)-1974 .... **CLC 20**
See also CA 117

Desnos, Robert 1900-1945 .... **TCLC 22**
See also CA 121; 151

Destouches, Louis-Ferdinand 1894-1961 **C L C
9, 15**
See also Celine, Louis-Ferdinand
See also CA 85-88; CANR 28; MTCW

de Tolignac, Gaston
See Griffith, D(avid Lewelyn) W(ark)

Deutsch, Babette 1895-1982 .... **CLC 18**
See also CA 1-4R; 108; CANR 4; DLB 45;
SATA 1; SATA-Obit 33

Devenant, William 1606-1649 .... **LC 13**

Devkota, Laxmiprasad 1909-1959 . **TCLC 23**
See also CA 123

De Voto, Bernard (Augustine) 1897-1955
TCLC 29
See also CA 113; 160; DLB 9

De Vries, Peter 1910-1993 **CLC 1, 2, 3, 7, 10,
28, 46; DAM NOV**
See also CA 17-20R; 142; CANR 41; DLB 6;
DLBY 82; MTCW

Dexter, John
See Bradley, Marion Zimmer

Dexter, Martin
See Faust, Frederick (Schiller)

Dexter, Pete 1943- ... **CLC 34, 55; DAM POP**
See also BEST 89:2; CA 127; 131; INT 131;
MTCW

Diamano, Silmang
See Senghor, Leopold Sedar

Diamond, Neil 1941- .... **CLC 30**
See also CA 108

Diaz del Castillo, Bernal 1496-1584 ... **LC 31**

di Bassetto, Corno
See Shaw, George Bernard

Dick, Philip K(indred) 1928-1982 **CLC 10, 30,
72; DAM NOV, POP**
See also AAYA 24; CA 49-52; 106; CANR 2,
16; DLB 8; MTCW

Dickens, Charles (John Huffam) 1812-1870
**NCLC 3, 8, 18, 26, 37, 50; DA; DAB; DAC;
DAM MST, NOV; SSC 17; WLC**
See also AAYA 23; CDBLB 1832-1890; DLB
21, 55, 70, 159, 166; JRDA; MAICYA; SATA
15

Dickey, James (Lafayette) 1923-1997 **CLC 1,
2, 4, 7, 10, 15, 47, 109; DAM NOV, POET,
POP**
See also AITN 1, 2; CA 9-12R; 156; CABS 2;
CANR 10, 48, 61; CDALB 1968-1988; DLB
5, 193; DLBD 7; DLBY 82, 93, 96, 97; INT
CANR-10; MTCW

Dickey, William 1928-1994 .... **CLC 3, 28**
See also CA 9-12R; 145; CANR 24; DLB 5

Dickinson, Charles 1951- .... **CLC 49**
See also CA 128

Dickinson, Emily (Elizabeth) 1830-1886
**NCLC 21; DA; DAB; DAC; DAM MST,
POET; PC 1; WLC**
See also AAYA 22; CDALB 1865-1917; DLB
1; SATA 29

Dickinson, Peter (Malcolm) 1927- **CLC 12, 35**
See also AAYA 9; CA 41-44R; CANR 31, 58;
CLR 29; DLB 87, 161; JRDA; MAICYA;
SATA 5, 62, 95

Dickson, Carr
See Carr, John Dickson

Dickson, Carter
See Carr, John Dickson

Diderot, Denis 1713-1784 .... **LC 26**

Didion, Joan 1934- **CLC 1, 3, 8, 14, 32; DAM
NOV**
See also AITN 1; CA 5-8R; CANR 14, 52;
CDALB 1968-1988; DLB 2, 173, 185;
DLBY 81, 86; MTCW

Dietrich, Robert
See Hunt, E(verette) Howard, (Jr.)

Dillard, Annie 1945- . **CLC 9, 60; DAM NOV**
See also AAYA 6; CA 49-52; CANR 3, 43, 62;
DLBY 80; MTCW; SATA 10

Dillard, R(ichard) H(enry) W(ilde) 1937-
CLC 5
See also CA 21-24R; CAAS 7; CANR 10; DLB
5

Dillon, Eilis 1920-1994 .... **CLC 17**
See also CA 9-12R; 147; CAAS 3; CANR 4,
38; CLR 26; MAICYA; SATA 2, 74; SATA-
Obit 83

Dimont, Penelope
See Mortimer, Penelope (Ruth)

Dinesen, Isak .... **CLC 10, 29, 95; SSC 7**
See also Blixen, Karen (Christentze Dinesen)

Ding Ling .... **CLC 68**
See also Chiang Pin-chin

Disch, Thomas M(ichael) 1940- ... **CLC 7, 36**
See also AAYA 17; CA 21-24R; CAAS 4;
CANR 17, 36, 54; CLR 18; DLB 8;
MAICYA; MTCW; SAAS 15; SATA 92

Disch, Tom
See Disch, Thomas M(ichael)

d'Isly, Georges
See Simenon, Georges (Jacques Christian)

Disraeli, Benjamin 1804-1881 ....**NCLC 2, 39**
See also DLB 21, 55

Ditcum, Steve
See Crumb, R(obert)

Dixon, Paige
See Corcoran, Barbara

Dixon, Stephen 1936- .... **CLC 52; SSC 16**
See also CA 89-92; CANR 17, 40, 54; DLB 130

Doak, Annie
See Dillard, Annie

Dobell, Sydney Thompson 1824-1874 **N C L C
43**
See also DLB 32

Doblin, Alfred .... **TCLC 13**
See also Doeblin, Alfred

Dobrolyubov, Nikolai Alexandrovich 1836-1861
NCLC 5

Dobson, Austin 1840-1921 .... **TCLC 79**
See also DLB 35; 144

Dobyns, Stephen 1941- .... **CLC 37**
See also CA 45-48; CANR 2, 18

Doctorow, E(dgar) L(aurence) 1931- **CLC 6,
11, 15, 18, 37, 44, 65; DAM NOV, POP**
See also AAYA 22; AITN 2; BEST 89:3; CA
45-48; CANR 2, 33, 51; CDALB 1968-1988;

DRAM, NOV
See also CA 5-8R; CANR 30, 69; DLB 13, 14, 194; MTCW

Fraze, Candida (Merrill) 1945- .... **CLC 50**
See also CA 126

Frazer, J(ames) G(eorge) 1854-1941**TCLC 32**
See also CA 118

Frazer, Robert Caine
See Creasey, John

Frazer, Sir James George
See Frazer, J(ames) G(eorge)

Frazier, Charles 1950- .... **CLC 109**
See also CA 161

Frazier, Ian 1951- .... **CLC 46**
See also CA 130; CANR 54

Frederic, Harold 1856-1898 .... **NCLC 10**
See also DLB 12, 23; DLBD 13

Frederick, John
See Faust, Frederick (Schiller)

Frederick the Great 1712-1786 .... **LC 14**

Fredro, Aleksander 1793-1876 .... **NCLC 8**

Freeling, Nicolas 1927- .... **CLC 38**
See also CA 49-52; CAAS 12; CANR 1, 17, 50; DLB 87

Freeman, Douglas Southall 1886-1953**T C L C 11**
See also CA 109; DLB 17

Freeman, Judith 1946- .... **CLC 55**
See also CA 148

Freeman, Mary Eleanor Wilkins 1852-1930 **TCLC 9; SSC 1**
See also CA 106; DLB 12, 78

Freeman, R(ichard) Austin 1862-1943 **T C L C 21**
See also CA 113; DLB 70

French, Albert 1943- .... **CLC 86**

French, Marilyn 1929-**CLC 10, 18, 60; DAM DRAM, NOV, POP**
See also CA 69-72; CANR 3, 31; INT CANR-31; MTCW

French, Paul
See Asimov, Isaac

Freneau, Philip Morin 1752-1832 .... **NCLC 1**
See also DLB 37, 43

Freud, Sigmund 1856-1939 .... **TCLC 52**
See also CA 115; 133; CANR 69; MTCW

Friedan, Betty (Naomi) 1921- .... **CLC 74**
See also CA 65-68; CANR 18, 45; MTCW

Friedlander, Saul 1932- .... **CLC 90**
See also CA 117; 130

Friedman, B(ernard) H(arper) 1926- . **CLC 7**
See also CA 1-4R; CANR 3, 48

Friedman, Bruce Jay 1930- ...... **CLC 3, 5, 56**
See also CA 9-12R; CANR 25, 52; DLB 2, 28; INT CANR-25

Friel, Brian 1929- .... **CLC 5, 42, 59; DC 8**
See also CA 21-24R; CANR 33, 69; DLB 13; MTCW

Friis-Baastad, Babbis Ellinor 1921-1970**C L C 12**
See also CA 17-20R; 134; SATA 7

Frisch, Max (Rudolf) 1911-1991**CLC 3, 9, 14, 18, 32, 44; DAM DRAM, NOV**
See also CA 85-88; 134; CANR 32; DLB 69, 124; MTCW

Fromentin, Eugene (Samuel Auguste) 1820-1876 .... **NCLC 10**
See also DLB 123

Frost, Frederick
See Faust, Frederick (Schiller)

Frost, Robert (Lee) 1874-1963**CLC 1, 3, 4, 9, 10, 13, 15, 26, 34, 44; DA; DAB; DAC; DAM MST, POET; PC 1; WLC**

See also AAYA 21; CA 89-92; CANR 33; CDALB 1917-1929; DLB 54; DLBD 7; MTCW; SATA 14

Froude, James Anthony 1818-1894**NCLC 43**
See also DLB 18, 57, 144

Froy, Herald
See Waterhouse, Keith (Spencer)

Fry, Christopher 1907- **CLC 2, 10, 14; DAM DRAM**
See also CA 17-20R; CAAS 23; CANR 9, 30; DLB 13; MTCW; SATA 66

Frye, (Herman) Northrop 1912-1991**CLC 24, 70**
See also CA 5-8R; 133; CANR 8, 37; DLB 67, 68; MTCW

Fuchs, Daniel 1909-1993 .... **CLC 8, 22**
See also CA 81-84; 142; CAAS 5; CANR 40; DLB 9, 26, 28; DLBY 93

Fuchs, Daniel 1934- .... **CLC 34**
See also CA 37-40R; CANR 14, 48

Fuentes, Carlos 1928-**CLC 3, 8, 10, 13, 22, 41, 60; DA; DAB; DAC; DAM MST, MULT, NOV; HLC; SSC 24; WLC**
See also AAYA 4; AITN 2; CA 69-72; CANR 10, 32, 68; DLB 113; HW; MTCW

Fuentes, Gregorio Lopez y
See Lopez y Fuentes, Gregorio

Fugard, (Harold) Athol 1932-**CLC 5, 9, 14, 25, 40, 80; DAM DRAM; DC 3**
See also AAYA 17; CA 85-88; CANR 32, 54; MTCW

Fugard, Sheila 1932- .... **CLC 48**
See also CA 125

Fuller, Charles (H., Jr.) 1939-**CLC 25; BLC 2; DAM DRAM, MULT; DC 1**
See also BW 2; CA 108; 112; DLB 38; INT 112; MTCW

Fuller, John (Leopold) 1937- .... **CLC 62**
See also CA 21-24R; CANR 9, 44; DLB 40

Fuller, Margaret .... **NCLC 5, 50**
See also Ossoli, Sarah Margaret (Fuller marchesa d')

Fuller, Roy (Broadbent) 1912-1991**CLC 4, 28**
See also CA 5-8R; 135; CAAS 10; CANR 53; DLB 15, 20; SATA 87

Fulton, Alice 1952- .... **CLC 52**
See also CA 116; CANR 57; DLB 193

Furphy, Joseph 1843-1912 .... **TCLC 25**
See also CA 163

Fussell, Paul 1924- .... **CLC 74**
See also BEST 90:1; CA 17-20R; CANR 8, 21, 35, 69; INT CANR-21; MTCW

Futabatei, Shimei 1864-1909 .... **TCLC 44**
See also CA 162; DLB 180

Futrelle, Jacques 1875-1912 .... **TCLC 19**
See also CA 113; 155

Gaboriau, Emile 1835-1873 .... **NCLC 14**

Gadda, Carlo Emilio 1893-1973 .... **CLC 11**
See also CA 89-92; DLB 177

Gaddis, William 1922- **CLC 1, 3, 6, 8, 10, 19, 43, 86**
See also CA 17-20R; CANR 21, 48; DLB 2; MTCW

Gage, Walter
See Inge, William (Motter)

Gaines, Ernest J(ames) 1933- **CLC 3, 11, 18, 86; BLC 2; DAM MULT**
See also AAYA 18; AITN 1; BW 2; CA 9-12R; CANR 6, 24, 42; CDALB 1968-1988; DLB 2, 33, 152; DLBY 80; MTCW; SATA 86

Gaitskill, Mary 1954- .... **CLC 69**
See also CA 128; CANR 61

Galdos, Benito Perez
See Perez Galdos, Benito

Gale, Zona 1874-1938**TCLC 7; DAM DRAM**
See also CA 105; 153; DLB 9, 78

Galeano, Eduardo (Hughes) 1940- ... **CLC 72**
See also CA 29-32R; CANR 13, 32; HW

Galiano, Juan Valera y Alcala
See Valera y Alcala-Galiano, Juan

Gallagher, Tess 1943- ...... **CLC 18, 63; DAM POET; PC 9**
See also CA 106; DLB 120

Gallant, Mavis 1922- ... **CLC 7, 18, 38; DAC; DAM MST; SSC 5**
See also CA 69-72; CANR 29, 69; DLB 53; MTCW

Gallant, Roy A(rthur) 1924- .... **CLC 17**
See also CA 5-8R; CANR 4, 29, 54; CLR 30; MAICYA; SATA 4, 68

Gallico, Paul (William) 1897-1976 ..... **CLC 2**
See also AITN 1; CA 5-8R; 69-72; CANR 23; DLB 9, 171; MAICYA; SATA 13

Gallo, Max Louis 1932- .... **CLC 95**
See also CA 85-88

Gallois, Lucien
See Desnos, Robert

Gallup, Ralph
See Whitemore, Hugh (John)

Galsworthy, John 1867-1933**TCLC 1, 45; DA; DAB; DAC; DAM DRAM, MST, NOV; SSC 22; WLC 2**
See also CA 104; 141; CDBLB 1890-1914; DLB 10, 34, 98, 162; DLBD 16

Galt, John 1779-1839 .... **NCLC 1**
See also DLB 99, 116, 159

Galvin, James 1951- .... **CLC 38**
See also CA 108; CANR 26

Gamboa, Federico 1864-1939 .... **TCLC 36**

Gandhi, M. K.
See Gandhi, Mohandas Karamchand

Gandhi, Mahatma
See Gandhi, Mohandas Karamchand

Gandhi, Mohandas Karamchand 1869-1948 **TCLC 59; DAM MULT**
See also CA 121; 132; MTCW

Gann, Ernest Kellogg 1910-1991 ...... **CLC 23**
See also AITN 1; CA 1-4R; 136; CANR 1

Garcia, Cristina 1958- .... **CLC 76**
See also CA 141

Garcia Lorca, Federico 1898-1936**TCLC 1, 7, 49; DA; DAB; DAC; DAM DRAM, MST, MULT, POET; DC 2; HLC; PC 3; WLC**
See also CA 104; 131; DLB 108; HW; MTCW

Garcia Marquez, Gabriel (Jose) 1928-**CLC 2, 3, 8, 10, 15, 27, 47, 55, 68; DA; DAB; DAC; DAM MST, MULT, NOV, POP; HLC; SSC 8; WLC**
See also AAYA 3; BEST 89:1, 90:4; CA 33-36R; CANR 10, 28, 50; DLB 113; HW; MTCW

Gard, Janice
See Latham, Jean Lee

Gard, Roger Martin du
See Martin du Gard, Roger

Gardam, Jane 1928- .... **CLC 43**
See also CA 49-52; CANR 2, 18, 33, 54; CLR 12; DLB 14, 161; MAICYA; MTCW; SAAS 9; SATA 39, 76; SATA-Brief 28

Gardner, Herb(ert) 1934- .... **CLC 44**
See also CA 149

Gardner, John (Champlin), Jr. 1933-1982 **CLC 2, 3, 5, 7, 8, 10, 18, 28, 34; DAM NOV, POP; SSC 7**
See also AITN 1; CA 65-68; 107; CANR 33; DLB 2; DLBY 82; MTCW; SATA 40; SATA-

Obit 31

Gardner, John (Edmund) 1926-**CLC 30; DAM POP**
See also CA 103; CANR 15, 69; MTCW

Gardner, Miriam
See Bradley, Marion Zimmer

Gardner, Noel
See Kuttner, Henry

Gardons, S. S.
See Snodgrass, W(illiam) D(e Witt)

Garfield, Leon 1921-1996 .... **CLC 12**
See also AAYA 8; CA 17-20R; 152; CANR 38, 41; CLR 21; DLB 161; JRDA; MAICYA; SATA 1, 32, 76; SATA-Obit 90

Garland, (Hannibal) Hamlin 1860-1940
TCLC 3; SSC 18
See also CA 104; DLB 12, 71, 78, 186

Garneau, (Hector de) Saint-Denys 1912-1943
TCLC 13
See also CA 111; DLB 88

Garner, Alan 1934-**CLC 17; DAB; DAM POP**
See also AAYA 18; CA 73-76; CANR 15, 64; CLR 20; DLB 161; MAICYA; MTCW; SATA 18, 69

Garner, Hugh 1913-1979 .... **CLC 13**
See also CA 69-72; CANR 31; DLB 68

Garnett, David 1892-1981 ....**CLC 3**
See also CA 5-8R; 103; CANR 17; DLB 34

Garos, Stephanie
See Katz, Steve

Garrett, George (Palmer) 1929-**CLC 3, 11, 51; SSC 30**
See also CA 1-4R; CAAS 5; CANR 1, 42, 67; DLB 2, 5, 130, 152; DLBY 83

Garrick, David 1717-1779 ....**LC 15; DAM DRAM**
See also DLB 84

Garrigue, Jean 1914-1972 .... **CLC 2, 8**
See also CA 5-8R; 37-40R; CANR 20

Garrison, Frederick
See Sinclair, Upton (Beall)

Garth, Will
See Hamilton, Edmond; Kuttner, Henry

Garvey, Marcus (Moziah, Jr.) 1887-1940
TCLC 41; BLC 2; DAM MULT
See also BW 1; CA 120; 124

Gary, Romain .... **CLC 25**
See also Kacew, Romain
See also DLB 83

Gascar, Pierre .... **CLC 11**
See also Fournier, Pierre

Gascoyne, David (Emery) 1916- ...... **CLC 45**
See also CA 65-68; CANR 10, 28, 54; DLB 20; MTCW

Gaskell, Elizabeth Cleghorn 1810-1865**NCLC 70; DAB; DAM MST; SSC 25**
See also CDBLB 1832-1890; DLB 21, 144, 159

Gass, William H(oward) 1924-**CLC 1, 2, 8, 11, 15, 39; SSC 12**
See also CA 17-20R; CANR 30; DLB 2; MTCW

Gasset, Jose Ortega y
See Ortega y Gasset, Jose

Gates, Henry Louis, Jr. 1950-**CLC 65; BLCS; DAM MULT**
See also BW 2; CA 109; CANR 25, 53; DLB 67

Gautier, Theophile 1811-1872 .. **NCLC 1, 59; DAM POET; PC 18; SSC 20**
See also DLB 119

Gawsworth, John
See Bates, H(erbert) E(rnest)

Gay, Oliver
See Gogarty, Oliver St. John

Gaye, Marvin (Penze) 1939-1984 .....**CLC 26**
See also CA 112

Gebler, Carlo (Ernest) 1954- ....**CLC 39**
See also CA 119; 133

Gee, Maggie (Mary) 1948- ....**CLC 57**
See also CA 130

Gee, Maurice (Gough) 1931-............**CLC 29**
See also CA 97-100; CANR 67; SATA 46

Gelbart, Larry (Simon) 1923-.... **CLC 21, 61**
See also CA 73-76; CANR 45

Gelber, Jack 1932- .... **CLC 1, 6, 14, 79**
See also CA 1-4R; CANR 2; DLB 7

Gellhorn, Martha (Ellis) 1908-1998 **CLC 14, 60**
See also CA 77-80; 164; CANR 44; DLBY 82

Genet, Jean 1910-1986**CLC 1, 2, 5, 10, 14, 44, 46; DAM DRAM**
See also CA 13-16R; CANR 18; DLB 72; DLBY 86; MTCW

Gent, Peter 1942-...............................**CLC 29**
See also AITN 1; CA 89-92; DLBY 82

Gentlewoman in New England, A
See Bradstreet, Anne

Gentlewoman in Those Parts, A
See Bradstreet, Anne

George, Jean Craighead 1919- ....**CLC 35**
See also AAYA 8; CA 5-8R; CANR 25; CLR 1; DLB 52; JRDA; MAICYA; SATA 2, 68

George, Stefan (Anton) 1868-1933**TCLC 2, 14**
See also CA 104

Georges, Georges Martin
See Simenon, Georges (Jacques Christian)

Gerhardi, William Alexander
See Gerhardie, William Alexander

Gerhardie, William Alexander 1895-1977
CLC 5
See also CA 25-28R; 73-76; CANR 18; DLB 36

Gerstler, Amy 1956- ....**CLC 70**
See also CA 146

Gertler, T. ....**CLC 34**
See also CA 116; 121; INT 121

Ghalib ....**NCLC 39**
See also Ghalib, Hsadullah Khan

Ghalib, Hsadullah Khan 1797-1869
See Ghalib
See also DAM POET

Ghelderode, Michel de 1898-1962**CLC 6, 11; DAM DRAM**
See also CA 85-88; CANR 40

Ghiselin, Brewster 1903- ....**CLC 23**
See also CA 13-16R; CAAS 10; CANR 13

Ghose, Zulfikar 1935- ....**CLC 42**
See also CA 65-68; CANR 67

Ghosh, Amitav 1956-........................**CLC 44**
See also CA 147

Giacosa, Giuseppe 1847-1906 ....**TCLC 7**
See also CA 104

Gibb, Lee
See Waterhouse, Keith (Spencer)

Gibbon, Lewis Grassic ....**TCLC 4**
See also Mitchell, James Leslie

Gibbons, Kaye 1960-**CLC 50, 88; DAM POP**
See also CA 151

Gibran, Kahlil 1883-1931 . **TCLC 1, 9; DAM POET, POP; PC 9**
See also CA 104; 150

Gibran, Khalil
See Gibran, Kahlil

Gibson, William 1914- .. **CLC 23; DA; DAB; DAC; DAM DRAM, MST**
See also CA 9-12R; CANR 9, 42; DLB 7; SATA 66

Gibson, William (Ford) 1948- ... **CLC 39, 63; DAM POP**
See also AAYA 12; CA 126; 133; CANR 52

Gide, Andre (Paul Guillaume) 1869-1951
TCLC 5, 12, 36; DA; DAB; DAC; DAM MST, NOV; SSC 13; WLC
See also CA 104; 124; DLB 65; MTCW

Gifford, Barry (Colby) 1946- .... **CLC 34**
See also CA 65-68; CANR 9, 30, 40

Gilbert, Frank
See De Voto, Bernard (Augustine)

Gilbert, W(illiam) S(chwenck) 1836-1911
TCLC 3; DAM DRAM, POET
See also CA 104; SATA 36

Gilbreth, Frank B., Jr. 1911- .... **CLC 17**
See also CA 9-12R; SATA 2

Gilchrist, Ellen 1935-**CLC 34, 48; DAM POP; SSC 14**
See also CA 113; 116; CANR 41, 61; DLB 130; MTCW

Giles, Molly 1942- .... **CLC 39**
See also CA 126

Gill, Patrick
See Creasey, John

Gilliam, Terry (Vance) 1940- .... **CLC 21**
See also Monty Python
See also AAYA 19; CA 108; 113; CANR 35; INT 113

Gillian, Jerry
See Gilliam, Terry (Vance)

Gilliatt, Penelope (Ann Douglass) 1932-1993
CLC 2, 10, 13, 53
See also AITN 2; CA 13-16R; 141; CANR 49; DLB 14

Gilman, Charlotte (Anna) Perkins (Stetson) 1860-1935 .... **TCLC 9, 37; SSC 13**
See also CA 106; 150

Gilmour, David 1949- .... **CLC 35**
See also CA 138, 147

Gilpin, William 1724-1804 .... **NCLC 30**

Gilray, J. D.
See Mencken, H(enry) L(ouis)

Gilroy, Frank D(aniel) 1925-...............**CLC 2**
See also CA 81-84; CANR 32, 64; DLB 7

Gilstrap, John 1957(?)- .... **CLC 99**
See also CA 160

Ginsberg, Allen 1926-1997**CLC 1, 2, 3, 4, 6, 13, 36, 69, 109; DA; DAB; DAC; DAM MST, POET; PC 4; WLC 3**
See also AITN 1; CA 1-4R; 157; CANR 2, 41, 63; CDALB 1941-1968; DLB 5, 16, 169; MTCW

Ginzburg, Natalia 1916-1991**CLC 5, 11, 54, 70**
See also CA 85-88; 135; CANR 33; DLB 177; MTCW

Giono, Jean 1895-1970 .... **CLC 4, 11**
See also CA 45-48; 29-32R; CANR 2, 35; DLB 72; MTCW

Giovanni, Nikki 1943-**CLC 2, 4, 19, 64; BLC 2; DA; DAB; DAC; DAM MST, MULT, POET; PC 19; WLCS**
See also AAYA 22; AITN 1; BW 2; CA 29-32R; CAAS 6; CANR 18, 41, 60; CLR 6; DLB 5, 41; INT CANR-18; MAICYA; MTCW; SATA 24

Giovene, Andrea 1904- ....**CLC 7**
See also CA 85-88

Gippius, Zinaida (Nikolayevna) 1869-1945
See Hippius, Zinaida
See also CA 106

Giraudoux, (Hippolyte) Jean 1882-1944
TCLC 2, 7; DAM DRAM
See also CA 104; DLB 65

Gironella, Jose Maria 1917- .... **CLC 11**
   See also CA 101
Gissing, George (Robert) 1857-1903**TCLC 3, 24, 47**
   See also CA 105; DLB 18, 135, 184
Giurlani, Aldo
   See Palazzeschi, Aldo
Gladkov, Fyodor (Vasilyevich) 1883-1958 **TCLC 27**
Glanville, Brian (Lester) 1931- .... **CLC 6**
   See also CA 5-8R; CAAS 9; CANR 3; DLB 15, 139; SATA 42
Glasgow, Ellen (Anderson Gholson) 1873-1945 **TCLC 2, 7**
   See also CA 104; 164; DLB 9, 12
Glaspell, Susan 1882(?)-1948 .... **TCLC 55**
   See also CA 110; 154; DLB 7, 9, 78; YABC 2
Glassco, John 1909-1981 .... **CLC 9**
   See also CA 13-16R; 102; CANR 15; DLB 68
Glasscock, Amnesia
   See Steinbeck, John (Ernst)
Glasser, Ronald J. 1940(?)- .... **CLC 37**
Glassman, Joyce
   See Johnson, Joyce
Glendinning, Victoria 1937- .... **CLC 50**
   See also CA 120; 127; CANR 59; DLB 155
Glissant, Edouard 1928- . **CLC 10, 68; DAM MULT**
   See also CA 153
Gloag, Julian 1930- .... **CLC 40**
   See also AITN 1; CA 65-68; CANR 10
Glowacki, Aleksander
   See Prus, Boleslaw
Gluck, Louise (Elisabeth) 1943-**CLC 7, 22, 44, 81; DAM POET; PC 16**
   See also CA 33-36R; CANR 40, 69; DLB 5
Glyn, Elinor 1864-1943 .... **TCLC 72**
   See also DLB 153
Gobineau, Joseph Arthur (Comte) de 1816-1882 .... **NCLC 17**
   See also DLB 123
Godard, Jean-Luc 1930- .... **CLC 20**
   See also CA 93-96
Godden, (Margaret) Rumer 1907-... **CLC 53**
   See also AAYA 6; CA 5-8R; CANR 4, 27, 36, 55; CLR 20; DLB 161; MAICYA; SAAS 12; SATA 3, 36
Godoy Alcayaga, Lucila 1889-1957
   See Mistral, Gabriela
   See also BW 2; CA 104; 131; DAM MULT; HW; MTCW
Godwin, Gail (Kathleen) 1937- **CLC 5, 8, 22, 31, 69; DAM POP**
   See also CA 29-32R; CANR 15, 43, 69; DLB 6; INT CANR-15; MTCW
Godwin, William 1756-1836 .... **NCLC 14**
   See also CDBLB 1789-1832; DLB 39, 104, 142, 158, 163
Goebbels, Josef
   See Goebbels, (Paul) Joseph
Goebbels, (Paul) Joseph 1897-1945 **TCLC 68**
   See also CA 115; 148
Goebbels, Joseph Paul
   See Goebbels, (Paul) Joseph
Goethe, Johann Wolfgang von 1749-1832 **NCLC 4, 22, 34; DA; DAB; DAC; DAM DRAM, MST, POET; PC 5; WLC 3**
   See also DLB 94
Gogarty, Oliver St. John 1878-1957**TCLC 15**
   See also CA 109; 150; DLB 15, 19
Gogol, Nikolai (Vasilyevich) 1809-1852**NCLC 5, 15, 31; DA; DAB; DAC; DAM DRAM, MST; DC 1; SSC 4, 29; WLC**

Goines, Donald 1937(?)-1974**CLC 80; BLC 2; DAM MULT, POP**
   See also AITN 1; BW 1; CA 124; 114; DLB 33
Gold, Herbert 1924- .... **CLC 4, 7, 14, 42**
   See also CA 9-12R; CANR 17, 45; DLB 2; DLBY 81
Goldbarth, Albert 1948- .... **CLC 5, 38**
   See also CA 53-56; CANR 6, 40; DLB 120
Goldberg, Anatol 1910-1982 .... **CLC 34**
   See also CA 131; 117
Goldemberg, Isaac 1945- .... **CLC 52**
   See also CA 69-72; CAAS 12; CANR 11, 32; HW
Golding, William (Gerald) 1911-1993**CLC 1, 2, 3, 8, 10, 17, 27, 58, 81; DA; DAB; DAC; DAM MST, NOV; WLC**
   See also AAYA 5; CA 5-8R; 141; CANR 13, 33, 54; CDBLB 1945-1960; DLB 15, 100; MTCW
Goldman, Emma 1869-1940 .... **TCLC 13**
   See also CA 110; 150
Goldman, Francisco 1954- .... **CLC 76**
   See also CA 162
Goldman, William (W.) 1931- ...... **CLC 1, 48**
   See also CA 9-12R; CANR 29, 69; DLB 44
Goldmann, Lucien 1913-1970 .... **CLC 24**
   See also CA 25-28; CAP 2
Goldoni, Carlo 1707-1793**LC 4; DAM DRAM**
Goldsberry, Steven 1949- .... **CLC 34**
   See also CA 131
Goldsmith, Oliver 1728-1774**LC 2; DA; DAB; DAC; DAM DRAM, MST, NOV, POET; DC 8; WLC**
   See also CDBLB 1660-1789; DLB 39, 89, 104, 109, 142; SATA 26
Goldsmith, Peter
   See Priestley, J(ohn) B(oynton)
Gombrowicz, Witold 1904-1969**CLC 4, 7, 11, 49; DAM DRAM**
   See also CA 19-20; 25-28R; CAP 2
Gomez de la Serna, Ramon 1888-1963**CLC 9**
   See also CA 153; 116; HW
Goncharov, Ivan Alexandrovich 1812-1891 **NCLC 1, 63**
Goncourt, Edmond (Louis Antoine Huot) de 1822-1896 .... **NCLC 7**
   See also DLB 123
Goncourt, Jules (Alfred Huot) de 1830-1870 **NCLC 7**
   See also DLB 123
Gontier, Fernande 19(?)- .... **CLC 50**
Gonzalez Martinez, Enrique 1871-1952 **TCLC 72**
   See also CA 166; HW
Goodman, Paul 1911-1972 ...... **CLC 1, 2, 4, 7**
   See also CA 19-20; 37-40R; CANR 34; CAP 2; DLB 130; MTCW
Gordimer, Nadine 1923-**CLC 3, 5, 7, 10, 18, 33, 51, 70; DA; DAB; DAC; DAM MST, NOV; SSC 17; WLCS**
   See also CA 5-8R; CANR 3, 28, 56; INT CANR-28; MTCW
Gordon, Adam Lindsay 1833-1870 **NCLC 21**
Gordon, Caroline 1895-1981**CLC 6, 13, 29, 83; SSC 15**
   See also CA 11-12; 103; CANR 36; CAP 1; DLB 4, 9, 102; DLBY 81; MTCW
Gordon, Charles William 1860-1937
   See Connor, Ralph
   See also CA 109
Gordon, Mary (Catherine) 1949-**CLC 13, 22**
   See also CA 102; CANR 44; DLB 6; DLBY 81; INT 102; MTCW

Gordon, N. J.
   See Bosman, Herman Charles
Gordon, Sol 1923- .... **CLC 26**
   See also CA 53-56; CANR 4; SATA 11
Gordone, Charles 1925-1995**CLC 1, 4; DAM DRAM; DC 8**
   See also BW 1; CA 93-96; 150; CANR 55; DLB 7; INT 93-96; MTCW
Gore, Catherine 1800-1861 .... **NCLC 65**
   See also DLB 116
Gorenko, Anna Andreevna
   See Akhmatova, Anna
Gorky, Maxim 1868-1936**TCLC 8; DAB; SSC 28; WLC**
   See also Peshkov, Alexei Maximovich
Goryan, Sirak
   See Saroyan, William
Gosse, Edmund (William) 1849-1928**TCLC 28**
   See also CA 117; DLB 57, 144, 184
Gotlieb, Phyllis Fay (Bloom) 1926- .. **CLC 18**
   See also CA 13-16R; CANR 7; DLB 88
Gottesman, S. D.
   See Kornbluth, C(yril) M.; Pohl, Frederik
Gottfried von Strassburg fl. c. 1210- . **CMLC 10**
   See also DLB 138
Gould, Lois .... **CLC 4, 10**
   See also CA 77-80; CANR 29; MTCW
Gourmont, Remy (-Marie-Charles) de 1858-1915 .... **TCLC 17**
   See also CA 109; 150
Govier, Katherine 1948- .... **CLC 51**
   See also CA 101; CANR 18, 40
Goyen, (Charles) William 1915-1983**CLC 5, 8, 14, 40**
   See also AITN 2; CA 5-8R; 110; CANR 6; DLB 2; DLBY 83; INT CANR-6
Goytisolo, Juan 1931- . **CLC 5, 10, 23; DAM MULT; HLC**
   See also CA 85-88; CANR 32, 61; HW; MTCW
Gozzano, Guido 1883-1916 .... **PC 10**
   See also CA 154; DLB 114
Gozzi, (Conte) Carlo 1720-1806 .... **NCLC 23**
Grabbe, Christian Dietrich 1801-1836**NCLC 2**
   See also DLB 133
Grace, Patricia 1937- .... **CLC 56**
Gracian y Morales, Baltasar 1601-1658**LC 15**
Gracq, Julien .... **CLC 11, 48**
   See also Poirier, Louis
   See also DLB 83
Grade, Chaim 1910-1982 .... **CLC 10**
   See also CA 93-96; 107
Graduate of Oxford, A
   See Ruskin, John
Grafton, Garth
   See Duncan, Sara Jeannette
Graham, John
   See Phillips, David Graham
Graham, Jorie 1951- .... **CLC 48**
   See also CA 111; CANR 63; DLB 120
Graham, R(obert) B(ontine) Cunninghame
   See Cunninghame Graham, R(obert) B(ontine)
   See also DLB 98, 135, 174
Graham, Robert
   See Haldeman, Joe (William)
Graham, Tom
   See Lewis, (Harry) Sinclair
Graham, W(illiam) S(ydney) 1918-1986**CLC 29**
   See also CA 73-76; 118; DLB 20
Graham, Winston (Mawdsley) 1910-**CLC 23**
   See also CA 49-52; CANR 2, 22, 45, 66; DLB

See also DLB 90
Heidegger, Martin 1889-1976 .... **CLC 24**
See also CA 81-84; 65-68; CANR 34; MTCW
Heidenstam, (Carl Gustaf) Verner von 1859-
1940 .... **TCLC 5**
See also CA 104
Heifner, Jack 1946- .... **CLC 11**
See also CA 105; CANR 47
Heijermans, Herman 1864-1924 .... **TCLC 24**
See also CA 123
Heilbrun, Carolyn G(old) 1926- ...... **CLC 25**
See also CA 45-48; CANR 1, 28, 58
Heine, Heinrich 1797-1856 .... **NCLC 4, 54**
See also DLB 90
Heinemann, Larry (Curtiss) 1944- .. **CLC 50**
See also CA 110; CAAS 21; CANR 31; DLBD
9; INT CANR-31
Heiney, Donald (William) 1921-1993
See Harris, MacDonald
See also CA 1-4R; 142; CANR 3, 58
Heinlein, Robert A(nson) 1907-1988**CLC 1, 3,
8, 14, 26, 55; DAM POP**
See also AAYA 17; CA 1-4R; 125; CANR 1,
20, 53; DLB 8; JRDA; MAICYA; MTCW;
SATA 9, 69; SATA-Obit 56
Helforth, John
See Doolittle, Hilda
Hellenhofferu, Vojtech Kapristian z
See Hasek, Jaroslav (Matej Frantisek)
Heller, Joseph 1923-**CLC 1, 3, 5, 8, 11, 36, 63;
DA; DAB; DAC; DAM MST, NOV, POP;
WLC**
See also AAYA 24; AITN 1; CA 5-8R; CABS
1; CANR 8, 42, 66; DLB 2, 28; DLBY 80;
INT CANR-8; MTCW
Hellman, Lillian (Florence) 1906-1984**CLC 2,
4, 8, 14, 18, 34, 44, 52; DAM DRAM; DC 1**
See also AITN 1, 2; CA 13-16R; 112; CANR
33; DLB 7; DLBY 84; MTCW
Helprin, Mark 1947-**CLC 7, 10, 22, 32; DAM
NOV, POP**
See also CA 81-84; CANR 47, 64; DLBY 85;
MTCW
Helvetius, Claude-Adrien 1715-1771 . **LC 26**
Helyar, Jane Penelope Josephine 1933-
See Poole, Josephine
See also CA 21-24R; CANR 10, 26; SATA 82
Hemans, Felicia 1793-1835 .... **NCLC 29**
See also DLB 96
Hemingway, Ernest (Miller) 1899-1961 **C L C
1, 3, 6, 8, 10, 13, 19, 30, 34, 39, 41, 44, 50,
61, 80; DA; DAB; DAC; DAM MST, NOV;
SSC 25; WLC**
See also AAYA 19; CA 77-80; CANR 34;
CDALB 1917-1929; DLB 4, 9, 102; DLBD
1, 15, 16; DLBY 81, 87, 96; MTCW
Hempel, Amy 1951- .... **CLC 39**
See also CA 118; 137
Henderson, F. C.
See Mencken, H(enry) L(ouis)
Henderson, Sylvia
See Ashton-Warner, Sylvia (Constance)
Henderson, Zenna (Chlarson) 1917-1983**S S C
29**
See also CA 1-4R; 133; CANR 1; DLB 8; SATA
5
Henley, Beth .... **CLC 23; DC 6**
See also Henley, Elizabeth Becker
See also CABS 3; DLBY 86
Henley, Elizabeth Becker 1952-
See Henley, Beth
See also CA 107; CANR 32; DAM DRAM,
MST; MTCW

Henley, William Ernest 1849-1903 .. **TCLC 8**
See also CA 105; DLB 19
Hennissart, Martha
See Lathen, Emma
See also CA 85-88; CANR 64
Henry, O. .... **TCLC 1, 19; SSC 5; WLC**
See also Porter, William Sydney
Henry, Patrick 1736-1799 .... **LC 25**
Henryson, Robert 1430(?)-1506(?) ..... **LC 20**
See also DLB 146
Henry VIII 1491-1547 .... **LC 10**
Henschke, Alfred
See Klabund
Hentoff, Nat(han Irving) 1925- .... **CLC 26**
See also AAYA 4; CA 1-4R; CAAS 6; CANR
5, 25; CLR 1; INT CANR-25; JRDA;
MAICYA; SATA 42, 69; SATA-Brief 27
Heppenstall, (John) Rayner 1911-1981 . **C L C
10**
See also CA 1-4R; 103; CANR 29
Heraclitus c. 540B.C.-c. 450B.C. .... **CMLC 22**
See also DLB 176
Herbert, Frank (Patrick) 1920-1986**CLC 12,
23, 35, 44, 85; DAM POP**
See also AAYA 21; CA 53-56; 118; CANR 5,
43; DLB 8; INT CANR-5; MTCW; SATA 9,
37; SATA-Obit 47
Herbert, George 1593-1633 ..... **LC 24; DAB;
DAM POET; PC 4**
See also CDBLB Before 1660; DLB 126
Herbert, Zbigniew 1924- ...**CLC 9, 43; DAM
POET**
See also CA 89-92; CANR 36; MTCW
Herbst, Josephine (Frey) 1897-1969 . **CLC 34**
See also CA 5-8R; 25-28R; DLB 9
Hergesheimer, Joseph 1880-1954 .. **TCLC 11**
See also CA 109; DLB 102, 9
Herlihy, James Leo 1927-1993 .... **CLC 6**
See also CA 1-4R; 143; CANR 2
Hermogenes fl. c. 175- .... **CMLC 6**
Hernandez, Jose 1834-1886 .... **NCLC 17**
Herodotus c. 484B.C.-429B.C. ...... **CMLC 17**
See also DLB 176
Herrick, Robert 1591-1674**LC 13; DA; DAB;
DAC; DAM MST, POP; PC 9**
See also DLB 126
Herring, Guilles
See Somerville, Edith
Herriot, James 1916-1995**CLC 12; DAM POP**
See also Wight, James Alfred
See also AAYA 1; CA 148; CANR 40; SATA
86
Herrmann, Dorothy 1941- .... **CLC 44**
See also CA 107
Herrmann, Taffy
See Herrmann, Dorothy
Hersey, John (Richard) 1914-1993**CLC 1, 2, 7,
9, 40, 81, 97; DAM POP**
See also CA 17-20R; 140; CANR 33; DLB 6,
185; MTCW; SATA 25; SATA-Obit 76
Herzen, Aleksandr Ivanovich 1812-1870
NCLC 10, 61
Herzl, Theodor 1860-1904 .... **TCLC 36**
Herzog, Werner 1942- .... **CLC 16**
See also CA 89-92
Hesiod c. 8th cent. B.C.- .... **CMLC 5**
See also DLB 176
Hesse, Hermann 1877-1962**CLC 1, 2, 3, 6, 11,
17, 25, 69; DA; DAB; DAC; DAM MST,
NOV; SSC 9; WLC**
See also CA 17-18; CAP 2; DLB 66; MTCW;
SATA 50
Hewes, Cady

See De Voto, Bernard (Augustine)
Heyen, William 1940- .... **CLC 13, 18**
See also CA 33-36R; CAAS 9; DLB 5
Heyerdahl, Thor 1914- .... **CLC 26**
See also CA 5-8R; CANR 5, 22, 66; MTCW;
SATA 2, 52
Heym, Georg (Theodor Franz Arthur) 1887-
1912 .... **TCLC 9**
See also CA 106
Heym, Stefan 1913- .... **CLC 41**
See also CA 9-12R; CANR 4; DLB 69
Heyse, Paul (Johann Ludwig von) 1830-1914
TCLC 8
See also CA 104; DLB 129
Heyward, (Edwin) DuBose 1885-1940 **T C L C
59**
See also CA 108; 157; DLB 7, 9, 45; SATA 21
Hibbert, Eleanor Alice Burford 1906-1993
CLC 7; DAM POP
See also BEST 90:4; CA 17-20R; 140; CANR
9, 28, 59; SATA 2; SATA-Obit 74
Hichens, Robert (Smythe) 1864-1950 . **T C L C
64**
See also CA 162; DLB 153
Higgins, George V(incent) 1939-**CLC 4, 7, 10,
18**
See also CA 77-80; CAAS 5; CANR 17, 51;
DLB 2; DLBY 81; INT CANR-17; MTCW
Higginson, Thomas Wentworth 1823-1911
TCLC 36
See also CA 162; DLB 1, 64
Highet, Helen
See MacInnes, Helen (Clark)
Highsmith, (Mary) Patricia 1921-1995**CLC 2,
4, 14, 42, 102; DAM NOV, POP**
See also CA 1-4R; 147; CANR 1, 20, 48, 62;
MTCW
Highwater, Jamake (Mamake) 1942(?)- **C L C
12**
See also AAYA 7; CA 65-68; CAAS 7; CANR
10, 34; CLR 17; DLB 52; DLBY 85; JRDA;
MAICYA; SATA 32, 69; SATA-Brief 30
Highway, Tomson 1951-**CLC 92; DAC; DAM
MULT**
See also CA 151; NNAL
Higuchi, Ichiyo 1872-1896 .... **NCLC 49**
Hijuelos, Oscar 1951- **CLC 65; DAM MULT,
POP; HLC**
See also AAYA 25; BEST 90:1; CA 123; CANR
50; DLB 145; HW
Hikmet, Nazim 1902(?)-1963 .... **CLC 40**
See also CA 141; 93-96
Hildegard von Bingen 1098-1179 . **CMLC 20**
See also DLB 148
Hildesheimer, Wolfgang 1916-1991 .. **CLC 49**
See also CA 101; 135; DLB 69, 124
Hill, Geoffrey (William) 1932- **CLC 5, 8, 18,
45; DAM POET**
See also CA 81-84; CANR 21; CDBLB 1960
to Present; DLB 40; MTCW
Hill, George Roy 1921- .... **CLC 26**
See also CA 110; 122
Hill, John
See Koontz, Dean R(ay)
Hill, Susan (Elizabeth) 1942- . **CLC 4; DAB;
DAM MST, NOV**
See also CA 33-36R; CANR 29, 69; DLB 14,
139; MTCW
Hillerman, Tony 1925- .. **CLC 62; DAM POP**
See also AAYA 6; BEST 89:1; CA 29-32R;
CANR 21, 42, 65; SATA 6
Hillesum, Etty 1914-1943 .... **TCLC 49**
See also CA 137

See McAuley, James Phillip
Mallowan, Agatha Christie
  See Christie, Agatha (Mary Clarissa)
Maloff, Saul 1922- .... **CLC 5**
  See also CA 33-36R
Malone, Louis
  See MacNeice, (Frederick) Louis
Malone, Michael (Christopher) 1942-**CLC 43**
  See also CA 77-80; CANR 14, 32, 57
Malory, (Sir) Thomas 1410(?)-1471(?)**LC 11;**
  DA; DAB; DAC; DAM MST; WLCS
  See also CDBLB Before 1660; DLB 146; SATA
  59; SATA-Brief 33
Malouf, (George Joseph) David 1934-**CLC 28,
  86**
  See also CA 124; CANR 50
Malraux, (Georges-)Andre 1901-1976**CLC 1,
  4, 9, 13, 15, 57; DAM NOV**
  See also CA 21-22; 69-72; CANR 34, 58; CAP
  2; DLB 72; MTCW
Malzberg, Barry N(athaniel) 1939- .... **CLC 7**
  See also CA 61-64; CAAS 4; CANR 16; DLB
  8
Mamet, David (Alan) 1947-**CLC 9, 15, 34, 46,
  91; DAM DRAM; DC 4**
  See also AAYA 3; CA 81-84; CABS 3; CANR
  15, 41, 67; DLB 7; MTCW
Mamoulian, Rouben (Zachary) 1897-1987
  CLC 16
  See also CA 25-28R; 124
Mandelstam, Osip (Emilievich) 1891(?)-1938(?)
  TCLC 2, 6; PC 14
  See also CA 104; 150
Mander, (Mary) Jane 1877-1949 ... **TCLC 31**
  See also CA 162
Mandeville, John fl. 1350- .... **CMLC 19**
  See also DLB 146
Mandiargues, Andre Pieyre de .... **CLC 41**
  See also Pieyre de Mandiargues, Andre
  See also DLB 83
Mandrake, Ethel Belle
  See Thurman, Wallace (Henry)
Mangan, James Clarence 1803-1849**NCLC 27**
Maniere, J.-E.
  See Giraudoux, (Hippolyte) Jean
Manley, (Mary) Delariviere 1672(?)-1724 **L C
  1**
  See also DLB 39, 80
Mann, Abel
  See Creasey, John
Mann, Emily 1952- .... **DC 7**
  See also CA 130; CANR 55
Mann, (Luiz) Heinrich 1871-1950 ... **TCLC 9**
  See also CA 106; 164; DLB 66
Mann, (Paul) Thomas 1875-1955 **TCLC 2, 8,
  14, 21, 35, 44, 60; DA; DAB; DAC; DAM
  MST, NOV; SSC 5; WLC**
  See also CA 104; 128; DLB 66; MTCW
Mannheim, Karl 1893-1947 .... **TCLC 65**
Manning, David
  See Faust, Frederick (Schiller)
Manning, Frederic 1887(?)-1935 ... **TCLC 25**
  See also CA 124
Manning, Olivia 1915-1980 .... **CLC 5, 19**
  See also CA 5-8R; 101; CANR 29; MTCW
Mano, D. Keith 1942- .... **CLC 2, 10**
  See also CA 25-28R; CAAS 6; CANR 26, 57;
  DLB 6
Mansfield, Katherine—**TCLC 2, 8, 39; DAB; SSC
  9, 23; WLC**
  See also Beauchamp, Kathleen Mansfield
  See also DLB 162
Manso, Peter 1940-........................... **CLC 39**

See also CA 29-32R; CANR 44
Mantecon, Juan Jimenez
  See Jimenez (Mantecon), Juan Ramon
Manton, Peter
  See Creasey, John
Man Without a Spleen, A
  See Chekhov, Anton (Pavlovich)
Manzoni, Alessandro 1785-1873 .... **NCLC 29**
Mapu, Abraham (ben Jekutiel) 1808-1867
  NCLC 18
Mara, Sally
  See Queneau, Raymond
Marat, Jean Paul 1743-1793 .... **LC 10**
Marcel, Gabriel Honore 1889-1973 ..**CLC 15**
  See also CA 102; 45-48; MTCW
Marchbanks, Samuel
  See Davies, (William) Robertson
Marchi, Giacomo
  See Bassani, Giorgio
Margulies, Donald .... **CLC 76**
Marie de France c. 12th cent. - **CMLC 8; PC
  22**
Marie de l'Incarnation 1599-1672 ...... **LC 10**
Marier, Captain Victor
  See Griffith, D(avid Lewelyn) W(ark)
Mariner, Scott
  See Pohl, Frederik
Marinetti, Filippo Tommaso 1876-1944**TCLC
  10**
  See also CA 107; DLB 114
Marivaux, Pierre Carlet de Chamblain de 1688-
  1763 .... **LC 4; DC 7**
Markandaya, Kamala .... **CLC 8, 38**
  See also Taylor, Kamala (Purnaiya)
Markfield, Wallace 1926- .... **CLC 8**
  See also CA 69-72; CAAS 3; DLB 2, 28
Markham, Edwin 1852-1940 .... **TCLC 47**
  See also CA 160; DLB 54, 186
Markham, Robert
  See Amis, Kingsley (William)
Marks, J
  See Highwater, Jamake (Mamake)
Marks-Highwater, J
  See Highwater, Jamake (Mamake)
Markson, David M(errill) 1927- .... **CLC 67**
  See also CA 49-52; CANR 1
Marley, Bob .... **CLC 17**
  See also Marley, Robert Nesta
Marley, Robert Nesta 1945-1981
  See Marley, Bob
  See also CA 107; 103
Marlowe, Christopher 1564-1593**LC 22; DA;
  DAB; DAC; DAM DRAM, MST; DC 1;
  WLC**
  See also CDBLB Before 1660; DLB 62
Marlowe, Stephen 1928-
  See Queen, Ellery
  See also CA 13-16R; CANR 6, 55
Marmontel, Jean-Francois 1723-1799 . **LC 2**
Marquand, John P(hillips) 1893-1960**CLC 2,
  10**
  See also CA 85-88; DLB 9, 102
Marques, Rene 1919-1979 ..... **CLC 96; DAM
  MULT; HLC**
  See also CA 97-100; 85-88; DLB 113; HW
Marquez, Gabriel (Jose) Garcia
  See Garcia Marquez, Gabriel (Jose)
Marquis, Don(ald Robert Perry) 1878-1937
  TCLC 7
  See also CA 104; 166; DLB 11, 25
Marric, J. J.
  See Creasey, John
Marryat, Frederick 1792-1848 .... **NCLC 3**

See also DLB 21, 163
Marsden, James
  See Creasey, John
Marsh, (Edith) Ngaio 1899-1982 **CLC 7, 53;
  DAM POP**
  See also CA 9-12R; CANR 6, 58; DLB 77;
  MTCW
Marshall, Garry 1934- .... **CLC 17**
  See also AAYA 3; CA 111; SATA 60
Marshall, Paule 1929- .. **CLC 27, 72; BLC 3;
  DAM MULT; SSC 3**
  See also BW 2; CA 77-80; CANR 25; DLB 157;
  MTCW
Marsten, Richard
  See Hunter, Evan
Marston, John 1576-1634**LC 33; DAM DRAM**
  See also DLB 58, 172
Martha, Henry
  See Harris, Mark
Marti, Jose 1853-1895**NCLC 63; DAM MULT;
  HLC**
Martial c. 40-c. 104 .... **PC 10**
Martin, Ken
  See Hubbard, L(afayette) Ron(ald)
Martin, Richard
  See Creasey, John
Martin, Steve 1945- .... **CLC 30**
  See also CA 97-100; CANR 30; MTCW
Martin, Valerie 1948- .... **CLC 89**
  See also BEST 90:2; CA 85-88; CANR 49
Martin, Violet Florence 1862-1915 **TCLC 51**
Martin, Webber
  See Silverberg, Robert
Martindale, Patrick Victor
  See White, Patrick (Victor Martindale)
Martin du Gard, Roger 1881-1958 **TCLC 24**
  See also CA 118; DLB 65
Martineau, Harriet 1802-1876 .... **NCLC 26**
  See also DLB 21, 55, 159, 163, 166, 190; YABC
  2
Martines, Julia
  See O'Faolain, Julia
Martinez, Enrique Gonzalez
  See Gonzalez Martinez, Enrique
Martinez, Jacinto Benavente y
  See Benavente (y Martinez), Jacinto
Martinez Ruiz, Jose 1873-1967
  See Azorin; Ruiz, Jose Martinez
  See also CA 93-96; HW
Martinez Sierra, Gregorio 1881-1947**TCLC 6**
  See also CA 115
Martinez Sierra, Maria (de la O'LeJarraga)
  1874-1974 .... **TCLC 6**
  See also CA 115
Martinsen, Martin
  See Follett, Ken(neth Martin)
Martinson, Harry (Edmund) 1904-1978**C L C
  14**
  See also CA 77-80; CANR 34
Marut, Ret
  See Traven, B.
Marut, Robert
  See Traven, B.
Marvell, Andrew 1621-1678 ... **LC 4, 43; DA;
  DAB; DAC; DAM MST, POET; PC 10;
  WLC**
  See also CDBLB 1660-1789; DLB 131
Marx, Karl (Heinrich) 1818-1883 . **NCLC 17**
  See also DLB 129
Masaoka Shiki .... **TCLC 18**
  See also Masaoka Tsunenori
Masaoka Tsunenori 1867-1902
  See Masaoka Shiki

McIlwraith, Maureen Mollie Hunter
See Hunter, Mollie
See also SATA 2
McInerney, Jay 1955- ... **CLC 34; DAM POP**
See also AAYA 18; CA 116; 123; CANR 45, 68; INT 123
McIntyre, Vonda N(eel) 1948- .... **CLC 18**
See also CA 81-84; CANR 17, 34, 69; MTCW
McKay, Claude **TCLC 7, 41; BLC 3; DAB; PC 2**
See also McKay, Festus Claudius
See also DLB 4, 45, 51, 117
McKay, Festus Claudius 1889-1948
See McKay, Claude
See also BW 1; CA 104; 124; DA; DAC; DAM MST, MULT, NOV, POET; MTCW; WLC
McKuen, Rod 1933- .... **CLC 1, 3**
See also AITN 1; CA 41-44R; CANR 40
McLoughlin, R. B.
See Mencken, H(enry) L(ouis)
McLuhan, (Herbert) Marshall 1911-1980 **CLC 37, 83**
See also CA 9-12R; 102; CANR 12, 34, 61; DLB 88; INT CANR-12; MTCW
McMillan, Terry (L.) 1951- .... **CLC 50, 61; BLCS; DAM MULT, NOV, POP**
See also AAYA 21; BW 2; CA 140; CANR 60
McMurtry, Larry (Jeff) 1936- **CLC 2, 3, 7, 11, 27, 44; DAM NOV, POP**
See also AAYA 15; AITN 2; BEST 89:2; CA 5-8R; CANR 19, 43, 64; CDALB 1968-1988; DLB 2, 143; DLBY 80, 87; MTCW
McNally, T. M. 1961- .... **CLC 82**
McNally, Terrence 1939- ... **CLC 4, 7, 41, 91; DAM DRAM**
See also CA 45-48; CANR 2, 56; DLB 7
McNamer, Deirdre 1950- .... **CLC 70**
McNeile, Herman Cyril 1888-1937
See Sapper
See also DLB 77
McNickle, (William) D'Arcy 1904-1977 **C L C 89; DAM MULT**
See also CA 9-12R; 85-88; CANR 5, 45; DLB 175; NNAL; SATA-Obit 22
McPhee, John (Angus) 1931- .... **CLC 36**
See also BEST 90:1; CA 65-68; CANR 20, 46, 64, 69; DLB 185; MTCW
McPherson, James Alan 1943- .. **CLC 19, 77; BLCS**
See also BW 1; CA 25-28R; CAAS 17; CANR 24; DLB 38; MTCW
McPherson, William (Alexander) 1933- **C L C 34**
See also CA 69-72; CANR 28; INT CANR-28
Mead, Margaret 1901-1978 .... **CLC 37**
See also AITN 1; CA 1-4R; 81-84; CANR 4; MTCW; SATA-Obit 20
Meaker, Marijane (Agnes) 1927-
See Kerr, M. E.
See also CA 107; CANR 37, 63; INT 107; JRDA; MAICYA; MTCW; SATA 20, 61
Medoff, Mark (Howard) 1940- ... **CLC 6, 23; DAM DRAM**
See also AITN 1; CA 53-56; CANR 5; DLB 7; INT CANR-5
Medvedev, P. N.
See Bakhtin, Mikhail Mikhailovich
Meged, Aharon
See Megged, Aharon
Meged, Aron
See Megged, Aharon
Megged, Aharon 1920- .... **CLC 9**
See also CA 49-52; CAAS 13; CANR 1

Mehta, Ved (Parkash) 1934- .... **CLC 37**
See also CA 1-4R; CANR 2, 23, 69; MTCW
Melanter
See Blackmore, R(ichard) D(oddridge)
Melikow, Loris
See Hofmannsthal, Hugo von
Melmoth, Sebastian
See Wilde, Oscar (Fingal O'Flahertie Wills)
Meltzer, Milton 1915- .... **CLC 26**
See also AAYA 8; CA 13-16R; CANR 38; CLR 13; DLB 61; JRDA; MAICYA; SAAS 1; SATA 1, 50, 80
Melville, Herman 1819-1891 **NCLC 3, 12, 29, 45, 49; DA; DAB; DAC; DAM MST, NOV; SSC 1, 17; WLC**
See also AAYA 25; CDALB 1640-1865; DLB 3, 74; SATA 59
Menander c. 342B.C.-c. 292B.C. ... **CMLC 9; DAM DRAM; DC 3**
See also DLB 176
Mencken, H(enry) L(ouis) 1880-1956 **T C L C 13**
See also CA 105; 125; CDALB 1917-1929; DLB 11, 29, 63, 137; MTCW
Mendelsohn, Jane 1965(?)- .... **CLC 99**
See also CA 154
Mercer, David 1928-1980 **CLC 5; DAM DRAM**
See also CA 9-12R; 102; CANR 23; DLB 13; MTCW
Merchant, Paul
See Ellison, Harlan (Jay)
Meredith, George 1828-1909 .. **TCLC 17, 43; DAM POET**
See also CA 117; 153; CDBLB 1832-1890; DLB 18, 35, 57, 159
Meredith, William (Morris) 1919- **CLC 4, 13, 22, 55; DAM POET**
See also CA 9-12R; CAAS 14; CANR 6, 40; DLB 5
Merezhkovsky, Dmitry Sergeyevich 1865-1941 **TCLC 29**
Merimee, Prosper 1803-1870 **NCLC 6, 65; SSC 7**
See also DLB 119, 192
Merkin, Daphne 1954- .... **CLC 44**
See also CA 123
Merlin, Arthur
See Blish, James (Benjamin)
Merrill, James (Ingram) 1926-1995 **CLC 2, 3, 6, 8, 13, 18, 34, 91; DAM POET**
See also CA 13-16R; 147; CANR 10, 49, 63; DLB 5, 165; DLBY 85; INT CANR-10; MTCW
Merriman, Alex
See Silverberg, Robert
Merriman, Brian 1747-1805 .... **NCLC 70**
Merritt, E. B.
See Waddington, Miriam
Merton, Thomas 1915-1968 **CLC 1, 3, 11, 34, 83; PC 10**
See also CA 5-8R; 25-28R; CANR 22, 53; DLB 48; DLBY 81; MTCW
Merwin, W(illiam) S(tanley) 1927- **CLC 1, 2, 3, 5, 8, 13, 18, 45, 88; DAM POET**
See also CA 13-16R; CANR 15, 51; DLB 5, 169; INT CANR-15; MTCW
Metcalf, John 1938- .... **CLC 37**
See also CA 113; DLB 60
Metcalf, Suzanne
See Baum, L(yman) Frank
Mew, Charlotte (Mary) 1870-1928 .. **TCLC 8**
See also CA 105; DLB 19, 135
Mewshaw, Michael 1943- .... **CLC 9**

See also CA 53-56; CANR 7, 47; DLBY 80
Meyer, June
See Jordan, June
Meyer, Lynn
See Slavitt, David R(ytman)
Meyer-Meyrink, Gustav 1868-1932
See Meyrink, Gustav
See also CA 117
Meyers, Jeffrey 1939- .... **CLC 39**
See also CA 73-76; CANR 54; DLB 111
Meynell, Alice (Christina Gertrude Thompson) 1847-1922 .... **TCLC 6**
See also CA 104; DLB 19, 98
Meyrink, Gustav .... **TCLC 21**
See also Meyer-Meyrink, Gustav
See also DLB 81
Michaels, Leonard 1933- **CLC 6, 25; SSC 16**
See also CA 61-64; CANR 21, 62; DLB 130; MTCW
Michaux, Henri 1899-1984 .... **CLC 8, 19**
See also CA 85-88; 114
Micheaux, Oscar 1884-1951 .... **TCLC 76**
See also DLB 50
Michelangelo 1475-1564 .... **LC 12**
Michelet, Jules 1798-1874 .... **NCLC 31**
Michener, James A(lbert) 1907(?)-1997 **C L C 1, 5, 11, 29, 60, 109; DAM NOV, POP**
See also AITN 1; BEST 90:1; CA 5-8R; 161; CANR 21, 45, 68; DLB 6; MTCW
Mickiewicz, Adam 1798-1855 .... **NCLC 3**
Middleton, Christopher 1926- .... **CLC 13**
See also CA 13-16R; CANR 29, 54; DLB 40
Middleton, Richard (Barham) 1882-1911 **TCLC 56**
See also DLB 156
Middleton, Stanley 1919- .... **CLC 7, 38**
See also CA 25-28R; CAAS 23; CANR 21, 46; DLB 14
Middleton, Thomas 1580-1627 **LC 33; DAM DRAM, MST; DC 5**
See also DLB 58
Migueis, Jose Rodrigues 1901- .... **CLC 10**
Mikszath, Kalman 1847-1910 .... **TCLC 31**
Miles, Jack .... **CLC 100**
Miles, Josephine (Louise) 1911-1985 **CLC 1, 2, 14, 34, 39; DAM POET**
See also CA 1-4R; 116; CANR 2, 55; DLB 48
Militant
See Sandburg, Carl (August)
Mill, John Stuart 1806-1873 .... **NCLC 11, 58**
See also CDBLB 1832-1890; DLB 55, 190
Millar, Kenneth 1915-1983 .... **CLC 14; DAM POP**
See also Macdonald, Ross
See also CA 9-12R; 110; CANR 16, 63; DLB 2; DLBD 6; DLBY 83; MTCW
Millay, E. Vincent
See Millay, Edna St. Vincent
Millay, Edna St. Vincent 1892-1950 **TCLC 4, 49; DA; DAB; DAC; DAM MST, POET; PC 6; WLCS**
See also CA 104; 130; CDALB 1917-1929; DLB 45; MTCW
Miller, Arthur 1915- **CLC 1, 2, 6, 10, 15, 26, 47, 78; DA; DAB; DAC; DAM DRAM, MST; DC 1; WLC**
See also AAYA 15; AITN 1; CA 1-4R; CABS 3; CANR 2, 30, 54; CDALB 1941-1968; DLB 7; MTCW
Miller, Henry (Valentine) 1891-1980 **CLC 1, 2, 4, 9, 14, 43, 84; DA; DAB; DAC; DAM MST, NOV; WLC**
See also CA 9-12R; 97-100; CANR 33, 64;

See also Blair, Eric (Arthur)
See also CDBLB 1945-1960; DLB 15, 98, 195
Osborne, David
See Silverberg, Robert
Osborne, George
See Silverberg, Robert
Osborne, John (James) 1929-1994**CLC 1, 2, 5, 11, 45; DA; DAB; DAC; DAM DRAM, MST; WLC**
See also CA 13-16R; 147; CANR 21, 56; CDBLB 1945-1960; DLB 13; MTCW
Osborne, Lawrence 1958- .... **CLC 50**
Oshima, Nagisa 1932- .... **CLC 20**
See also CA 116; 121
Oskison, John Milton 1874-1947 . **TCLC 35; DAM MULT**
See also CA 144; DLB 175; NNAL
Ossoli, Sarah Margaret (Fuller marchesa d') 1810-1850
See Fuller, Margaret
See also SATA 25
Ostrovsky, Alexander 1823-1886**NCLC 30, 57**
Otero, Blas de 1916-1979 .... **CLC 11**
See also CA 89-92; DLB 134
Otto, Whitney 1955- .... **CLC 70**
See also CA 140
Ouida .... **TCLC 43**
See also De La Ramee, (Marie) Louise
See also DLB 18, 156
Ousmane, Sembene 1923- .... **CLC 66; BLC 3**
See also BW 1; CA 117; 125; MTCW
Ovid 43B.C.-18(?)**CMLC 7; DAM POET; PC 2**
Owen, Hugh
See Faust, Frederick (Schiller)
Owen, Wilfred (Edward Salter) 1893-1918 **TCLC 5, 27; DA; DAB; DAC; DAM MST, POET; PC 19; WLC**
See also CA 104; 141; CDBLB 1914-1945; DLB 20
Owens, Rochelle 1936- ....**CLC 8**
See also CA 17-20R; CAAS 2; CANR 39
Oz, Amos 1939-**CLC 5, 8, 11, 27, 33, 54; DAM NOV**
See also CA 53-56; CANR 27, 47, 65; MTCW
Ozick, Cynthia 1928-**CLC 3, 7, 28, 62; DAM NOV, POP; SSC 15**
See also BEST 90:1; CA 17-20R; CANR 23, 58; DLB 28, 152; DLBY 82; INT CANR-23; MTCW
Ozu, Yasujiro 1903-1963 .... **CLC 16**
See also CA 112
Pacheco, C.
See Pessoa, Fernando (Antonio Nogueira)
Pa Chin .... **CLC 18**
See also Li Fei-kan
Pack, Robert 1929- .... **CLC 13**
See also CA 1-4R; CANR 3, 44; DLB 5
Padgett, Lewis
See Kuttner, Henry
Padilla (Lorenzo), Heberto 1932- .... **CLC 38**
See also AITN 1; CA 123; 131; HW
Page, Jimmy 1944- .... **CLC 12**
Page, Louise 1955-........................... **CLC 40**
See also CA 140
Page, P(atricia) K(athleen) 1916- **CLC 7, 18; DAC; DAM MST; PC 12**
See also CA 53-56; CANR 4, 22, 65; DLB 68; MTCW
Page, Thomas Nelson 1853-1922 .... **SSC 23**
See also CA 118; DLB 12, 78; DLBD 13
Pagels, Elaine Hiesey 1943-............ **CLC 104**
See also CA 45-48; CANR 2, 24, 51

Paget, Violet 1856-1935
See Lee, Vernon
See also CA 104; 166
Paget-Lowe, Henry
See Lovecraft, H(oward) P(hillips)
Paglia, Camille (Anna) 1947- .... **CLC 68**
See also CA 140
Paige, Richard
See Koontz, Dean R(ay)
Paine, Thomas 1737-1809 .... **NCLC 62**
See also CDALB 1640-1865; DLB 31, 43, 73, 158
Pakenham, Antonia
See Fraser, (Lady) Antonia (Pakenham)
Palamas, Kostes 1859-1943 .... **TCLC 5**
See also CA 105
Palazzeschi, Aldo 1885-1974 .... **CLC 11**
See also CA 89-92; 53-56; DLB 114
Paley, Grace 1922-**CLC 4, 6, 37; DAM POP; SSC 8**
See also CA 25-28R; CANR 13, 46; DLB 28; INT CANR-13; MTCW
Palin, Michael (Edward) 1943- .... **CLC 21**
See also Monty Python
See also CA 107; CANR 35; SATA 67
Palliser, Charles 1947- .... **CLC 65**
See also CA 136
Palma, Ricardo 1833-1919 .... **TCLC 29**
Pancake, Breece Dexter 1952-1979
See Pancake, Breece D'J
See also CA 123; 109
Pancake, Breece D'J .... **CLC 29**
See also Pancake, Breece Dexter
See also DLB 130
Panko, Rudy
See Gogol, Nikolai (Vasilyevich)
Papadiamantis, Alexandros 1851-1911**TCLC 29**
Papadiamantopoulos, Johannes 1856-1910
See Moreas, Jean
See also CA 117
Papini, Giovanni 1881-1956 .... **TCLC 22**
See also CA 121
Paracelsus 1493-1541 .... **LC 14**
See also DLB 179
Parasol, Peter
See Stevens, Wallace
Pardo Bazán, Emilia 1851-1921 .... **SSC 30**
Pareto, Vilfredo 1848-1923 .... **TCLC 69**
Parfenie, Maria
See Codrescu, Andrei
Parini, Jay (Lee) 1948- .... **CLC 54**
See also CA 97-100; CAAS 16; CANR 32
Park, Jordan
See Kornbluth, C(yril) M.; Pohl, Frederik
Park, Robert E(zra) 1864-1944 ...... **TCLC 73**
See also CA 122; 165
Parker, Bert
See Ellison, Harlan (Jay)
Parker, Dorothy (Rothschild) 1893-1967**CLC 15, 68; DAM POET; SSC 2**
See also CA 19-20; 25-28R; CAP 2; DLB 11, 45, 86; MTCW
Parker, Robert B(rown) 1932-**CLC 27; DAM NOV, POP**
See also BEST 89:4; CA 49-52; CANR 1, 26, 52; INT CANR-26; MTCW
Parkin, Frank 1940- .... **CLC 43**
See also CA 147
Parkman, Francis, Jr. 1823-1893 ... **NCLC 12**
See also DLB 1, 30, 186
Parks, Gordon (Alexander Buchanan) 1912- **CLC 1, 16; BLC 3; DAM MULT**

See also AITN 2; BW 2; CA 41-44R; CANR 26, 66; DLB 33; SATA 8
Parmenides c. 515B.C.-c. 450B.C. **CMLC 22**
See also DLB 176
Parnell, Thomas 1679-1718 .... **LC 3**
See also DLB 94
Parra, Nicanor 1914- ...... **CLC 2, 102; DAM MULT; HLC**
See also CA 85-88; CANR 32; HW; MTCW
Parrish, Mary Frances
See Fisher, M(ary) F(rances) K(ennedy)
Parson
See Coleridge, Samuel Taylor
Parson Lot
See Kingsley, Charles
Partridge, Anthony
See Oppenheim, E(dward) Phillips
Pascal, Blaise 1623-1662 .... **LC 35**
Pascoli, Giovanni 1855-1912 .... **TCLC 45**
Pasolini, Pier Paolo 1922-1975 . **CLC 20, 37, 106; PC 17**
See also CA 93-96; 61-64; CANR 63; DLB 128, 177; MTCW
Pasquini
See Silone, Ignazio
Pastan, Linda (Olenik) 1932- **CLC 27; DAM POET**
See also CA 61-64; CANR 18, 40, 61; DLB 5
Pasternak, Boris (Leonidovich) 1890-1960 **CLC 7, 10, 18, 63; DA; DAB; DAC; DAM MST, NOV, POET; PC 6; WLC**
See also CA 127; 116; MTCW
Patchen, Kenneth 1911-1972 ... **CLC 1, 2, 18; DAM POET**
See also CA 1-4R; 33-36R; CANR 3, 35; DLB 16, 48; MTCW
Pater, Walter (Horatio) 1839-1894 ..**NCLC 7**
See also CDBLB 1832-1890; DLB 57, 156
Paterson, A(ndrew) B(arton) 1864-1941 **TCLC 32**
See also CA 155; SATA 97
Paterson, Katherine (Womeldorf) 1932-**CLC 12, 30**
See also AAYA 1; CA 21-24R; CANR 28, 59; CLR 7, 50; DLB 52; JRDA; MAICYA; MTCW; SATA 13, 53, 92
Patmore, Coventry Kersey Dighton 1823-1896 **NCLC 9**
See also DLB 35, 98
Paton, Alan (Stewart) 1903-1988 **CLC 4, 10, 25, 55, 106; DA; DAB; DAC; DAM MST, NOV; WLC**
See also CA 13-16; 125; CANR 22; CAP 1; MTCW; SATA 11; SATA-Obit 56
Paton Walsh, Gillian 1937-
See Walsh, Jill Paton
See also CANR 38; JRDA; MAICYA; SAAS 3; SATA 4, 72
Patton, George S. 1885-1945 .... **TCLC 79**
Paulding, James Kirke 1778-1860 ... **NCLC 2**
See also DLB 3, 59, 74
Paulin, Thomas Neilson 1949-
See Paulin, Tom
See also CA 123; 128
Paulin, Tom .... **CLC 37**
See also Paulin, Thomas Neilson
See also DLB 40
Paustovsky, Konstantin (Georgievich) 1892-1968 .... **CLC 40**
See also CA 93-96; 25-28R
Pavese, Cesare 1908-1950 ... **TCLC 3; PC 13; SSC 19**
See also CA 104; DLB 128, 177

See also CA 53-56; CANR 42; MTCW; SATA 39

Pisarev, Dmitry Ivanovich 1840-1868 **N C L C 25**

Pix, Mary (Griffith) 1666-1709 .... **LC 8**
See also DLB 80

Pixerecourt, (Rene Charles) Guilbert de 1773-1844 .... **NCLC 39**
See also DLB 192

Plaatje, Sol(omon) T(shekisho) 1876-1932 **TCLC 73; BLCS**
See also BW 2; CA 141

Plaidy, Jean
See Hibbert, Eleanor Alice Burford

Planche, James Robinson 1796-1880**NCLC 42**

Plant, Robert 1948- .... **CLC 12**

Plante, David (Robert) 1940- **CLC 7, 23, 38; DAM NOV**
See also CA 37-40R; CANR 12, 36, 58; DLBY 83; INT CANR-12; MTCW

Plath, Sylvia 1932-1963 **CLC 1, 2, 3, 5, 9, 11, 14, 17, 50, 51, 62, 111; DA; DAB; DAC; DAM MST, POET; PC 1; WLC**
See also AAYA 13; CA 19-20; CANR 34; CAP 2; CDALB 1941-1968; DLB 5, 6, 152; MTCW; SATA 96

Plato 428(?)B.C.-348(?)B.C. .... **CMLC 8; DA; DAB; DAC; DAM MST; WLCS**
See also DLB 176

Platonov, Andrei .... **TCLC 14**
See also Klimentov, Andrei Platonovich

Platt, Kin 1911- .... **CLC 26**
See also AAYA 11; CA 17-20R; CANR 11; JRDA; SAAS 17; SATA 21, 86

Plautus c. 251B.C.-184B.C. .. **CMLC 24; DC 6**

Plick et Plock
See Simenon, Georges (Jacques Christian)

Plimpton, George (Ames) 1927- .... **CLC 36**
See also AITN 1; CA 21-24R; CANR 32; DLB 185; MTCW; SATA 10

Pliny the Elder c. 23-79 .... **CMLC 23**

Plomer, William Charles Franklin 1903-1973 **CLC 4, 8**
See also CA 21-22; CANR 34; CAP 2; DLB 20, 162, 191; MTCW; SATA 24

Plowman, Piers
See Kavanagh, Patrick (Joseph)

Plum, J.
See Wodehouse, P(elham) G(renville)

Plumly, Stanley (Ross) 1939- .... **CLC 33**
See also CA 108; 110; DLB 5, 193; INT 110

Plumpe, Friedrich Wilhelm 1888-1931**T C L C 53**
See also CA 112

Po Chu-i 772-846 .... **CMLC 24**

Poe, Edgar Allan 1809-1849**NCLC 1, 16, 55; DA; DAB; DAC; DAM MST, POET; PC 1; SSC 1, 22; WLC**
See also AAYA 14; CDALB 1640-1865; DLB 3, 59, 73, 74; SATA 23

Poet of Titchfield Street, The
See Pound, Ezra (Weston Loomis)

Pohl, Frederik 1919- .... **CLC 18; SSC 25**
See also AAYA 24; CA 61-64; CAAS 1; CANR 11, 37; DLB 8; INT CANR-11; MTCW; SATA 24

Poirier, Louis 1910-
See Gracq, Julien
See also CA 122; 126

Poitier, Sidney 1927- .... **CLC 26**
See also BW 1; CA 117

Polanski, Roman 1933- .... **CLC 16**
See also CA 77-80

Poliakoff, Stephen 1952- .... **CLC 38**
See also CA 106; DLB 13

Police, The
See Copeland, Stewart (Armstrong); Summers, Andrew James; Sumner, Gordon Matthew

Polidori, John William 1795-1821 . **NCLC 51**
See also DLB 116

Pollitt, Katha 1949- .... **CLC 28**
See also CA 120; 122; CANR 66; MTCW

Pollock, (Mary) Sharon 1936-**CLC 50; DAC; DAM DRAM, MST**
See also CA 141; DLB 60

Polo, Marco 1254-1324 .... **CMLC 15**

Polonsky, Abraham (Lincoln) 1910- **CLC 92**
See also CA 104; DLB 26; INT 104

Polybius c. 200B.C.-c. 118B.C. ...... **CMLC 17**
See also DLB 176

Pomerance, Bernard 1940- .... **CLC 13; DAM DRAM**
See also CA 101; CANR 49

Ponge, Francis (Jean Gaston Alfred) 1899-1988 **CLC 6, 18; DAM POET**
See also CA 85-88; 126; CANR 40

Pontoppidan, Henrik 1857-1943 .... **TCLC 29**

Poole, Josephine .... **CLC 17**
See also Helyar, Jane Penelope Josephine
See also SAAS 2; SATA 5

Popa, Vasko 1922-1991 .... **CLC 19**
See also CA 112; 148; DLB 181

Pope, Alexander 1688-1744 **LC 3; DA; DAB; DAC; DAM MST, POET; WLC**
See also CDBLB 1660-1789; DLB 95, 101

Porter, Connie (Rose) 1959(?)- .... **CLC 70**
See also BW 2; CA 142; SATA 81

Porter, Gene(va Grace) Stratton 1863(?)-1924 **TCLC 21**
See also CA 112

Porter, Katherine Anne 1890-1980**CLC 1, 3, 7, 10, 13, 15, 27, 101; DA; DAB; DAC; DAM MST, NOV; SSC 4**
See also AITN 2; CA 1-4R; 101; CANR 1, 65; DLB 4, 9, 102; DLBD 12; DLBY 80; MTCW; SATA 39; SATA-Obit 23

Porter, Peter (Neville Frederick) 1929-**CLC 5, 13, 33**
See also CA 85-88; DLB 40

Porter, William Sydney 1862-1910
See Henry, O.
See also CA 104; 131; CDALB 1865-1917; DA; DAB; DAC; DAM MST; DLB 12, 78, 79; MTCW; YABC 2

Portillo (y Pacheco), Jose Lopez
See Lopez Portillo (y Pacheco), Jose

Post, Melville Davisson 1869-1930 **TCLC 39**
See also CA 110

Potok, Chaim 1929- . **CLC 2, 7, 14, 26; DAM NOV**
See also AAYA 15; AITN 1, 2; CA 17-20R; CANR 19, 35, 64; DLB 28, 152; INT CANR-19; MTCW; SATA 33

Potter, (Helen) Beatrix 1866-1943
See Webb, (Martha) Beatrice (Potter)
See also MAICYA

Potter, Dennis (Christopher George) 1935-1994 **CLC 58, 86**
See also CA 107; 145; CANR 33, 61; MTCW

Pound, Ezra (Weston Loomis) 1885-1972**CLC 1, 2, 3, 4, 5, 7, 10, 13, 18, 34, 48, 50; DA; DAB; DAC; DAM MST, POET; PC 4; WLC**
See also CA 5-8R; 37-40R; CANR 40; CDALB 1917-1929; DLB 4, 45, 63; DLBD 15; MTCW

Povod, Reinaldo 1959-1994 .... **CLC 44**
See also CA 136; 146

Powell, Adam Clayton, Jr. 1908-1972**CLC 89; BLC 3; DAM MULT**
See also BW 1; CA 102; 33-36R

Powell, Anthony (Dymoke) 1905-**CLC 1, 3, 7, 9, 10, 31**
See also CA 1-4R; CANR 1, 32, 62; CDBLB 1945-1960; DLB 15; MTCW

Powell, Dawn 1897-1965 .... **CLC 66**
See also CA 5-8R; DLBY 97

Powell, Padgett 1952- .... **CLC 34**
See also CA 126; CANR 63

Power, Susan 1961- .... **CLC 91**

Powers, J(ames) F(arl) 1917-**CLC 1, 4, 8, 57; SSC 4**
See also CA 1-4R; CANR 2, 61; DLB 130; MTCW

Powers, John J(ames) 1945-
See Powers, John R.
See also CA 69-72

Powers, John R. .... **CLC 66**
See also Powers, John J(ames)

Powers, Richard (S.) 1957- .... **CLC 93**
See also CA 148

Pownall, David 1938- .... **CLC 10**
See also CA 89-92; CAAS 18; CANR 49; DLB 14

Powys, John Cowper 1872-1963**CLC 7, 9, 15, 46**
See also CA 85-88; DLB 15; MTCW

Powys, T(heodore) F(rancis) 1875-1953 **TCLC 9**
See also CA 106; DLB 36, 162

Prado (Calvo), Pedro 1886-1952 .... **TCLC 75**
See also CA 131; HW

Prager, Emily 1952- .... **CLC 56**

Pratt, E(dwin) J(ohn) 1883(?)-1964 **CLC 19; DAC; DAM POET**
See also CA 141; 93-96; DLB 92

Premchand .... **TCLC 21**
See also Srivastava, Dhanpat Rai

Preussler, Otfried 1923- .... **CLC 17**
See also CA 77-80; SATA 24

Prevert, Jacques (Henri Marie) 1900-1977 **CLC 15**
See also CA 77-80; 69-72; CANR 29, 61; MTCW; SATA-Obit 30

Prevost, Abbe (Antoine Francois) 1697-1763 **LC 1**

Price, (Edward) Reynolds 1933-**CLC 3, 6, 13, 43, 50, 63; DAM NOV; SSC 22**
See also CA 1-4R; CANR 1, 37, 57; DLB 2; INT CANR-37

Price, Richard 1949- .... **CLC 6, 12**
See also CA 49-52; CANR 3; DLBY 81

Prichard, Katharine Susannah 1883-1969 **CLC 46**
See also CA 11-12; CANR 33; CAP 1; MTCW; SATA 66

Priestley, J(ohn) B(oynton) 1894-1984**CLC 2, 5, 9, 34; DAM DRAM, NOV**
See also CA 9-12R; 113; CANR 33; CDBLB 1914-1945; DLB 10, 34, 77, 100, 139; DLBY 84; MTCW

Prince 1958(?)- .... **CLC 35**

Prince, F(rank) T(empleton) 1912- .. **CLC 22**
See also CA 101; CANR 43; DLB 20

Prince Kropotkin
See Kropotkin, Peter (Aleksieevich)

Prior, Matthew 1664-1721 .... **LC 4**
See also DLB 95

Prishvin, Mikhail 1873-1954 .... **TCLC 75**

Shelley, Mary Wollstonecraft (Godwin) 1797-1851NCLC **14, 59; DA; DAB; DAC; DAM MST, NOV; WLC**
See also AAYA 20; CDBLB 1789-1832; DLB 110, 116, 159, 178; SATA 29

Shelley, Percy Bysshe 1792-1822 . **NCLC 18; DA; DAB; DAC; DAM MST, POET; PC 14; WLC**
See also CDBLB 1789-1832; DLB 96, 110, 158

Shepard, Jim 1956- .... **CLC 36**
See also CA 137; CANR 59; SATA 90

Shepard, Lucius 1947- .... **CLC 34**
See also CA 128; 141

Shepard, Sam 1943- CLC **4, 6, 17, 34, 41, 44; DAM DRAM; DC 5**
See also AAYA 1; CA 69-72; CABS 3; CANR 22; DLB 7; MTCW

Shepherd, Michael
See Ludlum, Robert

Sherburne, Zoa (Morin) 1912- .... **CLC 30**
See also AAYA 13; CA 1-4R; CANR 3, 37; MAICYA; SAAS 18; SATA 3

Sheridan, Frances 1724-1766 .... **LC 7**
See also DLB 39, 84

Sheridan, Richard Brinsley 1751-1816N C L C **5; DA; DAB; DAC; DAM DRAM, MST; DC 1; WLC**
See also CDBLB 1660-1789; DLB 89

Sherman, Jonathan Marc .... **CLC 55**

Sherman, Martin 1941(?)- .... **CLC 19**
See also CA 116; 123

Sherwin, Judith Johnson 1936- ... **CLC 7, 15**
See also CA 25-28R; CANR 34

Sherwood, Frances 1940- .... **CLC 81**
See also CA 146

Sherwood, Robert E(mmet) 1896-1955T C L C **3; DAM DRAM**
See also CA 104; 153; DLB 7, 26

Shestov, Lev 1866-1938 .... **TCLC 56**

Shevchenko, Taras 1814-1861 .... **NCLC 54**

Shiel, M(atthew) P(hipps) 1865-1947TCLC **8**
See also Holmes, Gordon
See also CA 106; 160; DLB 153

Shields, Carol 1935- .... **CLC 91; DAC**
See also CA 81-84; CANR 51

Shields, David 1956- .... **CLC 97**
See also CA 124; CANR 48

Shiga, Naoya 1883-1971 ..... **CLC 33; SSC 23**
See also CA 101; 33-36R; DLB 180

Shilts, Randy 1951-1994 .... **CLC 85**
See also AAYA 19; CA 115; 127; 144; CANR 45; INT 127

Shimazaki, Haruki 1872-1943
See Shimazaki Toson
See also CA 105; 134

Shimazaki Toson 1872-1943 .... **TCLC 5**
See also Shimazaki, Haruki
See also DLB 180

Sholokhov, Mikhail (Aleksandrovich) 1905-1984 .... **CLC 7, 15**
See also CA 101; 112; MTCW; SATA-Obit 36

Shone, Patric
See Hanley, James

Shreve, Susan Richards 1939- .... **CLC 23**
See also CA 49-52; CAAS 5; CANR 5, 38, 69; MAICYA; SATA 46, 95; SATA-Brief 41

Shue, Larry 1946-1985CLC **52; DAM DRAM**
See also CA 145; 117

Shu-Jen, Chou 1881-1936
See Lu Hsun
See also CA 104

Shulman, Alix Kates 1932- .... **CLC 2, 10**
See also CA 29-32R; CANR 43; SATA 7

Shuster, Joe 1914- .... **CLC 21**

Shute, Nevil .... **CLC 30**
See also Norway, Nevil Shute

Shuttle, Penelope (Diane) 1947- .... **CLC 7**
See also CA 93-96; CANR 39; DLB 14, 40

Sidney, Mary 1561-1621 .... **LC 19, 39**

Sidney, Sir Philip 1554-1586 **LC 19, 39; DA; DAB; DAC; DAM MST, POET**
See also CDBLB Before 1660; DLB 167

Siegel, Jerome 1914-1996 .... **CLC 21**
See also CA 116; 151

Siegel, Jerry
See Siegel, Jerome

Sienkiewicz, Henryk (Adam Alexander Pius) 1846-1916 .... **TCLC 3**
See also CA 104; 134

Sierra, Gregorio Martinez
See Martinez Sierra, Gregorio

Sierra, Maria (de la O'LeJarraga) Martinez
See Martinez Sierra, Maria (de la O'LeJarraga)

Sigal, Clancy 1926- .... **CLC 7**
See also CA 1-4R

Sigourney, Lydia Howard (Huntley) 1791-1865 **NCLC 21**
See also DLB 1, 42, 73

Siguenza y Gongora, Carlos de 1645-1700L C **8**

Sigurjonsson, Johann 1880-1919 ... **TCLC 27**

Sikelianos, Angelos 1884-1951 .... **TCLC 39**

Silkin, Jon 1930- .... **CLC 2, 6, 43**
See also CA 5-8R; CAAS 5; DLB 27

Silko, Leslie (Marmon) 1948-CLC **23, 74; DA; DAC; DAM MST, MULT, POP; WLCS**
See also AAYA 14; CA 115; 122; CANR 45, 65; DLB 143, 175; NNAL

Sillanpaa, Frans Eemil 1888-1964 .... **CLC 19**
See also CA 129; 93-96; MTCW

Sillitoe, Alan 1928- .... CLC **1, 3, 6, 10, 19, 57**
See also AITN 1; CA 9-12R; CAAS 2; CANR 8, 26, 55; CDBLB 1960 to Present; DLB 14, 139; MTCW; SATA 61

Silone, Ignazio 1900-1978 .... **CLC 4**
See also CA 25-28; 81-84; CANR 34; CAP 2; MTCW

Silver, Joan Micklin 1935- .... **CLC 20**
See also CA 114; 121; INT 121

Silver, Nicholas
See Faust, Frederick (Schiller)

Silverberg, Robert 1935- CLC **7; DAM POP**
See also AAYA 24; CA 1-4R; CAAS 3; CANR 1, 20, 36; DLB 8; INT CANR-20; MAICYA; MTCW; SATA 13, 91

Silverstein, Alvin 1933- .... **CLC 17**
See also CA 49-52; CANR 2; CLR 25; JRDA; MAICYA; SATA 8, 69

Silverstein, Virginia B(arbara Opshelor) 1937- **CLC 17**
See also CA 49-52; CANR 2; CLR 25; JRDA; MAICYA; SATA 8, 69

Sim, Georges
See Simenon, Georges (Jacques Christian)

Simak, Clifford D(onald) 1904-1988CLC **1, 55**
See also CA 1-4R; 125; CANR 1, 35; DLB 8; MTCW; SATA-Obit 56

Simenon, Georges (Jacques Christian) 1903-1989 .. CLC **1, 2, 3, 8, 18, 47; DAM POP**
See also CA 85-88; 129; CANR 35; DLB 72; DLBY 89; MTCW

Simic, Charles 1938- .... CLC **6, 9, 22, 49, 68; DAM POET**
See also CA 29-32R; CAAS 4; CANR 12, 33, 52, 61; DLB 105

Simmel, Georg 1858-1918 .... **TCLC 64**

See also CA 157

Simmons, Charles (Paul) 1924- .... **CLC 57**
See also CA 89-92; INT 89-92

Simmons, Dan 1948- ...... CLC **44; DAM POP**
See also AAYA 16; CA 138; CANR 53

Simmons, James (Stewart Alexander) 1933- **CLC 43**
See also CA 105; CAAS 21; DLB 40

Simms, William Gilmore 1806-1870 **NCLC 3**
See also DLB 3, 30, 59, 73

Simon, Carly 1945- .... **CLC 26**
See also CA 105

Simon, Claude 1913-1984 .. CLC **4, 9, 15, 39; DAM NOV**
See also CA 89-92; CANR 33; DLB 83; MTCW

Simon, (Marvin) Neil 1927-CLC **6, 11, 31, 39, 70; DAM DRAM**
See also AITN 1; CA 21-24R; CANR 26, 54; DLB 7; MTCW

Simon, Paul (Frederick) 1941(?)- .... **CLC 17**
See also CA 116; 153

Simonon, Paul 1956(?)- .... **CLC 30**

Simpson, Harriette
See Arnow, Harriette (Louisa) Simpson

Simpson, Louis (Aston Marantz) 1923-CLC **4, 7, 9, 32; DAM POET**
See also CA 1-4R; CAAS 4; CANR 1, 61; DLB 5; MTCW

Simpson, Mona (Elizabeth) 1957- .... **CLC 44**
See also CA 122; 135; CANR 68

Simpson, N(orman) F(rederick) 1919-CLC **29**
See also CA 13-16R; DLB 13

Sinclair, Andrew (Annandale) 1935- .CLC **2, 14**
See also CA 9-12R; CAAS 5; CANR 14, 38; DLB 14; MTCW

Sinclair, Emil
See Hesse, Hermann

Sinclair, Iain 1943- .... **CLC 76**
See also CA 132

Sinclair, Iain MacGregor
See Sinclair, Iain

Sinclair, Irene
See Griffith, D(avid Lewelyn) W(ark)

Sinclair, Mary Amelia St. Clair 1865(?)-1946
See Sinclair, May
See also CA 104

Sinclair, May 1863-1946 .... **TCLC 3, 11**
See also Sinclair, Mary Amelia St. Clair
See also CA 166; DLB 36, 135

Sinclair, Roy
See Griffith, D(avid Lewelyn) W(ark)

Sinclair, Upton (Beall) 1878-1968 CLC **1, 11, 15, 63; DA; DAB; DAC; DAM MST, NOV; WLC**
See also CA 5-8R; 25-28R; CANR 7; CDALB 1929-1941; DLB 9; INT CANR-7; MTCW; SATA 9

Singer, Isaac
See Singer, Isaac Bashevis

Singer, Isaac Bashevis 1904-1991CLC **1, 3, 6, 9, 11, 15, 23, 38, 69, 111; DA; DAB; DAC; DAM MST, NOV; SSC 3; WLC**
See also AITN 1, 2; CA 1-4R; 134; CANR 1, 39; CDALB 1941-1968; CLR 1; DLB 6, 28, 52; DLBY 91; JRDA; MAICYA; MTCW; SATA 3, 27; SATA-Obit 68

Singer, Israel Joshua 1893-1944 .... **TCLC 33**

Singh, Khushwant 1915- .... **CLC 11**
See also CA 9-12R; CAAS 9; CANR 6

Singleton, Ann
See Benedict, Ruth (Fulton)

Sinjohn, John

See also BW 2; CA 13-16R; CANR 27, 39; DLB 125; MTCW

Spackman, W(illiam) M(ode) 1905-1990**C L C 46**
See also CA 81-84; 132

Spacks, Barry (Bernard) 1931- .... **CLC 14**
See also CA 154; CANR 33; DLB 105

Spanidou, Irini 1946- .... **CLC 44**

Spark, Muriel (Sarah) 1918-**CLC 2, 3, 5, 8, 13, 18, 40, 94; DAB; DAC; DAM MST, NOV; SSC 10**
See also CA 5-8R; CANR 12, 36; CDBLB 1945-1960; DLB 15, 139; INT CANR-12; MTCW

Spaulding, Douglas
See Bradbury, Ray (Douglas)

Spaulding, Leonard
See Bradbury, Ray (Douglas)

Spence, J. A. D.
See Eliot, T(homas) S(tearns)

Spencer, Elizabeth 1921- .... **CLC 22**
See also CA 13-16R; CANR 32, 65; DLB 6; MTCW; SATA 14

Spencer, Leonard G.
See Silverberg, Robert

Spencer, Scott 1945- .... **CLC 30**
See also CA 113; CANR 51; DLBY 86

Spender, Stephen (Harold) 1909-1995**CLC 1, 2, 5, 10, 41, 91; DAM POET**
See also CA 9-12R; 149; CANR 31, 54; CDBLB 1945-1960; DLB 20; MTCW

Spengler, Oswald (Arnold Gottfried) 1880-1936 **TCLC 25**
See also CA 118

Spenser, Edmund 1552(?)-1599**LC 5, 39; DA; DAB; DAC; DAM MST, POET; PC 8; WLC**
See also CDBLB Before 1660; DLB 167

Spicer, Jack 1925-1965 **CLC 8, 18, 72; DAM POET**
See also CA 85-88; DLB 5, 16, 193

Spiegelman, Art 1948- .... **CLC 76**
See also AAYA 10; CA 125; CANR 41, 55

Spielberg, Peter 1929- ....**CLC 6**
See also CA 5-8R; CANR 4, 48; DLBY 81

Spielberg, Steven 1947- .... **CLC 20**
See also AAYA 8, 24; CA 77-80; CANR 32; SATA 32

Spillane, Frank Morrison 1918-
See Spillane, Mickey
See also CA 25-28R; CANR 28, 63; MTCW; SATA 66

Spillane, Mickey .... **CLC 3, 13**
See also Spillane, Frank Morrison

Spinoza, Benedictus de 1632-1677........ **LC 9**

Spinrad, Norman (Richard) 1940- .. **CLC 46**
See also CA 37-40R; CAAS 19; CANR 20; DLB 8; INT CANR-20

Spitteler, Carl (Friedrich Georg) 1845-1924 **TCLC 12**
See also CA 109; DLB 129

Spivack, Kathleen (Romola Drucker) 1938- **CLC 6**
See also CA 49-52

Spoto, Donald 1941- .... **CLC 39**
See also CA 65-68; CANR 11, 57

Springsteen, Bruce (F.) 1949- .... **CLC 17**
See also CA 111

Spurling, Hilary 1940- .... **CLC 34**
See also CA 104; CANR 25, 52

Spyker, John Howland
See Elman, Richard (Martin)

Squires, (James) Radcliffe 1917-1993**CLC 51**
See also CA 1-4R; 140; CANR 6, 21

Srivastava, Dhanpat Rai 1880(?)-1936
See Premchand
See also CA 118

Stacy, Donald
See Pohl, Frederik

Stael, Germaine de 1766-1817
See Stael-Holstein, Anne Louise Germaine Necker Baronn
See also DLB 119

Stael-Holstein, Anne Louise Germaine Necker Baronn 1766-1817 ....
NCLC 3
See also Stael, Germaine de
See also DLB 192

Stafford, Jean 1915-1979**CLC 4, 7, 19, 68; SSC 26**
See also CA 1-4R; 85-88; CANR 3, 65; DLB 2, 173; MTCW; SATA-Obit 22

Stafford, William (Edgar) 1914-1993 **CLC 4, 7, 29; DAM POET**
See also CA 5-8R; 142; CAAS 3; CANR 5, 22; DLB 5; INT CANR-22

Stagnelius, Eric Johan 1793-1823 . **NCLC 61**

Staines, Trevor
See Brunner, John (Kilian Houston)

Stairs, Gordon
See Austin, Mary (Hunter)

Stannard, Martin 1947- .... **CLC 44**
See also CA 142; DLB 155

Stanton, Elizabeth Cady 1815-1902**TCLC 73**
See also DLB 79

Stanton, Maura 1946- .... **CLC 9**
See also CA 89-92; CANR 15; DLB 120

Stanton, Schuyler
See Baum, L(yman) Frank

Stapledon, (William) Olaf 1886-1950 . **T C L C 22**
See also CA 111; 162; DLB 15

Starbuck, George (Edwin) 1931-1996**CLC 53; DAM POET**
See also CA 21-24R; 153; CANR 23

Stark, Richard
See Westlake, Donald E(dwin)

Staunton, Schuyler
See Baum, L(yman) Frank

Stead, Christina (Ellen) 1902-1983 **CLC 2, 5, 8, 32, 80**
See also CA 13-16R; 109; CANR 33, 40; MTCW

Stead, William Thomas 1849-1912 **TCLC 48**

Steele, Richard 1672-1729 .... **LC 18**
See also CDBLB 1660-1789; DLB 84, 101

Steele, Timothy (Reid) 1948- .... **CLC 45**
See also CA 93-96; CANR 16, 50; DLB 120

Steffens, (Joseph) Lincoln 1866-1936 . **T C L C 20**
See also CA 117

Stegner, Wallace (Earle) 1909-1993**CLC 9, 49, 81; DAM NOV; SSC 27**
See also AITN 1; BEST 90:3; CA 1-4R; 141; CAAS 9; CANR 1, 21, 46; DLB 9; DLBY 93; MTCW

Stein, Gertrude 1874-1946**TCLC 1, 6, 28, 48; DA; DAB; DAC; DAM MST, NOV, POET; PC 18; WLC**
See also CA 104; 132; CDALB 1917-1929; DLB 4, 54, 86; DLBD 15; MTCW

Steinbeck, John (Ernst) 1902-1968**CLC 1, 5, 9, 13, 21, 34, 45, 75; DA; DAB; DAC; DAM DRAM, MST, NOV; SSC 11; WLC**
See also AAYA 12; CA 1-4R; 25-28R; CANR 1, 35; CDALB 1929-1941; DLB 7, 9; DLBD 2; MTCW; SATA 9

Steinem, Gloria 1934- .... **CLC 63**
See also CA 53-56; CANR 28, 51; MTCW

Steiner, George 1929- ... **CLC 24; DAM NOV**
See also CA 73-76; CANR 31, 67; DLB 67; MTCW; SATA 62

Steiner, K. Leslie
See Delany, Samuel R(ay, Jr.)

Steiner, Rudolf 1861-1925 .... **TCLC 13**
See also CA 107

Stendhal 1783-1842**NCLC 23, 46; DA; DAB; DAC; DAM MST, NOV; SSC 27; WLC**
See also DLB 119

Stephen, Adeline Virginia
See Woolf, (Adeline) Virginia

Stephen, SirLeslie 1832-1904 .... **TCLC 23**
See also CA 123; DLB 57, 144, 190

Stephen, Sir Leslie
See Stephen, SirLeslie

Stephen, Virginia
See Woolf, (Adeline) Virginia

Stephens, James 1882(?)-1950 .... **TCLC 4**
See also CA 104; DLB 19, 153, 162

Stephens, Reed
See Donaldson, Stephen R.

Steptoe, Lydia
See Barnes, Djuna

Sterchi, Beat 1949- .... **CLC 65**

Sterling, Brett
See Bradbury, Ray (Douglas); Hamilton, Edmond

Sterling, Bruce 1954- ....**CLC 72**
See also CA 119; CANR 44

Sterling, George 1869-1926 .... **TCLC 20**
See also CA 117; 165; DLB 54

Stern, Gerald 1925- .... **CLC 40, 100**
See also CA 81-84; CANR 28; DLB 105

Stern, Richard (Gustave) 1928- ... **CLC 4, 39**
See also CA 1-4R; CANR 1, 25, 52; DLBY 87; INT CANR-25

Sternberg, Josef von 1894-1969 ....**CLC 20**
See also CA 81-84

Sterne, Laurence 1713-1768**LC 2; DA; DAB; DAC; DAM MST, NOV; WLC**
See also CDBLB 1660-1789; DLB 39

Sternheim, (William Adolf) Carl 1878-1942 **TCLC 8**
See also CA 105; DLB 56, 118

Stevens, Mark 1951- ....**CLC 34**
See also CA 122

Stevens, Wallace 1879-1955 **TCLC 3, 12, 45; DA; DAB; DAC; DAM MST, POET; PC 6; WLC**
See also CA 104; 124; CDALB 1929-1941; DLB 54; MTCW

Stevenson, Anne (Katharine) 1933-**CLC 7, 33**
See also CA 17-20R; CAAS 9; CANR 9, 33; DLB 40; MTCW

Stevenson, Robert Louis (Balfour) 1850-1894 **NCLC 5, 14, 63; DA; DAB; DAC; DAM MST, NOV; SSC 11; WLC**
See also AAYA 24; CDBLB 1890-1914; CLR 10, 11; DLB 18, 57, 141, 156, 174; DLBD 13; JRDA; MAICYA; YABC 2

Stewart, J(ohn) I(nnes) M(ackintosh) 1906-1994 .... **CLC 7, 14, 32**
See also CA 85-88; 147; CAAS 3; CANR 47; MTCW

Stewart, Mary (Florence Elinor) 1916-**CLC 7, 35; DAB**
See also CA 1-4R; CANR 1, 59; SATA 12

Stewart, Mary Rainbow
See Stewart, Mary (Florence Elinor)

Stifle, June

Symonds, John Addington 1840-1893 N C L C
34
See also DLB 57, 144

Symons, Arthur 1865-1945 .... TCLC 11
See also CA 107; DLB 19, 57, 149

Symons, Julian (Gustave) 1912-1994 CLC 2,
14, 32
See also CA 49-52; 147; CAAS 3; CANR 3,
33, 59; DLB 87, 155; DLBY 92; MTCW

Synge, (Edmund) J(ohn) M(illington) 1871-
1909 .. TCLC 6, 37; DAM DRAM; DC 2
See also CA 104; 141; CDBLB 1890-1914;
DLB 10, 19

Syruc, J.
See Milosz, Czeslaw

Szirtes, George 1948- .... CLC 46
See also CA 109; CANR 27, 61

Szymborska, Wislawa 1923-............. CLC 99
See also CA 154; DLBY 96

T. O., Nik
See Annensky, Innokenty (Fyodorovich)

Tabori, George 1914- .... CLC 19
See also CA 49-52; CANR 4, 69

Tagore, Rabindranath 1861-1941TCLC 3, 53;
DAM DRAM, POET; PC 8
See also CA 104; 120; MTCW

Taine, Hippolyte Adolphe 1828-1893 . N C L C
15

Talese, Gay 1932- .... CLC 37
See also AITN 1; CA 1-4R; CANR 9, 58; DLB
185; INT CANR-9; MTCW

Tallent, Elizabeth (Ann) 1954- .... CLC 45
See also CA 117; DLB 130

Tally, Ted 1952- .... CLC 42
See also CA 120; 124; INT 124

Tamayo y Baus, Manuel 1829-1898 . NCLC 1

Tammsaare, A(nton) H(ansen) 1878-1940
TCLC 27
See also CA 164

Tam'si, Tchicaya U
See Tchicaya, Gerald Felix

Tan, Amy (Ruth) 1952-CLC 59; DAM MULT,
NOV, POP
See also AAYA 9; BEST 89:3; CA 136; CANR
54; DLB 173; SATA 75

Tandem, Felix
See Spitteler, Carl (Friedrich Georg)

Tanizaki, Jun'ichiro 1886-1965CLC 8, 14, 28;
SSC 21
See also CA 93-96; 25-28R; DLB 180

Tanner, William
See Amis, Kingsley (William)

Tao Lao
See Storni, Alfonsina

Tarassoff, Lev
See Troyat, Henri

Tarbell, Ida M(inerva) 1857-1944 . TCLC 40
See also CA 122; DLB 47

Tarkington, (Newton) Booth 1869-1946TCLC
9
See also CA 110; 143; DLB 9, 102; SATA 17

Tarkovsky, Andrei (Arsenyevich) 1932-1986
CLC 75
See also CA 127

Tartt, Donna 1964(?)- .... CLC 76
See also CA 142

Tasso, Torquato 1544-1595 .... LC 5

Tate, (John Orley) Allen 1899-1979CLC 2, 4,
6, 9, 11, 14, 24
See also CA 5-8R; 85-88; CANR 32; DLB 4,
45, 63; MTCW

Tate, Ellalice
See Hibbert, Eleanor Alice Burford

Tate, James (Vincent) 1943- ..... CLC 2, 6, 25
See also CA 21-24R; CANR 29, 57; DLB 5,
169

Tavel, Ronald 1940- .... CLC 6
See also CA 21-24R; CANR 33

Taylor, C(ecil) P(hilip) 1929-1981 ..... CLC 27
See also CA 25-28R; 105; CANR 47

Taylor, Edward 1642(?)-1729 ..... LC 11; DA;
DAB; DAC; DAM MST, POET
See also DLB 24

Taylor, Eleanor Ross 1920- .... CLC 5
See also CA 81-84

Taylor, Elizabeth 1912-1975 ..... CLC 2, 4, 29
See also CA 13-16R; CANR 9; DLB 139;
MTCW; SATA 13

Taylor, Frederick Winslow 1856-1915 T C L C
76

Taylor, Henry (Splawn) 1942- ....CLC 44
See also CA 33-36R; CAAS 7; CANR 31; DLB
5

Taylor, Kamala (Purnaiya) 1924-
See Markandaya, Kamala
See also CA 77-80

Taylor, Mildred D. ....CLC 21
See also AAYA 10; BW 1; CA 85-88; CANR
25; CLR 9; DLB 52; JRDA; MAICYA; SAAS
5; SATA 15, 70

Taylor, Peter (Hillsman) 1917-1994CLC 1, 4,
18, 37, 44, 50, 71; SSC 10
See also CA 13-16R; 147; CANR 9, 50; DLBY
81, 94; INT CANR-9; MTCW

Taylor, Robert Lewis 1912- ....CLC 14
See also CA 1-4R; CANR 3, 64; SATA 10

Tchekhov, Anton
See Chekhov, Anton (Pavlovich)

Tchicaya, Gerald Felix 1931-1988 . CLC 101
See also CA 129; 125

Tchicaya U Tam'si
See Tchicaya, Gerald Felix

Teasdale, Sara 1884-1933 .... TCLC 4
See also CA 104; 163; DLB 45; SATA 32

Tegner, Esaias 1782-1846 .... NCLC 2

Teilhard de Chardin, (Marie Joseph) Pierre
1881-1955 .... TCLC 9
See also CA 105

Temple, Ann
See Mortimer, Penelope (Ruth)

Tennant, Emma (Christina) 1937-CLC 13, 52
See also CA 65-68; CAAS 9; CANR 10, 38,
59; DLB 14

Tenneshaw, S. M.
See Silverberg, Robert

Tennyson, Alfred 1809-1892 ... NCLC 30, 65;
DA; DAB; DAC; DAM MST, POET; PC
6; WLC
See also CDBLB 1832-1890; DLB 32

Teran, Lisa St. Aubin de .... CLC 36
See also St. Aubin de Teran, Lisa

Terence 195(?)B.C.-159B.C. CMLC 14; DC 7

Teresa de Jesus, St. 1515-1582 .... LC 18

Terkel, Louis 1912-
See Terkel, Studs
See also CA 57-60; CANR 18, 45, 67; MTCW

Terkel, Studs ....CLC 38
See also Terkel, Louis
See also AITN 1

Terry, C. V.
See Slaughter, Frank G(ill)

Terry, Megan 1932- ....CLC 19
See also CA 77-80; CABS 3; CANR 43; DLB 7

Tertz, Abram
See Sinyavsky, Andrei (Donatevich)

Tesich, Steve 1943(?)-1996 .... CLC 40, 69

See also CA 105; 152; DLBY 83

Teternikov, Fyodor Kuzmich 1863-1927
See Sologub, Fyodor
See also CA 104

Tevis, Walter 1928-1984 .... CLC 42
See also CA 113

Tey, Josephine .... TCLC 14
See also Mackintosh, Elizabeth
See also DLB 77

Thackeray, William Makepeace 1811-1863
NCLC 5, 14, 22, 43; DA; DAB; DAC; DAM
MST, NOV; WLC
See also CDBLB 1832-1890; DLB 21, 55, 159,
163; SATA 23

Thakura, Ravindranatha
See Tagore, Rabindranath

Tharoor, Shashi 1956- ....CLC 70
See also CA 141

Thelwell, Michael Miles 1939- ....CLC 22
See also BW 2; CA 101

Theobald, Lewis, Jr.
See Lovecraft, H(oward) P(hillips)

Theodorescu, Ion N. 1880-1967
See Arghezi, Tudor
See also CA 116

Theriault, Yves 1915-1983 .... CLC 79; DAC;
DAM MST
See also CA 102; DLB 88

Theroux, Alexander (Louis) 1939-CLC 2, 25
See also CA 85-88; CANR 20, 63

Theroux, Paul (Edward) 1941- CLC 5, 8, 11,
15, 28, 46; DAM POP
See also BEST 89:4; CA 33-36R; CANR 20,
45; DLB 2; MTCW; SATA 44

Thesen, Sharon 1946- ....CLC 56
See also CA 163

Thevenin, Denis
See Duhamel, Georges

Thibault, Jacques Anatole Francois 1844-1924
See France, Anatole
See also CA 106; 127; DAM NOV; MTCW

Thiele, Colin (Milton) 1920- ....CLC 17
See also CA 29-32R; CANR 12, 28, 53; CLR
27; MAICYA; SAAS 2; SATA 14, 72

Thomas, Audrey (Callahan) 1935-CLC 7, 13,
37, 107; SSC 20
See also AITN 2; CA 21-24R; CAAS 19; CANR
36, 58; DLB 60; MTCW

Thomas, D(onald) M(ichael) 1935-. CLC 13,
22, 31
See also CA 61-64; CAAS 11; CANR 17, 45;
CDBLB 1960 to Present; DLB 40; INT
CANR-17; MTCW

Thomas, Dylan (Marlais) 1914-1953TCLC 1,
8, 45; DA; DAB; DAC; DAM DRAM,
MST, POET; PC 2; SSC 3; WLC
See also CA 104; 120; CANR 65; CDBLB
1945-1960; DLB 13, 20, 139; MTCW; SATA
60

Thomas, (Philip) Edward 1878-1917 . T C L C
10; DAM POET
See also CA 106; 153; DLB 19

Thomas, Joyce Carol 1938- ....CLC 35
See also AAYA 12; BW 2; CA 113; 116; CANR
48; CLR 19; DLB 33; INT 116; JRDA;
MAICYA; MTCW; SAAS 7; SATA 40, 78

Thomas, Lewis 1913-1993 .... CLC 35
See also CA 85-88; 143; CANR 38, 60; MTCW

Thomas, Paul
See Mann, (Paul) Thomas

Thomas, Piri 1928- ....CLC 17
See also CA 73-76; HW

Thomas, R(onald) S(tuart) 1913- CLC 6, 13,

48; DAB; DAM POET
See also CA 89-92; CAAS 4; CANR 30;
CDBLB 1960 to Present; DLB 27; MTCW

Thomas, Ross (Elmore) 1926-1995 .. CLC 39
See also CA 33-36R; 150; CANR 22, 63

Thompson, Francis Clegg
See Mencken, H(enry) L(ouis)

Thompson, Francis Joseph 1859-1907TCLC 4
See also CA 104; CDBLB 1890-1914; DLB 19

Thompson, Hunter S(tockton) 1939- CLC 9,
17, 40, 104; DAM POP
See also BEST 89:1; CA 17-20R; CANR 23,
46; DLB 185; MTCW

Thompson, James Myers
See Thompson, Jim (Myers)

Thompson, Jim (Myers) 1906-1977(?)CLC 69
See also CA 140

Thompson, Judith .... CLC 39

Thomson, James 1700-1748 .... LC 16, 29, 40;
DAM POET
See also DLB 95

Thomson, James 1834-1882 NCLC 18; DAM
POET
See also DLB 35

Thoreau, Henry David 1817-1862NCLC 7, 21,
61; DA; DAB; DAC; DAM MST; WLC
See also CDALB 1640-1865; DLB 1

Thornton, Hall
See Silverberg, Robert

Thucydides c. 455B.C.-399B.C. ...... CMLC 17
See also DLB 176

Thurber, James (Grover) 1894-1961 CLC 5,
11, 25; DA; DAB; DAC; DAM DRAM,
MST, NOV; SSC 1
See also CA 73-76; CANR 17, 39; CDALB
1929-1941; DLB 4, 11, 22, 102; MAICYA;
MTCW; SATA 13

Thurman, Wallace (Henry) 1902-1934T C L C
6; BLC 3; DAM MULT
See also BW 1; CA 104; 124; DLB 51

Ticheburn, Cheviot
See Ainsworth, William Harrison

Tieck, (Johann) Ludwig 1773-1853 NCLC 5,
46
See also DLB 90

Tiger, Derry
See Ellison, Harlan (Jay)

Tilghman, Christopher 1948(?)- ...... CLC 65
See also CA 159

Tillinghast, Richard (Williford) 1940-CLC 29
See also CA 29-32R; CAAS 23; CANR 26, 51

Timrod, Henry 1828-1867 .... NCLC 25
See also DLB 3

Tindall, Gillian (Elizabeth) 1938-....... CLC 7
See also CA 21-24R; CANR 11, 65

Tiptree, James, Jr. .... CLC 48, 50
See also Sheldon, Alice Hastings Bradley
See also DLB 8

Titmarsh, Michael Angelo
See Thackeray, William Makepeace

Tocqueville, Alexis (Charles Henri Maurice
Clerel Comte) 1805-1859 ...NCLC 7, 63

Tolkien, J(ohn) R(onald) R(euel) 1892-1973
CLC 1, 2, 3, 8, 12, 38; DA; DAB; DAC;
DAM MST, NOV, POP; WLC
See also AAYA 10; AITN 1; CA 17-18; 45-48;
CANR 36; CAP 2; CDBLB 1914-1945; DLB
15, 160; JRDA; MAICYA; MTCW; SATA 2,
32; SATA-Obit 24

Toller, Ernst 1893-1939 .... TCLC 10
See also CA 107; DLB 124

Tolson, M. B.
See Tolson, Melvin B(eaunorus)

Tolson, Melvin B(eaunorus) 1898(?)-1966
CLC 36, 105; BLC 3; DAM MULT, POET
See also BW 1; CA 124; 89-92; DLB 48, 76

Tolstoi, Aleksei Nikolaevich
See Tolstoy, Alexey Nikolaevich

Tolstoy, Alexey Nikolaevich 1882-1945T C L C
18
See also CA 107; 158

Tolstoy, Count Leo
See Tolstoy, Leo (Nikolaevich)

Tolstoy, Leo (Nikolaevich) 1828-1910TCLC 4,
11, 17, 28, 44, 79; DA; DAB; DAC; DAM
MST, NOV; SSC 9, 30; WLC
See also CA 104; 123; SATA 26

Tomasi di Lampedusa, Giuseppe 1896-1957
See Lampedusa, Giuseppe (Tomasi) di
See also CA 111

Tomlin, Lily ....CLC 17
See also Tomlin, Mary Jean

Tomlin, Mary Jean 1939(?)-
See Tomlin, Lily
See also CA 117

Tomlinson, (Alfred) Charles 1927-CLC 2, 4, 6,
13, 45; DAM POET; PC 17
See also CA 5-8R; CANR 33; DLB 40

Tomlinson, H(enry) M(ajor) 1873-1958TCLC
71
See also CA 118; 161; DLB 36, 100, 195

Tonson, Jacob
See Bennett, (Enoch) Arnold

Toole, John Kennedy 1937-1969 CLC 19, 64
See also CA 104; DLBY 81

Toomer, Jean 1894-1967CLC 1, 4, 13, 22; BLC
3; DAM MULT; PC 7; SSC 1; WLCS
See also BW 1; CA 85-88; CDALB 1917-1929;
DLB 45, 51; MTCW

Torley, Luke
See Blish, James (Benjamin)

Tornimparte, Alessandra
See Ginzburg, Natalia

Torre, Raoul della
See Mencken, H(enry) L(ouis)

Torrey, E(dwin) Fuller 1937- .... CLC 34
See also CA 119

Torsvan, Ben Traven
See Traven, B.

Torsvan, Benno Traven
See Traven, B.

Torsvan, Berick Traven
See Traven, B.

Torsvan, Berwick Traven
See Traven, B.

Torsvan, Bruno Traven
See Traven, B.

Torsvan, Traven
See Traven, B.

Tournier, Michel (Edouard) 1924-CLC 6, 23,
36, 95
See also CA 49-52; CANR 3, 36; DLB 83;
MTCW; SATA 23

Tournimparte, Alessandra
See Ginzburg, Natalia

Towers, Ivar
See Kornbluth, C(yril) M.

Towne, Robert (Burton) 1936(?)-....... CLC 87
See also CA 108; DLB 44

Townsend, Sue .... CLC 61
See also Townsend, Susan Elaine
See also SATA 55, 93; SATA-Brief 48

Townsend, Susan Elaine 1946-
See Townsend, Sue
See also CA 119; 127; CANR 65; DAB; DAC;
DAM MST

Townshend, Peter (Dennis Blandford) 1945-
CLC 17, 42
See also CA 107

Tozzi, Federigo 1883-1920 .... TCLC 31
See also CA 160

Traill, Catharine Parr 1802-1899 ..NCLC 31
See also DLB 99

Trakl, Georg 1887-1914 .... TCLC 5; PC 20
See also CA 104; 165

Transtroemer, Tomas (Goesta) 1931-CLC 52,
65; DAM POET
See also CA 117; 129; CAAS 17

Transtromer, Tomas Gosta
See Transtroemer, Tomas (Goesta)

Traven, B. (?)-1969 ....CLC 8, 11
See also CA 19-20; 25-28R; CAP 2; DLB 9,
56; MTCW

Treitel, Jonathan 1959- .... CLC 70

Tremain, Rose 1943-........................... CLC 42
See also CA 97-100; CANR 44; DLB 14

Tremblay, Michel 1942- CLC 29, 102; DAC;
DAM MST
See also CA 116; 128; DLB 60; MTCW

Trevanian .... CLC 29
See also Whitaker, Rod(ney)

Trevor, Glen
See Hilton, James

Trevor, William 1928- ..CLC 7, 9, 14, 25, 71;
SSC 21
See also Cox, William Trevor
See also DLB 14, 139

Trifonov, Yuri (Valentinovich) 1925-1981
CLC 45
See also CA 126; 103; MTCW

Trilling, Lionel 1905-1975 ...... CLC 9, 11, 24
See also CA 9-12R; 61-64; CANR 10; DLB 28,
63; INT CANR-10; MTCW

Trimball, W. H.
See Mencken, H(enry) L(ouis)

Tristan
See Gomez de la Serna, Ramon

Tristram
See Housman, A(lfred) E(dward)

Trogdon, William (Lewis) 1939-
See Heat-Moon, William Least
See also CA 115; 119; CANR 47; INT 119

Trollope, Anthony 1815-1882NCLC 6, 33; DA;
DAB; DAC; DAM MST, NOV; SSC 28;
WLC
See also CDBLB 1832-1890; DLB 21, 57, 159;
SATA 22

Trollope, Frances 1779-1863 ....NCLC 30
See also DLB 21, 166

Trotsky, Leon 1879-1940 .... TCLC 22
See also CA 118

Trotter (Cockburn), Catharine 1679-1749L C
8
See also DLB 84

Trout, Kilgore
See Farmer, Philip Jose

Trow, George W. S. 1943- .... CLC 52
See also CA 126

Troyat, Henri 1911- .... CLC 23
See also CA 45-48; CANR 2, 33, 67; MTCW

Trudeau, G(arretson) B(eekman) 1948-
See Trudeau, Garry B.
See also CA 81-84; CANR 31; SATA 35

Trudeau, Garry B. .... CLC 12
See also Trudeau, G(arretson) B(eekman)
See also AAYA 10; AITN 2

Truffaut, Francois 1932-1984 .. CLC 20, 101
See also CA 81-84; 113; CANR 34

Trumbo, Dalton 1905-1976 .... CLC 19

Vasiliu, Gheorghe 1881-1957
   See Bacovia, George
   See also CA 123
Vassa, Gustavus
   See Equiano, Olaudah
Vassilikos, Vassilis 1933- .... **CLC 4, 8**
   See also CA 81-84
Vaughan, Henry 1621-1695 .... **LC 27**
   See also DLB 131
Vaughn, Stephanie .... **CLC 62**
Vazov, Ivan (Minchov) 1850-1921 . **TCLC 25**
   See also CA 121; DLB 147
Veblen, Thorstein (Bunde) 1857-1929 **T C L C 31**
   See also CA 115; 165
Vega, Lope de 1562-1635 .... **LC 23**
Venison, Alfred
   See Pound, Ezra (Weston Loomis)
Verdi, Marie de
   See Mencken, H(enry) L(ouis)
Verdu, Matilde
   See Cela, Camilo Jose
Verga, Giovanni (Carmelo) 1840-1922**T C L C 3; SSC 21**
   See also CA 104; 123
Vergil 70B.C.-19B.C. .... **CMLC 9; DA; DAB; DAC; DAM MST, POET; PC 12; WLCS**
Verhaeren, Emile (Adolphe Gustave) 1855-1916 **TCLC 12**
   See also CA 109
Verlaine, Paul (Marie) 1844-1896**NCLC 2, 51; DAM POET; PC 2**
Verne, Jules (Gabriel) 1828-1905**TCLC 6, 52**
   See also AAYA 16; CA 110; 131; DLB 123; JRDA; MAICYA; SATA 21
Very, Jones 1813-1880 .... **NCLC 9**
   See also DLB 1
Vesaas, Tarjei 1897-1970 .... **CLC 48**
   See also CA 29-32R
Vialis, Gaston
   See Simenon, Georges (Jacques Christian)
Vian, Boris 1920-1959 .... **TCLC 9**
   See also CA 106; 164; DLB 72
Viaud, (Louis Marie) Julien 1850-1923
   See Loti, Pierre
   See also CA 107
Vicar, Henry
   See Felsen, Henry Gregor
Vicker, Angus
   See Felsen, Henry Gregor
Vidal, Gore 1925-**CLC 2, 4, 6, 8, 10, 22, 33, 72; DAM NOV, POP**
   See also AITN 1; BEST 90:2; CA 5-8R; CANR 13, 45, 65; DLB 6, 152; INT CANR-13; MTCW
Viereck, Peter (Robert Edwin) 1916- . **CLC 4**
   See also CA 1-4R; CANR 1, 47; DLB 5
Vigny, Alfred (Victor) de 1797-1863**NCLC 7; DAM POET**
   See also DLB 119, 192
Vilakazi, Benedict Wallet 1906-1947**TCLC 37**
Villa, Jose Garcia 1904-1997 .... **PC 22**
   See also CA 25-28R; CANR 12
Villaurrutia, Xavier 1903-1950 ...... **TCLC 80**
   See also HW
Villiers de l'Isle Adam, Jean Marie Mathias Philippe Auguste, Comte de 1838-1889 **NCLC 3; SSC 14**
   See also DLB 123
Villon, Francois 1431-1463(?) .... **PC 13**
Vinci, Leonardo da 1452-1519 .... **LC 12**
Vine, Barbara .... **CLC 50**
   See also Rendell, Ruth (Barbara)

See also BEST 90:4
Vinge, Joan D(ennison) 1948-**CLC 30; SSC 24**
   See also CA 93-96; SATA 36
Violis, G.
   See Simenon, Georges (Jacques Christian)
Virgil
   See Vergil
Visconti, Luchino 1906-1976 .... **CLC 16**
   See also CA 81-84; 65-68; CANR 39
Vittorini, Elio 1908-1966 .... **CLC 6, 9, 14**
   See also CA 133; 25-28R
Vizenor, Gerald Robert 1934-**CLC 103; DAM MULT**
   See also CA 13-16R; CAAS 22; CANR 5, 21, 44, 67; DLB 175; NNAL
Vizinczey, Stephen 1933- .... **CLC 40**
   See also CA 128; INT 128
Vliet, R(ussell) G(ordon) 1929-1984 . **CLC 22**
   See also CA 37-40R; 112; CANR 18
Vogau, Boris Andreyevich 1894-1937(?)
   See Pilnyak, Boris
   See also CA 123
Vogel, Paula A(nne) 1951- .... **CLC 76**
   See also CA 108
Voight, Ellen Bryant 1943- .... **CLC 54**
   See also CA 69-72; CANR 11, 29, 55; DLB 120
Voigt, Cynthia 1942- .... **CLC 30**
   See also AAYA 3; CA 106; CANR 18, 37, 40; CLR 13,48; INT CANR-18; JRDA; MAICYA; SATA 48, 79; SATA-Brief 33
Voinovich, Vladimir (Nikolaevich) 1932-**C L C 10, 49**
   See also CA 81-84; CAAS 12; CANR 33, 67; MTCW
Vollmann, William T. 1959-... **CLC 89; DAM NOV, POP**
   See also CA 134; CANR 67
Voloshinov, V. N.
   See Bakhtin, Mikhail Mikhailovich
Voltaire 1694-1778 **LC 14; DA; DAB; DAC; DAM DRAM, MST; SSC 12; WLC**
von Daeniken, Erich 1935- .... **CLC 30**
   See also AITN 1; CA 37-40R; CANR 17, 44
von Daniken, Erich
   See von Daeniken, Erich
von Heidenstam, (Carl Gustaf) Verner
   See Heidenstam, (Carl Gustaf) Verner von
von Heyse, Paul (Johann Ludwig)
   See Heyse, Paul (Johann Ludwig von)
von Hofmannsthal, Hugo
   See Hofmannsthal, Hugo von
von Horvath, Odon
   See Horvath, Oedoen von
von Horvath, Oedoen
   See Horvath, Oedoen von
von Liliencron, (Friedrich Adolf Axel) Detlev
   See Liliencron, (Friedrich Adolf Axel) Detlev von
Vonnegut, Kurt, Jr. 1922-**CLC 1, 2, 3, 4, 5, 8, 12, 22, 40, 60, 111; DA; DAB; DAC; DAM MST, NOV, POP; SSC 8; WLC**
   See also AAYA 6; AITN 1; BEST 90:4; CA 1-4R; CANR 1, 25, 49; CDALB 1968-1988; DLB 2, 8, 152; DLBD 3; DLBY 80; MTCW
Von Rachen, Kurt
   See Hubbard, L(afayette) Ron(ald)
von Rezzori (d'Arezzo), Gregor
   See Rezzori (d'Arezzo), Gregor von
von Sternberg, Josef
   See Sternberg, Josef von
Vorster, Gordon 1924- .... **CLC 34**
   See also CA 133
Vosce, Trudie

See Ozick, Cynthia
Voznesensky, Andrei (Andreievich) 1933-**CLC 1, 15, 57; DAM POET**
   See also CA 89-92; CANR 37; MTCW
Waddington, Miriam 1917- .... **CLC 28**
   See also CA 21-24R; CANR 12, 30; DLB 68
Wagman, Fredrica 1937- .... **CLC 7**
   See also CA 97-100; INT 97-100
Wagner, Linda W.
   See Wagner-Martin, Linda (C.)
Wagner, Linda Welshimer
   See Wagner-Martin, Linda (C.)
Wagner, Richard 1813-1883 .... **NCLC 9**
   See also DLB 129
Wagner-Martin, Linda (C.) 1936- ... **CLC 50**
   See also CA 159
Wagoner, David (Russell) 1926- **CLC 3, 5, 15**
   See also CA 1-4R; CAAS 3; CANR 2; DLB 5; SATA 14
Wah, Fred(erick James) 1939- .... **CLC 44**
   See also CA 107; 141; DLB 60
Wahloo, Per 1926-1975 .... **CLC 7**
   See also CA 61-64
Wahloo, Peter
   See Wahloo, Per
Wain, John (Barrington) 1925-1994 . **CLC 2, 11, 15, 46**
   See also CA 5-8R; 145; CAAS 4; CANR 23, 54; CDBLB 1960 to Present; DLB 15, 27, 139, 155; MTCW
Wajda, Andrzej 1926- .... **CLC 16**
   See also CA 102
Wakefield, Dan 1932- .... **CLC 7**
   See also CA 21-24R; CAAS 7
Wakoski, Diane 1937-. **CLC 2, 4, 7, 9, 11, 40; DAM POET; PC 15**
   See also CA 13-16R; CAAS 1; CANR 9, 60; DLB 5; INT CANR-9
Wakoski-Sherbell, Diane
   See Wakoski, Diane
Walcott, Derek (Alton) 1930-**CLC 2, 4, 9, 14, 25, 42, 67, 76; BLC 3; DAB; DAC; DAM MST, MULT, POET; DC 7**
   See also BW 2; CA 89-92; CANR 26, 47; DLB 117; DLBY 81; MTCW
Waldman, Anne (Lesley) 1945- .... **CLC 7**
   See also CA 37-40R; CAAS 17; CANR 34, 69; DLB 16
Waldo, E. Hunter
   See Sturgeon, Theodore (Hamilton)
Waldo, Edward Hamilton
   See Sturgeon, Theodore (Hamilton)
Walker, Alice (Malsenior) 1944- **CLC 5, 6, 9, 19, 27, 46, 58, 103; BLC 3; DA; DAB; DAC; DAM MST, MULT, NOV, POET, POP; SSC 5; WLCS**
   See also AAYA 3; BEST 89:4; BW 2; CA 37-40R; CANR 9, 27, 49, 66; CDALB 1968-1988; DLB 6, 33, 143; INT CANR-27; MTCW; SATA 31
Walker, David Harry 1911-1992 ...... **CLC 14**
   See also CA 1-4R; 137; CANR 1; SATA 8; SATA-Obit 71
Walker, Edward Joseph 1934-
   See Walker, Ted
   See also CA 21-24R; CANR 12, 28, 53
Walker, George F. 1947- . **CLC 44, 61; DAB; DAC; DAM MST**
   See also CA 103; CANR 21, 43, 59; DLB 60
Walker, Joseph A. 1935- .... **CLC 19; DAM DRAM, MST**
   See also BW 1; CA 89-92; CANR 26; DLB 38
Walker, Margaret (Abigail) 1915- **CLC 1, 6;**

BLC; DAM MULT; PC 20
See also BW 2; CA 73-76; CANR 26, 54; DLB 76, 152; MTCW

Walker, Ted .... CLC 13
See also Walker, Edward Joseph
See also DLB 40

Wallace, David Foster 1962- .... CLC 50
See also CA 132; CANR 59

Wallace, Dexter
See Masters, Edgar Lee

Wallace, (Richard Horatio) Edgar 1875-1932
TCLC 57
See also CA 115; DLB 70

Wallace, Irving 1916-1990 . CLC 7, 13; DAM NOV, POP
See also AITN 1; CA 1-4R; 132; CAAS 1; CANR 1, 27; INT CANR-27; MTCW

Wallant, Edward Lewis 1926-1962CLC 5, 10
See also CA 1-4R; CANR 22; DLB 2, 28, 143; MTCW

Walley, Byron
See Card, Orson Scott

Walpole, Horace 1717-1797 .... LC 2
See also DLB 39, 104

Walpole, Hugh (Seymour) 1884-1941TCLC 5
See also CA 104; 165; DLB 34

Walser, Martin 1927- .... CLC 27
See also CA 57-60; CANR 8, 46; DLB 75, 124

Walser, Robert 1878-1956 TCLC 18; SSC 20
See also CA 118; 165; DLB 66

Walsh, Jill Paton .... CLC 35
See also Paton Walsh, Gillian
See also AAYA 11; CLR 2; DLB 161; SAAS 3

Walter, William Christian
See Andersen, Hans Christian

Wambaugh, Joseph (Aloysius, Jr.) 1937-CLC 3, 18; DAM NOV, POP
See also AITN 1; BEST 89:3; CA 33-36R; CANR 42, 65; DLB 6; DLBY 83; MTCW

Wang Wei 699(?)-761(?) .... PC 18

Ward, Arthur Henry Sarsfield 1883-1959
See Rohmer, Sax
See also CA 108

Ward, Douglas Turner 1930- .... CLC 19
See also BW 1; CA 81-84; CANR 27; DLB 7, 38

Ward, Mary Augusta
See Ward, Mrs. Humphry

Ward, Mrs. Humphry 1851-1920 .. TCLC 55
See also DLB 18

Ward, Peter
See Faust, Frederick (Schiller)

Warhol, Andy 1928(?)-1987 .... CLC 20
See also AAYA 12; BEST 89:4; CA 89-92; 121; CANR 34

Warner, Francis (Robert le Plastrier) 1937-
CLC 14
See also CA 53-56; CANR 11

Warner, Marina 1946- .... CLC 59
See also CA 65-68; CANR 21, 55; DLB 194

Warner, Rex (Ernest) 1905-1986 ..... CLC 45
See also CA 89-92; 119; DLB 15

Warner, Susan (Bogert) 1819-1885 NCLC 31
See also DLB 3, 42

Warner, Sylvia (Constance) Ashton
See Ashton-Warner, Sylvia (Constance)

Warner, Sylvia Townsend 1893-1978 CLC 7, 19; SSC 23
See also CA 61-64; 77-80; CANR 16, 60; DLB 34, 139; MTCW

Warren, Mercy Otis 1728-1814 ...... NCLC 13
See also DLB 31

Warren, Robert Penn 1905-1989CLC 1, 4, 6,

8, 10, 13, 18, 39, 53, 59; DA; DAB; DAC; DAM MST, NOV, POET; SSC 4; WLC
See also AITN 1; CA 13-16R; 129; CANR 10, 47; CDALB 1968-1988; DLB 2, 48, 152; DLBY 80, 89; INT CANR-10; MTCW; SATA 46; SATA-Obit 63

Warshofsky, Isaac
See Singer, Isaac Bashevis

Warton, Thomas 1728-1790 ..... LC 15; DAM POET
See also DLB 104, 109

Waruk, Kona
See Harris, (Theodore) Wilson

Warung, Price 1855-1911 .... TCLC 45

Warwick, Jarvis
See Garner, Hugh

Washington, Alex
See Harris, Mark

Washington, Booker T(aliaferro) 1856-1915
TCLC 10; BLC 3; DAM MULT
See also BW 1; CA 114; 125; SATA 28

Washington, George 1732-1799 .... LC 25
See also DLB 31

Wassermann, (Karl) Jakob 1873-1934T C L C
6
See also CA 104; DLB 66

Wasserstein, Wendy 1950- ... CLC 32, 59, 90; DAM DRAM; DC 4
See also CA 121; 129; CABS 3; CANR 53; INT 129; SATA 94

Waterhouse, Keith (Spencer) 1929-..CLC 47
See also CA 5-8R; CANR 38, 67; DLB 13, 15; MTCW

Waters, Frank (Joseph) 1902-1995 ...CLC 88
See also CA 5-8R; 149; CAAS 13; CANR 3, 18, 63; DLBY 86

Waters, Roger 1944- .... CLC 35

Watkins, Frances Ellen
See Harper, Frances Ellen Watkins

Watkins, Gerrold
See Malzberg, Barry N(athaniel)

Watkins, Gloria 1955(?)-
See hooks, bell
See also BW 2; CA 143

Watkins, Paul 1964- .... CLC 55
See also CA 132; CANR 62

Watkins, Vernon Phillips 1906-1967 CLC 43
See also CA 9-10; 25-28R; CAP 1; DLB 20

Watson, Irving S.
See Mencken, H(enry) L(ouis)

Watson, John H.
See Farmer, Philip Jose

Watson, Richard F.
See Silverberg, Robert

Waugh, Auberon (Alexander) 1939- ..CLC 7
See also CA 45-48; CANR 6, 22; DLB 14, 194

Waugh, Evelyn (Arthur St. John) 1903-1966
CLC 1, 3, 8, 13, 19, 27, 44, 107; DA; DAB; DAC; DAM MST, NOV, POP; WLC
See also CA 85-88; 25-28R; CANR 22; CDBLB 1914-1945; DLB 15, 162, 195; MTCW

Waugh, Harriet 1944- .... CLC 6
See also CA 85-88; CANR 22

Ways, C. R.
See Blount, Roy (Alton), Jr.

Waystaff, Simon
See Swift, Jonathan

Webb, (Martha) Beatrice (Potter) 1858-1943
TCLC 22
See also Potter, (Helen) Beatrix
See also CA 117

Webb, Charles (Richard) 1939- .... CLC 7
See also CA 25-28R

Webb, James H(enry), Jr. 1946- .... CLC 22
See also CA 81-84

Webb, Mary (Gladys Meredith) 1881-1927
TCLC 24
See also CA 123; DLB 34

Webb, Mrs. Sidney
See Webb, (Martha) Beatrice (Potter)

Webb, Phyllis 1927-.......................... CLC 18
See also CA 104; CANR 23; DLB 53

Webb, Sidney (James) 1859-1947 .. TCLC 22
See also CA 117; 163; DLB 190

Webber, Andrew Lloyd .... CLC 21
See also Lloyd Webber, Andrew

Weber, Lenora Mattingly 1895-1971 CLC 12
See also CA 19-20; 29-32R; CAP 1; SATA 2; SATA-Obit 26

Weber, Max 1864-1920 .... TCLC 69
See also CA 109

Webster, John 1579(?)-1634(?) ... LC 33; DA; DAB; DAC; DAM DRAM, MST; DC 2; WLC
See also CDBLB Before 1660; DLB 58

Webster, Noah 1758-1843 .... NCLC 30

Wedekind, (Benjamin) Frank(lin) 1864-1918
TCLC 7; DAM DRAM
See also CA 104; 153; DLB 118

Weidman, Jerome 1913- ....CLC 7
See also AITN 2; CA 1-4R; CANR 1; DLB 28

Weil, Simone (Adolphine) 1909-1943TCLC 23
See also CA 117; 159

Weinstein, Nathan
See West, Nathanael

Weinstein, Nathan von Wallenstein
See West, Nathanael

Weir, Peter (Lindsay) 1944- .... CLC 20
See also CA 113; 123

Weiss, Peter (Ulrich) 1916-1982CLC 3, 15, 51; DAM DRAM
See also CA 45-48; 106; CANR 3; DLB 69, 124

Weiss, Theodore (Russell) 1916-CLC 3, 8, 14
See also CA 9-12R; CAAS 2; CANR 46; DLB 5

Welch, (Maurice) Denton 1915-1948TCLC 22
See also CA 121; 148

Welch, James 1940- ..... CLC 6, 14, 52; DAM MULT, POP
See also CA 85-88; CANR 42, 66; DLB 175; NNAL

Weldon, Fay 1931-..CLC 6, 9, 11, 19, 36, 59; DAM POP
See also CA 21-24R; CANR 16, 46, 63; CDBLB 1960 to Present; DLB 14, 194; INT CANR-16; MTCW

Wellek, Rene 1903-1995 .... CLC 28
See also CA 5-8R; 150; CAAS 7; CANR 8; DLB 63; INT CANR-8

Weller, Michael 1942- .... CLC 10, 53
See also CA 85-88

Weller, Paul 1958- ....CLC 26

Wellershoff, Dieter 1925-...................CLC 46
See also CA 89-92; CANR 16, 37

Welles, (George) Orson 1915-1985CLC 20, 80
See also CA 93-96; 117

Wellman, John McDowell 1945-
See Wellman, Mac
See also CA 166

Wellman, Mac 1945- ....CLC 65
See also Wellman, John McDowell; Wellman, John McDowell

Wellman, Manly Wade 1903-1986 ....CLC 49
See also CA 1-4R; 118; CANR 6, 16, 44; SATA 6; SATA-Obit 47

Wells, Carolyn 1869(?)-1942 .... TCLC 35

Literary Criticism Series
Cumulative Topic Index

This index lists all topic entries in Gale's *Classical and Medieval Literature Criticism, Contemporary Literary Criticism, Literature Criticism from 1400 to 1800, Nineteenth-Century Literature Criticism,* and *Twentieth-Century Literary Criticism.*

Topic Index

Topic Index

Contemporary Literary Criticism
Cumulative Nationality Index

Nationality Index

515

Nationality Index

Nationality Index

Nationality Index

Nationality Index

CLC-111 Title Index

Title Index

ISBN 0-7876-2208-7

90000

9 780787 622084